Collins
French
Dictionary

Collins
French
Dictionary

HarperCollins Publishers
Westerhill Road
Bishopbriggs
Glasgow
G64 2QT
Great Britain

Second Edition 2006

© HarperCollins Publishers 2005, 2006

ISBN-13 978-0-00-719162-8
ISBN-10 0-00-719162-6

Collins® and Bank of English® are registered trademarks of HarperCollins Publishers Limited

www.collins.co.uk

A catalogue record for this book is available from the British Library

Typeset by Wordcraft, Glasgow

Printed in Italy by Amadeus S.r.l.

Acknowledgements
We would like to thank those authors and publishers who kindly gave permission for copyright material to be used in the Collins Word Web. We would also like to thank Times Newspapers Ltd for providing valuable data.

Pierre-Henri Cousin
Lorna Sinclair Knight
Lesley Robertson

CONTRIBUTORS
Claude Nimmo
Philippe Patry
Hélène Lewis
Elisabeth Campbell
Renée Birks
Jean-François Allain
Christine Penman
Sabine Citron

EDITORIAL STAFF
Catherine Love
Angela Campbell
Stephen Clarke
Joyce Littlejohn
Megan Thomson
Linda Chestnutt

EDITORIAL MANAGEMENT
Vivian Marr

CONTRIBUTORS TO SECOND EDITION
Catherine E. Love
Jennifer Baird
Stewart C. Russell
Wendy Lee
Callum Brines
Jill Williams

INTRODUCTION

We are delighted you have decided to buy this dictionary. It is designed to give you, in one handy volume, comprehensive and authoritative answers to all your vocabulary and grammar queries.

In the Dictionary section you will find:

● in-depth vocabulary coverage which will more than meet your examination needs

● clear signposting of meanings and subject areas to guide you to the most appropriate translation

● modern, idiomatic phrases showing words in their context

● the most common words in each language highlighted and treated in depth

The Grammar section contains further essential information on all the basic rules and structures of French, as well as all you need to know about French verbs.

We hope you will enjoy using this book and that it will be an invaluable reference tool for all your French language studies.

CONTENTS

Note on trademarks

Words which we have reason to believe constitute trademarks have been designated as such. However, neither the presence nor the absence of such designation should be regarded as affecting the legal status of any trademark.

HOW TO USE THE DICTIONARY

Below you will find an outline of how information is presented in your dictionary. Our aim is to give you the maximum amount of detail in the clearest and most helpful way.

Entries

A typical entry in your dictionary will be made up of the following elements:

Phonetic transcription

Phonetics appear in square brackets immediately after the headword. They are shown using the International Phonetic Alphabet (IPA), and a complete list of the symbols used in this system can be found on pages viii and ix.

Grammatical information

All words belong to one of the following parts of speech: noun, verb, adjective, adverb, pronoun, article, conjunction, preposition, abbreviation. Nouns can be singular or plural and, in French, masculine or feminine. Verbs can be transitive, intransitive, reflexive or impersonal. Parts of speech appear in *italics* immediately after the phonetic spelling of the headword. The gender of the translation also appears in *italics* immediately following the key element of the translation.

Often a word can have more than one part of speech. Just as the English word **chemical** can be an adjective or a noun, the French word **rose** can be an adjective ("pink") or a feminine noun ("rose"). In the same way the verb **to walk** is sometimes transitive, ie it takes an object ("to walk the dog") and sometimes intransitive, ie it doesn't take an object ("to walk to school"). To help you find the meaning you are looking for quickly and for clarity of presentation, the different part of speech categories are separated by a black lozenge ♦.

Meaning divisions

Most words have more than one meaning. Take, for example, **punch** which can be, amongst other things, a blow with the fist or an object used for making holes. Other words are translated differently depending on the context in which they are used. The transitive verb **to roll up**, for example, can be translated by "rouler" or "retrousser" depending on *what* it is you are rolling up. To help you select the most appropriate translation in every context, entries are divided according to meaning. Different meanings are introduced by an "indicator" in *italics* and in brackets. Thus, the examples given above will be shown as follows:

> **punch** *n* (*blow*) coup *m* de poing; (*tool*) poinçon *m*
> **roll up** *vt* (*carpet, cloth, map*) rouler; (*sleeves*) retrousser

Likewise, some words can have a different meaning when used to talk about a specific subject area or field. For example, **bishop**, which we generally use to mean a high-ranking clergyman, is also the name of a chess piece. To show English speakers which translation to use, we have added "subject field labels" in capitals and in brackets, in this case (*CHESS*):

> **bishop** *n* évêque *m*; (*CHESS*) fou *m*

Field labels are often shortened to save space. You will find a complete list of abbreviations used in the dictionary on pages vi and vii.

Translations

Most English words have a direct translation in French and vice versa, as shown in the examples given above. Sometimes, however, no exact equivalent exists in the target language. In such cases we have given an approximate equivalent, indicated by the sign $\simeq$. An example is **National Insurance**, the French equivalent of which is "Sécurité Sociale". There is no exact equivalent since the systems of the two countries are quite different:

> **National Insurance** *n* (*BRIT*) $\simeq$ Sécurité Sociale

On occasion it is impossible to find even an approximate equivalent. This may be the case, for example, with the names of types of food:

> **mince pie** *n sorte de tarte aux fruits secs*

Here the translation (which doesn't exist) is replaced by an explanation. For increased clarity the explanation, or "gloss", is shown in *italics*.

It is often the case that a word, or a particular meaning of a word, cannot be translated in isolation. The translation of **Dutch**, for example, is "hollandais(e), néerlandais(e)". However, the phrase **to go Dutch** is rendered by "partager les frais". Even an expression as simple as **washing powder** needs a separate translation since it translates as "lessive (en poudre)", not "poudre à laver". This is where your dictionary will prove to be particularly informative and useful since it contains an abundance of compounds, phrases and idiomatic expressions.

Levels of formality and familiarity

In English you instinctively know when to say **I don't have any money** and when to say **I'm broke** or **I'm a bit short of cash**. When you are trying to understand someone who is speaking French, however, or when you yourself try to speak French, it is important to know what is polite and what is less so, and what you can say in a relaxed situation but not in a formal context. To help you with this, on the French-English side we have added the label (*fam*) to show that a French meaning or expression is colloquial, while those meanings or expressions which are vulgar are given an exclamation mark (*fam!*), warning you they can cause serious offence. Note also that on the English-French side, translations which are vulgar are followed by an exclamation mark in brackets.

Keywords

Words labelled in the text as KEYWORDS, such as **be** and **do** or their French equivalents **être** and **faire**, have been given special treatment because they form the basic elements of the language. This extra help will ensure that you know how to use these complex words with confidence.

Cultural information

Entries which appear separated from the main text by a line above and below them explain aspects of culture in French and English-speaking countries. Subject areas covered include politics, education, media and national festivals, for example **Assemblée nationale**, **baccalauréat**, **BBC** and **Hallowe'en**.

ABRÉVIATIONS

ABBREVIATIONS

abréviation	*ab(b)r*	abbreviation
adjectif, locution adjective	*adj*	adjective, adjectival phrase
administration	*ADMIN*	administration
adverbe, locution adverbiale	*adv*	adverb, adverbial phrase
agriculture	*AGR*	agriculture
anatomie	*ANAT*	anatomy
architecture	*ARCH*	architecture
article défini	*art déf*	definite article
article indéfini	*art indéf*	indefinite article
automobile	*AUT(O)*	the motor car and motoring
aviation, voyages aériens	*AVIAT*	flying, air travel
biologie	*BIO(L)*	biology
botanique	*BOT*	botany
anglais de Grande-Bretagne	*BRIT*	British English
chimie	*CHIMIE, CHEM*	chemistry
cinéma	*CINÉ, CINE*	cinema
langue familière (! emploi vulgaire)	*col(!)*	colloquial usage (! particularly offensive)
commerce, finance, banque	*COMM*	commerce, finance, banking
informatique	*COMPUT*	computing
conjonction	*conj*	conjunction
construction	*CONSTR*	building
nom utilisé comme adjectif, ne peut s'employer ni comme attribut , ni après le nom qualifié	*cpd*	compound element: noun used as an adjective and which cannot follow the noun it qualifies
cuisine, art culinaire	*CULIN*	cookery
article défini	*def art*	definite article
déterminant: adjectif démonstratif, indéfini etc	*dét*	determiner: demonstrative etc.
économie	*ECON*	economics
électricité, électronique	*ELEC*	electricity, electronics
exclamation, interjection	*excl*	exclamation, interjection
féminin	*f*	feminine
langue familière (! emploi vulgaire)	*fam(!)*	colloquial usage (! particularly offensive)
emploi figuré	*fig*	figurative use
(verbe anglais) dont la particule est inséparable du verbe	*fus*	(phrasal verb) where the particle cannot be separated from the main verb
dans la plupart des sens; généralement	*gén, gen*	in most or all senses; generally
géographie, géologie	*GEO*	geography, geology
géométrie	*GEOM*	geometry
histoire	*HIST*	history
article indéfini	*indef art*	indefinite article
informatique	*INFORM*	computing
invariable	*inv*	invariable
irrégulier	*irrég, irreg*	irregular
domaine juridique	*JUR*	law

ABRÉVIATIONS / ABBREVIATIONS

grammaire, linguistique	*LING*	grammar, linguistics
masculin	*m*	masculine
mathématiques, algèbre	*MATH*	mathematics, calculus
médecine	*MÉD, MED*	medical term, medicine
masculin ou féminin, suivant le sexe	*m/f*	either masculine or feminine depending on sex
domaine militaire, armée	*MIL*	military matters
musique	*MUS*	music
nom	*n*	noun
navigation, nautisme	*NAVIG, NAUT*	sailing, navigation
nom non comptable: ne peut s'utiliser au pluriel	*no pl*	collective (uncountable) noun: is not used in the plural
nom ou adjectif numéral	*num*	numeral adjective or noun
	o.s.	oneself
péjoratif	*péj, pej*	derogatory, pejorative
photographie	*PHOT(O)*	photography
physiologie	*PHYSIOL*	physiology
pluriel	*pl*	plural
politique	*POL*	politics
participe passé	*pp*	past participle
préposition	*prép, prep*	preposition
psychologie, psychiatrie	*PSYCH*	psychology, psychiatry
temps du passé	*pt*	past tense
quelque chose	*qch*	
quelqu'un	*qn*	
religions, domaine ecclésiastique	*REL*	religions, church service
	sb	somebody
enseignement, système scolaire et universitaire	*SCOL*	schooling, schools and universities
singulier	*sg*	singular
	sth	something
subjonctif	*sub*	subjunctive
sujet (grammatical)	*su(b)j*	(grammatical) subject
techniques, technologie	*TECH*	technical term, technology
télécommunications	*TEL*	telecommunications
théâtre	*THÉÂT, THEAT*	theatre
télévision	*TV*	television
typographie	*TYP(O)*	typography, printing
anglais des USA	*US*	American English
verbe	*vb*	verb
verbe ou groupe verbal à fonction intransitive	*vi*	verb or phrasal verb used intransitively
verbe ou groupe verbal à fonction transitive	*vt*	verb or phrasal verb used transitively
zoologie	*ZOOL*	zoology
marque déposée	®	registered trademark
indique une équivalence culturelle	≃	introduces a cultural equivalent
pas de liaison devant h aspiré	'	no liaison before aspirate h

TRANSCRIPTION PHONÉTIQUE

Consonnes

NB. p, b, t, d, k, g sont suivis
d'une aspiration en anglais.

Consonants

NB. p, b, t, d, k, g are not
aspirated in French.

poupée	p	puppy
bombe	b	baby
tente thermal	t	tent
dinde	d	daddy
coq qui képi	k	cork kiss chord
gag bague	g	gag guess
sale ce nation	s	so rice kiss
zéro rose	z	cousin buzz
tache chat	ʃ	sheep sugar
gilet juge	ʒ	pleasure beige
	tʃ	church
	dʒ	judge general
fer phare	f	farm raffle
valve	v	very rev
	θ	thin maths
	ð	that other
lent salle	l	little ball
rare rentrer	ʀ	
	r	rat rare
maman femme	m	mummy comb
non nonne	n	no ran
agneau vigne	ɲ	
	ŋ	singing bank
hop!	h	hat reheat
yeux paille pied	j	yet
nouer oui	w	wall bewail
huile lui	ɥ	
	x	loch

Divers

pour l'anglais: le r final se
prononce en liaison devant
une voyelle   *

pour l'anglais: précède la   '
syllabe accentuée

Miscellaneous

in French transcription: no
liaison before aspirate h

En règle générale, la prononciation est donnée entre crochets après chaque entrée.
Toutefois, du côté anglais-français et dans le cas des expressions composées de deux ou
plusieurs mots non réunis par un trait d'union et faisant l'objet d'une entrée séparée, la
prononciation doit être cherchée sous chacun des mots constitutifs de l'expression en
question.

PHONETIC TRANSCRIPTION

Voyelles

NB. La mise en équivalence de certains sons n'indique qu'une ressemblance approximative.

Vowels

NB. The pairing of some vowel sounds only indicates approximate equivalence.

ici vie lyre	i iː	**heel bead**
	ɪ	**hit pity**
jou**er été**	e	
lait jou**et merci**	ɛ	**set tent**
pl**at a**mour	a æ	**bat apple**
bas pâte	ɑ ɑː	**after car calm**
	ʌ	**fun cousin**
le premier	ə	**over above**
beurre peur	œ	
peu deux	ø əː	**urn fern work**
or homme	ɔ	**wash pot**
mot eau gauche	o ɔː	**born cork**
genou roue	u	**full soot**
	uː	**boon lewd**
rue urne	y	

Diphtongues

Diphthongs

	ɪə	**beer tier**
	ɛə	**tear fair there**
	eɪ	**date plaice day**
	aɪ	**life buy cry**
	au	**owl foul now**
	əu	**low no**
	ɔɪ	**boil boy oily**
	uə	**poor tour**

Nasales

Nasal Vowels

mat**in** pl**ein**	ɛ̃
br**un**	œ̃
s**ang an** d**ans**	ɑ̃
n**on** p**ont**	ɔ̃

In general, we give the pronunciation of each entry in square brackets after the word in question. However, on the English-French side, where the entry is composed of two or more unhyphenated words, each of which is given elsewhere in this dictionary, you will find the pronunciation of each word in its alphabetical position.

FRENCH VERB FORMS

1 Participe présent *2* Participe passé *3* Présent *4* Imparfait *5* Futur *6* Conditionnel
7 Subjonctif présent

acquérir *1* acquérant *2* acquis
  3 acquiers, acquérons, acquièrent
  4 acquérais *5* acquerrai *7* acquière
ALLER *1* allant *2* allé *3* vais, vas, va,
  allons, allez, vont *4* allais *5* irai *6* irais
  7 aille
asseoir *1* asseyant *2* assis *3* assieds,
  asseyons, asseyez, asseyent
  4 asseyais *5* assiérai *7* asseye
atteindre *1* atteignant *2* atteint
  3 atteins, atteignons *4* atteignais
  7 atteigne
AVOIR *1* ayant *2* eu *3* ai, as, a, avons,
  avez, ont *4* avais *5* aurai *6* aurais
  7 aie, aies, ait, ayons, ayez, aient
battre *1* battant *2* battu *3* bats, bat,
  battons *4* battais *7* batte
boire *1* buvant *2* bu *3* bois, buvons,
  boivent *4* buvais *7* boive
bouillir *1* bouillant *2* bouilli *3* bous,
  bouillons *4* bouillais *7* bouille
conclure *1* concluant *2* conclu
  3 conclus, concluons *4* concluais
  7 conclue
conduire *1* conduisant *2* conduit
  3 conduis, conduisons *4* conduisais
  7 conduise
connaître *1* connaissant *2* connu
  3 connais, connaît, connaissons
  4 connaissais *7* connaisse
coudre *1* cousant *2* cousu *3* couds,
  cousons, cousez, cousent *4* cousais
  7 couse
courir *1* courant *2* couru *3* cours,
  courons, courez *5* courrai *7* coure
couvrir *1* couvrant *2* couvert
  3 couvre, couvrons *4* couvrais
  7 couvre
craindre *1* craignant *2* craint *3* crains,
  craignons *4* craignais *7* craigne
croire *1* croyant *2* cru *3* crois, croyons,
  croient *4* croyais *7* croie

croître *1* croissant *2* crû, crue, crus,
  crues *3* croîs, croissons *4* croissais
  7 croisse
cueillir *1* cueillant *2* cueilli *3* cueille,
  cueillons *4* cueillais *5* cueillerai
  7 cueille
devoir *1* devant *2* dû, due, dus, dues
  3 dois, devons, doivent *4* devais
  5 devrai *7* doive
dire *1* disant *2* dit *3* dis, disons, dites,
  disent *4* disais *7* dise
dormir *1* dormant *2* dormi *3* dors,
  dormons *4* dormais *7* dorme
écrire *1* écrivant *2* écrit *3* écris,
  écrivons *4* écrivais *7* écrive
ÊTRE *1* étant *2* été *3* suis, es, est,
  sommes, êtes, sont *4* étais *5* serai
  6 serais *7* sois, sois, soit, soyons,
  soyez, soient
FAIRE *1* faisant *2* fait *3* fais, fais, fait,
  faisons, faites, font *4* faisais *5* ferai
  6 ferais *7* fasse
falloir *2* fallu *3* faut *4* fallait *5* faudra
  7 faille
FINIR *1* finissant *2* fini *3* finis, finis,
  finit, finissons, finissez, finissent
  4 finissais *5* finirai *6* finirais *7* finisse
fuir *1* fuyant *2* fui *3* fuis, fuyons, fuient
  4 fuyais *7* fuie
joindre *1* joignant *2* joint *3* joins,
  joignons *4* joignais *7* joigne
lire *1* lisant *2* lu *3* lis, lisons *4* lisais
  7 lise
luire *1* luisant *2* lui *3* luis, luisons
  4 luisais *7* luise
maudire *1* maudissant *2* maudit
  3 maudis, maudissons *4* maudissait
  7 maudisse
mentir *1* mentant *2* menti *3* mens,
  mentons *4* mentais *7* mente
mettre *1* mettant *2* mis *3* mets,
  mettons *4* mettais *7* mette

1 Participe présent **2** Participe passé **3** Présent **4** Imparfait **5** Futur **6** Conditionnel **7** Subjonctif présent

mourir 1 mourant **2** mort **3** meurs, mourons, meurent **4** mourais **5** mourrai **7** meure

naître 1 naissant **2** né **3** nais, naît, naissons **4** naissais **7** naisse

offrir 1 offrant **2** offert **3** offre, offrons **4** offrais **7** offre

PARLER 1 parlant **2** parlé **3** parle, parles, parle, parlons, parlez, parlent **4** parlais, parlais, parlait, parlions, parliez, parlaient **5** parlerai, parleras, parlera, parlerons, parlerez, parleront **6** parlerais, parlerais, parlerait, parlerions, parleriez, parleraient **7** parle, parles, parle, parlions, parliez, parlent *impératif* parle! parlez!

partir 1 partant **2** parti **3** pars, partons **4** partais **7** parte

plaire 1 plaisant **2** plu **3** plais, plaît, plaisons **4** plaisais **7** plaise

pleuvoir 1 pleuvant **2** plu **3** pleut, pleuvent **4** pleuvait **5** pleuvra **7** pleuve

pourvoir 1 pourvoyant **2** pourvu **3** pourvois, pourvoyons, pourvoient **4** pourvoyais **7** pourvoie

pouvoir 1 pouvant **2** pu **3** peux, peut, pouvons, peuvent **4** pouvais **5** pourrai **7** puisse

prendre 1 prenant **2** pris **3** prends, prenons, prennent **4** prenais **7** prenne

prévoir *like voir* **5** prévoirai

RECEVOIR 1 recevant **2** reçu **3** reçois, reçois, reçoit, recevons, recevez, reçoivent **4** recevais **5** recevrai **6** recevrais **7** reçoive

RENDRE 1 rendant **2** rendu **3** rends, rends, rend, rendons, rendez, rendent **4** rendais **5** rendrai **6** rendrais **7** rende

résoudre 1 résolvant **2** résolu **3** résous, résout, résolvons **4** résolvais **7** résolve

rire 1 riant **2** ri **3** ris, rions **4** riais **7** rie

savoir 1 sachant **2** su **3** sais, savons, savent **4** savais **5** saurai **7** sache *impératif* sache, sachons, sachez

servir 1 servant **2** servi **3** sers, servons **4** servais **7** serve

sortir 1 sortant **2** sorti **3** sors, sortons **4** sortais **7** sorte

souffrir 1 souffrant **2** souffert **3** souffre, souffrons **4** souffrais **7** souffre

suffire 1 suffisant **2** suffi **3** suffis, suffisons **4** suffisais **7** suffise

suivre 1 suivant **2** suivi **3** suis, suivons **4** suivais **7** suive

taire 1 taisant **2** tu **3** tais, taisons **4** taisais **7** taise

tenir 1 tenant **2** tenu **3** tiens, tenons, tiennent **4** tenais **5** tiendrai **7** tienne

vaincre 1 vainquant **2** vaincu **3** vaincs, vainc, vainquons **4** vainquais **7** vainque

valoir 1 valant **2** valu **3** vaux, vaut, valons **4** valais **5** vaudrai **7** vaille

venir 1 venant **2** venu **3** viens, venons, viennent **4** venais **5** viendrai **7** vienne

vivre 1 vivant **2** vécu **3** vis, vivons **4** vivais **7** vive

voir 1 voyant **2** vu **3** vois, voyons, voient **4** voyais **5** verrai **7** voie

vouloir 1 voulant **2** voulu **3** veux, veut, voulons, veulent **4** voulais **5** voudrai **7** veuille *impératif* veuillez

For additional information on French verb formation, see pp. 6-75 of Grammar section.

LES NOMBRES

un (une)	**1**
deux	**2**
trois	**3**
quatre	**4**
cinq	**5**
six	**6**
sept	**7**
huit	**8**
neuf	**9**
dix	**10**
onze	**11**
douze	**12**
treize	**13**
quatorze	**14**
quinze	**15**
seize	**16**
dix-sept	**17**
dix-huit	**18**
dix-neuf	**19**
vingt	**20**
vingt et un (une)	**21**
vingt-deux	**22**
trente	**30**
quarante	**40**
cinquante	**50**
soixante	**60**
soixante-dix	**70**
soixante et onze	**71**
soixante-douze	**72**
quatre-vingts	**80**
quatre-vingt-un (-une)	**81**
quatre-vingt-dix	**90**
quatre-vingt-onze	**91**
cent	**100**
cent un (une)	**101**
trois cents	**300**
trois cent un (une)	**301**
mille	**1 000**
un million	**1 000 000**

NUMBERS

one
two
three
four
five
six
seven
eight
nine
ten
eleven
twelve
thirteen
fourteen
fifteen
sixteen
seventeen
eighteen
nineteen
twenty
twenty-one
twenty-two
thirty
forty
fifty
sixty
seventy
seventy-one
seventy-two
eighty
eighty-one
ninety
ninety-one
a hundred
a hundred and one
three hundred
three hundred and one
a thousand
a million

LES NOMBRES

premier (première), 1er
deuxième, 2e or 2ème
troisième, 3e or 3ème
quatrième
cinquième
sixième
septième
huitième
neuvième
dixième
onzième
douzième
treizième
quatorzième
quinzième
seizième
dix-septième
dix-huitième
dix-neuvième
vingtième
vingt-et-unième
vingt-deuxième
trentième
centième
cent-unième
millième

NUMBERS

first, 1st
second, 2nd
third, 3rd
fourth, 4th
fifth, 5th
sixth, 6th
seventh
eighth
ninth
tenth
eleventh
twelfth
thirteenth
fourteenth
fifteenth
sixteenth
seventeenth
eighteenth
nineteenth
twentieth
twenty-first
twenty-second
thirtieth
hundredth
hundred-and-first
thousandth

L'HEURE

quelle heure est-il?

il est …

minuit
une heure (du matin)

une heure cinq
une heure dix
une heure et quart
une heure vingt-cinq

une heure et demie, une heure trente
deux heures moins vingt-cinq, une heure trente-cinq
deux heures moins vingt, une heure quarante
deux heures moins le quart, une heure quarante-cinq
deux heures moins dix, une heure cinquante
midi
deux heures (de l'après-midi)

sept heures (du soir)

à quelle heure?

à minuit
à sept heures
à une heure
dans vingt minutes
il y a dix minutes

LA DATE

aujourd'hui
demain
après-demain
hier
avant-hier
la veille

THE TIME

what time is it?

it's …

midnight
one o'clock (in the morning), one (am)

five past one
ten past one
a quarter past one, one fifteen
twenty-five past one, one twenty-five

half past one, one thirty

twenty-five to two, one thirty-five

twenty to two, one forty

a quarter to two, one forty-five

ten to two, one fifty

twelve o'clock, midday, noon
two o'clock (in the afternoon), two (pm)

seven o'clock (in the evening), seven (pm)

at what time?

at midnight
at seven o'clock
at one o'clock
in twenty minutes
ten minutes ago

THE DATE

today
tomorrow
the day after tomorrow
yesterday
the day before yesterday
the day before, the previous day

le lendemain	the next *or* following day
le matin	morning
le soir	evening
ce matin	this morning
ce soir	this evening
cet après-midi	this afternoon
hier matin	yesterday morning
hier soir	yesterday evening
demain matin	tomorrow morning
demain soir	tomorrow evening
dans la nuit du samedi au dimanche	during Saturday night, during the night of Saturday to Sunday
il viendra samedi	he's coming on Saturday
le samedi	on Saturdays
tous les samedis	every Saturday
samedi passé *ou* dernier	last Saturday
samedi prochain	next Saturday
samedi en huit	a week on Saturday
samedi en quinze	a fortnight *or* two weeks on Saturday
du lundi au samedi	from Monday to Saturday
tous les jours	every day
une fois par semaine	once a week
une fois par mois	once a month
deux fois par semaine	twice a week
il y a une semaine *ou* huit jours	a week ago
il y a quinze jours	a fortnight *or* two weeks ago
l'année passée *ou* dernière	last year
dans deux jours	in two days
dans huit jours *ou* une semaine	in a week
dans quinze jours	in a fortnight *or* two weeks
le mois prochain	next month
l'année prochaine	next year

quel jour sommes-nous?

what day is it?

le 1er/24 octobre 1996	the 1st/24th of October 1996, October 1st/24th 1996
en 1996	in 1996
mille neuf cent quatre-vingt seize	nineteen ninety-six
44 av. J.-C.	44 BC
14 apr. J.-C.	14 AD
au XIXe (siècle)	in the nineteenth century
dans les années trente	in the thirties
il était une fois …	once upon a time …

FRANÇAIS-ANGLAIS
FRENCH-ENGLISH

— A a —

a [a] *vb voir* **avoir**

$\boxed{\text{MOT CLÉ}}$

à [a] (*à + le =* **au**, *à + les =* **aux**) *prép* **1** (*endroit, situation*) at, in; **être à Paris/au Portugal** to be in Paris/Portugal; **être à la maison/à l'école** to be at home/at school; **à la campagne** in the country; **c'est à 10 m/km/à 20 minutes (d'ici)** it's 10 m/km/20 minutes away
2 (*direction*) to; **aller à Paris/au Portugal** to go to Paris/Portugal; **aller à la maison/à l'école** to go home/to school; **à la campagne** to the country
3 (*temps*): **à 3 heures/minuit** at 3 o'clock/midnight; **au printemps** in the spring; **au mois de juin** in June; **au départ** at the start, at the outset; **à demain/la semaine prochaine!** see you tomorrow/next week!; **visites de 5 heures à 6 heures** visiting from 5 to *ou* till 6 o'clock
4 (*attribution, appartenance*) to; **le livre est à Paul/à lui/à nous** this book is Paul's/his/ours; **donner qch à qn** to give sth to sb; **un ami à moi** a friend of mine; **c'est à moi de le faire** it's up to me to do it
5 (*moyen*) with; **se chauffer au gaz** to have gas heating; **à bicyclette** on a *ou* by bicycle; **à la main/machine** by hand/machine; **à la télévision/la radio** on television/the radio
6 (*provenance*) from; **boire à la bouteille** to drink from the bottle
7 (*caractérisation, manière*): **l'homme aux yeux bleus** the man with the blue eyes; **à la russe** the Russian way; **glace à la framboise** raspberry ice cream
8 (*but, destination*): **tasse à café** coffee cup; **maison à vendre** house for sale; **problème à régler** problem to sort out
9 (*rapport, évaluation, distribution*): **100 km/unités à l'heure** 100 km/units per *ou* an hour; **payé à l'heure** paid by the hour; **cinq à six** five to six
10 (*conséquence, résultat*): **à ce qu'il prétend** according to him; **à leur grande surprise** much to their surprise; **à nous trois nous n'avons pas su le faire** we couldn't do it even between the three of us; **ils sont arrivés à 4** 4 of them arrived (together)

abaisser [abese] *vt* to lower, bring down; (*manette*) to pull down; (*fig*) to debase; to humiliate; **s'abaisser** *vi* to go down; (*fig*) to demean o.s.; **s'abaisser à faire/à qch** to stoop *ou* descend to doing/to sth

abandon [abɑ̃dɔ̃] *nm* abandoning; deserting; giving up; withdrawal; surrender, relinquishing; (*fig*) lack of constraint; relaxed pose *ou* mood; **être à l'abandon** to be in a state of neglect; **laisser à l'abandon** to abandon

abandonner [abɑ̃dɔne] *vt* to leave, abandon, desert; (*projet, activité*) to abandon, give up; (*SPORT*) to retire *ou* withdraw from; (*céder*) to surrender, relinquish; **s'abandonner** *vi* to let o.s. go; **s'abandonner à** (*paresse, plaisirs*) to give o.s. up to; **abandonner qch à qn** to give sth up to sb

abasourdir [abazurdir] *vt* to stun, stagger

abat-jour [abaʒur] *nm inv* lampshade

abats [aba] *vb voir* **abattre ♦** *nmpl* (*de bœuf, porc*) offal *sg* (*BRIT*), entrails (*US*); (*de volaille*) giblets

abattement [abatmɑ̃] *nm* (*physique*) enfeeblement; (*moral*) dejection, despondency; (*déduction*) reduction; **abattement fiscal** = tax allowance

abattoir [abatwar] *nm* abattoir (*BRIT*), slaughterhouse

abattre [abatr(ə)] *vt* (*arbre*) to cut down, fell; (*mur, maison*) to pull down; (*avion, personne*) to shoot down; (*animal*) to shoot, kill; (*fig: physiquement*) to wear out, tire out; (*: moralement*) to demoralize; **s'abattre** *vi* to crash down; **s'abattre sur** (*pluie*) to beat down on; (*: coups, injures*) to rain down on; **abattre ses cartes** (*aussi fig*) to lay one's cards on the table; **abattre du travail** *ou* **de la besogne** to get through a lot of work

abbaye [abei] *nf* abbey

abbé [abe] *nm* priest; (*d'une abbaye*) abbot; **M l'abbé** Father

abcès [apsɛ] *nm* abscess

abdiquer [abdike] *vi* to abdicate **♦** *vt* to renounce, give up

abdominal, e, aux [abdɔminal, -o] *adj* abdominal **♦** *nmpl*: **faire des abdominaux** to do exercises for the stomach muscles

abeille [abɛj] *nf* bee

aberrant, e [aberɑ̃, -ɑ̃t] *adj* absurd

aberration [abeʀɑsjɔ̃] *nf* aberration

abêtir [abetiʀ] *vt* to make morons (*ou* a moron) of

abîme [abim] *nm* abyss, gulf

abîmer [abime] *vt* to spoil, damage; **s'abîmer** *vi* to get spoilt *ou* damaged; (*fruits*) to spoil; (*tomber*) to sink, founder; **s'abîmer les yeux** to ruin one's eyes *ou* eyesight

ablation [ablɑsjɔ̃] *nf* removal

aboiement [abwamɑ̃] *nm* bark, barking *no pl*

abois [abwa] *nmpl*: **aux abois** at bay

abolir [abɔliʀ] *vt* to abolish

abominable [abɔminabl(ə)] *adj* abominable

abondance [abɔ̃dɑ̃s] *nf* abundance; (*richesse*) affluence; **en abondance** in abundance

abondant, e [abɔ̃dɑ̃, -ɑ̃t] *adj* plentiful, abundant, copious

abonder [abɔ̃de] *vi* to abound, be plentiful; **abonder en** to be full of, abound in; **abonder dans le sens de qn** to concur with sb

abonné, e [abɔne] *nm/f* subscriber; season ticket holder ◆ *adj*: **être abonné à un journal** to subscribe to *ou* have a subscription to a periodical; **être abonné au téléphone** to be on the (tele)phone

abonnement [abɔnmɑ̃] *nm* subscription; (*pour transports en commun, concerts*) season ticket

abonner [abɔne] *vt*: **s'abonner à** to subscribe to, take out a subscription to

abord [abɔʀ] *nm*: **être d'un abord facile** to be approachable; **être d'un abord difficile** (*personne*) to be unapproachable; (*lieu*) to be hard to reach *ou* difficult to get to; **de prime abord, au premier abord** at first sight; **d'abord** *adv* first; **tout d'abord** first of all

abordable [abɔʀdabl(ə)] *adj* (*personne*) approachable; (*marchandise*) reasonably priced; (*prix*) affordable, reasonable

aborder [abɔʀde] *vi* to land ◆ *vt* (*sujet, difficulté*) to tackle; (*personne*) to approach; (*rivage etc*) to reach; (*NAVIG: attaquer*) to board; (*: heurter*) to collide with

aboutir [abutiʀ] *vi* (*négociations etc*) to succeed; (*abcès*) to come to a head; **aboutir à/dans/sur** to end up at/in/on

aboyer [abwaje] *vi* to bark

abréger [abʀeʒe] *vt* (*texte*) to shorten, abridge; (*mot*) to shorten, abbreviate; (*réunion, voyage*) to cut short, shorten

abreuver [abʀœve] *vt* to water; (*fig*): **abreuver qn de** to shower *ou* swamp sb with; (*injures etc*) to shower sb with; **s'abreuver** *vi* to drink

abreuvoir [abʀœvwaʀ] *nm* watering place

abréviation [abʀevjɑsjɔ̃] *nf* abbreviation

abri [abʀi] *nm* shelter; **à l'abri** under cover; **être/se mettre à l'abri** to be/get under cover *ou* shelter; **à l'abri de** sheltered from; (*fig*) safe from

abricot [abʀiko] *nm* apricot

abriter [abʀite] *vt* to shelter; (*loger*) to accommo-date; **s'abriter** to shelter, take cover

abrupt, e [abʀypt] *adj* sheer, steep; (*ton*) abrupt

abruti [abʀyti] *nm/f* (*fam*) idiot, moron

absence [apsɑ̃s] *nf* absence; (*MÉD*) blackout; (*distraction*) mental blank; **en l'absence de** in the absence of

absent, e [apsɑ̃, -ɑ̃t] *adj* absent; (*chose*) missing, lacking; (*distrait: air*) vacant, faraway ◆ *nm/f* absentee

absenter [apsɑ̃te]: **s'absenter** *vi* to take time off work; (*sortir*) to leave, go out

absolu, e [apsɔly] *adj* absolute; (*caractère*) rigid, uncompromising ◆ *nm* (*PHILOSOPHIE*): **l'absolu** the Absolute; **dans l'absolu** in the absolute, in a vacuum

absolument [apsɔlymɑ̃] *adv* absolutely

absorbant, e [apsɔʀbɑ̃, -ɑ̃t] *adj* absorbent; (*tâche*) absorbing, engrossing

absorber [apsɔʀbe] *vt* to absorb; (*gén MÉD: manger, boire*) to take; (*ÉCON: firme*) to take over, absorb

abstenir [apstəniʀ]: **s'abstenir** *vi* (*POL*) to abstain; **s'abstenir de qch/de faire** to refrain from sth/from doing

abstraction [apstʀaksjɔ̃] *nf* abstraction; **faire abstraction de** to set *ou* leave aside; **abstraction faite de …** leaving aside …

abstrait, e [apstʀɛ, -ɛt] *pp de* **abstraire** ◆ *adj* abstract ◆ *nm*: **dans l'abstrait** in the abstract

absurde [apsyʀd(ə)] *adj* absurd ◆ *nm* absurdity; (*PHILOSOPHIE*): **l'absurde** absurd; **par l'absurde** ad absurdio

abus [aby] *nm* (*excès*) abuse, misuse; (*injustice*) abuse; **abus de confiance** breach of trust; (*détournement de fonds*) embezzlement

abuser [abyze] *vi* to go too far, overstep the mark ◆ *vt* to deceive, mislead; **s'abuser** *vi* (*se méprendre*) to be mistaken; **abuser de** *vt* (*force, droit*) to misuse; (*alcool*) to take to excess; (*violer, duper*) to take advantage of

abusif, ive [abyzif, -iv] *adj* exorbitant; (*punition*) excessive; (*pratique*) improper

acabit [akabi] *nm*: **du même acabit** of the same type

académie [akademi] *nf* (*société*) learned society; (*école: d'art, de danse*) academy; (*ART: nu*) nude; (*SCOL: circonscription*) = regional education authority; **l'Académie (française)** the French Academy; *see boxed note*

ACADÉMIE FRANÇAISE

The **Académie française** was founded by Cardinal Richelieu in 1635, during the reign of Louis XIII. It is made up of forty elected scholars and writers who are known as 'les Quarante' or 'les Immortels'. One of the **Académie's** functions is to keep an eye on the development of the French language, and its recommendations are frequently the subject of lively public debate. It has produced several editions of its famous dictionary and also awards various literary prizes.

acajou [akaʒu] *nm* mahogany

acariâtre [akarjatr(ə)] *adj* sour(-tempered) (*BRIT*), cantankerous

accablant, e [akablã, -ãt] *adj* (*témoignage, preuve*) overwhelming

accablement [akabləmã] *nm* deep despondency

accabler [akable] *vt* to overwhelm, overcome; (*suj: témoignage*) to condemn, damn; **accabler qn d'injures** to heap ou shower abuse on sb; **accabler qn de travail** to overburden sb with work; **accablé de dettes/soucis** weighed down with debts/cares

accalmie [akalmi] *nf* lull

accaparer [akapare] *vt* to monopolize; (*suj: travail etc*) to take up (all) the time ou attention of

accéder [aksede]: **accéder à** *vt* (*lieu*) to reach; (*fig: pouvoir*) to accede to; (: *poste*) to attain; (*accorder: requête*) to grant, accede to

accélérateur [akseleratœr] *nm* accelerator

accélération [akselerasjõ] *nf* speeding up; acceleration

accélérer [akselere] *vt* (*mouvement, travaux*) to speed up ♦ *vi* (*AUTO*) to accelerate

accent [aksã] *nm* accent; (*inflexions expressives*) tone (of voice); (*PHONÉTIQUE, fig*) stress; **aux accents de** (*musique*) to the strains of; **mettre l'accent sur** (*fig*) to stress; **accent aigu/grave/circonflexe** acute/grave/circumflex accent

accentuer [aksãtɥe] *vt* (*LING: orthographe*) to accent; (: *phonétique*) to stress, accent; (*fig*) to accentuate, emphasize; (: *effort, pression*) to increase; **s'accentuer** *vi* to become more marked ou pronounced

acceptation [akseptasjõ] *nf* acceptance

accepter [aksepte] *vt* to accept; (*tolérer*): **accepter que qn fasse** to agree to sb doing; **accepter de faire** to agree to do

accès [akse] *nm* (*à un lieu, INFORM*) access; (*MÉD*) attack; (: *de toux*) fit, bout ♦ *nmpl* (*routes etc*) means of access, approaches; **d'accès facile/malaisé** easily/not easily accessible; **donner accès à** (*lieu*) to give access to; (*carrière*) to open the door to; **avoir accès auprès de qn** to have access to sb; **l'accès aux quais est interdit aux personnes non munies d'un billet** ticket-holders only on platforms, no access to platforms without a ticket; **accès de colère** fit of anger; **accès de joie** burst of joy

accessible [aksesibl(ə)] *adj* accessible; (*personne*) approachable; (*livre, sujet*): **accessible à qn** within the reach of sb; (*sensible*): **accessible à la pitié/l'amour** open to pity/love

accessoire [akseswar] *adj* secondary, of secondary importance; (*frais*) incidental ♦ *nm* accessory; (*THÉÂT*) prop

accident [aksidã] *nm* accident; **par accident** by chance; **accident de parcours** mishap; **accident de la route** road accident; **accident du travail** accident at work; industrial injury ou accident; **accidents de terrain** unevenness of the ground

accidenté, e [aksidãte] *adj* damaged ou injured (in an accident); (*relief, terrain*) uneven; hilly

accidentel, le [aksidãtel] *adj* accidental

acclamation [aklamasjõ] *nf*: **par acclamation** (*vote*) by acclamation; **acclamations** *nfpl* cheers, cheering *sg*

acclamer [aklame] *vt* to cheer, acclaim

acclimater [aklimate] *vt* to acclimatize; **s'acclimater** *vi* to become acclimatized

accolade [akɔlad] *nf* (*amicale*) embrace; (*signe*) brace; **donner l'accolade à qn** to embrace sb

accommodant, e [akɔmɔdã, -ãt] *adj* accommodating, easy-going

accommoder [akɔmɔde] *vt* (*CULIN*) to prepare; (*points de vue*) to reconcile; **accommoder qch à** (*adapter*) to adapt sth to; **s'accommoder de** to put up with; (*se contenter de*) to make do with; **s'accommoder à** (*s'adapter*) to adapt to

accompagnateur, trice [akɔ̃paɲatœr, -tris] *nm/f* (*MUS*) accompanist; (*de voyage*) guide; (*de voyage organisé*) courier; (*d'enfants*) accompanying adult

accompagner [akɔ̃paɲe] *vt* to accompany, be ou go ou come with; (*MUS*) to accompany; **s'accompagner de** to bring, be accompanied by

accompli, e [akɔ̃pli] *adj* accomplished

accomplir [akɔ̃plir] *vt* (*tâche, projet*) to carry out; (*souhait*) to fulfil; **s'accomplir** *vi* to be fulfilled

accord [akɔr] *nm* (*entente, convention, LING*) agreement; (*entre des styles, tons etc*) harmony; (*consentement*) agreement, consent; (*MUS*) chord; **donner son accord** to give one's agreement; **mettre 2 personnes d'accord** to make 2 people come to an agreement, reconcile 2 people; **se mettre d'accord** to come to an agreement (with each other); **être d'accord** to agree; **être d'accord avec qn** to agree with sb; **d'accord!** OK!, right!; **d'un commun accord** of one accord; **accord parfait** (*MUS*) tonic chord

accordéon [akɔrdeõ] *nm* (*MUS*) accordion

accorder [akɔrde] *vt* (*faveur, délai*) to grant; (*attribuer*): **accorder de l'importance/de la valeur à qch** to attach importance/value to sth; (*harmoniser*) to match; (*MUS*) to tune; **s'accorder** to get on together; (*être d'accord*) to agree; (*couleurs, caractères*) to go together, match; (*LING*) to agree; **je vous accorde que ...** I grant you that ...

accoster [akɔste] *vt* (*NAVIG*) to draw alongside; (*personne*) to accost ♦ *vi* (*NAVIG*) to berth

accotement [akɔtmã] *nm* (*de route*) verge (*BRIT*), shoulder; **accotement stabilisé/non stabilisé** hard shoulder/soft verge ou shoulder

accouchement [akuʃmã] *nm* delivery, (child)birth; (*travail*) labour (*BRIT*), labor (*US*); **accouchement à terme** delivery at (full) term; **accouchement sans douleur** natural childbirth

accoucher [akuʃe] *vi* to give birth, have a baby; (*être en travail*) to be in labour (*BRIT*) *ou* labor (*US*) ◆ *vt* to deliver; **accoucher d'un garçon** to give birth to a boy

accoucheur [akuʃœʀ] *nm*: **(médecin) accoucheur** obstetrician

accouder [akude]: **s'accouder** *vi*: **s'accouder à/ contre/sur** to rest one's elbows on/against/on; **accoudé à la fenêtre** leaning on the windowsill

accoudoir [akudwaʀ] *nm* armrest

accoupler [akuple] *vt* to couple; (*pour la reproduction*) to mate; **s'accoupler** to mate

accourir [akuʀiʀ] *vi* to rush *ou* run up

accoutrement [akutʀəmã] *nm* (*péj*) getup (*BRIT*), outfit

accoutumance [akutymãs] *nf* (*gén*) adaptation; (*MÉD*) addiction

accoutumé, e [akutyme] *adj* (*habituel*) customary, usual; **comme à l'accoutumée** as is customary *ou* usual

accoutumer [akutyme] *vt*: **accoutumer qn à qch/faire** to accustom sb to sth/to doing; **s'accoutumer à** to get accustomed *ou* used to

accréditer [akʀedite] *vt* (*nouvelle*) to substantiate; **accréditer qn (auprès de)** to accredit sb (to)

accroc [akʀo] *nm* (*déchirure*) tear; (*fig*) hitch, snag; **sans accroc** without a hitch; **faire un accroc à** (*vêtement*) to make a tear in, tear; (*fig: règle etc*) to infringe

accrochage [akʀɔʃaʒ] *nm* hanging (up); hitching (up); (*AUTO*) (minor) collision; (*MIL*) encounter, engagement; (*dispute*) clash, brush

accrocher [akʀɔʃe] *vt* (*suspendre*): **accrocher qch à** to hang sth (up) on; (*attacher: remorque*): **accrocher qch à** to hitch sth (up) to; (*heurter*) to catch; to hit; (*déchirer*): **accrocher qch (à)** to catch sth (on); (*fig*) to engage; (*fig*) to catch, attract ◆ *vi* to stick, get stuck; (*fig: pourparlers etc*) to hit a snag; (*plaire: disque etc*) to catch on; **s'accrocher** (*se disputer*) to have a clash *ou* brush; (*ne pas céder*) to hold one's own, hang on in (*fam*); **s'accrocher à** (*rester pris à*) to catch on; (*agripper, fig*) to hang on *ou* cling to

accroissement [akʀwasmã] *nm* increase

accroître [akʀwatʀ(ə)] *vt*, **s'accroître** *vi* to increase

accroupir [akʀupiʀ]: **s'accroupir** *vi* to squat, crouch (down)

accru, e [akʀy] *pp de* **accroître**

accueil [akœj] *nm* welcome; (*endroit*) reception (desk); (: *dans une gare*) information kiosk; **comité/ centre d'accueil** reception committee/centre

accueillant, e [akœjã, -ãt] *adj* welcoming, friendly

accueillir [akœjiʀ] *vt* to welcome; (*loger*) to accommodate

acculer [akyle] *vt*: **acculer qn à** *ou* **contre** to drive sb back against; **acculer qn dans** to corner sb in;

acculer qn à (*faillite*) to drive sb to the brink of

accumuler [akymyle] *vt* to accumulate, amass; **s'accumuler** *vi* to accumulate; to pile up

accusation [akyzasjɔ̃] *nf* (*gén*) accusation; (*JUR*) charge; (*partie*): **l'accusation** the prosecution; **mettre en accusation** to indict; **acte d'accusation** bill of indictment

accusé, e [akyze] *nm/f* accused; (*prévenu(e)*) defendant ◆ *nm*: **accusé de réception** acknowledgement of receipt

accuser [akyze] *vt* to accuse; (*fig*) to emphasize, bring out; (: *montrer*) to show; **s'accuser** *vi* (*s'accentuer*) to become more marked; **accuser qn de** to accuse sb of; (*JUR*) to charge sb with; **accuser qn/ qch de qch** (*rendre responsable*) to blame sb/sth for sth; **s'accuser de qch/d'avoir fait qch** to admit sth/having done sth; to blame o.s. for sth/for having done sth; **accuser réception de** to acknowledge receipt of; **accuser le coup** (*aussi fig*) to be visibly affected

acerbe [asɛʀb(ə)] *adj* caustic, acid

acéré, e [aseʀe] *adj* sharp

acharné, e [aʃaʀne] *adj* (*lutte, adversaire*) fierce, bitter; (*travail*) relentless, unremitting

acharner [aʃaʀne]: **s'acharner** *vi*: **s'acharner sur** to go at fiercely, hound; **s'acharner contre** to set o.s. against; to dog, pursue; (*suj: malchance*) to hound; **s'acharner à faire** to try doggedly to do; to persist in doing

achat [aʃa] *nm* buying *no pl*; (*article acheté*) purchase; **faire l'achat de** to buy, purchase; **faire des achats** to go some shopping, buy a few things

acheminer [aʃmine] *vt* (*courrier*) to forward, dispatch; (*troupes*) to convey, transport; (*train*) to route; **s'acheminer vers** to head for

acheter [aʃte] *vt* to buy, purchase; (*soudoyer*) to buy, bribe; **acheter qch à** (*marchand*) to buy *ou* purchase sth from; (*ami etc: offrir*) to buy sth for; **acheter à crédit** to buy on credit

acheteur, euse [aʃtœʀ, -øz] *nm/f* buyer; shopper; (*COMM*) buyer; (*JUR*) vendee, purchaser

achever [aʃve] *vt* to complete, finish; (*blessé*) to finish off; **s'achever** *vi* to end

acide [asid] *adj* sour, sharp; (*ton*) acid, biting; (*CHIMIE*) acid(ic) ◆ *nm* acid

acidulé, e [asidyle] *adj* slightly acid; **bonbons acidulés** acid drops (*BRIT*), ≈ lemon drops (*US*)

acier [asje] *nm* steel; **acier inoxydable** stainless steel

aciérie [asjeʀi] *nf* steelworks *sg*

acné [akne] *nf* acne

acolyte [akɔlit] *nm* (*péj*) associate

acompte [akɔ̃t] *nm* deposit; (*versement régulier*) instalment; (*sur somme due*) payment on account; (*sur salaire*) advance; **un acompte de 15 €** 15 € on account

à-côté [akote] *nm* side-issue; (*argent*) extra

à-coup [aku] *nm* (*du moteur*) (hic)cough; (*fig*) jolt;

sans à-coups smoothly; **par à-coups** by fits and starts

acoustique [akustik] *nf* (*d'une salle*) acoustics *pl*; (*science*) acoustics *sg* ♦ *adj* acoustic

acquéreur [akeʀœʀ] *nm* buyer, purchaser; **se porter/se rendre acquéreur de qch** to announce one's intention to purchase/to purchase sth

acquérir [akeʀiʀ] *vt* to acquire; (*par achat*) to purchase, acquire; (*valeur*) to gain; (*résultats*) to achieve; **ce que ses efforts lui ont acquis** what his efforts have won *ou* gained (for) him

acquis, e [aki, -iz] *pp de* **acquérir** ♦ *nm* (accumulated) experience; (*avantage*) gain ♦ *adj* (*voir acquérir*) acquired; gained; achieved; **être acquis à** (*plan, idée*) to be in full agreement with; **son aide nous est acquise** we can count on *ou* be sure of his help; **tenir qch pour acquis** to take sth for granted

acquit [aki] *vb voir* **acquérir** ♦ *nm* (*quittance*) receipt; **pour acquit** received; **par acquit de conscience** to set one's mind at rest

acquitter [akite] *vt* (*JUR*) to acquit; (*facture*) to pay, settle; **s'acquitter de** to discharge; (*promesse, tâche*) to fulfil (*BRIT*), fulfill (*US*), carry out

âcre [ɑkʀ(ə)] *adj* acrid, pungent

acrobate [akʀɔbat] *nm/f* acrobat

acrobatie [akʀɔbasi] *nf* (*art*) acrobatics *sg*; (*exercice*) acrobatic feat; **acrobatie aérienne** aerobatics *sg*

acte [akt(ə)] *nm* act, action; (*THÉÂT*) act; **actes** *nmpl* (*compte-rendu*) proceedings; **prendre acte de** to note, take note of; **faire acte de présence** to put in an appearance; **faire acte de candidature** to submit an application; **acte d'accusation** charge (*BRIT*), bill of indictment; **acte de baptême** baptismal certificate; **acte de mariage/naissance** marriage/birth certificate; **acte de vente** bill of sale

acteur [aktœʀ] *nm* actor

actif, ive [aktif, -iv] *adj* active ♦ *nm* (*COMM*) assets *pl*; (*LING*) active (voice); (*fig*): **avoir à son actif** to have to one's credit; **actifs** *nmpl* people in employment; **mettre à son actif** to add to one's list of achievements; **l'actif et le passif** assets and liabilities; **prendre une part active à qch** to take an active part in sth; **population active** working population

action [aksjɔ̃] *nf* (*gén*) action; (*COMM*) share; **une bonne/mauvaise action** a good/an unkind deed; **mettre en action** to put into action; **passer à l'action** to take action; **sous l'action de** under the effect of; **l'action syndicale** (the) union action; **un film d'action** an action film *ou* movie; **action en diffamation** libel action; **action de grâce(s)** (*REL*) thanksgiving

actionnaire [aksjɔnɛʀ] *nm/f* shareholder

actionner [aksjɔne] *vt* to work; to activate; to operate

activer [aktive] *vt* to speed up; (*CHIMIE*) to activate;

s'activer *vi* (*s'affairer*) to bustle about; (*se hâter*) to hurry up

activité [aktivite] *nf* activity; **en activité** (*volcan*) active; (*fonctionnaire*) in active life; (*militaire*) on active service

actrice [aktʀis] *nf* actress

actualiser [aktualize] *vt* to actualize; (*mettre à jour*) to bring up to date

actualité [aktualite] *nf* (*d'un problème*) topicality; (*événements*): **l'actualité** current events; **les actualités** (*CINÉ*, *TV*) the news; **l'actualité politique/sportive** the political/sports *ou* sporting news; **les actualités télévisées** the television news; **d'actualité** topical

actuel, le [aktuɛl] *adj* (*présent*) present; (*d'actualité*) topical; (*non virtuel*) actual; **à l'heure actuelle** at this moment in time, at the moment

actuellement [aktuɛlmɑ̃] *adv* at present, at the present time

acuité [akuite] *nf* acuteness

acuponcteur, acupuncteur [akypɔ̃ktœʀ] *nm* acupuncturist

acuponcture, acupuncture [akypɔ̃ktyʀ] *nf* acupuncture

adaptateur, trice [adaptatœʀ, -tʀis] *nm/f* adapter

adapter [adapte] *vt* to adapt; **s'adapter (à)** (*suj: personne*) to adapt (to); (: *objet, prise etc*) to apply (to); **adapter qch à** (*approprier*) to adapt sth to (fit); **adapter qch sur/dans/à** (*fixer*) to fit sth on/into/to

additif [aditif] *nm* additional clause; (*substance*) additive; **additif alimentaire** food additive

addition [adisjɔ̃] *nf* addition; (*au café*) bill

additionner [adisjɔne] *vt* to add (up); **s'additionner** *vi* to add up; **additionner un produit d'eau** to add water to a product

adepte [adɛpt(ə)] *nm/f* follower

adéquat, e [adekwa, -at] *adj* appropriate, suitable

adhérent, e [adeʀɑ̃, -ɑ̃t] *nm/f* (*de club*) member

adhérer [adeʀe] *vi* (*coller*) to adhere, stick; **adhérer à** (*coller*) to adhere *ou* stick to; (*se rallier à: parti, club*) to join; to be a member of; (: *opinion, mouvement*) to support

adhésif, ive [adezif, -iv] *adj* adhesive, sticky ♦ *nm* adhesive

adhésion [adezjɔ̃] *nf* (*à un club*) joining; membership; (*à une opinion*) support

adieu, x [adjø] *excl* goodbye ♦ *nm* farewell; **dire adieu à qn** to say goodbye *ou* farewell to sb; **dire adieu à qch** (*renoncer*) to say *ou* wave goodbye to sth

adjectif [adʒɛktif] *nm* adjective; **adjectif attribut** adjectival complement; **adjectif épithète** attributive adjective

adjoindre [adʒwɛ̃dʀ(ə)] *vt*: **adjoindre qch à** to attach sth to; (*ajouter*) to add sth to; **adjoindre qn à** (*personne*) to appoint sb as an assistant to; (*comité*) to appoint sb to, attach sb to; **s'adjoindre**

vt (*collaborateur etc*) to take on, appoint

adjoint, e [adʒwɛ̃, -wɛt] *pp de* **adjoindre ♦** *nm/f* assistant; **directeur adjoint** assistant manager

adjudant [adʒydɑ̃] *nm* (*MIL*) warrant officer; **adjudant-chef** = warrant officer 1st class (*BRIT*), ≈ chief warrant officer (*US*)

adjuger [adʒyʒe] *vt* (*prix, récompense*) to award; (*lors d'une vente*) to auction (off); **s'adjuger** *vt* to take for o.s.; **adjugé!** (*vendu*) gone!, sold!

adjurer [adʒyʀe] *vt*: **adjurer qn de faire** to implore *ou* beg sb to do

admettre [admɛtʀ(ə)] *vt* (*visiteur, nouveau-venu*) to admit, let in; (*candidat*: *SCOL*) to pass; (*TECH*: *gaz, eau, air*) to admit; (*tolérer*) to allow, accept; (*reconnaître*) to admit, acknowledge; (*supposer*) to suppose; **j'admets que ...** I admit that ...; **je n'admets pas que tu fasses cela** I won't allow you to do that; **admettons que ...** let's suppose that ...; **admettons** let's suppose so

administrateur, trice [administratœʀ, -tʀis] *nm/f* (*COMM*) director; (*ADMIN*) administrator; **administrateur délégué** managing director; **administrateur judiciaire** receiver

administration [administʀasjɔ̃] *nf* administration; **l'Administration** = the Civil Service

administrer [administʀe] *vt* (*firme*) to manage, run; (*biens, remède, sacrement etc*) to administer

admirable [admiʀabl(ə)] *adj* admirable, wonderful

admirateur, trice [admiʀatœʀ, -tʀis] *nm/f* admirer

admiration [admiʀasjɔ̃] *nf* admiration; **être en admiration devant** to be lost in admiration before

admirer [admiʀe] *vt* to admire

admis, e [admi, -iz] *pp de* **admettre**

admissible [admisibl(ə)] *adj* (*candidat*) eligible; (*comportement*) admissible, acceptable; (*JUR*) receivable

admission [admisjɔ̃] *nf* admission; **tuyau d'admission** intake pipe; **demande d'admission** application for membership; **service des admissions** admissions

ADN *sigle m* (= *acide désoxyribonucléique*) DNA

adolescence [adɔlesɑ̃s] *nf* adolescence

adolescent, e [adɔlesɑ̃, -ɑ̃t] *nm/f* adolescent, teenager

adonner [adɔne]: **s'adonner à** *vt* (*sport*) to devote o.s. to; (*boisson*) to give o.s. over to

adopter [adɔpte] *vt* to adopt; (*projet de loi etc*) to pass

adoptif, ive [adɔptif, -iv] *adj* (*parents*) adoptive; (*fils, patrie*) adopted

adorable [adɔʀabl(ə)] *adj* adorable

adorer [adɔʀe] *vt* to adore; (*REL*) to worship

adosser [adose] *vt*: **adosser qch à** *ou* **contre** to stand sth against; **s'adosser à** *ou* **contre** to lean with one's back against; **être adossé à** *ou* **contre** to be leaning with one's back against

adoucir [adusiʀ] *vt* (*goût, température*) to make milder; (*avec du sucre*) to sweeten; (*peau, voix, eau*) to soften; (*caractère, personne*) to mellow; (*peine*) to soothe, allay; **s'adoucir** *vi* to become milder; to soften; to mellow

adresse [adʀɛs] *nf* (*voir adroit*) skill, dexterity; (*domicile, INFORM*) address; **à l'adresse de** (*pour*) for the benefit of

adresser [adʀɛse] *vt* (*lettre*: *expédier*) to send; (: *écrire l'adresse sur*) to address; (*injure, compliments*) to address; **adresser qn à un docteur/ bureau** to refer *ou* send sb to a doctor/an office; **adresser la parole à qn** to speak to *ou* address sb; **s'adresser à** (*parler à*) to speak to, address; (*s'informer auprès de*) to go and see, go and speak to; (: *bureau*) to enquire at; (*suj*: *livre, conseil*) to be aimed at

adroit, e [adʀwa, -wat] *adj* (*joueur, mécanicien*) skilful (*BRIT*), skillful (*US*), dext(e)rous; (*politicien etc*) shrewd, skilled

adulte [adylt(ə)] *nm/f* adult, grown-up ♦ *adj* (*personne, attitude*) adult, grown-up; (*chien, arbre*) fully-grown, mature; **l'âge adulte** adulthood; **formation/film pour adultes** adult training/film

adultère [adyltɛʀ] *adj* adulterous ♦ *nm/f* adulterer/adulteress ♦ *nm* (*acte*) adultery

advenir [advəniʀ] *vi* to happen; **qu'est-il advenu de?** what has become of?; **quoi qu'il advienne** whatever befalls *ou* happens

adverbe [advɛʀb(ə)] *nm* adverb; **adverbe de manière** adverb of manner

adversaire [advɛʀsɛʀ] *nm/f* (*SPORT, gén*) opponent, adversary; (*MIL*) adversary, enemy

adverse [advɛʀs(ə)] *adj* opposing

aération [aeʀasjɔ̃] *nf* airing; (*circulation de l'air*) ventilation; **conduit d'aération** ventilation shaft; **bouche d'aération** air vent

aérer [aeʀe] *vt* to air; (*fig*) to lighten; **s'aérer** *vi* to get some (fresh) air

aérien, ne [aeʀjɛ̃, -ɛn] *adj* (*AVIAT*) air *cpd*, aerial; (*câble, métro*) overhead; (*fig*) light; **compagnie aérienne** airline (company); **ligne aérienne** airline

aérobic [aeʀɔbik] *nf* aerobics *sg*

aérogare [aeʀɔgaʀ] *nf* airport (buildings); (*en ville*) air terminal

aéroglisseur [aeʀɔglisœʀ] *nm* hovercraft

Aéronavale [aeʀɔnaval] *nf* = Fleet Air Arm (*BRIT*), = Naval Air Force (*US*)

aérophagie [aeʀɔfaʒi] *nf* aerophagy

aéroport [aeʀɔpɔʀ] *nm* airport; **aéroport d'embarquement** departure airport

aéroporté, e [aeʀɔpɔʀte] *adj* airborne, airlifted

aérosol [aeʀɔsɔl] *nm* aerosol

affable [afabl(ə)] *adj* affable

affaiblir [afebliʀ] *vt* to weaken; **s'affaiblir** *vi* to weaken, grow weaker; (*vue*) to grow dim

affaire [afɛʀ] *nf* (*problème, question*) matter; (*criminelle, judiciaire*) case; (*scandaleuse etc*) affair;

(*entreprise*) business; (*marché, transaction*) (business) deal, (piece of) business *no pl*; (*occasion intéressante*) good deal; **affaires** *nfpl* affairs; (*activité commerciale*) business *sg*; (*effets personnels*) things, belongings; **tirer qn/se tirer d'affaire** to get sb/o.s. out of trouble; **ceci fera l'affaire** this will do (nicely); **avoir affaire à** (*comme adversaire*) to be faced with; (*en contact*) to be dealing with; **tu auras affaire à moi!** (*menace*) you'll have me to contend with!; **c'est une affaire de goût/d'argent** it's a question *ou* matter of taste/money; **c'est l'affaire d'une minute/heure** it'll only take a minute/an hour; **ce sont mes affaires** (*cela me concerne*) that's my business; **toutes affaires cessantes** forthwith; **les affaires étrangères** (*POL*) foreign affairs

affairer [afeʀe]: **s'affairer** *vi* to busy o.s., bustle about

affaisser [afese]: **s'affaisser** *vi* (*terrain, immeuble*) to subside, sink; (*personne*) to collapse

affaler [afale]: **s'affaler dans/sur** to collapse *ou* slump into/onto

affamé, e [afame] *adj* starving, famished

affectation [afɛktasjɔ̃] *nf* (*voir affecter*) allotment; appointment; posting; affectedness

affecter [afɛkte] *vt* (*émouvoir*) to affect, move; (*feindre*) to affect, feign; (*telle ou telle forme etc*) to take on, assume; **affecter qch à** to allocate *ou* allot sth to; **affecter qn à** to appoint sb to; (*diplomate*) to post sb to; **affecter qch de** (*de coefficient*) to modify sth by

affectif, ive [afɛktif, -iv] *adj* emotional, affective

affection [afɛksjɔ̃] *nf* affection; (*mal*) ailment; **avoir de l'affection pour** to feel affection for; **prendre en affection** to become fond of

affectionner [afɛksjɔne] *vt* to be fond of

affectueusement [afɛktɥøzmɑ̃] *adv* affectionately

affectueux, euse [afɛktɥø, -øz] *adj* affectionate

affermir [afɛʀmiʀ] *vt* to consolidate, strengthen

affichage [afiʃaʒ] *nm* billposting, billsticking; (*électronique*) display; **"affichage interdit"** "stick no bills", "billsticking prohibited"; **affichage à cristaux liquides** liquid crystal display, LCD; **affichage numérique** *ou* **digital** digital display

affiche [afiʃ] *nf* poster; (*officielle*) (public) notice; (*THÉÂT*) bill; **être à l'affiche** (*THÉÂT*) to be on; **tenir l'affiche** to run

afficher [afiʃe] *vt* (*affiche*) to put up, post up; (*réunion*) to put up a notice about; (*électroniquement*) to display; (*fig*) to exhibit, display; **s'afficher** (*péj*) to flaunt o.s.; **"défense d'afficher"** "stick no bills"

affilée [afile]: **d'affilée** *adv* at a stretch

affiler [afile] *vt* to sharpen

affilier [afilje] *vt*: **s'affilier à** to become affiliated to

affiner [afine] *vt* to refine; **s'affiner** *vi* to become (more) refined

affirmatif, ive [afiʀmatif, -iv] *adj* affirmative ◆ *nf*: **répondre par l'affirmative** to reply in the affirmative; **dans l'affirmative** (*si oui*) if (the answer is) yes …, if he does (*ou* you do *etc*) …

affirmation [afiʀmasjɔ̃] *nf* assertion

affirmer [afiʀme] *vt* (*prétendre*) to maintain, assert; (*autorité etc*) to assert; **s'affirmer** to assert o.s.; to assert itself

affligé, e [afliʒe] *adj* distressed, grieved; **affligé de** (*maladie, tare*) afflicted with

affliger [afliʒe] *vt* (*peiner*) to distress, grieve

affluence [aflyɑ̃s] *nf* crowds *pl*; **heures d'affluence** rush hour *sg*; **jours d'affluence** busiest days

affluent [aflyɑ̃] *nm* tributary

affluer [aflye] *vi* (*secours, biens*) to flood in, pour in; (*sang*) to rush, flow

affolant, e [afɔlɑ̃, -ɑ̃t] *adj* terrifying

affolement [afɔlmɑ̃] *nm* panic

affoler [afɔle] *vt* to throw into a panic; **s'affoler** *vi* to panic

affranchir [afʀɑ̃ʃiʀ] *vt* to put a stamp *ou* stamps on; (*à la machine*) to frank (*BRIT*), meter (*US*); (*esclave*) to enfranchise, emancipate; (*fig*) to free, liberate; **s'affranchir de** to free o.s. from; **machine à affranchir** franking machine, postage meter

affranchissement [afʀɑ̃ʃismɑ̃] *nm* franking (*BRIT*), metering (*US*); freeing; (*POSTES: prix payé*) postage; **tarifs d'affranchissement** postage rates

affréter [afʀete] *vt* to charter

affreux, euse [afʀø, -øz] *adj* dreadful, awful

affront [afʀɔ̃] *nm* affront

affrontement [afʀɔ̃tmɑ̃] *nm* (*MIL, POL*) clash, confrontation

affronter [afʀɔ̃te] *vt* to confront, face; **s'affronter** to confront each other

affubler [afyble] *vt* (*péj*): **affubler qn de** to rig *ou* deck sb out in; (*surnom*) to attach to sb

affût [afy] *nm* (*de canon*) gun carriage; **à l'affût (de)** (*gibier*) lying in wait (for); (*fig*) on the look-out (for)

affûter [afyte] *vt* to sharpen, grind

afin [afɛ̃]: **afin que** *conj* so that, in order that; **afin de faire** in order to do, so as to do

africain, e [afʀikɛ̃, -ɛn] *adj* African ◆ *nm/f*: **Africain, e** African

Afrique [afʀik] *nf*: **l'Afrique** Africa; **l'Afrique australe/du Nord/du Sud** southern/North/South Africa

agacer [agase] *vt* to pester, tease; (*involontairement*) to irritate, aggravate; (*aguicher*) to excite, lead on

âge [ɑʒ] *nm* age; **quel âge as-tu?** how old are you?; **une femme d'un certain âge** a middle-aged woman, a woman who is getting on (in years); **bien porter son âge** to wear well; **prendre de l'âge** to be getting on (in years), grow older; **limite d'âge**

age limit; **dispense d'âge** special exemption from age limit; **troisième âge** (*période*) retirement; (*personnes âgées*) senior citizens; **l'âge ingrat** the awkward *ou* difficult age; **âge légal** legal age; **âge mental** mental age; **l'âge mûr** maturity, middle age; **âge de raison** age of reason

âgé, e [ɑʒe] *adj* old, elderly; **âgé de 10 ans** 10 years old

agence [aʒɑ̃s] *nf* agency, office; (*succursale*) branch; **agence immobilière** estate agent's (office), (*BRIT*), real estate office (*US*); **agence matrimoniale** marriage bureau; **agence de placement** employment agency; **agence de publicité** advertising agency; **agence de voyages** travel agency

agencer [aʒɑ̃se] *vt* to put together; (*local*) to arrange, lay out

agenda [aʒɛ̃da] *nm* diary

agenouiller [aʒnuje]: **s'agenouiller** *vi* to kneel (down)

agent [aʒɑ̃] *nm* (*aussi*: **agent de police**) policeman; (*ADMIN*) official, officer; (*fig*: *élément, facteur*) agent; **agent d'assurances** insurance broker; **agent de change** stockbroker; **agent commercial** sales representative; **agent immobilier** estate agent (*BRIT*), realtor (*US*); **agent (secret)** (secret) agent

agglomération [aglɔmeʀasjɔ̃] *nf* town; (*AUTO*) built-up area; **l'agglomération parisienne** the urban area of Paris

aggloméré [aglɔmeʀe] *nm* (*bois*) chipboard; (*pierre*) conglomerate

aggraver [agʀave] *vt* to worsen, aggravate; (*JUR*: *peine*) to increase; **s'aggraver** *vi* to worsen; **aggraver son cas** to make one's case worse

agile [aʒil] *adj* agile, nimble

agir [aʒiʀ] *vi* (*se comporter*) to behave, act; (*faire quelque chose*) to act, take action; (*avoir de l'effet*) to act; **il s'agit de** it's a matter *ou* question of; it is about; (*il importe que*): **il s'agit de faire** we (*ou* you *etc*) must do; **de quoi s'agit-il?** what is it about?

agitation [aʒitasjɔ̃] *nf* (hustle and) bustle; (*trouble*) agitation, excitement; (*politique*) unrest, agitation

agité, e [aʒite] *adj* (*remuant*) fidgety, restless; (*troublé*) agitated, perturbed; (*journée*) hectic; (*mer*) rough; (*sommeil*) disturbed, broken

agiter [aʒite] *vt* (*bouteille, chiffon*) to shake; (*bras, mains*) to wave; (*préoccuper, exciter*) to trouble, perturb; **s'agiter** *vi* to bustle about; (*dormeur*) to toss and turn; (*enfant*) to fidget; (*POL*) to grow restless; **"agiter avant l'emploi"** "shake before use"

agneau, x [aɲo] *nm* lamb; (*toison*) lambswool

agonie [agɔni] *nf* mortal agony, death pangs *pl*; (*fig*) death throes *pl*

agrafe [agʀaf] *nf* (*de vêtement*) hook, fastener; (*de bureau*) staple; (*MÉD*) clip

agrafer [agʀafe] *vt* to fasten; to staple

agrafeuse [agʀaføz] *nf* stapler

agrandir [agʀɑ̃diʀ] *vt* (*magasin, domaine*) to extend, enlarge; (*trou*) to enlarge, make bigger; (*PHOTO*) to enlarge, blow up; **s'agrandir** *vi* to be extended; to be enlarged

agrandissement [agʀɑ̃dismɑ̃] *nm* extension; enlargement; (*photographie*) enlargement

agréable [agʀeabl(ə)] *adj* pleasant, nice

agréé, e [agʀee] *adj*: **concessionnaire agréé** registered dealer; **magasin agréé** registered dealer('s)

agréer [agʀee] *vt* (*requête*) to accept; **agréer à** *vt* to please, suit; **veuillez agréer ...** (*formule épistolaire*) yours faithfully

agrégation [agʀegasjɔ̃] *nf* highest teaching diploma in France; *see boxed note*

AGRÉGATION

The **agrégation**, informally known as the '**agrég**', is a prestigious competitive examination for the recruitment of secondary school teachers in France. The number of candidates always far exceeds the number of vacant posts. Most teachers of 'classes préparatoires' and most university lecturers have passed the **agrégation**.

---

agrégé, e [agʀeʒe] *nm/f* holder of the *agrégation*

agrément [agʀemɑ̃] *nm* (*accord*) consent, approval; (*attraits*) charm, attractiveness; (*plaisir*) pleasure; **voyage d'agrément** pleasure trip

agrémenter [agʀemɑ̃te] *vt*: **agrémenter (de)** to embellish (with), adorn (with)

agresser [agʀese] *vt* to attack

agresseur [agʀesœʀ] *nm* aggressor

agressif, ive [agʀesif, -iv] *adj* aggressive

agricole [agʀikɔl] *adj* agricultural, farm *cpd*

agriculteur, trice [agʀikyltœʀ, -tʀis] *nm/f* farmer

agriculture [agʀikyltyʀ] *nf* agriculture; farming

agripper [agʀipe] *vt* to grab, clutch; (*pour arracher*) to snatch, grab; **s'agripper à** to cling (on) to, clutch, grip

agroalimentaire [agʀɔalimɑ̃tɛʀ] *adj* farming *cpd* ♦ *nm*: **l'agroalimentaire** agribusiness

agrumes [agʀym] *nmpl* citrus fruit(s)

aguerrir [ageʀiʀ] *vt* to harden; **s'aguerrir (contre)** to become hardened (to)

aguets [agɛ]: **aux aguets** *adv*: **être aux aguets** to be on the look-out

aguicher [agiʃe] *vt* to entice

ahuri, e [ayʀi] *adj* (*stupéfait*) flabbergasted; (*idiot*) dim-witted

ai [e] *vb voir* **avoir**

aide [ɛd] *nm/f* assistant ♦ *nf* assistance, help; (*secours financier*) aid; **à l'aide de** with the help *ou* aid of; **aller à l'aide de qn** to go to sb's aid, go to help sb; **venir en aide à qn** to help sb, come to sb's assistance; **appeler (qn) à l'aide** to call for help (from sb); **à l'aide!** help!; **aide de camp** nm aide-de-camp; **aide comptable** nm accountant's assistant; **aide électricien** nm electrician's mate; **aide familiale** nf mother's help, ≃ home help; **aide judiciaire** nf legal aid; **aide ménagère** nf ≃ home help; **aide sociale** nf (assistance) state aid; **aide soignant, e** nm/f auxiliary nurse; **aide technique** nf ≃ VSO (BRIT), ≃ Peace Corps (US)

aide-mémoire [ɛdmemwaʀ] nm inv (key facts) handbook

aider [ede] vt to help; **aider à qch** to help (towards) sth; **aider qn à faire qch** to help sb to do sth; **s'aider de** (se servir de) to use, make use of

aie etc [ɛ] vb voir **avoir**

aïe [aj] excl ouch!

aïeul, e [ajœl] nm/f grandparent, grandfather/grandmother; (ancêtre) forebear

aïeux [ajø] nmpl grandparents; forebears, forefathers

aigle [ɛgl(ə)] nm eagle

aigre [ɛgʀ(ə)] adj sour, sharp; (fig) sharp, cutting; **tourner à l'aigre** to turn sour

aigre-doux, -douce [ɛgʀədu, -dus] adj (fruit) bitter-sweet; (sauce) sweet and sour

aigreur [ɛgʀœʀ] nf sourness; sharpness; **aigreurs d'estomac** heartburn sg

aigrir [ɛgʀiʀ] vt (personne) to embitter; (caractère) to sour; **s'aigrir** vi to become embittered; to sour; (lait etc) to turn sour

aigu, ë [egy] adj (objet, arête) sharp, pointed; (son, voix) high-pitched, shrill; (note) high(-pitched); (douleur, intelligence) acute, sharp

aiguille [egɥij] nf needle; (de montre) hand; **aiguille à tricoter** knitting needle

aiguiller [egɥije] vt (orienter) to direct; (RAIL) to shunt

aiguilleur [egɥijœʀ] nm: **aiguilleur du ciel** air traffic controller

aiguillon [egɥijɔ̃] nm (d'abeille) sting; (fig) spur, stimulus

aiguillonner [egɥijɔne] vt to spur ou goad on

aiguiser [egize] vt to sharpen, grind; (fig) to stimulate; (: esprit) to sharpen; (: sens) to excite

ail [aj] nm garlic

aile [ɛl] nf wing; (de voiture) wing (BRIT), fender (US); **battre de l'aile** (fig) to be in a sorry state; **voler de ses propres ailes** to stand on one's own two feet; **aile libre** hang-glider

aileron [ɛlʀɔ̃] nm (de requin) fin; (d'avion) aileron

ailier [elje] nm (SPORT) winger

aille etc [aj] vb voir **aller**

ailleurs [ajœʀ] adv elsewhere, somewhere else; **partout/nulle part ailleurs** everywhere/nowhere else; **d'ailleurs** adv (du reste) moreover, besides; **par ailleurs** adv (d'autre part) moreover, furthermore

aimable [ɛmabl(ə)] adj kind, nice; **vous êtes bien aimable** that's very nice ou kind of you, how kind (of you)!

aimant [ɛmɑ̃] nm magnet

aimer [eme] vt to love; (d'amitié, affection, par goût) to like; (souhait): **j'aimerais ...** I would like ...; **s'aimer** to love each other; to like each other; **je n'aime pas beaucoup Paul** I don't like Paul much, I don't care much for Paul; **aimer faire qch** to like doing sth, to like to do sth; **aimeriez-vous que je vous accompagne?** would you like me to come with you?; **j'aimerais (bien) m'en aller** I should (really) like to go; **bien aimer qn/qch** to like sb/sth; **j'aime mieux Paul (que Pierre)** I prefer Paul (to Pierre); **j'aime mieux ou autant vous dire que** I may as well tell you that; **j'aimerais autant ou mieux y aller maintenant** I'd sooner ou rather go now; **j'aime assez aller au cinéma** I quite like going to the cinema; **j'aime faire du ski** I like skiing; **je t'aime** I love you

aine [ɛn] nf groin

aîné, e [ene] adj elder, older; (le plus âgé) eldest, oldest ♦ nm/f oldest child ou one, oldest boy ou son/girl ou daughter; **aînés** nmpl (fig: anciens) elders; **il est mon aîné (de 2 ans)** he's (2 years) older than me, he's (2 years) my senior

ainsi [ɛ̃si] adv (de cette façon) like this, in this way, thus; (ce faisant) thus ♦ conj thus, so; **ainsi que** (comme) (just) as; (et aussi) as well as; **pour ainsi dire** so to speak, as it were; **ainsi donc** and so; **ainsi soit-il** (REL) so be it; **et ainsi de suite** and so on (and so forth)

aïoli [ajɔli] nm = garlic mayonnaise

air [ɛʀ] nm air; (mélodie) tune; (expression) look, air; (atmosphère, ambiance): **dans l'air** in the air (fig) **prendre de grands airs (avec qn)** to give o.s. airs (with sb); **en l'air** (up) into the air; **tirer en l'air** to fire shots in the air; **paroles/menaces en l'air** idle words/threats; **prendre l'air** to get some (fresh) air; (avion) to take off; **avoir l'air triste** to look ou seem sad; **avoir l'air de qch** to look like sth; **avoir l'air de faire** to look as though one is doing, appear to be doing; **courant d'air** draught (BRIT), draft (US); **le grand air** the open air; **mal de l'air** air-sickness; **tête en l'air** scatterbrain; **air comprimé** compressed air; **air conditionné** air-conditioning

aisance [ɛzɑ̃s] nf ease; (COUTURE) easing, freedom of movement; (richesse) affluence; **être dans l'aisance** to be well-off ou affluent

aise [ɛz] nf comfort ♦ adj: **être bien aise de/que** to be delighted to/that; **aises** nfpl: **aimer ses aises** to like one's (creature) comforts; **prendre ses aises** to make o.s. comfortable; **frémir d'aise** to shudder with pleasure; **être à l'aise** ou **à son aise** to be comfortable; (pas embarrassé) to be at ease; (financièrement) to be comfortably off; **se mettre à l'aise** to make o.s. comfortable; **être mal à l'aise** ou **à son aise** to be uncomfortable; (gêné) to be ill at ease; **mettre qn à l'aise** to put sb at his (ou her) ease; **mettre qn mal à l'aise** to make sb feel ill at ease; **à**

votre aise please yourself, just as you like; **en faire à son aise** to do as one likes; **en prendre à son aise avec qch** to be free and easy with sth, do as one likes with sth

aisé, e [eze] adj easy; (assez riche) well-to-do, well-off

aisselle [esεl] nf armpit

ait [ε] vb voir **avoir**

ajonc [aʒɔ̃] nm gorse no pl

ajourner [aʒuʀne] vt (réunion) to adjourn; (décision) to defer, postpone; (candidat) to refer; (conscrit) to defer

ajouter [aʒute] vt to add; (INFORM) to append; **ajouter à** vt (accroître) to add to; **s'ajouter à** to add to; **ajouter que** to add that; **ajouter foi à** to lend ou give credence to

ajusté, e [aʒyste] adj: **bien ajusté** (robe etc) close-fitting

ajuster [aʒyste] vt (régler) to adjust; (vêtement) to alter; (arranger): **ajuster sa cravate** to adjust one's tie; (coup de fusil) to aim; (cible) to aim at; (adapter): **ajuster qch à** to fit sth to

alarme [alaʀm(ə)] nf alarm; **donner l'alarme** to give ou raise the alarm; **jeter l'alarme** to cause alarm

alarmer [alaʀme] vt to alarm; **s'alarmer** vi to become alarmed

alarmiste [alaʀmist(ə)] adj alarmist

album [albɔm] nm album; **album à colorier** colouring book; **album de timbres** stamp album

albumine [albymin] nf albumin; **avoir** ou **faire de l'albumine** to suffer from albuminuria

alcool [alkɔl] nm: **l'alcool** alcohol; **un alcool** a spirit, a brandy; **alcool à brûler** methylated spirits (BRIT), wood alcohol (US); **alcool à 90°** surgical spirit; **alcool camphré** camphorated alcohol; **alcool de prune** etc plum etc brandy

alcoolique [alkɔlik] adj, nm/f alcoholic

alcoolisé, e [alkɔlize] adj alcoholic

alcoolisme [alkɔlism(ə)] nm alcoholism

alco(o)test® [alkɔtεst] nm (objet) Breathalyser®; (test) breath-test; **faire subir l'alco(o)test à qn** to Breathalyze® sb

aléas [alea] nmpl hazards

aléatoire [aleatwaʀ] adj uncertain; (INFORM, STATISTIQUE) random

alentour [alɑ̃tuʀ] adv around (about); **alentours** nmpl surroundings; **aux alentours de** in the vicinity ou neighbourhood of, around about; (temps) around about

alerte [alεʀt(ə)] adj agile, nimble; (style) brisk, lively ♦ nf alert; warning; **donner l'alerte** to give the alert; **à la première alerte** at the first sign of trouble ou danger; **alerte à la bombe** bomb scare

alerter [alεʀte] vt to alert

algèbre [alʒεbʀ(ə)] nf algebra

Alger [alʒe] n Algiers

Algérie [alʒeʀi] nf: **l'Algérie** Algeria

algérien, ne [alʒeʀjɛ̃, -εn] adj Algerian ♦ nm/f: **Algérien, ne** Algerian

algue [alg(ə)] nf (gén) seaweed no pl; (BOT) alga (pl -ae)

alibi [alibi] nm alibi

aliéné, e [aljene] nm/f insane person, lunatic (péj)

aligner [aliɲe] vt to align, line up; (idées, chiffres) to string together; (adapter): **aligner qch sur** to bring sth into alignment with; **s'aligner** (soldats etc) to line up; **s'aligner sur** (POL) to align o.s. with

aliment [alimɑ̃] nm food; **aliment complet** whole food

alimentaire [alimɑ̃tεʀ] adj food cpd; (péj: besogne) done merely to earn a living; **produits alimentaires** foodstuffs, foods

alimentation [alimɑ̃tasjɔ̃] nf feeding; supplying, supply; (commerce) food trade; (produits) groceries pl; (régime) diet; (INFORM) feed; **alimentation (générale)** (general) grocer's; **alimentation de base** staple diet; **alimentation en feuilles/en continu/en papier** form/stream/sheet feed

alimenter [alimɑ̃te] vt to feed; (TECH): **alimenter (en)** to supply (with), feed (with); (fig) to sustain, keep going

alinéa [alinea] nm paragraph; **"nouvel alinéa"** "new line"

aliter [alite]: **s'aliter** vi to take to one's bed; **infirme alité** bedridden person ou invalid

allaiter [alete] vt (suj: femme) to (breast-)feed, nurse; (suj: animal) to suckle; **allaiter au biberon** to bottle-feed

allant [alɑ̃] nm drive, go

alléchant, e [aleʃɑ̃, -ɑ̃t] adj tempting, enticing

allécher [aleʃe] vt: **allécher qn** to make sb's mouth water; to tempt sb, entice sb

allée [ale] nf (de jardin) path; (en ville) avenue, drive; **allées et venues** comings and goings

allégé, e [aleʒe] adj (yaourt etc) low-fat

alléger [aleʒe] vt (voiture) to make lighter; (chargement) to lighten; (souffrance) to alleviate, soothe

allègre [alεgʀ(ə)] adj lively, jaunty (BRIT); (personne) gay, cheerful

alléguer [alege] vt to put forward (as proof ou as excuse)

Allemagne [aləmaɲ] nf: **l'Allemagne** Germany; **l'Allemagne de l'Est/Ouest** East/West Germany; **l'Allemagne fédérale (RFA)** the Federal Republic of Germany (FRG)

allemand, e [almɑ̃, -ɑ̃d] adj German ♦ nm (LING) German ♦ nm/f: **Allemand, e** German; **Allemand de l'Est/l'Ouest** East/West German

aller [ale] nm (trajet) outward journey; (billet): **aller (simple)** single (BRIT) ou one-way ticket; **aller (et) retour (AR)** (trajet) return trip ou journey (BRIT), round trip (US); (billet) return (BRIT) ou round-trip (US) ticket ♦ vi (gén) to go; **aller à** (convenir) to suit; (suj: forme, pointure etc) to fit; **cela me va** (couleur) that suits me; (vêtement) that suits me; that fits me; (projet, disposition) that suits me, that's fine ou OK by me; **aller à la chasse/pêche** to go hunting/fishing; **aller avec** (couleurs, style etc) to go (well) with; **je vais le faire/me fâcher** I'm going to do it/to get angry; **aller voir/chercher qn** to go and see/look for sb; **comment allez-vous?** how are you?; **comment ça va?** how are you?; **ça va? – oui (ça va)!** how are things? – fine!; **pour aller à** how do I get to; **ça va (comme ça)** that's fine (as it is); **il va bien/mal** he's well/ not well, he's fine/ill; **ça va bien/mal** (affaires etc) it's going well/not going well; **tout va bien** everything's fine; **ça ne va pas!** (mauvaise humeur etc) that's not on!, hey, come on!; **ça ne va pas sans difficultés** it's not without difficulties; **aller mieux** to be better; **il y a de leur vie** their lives are at stake; **se laisser aller** to let o.s. go; **s'en aller** vi (partir) to be off, go, leave; (disparaître) to go away; **aller jusqu'à** to go as far as; **ça va de soi, ça va sans dire** that goes without saying; **allez!** go on!; come on!; **allons-y!** let's go!; **allez, au revoir** right ou OK then, bye-bye!

allergique [alɛrʒik] adj allergic; **allergique à** allergic to

alliage [aljaʒ] nm alloy

alliance [aljɑ̃s] nf (MIL, POL) alliance; (mariage) marriage; (bague) wedding ring; **neveu par alliance** nephew by marriage

allier [alje] vt (métaux) to alloy; (POL, gén) to ally; (fig) to combine; **s'allier** to become allies; (éléments, caractéristiques) to combine; **s'allier à** to become allied to ou with

allô [alo] excl hullo, hallo

allocation [alɔkasjɔ̃] nf allowance; **allocation (de) chômage** unemployment benefit; **allocation (de) logement** rent allowance; **allocations familiales** = child benefit no pl; **allocations de maternité** maternity allowance

allocution [alɔkysjɔ̃] nf short speech

allonger [alɔ̃ʒe] vt (vêtement) to lengthen, make longer; (étendre: bras, jambe) to stretch (out); (sauce) to spin out, make go further; **s'allonger** vi to get longer; (se coucher) to lie down, stretch out

allouer [alwe] vt: **allouer qch à** to allocate sth to, allot sth to

allumage [alymaʒ] nm (AUTO) ignition

allume-cigare [alymsigar] nm inv cigar lighter

allumer [alyme] vt (lampe, phare, radio) to put ou switch on; (pièce) to put ou switch the light(s) on in; (feu, bougie, cigare, pipe, gaz) to light; (chauffage) to put on; **s'allumer** vi (lumière, lampe) to come ou go on; **allumer (la lumière ou l'électricité)** to put on the light

allumette [alymɛt] nf match; (morceau de bois) matchstick; (CULIN): **allumette au fromage** cheese straw; **allumette de sûreté** safety match

allure [alyr] nf (vitesse) speed; (: à pied) pace;

(démarche) walk; (maintien) bearing; (aspect, air) look; **avoir de l'allure** to have style ou a certain elegance; **à toute allure** at top ou full speed

allusion [alyzjɔ̃] nf allusion; (sous-entendu) hint; **faire allusion à** to allude ou refer to; to hint at

---

MOT-CLÉ

alors [alɔr] adv 1 (à ce moment-là) then, at that time; **il habitait alors à Paris** he lived in Paris at that time; **jusqu'alors** up till ou until then

2 (par conséquent) then; **tu as fini? alors je m'en vais** have you finished? I'm going then

3 (expressions): **alors? quoi de neuf?** well ou so? what's new?; **et alors?** so (what)?; **ça alors!** (well) really!

alors que conj 1 (au moment où) when, as; **il est arrivé alors que je partais** he arrived as I was leaving

2 (pendant que) while, when; **alors qu'il était à Paris, il a visité ...** while ou when he was in Paris, he visited ...

3 (tandis que) whereas, while; **alors que son frère travaillait dur, lui se reposait** while his brother was working hard, HE would rest

---

alouette [alwɛt] nf (sky)lark

alourdir [alurdir] vt to weigh down, make heavy; **s'alourdir** vi to grow heavy ou heavier

aloyau [alwajo] nm sirloin

Alpes [alp(ə)] nfpl: **les Alpes** the Alps

alphabet [alfabɛ] nm alphabet; (livre) ABC (book), primer

alphabétique [alfabetik] adj alphabetic(al); **par ordre alphabétique** in alphabetical order

alphabétiser [alfabetize] vt to teach to read and write; (pays) to eliminate illiteracy in

alpinisme [alpinism(ə)] nm mountaineering, climbing

alpiniste [alpinist(ə)] nm/f mountaineer, climber

Alsace [alzas] nf: **l'Alsace** Alsace

alsacien, ne [alzasjɛ̃, -ɛn] adj Alsatian

altérer [altere] vt (faits, vérité) to falsify, distort; (qualité) to debase, impair; (données) to corrupt; (donner soif à) to make thirsty; **s'altérer** vi to deteriorate; to spoil

altermondialisme [altɛrmɔ̃djalism] nm antiglobalism

altermondialiste [altɛrmɔ̃djalist] adj, nm/f antiglobalist

alternateur [altɛrnatœr] nm alternator

alternatif, ive [altɛrnatif, -iv] adj alternating ♦ nf alternative

alterner [altɛrne] vt to alternate ♦ vi: **alterner (avec)** to alternate (with); **(faire) alterner qch avec qch** to alternate sth with sth

Altesse [altɛs] nf Highness

altitude [altityd] nf altitude, height; **à 1 000 m d'altitude** at a height ou an altitude of 1000 m; **en**

altitude at high altitudes; **perdre/prendre de l'altitude** to lose/gain height; **voler à haute/ basse altitude** to fly at a high/low altitude

alto [alto] *nm* (*instrument*) viola ♦ *nf* (contr)alto

aluminium [alyminjɔm] *nm* aluminium (*BRIT*), aluminum (*US*)

amabilité [amabilite] *nf* kindness; **il a eu l'amabilité de** he was kind *ou* good enough to

amadouer [amadwe] *vt* to coax, cajole; (*adoucir*) to mollify, soothe

amaigrir [amegʀiʀ] *vt* to make thin *ou* thinner

amaigrissant, e [amegʀisɑ̃, -ɑ̃t] *adj*: **régime amaigrissant** slimming (*BRIT*) *ou* weight-reduction (*US*) diet

amalgame [amalgam] *nm* amalgam; (*fig: de gens, d'idées*) hotch-potch, mixture

amande [amɑ̃d] *nf* (*de l'amandier*) almond; (*de noyau de fruit*) kernel; **en amande** (*yeux*) almond *cpd*, almond-shaped

amandier [amɑ̃dje] *nm* almond (tree)

amant [amɑ̃] *nm* lover

amarrer [amaʀe] *vt* (*NAVIG*) to moor; (*gén*) to make fast

amas [amɑ] *nm* heap, pile

amasser [amɑse] *vt* to amass; **s'amasser** *vi* to pile up, accumulate; (*foule*) to gather

amateur [amatœʀ] *nm* amateur; **en amateur** (*péj*) amateurishly; **musicien/sportif amateur** amateur musician/sportsman; **amateur de musique/sport** *etc* music/sport *etc* lover

amazone [amazɔn] *nf* horsewoman; **en amazone** side-saddle

ambassade [ɑ̃basad] *nf* embassy; (*mission*): **en ambassade** on a mission

ambassadeur, drice [ɑ̃basadœʀ, -dʀis] *nm/f* ambassador/ambassadress

ambiance [ɑ̃bjɑ̃s] *nf* atmosphere; **il y a de l'ambiance** everyone's having a good time

ambiant, e [ɑ̃bjɑ̃, -ɑ̃t] *adj* (*air, milieu*) surrounding; (*température*) ambient

ambigu, ë [ɑ̃bigy] *adj* ambiguous

ambitieux, euse [ɑ̃bisjø, -øz] *adj* ambitious

ambition [ɑ̃bisjɔ̃] *nf* ambition

ambulance [ɑ̃bylɑ̃s] *nf* ambulance

ambulancier, ière [ɑ̃bylɑ̃sje, -jɛʀ] *nm/f* ambulanceman/woman (*BRIT*), paramedic (*US*)

ambulant, e [ɑ̃bylɑ̃, -ɑ̃t] *adj* travelling, itinerant

âme [ɑm] *nf* soul; **rendre l'âme** to give up the ghost; **bonne âme** (*aussi ironique*) kind soul; **un joueur/tricheur dans l'âme** a gambler/cheat through and through; **âme sœur** kindred spirit

amélioration [ameljɔʀasjɔ̃] *nf* improvement

améliorer [ameljɔʀe] *vt* to improve; **s'améliorer** *vi* to improve, get better

aménager [amenaʒe] *vt* (*agencer: espace, local*) to fit out; (: *terrain*) to lay out; (: *quartier, territoire*) to develop; (*installer*) to fix up, put in; **ferme amé-**

nagée converted farmhouse

amende [amɑ̃d] *nf* fine; **mettre à l'amende** to penalize; **faire amende honorable** to make amends

amener [amne] *vt* to bring; (*causer*) to bring about; (*baisser: drapeau, voiles*) to strike; **s'amener** *vi* (*fam*) to show up, turn up; **amener qn à qch/à faire** to lead sb to sth/to do

amenuiser [amənɥize]: **s'amenuiser** *vi* to dwindle; (*chances*) to grow slimmer, lessen

amer, amère [amɛʀ] *adj* bitter

américain, e [ameʀikɛ̃, -ɛn] *adj* American ♦ *nm* (*LING*) American (English) ♦ *nm/f*: **Américain, e** American; **en vedette américaine** as a special guest (star)

Amérique [ameʀik] *nf* America; **l'Amérique centrale** Central America; **l'Amérique latine** Latin America; **l'Amérique du Nord** North America; **l'Amérique du Sud** South America

amertume [ameʀtym] *nf* bitterness

ameublement [amœbləmɑ̃] *nm* furnishing; (*meubles*) furniture; **articles d'ameublement** furnishings; **tissus d'ameublement** soft furnishings, furnishing fabrics

ameuter [amøte] *vt* (*badauds*) to draw a crowd of; (*peuple*) to rouse, stir up

ami, e [ami] *nm/f* friend; (*amant/maîtresse*) boyfriend/girlfriend ♦ *adj*: **pays/groupe ami** friendly country/group; **être (très) ami avec qn** to be (very) friendly with sb; **être ami de l'ordre** to be a lover of order; **un ami des arts** a patron of the arts; **un ami des chiens** a dog lover; **petit ami/ petite amie** (*fam*) boyfriend/girlfriend

amiable [amjabl(ə)]: **à l'amiable** *adv* (*JUR*) out of court; (*gén*) amicably

amiante [amjɑ̃t] *nm* asbestos

amical, e, aux [amikal, -o] *adj* friendly ♦ *nf* (*club*) association

amicalement [amikalmɑ̃] *adv* in a friendly way; (*formule épistolaire*) regards

amidon [amidɔ̃] *nm* starch

amincir [amɛ̃siʀ] *vt* (*objet*) to thin (down); **s'amincir** *vi* to get thinner *ou* slimmer; **amincir qn** to make sb thinner *ou* slimmer

amincissant, e [amɛ̃sisɑ̃, -ɑ̃t] *adj* slimming

amiral, aux [amiʀal, -o] *nm* admiral

amitié [amitje] *nf* friendship; **prendre en amitié** to take a liking to; **faire** *ou* **présenter ses amitiés à qn** to send sb one's best wishes; **amitiés** (*formule épistolaire*) (with) best wishes

ammoniaque [amɔnjak] *nf* ammonia (water)

amnistie [amnisti] *nf* amnesty

amoindrir [amwɛ̃dʀiʀ] *vt* to reduce

amollir [amɔliʀ] *vt* to soften

amonceler [amɔ̃sle] *vt*, **s'amonceler** *vi* to pile ou heap up; (*fig*) to accumulate

amont [amɔ̃]: **en amont** *adv* upstream; (*sur une*

pente) uphill; **en amont de** *prép* upstream from; uphill from, above

amorce [amɔʀs(ə)] *nf* (*sur un hameçon*) bait; (*explosif*) cap; (*tube*) primer; (: *contenu*) priming; (*fig*: *début*) beginning(s), start

amorcer [amɔʀse] *vt* to bait; to prime; (*commencer*) to begin, start

amorphe [amɔʀf(ə)] *adj* passive, lifeless

amortir [amɔʀtiʀ] *vt* (*atténuer*: *choc*) to absorb, cushion; (: *bruit, douleur*) to deaden; (*COMM*: *dette*) to pay off, amortize; (: *mise de fonds, matériel*) to write off; **amortir un abonnement** to make a season ticket pay (for itself)

amortisseur [amɔʀtisœʀ] *nm* shock absorber

amour [amuʀ] *nm* love; (*liaison*) love affair, love; (*statuette etc*) cupid; **un amour de** a lovely little; **faire l'amour** to make love

amouracher [amuʀaʃe]: **s'amouracher de** *vt* (*péj*) to become infatuated with

amoureux, euse [amuʀø, -øz] *adj* (*regard, tempérament*) amorous; (*vie, problèmes*) love *cpd*; (*personne*): **amoureux (de qn)** in love (with sb) ♦ *nm/f* lover ♦ *nmpl* courting couple(s); **tomber amoureux de qn** to fall in love sb; **être amoureux de qch** to be passionately fond of sth; **un amoureux de la nature** a nature lover

amour-propre, *pl* **amours-propres** [amuʀpʀɔpʀ(ə)] *nm* self-esteem

amovible [amɔvibl(ə)] *adj* removable, detachable

ampère [ɑ̃pɛʀ] *nm* amp(ere)

amphithéâtre [ɑ̃fiteatʀ(ə)] *nm* amphitheatre; (*d'université*) lecture hall *ou* theatre

ample [ɑ̃pl(ə)] *adj* (*vêtement*) roomy, ample; (*gestes, mouvement*) broad; (*ressources*) ample; **jusqu'à plus ample informé** (*ADMIN*) until further details are available

amplement [ɑ̃pləmɑ̃] *adv* amply; **amplement suffisant** ample, more than enough

ampleur [ɑ̃plœʀ] *nf* scale, size; extent, magnitude

amplificateur [ɑ̃plifikatœʀ] *nm* amplifier

amplifier [ɑ̃plifje] *vt* (*son, oscillation*) to amplify; (*fig*) to expand, increase

ampoule [ɑ̃pul] *nf* (*électrique*) bulb; (*de médicament*) phial; (*aux mains, pieds*) blister

ampoulé, e [ɑ̃pule] *adj* (*péj*) pompous, bombastic

amputer [ɑ̃pyte] *vt* (*MÉD*) to amputate; (*fig*) to cut *ou* reduce drastically; **amputer qn d'un bras/pied** to amputate sb's arm/foot

amusant, e [amyzɑ̃, -ɑ̃t] *adj* (*divertissant, spirituel*) entertaining, amusing; (*comique*) funny, amusing

amuse-gueule [amyzgœl] *nm inv* appetizer, snack

amusement [amyzmɑ̃] *nm* (*voir amusé*) amusement; (*voir amuser*) entertaining, amusing; (*jeu etc*) pastime, diversion

amuser [amyze] *vt* (*divertir*) to entertain, amuse; (*égayer, faire rire*) to amuse; (*détourner l'attention*

de) to distract; **s'amuser** *vi* (*jouer*) to amuse o.s., play; (*se divertir*) to enjoy o.s., have fun; (*fig*) to mess around; **s'amuser de qch** (*trouver comique*) to find sth amusing; **s'amuser avec** *ou* **de qn** (*duper*) to make a fool of sb

amygdale [amidal] *nf* tonsil; **opérer qn des amygdales** to take sb's tonsils out

an [ɑ̃] *nm* year; **être âgé de** *ou* **avoir 3 ans** to be 3 (years old); **en l'an 1980** in the year 1980; **le jour de l'an, le premier de l'an, le nouvel an** New Year's Day

analogique [analɔʒik] *adj* (*LOGIQUE*: *raisonnement*) analogical; (*calculateur, montre etc*) analogue; (*INFORM*) analog

analogue [analɔg] *adj*: **analogue (à)** analogous (to), similar (to)

analphabète [analfabet] *nm/f* illiterate

analyse [analiz] *nf* analysis; (*MÉD*) test; **faire l'analyse de** to analyse; **une analyse approfondie** an in-depth analysis; **en dernière analyse** in the last analysis; **avoir l'esprit d'analyse** to have an analytical turn of mind; **analyse grammaticale** grammatical analysis, parsing (*SCOL*)

analyser [analize] *vt* to analyse; (*MÉD*) to test

ananas [anana] *nm* pineapple

anarchie [anaʀʃi] *nf* anarchy

anatomie [anatɔmi] *nf* anatomy

ancêtre [ɑ̃sɛtʀ(ə)] *nm/f* ancestor; (*fig*): **l'ancêtre de** the forerunner of

anchois [ɑ̃ʃwa] *nm* anchovy

ancien, ne [ɑ̃sjɛ̃, -en] *adj* old; (*de jadis, de l'antiquité*) ancient; (*précédent, ex-*) former, old ♦ *nm* (*mobilier ancien*): **l'ancien** antiques *pl* ♦ *nm/f* (*dans une tribu etc*) elder; **un ancien ministre** a former minister; **mon ancienne voiture** my previous car; **être plus ancien que qn dans une maison** to have been in a firm longer than sb; (*dans l'hiérarchie*) to be senior to sb in a firm; **ancien combattant** ex-serviceman; **ancien (élève)** (*SCOL*) ex-pupil (*BRIT*), alumnus (*US*)

anciennement [ɑ̃sjɛnmɑ̃] *adv* formerly

ancienneté [ɑ̃sjɛnte] *nf* oldness; antiquity; (*ADMIN*) (length of) service; seniority

ancre [ɑ̃kʀ(ə)] *nf* anchor; **jeter/lever l'ancre** to cast/weigh anchor; **à l'ancre** at anchor

ancrer [ɑ̃kʀe] *vt* (*CONSTR*) to anchor; (*fig*) to fix firmly; **s'ancrer** *vi* (*NAVIG*) to (cast) anchor

Andorre [ɑ̃dɔʀ] *nf* Andorra

andouille [ɑ̃duj] *nf* (*CULIN*) sausage made of chitterlings; (*fam*) clot, nit

âne [ɑn] *nm* donkey, ass; (*péj*) dunce, fool

anéantir [aneɑ̃tiʀ] *vt* to annihilate, wipe out; (*fig*) to obliterate, destroy; (*déprimer*) to overwhelm

anémie [anemi] *nf* anaemia

anémique [anemik] *adj* anaemic

ânerie [ɑnʀi] *nf* stupidity; (*parole etc*) stupid *ou* idiotic comment *etc*

anesthésie [anɛstezi] *nf* anaesthesia; **sous anesthésie** under anaesthetic; **anesthésie générale/locale** general/local anaesthetic; **faire une anesthésie locale à qn** to give sb a local anaesthetic

ange [ãʒ] *nm* angel; **être aux anges** to be over the moon; **ange gardien** guardian angel

angélus [ãʒelys] *nm* angelus; (*cloches*) evening bells *pl*

angine [ãʒin] *nf* sore throat, throat infection; **angine de poitrine** angina (pectoris)

anglais, e [ãglɛ, -ɛz] *adj* English ◆ *nm* (LING) English ◆ *nm/f*: **Anglais, e** Englishman/woman; **les Anglais** the English; **filer à l'anglaise** to take French leave; **à l'anglaise** (CULIN) boiled

angle [ãgl(ə)] *nm* angle; (*coin*) corner; **angle droit/obtus/aigu/mort** right/obtuse/acute/dead angle

Angleterre [ãglətɛʀ] *nf*: **l'Angleterre** England

anglophone [ãglɔfɔn] *adj* English-speaking

angoisse [ãgwas] *nf*: **l'angoisse** anguish *no pl*

angoissé, e [ãgwase] *adj* anguished; (*personne*) full of anxieties *ou* hang-ups (*fam*)

angoisser [ãgwase] *vt* to harrow, cause anguish to ◆ *vi* to worry, fret

anguille [ãgij] *nf* eel; **anguille de mer** conger (eel); **il y a anguille sous roche** (*fig*) there's something going on, there's something beneath all this

anicroche [anikʀɔʃ] *nf* hitch, snag

animal, e, aux [animal, -o] *adj, nm* animal; **animal domestique/sauvage** domestic/wild animal

animateur, trice [animatœʀ, -tʀis] *nm/f* (*de télévision*) host; (*de music-hall*) compère; (*de groupe*) leader, organizer; (CINÉ: *technicien*) animator

animation [animasjɔ̃] *nf* (*voir animé*) busyness; liveliness; (CINÉ: *technique*) animation; **animations** *nfpl* (*activité*) activities; **centre d'animation** = community centre

animé, e [anime] *adj* (*rue, lieu*) busy, lively; (*conversation, réunion*) lively, animated; (*opposé à inanimé, aussi* LING) animate

animer [anime] *vt* (*ville, soirée*) to liven up, enliven; (*mettre en mouvement*) to drive; (*stimuler*) to drive, impel; **s'animer** *vi* to liven up, come to life

anis [ani] *nm* (CULIN) aniseed; (BOT) anise

ankyloser [ãkiloze]: **s'ankyloser** *vi* to get stiff, ankylose

anneau, x [ano] *nm* ring; (*de chaîne*) link; (SPORT): **exercices aux anneaux** ring exercises

année [ane] *nf* year; **souhaiter la bonne année à qn** to wish sb a Happy New Year; **tout au long de l'année** all year long; **d'une année à l'autre** from one year to the next; **d'année en année** from year to year; **l'année scolaire/fiscale** the school/tax year

annexe [anɛks(ə)] *adj* (*problème*) related; (*document*) appended; (*salle*) adjoining ◆ *nf* (*bâtiment*) annex(e); (*de document, ouvrage*) annex, appendix;
(*jointe à une lettre, un dossier*) enclosure

anniversaire [anivɛʀsɛʀ] *nm* birthday; (*d'un événement, bâtiment*) anniversary ◆ *adj*: **jour anniversaire** anniversary

annonce [anɔ̃s] *nf* announcement; (*signe, indice*) sign; (*aussi*: **annonce publicitaire**) advertisement; (CARTES) declaration; **annonce personnelle** personal message; **les petites annonces** the small *ou* classified ads

annoncer [anɔ̃se] *vt* to announce; (*être le signe de*) to herald; (CARTES) to declare; **je vous annonce que …** I wish to tell you that …; **s'annoncer bien/difficile** to look promising/difficult; **annoncer la couleur** (*fig*) to lay one's cards on the table

annonceur, euse [anɔ̃sœʀ, -øz] *nm/f* (TV, RADIO: *speaker*) announcer; (*publicitaire*) advertiser

annuaire [anɥɛʀ] *nm* yearbook, annual; **annuaire téléphonique** (telephone) directory, phone book

annuel, le [anɥɛl] *adj* annual, yearly

annuité [anɥite] *nf* annual instalment

annulation [anylasjɔ̃] *nf* cancellation; annulment; quashing, repeal

annuler [anyle] *vt* (*rendez-vous, voyage*) to cancel, call off; (*mariage*) to annul; (*jugement*) to quash (BRIT), repeal (US); (*résultats*) to declare void; (MATH, PHYSIQUE) to cancel out; **s'annuler** to cancel each other out

anodin, e [anɔdɛ̃, -in] *adj* harmless; (*sans importance*) insignificant, trivial

anonymat [anɔnima] *nm* anonymity; **garder l'anonymat** to remain anonymous

anonyme [anɔnim] *adj* anonymous; (*fig*) impersonal

anorak [anɔʀak] *nm* anorak

anorexie [anɔʀɛksi] *nf* anorexia

anormal, e, aux [anɔʀmal, -o] *adj* abnormal; (*insolite*) unusual, abnormal

ANPE *sigle f* (= Agence nationale pour l'emploi) national employment agency (*functions include job creation*)

anse [ãs] *nf* handle; (GÉO) cove

antan [ãtã]: **d'antan** *adj* of yesteryear, of long ago

antarctique [ãtaʀktik] *adj* Antarctic ◆ *nm*: **l'Antarctique** the Antarctic; **le cercle Antarctique** the Antarctic Circle; **l'océan Antarctique** the Antarctic Ocean

antécédent [ãtesedã] *nm* (LING) antecedent; **antécédents** *nmpl* (MÉD *etc*) past history *sg*; **antécédents professionnels** record, career to date

antenne [ãtɛn] *nf* (*de radio, télévision*) aerial; (*d'insecte*) antenna (*pl* -ae), feeler; (*poste avancé*) outpost; (*petite succursale*) sub-branch; **sur l'antenne** on the air; **passer à/avoir l'antenne** to go/be on the air; **2 heures d'antenne** 2 hours' broadcasting time; **hors antenne** off the air; **antenne chirurgicale** (MIL) advance surgical unit

antérieur, e [ɑ̃teʀjœʀ] *adj (d'avant)* previous, earlier; *(de devant)* front; **antérieur à** prior ou previous to; **passé/futur antérieur** *(LING)* past/future anterior

antialcoolique [ɑ̃tialkɔlik] *adj* anti-alcohol; **ligue antialcoolique** temperance league

antiatomique [ɑ̃tiatɔmik] *adj*: **abri anti-atomique** fallout shelter

antibiotique [ɑ̃tibjɔtik] *nm* antibiotic

antibrouillard [ɑ̃tibʀujaʀ] *adj*: **phare antibrouillard** fog lamp

anticipation [ɑ̃tisipasjɔ̃] *nf* anticipation; *(COMM)* payment in advance; **par anticipation** in anticipation, in advance; **livre/film d'anticipation** science fiction book/film

anticipé, e [ɑ̃tisipe] *adj (règlement, paiement)* early, in advance; *(joie etc)* anticipated, early; **avec mes remerciements anticipés** thanking you in advance ou anticipation

anticiper [ɑ̃tisipe] *vt* to anticipate, foresee; *(paiement)* to pay ou make in advance ◆ *vi* to look ou think ahead; *(en racontant)* to jump ahead; *(prévoir)* to anticipate; **anticiper sur** to anticipate

anticonceptionnel, le [ɑ̃tikɔ̃sepsjɔnel] *adj* contraceptive

anticorps [ɑ̃tikɔʀ] *nm* antibody

antidote [ɑ̃tidɔt] *nm* antidote

antigel [ɑ̃tiʒel] *nm* antifreeze

antihistaminique [ɑ̃tiistaminik] *nm* antihistamine

antillais, e [ɑ̃tijɛ, -ɛz] *adj* West Indian

Antilles [ɑ̃tij] *nfpl*: **les Antilles** the West Indies; **les Grandes/Petites Antilles** the Greater/Lesser Antilles

antilope [ɑ̃tilɔp] *nf* antelope

antimite(s) [ɑ̃timit] *adj, nm*: **(produit) antimite(s)** mothproofer, moth repellent

antipathique [ɑ̃tipatik] *adj* unpleasant, disagreeable

antipelliculaire [ɑ̃tipelikylɛʀ] *adj* anti-dandruff

antipodes [ɑ̃tipɔd] *nmpl (GÉO)*: **les antipodes** the antipodes; *(fig)*: **être aux antipodes de** to be the opposite extreme of

antiquaire [ɑ̃tikɛʀ] *nm/f* antique dealer

antique [ɑ̃tik] *adj* antique; *(très vieux)* ancient, antiquated

antiquité [ɑ̃tikite] *nf (objet)* antique; **l'Antiquité** Antiquity; **magasin/marchand d'antiquités** antique shop/dealer

antirabique [ɑ̃tiʀabik] *adj* rabies *cpd*

antirouille [ɑ̃tiʀuj] *adj inv*: **peinture antirouille** antirust paint; **traitement antirouille** rustproofing

antisémite [ɑ̃tisemit] *adj* anti-Semitic

antiseptique [ɑ̃tiseptik] *adj, nm* antiseptic

antivol [ɑ̃tivɔl] *adj, nm*: **(dispositif) antivol** antitheft device; *(pour vélo)* padlock

antre [ɑ̃tʀ(ə)] *nm* den, lair

anxiété [ɑ̃ksjete] *nf* anxiety

anxieux, euse [ɑ̃ksjø, -øz] *adj* anxious, worried; **être anxieux de faire** to be anxious to do

AOC *sigle f* (= Appellation d'origine contrôlée) guarantee of quality of wine; *see boxed note*

AOC

AOC ('appellation d'origine contrôlée') is the highest French wine classification. It indicates that the wine meets strict requirements concerning vineyard of origin, type of grape, method of production and alcoholic strength.

---

août [u] *nm* August; *voir aussi* **juillet**, **Assomption**

apaiser [apeze] *vt (colère)* to calm, quell, soothe; *(faim)* to appease, assuage; *(douleur)* to soothe; *(personne)* to calm (down), pacify; **s'apaiser** *vi (tempête, bruit)* to die down, subside

apanage [apanaʒ] *nm*: **être l'apanage de** to be the privilege ou prerogative of

aparté [apaʀte] *nm (THÉÂT)* aside; *(entretien)* private conversation; **en aparté** *adv* in an aside *(BRIT)*; *(entretien)* in private

apathique [apatik] *adj* apathetic

apatride [apatʀid] *nm/f* stateless person

apercevoir [apɛʀsəvwaʀ] *vt* to see; **s'apercevoir de** *vt* to notice; **s'apercevoir que** to notice that; **sans s'en apercevoir** without realizing ou noticing

aperçu, e [apɛʀsy] *pp de* **apercevoir** ◆ *nm (vue d'ensemble)* general survey; *(intuition)* insight

apéritif, ive [apeʀitif, -iv] *adj* which stimulates the appetite ◆ *nm (boisson)* aperitif; *(réunion)* (pre-lunch ou -dinner) drinks *pl*; **prendre l'apéritif** to have drinks (before lunch ou dinner) ou an aperitif

à-peu-près [apøpʀɛ] *nm inv (péj)* vague approximation

apeuré, e [apœʀe] *adj* frightened, scared

aphte [aft(ə)] *nm* mouth ulcer

apiculture [apikyltyʀ] *nf* beekeeping, apiculture

apitoyer [apitwaje] *vt* to move to pity; **apitoyer qn sur qn/qch** to move sb to pity for sb/over sth; **s'apitoyer (sur qn/qch)** to feel pity ou compassion (for sb/over sth)

aplanir [aplaniʀ] *vt* to level; *(fig)* to smooth away, iron out

aplatir [aplatiʀ] *vt* to flatten; **s'aplatir** *vi* to become flatter; *(écrasé)* to be flattened; *(fig)* to lie flat on the ground; *(fam)* to fall flat on one's face; *(: péj)* to grovel

aplomb [aplɔ̃] *nm (équilibre)* balance, equilibrium; *(fig)* self-assurance; *(: péj)* nerve; **d'aplomb** *adv* steady; *(CONSTR)* plumb

apogée [apɔʒe] *nm (fig)* peak, apogee

apologie [apɔlɔʒi] *nf* praise; *(JUR)* vindication

a posteriori [apɔsteʀjɔʀi] *adv* after the event, with hindsight, a posteriori

apostrophe [apɔstʀɔf] *nf* (*signe*) apostrophe; (*appel*) interpellation

apostropher [apɔstʀɔfe] *vt* (*interpeller*) to shout at, address sharply

apothéose [apɔteoz] *nf* pinnacle (of achievement); (*MUS etc*) grand finale

apôtre [apotʀ(ə)] *nm* apostle, disciple

apparaître [apaʀɛtʀ(ə)] *vi* to appear ♦ *vb avec attribut* to appear, seem

apparat [apaʀa] *nm*: **tenue/dîner d'apparat** ceremonial dress/dinner

appareil [apaʀɛj] *nm* (*outil, machine*) piece of apparatus, device; (*électrique etc*) appliance; (*politique, syndical*) machinery; (*avion*) (aero)plane (*BRIT*), (air)plane (*US*), aircraft *inv*; (*téléphonique*) telephone; (*dentier*) brace (*BRIT*), braces (*US*); **appareil digestif/reproducteur** digestive/reproductive system *ou* apparatus; **l'appareil productif** the means of production; **qui est à l'appareil?** who's speaking?; **dans le plus simple appareil** in one's birthday suit; **appareil (photographique)** camera; **appareil 24 x 36** *ou* **petit format** 35 mm camera

appareiller [apaʀeje] *vi* (*NAVIG*) to cast off, get under way ♦ *vt* (*assortir*) to match up

appareil-photo, *pl* **appareils-photos** [apaʀɛj-fɔto] *nm* camera

apparemment [apaʀamɑ̃] *adv* apparently

apparence [apaʀɑ̃s] *nf* appearance; **malgré les apparences** despite appearances; **en apparence** apparently, seemingly

apparent, e [apaʀɑ̃, -ɑ̃t] *adj* visible; (*évident*) obvious; (*superficiel*) apparent; **coutures apparentes** topstitched seams; **poutres apparentes** exposed beams

apparenté, e [apaʀɑ̃te] *adj*: **apparenté à** related to; (*fig*) similar to

apparition [apaʀisjɔ̃] *nf* appearance; (*surnaturelle*) apparition; **faire son apparition** to appear

appartement [apaʀtəmɑ̃] *nm* flat (*BRIT*), apartment (*US*)

appartenir [apaʀtəniʀ]: **appartenir à** *vt* to belong to; (*faire partie de*) to belong to, be a member of; **il lui appartient de** it is up to him to

apparu, e [apaʀy] *pp de* **apparaître**

appât [apɑ] *nm* (*PÊCHE*) bait; (*fig*) lure, bait

appâter [apɑte] *vt* (*hameçon*) to bait; (*poisson, fig*) to lure, entice

appauvrir [apovʀiʀ] *vt* to impoverish; **s'appauvrir** *vi* to grow poorer, become impoverished

appel [apɛl] *nm* call; (*nominal*) roll call; (: *SCOL*) register; (*MIL*: *recrutement*) call-up; (*JUR*) appeal; **faire appel à** (*invoquer*) to appeal to; (*avoir recours à*) to call on; (*nécessiter*) to call for, require; **faire** *ou* **interjeter appel** (*JUR*) to appeal, lodge an appeal; **faire l'appel** to call the roll; to call the register; **indicatif d'appel** call sign; **numéro d'appel** (*TÉL*) number; **produit d'appel** (*COMM*) loss leader; **sans appel**

(*fig*) final, irrevocable; **appel d'air** in-draught; **appel d'offres** (*COMM*) invitation to tender; **faire un appel de phares** to flash one's headlights; **appel (téléphonique)** (tele)phone call

appelé [aple] *nm* (*MIL*) conscript

appeler [aple] *vt* to call; (*TÉL*) to call, ring; (*faire venir*: *médecin etc*) to call, send for; (*fig*: *nécessiter*) to call for, demand; **appeler au secours** to call for help; **appeler qn à l'aide** *ou* **au secours** to call to sb for help; **appeler qn à un poste/des fonctions** to appoint sb to a post/assign duties to sb; **être appelé à** (*fig*) to be destined to; **appeler qn à comparaître** (*JUR*) to summon sb to appear; **en appeler à** to appeal to; **s'appeler**: **elle s'appelle Gabrielle** her name is Gabrielle, she's called Gabrielle; **comment ça s'appelle?** what is it *ou* that called?

appendice [apɛ̃dis] *nm* appendix

appendicite [apɛ̃disit] *nf* appendicitis

appentis [apɑ̃ti] *nm* lean-to

appesantir [apzɑ̃tiʀ]: **s'appesantir** *vi* to grow heavier; **s'appesantir sur** (*fig*) to dwell at length on

appétissant, e [apetisɑ̃, -ɑ̃t] *adj* appetizing, mouth-watering

appétit [apeti] *nm* appetite; **couper l'appétit à qn** to take away sb's appetite; **bon appétit!** enjoy your meal!

applaudir [aplodiʀ] *vt* to applaud ♦ *vi* to applaud, clap; **applaudir à** *vt* (*décision*) to applaud, commend

applaudissements [aplodismɑ̃] *nmpl* applause *sg*, clapping *sg*

application [aplikasjɔ̃] *nf* application; (*d'une loi*) enforcement; **mettre en application** to implement

applique [aplik] *nf* wall lamp

appliquer [aplike] *vt* to apply; (*loi*) to enforce; (*donner*: *gifle, châtiment*) to give; **s'appliquer** *vi* (*suj*: *élève etc*) to apply o.s.; **s'appliquer à** (*loi, remarque*) to apply to; **s'appliquer à faire qch** to apply o.s. to doing sth, take pains to do sth; **s'appliquer sur** (*coïncider avec*) to fit over

appoint [apwɛ̃] *nm* (*extra*) contribution *ou* help; **avoir/faire l'appoint** (*en payant*) to have/give the right change *ou* money; **chauffage d'appoint** extra heating

appointements [apwɛ̃tmɑ̃] *nmpl* salary *sg*, stipend (*surtout REL*)

apport [apɔʀ] *nm* supply; (*argent, biens etc*) contribution

apporter [apɔʀte] *vt* to bring; (*preuve*) to give, provide; (*modification*) to make; (*suj*: *remarque*) to contribute, add

apposer [apoze] *vt* to append; (*sceau etc*) to affix

appréciable [apʀesjabl(ə)] *adj* (*important*) appreciable, significant

apprécier [apʀesje] *vt* to appreciate; (*évaluer*) to estimate, assess; **j'apprécierais que tu ...** I should appreciate (it) if you …

appréhender [apreɑ̃de] *vt* (*craindre*) to dread; (*arrêter*) to apprehend; **appréhender que** to fear that; **appréhender de faire** to dread doing

appréhension [apreɑ̃sjɔ̃] *nf* apprehension

apprendre [aprɑ̃dr(ə)] *vt* to learn; (*événement, résultats*) to learn of, hear of; **apprendre qch à qn** (*informer*) to tell sb (of) sth; (*enseigner*) to teach sb sth; **tu me l'apprends!** that's news to me!; **apprendre à faire qch** to learn to do sth; **apprendre à qn à faire qch** to teach sb to do sth

apprenti, e [aprɑ̃ti] *nm/f* apprentice; (*fig*) novice, beginner

apprentissage [aprɑ̃tisaʒ] *nm* learning; (*COMM, SCOL: période*) apprenticeship; **école** *ou* **centre d'apprentissage** training school *ou* centre; **faire l'apprentissage de qch** (*fig*) to be initiated into sth

apprêté, e [aprete] *adj* (*fig*) affected

apprêter [aprete] *vt* to dress, finish; **s'apprêter** *vi*: **s'apprêter à qch/à faire qch** to prepare for sth/for doing sth

appris, e [apri, -iz] *pp de* **apprendre**

apprivoiser [aprivwaze] *vt* to tame

approbation [aprɔbasjɔ̃] *nf* approval; **digne d'approbation** (*conduite, travail*) praiseworthy, commendable

approchant, e [aprɔʃɑ̃, -ɑ̃t] *adj* similar, close; **quelque chose d'approchant** something similar

approche [aprɔʃ] *nf* approaching; (*arrivée, attitude*) approach; **approches** *nfpl* (*abords*) surroundings; **à l'approche du bateau/de l'ennemi** as the ship/enemy approached *ou* drew near; **l'approche d'un problème** the approach to a problem; **travaux d'approche** (*fig*) manoeuvrings

approcher [aprɔʃe] *vi* to approach, come near ◆ *vt* (*vedette, artiste*) to come close to, approach; (*rapprocher*) **approcher qch (de qch)** to bring *ou* put *ou* move sth near (to sth); **s'approcher de** *vt* to approach, go *ou* come *ou* move near to; **approchez-vous** come *ou* go nearer

approfondir [aprɔfɔ̃dir] *vt* to deepen; (*question*) to go further into; **sans approfondir** without going too deeply into it

approprié, e [aprɔprije] *adj*: **approprié (à)** appropriate (to), suited to

approprier [aprɔprije] *vt* (*adapter*) adapt; **s'approprier** *vt* to appropriate, take over

approuver [apruve] *vt* to agree with; (*autoriser: loi, projet*) to approve, pass; (*trouver louable*) to approve of; **je vous approuve entièrement/ne vous approuve pas** I agree with you entirely/don't agree with you; **lu et approuvé** (read and) approved

approvisionner [aprɔvizjɔne] *vt* to supply; (*compte bancaire*) to pay funds into; **approvisionner qn en** to supply sb with; **s'approvisionner** *vi*: **s'approvisionner dans un certain magasin/au marché** to shop in a certain shop/at the market; **s'approvisionner en** to stock up with

approximatif, ive [aprɔksimatif, -iv] *adj* approximate, rough; (*imprécis*) vague

appt *abr* = **appartement**

appui [apɥi] *nm* support; **prendre appui sur** to lean on; (*suj: objet*) to rest on; **point d'appui** fulcrum; (*fig*) something to lean on; **à l'appui de** (*pour prouver*) in support of; **à l'appui** *adv* to support one's argument; **l'appui de la fenêtre** the windowsill, the window ledge

appui-tête, appuie-tête [apɥitet] *nm inv* headrest

appuyer [apɥije] *vt* (*poser*): **appuyer qch sur/ contre/à** to lean *ou* rest sth on/against/on; (*soutenir: personne, demande*) to support, back (up) ◆ *vi*: **appuyer sur** (*bouton, frein*) to press, push; (*mot, détail*) to stress, emphasize; (*suj: chose: peser sur*) to rest (heavily) on, press against; **s'appuyer sur** *vt* to lean on; (*compter sur*) to rely on; **s'appuyer sur qn** to lean on sb; **appuyer contre** (*toucher: mur, porte*) to lean *ou* rest against; **appuyer à droite** *ou* **sur sa droite** to bear (to the) right; **appuyer sur le champignon** to put one's foot down

âpre [ɑpr] *adj* acrid, pungent; (*fig*) harsh; (*lutte*) bitter; **âpre au gain** grasping, greedy

après [apre] *prép* ◆ *adv* afterwards; **2 heures après** 2 hours later; **après qu'il est parti/ avoir fait** after he left/having done; **courir après qn** to run after sb; **crier après qn** to shout at sb; **être toujours après qn** (*critiquer etc*) to be always on at sb; **après quoi** after which; **d'après** *prép* (*selon*) according to; **d'après lui** according to him; **d'après moi** in my opinion; **après coup** *adv* after the event, afterwards; **après tout** *adv* (*au fond*) after all; **et (puis) après?** so what?

après-demain [apredmɛ̃] *adv* the day after tomorrow

après-guerre [apreɡɛr] *nm* post-war years *pl*; **d'après-guerre** *adj* post-war

après-midi [apremidi] *nm ou nf inv* afternoon

après-rasage [aprerazaʒ] *nm inv*: **(lotion) après-rasage** after-shave (lotion)

après-shampooing [apreʃɑ̃pwɛ̃] *nm inv* conditioner

après-ski [apreski] *nm inv* (*chaussure*) snow boot; (*moment*) après-ski

à-propos [apropo] *nm* (*d'une remarque*) aptness; **faire preuve d'à-propos** to show presence of mind, do the right thing; **avec à-propos** suitably, aptly

apte [apt(ə)] *adj*: **apte à qch/faire qch** capable of sth/doing sth; **apte (au service)** (*MIL*) fit (for service)

aquarelle [akwarɛl] *nf* (*tableau*) watercolour (*BRIT*), watercolor (*US*); (*genre*) watercolo(u)rs *pl*, aquarelle

aquarium [akwaʀjɔm] *nm* aquarium

arabe [aʀab] *adj* Arabic; (*désert, cheval*) Arabian; (*nation, peuple*) Arab ♦ *nm* (*LING*) Arabic ♦ *nm/f*: **Arabe** Arab

Arabie [aʀabi] *nf*: **l'Arabie** Arabia; **l'Arabie Saoudite** *ou* **Séoudite** Saudi Arabia

arachide [aʀaʃid] *nf* groundnut (plant); (*graine*) peanut, groundnut

araignée [aʀeɲe] *nf* spider; **araignée de mer** spider crab

arbitraire [aʀbitʀɛʀ] *adj* arbitrary

arbitre [aʀbitʀ(ə)] *nm* (*SPORT*) referee; (: *TENNIS, CRICKET*) umpire; (*fig*) arbiter, judge; (*JUR*) arbitrator

arbitrer [aʀbitʀe] *vt* to referee; to umpire; to arbitrate

arborer [aʀbɔʀe] *vt* to bear, display; (*avec ostentation*) to sport

arbre [aʀbʀ(ə)] *nm* tree; (*TECH*) shaft; **arbre à cames** (*AUTO*) camshaft; **arbre fruitier** fruit tree; **arbre généalogique** family tree; **arbre de Noël** Christmas tree; **arbre de transmission** (*AUTO*) driveshaft

arbuste [aʀbyst(ə)] *nm* small shrub, bush

arc [aʀk] *nm* (*arme*) bow; (*GÉOM*) arc; (*ARCHIT*) arch; **arc de cercle** arc of a circle; **en arc de cercle** *adj* semi-circular

arcade [aʀkad] *nf* arch(way); **arcades** *nfpl*, arcade *sg*, arches; **arcade sourcilière** arch of the eyebrows

arcanes [aʀkan] *nmpl* mysteries

arc-boutant, *pl* **arcs-boutants** [aʀkbutɑ̃] *nm* flying buttress

arceau, x [aʀso] *nm* (*métallique etc*) hoop

arc-en-ciel, *pl* **arcs-en-ciel** [aʀkɑ̃sjɛl] *nm* rainbow

arche [aʀʃ(ə)] *nf* arch; **arche de Noé** Noah's Ark

archéologie [aʀkeɔlɔʒi] *nf* arch(a)eology

archéologue [aʀkeɔlɔg] *nm/f* arch(a)eologist

archet [aʀʃɛ] *nm* bow

archevêque [aʀʃəvɛk] *nm* archbishop

archipel [aʀʃipɛl] *nm* archipelago

architecte [aʀʃitɛkt(ə)] *nm* architect

architecture [aʀʃitɛktyʀ] *nf* architecture

archive [aʀʃiv] *nf* file; **archives** *nfpl* archives

arctique [aʀktik] *adj* Arctic ♦ *nm*: **l'Arctique** the Arctic; **le cercle Arctique** the Arctic Circle; **l'océan Arctique** the Arctic Ocean

ardemment [aʀdamɑ̃] *adv* ardently, fervently

ardent, e [aʀdɑ̃, -ɑ̃t] *adj* (*soleil*) blazing; (*fièvre*) raging; (*amour*) ardent, passionate; (*prière*) fervent

ardeur [aʀdœʀ] *nf* blazing heat; (*fig*) fervour, ardour

ardoise [aʀdwaz] *nf* slate

ardu, e [aʀdy] *adj* arduous, difficult; (*pente*) steep, abrupt

arène [aʀɛn] *nf* arena; (*fig*): **l'arène politique** the politicalr arena; **arènes** *nfpl* bull-ring *sg*

arête [aʀɛt] *nf* (*de poisson*) bone; (*d'une montagne*) ridge; (*GÉOM etc*) edge (*where two faces meet*)

argent [aʀʒɑ̃] *nm* (*métal*) silver; (*monnaie*) money; (*couleur*) silver; **en avoir pour son argent** to get money for money; **gagner beaucoup d'argent** to earn a lot of money; **argent comptant** (hard) cash; **argent liquide** ready money, (ready) cash; **argent de poche** pocket money

argenté, e [aʀʒɑ̃te] *adj* silver(y); (*métal*) silver-plated

argenterie [aʀʒɑ̃tʀi] *nf* silverware; (*en métal argenté*) silver plate

argentin, e [aʀʒɑ̃tɛ̃, -in] *adj* Argentinian, Argentine ♦ *nm/f*: **Argentin, e** Argentinian, Argentine

Argentine [aʀʒɑ̃tin] *nf*: **l'Argentine** Argentina, the Argentine

argentique [aʀʒɑ̃tik] *adj* (*appareil-photo*) film (*cpd*)

argile [aʀʒil] *nf* clay

argot [aʀgo] *nm* slang; *see boxed note*

ARGOT

Argot was the term originally used to describe the jargon of the criminal underworld, characterized by colourful images and distinctive intonation and designed to confuse the outsider. Some French authors write in **argot** and so have helped it spread and grow. More generally, the special vocabulary used by any social or professional group is also known as **argot**.

---

argotique [aʀgɔtik] *adj* slang *cpd*; (*très familier*) slangy

argument [aʀgymɑ̃] *nm* argument

argumentaire [aʀgymɑ̃tɛʀ] *nm* list of sales points; (*brochure*) sales leaflet

argumenter [aʀgymɑ̃te] *vi* to argue

argus [aʀgys] *nm* guide to second-hand car etc prices

aride [aʀid] *adj* arid

aristocratie [aʀistɔkʀasi] *nf* aristocracy

aristocratique [aʀistɔkʀatik] *adj* aristocratic

arithmétique [aʀitmetik] *adj* arithmetic(al) ♦ *nf* arithmetic

armateur [aʀmatœʀ] *nm* shipowner

armature [aʀmatyʀ] *nf* framework; (*de tente etc*) frame; (*de corset*) bone; (*de soutien-gorge*) wiring

arme [aʀm(ə)] *nf* weapon; (*section de l'armée*) arm; **armes** *nfpl* weapons, arms; (*blason*) (coat of) arms; **les armes** (*profession*) soldiering *sg*; **à armes égales** on equal terms; **en armes** up in arms; **passer par les armes** to execute (by firing squad); **prendre/présenter les armes** to take up/present arms; **se battre à l'arme blanche** to fight with blades; **arme à feu** firearm

armée [aʀme] *nf* army; **armée de l'air** Air Force; **l'armée du Salut** the Salvation Army; **armée de**

terre Army

armement [aʀməmɑ̃] *nm* (*matériel*) arms *pl*, weapons *pl*; (: *d'un pays*) arms *pl*, armament; (*action d'équiper: d'un navire*) fitting out; **armements nucléaires** nuclear armaments; **course aux armements** arms race

armer [aʀme] *vt* to arm; (*arme à feu*) to cock; (*appareil-photo*) to wind on; **armer qch de** to fit sth with; (*renforcer*) to reinforce sth with; **armer qn de** to arm *ou* equip sb with; **s'armer de** to arm o.s. with

armistice [aʀmistis] *nm* armistice; **l'Armistice** ≈ Remembrance (*BRIT*) *ou* Veterans (*US*) Day

armoire [aʀmwaʀ] *nf* (tall) cupboard; (*penderie*) wardrobe (*BRIT*), closet (*US*); **armoire à pharmacie** medicine chest

armoiries [aʀmwaʀi] *nfpl* coat of arms *sg*

armure [aʀmyʀ] *nf* armour *no pl*, suit of armour

armurier [aʀmyʀje] *nm* gunsmith; (*MIL, d'armes blanches*) armourer

arnaque [aʀnak] *nf*: **de l'arnaque** daylight robbery

arnaquer [aʀnake] *vt* to do (*fam*), swindle; **se faire arnaquer** to be had (*fam*) *ou* done (*fam*)

arobase [aʀobaz] *nf* at symbol, @

aromates [aʀomat] *nmpl* seasoning *sg*, herbs (and spices)

aromathérapie [aʀomateʀapi] *nf* aromatherapy

aromatisé, e [aʀomatize] *adj* flavoured

arôme [aʀom] *nm* aroma; (*d'une fleur etc*) fragrance

arpenter [aʀpɑ̃te] *vt* to pace up and down

arpenteur [aʀpɑ̃tœʀ] *nm* land surveyor

arqué, e [aʀke] *adj* arched; (*jambes*) bow *cpd*, bandy

arrache-pied [aʀaʃpje]: **d'arrache-pied** *adv* relentlessly

arracher [aʀaʃe] *vt* to pull out; (*page etc*) to tear off, tear out; (*déplanter: légume*) to lift; (: *herbe, souche*) to pull up; (*bras etc: par explosion*) to blow off; (: *par accident*) to tear off; **s'arracher** *vt* (*article très recherché*) to fight over; **arracher qch à qn** to snatch sth from sb; (*fig*) to wring sth out of sb, wrest sth from sb; **arracher qn à** (*solitude, rêverie*) to drag sb out of; (*famille etc*) to tear *ou* wrench sb away from; **se faire arracher une dent** to have a tooth out *ou* pulled (*US*)

arraisonner [aʀezɔne] *vt* to board and search

arrangeant, e [aʀɑ̃ʒɑ̃, -ɑ̃t] *adj* accommodating, obliging

arrangement [aʀɑ̃ʒmɑ̃] *nm* arrangement

arranger [aʀɑ̃ʒe] *vt* to arrange; (*réparer*) to fix, put right; (*régler*) to settle, sort out; (*convenir à*) to suit, be convenient for; **s'arranger** (*se mettre d'accord*) to come to an agreement *ou* arrangement; (*s'améliorer: querelle, situation*) to be sorted out; (*se débrouiller*): **s'arranger pour que ...** to arrange things so that ...; **je vais m'arranger** I'll manage;

ça va s'arranger it'll sort itself out; **s'arranger pour faire** to make sure that *ou* see to it that one can do

arrestation [aʀestasjɔ̃] *nf* arrest

arrêt [aʀe] *nm* stopping; (*de bus etc*) stop; (*JUR*) judgment, decision; (*FOOTBALL*) save; **arrêts** *nmpl* (*MIL*) arrest *sg*; **être à l'arrêt** to be stopped, have come to a halt; **rester** *ou* **tomber en arrêt devant** to stop short in front of; **sans arrêt** without stopping, non-stop; (*fréquemment*) continually; **arrêt d'autobus** bus stop; **arrêt facultatif** request stop; **arrêt de mort** capital sentence; **arrêt de travail** stoppage (of work)

arrêté, e [aʀete] *adj* (*idées*) firm, fixed ♦ *nm* order, decree; **arrêté municipal** ≈ bylaw, byelaw

arrêter [aʀete] *vt* to stop; (*chauffage etc*) to turn off, switch off; (*COMM: compte*) to settle; (*COUTURE: point*) to fasten off; (*fixer: date etc*) to appoint, decide on; (*criminel, suspect*) to arrest; **s'arrêter** *vi* to stop; (*s'interrompre*) to stop o.s.; **arrêter de faire** to stop doing; **arrête de te plaindre** stop complaining; **ne pas arrêter de faire** to keep on doing; **s'arrêter de faire** to stop doing; **s'arrêter sur** (*suj: choix, regard*) to fall on

arrhes [aʀ] *nfpl* deposit *sg*

arrière [aʀjeʀ] *nm* back; (*SPORT*) fullback ♦ *adj inv*: **siège/roue arrière** back *ou* rear seat/wheel; **arrières** *nmpl* (*fig*): **protéger ses arrières** to protect the rear; **à l'arrière** *adv* behind, at the back; **en arrière** *adv* behind; (*regarder*) back, behind; (*tomber, aller*) backwards; **en arrière de** *prép* behind

arriéré, e [aʀjeʀe] *adj* (*péj*) backward ♦ *nm* (*d'argent*) arrears *pl*

arrière-goût [aʀjeʀgu] *nm* aftertaste

arrière-grand-mère, *pl* **arrière-grands-mères** [aʀjeʀgʀɑ̃meʀ] *nf* great-grandmother

arrière-grand-père, *pl* **arrière-grands-pères** [aʀjeʀgʀɑ̃peʀ] *nm* great-grandfather

arrière-pays [aʀjeʀpei] *nm inv* hinterland

arrière-pensée [aʀjeʀpɑ̃se] *nf* ulterior motive; (*doute*) mental reservation

arrière-plan [aʀjeʀplɑ̃] *nm* background; **d'arrière-plan** *adj* (*INFORM*) background *cpd*

arrière-saison [aʀjeʀsezɔ̃] *nf* late autumn

arrière-train [aʀjeʀtʀɛ̃] *nm* hindquarters *pl*

arrimer [aʀime] *vt* to stow; (*fixer*) to secure, fasten securely

arrivage [aʀivaʒ] *nm* arrival

arrivée [aʀive] *nf* arrival; (*ligne d'arrivée*) finish; **arrivée d'air/de gaz** air/gas inlet; **courrier à l'arrivée** incoming mail; **à mon arrivée** when I arrived

arriver [aʀive] *vi* to arrive; (*survenir*) to happen, occur; **j'arrive!** (I'm) just coming!; **il arrive à Paris à 8 h** he gets to *ou* arrives in Paris at 8; **arriver à destination** to arrive at one's destination; **arriver à** (*atteindre*) to reach; **arriver à (faire) qch** (*réussir*) to manage (to do) sth; **arriver à échéance** to fall due;

en arriver à faire to end up doing, get to the point of doing; **il arrive que** it happens that; **il lui arrive de faire** he sometimes does

arriviste [aʀivist(ə)] nm/f go-getter

arrogance [aʀɔgɑ̃s] nf arrogance

arrogant, e [aʀɔgɑ̃, -ɑ̃t] adj arrogant

arrondir [aʀɔ̃diʀ] vt (forme, objet) to round; (somme) to round off; **s'arrondir** vi to become round(ed); **arrondir ses fins de mois** to supplement one's pay

arrondissement [aʀɔ̃dismɑ̃] nm (ADMIN) ≈ district

arroser [aʀoze] vt to water; (victoire etc) to celebrate (over a drink); (CULIN) to baste

arrosoir [aʀozwaʀ] nm watering can

arsenal, aux [aʀsənal, -o] nm (NAVIG) naval dockyard; (MIL) arsenal; (fig) gear, paraphernalia

art [aʀ] nm art; **avoir l'art de faire** (fig: personne) to have a talent for doing; **les arts** the arts; **livre/critique d'art** art book/critic; **objet d'art** objet d'art; **art dramatique** dramatic art; **arts martiaux** martial arts; **arts et métiers** applied arts and crafts; **arts ménagers** home economics sg; **arts plastiques** plastic arts

artère [aʀtɛʀ] nf (ANAT) artery; (rue) main road

arthrite [aʀtʀit] nf arthritis

artichaut [aʀtiʃo] nm artichoke

article [aʀtikl(ə)] nm article; (COMM) item, article; (INFORM) record, item; **faire l'article** (COMM) to do one's sales spiel; **faire l'article de** (fig) to sing the praises of; **à l'article de la mort** at the point of death; **article défini/indéfini** definite/indefinite article; **article de fond** (PRESSE) feature article; **articles de bureau** office equipment; **articles de voyage** travel goods ou items

articulation [aʀtikylasjɔ̃] nf articulation; (ANAT) joint

articuler [aʀtikyle] vt to articulate; **s'articuler (sur)** (ANAT, TECH) to articulate (with); **s'articuler autour de** (fig) to centre around ou on, turn on

artifice [aʀtifis] nm device, trick

artificiel, le [aʀtifisjɛl] adj artificial

artisan [aʀtizɑ̃] nm artisan, (self-employed) craftsman; **l'artisan de la victoire/du malheur** the architect of victory/of the disaster

artisanal, e, aux [aʀtizanal, -o] adj of ou made by craftsmen; (péj) cottage industry cpd, unsophisticated

artisanat [aʀtizana] nm arts and crafts pl

artiste [aʀtist(ə)] nm/f artist; (THÉAT, MUS) artist, performer; (: de variétés) entertainer

artistique [aʀtistik] adj artistic

as vb [a] voir **avoir** ♦ nm [ɑs] ace

ascendance [asɑ̃dɑ̃s] nf (origine) ancestry; (ASTROLOGIE) ascendant

ascendant, e [asɑ̃dɑ̃, -ɑ̃t] adj upward ♦ nm influence; **ascendants** nmpl ascendants

ascenseur [asɑ̃sœʀ] nm lift (BRIT), elevator (US)

ascension [asɑ̃sjɔ̃] nf ascent; climb; **l'Ascension** (REL) the Ascension; (: jour férié) Ascension (Day); **(île de) l'Ascension** Ascension Island; see boxed note

FÊTE DE L'ASCENSION

The **fête de l'Ascension** is a public holiday in France. It always falls on a Thursday, usually in May. Many French people take the following Friday off work too and enjoy a long weekend.

aseptisé, e [aseptize] (péj) adj sanitized

asiatique [azjatik] adj Asian, Asiatic ♦ nm/f: **Asiatique** Asian

Asie [azi] nf: **l'Asie** Asia

asile [azil] nm (refuge) refuge, sanctuary; (POL): **droit d'asile** (political) asylum; (pour malades, vieillards etc) home; **accorder l'asile politique à qn** to grant ou give sb political asylum; **chercher/trouver asile quelque part** to seek/find refuge somewhere

aspect [aspɛ] nm appearance, look; (fig) aspect, side; (LING) aspect; **à l'aspect de** at the sight of

asperge [aspɛʀʒ(ə)] nf asparagus no pl

asperger [aspɛʀʒe] vt to spray, sprinkle

aspérité [asperite] nf excrescence, protruding bit (of rock etc)

asphalte [asfalt(ə)] nm asphalt

asphyxier [asfiksje] vt to suffocate, asphyxiate; (fig) to stifle; **mourir asphyxié** to die of suffocation ou asphyxiation

aspirateur [aspiʀatœʀ] nm vacuum cleaner, hoover®

aspirer [aspiʀe] vt (air) to inhale; (liquide) to suck (up); (suj: appareil) to suck ou draw up; **aspirer à** vt to aspire to

aspirine [aspiʀin] nf aspirin

assagir [asaʒiʀ] vt: **s'assagir** vi to quieten down, sober down

assaillir [asajiʀ] vt to assail, attack; **assaillir qn de** (questions) to assail ou bombard sb with

assainir [aseniʀ] vt to clean up; (eau, air) to purify

assaisonnement [asɛzɔnmɑ̃] nm seasoning

assaisonner [asɛzɔne] vt to season; **bien assaisonné** highly seasoned

assassin [asasɛ̃] nm murderer; assassin

assassiner [asasine] vt to murder; (surtout POL) to assassinate

assaut [aso] nm assault, attack; **prendre d'assaut** to (take by) storm, assault; **donner l'assaut (à)** to attack; **faire assaut de** (rivaliser) to vie with ou rival each other in

assécher [aseʃe] vt to drain

assemblage [asɑ̃blaʒ] nm assembling; (MENUISERIE) joint; **un assemblage de** (fig) a collection of; **langage d'assemblage** (INFORM) assembly language

assemblée [asɑ̃ble] nf (réunion) meeting; (public,

assistance) gathering; assembled people; (*POL*) assembly; (*REL*) **l'assemblée des fidèles** the congregation; **l'Assemblée nationale (AN)** the (French) National Assembly; *see boxed note*

ASSEMBLÉE NATIONALE

The **Assemblée nationale** is the lower house of the French Parliament, the upper house being the 'Sénat'. It is housed in the Palais Bourbon in Paris. Its members, or 'députés', are elected every five years.

---

assembler [asᾶble] *vt* (*joindre, monter*) to assemble, put together; (*amasser*) to gather (together), collect (together); **s'assembler** *vi* to gather, collect

assener, asséner [asene] *vt*: **assener un coup à qn** to deal sb a blow

assentiment [asᾶtimᾶ] *nm* assent, consent; (*approbation*) approval

asseoir [aswar] *vt* (*malade, bébé*) to sit up; (*personne debout*) to sit down; (*autorité, réputation*) to establish; **s'asseoir** *vi* to sit (o.s.) up; to sit (o.s.) down; **faire asseoir qn** to ask sb to sit down; **asseyez-vous!, assieds-toi!** sit down!; **asseoir qch sur** to build sth on; (*appuyer*) to base sth on

assermenté, e [asεRmᾶte] *adj* sworn, on oath

asservir [asεRviR] *vt* to subjugate, enslave

assez [ase] *adv* (*suffisamment*) enough, sufficiently; (*passablement*) rather, quite, fairly; **assez!** enough!, that'll do!; **assez/pas assez cuit** well enough done/underdone; **est-il assez fort/rapide?** is he strong/fast enough?; **il est passé assez vite** he went past rather *ou* quite *ou* fairly fast; **assez de pain/livres** enough *ou* sufficient bread/ books; **vous en avez assez?** have you got enough?; **en avoir assez de qch** (*en être fatigué*) to have had enough of sth; **travailler assez** to work (hard) enough

assidu, e [asidy] *adj* assiduous, painstaking; (*régulier*) regular; **assidu auprès de qn** attentive towards sb

assied *etc* [asje] *vb voir* **asseoir**

assiéger [asjeʒe] *vt* to besiege, lay siege to; (*suj: foule, touristes*) to mob, besiege

assiérai *etc* [asjeʀe] *vb voir* **asseoir**

assiette [asjεt] *nf* plate; (*contenu*) plate(ful); (*équilibre*) seat; (*de colonne*) seating; (*de navire*) trim; **assiette anglaise** assorted cold meats; **assiette creuse** (soup) dish, soup plate; **assiette à dessert** dessert *ou* side plate; **assiette de l'impôt** basis of (tax) assessment; **assiette plate** (dinner) plate

assigner [asiɲe] *vt*: **assigner qch à** to assign *ou* allot sth to; (*valeur, importance*) to attach sth to; (*somme*) to allocate sth to; (*limites*) to set *ou* fix sth to; (*cause, effet*) to ascribe *ou* attribute sth to; **assigner qn à** (*affecter*) to assign sb to; **assigner qn à résidence** (*JUR*) to give sb a compulsory order of residence

assimiler [asimile] *vt* to assimilate, absorb; (*comparer*): **assimiler qch/qn à** to liken *ou* compare sth/ sb to; **s'assimiler** *vi* (*s'intégrer*) to be assimilated *ou* absorbed; **ils sont assimilés aux infirmières** (*ADMIN*) they are classed as nurses

assis, e [asi, -iz] *pp de* **asseoir** ♦ *adj* sitting (down), seated ♦ *nf* (*CONSTR*) course; (*GÉO*) stratum (*pl* -a); (*fig*) basis (*pl* bases), foundation; **assis en tailleur** sitting cross-legged

assises [asiz] *nfpl* (*JUR*) assizes; (*congrès*) (annual) conference

assistance [asistᾶs] *nf* (*public*) audience; (*aide*) assistance; **porter** *ou* **prêter assistance à qn** to give sb assistance; **Assistance publique (AP)** *public health service*; **enfant de l'Assistance (publique)** (*formerly*) child in care; **assistance technique** technical aid

assistant, e [asistᾶ, -ᾶt] *nm/f* assistant; (*d'université*) probationary lecturer; **les assistants** *nmpl* (*auditeurs etc*) those present; **assistante sociale** social worker

assisté, e [asiste] *adj* (*AUTO*) power assisted ♦ *nm/f* person receiving aid from the State

assister [asiste] *vt* to assist; **assister à** *vt* (*scène, événement*) to witness; (*conférence*) to attend, be (present) at; (*spectacle, match*) to be at, see

association [asɔsjasjɔ̃] *nf* association; (*COMM*) partnership; **association d'idées/images** association of ideas/images

associé, e [asɔsje] *nm/f* associate; (*COMM*) partner

associer [asɔsje] *vt* to associate; **associer qn à** (*profits*) to give sb a share of; (*affaire*) to make sb a partner in; (*joie, triomphe*) to include sb in; **associer qch à** (*joindre, allier*) to combine sth with; **s'associer** *vi* to join together; (*COMM*) to form a partnership ♦ *vt* (*collaborateur*) to take on (as a partner); **s'associer à** to be combined with; (*opinions, joies de qn*) to share in; **s'associer à** *ou* **avec qn pour faire** to join (forces) *ou* join together with sb to do

assoiffé, e [aswafe] *adj* thirsty; (*fig*): **assoiffé de** (*sang*) thirsting for; (*gloire*) thirsting after

assombrir [asɔ̃bRiR] *vt* to darken; (*fig*) to fill with gloom; **s'assombrir** *vi* to darken; (*devenir nuageux, fig: visage*) to cloud over; (*fig*) to become gloomy

assommer [asɔme] *vt* (*étourdir, abrutir*) to knock out, stun; (*fam: ennuyer*) to bore stiff

Assomption [asɔ̃psjɔ̃] *nf*: **l'Assomption** the Assumption; *see boxed note*

FÊTE DE L'ASSOMPTION

The **fête de l'Assomption**, more commonly known as 'le 15 août', is a national holiday in France. Traditionally, large numbers of holiday-makers leave home on 15 August, frequently causing chaos on the roads.

---

assorti, e [asɔRti] *adj* matched, matching; **fro-**

mages/légumes assortis assorted cheeses/vegetables; **assorti à** matching; **assorti de** accompanied with; (conditions, conseils) coupled with; **bien/mal assorti** well/ill-matched

assortiment [asɔʀtimɑ̃] nm (choix) assortment, selection; (harmonie de couleurs, formes) arrangement; (COMM: lot, stock) selection

assortir [asɔʀtiʀ] vt to match; **s'assortir** to go well together, match; **assortir qch à** to match sth with; **assortir qch de** to accompany sth with; **s'assortir de** to be accompanied by

assoupi, e [asupi] adj dozing, sleeping; (fig) (be)numbed; (sens) dulled

assoupir [asupiʀ]: **s'assoupir** vi (personne) to doze off; (sens) to go numb

assouplir [asupliʀ] vt to make supple, soften; (membres, corps) to limber up, make supple; (fig) to relax; (: caractère) to soften, make more flexible; **s'assouplir** vi to soften; to limber up; to relax; to become more flexible

assouplissant [asuplisɑ̃] nm (fabric) softener

assourdir [asuʀdiʀ] vt (bruit) to deaden, muffle; (suj: bruit) to deafen

assouvir [asuviʀ] vt to satisfy, appease

assujettir [asyʒetiʀ] vt to subject, subjugate; (fixer: planches, tableau) to fix securely; **assujettir qn à** (règle, impôt) to subject sb to

assumer [asyme] vt (fonction, emploi) to assume, take on; (accepter: conséquence, situation) to accept

assurance [asyʀɑ̃s] nf (certitude) assurance; (confiance en soi) (self-)confidence; (contrat) insurance (policy); (secteur commercial) insurance; **prendre une assurance contre** to take out insurance ou an insurance policy against; **assurance contre l'incendie** fire insurance; **assurance contre le vol** insurance against theft; **société d'assurance, compagnie d'assurances** insurance company; **assurance maladie (AM)** health insurance; **assurance au tiers** third party insurance; **assurance tous risques** (AUTO) comprehensive insurance; **assurances sociales (AS)** ≈ National Insurance (BRIT), ≈ Social Security (US)

assurance-vie, pl **assurances-vie** [asyʀɑ̃svi] nf life assurance ou insurance

assuré, e [asyʀe] adj (victoire etc) certain, sure; (démarche, voix) assured, (self-)confident; (certain): **assuré de** confident of; (ASSURANCES) insured ♦ nm/f insured (person); **assuré social** ≈ member of the National Insurance (BRIT) ou Social Security (US) scheme

assurément [asyʀemɑ̃] adv assuredly, most certainly

assurer [asyʀe] vt (COMM) to insure; (stabiliser) to steady, stabilize; (victoire etc) to ensure, make certain; (frontières, pouvoir) to make secure; (service, garde) to provide, operate; **assurer qch à qn** (garantir) to secure ou guarantee sth for sb; (certifier) to assure sb of sth; **assurer à qn que** to assure

sb that; **je vous assure que non/si** I assure you that that is not the case/is the case; **assurer qn de** to assure sb of that; **assurer ses arrières** (fig) to be sure one has something to fall back on; **s'assurer (contre)** (COMM) to insure o.s. (against); **s'assurer de/que** (vérifier) to make sure of/that; **s'assurer (de)** (aide de qn) to secure; **s'assurer sur la vie** to take out a life insurance; **s'assurer le concours/la collaboration de qn** to secure sb's aid/collaboration

assureur [asyʀœʀ] nm insurance agent; (société) insurers pl

asthmatique [asmatik] adj asthmatic

asthme [asm(ə)] nm asthma

asticot [astiko] nm maggot

astiquer [astike] vt to polish, shine

astre [astʀ(ə)] nm star

astreignant, e [astʀɛɲɑ̃, -ɑ̃t] adj demanding

astreindre [astʀɛ̃dʀ(ə)] vt: **astreindre qn à qch** to force sth upon sb; **astreindre qn à faire** to compel ou force sb to do; **s'astreindre à** to compel ou force o.s. to

astrologie [astʀɔlɔʒi] nf astrology

astronaute [astʀɔnot] nm/f astronaut

astronomie [astʀɔnɔmi] nf astronomy

astuce [astys] nf shrewdness, astuteness; (truc) trick, clever way; (plaisanterie) wisecrack

astucieux, euse [astysjø, -øz] adj shrewd, clever, astute

atelier [atəlje] nm workshop; (de peintre) studio

athée [ate] adj atheistic ♦ nm/f atheist

Athènes [atɛn] n Athens

athlète [atlɛt] nm/f (SPORT) athlete; (costaud) muscleman

athlétisme [atletism(ə)] nm athletics sg; **faire de l'athlétisme** to do athletics; **tournoi d'athlétisme** athletics meeting

atlantique [atlɑ̃tik] adj Atlantic ♦ nm: **l'(océan) Atlantique** the Atlantic (Ocean)

atlas [atlɑs] nm atlas

atmosphère [atmɔsfɛʀ] nf atmosphere

atome [atom] nm atom

atomique [atɔmik] adj atomic, nuclear; (usine) nuclear; (nombre, masse) atomic

atomiseur [atɔmizœʀ] nm atomizer

atout [atu] nm trump; (fig) asset; (: plus fort) trump card; **"atout pique/trèfle"** "spades/clubs are trumps"

âtre [ɑtʀ(ə)] nm hearth

atroce [atʀɔs] adj atrocious, horrible

attabler [atable]: **s'attabler** vi to sit down at (the) table; **s'attabler à la terrasse** to sit down (at a table) on the terrace

attachant, e [ataʃɑ̃, -ɑ̃t] adj engaging, likeable

attache [ataʃ] nf clip, fastener; (fig) tie; **attaches** nfpl (relations) connections; **à l'attache** (chien) tied up

attacher [ataʃe] vt to tie up; (étiquette) to attach,

tie on; (*souliers*) to do up ♦ *vi* (*poêle, riz*) to stick; **s'attacher** (*robe etc*) to do up; **s'attacher à** (*par affection*) to become attached to; **s'attacher à faire qch** to endeavour to do sth; **attacher qch à** to tie ou fasten ou attach sth to; **attacher qn à** (*fig: lier*) to attach sb to; **attacher du prix/de l'importance à** to attach great value/attach importance to

attaque [atak] *nf* attack; (*cérébrale*) stroke; (*d'épilepsie*) fit; **être/se sentir d'attaque** to be/feel on form; **attaque à main armée** armed attack

attaquer [atake] *vt* to attack; (*en justice*) to bring an action against, sue; (*travail*) to tackle, set about ♦ *vi* to attack; **s'attaquer à** to attack; (*épidémie, misère*) to tackle, attack

attardé, e [ataʀde] *adj* (*passants*) late; (*enfant*) backward; (*conceptions*) old-fashioned

attarder [ataʀde]: **s'attarder** *vi* (*sur qch, en chemin*) to linger; (*chez qn*) to stay on

atteindre [atɛ̃dʀ(ə)] *vt* to reach; (*blesser*) to hit; (*contacter*) to reach, contact, get in touch with; (*émouvoir*) to affect

atteint, e [atɛ̃, -ɛ̃t] *pp de* **atteindre** ♦ *adj* (*MÉD*): **être atteint de** to be suffering from ♦ *nf* attack; **hors d'atteinte** out of reach; **porter atteinte à** to strike a blow at, undermine

atteler [atle] *vt* (*cheval, bœufs*) to hitch up; (*wagons*) to couple; **s'atteler à** (*travail*) to buckle down to

attelle [atɛl] *nf* splint

attenant, e [atnɑ̃, -ɑ̃t] *adj*: **attenant (à)** adjoining

attendant [atɑ̃dɑ̃]: **en attendant** *adv* (*dans l'intervalle*) meanwhile, in the meantime

attendre [atɑ̃dʀ(ə)] *vt* to wait for; (*être destiné ou réservé à*) to await, be in store for ♦ *vi* to wait; **je n'attends plus rien (de la vie)** I expect nothing more (from life); **attendez que je réfléchisse** wait while I think; **s'attendre à (ce que)** (*escompter*) to expect (that); **je ne m'y attendais pas** I didn't expect that; **ce n'est pas ce à quoi je m'attendais** that's not what I expected; **attendre un enfant** to be expecting a baby; **attendre de pied ferme** to wait determinedly; **attendre de faire/d'être** to wait until one does/is; **attendre que** to wait until; **attendre qch de** to expect sth (of); **faire attendre qn** to keep sb waiting; **se faire attendre** to keep people (ou us etc) waiting; **en attendant** *adv* voir **attendant**

attendrir [atɑ̃dʀiʀ] *vt* to move (to pity); (*viande*) to tenderize; **s'attendrir (sur)** to be moved ou touched (by)

attendrissant, e [atɑ̃dʀisɑ̃, -ɑ̃t] *adj* moving, touching

attendu, e [atɑ̃dy] *pp de* **attendre** ♦ *adj* long-awaited; (*prévu*) expected ♦ *nm*: **attendus** reasons adduced for a judgment; **attendu que** *conj* considering that, since

attentat [atɑ̃ta] *nm* (*contre une personne*) assassination attempt; (*contre un bâtiment*) attack; **atten-**

tat à la bombe bomb attack; **attentat à la pudeur** (*exhibitionnisme*) indecent exposure no pl; (*agression*) indecent assault no pl

attente [atɑ̃t] *nf* wait; (*espérance*) expectation; **contre toute attente** contrary to (all) expectations

attenter [atɑ̃te]: **attenter à** *vt* (*liberté*) to violate; **attenter à la vie de qn** to make an attempt on sb's life; **attenter à ses jours** to make an attempt on one's life

attentif, ive [atɑ̃tif, -iv] *adj* (*auditeur*) attentive; (*soin*) scrupulous; (*travail*) careful; **attentif à** paying attention to; (*devoir*) mindful of; **attentif à faire** careful to do

attention [atɑ̃sjɔ̃] *nf* attention; (*prévenance*) attention, thoughtfulness no pl; **mériter attention** to be worthy of attention; **à l'attention de** for the attention of; **porter qch à l'attention de qn** to bring sth to sb's attention; **attirer l'attention de qn sur qch** to draw sb's attention to sth; **faire attention (à)** to be careful (of); **faire attention (à ce) que** to be ou make sure that; **attention!** careful!, watch!, watch ou mind (*BRIT*) out!; **attention, si vous ouvrez cette lettre** (*sanction*) just watch out, if you open that letter; **attention, respectez les consignes de sécurité** be sure to observe the safety instructions

attentionné, e [atɑ̃sjɔne] *adj* thoughtful, considerate

atténuer [atenɥe] *vt* to alleviate, ease; (*diminuer*) to lessen; (*amoindrir*) to mitigate the effects of; **s'atténuer** *vi* to ease; (*violence etc*) to abate

atterrer [ateʀe] *vt* to dismay, appal

atterrir [ateʀiʀ] *vi* to land

atterrissage [ateʀisaʒ] *nm* landing; **atterrissage sur le ventre/sans visibilité/forcé** belly/blind/forced landing

attestation [atɛstasjɔ̃] *nf* certificate, testimonial; **attestation médicale** doctor's certificate

attester [atɛste] *vt* to testify to, vouch for; (*démontrer*) to attest, testify to; **attester que** to testify that

attirail [atiʀaj] *nm* gear; (*péj*) paraphernalia

attirant, e [atiʀɑ̃, -ɑ̃t] *adj* attractive, appealing

attirer [atiʀe] *vt* to attract; (*appâter*) to lure, entice; **attirer qn dans un coin/vers soi** to draw sb into a corner/towards one; **attirer l'attention de qn** to attract sb's attention; **attirer l'attention de qn sur qch** to draw sb's attention to sth; **attirer des ennuis à qn** to make trouble for sb; **s'attirer des ennuis** to bring trouble upon o.s., get into trouble

attiser [atize] *vt* (*feu*) to poke (up), stir up; (*fig*) to fan the flame of, stir up

attitré, e [atitʀe] *adj* qualified; (*agréé*) accredited, appointed

attitude [atityd] *nf* attitude; (*position du corps*) bearing

attouchements [atuʃmɑ̃] *nmpl* touching *sg*; (*sexuels*) fondling *sg*, stroking *sg*

attraction [atʀaksjɔ̃] *nf* attraction; (*de cabaret, cirque*) number

attrait [atʀɛ] *nm* appeal, attraction; (*plus fort*) lure; **attraits** *nmpl* attractions; **éprouver de l'attrait pour** to be attracted to

attrape-nigaud [atʀapnigo] *nm* con

attraper [atʀape] *vt* to catch; (*habitude, amende*) to get, pick up; (*fam: duper*) to take in (*BRIT*), con

attrayant, e [atʀɛjɑ̃, -ɑ̃t] *adj* attractive

attribuer [atʀibɥe] *vt* (*prix*) to award; (*rôle, tâche*) to allocate, assign; (*imputer*): **attribuer qch à** to attribute sth to, ascribe sth to, put sth down to; **s'attribuer** *vt* (*s'approprier*) to claim for o.s.

attribut [atʀiby] *nm* attribute; (*LING*) complement

attrister [atʀiste] *vt* to sadden; **s'attrister de qch** to be saddened by sth

attroupement [atʀupmɑ̃] *nm* crowd, mob

attrouper [atʀupe]: **s'attrouper** *vi* to gather

au [o] *prép + dét voir* **à**

aubaine [obɛn] *nf* godsend; (*financière*) windfall; (*COMM*) bonanza

aube [ob] *nf* dawn, daybreak; (*REL*) alb; **à l'aube** at dawn *ou* daybreak; **à l'aube de** (*fig*) at the dawn of

aubépine [obepin] *nf* hawthorn

auberge [obɛʀʒ(ə)] *nf* inn; **auberge de jeunesse** youth hostel

aubergine [obɛʀʒin] *nf* aubergine (*BRIT*), eggplant (*US*)

aubergiste [obɛʀʒist(ə)] *nm/f* inn-keeper, hotel-keeper

aucun, e [okœ̃, -yn] *dét* no, *tournure négative +* any; (*positif*) any ♦ *pron* none, *tournure négative +* any; (*positif*) any(one); **il n'y a aucun livre** there isn't any book, there is no book; **je n'en vois aucun qui** I can't see any which, I (can) see none which; **aucun homme** no man; **sans aucun doute** without any doubt; **sans aucune hésitation** without hesitation; **plus qu'aucun autre** more than any other; **plus qu'aucun de ceux qui ...** more than any of those who ...; **en aucune façon** in no way at all; **aucun des deux** neither of the two; **aucun d'entre eux** none of them; **d'aucuns** (*certains*) some

aucunement [okynmɑ̃] *adv* in no way, not in the least

audace [odas] *nf* daring, boldness; (*péj*) audacity; **il a eu l'audace de ...** he had the audacity to ...; **vous ne manquez pas d'audace!** you're not lacking in nerve *ou* cheek!

audacieux, euse [odasjø, -øz] *adj* daring, bold

au-delà [odla] *adv* beyond ♦ *nm*: **l'au-delà** the hereafter; **au-delà de** *prép* beyond

au-dessous [odsu] *adv* underneath; below; **au-dessous de** *prép* under(neath), below; (*limite, somme etc*) below, under; (*dignité, condition*) below

au-dessus [odsy] *adv* above; **au-dessus de** *prép* above

au-devant [odvɑ̃]: **au-devant de** *prép*: **aller au-devant de** to go (out) and meet; (*souhaits de qn*) to anticipate

audience [odjɑ̃s] *nf* audience; (*JUR: séance*) hearing; **trouver audience auprès de** to arouse much interest among, get the (interested) attention of

audimat [odimat] *nm* (*taux d'écoute*) ratings *pl*

audio-visuel, le [odjovizɥɛl] *adj* audio-visual ♦ *nm* (*équipement*) audio-visual aids *pl*; (*méthodes*) audio-visual methods *pl*; **l'audio-visuel** radio and television

auditeur, trice [oditœʀ, -tʀis] *nm/f* (*à la radio*) listener; (*à une conférence*) member of the audience, listener; **auditeur libre** unregistered student (*attending lectures*) auditor (*US*)

audition [odisjɔ̃] *nf* (*ouïe, écoute*) hearing; (*JUR: de témoins*) examination; (*MUS, THÉÂT: épreuve*) audition

auditoire [oditwaʀ] *nm* audience

auge [oʒ] *nf* trough

augmentation [oɡmɑ̃tasjɔ̃] *nf* (*action*) increasing; raising; (*résultat*) increase; **augmentation (de salaire)** rise (in salary) (*BRIT*), (pay) raise (*US*)

augmenter [oɡmɑ̃te] *vt* to increase; (*salaire, prix*) to increase, raise, put up; (*employé*) to increase the salary of, give a (salary) rise (*BRIT*) *ou* (pay) raise (*US*) to ♦ *vi* to increase; **augmenter de poids/volume** to gain (in) weight/volume

augure [oɡyʀ] *nm* soothsayer, oracle; **de bon/mauvais augure** of good/ill omen

augurer [oɡyʀe] *vt*: **augurer qch de** to foresee sth (coming) from *ou* out of; **augurer bien de** to augur well for

aujourd'hui [oʒuʀdɥi] *adv* today; **aujourd'hui en huit/quinze** a week/two weeks today, a week/two weeks from now; **à dater** *ou* **partir d'aujourd'hui** from today('s date)

aumône [omon] *nf* alms *sg* (*pl inv*); **faire l'aumône (à qn)** to give alms (to sb); **faire l'aumône de qch à qn** (*fig*) to favour sb with sth

aumônier [omonje] *nm* chaplain

auparavant [opaʀavɑ̃] *adv* before(hand)

auprès [opʀɛ]: **auprès de** *prép* next to, close to; (*recourir, s'adresser*) to; (*en comparaison de*) compared with, next to; (*dans l'opinion de*) in the opinion of

auquel [okɛl] *prép + pron voir* **lequel**

aurai *etc* [ɔʀe] *vb voir* **avoir**

auréole [ɔʀeɔl] *nf* halo; (*tache*) ring

aurons *etc* [ɔʀɔ̃] *vb voir* **avoir**

aurore [ɔʀɔʀ] *nf* dawn, daybreak; **aurore boréale** northern lights *pl*

ausculter [ɔskylte] *vt* to sound

aussi [osi] *adv* (*également*) also, too; (*de comparaison*) as ♦ *conj* therefore, consequently; **aussi fort que** as strong as; **lui aussi** he too; (*objet*) him too; **aussi bien que** (*de même que*) as well as

aussitôt [osito] *adv* straight away, immediately;

aussitôt que as soon as; **aussitôt envoyé** as soon as it is (ou was) sent; **aussitôt fait** no sooner done

austère [ɔstɛʀ] adj austere; (sévère) stern

austral, e [ɔstʀal] adj southern; **l'océan Austral** the Antarctic Ocean; **les Terres Australes** Antarctica

Australie [ɔstʀali] nf: **l'Australie** Australia

australien, ne [ɔstʀaljɛ̃, -ɛn] adj Australian ♦ nm/f: **Australien, ne** Australian

autant [otɑ̃] adv so much; (comparatif): **autant (que)** as much (as); (nombre) as many (as); **autant (de)** so much (ou many); as much (ou many); **n'importe qui aurait pu en faire autant** anyone could have done the same ou as much; **autant partir** we (ou you etc) may as well leave; **autant ne rien dire** best not say anything; **autant dire que ...** one might as well say that ...; **fort autant que courageux** as strong as he is brave; **il n'est pas découragé pour autant** he isn't discouraged for all that; **pour autant que** conj assuming, as long as; **d'autant** adv accordingly, in proportion; **d'autant plus/mieux (que)** all the more/the better (since)

autel [otɛl] nm altar

auteur [otœʀ] nm author; **l'auteur de cette remarque** the person who said that; **droit d'auteur** copyright

authenticité [otɑ̃tisite] nf authenticity

authentique [otɑ̃tik] adj authentic, genuine

auto [oto] nf car; **autos tamponneuses** bumper cars, dodgems

autobiographie [otobjɔgʀafi] nf autobiography

autobronzant [otobʀɔ̃zɑ̃] nm self-tanning cream (or lotion etc)

autobus [otobys] nm bus

autocar [otokaʀ] nm coach

autochtone [otoktɔn] nm/f native

autocollant, e [otokɔlɑ̃, -ɑ̃t] adj self-adhesive; (enveloppe) self-seal ♦ nm sticker

auto-couchettes [otokuʃɛt] adj inv: **train auto-couchettes** car sleeper train, motorail® train (BRIT)

autocuiseur [otokwizœʀ] nm (CULIN) pressure cooker

autodéfense [otodefɑ̃s] nf self-defence; **groupe d'autodéfense** vigilante committee

autodidacte [otodidakt] nm/f self-taught person

auto-école [otoekɔl] nf driving school

autographe [otogʀaf] nm autograph

automate [otomat] nm (robot) automaton; (machine) (automatic) machine

automatique [otomatik] adj, nm automatic; **l'automatique** (TÉL) ≈ direct dialling

automatiquement [otomatikmɑ̃] adv automatically

automatiser [otomatize] vt to automate

automne [otɔn] nm autumn (BRIT), fall (US)

automobile [otomɔbil] adj motor cpd ♦ nf (motor) car; **l'automobile** motoring; (industrie) the car ou automobile (US) industry

automobiliste [otomɔbilist(ə)] nm/f motorist

autonome [otonɔm] adj autonomous; (INFORM) stand-alone; **(en mode) autonome** off line

autonomie [otonɔmi] nf autonomy; (POL) self-government, autonomy; **autonomie de vol** range

autopsie [otopsi] nf post-mortem (examination), autopsy

autoradio [otoʀadjo] nf car radio

autorisation [otoʀizasjɔ̃] nf permission, authorization; (papiers) permit; **donner à qn l'autorisation de** to give sb permission to, authorize sb to; **avoir l'autorisation de faire** to be allowed ou have permission to do, be authorized to do

autorisé, e [otoʀize] adj (opinion, sources) authoritative; (permis): **autorisé à faire** authorized ou permitted to do; **dans les milieux autorisés** in official circles

autoriser [otoʀize] vt to give permission for, authorize; (fig) to allow (of), sanction; **autoriser qn à faire** to give permission to sb to do, authorize sb to do

autoritaire [otoʀitɛʀ] adj authoritarian

autorité [otoʀite] nf authority; **faire autorité** to be authoritative; **autorités constituées** constitutional authorities

autoroute [otoʀut] nf motorway (BRIT), expressway (US); **autoroute de l'information** (TEL) information highway

auto-stop [otostɔp] nm: **l'auto-stop** hitch-hiking; **faire de l'auto-stop** to hitch-hike; **prendre qn en auto-stop** to give sb a lift

auto-stoppeur, euse [otostopœʀ, -øz] nm/f hitch-hiker, hitcher (BRIT)

autour [otuʀ] adv around; **autour de** prép around; (environ) around, about; **tout autour** adv all around

---

MOT CLÉ

---

autre [otʀ(ə)] adj 1 (différent) other, different; **je préférerais un autre verre** I'd prefer another ou a different glass; **d'autres verres** different glasses; **se sentir autre** to feel different; **la difficulté est autre** the difficulty is ou lies elsewhere 2 (supplémentaire) other; **je voudrais un autre verre d'eau** I'd like another glass of water

3: **autre chose** something else; **autre part** somewhere else; **d'autre part** on the other hand ♦ pron 1: **un autre** another (one); **nous/vous autres** us/you; **d'autres** others; **l'autre** the other (one); **les autres** the others; (autrui) others; **l'un et l'autre** both of them; **ni l'un ni l'autre** neither of them; **se détester l'un l'autre/les uns les autres** to hate each other ou one another; **d'une semaine/minute à l'autre** from one week/minute ou moment to the next; (incessamment) any week/minute ou moment now; **de temps à**

autre from time to time; **entre autres** among other things

2 (expressions): **j'en ai vu d'autres** I've seen worse; **à d'autres!** pull the other one!

autrefois [otʀǝfwa] *adv* in the past

autrement [otʀǝmɑ̃] *adv* differently; *(d'une manière différente)* in another way; *(sinon)* otherwise; **je n'ai pas pu faire autrement** I couldn't do anything else, I couldn't do otherwise; **autrement dit** in other words; *(c'est-à-dire)* that is to say

Autriche [otʀiʃ] *nf*: **l'Autriche** Austria

autrichien, ne [otʀiʃjɛ̃, -ɛn] *adj* Austrian ◆ *nm/f*: **Autrichien, ne** Austrian

autruche [otʀyʃ] *nf* ostrich; **faire l'autruche** *(fig)* to bury one's head in the sand

autrui [otʀɥi] *pron* others

auvent [ovɑ̃] *nm* canopy

aux [o] *prép + dét voir* **à**

auxiliaire [ɔksiljɛʀ] *adj, nm/f* auxiliary

auxquels, auxquelles [okɛl] *prép + pron voir* **lequel**

avachi, e [avaʃi] *adj* limp, flabby; *(chaussure, vêtement)* out-of-shape; *(personne)*: **avachi sur qch** slumped on *ou* across sth

aval [aval] *nm* (*accord*) endorsement, backing; *(GÉO)*: **en aval** downstream, downriver; *(sur une pente)* downhill; **en aval de** downstream *ou* downriver from; downhill from

avalanche [avalɑ̃ʃ] *nf* avalanche; **avalanche poudreuse** powder snow avalanche

avaler [avale] *vt* to swallow

avance [avɑ̃s] *nf* (*de troupes etc*) advance; *(progrès)* progress; *(d'argent)* advance; *(opposé à retard)* lead; being ahead of schedule; **avances** *nfpl* overtures; *(amoureuses)* advances; **une avance de 300 m/4 h** *(SPORT)* a 300 m/4 hour lead; **(être) en avance** (to be) early; *(sur un programme)* (to be) ahead of schedule; **on n'est pas en avance!** we're kind of late!; **être en avance sur qn** to be ahead of sb; **d'avance, à l'avance, par avance** in advance; **avance (du) papier** *(INFORM)* paper advance

avancé, e [avɑ̃se] *adj* advanced; *(travail etc)* well on, well under way; *(fruit, fromage)* overripe ◆ *nf* projection; overhang; **il est avancé pour son âge** he is advanced for his age

avancement [avɑ̃smɑ̃] *nm* (*professionnel*) promotion; *(de travaux)* progress

avancer [avɑ̃se] *vi* to move forward, advance; *(projet, travail)* to make progress; *(être en saillie)* to overhang; to project; *(montre, réveil)* to be fast; *(: d'habitude)* to gain ◆ *vt* to move forward, advance; *(argent)* to advance; *(montre, pendule)* to put forward; *(faire progresser: travail etc)* to advance, move on; **s'avancer** *vi* to move forward, advance; *(fig)* to commit o.s.; *(faire saillie)* to overhang; to project; **j'avance (d'une heure)** I'm (an hour) fast

avant [avɑ̃] *prép* before ◆ *adv*: **trop/plus avant** too far/further forward ◆ *adj inv*: **siège/roue avant** front seat/wheel ◆ *nm* front; *(SPORT: joueur)* forward; **avant qu'il parte/de partir** before he leaves/leaving; **avant qu'il (ne) pleuve** before it rains *(ou* rained*)*; **avant tout** *(surtout)* above all; **à l'avant** *(dans un véhicule)* in (the) front; **en avant** *adv* forward(s); **en avant de** *prép* in front of; **aller de l'avant** to steam ahead *(fig)*, make good progress

avantage [avɑ̃taʒ] *nm* advantage; *(TENNIS)*: **avantage service/dehors** advantage *ou* van *(BRIT) ou* ad *(US)* in/out; **tirer avantage de** to take advantage of; **vous auriez avantage à faire** you would be well-advised to do, it would be to your advantage to do; **à l'avantage de qn** to sb's advantage; **être à son avantage** to be at one's best; **avantages en nature** benefits in kind; **avantages sociaux** fringe benefits

avantager [avɑ̃taʒe] *vt* (*favoriser*) to favour; *(embellir)* to flatter

avantageux, euse [avɑ̃taʒø, -øz] *adj* attractive; *(intéressant)* attractively priced; *(portrait, coiffure)* flattering; **conditions avantageuses** favourable terms

avant-bras [avɑ̃bʀa] *nm inv* forearm

avant-coureur [avɑ̃kuʀœʀ] *adj inv* (*bruit etc*) precursory; **signe avant-coureur** advance indication *ou* sign

avant-dernier, ière [avɑ̃dɛʀnje, -jɛʀ] *adj, nm/f* next to last, last but one

avant-goût [avɑ̃gu] *nm* foretaste

avant-hier [avɑ̃tjɛʀ] *adv* the day before yesterday

avant-première [avɑ̃pʀǝmjɛʀ] *nf* (*de film*) preview; **en avant-première** as a preview, in a preview showing

avant-projet [avɑ̃pʀɔʒɛ] *nm* preliminary draft

avant-propos [avɑ̃pʀɔpo] *nm* foreword

avant-veille [avɑ̃vɛj] *nf*: **l'avant-veille** two days before

avare [avaʀ] *adj* miserly, avaricious ◆ *nm/f* miser; **avare de compliments** stingy *ou* sparing with one's compliments

avarié, e [avaʀje] *adj* (*viande, fruits*) rotting, going off *(BRIT)*; *(NAVIG: navire)* damaged

avaries [avaʀi] *nfpl* (*NAVIG*) damage *sg*

avec [avɛk] *prép* with; *(à l'égard de)* to(wards), with ◆ *adv* (*fam*) with it *(ou* him *etc)*; **avec habileté/lenteur** skilfully/slowly; **avec eux/ces maladies** with them/these diseases; **avec ça** *(malgré ça)* for all that; **et avec ça?** *(dans un magasin)* anything *ou* something else?

avenant, e [avnɑ̃, -ɑ̃t] *adj* pleasant ◆ *nm* (*ASSURANCES*) additional clause; **à l'avenant** *adv* in keeping

avènement [avɛnmɑ̃] *nm* (*d'un roi*) accession, succession; *(d'un changement)* advent; *(d'une politique, idée)* coming

avenir [avniʀ] *nm*: **l'avenir** the future; **à l'avenir** in future; **sans avenir** with no future, without a future; **carrière/politicien d'avenir** career/politician with prospects *ou* a future

aventure [avɑ̃tyʀ] *nf*: **l'aventure** adventure; **une aventure** an adventure; (*amoureuse*) an affair; **partir à l'aventure** to go off in search of adventure; (*au hasard*) to go where one's fancy takes one; **roman/film d'aventure** adventure story/film

aventurer [avɑ̃tyʀe] *vt* (*somme, réputation, vie*) to stake; (*remarque, opinion*) to venture; **s'aventurer** *vi* to venture; **s'aventurer à faire qch** to venture into sth

aventureux, euse [avɑ̃tyʀø, -øz] *adj* adventurous, venturesome; (*projet*) risky, chancy

avenue [avny] *nf* avenue

avérer [aveʀe]: **s'avérer** *vb avec attribut*: **s'avérer faux/coûteux** to prove (to be) wrong/expensive

averse [avɛʀs(ə)] *nf* shower

averti, e [avɛʀti] *adj* (well-)informed

avertir [avɛʀtiʀ] *vt*: **avertir qn (de qch/que)** to warn sb (of sth/that); (*renseigner*) to inform sb (of sth/that); **avertir qn de ne pas faire qch** to warn sb not to do sth

avertissement [avɛʀtismɑ̃] *nm* warning

avertisseur [avɛʀtisœʀ] *nm* horn, siren; **avertisseur (d'incendie)** (fire) alarm

aveu, x [avø] *nm* confession; **passer aux aveux** to make a confession; **de l'aveu de** according to

aveugle [avœgl(ə)] *adj* blind ◆ *nm/f* blind person; **les aveugles** the blind; **test en (double) aveugle** (double) blind test

aveuglément [avœglemɑ̃] *adv* blindly

aveugler [avœgle] *vt* to blind

aviateur, trice [avjatœʀ, -tʀis] *nm/f* aviator, pilot

aviation [avjɑsjɔ̃] *nf* (*secteur commercial*) aviation; (*sport, métier de pilote*) flying; (MIL) air force; **terrain d'aviation** airfield; **aviation de chasse** fighter force

avide [avid] *adj* eager; (*péj*) greedy, grasping; **avide de** (*sang etc*) thirsting for; **avide d'honneurs/d'argent** greedy for honours/money; **avide de connaître/d'apprendre** eager to know/learn

avilir [aviliʀ] *vt* to debase

avion [avjɔ̃] *nm* (aero)plane (BRIT), (air)plane (US); **aller (quelque part) en avion** to go (somewhere) by plane, fly (somewhere); **par avion** by airmail; **avion de chasse** fighter; **avion de ligne** airliner; **avion à réaction** jet (plane)

aviron [aviʀɔ̃] *nm* oar; (*sport*): **l'aviron** rowing

avis [avi] *nm* opinion; (*notification*) notice; (COMM): **avis de crédit/débit** credit/debit advice; **à mon avis** in my opinion; **je suis de votre avis** I share your opinion, I am of your opinion; **être d'avis que** to be of the opinion that; **changer d'avis** to change one's mind; **sauf avis contraire** unless you hear to the contrary; **sans avis préalable** without notice; **jusqu'à nouvel avis** until further notice;

avis de décès death announcement

avisé, e [avize] *adj* sensible, wise; **être bien/mal avisé de faire** to be well-/ill-advised to do

aviser [avize] *vt* (*voir*) to notice, catch sight of; (*informer*): **aviser qn de/que** to advise *ou* inform *ou* notify sb of/that ◆ *vi* to think about things, assess the situation; **s'aviser de qch/que** to become suddenly aware of sth/that; **s'aviser de faire** to take it into one's head to do

avocat, e [avɔka, -at] *nm/f* (JUR) ≈ barrister (BRIT), lawyer; (*fig*) advocate, champion ◆ *nm* (CULIN) avocado (pear); **se faire l'avocat du diable** to be the devil's advocate; **l'avocat de la défense/partie civile** the counsel for the defence/plaintiff; **avocat d'affaires** business lawyer; **avocat général** assistant public prosecutor

avoine [avwan] *nf* oats *pl*

MOT CLÉ

avoir [avwaʀ] *nm* assets *pl*, resources *pl*; (COMM) credit; **avoir fiscal** tax credit

◆ *vt* **1** (*posséder*) to have; **elle a 2 enfants/une belle maison** she has (got) 2 children/a lovely house; **il a les yeux bleus** he has (got) blue eyes

2 (*éprouver*): **qu'est-ce que tu as?, qu'as-tu?** what's wrong?, what's the matter?; *voir aussi* **faim, peur** *etc*

3 (*âge, dimensions*) to be; **il a 3 ans** he is 3 (years old); **le mur a 3 mètres de haut** the wall is 3 metres high

4 (*fam: duper*) to have; **on vous a eu!** you've been done *ou* had!

5: **en avoir contre qn** to have a grudge against sb; **en avoir assez** to be fed up; **j'en ai pour une demi-heure** it'll take me half an hour; **n'avoir que faire de qch** to have no use for sth

◆ *vb aux* **1** to have; **avoir mangé/dormi** to have eaten/slept; **hier je n'ai pas mangé** I didn't eat yesterday

2 (*avoir +à +infinitif*): **avoir à faire qch** to have to do sth; **vous n'avez qu'à lui demander** you only have to ask him; **tu n'as pas à me poser des questions** it's not for you to ask me questions

◆ *vb impers* **1**: **il y a** (+ *singulier*) there is; (+ *pluriel*) there are; **qu'y-a-t-il?, qu'est-ce qu'il y a?** what's the matter?, what is it?; **il doit y avoir une explication** there must be an explanation; **il n'y a qu'à …** we (*ou* you *etc*) will just have to …; **il ne peut y en avoir qu'un** there can only be one

2 (*temporel*): **il y a 10 ans** 10 years ago; **il y a 10 ans/longtemps que je le connais** I've known him for 10 years/a long time; **il y a 10 ans qu'il est arrivé** it's 10 years since he arrived

---

avoisiner [avwazine] *vt* to be near *ou* close to; (*fig*) to border *ou* verge on

avortement [avɔʀtəmɑ̃] *nm* abortion

avorter [avɔʀte] *vi* (MÉD) to have an abortion; (*fig*) to fail; **faire avorter** to abort; **se faire avorter** to have an abortion

avoué, e [avwe] *adj* avowed ♦ *nm* (*JUR*) ≈ solicitor (*BRIT*), lawyer

avouer [avwe] *vt* (*crime, défaut*) to confess (to) ♦ *vi* (*se confesser*) to confess; (*admettre*) to admit; **avouer avoir fait/que** to admit *ou* confess to having done/that; **avouer que oui/non** to admit that is so/not so

avril [avril] *nm* April; *voir aussi* **juillet**; *see boxed note*

POISSON D'AVRIL

The traditional April Fools' Day prank in France involves attaching a cut-out paper fish, known as a '**poisson d'avril**', to the back of one's victim, without being caught.

axe [aks(ə)] *nm* axis (*pl* axes); (*de roue etc*) axle: **dans l'axe de** directly in line with; (*fig*) main line; **axe routier** trunk road, main road

axer [akse] *vt*: **axer qch sur** to centre sth on

ayons *etc* [ɛjɔ̃] *vb voir* **avoir**

azote [azɔt] *nm* nitrogen

— B b —

baba [baba] *adj inv*: **en être baba** (*fam*) to be flabbergasted ♦ *nm*: **baba au rhum** rum baba

babines [babin] *nfpl* chops

babiole [babjɔl] *nf* (*bibelot*) trinket; (*vétille*) trifle

bâbord [babɔʁ] *nm*: **à** *ou* **par bâbord** to port, on the port side

baby-foot [babifut] *nm inv* table football

baby-sitting [babisitiŋ] *nm* baby-sitting; **faire du baby-sitting** to baby-sit

bac [bak] *nm* (*SCOL*) = **baccalauréat**; (*bateau*) ferry; (*récipient*) tub; (: *PHOTO etc*) tray; (: *INDUSTRIE*) tank; **bac à glace** ice-tray; **bac à légumes** vegetable compartment *ou* rack

baccalauréat [bakalɔʁea] *nm* ≈ GCE A-levels *pl* (*BRIT*), ≈ high school diploma (*US*); *see boxed note*

BACCALAURÉAT

The **baccalauréat** or 'bac' is the school-leaving examination taken at a French 'lycée' at the age of 17 or 18; it marks the end of seven years' secondary education. Several subject combinations are available, although in all cases a broad range is studied. Successful candidates can go on to university, if they so wish.

bâche [baʃ] *nf* tarpaulin, canvas sheet

bachelier, ière [baʃəlje, -jɛʁ] *nm/f* holder of the baccalauréat

bâcler [bakle] *vt* to botch (up)

badaud, e [bado, -od] *nm/f* idle onlooker

badigeonner [badiʒɔne] *vt* to distemper; to colourwash; (*péj: barbouiller*) to daub; (*MÉD*) to paint

badiner [badine] *vi*: **badiner avec qch** to treat sth lightly; **ne pas badiner avec qch** not to trifle with sth

baffe [baf] *nf* (*fam*) slap, clout

baffle [bafl(ə)] *nm* baffle (board)

bafouer [bafwe] *vt* to deride, ridicule

bafouiller [bafuje] *vi, vt* to stammer

bâfrer [bafʁe] *vi, vt* (*fam*) to guzzle, gobble

bagages [bagaʒ] *nmpl* luggage *sg*, baggage; **faire ses bagages** to pack (one's bags); **bagage littéraire** (stock of) literary knowledge; **bagages à main** hand-luggage

bagarre [bagaʁ] *nf* fight, brawl; **il aime la bagarre** he loves a fight, he likes fighting

bagarrer [bagaʁe]: **se bagarrer** *vi* to (have a) fight

bagatelle [bagatɛl] *nf* trifle, trifling sum (*ou* matter)

bagne [baɲ] *nm* penal colony; **c'est le bagne** (*fig*) it's forced labour

bagnole [baɲɔl] *nf* (*fam*) car, wheels *pl* (*BRIT*)

bagout [bagu] *nm* glibness; **avoir du bagout** to have the gift of the gab

bague [bag] *nf* ring; **bague de fiançailles** engagement ring; **bague de serrage** clip

baguette [bagɛt] *nf* stick; (*cuisine chinoise*) chopstick; (*de chef d'orchestre*) baton; (*pain*) stick of (French) bread; (*CONSTR: moulure*) beading; **mener qn à la baguette** to rule sb with a rod of iron; **baguette magique** magic wand; **baguette de sourcier** divining rod; **baguette de tambour** drumstick

baie [bɛ] *nf* (*GÉO*) bay; (*fruit*) berry; **baie (vitrée)** picture window

baignade [bɛɲad] *nf* (*action*) bathing; (*bain*) bathe; (*endroit*) bathing place

baigner [beɲe] *vt* (*bébé*) to bath ♦ *vi*: **baigner dans son sang** to lie in a pool of blood; **baigner dans la brume** to be shrouded in mist; **se baigner** *vi* to go swimming *ou* bathing; (*dans une baignoire*) to have a bath; **ça baigne!** (*fam*) everything's great!

baignoire [beɲwaʁ] *nf* bath(tub); (*THÉÂT*) ground-floor box

bail, baux [baj, bo] *nm* lease; **donner** *ou* **prendre qch à bail** to lease sth

bâillement [bajmɑ̃] *nm* yawn

bâiller [baje] *vi* to yawn; (*être ouvert*) to gape

bâillonner [bajɔne] *vt* to gag

bain [bɛ̃] *nm* (*dans une baignoire, PHOTO, TECH*) bath; (*dans la mer, une piscine*) swim; **costume de bain**

bathing costume (BRIT), swimsuit; **prendre un bain** to have a bath; **se mettre dans le bain** (fig) to get into (the way of) it ou things; **bain de bouche** mouthwash; **bain de foule** walkabout; **bain de pieds** footbath; (au bord de la mer) paddle; **bain de siège** hip bath; **bain de soleil** sunbathing no pl; **prendre un bain de soleil** to sunbathe; **bains de mer** sea bathing sg; **bains(-douches) municipaux** public baths

bain-marie, pl **bains-marie** [bɛ̃mari] nm double boiler; **faire chauffer au bain-marie** (boîte etc) to immerse in boiling water

baiser [beze] nm kiss ♦ vt (main, front) to kiss; (fam!) to screw (!)

baisse [bɛs] nf fall, drop; (COMM): **"baisse sur la viande"** "meat prices down"; **en baisse** (cours, action) falling; **à la baisse** downwards

baisser [bese] vt to lower; (radio, chauffage) to turn down; (AUTO: phares) to dip (BRIT), lower (US) ♦ vi to fall, drop, go down; **se baisser** vi to bend down

bal [bal] nm dance; (grande soirée) ball; **bal costumé/masqué** fancy-dress/masked ball; **bal musette** dance (with accordion accompaniment)

balade [balad] nf walk, stroll; (en voiture) drive; **faire une balade** to go for a walk ou stroll; to go for a drive

balader [balade] vt (traîner) to trail around; **se balader** vi to go for a walk ou stroll; to go for a drive

baladeur [baladœr] nm personal stereo

balafre [balafr(ə)] nf gash, slash; (cicatrice) scar

balai [bale] nm broom, brush; (AUTO: d'essuie-glace) blade; (MUS: de batterie etc) brush; **donner un coup de balai** to give the floor a sweep; **balai mécanique** carpet sweeper

balai-brosse, pl **balais-brosses** [balebrɔs] nm (long-handled) scrubbing brush

balance [balɑ̃s] nf (à plateaux) scales pl; (de précision) balance; (COMM, POL): **balance des comptes** ou **paiements** balance of payments; (signe): **la Balance** Libra, the Scales; **être de la Balance** to be Libra; **balance commerciale** balance of trade; **balance des forces** balance of power; **balance romaine** steelyard

balancer [balɑ̃se] vt to swing; (lancer) to fling, chuck; (renvoyer, jeter) to chuck out ♦ vi to swing; **se balancer** vi to swing; (bateau) to rock; (branche) to sway; **se balancer de qch** (fam) not to give a toss about sth

balançoire [balɑ̃swar] nf swing; (sur pivot) seesaw

balayer [baleje] vt (feuilles etc) to sweep up, brush up; (pièce, cour) to sweep; (chasser) to sweep away ou aside; (suj: radar) to scan; (: phares) to sweep across

balayeur, euse [balejœr, -øz] nm/f roadsweeper ♦ nf (engin) roadsweeper

balbutier [balbysje] vi, vt to stammer

balcon [balkɔ̃] nm balcony; (THÉÂT) dress circle

baleine [balɛn] nf whale; (de parapluie) rib; (de corset) bone

balise [baliz] nf (NAVIG) beacon, (marker) buoy; (AVIAT) runway light, beacon; (AUTO, SKI) sign, marker

baliser [balize] vt to mark out (with beacons ou lights etc)

balivernes [balivern(ə)] nfpl twaddle sg (BRIT), nonsense sg

ballant, e [balɑ̃, -ɑ̃t] adj dangling

balle [bal] nf (de fusil) bullet; (de sport) ball; (du blé) chaff; (paquet) bale; (fam: franc) franc; **balle perdue** stray bullet

ballerine [balrin] nf ballet dancer; (chaussure) pump, ballerina

ballet [balɛ] nm ballet; (fig): **ballet diplomatique** diplomatic to-ings and fro-ings

ballon [balɔ̃] nm (de sport) ball; (jouet, AVIAT, de bande dessinée) balloon; (de vin) glass; **ballon d'essai** (météorologique) pilot balloon; (fig) feeler(s); **ballon de football** football; **ballon d'oxygène** oxygen bottle

ballot [balo] nm bundle; (péj) nitwit

ballottage [balɔtaʒ] nm (POL) second ballot

ballotter [balɔte] vi to roll around; (bateau etc) to toss ♦ vt to shake ou throw about; to toss; **être ballotté entre** (fig) to be shunted between; (: indécis) to be torn between

balnéaire [balneɛr] adj seaside cpd

balourd, e [balur, -urd(ə)] adj clumsy ♦ nm/f clodhopper

balustrade [balystrad] nf railings pl, handrail

bambin [bɑ̃bɛ̃] nm little child

bambou [bɑ̃bu] nm bamboo

ban [bɑ̃] nm round of applause, cheer; **être/mettre au ban de** to be outlawed/to outlaw from; **le ban et l'arrière-ban de sa famille** every last one of his relatives; **bans (de mariage)** banns, bans

banal, e [banal] adj banal, commonplace; (péj) trite; **four/moulin banal** village oven/mill

banalité [banalite] nf banality; (remarque) truism, trite remark

banane [banan] nf banana

banc [bɑ̃] nm seat, bench; (de poissons) shoal; **banc des accusés** dock; **banc d'essai** (fig) testing ground; **banc de sable** sandbank; **banc des témoins** witness box; **banc de touche** dugout

bancaire [bɑ̃kɛr] adj banking, bank cpd

bancal, e [bɑ̃kal] adj wobbly; (personne) bowlegged; (fig: projet) shaky

bandage [bɑ̃daʒ] nm bandaging; (pansement) bandage; **bandage herniaire** truss

bande [bɑ̃d] nf (de tissu etc) strip; (MÉD) bandage; (motif, dessin) stripe; (CINÉ) film; (INFORM) tape; (RADIO, groupe) band; (péj): **une bande de** a bunch ou crowd of; **par la bande** in a roundabout way; **donner de la bande** to list; **faire bande à part** to keep to o.s.; **bande dessinée (BD)** strip cartoon (BRIT), comic strip; **bande magnétique** magnetic tape; **bande perforée** punched tape; **bande de roulement** (de pneu) tread; **bande sonore** sound track; **bande de terre** strip of land; **bande Velpeau®** (MÉD) crêpe bandage; see boxed note

BANDE DESSINÉE

The **bande dessinée** or 'BD' enjoys a huge following amongst adults as well as children in France, where the comic strip is accorded both literary and artistic status. Every year, an international exhibition takes place in Angoulême at the end of January. Astérix, Tintin, Lucky Luke and Gaston Lagaffe are some of the most famous cartoon characters.

bandeau, x [bɑ̃do] nm headband; (sur les yeux) blindfold; (MÉD) head bandage

bander [bɑ̃de] vt to bandage; (muscle) to tense; (arc) to bend ♦ vi (fam!) to have a hard on (!); **bander les yeux à qn** to blindfold sb

banderole [bɑ̃dʀɔl] nf banderole; (dans un défilé etc) streamer

bandit [bɑ̃di] nm bandit

banditisme [bɑ̃ditism(ə)] nm violent crime, armed robberies pl

bandoulière [bɑ̃duljɛʀ] nf: **en bandoulière** (slung ou worn) across the shoulder

banlieue [bɑ̃ljø] nf suburbs pl; **quartiers de banlieue** suburban areas; **trains de banlieue** commuter trains

banlieusard, e [bɑ̃ljøzaʀ, -aʀd(ə)] nm/f suburbanite

bannière [banjɛʀ] nf banner

bannir [baniʀ] vt to banish

banque [bɑ̃k] nf bank; (activités) banking; **banque des yeux/du sang** eye/blood bank; **banque d'affaires** merchant bank; **banque de dépôt** deposit bank; **banque de données** (INFORM) data bank; **banque d'émission** bank of issue

banqueroute [bɑ̃kʀut] nf bankruptcy

banquet [bɑ̃kɛ] nm (de club) dinner; (de noces) reception; (d'apparat) banquet

banquette [bɑ̃kɛt] nf seat

banquier [bɑ̃kje] nm banker

banquise [bɑ̃kiz] nf ice field

baptême [batɛm] nm (sacrement) baptism; (cérémonie) christening, baptism; (d'un navire) launching; (d'une cloche) consecration, dedication; **baptême de l'air** first flight

baptiser [batize] vt to christen; to baptize; to launch; to consecrate, dedicate

baquet [bakɛ] nm tub, bucket

bar [baʀ] nm bar; (poisson) bass

baraque [baʀak] nf shed; (fam) house; **baraque foraine** fairground stand

baraqué, e [baʀake] adj well-built, hefty

baraquements [baʀakmɑ̃] nmpl huts (for refugees, workers etc)

baratin [baʀatɛ̃] nm (fam) smooth talk, patter

baratiner [baʀatine] vt to chat up

barbant, e [baʀbɑ̃, -ɑ̃t] adj (fam) deadly (boring)

barbare [baʀbaʀ] adj barbaric ♦ nm/f barbarian

barbarie [baʀbaʀi] nf barbarism; (cruauté) barbarity

barbe [baʀb(ə)] nf beard; **(au nez et) à la barbe de qn** (fig) under sb's very nose; **quelle barbe!** (fam) what a drag ou bore!; **barbe à papa** candyfloss (BRIT), cotton candy (US)

barbelé [baʀbəle] nm barbed wire no pl

barber [baʀbe] vt (fam) to bore stiff

barbiturique [baʀbityʀik] nm barbiturate

barboter [baʀbɔte] vi to paddle, dabble ♦ vt (fam) to filch

barbouiller [baʀbuje] vt to daub; (péj: écrire, dessiner) to scribble; **avoir l'estomac barbouillé** to feel queasy ou sick

barbu, e [baʀby] adj bearded

barda [baʀda] nm (fam) kit, gear

barder [baʀde] vt (CULIN: rôti, volaille) to bard ♦ vi (fam): **ça va barder** sparks will fly

barème [baʀɛm] nm scale; (liste) table; **barème des salaires** salary scale

baril [baʀil] nm (tonneau) barrel; (de poudre) keg

bariolé, e [baʀjɔle] adj many-coloured, rainbow-coloured

baromètre [baʀɔmɛtʀ(ə)] nm barometer; **baromètre anéroïde** aneroid barometer

baron [baʀɔ̃] nm baron

baroque [baʀɔk] adj (ART) baroque; (fig) weird

barque [baʀk(ə)] nf small boat

barquette [baʀkɛt] nf small boat-shaped tart; (récipient: en aluminium) tub; (: en bois) basket

barrage [baʀaʒ] nm dam; (sur route) roadblock, barricade; **barrage de police** police roadblock

barre [baʀ] nf (de fer etc) rod, bar; (NAVIG) helm; (écrite) line, stroke; (DANSE) barre; (niveau): **la livre a franchi la barre des 10 frs** the pound has broken the 10 frs barrier; (JUR): **comparaître à la barre** to appear as a witness; **être à** ou **tenir la barre** (NAVIG) to be at the helm; **coup de barre** (fig): **c'est le coup de barre!** it's daylight robbery!; **j'ai le coup de barre!** I'm all in!; **barre fixe** (GYM) horizontal bar; **barre de mesure** (MUS) bar line; **barre à mine** crowbar; **barres parallèles/asymétriques** (GYM) parallel/asymmetric bars

barreau, x [baʀo] nm bar; (JUR): **le barreau** the Bar

barrer [baʀe] vt (route etc) to block; (mot) to cross out; (chèque) to cross (BRIT); (NAVIG) to steer; **se barrer** vi (fam) to clear off

barrette [baʀɛt] nf (pour cheveux) (hair) slide (BRIT) ou clip (US); (REL: bonnet) biretta; (broche) brooch

barricader [baʀikade] *vt* to barricade; **se barricader chez soi** (*fig*) to lock o.s. in

barrière [baʀjɛʀ] *nf* fence; (*obstacle*) barrier; (*porte*) gate; **la Grande Barrière** the Great Barrier Reef; **barrière de dégel** (ADMIN: *on roadsigns*) no heavy vehicles – road liable to subsidence due to thaw; **barrières douanières** trade barriers

barrique [baʀik] *nf* barrel, cask

bar-tabac [baʀtaba] *nm* bar (*which sells tobacco and stamps*)

bas, basse [ba, bas] *adj* low; (*action*) low, ignoble ♦ *nm* (*vêtement*) stocking; (*partie inférieure*): **le bas de** the lower part *ou* foot *ou* bottom of ♦ *nf* (MUS) bass ♦ *adv* low; (*parler*) softly; **plus bas** lower down; more softly; (*dans un texte*) further on, below; **la tête basse** with lowered head; (*fig*) with head hung low; **avoir la vue basse** to be short-sighted; **au bas mot** at the lowest estimate; **enfant en bas âge** infant, young child; **en bas** down below; at (*ou* to) the bottom; (*dans une maison*) downstairs; **en bas de** at the bottom of; **de bas en haut** upwards; from the bottom to the top; **des hauts et des bas** ups and downs; **un bas de laine** (*fam: économies*) money under the mattress (*fig*); **mettre bas** *vi* to give birth; **à bas la dictature!** down with dictatorship!; **bas morceaux** (*viande*) cheap cuts

basané, e [bazane] *adj* tanned, bronzed; (*immigré etc*) swarthy

bas-côté [bakote] *nm* (*de route*) verge (BRIT), shoulder (US); (*d'église*) (side) aisle

bascule [baskyl] *nf*: **(jeu de) bascule** seesaw; **(balance à) bascule** scales *pl*; **fauteuil à bascule** rocking chair; **système à bascule** tip-over device; rocker device

basculer [baskyle] *vi* to fall over, topple (over); (*benne*) to tip up ♦ *vt* (*aussi:* **faire basculer**) to topple over; to tip out, tip up

base [baz] *nf* base; (POL): **la base** the rank and file, the grass roots; (*fondement, principe*) basis (*pl* bases); **jeter les bases de** to lay the foundations of; **à la base de** (*fig*) at the root of; **sur la base de** (*fig*) on the basis of; **de base** basic; **à base de café** *etc* coffee *etc* -based; **base de données** (INFORM) database; **base de lancement** launching site

baser [baze] *vt*: **baser qch sur** to base sth on; **se baser sur** (*données, preuves*) to base one's argument on; **être basé à/dans** (MIL) to be based at/in

bas-fond [bafɔ̃] *nm* (NAVIG) shallow; **bas-fonds** *nmpl* (*fig*) dregs

basilic [bazilik] *nm* (CULIN) basil

basket(-ball) [basket(bol)] *nm* basketball

basque [bask(ə)] *adj, nm* (LING) Basque ♦ *nm/f*: **Basque** Basque; **le Pays basque** the Basque country

basse [bas] *adj f, nf voir* **bas**

basse-cour, *pl* basses-cours [baskuʀ] *nf* farm-yard; (*animaux*) farmyard animals

bassin [basɛ̃] *nm* (*cuvette*) bowl; (*pièce d'eau*) pond, pool; (*de fontaine*, GÉO) basin; (ANAT) pelvis; (*portuaire*) dock; **bassin houiller** coalfield

bassine [basin] *nf* basin; (*contenu*) bowl, bowlful

basson [basɔ̃] *nm* bassoon

bas-ventre [bavɑ̃tʀ(ə)] *nm* (*lower part of the*) stomach

bataille [bataj] *nf* battle; **en bataille** (*en travers*) at an angle; (*en désordre*) awry; **bataille rangée** pitched battle

bâtard, e [batɑʀ, -aʀd(ə)] *adj* (*enfant*) illegitimate; (*fig*) hybrid ♦ *nm/f* illegitimate child, bastard (*péj*) ♦ *nm* (BOULANGERIE) ≈ Vienna loaf; **chien bâtard** mongrel

bateau, x [bato] *nm* boat; (*grand*) ship ♦ *adj inv* (*banal, rebattu*) hackneyed; **bateau de pêche/à moteur/à voiles** fishing/motor/sailing boat

bateau-mouche [batomuʃ] *nm* (*passenger*) pleasure boat (*on the seine*)

bâti, e [bati] *adj* (*terrain*) developed ♦ *nm* (*armature*) frame; (COUTURE) tacking; **bien bâti** (*personne*) well-built

batifoler [batifɔle] *vi* to frolic *ou* lark about

bâtiment [batimɑ̃] *nm* building; (NAVIG) ship, ves-sel; (*industrie*): **le bâtiment** the building trade

bâtir [batiʀ] *vt* to build; (COUTURE: *jupe, ourlet*) to tack; **fil à bâtir** (COUTURE) tacking thread

bâtisse [batis] *nf* building

bâton [batɔ̃] *nm* stick; **mettre des bâtons dans les roues à qn** to put a spoke in sb's wheel; **à bâtons rompus** informally; **bâton de rouge (à lèvres)** lipstick; **bâton de ski** ski stick

bats [ba] *vb voir* **battre**

battage [bataʒ] *nm* (*publicité*) (hard) plugging

battant, e [batɑ̃, -ɑ̃t] *vb voir* **battre** ♦ *adj*: **pluie battante** lashing rain ♦ *nm* (*de cloche*) clapper; (*de volets*) shutter, flap (*de porte*), side; (*fig: personne*) fighter; **porte à double battant** double door; **tam-bour battant** briskly

battement [batmɑ̃] *nm* (*de cœur*) beat; (*inter-valle*) interval (*between classes, trains etc*) **batte-ment de paupières** blinking *no pl* (*of eyelids*); **un battement de 10 minutes, 10 minutes de batte-ment** 10 minutes to spare

batterie [batʀi] *nf* (MIL, ÉLEC) battery; (MUS) drums *pl*, drum kit; **batterie de cuisine** kitchen utensils *pl*; (*casseroles etc*) pots and pans *pl*; **une batterie de tests** a string of tests

batteur [batœʀ] *nm* (MUS) drummer; (*appareil*) whisk

battre [batʀ(ə)] *vt* to beat; (*pluie, vagues*) to beat *ou* lash against; (*œufs etc*) to beat up, whisk; (*blé*) to thresh; (*cartes*) to shuffle; (*passer au peigne fin*) to scour ♦ *vi* (*cœur*) to beat; (*volets etc*) to bang, rattle; **se battre** *vi* to fight; **battre la mesure** to beat time; **battre en brèche** (MIL: *mur*) to batter; (*fig: théorie*) to demolish; (: *institution etc*) to attack; **bat-**

tre son plein to be at its height, be going full swing; **battre pavillon britannique** to fly the British flag; **battre des mains** to clap one's hands; **battre des ailes** to flap its wings; **battre de l'aile** (*fig*) to be in a bad way *ou* in bad shape; **battre la semelle** to stamp one's feet; **battre en retraite** to beat a retreat

baume [bom] *nm* balm

bavard, e [bavar, -ard(ə)] *adj* (very) talkative; gossipy

bavarder [bavarde] *vi* to chatter; (*indiscrètement*) to gossip; (: *révéler un secret*) to blab

bave [bav] *nf* dribble; (*de chien etc*) slobber, slaver (*BRIT*), drool (*US*); (*d'escargot*) slime

baver [bave] *vi* to dribble; to slobber, slaver (*BRIT*), drool (*US*); (*encre, couleur*) to run; **en baver** (*fam*) to have a hard time (of it)

baveux, euse [bavø, -øz] *adj* dribbling; (*omelette*) runny

bavoir [bavwar] *nm* (*de bébé*) bib

bavure [bavyr] *nf* smudge; (*fig*) hitch; blunder

bayer [baje] *vi*: **bayer aux corneilles** to stand gaping

bazar [bazar] *nm* general store; (*fam*) jumble

bazarder [bazarde] *vt* (*fam*) to chuck out

BCBG *sigle a* (= *bon chic bon genre*) = preppy

BD *sigle f* = *bande dessinée*; (= *base de données*) DB

bd *abr* = *boulevard*

béant, e [beã, -ãt] *adj* gaping

béat, e [bea, -at] *adj* showing open-eyed wonder; (*sourire etc*) blissful

béatitude [beatityd] *nf* bliss

beau (bel), belle, beaux [bo, bɛl] *adj* beautiful, lovely; (*homme*) handsome ♦ *nf* (*SPORT*) decider ♦ *adv*: **il fait beau** the weather's fine ♦ *nm*: **avoir le sens du beau** to have an aesthetic sense; **le temps est au beau** the weather is set fair; **un beau geste** (*fig*) a fine gesture; **un beau salaire** a good salary; **un beau gâchis/rhume** a fine mess/nasty cold; **en faire/dire de belles** to do/say (some) stupid things; **le beau monde** high society; **beau parleur** smooth talker; **un beau jour** one (fine) day; **de plus belle** more than ever, even more; **bel et bien** well and truly; (*vraiment*) really (and truly); **le plus beau c'est que ...** the best of it is that ...; **c'est du beau!** that's great, that is!; **on a beau essayer** however hard *ou* no matter how hard we try; **il a beau jeu de protester** *etc* it's easy for him to protest *etc*; **faire le beau** (*chien*) to sit up and beg

┌─────────────┐
│ MOT CLÉ │
└─────────────┘

beaucoup [boku] *adv* **1** a lot; **il boit beaucoup** he drinks a lot; **il ne boit pas beaucoup** he doesn't drink much *ou* a lot

2 (*suivi de plus, trop etc*) much, a lot, far; **il est beaucoup plus grand** he is much *ou* a lot *ou* far taller

3: **beaucoup de** (*nombre*) many, a lot of; (*quantité*) a lot of; **pas beaucoup de** (*nombre*) not many, not a lot of; (*quantité*) not much, not a lot of; **beaucoup d'étudiants/de touristes** a lot of *ou* many students/tourists; **beaucoup de courage** a lot of courage; **il n'a pas beaucoup d'argent** he hasn't got much *ou* a lot of money; **il n'y a pas beaucoup de touristes** there aren't many *ou* a lot of tourists

4: **de beaucoup** by far

♦ *pron*: **beaucoup le savent** lots of people know that

beau-fils, *pl* **beaux-fils** [bofis] *nm* son-in-law; (*remariage*) stepson

beau-frère, *pl* **beaux-frères** [bofrɛr] *nm* brother-in-law

beau-père, *pl* **beaux-pères** [boper] *nm* father-in-law; (*remariage*) stepfather

beauté [bote] *nf* beauty; **de toute beauté** beautiful; **en beauté** *adv* with a flourish, brilliantly

beaux-arts [bozar] *nmpl* fine arts

beaux-parents [boparã] *nmpl* wife's/husband's family *sg ou pl*, in-laws

bébé [bebe] *nm* baby

bec [bɛk] *nm* beak, bill; (*de plume*) nib; (*de cafetière etc*) spout; (*de casserole etc*) lip; (*d'une clarinette etc*) mouthpiece; (*fam*) mouth; **clouer le bec à qn** (*fam*) to shut sb up; **ouvrir le bec** (*fam*) to open one's mouth; **bec de gaz** (street) gaslamp; **bec verseur** pouring lip

bécane [bekan] *nf* (*fam*) bike

bec-de-lièvre, *pl* **becs-de-lièvre** [bɛkdəljɛvr(ə)] *nm* harelip

bêche [bɛʃ] *nf* spade

bêcher [beʃe] *vt* (*terre*) to dig; (*personne: critiquer*) to slate; (: *snober*) to look down on

bécoter [bekɔte]: **se bécoter** *vi* to smooch

becqueter [bɛkte] *vt* (*fam*) to eat

bedaine [bədɛn] *nf* paunch

bedonnant, e [bədɔnã, -ãt] *adj* paunchy, potbellied

bée [be] *adj*: **bouche bée** gaping

beffroi [befrwa] *nm* belfry

bégayer [begeje] *vt, vi* to stammer

bègue [bɛg] *nm/f*: **être bègue** to have a stammer

beige [bɛʒ] *adj* beige

beignet [bɛɲɛ] *nm* fritter

bel [bɛl] *adj m voir* **beau**

bêler [bele] *vi* to bleat

belette [bəlɛt] *nf* weasel

belge [bɛlʒ(ə)] *adj* Belgian ♦ *nm/f*: **Belge** Belgian; *see boxed note*

Belgique [bɛlʒik] *nf*: **la Belgique** Belgium

bélier [belje] *nm* ram; (*engin*) (battering) ram; (*signe*): **le Bélier** Aries, the Ram; **être du Bélier** to be Aries

belle [bɛl] *adj f*, *nf voir* **beau**

belle-fille, *pl* **belles-filles** [bɛlfij] *nf* daughter-in-law; (*remariage*) stepdaughter

belle-mère, *pl* **belles-mères** [bɛlmɛʀ] *nf* mother-in-law; (*remariage*) stepmother

belle-sœur, *pl* **belles-sœurs** [bɛlsœʀ] *nf* sister-in-law

belliqueux, euse [belikø, -øz] *adj* aggressive, warlike

belvédère [bɛlvedɛʀ] *nm* panoramic viewpoint (*or small building there*)

bémol [bemɔl] *nm* (*MUS*) flat

bénédiction [benediksjɔ̃] *nf* blessing

bénéfice [benefis] *nm* (*COMM*) profit; (*avantage*) benefit; **au bénéfice de** in aid of

bénéficier [benefisje] *vi*: **bénéficier de** to enjoy; (*profiter*) to benefit from *ou* by; (*obtenir*) to get, be given

bénéfique [benefik] *adj* beneficial

bénévole [benevɔl] *adj* voluntary, unpaid

bénin, igne [benɛ̃, -iɲ] *adj* minor, mild; (*tumeur*) benign

bénir [beniʀ] *vt* to bless

bénit, e [beni, -it] *adj* consecrated; **eau bénite** holy water

benjamin, e [bɛ̃ʒamɛ̃, -in] *nm/f* youngest child; (*SPORT*) under-13

benne [bɛn] *nf* skip; (*de téléphérique*) (cable) car; **benne basculante** tipper (*BRIT*), dump *ou* dumper truck

BEP *sigle m* (= *Brevet d'études professionnelles*) *school-leaving diploma, taken at approx. 18 years'*

béquille [bekij] *nf* crutch; (*de bicyclette*) stand

berceau, x [bɛʀso] *nm* cradle, crib

bercer [bɛʀse] *vt* to rock, cradle; (*suj: musique etc*) to lull; **bercer qn de** (*promesses etc*) to delude sb with

berceuse [bɛʀsøz] *nf* (*chanson*) lullaby

béret (basque) [beʀe(bask(ə))] *nm* beret

berge [bɛʀʒ(ə)] *nf* bank

berger, ère [bɛʀʒe, -ɛʀ] *nm/f* shepherd/shepherdess; **berger allemand** (*chien*) alsatian (dog) (*BRIT*), German shepherd (dog) (*US*)

berlingot [bɛʀlɛ̃go] *nm* (*emballage*) carton (*pyramid shaped*); (*bonbon*) lozenge

berlue [bɛʀly] *nf*: **j'ai la berlue** I must be seeing things

berner [bɛʀne] *vt* to fool

besogne [bəzɔɲ] *nf* work *no pl*, job

besoin [bazwɛ̃] *nm* need; (*pauvreté*): **le besoin** need, want; **le besoin d'argent/de gloire** the need for money/glory; **besoins (naturels)** nature's needs; **faire ses besoins** to relieve o.s.; **avoir**

besoin de qch/faire qch to need sth/to do sth; **il n'y a pas besoin de (faire)** there is no need to (do); **au besoin, si besoin est** if need be; **pour les besoins de la cause** for the purpose in hand

bestial, e, aux [bɛstjal, -o] *adj* bestial, brutish
♦ *nmpl* cattle

bestiole [bɛstjɔl] *nf* (tiny) creature

bétail [betaj] *nm* livestock, cattle *pl*

bête [bɛt] *nf* animal; (*bestiole*) insect, creature
♦ *adj* stupid, silly; **les bêtes** (the) animals; **chercher la petite bête** to nit-pick; **bête noire** pet hate, bugbear (*BRIT*); **bête sauvage** wild beast; **bête de somme** beast of burden

bêtement [bɛtmɑ̃] *adv* stupidly; **tout bêtement** quite simply

bêtise [betiz] *nf* stupidity; (*action, remarque*) stupid thing (to say *ou* do); (*bonbon*) type of mint sweet (*BRIT*) *ou* candy (*US*); **faire/dire une bêtise** to do/say something stupid

béton [betɔ̃] *nm* concrete; **(en) béton** (*fig: alibi, argument*) cast iron; **béton armé** reinforced concrete; **béton précontraint** prestressed concrete

bétonnière [betɔnjɛʀ] *nf* cement mixer

betterave [bɛtʀav] *nf* (*rouge*) beetroot (*BRIT*), beet (*US*); **betterave fourragère** mangel-wurzel; **betterave sucrière** sugar beet

beugler [bøgle] *vi* to low; (*péj: radio etc*) to blare
♦ *vt* (*péj: chanson etc*) to bawl out

Beur [bœʀ] *adj*, *nm/f see boxed note*

beurre [bœʀ] *nm* butter; **mettre du beurre dans les épinards** (*fig*) to add a little to the kitty; **beurre de cacao** cocoa butter; **beurre noir** brown butter (sauce)

beurrer [bœʀe] *vt* to butter

beurrier [bœʀje] *nm* butter dish

beuverie [bœvʀi] *nf* drinking session

bévue [bevy] *nf* blunder

Beyrouth [beʀut] *n* Beirut

biais [bjɛ] *nm* (*moyen*) device, expedient; (*aspect*) angle; (*bande de tissu*) piece of cloth cut on the bias; **en biais, de biais** (*obliquement*) at an angle; (*fig*) indirectly

biaiser [bjeze] *vi* (*fig*) to sidestep the issue

bibelot [biblo] *nm* trinket, curio

biberon [bibʀɔ̃] *nm* (feeding) bottle; **nourrir au biberon** to bottle-feed

bible [bibl(ə)] *nf* bible

bibliobus [biblijɔbys] *nm* mobile library van

bibliographie [biblijɔgrafi] *nf* bibliography
bibliothécaire [biblijɔtekɛʀ] *nm/f* librarian
bibliothèque [biblijɔtɛk] *nf* library; *(meuble)*
bookcase; **bibliothèque municipale** public library
bic® [bik] *nm* Biro®
bicarbonate [bikaʀbɔnat] *nm*: **bicarbonate (de
soude)** bicarbonate of soda
biceps [bisɛps] *nm* biceps
biche [biʃ] *nf* doe
bichonner [biʃɔne] *vt* to groom
bicolore [bikɔlɔʀ] *adj* two-coloured (BRIT), two-
colored (US)
bicoque [bikɔk] *nf* (*péj*) shack, dump
bicyclette [bisiklɛt] *nf* bicycle
bide [bid] *nm* (*fam: ventre*) belly; (*THÉÂT*) flop
bidet [bidɛ] *nm* bidet
bidon [bidɔ̃] *nm* can ♦ *adj inv* (*fam*) phoney
bidonville [bidɔ̃vil] *nm* shanty town
bidule [bidyl] *nm* (*fam*) thingamajig

MOT-CLÉ
---

bien [bjɛ̃] *nm* **1** (*avantage, profit*): **faire le bien**
to do good; **faire du bien à qn** to do sb good; **ça
fait du bien de faire** it does you good to do;
dire du bien de to speak well of; **c'est pour son
bien** it's for his own good; **changer en bien** to
change for the better; **le bien public** the public
good; **vouloir du bien à qn** (*vouloir aider*) to
have sb's (best) interests at heart; **je te veux du
bien** (*pour mettre en confiance*) I don't wish you
any harm
2 (*possession, patrimoine*) possession, property;
son bien le plus précieux his most treasured
possession; **avoir du bien** to have property;
biens (de consommation *etc*) (consumer *etc*)
goods; **biens durables** (consumer) durables
3 (*moral*): **le bien** good; **distinguer le bien du
mal** to tell good from evil
♦ *adv* **1** (*de façon satisfaisante*) well; **elle tra-
vaille/mange bien** she works/eats well; **aller** *or*
se porter bien to be well; **croyant bien faire, je/
il ...** thinking I/he was doing the right thing,
I/he ...
2 (*valeur intensive*) quite; **bien jeune** quite
young; **bien assez** quite enough; **bien mieux**
(very) much better; **bien du temps/des gens**
quite a time/a number of people; **j'espère bien
y aller** I do hope to go; **je veux bien le faire**
(*concession*) I'm quite willing to do it; **il faut bien
le faire** it has to be done; **il y a bien 2 ans** at
least 2 years ago; **il semble bien que** it really
seems that; **peut-être bien** it could well be;
aimer bien to like; **Paul est bien venu, n'est-ce
pas?** Paul HAS come, hasn't he?; **où peut-il bien
être passé?** where on earth can he have got to?
3 (*conséquence, résultat*): **si bien que** with the
result that; **on verra bien** we'll see; **faire bien de
...** to be right to ...

♦ *excl* right!, OK!, fine!; **eh bien!** well!; **(c'est)
bien fait!** it serves you (*ou* him *etc*) right!; **bien
sûr!, bien entendu!** certainly!, of course!
♦ *adj inv* **1** (*en bonne forme, à l'aise*): **je me sens
bien, je suis bien** I feel fine; **je ne me sens pas
bien, je ne suis pas bien** I don't feel well; **on est
bien dans ce fauteuil** this chair is very comfortable
2 (*joli, beau*) good-looking; **tu es bien dans cette
robe** you look good in that dress
3 (*satisfaisant*) good; **elle est bien, cette mai-
son/secrétaire** it's a good house/she's a good
secretary; **c'est très bien (comme ça)** it's fine
(like that); **ce n'est pas si bien que ça** it's not as
good *ou* great as all that; **c'est bien?** is that all
right?
4 (*moralement*) right; (: *personne*) good, nice;
(*respectable*) respectable; **ce n'est pas bien de
...** it's not right to ...; **elle est bien, cette femme**
she's a nice woman, she's a good sort; **des gens
bien** respectable people
5 (*en bons termes*): **être bien avec qn** to be on
good terms with sb

---

bienséant, e [bjɛ̃seɑ̃, -ɑ̃t] *adj* proper, seemly
bientôt [bjɛ̃to] *adv* soon; **à bientôt** see you soon
bienveillant, e [bjɛ̃vɛjɑ̃, -ɑ̃t] *adj* kindly
bienvenu, e [bjɛ̃vny] *adj* welcome ♦ *nm/f*: **être
le bienvenu/la bienvenue** to be welcome ♦ *nf*:
souhaiter la bienvenue à to welcome; **bienvenue
à** welcome to
bière [bjɛʀ] *nf* (*boisson*) beer; (*cercueil*) bier; **bière
blonde** lager; **bière brune** brown ale; **bière (à la)
pression** draught beer
biffer [bife] *vt* to cross out
bifteck [biftɛk] *nm* steak
bifurquer [bifyʀke] *vi* (*route*) to fork; (*véhicule*) to
turn off
bigarré, e [bigaʀe] *adj* multicoloured (BRIT), multi-
colored (US); (*disparate*) motley
bigorneau, x [bigɔʀno] *nm* winkle
bigot, e [bigo, -ɔt] (*péj*) *adj* bigoted ♦ *nm/f*
bigot
bigoudi [bigudi] *nm* curler
bijou, x [biʒu] *nm* jewel
bijouterie [biʒutʀi] *nf* (*magasin*) jeweller's (shop)
(BRIT), jewelry store (US); (*bijoux*) jewellery, jewelry
bijoutier, ière [biʒutje, -jɛʀ] *nm/f* jeweller (BRIT),
jeweler (US)
bikini [bikini] *nm* bikini
bilan [bilɑ̃] *nm* (*COMM*) balance sheet(s); (*annuel*)
end of year statement; (*fig*) (net) outcome; (: *de victimes*) toll; **faire le bilan de** to assess; to review;
déposer son bilan to file a bankruptcy statement;
bilan de santé (*MÉD*) check-up; **bilan social** *statement of a firm's policies towards its employees*
bile [bil] *nf* bile; **se faire de la bile** (*fam*) to worry
o.s. sick

bilieux, euse [biljø, -øz] *adj* bilious; (*fig: colérique*) testy

bilingue [bilɛ̃g] *adj* bilingual

billard [bijar] *nm* billiards *sg*; (*table*) billiard table; **c'est du billard** (*fam*) it's a cinch; **passer sur le billard** (*fam*) to have an (*ou* one's) operation; **billard électrique** pinball

bille [bij] *nf* ball; (*du jeu de billes*) marble; (*de bois*) log; **jouer aux billes** to play marbles

billet [bijɛ] *nm* (*aussi*: **billet de banque**) (bank)note; (*de cinéma, de bus etc*) ticket; (*courte lettre*) note; **billet à ordre** *ou* **de commerce** (*COMM*) promissory note, IOU; **billet d'avion/de train** plane/train ticket; **billet circulaire** round-trip ticket; **billet doux** love letter; **billet de faveur** complimentary ticket; **billet de loterie** lottery ticket; **billet de quai** platform ticket

billetterie [bijɛtʀi] *nf* ticket office; (*distributeur*) ticket dispenser; (*BANQUE*) cash dispenser

billion [biljɔ̃] *nm* billion (*BRIT*), trillion (*US*)

billot [bijo] *nm* block

bimensuel, le [bimɑ̃sɥɛl] *adj* bimonthly, twice-monthly

binette [binɛt] *nf* (*outil*) hoe

biochimie [bjɔʃimi] *nf* biochemistry

biodiversité [bjodivɛʀsite] *nf* biodiversity

bioéthique [bjoetik] *nf* bioethics *sg*

biographie [bjɔgʀafi] *nf* biography

biologie [bjɔlɔʒi] *nf* biology

biologique [bjɔlɔʒik] *adj* biological

biologiste [bjɔlɔʒist(ə)] *nm/f* biologist

Birmanie [biʀmani] *nf*: **la Birmanie** Burma

bis, e [bi, biz] *adj* (*couleur*) greyish brown ♦ *adv* [bis]: **12 bis** 12a *ou* A ♦ *excl, nm* [bis] encore ♦ *nf* (*baiser*) kiss; (*vent*) North wind; **faire une** *ou* **la bise à qn** to kiss sb

bisannuel, le [bizanɥɛl] *adj* biennial

biscornu, e [biskɔʀny] *adj* crooked; (*bizarre*) weird(-looking)

biscotte [biskɔt] *nf* (*breakfast*) rusk

biscuit [biskɥi] *nm* biscuit (*BRIT*), cookie (*US*); (*gateau*) sponge cake; **biscuit à la cuiller** sponge finger

bise [biz] *adj f, nf voir* **bis**

bisou [bizu] *nm* (*fam*) kiss

bissextile [bisɛkstil] *adj*: **année bissextile** leap year

bistouri [bisturi] *nm* lancet

bistro(t) [bistro] *nm* bistro, café

bitume [bitym] *nm* asphalt

bizarre [bizaʀ] *adj* strange, odd

blafard, e [blafaʀ, -aʀd(ə)] *adj* wan

blague [blag] *nf* (*propos*) joke; (*farce*) trick; **sans blague!** no kidding!; **blague à tabac** tobacco pouch

blaguer [blage] *vi* to joke ♦ *vt* to tease

blaireau, x [blɛʀo] *nm* (*ZOOL*) badger; (*brosse*) shaving brush

blairer [blɛʀe] *vt*: **je ne peux pas le blairer** I can't bear *ou* stand him

blâme [blɑm] *nm* blame; (*sanction*) reprimand

blâmer [blɑme] *vt* (*réprouver*) to blame; (*réprimander*) to reprimand

blanc, blanche [blɑ̃, blɑ̃ʃ] *adj* white; (*non imprimé*) blank; (*innocent*) pure ♦ *nm/f* white, white man/woman ♦ *nm* (*couleur*) white; (*linge*): **le blanc** whites *pl*; (*espace non écrit*) blank; (*aussi*: **blanc d'œuf**) (egg-)white; (*aussi*: **blanc de poulet**) breast, white meat; (*aussi*: **vin blanc**) white wine ♦ *nf* (*MUS*) minim (*BRIT*), half-note (*US*); (*fam: drogue*) smack; **d'une voix blanche** in a toneless voice; **aux cheveux blancs** white-haired; **le blanc de l'œil** the white of the eye; **laisser en blanc** to leave blank; **chèque en blanc** blank cheque; **à blanc** *adv* (*chauffer*) white-hot; (*tirer, charger*) with blanks; **saigner à blanc** to bleed white; **blanc cassé** off-white

blancheur [blɑ̃ʃœʀ] *nf* whiteness

blanchir [blɑ̃ʃiʀ] *vt* (*gén*) to whiten; (*linge, fig: argent*) to launder; (*CULIN*) to blanch; (*fig: disculper*) to clear ♦ *vi* to grow white; (*cheveux*) to go white; **blanchi à la chaux** whitewashed

blanchisserie [blɑ̃ʃisʀi] *nf* laundry

blason [blazɔ̃] *nm* coat of arms

blasphème [blasfɛm] *nm* blasphemy

blazer [blazɛʀ] *nm* blazer

blé [ble] *nm* wheat; **blé en herbe** wheat on the ear; **blé noir** buckwheat

bled [blɛd] *nm* (*péj*) hole; (*en Afrique du Nord*): **le bled** the interior

blême [blɛm] *adj* pale

blessant, e [blesɑ̃, -ɑ̃t] *adj* hurtful

blessé, e [blese] *adj* injured ♦ *nm/f* injured person, casualty; **un blessé grave, un grand blessé** a seriously injured *ou* wounded person

blesser [blese] *vt* to injure; (*délibérément*: *MIL etc*) to wound; (*suj: souliers etc, offenser*) to hurt; **se blesser** to injure o.s.; **se blesser au pied** *etc* to injure one's foot *etc*

blessure [blesyʀ] *nf* injury; wound

bleu, e [blø] *adj* blue; (*bifteck*) very rare ♦ *nm* (*couleur*) blue; (*novice*) greenhorn; (*contusion*) bruise; (*vêtement, aussi*: **bleus**) overalls *pl* (*BRIT*), coveralls *pl* (*US*); **avoir une peur bleue** to be scared stiff; **zone bleue** ≈ restricted parking area; **fromage bleu** blue cheese; **au bleu** (*CULIN*) au bleu; **bleu (de lessive)** ≈ blue bag; **bleu de méthylène** (*MÉD*) methylene blue; **bleu marine/nuit/roi** navy/midnight/royal blue

bleuet [bløɛ] *nm* cornflower

bleuté, e [bløte] *adj* blue-shaded

blinder [blɛ̃de] *vt* to armour (*BRIT*), armor (*US*); (*fig*) to harden

bloc [blɔk] *nm* (*de pierre etc, INFORM*) block; (*de papier à lettres*) pad; (*ensemble*) group, block; **serré à**

bloc tightened right down; **en bloc** as a whole; wholesale; **faire bloc** to unite; **bloc opératoire** operating *ou* theatre block; **bloc sanitaire** toilet block; **bloc sténo** shorthand notebook

blocage [blɔkaʒ] *nm* (*voir bloquer*) blocking; jamming; freezing; (*PSYCH*) hang-up

bloc-notes, *pl* **blocs-notes** [blɔknɔt] *nm* note pad

blocus [blɔkys] *nm* blockade

blog [blɔg] (*INFORM*) *nm* blog

blond, e [blɔ̃, -ɔ̃d] *adj* fair; (*plus clair*) blond; (*sable, blés*) golden ♦ *nm/f* fair-haired *ou* blond man/woman; **blond cendré** ash blond

bloquer [blɔke] *vt* (*passage*) to block; (*pièce mobile*) to jam; (*crédits, compte*) to freeze; (*personne, négociations etc*) to hold up; (*regrouper*) to group; **bloquer les freins** to jam on the brakes

blottir [blɔtiʀ]: **se blottir** *vi* to huddle up

blouse [bluz] *nf* overall

blouson [bluzɔ̃] *nm* blouson (jacket)

blue-jean(s) [bludʒin(s)] *nm* jeans

bluff [blœf] *nm* bluff

bluffer [blœfe] *vi*, *vt* to bluff

bobard [bɔbaʀ] *nm* (*fam*) tall story

bobine [bɔbin] *nf* (*de fil*) reel; (*de machine à coudre*) spool; (*de machine à écrire*) ribbon; (*ELEC*) coil; **bobine (d'allumage)** (*AUTO*) coil; **bobine de pellicule** (*PHOTO*) roll of film

bocal, aux [bɔkal, -o] *nm* jar

bock [bɔk] *nm* (beer) glass; (*contenu*) glass of beer

body [bɔdi] *nm* body(suit); (*SPORT*) leotard

bœuf [bœf] *nm* ox (*pl* oxen), steer; (*CULIN*) beef; (*MUS, fam*) jam session

bof [bɔf] *excl* (*fam: indifférence*) don't care!; (: *pas terrible*) nothing special

bogue [bɔg] *nf* (*BOT*) husk ♦ *nm* (*ORDIN*) bug

bohème [bɔɛm] *adj* happy-go-lucky, unconventional

bohémien, ne [bɔemjɛ̃, -ɛn] *adj* Bohemian ♦ *nm/f* gipsy

boire [bwaʀ] *vt* to drink; (*s'imprégner de*) to soak up; **boire un coup** to have a drink

bois [bwa] *vb voir* **boire** ♦ *nm* wood; (*ZOOL*) antler; (*MUS*): **les bois** the woodwind; **de bois, en bois** wooden; **bois vert** green wood; **bois mort** deadwood; **bois de lit** bedstead

boisé, e [bwaze] *adj* woody, wooded

boisson [bwasɔ̃] *nf* drink; **pris de boisson** drunk, intoxicated; **boissons alcoolisées** alcoholic beverages *ou* drinks; **boissons non alcoolisées** soft drinks

boîte [bwat] *nf* box; (*fam: entreprise*) firm, company; **aliments en boîte** canned *ou* tinned (*BRIT*) foods; **boîte de sardines/petits pois** can *ou* tin (*BRIT*) of sardines/peas; **mettre qn en boîte** (*fam*) to have a laugh at sb's expense; **boîte d'allumettes** box of matches; (*vide*) matchbox; **boîte de con-**

serves can *ou* tin (*BRIT*) (of food); **boîte crânienne** cranium; **boîte à gants** glove compartment; **boîte aux lettres** letter box, mailbox (*US*); (*INFORM*) mailbox; **boîte à musique** musical box; **boîte noire** (*AVIAT*) black box; **boîte de nuit** night club; **boîte à ordures** dustbin (*BRIT*), trash can (*US*); **boîte postale (BP)** PO box; **boîte de vitesses** gear box; **boîte vocale** voice mail

boiter [bwate] *vi* to limp; (*fig*) to wobble; (*raisonnement*) to be shaky

boîtier [bwatje] *nm* case; (*d'appareil-photo*) body; **boîtier de montre** watch case

boive *etc* [bwav] *vb voir* **boire**

bol [bɔl] *nm* bowl; (*contenu*): **un bol de café** *etc* a bowl of coffee *etc*; **un bol d'air** a breath of fresh air; **en avoir ras le bol** (*fam*) to have had a bellyful

bolide [bɔlid] *nm* racing car; **comme un bolide** like a rocket

bombardement [bɔ̃baʀdəmɑ̃] *nm* bombing

bombarder [bɔ̃baʀde] *vt* to bomb; **bombarder qn de** (*cailloux, lettres*) to bombard sb with; **bombarder qn directeur** to thrust sb into the director's seat

bombe [bɔ̃b] *nf* bomb; (*atomiseur*) (aerosol) spray; (*ÉQUITATION*) riding cap; **faire la bombe** (*fam*) to go on a binge; **bombe atomique** atomic bomb; **bombe à retardement** time bomb

bombé, e [bɔ̃be] *adj* rounded; (*mur*) bulging; (*front*) domed; (*route*) steeply cambered

bomber [bɔ̃be] *vi* to bulge; (*route*) to camber ♦ *vt*: **bomber le torse** to swell out one's chest

---

MOT-CLÉ

bon, bonne [bɔ̃, bɔn] *adj* **1** (*agréable, satisfaisant*) good; **un bon repas/restaurant** a good meal/restaurant; **être bon en maths** to be good at maths

2 (*charitable*): **être bon (envers)** to be good (to), to be kind (to); **vous êtes trop bon** you're too kind

3 (*correct*) right; **le bon numéro/moment** the right number/moment

4 (*souhaits*): **bon anniversaire** happy birthday; **bon courage** good luck; **bon séjour** enjoy your stay; **bon voyage** have a good trip; **bon weekend** have a good weekend; **bonne année** happy New Year; **bonne chance** good luck; **bonne fête** happy holiday; **bonne nuit** good night

5 (*approprié*): **bon à/pour** fit to/for; **bon à jeter** fit for the bin; **c'est bon à savoir** that's useful to know; **à quoi bon (...)?** what's the point *ou* use (of ...)?

6 (*intensif*): **ça m'a pris 2 bonnes heures** it took me a good 2 hours; **un bon nombre de** a good number of

7: **bon enfant** *adj inv* accommodating, easy-going; **bonne femme** (*péj*) woman; **de bonne heure** early; **bon marché** cheap; **bon mot** witticism; **pour faire bon poids ...** to make up for it

...; **bon sens** common sense; **bon vivant** jovial chap; **bonnes œuvres** charitable works, charities; **bonne sœur** nun

◆ *nm* 1 (*billet*) voucher; (*aussi*: **bon cadeau**) gift voucher; **bon de caisse** cash voucher; **bon d'essence** petrol coupon; **bon à tirer** pass for press; **bon du Trésor** Treasury bond

2: **avoir du bon** to have its good points; **il y a du bon dans ce qu'il dit** there's some sense in what he says; **pour le bon** for good

◆ *nm/f*: **un bon à rien** a good-for-nothing

◆ *adv*: **il fait bon** it's *ou* the weather is fine; **sentir bon** to smell good; **tenir bon** to stand firm; **juger bon de faire ...** to think fit to do ...

◆ *excl* right!, good!; **ah bon?** really?; **bon, je reste** right, I'll stay; *voir aussi* **bonne**

bonbon [bɔ̃bɔ̃] *nm* (boiled) sweet
bonbonne [bɔ̃bɔn] *nf* demijohn; carboy
bond [bɔ̃] *nm* leap; (*d'une balle*) rebound, ricochet; **faire un bond** to leap in the air; **d'un seul bond** in one bound, with one leap; **bond en avant** (*fig: progrès*) leap forward
bondé, e [bɔ̃de] *adj* packed (full)
bondir [bɔ̃diʀ] *vi* to leap; **bondir de joie** (*fig*) to jump for joy; **bondir de colère** (*fig*) to be hopping mad
bonheur [bɔnœʀ] *nm* happiness; **avoir le bonheur de** to have the good fortune to; **porter bonheur (à qn)** to bring sb luck; **au petit bonheur** haphazardly; **par bonheur** fortunately
bonhomie [bɔnɔmi] *nf* goodnaturedness
bonhomme [bɔnɔm], *pl* **bonshommes** [bɔ̃zɔm] *nm* fellow ◆ *adj* good-natured; **un vieux bonhomme** an old chap; **aller son bonhomme de chemin** to carry on in one's own sweet way; **bonhomme de neige** snowman
bonifier [bɔnifje] *vt*: **se bonifier** *vi* to improve
boniment [bɔnimɑ̃] *nm* patter *no pl*
bonjour [bɔ̃ʒuʀ] *excl*, *nm* hello; (*selon l'heure*) good morning (*ou* afternoon); **donner** *ou* **souhaiter le bonjour à qn** to bid sb good morning *ou* afternoon
bonne [bɔn] *adj f voir* **bon** ◆ *nf* (*domestique*) maid; **bonne à tout faire** general help; **bonne d'enfant** nanny
bonnement [bɔnmɑ̃] *adv*: **tout bonnement** quite simply
bonnet [bɔnɛ] *nm* bonnet, hat; (*de soutien-gorge*) cup; **bonnet d'âne** dunce's cap; **bonnet de bain** bathing cap; **bonnet de nuit** nightcap
bonsoir [bɔ̃swaʀ] *excl* good evening
bonté [bɔ̃te] *nf* kindness *no pl*; **avoir la bonté de** to be kind *ou* good enough to
bonus [bɔnys] *nm* (*assurances*) no-claims bonus
bord [bɔʀ] *nm* (*de table, verre, falaise*) edge; (*de rivière, lac*) bank; (*de route*) side; (*de vêtement*) edge, border; (*de chapeau*) brim; **(monter) à bord** (to go)

on board; **jeter par-dessus bord** to throw overboard; **le commandant du bord/les hommes du bord** the ship's master/crew; **du même bord** (*fig*) of the same opinion; **au bord de la mer/route** at the seaside/roadside; **être au bord des larmes** to be on the verge of tears; **virer de bord** (*NAVIG*) to tack; **sur les bords** (*fig*) slightly; **de tous bords** on all sides; **bord du trottoir** kerb (*BRIT*), curb (*US*)
bordeaux [bɔʀdo] *nm* Bordeaux ◆ *adj inv* maroon
bordel [bɔʀdɛl] *nm* brothel; (*fam!*) bloody (*BRIT*) *ou* goddamn (*US*) mess (!) ◆ *excl* hell!
bordelais, e [bɔʀdəlɛ, -ez] *adj* of *ou* from Bordeaux
border [bɔʀde] *vt* (*être le long de*) to border, line; (*garnir*): **border qch de** to line sth with; to trim sth with; (*qn dans son lit*) to tuck up
bordereau, x [bɔʀdəʀo] *nm* docket, slip
bordure [bɔʀdyʀ] *nf* border; (*sur un vêtement*) trim(ming), border; **en bordure de** on the edge of
borgne [bɔʀɲ(ə)] *adj* one-eyed; **hôtel borgne** shady hotel; **fenêtre borgne** obstructed window
borne [bɔʀn(ə)] *nf* boundary stone; (*aussi*: **borne kilométrique**) kilometre-marker, = milestone; **bornes** *nfpl* (*fig*) limits; **dépasser les bornes** to go too far; **sans borne(s)** boundless
borné, e [bɔʀne] *adj* narrow; (*obtus*) narrowminded
borner [bɔʀne] *vt* (*délimiter*) to limit; (*limiter*) to confine; **se borner à faire** to content o.s. with doing; to limit o.s. to doing
bosquet [bɔske] *nm* copse (*BRIT*), grove
bosse [bɔs] *nf* (*de terrain etc*) bump; (*enflure*) lump; (*du bossu, du chameau*) hump; **avoir la bosse des maths** *etc* to have a gift for maths *etc*; **il a roulé sa bosse** he's been around
bosser [bɔse] *vi* (*fam*) to work; (*: dur*) to slog (hard) (*BRIT*), slave (away)
bossu, e [bɔsy] *nm/f* hunchback
botanique [bɔtanik] *nf* botany ◆ *adj* botanic(al)
botte [bɔt] *nf* (*soulier*) (high) boot; (*ESCRIME*) thrust; (*gerbe*): **botte de paille** bundle of straw; **botte de radis/d'asperges** bunch of radishes/asparagus; **bottes de caoutchouc** wellington boots
botter [bɔte] *vt* to put boots on; (*donner un coup de pied à*) to kick; (*fam*): **ça me botte** I fancy that
bottin® [bɔtɛ̃] *nm* directory
bottine [bɔtin] *nf* ankie boot
bouc [buk] *nm* goat; (*barbe*) goatee; **bouc émissaire** scapegoat
boucan [bukɑ̃] *nm* din, racket
bouche [buʃ] *nf* mouth; **une bouche à nourrir** a mouth to feed; **les bouches inutiles** the nonproductive members of the population; **faire du bouche à bouche à qn** to give sb the kiss of life (*BRIT*), give sb mouth-to- mouth resuscitation; **de bouche à oreille** confidentially; **pour la bonne bouche** (*pour la fin*) till last; **faire venir l'eau à la**

bouche to make one's mouth water; **bouche cousue!** mum's the word!; **bouche d'aération** air vent; **bouche de chaleur** hot air vent; **bouche d'égout** manhole; **bouche d'incendie** fire hydrant; **bouche de métro** métro entrance

bouché, e [buʃe] *adj* (*flacon etc*) stoppered; (*temps, ciel*) overcast; (*carrière*) blocked; (*péj: personne*) thick; (*trompette*) muted; **avoir le nez bouché** to have a blocked(-up) nose

bouchée [buʃe] *nf* mouthful; **ne faire qu'une bouchée de** (*fig*) to make short work of; **pour une bouchée de pain** (*fig*) for next to nothing; **bouchées à la reine** chicken vol-au-vents

boucher [buʃe] *nm* butcher ♦ *vt* (*pour colmater*) to stop up; to fill up; (*obstruer*) to block (up); **se boucher** (*tuyau etc*) to block up, get blocked up; **se boucher le nez** to hold one's nose

boucherie [buʃʀi] *nf* butcher's (shop); (*métier*) butchery; (*fig*) slaughter, butchery

bouche-trou [buʃtʀu] *nm* (*fig*) stop-gap

bouchon [buʃɔ̃] *nm* (*en liège*) cork; (*autre matière*) stopper; (*fig: embouteillage*) holdup; (*PÊCHE*) float; **bouchon doseur** measuring cap

boucle [bukl(ə)] *nf* (*forme, figure, aussi INFORM*) loop; (*objet*) buckle; **boucle (de cheveux)** curl; **boucle d'oreilles** earring

bouclé, e [bukle] *adj* curly; (*tapis*) uncut

boucler [bukle] *vt* (*fermer: ceinture etc*) to fasten; (: *magasin*) to shut; (*terminer*) to finish off; (: *circuit*) to complete; (*budget*) to balance; (*enfermer*) to shut away; (: *condamné*) to lock up; (: *quartier*) to seal off ♦ *vi* to curl; **faire boucler** (*cheveux*) to curl; **boucler la boucle** (*AVIAT*) to loop the loop

bouclier [buklije] *nm* shield

bouddhiste [budist(ə)] *nm/f* Buddhist

bouder [bude] *vi* to sulk ♦ *vt* (*chose*) to turn one's nose up at; (*personne*) to refuse to have anything to do with

boudin [budɛ̃] *nm* (*CULIN*) black pudding; (*TECH*) roll; **boudin blanc** white pudding

boue [bu] *nf* mud

bouée [bwe] *nf* buoy; (*de baigneur*) rubber ring; **bouée (de sauvetage)** lifebuoy; (*fig*) lifeline

boueux, euse [bwø, -øz] *adj* muddy ♦ *nm* (*fam*) refuse (*BRIT*) *ou* garbage (*US*) collector

bouffe [buf] *nf* (*fam*) grub, food

bouffée [bufe] *nf* puff; **bouffée de chaleur** (*gén*) blast of hot air; (*MÉD*) hot flush (*BRIT*) *ou* flash (*US*); **bouffée de fièvre/de honte** flush of fever/shame; **bouffée d'orgueil** fit of pride

bouffer [bufe] *vi* (*fam*) to eat; (*COUTURE*) to puff out ♦ *vt* (*fam*) to eat

bouffi, e [bufi] *adj* swollen

bougeoir [buʒwaʀ] *nm* candlestick

bougeotte [buʒɔt] *nf*: **avoir la bougeotte** to have the fidgets

bouger [buʒe] *vi* to move; (*dent etc*) to be loose; (*changer*) to alter; (*agir*) to stir ♦ *vt* to move; **se**

bouger (*fam*) to move (oneself)

bougie [buʒi] *nf* candle; (*AUTO*) spark(ing) plug

bougon, ne [bugɔ̃, -ɔn] *adj* grumpy

bougonner [bugɔne] *vi, vt* to grumble

bouillabaisse [bujabɛs] *nf* type of fish soup

bouillant, e [bujɑ̃, -ɑ̃t] *adj* (*qui bout*) boiling; (*très chaud*) boiling (hot); (*fig: ardent*) hot-headed; **bouillant de colère** *etc* seething with anger *etc*

bouillie [buji] *nf* gruel; (*de bébé*) cereal; **en bouillie** (*fig*) crushed

bouillir [bujiʀ] *vi* to boil ♦ *vt* (*aussi*: **faire bouillir**: *CULIN*) to boil; **bouillir de colère** *etc* to seethe with anger *etc*

bouilloire [bujwaʀ] *nf* kettle

bouillon [bujɔ̃] *nm* (*CULIN*) stock *no pl*; (*bulles, écume*) bubble; **bouillon de culture** culture medium

bouillonner [bujɔne] *vi* to bubble; (*fig*) to bubble up; (*torrent*) to foam

bouillotte [bujɔt] *nf* hot-water bottle

boulanger, ère [bulɑ̃ʒe, -ɛʀ] *nm/f* baker ♦ *nf* (*femme du boulanger*) baker's wife

boulangerie [bulɑ̃ʒʀi] *nf* bakery, baker's (shop); (*commerce*) bakery; **boulangerie industrielle** bakery

boulangerie-pâtisserie, *pl* **boulangeries-pâtisseries** [bulɑ̃ʒʀipatisʀi] *nf* baker's and confectioner's (shop)

boule [bul] *nf* (*gén*) ball; (*pour jouer*) bowl; (*de machine à écrire*) golf ball; **roulé en boule** curled up in a ball; **se mettre en boule** (*fig*) to fly off the handle, blow one's top; **perdre la boule** (*fig: fam*) to go off one's rocker; **boule de gomme** (*bonbon*) gum(drop), pastille; **boule de neige** snowball; **faire boule de neige** (*fig*) to snowball

bouleau, x [bulo] *nm* (silver) birch

bouledogue [buldɔg] *nm* bulldog

boulet [bulɛ] *nm* (*aussi*: **boulet de canon**) cannonball; (*de bagnard*) ball and chain; (*charbon*) (coal) nut

boulette [bulɛt] *nf* ball

boulevard [bulvaʀ] *nm* boulevard

bouleversant, e [bulvɛʀsɑ̃, -ɑ̃t] *adj* (*récit*) deeply distressing; (*nouvelle*) shattering

bouleversement [bulvɛʀsəmɑ̃] *nm* (*politique, social*) upheaval

bouleverser [bulvɛʀse] *vt* (*émouvoir*) to overwhelm; (*causer du chagrin à*) to distress; (*pays, vie*) to disrupt; (*papiers, objets*) to turn upside down, upset

boulon [bulɔ̃] *nm* bolt

boulot [bulo] *nm* (*fam: travail*) work

boulot, te [bulo, -ɔt] *adj* plump, tubby

boum [bum] *nm* bang ♦ *nf* party

bouquet [bukɛ] *nm* (*de fleurs*) bunch (of flowers), bouquet; (*de persil etc*) bunch; (*parfum*) bouquet; (*fig*) crowning piece; **c'est le bouquet!** that's the last strawl;; **bouquet garni** (*CULIN*) bouquet garni

bouquin [bukɛ̃] *nm* (*fam*) book

bouquiner [bukine] *vi* (*fam*) to read

bouquiniste [bukinist(ə)] *nm/f* bookseller

bourbeux, euse [buʀbø, -øz] *adj* muddy

bourbier [buʀbje] *nm* (quag)mire

bourde [buʀd(ə)] *nf* (*erreur*) howler; (*gaffe*) blunder

bourdon [buʀdɔ̃] *nm* bumblebee

bourdonner [buʀdɔne] *vi* to buzz; (*moteur*) to hum

bourg [buʀ] *nm* small market town (*ou* village)

bourgeois, e [buʀʒwa, -waz] *adj* (*péj*) ≃ (upper) middle class; bourgeois; (*maison etc*) very comfortable ♦ *nm/f* (*autrefois*) burgher

bourgeoisie [buʀʒwazi] *nf* ≃ upper middle classes *pl*; bourgeoisie; **petite bourgeoisie** middle classes

bourgeon [buʀʒɔ̃] *nm* bud

Bourgogne [buʀgɔɲ] *nf*: **la Bourgogne** Burgundy ♦ *nm*: **bourgogne** burgundy (wine)

bourguignon, ne [buʀgiɲɔ̃, -ɔn] *adj* *ou* from Burgundy, Burgundian; **bœuf bourguignon** bœuf bourguignon

bourlinguer [buʀlɛ̃ge] *vi* to knock about a lot, get around a lot

bourrade [buʀad] *nf* shove, thump

bourrage [buʀaʒ] *nm* (*papier*) jamming; **bourrage de crâne** brainwashing; (*SCOL*) cramming

bourrasque [buʀask(ə)] *nf* squall

bourratif, ive [buʀatif, -iv] *adj* filling, stodgy

bourré, e [buʀe] *adj* (*rempli*): **bourré de** crammed full of; (*fam: ivre*) pickled, plastered

bourreau, x [buʀo] *nm* executioner; (*fig*) torturer; **bourreau de travail** workaholic, glutton for work

bourrelet [buʀlɛ] *nm* draught (*BRIT*) *ou* draft (*US*) excluder; (*de peau*) fold *ou* roll (of flesh)

bourrer [buʀe] *vt* (*pipe*) to fill; (*poêle*) to pack; (*valise*) to cram (full); **bourrer de** to cram (full) with, stuff with; **bourrer de coups** to hammer blows on, pummel; **bourrer le crâne à qn** to pull the wool over sb's eyes; (*endoctriner*) to brainwash sb

bourrique [buʀik] *nf* (*âne*) ass

bourru, e [buʀy] *adj* surly, gruff

bourse [buʀs(ə)] *nf* (*subvention*) grant; (*porte-monnaie*) purse; **sans bourse délier** without spending a penny; **la Bourse** the Stock Exchange; **bourse du travail** ≃ trades union council (regional headquarters)

boursier, ière [buʀsje, -jɛʀ] *adj* (*COMM*) Stock Market *cpd* ♦ *nm/f* (*SCOL*) grant-holder

boursoufler [buʀsufle] *vt* to puff up, bloat; **se boursoufler** *vi* (*visage*) to swell *ou* puff up; (*peinture*) to blister

bous [bu] *vb voir* **bouillir**

bousculade [buskylad] *nf* (*hâte*) rush; (*poussée*) crush

bousculer [buskyle] *vt* to knock over; to knock into; (*fig*) to push, rush

bouse [buz] *nf*: **bouse (de vache)** (cow) dung *no pl* (*BRIT*), manure *no pl*

bousiller [buzije] *vt* (*fam*) to wreck

boussole [busɔl] *nf* compass

bout [bu] *vb voir* **bouillir** ♦ *nm* bit; (*extrémité: d'un bâton etc*) tip; (: *d'une ficelle, table, rue, période*) end; **au bout de** at the end of, after; **au bout du compte** at the end of the day; **pousser qn à bout** to push sb to the limit (of his patience); **venir à bout de** to manage to finish (off) *ou* overcome; **bout à bout** end to end; **à tout bout de champ** at every turn; **d'un bout à l'autre, de bout en bout** from one end to the other; **à bout portant** at point-blank range; **un bout de chou** (*enfant*) a little tot; **bout d'essai** (*CINÉ etc*) screen test; **bout filtre** filter tip

boutade [butad] *nf* quip, sally

boute-en-train [butɑ̃trɛ̃] *nm inv* live wire (*fig*)

bouteille [butɛj] *nf* bottle; (*de gaz butane*) cylinder

boutique [butik] *nf* shop (*BRIT*), store (*US*); (*de grand couturier, de mode*) boutique

bouton [butɔ̃] *nm* (*de vêtement, électrique etc*) button; (*BOT*) bud; (*sur la peau*) spot; (*de porte*) knob; **bouton de manchette** cuff-link; **bouton d'or** buttercup

boutonner [butɔne] *vt* to button up, do up; **se boutonner** to button one's clothes up

boutonnière [butɔnjɛʀ] *nf* buttonhole

bouton-pression, *pl* **boutons-pression** [butɔ̃pʀesjɔ̃] *nm* press stud, snap fastener

bouture [butyʀ] *nf* cutting; **faire des boutures** to take cuttings

bovins [bɔvɛ̃] *nm* cattle

bowling [bɔliŋ] *nm* (tenpin) bowling; (*salle*) bowling alley

box [bɔks] *nm* lock-up (garage); (*de salle, dortoir*) cubicle; (*d'écurie*) loose-box; **le box des accusés** the dock

boxe [bɔks(ə)] *nf* boxing

boxeur [bɔksœʀ] *nm* boxer

boyaux [bwajo] *nmpl* (*viscères*) entrails, guts

BP *sigle f* = **boîte postale**

bracelet [bʀaslɛ] *nm* bracelet

braconnier [bʀakɔnje] *nm* poacher

brader [bʀade] *vt* to sell off, sell cheaply

braderie [bʀadʀi] *nf* clearance sale; (*par des particuliers*) ≃ car boot sale (*BRIT*), ≃ garage sale (*US*); (*magasin*) discount store; (*sur marché*) cut-price (*BRIT*) *ou* cut-rate (*US*) stall

braguette [bʀagɛt] *nf* fly, flies *pl* (*BRIT*), zipper (*US*)

brailler [bʀaje] *vi* to bawl, yell ♦ *vt* to bawl out,

yell out

braire [bʀɛʀ] *vi* to bray

braise [bʀɛz] *nf* embers *pl*

brancard [bʀɑ̃kaʀ] *nm* (*civière*) stretcher; (*bras, perche*) shaft

brancardier [bʀɑ̃kaʀdje] *nm* stretcher-bearer

branchages [bʀɑ̃ʃaʒ] *nmpl* branches, boughs

branche [bʀɑ̃ʃ] *nf* branch; (*de lunettes*) side(-piece)

branché, e [bʀɑ̃ʃe] *adj* (*fam*) switched-on, trendy ◆ *nm/f* (*fam*) trendy

brancher [bʀɑ̃ʃe] *vt* to connect (up); (*en mettant la prise*) to plug in; **brancher qn/qch sur** (*fig*) to get sb/sth launched onto

brandir [bʀɑ̃diʀ] *vt* (*arme*) to brandish, wield; (*document*) to flourish, wave

branle [bʀɑ̃l] *nm*: **mettre en branle** to set swinging; **donner le branle à** to set in motion

branle-bas [bʀɑ̃lba] *nm inv* commotion

braquer [bʀake] *vi* (*AUTO*) to turn (the wheel) ◆ *vt* (*revolver etc*): **braquer qch sur** to aim sth at, point sth at; (*mettre en colère*): **braquer qn** to antagonize sb, put sb's back up; **braquer son regard sur** to fix one's gaze on; **se braquer** *vi*: **se braquer (contre)** to take a stand (against)

bras [bʀɑ] *nm* arm; (*de fleuve*) branch ◆ *nmpl* (*fig: travailleurs*) labour *sg* (*BRIT*), labor *sg* (*US*), hands; **bras dessus bras dessous** arm in arm; **à bras raccourcis** with fists flying; **à tour de bras** with all one's might; **baisser les bras** to give up; **bras droit** (*fig*) right hand man; **bras de fer** arm-wrestling; **une partie de bras de fer** (*fig*) a trial of strength; **bras de levier** lever arm; **bras de mer** arm of the sea, sound

brasier [bʀazje] *nm* blaze, (blazing) inferno; (*fig*) inferno

bras-le-corps [bʀalkɔʀ]: **à bras-le-corps** *adv* (a)round the waist

brassard [bʀasaʀ] *nm* armband

brasse [bʀas] *nf* (*nage*) breast-stroke; (*mesure*) fathom; **brasse papillon** butterfly(-stroke)

brassée [bʀase] *nf* armful; **une brassée de** (*fig*) a number of

brasser [bʀase] *vt* (*bière*) to brew; (*remuer: salade*) to toss; (: *cartes*) to shuffle; (*fig*) to mix; **brasser l'argent/les affaires** to handle a lot of money/ business

brasserie [bʀasʀi] *nf* (*restaurant*) bar (*selling food*), brasserie; (*usine*) brewery

brave [bʀav] *adj* (*courageux*) brave; (*bon, gentil*) good, kind

braver [bʀave] *vt* to defy

bravo [bʀavo] *excl* bravo! ◆ *nm* cheer

bravoure [bʀavuʀ] *nf* bravery

break [bʀɛk] *nm* (*AUTO*) estate car (*BRIT*), station wagon (*US*)

brebis [bʀəbi] *nf* ewe; **brebis galeuse** black sheep

brèche [bʀɛʃ] *nf* breach, gap; **être sur la brèche** (*fig*) to be on the go

bredouille [bʀəduj] *adj* empty-handed

bredouiller [bʀəduje] *vi*, *vt* to mumble, stammer

bref, brève [bʀɛf, bʀɛv] *adj* short, brief ◆ *adv* in short ◆ *nf* (*voyelle*) short vowel; (*information*) brief news item; **d'un ton bref** sharply, curtly; **en bref** in short, in brief; **à bref délai** shortly

Brésil [bʀezil] *nm*: **le Brésil** Brazil

brésilien, ne [bʀeziljɛ̃, -ɛn] *adj* Brazilian ◆ *nm/f*: **Brésilien, ne** Brazilian

Bretagne [bʀətaɲ] *nf*: **la Bretagne** Brittany

bretelle [bʀətɛl] *nf* (*de fusil etc*) sling; (*de vêtement*) strap; (*d'autoroute*) slip road (*BRIT*), entrance ou exit ramp (*US*); **bretelles** *nfpl* (*pour pantalon*) braces (*BRIT*), suspenders (*US*); **bretelle de contournement** (*AUTO*) bypass; **bretelle de raccordement** (*AUTO*) access road

breton, ne [bʀətɔ̃, -ɔn] *adj* Breton ◆ *nm* (*LING*) Breton ◆ *nm/f*: **Breton, ne** Breton

breuvage [bʀœvaʒ] *nm* beverage, drink

brève [bʀɛv] *adj f*, *nf voir* **bref**

brevet [bʀəvɛ] *nm* diploma, certificate; **brevet (d'invention)** patent; **brevet d'apprentissage** certificate of apprenticeship; **brevet (des collèges)** school certificate, taken at approx. 16 years

breveté, e [bʀəvte] *adj* patented; (*diplômé*) qualified

bribes [bʀib] *nfpl* bits, scraps; (*d'une conversation*) snatches; **par bribes** piecemeal

bricolage [bʀikɔlaʒ] *nm*: **le bricolage** do-it-yourself (jobs); (*péj*) patched-up job

bricole [bʀikɔl] *nf* (*babiole, chose insignifiante*) trifle; (*petit travail*) small job

bricoler [bʀikɔle] *vi* to do odd jobs; (*en amateur*) to do DIY jobs; (*passe-temps*) to potter about ◆ *vt* (*réparer*) to fix up; (*mal réparer*) to tinker with; (*trafiquer: voiture etc*) to doctor, fix

bricoleur, euse [bʀikɔlœʀ, -øz] *nm/f* handyman/woman, DIY enthusiast

bride [bʀid] *nf* bridle; (*d'un bonnet*) string, tie; **à bride abattue** flat out, hell for leather; **tenir en bride** to keep in check; **lâcher la bride à, laisser la bride sur le cou à** to give free rein to

bridé, e [bʀide] *adj*: **yeux bridés** slit eyes

bridge [bʀidʒ(ə)] *nm* bridge

brièvement [bʀijɛvmɑ̃] *adv* briefly

brigade [bʀigad] *nf* squad; (*MIL*) brigade

brigadier [bʀigadje] *nm* (*POLICE*) ≈ sergeant; (*MIL*) bombardier; corporal

brigandage [bʀigɑ̃daʒ] *nm* robbery

briguer [bʀige] *vt* to aspire to; (*suffrages*) to canvass

brillamment [bʀijamɑ̃] *adv* brilliantly

brillant, e [bʀijɑ̃, -ɑ̃t] *adj* brilliant; bright; (*luisant*) shiny, shining ◆ *nm* (*diamant*) brilliant

briller [bʀije] *vi* to shine

brimer [bʀime] *vt* to harass; to bully

brin [bʀɛ̃] *nm* (*de laine, ficelle etc*) strand; (*fig*): **un brin de** a bit of; **un brin mystérieux** *etc* (*fam*) a weeny bit mysterious *etc*; **brin d'herbe** blade of grass; **brin de muguet** sprig of lily of the valley; **brin de paille** wisp of straw

brindille [bʀɛ̃dij] *nf* twig

brio [bʀijo] *nm* brilliance; (*MUS*) brio; **avec brio** brilliantly, with panache

brioche [bʀijɔʃ] *nf* brioche (bun); (*fam: ventre*) paunch

brique [bʀik] *nf* brick; (*fam*) 10,000 francs ♦ *adj inv* brick red

briquer [bʀike] *vt* (*fam*) to polish up

briquet [bʀikɛ] *nm* (cigarette) lighter

brise [bʀiz] *nf* breeze

briser [bʀize] *vt* to break; **se briser** *vi* to break

britannique [bʀitanik] *adj* British ♦ *nm/f*: **Britannique** Briton, British person; **les Britanniques** the British

brocante [bʀɔkɑ̃t] *nf* (*objets*) secondhand goods *pl*, junk; (*commerce*) secondhand trade; junk dealing

brocanteur, euse [bʀɔkɑ̃tœʀ, -øz] *nm/f* junkshop owner; junk dealer

broche [bʀɔʃ] *nf* brooch; (*CULIN*) spit; (*fiche*) spike, peg; (*MÉD*) pin; **à la broche** spit-roasted, roasted on a spit

broché, e [bʀɔʃe] *adj* (*livre*) paper-backed; (*tissu*) brocaded

brochet [bʀɔʃɛ] *nm* pike *inv*

brochette [bʀɔʃɛt] *nf* skewer; **brochette de décorations** row of medals

brochure [bʀɔʃyʀ] *nf* pamphlet, brochure, booklet

broder [bʀɔde] *vt* to embroider ♦ *vi*: **broder (sur des faits** *ou* **une histoire)** to embroider the facts

broderie [bʀɔdʀi] *nf* embroidery

broncher [bʀɔ̃ʃe] *vi*: **sans broncher** without flinching, without turning a hair

bronches [bʀɔ̃ʃ] *nfpl* bronchial tubes

bronchite [bʀɔ̃ʃit] *nf* bronchitis

bronze [bʀɔ̃z] *nm* bronze

bronzer [bʀɔ̃ze] *vt* to tan ♦ *vi* to get a tan; **se bronzer** to sunbathe

brosse [bʀɔs] *nf* brush; **donner un coup de brosse à qch** to give sth a brush; **coiffé en brosse** with a crewcut; **brosse à cheveux** hairbrush; **brosse à dents** toothbrush; **brosse à habits** clothesbrush

brosser [bʀɔse] *vt* (*nettoyer*) to brush; (*fig: tableau etc*) to paint; to draw; **se brosser** to brush one's clothes; **se brosser les dents** to brush one's teeth; **tu peux te brosser!** (*fam*) you can sing for it!

brouette [bʀuɛt] *nf* wheelbarrow

brouhaha [bʀuaa] *nm* hubbub

brouillard [bʀujaʀ] *nm* fog; **être dans le brouillard** (*fig*) to be all at sea

brouille [bʀuj] *nf* quarrel

brouiller [bʀuje] *vt* to mix up; to confuse; (*RADIO*) to cause interference to; (: *délibérément*) to jam; (*rendre trouble*) to cloud; (*désunir: amis*) to set at odds; **se brouiller** *vi* (*ciel, vue*) to cloud over; (*détails*) to become confused; **se brouiller (avec)** to fall out (with); **brouiller les pistes** to cover one's tracks; (*fig*) to confuse the issue

brouillon, ne [bʀujɔ̃, -ɔn] *adj* disorganized, unmethodical ♦ *nm* (first) draft; **cahier de brouillon** rough (work) book

broussailles [bʀusɑj] *nfpl* undergrowth *sg*

broussailleux, euse [bʀusɑjø, -øz] *adj* bushy

brousse [bʀus] *nf*: **la brousse** the bush

brouter [bʀute] *vt* to graze on ♦ *vi* to graze; (*AUTO*) to judder

broutille [bʀutij] *nf* trifle

broyer [bʀwaje] *vt* to crush; **broyer du noir** to be down in the dumps

bru [bʀy] *nf* daughter-in-law

brugnon [bʀyɲɔ̃] *nm* nectarine

bruiner [bʀɥine] *vb impers*: **il bruine** it's drizzling, there's a drizzle

bruire [bʀɥiʀ] *vi* (*eau*) to murmur; (*feuilles, étoffe*) to rustle

bruit [bʀɥi] *nm*: **un bruit** a noise, a sound; (*fig: rumeur*) a rumour (*BRIT*), a rumor (*US*); **le bruit** noise; **pas/trop de bruit** no/too much noise; **sans bruit** without a sound, noiselessly; **faire du bruit** to make a noise; **bruit de fond** background noise

bruitage [bʀɥitaʒ] *nm* sound effects *pl*

brûlant, e [bʀylɑ̃, -ɑ̃t] *adj* burning (hot); (*liquide*) boiling (hot); (*regard*) fiery; (*sujet*) red-hot

brûlé, e [bʀyle] *adj* (*fig: démasqué*) blown; (: *homme politique etc*) discredited ♦ *nm*: **odeur de brûlé** smell of burning

brûle-pourpoint [bʀylpuʀpwɛ̃]: **à brûle-pourpoint** *adv* point-blank

brûler [bʀyle] *vt* to burn; (*suj: eau bouillante*) to scald; (*consommer: électricité, essence*) to use; (*feu rouge, signal*) to go through (without stopping) ♦ *vi* to burn; (*jeu*): **tu brûles** you're getting warm *ou* hot; **se brûler** to burn o.s.; to scald o.s.; **se brûler la cervelle** to blow one's brains out; **brûler les étapes** to make rapid progress; (*aller trop vite*) to cut corners; **brûler (d'impatience) de faire qch** to burn with impatience to do sth, be dying to do sth

brûlure [bʀylyʀ] *nf* (*lésion*) burn; (*sensation*) burning *no pl*, burning sensation; **brûlures d'estomac** heartburn *sg*

brume [bʀym] *nf* mist

brumeux, euse [bʀymø, -øz] *adj* misty; (*fig*) hazy

brumisateur [bʀymizatœʀ] *nm* atomizer

brun, e [bʀœ̃, -yn] *adj* brown; (*cheveux, personne*) dark ♦ *nm* (*couleur*) brown ♦ *nf* (*cigarette*) cigarette *made of dark tobacco*; (*bière*) ≈ brown ale, ≈ stout

brunch [bʀœntʃ] *nm* brunch

brunir [bʀyniʀ] *vi*: **se brunir** to get a tan ♦ *vt* to tan

brushing [bʀœʃiŋ] *nm* blow-dry

brusque [bʀysk(ə)] *adj* (*soudain*) abrupt, sudden; (*rude*) abrupt, brusque

brusquer [bʀyske] *vt* to rush

brut, e [bʀyt] *adj* raw, crude, rough; (*diamant*) uncut; (*soie, minéral,* INFORM: *données*) raw; (COMM) gross ♦ *nf* brute; (**champagne**) **brut** brut champagne; (**pétrole**) **brut** crude (oil)

brutal, e, aux [bʀytal, -o] *adj* brutal

brutaliser [bʀytalize] *vt* to handle roughly, manhandle

Bruxelles [bʀysɛl] *n* Brussels

bruyamment [bʀɥijamɑ̃] *adv* noisily

bruyant, e [bʀɥijɑ̃, -ɑ̃t] *adj* noisy

bruyère [bʀɥijɛʀ] *nf* heather

BTS *sigle m* (= *Brevet de technicien supérieur*) *vocational training certificate taken at end of 2-year higher education course*

bu, e [by] *pp de* **boire**

buccal, e, aux [bykal, -o] *adj*: **par voie buccale** orally

bûche [byʃ] *nf* log; **prendre une bûche** (*fig*) to come a cropper (BRIT), fall flat on one's face; **bûche de Noël** Yule log

bûcher [byʃe] *nm* pyre; bonfire ♦ *vi* (fam: *étudier*) to swot (BRIT), grind (US) ♦ *vt* to swot up (BRIT), cram

bûcheron [byʃʀɔ̃] *nm* woodcutter

bûcheur, euse [byʃœʀ, -øz] *nm/f* (fam: *étudiant*) swot (BRIT), grind (US)

budget [bydʒɛ] *nm* budget

buée [bɥe] *nf* (*sur une vitre*) mist; (*de l'haleine*) steam

buffet [byfɛ] *nm* (*meuble*) sideboard; (*de réception*) buffet; **buffet (de gare)** (station) buffet, snack bar

buffle [byfl(ə)] *nm* buffalo

buis [bɥi] *nm* box tree; (*bois*) box(wood)

buisson [bɥisɔ̃] *nm* bush

buissonnière [bɥisɔnjɛʀ] *adj f*: **faire l'école buissonnière** (BRIT) to play truant, skip school

bulbe [bylb(ə)] *nm* (BOT, ANAT) bulb; (*coupole*) onion-shaped dome

Bulgarie [bylgaʀi] *nf*: **la Bulgarie** Bulgaria

bulle [byl] *adj, nm*: (**papier**) **bulle** manil(l)a paper ♦ *nf* bubble; (*de bande dessinée*) balloon; (*papale*) bull; **bulle de savon** soap bubble

bulletin [byltɛ̃] *nm* (*communiqué, journal*) bulletin; (*papier*) form; (*de bagages*) ticket; (SCOL) report; **bulletin d'informations** news bulletin; **bulletin météorologique** weather report; **bulletin de naissance** birth certificate; **bulletin de salaire** pay slip; **bulletin de santé** medical bulletin; **bulletin (de vote)** ballot paper

bureau, x [byʀo] *nm* (*meuble*) desk; (*pièce, service*) office; **bureau de change** (foreign) exchange office ou bureau; **bureau d'embauche** ≈ job centre; **bureau d'études** design office; **bureau de location** box office; **bureau des objets trouvés** lost property office (BRIT), lost and found (US); **bureau de placement** employment agency; **bureau de poste** post office; **bureau de tabac** tobacconist's (shop), smoke shop (US); **bureau de vote** polling station

bureaucratie [byʀokʀasi] *nf* bureaucracy

burin [byʀɛ̃] *nm* cold chisel; (ART) burin

burlesque [byʀlɛsk(ə)] *adj* ridiculous; (LITTÉRATURE) burlesque

bus *vb* [by] *voir* **boire** ♦ *nm* [bys] (*véhicule, aussi* INFORM) bus

busqué, e [byske] *adj*: **nez busqué** hook(ed) nose

buste [byst(ə)] *nm* (ANAT) chest; (: *de femme*) bust; (*sculpture*) bust

but [by] *vb voir* **boire** ♦ *nm* (*cible*) target; (*fig*) goal, aim; (FOOTBALL etc) goal; **de but en blanc** point-blank; **avoir pour but de faire** to aim to do; **dans le but de** with the intention of

butane [bytan] *nm* butane; (*domestique*) Calor gas® (BRIT), butane

buté, e [byte] *adj* stubborn, obstinate ♦ *nf* (ARCHIT) abutment; (TECH) stop

buter [byte] *vi*: **buter contre** ou **sur** to bump into; (*trébucher*) to stumble against ♦ *vt* to antagonize; **se buter** *vi* to get obstinate, dig in one's heels

butin [bytɛ̃] *nm* booty, spoils *pl*; (*d'un vol*) loot

butiner [bytine] *vi* to gather nectar

butte [byt] *nf* mound, hillock; **être en butte à** to be exposed to

buvais etc [byvɛ] *vb voir* **boire**

buvard [byvaʀ] *nm* blotter

buvette [byvɛt] *nf* refreshment room ou stall; (*comptoir*) bar

buveur, euse [byvœʀ, -øz] *nm/f* drinker

— C c —

c' [s] *dét voir* **ce**

CA *sigle m* = **chiffre d'affaires, conseil d'administration, corps d'armée** ♦ *sigle f* = **chambre d'agriculture**

ça [sa] *pron* (*pour désigner*) this; (: *plus loin*) that; (*comme sujet indéfini*) it; **ça m'étonne que** it surprises me that; **ça va?** how are you?; how are things?; (*d'accord*) OK?, all right?; **ça alors!** (*désapprobation*) well!, really!; (*étonnement*) heavens!; **c'est ça** that's right

çà [sa] *adv*: **çà et là** here and there

cabane [kaban] *nf* hut, cabin

cabaret [kabaʀɛ] *nm* night club

cabas [kaba] *nm* shopping bag

cabillaud [kabijo] *nm* cod *inv*

cabine [kabin] *nf* (*de bateau*) cabin; (*de plage*) (beach) hut; (*de piscine etc*) cubicle; (*de camion, train*) cab; (*d'avion*) cockpit; **cabine (d'ascenseur)** lift cage; **cabine d'essayage** fitting room; **cabine de projection** projection room; **cabine spatiale** space capsule; **cabine (téléphonique)** call *ou* (tele)phone box, (tele)phone booth

cabinet [kabinɛ] *nm* (*petite pièce*) closet; (*de médecin*) surgery (*BRIT*), office (*US*); (*de notaire etc*) office; (: *clientèle*) practice; (*POL*) cabinet; (*d'un ministre*) advisers *pl*; **cabinets** *nmpl* (*w.-c.*) toilet *sg*, loo *sg* (*fam BRIT*); **cabinet d'affaires** business consultants' (bureau), business partnership; **cabinet de toilette** toilet; **cabinet de travail** study

câble [kɑbl(ə)] *nm* cable; **le câble** (*TV*) cable television, cablevision (*US*)

cabosser [kabɔse] *vt* to dent

cabrer [kabʀe]: **se cabrer** *vi* (*cheval*) to rear up; (*avion*) to nose up; (*fig*) to revolt, rebel; to jib

cabriole [kabʀijɔl] *nf* caper; (*gymnastique etc*) somersault

cacahuète [kakaɥɛt] *nf* peanut

cacao [kakao] *nm* cocoa (powder); (*boisson*) cocoa

cache [kaʃ] *nm* mask, card (*for masking*) ♦ *nf* hiding place

cache-cache [kaʃkaʃ] *nm*: **jouer à cache-cache** to play hide-and-seek

cachemire [kaʃmiʀ] *nm* cashmere ♦ *adj*: **dessin cachemire** paisley pattern; **le Cachemire** Kashmir

cache-nez [kaʃne] *nm inv* scarf (*pl* scarves), muffler

cacher [kaʃe] *vt* to hide, conceal; **cacher qch à qn** to hide *ou* conceal sth from sb; **se cacher** to hide; to be hidden *ou* concealed; **il ne s'en cache pas** he makes no secret of it

cachet [kaʃɛ] *nm* (*comprimé*) tablet; (*sceau: du roi*) seal; (: *de la poste*) postmark; (*rétribution*) fee; (*fig*) style, character

cacheter [kaʃte] *vt* to seal; **vin cacheté** vintage wine

cachette [kaʃɛt] *nf* hiding place; **en cachette** on the sly, secretly

cachot [kaʃo] *nm* dungeon

cachotterie [kaʃɔtʀi] *nf* mystery; **faire des cachotteries** to be secretive

cactus [kaktys] *nm* cactus

cadavre [kadavʀ(ə)] *nm* corpse, (dead) body

Caddie® [kadi] *nm* (*supermarket*) trolley

cadeau, x [kado] *nm* present, gift; **faire un cadeau à qn** to give sb a present *ou* gift; **faire cadeau de qch à qn** to make a present of sth to sb, give sth as a present

cadenas [kadnɑ] *nm* padlock

cadence [kadɑ̃s] *nf* (*MUS*) cadence; (: *rythme*) rhythm; (*de travail etc*) rate; **cadences** *nfpl* (*en usine*) production rate *sg*; **en cadence** rhythmically; in time

cadet, te [kadɛ, -ɛt] *adj* younger; (*le plus jeune*) youngest ♦ *nm/f* youngest child *ou* one, youngest boy *ou* son/girl *ou* daughter; **il est mon cadet de deux ans** he's 2 years younger than me, he's 2 years my junior; **les cadets** (*SPORT*) the minors (*15 – 17 years*); **le cadet de mes soucis** the least of my worries

cadran [kadʀɑ̃] *nm* dial; **cadran solaire** sundial

cadre [kadʀ(ə)] *nm* frame; (*environnement*) surroundings *pl*; (*limites*) scope ♦ *nm/f* (*ADMIN*) managerial employee, executive ♦ *adj*: **loi cadre** outline *ou* blueprint law; **cadre moyen/supérieur** (*ADMIN*) middle/senior management employee, junior/senior executive; **rayer qn des cadres** to discharge sb; to dismiss sb; **dans le cadre de** (*fig*) within the framework *ou* context of

cadrer [kadʀe] *vi*: **cadrer avec** to tally *ou* correspond with ♦ *vt* (*CINÉ, PHOTO*) to frame

cafard [kafaʀ] *nm* cockroach; **avoir le cafard** to be down in the dumps, be feeling low

café [kafe] *nm* coffee; (*bistro*) café ♦ *adj inv* coffee *cpd*; **café crème** coffee with cream; **café au lait** white coffee; **café noir** black coffee; **café en grains** coffee beans; **café en poudre** instant coffee; **café tabac** tobacconist's *or* newsagent's also serving coffee and spirits; **café liégeois** coffee ice cream with whipped cream

cafétéria [kafeteʀja] *nf* cafeteria

cafetière [kaftjɛʀ] *nf* (*pot*) coffee-pot

cafouiller [kafuje] *vi* to get in a shambles; (*machine etc*) to work in fits and starts

cage [kaʒ] *nf* cage; **cage (des buts)** goal; **en cage** in a cage, caged up *ou* in; **cage d'ascenseur** lift shaft; **cage d'escalier** (stair)well; **cage thoracique** rib cage

cageot [kaʒo] *nm* crate

cagibi [kaʒibi] *nm* shed

cagnotte [kaɲɔt] *nf* kitty

cagoule [kagul] *nf* cowl; hood; (*SKI etc*) cagoule

cahier [kaje] *nm* notebook; (*TYPO*) signature; (*revue*): **cahiers** journal; **cahier de revendications/doléances** list of claims/grievances; **cahier de brouillons** roughbook, jotter; **cahier des charges** specification; **cahier d'exercices** exercise book

cahot [kao] *nm* jolt, bump

caïd [kaid] *nm* big chief, boss

caille [kaj] *nf* quail

cailler [kaje] *vi* (*lait*) to curdle; (*sang*) to clot; (*fam*) to be cold

caillot [kajo] *nm* (blood) clot

caillou, x [kaju] *nm* (little) stone

caillouteux, euse [kajutø, -øz] *adj* stony; pebbly

Caire [kɛʀ] *nm*: **le Caire** Cairo

caisse [kɛs] *nf* box; (*où l'on met la recette*) cashbox; (: *machine*) till; (*où l'on paye*) cash desk (*BRIT*), checkout counter; (: *au supermarché*) checkout; (*de banque*) cashier's desk; (*TECH*) case, casing; **faire sa caisse** (*COMM*) to count the takings; **caisse claire** (*MUS*) side *ou* snare drum; **caisse éclair** express checkout; **caisse enregistreuse** cash register; **caisse d'épargne** (**CE**) savings bank; **caisse noire** slush fund; **caisse de retraite** pension fund; **caisse de sortie** checkout *voir* **grosse**

caissier, ière [kesje, -jɛʀ] *nm/f* cashier

cajoler [kaʒɔle] *vt* to wheedle, coax; to surround with love and care, make a fuss of

cake [kɛk] *nm* fruit cake

calandre [kalɑ̃dʀ(ə)] *nf* radiator grill; (*machine*) calender, mangle

calanque [kalɑ̃k] *nf* rocky inlet

calcaire [kalkɛʀ] *nm* limestone ♦ *adj* (*eau*) hard; (*GÉO*) limestone *cpd*

calciné, e [kalsine] *adj* burnt to ashes

calcul [kalkyl] *nm* calculation; **le calcul** (*SCOL*) arithmetic; **calcul différentiel/intégral** differential/integral calculus; **calcul mental** mental arithmetic; **calcul (biliaire)** (gall)stone; **calcul (rénal)** (kidney) stone; **d'après mes calculs** by my reckoning

calculer [kalkyle] *vt* to calculate, work out, reckon; (*combiner*) to calculate; **calculer qch de tête** to work sth out in one's head

calculette [kalkylɛt] *nf* (pocket) calculator

cale [kal] *nf* (*de bateau*) hold; (*en bois*) wedge, chock; **cale sèche** *ou* **de radoub** dry dock

calé, e [kale] *adj* (*fam*) clever, bright

caleçon [kalsɔ̃] *nm* pair of underpants, trunks *pl*; **caleçon de bain** bathing trunks *pl*

calembour [kalɑ̃buʀ] *nm* pun

calendrier [kalɑ̃dʀije] *nm* calendar; (*fig*) timetable

calepin [kalpɛ̃] *nm* notebook

caler [kale] *vt* to wedge, chock up; **caler (son moteur/véhicule)** to stall (one's engine/vehicle); **se caler dans un fauteuil** to make o.s. comfortable in an armchair

calfeutrer [kalføtʀe] *vt* to (make) draughtproof (*BRIT*) *ou* draftproof (*US*); **se calfeutrer** to make o.s. snug and comfortable

calibre [kalibʀ(ə)] *nm* (*d'un fruit*) grade; (*d'une arme*) bore, calibre (*BRIT*), caliber (*US*); (*fig*) calibre, caliber

califourchon [kalifuʀʃɔ̃]: **à califourchon** *adv* astride; **à califourchon sur** astride, straddling

câlin, e [kɑlɛ̃, -in] *adj* cuddly, cuddlesome; tender

câliner [kɑline] *vt* to fondle, cuddle

calmant [kalmɑ̃] *nm* tranquillizer, sedative; (*contre la douleur*) painkiller

calme [kalm(ə)] *adj* calm, quiet ♦ *nm* calm(ness),

quietness; **sans perdre son calme** without losing one's cool *ou* calmness; **calme plat** (*NAVIG*) dead calm

calmer [kalme] *vt* to calm (down); (*douleur, inquiétude*) to ease, soothe; **se calmer** to calm down

calomnie [kalɔmni] *nf* slander; (*écrite*) libel

calomnier [kalɔmnje] *vt* to slander; to libel

calorie [kalɔʀi] *nf* calorie

calotte [kalɔt] *nf* (*coiffure*) skullcap; (*gifle*) slap; **la calotte** (*péj: clergé*) the cloth, the clergy; **calotte glaciaire** icecap

calquer [kalke] *vt* to trace; (*fig*) to copy exactly

calvaire [kalvɛʀ] *nm* (*croix*) wayside cross, calvary; (*souffrances*) suffering, martyrdom

calvitie [kalvisi] *nf* baldness

camarade [kamaʀad] *nm/f* friend, pal; (*POL*) comrade

camaraderie [kamaʀadʀi] *nf* friendship

cambouis [kɑ̃bwi] *nm* dirty oil *ou* grease

cambrer [kɑ̃bʀe] *vt* to arch; **se cambrer** to arch one's back; **cambrer la taille** *ou* **les reins** to arch one's back

cambriolage [kɑ̃bʀijɔlaʒ] *nm* burglary

cambrioler [kɑ̃bʀijɔle] *vt* to burgle (*BRIT*), burglarize (*US*)

cambrioleur, euse [kɑ̃bʀijɔlœʀ, -øz] *nm/f* burglar

camelote [kamlɔt] *nf* rubbish, trash, junk

caméra [kameʀa] *nf* (*CINÉ, TV*) camera; (*d'amateur*) cine-camera

caméscope® [kameskɔp] *nm* camcorder

camion [kamjɔ̃] *nm* lorry (*BRIT*), truck; (*plus petit, fermé*) van; (*charge*): **camion de sable/cailloux** lorry-load (*BRIT*) *ou* truck-load of sand/stones; **camion de dépannage** breakdown (*BRIT*) *ou* tow (*US*) truck

camion-citerne, *pl* **camions-citernes** [kamjɔ̃sitɛʀn(ə)] *nm* tanker

camionnette [kamjɔnɛt] *nf* (small) van

camionneur [kamjɔnœʀ] *nm* (*entrepreneur*) haulage contractor (*BRIT*), trucker (*US*); (*chauffeur*) lorry (*BRIT*) *ou* truck driver; van driver

camisole [kamizɔl] *nf*: **camisole (de force)** straitjacket

camomille [kamɔmij] *nf* camomile; (*boisson*) camomile tea

camoufler [kamufle] *vt* to camouflage; (*fig*) to conceal, cover up

camp [kɑ̃] *nm* camp; (*fig*) side; **camp de nudistes/vacances** nudist/holiday camp; **camp de concentration** concentration camp

campagnard, e [kɑ̃paɲaʀ, -aʀd(ə)] *adj* country *cpd* ♦ *nm/f* countryman/woman

campagne [kɑ̃paɲ] *nf* country, countryside; (*MIL, POL, COMM*) campaign; **en campagne** (*MIL*) in the field; **à la campagne** in/to the country; **faire campagne pour** to campaign for; **campagne élec-**

torale election campaign; **campagne de publicité** advertising campaign

camper [kɑ̃pe] *vi* to camp ♦ *vt* (*chapeau etc*) to pull *ou* put on firmly; (*dessin*) to sketch; **se camper devant** to plant o.s. in front of

campeur, euse [kɑ̃pœʀ, -øz] *nm/f* camper

camping [kɑ̃piŋ] *nm* camping; (**terrain de**) **camping** campsite, camping site; **faire du camping** to go camping; **faire du camping sauvage** to camp rough

camping-car [kɑ̃piŋkaʀ] *nm* caravanette, camper (*US*)

camping-gaz® [kɑ̃piŋgaz] *nm inv* camp(ing) stove

Canada [kanada] *nm*: **le Canada** Canada

canadien, ne [kanadjɛ̃, -ɛn] *adj* Canadian ♦ *nm/f*: **Canadien, ne** Canadian ♦ *nf* (*veste*) furlined jacket

canaille [kanɑj] *nf* (*péj*) scoundrel; (*populace*) riffraff ♦ *adj* raffish, rakish

canal, aux [kanal, -o] *nm* canal; (*naturel*) channel; (*ADMIN*): **par le canal de** through (the medium of), via; **canal de distribution/télévision** distribution/television channel; **canal de Panama/Suez** Panama/Suez Canal

canalisation [kanalizɑsjɔ̃] *nf* (*tuyau*) pipe

canaliser [kanalize] *vt* to canalize; (*fig*) to channel

canapé [kanape] *nm* settee, sofa; (*CULIN*) canapé, open sandwich

canard [kanaʀ] *nm* duck

canari [kanaʀi] *nm* canary

cancans [kɑ̃kɑ̃] *nmpl* (malicious) gossip *sg*

cancer [kɑ̃sɛʀ] *nm* cancer; (*signe*): **le Cancer** Cancer, the Crab; **être du Cancer** to be Cancer; **il a un cancer** he has cancer

cancre [kɑ̃kʀ(ə)] *nm* dunce

candeur [kɑ̃dœʀ] *nf* ingenuousness

candidat, e [kɑ̃dida, -at] *nm/f* candidate; (*à un poste*) applicant, candidate

candidature [kɑ̃didatyʀ] *nf* candidacy; application; **poser sa candidature** to submit an application, apply

candide [kɑ̃did] *adj* ingenuous, guileless, naïve

cane [kan] *nf* (female) duck

caneton [kantɔ̃] *nm* duckling

canette [kanɛt] *nf* (*de bière*) (flip-top) bottle; (*de machine à coudre*) spool

canevas [kanva] *nm* (*COUTURE*) canvas (for tapestry work); (*fig*) framework, structure

caniche [kaniʃ] *nm* poodle

canicule [kanikyl] *nf* scorching heat; midsummer heat, dog days *pl*

canif [kanif] *nm* penknife, pocket knife

canine [kanin] *nf* canine (tooth), eye tooth

caniveau, x [kanivo] *nm* gutter

canne [kan] *nf* (walking) stick; **canne à pêche** fishing rod; **canne à sucre** sugar cane; **les cannes**

blanches (*les aveugles*) the blind

cannelle [kanɛl] *nf* cinnamon

canoë [kanɔe] *nm* canoe; (*sport*) canoeing; **canoë (kayak)** kayak

canon [kanɔ̃] *nm* (*arme*) gun; (*HIST*) cannon; (*d'une arme: tube*) barrel; (*fig*) model; (*MUS*) canon ♦ *adj*: **droit canon** canon law; **canon rayé** rifled barrel

canot [kano] *nm* boat, dingh(e)y; **canot pneumatique** rubber *ou* inflatable ding(h)y; **canot de sauvetage** lifeboat

canotier [kanɔtje] *nm* boater

cantatrice [kɑ̃tatʀis] *nf* (opera) singer

cantine [kɑ̃tin] *nf* canteen; (*réfectoire d'école*) dining hall

cantique [kɑ̃tik] *nm* hymn

canton [kɑ̃tɔ̃] *nm* district (*consisting of several communes*); (*en Suisse*) canton; *see boxed note*

CANTON

A French **canton** is the administrative division represented by a councillor in the 'Conseil général'. It comprises a number of 'communes' and is, in turn, a subdivision of an 'arrondissement'. In Switzerland the **cantons** are the 23 autonomous political divisions which make up the Swiss confederation.

cantonade [kɑ̃tɔnad]: **à la cantonade** *adv* to everyone in general; (*crier*) from the rooftops

cantonner [kɑ̃tɔne] *vt* (*MIL*) to billet (*BRIT*), quarter; to station; **se cantonner dans** to confine o.s. to

cantonnier [kɑ̃tɔnje] *nm* roadmender

canular [kanylaʀ] *nm* hoax

caoutchouc [kautʃu] *nm* rubber; **caoutchouc mousse** foam rubber; **en caoutchouc** rubber *cpd*

CAP *sigle m* (= *Certificat d'aptitude professionnelle*) vocational training certificate taken at secondary school

cap [kap] *nm* (*GÉO*) cape; headland; (*fig*) hurdle; watershed; (*NAVIG*): **changer de cap** to change course; **mettre le cap sur** to head *ou* steer for; **doubler** *ou* **passer le cap** (*fig*) to get over the worst; **Le Cap** Cape Town; **le cap de Bonne Espérance** the Cape of Good Hope; **le cap Horn** Cape Horn; **les îles du Cap Vert** (*aussi*: **le Cap-Vert**) the Cape Verde Islands

capable [kapabl(ə)] *adj* able, capable; **capable de qch/faire** capable of sth/doing; **il est capable d'oublier** he could easily forget; **spectacle capable d'intéresser** show likely to be of interest

capacité [kapasite] *nf* (*compétence*) ability; (*JUR, INFORM, d'un récipient*) capacity; **capacité (en droit)** basic legal qualification

cape [kap] *nf* cape, cloak; **rire sous cape** to laugh up one's sleeve

CAPES [kapɛs] *sigle m* (= *Certificat d'aptitude au professorat de l'enseignement du second degré*) sec-

ondary teaching diploma; see boxed note

CAPES

The French **CAPES** ('certificat d'aptitude au professorat de l'enseignement du second degré') is a competitive examination sat by prospective secondary school teachers after the 'licence'. Successful candidates become fully qualified teachers ('professeurs certifiés').

capillaire [kapilɛʀ] *adj* (*soins, lotion*) hair *cpd*; (*vaisseau etc*) capillary; **artiste capillaire** hair artist *ou* designer

capitaine [kapitɛn] *nm* captain; **capitaine des pompiers** fire chief (*BRIT*), fire marshal (*US*); **capitaine au long cours** master mariner

capital, e, aux [kapital, -o] *adj* major; fundamental; (*JUR*) capital ♦ *nm* capital; (*fig*) stock; asset ♦ *nf* (*ville*) capital; (*lettre*) capital (letter) ♦ *nmpl* (*fonds*) capital *sg*, monies *sg*; **les sept péchés capitaux** the seven deadly sins; **peine capitale** capital punishment; **capital (social)** authorized capital; **capital d'exploitation** working capital

capitalisme [kapitalism(ə)] *nm* capitalism

capitaliste [kapitalist(ə)] *adj, nm/f* capitalist

capitonné, e [kapitɔne] *adj* padded

caporal, aux [kapɔʀal, -o] *nm* lance corporal

capot [kapo] *nm* (*AUTO*) bonnet (*BRIT*), hood (*US*)

capote [kapɔt] *nf* (*de voiture*) hood (*BRIT*), top (*US*); (*de soldat*) greatcoat; **capote (anglaise)** (*fam*) rubber, condom

capoter [kapɔte] *vi* to overturn; (*négociations*) to founder

câpre [kɑpʀ(ə)] *nf* caper

caprice [kapʀis] *nm* whim, caprice; passing fancy; **caprices** *nmpl* (*de la mode etc*) vagaries; **faire un caprice** to throw a tantrum; **faire des caprices** to be temperamental

capricieux, euse [kapʀisjø, -øz] *adj* capricious; whimsical; temperamental

Capricorne [kapʀikɔʀn] *nm:* **le Capricorne** Capricorn, the Goat; **être du Capricorne** to be Capricorn

capsule [kapsyl] *nf* (*de bouteille*) cap; (*amorce*) primer; cap; (*BOT etc, spatiale*) capsule

capter [kapte] *vt* (*ondes radio*) to pick up; (*eau*) to harness; (*fig*) to win, capture

captivant, e [kaptivɑ̃, -ɑ̃t] *adj* captivating

captivité [kaptivite] *nf* captivity; **en captivité** in captivity

capturer [kaptyʀe] *vt* to capture, catch

capuche [kapyʃ] *nf* hood

capuchon [kapyʃɔ̃] *nm* hood; (*de stylo*) cap, top

capucine [kapysin] *nf* (*BOT*) nasturtium

caquet [kakɛ] *nm:* **rabattre le caquet à qn** to bring sb down a peg or two

caqueter [kakte] *vi* (*poule*) to cackle; (*fig*) to prattle

car [kaʀ] *nm* coach (*BRIT*), bus ♦ *conj* because, for; **car de police** police van; **car de reportage** broadcasting *ou* radio van

carabine [kaʀabin] *nf* carbine, rifle; **carabine à air comprimé** airgun

caractère [kaʀaktɛʀ] *nm* (*gén*) character; **en caractères gras** in bold type; **en petits caractères** in small print; **en caractères d'imprimerie** in block capitals; **avoir du caractère** to have character; **avoir bon/mauvais caractère** to be good-/ill-natured *ou* tempered; **caractère de remplacement** wild card; **caractères/seconde (cps)** characters per second (cps)

caractériel, le [kaʀakteʀjɛl] *adj* (*enfant*) (emotionally) disturbed ♦ *nm/f* problem child; **troubles caractériels** emotional stress

caractérisé, e [kaʀakteʀize] *adj:* **c'est une grippe/de l'insubordination caractérisée** it is a clear(-cut) case of flu/insubordination

caractériser [kaʀakteʀize] *vt* to characterize; **se caractériser par** to be characterized *ou* distinguished by

caractéristique [kaʀakteʀistik] *adj, nf* characteristic

carafe [kaʀaf] *nf* decanter; carafe

caraïbe [kaʀaib] *adj* Caribbean; **les Caraïbes** *nfpl* the Caribbean (Islands); **la mer des Caraïbes** the Caribbean Sea

carambolage [kaʀɑ̃bɔlaʒ] *nm* multiple crash, pileup

caramel [kaʀamɛl] *nm* (*bonbon*) caramel, toffee; (*substance*) caramel

carapace [kaʀapas] *nf* shell

caravane [kaʀavan] *nf* caravan

caravaning [kaʀavaniŋ] *nm* caravanning; (*emplacement*) caravan site

carbone [kaʀbɔn] *nm* carbon; (*feuille*) carbon, sheet of carbon paper; (*double*) carbon (copy)

carbonique [kaʀbɔnik] *adj:* **gaz carbonique** carbon dioxide; **neige carbonique** dry ice

carbonisé, e [kaʀbɔnize] *adj* charred; **mourir carbonisé** to be burned to death

carburant [kaʀbyʀɑ̃] *nm* (motor) fuel

carburateur [kaʀbyʀatœʀ] *nm* carburettor

carcan [kaʀkɑ̃] *nm* (*fig*) yoke, shackles *pl*

carcasse [kaʀkas] *nf* carcass; (*de véhicule etc*) shell

cardiaque [kaʀdjak] *adj* cardiac, heart *cpd* ♦ *nm/f* heart patient; **être cardiaque** to have a heart condition

cardigan [kaʀdigɑ̃] *nm* cardigan

cardiologue [kaʀdjɔlɔg] *nm/f* cardiologist, heart specialist

carême [kaʀɛm] *nm:* **le Carême** Lent

carence [kaʀɑ̃s] *nf* incompetence, inadequacy; (*manque*) deficiency; **carence vitaminique** vitamin deficiency

caresse [kaʀɛs] *nf* caress

caresser [kaʀese] *vt* to caress, stroke, fondle; (*fig: projet, espoir*) to toy with

cargaison [kaʀgɛzɔ̃] *nf* cargo, freight

cargo [kaʀgo] *nm* cargo boat, freighter; **cargo mixte** cargo and passenger ship

caricature [kaʀikatyʀ] *nf* caricature; (*politique etc*) (satirical) cartoon

carie [kaʀi] *nf*: **la carie (dentaire)** tooth decay; **une carie** a bad tooth

carillon [kaʀijɔ̃] *nm* (*d'église*) bells *pl*; (*de pendule*) chimes *pl*; (*de porte*): **carillon (électrique)** (electric) door chime *ou* bell

caritatif, ive [kaʀitatif, -iv] *adj* charitable

carnassier, ière [kaʀnasje, -jɛʀ] *adj* carnivorous ♦ *nm* carnivore

carnaval [kaʀnaval] *nm* carnival

carnet [kaʀnɛ] *nm* (*calepin*) notebook; (*de tickets, timbres etc*) book; (*d'école*) school report; (*journal intime*) diary; **carnet d'adresses** address book; **carnet de chèques** cheque book (*BRIT*), checkbook (*US*); **carnet de commandes** order book; **carnet de notes** (*SCOL*) (school) report; **carnet à souches** counterfoil book

carotte [kaʀɔt] *nf* (*aussi fig*) carrot

carpette [kaʀpɛt] *nf* rug

carré, e [kaʀe] *adj* square; (*fig: franc*) straightforward ♦ *nm* (*de terrain, jardin*) patch, plot; (*NAVIG: salle*) wardroom; (*MATH*) square; (*CARTES*): **carré d'as/ de rois** four aces/kings; **élever un nombre au carré** to square a number; **mètre/kilomètre carré** square metre/kilometre; **carré de soie** silk headsquare *ou* headscarf; **carré d'agneau** loin of lamb

carreau, x [kaʀo] *nm* (*en faïence etc*) (floor) tile; (*wall*) tile; (*de fenêtre*) (window) pane; (*motif*) check, square; (*CARTES: couleur*) diamonds *pl*; (*: carte*) diamond; **tissu à carreaux** checked fabric; **papier à carreaux** squared paper

carrefour [kaʀfuʀ] *nm* crossroads *sg*

carrelage [kaʀlaʒ] *nm* tiling; (tiled) floor

carrelet [kaʀlɛ] *nm* (*poisson*) plaice

carrément [kaʀemɑ̃] *adv* (*franchement*) straight out, bluntly; (*sans détours, sans hésiter*) straight; (*nettement*) definitely; **il l'a carrément mis à la porte** he threw him straight out

carrière [kaʀjɛʀ] *nf* (*de roches*) quarry; (*métier*) career; **militaire de carrière** professional soldier; **faire carrière dans** to make one's career in

carrossable [kaʀɔsabl(ə)] *adj* suitable for (motor) vehicles

carrosse [kaʀɔs] *nm* (horse-drawn) coach

carrosserie [kaʀɔsʀi] *nf* body, bodywork *no pl* (*BRIT*); (*activité, commerce*) coachwork (*BRIT*), (car) body manufacturing; **atelier de carrosserie** (*pour réparations*) body shop, panel beaters' (yard) (*BRIT*)

carrure [kaʀyʀ] *nf* build; (*fig*) stature

cartable [kaʀtabl(ə)] *nm* (*d'écolier*) satchel, (school) bag

carte [kaʀt(ə)] *nf* (*de géographie*) map; (*marine, du ciel*) chart; (*de fichier, d'abonnement etc, à jouer*) card; (*au restaurant*) menu; (*aussi*: **carte postale**) (post)card; (*aussi*: **carte de visite**) (visiting) card; **avoir/donner carte blanche** to have/give carte blanche *ou* a free hand; **tirer les cartes à qn** to read sb's cards; **jouer aux cartes** to play cards; **jouer cartes sur table** (*fig*) to put one's cards on the table; **à la carte** (*au restaurant*) à la carte; **carte bancaire** cash card; **carte à circuit imprimé** printed circuit; **carte à puce** smartcard; **carte de crédit** credit card; **carte d'état-major** ≈ Ordnance (*BRIT*) *ou* Geological (*US*) Survey map; **la carte grise** (*AUTO*) ≈ (the (car) registration document; **carte d'identité** identity card; **carte jeune** young person's railcard; **carte perforée** punch(ed) card; **carte de séjour** residence permit; **carte routière** road map; **la carte verte** (*AUTO*) the green card; **la carte des vins** the wine list

carter [kaʀtɛʀ] *nm* (*AUTO: d'huile*) sump (*BRIT*), oil pan (*US*); (*: de la boîte de vitesses*) casing; (*de bicyclette*) chain guard

carton [kaʀtɔ̃] *nm* (*matériau*) cardboard; (*boîte*) (cardboard) box; (*d'invitation*) invitation card; (*ART*) sketch; cartoon; **en carton** cardboard *cpd*; **faire un carton** (*au tir*) to have a go at the rifle range; to score a hit; **carton (à dessin)** portfolio

carton-pâte [kaʀtɔ̃pɑt] *nm* pasteboard; **de carton-pâte** (*fig*) cardboard *cpd*

cartouche [kaʀtuʃ] *nf* cartridge; (*de cigarettes*) carton

cas [kɑ] *nm* case; **faire peu de cas/grand cas de** to attach little/great importance to; **le cas échéant** if need be; **en aucun cas** on no account, under no circumstances (whatsoever); **au cas où** in case; **dans ce cas** in that case; **en cas de** in case of, in the event of; **en cas de besoin** if need be; **en cas d'urgence** in an emergency; **en cas** in that case; **en tout cas** in any case, at any rate; **cas de conscience** matter of conscience; **cas de force majeure** case of absolute necessity; (*ASSURANCES*) act of God; **cas limite** borderline case; **cas social** social problem

casanier, ière [kazanje, -jɛʀ] *adj* stay-at-home

cascade [kaskad] *nf* waterfall, cascade; (*fig*) stream, torrent

cascadeur, euse [kaskadœʀ, -øz] *nm/f* stuntman/girl

case [kɑz] *nf* (*hutte*) hut; (*compartiment*) compartment; (*pour le courrier*) pigeonhole; (*mots croisés, d'échiquier*) square; (*sur un formulaire*) box

caser [kɑze] *vt* (*mettre*) to put; (*loger*) to put up; (*péj*) to find a job for; to marry off; **se caser** (*personne*) to settle down

caserne [kazɛʀn(ə)] *nf* barracks

cash [kaʃ] *adv*: **payer cash** to pay cash down

casier [kɑzje] *nm* (*à journaux etc*) rack; (*de bureau*) filing cabinet; (: *à cases*) set of pigeonholes; (*case*) compartment; pigeonhole; (: *à clef*) locker; (*PÊCHE*) lobster pot; **casier à bouteilles** bottle rack; **casier judiciaire** police record

casino [kazino] *nm* casino

casque [kask(ə)] *nm* helmet; (*chez le coiffeur*) (hair-)dryer; (*pour audition*) (head-)phones *pl*, headset; **les Casques bleus** the UN peacekeeping force

casquette [kasket] *nf* cap

cassant, e [kɑsɑ̃, -ɑ̃t] *adj* brittle; (*fig*) brusque, abrupt

cassation [kasɑsjɔ̃] *nf*: **se pourvoir en cassation** to lodge an appeal; **recours en cassation** appeal to the Supreme Court

casse [kas] *nf* (*pour voitures*): **mettre à la casse** to scrap, send to the breakers; (*dégâts*): **il y a eu de la casse** there were a lot of breakages; (*TYPO*): **haut/bas de casse** upper/lower case

casse-cou [kasku] *adj inv* daredevil, reckless; **crier casse-cou à qn** to warn sb (*against a risky undertaking*)

casse-croûte [kaskrut] *nm inv* snack

casse-noisettes [kasnwazet], **casse-noix** [kasnwa] *nm inv* nutcrackers *pl*

casse-pieds [kaspje] *adj, nm/f inv* (*fam*): **il est casse-pieds, c'est un casse-pieds** he's a pain (in the neck)

casser [kase] *vt* to break; (*ADMIN: gradé*) to demote; (*JUR*) to quash; (*COMM*): **casser les prix** to slash prices; **se casser** *vi* to break; (*fam*) to go, leave ◆ *vt*: **se casser la jambe/une jambe** to break one's leg/ a leg; **à tout casser** fantastic, brilliant; **se casser net** to break clean off

casserole [kasrɔl] *nf* saucepan; **à la casserole** (*CULIN*) braised

casse-tête [kastet] *nm inv* (*fig*) brain teaser; (*difficultés*) headache (*fig*)

cassette [kaset] *nf* (*bande magnétique*) cassette; (*coffret*) casket; **cassette numérique** digital compact cassette; **cassette vidéo** video

casseur [kasœr] *nm* hooligan; rioter

cassis [kasis] *nm* blackcurrant; (*de la route*) dip, bump

cassoulet [kasule] *nm* sausage and bean hotpot

cassure [kasyr] *nf* break, crack

castor [kastɔr] *nm* beaver

castrer [kastre] *vt* (*mâle*) to castrate; (*femelle*) to spay; (*cheval*) to geld; (*chat, chien*) to doctor (*BRIT*), fix (*US*)

catalogue [katalɔg] *nm* catalogue

cataloguer [katalɔge] *vt* to catalogue, list; (*péj*) to put a label on

catalyseur [katalizœr] *nm* catalyst

catalytique [katalitik] *adj* catalytic

catastrophe [katastrɔf] *nf* catastrophe, disaster;

atterrir en catastrophe to make an emergency landing; **partir en catastrophe** to rush away

catch [katʃ] *nm* (all-in) wrestling

catéchisme [kateʃism(ə)] *nm* catechism

catégorie [kategɔri] *nf* category; (*BOUCHERIE*): **morceaux de première/deuxième catégorie** prime/second cuts

catégorique [kategɔrik] *adj* categorical

cathédrale [katedral] *nf* cathedral

catholique [katɔlik] *adj, nm/f* (Roman) Catholic; **pas très catholique** a bit shady *ou* fishy

catimini [katimini]: **en catimini** *adv* on the sly, on the quiet

cauchemar [koʃmar] *nm* nightmare

cause [koz] *nf* cause; (*JUR*) lawsuit, case; brief; **faire cause commune avec qn** to take sides with sb; **être cause de** to be the cause of; **à cause de** because of, owing to; **pour cause de** on account of; owing to; **(et) pour cause** and for (a very) good reason; **être en cause** (*intérêts*) to be at stake; (*personne*) to be involved; (*qualité*) to be in question; **mettre en cause** to implicate; to call into question; **remettre en cause** to challenge, call into question; **c'est hors de cause** it's out of the question; **en tout état de cause** in any case

causer [koze] *vt* to cause ◆ *vi* to chat, talk

causerie [kozri] *nf* talk

causette [kozet] *nf*: **faire la** *ou* **un brin de causette** to have a chat

caution [kosjɔ̃] *nf* guarantee, security; deposit; (*JUR*) bail (bond); (*fig*) backing, support; **payer la caution de qn** to stand bail for sb; **se porter caution pour qn** to stand security for sb; **libéré sous caution** released on bail; **sujet à caution** unconfirmed

cautionner [kosjɔne] *vt* to guarantee; (*soutenir*) to support

cavalcade [kavalkad] *nf* (*fig*) stampede

cavalier, ière [kavalje, -jɛr] *adj* (*désinvolte*) offhand ◆ *nm/f* rider; (*au bal*) partner ◆ *nm* (*ÉCHECS*) knight; **faire cavalier seul** to go it alone; **allée** *ou* **piste cavalière** riding path

cave [kav] *nf* cellar; (*cabaret*) (cellar) nightclub ◆ *adj*: **yeux caves** sunken eyes; **joues caves** hollow cheeks

caveau, x [kavo] *nm* vault

caverne [kavɛrn(ə)] *nf* cave

CCP *sigle m* = **compte chèque postal**

CD *sigle m* (= *chemin départemental*) secondary road, = B road (*BRIT*); (= *compact disc*) CD; (= *comité directeur*) steering committee; (*POL*) = **corps diplomatique**

CD-ROM [sederɔm] *nm inv* (= *Compact Disc Read Only Memory*) CD-ROM

CE *sigle f* (= *Communauté européenne*) EC; (*COMM*) = **caisse d'épargne** ◆ *sigle m* (*INDUSTRIE*) = **comité d'entreprise**; (*SCOL*) = **cours élémentaire**

MOT CLÉ

ce, cette [sə, sɛt] (*devant nm* **cet** + *voyelle ou h aspiré; pl* **ces**) *dét* (*proximité*) this; these *pl*; (*non-proximité*) that; those *pl*; **cette maison(-ci-là)** this/that house; **cette nuit** (*qui vient*) tonight; (*passée*) last night

◆ *pron* **1: c'est** it's, it is; **c'est petit/grand/un livre** it's *ou* it is small/big/a book; **c'est un peintre** he's *ou* he is a painter; **ce sont des peintres** they're *ou* they are painters; **c'est le facteur** *etc* (*à la porte*) it's the postman *etc*; **qui est-ce?** who is it?; (*en désignant*) who is he/she?; **qu'est-ce?** what is it?; **c'est toi qui lui as parlé** it was you who spoke to him

2: c'est que: c'est qu'il est lent/qu'il n'a pas faim the fact is, he's slow/he's not hungry

3 (*expressions*): **c'est ça** (*correct*) that's it, that's right; **c'est toi qui le dis!** that's what YOU say!; *voir aussi* **c'est-à-dire; -ci; est-ce que; n'est-ce pas**

4: ce qui, ce que what; (*chose qui*): **il est bête, ce qui me chagrine** he's stupid, which saddens me; **tout ce qui bouge** everything that *ou* which moves; **tout ce que je sais** all I know; **ce dont j'ai parlé** what I talked about; **ce que c'est grand!** it's so big!

---

ceci [səsi] *pron* this

cécité [sesite] *nf* blindness

céder [sede] *vt* to give up ◆ *vi* (*pont, barrage*) to give way; (*personne*) to give in; **céder à** to yield to, give in to

cédérom [sederɔm] *nm* CD-ROM

CEDEX [sedɛks] *sigle m* (= *courrier d'entreprise à distribution exceptionnelle*) accelerated postal service for bulk users

cédille [sedij] *nf* cedilla

cèdre [sɛdʀ(ə)] *nm* cedar

CEI *sigle f* (= *Communauté des États indépendants*) CIS

ceinture [sɛtyʀ] *nf* belt; (*taille*) waist; (*fig*) ring; belt; circle; **ceinture de sauvetage** lifebelt (*BRIT*), life preserver (*US*); **ceinture de sécurité** safety *ou* seat belt; **ceinture (de sécurité) à enrouleur** inertia reel seat belt; **ceinture verte** green belt

cela [səla] *pron* that; (*comme sujet indéfini*) it; **cela m'étonne que** it surprises me that; **quand/où cela?** when/where (was that)?

célèbre [selɛbʀ(ə)] *adj* famous

célébrer [selebʀe] *vt* to celebrate; (*louer*) to extol

céleri [sɛlʀi] *nm*: **céleri(-rave)** celeriac; **céleri (en branche)** celery

célibat [seliba] *nm* celibacy, bachelor/spinsterhood

célibataire [selibatɛʀ] *adj* single, unmarried ◆ *nm/f* bachelor/unmarried *ou* single woman; **mère célibataire** single *ou* unmarried mother

celle, celles [sɛl] *pron voir* **celui**

cellier [selje] *nm* storeroom

cellule [selyl] *nf* (*gén*) cell; **cellule (photo-électrique)** electronic eye

cellulite [selylit] *nf* cellulite

MOT CLÉ

celui, celle [səlɥi, sɛl] (*mpl* **ceux**, *fpl* **celles**) *pron* **1: celui-ci/là, celle-ci/là** this one/that one; **ceux-ci, celles-ci** these (ones); **ceux-là, celles-là** those (ones); **celui de mon frère** my brother's; **celui du salon/du dessous** the one in (*ou* from) the lounge/below

2: celui qui bouge the one which *ou* that moves; (*personne*) the one who moves; **celui que je vois** the one (which *ou* that) I see; (*personne*) the one (whom) I see; **celui dont je parle** the one I'm talking about

3 (*valeur indéfinie*): **celui qui veut** whoever wants

---

cendre [sɑ̃dʀ(ə)] *nf* ash; **cendres** (*d'un foyer*) ash(es), cinders; (*volcaniques*) ash *sg*; (*d'un défunt*) ashes; **sous la cendre** (*CULIN*) in (the) embers

cendrier [sɑ̃dʀije] *nm* ashtray

cène [sɛn] *nf*: **la cène** (Holy) Communion; (*ART*) the Last Supper

censé, e [sɑ̃se] *adj*: **être censé faire** to be supposed to do

censeur [sɑ̃sœʀ] *nm* (*SCOL*) deputy-head (*BRIT*), vice-principal (*US*); (*CINÉ, POL*) censor

censure [sɑ̃syʀ] *nf* censorship

censurer [sɑ̃syʀe] *vt* (*CINÉ, PRESSE*) to censor; (*POL*) to censure

cent [sɑ̃] *num* a hundred, one hundred; **pour cent (%)** per cent (%); **faire les cent pas** to pace up and down ◆ *nm* (US, Canada, partie de l'euro etc) cent

centaine [sɑ̃tɛn] *nf*: **une centaine (de)** about a hundred, a hundred or so; (*COMM*) a hundred; **plusieurs centaines (de)** several hundred; **des centaines (de)** hundreds (of)

centenaire [sɑ̃tnɛʀ] *adj* hundred-year-old ◆ *nm/f* centenarian ◆ *nm* (*anniversaire*) centenary

centième [sɑ̃tjɛm] *num* hundredth

centigrade [sɑ̃tigʀad] *nm* centigrade

centilitre [sɑ̃tilitʀ(ə)] *nm* centilitre (*BRIT*), centiliter (*US*)

centime [sɑ̃tim] *nm* centime

centimètre [sɑ̃timɛtʀ(ə)] *nm* centimetre (*BRIT*), centimeter (*US*); (*ruban*) tape measure, measuring tape

central, e, aux [sɑ̃tʀal, -o] *adj* central ◆ *nm*: **central (téléphonique)** (telephone) exchange ◆ *nf*: **centrale d'achat** (*COMM*) central buying service; **centrale électrique/nucléaire** electric/nuclear power station; **centrale syndicale** group of affiliated trade unions

centre [sɑ̃tʀ(ə)] *nm* centre (*BRIT*), center (*US*); **centre commercial/sportif/culturel** shopping/sports/

arts centre; **centre aéré** outdoor centre; **centre d'appels** call centre; **centre d'apprentissage** training college; **centre d'attraction** centre of attraction; **centre de gravité** centre of gravity; **centre de loisirs** leisure centre; **centre d'enfouissement des déchets** landfill site; **centre hospitalier** hospital complex; **centre de tri** (POSTES) sorting office; **centres nerveux** (ANAT) nerve centres

centre-ville, pl **centres-villes** [sɑ̃trəvil] nm town centre (BRIT) ou center (US), downtown (area) (US)

centuple [sɑ̃typl(ə)] nm: **le centuple de qch** a hundred times sth; **au centuple** a hundredfold

cep [sɛp] nm (vine) stock

cèpe [sɛp] nm (edible) boletus

cependant [səpɑ̃dɑ̃] adv however, nevertheless

céramique [seramik] adj ceramic ♦ nf ceramic; (art) ceramics sg

cercle [sɛrkl(ə)] nm circle; (objet) band, hoop; **décrire un cercle** (avion) to circle; (projectile) to describe a circle; **cercle d'amis** circle of friends; **cercle de famille** family circle; **cercle vicieux** vicious circle

cercueil [sɛrkœj] nm coffin

céréale [sereal] nf cereal

cérémonie [seremɔni] nf ceremony; **cérémonies** nfpl (péj) fuss sg, to-do sg

cerf [sɛr] nm stag

cerfeuil [sɛrfœj] nm chervil

cerf-volant [sɛrvɔlɑ̃] nm kite; **jouer au cerf-volant** to fly a kite

cerise [səriz] nf cherry

cerisier [sərizje] nm cherry (tree)

cerner [sɛrne] vt (MIL etc) to surround; (fig: problème) to delimit, define

cernes [sɛrn(ə)] nfpl (dark) rings, shadows (under the eyes)

certain, e [sɛrtɛ̃, -ɛn] adj certain; (sûr): **certain (de/que)** certain ou sure (of/ that) ♦ dét certain; **d'un certain âge** past one's prime, not so young; **un certain temps** (quite) some time; **sûr et certain** absolutely certain; **certains** pron some

certainement [sɛrtɛnmɑ̃] adv (probablement) most probably ou likely; (bien sûr) certainly, of course

certes [sɛrt(ə)] adv admittedly; of course; indeed (yes)

certificat [sɛrtifika] nm certificate; **Certificat d'études (primaires) (CEP)** former school leaving certificate (taken at the end of primary education); **Certificat de fin d'études secondaires (CFES)** school leaving certificate

certifier [sɛrtifje] vt to certify, guarantee; **certifier à qn que** to assure sb that, guarantee to sb that; **certifier qch à qn** to guarantee sth to sb

certitude [sɛrtityd] nf certainty

cerveau, x [sɛrvo] nm brain; **cerveau électro-** **nique** electronic brain

cervelas [sɛrvəla] nm saveloy

cervelle [sɛrvɛl] nf (ANAT) brain; (CULIN) brain(s); **se creuser la cervelle** to rack one's brains

CES sigle m (= Collège d'enseignement secondaire) ≈ (junior) secondary school (BRIT), ≈ junior high school (US)

ces [se] dét voir **ce**

cesse [sɛs]: **sans cesse** adv continually, constantly; continuously; **il n'avait de cesse que** he would not rest until

cesser [sese] vt to stop ♦ vi to stop, cease; **cesser de faire** to stop doing; **faire cesser** (bruit, scandale) to put a stop to

cessez-le-feu [seselfø] nm inv ceasefire

c'est-à-dire [sɛtadir] adv that is (to say); (demander de préciser): **c'est-à-dire?** what does that mean?; **c'est-à-dire que ...** (en conséquence) which means that ...; (manière d'excuse) well, in fact ...

cet, cette [sɛt] dét voir **ce**

ceux [sø] pron voir **celui**

CFC sigle mpl (= chlorofluorocarbures) CFC

CFDT sigle f (= Confédération française démocratique du travail) trade union

CGT sigle f (= Confédération générale du travail) trade union

chacun, e [ʃakœ̃, -yn] pron each; (indéfini) everyone, everybody

chagrin, e [ʃagrɛ̃, -in] adj morose ♦ nm grief, sorrow; **avoir du chagrin** to be grieved ou sorrowful

chagriner [ʃagrine] vt to grieve, distress; (contrarier) to bother, worry

chahut [ʃay] nm uproar

chahuter [ʃayte] vt to rag, bait ♦ vi to make an uproar

chaîne [ʃɛn] nf chain; (RADIO, TV) channel; (INFORM) string; **chaînes** nfpl (liens, asservissement) fetters, bonds; **travail à la chaîne** production line work; **réactions en chaîne** chain reactions; **faire la chaîne** to form a (human) chain; **chaîne alimentaire** food chain; **chaîne compacte** music centre; **chaîne d'entraide** mutual aid association; **chaîne (haute-fidélité ou hi-fi)** hi-fi system; **chaîne (de montage ou de fabrication)** production ou assembly line; **chaîne (de montagnes)** (mountain) range; **chaîne de solidarité** solidarity network; **chaîne (stéréo ou audio)** stereo (system)

chaînette [ʃɛnɛt] nf (small) chain

chair [ʃɛr] nf flesh ♦ adj: (couleur) chair flesh-coloured; **avoir la chair de poule** to have goosepimples ou gooseflesh; **bien en chair** plump, well-padded; **en chair et en os** in the flesh; **chair à saucisses** sausage meat

chaire [ʃɛr] nf (d'église) pulpit; (d'université) chair

chaise [ʃez] nf chair; **chaise de bébé** high chair; **chaise électrique** electric chair; **chaise longue** deckchair

châle [ʃɑl] *nm* shawl

chaleur [ʃalœʀ] *nf* heat; (*fig*) warmth; fire, fervour (*BRIT*), fervor (*US*); heat; **en chaleur** (*ZOOL*) on heat

chaleureux, euse [ʃalœʀø, -øz] *adj* warm

chaloupe [ʃalup] *nf* launch; (*de sauvetage*) lifeboat

chalumeau, x [ʃalymo] *nm* blowlamp (*BRIT*), blowtorch

chalutier [ʃalytje] *nm* trawler; (*pêcheur*) trawlerman

chamailler [ʃamaje]: **se chamailler** *vi* to squabble, bicker

chambouler [ʃɑ̃bule] *vt* to disrupt, turn upside down

chambre [ʃɑ̃bʀ(ə)] *nf* bedroom; (*TECH*) chamber; (*POL*) chamber, house; (*JUR*) court; (*COMM*) chamber; federation; **faire chambre à part** to sleep in separate rooms; **stratège/alpiniste en chambre** armchair strategist/mountaineer; **chambre à un lit/deux lits** single/twin-bedded room; **chambre pour une/deux personne(s)** single/double room; **chambre d'accusation** court of criminal appeal; **chambre d'agriculture** *body responsible for the agricultural interests of a département*; **chambre à air** (*de pneu*) (inner) tube; **chambre d'amis** spare *ou* guest room; **chambre de combustion** combustion chamber; **chambre de commerce et d'industrie (CCI)** chamber of commerce and industry; **chambre à coucher** bedroom; **la Chambre des députés** the Chamber of Deputies, ≈ the House (of Commons) (*BRIT*), ≈ the House of Representatives (*US*); **chambre forte** strongroom; **chambre froide** *ou* **frigorifique** cold room; **chambre à gaz** gas chamber; **chambre d'hôte** ≈ bed and breakfast (*in private home*); **chambre des machines** engine-room; **chambre des métiers (CM)** *chamber of commerce for trades*; **chambre meublée** bedsit(ter) (*BRIT*), furnished room; **chambre noire** (*PHOTO*) dark room

chambrer [ʃɑ̃bʀe] *vt* (*vin*) to bring to room temperature

chameau, x [ʃamo] *nm* camel

chamois [ʃamwa] *nm* chamois ♦ *adj*: (**couleur**) **chamois** fawn, buff

champ [ʃɑ̃] *nm* (*aussi INFORM*) field; (*PHOTO: aussi*: **dans le champ**) in the picture; **prendre du champ** to draw back; **laisser le champ libre à qn** to leave sb a clear field; **champ d'action** sphere of operation(s); **champ de bataille** battlefield; **champ de courses** racecourse; **champ d'honneur** field of honour; **champ de manœuvre** (*MIL*) parade ground; **champ de mines** minefield; **champ de tir** shooting *ou* rifle range; **champ visuel** field of vision

champagne [ʃɑ̃paɲ] *nm* champagne

champêtre [ʃɑ̃petʀ(ə)] *adj* country *cpd*, rural

champignon [ʃɑ̃piɲɔ̃] *nm* mushroom; (*terme générique*) fungus (*pl* -i); (*fam: accélérateur*) accel-

erator, gas pedal (*US*); **champignon de couche** *ou* **de Paris** button mushroom; **champignon vénéneux** toadstool, poisonous mushroom

champion, ne [ʃɑ̃pjɔ̃, -ɔn] *adj, nm/f* champion

championnat [ʃɑ̃pjɔna] *nm* championship

chance [ʃɑ̃s] *nf*: **la chance** luck; **une chance** a stroke *ou* piece of luck *ou* good fortune; (*occasion*) a lucky break; **chances** *nfpl* (*probabilités*) chances; **avoir de la chance** to be lucky; **il a des chances de gagner** he has a chance of winning; **il y a de fortes chances pour que Paul soit malade** it's highly probable that Paul is ill; **bonne chance!** good luck!; **encore une chance que tu viennes!** it's lucky you're coming; **je n'ai pas de chance** I'm out of luck; (*toujours*) I never have any luck; **donner sa chance à qn** to give sb a chance

chanceler [ʃɑ̃sle] *vi* to totter

chancelier [ʃɑ̃səlje] *nm* (*allemand*) chancellor; (*d'ambassade*) secretary

chanceux, euse [ʃɑ̃sø, -øz] *adj* lucky, fortunate

chandail [ʃɑ̃daj] *nm* (thick) jumper *ou* sweater

Chandeleur [ʃɑ̃dlœʀ] *nf*: **la Chandeleur** Candlemas

chandelier [ʃɑ̃dəlje] *nm* candlestick; (*à plusieurs branches*) candelabra

chandelle [ʃɑ̃dɛl] *nf* (tallow) candle; (*TENNIS*): **faire une chandelle** to lob; (*AVIAT*): **monter en chandelle** to climb vertically; **tenir la chandelle** to play gooseberry; **dîner aux chandelles** candlelight dinner

change [ʃɑ̃ʒ] *nm* (*COMM*) exchange; **opérations de change** (foreign) exchange transactions; **contrôle des changes** exchange control; **gagner/perdre au change** to be better/worse off (for it); **donner le change à qn** (*fig*) to lead sb up the garden path

changement [ʃɑ̃ʒmɑ̃] *nm* change; **changement de vitesse** (*dispositif*) gears *pl*; (*action*) gear change

changer [ʃɑ̃ʒe] *vt* (*modifier*) to change, alter; (*remplacer, COMM, rhabiller*) to change ♦ *vi* to change, alter; **se changer** to change (o.s.); **changer de** (*remplacer: adresse, nom, voiture etc*) to change one's; (*échanger, alterner: côté, place, train etc*) to change + *npl*; **changer d'air** to get a change of air; **changer de couleur/direction** to change colour/direction; **changer d'idée** to change one's mind; **changer de place avec qn** to change places with sb; **changer de vitesse** (*AUTO*) to change gear; **changer qn/qch de place** to move sb/sth to another place; **changer (de train** *etc*) to change (trains *etc*); **changer qch en** to change sth into

chanson [ʃɑ̃sɔ̃] *nf* song

chant [ʃɑ̃] *nm* song; (*art vocal*) singing; (*d'église*) hymn; (*de poème*) canto; (*TECH*): **posé de** *ou* **sur chant** placed edgeways; **chant de Noël** Christmas carol

chantage [ʃɑ̃taʒ] *nm* blackmail; **faire du chan-**

tage to use blackmail; **soumettre qn à un chantage** to blackmail sb

chanter [ʃɑ̃te] *vt, vi* to sing; **chanter juste/faux** to sing in tune/out of tune; **si cela lui chante** (*fam*) if he feels like it *ou* fancies it

chanteur, euse [ʃɑ̃tœʀ, -øz] *nm/f* singer; **chanteur de charme** crooner

chantier [ʃɑ̃tje] *nm* (building) site; (*sur une route*) roadworks *pl*; **mettre en chantier** to start work on; **chantier naval** shipyard

chantilly [ʃɑ̃tiji] *nf voir* **crème**

chantonner [ʃɑ̃tɔne] *vi, vt* to sing to oneself, hum

chanvre [ʃɑ̃vʀ(ə)] *nm* hemp

chaparder [ʃapaʀde] *vt* to pinch

chapeau, x [ʃapo] *nm* hat; (*PRESSE*) introductory paragraph; **chapeau!** well done!; **chapeau melon** bowler hat; **chapeau mou** trilby; **chapeaux de roues** hub caps

chapelet [ʃaplɛ] *nm* (*REL*) rosary; (*fig*): **un chapelet de** a string of; **dire son chapelet** to tell one's beads

chapelle [ʃapɛl] *nf* chapel; **chapelle ardente** chapel of rest

chapelure [ʃaplyʀ] *nf* (dried) breadcrumbs *pl*

chapiteau, x [ʃapito] *nm* (*ARCHIT*) capital; (*de cirque*) marquee, big top

chapitre [ʃapitʀ(ə)] *nm* chapter; (*fig*) subject, matter; **avoir voix au chapitre** to have a say in the matter

chaque [ʃak] *dét* each, every; (*indéfini*) every

char [ʃaʀ] *nm* (*à foin etc*) cart, waggon; (*de carnaval*) float; **char (d'assaut)** tank

charabia [ʃaʀabja] *nm* (*péj*) gibberish, gobbledygook (*BRIT*)

charade [ʃaʀad] *nf* riddle; (*mimée*) charade

charbon [ʃaʀbɔ̃] *nm* coal; **charbon de bois** charcoal

charcuterie [ʃaʀkytʀi] *nf* (*magasin*) pork butcher's shop and delicatessen; (*produits*) cooked pork meats *pl*

charcutier, ière [ʃaʀkytje, -jɛʀ] *nm/f* pork butcher

chardon [ʃaʀdɔ̃] *nm* thistle

charge [ʃaʀʒ(ə)] *nf* (*fardeau*) load; (*explosif, ÉLEC, MIL, JUR*) charge; (*rôle, mission*) responsibility; **charges** *nfpl* (*du loyer*) service charges; **à la charge de** (*dépendant de*) dependent upon, supported by; (*aux frais de*) chargeable to, payable by; **j'accepte, à charge de revanche** I accept, provided I can do the same for you (in return) one day; **prendre en charge** to take charge of; (*suj: véhicule*) to take on; (*dépenses*) to take care of; **charge utile** (*AUTO*) live load; (*COMM*) payload; **charges sociales** social security contributions

chargé [ʃaʀʒe] *adj* (*voiture, animal, personne*) laden; (*fusil, batterie, caméra*) loaded; (*occupé: emploi du temps, journée*) busy, full; (*estomac*) heavy,

full; (*langue*) furred; (*décoration, style*) heavy, ornate ◆ *nm*: **chargé d'affaires** chargé d'affaires; **chargé de cours** ≃ lecturer; **chargé de** (*responsable de*) responsible for

chargement [ʃaʀʒəmɑ̃] *nm* (*action*) loading; charging; (*objets*) load

charger [ʃaʀʒe] *vt* (*voiture, fusil, caméra, INFORM*) to load; (*batterie*) to charge ◆ *vi* (*MIL etc*) to charge; **se charger de** *vt* to see to, take care of; **charger qn de qch/faire qch** to give sb the responsibility of sth/of doing sth; to put sb in charge of sth/doing sth; **se charger de faire qch** to take it upon o.s. to do sth

chariot [ʃaʀjo] *nm* trolley; (*charrette*) waggon; (*de machine à écrire*) carriage; **chariot élévateur** forklift truck

charité [ʃaʀite] *nf* charity; **faire la charité** to give to charity; to do charitable works; **faire la charité à** to give (something) to; **fête/vente de charité** fête/sale in aid of charity

charmant, e [ʃaʀmɑ̃, -ɑ̃t] *adj* charming

charme [ʃaʀm(ə)] *nm* charm; **charmes** *nmpl* (*appas*) charms; **c'est ce qui en fait le charme** that is its attraction; **faire du charme** to be charming, turn on the charm; **aller** *ou* **se porter comme un charme** to be in the pink

charmer [ʃaʀme] *vt* to charm; **je suis charmé de** I'm delighted to

charnel, le [ʃaʀnɛl] *adj* carnal

charnière [ʃaʀnjɛʀ] *nf* hinge; (*fig*) turning-point

charnu, e [ʃaʀny] *adj* fleshy

charpente [ʃaʀpɑ̃t] *nf* frame(work); (*fig*) structure, framework; (*carrure*) build, frame

charpentier [ʃaʀpɑ̃tje] *nm* carpenter

charpie [ʃaʀpi] *nf*: **en charpie** (*fig*) in shreds *ou* ribbons

charrette [ʃaʀɛt] *nf* cart

charrier [ʃaʀje] *vt* to carry (along); to cart, carry ◆ *vi* (*fam*) to exaggerate

charrue [ʃaʀy] *nf* plough (*BRIT*), plow (*US*)

charter [tʃaʀtœʀ] *nm* (*vol*) charter flight; (*avion*) charter plane

chasse [ʃas] *nf* hunting; (*au fusil*) shooting; (*poursuite*) chase; (*aussi:* **chasse d'eau**) flush; **la chasse est ouverte** the hunting season is open; **la chasse est fermée** it is the close (*BRIT*) *ou* closed (*US*) season; **aller à la chasse** to go hunting; **prendre en chasse, donner la chasse à** to give chase to; **tirer la chasse (d'eau)** to flush the toilet, pull the chain; **chasse aérienne** aerial pursuit; **chasse à courre** hunting; **chasse à l'homme** manhunt; **chasse gardée** private hunting grounds *pl*; **chasse sous-marine** underwater fishing

chasse-neige [ʃasnɛʒ] *nm inv* snowplough (*BRIT*), snowplow (*US*)

chasser [ʃase] *vt* to hunt; (*expulser*) to chase away *ou* out, drive away *ou* out; (*dissiper*) to chase *ou* sweep away; to dispel, drive away

chasseur, euse [ʃasœʀ, -øz] *nm/f* hunter ♦ *nm* (*avion*) fighter; (*domestique*) page (boy), messenger (boy); **chasseur d'images** roving photographer; **chasseur de têtes** (*fig*) headhunter; **chasseurs alpins** mountain infantry

châssis [ʃasi] *nm* (*AUTO*) chassis; (*cadre*) frame; (*de jardin*) cold frame

chat [ʃa] *nm* cat; **chat sauvage** wildcat

châtaigne [ʃatɛɲ] *nf* chestnut

châtaignier [ʃatɛɲe] *nm* chestnut (tree)

châtain [ʃatɛ̃] *adj inv* chestnut (brown); (*personne*) chestnut-haired

château, x [ʃato] *nm* castle; **château d'eau** water tower; **château fort** stronghold, fortified castle; **château de sable** sandcastle

châtier [ʃatje] *vt* to punish, castigate; (*fig: style*) to polish, refine

châtiment [ʃatimã] *nm* punishment, castigation; **châtiment corporel** corporal punishment

chaton [ʃatɔ̃] *nm* (*ZOOL*) kitten; (*BOT*) catkin; (*de bague*) bezel; stone

chatouiller [ʃatuje] *vt* to tickle; (*l'odorat, le palais*) to titillate

chatouilleux, euse [ʃatujø, -øz] *adj* ticklish; (*fig*) touchy, over-sensitive

chatoyer [ʃatwaje] *vi* to shimmer

châtrer [ʃatʀe] *vt* (*mâle*) to castrate; (*femelle*) to spay; (*cheval*) to geld; (*chat, chien*) to doctor (*BRIT*), fix (*US*); (*fig*) to mutilate

chatte [ʃat] *nf* (she-)cat

chaud, e [ʃo, -od] *adj* (*gén*) warm; (*très chaud*) hot; (*fig: félicitations*) hearty; (*discussion*) heated; **il fait chaud** it's warm; it's hot; **manger chaud** to have something hot to eat; **avoir chaud** to be warm; to be hot; **tenir chaud** to keep hot; **ça me tient chaud** it keeps me warm; **tenir au chaud** to keep in a warm place; **rester au chaud** to stay in the warm

chaudière [ʃodjɛʀ] *nf* boiler

chaudron [ʃodʀɔ̃] *nm* cauldron

chauffage [ʃofaʒ] *nm* heating; **chauffage au gaz/à l'électricité/au charbon** gas/electric/solid fuel heating; **chauffage central** central heating; **chauffage par le sol** underfloor heating

chauffard [ʃofaʀ] *nm* (*péj*) reckless driver; roadhog; (*après un accident*) hit-and-run driver

chauffe-eau [ʃofo] *nm inv* water heater

chauffer [ʃofe] *vt* to heat ♦ *vi* to heat up, warm up; (*trop chauffer: moteur*) to overheat; **se chauffer** (*se mettre en train*) to warm up; (*au soleil*) to warm o.s.

chauffeur [ʃofœʀ] *nm* driver; (*privé*) chauffeur; **voiture avec/sans chauffeur** chauffeur-driven/self-drive car; **chauffeur de taxi** taxi driver

chaume [ʃom] *nm* (*du toit*) thatch; (*tiges*) stubble

chaumière [ʃomjɛʀ] *nf* (thatched) cottage

chaussée [ʃose] *nf* road(way); (*digue*) causeway

chausse-pied [ʃospje] *nm* shoe-horn

chausser [ʃose] *vt* (*bottes, skis*) to put on; (*enfant*) to put shoes on; (*suj: soulier*) to fit; **chausser du 38/42** to take size 38/42; **chausser grand/bien** to be big-/well-fitting; **se chausser** to put one's shoes on

chaussette [ʃosɛt] *nf* sock

chausson [ʃosɔ̃] *nm* slipper; (*de bébé*) bootee; **chausson (aux pommes)** (apple) turnover

chaussure [ʃosyʀ] *nf* shoe; (*commerce*): **la chaussure** the shoe industry *ou* trade; **chaussures basses** flat shoes; **chaussures montantes** ankle boots; **chaussures de ski** ski boots

chauve [ʃov] *adj* bald

chauve-souris, *pl* **chauves-souris** [ʃovsuʀi] *nf* bat

chauvin, e [ʃovɛ̃, -in] *adj* chauvinistic; jingoistic

chaux [ʃo] *nf* lime; **blanchi à la chaux** whitewashed

chavirer [ʃaviʀe] *vi* to capsize, overturn

chef [ʃɛf] *nm* head, leader; (*patron*) boss; (*de cuisine*) chef; **au premier chef** extremely, to the nth degree; **de son propre chef** on his *ou* her own initiative; **général/commandant en chef** general-/commander-in-chief; **chef d'accusation** (*JUR*) charge, count (of indictment); **chef d'atelier** (shop) foreman; **chef de bureau** head clerk; **chef de clinique** senior hospital lecturer; **chef d'entreprise** company head; **chef d'équipe** team leader; **chef d'état** head of state; **chef de famille** head of the family; **chef de file** (*de parti etc*) leader; **chef de gare** station master; **chef d'orchestre** conductor (*BRIT*), leader (*US*); **chef de rayon** department(al) supervisor; **chef de service** departmental head

chef-d'œuvre, *pl* **chefs-d'œuvre** [ʃɛdœvʀ(ə)] *nm* masterpiece

chef-lieu, *pl* **chefs-lieux** [ʃɛfljø] *nm* county town

chemin [ʃ(ə)mɛ̃] *nm* path; (*itinéraire, direction, trajet*) way; **en chemin, chemin faisant** on the way; **chemin de fer** railway (*BRIT*), railroad (*US*); **par chemin de fer** by rail; **les chemins de fer** the railways (*BRIT*), the railroad (*US*); **chemin de terre** dirt track

cheminée [ʃ(ə)mine] *nf* chimney; (*à l'intérieur*) chimney piece, fireplace; (*de bateau*) funnel

cheminement [ʃəminmã] *nm* progress; course

cheminot [ʃ(ə)mino] *nm* railwayman (*BRIT*), railroad worker (*US*)

chemise [ʃ(ə)miz] *nf* shirt; (*dossier*) folder; **chemise de nuit** nightdress

chemisier [ʃ(ə)mizje] *nm* blouse

chenal, aux [ʃ(ə)nal, -o] *nm* channel

chêne [ʃɛn] *nm* oak (tree); (*bois*) oak

chenil [ʃ(ə)nil] *nm* kennels *pl*

chenille [ʃ(ə)nij] *nf* (*ZOOL*) caterpillar; (*AUTO*) caterpillar track; **véhicule à chenilles** tracked vehicle, caterpillar

chèque [ʃɛk] *nm* cheque (*BRIT*), check (*US*); **faire/toucher un chèque** to write/cash a cheque; **par**

chèque by cheque; **chèque barré/sans provision** crossed (*BRIT*) /bad cheque; **chèque en blanc** blank cheque; **chèque au porteur** cheque to bearer; **chèque postal** post office cheque, ≈ giro cheque (*BRIT*); **chèque de voyage** traveller's cheque

chéquier [ʃekje] *nm* cheque book (*BRIT*), checkbook (*US*)

cher, ère [ʃɛr] *adj* (*aimé*) dear; (*coûteux*) expensive, dear ♦ *adv*: **coûter/payer cher** to cost/pay a lot ♦ *nf*: **la bonne chère** good food; **cela coûte cher** it's expensive, it costs a lot of money; **mon cher, ma chère** my dear

chercher [ʃɛrʃe] *vt* to look for; (*gloire etc*) to seek; (*INFORM*) to search; **chercher des ennuis/la bagarre** to be looking for trouble/a fight; **aller chercher** to go for, go and fetch; **chercher à faire** to try to do

chercheur, euse [ʃɛrʃœr, -øz] *nm/f* researcher, research worker; **chercheur de** seeker of; hunter of; **chercheur d'or** gold digger

chère [ʃɛr] *adj f, nf voir* **cher**

chéri, e [ʃeri] *adj* beloved, dear; **(mon) chéri** darling

chérir [ʃerir] *vt* to cherish

cherté [ʃɛrte] *nf*: **la cherté de la vie** the high cost of living

chétif, ive [ʃetif, -iv] *adj* puny, stunted

cheval, aux [ʃəval, -o] *nm* horse; (*AUTO*): **cheval (vapeur) (CV)** horsepower *no pl*; **50 chevaux (au frein)** 50 brake horsepower, 50 b.h.p.; **10 chevaux (fiscaux)** 10 horsepower (*for tax purposes*); **faire du cheval** to ride; **à cheval** on horseback; **à cheval sur** astride, straddling; (*fig*) overlapping; **cheval d'arçons** vaulting horse; **cheval à bascule** rocking horse; **cheval de bataille** charger; (*fig*) hobby-horse; **cheval de course** race horse; **chevaux de bois** (*des manèges*) wooden (fairground) horses; (*manège*) merry-go-round

chevalet [ʃəvalɛ] *nm* easel

chevalier [ʃəvalje] *nm* knight; **chevalier servant** escort

chevalière [ʃəvaljɛr] *nf* signet ring

chevalin, e [ʃəvalɛ̃, -in] *adj* of horses, equine; (*péj*) horsy; **boucherie chevaline** horse-meat butcher's

chevaucher [ʃəvoʃe] *vi* (*aussi*: **se chevaucher**) to overlap (each other) ♦ *vt* to be astride, straddle

chevaux [ʃəvo] *nmpl voir* **cheval**

chevelu, e [ʃəvly] *adj* with a good head of hair, hairy (*péj*)

chevelure [ʃəvlyr] *nf* hair *no pl*

chevet [ʃəvɛ] *nm*: **au chevet de qn** at sb's bedside; **lampe de chevet** bedside lamp

cheveu, x [ʃəvø] *nm* hair ♦ *nmpl* (*chevelure*) hair *sg*; **avoir les cheveux courts/en brosse** to have short hair/a crew cut; **se faire couper les cheveux** to get *ou* have one's hair cut; **tiré par les cheveux** (*histoire*) far-fetched

cheville [ʃəvij] *nf* (*ANAT*) ankle; (*de bois*) peg; (*pour enfoncer une vis*) plug; **être en cheville avec qn** to be in cahoots with sb; **cheville ouvrière** (*fig*) kingpin

chèvre [ʃɛvr(ə)] *nf* (she-)goat; **ménager la chèvre et le chou** to try to please everyone

chevreau, x [ʃəvro] *nm* kid

chèvrefeuille [ʃɛvrəfœj] *nm* honeysuckle

chevreuil [ʃəvrœj] *nm* roe deer *inv*; (*CULIN*) venison

chevronné, e [ʃəvrɔne] *adj* seasoned, experienced

┌─────────────┐
│ *MOT CLÉ* │
└─────────────┘

chez [ʃe] *prép* **1** (*à la demeure de*) at; (*: direction*) to; **chez qn** at/to sb's house *ou* place; **chez moi** at home; (*direction*) home

2 (*à l'entreprise de*): **il travaille chez Renault** he works for Renault, he works at Renault('s)

3 (+*profession*) at; (*: direction*) to; **chez le boulanger/dentiste** at *ou* to the baker's/dentist's

4 (*dans le caractère, l'œuvre de*) in; **chez les renards/Racine** in foxes/Racine; **chez les Français** among the French; **chez lui, c'est un devoir** for him, it's a duty

♦ *nm inv*: **mon chez moi/ton chez toi** *etc* my/your *etc* home *ou* place

---

chez-soi [ʃeswa] *nm inv* home

chic [ʃik] *adj inv* chic, smart; (*généreux*) nice, decent ♦ *nm* stylishness; **avoir le chic de** *ou* **pour** to have the knack of *ou* for; **de chic** *adv* off the cuff; **chic!** great!, terrific!

chicane [ʃikan] *nf* (*obstacle*) zigzag; (*querelle*) squabble

chicaner [ʃikane] *vi* (*ergoter*): **chicaner sur** to quibble about

chiche [ʃiʃ] *adj* (*mesquin*) niggardly, mean; (*pauvre*) meagre (*BRIT*), meager (*US*) ♦ *excl* (*en réponse à un défi*) you're on!; **tu n'es pas chiche de lui parler!** you wouldn't (dare) speak to her!

chichis [ʃiʃi] (*fam*) *nmpl* fuss *sg*

chicorée [ʃikɔre] *nf* (*café*) chicory; (*salade*) endive; **chicorée frisée** curly endive

chien [ʃjɛ̃] *nm* dog; (*de pistolet*) hammer; **temps de chien** rotten weather; **vie de chien** dog's life; **couché en chien de fusil** curled up; **chien d'aveugle** guide dog; **chien de chasse** gun dog; **chien de garde** guard dog; **chien policier** police dog; **chien de race** pedigree dog; **chien de traîneau** husky

chiendent [ʃjɛ̃dɑ̃] *nm* couch grass

chien-loup, *pl* **chiens-loups** [ʃjɛ̃lu] *nm* wolfhound

chienne [ʃjɛn] *nf* (she-)dog, bitch

chier [ʃje] *vi* (*fam!*) to crap (*!*), shit (*!*); **faire chier qn** (*importuner*) to bug sb; (*causer des ennuis à*) to piss sb around (*!*); **se faire chier** (*s'ennuyer*) to be bored rigid

chiffon [ʃifɔ̃] *nm* (piece of) rag

chiffonner [ʃifɔne] *vt* to crumple, crease; (*tracasser*) to concern

chiffre [ʃifʀ(ə)] *nm* (*représentant un nombre*) figure; numeral; (*montant, total*) total, sum; (*d'un code*) code, cipher; **chiffres romains/arabes** roman/arabic figures *ou* numerals; **en chiffres ronds** in round figures; **écrire un nombre en chiffres** to write a number in figures; **chiffre d'affaires (CA)** turnover; **chiffre de ventes** sales figures

chiffrer [ʃifʀe] *vt* (*dépense*) to put a figure to, assess; (*message*) to (en)code, cipher ♦ *vi*: **chiffrer à, se chiffrer à** to add up to

chignon [ʃiɲɔ̃] *nm* chignon, bun

Chili [ʃili] *nm*: **le Chili** Chile

chilien, ne [ʃiljɛ̃, -ɛn] *adj* Chilean ♦ *nm/f*: **Chilien,ne** Chilean

chimie [ʃimi] *nf* chemistry

chimique [ʃimik] *adj* chemical; **produits chimiques** chemicals

chimpanzé [ʃɛ̃pɑ̃ze] *nm* chimpanzee

Chine [ʃin] *nf*: **la Chine** China; **la Chine libre, la république de Chine** the Republic of China, Nationalist China (*Taiwan*)

chine [ʃin] *nm* rice paper; (*porcelaine*) china (vase)

chinois, e [ʃinwa, -waz] *adj* Chinese; (*fig: péj*) pernickety, fussy ♦ *nm* (*LING*) Chinese ♦ *nm/f*: **Chinois,e** Chinese

chiot [ʃjo] *nm* pup(py)

chiper [ʃipe] *vt* (*fam*) to pinch

chipoter [ʃipɔte] *vi* (*manger*) to nibble; (*ergoter*) to quibble, haggle

chips [ʃips] *nfpl* (*aussi*: **pommes chips**) crisps (*BRIT*), (potato) chips (*US*)

chiquenaude [ʃiknod] *nf* flick, flip

chirurgical, e, aux [ʃiʀyʀʒikal, -o] *adj* surgical

chirurgie [ʃiʀyʀʒi] *nf* surgery; **chirurgie esthétique** cosmetic *ou* plastic surgery

chirurgien [ʃiʀyʀʒjɛ̃] *nm* surgeon; **chirurgien dentiste** dental surgeon

chlore [klɔʀ] *nm* chlorine

choc [ʃɔk] *nm* impact; shock; crash; (*moral*) shock; (*affrontement*) clash ♦ *adj*: **prix choc** amazing *ou* incredible price/prices; **de choc** (*troupe, traitement*) shock *cpd*; (*patron etc*) high-powered; **choc opératoire/nerveux** post-operative/nervous shock; **choc en retour** return shock; (*fig*) backlash

chocolat [ʃɔkɔla] *nm* chocolate; (*boisson*) (hot) chocolate; **chocolat chaud** hot chocolate; **chocolat à cuire** cooking chocolate; **chocolat au lait** milk chocolate; **chocolat en poudre** drinking chocolate

chœur [kœʀ] *nm* (*chorale*) choir; (*OPÉRA, THÉÂT*) chorus; (*ARCHIT*) choir, chancel; **en chœur** in chorus

choisir [ʃwaziʀ] *vt* to choose; (*entre plusieurs*) to choose, select; **choisir de faire qch** to choose *ou* opt to do sth

choix [ʃwa] *nm* choice; selection; **avoir le choix** to have the choice; **je n'avais pas le choix** I had no choice; **de premier choix** (*COMM*) class *ou* grade one; **de choix** choice *cpd*, selected; **au choix** as you wish *ou* prefer; **de mon/son choix** of my/his *ou* her choosing

chômage [ʃomaʒ] *nm* unemployment; **mettre au chômage** to make redundant, put out of work; **être au chômage** to be unemployed *ou* out of work; **chômage partiel** short-time working; **chômage structurel** structural unemployment; **chômage technique** lay-offs *pl*

chômeur, euse [ʃomœʀ, -øz] *nm/f* unemployed person, person out of work

chope [ʃɔp] *nf* tankard

choper [ʃɔpe] (*fam*) *vt* (*objet, maladie*) to catch

choquer [ʃɔke] *vt* (*offenser*) to shock; (*commotionner*) to shake (up)

chorale [kɔʀal] *nf* choral society, choir

choriste [kɔʀist(ə)] *nm/f* choir member; (*OPÉRA*) chorus member

chose [ʃoz] *nf* thing ♦ *nm* (*fam: machin*) thingamajig ♦ *adj inv*: **être/se sentir tout chose** (*bizarre*) to be/feel a bit odd; (*malade*) to be/feel out of sorts; **dire bien des choses à qn** to give sb's regards to sb; **parler de chose(s) et d'autre(s)** to talk about one thing and another; **c'est peu de chose** it's nothing much

chou, x [ʃu] *nm* cabbage ♦ *adj inv* cute; **mon petit chou** (my) sweetheart; **faire chou blanc** to draw a blank; **feuille de chou** (*fig: journal*) rag; **chou à la crème** cream bun (*made of choux pastry*); **chou de Bruxelles** Brussels sprout

chouchou, te [ʃuʃu, -ut] *nm/f* (*SCOL*) teacher's pet

choucroute [ʃukʀut] *nf* sauerkraut; **choucroute garnie** sauerkraut with cooked meats and potatoes

chouette [ʃwɛt] *nf* owl ♦ *adj* (*fam*) great, smashing

chou-fleur, pl choux-fleurs [ʃuflœʀ] *nm* cauliflower

choyer [ʃwaje] *vt* to cherish; to pamper

chrétien, ne [kʀetjɛ̃, -ɛn] *adj, nm/f* Christian

Christ [kʀist] *nm*: **le Christ** Christ; **christ** (*crucifix etc*) figure of Christ; **Jésus Christ** Jesus Christ

christianisme [kʀistjanism(ə)] *nm* Christianity

chrome [kʀom] *nm* chromium; (*revêtement*) chrome, chromium

chromé, e [kʀome] *adj* chrome-plated, chromium-plated

chronique [kʀɔnik] *adj* chronic ♦ *nf* (*de journal*) column, page; (*historique*) chronicle; (*RADIO, TV*): **la chronique sportive/théâtrale** the sports/theatre review; **la chronique locale** local news and gossip

chronologique [kʀɔnɔlɔʒik] *adj* chronological

chronomètre [kʀɔnɔmɛtʀ(ə)] *nm* stopwatch

chronométrer [kʀɔnɔmetʀe] *vt* to time

chrysanthème [kʀizɑ̃tɛm] *nm* chrysanthemum

chuchotement [ʃyʃɔtmɑ̃] *nm* whisper

chuchoter [ʃyʃɔte] *vt, vi* to whisper

chut *excl* [ʃyt] ♦ *vb* [ʃy] *voir* **choir**

chute [ʃyt] *nf* fall; (*de bois, papier: déchet*) scrap; **la chute des cheveux** hair loss; **faire une chute (de 10 m)** to fall (10 m); **chutes de pluie/neige/snowfalls**; **chute (d'eau)** waterfall; **chute du jour** nightfall; **chute libre** free fall; **chute des reins** small of the back

Chypre [ʃipʀ] *nm*: **le Chypre** Cyprus

-ci, ci- [si] *adv voir* **par, ci-contre, ci-joint** *etc* ♦ *dét*: **ce garçon-ci/-là** this/that boy; **ces femmes-ci/-là** these/those women

cible [sibl(ə)] *nf* target

ciboulette [sibulɛt] *nf* (small) chive

cicatrice [sikatʀis] *nf* scar

cicatriser [sikatʀize] *vt* to heal; **se cicatriser** to heal (up) form a scar

ci-contre [sikɔ̃tʀ(ə)] *adv* opposite

ci-dessous [sidəsu] *adv* below

ci-dessus [sidəsy] *adv* above

cidre [sidʀ(ə)] *nm* cider

Cie *abr* (= **compagnie**) Co.

ciel [sjɛl] *nm* sky; (*REL*) heaven; **ciels** *nmpl* (*PEINTURE etc*) skies; **cieux** *nmpl* sky *sg*, skies; (*REL*) heaven *sg*; **à ciel ouvert** open-air; (*mine*) opencast; **tomber du ciel** (*arriver à l'improviste*) to appear out of the blue; (*être stupéfait*) to be unable to believe one's eyes; **Ciel!** good heavens!; **ciel de lit** canopy

cierge [sjɛʀʒ(ə)] *nm* candle; **cierge pascal** Easter candle

cieux [sjø] *nmpl voir* **ciel**

cigale [sigal] *nf* cicada

cigare [sigaʀ] *nm* cigar

cigarette [sigaʀɛt] *nf* cigarette; **cigarette (à) bout filtre** filter cigarette

ci-gît [siʒi] *adv* here lies

cigogne [sigɔɲ] *nf* stork

ci-inclus, e [siɛ̃kly, -yz] *adj, adv* enclosed

ci-joint, e [siʒwɛ̃, -ɛt] *adj, adv* enclosed; **veuillez trouver ci-joint** please find enclosed

cil [sil] *nm* (eye)lash

cime [sim] *nf* top; (*montagne*) peak

ciment [simɑ̃] *nm* cement; **ciment armé** reinforced concrete

cimetière [simtjɛʀ] *nm* cemetery; (*d'église*) churchyard; **cimetière de voitures** scrapyard

cinéaste [sineast(ə)] *nm/f* film-maker

cinéma [sinema] *nm* cinema; **aller au cinéma** to go to the cinema *ou* pictures *ou* movies; **cinéma d'animation** cartoon (film)

cinématographique [sinematɔgʀafik] *adj* film *cpd*, cinema *cpd*

cinglant, e [sɛ̃glɑ̃, -ɑ̃t] *adj* (*propos, ironie*) scathing, biting; (*échec*) crushing

cinglé, e [sɛ̃gle] *adj* (*fam*) crazy

cinq [sɛ̃k] *num* five

cinquantaine [sɛ̃kɑ̃tɛn] *nf*: **une cinquantaine (de)** about fifty; **avoir la cinquantaine** (*âge*) to be around fifty

cinquante [sɛ̃kɑ̃t] *num* fifty

cinquantenaire [sɛ̃kɑ̃tnɛʀ] *adj, nm/f* fifty-year-old

cinquième [sɛ̃kjɛm] *num* fifth

cintre [sɛ̃tʀ(ə)] *nm* coat-hanger; (*ARCHIT*) arch; **plein cintre** semicircular arch

cintré, e [sɛ̃tʀe] *adj* curved; (*chemise*) fitted, slim-fitting

cirage [siʀaʒ] *nm* (shoe) polish

circonflexe [siʀkɔ̃flɛks(ə)] *adj*: **accent circonflexe** circumflex accent

circonscription [siʀkɔ̃skʀipsjɔ̃] *nf* district; **circonscription électorale** (*d'un député*) constituency; **circonscription militaire** military area

circonscrire [siʀkɔ̃skʀiʀ] *vt* to define, delimit; (*incendie*) to contain; (*propriété*) to mark out; (*sujet*) to define

circonstance [siʀkɔ̃stɑ̃s] *nf* circumstance; (*occasion*) occasion; **œuvre de circonstance** occasional work; **air de circonstance** fitting air; **tête de circonstance** appropriate demeanour (*BRIT*) *ou* demeanor (*US*); **circonstances atténuantes** mitigating circumstances

circuit [siʀkɥi] *nm* (*trajet*) tour, (round) trip; (*ÉLEC, TECH*) circuit; **circuit automobile** motor circuit; **circuit de distribution** distribution network; **circuit fermé** closed circuit; **circuit intégré** integrated circuit

circulaire [siʀkylɛʀ] *adj, nf* circular

circulation [siʀkylasjɔ̃] *nf* circulation; (*AUTO*): **la circulation** (the) traffic; **bonne/mauvaise circulation** good/bad circulation; **mettre en circulation** to put into circulation

circuler [siʀkyle] *vi* to drive (along); to walk along; (*train etc*) to run; (*sang, devises*) to circulate; **faire circuler** (*nouvelle*) to spread (about), circulate; (*badauds*) to move on

cire [siʀ] *nf* wax; **cire à cacheter** sealing wax

ciré [siʀe] *nm* oilskin

cirer [siʀe] *vt* to wax, polish

cirque [siʀk(ə)] *nm* circus; (*arène*) amphitheatre (*BRIT*), amphitheater (*US*); (*GÉO*) cirque; (*fig: désordre*) chaos, bedlam; (*: chichis*) carry-on

cisaille(s) [sizaj] *nf(pl)* (gardening) shears *pl*

ciseau, x [sizo] *nm*: **ciseau (à bois)** chisel ♦ *nmpl* (pair of) scissors; **sauter en ciseaux** to do a scissors jump; **ciseau à froid** cold chisel

ciseler [sizle] *vt* to chisel, carve

citadin, e [sitadɛ̃, -in] *nm/f* city dweller ♦ *adj* town *cpd*, city *cpd*, urban

citation [sitasjɔ̃] *nf* (*d'auteur*) quotation; (*JUR*) summons *sg*; (*MIL: récompense*) mention

cité [site] *nf* town; (*plus grande*) city; **cité ouvrière** (workers') housing estate; **cité universitaire** students' residences *pl*

citer [site] *vt* (*un auteur*) to quote (from); (*nommer*) to name; (*JUR*) to summon; **citer (en exemple)** (*personne*) to hold up (as an example); **je ne veux citer personne** I don't want to name names

citerne [sitɛʀn(ə)] *nf* tank

citoyen, ne [sitwajɛ̃, -ɛn] *nm/f* citizen

citron [sitʀɔ̃] *nm* lemon; **citron pressé** (fresh) lemon juice; **citron vert** lime

citronnade [sitʀɔnad] *nf* lemonade

citrouille [sitʀuj] *nf* pumpkin

civet [sivɛ] *nm* stew; **civet de lièvre** jugged hare

civière [sivjɛʀ] *nf* stretcher

civil, e [sivil] *adj* (*JUR, ADMIN, poli*) civil; (*non militaire*) civilian ♦ *nm* civilian; **en civil** in civilian clothes; **dans le civil** in civilian life

civilisation [sivilizasjɔ̃] *nf* civilization

clair, e [klɛʀ] *adj* light; (*chambre*) light, bright; (*eau, son, fig*) clear ♦ *adv*: **voir clair** to see clearly ♦ *nm*: **mettre au clair** (*notes etc*) to tidy up; **tirer qch au clair** to clear sth up, clarify sth; **bleu clair** light blue; **pour être clair** so as to make it plain; **y voir clair** (*comprendre*) to understand, see; **le plus clair de son temps/argent** the better part of his time/ money; **en clair** (*non codé*) in clear; **clair de lune** moonlight

clairement [klɛʀmɑ̃] *adv* clearly

clairière [klɛʀjɛʀ] *nf* clearing

clairon [klɛʀɔ̃] *nm* bugle

claironner [klɛʀɔne] *vt* (*fig*) to trumpet, shout from the rooftops

clairsemé, e [klɛʀsəme] *adj* sparse

clairvoyant, e [klɛʀvwajɑ̃, -ɑ̃t] *adj* perceptive, clear-sighted

clandestin, e [klɑ̃dɛstɛ̃, -in] *adj* clandestine, covert; (*POL*) underground, clandestine; **passager clandestin** stowaway

clapier [klapje] *nm* (rabbit) hutch

clapoter [klapɔte] *vi* to lap

claque [klak] *nf* (*gifle*) slap; (*THÉAT*) claque ♦ *nm* (*chapeau*) opera hat

claquer [klake] *vi* (*drapeau*) to flap; (*porte*) to bang, slam; (*coup de feu*) to ring out ♦ *vt* (*porte*) to slam, bang; (*doigts*) to snap; **elle claquait des dents** her teeth were chattering; **se claquer un muscle** to pull ou strain a muscle

claquettes [klakɛt] *nfpl* tap-dancing *sg*

clarinette [klaʀinɛt] *nf* clarinet

clarté [klaʀte] *nf* lightness; brightness; (*d'un son, de l'eau*) clearness; (*d'une explication*) clarity

classe [klas] *nf* (*gén*) class; (*SCOL: local*) class(room); (: *leçon*) class; (: *élèves*) class, form; **1ère/2ème classe** 1st/2nd class; **un (soldat de) deuxième classe** (*MIL: armée de terre*) ≃ private (soldier); (: *armée de l'air*) ≃ aircraftman (*BRIT*), ≃ airman basic (*US*); **de classe** luxury *cpd*; **faire ses classes** (*MIL*) to do one's (recruit's) training; **faire la classe** (*SCOL*) to be a *ou* the teacher; to teach; **aller en classe** to go to school; **aller en classe verte/ neige/de mer** to go to the countryside/skiing/to the seaside with the school; **classe préparatoire** class which prepares students for the Grandes Écoles entry exams; *see boxed note*; **classe sociale** social class; **classe touriste** economy class

---

CLASSES PRÉPARATOIRES

Classes préparatoires are the two years of intensive study which coach students for the competitive entry examinations to the 'grandes écoles'. These extremely demanding courses follow the 'baccalauréat' and are usually done at a 'lycée'. Schools which provide such classes are more highly regarded than those which do not.

---

classement [klasmɑ̃] *nm* classifying; filing; grading; closing; (*rang: SCOL*) place; (: *SPORT*) placing; (*liste: SCOL*) class list (in order of merit); (: *SPORT*) placings *pl*; **premier au classement général** (*SPORT*) first overall

classer [klase] *vt* (*idées, livres*) to classify; (*papiers*) to file; (*candidat, concurrent*) to grade; (*personne: juger: péj*) to rate; (*JUR: affaire*) to close; **se classer premier/dernier** to come first/last; (*SPORT*) to finish first/last

classeur [klasœʀ] *nm* file; (*meuble*) filing cabinet; **classeur à feuillets mobiles** ring binder

classique [klasik] *adj* classical; (*habituel*) standard, classic ♦ *nm* classic; classical author; **études classiques** classical studies, classics

clause [kloz] *nf* clause

clavecin [klavsɛ̃] *nm* harpsichord

clavicule [klavikyl] *nf* clavicle, collarbone

clavier [klavje] *nm* keyboard

clé, clef [kle] *nf* key; (*MUS*) clef; (*de mécanicien*) spanner, wrench (*US*) ♦ *adj*: **problème/position clé** key problem/position; **mettre sous clé** to place under lock and key; **prendre la clé des champs** to run away, make off; **prix clés en main** (*d'une voiture*) on-the-road price; (*d'un appartement*) price with immediate entry; **clé de sol/de fa/ d'ut** treble/bass/alto clef; **livre/film** etc **à clé** book/ film etc in which real people are depicted under fictitious names; **à la clé** (*à la fin*) at the end of it all; **clé anglaise** = **clé à molette**; **clé de contact** ignition key; **clé à molette** adjustable spanner (*BRIT*) ou wrench, monkey wrench; **clé de voûte** keystone

clément, e [klemɑ̃, -ɑ̃t] *adj* (*temps*) mild; (*indulgent*) lenient

clerc [klɛʀ] *nm*: **clerc de notaire** ou **d'avoué** lawyer's clerk

clergé [klɛʀʒe] *nm* clergy

cliché [klife] *nm* (*PHOTO*) negative; print; (*TYPO*) (printing) plate; (*LING*) cliché

client, e [klijã, -ãt] *nm/f* (*acheteur*) customer, client; (*d'hôtel*) guest, patron; (*du docteur*) patient; (*de l'avocat*) client

clientèle [klijãtɛl] *nf* (*du magasin*) customers *pl*, clientèle; (*du docteur, de l'avocat*) practice; **accorder sa clientèle à** to give one's custom to; **retirer sa clientèle à** to take one's business away from

cligner [kliɲe] *vi*: **cligner des yeux** to blink (one's eyes); **cligner de l'œil** to wink

clignotant [kliɲɔtã] *nm* (*AUTO*) indicator

clignoter [kliɲɔte] *vi* (*étoiles etc*) to twinkle; (*lumière: à intervalles réguliers*) to flash; (: *vaciller*) to flicker; (*yeux*) to blink

climat [klima] *nm* climate

climatisation [klimatizasjɔ̃] *nf* air conditioning

climatisé, e [klimatize] *adj* air-conditioned

clin d'œil [klɛ̃dœj] *nm* wink; **en un clin d'œil** in a flash

clinique [klinik] *adj* clinical ♦ *nf* nursing home, private) clinic

clinquant, e [klɛ̃kɑ̃, -ãt] *adj* flashy

clip [klip] *nm* (*pince*) clip; (*vidéo*) pop (*ou* promotional) video

cliquer [klike] *vi* (*INFORM*) to click

cliqueter [klikte] *vi* to clash; (*ferraille, clefs, monnaie*) to jangle, jingle; (*verres*) to chink

clochard, e [klɔʃaʀ, -aʀd(ə)] *nm/f* tramp

cloche [klɔʃ] *nf* (*d'église*) bell; (*fam*) clot; (*chapeau*) cloche (hat); **cloche à fromage** cheese-cover

cloche-pied [klɔʃpje]: **à cloche-pied** *adv* on one leg, hopping (along)

clocher [klɔʃe] *nm* church tower; (*en pointe*) steeple ♦ *vi* (*fam*) to be *ou* go wrong; **de clocher** (*péj*) parochial

cloison [klwazɔ̃] *nf* partition (wall); **cloison étanche** (*fig*) impenetrable barrier, brick wall (*fig*)

cloître [klwatʀ(ə)] *nm* cloister

cloîtrer [klwatʀe] *vt*: **se cloîtrer** to shut o.s. away; (*REL*) to enter a convent *ou* monastery

cloque [klɔk] *nf* blister

clore [klɔʀ] *vt* to close; **clore une session** (*INFORM*) to log out

clos, e [klo, -oz] *pp de* **clore** ♦ *adj voir* **maison, huis, vase** ♦ *nm* (enclosed) field

clôture [klotyʀ] *nf* closure, closing; (*barrière*) enclosure, fence

clôturer [klotyʀe] *vt* (*terrain*) to enclose, close off; (*festival, débats*) to close

clou [klu] *nm* nail; (*MÉD*) boil; **clous** *nmpl* = **passage clouté; pneus à clous** studded tyres; **le clou du spectacle** the highlight of the show; **clou de girofle** clove

clouer [klue] *vt* to nail down (*ou* up); (*fig*): **clouer sur/contre** to pin to/against

clown [klun] *nm* clown; **faire le clown** (*fig*) to clown (about), play the fool

club [klœb] *nm* club

CMU *sigle f* (= *couverture maladie universelle*) system of free health care for those on low incomes

CNRS *sigle m* = *Centre national de la recherche scientifique*

coaguler [kɔagyle] *vi, vt*: **se coaguler** *vi* to coagulate

coasser [kɔase] *vi* to croak

cobaye [kɔbaj] *nm* guinea-pig

coca® [kɔka] *nm* Coke®

cocaïne [kɔkain] *nf* cocaine

cocasse [kɔkas] *adj* comical, funny

coccinelle [kɔksinɛl] *nf* ladybird (*BRIT*), ladybug (*US*)

cocher [kɔʃe] *nm* coachman ♦ *vt* to tick off; (*entailler*) to notch

cochère [kɔʃɛʀ] *adj f*: **porte cochère** carriage entrance

cochon, ne [kɔʃɔ̃, -ɔn] *nm* pig ♦ *nm/f* (*péj: sale*) (filthy) pig; (: *méchant*) swine ♦ *adj* (*fam*) dirty, smutty; **cochon d'Inde** guinea-pig; **cochon de lait** (*CULIN*) sucking pig

cochonnerie [kɔʃɔnʀi] *nf* (*fam: saleté*) filth; (: *marchandises*) rubbish, trash

cocktail [kɔktɛl] *nm* cocktail; (*réception*) cocktail party

coco [kɔko] *nm voir* **noix**

cocorico [kɔkɔriko] *excl, nm* cock-a-doodle-do

cocotier [kɔkɔtje] *nm* coconut palm

cocotte [kɔkɔt] *nf* (*en fonte*) casserole; **ma cocotte** (*fam*) sweetie (*pie*); **cocotte (minute)**® pressure cooker; **cocotte en papier** paper shape

cocu [kɔky] *nm* cuckold

code [kɔd] *nm* code; **se mettre en code(s)** to dip (*BRIT*) *ou* dim (*US*) one's (head)lights; **code à barres** bar code; **code de caractère** (*INFORM*) character code; **code civil** Common Law; **code machine** machine code; **code pénal** penal code; **code postal** (*numéro*) postcode (*BRIT*), zip code (*US*); **code de la route** highway code; **code secret** cipher

cœur [kœʀ] *nm* heart; (*CARTES: couleur*) hearts *pl*; (: *carte*) heart; (*CULIN*): **cœur de laitue/d'artichaut** lettuce/artichoke heart; (*fig*): **cœur du débat** heart of the debate; **cœur de l'été** height of summer; **cœur de la forêt** depths *pl* of the forest; **affaire de cœur** love affair; **avoir bon cœur** to be kind-hearted; **avoir mal au cœur** to feel sick; **contre** *ou* **sur son cœur** to one's breast; **opérer qn à cœur ouvert** to perform open-heart surgery on sb; **recevoir qn à cœur ouvert** to welcome sb with open arms; **parler à cœur ouvert** to open one's heart; **de tout son cœur** with all one's heart; **avoir le cœur gros** *ou* **serré** to have a heavy heart; **en avoir le cœur net** to be clear in one's own mind (about it); **par cœur** by heart; **de bon cœur** willingly; **avoir à cœur de faire** to be very keen to do; **cela lui tient à cœur** that's (very) close to his heart;

prendre les choses à cœur to take things to heart; **à cœur joie** to one's heart's content; **être de tout cœur avec qn** to be (completely) in accord with sb

coffre [kɔfʀ(ə)] *nm* (*meuble*) chest; (*coffre-fort*) safe; (*d'auto*) boot (*BRIT*), trunk (*US*); **avoir du coffre** (*fam*) to have a lot of puff

coffre-fort, *pl* **coffres-forts** [kɔfʀəfɔʀ] *nm* safe

coffret [kɔfʀɛ] *nm* casket; **coffret à bijoux** jewel box

cognac [kɔɲak] *nm* brandy, cognac

cogner [kɔɲe] *vi* to knock, bang; **se cogner** to bump o.s.

cohérent, e [kɔeʀɑ̃, -ɑ̃t] *adj* coherent

cohorte [kɔɔʀt(ə)] *nf* troop

cohue [kɔy] *nf* crowd

coi, coite [kwa, kwat] *adj*: **rester coi** to remain silent

coiffe [kwaf] *nf* headdress

coiffé, e [kwafe] *adj*: **bien/mal coiffé** with tidy/untidy hair; **coiffé d'un béret** wearing a beret; **coiffé en arrière** with one's hair brushed *ou* combed back; **coiffé en brosse** with a crew cut

coiffer [kwafe] *vt* (*fig*) to cover, top; **coiffer qn** to do sb's hair; **coiffer qn d'un béret** to put a beret on sb; **se coiffer** to do one's hair; to put on a *ou* one's hat

coiffeur, euse [kwafœʀ, -øz] *nm/f* hairdresser ♦ *nf* (*table*) dressing table

coiffure [kwafyʀ] *nf* (*cheveux*) hairstyle, hairdo; (*chapeau*) hat, headgear *no pl*; (*art*): **la coiffure** hairdressing

coin [kwɛ̃] *nm* corner; (*pour graver*) die; (*pour coincer*) wedge; (*poinçon*) hallmark; **l'épicerie du coin** the local grocer; **dans le coin** (*aux alentours*) in the area, around about; locally; **au coin du feu** by the fireside; **du coin de l'œil** out of the corner of one's eye; **regard en coin** side(ways) glance; **sourire en coin** half-smile

coincé, e [kwɛ̃se] *adj* stuck, jammed; (*fig: inhibé*) inhibited, with hang-ups

coincer [kwɛ̃se] *vt* to jam; (*fam*) to catch (out); to nab; **se coincer** to get stuck *ou* jammed

coïncidence [kɔɛ̃sidɑ̃s] *nf* coincidence

coïncider [kɔɛ̃side] *vi*: **coïncider (avec)** to coincide (with); (*correspondre: témoignage etc*) to correspond *ou* tally (with)

coing [kwɛ̃] *nm* quince

col [kɔl] *nm* (*de chemise*) collar; (*encolure, cou*) neck; (*de montagne*) pass; **col roulé** polo-neck; **col de l'utérus** cervix

colère [kɔlɛʀ] *nf* anger; **une colère** a fit of anger; **être en colère (contre qn)** to be angry (with sb); **mettre qn en colère** to make sb angry; **se mettre en colère** to get angry

coléreux, euse [kɔleʀø, -øz] *adj*, **colérique** [kɔleʀik] *adj* quick-tempered, irascible

colifichet [kɔlifiʃɛ] *nm* trinket

colimaçon [kɔlimasɔ̃] *nm*: **escalier en colimaçon** spiral staircase

colin [kɔlɛ̃] *nm* hake

colique [kɔlik] *nf* diarrhoea (*BRIT*), diarrhea (*US*); (*douleurs*) colic (*pains pl*); (*fam: personne ou chose ennuyeuse*) pain

colis [kɔli] *nm* parcel; **par colis postal** by parcel post

collaborateur, trice [kɔlabɔʀatœʀ, -tʀis] *nm/f* (*aussi POL*) collaborator; (*d'une revue*) contributor

collaborer [kɔlabɔʀe] *vi* to collaborate; (*aussi*: **collaborer à**) to collaborate on; (*revue*) to contribute to

collant, e [kɔlɑ̃, -ɑ̃t] *adj* sticky; (*robe etc*) clinging, skintight; (*péj*) clinging ♦ *nm* (*bas*) tights *pl*

collation [kɔlasjɔ̃] *nf* light meal

colle [kɔl] *nf* glue; (*à papiers peints*) (wallpaper) paste; (*devinette*) teaser, riddle; (*SCOL fam*) detention; **colle forte** superglue®

collecte [kɔlɛkt(ə)] *nf* collection; **faire une collecte** to take up a collection

collectif, ive [kɔlɛktif, -iv] *adj* collective; (*visite, billet etc*) group *cpd* ♦ *nm*: **collectif budgétaire** mini-budget (*BRIT*), mid-term budget; **immeuble collectif** block of flats

collection [kɔlɛksjɔ̃] *nf* collection; (*ÉDITION*) series; **pièce de collection** collector's item; **faire (la) collection de** to collect; **(toute) une collection de ...** (*fig*) a (complete) set of ...

collectionner [kɔlɛksjɔne] *vt* (*tableaux, timbres*) to collect

collectionneur, euse [kɔlɛksjɔnœʀ, -øz] *nm/f* collector

collectivité [kɔlɛktivite] *nf* group; **la collectivité** the community, the collectivity; **les collectivités locales** local authorities

collège [kɔlɛʒ] *nm* (*école*) (secondary) school; (*assemblée*) body; **collège électoral** electoral college; **collège d'enseignement secondaire (CES)** ≈ junior secondary school (*BRIT*), ≈ junior high school (*US*); *see boxed note*

COLLÈGE

A **collège** is a state secondary school for children between 11 and 15 years of age. Pupils follow a national curriculum which prescribes a common core along with several options. Schools are free to arrange their own timetable and choose their own teaching methods. Before leaving this phase of their education, students are assessed by examination and course work for their 'brevet des collèges'.

---

collégien, ne [kɔleʒjɛ̃, -ɛn] *nm/f* secondary school pupil (*BRIT*), high school student (*US*)

collègue [kɔleg] *nm/f* colleague

coller [kɔle] *vt* (*papier, timbre*) to stick (on); (*affiche*) to stick up; (*appuyer, placer contre*): **coller son front à la vitre** to press one's face to the window; (*enveloppe*) to stick down; (*morceaux*) to stick *ou* glue together; (*fam: mettre, fourrer*) to stick, shove; (*SCOL fam*) to keep in, give detention to ♦ *vi* (*être collant*) to be sticky; (*adhérer*) to stick; **coller qch sur** to stick (*ou* paste *ou* glue) sth on(to); **coller à** to stick to; (*fig*) to cling to

collet [kɔlɛ] *nm* (*piège*) snare, noose; (*cou*): **prendre qn au collet** to grab sb by the throat; **collet monté** *adj inv* straight-laced

collier [kɔlje] *nm* (*bijou*) necklace; (*de chien, TECH*) collar; **collier (de barbe), barbe en collier** narrow beard along the line of the jaw; **collier de serrage** choke collar

collimateur [kɔlimatœR] *nm*: **être dans le collimateur** (*fig*) to be in the firing line; **avoir qn/qch dans le collimateur** (*fig*) to have sb/sth in one's sights

colline [kɔlin] *nf* hill

collision [kɔlizjɔ̃] *nf* collision, crash; **entrer en collision (avec)** to collide (with)

colloque [kɔlɔk] *nm* colloquium, symposium

collyre [kɔliʀ] *nm* (*MÉD*) eye lotion

colmater [kɔlmate] *vt* (*fuite*) to seal off; (*brèche*) to plug, fill in

colombe [kɔlɔ̃b] *nf* dove

Colombie [kɔlɔ̃bi] *nf*: **la Colombie** Colombia

colon [kɔlɔ̃] *nm* settler; (*enfant*) boarder (*in children's holiday camp*)

colonel [kɔlɔnɛl] *nm* colonel; (*de l'armée de l'air*) group captain

colonie [kɔlɔni] *nf* colony; **colonie (de vacances)** holiday camp (*for children*)

colonne [kɔlɔn] *nf* column; **se mettre en colonne par deux/quatre** to get into twos/fours; **en colonne par deux** in double file; **colonne de secours** rescue party; **colonne (vertébrale)** spine, spinal column

colorant [kɔlɔʀɑ̃] *nm* colo(u)ring

colorer [kɔlɔʀe] *vt* to colour (*BRIT*), color (*US*); **se colorer** *vi* to turn red; to blush

colorier [kɔlɔʀje] *vt* to colo(u)r (in); **album à colorier** colouring book

coloris [kɔlɔʀi] *nm* colo(u)r, shade

colporter [kɔlpɔʀte] *vt* to peddle

colza [kɔlza] *nm* rape(seed)

coma [kɔma] *nm* coma; **être dans le coma** to be in a coma

combat [kɔ̃ba] *vb voir* **combattre** ♦ *nm* fight; fighting *no pl*; **combat de boxe** boxing match; **combat de rues** street fighting *no pl*; **combat singulier** single combat

combattant [kɔ̃batɑ̃] *vb voir* **combattre** ♦ *nm* combatant; (*d'une rixe*) brawler; **ancien combat-**

tant war veteran

combattre [kɔ̃batʀ(ə)] *vi* to fight ♦ *vt* to fight; (*épidémie, ignorance*) to combat

combien [kɔ̃bjɛ̃] *adv* (*quantité*) how much; (*nombre*) how many; (*exclamatif*) how; **combien de** how much; how many; **combien de temps** how long, how much time; **c'est combien?, ça fait combien?** how much is it?; **combien coûte/pèse ceci?** how much does this cost/weigh?; **vous mesurez combien?** what size are you?; **ça fait combien en largeur?** how wide is that?

combinaison [kɔ̃binezɔ̃] *nf* combination; (*astuce*) device, scheme; (*de femme*) slip; (*d'aviateur*) flying suit; (*d'homme-grenouille*) wetsuit; (*bleu de travail*) boilersuit (*BRIT*), coveralls *pl* (*US*)

combine [kɔ̃bin] *nf* trick; (*péj*) scheme, fiddle (*BRIT*)

combiné [kɔ̃bine] *nm* (*aussi*: **combiné téléphonique**) receiver; (*SKI*) combination (event); (*vêtement de femme*) corselet

combiner [kɔ̃bine] *vt* to combine; (*plan, horaire*) to work out, devise

comble [kɔ̃bl(ə)] *adj* (*salle*) packed (full) ♦ *nm* (*du bonheur, plaisir*) height; **combles** *nmpl* (*CONSTR*) attic *sg*, loft *sg*; **de fond en comble** from top to bottom; **pour comble de malchance** to cap it all; **c'est le comble!** that beats everything!, that takes the biscuit! (*BRIT*); **sous les combles** in the attic

combler [kɔ̃ble] *vt* (*trou*) to fill in; (*besoin, lacune*) to fill; (*déficit*) to make good; (*satisfaire*) to gratify, fulfil (*BRIT*), fulfill (*US*); **combler qn de joie** to fill sb with joy; **combler qn d'honneurs** to shower sb with honours

combustible [kɔ̃bystibl(ə)] *adj* combustible ♦ *nm* fuel

comédie [kɔmedi] *nf* comedy; (*fig*) playacting *no pl*; **jouer la comédie** (*fig*) to put on an act; **comédie musicale** musical; *see boxed note*

COMÉDIE FRANÇAISE

Founded in 1680 by Louis XIV, the **Comédie française** is the French national theatre. The company is subsidized by the state and mainly performs in the Palais Royal in Paris, tending to concentrate on classical French drama.

---

comédien, ne [kɔmedjɛ̃, -ɛn] *nm/f* actor/actress; (*comique*) comedy actor/actress, comedian/comedienne; (*fig*) sham

comestible [kɔmɛstibl(ə)] *adj* edible; **comestibles** *nmpl* foods

comique [kɔmik] *adj* (*drôle*) comical; (*THÉÂT*) comic ♦ *nm* (*artiste*) comic, comedian; **le comique de qch** the funny *ou* comical side of sth

comité [kɔmite] *nm* committee; **petit comité** select group; **comité directeur** management committee; **comité d'entreprise (CE)** works council;

comité des fêtes festival committee
commandant [kɔmɑ̃dɑ̃] *nm* (*gén*) commander, commandant; (*MIL: grade*) major; (: *armée de l'air*) squadron leader; (*NAVIG*) captain; **commandant (de bord)** (*AVIAT*) captain
commande [kɔmɑ̃d] *nf* (*COMM*) order; (*INFORM*) command; **commandes** *nfpl* (*AVIAT etc*) controls; **passer une commande (de)** to put in an order (for); **sur commande** to order; **commande à distance** remote control; **véhicule à double commande** vehicle with dual controls
commandement [kɔmɑ̃dmɑ̃] *nm* command; (*ordre*) command, order; (*REL*) commandment
commander [kɔmɑ̃de] *vt* (*COMM*) to order; (*diriger, ordonner*) to command; **commander à** (*MIL*) to command; (*contrôler, maîtriser*) to have control over; **commander à qn de faire** to command *ou* order sb to do
commando [kɔmɑ̃do] *nm* commando (squad)

MOT-CLÉ
---

comme [kɔm] *prép* **1** (*comparaison*) like; **tout comme son père** just like his father; **fort comme un bœuf** as strong as an ox; **joli comme tout** ever so pretty
2 (*manière*) like; **faites-le comme ça** do it like this, do it this way; **comme ça ou cela on n'aura pas d'ennuis** that way we won't have any problems; **comme ci, comme ça** so-so, middling; **comment ça va? – comme ça** how are things? – OK; **comme on dit** as they say
3 (*en tant que*) as a; **donner comme prix** to give as a prize; **travailler comme secrétaire** to work as a secretary
4: **comme quoi** (*d'où il s'ensuit que*) which shows that; **il a écrit une lettre comme quoi il …** he's written a letter saying that …
5: **comme il faut** *phr adv* properly; *phr adj* (*correct*) proper, correct
◆ *conj* **1** (*ainsi que*) as; **elle écrit comme elle parle** she writes as she talks; **comme si** as if
2 (*au moment où, alors que*) as; **il est parti comme j'arrivais** he left as I arrived
3 (*parce que, puisque*) as, since; **comme il était en retard, il …** as he was late, he …
◆ *adv*: **comme il est fort/c'est bon!** he's so strong/it's so good!; **il est malin comme c'est pas permis** he's as smart as anything

commémorer [kɔmemɔre] *vt* to commemorate
commencement [kɔmɑ̃smɑ̃] *nm* beginning, start, commencement; **commencements** *nmpl* (*débuts*) beginnings
commencer [kɔmɑ̃se] *vt* to begin, start, commence ◆ *vi* to begin, start, commence; **commencer à ou de faire** to begin *ou* start doing; **commencer par qch** to begin with sth; **commencer par faire qch** to begin by doing sth
comment [kɔmɑ̃] *adv* how; **comment?** (*que dites-vous*) (I beg your) pardon?; **comment!** what! ◆ *nm*: **le comment et le pourquoi** the whys and wherefores; **et comment!** and how!; **comment donc!** of course!; **comment faire?** how will we do it?; **comment se fait-il que?** how is it that?
commentaire [kɔmɑ̃tɛr] *nm* comment; remark; **commentaire (de texte)** (*SCOL*) commentary; **commentaire sur image** voice-over
commenter [kɔmɑ̃te] *vt* (*jugement, événement*) to comment (up)on; (*RADIO, TV: match, manifestation*) to cover, give a commentary on
commérages [kɔmeraʒ] *nmpl* gossip *sg*
commerçant, e [kɔmɛrsɑ̃, -ɑ̃t] *adj* commercial; trading; (*rue*) shopping *cpd*; (*personne*) commercially shrewd ◆ *nm/f* shopkeeper, trader
commerce [kɔmɛrs(ə)] *nm* (*activité*) trade, commerce; (*boutique*) business; **le petit commerce** small shopowners *pl*, small traders *pl*; **faire commerce de** to trade in; (*fig: péj*) to trade on; **chambre de commerce** Chamber of Commerce; **livres de commerce** (account) books; **vendu dans le commerce** sold in the shops; **vendu hors-commerce** sold directly to the public; **commerce en ou de gros/détail** wholesale/retail trade; **commerce électronique** e-commerce; **commerce équitable** fair trade; **commerce intérieur/extérieur** home/foreign trade
commercial, e, aux [kɔmɛrsjal, -o] *adj* commercial, trading; (*péj*) commercial ◆ *nm*: **les commerciaux** the commercial people
commercialiser [kɔmɛrsjalize] *vt* to market
commère [kɔmɛr] *nf* gossip
commettre [kɔmɛtr(ə)] *vt* to commit; **se commettre** to compromise one's good name
commis [kɔmi] *vb voir* **commettre** ◆ *nm* (*de magasin*) (shop) assistant (*BRIT*), sales clerk (*US*); (*de banque*) clerk; **commis voyageur** commercial traveller (*BRIT*) *ou* traveler (*US*)
commis, e [kɔmi, -iz] *pp de* **commettre**
commissaire [kɔmisɛr] *nm* (*de police*) ≈ (police) superintendent (*BRIT*), ≈ (police) captain (*US*); (*de rencontre sportive etc*) steward; **commissaire du bord** (*NAVIG*) purser; **commissaire aux comptes** (*ADMIN*) auditor
commissaire-priseur, *pl* **commissaires-priseurs** [kɔmisɛrprizœr] *nm* (*official*) auctioneer
commissariat [kɔmisarja] *nm*: **commissariat (de police)** police station; (*ADMIN*) commissionership
commission [kɔmisjɔ̃] *nf* (*comité, pourcentage*) commission; (*message*) message; (*course*) errand; **commissions** *nfpl* (*achats*) shopping *sg*; **commission d'examen** examining board
commode [kɔmɔd] *adj* (*pratique*) convenient, handy; (*facile*) easy; (*air, personne*) easy-going; (*personne*): **pas commode** awkward (to deal with) ◆ *nf* chest of drawers
commodité [kɔmɔdite] *nf* convenience
commotion [kɔmosjɔ̃] *nf*: **commotion**

(cérébrale) concussion

commotionné, e [kɔmosjɔne] *adj* shocked, shaken

commun, e [kɔmœ̃, -yn] *adj* common; *(pièce)* communal, shared; *(réunion, effort)* joint ◆ *nf* *(ADMIN)* commune, ≈ district; *(: urbaine)* ≈ borough; **communs** *nmpl (bâtiments)* outbuildings; **cela sort du commun** it's out of the ordinary; **le commun des mortels** the common run of people; **sans commune mesure** incomparable; **être commun à** *(suj: chose)* to be shared by; **en commun (faire)** jointly; **mettre en commun** to pool, share; **peu commun** unusual; **d'un commun accord** of one accord; with one accord

communauté [kɔmynote] *nf* community; *(JUR)*: **régime de la communauté** communal estate settlement

commune [kɔmyn] *adj f, nf voir* **commun**

communicatif, ive [kɔmynikatif, -iv] *adj (personne)* communicative; *(rire)* infectious

communication [kɔmynikasjɔ̃] *nf* communication; **communication (téléphonique)** (telephone) call; **avoir la communication (avec)** to get *ou* be through (to); **vous avez la communication** you're through; **donnez-moi la communication avec** put me through to; **mettre qn en communication avec qn** *(en contact)* to put sb in touch with sb; *(au téléphone)* to connect sb with sb; **communication interurbaine** long-distance call; **communication en PCV** reverse charge *(BRIT) ou* collect *(US)* call; **communication avec préavis** personal call

communier [kɔmynje] *vi (REL)* to receive communion; *(fig)* to be united

communion [kɔmynjɔ̃] *nf* communion

communiquer [kɔmynike] *vt (nouvelle, dossier)* to pass on, convey; *(maladie)* to pass on; *(peur etc)* to communicate; *(chaleur, mouvement)* to transmit ◆ *vi* to communicate; **communiquer avec** *(suj: salle)* to communicate with; **se communiquer à** *(se propager)* to spread to

communisme [kɔmynism(ə)] *nm* communism

communiste [kɔmynist(ə)] *adj, nm/f* communist

commutateur [kɔmytatœR] *nm (ÉLEC)* (change-over) switch, commutator

compact, e [kɔpakt] *adj* dense; compact

compagne [kɔpaɲ] *nf* companion

compagnie [kɔpaɲi] *nf (firme, MIL)* company; *(groupe)* gathering; *(présence)*: **la compagnie de qn** sb's company; **homme/femme de compagnie** escort; **tenir compagnie à qn** to keep sb company; **fausser compagnie à qn** to give sb the slip, slip *ou* sneak away from sb; **en compagnie de** in the company of sb; **Dupont et compagnie, Dupont et Cie** Dupont and Company, Dupont and Co.; **compagnie aérienne** airline (company)

compagnon [kɔpaɲɔ̃] *nm* companion; *(autrefois: ouvrier)* craftsman; journeyman

comparable [kɔparabl(ə)] *adj*: **comparable (à)** comparable (to)

comparaison [kɔparɛzɔ̃] *nf* comparison; *(métaphore)* simile; **en comparaison (de)** in comparison (with); **par comparaison (à)** by comparison (with)

comparaître [kɔparɛtr(ə)] *vi*: **comparaître (devant)** to appear (before)

comparer [kɔpare] *vt* to compare; **comparer qch/qn à** *ou* **et** *(pour choisir)* to compare sth/sb with *ou* and; *(pour établir une similitude)* to compare sth/sb to *ou* and

compartiment [kɔpartimã] *nm* compartment

comparution [kɔparysjɔ̃] *nf* appearance

compas [kɔpa] *nm (GÉOM)* (pair of) compasses *pl*; *(NAVIG)* compass

compatible [kɔpatibl(ə)] *adj*: **compatible (avec)** compatible (with)

compatir [kɔpatir] *vi*: **compatir (à)** to sympathize (with)

compatriote [kɔpatrijɔt] *nm/f* compatriot, fellow countryman/woman

compensation [kɔpɑ̃sasjɔ̃] *nf* compensation; *(BANQUE)* clearing; **en compensation** in *ou* as compensation

compenser [kɔpɑ̃se] *vt* to compensate for, make up for

compère [kɔpɛR] *nm* accomplice; fellow musician *ou* comedian *etc*

compétence [kɔpetɑ̃s] *nf* competence

compétent, e [kɔpetɑ̃, -ɑ̃t] *adj (apte)* competent, capable; *(JUR)* competent

compétition [kɔpetisjɔ̃] *nf (gén)* competition; *(SPORT: épreuve)* event; **la compétition** competitive sport; **être en compétition avec** to be competing with; **la compétition automobile** motor racing

complainte [kɔplɛ̃t] *nf* lament

complaire [kɔplɛR]: **se complaire** *vi*: **se complaire dans/parmi** to take pleasure in/in being among

complaisance [kɔplɛzɑ̃s] *nf* kindness; *(péj)* indulgence; *(: fatuité)* complacency; **attestation de complaisance** certificate produced to oblige a patient *etc*; **pavillon de complaisance** flag of convenience

complaisant, e [kɔplɛzɑ̃, -ɑ̃t] *vb voir* **complaire** ◆ *adj (aimable)* kind, obliging; *(péj)* accommodating; *(: fat)* complacent

complément [kɔplemɑ̃] *nm* complement; *(reste)* remainder; *(LING)* complement; **complément d'information** *(ADMIN)* supplementary *ou* further information; **complément d'agent** agent; **complément (d'objet) direct/indirect** direct/indirect object; **complément (circonstanciel) de lieu/temps** adverbial phrase of place/time; **complément de nom** possessive phrase

complémentaire [kɔplemɑ̃tɛR] *adj* complementary; *(additionnel)* supplementary

complet, ète [kɔplɛ, -ɛt] *adj* complete; *(plein:*

hôtel etc) full ♦ *nm* (*aussi:* **complet-veston**) suit; **au (grand) complet** all together

complètement [kɔ̃plεtmɑ̃] *adv* (*en entier*) completely; (*absolument: fou, faux etc*) absolutely; (*à fond: étudier etc*) fully, in depth

compléter [kɔ̃plete] *vt* (*porter à la quantité voulue*) to complete; (*augmenter*) to complement, supplement; to add to; **se compléter** (*personnes*) to complement one another; (*collection etc*) to become complete

complexe [kɔ̃plεks(ə)] *adj* complex ♦ *nm* (*PSYCH*) complex, hang-up; (*bâtiments*): **complexe hospitalier/industriel** hospital/industrial complex

complexé, e [kɔ̃plεkse] *adj* mixed-up, hung-up

complication [kɔ̃plikasjɔ̃] *nf* complexity, intricacy; (*difficulté, ennui*) complication; **complications** *nfpl* (*MÉD*) complications

complice [kɔ̃plis] *nm* accomplice

complicité [kɔ̃plisite] *nf* complicity

compliment [kɔ̃plimɑ̃] *nm* (*louange*) compliment; **compliments** *nmpl* (*félicitations*) congratulations

compliqué, e [kɔ̃plike] *adj* complicated, complex, intricate; (*personne*) complicated

compliquer [kɔ̃plike] *vt* to complicate; **se compliquer** *vi* (*situation*) to become complicated; **se compliquer la vie** to make life difficult *ou* complicated for o.s

complot [kɔ̃plo] *nm* plot

comportement [kɔ̃pɔrtəmɑ̃] *nm* behaviour (*BRIT*), behavior (*US*); (*TECH: d'une pièce, d'un véhicule*) behavio(u)r, performance

comporter [kɔ̃pɔrte] *vt* to be composed of, consist of, comprise; (*être équipé de*) to have; (*impliquer*) to entail, involve; **se comporter** *vi* to behave; (*TECH*) to behave, perform

composant [kɔ̃pozɑ̃] *nm* component, constituent

composé, e [kɔ̃poze] *adj* (*visage, air*) studied; (*BIO, CHIMIE, LING*) compound ♦ *nm* (*CHIMIE, LING*) compound; **composé de** made up of

composer [kɔ̃poze] *vt* (*musique, texte*) to compose; (*mélange, équipe*) to make up; (*faire partie de*) to make up, form; (*TYPO*) to (type)set ♦ *vi* (*SCOL*) to sit *ou* do a test; (*transiger*) to come to terms; **se composer de** to be composed of, be made up of; **composer un numéro** (*au téléphone*) to dial a number

compositeur, trice [kɔ̃pozitœr, -tris] *nm/f* (*MUS*) composer; (*TYPO*) compositor, typesetter

composition [kɔ̃pozisjɔ̃] *nf* composition; (*SCOL*) test; (*TYPO*) (type)setting, composition; **de bonne composition** (*accommodant*) easy to deal with; **amener qn à composition** to get sb to come to terms; **composition française** (*SCOL*) French essay

composter [kɔ̃pɔste] *vt* to date-stamp; to punch

compote [kɔ̃pɔt] *nf* stewed fruit *no pl*; **compote de pommes** stewed apples

compréhensible [kɔ̃preɑ̃sibl(ə)] *adj* compre-

hensible; (*attitude*) understandable

compréhensif, ive [kɔ̃preɑ̃sif, -iv] *adj* understanding

comprendre [kɔ̃prɑ̃dr(ə)] *vt* to understand; (*se composer de*) to comprise, consist of; (*inclure*) to include; **se faire comprendre** to make o.s. understood; to get one's ideas across; **mal comprendre** to misunderstand

compresse [kɔ̃prεs] *nf* compress

compression [kɔ̃presjɔ̃] *nf* compression; (*d'un crédit etc*) reduction

comprimé, e [kɔ̃prime] *adj*: **air comprimé** compressed air ♦ *nm* tablet

comprimer [kɔ̃prime] *vt* to compress; (*fig: crédit etc*) to reduce, cut down

compris, e [kɔ̃pri, -iz] *pp de* **comprendre** ♦ *adj* (*inclus*) included; **compris?** understood?, is that clear?; **compris entre** (*situé*) contained between; **la maison comprise/non comprise, y/non compris la maison** including/excluding the house; **service compris** service (charge) included; **100 € tout compris** 100 € all inclusive *ou* all-in

compromettre [kɔ̃prɔmεtr(ə)] *vt* to compromise

compromis [kɔ̃prɔmi] *vb voir* **compromettre** ♦ *nm* compromise

comptabilité [kɔ̃tabilite] *nf* (*activité, technique*) accounting, accountancy; (*d'une société: comptes*) accounts *pl*, books *pl*; (*: service*) accounts office *ou* department; **comptabilité à partie double** double-entry book-keeping

comptable [kɔ̃tabl(ə)] *nm/f* accountant ♦ *adj* accounts *cpd*, accounting

comptant [kɔ̃tɑ̃] *adv*: **payer comptant** to pay cash; **acheter comptant** to buy for cash

compte [kɔ̃t] *nm* count, counting; (*total, montant*) count, (right) number; (*bancaire, facture*) account; **comptes** *nmpl* accounts, books; (*fig*) explanation *sg*; **ouvrir un compte** to open an account; **rendre des comptes à qn** (*fig*) to be answerable to sb; **faire le compte de** to count up, make a count of; **tout compte fait** on the whole; **à ce compte-là** (*dans ce cas*) in that case; (*à ce train-là*) at that rate; **en fin de compte** (*fig*) all things considered, weighing it all up; **au bout du compte** in the final analysis; **à bon compte** at a favourable price; (*fig*) lightly; **avoir son compte** (*fig: fam*) to have had it; **pour le compte de** on behalf of; **pour son propre compte** for one's own benefit; **sur le compte de qn** (*à son sujet*) about sb; **travailler à son compte** to work for oneself; **mettre qch sur le compte de qn** (*le rendre responsable*) to attribute sth to sb; **prendre qch à son compte** to take responsibility for sth; **trouver son compte à qch** to do well out of sth; **régler un compte** (*s'acquitter de qch*) to settle an account; (*se venger*) to get one's own back; **rendre compte (à qn) de qch** to give (sb) an account of sth; **tenir compte de qch** to take sth into account; **compte tenu de** taking into account;

compte en banque bank account; **compte chèque(s)** current account; **compte chèque postal (CCP)** Post Office account; **compte client** (*sur bilan*) accounts receivable; **compte courant (CC)** current account; **compte de dépôt** deposit account; **compte d'exploitation** operating account; **compte fournisseur** (*sur bilan*) accounts payable; **compte à rebours** countdown; **compte rendu** account, report; (*de film, livre*) review; *voir aussi* **rendre**

compte-gouttes [kɔ̃tgut] *nm inv* dropper

compter [kɔ̃te] *vt* to count; (*facturer*) to charge for; (*avoir à son actif, comporter*) to have; (*prévoir*) to allow, reckon; (*tenir compte de, inclure*) to include; (*penser, espérer*): **compter réussir/revenir** to expect to succeed/return ♦ *vi* to count; (*être économe*) to economize; (*être non négligeable*) to count, matter; (*valoir*): **compter pour** to count for; (*figurer*): **compter parmi** to be *ou* rank among; **compter sur** to count (up)on; **compter avec qch/qn** to reckon with *ou* take account of sth/sb; **compter sans qch/qn** to reckon without sth/sb; **sans compter que** besides which; **à compter du 10 janvier** (*COMM*) (as) from 10th January

compteur [kɔ̃tœʀ] *nm* meter; **compteur de vitesse** speedometer

comptine [kɔ̃tin] *nf* nursery rhyme

comptoir [kɔ̃twaʀ] *nm* (*de magasin*) counter; (*de café*) counter, bar; (*colonial*) trading post

compulser [kɔ̃pylse] *vt* to consult

comte, comtesse [kɔ̃t, kɔ̃tɛs] *nm/f* count/countess

con, ne [kɔ̃, kɔn] *adj* (*fam!*) bloody (*BRIT*) *ou* damned stupid (*!*)

concéder [kɔ̃sede] *vt* to grant; (*défaite, point*) to concede; **concéder que** to concede that

concentré [kɔ̃sɑ̃tʀe] *nm* concentrate; **concentré de tomates** tomato purée

concentrer [kɔ̃sɑ̃tʀe] *vt* to concentrate; **se concentrer** to concentrate

concept [kɔ̃sɛpt] *nm* concept

conception [kɔ̃sɛpsjɔ̃] *nf* conception; (*d'une machine etc*) design

concerner [kɔ̃sɛʀne] *vt* to concern; **en ce qui me concerne** as far as I am concerned; **en ce qui concerne ceci** as far as this is concerned, with regard to this

concert [kɔ̃sɛʀ] *nm* concert; **de concert** *adv* in unison; together

concerter [kɔ̃sɛʀte] *vt* to devise; **se concerter** *vi* (*collaborateurs etc*) to put our (*ou* their *etc*) heads together, consult (each other)

concession [kɔ̃sesjɔ̃] *nf* concession

concessionnaire [kɔ̃sesjɔnɛʀ] *nm/f* agent, dealer

concevoir [kɔ̃svwaʀ] *vt* (*idée, projet*) to conceive (of); (*méthode, plan d'appartement, décoration etc*) to plan, design; (*enfant*) to conceive; **maison bien/mal conçue** well-/badly-designed *ou* -planned house

concierge [kɔ̃sjɛʀʒ(ə)] *nm/f* caretaker; (*d'hôtel*) head porter

conciliabules [kɔ̃siljabyl] *nmpl* (private) discussions, confabulations (*BRIT*)

concilier [kɔ̃silje] *vt* to reconcile; **se concilier qn/l'appui de qn** to win sb over/sb's support

concis, e [kɔ̃si, -iz] *adj* concise

concitoyen, ne [kɔ̃sitwajɛ̃, -ɛn] *nm/f* fellow citizen

concluant, e [kɔ̃klyɑ̃, -ɑ̃t] *vb voir* **conclure** ♦ *adj* conclusive

conclure [kɔ̃klyʀ] *vt* to conclude; (*signer: accord, pacte*) to enter into; (*déduire*) to deduce sth from sth; **conclure à l'acquittement** to decide in favour of an acquittal; **conclure au suicide** to come to the conclusion (*ou JUR*) to pronounce) that it is a case of suicide; **conclure un marché** to clinch a deal; **j'en conclus que** from that I conclude that

conclusion [kɔ̃klyzjɔ̃] *nf* conclusion; **conclusions** *nfpl* (*JUR*) submissions; findings; **en conclusion** in conclusion

conçois [kɔ̃swa], **conçoive** etc [kɔ̃swav] *vb voir* **concevoir**

concombre [kɔ̃kɔ̃bʀ(ə)] *nm* cucumber

concorder [kɔ̃kɔʀde] *vi* to tally, agree

concourir [kɔ̃kuʀiʀ] *vi* (*SPORT*) to compete; **concourir à** *vt* (*effet etc*) to work towards

concours [kɔ̃kuʀ] *vb voir* **concourir** ♦ *nm* competition; (*SCOL*) competitive examination; (*assistance*) aid, help; **recrutement par voie de concours** recruitment by (competitive) examination; **apporter son concours à** to give one's support to; **concours de circonstances** combination of circumstances; **concours hippique** horse show; *voir* **hors**

concret, ète [kɔ̃kʀɛ, -ɛt] *adj* concrete

concrétiser [kɔ̃kʀetize] *vt* to realize; **se concrétiser** *vi* to materialize

conçu, e [kɔ̃sy] *pp de* **concevoir**

concubinage [kɔ̃kybinaʒ] *nm* (*JUR*) cohabitation

concurrence [kɔ̃kyʀɑ̃s] *nf* competition; **jusqu'à concurrence de** up to; **concurrence déloyale** unfair competition

concurrent, e [kɔ̃kyʀɑ̃, -ɑ̃t] *adj* competing ♦ *nm/f* (*SPORT, ÉCON etc*) competitor; (*SCOL*) candidate

condamner [kɔ̃dane] *vt* (*blâmer*) to condemn; (*JUR*) to sentence; (*porte, ouverture*) to fill in, block up; (*malade*) to give up (hope for); (*obliger*): **condamner qn à qch/à faire** to condemn sb to sth/to do; **condamner qn à 2 ans de prison** to sentence sb to 2 years' imprisonment; **condamner qn à une amende** to impose a fine on sb

condensation [kɔ̃dɑ̃sasjɔ̃] *nf* condensation

condenser [kɔ̃dɑ̃se] *vt*: **se condenser** *vi* to condense

condisciple [kɔ̃disipl(ə)] *nm/f* school fellow, fellow student

condition [kɔ̃disjɔ̃] *nf* condition; **conditions** *nfpl* (*tarif, prix*) terms; (*circonstances*) conditions; **sans condition** *adj* unconditional ♦ *adv* unconditionally; **sous condition que** on condition that; **à condition de** *ou* **que** provided that; **en bonne condition** in good condition; **mettre en condition** (*SPORT etc*) to get fit; (*PSYCH*) to condition (mentally); **conditions de vie** living conditions

conditionnel, le [kɔ̃disjɔnɛl] *adj* conditional ♦ *nm* conditional (tense)

conditionnement [kɔ̃disjɔnmɑ̃] *nm* (*emballage*) packaging; (*fig*) conditioning

conditionner [kɔ̃disjɔne] *vt* (*déterminer*) to determine, (*COMM: produit*) to package; (*fig: personne*) to condition; **air conditionné** air conditioning; **réflexe conditionné** conditioned reflex

condoléances [kɔ̃dɔleɑ̃s] *nfpl* condolences

conducteur, trice [kɔ̃dyktœr, -tris] *adj* (*ÉLEC*) conducting ♦ *nm/f* (*AUTO etc*) driver; (*de* or *d'une*) *machine*) operator ♦ *nm* (*ÉLEC etc*) conductor

conduire [kɔ̃dɥir] *vt* (*véhicule, passager*) to drive; (*délégation, troupeau*) to lead; **se conduire** *vi* to behave; **conduire vers/à** to lead towards/to; **conduire qn quelque part** to take sb somewhere; to drive sb somewhere

conduite [kɔ̃dɥit] *nf* (*en auto*) driving; (*comportement*) behaviour (*BRIT*), behavior (*US*); (*d'eau, de gaz*) pipe; **sous la conduite de** led by; **conduite forcée** pressure pipe; **conduite à gauche** left-hand drive; **conduite intérieure** saloon (car)

cône [kon] *nm* cone; **en forme de cône** cone-shaped

confection [kɔ̃fɛksjɔ̃] *nf* (*fabrication*) making; (*COUTURE*): **la confection** the clothing industry, the rag trade (*fam*); **vêtement de confection** ready-to-wear *ou* off-the-peg garment

confectionner [kɔ̃fɛksjɔne] *vt* to make

conférence [kɔ̃ferɑ̃s] *nf* (*exposé*) lecture; (*pourparlers*) conference; **conférence de presse** press conference; **conférence au sommet** summit (conference)

conférencier, ière [kɔ̃ferɑ̃sje, -jɛr] *nm/f* lecturer

confesser [kɔ̃fese] *vt* to confess; **se confesser** *vi* (*REL*) to go to confession

confession [kɔ̃fesjɔ̃] *nf* confession; (*culte: catholique etc*) denomination

confiance [kɔ̃fjɑ̃s] *nf* confidence, trust; faith; **avoir confiance en** to have confidence *ou* faith in, trust; **faire confiance à** to trust; **en toute confiance** with complete confidence; **de confiance** trustworthy, reliable; **mettre qn en confiance** to win sb's trust; **vote de confiance** (*POL*) vote of confidence; **inspirer confiance à** to inspire confidence in; **confiance en soi** self-confidence *voir* **question**

confiant, e [kɔ̃fjɑ̃, -ɑ̃t] *adj* confident; trusting

confidence [kɔ̃fidɑ̃s] *nf* confidence

confidentiel, le [kɔ̃fidɑ̃sjɛl] *adj* confidential

confier [kɔ̃fje] *vt*: **confier à qn** (*objet en dépôt, travail etc*) to entrust to sb; (*secret, pensée*) to confide to sb; **se confier à qn** to confide in sb

confins [kɔ̃fɛ̃] *nmpl*: **aux confins de** on the borders of

confirmation [kɔ̃firmasjɔ̃] *nf* confirmation

confirmer [kɔ̃firme] *vt* to confirm; **confirmer qn dans une croyance/ses fonctions** to strengthen sb in a belief/his duties

confiserie [kɔ̃fizri] *nf* (*magasin*) confectioner's *ou* sweet shop (*BRIT*), candy store (*US*); **confiseries** *nfpl* (*bonbons*) confectionery *sg*, sweets, candy *no pl*

confisquer [kɔ̃fiske] *vt* to confiscate

confit, e [kɔ̃fi, -it] *adj*: **fruits confits** crystallized fruits ♦ *nm*: **confit d'oie** potted goose

confiture [kɔ̃fityr] *nf* jam; **confiture d'oranges** (orange) marmalade

conflit [kɔ̃fli] *nm* conflict

confondre [kɔ̃fɔ̃dr(ə)] *vt* (*jumeaux, faits*) to confuse, mix up; (*témoin, menteur*) to confound; **se confondre** *vi* to merge; **se confondre en excuses** to offer profuse apologies, apologize profusely; **confondre qch/qn avec qch/qn d'autre** to mistake sth/sb for sth/sb else

confondu, e [kɔ̃fɔ̃dy] *pp de* **confondre** ♦ *adj* (*stupéfait*) speechless, overcome; **toutes catégories confondues** taking all categories together

conforme [kɔ̃fɔrm(ə)] *adj*: **conforme à** (*en accord avec*) in accordance with, in keeping with; (*identique à*) true to; **copie certifiée conforme** (*ADMIN*) certified copy; **conforme à la commande** as per order

conformément [kɔ̃fɔrmemɑ̃] *adv*: **conformément à** in accordance with

conformer [kɔ̃fɔrme] *vt*: **conformer qch à** to model sth on; **se conformer à** to conform to

confort [kɔ̃fɔr] *nm* comfort; **tout confort** (*COMM*) with all mod cons (*BRIT*) *ou* modern conveniences

confortable [kɔ̃fɔrtabl(ə)] *adj* comfortable

confrère [kɔ̃frɛr] *nm* colleague; fellow member

confronter [kɔ̃frɔ̃te] *vt* to confront; (*textes*) to compare, collate

confus, e [kɔ̃fy, -yz] *adj* (*vague*) confused; (*embarrassé*) embarrassed

confusion [kɔ̃fyzjɔ̃] *nf* (*voir confus*) confusion; embarrassment; (*voir confondre*) confusion; mixing up; (*erreur*) confusion; **confusion des peines** (*JUR*) concurrency of sentences

congé [kɔ̃ʒe] *nm* (*vacances*) holiday; (*arrêt de travail*) time off *no pl*; leave *no pl*; (*MIL*) leave *no pl*; (*avis de départ*) notice; **en congé** on holiday; off (work); on leave; **semaine/jour de congé** week/day off; **prendre congé de qn** to take one's leave of sb; **donner son congé à** to hand *ou* give in one's notice to; **congé de maladie** sick leave; **congé de maternité** maternity leave; **congés payés** paid holiday *ou* leave

congédier [kɔ̃ʒedje] *vt* to dismiss

congélateur [kɔ̃ʒelatœʀ] *nm* freezer, deep freeze

congeler [kɔ̃ʒle] *vt*: **se congeler** *vi* to freeze

congestion [kɔ̃ʒεstjɔ̃] *nf* congestion; **congestion cérébrale** stroke; **congestion pulmonaire** congestion of the lungs

congestionner [kɔ̃ʒεstjɔne] *vt* to congest; (*MÉD*) to flush

congrès [kɔ̃gʀε] *nm* congress

conifère [kɔnifεʀ] *nm* conifer

conjecture [kɔ̃ʒεktyʀ] *nf* conjecture, speculation *no pl*

conjoint, e [kɔ̃ʒwε̃, -wε̃t] *adj* joint ♦ *nm/f* spouse

conjonction [kɔ̃ʒɔ̃ksjɔ̃] *nf* (*LING*) conjunction

conjonctivite [kɔ̃ʒɔ̃ktivit] *nf* conjunctivitis

conjoncture [kɔ̃ʒɔ̃ktyʀ] *nf* circumstances *pl*; **la conjoncture (économique)** the economic climate *ou* situation

conjugaison [kɔ̃ʒygεzɔ̃] *nf* (*LING*) conjugation

conjuguer [kɔ̃ʒyge] *vt* (*LING*) to conjugate; (*efforts etc*) to combine

conjuration [kɔ̃ʒyʀasjɔ̃] *nf* conspiracy

conjurer [kɔ̃ʒyʀe] *vt* (*sort, maladie*) to avert; (*implorer*): **conjurer qn de faire qch** to beseech *ou* entreat sb to do sth

connaissance [kɔnεsɑ̃s] *nf* (*savoir*) knowledge *no pl*; (*personne connue*) acquaintance; (*conscience*) consciousness; **connaissances** *nfpl* knowledge *no pl*; **être sans connaissance** to be unconscious; **perdre/reprendre connaissance** to lose/regain consciousness; **à ma/sa connaissance** to (the best of) my/his knowledge; **faire connaissance avec qn** *ou* **la connaissance de qn** (*rencontrer*) to meet sb; (*apprendre à connaître*) to get to know sb; **avoir connaissance de** to be aware of; **prendre connaissance de** (*document etc*) to peruse; **en connaissance de cause** with full knowledge of the facts; **de connaissance** (*personne, visage*) familiar

connaisseur, euse [kɔnεsœʀ, -øz] *nm/f* connoisseur ♦ *adj* expert

connaître [kɔnεtʀ(ə)] *vt* to know; (*éprouver*) to experience; (*avoir*) to enjoy; **connaître de nom/vue** to know by name/sight; **se connaître** to know each other; (*soi-même*) to know o.s.; **ils se sont connus à Genève** they (first) met in Geneva; **s'y connaître en qch** to know about sth

connecter [kɔnεkte] *vt* to connect

connerie [kɔnʀi] *nf* (*fam*) (bloody) stupid (*BRIT*) *ou* damn-fool (*US*) thing to do *ou* say

connu, e [kɔny] *pp de* **connaître** ♦ *adj* (*célèbre*) well-known

conquérir [kɔ̃keʀiʀ] *vt* to conquer, win

conquête [kɔ̃kεt] *nf* conquest

consacrer [kɔ̃sakʀe] *vt* (*REL*): **consacrer qch (à)** to consecrate sth (to); (*fig: usage etc*) to sanction,

establish; (*employer*): **consacrer qch à** to devote *ou* dedicate sth to; **se consacrer à qch/faire** to dedicate *ou* devote o.s. to sth/to doing

conscience [kɔ̃sjɑ̃s] *nf* conscience; (*perception*) consciousness; **avoir/prendre conscience de** to be/become aware of; **perdre/reprendre conscience** to lose/regain consciousness; **avoir bonne/mauvaise conscience** to have a clear/ guilty conscience; **en (toute) conscience** in all conscience

consciencieux, euse [kɔ̃sjɑ̃sjø, -øz] *adj* conscientious

conscient, e [kɔ̃sjɑ̃, -ɑ̃t] *adj* conscious; **conscient de** aware *ou* conscious of

conscrit [kɔ̃skʀi] *nm* conscript

consécutif, ive [kɔ̃sekytif, -iv] *adj* consecutive; **consécutif à** following upon

conseil [kɔ̃sεj] *nm* (*avis*) piece of advice, advice *no pl*; (*assemblée*) council; (*expert*): **conseil en recrutement** recruitment consultant ♦ *adj*: **ingénieur-conseil** engineering consultant; **tenir conseil** to hold a meeting; to deliberate; **donner un conseil** *ou* **des conseils à qn** to give sb (a piece of) advice; **demander conseil à qn** to ask sb's advice; **prendre conseil (auprès de qn)** to take advice (from sb); **conseil d'administration (CA)** board (of directors); **conseil de classe** (*SCOL*) meeting of teachers, parents and class representatives to discuss pupils' progress; **conseil de discipline** disciplinary committee; **conseil général** regional council; *see boxed note*; **conseil de guerre** court-martial; **le conseil des ministres** ≃ the Cabinet; **conseil municipal (CM)** town council; **conseil régional** *regional board of elected representatives*; **conseil de révision** recruitment *ou* draft (*US*) board

---

CONSEIL GÉNÉRAL

Each 'département' of France is run by a **Conseil général**, whose remit covers personnel, transport infrastructure, housing, school grants and economic development. The council is made up of 'conseillers généraux', each of whom represents a 'canton' and is elected for a six-year term. Half of the council's membership are elected every three years.

---

conseiller[1] [kɔ̃seje] *vt* (*personne*) to advise; (*méthode, action*) to recommend, advise; **conseiller qch à qn** to recommend sth to sb; **conseiller à qn de faire qch** to advise sb to do sth

conseiller[2]**, ère** [kɔ̃seje, -εʀ] *nm/f* adviser; **conseiller général** regional councillor; **conseiller matrimonial** marriage guidance counsellor; **conseiller municipal** town councillor; **conseiller d'orientation** (*SCOL*) careers adviser (*BRIT*), (school) counselor (*US*)

consentement [kɔ̃sɑ̃tmɑ̃] *nm* consent

consentir [kɔ̃sɑ̃tiʀ] *vt*: **consentir (à qch/faire)** to agree *ou* consent (to sth/to doing); **consentir qch à qn** to grant sb sth

conséquence [kɔ̃sekɑ̃s] *nf* consequence, outcome; **conséquences** *nfpl*/consequences, repercussions; **en conséquence** (*donc*) consequently; (*de façon appropriée*) accordingly; **ne pas tirer à conséquence** to be unlikely to have any repercussions; **sans conséquence** unimportant; **de conséquence** important

conséquent, e [kɔ̃sekɑ̃, -ɑ̃t] *adj* logical, rational; (*fam: important*) substantial; **par conséquent** consequently

conservateur, trice [kɔ̃sɛʀvatœʀ, -tʀis] *adj* conservative ♦ *nm/f* (*POL*) conservative; (*de musée*) curator

conservatoire [kɔ̃sɛʀvatwaʀ] *nm* academy; (*ÉCOLOGIE*) conservation area

conserve [kɔ̃sɛʀv(ə)] *nf* (*gén pl*) canned *ou* tinned (*BRIT*) food; **conserves de poisson** canned *ou* tinned (*BRIT*) fish; **en conserve** canned, tinned (*BRIT*); **de conserve** (*ensemble*) in concert; (*naviguer*) in convoy

conserver [kɔ̃sɛʀve] *vt* (*faculté*) to retain, keep; (*habitude*) to keep up; (*amis, livres*) to keep; (*préserver, CULIN*) to preserve; **se conserver** *vi* (*aliments*) to keep; **"conserver au frais"** "store in a cool place"

considérable [kɔ̃sideʀabl(ə)] *adj* considerable, significant, extensive

considération [kɔ̃sideʀasjɔ̃] *nf* consideration; (*estime*) esteem, respect; **considérations** *nfpl* (*remarques*) reflections; **prendre en considération** to take into consideration *ou* account; **ceci mérite considération** this is worth considering; **en considération de** given, because of

considérer [kɔ̃sideʀe] *vt* to consider; (*regarder*) to consider, study; **considérer qch comme** to regard sth as

consigne [kɔ̃siɲ] *nf* (*COMM*) deposit; (*de gare*) left luggage (office) (*BRIT*), checkroom (*US*); (*punition: SCOL*) detention; (: *MIL*) confinement to barracks; (*ordre, instruction*) instructions *pl*; **consigne automatique** left-luggage locker; **consignes de sécurité** safety instructions

consigner [kɔ̃siɲe] *vt* (*note, pensée*) to record; (*marchandises*) to deposit; (*punir: MIL*) to confine to barracks; (: *élève*) to put in detention; (*COMM*) to put a deposit on

consistant, e [kɔ̃sistɑ̃, -ɑ̃t] *adj* thick; solid

consister [kɔ̃siste] *vi*: **consister en/dans/à faire** to consist of/in/in doing

consœur [kɔ̃sœʀ] *nf* (lady) colleague; fellow member

console [kɔ̃sɔl] *nf* console; **console graphique** *ou* **de visualisation** (*INFORM*) visual display unit, VDU; **console de jeux vidéo** games console

consoler [kɔ̃sɔle] *vt* to console; **se consoler (de qch)** to console o.s. (for sth)

consolider [kɔ̃sɔlide] *vt* to strengthen, reinforce; (*fig*) to consolidate; **bilan consolidé** consolidated balance sheet

consommateur, trice [kɔ̃sɔmatœʀ, -tʀis] *nm/f* (*ÉCON*) consumer; (*dans un café*) customer

consommation [kɔ̃sɔmasjɔ̃] *nf* consumption; (*JUR*) consummation; (*boisson*) drink; **consommation aux 100 km** (*AUTO*) (fuel) consumption per 100 km, ≈ miles per gallon (mpg), ≈ gas mileage (*US*); **de consommation** (*biens, société*) consumer *cpd*

consommer [kɔ̃sɔme] *vt* (*personne*) to eat *ou* drink, consume; (*voiture, usine, poêle*) to use, consume; (*JUR*) to consummate ♦ *vi* (*dans un café*) to (have a) drink

consonne [kɔ̃sɔn] *nf* consonant

conspirer [kɔ̃spiʀe] *vi* to conspire, plot; **conspirer à** (*tendre à*) to conspire to

constamment [kɔ̃stamɑ̃] *adv* constantly

constant, e [kɔ̃stɑ̃, -ɑ̃t] *adj* constant; (*personne*) steadfast ♦ *nf* constant

constat [kɔ̃sta] *nm* (*d'huissier*) certified report (by bailiff); (*de police*) report; (*observation*) (observed) fact, observation; (*affirmation*) statement; **constat (à l'amiable)** (*jointly agreed*) statement for insurance purposes

constatation [kɔ̃statasjɔ̃] *nf* noticing; certifying; (*remarque*) observation

constater [kɔ̃state] *vt* (*remarquer*) to note, notice; (*ADMIN, JUR: attester*) to certify; (*dégâts*) to note; **constater que** (*dire*) to state that

consterner [kɔ̃stɛʀne] *vt* to dismay

constipé, e [kɔ̃stipe] *adj* constipated; (*fig*) stiff

constitué, e [kɔ̃stitɥe] *adj*: **constitué de** made up *ou* composed of; **bien constitué** of sound constitution; well-formed

constituer [kɔ̃stitɥe] *vt* (*comité, équipe*) to set up, form; (*dossier, collection*) to put together, build up; (*suj: éléments, parties: composer*) to make up, constitute; (*représenter, être*) to constitute; **se constituer prisonnier** to give o.s. up; **se constituer partie civile** to bring an independent action for damages

constitution [kɔ̃stitysjɔ̃] *nf* setting up; building up; (*composition*) composition, make-up; (*santé, POL*) constitution

constructeur [kɔ̃stʀyktœʀ] *nm* manufacturer, builder

constructif, ive [kɔ̃stʀyktif, -iv] *adj* (*positif*) constructive

construction [kɔ̃stʀyksjɔ̃] *nf* construction, building

construire [kɔ̃stʀɥiʀ] *vt* to build, construct; **se construire: l'immeuble s'est construit très vite** the building went up *ou* was built very quickly

consul [kɔ̃syl] *nm* consul

consulat [kɔ̃syla] *nm* consulate

consultant, e [kɔ̃syltɑ̃, -ɑ̃t] *adj* consultant

consultation [kɔ̃syltasjɔ̃] *nf* consultation; **con-**

sultations *nfpl* (*POL*) talks; **être en consultation** (*délibération*) to be in consultation; (*médecin*) to be consulting; **aller à la consultation** (*MÉD*) to go to the surgery (*BRIT*) *ou* doctor's office (*US*); **heures de consultation** (*MÉD*) surgery (*BRIT*) *ou* office (*US*) hours

consulter [kɔ̃sylte] *vt* to consult ♦ *vi* (*médecin*) to hold surgery (*BRIT*), be in (the office) (*US*); **se consulter** to confer

consumer [kɔ̃syme] *vt* to consume; **se consumer** *vi* to burn; **se consumer de chagrin/douleur** to be consumed with sorrow/grief

contact [kɔ̃takt] *nm* contact; **au contact de** (*air, peau*) on contact with; (*gens*) through contact with; **mettre/couper le contact** (*AUTO*) to switch on/off the ignition; **entrer en contact** (*fils, objets*) to come into contact, make contact; **se mettre en contact avec** (*RADIO*) to make contact with; **prendre contact avec** (*relation d'affaires, connaissance*) to get in touch *ou* contact with

contacter [kɔ̃takte] *vt* to contact, get in touch with

contagieux, euse [kɔ̃taʒjø, -øz] *adj* contagious; infectious

contaminer [kɔ̃tamine] *vt* (*par un virus*) to infect; (*par des radiations*) to contaminate

conte [kɔ̃t] *nm* tale; **conte de fées** fairy tale

contempler [kɔ̃tɑ̃ple] *vt* to contemplate, gaze at

contemporain, e [kɔ̃tɑ̃pɔʀɛ̃, -ɛn] *adj, nm/f* contemporary

contenance [kɔ̃tnɑ̃s] *nf* (*d'un récipient*) capacity; (*attitude*) bearing, attitude; **perdre contenance** to lose one's composure; **se donner une contenance** to give the impression of composure; **faire bonne contenance (devant)** to put on a bold front (in the face of)

conteneur [kɔ̃tnœʀ] *nm* container; **conteneur (de bouteilles)** bottle bank

contenir [kɔ̃tniʀ] *vt* to contain; (*avoir une capacité de*) to hold; **se contenir** (*se retenir*) to control o.s. *ou* one's emotions, contain o.s.

content, e [kɔ̃tɑ̃, -ɑ̃t] *adj* pleased, glad; **content de** pleased with; **je serais content que tu ...** I would be pleased if you ...

contenter [kɔ̃tɑ̃te] *vt* to satisfy, please; (*envie*) to satisfy; **se contenter de** to content o.s. with

contentieux [kɔ̃tɑ̃sjø] *nm* (*COMM*) litigation; (: *service*) litigation department; (*POL etc*) contentious issues *pl*

contenu, e [kɔ̃tny] *pp de* **contenir** ♦ *nm* (*d'un bol*) contents *pl*; (*d'un texte*) content

conter [kɔ̃te] *vt* to recount, relate; **en conter de belles à qn** to tell tall stories to sb

contestable [kɔ̃tɛstabl(ə)] *adj* questionable

contestation [kɔ̃tɛstasjɔ̃] *nf* questioning, contesting; (*POL*): **la contestation** anti-establishment activity, protest

conteste [kɔ̃tɛst(ə)]: **sans conteste** *adv* unques-

tionably, indisputably

contester [kɔ̃tɛste] *vt* to question, contest ♦ *vi* (*POL*: *gén*) to protest, rebel (against established authority)

contexte [kɔ̃tɛkst(ə)] *nm* context

contigu, ë [kɔ̃tigy] *adj*: **contigu (à)** adjacent (to)

continent [kɔ̃tinɑ̃] *nm* continent

continu, e [kɔ̃tiny] *adj* continuous; **(courant) continu** direct current, DC

continuel, le [kɔ̃tinɥɛl] *adj* (*qui se répète*) constant, continual; (*continu*) continuous

continuer [kɔ̃tinɥe] *vt* (*travail, voyage etc*) to continue (with), carry on (with), go on with; (*prolonger: alignement, rue*) to continue ♦ *vi* (*pluie, vie, bruit*) to continue, go on; (*voyageur*) to go on; **se continuer** *vi* to carry on; **continuer à** *ou* **de faire** to go on *ou* continue doing

contorsionner [kɔ̃tɔʀsjɔne]: **se contorsionner** *vi* to contort o.s., writhe about

contour [kɔ̃tuʀ] *nm* outline, contour; **contours** *nmpl* (*d'une rivière etc*) windings

contourner [kɔ̃tuʀne] *vt* to bypass, walk (*ou* drive) round

contraceptif, ive [kɔ̃tʀaseptif, -iv] *adj, nm* contraceptive

contraception [kɔ̃tʀasɛpsjɔ̃] *nf* contraception

contracté, e [kɔ̃tʀakte] *adj* (*muscle*) tense, contracted; (*personne: tendu*) tense, tensed up; **article contracté** (*LING*) contracted article

contracter [kɔ̃tʀakte] *vt* (*muscle etc*) to tense, contract; (*maladie, dette, obligation*) to contract; (*assurance*) to take out; **se contracter** *vi* (*suj: métal, muscles*) to contract

contractuel, le [kɔ̃tʀaktɥɛl] *adj* contractual ♦ *nm/f* (*agent*) traffic warden; (*employé*) contract employee

contradiction [kɔ̃tʀadiksjɔ̃] *nf* contradiction

contradictoire [kɔ̃tʀadiktwaʀ] *adj* contradictory, conflicting; **débat contradictoire** (open) debate

contraignant, e [kɔ̃tʀɛɲɑ̃, -ɑ̃t] *vb voir* **contraindre** ♦ *adj* restricting

contraindre [kɔ̃tʀɛ̃dʀ(ə)] *vt*: **contraindre qn à faire** to force *ou* compel sb to do

contrainte [kɔ̃tʀɛ̃t] *nf* constraint; **sans contrainte** unrestrainedly, unconstrainedly

contraire [kɔ̃tʀɛʀ] *adj, nm* opposite; **contraire à** contrary to; **au contraire** *adv* on the contrary

contrarier [kɔ̃tʀaʀje] *vt* (*personne*) to annoy, bother; (*fig*) to impede; to thwart, frustrate

contrariété [kɔ̃tʀaʀjete] *nf* annoyance

contraste [kɔ̃tʀast(ə)] *nm* contrast

contrat [kɔ̃tʀa] *nm* contract; (*fig: accord, pacte*) agreement; **contrat de travail** employment contract

contravention [kɔ̃tʀavɑ̃sjɔ̃] *nf* (*infraction*): **contravention à** contravention of; (*amende*) fine; (*PV pour stationnement interdit*) parking ticket; **dresser**

contravention à (*automobiliste*) to book; to write out a parking ticket for

contre [kɔ̃tr(ə)] *prép* against; (*en échange*) (in exchange) for; **par contre** on the other hand

contrebande [kɔ̃trəbɑ̃d] *nf* (*trafic*) contraband, smuggling; (*marchandise*) contraband, smuggled goods *pl*; **faire la contrebande de** to smuggle

contrebandier, ière [kɔ̃trəbɑ̃dje, -jɛr] *nm/f* smuggler

contrebas [kɔ̃trəba]: **en contrebas** *adv* (down) below

contrebasse [kɔ̃trəbas] *nf* (double) bass

contrecarrer [kɔ̃trəkare] *vt* to thwart

contrecœur [kɔ̃trəkœr]: **à contrecœur** *adv* (be)grudgingly, reluctantly

contrecoup [kɔ̃trəku] *nm* repercussions *pl*; **par contrecoup** as an indirect consequence

contredire [kɔ̃trədir] *vt* (*personne*) to contradict; (*témoignage, assertion, faits*) to refute; **se contredire** to contradict o.s

contrée [kɔ̃tre] *nf* region; land

contrefaçon [kɔ̃trəfasɔ̃] *nf* forgery; **contrefaçon de brevet** patent infringement

contrefaire [kɔ̃trəfɛr] *vt* (*document, signature*) to forge, counterfeit; (*personne, démarche*) to mimic; (*dénaturer: sa voix etc*) to disguise

contre-indication [kɔ̃trɛ̃dikasjɔ̃] *nf* contra-indication

contre-indiqué, e [kɔ̃trɛ̃dike] *adj* (*MÉD*) contraindicated

contre-jour [kɔ̃trəʒur]: **à contre-jour** *adv* against the light

contremaître [kɔ̃trəmɛtr(ə)] *nm* foreman

contrepartie [kɔ̃trəparti] *nf* compensation; **en contrepartie** in compensation, in return

contre-pied [kɔ̃trəpje] *nm* (*inverse, opposé*): **le contre-pied de ...** the exact opposite of ...; **prendre le contre-pied de** to take the opposing view of; to take the opposite course to; **prendre qn à contre-pied** (*SPORT*) to wrong-foot sb

contre-plaqué [kɔ̃trəplake] *nm* plywood

contrepoids [kɔ̃trəpwa] *nm* counterweight, counterbalance; **faire contrepoids** to act as a counterbalance

contrepoison [kɔ̃trəpwazɔ̃] *nm* antidote

contrer [kɔ̃tre] *vt* to counter

contresens [kɔ̃trəsɑ̃s] *nm* misinterpretation; (*mauvaise traduction*) mistranslation; (*absurdité*) nonsense *no pl*; **à contresens** *adv* the wrong way

contretemps [kɔ̃trətɑ̃] *nm* hitch, contretemps; **à contretemps** *adv* (*MUS*) out of time; (*fig*) at an inopportune moment

contrevenir [kɔ̃trəvnir]: **contrevenir à** *vt* to contravene

contribuable [kɔ̃tribɥabl(ə)] *nm/f* taxpayer

contribuer [kɔ̃tribɥe]: **contribuer à** *vt* to contribute towards

contribution [kɔ̃tribysjɔ̃] *nf* contribution; **les contributions** (*bureaux*) the tax office; **mettre à contribution** to call upon; **contributions directes/indirectes** direct/indirect taxation

contrôle [kɔ̃trol] *nm* checking *no pl*, check; supervision; monitoring; (*test*) test, examination; **perdre le contrôle de son véhicule** to lose control of one's vehicle; **contrôle des changes** (*COMM*) exchange controls; **contrôle continu** (*SCOL*) continuous assessment; **contrôle d'identité** identity check; **contrôle des naissances** birth control; **contrôle des prix** price control

contrôler [kɔ̃trole] *vt* (*vérifier*) to check; (*surveiller*) to supervise; to monitor, control; (*maîtriser*, *COMM: firme*) to control; **se contrôler** to control o.s

contrôleur, euse [kɔ̃trolœr, -øz] *nm/f* (*de train*) (ticket) inspector; (*de bus*) (bus) conductor/tress; **contrôleur de la navigation aérienne, contrôleur aérien** air traffic controller; **contrôleur financier** financial controller

contrordre [kɔ̃trɔrdr(ə)] *nm* counter-order, countermand; **sauf contrordre** unless otherwise directed

controversé, e [kɔ̃trɔverse] *adj* (*personnage, question*) controversial

contusion [kɔ̃tyzjɔ̃] *nf* bruise, contusion

convaincre [kɔ̃vɛ̃kr(ə)] *vt*: **convaincre qn (de qch)** to convince sb (of sth); **convaincre qn (de faire)** to persuade sb (to do); **convaincre qn de** (*JUR: délit*) to convict sb of

convalescence [kɔ̃valesɑ̃s] *nf* convalescence; **maison de convalescence** convalescent home

convenable [kɔ̃vnabl(ə)] *adj* suitable; (*décent*) acceptable, proper; (*assez bon*) decent, acceptable, adequate, passable

convenance [kɔ̃vnɑ̃s] *nf*: **à ma/votre convenance** to my/your liking; **convenances** *nfpl* proprieties

convenir [kɔ̃vnir] *vt* to be suitable; **convenir à** to suit; **il convient de** it is advisable to; (*bienséant*) it is right *ou* proper to; **convenir de** (*bien-fondé de qch*) to admit (to), acknowledge; (*date, somme etc*) to agree upon; **convenir que** (*admettre*) to admit that, acknowledge the fact that; **convenir de faire qch** to agree to do sth; **il a été convenu que** it has been agreed that; **comme convenu** as agreed

convention [kɔ̃vɑ̃sjɔ̃] *nf* convention; **conventions** *nfpl* (*convenances*) convention *sg*, social conventions; **de convention** conventional; **convention collective** (*ÉCON*) collective agreement

conventionné, e [kɔ̃vɑ̃sjɔne] *adj* (*ADMIN*) applying charges laid down by the state

convenu, e [kɔ̃vny] *pp de* **convenir** ♦ *adj* agreed

conversation [kɔ̃vɛrsasjɔ̃] *nf* conversation; **avoir de la conversation** to be a good conversationalist

convertir [kɔ̃vɛrtir] *vt*: **convertir qn (à)** to convert sb (to); **convertir qch en** to convert sth into; **se convertir (à)** to be converted (to)

conviction [kɔ̃viksjɔ̃] *nf* conviction

convier [kɔ̃vje] *vt*: **convier qn à** (*dîner etc*) to (cordially) invite sb to; **convier qn à faire** to urge sb to do

convive [kɔ̃viv] *nm/f* guest (*at table*)

convivial, e [kɔ̃vivjal] *adj* (*INFORM*) user-friendly

convocation [kɔ̃vɔkasjɔ̃] *nf* (*voir convoquer*) convening, convoking; summoning; invitation; (*document*) notification to attend; summons *sg*

convoi [kɔ̃vwa] *nm* (*de voitures, prisonniers*) convoy; (*train*) train; **convoi (funèbre)** funeral procession

convoiter [kɔ̃vwate] *vt* to covet

convoquer [kɔ̃vɔke] *vt* (*assemblée*) to convene, convoke; (*subordonné, témoin*) to summon; (*candidat*) to ask to attend; **convoquer qn (à)** (*réunion*) to invite sb (to attend)

convoyeur [kɔ̃vwajœR] *nm* (*NAVIG*) escort ship; **convoyeur de fonds** security guard

coopération [kɔɔpeRasjɔ̃] *nf* co-operation; (*ADMIN*): **la Coopération** = Voluntary Service Overseas (*BRIT*) *ou* the Peace Corps (*US*) (*done as alternative to military service*)

coopérer [kɔɔpeRe] *vi*: **coopérer (à)** to co-operate (in)

coordonnées [kɔɔRdɔne] *nfpl*: **donnez-moi vos coordonnées** (*fam*) can I have your details please?

coordonner [kɔɔRdɔne] *vt* to coordinate

copain, copine [kɔpɛ̃, kɔpin] *nm/f* mate (*BRIT*), pal ♦ *adj*: **être copain avec** to be pally with

copeau, x [kɔpo] *nm* shaving; (*de métal*) turning

copie [kɔpi] *nf* copy; (*SCOL*) script, paper; exercise; **copie certifiée conforme** certified copy; **copie papier** (*INFORM*) hard copy

copier [kɔpje] *vt, vi* to copy; **copier sur** to copy from

copieur [kɔpjœR] *nm* (photo)copier

copieux, euse [kɔpjø, -øz] *adj* copious, hearty

copine [kɔpin] *nf voir* **copain**

copropriété [kɔpRɔpRijete] *nf* co-ownership, joint ownership; **acheter en copropriété** to buy on a co-ownership basis

coq [kɔk] *nm* cock, rooster ♦ *adj inv* (*BOXE*): **poids coq** bantamweight; **coq de bruyère** grouse; **coq du village** (*fig:péj*) ladykiller; **coq au vin** coq au vin

coq-à-l'âne [kɔkalɑn] *nm inv* abrupt change of subject

coque [kɔk] *nf* (*de noix, mollusque*) shell; (*de bateau*) hull; **à la coque** (*CULIN*) (soft-)boiled

coquelicot [kɔkliko] *nm* poppy

coqueluche [kɔklyʃ] *nf* whooping-cough; (*fig*): **être la coqueluche de qn** to be sb's flavour of the month

coquet, te [kɔkɛ, -ɛt] *adj* appearance-conscious; (*joli*) pretty

coquetier [kɔktje] *nm* egg-cup

coquillage [kɔkijaʒ] *nm* (*mollusque*) shellfish *inv*; (*coquille*) shell

coquille [kɔkij] *nf* shell; (*TYPO*) misprint; **coquille de beurre** shell of butter; **coquille d'œuf** *adj* (*couleur*) eggshell; **coquille de noix** nutshell; **coquille St Jacques** scallop

coquin, e [kɔkɛ̃, -in] *adj* mischievous, roguish; (*polisson*) naughty ♦ *nm/f* (*péj*) rascal

cor [kɔR] *nm* (*MUS*) horn; (*MÉD*): **cor (au pied)** corn; **réclamer à cor et à cri** to clamour for; **cor anglais** cor anglais; **cor de chasse** hunting horn

corail, aux [kɔRaj, -o] *nm* coral *no pl*

Coran [kɔRɑ̃] *nm*: **le Coran** the Koran

corbeau, x [kɔRbo] *nm* crow

corbeille [kɔRbɛj] *nf* basket; (*BOURSE*): **la corbeille** = the floor (of the Stock Exchange); **corbeille de mariage** (*fig*) wedding presents *pl*; **corbeille à ouvrage** work-basket; **corbeille à pain** breadbasket; **corbeille à papier** waste paper basket *ou* bin

corbillard [kɔRbijaR] *nm* hearse

corde [kɔRd(ə)] *nf* rope; (*de violon, raquette, d'arc*) string; (*trame*): **la corde** the thread; (*ATHLÉTISME, AUTO*): **la corde** the rails *pl*; **les cordes** (*BOXE*) the ropes; **les (instruments à) cordes** (*MUS*) the strings, the stringed instruments; **semelles de corde** rope soles; **tenir la corde** (*ATHLÉTISME, AUTO*) to be in the inside lane; **tomber des cordes** to rain cats and dogs; **tirer sur la corde** to go too far; **la corde sensible** the right chord; **usé jusqu'à la corde** threadbare; **corde à linge** washing *ou* clothes line; **corde lisse** (climbing) rope; **corde à nœuds** knotted climbing rope; **corde raide** tightrope; **corde à sauter** skipping rope; **cordes vocales** vocal cords

cordée [kɔRde] *nf* (*d'alpinistes*) rope, roped party

cordialement [kɔRdjalmɑ̃] *adv* cordially, heartily; (*formule épistolaire*) (kind) regards

cordon [kɔRdɔ̃] *nm* cord, string; **cordon sanitaire/de police** sanitary/police cordon; **cordon littoral** sandbank, sandbar; **cordon ombilical** umbilical cord

cordonnerie [kɔRdɔnRi] *nf* shoe repairer's *ou* mender's (shop)

cordonnier [kɔRdɔnje] *nm* shoe repairer *ou* mender, cobbler

Corée [kɔRe] *nf*: **la Corée** Korea; **la Corée du Sud/du Nord** South/North Korea; **la République (démocratique populaire) de Corée** the (Democratic People's) Republic of Korea

coriace [kɔRjas] *adj* tough

corne [kɔRn(ə)] *nf* horn; (*de cerf*) antler; (*de la peau*) callus; **corne d'abondance** horn of plenty; **corne de brume** (*NAVIG*) foghorn

cornée [kɔRne] *nf* cornea

corneille [kɔRnɛj] *nf* crow

cornemuse [kɔRnəmyz] *nf* bagpipes *pl*; **joueur de cornemuse** piper

cornet [kɔRnɛ] *nm* (paper) cone; (*de glace*) cornet, cone; **cornet à pistons** cornet

corniche [kɔʀniʃ] nf (de meuble, neigeuse) cornice; (route) coast road

cornichon [kɔʀniʃɔ̃] nm gherkin

Cornouailles [kɔʀnwaj] nf(pl) Cornwall

corporation [kɔʀpɔʀasjɔ̃] nf corporate body; (au Moyen-Âge) guild

corporel, le [kɔʀpɔʀɛl] adj bodily; (punition) corporal; **soins corporels** care sg of the body

corps [kɔʀ] nm (gén) body; (cadavre) (dead) body; **à son corps défendant** against one's will; **à corps perdu** headlong; **perdu corps et biens** lost with all hands; **prendre corps** to take shape; **faire corps avec** to be joined to; to form one body with; **corps d'armée** (CA) army corps; **corps de ballet** corps de ballet; **corps constitués** (POL) constitutional bodies; **le corps consulaire** (CC) the consular corps; **corps à corps** adv hand-to-hand ♦ nm clinch; **le corps du délit** (JUR) corpus delicti; **le corps diplomatique** (CD) the diplomatic corps; **le corps électoral** the electorate; **le corps enseignant** the teaching profession; **corps étranger** (MÉD) foreign body; **corps expéditionnaire** task force; **corps de garde** guardroom; **corps législatif** legislative body; **le corps médical** the medical profession

corpulent, e [kɔʀpylɑ̃, -ɑ̃t] adj stout (BRIT), corpulent

correct, e [kɔʀɛkt] adj (exact) accurate, correct; (bienséant, honnête) correct; (passable) adequate

correcteur, trice [kɔʀɛktœʀ, -tʀis] nm/f (SCOL) examiner, marker; (TYPO) proofreader

correction [kɔʀɛksjɔ̃] nf (voir corriger) correction; marking; (voir correct) correctness; (rature, surcharge) correction, emendation; (coups) thrashing; **correction sur écran** (INFORM) screen editing; **correction (des épreuves)** proofreading

correctionnel, le [kɔʀɛksjɔnɛl] adj (JUR): **tribunal correctionnel** ≈ criminal court

correspondance [kɔʀɛspɔ̃dɑ̃s] nf correspondence; (de train, d'avion) connection; **ce train assure la correspondance avec l'avion de 10 heures** this train connects with the 10 o'clock plane; **cours par correspondance** correspondence course; **vente par correspondance** mail-order business

correspondant, e [kɔʀɛspɔ̃dɑ̃, -ɑ̃t] nm/f correspondent; (TÉL) person phoning (ou being phoned)

correspondre [kɔʀɛspɔ̃dʀ(ə)] vi (données, témoignages) to correspond, tally; (chambres) to communicate; **correspondre à** to correspond to; **correspondre avec qn** to correspond with sb

corrida [kɔʀida] nf bullfight

corridor [kɔʀidɔʀ] nm corridor, passage

corrigé [kɔʀiʒe] nm (SCOL) correct version; fair copy

corriger [kɔʀiʒe] vt (devoir) to correct, mark; (texte) to correct, emend; (erreur, défaut) to correct, put right; (punir) to thrash; **corriger qn de** (défaut)

to cure sb of; **se corriger de** to cure o.s. of

corroborer [kɔʀɔbɔʀe] vt to corroborate

corrompre [kɔʀɔ̃pʀ(ə)] vt (dépraver) to corrupt; (acheter: témoin etc) to bribe

corruption [kɔʀypsjɔ̃] nf corruption; bribery

corsage [kɔʀsaʒ] nm (d'une robe) bodice; (chemisier) blouse

corsaire [kɔʀsɛʀ] nm pirate, corsair; privateer

corse [kɔʀs(ə)] adj Corsican ♦ nm/f: **Corse** Corsican ♦ nf: **la Corse** Corsica

corsé, e [kɔʀse] adj vigorous; (café etc) full-flavoured (BRIT) ou -flavored (US); (goût) full; (fig) spicy; tricky

corset [kɔʀsɛ] nm corset; (d'une robe) bodice; **corset orthopédique** surgical corset

cortège [kɔʀtɛʒ] nm procession

cortisone [kɔʀtizon] nf (MÉD) cortisone

corvée [kɔʀve] nf chore, drudgery no pl; (MIL) fatigue (duty)

cosmétique [kɔsmetik] nm (pour les cheveux) hair-oil; (produit de beauté) beauty care product

cosmopolite [kɔsmɔpɔlit] adj cosmopolitan

cossu, e [kɔsy] adj opulent-looking, well-to-do

costaud, e [kɔsto, -od] adj strong, sturdy

costume [kɔstym] nm (d'homme) suit; (de théâtre) costume

costumé, e [kɔstyme] adj dressed up

cote [kɔt] nf (en Bourse etc) quotation; quoted value; (d'un cheval): **la cote de** the odds pl on; (d'un candidat etc) rating; (mesure: sur une carte) spot height; (: sur un croquis) dimension; (de classement) (classification) mark; reference number; **avoir la cote** to be very popular; **inscrit à la cote** quoted on the Stock Exchange; **cote d'alerte** danger ou flood level; **cote mal taillée** (fig) compromise; **cote de popularité** popularity rating

coté, e [kɔte] adj: **être coté** to be listed ou quoted; **être coté en Bourse** to be quoted on the Stock Exchange; **être bien/mal coté** to be highly/poorly rated

côte [kot] nf (rivage) coast(line); (pente) slope; (: sur une route) hill; (ANAT) rib; (d'un tricot, tissu) rib, ribbing no pl; **côte à côte** adv side by side; **la Côte (d'Azur)** the (French) Riviera; **la Côte d'Ivoire** the Ivory Coast; **côte de porc** pork chop

côté [kote] nm (gén) side; (direction) way, direction; **de chaque côté (de)** on each side of; **de tous les côtés** from all directions; **de quel côté est-il parti?** which way ou in which direction did he go?; **de ce/de l'autre côté** this/the other way; **d'un côté ... de l'autre côté** (alternative) on (the) one hand ... on the other (hand); **du côté de** (provenance) from; (direction) towards; **du côté de Lyon** (proximité) near Lyons; **du côté gauche** on the left-hand side; **de côté** adv sideways; on one side; to one side; aside; **laisser de côté** to leave on one side; **mettre de côté** to put on one side, put aside; **de mon côté** (quant à moi) for my part; **à côté** adv (right) nearby; beside; next door; (*d'autre part*) besides; **à côté de** beside; next to; (*fig*) in comparison to; **à côté (de la cible)** off target, wide (of the mark); **être aux côtés de** to be by the side of

coteau, x [kɔto] *nm* hill

côtelette [kotlɛt] *nf* chop

côtier, ière [kotje, -jɛʀ] *adj* coastal

cotisation [kotizasjɔ̃] *nf* subscription, dues *pl*; (*pour une pension*) contributions *pl*

cotiser [kotize] *vi*: **cotiser (à)** to pay contributions (to); (*à une association*) to subscribe (to); **se cotiser** to club together

coton [kɔtɔ̃] *nm* cotton; **coton hydrophile** cotton wool (*BRIT*), absorbent cotton (*US*)

Coton-Tige® [kɔtɔ̃tiʒ] *nm* cotton bud

côtoyer [kotwaje] *vt* to be close to; (*rencontrer*) to rub shoulders with; (*longer*) to run alongside; (*fig: friser*) to be bordering *ou* verging on

cou [ku] *nm* neck

couchant [kuʃɑ̃] *adj*: **soleil couchant** setting sun

couche [kuʃ] *nf* (*strate: gén*), *GÉO*) layer, stratum (*pl* -a); (*de peinture, vernis*) coat; (*de poussière, crème*) layer; (*de bébé*) nappy (*BRIT*), diaper (*US*); **couche d'o-zone** ozone layer; **couches** *nfpl* (*MÉD*) confinement *sg*; **couches sociales** social levels *ou* strata

couché, e [kuʃe] *adj* (*étendu*) lying down; (*au lit*) in bed

coucher [kuʃe] *nm* (*du soleil*) setting ◆ *vt* (*personne*) to put to bed; (*: loger*) to put up; (*objet*) to lay on its side; (*écrire*) to inscribe, couch ◆ *vi* (*dormir*) to sleep, spend the night; **coucher avec qn** to sleep with sb, go to bed with sb; **se coucher** *vi* (*pour dormir*) to go to bed; (*pour se reposer*) to lie down; (*soleil*) to set, go down; **à prendre avant le coucher** (*MÉD*) take at night *ou* before going to bed; **coucher de soleil** sunset

couchette [kuʃɛt] *nf* couchette; (*de marin*) bunk

coucou [kuku] *nm* cuckoo ◆ *excl* peek-a-boo

coude [kud] *nm* (*ANAT*) elbow; (*de tuyau, de la route*) bend; **coude à coude** *adv* shoulder to shoulder, side by side

coudre [kudʀ(ə)] *vt* (*bouton*) to sew on; (*robe*) to sew (up) ◆ *vi* to sew

couenne [kwan] *nf* (*de lard*) rind

couette [kwɛt] *nf* duvet, (continental) quilt; **couettes** *nfpl* (*cheveux*) bunches

couffin [kufɛ̃] *nm* Moses basket; (straw) basket

couler [kule] *vi* to flow, run; (*fuir: stylo, récipient*) to leak; (*sombrer: bateau*) to sink ◆ *vt* (*cloche, sculpture*) to cast; (*bateau*) to sink; (*fig*) to ruin, bring down; (*: passer*): **couler une vie heureuse** to enjoy a happy life; **se couler dans** (*interstice etc*) to slip into; **faire couler** (*eau*) to run; **faire couler un bain** to run a bath; **il a coulé une bielle** (*AUTO*) his big end went; **couler de source** to follow on naturally; **couler à pic** to sink *ou* go straight to the bottom

couleur [kulœʀ] *nf* colour (*BRIT*), color (*US*); (*CARTES*) suit; **couleurs** *nfpl* (*du teint*) colo(u)r *sg*; **les**

couleurs (*MIL*) the colo(u)rs; **en couleurs** (*film*) in colo(u)r; **télévision en couleurs** colo(u)r television; **de couleur** (*homme, femme*) colo(u)red; **sous couleur de** on the pretext of; **de quelle couleur** of what colo(u)r

couleuvre [kulœvʀ(ə)] *nf* grass snake

coulisse [kulis] *nf* (*TECH*) runner; **coulisses** *nfpl* (*THÉÂT*) wings; (*fig*): **dans les coulisses** behind the scenes; **porte à coulisse** sliding door

coulisser [kulise] *vi* to slide, run

couloir [kulwaʀ] *nm* corridor, passage; (*d'avion*) aisle; (*de bus*) gangway; (*: sur la route*) bus lane; (*SPORT: de piste*) lane; (*GÉO*) gully; **couloir aérien** air corridor *ou* lane; **couloir de navigation** shipping lane

coup [ku] *nm* (*heurt, choc*) knock; (*affectif*) blow, shock; (*agressif*) blow; (*avec arme à feu*) shot; (*de l'horloge*) chime; (*SPORT*) stroke; shot; blow; (*fam: fois*) time; (*ÉCHECS*) move; **coup de coude/genou** nudge (with the elbow)/ with the knee; **à coups de hache/marteau** (hitting) with an axe/a hammer; **coup de tonnerre** clap of thunder; **coup de sonnette** ring of the bell; **coup de crayon/pinceau** stroke of the pencil/brush; **donner un coup de balai** to sweep up, give the floor a sweep; **donner un coup de chiffon** to go round with the duster; **avoir le coup** (*fig*) to have the knack; **être dans le/hors du coup** to be/not to be in on it; **boire un coup** to have a drink; **d'un seul coup** (*subitement*) suddenly; (*à la fois*) at one go; in one blow; **du coup** so (you see); **du premier coup** first time *ou* go, at the first attempt; **du même coup** at the same time; **à coup sûr** definitely, without fail; **après coup** afterwards; **coup sur coup** in quick succession; **être sur un coup** to be on to something; **sur le coup** outright; **sous le coup de** (*surprise etc*) under the influence of; **tomber sous le coup de la loi** to constitute a statutory offence; **à tous les coups** every time; **il a raté son coup** he missed his turn; **pour le coup** for once; **coup bas** (*fig*): **donner un coup bas à qn** to hit sb below the belt; **coup de chance** stroke of luck; **coup de chapeau** (*fig*) pat on the back; **coup de couteau** stab (of a knife); **coup dur** hard blow; **coup d'éclat** (great) feat; **coup d'envoi** kick-off; **coup d'essai** first attempt; **coup d'état** coup d'état; **coup de feu** shot; **coup de filet** (*POLICE*) haul; **coup de foudre** (*fig*) love at first sight; **coup fourré** stab in the back; **coup franc** free kick; **coup de frein** (sharp) braking *no pl*; **coup de fusil** rifle shot; **coup de grâce** coup de grâce; **coup du lapin** (*AUTO*) whiplash; **coup de main**: **donner un coup de main à qn** to give sb a (helping) hand; **coup de maître** master stroke; **coup d'œil** glance; **coup de poid** kick; **coup de poing** punch; **coup de soleil** sunburn *no pl*; **coup de téléphone** phone call; **coup de tête** (*fig*) (sudden) impulse; **coup de théâtre** (*fig*) dramatic turn of events; **coup de vent** gust of wind; **en coup de vent** (*rapidement*) in a tearing hurry

coupable [kupabl(ə)] *adj* guilty; (*pensée*) guilty, culpable ♦ *nm/f* (*gén*) culprit; (*JUR*) guilty party; **coupable de** guilty of

coupe [kup] *nf* (*verre*) goblet; (*à fruits*) dish; (*SPORT*) cup; (*de cheveux, de vêtement*) cut; (*graphique, plan*) (cross) section; **être sous la coupe de** to be under the control of; **faire des coupes sombres dans** to make drastic cuts in

coupe-papier [kuppapje] *nm inv* paper knife

couper [kupe] *vt* to cut; (*retrancher*) to cut (out), take out; (*route, courant*) to cut off; (*appétit*) to take away; (*fièvre*) to take down, reduce; (*vin, cidre*) to blend; (: *à table*) to dilute (with water) ♦ *vi* to cut; (*prendre un raccourci*) to take a short-cut; (*CARTES: diviser le paquet*) to cut; (: *avec l'atout*) to trump; **se couper** (*se blesser*) to cut o.s.; (*en témoignant etc*) to give o.s. away; **couper l'appétit à qn** to spoil sb's appetite; **couper la parole à qn** to cut sb short; **couper les vivres à qn** to cut off sb's vital supplies; **couper le contact** *ou* **l'allumage** (*AUTO*) to turn off the ignition; **couper les ponts avec qn** to break with sb; **se faire couper les cheveux** to have *ou* get one's hair cut

couple [kupl(ə)] *nm* couple; **couple de torsion** torque

couplet [kuplɛ] *nm* verse

coupole [kupɔl] *nf* dome; cupola

coupon [kupɔ̃] *nm* (*ticket*) coupon; (*de tissu*) remnant; roll

coupon-réponse, *pl* **coupons-réponses** [kupɔ̃repɔ̃s] *nm* reply coupon

coupure [kupyʀ] *nf* cut; (*billet de banque*) note; (*de journal*) cutting; **coupure de courant** power cut

cour [kuʀ] *nf* (*de ferme, jardin*) (court)yard; (*d'immeuble*) back yard; (*JUR, royale*) court; **faire la cour à qn** to court sb; **cour d'appel** appeal court (*BRIT*), appellate court (*US*); **cour d'assises** court of assizes, = Crown Court (*BRIT*); **cour de cassation** final court of appeal; **cour des comptes** (*ADMIN*) revenue court; **cour martiale** court-martial; **cour de récréation** (*SCOL*) schoolyard, playground

courage [kuʀaʒ] *nm* courage, bravery

courageux, euse [kuʀaʒø, -øz] *adj* brave, courageous

couramment [kuʀamɑ̃] *adv* commonly; (*parler*) fluently

courant, e [kuʀɑ̃, -ɑ̃t] *adj* (*fréquent*) common; (*COMM, gén: normal*) standard; (*en cours*) current ♦ *nm* current; (*fig*) movement; trend; **être au courant (de)** (*fait, nouvelle*) to know (about); **mettre qn au courant (de)** (*fait, nouvelle*) to tell sb (about); (*nouveau travail etc*) to teach sb the basics (of), brief sb (about); **se tenir au courant (de)** (*techniques etc*) to keep o.s. up-to-date (on); **dans le courant de** (*pendant*) in the course of; **courant octobre etc** in the course of October etc; **le 10 courant** (*COMM*) the 10th inst; **courant d'air**

draught (*BRIT*), draft (*US*); **courant électrique** (electric) current, power

courbature [kuʀbatyʀ] *nf* ache

courbe [kuʀb(ə)] *adj* curved ♦ *nf* curve; **courbe de niveau** contour line

courber [kuʀbe] *vt* to bend; **courber la tête** to bow one's head; **se courber** *vi* (*branche etc*) to bend, curve; (*personne*) to bend (down)

coureur, euse [kuʀœʀ, -øz] *nm/f* (*SPORT*) runner (*ou* driver); (*péj*) womanizer/manhunter; **coureur cycliste/automobile** racing cyclist/driver

courge [kuʀʒ(ə)] *nf* (*BOT*) gourd; (*CULIN*) marrow

courgette [kuʀʒɛt] *nf* courgette (*BRIT*), zucchini (*US*)

courir [kuʀiʀ] *vi* (*gén*) to run; (*se dépêcher*) to rush; (*fig: rumeurs*) to go round; (*COMM: intérêt*) to accrue ♦ *vt* (*SPORT: épreuve*) to compete in; (*risque*) to run; (*danger*) to face; **courir les cafés/bals** to do the rounds of the cafés/ dances; **le bruit court que** the rumour is going round that; **par les temps qui courent** at the present time; **courir après qn** to run after sb, chase (after) sb; **laisser courir** to let things alone; **faire courir qn** to make sb run around (all over the place); **tu peux (toujours) courir!** you've got a hope!

couronne [kuʀɔn] *nf* crown; (*de fleurs*) wreath, circlet; **couronne (funéraire** *ou* **mortuaire)** (funeral) wreath

courons [kuʀɔ̃], **courrai** etc [kuʀe] *vb voir* **courir**

courrier [kuʀje] *nm* mail, post; (*lettres à écrire*) letters *pl*; (*rubrique*) column; **qualité courrier** letter quality; **long/moyen courrier** *adj* (*AVIAT*) long-/medium-haul; **courrier du cœur** problem page; **courrier électronique** electronic mail, E-mail

courroie [kuʀwa] *nf* strap; (*TECH*) belt; **courroie de transmission/de ventilateur** driving/fan belt

courrons etc [kuʀɔ̃] *vb voir* **courir**

cours [kuʀ] *vb voir* **courir** ♦ *nm* (*leçon*) lesson; class; (*série de leçons*) course; (*cheminement*) course; (*écoulement*) flow; (*avenue*) walk; (*COMM*) rate; price; (*BOURSE*) quotation; **donner libre cours à** to give free expression to; **avoir cours** (*monnaie*) to be legal tender; (*fig*) to be current; (*SCOL*) to have a class *ou* lecture; **en cours** (*année*) current; (*travaux*) in progress; **en cours de route** on the way; **au cours de** in the course of, during; **le cours du change** the exchange rate; **cours d'eau** waterway; **cours élémentaire (CE)** 2nd and 3rd years of primary school; **cours moyen (CM)** 4th and 5th years of primary school; **cours préparatoire** = infants' class (*BRIT*), = 1st grade (*US*); **cours du soir** night school

course [kuʀs(ə)] *nf* running; (*SPORT: épreuve*) race; (*trajet: du soleil*) course; (: *d'un projectile*) flight; (: *d'une pièce mécanique*) travel; (*excursion*) outing; climb; (*d'un taxi, autocar*) journey, trip; (*petite mission*) errand; **courses** *nfpl* (*achats*) shopping *sg*; (*HIPPISME*) races; **faire les** *ou* **ses courses** to go shopping; **jouer aux courses** to bet on the races; **à bout de course** (*épuisé*) exhausted; **course auto-**

mobile car race; **course de côte** (*AUTO*) hill climb; **course par étapes** *ou* **d'étapes** race in stages; **course d'obstacles** obstacle race; **course à pied** walking race; **course de vitesse** sprint; **courses de chevaux** horse racing

court, e [kuʀ, kuʀt(ə)] *adj* short ♦ *adv* short ♦ *nm*: **court (de tennis)** (tennis) court; **tourner court** to come to a sudden end; **couper court à** to cut short; **à court de** short of; **prendre qn de court** to catch sb unawares; **pour Faire court** briefly, to cut a long story short; **ça fait court** that's not very long; **tirer à la courte paille** to draw lots; **faire la courte échelle à qn** to give sb a leg up; **court métrage** (*CINÉ*) short (film)

court-circuit, *pl* **courts-circuits** [kuʀsiʀkɥi] *nm* short-circuit

courtier, ière [kuʀtje, -jɛʀ] *nm/f* broker

courtiser [kuʀtize] *vt* to court, woo

courtois, e [kuʀtwa, -waz] *adj* courteous

courtoisie [kuʀtwazi] *nf* courtesy

couru, e [kuʀy] *pp de* **courir** ♦ *adj* (*spectacle etc*) popular; **c'est couru (d'avance)!** (*fam*) it's a safe bet!

cousais *etc* [kuze] *vb voir* **coudre**

couscous [kuskus] *nm* couscous

cousin, e [kuzɛ̃, -in] *nm/f* cousin ♦ *nm* (*ZOOL*) mosquito; **cousin germain** first cousin

coussin [kusɛ̃] *nm* cushion; **coussin d'air** (*TECH*) air cushion

cousu, e [kuzy] *pp de* **coudre** ♦ *adj*: **cousu d'or** rolling in riches

coût [ku] *nm* cost; **le coût de la vie** the cost of living

coûtant [kutɑ̃] *adj m*: **au prix coûtant** at cost price

couteau, x [kuto] *nm* knife; **couteau à cran d'arrêt** flick-knife; **couteau de cuisine** kitchen knife; **couteau à pain** bread knife; **couteau de poche** pocket knife

coûter [kute] *vt* to cost ♦ *vi*: **coûter à qn** to cost sb a lot; **coûter cher** to be expensive; **coûter cher à qn** (*fig*) to cost sb dear or dearly; **combien ça coûte?** how much is it?, what does it cost?; **coûte que coûte** at all costs

coûteux, euse [kutø, -øz] *adj* costly, expensive

coutume [kutym] *nf* custom; **de coutume** usual, customary

couture [kutyʀ] *nf* sewing; dress-making; (*points*) seam

couturier [kutyʀje] *nm* fashion designer, couturier

couturière [kutyʀjɛʀ] *nf* dressmaker

couvée [kuve] *nf* brood, clutch

couvent [kuvɑ̃] *nm* (*de sœurs*) convent; (*de frères*) monastery; (*établissement scolaire*) convent (school)

couver [kuve] *vt* to hatch; (*maladie*) to be sicken-ing for ♦ *vi* (*feu*) to smoulder (*BRIT*), smolder (*US*); (*révolte*) to be brewing; **couver qn/qch des yeux** to look lovingly at sb/sth; (*convoiter*) to look longingly at sb/sth

couvercle [kuvɛʀkl(ə)] *nm* lid; (*de bombe aérosol etc, qui se visse*) cap, top

couvert, e [kuvɛʀ, -ɛʀt(ə)] *pp de* **couvrir** ♦ *adj* (*ciel*) overcast; (*coiffé d'un chapeau*) wearing a hat ♦ *nm* place setting; (*place à table*) place; (*au restaurant*) cover charge; **couverts** *nmpl* place settings; cutlery *sg*; **couvert de** covered with *ou* in; **bien couvert** (*habillé*) well wrapped up; **mettre le couvert** to lay the table; **à couvert** under cover; **sous le couvert de** under the shelter of; (*fig*) under cover of

couverture [kuvɛʀtyʀ] *nf* (*de lit*) blanket; (*de bâti-ment*) roofing; (*de livre, fig: d'un espion etc*), *ASSU-RANCES*) cover; (*PRESSE*) coverage; **de couverture** (*let-tre etc*) covering; **couverture chauffante** electric blanket

couveuse [kuvøz] *nf* (*à poules*) sitter, brooder; (*de maternité*) incubator

couvre-feu, x [kuvʀəfø] *nm* curfew

couvre-lit [kuvʀəli] *nm* bedspread

couvreur [kuvʀœʀ] *nm* roofer

couvrir [kuvʀiʀ] *vt* to cover; (*dominer, étouffer: voix, pas*) to drown out; (*erreur*) to cover up; (*ZOOL: s'accoupler à*) to cover; **se couvrir** (*ciel*) to cloud over; (*s'habiller*) to cover up, wrap up; (*se coiffer*) to put on one's hat; (*par une assurance*) to cover o.s.; **se couvrir de** (*fleurs, boutons*) to become covered in

cow-boy [kɔbɔj] *nm* cowboy

crabe [kʀab] *nm* crab

cracher [kʀaʃe] *vi* to spit ♦ *vt* to spit out; (*fig: lave etc*) to belch (out); **cracher du sang** to spit blood

crachin [kʀaʃɛ̃] *nm* drizzle

crack [kʀak] *nm* (*intellectuel*) whizzkid; (*sportif*) ace; (*poulain*) hot favourite (*BRIT*) *ou* favorite (*US*)

craie [kʀɛ] *nf* chalk

craindre [kʀɛ̃dʀ(ə)] *vt* to fear, be afraid of; (*être sensible à: chaleur, froid*) to be easily damaged by; **craindre de/que** to be afraid of/that; **je crains qu'il (ne) vienne** I am afraid he may come

crainte [kʀɛ̃t] *nf* fear; **de crainte de/que** for fear of/that

craintif, ive [kʀɛ̃tif, -iv] *adj* timid

cramoisi, e [kʀamwazi] *adj* crimson

crampe [kʀɑ̃p] *nf* cramp; **crampe d'estomac** stomach cramp

crampon [kʀɑ̃pɔ̃] *nm* (*de semelle*) stud; (*ALPINISME*) crampon

cramponner [kʀɑ̃pɔne]: **se cramponner** *vi*: **se cramponner (à)** to hang *ou* cling on (to)

cran [kʀɑ̃] *nm* (*entaille*) notch; (*de courroie*) hole; (*courage*) guts *pl*; **cran d'arrêt/de sûreté** safety catch; **cran de mire** bead

crâne [kʀɑn] *nm* skull

crâner [kʀɑne] vi (fam) to swank, show off

crapaud [kʀapo] nm toad

crapule [kʀapyl] nf villain

craquement [kʀakmɑ̃] nm crack, snap; (du plancher) creak, creaking no pl

craquer [kʀake] vi (bois, plancher) to creak; (fil, branche) to snap; (couture) to come apart, burst; (fig) to break down, fall apart; (: être enthousiasmé) to go wild ♦ vt: **craquer une allumette** to strike a match

crasse [kʀas] nf grime, filth ♦ adj (fig: ignorance) crass

crasseux, euse [kʀaso, øz] adj filthy

cravache [kʀavaʃ] nf (riding) crop

cravate [kʀavat] nf tie

crawl [kʀol] nm crawl

crayon [kʀejɔ̃] nm pencil; (de rouge à lèvres etc) stick, pencil; **écrire au crayon** to write in pencil; **crayon à bille** ball-point pen; **crayon de couleur** crayon; **crayon optique** light pen

crayon-feutre, pl **crayons-feutres** [kʀejɔ̃føtʀ(ə)] nm felt(-tip) pen

créancier, ière [kʀeɑ̃sje, -jɛʀ] nm/f creditor

création [kʀeɑsjɔ̃] nf creation

créature [kʀeatyʀ] nf creature

crèche [kʀɛʃ] nf (de Noël) crib; (garderie) crèche, day nursery; see boxed note

crédit [kʀedi] nm (gén) credit; **crédits** nmpl: **acheter à crédit** to buy on credit ou on easy terms; **faire crédit à qn** to give sb credit; **crédit municipal** pawnshop; **crédit relais** bridging loan

créditer [kʀedite] vt: **créditer un compte (de)** to credit an account (with)

crédule [kʀedyl] adj credulous, gullible

créer [kʀee] vt to create; (THÉÂT: pièce) to produce (for the first time); (: rôle) to create

crémaillère [kʀemajɛʀ] nf (RAIL) rack; (tige crantée) trammel; **direction à crémaillère** (AUTO) rack and pinion steering; **pendre la crémaillère** to have a house-warming party

crématoire [kʀematwaʀ] adj: **four crématoire** crematorium

crème [kʀɛm] nf cream; (entremets) cream dessert ♦ adj inv cream; **un (café) crème** = a white coffee; **crème chantilly** whipped cream, crème Chantilly; **crème fouettée** whipped cream; **crème glacée** ice cream; **crème à raser** shaving cream;

crème solaire sun cream

crémerie [kʀɛmʀi] nf dairy; (tearoom) teashop

crémeux, euse [kʀemø, -øz] adj creamy

créneau, x [kʀeno] nm (de fortification) crenel(le); (fig, aussi COMM) gap, slot; (AUTO): **faire un créneau** to reverse into a parking space (between cars alongside the kerb)

crêpe [kʀɛp] nf (galette) pancake ♦ nm (tissu) crêpe; (de deuil) black mourning crêpe; (ruban) black armband (ou hatband ou ribbon); **semelle (de) crêpe** crêpe sole; **crêpe de Chine** crêpe de Chine

crêpé, e [kʀepe] adj (cheveux) backcombed

crêperie [kʀepʀi] nf pancake shop ou restaurant

crépiter [kʀepite] vi to sputter, splutter, crackle

crépu, e [kʀepy] adj frizzy, fuzzy

crépuscule [kʀepyskyl] nm twilight, dusk

cresson [kʀesɔ̃] nm watercress

crête [kʀɛt] nf (de coq) comb; (de vague, montagne) crest

creuser [kʀøze] vt (trou, tunnel) to dig; (sol) to dig a hole in; (bois) to hollow out; (fig) to go (deeply) into; **ça creuse** that gives you a real appetite; **se creuser (la cervelle)** to rack one's brains

creux, euse [kʀø, -øz] adj hollow ♦ nm hollow; (fig: sur graphique etc) trough; **heures creuses** slack periods; off-peak periods; **le creux de l'estomac** the pit of the stomach

crevaison [kʀəvɛzɔ̃] nf puncture, flat

crevasse [kʀəvas] nf (dans le sol) crack, fissure; (de glacier) crevasse; (de la peau) crack

crevé, e [kʀəve] adj (fam: fatigué) worn out, dead beat

crever [kʀəve] vt (papier) to tear, break; (tambour, ballon) to burst ♦ vi (pneu) to burst; (automobiliste) to have a puncture (BRIT) ou a flat (tire) (US); (abcès, outre, nuage) to burst (open); (fam) to die; **cela lui a crevé un œil** it blinded him in one eye; **crever l'écran** to have real screen presence

crevette [kʀəvɛt] nf: **crevette (rose)** prawn; **crevette grise** shrimp

cri [kʀi] nm cry, shout; (d'animal: spécifique) cry, call; **à grands cris** at the top of one's voice; **c'est le dernier cri** (fig) it's the latest fashion

criant, e [kʀijɑ̃, -ɑ̃t] adj (injustice) glaring

criard, e [kʀijaʀ, -aʀd(ə)] adj (couleur) garish, loud; (voix) yelling

crible [kʀibl(ə)] nm riddle; (mécanique) screen, jig; **passer qch au crible** to put sth through a riddle; (fig) to go over sth with a fine-tooth comb

criblé, e [kʀible] adj: **criblé de** riddled with

cric [kʀik] nm (AUTO) jack

crier [kʀije] vi (pour appeler) to shout, cry (out); (de peur, de douleur etc) to scream, yell; (fig: grincer) to squeal, screech ♦ vt (ordre, injure) to shout (out), yell (out); **sans crier gare** without warning; **crier grâce** to cry for mercy; **crier au secours** to shout for help

crime [kʀim] *nm* crime; (*meurtre*) murder

criminel, le [kʀiminɛl] *adj* criminal ♦ *nm/f* criminal; murderer; **criminel de guerre** war criminal

crin [kʀɛ̃] *nm* hair *no pl*; (*fibre*) horsehair; **à tous crins, à tout crin** diehard, out-and-out

crinière [kʀinjɛʀ] *nf* mane

crique [kʀik] *nf* creek, inlet

criquet [kʀikɛ] *nm* grasshopper

crise [kʀiz] *nf* crisis (*pl* crises); (*MÉD*) attack; fit; **crise cardiaque** heart attack; **crise de foi** crisis of belief; **crise de foie** bilious attack; **crise de nerfs** attack of nerves

crisper [kʀispe] *vt* to tense; (*poings*) to clench; **se crisper** to tense; to clench; (*personne*) to get tense

crisser [kʀise] *vi* (*neige*) to crunch; (*tissu*) to rustle; (*pneu*) to screech

cristal, aux [kʀistal, -o] *nm* crystal ♦ *nmpl* (*objets*) crystal(ware) *sg*; **cristal de plomb** (lead) crystal; **cristal de roche** rock-crystal; **cristaux de soude** washing soda *sg*

cristallin, e [kʀistalɛ̃, -in] *adj* crystal-clear ♦ *nm* (*ANAT*) crystalline lens

critère [kʀitɛʀ] *nm* criterion (*pl* -ia)

critiquable [kʀitikabl(ə)] *adj* open to criticism

critique [kʀitik] *adj* critical ♦ *nm/f* (*de théâtre, musique*) critic ♦ *nf* criticism; (*THÉAT etc: article*) review; **la critique** (*activité*) criticism; (*personnes*) the critics *pl*

critiquer [kʀitike] *vt* (*dénigrer*) to criticize; (*évaluer, juger*) to assess, examine (critically)

croasser [kʀoase] *vi* to caw

Croatie [kʀoasi] *nf*: **la Croatie** Croatia

croc [kʀo] *nm* (*dent*) fang; (*de boucher*) hook

croc-en-jambe *pl* **crocs-en-jambe** [kʀokɑ̃ʒɑ̃b] *nm*: **faire un croc-en-jambe à qn** to trip sb up

croche [kʀɔʃ] *nf* (*MUS*) quaver (*BRIT*), eighth note (*US*); **double croche** semiquaver (*BRIT*), sixteenth note (*US*)

croche-pied [kʀɔʃpje] *nm* = **croc-en-jambe**

crochet [kʀɔʃɛ] *nm* hook; (*clef*) picklock; (*détour*) detour; (*BOXE*): **crochet du gauche** left hook; (*TRICOT: aiguille*) crochet hook; (: *technique*) crochet; **crochets** *nmpl* (*TYPO*) square brackets; **vivre aux crochets de qn** to live ou sponge off sb

crochu, e [kʀɔʃy] *adj* hooked; claw-like

crocodile [kʀɔkɔdil] *nm* crocodile

croire [kʀwaʀ] *vt* to believe; (*être honnête*) to believe sb (to be) honest; **se croire fort** to think one is strong; **croire que** to believe ou think that; **vous croyez?** do you think so?; **croire être/faire** to think one is/does; **croire à, croire en** to believe in

crois *etc* [kʀwa] *vb voir* **croître**

croisade [kʀwazad] *nf* crusade

croisé, e [kʀwaze] *adj* (*veston*) double-breasted ♦ *nm* (*guerrier*) crusader ♦ *nf* (*fenêtre*) window, casement; **croisée d'ogives** intersecting ribs; **à la**

croisée des chemins at the crossroads

croisement [kʀwazmɑ̃] *nm* (*carrefour*) crossroads *sg*; (*BIO*) crossing; crossbreed

croiser [kʀwaze] *vt* (*personne, voiture*) to pass; (*route*) to cross, cut across; (*BIO*) to cross ♦ *vi* (*NAVIG*) to cruise; **croiser les jambes/bras** to cross one's legs/ fold one's arms; **se croiser** (*personnes, véhicules*) to pass each other; (*routes*) to cross, intersect; (*lettres*) to cross (in the post); (*regards*) to meet; **se croiser les bras** (*fig*) to twiddle one's thumbs

croisière [kʀwazjɛʀ] *nf* cruise; **vitesse de croisière** (*AUTO etc*) cruising speed

croissance [kʀwasɑ̃s] *nf* growing, growth; **troubles de la croissance** growing pains; **maladie de croissance** growth disease; **croissance économique** economic growth

croissant, e [kʀwasɑ̃, -ɑ̃t] *vb voir* **croître** ♦ *adj* growing; rising ♦ *nm* (*à manger*) croissant; (*motif*) crescent; **croissant de lune** crescent moon

croître [kʀwatʀ(ə)] *vi* to grow; (*lune*) to wax

croix [kʀwa] *nf* cross; **en croix** *adj, adv* in the form of a cross; **la Croix Rouge** the Red Cross

croque-madame [kʀɔkmadam] *nm inv* toasted cheese sandwich with a fried egg on top

croque-monsieur [kʀɔkməsjø] *nm inv* toasted ham and cheese sandwich

croquer [kʀɔke] *vt* (*manger*) to crunch; to munch; (*dessiner*) to sketch ♦ *vi* to be crisp ou crunchy; **chocolat à croquer** plain dessert chocolate

croquis [kʀɔki] *nm* sketch

cross(-country), *pl* **cross(-countries)** [kʀɔs (-kuntʀi)] *nm* cross-country race ou run; cross-country racing ou running

crosse [kʀɔs] *nf* (*de fusil*) butt; (*de revolver*) grip; (*d'évêque*) crook, crosier; (*de hockey*) hockey stick

crotte [kʀɔt] *nf* droppings *pl*; **crotte!** (*fam*) damn!

crotté, e [kʀɔte] *adj* muddy, mucky

crottin [kʀɔtɛ̃] *nm*: **crottin (de cheval)** (horse) dung ou manure

crouler [kʀule] *vi* (*s'effondrer*) to collapse; (*être délabré*) to be crumbling

croupe [kʀup] *nf* croup, rump; **en croupe** pillion

croupir [kʀupiʀ] *vi* to stagnate

croustillant, e [kʀustijɑ̃, -ɑ̃t] *adj* crisp; (*fig*) spicy

croûte [kʀut] *nf* crust; (*du fromage*) rind; (*de vol-au-vent*) case; (*MÉD*) scab; **en croûte** (*CULIN*) in pastry, in a pie; **croûte aux champignons** mushrooms on toast; **croûte au fromage** cheese on toast *no pl*; **croûte de pain** (*morceau*) crust (of bread); **croûte terrestre** earth's crust

croûton [kʀutɔ̃] *nm* (*CULIN*) crouton; (*bout du pain*) crust, heel

croyable [kʀwajabl(ə)] *adj* believable, credible

croyant, e [kʀwajɑ̃, -ɑ̃t] *vb voir* **croire** ♦ *adj*: **être/ ne pas être croyant** to be/not to be a believer ♦ *nm/f* believer

CRS *sigle fpl* (= *Compagnies républicaines de sécu-*

rité) state security police force ◆ *sigle m* member of the CRS

cru, e [kRy] *pp de* **croire** ◆ *adj (non cuit)* raw; *(lumière, couleur)* harsh; *(description)* crude; *(paroles, langage: franc)* blunt; *(: grossier)* crude ◆ *nm (vignoble)* vineyard; *(vin)* wine ◆ *nf (d'un cours d'eau)* swelling, rising; **de son (propre) cru** *(fig)* of his own devising; **monter à cru** to ride bareback; **du cru** local; **en crue** in spate

crû [kRy] *pp de* **croître**

cruauté [kRyote] *nf* cruelty

cruche [kRyʃ] *nf* pitcher, (earthenware) jug

crucifix [kRysifi] *nm* crucifix

crucifixion [kRysifiksjɔ̃] *nf* crucifixion

crudité [kRydite] *nf* crudeness *no pl*; harshness *no pl*; **crudités** *nfpl (CULIN)* mixed salads *(as hors-d'œuvre)*

crue [kRy] *nf voir* **cru**

cruel, le [kRyɛl] *adj* cruel

crus, crûs [kRy etc] *vb voir* **croire, croître**

crustacés [kRystase] *nmpl* shellfish

Cuba [kyba] *nm*: **le Cuba** Cuba

cubain, e [kybɛ̃, -ɛn] *adj* Cuban ◆ *nm/f*: **Cubain,e** Cuban

cube [kyb] *nm* cube; *(jouet)* brick, building block; **gros cube** powerful motorbike; **mètre cube** cubic metre; **2 au cube = 8** 2 cubed is 8; **élever au cube** to cube

cueillette [kœjɛt] *nf* picking, gathering; harvest ou crop (of fruit)

cueillir [kœjiR] *vt (fruits, fleurs)* to pick, gather; *(fig)* to catch

cuiller, cuillère [kɥijɛR] *nf* spoon; **cuiller à café** coffee spoon; *(CULIN)* = teaspoonful; **cuiller à soupe** soup spoon; *(CULIN)* = tablespoonful

cuillerée [kɥijRe] *nf* spoonful; *(CULIN)*: **cuillerée à soupe/café** tablespoonful/teaspoonful

cuir [kɥiR] *nm* leather; *(avant tannage)* hide; **cuir chevelu** scalp

cuire [kɥiR] *vt*: **(faire) cuire** *(aliments)* to cook; *(au four)* to bake; *(poterie)* to fire ◆ *vi* to cook; *(picoter)* to smart, sting, burn; **bien cuit** *(viande)* well done; **trop cuit** overdone; **pas assez cuit** underdone; **cuit à point** medium done; done to a turn

cuisant, e [kɥizɑ̃, -ɑ̃t] *vb voir* **cuire** ◆ *adj (douleur)* smarting, burning; *(fig: souvenir, échec)* bitter

cuisine [kɥizin] *nf (pièce)* kitchen; *(art culinaire)* cookery, cooking; *(nourriture)* cooking, food; **faire la cuisine** to cook

cuisiné, e [kɥizine] *adj*: **plat cuisiné** ready-made meal ou dish

cuisiner [kɥizine] *vt* to cook; *(fam)* to grill ◆ *vi* to cook

cuisinier, ière [kɥizinje, -jɛR] *nm/f* cook ◆ *nf (poêle)* cooker; **cuisinière électrique/à gaz** electric/gas cooker

cuisse [kɥis] *nf (ANAT)* thigh; *(CULIN)* leg

cuisson [kɥisɔ̃] *nf* cooking; *(de poterie)* firing

cuit, e [kɥi, -it] *pp de* **cuire** ◆ *nf (fam)*: **prendre une cuite** to get plastered ou smashed

cuivre [kɥivR(ə)] *nm* copper; **les cuivres** *(MUS)* the brass; **cuivre rouge** copper; **cuivre jaune** brass

cul [ky] *nm (fam!)* arse *(BRIT!)*, ass *(US!)*, bum *(BRIT)*; **cul de bouteille** bottom of a bottle

culbute [kylbyt] *nf* somersault; *(accidentelle)* tumble, fall

culminant, e [kylminɑ̃, -ɑ̃t] *adj*: **point culminant** highest point; *(fig)* height, climax

culminer [kylmine] *vi* to reach its highest point; to tower

culot [kylo] *nm (d'ampoule)* cap; *(effronterie)* cheek, nerve

culotte [kylɔt] *nf (de femme)* panties *pl*, knickers *pl (BRIT)*; *(d'homme)* underpants *pl*; *(pantalon)* trousers *pl (BRIT)*, pants *pl (US)*; **culotte de cheval** riding breeches *pl*

culpabilité [kylpabilite] *nf* guilt

culte [kylt(ə)] *adj*: **livre/film culte** cult film/book ◆ *nm (religion)* religion; *(hommage, vénération)* worship; *(protestant)* service

cultivateur, trice [kyltivatœR, -tRis] *nm/f* farmer

cultivé, e [kyltive] *adj (personne)* cultured, cultivated

cultiver [kyltive] *vt* to cultivate; *(légumes)* to grow, cultivate

culture [kyltyR] *nf* cultivation; growing; *(connaissances etc)* culture; **(champs de) cultures** land(s) under cultivation; **culture physique** physical training

culturel, le [kyltyRɛl] *adj* cultural

culturisme [kyltyRism(ə)] *nm* body-building

cumin [kymɛ̃] *nm (CULIN)* cumin

cumuler [kymyle] *vt (emplois, honneurs)* to hold concurrently; *(salaires)* to draw concurrently; *(JUR: droits)* to accumulate

cupide [kypid] *adj* greedy, grasping

cure [kyR] *nf (MÉD)* course of treatment; *(REL)* cure, = living; presbytery, = vicarage; **faire une cure de fruits** to go on a fruit cure ou diet; **faire une cure thermale** to take the waters; **n'avoir cure de** to pay no attention to; **cure d'amaigrissement** slimming course; **cure de repos** rest cure; **cure de sommeil** sleep therapy *no pl*

curé [kyRe] *nm* parish priest; **M le curé** = Vicar

cure-dent [kyRdɑ̃] *nm* toothpick

cure-pipe [kyRpip] *nm* pipe cleaner

curer [kyRe] *vt* to clean out; **se curer les dents** to pick one's teeth

curieusement [kyRjøzmɑ̃] *adv* oddly

curieux, euse [kyRjø, -øz] *adj (étrange)* strange, curious; *(indiscret)* curious, inquisitive; *(intéressé)* inquiring, curious ◆ *nmpl (badauds)* onlookers, bystanders

curiosité [kyRjozite] *nf* curiosity, inquisitiveness;

(*objet*) curio(sity); (*site*) unusual feature *ou* sight

curriculum vitae (CV) [kyʀikylɔmvite] *nm inv* curriculum vitae (CV)

curseur [kyʀsœʀ] *nm* (*INFORM*) cursor; (*de règle*) slide; (*de fermeture-éclair*) slider

cutané, e [kytane] *adj* cutaneous, skin *cpd*

cuti-réaction [kytiʀeaksjɔ̃] *nf* (*MÉD*) skin-test

cuve [kyv] *nf* vat; (*à mazout etc*) tank

cuvée [kyve] *nf* vintage

cuvette [kyvɛt] *nf* (*récipient*) bowl, basin; (*du lavabo*) (wash)basin; (*des w.-c.*) pan; (*GÉO*) basin

CV *sigle m* (*AUTO*) = **cheval vapeur**; (*ADMIN*) = **curriculum vitae**

cyanure [sjanyʀ] *nm* cyanide

cybercafé [sibɛʀkafe] *nm* cybercafé

cyclable [siklabl(ə)] *adj*: **piste cyclable** cycle track

cycle [sikl(ə)] *nm* cycle; (*SCOL*): **premier/second cycle** ≃ middle/upper school (*BRIT*), ≃ junior/senior high school (*US*)

cyclisme [siklism(ə)] *nm* cycling

cycliste [siklist(ə)] *nm/f* cyclist ♦ *adj* cycle *cpd*; **coureur cycliste** racing cyclist

cyclomoteur [siklɔmɔtœʀ] *nm* moped

cyclone [siklon] *nm* hurricane

cygne [siɲ] *nm* swan

cylindre [silɛ̃dʀ(ə)] *nm* cylinder; **moteur à 4 cylindres en ligne** straight-4 engine

cylindrée [silɛ̃dʀe] *nf* (*AUTO*) (cubic) capacity; **une (voiture de) grosse cylindrée** a big-engined car

cymbale [sɛ̃bal] *nf* cymbal

cynique [sinik] *adj* cynical

cystite [sistit] *nf* cystitis

— D d —

d' *prép*, *dét voir* **de**

dactylo [daktilo] *nf* (*aussi*: **dactylographe**) typist; (*aussi*: **dactylographie**) typing, typewriting

dactylographier [daktilɔgʀafje] *vt* to type (out)

dada [dada] *nm* hobby-horse

daigner [deɲe] *vt* to deign

daim [dɛ̃] *nm* (fallow) deer *inv*; (*peau*) buckskin; (*imitation*) suede

dalle [dal] *nf* slab; (*au sol*) paving stone, flag (stone); **que dalle** nothing at all, damn all (*BRIT*)

daltonien, ne [daltɔnjɛ̃, -ɛn] *adj* colour-blind (*BRIT*), color-blind (*US*)

dam [dam] *nm*: **au grand dam de** much to the detriment (*ou* annoyance) of

dame [dam] *nf* lady; (*CARTES, ÉCHECS*) queen; **dames** *nfpl* (*jeu*) draughts *sg* (*BRIT*), checkers *sg* (*US*); **les (toilettes des) dames** the ladies' (toilets); **dame de charité** benefactress; **dame de compagnie** lady's companion

damner [dane] *vt* to damn

dancing [dɑ̃siŋ] *nm* dance hall

Danemark [danmaʀk] *nm*: **le Danemark** Denmark

danger [dɑ̃ʒe] *nm* danger; **mettre en danger** to endanger, put in danger; **être en danger de mort** to be in peril of one's life; **être hors de danger** to be out of danger

dangereux, euse [dɑ̃ʒʀø, -øz] *adj* dangerous

danois, e [danwa, -waz] *adj* Danish ♦ *nm* (*LING*) Danish ♦ *nm/f*: **Danois, e** Dane

---

MOT-CLÉ

dans [dɑ̃] *prép* **1** (*position*) in; (*à l'intérieur de*) inside; **c'est dans le tiroir/le salon** it's in the drawer/lounge; **dans la boîte** in *ou* inside the box; **marcher dans la ville/la rue** to walk about the town/along the street; **je l'ai lu dans le journal** I read it in the newspaper; **être dans les meilleurs** to be among *ou* one of the best

2 (*direction*) into; **elle a couru dans le salon** she ran into the lounge

3 (*provenance*) out of, from; **je l'ai pris dans le tiroir/salon** I took it out of *ou* from the drawer/lounge; **boire dans un verre** to drink out of *ou* from a glass

4 (*temps*) in; **dans 2 mois** in 2 months, in 2 months' time

5 (*approximation*) about; **dans les 20 €** about 20 €

---

danse [dɑ̃s] *nf*: **la danse** dancing; (*classique*) (ballet) dancing; **une danse** a dance; **danse du ventre** belly dancing

danser [dɑ̃se] *vi*, *vt* to dance

danseur, euse [dɑ̃sœʀ, -øz] *nm/f* ballet dancer; (*au bal etc*) dancer; (: *cavalier*) partner; **danseur de claquettes** tap-dancer; **en danseuse** (*à vélo*) standing on the pedals

dard [daʀ] *nm* sting (*organ*)

date [dat] *nf* date; **faire date** to mark a milestone; **de longue date** *adj* longstanding; **date de naissance** date of birth; **date limite** deadline; (*d'un aliment*: *aussi*: **date limite de vente**) sell-by date

dater [date] *vt*, *vi* to date; **dater de** to date from, go back to; **à dater de** (as) from

datte [dat] *nf* date

dauphin [dofɛ̃] *nm* (*ZOOL*) dolphin; (*du roi*) dauphin; (*fig*) heir apparent

davantage [davɑ̃taʒ] *adv* more; (*plus longtemps*) longer; **davantage de** more; **davantage que** more than

---

MOT-CLÉ

de, (d') (*de* + *le* = **du**, *de* + *les* = **des**) *prép* **1** (*appartenance*) of; **le toit de la maison** the roof of the house; **la voiture d'Elisabeth/de mes parents** Elizabeth's/my parents' car

2 (*provenance*) from; **il vient de Londres** he comes from London; **de Londres à Paris** from London to Paris; **elle est sortie du cinéma** she came out of the cinema

3 (*moyen*) with; **je l'ai fait de mes propres mains** I did it with my own two hands

4 (*caractérisation, mesure*): **un mur de brique/bureau d'acajou** a brick wall/mahogany desk; **un billet de 10 €** a 10 € note; **une pièce de 2 m de large** *ou* **large de 2 m** a room 2 m wide, a 2m-wide room; **un bébé de 10 mois** a 10-month-old baby; **12 mois de crédit/travail** 12 months' credit/work; **elle est payée 4 € de l'heure** she's paid 4 € an hour *ou* per hour; **augmenter de 10 €** to increase by 10 €; **3 jours de libres** 3 free days, 3 days free; **un verre d'eau** a glass of water; **il mange de tout** he'll eat anything

5 (*rapport*) from; **de 4 à 6** from 4 to 6

6 (*de la part de*): **estimé de ses collègues** respected by his colleagues

7 (*cause*): **mourir de faim** to die of hunger; **rouge de colère** red with fury

8 (*vb +de +infin*) to; **il m'a dit de rester** he told me to stay

9 (*en apposition*): **cet imbécile de Paul** that idiot Paul; **le terme de franglais** the term "franglais"
◆ *dét* **1** (*phrases affirmatives*) some (*souvent omis*); **du vin, de l'eau, des pommes** (some) wine, (some) water, (some) apples; **des enfants sont venus** some children came; **pendant des mois** for months

2 (*phrases interrogatives et négatives*) any; **a-t-il du vin?** has he got any wine?; **il n'a pas de pommes/d'enfants** he hasn't (got) any apples/children, he has no apples/children

dé [de] *nm* (*à jouer*) die *ou* dice (*pl* dice); (*aussi*: **dé à coudre**) thimble; **dés** *nmpl* (*jeu*) (game of) dice; **un coup de dés** a throw of the dice; **couper en dés** (*CULIN*) to dice

dealer [dilœʀ] *nm* (*fam*) (drug) pusher

déambuler [deɑ̃byle] *vi* to stroll about

débâcle [debɑkl(ə)] *nf* rout

déballer [debale] *vt* to unpack

débandade [debɑ̃dad] *nf* scattering; (*déroute*) rout

débarbouiller [debaʀbuje] *vt* to wash; **se débarbouiller** to wash (one's face)

débarcadère [debaʀkadɛʀ] *nm* landing stage (*BRIT*), wharf

débardeur [debaʀdœʀ] *nm* docker, stevedore; (*maillot*) slipover, tank top

débarquer [debaʀke] *vt* to unload, land ◆ *vi* to disembark; (*fig*) to turn up

débarras [debaʀa] *nm* lumber room; (*placard*) junk cupboard; (*remise*) outhouse; **bon débarras!** good riddance!

débarrasser [debaʀase] *vt* to clear ◆ *vi* (*enlever le couvert*) to clear away; **débarrasser qn de** (*vête-*

ments, paquets) to relieve sb of; (*habitude, ennemi*) to rid sb of; **débarrasser qch de** (*fouillis etc*) to clear sth of; **se débarrasser de** *vt* to get rid of; to rid o.s. of

débat [deba] *vb voir* **débattre** ◆ *nm* discussion, debate; **débats** *nmpl* (*POL*) proceedings, debates

débattre [debatʀ(ə)] *vt* to discuss, debate; **se débattre** *vi* to struggle

débaucher [deboʃe] *vt* (*licencier*) to lay off, dismiss; (*salarié d'une autre entreprise*) to poach; (*entraîner*) to lead astray, debauch; (*inciter à la grève*) to incite

débile [debil] *adj* weak, feeble; (*fam: idiot*) dimwitted ◆ *nm/f*: **débile mental** retarded person

débit [debi] *nm* (*d'un liquide, fleuve*) (rate of) flow; (*d'un magasin*) turnover (of goods); (*élocution*) delivery; (*bancaire*) debit; **avoir un débit de 10 €** to be 10 € in debit; **débit de boissons** drinking establishment; **débit de tabac** tobacconist's (shop) (*BRIT*), tobacco *ou* smoke shop (*US*)

débiter [debite] *vt* (*compte*) to debit; (*liquide, gaz*) to yield, produce, give out; (*couper: bois, viande*) to cut up; (*vendre*) to retail; (*péj: paroles etc*) to come out with, churn out

débiteur, trice [debitœʀ, -tʀis] *nm/f* debtor ◆ *adj* in debit; (*compte*) debit *cpd*

déblayer [debleje] *vt* to clear; **déblayer le terrain** (*fig*) to clear the ground

débloquer [debloke] *vt* (*frein, fonds*) to release; (*prix*) to unfreeze ◆ *vi* (*fam*) to talk rubbish

déboires [debwaʀ] *nmpl* setbacks

déboiser [debwaze] *vt* to clear of trees; (*région*) to deforest; **se déboiser** *vi* (*colline, montagne*) to become bare of trees

déboîter [debwate] *vt* (*AUTO*) to pull out; **se déboîter le genou** *etc* to dislocate one's knee *etc*

débonnaire [debɔnɛʀ] *adj* easy-going, good-natured

débordé, e [debɔʀde] *adj*: **être débordé de** (*travail, demandes*) to be snowed under with

déborder [debɔʀde] *vi* to overflow; (*lait etc*) to boil over ◆ *vt* (*MIL, SPORT*) to outflank; **déborder (de) qch** (*dépasser*) to extend beyond sth; **déborder de** (*joie, zèle*) to be brimming over with *ou* bursting with

débouché [debuʃe] *nm* (*pour vendre*) outlet; (*perspective d'emploi*) opening; (*sortie*): **au débouché de la vallée** where the valley opens out (onto the plain)

déboucher [debuʃe] *vt* (*évier, tuyau etc*) to unblock; (*bouteille*) to uncork, open ◆ *vi*: **déboucher de** to emerge from, come out of; **déboucher sur** to come out onto; to open out onto; (*fig*) to arrive at, lead up to

débourser [debuʀse] *vt* to pay out, lay out

déboussoler [debusole] *vt* to disorientate, disori-

debout [dəbu] *adv*: **être debout** (*personne*) to be standing, stand; (*levé, éveillé*) to be up (and about); (*chose*) to be upright; **être encore debout** (*fig: en état*) to be still going; to be still standing; to be still up; **mettre qn debout** to get sb to his feet; **mettre qch debout** to stand sth up; **se mettre debout** to get up (on one's feet); **se tenir debout** to stand; **debout!** get up!; **cette histoire ne tient pas debout** this story doesn't hold water

déboutonner [debutɔne] *vt* to undo, unbutton; **se déboutonner** *vi* to come undone *ou* unbuttoned

débraillé, e [debRaje] *adj* slovenly, untidy

débrancher [debRɑ̃ʃe] *vt* (*appareil électrique*) to unplug; (*téléphone, courant électrique*) to disconnect, cut off

débrayage [debReʒaʒ] *nm* (AUTO) clutch; (: *action*) disengaging the clutch; (*grève*) stoppage; **faire un double débrayage** to double-declutch

débrayer [debReje] *vi* (AUTO) to declutch, disengage the clutch; (*cesser le travail*) to stop work

débris [debRi] *nm* (*fragment*) fragment ♦ *nmpl* (*déchets*) pieces, debris *sg*; rubbish *sg* (BRIT), garbage *sg* (US)

débrouillard, e [debRujaR, -aRd(ə)] *adj* smart, resourceful

débrouiller [debRuje] *vt* to disentangle, untangle; (*fig*) to sort out, unravel; **se débrouiller** *vi* to manage

début [deby] *nm* beginning, start; **débuts** *nmpl* beginnings; (*de carrière*) début *sg*; **faire ses débuts** to start up; **au début** in *ou* at the beginning, at first; **au début de** at the beginning *ou* start of; **dès le début** from the start

débutant, e [debytɑ̃, -ɑ̃t] *nm/f* beginner, novice

débuter [debyte] *vi* to begin, start; (*faire ses débuts*) to start out

deçà [dəsa]: **en deçà de** *prép* this side of; **en deçà** *adv* on this side

décadence [dekadɑ̃s] *nf* decadence; decline

décaféiné, e [dekafeine] *adj* decaffeinated, caffeine-free

décalage [dekalaʒ] *nm* move forward *ou* back; shift forward *ou* back; (*écart*) gap; (*désaccord*) discrepancy; **décalage horaire** time difference (between time zones), time-lag

décaler [dekale] *vt* (*dans le temps: avancer*) to bring forward; (: *retarder*) to put back; (*changer de position*) to shift forward *ou* back; **décaler de 10 cm** to move forward *ou* back by 10 cm; **décaler de 2 h** to bring *ou* move forward 2 hours; to put back 2 hours

décalquer [dekalke] *vt* to trace; (*par pression*) to transfer

décamper [dekɑ̃pe] *vi* to clear out *ou* off

décaper [dekape] *vt* to strip; (*avec abrasif*) to scour; (*avec papier de verre*) to sand

décapiter [dekapite] *vt* to behead; (*par accident*) to decapitate; (*fig*) to cut the top off; (: *organisation*) to remove the top people from

décapotable [dekapɔtabl(ə)] *adj* convertible

décapsuleur [dekapsylœR] *nm* bottle-opener

décarcasser [dekaRkase] *vt*: **se décarcasser pour qn/pour faire qch** (*fam*) to slog one's guts out for sb/to do sth

décédé, e [desede] *adj* deceased

décéder [desede] *vi* to die

déceler [desle] *vt* to discover, detect; (*révéler*) to indicate, reveal

décembre [desɑ̃bR(ə)] *nm* December; *voir aussi* **juillet**

décemment [desamɑ̃] *adv* decently

décennie [desni] *nf* decade

décent, e [desɑ̃, -ɑ̃t] *adj* decent

déception [desɛpsjɔ̃] *nf* disappointment

décerner [deseRne] *vt* to award

décès [desɛ] *nm* death, decease; **acte de décès** death certificate

décevant, e [desvɑ̃, -ɑ̃t] *adj* disappointing

décevoir [desvwaR] *vt* to disappoint

déchaîner [deʃene] *vt* (*passions, colère*) to unleash; (*rires etc*) to give rise to, arouse; **se déchaîner** *vi* to be unleashed; (*rires*) to burst out; (*se mettre en colère*) to fly into a rage; **se déchaîner contre qn** to unleash one's fury on sb

déchanter [deʃɑ̃te] *vi* to become disillusioned

décharge [deʃaRʒ(ə)] *nf* (*dépôt d'ordures*) rubbish tip *ou* dump; (*électrique*) electrical discharge; (*salve*) volley of shots; **à la décharge de** in defence of

décharger [deʃaRʒe] *vt* (*marchandise, véhicule*) to unload; (ÉLEC) to discharge; (*arme: neutraliser*) to unload; (: *faire feu*) to discharge, fire; **décharger qn de** (*responsabilité*) to relieve sb of, release sb from; **décharger sa colère (sur)** to vent one's anger (on); **décharger sa conscience** to unburden one's conscience; **se décharger dans** (*se déverser*) to flow into; **se décharger d'une affaire sur qn** to hand a matter over to sb

décharné, e [deʃaRne] *adj* bony, emaciated, fleshless

déchausser [deʃose] *vt* (*personne*) to take the shoes off; (*skis*) to take off; **se déchausser** to take off one's shoes; (*dent*) to come *ou* work loose

déchéance [deʃeɑ̃s] *nf* (*déclin*) degeneration, decay, decline; (*chute*) fall

déchet [deʃɛ] *nm* (*de bois, tissu etc*) scrap; (*perte: gén* COMM) wastage, waste; **déchets** *nmpl* (*ordures*) refuse *sg*, rubbish *sg* (BRIT), garbage *sg* (US); **déchets radioactifs** radioactive waste

déchiffrer [deʃifRe] *vt* to decipher

déchiqueter [deʃikte] *vt* to tear *ou* pull to pieces

déchirant, e [deʃiRɑ̃, -ɑ̃t] *adj* heart-breaking, heart-rending

déchirement [deʃiRmɑ̃] *nm* (*chagrin*) wrench, heartbreak; (*gén pl: conflit*) rift, split

déchirer [deʃiʀe] *vt* to tear, rip; (*mettre en morceaux*) to tear up; (*pour ouvrir*) to tear off; (*arracher*) to tear out; (*fig*) to tear apart; **se déchirer** *vi* to tear, rip; **se déchirer un muscle/tendon** to tear a muscle/ tendon

déchirure [deʃiʀyʀ] *nf* (*accroc*) tear, rip; **déchirure musculaire** torn muscle

déchoir [deʃwaʀ] *vi* (*personne*) to lower o.s., demean o.s.; **déchoir de** to fall from

déchu, e [deʃy] *pp de* **déchoir** ◆ *adj* fallen; (*roi*) deposed

décidé, e [deside] *adj* (*personne, air*) determined; **c'est décidé** it's decided; **être décidé à faire** to be determined to do

décidément [desidemã] *adv* undoubtedly; really

décider [deside] *vt*: **décider qch** to decide on sth; **décider de faire/que** to decide to do/that; **décider qn (à faire qch)** to persuade *ou* induce sb (to do sth); **décider de qch** to decide upon sth; (*suj: chose*) to determine sth; **se décider** *vi* (*personne*) to decide, make up one's mind; (*problème, affaire*) to be resolved; **se décider à qch** to decide on sth; **se décider à faire** to decide *ou* make up one's mind to do; **se décider pour qch** to decide on *ou* in favour of sth

décimal, e, aux [desimal, -o] *adj, nf* decimal

décimètre [desimetʀ(ə)] *nm* decimetre (*BRIT*), decimeter (*US*); **double décimètre (20 cm)** ruler

décisif, ive [desizif, -iv] *adj* decisive; (*qui l'emporte*): **le facteur/l'argument décisif** the deciding factor/argument

décision [desizjɔ̃] *nf* decision; (*fermeté*) decisiveness, decision; **prendre une décision** to make a decision; **prendre la décision de faire** to take the decision to do; **emporter** *ou* **faire la décision** to be decisive

déclaration [deklaʀasjɔ̃] *nf* declaration; registration; (*discours: POL etc*) statement; (*compte rendu*) report; **fausse déclaration** misrepresentation; **déclaration (d'amour)** declaration; **déclaration de décès** registration of death; **déclaration de guerre** declaration of war; **déclaration (d'impôts)** statement of income, tax declaration, ≈ tax return; **déclaration (de sinistre)** (insurance) claim; **déclaration de revenus** statement of income

déclarer [deklaʀe] *vt* to declare, announce; (*revenus, employés, marchandises*) to declare; (*décès, naissance*) to register; (*vol etc: à la police*) to report; **rien à déclarer** nothing to declare; **se déclarer** *vi* (*feu, maladie*) to break out; **déclarer la guerre** to declare war

déclencher [deklãʃe] *vt* (*mécanisme etc*) to release; (*sonnerie*) to set off, activate; (*attaque, grève*) to launch; (*provoquer*) to trigger off; **se déclencher** *vi* to release itself; to go off

déclic [deklik] *nm* trigger mechanism; (*bruit*) click

décliner [dekline] *vi* to decline ◆ *vt* (*invitation*) to decline, refuse; (*responsabilité*) to refuse to accept; (*nom, adresse*) to state; (*LING*) to decline; **se décliner** (*LING*) to decline

décocher [dekɔʃe] *vt* to hurl; (*flèche, regard*) to shoot

décoiffer [dekwafe] *vt*: **décoiffer qn** to disarrange *ou* mess up sb's hair; to take sb's hat off; **se décoiffer** to take off one's hat

déçois [deswa] *etc*, **déçoive** [deswav] *etc vb voir* **décevoir**

décollage [dekɔlaʒ] *nm* (*AVIAT, ÉCON*) takeoff

décoller [dekɔle] *vt* to unstick ◆ *vi* to take off; (*projet, entreprise*) to take off, get off the ground; **se décoller** *vi* to come unstuck

décolleté, e [dekɔlte] *adj* low-necked, low-cut; (*femme*) wearing a low-cut dress ◆ *nm* low neck (line); (*épaules*) (bare) neck and shoulders; (*plongeant*) cleavage

décolorer [dekɔlɔʀe] *vt* (*tissu*) to fade; (*cheveux*) to bleach, lighten; **se décolorer** *vi* to fade

décombres [dekɔ̃bʀ(ə)] *nmpl* rubble *sg*, debris *sg*

décommander [dekɔmãde] *vt* to cancel; (*invités*) to put off; **se décommander** to cancel, cry off

décomposé, e [dekɔ̃poze] *adj* (*pourri*) decomposed; (*visage*) haggard, distorted

décompte [dekɔ̃t] *nm* deduction; (*facture*) breakdown (of an account), detailed account

déconcerter [dekɔ̃seʀte] *vt* to disconcert, confound

déconfit, e [dekɔ̃fi, -it] *adj* crestfallen, downcast

décongeler [dekɔ̃ʒle] *vt* to thaw (out)

déconner [dekɔne] *vi* (*fam!: en parlant*) to talk (a load of) rubbish (*BRIT*) *ou* garbage (*US*); (: *faire des bêtises*) to muck about; **sans déconner** no kidding

déconseiller [dekɔ̃seje] *vt*: **déconseiller qch (à qn)** to advise (sb) against sth; **déconseiller à qn de faire** to advise sb against doing; **c'est déconseillé** it's not advised *ou* advisable

décontracté, e [dekɔ̃tʀakte] *adj* relaxed

décontracter [dekɔ̃tʀakte] *vt*: **se décontracter** *vi* to relax

déconvenue [dekɔ̃vny] *nf* disappointment

décor [dekɔʀ] *nm* décor; (*paysage*) scenery; **décors** *nmpl* (*THÉÂT*) scenery *sg*, decor *sg*; (*CINÉ*) set *sg*; **changement de décor** (*fig*) change of scene; **entrer dans le décor** (*fig*) to run off the road; **en décor naturel** (*CINÉ*) on location

décorateur, trice [dekɔʀatœʀ, -tʀis] *nm/f* (interior) decorator; (*CINÉ*) set designer

décoration [dekɔʀasjɔ̃] *nf* decoration

décorer [dekɔʀe] *vt* to decorate

décortiquer [dekɔʀtike] *vt* to shell; (*riz*) to hull; (*fig*) to dissect

découcher [dekuʃe] *vi* to spend the night away

découdre [dekudʀ(ə)] *vt* (*vêtement, couture*) to unpick, take the stitching out of; (*bouton*) to take off; **se découdre** *vi* to come unstitched; (*bouton*) to come off; **en découdre** (*fig*) to fight, do battle

découler [dekule] *vi*: **découler de** to ensue *ou* follow from

découper [dekupe] *vt* (*papier, tissu etc*) to cut up; (*volaille, viande*) to carve; (*détacher: manche, article*) to cut out; **se découper sur** (*ciel, fond*) to stand out against

décourager [dekuRaʒe] *vt* to discourage, dishearten; (*dissuader*) to discourage, put off; **se décourager** *vi* to lose heart, become discouraged; **décourager qn de faire/de qch** to discourage sb from doing/from sth, put sb off doing/sth

décousu, e [dekuzy] *pp de* **découdre** ♦ *adj* unstitched; (*fig*) disjointed, disconnected

découvert, e [dekuvɛR, -ɛRt(ə)] *pp de* **découvrir** ♦ *adj* (*tête*) bare, uncovered; (*lieu*) open, exposed ♦ *nm* (*bancaire*) overdraft ♦ *nf* discovery; **à découvert** *adv* (*MIL*) exposed, without cover; (*fig*) openly ♦ *adj* (*COMM*) overdrawn; **à visage découvert** openly; **aller à la découverte de** to go in search of

découvrir [dekuvRiR] *vt* to discover; (*apercevoir*) to see; (*enlever ce qui couvre ou protège*) to uncover; (*montrer, dévoiler*) to reveal; **se découvrir** to take off one's hat; (*se déshabiller*) to take something off; (*au lit*) to uncover o.s.; (*ciel*) to clear; **se découvrir des talents** to find hidden talents in o.s.

décret [dekRe] *nm* decree

décréter [dekRete] *vt* to decree; (*ordonner*) to order

décrié, e [dekRije] *adj* disparaged

décrire [dekRiR] *vt* to describe; (*courbe, cercle*) to follow, describe

décrocher [dekRɔʃe] *vt* (*dépendre*) to take down; (*téléphone*) to take off the hook; (*: pour répondre*): **décrocher (le téléphone)** to pick up *ou* lift the receiver; (*fig: contrat etc*) to get, land ♦ *vi* to drop out; to switch off; **se décrocher** *vi* (*tableau, rideau*) to fall down

décroître [dekRwatR(ə)] *vi* to decrease, decline, diminish

décrypter [dekRipte] *vt* to decipher

déçu, e [desy] *pp de* **décevoir** ♦ *adj* disappointed

décupler [dekyple] *vt, vi* to increase tenfold

dédaigner [dedeɲe] *vt* to despise, scorn; (*négliger*) to disregard, spurn; **dédaigner de faire** to consider it beneath one to do, not deign to do

dédaigneux, euse [dedeɲø, -øz] *adj* scornful, disdainful

dédain [dedɛ̃] *nm* scorn, disdain

dédale [dedal] *nm* maze

dedans [dədɑ̃] *adv* inside; (*pas en plein air*) indoors, inside ♦ *nm* inside; **au dedans** on the inside; inside; **en dedans** (*vers l'intérieur*) inwards; *voir aussi* **là**

dédicacer [dedikase] *vt*: **dédicacer (à qn)** to sign (for sb), autograph (for sb), inscribe (to sb)

dédier [dedje] *vt* to dedicate

dédire [dediR]: **se dédire** *vi* to go back on one's word; (*se rétracter*) to retract, recant

dédommagement [dedɔmaʒmɑ̃] *nm* compensation

dédommager [dedɔmaʒe] *vt*: **dédommager qn (de)** to compensate sb (for); (*fig*) to repay sb (for)

dédouaner [dedwane] *vt* to clear through customs

dédoubler [deduble] *vt* (*classe, effectifs*) to split (into two); (*couverture etc*) to unfold; (*manteau*) to remove the lining of; **dédoubler un train/les trains** to run a relief train/additional trains; **se dédoubler** *vi* (*PSYCH*) to have a split personality

déduire [dedɥiR] *vt*: **déduire qch (de)** (*ôter*) to deduct sth (from); (*conclure*) to deduce *ou* infer sth (from)

déesse [dees] *nf* goddess

défaillance [defajɑ̃s] *nf* (*syncope*) blackout; (*fatigue*) (sudden) weakness *no pl*; (*technique*) fault, failure; (*morale etc*) weakness; **défaillance cardiaque** heart failure

défaillir [defajiR] *vi* to faint; to feel faint; (*mémoire etc*) to fail

défaire [defɛR] *vt* (*installation, échafaudage*) to take down, dismantle; (*paquet etc, nœud, vêtement*) to undo; (*bagages*) to unpack; (*ouvrage*) to undo, unpick; (*cheveux*) to take out; **se défaire** *vi* to come undone; **se défaire de** *vt* (*se débarrasser de*) to get rid of; (*se séparer de*) to part with; **défaire le lit** (*pour changer les draps*) to strip the bed; (*pour se coucher*) to turn back the bedclothes

défait, e [defe, -ɛt] *pp de* **défaire** ♦ *adj* (*visage*) haggard, ravaged ♦ *nf* defeat

défalquer [defalke] *vt* to deduct

défaut [defo] *nm* (*moral*) fault, failing, defect; (*d'étoffe, métal*) fault, flaw, defect; (*manque, carence*): **défaut de** lack of; shortage of; (*INFORM*) bug; **défaut de la cuirasse** (*fig*) chink in the armour (*BRIT*) *ou* armor (*US*); **en défaut** at fault; in the wrong; **faire défaut** (*manquer*) to be lacking; **à défaut** *adv* failing that; **à défaut de** for lack *ou* want of; **par défaut** (*JUR*) in his (*ou* her *etc*) absence

défavorable [defavɔRabl(ə)] *adj* unfavourable (*BRIT*), unfavorable (*US*)

défavoriser [defavɔRize] *vt* to put at a disadvantage

défection [defɛksjɔ̃] *nf* defection, failure to give support *ou* assistance; failure to appear; **faire défection** (*d'un parti etc*) to withdraw one's support, leave

défectueux, euse [defɛktɥø, -øz] *adj* faulty, defective

défendre [defɑ̃dR(ə)] *vt* to defend; (*interdire*) to forbid; **défendre à qn qch/de faire** to forbid sb sth/to do; **il est défendu de cracher** spitting is prohibited *ou* is not allowed; **c'est défendu** it is forbidden; **se défendre** to defend o.s.; **il se défend** (*fig*) he can hold his own; **ça se défend** (*fig*) it holds together; **se défendre de/contre** (*se protéger*) to protect o.s. from/against; **se défendre de** (*se* *garder de)* to refrain from; *(nier)*: **se défendre de vouloir** to deny wanting

défense [defɑ̃s] *nf* defence *(BRIT)*, defense *(US)*; *(d'éléphant etc)* tusk; **ministre de la défense** Minister of Defence *(BRIT)*, Defence Secretary; **la défense nationale** defence, the defence of the realm *(BRIT)*; **la défense contre avions** anti-aircraft defence; **"défense de fumer/cracher"** "no smoking/spitting", "smoking/spitting prohibited"; **prendre la défense de qn** to stand up for sb; **défense des consommateurs** consumerism

déférer [defeʀe] *vt (JUR)* to refer; **déférer à** *vt (requête, décision)* to defer to; **déférer qn à la justice** to hand sb over to justice

déferler [defeʀle] *vi (vagues)* to break; *(fig)* to surge

défi [defi] *nm (provocation)* challenge; *(bravade)* defiance; **mettre qn au défi de faire qch** to challenge sb to do sth; **relever un défi** to take up *ou* accept a challenge

déficit [defisit] *nm (COMM)* deficit; *(PSYCH etc: manque)* defect; **déficit budgétaire** budget deficit; **être en déficit** to be in deficit

déficitaire [defisiteʀ] *adj (année, récolte)* bad; **entreprise/budget déficitaire** business/budget in deficit

défier [defje] *vt (provoquer)* to challenge; *(fig)* to defy, brave; **se défier de** *(se méfier de)* to distrust, mistrust; **défier qn de faire** to challenge *ou* defy sb to do; **défier qn à** to challenge sb to; **défier toute comparaison/concurrence** to be incomparable/unbeatable

défigurer [defigyʀe] *vt* to disfigure; *(boutons etc)* to mar *ou* spoil (the looks of); *(fig: œuvre)* to mutilate, deface

défilé [defile] *nm (GÉO)* (narrow) gorge *ou* pass; *(soldats)* parade; *(manifestants)* procession, march; **un défilé de** *(voitures, visiteurs etc)* a stream of

défiler [defile] *vi (troupes)* to march past; *(sportifs)* to parade; *(manifestants)* to march; *(visiteurs)* to pour, stream; **se défiler** *vi (se dérober)* to slip away, sneak off; **faire défiler** *(bande, film)* to put on; *(INFORM)* to scroll

définir [definiʀ] *vt* to define

définitif, ive [definitif, -iv] *adj (final)* final, definitive; *(pour longtemps)* permanent, definitive; *(sans appel)* final, definite ♦ *nf*: **en définitive** eventually; *(somme toute)* when all is said and done

définitivement [definitivmɑ̃] *adv* definitively; permanently; definitely

défoncer [defɔ̃se] *vt (caisse)* to stave in; *(porte)* to smash in *ou* down; *(lit, fauteuil)* to burst (the springs of); *(terrain, route)* to rip *ou* plough up; **se défoncer** *vi (se donner à fond)* to give it all one's got

déformer [defɔʀme] *vt* to put out of shape; *(corps)* to deform; *(pensée, fait)* to distort; **se déformer** *vi* to lose its shape

défouler [defule]: **se défouler** *vi (PSYCH)* to work off one's tensions, release one's pent-up feelings; *(gén)* to unwind, let off steam

défraîchir [defʀeʃiʀ]: **se défraîchir** *vi* to fade; to become shop-soiled

défricher [defʀiʃe] *vt* to clear (for cultivation)

défunt, e [defœ̃, -œ̃t] *adj*: **son défunt père** his late father ♦ *nm/f* deceased

dégagé, e [degaʒe] *adj* clear; *(ton, air)* casual, jaunty

dégagement [degaʒmɑ̃] *nm* emission; freeing; clearing; *(espace libre)* clearing; passage; clearance; *(FOOTBALL)* clearance; **voie de dégagement** slip road; **itinéraire de dégagement** alternative route *(to relieve traffic congestion)*

dégager [degaʒe] *vt (exhaler)* to give off, emit; *(délivrer)* to free, extricate; *(MIL: troupes)* to relieve; *(désencombrer)* to clear; *(isoler, mettre en valeur)* to bring out; *(crédits)* to release; **se dégager** *vi (odeur)* to emanate, be given off; *(passage, ciel)* to clear; **dégager qn de** *(engagement, parole etc)* to release *ou* free sb from; **se dégager de** *(fig: engagement etc)* to get out of; *(: promesse)* to go back on

dégarnir [degaʀniʀ] *vt (vider)* to empty, clear; **se dégarnir** *vi* to empty; to be cleaned out *ou* cleared; *(tempes, crâne)* to go bald

dégâts [dega] *nmpl* damage *sg*; **faire des dégâts** to damage

dégel [deʒɛl] *nm* thaw; *(fig: des prix etc)* unfreezing

dégeler [deʒle] *vt* to thaw (out); *(fig)* to unfreeze ♦ *vi* to thaw (out); **se dégeler** *vi (fig)* to thaw out

dégénérer [deʒeneʀe] *vi* to degenerate; *(empirer)* to go from bad to worse; *(devenir)*: **dégénérer en** to degenerate into

dégingandé, e [deʒɛ̃gɑ̃de] *adj* gangling, lanky

dégivrer [deʒivʀe] *vt (frigo)* to defrost; *(vitres)* to de-ice

dégonflé, e [degɔ̃fle] *adj (pneu)* flat; *(fam)* chicken ♦ *nm/f (fam)* chicken

dégonfler [degɔ̃fle] *vt (pneu, ballon)* to let down, deflate ♦ *vi (désenfler)* to go down; **se dégonfler** *vi (fam)* to chicken out

dégouliner [deguline] *vi* to trickle, drip; **dégouliner de** to be dripping with

dégourdi, e [deguʀdi] *adj* smart, resourceful

dégourdir [deguʀdiʀ] *vt* to warm (up); **se dégourdir (les jambes)** to stretch one's legs

dégoût [degu] *nm* disgust, distaste

dégoûtant, e [degutɑ̃, -ɑ̃t] *adj* disgusting

dégoûté, e [degute] *adj* disgusted; **dégoûté de** sick of

dégoûter [degute] *vt* to disgust; **cela me dégoûte** I find this disgusting *ou* revolting; **dégoûter qn de qch** to put sb off sth; **se dégoûter de** to get *ou* become sick of

dégrader [degʀade] *vt (MIL: officier)* to degrade; *(abîmer)* to damage, deface; *(avilir)* to degrade, debase; **se dégrader** *vi* (*relations, situation*) to deteriorate

dégrafer [degʀafe] *vt* to unclip, unhook, unfasten

degré [dagʀe] *nm* degree; (*d'escalier*) step; **brûlure au 1er/2ème degré** 1st/2nd degree burn; **équation du 1er/2ème degré** linear/quadratic equation; **le premier degré** (*SCOL*) primary level; **alcool à 90 degrés** surgical spirit; **vin de 10 degrés** 10° wine (*on Gay-Lussac scale*); **par degré(s)** *adv* by degrees, gradually

dégressif, ive [degʀesif, -iv] *adj* on a decreasing scale, degressive; **tarif dégressif** decreasing rate of charge

dégringoler [degʀɛ̃gɔle] *vi* to tumble (down); (*fig: prix, monnaie etc*) to collapse

dégrossir [degʀosiʀ] *vt* (*bois*) to trim; (*fig*) to work out roughly; (: *personne*) to knock the rough edges off

déguenillé, e [dɛgnije] *adj* ragged, tattered

déguerpir [degɛʀpiʀ] *vi* to clear off

dégueulasse [degœlas] *adj* (*fam*) disgusting

dégueuler [degœle] *vi* (*fam*) to puke, throw up

déguisement [degizmɑ̃] *nm* disguise; (*habits: pour s'amuser*) dressing-up clothes; (: *pour tromper*) disguise

déguiser [degize] *vt* to disguise; **se déguiser (en)** (*se costumer*) to dress up (as); (*pour tromper*) to disguise o.s. (as)

dégustation [degystasjɔ̃] *nf* tasting; sampling; savouring (*BRIT*), savoring (*US*); (*séance*): **dégustation de vin(s)** wine-tasting

déguster [degyste] *vt* (*vins*) to taste; (*fromages etc*) to sample; (*savourer*) to enjoy, savour (*BRIT*), savor (*US*)

dehors [dəɔʀ] *adv* outside; (*en plein air*) outdoors, outside ♦ *nm* outside ♦ *nmpl* (*apparences*) appearances, exterior *sg*; **mettre** *ou* **jeter dehors** to throw out; **au dehors** outside; (*en apparence*) outwardly; **au dehors de** outside; **de dehors** from outside; **en dehors** outside; outwards; **en dehors de** apart from

déjà [deʒa] *adv* already; (*auparavant*) before, already; **as-tu déjà été en France?** have you been to France before?; **c'est déjà pas mal** that's not too bad (at all); **c'est déjà quelque chose** (at least) it's better than nothing; **quel nom, déjà?** what was the name again?

déjeuner [deʒœne] *vi* to (have) lunch; (*le matin*) to have breakfast ♦ *nm* lunch; (*petit déjeuner*) breakfast; **déjeuner d'affaires** business lunch

déjouer [deʒwe] *vt* to elude, to foil, thwart

delà [dəla] *adv*: **par delà, en delà (de), au delà (de)** beyond

délabrer [delabʀe] *vb*: **se délabrer** *vi* to fall into decay, become dilapidated

délacer [delase] *vt* to unlace, undo

délai [delɛ] *nm* (*attente*) waiting period; (*sursis*) extension (of time); (*temps accordé; aussi*: **délais**) time limit; **sans délai** without delay; **à bref délai** shortly, very soon; at short notice; **dans les délais** within the time limit; **un délai de 30 jours** a period of 30 days; **comptez un délai de livraison de 10 jours** allow 10 days for delivery

délaisser [delese] *vt* (*abandonner*) to abandon, desert; (*négliger*) to neglect

délasser [delase] *vt* (*reposer*) to relax; (*divertir*) to divert, entertain; **se délasser** *vi* to relax

délavé, e [delave] *adj* faded

délayer [deleje] *vt* (*CULIN*) to mix (with water *etc*); (*peinture*) to thin down; (*fig*) to pad out, spin out

delco® [dɛlko] *nm* (*AUTO*) distributor; **tête de delco** distributor cap

délecter [delɛkte]: **se délecter** *vi*: **se délecter de** to revel *ou* delight in

délégué, e [delege] *adj* delegated ♦ *nm/f* delegate; representative; **ministre délégué à** minister with special responsibility for

déléguer [delege] *vt* to delegate

délibéré, e [delibeʀe] *adj* (*conscient*) deliberate; (*déterminé*) determined, resolute; **de propos délibéré** (*à dessein, exprès*) intentionally

délibérer [delibeʀe] *vi* to deliberate

délicat, e [delika, -at] *adj* delicate; (*plein de tact*) tactful; (*attentionné*) thoughtful; (*exigeant*) fussy, particular; **procédés peu délicats** unscrupulous methods

délicatement [delikatmɑ̃] *adv* delicately; (*avec douceur*) gently

délice [delis] *nm* delight

délicieux, euse [delisjø, -øz] *adj* (*au goût*) delicious; (*sensation, impression*) delightful

délimiter [delimite] *vt* to delimit

délinquance [delɛ̃kɑ̃s] *nf* criminality; **délinquance juvénile** juvenile delinquency

délinquant, e [delɛ̃kɑ̃, -ɑ̃t] *adj, nm/f* delinquent

délirant, e [deliʀɑ̃, -ɑ̃t] *adj* (*MÉD: fièvre*) delirious; (*imagination*) frenzied; (*fam: déraisonnable*) crazy

délirer [deliʀe] *vi* to be delirious; (*fig*) to be raving

délit [deli] *nm* (*criminal*) offence; **délit de droit commun** violation of common law; **délit de fuite** failure to stop after an accident; **délit d'initiés** insider dealing *ou* trading; **délit de presse** violation of the press laws

délivrer [delivʀe] *vt* (*prisonnier*) to (set) free, release; (*passeport, certificat*) to issue; **délivrer qn de** (*ennemis*) to set sb free from; (*fig*) to rid sb of

déloger [delɔʒe] *vt* (*locataire*) to turn out; (*objet coincé, ennemi*) to dislodge

déloyal, e, aux [delwajal, -o] *adj* (*personne, conduite*) disloyal; (*procédé*) unfair

deltaplane® [dɛltaplan] *nm* hang-glider

déluge [delyʒ] *nm* (*biblique*) Flood, Deluge; (*grosse pluie*) downpour, deluge; (*grand nombre*): **déluge de** flood of

déluré, e [delyʀe] *adj* smart, resourceful; (*péj*) forward, pert

demain [dəmɛ̃] *adv* tomorrow; **demain matin/ soir** tomorrow morning/evening; **demain midi** tomorrow at midday; **à demain!** see you tomorrow!

demande [dəmɑ̃d] *nf* (*requête*) request; (*revendication*) demand; (*ADMIN, formulaire*) application; (*ÉCON*): **la demande** demand; "**demandes d'emploi**" "situations wanted"; **à la demande générale** by popular request; **demande en mariage** (marriage) proposal; **faire sa demande (en mariage)** to propose (marriage); **demande de naturalisation** application for naturalization; **demande de poste** job application

demandé, e [dəmɑ̃de] *adj* (*article etc*): **très demandé** (very) much in demand

demander [dəmɑ̃de] *vt* to ask for; (*question: date, heure, chemin*) to ask; (*requérir, nécessiter*) to require, demand; **demander qch à qn** to ask sb for sth, ask sb sth; **ils demandent 2 secrétaires et un ingénieur** they're looking for 2 secretaries and an engineer; **demander la main de qn** to ask for sb's hand (in marriage); **demander pardon à qn** to apologize to sb; **demander à** *ou* **de voir/faire** to ask to see/ask if one can do; **demander à qn de faire** to ask sb to do; **demander que/pourquoi** to ask that/why; **se demander si/pourquoi** *etc* to wonder if/why *etc*; (*sens purement réfléchi*) to ask o.s. if/why *etc*; **on vous demande au téléphone** you're wanted on the phone, there's someone for you on the phone; **il ne demande que ça** that's all he wants; **je ne demande pas mieux** I'm asking nothing more; **il ne demande qu'à faire** all he wants is to do

demandeur, euse [dəmɑ̃dœʀ, -øz] *nm/f*: **demandeur d'emploi** job-seeker

démangeaison [demɑ̃ʒɛzɔ̃] *nf* itching

démanger [demɑ̃ʒe] *vi* to itch; **la main me démange** my hand is itching; **l'envie** *ou* **ça me démange de faire** I'm itching to do

démanteler [demɑ̃tle] *vt* to break up; to demolish

démaquillant [demakijɑ̃] *nm* make-up remover
démaquiller [demakije] *vt*: **se démaquiller** to remove one's make-up

démarche [demaʀʃ(ə)] *nf* (*allure*) gait, walk; (*intervention*) step; approach; (*fig: intellectuelle*) thought processes *pl*; approach; **faire** *ou* **entreprendre des démarches** to take action; **faire des démarches auprès de qn** to approach sb

démarcheur, euse [demaʀʃœʀ, -øz] *nm/f* (*COMM*) door-to-door salesman/woman; (*POL etc*) canvasser

démarque [demaʀk(ə)] *nf* (*COMM: d'un article*) mark-down

démarrage [demaʀaʒ] *nm* starting *no pl*, start; **démarrage en côte** hill start

démarrer [demaʀe] *vt* to start up ♦ *vi* (*conduc-*

teur) to start (up); (*véhicule*) to move off; (*travaux, affaire*) to get moving; (*coureur: accélérer*) to pull away

démarreur [demaʀœʀ] *nm* (*AUTO*) starter

démêlant, e [demelɑ̃, -ɑ̃t] *adj*: **baume démêlant, crème démêlante** (hair) conditioner

démêler [demele] *vt* to untangle, disentangle

démêlés [demele] *nmpl* problems

déménagement [demenaʒmɑ̃] *nm* (*du point de vue du locataire etc*) move; (: *du déménageur*) removal (*BRIT*), moving (*US*); **entreprise/camion de déménagement** removal (*BRIT*) *ou* moving (*US*) firm/van

déménager [demenaʒe] *vt* (*meubles*) to (re)move ♦ *vi* to move (house)

déménageur [demenaʒœʀ] *nm* removal man (*BRIT*), (furniture) mover (*US*); (*entrepreneur*) furniture remover

démener [demne]: **se démener** *vi* to thrash about; (*fig*) to exert o.s.

dément, e [demɑ̃, -ɑ̃t] *vb voir* **démentir** ♦ *adj* (*fou*) mad (*BRIT*), crazy; (*fam*) brilliant, fantastic

démentiel, le [demɑ̃sjɛl] *adj* insane

démentir [demɑ̃tiʀ] *vt* (*nouvelle, témoin*) to refute; (*faits etc*) to belie, refute; **démentir que** to deny that; **ne pas se démentir** not to fail, keep up

démerder [demɛʀde]: **se démerder** *vi* (*fam!*) to bloody well manage for o.s.

démesuré, e [deməzyʀe] *adj* immoderate, disproportionate

démettre [demɛtʀ(ə)] *vt*: **démettre qn de** (*fonction, poste*) to dismiss sb from; **se démettre (de ses fonctions)** to resign (from) one's duties; **se démettre l'épaule** *etc* to dislocate one's shoulder *etc*

demeurant [dəmœʀɑ̃]: **au demeurant** *adv* for all that

demeure [dəmœʀ] *nf* residence; **dernière demeure** (*fig*) last resting place; **mettre qn en demeure de faire** to enjoin *ou* order sb to do; **à demeure** *adv* permanently

demeurer [dəmœʀe] *vi* (*habiter*) to live; (*séjourner*) to stay; (*rester*) to remain; **en demeurer là** (*suj: personne*) to leave it at that; (: *choses*) to be left at that

demi, e [dəmi] *adj*: **et demi: trois heures/ bouteilles et demies** three and a half hours/bottles, three hours/bottles and a half ♦ *nm* (*bière: = 0.25 litre*) ≈ half-pint; (*FOOTBALL*) half-back; **il est 2 heures et demie** it's half past 2; **il est midi et demi** it's half past 12; **demi de mêlée/d'ouverture** (*RUGBY*) scrum/fly half; **à demi** *adv* half-; **ouvrir à demi** to half-open; **faire les choses à demi** to do things by halves; **à la demie** (*heure*) on the half-hour

demi-cercle [dəmisɛʀkl(ə)] *nm* semicircle; **en demi-cercle** *adj* semicircular ♦ *adv* in a semicircle
demi-douzaine [dəmiduzɛn] *nf* half-dozen, half a dozen

demi-finale [dəmifinal] *nf* semifinal

demi-frère [dəmifʀɛʀ] *nm* half-brother

demi-heure [dəmijœʀ] *nf*: **une demi-heure** a half-hour, half an hour

demi-journée [dəmiʒuʀne] *nf* half-day, half a day

demi-litre [dəmilitʀ(ə)] *nm* half-litre (*BRIT*), half-liter (*US*), half a litre *ou* liter

demi-livre [dəmilivʀ(ə)] *nf* half-pound, half a pound

demi-mot [dəmimo]: **à demi-mot** *adv* without having to spell things out

demi-pension [dəmipɑ̃sjɔ̃] *nf* half-board; **être en demi-pension** (*SCOL*) to take school meals

demi-pensionnaire [dəmipɑ̃sjɔnɛʀ] *nm/f* (*SCOL*) half-boarder

demi-place [dəmiplas] *nf* half-price; (*TRANSPORTS*) half-fare

démis, e [demi, -iz] *pp de* **démettre** ♦ *adj* (*épaule etc*) dislocated

demi-sel [dəmisɛl] *adj inv* slightly salted

demi-sœur [dəmisœʀ] *nf* half-sister

démission [demisjɔ̃] *nf* resignation; **donner sa démission** to give *ou* hand in one's notice, hand in one's resignation

démissionner [demisjɔne] *vi* (*de son poste*) to resign, give *ou* hand in one's notice

demi-tarif [dəmitaʀif] *nm* half-price; (*TRANSPORTS*) half-fare

demi-tour [dəmituʀ] *nm* about-turn; **faire un demi-tour** (*MIL etc*) to make an about-turn; **faire demi-tour** to turn (and go) back; (*AUTO*) to do a U-turn

démocratie [demɔkʀasi] *nf* democracy; **démocratie populaire/libérale** people's/liberal democracy

démocratique [demɔkʀatik] *adj* democratic

démodé, e [demɔde] *adj* old-fashioned

demoiselle [dəmwazɛl] *nf* (*jeune fille*) young lady; (*célibataire*) single lady, maiden lady; **demoiselle d'honneur** bridesmaid

démolir [demɔliʀ] *vt* to demolish; (*fig: personne*) to do for

démon [demɔ̃] *nm* demon, fiend; evil spirit; (*enfant turbulent*) devil, demon; **le démon du jeu/des femmes** a mania for gambling/women; **le Démon** the Devil

démonstration [demɔ̃stʀasjɔ̃] *nf* demonstration; (*aérienne, navale*) display

démonté, e [demɔ̃te] *adj* (*fig*) raging, wild

démonter [demɔ̃te] *vt* (*machine etc*) to take down, dismantle; (*pneu, porte*) to take off; (*cavalier*) to throw, unseat; (*fig: personne*) to disconcert; **se démonter** *vi* (*personne*) to lose countenance

démontrer [demɔ̃tʀe] *vt* to demonstrate, show

démordre [demɔʀdʀ(ə)] *vi* (*aussi*: **ne pas démordre de**) to refuse to give up, stick to

démouler [demule] *vt* (*gâteau*) to turn out

démuni, e [demyni] *adj* (*sans argent*) impoverished; **démuni de** without, lacking in

démunir [demyniʀ] *vt*: **démunir qn de** to deprive sb of; **se démunir de** to part with, give up

dénaturer [denatyʀe] *vt* (*goût*) to alter (completely); (*pensée, fait*) to distort, misrepresent

dénicher [deniʃe] *vt* to unearth

dénier [denje] *vt* to deny; **dénier qch à qn** to deny sb sth

dénigrer [denigʀe] *vt* to denigrate, run down

dénivellation [denivɛlasjɔ̃] *nf*, **dénivellement** [denivɛlmɑ̃] *nm* difference in level; (*pente*) ramp; (*creux*) dip

dénombrer [denɔ̃bʀe] *vt* (*compter*) to count; (*énumérer*) to enumerate, list

dénomination [denɔminasjɔ̃] *nf* designation, appellation

dénommé, e [denɔme] *adj*: **le dénommé Dupont** the man by the name of Dupont

dénoncer [denɔ̃se] *vt* to denounce; **se dénoncer** to give o.s. up, come forward

dénouement [denumɑ̃] *nm* outcome, conclusion; (*THÉÂT*) dénouement

dénouer [denwe] *vt* to unknot, undo

dénoyauter [denwajote] *vt* to stone; **appareil à dénoyauter** stoner

denrée [dɑ̃ʀe] *nf* commodity; (*aussi*: **denrée alimentaire**) food(stuff)

dense [dɑ̃s] *adj* dense

densité [dɑ̃site] *nf* denseness; (*PHYSIQUE*) density

dent [dɑ̃] *nf* tooth (*pl* teeth); **avoir/garder une dent contre qn** to have/hold a grudge against sb; **se mettre qch sous la dent** to eat sth; **être sur les dents** to be on one's last legs; **faire ses dents** to teethe, cut (one's) teeth; **en dents de scie** serrated; (*irrégulier*) jagged; **avoir les dents longues** (*fig*) to be ruthlessly ambitious; **dent de lait/sagesse** milk/wisdom tooth

dentaire [dɑ̃tɛʀ] *adj* dental; **cabinet dentaire** dental surgery; **école dentaire** dental school

dentelé, e [dɑ̃tle] *adj* jagged, indented

dentelle [dɑ̃tɛl] *nf* lace *no pl*

dentier [dɑ̃tje] *nm* denture

dentifrice [dɑ̃tifʀis] *adj*, *nm*: **(pâte) dentifrice** toothpaste; **eau dentifrice** mouthwash

dentiste [dɑ̃tist(ə)] *nm/f* dentist

dentition [dɑ̃tisjɔ̃] *nf* teeth *pl*, dentition

dénuder [denyde] *vt* to bare; **se dénuder** (*personne*) to strip

dénué, e [denɥe] *adj*: **dénué de** lacking in; (*intérêt*) devoid of

dénuement [denymɑ̃] *nm* destitution

déodorant [deɔdɔʀɑ̃] *nm* deodorant

déontologie [deɔ̃tɔlɔʒi] *nf* code of ethics; (*professionnelle*) (professional) code of practice

dépannage [depanaʒ] *nm*: **service/camion de**

dépannage (*AUTO*) breakdown service/truck

dépanner [depane] *vt* (*voiture, télévision*) to tix, repair; (*fig*) to bail out, help out

dépanneuse [depanøz] *nf* breakdown lorry (*BRIT*), tow truck (*US*)

dépareillé, e [depareje] *adj* (*collection, service*) incomplete; (*gant, volume, objet*) odd

départ [depar] *nm* leaving *no pl*, departure; (*SPORT*) start; (*sur un horaire*) departure; **à son départ** when he left; **au départ** (*au début*) initially, at the start; **courrier au départ** outgoing mail

départager [departaʒe] *vt* to decide between

département [departəmɑ̃] *nm* department; *see boxed note*

DÉPARTEMENT

France is divided into 96 administrative units called **départements**. These local government divisions are headed by a state-appointed 'préfet', and administered by an elected 'Conseil général'. **Départements** are usually named after prominent geographical features such as rivers or mountain ranges.

---

dépassé, e [depase] *adj* superseded, outmoded; (*fig*) out of one's depth

dépasser [depase] *vt* (*véhicule, concurrent*) to overtake; (*endroit*) to pass, go past; (*somme, limite*) to exceed; (*fig: en beauté etc*) to surpass, outshine; (*être en saillie sur*) to jut out above (*ou* in front of); (*dérouter*): **cela me dépasse** it's beyond me ♦ *vi* (*AUTO*) to overtake; (*jupon*) to show; **se dépasser** to excel o.s.

dépaysé, e [depeize] *adj* disorientated

dépaysement [depeizmɑ̃] *nm* disorientation; change of scenery

dépecer [depəse] *vt* (*suj: boucher*) to joint, cut up; (*suj: animal*) to dismember

dépêche [depɛʃ] *nf* dispatch; **dépêche (télégraphique)** telegram, wire

dépêcher [depɛʃe] *vt* to dispatch; **se dépêcher** *vi* to hurry; **se dépêcher de faire qch** to hasten to do sth, hurry (in order) to do sth

dépeindre [depɛ̃dʀ(ə)] *vt* to depict

dépendance [depɑ̃dɑ̃s] *nf* (*interdépendance*) dependence *no pl*, dependency; (*bâtiment*) outbuilding

dépendre [depɑ̃dʀ(ə)] *vt* (*tableau*) to take down; **dépendre de** *vt* to depend on, to be dependent on; (*appartenir*) to belong to; **ça dépend** it depends

dépens [depɑ̃] *nmpl*: **aux dépens de** at the expense of

dépense [depɑ̃s] *nf* spending *no pl*, expense, expenditure *no pl*; (*fig*) consumption; (*: de temps, de forces*) expenditure; **pousser qn à la dépense** to make sb incur an expense; **dépense physique**

(physical) exertion; **dépenses de fonctionnement** revenue expenditure; **dépenses d'investissement** capital expenditure; **dépenses publiques** public expenditure

dépenser [depɑ̃se] *vt* to spend; (*gaz, eau*) to use; (*fig*) to expend, use up; **se dépenser** (*se fatiguer*) to exert o.s.

dépensier, ière [depɑ̃sje, -jɛʀ] *adj*: **il est dépensier** he's a spendthrift

dépérir [deperiʀ] *vi* (*personne*) to waste away; (*plante*) to wither

dépêtrer [depetʀe] *vt*: **se dépêtrer de** (*situation*) to extricate o.s. from

dépeupler [depœple] *vt* to depopulate; **se dépeupler** to be depopulated

dépilatoire [depilatwaʀ] *adj* depilatory, hairremoving

dépister [depiste] *vt* to detect; (*MÉD*) to screen; (*voleur*) to track down; (*poursuivants*) to throw off the scent

dépit [depi] *nm* vexation, frustration; **en dépit de** *prép* in spite of; **en dépit du bon sens** contrary to all good sense

dépité, e [depite] *adj* vexed, frustrated

déplacé, e [deplase] *adj* (*propos*) out of place, uncalled-for; **personne déplacée** displaced person

déplacement [deplasmɑ̃] *nm* moving; shifting; transfer; (*voyage*) trip, travelling *no pl* (*BRIT*), traveling *no pl* (*US*); **en déplacement** away (on a trip); **déplacement d'air** displacement of air; **déplacement de vertèbre** slipped disc

déplacer [deplase] *vt* (*table, voiture*) to move, shift; (*employé*) to transfer, move; **se déplacer** *vi* (*objet*) to move; (*organe*) to become displaced; (*personne: bouger*) to move, walk; (*: voyager*) to travel ♦ *vt* (*vertèbre etc*) to displace

déplaire [deplɛʀ] *vi*: **ceci me déplaît** I don't like this, I dislike this; **il cherche à nous déplaire** he's trying to displease us *ou* be disagreeable to us; **se déplaire quelque part** to dislike it *ou* be unhappy somewhere

déplaisant, e [deplɛzɑ̃, -ɑ̃t] *vb voir* **déplaire** ♦ *adj* disagreeable, unpleasant

dépliant [deplijɑ̃] *nm* leaflet

déplier [deplije] *vt* to unfold; **se déplier** (*parachute*) to open

déplorer [deplɔʀe] *vt* (*regretter*) to deplore; (*pleurer sur*) to lament

déployer [deplwaje] *vt* to open out, spread; (*MIL*) to deploy; (*montrer*) to display, exhibit

déporter [depɔʀte] *vt* (*POL*) to deport; (*dévier*) to carry off course; **se déporter** *vi* (*voiture*) to swerve

déposer [depoze] *vt* (*gén: mettre, poser*) to lay down, put down, set down; (*à la banque, à la consigne*) to deposit; (*caution*) to put down; (*passager*) to drop (off), set down; (*démonter: serrure, moteur*) to take out; (*: rideau*) to take down; (*roi*) to depose;

(ADMIN: faire enregistrer) to file; to register ♦ vi to form a sediment ou deposit; (JUR): **déposer (contre)** to testify ou give evidence (against); **se déposer** vi to settle; **déposer son bilan** (COMM) to go into (voluntary) liquidation

dépositaire [depozitɛʀ] nm/f (JUR) depository; (COMM) agent; **dépositaire agréé** authorized agent

déposition [depozisjɔ̃] nf (JUR) deposition

dépôt [depo] nm (à la banque, sédiment) deposit; (entrepôt, réserve) warehouse, store; (gare) depot; (prison) cells pl; **dépôt d'ordures** rubbish (BRIT) ou garbage (US) dump, tip (BRIT); **dépôt de bilan** (voluntary) liquidation; **dépôt légal** registration of copyright

dépotoir [depɔtwaʀ] nm dumping ground, rubbish (BRIT) ou garbage (US) dump; **dépotoir nucléaire** nuclear (waste) dump

dépouiller [depuje] vt (animal) to skin; (spolier) to deprive of one's possessions; (documents) to go through, peruse; **dépouiller qn/qch de** to strip sb/sth of; **dépouiller le scrutin** to count the votes

dépourvu, e [depuʀvy] adj: **dépourvu de** lacking in, without; **au dépourvu** adv: **prendre qn au dépourvu** to catch sb unawares

déprécier [depʀesje] vt: **se déprécier** vi to depreciate

dépression [depʀesjɔ̃] nf depression; **dépression (nerveuse)** (nervous) breakdown

déprimant, e [depʀimɑ̃, -ɑ̃t] adj depressing

déprimer [depʀime] vt to depress

MOT CLÉ

depuis [dəpɥi] prép 1 (point de départ dans le temps) since; **il habite Paris depuis 1983/l'an dernier** he has been living in Paris since 1983/last year; **depuis quand?** since when?; **depuis quand le connaissez-vous?** how long have you known him?; **depuis lors** since then

2 (temps écoulé) for; **il habite Paris depuis 5 ans** he has been living in Paris for 5 years; **je le connais depuis 3 ans** I've known him for 3 years; **depuis combien de temps êtes-vous ici?** how long have you been here?

3 (lieu): **il a plu depuis Metz** it's been raining since Metz; **elle a téléphoné depuis Valence** she rang from Valence

4 (quantité, rang) from; **depuis les plus petits jusqu'aux plus grands** from the youngest to the oldest

♦ adv (temps) since (then); **je ne lui ai pas parlé depuis** I haven't spoken to him since (then); **depuis que** conj (ever) since; **depuis qu'il m'a dit ça** (ever) since he said that to me

---

député, e [depyte] nm/f (POL) deputy, ≈ Member of Parliament (BRIT), ≈ Congressman/woman (US)

députer [depyte] vt to delegate; **députer qn auprès de** to send sb (as a representative) to

déraciner [deʀasine] vt to uproot

dérailler [deʀaje] vi (train) to be derailed, go off ou jump the rails; (fam) to be completely off the track; **faire dérailler** to derail

déraisonner [deʀɛzɔne] vi to talk nonsense, rave

dérangement [deʀɑ̃ʒmɑ̃] nm (gêne, déplacement) trouble; (gastrique etc) disorder; (mécanique) breakdown; **en dérangement** (téléphone) out of order

déranger [deʀɑ̃ʒe] vt (personne) to trouble, bother, disturb; (projets) to disrupt, upset; (objets, vêtements) to disarrange; **se déranger** to put o.s. out; (se déplacer) to (take the trouble to) come (ou go) out; **est-ce que cela vous dérange si ...?** do you mind if ...?; **ça te dérangerait de faire ...?** would you mind doing ...?; **ne vous dérangez pas** don't go to any trouble; don't disturb yourself

déraper [deʀape] vi (voiture) to skid; (personne, semelles, couteau) to slip; (fig: économie etc) to go out of control

dérégler [deʀegle] vt (mécanisme) to put out of order, cause to break down; (estomac) to upset; **se dérégler** vi to break down, go wrong

dérider [deʀide] vt: **se dérider** vi to brighten ou cheer up

dérision [deʀizjɔ̃] nf derision; **tourner en dérision** to deride; **par dérision** in mockery

dérisoire [deʀizwaʀ] adj derisory

dérive [deʀiv] nf (de dériveur) centre-board; **aller à la dérive** (NAVIG, fig) to drift; **dérive des continents** (GÉO) continental drift

dérivé, e [deʀive] adj derived ♦ nm (LING) derivative; (TECH) by-product ♦ nf (MATH) derivative

dériver [deʀive] vt (MATH) to derive; (cours d'eau etc) to divert ♦ vi (bateau) to drift; **dériver de** to derive from

dermatologue [dɛʀmatɔlɔg] nm/f dermatologist

dernier, ière [dɛʀnje, -jɛʀ] adj (dans le temps, l'espace) last; (le plus récent: gén avant n) latest, last; (final, ultime: effort) final; (échelon, grade) top, highest ♦ nm (étage) top floor; **lundi/le mois dernier** last Monday/month; **du dernier chic** extremely smart; **le dernier cri** the last word (in fashion); **les derniers honneurs** the last tribute; **le dernier soupir**: **rendre le dernier soupir** to breathe one's last; **en dernier** adv last; **ce dernier, cette dernière** the latter

dernièrement [dɛʀnjɛʀmɑ̃] adv recently

dérobé, e [deʀɔbe] adj (porte) secret, hidden; **à la dérobée** surreptitiously

dérober [deʀɔbe] vt to steal; (cacher): **dérober qch à (la vue de) qn** to conceal ou hide sth from sb('s view); **se dérober** vi (s'esquiver) to slip away; (fig) to shy away; **se dérober sous** (s'effondrer) to give way beneath; **se dérober à** (justice, regards) to hide from; (obligation) to shirk

dérogation [deʀɔgasjɔ̃] nf (special) dispensation

déroger [deʀɔʒe]: **déroger à** vt to go against,

depart from

dérouiller [deʀuje] *vt*: **se dérouiller les jambes** to stretch one's legs

déroulement [deʀulmɑ̃] *nm* (*d'une opération etc*) progress

dérouler [deʀule] *vt* (*ficelle*) to unwind; (*papier*) to unroll; **se dérouler** *vi* to unwind; to unroll, come unrolled; (*avoir lieu*) to take place; (*se passer*) to go

dérouter [deʀute] *vt* (*avion, train*) to reroute, divert; (*étonner*) to disconcert, throw (out)

derrière [deʀjeʀ] *adv, prép* behind ♦ *nm* (*d'une maison*) back; (*postérieur*) behind, bottom; **les pattes de derrière** the back legs, the hind legs; **par derrière** from behind; (*fig*) in an underhand way, behind one's back

des [de] *dét, prép* + *dét voir* **de**

dès [dɛ] *prép* from; **dès que** *conj* as soon as; **dès à présent** here and now; **dès son retour** as soon as he was (*ou* is) back; **dès réception** upon receipt; **dès lors** *adv* from then on; **dès lors que** *conj* from the moment (that)

désabusé, e [dezabyze] *adj* disillusioned

désaccord [dezakɔʀ] *nm* disagreement

désaccordé, e [dezakɔʀde] *adj* (*MUS*) out of tune

désaffecté, e [dezafɛkte] *adj* disused

désagréable [dezagʀeablə] *adj* unpleasant, disagreeable

désagréger [dezagʀeʒe]: **se désagréger** *vi* to disintegrate, break up

désagrément [dezagʀemɑ̃] *nm* annoyance, trouble *no pl*

désaltérer [dezalteʀe] *vt*: **se désaltérer** to quench one's thirst; **ça désaltère** it's thirst-quenching, it quenches your thirst

désapprobateur, trice [dezapʀɔbatœʀ, -tʀis] *adj* disapproving

désapprouver [dezapʀuve] *vt* to disapprove of

désarmant, e [dezaʀmɑ̃, -ɑ̃t] *adj* disarming

désarroi [dezaʀwa] *nm* helplessness, disarray

désastre [dezastʀ(ə)] *nm* disaster

désastreux, euse [dezastʀø, -øz] *adj* disastrous

désavantage [dezavɑ̃taʒ] *nm* disadvantage; (*inconvénient*) drawback, disadvantage

désavantager [dezavɑ̃taʒe] *vt* to put at a disadvantage

descendre [desɑ̃dʀ(ə)] *vt* (*escalier, montagne*) to go (*ou* come) down; (*valise, paquet*) to take *ou* get down; (*étagère etc*) to lower; (*fam: abattre*) to shoot down; (: *boire*) to knock back ♦ *vi* to go (*ou* come) down; (*passager: s'arrêter*) to get out, alight; (*niveau, température*) to go *ou* come down, fall, drop; (*marée*) to go out; **descendre à pied/en voiture** to walk/drive down, go down on foot/by car; **descendre de** (*famille*) to be descended from; **descendre du train** to get out of *ou* off the train; **descendre d'un arbre** to climb down from a tree; **descendre de cheval** to dismount, get off one's horse; **descendre à l'hôtel** to stay at a hotel;

descendre dans la rue (*manifester*) to take to the streets; **descendre en ville** to go into town, go down town

descente [desɑ̃t] *nf* descent, going down; (*chemin*) way down; (*SKI*) downhill (race); **au milieu de la descente** halfway down; **freinez dans les descentes** use the brakes going downhill; **descente de lit** bedside rug; **descente (de police)** (police) raid

description [deskʀipsjɔ̃] *nf* description

désemparé, e [dezɑ̃paʀe] *adj* bewildered, distraught; (*bateau, avion*) crippled

désemplir [dezɑ̃pliʀ] *vi*: **ne pas désemplir** to be always full

déséquilibre [dezekilibʀ(ə)] *nm* (*position*): **être en déséquilibre** to be unsteady; (*fig: des forces, du budget*) imbalance; (*PSYCH*) unbalance

déséquilibré, e [dezekilibʀe] *nm/f* (*PSYCH*) unbalanced person

déséquilibrer [dezekilibʀe] *vt* to throw off balance

désert, e [dezeʀ, -ɛʀt(ə)] *adj* deserted ♦ *nm* desert

déserter [dezeʀte] *vi, vt* to desert

désertique [dezeʀtik] *adj* desert *cpd*; (*inculte*) barren, empty

désespéré, e [dezespeʀe] *adj* desperate; (*regard*) despairing; **état désespéré** (*MED*) hopeless condition

désespérer [dezespeʀe] *vt* to drive to despair ♦ *vi*: **se désespérer** *vi* to despair; **désespérer de** to despair of

désespoir [dezespwaʀ] *nm* despair; **être ou faire le désespoir de qn** to be the despair of sb; **en désespoir de cause** in desperation

déshabiller [dezabije] *vt* to undress; **se déshabiller** to undress (o.s.)

déshérité, e [dezeʀite] *adj* disinherited ♦ *nm/f*: **les déshérités** (*pauvres*) the underprivileged, the deprived

déshériter [dezeʀite] *vt* to disinherit

déshonneur [dezɔnœʀ] *nm* dishonour (*BRIT*), dishonor (*US*), disgrace

déshydraté, e [dezidʀate] *adj* dehydrated

desiderata [dezideʀata] *nmpl* requirements

désigner [dezine] *vt* (*montrer*) to point out, indicate; (*dénommer*) to denote, refer to; (*nommer: candidat etc*) to name, appoint

désinfectant, e [dezɛ̃fɛktɑ̃, -ɑ̃t] *adj, nm* disinfectant

désinfecter [dezɛ̃fɛkte] *vt* to disinfect

désintégrer [dezɛ̃tegʀe] *vt*: **se désintégrer** *vi* to disintegrate

désintéressé, e [dezɛ̃teʀese] *adj* (*généreux, bénévole*) disinterested, unselfish

désintéresser [dezɛ̃teʀese] *vt*: **se désintéresser (de)** to lose interest (in)

désintoxication [dezɛ̃tɔksikasjɔ̃] *nf* treatment for alcoholism (*ou* drug addiction); **faire une cure**

de désintoxication to have *ou* undergo treatment for alcoholism (*ou* drug addiction)

désinvolte [dezɛ̃vɔlt(ə)] *adj* casual, off-hand

désinvolture [dezɛ̃vɔltyʀ] *nf* casualness

désir [deziʀ] *nm* wish; (*fort, sensuel*) desire

désirer [deziʀe] *vt* to want, wish for; (*sexuellement*) to desire; **je désire ...** (*formule de politesse*) I would like ...; **il désire que tu l'aides** he would like *ou* he wants you to help him; **désirer faire** to want *ou* wish to do; **ça laisse à désirer** it leaves something to be desired

désister [deziste]: **se désister** *vi* to stand down, withdraw

désobéir [dezɔbeiʀ] *vi*: **désobéir (à qn/qch)** to disobey (sb/sth)

désobéissant, e [dezɔbeisɑ̃, -ɑ̃t] *adj* disobedient

désobligeant, e [dezɔbliʒɑ̃, -ɑ̃t] *adj* disagreeable, unpleasant

désodorisant [dezɔdɔʀizɑ̃] *nm* air freshener, deodorizer

désœuvré, e [dezœvʀe] *adj* idle

désolé, e [dezɔle] *adj* (*paysage*) desolate; **je suis désolé** I'm sorry

désoler [dezɔle] *vt* to distress, grieve; **se désoler** to be upset

désopilant, e [dezɔpilɑ̃, -ɑ̃t] *adj* screamingly funny, hilarious

désordonné, e [dezɔʀdɔne] *adj* untidy, disorderly

désordre [dezɔʀdʀ(ə)] *nm* disorder(liness), untidiness; (*anarchie*) disorder; **désordres** *nmpl* (*POL*) disturbances, disorder *sg*; **en désordre** in a mess, untidy

désorienté, e [dezɔʀjɑ̃te] *adj* disorientated; (*fig*) bewildered

désormais [dezɔʀmɛ] *adv* in future, from now on

désosser [dezɔse] *vt* to bone

desquels, desquelles [dekɛl] *prép + pron voir* **lequel**

desséché, e [deseʃe] *adj* dried up

dessécher [deseʃe] *vt* (*terre, plante*) to dry out, parch; (*peau*) to dry out; (*volontairement: aliments etc*) to dry, dehydrate; (*fig: cœur*) to harden; **se dessécher** *vi* to dry out; (*peau, lèvres*) to go dry

dessein [desɛ̃] *nm* design; **dans le dessein de** with the intention of; **à dessein** intentionally, deliberately

desserrer [deseʀe] *vt* to loosen; (*frein*) to release; (*poing, dents*) to unclench; (*objets alignés*) to space out; **ne pas desserrer les dents** not to open one's mouth

dessert [desɛʀ] *vb voir* **desservir** ♦ *nm* dessert, pudding

desserte [desɛʀt(ə)] *nf* (*table*) side table; (*transport*): **la desserte du village est assurée par autocar** there is a coach service to the village; **chemin** *ou* **voie de desserte** service road

desservir [desɛʀviʀ] *vt* (*ville, quartier*) to serve;

(: *suj: voie de communication*) to lead into; (*suj: vicaire: paroisse*) to serve; (*nuire à: personne*) to do a disservice to; (*débarrasser*): **desservir (la table)** to clear the table

dessin [desɛ̃] *nm* (*œuvre, art*) drawing; (*motif*) pattern, design; (*contour*) (out)line; **le dessin industriel** draughtsmanship (*BRIT*), draftsmanship (*US*); **dessin animé** cartoon (film); **dessin humoristique** cartoon

dessinateur, trice [desinatœʀ, -tʀis] *nm/f* drawer; (*de bandes dessinées*) cartoonist; (*industriel*) draughtsman (*BRIT*), draftsman (*US*); **dessinatrice de mode** fashion designer

dessiner [desine] *vt* to draw; (*concevoir: carrosserie, maison*) to design; (*suj: robe: taille*) to show off; **se dessiner** *vi* (*forme*) to be outlined; (*fig: solution*) to emerge

dessous [dəsu] *adv* underneath, beneath ♦ *nm* underside; (*étage inférieur*): **les voisins du dessous** the downstairs neighbours ♦ *nmpl* (*sous-vêtements*) underwear *sg*; (*fig*) hidden aspects; **en dessous** underneath; below; (*fig: en catimini*) slyly, on the sly; **par dessous** underneath; below; **de dessous le lit** from under the bed; **au-dessous** *adv* below; **au-dessous de** *prép* below; (*peu digne de*) beneath; **au-dessous de tout** the (absolute) limit; **avoir le dessous** to get the worst of it

dessous-de-plat [dəsudpla] *nm inv* tablemat

dessus [dəsy] *adv* on top; (*collé, écrit*) on it ♦ *nm* top; (*étage supérieur*): **les voisins/l'appartement du dessus** the upstairs neighbours/flat; **en dessus** above; **par dessus** *adv* over it ♦ *prép* over; **au-dessus** above; **au-dessus de** above; **avoir/prendre le dessus** to have/get the upper hand; **reprendre le dessus** to get over it; **bras dessus bras dessous** arm in arm; **sens dessus dessous** upside down; *voir* **ci-**, **là-**

dessus-de-lit [dəsydli] *nm inv* bedspread

destin [destɛ̃] *nm* fate; (*avenir*) destiny

destinataire [destinatɛʀ] *nm/f* (*POSTES*) addressee; (*d'un colis*) consignee; (*d'un mandat*) payee; **aux risques et périls du destinataire** at owner's risk

destination [destinasjɔ̃] *nf* (*lieu*) destination; (*usage*) purpose; **à destination de** (*avion etc*) bound for; (*voyageur*) bound for, travelling to

destinée [destine] *nf* fate; (*existence, avenir*) destiny

destiner [destine] *vt*: **destiner qn à** (*poste, sort*) to destine sb for, intend sb to + *verbe*; **destiner qn/qch à** (*prédestiner*) to mark sb/sth out for, destine sb/sth to + *verbe*; **destiner qch à** (*envisager d'affecter*) to intend to use sth for; **destiner qch à qn** (*envisager de donner*) to intend to give sth to sb, intend sb to have sth; (*adresser*) to intend sth for sb; **se destiner à l'enseignement** to intend to become a teacher; **être destiné à** (*sort*) to be destined to + *verbe*; (*usage*) to be intended *ou* meant for; (*suj: sort*) to be in store for

destruction [destʀyksjɔ̃] *nf* destruction

désuet, ète [desɥɛ, -ɛt] *adj* outdated, outmoded

détachant [detaʃɑ̃] *nm* stain remover

détachement [detaʃmɑ̃] *nm* detachment; (*fonctionnaire, employé*): **être en détachement** to be on secondment (*BRIT*) *ou* a posting

détacher [detaʃe] *vt* (*enlever*) to detach, remove; (*délier*) to untie; (*ADMIN*): **détacher qn (auprès de** *ou* **à)** to send sb on secondment (to) (*BRIT*), post sb (to); (*MIL*) to detail; (*vêtement: nettoyer*) to remove the stains from; **se détacher** *vi* (*tomber*) to come off; to come out; (*se défaire*) to come undone; (*SPORT*) to pull *ou* break away; (*se délier: chien, prisonnier*) to break loose; **se détacher sur** to stand out against; **se détacher de** (*se désintéresser*) to grow away from

détail [detaj] *nm* detail; (*COMM*): **le détail** retail; **prix de détail** retail price; **au détail** *adv* (*COMM*) retail; (: *individuellement*) separately; **donner le détail de** to give a detailed account of; (*compte*) to give a breakdown of; **en détail** in detail

détaillant, e [detajɑ̃, -ɑ̃t] *nm/f* retailer

détaillé, e [detaje] *adj* (*récit*) detailed

détailler [detaje] *vt* (*COMM*) to sell retail; to sell separately; (*expliquer*) to explain in detail; to detail; (*examiner*) to look over, examine

détaler [detale] *vi* (*lapin*) to scamper off; (*fam: personne*) to make off, scarper (*fam*)

détartrant [detartrɑ̃] *nm* descaling agent (*BRIT*), scale remover

détaxer [detakse] *vt* (*réduire*) to reduce the tax on; (*ôter*) to remove the tax on

détecter [detɛkte] *vt* to detect

détective [detɛktiv] *nm* (*BRIT POLICIER*) detective; **détective (privé)** private detective *ou* investigator

déteindre [detɛ̃dʀ(ə)] *vi* to fade; (*fig*): **déteindre sur** to rub off on

détendre [detɑ̃dʀ(ə)] *vt* (*fil*) to slacken, loosen; (*personne, atmosphère*) to relax; (: *situation*) to relieve; **se détendre** *vi* to lose its tension; to relax

détenir [detnir] *vt* (*fortune, objet, secret*) to be in possession of; (*prisonnier*) to detain; (*record*) to hold; **détenir le pouvoir** to be in power

détente [detɑ̃t] *nf* relaxation; (*POL*) détente; (*d'une arme*) trigger; (*d'un athlète qui saute*) spring

détention [detɑ̃sjɔ̃] *nf* (*voir détenir*) possession; detention; holding; **détention préventive** (pretrial) custody

détenu, e [detny] *pp de* **détenir** ◆ *nm/f* prisoner

détergent [detɛʀʒɑ̃] *nm* detergent

détériorer [deteʀjɔʀe] *vt* to damage; **se détériorer** *vi* to deteriorate

déterminé, e [detɛʀmine] *adj* (*résolu*) determined; (*précis*) specific, definite

déterminer [detɛʀmine] *vt* (*fixer*) to determine; (*décider*): **déterminer qn à faire** to decide sb to do; **se déterminer à faire** to make up one's mind to do

déterrer [deteʀe] *vt* to dig up

détestable [detɛstabl(ə)] *adj* foul, detestable

détester [detɛste] *vt* to hate, detest

détonner [detɔne] *vi* (*MUS*) to go out of tune; (*fig*) to clash

détour [detur] *nm* detour; (*tournant*) bend, curve; (*fig: subterfuge*) roundabout means; **sans détour** (*fig*) plainly

détourné, e [deturne] *adj* (*sentier, chemin, moyen*) roundabout

détournement [deturnəmɑ̃] *nm* diversion, rerouting; **détournement d'avion** hijacking; **détournement (de fonds)** embezzlement *ou* misappropriation (of funds); **détournement de mineur** corruption of a minor

détourner [deturne] *vt* to divert; (*avion*) to divert, reroute; (: *par la force*) to hijack; (*yeux, tête*) to turn away; (*de l'argent*) to embezzle, misappropriate; **se détourner** to turn away; **détourner la conversation** to change the subject; **détourner qn de son devoir** to divert sb from his duty; **détourner l'attention (de qn)** to distract *ou* divert (sb's) attention

détracteur, trice [detraktœr, -tris] *nm/f* disparager, critic

détraquer [detrake] *vt* to put out of order; (*estomac*) to upset; **se détraquer** *vi* to go wrong

détrempé, e [detrɑ̃pe] *adj* (*sol*) sodden, waterlogged

détresse [detres] *nf* distress; **en détresse** (*avion etc*) in distress; **appel/signal de détresse** distress call/signal

détriment [detrimɑ̃] *nm*: **au détriment de** to the detriment of

détritus [detritys] *nmpl* rubbish *sg*, refuse *sg*, garbage *sg* (*US*)

détroit [detrwa] *nm* strait; **le détroit de Bering** *ou* **Behring** the Bering Strait; **le détroit de Gibraltar** the Straits of Gibraltar; **le détroit du Bosphore** the Bosphorus; **le détroit de Magellan** the Strait of Magellan, the Magellan Strait

détromper [detrɔ̃pe] *vt* to disabuse; **se détromper**: **détrompez-vous** don't believe it

détruire [detrɥir] *vt* to destroy; (*fig: santé, réputation*) to ruin; (*documents*) to shred

dette [dɛt] *nf* debt; **dette publique** *ou* **de l'État** national debt

DEUG [døg] *sigle m = Diplôme d'études universitaires générales; see boxed note*

deuil [dœj] *nm* (*perte*) bereavement; (*période*) mourning; (*chagrin*) grief; **porter le deuil** to wear mourning; **prendre le/être en deuil** to go into/be in mourning

deux [dø] *num* two; **les deux** both; **ses deux mains** both his hands, his two hands; **à deux pas** a short distance away; **tous les deux mois** every two months, every other month

deuxième [døzjɛm] *num* second

deuxièmement [døzjɛmmã] *adv* secondly, in the second place

deux-pièces [døpjɛs] *nm inv* (*tailleur*) two-piece (suit); (*de bain*) two-piece (swimsuit); (*appartement*) two-roomed flat (BRIT) ou apartment (US)

deux-points [døpwɛ̃] *nm inv* colon *sg*

deux-roues [døRu] *nm inv* two-wheeled vehicle

devais *etc* [dəvɛ] *vb voir* **devoir**

dévaler [devale] *vt* to hurtle down

dévaliser [devalize] *vt* to rob, burgle

dévaloriser [devalɔrize] *vt*: **se dévaloriser** *vi* to depreciate

dévaluation [devalɥasjɔ̃] *nf* depreciation; (ÉCON: *mesure*) devaluation

devancer [dəvɑ̃se] *vt* to be ahead of; (*distancer*) to get ahead of; (*arriver avant*) to arrive before; (*prévenir*) to anticipate; **devancer l'appel** (MIL) to enlist before call-up

devant [dəvɑ̃] *vb voir* **devoir** ♦ *adv* in front; (*à distance: en avant*) ahead ♦ *prép* in front of; ahead of; (*avec mouvement: passer*) past; (*fig*) before, in front of; (: *face à*) faced with, in the face of; (: *vu*) in view of ♦ *nm* front; **prendre les devants** to make the first move; **de devant** (*roue, porte*) front; **les pattes de devant** the front legs, the forelegs; **par devant** (*boutonner*) at the front; (*entrer*) the front way; **par-devant notaire** in the presence of a notary; **aller au-devant de qn** to go out to meet sb; **aller au-devant de** (*désirs de qn*) to anticipate; **aller au-devant des ennuis** ou **difficultés** to be asking for trouble

devanture [dəvɑ̃tyR] *nf* (*façade*) (shop) front; (*étalage*) display; (shop) window

déveine [devɛn] *nf* rotten luck *no pl*

développement [devlɔpmɑ̃] *nm* development

développer [devlɔpe] *vt*: **se développer** *vi* to develop

devenir [dəvniR] *vb avec attribut* to become; **devenir instituteur** to become a teacher; **que sont-ils devenus?** what has become of them?

dévergondé, e [deverɡɔ̃de] *adj* wild, shameless

déverser [deverse] *vt* (*liquide*) to pour (out); (*ordures*) to tip (out); **se déverser dans** (*fleuve, mer*) to flow into

dévêtir [devetiR] *vt*: **se dévêtir** *vi* to undress

devez [dəve] *vb voir* **devoir**

déviation [devjasjɔ̃] *nf* deviation; (AUTO) diversion (BRIT), detour (US); **déviation de la colonne (vertébrale)** curvature of the spine

dévier [devje] *vt* (*fleuve, circulation*) to divert; (*coup*) to deflect ♦ *vi* to veer (off course); (**faire**) **dévier** (*projectile*) to deflect; (*véhicule*) to push off course

devin [dəvɛ̃] *nm* soothsayer, seer

deviner [dəvine] *vt* to guess; (*prévoir*) to foretell, foresee; (*apercevoir*) to distinguish

devinette [dəvinɛt] *nf* riddle

devis [dəvi] *nm* estimate, quotation; **devis descriptif/estimatif** detailed/preliminary estimate

dévisager [devizaʒe] *vt* to stare at

devise [dəviz] *nf* (*formule*) motto, watchword; (ÉCON: *monnaie*) currency; **devises** *nfpl* (*argent*) currency *sg*

deviser [dəvize] *vi* to converse

dévisser [devise] *vt* to unscrew, undo; **se dévisser** *vi* to come unscrewed

dévoiler [devwale] *vt* to unveil

devoir [dəvwaR] *nm* duty; (SCOL) piece of homework, homework *no pl*; (: *en classe*) exercise ♦ *vt* (*argent, respect*): **devoir qch (à qn)** to owe (sb) sth; (*suivi de l'infinitif: obligation*): **il doit le faire** he has to do it, he must do it; (: *fatalité*): **cela devait arriver un jour** it was bound to happen; (: *intention*): **il doit partir demain** he is (due) to leave tomorrow; (: *probabilité*): **il doit être tard** it must be late; **se faire un devoir de faire qch** to make it one's duty to do sth; **devoirs de vacances** homework set for the holidays; **se devoir de faire qch** to be duty bound to do sth; **je devrais faire** I ought to ou should do; **tu n'aurais pas dû** you ought not to have ou shouldn't have; **comme il se doit** (*comme il faut*) as is right and proper

dévolu, e [devɔly] *adj*: **dévolu à** allotted to ♦ *nm*: **jeter son dévolu sur** to fix one's choice on

dévorer [devɔre] *vt* to devour; (*suj: feu, soucis*) to consume; **dévorer qn/qch des yeux** ou **du regard** (*fig*) to eye sb/sth intently; (: *convoitise*) to eye sb/sth greedily

dévot, e [devo, -ɔt] *adj* devout, pious ♦ *nm/f* devout person; **un faux dévot** a falsely pious person

dévotion [devosjɔ̃] *nf* devoutness; **être à la dévotion de qn** to be totally devoted to sb; **avoir une dévotion pour qn** to worship sb

dévoué, e [devwe] *adj* devoted

dévouement [devumɑ̃] *nm* devotion, dedication

dévouer [devwe]: **se dévouer** *vi* (*se sacrifier*): **se dévouer (pour)** to sacrifice o.s. (for); (*se consacrer*): **se dévouer à** to devote ou dedicate o.s. to

dévoyé, e [devwaje] *adj* delinquent

devrai *etc* [dəvRe] *vb voir* **devoir**

diabète [djabɛt] *nm* diabetes *sg*

diabétique [djabetik] *nm/f* diabetic

diable [djabl(ə)] *nm* devil; **une musique du diable** an unholy racket; **il fait une chaleur du diable**

it's fiendishly hot; **avoir le diable au corps** to be the very devil

diabolo [djabɔlo] *nm* (*jeu*) diabolo; (*boisson*) lemonade and fruit cordial; **diabolo(-menthe)** lemonade and mint cordial

diagnostic [djagnɔstik] *nm* diagnosis *sg*

diagnostiquer [djagnɔstike] *vt* to diagnose

diagonal, e, aux [djagɔnal, -o] *adj, nf* diagonal; **en diagonale** diagonally; **lire en diagonale** (*fig*) to skim through

diagramme [djagram] *nm* chart, graph

dialecte [djalɛkt(ə)] *nm* dialect

dialogue [djalɔg] *nm* dialogue; **dialogue de sourds** dialogue of the deaf

diamant [djamɑ̃] *nm* diamond

diamètre [djamɛtʀ(ə)] *nm* diameter

diapason [djapazɔ̃] *nm* tuning fork; (*fig*): **être/se mettre au diapason (de)** to be/get in tune (with)

diaphragme [djafʀagm(ə)] *nm* (*ANAT, PHOTO*) diaphragm; (*contraceptif*) diaphragm, cap; **ouverture du diaphragme** (*PHOTO*) aperture

diapo [djapo], **diapositive** [djapozitiv] *nf* transparency, slide

diarrhée [djaʀe] *nf* diarrhoea (*BRIT*), diarrhea (*US*)

dictateur [diktatœʀ] *nm* dictator

dictature [diktatyʀ] *nf* dictatorship

dictée [dikte] *nf* dictation; **prendre sous dictée** to take down (*sth dictated*)

dicter [dikte] *vt* to dictate

dictionnaire [diksjɔnɛʀ] *nm* dictionary; **dictionnaire géographique** gazetteer

dicton [diktɔ̃] *nm* saying, dictum

dièse [djɛz] *nm* (*MUS*) sharp

diesel [djezɛl] *nm, adj inv* diesel

diète [djɛt] *nf* diet; **être à la diète** to be on a diet

diététique [djetetik] *nf* dietetics *sg* ♦ *adj*: **magasin diététique** health food shop (*BRIT*) *ou* store (*US*)

dieu, x [djø] *nm* god; **Dieu** God; **le bon Dieu** the good Lord; **mon Dieu!** good heavens!

diffamation [difamɑsjɔ̃] *nf* slander; (*écrite*) libel; **attaquer qn en diffamation** to sue sb for slander (*ou* libel)

différé [difeʀe] *adj* (*INFORM*): **traitement différé** batch processing; **crédit différé** deferred credit ♦ *nm* (*TV*): **en différé** (pre-)recorded

différemment [difeʀamɑ̃] *adv* differently

différence [difeʀɑ̃s] *nf* difference; **à la différence de** unlike

différencier [difeʀɑ̃sje] *vt* to differentiate; **se différencier** *vi* (*organisme*) to become differentiated; **se différencier de** to differentiate o.s. from; (*être différent*) to differ from

différend [difeʀɑ̃] *nm* difference (of opinion), disagreement

différent, e [difeʀɑ̃, -ɑ̃t] *adj*: **différent (de)** different (from); **différents objets** different *ou* various objects; **à différentes reprises** on various occa-sions

différer [difeʀe] *vt* to postpone, put off ♦ *vi*: **différer (de)** to differ (from); **différer de faire** (*tarder*) to delay doing

difficile [difisil] *adj* difficult; (*exigeant*) hard to please, difficult (to please); **faire le** *ou* **la difficile** to be hard to please, be difficult

difficilement [difisilmɑ̃] *adv* (*marcher, s'expliquer etc*) with difficulty; **difficilement lisible/compréhensible** difficult *ou* hard to read/understand

difficulté [difikylte] *nf* difficulty; **en difficulté** (*bateau, alpiniste*) in trouble *ou* difficulties; **avoir de la difficulté à faire** to have difficulty (in) doing

difforme [difɔʀm(ə)] *adj* deformed, misshapen

diffuser [difyze] *vt* (*chaleur, bruit, lumière*) to diffuse; (*émission, musique*) to broadcast; (*nouvelle, idée*) to circulate; (*COMM: livres, journaux*) to distribute

digérer [diʒeʀe] *vt* (*suj: personne*) to digest; (*: machine*) to process; (*fig: accepter*) to stomach, put up with

digestif, ive [diʒɛstif, -iv] *adj* digestive ♦ *nm* (after-dinner) liqueur

digestion [diʒɛstjɔ̃] *nf* digestion

digne [diɲ] *adj* dignified; **digne de** worthy of; **digne de foi** trustworthy

dignité [diɲite] *nf* dignity

digue [dig] *nf* dike, dyke; (*pour protéger la côte*) sea wall

dilapider [dilapide] *vt* to squander, waste; (*détourner: biens, fonds publics*) to embezzle, misappropriate

dilemme [dilɛm] *nm* dilemma

dilettante [diletɑ̃t] *nm/f* dilettante; **en dilettante** in a dilettantish way

diligence [diliʒɑ̃s] *nf* stagecoach, diligence; (*empressement*) despatch; **faire diligence** to make haste

diluer [dilɥe] *vt* to dilute

diluvien, ne [dilyvjɛ̃, -ɛn] *adj*: **pluie diluvienne** torrential rain

dimanche [dimɑ̃ʃ] *nm* Sunday; **le dimanche des Rameaux/de Pâques** Palm/Easter Sunday; *voir aussi* **lundi**

dimension [dimɑ̃sjɔ̃] *nf* (*grandeur*) size; (*gén pl: cotes, MATH: de l'espace*) dimension

diminué, e [diminɥe] *adj* (*personne: physiquement*) run-down; (*: mentalement*) less alert

diminuer [diminɥe] *vt* to reduce, decrease; (*ardeur etc*) to lessen; (*personne: physiquement*) to undermine; (*dénigrer*) to belittle ♦ *vi* to decrease, diminish

diminutif [diminytif] *nm* (*LING*) diminutive; (*surnom*) pet name

diminution [diminysjɔ̃] *nf* decreasing, diminishing

dinde [dɛ̃d] *nf* turkey; (*femme stupide*) goose

dindon [dɛ̃dɔ̃] *nm* turkey

dîner [dine] *nm* dinner ♦ *vi* to have dinner; **dîner d'affaires/de famille** business/family dinner

dingue [dɛ̃g] *adj* (*fam*) crazy

dinosaure [dinozɔR] *nm* dinosaur

diplomate [diplɔmat] *adj* diplomatic ♦ *nm* diplomat; (*fig: personne habile*) diplomatist; (*CULIN: gâteau*) dessert made of sponge cake, candied fruit and custard, ≈ trifle (*BRIT*)

diplomatie [diplɔmasi] *nf* diplomacy

diplôme [diplom] *nm* diploma certificate; (*examen*) (diploma) examination

diplômé, e [diplome] *adj* qualified

dire [diR] *nm*: **au dire de** according to; **leurs dires** what they say ♦ *vt* to say; (*secret, mensonge*) to tell; **dire l'heure/la vérité** to tell the time/the truth; **dis pardon/merci** say sorry/thank you; **dire qch à qn** to tell sb sth; **dire à qn qu'il fasse** *ou* **de faire** to tell sb to do; **dire que** to say that; **on dit que** they say that; **comme on dit** as they say; **on dirait que** it looks (*ou* sounds *etc*) as though; **on dirait du vin** you'd *ou* one would think it was wine; **que dites-vous de** (*penser*) what do you think of; **si cela lui dit** if he feels like it, if he fancies it; **cela ne me dit rien** that doesn't appeal to me; **à vrai dire** truth to tell; **pour ainsi dire** so to speak; **cela va sans dire** that goes without saying; **dis donc!, dites donc!** (*pour attirer l'attention*) hey!; (*au fait*) by the way; **et dire que ...** and to think that ...; **ceci** *ou* **cela dit** that being said; (*à ces mots*) whereupon; **c'est dit, voilà qui est dit** so that's settled; **il n'y a pas à dire** there's no getting away from it; **c'est dire si ...** that just shows that ...; **c'est beaucoup/peu dire** that's saying a lot/not saying much; **se dire** (*à soi-même*) to say to oneself; (*se prétendre*): **se dire malade** *etc* to say (that) one is ill *etc*; **ça se dit ... en anglais** that is ... in English; **cela ne se dit pas comme ça** you don't say it like that; **se dire au revoir** to say goodbye (to each other)

direct, e [diRɛkt] *adj* direct ♦ *nm* (*train*) through train; **en direct** (*émission*) live; **train/bus direct** express train/bus

directement [diRɛktəmɑ̃] *adv* directly

directeur, trice [diRɛktœr, -tris] *nm/f* (*d'entreprise*) director; (*de service*) manager/eress; (*d'école*) head(teacher) (*BRIT*), principal (*US*); **comité directeur** management *ou* steering committee; **directeur général** general manager; **directeur de thèse** ≈ PhD supervisor

direction [diRɛksjɔ̃] *nf* management; conducting; supervision; (*AUTO*) steering; (*sens*) direction; **sous la direction de** (*MUS*) conducted by; **en direction de** (*avion, train, bateau*) for; **"toutes directions"** (*AUTO*) "all routes"

dirent [diR] *vb voir* **dire**

dirigeant, e [diRiʒɑ̃, -ɑ̃t] *adj* managerial; (*classes*) ruling ♦ *nm/f* (*d'un parti etc*) leader; (*d'entreprise*) manager, member of the management

diriger [diRiʒe] *vt* (*entreprise*) to manage, run; (*véhicule*) to steer; (*orchestre*) to conduct; (*recherches, travaux*) to supervise, be in charge of; (*braquer: regard, arme*): **diriger sur** to point *ou* level *ou* aim at; (*fig: critiques*): **diriger contre** to aim at; **se diriger** (*s'orienter*) to find one's way; **se diriger vers** *ou* **sur** to make *ou* head for

dis [di], **disais** [dize] *etc vb voir* **dire**

discernement [disɛRnəmɑ̃] *nm* discernment, judgment

discerner [disɛRne] *vt* to discern, make out

discipline [disiplin] *nf* discipline

discipliner [disipline] *vt* to discipline; (*cheveux*) to control

discontinu, e [diskɔ̃tiny] *adj* intermittent; (*bande: sur la route*) broken

discontinuer [diskɔ̃tinɥe] *vi*: **sans discontinuer** without stopping, without a break

discordant, e [diskɔRdɑ̃, -ɑ̃t] *adj* discordant; conflicting

discothèque [diskɔtek] *nf* (*disques*) record collection; (: *dans une bibliothèque*): **discothèque (de prêt)** record library; (*boîte de nuit*) disco(thèque)

discours [diskuR] *vb voir* **discourir** ♦ *nm* speech; **discours direct/indirect** (*LING*) direct/indirect *ou* reported speech

discret, ète [diskRɛ, -ɛt] *adj* discreet; (*fig: musique, style*) unobtrusive; (: *endroit*) quiet

discrétion [diskResjɔ̃] *nf* discretion; **à la discrétion de qn** at sb's discretion; in sb's hands; **à discrétion** (*boisson etc*) unlimited, as much as one wants

discrimination [diskRiminasjɔ̃] *nf* discrimination; **sans discrimination** indiscriminately

disculper [diskylpe] *vt* to exonerate

discussion [diskysjɔ̃] *nf* discussion

discutable [diskytabl(ə)] *adj* (*contestable*) doubtful; (*à débattre*) debatable

discuté, e [diskyte] *adj* controversial

discuter [diskyte] *vt* (*contester*) to question, dispute; (*débattre: prix*) to discuss ♦ *vi* to talk; (*ergoter*) to argue; **discuter de** to discuss

dise *etc* [diz] *vb voir* **dire**

diseuse [dizøz] *nf*: **diseuse de bonne aventure** fortuneteller

disgracieux, euse [disgRasjø, -øz] *adj* ungainly, awkward

disjoindre [disʒwɛ̃dR(ə)] *vt* to take apart; **se disjoindre** *vi* to come apart

disjoncteur [disʒɔ̃ktœR] *nm* (*ÉLEC*) circuit breaker

disloquer [dislɔke] *vt* (*membre*) to dislocate; (*chaise*) to dismantle; (*troupe*) to disperse; **se disloquer** *vi* (*parti, empire*) to break up; **se disloquer l'épaule** to dislocate one's shoulder

disons *etc* [dizɔ̃] *vb voir* **dire**

disparaître [disparetR(ə)] *vi* to disappear; (*à la vue*) to vanish, disappear; to be hidden *ou* concealed; (*être manquant*) to go missing, disappear; (*se perdre: traditions etc*) to die out; (*personne: mourir*) to die; **faire disparaître** (*objet, tache, trace*) to remove; (*personne*) to get rid of

disparition [dispaʀisjɔ̃] *nf* disappearance

disparu, e [dispaʀy] *pp de* **disparaître** ♦ *nm/f* missing person; (*défunt*) departed; **être porté disparu** to be reported missing

dispensaire [dispɑ̃sɛʀ] *nm* community clinic

dispenser [dispɑ̃se] *vt* (*donner*) to lavish, bestow; (*exempter*): **dispenser qn de** to exempt sb from; **se dispenser de** *vt* to avoid, get out of

disperser [dispɛʀse] *vt* to scatter; (*fig: son attention*) to dissipate; **se disperser** *vi* to scatter; (*fig*) to dissipate one's efforts

disponibilité [disponibilite] *nf* availability; (*ADMIN*): **être en disponibilité** to be on leave of absence; **disponibilités** *nfpl* (*COMM*) liquid assets

disponible [disponibl(ə)] *adj* available

dispos [dispo] *adj m*: **(frais et) dispos** fresh (as a daisy)

disposé, e [dispoze] *adj* (*d'une certaine manière*) arranged, laid-out; **bien/mal disposé** (*humeur*) in a good/bad mood; **bien/mal disposé pour** *ou* **envers qn** well/badly disposed towards sb; **disposé à** (*prêt à*) willing *ou* prepared to

disposer [dispoze] *vt* (*arranger, placer*) to arrange; (*inciter*): **disposer qn à qch/faire qch** to dispose *ou* incline sb towards sth/to do sth ♦ *vi*: **vous pouvez disposer** you may leave; **disposer de** *vt* to have (at one's disposal); **se disposer à faire** to prepare to do, be about to do

dispositif [dispozitif] *nm* device; (*fig*) system, plan of action; set-up; (*d'un texte de loi*) operative part; **dispositif de sûreté** safety device

disposition [dispozisjɔ̃] *nf* (*arrangement*) arrangement, layout; (*humeur*) mood; (*tendance*) tendency; **dispositions** *nfpl* (*mesures*) steps, measures; (*préparatifs*) arrangements; (*de loi, testament*) provisions; (*aptitudes*) bent *sg*, aptitude *sg*; **à la disposition de qn** at sb's disposal

disproportionné, e [dispʀɔpɔʀsjɔne] *adj* disproportionate, out of all proportion

dispute [dispyt] *nf* quarrel, argument

disputer [dispyte] *vt* (*match*) to play; (*combat*) to fight; (*course*) to run; **se disputer** *vi* to quarrel, have a quarrel; (*match, combat, course*) to take place; **disputer qch à qn** to fight with sb for *ou* over sth

disquaire [diskɛʀ] *nm/f* record dealer

disqualifier [diskalifje] *vt* to disqualify; **se disqualifier** *vi* to bring discredit on o.s.

disque [disk(ə)] *nm* (*MUS*) record; (*INFORM*) disk, disc; (*forme, pièce*) disc; (*SPORT*) discus; **disque compact** compact disc; **disque dur** hard disk; **disque d'embrayage** (*AUTO*) clutch plate; **disque laser** compact disc; **disque de stationnement** parking disc; **disque système** system disk

disquette [diskɛt] *nf* diskette, floppy (disk); **disquette (à) simple/double densité** single/double density disk; **disquette une face/double face** single-/double-sided disk

disséminer [disemine] *vt* to scatter; (*troupes: sur un territoire*) to disperse

disséquer [diseke] *vt* to dissect

dissertation [disɛʀtasjɔ̃] *nf* (*SCOL*) essay

dissimuler [disimyle] *vt* to conceal; **se dissimuler** to conceal o.s.; to be concealed

dissipé, e [disipe] *adj* (*indiscipliné*) unruly

dissiper [disipe] *vt* to dissipate; (*fortune*) to squander, fritter away; **se dissiper** *vi* (*brouillard*) to clear, disperse; (*doutes*) to disappear, melt away; (*élève*) to become undisciplined *ou* unruly

dissolvant, e [disɔlvɑ̃, -ɑ̃t] *vb voir* **dissoudre** ♦ *nm* (*CHIMIE*) solvent; **dissolvant (gras)** nail polish remover

dissonant, e [disɔnɑ̃, -ɑ̃t] *adj* discordant

dissoudre [disudʀ(ə)] *vt*: **se dissoudre** *vi* to dissolve

dissuader [disɥade] *vt*: **dissuader qn de faire/ de qch** to dissuade sb from doing/from sth

dissuasion [disɥazjɔ̃] *nf* dissuasion; **force de dissuasion** deterrent power

distance [distɑ̃s] *nf* distance; (*fig: écart*) gap; **à distance** at *ou* from a distance; (*mettre en marche, commander*) by remote control; (**situé) à distance** (*INFORM*) remote; **tenir qn à distance** to keep sb at a distance; **se tenir à distance** to keep one's distance; **à une distance de 10 km, à 10 km de distance** 10 km away, at a distance of 10 km; **à 2 ans de distance** with a gap of 2 years; **prendre ses distances** to space out; **garder ses distances** to keep one's distance; **tenir la distance** (*SPORT*) to cover the distance, last the course; **distance focale** (*PHOTO*) focal length

distancer [distɑ̃se] *vt* to outdistance, leave behind

distant, e [distɑ̃, -ɑ̃t] *adj* (*réservé*) distant, aloof; (*éloigné*) distant, far away; **distant de** (*lieu*) far away *ou* a long way from; **distant de 5 km (d'un lieu)** 5 km away (from a place)

distendre [distɑ̃dʀ(ə)] *vt*, **se distendre** *vi* to distend

distillerie [distilʀi] *nf* distillery

distinct, e [distɛ̃(kt), distɛ̃kt(ə)] *adj* distinct

distinctement [distɛ̃ktəmɑ̃] *adv* distinctly

distinctif, ive [distɛ̃ktif, -iv] *adj* distinctive

distingué, e [distɛ̃ge] *adj* distinguished

distinguer [distɛ̃ge] *vt* to distinguish; **se distinguer** *vi* (*s'illustrer*) to distinguish o.s.; (*différer*): **se distinguer (de)** to distinguish o.s. *ou* be distinguished (from)

distraction [distʀaksjɔ̃] *nf* (*manque d'attention*) absent-mindedness; (*oubli*) lapse (in concentration *ou* attention); (*détente*) diversion, recreation; (*passe-temps*) distraction, entertainment

distraire [distʀɛʀ] *vt* (*déranger*) to distract; (*divertir*) to entertain, divert; (*détourner: somme d'argent*) to divert, misappropriate; **se distraire** to amuse *ou* enjoy o.s.

distrait, e [distʀɛ, -ɛt] *pp de* **distraire** ♦ *adj* absent-minded

distrayant, e [distʀɛjɑ̃, -ɑ̃t] *vb voir* **distraire** ♦ *adj* entertaining

distribuer [distʀibɥe] *vt* to distribute; to hand out; (*CARTES*) to deal out; (*courrier*) to deliver

distributeur [distʀibytœʀ] *nm* (*AUTO, COMM*) distributor; (*automatique*) (vending) machine; **distributeur de billets** (*RAIL*) ticket machine; (*BANQUE*) cash dispenser

distribution [distʀibysjɔ̃] *nf* distribution; (*postale*) delivery; (*choix d'acteurs*) casting; **circuits de distribution** (*COMM*) distribution network; **distribution des prix** (*SCOL*) prize giving

dit, e [di, dit] *pp de* **dire** ♦ *adj* (*fixé*): **le jour dit** the arranged day; (*surnommé*): **X, dit Pierrot** X, known as *ou* called Pierrot

dites [dit] *vb voir* **dire**

divaguer [divage] *vi* to ramble; (*malade*) to rave

divan [divɑ̃] *nm* divan

diverger [divɛʀʒe] *vi* to diverge

divers, e [divɛʀ, -ɛʀs(ə)] *adj* (*varié*) diverse, varied; (*différent*) different, various ♦ *dét* (*plusieurs*) various, several; **(frais) divers** (*COMM*) sundries, miscellaneous (expenses); **"divers"** (*rubrique*) "miscellaneous"

diversifier [divɛʀsifje] *vt*: **se diversifier** *vi* to diversify

diversité [divɛʀsite] *nf* diversity, variety

divertir [divɛʀtiʀ] *vt* to amuse, entertain; **se divertir** to amuse *ou* enjoy o.s.

divertissement [divɛʀtismɑ̃] *nm* entertainment; (*MUS*) divertimento, divertissement

divin, e [divɛ̃, -in] *adj* divine; (*fig: excellent*) heavenly, divine

diviser [divize] *vt* (*gén, MATH*) to divide; (*morceler, subdiviser*) to divide (up), split (up); **se diviser en** to divide into; **diviser par** to divide by

division [divizjɔ̃] *nf* (*gén*) division; **division du travail** (*ÉCON*) division of labour

divorce [divɔʀs(ə)] *nm* divorce

divorcé, e [divɔʀse] *nm/f* divorcee

divorcer [divɔʀse] *vi* to get a divorce, get divorced; **divorcer de** *ou* **d'avec qn** to divorce sb

divulguer [divylge] *vt* to divulge, disclose

dix [di, dis, diz] *num* ten

dixième [dizjɛm] *num* tenth

dizaine [dizɛn] *nf* (*10*) ten; (*environ 10*): **une dizaine (de)** about ten, ten or so

do [do] *nm* (*note*) C; (*en chantant la gamme*) do(h)

docile [dɔsil] *adj* docile

dock [dɔk] *nm* dock; (*hangar, bâtiment*) warehouse

docker [dɔkɛʀ] *nm* docker

docteur [dɔktœʀ] *nm* doctor; **docteur en médecine** doctor of medicine

doctorat [dɔktɔʀa] *nm*: **doctorat (d'Université)** = doctorate; **doctorat d'État** = PhD; **doctorat de troisième cycle** = doctorate

doctoresse [dɔktɔʀɛs] *nf* lady doctor

doctrine [dɔktʀin] *nf* doctrine

document [dɔkymɑ̃] *nm* document

documentaire [dɔkymɑ̃tɛʀ] *adj, nm* documentary

documentaliste [dɔkymɑ̃talist(ə)] *nm/f* archivist; (*PRESSE, TV*) researcher

documentation [dɔkymɑ̃tasjɔ̃] *nf* documentation, literature; (*PRESSE, TV: service*) research

documenter [dɔkymɑ̃te] *vt*: **se documenter (sur)** to gather information *ou* material (on *ou* about)

dodo [dodo] *nm*: **aller faire dodo** to go to beddy-byes

dodu, e [dody] *adj* plump

dogue [dɔg] *nm* mastiff

doigt [dwa] *nm* finger; **à deux doigts de** within an ace (*BRIT*) *ou* an inch of; **un doigt de lait/whisky** a drop of milk/whisky; **désigner** *ou* **montrer du doigt** to point at; **au doigt et à l'œil** to the letter; **connaître qch sur le bout du doigt** to know sth backwards; **mettre le doigt sur la plaie** (*fig*) to find the sensitive spot; **doigt de pied** toe

doigté [dwate] *nm* (*MUS*) fingering; (*fig: habileté*) diplomacy, tact

doit *etc* [dwa] *vb voir* **devoir**

doléances [dɔleɑ̃s] *nfpl* complaints; (*réclamations*) grievances

dollar [dɔlaʀ] *nm* dollar

domaine [dɔmɛn] *nm* estate, property; (*fig*) domain, field; **tomber dans le domaine public** (*livre etc*) to be out of copyright; **dans tous les domaines** in all areas

domestique [dɔmɛstik] *adj* domestic ♦ *nm/f* servant, domestic

domestiquer [dɔmɛstike] *vt* to domesticate; (*vent, marées*) to harness

domicile [dɔmisil] *nm* home, place of residence; **à domicile** at home; **élire domicile à** to take up residence in; **sans domicile fixe** of no fixed abode; **domicile conjugal** marital home; **domicile légal** domicile

domicilié, e [dɔmisilje] *adj*: **être domicilié à** to have one's home in *ou* at

dominant, e [dɔminɑ̃, -ɑ̃t] *adj* dominant; (*plus important*) predominant ♦ *nf* (*caractéristique*) dominant characteristic; (*couleur*) dominant colour

dominer [dɔmine] *vt* to dominate; (*passions etc*) to control, master; (*surpasser*) to outclass, surpass; (*surplomber*) to tower above, dominate ♦ *vi* to be in the dominant position; **se dominer** to control o.s.

domino [dɔmino] *nm* domino; **dominos** *nmpl* (*jeu*) dominoes *sg*

dommage [dɔmaʒ] *nm* (*préjudice*) harm, injury; (*dégâts, pertes*) damage *no pl*; **c'est dommage de faire/que** it's a shame ou pity to do/that; **quel dommage!** what a pity ou shame!; **dommages corporels** physical injury

dommages-intérêts [dɔmaʒ(əz)ēteʀe] *nmpl* damages

dompter [dɔ̃te] *vt* to tame

dompteur, euse [dɔ̃tœʀ, -øz] *nm/f* trainer; (*de lion*) liontamer

DOM-ROM [dɔmʀɔm] *sigle m ou mpl* (= *Département(s) d'outre-mers/Régions d'outre-mers*) *French overseas departments and regions*

don [dɔ̃] *nm* (*cadeau*) gift; (*charité*) donation; (*aptitude*) gift, talent; **avoir des dons pour** to have a gift ou talent for; **faire don de** to make a gift of; **don en argent** cash donation

donc [dɔ̃k] *conj* therefore, so; (*après une digression*) so, then; (*intensif*): **voilà donc la solution** so there's the solution; **je disais donc que ...** as I was saying, ...; **venez donc dîner à la maison** do come for dinner; **allons donc!** come now!; **faites donc** go ahead

donjon [dɔ̃ʒɔ̃] *nm* keep

donné, e [dɔne] *adj* (*convenu*) given; (*pas cher*) very cheap ♦ *nf* (*MATH, INFORM, gén*) datum (*pl* data); **c'est donné** it's a gift; **étant donné ...** given ...

données [dɔne] *nfpl* data

donner [dɔne] *vt* to give; (*vieux habits etc*) to give away; (*spectacle*) to put on; (*film*) to show; **donner qch à qn** to give sb sth, give sth to sb; **donner sur** (*suj: fenêtre, chambre*) to look (out) onto; **donner dans** (*piège etc*) to fall into; **faire donner l'infanterie** (*MIL*) to send in the infantry; **donner l'heure à qn** to tell sb the time; **donner le ton** (*fig*) to set the tone; **donner à penser/entendre que ...** to make one think/give one to understand that ...; **se donner à fond (à son travail)** to give one's all (to one's work); **se donner du mal** ou **de la peine (pour faire qch)** to go to a lot of trouble (to do sth); **s'en donner à cœur joie** (*fam*) to have a great time (of it)

MOT-CLÉ

---

dont [dɔ̃] *pron relatif* **1** (*appartenance: objets*) whose, of which; (*: êtres animés*) whose; **la maison dont le toit est rouge** the house whose roof ou of which is red, the house whose roof is red; **l'homme dont je connais la sœur** the man whose sister I know

2 (*parmi lesquel(le)s*): **2 livres, dont l'un est ...** 2 books, one of which is ...; **il y avait plusieurs personnes, dont Gabrielle** there were several people, among them Gabrielle; **10 blessés, dont 2 grièvement** 10 injured, 2 of them seriously

3 (*complément d'adjectif, de verbe*): **le fils dont il est si fier** the son he's so proud of; **ce dont je parle** what I'm talking about; **la façon dont il l'a fait** the way (in which) he did it

---

doré, e [dɔʀe] *adj* golden; (*avec dorure*) gilt, gilded

dorénavant [dɔʀenavɑ̃] *adv* from now on, henceforth

dorer [dɔʀe] *vt* (*cadre*) to gild; **(faire) dorer** (*CULIN*) to brown; (*: gâteau*) to glaze; **se dorer au soleil** to sunbathe; **dorer la pilule à qn** to sugar the pill for sb

dorloter [dɔʀlɔte] *vt* to pamper, cosset (*BRIT*); **se faire dorloter** to be pampered ou cosseted

dormir [dɔʀmiʀ] *vi* to sleep; (*être endormi*) to be asleep; **dormir à poings fermés** to sleep very soundly

dortoir [dɔʀtwaʀ] *nm* dormitory

dorure [dɔʀyʀ] *nf* gilding

dos [do] *nm* back; (*de livre*) spine; **"voir au dos"** "see over"; **robe décolletée dans le dos** low-backed dress; **de dos** from the back, from behind; **dos à dos** back to back; **sur le dos** on one's back; **à dos de chameau** riding on a camel; **avoir bon dos** to be a good excuse; **se mettre qn à dos** to turn sb against one

dosage [dozaʒ] *nm* mixture

dose [doz] *nf* (*MÉD*) dose; **forcer la dose** (*fig*) to overstep the mark

doser [doze] *vt* to measure out; (*mélanger*) to mix in the correct proportions; (*fig*) to expend in the right amounts ou proportions; to strike a balance between

dossard [dosaʀ] *nm* number (*worn by competitor*)

dossier [dosje] *nm* (*renseignements, fichier*) file; (*enveloppe*) folder, file; (*de chaise*) back; (*PRESSE*) feature; **le dossier social/monétaire** (*fig*) the social/financial question; **dossier suspendu** suspension file

dot [dɔt] *nf* dowry

doter [dɔte] *vt*: **doter qn/qch de** to equip sb/sth with

douane [dwan] *nf* (*poste, bureau*) customs *pl*; (*taxes*) (customs) duty; **passer la douane** to go through customs; **en douane** (*marchandises, entrepôt*) bonded

douanier, ière [dwanje, -jɛʀ] *adj* customs *cpd* ♦ *nm* customs officer

double [dubl(ə)] *adj, adv* double ♦ *nm* (*2 fois plus*): **le double (de)** twice as much (ou many) (as), double the amount (ou number) (of); (*autre exemplaire*) duplicate, copy; (*sosie*) double; (*TENNIS*) doubles *sg*; **voir double** to see double; **en double (exemplaire)** in duplicate; **faire double emploi** to be redundant; **à double sens** with a double meaning; **à double tranchant** two-edged; **double carburateur** twin carburettor; **à doubles commandes** dual-control; **double messieurs/mixte** men's/

mixed doubles *sg*; **double toit** (*de tente*) fly sheet; **double vue** second sight

double-cliquer [dubl(ə)klike] *vi* (*INFORM*) to double-click

doubler [duble] *vt* (*multiplier par 2*) to double; (*vêtement*) to line; (*dépasser*) to overtake, pass; (*film*) to dub; (*acteur*) to stand in for ♦ *vi* to double, increase twofold; **se doubler de** to be coupled with; **doubler (la classe)** (*SCOL*) to repeat a year; **doubler un cap** (*NAVIG*) to round a cape; (*fig*) to get over a hurdle

doublure [dublyʀ] *nf* lining; (*CINÉ*) stand-in

douce [dus] *adj f voir* **doux**

douceâtre [dusɑtʀ(ə)] *adj* sickly sweet

doucement [dusmɑ̃] *adv* gently; (*à voix basse*) softly; (*lentement*) slowly

doucereux, euse [dusʀø, -øz] *adj* (*péj*) sugary

douceur [dusœʀ] *nf* softness; sweetness; mildness; gentleness; **douceurs** *nfpl* (*friandises*) sweets (*BRIT*), candy *sg* (*US*); **en douceur** gently

douche [duʃ] *nf* shower; **douches** *nfpl* shower room *sg*; **prendre une douche** to have *ou* take a shower; **douche écossaise** (*fig*), **douche froide** (*fig*) let-down

doucher [duʃe] *vt*: **doucher qn** to give sb a shower; (*mouiller*) to drench sb; (*fig*) to give sb a telling-off; **se doucher** to have *ou* take a shower

doudoune [dudun] *nf* padded jacket; (*fam*) boob

doué, e [dwe] *adj* gifted, talented; **doué de** endowed with; **être doué pour** to have a gift for

douille [duj] *nf* (*ÉLEC*) socket; (*de projectile*) case

douillet, te [dujɛ, -ɛt] *adj* cosy; (*péj*) soft

douleur [dulœʀ] *nf* pain; (*chagrin*) grief, distress; **ressentir des douleurs** to feel pain; **il a eu la douleur de perdre son père** he suffered the grief of losing his father

douloureux, euse [duluʀø, -øz] *adj* painful

doute [dut] *nm* doubt; **sans doute** *adv* no doubt; (*probablement*) probably; **sans nul** *ou* **aucun doute** without (a) doubt; **hors de doute** beyond doubt; **nul doute que** there's no doubt that; **mettre en doute** to call into question; **mettre en doute que** to question whether

douter [dute] *vt* to doubt; **douter de** *vt* (*allié*) to doubt, have (one's) doubts about; (*résultat*) to be doubtful of; **douter que** to doubt whether *ou* if; **j'en doute** I have my doubts; **se douter de qch/que** to suspect sth/that; **je m'en doutais** I suspected as much; **il ne se doutait de rien** he didn't suspect a thing

douteux, euse [dutø, -øz] *adj* (*incertain*) doubtful; (*discutable*) dubious, questionable; (*péj*) dubious-looking

Douvres [duvʀ(ə)] *n* Dover

doux, douce [du, dus] *adj* (*lisse, moelleux, pas vif*: *couleur, non calcaire*: *eau*) soft; (*sucré, agréable*) sweet; (*peu fort*: *moutarde etc, clément*: *climat*) mild;

(*pas brusque*) gentle; **en douce** (*partir etc*) on the quiet

douzaine [duzɛn] *nf* (*12*) dozen; (*environ 12*): **douzaine (de)** a dozen or so, twelve or so

douze [duz] *num* twelve; **les Douze** (*membres de la CE*) the Twelve

douzième [duzjɛm] *num* twelfth

doyen, ne [dwajɛ̃, -ɛn] *nm/f* (*en âge, ancienneté*) most senior member; (*de faculté*) dean

dragée [dʀaʒe] *nf* sugared almond; (*MÉD*) (sugar-coated) pill

dragon [dʀagɔ̃] *nm* dragon

draguer [dʀage] *vt* (*rivière*: *pour nettoyer*) to dredge; (*: pour trouver qch*) to drag; (*fam*) to try and pick up, chat up (*BRIT*) ♦ *vi* (*fam*) to try and pick sb up, chat sb up (*BRIT*)

dramatique [dʀamatik] *adj* dramatic; (*tragique*) tragic ♦ *nf* (*TV*) (television) drama

dramaturge [dʀamatyʀʒ(ə)] *nm* dramatist, playwright

drame [dʀam] *nm* (*THÉÂT*) drama; (*catastrophe*) drama, tragedy; **drame familial** family drama

drap [dʀa] *nm* (*de lit*) sheet; (*tissu*) woollen fabric; **drap de plage** beach towel

drapeau, x [dʀapo] *nm* flag; **sous les drapeaux** with the colours (*BRIT*) *ou* colors (*US*), in the army

drap-housse, *pl* **draps-housses** [dʀaus] *nm* fitted sheet

dresser [dʀese] *vt* (*mettre vertical, monter*: *tente*) to put up, erect; (*fig*: *liste, bilan, contrat*) to draw up; (*animal*) to train; **se dresser** *vi* (*falaise, obstacle*) to stand; (*avec grandeur, menace*) to tower (up); (*personne*) to draw o.s. up; **dresser l'oreille** to prick up one's ears; **dresser la table** to set *ou* lay the table; **dresser qn contre qn d'autre** to set sb against sb else; **dresser un procès-verbal** *ou* **une contravention à qn** to book sb

drogue [dʀɔg] *nf* drug; **la drogue** drugs *pl*; **drogue dure/douce** hard/soft drugs *pl*

drogué, e [dʀɔge] *nm/f* drug addict

droguer [dʀɔge] *vt* (*victime*) to drug; (*malade*) to give drugs to; **se droguer** (*aux stupéfiants*) to take drugs; (*péj*: *de médicaments*) to dose o.s. up

droguerie [dʀɔgʀi] *nf* ≃ hardware shop (*BRIT*) *ou* store (*US*)

droguiste [dʀɔgist(ə)] *nm* ≃ keeper (*ou* owner) of a hardware shop *ou* store

droit, e [dʀwa, dʀwat] *adj* (*non courbe*) straight; (*vertical*) upright, straight; (*fig*: *loyal, franc*) upright, straight(forward)); (*opposé à gauche*) right, right-hand ♦ *adv* straight ♦ *nm* (*prérogative, BOXE*) right; (*taxe*) duty, tax; (*: d'inscription*) fee; (*lois, branche*): **le droit** law ♦ *nf* (*POL*) right (wing); (*ligne*) straight line; **droit au but** *ou* **au fait/cœur** straight to the point/heart; **avoir le droit de** to be allowed to; **avoir droit à** to be entitled to; **être en droit de** to have a *ou* the right to; **faire droit à** to grant, accede to; **être dans son droit** to be within one's rights; **à bon droit** (*justement*) with good reason; **de quel droit?** by what right?; **à qui de droit** to whom it may concern; **à droite** on the right; (*direction*) (to the) right; **à droite de** to the right of; **de droite, sur votre droite** on your right; (*POL*) right-wing; **droit d'auteur** copyright; **avoir droit de cité (dans)** (*fig*) to belong (to); **droit coutumier** common law; **droit de regard** right of access *ou* inspection; **droit de réponse** right to reply; **droit de visite** (right of) access; **droit de vote** (right to) vote; **droits d'auteur** royalties; **droits de douane** customs duties; **droits de l'homme** human rights; **droits d'inscription** enrolment *ou* registration fees

droitier, ière [dʀwatje, -jɛʀ] *nm/f* right-handed person

droiture [dʀwatyʀ] *nf* uprightness, straightness

drôle [dʀol] *adj* (*amusant*) funny, amusing; (*bizarre*) funny, peculiar; **un drôle de ...** (*bizarre*) a strange *ou* funny ...; (*intensif*) an incredible ..., a terrific ...

drôlement [dʀolmɑ̃] *adv* funnily; peculiarly; (*très*) terribly, awfully; **il fait drôlement froid** it's awfully cold

dromadaire [dʀɔmadɛʀ] *nm* dromedary

dru, e [dʀy] *adj* (*cheveux*) thick, bushy; (*pluie*) heavy ♦ *adv* (*pousser*) thickly; (*tomber*) heavily

du [dy] *prép* + *dét*, *dét voir* **de**

dû, due [dy] *pp de* **devoir** ♦ *adj* (*somme*) owing, owed; (: *venant à échéance*) due; (*causé par*): **dû à** due to ♦ *nm* due; (*somme*) dues *pl*

duc [dyk] *nm* duke

duchesse [dyʃɛs] *nf* duchess

dûment [dymɑ̃] *adv* duly

dune [dyn] *nf* dune

Dunkerque [dœ̃kɛʀk] *n* Dunkirk

duo [dɥo] *nm* (*MUS*) duet; (*fig: couple*) duo, pair

dupe [dyp] *nf* dupe ♦ *adj*: **(ne pas) être dupe de** (not) to be taken in by

duplex [dyplɛks] *nm* (*appartement*) split-level apartment, duplex; (*TV*): **émission en duplex** link-up

duplicata [dyplikata] *nm* duplicate

duquel [dykɛl] *prép* + *pron voir* **lequel**

dur, e [dyʀ] *adj* (*pierre, siège, travail, problème*) hard; (*lumière, voix, climat*) harsh; (*sévère*) hard, harsh; (*cruel*) hard(-hearted); (*porte, col*) stiff; (*viande*) tough ♦ *adv* hard ♦ *nf*: **à la dure** rough; **mener la vie dure à qn** to give sb a hard time; **dur d'oreille** hard of hearing

durant [dyʀɑ̃] *prép* (*au cours de*) during; (*pendant*) for; **durant des mois, des mois durant** for months

durcir [dyʀsiʀ] *vt*, *vi*: **se durcir** *vi* to harden

durée [dyʀe] *nf* length; (*d'une pile etc*) life; (*déroulement: des opérations etc*) duration; **pour une durée illimitée** for an unlimited length of

time; **de courte durée** (*séjour, répit*) brief, short-term; **de longue durée** (*effet*) long-term; **pile de longue durée** long-life battery

durement [dyʀmɑ̃] *adv* harshly

durer [dyʀe] *vi* to last

dureté [dyʀte] *nf* (*voir dur*) hardness; harshness; stiffness; toughness

durit® [dyʀit] *nf* (car radiator) hose

duvet [dyvɛ] *nm* down; **(sac de couchage en) duvet** down-filled sleeping bag

DVD *sigle m* (= *digital versatile disc*) DVD

dynamique [dinamik] *adj* dynamic

dynamisme [dinamism(ə)] *nm* dynamism

dynamite [dinamit] *nf* dynamite

dynamo [dinamo] *nf* dynamo

dyslexie [dislɛksi] *nf* dyslexia, word blindness

— *E e* —

eau, x [o] *nf* water ♦ *nfpl* waters; **prendre l'eau** (*chaussure etc*) to leak, let in water; **prendre les eaux** to take the waters; **faire eau** to leak; **tomber à l'eau** (*fig*) to fall through; **à l'eau de rose** slushy, sentimental; **eau bénite** holy water; **eau de Cologne** eau de Cologne; **eau courante** running water; **eau distillée** distilled water; **eau douce** fresh water; **eau de Javel** bleach; **eau lourde** heavy water; **eau minérale** mineral water; **eau oxygénée** hydrogen peroxide; **eau plate** still water; **eau de pluie** rainwater; **eau salée** salt water; **eau de toilette** toilet water; **eaux ménagères** dirty water (*from washing up etc*) **eaux territoriales** territorial waters; **eaux usées** liquid waste

eau-de-vie, *pl* **eaux-de-vie** [odvi] *nf* brandy

eau-forte, *pl* **eaux-fortes** [ofɔʀt(ə)] *nf* etching

ébahi, e [ebai] *adj* dumbfounded, flabbergasted

ébattre [ebatʀ(ə)]: **s'ébattre** *vi* to frolic

ébaucher [eboʃe] *vt* to sketch out, outline; (*fig*): **ébaucher un sourire/geste** to give a hint of a smile/make a slight gesture; **s'ébaucher** *vi* to take shape

ébène [ebɛn] *nf* ebony

ébéniste [ebenist(ə)] *nm* cabinetmaker

éberlué, e [ebɛʀlɥe] *adj* astounded, flabbergasted

éblouir [ebluiʀ] *vt* to dazzle

éborgner [ebɔʀɲe] *vt*: **éborgner qn** to blind sb in one eye

éboueur [ebwœʀ] *nm* dustman (*BRIT*), garbageman (*US*)

ébouillanter [ebujɑ̃te] *vt* to scald; (*CULIN*) to blanch; **s'ébouillanter** to scald o.s

éboulement [ebulmɑ̃] *nm* falling rocks *pl*, rock

fall; (*amas*) heap of boulders *etc*

ébouler [ebule]: **s'ébouler** *vi* to crumble, collapse

éboulis [ebuli] *nmpl* fallen rocks

ébouriffé, e [eburife] *adj* tousled, ruffled

ébranler [ebrɑ̃le] *vt* to shake; (*rendre instable: mur, santé*) to weaken; **s'ébranler** *vi* (*partir*) to move off

ébrécher [ebreʃe] *vt* to chip

ébriété [ebrijete] *nf*: **en état d'ébriété** in a state of intoxication

ébrouer [ebrue]: **s'ébrouer** *vi* (*souffler*) to snort; (*s'agiter*) to shake o.s.

ébruiter [ebrɥite] *vt*: **s'ébruiter** *vi* to spread

ébullition [ebylisjɔ̃] *nf* boiling point; **en ébullition** boiling; (*fig*) in an uproar

écaille [ekaj] *nf* (*de poisson*) scale; (*de coquillage*) shell; (*matière*) tortoiseshell; (*de roc etc*) flake

écailler [ekaje] *vt* (*poisson*) to scale; (*huître*) to open; **s'écailler** *vi* to flake *ou* peel (off)

écarlate [ekarlat] *adj* scarlet

écarquiller [ekarkije] *vt*: **écarquiller les yeux** to stare wide-eyed

écart [ekar] *nm* gap; (*embardée*) swerve; (*saut*) sideways leap; (*fig*) departure, deviation; **à l'écart** *adv* out of the way; **à l'écart de** *prép* away from; (*fig*) out of; **faire le grand écart** (*DANSE, GYMNASTIQUE*) to do the splits; **écart de conduite** misdemeanour

écarté, e [ekarte] *adj* (*lieu*) out-of-the-way, remote; (*ouvert*): **les jambes écartées** legs apart; **les bras écartés** arms outstretched

écarter [ekarte] *vt* (*séparer*) to move apart, separate; (*éloigner*) to push back, move away; (*ouvrir: bras, jambes*) to spread, open; (*: rideau*) to draw (back); (*éliminer: candidat, possibilité*) to dismiss; (*CARTES*) to discard; **s'écarter** *vi* to part; (*personne*) to move away; **s'écarter de** to wander from

écervelé, e [esɛrvale] *adj* scatterbrained, feather-brained

échafaud [eʃafo] *nm* scaffold

échafaudage [eʃafodaʒ] *nm* scaffolding; (*fig*) heap, pile

échafauder [eʃafode] *vt* (*plan*) to construct

échalote [eʃalɔt] *nf* shallot

échancrure [eʃɑ̃kryr] *nf* (*de robe*) scoop neckline; (*de côte, arête rocheuse*) indentation

échange [eʃɑ̃ʒ] *nm* exchange; **en échange** in exchange; **en échange de** in exchange *ou* return for; **libre échange** free trade; **échange de lettres/politesses/vues** exchange of letters/civilities/views; **échanges commerciaux** trade; **échanges culturels** cultural exchanges

échanger [eʃɑ̃ʒe] *vt*: **échanger qch (contre)** to exchange sth (for)

échangeur [eʃɑ̃ʒœr] *nm* (*AUTO*) interchange

échantillon [eʃɑ̃tijɔ̃] *nm* sample

échappement [eʃapmɑ̃] *nm* (*AUTO*) exhaust; **échappement libre** cutout

échapper [eʃape]: **échapper à** *vt* (*gardien*) to escape (from); (*punition, péril*) to escape; **échapper à qn** (*détail, sens*) to escape sb; (*objet qu'on tient*) *aussi*: **échapper des mains de qn**) to slip out of sb's hands; **laisser échapper** to let fall; (*cri etc*) to let out; **s'échapper** *vi* to escape; **l'échapper belle** to have a narrow escape

écharde [eʃard(ə)] *nf* splinter (of wood)

écharpe [eʃarp(ə)] *nf* scarf (*pl* scarves); (*de maire*) sash; (*MÉD*) sling; **prendre en écharpe** (*dans une collision*) to hit sideways on

échasse [eʃas] *nf* stilt

échassier [eʃasje] *nm* wader

échauffer [eʃofe] *vt* (*métal, moteur*) to overheat; (*fig: exciter*) to fire, excite; **s'échauffer** *vi* (*SPORT*) to warm up; (*discussion*) to become heated

échéance [eʃeɑ̃s] *nf* (*d'un paiement: date*) settlement date; (*: somme due*) financial commitment(s); (*fig*) deadline; **à brève/longue échéance** *adj* short-/long-term ♦ *adv* in the short/long term

échéant [eʃeɑ̃]: **le cas échéant** *adv* if the case arises

échec [eʃɛk] *nm* failure; (*ÉCHECS*): **échec et mat/au roi** checkmate/check; **échecs** *nmpl* (*jeu*) chess *sg*; **mettre en échec** to put in check; **tenir en échec** to hold in check; **faire échec à** to foil, thwart

échelle [eʃɛl] *nf* ladder; (*fig, d'une carte*) scale; **à l'échelle de** on the scale of; **sur une grande/petite échelle** on a large/small scale; **faire la courte échelle à qn** to give sb a leg up; **échelle de corde** rope ladder

échelon [eʃlɔ̃] *nm* (*d'échelle*) rung; (*ADMIN*) grade

échelonner [eʃlɔne] *vt* to space out, spread out; (*versement*) **échelonné** (payment) by instalments

échevelé, e [eʃəvle] *adj* tousled, dishevelled; (*fig*) wild, frenzied

échine [eʃin] *nf* backbone, spine

échiquier [eʃikje] *nm* chessboard

écho [eko] *nm* echo; **échos** *nmpl* (*potins*) gossip *sg*, rumours; (*PRESSE: rubrique*) "news in brief"; **rester sans écho** (*suggestion etc*) to come to nothing; **se faire l'écho de** to repeat, spread about

échographie [ekɔɡrafi] *nf* ultrasound (scan)

échoir [eʃwar] *vi* (*dette*) to fall due; (*délais*) to expire; **échoir à** *vt* to fall to

échouer [eʃwe] *vi* to fail; (*débris etc: sur la plage*) to be washed up; (*aboutir: personne dans un café etc*) to arrive ♦ *vt* (*bateau*) to ground; **s'échouer** *vi* to run aground

échu, e [eʃy] *pp de* **échoir** ♦ *adj* due, mature

éclabousser [eklabuse] *vt* to splash; (*fig*) to tarnish

éclair [eklɛr] *nm* (*d'orage*) flash of lightning, lightning *no pl*; (*PHOTO: de flash*) flash; (*fig*) flash, spark; (*gâteau*) éclair

éclairage [eklɛraʒ] *nm* lighting

éclaircie [eklɛʀsi] *nf* bright *ou* sunny interval

éclaircir [eklɛʀsiʀ] *vt* to lighten; (*fig*) to clear up, clarify; (*CULIN*) to thin (down); **s'éclaircir** *vi* (*ciel*) to brighten up, clear; (*cheveux*) to go thin; (*situation etc*) to become clearer; **s'éclaircir la voix** to clear one's throat

éclaircissement [eklɛʀsismɑ̃] *nm* clearing up, clarification

éclairer [eklere] *vt* (*lieu*) to light (up); (*personne: avec une lampe de poche etc*) to light the way for; (*fig: instruire*) to enlighten; (: *rendre comprehensible*) to shed light on ♦ *vi*: **éclairer mal/bien** to give a poor/good light; **s'éclairer** *vi* (*phare, rue*) to light up; (*situation etc*) to become clearer; **s'éclairer à la bougie/l'électricité** to use candlelight/have electric lighting

éclaireur, euse [eklɛʀœʀ, -øz] *nm/f* (*scout*) (boy) scout/(girl) guide ♦ *nm* (*MIL*) scout; **partir en éclaireur** to go off to reconnoitre

éclat [ekla] *nm* (*de bombe, de verre*) fragment; (*du soleil, d'une couleur etc*) brightness, brilliance; (*d'une cérémonie*) splendour; (*scandale*): **faire un éclat** to cause a commotion; **action d'éclat** outstanding action; **voler en éclats** to shatter; **des éclats de verre** broken glass; flying glass; **éclat de rire** burst *ou* roar of laughter; **éclat de voix** shout

éclatant, e [eklatɑ̃, -ɑ̃t] *adj* brilliant, bright; (*succès*) resounding; (*revanche*) devastating

éclater [eklate] *vi* (*pneu*) to burst; (*bombe*) to explode; (*guerre, épidémie*) to break out; (*groupe, parti*) to break up; **éclater de rire/en sanglots** to burst out laughing/sobbing

éclipser [eklipse] *vt* to eclipse; **s'éclipser** *vi* to slip away

éclore [eklɔʀ] *vi* (*suj: œuf*) to hatch; (*fleur*) to open (out)

écluse [eklyz] *nf* lock

écœurant, e [ekœʀɑ̃, -ɑ̃t] *adj* sickening; (*gâteau etc*) sickly

écœurer [ekœʀe] *vt*: **écœurer qn** to make sb feel sick; (*fig: démoraliser*) to disgust sb

école [ekɔl] *nf* school; **aller à l'école** to go to school; **faire école** to collect a following; **les grandes écoles** *prestige university-level colleges with competitive entrance examinations*; **école maternelle** nursery school; **école primaire** primary (*BRIT*) *ou* grade (*US*) school; **école secondaire** secondary (*BRIT*) *ou* high (*US*) school; **école privée/publique/élémentaire** private/state/elementary school; **école de dessin/danse/musique** art/dancing/music school; **école hôtelière** catering college; **école normale (d'instituteurs) (ENI)** *primary school teachers' training college*; **école normale supérieure (ENS)** *grande école for training secondary school teachers*; **école de secrétariat** secretarial college; *see boxed note*

écolier, ière [ekɔlje, -jɛʀ] *nm/f* schoolboy/girl

écologie [ekɔlɔʒi] *nf* ecology; (*sujet scolaire*) environmental studies *pl*

écologique [ekɔlɔʒik] *adj* ecological; environmental

écologiste [ekɔlɔʒist(ə)] *nm/f* ecologist; environmentalist

éconduire [ekɔ̃dɥiʀ] *vt* to dismiss

économe [ekɔnɔm] *adj* thrifty ♦ *nm/f* (*de lycée etc*) bursar (*BRIT*), treasurer (*US*)

économie [ekɔnɔmi] *nf* (*vertu*) economy, thrift; (*gain: d'argent, de temps etc*) saving; (*science*) economics *sg*; (*situation économique*) economy; **économies** *nfpl* (*pécule*) savings; **faire des économies** to save up; **une économie de temps/d'argent** a saving in time/of money; **économie dirigée** planned economy; **économie de marché** market economy

économique [ekɔnɔmik] *adj* (*avantageux*) economical; (*ÉCON*) economic

économiser [ekɔnɔmize] *vt, vi* to save

écoper [ekɔpe] *vi* to bale out; (*fig*) to cop it; **écoper (de)** *vt* to get

écorce [ekɔʀs(ə)] *nf* bark; (*de fruit*) peel

écorcher [ekɔʀʃe] *vt* (*animal*) to skin; (*égratigner*) to graze; **écorcher une langue** to speak a language brokenly; **s'écorcher le genou** *etc* to scrape *ou* graze one's knee *etc*

écorchure [ekɔʀʃyʀ] *nf* graze

Écosse [ekɔs] *nf*: **l'Écosse** Scotland

écossais, e [ekɔse, -ez] *adj* Scottish, Scots; (*whisky, confiture*) Scotch; (*écharpe, tissu*) tartan ♦ *nm* (*LING*) Scots; (: *gaélique*) Gaelic; (*tissu*) tartan (cloth) ♦ *nm/f*: **Écossais, e** Scot, Scotsman/woman; **les Écossais** the Scots

écosser [ekɔse] *vt* to shell

écoulement [ekulmɑ̃] *nm* (*de faux billets*) circulation; (*de stock*) selling

écouler [ekule] *vt* to dispose of; **s'écouler** *vi* (*eau*) to flow (out); (*foule*) to drift away; (*jours, temps*) to pass (by)

écourter [ekuʀte] *vt* to curtail, cut short

écoute [ekut] *nf* (*NAVIG: cordage*) sheet; (*RADIO, TV*): **temps d'écoute** (listening *ou* viewing) time; **heure de grande écoute** peak listening *ou* viewing time; **prendre l'écoute** to tune in; **rester à l'écoute (de)** to stay tuned in (to); **écoutes téléphoniques**

phone tapping *sg*

écouter [ekute] *vt* to listen to

écouteur [ekutœʀ] *nm* (*TÉL*) (additional) earpiece; **écouteurs** *nmpl* (*RADIO*) headphones, headset *sg*

écoutille [ekutij] *nf* hatch

écran [ekʀɑ̃] *nm* screen; (*INFORM*) VDU, screen; **écran de fumée/d'eau** curtain of smoke/water; **porter à l'écran** (*CINÉ*) to adapt for the screen; **le petit écran** television, the small screen

écrasant, e [ekʀɑzɑ̃, -ɑ̃t] *adj* overwhelming

écraser [ekʀɑze] *vt* to crush; (*piéton*) to run over; (*INFORM*) to overwrite; **se faire écraser** to be run over; **écrase(-toi)!** shut up!; **s'écraser (au sol)** to crash; **s'écraser contre** to crash into

écrémé, e [ekʀeme] *adj* (*lait*) skimmed

écrevisse [ekʀavis] *nf* crayfish *inv*

écrier [ekʀije]: **s'écrier** *vi* to exclaim

écrin [ekʀɛ̃] *nm* case, box

écrire [ekʀiʀ] *vt, vi* to write ◆ *vi*: **ça s'écrit comment?** how is it spelt?; **écrire à qn que** to write and tell sb that; **s'écrire** to write to one another

écrit, e [ekʀi, -it] *pp de* **écrire** ◆ *adj*: **bien/mal écrit** well/badly written ◆ *nm* document; (*examen*) written paper; **par écrit** in writing

écriteau, x [ekʀito] *nm* notice, sign

écriture [ekʀityʀ] *nf* writing; (*COMM*) entry; **écritures** *nfpl* (*COMM*) accounts, books; **l'Écriture (sainte), les Écritures** the Scriptures

écrivain [ekʀivɛ̃] *nm* writer

écrou [ekʀu] *nm* nut

écrouer [ekʀue] *vt* to imprison; (*provisoirement*) to remand in custody

écrouler [ekʀule]: **s'écrouler** *vi* to collapse

écru, e [ekʀy] *adj* (*toile*) raw, unbleached; (*couleur*) off-white, écru

écueil [ekœj] *nm* reef; (*fig*) pitfall; stumbling block

éculé, e [ekyle] *adj* (*chaussure*) down-at-heel; (*fig: péj*) hackneyed

écume [ekym] *nf* foam; (*CULIN*) scum; **écume de mer** meerschaum

écumer [ekyme] *vt* (*CULIN*) to skim; (*fig*) to plunder ◆ *vi* (*mer*) to foam; (*fig*) to boil with rage

écumoire [ekymwaʀ] *nf* skimmer

écureuil [ekyʀœj] *nm* squirrel

écurie [ekyʀi] *nf* stable

écusson [ekysɔ̃] *nm* badge

écuyer, ère [ekɥije, -ɛʀ] *nm/f* rider

eczéma [egzema] *nm* eczema

édenté, e [edɑ̃te] *adj* toothless

EDF *sigle f* (= *Électricité de France*) national electricity company

édifice [edifis] *nm* building, edifice

édifier [edifje] *vt* to build, erect; (*fig*) to edify

Édimbourg [edɛ̃buʀ] *n* Edinburgh

éditer [edite] *vt* (*publier*) to publish; (: *disque*) to produce; (*préparer: texte, INFORM*) to edit

éditeur, trice [editœʀ, -tʀis] *nm/f* publisher; editor

édition [edisjɔ̃] *nf* editing *no pl*; (*série d'exemplaires*) edition; (*industrie du livre*): **l'édition** publishing; **édition sur écran** (*INFORM*) screen editing

édredon [edʀadɔ̃] *nm* eiderdown, comforter (*US*)

éducateur, trice [edykatœʀ, -tʀis] *nm/f* teacher; **éducateur spécialisé** specialist teacher

éducatif, ive [edykatif, -iv] *adj* educational

éducation [edykasjɔ̃] *nf* education; (*familiale*) upbringing; (*manières*) (good) manners *pl*; **bonne/mauvaise éducation** good/bad upbringing; **sans éducation** bad-mannered, ill-bred; **l'Éducation (nationale)** ≃ the Department for Education; **éducation permanente** continuing education; **éducation physique** physical education

édulcorant [edylkɔʀɑ̃] *nm* sweetener

éduquer [edyke] *vt* to educate; (*élever*) to bring up; (*faculté*) to train; **bien/mal éduqué** well/badly brought up

effacé, e [efase] *adj* (*fig*) retiring, unassuming

effacer [efase] *vt* to erase, rub out; (*bande magnétique*) to erase; (*INFORM: fichier, fiche*) to delete, erase; **s'effacer** *vi* (*inscription etc*) to wear off; (*pour laisser passer*) to step aside; **effacer le ventre** to pull one's stomach in

effarant, e [efaʀɑ̃, -ɑ̃t] *adj* alarming

effarer [efaʀe] *vt* to alarm

effaroucher [efaʀuʃe] *vt* to frighten *ou* scare away; (*personne*) to alarm

effectif, ive [efɛktif, -iv] *adj* real; effective ◆ *nm* (*MIL*) strength; (*SCOL*) total number of pupils; size; **effectifs** numbers, strength *sg*; (*COMM*) manpower *sg*; **réduire l'effectif de** to downsize

effectivement [efɛktivmɑ̃] *adv* effectively, (*réellement*) actually, really; (*en effet*) indeed

effectuer [efɛktɥe] *vt* (*opération, mission*) to carry out; (*déplacement, trajet*) to make, complete; (*mouvement*) to execute, make; **s'effectuer** to be carried out

efféminé, e [efemine] *adj* effeminate

effervescent, e [efɛʀvesɑ̃, -ɑ̃t] *adj* (*cachet, boisson*) effervescent; (*fig*) agitated, in a turmoil

effet [efɛ] *nm* (*résultat, artifice*) effect; (*impression*) impression; (*COMM*) bill; (*JUR: d'une loi, d'un jugement*): **avec effet rétroactif** applied retrospectively; **effets** *nmpl* (*vêtements etc*) things; **effet de style/couleur/lumière** stylistic/colour/lighting effect; **effets de voix** dramatic effects with one's voice; **faire de l'effet** (*médicament, menace*) to have an effect, be effective; **sous l'effet de** under the effect of; **donner de l'effet à une balle** (*TENNIS*) to put some spin on a ball; **à cet effet** to that end; **en effet** *adv* indeed; **effet (de commerce)** bill of exchange; **effet de serre** greenhouse effect; **effets spéciaux** (*CINÉ*) special effects

efficace [efikas] *adj* (*personne*) efficient; (*action, médicament*) effective

efficacité [efikasite] *nf* efficiency; effectiveness

effilocher [efiloʃe]: **s'effilocher** *vi* to fray

efflanqué, e [eflɑ̃ke] *adj* emaciated

effleurer [eflœʀe] *vt* to brush (against); (*sujet*) to touch upon; (*suj: idée, pensée*): **effleurer qn** to cross sb's mind

effluves [eflyv] *nmpl* exhalation(s)

effondrer [efɔ̃dʀe]: **s'effondrer** *vi* to collapse

efforcer [efɔʀse]: **s'efforcer de** *vt*: **s'efforcer de faire** to try hard to do

effort [efɔʀ] *nm* effort; **faire un effort** to make an effort; **faire tous ses efforts** to try one's hardest; **faire l'effort de ...** to make the effort to ...; **sans effort** *adj* effortless ♦ *adv* effortlessly; **effort de mémoire** attempt to remember; **effort de volonté** effort of will

effraction [efʀaksjɔ̃] *nf* breaking-in; **s'introduire par effraction dans** to break into

effrayant, e [efʀejɑ̃, -ɑ̃t] *adj* frightening, fearsome; (*sens affaibli*) dreadful

effrayer [efʀeje] *vt* to frighten, scare; (*rebuter*) to put off; **s'effrayer (de)** to be frightened *ou* scared (by)

effréné, e [efʀene] *adj* wild

effriter [efʀite]: **s'effriter** *vi* to crumble; (*monnaie*) to be eroded; (*valeurs*) to slacken off

effroi [efʀwa] *nm* terror, dread *no pl*

effronté, e [efʀɔ̃te] *adj* insolent

effroyable [efʀwajabl(ə)] *adj* horrifying, appalling

effusion [efyzjɔ̃] *nf* effusion; **sans effusion de sang** without bloodshed

égal, e, aux [egal, -o] *adj* (*identique, ayant les mêmes droits*) equal; (*plan: surface*) even, level; (*constant: vitesse*) steady; (*équitable*) even ♦ *nm/f* equal; **être égal à** (*prix, nombre*) to be equal to; **ça m'est égal** it's all the same to me, it doesn't matter to me, I don't mind; **c'est égal, ...** all the same, ...; **sans égal** matchless, unequalled; **à l'égal de** (*comme*) just like; **d'égal à égal** as equals

également [egalmɑ̃] *adv* equally; evenly; steadily; (*aussi*) too, as well

égaler [egale] *vt* to equal

égaliser [egalize] *vt* (*sol, salaires*) to level (out); (*chances*) to equalize ♦ *vi* (*SPORT*) to equalize

égalité [egalite] *nf* equality; evenness; steadiness; (*MATH*) identity : **être à égalité (de points)** to be level; **égalité de droits** equality of rights; **égalité d'humeur** evenness of temper

égard [egaʀ] *nm*: **égards** *nmpl* consideration *sg*; **à cet égard** in this respect; **à certains égards/tous égards** in certain respects/all respects; **eu égard à** in view of; **par égard pour** out of consideration for; **sans égard pour** without regard for; **à l'égard de** *prép* towards; (*en ce qui concerne*) concerning, as regards

égarement [egaʀmɑ̃] *nm* distraction; aberration

égarer [egaʀe] *vt* (*objet*) to mislay; (*moralement*) to lead astray; **s'égarer** *vi* to get lost, lose one's way; (*objet*) to go astray; (*fig: dans une discussion*) to wander

égayer [egeje] *vt* (*personne*) to amuse; (: *remonter*) to cheer up; (*récit, endroit*) to brighten up, liven up

églantine [eglɑ̃tin] *nf* wild *ou* dog rose

églefin [egləfɛ̃] *nm* haddock

église [egliz] *nf* church

égoïsme [egɔism(ə)] *nm* selfishness, egoism

égoïste [egɔist(ə)] *adj* selfish, egoistic ♦ *nm/f* egoist

égorger [egɔʀʒe] *vt* to cut the throat of

égosiller [egozije]: **s'égosiller** *vi* to shout o.s. hoarse

égout [egu] *nm* sewer; **eaux d'égout** sewage

égoutter [egute] *vt* (*linge*) to wring out; (*vaisselle, fromage*) to drain ♦ *vi*: **s'égoutter** *vi* to drip

égouttoir [egutwaʀ] *nm* draining board; (*mobile*) draining rack

égratigner [egʀatiɲe] *vt* to scratch; **s'égratigner** to scratch o.s.

égratignure [egʀatiɲyʀ] *nf* scratch

Égypte [eʒipt] *nf*: **l'Égypte** Egypt

égyptien, ne [eʒipsjɛ̃, -ɛn] *adj* Egyptian ♦ *nm/f*: **Égyptien, ne** Egyptian

eh [e] *excl* hey!; **eh bien** well

éhonté, e [eɔ̃te] *adj* shameless, brazen (*BRIT*)

éjecter [eʒɛkte] *vt* (*TECH*) to eject; (*fam*) to kick *ou* chuck out

élaborer [elabɔʀe] *vt* to elaborate; (*projet, stratégie*) to work out; (*rapport*) to draft

élan [elɑ̃] *nm* (*ZOOL*) elk, moose; (*SPORT: avant le saut*) run up; (*de véhicule*) momentum; (*fig: de tendresse etc*) surge; **prendre son élan/de l'élan** to take a run up/gather speed; **perdre son élan** to lose one's momentum

élancé, e [elɑ̃se] *adj* slender

élancement [elɑ̃smɑ̃] *nm* shooting pain

élancer [elɑ̃se]: **s'élancer** *vi* to dash, hurl o.s.; (*fig: arbre, clocher*) to soar (upwards)

élargir [elaʀʒiʀ] *vt* to widen; (*vêtement*) to let out; (*JUR*) to release; **s'élargir** *vi* to widen; (*vêtement*) to stretch

élastique [elastik] *adj* elastic ♦ *nm* (*de bureau*) rubber band; (*pour la couture*) elastic *no pl*

électeur, trice [elɛktœʀ, -tʀis] *nm/f* elector, voter

élection [elɛksjɔ̃] *nf* election; **élections** *nfpl* (*POL*) election(s); **sa terre/patrie d'élection** the land/country of one's choice; **élection partielle** ≃ by-election; **élections législatives/présidentielles** general/presidential election *sg*; *see boxed note*

ÉLECTIONS LÉGISLATIVES

Élections législatives are held in France every five years to elect 'députés' to the 'Assemblée nationale'. The president is chosen in the 'élection présidentielle', which comes round every five years. Voting is by direct universal suffrage and is divided into two rounds. The ballots always take place on a Sunday.

électorat [elɛktɔʀa] *nm* electorate

électricien, ne [elɛktʀisjɛ̃, -ɛn] *nm/f* electrician

électricité [elɛktʀisite] *nf* electricity; **électricité statique** static electricity

électrique [elɛktʀik] *adj* electric(al)

électrocuter [elɛktʀɔkyte] *vt* to electrocute

électroménager [elɛktʀɔmenaʒe] *adj*: **appareils électroménagers** domestic (electrical) appliances ◆ *nm*: **l'électroménager** household appliances

électronique [elɛktʀɔnik] *adj* electronic ◆ *nf* (*science*) electronics *sg*

électrophone [elɛktʀɔfɔn] *nm* record player

élégance [elegɑ̃s] *nf* elegance

élégant, e [elegɑ̃, -ɑ̃t] *adj* elegant; (*solution*) neat, elegant; (*attitude, procédé*) courteous, civilized

élément [elemɑ̃] *nm* element; (*pièce*) component, part; **éléments** *nmpl* elements

élémentaire [elemɑ̃tɛʀ] *adj* elementary; (*CHIMIE*) elemental

éléphant [elefɑ̃] *nm* elephant; **éléphant de mer** elephant seal

élevage [ɛlvaʒ] *nm* breeding; (*de bovins*) cattle breeding *ou* rearing; (*ferme*) cattle farm

élévation [elevasjɔ̃] *nf* (*gén*) elevation; (*voir élever*) raising; (*voir s'élever*) rise

élevé, e [ɛlve] *adj* (*prix, sommet*) high; (*fig: noble*) elevated; **bien/mal élevé** well-/ill-mannered

élève [elɛv] *nm/f* pupil; **élève infirmière** student nurse

élever [ɛlve] *vt* (*enfant*) to bring up, raise; (*bétail, volaille*) to breed; (*abeilles*) to keep; (*hausser: taux, niveau*) to raise; (*fig: âme, esprit*) to elevate; (*édifier: monument*) to put up, erect; **s'élever** *vi* (*avion, alpiniste*) to go up; (*niveau, température, aussi: cri etc*) to rise; (*survenir: difficultés*) to arise; **s'élever à** (*suj: frais, dégâts*) to amount to, add up to; **s'élever contre** to rise up against; **élever une protestation/critique** to raise a protest/make a criticism; **élever qn au rang de** to raise *ou* elevate sb to the rank of; **élever un nombre au carré/au cube** to square/cube a number

éleveur, euse [ɛlvœʀ, -øz] *nm/f* stock breeder

élimé, e [elime] *adj* worn (thin), threadbare

éliminatoire [eliminatwaʀ] *adj* eliminatory; (*SPORT*) disqualifying ◆ *nf* (*SPORT*) heat

éliminer [elimine] *vt* to eliminate

élire [eliʀ] *vt* to elect; **élire domicile à** to take up residence in *ou* at

elle [ɛl] *pron* (*sujet*) she; (: *chose*) it; (*complément*) her; it; **elles** (*sujet*) they; (*complément*) them; **elle-même** herself; itself; **elles-mêmes** themselves; *voir* **il**

élocution [elɔkysjɔ̃] *nf* delivery; **défaut d'élocution** speech impediment

éloge [elɔʒ] *nm* praise *gén no pl*; **faire l'éloge de** to praise

élogieux, euse [elɔʒjø, -øz] *adj* laudatory, full of praise

éloigné, e [elwaɲe] *adj* distant, far-off

éloignement [elwaɲmɑ̃] *nm* removal; putting off; estrangement; (*fig: distance*) distance

éloigner [elwaɲe] *vt* (*objet*): **éloigner qch (de)** to move *ou* take sth away (from); (*personne*): **éloigner qn (de)** to take sb away *ou* remove sb (from); (*échéance*) to put off, postpone; (*soupçons, danger*) to ward off; **s'éloigner (de)** (*personne*) to go away (from); (*véhicule*) to move away (from); (*affectivement*) to become estranged (from)

élu, e [ely] *pp de* **élire** ◆ *nm/f* (*POL*) elected representative

éluder [elyde] *vt* to evade

Élysée [elize] *nm*: (**le palais de) l'Élysée** the Élysée palace; **les Champs Élysées** the Champs Élysées; *see boxed note*

PALAIS DE L'ÉLYSÉE

The **palais de l'Élysée**, situated in the heart of Paris just off the Champs Élysées, is the official residence of the French President. Built in the eighteenth century, it has performed its present function since 1876. A shorter form of its name, 'l'Élysée' is frequently used to refer to the presidency itself.

émacié, e [emasje] *adj* emaciated

e-mail [imel] *nm* (*INFORM*) email

émail, aux [emaj, -o] *nm* enamel

émaillé, e [emaje] *adj* enamelled; (*fig*): **émaillé de** dotted with

émanciper [emɑ̃sipe] *vt* to emancipate; **s'émanciper** (*fig*) to become emancipated *ou* liberated

émaner [emane]: **émaner de** *vt* to emanate from; (*ADMIN*) to proceed from

emballage [ɑ̃balaʒ] *nm* wrapping; packing; (*papier*) wrapping; (*carton*) packaging

emballer [ɑ̃bale] *vt* to wrap (up); (*dans un carton*) to pack (up); (*fig: fam*) to thrill to bits); **s'emballer** *vi* (*moteur*) to race; (*cheval*) to bolt; (*fig: personne*) to get carried away

embarcadère [ɑ̃baʀkadɛʀ] *nm* landing stage (*BRIT*), pier

embarcation [ɑ̃baʀkasjɔ̃] *nf* (small) boat, (small) craft *inv*

embardée [ɑ̃baʀde] *nf* swerve; **faire une embardée** to swerve

embarquement [ɑ̃baʀkəmɑ̃] *nm* embarkation; loading; boarding

embarquer [ɑ̃baʀke] *vt* (*personne*) to embark; (*marchandise*) to load; (*fam*) to cart off; (: *arrêter*) to nick ◆ *vi* (*passager*) to board; (*NAVIG*) to ship water; **s'embarquer** *vi* to board; **s'embarquer dans** (*affaire, aventure*) to embark upon

embarras [ɑ̃baʀa] *nm* (*obstacle*) hindrance; (*confusion*) embarrassment; (*ennuis*): **être dans l'embarras** to be in a predicament *ou* an awkward position; (*gêne financière*) to be in difficulties; **embarras gastrique** stomach upset

embarrassant, e [ɑ̃baʀasɑ̃, -ɑ̃t] *adj* cumbersome; embarrassing; awkward

embarrasser [ɑ̃baʀase] *vt* (*encombrer*) to clutter (up); (*gêner*) to hinder, hamper; (*fig*) to cause embarrassment to; to put in an awkward position; **s'embarrasser de** to burden o.s. with

embauche [ɑ̃boʃ] *nf* hiring; **bureau d'embauche** labour office

embaucher [ɑ̃boʃe] *vt* to take on, hire; **s'embaucher comme** to get (o.s.) a job as

embaumer [ɑ̃bome] *vt* to embalm; (*parfumer*) to fill with its fragrance; **embaumer la lavande** to be fragrant with (the scent of) lavender

embellie [ɑ̃beli] *nf* bright spell, brighter period

embellir [ɑ̃beliʀ] *vt* to make more attractive; (*une histoire*) to embellish ◆ *vi* to grow lovelier *ou* more attractive

embêtant, e [ɑ̃bɛtɑ̃, -ɑ̃t] *adj* annoying

embêtement [ɑ̃bɛtmɑ̃] *nm* problem, difficulty; **embêtements** *nmpl* trouble *sg*

embêter [ɑ̃bɛte] *vt* to bother; **s'embêter** *vi* (*s'ennuyer*) to be bored; **ça m'embête** it bothers me; **il ne s'embête pas!** (*ironique*) he does all right for himself!

emblée [ɑ̃ble]: **d'emblée** *adv* straightaway

embobiner [ɑ̃bɔbine] *vt* (*enjôler*): **embobiner qn** to get round sb

emboîter [ɑ̃bwate] *vt* to fit together; **s'emboîter dans** to fit into; **s'emboîter (l'un dans l'autre)** to fit together; **emboîter le pas à qn** to follow in sb's footsteps

embonpoint [ɑ̃bɔ̃pwɛ̃] *nm* stoutness (*BRIT*), corpulence; **prendre de l'embonpoint** to grow stout (*BRIT*) *ou* corpulent

embouchure [ɑ̃buʃyʀ] *nf* (*GÉO*) mouth; (*MUS*) mouthpiece

embourber [ɑ̃buʀbe]: **s'embourber** *vi* to get stuck in the mud; (*fig*): **s'embourber dans** to sink into

embourgeoiser [ɑ̃buʀʒwaze]: **s'embourgeoiser** *vi* to adopt a middle-class outlook

embouteillage [ɑ̃butejaʒ] *nm* traffic jam, (traffic) holdup (*BRIT*)

emboutir [ɑ̃butiʀ] *vt* (*TECH*) to stamp; (*heurter*) to crash into, ram

embranchement [ɑ̃bʀɑ̃ʃmɑ̃] *nm* (*routier*) junction; (*classification*) branch

embraser [ɑ̃bʀaze]: **s'embraser** *vi* to flare up

embrasser [ɑ̃bʀase] *vt* to kiss; (*sujet, période*) to embrace, encompass; (*carrière*) to embark on; (*métier*) to go in for, take up; **embrasser du regard** to take in (with eyes); **s'embrasser** to kiss (each other)

embrasure [ɑ̃bʀazyʀ] *nf*: **dans l'embrasure de la porte** in the door(way)

embrayage [ɑ̃bʀejaʒ] *nm* clutch

embrayer [ɑ̃bʀeje] *vi* (*AUTO*) to let in the clutch ◆ *vt* (*fig: affaire*) to set in motion; **embrayer sur qch** to begin on sth

embrocher [ɑ̃bʀɔʃe] *vt* to (put on a) spit (*ou* skewer)

embrouiller [ɑ̃bʀuje] *vt* (*fils*) to tangle (up); (*fiches, idées, personne*) to muddle up; **s'embrouiller** *vi* to get in a muddle

embruns [ɑ̃bʀœ̃] *nmpl* sea spray *sg*

embryon [ɑ̃bʀijɔ̃] *nm* embryo

embûches [ɑ̃byʃ] *nfpl* pitfalls, traps

embué, e [ɑ̃bɥe] *adj* misted up; **yeux embués de larmes** eyes misty with tears

embuscade [ɑ̃byskad] *nf* ambush; **tendre une embuscade à** to lay an ambush for

éméché, e [emeʃe] *adj* tipsy, merry

émeraude [emʀod] *nf* emerald ◆ *adj inv* emerald-green

émerger [emɛʀʒe] *vi* to emerge; (*faire saillie, aussi fig*) to stand out

émeri [emʀi] *nm*: **toile** *ou* **papier émeri** emery paper

émerveillement [emɛʀvejmɑ̃] *nm* wonderment

émerveiller [emɛʀveje] *vt* to fill with wonder; **s'émerveiller de** to marvel at

émettre [emɛtʀ(ə)] *vt* (*son, lumière*) to give out, emit; (*message etc: RADIO*) to transmit; (*billet, timbre, emprunt, chèque*) to issue; (*hypothèse, avis*) to voice, put forward; (*vœu*) to express ◆ *vi*: **émettre sur ondes courtes** to broadcast on short wave

émeus *etc* [emø] *vb voir* **émouvoir**

émeute [emøt] *nf* riot

émietter [emjete] *vt* (*pain, terre*) to crumble; (*fig*) to split up, disperse; **s'émietter** *vi* (*pain, terre*) to crumble

émigrer [emigʀe] *vi* to emigrate

émincer [emɛ̃se] *vt* (*CULIN*) to slice thinly

éminent, e [eminɑ̃, -ɑ̃t] *adj* distinguished

émission [emisjɔ̃] *nf* (*voir émettre*) emission; transmission; issue; (*RADIO, TV*) programme, broadcast

emmagasiner [ɑ̃magazine] *vt* to (put into) store; (*fig*) to store up

emmanchure [ɑ̃mɑ̃ʃyʀ] *nf* armhole

emmêler [ɑ̃mele] *vt* to tangle (up); (*fig*) to muddle up; **s'emmêler** to get into a tangle

emménager [ɑ̃menaʒe] *vi* to move in; **emménager dans** to move into

emmener [ɑ̃mne] *vt* to take (with one); (*comme otage, capture*) to take away; **emmener qn au concert** to take sb to a concert

emmerder [ɑ̃mɛʀde] (*fam!*) *vt* to bug, bother; **s'emmerder** *vi* (*s'ennuyer*) to be bored stiff; **je t'emmerde!** to hell with you!

emmitoufler [ɑ̃mitufle] *vt* to wrap up (warmly); **s'emmitoufler** to wrap (o.s.) up (warmly)

émoi [emwa] *nm* (*agitation, effervescence*) commotion; (*trouble*) agitation; **en émoi** (*sens*) excited, stirred

émotif, ive [emɔtif, -iv] *adj* emotional

émotion [emosjɔ̃] *nf* emotion; **avoir des émotions** (*fig*) to get a fright; **donner des émotions à** to give a fright to; **sans émotion** without emotion, coldly

émousser [emuse] *vt* to blunt; (*fig*) to dull

émouvoir [emuvwaʀ] *vt* (*troubler*) to stir, affect; (*toucher, attendrir*) to move; (*indigner*) to rouse; (*effrayer*) to disturb, worry; **s'émouvoir** *vi* to be affected or be moved; to be roused; to be disturbed or worried

empailler [ɑ̃paje] *vt* to stuff

empaqueter [ɑ̃pakte] *vt* to pack up

emparer [ɑ̃paʀe]: **s'emparer de** *vt* (*objet*) to seize, grab; (*comme otage, MIL*) to seize; (*suj: peur etc*) to take hold of

empâter [ɑ̃pɑte]: **s'empâter** *vi* to thicken out

empêchement [ɑ̃pɛʃmɑ̃] *nm* (unexpected) obstacle, hitch

empêcher [ɑ̃peʃe] *vt* to prevent; **empêcher qn de faire** to prevent or stop sb (from) doing; **empêcher que qch (n')arrive/qn (ne) fasse** to prevent sth from happening/sb from doing; **il n'empêche que** nevertheless, be that as it may; **il n'a pas pu s'empêcher de rire** he couldn't help laughing

empereur [ɑ̃pʀœʀ] *nm* emperor

empester [ɑ̃pɛste] *vt* (*lieu*) to stink out ♦ *vi* to stink, reek; **empester le tabac/le vin** to stink or reek of tobacco/wine

empêtrer [ɑ̃petʀe] *vt*: **s'empêtrer dans** (*fils etc, aussi fig*) to get tangled up in

emphase [ɑ̃faz] *nf* pomposity, bombast; **avec emphase** pompously

empiéter [ɑ̃pjete]: **empiéter sur** *vt* to encroach upon

empiffrer [ɑ̃pifʀe]: **s'empiffrer** *vi* (*péj*) to stuff o.s.

empiler [ɑ̃pile] *vt* to pile (up), stack (up); **s'empiler** *vi* to pile up

empire [ɑ̃piʀ] *nm* empire; (*fig*) influence; **style Empire** Empire style; **sous l'empire de** in the grip of

empirer [ɑ̃piʀe] *vi* to worsen, deteriorate

emplacement [ɑ̃plasmɑ̃] *nm* site; **sur l'emplacement de** on the site of

emplette [ɑ̃plɛt] *nf*: **faire l'emplette de** to purchase; **emplettes** shopping *sg*; **faire des emplettes** to go shopping

emplir [ɑ̃pliʀ] *vt* to fill; **s'emplir (de)** to fill (with)

emploi [ɑ̃plwa] *nm* use; (*COMM, ÉCON*): **l'emploi** employment; (*poste*) job, situation; **d'emploi facile** easy to use; **le plein emploi** full employment; **emploi du temps** timetable, schedule

employé, e [ɑ̃plwaje] *nm/f* employee; **employé de bureau/banque** office/bank employee or clerk; **employé de maison** domestic (servant)

employer [ɑ̃plwaje] *vt* (*outil, moyen, méthode, mot*) to use; (*ouvrier, main-d'œuvre*) to employ; **s'employer à qch/à faire** to apply or devote o.s. to sth/to doing

employeur, euse [ɑ̃plwajœʀ, -øz] *nm/f* employer

empocher [ɑ̃pɔʃe] *vt* to pocket

empoigner [ɑ̃pwaɲe] *vt* to grab; **s'empoigner** (*fig*) to have a row or set-to

empoisonner [ɑ̃pwazɔne] *vt* to poison; (*empester: air, pièce*) to stink out; (*fam*): **empoisonner qn** to drive sb mad; **s'empoisonner** to poison o.s.; **empoisonner l'atmosphère** (*aussi fig*) to poison the atmosphere; (*aussi*: **il nous empoisonne l'existence**) he's the bane of our life

emporté, e [ɑ̃pɔʀte] *adj* (*personne, caractère*) fiery

emporter [ɑ̃pɔʀte] *vt* to take (with one); (*en dérobant ou en levant, emmener: blessés, voyageurs*) to take away; (*entraîner*) to carry away ou along; (*arracher*) to tear off; (*rivière, vent*) to carry away; (*MIL: position*) to take; (*avantage, approbation*) to win; **s'emporter** *vi* (*de colère*) to fly into a rage, lose one's temper; **la maladie qui l'a emporté** the illness which caused his death; **l'emporter** to gain victory; **l'emporter (sur)** to get the upper hand (of); (*méthode etc*) to prevail (over); **boissons à emporter** take-away drinks

empreint, e [ɑ̃pʀɛ̃, -ɛ̃t] *adj*: **empreint de** marked with; tinged with ♦ *nf* (*de pied, main*) print; (*fig*) stamp, mark; **empreinte (digitale)** fingerprint

empressé, e [ɑ̃pʀese] *adj* attentive; (*péj*) overanxious to please, overattentive

empressement [ɑ̃pʀesmɑ̃] *nm* eagerness

empresser [ɑ̃pʀese]: **s'empresser** *vi*: **s'empresser auprès de qn** to surround sb with attentions; **s'empresser de faire** to hasten to do

emprise [ɑ̃pʀiz] *nf* hold, ascendancy; **sous l'emprise de** under the influence of

emprisonnement [ɑ̃pʀizɔnmɑ̃] *nm* imprisonment

emprisonner [ɑ̃pʀizɔne] *vt* to imprison, jail

emprunt [ɑ̃pʀœ̃] *nm* borrowing *no pl*, loan (*from debtor's point of view*); (*LING etc*) borrowing; **nom**

d'emprunt assumed name; **emprunt d'État** government ou state loan; **emprunt public à 5%** 5% public loan

emprunté, e [ɑ̃pʀœte] adj (fig) ill-at-ease, awkward

emprunter [ɑ̃pʀœte] vt to borrow; (itinéraire) to take, follow; (style, manière) to adopt, assume

ému, e [emy] pp de **émouvoir** ♦ adj excited; touched; moved

---
MOT CLÉ
---

en [ɑ̃] prép **1** (endroit, pays) in; (direction) to; **habiter en France/ville** to live in France/town; **aller en France/ville** to go to France/town
2 (moment, temps) in; **en été/juin** in summer/June; **en 3 jours/20 ans** in 3 days/20 years
3 (moyen) by; **en avion/taxi** by plane/taxi
4 (composition) made of; **c'est en verre/coton/laine** it's (made of) glass/cotton/wool; **en metal/plastique** made of metal/plastic; **un collier en argent** a silver necklace; **en 2 volumes/une pièce** in 2 volumes/one piece
5 (description, état): **une femme (habillée) en rouge** a woman (dressed) in red; **peindre qch en rouge** to paint sth red; **en T/étoile** T-/star-shaped; **en chemise/chaussettes** in one's shirt sleeves/socks; **en soldat** as a soldier; **en civil** in civilian clothes; **cassé en plusieurs morceaux** broken into several pieces; **en réparation** being repaired, under repair; **en vacances** on holiday; **en bonne santé** healthy, in good health; **en deuil** in mourning; **le même en plus grand** the same but ou only bigger
6 (avec gérondif) while; on; **en dormant** while sleeping, as one sleeps; **en sortant** on going out, as he etc went out; **sortir en courant** to run out; **en apprenant la nouvelle, il s'est évanoui** he fainted at the news ou when he heard the news
7 (matière): **fort en math** good at maths; **expert en** expert in
8 (conformité): **en tant que** as; **en bon politicien, il ...** good politician that he is, he ..., like a good ou true politician, he ...; **je te parle en ami** I'm talking to you as a friend
♦ pron **1** (indéfini): **j'en ai/veux** I have/want some; **en as-tu?** have you got any?; **il n'y en a pas** there isn't ou aren't any; **je n'en veux pas** I don't want any; **j'en ai 2** I've got 2; **combien y en a-t-il?** how many (of them) are there?; **j'en ai assez** I've got enough (of it ou them); (j'en ai marre) I've had enough; **où en étais-je?** where was I?
2 (provenance) from there; **j'en viens** I've come from there
3 (cause): **il en est malade/perd le sommeil** he is ill/can't sleep because of it
4 (de la part de): **elle en est aimée** she is loved by him (ou them etc)
5 (complément de nom, d'adjectif, de verbe): **j'en**

connais les dangers I know its ou the dangers; **j'en suis fier/ai besoin** I am proud of it/need it; **il en est ainsi** ou **de même pour moi** it's the same for me, same here

---

ENA [ena] sigle f (= École nationale d'administration) grande école for training civil servants

encadrement [ɑ̃kɑdʀəmɑ̃] nm framing; training; (de porte) frame; **encadrement du crédit** credit restrictions

encadrer [ɑ̃kɑdʀe] vt (tableau, image) to frame; (fig: entourer) to surround; (personnel, soldats etc) to train; (COMM: crédit) to restrict

encaissé, e [ɑ̃kese] adj (vallée) steep-sided; (rivière) with steep banks

encaisser [ɑ̃kese] vt (chèque) to cash; (argent) to collect; (fig: coup, défaite) to take

encart [ɑ̃kaʀ] nm insert; **encart publicitaire** publicity insert

en-cas [ɑ̃kɑ] nm inv snack

encastré, e [ɑ̃kɑstʀe] adj (four, baignoire) built-in

enceinte [ɑ̃sɛ̃t] adj f: **enceinte (de 6 mois)** (6 months) pregnant ♦ nf (mur) wall; (espace) enclosure; **enceinte (acoustique)** speaker

encens [ɑ̃sɑ̃] nm incense

encercler [ɑ̃sɛʀkle] vt to surround

enchaîner [ɑ̃ʃene] vt to chain up; (mouvements, séquences) to link (together) ♦ vi to carry on

enchanté, e [ɑ̃ʃɑ̃te] adj (ravi) delighted; (ensorcelé) enchanted; **enchanté (de faire votre connaissance)** pleased to meet you, how do you do?

enchantement [ɑ̃ʃɑ̃tmɑ̃] nm delight; (magie) enchantment; **comme par enchantement** as if by magic

enchère [ɑ̃ʃɛʀ] nf bid; **faire une enchère** to (make a) bid; **mettre/vendre aux enchères** to put up for (sale by)/sell by auction; **les enchères montent** the bids are rising; **faire monter les enchères** (fig) to raise the bidding

enchevêtrer [ɑ̃ʃvetʀe] vt to tangle (up)

enclencher [ɑ̃klɑ̃ʃe] vt (mécanisme) to engage; (fig: affaire) to set in motion; **s'enclencher** vi to engage

enclin, e [ɑ̃klɛ̃, -in] adj: **enclin à qch/à faire** inclined ou prone to sth/to do

enclos [ɑ̃klo] nm enclosure; (clôture) fence

enclume [ɑ̃klym] nf anvil

encoche [ɑ̃kɔʃ] nf notch

encoignure [ɑ̃kɔɲyʀ] nf corner

encolure [ɑ̃kɔlyʀ] nf (tour de cou) collar size; (col, cou) neck

encombrant, e [ɑ̃kɔ̃bʀɑ̃, -ɑ̃t] adj cumbersome, bulky

encombre [ɑ̃kɔ̃bʀ(ə)]: **sans encombre** adv without mishap ou incident

encombrement [ɑ̃kɔ̃bʀəmɑ̃] nm (d'un lieu) cluttering (up); (d'un objet: dimensions) bulk

encombrer [ãkɔ̃bʀe] vt to clutter (up); (gêner) to hamper; **s'encombrer de** (bagages etc) to load ou burden o.s. with; **encombrer le passage** to block ou obstruct the way

encontre [ãkɔ̃tʀ(ə)]: **à l'encontre de** prép against, counter to

---
MOT CLÉ
---

encore [ãkɔʀ] adv 1 (continuation) still; **il y travaille encore** he's still working on it; **pas encore** not yet

2 (de nouveau) again; **j'irai encore demain** I'll go again tomorrow; **encore une fois** (once) again; **encore un effort** one last effort; **encore deux jours** two more days

3 (intensif) even, still; **encore plus fort/mieux** even louder/better, louder/better still; **hier encore** even yesterday; **non seulement ..., mais encore ...** not only ..., but also ...; **encore!** (insatisfaction) not again!; **quoi encore?** what now?

4 (restriction) even so ou then, only; **encore pourrais-je le faire si ...** even so, I might be able to do it if ...; **si encore** if only; **encore que** conj although

---

encouragement [ãkuʀaʒmã] nm encouragement; (récompense) incentive

encourager [ãkuʀaʒe] vt to encourage; **encourager qn à faire qch** to encourage sb to do sth

encourir [ãkuʀiʀ] vt to incur

encrasser [ãkʀase] vt to foul up; (AUTO etc) to soot up

encre [ãkʀ(ə)] nf ink; **encre de Chine** Indian ink; **encre indélébile** indelible ink; **encre sympathique** invisible ink

encrier [ãkʀije] nm inkwell

encroûter [ãkʀute]: **s'encroûter** vi (fig) to get into a rut, get set in one's ways

encyclopédie [ãsiklɔpedi] nf encyclopaedia (BRIT), encyclopedia (US)

endetter [ãdete] vt: **s'endetter** vi to get into debt

endiablé, e [ãdjable] adj furious; (enfant) boisterous

endimanché, e [ãdimãʃe] adj in one's Sunday best

endive [ãdiv] nf chicory no pl

endoctriner [ãdɔktʀine] vt to indoctrinate

endommager [ãdɔmaʒe] vt to damage

endormi, e [ãdɔʀmi] pp de **endormir** ♦ adj (personne) asleep; (fig: indolent, lent) sluggish; (engourdi: main, pied) numb

endormir [ãdɔʀmiʀ] vt to put to sleep; (chaleur etc) to send to sleep; (MÉD: dent, nerf) to anaesthetize; (fig: soupçons) to allay; **s'endormir** vi to fall asleep, go to sleep

endosser [ãdose] vt (responsabilité) to take,

shoulder; (chèque) to endorse; (uniforme, tenue) to put on, don

endroit [ãdʀwa] nm place; (localité): **les gens de l'endroit** the local people; (opposé à l'envers) right side; **à cet endroit** in this place; **à l'endroit** right side out; the right way up; (vêtement) the right way out; **à l'endroit de** prép regarding, with regard to; **par endroits** in places

enduire [ãdɥiʀ] vt to coat; **enduire qch de** to coat sth with

enduit, e [ãdɥi, -it] pp de **enduire** ♦ nm coating

endurance [ãdyʀãs] nf endurance

endurant, e [ãdyʀã, -ãt] adj tough, hardy

endurcir [ãdyʀsiʀ] vt (physiquement) to toughen; (moralement) to harden; **s'endurcir** vi to become tougher; to become hardened

endurer [ãdyʀe] vt to endure, bear

énergétique [enɛʀʒetik] adj (ressources etc) energy cpd; (aliment) energizing

énergie [enɛʀʒi] nf (PHYSIQUE) energy; (TECH) power; (fig: physique) energy; (: morale) vigour, spirit; **énergie éolienne/solaire** wind/solar power

énergique [enɛʀʒik] adj energetic; vigorous; (mesures) drastic, stringent

énervant, e [enɛʀvã, -ãt] adj irritating

énervé, e [enɛʀve] adj nervy, on edge; (agacé) irritated

énerver [enɛʀve] vt to irritate, annoy; **s'énerver** vi to get excited, get worked up

enfance [ãfãs] nf (âge) childhood; (fig) infancy; (enfants) children pl; **c'est l'enfance de l'art** it's child's play; **petite enfance** infancy; **souvenir/ami d'enfance** childhood memory/friend; **retomber en enfance** to lapse into one's second childhood

enfant [ãfã] nm/f child (pl children); **enfant adoptif/naturel** adopted/natural child; **bon enfant** adj good-natured, easy-going; **enfant de chœur** nm (REL) altar boy; **enfant prodige** child prodigy; **enfant unique** only child

enfantillage [ãfãtijaʒ] nm (péj) childish behaviour no pl

enfantin, e [ãfãtɛ̃, -in] adj childlike; (péj) childish; (langage) child cpd

enfer [ãfɛʀ] nm hell; **allure/bruit d'enfer** horrendous speed/noise

enfermer [ãfɛʀme] vt to shut up; (à clef, interner) to lock up; **s'enfermer** vi to shut o.s. away; **s'enfermer à clé** to lock o.s. in; **s'enfermer dans la solitude/le mutisme** to retreat into solitude/silence

enfiévré, e [ãfjevʀe] adj (fig) feverish

enfiler [ãfile] vt (vêtement): **enfiler qch** to slip sth on, slip into sth; (insérer): **enfiler qch dans** to stick sth into; (rue, couloir) to take; (perles) to string; (aiguille) to thread; **s'enfiler dans** to disappear into

enfin [ãfɛ̃] adv at last; (en énumérant) lastly; (de restriction, résignation) still; (eh bien) well; (pour conclure) in a word

enflammer [ɑ̃flame] *vt* to set fire to; (*MÉD*) to inflame; **s'enflammer** *vi* to catch fire; to become inflamed

enflé, e [ɑ̃fle] *adj* swollen; (*péj: style*) bombastic, turgid

enfler [ɑ̃fle] *vi* to swell (up); **s'enfler** *vi* to swell

enfoncer [ɑ̃fɔ̃se] *vt* (*clou*) to drive in; (*faire pénétrer*): **enfoncer qch dans** to push (*ou* drive) sth into; (*forcer: porte*) to break open; (*: plancher*) to cause to cave in; (*défoncer: côtes etc*) to smash; (*fam: surpasser*) to lick, beat (hollow) ◆ *vi* (*dans la vase etc*) to sink in; (*sol, surface porteuse*) to give way; **s'enfoncer** *vi* to sink; **s'enfoncer dans** to sink into; (*forêt, ville*) to disappear into; **enfoncer un chapeau sur la tête** to cram *ou* jam a hat on one's head; **enfoncer qn dans la dette** to drag sb into debt

enfouir [ɑ̃fwiʀ] *vt* (*dans le sol*) to bury; (*dans un tiroir etc*) to tuck away; **s'enfouir dans/sous** to bury o.s. in/under

enfourcher [ɑ̃fuʀʃe] *vt* to mount; **enfourcher son dada** (*fig*) to get on one's hobby-horse

enfreindre [ɑ̃fʀɛ̃dʀ(ə)] *vt* to infringe, break

enfuir [ɑ̃fɥiʀ]: **s'enfuir** *vi* to run away *ou* off

enfumer [ɑ̃fyme] *vt* to smoke out

engageant, e [ɑ̃gaʒɑ̃, -ɑ̃t] *adj* attractive, appealing

engagement [ɑ̃gaʒmɑ̃] *nm* taking on, engaging; starting; investing; (*promesse*) commitment; (*MIL: combat*) engagement; (*: recrutement*) enlistment; (*SPORT*) entry; **prendre l'engagement de faire** to undertake to do; **sans engagement** (*COMM*) without obligation

engager [ɑ̃gaʒe] *vt* (*embaucher*) to take on, engage; (*commencer*) to start; (*lier*) to bind, commit; (*impliquer, entraîner*) to involve; (*investir*) to invest, lay out; (*faire intervenir*) to engage; (*SPORT: concurrents, chevaux*) to enter; (*inciter*): **engager qn à faire** to urge sb to do; (*faire pénétrer*): **engager qch dans** to insert sth into; **engager qn à qch** to urge sth on sb; **s'engager** to get taken on; (*MIL*) to enlist; (*promettre, politiquement*) to commit o.s.; (*débuter*) to start (up); **s'engager à faire** to undertake to do; **s'engager dans** (*rue, passage*) to enter, turn into; (*s'emboîter*) to engage *ou* fit into; (*fig: affaire, discussion*) to enter into, embark on

engelures [ɑ̃ʒlyʀ] *nfpl* chilblains

engendrer [ɑ̃ʒɑ̃dʀe] *vt* to father; (*fig*) to create, breed

engin [ɑ̃ʒɛ̃] *nm* machine instrument; vehicle; (*péj*) gadget; (*AVIAT: avion*) aircraft *inv*; (*: missile*) missile; **engin blindé** armoured vehicle; **engin (explosif)** (explosive) device; **engins (spéciaux)** missiles

englober [ɑ̃glɔbe] *vt* to include

engloutir [ɑ̃glutiʀ] *vt* to swallow up; (*fig: dépenses*) to devour; **s'engloutir** to be engulfed

engoncé, e [ɑ̃gɔ̃se] *adj*: **engoncé dans** cramped in

engorger [ɑ̃gɔʀʒe] *vt* to obstruct, block; **s'en-**

gorger *vi* to become blocked

engouement [ɑ̃gumɑ̃] *nm* (sudden) passion

engouffrer [ɑ̃gufʀe] *vt* to swallow up, devour; **s'engouffrer dans** to rush into

engourdir [ɑ̃guʀdiʀ] *vt* to numb; (*fig*) to dull, blunt; **s'engourdir** *vi* to go numb

engrais [ɑ̃gʀɛ] *nm* manure; **engrais (chimique)** (chemical) fertilizer; **engrais organique/inorganique** organic/inorganic fertilizer

engraisser [ɑ̃gʀese] *vt* to fatten (up); (*terre: fertiliser*) to fertilize ◆ *vi* (*péj*) to get fat(ter)

engrenage [ɑ̃gʀənaʒ] *nm* gears *pl*, gearing; (*fig*) chain

engueuler [ɑ̃gœle] *vt* (*fam*) to bawl at *ou* out

enhardir [ɑ̃aʀdiʀ]: **s'enhardir** *vi* to grow bolder

énigme [enigm(ə)] *nf* riddle

enivrer [ɑ̃nivʀe] *vt*: **s'enivrer** to get drunk; **s'enivrer de** (*fig*) to become intoxicated with

enjambée [ɑ̃ʒɑ̃be] *nf* stride; **d'une enjambée** with one stride

enjamber [ɑ̃ʒɑ̃be] *vt* to stride over; (*pont etc*) to span, straddle

enjeu, x [ɑ̃ʒø] *nm* stakes *pl*

enjôler [ɑ̃ʒole] *vt* to coax, wheedle

enjoliver [ɑ̃ʒɔlive] *vt* to embellish

enjoliveur [ɑ̃ʒɔlivœʀ] *nm* (*AUTO*) hub cap

enjoué, e [ɑ̃ʒwe] *adj* playful

enlacer [ɑ̃lase] *vt* (*étreindre*) to embrace, hug; (*suj: lianes*) to wind round, entwine

enlaidir [ɑ̃lediʀ] *vt* to make ugly ◆ *vi* to become ugly

enlèvement [ɑ̃lɛvmɑ̃] *nm* removal; (*rapt*) abduction, kidnapping; **l'enlèvement des ordures ménagères** refuse collection

enlever [ɑ̃lve] *vt* (*ôter: gén*) to remove; (*: vêtement, lunettes*) to take off; (*: MÉD: organe*) to remove; (*emporter: ordures etc*) to collect, take away; (*kidnapper*) to abduct, kidnap; (*obtenir: prix, contrat*) to win; (*MIL: position*) to take; (*morceau de piano etc*) to execute with spirit *ou* brio; (*prendre*): **enlever qch à qn** to take sth (away) from sb; **s'enlever** (*tache*) to come out *ou* off; **la maladie qui nous l'a enlevé** (*euphémisme*) the illness which took him from us

enliser [ɑ̃lize]: **s'enliser** *vi* to sink, get stuck; (*dialogue etc*) to get bogged down

enneigé, e [ɑ̃neʒe] *adj* snowy; (*col*) snowed-up; (*maison*) snowed-in

ennemi, e [enmi] *adj* hostile; (*MIL*) enemy *cpd* ◆ *nm/f* enemy; **être ennemi de** to be strongly averse *ou* opposed to

ennui [ɑ̃nɥi] *nm* (*lassitude*) boredom; (*difficulté*) trouble *no pl*; **avoir des ennuis** to have problems; **s'attirer des ennuis** to cause problems for o.s.

ennuyer [ɑ̃nɥije] *vt* to bother; (*lasser*) to bore; **s'ennuyer** *vi* to be bored; **s'ennuyer de** (*regretter*) to miss; **si cela ne vous ennuie pas** if it's no trouble to you

ennuyeux, euse [ãnɥijø, -øz] *adj* boring, tedious; (*agaçant*) annoying

énoncé [enɔ̃se] *nm* terms *pl*; wording; (*LING*) utterance

énoncer [enɔ̃se] *vt* to say, express; (*conditions*) to set out, lay down, state

enorgueillir [ãnɔʀgœjiʀ]: **s'enorgueillir de** *vt* pride o.s. on; to boast

énorme [enɔʀm(ə)] *adj* enormous, huge

énormément [enɔʀmemɑ̃] *adv* enormously, tremendously; **énormément de neige/gens** an enormous amount of snow/number of people

énormité [enɔʀmite] *nf* enormity, hugeness; (*propos*) outrageous remark

enquérir [ãkeʀiʀ]: **s'enquérir de** *vt* to inquire about

enquête [ãkɛt] *nf* (*de journaliste, de police*) investigation; (*judiciaire, administrative*) inquiry; (*sondage d'opinion*) survey

enquêter [ãkete] *vi* to investigate; to hold an inquiry; (*faire un sondage*): **enquêter (sur)** to do a survey (on), carry out an opinion poll (on)

enquiers, enquière *etc* [ãkjɛʀ] *vb voir* **enquérir**

enquiquiner [ãkikine] *vt* to rile, irritate

enraciné, e [ãʀasine] *adj* deep-rooted

enragé, e [ãʀaʒe] *adj* (*MÉD*) rabid, with rabies; (*furieux*) furiously angry; (*fig*) fanatical; **enragé de** wild about

enrageant, e [ãʀaʒã, -ãt] *adj* infuriating

enrager [ãʀaʒe] *vi* to be furious, be in a rage; **faire enrager qn** to make sb wild with anger

enrayer [ãʀeje] *vt* to check, stop; **s'enrayer** *vi* (*arme à feu*) to jam

enregistrement [ãʀʒistʀəmɑ̃] *nm* recording; (*ADMIN*) registration; **enregistrement des bagages** (*à l'aéroport*) baggage check-in; **enregistrement magnétique** tape-recording

enregistrer [ãʀʒistʀe] *vt* (*MUS, INFORM ETC*) to record; (*remarquer, noter*) to note, record; (*COMM: commande*) to note, enter; (*fig: mémoriser*) to make a mental note of; (*ADMIN*) to register; (*aussi:* **faire enregistrer**: *bagages: par train*) to register; (: *à l'aéroport*) to check in

enrhumé, e [ãʀyme] *adj*: **il est enrhumé** he has a cold

enrhumer [ãʀyme]: **s'enrhumer** *vi* to catch a cold

enrichir [ãʀiʃiʀ] *vt* to make rich(er); (*fig*) to enrich; **s'enrichir** to get rich(er)

enrober [ãʀɔbe] *vt*: **enrober qch de** to coat sth with; (*fig*) to wrap sth up in

enrôler [ãʀole] *vt* to enlist; **s'enrôler (dans)** to enlist (in)

enrouer [ãʀwe]: **s'enrouer** *vi* to go hoarse

enrouler [ãʀule] *vt* (*fil, corde*) to wind (up); **s'en-**

rouler to coil up; **enrouler qch autour de** to wind sth (a)round

ensanglanté, e [ãsãglãte] *adj* covered with blood

enseignant, e [ãsɛɲã, -ãt] *adj* teaching ♦ *nm/f* teacher

enseigne [ãsɛɲ] *nf* sign ♦ *nm*: **enseigne de vaisseau** lieutenant; **à telle enseigne que** so much so that; **être logés à la même enseigne** (*fig*) to be in the same boat; **enseigne lumineuse** neon sign

enseignement [ãsɛɲmɑ̃] *nm* teaching; **enseignement ménager** home economics; **enseignement primaire** primary (*BRIT*) *ou* grade school (*US*) education; **enseignement secondaire** secondary (*BRIT*) *ou* high school (*US*) education

enseigner [ãsɛɲe] *vt, vi* to teach; **enseigner qch à qn/à qn que** to teach sb sth/sb that

ensemble [ãsãbl(ə)] *adv* together ♦ *nm* (*assemblage, MATH*) set; (*totalité*): **l'ensemble du/de la** whole *ou* entire; (*vêtement féminin*) ensemble, suit; (*unité, harmonie*) unity; (*résidentiel*) housing development; **aller ensemble** to go together; **impression/idée d'ensemble** overall *ou* general impression/idea; **dans l'ensemble** (*en gros*) on the whole; **dans son ensemble** overall, in general; **ensemble vocal/musical** vocal/musical ensemble

ensemencer [ãsmãse] *vt* to sow

ensevelir [ãsəvliʀ] *vt* to bury

ensoleillé, e [ãsɔleje] *adj* sunny

ensommeillé, e [ãsɔmeje] *adj* sleepy, drowsy

ensorceler [ãsɔʀsəle] *vt* to enchant, bewitch

ensuite [ãsɥit] *adv* then, next; (*plus tard*) afterwards, later; **ensuite de quoi** after which

ensuivre [ãsɥivʀ(ə)]: **s'ensuivre** *vi* to follow, ensue; **il s'ensuit que ...** it follows that ...; **et tout ce qui s'ensuit** and all that goes with it

entaille [ãtaj] *nf* (*encoche*) notch; (*blessure*) cut; **se faire une entaille** to cut o.s.

entamer [ãtame] *vt* to start; (*hostilités, pourparlers*) to open; (*fig: altérer*) to make a dent in; to damage

entasser [ãtase] *vt* (*empiler*) to pile up, heap up; (*tenir à l'étroit*) to cram together; **s'entasser** *vi* to pile up; to cram; **s'entasser dans** to cram into

entendre [ãtãdʀ(ə)] *vt* to hear; (*comprendre*) to understand; (*vouloir dire*) to mean; (*vouloir*): **entendre être obéi/que** to intend *ou* mean to be obeyed/that; **j'ai entendu dire que** I've heard (it said) that; **je suis heureux de vous l'entendre dire** I'm pleased to hear you say it; **entendre parler de** to hear of; **laisser entendre que, donner à entendre que** to let it be understood that; **entendre raison** to see sense, listen to reason; **qu'à cela ne tienne pas entendre!** whatever next!; **j'ai mal entendu** I didn't catch what was said; **je vous entends très mal** I can hardly hear you; **s'entendre** *vi* (*sympathiser*) to get on; (*se mettre d'accord*) to agree; **s'entendre à qch/à faire** (*être compétent*) to be good at sth/doing; **ça s'entend** (*est audible*) it's audible; **je m'entends** I mean; **entendons-nous!** let's be clear what we mean

entendu, e [ãtãdy] *pp de* **entendre ♦** *adj* (*réglé*) agreed; (*au courant: air*) knowing; **étant entendu que** since (it's understood *ou* agreed that); **(c'est) entendu** all right, agreed; **c'est entendu** (*concession*) all right, granted; **bien entendu** of course

entente [ãtãt] *nf* (*entre amis, pays*) understanding, harmony; (*accord, traité*) agreement, understanding; **à double entente** (*sens*) with a double meaning

entériner [ãterine] *vt* to ratify, confirm

enterrement [ãtɛrmã] *nm* burying; (*cérémonie*) funeral, burial; (*cortège funèbre*) funeral procession

enterrer [ãtere] *vt* to bury

entêtant, e [ãtetã, -ãt] *adj* heady

entêté, e [ãtete] *adj* stubborn

en-tête [ãtɛt] *nm* heading; (*de papier à lettres*) letterhead; **papier à en-tête** headed notepaper

entêter [ãtete]: **s'entêter** *vi*: **s'entêter (à faire)** to persist (in doing)

enthousiasme [ãtuzjasm(ə)] *nm* enthusiasm; **avec enthousiasme** enthusiastically

enthousiasmer [ãtuzjasme] *vt* to fill with enthusiasm; **s'enthousiasmer (pour qch)** to get enthusiastic (about sth)

enthousiaste [ãtuzjast(ə)] *adj* enthusiastic

enticher [ãtiʃe]: **s'enticher de** *vt* to become infatuated with

entier, ière [ãtje, -jɛr] *adj* (*non entamé, en totalité*) whole; (*total, complet*) complete; (*fig: caractère*) unbending, averse to compromise **♦** *nm* (*MATH*) whole; **en entier** totally; in its entirety; **se donner tout entier à qch** to devote o.s. completely to sth; **lait entier** full-cream milk; **pain entier** wholemeal bread; **nombre entier** whole number

entièrement [ãtjɛrmã] *adv* entirely, completely, wholly

entonner [ãtɔne] *vt* (*chanson*) to strike up

entonnoir [ãtɔnwar] *nm* (*ustensile*) funnel; (*trou*) shell-hole, crater

entorse [ãtɔrs(ə)] *nf* (*MÉD*) sprain; (*fig*): **entorse à la loi/au règlement** infringement of the law/rule; **se faire une entorse à la cheville/au poignet** to sprain one's ankle/wrist

entortiller [ãtɔrtije] *vt* (*envelopper*): **entortiller qch dans/avec** to wrap sth in/with; (*enrouler*): **entortiller qch autour de** to twist *ou* wind sth (a)round; (*fam*): **entortiller qn** to get (a)round sb; (: *duper*) to hoodwink sb (*BRIT*), trick sb; **s'entortiller dans** (*draps*) to roll o.s. up in; (*fig: réponses*) to get tangled up in

entourage [ãturaʒ] *nm* circle; family (circle); (*d'une vedette etc*) entourage; (*ce qui enclôt*) surround

entouré, e [ãture] *adj* (*recherché, admiré*) popular; **entouré de** surrounded by

entourer [ãture] *vt* to surround; (*apporter son soutien à*) to rally round; **entourer de** to surround with; (*trait*) to encircle with; **s'entourer de** to surround o.s. with; **s'entourer de précautions** to take all possible precautions

entracte [ãtrakt(ə)] *nm* interval

entraide [ãtrɛd] *nf* mutual aid *ou* assistance

entrain [ãtrɛ̃] *nm* spirit; **avec entrain** (*répondre, travailler*) energetically; **faire qch sans entrain** to do sth half-heartedly *ou* without enthusiasm

entraînement [ãtrɛnmã] *nm* training; (*TECH*): **entraînement à chaîne/galet** chain/wheel drive; **manquer d'entraînement** to be unfit; **entraînement par ergots/friction** (*INFORM*) tractor/friction feed

entraîner [ãtrene] *vt* (*tirer: wagons*) to pull; (*charrier*) to carry *ou* drag along; (*TECH*) to drive; (*emmener: personne*) to take (off); (*mener à l'assaut, influencer*) to lead; (*SPORT*) to train; (*impliquer*) to entail; (*causer*) to lead to, bring about; **entraîner qn à faire** (*inciter*) to lead sb to do; **s'entraîner** (*SPORT*) to train; **s'entraîner à qch/à faire** to train o.s. for sth/to do

entraîneur [ãtrenœr] *nm* (*SPORT*) coach, trainer; (*HIPPISME*) trainer

entraver [ãtrave] *vt* (*circulation*) to hold up; (*action, progrès*) to hinder, hamper

entre [ãtr(ə)] *prép* between; (*parmi*) among(st); **l'un d'entre eux/nous** one of them/us; **le meilleur d'entre eux/nous** the best of them/us; **ils préfèrent rester entre eux** they prefer to keep to themselves; **entre autres (choses)** among other things; **entre nous, ...** between ourselves ..., between you and me ...; **ils se battent entre eux** they are fighting among(st) themselves

entrebâillé, e [ãtrəbaje] *adj* half-open, ajar

entrechoquer [ãtrəʃɔke]: **s'entrechoquer** *vi* to knock *ou* bang together

entrecôte [ãtrəkot] *nf* entrecôte *ou* rib steak

entrecouper [ãtrəkupe] *vt*: **entrecouper qch de** to intersperse sth with; **entrecouper un récit/voyage de** to interrupt a story/journey with; **s'entrecouper** (*traits, lignes*) to cut across each other

entrecroiser [ãtrəkrwaze] *vt*: **s'entrecroiser** *vi* to intertwine

entrée [ãtre] *nf* entrance; (*accès: au cinéma etc*) admission; (*billet*) (admission) ticket; (*CULIN*) first course; (*COMM: de marchandises*) entry; (*INFORM*) entry, input; **entrées** *nfpl*: **avoir ses entrées chez** *ou* **auprès de** to be a welcome visitor to; **d'entrée** *adv* from the outset; **erreur d'entrée** input error; **"entrée interdite"** "no admittance *ou* entry"; **entrée des artistes** stage door; **entrée en matière** introduction; **entrée principale** main entrance; **entrée en scène** entrance; **entrée de service** service entrance

entrefaites [ãtrəfɛt]: **sur ces entrefaites** *adv* at this juncture

entrefilet [ɑ̃trəfilε] *nm* (*article*) paragraph, short report

entrejambes [ɑ̃trəʒɑ̃b] *nm inv* crotch

entrelacer [ɑ̃trəlase] *vt*: **s'entrelacer** *vi* to intertwine

entremêler [ɑ̃trəmele] *vt*: **entremêler qch de** to (inter)mingle sth with

entremets [ɑ̃trəmε] *nm* (cream) dessert

entremise [ɑ̃trəmiz] *nf* intervention; **par l'entremise de** through

entreposer [ɑ̃trəpoze] *vt* to store, put into storage

entrepôt [ɑ̃trəpo] *nm* warehouse

entreprenant, e [ɑ̃trəprənɑ̃, -ɑ̃t] *vb voir* **entreprendre** ♦ *adj* (*actif*) enterprising; (*trop galant*) forward

entreprendre [ɑ̃trəprɑ̃dr(ə)] *vt* (*se lancer dans*) to undertake; (*commencer*) to begin *ou* start (upon); (*personne*) to buttonhole; **entreprendre qn sur un sujet** to tackle sb on a subject; **entreprendre de faire** to undertake to do

entrepreneur [ɑ̃trəprənœr] *nm*: **entrepreneur (en bâtiment)** (building) contractor; **entrepreneur de pompes funèbres** funeral director, undertaker

entreprise [ɑ̃trəpriz] *nf* (*société*) firm, business; (*action*) undertaking, venture

entrer [ɑ̃tre] *vi* to go (*ou* come) in, enter ♦ *vt* (*INFORM*) to input, enter; **(faire) entrer qch dans** to get sth into; **entrer dans** (*gén*) to enter; (*pièce*) to go (*ou* come) into, enter; (*club*) to join; (*heurter*) to run into; (*partager: vues, craintes de qn*) to share; (*être une composante de*) to go into; (*faire partie de*) to form part of; **entrer au couvent** to enter a convent; **entrer à l'hôpital** to go into hospital; **entrer dans le système** (*INFORM*) to log in; **entrer en fureur** to become angry; **entrer en ébullition** to start to boil; **entrer en scène** to come on stage; **laisser entrer qn/qch** to let sb/sth in; **faire entrer** (*visiteur*) to show in

entresol [ɑ̃trəsɔl] *nm* entresol, mezzanine

entre-temps [ɑ̃trətɑ̃] *adv* meanwhile, (in the) meantime

entretenir [ɑ̃trətnir] *vt* to maintain; (*amitié*) to keep alive; (*famille, maîtresse*) to support, keep; **entretenir qn (de)** to speak to sb (about); **s'entretenir (de)** to converse (about); **entretenir qn dans l'erreur** to let sb remain in ignorance

entretien [ɑ̃trətjɛ̃] *nm* maintenance; (*discussion*) discussion, talk; (*audience*) interview; **frais d'entretien** maintenance charges

entrevoir [ɑ̃trəvwar] *vt* (*à peine*) to make out; (*brièvement*) to catch a glimpse of

entrevue [ɑ̃trəvy] *nf* meeting; (*audience*) interview

entrouvert, e [ɑ̃truvεr, -εrt(ə)] *adj* half-open

énumérer [enymere] *vt* to list, enumerate

envahir [ɑ̃vair] *vt* to invade; (*suj: inquiétude, peur*) to come over

envahissant, e [ɑ̃vaisɑ̃, -ɑ̃t] *adj* (*péj: personne*) interfering, intrusive

enveloppe [ɑ̃vlɔp] *nf* (*de lettre*) envelope; (*TECH*) casing; outer layer; **mettre sous enveloppe** to put in an envelope; **enveloppe autocollante** self-seal envelope; **enveloppe budgétaire** budget; **enveloppe à fenêtre** window envelope

envelopper [ɑ̃vlɔpe] *vt* to wrap; (*fig*) to envelop, shroud; **s'envelopper dans un châle/une couverture** to wrap o.s. in a shawl/blanket

envenimer [ɑ̃vnime] *vt* to aggravate; **s'envenimer** *vi* (*plaie*) to fester; (*situation, relations*) to worsen

envergure [ɑ̃vεrgyr] *nf* (*d'un oiseau, avion*) wingspan; (*fig: étendue*) scope; (: *valeur*) calibre

enverrai *etc* [ɑ̃vεr] *vb voir* **envoyer**

envers [ɑ̃vεr] *prép* towards, to ♦ *nm* other side; (*d'une étoffe*) wrong side; **à l'envers** upside down; back to front; (*vêtement*) inside out; **envers et contre tous** *ou* **tout** against all opposition

envie [ɑ̃vi] *nf* (*sentiment*) envy; (*souhait*) desire, wish; (*tache sur la peau*) birthmark; (*filet de peau*) hangnail; **avoir envie de** to feel like; (*désir plus fort*) to want; **avoir envie de faire** to feel like doing; to want to do; **avoir envie que** to wish that; **donner à qn l'envie de faire** to make sb want to do; **ça lui fait envie** he would like that

envier [ɑ̃vje] *vt* to envy; **envier qch à qn** to envy sb sth; **n'avoir rien à envier à** to have no cause to be envious of

envieux, euse [ɑ̃vjø, -øz] *adj* envious

environ [ɑ̃virɔ̃] *adv*: **environ 3 h/2 km, 3 h/2km environ** (around) about 3 o'clock/2 km, 3 o'clock/2 km or so

environnant, e [ɑ̃virɔnɑ̃, -ɑ̃t] *adj* surrounding

environnement [ɑ̃virɔnmɑ̃] *nm* environment

environs [ɑ̃virɔ̃] *nmpl* surroundings; **aux environs de** around

envisager [ɑ̃vizaʒe] *vt* (*examiner, considérer*) to view, contemplate; (*avoir en vue*) to envisage; **envisager de faire** to consider doing

envoi [ɑ̃vwa] *nm* sending; (*paquet*) parcel, consignment; **envoi contre remboursement** (*COMM*) cash on delivery

envoler [ɑ̃vɔle]: **s'envoler** *vi* (*oiseau*) to fly away *ou* off; (*avion*) to take off; (*papier, feuille*) to blow away; (*fig*) to vanish (into thin air)

envoûter [ɑ̃vute] *vt* to bewitch

envoyé, e [ɑ̃vwaje] *nm/f* (*POL*) envoy; (*PRESSE*) correspondent ♦ *adj*: **bien envoyé** (*remarque, réponse*) well-aimed

envoyer [ɑ̃vwaje] *vt* to send; (*lancer*) to hurl, throw; **envoyer une gifle/un sourire à qn** to aim a blow/flash a smile at sb; **envoyer les couleurs** to run up the colours; **envoyer chercher** to send for; **envoyer par le fond** (*bateau*) to send to the bottom

ÉOLE [eɔl] sigle m (= est-ouest-liaison-express) Paris high-speed, east-west subway service

épagneul, e [epaɲœl] nm/f spaniel

épais, se [epɛ, -ɛs] adj thick

épaisseur [epesœʀ] nf thickness

épancher [epɑ̃ʃe] vt to give vent to; **s'épancher** vi to open one's heart; (liquide) to pour out

épanouir [epanwiʀ]: **s'épanouir** vi (fleur) to bloom, open out; (visage) to light up; (fig: se développer) to blossom (out); (: mentalement) to open up

épargne [epaʀɲ(ə)] nf saving; **l'épargne-logement** property investment

épargner [epaʀɲe] vt to save; (ne pas tuer ou endommager) to spare ♦ vi to save; **épargner qch à qn** to spare sb sth

éparpiller [epaʀpije] vt to scatter; (pour répartir) to disperse; (fig: efforts) to dissipate; **s'éparpiller** vi to scatter; (fig) to dissipate one's efforts

épars, e [epaʀ, -aʀs(ə)] adj (maisons) scattered; (cheveux) sparse

épatant, e [epatɑ̃, -ɑ̃t] adj (fam) super, splendid

épater [epate] vt to amaze; (impressionner) to impress

épaule [epol] nf shoulder

épauler [epole] vt (aider) to back up, support; (arme) to raise (to one's shoulder) ♦ vi to (take) aim

épaulette [epolɛt] nf (MIL, d'un veston) epaulette; (de combinaison) shoulder strap

épave [epav] nf wreck

épée [epe] nf sword

épeler [eple] vt to spell

éperdu, e [epɛʀdy] adj (personne) overcome; (sentiment) passionate; (fuite) frantic

éperon [epʀɔ̃] nm spur

épervier [epɛʀvje] nm (ZOOL) sparrowhawk; (PÊCHE) casting net

épi [epi] nm (de blé, d'orge) ear; **épi de cheveux** tuft of hair; **stationnement/se garer en épi** parking/to park at an angle to the kerb

épice [epis] nf spice

épicé, e [epise] adj highly spiced, spicy; (fig) spicy

épicer [epise] vt to spice; (fig) to add spice to

épicerie [episʀi] nf (magasin) grocer's shop; (denrées) groceries pl; **épicerie fine** delicatessen (shop)

épicier, ière [episje, -jɛʀ] nm/f grocer

épidémie [epidemi] nf epidemic

épiderme [epidɛʀm(ə)] nm skin, epidermis

épier [epje] vt to spy on, watch closely; (occasion) to look out for

épilepsie [epilɛpsi] nf epilepsy

épiler [epile] vt (jambes) to remove the hair from; (sourcils) to pluck; **s'épiler les jambes** to remove the hair from one's legs; **s'épiler les sourcils** to pluck one's eyebrows; **se faire épiler** to get unwanted hair removed; **crème à épiler** hair-removing ou depilatory cream; **pince à épiler** eyebrow tweezers

épilogue [epilɔg] nm (fig) conclusion, dénouement

épiloguer [epilɔge] vi: **épiloguer sur** to hold forth on

épinards [epinaʀ] nmpl spinach sg

épine [epin] nf thorn, prickle; (d'oursin etc) spine, prickle; **épine dorsale** backbone

épineux, euse [epinø, -øz] adj thorny, prickly

épingle [epɛ̃gl(ə)] nf pin; **tirer son épingle du jeu** to play one's game well; **tiré à quatre épingles** well turned-out; **monter qch en épingle** to build sth up, make a thing of sth (fam) **épingle à chapeau** hatpin; **épingle à cheveux** hairpin; **virage en épingle à cheveux** hairpin bend; **épingle de cravate** tie pin; **épingle de nourrice** ou **de sûreté** ou **double** safety pin, nappy (BRIT) ou diaper (US) pin

épingler [epɛ̃gle] vt (badge, décoration): **épingler qch sur** to pin sth on(to); (COUTURE: tissu, robe) to pin together; (fam) to catch, nick

épique [epik] adj epic

épisode [epizɔd] nm episode; **film/roman à épisodes** serialized film/novel, serial

épisodique [epizɔdik] adj occasional

éploré, e [eplɔʀe] adj in tears, tearful

épluche-légumes [eplyʃlegym] nm inv potato peeler

éplucher [eplyʃe] vt (fruit, légumes) to peel; (comptes, dossier) to go over with a fine-tooth comb

épluchures [eplyʃyʀ] nfpl peelings

éponge [epɔ̃ʒ] nf sponge; **passer l'éponge (sur)** (fig) to let bygones be bygones (with regard to); **jeter l'éponge** (fig) to throw in the towel; **éponge métallique** scourer

éponger [epɔ̃ʒe] vt (liquide) to mop ou sponge up; (surface) to sponge; (fig: déficit) to soak up, absorb; **s'éponger le front** to mop one's brow

épopée [epɔpe] nf epic

époque [epɔk] nf (de l'histoire) age, era; (de l'année, la vie) time; **d'époque** adj (meuble) period cpd; **à cette époque** at this (ou that) time ou period; **faire époque** to make history

époumoner [epumɔne]: **s'époumoner** vi to shout (ou sing) o.s. hoarse

épouse [epuz] nf wife (pl wives)

épouser [epuze] vt to marry; (fig: idées) to espouse; (: forme) to fit

épousseter [epuste] vt to dust

époustouflant, e [epustuflɑ̃, -ɑ̃t] adj staggering, mind-boggling

épouvantable [epuvɑ̃tabl(ə)] adj appalling, dreadful

épouvantail [epuvɑ̃taj] nm (à moineaux) scarecrow; (fig) bog(e)y; bugbear

épouvante [epuvɑ̃t] nf terror; **film d'épouvante** horror film

épouvanter [epuvɑ̃te] vt to terrify

époux [epu] *nm* husband ♦ *nmpl*: **les époux** the (married) couple, the husband and wife

éprendre [eprɑ̃dr(ə)]: **s'éprendre de** *vt* to fall in love with

épreuve [eprœv] *nf* (*d'examen*) test; (*malheur, difficulté*) trial, ordeal; (*PHOTO*) print; (*TYPO*) proof; (*SPORT*) event; **à l'épreuve des balles/du feu** (*vêtement*) bulletproof/fireproof; **à toute épreuve** unfailing; **mettre à l'épreuve** to put to the test; **épreuve de force** trial of strength; (*fig*) showdown; **épreuve de résistance** test of resistance; **épreuve de sélection** (*SPORT*) heat

épris, e [epri, -iz] *vb voir* **éprendre** ♦ *adj*: **épris de** in love with

éprouvant, e [epruvɑ̃, -ɑ̃t] *adj* trying

éprouver [epruve] *vt* (*tester*) to test; (*mettre à l'épreuve*) to put to the test; (*marquer, faire souffrir*) to afflict, distress; (*ressentir*) to experience

éprouvette [epruvɛt] *nf* test tube

épuisé, e [epɥize] *adj* exhausted; (*livre*) out of print

épuisement [epɥizmɑ̃] *nm* exhaustion; **jusqu'à épuisement des stocks** while stocks last

épuiser [epɥize] *vt* (*fatiguer*) to exhaust, wear *ou* tire out; (*stock, sujet*) to exhaust; **s'épuiser** *vi* to wear *ou* tire o.s. out, exhaust o.s.; (*stock*) to run out

épuisette [epɥizɛt] *nf* landing net; shrimping net

épurer [epyre] *vt* (*liquide*) to purify; (*parti, administration*) to purge; (*langue, texte*) to refine

équateur [ekwatœr] *nm* equator; **(la république de) l'Équateur** Ecuador

équation [ekwasjɔ̃] *nf* equation; **mettre en équation** to equate; **équation du premier/second degré** simple/quadratic equation

équerre [ekɛr] *nf* (*à dessin*) (set) square; (*pour fixer*) brace; **en équerre** at right angles; **à l'équerre, d'équerre** straight; **double équerre** T-square

équilibre [ekilibr(ə)] *nm* balance; (*d'une balance*) equilibrium; **équilibre budgétaire** balanced budget; **garder/perdre l'équilibre** to keep/lose one's balance; **être en équilibre** to be balanced; **mettre en équilibre** to make steady; **avoir le sens de l'équilibre** to be well-balanced

équilibré, e [ekilibre] *adj* (*fig*) well-balanced, stable

équilibrer [ekilibre] *vt* to balance; **s'équilibrer** (*poids*) to balance; (*fig: défauts etc*) to balance each other out

équipage [ekipaʒ] *nm* crew; **en grand équipage** in great array

équipe [ekip] *nf* team; (*bande: parfois péj*) bunch; **travailler par équipes** to work in shifts; **travailler en équipe** to work as a team; **faire équipe avec** to team up with; **équipe de chercheurs** research team; **équipe de secours** *ou* **de sauvetage** rescue team

équipé, e [ekipe] *adj* (*cuisine etc*) equipped, fitted

(-out) ♦ *nf* escapade

équipement [ekipmɑ̃] *nm* equipment; **équipements** *nmpl* amenities, facilities; installations; **biens/dépenses d'équipement** capital goods/expenditure; **ministère de l'Équipement** department of public works; **équipements sportifs/collectifs** sports/community facilities *ou* resources

équiper [ekipe] *vt* to equip; (*voiture, cuisine*) to equip, fit out; **équiper qn/qch de** to equip sb/sth with; **s'équiper** (*suj: sportif*) to equip o.s., kit o.s. out

équipier, ière [ekipje, -jɛr] *nm/f* team member

équitable [ekitabl(ə)] *adj* fair

équitation [ekitasjɔ̃] *nf* (horse-)riding; **faire de l'équitation** to go (horse-)riding

équivalent, e [ekivalɑ̃, -ɑ̃t] *adj, nm* equivalent

équivaloir [ekivalwar]: **équivaloir à** *vt* to be equivalent to; (*représenter*) to amount to

équivoque [ekivɔk] *adj* equivocal, ambiguous; (*louche*) dubious ♦ *nf* ambiguity

érable [erabl(ə)] *nm* maple

érafler [erafle] *vt* to scratch; **s'érafler la main/les jambes** to scrape *ou* scratch one's hand/legs

éraflure [eraflyr] *nf* scratch

éraillé, e [eraje] *adj* (*voix*) rasping, hoarse

ère [ɛr] *nf* era; **en l'an 1050 de notre ère** in the year 1050 A.D.

érection [erɛksjɔ̃] *nf* erection

éreinter [erɛ̃te] *vt* to exhaust, wear out; (*fig: critiquer*) to slate; **s'éreinter (à faire qch/à qch)** to wear o.s. out (doing sth/with sth)

ériger [eriʒe] *vt* (*monument*) to erect; **ériger qch en principe/loi** to make sth a principle/law; **s'ériger en critique (de)** to set o.s. up as a critic (of)

ermite [ermit] *nm* hermit

éroder [erɔde] *vt* to erode

érotique [erɔtik] *adj* erotic

errer [ere] *vi* to wander

erreur [erœr] *nf* mistake, error; (*INFORM: de programme*) bug; (*morale*): **erreurs** *nfpl* errors; **être dans l'erreur** to be wrong; **induire qn en erreur** to mislead sb; **par erreur** by mistake; **sauf erreur** unless I'm mistaken; **faire erreur** to be mistaken; **erreur de date** mistake in the date; **erreur de fait** error of fact; **erreur d'impression** (*TYPO*) misprint; **erreur judiciaire** miscarriage of justice; **erreur de jugement** error of judgment; **erreur matérielle** *ou* **d'écriture** clerical error; **erreur tactique** tactical error

érudit, e [erydi, -it] *adj* erudite, learned ♦ *nm/f* scholar

éruption [erypsjɔ̃] *nf* eruption; (*cutanée*) outbreak; (: *boutons*) rash; (*fig: de joie, colère, folie*) outburst

es [ɛ] *vb voir* **être**

ès [ɛs] *prép*: **licencié ès lettres/sciences** ≃

Bachelor of Arts/Science; **docteur ès lettres** ≃ doctor of philosophy, ≃ PhD

escabeau, x [ɛskabo] *nm* (*tabouret*) stool; (*échelle*) stepladder

escadron [ɛskadʀɔ̃] *nm* squadron

escalade [ɛskalad] *nf* climbing *no pl*; (POL etc) escalation

escalader [ɛskalade] *vt* to climb, scale

escale [ɛskal] *nf* (NAVIG) call; (: *port*) port of call; (AVIAT) stop(over); **faire escale à** to put in at, call in at; to stop over at; **escale technique** (AVIAT) refuelling stop

escalier [ɛskalje] *nm* stairs *pl*; **dans l'escalier** *ou* **les escaliers** on the stairs; **descendre l'escalier** *ou* **les escaliers** to go downstairs; **escalier mécanique** *ou* **roulant** escalator; **escalier de secours** fire escape; **escalier de service** backstairs; **escalier à vis** *ou* **en colimaçon** spiral staircase

escamoter [ɛskamɔte] *vt* (*esquiver*) to get round, evade; (*faire disparaître*) to conjure away; (*dérober: portefeuille etc*) to snatch; (*train d'atterrissage*) to retract; (*mots*) to miss out

escapade [ɛskapad] *nf*: **faire une escapade** to go on a jaunt; (*s'enfuir*) to run away *ou* off

escargot [ɛskaʀgo] *nm* snail

escarpé, e [ɛskaʀpe] *adj* steep

escarpin [ɛskaʀpɛ̃] *nm* flat(-heeled) shoe

escient [esjɑ̃] *nm*: **à bon escient** advisedly

esclaffer [ɛsklafe]: **s'esclaffer** *vi* to guffaw

esclandre [ɛsklɑ̃dʀ(ə)] *nm* scene, fracas

esclavage [ɛsklavaʒ] *nm* slavery

esclave [ɛsklav] *nm/f* slave; **être esclave de** (*fig*) to be a slave of

escompte [ɛskɔ̃t] *nm* discount

escompter [ɛskɔ̃te] *vt* (COMM) to discount; (*espérer*) to expect, reckon upon; **escompter que** to reckon *ou* expect that

escorte [ɛskɔʀt(ə)] *nf* escort; **faire escorte à** to escort

escorter [ɛskɔʀte] *vt* to escort

escouade [ɛskwad] *nf* squad; (*fig: groupe de personnes*) group

escrime [ɛskʀim] *nf* fencing; **faire de l'escrime** to fence

escrimer [ɛskʀime]: **s'escrimer** *vi*: **s'escrimer à faire** to wear o.s. out doing

escroc [ɛskʀo] *nm* swindler, con-man

escroquer [ɛskʀɔke] *vt*: **escroquer qn (de qch)/ qch à qn** to swindle sb (out of sth)/sth out of sb

escroquerie [ɛskʀɔkʀi] *nf* swindle

espace [ɛspas] *nm* space; **espace publicitaire** advertising space; **espace vital** living space

espacer [ɛspase] *vt* to space out; **s'espacer** *vi* (*visites etc*) to become less frequent

espadon [ɛspadɔ̃] *nm* swordfish *inv*

espadrille [ɛspadʀij] *nf* rope-soled sandal

Espagne [ɛspaɲ(ə)] *nf*: **l'Espagne** Spain

espagnol, e [ɛspaɲɔl] *adj* Spanish ♦ *nm* (LING) Spanish ♦ *nm/f*: **Espagnol, e** Spaniard

espèce [ɛspɛs] *nf* (BIO, BOT, ZOOL) species *inv*; (*gén: sorte*) sort, kind, type; (*péj*): **espèce de maladroit/ de brute!** you clumsy oaf/you brute!; **espèces** *nfpl* (COMM) cash *sg*; (REL) species; **de toute espèce** of all kinds *ou* sorts; **en l'espèce** *adv* in the case in point; **payer en espèces** to pay (in) cash; **cas d'espèce** individual case; **l'espèce humaine** humankind

espérance [ɛsperɑ̃s] *nf* hope; **espérance de vie** life expectancy

espérer [ɛspere] *vt* to hope for; **j'espère (bien)** I hope so; **espérer que/faire** to hope that/to do; **espérer en** to trust in

espiègle [ɛspjɛgl(ə)] *adj* mischievous

espion, ne [ɛspjɔ̃, -ɔn] *nm/f* spy; **avion espion** spy plane

espionnage [ɛspjɔnaʒ] *nm* espionage, spying; **film/roman d'espionnage** spy film/novel

espionner [ɛspjɔne] *vt* to spy (up)on

esplanade [ɛsplanad] *nf* esplanade

espoir [ɛspwaʀ] *nm* hope; **l'espoir de qch/de faire qch** the hope of sth/of doing sth; **avoir bon espoir que ...** to have high hopes that ...; **garder l'espoir que ...** to remain hopeful that ...; **un espoir de la boxe/du ski** one of boxing's/skiing's hopefuls, one of the hopes of boxing/skiing; **sans espoir** *adj* hopeless

esprit [ɛspʀi] *nm* (*pensée, intellect*) mind; (*humour, ironie*) wit; (*mentalité, d'une loi etc, fantôme etc*) spirit; **l'esprit d'équipe de compétition** team/competitive spirit; **faire de l'esprit** to try to be witty; **reprendre ses esprits** to come to; **perdre l'esprit** to lose one's mind; **avoir bon/mauvais esprit** to be of a good/bad disposition; **avoir l'esprit à faire qch** to have a mind to do sth; **avoir l'esprit critique** to be critical; **esprit de contradiction** contrariness; **esprit de corps** esprit de corps; **esprit de famille** family loyalty; **l'esprit malin** (*le diable*) the Evil One; **esprits chagrins** faultfinders

esquimau, de, x [ɛskimo, -od] *adj* Eskimo ♦ *nm* (LING) Eskimo; (*glace*): **Esquimau®** ice lolly (BRIT), popsicle (US) ♦ *nm/f*: **Esquimau, de** Eskimo; **chien esquimau** husky

esquinter [ɛskɛ̃te] *vt* (*fam*) to mess up; **s'esquinter** *vi*: **s'esquinter à faire qch** to knock o.s. out doing sth

esquisse [ɛskis] *nf* sketch; **l'esquisse d'un sourire/changement** a hint of a smile/of change

esquisser [ɛskise] *vt* to sketch; **s'esquisser** *vi* (*amélioration*) to begin to be detectable; **esquisser un sourire** to give a hint of a smile

esquiver [ɛskive] *vt* to dodge; **s'esquiver** *vi* to slip away

essai [ese] *nm* trying; (*tentative*) attempt, try; (RUGBY) try; (LITTÉRATURE) essay; **essais** *nmpl* (AUTO) trials; **à l'essai** on a trial basis; **essai gratuit** (COMM) free trial

essaim [esɛ̃] *nm* swarm

essayer [eseje] *vt* (*gén*) to try; (*vêtement, chaussures*) to try (on); (*restaurant, méthode, voiture*) to try (out) ♦ *vi* to try; **essayer de faire** to try *ou* attempt to do; **s'essayer à faire** to try one's hand at doing; **essayez un peu!** (*menace*) just you try!

essence [esɑ̃s] *nf* (*de voiture*) petrol (*BRIT*), gas(oline) (*US*); (*extrait de plante, PHILOSOPHIE*) essence; (*espèce: d'arbre*) species *inv*; **prendre de l'essence** to get (some) petrol *ou* gas; **par essence** (*essentiellement*) essentially; **essence de citron/rose** lemon/rose oil; **essence sans plomb** unleaded petrol; **essence de térébenthine** turpentine

essentiel, le [esɑ̃sjɛl] *adj* essential ♦ *nm*: **l'essentiel d'un discours/d'une œuvre** the essence of a speech/work of art; **emporter l'essentiel** to take the essentials; **c'est l'essentiel** (*ce qui importe*) that's the main thing; **l'essentiel de** (*la majeure partie*) the main part of

essieu, x [esjø] *nm* axle

essor [esɔʀ] *nm* (*de l'économie etc*) rapid expansion; **prendre son essor** (*oiseau*) to fly off

essorer [esɔʀe] *vt* (*en tordant*) to wring (out); (*par la force centrifuge*) to spin-dry; (*salade*) to spin; (*: en secouant*) to shake dry

essoreuse [esɔʀøz] *nf* mangle, wringer; (*à tambour*) spin-dryer

essoufflé, e [esufle] *adj* out of breath, breathless

essouffler [esufle] *vt* to make breathless; **s'essouffler** *vi* to get out of breath; (*fig: économie*) to run out of steam

essuie-glace [esɥiglas] *nm* windscreen (*BRIT*) *ou* windshield (*US*) wiper

essuyer [esɥije] *vt* to wipe; (*fig: subir*) to suffer; **s'essuyer** (*après le bain*) to dry o.s.; **essuyer la vaisselle** to dry up, dry the dishes

est [ɛ] *vb voir* **être** ♦ [ɛst] *nm* [ɛst]: **l'est** the east ♦ *adj inv* east; (*région*) east(ern); **à l'est** in the east; (*direction*) to the east, east(wards); **à l'est de** (to the) east of; **les pays de l'Est** the eastern countries

estampe [estɑ̃p] *nf* print, engraving

est-ce que [ɛskə] *adv*: **est-ce que c'est cher/c'était bon?** is it expensive/was it good?; **quand est-ce qu'il part?** when does he leave?, when is he leaving?; **où est-ce qu'il va?** where's he going?; **qui est-ce qui le connaît/a fait ça?** who knows him/did that?; *voir aussi* **que**

esthéticienne [estetisjɛn] *nf* beautician

esthétique [estetik] *adj* (*sens, jugement*) aesthetic; (*beau*) attractive, aesthetically pleasing ♦ *nf* aesthetics *sg*; **l'esthétique industrielle** industrial design

estimation [estimasjɔ̃] *nf* valuation; assessment; **d'après mes estimations** according to my calculations

estime [estim] *nf* esteem, regard; **avoir de l'estime pour qn** to think highly of sb

estimer [estime] *vt* (*respecter*) to esteem, hold in high regard; (*expertiser*) to value; (*évaluer*) to assess, estimate; (*penser*): **estimer que/être** to consider that/o.s. to be; **s'estimer satisfait/heureux** to feel satisfied/happy; **j'estime la distance à 10 km** I reckon the distance to be 10 km

estival, e, aux [estival, -o] *adj* summer *cpd*; **station estivale** (summer) holiday resort

estivant, e [estivɑ̃, -ɑ̃t] *nm/f* (summer) holidaymaker

estomac [estɔma] *nm* stomach; **avoir mal à l'estomac** to have stomach ache; **avoir l'estomac creux** to have an empty stomach

estomaqué, e [estɔmake] *adj* flabbergasted

estomper [estɔ̃pe] *vt* (*ART*) to shade off; (*fig*) to blur, dim; **s'estomper** *vi* (*sentiments*) to soften; (*contour*) to become blurred

estrade [estʀad] *nf* platform, rostrum

estragon [estʀagɔ̃] *nm* tarragon

estuaire [estɥɛʀ] *nm* estuary

et [e] *conj* and; **et lui?** what about him?; **et alors?, et (puis) après?** so what?; (*ensuite*) and then?

étable [etablə] *nf* cowshed

établi, e [etabli] *adj* established ♦ *nm* (work)bench

établir [etablir] *vt* (*papiers d'identité, facture*) to make out; (*liste, programme*) to draw up; (*gouvernement, artisan etc: aider à s'installer*) to set up, establish; (*entreprise, atelier, camp*) to set up; (*réputation, usage, fait, culpabilité, relations*) to establish; (*SPORT: record*) to set; **s'établir** *vi* (*se faire: entente etc*) to be established; **s'établir (à son compte)** to set up in business; **s'établir à/près de** to settle in/near

établissement [etablismɑ̃] *nm* making out; drawing up; setting up, establishing; (*entreprise, institution*) establishment; **établissement de crédit** credit institution; **établissement hospitalier** hospital complex; **établissement industriel** industrial plant, factory; **établissement scolaire** school, educational establishment

étage [etaʒ] *nm* (*d'immeuble*) storey (*BRIT*), story (*US*), floor; (*de fusée*) stage; (*GÉO: de culture, végétation*) level; **au 2ème étage** on the 2nd (*BRIT*) *ou* 3rd (*US*) floor; **à l'étage** upstairs; **maison à deux étages** two-storey *ou* -story house; **de bas étage** *adj* low-born; (*médiocre*) inferior

étagère [etaʒɛʀ] *nf* (*rayon*) shelf; (*meuble*) shelves *pl*, set of shelves

étai [ete] *nm* stay, prop

étain [etɛ̃] *nm* tin; (*ORFÈVRERIE*) pewter *no pl*

étais *etc* [ete] *vb voir* **être**

étal [etal] *nm* stall

étalage [etalaʒ] *nm* display; (*vitrine*) display window; **faire étalage de** to show off, parade

étaler [etale] *vt* (*carte, nappe*) to spread (out); (*peinture, liquide*) to spread; (*échelonner: paiements, dates, vacances*) to spread, stagger; (*exposer: marchandises*) to display; (*richesses, connaissances*) to parade; **s'étaler** *vi* (*liquide*) to spread out; (*fam*) to come a cropper (BRIT), fall flat on one's face; **s'é-taler sur** (paiements etc) to be spread over

étalon [etalɔ̃] nm (mesure) standard; (cheval) stallion; **l'étalon-or** the gold standard

étanche [etɑ̃ʃ] adj (récipient, aussi fig) watertight; (montre, vêtement) waterproof; **étanche à l'air** airtight

étancher [etɑ̃ʃe] vt (liquide) to stop (flowing); **étancher sa soif** to quench ou slake one's thirst

étang [etɑ̃] nm pond

étant [etɑ̃] vb voir **être**, **donné**

étape [etap] nf stage; (lieu d'arrivée) stopping place; (CYCLISME) staging point; **faire étape à** to stop off at; **brûler les étapes** (fig) to cut corners

état [eta] nm (POL, condition) state; (d'un article d'occasion etc) condition, state; (liste) inventory, statement; (condition: professionnelle) profession, trade; (: sociale) status; **en bon/mauvais état** in good/poor condition; **en état (de marche)** in (working) order; **remettre en état** to repair; **hors d'état** out of order; **être en état/hors d'état de faire** to be in a state/in no fit state to do; **en tout état de cause** in any event; **être dans tous ses états** to be in a state; **faire état de** (alléguer) to put forward; **état d'arrestation** under arrest; **état de grâce** (REL) state of grace; (fig) honeymoon period; **en état de grâce** (fig) inspired; **en état d'ivresse** under the influence of drink; **état de choses** (situation) state of affairs; **état civil** civil status; (bureau) registry office (BRIT); **état d'esprit** frame of mind; **état des lieux** inventory of fixtures; **état de santé** state of health; **état de siège/d'urgence** state of siege/emergency; **état de veille** (PSYCH) waking state; **états d'âme** moods; **les États barbaresques** the Barbary States; **les États du Golfe** the Gulf States; **états de service** service record sg

étatiser [etatize] vt to bring under state control

état-major, pl **états-majors** [etamaʒɔr] nm (MIL) staff; (d'un parti etc) top advisers pl; (d'une entreprise) top management

États-Unis [etazyni] nmpl: **les États-Unis (d'Amérique)** the United States (of America)

étau, x [eto] nm vice (BRIT), vise (US)

étayer [eteje] vt to prop ou shore up; (fig) to back up

et c(a)etera [ɛtsetera], **etc.** adv et cetera, and so on, etc

été [ete] pp de **être** ♦ nm summer; **en été** in summer

éteindre [etɛ̃dr(ə)] vt (lampe, lumière, radio, chauffage) to turn ou switch off; (cigarette, incendie, bougie) to put out, extinguish; (JUR: dette) to extinguish; **s'éteindre** vi to go off; to go out; (mourir) to pass away

éteint, e [etɛ̃, -ɛ̃t] pp de **éteindre** ♦ adj (fig) lacklustre, dull; (volcan) extinct; **tous feux éteints** (AUTO: rouler) without lights

étendard [etɑ̃dar] nm standard

étendre [etɑ̃dr(ə)] vt (appliquer: pâte, liquide) to spread; (déployer: carte etc) to spread out; (sur un fil: lessive, linge) to hang up ou out; (bras, jambes, par terre: blessé) to stretch out; (diluer) to dilute, thin; (fig: agrandir) to extend; (fam: adversaire) to floor; **s'étendre** vi (augmenter, se propager) to spread; (terrain, forêt etc): **s'étendre jusqu'à/de ... à** to stretch as far as/from ... to; **s'étendre (sur)** (s'allonger) to stretch out (upon); (se coucher) to lie down (on); (fig: expliquer) to elaborate ou enlarge (upon)

étendu, e [etɑ̃dy] adj extensive ♦ nf (d'eau, de sable) stretch, expanse; (importance) extent

éternel, le [etɛrnɛl] adj eternal; **les neiges éternelles** perpetual snow

éterniser [etɛrnize]: **s'éterniser** vi to last for ages; (personne) to stay for ages

éternité [etɛrnite] nf eternity; **il y a ou ça fait une éternité que** it's ages since; **de toute éternité** from time immemorial

éternuement [etɛrnymɑ̃] nm sneeze

éternuer [etɛrnɥe] vi to sneeze

êtes [ɛt] vb voir **être**

éthique [etik] adj ethical ♦ nf ethics sg

ethnie [etni] nf ethnic group

éthylisme [etilism(ə)] nm alcoholism

étiez [etje] vb voir **être**

étinceler [etɛ̃sle] vi to sparkle

étincelle [etɛ̃sɛl] nf spark

étiqueter [etikte] vt to label

étiquette [etiket] vb voir **étiqueter** ♦ nf label; (protocole): **l'étiquette** etiquette

étirer [etire] vt to stretch; (ressort) to stretch out; **s'étirer** vi (personne) to stretch; (convoi, route): **s'étirer sur** to stretch out over

étoffe [etɔf] nf material, fabric; **avoir l'étoffe d'un chef** etc to be cut out to be a leader etc; **avoir de l'étoffe** to be a forceful personality

étoffer [etɔfe] vt: **s'étoffer** vi to fill out

étoile [etwal] nf star ♦ adj: **danseuse ou danseur étoile** leading dancer; **la bonne/mauvaise étoile de qn** sb's lucky/unlucky star; **à la belle étoile** (out) in the open; **étoile filante** shooting star; **étoile de mer** starfish; **étoile polaire** pole star

étoilé, e [etwale] adj starry

étonnant, e [etɔnɑ̃, -ɑ̃t] adj surprising

étonnement [etɔnmɑ̃] nm surprise; **à mon grand étonnement ...** to my great surprise ou amazement ...

étonner [etɔne] vt to surprise; **s'étonner que/de** to be surprised that/at; **cela m'étonnerait (que)** (j'en doute) I'd be (very) surprised (if)

étouffant, e [etufɑ̃, -ɑ̃t] adj stifling

étouffée [etufe] nf: **à l'étouffée** (CULIN: poisson, légumes) steamed; (: viande) braised

étouffer [etufe] vt to suffocate; (bruit) to muffle;

(scandale) to hush up ♦ *vi* to suffocate; *(avoir trop chaud; aussi fig)* to feel stifled; **s'étouffer** *vi (en mangeant etc)* to choke

étourderie [etuʀdəʀi] *nf* heedlessness *no pl*; thoughtless blunder; **faute d'étourderie** careless mistake

étourdi, e [etuʀdi] *adj (distrait)* scatterbrained, heedless

étourdir [etuʀdiʀ] *vt (assommer)* to stun, daze; *(griser)* to make dizzy *ou* giddy

étourdissement [etuʀdismɑ̃] *nm* dizzy spell

étourneau, x [etuʀno] *nm* starling

étrange [etʀɑ̃ʒ] *adj* strange

étranger, ère [etʀɑ̃ʒe, -ɛʀ] *adj* foreign; *(pas de la famille, non familier)* strange ♦ *nm/f* foreigner; stranger ♦ *nm:* **l'étranger** foreign countries; **à l'étranger** abroad; **de l'étranger** from abroad; **étranger à** *(mal connu)* unfamiliar to; *(sans rapport)* irrelevant to

étrangler [etʀɑ̃gle] *vt* to strangle; *(fig: presse, libertés)* to stifle; **s'étrangler** *vi (en mangeant etc)* to choke; *(se resserrer)* to make a bottleneck

---

MOT CLÉ

être [etʀ(ə)] *nm* being; **être humain** human being

♦ *vb +attrib* **1** *(état, description)* to be; **il est instituteur** he is *ou* he's a teacher; **vous êtes grand/intelligent/fatigué** you are *ou* you're tall/clever/tired

2 *(+à: appartenir)* to be; **le livre est à Paul** the book is Paul's *ou* belongs to Paul; **c'est à moi/eux** it's *ou* it's mine/theirs

3 *(+de: provenance)*: **il est de Paris** he is from Paris; *(appartenance)*: **il est des nôtres** he is one of us

4 *(date)*: **nous sommes le 10 janvier** it's the 10th of January (today)

♦ *vi* to be; **je ne serai pas ici demain** I won't be here tomorrow

♦ *vb aux* **1** to have; to be; **être arrivé/allé** to have arrived/gone; **il est parti** he has left, he has gone

2 *(forme passive)* to be; **être fait par** to be made by; **il a été promu** he has been promoted

3 *(+à +inf: obligation, but)*: **c'est à réparer** it needs repairing; **c'est à essayer** it should be tried; **il est à espérer que ...** it is *ou* it's to be hoped that ...

♦ *vb impers* **1**: **il est** + *adjective* it is *(+ adjectif)*; **il est impossible de le faire** it's impossible to do it

2 *(heure, date)*: **il est 10 heures** it is *ou* it's 10 o'clock

3 *(emphatique)*: **c'est moi** it's me; **c'est à lui de le faire** it's up to him to do it; *voir aussi* **est-ce que, n'est-ce pas, c'est-à-dire, ce**

étreindre [etʀɛ̃dʀ(ə)] *vt* to clutch, grip; *(amoureusement, amicalement)* to embrace;

s'étreindre to embrace

étrenner [etʀene] *vt* to use *(ou* wear) for the first time

étrennes [etʀɛn] *nfpl (cadeaux)* New Year's present; *(gratifications)* ≈ Christmas box *sg*, ≈ Christmas bonus

étrier [etʀije] *nm* stirrup

étriqué, e [etʀike] *adj* skimpy

étroit, e [etʀwa, -wat] *adj* narrow; *(vêtement)* tight; *(fig: serré)* close, tight; **à l'étroit** cramped; **étroit d'esprit** narrow-minded

étude [etyd] *nf* studying; *(ouvrage, rapport, MUS)* study; *(de notaire: bureau)* office; *(: charge)* practice; *(SCOL: salle de travail)* study room; **études** *nfpl (SCOL)* studies; **être à l'étude** *(projet etc)* to be under consideration; **faire des études (de droit/médecine)** to study (law/medicine); **études secondaires/supérieures** secondary/higher education; **étude de cas** case study; **étude de faisabilité** feasibility study; **étude de marché** *(ÉCON)* market research

étudiant, e [etydjɑ̃, -ɑ̃t] *adj, nm/f* student

étudier [etydje] *vt, vi* to study

étui [etɥi] *nm* case

étuve [etyv] *nf* steamroom; *(appareil)* sterilizer

étuvée [etyve]: **à l'étuvée** *adv* braised

eu, eue [y] *pp de* **avoir**

euh [ø] *excl* er

euro [øʀo] *nm* euro

Euroland [øʀɔlɑ̃d] *nm* Euroland

Europe [øʀɔp] *nf:* **l'Europe** Europe; **l'Europe centrale** Central Europe; **l'Europe verte** European agriculture

européen, ne [øʀɔpeɛ̃, -ɛn] *adj* European ♦ *nm/f:* **Européen, ne** European

eus *etc* [y] *vb voir* **avoir**

eux [ø] *pron (sujet)* they; *(objet)* them; **eux, ils ont fait ...** THEY did ...

évacuer [evakɥe] *vt (salle, région)* to evacuate, clear; *(occupants, population)* to evacuate; *(toxine etc)* to evacuate, discharge

évader [evade]: **s'évader** *vi* to escape

évaluer [evalɥe] *vt* to assess, evaluate

évangile [evɑ̃ʒil] *nm* gospel; *(texte de la Bible)*: **Évangile** Gospel; **ce n'est pas l'Évangile** *(fig)* it's not gospel

évanouir [evanwiʀ]: **s'évanouir** *vi* to faint, pass out; *(disparaître)* to vanish, disappear

évanouissement [evanwismɑ̃] *nm (syncope)* fainting fit; *(MÉD)* loss of consciousness

évaporer [evapɔʀe]: **s'évaporer** *vi* to evaporate

évasé, e [evaze] *adj (jupe etc)* flared

évasif, ive [evazif, -iv] *adj* evasive

évasion [evazjɔ̃] *nf* escape; **littérature d'évasion** escapist literature; **évasion des capitaux** *(ÉCON)* flight of capital; **évasion fiscale** tax avoidance

évêché [eveʃe] *nm (fonction)* bishopric; *(palais)* bishop's palace

éveil [evɛj] *nm* awakening; **être en éveil** to be alert; **mettre qn en éveil, donner l'éveil à qn** to arouse sb's suspicions; **activités d'éveil** early-learning activities

éveillé, e [eveje] *adj* awake; (*vif*) alert, sharp

éveiller [eveje] *vt* to (a)waken; **s'éveiller** *vi* to (a)waken; (*fig*) to be aroused

événement [evɛnmɑ̃] *nm* event

éventail [evɑ̃taj] *nm* fan; (*choix*) range; **en éventail** fanned out; fan-shaped

éventaire [evɑ̃tɛʀ] *nm* stall, stand

éventer [evɑ̃te] *vt* (*secret, complot*) to uncover; (*avec un éventail*) to fan; **s'éventer** *vi* (*parfum, vin*) to go stale

éventualité [evɑ̃tɥalite] *nf* eventuality; possibility; **dans l'éventualité de** in the event of; **parer à toute éventualité** to guard against all eventualities

éventuel, le [evɑ̃tɥɛl] *adj* possible

éventuellement [evɑ̃tɥɛlmɑ̃] *adv* possibly

évêque [evɛk] *nm* bishop

évertuer [evɛʀtɥe]: **s'évertuer** *vi*: **s'évertuer à faire** to try very hard to do

éviction [eviksjɔ̃] *nf* ousting, supplanting; (*de locataire*) eviction

évidemment [evidamɑ̃] *adv* obviously

évidence [evidɑ̃s] *nf* obviousness; (*fait*) obvious fact; **se rendre à l'évidence** to bow before the evidence; **nier l'évidence** to deny the evidence; **à l'évidence** evidently; **de toute évidence** quite obviously *ou* evidently; **en évidence** conspicuous; **mettre en évidence** to bring to the fore

évident, e [evidɑ̃, -ɑ̃t] *adj* obvious, evident; **ce n'est pas évident** (*cela pose des problèmes*) it's not (all that) straightforward, it's not as simple as all that

évider [evide] *vt* to scoop out

évier [evje] *nm* (kitchen) sink

évincer [evɛ̃se] *vt* to oust, supplant

éviter [evite] *vt* to avoid; **éviter de faire/que qch ne se passe** to avoid doing/sth happening; **éviter qch à qn** to spare sb sth

évolué, e [evɔlɥe] *adj* advanced; (*personne*) broad-minded

évoluer [evɔlɥe] *vi* (*enfant, maladie*) to develop; (*situation, moralement*) to evolve, develop; (*aller et venir: danseur etc*) to move about, circle

évolution [evɔlysjɔ̃] *nf* development; evolution; **évolutions** *nfpl* movements

évoquer [evɔke] *vt* to call to mind, evoke; (*mentionner*) to mention

exact, e [egzakt] *adj* (*précis*) exact, accurate, precise; (*correct*) correct; (*ponctuel*) punctual; **l'heure exacte** the right *ou* exact time

exactement [egzaktəmɑ̃] *adv* exactly, accurately, precisely; correctly; (*c'est cela même*) exactly

ex aequo [egzeko] *adj* equally placed; **classé 1er ex aequo** placed equal first

exagéré, e [egzaʒere] *adj* (*prix etc*) excessive

exagérer [egzaʒere] *vt* to exaggerate ♦ *vi* (*abuser*) to go too far; (*dépasser les bornes*) to overstep the mark; (*déformer les faits*) to exaggerate; **s'exagérer qch** to exaggerate sth

exalter [egzalte] *vt* (*enthousiasmer*) to excite, elate; (*glorifier*) to exalt

examen [egzamɛ̃] *nm* examination; (*SCOL*) exam, examination; **à l'examen** (*dossier, projet*) under consideration; (*COMM*) on approval; **examen blanc** mock exam(ination); **examen de la vue** sight test

examinateur, trice [egzaminatœʀ, -tʀis] *nm/f* examiner

examiner [egzamine] *vt* to examine

exaspérant, e [egzaspeʀɑ̃, -ɑ̃t] *adj* exasperating

exaspérer [egzaspeʀe] *vt* to exasperate; (*aggraver*) to exacerbate

exaucer [egzose] *vt* (*vœu*) to grant, fulfil; **exaucer qn** to grant sb's wishes

excédent [eksedɑ̃] *nm* surplus; **en excédent** surplus; **payer 100 € d'excédent** (*de bagages*) to pay 100 € excess luggage; **excédent de bagages** excess luggage; **excédent commercial** trade surplus

excéder [eksede] *vt* (*dépasser*) to exceed; (*agacer*) to exasperate; **excédé de fatigue** exhausted; **excédé de travail** worn out with work

excellent, e [ekselɑ̃, -ɑ̃t] *adj* excellent

excentrique [eksɑ̃tʀik] *adj* eccentric; (*quartier*) outlying ♦ *nm/f* eccentric

excepté, e [eksepte] *adj*, *prép*: **les élèves exceptés, excepté les élèves** except for *ou* apart from the pupils; **excepté si/quand** except if/when; **excepté que** except that

exception [eksepsjɔ̃] *nf* exception; **faire exception** to be an exception; **faire une exception** to make an exception; **sans exception** without exception; **à l'exception de** except for, with the exception of; **d'exception** (*mesure, loi*) special, exceptional

exceptionnel, le [eksepsjɔnɛl] *adj* exceptional; (*prix*) special

exceptionnellement [eksepsjɔnɛlmɑ̃] *adv* exceptionally; (*par exception*) by way of an exception, on this occasion

excès [eksɛ] *nm* surplus ♦ *nmpl* excesses; **à l'excès** (*méticuleux, généreux*) to excess; **avec excès** to excess; **sans excès** in moderation; **tomber dans l'excès inverse** to go to the opposite extreme; **excès de langage** immoderate language; **excès de pouvoir** abuse of power; **excès de vitesse** speeding *no pl*, exceeding the speed limit; **excès de zèle** overzealousness *no pl*

excessif, ive [eksesif, -iv] *adj* excessive

excitant, e [eksitɑ̃, -ɑ̃t] *adj* exciting ♦ *nm* stimulant

excitation [eksitasjɔ̃] *nf* (*état*) excitement

exciter [ɛksite] *vt* to excite; (*suj: café etc*) to stimulate; **s'exciter** *vi* to get excited; **exciter qn à** (*révolte etc*) to incite sb to

exclamation [ɛksklamɑsjɔ̃] *nf* exclamation

exclamer [ɛksklame]: **s'exclamer** *vi* to exclaim

exclure [ɛksklyʀ] *vt* (*faire sortir*) to expel; (*ne pas compter*) to exclude, leave out; (*rendre impossible*) to exclude, rule out

exclusif, ive [ɛksklyzif, -iv] *adj* exclusive; **avec la mission exclusive/dans le but exclusif de ...** with the sole mission/aim of ...; **agent exclusif** sole agent

exclusion [ɛksklyzjɔ̃] *nf* expulsion; **à l'exclusion de** with the exclusion ou exception of

exclusivité [ɛksklyzivite] *nf* exclusiveness; (*COMM*) exclusive rights *pl*; **passer en exclusivité** (*film*) to go on general release

excursion [ɛkskyʀsjɔ̃] *nf* (*en autocar*) excursion, trip; (*à pied*) walk, hike; **faire une excursion** to go on an excursion ou a trip; to go on a walk ou hike

excuse [ɛkskyz] *nf* excuse; **excuses** *nfpl* apology *sg*, apologies; **faire des excuses** to apologize; **faire ses excuses** to offer one's apologies; **mot d'excuse** (*SCOL*) note from one's parent(s) (*to explain absence etc*); **lettre d'excuses** letter of apology

excuser [ɛkskyze] *vt* to excuse; **excuser qn de qch** (*dispenser*) to excuse sb from sth; **s'excuser (de)** to apologize (for); **"excusez-moi"** "I'm sorry"; (*pour attirer l'attention*) "excuse me"; **se faire excuser** to ask to be excused

exécrable [ɛgzekʀabl(ə)] *adj* atrocious

exécuter [ɛgzekyte] *vt* (*prisonnier*) to execute; (*tâche etc*) to execute, carry out; (*MUS: jouer*) to perform, execute; (*INFORM*) to run; **s'exécuter** *vi* to comply

exécutif, ive [ɛgzekytif, -iv] *adj, nm* (*POL*) executive

exécution [ɛgzekysjɔ̃] *nf* execution; carrying out; **mettre à exécution** to carry out

exemplaire [ɛgzɑ̃plɛʀ] *adj* exemplary ♦ *nm* copy

exemple [ɛgzɑ̃pl(ə)] *nm* example; **par exemple** for instance, for example; (*valeur intensive*) really!; **sans exemple** (*bêtise, gourmandise etc*) unparalleled; **donner l'exemple** to set an example; **prendre exemple sur** to take as a model; **à l'exemple de** just like; **pour l'exemple** (*punir*) as an example

exempt, e [ɛgzɑ̃, -ɑ̃t] *adj*: **exempt de** (*dispensé de*) exempt from; (*sans*) free from; **exempt de taxes** tax-free

exercer [ɛgzɛʀse] *vt* (*pratiquer*) to exercise, practise; (*faire usage de: prérogative*) to exercise; (*effectuer: influence, contrôle, pression*) to exert; (*former*) to exercise, train ♦ *vi* (*médecin*) to be in practice; **s'exercer** (*sportif, musicien*) to practise; (*se faire sentir: pression etc*): **s'exercer (sur** ou **contre)** to be exerted (on); **s'exercer à faire qch** to train o.s. to do sth

exercice [ɛgzɛʀsis] *nm* practice; exercising; (*tâche,*

travail) exercise; (*COMM, ADMIN: période*) accounting period; **l'exercice** (*sportive etc*) exercise; (*MIL*) drill; **en exercice** (*juge*) in office; (*médecin*) practising; **dans l'exercice de ses fonctions** in the discharge of his duties; **exercices d'assouplissement** limbering-up (exercises)

exhaustif, ive [ɛgzostif, -iv] *adj* exhaustive

exhiber [ɛgzibe] *vt* (*montrer: papiers, certificat*) to present, produce; (*péj*) to display, flaunt; **s'exhiber** (*personne*) to parade; (*exhibitionniste*) to expose o.s.

exhibitionniste [ɛgzibisjɔnist(ə)] *nm/f* exhibitionist

exhorter [ɛgzɔʀte] *vt*: **exhorter qn à faire** to urge sb to do

exigeant, e [ɛgziʒɑ̃, -ɑ̃t] *adj* demanding; (*péj*) hard to please

exigence [ɛgziʒɑ̃s] *nf* demand, requirement

exiger [ɛgziʒe] *vt* to demand, require

exigu, ë [ɛgzigy] *adj* cramped, tiny

exil [ɛgzil] *nm* exile; **en exil** in exile

exiler [ɛgzile] *vt* to exile; **s'exiler** to go into exile

existence [ɛgzistɑ̃s] *nf* existence; **dans l'existence** in life

exister [ɛgziste] *vi* to exist; **il existe un/des** there is a/are (some)

exonérer [ɛgzɔneʀe] *vt*: **exonérer de** to exempt from

exorbitant, e [ɛgzɔʀbitɑ̃, -ɑ̃t] *adj* exorbitant

exorbité, e [ɛgzɔʀbite] *adj*: **yeux exorbités** bulging eyes

exotique [ɛgzɔtik] *adj* exotic

expatrier [ɛkspatʀije] *vt* (*argent*) to take ou send out of the country; **s'expatrier** to leave one's country

expectative [ɛkspɛktativ] *nf*: **être dans l'expectative** to be waiting to see

expédient [ɛkspedjɑ̃] *nm* (*parfois péj*) expedient; **vivre d'expédients** to live by one's wits

expédier [ɛkspedje] *vt* (*lettre, paquet*) to send; (*troupes, renfort*) to dispatch; (*péj: travail etc*) to dispose of, dispatch

expéditeur, trice [ɛkspeditœʀ, -tʀis] *nm/f* (*POSTES*) sender

expédition [ɛkspedisjɔ̃] *nf* sending; (*scientifique, sportive, MIL*) expedition; **expédition punitive** punitive raid

expérience [ɛkspeʀjɑ̃s] *nf* (*de la vie, des choses*) experience; (*scientifique*) experiment; **avoir de l'expérience** to have experience, be experienced; **avoir l'expérience de** to have experience of; **faire l'expérience de qch** to experience sth; **expérience de chimie/d'électricité** chemical/electrical experiment

expérimenté, e [ɛkspeʀimɑ̃te] *adj* experienced

expérimenter [ɛkspeʀimɑ̃te] *vt* (*machine, technique*) to test out, experiment with

expert, e [ɛkspɛʀ, -ɛʀt(ə)] *adj*: **expert en** expert in ◆ *nm* (*spécialiste*) expert; **expert en assurances** insurance valuer

expert-comptable, *pl* **experts-comptables** [ɛkspɛʀkɔ̃tabl(ə)] *nm* = chartered (*BRIT*) *ou* certified public (*US*) accountant

expertise [ɛkspɛʀtiz] *nf* valuation; assessment; valuer's (*ou* assessor's) report; (*JUR*) (forensic) examination

expertiser [ɛkspɛʀtize] *vt* (*objet de valeur*) to value; (*voiture accidentée etc*) to assess damage to

expier [ɛkspje] *vt* to expiate, atone for

expirer [ɛkspiʀe] *vi* (*prendre fin, littéraire: mourir*) to expire; (*respirer*) to breathe out

explicatif, ive [ɛksplikatif, -iv] *adj* (*mot, texte, note*) explanatory

explication [ɛksplikasjɔ̃] *nf* explanation; (*discussion*) discussion; **explication de texte** (*SCOL*) critical analysis (of a text)

explicite [ɛksplisit] *adj* explicit

expliquer [ɛksplike] *vt* to explain; **expliquer (à qn)** to point out *ou* explain (to sb) how/that; **s'expliquer** (*se faire comprendre: personne*) to explain o.s.; (*discuter*) to discuss things; (*se disputer*) to have it out; (*comprendre*) **je m'explique son retard/absence** I understand his lateness/absence; **son erreur s'explique** one can understand his mistake

exploit [ɛksplwa] *nm* exploit, feat

exploitant [ɛksplwatɑ̃] *nm* farmer

exploitation [ɛksplwatasjɔ̃] *nf* exploitation; running; (*entreprise*): **exploitation agricole** farming concern

exploiter [ɛksplwate] *vt* to exploit; (*entreprise, ferme*) to run, operate

explorer [ɛksplɔʀe] *vt* to explore

exploser [ɛksploze] *vi* to explode, blow up; (*engin explosif*) to go off; (*fig: joie, colère*) to burst out, explode; (: *personne: de colère*) to explode, flare up; **faire exploser** (*bombe*) to explode, detonate; (*bâtiment, véhicule*) to blow up

explosif, ive [ɛksplozif, -iv] *adj, nm* explosive

explosion [ɛksplozjɔ̃] *nf* explosion; **explosion de joie/colère** outburst of joy/rage; **explosion démographique** population explosion

exportateur, trice [ɛkspɔʀtatœʀ, -tʀis] *adj* exporting ◆ *nm* exporter

exportation [ɛkspɔʀtasjɔ̃] *nf* export

exporter [ɛkspɔʀte] *vt* to export

exposant [ɛkspozɑ̃] *nm* exhibitor; (*MATH*) exponent

exposé, e [ɛkspoze] *nm* (*écrit*) exposé; (*oral*) talk ◆ *adj*: **exposé au sud** facing south, with a southern aspect; **bien exposé** well situated; **très exposé** very exposed

exposer [ɛkspoze] *vt* (*montrer: marchandise*) to display; (: *peinture*) to exhibit, show; (*parler de: problème, situation*) to explain, expose, set out; (*mettre en danger, orienter: maison etc*) to expose; **exposer qn/qch à** to expose sb/sth to; **exposer sa vie** to risk one's life; **s'exposer à** (*soleil, danger*) to expose o.s. to; (*critiques, punition*) to lay o.s. open to

exposition [ɛkspozisjɔ̃] *nf* (*voir exposer*) displaying; exhibiting; explanation, exposition; exposure; (*voir exposé*) aspect, situation; (*manifestation*) exhibition; (*PHOTO*) exposure; (*introduction*) exposition

exprès [ɛkspʀɛ] *adv* (*délibérément*) on purpose; (*spécialement*) specially; **faire exprès de faire qch** to do sth on purpose

exprès, esse [ɛkspʀɛs] *adj* (*ordre, défense*) express, formal ◆ *adj inv, adv* (*POSTES*) express; **envoyer qch en exprès** to send sth express

express [ɛkspʀɛs] *adj, nm*: **(café) express** espresso; **(train) express** fast train

expressément [ɛkspʀɛsemɑ̃] *adv* expressly, specifically

expressif, ive [ɛkspʀesif, -iv] *adj* expressive

expression [ɛkspʀesjɔ̃] *nf* expression; **réduit à sa plus simple expression** reduced to its simplest terms; **liberté/moyens d'expression** freedom/means of expression; **expression toute faite** set phrase

exprimer [ɛkspʀime] *vt* (*sentiment, idée*) to express; (*faire sortir: jus, liquide*) to press out; **s'exprimer** *vi* (*personne*) to express o.s.

exproprier [ɛkspʀɔpʀije] *vt* to buy up (*ou* buy the property of) by compulsory purchase, expropriate

expulser [ɛkspylse] *vt* (*d'une salle, d'un groupe*) to expel; (*locataire*) to evict; (*FOOTBALL*) to send off

exquis, e [ɛkski, -iz] *adj* (*gâteau, parfum, élégance*) exquisite; (*personne, temps*) delightful

extase [ɛkstaz] *nf* ecstasy; **être en extase** to be in raptures

extasier [ɛkstazje]: **s'extasier** *vi*: **s'extasier sur** to go into raptures over

extension [ɛkstɑ̃sjɔ̃] *nf* (*d'un muscle, ressort*): stretching; (*MÉD*): **à l'extension** in traction; (*fig*) extension; expansion

exténuer [ɛkstenɥe] *vt* to exhaust

extérieur, e [ɛksteʀjœʀ] *adj* (*de dehors: porte, mur etc*) outer, outside; (: *commerce, politique*) foreign; (: *influences, pressions*) external; (*au dehors: escalier, w.-c.*) outside; (*apparent: calme, gaieté etc*) outer ◆ *nm* (*d'une maison, d'un récipient etc*) outside, exterior; (*d'une personne: apparence*) exterior; (*d'un pays, d'un groupe social*): **l'extérieur** the outside world; **à l'extérieur** (*dehors*) outside; (*fig: à l'étranger*) abroad

extérieurement [ɛksteʀjœʀmɑ̃] *adv* (*de dehors*) on the outside; (*en apparence*) on the surface

exterminer [ɛkstɛʀmine] *vt* to exterminate, wipe out

externat [ɛkstɛʀna] *nm* day school

externe [ɛkstɛʀn(ə)] *adj* external, outer ◆ *nm/f* (*MÉD*) non-resident medical student, extern (*US*); (*SCOL*) day pupil

extincteur [ɛkstɛ̃ktœʀ] *nm* (fire) extinguisher

extinction [ɛkstɛ̃ksjɔ̃] *nf* extinction; (*JUR: d'une dette*) extinguishment; **extinction de voix** (*MÉD*) loss of voice

extorquer [ɛkstɔʀke] *vt* (*de l'argent, un renseignement*): **extorquer qch à qn** to extort sth from sb

extra [ɛkstʀa] *adj inv* first-rate; (*marchandises*) top-quality ♦ *nm inv* extra help ♦ *préfixe* extra(-)

extrader [ɛkstʀade] *vt* to extradite

extraire [ɛkstʀɛʀ] *vt* to extract

extrait, e [ɛkstʀɛ, -ɛt] *pp de* **extraire** ♦ *nm* (*de plante*) extract; (*de film, livre*) extract, excerpt; **extrait de naissance** birth certificate

extraordinaire [ɛkstʀaɔʀdinɛʀ] *adj* extraordinary; (*POL, ADMIN*) special; **ambassadeur extraordinaire** ambassador extraordinary; **assemblée extraordinaire** extraordinary meeting; **par extraordinaire** by some unlikely chance

extravagant, e [ɛkstʀavagɑ̃, -ɑ̃t] *adj* (*personne, attitude*) extravagant; (*idée*) wild

extraverti, e [ɛkstʀavɛʀti] *adj* extrovert

extrême [ɛkstʀɛm] *adj, nm* extreme; (*intensif*): **d'une extrême simplicité/brutalité** extremely simple/brutal; **d'un extrême à l'autre** from one extreme to another; **à l'extrême** in the extreme; **à l'extrême rigueur** in the absolute extreme

extrêmement [ɛkstʀɛmmɑ̃] *adv* extremely

extrême-onction, *pl* **extrêmes-onctions** [ɛkstʀɛmɔ̃ksjɔ̃] *nf* (*REL*) last rites *pl*, Extreme Unction

Extrême-Orient [ɛkstʀɛmɔʀjɑ̃] *nm*: **l'Extrême-Orient** the Far East

extrémité [ɛkstʀemite] *nf* (*bout*) end; (*situation*) straits *pl*, plight; (*geste désespéré*) extreme action; **extrémités** *nfpl* (*pieds et mains*) extremities; **à la dernière extrémité** (*à l'agonie*) on the point of death

exubérant, e [ɛgzybeʀɑ̃, -ɑ̃t] *adj* exuberant

exutoire [ɛgzytwaʀ] *nm* outlet, release

— **F f** —

F, f [ɛf] *nm inv* F, f ♦ *abr* = **féminin**; (= *franc*) fr.; (= *Fahrenheit*) F; (= *frère*) Br(o).; (= *femme*) W; (*appartement*): **un F2/F3** a 2-/3-roomed flat (*BRIT*) *ou* apartment (*US*); **F comme François** F for Frederick (*BRIT*) *ou* Fox (*US*)

fa [fa] *nm inv* (*MUS*) F; (*en chantant la gamme*) fa

fable [fabl(ə)] *nf* fable; (*mensonge*) story, tale

fabricant [fabʀikɑ̃] *nm* manufacturer, maker

fabrication [fabʀikasjɔ̃] *nf* manufacture, making

fabrique [fabʀik] *nf* factory

fabriquer [fabʀike] *vt* to make; (*industriellement*) to manufacture, make; (*construire: voiture*) to manufacture, build; (: *maison*) to build; (*fig: inventer: histoire, alibi*) to make up; (*fam*): **qu'est-ce qu'il fabrique?** what is he up to?; **fabriquer en série** to mass-produce

fabulation [fabylasjɔ̃] *nf* (*PSYCH*) fantasizing

fac [fak] *abr f* (*fam:* = *faculté*) Uni (*BRIT fam*), ≈ college (*US*)

façade [fasad] *nf* front, façade; (*fig*) façade

face [fas] *nf* face; (*fig: aspect*) side ♦ *adj*: **le côté face** heads; **perdre/sauver la face** to lose/save face; **regarder qn en face** to look sb in the face; **la maison/le trottoir d'en face** the house/pavement opposite; **en face de** *prép* opposite; (*fig*) in front of; **de face** *adv* from the front; face on; **face à** *prép* facing; (*fig*) faced with, in the face of; **faire face à** to face; **faire face à la demande** (*COMM*) to meet the demand; **face à face** *adv* facing each other ♦ *nm inv* encounter

fâché, e [fɑʃe] *adj* angry; (*désolé*) sorry

fâcher [fɑʃe] *vt* to anger; **se fâcher** *vi* to get angry; **se fâcher avec** (*se brouiller*) to fall out with

fâcheux, euse [fɑʃø, -øz] *adj* unfortunate, regrettable

facile [fasil] *adj* easy; (*accommodant*) easy-going; **facile d'emploi** (*INFORM*) user-friendly

facilement [fasilmɑ̃] *adv* easily

facilité [fasilite] *nf* easiness; (*disposition, don*) aptitude; (*moyen, occasion, possibilité*): **il a la facilité de rencontrer les gens** he has every opportunity to meet people; **facilités** *nfpl* facilities; (*COMM*) terms; **facilités de crédit** credit terms; **facilités de paiement** easy terms

faciliter [fasilite] *vt* to make easier

façon [fasɔ̃] *nf* (*manière*) way; (*d'une robe etc*) making-up; cut; (*d'une œuvre*) labour (*BRIT*), labor (*US*); (*imitation*): **châle façon cachemire** cashmere-style shawl; **façons** *nfpl* (*péj*) fuss *sg*; **faire des façons** (*péj: être affecté*) to be affected; (: *faire des histoires*) to make a fuss; **de quelle façon?** (in) what way?; **sans façon** *adv* without fuss ♦ *adj* unaffected; **d'une autre façon** in another way; **en aucune façon** in no way; **de façon à** so as to; **de façon à ce que, de (telle) façon que** so that; **de toute façon** anyway, in any case; **(c'est une) façon de parler** it's a way of putting it; **travail à façon** tailoring

façonner [fasɔne] *vt* (*fabriquer*) to manufacture; (*travailler: matière*) to shape, fashion; (*fig*) to mould, shape

facteur, trice [faktœʀ, -tʀis] *nm/f* postman/woman (*BRIT*), mailman/woman (*US*) ♦ *nm* (*MATH, gén*) factor; **facteur d'orgues** organ builder; **facteur de pianos** piano maker; **facteur rhésus** rhesus factor

factice [faktis] *adj* artificial

faction [faksjɔ̃] *nf* (*groupe*) faction; (*MIL*) guard *ou* sentry (duty); watch; **en faction** on guard; standing watch

facture [faktyʀ] *nf* (*à payer: gén*) bill; (: *COMM*) invoice; (*d'un artisan, artiste*) technique, workmanship

facturer [faktyʀe] *vt* to invoice

facultatif, ive [fakyltatif, -iv] *adj* optional; (*arrêt de bus*) request *cpd*

faculté [fakylte] *nf* (*intellectuelle, d'université*) faculty; (*pouvoir, possibilité*) power

fade [fad] *adj* insipid

fagot [fago] *nm* (*de bois*) bundle of sticks

faible [fɛbl(ə)] *adj* weak; (*voix, lumière, vent*) faint; (*élève, copie*) poor; (*rendement, intensité, revenu etc*) low ♦ *nm* weak point; (*pour quelqu'un*) weakness, soft spot; **faible d'esprit** feeble-minded

faiblesse [fɛbles] *nf* weakness

faiblir [fɛbliʀ] *vi* to weaken; (*lumière*) to dim; (*vent*) to drop

faïence [fajɑ̃s] *nf* earthenware *no pl*; (*objet*) piece of earthenware

faignant, e [fɛɲɑ̃, -ɑ̃t] *nm/f* = **fainéant, e**

faille [faj] *vb voir* **falloir** ♦ *nf* (GÉO) fault; (*fig*) flaw, weakness

faillir [fajiʀ] *vi:* **j'ai failli tomber/lui dire** I almost *ou* nearly fell/told him; **faillir à une promesse/un engagement** to break a promise/an agreement

faillite [fajit] *nf* bankruptcy; (*échec: d'une politique etc*) collapse; **être en faillite** to be bankrupt; **faire faillite** to go bankrupt

faim [fɛ̃] *nf* hunger; (*fig*): **faim d'amour/de richesse** hunger *ou* yearning for love/wealth; **avoir faim** to be hungry; **rester sur sa faim** (*aussi fig*) to be left wanting more

fainéant, e [fɛneɑ̃, -ɑ̃t] *nm/f* idler, loafer

MOT CLÉ

---

faire [fɛʀ] *vt* **1** (*fabriquer, être l'auteur de*) to make; (*produire*) to produce; (*construire: maison, bateau*) to build; **faire du vin/une offre/un film** to make wine/an offer/a film; **faire du bruit** to make a noise

2 (*effectuer: travail, opération*) to do; **que faites-vous?** (*quel métier etc*) what do you do?; (*quelle activité: au moment de la question*) what are you doing?; **que faire?** what are we going to do?, what can be done (about it)?; **faire la lessive/le ménage** to do the washing/the housework

3 (*études*) (*sport, musique*) to play; **faire du droit/du français** to do law/French; **faire du rugby/piano** to play rugby/the piano; **faire du cheval/du ski** to go riding/skiing

4 (*visiter*): **faire les magasins** to go shopping; **faire l'Europe** to tour *ou* do Europe

5 (*simuler*): **faire le malade/l'ignorant** to act the invalid/the fool

6 (*transformer, avoir un effet sur*): **faire de qn un frustré/avocat** to make sb frustrated/a lawyer; **ça ne me fait rien** (*m'est égal*) I don't care *ou* mind; (*me laisse froid*) it has no effect on me; **ça ne fait rien** it doesn't matter; **faire que** (*impliquer*) to mean that

7 (*calculs, prix, mesures*): **2 et 2 font 4** 2 and 2 are *ou* make 4; **ça fait 10 m/15F** it's 10 m/15F; **je vous le fais 10F** I'll let you have it for 10F

8 (*vb +de*): **qu'a-t-il fait de sa valise/de sa sœur?** what has he done with his case/his sister?

9: **ne faire que, il ne fait que critiquer** (*sans cesse*) all he (ever) does is criticize; (*seulement*) he's only criticizing

10 (*dire*) to say; **vraiment? fit-il** really? he said

11 (*maladie*) to have; **faire du diabète/de la tension** to have diabetes *sg*/high blood pressure

♦ *vi* **1** (*agir, s'y prendre*) to act, do; **il faut faire vite** we (*ou* you etc) must act quickly; **comment a-t-il fait pour?** how did he manage to?; **faites comme chez vous** make yourself at home; **je n'ai pas pu faire autrement** there was nothing else I could do

2 (*paraître*) to look; **faire vieux/démodé** to look old/old-fashioned; **ça fait bien** it looks good; **tu fais jeune dans cette robe** that dress makes you look young(er)

♦ *vb substitut* to do; **ne le casse pas comme je l'ai fait** don't break it as I did; **je peux le voir? – faites!** can I see it? – please do!; **remets-le en place – je viens de le faire** put it back in its place – I just have (done)

♦ *vb impers* **1**: **il fait beau** *etc* the weather is fine *etc*; *voir aussi* **jour**; **froid** *etc*

2 (*temps écoulé, durée*): **ça fait 2 ans qu'il est parti** it's 2 years since he left; **ça fait 2 ans qu'il y est** he's been there for 2 years

♦ *vb semi-aux* **1**: **faire** + *infinitif* (*action directe*) to make; **faire tomber/bouger qch** to make sth fall/move; **faire démarrer un moteur/chauffer de l'eau** to start up an engine/heat some water; **cela fait dormir** it makes you sleep; **faire travailler les enfants** to make the children work *ou* get the children to work; **il m'a fait traverser la rue** he helped me to cross the road

2 (*indirectement, par un intermédiaire*): **faire réparer qch** to get *ou* have sth repaired; **faire punir les enfants** to have the children punished; **il m'a fait ouvrir la porte** he got me to open the door;

se faire *vi* **1** (*vin, fromage*) to mature

2: **cela se fait beaucoup/ne se fait pas** it's done a lot/not done

3 (+*nom ou pron*): **se faire une jupe** to make o.s. a skirt; **se faire des amis** to make friends; **se faire du souci** to worry; **se faire des illusions** to delude o.s.; **se faire beaucoup d'argent** to make a lot of money; **il ne s'en fait pas** he doesn't worry

4 (+*adj*) (*devenir*): **se faire vieux** to be getting old; (*délibérément*): **se faire beau** to do o.s. up

5: **se faire à** (*s'habituer*) to get used to; **je n'arrive pas à me faire à la nourriture/au climat** I can't get used to the food/climate

6 (+*infinitif*): **se faire examiner la vue/opérer** to have one's eyes tested/have an operation; **se**

faire couper les cheveux to get one's hair cut; **il va se faire tuer/punir** he's going to get himself killed/get (himself) punished; **il s'est fait aider** he got somebody to help him; **il s'est fait aider par Simon** he got Simon to help him; **se faire faire un vêtement** to get a garment made for o.s.

7 (*impersonnel*): **comment se fait-il/faisait-il que?** how is it/was it that?; **il peut se faire que nous utilisions ...** it's possible that we could use ...

faire-part [fɛʀpaʀ] *nm inv* announcement (*of birth, marriage etc*)

faisable [fəzabl(ə)] *adj* feasible

faisan, e [fəzɑ̃, -an] *nm/f* pheasant

faisandé, e [fəzɑ̃de] *adj* high (*bad*); (*fig péj*) corrupt, decadent

faisceau, x [fɛso] *nm* (*de lumière etc*) beam; (*de branches etc*) bundle

faisons *etc* [fəzɔ̃] *vb voir* **faire**

fait¹ [fɛ] *vb voir* **faire** ♦ *nm* (*événement*) event, occurrence; (*réalité, donnée*) fact; **le fait que/de manger** the fact that/of eating; **être le fait de** (*causé par*) to be the work of; **être au fait (de)** to be informed (of); **mettre qn au fait** to inform sb, put sb in the picture; **au fait** (*à propos*) by the way; **en venir au fait** to get to the point; **de fait** *adj* (*opposé à: de droit*) de facto; *adv* in fact; **du fait de ceci/qu'il a menti** because of *ou* on account of this/his having lied; **de ce fait** therefore, for this reason; **en fait** in fact; **en fait de repas** by way of a meal; **prendre fait et cause pour qn** to support sb, side with sb; **prendre qn sur le fait** to catch sb in the act; **dire à qn son fait** to give sb a piece of one's mind; **hauts faits** (*exploits*) exploits; **fait d'armes** feat of arms; **fait divers** (short) news item; **les faits et gestes de qn** sb's actions *ou* doings

fait², e [fɛ, fɛt] *pp de* **faire** ♦ *adj* (*mûr: fromage, melon*) ripe; (*maquillé: yeux*) made-up; (*vernis: ongles*) painted, polished; **un homme fait** a grown man; **tout(e) fait(e)** (*préparé à l'avance*) ready-made; **c'en est fait de notre tranquillité** that's the end of our peace; **c'est bien fait (pour lui *ou* eux *etc*)** it serves him (*ou* them *etc*) right

faîte [fɛt] *nm* top; (*fig*) pinnacle, height

faites [fɛt] *vb voir* **faire**

faitout [fɛtu] *nm* stewpot

falaise [falɛz] *nf* cliff

falloir [falwaʀ] *vb impers*: **il faut faire les lits** we (*ou* you *etc*) have to *ou* must make the beds; **il faut que je fasse les lits** I have to *ou* must make the beds; **il a fallu qu'il parte** he had to leave; **il faudrait qu'elle rentre** she ought to go home; **il va falloir 15 €** we'll (*ou* I'll *etc*) need 15 €; **il doit falloir du temps** that must take time; **il vous faut tourner à gauche après l'église** you have to turn left past the church; **nous avons ce qu'il (nous)**

faut we have what we need; **il faut qu'il ait oublié** he must have forgotten; **il a fallu qu'il l'apprenne** he would have to hear about it; **il ne fallait pas** (*pour remercier*) you shouldn't have (done); **faut le faire!** (it) takes some doing! ♦ *vi*: **s'en falloir, il s'en est fallu de 100 €/5 minutes** we (*ou* they *etc*) were 100 € short/5 minutes late (*ou* early); **il s'en faut de beaucoup qu'il soit ...** he is far from being ...; **il s'en est fallu de peu que cela n'arrive** it very nearly happened; **ou peu s'en faut** or just about, or as good as; **comme il faut** *adj* proper, *adv* properly

falsifier [falsifje] *vt* to falsify

famé, e [fame] *adj*: **mal famé** disreputable, of ill repute

famélique [famelik] *adj* half-starved

fameux, euse [famø, -øz] *adj* (*illustre: parfois péj*) famous; (*bon: repas, plat etc*) first-rate, first-class; (*intensif*): **un fameux problème** *etc* a real problem *etc*; **pas fameux** not great, not much good

familial, e, aux [familjal, -o] *adj* family *cpd* ♦ *nf* (*AUTO*) family estate car (*BRIT*), station wagon (*US*)

familiarité [familjaʀite] *nf* familiarity; informality; **familiarités** *nfpl* familiarities; **familiarité avec** (*sujet, science*) familiarity with

familier, ière [familje, -jɛʀ] *adj* (*connu, impertinent*) familiar; (*dénotant une certaine intimité*) informal, friendly; (*LING*) informal, colloquial ♦ *nm* regular (visitor)

famille [famij] *nf* family; **il a de la famille à Paris** he has relatives in Paris

famine [famin] *nf* famine

fana [fana] *adj, nm/f* (*fam*) = **fanatique**

fanatique [fanatik] *adj*: **fanatique (de)** fanatical (about) ♦ *nm/f* fanatic

fanatisme [fanatism(ə)] *nm* fanaticism

faner [fane]: **se faner** *vi* to fade

fanfare [fɑ̃faʀ] *nf* (*orchestre*) brass band; (*musique*) fanfare; **en fanfare** (*avec bruit*) noisily

fanfaron, ne [fɑ̃faʀɔ̃, -ɔn] *nm/f* braggart

fantaisie [fɑ̃tezi] *nf* (*spontanéité*) fancy, imagination; (*caprice*) whim; extravagance; (*MUS*) fantasia ♦ *adj*: **bijou (de) fantaisie** (piece of) costume jewellery (*BRIT*) *ou* jewelry (*US*); **pain (de) fantaisie** fancy bread

fantaisiste [fɑ̃tezist(ə)] *adj* (*péj*) unorthodox, eccentric ♦ *nm/f* (*de music-hall*) variety artist *ou* entertainer

fantasme [fɑ̃tasm(ə)] *nm* fantasy

fantasque [fɑ̃task(ə)] *adj* whimsical, capricious; fantastic

fantastique [fɑ̃tastik] *adj* fantastic

fantôme [fɑ̃tom] *nm* ghost, phantom

faon [fɑ̃] *nm* fawn (*deer*)

farce [faʀs(ə)] *nf* (*viande*) stuffing; (*blague*) (practical) joke; (*THÉÂT*) farce; **faire une farce à qn** to play a (practical) joke on sb; **farces et attrapes** jokes and novelties

farcir [faʀsiʀ] *vt* (*viande*) to stuff; (*fig*): **farcir qch de** to stuff sth with; **se farcir** (*fam*): **je me suis farci la vaisselle** I've got stuck *ou* landed with the washing-up

fardeau, x [faʀdo] *nm* burden

farder [faʀde] *vt* to make up; (*vérité*) to disguise; **se farder** to make o.s. up

farfelu, e [faʀfəly] *adj* wacky (*fam*), hare-brained

farine [faʀin] *nf* flour; **farine de blé** wheatflour; **farine de maïs** cornflour (*BRIT*), cornstarch (*US*); **farine lactée** (*pour bouillie*) baby cereal

farineux, euse [faʀinø, -øz] *adj* (*sauce, pomme*) floury ♦ *nmpl* (*aliments*) starchy foods

farouche [faʀuʃ] *adj* shy, timid; (*sauvage*) savage, wild; (*violent*) fierce

fart [faʀ(t)] *nm* (ski) wax

fascicule [fasikyl] *nm* volume

fascination [fasinɑsjɔ̃] *nf* fascination

fasciner [fasine] *vt* to fascinate

fascisme [faʃism(ə)] *nm* fascism

fasse *etc* [fas] *vb voir* **faire**

faste [fast(ə)] *nm* splendour (*BRIT*), splendor (*US*) ♦ *adj*: **c'est un jour faste** it's his (*ou* our *etc*) lucky day

fastidieux, euse [fastidjø, -øz] *adj* tedious, tiresome

fastueux, euse [fastɥø, -øz] *adj* sumptuous, luxurious

fatal, e [fatal] *adj* fatal; (*inévitable*) inevitable

fatalité [fatalite] *nf* (*destin*) fate; (*coïncidence*) fateful coincidence; (*caractère inévitable*) inevitability

fatidique [fatidik] *adj* fateful

fatigant, e [fatigɑ̃, -ɑ̃t] *adj* tiring; (*agaçant*) tiresome

fatigue [fatig] *nf* tiredness, fatigue; (*détérioration*) fatigue; **les fatigues du voyage** the wear and tear of the journey

fatigué, e [fatige] *adj* tired

fatiguer [fatige] *vt* to tire, make tired; (*TECH*) to put a strain on, strain; (*fig: importuner*) to wear out ♦ *vi* (*moteur*) to labour (*BRIT*), labor (*US*), strain; **se fatiguer** *vi* to get tired; to tire o.s. (out); **se fatiguer à faire qch** to tire o.s. out doing sth

fatras [fatʀa] *nm* jumble, hotchpotch

faubourg [fobuʀ] *nm* suburb

fauché, e [foʃe] *adj* (*fam*) broke

faucher [foʃe] *vt* (*herbe*) to cut; (*champs, blés*) to reap; (*fig*) to cut down; to mow down; (*fam: voler*) to pinch, nick

faucille [fosij] *nf* sickle

faucon [fokɔ̃] *nm* falcon, hawk

faudra *etc* [fodʀa] *vb voir* **falloir**

faufiler [fofile] *vt* to tack, baste; **se faufiler** *vi*: **se faufiler dans** to edge one's way into; **se faufiler parmi/entre** to thread one's way among/between

faune [fon] *nf* (*ZOOL*) wildlife, fauna; (*fig péj*) set, crowd ♦ *nm* faun; **faune marine** marine (animal) life

faussaire [fosɛʀ] *nm/f* forger

fausse [fos] *adj f voir* **faux²**

faussement [fosmɑ̃] *adv* (*accuser*) wrongly, wrongfully; (*croire*) falsely, erroneously

fausser [fose] *vt* (*objet*) to bend, buckle; (*fig*) to distort; **fausser compagnie à qn** to give sb the slip

faut [fo] *vb voir* **falloir**

faute [fot] *nf* (*erreur*) mistake, error; (*péché, manquement*) misdemeanour; (*FOOTBALL etc*) offence; (*TENNIS*) fault; (*responsabilité*): **par la faute de** through the fault of, because of; **c'est de sa/ma faute** it's his/my fault; **être en faute** to be in the wrong; **prendre qn en faute** to catch sb out; **faute de** (*temps, argent*) for *ou* through lack of; **faute de mieux** for want of anything *ou* something better; **sans faute** *adv* without fail; **faute de frappe** typing error; **faute d'inattention** careless mistake; **faute d'orthographe** spelling mistake; **faute professionnelle** professional misconduct *no pl*

fauteuil [fotœj] *nm* armchair; **fauteuil à bascule** rocking chair; **fauteuil club** (big) easy chair; **fauteuil d'orchestre** seat in the front stalls (*BRIT*) *ou* the orchestra (*US*); **fauteuil roulant** wheelchair

fauteur [fotœʀ] *nm*: **fauteur de troubles** trouble-maker

fautif, ive [fotif, -iv] *adj* (*incorrect*) incorrect, inaccurate; (*responsable*) at fault, in the wrong; (*coupable*) guilty ♦ *nm/f* culprit

fauve [fov] *nm* wildcat; (*peintre*) Fauve ♦ *adj* (*couleur*) fawn

faux¹ [fo] *nf* scythe

faux², fausse [fo, fos] *adj* (*inexact*) wrong; (*piano, voix*) out of tune; (*falsifié*) fake, forged; (*sournois, postiche*) false ♦ *adv* (*MUS*) out of tune ♦ *nm* (*copie*) fake, forgery; (*opposé au vrai*): **le faux** falsehood; **le faux numéro/la fausse clé** the wrong number/key; **faire fausse route** to go the wrong way; **faire faux bond à qn** to let sb down; **faux ami** (*LING*) faux ami; **faux col** detachable collar; **faux départ** (*SPORT, fig*) false start; **faux frais** *nmpl* extras, incidental expenses; **faux frère** (*fig péj*) false friend; **faux mouvement** awkward movement; **faux nez** false nose; **faux nom** assumed name; **faux pas** tripping *no pl*; (*fig*) faux pas; **faux témoignage** (*délit*) perjury; **fausse alerte** false alarm; **fausse clé** skeleton key; **fausse couche** (*MÉD*) miscarriage; **fausse joie** vain joy; **fausse note** wrong note

faux-filet [fofile] *nm* sirloin

faux-monnayeur [fomɔnejœʀ] *nm* counterfeiter, forger

faveur [favœʀ] *nf* favour (*BRIT*), favor (*US*); **traitement de faveur** preferential treatment; **à la faveur de** under cover of; (*grâce à*) thanks to; **en faveur de** in favo(u)r of

favorable [favɔʀabl(ə)] *adj* favo(u)rable

favori, te [favɔʀi, -it] *adj*, *nm/f* favo(u)rite

favoriser [favɔʀize] *vt* to favour (*BRIT*), favor (*US*)

fax [faks] *nm* fax

FB *abr* (= *franc belge*) BF, FB

fébrile [febʀil] *adj* feverish, febrile; **capitaux fébriles** (*ÉCON*) hot money

fécond, e [fekɔ̃, -ɔ̃d] *adj* fertile

féconder [fekɔ̃de] *vt* to fertilize

fécondité [fekɔ̃dite] *nf* fertility

fécule [fekyl] *nf* potato flour

féculent [fekylɑ̃] *nm* starchy food

fédéral, e, aux [federal, -o] *adj* federal

fée [fe] *nf* fairy

féerique [feʀik] *adj* magical, fairytale *cpd*

feignant, e [fɛɲɑ̃, -ɑ̃t] *nm/f* = **fainéant, e**

feindre [fɛ̃dʀ(ə)] *vt* to feign ♦ *vi* to dissemble; **feindre de faire** to pretend to do

feint, e [fɛ̃, fɛ̃t] *pp de* **feindre** ♦ *adj* feigned ♦ *nf* (*SPORT: escrime*) feint; (: *football, rugby*) dummy (*BRIT*), fake (*US*); (*fam: ruse*) sham

fêler [fele] *vt* to crack

félicitations [felisitasjɔ̃] *nfpl* congratulations

féliciter [felisite] *vt*: **féliciter qn (de)** to congratulate sb (on)

félin, e [felɛ̃, -in] *adj* feline ♦ *nm* (big) cat

fêlure [felyʀ] *nf* crack

femelle [fəmɛl] *adj* (*aussi ÉLEC, TECH*) female ♦ *nf* female

féminin, e [feminɛ̃, -in] *adj* feminine; (*sexe*) female; (*équipe, vêtements etc*) women's; (*parfois péj: homme*) effeminate ♦ *nm* (*LING*) feminine

féministe [feminist(ə)] *adj, nf* feminist

femme [fam] *nf* woman; (*épouse*) wife (*pl* wives); **être très femme** to be very much a woman; **devenir femme** to attain womanhood; **femme d'affaires** businesswoman; **femme de chambre** chambermaid; **femme fatale** femme fatale; **femme au foyer** housewife; **femme d'intérieur** (real) homemaker; **femme de ménage** domestic help, cleaning lady; **femme du monde** society woman; **femme-objet** sex object; **femme de tête** determined, intellectual woman

fémur [femyʀ] *nm* femur, thighbone

fendre [fɑ̃dʀ(ə)] *vt* (*couper en deux*) to split; (*fissurer*) to crack; (*fig: traverser*) to cut through; to push one's way through; **se fendre** *vi* to crack

fenêtre [fənɛtʀ(ə)] *nf* window; **fenêtre à guillotine** sash window

fenouil [fənuj] *nm* fennel

fente [fɑ̃t] *nf* slit; (*fissure*) crack

féodal, e, aux [feɔdal, -o] *adj* feudal

fer [fɛʀ] *nm* iron; (*de cheval*) shoe; **fers** *pl* (*MÉD*) forceps; **mettre aux fers** (*enchaîner*) to put in chains; **au fer rouge** with a red-hot iron; **santé/main de fer** iron constitution/hand; **fer à cheval** horseshoe; **en fer à cheval** (*fig*) horseshoe-shaped; **fer forgé** wrought iron; **fer à friser** curling tongs; **fer de lance** spearhead; **fer (à repasser)** iron; **fer à sou-**der soldering iron

fer-blanc [fɛʀblɑ̃] *nm* tin(plate)

férié, e [feʀje] *adj*: **jour férié** public holiday

ferions *etc* [faʀjɔ̃] *vb voir* **faire**

ferme [fɛʀm(ə)] *adj* firm ♦ *adv* (*travailler etc*) hard; (*discuter*) ardently ♦ *nf* (*exploitation*) farm; (*maison*) farmhouse; **tenir ferme** to stand firm

fermé, e [fɛʀme] *adj* closed, shut; (*gaz, eau etc*) off; (*fig: personne*) uncommunicative; (: *milieu*) exclusive

fermenter [fɛʀmɑ̃te] *vi* to ferment

fermer [fɛʀme] *vt* to close, shut; (*cesser l'exploitation de*) to close down, shut down; (*eau, lumière, électricité, robinet*) to put off, turn off; (*aéroport, route*) to close ♦ *vi* to close, shut; to close down, shut down; **se fermer** *vi* (*yeux*) to close, shut; (*fleur, blessure*) to close up; **fermer à clef** to lock; **fermer au verrou** to bolt; **fermer les yeux (sur qch)** (*fig*) to close one's eyes (to sth); **se fermer à** (*pitié, amour*) to close one's heart ou mind to

fermeté [fɛʀməte] *nf* firmness

fermeture [fɛʀmətyʀ] *nf* (*voir fermer*) closing; shutting; closing ou shutting down; putting ou turning off; (*dispositif*) catch; fastening, fastener; **heure de fermeture** (*COMM*) closing time; **jour de fermeture** (*COMM*) day on which the shop (*etc*) is closed; **fermeture éclair®** ou **à glissière** zip (fastener) (*BRIT*), zipper

fermier, ière [fɛʀmje, -jɛʀ] *nm/f* farmer ♦ *nf* (*femme de fermier*) farmer's wife ♦ *adj*: **beurre/ cidre fermier** farm butter/cider

fermoir [fɛʀmwaʀ] *nm* clasp

féroce [feʀɔs] *adj* ferocious, fierce

ferons *etc* [faʀɔ̃] *vb voir* **faire**

ferraille [feʀɑj] *nf* scrap iron; **mettre à la ferraille** to scrap; **bruit de ferraille** clanking

ferrer [feʀe] *vt* (*cheval*) to shoe; (*chaussure*) to nail; (*canne*) to tip; (*poisson*) to strike

ferronnerie [feʀɔnʀi] *nf* ironwork; **ferronnerie d'art** wrought iron work

ferroviaire [feʀɔvjɛʀ] *adj* rail *cpd*, railway *cpd* (*BRIT*), railroad *cpd* (*US*)

ferry(-boat) [feʀe(bot)] *nm* ferry

fertile [feʀtil] *adj* fertile; **fertile en incidents** eventful, packed with incidents

féru, e [feʀy] *adj*: **féru de** with a keen interest in

fervent, e [fɛʀvɑ̃, -ɑ̃t] *adj* fervent

fesse [fɛs] *nf* buttock; **les fesses** the bottom *sg*, the buttocks

fessée [fese] *nf* spanking

festin [fɛstɛ̃] *nm* feast

festival [fɛstival] *nm* festival

festivités [fɛstivite] *nfpl* festivities, merrymaking *sg*

festoyer [fɛstwaje] *vi* to feast

fêtard [fɛtaʀ] *nm* (*péj*) high liver, merrymaker

fête [fɛt] *nf* (*religieuse*) feast; (*publique*) holiday;

(*en famille etc*) celebration; (*kermesse*) fête, fair, festival; (*du nom*) feast day, name day; **faire la fête** to live it up; **faire fête à qn** to give sb a warm welcome; **se faire une fête de** to look forward to; to enjoy; **ça va être sa fête!** (*fam*) he's going to get it!; **jour de fête** holiday; **les fêtes (de fin d'année)** the festive season; **la salle/le comité des fêtes** the village hall/festival committee; **la fête des Mères/Pères** Mother's/Father's Day; **fête de charité** charity fair *ou* fête; **fête foraine** (fun)fair; **fête mobile** movable feast (day); **la Fête Nationale** the national holiday; *see boxed note*

FÊTE DE LA MUSIQUE

The **fête de la Musique** is a music festival which has taken place every year since 1981. On 21 June throughout France local musicians perform free of charge in parks, streets and squares.

---

fêter [fete] *vt* to celebrate; (*personne*) to have a celebration for

feu, x [fø] *nm* (*gén*) fire; (*signal lumineux*) light; (*de cuisinière*) ring; (*sensation de brûlure*) burning (sensation); **feux** *nmpl* fire *sg*; (*AUTO*) (traffic) lights; **tous feux éteints** (*NAVIG, AUTO*) without lights; **au feu!** (*incendie*) fire!; **à feu doux/vif** over a slow/brisk heat; **à petit feu** (*CULIN*) over a gentle heat; (*fig*) slowly; **faire feu** to fire; **ne pas faire long feu** (*fig*) not to last long; **commander le feu** (*MIL*) to give the order to (open) fire; **tué au feu** (*MIL*) killed in action; **mettre à feu** (*fusée*) to fire off; **pris entre deux feux** caught in the crossfire; **en feu** on fire; **être tout feu tout flamme (pour)** (*passion*) to be aflame with passion (for); (*enthousiasme*) to be fired with enthusiasm (for); **prendre feu** to catch fire; **mettre le feu à** to set fire to, set on fire; **faire du feu** to make a fire; **avez-vous du feu?** (*pour cigarette*) have you (got) a light?; **feu rouge/vert/orange** (*AUTO*) red/green/amber (*BRIT*) *ou* yellow (*US*) light; **donner le feu vert à qch/qn** (*fig*) to give sb/sb the go-ahead *ou* green light; **feu arrière** (*AUTO*) rear light; **feu d'artifice** firework; (*spectacle*) fireworks *pl*; **feu de camp** campfire; **feu de cheminée** chimney fire; **feu de joie** bonfire; **feu de paille** (*fig*) flash in the pan; **feux de brouillard** (*AUTO*) fog lights *ou* lamps; **feux de croisement** (*AUTO*) dipped (*BRIT*) *ou* dimmed (*US*) headlights; **feux de position** (*AUTO*) sidelights; **feux de route** (*AUTO*) headlights (on full (*BRIT*) *ou* high (*US*) beam); **feux de stationnement** parking lights

feuillage [fœjaʒ] *nm* foliage, leaves *pl*

feuille [fœj] *nf* (*d'arbre*) leaf (*pl* leaves); **feuille (de papier)** sheet (of paper); **rendre feuille blanche** (*SCOL*) to give in a blank paper; **feuille d'or/de métal** gold/metal leaf; **feuille de chou** (*péj: journal*) rag; **feuille d'impôts** tax form; **feuille de maladie** medical expenses claim form; **feuille morte**

dead leaf; **feuille de paye** pay slip; **feuille de présence** attendance sheet; **feuille de température** temperature chart; **feuille de vigne** (*BOT*) vine leaf; (*sur statue*) fig leaf; **feuille volante** loose sheet

feuillet [fœjɛ] *nm* leaf (*pl* leaves) page

feuilleté, e [fœjte] *adj* (*CULIN*) flaky; (*verre*) laminated

feuilleter [fœjte] *vt* (*livre*) to leaf through

feuilleton [fœjtɔ̃] *nm* serial

feutre [føtʀ(ə)] *nm* felt; (*chapeau*) felt hat; (*stylo*) felt-tip(ped pen)

feutré, e [føtʀe] *adj* feltlike; (*pas, voix*) muffled

fève [fɛv] *nf* broad bean; (*dans la galette des Rois*) charm (*hidden in cake eaten on Twelfth Night*)

février [fevʀije] *nm* February; *voir aussi* **juillet**

FF *abr* (= franc français) FF

fiable [fjabl(ə)] *adj* reliable

fiançailles [fjɑ̃saj] *nfpl* engagement *sg*

fiancé, e [fjɑ̃se] *nm/f* fiancé/fiancée ♦ *adj*: **être fiancé (à)** to be engaged (to)

fiancer [fjɑ̃se]: **se fiancer** *vi*: **se fiancer (avec)** to become engaged (to)

fibre [fibʀ(ə)] *nf* fibre, fiber (*US*); **avoir la fibre paternelle/militaire** to be a born father/soldier; **fibre optique** optical fibre *ou* fiber; **fibre de verre** fibreglass (*BRIT*), fiberglass (*US*), glass fibre *ou* fiber

ficeler [fisle] *vt* to tie up

ficelle [fisɛl] *nf* string *no pl*; (*morceau*) piece *ou* length of string; (*pain*) stick of French bread; **ficelles** *pl* (*fig*) strings; **tirer sur la ficelle** (*fig*) to go too far

fiche [fiʃ] *nf* (*carte*) (index) card; (*INFORM*) record; (*formulaire*) form; (*ÉLEC*) plug; **fiche de paye** pay slip; **fiche signalétique** (*POLICE*) identification card; **fiche technique** data sheet, specification *ou* spec sheet

ficher [fiʃe] *vt* (*dans un fichier*) to file; (: *POLICE*) to put on file; (*fam*) to do; (: *donner*) to give; (: *mettre*) to stick *ou* shove; (*planter*): **ficher qch dans** to stick *ou* drive sth into; **ficher qn à la porte** (*fam*) to chuck sb out; **fiche(-moi) le camp** (*fam*) clear off; **fiche-moi la paix** (*fam*) leave me alone; **se ficher dans** (*s'enfoncer*) to get stuck in, embed itself in; **se ficher de** (*fam*) to make fun of; not to care about

fichier [fiʃje] *nm* (*gén, INFORM*) file; (*à cartes*) card index; **fichier actif** *ou* **en cours d'utilisation** (*INFORM*) active file; **fichier d'adresses** mailing list; **fichier d'archives** (*INFORM*) archive file

fichu, e [fiʃy] *pp de* **ficher** (*fam*) ♦ *adj* (*fam: fini, inutilisable*) bust, done for; (: *intensif*) wretched, darned ♦ *nm* (*foulard*) (head)scarf (*pl* -scarves); **être fichu de** to be capable of; **mal fichu** feeling lousy; useless; **bien fichu** great

fictif, ive [fiktif, -iv] *adj* fictitious

fiction [fiksjɔ̃] *nf* fiction; (*fait imaginé*) invention

fidèle [fidɛl] *adj*: **fidèle (à)** faithful (to) ♦ *nm/f* (*REL*): **les fidèles** the faithful; (*à l'église*) the congregation

fidélité [fidelite] *nf* faithfulness

fier¹ [fje]: **se fier à** *vt* to trust

fier², fière [fjɛʀ] *adj* proud; **fier de** proud of; **avoir fière allure** to cut a fine figure

fierté [fjɛʀte] *nf* pride

fièvre [fjɛvʀ(ə)] *nf* fever; **avoir de la fièvre/39 de fièvre** to have a high temperature/a temperature of 39° C; **fièvre typhoïde** typhoid fever

fiévreux, euse [fjevʀø, -øz] *adj* feverish

figé, e [fiʒe] *adj* (*manières*) stiff; (*société*) rigid; (*sourire*) set

figer [fiʒe] *vt* to congeal; (*fig: personne*) to freeze, root to the spot; **se figer** *vi* to congeal; to freeze; (*institutions etc*) to become set, stop evolving

fignoler [fiɲɔle] *vt* to put the finishing touches to

figue [fig] *nf* fig

figuier [figje] *nm* fig tree

figurant, e [figyʀɑ̃, -ɑ̃t] *nm/f* (*THÉÂT*) walk-on; (*CINÉ*) extra

figure [figyʀ] *nf* (*visage*) face; (*image, tracé, forme, personnage*) figure; (*illustration*) picture, diagram; **faire figure de** to look like; **faire bonne figure** to put up a good show; **faire triste figure** to be a sorry sight; **figure de rhétorique** figure of speech

figuré, e [figyʀe] *adj* (*sens*) figurative

figurer [figyʀe] *vi* to appear ♦ *vt* to represent; **se figurer que** to imagine that; **figurez-vous que ...** would you believe that ...?

fil [fil] *nm* (*brin, fig: d'une histoire*) thread; (*du téléphone*) cable, wire; (*textile de lin*) linen; (*d'un couteau: tranchant*) edge; **au fil des années** with the passing of the years; **au fil de l'eau** with the stream *ou* current; **de fil en aiguille** one thing leading to another; **ne tenir qu'à un fil** (*vie, réussite etc*) to hang by a thread; **donner du fil à retordre à qn** to make life difficult for sb; **donner/recevoir un coup de fil** to make/get a phone call; **fil à coudre** (sewing) thread *ou* yarn; **fil dentaire** dental floss; **fil électrique** electric wire; **fil de fer** wire; **fil de fer barbelé** barbed wire; **fil à pêche** fishing line; **fil à plomb** plumbline; **fil à souder** soldering wire

filament [filamɑ̃] *nm* (*ÉLEC*) filament; (*de liquide*) trickle, thread

filandreux, euse [filɑ̃dʀø, -øz] *adj* stringy

filature [filatyʀ] *nf* (*fabrique*) mill; (*policière*) shadowing *no pl*, tailing *no pl*; **prendre qn en filature** to shadow *ou* tail sb

file [fil] *nf* line; **file (d'attente)** queue (*BRIT*), line (*US*); **prendre la file** to join the (end of the) queue *ou* line; **prendre la file de droite** (*AUTO*) to move into the right-hand lane; **se mettre en file** to form a line; (*AUTO*) to get into lane; **stationner en double file** (*AUTO*) to double-park; **à la file** *adv* (*d'affilée*) in succession; (*à la suite*) one after another; **à la** *ou* **en file indienne** in single file

filer [file] *vt* (*tissu, toile, verre*) to spin; (*dérouler:*

câble etc) to pay *ou* let out; (*prendre en filature*) to shadow, tail; (*fam: donner*) to give; **filer qch à qn** to slip sb sth ♦ *vi* (*bas, maille, liquide, pâte*) to run; (*aller vite*) to fly past *ou* by; (*fam: partir*) to make off; **filer à l'anglaise** to take French leave; **filer doux** to behave o.s., toe the line; **filer un mauvais coton** to be in a bad way

filet [file] *nm* net; (*CULIN*) fillet; (*d'eau, de sang*) trickle; **tendre un filet** (*police*) to set a trap; **filet (à bagages)** (*RAIL*) luggage rack; **filet (à provisions)** string bag

filiale [filjal] *nf* (*COMM*) subsidiary; affiliate

filière [filjɛʀ] *nf*: **passer par la filière** to go through the (administrative) channels; **suivre la filière** to work one's way up (through the hierarchy)

filiforme [filifɔʀm(ə)] *adj* spindly; threadlike

filigrane [filigʀan] *nm* (*d'un billet, timbre*) watermark; **en filigrane** (*fig*) showing just beneath the surface

fille [fij] *nf* girl; (*opposé à fils*) daughter; **vieille fille** old maid; **fille de joie** prostitute; **fille de salle** waitress

fillette [fijɛt] *nf* (little) girl

filleul, e [fijœl] *nm/f* godchild, godson/daughter

film [film] *nm* (*pour photo*) (roll of) film; (*œuvre*) film, picture, movie; (*couche*) film; **film muet/parlant** silent/talking picture *ou* movie; **film alimentaire** clingfilm; **film d'amour/d'animation/d'horreur** romantic/animated/horror film; **film comique** comedy; **film policier** thriller

filon [filɔ̃] *nm* vein, lode; (*fig*) lucrative line, moneyspinner

fils [fis] *nm* son; **fils de famille** moneyed young man; **fils à papa** (*péj*) daddy's boy

filtre [filtʀ(ə)] *nm* filter; **"filtre ou sans filtre?"** (*cigarettes*) "tipped or plain?"; **filtre à air** air filter

filtrer [filtʀe] *vt* to filter; (*fig: candidats, visiteurs*) to screen ♦ *vi* to filter (through)

fin¹ [fɛ̃] *nf* end; **fins** *nfpl* (*but*) ends; **à (la) fin mai, fin mai** at the end of May; **en fin de semaine** at the end of the week; **prendre fin** to come to an end; **toucher à sa fin** to be drawing to a close; **mettre fin à** to put an end to; **mener à bonne fin** to bring to a successful conclusion; **à cette fin** to this end; **à toutes fins utiles** for your information; **à la fin** in the end, eventually; **sans fin** *adj* endless, *adv* endlessly; **fin de non-recevoir** (*JUR, ADMIN*) objection; **fin de section** (*de ligne d'autobus*) (fare) stage

fin², e [fɛ̃, fin] *adj* (*papier, couche, fil*) thin; (*cheveux, poudre, pointe, visage*) fine; (*taille*) neat, slim; (*esprit, remarque*) subtle; shrewd ♦ *adv* (*moudre, couper*) finely ♦ *nm*: **vouloir jouer au plus fin (avec qn)** to try to outsmart sb ♦ *nf* (*alcool*) liqueur brandy; **c'est fin!** (*ironique*) how clever!; **fin prêt/soûl** quite ready/drunk; **un fin gourmet** a gourmet; **un fin tireur** a crack shot;

avoir la vue/l'ouïe fine to have sharp eyes/ears, have keen eyesight/hearing; **or/linge/vin fin** fine gold/linen/wine; **le fin fond de** the very depths of; **le fin mot de** the real story behind; **la fine fleur de** the flower of; **une fine mouche** *(fig)* a sharp customer; **fines herbes** mixed herbs

final, e [final] *adj, nf* final ♦ *nm (MUS)* finale; **quarts de finale** quarter finals; **8èmes/16èmes de finale** 2nd/1st round *(in 5 round knock-out competition)*

finalement [finalmɑ̃] *adv* finally, in the end; *(après tout)* after all

finance [finɑ̃s] *nf* finance; **finances** *nfpl (situation financière)* finances; *(activités financières)* finance *sg;* **moyennant finance** for a fee *ou* consideration

financer [finɑ̃se] *vt* to finance

financier, ière [finɑ̃sje, -jɛʀ] *adj* financial ♦ *nm* financier

finaud, e [fino, -od] *adj* wily

finesse [fines] *nf* thinness; fineness; neatness; slimness; subtlety; shrewdness; **finesses** *nfpl (subtilités)* niceties; finer points

fini, e [fini] *adj* finished; *(MATH)* finite; *(intensif):* **un menteur fini** a liar through and through ♦ *nm (d'un objet manufacturé)* finish

finir [finiʀ] *vt* to finish ♦ *vi* to finish, end; **finir quelque part** to end *ou* finish up somewhere; **finir de faire** to finish doing; *(cesser)* to stop doing; **finir par faire** to end *ou* finish up doing; **il finit par m'agacer** he's beginning to get on my nerves; **finir en pointe/tragédie** to end in a point/in tragedy; **en finir avec** to be *ou* have done with; **à n'en plus finir** *(route, discussions)* never-ending; **il va mal finir** he will come to a bad end; **c'est bientôt fini?** *(reproche)* have you quite finished?

finition [finisjɔ̃] *nf* finishing; finish

finlandais, e [fɛ̃lɑ̃dɛ, -ɛz] *adj* Finnish ♦ *nm/f:* **Finlandais, e** Finn

Finlande [fɛ̃lɑ̃d] *nf:* **la Finlande** Finland

fiole [fjɔl] *nf* phial

firme [fiʀm(ə)] *nf* firm

fis [fi] *vb voir* **faire**

fisc [fisk] *nm* tax authorities *pl,* ≈ Inland Revenue *(BRIT),* ≈ Internal Revenue Service *(US)*

fiscal, e, aux [fiskal, -o] *adj* tax *cpd,* fiscal

fiscalité [fiskalite] *nf* tax system; *(charges)* taxation

fissure [fisyʀ] *nf* crack

fissurer [fisyʀe] *vt:* **se fissurer** *vi* to crack

fiston [fistɔ̃] *nm (fam)* son, lad

fit [fi] *vb voir* **faire**

fixation [fiksɑsjɔ̃] *nf* fixing; fastening; setting; *(de ski)* binding; *(PSYCH)* fixation

fixe [fiks(ə)] *adj, nm (salaire)* basic salary; *(téléphone)* landline; **à heure fixe** at a set time; **menu à prix fixe** set menu

fixé, e [fikse] *adj (heure, jour)* appointed; **être fixé (sur)** to have made up one's mind (about); to know for certain (about)

fixer [fikse] *vt (attacher):* **fixer qch (à/sur)** to fix *ou* fasten sth (to/onto); *(déterminer)* to fix, set; *(CHIMIE, PHOTO)* to fix; *(poser son regard sur)* to look hard at, stare at; **se fixer** *(s'établir)* to settle down; **fixer son choix sur qch** to decide on sth; **se fixer sur** *(suj: attention)* to focus on

flacon [flakɔ̃] *nm* bottle

flageoler [flaʒɔle] *vi* to have knees like jelly

flageolet [flaʒɔlɛ] *nm (MUS)* flageolet; *(CULIN)* dwarf kidney bean

flagrant, e [flagrɑ̃, -ɑ̃t] *adj* flagrant, blatant; **en flagrant délit** in the act, in flagrante delicto

flair [flɛʀ] *nm* sense of smell; *(fig)* intuition

flairer [fleʀe] *vt (humer)* to sniff (at); *(détecter)* to scent

flamand, e [flamɑ̃, -ɑ̃d] *adj* Flemish ♦ *nm (LING)* Flemish ♦ *nm/f:* **Flamand, e** Fleming; **les Flamands** the Flemish

flamant [flamɑ̃] *nm* flamingo

flambant [flɑ̃bɑ̃] *adv:* **flambant neuf** brand new

flambé, e [flɑ̃be] *adj (CULIN)* flambé ♦ *nf* blaze; *(fig)* flaring-up, explosion

flambeau, x [flɑ̃bo] *nm (flaming)* torch; **se passer le flambeau** *(fig)* to hand down the *(ou* a) tradition

flambée [flɑ̃be] *nf (feu)* blaze; *(COMM):* **flambée des prix** (sudden) shooting up of prices

flamber [flɑ̃be] *vi* to blaze (up) ♦ *vt (poulet)* to singe; *(aiguille)* to sterilize

flamboyer [flɑ̃bwaje] *vi* to blaze (up); *(fig)* to flame

flamme [flam] *nf* flame; *(fig)* fire, fervour; **en flammes** on fire, ablaze

flan [flɑ̃] *nm (CULIN)* custard tart *ou* pie

flanc [flɑ̃] *nm* side; *(MIL)* flank; **à flanc de colline** on the hillside; **prêter le flanc à** *(fig)* to lay o.s. open to

flancher [flɑ̃ʃe] *vi (cesser de fonctionner)* to fail, pack up; *(armée)* to quit

flanelle [flanɛl] *nf* flannel

flâner [flɑne] *vi* to stroll

flânerie [flɑnʀi] *nf* stroll

flanquer [flɑ̃ke] *vt* to flank; *(fam: jeter):* **flanquer par terre/à la porte** to fling to the ground/chuck out; *(: donner):* **flanquer la frousse à qn** to put the wind up sb, give sb an awful fright

flaque [flak] *nf (d'eau)* puddle; *(d'huile, de sang etc)* pool

flash, pl flashes [flaʃ] *nm (PHOTO)* flash; **flash (d'information)** newsflash

flasque [flask(ə)] *adj* flabby ♦ *nf (flacon)* flask

flatter [flate] *vt* to flatter; *(caresser)* to stroke; **se flatter de qch** to pride o.s. on sth

flatterie [flatʀi] *nf* flattery

flatteur, euse [flatœʀ, -øz] *adj* flattering ♦ *nm/f* flatterer

fléau, x [fleo] *nm* scourge, curse; (*de balance*) beam; (*pour le blé*) flail

flèche [flɛʃ] *nf* arrow; (*de clocher*) spire; (*de grue*) jib; (*trait d'esprit, critique*) shaft; **monter en flèche** (*fig*) to soar, rocket; **partir en flèche** (*fig*) to be off like a shot; **à flèche variable** (*avion*) swing-wing *cpd*

fléchette [fleʃɛt] *nf* dart; **fléchettes** *nfpl* (*jeu*) darts *sg*

fléchir [fleʃiʀ] *vt* (*corps, genou*) to bend; (*fig*) to sway, weaken ♦ *vi* (*poutre*) to sag, bend; (*fig*) to weaken, flag; (: *baisser: prix*) to fall off

flemmard, e [flemaʀ, -aʀd(ə)] *nm/f* lazybones *sg*, loafer

flemme [flɛm] *nf* (*fam*): **j'ai la flemme de le faire** I can't be bothered

flétrir [fletʀiʀ] *vt* to wither; (*stigmatiser*) to condemn (in the most severe terms); **se flétrir** *vi* to wither

fleur [flœʀ] *nf* flower; (*d'un arbre*) blossom; **être en fleur** (*arbre*) to be in blossom; **tissu à fleurs** flowered *ou* flowery fabric; **la (fine) fleur de** (*fig*) the flower of; **être fleur bleue** to be soppy *ou* sentimental; **à fleur de terre** just above the ground; **faire une fleur à qn** to do sb a favour (*BRIT*) *ou* favor (*US*); **fleur de lis** fleur-de-lis

fleuri, e [flœʀi] *adj* in flower *ou* bloom, surrounded by flowers; (*fig: style*) flowery; (: *teint*) glowing

fleurir [flœʀiʀ] *vi* (*rose*) to flower; (*arbre*) to blossom; (*fig*) to flourish ♦ *vt* (*tombe*) to put flowers on; (*chambre*) to decorate with flowers

fleuriste [flœʀist(ə)] *nm/f* florist

fleuve [flœv] *nm* river; **roman-fleuve** saga; **discours-fleuve** interminable speech

flexible [flɛksibl(ə)] *adj* flexible

flic [flik] *nm* (*fam: péj*) cop

flipper *nm* [flipœʀ] pinball (machine) ♦ *vi* [flipe] (*fam: être déprimé*) to feel down, be on a downer; (: *être exalté*) to freak out

flirter [flœʀte] *vi* to flirt

flocon [flɔkɔ̃] *nm* flake; (*de laine etc: boulette*) flock; **flocons d'avoine** oatflakes, porridge oats

flopée [flɔpe] *nf*: **une flopée de** loads of

floraison [flɔʀɛzɔ̃] *nf* (*voir fleurir*) flowering; blossoming; flourishing

flore [flɔʀ] *nf* flora

florissant, e [flɔʀisɑ̃, -ɑ̃t] *vb voir* **fleurir** ♦ *adj* flourishing; (*santé, teint, mine*) blooming

flot [flo] *nm* flood, stream; (*marée*) flood tide; **flots** *nmpl* (*de la mer*) waves; **être à flot** (*NAVIG*) to be afloat; (*fig*) to be on an even keel; **à flots** (*couler*) in torrents; **entrer à flots** to stream *ou* pour in

flottant, e [flɔtɑ̃, -ɑ̃t] *adj* (*vêtement*) loose (-fitting); (*cours, barème*) floating

flotte [flɔt] *nf* (*NAVIG*) fleet; (*fam*) water; rain

flottement [flɔtmɑ̃] *nm* (*fig*) wavering, hesitation; (*ÉCON*) floating

flotter [flɔte] *vi* to float; (*nuage, odeur*) to drift; (*drapeau*) to fly; (*vêtements*) to hang loose ♦ *vb impers* (*fam: pleuvoir*): **il flotte** it's raining ♦ *vt* to float; **faire flotter** to float

flotteur [flɔtœʀ] *nm* float

flou, e [flu] *adj* fuzzy, blurred; (*fig*) woolly (*BRIT*), vague; (*non ajusté: robe*) loose(-fitting)

fluctuation [flyktɥasjɔ̃] *nf* fluctuation

fluet, te [flyɛ, -ɛt] *adj* thin, slight; (*voix*) thin

fluide [flɥid] *adj* fluid; (*circulation etc*) flowing freely ♦ *nm* fluid; (*force*) (mysterious) power

fluor [flyɔʀ] *nm* fluorine

fluorescent, e [flyɔʀesɑ̃, -ɑ̃t] *adj* fluorescent

flûte [flyt] *nf* (*aussi*: **flûte traversière**) flute; (*verre*) flute glass; (*pain*) long loaf (*pl* loaves); **petite flûte** piccolo (*pl* -s); **flûte!** drat it!; **flûte (à bec)** recorder; **flûte de Pan** panpipes *pl*

flux [fly] *nm* incoming tide; (*écoulement*) flow; **le flux et le reflux** the ebb and flow

FM *sigle f* (= frequency modulation) FM

foc [fɔk] *nm* jib

foi [fwa] *nf* faith; **sous la foi du serment** under *ou* on oath; **ajouter foi à** to lend credence to; **faire foi** (*prouver*) to be evidence; **digne de foi** reliable; **sur la foi de** on the word *ou* strength of; **être de bonne/mauvaise foi** to be in good faith/not to be in good faith; **ma foi!** well!

foie [fwa] *nm* liver; **foie gras** foie gras

foin [fwɛ̃] *nm* hay; **faire les foins** to make hay; **faire du foin** (*fam*) to kick up a row

foire [fwaʀ] *nf* fair; (*fête foraine*) (fun) fair; (*fig: désordre, confusion*) bear garden; **faire la foire** to whoop it up; **foire (exposition)** trade fair

fois [fwa] *nf* time; **une/deux fois** once/twice; **trois/vingt fois** three/twenty times; **2 fois 2** 2 times 2; **deux/quatre fois plus grand (que)** twice/four times as big (as); **une fois** (*passé*) once; (*futur*) sometime; **une (bonne) fois pour toutes** once and for all; **encore une fois** again, once more; **il était une fois** once upon a time; **une fois que c'est fait** once it's done; **une fois parti** once he (*ou* I *etc*) had left; **des fois** (*parfois*) sometimes; **si des fois ...** (*fam*) if ever ...; **non mais des fois!** (*fam*) (now) look here!; **à la fois** (*ensemble*) (all) at once; **à la fois grand et beau** both tall and handsome

foison [fwazɔ̃] *nf*: **une foison de** an abundance of; **à foison** *adv* in plenty

foisonner [fwazɔne] *vi* to abound; **foisonner en** *ou* **de** to abound in

fol [fɔl] *adj m voir* **fou**

folie [fɔli] *nf* (*d'une décision, d'un acte*) madness, folly; (*état*) madness, insanity; (*acte*) folly; **la folie des grandeurs** delusions of grandeur; **faire des folies** (*en dépenses*) to be extravagant

folklorique [fɔlklɔʀik] *adj* folk *cpd*; (*fam*) weird

folle [fɔl] *adj f, nf* voir **fou**

follement [fɔlmɑ̃] *adv* (*très*) madly, wildly

foncé, e [fɔ̃se] *adj* dark; **bleu foncé** dark blue

foncer [fɔ̃se] *vt* to make darker; (*CULIN: moule etc*) to line ◆ *vi* to go darker; (*fam: aller vite*) to tear *ou* belt along; **foncer sur** to charge at

foncier, ière [fɔ̃sje, -jɛʀ] *adj* (*honnêteté etc*) basic, fundamental; (*malhonnêteté*) deep-rooted; (*COMM*) real estate *cpd*

fonction [fɔ̃ksjɔ̃] *nf* (*rôle*, *MATH, LING*) function; (*emploi, poste*) post, position; **fonctions** (*professionnelles*) duties; **entrer en fonctions** to take up one's post *ou* duties; to take up office; **voiture de fonction** company car; **être fonction de** (*dépendre de*) to depend on; **en fonction de** (*par rapport à*) according to; **faire fonction de** to serve as; **la fonction publique** the state *ou* civil (*BRIT*) service

fonctionnaire [fɔ̃ksjɔnɛʀ] *nm/f* state employee *ou* official; (*dans l'administration*) ≈ civil servant (*BRIT*)

fonctionner [fɔ̃ksjɔne] *vi* to work, function; (*entreprise*) to operate, function; **faire fonctionner** to work, operate

fond [fɔ̃] *nm; voir aussi* **fonds**; (*d'un récipient, trou*) bottom; (*d'une salle, scène*) back; (*d'un tableau, décor*) background; (*opposé à la forme*) content; (*petite quantité*): **un fond de verre** a drop; (*SPORT*): **le fond** long distance (running); **course/épreuve de fond** long-distance race/trial; **au fond de** at the bottom of; at the back of; **aller au fond des choses** to get to the root of things; **le fond de sa pensée** his (*ou* her) true thoughts *ou* feelings; **sans fond** *adj* bottomless; **envoyer par le fond** (*NAVIG: couler*) to sink, scuttle; **à fond** (*connaître, soutenir*) thoroughly; (*appuyer, visser*) right down *ou* home; **à fond (de train)** *adv* (*fam*) full tilt; **dans le fond, au fond** (*en somme*) basically, really; **de fond en comble** *adv* from top to bottom; **fond sonore** background noise; background music; **fond de teint** (make-up) foundation

fondamental, e, aux [fɔ̃damɑ̃tal, -o] *adj* fundamental

fondant, e [fɔ̃dɑ̃, -ɑ̃t] *adj* (*neige*) melting; (*poire*) that melts in the mouth; (*chocolat*) fondant

fondateur, trice [fɔ̃datœʀ, -tʀis] *nm/f* founder; **membre fondateur** founder (*BRIT*) *ou* founding (*US*) member

fondation [fɔ̃dasjɔ̃] *nf* founding; (*établissement*) foundation; **fondations** *nfpl* (*d'une maison*) foundations; **travail de fondation** foundation works *pl*

fondé, e [fɔ̃de] *adj* (*accusation etc*) well-founded ◆ *nm*: **fondé de pouvoir** authorized representative; **mal fondé** unfounded; **être fondé à croire** to have grounds for believing *ou* good reason to believe

fondement [fɔ̃dmɑ̃] *nm* (*derrière*) behind; **fondements** *nmpl* foundations; **sans fondement** *adj* (*rumeur etc*) groundless, unfounded

fonder [fɔ̃de] *vt* to found; (*fig*): **fonder qch sur** to base sth on; **se fonder sur** (*suj: personne*) to base o.s. on; **fonder un foyer** (*se marier*) to set up home

fonderie [fɔ̃dʀi] *nf* smelting works *sg*

fondre [fɔ̃dʀ(ə)] *vt* to melt; (*dans l'eau: sucre, sel*) to dissolve; (*fig: mélanger*) to merge, blend ◆ *vi* to melt; to dissolve; (*fig*) to melt away; (*se précipiter*): **fondre sur** to swoop down on; **se fondre** *vi* (*se combiner, se confondre*) to merge into each other; to dissolve; **fondre en larmes** to dissolve into tears

fonds [fɔ̃] *nm* (*de bibliothèque*) collection; (*COMM*): **fonds (de commerce)** business; (*fig*): **fonds de probité** *etc* fund of integrity *etc* ◆ *nmpl* (*argent*) funds; **à fonds perdus** *adv* with little or no hope of getting the money back; **être en fonds** to be in funds; **mise de fonds** investment, (capital) outlay; **Fonds monétaire international (FMI)** International Monetary Fund (IMF); **fonds de roulement** *nm* float

fondu, e [fɔ̃dy] *adj* (*beurre, neige*) melted; (*métal*) molten ◆ *nm* (*CINE*): **fondu (enchaîné)** dissolve ◆ *nf* (*CULIN*) fondue

font [fɔ̃] *vb voir* **faire**

fontaine [fɔ̃tɛn] *nf* fountain; (*source*) spring

fonte [fɔ̃t] *nf* melting; (*métal*) cast iron; **la fonte des neiges** the (spring) thaw

foot(ball) [fut(bol)] *nm* football, soccer

footballeur, euse [futbolœʀ, -øz] *nm/f* footballer (*BRIT*), football *ou* soccer player

footing [futiŋ] *nm* jogging; **faire du footing** to go jogging

for [fɔʀ] *nm*: **dans** *ou* **en son for intérieur** in one's heart of hearts

forain, e [fɔʀɛ̃, -ɛn] *adj* fairground *cpd* ◆ *nm* (*marchand*) stallholder; (*acteur etc*) fairground entertainer

forçat [fɔʀsa] *nm* convict

force [fɔʀs(ə)] *nf* strength; (*puissance: surnaturelle etc*) power; (*PHYSIQUE, MÉCANIQUE*) force; **forces** *nfpl* (*physiques*) strength *sg*; (*MIL*) forces; (*effectifs*): **d'importantes forces de police** large contingents of police; **avoir de la force** to be strong; **être à bout de force** to have no strength left; **à la force du poignet** (*fig*) by the sweat of one's brow; **à force de faire** by dint of doing; **arriver en force** (*nombreux*) to arrive in force; **cas de force majeure** case of absolute necessity; (*ASSURANCES*) act of God; **force de la nature** natural force; **de force** *adv* forcibly, by force; **de toutes mes/ses forces** with all my/his strength; **par la force** using force; **par la force des choses/d'habitude** by force of circumstances/habit; **à toute force** (*absolument*) at all costs; **faire force de rames/voiles** to ply the oars/cram on sail; **être de force à faire** to be up to doing; **de première force** first class; **la force armée** (*les troupes*) the army; **force d'âme** fortitude; **force de frappe** strike force; **force d'inertie** force of inertia; **la force publique** the authorities responsible for public order; **forces d'intervention** (MIL, POLICE) peace-keeping force sg; **les forces de l'ordre** the police

forcé, e [fɔʀse] adj forced; (bain) unintended; (inevitable): **c'est forcé!** it's inevitable!, it HAS to be!

forcément [fɔʀsemɑ̃] adv necessarily, inevitably; (bien sûr) of course

forcené, e [fɔʀsəne] adj frenzied ♦ nm/f maniac

forcer [fɔʀse] vt (contraindre): **forcer qn à faire** to force sb to do; (porte, serrure, plante) to force; (moteur, voix) to strain ♦ vi (SPORT) to strain; **forcer à faire qch** to force o.s. to do sth; **forcer la dose/l'allure** to overdo it/increase the pace; **forcer l'attention/le respect** to command attention/respect; **forcer la consigne** to bypass orders

forcir [fɔʀsiʀ] vi (grossir) to broaden out; (vent) to freshen

forer [fɔʀe] vt to drill, bore

forestier, ière [fɔʀɛstje, -jɛʀ] adj forest cpd

forêt [fɔʀɛ] nf forest; **Office National des Forêts** (ADMIN) ≈ Forestry Commission (BRIT), ≈ National Forest Service (US); **la Forêt Noire** the Black Forest

forfait [fɔʀfɛ] nm (COMM) fixed ou set price; all-in deal ou price; (crime) infamy; **déclarer forfait** to withdraw; **gagner par forfait** to win by a walkover; **travailler à forfait** to work for a lump sum

forfaitaire [fɔʀfetɛʀ] adj set; inclusive

forge [fɔʀʒ(ə)] nf forge, smithy

forger [fɔʀʒe] vt to forge; (fig: personnalité) to form; (: prétexte) to contrive, make up

forgeron [fɔʀʒəʀɔ̃] nm (black)smith

formaliser [fɔʀmalize]: **se formaliser** vi: **se formaliser (de)** to take offence (at)

formalité [fɔʀmalite] nf formality

format [fɔʀma] nm size; **petit format** small size; (PHOTO) 35 mm (film)

formater [fɔʀmate] vt (disque) to format; **non formaté** unformatted

formation [fɔʀmasjɔ̃] nf forming; (éducation) training; (MUS) group; (MIL, AVIAT, GÉO) formation; **la formation permanente** ou **continue** continuing education; **la formation professionnelle** vocational training

forme [fɔʀm(ə)] nf (gén) form; (d'un objet) shape, form; **formes** nfpl (bonnes manières) proprieties; (d'une femme) figure sg; **en forme de poire** pear-shaped, in the shape of a pear; **sous forme de** in the form of; in the guise of; **sous forme de cachets** in the form of tablets; **être en (bonne** ou **pleine) forme** avoir la forme; (SPORT etc) to be on form; **en bonne et due forme** in due form; **pour la forme** for the sake of form; **sans autre forme de procès** (fig) without further ado; **prendre forme** to take shape

formel, le [fɔʀmɛl] adj (preuve, décision) definite, positive; (logique) formal

formellement [fɔʀmɛlmɑ̃] adv (interdit) strictly

former [fɔʀme] vt (gén) to form; (éduquer: soldat,

ingénieur etc) to train; **se former** to form; to train

formidable [fɔʀmidabl(ə)] adj tremendous

formulaire [fɔʀmylɛʀ] nm form

formule [fɔʀmyl] nf (gén) formula; (formulaire) form; **selon la formule consacrée** as one says; **formule de politesse** polite phrase; (en fin de lettre) letter ending

formuler [fɔʀmyle] vt (émettre: réponse, vœux) to formulate; (expliciter: sa pensée) to express

fort, e [fɔʀ, fɔʀt(ə)] adj strong; (intensité, rendement) high, great; (corpulent) large; (doué): **être fort (en)** to be good (at) ♦ adv (serrer, frapper) hard; (sonner) loud(ly); (beaucoup) greatly, very much; (très) very ♦ nm (édifice) fort; (point fort) strong point, forte; (gén pl: personne, pays): **le fort, les forts** the strong; **c'est un peu fort!** it's a bit much!; **à plus forte raison** even more so, all the more reason; **avoir fort à faire avec qn** to have a hard job with sb; **se faire fort de faire** to claim one can do; **fort bien/peu** very well/few; **au plus fort de** (au milieu de) in the thick of, at the height of; **forte tête** rebel

forteresse [fɔʀtəʀɛs] nf fortress

fortifiant [fɔʀtifjɑ̃] nm tonic

fortifier [fɔʀtifje] vt to strengthen, fortify; (MIL) to fortify; **se fortifier** vi (personne, santé) to grow stronger

fortiori [fɔʀtjɔʀi]: **à fortiori** adv all the more so

fortuit, e [fɔʀtɥi, -it] adj fortuitous, chance cpd

fortune [fɔʀtyn] nf fortune; **faire fortune** to make one's fortune; **de fortune** adj makeshift; (compagnon) chance cpd

fortuné, e [fɔʀtyne] adj wealthy, well-off

fosse [fos] nf (grand trou) pit; (tombe) grave; **la fosse aux lions/ours** the lions' den/bear pit; **fosse commune** common ou communal grave; **fosse (d'orchestre)** (orchestra) pit; **fosse à purin** cesspit; **fosse septique** septic tank; **fosses nasales** nasal fossae

fossé [fose] nm ditch; (fig) gulf, gap

fossette [fosɛt] nf dimple

fossile [fosil] nm fossil ♦ adj fossilized, fossil cpd

fossoyeur [foswajœʀ] nm gravedigger

fou, fol, folle [fu, fɔl] adj mad, crazy; (déréglé etc) wild, erratic; (mèche) stray; (herbe) wild; (fam: extrême, très grand) terrific, tremendous ♦ nm/f madman/woman ♦ nm (du roi) jester, fool; (ÉCHECS) bishop; **fou à lier, fou furieux (folle furieuse)** raving mad; **être fou de** to be mad ou crazy about; (chagrin, joie, colère) to be wild with; **faire le fou** to play ou act the fool; **avoir le fou rire** to have the giggles

foudre [fudʀ(ə)] nf lightning; **foudres** nfpl (fig: colère) wrath sg

foudroyant, e [fudʀwajɑ̃, -ɑ̃t] adj devastating; (maladie, poison) violent

foudroyer [fudʀwaje] vt to strike down; **foudroyer qn du regard** to look daggers at sb; **il a été**

foudroyé he was struck by lightning

fouet [fwɛ] *nm* whip; (*CULIN*) whisk; **de plein fouet** *adv* head on

fouetter [fwete] *vt* to whip; to whisk

fougère [fuʒɛʀ] *nf* fern

fougue [fug] *nf* ardour (*BRIT*), ardor (*US*), spirit

fougueux, euse [fugø, -øz] *adj* fiery, ardent

fouille [fuj] *nf* search; **fouilles** *nfpl* (*archéologiques*) excavations; **passer à la fouille** to be searched

fouiller [fuje] *vt* to search; (*creuser*) to dig; (: *suj: archéologue*) to excavate; (*approfondir: étude etc*) to go into ♦ *vi* (*archéologue*) to excavate; **fouiller dans/parmi** to rummage in/among

fouillis [fuji] *nm* jumble, muddle

fouiner [fwine] *vi* (*péj*): **fouiner dans** to nose around *ou* about in

foulard [fulaʀ] *nm* scarf (*pl* scarves)

foule [ful] *nf* crowd; **une foule de** masses of; **venir en foule** to come in droves

foulée [fule] *nf* stride; **dans la foulée de** on the heels of

fouler [fule] *vt* to press; (*sol*) to tread upon; **se fouler** *vi* (*fam*) to overexert o.s.; **se fouler la cheville** to sprain one's ankle; **fouler aux pieds** to trample underfoot

foulure [fulyʀ] *nf* sprain

four [fuʀ] *nm* oven; (*de potier*) kiln; (*THÉÂT: échec*) flop; **allant au four** ovenproof

fourbe [fuʀb(ə)] *adj* deceitful

fourbu, e [fuʀby] *adj* exhausted

fourche [fuʀʃ(ə)] *nf* pitchfork; (*de bicyclette*) fork

fourchette [fuʀʃet] *nf* fork; (*STATISTIQUE*) bracket, margin

fourgon [fuʀgɔ̃] *nm* van; (*RAIL*) wag(g)on; **fourgon mortuaire** hearse

fourgonnette [fuʀgɔnet] *nf* (delivery) van

fourmi [fuʀmi] *nf* ant; **avoir des fourmis** (*fig*) to have pins and needles

fourmilière [fuʀmiljeʀ] *nf* ant-hill; (*fig*) hive of activity

fourmiller [fuʀmije] *vi* to swarm; **fourmiller de** to be teeming with, be swarming with

fournaise [fuʀnez] *nf* blaze; (*fig*) furnace, oven

fourneau, x [fuʀno] *nm* stove

fournée [fuʀne] *nf* batch

fourni, e [fuʀni] *adj* (*barbe, cheveux*) thick; (*magasin*): **bien fourni (en)** well stocked (with)

fournir [fuʀniʀ] *vt* to supply; (*preuve, exemple*) to provide, supply; (*effort*) to put in; **fournir qch à qn** to supply sth to sb, supply *ou* provide sb with sth; **fournir qn en** to supply sb with; **se fournir chez** to shop at

fournisseur, euse [fuʀnisœʀ, -øz] *nm/f* supplier; (*INTERNET*): **fournisseur d'accès à Internet** (Internet) service provider

fourniture [fuʀnityʀ] *nf* supply(ing); **fournitures** *nfpl* supplies; **fournitures de bureau** office supplies, stationery; **fournitures scolaires** school stationery

fourrage [fuʀaʒ] *nm* fodder

fourré, e [fuʀe] *adj* (*bonbon, chocolat*) filled; (*manteau, botte*) fur-lined ♦ *nm* thicket

fourrer [fuʀe] *vt* (*fam*): **fourrer qch dans** to stick *ou* shove sth into; **se fourrer dans/sous** to get into/under; **se fourrer dans** (*une mauvaise situation*) to land o.s. in

fourre-tout [fuʀtu] *nm inv* (*sac*) holdall; (*péj*) junk room (*ou* cupboard); (*fig*) rag-bag

fourrière [fuʀjeʀ] *nf* pound

fourrure [fuʀyʀ] *nf* fur; (*sur l'animal*) coat; **manteau/col de fourrure** fur coat/collar

fourvoyer [fuʀvwaje]: **se fourvoyer** *vi* to go astray, stray; **se fourvoyer dans** to stray into

foutre [futʀ(ə)] *vt* (*fam!*) = **ficher** (*fam*)

foutu, e [futy] *adj* (*fam!*) = **fichu**

foyer [fwaje] *nm* (*de cheminée*) hearth; (*fig*) seat, centre; (*famille*) family; (*domicile*) home; (*local de réunion*) (social) club; (*résidence*) hostel; (*salon*) foyer; (*OPTIQUE, PHOTO*) focus; **lunettes à double foyer** bi-focal glasses

fracas [fʀaka] *nm* din; crash

fracassant, e [fʀakasɑ̃, -ɑ̃t] *adj* sensational, staggering

fracasser [fʀakase] *vt* to smash; **se fracasser contre** *ou* **sur** to crash against

fraction [fʀaksjɔ̃] *nf* fraction

fractionner [fʀaksjɔne] *vt* to divide (up), split (up)

fracture [fʀaktyʀ] *nf* fracture; **fracture du crâne** fractured skull; **fracture de la jambe** broken leg

fracturer [fʀaktyʀe] *vt* (*coffre, serrure*) to break open; (*os, membre*) to fracture

fragile [fʀaʒil] *adj* fragile, delicate; (*fig*) frail

fragilité [fʀaʒilite] *nf* fragility

fragment [fʀagmɑ̃] *nm* (*d'un objet*) fragment, piece; (*d'un texte*) passage, extract

fraîche [fʀɛʃ] *adj f voir* **frais**

fraîcheur [fʀɛʃœʀ] *nf* (*voir frais*) coolness; freshness

fraîchir [fʀɛʃiʀ] *vi* to get cooler; (*vent*) to freshen

frais, fraîche [fʀɛ, fʀɛʃ] *adj* (*air, eau, accueil*) cool; (*petit pois, œufs, nouvelles, couleur, troupes*) fresh; **le voilà frais!** he's in a (right) mess! ♦ *adv* (*récemment*) newly, fresh(ly); **il fait frais** it's cool; **servir frais** chill before serving, serve chilled ♦ *nm*: **mettre au frais** to put in a cool place; **prendre le frais** to take a breath of cool air ♦ *nmpl* (*débours*) expenses; (*COMM*) costs; charges; **faire des frais** to spend; to go to a lot of expense; **faire les frais de** to bear the brunt of; **faire les frais de la conversation** (*parler*) to do most of the talking; (*en être le sujet*) to be the topic of conversation; **il en a été pour ses frais** he could have spared himself the trouble; **rentrer dans ses frais** to recover one's expenses; **frais de déplacement** travel(ling) expenses; **frais d'entretien** upkeep; **frais généraux** overheads; **frais de scolarité** school fees, tuition (*US*)

fraise [fʀɛz] *nf* strawberry; (*TECH*) countersink (bit); (*de dentiste*) drill; **fraise des bois** wild strawberry

framboise [fʀɑ̃bwaz] *nf* raspberry

franc, franche [fʀɑ̃, fʀɑ̃ʃ] *adj* (*personne*) frank, straightforward; (*visage*) open; (*net: refus, couleur*) clear; (: *coupure*) clean; (*intensif*) downright; (*exempt*): **franc de port** post free, postage paid; (*zone, port*) free; (*boutique*) duty-free ♦ *adv*: **parler franc** to be frank *ou* candid ♦ *nm* franc

français, e [fʀɑ̃sɛ, -ɛz] *adj* French ♦ *nm* (*LING*) French ♦ *nm/f*: **Français, e** Frenchman/woman; **les Français** the French

France [fʀɑ̃s] *nf*: **la France** France; **en France** in France

franche [fʀɑ̃ʃ] *adj f voir* **franc**

franchement [fʀɑ̃ʃmɑ̃] *adv* (*voir franc*) frankly; clearly; (*tout à fait*) downright ♦ *excl* well, really!

franchir [fʀɑ̃ʃiʀ] *vt* (*obstacle*) to clear, get over; (*seuil, ligne, rivière*) to cross; (*distance*) to cover

franchise [fʀɑ̃ʃiz] *nf* frankness; (*douanière, d'impôt*) exemption; (*ASSURANCES*) excess; (*COMM*) franchise; **franchise de bagages** baggage allowance

franc-maçon, *pl* **francs-maçons** [fʀɑ̃masɔ̃] *nm* Freemason

franco [fʀɑ̃ko] *adv* (*COMM*): **franco (de port)** postage paid

francophone [fʀɑ̃kɔfɔn] *adj* French-speaking ♦ *nm/f* French speaker

franc-parler [fʀɑ̃paʀle] *nm inv* outspokenness

frange [fʀɑ̃ʒ] *nf* fringe; (*cheveux*) fringe (*BRIT*), bangs (*US*)

frangipane [fʀɑ̃ʒipan] *nf* almond paste

franquette [fʀɑ̃kɛt]: **à la bonne franquette** *adv* without any fuss

frappant, e [fʀapɑ̃, -ɑ̃t] *adj* striking

frappé, e [fʀape] *adj* (*CULIN*) iced; **frappé de panique** panic-stricken; **frappé de stupeur** thunderstruck, dumbfounded

frapper [fʀape] *vt* to hit, strike; (*étonner*) to strike; (*monnaie*) to strike, stamp; **se frapper** *vi* (*s'inquiéter*) to get worked up; **frapper à la porte** to knock at the door; **frapper dans ses mains** to clap one's hands; **frapper du poing sur** to bang one's fist on; **frapper un grand coup** (*fig*) to strike a blow

frasques [fʀask(ə)] *nfpl* escapades; **faire des frasques** to get up to mischief

fraternel, le [fʀatɛʀnɛl] *adj* brotherly, fraternal

fraternité [fʀatɛʀnite] *nf* brotherhood

fraude [fʀod] *nf* fraud; (*SCOL*) cheating; **passer qch en fraude** to smuggle sth in (*ou* out); **fraude fiscale** tax evasion

frauder [fʀode] *vi, vt* to cheat; **frauder le fisc** to evade paying tax(es)

frauduleux, euse [fʀodylø, -øz] *adj* fraudulent

frayer [fʀeje] *vt* to open up, clear ♦ *vi* to spawn; (*fréquenter*): **frayer avec** to mix *ou* associate with; **se frayer un passage dans** to clear a path through, force one's way through

frayeur [fʀejœʀ] *nf* fright

fredonner [fʀədɔne] *vt* to hum

freezer [fʀizœʀ] *nm* freezing compartment

frein [fʀɛ̃] *nm* brake; **mettre un frein à** (*fig*) to put a brake on, check; **sans frein** (*sans limites*) unchecked; (*de jeu*) handbrake; **frein à main** handbrake; **frein moteur** engine braking; **freins à disques** disc brakes; **freins à tambour** drum brakes

freiner [fʀene] *vi* to brake ♦ *vt* (*progrès etc*) to check

frêle [fʀɛl] *adj* frail, fragile

frelon [fʀəlɔ̃] *nm* hornet

frémir [fʀemiʀ] *vi* (*de froid, de peur*) to tremble, shiver; (*de joie*) to quiver; (*eau*) to (begin to) bubble

frêne [fʀɛn] *nm* ash (tree)

frénétique [fʀenetik] *adj* frenzied, frenetic

fréquemment [fʀekamɑ̃] *adv* frequently

fréquent, e [fʀekɑ̃, -ɑ̃t] *adj* frequent

fréquentation [fʀekɑ̃tasjɔ̃] *nf* frequenting; seeing; **fréquentations** *nfpl* company *sg*

fréquenté, e [fʀekɑ̃te] *adj*: **très fréquenté** (very) busy; **mal fréquenté** patronized by disreputable elements

fréquenter [fʀekɑ̃te] *vt* (*lieu*) to frequent; (*personne*) to see; **se fréquenter** to see a lot of each other

frère [fʀɛʀ] *nm* brother ♦ *adj*: **partis/pays frères** sister parties/countries

fresque [fʀɛsk(ə)] *nf* (*ART*) fresco

fret [fʀɛ] *nm* freight

frétiller [fʀetije] *vi* to wriggle; to quiver; **frétiller de la queue** to wag its tail

fretin [fʀətɛ̃] *nm*: **le menu fretin** the small fry

friable [fʀijabl(ə)] *adj* crumbly

friand, e [fʀijɑ̃, -ɑ̃d] *adj*: **friand de** very fond of ♦ *nm* (*CULIN*) small minced-meat (*BRIT*) *ou* ground-meat (*US*) pie; (: *sucré*) small almond cake

friandise [fʀijɑ̃diz] *nf* sweet

fric [fʀik] *nm* (*fam*) cash, bread

friche [fʀiʃ]: **en friche** *adj, adv* (lying) fallow

friction [fʀiksjɔ̃] *nf* (*massage*) rub, rub-down; (*chez le coiffeur*) scalp massage; (*TECH, fig*) friction

frictionner [fʀiksjɔne] *vt* to rub (down); to massage

frigidaire® [fʀiʒidɛʀ] *nm* refrigerator

frigide [fʀiʒid] *adj* frigid

frigo [fʀigo] *nm* (= *frigidaire*) fridge

frigorifique [fʀigɔʀifik] *adj* refrigerating

frileux, euse [fʀilø, -øz] *adj* sensitive to (the) cold; (*fig*) overcautious

frime [fʀim] *nf* (*fam*): **c'est de la frime** it's all put on; **pour la frime** just for show

frimer [fʀime] *vi* to put on an act

frimousse [fʀimus] *nf* (sweet) little face

fringale [fʀɛ̃gal] *nf*: **avoir la fringale** to be ravenous

fringant, e [fʀɛ̃gɑ̃, -ɑ̃t] *adj* dashing

fringues [fʀɛ̃g] *nfpl* (fam) clothes, gear *no pl*

fripé, e [fʀipe] *adj* crumpled

fripon, ne [fʀipɔ̃, -ɔn] *adj* roguish, mischievous ♦ *nm/f* rascal, rogue

fripouille [fʀipuj] *nf* scoundrel

frire [fʀiʀ] *vt* (*aussi*: **faire frire**), *vi* to fry

frisé, e [fʀize] *adj* curly, curly-haired ♦ *nf*: **(chicorée) frisée** curly endive

frisson [fʀisɔ̃], **frissonnement** [fʀisɔnmɑ̃] *nm* shudder, shiver; quiver

frissonner [fʀisɔne] *vi* (*personne*) to shudder, shiver; (*feuilles*) to quiver

frit, e [fʀi, fʀit] *pp de* **frire** ♦ *adj* fried ♦ *nf*: **(pommes) frites** chips (BRIT), French fries

friteuse [fʀitøz] *nf* chip pan (BRIT), deep (fat) fryer

friture [fʀityʀ] *nf* (*huile*) (deep) fat; (*plat*): **friture (de poissons)** fried fish; (RADIO) crackle, crackling *no pl*; **fritures** *nfpl* (*aliments frits*) fried food *sg*

frivole [fʀivɔl] *adj* frivolous

froid, e [fʀwa, fʀwad] *adj* cold ♦ *nm* cold; (*absence de sympathie*) coolness *no pl*; **il fait froid** it's cold; **avoir froid** to be cold; **prendre froid** to catch a chill *ou* cold; **à froid** *adv* (*démarrer*) (from) cold; **(pendant) les grands froids** (in) the depths of winter, (during) the cold season; **jeter un froid** (*fig*) to cast a chill; **être en froid avec** to be on bad terms with; **battre froid à qn** to give sb the cold shoulder

froidement [fʀwadmɑ̃] *adv* (*accueillir*) coldly; (*décider*) coolly

froideur [fʀwadœʀ] *nf* coolness *no pl*

froisser [fʀwase] *vt* to crumple (up), crease; (*fig*) to hurt, offend; **se froisser** *vi* to crumple, crease; to take offence (BRIT) *ou* offense (US); **se froisser un muscle** to strain a muscle

frôler [fʀole] *vt* to brush against; (*suj: projectile*) to skim past; (*fig*) to come within a hair's breadth of, come very close to

fromage [fʀɔmaʒ] *nm* cheese; **fromage blanc** soft white cheese; **fromage de tête** pork brawn

froment [fʀɔmɑ̃] *nm* wheat

froncer [fʀɔ̃se] *vt* to gather; **froncer les sourcils** to frown

frondaisons [fʀɔ̃dɛzɔ̃] *nfpl* foliage *sg*

front [fʀɔ̃] *nm* forehead, brow; (MIL, MÉTÉOROLOGIE, POL) front; **avoir le front de faire** to have the effrontery *ou* front to do; **de front** *adv* (*se heurter*) head-on; (*rouler*) together (*i.e. 2 or 3 abreast*); (*simultanément*) at once; **faire front à** to face up to; **front de mer** (sea) front

frontalier, ière [fʀɔ̃talje, -jɛʀ] *adj* border *cpd*,

frontier *cpd* ♦ *nm/f*: **(travailleurs) frontaliers** workers who cross the border to go to work, commuters from across the border

frontière [fʀɔ̃tjɛʀ] *nf* (GÉO, POL) frontier, border; (*fig*) frontier, boundary

frotter [fʀɔte] *vi* to rub, scrape ♦ *vt* to rub; (*pour nettoyer*) to rub (up); (: *avec une brosse*) to scrub; **frotter une allumette** to strike a match; **se frotter à qn** to cross swords with sb; **se frotter à qch** to come up against sth; **se frotter les mains** (*fig*) to rub one's hands (gleefully)

fructifier [fʀyktifje] *vi* to yield a profit; **faire fructifier** to turn to good account

fructueux, euse [fʀyktɥø, -øz] *adj* fruitful; profitable

frugal, e, aux [fʀygal, -o] *adj* frugal

fruit [fʀɥi] *nm* fruit *gén no pl*; **fruits de mer** (CULIN) seafood(s); **fruits secs** dried fruit *sg*

fruité, e [fʀɥite] *adj* (*vin*) fruity

fruitier, ière [fʀɥitje, -jɛʀ] *adj*: **arbre fruitier** fruit tree ♦ *nm/f* fruiterer (BRIT), fruit merchant (US)

fruste [fʀyst(ə)] *adj* unpolished, uncultivated

frustrer [fʀystʀe] *vt* to frustrate; (*priver*): **frustrer qn de qch** to deprive sb of sth

FS *abr* (= *franc suisse*) FS, SF

fuel(-oil) [fjul(ɔjl)] *nm* fuel oil; (*pour chauffer*) heating oil

fugace [fygas] *adj* fleeting

fugitif, ive [fyʒitif, -iv] *adj* (*lueur, amour*) fleeting; (*prisonnier etc*) runaway ♦ *nm/f* fugitive, runaway

fugue [fyg] *nf* (*d'un enfant*) running away *no pl*; (MUS) fugue; **faire une fugue** to run away, abscond

fuir [fɥiʀ] *vt* to flee from; (*éviter*) to shun ♦ *vi* to run away; (*gaz, robinet*) to leak

fuite [fɥit] *nf* flight; (*écoulement*) leak, leakage; (*divulgation*) leak; **être en fuite** to be on the run; **mettre en fuite** to put to flight; **prendre la fuite** to take flight

fulgurant, e [fylgyʀɑ̃, -ɑ̃t] *adj* lightning *cpd*, dazzling

fulminer [fylmine] *vi*: **fulminer (contre)** to thunder forth (against)

fumé, e [fyme] *adj* (CULIN) smoked; (*verre*) tinted ♦ *nf* smoke; **partir en fumée** to go up in smoke

fumer [fyme] *vi* to smoke; (*liquide*) to steam ♦ *vt* to smoke; (*terre, champ*) to manure

fûmes [fym] *vb voir* **être**

fumet [fyme] *nm* aroma

fumeur, euse [fymœʀ, -øz] *nm/f* smoker; **(compartiment) fumeurs** smoking compartment

fumeux, euse [fymø, -øz] *adj* (*péj*) woolly (BRIT), hazy

fumier [fymje] *nm* manure

fumiste [fymist(ə)] *nm* (*ramoneur*) chimney sweep ♦ *nm/f* (*péj: paresseux*) shirker; (*charlatan*) phoney

funèbre [fynɛbʀ(ə)] *adj* funeral *cpd*; (*fig*) doleful;

funereal

funérailles [fyneʀaj] *nfpl* funeral *sg*

funeste [fynɛst(ə)] *adj* disastrous; deathly

fur [fyʀ]: **au fur et à mesure** *adv* as one goes along; **au fur et à mesure que** as; **au fur et à mesure de leur progression** as they advance (*ou* advanced)

furet [fyʀɛ] *nm* ferret

fureter [fyʀte] *vi* (*péj*) to nose about

fureur [fyʀœʀ] *nf* fury; (*passion*): **fureur de passion** for; **faire fureur** to be all the rage

furibond, e [fyʀibɔ̃, -ɔ̃d] *adj* livid, absolutely furious

furie [fyʀi] *nf* fury; (*femme*) shrew, vixen; **en furie** (*mer*) raging

furieux, euse [fyʀjø, -øz] *adj* furious

furoncle [fyʀɔ̃kl(ə)] *nm* boil

furtif, ive [fyʀtif, -iv] *adj* furtive

fus [fy] *vb voir* **être**

fusain [fyzɛ̃] *nm* (*BOT*) spindle-tree; (*ART*) charcoal

fuseau, x [fyzo] *nm* (*pantalon*) (ski-)pants *pl*; (*pour filer*) spindle; **en fuseau** (*jambes*) tapering; (*colonne*) bulging; **fuseau horaire** time zone

fusée [fyze] *nf* rocket; **fusée éclairante** flare

fuser [fyze] *vi* (*rires etc*) to burst forth

fusible [fyzibl(ə)] *nm* (*ÉLEC: fil*) fuse wire; (: *fiche*) fuse

fusil [fyzi] *nm* (*de guerre, à canon rayé*) rifle, gun; (*de chasse, à canon lisse*) shotgun, gun; **fusil à deux coups** double-barrelled rifle *ou* shotgun; **fusil sous-marin** spear-gun

fusillade [fyzijad] *nf* gunfire *no pl*, shooting *no pl*; (*combat*) gun battle

fusiller [fyzije] *vt* to shoot; **fusiller qn du regard** to look daggers at sb

fusil-mitrailleur, *pl* **fusils-mitrailleurs** [fyzimitʀajœʀ] *nm* machine gun

fusionner [fyzjɔne] *vi* to merge

fut [fy] *vb voir* **être**

fût [fy] *vb voir* **être** ♦ *nm* (*tonneau*) barrel, cask; (*de canon*) stock; (*d'arbre*) bole, trunk; (*de colonne*) shaft

futé, e [fyte] *adj* crafty

futile [fytil] *adj* (*inutile*) futile; (*frivole*) frivolous

futur, e [fytyʀ] *adj, nm* future; **son futur époux** her husband-to-be; **au futur** (*LING*) in the future

fuyant, e [fɥijɑ̃, -ɑ̃t] *vb voir* **fuir** ♦ *adj* (*regard etc*) evasive; (*lignes etc*) receding; (*perspective*) vanishing

fuyard, e [fɥijaʀ, -aʀd(ə)] *nm/f* runaway

— *G g* —

gâcher [ɡɑʃe] *vt* (*gâter*) to spoil, ruin; (*gaspiller*) to waste; (*plâtre*) to temper; (*mortier*) to mix

gâchis [ɡɑʃi] *nm* (*désordre*) mess; (*gaspillage*) waste *no pl*

gadoue [ɡadu] *nf* sludge

gaffe [ɡaf] *nf* (*instrument*) boat hook; (*fam: erreur*) blunder; **faire gaffe** (*fam*) to watch out

gage [ɡaʒ] *nm* (*dans un jeu*) forfeit; (*fig: de fidélité*) token; **gages** *nmpl* (*salaire*) wages; (*garantie*) guarantee *sg*; **mettre en gage** to pawn; **laisser en gage** to leave as security

gageure [ɡaʒyʀ] *nf*: **c'est une gageure** it's attempting the impossible

gagnant, e [ɡaɲɑ̃, -ɑ̃t] *adj*: **billet/numéro gagnant** winning ticket/number ♦ *adv*: **jouer gagnant** (*aux courses*) to be bound to win ♦ *nm/f* winner

gagne-pain [ɡaɲpɛ̃] *nm inv* job

gagner [ɡaɲe] *vt* (*concours, procès, pari*) to win; (*somme d'argent, revenu*) to earn; (*aller vers, atteindre*) to reach; (*s'emparer de*) to overcome; (*envahir*) to spread to; (*se concilier*): **gagner qn** to win sb over ♦ *vi* to win; (*fig*) to gain; **gagner du temps/de la place** to gain time/save space; **gagner sa vie** to earn one's living; **gagner du terrain** (*aussi fig*) to gain ground; **gagner qn de vitesse** to outstrip sb; (*aussi fig*) **gagner à faire** (*s'en trouver bien*) to be better off doing; **il y gagne** it's in his interest, it's to his advantage

gai, e [ɡe] *adj* cheerful; (*livre, pièce de théâtre*) light-hearted; (*un peu ivre*) merry

gaiement [ɡemɑ̃] *adv* cheerfully

gaieté [ɡete] *nf* cheerfulness; **gaietés** *nfpl* (*souvent ironique*) delights; **de gaieté de cœur** with a light heart

gaillard, e [ɡajaʀ, -aʀd(ə)] *adj* (*robuste*) sprightly; (*grivois*) bawdy, ribald ♦ *nm/f* (*strapping*) fellow/ wench

gain [ɡɛ̃] *nm* (*revenu*) earnings *pl*; (*bénéfice: gén pl*) profits *pl*; (*au jeu: gén pl*) winnings *pl*; (*fig: de temps, place*) saving; (: *avantage*) benefit; (: *lucre*) gain; **avoir gain de cause** to win the case; (*fig*) to be proved right; **obtenir gain de cause** (*fig*) to win out

gaine [ɡɛn] *nf* (*corset*) girdle; (*fourreau*) sheath; (*de fil électrique etc*) outer covering

gala [ɡala] *nm* official reception; **soirée de gala** gala evening

galant, e [ɡalɑ̃, -ɑ̃t] *adj* (*courtois*) courteous, gentlemanly; (*entreprenant*) flirtatious, gallant; (*aventure, poésie*) amorous; **en galante compagnie** (*homme*) with a lady friend; (*femme*) with a gentleman friend

galère [ɡalɛʀ] *nf* galley

galérer [galeʀe] *vi (fam)* to work hard, slave (away)

galerie [galʀi] *nf* gallery; *(THÉÂT)* circle; *(de voiture)* roof rack; *(fig: spectateurs)* audience; **galerie marchande** shopping mall; **galerie de peinture** (private) art gallery

galet [galɛ] *nm* pebble; *(TECH)* wheel; **galets** *nmpl* pebbles, shingle *sg*

galette [galɛt] *nf (gâteau)* flat pastry cake; *(crêpe)* savoury pancake; **la galette des Rois** *cake traditionally eaten on Twelfth Night*

galipette [galipɛt] *nf:* **faire des galipettes** to turn somersaults

Galles [gal] *nfpl:* **le pays de Galles** Wales

gallois, e [galwa, -waz] *adj* Welsh ♦ *nm (LING)* Welsh ♦ *nm/f:* **Gallois, e** Welshman/woman

galon [galɔ̃] *nm (MIL)* stripe; *(décoratif)* piece of braid; **prendre du galon** to be promoted

galop [galo] *nm* gallop; **au galop** at a gallop; **galop d'essai** *(fig)* trial run

galoper [galɔpe] *vi* to gallop

galopin [galɔpɛ̃] *nm* urchin, ragamuffin

gambader [gɑ̃bade] *vi* to skip *ou* frisk about

gamin, e [gamɛ̃, -in] *nm/f* kid ♦ *adj* mischievous, playful

gamme [gam] *nf (MUS)* scale; *(fig)* range

gammé, e [game] *adj:* **croix gammée** swastika

gang [gɑ̃g] *nm* gang

gant [gɑ̃] *nm* glove; **prendre des gants** *(fig)* to handle the situation with kid gloves; **relever le gant** *(fig)* to take up the gauntlet; **gant de crin** massage glove; **gant de toilette** (face) flannel *(BRIT)*, face cloth; **gants de boxe** boxing gloves; **gants de caoutchouc** rubber gloves

garage [gaʀaʒ] *nm* garage; **garage à vélos** bicycle shed

garagiste [gaʀaʒist(ə)] *nm/f (propriétaire)* garage owner; *(mécanicien)* garage mechanic

garantie [gaʀɑ̃ti] *nf* guarantee, warranty; *(gage)* security, surety; **(bon de) garantie** guarantee *ou* warranty slip; **garantie de bonne exécution** performance bond

garantir [gaʀɑ̃tiʀ] *vt* to guarantee; *(protéger):* **garantir de** to protect from; **je vous garantis que** I can assure you that; **garanti pure laine/2 ans** guaranteed pure wool/for 2 years

garce [gaʀs(ə)] *nf (péj)* bitch

garçon [gaʀsɔ̃] *nm* boy; *(célibataire)* bachelor; *(jeune homme)* boy, lad; *(aussi:* **garçon de café**) waiter; **garçon boucher/coiffeur** butcher's/hairdresser's assistant; **garçon de courses** messenger; **garçon d'écurie** stable lad; **garçon manqué** tomboy

garçonnière [gaʀsɔnjɛʀ] *nf* bachelor flat

garde [gaʀd(ə)] *nm (de prisonnier)* guard; *(de domaine etc)* warden; *(soldat, sentinelle)* guardsman ♦ *nf* guarding; looking after; *(soldats, BOXE, ESCRIME)* guard; *(faction)* watch; *(d'une arme)* hilt; *(TYPO: aussi:* **page** *ou* **feuille de garde**) flyleaf; *(: collée)* endpaper; **de garde** *adj, adv* on duty; **monter la garde** to stand guard; **être sur ses gardes** to be on one's guard; **mettre en garde** to warn; **mise en garde** warning; **prendre garde (à)** to be careful (of); **avoir la garde des enfants** *(après divorce)* to have custody of the children; **garde champêtre** *nm* rural policeman; **garde du corps** *nm* bodyguard; **garde d'enfants** *nf* child minder; **garde forestier** *nm* forest warden; **garde mobile** *nm, nf* mobile guard; **garde des Sceaux** *nm* ≃ Lord Chancellor *(BRIT),* ≃ Attorney General *(US);* **garde à vue** *nf (JUR)* ≃ police custody

garde-à-vous [gaʀdavu] *nm inv:* **être/se mettre au garde-à-vous** to be at/stand to attention; **garde-à-vous (fixe)!** *(MIL)* attention!

garde-barrière, *pl* **gardes-barrière(s)** [gaʀdəbaʀjɛʀ] *nm/f* level-crossing keeper

garde-boue [gaʀdəbu] *nm inv* mudguard

garde-chasse, *pl* **gardes-chasse(s)** [gaʀdəʃas] *nm* gamekeeper

garde-malade, *pl* **gardes-malade(s)** [gaʀdəmalad] *nf* home nurse

garde-manger [gaʀdmɑ̃ʒe] *nm inv (boîte)* meat safe; *(placard)* pantry, larder

garder [gaʀde] *vt (conserver)* to keep; *(: sur soi: vêtement, chapeau)* to keep on; *(surveiller: enfants)* to look after; *(: immeuble, lieu, prisonnier)* to guard; **se garder** *vi (aliment: se conserver)* to keep; **se garder de faire** to be careful not to do; **garder le lit/la chambre** to stay in bed/indoors; **garder le silence** to keep silent *ou* quiet; **garder la ligne** to keep one's figure; **garder à vue** to keep in custody; **pêche/chasse gardée** private fishing/hunting (ground)

garderie [gaʀdəʀi] *nf* day nursery, crèche

garde-robe [gaʀdəʀɔb] *nf* wardrobe

gardien, ne [gaʀdjɛ̃, -ɛn] *nm/f (garde)* guard; *(de prison)* warder; *(de domaine, réserve)* warden; *(de musée etc)* attendant; *(de phare, cimetière)* keeper; *(d'immeuble)* caretaker; *(fig)* guardian; **gardien de but** goalkeeper; **gardien de nuit** night watchman; **gardien de la paix** policeman

gare [gaʀ] *nf (railway)* station, train station *(US)* ♦ *excl:* **gare à ...** mind ...!, watch out for ...!; **gare à ne pas ...** mind you don't ...; **gare à toi!** watch out!; **sans crier gare** without warning; **gare maritime** harbour station; **gare routière** coach *(BRIT) ou* bus station; *(de camions)* haulage *(BRIT) ou* trucking *(US)* depot; **gare de triage** marshalling yard

garer [gaʀe] *vt* to park; **se garer** to park; *(pour laisser passer)* to draw into the side

gargariser [gaʀgaʀize]: **se gargariser** *vi* to gargle; **se gargariser de** *(fig)* to revel in

gargote [gaʀgɔt] *nf* cheap restaurant, greasy spoon *(fam)*

gargouille [gaʀguj] *nf* gargoyle

gargouiller [gaʀguje] vi (*estomac*) to rumble; (*eau*) to gurgle

garnement [gaʀnəmã] nm rascal, scallywag

garni, e [gaʀni] adj (*plat*) served with vegetables (*and chips or pasta or rice*) ♦ nm (*appartement*) furnished accommodation no pl (BRIT) ou accommodations pl (US)

garnison [gaʀnizɔ̃] nf garrison

garniture [gaʀnityʀ] nf (CULIN: *légumes*) vegetables pl; (: *persil etc*) garnish; (: *farce*) filling; (*décoration*) trimming; (*protection*) fittings pl; **garniture de cheminée** mantelpiece ornaments pl; **garniture de frein** (AUTO) brake lining; **garniture intérieure** (AUTO) interior trim; **garniture périodique** sanitary towel (BRIT) ou napkin (US)

gars [ga] nm lad; (*type*) guy

Gascogne [gaskɔɲ] nf: **la Gascogne** Gascony

gas-oil [gazɔjl] nm diesel oil

gaspiller [gaspije] vt to waste

gastronome [gastʀɔnɔm] nm/f gourmet

gastronomie [gastʀɔnɔmi] nf gastronomy

gastronomique [gastʀɔnɔmik] adj: **menu gastronomique** gourmet menu

gâteau, x [gato] nm cake ♦ adj inv (fam: *trop indulgent*): **papa-/maman-gâteau** doting father/mother; **gâteau d'anniversaire** birthday cake; **gâteau de riz** = rice pudding; **gâteau sec** biscuit

gâter [gate] vt to spoil; **se gâter** vi (*dent, fruit*) to go bad; (*temps, situation*) to change for the worse

gâterie [gatʀi] nf little treat

gâteux, euse [gatø, -øz] adj senile

gauche [goʃ] adj left, left-hand; (*maladroit*) awkward, clumsy ♦ nf (POL) left (wing); (BOXE) left; **à gauche** on the left; (*direction*) (to the) left; **à gauche de** (on ou to the) left of; **à la gauche de** to the left of; **sur votre gauche** on your left; **de gauche** (POL) left-wing

gaucher, ère [goʃe, -ɛʀ] adj left-handed

gauchiste [goʃist(ə)] adj, nm/f leftist

gaufre [gofʀ(ə)] nf (*pâtisserie*) waffle; (*de cire*) honeycomb

gaufrette [gofʀɛt] nf wafer

gaulois, e [golwa, -waz] adj Gallic; (*grivois*) bawdy ♦ nm/f: **Gaulois, e** Gaul

gaver [gave] vt to force-feed; (*fig*): **gaver de** to cram with, fill up with; (*personne*): **se gaver de** to stuff o.s. with

gaz [gaz] nm inv gas; **mettre les gaz** (AUTO) to put one's foot down; **chambre/masque à gaz** gas chamber/mask; **gaz en bouteille** bottled gas; **gaz butane** Calor gas® (BRIT); **gaz carbonique** carbon dioxide; **gaz hilarant** laughing gas; **gaz lacrymogène** tear gas; **gaz naturel** natural gas; **gaz de ville** town gas (BRIT), manufactured domestic gas

gaze [gaz] nf gauze

gazer [gaze] vt to gas ♦ vi (fam) to be going ou working well

gazette [gazɛt] nf news sheet

gazeux, euse [gazø, -øz] adj gaseous; (*eau*) sparkling; (*boisson*) fizzy

gazoduc [gazɔdyk] nm gas pipeline

gazon [gazɔ̃] nm (*herbe*) turf, grass; (*pelouse*) lawn

gazouiller [gazuje] vi (*oiseau*) to chirp; (*enfant*) to babble

GDF sigle m (= Gaz de France) national gas company

geai [ʒɛ] nm jay

géant, e [ʒeã, -ãt] adj gigantic, giant; (COMM) giant-size ♦ nm/f giant

geindre [ʒɛ̃dʀ(ə)] vi to groan, moan

gel [ʒɛl] nm frost; (*de l'eau*) freezing; (*fig: des salaires, prix*) freeze; freezing; (*produit de beauté*) gel

gélatine [ʒelatin] nf gelatine

gelé, e [ʒ(ə)le] adj frozen ♦ nf jelly; (*gel*) frost; **gelée blanche** hoarfrost, white frost

geler [ʒ(ə)le] vt, vi to freeze; **il gèle** it's freezing

gélule [ʒelyl] nf capsule

gelures [ʒəlyʀ] nfpl frostbite sg

Gémeaux [ʒemo] nmpl: **les Gémeaux** Gemini, the Twins; **être des Gémeaux** to be Gemini

gémir [ʒemiʀ] vi to groan, moan

gênant, e [ʒenã, -ãt] adj (*objet*) awkward, in the way; (*histoire, personne*) embarrassing

gencive [ʒãsiv] nf gum

gendarme [ʒãdaʀm(ə)] nm gendarme

gendarmerie [ʒãdaʀməʀi] nf military police force in countryside and small towns; their police station or barracks

gendre [ʒãdʀ(ə)] nm son-in-law

gêné, e [ʒene] adj embarrassed; (*dépourvu d'argent*) short (of money)

gêner [ʒene] vt (*incommoder*) to bother; (*encombrer*) to hamper; (*bloquer le passage*) to be in the way of; (*déranger*) to bother; (*embarrasser*): **gêner qn** to make sb feel ill-at-ease; **se gêner** to put o.s. out; **ne vous gênez pas!** (*ironique*) go right ahead!, don't mind me!; **je vais me gêner!** (*ironique*) why should I care?

général, e, aux [ʒeneʀal, -o] adj, nm general ♦ nf: **(répétition) générale** final dress rehearsal; **en général** usually, in general; **à la satisfaction générale** to everyone's satisfaction

généralement [ʒeneʀalmã] adv generally

généraliser [ʒeneʀalize] vt, vi to generalize; **se généraliser** vi to become widespread

généraliste [ʒeneʀalist(ə)] nm/f (MÉD) general practitioner, GP

génération [ʒeneʀasjɔ̃] nf (*aussi* INFORM) generation

généreux, euse [ʒeneʀø, -øz] adj generous

générique [ʒeneʀik] adj generic ♦ nm (CINÉ, TV) credits pl, credit titles pl

générosité [ʒeneʀozite] *nf* generosity

genêt [ʒənɛ] *nm* (*BOT*) broom *no pl*

génétique [ʒenetik] *adj* genetic ♦ *nf* genetics *sg*

Genève [ʒənɛv] Geneva

génial, e, aux [ʒenjal, -o] *adj* of genius; (*fam*) fantastic, brilliant

génie [ʒeni] *nm* genius; (*MIL*): **le génie** = the Engineers *pl*; **avoir du génie** to have genius; **génie civil** civil engineering; **génie génétique** genetic engineering

genièvre [ʒənjɛvʀ(ə)] *nm* (*BOT*) juniper (tree); (*boisson*) geneva; **grain de genièvre** juniper berry

génisse [ʒenis] *nf* heifer; **foie de génisse** ox liver

génital, e, aux [ʒenital, -o] *adj* genital

génoise [ʒenwaz] *nf* (*gâteau*) = sponge cake

genou, x [ʒnu] *nm* knee; **à genoux** on one's knees; **se mettre à genoux** to kneel down

genre [ʒɑ̃ʀ] *nm* (*espèce, sorte*) kind, type, sort; (*allure*) style; (*LING*) gender; (*ART*) genre; (*ZOOL etc*) genus; **se donner du genre** to give o.s. airs; **avoir bon genre** to have style; **avoir mauvais genre** to be ill-mannered

gens [ʒɑ̃] *nmpl* (*f in some phrases*) people *pl*; **les gens d'Église** the clergy; **les gens du monde** society people; **gens de maison** domestics

gentil, le [ʒɑ̃ti, -ij] *adj* kind; (*enfant: sage*) good; (*sympa: endroit etc*) nice; **c'est très gentil à vous** it's very kind *ou* good *ou* nice of you

gentillesse [ʒɑ̃tijɛs] *nf* kindness

gentiment [ʒɑ̃timɑ̃] *adv* kindly

géo [ʒeo] *abbr* (= *géographie*) geography

géographie [ʒeɔgʀafi] *nf* geography

geôlier [ʒolje] *nm* jailer

géologie [ʒeɔlɔʒi] *nf* geology

géomètre [ʒeɔmɛtʀ(ə)] *nm*: **(arpenteur) géomètre** (land) surveyor

géométrie [ʒeɔmetʀi] *nf* geometry; **à géométrie variable** (*AVIAT*) swing-wing

géométrique [ʒeɔmetʀik] *adj* geometric

géranium [ʒeʀanjɔm] *nm* geranium

gérant, e [ʒeʀɑ̃, -ɑ̃t] *nm/f* manager/manageress; **gérant d'immeuble** managing agent

gerbe [ʒɛʀb(ə)] *nf* (*de fleurs, d'eau*) spray; (*de blé*) sheaf (*pl* sheaves); (*fig*) shower, burst

gercé, e [ʒɛʀse] *adj* chapped

gerçure [ʒɛʀsyʀ] *nf* crack

gérer [ʒeʀe] *vt* to manage

germain, e [ʒɛʀmɛ̃, -ɛn] *adj*: **cousin germain** first cousin

germe [ʒɛʀm(ə)] *nm* germ

germer [ʒɛʀme] *vi* to sprout; (*semence, aussi fig*) to germinate

geste [ʒɛst(ə)] *nm* gesture; move; motion; **il fit un geste de la main pour m'appeler** he signed to me to come over, he waved me over; **ne faites pas un geste** (*ne bougez pas*) don't move

gestion [ʒɛstjɔ̃] *nf* management; **gestion des disques** (*INFORM*) housekeeping; **gestion de fichier(s)** (*INFORM*) file management

ghetto [geto] *nm* ghetto

gibet [ʒibɛ] *nm* gallows *pl*

gibier [ʒibje] *nm* (*animaux*) game; (*fig*) prey

giboulée [ʒibule] *nf* sudden shower

gicler [ʒikle] *vi* to spurt, squirt

gifle [ʒifl(ə)] *nf* slap (in the face)

gifler [ʒifle] *vt* to slap (in the face)

gigantesque [ʒigɑ̃tɛsk(ə)] *adj* gigantic

gigogne [ʒigɔɲ] *adj*: **lits gigognes** truckle (*BRIT*) *ou* trundle (*US*) beds; **tables/poupées gigognes** nest of tables/dolls

gigot [ʒigo] *nm* leg (of mutton *ou* lamb)

gigoter [ʒigɔte] *vi* to wriggle (about)

gilet [ʒilɛ] *nm* waistcoat; (*pull*) cardigan; (*de corps*) vest; **gilet pare-balles** bulletproof jacket; **gilet de sauvetage** life jacket

gin [dʒin] *nm* gin

gingembre [ʒɛ̃ʒɑ̃bʀ(ə)] *nm* ginger

girafe [ʒiʀaf] *nf* giraffe

giratoire [ʒiʀatwaʀ] *adj*: **sens giratoire** roundabout

girofle [ʒiʀɔfl(ə)] *nm*: **clou de girofle** clove

girouette [ʒiʀwɛt] *nf* weather vane *ou* cock

gitan, e [ʒitɑ̃, -ɑn] *nm/f* gipsy

gîte [ʒit] *nm* home; shelter; (*du lièvre*) form; **gîte (rural)** (country) holiday cottage *ou* apartment

givre [ʒivʀ(ə)] *nm* (hoar)frost

givré, e [ʒivʀe] *adj*: **citron givré/orange givrée** lemon/orange sorbet (*served in fruit skin*)

glace [glas] *nf* ice; (*crème glacée*) ice cream; (*verre*) sheet of glass; (*miroir*) mirror; (*de voiture*) window; **glaces** *nfpl* (*GÉO*) ice sheets, ice *sg*; **de glace** (*fig: accueil, visage*) frosty, icy; **rester de glace** to remain unmoved

glacé, e [glase] *adj* icy; (*boisson*) iced

glacer [glase] *vt* to freeze; (*boisson*) to chill, ice; (*gâteau*) to ice (*BRIT*), frost (*US*); (*papier, tissu*) to glaze; (*fig*): **glacer qn** to chill sb; (*fig*) to make sb's blood run cold

glacial, e [glasjal] *adj* icy

glacier [glasje] *nm* (*GÉO*) glacier; (*marchand*) ice-cream maker

glacière [glasjɛʀ] *nf* icebox

glaçon [glasɔ̃] *nm* icicle; (*pour boisson*) ice cube

glaïeul [glajœl] *nm* gladiola

glaise [glɛz] *nf* clay

gland [glɑ̃] *nm* (*de chêne*) acorn; (*décoration*) tassel; (*ANAT*) glans

glande [glɑ̃d] *nf* gland

glander [glɑ̃de] *vi* (*fam*) to fart around (*BRIT!*), screw around (*US!*)

glauque [glok] *adj* dull blue-green

glissade [glisad] *nf* (*par jeu*) slide; (*chute*) slip; (*dérapage*) skid; **faire des glissades** to slide

glissant, e [glisɑ̃, -ɑ̃t] *adj* slippery

glissement [glismɑ̃] *nm* sliding; (*fig*) shift; **glissement de terrain** landslide

glisser [glise] *vi* (*avancer*) to glide *ou* slide along; (*coulisser, tomber*) to slide; (*déraper*) to slip; (*être glissant*) to be slippery ♦ *vt*: **glisser qch sous/dans/à** to slip sth under/into/to; **glisser sur** (*fig*: *détail etc*) to skate over; **se glisser dans/entre** to slip into/between

global, e, aux [glɔbal, -o] *adj* overall

globe [glɔb] *nm* globe; **sous globe** under glass; **globe oculaire** eyeball; **le globe terrestre** the globe

globule [glɔbyl] *nm* (*du sang*): **globule blanc/rouge** white/red corpuscle

globuleux, euse [glɔbylø, -øz] *adj*: **yeux globuleux** protruding eyes

gloire [glwaʀ] *nf* glory; (*mérite*) distinction, credit; (*personne*) celebrity

glorieux, euse [glɔʀjø, -øz] *adj* glorious

gloussement [glusmɑ̃] *nm* (*de poule*) cluck; (*rire*) chuckle

glousser [gluse] *vi* to cluck; (*rire*) to chuckle

glouton, ne [glutɔ̃, -ɔn] *adj* gluttonous, greedy

gluant, e [glyɑ̃, -ɑ̃t] *adj* sticky, gummy

glucose [glykoz] *nm* glucose

glycine [glisin] *nf* wisteria

GO *sigle fpl* (= grandes ondes) LW ♦ *sigle m* (= gentil organisateur) *title given to leaders on Club Méditerranée holidays; extended to refer to easy-going leader of any group*

goal [gol] *nm* goalkeeper

gobelet [gɔblɛ] *nm* (*en métal*) tumbler; (*en plastique*) beaker; (*à dés*) cup

gober [gɔbe] *vt* to swallow

godasse [gɔdas] *nf* (*fam*) shoe

godet [gɔdɛ] *nm* pot; (*COUTURE*) unpressed pleat

goéland [gɔelɑ̃] *nm* (sea)gull

goélette [gɔelɛt] *nf* schooner

gogo [gɔgo] *nm* (*péj*) mug, sucker; **à gogo** *adv* galore

goguenard, e [gɔgnaʀ, -aʀd(ə)] *adj* mocking

goinfre [gwɛ̃fʀ(ə)] *nm* glutton

golf [gɔlf] *nm* (*jeu*) golf; (*terrain*) golf course; **golf miniature** crazy *ou* miniature golf

golfe [gɔlf(ə)] *nm* gulf; bay; **le golfe d'Aden** the Gulf of Aden; **le golfe de Gascogne** the Bay of Biscay; **le golfe du Lion** the Gulf of Lions; **le golfe Persique** the Persian Gulf

gomme [gɔm] *nf* (*à effacer*) rubber (*BRIT*), eraser; (*résine*) gum; **boule** *ou* **pastille de gomme** throat pastille

gommer [gɔme] *vt* (*effacer*) to rub out (*BRIT*), erase; (*enduire de gomme*) to gum

gond [gɔ̃] *nm* hinge; **sortir de ses gonds** (*fig*) to fly off the handle

gondoler [gɔ̃dɔle]: **se gondoler** *vi* to warp, buck-le; (*fam: rire*) to hoot with laughter; to be in stitches

gonflé, e [gɔ̃fle] *adj* swollen; (*ventre*) bloated; (*fam: culotté*): **être gonflé** to have a nerve

gonfler [gɔ̃fle] *vt* (*pneu, ballon*) to inflate, blow up; (*nombre, importance*) to inflate ♦ *vi* (*pied etc*) to swell (up); (*CULIN: pâte*) to rise

gonfleur [gɔ̃flœʀ] *nm* air pump

gonzesse [gɔ̃zɛs] *nf* (*fam*) chick, bird (*BRIT*)

goret [gɔʀɛ] *nm* piglet

gorge [gɔʀʒ(ə)] *nf* (*ANAT*) throat; (*poitrine*) breast; (*GÉO*) gorge; (*rainure*) groove; **avoir mal à la gorge** to have a sore throat; **avoir la gorge serrée** to have a lump in one's throat

gorgé, e [gɔʀʒe] *adj*: **gorgé de** filled with; (*eau*) saturated with ♦ *nf* mouthful; sip; gulp; **boire à petites/grandes gorgées** to take little sips/big gulps

gorille [gɔʀij] *nm* gorilla; (*fam*) bodyguard

gosier [gozje] *nm* throat

gosse [gɔs] *nm/f* kid

goudron [gudʀɔ̃] *nm* (*asphalte*) tar(mac) (*BRIT*), asphalt; (*du tabac*) tar

goudronner [gudʀɔne] *vt* to tar(mac) (*BRIT*), asphalt

gouffre [gufʀ(ə)] *nm* abyss, gulf

goujat [guʒa] *nm* boor

goulot [gulo] *nm* neck; **boire au goulot** to drink from the bottle

goulu, e [guly] *adj* greedy

gourd, e [guʀ, guʀd(ə)] *adj* numb (with cold); (*fam*) oafish

gourde [guʀd(ə)] *nf* (*récipient*) flask; (*fam*) (*clumsy*) clot *ou* oaf

gourer [guʀe] (*fam*): **se gourer** *vi* to boob

gourdin [guʀdɛ̃] *nm* club, bludgeon

gourmand, e [guʀmɑ̃, -ɑ̃d] *adj* greedy

gourmandise [guʀmɑ̃diz] *nf* greed; (*bonbon*) sweet (*BRIT*), piece of candy (*US*)

gourmet [guʀmɛ] *nm* epicure

gourmette [guʀmɛt] *nf* chain bracelet

gousse [gus] *nf* (*de vanille etc*) pod; **gousse d'ail** clove of garlic

goût [gu] *nm* taste; (*fig: appréciation*) taste, liking; **le (bon) goût** good taste; **de bon goût** in good taste, tasteful; **de mauvais goût** in bad taste, tasteless; **avoir bon/mauvais goût** (*aliment*) to taste nice/ nasty; (*personne*) to have good/bad taste; **avoir du/manquer de goût** to have/lack taste; **avoir du goût pour** to have a liking for; **prendre goût à** to develop a taste *ou* a liking for

goûter [gute] *vt* (*essayer*) to taste; (*apprécier*) to enjoy ♦ *vi* to have (afternoon) tea ♦ *nm* (afternoon) tea; **goûter à** to taste, sample; **goûter de** to have a taste of; **goûter d'enfants/d'anniversaire** children's tea/birthday party

goutte [gut] *nf* drop; (*MÉD*) gout; (*alcool*) nip (*BRIT*), tot (*BRIT*), drop (*US*); **gouttes** *nfpl* (*MÉD*) drops;

goutte à goutte *adv* a drop at a time; **tomber goutte à goutte** to drip

goutte-à-goutte [gutagut] *nm inv* (*MÉD*) drip; **alimenter au goutte-à-goutte** to drip-feed

gouttelette [gutlɛt] *nf* droplet

gouttière [gutjɛʁ] *nf* gutter

gouvernail [guvɛʁnaj] *nm* rudder; (*barre*) helm, tiller

gouvernante [guvɛʁnɑ̃t] *nf* housekeeper; (*d'un enfant*) governess

gouvernement [guvɛʁnəmɑ̃] *nm* government

gouverner [guvɛʁne] *vt* to govern; (*diriger*) to steer; (*fig*) to control

grâce [gʁɑs] *nf* grace; (*faveur*) favour; (*JUR*) pardon; **grâces** *nfpl* (*REL*) grace *sg*; **de bonne/mauvaise grâce** with (a) good/bad grace; **dans les bonnes grâces de qn** in favour with sb; **faire grâce à qn de qch** to spare sb sth; **rendre grâce(s) à** to give thanks to; **demander grâce** to beg for mercy; **droit de grâce** right of reprieve; **recours en grâce** plea for pardon; **grâce à** *prép* thanks to

gracier [gʁasje] *vt* to pardon

gracieux, euse [gʁasjø, -øz] *adj* (*charmant, élégant*) graceful; (*aimable*) gracious, kind; **à titre gracieux** free of charge

grade [gʁad] *nm* (*MIL*) rank; (*SCOL*) degree; **monter en grade** to be promoted

gradin [gʁadɛ̃] *nm* (*dans un théâtre*) tier; (*de stade*) step; **gradins** *nmpl* (*de stade*) terracing *no pl* (*BRIT*), standing area; **en gradins** terraced

gradué, e [gʁadɥe] *adj* (*exercices*) graded (for difficulty); (*thermomètre, verre*) graduated

graduel, le [gʁadɥɛl] *adj* gradual; progressive

graduer [gʁadɥe] *vt* (*effort etc*) to increase gradually; (*règle, verre*) to graduate

graffiti [gʁafiti] *nmpl* graffiti

grain [gʁɛ̃] *nm* (*gén*) grain; (*de chapelet*) bead; (*NAVIG*) squall; (*averse*) heavy shower; (*fig: petite quantité*) **un grain de** a touch of; **grain de beauté** beauty spot; **grain de café** coffee bean; **grain de poivre** peppercorn; **grain de poussière** speck of dust; **grain de raisin** grape

graine [gʁɛn] *nf* seed; **mauvaise graine** (*mauvais sujet*) bad lot; **une graine de voyou** a hooligan in the making

graissage [gʁɛsaʒ] *nm* lubrication, greasing

graisse [gʁɛs] *nf* fat; (*lubrifiant*) grease; **graisse saturée** saturated fat

graisser [gʁese] *vt* to lubricate, grease; (*tacher*) to make greasy

graisseux, euse [gʁesø, -øz] *adj* greasy; (*ANAT*) fatty

grammaire [gʁamɛʁ] *nf* grammar

grammatical, e, aux [gʁamatikal, -o] *adj* grammatical

gramme [gʁam] *nm* gramme

grand, e [gʁɑ̃, gʁɑ̃d] *adj* (*haut*) tall; (*gros, vaste, large*) big, large; (*long*) long; (*sens abstraits*) great ♦ *adv*: **grand ouvert** wide open; **un grand buveur** a heavy drinker; **un grand homme** a great man; **son grand frère** his big *ou* older brother; **avoir grand besoin de** to be in dire *ou* desperate need of; **il est grand temps de** it's high time to; **il est assez grand pour** he's big *ou* old enough to; **voir grand** to think big; **en grand** on a large scale; **au grand air** in the open (air); **les grands blessés/brûlés** the severely injured/burned; **de grand matin** at the crack of dawn; **grand écart** splits *pl*; **grand ensemble** housing scheme; **grand jour** broad daylight; **grand livre** (*COMM*) ledger; **grand magasin** department store; **grand malade** very sick person; **grand public** general public; **grande personne** grown-up; **grande surface** hypermarket, superstore; **grandes écoles** *prestige university-level colleges with competitive entrance examinations*; **grandes lignes** (*RAIL*) main lines; **grandes vacances** summer holidays; *see boxed note*

GRANDES ÉCOLES

The **grandes écoles** are highly-respected institutes of higher education which train students for specific careers. Students who have spent two years after the 'baccalauréat' in the 'classes préparatoires' are recruited by competitive entry examination. The prestigious **grandes écoles** have a strong corporate identity and tend to furnish France with its intellectual, administrative and political élite.

---

grand-chose [gʁɑ̃ʃoz] *nm/f inv*: **pas grand-chose** not much

Grande-Bretagne [gʁɑ̃dbʁətaɲ] *nf*: **la Grande-Bretagne** (Great) Britain; **en Grande-Bretagne** in (Great) Britain

grandeur [gʁɑ̃dœʁ] *nf* (*dimension*) size; (*fig: ampleur, importance*) magnitude; (: *gloire, puissance*) greatness; **grandeur nature** *adj* life-size

grandiose [gʁɑ̃djoz] *adj* (*paysage, spectacle*) imposing

grandir [gʁɑ̃diʁ] *vi* (*enfant, arbre*) to grow; (*bruit, hostilité*) to increase, grow ♦ *vt*: **grandir qn** (*suj: vêtement, chaussure*) to make sb look taller; (*fig*) to make sb grow in stature

grand-mère, *pl* **grands-mères** [gʁɑ̃mɛʁ] *nf* grandmother

grand-messe [gʁɑ̃mɛs] *nf* high mass

grand-peine [gʁɑ̃pɛn]: **à grand-peine** *adv* with (great) difficulty

grand-père, *pl* **grands-pères** [gʁɑ̃pɛʁ] *nm* grandfather

grand-route [gʁɑ̃ʁut] *nf* main road

grands-parents [gʁɑ̃paʁɑ̃] *nmpl* grandparents

grange [gʁɑ̃ʒ] *nf* barn

granit(e) [gʁanit] *nm* granite

graphique [gʀafik] *adj* graphic ♦ *nm* graph

grappe [gʀap] *nf* cluster; **grappe de raisin** bunch of grapes

gras, se [gʀɑ, gʀɑs] *adj* (*viande, soupe*) fatty; (*personne*) fat; (*surface, main, cheveux*) greasy; (*terre*) sticky; (*toux*) loose, phlegmy; (*rire*) throaty; (*plaisanterie*) coarse; (*crayon*) soft-lead; (*TYPO*) bold ♦ *nm* (*CULIN*) fat; **faire la grasse matinée** to have a lie-in (*BRIT*), sleep late; **matière grasse** fat (content)

grassement [gʀasmɑ̃] *adv* (*généreusement*): **grassement payé** handsomely paid; (*grossièrement: rire*) coarsely

grassouillet, te [gʀasujɛ, -ɛt] *adj* podgy, plump

gratifiant, e [gʀatifjɑ̃, -ɑ̃t] *adj* gratifying, rewarding

gratin [gʀatɛ̃] *nm* (*CULIN*) cheese- (*ou* crumb-) topped dish; (: *croûte*) topping; **au gratin** au gratin; **tout le gratin parisien** all the best people of Paris

gratiné [gʀatine] *adj* (*CULIN*) au gratin; (*fam*) hellish ♦ *nf* (*soupe*) onion soup au gratin

gratis [gʀatis] *adv, adj* free

gratitude [gʀatityd] *nf* gratitude

gratte-ciel [gʀatsjɛl] *nm inv* skyscraper

gratte-papier [gʀatpapje] *nm inv* (*péj*) pen-pusher

gratter [gʀate] *vt* (*frotter*) to scrape; (*enlever*) to scrape off; (*bras, bouton*) to scratch; **se gratter** to scratch o.s.

gratuit, e [gʀatɥi, -ɥit] *adj* (*entrée*) free; (*billet*) free, complimentary; (*fig*) gratuitous

gravats [gʀava] *nmpl* rubble *sg*

grave [gʀav] *adj* (*dangereux: maladie, accident*) serious, bad; (*sérieux: sujet, problème*) serious, grave; (*personne, air*) grave, solemn; (*voix, son*) deep, low-pitched ♦ *nm* (*MUS*) low register; **ce n'est pas grave!** it's all right, don't worry; **blessé grave** seriously injured person

gravement [gʀavmɑ̃] *adv* seriously; badly; gravely

graver [gʀave] *vt* (*plaque, nom*) to engrave; (*CD, DVD*) to burn; (*fig*): **graver qch dans son esprit/sa mémoire** to etch sth in one's mind/memory

graveur [gʀavœʀ] *nm* (*de CD, DVD*) burner

gravier [gʀavje] *nm* (*loose*) gravel *no pl*

gravillons [gʀavijɔ̃] *nmpl* gravel *sg*, loose chippings *ou* gravel

gravir [gʀaviʀ] *vt* to climb (up)

gravité [gʀavite] *nf* (*voir grave*) seriousness; gravity; (*PHYSIQUE*) gravity

graviter [gʀavite] *vi*: **graviter autour de** to revolve around

gravure [gʀavyʀ] *nf* engraving; (*reproduction*) print; plate

gré [gʀe] *nm*: **à son gré** *adj* to his liking ♦ *adv* as he pleases; **au gré de** according to, following; **contre le gré de qn** against sb's will; **de son (plein) gré** of one's own free will; **de gré ou de force**

whether one likes it or not; **de bon gré** willingly; **bon gré mal gré** like it or not; willy-nilly; **de gré à gré** (*COMM*) by mutual agreement; **savoir (bien) gré à qn de qch** to be (most) grateful to sb for sth

grec, grecque [gʀɛk] *adj* Greek; (*classique: vase etc*) Grecian ♦ *nm* (*LING*) Greek ♦ *nm/f*: **Grec, Grecque** Greek

Grèce [gʀɛs] *nf*: **la Grèce** Greece

greffe [gʀɛf] *nf* graft; transplant ♦ *nm* (*JUR*) office

greffer [gʀefe] *vt* (*BOT, MÉD: tissu*) to graft; (*MÉD: organe*) to transplant

greffier [gʀefje] *nm* clerk of the court

grêle [gʀɛl] *adj* (very) thin ♦ *nf* hail

grêler [gʀele] *vb impers*: **il grêle** it's hailing ♦ *vt*: **la région a été grêlée** the region was damaged by hail

grêlon [gʀelɔ̃] *nm* hailstone

grelot [gʀəlo] *nm* little bell

grelotter [gʀəlɔte] *vi* (*trembler*) to shiver

grenade [gʀənad] *nf* (*explosive*) grenade; (*BOT*) pomegranate; **grenade lacrymogène** teargas grenade

grenadine [gʀənadin] *nf* grenadine

grenat [gʀəna] *adj inv* dark red

grenier [gʀənje] *nm* (*de maison*) attic; (*de ferme*) loft

grenouille [gʀənuj] *nf* frog

grès [gʀɛ] *nm* (*roche*) sandstone; (*poterie*) stoneware

grésiller [gʀezije] *vi* to sizzle; (*RADIO*) to crackle

grève [gʀɛv] *nf* (*d'ouvriers*) strike; (*plage*) shore; **se mettre en/faire grève** to go on/be on strike; **grève bouchon** partial strike (*in key areas of a company*); **grève de la faim** hunger strike; **grève perlée** go-slow (*BRIT*), slowdown (*US*); **grève sauvage** wildcat strike; **grève de solidarité** sympathy strike; **grève surprise** lightning strike; **grève sur le tas** sit down strike; **grève tournante** strike by rota; **grève du zèle** work-to-rule (*BRIT*), slowdown (*US*)

gréviste [gʀevist(ə)] *nm/f* striker

gribouiller [gʀibuje] *vt* to scribble, scrawl ♦ *vi* to doodle

grièvement [gʀijɛvmɑ̃] *adv* seriously

griffe [gʀif] *nf* claw; (*fig*) signature; (: *d'un couturier, parfumeur*) label, signature

griffer [gʀife] *vt* to scratch

grignoter [gʀiɲɔte] *vt, vi* to nibble

gril [gʀil] *nm* steak *ou* grill pan

grillade [gʀijad] *nf* grill

grillage [gʀijaʒ] *nm* (*treillis*) wire netting; (*clôture*) wire fencing

grille [gʀij] *nf* (*portail*) (metal) gate; (*clôture*) railings *pl*; (*d'égout*) (metal) grate; (*fig*) grid

grille-pain [gʀijpɛ̃] *nm inv* toaster

griller [gʀije] *vt* (*aussi*: **faire griller**: *pain*) to toast; (: *viande*) to grill (*BRIT*), broil (*US*); (: *café*) to roast; (*fig: ampoule etc*) to burn out, blow; **griller un feu**

rouge to jump the lights (*BRIT*), run a stoplight (*US*) ◆ *vi* (*brûler*) to be roasting

grillon [gʀijɔ̃] *nm* (*ZOOL*) cricket

grimace [gʀimas] *nf* grimace; (*pour faire rire*): **faire des grimaces** to pull *ou* make faces

grimper [gʀɛ̃pe] *vi, vt* to climb ◆ *nm*: **le grimper** (*SPORT*) rope-climbing; **grimper à/sur** to climb (up)/climb onto

grincer [gʀɛ̃se] *vi* (*porte, roue*) to grate; (*plancher*) to creak; **grincer des dents** to grind one's teeth

grincheux, euse [gʀɛ̃ʃø, -øz] *adj* grumpy

grippe [gʀip] *nf* flu, influenza; **avoir la grippe** to have (the) flu; **prendre qn/qch en grippe** (*fig*) to take a sudden dislike to sb/sth

grippé, e [gʀipe] *adj*: **être grippé** to have (the) flu; (*moteur*) to have seized up (*BRIT*) *ou* jammed

gris, e [gʀi, gʀiz] *adj* grey (*BRIT*), gray (*US*); (*ivre*) tipsy ◆ *nm* (*couleur*) grey (*BRIT*), gray (*US*); **il fait gris** it's a dull *ou* grey day; **faire grise mine** to look miserable *ou* morose; **faire grise mine à qn** to give sb a cool reception

grisaille [gʀizaj] *nf* greyness (*BRIT*), grayness (*US*), dullness

griser [gʀize] *vt* to intoxicate; **se griser de** (*fig*) to become intoxicated with

grisonner [gʀizɔne] *vi* to be going grey (*BRIT*) *ou* gray (*US*)

grisou [gʀizu] *nm* firedamp

grive [gʀiv] *nf* (*ZOOL*) thrush

grivois, e [gʀivwa, -waz] *adj* saucy

Groenland [gʀɔɛnlɑ̃d] *nm*: **le Groenland** Greenland

grogner [gʀɔɲe] *vi* to growl; (*fig*) to grumble

grognon, ne [gʀɔɲɔ̃, -ɔn] *adj* grumpy, grouchy

groin [gʀwɛ̃] *nm* snout

grommeler [gʀɔmle] *vi* to mutter to o.s.

gronder [gʀɔ̃de] *vi* (*canon, moteur, tonnerre*) to rumble; (*animal*) to growl; (*fig: révolte*) to be brewing ◆ *vt* to scold

groom [gʀum] *nm* page, bellhop (*US*)

gros, se [gʀo, gʀos] *adj* big, large; (*obèse*) fat; (*problème, quantité*) great; (*travaux, dégâts*) extensive; (*large: trait, fil*) thick, heavy ◆ *adv*: **risquer/gagner gros** to risk/win a lot ◆ *nm* (*COMM*): **le gros** the wholesale business; **écrire gros** to write in big letters; **prix de gros** wholesale price; **par gros temps/grosse mer** in rough weather/heavy seas; **le gros de** the main body of; (*du travail etc*) the bulk of; **en avoir gros sur le cœur** to be upset; **en gros** roughly; (*COMM*) wholesale; **gros intestin** large intestine; **gros lot** jackpot; **gros mot** coarse word, vulgarity; **gros œuvre** shell (of building); **gros plan** (*PHOTO*) close-up; **gros porteur** wide-bodied aircraft, jumbo (jet); **gros sel** cooking salt; **gros titre** headline; **grosse caisse** big drum

groseille [gʀozɛj] *nf*: **groseille (rouge)/(blanche)** red/white currant; **groseille à maquereau** gooseberry

grosse [gʀos] *adj f voir* **gros** ◆ *nf* (*COMM*) gross

grossesse [gʀoses] *nf* pregnancy; **grossesse nerveuse** phantom pregnancy

grosseur [gʀosœʀ] *nf* size; fatness; (*tumeur*) lump

grossier, ière [gʀosje, -jɛʀ] *adj* coarse; (*travail*) rough; crude; (*évident: erreur*) gross

grossièrement [gʀosjɛʀmɑ̃] *adv* coarsely; roughly; crudely; (*en gros*) roughly

grossièreté [gʀosjɛʀte] *nf* coarseness; rudeness

grossir [gʀosiʀ] *vi* (*suj: personne*) to put on weight; (*fig*) to grow, get bigger; (*rivière*) to swell ◆ *vt* to increase; (*exagérer*) to exaggerate; (*au microscope*) to magnify, enlarge; (*suj: vêtement*): **grossir qn** to make sb look fatter

grossiste [gʀosist(ə)] *nm/f* wholesaler

grosso modo [gʀosomɔdo] *adv* roughly

grotesque [gʀɔtɛsk(ə)] *adj* grotesque

grotte [gʀɔt] *nf* cave

grouiller [gʀuje] *vi* (*foule*) to mill about; (*fourmis*) to swarm about; **grouiller de** to be swarming with

groupe [gʀup] *nm* group; **cabinet de groupe** group practice; **médecine de groupe** group practice; **groupe électrogène** generator; **groupe de pression** pressure group; **groupe sanguin** blood group; **groupe scolaire** school complex

groupement [gʀupmɑ̃] *nm* grouping; (*groupe*) group; **groupement d'intérêt économique (GIE)** = trade association

grouper [gʀupe] *vt* to group; (*ressources, moyens*) to pool; **se grouper** to get together

grue [gʀy] *nf* crane; **faire le pied de grue** (*fam*) to hang around (waiting), kick one's heels (*BRIT*)

grumeaux [gʀymo] *nmpl* (*CULIN*) lumps

guenilles [gənij] *nfpl* rags

guenon [gənɔ̃] *nf* female monkey

guépard [gepaʀ] *nm* cheetah

guêpe [gɛp] *nf* wasp

guêpier [gepje] *nm* (*fig*) trap

guère [gɛʀ] *adv* (*avec adjectif, adverbe*): **ne ... guère** hardly; (*avec verbe*): **ne ... guère** *tournure négative* + much; hardly ever; *tournure négative* + (very) long; **il n'y a guère que/de** there's hardly anybody (*ou* anything) but/hardly any

guéridon [geʀidɔ̃] *nm* pedestal table

guérilla [geʀija] *nf* guerrilla warfare

guérillero [geʀijeʀo] *nm* guerrilla

guérir [geʀiʀ] *vt* (*personne, maladie*) to cure; (*membre, plaie*) to heal ◆ *vi* (*personne*) to recover, be cured; (*plaie, chagrin*) to heal; **guérir de** to be cured of, recover from; **guérir qn de** to cure sb of

guérison [geʀizɔ̃] *nf* curing; healing; recovery

guérisseur, euse [geʀisœʀ, -øz] *nm/f* healer

guerre [gɛʀ] *nf* war; (*méthode*): **guerre atomique/de tranchées** atomic/trench warfare *no pl*; **en guerre** at war; **faire la guerre à** to wage war against; **de guerre lasse** (*fig*) tired of fighting *ou* resisting; **de bonne guerre** fair and square; **guerre**

civile/mondiale civil/world war; **guerre froide/ sainte** cold/holy war; **guerre d'usure** war of attrition

guerrier, ière [gɛʀje, -jɛʀ] *adj* warlike ♦ *nm/f* warrior

guet [gɛ] *nm*: **faire le guet** to be on the watch *ou* look-out

guet-apens, *pl* **guets-apens** [gɛtapɑ̃] *nm* ambush

guetter [gete] *vt* (*épier*) to watch (intently); (*attendre*) to watch (out) for; (: *pour surprendre*) to be lying in wait for

gueule [gœl] *nf* mouth; (*fam: visage*) mug; (: *bouche*) gob (!), mouth; **ta gueule!** (*fam*) shut up!; **gueule de bois** (*fam*) hangover

gueuler [gœle] *vi* (*fam*) to bawl

gueuleton [gœltɔ̃] *nm* (*fam*) blowout (*BRIT*), big meal

gui [gi] *nm* mistletoe

guichet [giʃɛ] *nm* (*de bureau, banque*) counter, window; (*d'une porte*) wicket, hatch; **les guichets** (*à la gare, au théâtre*) the ticket office; **jouer à guichets fermés** to play to a full house

guide [gid] *nm* guide; (*livre*) guide(book) ♦ *nf* (*fille scout*) (girl) guide (*BRIT*), girl scout (*US*); **guides** *nfpl* (*d'un cheval*) reins

guider [gide] *vt* to guide

guidon [gidɔ̃] *nm* handlebars *pl*

guignol [giɲɔl] *nm* ≈ Punch and Judy show; (*fig*) clown

guillemets [gijme] *nmpl*: **entre guillemets** in inverted commas *ou* quotation marks; **guillemets de répétition** ditto marks

guillotiner [gijɔtine] *vt* to guillotine

guindé, e [gɛ̃de] *adj* stiff, starchy

guirlande [giʀlɑ̃d] *nf* garland; (*de papier*) paper chain; **guirlande lumineuse** (fairy (*BRIT*)) lights *pl*; **guirlande de Noël** tinsel *no pl*

guise [giz] *nf*: **à votre guise** as you wish *ou* please; **en guise de** by way of

guitare [gitaʀ] *nf* guitar

gym [ʒim] *nf* (*exercices*) gym

gymnase [ʒimnɑz] *nm* gym(nasium)

gymnaste [ʒimnast(ə)] *nm/f* gymnast

gymnastique [ʒimnastik] *nf* gymnastics *sg*; (*au réveil etc*) keep-fit exercises *pl*; **gymnastique corrective** remedial gymnastics

gynécologie [ʒinekɔlɔʒi] *nf* gynaecology (*BRIT*), gynecology (*US*)

gynécologique [ʒinekɔlɔʒik] *adj* gynaecological (*BRIT*), gynecological (*US*)

gynécologue [ʒinekɔlɔg] *nm/f* gynaecologist (*BRIT*), gynecologist (*US*)

— H h —

habile [abil] *adj* skilful; (*malin*) clever

habileté [abilte] *nf* skill, skilfulness; cleverness

habillé, e [abije] *adj* dressed; (*chic*) dressy; (*TECH*): **habillé de** covered with; encased in

habillement [abijmɑ̃] *nm* clothes *pl*; (*profession*) clothing industry

habiller [abije] *vt* to dress; (*fournir en vêtements*) to clothe; **s'habiller** to dress (o.s.); (*se déguiser, mettre des vêtements chic*) to dress up; **s'habiller de/en** to dress in/dress up as; **s'habiller chez/à** to buy one's clothes from/at

habit [abi] *nm* outfit; **habits** *nmpl* (*vêtements*) clothes; **habit (de soirée)** tails *pl*; evening dress; **prendre l'habit** (*REL: entrer en religion*) to enter (holy) orders

habitant, e [abitɑ̃, -ɑ̃t] *nm/f* inhabitant; (*d'une maison*) occupant, occupier; **loger chez l'habitant** to stay with the locals

habitation [abitasjɔ̃] *nf* living; (*demeure*) residence, home; (*maison*) house; **habitations à loyer modéré (HLM)** low-rent, state-owned housing, ≈ council housing *sg* (*BRIT*), ≈ public housing units (*US*)

habiter [abite] *vt* to live in; (*suj: sentiment*) to dwell in ♦ *vi*: **habiter à/dans** to live in *ou* at/in; **habiter chez** *ou* **avec qn** to live with sb; **habiter 16 rue Montmartre** to live at number 16 rue Montmartre; **habiter rue Montmartre** to live in rue Montmartre

habitude [abityd] *nf* habit; **avoir l'habitude de faire** to be in the habit of doing; **avoir l'habitude des enfants** to be used to children; **prendre l'habitude de faire qch** to get into the habit of doing sth; **perdre une habitude** to get out of a habit; **d'habitude** usually; **comme d'habitude** as usual; **par habitude** out of habit

habitué, e [abitye] *adj*: **être habitué à** to be used *ou* accustomed to ♦ *nm/f* regular visitor; (*client*) regular (customer)

habituel, le [abityɛl] *adj* usual

habituer [abitye] *vt*: **habituer qn à** to get sb used to; **s'habituer à** to get used to

'hache [ˈaʃ] *nf* axe

'hacher [ˈaʃe] *vt* (*viande*) to mince (*BRIT*), grind (*US*); (*persil*) to chop; **hacher menu** to mince *ou* grind finely; to chop finely

'hachis [ˈaʃi] *nm* mince *no pl* (*BRIT*), hamburger meat (*US*); **hachis de viande** minced (*BRIT*) *ou* ground (*US*) meat

'hachisch [ˈaʃiʃ] *nm* hashish

'hachoir [ˈaʃwaʀ] *nm* chopper; (*meat*) mincer (*BRIT*) *ou* grinder (*US*); (*planche*) chopping board

'hagard, e [ˈagaʀ, -aʀd(ə)] *adj* wild, distraught

'haie [ˈɛ] *nf* hedge; (*SPORT*) hurdle; (*fig: rang*) line, row; **200 m haies** 200 m hurdles; **haie d'honneur** guard of honour

'haillons [ˈɑjɔ̃] *nmpl* rags

'haine [ˈɛn] *nf* hatred

'haïr [ˈaiʀ] *vt* to detest, hate; **se haïr** to hate each other

'hâlé, e [ˈɑle] *adj* (sun)tanned, sunburnt

haleine [alɛn] *nf* breath; **perdre haleine** to get out of breath; **à perdre haleine** until one is gasping for breath; **avoir mauvaise haleine** to have bad breath; **reprendre haleine** to get one's breath back; **hors d'haleine** out of breath; **tenir en haleine** to hold spellbound; (*en attente*) to keep in suspense; **de longue haleine** *adj* long-term

'haleter [ˈalte] *vi* to pant

'hall [ˈol] *nm* hall

'halle [ˈal] *nf* (covered) market; **halles** *nfpl* central food market *sg*

hallucinant, e [alysinɑ̃, -ɑ̃t] *adj* staggering

hallucination [alysinasjɔ̃] *nf* hallucination

'halte [ˈalt(ə)] *nf* stop, break; (*escale*) stopping place; (*RAIL*) halt ◆ *excl* stop!; **faire halte** to stop

haltère [altɛʀ] *nm* (*à boules, disques*) dumbbell, barbell; **(poids et) haltères** weightlifting

haltérophilie [alteʀɔfili] *nf* weightlifting

'hamac [ˈamak] *nm* hammock

'hamburger [ˈɑ̃buʀgœʀ] *nm* hamburger

'hameau, x [ˈamo] *nm* hamlet

hameçon [amsɔ̃] *nm* (fish) hook

'hamster [ˈamstɛʀ] *nm* hamster

'hanche [ˈɑ̃ʃ] *nf* hip

'hand-ball [ˈɑdbal] *nm* handball

'handicapé, e [ˈɑ̃dikape] *adj* handicapped ◆ *nm/f* physically (*ou* mentally) handicapped person; **handicapé moteur** spastic

'hangar [ˈɑ̃gaʀ] *nm* shed; (*AVIAT*) hangar

'hanneton [ˈantɔ̃] *nm* cockchafer

'hanter [ˈɑ̃te] *vt* to haunt

'hantise [ˈɑ̃tiz] *nf* obsessive fear

'happer [ˈape] *vt* to snatch; (*suj: train etc*) to hit

'haras [ˈaʀɑ] *nm* stud farm

'harassant, e [ˈaʀasɑ̃, -ɑ̃t] *adj* exhausting

'harcèlement [ˈaʀsɛlmɑ̃] *nm* harassment; **harcèlement sexuel** sexual harassment

'harceler [ˈaʀsəle] *vt* (*MIL, CHASSE*) to harass, harry; (*importuner*) to plague

'hardi, e [ˈaʀdi] *adj* bold, daring

'hareng [ˈaʀɑ̃] *nm* herring

'hargne [ˈaʀɲ(ə)] *nf* aggressivity, aggressiveness

'hargneux, euse [ˈaʀɲø, -øz] *adj* (*propos, personne*) belligerent, aggressive; (*chien*) fierce

'haricot [ˈaʀiko] *nm* bean; **haricot blanc/rouge** haricot/kidney bean; **haricot vert** French (*BRIT*) *ou* green bean

harmonica [aʀmɔnika] *nm* mouth organ

harmonie [aʀmɔni] *nf* harmony

harmonieux, euse [aʀmɔnjø, -øz] *adj* harmonious

'harnacher [ˈaʀnaʃe] *vt* to harness

'harnais [ˈaʀnɛ] *nm* harness

'harpe [ˈaʀp(ə)] *nf* harp

'harponner [ˈaʀpɔne] *vt* to harpoon; (*fam*) to collar

'hasard [ˈazaʀ] *nm*: **le hasard** chance, fate; **un hasard** a coincidence; (*aubaine, chance*) a stroke of luck; **au hasard** (*sans but*) aimlessly; (*à l'aveuglette*) at random, haphazardly; **par hasard** by chance; **comme par hasard** as if by chance; **à tout hasard** on the off chance; (*en cas de besoin*) just in case

'hasarder [ˈazaʀde] *vt* (*mot*) to venture; (*fortune*) to risk; **se hasarder à faire** to risk doing, venture to do

'hâte [ˈɑt] *nf* haste; **à la hâte** hurriedly, hastily; **en hâte** posthaste, with all possible speed; **avoir hâte de** to be eager *ou* anxious to

'hâter [ˈɑte] *vt* to hasten; **se hâter** to hurry; **se hâter de** to hurry *ou* hasten to

'hâtif, ive [ˈɑtif, -iv] *adj* (*travail*) hurried; (*décision*) hasty; (*légume*) early

'hausse [ˈos] *nf* rise, increase; (*de fusil*) backsight adjuster; **à la hausse** upwards; **en hausse** rising

'hausser [ˈose] *vt* to raise; **hausser les épaules** to shrug (one's shoulders); **se hausser sur la pointe des pieds** to stand (up) on tiptoe *ou* tippy-toe (*US*)

'haut, e [ˈo, ˈot] *adj* high; (*grand*) tall; (*son, voix*) high(-pitched) ◆ *adv* high ◆ *nm* top (part); **de 3 m de haut, haut de 3 m** 3 m high, 3 m in height; **en haute montagne** high up in the mountains; **en haut lieu** in high places; **à haute voix, (tout) haut** aloud, out loud; **des hauts et des bas** ups and downs; **du haut de** from the top of; **tomber de haut** to fall from a height; (*fig*) to have one's hopes dashed; **dire qch bien haut** to say sth plainly; **prendre qch de (très) haut** to react haughtily to sth; **traiter qn de haut** to treat sb with disdain; **de haut en bas** from top to bottom; downwards; **haut en couleur** (*chose*) highly coloured; (*personne*): **un personnage haut en couleur** a colourful character; **plus haut** higher up, further up; (*dans un texte*) above; (*parler*) louder; **en haut** up above; at (*ou* to) the top; (*dans une maison*) upstairs; **haut les mains!** hands up!, stick 'em up!; **la haute couture/coiffure** haute couture/coiffure; **haute fidélité** hi-fi, high fidelity; **la haute finance** high finance; **haut débit** broadband; **haute trahison** high treason

'hautain, e [ˈotɛ̃, -ɛn] *adj* (*personne, regard*) haughty

'hautbois [ˈobwa] *nm* oboe

'haut-de-forme, *pl* **hauts-de-forme** [ˈod-fɔʀm(ə)] *nm* top hat

'hauteur [ˈotœʀ] *nf* height; (*GÉO*) height, hill; (*fig*) loftiness; haughtiness; **à hauteur de** up to (the level of); **à hauteur des yeux** at eye level; **à la**

hauteur de (*sur la même ligne*) level with; by; (*fig*) equal to; **à la hauteur** (*fig*) up to it, equal to the task

'haut-fourneau, *pl* **hauts-fourneaux** ['ofurno] *nm* blast *ou* smelting furnace

'haut-le-cœur ['olkœr] *nm inv* retch, heave

'haut-parleur, *pl* **haut-parleurs** ['oparlœr] *nm* (loud)speaker

'havre ['ɑvr(ə)] *nm* haven

'Haye ['ɛ] *n*: **la Haye** the Hague

hebdo [ɛbdo] *nm* (*fam*) weekly

hebdomadaire [ɛbdɔmadɛr] *adj, nm* weekly

hébergement [ebɛrʒəmɑ̃] *nm* accommodation, lodging; taking in

héberger [ebɛrʒe] *vt* to accommodate, lodge; (*réfugiés*) to take in

hébergeur [ebɛrʒœr] *nm* (*Internet*) host

hébété, e [ebete] *adj* dazed

hébreu, x [ebrø] *adj m, nm* Hebrew

hécatombe [ekatɔ̃b] *nf* slaughter

hectare [ɛktar] *nm* hectare, 10,000 square metres

'hein ['ɛ̃] *excl* eh?; (*sollicitant l'approbation*): **tu m'approuves, hein?** so I did the right thing then?; **Paul est venu, hein?** Paul came, did he?; **que fais-tu, hein?** hey! what are you doing?

'hélas ['elas] *excl* alas! ♦ *adv* unfortunately

'héler [ele] *vt* to hail

hélice [elis] *nf* propeller

hélicoptère [elikɔptɛr] *nm* helicopter

helvétique [ɛlvetik] *adj* Swiss

hématome [ematom] *nm* haematoma

hémicycle [emisikl(ə)] *nm* semicircle; (*POL*): **l'hémicycle** the benches (in french parliament)

hémisphère [emisfɛr] *nf*: **hémisphère nord/ sud** northern/southern hemisphere

hémorragie [emɔraʒi] *nf* bleeding *no pl*, haemorrhage (*BRIT*), hemorrhage (*US*); **hémorragie cérébrale** cerebral haemorrhage; **hémorragie interne** internal bleeding *ou* haemorrhage

hémorroïdes [emɔrɔid] *nfpl* piles, haemorrhoids (*BRIT*), hemorrhoids (*US*)

'hennir ['enir] *vi* to neigh, whinny

'hennissement ['enismɑ̃] *nm* neighing, whinnying

hépatite [epatit] *nf* hepatitis, liver infection

herbe [ɛrb(ə)] *nf* grass; (*CULIN, MÉD*) herb; **en herbe** unripe; (*fig*) budding; **touffe/brin d'herbe** clump/ blade of grass

herbicide [ɛrbisid] *nm* weed-killer

herboriste [ɛrbɔrist(ə)] *nm/f* herbalist

'hère ['ɛr] *nm*: **pauvre hère** poor wretch

héréditaire [erediter] *adj* hereditary

'hérisser ['erise] *vt*: **hérisser qn** (*fig*) to ruffle sb; **se hérisser** *vi* to bristle, bristle up

'hérisson ['erisɔ̃] *nm* hedgehog

héritage [eritaʒ] *nm* inheritance; (*fig*) heritage; (: *legs*) legacy; **faire un (petit) héritage** to come

into (a little) money

hériter [erite] *vi*: **hériter de qch (de qn)** to inherit sth (from sb); **hériter de qn** to inherit sb's property

héritier, ière [eritje, -jɛr] *nm/f* heir/heiress

hermétique [ɛrmetik] *adj* (*à l'air*) airtight; (*à l'eau*) watertight; (*fig: écrivain, style*) abstruse; (: *visage*) impenetrable

hermine [ɛrmin] *nf* ermine

'hernie ['ɛrni] *nf* hernia

héroïne [erɔin] *nf* heroine; (*drogue*) heroin

héroïque [erɔik] *adj* heroic

'héron ['erɔ̃] *nm* heron

'héros ['ero] *nm* hero

hésitant, e [ezitɑ̃, -ɑ̃t] *adj* hesitant

hésitation [ezitasjɔ̃] *nf* hesitation

hésiter [ezite] *vi*: **hésiter (à faire)** to hesitate (to do); **hésiter sur qch** to hesitate over sth

hétéroclite [eterɔklit] *adj* heterogeneous; (*objets*) sundry

hétérogène [eterɔʒɛn] *adj* heterogeneous

hétérosexuel, le [eterɔsɛkɥɛl] *adj* heterosexual

'hêtre ['ɛtr(ə)] *nm* beech

heure [œr] *nf* hour; (*SCOL*) period; (*moment, moment fixé*) time; **c'est l'heure** it's time; **pourriez-vous me donner l'heure, s'il vous plaît?** could you tell me the time, please?; **quelle heure est-il?** what time is it?; **2 heures (du matin)** 2 o'clock (in the morning); **à la bonne heure!** (*parfois ironique*) splendid!; **être à l'heure** to be on time; (*montre*) to be right; **le bus passe à l'heure** the bus runs on the hour; **mettre à l'heure** to set right; **100 km à l'heure** ≈ 60 miles an *ou* per hour; **à toute heure** at any time; **24 heures sur 24** round the clock, 24 hours a day; **à l'heure qu'il est** at this time (of day); (*fig*) now; **à l'heure actuelle** at the present time; **sur l'heure** at once; **pour l'heure** for the time being; **d'heure en heure** from one hour to the next; (*régulièrement*) hourly; **d'une heure à l'autre** from hour to hour; **de bonne heure** early; **2 heures de marche/travail** 2 hours' walking/ work; **une heure d'arrêt** an hour's break *ou* stop; **heure d'été** summer time (*BRIT*), daylight saving time (*US*); **heure de pointe** rush hour; **heures de bureau** office hours; **heures supplémentaires** overtime *sg*

heureusement [œrøzmɑ̃] *adv* (*par bonheur*) fortunately, luckily; **heureusement que ...** it's a good job that ..., fortunately ...

heureux, euse [œrø, -øz] *adj* happy; (*chanceux*) lucky, fortunate; (*judicieux*) felicitous, fortunate; **être heureux de qch** to be pleased *ou* happy about sth; **être heureux de faire/que** to be pleased *ou* happy to do/that; **s'estimer heureux de qch/que** to consider o.s. fortunate with sth/ that; **encore heureux que ...** just as well that ...

'heurt ['œr] *nm* (*choc*) collision; **heurts** *nmpl* (*fig*) clashes

'heurter ['œrte] *vt* (*mur*) to strike, hit; (*personne*) to collide with; (fig) to go against, upset; **se heurter** (couleurs, tons) to clash; **se heurter à** to collide with; (fig) to come up against; **heurter qn de front** to clash head-on with sb

hexagone [ɛgzagɔn] nm hexagon; (la France) France (because of its roughly hexagonal shape)

hiberner [ibɛʀne] vi to hibernate

'**hibou, x** ['ibu] nm owl

'**hideux, euse** ['idø, -øz] adj hideous

hier [jɛʀ] adv yesterday; **hier matin/soir/midi** yesterday morning/evening/at midday; **toute la journée d'hier** all day yesterday; **toute la matinée d'hier** all yesterday morning

'**hiérarchie** ['jeʀaʀʃi] nf hierarchy

'**hi-fi** ['ifi] nf inv hi-fi

hilare [ilaʀ] adj mirthful

hindou, e [ɛ̃du] adj, nm/f Hindu; (Indien) Indian

hippique [ipik] adj equestrian, horse cpd

hippisme [ipism(ə)] nm (horse-)riding

hippodrome [ipɔdʀom] nm racecourse

hippopotame [ipɔpɔtam] nm hippopotamus

hirondelle [iʀɔ̃dɛl] nf swallow

hirsute [iʀsyt] adj (personne) hairy; (barbe) shaggy; (tête) tousled

'**hisser** ['ise] vt to hoist, haul up; **se hisser sur** to haul o.s. up onto

histoire [istwaʀ] nf (science, événements) history; (anecdote, récit, mensonge) story; (affaire) business no pl; (chichis: gén pl) fuss no pl; **histoires** nfpl (ennuis) trouble sg; **l'histoire de France** French history, the history of France; **l'histoire sainte** biblical history; **une histoire de** (fig) a question of

historique [istɔʀik] adj historical; (important) historic ♦ nm (exposé, récit): **faire l'historique de** to give the background to

'**hit-parade** ['itpaʀad] nm: **le hit-parade** the charts

hiver [ivɛʀ] nm winter; **en hiver** in winter

hivernal, e, aux [ivɛʀnal, -o] adj (de l'hiver) winter cpd; (comme en hiver) wintry

hiverner [ivɛʀne] vi to winter

HLM sigle m ou f (= habitations à loyer modéré) low-rent, state-owned housing; **un(e) HLM** ≈ a council flat (ou house) (BRIT), ≈ a public housing unit (US)

'**hobby** ['ɔbi] nm hobby

'**hocher** ['ɔʃe] vt: **hocher la tête** to nod; (signe négatif ou dubitatif) to shake one's head

'**hochet** ['ɔʃɛ] nm rattle

'**hockey** ['ɔkɛ] nm: **hockey (sur glace/gazon)** (ice/field) hockey

'**hold-up** ['ɔldœp] nm inv hold-up

'**hollandais, e** ['ɔlɑ̃dɛ, -ɛz] adj Dutch ♦ nm (LING) Dutch ♦ nm/f: **Hollandais, e** Dutchman/woman; **les Hollandais** the Dutch

'**Hollande** ['ɔlɑ̃d] nf: **la Hollande** Holland ♦ nm: **hollande** (fromage) Dutch cheese

'**homard** ['ɔmaʀ] nm lobster

homéopathique [ɔmeɔpatik] adj homoeopathic

homicide [ɔmisid] nm murder ♦ nm/f murderer/eress; **homicide involontaire** manslaughter

hommage [ɔmaʒ] nm tribute; **hommages** nmpl: **présenter ses hommages** to pay one's respects; **rendre hommage à** to pay tribute ou homage to; **en hommage de** as a token of; **faire hommage de qch à qn** to present sb with sth

homme [ɔm] nm man; (espèce humaine): **l'homme**, man, mankind; **homme d'affaires** businessman; **homme des cavernes** caveman; **homme d'Église** churchman, clergyman; **homme d'État** statesman; **homme de loi** lawyer; **homme de main** hired man; **homme de paille** stooge; **homme politique** politician; **l'homme de la rue** the man in the street; **homme à tout faire** odd-job man

homme-grenouille, pl **hommes-grenouilles** [ɔmgʀənuj] nm frogman

homogène [ɔmɔʒɛn] adj homogeneous

homologue [ɔmɔlɔg] nm/f counterpart, opposite number

homologué, e [ɔmɔlɔge] adj (SPORT) officially recognized, ratified; (tarif) authorized

homonyme [ɔmɔnim] nm (LING) homonym; (d'une personne) namesake

homosexuel, le [ɔmɔsɛksɥɛl] adj homosexual

'**Hongrie** ['ɔ̃gʀi] nf: **la Hongrie** Hungary

'**hongrois, e** ['ɔ̃gʀwa, -waz] adj Hungarian ♦ nm (LING) Hungarian ♦ nm/f: **Hongrois, e** Hungarian

honnête [ɔnɛt] adj (intègre) honest; (juste, satisfaisant) fair

honnêtement [ɔnɛtmɑ̃] adv honestly

honnêteté [ɔnɛtte] nf honesty

honneur [ɔnœʀ] nm honour; (mérite): **l'honneur lui revient** the credit is his; **à qui ai-je l'honneur** to whom have I the pleasure of speaking?; "**j'ai l'honneur de …**" "I have the honour of …"; **en l'honneur de** (personne) in honour of; (événement) on the occasion of; **faire honneur à** (engagements) to honour; (famille, professeur) to be a credit to; (fig: repas etc) to do justice to; **être à l'honneur** to be in the place of honour; **être en honneur** to be in favour; **membre d'honneur** honorary member; **table d'honneur** top table

honorable [ɔnɔʀabl(ə)] adj worthy, honourable; (suffisant) decent

honoraire [ɔnɔʀɛʀ] adj honorary; **honoraires** nmpl fees; **professeur honoraire** professor emeritus

honorer [ɔnɔʀe] vt to honour; (estimer) to hold in high regard; (faire honneur à) to do credit to; **honorer qn de** to honour sb with; **s'honorer de** to pride o.s. upon

honorifique [ɔnɔʀifik] adj honorary

'**honte** ['ɔ̃t] nf shame; **avoir honte de** to be

ashamed of; **faire honte à qn** to make sb (feel) ashamed

'**honteux, euse** [ˈɔ̃tø, -øz] *adj* ashamed; (*conduite, acte*) shameful, disgraceful

hôpital, aux [ɔpital, -o] *nm* hospital

'**hoquet** [ˈɔke] *nm* hiccough; **avoir le hoquet** to have (the) hiccoughs

'**hoqueter** [ˈɔkte] *vi* to hiccough

horaire [ɔRER] *adj* hourly ♦ *nm* timetable, schedule; **horaires** *nmpl* (*heures de travail*) hours; **horaire flexible** *ou* **mobile** *ou* **à la carte** *ou* **souple** flex(i)time

horizon [ɔRizɔ̃] *nm* horizon; (*paysage*) landscape, view; **sur l'horizon** on the skyline *ou* horizon

horizontal, e, aux [ɔRizɔ̃tal, -o] *adj* horizontal ♦ *nf:* **à l'horizontale** on the horizontal

horloge [ɔRlɔʒ] *nf* clock; **l'horloge parlante** the speaking clock; **horloge normande** grandfather clock; **horloge physiologique** biological clock

horloger, ère [ɔRlɔʒe, -ER] *nm/f* watchmaker; clockmaker

'**hormis** [ˈɔRmi] *prép* save

horoscope [ˈɔskɔp] *nm* horoscope

horreur [ɔRœR] *nf* horror; **avoir horreur de** to loathe, detest; **quelle horreur!** how awful!; **cela me fait horreur** I find that awful

horrible [ɔRibl(ə)] *adj* horrible

horrifier [ɔRifje] *vt* to horrify

horripiler [ɔRipile] *vt* to exasperate

'**hors** [ˈɔR] *prép* except (for); **hors de** out of; **hors ligne, hors pair** outstanding; **hors de propos** inopportune; **hors série** (*sur mesure*) made-to-order; (*exceptionnel*) exceptional; **hors service (HS), hors d'usage** out of service; **être hors de soi** to be beside o.s.

'**hors-bord** [ˈɔRbɔR] *nm inv* outboard motor; (*canot*) speedboat (with outboard motor)

'**hors-d'œuvre** [ˈɔRdœvR(ə)] *nm inv* hors d'œuvre

'**hors-jeu** [ˈɔRʒø] *nm inv* being offside *no pl*

'**hors-la-loi** [ˈɔRlalwa] *nm inv* outlaw

hors-taxe [ɔRtaks] *adj* (*sur une facture, prix*) excluding VAT; (*boutique, marchandises*) duty-free

hortensia [ɔRtɑ̃sja] *nm* hydrangea

hospice [ɔspis] *nm* (*de vieillards*) home; (*asile*) hospice

hospitalier, ière [ɔspitalje, -jER] *adj* (*accueillant*) hospitable; (*MÉD: service, centre*) hospital *cpd*

hospitaliser [ɔspitalize] *vt* to take (*ou* send) to hospital, hospitalize

hospitalité [ɔspitalite] *nf* hospitality

hostie [ɔsti] *nf* host (*REL*)

hostile [ɔstil] *adj* hostile

hostilité [ɔstilite] *nf* hostility; **hostilités** *nfpl* hostilities

hôte [ot] *nm* (*maître de maison*) host; (*client*) patron; (*fig*) inhabitant, occupant ♦ *nm/f* (*invité*) guest; **hôte payant** paying guest

hôtel [otel] *nm* hotel; **aller à l'hôtel** to stay in a hotel; **hôtel (particulier)** (private) mansion; **hôtel de ville** town hall

hôtelier, ière [otəlje, -jER] *adj* hotel *cpd* ♦ *nm/f* hotelier, hotel-keeper

hôtellerie [otelRi] *nf* (*profession*) hotel business; (*auberge*) inn

hôtesse [otes] *nf* hostess; **hôtesse de l'air** air hostess (*BRIT*) *ou* stewardess; **hôtesse (d'accueil)** receptionist

'**hotte** [ˈɔt] *nf* (*panier*) basket (*carried on the back*); (*de cheminée*) hood; **hotte aspirante** cooker hood

'**houblon** [ˈublɔ̃] *nm* (*BOT*) hop; (*pour la bière*) hops *pl*

'**houille** [ˈuj] *nf* coal; **houille blanche** hydroelectric power

'**houle** [ˈul] *nf* swell

'**houleux, euse** [ˈulø, -øz] *adj* heavy, swelling; (*fig*) stormy, turbulent

'**hourra** [ˈuRa] *nm* cheer ♦ *excl* hurrah!

'**houspiller** [ˈuspije] *vt* to scold

'**housse** [ˈus] *nf* cover; (*pour protéger provisoirement*) dust cover; (*pour recouvrir à neuf*) loose *ou* stretch cover; **housse (penderie)** hanging wardrobe

'**houx** [ˈu] *nm* holly

hovercraft [ovœRkRaft] *nm* hovercraft

'**hublot** [ˈyblo] *nm* porthole

'**huche** [ˈyʃ] *nf:* **huche à pain** bread bin

'**huer** [ˈɥe] *vt* to boo; (*hibou, chouette*) to hoot

huile [ɥil] *nf* oil; (*ART*) oil painting; (*fam*) bigwig; **mer d'huile** (*très calme*) glassy sea, sea of glass; **faire tache d'huile** (*fig*) to spread; **huile d'arachide** groundnut oil; **huile essentielle** essential oil; **huile de foie de morue** cod-liver oil; **huile de ricin** castor oil; **huile solaire** suntan oil; **huile de table** salad oil

huiler [ɥile] *vt* to oil

huileux, euse [ɥilø, -øz] *adj* oily

huis [ɥi] *nm:* **à huis clos** in camera

huissier [ɥisje] *nm* usher; (*JUR*) ≈ bailiff

'**huit** [ˈɥi(t)] *num* eight; **samedi en huit** a week on Saturday; **dans huit jours** in a week('s time)

'**huitaine** [ˈɥiten] *nf:* **une huitaine de** about eight, eight or so; **une huitaine de jours** a week or so

'**huitième** [ˈɥitjem] *num* eighth

huître [ɥitR(ə)] *nf* oyster

humain, e [ymɛ̃, -en] *adj* human; (*compatissant*) humane ♦ *nm* human (being)

humanitaire [ymaniter] *adj* humanitarian

humanité [ymanite] *nf* humanity

humble [œ̃bl(ə)] *adj* humble

humecter [ymekte] *vt* to dampen; **s'humecter les lèvres** to moisten one's lips

'**humer** [ˈyme] *vt* to inhale; (*pour sentir*) to smell

humeur [ymœʀ] *nf* mood; (*tempérament*) temper; (*irritation*) bad temper; **de bonne/mauvaise humeur** in a good/bad mood; **être d'humeur à faire qch** to be in the mood for doing sth

humide [ymid] *adj* (*linge*) damp; (*main, yeux*) moist; (*climat, chaleur*) humid; (*saison, route*) wet

humilier [ymilje] *vt* to humiliate; **s'humilier devant qn** to humble o.s. before sb

humilité [ymilite] *nf* humility

humoristique [ymɔʀistik] *adj* humorous; humoristic

humour [ymuʀ] *nm* humour; **avoir de l'humour** to have a sense of humour; **humour noir** sick humour

'huppé, e [ˈype] *adj* crested; (*fam*) posh

'hurlement [ˈyʀləmɑ̃] *nm* howling *no pl*, howl; yelling *no pl*, yell

'hurler [ˈyʀle] *vi* to howl, yell; (*fig: vent*) to howl; (*: couleurs etc*) to clash; **hurler à la mort** (*suj: chien*) to bay at the moon

hurluberlu [yʀlybɛʀly] *nm* (*péj*) crank ♦ *adj* cranky

'hutte [ˈyt] *nf* hut

hybride [ibʀid] *adj* hybrid

hydratant, e [idʀatɑ̃, -ɑ̃t] *adj* (*crème*) moisturizing

hydraulique [idʀolik] *adj* hydraulic

hydravion [idʀavjɔ̃] *nm* seaplane, hydroplane

hydrogène [idʀɔʒɛn] *nm* hydrogen

hydroglisseur [idʀɔɡlisœʀ] *nm* hydroplane

hyène [jɛn] *nf* hyena

hygiène [iʒjɛn] *nf* hygiene; **hygiène intime** personal hygiene

hygiénique [iʒenik] *adj* hygienic

hymne [imn(ə)] *nm* hymn; **hymne national** national anthem

hypermarché [ipɛʀmaʀʃe] *nm* hypermarket

hypermétrope [ipɛʀmetʀɔp] *adj* long-sighted

hypertension [ipɛʀtɑ̃sjɔ̃] *nf* high blood pressure, hypertension

hypertexte [ipɛʀtɛkst] *nm* (*INFORM*) hypertext

hypnose [ipnoz] *nf* hypnosis

hypnotiser [ipnɔtize] *vt* to hypnotize

hypnotiseur [ipnɔtizœʀ] *nm* hypnotist

hypocrisie [ipɔkʀizi] *nf* hypocrisy

hypocrite [ipɔkʀit] *adj* hypocritical ♦ *nm/f* hypocrite

hypothèque [ipɔtɛk] *nf* mortgage

hypothèse [ipɔtɛz] *nf* hypothesis; **dans l'hypothèse où** assuming that

hystérique [isteʀik] *adj* hysterical

— I i —

iceberg [isbɛʀɡ] *nm* iceberg

ici [isi] *adv* here; **jusqu'ici** as far as this; (*temporel*) until now; **d'ici là** by then; (*en attendant*) in the meantime; **d'ici peu** before long

icône [ikon] *nf* (*aussi INFORM*) icon

idéal, e, aux [ideal, -o] *adj* ideal ♦ *nm* ideal; (*système de valeurs*) ideals *pl*

idéaliste [idealist(ə)] *adj* idealistic ♦ *nm/f* idealist

idée [ide] *nf* idea; (*illusion*): **se faire des idées** to imagine things, get ideas into one's head; **avoir dans l'idée que** to have an idea that; **mon idée, c'est que …** I suggest that …, I think that …; **à l'idée de/que** at the idea of/that, at the thought of/that; **je n'ai pas la moindre idée** I haven't the faintest idea; **avoir idée que** to have an idea that; **avoir des idées larges/étroites** to be broad-/narrow-minded; **venir à l'idée de qn** to occur to sb; **en voilà des idées!** the very ideal; **idée fixe** idée fixe, obsession; **idées noires** black *ou* dark thoughts; **idées reçues** accepted ideas *ou* wisdom

identifier [idɑ̃tifje] *vt* to identify; **identifier qch/ qn à** to identify sth/sb with; **s'identifier avec** *ou* **à qn/qch** (*héros etc*) to identify with sb/sth

identique [idɑ̃tik] *adj*: **identique (à)** identical (to)

identité [idɑ̃tite] *nf* identity; **identité judiciaire** (*POLICE*) = Criminal Records Office

idiot, e [idjo, idjɔt] *adj* idiotic ♦ *nm/f* idiot

idiotie [idjɔsi] *nf* idiocy; (*propos*) idiotic remark *etc*

idole [idɔl] *nf* idol

if [if] *nm* yew

igloo [iglu] *nm* igloo

ignare [iɲaʀ] *adj* ignorant

ignoble [iɲɔbl(ə)] *adj* vile

ignorant, e [iɲɔʀɑ̃, -ɑ̃t] *adj* ignorant ♦ *nm/f*: **faire l'ignorant** to pretend one doesn't know; **ignorant de** ignorant of, not aware of; **ignorant en** ignorant of, knowing nothing of

ignorer [iɲɔʀe] *vt* (*ne pas connaître*) not to know, be unaware *ou* ignorant of; (*être sans expérience de: plaisir, guerre etc*) not to know about, have no experience of; (*bouder: personne*) to ignore; **j'ignore comment/si** I do not know how/if; **ignorer que** to be unaware that, not to know that; **je n'ignore pas que …** I'm not forgetting that …, I'm not unaware that …; **je l'ignore** I don't know

il [il] *pron* he; (*animal, chose, en tournure impersonnelle*) it; *NB: en anglais les navires et les pays sont en général assimilés aux femelles, et les bébés aux choses, si le sexe n'est pas spécifié;* **ils** they; **il neige** it's snowing; *voir aussi* **avoir**

île [il] *nf* island; **les îles** the West Indies; **l'île de Beauté** Corsica; **l'île Maurice** Mauritius; **les îles**

anglo-normandes the Channel Islands; **les îles Britanniques** the British Isles; **les îles Cocos** ou **Keeling** the Cocos ou Keeling Islands; **les îles Cook** the Cook Islands; **les îles Scilly** the Scilly Isles, the Scillies; **les îles Shetland** the Shetland Islands, Shetland; **les îles Sorlingues = les îles Scilly; les îles Vierges** the Virgin Islands

illégal, e, aux [ilegal, -o] *adj* illegal, unlawful (*ADMIN*)

illégitime [ileʒitim] *adj* illegitimate; (*optimisme, sévérité*) unjustified, unwarranted

illettré, e [iletre] *adj, nm/f* illiterate

illimité, e [ilimite] *adj* (*immense*) boundless, unlimited; (*congé, durée*) indefinite, unlimited

illisible [ilizibl(ə)] *adj* illegible; (*roman*) unreadable

illogique [ilɔʒik] *adj* illogical

illumination [ilyminɑsjɔ̃] *nf* illumination, floodlighting; (*inspiration*) flash of inspiration; **illuminations** *nfpl* illuminations, lights

illuminer [ilymine] *vt* to light up; (*monument, rue: pour une fête*) to illuminate, floodlight; **s'illuminer** *vi* to light up

illusion [ilyzjɔ̃] *nf* illusion; **se faire des illusions** to delude o.s.; **faire illusion** to delude ou fool people; **illusion d'optique** optical illusion

illusionniste [ilyzjɔnist(ə)] *nm/f* conjuror

illustration [ilystrɑsjɔ̃] *nf* illustration; (*d'un ouvrage: photos*) photos *pl*

illustre [ilystr(ə)] *adj* illustrious, renowned

illustré, e [ilystre] *adj* illustrated ◆ *nm* illustrated magazine; (*pour enfants*) comic

illustrer [ilystre] *vt* to illustrate; **s'illustrer** to become famous, win fame

îlot [ilo] *nm* small island, islet; (*de maisons*) block; (*petite zone*): **un îlot de verdure** an island of greenery, a patch of green

ils [il] *pron voir* **il**

image [imaʒ] *nf* (*gén*) picture; (*comparaison, ressemblance, OPTIQUE*) image; **image de** picture ou image of; **image d'Épinal** (*social*) stereotype; **image de marque** brand image; (*d'une personne*) (public) image; (*d'une entreprise*) corporate image; **image pieuse** holy picture

imagé, e [imaʒe] *adj* full of imagery

imaginaire [imaʒinɛr] *adj* imaginary

imagination [imaʒinɑsjɔ̃] *nf* imagination; (*chimère*) fancy, imagining; **avoir de l'imagination** to be imaginative, have a good imagination

imaginer [imaʒine] *vt* to imagine; (*croire*): **qu'allez-vous imaginer là?** what on earth are you thinking of?; (*inventer: expédient, mesure*) to devise, think up; **s'imaginer** *vt* (*se figurer: scène etc*) to imagine, picture; **s'imaginer à 60 ans** to picture ou imagine o.s. at 60; **s'imaginer que** to imagine that; **s'imaginer pouvoir faire qch** to think one can do sth; **j'imagine qu'il a voulu plaisanter** I suppose he was joking; **imaginer de faire** (*se mettre dans*

l'idée de) to dream up the idea of doing

imbattable [ɛ̃batabl(ə)] *adj* unbeatable

imbécile [ɛ̃besil] *adj* idiotic ◆ *nm/f* idiot; (*MÉD*) imbecile

imbécillité [ɛ̃besilite] *nf* idiocy; imbecility; idiotic action (*ou* remark *etc*)

imbiber [ɛ̃bibe] *vt*: **imbiber qch de** to moisten ou wet sth with; **s'imbiber de** to become saturated with; **imbibé(e) d'eau** (*chaussures, étoffe*) saturated; (*terre*) waterlogged

imbu, e [ɛ̃by] *adj*: **imbu de** full of; **imbu de soi-même/sa supériorité** full of oneself/one's superiority

imbuvable [ɛ̃byvabl(ə)] *adj* undrinkable

imitateur, trice [imitatœr, -tris] *nm/f* (*gén*) imitator; (*MUSIC-HALL: d'une personnalité*) impersonator

imitation [imitɑsjɔ̃] *nf* imitation; impersonation; **sac imitation cuir** bag in imitation ou simulated leather; **à l'imitation de** in imitation of

imiter [imite] *vt* to imitate; (*personne*) to imitate, impersonate; (*contrefaire: signature, document*) to forge, copy; (*ressembler à*) to look like; **il se leva et je l'imitai** he got up and I did likewise

immaculé, e [imakyle] *adj* spotless, immaculate; **l'Immaculée Conception** (*REL*) the Immaculate Conception

immangeable [ɛ̃mɑ̃ʒabl(ə)] *adj* inedible, uneatable

immatriculation [imatrikylɑsjɔ̃] *nf* registration

immatriculer [imatrikyle] *vt* to register; **faire/se faire immatriculer** to register; **voiture immatriculée dans la Seine** car with a Seine registration (number)

immédiat, e [imedja, -at] *adj* immediate ◆ *nm*: **dans l'immédiat** for the time being; **dans le voisinage immédiat de** in the immediate vicinity of

immédiatement [imedjatmɑ̃] *adv* immediately

immense [imɑ̃s] *adj* immense

immerger [imɛrʒe] *vt* to immerse, submerge; (*câble etc*) to lay under water; (*déchets*) to dump at sea; **s'immerger** *vi* (*sous-marin*) to dive, submerge

immeuble [imœbl(ə)] *nm* building ◆ *adj* (*JUR*) immovable, real; **immeuble locatif** block of rented flats (*BRIT*), rental building (*US*); **immeuble de rapport** investment property

immigration [imigrɑsjɔ̃] *nf* immigration

immigré, e [imigre] *nm/f* immigrant

imminent, e [iminɑ̃, -ɑ̃t] *adj* imminent, impending

immiscer [imise]: **s'immiscer** *vi*: **s'immiscer dans** to interfere in ou with

immobile [imɔbil] *adj* still, motionless; (*pièce de machine*) fixed; (*fig*) unchanging; **rester/se tenir immobile** to stay/keep still

immobilier, ière [imɔbilje, -jɛr] *adj* property *cpd*, in real estate ◆ *nm*: **l'immobilier** the property ou the real estate business

immobiliser [imɔbilize] *vt* (*gén*) to immobilize; (*circulation, véhicule, affaires*) to bring to a standstill; **s'immobiliser** (*personne*) to stand still; (*machine, véhicule*) to come to a halt *ou* a standstill

immonde [imɔ̃d] *adj* foul; (*sale: ruelle, taudis*) squalid

immoral, e, aux [imɔral, -o] *adj* immoral

immortel, le [imɔrtɛl] *adj* immortal ♦ *nf* (*BOT*) everlasting (flower)

immuable [imɥabl(ə)] *adj* (*inébranlable*) immutable; (*qui ne change pas*) unchanging; (*personne*): **immuable dans ses convictions** immoveable (in one's convictions)

immunisé, e [im(m)ynize] *adj*: **immunisé contre** immune to

immunité [imynite] *nf* immunity; **immunité diplomatique** diplomatic immunity; **immunité parlementaire** parliamentary privilege

impact [ɛ̃pakt] *nm* impact; **point d'impact** point of impact

impair, e [ɛ̃pɛr] *adj* odd ♦ *nm* faux pas, blunder; **numéros impairs** odd numbers

impardonnable [ɛ̃pardɔnabl(ə)] *adj* unpardonable, unforgivable; **vous êtes impardonnable d'avoir fait cela** it's unforgivable of you to have done that

imparfait, e [ɛ̃parfɛ, -ɛt] *adj* imperfect ♦ *nm* (*LING*) imperfect (tense)

impartial, e, aux [ɛ̃parsjal, -o] *adj* impartial, unbiased

impasse [ɛ̃pɑs] *nf* dead-end, cul-de-sac; (*fig*) deadlock; **être dans l'impasse** (*négociations*) to have reached deadlock; **impasse budgétaire** budget deficit

impassible [ɛ̃pasibl(ə)] *adj* impassive

impatience [ɛ̃pasjɑ̃s] *nf* impatience

impatient, e [ɛ̃pasjɑ̃, -ɑ̃t] *adj* impatient; **impatient de faire qch** keen *ou* impatient to do sth

impatienter [ɛ̃pasjɑ̃te] *vt* to irritate, annoy; **s'impatienter** *vi* to get impatient; **s'impatienter de/contre** to lose patience at/with, grow impatient at/with

impeccable [ɛ̃pekabl(ə)] *adj* faultless, impeccable; (*propre*) spotlessly clean; (*chic*) impeccably dressed; (*fam*) smashing

impensable [ɛ̃pɑ̃sabl(ə)] *adj* unthinkable, unbelievable

imper [ɛ̃pɛr] *nm* (*imperméable*) mac

impératif, ive [ɛ̃peratif, -iv] *adj* imperative; (*JUR*) mandatory ♦ *nm* (*LING*) imperative; **impératifs** *nmpl* requirements; demands

impératrice [ɛ̃peratris] *nf* empress

imperceptible [ɛ̃pɛrsɛptibl(ə)] *adj* imperceptible

impérial, e, aux [ɛ̃perjal, -o] *adj* imperial ♦ *nf* upper deck; **autobus à impériale** double-decker bus

impérieux, euse [ɛ̃perjø, -øz] *adj* (*caractère, ton*) imperious; (*obligation, besoin*) pressing, urgent

impérissable [ɛ̃perisabl(ə)] *adj* undying, imperishable

imperméable [ɛ̃pɛrmeabl(ə)] *adj* waterproof; (*GÉO*) impermeable; (*fig*): **imperméable à** impervious to ♦ *nm* raincoat; **imperméable à l'air** airtight

impertinent, e [ɛ̃pɛrtinɑ̃, -ɑ̃t] *adj* impertinent

imperturbable [ɛ̃pɛrtyrbabl(ə)] *adj* (*personne*) imperturbable; (*sang-froid*) unshakeable; **rester imperturbable** to remain unruffled

impétueux, euse [ɛ̃petyø, -øz] *adj* fiery

impitoyable [ɛ̃pitwajabl(ə)] *adj* pitiless, merciless

implanter [ɛ̃plɑ̃te] *vt* (*usine, industrie, usage*) to establish; (*colons etc*) to settle; (*idée, préjugé*) to implant; **s'implanter dans** to be established in; to settle in; to become implanted in

impliquer [ɛ̃plike] *vt* to imply; **impliquer qn (dans)** to implicate sb (in)

impoli, e [ɛ̃pɔli] *adj* impolite, rude

impopulaire [ɛ̃pɔpylɛr] *adj* unpopular

importance [ɛ̃pɔrtɑ̃s] *nf* importance; **avoir de l'importance** to be important; **sans importance** unimportant; **d'importance** important, considerable; **quelle importance?** what does it matter?

important, e [ɛ̃pɔrtɑ̃, -ɑ̃t] *adj* important; (*en quantité*) considerable, sizeable; (: *gamme, dégâts*) extensive; (*péj: airs, ton*) self-important ♦ *nm*: **l'important** the important thing

importateur, trice [ɛ̃pɔrtatœr, -tris] *adj* importing ♦ *nm/f* importer; **pays importateur de blé** wheat-importing country

importation [ɛ̃pɔrtasjɔ̃] *nf* import; introduction; (*produit*) import

importer [ɛ̃pɔrte] *vt* (*COMM*) to import; (*maladies, plantes*) to introduce ♦ *vi* (*être important*) to matter; **importer à qn** to matter to sb; **il importe de** it is important to; **il importe qu'il fasse** he must do, it is important that he should do; **peu m'importe** I don't mind, I don't care; **peu importe** it doesn't matter; **peu importe (que)** it doesn't matter (if); **peu importe le prix** never mind the price; *voir aussi* **n'importe**

importun, e [ɛ̃pɔrtœ̃, -yn] *adj* irksome, importunate; (*arrivée, visite*) inopportune, ill-timed ♦ *nm* intruder

importuner [ɛ̃pɔrtyne] *vt* to bother

imposable [ɛ̃pozabl(ə)] *adj* taxable

imposant, e [ɛ̃pozɑ̃, -ɑ̃t] *adj* imposing

imposer [ɛ̃poze] *vt* (*taxer*) to tax; (*REL*): **imposer les mains** to lay on hands; **imposer qch à qn** to impose sth on sb; **s'imposer** (*être nécessaire*) to be imperative; (*montrer sa proéminence*) to stand out, emerge; (*artiste: se faire connaître*) to win recognition, come to the fore; **en imposer** to be imposing; **en imposer à** to impress; **ça s'impose** it's essential, it's vital

impossibilité [ɛ̃pɔsibilite] *nf* impossibility; **être dans l'impossibilité de faire** to be unable to do, find it impossible to do

impossible [ɛ̃pɔsibl(ə)] *adj* impossible ♦ *nm*: **l'impossible** the impossible; **impossible à faire** impossible to do; **il m'est impossible de le faire** it is impossible for me to do it, I can't possibly do it; **faire l'impossible (pour que)** to do one's utmost (so that); **si, par impossible ...** if, by some miracle ...

imposteur [ɛ̃pɔstœʀ] *nm* impostor

impôt [ɛ̃po] *nm* tax; (*taxes*) taxation, taxes *pl*; **impôts** *nmpl* (*contributions*) (income) tax *sg*; **payer 200 € d'impôts** to pay 200 € in tax; **impôt direct/indirect** direct/indirect tax; **impôt sur le chiffre d'affaires** tax on turnover; **impôt foncier** land tax; **impôt sur la fortune** wealth tax; **impôt sur les plus-values** capital gains tax; **impôt sur le revenu** income tax; **impôt sur le RPP** personal income tax; **impôt sur les sociétés** tax on companies; **impôts locaux** rates, local taxes (*US*), ≈ council tax (*BRIT*)

impotent, e [ɛ̃pɔtɑ̃, -ɑ̃t] *adj* disabled

impraticable [ɛ̃pʀatikabl(ə)] *adj* (*projet*) impracticable, unworkable; (*piste*) impassable

imprécis, e [ɛ̃pʀesi, -iz] *adj* (*contours, souvenir*) imprecise, vague; (*tir*) inaccurate, imprecise

imprégner [ɛ̃pʀeɲe] *vt* (*tissu, tampon*) to: **imprégner (de)** to soak *ou* impregnate (with); (*lieu, air*): **imprégner (de)** to fill (with); (*amertume, ironie*) to pervade; **s'imprégner de** to become impregnated with; to be filled with; (*fig*) to absorb

imprenable [ɛ̃pʀənabl(ə)] *adj* (*forteresse*) impregnable; **vue imprenable** unimpeded outlook

impresario [ɛ̃pʀesaʀjo] *nm* manager, impresario

impression [ɛ̃pʀesjɔ̃] *nf* impression; (*d'un ouvrage, tissu*) printing; (*PHOTO*) exposure; **faire bonne impression** to make a good impression; **donner une impression de/l'impression que** to give the impression of/that; **avoir l'impression de/que** to have the impression of/that; **faire impression** to make an impression; **impressions de voyage** impressions of one's journey

impressionnant, e [ɛ̃pʀesjɔnɑ̃, -ɑ̃t] *adj* impressive; upsetting

impressionner [ɛ̃pʀesjɔne] *vt* (*frapper*) to impress; (*troubler*) to upset; (*PHOTO*) to expose

imprévisible [ɛ̃pʀevizibl(ə)] *adj* unforeseeable; (*réaction, personne*) unpredictable

imprévoyant, e [ɛ̃pʀevwajɑ̃, -ɑ̃t] *adj* lacking in foresight; (*en matière d'argent*) improvident

imprévu, e [ɛ̃pʀevy] *adj* unforeseen, unexpected ♦ *nm* unexpected incident; **l'imprévu** the unexpected; **en cas d'imprévu** if anything unexpected happens; **sauf imprévu** barring anything unexpected

imprimante [ɛ̃pʀimɑ̃t] *nf* (*INFORM*) printer; **imprimante à bulle d'encre** bubblejet printer; **imprimante à jet d'encre** ink-jet printer; **imprimante à laser** laser printer; **imprimante (ligne par) ligne** line printer; **imprimante à marguerite** daisy-wheel printer; **imprimante matricielle** dot-matrix printer; **imprimante thermique** thermal printer

imprimé [ɛ̃pʀime] *nm* (*formulaire*) printed form; (*POSTES*) printed matter *no pl*; (*tissu*) printed fabric; **un imprimé à fleurs/pois** (*tissu*) a floral/polka-dot print

imprimer [ɛ̃pʀime] *vt* to print; (*INFORM*) to print (out); (*apposer: visa, cachet*) to stamp; (*empreinte etc*) to imprint; (*publier*) to publish; (*communiquer: mouvement, impulsion*) to impart, transmit

imprimerie [ɛ̃pʀimʀi] *nf* printing; (*établissement*) printing works *sg*; (*atelier*) printing house, printery

imprimeur [ɛ̃pʀimœʀ] *nm* printer; **imprimeur-éditeur/-libraire** printer and publisher/bookseller

impromptu, e [ɛ̃pʀɔ̃pty] *adj* impromptu; (*départ*) sudden

impropre [ɛ̃pʀɔpʀ(ə)] *adj* inappropriate; **impropre à** unsuitable for

improviser [ɛ̃pʀɔvize] *vt, vi* to improvize; **s'improviser** (*secours, réunion*) to be improvized; **s'improviser cuisinier** to (decide to) act as cook; **improviser qn cuisinier** to get sb to act as cook

improviste [ɛ̃pʀɔvist(ə)]: **à l'improviste** *adv* unexpectedly, without warning

imprudence [ɛ̃pʀydɑ̃s] *nf* carelessness *no pl*; imprudence *no pl*; act of carelessness, foolish *ou* unwise action

imprudent, e [ɛ̃pʀydɑ̃, -ɑ̃t] *adj* (*conducteur, geste, action*) careless; (*remarque*) unwise, imprudent; (*projet*) foolhardy

impudent, e [ɛ̃pydɑ̃, -ɑ̃t] *adj* impudent

impudique [ɛ̃pydik] *adj* shameless

impuissant, e [ɛ̃pɥisɑ̃, -ɑ̃t] *adj* helpless; (*sans effet*) ineffectual; (*sexuellement*) impotent ♦ *nm* impotent man; **impuissant à faire qch** powerless to do sth

impulsif, ive [ɛ̃pylsif, -iv] *adj* impulsive

impulsion [ɛ̃pylsjɔ̃] *nf* (*ÉLEC, instinct*) impulse; (*élan, influence*) impetus

impunément [ɛ̃pynemɑ̃] *adv* with impunity

inabordable [inabɔʀdabl(ə)] *adj* (*lieu*) inaccessible; (*cher*) prohibitive

inacceptable [inakseptabl(ə)] *adj* unacceptable

inaccessible [inaksesibl(ə)] *adj* inaccessible; (*objectif*) unattainable; (*insensible*): **inaccessible à** impervious to

inachevé, e [inaʃve] *adj* unfinished

inactif, ive [inaktif, -iv] *adj* inactive, idle

inadapté, e [inadapte] *adj* (*PSYCH: adulte, enfant*) maladjusted ♦ *nm/f* (*péj: adulte: asocial*) misfit; **inadapté à** not adapted to, unsuited to

inadéquat, e [inadekwa, wat] *adj* inadequate

inadmissible [inadmisibl(ə)] *adj* inadmissible

inadvertance [inadvɛʀtɑ̃s]: **par inadvertance** *adv* inadvertently

inaltérable [inalteʀabl(ə)] *adj* (*matière*) stable;

(*fig*) unchanging; **inaltérable à** unaffected by; **couleur inaltérable (au lavage/à la lumière)** fast colour/fade-resistant colour

inanimé, e [inanime] *adj* (*matière*) inanimate; (*évanoui*) unconscious; (*sans vie*) lifeless

inanition [inanisjɔ̃] *nf*: **tomber d'inanition** to faint with hunger (and exhaustion)

inaperçu, e [inapɛʁsy] *adj*: **passer inaperçu** to go unnoticed

inapte [inapt(ə)] *adj*: **inapte à** incapable of; (*MIL*) unfit for

inattaquable [inatakabl(ə)] *adj* (*MIL*) unassailable; (*texte, preuve*) irrefutable

inattendu, e [inatɑ̃dy] *adj* unexpected ♦ *nm*: **l'inattendu** the unexpected

inattentif, ive [inatɑ̃tif, -iv] *adj* inattentive; **inattentif à** (*dangers, détails*) heedless of

inattention [inatɑ̃sjɔ̃] *nf* inattention; (*inadvertance*): **une minute d'inattention** a minute of inattention, a minute's carelessness; **par inattention** inadvertently; **faute d'inattention** careless mistake

inauguration [inɔgyʁasjɔ̃] *nf* unveiling; opening; **discours/cérémonie d'inauguration** inaugural speech/ceremony

inaugurer [inɔgyʁe] *vt* (*monument*) to unveil; (*exposition, usine*) to open; (*fig*) to inaugurate

inavouable [inavwabl(ə)] *adj* undisclosable; (*honteux*) shameful

incalculable [ɛ̃kalkylabl(ə)] *adj* incalculable; **un nombre incalculable de** countless numbers of

incandescence [ɛ̃kɑ̃desɑ̃s] *nf* incandescence; **en incandescence** incandescent, white-hot; **porter à incandescence** to heat white-hot; **lampe/manchon à incandescence** incandescent lamp/(gas) mantle

incapable [ɛ̃kapabl(ə)] *adj* incapable; **incapable de faire** incapable of doing; (*empêché*) unable to do

incapacité [ɛ̃kapasite] *nf* incapability; (*JUR*) incapacity; **être dans l'incapacité de faire** to be unable to do; **incapacité permanente/de travail** permanent/industrial disablement; **incapacité électorale** ineligibility to vote

incarcérer [ɛ̃kaʁseʁe] *vt* to incarcerate

incarné, e [ɛ̃kaʁne] *adj* incarnate; (*ongle*) ingrown

incarner [ɛ̃kaʁne] *vt* to embody, personify; (*THÉÂT*) to play; (*REL*) to incarnate; **s'incarner dans** (*REL*) to be incarnate in

incassable [ɛ̃kasabl(ə)] *adj* unbreakable

incendiaire [ɛ̃sɑ̃djɛʁ] *adj* incendiary; (*fig: discours*) inflammatory ♦ *nm/f* fire-raiser, arsonist

incendie [ɛ̃sɑ̃di] *nm* fire; **incendie criminel** arson *no pl*; **incendie de forêt** forest fire

incendier [ɛ̃sɑ̃dje] *vt* (*mettre le feu à*) to set fire to, set alight; (*brûler complètement*) to burn down

incertain, e [ɛ̃sɛʁtɛ̃, -ɛn] *adj* uncertain; (*temps*) uncertain, unsettled; (*imprécis: contours*) indistinct, blurred

incertitude [ɛ̃sɛʁtityd] *nf* uncertainty

incessamment [ɛ̃sesamɑ̃] *adv* very shortly

incident [ɛ̃sidɑ̃] *nm* incident; **incident de frontière** border incident; **incident de parcours** minor hitch *ou* setback; **incident technique** technical difficulties *pl*, technical hitch

incinérer [ɛ̃sineʁe] *vt* (*ordures*) to incinerate; (*mort*) to cremate

incisive [ɛ̃siziv] *nf* incisor

inciter [ɛ̃site] *vt*: **inciter qn à (faire) qch** to prompt *ou* encourage sb to do sth; (*à la révolte etc*) to incite sb to do sth

inclinable [ɛ̃klinabl(ə)] *adj* (*dossier etc*) tilting; **siège à dossier inclinable** reclining seat

inclinaison [ɛ̃klinɛzɔ̃] *nf* (*déclivité: d'une route etc*) incline; (: *d'un toit*) slope; (*état penché: d'un mur*) lean; (: *de la tête*) tilt; (: *d'un navire*) list

inclination [ɛ̃klinasjɔ̃] *nf* (*penchant*) inclination, tendency; **montrer de l'inclination pour les sciences** *etc* to show an inclination for the sciences *etc*; **inclinations égoïstes/altruistes** egoistic/ altruistic tendencies; **inclination de (la) tête** nod (of the head); **inclination (de buste)** bow

incliner [ɛ̃kline] *vt* (*bouteille*) to tilt; (*tête*) to incline; (*inciter*): **incliner qn à qch/à faire** to encourage sb towards sth/to do ♦ *vi*: **incliner à qch/à faire** (*tendre à, pencher pour*) to incline towards sth/doing, tend towards sth/doing; **s'incliner** (*route*) to slope; (*toit*) to be sloping; **s'incliner (devant)** to bow (before)

inclure [ɛ̃klyʁ] *vt* to include; (*joindre à un envoi*) to enclose; **jusqu'au 10 mars inclus** until 10th March inclusive

incognito [ɛ̃kɔɲito] *adv* incognito ♦ *nm*: **garder l'incognito** to remain incognito

incohérent, e [ɛ̃kɔeʁɑ̃, -ɑ̃t] *adj* inconsistent; incoherent

incollable [ɛ̃kɔlabl(ə)] *adj* (*riz*) that does not stick; (*fam: personne*): **il est incollable** he's got all the answers

incolore [ɛ̃kɔlɔʁ] *adj* colourless

incommoder [ɛ̃kɔmɔde] *vt*: **incommoder qn** to bother *ou* inconvenience sb; (*embarrasser*) to make sb feel uncomfortable *ou* ill at ease

incomparable [ɛ̃kɔ̃paʁabl(ə)] *adj* not comparable; (*inégalable*) incomparable, matchless

incompatible [ɛ̃kɔ̃patibl(ə)] *adj* incompatible

incompétent, e [ɛ̃kɔ̃petɑ̃, -ɑ̃t] *adj* (*ignorant*) inexpert; (*incapable*) incompetent, not competent

incomplet, ète [ɛ̃kɔ̃plɛ, -ɛt] *adj* incomplete

incompréhensible [ɛ̃kɔ̃pʁeɑ̃sibl(ə)] *adj* incomprehensible

incompris, e [ɛ̃kɔ̃pʁi, -iz] *adj* misunderstood

inconcevable [ɛ̃kɔ̃svabl(ə)] *adj* (*conduite etc*) inconceivable; (*mystère*) incredible

inconciliable [ɛ̃kɔ̃siljabl(ə)] *adj* irreconcilable

inconditionnel, le [ɛkɔ̃disjɔnɛl] *adj* unconditional; (*partisan*) unquestioning ◆ *nm/f* (*partisan*) unquestioning supporter

inconfort [ɛkɔ̃fɔR] *nm* lack of comfort, discomfort

inconfortable [ɛkɔ̃fɔRtabl(ə)] *adj* uncomfortable

incongru, e [ɛkɔ̃gRy] *adj* unseemly; (*remarque*) ill-chosen, incongruous

inconnu, e [ɛkɔny] *adj* unknown; (*sentiment, plaisir*) new, strange ◆ *nm/f* stranger; unknown person (*ou* artist *etc*) ◆ *nm*: **l'inconnu** the unknown ◆ *nf* (*MATH*) unknown; (*fig*) unknown factor

inconsciemment [ɛkɔ̃sjamɑ̃] *adv* unconsciously

inconscient, e [ɛkɔ̃sjɑ̃, -ɑ̃t] *adj* unconscious; (*irréfléchi*) reckless ◆ *nm* (*PSYCH*): **l'inconscient** the subconscious, the unconscious; **inconscient de** unaware of

inconsidéré, e [ɛkɔ̃sideRe] *adj* ill-considered

inconsistant, e [ɛkɔ̃sistɑ̃, -ɑ̃t] *adj* flimsy, weak; (*crème etc*) runny

inconsolable [ɛkɔ̃sɔlabl(ə)] *adj* inconsolable

incontestable [ɛkɔ̃tɛstabl(ə)] *adj* unquestionable, indisputable

incontinent, e [ɛkɔ̃tinɑ̃, -ɑ̃t] *adj* (*MÉD*) incontinent ◆ *adv* (*tout de suite*) forthwith

incontournable [ɛkɔ̃tuRnabl(ə)] *adj* unavoidable

incontrôlable [ɛkɔ̃tRolabl(ə)] *adj* unverifiable

inconvenant, e [ɛkɔ̃vnɑ̃, -ɑ̃t] *adj* unseemly, improper

inconvénient [ɛkɔ̃venjɑ̃] *nm* (*d'une situation, d'un projet*) disadvantage, drawback; (*d'un remède, changement etc*) risk, inconvenience; **si vous n'y voyez pas d'inconvénient** if you have no objections; **y a-t-il un inconvénient à …?** (*risque*) isn't there a risk in …?; (*objection*) is there any objection to …?

incorporer [ɛkɔRpɔRe] *vt*: **incorporer (à)** to mix in (with); (*paragraphe etc*): **incorporer (dans)** to incorporate (in); (*territoire, immigrants*): **incorporer (dans)** to incorporate (into); (*MIL: appeler*) to recruit, call up; (: *affecter*): **incorporer qn dans** to enlist sb into

incorrect, e [ɛkɔRɛkt] *adj* (*impropre, inconvenant*) improper; (*défectueux*) faulty; (*inexact*) incorrect; (*impoli*) impolite; (*déloyal*) underhand

incorrigible [ɛkɔRiʒibl(ə)] *adj* incorrigible

incrédule [ɛkRedyl] *adj* incredulous; (*REL*) unbelieving

increvable [ɛkRəvabl(ə)] *adj* (*pneu*) punctureproof; (*fam*) tireless

incriminer [ɛkRimine] *vt* (*personne*) to incriminate; (*action, conduite*) to bring under attack; (*bonne foi, honnêteté*) to call into question; **livre/ article incriminé** offending book/article

incroyable [ɛkRwajabl(ə)] *adj* incredible, unbelievable

incruster [ɛkRyste] *vt* (*ART*): **incruster qch dans/ qch de** to inlay sth into/sth with; (*radiateur etc*) to coat with scale *ou* fur; **s'incruster** *vi* (*invité*) to take root; (*radiateur etc*) to become coated with fur *ou* scale; **s'incruster dans** (*suj: corps étranger, caillou*) to become embedded in

inculpé, e [ɛkylpe] *nm/f* accused

inculper [ɛkylpe] *vt*: **inculper (de)** to charge (with)

inculquer [ɛkylke] *vt*: **inculquer qch à** to inculcate sth in, instil sth into

inculte [ɛkylt(ə)] *adj* uncultivated; (*esprit, peuple*) uncultured; (*barbe*) unkempt

Inde [ɛd] *nf*: **l'Inde** India

indécent, e [ɛdesɑ̃, -ɑ̃t] *adj* indecent

indéchiffrable [ɛdeʃifRabl(ə)] *adj* indecipherable

indécis, e [ɛdesi, -iz] *adj* indecisive; (*perplexe*) undecided

indéfendable [ɛdefɑ̃dabl(ə)] *adj* indefensible

indéfini, e [ɛdefini] *adj* (*imprécis, incertain*) undefined; (*illimité, LING*) indefinite

indéfiniment [ɛdefinimɑ̃] *adv* indefinitely

indéfinissable [ɛdefinisabl(ə)] *adj* indefinable

indélébile [ɛdelebil] *adj* indelible

indélicat, e [ɛdelika, -at] *adj* tactless; (*malhonnête*) dishonest

indemne [ɛdɛmn(ə)] *adj* unharmed

indemniser [ɛdɛmnize] *vt*: **indemniser qn (de)** to compensate sb (for); **se faire indemniser** to get compensation

indemnité [ɛdɛmnite] *nf* (*dédommagement*) compensation *no pl*; (*allocation*) allowance; **indemnité de licenciement** redundancy payment; **indemnité de logement** housing allowance; **indemnité parlementaire** ≈ MP's (*BRIT*) *ou* Congressman's (*US*) salary

indépendamment [ɛdepɑ̃damɑ̃] *adv* independently; **indépendamment de** independently of; (*abstraction faite de*) irrespective of; (*en plus de*) over and above

indépendance [ɛdepɑ̃dɑ̃s] *nf* independence; **indépendance matérielle** financial independence

indépendant, e [ɛdepɑ̃dɑ̃, -ɑ̃t] *adj* independent; **indépendant de** independent of; **chambre indépendante** room with private entrance; **travailleur indépendant** self-employed worker

indescriptible [ɛdeskRiptibl(ə)] *adj* indescribable

indésirable [ɛdezirabl(ə)] *adj* undesirable

indestructible [ɛdestRyktibl(ə)] *adj* indestructible; (*marque, impression*) indelible

indétermination [ɛdetɛRminasjɔ̃] *nf* indecision, indecisiveness

indéterminé, e [ɛdetɛRmine] *adj* unspecified; indeterminate; indeterminable

index [ɛdɛks] *nm* (*doigt*) index finger; (*d'un livre* *etc)* index; **mettre à l'index** to blacklist

indexé, e [ɛdekse] *adj (ÉCON):* **indexé (sur)** index-linked (to)

indicateur [ɛdikatœʀ] *nm (POLICE)* informer; (*livre*) guide; (*: liste*) directory; (*TECH*) gauge; indicator; (*ÉCON*) indicator ♦ *adj:* **poteau indicateur** signpost; **tableau indicateur** indicator (board); **indicateur des chemins de fer** railway timetable; **indicateur de direction** (*AUTO*) indicator; **indicateur immobilier** property gazette; **indicateur de niveau** level, gauge; **indicateur de pression** pressure gauge; **indicateur de rues** street directory; **indicateur de vitesse** speedometer

indicatif, ive [ɛdikatif, -iv] *adj:* **à titre indicatif** for (your) information ♦ *nm (LING)* indicative; (*d'une émission*) theme *ou* signature tune; (*TÉL*) dialling code; **indicatif d'appel** (*RADIO*) call sign

indication [ɛdikasjɔ̃] *nf (renseignement)* information *no pl;* **indications** *nfpl (directives)* instructions; **indication d'origine** (*COMM*) place of origin

indice [ɛdis] *nm (marque, signe)* indication, sign; (*POLICE: lors d'une enquête*) clue; (*JUR: présomption*) piece of evidence; (*SCIENCE, ÉCON, TECH*) index; (*ADMIN*) grading; rating; **indice du coût de la vie** cost-of-living index; **indice inférieur** subscript; **indice d'octane** octane rating; **indice des prix** price index; **indice de traitement** salary grading

indicible [ɛdisibl(ə)] *adj* inexpressible

indien, ne [ɛdjɛ̃, -ɛn] *adj* Indian ♦ *nm/f:* **Indien, ne** (*d'Amérique*) (American *ou* Red) Indian; (*d'Inde*) Indian

indifféremment [ɛdiferamɑ̃] *adv (sans distinction)* equally; indiscriminately

indifférence [ɛdiferɑ̃s] *nf* indifference

indifférent, e [ɛdiferɑ̃, -ɑ̃t] *adj (peu intéressé)* indifferent; **indifférent à** (*insensible à*) indifferent to, unconcerned about; (*peu intéressant pour*) indifferent to; immaterial to; **ça m'est indifférent (que ...)** it doesn't matter to me (whether ...)

indigence [ɛdiʒɑ̃s] *nf* poverty; **être dans l'indigence** to be destitute

indigène [ɛdiʒɛn] *adj* native, indigenous; (*de la région*) local ♦ *nm/f* native

indigeste [ɛdiʒɛst(ə)] *adj* indigestible

indigestion [ɛdiʒɛstjɔ̃] *nf* indigestion *no pl;* **avoir une indigestion** to have indigestion

indigne [ɛdiɲ] *adj:* **indigne (de)** unworthy (of)

indigner [ɛdiɲe] *vt* to make indignant; **s'indigner (de/contre)** to be (*ou* become) indignant (at)

indiqué, e [ɛdike] *adj (date, lieu)* given, appointed; (*adéquat*) appropriate, suitable; (*conseillé*) advisable; (*remède, traitement*) appropriate

indiquer [ɛdike] *vt (désigner):* **indiquer qch/qn à qn** to point sth/sb out to sb; (*suj: pendule, aiguille*) to show; (*suj: étiquette, plan*) to show, indicate; (*faire connaître: médecin, restaurant*): **indiquer qch/qn à qn** to tell sb of sth/sb; (*renseigner sur*) to point out,

tell; (*déterminer: date, lieu*) to give, state; (*dénoter*) to indicate, point to; **indiquer du doigt** to point out; **indiquer de la main** to indicate with one's hand; **indiquer du regard** to glance towards *ou* in the direction of; **pourriez-vous m'indiquer les toilettes/l'heure?** could you direct me to the toilets/tell me the time?

indirect, e [ɛdiʀɛkt] *adj* indirect

indiscipliné, e [ɛdisipline] *adj* undisciplined; (*fig*) unmanageable

indiscret, ète [ɛdiskʀɛ, -ɛt] *adj* indiscreet

indiscutable [ɛdiskytabl(ə)] *adj* indisputable

indispensable [ɛdispɑ̃sabl(ə)] *adj* indispensable, essential; **indispensable à qn/pour faire qch** essential for sb/to do sth

indisposé, e [ɛdispoze] *adj* indisposed, unwell

indisposer [ɛdispoze] *vt (incommoder)* to upset; (*déplaire à*) to antagonize

indistinct, e [ɛdistɛ̃, -ɛkt(ə)] *adj* indistinct

indistinctement [ɛdistɛ̃ktəmɑ̃] *adv (voir, prononcer)* indistinctly; (*sans distinction*) without distinction, indiscriminately

individu [ɛdividy] *nm* individual

individuel, le [ɛdividɥɛl] *adj (gén)* individual; (*opinion, livret, contrôle, avantages*) personal; **chambre individuelle** single room; **maison individuelle** detached house; **propriété individuelle** personal *ou* private property

indolore [ɛdɔlɔʀ] *adj* painless

indomptable [ɛdɔ̃tabl(ə)] *adj* untameable; (*fig*) invincible, indomitable

Indonésie [ɛdɔnezi] *nf:* **l'Indonésie** Indonesia

indu, e [ɛdy] *adj:* **à des heures indues** at an ungodly hour

induire [ɛdɥiʀ] *vt:* **induire qch de** to induce sth from; **induire qn en erreur** to lead sb astray, mislead sb

indulgent, e [ɛdylʒɑ̃, -ɑ̃t] *adj (parent, regard)* indulgent; (*juge, examinateur*) lenient

industrialisé, e [ɛdystʀijalize] *adj* industrialized

industrie [ɛdystʀi] *nf* industry; **industrie automobile/textile** car/textile industry; **industrie du spectacle** entertainment business

industriel, le [ɛdystʀijɛl] *adj* industrial; (*produit industriellement: pain etc*) mass-produced, factory-produced ♦ *nm* industrialist; (*fabricant*) manufacturer

inébranlable [inebʀɑ̃labl(ə)] *adj (masse, colonne)* solid; (*personne, certitude, foi*) steadfast, unwavering

inédit, e [inedi, -it] *adj (correspondance etc)* (hitherto) unpublished; (*spectacle, moyen*) novel, original

ineffaçable [inefasabl(ə)] *adj* indelible

inefficace [inefikas] *adj (remède, moyen)* ineffective; (*machine, employé*) inefficient

inégal, e, aux [inegal, -o] *adj* unequal; (*irrégulier*) uneven

inégalable [inegalabl(e)] *adj* matchless

inégalé, e [inegale] *adj* unmatched, unequalled

inégalité [inegalite] *nf* inequality; unevenness *no pl*; **inégalité de 2 hauteurs** difference *ou* disparity between 2 heights; **inégalités de terrain** uneven ground

inépuisable [inepɥizabl(ə)] *adj* inexhaustible

inerte [inɛʀt(ə)] *adj* lifeless; (*apathique*) passive, inert; (*PHYSIQUE, CHIMIE*) inert

inespéré, e [inɛspeʀe] *adj* unhoped-for, unexpected

inestimable [inɛstimabl(e)] *adj* priceless; (*fig: bienfait*) invaluable

inévitable [inevitabl(ə)] *adj* unavoidable; (*fatal, habituel*) inevitable

inexact, e [inɛgzakt] *adj* inaccurate, inexact; (*non ponctuel*) unpunctual

inexcusable [inɛkskyzabl(ə)] *adj* inexcusable, unforgivable

inexplicable [inɛksplikabl(ə)] *adj* inexplicable

in extremis [inɛkstremis] *adv* at the last minute ♦ *adj* last-minute; (*testament*) deathbed *cpd*

infaillible [ɛfajibl(ə)] *adj* infallible; (*instinct*) infallible, unerring

infâme [ɛfɑm] *adj* vile

infarctus [ɛfaʀktys] *nm*: **infarctus (du myocarde)** coronary (thrombosis)

infatigable [ɛfatigabl(ə)] *adj* tireless, indefatigable

infect, e [ɛfɛkt] *adj* vile, foul; (*repas, vin*) revolting, foul

infecter [ɛfɛkte] *vt* (*atmosphère, eau*) to contaminate; (*MÉD*) to infect; **s'infecter** to become infected *ou* septic

infection [ɛfɛksjɔ̃] *nf* infection

inférieur, e [ɛfeʀjœʀ] *adj* lower; (*en qualité, intelligence*) inferior ♦ *nm/f* inferior; **inférieur à** (*somme, quantité*) less *ou* smaller than; (*moins bon que*) inferior to; (*tâche: pas à la hauteur de*) unequal to

infernal, e, aux [ɛfɛʀnal, -o] *adj* (*chaleur, rythme*) infernal; (*méchanceté, complot*) diabolical

infidèle [ɛfidɛl] *adj* unfaithful; (*REL*) infidel

infiltrer [ɛfiltʀe]: **s'infiltrer** *vi*: **s'infiltrer dans** to penetrate into; (*liquide*) to seep into; (*fig: noyauter*) to infiltrate

infime [ɛfim] *adj* minute, tiny; (*inférieur*) lowly

infini, e [ɛfini] *adj* infinite ♦ *nm* infinity; **à l'infini** (*MATH*) to infinity; (*discourir*) ad infinitum, endlessly; (*agrandir, varier*) infinitely; (*à perte de vue*) endlessly (into the distance)

infiniment [ɛfinimɑ̃] *adv* infinitely; **infiniment grand/petit** (*MATH*) infinitely great/infinitesimal

infinité [ɛfinite] *nf*: **une infinité de** an infinite number of

infinitif, ive [ɛfinitif, -iv] *adj, nm* infinitive

infirme [ɛfiʀm(ə)] *adj* disabled ♦ *nm/f* disabled person; **infirme mental** mentally-handicapped person; **infirme moteur** spastic; **infirme de guerre** war cripple; **infirme du travail** industrially disabled person

infirmerie [ɛfiʀməʀi] *nf* sick bay

infirmier, ière [ɛfiʀmje, -jɛʀ] *nm/f* nurse ♦ *adj*: **élève infirmier** student nurse; **infirmière chef** sister; **infirmière diplômée** registered nurse; **infirmière visiteuse** visiting nurse, ≈ district nurse (*BRIT*)

infirmité [ɛfiʀmite] *nf* disability

inflammable [ɛflamabl(ə)] *adj* (in)flammable

inflation [ɛflasjɔ̃] *nf* inflation; **inflation rampante/galopante** creeping/galloping inflation

infliger [ɛfliʒe] *vt*: **infliger qch (à qn)** to inflict sth (on sb); (*amende, sanction*) to impose sth (on sb)

influençable [ɛflyɑ̃sabl(ə)] *adj* easily influenced

influence [ɛflyɑ̃s] *nf* influence; (*d'un médicament*) effect

influencer [ɛflyɑ̃se] *vt* to influence

influent, e [ɛflyɑ̃, -ɑ̃t] *adj* influential

informateur, trice [ɛfɔʀmatœʀ, -tʀis] *nm/f* informant

informaticien, ne [ɛfɔʀmatisjɛ̃, -ɛn] *nm/f* computer scientist

information [ɛfɔʀmasjɔ̃] *nf* (*renseignement*) piece of information; (*PRESSE, TV: nouvelle*) item of news; (*diffusion de renseignements, INFORM*) information; (*JUR*) inquiry, investigation; **informations** *nfpl* (*TV*) news *sg*; **voyage d'information** fact-finding trip; **agence d'information** news agency; **journal d'information** quality (*BRIT*) *ou* serious newspaper

informatique [ɛfɔʀmatik] *nf* (*technique*) data processing; (*science*) computer science ♦ *adj* computer *cpd*

informatiser [ɛfɔʀmatize] *vt* to computerize

informe [ɛfɔʀm(ə)] *adj* shapeless

informer [ɛfɔʀme] *vt*: **informer qn (de)** to inform sb (of) ♦ *vi* (*JUR*): **informer contre qn/sur qch** to initiate inquiries about sb/sth; **s'informer (sur)** to inform o.s. (about); **s'informer (de qch/si)** to inquire *ou* find out (about sth/whether *ou* if)

infos [ɛfo] *nfpl* (= *informations*) news

infraction [ɛfraksjɔ̃] *nf* offence; **infraction à** violation *ou* breach of; **être en infraction** to be in breach of the law

infranchissable [ɛfrɑ̃ʃisabl(ə)] *adj* impassable; (*fig*) insuperable

infrarouge [ɛfraruʒ] *adj, nm* infrared

infrastructure [ɛfrastryktyʀ] *nf* (*d'une route etc*) substructure; (*AVIAT, MIL*) ground installations *pl* (*touristique etc*) facilities *pl*

infuser [ɛfyze] *vt* (*aussi*: **faire infuser**: *thé*) to brew; (: *tisane*) to infuse ♦ *vi* to brew; to infuse; **laisser infuser** (to leave) to brew

infusion [ɛfyzjɔ̃] *nf* (*tisane*) infusion, herb tea

ingénier [ɛʒenje]: **s'ingénier** *vi*: **s'ingénier à**

faire to strive to do

ingénierie [ɛ̃ʒeniʀi] nf engineering

ingénieur [ɛ̃ʒenjœʀ] nm engineer; **ingénieur agronome/chimiste** agricultural/chemical engineer; **ingénieur conseil** consulting engineer; **ingénieur du son** sound engineer

ingénieux, euse [ɛ̃ʒenjø, -øz] adj ingenious, clever

ingénu, e [ɛ̃ʒeny] adj ingenuous, artless ♦ nf (THÉÂT) ingénue

ingérer [ɛ̃ʒeʀe]: **s'ingérer** vi: **s'ingérer dans** to interfere in

ingrat, e [ɛ̃gʀa, -at] adj (personne) ungrateful; (sol) poor; (travail, sujet) arid, thankless; (visage) unprepossessing

ingrédient [ɛ̃gʀedjɑ̃] nm ingredient

ingurgiter [ɛ̃gyʀʒite] vt to swallow; **faire ingurgiter qch à qn** to make sb swallow sth; (fig: connaissances) to force sth into sb

inhabitable [inabitabl(ə)] adj uninhabitable

inhabité, e [inabite] adj (régions) uninhabited; (maison) unoccupied

inhabituel, le [inabituɛl] adj unusual

inhibition [inibisjɔ̃] nf inhibition

inhumain, e [inymɛ̃, -ɛn] adj inhuman

inhumation [inymasjɔ̃] nf interment, burial

inhumer [inyme] vt to inter, bury

inimaginable [inimaʒinabl(ə)] adj unimaginable

ininterrompu, e [inɛ̃teʀɔ̃py] adj (file, série) unbroken; (flot, vacarme) uninterrupted, non-stop; (effort) unremitting, continuous

initial, e, aux [inisjal, -o] adj, nf initial; **initiales** nfpl, initials

initialiser [inisjalize] vt to initialize

initiation [inisjasjɔ̃] nf initiation

initiative [inisjativ] nf initiative; **prendre l'initiative de qch/de faire** to take the initiative for sth/of doing; **avoir de l'initiative** to have initiative, show enterprise; **esprit/qualités d'initiative** spirit/qualities of initiative; **à** ou **sur l'initiative de qn** on sb's initiative; **de sa propre initiative** on one's own initiative

initier [inisje] vt to initiate; **initier qn à** to initiate sb into; (faire découvrir: art, jeu) to introduce sb to; **s'initier à** (métier, profession, technique) to become initiated into

injecté, e [ɛ̃ʒekte] adj: **yeux injectés de sang** bloodshot eyes

injecter [ɛ̃ʒekte] vt to inject

injection [ɛ̃ʒeksjɔ̃] nf injection; **à injection** (AUTO) fuel injection cpd

injure [ɛ̃ʒyʀ] nf insult, abuse no pl

injurier [ɛ̃ʒyʀje] vt to insult, abuse

injurieux, euse [ɛ̃ʒyʀjø, -øz] adj abusive, insulting

injuste [ɛ̃ʒyst(ə)] adj unjust, unfair

injustice [ɛ̃ʒystis] nf injustice

inlassable [ɛ̃lasabl(ə)] adj tireless, indefatigable

inné, e [ine] adj innate, inborn

innocent, e [inɔsɑ̃, -ɑ̃t] adj innocent ♦ nm/f innocent person; **faire l'innocent** to play ou come the innocent

innocenter [inɔsɑ̃te] vt to clear, prove innocent

innombrable [inɔ̃bʀabl(ə)] adj innumerable

innommable [inɔmabl(ə)] adj unspeakable

innover [inɔve] vi: **innover en matière d'art** to break new ground in the field of art

inoccupé, e [inɔkype] adj unoccupied

inodore [inɔdɔʀ] adj (gaz) odourless; (fleur) scentless

inoffensif, ive [inɔfɑ̃sif, -iv] adj harmless, innocuous

inondation [inɔ̃dasjɔ̃] nf flooding no pl; (torrent, eau) flood

inonder [inɔ̃de] vt to flood; (fig) to inundate, overrun; **inonder de** (fig) to flood ou swamp with

inopiné, e [inɔpine] adj unexpected, sudden

inopportun, e [inɔpɔʀtœ̃, -yn] adj ill-timed, untimely; inappropriate; (moment) inopportune

inoubliable [inublijabl(ə)] adj unforgettable

inouï, e [inwi] adj unheard-of, extraordinary

inox [inɔks] adj, nm (= inoxydable) stainless (steel)

inqualifiable [ɛ̃kalifjabl(ə)] adj unspeakable

inquiet, ète [ɛ̃kjɛ, -ɛt] adj (par nature) anxious; (momentanément) worried; **inquiet de qch/au sujet de qn** worried about sth/sb

inquiétant, e [ɛ̃kjetɑ̃, -ɑ̃t] adj worrying, disturbing

inquiéter [ɛ̃kjete] vt to worry, disturb; (harceler) to harass; **s'inquiéter** to worry, become anxious; **s'inquiéter de** to worry about; (s'enquérir de) to inquire about

inquiétude [ɛ̃kjetyd] nf anxiety; **donner de l'inquiétude** ou **des inquiétudes à** to worry; **avoir de l'inquiétude** ou **des inquiétudes au sujet de** to feel anxious ou worried about

insaisissable [ɛ̃sezisabl(ə)] adj elusive

insalubre [ɛ̃salybʀ(ə)] adj unhealthy, insalubrious

insatisfait, e [ɛ̃satisfɛ, -ɛt] adj (non comblé) unsatisfied; (:passion, envie) unfulfilled; (mécontent) dissatisfied

inscription [ɛ̃skʀipsjɔ̃] nf (sur un mur, écriteau etc) inscription; (à une institution: voir s'inscrire) enrolment; registration

inscrire [ɛ̃skʀiʀ] vt (marquer: sur son calepin etc) to note ou write down; (: sur un mur, une affiche etc) to write; (: dans la pierre, le métal) to inscribe; (mettre: sur une liste, un budget etc) to put down; (enrôler: soldat) to enlist; **inscrire qn à** (club, école etc) to enrol sb at; **s'inscrire** (pour une excursion etc) to put one's name down; **s'inscrire (à)** (club, parti) to join; (université) to register ou enrol (at); (examen, concours) to register ou enter (for); **s'inscrire dans**

(*se situer: négociations etc*) to come within the scope of; **s'inscrire en faux contre** to deny (strongly); (*JUR*) to challenge

insecte [ɛ̃sɛkt(ə)] *nm* insect

insecticide [ɛ̃sɛktisid] *nm* insecticide

insensé, e [ɛ̃sɑ̃se] *adj* insane, mad

insensibiliser [ɛ̃sɑ̃sibilize] *vt* to anaesthetize; (*à une allergie*) to desensitize; **insensibiliser à qch** (*fig*) to cause to become insensitive to sth

insensible [ɛ̃sɑ̃sibl(ə)] *adj* (*nerf, membre*) numb; (*dur, indifférent*) insensitive; (*imperceptible*) imperceptible

inséparable [ɛ̃sepaʀabl(ə)] *adj*: **inséparable (de)** inseparable (from) ◆ *nmpl*: **inséparables** (*oiseaux*) lovebirds

insigne [ɛ̃siɲ] *nm* (*d'un parti, club*) badge ◆ *adj* distinguished; **insignes** *nmpl* (*d'une fonction*) insignia *pl*

insignifiant, e [ɛ̃siɲifjɑ̃, -ɑ̃t] *adj* insignificant; (*somme, affaire, détail*) trivial, insignificant

insinuer [ɛ̃sinɥe] *vt* to insinuate, imply; **s'insinuer dans** to seep into; (*fig*) to worm one's way into, creep into

insipide [ɛ̃sipid] *adj* insipid

insister [ɛ̃siste] *vi* to insist; (*s'obstiner*) to keep on; **insister sur** (*détail, note*) to stress; **insister pour qch/pour faire qch** to be insistent about sth/about doing sth

insolation [ɛ̃sɔlasjɔ̃] *nf* (*MÉD*) sunstroke *no pl*; (*ensoleillement*) period of sunshine

insolent, e [ɛ̃sɔlɑ̃, -ɑ̃t] *adj* insolent

insolite [ɛ̃sɔlit] *adj* strange, unusual

insomnie [ɛ̃sɔmni] *nf* insomnia *no pl*, sleeplessness *no pl*; **avoir des insomnies** to suffer from insomnia

insonoriser [ɛ̃sɔnɔʀize] *vt* to soundproof

insouciant, e [ɛ̃susjɑ̃, -ɑ̃t] *adj* carefree; (*imprévoyant*) heedless

insoumis, e [ɛ̃sumi, -iz] *adj* (*caractère, enfant*) rebellious, refractory; (*contrée, tribu*) unsubdued; (*MIL: soldat*) absent without leave ◆ *nm* (*MIL: soldat*) absentee

insoupçonnable [ɛ̃supsɔnabl(ə)] *adj* above suspicion

insoupçonné, e [ɛ̃supsɔne] *adj* unsuspected

insoutenable [ɛ̃sutnabl(ə)] *adj* (*argument*) untenable; (*chaleur*) unbearable

inspecter [ɛ̃spɛkte] *vt* to inspect

inspecteur, trice [ɛ̃spɛktœʀ, -tʀis] *nm/f* inspector; (*des assurances*) assessor; **inspecteur d'Académie** (regional) director of education; **inspecteur (de l'enseignement) primaire** primary school inspector; **inspecteur des finances** ≃ tax inspector (*BRIT*), ≃ Internal Revenue Service agent (*US*); **inspecteur (de police)** (police) inspector

inspection [ɛ̃spɛksjɔ̃] *nf* inspection

inspirer [ɛ̃spiʀe] *vt* (*gén*) to inspire ◆ *vi* (*aspirer*) to breathe in; **s'inspirer de** (*suj: artiste*) to draw one's inspiration from; (*suj: tableau*) to be inspired by; **inspirer qch à qn** (*œuvre, project, action*) to inspire sb with sth; (*dégoût, crainte, horreur*) to fill sb with sth; **ça ne m'inspire pas** I'm not keen on the idea

instable [ɛ̃stabl(ə)] *adj* (*meuble, équilibre*) unsteady; (*population, temps*) unsettled; (*paix, régime, caractère*) unstable

installation [ɛ̃stalasjɔ̃] *nf* installation; putting in *ou* up; fitting out; settling in; (*appareils etc*) fittings *pl*, installations *pl*; **installations** *nfpl* installations; (*industrielles*) plant *sg*; (*de loisirs*) facilities

installer [ɛ̃stale] *vt* (*loger*): **installer qn** to get sb settled, install sb; (*asseoir, coucher*) to settle (down); (*placer*) to put, place; (*meuble*) to put in; (*rideau, étagère, tente*) to put up; (*gaz, électricité etc*) to put in, install; (*appartement*) to fit out; (*aménager*): **installer une salle de bains dans une pièce** to fit out a room with a bathroom suite; **s'installer** (*s'établir: artisan, dentiste etc*) to set o.s. up; (*se loger*): **s'installer à l'hôtel/chez qn** to move into a hotel/in with sb; (*emménager*) to settle in; (*sur un siège, à un emplacement*) to settle (down); (*fig: maladie, grève*) to take a firm hold *ou* grip

instance [ɛ̃stɑ̃s] *nf* (*JUR: procédure*) (legal) proceedings *pl*; (*ADMIN: autorité*) authority; **instances** *nfpl* (*prières*) entreaties; **affaire en instance** matter pending; **courrier en instance** mail ready for posting; **être en instance de divorce** to be awaiting a divorce; **train en instance de départ** train on the point of departure; **tribunal de première instance** court of first instance; **en seconde instance** on appeal

instant [ɛ̃stɑ̃] *nm* moment, instant; **dans un instant** in a moment; **à l'instant** this instant; **je l'ai vu à l'instant** I've just this minute seen him, I saw him a moment ago; **à l'instant (même) où** at the (very) moment that *ou* when, (just) as; **à chaque instant, à tout instant** at any moment; constantly; **pour l'instant** for the moment, for the time being; **par instants** at times; **de tous les instants** perpetual; **dès l'instant où** *ou* **que ...** from the moment when ..., since that moment when ...

instantané, e [ɛ̃stɑ̃tane] *adj* (*lait, café*) instant; (*explosion, mort*) instantaneous ◆ *nm* snapshot

instar [ɛ̃staʀ]: **à l'instar de** *prép* following the example of, like

instaurer [ɛ̃stɔʀe] *vt* to institute; **s'instaurer** *vi* to set o.s. up; (*collaboration etc*) to be established

instinct [ɛ̃stɛ̃] *nm* instinct; **d'instinct** (*spontanément*) instinctively; **instinct grégaire** herd instinct; **instinct de conservation** instinct of self-preservation

instinctivement [ɛ̃stɛ̃ktivmɑ̃] *adv* instinctively

instit [ɛ̃stit] (*fam*) *nm/f* (primary school) teacher

instituer [ɛ̃stiɥe] *vt* to institute, set up; **s'instituer défenseur d'une cause** to set o.s. up as defender of a cause

institut [ɛstity] *nm* institute; **institut de beauté** beauty salon; **institut médico-légal** mortuary; **Institut universitaire de technologie (IUT)** technical college

instituteur, trice [ɛstitytœʀ, -tʀis] *nm/f* (primary (*BRIT*) *ou* grade (*US*) school) teacher

institution [ɛstitysjɔ̃] *nf* institution; (*collège*) private school

instructif, ive [ɛstʀyktif, -iv] *adj* instructive

instruction [ɛstʀyksjɔ̃] *nf* (*enseignement, savoir*) education; (*JUR*) (preliminary) investigation and hearing; (*directive*) instruction; (*ADMIN: document*) directive; **instructions** *nfpl* instructions; (*mode d'emploi*) directions, instructions; **instruction civique** civics *sg*; **instruction primaire/publique** primary/public education; **instruction religieuse** religious instruction; **instruction professionnelle** vocational training

instruire [ɛstʀɥiʀ] *vt* (*élèves*) to teach; (*recrues*) to train; (*JUR: affaire*) to conduct the investigation for; **s'instruire** to educate o.s.; **s'instruire auprès de qn de qch** (*s'informer*) to find sth out from sb; **instruire qn de qch** (*informer*) to inform *ou* advise sb of sth; **instruire contre qn** (*JUR*) to investigate sb

instruit, e [ɛstʀɥi, -it] *pp de* **instruire** ♦ *adj* educated

instrument [ɛstʀymɑ̃] *nm* instrument; **instrument à cordes/vent** stringed/wind instrument; **instrument de mesure** measuring instrument; **instrument de musique** musical instrument; **instrument de travail** (working) tool

insu [ɛsy] *nm*: **à l'insu de qn** without sb knowing

insubmersible [ɛsybmɛʀsibl(ə)] *adj* unsinkable

insuffisant, e [ɛsyfizɑ̃, -ɑ̃t] *adj* insufficient; (*élève, travail*) inadequate

insulaire [ɛsylɛʀ] *adj* island *cpd*; (*attitude*) insular

insuline [ɛsylin] *nf* insulin

insulte [ɛsylt(ə)] *nf* insult

insulter [ɛsylte] *vt* to insult

insupportable [ɛsypɔʀtabl(ə)] *adj* unbearable

insurger [ɛsyʀʒe]: **s'insurger** *vi*: **s'insurger (contre)** to rise up *ou* rebel (against)

insurmontable [ɛsyʀmɔ̃tabl(ə)] *adj* (*difficulté*) insuperable; (*aversion*) unconquerable

insurrection [ɛsyʀɛksjɔ̃] *nf* insurrection, revolt

intact, e [ɛtakt] *adj* intact

intangible [ɛtɑ̃ʒibl(ə)] *adj* intangible; (*principe*) inviolable

intarissable [ɛtaʀisabl(ə)] *adj* inexhaustible

intégral, e, aux [ɛtegʀal, -o] *adj* complete ♦ *nf* (*MATH*) integral; (*œuvres complètes*) complete works

intégralement [ɛtegʀalmɑ̃] *adv* in full, fully

intégralité [ɛtegʀalite] *nf* (*d'une somme, d'un revenu*) whole (*ou* full) amount; **dans son intégralité** in its entirety

intégrant, e [ɛtegʀɑ̃, -ɑ̃t] *adj*: **faire partie inté-**

grante de to be an integral part of, be part and parcel of

intègre [ɛtegʀ(ə)] *adj* perfectly honest, upright

intégrer [ɛtegʀe] *vt*: **intégrer qch à** *ou* **dans** to integrate sth into; **s'intégrer à** *ou* **dans** to become integrated into

intégrisme [ɛtegʀism(ə)] *nm* fundamentalism

intellectuel, le [ɛtelɛktɥel] *adj, nm/f* intellectual; (*péj*) highbrow

intelligence [ɛteliʒɑ̃s] *nf* intelligence; (*compréhension*): **l'intelligence de** the understanding of; (*complicité*): **regard d'intelligence** glance of complicity, meaningful *ou* knowing look; (*accord*): **vivre en bonne intelligence avec qn** to be on good terms with sb; **intelligences** *nfpl* (*MIL, fig*) secret contacts; **être d'intelligence** to have an understanding; **intelligence artificielle** artificial intelligence (A.I.)

intelligent, e [ɛteliʒɑ̃, -ɑ̃t] *adj* intelligent; (*capable*): **intelligent en affaires** competent in business

intelligible [ɛteliʒibl(ə)] *adj* intelligible

intempéries [ɛtɑ̃peʀi] *nfpl* bad weather *sg*

intempestif, ive [ɛtɑ̃pestif, -iv] *adj* untimely

intenable [ɛtnabl(ə)] *adj* unbearable

intendant, e [ɛtɑ̃dɑ̃, -ɑ̃t] *nm/f* (*MIL*) quartermaster; (*SCOL*) bursar; (*d'une propriété*) steward

intense [ɛtɑ̃s] *adj* intense

intensif, ive [ɛtɑ̃sif, -iv] *adj* intensive; **cours intensif** crash course; **intensif en main-d'œuvre** labour-intensive; **intensif en capital** capital-intensive

intenter [ɛtɑ̃te] *vt*: **intenter un procès contre** *ou* **à qn** to start proceedings against sb

intention [ɛtɑ̃sjɔ̃] *nf* intention; (*JUR*) intent; **avoir l'intention de faire** to intend to do, have the intention of doing; **dans l'intention de faire qch** with a view to doing sth; **à l'intention de** *prép* for; (*renseignement*) for the benefit *ou* information of; (*film, ouvrage*) aimed at; **à cette intention** with this aim in view; **sans intention** unintentionally; **faire qch sans mauvaise intention** to do sth without ill intent; **agir dans une bonne intention** to act with good intentions

intentionné, e [ɛtɑ̃sjɔne] *adj*: **bien intentionné** well-meaning *ou* -intentioned; **mal intentionné** ill-intentioned

interactif, ive [ɛteʀaktif, -iv] *adj* (*aussi INFORM*) interactive

intercalaire [ɛteʀkalɛʀ] *adj, nm*: **(feuillet) intercalaire** insert; **(fiche) intercalaire** divider

intercaler [ɛteʀkale] *vt* to insert; **s'intercaler entre** to come in between; to slip in between

intercepter [ɛteʀsepte] *vt* to intercept; (*lumière, chaleur*) to cut off

interchangeable [ɛteʀʃɑ̃ʒabl(ə)] *adj* interchangeable

interclasse [ɛteʀklɑs] *nm* (*SCOL*) break (between

classes)

interdiction [ɛ̃tɛʀdiksjɔ̃] *nf* ban; **interdiction de faire qch** ban on doing sth; **interdiction de séjour** (*JUR*) *order banning ex-prisoner from frequenting specified places*

interdire [ɛ̃tɛʀdiʀ] *vt* to forbid; (*ADMIN: stationnement, meeting, passage*) to ban, prohibit; (: *journal, livre*) to ban; **interdire qch à qn** to forbid sb sth; **interdire à qn de faire** to forbid sb to do, prohibit sb from doing; (*suj: empêchement*) to prevent *ou* preclude sb from doing; **s'interdire qch** (*éviter*) to refrain *ou* abstain from sth; (*se refuser*) **il s'interdit d'y penser** he doesn't allow himself to think about it

interdit, e [ɛ̃tɛʀdi, -it] *pp de* **interdire** ♦ *adj* (*stupéfait*) taken aback; (*défendu*) forbidden, prohibited ♦ *nm* interdict, prohibition; **film interdit aux moins de 18/13 ans** ≈ 18-/PG-rated film; **sens interdit** one way; **stationnement interdit** no parking; **interdit de chéquier** having cheque book facilities suspended; **interdit de séjour** subject to an *interdiction de séjour*

intéressant, e [ɛ̃teʀesɑ̃, -ɑ̃t] *adj* interesting; **faire l'intéressant** to draw attention to o.s.

intéressé, e [ɛ̃teʀese] *adj* (*parties*) involved, concerned; (*amitié, motifs*) self-interested ♦ *nm*: **l'intéressé** the interested party; **les intéressés** those concerned *ou* involved

intéresser [ɛ̃teʀese] *vt* to interest; (*toucher*) to be of interest *ou* concern to; (*ADMIN: concerner*) to affect, concern; (*COMM: travailleur*) to give a share in the profits to; (: *partenaire*) to interest (in the business); **s'intéresser à** to take an interest in, be interested in; **intéresser qn à qch** to get sb interested in sth

intérêt [ɛ̃teʀɛ] *nm* (*aussi COMM*) interest; (*égoïsme*) self-interest; **porter de l'intérêt à qn** to take an interest in sb; **agir par intérêt** to act out of self-interest; **avoir des intérêts dans** (*COMM*) to have a financial interest *ou* a stake in; **avoir intérêt à faire** to do well to do; **il y a intérêt à …** it would be a good thing to …; **intérêt composé** compound interest

intérieur, e [ɛ̃teʀjœʀ] *adj* (*mur, escalier, poche*) inside; (*commerce, politique*) domestic; (*cour, calme, vie*) inner; (*navigation*) inland ♦ *nm* (*d'une maison, d'un récipient etc*) inside; (*d'un pays, aussi: décor, mobilier*) interior; (*POL*): **l'Intérieur** (the Department of) the Interior ≈ the Home Office (*BRIT*); **à l'intérieur (de)** inside; (*fig*) within; **de l'intérieur** (*fig*) from the inside; **en intérieur** (*CINÉ*) in the studio; **vêtement d'intérieur** indoor garment

intérieurement [ɛ̃teʀjœʀmɑ̃] *adv* inwardly

intérim [ɛ̃teʀim] *nm* interim period; **assurer l'intérim (de)** to deputize (for); **par intérim** *adj* interim ♦ *adv* in a temporary capacity

intérimaire [ɛ̃teʀimɛʀ] *adj* temporary, interim ♦ *nm/f* (*secrétaire etc*) temporary, temp (*BRIT*); (*suppléant*) deputy

interlocuteur, trice [ɛ̃tɛʀlɔkytœʀ, -tʀis] *nm/f* speaker; (*POL*): **interlocuteur valable** valid representative; **son interlocuteur** the person he *ou* she was speaking to

interloquer [ɛ̃tɛʀlɔke] *vt* to take aback

intermède [ɛ̃tɛʀmɛd] *nm* interlude

intermédiaire [ɛ̃tɛʀmedjɛʀ] *adj* intermediate; middle; half-way ♦ *nm/f* intermediary; (*COMM*) middleman; **sans intermédiaire** directly; **par l'intermédiaire de** through

interminable [ɛ̃tɛʀminabl(ə)] *adj* never-ending

intermittence [ɛ̃tɛʀmitɑ̃s] *nf*: **par intermittence** intermittently, sporadically

internat [ɛ̃tɛʀna] *nm* (*SCOL*) boarding school

international, e, aux [ɛ̃tɛʀnasjɔnal, -o] *adj, nm/f* international

internaute [ɛ̃tɛʀnot] *nm/f* Internet surfer

interne [ɛ̃tɛʀn(ə)] *adj* internal ♦ *nm/f* (*SCOL*) boarder; (*MÉD*) houseman (*US*)

interner [ɛ̃tɛʀne] *vt* (*POL*) to intern; (*MÉD*) to confine to a mental institution

Internet [ɛ̃tɛʀnɛt] *nm*: **l'Internet** the Internet

interpeller [ɛ̃tɛʀpəle] *vt* (*appeler*) to call out to; (*apostropher*) to shout at; (*POLICE*) to take in for questioning; (*POL*) to question; **s'interpeller** to exchange insults

interphone [ɛ̃tɛʀfɔn] *nm* intercom

interposer [ɛ̃tɛʀpoze] *vt* to interpose; **s'interposer** *vi* to intervene; **par personnes interposées** through a third party

interprétation [ɛ̃tɛʀpʀetasjɔ̃] *nf* interpretation

interprète [ɛ̃tɛʀpʀɛt] *nm/f* interpreter; (*porte-parole*) spokesman

interpréter [ɛ̃tɛʀpʀete] *vt* to interpret

interrogateur, trice [ɛ̃teʀɔgatœʀ, -tʀis] *adj* questioning, inquiring ♦ *nm/f* (*SCOL*) (oral) examiner

interrogatif, ive [ɛ̃teʀɔgatif, -iv] *adj* (*LING*) interrogative

interrogation [ɛ̃teʀɔgasjɔ̃] *nf* question; (*SCOL*) (written *ou* oral) test

interrogatoire [ɛ̃teʀɔgatwaʀ] *nm* (*POLICE*) questioning *no pl*; (*JUR*) cross-examination, interrogation

interroger [ɛ̃teʀɔʒe] *vt* to question; (*INFORM*) to interrogate; (*SCOL: candidat*) to test; **interroger qn (sur qch)** to question sb (about sth); **interroger qn du regard** to look questioningly at sb, give sb a questioning look; **s'interroger sur qch** to ask o.s. about sth, ponder (about) sth

interrompre [ɛ̃teʀɔ̃pʀ(ə)] *vt* (*gén*) to interrupt; (*travail, voyage*) to break off, interrupt; **s'interrompre** to break off

interrupteur [ɛ̃teʀyptœʀ] *nm* switch

interruption [ɛ̃teʀypsjɔ̃] *nf* interruption; **sans interruption** without a break; **interruption de grossesse** termination of pregnancy; **interruption volontaire de grossesse** voluntary termination of pregnancy, abortion

intersection [ɛ̃tɛʀsɛksjɔ̃] *nf* intersection

interstice [ɛ̃tɛʀstis] *nm* crack, slit

interurbain [ɛ̃tɛʀyʀbɛ̃]; (TÉL) *nm* long-distance call service ◆ *adj* long-distance

intervalle [ɛ̃tɛʀval] *nm* (espace) space; (de temps) interval; **dans l'intervalle** in the meantime; **à 2 mois d'intervalle** after a space of 2 months; **à intervalles rapprochés** at close intervals; **par intervalles** at intervals

intervenir [ɛ̃tɛʀvǝniʀ] *vi* (gén) to intervene; (survenir) to take place; (faire une conférence) to give a talk *ou* lecture; **intervenir auprès de/en faveur de qn** to intervene with/on behalf of sb; **la police a dû intervenir** police had to step in *ou* intervene; **les médecins ont dû intervenir** the doctors had to operate

intervention [ɛ̃tɛʀvɑ̃sjɔ̃] *nf* intervention; (conférence) talk, paper; **intervention (chirurgicale)** operation

intervertir [ɛ̃tɛʀvɛʀtiʀ] *vt* to invert (the order of), reverse

interview [ɛ̃tɛʀvju] *nf* interview

interviewer [ɛ̃tɛʀvjuve] *vt* to interview ◆ *nm* [ɛ̃tɛʀvjuvœʀ] (journaliste) interviewer

intestin, e [ɛ̃tɛstɛ̃, -in] *adj* internal ◆ *nm* intestine; **intestin grêle** small intestine

intime [ɛ̃tim] *adj* intimate; (vie, journal) private; (convictions) inmost; (dîner, cérémonie) held among friends, quiet ◆ *nm/f* close friend

intimider [ɛ̃timide] *vt* to intimidate

intimité [ɛ̃timite] *nf* intimacy; (vie privée) privacy; private life; **dans l'intimité** in private; (sans formalités) with only a few friends, quietly

intitulé [ɛ̃tityle] *nm* title

intolérable [ɛ̃tɔleʀabl(ǝ)] *adj* intolerable

intox [ɛ̃tɔks] (fam) *nf* brainwashing

intoxication [ɛ̃tɔksikasjɔ̃] *nf* poisoning *no pl*; (toxicomanie) drug addiction; (fig) brainwashing; **intoxication alimentaire** food poisoning

intoxiquer [ɛ̃tɔksike] *vt* to poison; (fig) to brainwash; **s'intoxiquer** to poison o.s.

intraduisible [ɛ̃tʀadɥizibl(ǝ)] *adj* untranslatable; (fig) inexpressible

intraitable [ɛ̃tʀɛtabl(ǝ)] *adj* inflexible, uncompromising

intranet [ɛ̃tʀanet] *nm* intranet

intransigeant, e [ɛ̃tʀɑ̃ziʒɑ̃, -ɑ̃t] *adj* intransigent; (morale, passion) uncompromising

intransitif, ive [ɛ̃tʀɑ̃zitif, -iv] *adj* (LING) intransitive

intrépide [ɛ̃tʀepid] *adj* dauntless, intrepid

intrigue [ɛ̃tʀig] *nf* intrigue; (scénario) plot

intriguer [ɛ̃tʀige] *vi* to scheme ◆ *vt* to puzzle, intrigue

intrinsèque [ɛ̃tʀɛ̃sɛk] *adj* intrinsic

introduction [ɛ̃tʀɔdyksjɔ̃] *nf* introduction; **paroles/chapitre d'introduction** introductory words/chapter; **lettre/mot d'introduction** letter/note of introduction

introduire [ɛ̃tʀɔdɥiʀ] *vt* to introduce; (visiteur) to show in; (aiguille, clef): **introduire qch dans** to insert *ou* introduce sth into; (personne): **introduire à qch** to introduce to sth; (: présenter): **introduire qn à qn/dans un club** to introduce sb to sb/to a club; (INFORM) to input, enter; **s'introduire** (techniques, usages) to be introduced; **s'introduire dans** to gain entry into; to get o.s. accepted into; (eau, fumée) to get into; **introduire au clavier** to key in

introuvable [ɛ̃tʀuvabl(ǝ)] *adj* which cannot be found; (COMM) unobtainable

introverti, e [ɛ̃tʀɔvɛʀti] *nm/f* introvert

intrus, e [ɛ̃tʀy, -yz] *nm/f* intruder

intrusion [ɛ̃tʀyzjɔ̃] *nf* intrusion; (ingérence) interference

intuition [ɛ̃tɥisjɔ̃] *nf* intuition; **avoir une intuition** to have a feeling; **avoir l'intuition de qch** to have an intuition of sth; **avoir de l'intuition** to have intuition

inusable [inyzabl(ǝ)] *adj* hard-wearing

inusité, e [inyzite] *adj* rarely used

inutile [inytil] *adj* useless; (superflu) unnecessary

inutilement [inytilmɑ̃] *adv* needlessly

inutilisable [inytilizabl(ǝ)] *adj* unusable

invalide [ɛ̃valid] *adj* disabled ◆ *nm/f*: **invalide de guerre** disabled ex-serviceman; **invalide du travail** industrially disabled person

invariable [ɛ̃vaʀjabl(ǝ)] *adj* invariable

invasion [ɛ̃vazjɔ̃] *nf* invasion

invectiver [ɛ̃vɛktive] *vt* to hurl abuse at ◆ *vi*: **invectiver contre** to rail against

invendable [ɛ̃vɑ̃dabl(ǝ)] *adj* unsaleable, unmarketable

invendu, e [ɛ̃vɑ̃dy] *adj* unsold ◆ *nm* return; **invendus** *nmpl* unsold goods

inventaire [ɛ̃vɑ̃tɛʀ] *nm* inventory; (COMM: liste) stocklist; (: opération) stocktaking *no pl*; (fig) survey; **faire un inventaire** to make an inventory; (COMM) to take stock; **faire *ou* procéder à l'inventaire** to take stock

inventer [ɛ̃vɑ̃te] *vt* to invent; (subterfuge) to devise, invent; (histoire, excuse) to make up, invent; **inventer de faire** to hit on the idea of doing

inventeur, trice [ɛ̃vɑ̃tœʀ, -tʀis] *nm/f* inventor

inventif, ive [ɛ̃vɑ̃tif, -iv] *adj* inventive

invention [ɛ̃vɑ̃sjɔ̃] *nf* invention; (imagination, inspiration) inventiveness

inverse [ɛ̃vɛʀs(ǝ)] *adj* (ordre) reverse; (sens) opposite; (rapport) inverse ◆ *nm* reverse; inverse; **en proportion inverse** in inverse proportion; **dans le sens inverse des aiguilles d'une montre** anticlockwise; **en sens inverse** in (ou from) the opposite direction; **à l'inverse** conversely

inversement [ɛ̃vɛʀsǝmɑ̃] *adv* conversely

inverser [ɛ̃vɛʀse] *vt* to reverse, invert; (*ÉLEC*) to reverse

investigation [ɛ̃vɛstigasjɔ̃] *nf* investigation, inquiry

investir [ɛ̃vɛstiʀ] *vt* to invest; **s'investir** *vi* (*PSYCH*) to involve o.s.; **investir qn de** to vest *ou* invest sb with

investissement [ɛ̃vɛstismɑ̃] *nm* investment; (*PSYCH*) involvement

investiture [ɛ̃vɛstityʀ] *nf* investiture; (*à une élection*) nomination

invétéré, e [ɛ̃vetere] *adj* (*habitude*) ingrained; (*bavard, buveur*) inveterate

invisible [ɛ̃vizibl(ə)] *adj* invisible; (*fig: personne*) not available

invitation [ɛ̃vitasjɔ̃] *nf* invitation; **à/sur l'invitation de qn** at/on sb's invitation; **carte/lettre d'invitation** invitation card/letter

invité, e [ɛ̃vite] *nm/f* guest

inviter [ɛ̃vite] *vt* to invite; **inviter qn à faire qch** to invite sb to do sth; (*suj: chose*) to induce *ou* tempt sb to do sth

invivable [ɛ̃vivabl(ə)] *adj* unbearable, impossible

involontaire [ɛ̃vɔlɔ̃tɛʀ] *adj* (*mouvement*) involuntary; (*insulte*) unintentional; (*complice*) unwitting

invoquer [ɛ̃vɔke] *vt* (*Dieu, muse*) to call upon, invoke; (*prétexte*) to put forward (as an excuse); (*témoignage*) to call upon; (*loi, texte*) to refer to; **invoquer la clémence de qn** to beg sb *ou* appeal to sb for clemency

invraisemblable [ɛ̃vʀɛsɑ̃blabl(ə)] *adj* unlikely, improbable; (*bizarre*) incredible

iode [jɔd] *nm* iodine

irai *etc* [iʀe] *vb voir* **aller**

Irak [iʀak] *nm*: **l'Irak** Iraq *ou* Irak

irakien, ne [iʀakjɛ̃, -ɛn] *adj* Iraqi ♦ *nm/f*: **Irakien, ne** Iraqi

Iran [iʀɑ̃] *nm*: **l'Iran** Iran

iranien, ne [iʀanjɛ̃, -ɛn] *adj* Iranian ♦ *nm* (*LING*) Iranian ♦ *nm/f*: **Iranien, ne** Iranian

irascible [iʀasibl(ə)] *adj* short-tempered, irascible

irions *etc* [iʀjɔ̃] *vb voir* **aller**

iris [iʀis] *nm* iris

irlandais, e [iʀlɑ̃dɛ, -ɛz] *adj, nm* (*LING*) Irish ♦ *nm/f*: **Irlandais, e** Irishman/woman; **les Irlandais** the Irish

Irlande [iʀlɑ̃d] *nf*: **l'Irlande** (*pays*) Ireland; (*état*) the Irish Republic, the Republic of Ireland, Eire; **Irlande du Nord** Northern Ireland, Ulster; **Irlande du Sud** Southern Ireland, Irish Republic, Eire; **la mer d'Irlande** the Irish Sea

ironie [iʀɔni] *nf* irony

ironique [iʀɔnik] *adj* ironical

irons *etc* [iʀɔ̃] *vb voir* **aller**

irradier [iʀadje] *vi* to radiate ♦ *vt* to irradiate

irraisonné, e [iʀɛzɔne] *adj* irrational, unreasoned

irrationnel, le [iʀasjɔnɛl] *adj* irrational

irréalisable [iʀealizabl(ə)] *adj* unrealizable; (*projet*) impracticable

irrécupérable [iʀekypeʀabl(ə)] *adj* unreclaimable, beyond repair; (*personne*) beyond redemption *ou* recall

irréductible [iʀedyktibl(ə)] *adj* indomitable, implacable; (*MATH: fraction, équation*) irreducible

irréel, le [iʀeɛl] *adj* unreal

irréfléchi, e [iʀefleʃi] *adj* thoughtless

irrégularité [iʀegylaʀite] *nf* irregularity; unevenness *no pl*

irrégulier, ière [iʀegylje, -jɛʀ] *adj* irregular; (*surface, rythme, écriture*) uneven, irregular; (*élève, athlète*) erratic

irrémédiable [iʀemedjabl(ə)] *adj* irreparable

irremplaçable [iʀɑ̃plasabl(ə)] *adj* irreplaceable

irréparable [iʀepaʀabl(ə)] *adj* beyond repair, irreparable; (*fig*) irreparable

irréprochable [iʀepʀɔʃabl(ə)] *adj* irreproachable, beyond reproach; (*tenue, toilette*) impeccable

irrésistible [iʀezistibl(ə)] *adj* irresistible; (*preuve, logique*) compelling

irrésolu, e [iʀezɔly] *adj* irresolute

irrespectueux, euse [iʀɛspɛktɥø, -øz] *adj* disrespectful

irrespirable [iʀɛspiʀabl(ə)] *adj* unbreathable; (*fig*) oppressive, stifling

irresponsable [iʀɛspɔ̃sabl(ə)] *adj* irresponsible

irriguer [iʀige] *vt* to irrigate

irritable [iʀitabl(ə)] *adj* irritable

irriter [iʀite] *vt* (*agacer*) to irritate, annoy; (*MÉD: enflammer*) to irritate; **s'irriter contre qn/de qch** to get annoyed *ou* irritated with sb/at sth

irruption [iʀypsjɔ̃] *nf* irruption *no pl*; **faire irruption dans** to burst into

Islam [islam] *nm* Islam

islamique [islamik] *adj* Islamic

islamiste [islamist(ə)] *adj, nm/f* Islamic

islamophobie [islamɔfɔbi] *nf* Islamophobia

Islande [islɑ̃d] *nf*: **l'Islande** Iceland

isolant, e [izɔlɑ̃, -ɑ̃t] *adj* insulating; (*insonorisant*) soundproofing ♦ *nm* insulator

isolation [izɔlasjɔ̃] *nf* insulation; **isolation acoustique/thermique** sound/thermal insulation

isolé, e [izɔle] *adj* isolated; (*ÉLEC*) insulated

isoler [izɔle] *vt* to isolate; (*prisonnier*) to put in solitary confinement; (*ville*) to cut off, isolate; (*ÉLEC*) to insulate

isoloir [izɔlwaʀ] *nm* polling booth

Israël [isʀaɛl] *nm*: **l'Israël** Israel

israélien, ne [isʀaeljɛ̃, -ɛn] *adj* Israeli ♦ *nm/f*: **Israélien, ne** Israeli

israélite [isʀaelit] *adj* Jewish; (*dans l'Ancien Testament*) Israelite ♦ *nm/f*: **Israélite** Jew/Jewess; Israelite

issu, e [isy] *adj*: **issu de** descended from; (*fig*) stemming from ◆ *nf* (*ouverture, sortie*) exit; (*solution*) way out, solution; (*dénouement*) outcome; **à l'issue de** at the conclusion *ou* close of; **rue sans issue** dead end, no through road (*BRIT*), no outlet (*US*); **issue de secours** emergency exit

Italie [itali] *nf*: **l'Italie** Italy

italien, ne [italjɛ̃, -ɛn] *adj* Italian ◆ *nm* (*LING*) Italian ◆ *nm/f*: **Italien, ne** Italian

italique [italik] *nm*: **en italique(s)** in italics

itinéraire [itinerɛr] *nm* itinerary, route

IUT *sigle m* = **Institut universitaire de technologie**

IVG *sigle f* (= *interruption volontaire de grossesse*) abortion

ivoire [ivwaʀ] *nm* ivory

ivre [ivʀ(ə)] *adj* drunk; **ivre de** (*colère*) wild with; (*bonheur*) drunk *ou* intoxicated with; **ivre mort** dead drunk

ivresse [ivʀɛs] *nf* drunkenness; (*euphorie*) intoxication

ivrogne [ivʀɔɲ] *nm/f* drunkard

— *J j* —

j' [ʒ] *pron voir* **je**

jacasser [ʒakase] *vi* to chatter

jacinthe [ʒasɛ̃t] *nf* hyacinth; **jacinthe des bois** bluebell

jadis [ʒadis] *adv* in times past, formerly

jaillir [ʒajiʀ] *vi* (*liquide*) to spurt out, gush out; (*lumière*) to flood out; (*fig*) to burst out

jais [ʒɛ] *nm* jet; (**d'un noir) de jais** jet-black

jalousie [ʒaluzi] *nf* jealousy; (*store*) (venetian) blind

jaloux, ouse [ʒalu, -uz] *adj* jealous; **être jaloux de qn/qch** to be jealous of sb/sth

jamais [ʒamɛ] *adv* never; (*sans négation*) ever; **ne ... jamais** never; **jamais de la vie!** never!; **si jamais ...** if ever ...; **à (tout) jamais, pour jamais** for ever, for ever and ever

jambe [ʒɑ̃b] *nf* leg; **à toutes jambes** as fast as one's legs can carry one

jambon [ʒɑ̃bɔ̃] *nm* ham

jambonneau, x [ʒɑ̃bɔno] *nm* knuckle of ham

jante [ʒɑ̃t] *nf* (wheel) rim

janvier [ʒɑ̃vje] *nm* January; *voir aussi* **juillet**

Japon [ʒapɔ̃] *nm*: **le Japon** Japan

japonais, e [ʒapɔnɛ, -ɛz] *adj* Japanese ◆ *nm* (*LING*) Japanese ◆ *nm/f*: **Japonais, e** Japanese

japper [ʒape] *vi* to yap, yelp

jaquette [ʒakɛt] *nf* (*de cérémonie*) morning coat; (*de femme*) jacket; (*de livre*) dust cover, (dust) jacket

jardin [ʒaʀdɛ̃] *nm* garden; **jardin d'acclimatation** zoological gardens *pl*; **jardin botanique** botanical gardens *pl*; **jardin d'enfants** nursery school; **jardin potager** vegetable garden; **jardin public** (public) park, public gardens *pl*; **jardins suspendus** hanging gardens; **jardin zoologique** zoological gardens

jardinage [ʒaʀdinaʒ] *nm* gardening

jardiner [ʒaʀdine] *vi* to garden, do some gardening

jardinier, ière [ʒaʀdinje, -jɛʀ] *nm/f* gardener ◆ *nf* (*de fenêtre*) window box; **jardinière d'enfants** nursery school teacher; **jardinière (de légumes)** (*CULIN*) mixed vegetables

jargon [ʒaʀgɔ̃] *nm* (*charabia*) gibberish; (*publicitaire, scientifique etc*) jargon

jarret [ʒaʀɛ] *nm* back of knee; (*CULIN*) knuckle, shin

jarretelle [ʒaʀtɛl] *nf* suspender (*BRIT*), garter (*US*)

jarretière [ʒaʀtjɛʀ] *nf* garter

jaser [ʒaze] *vi* to chatter, prattle; (*indiscrètement*) to gossip

jatte [ʒat] *nf* basin, bowl

jauge [ʒoʒ] *nf* (*capacité*) capacity, tonnage; (*instrument*) gauge; **jauge (de niveau) d'huile** dipstick

jaune [ʒon] *adj, nm* yellow ◆ *nm/f* Asiatic; (*briseur de grève*) blackleg ◆ *adv* (*fam*): **rire jaune** to laugh on the other side of one's face; **jaune d'œuf** (egg) yolk

jaunir [ʒoniʀ] *vi, vt* to turn yellow

jaunisse [ʒonis] *nf* jaundice

Javel [ʒavɛl] *nf voir* **eau**

javelot [ʒavlo] *nm* javelin; (*SPORT*): **faire du javelot** to throw the javelin

J.-C. *abr* = **Jésus-Christ**

je, j' [ʒ(ə)] *pron* I

jean [dʒin] *nm* jeans *pl*

Jésus-Christ [ʒezykri(st)] *n* Jesus Christ; **600 avant/après Jésus-Christ** *ou* **J.-C.** 600 B.C./A.D.

jet¹ [ʒɛ] *nm* (*lancer*) throwing *no pl*, throw; (*jaillissement*) jet; spurt; (*de tuyau*) nozzle; (*fig*): **premier jet** (*ébauche*) rough outline; **arroser au jet** to hose; **d'un (seul) jet** (*d'un seul coup*) at (*ou* in) one go; **du premier jet** at the first attempt *ou* shot; **jet d'eau** spray; (*fontaine*) fountain

jet² [dʒɛt] *nm* (*avion*) jet

jetable [ʒətabl(ə)] *adj* disposable

jetée [ʒəte] *nf* jetty; pier

jeter [ʒəte] *vt* (*gén*) to throw; (*se défaire de*) to throw away *ou* out; (*son, lueur etc*) to give out; **jeter qch à qn** to throw sth to sb; (*de façon agressive*) to throw sth at sb; (*NAVIG*): **jeter l'ancre** to cast anchor; **jeter un coup d'œil (à)** to take a look (at); **jeter les bras en avant/la tête en arrière** to throw one's arms forward/one's head back(ward); **jeter l'effroi parmi** to spread fear among; **jeter un sort à qn** to cast a spell on sb; **jeter qn dans la misère** to reduce sb to poverty; **jeter qn dehors/en prison** to throw sb out/into prison; **jeter l'éponge** (*fig*) to throw in the towel; **jeter des fleurs à qn** (*fig*) to say lovely things to sb; **jeter la pierre à qn** (accuser, blâmer) to accuse sb; **se jeter sur** to throw o.s. onto; **se jeter dans** (suj: fleuve) to flow into; **se jeter par la fenêtre** to throw o.s. out of the window; **se jeter à l'eau** (fig) to take the plunge

jeton [ʒətɔ̃] nm (au jeu) counter; (de téléphone) token; **jetons de présence** (director's) fees

jette etc [ʒɛt] vb voir **jeter**

jeu, x [ʒø] nm (divertissement, TECH: d'une pièce) play; (défini par des règles, TENNIS: partie, FOOTBALL etc: façon de jouer) game; (THÉÂT etc) acting; (fonctionnement) working, interplay; (série d'objets, jouet) set; (CARTES) hand; (au casino): **le jeu** gambling; **cacher son jeu** (fig) to keep one's cards hidden, conceal one's hand; **c'est un jeu d'enfant!** (fig) it's child's play!; **en jeu** at stake; at work; (FOOTBALL) in play; **remettre en jeu** to throw in; **entrer/mettre en jeu** to come/bring into play; **par jeu** (pour s'amuser) for fun; **d'entrée de jeu** (tout de suite, dès le début) from the outset; **entrer dans le jeu/le jeu de qn** (fig) to play the game/sb's game; **jouer gros jeu** to play for high stakes; **se piquer/se prendre au jeu** to get excited over/get caught up in the game; **jeu d'arcade** video game; **jeu de boules** game of bowls; (endroit) bowling pitch; (boules) set of bowls; **jeu de cartes** card game; (paquet) pack of cards; **jeu de construction** building set; **jeu d'échecs** chess set; **jeu d'écritures** (COMM) paper transaction; **jeu électronique** electronic game; **jeu de hasard** game of chance; **jeu de mots** pun; **le jeu de l'oie** snakes and ladders sg; **jeu d'orgue(s)** organ stop; **jeu de patience** puzzle; **jeu de physionomie** facial expressions pl; **jeu de société** parlour game; **jeu télévisé** television game; **jeu vidéo** computer game; **jeux de lumière** lighting effects; **Jeux olympiques (JO)** Olympic Games

jeudi [ʒødi] nm Thursday; **jeudi saint** Maundy Thursday; voir aussi **lundi**

jeun [ʒœ̃]: **à jeun** adv on an empty stomach

jeune [ʒœn] adj young ◆ adv: **faire/s'habiller jeune** to look/dress young; **les jeunes** young people, the young; **jeune fille** nf girl; **jeune homme** nm young man; **jeune loup** nm (POL, ÉCON) young go-getter; **jeune premier** leading man; **jeunes gens** nmpl young people; **jeunes mariés** nmpl newly weds

jeûne [ʒøn] nm fast

jeunesse [ʒœnɛs] nf youth; (aspect) youthfulness; (jeunes) young people pl, youth

joaillerie [ʒɔajʀi] nf jewel trade; jewellery (BRIT), jewelry (US)

joaillier, ière [ʒɔaje, -jɛʀ] nm/f jeweller (BRIT), jeweler (US)

jogging [dʒɔgiŋ] nm tracksuit (BRIT), sweatsuit (US); **faire du jogging** to jog, go jogging

joie [ʒwa] nf joy

joindre [ʒwɛ̃dʀ(ə)] vt to join; (à une lettre): **joindre qch à** to enclose sth with; (contacter) to contact, get in touch with; **joindre les mains/talons** to put one's hands/heels together; **joindre les deux bouts** (fig: du mois) to make ends meet; **se joindre** (mains etc) to come together; **se joindre à qn** to join sb; **se joindre à qch** to join in sth

joint, e [ʒwɛ̃, -ɛ̃t] pp de **joindre** ◆ adj: **joint (à)** (lettre, paquet) attached (to), enclosed (with); **pièce jointe** enclosure ◆ nm joint; (ligne) join; (de ciment etc) pointing no pl; **chercher/trouver le joint** (fig) to look for/come up with the answer; **joint de cardan** cardan joint; **joint de culasse** cylinder head gasket; **joint de robinet** washer; **joint universel** universal joint

joker [ʒɔkɛʀ] nm (CARTES) joker; (INFORM): **(caractère m) joker** wildcard

joli, e [ʒɔli] adj pretty, attractive; **une jolie somme/situation** a nice little sum/situation; **un joli gâchis** etc a nice mess etc; **c'est du joli!** that's very nice!; **tout ça, c'est bien joli mais ...** that's all very well but ...

jonc [ʒɔ̃] nm (bul) rush; (bague, bracelet) band

jonction [ʒɔ̃ksjɔ̃] nf joining; (point de) jonction (de routes) junction; (de fleuves) confluence; **opérer une jonction** (MIL etc) to rendez-vous

jongleur, euse [ʒɔ̃glœʀ, -øz] nm/f juggler

jonquille [ʒɔ̃kij] nf daffodil

Jordanie [ʒɔʀdani] nf: **la Jordanie** Jordan

joue [ʒu] nf cheek; **mettre en joue** to take aim at

jouer [ʒwe] vt (partie, carte, coup, MUS: morceau) to play; (somme d'argent, réputation) to stake, wager; (pièce, rôle) to perform; (film) to show; (simuler: sentiment) to affect, feign ◆ vi to play; (THÉÂT, CINÉ) to act, perform; (bois, porte: se voiler) to warp; (clef, pièce: avoir du jeu) to be loose; (entrer ou être en jeu) to come into play, come into it; **jouer sur** (miser) to gamble on; **jouer de** (MUS) to play; **jouer du couteau/des coudes** to use knives/one's elbows; **jouer à** (jeu, sport, roulette) to play; **jouer au héros** to act ou play the hero; **jouer avec** (risquer) to gamble with; **se jouer de** (difficultés) to make light of; **se jouer de qn** to deceive ou dupe sb; **jouer un tour à qn** to play a trick on sb; **jouer la comédie** (fig) to put on an act, put it on; **jouer aux courses** to back horses, bet on horses; **jouer à la baisse/hausse** (BOURSE) to play for a fall/rise; **jouer serré** to play a close game; **jouer de malchance** to be dogged with ill-luck; **jouer sur les mots** to play with words; **à toi/nous de jouer** it's your/our go ou turn

jouet [ʒwɛ] nm toy; **être le jouet de** (illusion etc) to be the victim of

joueur, euse [ʒwœʀ, -øz] nm/f player ◆ adj (enfant, chat) playful; **être beau/mauvais joueur** to be a good/bad loser

joufflu, e [ʒufly] adj chubby(-cheeked)

joug [ʒu] nm yoke

jouir [ʒwiʀ]: **jouir de** vt to enjoy

jouissance [ʒwisɑ̃s] nf pleasure; (JUR) use

joujou [ʒuʒu] nm (fam) toy

jour [ʒuʀ] *nm* day; (*opposé à la nuit*) day, daytime; (*clarté*) daylight; (*fig: aspect*): **sous un jour favourable/nouveau** in a favourable/new light; (*ouverture*) opening; (*COUTURE*) openwork *no pl*; **au jour le jour** from day to day; **de nos jours** these days, nowadays; **tous les jours** every day; **de jour en jour** day by day; **d'un jour à l'autre** from one day to the next; **du jour au lendemain** overnight; **il fait jour** it's daylight; **en plein jour** in broad daylight; **au jour** in daylight; **au petit jour** at daybreak; **au grand jour** (*fig*) in the open; **mettre au jour** to uncover, disclose; **être à jour** to be up to date; **mettre à jour** to bring up to date, update; **mise à jour** updating; **donner le jour à** to give birth to; **voir le jour** to be born; **se faire jour** (*fig*) to become clear; **jour férié** public holiday; **le jour J** D-Day

journal, aux [ʒuʀnal, -o] *nm* (news)paper; (*personnel*) journal, diary; **journal de bord** log; **journal de mode** fashion magazine; **le Journal officiel (de la République française) (JO)** bulletin giving details of laws and official announcements; **journal parlé/télévisé** radio/television news *sg*

journalier, ière [ʒuʀnalje, -jɛʀ] *adj* daily; (*banal*) everyday ♦ *nm* day labourer

journalisme [ʒuʀnalism(ə)] *nm* journalism

journaliste [ʒuʀnalist(ə)] *nm/f* journalist

journée [ʒuʀne] *nf* day; **la journée continue** the 9 to 5 working day (*with short lunch break*)

journellement [ʒuʀnɛlmɑ̃] *adv* (*tous les jours*) daily; (*souvent*) every day

joyau, x [ʒwajo] *nm* gem, jewel

joyeux, euse [ʒwajø, -øz] *adj* joyful, merry; **joyeux Noël!** Merry *ou* Happy Christmas!; **joyeuses Pâques!** Happy Easter!; **joyeux anniversaire!** many happy returns!

jubiler [ʒybile] *vi* to be jubilant, exult

jucher [ʒyʃe] *vt*: **jucher qch sur** to perch sth (up)on ♦ *vi* (*oiseau*): **jucher sur** to perch (up)on; **se jucher sur** to perch o.s. (up)on

judas [ʒyda] *nm* (*trou*) spy-hole

judiciaire [ʒydisjɛʀ] *adj* judicial

judicieux, euse [ʒydisjø, -øz] *adj* judicious

judo [ʒydo] *nm* judo

juge [ʒyʒ] *nm* judge; **juge d'instruction** examining (*BRIT*) *ou* committing (*US*) magistrate; **juge de paix** justice of the peace; **juge de touche** linesman

jugé [ʒyʒe]: **au jugé** *adv* by guesswork

jugement [ʒyʒmɑ̃] *nm* judgment; (*JUR: au pénal*) sentence; (: *au civil*) decision; **jugement de valeur** value judgment

jugeote [ʒyʒɔt] *nf* (*fam*) gumption

juger [ʒyʒe] *vt* to judge ♦ *nm*: **au juger** by guesswork; **juger qn/qch satisfaisant** to consider sb/sth (to be) satisfactory; **juger que** to think *ou* consider that; **juger bon de faire** to consider it a good idea to do, see fit to do; **juger de** *vt* to judge; **juges**

de ma surprise imagine my surprise

juif, ive [ʒɥif, -iv] *adj* Jewish ♦ *nm/f*: **Juif, ive** Jew/Jewess *ou* Jewish woman

juillet [ʒɥije] *nm* July; **le premier juillet** the first of July (*BRIT*), July first (*US*); **le deux/onze juillet** the second/eleventh of July, July second/eleventh; **il est venu le 5 juillet** he came on 5th July *ou* July 5th; **en juillet** in July; **début/fin juillet** at the beginning/end of July; *see boxed note*

14 JUILLET

Le 14 juillet is a national holiday in France and commemorates the storming of the Bastille during the French Revolution. Throughout the country there are celebrations, which feature parades, music, dancing and firework displays. In Paris a military parade along the Champs-Élysées is attended by the President.

juin [ʒɥɛ̃] *nm* June; *voir aussi* **juillet**

jumeau, elle, x [ʒymo, -ɛl] *adj, nm/f* twin; **maisons jumelles** semidetached houses

jumelage [ʒymlaʒ] *nm* twinning

jumeler [ʒymle] *vt* to twin; **roues jumelées** double wheels; **billets de loterie jumelés** double series lottery tickets; **pari jumelé** double bet

jumelle [ʒymɛl] *adj f, nf voir* **jumeau** ♦ *vb voir* **jumeler**

jument [ʒymɑ̃] *nf* mare

jungle [ʒœ̃gl(ə)] *nf* jungle

jupe [ʒyp] *nf* skirt

jupon [ʒypɔ̃] *nm* waist slip *ou* petticoat

juré, e [ʒyʀe] *nm/f* juror ♦ *adj*: **ennemi juré** sworn *ou* avowed enemy

jurer [ʒyʀe] *vt* (*obéissance etc*) to swear, vow ♦ *vi* (*dire des jurons*) to swear, curse; (*dissoner*) **jurer (avec)** to clash (with); (*s'engager*): **jurer de faire/que** to swear *ou* vow to do/that; (*affirmer*): **jurer que** to swear *ou* vouch that; **jurer de qch** (*s'en porter garant*) to swear to sth; **ils ne jurent que par lui** they swear by him; **je vous jure!** honestly!

juridique [ʒyʀidik] *adj* legal

juron [ʒyʀɔ̃] *nm* curse, swearword

jury [ʒyʀi] *nm* (*JUR*) jury; (*SCOL*) board (of examiners), jury

jus [ʒy] *nm* juice; (*de viande*) gravy, (meat) juice; **jus de fruits** fruit juice; **jus de raisin/tomates** grape/tomato juice

jusque [ʒysk(ə)]: **jusqu'à** *prép* (*endroit*) as far as, (up) to; (*moment*) until, till; (*limite*) up to; **jusque sur/dans** up to, as far as; (*y compris*) even on/in; **jusque vers** until about; **jusqu'à ce que** *conj* until; **jusque-là** (*temps*) until then; (*espace*) up to there; **jusqu'ici** (*temps*) until now; (*espace*) up to here; **jusqu'à présent** until now, so far

justaucorps [ʒystokɔʀ] *nm inv* (*DANSE, SPORT*) leotard

juste [ʒyst(ə)] *adj* (*équitable*) just, fair; (*légitime*) just, justified; (*exact, vrai*) right; (*étroit, insuffisant*) tight ♦ *adv* right; tight; (*chanter*) in tune; (*seulement*) just; **juste assez/au-dessus** just enough/ above; **pouvoir tout juste faire** to be only just able to do; **au juste** exactly, actually; **comme de juste** of course, naturally; **le juste milieu** the happy medium; **à juste titre** rightfully

justement [ʒystəmɑ̃] *adv* rightly; justly; (*précisément*): **c'est justement ce qu'il fallait faire** that's just *ou* precisely what needed doing

justesse [ʒystɛs] *nf* (*précision*) accuracy; (*d'une remarque*) aptness; (*d'une opinion*) soundness; **de justesse** just, by a narrow margin

justice [ʒystis] *nf* (*équité*) fairness, justice; (*ADMIN*) justice; **rendre la justice** to dispense justice; **traduire en justice** to bring before the courts; **obtenir justice** to obtain justice; **rendre justice à qn** to do sb justice; **se faire justice** to take the law into one's own hands; (*se suicider*) to take one's life

justicier, ière [ʒystisje, -jɛʀ] *nm/f* judge, righter of wrongs

justificatif, ive [ʒystifikatif, -iv] *adj* (*document etc*) supporting ♦ *nm* supporting proof

justifier [ʒystifje] *vt* to justify; **justifier de** *vt* to prove; **non justifié** unjustified; **justifié à droite/ gauche** ranged right/left

juteux, euse [ʒytø, -øz] *adj* juicy

juvénile [ʒyvenil] *adj* young, youthful

— K k —

K, k [kɑ] *nm inv* K, k ♦ *abr* (= *kilo*) kg; (= *kilooctet*) K; **K comme Kléber** K for King

K 7 [kaset] *nf* cassette

kaki [kaki] *adj inv* khaki

kangourou [kɑ̃guʀu] *nm* kangaroo

karaté [kaʀate] *nm* karate

karting [kaʀtiŋ] *nm* go-carting, karting

kascher [kaʃɛʀ] *adj inv* kosher

kayak [kajak] *nm* kayak

képi [kepi] *nm* kepi

kermesse [kɛʀmɛs] *nf* bazaar, (charity) fête; village fair

kidnapper [kidnape] *vt* to kidnap

kilo [kilo] *nm* kilo

kilogramme [kilɔgʀam] *nm* kilo₊ramme (*BRIT*), kilogram (*US*)

kilométrage [kilɔmetʀaʒ] *nm* number of kilometres travelled, = mileage

kilomètre [kilɔmɛtʀ(ə)] *nm* kilometre (*BRIT*), kilo-

meter (*US*); **kilomètres-heure** kilometres per hour

kilométrique [kilɔmetʀik] *adj* (*distance*) in kilometres; **compteur kilométrique** = mileage indicator

kinésithérapeute [kineziteʀapøt] *nm/f* physiotherapist

kiosque [kjɔsk(ə)] *nm* kiosk, stall; (*TÉL etc*) telephone and/or videotext information service; **kiosque à journaux** newspaper kiosk

kir [kiʀ] *nm* kir (*white wine with blackcurrant liqueur*)

kit [kit] *nm*: **en kit** in kit form

kiwi [kiwi] *nm* (*ZOOL*) kiwi; (*BOT*) kiwi (fruit)

klaxon [klaksɔn] *nm* horn

klaxonner [klaksɔne] *vi, vt* to hoot (*BRIT*), honk (one's horn) (*US*)

km *abr* (= *kilomètre*) km

km/h *abr* (= *kilomètres/heure*) = mph

K.-O. [kao] *adj inv* (knocked) out, out for the count

K-way® [kawe] *nm* (lightweight nylon) cagoule

kyste [kist(ə)] *nm* cyst

— L l —

l' [l] *art déf voir* **le**

la [la] *art déf, pron voir* **le** ♦ *nm* (*MUS*) A; (*en chantant la gamme*) la

là [la] *adv* (*aussi*: **-ci, celui**) there; (*ici*) here; (*dans le temps*) then; **est-ce que Catherine est là?** is Catherine there (*ou* here)?; **c'est là que** this is where; **là où** where; **de là** (*fig*) hence; **par là** (*fig*) by that; **tout est là** (*fig*) that's what it's all about

là-bas [laba] *adv* there

label [label] *nm* stamp, seal

labeur [labœʀ] *nm* toil *no pl*, toiling *no pl*

labo [labo] *nm* (= *laboratoire*) lab

laboratoire [labɔʀatwaʀ] *nm* laboratory; **laboratoire de langues/d'analyses** language/(medical) analysis laboratory

laborieux, euse [labɔʀjø, -øz] *adj* (*tâche*) laborious; **classes laborieuses** working classes

labour [labuʀ] *nm* ploughing *no pl* (*BRIT*), plowing *no pl* (*US*); **labours** *nmpl* (*champs*) ploughed fields; **cheval de labour** plough- *ou* cart-horse; **bœuf de labour** ox (*pl* oxen)

labourer [labuʀe] *vt* to plough (*BRIT*), plow (*US*); (*fig*) to make deep gashes *ou* furrows in

labyrinthe [labiʀɛ̃t] *nm* labyrinth, maze

lac [lak] *nm* lake; **le lac Léman** Lake Geneva; **les Grands Lacs** the Great Lakes

lacer [lase] *vt* to lace *ou* do up

lacérer [laseʀe] *vt* to tear to shreds

lacet [lase] *nm* (*de chaussure*) lace; (*de route*) sharp bend; (*piège*) snare; **chaussures à lacets** lace-up *ou* lacing shoes

lâche [laʃ] *adj* (*poltron*) cowardly; (*desserré*) loose, slack; (*morale, mœurs*) lax ♦ *nm/f* coward

lâcher [laʃe] *nm* (*de ballons, oiseaux*) release ♦ *vt* to let go of; (*ce qui tombe, abandonner*) to drop; (*oiseau, animal: libérer*) to release, set free; (*fig: mot, remarque*) to let slip, come out with; (*SPORT: distancer*) to leave behind ♦ *vi* (*fil, amarres*) to break, give way; (*freins*) to fail; **lâcher les amarres** (*NAVIG*) to cast off (the moorings); **lâcher prise** to let go

lâcheté [laʃte] *nf* cowardice; (*bassesse*) lowness

lacrymogène [lakʀimɔʒɛn] *adj*: **grenade/gaz lacrymogène** tear gas grenade/tear gas

lacté, e [lakte] *adj* milk *cpd*

lacune [lakyn] *nf* gap

là-dedans [ladədɑ̃] *adv* inside (there), in it; (*fig*) in that

là-dessous [ladsu] *adv* underneath, under there; (*fig*) behind that

là-dessus [ladsy] *adv* on there; (*fig*) at that point; (*: à ce sujet*) about that

ladite [ladit] *dét voir* **ledit**

lagune [lagyn] *nf* lagoon

là-haut [lao] *adv* up there

laïc [laik] *adj, nm/f* = **laïque**

laid, e [lɛ, lɛd] *adj* ugly; (*fig: acte*) mean, cheap

laideur [lɛdœʀ] *nf* ugliness *no pl*; meanness *no pl*

lainage [lɛnaʒ] *nm* woollen garment; (*étoffe*) woollen material

laine [lɛn] *nf* wool; **laine peignée** worsted (wool); **laine à tricoter** knitting wool; **laine de verre** glass wool; **laine vierge** new wool

laïque [laik] *adj* lay, civil; (*SCOL*) state *cpd* (*as opposed to private and Roman Catholic*) ♦ *nm/f* layman/woman

laisse [lɛs] *nf* (*de chien*) lead, leash; **tenir en laisse** to keep on a lead *ou* leash

laisser [lese] *vt* to leave ♦ *vb aux*: **laisser qn faire** to let sb do; **se laisser exploiter** to let o.s. be exploited; **se laisser aller** to let o.s. go; **laisser qn tranquille** to let *ou* leave sb alone; **laisse-toi faire** let me (*ou* him) do it; **rien ne laisse penser que ...** there is no reason to think that ...; **cela ne laisse pas de surprendre** nonetheless it is surprising

laisser-aller [leseale] *nm* carelessness, slovenliness

laissez-passer [lesepase] *nm inv* pass

lait [lɛ] *nm* milk; **frère/sœur de lait** foster brother/sister; **lait écrémé/concentré/condensé** skimmed/condensed/evaporated milk; **lait en poudre** powdered milk, milk powder; **lait de chèvre/vache** goat's/cow's milk; **lait maternel** mother's milk; **lait démaquillant/de beauté** cleansing/beauty lotion

laitage [letaʒ] *nm* milk product

laiterie [letʀi] *nf* dairy

laitier, ière [letje, -jɛʀ] *adj* dairy ♦ *nm/f* milkman/dairywoman

laiton [letɔ̃] *nm* brass

laitue [lety] *nf* lettuce

laïus [lajys] *nm* (*péj*) spiel

lambeau, x [lɑ̃bo] *nm* scrap; **en lambeaux** in tatters, tattered

lambris [lɑ̃bʀi] *nm* panelling *no pl*

lame [lam] *nf* blade; (*vague*) wave; (*lamelle*) strip; **lame de fond** ground swell *no pl*; **lame de rasoir** razor blade

lamelle [lamɛl] *nf* (*lame*) small blade; (*morceau*) sliver; (*de champignon*) gill; **couper en lamelles** to slice thinly

lamentable [lamɑ̃tabl(ə)] *adj* (*déplorable*) appalling; (*pitoyable*) pitiful

lamenter [lamɑ̃te]: **se lamenter** *vi*: **se lamenter (sur)** to moan (over)

lampadaire [lɑ̃padɛʀ] *nm* (*de salon*) standard lamp; (*dans la rue*) street lamp

lampe [lɑ̃p(ə)] *nf* lamp; (*TECH*) valve; **lampe à alcool** spirit lamp; **lampe à bronzer** sunlamp; **lampe de poche** torch (*BRIT*), flashlight (*US*); **lampe à souder** blowlamp; **lampe témoin** warning light

lampion [lɑ̃pjɔ̃] *nm* Chinese lantern

lance [lɑ̃s] *nf* spear; **lance d'arrosage** garden hose; **lance à eau** water hose; **lance d'incendie** fire hose

lancée [lɑ̃se] *nf*: **être/continuer sur sa lancée** to be under way/keep going

lancement [lɑ̃smɑ̃] *nm* launching *no pl*, launch; **offre de lancement** introductory offer

lance-pierres [lɑ̃spjɛʀ] *nm inv* catapult

lancer [lɑ̃se] *nm* (*SPORT*) throwing *no pl*, throw; (*PÊCHE*) rod and reel fishing ♦ *vt* to throw; (*émettre, projeter*) to throw out, send out; (*produit, fusée, bateau, artiste*) to launch; (*injure*) to hurl, fling; (*proclamation, mandat d'arrêt*) to issue; (*emprunt*) to float; (*moteur*) to send roaring away; **lancer qch à qn** to throw sth to sb; (*de façon agressive*) to throw sth at sb; **lancer un cri** *ou* **un appel** to shout *ou* call out; **se lancer** *vi* (*prendre de l'élan*) to build up speed; (*se précipiter*): **se lancer sur** *ou* **contre** to rush at; **se lancer dans** (*discussion*) to launch into; (*aventure*) to embark on; (*les affaires, la politique*) to go into; **lancer du poids** *nm* putting the shot

lancinant, e [lɑ̃sinɑ̃, -ɑ̃t] *adj* (*regrets etc*) haunting; (*douleur*) shooting

landau [lɑ̃do] *nm* pram (*BRIT*), baby carriage (*US*)

lande [lɑ̃d] *nf* moor

langage [lɑ̃gaʒ] *nm* language; **langage d'assemblage** (*INFORM*) assembly language; **langage du corps** body language; **langage évolué/machine** (*INFORM*) high-level/machine language; **langage de programmation** (*INFORM*) programming language

langouste [lɑ̃gust(ə)] *nf* crayfish *inv*

langoustine [lɑ̃gustin] *nf* Dublin Bay prawn

langue [lɑ̃g] *nf* (ANAT, CULIN) tongue; (LING) language; (*bande*): **langue de terre** spit of land; **tirer la langue (à)** to stick out one's tongue (at); **donner sa langue au chat** to give up, give in; **de langue française** French-speaking; **langue de bois** officialese; **langue maternelle** native language, mother tongue; **langue verte** slang; **langue vivante** modern language

langueur [lɑ̃gœʀ] *nf* languidness

languir [lɑ̃giʀ] *vi* to languish; (*conversation*) to flag; **se languir** *vi* to be languishing; **faire languir qn** to keep sb waiting

lanière [lanjɛʀ] *nf* (*de fouet*) lash; (*de valise, bretelle*) strap

lanterne [lɑ̃tɛʀn(ə)] *nf* (*portable*) lantern; (*électrique*) light, lamp; (*de voiture*) (side)light; **lanterne rouge** (*fig*) tail-ender; **lanterne vénitienne** Chinese lantern

laper [lape] *vt* to lap up

lapidaire [lapidɛʀ] *adj* stone *cpd*; (*fig*) terse

lapin [lapɛ̃] *nm* rabbit; (*fourrure*) cony; **coup du lapin** rabbit punch; **poser un lapin à qn** to stand sb up; **lapin de garenne** wild rabbit

Laponie [lapɔni] *nf*: **la Laponie** Lapland

laps [laps] *nm*: **laps de temps** space of time, time *no pl*

laque [lak] *nf* lacquer; (*brute*) shellac; (*pour cheveux*) hair spray ♦ *nm* lacquer; piece of lacquer ware

laquelle [lakɛl] *pron voir* **lequel**

larcin [laʀsɛ̃] *nm* theft

lard [laʀ] *nm* (*graisse*) fat; (*bacon*) (streaky) bacon

lardon [laʀdɔ̃] *nm* (CULIN) piece of chopped bacon; (*fam*: *enfant*) kid

large [laʀʒ(ə)] *adj* wide; broad; (*fig*) generous ♦ *adv*: **calculer/voir large** to allow extra/think big ♦ *nm* (*largeur*): **5 m de large** 5 m wide *ou* in width; (*mer*): **le large** the open sea; **en large** *adv* sideways; **au large de** off; **large d'esprit** broad-minded; **ne pas en mener large** to have one's heart in one's boots

largement [laʀʒəmɑ̃] *adv* widely; (*de loin*) greatly; (*amplement, au minimum*) easily; (*sans compter*: *donner etc*) generously

largesse [laʀʒɛs] *nf* generosity; **largesses** *nfpl* liberalities

largeur [laʀʒœʀ] *nf* (*qu'on mesure*) width; (*impression visuelle*) wideness, width; breadth; broadness

larguer [laʀge] *vt* to drop; (*fam*: *se débarrasser de*) to get rid of; **larguer les amarres** to cast off (the moorings)

larme [laʀm(ə)] *nf* tear; (*fig*): **une larme de** a drop of; **en larmes** in tears; **pleurer à chaudes larmes** to cry one's eyes out, cry bitterly

larmoyer [laʀmwaje] *vi* (*yeux*) to water; (*se plaindre*) to whimper

larvé, e [laʀve] *adj* (*fig*) latent

laryngite [laʀɛ̃ʒit] *nf* laryngitis

las, lasse [lɑ, lɑs] *adj* weary

laser [lazɛʀ] *nm*: **(rayon) laser** laser (beam); **chaîne** *ou* **platine laser** compact disc (player); **disque laser** compact disc

lasse [lɑs] *adj f voir* **las**

lasser [lɑse] *vt* to weary, tire; **se lasser de** to grow weary *ou* tired of

latéral, e, aux [lateʀal, -o] *adj* side *cpd*, lateral

latin, e [latɛ̃, -in] *adj* Latin ♦ *nm* (LING) Latin ♦ *nm/f*: **Latin, e** Latin; **j'y perds mon latin** it's all Greek to me

latitude [latityd] *nf* latitude; (*fig*): **avoir la latitude de faire** to be left free *ou* at liberty to do; **à 48° de latitude Nord** at latitude 48° North; **sous toutes les latitudes** (*fig*) world-wide, throughout the world

latte [lat] *nf* lath, slat; (*de plancher*) board

lauréat, e [lɔʀea, -at] *nm/f* winner

laurier [lɔʀje] *nm* (BOT) laurel; (CULIN) bay leaves *pl*; **lauriers** *nmpl* (*fig*) laurels

lavable [lavabl(ə)] *adj* washable

lavabo [lavabo] *nm* washbasin; **lavabos** *nmpl* toilet *sg*

lavage [lavaʒ] *nm* washing *no pl*, wash; **lavage d'estomac/d'intestin** stomach/intestinal wash; **lavage de cerveau** brainwashing *no pl*

lavande [lavɑ̃d] *nf* lavender

lave [lav] *nf* lava *no pl*

lave-linge [lavlɛ̃ʒ] *nm inv* washing machine

laver [lave] *vt* to wash; (*tache*) to wash off; (*fig*: *affront*) to avenge; **se laver** to have a wash, wash; **se laver les mains/dents** to wash one's hands/clean one's teeth; **laver la vaisselle/le linge** to wash the dishes/clothes; **laver qn de** (*accusation*) to clear sb of

laverie [lavʀi] *nf*: **laverie (automatique)** launderette

lavette [lavɛt] *nf* (*chiffon*) dish cloth; (*brosse*) dish mop; (*fam*: *homme*) wimp, drip

laveur, euse [lavœʀ, -øz] *nm/f* cleaner

lave-vaisselle [lavvesɛl] *nm inv* dishwasher

lavoir [lavwaʀ] *nm* wash house; (*bac*) washtub

laxatif, ive [laksatif, -iv] *adj, nm* laxative

layette [lejɛt] *nf* layette

MOT CLÉ

le, l', la [l(ə)], *pl* **les** *art déf* **1** the; **le livre/la pomme/l'arbre** the book/the apple/the tree; **les étudiants** the students

2 (*noms abstraits*): **le courage/l'amour/la jeunesse** courage/love/youth

3 (*indiquant la possession*): **se casser la jambe** *etc*, to break one's leg *etc*; **levez la main** put your hand up; **avoir les yeux gris/le nez rouge** to have grey eyes/a red nose

4 (*temps*): **le matin/soir** in the morning/evening; mornings/evenings; **le jeudi** *etc* (*d'habitude*) on Thursdays *etc*; (*ce jeudi-là etc*) on (the) Thursday; **nous venons le 3 décembre** (*parlé*) we're coming on the 3rd of December *ou* on December the 3rd; (*écrit*) we're coming (on) 3rd *ou* 3 December

5 (*distribution, évaluation*) a, an; **2 € le mètre/kilo** 2 € a *ou* per metre/kilo; **le tiers/quart de** a third/quarter of

◆ *pron* **1** (*personne: mâle*) him; (: *femelle*) her; (: *pluriel*) them; **je le/la/les vois** I can see him/her/them

2 (*animal, chose: singulier*) it; (: *pluriel*) them; **je le** (*ou* **la**) **vois** I can see it; **je les vois** I can see them

3 (*remplaçant une phrase*): **je ne le savais pas** I didn't know (about it); **il était riche et ne l'est plus** he was once rich but no longer is

lécher [leʃe] *vt* to lick; (*laper: lait, eau*) to lick *ou* lap up; (*finir, polir*) to over-refine; **lécher les vitrines** to go window-shopping; **se lécher les doigts/lèvres** to lick one's fingers/lips

lèche-vitrines [lɛʃvitrin] *nm inv*: **faire du lèche-vitrines** to go window-shopping

leçon [ləsɔ̃] *nf* lesson; **faire la leçon** to teach; **faire la leçon à** (*fig*) to give a lecture to; **leçons de conduite** driving lessons; **leçons particulières** private lessons *ou* tuition *sg* (*BRIT*)

lecteur, trice [lɛktœʀ, -tʀis] *nm/f* reader; (*d'université*) (foreign language) assistant (*BRIT*), (foreign) teaching assistant (*US*) ◆ *nm* (*TECH*): **lecteur de cassettes** cassette player; (*INFORM*): **lecteur de disquette(s)** disk drive; **lecteur de CD/DVD** CD/DVD player; **lecteur MP3** MP3 player

lecture [lɛktyʀ] *nf* reading

ledit [lədi], **ladite** [ladit], *mpl* **lesdits** [ledi], **lesdites** [ledit] *dét* the aforesaid

légal, e, aux [legal, -o] *adj* legal

légaliser [legalize] *vt* to legalize

légalité [legalite] *nf* legality, lawfulness; **être dans/sortir de la légalité** to be within/step outside the law

légendaire [leʒɑ̃dɛʀ] *adj* legendary

légende [leʒɑ̃d] *nf* (*mythe*) legend; (*de carte, plan*) key, legend; (*de dessin*) caption

léger, ère [leʒe, -ɛʀ] *adj* light; (*bruit, retard*) slight; (*boisson, parfum*) weak; (*couche, étoffe*) thin; (*superficiel*) thoughtless; (*volage*) free and easy; flighty; (*peu sérieux*) lightweight; **blessé léger** slightly injured person; **à la légère** *adv* (*parler, agir*) rashly, thoughtlessly

légèrement [leʒɛʀmɑ̃] *adv* lightly; thoughtlessly, rashly; **légèrement plus grand** slightly bigger

légèreté [leʒɛʀte] *nf* lightness; thoughtlessness

législatif, ive [leʒislatif, -iv] *adj* legislative; **législatives** *nfpl* general election *sg*

légitime [leʒitim] *adj* (*JUR*) lawful, legitimate; (*enfant*) legitimate; (*fig*) rightful, legitimate; **en état**

de légitime défense in self-defence

legs [lɛg] *nm* legacy

léguer [lege] *vt*: **léguer qch à qn** (*JUR*) to bequeath sth to sb; (*fig*) to hand sth down *ou* pass sth on to sb

légume [legym] *nm* vegetable; **légumes verts** green vegetables; **légumes secs** pulses

lendemain [lɑ̃dmɛ̃] *nm*: **le lendemain** the next *ou* following day; **le lendemain matin/soir** the next *ou* following morning/evening; **le lendemain de** the day after; **au lendemain de** in the days following; in the wake of; **penser au lendemain** to think of the future; **sans lendemain** short-lived; **de beaux lendemains** bright prospects; **des lendemains qui chantent** a rosy future

lent, e [lɑ̃, lɑ̃t] *adj* slow

lentement [lɑ̃tmɑ̃] *adv* slowly

lenteur [lɑ̃tœʀ] *nf* slowness *no pl*; **lenteurs** *nfpl* (*actions, décisions lentes*) slowness *sg*

lentille [lɑ̃tij] *nf* (*OPTIQUE*) lens *sg*; (*BOT*) lentil; **lentille d'eau** duckweed; **lentilles de contact** contact lenses

léopard [leɔpaʀ] *nm* leopard

lèpre [lɛpʀ(ə)] *nf* leprosy

MOT-CLÉ

lequel, laquelle [ləkɛl, lakɛl] (*mpl* **lesquels**, *fpl* **lesquelles**; *à + lequel =* **auquel**, *de + lequel =* **duquel**) *pron* **1** (*interrogatif*) which, which one

2 (*relatif: personne: sujet*) who; (: *objet, après préposition*) whom; (*sujet: possessif*) whose; (: *chose*) which; **je l'ai proposé au directeur, lequel est d'accord** I suggested it to the director, who agrees; **la femme à laquelle j'ai acheté mon chien** the woman from whom I bought my dog; **le pont sur lequel nous sommes passés** the bridge (over) which we crossed; **un homme sur la compétence duquel on peut compter** a man whose competence one can count on

◆ *adj*: **auquel cas** in which case

---

les [le] *voir* **le**

lesbienne [lɛsbjɛn] *nf* lesbian

lesdits [ledi], **lesdites** [ledit] *dét voir* **ledit**

léser [leze] *vt* to wrong; (*MÉD*) to injure

lésiner [lezine] *vt*: **lésiner (sur)** to skimp (on)

lésion [lezjɔ̃] *nf* lesion, damage *no pl*; **lésions cérébrales** brain damage

lesquels, lesquelles [lekɛl] *pron voir* **lequel**

lessive [lesiv] *nf* (*poudre*) washing powder; (*linge*) washing *no pl*, wash; (*opération*) washing *no pl*; **faire la lessive** to do the washing

lessiver [lesive] *vt* to wash

lest [lɛst] *nm* ballast; **jeter** *ou* **lâcher du lest** (*fig*) to make concessions

leste [lɛst(ə)] *adj* (*personne, mouvement*) sprightly, nimble; (*désinvolte: manières*) offhand; (*osé: plaisanterie*) risqué

lettre [lɛtʀ(ə)] *nf* letter; **lettres** *nfpl* (*étude, culture*) literature *sg*; (*SCOL*) arts (subjects); **à la lettre** (*au sens propre*) literally; (*ponctuellement*) to the letter; **en lettres majuscules** *ou* **capitales** in capital letters, in capitals; **en toutes lettres** in words, in full; **lettre de change** bill of exchange; **lettre piégée** letter bomb; **lettre de voiture (aérienne)** (air) waybill, (air) bill of lading; **lettres de noblesse** pedigree

leucémie [løsemi] *nf* leukaemia

MOT CLÉ

leur [lœʀ] *adj possessif* their; **leur maison** their house; **leurs amis** their friends; **à leur approche** as they came near; **à leur vue** at the sight of them
♦ *pron* **1** (*objet indirect*) (to) them; **je leur ai dit la vérité** I told them the truth; **je le leur ai donné** I gave it to them, I gave it them
2 (*possessif*): **le(la) leur, les leurs** theirs

---

leurre [lœʀ] *nm* (*appât*) lure; (*fig*) delusion; (*: piège*) snare

leurrer [lœʀe] *vt* to delude, deceive

leurs [lœʀ] *adj voir* **leur**

levain [ləvɛ̃] *nm* leaven; **sans levain** unleavened

levé, e [ləve] *adj*: **être levé** to be up ♦ *nm*: **levé de terrain** land survey; **à mains levées** (*vote*) by a show of hands; **au pied levé** at a moment's notice

levée [ləve] *nf* (*POSTES*) collection; (*CARTES*) trick; **levée de boucliers** general outcry; **levée du corps** collection of the body from house of the deceased, before funeral; **levée d'écrou** release from custody; **levée de terre** levee; **levée de troupes** levy

lever [ləve] *vt* (*vitre, bras etc*) to raise; (*soulever de terre, supprimer: interdiction, siège*) to lift; (*: difficulté*) to remove; (*séance*) to close; (*impôts, armée*) to levy; (*CHASSE: lièvre*) to start; (*: perdrix*) to flush; (*fam: fille*) to pick up ♦ *vi* (*CULIN*) to rise ♦ *nm*: **au lever** on getting up; **se lever** *vi* to get up; (*soleil*) to rise; (*jour*) to break; (*brouillard*) to lift; **levez-vous!, lève-toi!** stand up!, get up!; **ça va se lever** the weather will clear; **lever du jour** daybreak; **lever du rideau** (*THÉÂT*) curtain; **lever de rideau** (*pièce*) curtain raiser; **lever de soleil** sunrise

levier [ləvje] *nm* lever; **faire levier sur** to lever up (*ou* off); **levier de changement de vitesse** gear lever

lèvre [lɛvʀ(ə)] *nf* lip; **lèvres** *nfpl* (*d'une plaie*) edges; **petites/grandes lèvres** labia minora/majora; **du bout des lèvres** half-heartedly

lévrier [levʀije] *nm* greyhound

levure [ləvyʀ] *nf* yeast; **levure chimique** baking powder

lexique [lɛksik] *nm* vocabulary, lexicon; (*glossaire*) vocabulary

lézard [lezaʀ] *nm* lizard; (*peau*) lizardskin

lézarde [lezaʀd(ə)] *nf* crack

liaison [ljɛzɔ̃] *nf* (*rapport*) connection, link; (*RAIL, AVIAT ETC*) link; (*relation: d'amitié*) friendship; (*: d'affaires*) relationship; (*: amoureuse*) affair; (*CULIN, PHONÉTIQUE*) liaison; **entrer/être en liaison avec** to get/be in contact with; **liaison radio** radio contact; **liaison (de transmission de données)** (*INFORM*) data link

liane [ljan] *nf* creeper

liant, e [ljɑ̃, -ɑ̃t] *adj* sociable

liasse [ljas] *nf* wad, bundle

Liban [libɑ̃] *nm*: **le Liban** (the) Lebanon

libanais [libanɛ, -ɛz] *adj* Lebanese ♦ *nm/f*: **Libanais, e** Lebanese

libeller [libele] *vt* (*chèque, mandat*): **libeller (au nom de)** to make out (to); (*lettre*) to word

libellule [libelyl] *nf* dragonfly

libéral, e, aux [liberal, -o] *adj, nm/f* liberal; **les professions libérales** the professions

libérer [libere] *vt* (*délivrer*) to free, liberate; (*: moralement, PSYCH*) to liberate; (*relâcher: prisonnier*) to release; (*: soldat*) to discharge; (*dégager: gaz, cran d'arrêt*) to release; (*ÉCON: échanges commerciaux*) to ease restrictions on; **se libérer** (*de rendez-vous*) to try and be free, get out of previous engagements; **libérer qn de** (*liens, dette*) to free sb from; (*promesse*) to release sb from

liberté [libɛʀte] *nf* freedom; (*loisir*) free time; **libertés** *nfpl* (*privautés*) liberties; **mettre/être en liberté** to set/be free; **en liberté provisoire/surveillée/conditionnelle** on bail/probation/parole; **liberté d'association** right of association; **liberté de conscience** freedom of conscience; **liberté du culte** freedom of worship; **liberté d'esprit** independence of mind; **liberté d'opinion** freedom of thought; **liberté de la presse** freedom of the press; **liberté de réunion** right to hold meetings; **liberté syndicale** union rights *pl*; **libertés individuelles** personal freedom *sg*; **libertés publiques** civil rights

libraire [libʀɛʀ] *nm/f* bookseller

librairie [libʀɛʀi] *nf* bookshop

libre [libʀ(ə)] *adj* free; (*route*) clear; (*place etc*) vacant, free; (*fig: propos, manières*) open; (*SCOL*) private and Roman Catholic (*as opposed to "laïque"*); **de libre** (*place*) free; **libre de qch/de faire** free from sth/to do; **vente libre** (*COMM*) unrestricted sale; **libre arbitre** free will; **libre concurrence** free-market economy; **libre entreprise** free enterprise

libre-échange [libʀeʃɑ̃ʒ] *nm* free trade

libre-service [libʀəsɛʀvis] *nm inv* (*magasin*) self-service store; (*restaurant*) self-service restaurant

Libye [libi] *nf*: **la Libye** Libya

licence [lisɑ̃s] *nf* (*permis*) permit; (*diplôme*) (first) degree; (*liberté*) liberty; (*poétique, orthographique*) licence (*BRIT*), license (*US*); (*des mœurs*) licentiousness; **licence ès lettres/en droit** arts/law degree; *see boxed note*

LICENCE

After the 'DEUG', French university students undertake a third year of study to complete their **licence**. This is roughly equivalent to a bachelor's degree in Britain.

---

licencié, e [lisãsje] *nm/f* (*SCOL*): **licencié ès lettres/en droit** ≃ Bachelor of Arts/Law, arts/law graduate; (*SPORT*) permit-holder

licenciement [lisãsimã] *nm* dismissal; redundancy; laying off *no pl*

licencier [lisãsje] *vt* (*renvoyer*) to dismiss; (*débaucher*) to make redundant; to lay off

licite [lisit] *adj* lawful

lie [li] *nf* dregs *pl*, sediment

lié, e [lje] *adj*: **très lié avec** (*fig*) very friendly with *ou* close to; **lié par** (*serment, promesse*) bound by; **avoir partie liée (avec qn)** to be involved (with sb)

liège [ljɛʒ] *nm* cork

lien [ljɛ̃] *nm* (*corde, fig: affectif, culturel*) bond; (*rapport*) link, connection; (*analogie*) link; **lien de parenté** family tie

lier [lje] *vt* (*attacher*) to tie up; (*joindre*) to link up; (*fig: unir, engager*) to bind; (*CULIN*) to thicken; **lier qch à** (*attacher*) to tie sth to; (*associer*) to link sth to; **lier conversation (avec)** to strike up a conversation (with); **se lier avec** to make friends with

lierre [ljɛʀ] *nm* ivy

liesse [ljɛs] *nf*: **être en liesse** to be jubilant

lieu, x [ljø] *nm* place; **lieux** *nmpl* (*locaux*) premises; (*endroit: d'un accident etc*) scene *sg*; **en lieu sûr** in a safe place; **en haut lieu** in high places; **vider** *ou* **quitter les lieux** to leave the premises; **arriver/être sur les lieux** to arrive/be on the scene; **en premier lieu** in the first place; **en dernier lieu** lastly; **avoir lieu** to take place; **avoir lieu de faire** to have grounds *ou* good reason for doing; **tenir lieu de** to take the place of; (*servir de*) to serve as; **donner lieu à** to give rise to, give cause for; **au lieu de** instead of; **au lieu qu'il y aille** instead of him going; **lieu commun** commonplace; **lieu géométrique** locus; **lieu de naissance** place of birth

lieu-dit, *pl* **lieux-dits** [ljødi] *nm* locality

lieutenant [ljøtnã] *nm* lieutenant; **lieutenant de vaisseau** (*NAVIG*) lieutenant

lièvre [ljɛvʀ(ə)] *nm* hare; (*coureur*) pacemaker; **lever un lièvre** (*fig*) to bring up a prickly subject

ligament [ligamã] *nm* ligament

ligne [liɲ] *nf* (*gén*) line; (*TRANSPORTS: liaison*) service; (: *trajet*) route; (*silhouette*): **garder la ligne** to keep one's figure; **en ligne** (*INFORM*) on line; **en ligne droite** as the crow flies; **"à la ligne"** "new paragraph"; **entrer en ligne de compte** to be taken into account; to come into it; **ligne de but/médiane** goal/halfway line; **ligne d'arrivée/de**

départ finishing/starting line; **ligne de conduite** course of action; **ligne directrice** guiding line; **ligne d'horizon** skyline; **ligne de mire** line of sight; **ligne de touche** touchline

lignée [liɲe] *nf* (*race, famille*) line, lineage; (*postérité*) descendants *pl*

ligoter [ligɔte] *vt* to tie up

ligue [lig] *nf* league

liguer [lige]: **se liguer** *vi* to form a league; **se liguer contre** (*fig*) to combine against

lilas [lila] *nm* lilac

limace [limas] *nf* slug

limande [limãd] *nf* dab

lime [lim] *nf* (*TECH*) file; (*BOT*) lime; **lime à ongles** nail file

limer [lime] *vt* (*bois, métal*) to file (down); (*ongles*) to file; (*fig: prix*) to pare down

limier [limje] *nm* (*ZOOL*) bloodhound; (*détective*) sleuth

limitation [limitasjɔ̃] *nf* limitation, restriction; **sans limitation de temps** with no time limit; **limitation des naissances** birth control; **limitation de vitesse** speed limit

limite [limit] *nf* (*de terrain*) boundary; (*partie ou point extrême*) limit; **dans la limite de** within the limits of; **à la limite** (*au pire*) if the worst comes (*ou* came) to the worst; **sans limites** (*bêtise, richesse, pouvoir*) limitless, boundless; **vitesse/charge limite** maximum speed/load; **cas limite** borderline case; **date limite** deadline; **date limite de vente/consommation** sell-by/best-before date; **prix limite** upper price limit; **limite d'âge** maximum age, age limit

limiter [limite] *vt* (*restreindre*) to limit, restrict; (*délimiter*) to border, form the boundary of; **se limiter (à qch/à faire)** (*personne*) to limit *ou* confine o.s. (to sth/to doing sth); **se limiter à** (*chose*) to be limited to

limitrophe [limitʀɔf] *adj* border *cpd*; **limitrophe de** bordering on

limoger [limɔʒe] *vt* to dismiss

limon [limɔ̃] *nm* silt

limonade [limɔnad] *nf* lemonade (*BRIT*), (lemon) soda (*US*)

lin [lɛ̃] *nm* (*BOT*) flax; (*tissu, toile*) linen

linceul [lɛ̃sœl] *nm* shroud

linge [lɛ̃ʒ] *nm* (*serviettes etc*) linen; (*pièce de tissu*) cloth; (*aussi*: **linge de corps**) underwear; (*aussi*: **linge de toilette**) towel; (*lessive*) washing; **linge sale** dirty linen

lingerie [lɛ̃ʒʀi] *nf* lingerie, underwear

lingot [lɛ̃go] *nm* ingot

linguistique [lɛ̃gɥistik] *adj* linguistic ◆ *nf* linguistics *sg*

lion, ne [ljɔ̃, ljɔn] *nm/f* lion/lioness; (*signe*): **le Lion** Leo, the Lion; **être du Lion** to be Leo; **lion de mer** sealion

lionceau, x [ljɔ̃so] *nm* lion cub

liqueur [likœʀ] *nf* liqueur

liquidation [likidasjɔ̃] *nf* liquidation; (*COMM*) clearance (sale); **liquidation judiciaire** compulsory liquidation

liquide [likid] *adj* liquid ♦ *nm* liquid; (*COMM*): **en liquide** in ready money *ou* cash

liquider [likide] *vt* (*société, biens, témoin gênant*) to liquidate; (*compte, problème*) to settle; (*COMM: articles*) to clear, sell off

liquidités [likidite] *nfpl* (*COMM*) liquid assets

lire [liʀ] *nf* (*monnaie*) lira ♦ *vt, vi* to read; **lire qch à qn** to read sth (out) to sb

lis *vb* [li] *voir* **lire** ♦ *nm* [lis] = **lys**

lisible [lizibl(ə)] *adj* legible; (*digne d'être lu*) readable

lisière [lizjɛʀ] *nf* (*de forêt*) edge; (*de tissu*) selvage

lisons [lizɔ̃] *vb voir* **lire**

lisse [lis] *adj* smooth

liste [list(ə)] *nf* list; (*INFORM*) listing; **faire la liste de** to list, make out a list of; **liste d'attente** waiting list; **liste civile** civil list; **liste électorale** electoral roll; **liste de mariage** wedding (present) list; **liste noire** hit list

listing [listiŋ] *nm* (*INFORM*) listing; **qualité listing** draft quality

lit [li] *nm* (*gén*) bed; **faire son lit** to make one's bed; **aller/se mettre au lit** to go to/get into bed; **chambre avec un grand lit** room with a double bed; **prendre le lit** to take to one's bed; **d'un premier lit** (*JUR*) of a first marriage; **lit de camp** campbed (*BRIT*), cot (*US*); **lit d'enfant** cot (*BRIT*), crib (*US*)

literie [litʀi] *nf* bedding; (*linge*) bedding, bedclothes *pl*

litière [litjɛʀ] *nf* litter

litige [litiʒ] *nm* dispute; **en litige** in contention

litre [litʀ(ə)] *nm* litre; (*récipient*) litre measure

littéraire [liteʀɛʀ] *adj* literary

littéral, e, aux [literal, -o] *adj* literal

littérature [literatyʀ] *nf* literature

littoral, e, aux [litɔʀal, -o] *adj* coastal ♦ *nm* coast

liturgie [lityʀʒi] *nf* liturgy

livide [livid] *adj* livid, pallid

livraison [livʀɛzɔ̃] *nf* delivery; **livraison à domicile** home delivery (service)

livre [livʀ(ə)] *nm* book; (*imprimerie etc*): **le livre** the book industry ♦ *nf* (*poids, monnaie*) pound; **traduire qch à livre ouvert** to translate sth off the cuff *ou* at sight; **livre blanc** official report (*prepared by independent body, following war, natural disaster etc*); **livre de bord** (*NAVIG*) logbook; **livre de comptes** account(s) book; **livre de cuisine** cookery book (*BRIT*), cookbook; **livre de messe** mass *ou* prayer book; **livre d'or** visitors' book; **livre de poche** paperback (*cheap and pocket size*); **livre sterling** pound sterling; **livre verte** green pound

livré, e [livʀe] *nf* livery ♦ *adj*: **livré à** (*l'anarchie etc*) given over to; **livré à soi-même** left to oneself *ou* one's own devices

livrer [livʀe] *vt* (*COMM*) to deliver; (*otage, coupable*) to hand over; (*secret, information*) to give away; **se livrer à** (*se confier*) to confide in; (*se rendre*) to give o.s. up to; (*s'abandonner à: débauche etc*) to give o.s. up *ou* over to; (*faire: pratiques, actes*) to indulge in; (*travail*) to be engaged in, engage in; (: *sport*) to practise; (: *enquête*) to carry out; **livrer bataille** to give battle

livret [livʀɛ] *nm* booklet; (*d'opéra*) libretto (*pl* librettos); **livret de caisse d'épargne** (savings) bank-book; **livret de famille** (official) family record book; **livret scolaire** (school) report book

livreur, euse [livʀœʀ, -øz] *nm/f* delivery boy *ou* man/girl *ou* woman

local, e, aux [lɔkal, -o] *adj* local ♦ *nm* (*salle*) premises *pl* ♦ *nmpl* premises

localiser [lɔkalize] *vt* (*repérer*) to locate, place; (*limiter*) to localize, confine

localité [lɔkalite] *nf* locality

locataire [lɔkatɛʀ] *nm/f* tenant; (*de chambre*) lodger

location [lɔkasjɔ̃] *nf* (*par le locataire*) renting; (*par l'usager: de voiture etc*) hiring (*BRIT*), renting (*US*); (*par le propriétaire*) renting out, letting; hiring out (*BRIT*); (*de billets, places*) booking; (*bureau*) booking office; **"location de voitures"** "car hire (*BRIT*) *ou* rental (*US*)"

locomotive [lɔkɔmɔtiv] *nf* locomotive, engine; (*fig*) pacesetter, pacemaker

locution [lɔkysjɔ̃] *nf* phrase

loge [lɔʒ] *nf* (*THÉÂT: d'artiste*) dressing room; (: *de spectateurs*) box; (*de concierge, franc-maçon*) lodge

logement [lɔʒmɑ̃] *nm* flat (*BRIT*), apartment (*US*); accommodation *no pl* (*BRIT*), accommodations *pl* (*US*); **le logement** housing; **chercher un logement** to look for a flat *ou* apartment, look for accommodation(s); **construire des logements bon marché** to build cheap housing *sg*; **crise du logement** housing shortage; **logement de fonction** (*ADMIN*) company flat *ou* apartment, accommodation(s) provided with one's job

loger [lɔʒe] *vt* to accommodate ♦ *vi* to live; **se loger: trouver à se loger** to find accommodation; **se loger dans** (*suj: balle, flèche*) to lodge itself in

logeur, euse [lɔʒœʀ, -øz] *nm/f* landlord/landlady

logiciel [lɔʒisjɛl] *nm* software

logique [lɔʒik] *adj* logical ♦ *nf* logic; **c'est logique** it stands to reason

logis [lɔʒi] *nm* home; abode, dwelling

logo [lɔgo], **logotype** [lɔgɔtip] *nm* logo

loi [lwa] *nf* law; **faire la loi** to lay down the law; **les lois de la mode** (*fig*) the dictates of fashion; **proposition de loi** (private member's) bill; **projet de loi** (government) bill

loin [lwɛ̃] *adv* far; (*dans le temps: futur*) a long way off; (: *passé*) a long time ago; **plus loin** further;

moins loin (que) not as far (as); **loin de** far from; **loin d'ici** a long way from here; **pas loin de 1 000 €** not far off 1000 €; **au loin** far off; **de loin** *adv* from a distance; (*fig: de beaucoup*) by far; **il vient de loin** he's come a long way; he comes from a long way away; **de loin en loin** here and there; (*de temps en temps*) (every) now and then; **loin de là** (*au contraire*) far from it

lointain, e [lwɛ̃tɛ̃, -ɛn] *adj* faraway, distant; (*dans le futur, passé*) distant, far-off; (*cause, parent*) remote, distant ♦ *nm:* **dans le lointain** in the distance

loir [lwaʀ] *nm* dormouse (*pl* dormice)

loisir [lwaziʀ] *nm:* **heures de loisir** spare time; **loisirs** *nmpl* leisure *sg;* (*activités*) leisure activities; **avoir le loisir de faire** to have the time *ou* opportunity to do; **(tout) à loisir** (*en prenant son temps*) at leisure; (*autant qu'on le désire*) at one's pleasure

londonien, ne [lɔ̃dɔnjɛ̃, -ɛn] *adj* London *cpd*, of London ♦ *nm/f:* **Londonien, ne** Londoner

Londres [lɔ̃dʀ(ə)] *n* London

long, longue [lɔ̃, lɔ̃g] *adj* long ♦ *adv:* **en savoir long** to know a great deal ♦ *nm:* **de 3 m de long** 3 m long, 3 m in length ♦ *nf:* **à la longue** in the end; **faire long feu** to fizzle out; **ne pas faire long feu** not to last long; **au long cours** (*NAVIG*) ocean *cpd*, ocean-going; **de longue date** *adj* long-standing; **longue durée** *adj* long-term; **de longue haleine** *adj* long-term; **être long à faire** to take a long time to do; **en long** *adv* lengthwise, lengthways; **(tout) le long de** (all) along; **tout au long de** (*année, vie*) throughout; **de long en large** (*marcher*) to and fro, up and down; **en long et en large** (*fig*) in every detail

longer [lɔ̃ʒe] *vt* to go (*ou* walk *ou* drive) along (side); (*suj: mur, route*) to border

longiligne [lɔ̃ʒiliɲ] *adj* long-limbed

longitude [lɔ̃ʒityd] *nf* longitude; **à 45° de longitude ouest** at 45° longitude west

longtemps [lɔ̃tɑ̃] *adv* (for) a long time, (for) long; **ça ne va pas durer longtemps** it won't last long; **avant longtemps** before long; **pour/pendant longtemps** for a long time; **je n'en ai pas pour longtemps** I shan't be long; **mettre longtemps à faire** to take a long time to do; **il en a pour longtemps** he'll be a long time; **il y a longtemps que je travaille** I have been working (for) a long time; **il n'y a pas longtemps que je l'ai rencontré** it's not long since I met him

longue [lɔ̃g] *adj f voir* **long**

longuement [lɔ̃gmɑ̃] *adv* (*longtemps: parler, regarder*) for a long time; (*en détail: expliquer, raconter*) at length

longueur [lɔ̃gœʀ] *nf* length; **longueurs** *nfpl* (*fig: d'un film etc*) tedious parts; **sur une longueur de 10 km** for *ou* over 10 km; **en longueur** *adv* lengthwise, lengthways; **tirer en longueur** to drag on; **à longueur de journée** all day long; **d'une longueur** (*gagner*) by a length; **longueur d'onde** wavelength

longue-vue [lɔ̃gvy] *nf* telescope

look [luk] (*fam*) *nm* look, image

lopin [lɔpɛ̃] *nm:* **lopin de terre** patch of land

loque [lɔk] *nf* (*personne*) wreck; **loques** *nfpl* (*habits*) rags; **être** *ou* **tomber en loques** to be in rags

loquet [lɔkɛ] *nm* latch

lorgner [lɔʀɲe] *vt* to eye; (*convoiter*) to have one's eye on

lors [lɔʀ]: **lors de** *prép* (*au moment de*) at the time of; (*pendant*) during; **lors même que** even though

lorsque [lɔʀsk(ə)] *conj* when, as

losange [lɔzɑ̃ʒ] *nm* diamond; (*GÉOM*) lozenge; **en losange** diamond-shaped

lot [lo] *nm* (*part*) share; (*de loterie*) prize; (*fig: destin*) fate, lot; (*COMM, INFORM*) batch; **lot de consolation** consolation prize

loterie [lɔtʀi] *nf* lottery; (*tombola*) raffle; **Loterie nationale** French national lottery

loti, e [lɔti] *adj:* **bien/mal loti** well-/badly off, lucky/unlucky

lotion [losjɔ̃] *nf* lotion; **lotion après rasage** aftershave (lotion); **lotion capillaire** hair lotion

lotissement [lɔtismɑ̃] *nm* (*groupe de maisons, d'immeubles*) housing development; (*parcelle*) (building) plot, lot

loto [lɔto] *nm* lotto; *see boxed note*

> ### LOTO
>
> **Le Loto** is a state-run national lottery with large cash prizes. Participants select seven numbers out of a possible 49. There is a sliding scale of winnings: if you have all seven numbers right you win top prize, if you have six right you win a smaller sum, and so on. The draw is shown on television twice weekly.

lotte [lɔt] *nf* (*ZOOL: de rivière*) burbot; (: *de mer*) monkfish

louable [lwabl(ə)] *adj* (*appartement, garage*) rentable; (*action, personne*) praiseworthy, commendable

louange [lwɑ̃ʒ] *nf:* **à la louange de** in praise of; **louanges** *nfpl* praise *sg*

loubar(d) [lubaʀ] *nm* (*fam*) lout

louche [luʃ] *adj* shady, dubious ♦ *nf* ladle

loucher [luʃe] *vi* to squint; (*fig*): **loucher sur** to have one's (beady) eye on

louer [lwe] *vt* (*maison: suj: propriétaire*) to let, rent (out); (: *locataire*) to rent; (*voiture etc*) to hire out (*BRIT*), rent (out); to hire (*BRIT*), rent; (*réserver*) to book; (*faire l'éloge de*) to praise; **"à louer"** "to let" (*BRIT*), "for rent" (*US*); **louer qn de** to praise sb for; **se louer de** to congratulate o.s. on

loup [lu] *nm* wolf (*pl* wolves); (*poisson*) bass; (*masque*) (eye) mask; **jeune loup** young go-getter; **loup de mer** (*marin*) old seadog

loupe [lup] *nf* magnifying glass; **loupe de noyer** burr walnut; **à la loupe** (*fig*) in minute detail

louper [lupe] *vt* (*fam: manquer*) to miss; (: *gâcher*) to mess up, bungle

lourd, e [luʀ, luʀd(ə)] *adj* heavy; (*chaleur, temps*) sultry; (*fig: personne, style*) heavy-handed ◆ *adv*: **peser lourd** to be heavy; **lourd de** (*menaces*) charged with; (*conséquences*) fraught with; **artillerie/industrie lourde** heavy artillery/industry

lourdaud, e [luʀdo, -od] *adj* oafish

lourdement [luʀdəmã] *adv* heavily; **se tromper lourdement** to make a big mistake

lourdeur [luʀdœʀ] *nf* heaviness; **lourdeur d'estomac** indigestion *no pl*

loutre [lutʀ(ə)] *nf* otter; (*fourrure*) otter skin

louveteau, x [luvto] *nm* (*ZOOL*) wolf-cub; (*scout*) cub (scout)

louvoyer [luvwaje] *vi* (*NAVIG*) to tack; (*fig*) to hedge, evade the issue

loyal, e, aux [lwajal, -o] *adj* (*fidèle*) loyal, faithful; (*fair-play*) fair

loyauté [lwajote] *nf* loyalty, faithfulness; fairness

loyer [lwaje] *nm* rent; **loyer de l'argent** interest rate

lu, e [ly] *pp de* **lire**

lubie [lybi] *nf* whim, craze

lubrifiant [lybʀifjã] *nm* lubricant

lubrifier [lybʀifje] *vt* to lubricate

lubrique [lybʀik] *adj* lecherous

lucarne [lykaʀn(ə)] *nf* skylight

lucide [lysid] *adj* (*conscient*) lucid, conscious; (*perspicace*) clear-headed

lucratif, ive [lykʀatif, -iv] *adj* lucrative; profitable; **à but non lucratif** non profit-making

lueur [lɥœʀ] *nf* (*chatoyante*) glimmer *no pl*; (*métallique, mouillée*) gleam *no pl*; (*rougeoyante*) glow *no pl*; (*pâle*) (faint) light; (*fig*) spark; (: *d'espérance*) glimmer, gleam

luge [lyʒ] *nf* sledge (*BRIT*), sled (*US*); **faire de la luge** to sledge (*BRIT*), sled (*US*), toboggan

lugubre [lygybʀ(ə)] *adj* gloomy; dismal

MOT CLÉ

lui [lɥi] *pp de* **luire**

◆ *pron* **1** (*objet indirect: mâle*) (to) him; (: *femelle*) (to) her; (: *chose, animal*) (to) it; **je lui ai parlé** I have spoken to him (*ou* to her); **il lui a offert un cadeau** he gave him (*ou* her) a present; **je le lui ai donné** I gave it to him (*ou* her)

2 (*après préposition, comparatif: personne*) him; (: *chose, animal*) it; **elle est contente de lui** she is pleased with him; **je la connais mieux que lui** I know her better than he does; **cette voiture est à lui** this car belongs to him, this is HIS car

3 (*sujet, forme emphatique*) he; **lui, il est à Paris** HE is in Paris; **c'est lui qui l'a fait** HE did it

---

luire [lɥiʀ] *vi* (*gén*) to shine, gleam; (*surface mouillée*) to glisten; (*reflets chauds, cuivrés*) to glow

lumière [lymjɛʀ] *nf* light; **lumières** *nfpl* (*d'une personne*) knowledge *sg*, wisdom *sg*; **à la lumière de** by the light of; (*fig: événements*) in the light of; **fais de la lumière** let's have some light, give us some light; **faire (toute) la lumière sur** (*fig*) to clarify (completely); **mettre en lumière** (*fig*) to highlight; **lumière du jour/soleil** day/sunlight

luminaire [lyminɛʀ] *nm* lamp, light

lumineux, euse [lyminø, -øz] *adj* (*émettant de la lumière*) luminous; (*éclairé*) illuminated; (*ciel, journée, couleur*) bright; (*relatif à la lumière: rayon etc*) of light, light *cpd*; (*fig: regard*) radiant

lunatique [lynatik] *adj* whimsical, temperamental

lundi [lœdi] *nm* Monday; **on est lundi** it's Monday; **le lundi 20 août** Monday 20th August; **il est venu lundi** he came on Monday; **le(s) lundi(s)** on Mondays; **à lundi!** see you (on) Monday!; **lundi de Pâques** Easter Monday; **lundi de Pentecôte** Whit Monday (*BRIT*)

lune [lyn] *nf* moon; **pleine/nouvelle lune** full/new moon; **être dans la lune** (*distrait*) to have one's head in the clouds; **lune de miel** honeymoon

lunette [lynɛt] *nf*: **lunettes** *nfpl* glasses, spectacles; (*protectrices*) goggles; **lunette d'approche** telescope; **lunette arrière** (*AUTO*) rear window; **lunettes noires** dark glasses; **lunettes de soleil** sunglasses

lus etc [ly] *vb voir* **lire**

lustre [lystʀ(ə)] *nm* (*de plafond*) chandelier; (*fig: éclat*) lustre

lustrer [lystʀe] *vt*: **lustrer qch** (*faire briller*) to make sth shine; (*user*) to make sth shiny

lut [ly] *vb voir* **lire**

luth [lyt] *nm* lute

lutin [lytɛ̃] *nm* imp, goblin

lutte [lyt] *nf* (*conflit*) struggle; (*SPORT*): **la lutte** wrestling; **de haute lutte** after a hard-fought struggle; **lutte des classes** class struggle; **lutte libre** (*SPORT*) all-in wrestling

lutter [lyte] *vi* to fight, struggle; (*SPORT*) to wrestle

luxe [lyks(ə)] *nm* luxury; **un luxe de** (*détails, précautions*) a wealth of; **de luxe** *adj* luxury *cpd*

Luxembourg [lyksãbuʀ] *nm*: **le Luxembourg** Luxembourg

luxembourgeois, e [lyksãbuʀʒwa, -waz] *adj* of *ou* from Luxembourg ◆ *nm/f*: **Luxembourgeois, e** inhabitant *ou* native of Luxembourg

luxer [lykse] *vt*: **se luxer l'épaule** to dislocate one's shoulder

luxueux, euse [lyksɥø, -øz] *adj* luxurious

luxure [lyksyʀ] *nf* lust

luxuriant, e [lyksyʀjã, -ãt] *adj* luxuriant, lush

lycée [lise] *nm* (state) secondary (*BRIT*) *ou* high (*US*) school; **lycée technique** technical secondary *ou* high school; *see boxed note*

lycéen, ne [liseɛ̃, -ɛn] *nm/f* secondary school pupil

lyophilisé, e [ljɔfilize] *adj* freeze-dried

lyrique [liʀik] *adj* lyrical; (*OPÉRA*) lyric; **artiste lyrique** opera singer; **comédie lyrique** comic opera; **théâtre lyrique** opera house (*for light opera*)

lys [lis] *nm* lily

— M m —

M, m [ɛm] *nm inv* M, m ♦ *abr* = **majeur, masculin, mètre, Monsieur;** (= *million*) M; **M comme Marcel** M for Mike

m' [m] *pron voir* **me**

ma [ma] *dét voir* **mon**

macaron [makaʀɔ̃] *nm* (*gâteau*) macaroon; (*insigne*) (round) badge

macaroni(s) [makaʀɔni] *nm(pl)* macaroni *sg*; **macaroni(s) au fromage** *ou* **au gratin** macaroni cheese (*BRIT*), macaroni and cheese (*US*)

macédoine [masedwan] *nf*: **macédoine de fruits** fruit salad; **macédoine de légumes** mixed vegetables *pl*

macérer [maseʀe] *vi, vt* to macerate; (*dans du vinaigre*) to pickle

mâcher [mɑʃe] *vt* to chew; **ne pas mâcher ses mots** not to mince one's words; **mâcher le travail à qn** (*fig*) to spoonfeed sb, do half sb's work for him

machin [maʃɛ̃] *nm* (*fam*) thingamajig, thing; (*personne*): **Machin** what's-his(*ou* -her)-name

machinal, e, aux [maʃinal, -o] *adj* mechanical, automatic

machinalement [maʃinalmɑ̃] *adv* mechanically, automatically

machination [maʃinasjɔ̃] *nf* scheming, frame-up

machine [maʃin] *nf* machine; (*locomotive; de navire etc*) engine; (*fig: rouages*) machinery; (*fam: personne*): **Machine** what's-her-name; **faire machine arrière** (*NAVIG*) to go astern; (*fig*) to back-pedal; **machine à laver/coudre/tricoter** washing/sewing/knitting machine; **machine à écrire** typewriter; **machine à sous** fruit machine; **machine à vapeur** steam engine

macho [matʃo] (*fam*) *nm* male chauvinist

mâchoire [mɑʃwaʀ] *nf* jaw; **mâchoire de frein** brake shoe

mâchonner [mɑʃɔne] *vt* to chew (at)

maçon [masɔ̃] *nm* bricklayer; (*constructeur*) builder

maçonnerie [masɔnʀi] *nf* (*murs: de brique*) brickwork; (: *de pierre*) masonry, stonework; (*activité*) bricklaying; building; **maçonnerie de béton** concrete

maculer [makyle] *vt* to stain; (*TYPO*) to mackle

Madame [madam], *pl* **Mesdames** [medam] *nf*: **Madame X** Mrs X ['mɪsɪz]; **occupez-vous de Madame/Monsieur/Mademoiselle** please serve this lady/gentleman/(young) lady; **bonjour Madame/Monsieur/Mademoiselle** good morning; (*ton déférent*) good morning Madam/Sir/Madam; (*le nom est connu*) good morning Mrs X/Mr X/Miss X; **Madame/Monsieur/Mademoiselle!** (*pour appeler*) excuse me!; (*ton déférent*) Madam/Sir/Miss!; **Madame/Monsieur/Mademoiselle** (*sur lettre*) Dear Madam/Sir/Madam; **chère Madame/cher Monsieur/chère Mademoiselle** Dear Mrs X/Mr X/Miss X; **Madame la Directrice** the director; the manageress; the headteacher; **Mesdames** Ladies

madeleine [madlɛn] *nf* madeleine, ≈ sponge finger cake

Mademoiselle [madmwazɛl], *pl* **Mesdemoiselles** [medmwazɛl] *nf* Miss; *voir aussi* **Madame**

Madère [madɛʀ] *nf* Madeira ♦ *nm*: **madère** Madeira (wine)

magasin [magazɛ̃] *nm* (*boutique*) shop; (*entrepôt*) warehouse; (*d'arme, appareil-photo*) magazine; **en magasin** (*COMM*) in stock; **faire les magasins** to go (a)round the shops, do the shops; **magasin d'alimentation** grocer's (shop) (*BRIT*), grocery store (*US*)

magazine [magazin] *nm* magazine

Maghreb [magʀeb] *nm*: **le Maghreb** the Maghreb, North(-West) Africa

maghrébin, e [magʀebɛ̃, -in] *adj* d' *ou* from the Maghreb ♦ *nm/f*: **Maghrébin, e** North African, Maghrebi

magicien, ne [maʒisjɛ̃, -ɛn] *nm/f* magician

magie [maʒi] *nf* magic; **magie noire** black magic

magique [maʒik] *adj* (*occulte*) magic; (*fig*) magical

magistral, e, aux [maʒistʀal, -o] *adj* (*œuvre, adresse*) masterly; (*ton*) authoritative; (*gifle etc*) sound, resounding; (*ex cathedra*): **enseignement magistral** lecturing, lectures *pl*; **cours magistral** lecture

magistrat [maʒistʀa] *nm* magistrate

magnat [magna] *nm* tycoon, magnate

magnétique [maɲetik] *adj* magnetic

magnétiser [maɲetize] *vt* to magnetize; (*fig*) to

mesmerize, hypnotize

magnétophone [maɲetɔfɔn] *nm* tape recorder; **magnétophone à cassettes** cassette recorder

magnétoscope [maɲetɔskɔp] *nm*: **magnétoscope (à cassette)** video (recorder)

magnifique [maɲifik] *adj* magnificent

magot [mago] *nm* (*argent*) pile (of money); (*économies*) nest egg

magouille [maguj] *nf* (*fam*) scheming

magret [magrɛ] *nm*: **magret de canard** duck steaklet

mai [mɛ] *nm* May; *voir aussi* **juillet**; *see boxed note*

LE PREMIER MAI

Le premier mai is a public holiday in France and commemorates the trades union demonstrations in the United States in 1886 when workers demanded the right to an eight-hour working day. Sprigs of lily of the valley are traditionally exchanged. **Le 8 mai** is also a public holiday and commemorates the surrender of the German army to Eisenhower on 7 May, 1945. It is marked by parades of ex-servicemen and ex-servicewomen in most towns. The social upheavals of May and June 1968, with their student demonstrations, workers' strikes and general rioting, are usually referred to as 'les événements de mai 68'. De Gaulle's Government survived, but reforms in education and a move towards decentralization ensued.

---

maigre [mɛgʀ(ə)] *adj* (very) thin, skinny; (*viande*) lean; (*fromage*) low-fat; (*végétation*) thin; (*fig*) poor, meagre, skimpy ♦ *adv*: **faire maigre** not to eat meat; **jours maigres** days of abstinence, fish days

maigreur [mɛgʀœʀ] *nf* thinness

maigrir [megʀiʀ] *vi* to get thinner, lose weight ♦ *vt*: **maigrir qn** (*suj: vêtement*) to make sb look slim(mer)

mail [mɛl] *nm* e-mail

maille [maj] *nf* (*boucle*) stitch; (*ouverture*) hole (in the mesh); **avoir maille à partir avec qn** to have a brush with sb; **maille à l'endroit/à l'envers** knit one/purl one; (*boucle*) plain/purl stitch

maillet [majɛ] *nm* mallet

maillon [majɔ̃] *nm* link

maillot [majo] *nm* (*aussi*: **maillot de corps**) vest; (*de danseur*) leotard; (*de sportif*) jersey; **maillot de bain** bathing costume (*BRIT*), swimsuit; (*d'homme*) bathing trunks *pl*; **maillot deux pièces** two-piece swimsuit, bikini; **maillot jaune** yellow jersey

main [mɛ̃] *nf* hand; **la main dans la main** hand in hand; **à deux mains** with both hands; **à une main** with one hand; **à la main** (*tenir, avoir*) in one's hand; (*faire, tricoter etc*) by hand; **se donner la main** to hold hands; **donner** *ou* **tendre la main à qn** to hold out one's hand to sb; **se serrer la main** to

shake hands; **serrer la main à qn** to shake hands with sb; **sous la main** to *ou* at hand; **haut les mains!** hands up!; **à main levée** (*ART*) freehand; **à mains levées** (*voter*) with a show of hands; **attaque à main armée** armed attack; **à main droite/gauche** to the right/left; **à remettre en mains propres** to be delivered personally; **de première main** (*renseignement*) first-hand; (*COMM*: *voiture etc*) with only one previous owner; **faire main basse sur** to help o.s. to; **mettre la dernière main à** to put the finishing touches to; **mettre la main à la pâte** (*fig*) to lend a hand; **avoir/passer la main** (*CARTES*) to lead/hand over the lead; **s'en laver les mains** (*fig*) to wash one's hands of it; **se faire/perdre la main** to get one's hand in/lose one's touch; **avoir qch bien en main** to have got the hang of sth; **en un tour de main** (*fig*) in the twinkling of an eye; **main courante** handrail

main-d'œuvre [mɛ̃dœvʀ(ə)] *nf* manpower, labour (*BRIT*), labor (*US*)

main-forte [mɛ̃fɔʀt(ə)] *nf*: **prêter main-forte à qn** to come to sb's assistance

mainmise [mɛ̃miz] *nf* seizure; (*fig*): **avoir la mainmise sur** to have a grip *ou* stranglehold on

maint, e [mɛ̃, mɛ̃t] *adj* many a; **maints** many; **à maintes reprises** time and (time) again

maintenant [mɛ̃tnɑ̃] *adv* now; (*actuellement*) nowadays

maintenir [mɛ̃tniʀ] *vt* (*retenir, soutenir*) to support; (*contenir*: *foule etc*) to keep in check, hold back; (*conserver*) to maintain, uphold; (*affirmer*) to maintain; **se maintenir** *vi* (*paix, temps*) to hold; (*préjugé*) to persist; (*malade*) to remain stable

maintien [mɛ̃tjɛ̃] *nm* maintaining, upholding; (*attitude*) bearing; **maintien de l'ordre** maintenance of law and order

maire [mɛʀ] *nm* mayor

mairie [meʀi] *nf* (*endroit*) town hall; (*administration*) town council

mais [mɛ] *conj* but; **mais non!** of course not!; **mais enfin** but after all; (*indignation*) look here!; **mais encore?** is that all?

maïs [mais] *nm* maize (*BRIT*), corn (*US*)

maison [mɛzɔ̃] *nf* (*bâtiment*) house; (*chez-soi*) home; (*COMM*) firm; (*famille*): **ami de la maison** friend of the family ♦ *adj inv* (*CULIN*) home-made; (: *au restaurant*) made by the chef; (*COMM*) in-house, own; (*fam*) first-rate; **à la maison** at home; (*direction*) home; **maison d'arrêt** (short-stay) prison; **maison centrale** prison; **maison close** brothel; **maison de correction** ≃ remand home (*BRIT*), ≃ reformatory (*US*); **maison de la culture** ≃ arts centre; **maison des jeunes** ≃ youth club; *see boxed note*; **maison mère** parent company; **maison de passe** = **maison close**; **maison de repos** convalescent home; **maison de retraite** old people's home; **maison de santé** mental home

MAISONS DES JEUNES

Maisons des jeunes et de la culture are centres for young people which combine the functions of youth club and community arts centre. They organize a wide range of sporting and cultural activities (theatre, music, exhibitions), and their members also help out in the community. The centres receive some of their funding from the state.

maisonnée [mɛzɔne] *nf* household, family

maisonnette [mɛzɔnet] *nf* small house, cottage

maître, esse [mɛtr(ə), metrɛs] *nm/f* master/mistress; (*scol*) teacher, schoolmaster/mistress ♦ *nm* (*peintre etc*) master; (*titre*): **Maître (Mᵉ)** Maître, *term of address for lawyers etc* ♦ *nf* (*amante*) mistress ♦ *adj* (*principal, essentiel*) main; **maison de maître** family seat; **être maître de** (*soi-même, situation*) to be in control of; **se rendre maître de** (*pays, ville*) to gain control of; (*situation, incendie*) to bring under control; **être passé maître dans l'art de** to be a (past) master in the art of; **une maîtresse femme** a forceful woman; **maître d'armes** fencing master; **maître auxiliaire (MA)** (*scol*) temporary teacher; **maître chanteur** blackmailer; **maître de chapelle** choirmaster; **maître de conférences** ≃ senior lecturer (*brit*), ≃ assistant professor (*us*); **maître/ maîtresse d'école** teacher, schoolmaster/mistress; **maître d'hôtel** (*domestique*) butler; (*d'hôtel*) head waiter; **maître de maison** host; **maître nageur** lifeguard; **maître d'œuvre** (*constr*) project manager; **maître d'ouvrage** (*constr*) client; **maître queux** chef; **maîtresse de maison** hostess; (*ménagère*) housewife (*pl* -wives)

maîtrise [metriz] *nf* (*aussi:* **maîtrise de soi**) self-control; (*habileté*) skill, mastery; (*suprématie*) mastery, command; (*diplôme*) ≃ master's degree; (*chefs d'équipe*) supervisory staff; *see boxed note*

MAÎTRISE

The **maîtrise** is a French degree which is awarded to university students if they successfully complete two more years' study after the 'DEUG'. Students wishing to go on to do research or to take the 'agrégation' must hold a **maîtrise**.

maîtriser [metrize] *vt* (*cheval, incendie*) to (bring under) control; (*sujet*) to master; (*émotion*) to control; **se maîtriser** to control o.s.

majestueux, euse [maʒestɥø, -øz] *adj* majestic

majeur, e [maʒœr] *adj* (*important*) major; (*jur*) of age; (*fig*) adult ♦ *nm/f* (*jur*) person who has come of age *ou* attained his (*ou* her) majority ♦ *nm* (*doigt*) middle finger; **en majeure partie** for the most part; **la majeure partie de** the major part of

majoration [maʒɔrasjɔ̃] *nf* increase

majorer [maʒɔre] *vt* to increase

majoritaire [maʒɔriter] *adj* majority *cpd*; **système/scrutin majoritaire** majority system/ballot

majorité [maʒɔrite] *nf* (*gén*) majority; (*parti*) party in power; **en majorité** (*composé etc*) mainly

majuscule [maʒyskyl] *adj, nf*: **(lettre) majuscule** capital (letter)

mal, maux [mal, mo] *nm* (*opposé au bien*) evil; (*tort, dommage*) harm; (*douleur physique*) pain, ache; (*maladie*) illness, sickness *no pl*; (*difficulté, peine*) trouble; (*souffrance morale*) pain ♦ *adv* badly ♦ *adj*: **c'est mal (de faire)** it's bad *ou* wrong (to do); **être mal** to be uncomfortable; **être mal avec qn** to be on bad terms with sb; **être au plus mal** (*malade*) to be very bad; (*brouillé*) to be at daggers drawn; **il comprend mal** he has difficulty in understanding; **il a mal compris** he misunderstood; **mal tourner** to go wrong; **dire/penser du mal de** to speak/think ill of; **ne vouloir de mal à personne** to wish nobody any ill; **il n'a rien fait de mal** he has done nothing wrong; **avoir du mal à faire qch** to have trouble doing sth; **se donner du mal pour faire qch** to go to a lot of trouble to do sth; **ne voir aucun mal à** to see no harm in, see nothing wrong with; **craignant mal faire** fearing he *etc* was doing the wrong thing; **sans penser** *ou* **songer à mal** without meaning any harm; **faire du mal à qn** to hurt sb; to harm sb; **se faire mal** to hurt o.s.; **se faire mal au pied** to hurt one's foot; **ça fait mal** it hurts; **j'ai mal (ici)** it hurts (here); **j'ai mal au dos** my back aches, I've got a pain in my back; **avoir mal à la tête/à la gorge** to have a headache/a sore throat; **avoir mal aux dents/à l'oreille** to have toothache/earache; **avoir le mal de l'air** to be airsick; **avoir le mal du pays** to be homesick; **mal de mer** seasickness; **mal de la route** carsickness; **mal en point** *adj inv* in a bad state; **maux de ventre** stomach ache *sg*; *voir aussi* **cœur**

malade [malad] *adj* ill, sick; (*poitrine, jambe*) bad; (*plante*) diseased; (*fig: entreprise, monde*) ailing ♦ *nm/f* invalid, sick person; (*à l'hôpital etc*) patient; **tomber malade** to fall ill; **être malade du cœur** to have heart trouble *ou* a bad heart; **grand malade** seriously ill person; **malade mental** mentally sick *ou* ill person

maladie [maladi] *nf* (*spécifique*) disease, illness; (*mauvaise santé*) illness, sickness; (*fig: manie*) mania; **être rongé par la maladie** to be wasting away (through illness); **maladie d'Alzheimer** Alzheimer's disease; **maladie de peau** skin disease

maladif, ive [maladif, -iv] *adj* sickly; (*curiosité, besoin*) pathological

maladresse [maladrɛs] *nf* clumsiness *no pl*; (*gaffe*) blunder

maladroit, e [maladrwa, -wat] *adj* clumsy

malaise [malɛz] *nm* (*méd*) feeling of faintness; feeling of discomfort; (*fig*) uneasiness, malaise; **avoir un malaise** to feel faint *ou* dizzy

malaisé, e [maleze] *adj* difficult

malaria [malaʁja] *nf* malaria

malaxer [malakse] *vt* (*pétrir*) to knead; (*mêler*) to mix

malchance [malʃɑ̃s] *nf* misfortune, ill luck *no pl*; **par malchance** unfortunately; **quelle malchance!** what bad luck!

malchanceux, euse [malʃɑ̃sø, -øz] *adj* unlucky

mâle [mal] *adj* (*aussi ÉLEC, TECH*) male; (*viril: voix, traits*) manly ◆ *nm* male

malédiction [malediksjɔ̃] *nf* curse

malencontreux, euse [malɑ̃kɔ̃trø, -øz] *adj* unfortunate, untoward

malentendant, e [malɑ̃tɑ̃dɑ̃, -ɑ̃t] *nm/f*: **les malentendants** the hard of hearing

malentendu [malɑ̃tɑ̃dy] *nm* misunderstanding

malfaçon [malfasɔ̃] *nf* fault

malfaisant, e [malfəzɑ̃, -ɑ̃t] *adj* evil, harmful

malfaiteur [malfɛtœr] *nm* lawbreaker, criminal; (*voleur*) thief (*pl* thieves)

malfamé, e [malfame] *adj* disreputable, of ill repute

malgache [malgaʃ] *adj* Malagasy, Madagascan ◆ *nm* (*LING*) Malagasy ◆ *nm/f*: **Malgache** Malagasy, Madagascan

malgré [malgre] *prép* in spite of, despite; **malgré tout** *adv* in spite of everything

malhabile [malabil] *adj* clumsy

malheur [malœr] *nm* (*situation*) adversity, misfortune; (*événement*) misfortune; (: *plus fort*) disaster, tragedy; **par malheur** unfortunately; **quel malheur!** what a shame ou pity!; **faire un malheur** (*fam: un éclat*) to do something desperate; (: *avoir du succès*) to be a smash hit

malheureusement [malœrøzmɑ̃] *adv* unfortunately

malheureux, euse [malœrø, -øz] *adj* (*triste*) unhappy, miserable; (*infortuné, regrettable*) unfortunate; (*malchanceux*) unlucky; (*insignifiant*) wretched ◆ *nm/f* (*infortuné, misérable*) poor soul; (*indigent, miséreux*) unfortunate creature; **les malheureux** the destitute; **avoir la main malheureuse** (*au jeu*) to be unlucky; (*tout casser*) to be ham-fisted

malhonnête [malɔnɛt] *adj* dishonest; (*impoli*) rude

malhonnêteté [malɔnɛtte] *nf* dishonesty; rudeness *no pl*

malice [malis] *nf* mischievousness; (*méchanceté*): **par malice** out of malice ou spite; **sans malice** guileless

malicieux, euse [malisjø, -øz] *adj* mischievous

malin, igne [malɛ̃, -iɲ] *adj* (*futé: f gén: **maline***) smart, shrewd; (: *sourire*) knowing; (*MÉD, influence*) malignant; **faire le malin** to show off; **éprouver un malin plaisir à** to take malicious pleasure in

malingre [malɛ̃gr(ə)] *adj* puny

malle [mal] *nf* trunk; (*AUTO*): **malle (arrière)** boot (*BRIT*), trunk (*US*)

mallette [malɛt] *nf* (*valise*) (small) suitcase; (*aussi*: **mallette de voyage**) overnight case; (*pour documents*) attaché case

malmener [malməne] *vt* to manhandle; (*fig*) to give a rough ride to

malodorant, e [malɔdɔrɑ̃, -ɑ̃t] *adj* foul-smelling

malotru [malɔtry] *nm* lout, boor

malpoli, e [malpɔli] *nm/f* rude individual

malpropre [malprɔpr(ə)] *adj* (*personne, vêtement*) dirty; (*travail*) slovenly; (*histoire, plaisanterie*) unsavoury (*BRIT*), unsavory (*US*), smutty; (*malhonnête*) dishonest

malsain, e [malsɛ̃, -ɛn] *adj* unhealthy

malt [malt] *nm* malt; **pur malt** (*whisky*) malt (whisky)

Malte [malt(ə)] *nf* Malta

maltraiter [maltrete] *vt* (*brutaliser*) to manhandle, ill-treat; (*critiquer, éreinter*) to slate (*BRIT*), roast

malveillance [malvejɑ̃s] *nf* (*animosité*) ill will; (*intention de nuire*) malevolence; (*JUR*) malicious intent *no pl*

malversation [malvɛrsasjɔ̃] *nf* embezzlement, misappropriation (of funds)

maman [mamɑ̃] *nf* mum(my) (*BRIT*), mom (*US*)

mamelle [mamɛl] *nf* teat

mamelon [mamlɔ̃] *nm* (*ANAT*) nipple; (*colline*) knoll, hillock

mamie [mami] *nf* (*fam*) granny

mammifère [mamifɛr] *nm* mammal

mammouth [mamut] *nm* mammoth

manche [mɑ̃ʃ] *nf* (*de vêtement*) sleeve; (*d'un jeu, tournoi*) round; (*GÉO*): **la Manche** the (English) Channel ◆ *nm* (*d'outil, casserole*) handle; (*de pelle, pioche etc*) shaft; (*de violon, guitare*) neck; (*fam*) clumsy oaf; **faire la manche** to pass the hat; **manche à air** *nf* (*AVIAT*) wind-sock; **manche à balai** *nm* broomstick; (*AVIAT, INFORM*) joystick

manchette [mɑ̃ʃɛt] *nf* (*de chemise*) cuff; (*coup*) forearm blow; (*titre*) headline

manchot [mɑ̃ʃo] *nm* one-armed man; armless man; (*ZOOL*) penguin

mandarine [mɑ̃darin] *nf* mandarin (orange), tangerine

mandat [mɑ̃da] *nm* (*postal*) postal ou money order; (*d'un député etc*) mandate; (*procuration*) power of attorney, proxy; (*POLICE*) warrant; **mandat d'amener** summons *sg*; **mandat d'arrêt** warrant for arrest; **mandat de dépôt** committal order; **mandat de perquisition** (*POLICE*) search warrant

mandataire [mɑ̃datɛr] *nm/f* (*représentant, délégué*) representative; (*JUR*) proxy

manège [manɛʒ] *nm* riding school; (*à la foire*) roundabout (*BRIT*), merry-go-round; (*fig*) game, ploy; **faire un tour de manège** to go for a ride on a ou the roundabout *etc*; **manège (de chevaux de bois)** roundabout (*BRIT*), merry-go-round

manette [manɛt] *nf* lever, tap; **manette de jeu** (*INFORM*) joystick

mangeable [mɑ̃ʒabl(ə)] *adj* edible, eatable

mangeoire [mɑ̃ʒwaʀ] *nf* trough, manger

manger [mɑ̃ʒe] *vt* to eat; (*ronger: suj: rouille etc*) to eat into *ou* away; (*utiliser, consommer*) to eat up ♦ *vi* to eat

mangeur, euse [mɑ̃ʒœʀ, -øz] *nm/f* eater

mangue [mɑ̃g] *nf* mango

maniable [manjabl(ə)] *adj* (*outil*) handy; (*voiture, voilier*) easy to handle; manoeuvrable (*BRIT*), maneuverable (*US*); (*fig: personne*) easily influenced, manipulable

maniaque [manjak] *adj* (*pointilleux, méticuleux*) finicky, fussy; (*atteint de manie*) suffering from a mania ♦ *nm/f* maniac

manie [mani] *nf* mania; (*tic*) odd habit

manier [manje] *vt* to handle; **se manier** *vi* (*fam*) to get a move on

manière [manjɛʀ] *nf* (*façon*) way, manner; (*genre, style*) style; **manières** *nfpl* (*attitude*) manners; (*chichis*) fuss *sg*; **de manière à** so as to; **de telle manière que** in such a way that; **de cette manière** in this way *ou* manner; **d'une manière générale** generally speaking, as a general rule; **de toute manière** in any case; **d'une certaine manière** in a (certain) way; **faire des manières** to put on airs; **employer la manière forte** to use strong-arm tactics; **adverbe de manière** adverb of manner

maniéré, e [manjere] *adj* affected

manif [manif] *nf* (*manifestation*) demo (*pl* -s)

manifestant, e [manifestɑ̃, -ɑ̃t] *nm/f* demonstrator

manifestation [manifestasjɔ̃] *nf* (*de joie, mécontentement*) expression, demonstration; (*symptôme*) outward sign; (*fête etc*) event; (*POL*) demonstration

manifeste [manifɛst(ə)] *adj* obvious, evident ♦ *nm* manifesto (*pl* -s)

manifester [manifɛste] *vt* (*volonté, intentions*) to show, indicate; (*joie, peur*) to express, show ♦ *vi* (*POL*) to demonstrate; **se manifester** *vi* (*émotion*) to show *ou* express itself; (*difficultés*) to arise; (*symptômes*) to appear; (*témoin etc*) to come forward

manigance [manigɑ̃s] *nf* scheme

manigancer [manigɑ̃se] *vt* to plot, devise

manipulation [manipylasjɔ̃] *nf* handling; manipulation

manipuler [manipyle] *vt* to handle; (*fig*) to manipulate

manivelle [manivɛl] *nf* crank

mannequin [mankɛ̃] *nm* (*COUTURE*) dummy; (*MODE*) model

manœuvre [manœvʀ(ə)] *nf* (*gén*) manoeuvre (*BRIT*), maneuver (*US*) ♦ *nm* (*ouvrier*) labourer (*BRIT*), laborer (*US*)

manœuvrer [manœvʀe] *vt* to manoeuvre (*BRIT*), maneuver (*US*); (*levier, machine*) to operate; (*personne*) to manipulate ♦ *vi* to manoeuvre *ou* maneuver

manoir [manwaʀ] *nm* manor *ou* country house

manque [mɑ̃k] *nm* (*insuffisance*): **manque de** lack of; (*vide*) emptiness, gap; (*MÉD*) withdrawal; **manques** *nmpl* (*lacunes*) faults, defects; **par manque de** for want of; **manque à gagner** loss of profit *ou* earnings

manqué [mɑ̃ke] *adj* failed; **garçon manqué** tomboy

manquer [mɑ̃ke] *vi* (*faire défaut*) to be lacking; (*être absent*) to be missing; (*échouer*) to fail ♦ *vt* to miss ♦ *vb impers*: **il (nous) manque encore 15 €** we are still 15 € short; **il manque des pages (au livre)** there are some pages missing *ou* some pages are missing (from the book); **l'argent qui leur manque** the money they need *ou* are short of; **le pied/la voix lui manqua** he missed his footing/his voice failed him; **manquer à qn** (*absent etc*): **il/cela me manque** I miss him/that; **manquer à** *vt* (*règles etc*) to be in breach of, fail to observe; **manquer de** *vt* to lack; (*COMM*) to be out of (stock of); **ne pas manquer de faire**: **il n'a pas manqué de le dire** he certainly said it; **manquer (de) faire**: **il a manqué (de) se tuer** he very nearly got killed; **il ne manquerait plus qu'il fasse** all we need now is for him to do; **je n'y manquerai pas** leave it to me, I'll definitely do it

mansarde [mɑ̃saʀd(ə)] *nf* attic

mansardé, e [mɑ̃saʀde] *adj* attic *cpd*

manteau, x [mɑ̃to] *nm* coat; **manteau de cheminée** mantelpiece; **sous le manteau** (*fig*) under cover

manucure [manykyʀ] *nf* manicurist

manuel, le [manɥɛl] *adj* manual ♦ *nm/f* manually gifted pupil *etc* (*as opposed to intellectually gifted*) ♦ *nm* (*ouvrage*) manual, handbook

manufacture [manyfaktyʀ] *nf* (*établissement*) factory; (*fabrication*) manufacture

manufacturé, e [manyfaktyʀe] *adj* manufactured

manuscrit, e [manyskʀi, -it] *adj* handwritten ♦ *nm* manuscript

manutention [manytɑ̃sjɔ̃] *nf* (*COMM*) handling; (*local*) storehouse

mappemonde [mapmɔ̃d] *nf* (*plane*) map of the world; (*sphère*) globe

maquereau, x [makʀo] *nm* mackerel *inv*; (*fam: proxénète*) pimp

maquette [makɛt] *nf* (*d'un décor, bâtiment, véhicule*) (scale) model; (*TYPO*) mockup; (: *d'une page illustrée, affiche*) paste-up; (: *prêt à la réproduction*) artwork

maquillage [makijaʒ] *nm* making up; faking; (*produits*) make-up

maquiller [makije] *vt* (*personne, visage*) to make up; (*truquer: passeport, statistique*) to fake; (: *voiture* *volée*) to do over (*respray etc*) **se maquiller** to make o.s. up

maquis [maki] *nm* (*GÉO*) scrub; (*fig*) tangle; (*MIL*) maquis, underground fighting *no pl*

maraîcher, ère [maʀɛʃe, maʀɛʃɛʀ] *adj*: **cultures maraîchères** market gardening *sg* ♦ *nm/f* market gardener

marais [maʀɛ] *nm* marsh, swamp; **marais salant** saltworks

marasme [maʀasm(ə)] *nm* (*POL, ÉCON*) stagnation, sluggishness; (*accablement*) dejection, depression

marathon [maʀatɔ̃] *nm* marathon

maraudeur, euse [maʀodœʀ, -øz] *nm/f* marauder; prowler

marbre [maʀbʀ(ə)] *nm* (*pierre, statue*) marble; (*d'une table, commode*) marble top; (*TYPO*) stone, bed; **rester de marbre** to remain stonily indifferent

marc [maʀ] *nm* (*de raisin, pommes*) marc; **marc de café** coffee grounds *pl ou* dregs *pl*

marchand, e [maʀʃɑ̃, -ɑ̃d] *nm/f* shopkeeper, tradesman/woman; (*au marché*) stallholder; (*spécifique*): **marchand de cycles/tapis** bicycle/carpet dealer; **marchand de charbon/vins** coal/wine merchant ♦ *adj*: **prix/valeur marchand(e)** market price/value; **qualité marchande** standard quality; **marchand en gros/au détail** wholesaler/retailer; **marchand de biens** real estate agent; **marchand de canons** (*péj*) arms dealer; **marchand de couleurs** ironmonger (*BRIT*), hardware dealer (*US*); **marchand/e de fruits** fruiterer (*BRIT*), fruit seller (*US*); **marchand/e de journaux** newsagent; **marchand/e de légumes** greengrocer (*BRIT*), produce dealer (*US*); **marchand/e de poisson** fishmonger (*BRIT*), fish seller (*US*); **marchand/e de(s) quatre-saisons** costermonger (*BRIT*), street vendor (selling fresh fruit and vegetables); **marchand de sable** (*fig*) sandman; **marchand de tableaux** art dealer

marchander [maʀʃɑ̃de] *vt* (*article*) to bargain *ou* haggle over; (*éloges*) to be sparing with ♦ *vi* to bargain, haggle

marchandise [maʀʃɑ̃diz] *nf* goods *pl*, merchandise *no pl*

marche [maʀʃ(ə)] *nf* (*d'escalier*) step; (*activité*) walking; (*promenade, trajet, allure*) walk; (*démarche*) walk, gait; (*MIL etc, MUS*) march; (*fonctionnement*) running; (*progression*) progress; course; **à une heure de marche** an hour's walk (away); **ouvrir/fermer la marche** to lead the way/bring up the rear; **dans le sens de la marche** (*RAIL*) facing the engine; **en marche** (*monter etc*) while the vehicle is moving *ou* in motion; **mettre en marche** to start; **remettre qch en marche** to set *ou* start sth going again; **se mettre en marche** (*personne*) to get moving; (*machine*) to start; **marche arrière** (*AUTO*) reverse (gear); **faire marche arrière** (*AUTO*) to reverse; (*fig*) to backtrack, back-pedal; **marche à suivre** (*correct*) procedure; (*sur notice*) (step by step) instructions *pl*

marché [maʀʃe] *nm* (*lieu, COMM, ÉCON*) market; (*ville*) trading centre; (*transaction*) bargain, deal; **par-dessus le marché** into the bargain; **faire son marché** to do one's shopping; **mettre le marché en main à qn** to tell sb to take it or leave it; **marché au comptant** (*BOURSE*) spot market; **Marché commun** Common Market; **marché aux fleurs** flower market; **marché noir** black market; **faire du marché noir** to buy and sell on the black market; **marché aux puces** flea market; **marché à terme** (*BOURSE*) forward market; **marché du travail** labour market

marchepied [maʀʃəpje] *nm* (*RAIL*) step; (*AUTO*) running board; (*fig*) stepping stone

marcher [maʀʃe] *vi* to walk; (*MIL*) to march; (*aller: voiture, train, affaires*) to go; (*prospérer*) to go well; (*fonctionner*) to work, run; (*fam*) to go along, agree; (: *croire naïvement*) to be taken in; **marcher sur** to walk on; (*mettre le pied sur*) to step on *ou* in; (*MIL*) to march upon; **marcher dans** (*herbe etc*) to walk in *ou* on; (*flaque*) to step in; **faire marcher qn** (*pour rire*) to pull sb's leg; (*pour tromper*) to lead sb up the garden path

marcheur, euse [maʀʃœʀ, -øz] *nm/f* walker

mardi [maʀdi] *nm* Tuesday; **Mardi gras** Shrove Tuesday; *voir aussi* **lundi**

mare [maʀ] *nf* pond; **mare de sang** pool of blood

marécage [maʀekaʒ] *nm* marsh, swamp

marécageux, euse [maʀekaʒø, -øz] *adj* marshy, swampy

maréchal, aux [maʀeʃal, -o] *nm* marshal; **maréchal des logis** (*MIL*) sergeant

maréchal-ferrant, *pl* **maréchaux-ferrants** [maʀeʃalferɑ̃, maʀeʃo-] *nm* blacksmith, farrier (*BRIT*)

marée [maʀe] *nf* tide; (*poissons*) fresh (sea) fish; **marée haute/basse** high/low tide; **marée montante/descendante** rising/ebb tide; **marée noire** oil slick

marelle [maʀɛl] *nf*: **(jouer à) la marelle** (to play) hopscotch

margarine [maʀgaʀin] *nf* margarine

marge [maʀʒ(ə)] *nf* margin; **en marge** in the margin; **en marge de** (*fig*) on the fringe of; (*en dehors de*) cut off from; (*qui se rapporte à*) connected with; **marge bénéficiaire** profit margin, mark-up; **marge de sécurité** safety margin

marginal, e, aux [maʀʒinal, -o] *adj* marginal ♦ *nm/f* dropout

marguerite [maʀgəʀit] *nf* marguerite, (oxeye) daisy; (*INFORM*) daisy wheel

mari [maʀi] *nm* husband

mariage [maʀjaʒ] *nm* (*union, état, fig*) marriage; (*noce*) wedding; **mariage civil/religieux** registry office (*BRIT*) *ou* civil/church wedding; **un mariage de raison/d'amour** a marriage of convenience/a love match; **mariage blanc** unconsummated marriage; **mariage en blanc** white wedding

marié, e [maʀje] *adj* married ♦ *nm/f* (bride)groom/bride; **les mariés** the bride and groom; **les (jeunes) mariés** the newly-weds

marier [maʀje] *vt* to marry; (*fig*) to blend; **se marier (avec)** to marry, get married (to); (*fig*) to blend (with)

marin, e [maʀɛ̃, -in] *adj* sea *cpd*, marine ◆ *nm* sailor ◆ *nf* navy; (*ART*) seascape; (*couleur*) navy (blue); **avoir le pied marin** to be a good sailor; (*garder son équilibre*) to have one's sea legs; **marine de guerre** navy; **marine marchande** merchant navy; **marine à voiles** sailing ships *pl*

marine [maʀin] *adj f, nf voir* **marin** ◆ *adj inv* navy (blue) ◆ *nm* (*MIL*) marine

mariner [maʀine] *vi, vt* to marinate, marinade

marionnette [maʀjɔnɛt] *nf* puppet

maritalement [maʀitalmɑ̃] *adv*: **vivre maritalement** to live together (as husband and wife)

maritime [maʀitim] *adj* sea *cpd*, maritime; (*ville*) coastal, seaside; (*droit*) shipping, maritime

mark [maʀk] *nm* (*monnaie*) mark

marmelade [maʀməlad] *nf* (*compote*) stewed fruit, compote; **marmelade d'oranges** (orange) marmalade; **en marmelade** (*fig*) crushed (to a pulp)

marmite [maʀmit] *nf* (cooking-)pot

marmonner [maʀmɔne] *vt, vi* to mumble, mutter

marmot [maʀmo] *nm* (*fam*) brat

marmotter [maʀmɔte] *vt* (*prière*) to mumble, mutter

Maroc [maʀɔk] *nm*: **le Maroc** Morocco

marocain, e [maʀɔkɛ̃, -ɛn] *adj* Moroccan ◆ *nm/f*: **Marocain, e** Moroccan

maroquinerie [maʀɔkinʀi] *nf* (*industrie*) leather craft; (*commerce*) leather shop; (*articles*) fine leather goods *pl*

marquant, e [maʀkɑ̃, -ɑ̃t] *adj* outstanding

marque [maʀk(ə)] *nf* mark; (*SPORT, JEU*) score; (*COMM: de produits*) brand, make; (: *de disques*) label; (*insigne: d'une fonction*) badge; (*fig*): **marque d'affection** token of affection; **marque de joie** sign of joy; **à vos marques!** (*SPORT*) on your marks!; **de marque** *adj* (*COMM*) brand-name *cpd*; proprietary; (*fig*) high-class; (: *personnage, hôte*) distinguished; **produit de marque** (*COMM*) quality product; **marque déposée** registered trademark; **marque de fabrique** trademark

marquer [maʀke] *vt* to mark; (*inscrire*) to write down; (*bétail*) to brand; (*SPORT: but etc*) to score; (: *joueur*) to mark; (*accentuer: taille etc*) to emphasize; (*manifester: refus, intérêt*) to show ◆ *vi* (*événement, personnalité*) to stand out, be outstanding; (*SPORT*) to score; **marquer qn de son influence/empreinte** to have an influence/leave its impression on sb; **marquer un temps d'arrêt** to pause momentarily; **marquer le pas** (*fig*) to mark time; **il a marqué ce jour-là d'une pierre blanche** that was a red-letter day for him; **marquer les points** (*tenir la marque*) to keep the score

marqueterie [maʀkətʀi] *nf* inlaid work, marquetry

marquis, e [maʀki, -iz] *nm/f* marquis *ou* marquess/marchioness ◆ *nf* (*auvent*) glass canopy *ou* awning

marraine [maʀɛn] *nf* godmother; (*d'un navire, d'une rose etc*) namer

marrant, e [maʀɑ̃, -ɑ̃t] *adj* (*fam*) funny

marre [maʀ] *adv* (*fam*): **en avoir marre de** to be fed up with

marrer [maʀe]: **se marrer** *vi* (*fam*) to have a (good) laugh

marron, ne [maʀɔ̃, -ɔn] *nm* (*fruit*) chestnut ◆ *adj inv* brown ◆ *adj* (*péj*) crooked; (: *faux*) bogus; **marrons glacés** marrons glacés

marronnier [maʀɔnje] *nm* chestnut (tree)

mars [maʀs] *nm* March; *voir aussi* **juillet**

marsouin [maʀswɛ̃] *nm* porpoise

marteau, x [maʀto] *nm* hammer; (*de porte*) knocker; **marteau pneumatique** pneumatic drill

marteau-piqueur, *pl* **marteaux-piqueurs** [maʀtopikœʀ] *nm* pneumatic drill

marteler [maʀtəle] *vt* to hammer; (*mots, phrases*) to rap out

martien, ne [maʀsjɛ̃, -ɛn] *adj* Martian, of *ou* from Mars

martyr, e [maʀtiʀ] *nm/f* martyr ◆ *adj* martyred; **enfants martyrs** battered children

martyre [maʀtiʀ] *nm* martyrdom; (*fig: sens affaibli*) agony, torture; **souffrir le martyre** to suffer agonies

martyriser [maʀtiʀize] *vt* (*REL*) to martyr; (*fig*) to bully; (: *enfant*) to batter

marxiste [maʀksist(ə)] *adj, nm/f* Marxist

mascara [maskaʀa] *nm* mascara

masculin, e [maskylɛ̃, -in] *adj* masculine; (*sexe, population*) male; (*équipe, vêtements*) men's; (*viril*) manly ◆ *nm* masculine

masochiste [mazɔʃist(ə)] *adj* masochistic ◆ *nm/f* masochist

masque [mask(ə)] *nm* mask; **masque de beauté** face pack; **masque à gaz** gas mask; **masque de plongée** diving mask

masquer [maske] *vt* (*cacher: porte, goût*) to hide, conceal; (*dissimuler: vérité, projet*) to mask, obscure

massacre [masakʀ(ə)] *nm* massacre, slaughter; **jeu de massacre** (*fig*) wholesale slaughter

massacrer [masakʀe] *vt* to massacre, slaughter; (*fig: adversaire*) to slaughter; (: *texte etc*) to murder

massage [masaʒ] *nm* massage

masse [mas] *nf* mass; (*péj*): **la masse** the masses *pl*; (*ÉLEC*) earth; (*maillet*) sledgehammer; **masses** *nfpl* masses; **une masse de, des masses de** (*fam*) masses *ou* loads of; **en masse** *adv* (*en bloc*) in bulk; (*en foule*) en masse ◆ *adj* (*exécutions, production*) mass *cpd*; **masse monétaire** (*ÉCON*) money supply; **masse salariale** (*COMM*) wage(s) bill

masser [mase] *vt* (*assembler*) to gather; (*pétrir*) to massage; **se masser** *vi* to gather

masseur, euse [masœʀ, -øz] *nm/f (personne)* masseur/euse ◆ *nm (appareil)* massager

massif, ive [masif, -iv] *adj (porte)* solid, massive; *(visage)* heavy, large; *(bois, or)* solid; *(dose)* massive; *(déportations etc)* mass *cpd* ◆ *nm (montagneux)* massif; *(de fleurs)* clump, bank

massue [masy] *nf* club, bludgeon ◆ *adj inv*: **argument massue** sledgehammer argument

mastic [mastik] *nm (pour vitres)* putty; *(pour fentes)* filler

mastiquer [mastike] *vt (aliment)* to chew, masticate; *(fente)* to fill; *(vitre)* to putty

mat, e [mat] *adj (couleur, métal)* mat(t); *(bruit, son)* dull ◆ *adj inv (ÉCHECS)*: **être mat** to be checkmate

mât [mɑ] *nm (NAVIG)* mast; *(poteau)* pole, post

match [matʃ] *nm* match; **match nul** draw, tie *(US)*; **faire match nul** to draw *(BRIT)*, tie *(US)*; **match aller** first leg; **match retour** second leg, return match

matelas [matla] *nm* mattress; **matelas pneumatique** air bed *ou* mattress; **matelas à ressorts** spring *ou* interior-sprung mattress

matelassé, e *adj (vêtement)* padded; *(tissu)* quilted

matelot [matlo] *nm* sailor, seaman

mater [mate] *vt (personne)* to bring to heel, subdue; *(révolte)* to put down; *(fam)* to watch, look at

matérialiser [mateʀjalize]: **se matérialiser** *vi* to materialize

matérialiste [mateʀjalist(ə)] *adj* materialistic ◆ *nm/f* materialist

matériau, x [mateʀjo] *nm* material; **matériaux** *nmpl* material(s); **matériaux de construction** building materials

matériel, le [mateʀjɛl] *adj* material; *(organisation, aide, obstacle)* practical; *(fig: péj: personne)* materialistic ◆ *nm* equipment *no pl; (de camping etc)* gear *no pl;* **il n'a pas le temps matériel de le faire** he doesn't have the time (needed) to do it; **matériel d'exploitation** *(COMM)* plant; **matériel roulant** rolling stock

maternel, le [mateʀnɛl] *adj (amour, geste)* motherly, maternal; *(grand-père, oncle)* maternal ◆ *nf (aussi: **école maternelle**)* (state) nursery school

maternité [mateʀnite] *nf (établissement)* maternity hospital; *(état de mère)* motherhood, maternity; *(grossesse)* pregnancy

mathématique [matematik] *adj* mathematical

mathématiques [matematik] *nfpl* mathematics *sg*

maths [mat] *nfpl* maths *(BRIT)*, math *(US)*

matière [matjɛʀ] *nf (PHYSIQUE)* matter; *(COMM, TECH)* material, matter *no pl; (fig: d'un livre etc)* subject matter; *(SCOL)* subject; **en matière de** as regards; **donner matière à** to give cause to; **matière plastique** plastic; **matières fécales** faeces; **matières grasses** fat (content) *sg*; **matières premières** raw materials

matin [matɛ̃] *nm, adv* morning; **le matin** *(pendant le matin)* in the morning; **demain matin** tomorrow morning; **le lendemain matin** (the) next morning; **du matin au soir** from morning till night; **une heure du matin** one o'clock in the morning; **de grand** *ou* **bon matin** early in the morning

matinal, e, aux [matinal, -o] *adj (toilette, gymnastique)* morning *cpd; (de bonne heure)* early; **être matinal** *(personne)* to be up early; *(: habituellement)* to be an early riser

matinée [matine] *nf* morning; *(spectacle)* matinée, afternoon performance

matou [matu] *nm* tom(cat)

matraque [matʀak] *nf (de malfaiteur)* cosh *(BRIT)*, club; *(de policier)* truncheon *(BRIT)*, billy *(US)*

matricule [matʀikyl] *nf (aussi: **registre matricule**)* roll, register ◆ *nm (aussi: **numéro matricule**: MIL)* regimental number; *(: ADMIN)* reference number

matrimonial, e, aux [matʀimɔnjal, -o] *adj* marital, marriage *cpd*

maudire [modiʀ] *vt* to curse

maudit, e [modi, -it] *adj (fam: satané)* blasted, confounded

maugréer [mogʀee] *vi* to grumble

maussade [mosad] *adj (air, personne)* sullen; *(ciel, temps)* dismal

mauvais, e [mɔvɛ, -ɛz] *adj* bad; *(faux)*: **le mauvais numéro** the wrong number; *(méchant, malveillant)* malicious, spiteful ◆ *nm*: **le mauvais** the bad side ◆ *adv*: **il fait mauvais** the weather is bad; **sentir mauvais** to have a nasty smell, smell bad *ou* nasty; **la mer est mauvaise** the sea is rough; **mauvais coucheur** awkward customer; **mauvais coup** *(fig)* criminal venture; **mauvais garçon** tough; **mauvais pas** tight spot; **mauvais plaisant** hoaxer; **mauvais traitements** ill treatment *sg*; **mauvaise herbe** weed; **mauvaise langue** gossip, scandalmonger *(BRIT)*; **mauvaise passe** difficult situation; *(période)* bad patch; **mauvaise tête** rebellious *ou* headstrong customer

mauve [mov] *adj (couleur)* mauve ◆ *nf (BOT)* mallow

maux [mo] *nmpl voir* **mal**

maximal, e, aux [maksimal, -o] *adj* maximal

maximum [maksimɔm] *adj, nm* maximum; **atteindre un/son maximum** to reach a/his peak; **au maximum** *adv (le plus possible)* to the full; as much as one can; *(tout au plus)* at the (very) most *ou* maximum

mayonnaise [majɔnɛz] *nf* mayonnaise

mazout [mazut] *nm (fuel) oil;* **chaudière/poêle à mazout** oil-fired boiler/stove

me, m' [m(ə)] *pron* me; *(réfléchi)* myself

mec [mɛk] *nm (fam)* guy, bloke *(BRIT)*

mécanicien, ne [mekanisjɛ̃, -ɛn] *nm/f* mechanic; *(RAIL)* (train *ou* engine) driver; **mécanicien navi-**

gant *ou* **de bord** *(AVIAT)* flight engineer

mécanique [mekanik] *adj* mechanical ♦ *nf (science)* mechanics *sg*; *(technologie)* mechanical engineering; *(mécanisme)* mechanism; engineering; works *pl*; **ennui mécanique** engine trouble *no pl*; **s'y connaître en mécanique** to be mechanically minded; **mécanique hydraulique** hydraulics *sg*; **mécanique ondulataire** wave mechanics *sg*

mécanisme [mekanism(ə)] *nm* mechanism; **mécanisme des taux de change** exchange rate mechanism

méchamment [meʃamɑ̃] *adv* nastily, maliciously, spitefully; viciously

méchanceté [meʃɑ̃ste] *nf (d'une personne, d'une parole)* nastiness, maliciousness, spitefulness; *(parole, action)* nasty *ou* spiteful *ou* malicious remark *(ou* action)

méchant, e [meʃɑ̃, -ɑ̃t] *adj* nasty, malicious, spiteful; *(enfant: pas sage)* naughty; *(animal)* vicious; *(avant le nom: valeur péjorative)* nasty; miserable; *(: intensive)* terrific

mèche [mɛʃ] *nf (de lampe, bougie)* wick; *(d'un explosif)* fuse; *(MÉD)* pack, dressing; *(de vilebrequin, perceuse)* bit; *(de dentiste)* drill; *(de fouet)* lash; *(de cheveux)* lock; **se faire faire des mèches** *(chez le coiffeur)* to have one's hair streaked, have highlights put in one's hair; **vendre la mèche** to give the game away; **de mèche avec** in league with

méchoui [meʃwi] *nm* whole sheep barbecue

méconnaissable [mekɔnɛsabl(ə)] *adj* unrecognizable

méconnaître [mekɔnɛtʀ(ə)] *vt (ignorer)* to be unaware of; *(mésestimer)* to misjudge

mécontent, e [mekɔ̃tɑ̃, -ɑ̃t] *adj*: **mécontent (de)** *(insatisfait)* discontented *ou* dissatisfied *ou* displeased (with); *(contrarié)* annoyed (at) ♦ *nm/f* malcontent, dissatisfied person

mécontentement [mekɔ̃tɑ̃tmɑ̃] *nm* dissatisfaction, discontent, displeasure; annoyance

médaille [medaj] *nf* medal

médaillon [medajɔ̃] *nm (portrait)* medallion; *(bijou)* locket; *(CULIN)* médaillon; **en médaillon** *adj (carte etc)* inset

médecin [medsɛ̃] *nm* doctor; **médecin du bord** *(NAVIG)* ship's doctor; **médecin généraliste** general practitioner, GP; **médecin légiste** forensic scientist *(BRIT)*, medical examiner *(US)*; **médecin traitant** family doctor, GP

médecine [medsin] *nf* medicine; **médecine générale** general medicine; **médecine infantile** paediatrics *sg (BRIT)*, pediatrics *sg (US)*; **médecine légale** forensic medicine; **médecine préventive** preventive medicine; **médecine du travail** occupational *ou* industrial medicine; **médecines parallèles** *ou* **douces** alternative medicine

médiatique [medjatik] *adj* media *cpd*

médiatisé, e [medjatize] *adj* reported in the media; **ce procès a été très médiatisé** *(péj)* this trial was turned into a media event

médical, e, aux [medikal, -o] *adj* medical; **visiteur** *ou* **délégué médical** medical rep *ou* representative

médicament [medikamɑ̃] *nm* medicine, drug

médiéval, e, aux [medjeval, -o] *adj* medieval

médiocre [medjɔkʀ(ə)] *adj* mediocre, poor

médire [mediʀ] *vi*: **médire de** to speak ill of

médisance [medizɑ̃s] *nf* scandalmongering *no pl (BRIT)*, mud-slinging *no pl*; *(propos)* piece of scandal *ou* malicious gossip

méditer [medite] *vt (approfondir)* to meditate on, ponder (over); *(combiner)* to meditate ♦ *vi* to meditate; **méditer de faire** to contemplate doing, plan to do

Méditerranée [mediteʀane] *nf*: **la (mer) Méditerranée** the Mediterranean (Sea)

méditerranéen, ne [mediteʀaneɛ̃, -ɛn] *adj* Mediterranean ♦ *nm/f*: **Méditerranéen, ne** Mediterranean

méduse [medyz] *nf* jellyfish

meeting [mitiŋ] *nm (POL, SPORT)* rally, meeting; **meeting d'aviation** air show

méfait [mefɛ] *nm (faute)* misdemeanour, wrongdoing; **méfaits** *nmpl (ravages)* ravages

méfiance [mefjɑ̃s] *nf* mistrust, distrust

méfiant, e [mefjɑ̃, -ɑ̃t] *adj* mistrustful, distrustful

méfier [mefje]: **se méfier** *vi* to be wary; *(faire attention)* to be careful; **se méfier de** *vt* to mistrust, distrust, be wary of; to be careful about

mégarde [megaʀd(ə)] *nf*: **par mégarde** accidentally; *(par erreur)* by mistake

mégère [meʒɛʀ] *nf (péj: femme)* shrew

mégot [mego] *nm* cigarette end *ou* butt

meilleur, e [mɛjœʀ] *adj, adv* better; *(valeur superlative)* best ♦ *nm*: **le meilleur** *(celui qui …)* the best (one); *(ce qui …)* the best ♦ *nf*: **la meilleure** the best (one); **le meilleur des deux** the better of the two; **de meilleure heure** earlier; **meilleur marché** cheaper

mél [mɛl] *nm* e-mail

mélancolie [melɑ̃kɔli] *nf* melancholy, gloom

mélancolique [melɑ̃kɔlik] *adj* melancholy

mélange [melɑ̃ʒ] *nm (opération)* mixing; blending; *(résultat)* mixture; blend; **sans mélange** unadulterated

mélanger [melɑ̃ʒe] *vt (substances)* to mix; *(vins, couleurs)* to blend; *(mettre en désordre, confondre)* to mix up, muddle (up); **se mélanger** *(liquides, couleurs)* to blend, mix

mélasse [melas] *nf* treacle, molasses *sg*

mêlée [mele] *nf (bataille, cohue)* mêlée, scramble; *(lutte, conflit)* tussle, scuffle; *(RUGBY)* scrum(mage)

mêler [mele] *vt (substances, odeurs, races)* to mix; *(embrouiller)* to muddle (up), mix up; **se mêler** to mix; *(se joindre, s'allier)* to mingle; **se mêler à** *(suj: personne)* to join; to mix with; *(: odeurs etc)* to mingle with; **se mêler de** (*suj: personne*) to meddle with, interfere in; **mêle-toi de tes affaires!** mind your own business!; **mêler à** *ou* **avec** *ou* **de** to mix with; to mingle with; **mêler qn à** (*affaire*) to get sb mixed up *ou* involved in

mélodie [melɔdi] *nf* melody

mélodieux, euse [melɔdjø, -øz] *adj* melodious, tuneful

melon [məlɔ̃] *nm* (*BOT*) (honeydew) melon; (*aussi*: **chapeau melon**) bowler (hat); **melon d'eau** watermelon

membre [mɑ̃bʀ(ə)] *nm* (*ANAT*) limb; (*personne, pays, élément*) member ♦ *adj* member; **être membre de** to be a member of; **membre (viril)** (*male*) organ

mémé [meme] *nf* (*fam*) granny; (: *vieille femme*) old dear

---
MOT CLÉ
---

même [mɛm] *adj* **1** (*avant le nom*) same; **en même temps** at the same time; **ils ont les mêmes goûts** they have the same *ou* similar tastes

2 (*après le nom: renforcement*): **il est la loyauté même** he is loyalty itself; **ce sont ses paroles/celles-là même** they are his very words/the very ones

♦ *pron*: **le(la) même** the same one

♦ *adv* **1** (*renforcement*): **il n'a même pas pleuré** he didn't even cry; **même lui l'a dit** even *HE* said it; **ici même** at this very place; **même si** even if

2: **à même: boire à même la bouteille** straight from the bottle; **à même la peau** next to the skin; **être à même de faire** to be in a position to do, be able to do; **mettre qn à même de faire** to enable sb to do

3: **de même** likewise; **faire de même** to do likewise *ou* the same; **lui de même** so does (*ou* did *ou* is) he; **de même que** just as; **il en va de même pour** the same goes for

---

mémo [memo] (*fam*) *nm* memo

mémoire [memwaʀ] *nf* memory ♦ *nm* (*ADMIN, JUR*) memorandum (*pl* -a); (*SCOL*) dissertation, paper; **avoir la mémoire des visages/chiffres** to have a (good) memory for faces/figures; **n'avoir aucune mémoire** to have a terrible memory; **avoir de la mémoire** to have a good memory; **à la mémoire de** to the *ou* in memory of; **pour mémoire** *adv* for the record; **de mémoire** *adv* from memory; **de mémoire d'homme** in living memory; **mettre en mémoire** (*INFORM*) to store; **mémoire morte** ROM; **mémoire rémanente** *ou* **non volatile** non-volatile memory; **mémoire vive** RAM

mémorable [memɔʀabl(ə)] *adj* memorable

menace [mənas] *nf* threat; **menace en l'air** empty threat

menacer [mənase] *vt* to threaten; **menacer qn de qch/de faire qch** to threaten sb with sth/to do

sth

ménage [menaʒ] *nm* (*travail*) housekeeping, housework; (*couple*) (married) couple; (*famille, ADMIN*) household; **faire le ménage** to do the housework; **faire des ménages** to work as a cleaner (*in people's homes*); **monter son ménage** to set up house; **se mettre en ménage (avec)** to set up house (with); **heureux en ménage** happily married; **faire bon ménage avec** to get on well with; **ménage de poupée** doll's kitchen set; **ménage à trois** love triangle

ménagement [menaʒmɑ̃] *nm* care and attention; **ménagements** *nmpl* (*égards*) consideration *sg*, attention *sg*

ménager [menaʒe] *vt* (*traiter avec mesure*) to handle with tact; to treat considerately; (*utiliser*) to use with care; (: *avec économie*) to use sparingly; (*prendre soin de*) to take (great) care of, look after; (*organiser*) to arrange; (*installer*) to put in; to make; **se ménager** to look after o.s.; **ménager qch à qn** (*réserver*) to have sth in store for sb

ménager, ère [menaʒe, -ɛʀ] *adj* household *cpd*, domestic ♦ *nf* (*femme*) housewife (*pl* -wives); (*couverts*) canteen (*of cutlery*)

mendiant, e [mɑ̃djɑ̃, -ɑ̃t] *nm/f* beggar

mendier [mɑ̃dje] *vi* to beg ♦ *vt* to beg (for); (*fig: éloges, compliments*) to fish for

mener [məne] *vt* to lead; (*enquête*) to conduct; (*affaires*) to manage, conduct, run ♦ *vi*: **mener (à la marque)** to lead, be in the lead; **mener à/dans** (*emmener*) to take to/into; **mener qch à bonne fin** *ou* **à terme** *ou* **à bien** to see sth through (to a successful conclusion), complete sth successfully

meneur, euse [mənœʀ, -øz] *nm/f* leader; (*péj: agitateur*) ringleader; **meneur d'hommes** born leader; **meneur de jeu** host, quizmaster (*BRIT*)

méningite [menɛ̃ʒit] *nf* meningitis *no pl*

ménopause [menɔpoz] *nf* menopause

menotte [mənɔt] *nf* (*langage enfantin*) handie; **menottes** *nfpl* handcuffs; **passer les menottes à** to handcuff

mensonge [mɑ̃sɔ̃ʒ] *nm*: **le mensonge** lying *no pl*; **un mensonge** a lie

mensonger, ère [mɑ̃sɔ̃ʒe, -ɛʀ] *adj* false

mensualité [mɑ̃sɥalite] *nf* (*somme payée*) monthly payment; (*somme perçue*) monthly salary

mensuel, le [mɑ̃sɥɛl] *adj* monthly ♦ *nm/f* (*employé*) employee paid monthly ♦ *nm* (*PRESSE*) monthly

mensurations [mɑ̃syʀasjɔ̃] *nfpl* measurements

mental, e, aux [mɑ̃tal, -o] *adj* mental

mentalité [mɑ̃talite] *nf* mentality

menteur, euse [mɑ̃tœʀ, -øz] *nm/f* liar

menthe [mɑ̃t] *nf* mint; **menthe (à l'eau)** peppermint cordial

mention [mɑ̃sjɔ̃] *nf* (*note*) note, comment; (*SCOL*): **mention (très) bien/passable** (*very*) good/satisfactory pass; **faire mention de** to mention; **"rayer**

la mention inutile" "delete as appropriate"
mentionner [mɑ̃sjɔne] vt to mention

mentir [mɑ̃tiʀ] vi to lie

menton [mɑ̃tɔ̃] nm chin

menu, e [məny] adj (mince) thin; (petit) tiny; (frais, difficulté) minor ♦ adv (couper, hacher) very fine ♦ nm menu; **par le menu** (raconter) in minute detail; **menu touristique** popular ou tourist menu; **menue monnaie** small change

menuiserie [mənɥizʀi] nf (travail) joinery, carpentry; (d'amateur) woodwork; (local) joiner's workshop; (ouvrages) woodwork no pl

menuisier [mənɥizje] nm joiner, carpenter

méprendre [mepʀɑ̃dʀ(ə)]: **se méprendre** vi: **se méprendre sur** to be mistaken about

mépris, e [mepʀi, -iz] pp de **méprendre** ♦ nm (dédain) contempt, scorn; (indifférence): **le mépris de** contempt ou disregard for; **au mépris de** regardless of, in defiance of

méprisable [mepʀizabl(ə)] adj contemptible, despicable

méprisant, e [mepʀizɑ̃, -ɑ̃t] adj contemptuous, scornful

méprise [mepʀiz] nf mistake, error; (malentendu) misunderstanding

mépriser [mepʀize] vt to scorn, despise; (gloire, danger) to scorn, spurn

mer [mɛʀ] nf sea; (marée) tide; **mer fermée** inland sea; **en mer** at sea; **prendre la mer** to put out to sea; **en haute ou pleine mer** off shore, on the open sea; **la mer Adriatique** the Adriatic (Sea); **la mer des Antilles ou des Caraïbes** the Caribbean (Sea); **la mer Baltique** the Baltic (Sea); **la mer Caspienne** the Caspian Sea; **la mer de Corail** the Coral Sea; **la mer Égée** the Aegean (Sea); **la mer Ionienne** the Ionian Sea; **la mer Morte** the Dead Sea; **la mer Noire** the Black Sea; **la mer du Nord** the North Sea; **la mer Rouge** the Red Sea; **la mer des Sargasses** the Sargasso Sea; **les mers du Sud** the South Seas; **la mer Tyrrhénienne** the Tyrrhenian Sea

mercenaire [mɛʀsənɛʀ] nm mercenary

mercerie [mɛʀsəʀi] nf (COUTURE) haberdashery (BRIT), notions pl (US); (boutique) haberdasher's (shop) (BRIT), notions store (US)

merci [mɛʀsi] excl thank you ♦ nf: **à la merci de qn/qch** at sb's mercy/the mercy of sth; **merci beaucoup** thank you very much; **merci de ou pour** thank you for; **sans merci** adj merciless ♦ adv mercilessly

mercredi [mɛʀkʀədi] nm Wednesday; **mercredi des Cendres** Ash Wednesday; voir aussi **lundi**

mercure [mɛʀkyʀ] nm mercury

merde [mɛʀd(ə)] (fam!) nf shit (!) ♦ excl (bloody) hell (!)

mère [mɛʀ] nf mother ♦ adj inv mother cpd; **mère célibataire** single parent, unmarried mother

merguez [mɛʀgɛz] nf spicy North African sausage

méridional, e, aux [meʀidjɔnal, -o] adj southern; (du midi de la France) Southern (French) ♦ nm/f Southerner

meringue [məʀɛ̃g] nf meringue

mérite [meʀit] nm merit; **le mérite (de ceci) lui revient** the credit (for this) is his

mériter [meʀite] vt to deserve; **mériter de réussir** to deserve to succeed; **il mérite qu'on fasse ...** he deserves people to do ...

merlan [mɛʀlɑ̃] nm whiting

merle [mɛʀl(ə)] nm blackbird

merveille [mɛʀvɛj] nf marvel, wonder; **faire merveille ou des merveilles** to work wonders; **à merveille** perfectly, wonderfully

merveilleux, euse [mɛʀvɛjø, -øz] adj marvellous, wonderful

mes [me] adj possessif voir **mon**

mésange [mezɑ̃ʒ] nf tit(mouse) (pl -mice); **mésange bleue** bluetit

mésaventure [mezavɑ̃tyʀ] nf misfortune

Mesdames [medam] nfpl voir **Madame**

Mesdemoiselles [medmwazɛl] nfpl voir **Mademoiselle**

mesquin, e [mɛskɛ̃, -in] adj mean, petty

mesquinerie [mɛskinʀi] nf meanness no pl, pettiness no pl

message [mesaʒ] nm message; **message d'erreur** (INFORM) error message; **message (de guidage)** (INFORM) prompt; **message publicitaire** ad, advertisement; **message SMS** text message; **message téléphoné** telegram dictated by telephone

messager, ère [mesaʒe, -ɛʀ] nm/f messenger

messagerie [mesaʒʀi] nf: **messagerie (électronique)** (electronic) bulletin board; **messagerie rose** lonely hearts and contact service on videotext; **messageries aériennes/maritimes** air freight/shipping service sg; **messageries de presse** press distribution service

messe [mɛs] nf mass; **aller à la messe** to go to mass; **messe de minuit** midnight mass; **faire des messes basses** (fig, péj) to mutter

Messieurs [mesjø] nmpl voir **Monsieur**

mesure [məzyʀ] nf (évaluation, dimension) measurement; (étalon, récipient, contenu) measure; (MUS: cadence) time, tempo; (: division) bar; (retenue) moderation; (disposition) measure, step; **unité/système de mesure** unit/system of measurement; **sur mesure** (costume) made-to-measure; (fig) personally adapted; **à la mesure de** (fig: personne) worthy of; (chambre etc) on the same scale as; **dans la mesure où** insofar as, inasmuch as; **dans une certaine mesure** to some ou a certain extent; **à mesure que** as; **en mesure** (MUS) in time ou tempo; **être en mesure de** to be in a position to; **dépasser la mesure** (fig) to overstep the mark

mesurer [məzyʀe] vt to measure; (juger) to weigh up, assess; (limiter) to limit, ration; (modérer) to moderate; (proportionner): **mesurer qch à** to match sth to, gear sth to; **se mesurer avec** to have a confrontation with; to tackle; **il mesure 1 m 80** he's 1 m 80 tall

met [mɛ] *vb voir* **mettre**

métal, aux [metal, -o] *nm* metal

métallique [metalik] *adj* metallic

météo [meteo] *nf* (*bulletin*) (weather) forecast; (*service*) ≃ Met Office (BRIT), ≃ National Weather Service (US)

météorologie [meteɔʀɔlɔʒi] *nf* (*étude*) meteorology; (*service*) ≃ Meteorological Office (BRIT), ≃ National Weather Service (US)

méthode [metɔd] *nf* method; (*livre, ouvrage*) manual, tutor

méticuleux, euse [metikylø, -øz] *adj* meticulous

métier [metje] *nm* (*profession: gén*) job; (: *manuel*) trade; (: *artisanal*) craft; (*technique, expérience*) (acquired) skill *ou* technique; (*aussi:* **métier à tisser**) (weaving) loom; **être du métier** to be in the trade *ou* profession

métis, se [metis] *adj, nm/f* half-caste, half-breed

métrage [metʀaʒ] *nm* (*de tissu*) length; (CINÉ) footage, length; **long/moyen/court métrage** feature *ou* full-length/medium-length/short film

mètre [mɛtʀ(ə)] *nm* metre (BRIT), meter (US); (*règle*) (metre *ou* meter) rule; (*ruban*) tape measure; **mètre carré/cube** square/cubic metre *ou* meter

métrique [metʀik] *adj* metric ♦ *nf* metrics *sg*

métro [metʀo] *nm* underground (BRIT), subway (US)

métropole [metʀɔpɔl] *nf* (*capitale*) metropolis; (*pays*) home country

mets [mɛ] *nm* dish ♦ *vb voir* **mettre**

metteur [metœʀ] *nm*: **metteur en scène** (THÉÂT) producer; (CINÉ) director; **metteur en ondes** (RADIO) producer

---

MOT CLÉ

mettre [metʀ(ə)] *vt* **1** (*placer*) to put; **mettre en bouteille/en sac** to bottle/put in bags *ou* sacks; **mettre qch à la poste** to post sth (BRIT), mail sth (US); **mettre en examen (pour)** to charge (with) (BRIT), indict (for) (US); **mettre une note gaie/amusante** to inject a cheerful/an amusing note; **mettre qn debout/assis** to help sb up *ou* to their feet/help sb to sit down

2 (*vêtements: revêtir*) to put on; (: *porter*) to wear; **mets ton gilet** put your cardigan on; **je ne mets plus mon manteau** I no longer wear my coat

3 (*faire fonctionner: chauffage, électricité*) to put on; (: *reveil, minuteur*) to set; (*installer: gaz, eau*) to put in, lay on; **mettre en marche** to start up

4 (*consacrer*): **mettre du temps/2 heures à faire qch** to take time/2 hours to do sth *ou* over sth; **y mettre du sien** to pull one's weight

5 (*noter, écrire*) to say, put (down); **qu'est-ce qu'il a mis sur la carte?** what did he say *ou* write on the card?; **mettez au pluriel ...** put ... into the

plural

6 (*supposer*): **mettons que ...** let's suppose *ou* say that ..

7 (*faire + vb*): **faire mettre le gaz/l'électricité** to have gas/electricity put in *ou* installed

se mettre ♦ *vi* **1** (*se placer*): **vous pouvez vous mettre là** you can sit (*ou* stand) there; **où ça se met?** where does it go?; **se mettre au lit** to get into bed; **se mettre au piano** to sit down at the piano; **se mettre à l'eau** to get into the water; **se mettre de l'encre sur les doigts** to get ink on one's fingers

2 (*s'habiller*): **se mettre en maillot de bain** to get into *ou* put on a swimsuit; **n'avoir rien à se mettre** to have nothing to wear

3 (*dans rapports*): **se mettre bien/mal avec qn** to get on the right/wrong side of sb; **se mettre qn à dos** to get on sb's bad side; **se mettre avec qn** (*prendre parti*) to side with sb; (*faire équipe*) to team up with sb; (*en ménage*) to move in with sb

4: **se mettre à** to begin, start; **se mettre à faire** to begin *ou* start doing *ou* to do; **se mettre au piano** to start learning the piano; **se mettre au régime** to go on a diet; **se mettre au travail/à l'étude** to get down to work/one's studies; **il est temps de s'y mettre** it's time we got down to it *ou* got on with it

---

meuble [mœbl(ə)] *nm* (*objet*) piece of furniture; (*ameublement*) furniture *no pl* ♦ *adj* (*terre*) loose, friable; (JUR): **biens meubles** movables

meublé [mœble] *nm* (*pièce*) furnished room; (*appartement*) furnished flat (BRIT) *ou* apartment (US)

meubler [mœble] *vt* to furnish; (*fig*): **meubler qch (de)** to fill sth (with); **se meubler** to furnish one's house

meugler [mœgle] *vi* to low, moo

meule [møl] *nf* (*à broyer*) millstone; (*à aiguiser*) grindstone; (*à polir*) buffwheel; (*de foin, blé*) stack; (*de fromage*) round

meunier, ière [mønje, -jɛʀ] *nm* miller ♦ *nf* miller's wife ♦ *adj f* (CULIN) meunière

meurtre [mœʀtʀ(ə)] *nm* murder

meurtrier, ière [mœʀtʀije, -jɛʀ] *adj* (*arme, épidémie, combat*) deadly; (*accident*) fatal; (*carrefour, route*) lethal; (*fureur, instincts*) murderous ♦ *nm/f* murderer/murderess ♦ *nf* (*ouverture*) loophole

meurtrir [mœʀtʀiʀ] *vt* to bruise; (*fig*) to wound

meurtrissure [mœʀtʀisyʀ] *nf* bruise; (*fig*) scar

meus [mœ] *etc vb voir* **mouvoir**

meute [møt] *nf* pack

mexicain, e [mɛksikɛ̃, -ɛn] *adj* Mexican ♦ *nm/f*: **Mexicain, e** Mexican

Mexico [mɛksiko] *n* Mexico City

Mexique [mɛksik] *nm*: **le Mexique** Mexico

Mgr *abr* = **Monseigneur**

mi [mi] *nm* (MUS) E; (*en chantant la gamme*) mi
miauler [mjole] *vi* to miaow
mi-bas [miba] *nm inv* knee-length sock
miche [miʃ] *nf* round ou cob loaf
mi-chemin [miʃmɛ̃]: **à mi-chemin** *adv* halfway, midway
mi-clos, e [miklo, -kloz] *adj* half-closed
micro [mikro] *nm* mike, microphone; (INFORM) micro; **micro cravate** lapel mike
microbe [mikrɔb] *nm* germ, microbe
micro-onde [mikrɔɔ̃d] *nf*: **four à micro-ondes** microwave oven
micro-ordinateur [mikrɔɔrdinatœr] *nm* microcomputer
microscope [mikrɔskɔp] *nm* microscope; **au microscope** under ou through the microscope
microscopique [mikrɔskɔpik] *adj* microscopic
midi [midi] *nm* (*milieu du jour*) midday, noon; (*moment du déjeuner*) lunchtime; (*sud*) south; (: *de la France*): **le Midi** the South (of France), the Midi; **à midi** at 12 (o'clock) ou midday ou noon; **tous les midis** every lunchtime; **le repas de midi** lunch; **en plein midi** (right) in the middle of the day; (*sud*) facing south
mie [mi] *nf* inside (of the loaf)
miel [mjɛl] *nm* honey; **être tout miel** (*fig*) to be all sweetness and light
mielleux, euse [mjɛlø, -øz] *adj* (*péj*) sugary, honeyed
mien, ne [mjɛ̃, mjɛn] *adj, pron*: **le (la) mien(ne)**, **les miens** mine; **les miens** (*ma famille*) my family
miette [mjɛt] *nf* (*de pain, gâteau*) crumb; (*fig: de la conversation etc*) scrap; **en miettes** (*fig*) in pieces ou bits

---

MOT CLÉ

mieux [mjø] *adv* **1** (*d'une meilleure façon*): **mieux (que)** better (than); **elle travaille/mange mieux** she works/eats better; **aimer mieux** to prefer; **j'attendais mieux de vous** I expected better of you; **elle va mieux** she is better; **de mieux en mieux** better and better

2 (*de la meilleure façon*) best; **ce que je sais le mieux** what I know best; **les livres les mieux faits** the best made books

3 (*intensif*): **vous feriez mieux de faire ...** you would be better to do ...; **crier à qui mieux mieux** to try to shout each other down

♦ *adj* **1** (*plus à l'aise, en meilleure forme*) better; **se sentir mieux** to feel better

2 (*plus satisfaisant*) better; **c'est mieux ainsi** it's better like this; **c'est le mieux des deux** it's the better of the two; **le(la) mieux, les mieux** the best; **demandez-lui, c'est le mieux** ask him, it's the best thing

3 (*plus joli*) better-looking; (*plus gentil*) nicer; **il est mieux que son frère** (*plus beau*) he's better-looking than his brother; (*plus gentil*) he's nicer

than his brother; **il est mieux sans moustache** he looks better without a moustache

4: **au mieux** at best; **au mieux avec** on the best of terms with; **pour le mieux** for the best; **qui mieux est** even better, better still

♦ *nm* **1** (*progrès*) improvement

2: **de mon/ton mieux** as best I/you can (*ou could*); **faire de son mieux** to do one's best; **du mieux qu'il peut** the best he can; **faute de mieux** for lack ou want of anything better, failing anything better

---

mièvre [mjɛvr(ə)] *adj* sickly sentimental
mignon, ne [miɲɔ̃, -ɔn] *adj* sweet, cute
migraine [migrɛn] *nf* headache; migraine
mijoter [miʒɔte] *vt* to simmer; (*préparer avec soin*) to cook lovingly; (*affaire, projet*) to plot, cook up ♦ *vi* to simmer
mil [mil] *num* = **mille**
milieu, x [miljø] *nm* (*centre*) middle; (*fig*) middle course ou way; (*aussi*: **juste milieu**) happy medium; (BIO, GÉO) environment; (*entourage social*) milieu; (*familial*) background; circle; (*pègre*): **le milieu** the underworld; **au milieu de** in the middle of; **au beau ou en plein milieu (de)** right in the middle (of); **milieu de terrain** (FOOTBALL: *joueur*) midfield player; (: *joueurs*) midfield
militaire [militɛr] *adj* military ♦ *nm* serviceman; **service militaire** military service
militant, e [militɑ̃, -ɑ̃t] *adj, nm/f* militant
militer [milite] *vi* to be a militant; **militer pour/contre** to militate in favour of/against
mille [mil] *num* a ou one thousand ♦ *nm* (*mesure*): **mille (marin)** nautical mile; **mettre dans le mille** to hit the bull's-eye; (*fig*) to be bang on (target)
millefeuille [milfœj] *nm* cream ou vanilla slice
millénaire [milenɛr] *nm* millennium ♦ *adj* thousand-year-old; (*fig*) ancient
mille-pattes [milpat] *nm inv* centipede
millésimé, e [milezime] *adj* vintage *cpd*
millet [mijɛ] *nm* millet
milliard [miljar] *nm* milliard, thousand million (BRIT), billion (US)
milliardaire [miljardɛr] *nm/f* multimillionaire (BRIT), billionaire (US)
millier [milje] *nm* thousand; **un millier (de)** a thousand or so, about a thousand; **par milliers** in (their) thousands, by the thousand
milligramme [miligram] *nm* milligramme (BRIT), milligram (US)
millimètre [milimɛtr(ə)] *nm* millimetre (BRIT), millimeter (US)
million [miljɔ̃] *nm* million; **deux millions de** two million; **riche à millions** worth millions
millionnaire [miljɔnɛr] *nm/f* millionaire
mime [mim] *nm/f* (*acteur*) mime(r); (*imitateur*) mimic ♦ *nm* (*art*) mime, miming

mimer [mime] *vt* to mime; (*singer*) to mimic, take off

mimique [mimik] *nf* (*funny*) face; (*signes*) gesticulations *pl*, sign language *no pl*

minable [minabl(ə)] *adj* (*personne*) shabby(-looking); (*travail*) pathetic

mince [mɛ̃s] *adj* thin; (*personne, taille*) slim; (*fig: profit, connaissances*) slight, small; (: *prétexte*) weak ♦ *excl*: **mince (alors)!** darn it!

minceur [mɛ̃sœʀ] *nf* thinness; slimness, slenderness

mincir [mɛ̃siʀ] *vi* to get slimmer *ou* thinner

mine [min] *nf* (*physionomie*) expression, look; (*extérieur*) exterior, appearance; (*de crayon*) lead; (*gisement, exploitation, explosif*) mine; **mines** *nfpl* (*péj*) simpering airs; **les Mines** (ADMIN) the national mining and geological service; the government vehicle testing department; **avoir bonne mine** (BRIT) (*personne*) to look well; (*ironique*) to look an utter idiot; **avoir mauvaise mine** to look unwell; **faire mine de faire** to make a pretence of doing; **ne pas payer de mine** to be not much to look at; **mine de rien** *adv* with a casual air; although you wouldn't think so; **mine de charbon** coalmine; **mine à ciel ouvert** opencast (BRIT) *ou* open-air (US) mine

miner [mine] *vt* (*saper*) to undermine, erode; (MIL) to mine

minerai [minʀɛ] *nm* ore

minéral, e, aux [mineʀal, -o] *adj* mineral; (CHIMIE) inorganic ♦ *nm* mineral

minéralogique [mineʀalɔʒik] *adj* mineralogical; **plaque minéralogique** number (BRIT) *ou* license (US) plate; **numéro minéralogique** registration (BRIT) *ou* license (US) number

minet, te [minɛ, -ɛt] *nm/f* (*chat*) pussy-cat; (*péj*) young trendy

mineur, e [minœʀ] *adj* minor ♦ *nm/f* (JUR) minor ♦ *nm* (*travailleur*) miner; (MIL) sapper; **mineur de fond** face worker

miniature [minjatyʀ] *adj, nf* miniature

minibus [minibys] *nm* minibus

mini-cassette [minikasɛt] *nf* cassette (recorder)

minier, ière [minje, -jɛʀ] *adj* mining

mini-jupe [miniʒyp] *nf* mini-skirt

minimal, e, aux [minimal, -o] *adj* minimum

minime [minim] *adj* minor, minimal ♦ *nm/f* (SPORT) junior

minimiser [minimize] *vt* to minimize; (*fig*) to play down

minimum [minimɔm] *adj, nm* minimum; **au minimum** at the very least; **minimum vital** (*salaire*) living wage; (*niveau de vie*) subsistance level

ministère [ministɛʀ] *nm* (*cabinet*) government; (*département*) ministry (BRIT), department; (REL) ministry; **ministère public** (JUR) Prosecution, State Prosecutor

ministre [ministʀ(ə)] *nm* minister (BRIT), secretary; (REL) minister; **ministre d'État** senior minister *ou* secretary

Minitel® [minitɛl] *nm* videotext terminal and service; see boxed note

MINITEL

Minitel is a computer system provided by France-Télécom to telephone subscribers. The terminal is supplied free of charge. The system serves as a computerized telephone directory as well as providing a wide variety of other services, including train timetables, stock market news and situations vacant. Services are accessed by dialling the relevant number on the telephone, and charges are added to the subscriber's telephone bill.

minoritaire [minɔʀitɛʀ] *adj* minority *cpd*

minorité [minɔʀite] *nf* minority; **être en minorité** to be in the *ou* a minority; **mettre en minorité** (POL) to defeat

minuit [minɥi] *nm* midnight

minuscule [minyskyl] *adj* minute, tiny ♦ *nf*: (*lettre*) **minuscule** small letter

minute [minyt] *nf* minute; (JUR: *original*) minute, draft ♦ *excl* just a minute!, hang on!; **à la minute** (*présent*) (just) this instant; (*passé*) there and then; **entrecôte** *ou* **steak minute** minute steak

minuter [minyte] *vt* to time

minuterie [minytʀi] *nf* time switch

minutieux, euse [minysjø, -øz] *adj* (*personne*) meticulous; (*inspection*) minutely detailed; (*travail*) requiring painstaking attention to detail

mirabelle [miʀabɛl] *nf* (*fruit*) (cherry) plum; (*eau-de-vie*) plum brandy

miracle [miʀakl(ə)] *nm* miracle

mirage [miʀaʒ] *nm* mirage

mire [miʀ] *nf* (*d'un fusil*) sight; (TV) test card; **point de mire** target; (*fig*) focal point; **ligne de mire** line of sight

miroir [miʀwaʀ] *nm* mirror

miroiter [miʀwate] *vi* to sparkle, shimmer; **faire miroiter qch à qn** to paint sth in glowing colours for sb, dangle sth in front of sb's eyes

mis, e [mi, miz] *pp de* **mettre** ♦ *adj* (*couvert, table*) set, laid; (*personne*): **bien mis** well dressed ♦ *nf* (*argent: au jeu*) stake; (*tenue*) clothing; attire; **être de mise** to be acceptable *ou* in season; **mise en bouteilles** bottling; **mise en examen** charging, indictment; **mise à feu** blast-off; **mise de fonds** capital outlay; **mise à jour** updating; **mise à mort** kill; **mise à pied** (*d'un employé*) suspension; lay-off; **mise sur pied** (*d'une affaire, entreprise*) setting up; **mise en plis** set; **mise au point** (PHOTO) focusing; (*fig*) clarification; **mise à prix** reserve (BRIT) *ou* upset price; **mise en scène** production

mise [miz] *adj f*, *nf voir* **mis**

miser [mize] *vt (enjeu)* to stake, bet; **miser sur** *vt (cheval, numéro)* to bet on; *(fig)* to bank *ou* count on

misérable [mizerabl(ə)] *adj (lamentable, malheureux)* pitiful, wretched; *(pauvre)* poverty-stricken; *(insignifiant, mesquin)* miserable ◆ *nm/f* wretch; *(miséreux)* poor wretch

misère [mizer] *nf (pauvreté)* (extreme) poverty, destitution; **misères** *nfpl (malheurs)* woes, miseries; *(ennuis)* little troubles; **être dans la misère** to be destitute *ou* poverty-stricken; **salaire de misère** starvation wage; **faire des misères à qn** to torment sb; **misère noire** utter destitution

missile [misil] *nm* missile

mission [misjɔ̃] *nf* mission; **partir en mission** *(ADMIN, POL)* to go on an assignment

missionnaire [misjɔnɛr] *nm/f* missionary

mit [mi] *vb voir* **mettre**

mité, e [mite] *adj* moth-eaten

mi-temps [mitɑ̃] *nf inv (SPORT: période)* half *(pl halves)*; *(: pause)* half-time; **à mi-temps** *adj, adv* part-time

miteux, euse [mitø, -øz] *adj* seedy, shabby

mitigé, e [mitiʒe] *adj (conviction, ardeur)* lukewarm; *(sentiments)* mixed

mitonner [mitɔne] *vt (préparer)* to cook with loving care; *(fig)* to cook up quietly

mitoyen, ne [mitwajɛ̃, -ɛn] *adj* common, party *cpd*; **maisons mitoyennes** semi-detached houses; *(plus de deux)* terraced *(BRIT) ou* row *(US)* houses

mitrailler [mitraje] *vt* to machine-gun; *(fig: photographier)* to snap away at; **mitrailler qn de** to pelt *ou* bombard sb with

mitraillette [mitrajɛt] *nf* submachine gun

mitrailleuse [mitrajøz] *nf* machine gun

mi-voix [mivwa]: **à mi-voix** *adv* in a low *ou* hushed voice

mixage [miksaʒ] *nm (CINÉ)* (sound) mixing

mixer, mixeur [miksœr] *nm (CULIN)* (food) mixer

mixte [mikst(ə)] *adj (gén)* mixed; *(SCOL)* mixed, coeducational; **à usage mixte** dual-purpose; **cuisinière mixte** combined gas and electric cooker; **équipe mixte** combined team

mixture [mikstyr] *nf* mixture; *(fig)* concoction

MJC *sigle f (= maison des jeunes et de la culture)* community arts centre and youth club

Mlle, *pl* **Mlles** *abr* = **Mademoiselle**

MM *abr* = **Messieurs**; *voir* **Monsieur**

Mme, *pl* **Mmes** *abr* = **Madame**

mobile [mɔbil] *adj* mobile; *(amovible)* loose, removable; *(pièce de machine)* moving; *(élément de meuble etc)* movable ◆ *nm (motif)* motive; *(fam: téléphone)* mobile; *(œuvre d'art)* mobile; *(PHYSIQUE)* moving object *ou* body

mobilier, ière [mɔbilje, -jɛr] *adj (JUR)* personal ◆ *nm (meubles)* furniture; **valeurs mobilières** transferable securities; **vente mobilière** sale of personal property *ou* chattels

mobiliser [mɔbilize] *vt (MIL, gén)* to mobilize

mobylette® [mɔbilɛt] *nf* moped

mocassin [mɔkasɛ̃] *nm* moccasin

moche [mɔʃ] *adj (fam: laid)* ugly; *(: mauvais, méprisable)* rotten

modalité [mɔdalite] *nf* form, mode; **modalités** *nfpl (d'un accord etc)* clauses, terms; **modalités de paiement** methods of payment

mode [mɔd] *nf* fashion; *(commerce)* fashion trade *ou* industry ◆ *nm (manière)* form, mode, method; *(LING)* mood; *(INFORM, MUS)* mode; **travailler dans la mode** to be in the fashion business; **à la mode** fashionable, in fashion; **mode dialogué** *(INFORM)* interactive *ou* conversational mode; **mode d'emploi** directions *pl* (for use); **mode de vie** way of life

modèle [mɔdɛl] *adj* model ◆ *nm* model; *(qui pose: de peintre)* sitter; *(type)* type; *(gabarit, patron)* pattern; **modèle courant** *ou* **de série** *(COMM)* production model; **modèle déposé** registered design; **modèle réduit** small-scale model

modeler [mɔdle] *vt (ART)* to model, mould; *(suj: vêtement, érosion)* to mould, shape; **modeler qch sur/d'après** to model sth on

modem [mɔdɛm] *nm* modem

modéré, e [mɔdere] *adj, nm/f* moderate

modérer [mɔdere] *vt* to moderate; **se modérer** *vi* to restrain o.s

moderne [mɔdɛrn(ə)] *adj* modern ◆ *nm (ART)* modern style; *(ameublement)* modern furniture

moderniser [mɔdɛrnize] *vt* to modernize

modeste [mɔdɛst(ə)] *adj* modest; *(origine)* humble, lowly

modestie [mɔdɛsti] *nf* modesty; **fausse modestie** false modesty

modifier [mɔdifje] *vt* to modify, alter; *(LING)* to modify; **se modifier** *vi* to alter

modique [mɔdik] *adj (salaire, somme)* modest

modiste [mɔdist(ə)] *nf* milliner

module [mɔdyl] *nm* module

moelle [mwal] *nf* marrow; *(fig)* pith, core; **moelle épinière** spinal chord

moelleux, euse [mwalø, -øz] *adj* soft; *(au goût, à l'ouïe)* mellow; *(gracieux, souple)* smooth

mœurs [mœr] *nfpl (conduite)* morals; *(manières)* manners; *(pratiques sociales)* habits; *(mode de vie)* life style *sg*; *(d'une espèce animale)* behaviour *sg (BRIT)*, behavior *sg (US)*; **femme de mauvaises mœurs** loose woman; **passer dans les mœurs** to become the custom; **contraire aux bonnes mœurs** contrary to proprieties

mohair [mɔɛr] *nm* mohair

moi [mwa] *pron* me; *(emphatique)*: **moi, je ...** for my part, I ..., I myself ... ◆ *nm inv (PSYCH)* ego, self; **à moi!** *(à l'aide)* help (me)!

moi-même [mwamɛm] *pron* myself; *(emphatique)* I myself

moindre [mwɛ̃dʀ(ə)] *adj* lesser; lower; **le(la) moindre, les moindres** the least; the slightest; **le (la) moindre de** the least of; **c'est la moindre des choses** it's nothing at all

moine [mwan] *nm* monk, friar

moineau, x [mwano] *nm* sparrow

MOT-CLÉ

---

moins [mwɛ̃] *adv* **1** (*comparatif*): **moins (que)** less (than); **moins grand que** less tall than, not as tall as; **il a 3 ans de moins que moi** he's 3 years younger than me; **il est moins intelligent que moi** he's not as clever as me, he's less clever than me; **moins je travaille, mieux je me porte** the less I work, the better I feel

2 (*superlatif*): **le moins** (the) least; **c'est ce que j'aime le moins** it's what I like (the) least; **le(la) moins doué(e)** the least gifted; **au moins, du moins** at least; **pour le moins** at the very least

3: **moins de** (*quantité*) less (than); (*nombre*) fewer (than); **moins de sable/d'eau** less sand/water; **moins de livres/gens** fewer books/people; **moins de 2 ans** less than 2 years; **moins de midi** not yet midday

4: **de moins, en moins: 100 €/3 jours de moins** 100 €/3 days less; **3 livres en moins** 3 books fewer; 3 books too few; **de l'argent en moins** less money; **le soleil en moins** but for the sun, minus the sun; **de moins en moins** less and less; **en moins de deux** in a flash *ou* a trice

5: **à moins de, à moins que** unless; **à moins de faire** unless we do (*ou* he does *etc*); **à moins que tu ne fasses** unless you do; **à moins d'un accident** barring any accident

♦ *prép*: **4 moins 2** 4 minus 2; **10 heures moins 5** 5 to 10; **il fait moins 5** it's 5 (degrees) below (freezing), it's minus 5; **il est moins 5** it's 5 to

♦ *nm* (*signe*) minus sign

---

mois [mwa] *nm* month; (*salaire, somme dû*) (monthly) pay *ou* salary; **treizième mois, double mois** extra month's salary

moisi, e [mwazi] *adj* mouldy (*BRIT*), moldy (*US*), mildewed ♦ *nm* mould, mold mildew; **odeur de moisi** musty smell

moisir [mwaziʀ] *vi* to go mouldy (*BRIT*) *ou* moldy (*US*); (*fig*) to rot; (*personne*) to hang about ♦ *vt* to make mouldy *ou* moldy

moisissure [mwazisyʀ] *nf* mould *no pl* (*BRIT*), mold *no pl* (*US*)

moisson [mwasɔ̃] *nf* harvest; (*époque*) harvest (time); (*fig*): **faire une moisson de** to gather a wealth of

moissonner [mwasɔne] *vt* to harvest, reap; (*fig*) to collect

moissonneur, euse [mwasɔnœʀ, -øz] *nm/f* harvester, reaper ♦ *nf* (*machine*) harvester

moite [mwat] *adj* (*peau, mains*) sweaty, sticky; (*atmosphère*) muggy

moitié [mwatje] *nf* half (*pl* halves); (*épouse*): **sa moitié** his better half; **la moitié** half; **la moitié de** half (of), half the amount (*ou* number) of; **la moitié du temps/des gens** half the time/the people; **à la moitié de** halfway through; **moitié moins grand** half as tall; **moitié plus long** half as long again, longer by half; **à moitié** half (*avant le verbe*), half- (*avant l'adjectif*); **à moitié prix** (at) half price, half-price; **de moitié** by half; **moitié moitié** half-and-half

moka [mɔka] *nm* (*café*) mocha coffee; (*gâteau*) mocha cake

mol [mɔl] *adj m voir* **mou**

molaire [mɔlɛʀ] *nf* molar

molester [mɔleste] *vt* to manhandle, maul (about)

molle [mɔl] *adj f voir* **mou**

mollement [mɔlmɑ̃] *adv* softly; (*péj*) sluggishly; (*protester*) feebly

mollet [mɔlɛ] *nm* calf (*pl* calves) ♦ *adj m*: **œuf mollet** soft-boiled egg

molletonné, e [mɔltɔne] *adj* (*gants etc*) fleece-lined

mollir [mɔliʀ] *vi* (*jambes*) to give way; (*NAVIG: vent*) to drop, die down; (*fig: personne*) to relent; (: *courage*) to fail, flag

mollusque [mɔlysk(ə)] *nm* (*ZOOL*) mollusc; (*fig: personne*) lazy lump

môme [mom] *nm/f* (*fam: enfant*) brat; (: *fille*) bird (*BRIT*), chick

moment [mɔmɑ̃] *nm* moment; (*occasion*): **profiter du moment** to take (advantage of) the opportunity; **ce n'est pas le moment** this is not the right time; **à un certain moment** at some point; **à un moment donné** at a certain point; **à quel moment?** when exactly?; **au même moment** at the same time; (*instant*) at the same moment; **pour un bon moment** for a good while; **pour le moment** for the moment, for the time being; **au moment de** at the time of; **au moment où** as; at a time when; **à tout moment** at any time *ou* moment; (*continuellement*) constantly, continually; **en ce moment** at the moment; (*aujourd'hui*) at present; **sur le moment** at the time; **par moments** now and then, at times; **d'un moment à l'autre** any time (now); **du moment où** *ou* **que** seeing that, since; **n'avoir pas un moment à soi** not to have a minute to oneself

momentané, e [mɔmɑ̃tane] *adj* temporary, momentary

momentanément [mɔmɑ̃tanemɑ̃] *adv* for a moment, for a while

momie [mɔmi] *nf* mummy

mon [mɔ̃], **ma** [ma], *pl* **mes** [me], *adj possessif* my

Monaco [mɔnako] *nm*: **le Monaco** Monaco

monarchie [mɔnaʀʃi] *nf* monarchy

monastère [mɔnastɛʀ] *nm* monastery

monceau, x [mɔ̃so] *nm* heap

mondain, e [mɔ̃dɛ̃, -ɛn] *adj* (*soirée, vie*) society

cpd; (*obligations*) social; (*peintre, écrivain*) fashionable; (*personne*) society *cpd* ♦ *nm/f* society man/woman, socialite ♦ *nf*: **la Mondaine, la police mondaine** ≃ the vice squad

monde [mɔ̃d] *nm* world; (*personnes mondaines*): **le monde** (high) society; (*milieu*): **être du même monde** to move in the same circles; (*gens*): **il y a du monde** (*beaucoup de gens*) there are a lot of people; (*quelques personnes*) there are some people; **y a-t-il du monde dans le salon?** is there anybody in the lounge?; **beaucoup/peu de monde** many/few people; **le meilleur** *etc* **du monde** the best *etc* in the world; **mettre au monde** to bring into the world; **pas le moins du monde** not in the least; **se faire un monde de qch** to make a great deal of fuss about sth; **tour du monde** round-the-world trip; **homme/femme du monde** society man/woman

mondial, e, aux [mɔ̃djal, -o] *adj* (*population*) world *cpd*; (*influence*) world-wide

mondialement [mɔ̃djalmɑ̃] *adv* throughout the world

mondialisation [mɔ̃djalizasjɔ̃] *nf* globalization

monégasque [mɔnegask(ə)] *adj* Monegasque, of *ou* from Monaco ♦ *nm/f*: **Monégasque** Monegasque

monétaire [mɔnetɛʀ] *adj* monetary

moniteur, trice [mɔnitœʀ, -tʀis] *nm/f* (*SPORT*) instructor/instructress; (*de colonie de vacances*) supervisor ♦ *nm* (*écran*) monitor; **moniteur cardiaque** cardiac monitor; **moniteur d'auto-école** driving instructor

monnaie [mɔnɛ] *nf* (*pièce*) coin; (*ÉCON: gén: moyen d'échange*) currency; (*petites pièces*): **avoir de la monnaie** to have (some) change; **faire de la monnaie** to get (some) change; **avoir/faire la monnaie de 20 €** to have change of/get change for 20 €; **faire** *ou* **donner à qn la monnaie de 20 €** to give sb change of 20 €, change 20 € for sb; **rendre à qn la monnaie (sur 20 €)** to give sb the change (from *ou* out of 20 €); **servir de monnaie d'échange** (*fig*) to be used as a bargaining counter *ou* as bargaining counters; **payer en monnaie de singe** to fob (sb) off with empty promises; **c'est monnaie courante** it's a common occurrence; **monnaie légale** legal tender

monnayer [mɔneje] *vt* to convert into cash; (*talent*) to capitalize on

monologue [mɔnɔlɔg] *nm* monologue, soliloquy; **monologue intérieur** stream of consciousness

monopole [mɔnɔpɔl] *nm* monopoly

monotone [mɔnɔtɔn] *adj* monotonous

Monsieur [məsjø], *pl* **Messieurs** [mesjø] *titre* Mr ['mɪstə*] ♦ *nm* (*homme quelconque*): **un/le monsieur** a/the gentleman; *voir aussi* **Madame**

monstre [mɔ̃stʀ(ə)] *nm* monster ♦ *adj* (*fam: effet, publicité*) massive; **un travail monstre** a fantastic amount of work; an enormous job; **monstre sacré** superstar

monstrueux, euse [mɔ̃stʀyø, -øz] *adj* monstrous

mont [mɔ̃] *nm*: **par monts et par vaux** up hill and down dale; **le Mont Blanc** Mont Blanc; **mont de Vénus** mons veneris

montage [mɔ̃taʒ] *nm* putting up; (*d'un bijou*) mounting, setting; (*d'une machine etc*) assembly; (*PHOTO*) photomontage; (*CINÉ*) editing; **montage sonore** sound editing

montagnard, e [mɔ̃taɲaʀ, -aʀd(ə)] *adj* mountain *cpd* ♦ *nm/f* mountain-dweller

montagne [mɔ̃taɲ] *nf* (*cime*) mountain; (*région*): **la montagne** the mountains *pl*; **la haute montagne** the high mountains; **les montagnes Rocheuses** the Rocky Mountains, the Rockies; **montagnes russes** big dipper *sg*, switchback *sg*

montagneux, euse [mɔ̃taɲø, -øz] *adj* mountainous; hilly

montant, e [mɔ̃tɑ̃, -ɑ̃t] *adj* (*mouvement, marée*) rising; (*chemin*) uphill; (*robe, corsage*) high-necked ♦ *nm* (*somme, total*) (sum) total, (total) amount; (*de fenêtre*) upright; (*de lit*) post

monte-charge [mɔ̃tʃaʀʒ(ə)] *nm inv* goods lift, hoist

montée [mɔ̃te] *nf* rising, rise; (*escalade*) ascent, climb; (*chemin*) way up; (*côte*) hill; **au milieu de la montée** halfway up; **le moteur chauffe dans les montées** the engine overheats going uphill

monter [mɔ̃te] *vt* (*escalier, côte*) to go (*ou* come) up; (*valise, paquet*) to take (*ou* bring) up; (*cheval*) to mount; (*femelle*) to cover, serve; (*tente, échafaudage*) to put up; (*machine*) to assemble; (*bijou*) to mount, set; (*COUTURE*) to sew on; (: *manche*) to set in; (*CINÉ*) to edit; (*THÉÂT*) to put on, stage; (*société, coup etc*) to set up; (*fournir, équiper*) to equip ♦ *vi* to go (*ou* come) up; (*avion, voiture*) to climb, go up; (*chemin, niveau, température, voix, prix*) to go up, rise; (*brouillard, bruit*) to rise, come up; (*passager*) to get on; (*à cheval*): **monter bien/mal** to ride well/badly; **monter à cheval/bicyclette** to get on *ou* mount a horse/bicycle; (*faire du cheval etc*) to ride (a horse); (: ride a) bicycle; **monter à pied/en voiture** to walk/ drive up, go up on foot/ by car; **monter dans le train/l'avion** to get into the train/plane, board the train/plane; **monter sur** to climb up onto; **monter sur** *ou* **à un arbre/une échelle** to climb (up) a tree/ladder; **monter à bord** to (get on) board; **monter à la tête de qn** to go to sb's head; **monter sur les planches** to go on the stage; **monter en grade** to be promoted; **se monter** (*s'équiper*) to equip o.s., get kitted out (*BRIT*); **se monter à** (*frais etc*) to add up to, come to; **monter qn contre qn** to set sb against sb; **monter la tête à qn** to give sb ideas

montre [mɔ̃tʀ(ə)] *nf* watch; (*ostentation*): **pour la montre** for show; **montre en main** exactly, to the minute; **faire montre de** to show, display; **contre**

la **montre** (*SPORT*) against the clock; **montre de plongée** diver's watch

montre-bracelet, *pl* **montres-bracelets** [mɔ̃trabraslɛ] *nf* wristwatch

montrer [mɔ̃tre] *vt* to show; **se montrer** to appear; **montrer qch à qn** to show sb sth; **montrer qch du doigt** to point to sth, point one's finger at sth; **se montrer intelligent** to prove (to be) intelligent

monture [mɔ̃tyʀ] *nf* (*bête*) mount; (*d'une bague*) setting; (*de lunettes*) frame

monument [mɔnymɑ̃] *nm* monument; **monument aux morts** war memorial

moquer [mɔke]: **se moquer de** *vt* to make fun of, laugh at; (*fam: se désintéresser de*) not to care about; (*tromper*): **se moquer de qn** to take sb for a ride

moquerie [mɔkri] *nf* mockery *no pl*

moquette [mɔkɛt] *nf* fitted carpet, wall-to-wall carpeting *no pl*

moqueur, euse [mɔkœr, -øz] *adj* mocking

moral, e, aux [mɔral, -o] *adj* moral ♦ *nm* morale ♦ *nf* (*conduite*) morals *pl*; (*règles*) moral code, ethic; (*valeurs*) moral standards *pl*; morality; (*science*) ethics *sg*, moral philosophy; (*conclusion: d'une fable etc*) moral; **au moral, sur le plan moral** morally; **avoir le moral à zéro** to be really down; **faire la morale à** to lecture, preach at

moralité [mɔralite] *nf* (*d'une action, attitude*) morality; (*conduite*) morals *pl*; (*conclusion, enseignement*) moral

morceau, x [mɔrso] *nm* piece, bit; (*d'une œuvre*) passage, extract; (*MUS*) piece; (*CULIN: de viande*) cut; **mettre en morceaux** to pull to pieces *ou* bits

morceler [mɔrsəle] *vt* to break up, divide up

mordant, e [mɔrdɑ̃, -ɑ̃t] *adj* scathing, cutting; (*froid*) biting ♦ *nm* (*dynamisme, énergie*) spirit; (*fougue*) bite, punch

mordiller [mɔrdije] *vt* to nibble at, chew at

mordre [mɔrdr(ə)] *vt* to bite; (*suj: lime, vis*) to bite into ♦ *vi* (*poisson*) to bite; **mordre dans** to bite into; **mordre sur** (*fig*) to go over into, overlap into; **mordre à qch** (*comprendre, aimer*) to take to; **mordre à l'hameçon** to bite, rise to the bait

mordu, e [mɔrdy] *pp de* **mordre** ♦ *adj* (*amoureux*) smitten ♦ *nm/f*: **un mordu du jazz/de la voile** a jazz/sailing fanatic *ou* buff

morfondre [mɔrfɔ̃dr(ə)]: **se morfondre** *vi* to mope

morgue [mɔrg(ə)] *nf* (*arrogance*) haughtiness; (*lieu: de la police*) morgue; (: *à l'hôpital*) mortuary

morne [mɔrn(ə)] *adj* (*personne, visage*) glum, gloomy; (*temps, vie*) dismal, dreary

morose [mɔroz] *adj* sullen, morose; (*marché*) sluggish

mors [mɔr] *nm* bit

morse [mɔrs(ə)] *nm* (*ZOOL*) walrus; (*TÉL*) Morse (code)

morsure [mɔrsyr] *nf* bite

mort¹ [mɔr] *nf* death; **se donner la mort** to take one's own life; **de mort** (*silence, pâleur*) deathly; **blessé à mort** fatally wounded *ou* injured; **à la vie, à la mort** for better, for worse; **mort clinique** brain death; **mort subite du nourrisson, mort au berceau** cot death

mort², e [mɔr, mɔrt(ə)] *pp de* **mourir** ♦ *adj* dead ♦ *nm/f* (*défunt*) dead man/woman; (*victime*): **il y a eu plusieurs morts** several people were killed, there were several killed ♦ *nm* (*CARTES*) dummy; **mort ou vif** dead or alive; **mort de peur/fatigue** frightened to death/dead tired; **morts et blessés** casualties; **faire le mort** to play dead; (*fig*) to lie low

mortalité [mɔrtalite] *nf* mortality, death rate

mortel, le [mɔrtɛl] *adj* (*poison etc*) deadly, lethal; (*accident, blessure*) fatal; (*REL: danger, frayeur*) mortal; (*fig: froid*) deathly; (: *ennui, soirée*) deadly (boring) ♦ *nm/f* mortal

mortier [mɔrtje] *nm* (*gén*) mortar

mort-né, e [mɔrne] *adj* (*enfant*) stillborn; (*fig*) abortive

mortuaire [mɔrtyer] *adj* funeral *cpd*; **avis mortuaires** death announcements, intimations; **chapelle mortuaire** mortuary chapel; **couronne mortuaire** (funeral) wreath; **domicile mortuaire** house of the deceased; **drap mortuaire** pall

morue [mɔry] *nf* (*ZOOL*) cod *inv*; (*CULIN: salée*) saltcod

mosaïque [mɔzaik] *nf* (*ART*) mosaic; (*fig*) patchwork

Moscou [mɔsku] *n* Moscow

mosquée [mɔske] *nf* mosque

mot [mo] *nm* word; (*message*) line, note; (*bon mot etc*) saying; **le mot de la fin** the last word; **mot à mot** *adj*, *adv* word for word; **mot pour mot** word for word, verbatim; **sur *ou* à ces mots** with these words; **en un mot** in a word; **à mots couverts** in veiled terms; **prendre qn au mot** to take sb at his word; **se donner le mot** to send the word round; **avoir son mot à dire** to have a say; **mot d'ordre** watchword; **mot de passe** password; **mots croisés** crossword (puzzle) *sg*

motard [mɔtar] *nm* biker; (*policier*) motorcycle cop

motel [mɔtɛl] *nm* motel

moteur, trice [mɔtœr, -tris] *adj* (*ANAT, PHYSIOL*) motor; (*TECH*) driving; (*AUTO*): **à 4 roues motrices** 4-wheel drive ♦ *nm* engine, motor; (*fig*) mover, mainspring; **à moteur** power-driven, motor *cpd*; **moteur à deux temps** two-stroke engine; **moteur à explosion** internal combustion engine; **moteur à réaction** jet engine; **moteur thermique** heat engine

motif [mɔtif] *nm* (*cause*) motive; (*décoratif*) design, pattern, motif; (*d'un tableau*) subject, motif; (*MUS*) figure, motif; **motifs** *nmpl* (*JUR*) grounds *pl*; **sans motif** *adj* groundless

motivation [mɔtivasjɔ̃] *nf* motivation

motiver [mɔtive] *vt* (*justifier*) to justify, account for; (ADMIN, JUR, PSYCH) to motivate

moto [mɔto] *nf* (motor)bike; **moto verte** *ou* **de trial** trail (BRIT) *ou* dirt (US) bike

motocyclette [mɔtɔsiklɛt] *nf* motorbike, motor-cycle

motocycliste [mɔtɔsiklist(ə)] *nm/f* motorcyclist

motorisé, e [mɔtɔrize] *adj* (*troupe*) motorized; (*personne*) having one's own transport

motrice [mɔtris] *adj f voir* **moteur**

motte [mɔt] *nf*: **motte de terre** lump of earth, clod (of earth); **motte de gazon** turf, sod; **motte de beurre** lump of butter

mou (mol), molle [mu, mɔl] *adj* soft; (*péj: visage, traits*) flabby; (: *geste*) limp; (: *personne*) sluggish; (: *résistance, protestations*) feeble ♦ *nm* (*homme mou*) wimp; (*abats*) lights *pl*, lungs *pl*; (*de la corde*): **avoir du mou** to be slack; **donner du mou** to slacken, loosen; **avoir les jambes molles** to be weak at the knees

mouche [muʃ] *nf* fly; (ESCRIME) button; (*de taffetas*) patch; **prendre la mouche** to go into a huff; **faire mouche** to score a bull's-eye

moucher [muʃe] *vt* (*enfant*) to blow the nose of; (*chandelle*) to snuff (out); **se moucher** to blow one's nose

moucheron [muʃrɔ̃] *nm* midge

mouchoir [muʃwar] *nm* handkerchief, hanky; **mouchoir en papier** tissue, paper hanky

moudre [mudr(ə)] *vt* to grind

moue [mu] *nf* pout; **faire la moue** to pout; (*fig*) to pull a face

mouette [mwɛt] *nf* (sea)gull

moufle [mufl(ə)] *nf* (*gant*) mitt(en); (TECH) pulley block

mouillé, e [muje] *adj* wet

mouiller [muje] *vt* (*humecter*) to wet, moisten; (*tremper*): **mouiller qn/qch** to make sb/sth wet; (CULIN: *ragoût*) to add stock *ou* wine to; (*couper, diluer*) to water down; (*mine etc*) to lay ♦ *vi* (NAVIG) to lie *ou* be at anchor; **se mouiller** to get wet; (*fam*) to commit o.s *ou* get (o.s.) involved; **mouiller l'ancre** to drop *ou* cast anchor

moulant, e [mulɑ̃, -ɑ̃t] *adj* figure-hugging

moule [mul] *vb voir* **moudre** ♦ *nf* (*mollusque*) mussel ♦ *nm* (*creux, CULIN*) mould (US); (*modèle plein*) cast; **moule à gâteau** *nm* cake tin (BRIT) *ou* pan (US); **moule à gaufre** *nm* waffle iron; **moule à tarte** *nm* pie *ou* flan dish

moulent [mul] *vb voir* **moudre, mouler**

mouler [mule] *vt* (*brique*) to mould (BRIT), mold (US); (*statue*) to cast; (*visage, bas-relief*) to make a cast of; (*lettre*) to shape with care; (*suj: vêtement*) to hug, fit closely round; **mouler qch sur** (*fig*) to model sth on

moulin [mulɛ̃] *nm* mill; (*fam*) engine; **moulin à café** coffee mill; **moulin à eau** watermill; **moulin à légumes** (vegetable) shredder; **moulin à paroles** (*fig*) chatterbox; **moulin à poivre** pepper mill; **moulin à prières** prayer wheel; **moulin à vent** windmill

moulinet [mulinɛ] *nm* (*de treuil*) winch; (*de canne à pêche*) reel; (*mouvement*): **faire des moulinets avec qch** to whirl sth around

moulinette® [mulinɛt] *nf* (vegetable) shredder

moulu, e [muly] *pp de* **moudre** ♦ *adj* (*café*) ground

mourant, e [murɑ̃, -ɑ̃t] *vb voir* **mourir** ♦ *adj* dying ♦ *nm/f* dying man/woman

mourir [murir] *vi* to die; (*civilisation*) to die out; **mourir assassiné** to be murdered; **mourir de froid/faim/vieillesse** to die of exposure/hunger/old age; **mourir de faim/d'ennui** (*fig*) to be starving/be bored to death; **s'ennuyer à mourir** to be bored to death

mousse [mus] *nf* (BOT) moss; (*écume: sur eau, bière*) froth, foam; (: *shampooing*) lather; (*de champagne*) bubbles *pl*; (CULIN) mousse; (*en caoutchouc etc*) foam ♦ *nm* (NAVIG) ship's boy; **bain de mousse** bubble bath; **bas mousse** stretch stockings; **balle mousse** rubber ball; **mousse carbonique** (fire-fighting) foam; **mousse de nylon** nylon foam; (*tissu*) stretch nylon; **mousse à raser** shaving foam

mousseline [muslin] *nf* (TEXTILES) muslin; chiffon; **pommes mousseline** (CULIN) creamed potatoes

mousser [muse] *vi* to foam; to lather

mousseux, euse [musø, -øz] *adj* (*chocolat*) frothy; (*eau*) foamy, frothy; (*vin*) sparkling ♦ *nm*: **(vin) mousseux** sparkling wine

mousson [musɔ̃] *nf* monsoon

moustache [mustaʃ] *nf* moustache; **moustaches** *nfpl* (*d'animal*) whiskers *pl*

moustachu, e [mustaʃy] *adj* wearing a moustache

moustiquaire [mustiker] *nf* (*rideau*) mosquito net; (*chassis*) mosquito screen

moustique [mustik] *nm* mosquito

moutarde [mutard(ə)] *nf* mustard ♦ *adj inv* mustard(-coloured)

mouton [mutɔ̃] *nm* (ZOOL, *péj*) sheep *inv*; (*peau*) sheepskin; (CULIN) mutton

mouvement [muvmɑ̃] *nm* (*gen, aussi: mécanisme*) movement; (*ligne courbe*) contours *pl*; (*fig: tumulte, agitation*) activity, bustle; (: *impulsion*) impulse; reaction; (*geste*) gesture; (MUS: *rythme*) tempo (*pl* -s *ou* tempi); **en mouvement** in motion; on the move; **mettre qch en mouvement** to set sth in motion, set sth going; **mouvement d'humeur** fit *ou* burst of temper; **mouvement d'opinion** trend of (public) opinion; **le mouvement perpétuel** perpetual motion

mouvementé, e [muvmɑ̃te] *adj* (*vie, poursuite*) eventful; (*réunion*) turbulent

mouvoir [muvwar] *vt* (*levier, membre*) to move; (*machine*) to drive; **se mouvoir** to move

moyen, ne [mwajɛ̃, -ɛn] *adj* average; *(tailles, prix)* medium; *(de grandeur moyenne)* medium-sized ◆ *nm (façon)* means *sg*, way ◆ *nf* average; *(STATISTIQUE)* mean; *(SCOL: à l'examen)* pass mark; *(AUTO)* average speed; **moyens** *nmpl (capacités)* means; **au moyen de** by means of; **y a-t-il moyen de …?** is it possible to …?, can one …?; **par quel moyen?** how?, which way?, by which means?; **par tous les moyens** by every possible means, every possible way; **avec les moyens du bord** *(fig)* with what's available *ou* what comes to hand; **employer les grands moyens** to resort to drastic measures; **par ses propres moyens** all by oneself; **en moyenne** on (an) average; **faire la moyenne** to work out the average; **moyen de locomotion/d'expression** means of transport/expression; **moyen âge** Middle Ages; **moyen de transport** means of transport; **moyenne d'âge** average age; **moyenne entreprise** *(COMM)* medium-sized firm

moyennant [mwajɛnɑ̃] *prép (somme)* for; *(service, conditions)* in return for; *(travail, effort)* with

Moyen-Orient [mwajɛnɔrjɑ̃] *nm*: **le Moyen-Orient** the Middle East

moyeu, x [mwajø] *nm* hub

MST *sigle f* (= *maladie sexuellement transmissible*) STD (= *sexually transmitted disease*)

mû, mue [my] *pp de* **mouvoir**

muer [mɥe] *vi (oiseau, mammifère)* to moult *(BRIT)*, molt *(US)*; *(serpent)* to slough (its skin); *(jeune garçon)*: **il mue** his voice is breaking; **se muer en** to transform into

muet, te [mɥɛ, -ɛt] *adj* dumb; *(fig)*: **muet d'admiration** *etc* speechless with admiration *etc*; *(joie, douleur, CINÉ)* silent; *(LING: lettre)* silent, mute; *(carte)* blank ◆ *nm/f* mute ◆ *nm*: **le muet** *(CINÉ)* the silent cinema *ou* *(esp US)* movies

mufle [myfl(ə)] *nm* muzzle; *(goujat)* boor ◆ *adj* boorish

mugir [myʒir] *vi (bœuf)* to bellow; *(vache)* to low, moo; *(fig)* to howl

muguet [mygɛ] *nm (BOT)* lily of the valley; *(MÉD)* thrush

mule [myl] *nf (ZOOL)* (she-)mule

mulet [mylɛ] *nm (ZOOL)* (he-)mule; *(poisson)* mullet

multinational, e, aux [myltinasjɔnal, -o] *adj, nf* multinational

multiple [myltipl(ə)] *adj* multiple, numerous; *(varié)* many, manifold ◆ *nm (MATH)* multiple

multiplication [myltiplikasjɔ̃] *nf* multiplication

multiplier [myltiplije] *vt* to multiply; **se multiplier** *vi* to multiply; *(fig: personne)* to be everywhere at once

municipal, e, aux [mynisipal, -o] *adj* municipal; town *cpd*

municipalité [mynisipalite] *nf (corps municipal)* town council, corporation; *(commune)* town, municipality

munir [mynir] *vt*: **munir qn/qch de** to equip sb/sth with; **se munir de** to provide o.s. with

munitions [mynisjɔ̃] *nfpl* ammunition *sg*

mur [myr] *nm* wall; *(fig)* stone *ou* brick wall; **faire le mur** *(interne, soldat)* to jump the wall; **mur du son** sound barrier

mûr, e [myr] *adj* ripe; *(personne)* mature ◆ *nf (de la ronce)* blackberry; *(du mûrier)* mulberry

muraille [myraj] *nf* (high) wall

mural, e, aux [myral, -o] *adj* wall *cpd* ◆ *nm (ART)* mural

mûre [myr] *nf voir* **mûr**

muret [myrɛ] *nm* low wall

mûrir [myrir] *vi (fruit, blé)* to ripen; *(abcès, furoncle)* to come to a head; *(fig: idée, personne)* to mature; *(projet)* to develop ◆ *vt (fruit, blé)* to ripen; *(personne)* to (make) mature; *(pensée, projet)* to nurture

murmure [myrmyr] *nm* murmur; **murmures** *nmpl (plaintes)* murmurings, mutterings

murmurer [myrmyre] *vi* to murmur; *(se plaindre)* to mutter, grumble

muscade [myskad] *nf (aussi*: **noix muscade**) nutmeg

muscat [myska] *nm (raisin)* muscat grape; *(vin)* muscatel (wine)

muscle [myskl(ə)] *nm* muscle

musclé, e [myskle] *adj (personne, corps)* muscular; *(fig: politique, régime etc)* strong-arm *cpd*

museau, x [myzo] *nm* muzzle

musée [myze] *nm* museum; *(de peinture)* art gallery

museler [myzle] *vt* to muzzle

muselière [myzəljɛr] *nf* muzzle

musette [myzɛt] *nf (sac)* lunchbag ◆ *adj inv (orchestre etc)* accordion *cpd*

musical, e, aux [myzikal, -o] *adj* musical

music-hall [myzikol] *nm* variety theatre; *(genre)* variety

musicien, ne [myzisjɛ̃, -ɛn] *adj* musical ◆ *nm/f* musician

musique [myzik] *nf* music; *(fanfare)* band; **faire de la musique** to make music; *(jouer d'un instrument)* to play an instrument; **musique de chambre** chamber music; **musique de fond** background music

musulman, e [myzylmɑ̃, -an] *adj, nm/f* Moslem, Muslim

mutation [mytasjɔ̃] *nf (ADMIN)* transfer; *(BIO)* mutation

muter [myte] *vt (ADMIN)* to transfer

mutilé, e [mytile] *nm/f* disabled person *(through loss of limbs)* **mutilé de guerre** disabled ex-serviceman; **grand mutilé** severely disabled person

mutiler [mytile] *vt* to mutilate, maim; *(fig)* to mutilate, deface

mutin, e [mytɛ̃, -in] *adj (enfant, air, ton)* mischievous, impish ◆ *nm/f (MIL, NAVIG)* mutineer

mutinerie [mytinri] *nf* mutiny

mutisme [mytism(ə)] *nm* silence

mutuel, le [mytɥɛl] *adj* mutual ♦ *nf* mutual benefit society

myope [mjɔp] *adj* short-sighted

myosotis [mjozɔtis] *nm* forget-me-not

myrtille [mirtij] *nf* bilberry (*BRIT*), blueberry (*US*), whortleberry

mystère [mistɛr] *nm* mystery

mystérieux, euse [misterjø, -øz] *adj* mysterious

mystifier [mistifje] *vt* to fool, take in; (*tromper*) to mystify

mythe [mit] *nm* myth

mythologie [mitɔlɔʒi] *nf* mythology

— *N n* —

n' [n] *adv voir* ne

nacre [nakr(ə)] *nf* mother-of-pearl

nage [naʒ] *nf* swimming; (*manière*) style of swimming, stroke; **traverser/s'éloigner à la nage** to swim across/away; **en nage** bathed in perspiration; **nage indienne** sidestroke; **nage libre** freestyle; **nage papillon** butterfly

nageoire [naʒwar] *nf* fin

nager [naʒe] *vi* to swim; (*fig: ne rien comprendre*) to be all at sea; **nager dans** to be swimming in; (*vêtements*) to be lost in; **nager dans le bonheur** to be overjoyed

nageur, euse [naʒœr, -øz] *nm/f* swimmer

naguère [nagɛr] *adv* (*il y a peu de temps*) not long ago; (*autrefois*) formerly

naïf, ïve [naif, naiv] *adj* naïve

nain, e [nɛ̃, nɛn] *adj, nm/f* dwarf

naissance [nɛsɑ̃s] *nf* birth; **donner naissance à** to give birth to; (*fig*) to give rise to; **prendre naissance** to originate; **aveugle de naissance** born blind; **Français de naissance** French by birth; **à la naissance des cheveux** at the roots of the hair; **lieu de naissance** place of birth

naître [nɛtr(ə)] *vi* to be born; (*conflit, complications*) **naître de** to arise from, be born out of; **naître à** (*amour, poésie*) to awaken to; **je suis né en 1960** I was born in 1960; **il naît plus de filles que de garçons** there are more girls born than boys; **faire naître** (*fig*) to give rise to, arouse

naïveté [naivte] *nf* naïvety

nana [nana] *nf* (*fam: fille*) bird (*BRIT*), chick

nantir [nɑ̃tir] *vt*: **nantir qn de** to provide sb with; **les nantis** the well-to-do

nappe [nap] *nf* tablecloth; (*fig*) sheet; layer; **nappe de mazout** oil slick; **nappe (phréatique)** water table

napperon [napʁɔ̃] *nm* table-mat; **napperon individuel** place mat

narcodollars [narkodɔlar] *nmpl* drug money *no pl*

narguer [narge] *vt* to taunt

narine [narin] *nf* nostril

narquois, e [narkwa, -waz] *adj* derisive, mocking

natal, e [natal] *adj* native

natalité [natalite] *nf* birth rate

natation [natasjɔ̃] *nf* swimming; **faire de la natation** to go swimming (*regularly*); **natation synchronisée** synchronized swimming

natif, ive [natif, -iv] *adj* native

nation [nɑsjɔ̃] *nf* nation; **les Nations unies (NU)** the United Nations (UN)

national, e, aux [nasjɔnal, -o] *adj* national ♦ *nf*: **(route) nationale** ≈ A road (*BRIT*), ≈ state highway (*US*); **obsèques nationales** state funeral

nationaliser [nasjɔnalize] *vt* to nationalize

nationalisme [nasjɔnalism(ə)] *nm* nationalism

nationalité [nasjɔnalite] *nf* nationality; **de nationalité française** of French nationality

natte [nat] *nf* (*tapis*) mat; (*cheveux*) plait

naturaliser [natyralize] *vt* to naturalize; (*empailler*) to stuff

nature [natyr] *nf* nature ♦ *adj, adv* (*CULIN*) plain, without seasoning or sweetening; (*café, thé: sans lait*) black; (: *sans sucre*) without sugar; **payer en nature** to pay in kind; **peint d'après nature** painted from life; **être de nature à faire qch** (*propre à*) to be the sort of thing (*ou* person) to do sth; **nature morte** still-life

naturel, le [natyrɛl] *adj* (*gén, aussi: enfant*) natural ♦ *nm* naturalness; (*caractère*) disposition, nature; (*autochtone*) native; **au naturel** (*CULIN*) in water; in its own juices

naturellement [natyrɛlmɑ̃] *adv* naturally; (*bien sûr*) of course

naufrage [nofraʒ] *nm* (*ship*)wreck; (*fig*) wreck; **faire naufrage** to be shipwrecked

nauséabond, e [nozeabɔ̃, -ɔ̃d] *adj* foul, nauseous

nausée [noze] *nf* nausea; **avoir la nausée** to feel sick; **avoir des nausées** to have waves of nausea, feel nauseous *ou* sick

nautique [notik] *adj* nautical, water *cpd*; **sports nautiques** water sports

naval, e [naval] *adj* naval

navet [navɛ] *nm* turnip; (*péj*) third-rate film

navette [navɛt] *nf* shuttle; (*en car etc*) shuttle (service); **faire la navette (entre)** to go to and fro (between), shuttle (between); **navette spatiale** space shuttle

navigateur [navigatœr] *nm* (*NAVIG*) seafarer, sailor; (*AVIAT*) navigator; (*INFORM*) browser

navigation [navigɑsjɔ̃] *nf* navigation, sailing; (*COMM*) shipping; **compagnie de navigation** shipping company; **navigation spatiale** space navigation

naviguer [navige] *vi* to navigate, sail

navire [navir] *nm* ship; **navire de guerre** warship; **navire marchand** merchantman

navrer [navre] *vt* to upset, distress; **je suis navré (de/de faire/que)** I'm so sorry (for/for doing/that)

ne, n' [n(ə)] *adv voir* **pas, plus, jamais** *etc*; (*explétif*) *non traduit*

né, e [ne] *pp de* **naître**; **né en 1960** born in 1960; **née Scott** née Scott; **né(e) de ... et de ...** son/daughter of ... and of ...; **né d'une mère française** having a French mother; **né pour commander** born to lead ♦ *adj*: **un comédien né** a born comedian

néanmoins [neãmwɛ̃] *adv* nevertheless, yet

néant [neã] *nm* nothingness; **réduire à néant** to bring to nought; (*espoir*) to dash

nécessaire [neseser] *adj* necessary ♦ *nm* necessary; (*sac*) kit; **faire le nécessaire** to do the necessary; **n'emporter que le strict nécessaire** to take only what is strictly necessary; **nécessaire de couture** sewing kit; **nécessaire de toilette** toilet bag; **nécessaire de voyage** overnight bag

nécessité [nesesite] *nf* necessity; **se trouver dans la nécessité de faire qch** to find it necessary to do sth; **par nécessité** out of necessity

nécessiter [nesesite] *vt* to require

nécrologique [nekrɔlɔʒik] *adj*: **article nécrologique** obituary; **rubrique nécrologique** obituary column

nectar [nɛktar] *nm* nectar

néerlandais, e [neɛrlãdɛ, -ɛz] *adj* Dutch, of the Netherlands ♦ *nm* (*LING*) Dutch ♦ *nm/f*: **Néerlandais, e** Dutchman/woman; **les Néerlandais** the Dutch

nef [nɛf] *nf* (*d'église*) nave

néfaste [nefast(ə)] *adj* baneful; ill-fated

négatif, ive [negatif, iv] *adj* negative ♦ *nm* (*PHOTO*) negative

négligé, e [negliʒe] *adj* (*en désordre*) slovenly ♦ *nm* (*tenue*) negligee

négligeable [negliʒabl(ə)] *adj* insignificant, negligible

négligent, e [negliʒã, -ãt] *adj* careless; (*JUR etc*) negligent

négliger [negliʒe] *vt* (*épouse, jardin*) to neglect; (*tenue*) to be careless about; (*avis, précautions*) to disregard, overlook; **négliger de faire** to fail to do, not bother to do; **se négliger** to neglect o.s.

négoce [negɔs] *nm* trade

négociant [negɔsjã] *nm* merchant

négociation [negɔsjasjɔ̃] *nf* negotiation; **négociations collectives** collective bargaining *sg*

négocier [negɔsje] *vi, vt* to negotiate

nègre [nɛgr(ə)] *nm* (*péj*) Negro; (*péj: écrivain*) ghost writer ♦ *adj* Negro

neige [nɛʒ] *nf* snow; **battre les œufs en neige** (*CULIN*) to whip ou beat the egg whites until stiff; **neige carbonique** dry ice; **neige fondue** (*par*

terre*) slush; (*qui tombe*) sleet; **neige poudreuse** powdery snow

neiger [neʒe] *vi* to snow

nénuphar [nenyfar] *nm* water-lily

néon [neɔ̃] *nm* neon

néo-zélandais, e [neɔzelãdɛ, -ɛz] *adj* New Zealand *cpd* ♦ *nm/f*: **Néo-zélandais, e** New Zealander

nerf [nɛr] *nm* nerve; (*fig*) spirit; (: *forces*) stamina; **nerfs** *nmpl* nerves; **être** ou **vivre sur les nerfs** to live on one's nerves; **être à bout de nerfs** to be at the end of one's tether; **passer ses nerfs sur qn** to take it out on sb

nerveux, euse [nɛrvø, -øz] *adj* nervous; (*cheval*) highly-strung; (*voiture*) nippy, responsive; (*tendineux*) sinewy

nervosité [nɛrvozite] *nf* nervousness; (*émotivité*) excitability

nervure [nɛrvyr] *nf* (*de feuille*) vein; (*ARCHIT, TECH*) rib

n'est-ce pas [nɛspa] *adv* isn't it?, won't you? *etc*, *selon le verbe qui précède*; **c'est bon, n'est-ce pas?** it's good, isn't it?; **il a peur, n'est-ce pas?** he's afraid, isn't he?; **n'est-ce pas que c'est bon?** don't you think it's good?; **lui, n'est-ce pas, il peut se le permettre** he, of course, can afford to do that, can't he?

net, nette [nɛt] *adj* (*sans équivoque, distinct*) clear; (*photo*) sharp; (*évident*) definite; (*propre*) neat, clean; (*COMM: prix, salaire, poids*) net ♦ *adv* (*refuser*) flatly ♦ *nm*: **mettre au net** to copy out; **s'arrêter net** to stop dead; **la lame a cassé net** the blade snapped clean through; **faire place nette** to make a clean sweep; **net d'impôt** tax free

Net [nɛt] *nm* (*INTERNET*): **le Net** the Net

nettement [nɛtmã] *adv* (*distinctement*) clearly; (*évidemment*) definitely; (*avec comparatif, superlatif*): **nettement mieux** definitely ou clearly better

netteté [nɛtte] *nf* clearness

nettoyage [nɛtwajaʒ] *nm* cleaning; **nettoyage à sec** dry cleaning

nettoyer [nɛtwaje] *vt* to clean; (*fig*) to clean out

neuf [nœf] *num* nine

neuf, neuve [nœf, nœv] *adj* new ♦ *nm*: **repeindre à neuf** to redecorate; **remettre à neuf** to do up (as good as new), refurbish; **n'acheter que du neuf** to buy everything new; **quoi de neuf?** what's new?

neutre [nøtr(ə)] *adj, nm* (*aussi LING*) neutral

neuve [nœv] *adj f voir* **neuf**

neuvième [nœvjɛm] *num* ninth

neveu, x [nəvø] *nm* nephew

névrosé, e [nevroze] *adj, nm/f* neurotic

nez [ne] *nm* nose; **rire au nez de qn** to laugh in sb's face; **avoir du nez** to have flair; **avoir le nez fin** to have foresight; **nez à nez avec** face to face with; **à vue de nez** roughly

ni [ni] *conj*: **ni l'un ni l'autre ne sont** *ou* **n'est** neither one nor the other is; **il n'a rien dit ni fait** he hasn't said or done anything

niais, e [njɛ, -ɛz] *adj* silly, thick

niche [niʃ] *nf (du chien)* kennel; *(de mur)* recess, niche; *(farce)* trick

nicher [niʃe] *vi* to nest; **se nicher dans** (*personne: se blottir)* to snuggle into; (: *se cacher)* to hide in; *(objet)* to lodge itself in

nid [ni] *nm* nest; *(fig: repaire etc)* den, lair; **nid d'abeilles** *(COUTURE, TEXTILE)* honeycomb stitch; **nid de poule** pothole

nièce [njɛs] *nf* niece

nier [nje] *vt* to deny

nigaud, e [nigo, -od] *nm/f* booby, fool

Nil [nil] *nm*: **le Nil** the Nile

n'importe [nɛ̃pɔʀt(ə)] *adv*: **n'importe!** no matter!; **n'importe qui/quoi/où** anybody/anything/anywhere; **n'importe quoi!** *(fam: désapprobation)* what rubbish!; **n'importe quand** any time; **n'importe quel/quelle** any; **n'importe lequel/laquelle** any (one); **n'importe comment** *(sans soin)* carelessly; **n'importe comment, il part ce soir** he's leaving tonight in any case

niveau, x [nivo] *nm* level; *(des élèves, études)* standard; **au niveau de** at the level of; *(personne)* on a level with; **de niveau (avec)** level (with); **le niveau de la mer** sea level; **niveau (à bulle)** spirit level; **niveau (d'eau)** water level; **niveau de vie** standard of living

niveler [nivle] *vt* to level

NN *abr* (= *nouvelle norme)* revised standard of hotel classification

noble [nɔbl(ə)] *adj* noble; *(de qualité: métal etc)* precious ♦ *nm/f* noble(man/woman)

noblesse [nɔblɛs] *nf (classe sociale)* nobility; *(d'une action etc)* nobleness

noce [nɔs] *nf* wedding; *(gens)* wedding party *(ou* guests *pl)*; **il l'a épousée en secondes noces** she was his second wife; **faire la noce** *(fam)* to go on a binge; **noces d'or/d'argent/de diamant** golden/silver/diamond wedding

nocif, ive [nɔsif, -iv] *adj* harmful, noxious

nocturne [nɔktyʀn(ə)] *adj* nocturnal ♦ *nf (SPORT)* floodlit fixture; *(d'un magasin)* late opening

Noël [nɔɛl] *nm* Christmas; **la (fête de) Noël** Christmas time

nœud [nø] *nm (de corde, du bois, NAVIG)* knot; *(ruban)* bow; *(fig: liens)* bond, tie; (: *d'une question)* crux; *(THÉÂT etc)*: **le nœud de l'action** the web of events; **nœud coulant** noose; **nœud gordien** Gordian knot; **nœud papillon** bow tie

noir, e [nwaʀ] *adj* black; *(obscur, sombre)* dark ♦ *nm/f* black man/woman, Negro/Negro woman ♦ *nm*: **dans le noir** in the dark ♦ *nf (MUS)* crotchet *(BRIT)*, quarter note *(US)*; **il fait noir** it is dark; **au noir** *adv (acheter, vendre)* on the black market; **travail au noir** moonlighting

noircir [nwaʀsiʀ] *vt, vi* to blacken

noisette [nwazɛt] *nf* hazelnut; *(morceau: de beurre etc)* small knob ♦ *adj (yeux)* hazel

noix [nwa] *nf* walnut; *(fam)* twit; *(CULIN)*: **une noix de beurre** a knob of butter; **à la noix** *(fam)* worthless; **noix de cajou** cashew nut; **noix de coco** coconut; **noix muscade** nutmeg; **noix de veau** *(CULIN)* round fillet of veal

nom [nɔ̃] *nm* name; *(LING)* noun; **connaître qn de nom** to know sb by name; **au nom de** in the name of; **nom d'une pipe** *ou* **d'un chien!** *(fam)* for goodness' sake!; **nom de Dieu!** *(fam!)* bloody hell! *(BRIT)*, my God!; **nom commun/propre** common/proper noun; **nom composé** *(LING)* compound noun; **nom déposé** trade name; **nom d'emprunt** assumed name; **nom de famille** surname; **nom de fichier** file name; **nom de jeune fille** maiden name

nomade [nɔmad] *adj* nomadic ♦ *nm/f* nomad

nombre [nɔ̃bʀ(ə)] *nm* number; **venir en nombre** to come in large numbers; **depuis nombre d'années** for many years; **ils sont au nombre de 3** there are 3 of them; **au nombre de mes amis** among my friends; **sans nombre** countless; **(bon) nombre de** *(beaucoup, plusieurs)* a (large) number of; **nombre premier/entier** prime/whole number

nombreux, euse [nɔ̃bʀø, -øz] *adj* many, numerous; *(avec nom sg: foule etc)* large; **peu nombreux** few; small; **de nombreux cas** many cases

nombril [nɔ̃bʀi] *nm* navel

nommer [nɔme] *vt (baptiser)* to name, give a name to; *(qualifier)* to call; *(mentionner)* to name, give the name of; *(élire)* to appoint, nominate; **se nommer**: **il se nomme Pascal** his name's Pascal, he's called Pascal

non [nɔ̃] *adv (réponse)* no; *(suivi d'un adjectif, adverbe)* not; **Paul est venu, non?** Paul came, didn't he?; **répondre** *ou* **dire que non** to say no; **non pas que** not that; **non plus**: **moi non plus** neither do I, I don't either; **je préférerais que non** I would prefer not; **il se trouve que non** perhaps not; **je pense que non** I don't think so; **non mais!** well really!; **non mais des fois!** you must be joking!; **non alcoolisé** non-alcoholic; **non loin/seulement** not far/only

nonante [nɔnɑ̃t] *num (Belgique, Suisse)* ninety

nonchalant, e [nɔ̃ʃalɑ̃, -ɑ̃t] *adj* nonchalant, casual

non-fumeur [nɔ̃fymœʀ] *nm* non-smoker

non-sens [nɔ̃sɑ̃s] *nm* absurdity

nord [nɔʀ] *nm* North ♦ *adj* northern; north; **au nord** *(situation)* in the north; *(direction)* to the north; **au nord de** north of, to the north of; **perdre le nord** to lose the place *(fig)*

nord-est [nɔʀɛst] *nm* North-East

nord-ouest [nɔʀwɛst] *nm* North-West

normal, e, aux [nɔʀmal, -o] *adj* normal ♦ *nf*: **la normale** the norm, the average

normalement [nɔʀmalmɑ̃] *adv* (*en général*) normally; (*comme prévu*): **normalement, il le fera demain** he should be doing it tomorrow, he's supposed to do it tomorrow

normand, e [nɔʀmɑ̃, -ɑ̃d] *adj* (*de Normandie*) Norman ♦ *nm/f*: **Normand, e** (*de Normandie*) Norman

Normandie [nɔʀmɑ̃di] *nf*: **la Normandie** Normandy

norme [nɔʀm(ə)] *nf* norm; (*TECH*) standard

Norvège [nɔʀvɛʒ] *nf*: **la Norvège** Norway

norvégien, ne [nɔʀveʒjɛ̃, -ɛn] *adj* Norwegian ♦ *nm* (*LING*) Norwegian ♦ *nm/f*: **Norvégien, ne** Norwegian

nos [no] *adj possessif voir* **notre**

nostalgie [nɔstalʒi] *nf* nostalgia

nostalgique [nɔstalʒik] *adj* nostalgic

notable [nɔtabl(ə)] *adj* notable, noteworthy; (*marqué*) noticeable, marked ♦ *nm* prominent citizen

notaire [nɔtɛʀ] *nm* notary; solicitor

notamment [nɔtamɑ̃] *adv* in particular, among others

note [nɔt] *nf* (*écrite, MUS*) note; (*SCOL*) mark (*BRIT*), grade; (*facture*) bill; **prendre des notes** to take notes; **prendre note de** to note; (*par écrit*) to note, write down; **dans la note** exactly right; **forcer la note** to exaggerate; **une note de tristesse/de gaieté** a sad/happy note; **note de service** memorandum

noté, e [nɔte] *adj*: **être bien/mal noté** (*employé etc*) to have a good/bad record

noter [nɔte] *vt* (*écrire*) to write down, note; (*remarquer*) to note, notice; (*SCOL, ADMIN: donner une appréciation*) to mark, give a grade to; **notez bien que ...** (please) note that ...

notice [nɔtis] *nf* summary, short article; (*brochure*): **notice explicative** explanatory leaflet, instruction booklet

notifier [nɔtifje] *vt*: **notifier qch à qn** to notify sb of sth, notify sth to sb

notion [nɔsjɔ̃] *nf* notion, idea; **notions** *nfpl* (*rudiments*) rudiments

notoire [nɔtwaʀ] *adj* widely known; (*en mal*) notorious; **le fait est notoire** the fact is common knowledge

notre, nos [nɔtʀ(ə), no] *adj possessif* our

nôtre [notʀ(ə)] *adj* ours ♦ *pron*: **le/la nôtre** ours; **les nôtres** ours; (*alliés etc*) our own people; **soyez des nôtres** join us

nouer [nwe] *vt* to tie, knot; (*fig: alliance etc*) to strike up; **nouer la conversation** to start a good conversation; **se nouer** *vi*: **c'est là où l'intrigue se noue** it's at that point that the strands of the plot come together; **ma gorge se noua** a lump came to my throat

noueux, euse [nwø, -øz] *adj* gnarled

nouille [nuj] *nf* (*pâtes*): **nouilles** noodles; pasta *sg*; (*fam*) noodle (*BRIT*), fathead

nourrice [nuʀis] *nf* ≈ baby-minder; (*autrefois*) wet-nurse

nourrir [nuʀiʀ] *vt* to feed; (*fig: espoir*) to harbour, nurse; **logé nourri** with board and lodging; **nourrir au sein** to breast-feed; **se nourrir de légumes** to live on vegetables

nourrissant, e [nuʀisɑ̃, -ɑ̃t] *adj* nourishing, nutritious

nourrisson [nuʀisɔ̃] *nm* (*unweaned*) infant

nourriture [nuʀityʀ] *nf* food

nous [nu] *pron* (*sujet*) we; (*objet*) us

nous-mêmes [numɛm] *pron* ourselves

nouveau (nouvel), elle, x [nuvo, -ɛl] *adj* new; (*original*) novel ♦ *nm/f* new pupil (*ou* employee) ♦ *nm*: **il y a du nouveau** there's something new ♦ *nf* (piece of) news *sg*; (*LITTÉRATURE*) short story; **nouvelles** *nfpl* (*PRESSE, TV*) news; **de nouveau à nouveau** again; **je suis sans nouvelles de lui** I haven't heard from him; **Nouvel An** New Year; **nouveau venu, nouvelle venue** newcomer; **nouveaux mariés** newly-weds; **nouvelle vague** new wave

nouveau-né, e [nuvone] *nm/f* newborn (baby)

nouveauté [nuvote] *nf* novelty; (*chose nouvelle*) innovation, something new; (*COMM*) new film (*ou* book *ou* creation *etc*)

nouvel *adj m*, **nouvelle** *adj f*, *nf* [nuvɛl] *voir* **nouveau**

Nouvelle-Calédonie [nuvɛlkaledɔni] *nf*: **la Nouvelle-Calédonie** New Caledonia

nouvellement [nuvɛlmɑ̃] *adv* (*arrivé etc*) recently, newly

Nouvelle-Zélande [nuvɛlzelɑ̃d] *nf*: **la Nouvelle-Zélande** New Zealand

novembre [nɔvɑ̃bʀ(ə)] *nm* November; *voir aussi* **juillet**; *see boxed note*

---

11 NOVEMBRE

Le 11 novembre is a public holiday in France commemorating the signing of the armistice, near Compiègne, at the end of World War I.

---

novice [nɔvis] *adj* inexperienced ♦ *nm/f* novice

noyade [nwajad] *nf* drowning *no pl*

noyau, x [nwajo] *nm* (*de fruit*) stone; (*BIO, PHYSIQUE*) nucleus; (*ÉLEC, GÉO, fig: centre*) core; (*fig: d'artistes etc*) group; (*de résistants etc*) cell

noyauter [nwajote] *vt* (*POL*) to infiltrate

noyer [nwaje] *nm* walnut (tree); (*bois*) walnut ♦ *vt* to drown; (*fig*) to flood; to submerge; (*AUTO: moteur*) to flood; **se noyer** to be drowned, drown; (*suicide*) to drown o.s.; **noyer son chagrin** to drown one's sorrows; **noyer le poisson** to duck the issue

nu, e [ny] *adj* naked; (*membres*) naked, bare; (*chambre, fil, plaine*) bare ♦ *nm* (*ART*) nude; **le nu intégral** total nudity; **se mettre nu** to strip; **mettre**

à nu to bare

nuage [nɥaʒ] *nm* cloud; **être dans les nuages** (*distrait*) to have one's head in the clouds; **nuage de lait** drop of milk

nuageux, euse [nɥaʒø, -øz] *adj* cloudy

nuance [nɥɑ̃s] *nf* (*de couleur, sens*) shade; **il y a une nuance (entre)** there's a slight difference (between); **une nuance de tristesse** a tinge of sadness

nuancer [nɥɑ̃se] *vt* (*pensée, opinion*) to qualify

nucléaire [nykleɛʀ] *adj* nuclear ◆ *nm* nuclear power

nudiste [nydist(ə)] *adj, nm/f* nudist

nuée [nɥe] *nf*: **une nuée de** a cloud *ou* host *ou* swarm of

nues [ny] *nfpl*: **tomber des nues** to be taken aback; **porter qn aux nues** to praise sb to the skies

nuire [nɥiʀ] *vi* to be harmful; **nuire à** to harm, do damage to

nuisible [nɥizibl(ə)] *adj* harmful; (*animal*) **nuisible** pest

nuit [nɥi] *nf* night; **payer sa nuit** to pay for one's overnight accommodation; **il fait nuit** it's dark; **cette nuit** (*hier*) last night; (*aujourd'hui*) tonight; **de nuit** (*vol, service*) night *cpd*; **nuit blanche** sleepless night; **nuit de noces** wedding night; **nuit de Noël** Christmas Eve

nul, nulle [nyl] *adj* (*aucun*) no; (*minime*) nil, nonexistent; (*non valable*) null; (*péj*) useless, hopeless ◆ *pron* none, no one; **résultat nul, match nul** draw; **nulle part** *adv* nowhere

nullement [nylmɑ̃] *adv* by no means

nullité [nylite] *nf* nullity; (*péj*) hopelessness; (:*personne*) hopeless individual, nonentity

numérique [nymeʀik] *adj* numerical; (*INFORM*) digital

numéro [nymeʀo] *nm* number; (*spectacle*) act, turn; **faire** *ou* **composer un numéro** to dial a number; **numéro d'identification personnel** personal identification number (PIN); **numéro d'immatriculation** *ou* **minéralogique** *ou* **de police** registration (*BRIT*) *ou* license (*US*) number; **numéro de téléphone** (tele)phone number; **numéro vert** ≈ Freefone® number (*BRIT*), ≈ toll-free number (*US*)

numéroter [nymeʀote] *vt* to number

nu-pieds [nypje] *nm inv* sandal ◆ *adj inv* barefoot

nuque [nyk] *nf* nape of the neck

nu-tête [nytɛt] *adj inv* bareheaded

nutritif, ive [nytʀitif, -iv] *adj* nutritional; (*aliment*) nutritious, nourishing

nylon [nilɔ̃] *nm* nylon

— O o —

oasis [ɔazis] *nf ou m* oasis (*pl* oases)

obéir [ɔbeiʀ] *vi* to obey; **obéir à** to obey; (*moteur, véhicule*) to respond to

obéissance [ɔbeisɑ̃s] *nf* obedience

obéissant, e [ɔbeisɑ̃, -ɑ̃t] *adj* obedient

obèse [ɔbɛz] *adj* obese

obésité [ɔbezite] *nf* obesity

objecter [ɔbʒɛkte] *vt* (*prétexter*) to plead, put forward as an excuse; **objecter qch à** (*argument*) to put forward sth against; **objecter (à qn) que** to object (to sb) that

objecteur [ɔbʒɛktœʀ] *nm*: **objecteur de conscience** conscientious objector

objectif, ive [ɔbʒɛktif, -iv] *adj* objective ◆ *nm* (*OPTIQUE, PHOTO*) lens *sg*; (*MIL, fig*) objective; **objectif grand angulaire/à focale variable** wide-angle/zoom lens

objection [ɔbʒɛksjɔ̃] *nf* objection; **objection de conscience** conscientious objection

objectivité [ɔbʒɛktivite] *nf* objectivity

objet [ɔbʒɛ] *nm* (*chose*) object; (*d'une discussion, recherche*) subject; **être** *ou* **faire l'objet de** (*discussion*) to be the subject of; (*soins*) to be given *ou* shown; **sans objet** *adj* purposeless; (*sans fondement*) groundless; **objet d'art** objet d'art; **objets personnels** personal items; **objets de toilette** toiletries; **objets trouvés** lost property *sg* (*BRIT*), lost-and-found *sg* (*US*); **objets de valeur** valuables

obligation [ɔbligɑsjɔ̃] *nf* obligation; (*gén pl*: *devoir*) duty; (*COMM*) bond, debenture; **sans obligation d'achat** with no obligation (to buy); **être dans l'obligation de faire** to be obliged to do; **avoir l'obligation de faire** to be under an obligation to do; **obligations familiales** family obligations *ou* responsibilities; **obligations militaires** military obligations *ou* duties

obligatoire [ɔbligatwaʀ] *adj* compulsory, obligatory

obligatoirement [ɔbligatwaʀmɑ̃] *adv* compulsorily; (*fatalement*) necessarily

obligé, e [ɔbliʒe] *adj* (*redevable*): **être très obligé à qn** to be most obliged to sb; (*contraint*): **je suis (bien) obligé (de le faire)** I have to (do it); (*nécessaire: conséquence*) necessary; **c'est obligé!** it's inevitable!

obligeance [ɔbliʒɑ̃s] *nf*: **avoir l'obligeance de** to be kind *ou* good enough to

obligeant, e [ɔbliʒɑ̃, -ɑ̃t] *adj* obliging; kind

obliger [ɔbliʒe] *vt* (*contraindre*): **obliger qn à faire** to force *ou* oblige sb to do; (*JUR: engager*) to bind; (*rendre service à*) to oblige

oblique [ɔblik] *adj* oblique; **regard oblique** sidelong glance; **en oblique** *adv* diagonally

obliquer [ɔblike] *vi*: **obliquer vers** to turn off towards

oblitérer [ɔblitere] *vt* (*timbre-poste*) to cancel; (*MÉD: canal, vaisseau*) to obstruct

obnubiler [ɔbnybile] *vt* to obsess

obscène [ɔpsɛn] *adj* obscene

obscur, e [ɔpskyʀ] *adj* (*sombre*) dark; (*fig: raisons*) obscure; (: *sentiment, malaise*) vague; (: *personne, vie*) humble, lowly

obscurcir [ɔpskyʀsiʀ] *vt* to darken; (*fig*) to obscure; **s'obscurcir** *vi* to grow dark

obscurité [ɔpskyʀite] *nf* darkness; **dans l'obscurité** in the dark, in darkness; (*anonymat, médiocrité*) in obscurity

obsédé, e [ɔpsede] *nm/f* fanatic; **obsédé(e) sexuel(le)** sex maniac

obséder [ɔpsede] *vt* to obsess, haunt

obsèques [ɔpsɛk] *nfpl* funeral *sg*

observateur, trice [ɔpsɛʀvatœʀ, -tʀis] *adj* observant, perceptive ♦ *nm/f* observer

observation [ɔpsɛʀvasjɔ̃] *nf* observation; (*d'un règlement etc*) observance; (*commentaire*) observation, remark; (*reproche*) reproof; **en observation** (*MÉD*) under observation

observatoire [ɔpsɛʀvatwaʀ] *nm* observatory; (*lieu élevé*) observation post, vantage point

observer [ɔpsɛʀve] *vt* (*regarder*) to observe, watch; (*examiner*) to examine; (*scientifiquement, aussi: règlement, jeûne etc*) to observe; (*surveiller*) to watch; (*remarquer*) to observe, notice; **faire observer qch à qn** (*dire*) to point out sth to sb; **s'observer** (*se surveiller*) to keep a check on o.s.

obsession [ɔpsesjɔ̃] *nf* obsession; **avoir l'obsession de** to have an obsession with

obstacle [ɔpstakl(ə)] *nm* obstacle; (*ÉQUITATION*) jump, hurdle; **faire obstacle à** (*lumière*) to block out; (*projet*) to hinder, put obstacles in the path of; **obstacles antichars** tank defences

obstiné, e [ɔpstine] *adj* obstinate

obstiner [ɔpstine]: **s'obstiner** *vi* to insist, dig one's heels in; **s'obstiner à faire** to persist (obstinately) in doing; **s'obstiner sur qch** to keep working at sth, labour away at sth

obstruer [ɔpstʀye] *vt* to block, obstruct; **s'obstruer** *vi* to become blocked

obtenir [ɔptəniʀ] *vt* to obtain, get; (*total*) to arrive at, reach; (*résultat*) to achieve, obtain; **obtenir de pouvoir faire** to obtain permission to do; **obtenir qch à qn** to obtain sth for sb; **obtenir de qn qu'il fasse** to get sb to agree to do(ing)

obturateur [ɔptyʀatœʀ] *nm* (*PHOTO*) shutter; **obturateur à rideau** focal plane shutter

obus [ɔby] *nm* shell; **obus explosif** high-explosive shell; **obus incendiaire** incendiary device, fire bomb

occasion [ɔkazjɔ̃] *nf* (*aubaine, possibilité*) opportunity; (*circonstance*) occasion; (*COMM: article non neuf*) secondhand buy; (: *acquisition avantageuse*) bargain; **à plusieurs occasions** on several occasions; **à la première occasion** at the first *ou* earliest opportunity; **avoir l'occasion de faire** to have the opportunity to do; **être l'occasion de** to occasion, give rise to; **à l'occasion** *adv* sometimes, on occasions; (*un jour*) some time; **à l'occasion de** on the occasion of; **d'occasion** *adj, adv* secondhand

occasionnel, le [ɔkazjɔnɛl] *adj* (*fortuit*) chance *cpd*; (*non régulier*) occasional; (: *travail*) casual

occasionnellement [ɔkazjɔnɛlmɑ̃] *adv* occasionally, from time to time

occasionner [ɔkazjɔne] *vt* to cause, bring about; **occasionner qch à qn** to cause sb sth

occident [ɔksidɑ̃] *nm*: **l'Occident** the West

occidental, e, aux [ɔksidɑ̃tal, -o] *adj* western; (*POL*) Western ♦ *nm/f* Westerner

occupation [ɔkypasjɔ̃] *nf* occupation; **l'Occupation** the Occupation (of France)

occupé, e [ɔkype] *adj* (*MIL, POL*) occupied; (*personne: affairé, pris*) busy; (*esprit: absorbé*) occupied; (*place, sièges*) taken; (*toilettes, ligne*) engaged

occuper [ɔkype] *vt* to occupy; (*poste, fonction*) to hold; (*main-d'œuvre*) to employ; **s'occuper (à qch)** to occupy o.s. *ou* keep o.s. busy (with sth); **s'occuper de** (*être responsable de*) to be in charge of; (: *se charger de: affaire*) to take charge of, deal with; (: *clients etc*) to attend to; (*s'intéresser à, pratiquer: politique etc*) to be involved in; **ça occupe trop de place** it takes up too much room

occurrence [ɔkyʀɑ̃s] *nf*: **en l'occurrence** in this case

océan [ɔseɑ̃] *nm* ocean; **l'océan Indien** the Indian Ocean

octante [ɔktɑ̃t] *num* (*Belgique, Suisse*) eighty

octet [ɔktɛ] *nm* byte

octobre [ɔktɔbʀ(ə)] *nm* October; *voir aussi* **juillet**

octroyer [ɔktʀwaje] *vt*: **octroyer qch à qn** to grant sth to sb, grant sb sth

oculiste [ɔkylist(ə)] *nm/f* eye specialist, oculist

odeur [ɔdœʀ] *nf* smell

odieux, euse [ɔdjø, -øz] *adj* odious, hateful

odorant, e [ɔdɔʀɑ̃, -ɑ̃t] *adj* sweet-smelling, fragrant

odorat [ɔdɔʀa] *nm* (sense of) smell; **avoir l'odorat fin** to have a keen sense of smell

œil [œj], *pl* **yeux** [jø] *nm* eye; **avoir un œil poché** *ou* **au beurre noir** to have a black eye; **à l'œil** (*fam*) for free; **à l'œil nu** with the naked eye; **tenir qn à l'œil** to keep an eye *ou* a watch on sb; **avoir l'œil à** to keep an eye on; **faire de l'œil à qn** to make eyes at sb; **voir qch d'un bon/mauvais œil** to view sth in a favourable/an unfavourable light; **à l'œil vif** with a lively expression; **à mes/ses yeux** in my/his eyes; **de ses propres yeux** with his own eyes; **fermer les yeux (sur)** (*fig*) to turn a blind eye (to); **les yeux fermés** (*aussi fig*) with one's eyes shut; **fermer l'œil** to get a moment's sleep; **œil pour œil, dent pour dent** an eye for an eye, a tooth for a tooth; **pour les beaux yeux de qn** (*fig*) for love of sb; **œil de verre** glass eye

œillères [œjɛʀ] *nfpl* blinkers (*BRIT*), blinders (*US*); **avoir des œillères** (*fig*) to be blinkered, wear blinders

œillet [œjɛ] *nm* (*BOT*) carnation; (*trou*) eyelet

œuf [œf, *pl* ø] *nm* egg; **étouffer dans l'œuf** to nip in the bud; **œuf à la coque/dur/mollet** boiled/hard-boiled/soft-boiled egg; **œuf au plat/poché** fried/poached egg; **œufs brouillés** scrambled eggs; **œuf de Pâques** Easter egg; **œuf à repriser** darning egg

œuvre [œvʀ(ə)] *nf* (*tâche*) task, undertaking; (*ouvrage achevé, livre, tableau etc*) work; (*ensemble de la production artistique*) works *pl*; (*organisation charitable*) charity ◆ *nm* (*d'un artiste*) works *pl*; (*CONSTR*): **le gros œuvre** the shell; **œuvres** *nfpl* (*actes*) deeds, works; **être/se mettre à l'œuvre** to be at/get (down) to work; **mettre en œuvre** (*moyens*) to make use of; (*plan, loi, projet etc*) to implement; **œuvre d'art** work of art; **bonnes œuvres** good works *ou* deeds; **œuvres de bienfaisance** charitable works

offense [ɔfɑ̃s] *nf* (*affront*) insult; (*REL*: *péché*) transgression, trespass

offenser [ɔfɑ̃se] *vt* to offend, hurt; (*principes, Dieu*) to offend against; **s'offenser de** to take offence (*BRIT*) *ou* offense (*US*) at

offert, e [ɔfɛʀ, -ɛʀt(ə)] *pp de* offrir

office [ɔfis] *nm* (*charge*) office; (*agence*) bureau, agency; (*REL*) service ◆ *nm ou f* (*pièce*) pantry; **faire office de** to act as; to do duty as; **d'office** *adv* automatically; **bons offices** (*PCL*) good offices; **office du tourisme** tourist bureau

officiel, le [ɔfisjɛl] *adj, nm/f* official

officier [ɔfisje] *nm* officer ◆ *vi* (*REL*) to officiate; **officier de l'état-civil** registrar; **officier ministériel** member of the legal profession; **officier de police** = police officer

officieux, euse [ɔfisjø, -øz] *adj* unofficial

offrande [ɔfʀɑ̃d] *nf* offering

offre [ɔfʀ(ə)] *vb voir* offrir ◆ *nf* offer; (*aux enchères*) bid; (*ADMIN*: *soumission*) tender; (*ÉCON*): **l'offre** supply; **offre d'emploi** job advertised; **"offres d'emploi"** "situations vacant"; **offre publique d'achat (OPA)** takeover bid; **offres de service** offer of service

offrir [ɔfʀiʀ] *vt*: **offrir (à qn)** to offer (to sb); (*faire cadeau*) to give (to sb); **s'offrir** *vi* (*se présenter*: *occasion, paysage*) to present itself ◆ *vt* (*se payer*: *vacances, voiture*) to treat o.s. to; **offrir (à qn) de faire qch** to offer to do sth (for sb); **offrir à boire à qn** to offer sb a drink; **s'offrir à faire qch** to offer *ou* volunteer to do sth; **s'offrir comme guide/en otage** to offer one's services as (a) guide/offer o.s. as (a) hostage; **s'offrir aux regards** (*suj*: *personne*) to expose o.s. to the public gaze

offusquer [ɔfyske] *vt* to offend; **s'offusquer de** to take offence (*BRIT*) *ou* offense (*US*) at, be offended by

OGM *sigle m* (= *organisme génétiquement modifié*) GMO

oie [wa] *nf* (*ZOOL*) goose (*pl* geese); **oie blanche** (*fig*) young innocent

oignon [ɔɲɔ̃] *nm* (*CULIN*) onion; (*de tulipe etc*: *bulbe*) bulb; (*MÉD*) bunion; **ce ne sont pas tes oignons** (*fam*) that's none of your business

oiseau, x [wazo] *nm* bird; **oiseau de proie** bird of prey

oisif, ive [wazif, -iv] *adj* idle ◆ *nm/f* (*péj*) man/lady of leisure

oléoduc [ɔleɔdyk] *nm* (oil) pipeline

olive [ɔliv] *nf* (*BOT*) olive ◆ *adj inv* olive(-green)

olivier [ɔlivje] *nm* olive (tree); (*bois*) olive (wood)

OLP *sigle f* (= *Organisation de libération de la Palestine*) PLO

olympique [ɔlɛ̃pik] *adj* Olympic

ombragé, e [ɔ̃bʀaʒe] *adj* shaded, shady

ombrageux, euse [ɔ̃bʀaʒø, -øz] *adj* (*cheval*) skittish, nervous; (*personne*) touchy, easily offended

ombre [ɔ̃bʀ(ə)] *nf* (*espace non ensoleillé*) shade; (*ombre portée, tache*) shadow; **à l'ombre** in the shade; (*fam*: *en prison*) behind bars; **à l'ombre de** in the shade of; (*tout près de, fig*) in the shadow of; **tu me fais de l'ombre** you're in my light; **ça nous donne de l'ombre** it gives us (some) shade; **il n'y a pas l'ombre d'un doute** there's not the shadow of a doubt; **dans l'ombre** in the shade; **vivre dans l'ombre** (*fig*) to live in obscurity; **laisser dans l'ombre** (*fig*) to leave in the dark; **ombre à paupières** eyeshadow; **ombre portée** shadow; **ombres chinoises** (*spectacle*) shadow show *sg*

ombrelle [ɔ̃bʀɛl] *nf* parasol, sunshade

omelette [ɔmlɛt] *nf* omelette; **omelette baveuse** runny omelette; **omelette au fromage/au jambon** cheese/ham omelette; **omelette aux herbes** omelette with herbs; **omelette norvégienne** baked Alaska

omettre [ɔmɛtʀ(ə)] *vt* to omit, leave out; **omettre de faire** to fail *ou* omit to do

omnibus [ɔmnibys] *nm* slow *ou* stopping train

omoplate [ɔmɔplat] *nf* shoulder blade

MOT CLÉ

on [ɔ̃] *pron* **1** (*indéterminé*) you, one; **on peut le faire ainsi** you *ou* one can do it like this, it can be done like this; **on dit que ...** they say that ..., it is said that ..

2 (*quelqu'un*): **on les a attaqués** they were attacked; **on vous demande au téléphone** there's a phone call for you, you're wanted on the phone; **on frappe à la porte** someone's knocking at the door

3 (*nous*) we; **on va y aller demain** we're going tomorrow

4 (*les gens*) they; **autrefois, on croyait ...** they used to believe ...

5: on ne peut plus *adv*: **on ne peut plus stupide** as stupid as can be

oncle [ɔ̃kl(ə)] *nm* uncle

onctueux, euse [ɔ̃ktɥø, -øz] *adj* creamy, smooth; (*fig*) smooth, unctuous

onde [ɔ̃d] *nf* (*PHYSIQUE*) wave; **sur l'onde** on the waters; **sur les ondes** on the radio; **mettre en ondes** to produce for the radio; **onde de choc** shock wave; **ondes courtes (OC)** short wave *sg*; **petites ondes (PO), ondes moyennes (OM)** medium wave *sg*; **grandes ondes (GO), ondes longues (OL)** long wave *sg*; **ondes sonores** sound waves

ondée [ɔ̃de] *nf* shower

on-dit [ɔ̃di] *nm inv* rumour

onduler [ɔ̃dyle] *vi* to undulate; (*cheveux*) to wave

onéreux, euse [ɔnerø, -øz] *adj* costly; **à titre onéreux** in return for payment

ongle [ɔ̃gl(ə)] *nm* (*ANAT*) nail; **manger** *ou* **ronger ses ongles** to bite one's nails; **se faire les ongles** to do one's nails

ont [ɔ̃] *vb voir* **avoir**

ONU [ɔny] *sigle f* (= *Organisation des Nations unies*) UN(O)

onze [ɔ̃z] *num* eleven

onzième [ɔ̃zjɛm] *num* eleventh

OPA *sigle f* = **offre publique d'achat**

opaque [ɔpak] *adj* (*vitre, verre*) opaque; (*brouillard, nuit*) impenetrable

opéra [ɔpera] *nm* opera; (*édifice*) opera house

opérateur, trice [ɔperatœr, -tris] *nm/f* operator; **opérateur (de prise de vues)** cameraman

opération [ɔperasjɔ̃] *nf* operation; (*COMM*) dealing; **salle/table d'opération** operating theatre/ table; **opération de sauvetage** rescue operation; **opération à cœur ouvert** open-heart surgery *no pl*

opératoire [ɔperatwaʀ] *adj* (*manœuvre, méthode*) operating; (*choc etc*) post-operative

opérer [ɔpere] *vt* (*MÉD*) to operate on; (*faire, exécuter*) to carry out, make ♦ *vi* (*remède: faire effet*) to act, work; (*procéder*) to proceed; (*MÉD*) to operate; **s'opérer** *vi* (*avoir lieu*) to occur, take place; **se faire opérer** to have an operation; **se faire opérer des amygdales/du cœur** to have one's tonsils out/ have a heart operation

opérette [ɔperet] *nf* operetta, light opera

ophtalmologie [ɔftalmɔlɔʒi] *nf* ophthalmology

opiner [ɔpine] *vi*: **opiner de la tête** to nod assent ♦ *vt*: **opiner à** to consent to

opinion [ɔpinjɔ̃] *nf* opinion; **l'opinion (publique)** public opinion; **avoir bonne/mauvaise opinion de** to have a high/low opinion of

opportun, e [ɔpɔʀtœ̃, -yn] *adj* timely, opportune; **en temps opportun** at the appropriate time

opportuniste [ɔpɔʀtynist(ə)] *adj, nm/f* opportunist

opposant, e [ɔpozɑ̃, -ɑ̃t] *adj* opposing ♦ *nm/f* opponent

opposé, e [ɔpoze] *adj* (*direction, rive*) opposite; (*faction*) opposing; (*couleurs*) contrasting; (*opinions, intérêts*) conflicting; (*contre*): **opposé à** opposed to, against ♦ *nm*: **l'opposé** the other *ou* opposite side (*ou* direction); (*contraire*) the opposite; **être opposé à** to be opposed to; **à l'opposé** (*fig*) on the other hand; **à l'opposé de** on the other *ou* opposite side from; (*fig*) contrary to, unlike

opposer [ɔpoze] *vt* (*meubles, objets*) to place opposite each other; (*personnes, armées, équipes*) to oppose; (*couleurs, termes, tons*) to contrast; (*comparer: livres, avantages*) to contrast; **opposer qch à** (*comme obstacle, défense*) to set sth against; (*comme objection*) to put sth forward against; (*en contraste*) to set sth opposite; to match sth with; **s'opposer** (*sens réciproque*) to conflict; to clash; to face each other; to contrast; **s'opposer à** (*interdire, empêcher*) to oppose; (*tenir tête à*) to rebel against; **sa religion s'y oppose** it's against his religion; **s'opposer à ce que qn fasse** to be opposed to sb's doing

opposition [ɔpozisjɔ̃] *nf* opposition; **par opposition** in contrast; **par opposition à** as opposed to, in contrast with; **entrer en opposition avec** to come into conflict with; **être en opposition avec** (*idées, conduite*) to be at variance with; **faire opposition à un chèque** to stop a cheque

oppressant, e [ɔpresɑ̃, -ɑ̃t] *adj* oppressive

oppresser [ɔprese] *vt* to oppress; **se sentir oppressé** to feel breathless

oppression [ɔpresjɔ̃] *nf* oppression; (*malaise*) feeling of suffocation

opprimer [ɔprime] *vt* (*asservir: peuple, faibles*) to oppress; (*étouffer: liberté, opinion*) to suppress, stifle; (*suj: chaleur etc*) to suffocate, oppress

opter [ɔpte] *vi*: **opter pour** to opt for; **opter entre** to choose between

opticien, ne [ɔptisjɛ̃, -ɛn] *nm/f* optician

optimisme [ɔptimism(ə)] *nm* optimism

optimiste [ɔptimist(ə)] *adj* optimistic ♦ *nm/f* optimist

option [ɔpsjɔ̃] *nf* option; (*AUTO: supplément*) optional extra; **matière à option** (*SCOL*) optional subject (*BRIT*), elective (*US*); **prendre une option sur** to take (out) an option on; **option par défaut** (*INFORM*) default (option)

optique [ɔptik] *adj* (*nerf*) optic; (*verres*) optical ♦ *nf* (*PHOTO: lentilles etc*) optics *pl*; (*science, industrie*) optics *sg*; (*fig: manière de voir*) perspective

opulent, e [ɔpylɑ̃, -ɑ̃t] *adj* wealthy, opulent; (*formes, poitrine*) ample, generous

or [ɔʀ] *nm* gold ♦ *conj* now, but; **d'or** (*fig*) golden; **en or** gold *cpd*; (*occasion*) golden; **un mari/enfant en or** a treasure; **une affaire en or** (*achat*) a real bargain; (*commerce*) a gold mine; **plaqué or** gold-

opportuniste [ɔpɔʀtynist(ə)] *adj, nm/f* opportunist

plated; **or noir** black gold

orage [ɔʀaʒ] *nm* (thunder)storm

orageux, euse [ɔʀaʒø, -øz] *adj* stormy

oral, e, aux [ɔʀal, -o] *adj* (*déposition, promesse*) oral, verbal; (*MÉD*): **par voie orale** by mouth, orally ♦ *nm* (*SCOL*) oral

orange [ɔʀɑ̃ʒ] *adj inv, nf* orange; **orange sanguine** blood orange; **orange pressée** freshly-squeezed orange juice

orangé, e [ɔʀɑ̃ʒe] *adj* orangey, orange-coloured

orangeade [ɔʀɑ̃ʒad] *nf* orangeade

oranger [ɔʀɑ̃ʒe] *nm* orange tree

orateur [ɔʀatœʀ] *nm* speaker; orator

orbite [ɔʀbit] *nf* (*ANAT*) (eye-)socket; (*PHYSIQUE*) orbit; **mettre sur orbite** to put into orbit; (*fig*) to launch; **dans l'orbite de** (*fig*) within the sphere of influence of

orchestre [ɔʀkɛstʀ(ə)] *nm* orchestra; (*de jazz, danse*) band; (*places*) stalls *pl* (*BRIT*), orchestra (*US*)

orchestrer [ɔʀkɛstʀe] *vt* (*MUS*) to orchestrate; (*fig*) to mount, stage-manage

orchidée [ɔʀkide] *nf* orchid

ordinaire [ɔʀdinɛʀ] *adj* ordinary; (*coutumier: maladresse etc*) usual; (*de tous les jours*) everyday; (*modèle, qualité*) standard ♦ *nm* ordinary; (*menus*) everyday fare ♦ *nf* (*essence*) = two-star (petrol) (*BRIT*), = regular (gas) (*US*); **d'ordinaire** usually, normally; **à l'ordinaire** usually, ordinarily

ordinateur [ɔʀdinatœʀ] *nm* computer; **mettre sur ordinateur** to computerize, put on computer; **ordinateur de bureau** desktop computer; **ordinateur domestique** home computer; **ordinateur individuel** *ou* **personnel** personal computer; **ordinateur portatif** laptop (computer)

ordonnance [ɔʀdɔnɑ̃s] *nf* organization; (*groupement, disposition*) layout; (*MÉD*) prescription; (*JUR*) order; (*MIL*) orderly, batman (*BRIT*); **d'ordonnance** (*MIL*) regulation *cpd*; **officier d'ordonnance** aide-de-camp

ordonné, e [ɔʀdɔne] *adj* tidy, orderly; (*MATH*) ordered ♦ *nf* (*MATH*) Y-axis, ordinate

ordonner [ɔʀdɔne] *vt* (*agencer*) to organize, arrange; (: *meubles, appartement*) to lay out, arrange; (*donner un ordre*): **ordonner à qn de faire** to order sb to do; (*MATH*) to (arrange in) order; (*REL*) to ordain; (*MÉD*) to prescribe; (*JUR*) to order; **s'ordonner** (*faits*) to organize themselves

ordre [ɔʀdʀ(ə)] *nm* (*gén*) order; (*propreté et soin*) orderliness, tidiness; (*association professionnelle, honorifique*) association; (*COMM*): **à l'ordre de** payable to; (*nature*): **d'ordre pratique** of a practical nature; **ordres** *nmpl* (*REL*) holy orders; **avoir de l'ordre** to be tidy *ou* orderly; **mettre en ordre** to tidy (up), put in order; **mettre bon ordre à** to put to rights, sort out; **procéder par ordre** to take things one at a time; **être aux ordres de qn/sous les ordres de qn** to be at sb's disposal/under sb's command; **rappeler qn à l'ordre** to call sb to

order; **jusqu'à nouvel ordre** until further notice; **dans le même ordre d'idées** in this connection; **par ordre d'entrée en scène** in order of appearance; **un ordre de grandeur** some idea of the size (*ou* amount); **de premier ordre** first-rate; **ordre de grève** strike call; **ordre du jour** (*d'une réunion*) agenda; (*MIL*) order of the day; **à l'ordre du jour** on the agenda; (*fig*) topical; (*MIL: citer*) in dispatches; **ordre de mission** (*MIL*) orders *pl*; **ordre public** law and order; **ordre de route** marching orders *pl*

ordure [ɔʀdyʀ] *nf* filth *no pl*; (*propos, écrit*) obscenity, (piece of) filth; **ordures** *nfpl* (*balayures, déchets*) rubbish *sg*, refuse *sg*; **ordures ménagères** household refuse

oreille [ɔʀɛj] *nf* (*ANAT*) ear; (*de marmite, tasse*) handle; (*TECH: d'un écrou*) wing; **avoir de l'oreille** to have a good ear (for music); **avoir l'oreille fine** to have good *ou* sharp ears; **l'oreille basse** crest-fallen, dejected; **se faire tirer l'oreille** to take a lot of persuading; **dire qch à l'oreille de qn** to have a word in sb's ear (about sth)

oreiller [ɔʀeje] *nm* pillow

oreillons [ɔʀɛjɔ̃] *nmpl* mumps *sg*

ores [ɔʀ]: **d'ores et déjà** *adv* already

orfèvrerie [ɔʀfɛvʀəʀi] *nf* (*art, métier*) goldsmith's (*ou* silversmith's) trade; (*ouvrage*) (silver *ou* gold) plate

organe [ɔʀgan] *nm* organ; (*véhicule, instrument*) instrument; (*voix*) voice; (*porte-parole*) representative, mouthpiece; **organes de commande** (*TECH*) controls; **organes de transmission** (*TECH*) transmission system *sg*

organigramme [ɔʀganigʀam] *nm* (*hiérarchie, structure*) organization chart; (*des opérations*) flow chart

organique [ɔʀganik] *adj* organic

organisateur, trice [ɔʀganizatœʀ, -tʀis] *nm/f* organizer

organisation [ɔʀganizasjɔ̃] *nf* organization; **Organisation des Nations unies (ONU)** United Nations (Organization) (UN, UNO); **Organisation mondiale de la santé (OMS)** World Health Organization (WHO); **Organisation du traité de l'Atlantique Nord (OTAN)** North Atlantic Treaty Organization (NATO)

organiser [ɔʀganize] *vt* to organize; (*mettre sur pied: service etc*) to set up; **s'organiser** to get organized

organisme [ɔʀganism(ə)] *nm* (*BIO*) organism; (*corps humain*) body; (*ADMIN, POL etc*) body, organism

organiste [ɔʀganist(ə)] *nm/f* organist

orgasme [ɔʀgasm(ə)] *nm* orgasm, climax

orge [ɔʀʒ(ə)] *nf* barley

orgue [ɔʀg(ə)] *nm* organ; **orgues** *nfpl* organ *sg*; **orgue de Barbarie** barrel *ou* street organ

orgueil [ɔʀgœj] *nm* pride

orgueilleux, euse [ɔʀgœjø, -øz] *adj* proud

Orient [ɔʀjɑ̃] *nm*: **l'Orient** the East, the Orient

oriental, e, aux [ɔʀjɑ̃tal, -o] *adj* oriental, eastern; (*frontière*) eastern ♦ *nm/f*: **Oriental, e** Oriental

orientation [ɔʀjɑ̃tasjɔ̃] *nf* positioning; adjustment; orientation; direction; (*d'une maison etc*) aspect; (*d'un journal*) leanings *pl*; **avoir le sens de l'orientation** to have a (good) sense of direction; **course d'orientation** orienteering exercise; **orientation professionnelle** careers advice *ou* guidance; (*service*) careers advisory service

orienté, e [ɔʀjɑ̃te] *adj* (*fig: article, journal*) slanted; **bien/mal orienté** (*appartement*) well/badly positioned; **orienté au sud** facing south, with a southern aspect

orienter [ɔʀjɑ̃te] *vt* (*situer*) to position; (*placer, disposer: pièce mobile*) to adjust, position; (*tourner*) to direct, turn; (*voyageur, touriste, recherches*) to direct; (*fig: élève*) to orientate; **s'orienter** (*se repérer*) to find one's bearings; **s'orienter vers** (*fig*) to turn towards

origan [ɔʀigɑ̃] *nm* oregano

originaire [ɔʀiʒinɛʀ] *adj* original; **être originaire de** (*pays, lieu*) to be a native of; (*provenir de*) to originate from; to be native to

original, e, aux [ɔʀiʒinal, -o] *adj* original; (*bizarre*) eccentric ♦ *nm/f* (*fam: excentrique*) eccentric; (*: fantaisiste*) joker ♦ *nm* (*document etc, ART*) original; (*dactylographie*) top copy

origine [ɔʀiʒin] *nf* origin; (*d'un message, appel téléphonique*) source; (*d'une révolution, réussite*) root; **origines** *nfpl* (*d'une personne*) origins; **d'origine** of origin; (*pneus etc*) original; (*bureau postal*) dispatching; **d'origine française** of French origin; **dès l'origine** at *ou* from the outset; **à l'origine** originally; **avoir son origine dans** to have its origins in, originate in

originel, le [ɔʀiʒinɛl] *adj* original

orme [ɔʀm(ə)] *nm* elm

ornement [ɔʀnəmɑ̃] *nm* ornament; (*fig*) embellishment, adornment; **ornements sacerdotaux** vestments

orner [ɔʀne] *vt* to decorate, adorn; **orner qch de** to decorate sth with

ornière [ɔʀnjɛʀ] *nf* rut; (*fig*): **sortir de l'ornière** (*routine*) to get out of the rut; (*impasse*) to get out of a spot

orphelin, e [ɔʀfəlɛ̃, -in] *adj* orphan(ed) ♦ *nm/f* orphan; **orphelin de père/mère** fatherless/motherless

orphelinat [ɔʀfəlina] *nm* orphanage

orteil [ɔʀtɛj] *nm* toe; **gros orteil** big toe

orthographe [ɔʀtɔgʀaf] *nf* spelling

ortie [ɔʀti] *nf* (stinging) nettle; **ortie blanche** white dead-nettle

os [ɔs, *pl* o] *nm* bone; **sans os** (*BOUCHERIE*) off the bone, boned; **os à moelle** marrowbone

osciller [ɔsile] *vi* (*pendule*) to swing; (*au vent etc*) to rock; (*TECH*) to oscillate; (*fig*): **osciller entre** to waver *ou* fluctuate between

osé, e [oze] *adj* daring, bold

oseille [ozɛj] *nf* sorrel

oser [oze] *vi, vt* to dare; **oser faire** to dare (to) do

osier [ozje] *nm* (*BOT*) willow; **d'osier en osier** wicker(work) *cpd*

ossature [ɔsatyʀ] *nf* (*ANAT: squelette*) frame, skeletal structure; (*: du visage*) bone structure; (*fig*) framework

osseux, euse [ɔsø, -øz] *adj* bony; (*tissu, maladie, greffe*) bone *cpd*

ostensible [ɔstɑ̃sibl(ə)] *adj* conspicuous

otage [ɔtaʒ] *nm* hostage; **prendre qn comme otage** to take sb hostage

OTAN [ɔtɑ̃] *sigle f* (= Organisation du traité de l'Atlantique Nord) NATO

otarie [ɔtaʀi] *nf* sea-lion

ôter [ote] *vt* to remove; (*soustraire*) to take away; **ôter qch à qn** to take sth (away) from sb; **ôter qch de** to remove sth from; **6 ôté de 10 égale 4** 6 from 10 equals *ou* is 4

otite [ɔtit] *nf* ear infection

ou [u] *conj* or; **ou ... ou** either ... or; **ou bien** or (else)

MOT CLÉ

où [u] *pron relatif* **1** (*position, situation*) where, that (*souvent omis*); **la chambre où il était** the room (that) he was in, the room where he was; **la ville où je l'ai rencontré** the town where I met him; **la pièce d'où il est sorti** the room he came out of; **le village d'où je viens** the village I come from; **les villes par où il est passé** the towns he went through

2 (*temps, état*) that (*souvent omis*); **le jour où il est parti** the day (that) he left; **au prix où c'est** at the price it is

♦ *adv* **1** (*interrogation*) where; **où est-il/va-t-il?** where is he/is he going?; **par où?** which way?; **d'où vient que ...?** how come ...?

2 (*position*) where; **je sais où il est** I know where he is; **où que l'on aille** wherever you go

---

ouate [wat] *nf* cotton wool (*BRIT*), cotton (*US*); (*bourre*) padding, wadding; **ouate (hydrophile)** cotton wool (*BRIT*), (absorbent) cotton (*US*)

oubli [ubli] *nm* (*acte*): **l'oubli de** forgetting; (*étourderie*) forgetfulness *no pl*; (*négligence*) omission, oversight; (*absence de souvenirs*) oblivion; **oubli de soi** self-effacement, self-negation

oublier [ublije] *vt* (*gén*) to forget; (*ne pas voir: erreurs etc*) to miss; (*ne pas mettre: virgule, nom*) to leave out, forget; (*laisser quelque part: chapeau etc*) to leave behind; **s'oublier** to forget o.s.; (*enfant, animal*) to have an accident (*euphemism*) **oublier l'heure** to forget (about) the time

oubliettes [ublijɛt] *nfpl* dungeon *sg*; (**jeter) aux oubliettes** (*fig*) (to put) completely out of mind

ouest [wɛst] *nm* west ♦ *adj inv* west; (*région*)

western; **à l'ouest** in the west, (to the) west, westwards; **à l'ouest de** (to the) west of; **vent d'ouest** westerly wind

ouf [uf] *excl* phew!

oui [wi] *adv* yes; **répondre (par) oui** to answer yes; **mais oui, bien sûr** yes, of course; **je pense que oui** I think so; **pour un oui ou pour un non** for no apparent reason

ouï-dire [widiʀ]: **par ouï-dire** *adv* by hearsay

ouïe [wi] *nf* hearing; **ouïes** *nfpl* (*de poisson*) gills; (*de violon*) sound-hole *sg*

ouragan [uʀagɑ̃] *nm* hurricane; (*fig*) storm

ourlet [uʀlɛ] *nm* hem; **faire un ourlet à** to hem

ours [uʀs] *nm* bear; **ours brun/blanc** brown/polar bear; **ours marin** fur seal; **ours mal léché** uncouth fellow; **ours (en peluche)** teddy (bear)

oursin [uʀsɛ̃] *nm* sea urchin

ourson [uʀsɔ̃] *nm* (bear-)cub

ouste [ust(ə)] *excl* hop it!

outil [uti] *nm* tool

outiller [utije] *vt* (*ouvrier, usine*) to equip

outrage [utʀaʒ] *nm* insult; **faire subir les derniers outrages à** (*femme*) to ravish; **outrage aux bonnes mœurs** (*JUR*) outrage to public decency; **outrage à magistrat** (*JUR*) contempt of court; **outrage à la pudeur** (*JUR*) indecent behaviour *no pl*

outrager [utʀaʒe] *vt* to offend gravely; (*fig: contrevenir à*) to outrage, insult

outrance [utʀɑ̃s] *nf* excessiveness *no pl*, excess; **à outrance** *adv* excessively, to excess

outre [utʀ(ə)] *nf* goatskin, water skin ◆ *prép* besides ◆ *adv*: **passer outre** to carry on regardless; **passer outre à** to disregard, take no notice of; **en outre** besides, moreover; **outre que** apart from the fact that; **outre mesure** immoderately; unduly

outre-Atlantique [utʀatlɑ̃tik] *adv* across the Atlantic

outre-Manche [utʀəmɑ̃ʃ] *adv* across the Channel

outre-mer [utʀəmɛʀ] *adv* overseas; **d'outre-mer** overseas

outrepasser [utʀəpase] *vt* to go beyond, exceed

ouvert, e [uvɛʀ, -ɛʀt(ə)] *pp de* ouvrir ◆ *adj* open; (*robinet, gaz etc*) on; **à bras ouverts** with open arms

ouvertement [uvɛʀtəmɑ̃] *adv* openly

ouverture [uvɛʀtyʀ] *nf* opening; (*MUS*) overture; (*POL*): **l'ouverture** the widening of the political spectrum; (*PHOTO*): **ouverture (du diaphragme)** aperture; **ouvertures** *nfpl* (*propositions*) overtures; **ouverture d'esprit** open-mindedness; **heures d'ouverture** (*COMM*) opening hours; **jours d'ouverture** (*COMM*) days of opening

ouvrable [uvʀabl(ə)] *adj*: **jour ouvrable** working day, weekday; **heures ouvrables** business hours

ouvrage [uvʀaʒ] *nm* (*tâche, de tricot etc, MIL*) work

no pl; (*objet*: COUTURE, ART) (piece of) work; (*texte, livre*) work; **ouvrage d'art** (*GÉNIE CIVIL*) bridge or tunnel *etc*

ouvragé, e [uvʀaʒe] *adj* finely embroidered (*ou* worked *ou* carved)

ouvre-boîte(s) [uvʀəbwat] *nm inv* tin (*BRIT*) *ou* can opener

ouvre-bouteille(s) [uvʀəbutɛj] *nm inv* bottle-opener

ouvreuse [uvʀøz] *nf* usherette

ouvrier, ière [uvʀije, -jɛʀ] *nm/f* worker ◆ *nf* (*ZOOL*) worker (bee) ◆ *adj* working-class; (*problèmes, conflit*) industrial, labour *cpd* (*BRIT*), labor *cpd* (*US*); (*revendications*) workers'; **classe ouvrière** working class; **ouvrier agricole** farmworker; **ouvrier qualifié** skilled worker; **ouvrier spécialisé (OS)** semiskilled worker; **ouvrier d'usine** factory worker

ouvrir [uvʀiʀ] *vt* (*gén*) to open; (*brèche, passage*) to open up; (*commencer l'exploitation de, créer*) to open (up); (*eau, électricité, chauffage, robinet*) to turn on; (*MÉD: abcès*) to open, cut open ◆ *vi* to open; to open up; (*CARTES*): **ouvrir à trèfle** to open in clubs; **s'ouvrir** *vi* to open; **s'ouvrir à** (*art etc*) to open one's mind to; **s'ouvrir à qn (de qch)** to open one's heart to sb (about sth); **s'ouvrir les veines** to slash *ou* cut one's wrists; **ouvrir sur** to open onto; **ouvrir l'appétit à qn** to whet sb's appetite; **ouvrir des horizons** to open up new horizons; **ouvrir l'esprit** to broaden one's horizons; **ouvrir une session** (*INFORM*) to log in

ovaire [ɔvɛʀ] *nm* ovary

ovale [ɔval] *adj* oval

OVNI [ɔvni] *sigle m* (= objet volant non identifié) UFO

oxyder [ɔkside]: **s'oxyder** *vi* to become oxidized

oxygène [ɔksiʒɛn] *nm* oxygen; (*fig*): **cure d'oxygène** fresh air cure

oxygéné, e [ɔksiʒene] *adj*: **eau oxygénée** hydrogen peroxide; **cheveux oxygénés** bleached hair

ozone [ozon] *nm* ozone; **trou dans la couche d'ozone** ozone hole

— P p —

pacifique [pasifik] *adj* (*personne*) peaceable; (*intentions, coexistence*) peaceful ◆ *nm*: **le Pacifique, l'océan Pacifique** the Pacific (Ocean)

pack [pak] *nm* pack

pacotille [pakɔtij] *nf* (*péj*) cheap goods *pl*; **de pacotille** cheap

PACS [paks] *sigle m* (*Pacte Civil de Solidarité*) contract of civil partnership

pacte [pakt(ə)] *nm* pact, treaty

pagaie [pagɛ] *nf* paddle

pagaille [pagaj] *nf* mess, shambles *sg*; **il y en a en pagaille** there are loads *ou* heaps of them

pagayer [pageje] *vi* to paddle

page [paʒ] *nf* page; (*passage: d'un roman*) passage ♦ *nm* page (boy); **mettre en pages** to make up (into pages); **mise en page** layout; **à la page** (*fig*) up-to-date; **page blanche** blank page; **page de garde** endpaper

paiement [pemɑ̃] *nm* = **payement**

païen, ne [pajɛ̃, -ɛn] *adj, nm/f* pagan, heathen

paillasson [pɑjasɔ̃] *nm* doormat

paille [pɑj] *nf* straw; (*défaut*) flaw; **être sur la paille** to be ruined; **paille de fer** steel wool

paillette [pɑjɛt] *nf* speck, flake; **paillettes** *nfpl* (*décoratives*) sequins, spangles; **lessive en paillettes** soapflakes *pl*

pain [pɛ̃] *nm* (*substance*) bread; (*unité*) loaf (*pl* loaves) (of bread); (*morceau*): **pain de cire etc** bar of wax *etc*; (*culin*) **pain de poisson/légumes** fish/ vegetable loaf; **petit pain** (bread) roll; **pain bis/ complet** brown/wholemeal (*BRIT*) *ou* wholewheat (*US*) bread; **pain de campagne** farmhouse bread; **pain d'épice** ≃ gingerbread; **pain grillé** toast; **pain de mie** sandwich loaf; **pain perdu** French toast; **pain de seigle** rye bread; **pain de sucre** sugar loaf

pair, e [pɛʁ] *adj* (*nombre*) even ♦ *nm* peer; **aller de pair (avec)** to go hand in hand *ou* together (with); **au pair** (*FINANCE*) at par; **valeur au pair** par value; **jeune fille au pair** au pair

paire [pɛʁ] *nf* pair; **une paire de lunettes/ tenailles** a pair of glasses/pincers; **faire la paire: les deux font la paire** they are two of a kind

paisible [pezibl(ə)] *adj* peaceful, quiet

paître [pɛtʁ(ə)] *vi* to graze

paix [pɛ] *nf* peace; (*fig*) peacefulness, peace; **faire la paix avec** to make peace with; **avoir la paix** to have peace (and quiet)

Pakistan [pakistɑ̃] *nm*: **le Pakistan** Pakistan

palace [palas] *nm* luxury hotel

palais [palɛ] *nm* palace; (*ANAT*) palate; **le Palais Bourbon** the seat of the French National Assembly; **le Palais de l'Élysée** the Élysée Palace; **palais des expositions** exhibition centre; **le Palais de Justice** the Law Courts *pl*

pâle [pɑl] *adj* pale; (*fig*): **une pâle imitation** a pale imitation; **bleu pâle** pale blue; **pâle de colère** white *ou* pale with anger

Palestine [palestin] *nf*: **la Palestine** Palestine

palet [palɛ] *nm* disc; (*HOCKEY*) puck

paletot [palto] *nm* (short) coat

palette [palɛt] *nf* palette; (*de produits*) range

pâleur [pɑlœʁ] *nf* paleness

palier [palje] *nm* (*d'escalier*) landing; (*fig*) level, plateau; (: *phase stable*) levelling (*BRIT*) *ou* leveling (*US*) off, new level; (*TECH*) bearing; **nos voisins de palier** our neighbo(u)rs across the landing (*BRIT*) *ou*

the hall (*US*); **en palier** *adv* level; **par paliers** in stages

pâlir [pɑliʁ] *vi* to turn *ou* go pale; (*couleur*) to fade; **faire pâlir qn** (*de jalousie*) to make sb green (with envy)

palissade [palisad] *nf* fence

pallier [palje] *vt*, **pallier à** *vt* to offset, make up for

palmarès [palmaʁɛs] *nm* record (of achievements); (*SCOL*) prize list; (*SPORT*) list of winners

palme [palm(ə)] *nf* (*BOT*) palm leaf (*pl* leaves); (*symbole*) palm; (*de plongeur*) flipper; **palmes (académiques)** *decoration for services to education*

palmé, e [palme] *adj* (*pattes*) webbed

palmier [palmje] *nm* palm tree

pâlot, te [pɑlo, -ɔt] *adj* pale, peaky

palourde [paluʁd(ə)] *nf* clam

palper [palpe] *vt* to feel, finger

palpitant, e [palpitɑ̃, -ɑ̃t] *adj* thrilling, gripping

palpiter [palpite] *vi* (*cœur, pouls*) to beat; (: *plus fort*) to pound, throb; (*narines, chair*) to quiver

paludisme [palydism(ə)] *nm* malaria

pamphlet [pɑ̃flɛ] *nm* lampoon, satirical tract

pamplemousse [pɑ̃pləmus] *nm* grapefruit

pan [pɑ̃] *nm* section, piece; (*côté: d'un prisme, d'une tour*) side, face ♦ *excl* bang!; **pan de chemise** shirt tail; **pan de mur** section of wall

panache [panaʃ] *nm* plume; (*fig*) spirit, panache

panaché, e [panaʃe] *adj*: **œillet panaché** variegated carnation; **glace panachée** mixed ice cream; **salade panachée** mixed salad; **bière panachée** shandy

pancarte [pɑ̃kaʁt(ə)] *nf* sign, notice; (*dans un défilé*) placard

pancréas [pɑ̃kʁeas] *nm* pancreas

pané, e [pane] *adj* fried in breadcrumbs

panier [panje] *nm* basket; (*à diapositives*) magazine; **mettre au panier** to chuck away; **panier de crabes: c'est un panier de crabes** (*fig*) they're constantly at one another's throats; **panier percé** (*fig*) spendthrift; **panier à provisions** shopping basket; **panier à salade** (*CULIN*) salad shaker; (*POLICE*) paddy wagon, police van

panier-repas, *pl* **paniers-repas** [panje(ʁ)əpɑ] *nm* packed lunch

panique [panik] *adj* panicky ♦ *nf* panic

paniquer [panike] *vi* to panic

panne [pan] *nf* (*d'un mécanisme, moteur*) breakdown; **être/tomber en panne** to have broken down/break down; **être en panne d'essence** *ou* **en panne sèche** to have run out of petrol (*BRIT*) *ou* gas (*US*); **mettre en panne** (*NAVIG*) to bring to; **panne d'électricité** *ou* **de courant** power *ou* electrical failure

panneau, x [pano] *nm* (*écriteau*) sign, notice; (*de boiserie, de tapisserie etc*) panel; **tomber dans le panneau** (*fig*) to walk into the trap; **panneau d'affichage** notice (*BRIT*) *ou* bulletin (*US*) board; **pan-**

neau électoral board for election poster; **panneau indicateur** signpost; **panneau publicitaire** hoarding (BRIT), billboard (US); **panneau de signalisation** roadsign; **panneau solaire** solar panel

panoplie [panɔpli] nf (jouet) outfit; (d'armes) display; (fig) array

panorama [panɔrama] nm (vue) all-round view, panorama; (peinture) panorama; (fig: étude complète) complete overview

panse [pɑ̃s] nf paunch

pansement [pɑ̃smɑ̃] nm dressing, bandage; **pansement adhésif** sticking plaster (BRIT), bandaid® (US)

panser [pɑ̃se] vt (plaie) to dress, bandage; (bras) to put a dressing on, bandage; (cheval) to groom

pantalon [pɑ̃talɔ̃] nm (aussi: **pantalons**, **paire de pantalons**) trousers pl (BRIT), pants pl (US), pair of trousers ou pants; **pantalon de ski** ski pants pl

panthère [pɑ̃tɛr] nf panther

pantin [pɑ̃tɛ̃] nm (jouet) jumping jack; (péj: personne) puppet

pantois [pɑ̃twa] adj m: **rester pantois** to be flabbergasted

pantoufle [pɑ̃tufl(ə)] nf slipper

paon [pɑ̃] nm peacock

papa [papa] nm dad(dy)

pape [pap] nm pope

paperasse [papras] nf (péj) bumf no pl, papers pl; forms pl

paperasserie [paprasri] nf (péj) red tape no pl; paperwork no pl

papeterie [papetri] nf (fabrication du papier) paper-making (industry); (usine) paper mill; (magasin) stationer's (shop (BRIT)); (articles) stationery

papetier, ière [paptje, -jɛr] nm/f paper-maker; stationer

papi [papi] nm (fam) granddad

papier [papje] nm paper; (feuille) sheet ou piece of paper; (article) article; (écrit officiel) document; **papiers** nmpl (aussi: **papiers d'identité**) (identity) papers; **sur le papier** (théoriquement) on paper; **noircir du papier** to write page after page; paper; **papier couché/glacé** art/glazed paper; **papier (d')aluminium** aluminium (BRIT) ou aluminum (US) foil, tinfoil; **papier d'Arménie** incense paper; **papier bible** India ou bible paper; **papier de brouillon** rough ou scrap paper; **papier bulle** manil(l)a paper; **papier buvard** blotting paper; **papier calque** tracing paper; **papier carbone** carbon paper; **papier collant** Sellotape® (BRIT), Scotch tape® (US), sticky tape; **papier en continu** continuous stationery; **papier à dessin** drawing paper; **papier d'emballage** wrapping paper; **papier gommé** gummed paper; **papier hygiénique** toilet paper; **papier journal** newsprint; (pour emballer) newspaper; **papier à lettres** writing paper, notepaper; **papier mâché** papier-mâché; **papier machine** typing paper; **papier peint** wallpaper;

papier pelure India paper; **papier à pliage accordéon** fanfold paper; **papier de soie** tissue paper; **papier thermique** thermal paper; **papier de tournesol** litmus paper; **papier de verre** sandpaper

papillon [papijɔ̃] nm butterfly; (fam: contravention) (parking) ticket; (TECH: écrou) wing ou butterfly nut; **papillon de nuit** moth

papillote [papijɔt] nf (pour cheveux) curlpaper; (de gigot) (paper) frill

papoter [papɔte] vi to chatter

paquebot [pakbo] nm liner

pâquerette [pakrɛt] nf daisy

Pâques [pak] nm, nfpl Easter; **faire ses Pâques** to do one's Easter duties; **l'île de Pâques** Easter Island

paquet [pakɛ] nm packet; (colis) parcel; (ballot) bundle; (dans négociations) package (deal); (fig: tas): **paquet de** pile ou heap of; **paquets** nmpl (bagages) bags; **mettre le paquet** (fam) to give one's all; **paquet de mer** big wave

paquet-cadeau, pl **paquets-cadeaux** [pakɛkado] nm gift-wrapped parcel

par [par] prép by; **finir** etc **par** to end etc with; **par amour** out of love; **passer par Lyon/la côte** to go via ou through Lyons/along by the coast; **par la fenêtre** (jeter, regarder) out of the window; **3 par jour/personne** 3 a ou per day/head; **deux par deux** two at a time; (marcher etc) in twos; **par où?** which way?; **par ici** this way; (dans le coin) round here; **par-ci, par-là** here and there

parabolique [parabɔlik] adj parabolic; **antenne parabolique** satellite dish

parachever [paraʃve] vt to perfect

parachute [paraʃyt] nm parachute

parachutiste [paraʃytist(ə)] nm/f parachutist; (MIL) paratrooper

parade [parad] nf (spectacle, défilé) parade; (ESCRIME, BOXE) parry; (ostentation): **faire parade de** to display, show off; (défense, riposte): **trouver la parade à une attaque** to find the answer to an attack; **de parade** adj ceremonial; (superficiel) superficial, outward

paradis [paradi] nm heaven, paradise; **Paradis terrestre** (REL) Garden of Eden; (fig) heaven on earth

paradoxe [paradɔks(ə)] nm paradox

paraffine [parafin] nf paraffin; paraffin wax

parages [paraʒ] nmpl (NAVIG) waters; **dans les parages (de)** in the area ou vicinity (of)

paragraphe [paragraf] nm paragraph

paraître [parɛtr(ə)] vb avec attribut to seem, look, appear ♦ vi to appear; (être visible) to show; (PRESSE, ÉDITION) to be published, come out, appear; (briller) to show off; **laisser paraître qch** to let (sth) show ♦ vb impers: **il paraît que** it seems ou appears that; **il me paraît que** it seems to me that; **il paraît absurde de** it seems absurd to; **il ne**

paraît pas son âge he doesn't look his age; **paraître en justice** to appear before the court(s); **paraître en scène/en public/à l'écran** to appear on stage/in public/on the screen

parallèle [paralɛl] *adj* parallel; (*police, marché*) unofficial; (*société, énergie*) alternative ◆ *nm* (*comparaison*): **faire un parallèle entre** to draw a parallel between; (*GÉO*) parallel ◆ *nf* parallel (line); **en parallèle** in parallel; **mettre en parallèle** (*choses opposées*) to compare; (*choses semblables*) to parallel

paralyser [paralize] *vt* to paralyze

paramédical, e, aux [paramedikal, -o] *adj* paramedical

paraphrase [parafraz] *nf* paraphrase

parapluie [paraplɥi] *nm* umbrella; **parapluie atomique** *ou* **nucléaire** nuclear umbrella; **parapluie pliant** telescopic umbrella

parasite [parazit] *nm* parasite ◆ *adj* (*BOT, BIO*) parasitic(al); **parasites** *nmpl* (*TÉL*) interference *sg*

parasol [parasɔl] *nm* parasol, sunshade

paratonnerre [paratɔnɛr] *nm* lightning conductor

paravent [paravā] *nm* folding screen; (*fig*) screen

parc [park] *nm* (*public*) park, gardens *pl*; (*de château etc*) grounds *pl*; (*pour le bétail*) pen, enclosure; (*d'enfant*) playpen; (*MIL*: *entrepôt*) depot; (*ensemble d'unités*) stock; (*de voitures etc*) fleet; **parc d'attractions** amusement park; **parc automobile** (*d'un pays*) number of cars on the roads; **parc à huîtres** oyster bed; **parc à thème** theme park; **parc national** national park; **parc naturel** nature reserve; **parc de stationnement** car park; **parc zoologique** zoological gardens *pl*

parcelle [parsɛl] *nf* fragment, scrap; (*de terrain*) plot, parcel

parce que [parskə] *conj* because

parchemin [parʃəmɛ̃] *nm* parchment

parc(o)mètre [park(ɔ)mɛtr(ə)] *nm* parking meter

parcourir [parkurir] *vt* (*trajet, distance*) to cover; (*article, livre*) to skim *ou* glance through; (*lieu*) to go all over, travel up and down; (*suj: frisson, vibration*) to run through; **parcourir des yeux** to run one's eye over

parcours [parkur] *vb voir* **parcourir** ◆ *nm* (*trajet*) journey; (*itinéraire*) route; (*SPORT: terrain*) course; (: *tour*) round; run; lap; **parcours du combattant** assault course

par-dessous [pardəsu] *prép*, *adv* under(neath)

pardessus [pardəsy] *nm* overcoat

par-dessus [pardəsy] *prép* over (the top of) ◆ *adv* over (the top); **par-dessus le marché** on top of it all

par-devant [pardəvā] *prép* in the presence of, before ◆ *adv* at the front; round the front

pardon [pardɔ̃] *nm* forgiveness *no pl* ◆ *excl* (*excuses*) (I'm) sorry; (*pour interpeller etc*) excuse me; (*demander de répéter*) (I beg your) pardon? (*BRIT*),

pardon me? (*US*)

pardonner [pardɔne] *vt* to forgive; **pardonner qch à qn** to forgive sb for sth; **qui ne pardonne pas** (*maladie, erreur*) fatal

paré, e [pare] *adj* ready, prepared

pare-balles [parbal] *adj inv* bulletproof

pare-brise [parbriz] *nm inv* windscreen (*BRIT*), windshield (*US*)

pare-chocs [parʃɔk] *nm inv* bumper (*BRIT*), fender (*US*)

pareil, le [parɛj] *adj* (*identique*) the same, alike; (*similaire*) similar; (*tel*): **un courage/livre pareil** such courage/a book, courage/a book like this; **de pareils livres** such books ◆ *adv*: **habillés pareil** dressed the same (way), dressed alike; **faire pareil** to do the same (thing); **j'en veux un pareil** I'd like one just like it; **rien de pareil** no (*ou* any) such thing, nothing (*ou* anything) like it; **ses pareils** one's fellow men; one's peers; **ne pas avoir son (sa) pareil(le)** to be second to none; **pareil à** the same as; similar to; **sans pareil** unparalleled, unequalled; **c'est du pareil au même** it comes to the same thing, it's six (of one) and half-a-dozen (of the other); **en pareil cas** in such a case; **rendre la pareille à qn** to pay sb back in his own coin

parent, e [parā, -āt] *nm/f*: **un/une parent/e** a relative *ou* relation ◆ *adj*: **être parent de** to be related to; **parents** *nmpl* (*père et mère*) parents; (*famille, proches*) relatives, relations; **parent unique** lone parent; **parents par alliance** relatives *ou* relations by marriage; **parents en ligne directe** blood relations

parenté [parāte] *nf* (*lien*) relationship; (*personnes*) relatives *pl*, relations *pl*

parenthèse [parātɛz] *nf* (*ponctuation*) bracket, parenthesis; (*MATH*) bracket; (*digression*) parenthesis, digression; **ouvrir/fermer la parenthèse** to open/close brackets; **entre parenthèses** in brackets; (*fig*) incidentally

parer [pare] *vt* to adorn; (*CULIN*) to dress, trim; (*éviter*) to ward off; **parer à** (*danger*) to ward off; (*inconvénient*) to deal with; **se parer de** (*fig: qualité, titre*) to assume; **parer à toute éventualité** to be ready for every eventuality; **parer au plus pressé** to attend to what's most urgent

paresse [parɛs] *nf* laziness

paresseux, euse [paresø, -øz] *adj* lazy; (*fig*) slow, sluggish ◆ *nm* (*ZOOL*) sloth

parfaire [parfɛr] *vt* to perfect, complete

parfait, e [parfɛ, -ɛt] *pp de* **parfaire** ◆ *adj* perfect ◆ *nm* (*LING*) perfect (tense); (*CULIN*) parfait ◆ *excl* fine, excellent

parfaitement [parfɛtmā] *adv* perfectly ◆ *excl* (most) certainly

parfois [parfwa] *adv* sometimes

parfum [parfœ̃] *nm* (*produit*) perfume, scent; (*odeur: de fleur*) scent, fragrance; (: *de tabac, vin*) aroma; (*goût: de glace, milk-shake*) flavour (*BRIT*), flavor (US)

parfumé, e [paʁfyme] *adj* (*fleur, fruit*) fragrant; (*papier à lettres etc*) scented; (*femme*) wearing perfume *ou* scent, perfumed; (*aromatisé*): **parfumé au café** coffee-flavoured (BRIT) *ou* -flavored (US)

parfumer [paʁfyme] *vt* (*suj: odeur, bouquet*) to perfume; (*mouchoir*) to put scent *ou* perfume on; (*crème, gâteau*) to flavour (BRIT), flavor (US) **se parfumer** to put on (some) perfume *ou* scent; (*d'habitude*) to use perfume *ou* scent

parfumerie [paʁfymʁi] *nf* (*commerce*) perfumery; (*produits*) perfumes *pl*; (*boutique*) perfume shop (BRIT) *ou* store (US)

pari [paʁi] *nm* bet, wager; (SPORT) bet; **pari mutuel urbain (PMU)** *system of betting on horses*

parier [paʁje] *vt* to bet; **j'aurais parié que si/non** I'd have said he (*ou* you *etc*) would/wouldn't

Paris [paʁi] *n* Paris

parisien, ne [paʁizjɛ̃, -ɛn] *adj* Parisian; (GÉO, ADMIN) Paris *cpd* ♦ *nm/f*: **Parisien, ne** Parisian

parjure [paʁʒyʁ] *nm* (*faux serment*) false oath, perjury; (*violation de serment*) breach of oath, perjury ♦ *nm/f* perjurer

parking [paʁkiŋ] *nm* (*lieu*) car park (BRIT), parking lot (US)

parlant, e [paʁlɑ̃, -ɑ̃t] *adj* (*fig*) graphic, vivid; (: *comparaison, preuve*) eloquent; (CINÉ) talking ♦ *adv*: **généralement parlant** generally speaking

parlement [paʁləmɑ̃] *nm* parliament; **le Parlement européen** the European Parliament

parlementaire [paʁləmɑ̃tɛʁ] *adj* parliamentary ♦ *nm/f* (*député*) ≃ Member of Parliament (BRIT) *ou* Congress (US) parliamentarian; (*négociateur*) negotiator, mediator

parlementer [paʁləmɑ̃te] *vi* (*ennemis*) to negotiate, parley; (*s'entretenir, discuter*) to argue at length, have lengthy talks

parler [paʁle] *nm* speech; dialect ♦ *vi* to speak, talk; (*avouer*) to talk; **parler (à qn) de** to talk (to sb) about; **parler pour qn** (*intercéder*) to speak for sb; **parler en l'air** to say the first thing that comes into one's head; **parler le/en français** to speak French/in French; **parler affaires** to talk business; **parler en dormant/du nez** to talk in one's sleep/through one's nose; **sans parler de** (*fig*) not to mention, to say nothing of; **tu parles!** you must be joking!; **n'en parlons plus!** let's forget it!

parloir [paʁlwaʁ] *nm* (*d'une prison, d'un hôpital*) visiting room; (REL) parlour (BRIT), parlor (US)

parmi [paʁmi] *prép* among(st)

paroi [paʁwa] *nf* wall; (*cloison*) partition; **paroi rocheuse** rock face

paroisse [paʁwas] *nf* parish

parole [paʁɔl] *nf* (*faculté*): **la parole** speech; (*mot, promesse*) word; (REL): **la bonne parole** the word of God; **paroles** *nfpl* (MUS) words, lyrics; **tenir parole** to keep one's word; **avoir la parole** to have the

floor; **n'avoir qu'une parole** to be true to one's word; **donner la parole à qn** to hand over to sb; **prendre la parole** to speak; **demander la parole** to ask for permission to speak; **perdre la parole** to lose the power of speech; (*fig*) to lose one's tongue; **je le crois sur parole** I'll take his word for it, I'll take him at his word; **temps de parole** (TV, RADIO *etc*) discussion time; **ma parole!** my word!, good heavens!; **parole d'honneur** word of honour (BRIT) *ou* honor (US)

parquer [paʁke] *vt* (*voiture, matériel*) to park; (*bestiaux*) to pen (in *ou* up); (*prisonniers*) to pack in

parquet [paʁke] *nm* (*parquet*) floor; (JUR: *bureau*) public prosecutor's office; **le parquet (général)** (*magistrats*) ≃ the Bench

parrain [paʁɛ̃] *nm* godfather; (*d'un navire*) namer; (*d'un nouvel adhérent*) sponsor, proposer

parrainer [paʁene] *vt* (*nouvel adhérent*) to sponsor, propose; (*entreprise*) to promote, sponsor

pars [paʁ] *vb voir* **partir**

parsemer [paʁsəme] *vt* (*suj: feuilles, papiers*) to be scattered over; **parsemer qch de** to scatter sth with

part [paʁ] *vb voir* **partir** ♦ *nf* (*qui revient à qn*) share; (*fraction, partie*) part; (*de gâteau, fromage*) portion; (FINANCE) (non-voting) share; **prendre part à** (*débat etc*) to take part in; (*soucis, douleur de qn*) to share in; **faire part de qch à qn** to announce sth to sb, inform sb of sth; **pour ma part** as for me, as far as I'm concerned; **à part entière** *adj* full; **de la part de** (*au nom de*) on behalf of; (*donné par*) from; **c'est de la part de qui?** (*au téléphone*) who's calling *ou* speaking (please)?; **de toute(s) part(s)** from all sides *ou* quarters; **de part et d'autre** on both sides, on either side; **de part en part** right through; **d'une part ... d'autre part** on the one hand ... on the other hand; **nulle/autre/quelque part** nowhere/elsewhere/somewhere; **à part** *adv* separately; (*de côté*) aside ♦ *prép* apart from, except for ♦ *adj* exceptional, special; **pour une large** *ou* **bonne part** to a great extent; **prendre qch en bonne/mauvaise part** to take sth well/badly; **faire la part des choses** to make allowances; **faire la part du feu** (*fig*) to cut one's losses; **faire la part (trop) belle à qn** to give sb more than his (*ou* her) share

partage [paʁtaʒ] *nm* (*voir partager*) sharing (out) *no pl*, share-out; sharing; dividing up; (POL: *de suffrages*) share; **recevoir qch en partage** to receive sth as one's share (*ou* lot); **sans partage** undivided

partager [paʁtaʒe] *vt* to share; (*distribuer, répartir*) to share (out); (*morceler, diviser*) to divide (up); **se partager** *vt* (*héritage etc*) to share between themselves (*ou* ourselves *etc*)

partance [paʁtɑ̃s]: **en partance** *adv* outbound, due to leave; **en partance pour** (bound) for

partenaire [paʁtənɛʁ] *nm/f* partner; **partenaires sociaux** management and workforce

parterre [paʁtɛʁ] *nm* (*de fleurs*) (flower) bed, border; (THÉÂT) stalls pl

parti [parti] nm (POL) party; (décision) course of action; (personne à marier) match; **tirer parti de** to take advantage of, turn to good account; **prendre le parti de faire** to make up one's mind to do, resolve to do; **prendre le parti de qn** to stand up for sb, side with sb; **prendre parti (pour/contre)** to take sides ou a stand (for/against); **prendre son parti de** to come to terms with; **parti pris** bias

partial, e, aux [parsjal, -o] adj biased, partial

participant, e [partisipã, -ãt] nm/f participant; (à un concours) entrant; (d'une société) member

participation [partisipasjɔ̃] nf participation; sharing; (COMM) interest; **la participation aux bénéfices** profit-sharing; **la participation ouvrière** worker participation; **"avec la participation de …"** "featuring …"

participer [partisipe]: **participer à** vt (course, réunion) to take part in; (profits etc) to share in; (frais etc) to contribute to; (entreprise: financièrement) to cooperate in; (chagrin, succès de qn) to share (in); **participer de** vt to partake of.

particularité [partikylarite] nf particularity; (distinctive) characteristic, feature

particulier, ière [partikylje, -jɛR] adj (personnel, privé) private; (spécial) special, particular; (caractéristique) characteristic, distinctive; (spécifique) particular ♦ nm (individu: ADMIN) private individual; **"particulier vend …"** (COMM) "for sale privately …", "for sale by owner …" (US); **particulier à** peculiar to; **en particulier** adv (surtout) in particular, particularly; (à part) separately; (en privé) in private

particulièrement [partikyljɛRmã] adv particularly

partie [parti] nf (gén) part; (profession, spécialité) field, subject; (JUR etc: protagonistes) party; (de cartes, tennis etc) game; (fig: lutte, combat) struggle, fight; **une partie de campagne/de pêche** an outing in the country/a fishing party ou trip; **en partie** adv partly, in part; **faire partie de** to belong to; (suj: chose) to be part of; **prendre qn à partie** to take sb to task; (malmener) to set on sb; **en grande partie** largely, in the main; **ce n'est que partie remise** it will be for another time ou the next time; **avoir partie liée avec qn** to be in league with sb; **partie civile** (JUR) party claiming damages in a criminal case

partiel, le [parsjel] adj partial ♦ nm (SCOL) class exam

partir [partiR] vi (gén) to go; (quitter) to go, leave; (s'éloigner) to go (ou drive etc) away ou off; (moteur) to start; (pétard) to go off; (bouchon) to come out; (bouton) to come off; **partir de** (lieu: quitter) to leave; (: commencer à) to start from; (date) to run ou start from; **partir pour/à** (lieu, pays etc) to leave for/go off to; **à partir de** from

partisan, e [partizã, -an] nm/f partisan; (d'un parti, régime etc) supporter ♦ adj (lutte, querelle) partisan, one-sided; **être partisan de qch/faire** to be in favour (BRIT) ou favor (US) of sth/doing

partition [partisjɔ̃] nf (MUS) score; (POL) partition

partout [partu] adv everywhere; **partout où il allait** everywhere ou wherever he went; **trente partout** (TENNIS) thirty all

paru [paRy] pp de **paraître**

parure [paRyR] nf (bijoux etc) finery no pl; jewellery no pl (BRIT), jewelry no pl (US); (assortiment) set

parution [paRysjɔ̃] nf publication, appearance

parvenir [paRvəniR]: **parvenir à** vt (atteindre) to reach; (obtenir, arriver à) to attain; (réussir): **parvenir à faire** to manage to do, succeed in doing; **faire parvenir qch à qn** to have sth sent to sb

---
MOT CLÉ
---

pas¹ [pɑ] adv 1 (en corrélation avec ne, non etc) not; **il ne pleure pas** (habituellement) he does not ou doesn't cry; (maintenant) he's not ou isn't crying; **je ne mange pas de viande** I don't ou do not eat meat; **il n'a pas pleuré/ne pleurera pas** he did not ou didn't/will not ou won't cry; **ils n'ont pas de voiture/d'enfants** they haven't got a car/any children, they have no car/children; **il m'a dit de ne pas le faire** he told me not to do it; **non pas que …** not that ..

2 (employé sans ne etc) not; **pas moi** not me, not I, I don't (ou can't etc); **elle travaille, (mais) lui pas** ou **pas lui** she works but he doesn't ou does not; **une pomme pas mûre** an apple which isn't ripe; **pas plus tard qu'hier** only yesterday; **pas du tout** not at all; **pas de sucre, merci** no sugar, thanks; **ceci est à vous ou pas?** is this yours or not?, is this yours or isn't it?

3: **pas mal** (joli: personne, maison) not bad; **pas mal fait** not badly done ou made; **comment ça va? – pas mal** how are things? – not bad; **pas mal de** quite a lot of

---

pas² [pɑ] nm (allure, mesure) pace; (démarche) tread; (enjambée, DANSE, fig: étape) step; (bruit) (foot)step; (trace) footprint; (allure) pace; (d'un cheval) walk; (mesure) pace; (TECH: de vis, d'écrou) thread; **pas à pas** step by step; **au pas** at a walking pace; **de ce pas** (à l'instant même) straightaway, at once; **marcher à grands pas** to stride along; **mettre qn au pas** to bring sb to heel; **au pas de gymnastique/de course** at a jog ou trot/at a run; **à pas de loup** stealthily; **faire les cent pas** to pace up and down; **faire les premiers pas** to make the first move; **retourner** ou **revenir sur ses pas** to retrace one's steps; **se tirer d'un mauvais pas** to get o.s. out of a tight spot; **sur le pas de la porte** on the doorstep; **le pas de Calais** (détroit) the Straits pl of Dover; **pas de porte** (fig) key money

passage [pɑsaʒ] nm (fait de passer) voir **passer**; (lieu, prix de la traversée, extrait de livre etc) passage; (chemin) way; (itinéraire): **sur le passage du cortège** along the route of the procession; **"laissez/n'obstruez pas le passage"** "keep clear/do not obstruct"; **au passage** (en passant) as I (ou he *etc*) went by; **de passage** (*touristes*) passing through; (*amants etc*) casual; **passage clouté** pedestrian crossing; **"passage interdit"** "no entry"; **passage à niveau** level (*BRIT*) *ou* grade (*US*) crossing; **"passage protégé"** right of way over secondary road(s) on your right; **passage souterrain** subway (*BRIT*), underpass; **passage à tabac** beating-up; **passage à vide** (*fig*) bad patch

passager, ère [pasaʒe, -ɛʀ] *adj* passing; (*hôte*) short-stay *cpd*; (*oiseau*) migratory ◆ *nm/f* passenger; **passager clandestin** stowaway

passant, e [pasɑ̃, -ɑ̃t] *adj* (*rue, endroit*) busy ◆ *nm/f* passer-by ◆ *nm* (*pour ceinture etc*) loop; **en passant: remarquer qch en passant** to notice sth in passing

passe [pas] *nf* (*SPORT, magnétique*) pass; (*NAVIG*) channel ◆ *nm* (*passe-partout*) master *ou* skeleton key; **être en passe de faire** to be on the way to doing; **être dans une bonne/mauvaise passe** (*fig*) to be going through a good/bad patch; **passe d'armes** (*fig*) heated exchange

passé, e [pase] *adj* (*événement, temps*) past; (*couleur, tapisserie*) faded; (*précédent*): **dimanche passé** last Sunday ◆ *prép* after ◆ *nm* past; (*LING*) past (tense); **il est passé midi** *ou* **midi passé** it's gone (*BRIT*) past twelve; **passé de mode** out of fashion; **passé composé** perfect (tense); **passé simple** past historic

passe-partout [paspaʀtu] *nm inv* master *ou* skeleton key ◆ *adj inv* all-purpose

passeport [paspɔʀ] *nm* passport

passer [pase] *vi* (*se rendre, aller*) to go; (*voiture, piétons: défiler*) to pass (by), go by; (*faire une halte rapide: facteur, laitier etc*) to come, call; (: *pour rendre visite*) to call *ou* drop in; (*courant, air, lumière, franchir un obstacle etc*) to get through; (*accusé, projet de loi*): **passer devant** to come before; (*film, émission*) to be on; (*temps, jours*) to pass, go by; (*liquide, café*) to go through; (*être digéré, avalé*) to go down; (*couleur, papier*) to fade; (*mode*) to die out; (*douleur*) to pass, go away; (*CARTES*) to pass; (*SCOL*) to go up (to the next class); (*devenir*): **passer président** to be appointed *ou* become president ◆ *vt* (*frontière, rivière etc*) to cross; (*douane*) to go through; (*examen*) to sit, take; (*visite médicale etc*) to have; (*journée, temps*) to spend; (*donner*): **passer qch à qn** to pass sth to sb; to give sb sth; (*transmettre*): **passer qch à qn** to pass sth on to sb; (*enfiler: vêtement*) to slip on; (*faire entrer, mettre*): **(faire) passer qch dans/par** to get sth into/through; (*café*) to pour the water on; (*thé, soupe*) to strain; (*film, pièce*) to show, put on; (*disque*) to play, put on; (*marché, accord*) to agree on; (*tolérer*): **passer qch à qn** to let sb get away with sth; **se passer** *vi* (*avoir lieu: scène, action*) to take place; (*se dérouler: entretien etc*) to go on; (*arriver*): **que s'est-il passé?** what happened?; (*s'écouler: semaine etc*) to pass, go by; **se passer de** *vt* to go *ou* do without; **se passer les mains sous l'eau/de l'eau sur le visage** to put one's hands under the

tap/run water over one's face; **en passant** in passing; **passer par** to go through; **passez devant/par ici** go in front/this way; **passer sur** *vt* (*faute, détail inutile*) to pass over; **passer dans les mœurs/l'usage** to become the custom/normal usage; **passer avant qch/qn** (*fig*) to come before sth/sb; **laisser passer** (*air, lumière, personne*) to let through; (*occasion*) to let slip, miss; (*erreur*) to overlook; **faire passer** (*message*) to get over *ou* across; **faire passer à qn le goût de qch** to cure sb of his (*ou* her) taste for sth; **passer à la radio/fouille** to be X-rayed/searched; **passer à la radio/télévision** to be on the radio/on television; **passer à table** to sit down to eat; **passer au salon** to go through to *ou* into the sitting room; **passer à l'opposition** to go over to the opposition; **passer aux aveux** to confess, make a confession; **passer à l'action** to go into action; **passer pour riche** to be taken for a rich man; **il passait pour avoir** he was said to have; **faire passer qn/qch pour** to make sb/sth out to be; **passe encore de le penser, mais de le dire!** it's one thing to think it, but to say it!; **passons!** let's say no more (about it); **et j'en passe!** and that's not all!; **passer en seconde, passer la seconde** (*AUTO*) to change into second; **passer qch en fraude** to smuggle sth in (*ou* out); **passer la main par la portière** to stick one's hand out of the door; **passer le balai/l'aspirateur** to sweep up/hoover; **passer commande/la parole à qn** to hand over to sb; **je vous passe M X** (*je vous mets en communication avec lui*) I'm putting you through to Mr X; (*je lui passe l'appareil*) here is Mr X, I'll hand you over to Mr X; **passer prendre** to (come and) collect

passerelle [pasʀɛl] *nf* footbridge; (*de navire, avion*) gangway; (*NAVIG*): **passerelle (de commandement)** bridge

passe-temps [pastɑ̃] *nm inv* pastime

passible [pasibl(ə)] *adj*: **passible de** liable to

passif, ive [pasif, -iv] *adj* passive ◆ *nm* (*LING*) passive; (*COMM*) liabilities *pl*

passion [pasjɔ̃] *nf* passion; **avoir la passion de** to have a passion for; **fruit de la passion** passion fruit

passionnant, e [pasjɔnɑ̃, -ɑ̃t] *adj* fascinating

passionné, e [pasjɔne] *adj* (*personne, tempérament*) passionate; (*description*) impassioned ◆ *nm/f*: **c'est un passionné d'échecs** he's a chess fanatic; **être passionné de** *ou* **pour qch** to have a passion for sth

passionner [pasjɔne] *vt* (*personne*) to fascinate, grip; (*débat, discussion*) to inflame; **se passionner pour** to take an avid interest in; to have a passion for

passoire [paswaʀ] *nf* sieve; (*à légumes*) colander; (*à thé*) strainer

pastèque [pastɛk] *nf* watermelon

pasteur [pastœʀ] *nm* (*protestant*) minister, pastor

pasteurisé, e [pastœʀize] *adj* pasteurized

pastille [pastij] *nf* (*à sucer*) lozenge, pastille; (*de papier etc*) (small) disc; **pastilles pour la toux**

cough drops ou lozenges

patate [patat] *nf* spud; **patate douce** sweet potato

patauger [patoʒe] *vi* (*pour s'amuser*) to splash about; (*avec effort*) to wade about; (*fig*) to flounder; **patauger dans** (*en marchant*) to wade through

pâte [pɑt] *nf* (*à tarte*) pastry; (*à pain*) dough; (*à frire*) batter; (*substance molle*) paste; cream; **pâtes** *nfpl* (*macaroni etc*) pasta *sg*; **fromage à pâte dure/molle** hard/soft cheese; **pâte d'amandes** almond paste; **pâte brisée** shortcrust (*BRIT*) ou pie crust (*US*) pastry; **pâte à choux/feuilletée** choux/puff ou flaky (*BRIT*) pastry; **pâte de fruits** crystallized fruit *no pl*; **pâte à modeler** modelling clay, Plasticine® (*BRIT*); **pâte à papier** paper pulp

pâté [pɑte] *nm* (*charcuterie: terrine*) pâté; (*tache*) ink blot; (*de sable*) sandpie; **pâté (en croûte)** ≈ meat pie; **pâté de foie** liver pâté; **pâté de maisons** block (of houses)

pâtée [pɑte] *nf* mash, feed

patente [patɑ̃t] *nf* (*COMM*) trading licence (*BRIT*) ou license (*US*)

paternel, le [patɛrnɛl] *adj* (*amour, soins*) fatherly; (*ligne, autorité*) paternal

pâteux, euse [pɑtø, -øz] *adj* thick; pasty; **avoir la bouche** ou **langue pâteuse** to have a furred (*BRIT*) ou coated tongue

pathétique [patetik] *adj* pathetic, moving

patience [pasjɑ̃s] *nf* patience; **être à bout de patience** to have run out of patience; **perdre/prendre patience** to lose (one's)/have patience

patient, e [pasjɑ̃, -ɑ̃t] *adj*, *nm/f* patient

patienter [pasjɑ̃te] *vi* to wait

patin [patɛ̃] *nm* skate; (*sport*) skating; (*de traîneau, luge*) runner; (*pièce de tissu*) cloth pad (*used as slippers to protect polished floor*); **patin (de frein)** brake block; **patins (à glace)** (ice) skates; **patins à roulettes** roller skates

patinage [patinaʒ] *nm* skating; **patinage artistique/de vitesse** figure/speed skating

patiner [patine] *vi* to skate; (*embrayage*) to slip; (*roue, voiture*) to spin; **se patiner** *vi* (*meuble, cuir*) to acquire a sheen, become polished

patineur, euse [patinœr, -øz] *nm/f* skater

patinoire [patinwar] *nf* skating rink, (ice) rink

pâtir [pɑtir] : **pâtir de** *vt* to suffer because of

pâtisserie [pɑtisri] *nf* (*boutique*) cake shop; (*métier*) confectionery; (*à la maison*) pastry- ou cake-making, baking; **pâtisseries** *nfpl* (*gâteaux*) pastries, cakes

pâtissier, ière [pɑtisje, -jɛr] *nm/f* pastrycook; confectioner

patois [patwa] *nm* dialect, patois

patraque [patrak] (*fam*) *adj* peaky, off-colour

patrie [patri] *nf* homeland

patrimoine [patrimwan] *nm* inheritance, patrimony; (*culture*) heritage; **patrimoine génétique** ou **héréditaire** genetic inheritance

patriotique [patrijɔtik] *adj* patriotic

patron, ne [patrɔ̃, -ɔn] *nm/f* (*chef*) boss, manager/eress; (*propriétaire*) owner, proprietor/tress; (*employeur*) employer; (*MÉD*) ≈ senior consultant; (*REL*) patron saint ◆ *nm* (*COUTURE*) pattern; **patron de thèse** supervisor (of postgraduate thesis)

patronat [patrɔna] *nm* employers *pl*

patronner [patrɔne] *vt* to sponsor, support

patrouille [patruj] *nf* patrol

patte [pat] *nf* (*jambe*) leg; (*pied: de chien, chat*) paw; (*: d'oiseau*) foot; (*languette*) strap; (*: de poche*) flap; (*favoris*): **pattes (de lapin)** (short) sideburns; **à pattes d'éléphant** *adj* (*pantalon*) flared; **pattes de mouche** (*fig*) spidery scrawl *sg*; **pattes d'oie** (*fig*) crow's feet

pâturage [pɑtyraʒ] *nm* pasture

paume [pom] *nf* palm

paumé, e [pome] *nm/f* (*fam*) drop-out

paumer [pome] *vt* (*fam*) to lose

paupière [popjɛr] *nf* eyelid

pause [poz] *nf* (*arrêt*) break; (*en parlant, MUS*) pause; **pause de midi** lunch break

pauvre [povr(ə)] *adj* poor ◆ *nm/f* poor man/woman; **les pauvres** the poor; **pauvre en calcium** low in calcium

pauvreté [povrəte] *nf* (*état*) poverty

pavaner [pavane] : **se pavaner** *vi* to strut about

pavé, e [pave] *adj* (*cour*) paved; (*rue*) cobbled ◆ *nm* (*bloc*) paving stone; cobblestone; (*pavage*) paving; (*bifteck*) slab of steak; (*fam: livre*) hefty tome; **être sur le pavé** (*sans domicile*) to be on the streets; (*sans emploi*) to be out of a job; **pavé numérique** (*INFORM*) keypad

pavillon [pavijɔ̃] *nm* (*de banlieue*) small (detached) house; (*kiosque*) lodge; pavilion; (*d'hôpital*) ward; (*MUS: de cor etc*) bell; (*ANAT: de l'oreille*) pavilion, pinna; (*NAVIG*) flag; **pavillon de complaisance** flag of convenience

pavoiser [pavwaze] *vt* to deck with flags ◆ *vi* to put out flags; (*fig*) to rejoice, exult

pavot [pavo] *nm* poppy

payant, e [pejɑ̃, -ɑ̃t] *adj* (*spectateurs etc*) paying; (*billet*) that you pay for, to be paid for; (*fig: entreprise*) profitable; **c'est payant** you have to pay, there is a charge

paye [pɛj] *nf* pay, wages *pl*

payer [peje] *vt* (*créancier, employé, loyer*) to pay; (*achat, réparations, fig: faute*) to pay for ◆ *vi* to pay; (*métier*) to pay, be well-paid; (*effort, tactique etc*) to pay off; **être bien/mal payé** to be well/badly paid; **il me l'a fait payer 10 €** he charged me 10 € for it; **payer qn de** (*ses efforts, peines*) to reward sb for; **payer qch à qn** to buy sth for sb, buy sb sth; **ils nous ont payé le voyage** they paid for our trip; **payer de sa personne** to give of oneself; **payer d'audace** to act with great daring; **payer cher qch** to pay dear(ly) for sth; **cela ne paie pas de mine** it doesn't look much; **se payer qch** to buy o.s. sth; **se**

payer de mots to shoot one's mouth off; **se payer la tête de qn** to take the mickey out of sb (*BRIT*), make a fool of sb; (*duper*) to take sb for a ride

pays [pei] *nm* (*territoire, habitants*) country, land; (*région*) region; (*village*) village; **du pays** *adj* local; **le pays de Galles** Wales

paysage [peizaʒ] *nm* landscape

paysan, ne [peizɑ̃, -an] *nm/f* countryman/woman; farmer; (*péj*) peasant ♦ *adj* country *cpd* farming, farmers'

Pays-Bas [peiba] *nmpl*: **les Pays-Bas** the Netherlands

PC *sigle m* (*POL*) = **parti communiste**; (*INFORM*: = personal computer) PC; (= prêt conventionné) type of loan for house purchase (*CONSTR*: = permis de construire); (*MIL*) = **poste de commandement**

PDG *sigle m* = **président directeur général**

péage [peaʒ] *nm* toll; (*endroit*) tollgate; **pont à péage** toll bridge

peau, x [po] *nf* skin; (*cuir*): **gants de peau** leather gloves; **être bien/mal dans sa peau** to be at ease/odds with oneself; **se mettre dans la peau de qn** to put o.s. in sb's place *ou* shoes; **faire peau neuve** (*se renouveler*) to change one's image; **peau de chamois** (*chiffon*) chamois leather, shammy; **peau d'orange** orange peel

Peau-Rouge [poRuʒ] *nm/f* Red Indian, red skin

péché [peʃe] *nm* sin; **péché mignon** weakness

pêche [pɛʃ] *nf* (*sport, activité*) fishing; (*poissons pêchés*) catch; (*fruit*) peach; **aller à la pêche** to go fishing; **avoir la pêche** (*fam*) to be on (top) form; **pêche à la ligne** (*en rivière*) angling; **pêche sous-marine** deep-sea fishing

pécher [peʃe] *vi* (*REL*) to sin; (*fig: personne*) to err; (: *chose*) to be flawed; **pécher contre la bienséance** to break the rules of good behaviour

pêcher [peʃe] *nm* peach tree ♦ *vi* to go fishing; (*en rivière*) to go angling ♦ *vt* (*attraper*) to catch, land; (*chercher*) to fish for; **pêcher au chalut** to trawl

pécheur, eresse [peʃœR, peʃRɛs] *nm/f* sinner

pêcheur [peʃœR] *nm* voir **pêcher** fisherman; angler; **pêcheur de perles** pearl diver

pécule [pekyl] *nm* savings *pl*, nest egg; (*d'un détenu*) earnings *pl* (*paid on release*)

pédagogie [pedagɔʒi] *nf* educational methods *pl*, pedagogy

pédagogique [pedagɔʒik] *adj* educational; **formation pédagogique** teacher training

pédale [pedal] *nf* pedal; **mettre la pédale douce** to soft-pedal

pédalo [pedalo] *nm* pedalo, pedal-boat

pédant, e [pedɑ̃, -ɑ̃t] *adj* (*péj*) pedantic ♦ *nm/f* pedant

pédestre [pedɛstR(ə)] *adj*: **tourisme pédestre** hiking; **randonnée pédestre** (*activité*) rambling; (*excursion*) ramble

pédiatre [pedjatR(ə)] *nm/f* paediatrician (*BRIT*),

pediatrician *ou* pediatrist (*US*), child specialist

pédicure [pedikyR] *nm/f* chiropodist

pègre [pɛgR(ə)] *nf* underworld

peignais [peɲɛ] *etc vb voir* **peindre**

peigne [pɛɲ] *vb voir* **peindre, peigner** ♦ *nm* comb

peigner [peɲe] *vt* to comb (the hair of); **se peigner** to comb one's hair

peignoir [peɲwaR] *nm* dressing gown; **peignoir de bain** bathrobe; **peignoir de plage** beach robe

peindre [pɛ̃dR(ə)] *vt* to paint; (*fig*) to portray, depict

peine [pɛn] *nf* (*affliction*) sorrow, sadness *no pl*; (*mal, effort*) trouble *no pl*, effort; (*difficulté*) difficulty; (*punition, châtiment*) punishment; (*JUR*) sentence; **faire de la peine à qn** to distress *ou* upset sb; **prendre la peine de faire** to go to the trouble of doing; **se donner de la peine** to make an effort; **ce n'est pas la peine de faire** there's no point in doing, it's not worth doing; **ce n'est pas la peine que vous fassiez** there's no point (in) you doing; **avoir de la peine à faire** to have difficulty doing; **donnez-vous** *ou* **veuillez-vous donner la peine d'entrer** please do come in; **c'est peine perdue** it's a waste of time (and effort); **à peine** *adv* scarcely, hardly, barely; **à peine ... que** hardly ... than; **c'est à peine si ...** it's (*ou* it was) a job to ...; **sous peine**: **sous peine d'être puni** for fear of being punished; **défense d'afficher sous peine d'amende** billposters will be fined; **peine capitale** capital punishment; **peine de mort** death sentence *ou* penalty

peiner [pene] *vi* to work hard; to struggle; (*moteur, voiture*) to labour (*BRIT*), labor (*US*) ♦ *vt* to grieve, sadden

peintre [pɛ̃tR(ə)] *nm* painter; **peintre en bâtiment** house painter, painter and decorator; **peintre d'enseignes** signwriter

peinture [pɛ̃tyR] *nf* painting; (*couche de couleur, couleur*) paint; (*surfaces peintes; aussi*: **peintures**) paintwork; **je ne peux pas la voir en peinture** I can't stand the sight of him; **peinture mate/brillante** matt/gloss paint; **"peinture fraîche"** "wet paint"

péjoratif, ive [peʒɔRatif, -iv] *adj* pejorative, derogatory

pelage [pəlaʒ] *nm* coat, fur

pêle-mêle [pɛlmɛl] *adv* higgledy-piggledy

peler [pəle] *vt, vi* to peel

pèlerin [pɛlRɛ̃] *nm* pilgrim

pèlerinage [pɛlRinaʒ] *nm* (*voyage*) pilgrimage; (*lieu*) place of pilgrimage, shrine

pelle [pɛl] *nf* shovel; (*d'enfant, de terrassier*) spade; **pelle à gâteau** cake slice; **pelle mécanique** mechanical digger

pellicule [pelikyl] *nf* film; **pellicules** *nfpl* (*MÉD*) dandruff *sg*

pelote [pəlɔt] *nf* (*de fil, laine*) ball; (*d'épingles*) pin cushion; **pelote basque** pelota

peloton [pəlɔtɔ̃] *nm* (*groupe: de personnes*) group; (: *de pompiers, gendarmes*) squad; (: *sport*) pack; (*de laine*) ball; **peloton d'exécution** firing squad

pelotonner [pəlɔtɔne]: **se pelotonner** *vi* to curl (o.s.) up

pelouse [pəluz] *nf* lawn; (*hippisme*) spectating area inside racetrack

peluche [pəlyʃ] *nf* (bit of) fluff; **animal en peluche** soft toy, fluffy animal

pelure [pəlyʀ] *nf* peeling, peel *no pl*; **pelure d'oignon** onion skin

pénal, e, aux [penal, -o] *adj* penal

pénalité [penalite] *nf* penalty

penaud, e [pəno, -od] *adj* sheepish, contrite

penchant [pɑ̃ʃɑ̃] *nm*: **un penchant à faire/à qch** a tendency to do/to sth; **un penchant pour qch** a liking *ou* fondness for sth

pencher [pɑ̃ʃe] *vi* to tilt, lean over ♦ *vt* to tilt; **se pencher** *vi* to lean over; (*se baisser*) to bend down; **se pencher sur** to bend over; (*fig: problème*) to look into; **se pencher au dehors** to lean out; **pencher pour** to be inclined to favour (*brit*) *ou* favor (*us*)

pendaison [pɑ̃dɛzɔ̃] *nf* hanging

pendant, e [pɑ̃dɑ̃, -ɑ̃t] *adj* hanging (out); (*admin, jur*) pending ♦ *nm* counterpart; matching piece ♦ *prép* during; **faire pendant à** to match; to be the counterpart of; **pendant que** while; **pendants d'oreilles** drop *ou* pendant earrings

pendentif [pɑ̃dɑ̃tif] *nm* pendant

penderie [pɑ̃dʀi] *nf* wardrobe; (*placard*) walk-in cupboard

pendre [pɑ̃dʀ(ə)] *vt, vi* to hang; **se pendre (à)** (*se suicider*) to hang o.s. (on); **se pendre à** (*se suspendre*) to hang from; **pendre à** to hang (down) from; **pendre qch à** (*mur*) to hang sth (up) on; (*plafond*) to hang sth (up) from

pendule [pɑ̃dyl] *nf* clock ♦ *nm* pendulum

pénétrer [penetre] *vi* to come *ou* get in ♦ *vt* to penetrate; **pénétrer dans** to enter; (*suj: froid, projectile*) to penetrate; (: *air, eau*) to come into, get into; (*mystère, secret*) to fathom; **se pénétrer de qch** to get sth firmly set in one's mind

pénible [penibl(ə)] *adj* (*astreignant*) hard; (*affligeant*) painful; (*personne, caractère*) tiresome; **il m'est pénible de ...** I'm sorry to ...

péniblement [penibləmɑ̃] *adv* with difficulty

péniche [peniʃ] *nf* barge; **péniche de débarquement** landing craft *inv*

pénicilline [penisilin] *nf* penicillin

péninsule [penɛ̃syl] *nf* peninsula

pénis [penis] *nm* penis

pénitence [penitɑ̃s] *nf* (*repentir*) penitence; (*peine*) penance; (*punition, châtiment*) punishment; **mettre un enfant en pénitence** ≈ to make a child stand in the corner; **faire pénitence** to do a penance

pénitencier [penitɑ̃sje] *nm* prison, penitentiary (*us*)

pénombre [penɔ̃bʀ(ə)] *nf* half-light

pensée [pɑ̃se] *nf* thought; (*démarche, doctrine*) thinking *no pl*; (*bot*) pansy; **se représenter qch par la pensée** to conjure up a mental picture of sth; **en pensée** in one's mind

penser [pɑ̃se] *vi* to think ♦ *vt* to think; (*concevoir: problème, machine*) to think out; **penser à** to think of; (*songer à: ami, vacances*) to think of *ou* about; (*réfléchir à: problème, offre*): **penser à qch** to think about sth, think sth over; **penser à faire qch** to think of doing sth; **penser faire qch** to be thinking of doing sth, intend to do sth; **faire penser à** to remind one of; **n'y pensons plus** let's forget it; **vous n'y pensez pas!** don't let it bother you!; **sans penser à mal** without meaning any harm; **je le pense aussi** I think so too; **je pense que oui/non** I think so/don't think so

pensif, ive [pɑ̃sif, -iv] *adj* pensive, thoughtful

pension [pɑ̃sjɔ̃] *nf* (*allocation*) pension; (*prix du logement*) board and lodging, bed and board; (*maison particulière*) boarding house; (*hôtel*) guesthouse, hotel; (*école*) boarding school; **prendre pension chez** to take board and lodging at; **prendre qn en pension** to take sb (in) as a lodger; **mettre en pension** to send to boarding school; **pension alimentaire** (*d'étudiant*) living allowance; (*de divorcée*) maintenance allowance; alimony; **pension complète** full board; **pension de famille** boarding house, guesthouse; **pension de guerre/ d'invalidité** war/disablement pension

pensionnaire [pɑ̃sjɔnɛʀ] *nm/f* boarder; guest

pensionnat [pɑ̃sjɔna] *nm* boarding school

pente [pɑ̃t] *nf* slope; **en pente** *adj* sloping

Pentecôte [pɑ̃tkot] *nf*: **la Pentecôte** Whitsun (*brit*), Pentecost; (*dimanche*) Whitsunday (*brit*); **lundi de Pentecôte** Whit Monday (*brit*)

pénurie [penyʀi] *nf* shortage; **pénurie de main-d'œuvre** undermanning

pépé [pepe] *nm* (*fam*) grandad

pépin [pepɛ̃] *nm* (*bot: graine*) pip; (*fam: ennui*) snag, hitch; (: *parapluie*) brolly (*brit*), umbrella

pépinière [pepinjɛʀ] *nf* nursery; (*fig*) nest, breeding-ground

perçant, e [pɛʀsɑ̃, -ɑ̃t] *adj* (*vue, regard, yeux*) sharp, keen; (*cri, voix*) piercing, shrill

percée [pɛʀse] *nf* (*trouée*) opening; (*mil, comm, fig*) breakthrough; (*sport*) break

perce-neige [pɛʀsəneʒ] *nm ou f inv* snowdrop

percepteur [pɛʀsɛptœʀ] *nm* tax collector

perception [pɛʀsɛpsjɔ̃] *nf* perception; (*d'impôts etc*) collection; (*bureau*) tax (collector's) office

percer [pɛʀse] *vt* to pierce; (*ouverture etc*) to make; (*mystère, énigme*) to penetrate ♦ *vi* to come through; (*réussir*) to break through; **percer une dent** to cut a tooth

perceuse [pɛʀsøz] *nf* drill; **perceuse à percus-**

sion hammer drill

percevoir [pɛʀsəvwaʀ] *vt* (*distinguer*) to perceive, detect; (*taxe, impôt*) to collect; (*revenu, indemnité*) to receive

perche [pɛʀʃ(ə)] *nf* (*ZOOL*) perch; (*bâton*) pole; **perche à son** (*sound*) boom

percher [pɛʀʃe] *vt*: **percher qch sur** to perch sth on ◆ *vi*: **se percher** *vi* (*oiseau*) to perch

perchoir [pɛʀʃwaʀ] *nm* perch; (*fig*) presidency of the French National Assembly

perçois [pɛʀswa] *etc vb voir* **percevoir**

percolateur [pɛʀkɔlatœʀ] *nm* percolator

perçu, e [pɛʀsy] *pp de* **percevoir**

percussion [pɛʀkysjɔ̃] *nf* percussion

percuter [pɛʀkyte] *vt* to strike; (*suj: véhicule*) to crash into ◆ *vi*: **percuter contre** to crash into

perdant, e [pɛʀdɑ̃, -ɑ̃t] *nm/f* loser ◆ *adj* losing

perdre [pɛʀdʀ(ə)] *vt* to lose; (*gaspiller: temps, argent*) to waste; (*personne: moralement etc*) to ruin ◆ *vi* to lose; (*sur une vente etc*) to lose out; (*récipient*) to leak; **se perdre** *vi* (*s'égarer*) to get lost, lose one's way; (*fig: se gâter*) to go to waste; (*disparaître*) to disappear, vanish; **il ne perd rien pour attendre** it can wait, it'll keep

perdrix [pɛʀdʀi] *nf* partridge

perdu, e [pɛʀdy] *pp de* **perdre** ◆ *adj* (*enfant, cause, objet*) lost; (*isolé*) out-of-the-way; (*COMM: emballage*) non-returnable; (*récolte etc*) ruined; (*malade*): **il est perdu** there's no hope left for him; **à vos moments perdus** in your spare time

père [pɛʀ] *nm* father; **pères** *nmpl* (*ancêtres*) forefathers; **de père en fils** from father to son; **père de famille** father; family man; **mon père** (*REL*) Father; **le père Noël** Father Christmas

perfection [pɛʀfɛksjɔ̃] *nf* perfection; **à la perfection** *adv* to perfection

perfectionné, e [pɛʀfɛksjɔne] *adj* sophisticated

perfectionner [pɛʀfɛksjɔne] *vt* to improve, perfect; **se perfectionner en anglais** to improve one's English

perforatrice [pɛʀfɔʀatʀis] *nf voir* **perforateur**

perforer [pɛʀfɔʀe] *vt* to perforate, punch a hole ou holes in; (*ticket, bande, carte*) to punch

performant, e [pɛʀfɔʀmɑ̃, -ɑ̃t] *adj* (*ÉCON: produit, entreprise*) high-return *cpd*; (*TECH: appareil, machine*) high-performance *cpd*

perfusion [pɛʀfyzjɔ̃] *nf* perfusion; **faire une perfusion à qn** to put sb on a drip

péricliter [peʀiklite] *vi* to go downhill

péril [peʀil] *nm* peril; **au péril de sa vie** at the risk of his life; **à ses risques et périls** at his (ou her) own risk

périmé, e [peʀime] *adj* (out)dated; (*ADMIN*) out-of-date, expired

périmètre [peʀimɛtʀ(ə)] *nm* perimeter

période [peʀjɔd] *nf* period

périodique [peʀjɔdik] *adj* (*phases*) periodic; (*publication*) periodical; (*MATH: fraction*) recurring ◆ *nm* periodical; **garniture** ou **serviette périodique** sanitary towel (*BRIT*) ou napkin (*US*)

péripéties [peʀipesi] *nfpl* events, episodes

périphérique [peʀifeʀik] *adj* (*quartiers*) outlying; (*ANAT, TECH*) peripheral; (*station de radio*) operating from a neighbouring country ◆ *nm* (*INFORM*) peripheral; (*AUTO*): **(boulevard) périphérique** ring road (*BRIT*), beltway (*US*)

périple [peʀipl(ə)] *nm* journey

périr [peʀiʀ] *vi* to die, perish

périssable [peʀisabl(ə)] *adj* perishable

perle [pɛʀl(ə)] *nf* pearl; (*de plastique, métal, sueur*) bead; (*personne, chose*) gem, treasure; (*erreur*) gem, howler

permanence [pɛʀmanɑ̃s] *nf* permanence; (*local*) (duty) office, strike headquarters; (*service des urgences*) emergency service; (*SCOL*) study room; **assurer une permanence** (*service public, bureaux*) to operate ou maintain a basic service; **être de permanence** to be on call ou duty; **en permanence** *adv* (*toujours*) permanently; (*continûment*) continuously

permanent, e [pɛʀmanɑ̃, -ɑ̃t] *adj* permanent; (*spectacle*) continuous; (*armée, comité*) standing ◆ *nf perm* ◆ *nm/f* (*d'un syndicat, parti*) paid official

perméable [pɛʀmeabl(ə)] *adj* (*terrain*) permeable; **perméable à** (*fig*) receptive ou open to

permettre [pɛʀmɛtʀ(ə)] *vt* to allow, permit; **permettre à qn de faire/qch** to allow sb to do/sth; **se permettre de faire qch** to take the liberty of doing sth; **permettez!** excuse me!

permis, e [pɛʀmi, -iz] *pp de* **permettre** ◆ *nm* permit, licence (*BRIT*), license (*US*); **permis de chasse** hunting permit; **permis (de conduire)** (driving) licence (*BRIT*), (driver's) license (*US*); **permis de construire** planning permission (*BRIT*), building permit (*US*); **permis d'inhumer** burial certificate; **permis poids lourds** ≃ HGV (driving) licence (*BRIT*), ≃ class E (driver's) license (*US*); **permis de séjour** residence permit; **permis de travail** work permit

permission [pɛʀmisjɔ̃] *nf* permission; (*MIL*) leave; (: *papier*) pass; **en permission** on leave; **avoir la permission de faire** to have permission to do, be allowed to do

permuter [pɛʀmyte] *vt* to change around, permutate ◆ *vi* to change, swap

Pérou [peʀu] *nm*: **le Pérou** Peru

perpétuel, le [pɛʀpetɥɛl] *adj* perpetual; (*ADMIN etc*) permanent; for life

perpétuité [pɛʀpetɥite] *nf*: **à perpétuité** *adj, adv* for life; **être condamné à perpétuité** to be sentenced to life imprisonment, receive a life sentence

perplexe [pɛʀplɛks(ə)] *adj* perplexed, puzzled

perquisitionner [pɛʀkizisjɔne] *vi* to carry out a search

perron [pɛʀɔ̃] *nm* steps *pl* (in front of mansion etc)

perroquet [peʀɔke] *nm* parrot

perruche [peʀyʃ] *nf* budgerigar (*BRIT*), budgie (*BRIT*), parakeet (*US*)

perruque [peʀyk] *nf* wig

persan, e [peʀsɑ̃, -an] *adj* Persian ♦ *nm* (*LING*) Persian

persécuter [peʀsekyte] *vt* to persecute

persévérer [peʀsevere] *vi* to persevere; **persévérer à croire que** to continue to believe that

persiennes [peʀsjɛn] *nfpl* (slatted) shutters

persil [peʀsi] *nm* parsley

Persique [peʀsik] *adj*: **le golfe Persique** the (Persian) Gulf

persistant, e [peʀsistɑ̃, -ɑ̃t] *adj* persistent; (*feuilles*) evergreen; **à feuillage persistant** evergreen

persister [peʀsiste] *vi* to persist; **persister à faire qch** to persist in doing sth

personnage [peʀsɔnaʒ] *nm* (*notable*) personality; figure; (*individu*) character, individual; (*THÉÂT*) character; (*PEINTURE*) figure

personnalité [peʀsɔnalite] *nf* personality; (*personnage*) prominent figure

personne [peʀsɔn] *nf* person ♦ *pron* nobody, no one; (*quelqu'un*) anybody, anyone; **personnes** *nfpl* people *pl*; **il n'y a personne** there's nobody in *ou* there, there isn't anybody in *ou* there; **10 € par personne** 10 € per person *ou* a head; **en personne** personally, in person; **personne âgée** elderly person; **personne à charge** (*JUR*) dependent; **personne morale** *ou* **civile** (*JUR*) legal entity

personnel, le [peʀsɔnɛl] *adj* personal; (*égoïste: personne*) selfish, self-centred; (*idée, opinion*): **j'ai des idées personnelles à ce sujet** I have my own ideas about that ♦ *nm* personnel, staff; **service du personnel** personnel department

personnellement [peʀsɔnɛlmɑ̃] *adv* personally

perspective [peʀspektiv] *nf* (*ART*) perspective; (*vue, coup d'œil*) view; (*point de vue*) viewpoint, angle; (*chose escomptée, envisagée*) prospect; **en perspective** in prospect

perspicace [peʀspikas] *adj* clear-sighted, gifted with *ou* showing insight

perspicacité [peʀspikasite] *nf* insight, perspicacity

persuader [peʀsɥade] *vt*: **persuader qn (de/de faire)** to persuade sb (of/to do); **j'en suis persuadé** I'm quite sure *ou* convinced (of it)

persuasif, ive [peʀsɥazif, -iv] *adj* persuasive

perte [peʀt(ə)] *nf* loss; (*de temps*) waste; (*fig: morale*) ruin; **pertes** *fpl* losses; (*COMM*) at a loss; **à perte de vue** as far as the eye can (*ou* could) see; (*fig*) interminably; **en pure perte** for absolutely nothing; **courir à sa perte** to be on the road to ruin; **être en perte de vitesse** (*fig*) to be losing momentum; **avec perte et fracas** forcibly; **perte de chaleur** heat loss; **perte sèche** dead loss; **pertes blanches** (vaginal) discharge *sg*

pertinemment [peʀtinamɑ̃] *adv* to the point;

(*savoir*) perfectly well, full well

pertinent, e [peʀtinɑ̃, -ɑ̃t] *adj* (*remarque*) apt, pertinent, relevant; (*analyse*) discerning, judicious

perturbation [peʀtyʀbasjɔ̃] *nf* (*dans un service public*) disruption; (*agitation, trouble*) perturbation; **perturbation (atmosphérique)** atmospheric disturbance

perturber [peʀtyʀbe] *vt* to disrupt; (*PSYCH*) to perturb, disturb

pervers, e [peʀveʀ, -ɛʀs(ə)] *adj* perverted, depraved; (*malfaisant*) perverse

pervertir [peʀveʀtiʀ] *vt* to pervert

pesant, e [pəzɑ̃, -ɑ̃t] *adj* heavy; (*fig*) burdensome ♦ *nm*: **valoir son pesant de** to be worth one's weight in

pèse-personne [pɛzpɛʀsɔn] *nm* (bathroom) scales *pl*

peser [pəze] *vt, vb avec attribut* to weigh; (*considérer, comparer*) to weigh up ♦ *vi* to be heavy; (*fig*) to carry weight; **peser sur** (*levier, bouton*) to press, push; (*fig: accabler*) to lie heavy on; (: *influencer*) to influence; **peser à qn** to weigh heavy on sb

pessimisme [pesimism(ə)] *nm* pessimism

pessimiste [pesimist(ə)] *adj* pessimistic ♦ *nm/f* pessimist

peste [pɛst(ə)] *nf* plague; (*fig*) pest, nuisance

pester [pɛste] *vi*: **pester contre** to curse

pétale [petal] *nm* petal

pétanque [petɑ̃k] *nf* type of bowls; *see boxed note*

PÉTANQUE

Pétanque is a version of the game of 'boules', played on a variety of hard surfaces. Standing with their feet together, players throw steel bowls at a wooden jack. **Pétanque** originated in the South of France and is still very much associated with that area.

---

pétarader [petaʀade] *vi* to backfire

pétard [petaʀ] *nm* (*feu d'artifice*) banger (*BRIT*), firecracker; (*de cotillon*) cracker; (*RAIL*) detonator

péter [pete] *vi* (*fam: casser, sauter*) to burst; to bust; (*fam!*) to fart (!)

pétillant, e [petijɑ̃, -ɑ̃t] *adj* sparkling

pétiller [petije] *vi* (*flamme, bois*) to crackle; (*mousse, champagne*) to bubble; (*pierre, métal*) to glisten; (*yeux*) to sparkle; (*fig*): **pétiller d'esprit** to sparkle with wit

petit, e [pəti, -it] *adj* (*gén*) small; (*main, objet, colline, en âge: enfant*) small, little; (*mince, fin: personne, taille, pluie*) slight; (*voyage*) short, little; (*bruit etc*) faint, slight; (*mesquin*) mean; (*peu important*) minor ♦ *nm/f* (*petit enfant*) little one, child ♦ *nmpl* (*d'un animal*) young *pl*; **faire des petits** to have kittens (*ou* puppies etc); **en petit** in miniature; **mon petit** son; little one; **ma petite** dear; little one; **pauvre petit** poor little thing; **la classe des petits** the infant class; **pour petits et grands** for children and adults; **les tout-petits** the little ones, the tiny tots; **petit à petit** bit by bit, gradually; **petit(e) ami/e** boyfriend/girlfriend; **les petites annonces** the small ads; **petit déjeuner** breakfast; **petit doigt** little finger; **le petit écran** the small screen; **petit four** petit four; **petit pain** (bread) roll; **petite monnaie** small change; **petite vérole** smallpox; **petits pois** petit pois *pl*, garden peas; **petites gens** people of modest means

petite-fille, *pl* **petites-filles** [pətitfij] *nf* grand-daughter

petit-fils, *pl* **petits-fils** [pətifis] *nm* grandson

pétition [petisjɔ̃] *nf* petition; **faire signer une pétition** to get up a petition

petits-enfants [pətizɑ̃fɑ̃] *nmpl* grandchildren

petit-suisse, *pl* **petits-suisses** [pətisɥis] *nm* small individual pot of cream cheese

pétrin [petʀɛ̃] *nm* kneading-trough; (*fig*): **dans le pétrin** in a jam *ou* fix

pétrir [petʀiʀ] *vt* to knead

pétrole [petʀɔl] *nm* oil; (*aussi*: **pétrole lampant**) paraffin (*BRIT*), kerosene (*US*)

pétrolier, ière [petʀɔlje, -jɛʀ] *adj* oil *cpd*; (*pays*) oil-producing ♦ *nm* (*navire*) oil tanker; (*financier*) oilman; (*technicien*) petroleum engineer

P et T *sigle fpl* = postes et télécommunications

MOT-CLÉ

peu [pø] *adv* **1** (*modifiant verbe, adjectif, adverbe*): **il boit peu** he doesn't drink (very) much; **il est peu bavard** he's not very talkative; **peu avant/après** shortly before/afterwards; **pour peu qu'il fasse** if he should do, if by any chance he does

2 (*modifiant nom*): **peu de: peu de gens/d'arbres** few *ou* not (very) many people/trees; **il a peu d'espoir** he hasn't (got) much hope, he has little hope; **pour peu de temps** for (only) a short while; **à peu de frais** for very little cost

3: **peu à peu** little by little; **à peu près** just about, more or less; **à peu près 10 kg/10 €** approximately 10 kg/10 €

♦ *nm* **1**: **le peu de gens qui** the few people who; **le peu de sable qui** what little sand, the little sand which

2: **un peu** a little; **un petit peu** a little bit; **un peu d'espoir** a little hope; **elle est un peu bavarde** she's rather talkative; **un peu plus/moins de** slightly more/less (*ou* fewer) than; **pour un peu il ..., un peu plus et il ...** he very nearly *ou* all but ...; **essayez un peu!** have a go!, just try it!

♦ *pron*: **peu le savent** few know (it); **avant** *ou* **sous peu** shortly, before long; **depuis peu** for a short *ou* little while; (*au passé*) a short *ou* little while ago; **de peu** (only) just; **c'est peu de chose** it's nothing; **il est de peu mon cadet** he's just a little *ou* bit younger than me

---

peuple [pœpl(ə)] *nm* people; (*masse*): **un peuple de vacanciers** a crowd of holiday-makers; **il y a du peuple** there are a lot of people

peupler [pœple] *vt* (*pays, région*) to populate; (*étang*) to stock; (*suj: hommes, poissons*) to inhabit; (*fig: imagination, rêves*) to fill; **se peupler** *vi* (*ville, région*) to become populated; (*fig: s'animer*) to fill (up), be filled

peuplier [pøplije] *nm* poplar (tree)

peur [pœʀ] *nf* fear; **avoir peur (de/de faire/que)** to be frightened *ou* afraid (of/of doing/that); **prendre peur** to take fright; **faire peur à** to frighten; **de peur de/que** for fear of/that; **j'ai peur qu'il ne soit trop tard** I'm afraid it might be too late; **j'ai peur qu'il (ne) vienne (pas)** I'm afraid he may (not) come

peureux, euse [pœʀø, -øz] *adj* fearful, timorous

peut [pø] *vb voir* **pouvoir**

peut-être [pøtɛtʀ(ə)] *adv* perhaps, maybe; **peut-être que** perhaps, maybe; **peut-être bien qu'il fera/est** he may well do/be

phare [faʀ] *nm* (*en mer*) lighthouse; (*d'aéroport*) beacon; (*de véhicule*) headlight, headlamp (*BRIT*) ♦ *adj*: **produit phare** leading product; **se mettre en phares, mettre ses phares** to put on one's headlights; **phares de recul** reversing (*BRIT*) *ou* back-up (*US*) lights

pharmacie [faʀmasi] *nf* (*science*) pharmacology; (*magasin*) chemist's (*BRIT*), pharmacy; (*officine*) dispensary; (*produits*) pharmaceuticals *pl*; (*armoire*) medicine chest *ou* cupboard, first-aid cupboard

pharmacien, ne [faʀmasjɛ̃, -ɛn] *nm/f* pharmacist, chemist (*BRIT*)

phénomène [fenɔmɛn] *nm* phenomenon (*pl* -a); (*monstre*) freak

philatélie [filateli] *nf* philately, stamp collecting

philosophe [filɔzɔf] *nm/f* philosopher ♦ *adj* philosophical

philosophie [filɔzɔfi] *nf* philosophy

phobie [fɔbi] *nf* phobia

phonétique [fɔnetik] *adj* phonetic ♦ *nf* phonetics *sg*

phoque [fɔk] *nm* seal; (*fourrure*) sealskin

phosphorescent, e [fɔsfɔʀesɑ̃, -ɑ̃t] *adj* luminous

photo [fɔto] *nf* (*photographie*) photo ♦ *adj*: **appareil/pellicule photo** camera/film; **en photo** *in ou* on a photo; **prendre en photo** to take a photo of; **aimer la/faire de la photo** to like taking/take photos; **photo en couleurs** colour photo; **photo d'identité** passport photo

photocopie [fɔtɔkɔpi] *nf* (*procédé*) photocopying; (*document*) photocopy

photocopier [fɔtɔkɔpje] *vt* to photocopy

photocopieur [fɔtɔkɔpjœʀ] *nm*, **photocopieuse** [fɔtɔkɔpjøz] *nf* (photo)copier

photographe [fɔtɔgʀaf] *nm/f* photographer

photographie [fɔtɔgʀafi] *nf* (*procédé, technique*) photography; (*cliché*) photograph; **faire de la photographie** to do photography as a hobby; (*comme métier*) to be a photographer

photographier [fɔtɔgʀafje] *vt* to photograph, take

phrase [fʀɑz] *nf* (LING) sentence; (*propos, MUS*) phrase; **phrases** *nfpl* (*péj*) flowery language *sg*

physicien, ne [fizisjɛ̃, -ɛn] *nm/f* physicist

physionomie [fizjɔnɔmi] *nf* face; (*d'un paysage etc*) physiognomy

physique [fizik] *adj* physical ♦ *nm* physique ♦ *nf* physics *sg*; **au physique** physically

physiquement [fizikmɑ̃] *adv* physically

piailler [pjaje] *vi* to squawk

pianiste [pjanist(ə)] *nm/f* pianist

piano [pjano] *nm* piano; **piano à queue** grand piano

pianoter [pjanɔte] *vi* to tinkle away (at the piano); (*tapoter*): **pianoter sur** to drum one's fingers on

pic [pik] *nm* (*instrument*) pick(axe); (*montagne*) peak; (ZOOL) woodpecker; **à pic** *adv* vertically; (*fig*) just at the right time; **couler à pic** (*bateau*) to go straight down; **pic à glace** ice pick

pichet [piʃɛ] *nm* jug

picorer [pikɔʀe] *vt* to peck

picoter [pikɔte] *vt* (*suj: oiseau*) to peck ♦ *vi* (*irriter*) to smart, prickle

pie [pi] *nf* magpie; (*fig*) chatterbox ♦ *adj inv*: **cheval pie** piebald; **vache pie** black and white cow

pièce [pjɛs] *nf* (*d'un logement*) room; (THÉÂT) play; (*de mécanisme, machine*) part; (*de monnaie*) coin; (COUTURE) patch; (*document*) document; (*de drap, fragment, d'une collection*) piece; (*de bétail*) head; **mettre en pièces** to smash to pieces; **dix francs pièce** ten francs each; **vendre à la pièce** to sell separately *ou* individually; **travailler/payer à la pièce** to do piecework/pay piece rate; **de toutes pièces : c'est inventé de toutes pièces** it's a complete fabrication; **un maillot une pièce** a one-piece swimsuit; **un deux-pièces cuisine** a two-room(ed) flat (BRIT) *ou* apartment (US) with kitchen; **tout d'une pièce** (*personne: franc*) blunt; (: *sans souplesse*) inflexible; **pièce à conviction** exhibit; **pièce d'eau** ornamental lake *ou* pond; **pièce d'identité : avez-vous une pièce d'identité?** have you got any (means of) identification?; **pièce montée** tiered cake; **pièce de rechange** spare (part); **pièce de résistance** pièce de résistance; (*plat*) main dish; **pièces détachées** spares, (spare) parts; **en pièces détachées** (*à monter*) in kit form; **pièces justificatives** supporting documents

pied [pje] *nm* foot (*pl* feet); (*de verre*) stem; (*de table*) leg; (*de lampe*) base; (*plante*) plant; **pieds nus** barefoot; **à pied** on foot; **à pied sec** without getting one's feet wet; **à pied d'œuvre** ready to start (work); **au pied de la lettre** literally; **au pied levé** at a moment's notice; **de pied en cap** from head to foot; **en pied** (*portrait*) full-length; **avoir pied** to be able to touch the bottom, not to be out of one's depth; **avoir le pied marin** to be a good sailor; **perdre pied** to lose one's footing; (*fig*) to get out of one's depth; **sur pied** on the stalk, uncut; (*debout, rétabli*) up and about; **mettre sur pied** (*entreprise*) to set up; **mettre à pied** to suspend; to lay off; **mettre qn au pied du mur** to get sb with his (*ou* her) back to the wall; **sur le pied de guerre** ready for action; **sur un pied d'égalité** on an equal footing; **sur pied d'intervention** on stand-by; **faire du pied à qn** (*prévenir*) to give sb a (warning) kick; (*galamment*) to play footsie with sb; **mettre les pieds quelque part** to set foot somewhere; **faire des pieds et des mains** (*fig*) to move heaven and earth, pull out all the stops; **c'est le pied!** (*fam*) it's terrific!; **se lever du bon pied/du mauvais pied ou du pied gauche** to get out of bed on the right/wrong side; **pied de lit** footboard; **pied de nez : faire un pied de nez à** to thumb one's nose at; **pied de vigne** vine

pied-noir, *pl* **pieds-noirs** [pjenwaʀ] *nm* Algerian-born Frenchman

piège [pjɛʒ] *nm* trap; **prendre au piège** to trap

piéger [pjeʒe] *vt* (*animal, fig*) to trap; (*avec une bombe*) to booby-trap; **lettre/voiture piégée** letter-/car-bomb

piercing [pjɛʀsiŋ] *nm* piercing

pierre [pjɛʀ] *nf* stone; **première pierre** (*d'un édifice*) foundation stone; **mur de pierres sèches** dry-stone wall; **faire d'une pierre deux coups** to kill two birds with one stone; **pierre à briquet** flint; **pierre fine** semiprecious stone; **pierre ponce** pumice stone; **pierre de taille** freestone *no pl*; **pierre tombale** tombstone, gravestone; **pierre de touche** touchstone

pierreries [pjɛʀʀi] *nfpl* gems, precious stones

piétiner [pjetine] *vi* (*trépigner*) to stamp (one's foot); (*marquer le pas*) to stand about; (*fig*) to be at a standstill ♦ *vt* to trample on

piéton, ne [pjetɔ̃, -ɔn] *nm/f* pedestrian ♦ *adj* pedestrian *cpd*

piétonnier, ière [pjetɔnje, -jɛʀ] *adj* pedestrian *cpd*

pieu, x [pjø] *nm* (*piquet*) post; (*pointu*) stake; (*fam: lit*) bed

pieuvre [pjœvʀ(ə)] *nf* octopus

pieux, euse [pjø, -øz] *adj* pious

piffer [pife] *vt* (*fam*): **je ne peux pas le piffer** I can't stand him

pigeon [piʒɔ̃] *nm* pigeon; **pigeon voyageur** homing pigeon

piger [piʒe] *vi* (*fam*) to get it ♦ *vt* (*fam*) to get, understand

pigiste [piʒist(ə)] *nm/f* (*typographe*) typesetter on piecework; (*journaliste*) freelance journalist (*paid by the line*)

pignon [piɲɔ̃] *nm* (*de mur*) gable; (*d'engrenage*) cog(wheel), gearwheel; (*graine*) pine kernel; **avoir**

pignon sur rue (*fig*) to have a prosperous business

pile [pil] *nf* (*tas, pilier*) pile; (*ÉLEC*) battery ♦ *adj*: **le côté pile** tails ♦ *adv* (*net, brusquement*) dead; (*à temps, à point nommé*) just at the right time; **à deux heures pile** at two on the dot; **jouer à pile ou face** to toss up (for it); **pile ou face?** heads or tails?

piler [pile] *vt* to crush, pound

pilier [pilje] *nm* (*colonne, support*) pillar; (*personne*) mainstay; (*RUGBY*) prop (forward)

piller [pije] *vt* to pillage, plunder, loot

pilote [pilɔt] *nm* pilot; (*de char, voiture*) driver ♦ *adj* pilot *cpd*; **usine/ferme pilote** experimental factory/farm; **pilote de chasse/d'essai/de ligne** fighter/test/airline pilot; **pilote de course** racing driver

piloter [pilɔte] *vt* (*navire*) to pilot; (*avion*) to fly; (*automobile*) to drive; (*fig*): **piloter qn** to guide sb round; **piloté par menu** (*INFORM*) menu-driven

pilule [pilyl] *nf* pill; **prendre la pilule** to be on the pill; **pilule du lendemain** morning-after pill

piment [pimã] *nm* (*BOT*) pepper, capsicum; (*fig*) spice, piquancy; **piment rouge** (*CULIN*) chilli

pimenté, e [pimãte] *adj* hot and spicy

pimpant, e [pɛ̃pã, -ãt] *adj* spruce

pin [pɛ̃] *nm* pine (tree); (*bois*) pine(wood)

pinard [pinar] *nm* (*fam*) (cheap) wine, plonk (*BRIT*)

pince [pɛ̃s] *nf* (*outil*) pliers *pl*; (*de homard, crabe*) pincer, claw; (*COUTURE: pli*) dart; **pince à sucre/glace** sugar/ice tongs *pl*; **pince à épiler** tweezers *pl*; **pince à linge** clothes peg (*BRIT*) ou pin (*US*); **pince universelle** (universal) pliers *pl*; **pinces de cycliste** bicycle clips

pincé, e [pɛ̃se] *adj* (*air*) stiff; (*mince: bouche*) pinched ♦ *nf*: **une pincée de** a pinch of

pinceau, x [pɛ̃so] *nm* (paint)brush

pincer [pɛ̃se] *vt* to pinch; (*MUS: cordes*) to pluck; (*COUTURE*) to dart, put darts in; (*fam*) to nab; **se pincer le doigt** to squeeze *ou* nip one's finger; **se pincer le nez** to hold one's nose

pinède [pinɛd] *nf* pinewood, pine forest

pingouin [pɛ̃gwɛ̃] *nm* penguin

ping-pong [piŋpɔ̃g] *nm* table tennis

pingre [pɛ̃gʀ(ə)] *adj* niggardly

pinson [pɛ̃sɔ̃] *nm* chaffinch

pintade [pɛ̃tad] *nf* guinea-fowl

pioche [pjɔʃ] *nf* pickaxe

piocher [pjɔʃe] *vt* to dig up (with a pickaxe); (*fam*) to swot (*BRIT*) *ou* grind (*US*) at; **piocher dans** to dig into

pion, ne [pjɔ̃, pjɔn] *nm/f* (*SCOL, péj*) student paid to supervise schoolchildren ♦ *nm* (*ÉCHECS*) pawn; (*DAMES*) piece, draught (*BRIT*), checker (*US*)

pionnier [pjɔnje] *nm* pioneer

pipe [pip] *nf* pipe; **fumer la** *ou* **une pipe** to smoke a pipe; **pipe de bruyère** briar pipe

pipeau, x [pipo] *nm* (reed-)pipe

piquant, e [pikã, -ãt] *adj* (*barbe, rosier etc*) prickly; (*saveur, sauce*) hot, pungent; (*fig: description, style*) racy; (: *mordant, caustique*) biting ♦ *nm* (*épine*) thorn, prickle; (*de hérisson*) quill, spine; (*fig*) spiciness, spice

pique [pik] *nf* (*arme*) pike; (*fig*): **envoyer** *ou* **lancer des piques à qn** to make cutting remarks to sb ♦ *nm* (*CARTES: couleur*) spades *pl*; (: *carte*) spade

pique-nique [piknik] *nm* picnic

pique-niquer [piknike] *vi* to (have a) picnic

piquer [pike] *vt* (*percer*) to prick; (*planter*): **piquer qch dans** to stick sth into; (*fixer*): **piquer qch à** *ou* **sur** to pin sth onto; (*MÉD*) to give an injection to; (: *animal blessé etc*) to put to sleep; (*suj: insecte, fumée, ortie*) to sting; (: *poivre*) to burn; (: *froid*) to bite; (*COUTURE*) to machine (stitch); (*intérêt etc*) to arouse; (*fam: prendre*) to pick up; (: *voler*) to pinch; (: *arrêter*) to nab ♦ *vi* (*oiseau, avion*) to go into a dive; (*saveur*) to be pungent; to be sour; **se piquer** (*avec une aiguille*) to prick o.s.; (*se faire une piqûre*) to inject o.s.; (*se vexer*) to get annoyed; **se piquer de faire** to pride o.s. on doing; **piquer sur** to swoop down on; to head straight for; **piquer du nez** (*avion*) to go into a nose-dive; **piquer une tête** (*plonger*) to dive headfirst; **piquer un galop/un cent mètres** to break into a gallop/put on a sprint; **piquer une crise** to throw a fit; **piquer au vif** (*fig*) to sting

piquet [pike] *nm* (*pieu*) post, stake; (*de tente*) peg; **mettre un élève au piquet** to make a pupil stand in the corner; **piquet de grève** (strike) picket; **piquet d'incendie** fire-fighting squad

piqûre [pikyʀ] *nf* (*d'épingle*) prick; (*d'ortie*) sting; (*de moustique*) bite; (*MÉD*) injection, shot (*US*); (*COUTURE*) (straight) stitch; straight stitching; (*de ver*) hole; (*tache*) (spot of) mildew; **faire une piqûre à qn** to give sb an injection

pirate [piʀat] *adj* pirate *cpd* ♦ *nm* pirate; (*fig: escroc*) crook, shark; **pirate de l'air** hijacker

pire [piʀ] *adj* (*comparatif*) worse; (*superlatif*): **le (la) pire ...** the worst ... ♦ *nm*: **le pire (de)** the worst (of)

pis [pi] *nm* (*de vache*) udder; (*pire*): **le pis** the worst ♦ *adj, adv* worse; **qui pis est** that is worse; **au pis aller** if the worst comes to the worst, at worst

piscine [pisin] *nf* (swimming) pool; **piscine couverte** indoor (swimming) pool

pissenlit [pisɑ̃li] *nm* dandelion

pistache [pistaʃ] *nf* pistachio (nut)

piste [pist(ə)] *nf* (*d'un animal, sentier*) track, trail; (*indice*) lead; (*de stade, de magnétophone, INFORM*) track; (*de cirque*) ring; (*de danse*) floor; (*de patinage*) rink; (*de ski*) run; (*AVIAT*) runway; **piste cavalière** bridle path; **piste cyclable** cycle track, bikeway (*US*); **piste sonore** sound track

pistolet [pistɔle] *nm* (*arme*) pistol, gun; (*à peinture*) spray gun; **pistolet à bouchon/air comprimé** popgun/airgun; **pistolet à eau** water pistol

pistolet-mitrailleur, *pl* **pistolets-mitrailleurs** [pistɔlɛmitRajœR] *nm* submachine gun

piston [pistɔ̃] *nm* (*TECH*) piston; (*MUS*) valve; (*fig: appui*) string-pulling

pistonner [pistɔne] *vt* (*candidat*) to pull strings for

piteux, euse [pitø, -øz] *adj* pitiful, sorry (*avant le nom*) **en piteux état** in a sorry state

pitié [pitje] *nf* pity; **sans pitié** *adj* pitiless, merciless; **faire pitié** to inspire pity; **il me fait pitié** I pity him, I feel sorry for him; **avoir pitié de** (*compassion*) to pity, feel sorry for; (*merci*) to have pity *ou* mercy on; **par pitié!** for pity's sake!

pitoyable [pitwajabl(ə)] *adj* pitiful

pitre [pitR(ə)] *nm* clown

pitrerie [pitRəRi] *nf* tomfoolery *no pl*

pittoresque [pitɔRɛsk(ə)] *adj* picturesque; (*expression, détail*) colourful (*BRIT*), colorful (*US*)

pivot [pivo] *nm* pivot; (*d'une dent*) post

pivoter [pivɔte] *vi* (*fauteuil*) to swivel; (*porte*) to revolve; **pivoter sur ses talons** to swing round

pizza [pidza] *nf* pizza

PJ *sigle f* = **police judiciaire** ♦ *sigle fpl* (= *pièces jointes*) encl.

placard [plakaR] *nm* (*armoire*) cupboard; (*affiche*) poster, notice; (*TYPO*) galley; **placard publicitaire** display advertisement

place [plas] *nf* (*emplacement, situation, classement*) place; (*de ville, village*) square; (*ÉCON*): **place financière/boursière** money/stock market; (*espace libre*) room, space; (*de parking*) space; (*siège: de train, cinéma, voiture*) seat; (*prix: au cinéma etc*) price; (: *dans un bus, taxi*) fare; (*emploi*) job; **en place** (*mettre*) in its place; **de place en place, par places** here and there, in places; **sur place** on the spot; **faire place à** to give way to; **faire de la place à** to make room for; **ça prend de la place** it takes up a lot of room *ou* space; **prendre la place de** to take one's place; **remettre qn à sa place** to put sb in his (*ou* her) place; **ne pas rester** *ou* **tenir en place** to be always on the go; **à la place de** in place of, instead of; **une quatre places** (*AUTO*) a four-seater; **il y a 20 places assises/debout** there are 20 seats/ there is standing room for 20; **place forte** fortified town; **place d'honneur** place (*ou* seat) of honour (*BRIT*) *ou* honor (*US*)

placé, e [plase] *adj* (*HIPPISME*) placed; **haut placé** (*fig*) high-ranking; **être bien/mal placé** to be well/ badly placed; (*spectateur*) to have a good/bad seat; **être bien/mal placé pour faire** to be in/not to be in a position to do

placement [plasmã] *nm* placing; (*FINANCE*) investment; **agence** *ou* **bureau de placement** employment agency

placer [plase] *vt* to place, put; (*convive, spectateur*) to seat; (*capital, argent*) to place, invest; (*dans la conversation*) to put *ou* get in; **placer qn chez** to get sb a job at (*ou* with); **se placer au premier rang** to go

and stand (*ou* sit) in the first row

plafond [plafɔ̃] *nm* ceiling

plage [plaʒ] *nf* beach; (*station*) (seaside) resort; (*fig*) band, bracket; (*de disque*) track, band; **plage arrière** (*AUTO*) parcel *ou* back shelf

plagiat [plaʒja] *nm* plagiarism

plaid [plɛd] *nm* (*tartan*) car rug, lap robe (*US*)

plaider [plede] *vi* (*avocat*) to plead; (*plaignant*) to go to court, litigate ♦ *vt* to plead; **plaider pour** (*fig*) to speak for

plaidoyer [pledwaje] *nm* (*JUR*) speech for the defence (*BRIT*) *ou* defense (*US*); (*fig*) plea

plaie [plɛ] *nf* wound

plaignant, e [plɛɲɑ̃, -ɑ̃t] *vb voir* **plaindre** ♦ *nm/f* plaintiff

plaindre [plɛ̃dR(ə)] *vt* to pity, feel sorry for; **se plaindre** *vi* (*gémir*) to moan; (*protester, rouspéter*) **se plaindre (à qn) (de)** to complain (to sb) (about); (*souffrir*) **se plaindre de** to complain of

plaine [plɛn] *nf* plain

plain-pied [plɛ̃pje]: **de plain-pied** *adv* at streetlevel; (*fig*) straight; **de plain-pied (avec)** on the same level (as)

plaint, e [plɛ̃, -ɛ̃t] *pp de* **plaindre** ♦ *nf* (*gémissement*) moan, groan; (*doléance*) complaint; **porter plainte** to lodge a complaint

plaire [plɛR] *vi* to be a success, be successful; to please; **plaire à: cela me plaît** I like it; **essayer de plaire à qn** (*en étant serviable etc*) to try and please sb; **elle plaît aux hommes** she's a success with men, men like her; **se plaire quelque part** to like being somewhere, like it somewhere; **se plaire à faire** to take pleasure in doing; **ce qu'il vous plaira** what(ever) you like *ou* wish; **s'il vous plaît** please

plaisance [plɛzɑ̃s] *nf* (*aussi*: **navigation de plaisance**) (pleasure) sailing, yachting

plaisant, e [plɛzɑ̃, -ɑ̃t] *adj* pleasant; (*histoire, anecdote*) amusing

plaisanter [plɛzɑ̃te] *vi* to joke ♦ *vt* (*personne*) to tease, make fun of; **pour plaisanter** for a joke; **on ne plaisante pas avec cela** that's no joking matter; **tu plaisantes!** you're joking *ou* kidding!

plaisanterie [plɛzɑ̃tRi] *nf* joke; joking *no pl*

plaise [plɛz] *etc vb voir* **plaire**

plaisir [plɛziR] *nm* pleasure; **faire plaisir à qn** (*délibérément*) to be nice to *ou* please sb; (*suj: cadeau, nouvelle etc*): **ceci me fait plaisir** I'm delighted *ou* very pleased with this; **prendre plaisir à/à faire** to take pleasure in/in doing; **j'ai le plaisir de ...** it is with great pleasure that I ...; **M. et Mme X ont le plaisir de vous faire part de ...** M. and Mme X are pleased to announce ...; **se faire un plaisir de faire qch** to be (only too) pleased to do sth; **faites-moi le plaisir de ...** would you mind ..., would you be kind enough to ...; **à plaisir** freely; for the sake of it; **au plaisir (de vous revoir)** (I hope) to see you again; **pour le** *ou* **pour son** *ou* **par plaisir** for pleasure

plaît [plɛ] *vb voir* **plaire**

plan, e [plɑ̃, -an] *adj* flat ♦ *nm* plan; (*GÉOM*) plane; (*fig*) level, plane; (*CINÉ*) shot; **au premier/second plan** in the foreground/middle distance; **à l'arrière plan** in the background; **mettre qch au premier plan** (*fig*) to consider sth to be of primary importance; **sur le plan sexuel** sexually, as far as sex is concerned; **laisser/rester en plan** to abandon/be abandoned; **plan d'action** plan of action; **plan directeur** (*ÉCON*) master plan; **plan d'eau** lake; pond; **plan de travail** work-top, work surface; **plan de vol** (*AVIAT*) flight plan

planche [plɑ̃ʃ] *nf* (*pièce de bois*) plank, (wooden) board; (*illustration*) plate; (*de salades, radis, poireaux*) bed; (*d'un plongeoir*) (diving) board; **les planches** (*THÉÂT*) the boards; **en planches** *adj* wooden; **faire la planche** (*dans l'eau*) to float on one's back; **avoir du pain sur la planche** to have one's work cut out; **planche à découper** chopping board; **planche à dessin** drawing board; **planche à pain** breadboard; **planche à repasser** ironing board; **planche (à roulettes)** (*planche*) skateboard; (*sport*) skateboarding; **planche de salut** (*fig*) sheet anchor; **planche à voile** (*planche*) windsurfer, sailboard; (*sport*) windsurfing

plancher [plɑ̃ʃe] *nm* floor; (*planches*) floorboards *pl*; (*fig*) minimum level ♦ *vi* to work hard

planer [plane] *vi* (*oiseau, avion*) to glide; (*fumée, vapeur*) to float, hover; (*drogué*) to be (on a) high; **planer sur** to hang over; to hover above

planète [planɛt] *nf* planet

planeur [planœʀ] *nm* glider

planification [planifikɑsjɔ̃] *nf* (economic) planning

planifier [planifje] *vt* to plan

planning [planiŋ] *nm* programme (*BRIT*), program (*US*), schedule; **planning familial** family planning

planque [plɑ̃k] *nf* (*fam: combine, filon*) cushy (*BRIT*) *ou* easy number; (: *cachette*) hideout

plant [plɑ̃] *nm* seedling, young plant

plante [plɑ̃t] *nf* plant; **plante d'appartement** house *ou* pot plant; **plante du pied** sole (of the foot); **plante verte** house plant

planter [plɑ̃te] *vt* (*plante*) to plant; (*enfoncer*) to hammer *ou* drive in; (*tente*) to put up, pitch; (*drapeau, échelle, décors*) to put up; (*fam: mettre*) to dump; (: *abandonner*): **planter là** to ditch; **se planter** *vi* (*fam: se tromper*) to get it wrong; **planter qch dans** to hammer *ou* drive sth into; to stick sth into; **se planter dans** to sink into; to get stuck in; **se planter devant** to plant o.s. in front of

plantureux, euse [plɑ̃tyʀø, -øz] *adj* (*repas*) copious, lavish; (*femme*) buxom

plaque [plak] *nf* plate; (*de verre*) sheet; (*de verglas, d'eczéma*) patch; (*dentaire*) plaque; (*avec inscription*) plaque; **plaque (minéralogique *ou* de police *ou* d'immatriculation)** number (*BRIT*) *ou* license (*US*) plate; **plaque de beurre** slab of butter; **plaque**

chauffante hotplate; **plaque de chocolat** bar of chocolate; **plaque de cuisson** hob; **plaque d'identité** identity disc; **plaque tournante** (*fig*) centre (*BRIT*), center (*US*)

plaqué, e [plake] *adj*: **plaqué or/argent** gold-/silver-plated ♦ *nm*: **plaqué or/argent** gold/silver plate; **plaqué acajou** with a mahogany veneer

plaquer [plake] *vt* (*bijou*) to plate; (*bois*) to veneer; (*aplatir*): **plaquer qch sur/contre** to make sth stick *ou* cling to; (*RUGBY*) to bring down; (*fam: laisser tomber*) to drop, ditch; **se plaquer contre** to flatten o.s. against; **plaquer qn contre** to pin sb to

plaquette [plakɛt] *nf* tablet; (*de chocolat*) bar; (*de beurre*) slab, packet; (*livre*) small volume; (*MÉD: de pilules, gélules*) pack, packet; (*INFORM*) circuit board; **plaquette de frein** (*AUTO*) brake pad

plastique [plastik] *adj* plastic ♦ *nm* plastic ♦ *nf* plastic arts *pl*; (*d'une statue*) modelling

plastiquer [plastike] *vt* to blow up

plat, e [pla, -at] *adj* flat; (*fade: vin*) flat-tasting, insipid; (*personne, livre*) dull ♦ *nm* (*récipient, CULIN*) dish; (*d'un repas*): **le premier plat** the first course; (*partie plate*): **le plat de la main** the flat of the hand; (: *d'une route*) flat (part); **à plat ventre** *adv* face down; (*tomber*) flat on one's face; **à plat** *adj* (*pneu, batterie*) flat; (*fam: fatigué*) dead beat, tired out; **plat cuisiné** pre-cooked meal (*ou* dish); **plat du jour** dish of the day; **plat principal** *ou* **de résistance** main course; **plats préparés** convenience food(s)

platane [platan] *nm* plane tree

plateau, x [plato] *nm* (*support*) tray; (*d'une table*) top; (*d'une balance*) pan; (*GÉO*) plateau; (*de tourne-disques*) turntable; (*CINÉ*) set; (*TV*): **nous avons 2 journalistes sur le plateau ce soir** we have 2 journalists with us tonight; **plateau à fromages** cheeseboard

plate-bande, *pl* **plates-bandes** [platbɑ̃d] *nf* flower bed

plate-forme, *pl* **plates-formes** [platfɔʀm(ə)] *nf* platform; **plate-forme de forage/pétrolière** drilling/oil rig

platine [platin] *nm* platinum ♦ *nf* (*d'un tourne-disque*) turntable; **platine disque/cassette** record/cassette deck; **platine laser** *ou* **compact-disc** compact disc (player)

plâtre [plɑtʀ(ə)] *nm* (*matériau*) plaster; (*statue*) plaster statue; (*MÉD*) (plaster) cast; **plâtres** *nmpl* plasterwork *sg*; **avoir un bras dans le plâtre** to have an arm in plaster

plein, e [plɛ̃, -ɛn] *adj* full; (*porte, roue*) solid; (*chienne, jument*) big (with young) ♦ *nm*: **faire le plein (d'essence)** to fill up (with petrol (*BRIT*) *ou* gas (*US*)) ♦ *prép*: **avoir de l'argent plein les poches** to have loads of money; **plein de** full of; **avoir les mains pleines** to have one's hands full; **à pleines mains** (*ramasser*) in handfuls; (*empoigner*) firmly; **à plein régime** at maximum revs; at full speed; **à plein temps** full-time; **en plein air** in the open air;

jeux en plein air outdoor games; **en pleine mer** on the open sea; **en plein soleil** in direct sunlight; **en pleine nuit/rue** in the middle of the night/ street; **en plein milieu** right in the middle; **en plein jour** in broad daylight; **les pleins** the down- strokes (*in handwriting*) **faire le plein des voix** to get the maximum number of votes possible; **en plein sur** right on; **en avoir plein le dos** (*fam*) to have had it up to here

pleurer [plœʀe] *vi* to cry; (*yeux*) to water ◆ *vt* to mourn (for); **pleurer sur** *vt* to lament (over), bemoan; **pleurer de rire** to laugh till one cries

pleurnicher [plœʀniʃe] *vi* to snivel, whine

pleurs [plœʀ] *nmpl*: **en pleurs** in tears

pleut [plø] *vb voir* **pleuvoir**

pleuvait [pløvɛ] *etc vb voir* **pleuvoir**

pleuvoir [pløvwaʀ] *vb impers* to rain ◆ *vi* (*fig*): **pleuvoir (sur)** to shower down (upon), be show- ered upon; **il pleut** it's raining; **il pleut des cordes** *ou* **à verse** *ou* **à torrents** it's pouring (down), it's raining cats and dogs

pli [pli] *nm* fold; (*de jupe*) pleat; (*de pantalon*) crease; (*aussi*: **faux pli**) crease; (*enveloppe*) en- velope; (*lettre*) letter; (*CARTES*) trick; **prendre le pli de faire** to get into the habit of doing; **ça ne fait pas un pli!** don't you worry!; **pli d'aisance** invert- ed pleat

pliant, e [plijɑ̃, -ɑ̃t] *adj* folding ◆ *nm* folding stool, campstool

plier [plije] *vt* to fold; (*pour ranger*) to fold up; (*table pliante*) to fold down; (*genou, bras*) to bend ◆ *vi* to bend; (*fig*) to yield; **se plier à** to submit to; **plier bagages** (*fig*) to pack up (and go)

plinthe [plɛ̃t] *nf* skirting board

plisser [plise] *vt* (*chiffonner: papier, étoffe*) to crease; (*rider: front*) to furrow, wrinkle; (: *bouche*) to pucker; (*jupe*) to put pleats in; **se plisser** *vi* (*vête- ment, étoffe*) to crease

plomb [plɔ̃] *nm* (*métal*) lead; (*d'une cartouche*) (lead) shot; (*PÊCHE*) sinker; (*sceau*) (lead) seal; (*ÉLEC*) fuse; **de plomb** (*soleil*) blazing; **sans plomb** (*essence*) unleaded; **sommeil de plomb** heavy *ou* very deep sleep; **mettre à plomb** to plumb

plombage [plɔ̃baʒ] *nm* (*de dent*) filling

plomberie [plɔ̃bʀi] *nf* plumbing

plombier [plɔ̃bje] *nm* plumber

plonge [plɔ̃ʒ] *nf*: **faire la plonge** to be a washer- up (*BRIT*) *ou* dishwasher (*person*)

plongeant, e [plɔ̃ʒɑ̃, -ɑ̃t] *adj* (*vue*) from above; (*tir, décolleté*) plunging

plongée [plɔ̃ʒe] *nf* (*SPORT*) diving *no pl*; (: *sans scaphandre*) skin diving; (*de sous-marin*) submer- sion, dive; **en plongée** (*sous-marin*) submerged; (*prise de vue*) high angle

plongeoir [plɔ̃ʒwaʀ] *nm* diving board

plongeon [plɔ̃ʒɔ̃] *nm* dive

plonger [plɔ̃ʒe] *vi* to dive ◆ *vt*: **plonger qch dans** to plunge sth into; **plonger dans un sommeil pro-**

fond to sink straight into a deep sleep; **plonger qn dans l'embarras** to throw sb into a state of confu- sion

plongeur, euse [plɔ̃ʒœʀ, -øz] *nm/f* diver; (*de café*) washer-up (*BRIT*), dishwasher (*person*)

ployer [plwaje] *vt* to bend ◆ *vi* to bend; (*planch- er*) to sag

plu [ply] *pp de* **plaire**, **pleuvoir**

pluie [plɥi] *nf* rain; (*averse, ondée*): **une pluie brève** a shower; (*fig*): **pluie de** shower of; **une pluie fine** fine rain; **retomber en pluie** to shower down; **sous la pluie** in the rain

plume [plym] *nf* feather; (*pour écrire*) (pen) nib; (*fig*) pen; **dessin à la plume** pen and ink drawing

plupart [plypaʀ]: **la plupart** *pron* the majority, most (of them); **la plupart des** most, the majority of; **la plupart du temps/d'entre nous** most of the time/of us; **pour la plupart** *adv* for the most part, mostly

pluriel [plyʀjɛl] *nm* plural; **au pluriel** in the plural

plus[1] [ply] *vb voir* **plaire**

┌─────────────┐
│ MOT CLÉ │
└─────────────┘

plus[2] [ply] *adv* **1** (*forme négative*): **ne ... plus** no more, no longer; **je n'ai plus d'argent** I've got no more money *ou* no money left; **il ne travaille plus** he's no longer working, he doesn't work any more

2 [ply, plyz +voyelle] (*comparatif*) more, ...+er; (*superlatif*): **le plus** the most, the ...+est; **plus grand/intelligent (que)** bigger/more intelligent (than); **le plus grand/intelligent** the biggest/ most intelligent; **tout au plus** at the very most

3 [plys] (*davantage*) more; **il travaille plus (que)** he works more (than); **plus il travaille, plus il est heureux** the more he works, the happier he is; **plus de pain** more bread; **plus de 10 person- nes/3 heures/4 kilos** more than *ou* over 10 peo- ple/3 hours/4 kilos; **3 heures de plus que** 3 hours more than; **plus de minuit** after *ou* past midnight; **de plus** what's more, moreover; **il a 3 ans de plus que moi** he's 3 years older than me; **3 kilos en plus** 3 kilos more; **en plus de** in addi- tion to; **de plus en plus** more and more; **en plus de cela ...** what is more ...; **plus ou moins** more or less; **ni plus ni moins** no more, no less; **sans plus** (but) no more than that, (but) that's all; **qui plus est** what is more

◆ *prép* [plys]: **4 plus 2** 4 plus 2

---

plusieurs [plyzjœʀ] *dét, pron* several; **ils sont plusieurs** there are several of them

plus-value [plyvaly] *nf* (*d'un bien*) appreciation; (*bénéfice*) capital gain; (*budgétaire*) surplus

plut [ply] *vb voir* **plaire**, **pleuvoir**

plutôt [plyto] *adv* rather; **je ferais plutôt ceci** I'd rather *ou* sooner do this; **fais plutôt comme ça** try this way instead; **plutôt que (de) faire** rather than *ou* instead of doing

pluvieux, euse [plyvjø, -øz] *adj* rainy, wet

PME *sigle fpl* = petites et moyennes entreprises

PMU *sigle m* = pari mutuel urbain; (*café*) betting agency

PNB *sigle m* (= produit national brut) GNP

pneu [pnø] *nm* (*de roue*) tyre (*BRIT*), tire (*US*); (*message*) letter sent by pneumatic tube

pneumonie [pnømɔni] *nf* pneumonia

poche [pɔʃ] *nf* pocket; (*déformation*): **faire une/ des poche(s)** to bag; (*sous les yeux*) bag, pouch; (*ZOOL*) pouch ◆ *nm* (= livre de poche) (pocket-size) paperback; **de poche** pocket *cpd*; **en être de sa poche** to be out of pocket; **c'est dans la poche** it's in the bag

pocher [pɔʃe] *vt* (*CULIN*) to poach; (*ART*) to sketch ◆ *vi* (*vêtement*) to bag

pochette [pɔʃɛt] *nf* (*de timbres*) wallet, envelope; (*d'aiguilles etc*) case; (*sac: de femme*) clutch bag, purse; (: *d'homme*) (*sur veston*) breast pocket; (*mouchoir*) breast pocket handkerchief; **pochette d'allumettes** book of matches; **pochette de disque** record sleeve; **pochette surprise** lucky bag

poêle [pwal] *nm* stove ◆ *nf*: **poêle (à frire)** frying pan

poème [pɔɛm] *nm* poem

poésie [pɔezi] *nf* (*poème*) poem; (*art*): **la poésie** poetry

poète [pɔɛt] *nm* poet; (*fig*) dreamer ◆ *adj* poetic

poids [pwa] *nm* weight; (*SPORT*) shot; **vendre au poids** to sell by weight; **de poids** *adj* (*argument etc*) weighty; **prendre du poids** to put on weight; **faire le poids** (*fig*) to measure up; **poids plume/ mouche/coq/moyen** (*BOXE*) feather/fly/bantam/ middleweight; **poids et haltères** *nmpl* weight lifting *sg*; **poids lourd** (*BOXE*) heavyweight; (*camion; aussi*: **PL**) (big) lorry (*BRIT*), truck (*US*); (: *ADMIN*) large goods vehicle (*BRIT*), truck (*US*); **poids mort** dead weight; **poids utile** net weight

poignant, e [pwaɲɑ̃, -ɑ̃t] *adj* poignant, harrowing

poignard [pwaɲar] *nm* dagger

poignarder [pwaɲarde] *vt* to stab, knife

poigne [pwaɲ] *nf* grip; (*fig*) firm-handedness; **à poigne** firm-handed

poignée [pwaɲe] *nf* (*de sel etc, fig*) handful; (*de couvercle, porte*) handle; **poignée de main** handshake

poignet [pwaɲɛ] *nm* (*ANAT*) wrist; (*de chemise*) cuff

poil [pwal] *nm* (*ANAT*) hair; (*de pinceau, brosse*) bristle; (*de tapis, tissu*) strand; (*pelage*) coat; (*ensemble des poils*): **avoir du poil sur la poitrine** to have hair(s) on one's chest, have a hairy chest; **à poil** *adj* (*fam*) starkers; **au poil** *adj* (*fam*) hunky-dory; **de tout poil** of all kinds; **être de bon/mauvais poil** to be in a good/bad mood; **poil à gratter** itching powder

poilu, e [pwaly] *adj* hairy

poinçon [pwɛ̃sɔ̃] *nm* awl; bodkin; (*marque*) hall- mark

poinçonner [pwɛ̃sɔne] *vt* (*marchandise*) to stamp; (*bijou etc*) to hallmark; (*billet, ticket*) to clip, punch

poing [pwɛ̃] *nm* fist; **dormir à poings fermés** to sleep soundly

point [pwɛ̃] *vb voir* **poindre** ◆ *nm* (*marque, signe*) dot; (: *de ponctuation*) full stop, period (*US*); (*moment, de score etc, fig: question*) point; (*endroit*) spot; (*COUTURE, TRICOT*) stitch ◆ *adv* = **pas**; **ne ... point** not (at all); **faire le point** (*NAVIG*) to take a bearing; (*fig*) to take stock (of the situation); **faire le point sur** to review; **en tout point** in every respect; **sur le point de faire** (just) about to do; **au point que, à tel point que** so much so that; **mettre au point** (*mécanisme, procédé*) to develop; (*appareil-photo*) to focus; (*affaire*) to settle; **à point** (*CULIN*) just right; (: *viande*) medium; **à point (nommé)** just at the right time; **point de croix/tige/chaînette** (*COUTURE*) cross/stem/chain stitch; **point mousse/jersey** (*TRICOT*) garter/stocking stitch; **point de départ/d'arrivée/d'arrêt** departure/arrival/stopping point; **point chaud** (*MIL, POL*) hot spot; **point de chute** landing place; (*fig*) stopping-off point; **point (de côté)** stitch (*pain*); **point culminant** summit; (*fig*) height, climax; **point d'eau** spring; water point; **point d'exclamation** exclamation mark; **point faible** weak spot; **point final** full stop, period (*US*); **point d'interrogation** question mark; **point mort** (*FINANCE*) break-even point; **au point mort** (*AUTO*) in neutral; (*affaire, entreprise*) at a standstill; **point noir** (*sur le visage*) blackhead; (*AUTO*) accident black spot; **point de non-retour** point of no return; **point de repère** landmark; (*dans le temps*) point of reference; **point de vente** retail outlet; **point de vue** viewpoint; (*fig: opinion*) point of view; **du point de vue de** from the point of view of; **points cardinaux** points of the compass, cardinal points; **points de suspension** suspension points

pointe [pwɛ̃t] *nf* point; (*de la côte*) headland; (*allusion*) dig; sally; (*fig*): **une pointe d'ail/d'accent** a touch *ou* hint of garlic/of an accent; **pointes** *nfpl* (*DANSE*) points, point shoes; **être à la pointe de** (*fig*) to be in the forefront of; **faire *ou* pousser une pointe jusqu'à ...** to press on as far as ...; **sur la pointe des pieds** on tiptoe; **en pointe** *adv* (*tailler*) into a point ◆ *adj* pointed, tapered; **de pointe** *adj* (*technique etc*) leading; (*vitesse*) maximum, top; **heures/jours de pointe** peak hours/days; **faire du 180 en pointe** (*AUTO*) to have a top *ou* maximum speed of 180; **faire des pointes** (*DANSE*) to dance on points; **pointe d'asperge** asparagus tip; **pointe de courant** surge (of current); **pointe de tension** (*INFORM*) spike; **pointe de vitesse** burst of speed

pointer [pwɛ̃te] *vt* (*cocher*) to tick off; (*employés etc*) to check in; (*diriger: canon, longue-vue, doigt*): **pointer vers qch** to point at sth; (*MUS: note*) to dot ◆ *vi* (*employé*) to clock in *ou* on; (*pousses*) to come through; (*jour*) to break; **pointer les oreilles** (*chien*) to prick up its ears

pointillé [pwɛtije] *nm* (*trait*) dotted line; (*ART*) stippling *no pl*

pointilleux, euse [pwɛtijø, -øz] *adj* particular, pernickety

pointu, e [pwɛty] *adj* pointed; (*clou*) sharp; (*voix*) shrill; (*analyse*) precise

pointure [pwɛtyʀ] *nf* size

point-virgule, *pl* **points-virgules** [pwɛviʀgyl] *nm* semi-colon

poire [pwaʀ] *nf* pear; (*fam: péj*) mug; **poire électrique** (*pear-shaped*) switch; **poire à injections** syringe

poireau, x [pwaʀo] *nm* leek

poireauter [pwaʀote] *vi* (*fam*) to hang about (waiting)

poirier [pwaʀje] *nm* pear tree; (*GYMNASTIQUE*): **faire le poirier** to do a headstand

pois [pwa] *nm* (*BOT*) pea; (*sur une étoffe*) dot, spot; **à pois** (*cravate etc*) spotted, polka-dot *cpd*; **pois chiche** chickpea; **pois de senteur** sweet pea; **pois cassés** split peas

poison [pwazɔ̃] *nm* poison

poisse [pwas] *nf* rotten luck

poisseux, euse [pwasø, -øz] *adj* sticky

poisson [pwasɔ̃] *nm* fish *gén inv*; **les Poissons** (*ASTROL: signe*) Pisces, the Fish; **être des Poissons** to be Pisces; **pêcher** *ou* **prendre du poisson** *ou* **des poissons** to fish; **poisson d'avril** April fool; (*blague*) April fool's day trick; **poisson rouge** goldfish

poissonnerie [pwasɔnʀi] *nf* fishmonger's (*BRIT*), fish store (*US*)

poissonnier, ière [pwasɔnje, -jɛʀ] *nm/f* fishmonger (*BRIT*), fish merchant (*US*) ◆ *nf* (*ustensile*) fish kettle

poitrine [pwatʀin] *nf* (*ANAT*) chest; (*seins*) bust, bosom; (*CULIN*) breast; **poitrine de bœuf** brisket

poivre [pwavʀ(ə)] *nm* pepper; **poivre en grains/moulu** whole/ground pepper; **poivre de cayenne** cayenne (pepper); **poivre et sel** *adj* (*cheveux*) pepper-and-salt

poivron [pwavʀɔ̃] *nm* pepper, capsicum; **poivron vert/rouge** green/red pepper

polaire [pɔlɛʀ] *adj* polar

polar [pɔlaʀ] (*fam*) *nm* detective novel

pôle [pol] *nm* (*GÉO, ÉLEC*) pole; **le pôle Nord/Sud** the North/South Pole; **pôle d'attraction** (*fig*) centre of attraction

poli, e [pɔli] *adj* polite; (*lisse*) smooth; polished

police [pɔlis] *nf* police; (*discipline*): **assurer la police de** *ou* **dans** to keep order in; **peine de simple police** sentence given by a magistrates' or police court; **police (d'assurance)** (*insurance*) policy; **police (de caractères)** (*TYPO, INFORM*) typeface; **police judiciaire (PJ)** ≃ Criminal Investigation Department (CID) (*BRIT*), ≃ Federal Bureau of Investigation (FBI) (*US*); **police des mœurs** ≃ vice squad; **police secours** ≃ emergency services *pl*

policier, ière [pɔlisje, -jɛʀ] *adj* police *cpd* ◆ *nm* policeman; (*aussi:* **roman policier**) detective novel

polio(myélite) [pɔljɔ(mjelit)] *nf* polio(myelitis)

polio(myélitique) [pɔljɔ(mjelitik)] *nm/f* polio patient *ou* case

polir [pɔliʀ] *vt* to polish

polisson, ne [pɔlisɔ̃, -ɔn] *adj* naughty

politesse [pɔlitɛs] *nf* politeness; **politesses** *nfpl* (exchange of) courtesies; **rendre une politesse à qn** to return sb's favour (*BRIT*) *ou* favor (*US*)

politicien, ne [pɔlitisjɛ̃, -ɛn] *adj* political ◆ *nm/f* politician

politique [pɔlitik] *adj* political ◆ *nf* (*science, activité*) politics *sg*; (*principes, tactique*) policy, policies *pl* ◆ *nm* (*politicien*) politician; **politique étrangère/intérieure** foreign/domestic policy

pollen [pɔlɛn] *nm* pollen

polluant, e [pɔlɥɑ̃, -ɑ̃t] *adj* polluting ◆ *nm* polluting agent, pollutant

polluer [pɔlɥe] *vt* to pollute

pollution [pɔlysjɔ̃] *nf* pollution

polo [pɔlo] *nm* (*sport*) polo; (*tricot*) polo shirt

Pologne [pɔlɔɲ] *nf*: **la Pologne** Poland

polonais, e [pɔlɔnɛ, -ɛz] *adj* Polish ◆ *nm* (*LING*) Polish ◆ *nm/f*: **Polonais, e** Pole

poltron, ne [pɔltʀɔ̃, -ɔn] *adj* cowardly

polycopier [pɔlikɔpje] *vt* to duplicate

Polynésie [pɔlinezi] *nf*: **la Polynésie** Polynesia; **la Polynésie française** French Polynesia

polyvalent, e [pɔlivalɑ̃, -ɑ̃t] *adj* (*vaccin*) polyvalent; (*personne*) versatile; (*salle*) multi-purpose ◆ *nm* = tax inspector

pommade [pɔmad] *nf* ointment, cream

pomme [pɔm] *nf* (*BOT*) apple; (*boule décorative*) knob; (*pomme de terre*): **pommes frites** steak pommes (frites) steak and chips (*BRIT*) *ou* (French) fries (*US*); **tomber dans les pommes** (*fam*) to pass out; **pomme d'Adam** Adam's apple; **pommes allumettes** French fries (*thin-cut*); **pomme d'arrosoir** (*sprinkler*) rose; **pomme de pin** pine *ou* fir cone; **pomme de terre** potato; **pommes vapeur** boiled potatoes

pommeau, x [pɔmo] *nm* (*boule*) knob; (*de selle*) pommel

pommette [pɔmɛt] *nf* cheekbone

pommier [pɔmje] *nm* apple tree

pompe [pɔ̃p] *nf* (*faste*) pomp (and ceremony); **pompe à eau/essence** water/petrol pump; **pompe à huile** oil pump; **pompe à incendie** (*apparatus*) fire engine **pompes funèbres** undertaker's *sg*, funeral parlour *sg* (*BRIT*), mortician's *sg* (*US*)

pomper [pɔ̃pe] *vt* to pump; (*évacuer*) to pump

out; (*aspirer*) to pump up; (*absorber*) to soak up ♦ *vi* to pump

pompeux, euse [pɔ̃pø, -øz] *adj* pompous

pompier [pɔ̃pje] *nm* fireman ♦ *adj m* (*style*) pretentious, pompous

pompiste [pɔ̃pist(ə)] *nm/f* petrol (*BRIT*) *ou* gas (*US*) pump attendant

poncer [pɔ̃se] *vt* to sand (down)

ponctuation [pɔ̃ktɥasjɔ̃] *nf* punctuation

ponctuel, le [pɔ̃ktɥɛl] *adj* (*à l'heure, TECH*) punctual; (*fig: opération etc*) one-off, single; (*scrupuleux*) punctilious, meticulous

pondéré, e [pɔ̃dere] *adj* level-headed, composed

pondre [pɔ̃dʀ(ə)] *vt* to lay; (*fig*) to produce ♦ *vi* to lay

poney [pɔnɛ] *nm* pony

pont [pɔ̃] *nm* bridge; (*AUTO*): **pont arrière/avant** rear/front axle; (*NAVIG*) deck; **faire le pont** to take the extra day off; **faire un pont d'or à qn** to offer sb a fortune to take a job; **pont aérien** airlift; **pont basculant** bascule bridge; **pont d'envol** flight deck; **pont élévateur** hydraulic ramp; **pont de graissage** (*in garage*) ramp **pont à péage** tollbridge; **pont roulant** travelling crane; **pont suspendu** suspension bridge; **pont tournant** swing bridge; **Ponts et Chaussées** highways department; *see boxed note*

FAIRE LE PONT

The expression **'faire le pont'** refers to the practice of taking a Monday or Friday off to make a long weekend if a public holiday falls on a Tuesday or Thursday. The French commonly take an extra day off work to give four consecutive days' holiday at 'l'Ascension,' 'le 14 juillet' and le '15 août'.

---

pont-levis, *pl* **ponts-levis** [pɔ̃lvi] *nm* drawbridge

pop [pɔp] *adj inv* pop ♦ *nm*: **le pop** pop (music)

populace [pɔpylas] *nf* (*péj*) rabble

populaire [pɔpylɛʀ] *adj* popular; (*manifestation*) mass *cpd*, of the people; (*milieux, clientèle*) working-class; (*LING: mot etc*) used by the lower classes (of society)

popularité [pɔpylaʀite] *nf* popularity

population [pɔpylasjɔ̃] *nf* population; **population active/agricole** working/farming population

populeux, euse [pɔpylø, -øz] *adj* densely populated

porc [pɔʀ] *nm* (*ZOOL*) pig; (*CULIN*) pork; (*peau*) pigskin

porcelaine [pɔʀsəlɛn] *nf* (*substance*) porcelain, china; (*objet*) piece of china(ware)

porc-épic, *pl* **porcs-épics** [pɔʀkepik] *nm* porcupine

porche [pɔʀʃ(ə)] *nm* porch

porcherie [pɔʀʃəʀi] *nf* pigsty

pore [pɔʀ] *nm* pore

porno [pɔʀno] *adj* porno ♦ *nm* porn

port [pɔʀ] *nm* (*NAVIG*) harbour (*BRIT*), harbor (*US*), port; (*ville, aussi INFORM*) port; (*de l'uniforme etc*) wearing; (*pour lettre*) postage; (*pour colis, aussi: posture*) carriage; **port de commerce/de pêche** commercial/fishing port; **arriver à bon port** to arrive safe and sound; **port d'arme** (*JUR*) carrying of a firearm; **port d'attache** (*NAVIG*) port of registry; (*fig*) home base; **port d'escale** port of call; **port franc** free port

portable [pɔʀtabl(ə)] *adj* (*portatif*) transportable; (*téléphone*) mobile; (*vêtement*) wearable; ♦ *nm* (*COMPUT*) laptop (computer); (*téléphone*) mobile (phone)

portail [pɔʀtaj] *nm* gate; (*de cathédrale*) portal

portant, e [pɔʀtɑ̃, -ɑ̃t] *adj* (*murs*) structural, supporting; (*roues*) running; **bien/mal portant** in good/poor health

portatif, ive [pɔʀtatif, -iv] *adj* portable

porte [pɔʀt(ə)] *nf* door; (*de ville, forteresse, SKI*) gate; **mettre à la porte** to throw out; **prendre la porte** to leave, go away; **à ma/sa porte** (*tout près*) on my/his (*ou* her) doorstep; **porte (d'embarquement)** (*AVIAT*) (departure) gate; **porte d'entrée** front door; **porte à porte** *nm* door-to-door selling; **porte de secours** emergency exit; **porte de service** service entrance

porté, e [pɔʀte] *adj*: **être porté à faire qch** to be apt to do sth, tend to do sth; **être porté sur qch** to be partial to sth

porte-avions [pɔʀtavjɔ̃] *nm inv* aircraft carrier

porte-bagages [pɔʀtbagaʒ] *nm inv* luggage rack (*ou* basket *etc*)

porte-bonheur [pɔʀtbɔnœʀ] *nm inv* lucky charm

porte-clefs [pɔʀtəkle] *nm inv* key ring

porte-documents [pɔʀtdɔkymɑ̃] *nm inv* attaché *ou* document case

portée [pɔʀte] *nf* (*d'une arme*) range; (*fig: importance*) impact, import; (*: capacités*) scope, capability; (*de chatte etc*) litter; (*MUS*) stave, staff (*pl* staves); **à/hors de portée (de)** within/out of reach (of); **à portée de (la) main** within (arm's) reach; **à portée de voix** within earshot; **à la portée de qn** (*fig*) at sb's level, within sb's capabilities; **à la portée de toutes les bourses** to suit every pocket, within everyone's means

porte-fenêtre, *pl* **portes-fenêtres** [pɔʀtfənɛtʀ(ə)] *nf* French window

portefeuille [pɔʀtəfœj] *nm* wallet; (*POL, BOURSE*) portfolio; **faire un lit en portefeuille** to make an apple-pie bed

portemanteau, x [pɔʀtmɑ̃to] *nm* coat rack

porte-monnaie [pɔʀtmɔnɛ] *nm inv* purse

porte-parole [pɔʀtparɔl] *nm inv* spokesman

porter [pɔʀte] *vt* (*charge ou sac etc, aussi: foetus*) to carry; (*sur soi: vêtement, barbe, bague*) to wear; (*fig: responsabilité etc*) to bear, carry; (*inscription, marque, titre, patronyme: suj: arbre: fruits, fleurs*) to bear;

(*jugement*) to pass; (*apporter*): **porter qch quelque part/à qn** to take sth somewhere/to sb; (*inscrire*): **porter qch sur** to put sth down on; to enter sth in ♦ *vi* (*voix, regard, canon*) to carry; (*coup, argument*) to hit home; **se porter** *vi* (*se sentir*): **se porter bien/ mal** to be well/unwell; (*aller*): **se porter vers** to go towards; **porter sur** (*peser*) to rest on; (*accent*) to fall on; (*conférence etc*) to concern; (*heurter*) to strike; **être porté à faire** to be apt *ou* inclined to do; **elle portait le nom de Rosalie** she was called Rosalie; **porter qn au pouvoir** to bring sb to power; **porter bonheur à qn** to bring sb luck; **porter qn à croire** to lead sb to believe; **porter son âge** to look one's age; **porter un toast** to drink a toast; **porter de l'argent au crédit d'un compte** to credit an account with some money; **se porter partie civile** to associate in a court action with the public prosecutor; **se porter garant de qch** to guarantee sth, vouch for sth; **se porter candidat à la députation** ≃ to stand for Parliament (*BRIT*), ≃ run for Congress (*US*); **se faire porter malade** to report sick; **porter la main à son chapeau** to raise one's hand to one's hat; **porter son effort sur** to direct one's efforts towards; **porter un fait à la connaissance de qn** to bring a fact to sb's attention *ou* notice

porteur, euse [pɔʀtœʀ, -øz] *adj* (*COMM*) strong, promising; (*nouvelle, chèque etc*): **être porteur de** to be the bearer of ♦ *nm/f* (*de messages*) bearer ♦ *nm* (*de bagages*) porter; (*COMM: de chèque*) bearer; (: *d'actions*) holder; (**avion**) **gros porteur** wide-bodied aircraft, jumbo (jet)

porte-voix [pɔʀtəvwa] *nm inv* megaphone, loudhailer (*BRIT*)

portier [pɔʀtje] *nm* doorman, commissionnaire (*BRIT*)

portière [pɔʀtjɛʀ] *nf* door

portillon [pɔʀtijɔ̃] *nm* gate

portion [pɔʀsjɔ̃] *nf* (*part*) portion, share; (*partie*) portion, section

porto [pɔʀto] *nm* port (wine)

portrait [pɔʀtʀɛ] *nm* portrait; (*photographie*) photograph; (*fig*): **elle est le portrait de sa mère** she's the image of her mother

portrait-robot [pɔʀtʀɛʀɔbo] *nm* Identikit® *ou* Photo-fit® (*BRIT*) picture

portuaire [pɔʀtɥɛʀ] *adj* port *cpd*, harbour *cpd* (*BRIT*), harbor *cpd* (*US*)

portugais, e [pɔʀtɥgɛ, -ɛz] *adj* Portuguese ♦ *nm* (*LING*) Portuguese ♦ *nm/f*: **Portugais, e** Portuguese

Portugal [pɔʀtygal] *nm*: **le Portugal** Portugal

pose [poz] *nf* (*de moquette*) laying; (*de rideaux, papier peint*) hanging; (*attitude, d'un modèle*) pose; (*PHOTO*) exposure

posé, e [poze] *adj* calm, unruffled

poser [poze] *vt* (*déposer*): **poser qch (sur)/qn à** to put sth down (on)/drop sb at; (*placer*): **poser qch sur/quelque part** to put sth on/somewhere; (*installer: moquette, carrelage*) to lay; (*rideaux, papier peint*) to hang; (*MATH: chiffre*) to put (down); (*question*) to ask; (*principe, conditions*) to lay *ou* set down; (*problème*) to formulate; (*difficulté*) to pose; (*personne: mettre en valeur*) to give standing to ♦ *vi* (*modèle*) to pose; to sit; **se poser** (*oiseau, avion*) to land; (*question*) to arise; **se poser en** to pass o.s off as, pose as; **poser son** *ou* **un regard sur qn/qch** to turn one's gaze on sb/sth; **poser sa candidature** to apply; (*POL*) to put o.s. up for election

positif, ive [pozitif, -iv] *adj* positive

position [pozisjɔ̃] *nf* position; **prendre position** (*fig*) to take a stand

posologie [pozɔlɔʒi] *nf* directions *pl* for use, dosage

posséder [posede] *vt* to own, possess; (*qualité, talent*) to have, possess; (*bien connaître: métier, langue*) to have mastered, have a thorough knowledge of; (*sexuellement, aussi: suj: colère etc*) to possess; (*fam: duper*) to take in

possession [posesjɔ̃] *nf* ownership *no pl*; possession; **être/entrer en possession de qch** to be in/ take possession of sth

possibilité [posibilite] *nf* possibility; **possibilités** *nfpl* (*moyens*) means; (*potentiel*) potential *sg*; **avoir la possibilité de faire** to be in a position to do; to have the opportunity to do

possible [posibl(ə)] *adj* possible; (*projet, entreprise*) feasible ♦ *nm*: **faire son possible** to do all one can, do one's utmost; **(ce n'est) pas possible!** impossible!; **le plus/moins de livres possible** as many/few books as possible; **dès que possible** as soon as possible; **gentil etc au possible** as nice *etc* as it is possible to be

postal, e, aux [postal, -o] *adj* postal, post office *cpd*; **sac postal** mailbag, postbag

poste [post(ə)] *nf* (*service*) post, postal service; (*administration, bureau*) post office ♦ *nm* (*fonction, MIL*) post; (*TÉL*) extension; (*de radio etc*) set; (*de budget*) item; **postes** *nfpl* post office *sg*; **Postes télécommunications et télédiffusion (PTT)** *postal and telecommunications service*; **agent** *ou* **employé des postes** post office worker; **mettre à la poste** to post; **poste de commandement (PC)** *nm* (*MIL etc*) headquarters; **poste de contrôle** *nm* checkpoint; **poste de douane** *nm* customs post; **poste émetteur** *nm* transmitting set; **poste d'essence** *nm* filling station; **poste d'incendie** *nm* fire point; **poste de péage** *nm* tollgate; **poste de pilotage** *nm* cockpit; **poste (de police)** *nm* police station; **poste de radio** *nm* radio set; **poste restante (PR)** *nf* poste restante (*BRIT*), general delivery (*US*); **poste de secours** *nm* first-aid post; **poste de télévision** *nm* television set; **poste de travail** *nm* work station

poster *vt* [poste] to post ♦ *nm* [postɛʀ] poster; **se poster** to position o.s.

postérieur, e [posteʀjœʀ] *adj* (*date*) later; (*partie*) back ♦ *nm* (*fam*) behind

posthume [pɔstym] *adj* posthumous

postulant, e [pɔstylɑ̃, -ɑ̃t] *nm/f* (*candidat*) applicant; (*REL*) postulant

postuler [pɔstyle] *vt* (*emploi*) to apply for, put in for

posture [pɔstyʀ] *nf* posture, position; (*fig*) position

pot [po] *nm* jar, pot; (*en plastique, carton*) carton; (*en métal*) tin; (*fam*): **avoir du pot** to be lucky; **boire** *ou* **prendre un pot** (*fam*) to have a drink; **découvrir le pot aux roses** to find out what's been going on; **pot catalytique** catalytic converter; **pot (de chambre)** (chamber)pot; **pot d'échappement** exhaust pipe; **pot de fleurs** plant pot, flowerpot; (*plante*) pot plant; **pot à tabac** tobacco jar

potable [pɔtabl(ə)] *adj* (*fig: boisson*) drinkable; (: *travail, devoir*) decent; **eau (non) potable** (not) drinking water

potage [pɔtaʒ] *nm* soup

potager, ère [pɔtaʒe, -ɛʀ] *adj* (*plante*) edible, vegetable *cpd*; **(jardin) potager** kitchen *ou* vegetable garden

pot-au-feu [pɔtofø] *nm inv* (beef) stew; (*viande*) stewing beef ♦ *adj* (*fam: personne*) stay-at-home

pot-de-vin, *pl* **pots-de-vin** [podvɛ̃] *nm* bribe

pote [pɔt] *nm* (*fam*) mate (*BRIT*), pal

poteau, x [pɔto] *nm* post; **poteau de départ/arrivée** starting/finishing post; **poteau (d'exécution)** execution post, stake; **poteau indicateur** signpost; **poteau télégraphique** telegraph pole; **poteaux (de but)** goal-posts

potelé, e [pɔtle] *adj* plump, chubby

potence [pɔtɑ̃s] *nf* gallows *sg*; **en potence** T-shaped

potentiel, le [pɔtɑ̃sjɛl] *adj, nm* potential

poterie [pɔtri] *nf* (*fabrication*) pottery; (*objet*) piece of pottery

potier [pɔtje] *nm* potter

potins [pɔtɛ̃] *nmpl* gossip *sg*

potiron [pɔtirɔ̃] *nm* pumpkin

pou, x [pu] *nm* louse (*pl* lice)

poubelle [pubɛl] *nf* (dust)bin

pouce [pus] *nm* thumb; **se tourner** *ou* **se rouler les pouces** (*fig*) to twiddle one's thumbs; **manger sur le pouce** to eat on the run, snatch something to eat

poudre [pudʀ(ə)] *nf* powder; (*fard*) (face) powder; (*explosif*) gunpowder; **en poudre: café en poudre** instant coffee; **savon en poudre** soap powder; **lait en poudre** dried *ou* powdered milk; **poudre à canon** gunpowder; **poudre à éternuer** sneezing powder; **poudre à récurer** scouring powder; **poudre de riz** face powder

poudreux, euse [pudʀø, -øz] *adj* dusty; (*neige*) powdery, powder *cpd*

poudrier [pudʀije] *nm* (powder) compact

pouffer [pufe] *vi*: **pouffer (de rire)** to snigger; to giggle

poulailler [pulaje] *nm* henhouse; (*THÉÂT*): **le poulailler** the gods *sg*

poulain [pulɛ̃] *nm* foal; (*fig*) protégé

poule [pul] *nf* (*ZOOL*) hen; (*CULIN*) (boiling) fowl; (*SPORT*) (round-robin) tournament; (*RUGBY*) group; (*fam*) bird (*BRIT*), chick, broad (*US*); (*prostituée*) tart; **poule d'eau** moorhen; **poule mouillée** coward; **poule pondeuse** laying hen, layer; **poule au riz** chicken and rice

poulet [pulɛ] *nm* chicken; (*fam*) cop

poulie [puli] *nf* pulley

pouls [pu] *nm* pulse (*ANAT*); **prendre le pouls de qn** to take sb's pulse

poumon [pumɔ̃] *nm* lung; **poumon d'acier** *ou* **artificiel** iron *ou* artificial lung

poupe [pup] *nf* stern; **en poupe** astern

poupée [pupe] *nf* doll; **jouer à la poupée** to play with one's doll (*ou* dolls); **de poupée** (*très petit*): **jardin de poupée** doll's garden, pocket-handkerchief-sized garden

pouponnière [pupɔnjɛʀ] *nf* crèche, day nursery

pour [puʀ] *prép* for ♦ *nm*: **le pour et le contre** the pros and cons; **pour faire** (so as) to do, in order to do; **pour avoir fait** for having done; **pour que** so that, in order that; **pour moi** (*à mon avis, pour ma part*) for my part, personally; **pour riche qu'il soit** rich though he may be; **pour 50 € d'essence** 50 € worth of petrol; **pour cent** per cent; **pour ce qui est de** as for; **y être pour quelque chose** to have something to do with it

pourboire [puʀbwaʀ] *nm* tip

pourcentage [puʀsɑ̃taʒ] *nm* percentage; **travailler au pourcentage** to work on commission

pourchasser [puʀʃase] *vt* to pursue

pourparlers [puʀpaʀle] *nmpl* talks, negotiations; **être en pourparlers avec** to be having talks with

pourpre [puʀpʀ(ə)] *adj* crimson

pourquoi [puʀkwa] *adv, conj* why ♦ *nm inv*: **le pourquoi (de)** the reason (for)

pourrai [puʀe] *etc vb voir* **pouvoir**

pourri, e [puʀi] *adj* rotten; (*roche, pierre*) crumbling; (*temps, climat*) filthy, foul ♦ *nm*: **sentir le pourri** to smell rotten

pourrir [puʀiʀ] *vi* to rot; (*fruit*) to go rotten *ou* bad; (*fig: situation*) to deteriorate ♦ *vt* to rot; (*fig: corrompre: personne*) to corrupt; (: *gâter: enfant*) to spoil thoroughly

pourriture [puʀityʀ] *nf* rot

pourrons [puʀɔ̃] *etc vb voir* **pouvoir**

poursuite [puʀsɥit] *nf* pursuit, chase; **poursuites** *nfpl* (*JUR*) legal proceedings; **(course) poursuite** track race; (*fig*) chase

poursuivre [puʀsɥivʀ(ə)] *vt* to pursue, chase (after); (*relancer*) to hound, harry; (*obséder*) to haunt; (*JUR*) to bring proceedings against, prosecute; (: *au civil*) to sue; (*but*) to strive towards; (*voyage, études*) to carry on with, continue ♦ *vi* to carry on, go on; **se poursuivre** *vi* to go on, continue

pourtant [puʀtɑ̃] *adv* yet; **mais pourtant** but

nevertheless, but even so; **c'est pourtant facile** (and) yet it's easy

pourtour [puʀtuʀ] *nm* perimeter

pourvoir [puʀvwaʀ] *nm* (COMM) supply ◆ *vt:* **pourvoir qch/qn de** to equip sth/sb with ◆ *vi:* **pourvoir à** to provide for; (*emploi*) to fill; **se pourvoir** (JUR): **se pourvoir en cassation** to take one's case to the Court of Appeal

pourvoyeur, euse [puʀvwajœʀ, -øz] *nm/f* supplier

pourvu, e [puʀvy] *pp de* **pourvoir** ◆ *adj:* **pourvu de** equipped with; **pourvu que** (*si*) provided that, so long as; (*espérons que*) let's hope (that)

pousse [pus] *nf* growth; (*bourgeon*) shoot

poussé, e [puse] *adj* sophisticated, advanced; (*moteur*) souped-up

poussée [puse] *nf* thrust; (*coup*) push; (MÉD) eruption; (*fig*) upsurge

pousser [puse] *vt* to push; (*inciter*): **pousser qn à** to urge *ou* press sb to + *infinitif*; (*acculer*): **pousser qn à** to drive sb to; (*moteur, voiture*) to drive hard; (*émettre: cri etc*) to give; (*stimuler*) to urge on; to drive hard; (*poursuivre*) to carry on ◆ *vi* to push; (*croître*) to grow; (*aller*): **pousser plus loin** to push on a bit further; **se pousser** *vi* to move over; **faire pousser** (*plante*) to grow; **pousser le dévouement** *etc* **jusqu'à ...** to take devotion *etc* as far as ...

poussette [pusεt] *nf* (*voiture d'enfant*) pushchair (BRIT), stroller (US)

poussière [pusjεʀ] *nf* dust; (*grain*) speck of dust; **et des poussières** (*fig*) and a bit; **poussière de charbon** coaldust

poussiéreux, euse [pusjeʀø, -øz] *adj* dusty

poussin [pusɛ̃] *nm* chick

poutre [putʀ(ə)] *nf* beam; (*en fer, ciment armé*) girder; **poutres apparentes** exposed beams

---

MOT CLÉ

pouvoir [puvwaʀ] *nm* power; (POL: *dirigeants*): **le pouvoir** those in power; **les pouvoirs publics** the authorities; **avoir pouvoir de faire** (*autorisation*) to have (the) authority to do; (*droit*) to have the right to do; **pouvoir absolu** absolute power; **pouvoir absorbant** absorbency; **pouvoir d'achat** purchasing power; **pouvoir calorifique** calorific value

◆ *vb semi-aux* **1** (*être en état de*) can, be able to; **je ne peux pas le réparer** I can't *ou* I am not able to repair it; **déçu de ne pas pouvoir le faire** disappointed not to be able to do it

2 (*avoir la permission*) can, may, be allowed to; **vous pouvez aller au cinéma** you can *ou* may go to the pictures

3 (*probabilité, hypothèse*) may, might, could; **il a pu avoir un accident** he may *ou* might *ou* could have had an accident; **il aurait pu le dire!** he might *ou* could have said (so)!

4 (*expressions*): **tu ne peux pas savoir!** you have no idea!; **tu peux le dire!** you can say that again!

◆ *vb impers* may, might, could; **il peut arriver que** it may *ou* might *ou* could happen that; **il pourrait pleuvoir** it might rain

◆ *vt* **1** can, be able to; **j'ai fait tout ce que j'ai pu** I did all I could; **je n'en peux plus** (*épuisé*) I'm exhausted; (*à bout*) I've had enough

2 (*vb +adj ou adv comparatif*): **je me porte on ne peut mieux** I'm absolutely fine, I couldn't be better; **elle est on ne peut plus gentille** she couldn't be nicer, she's as nice as can be

se pouvoir *vi:* **il se peut que** it may *ou* might be that; **cela se pourrait** that's quite possible

---

prairie [pʀeʀi] *nf* meadow

praline [pʀalin] *nf* (*bonbon*) sugared almond; (*au chocolat*) praline

praticable [pʀatikabl(ə)] *adj* (*route etc*) passable, practicable; (*projet*) practicable

pratiquant, e [pʀatikɑ̃, -ɑ̃t] *adj* practising (BRIT), practicing (US)

pratique [pʀatik] *nf* practice ◆ *adj* practical; (*commode: horaire etc*) convenient; (: *outil*) handy, useful; **dans la pratique** in (actual) practice; **mettre en pratique** to put into practice

pratiquement [pʀatikmɑ̃] *adv* (*dans la pratique*) in practice; (*pour ainsi dire*) practically, virtually

pratiquer [pʀatike] *vt* to practise (BRIT), practice (US); (SPORT *etc*) to go in for, play; (*appliquer: méthode, théorie*) to apply; (*intervention, opération*) to carry out; (*ouverture, abri*) to make ◆ *vi* (REL) to be a churchgoer

pré [pʀe] *nm* meadow

préalable [pʀealabl(ə)] *adj* preliminary; **condition préalable (de)** precondition (for), prerequisite (for); **sans avis préalable** without prior *ou* previous notice; **au préalable** first, beforehand

préambule [pʀeɑ̃byl] *nm* preamble; (*fig*) prelude; **sans préambule** straight away

préau, x [pʀeo] *nm* (*d'une cour d'école*) covered playground; (*d'un monastère, d'une prison*) inner courtyard

préavis [pʀeavi] *nm* notice; **préavis de congé** notice; **communication avec préavis** (TÉL) personal *ou* person-to-person call

précaution [pʀekosjɔ̃] *nf* precaution; **avec précaution** cautiously; **prendre des** *ou* **ses précautions** to take precautions; **par précaution** as a precaution; **pour plus de précaution** to be on the safe side; **précautions oratoires** carefully phrased remarks

précédemment [pʀesedamɑ̃] *adv* before, previously

précédent, e [pʀesedɑ̃, -ɑ̃t] *adj* previous ◆ *nm* precedent; **sans précédent** unprecedented; **le jour précédent** the day before, the previous day

précéder [pʀesede] *vt* to precede; (*marcher ou rouler devant*) to be in front of; (*arriver avant*) to get ahead of

précepteur, trice [pʀesεptœʀ, -tʀis] *nm/f* (private) tutor

prêcher [pʀeʃe] *vt, vi* to preach

précieux, euse [pʀesjø, -øz] *adj* precious; (*collaborateur, conseils*) invaluable; (*style, écrivain*) précieux, precious

précipice [pʀesipis] *nm* drop, chasm; (*fig*) abyss; **au bord du précipice** at the edge of the precipice

précipitamment [pʀesipitamɑ̃] *adv* hurriedly, hastily

précipitation [pʀesipitasjɔ̃] *nf* (*hâte*) haste; **précipitations (atmosphériques)** *nfpl* precipitation *sg*

précipité, e [pʀesipite] *adj* (*respiration*) fast; (*pas*) hurried; (*départ*) hasty

précipiter [pʀesipite] *vt* (*faire tomber*): **précipiter qn/qch du haut de** to throw *ou* hurl sb/sth off *ou* from; (*hâter: marche*) to quicken; (: *départ*) to hasten; **se précipiter** *vi* (*événements*) to move faster; (*respiration*) to speed up; **se précipiter sur/vers** to rush at/towards; **se précipiter au-devant de qn** to throw o.s. before sb

précis, e [pʀesi, -iz] *adj* precise; (*tir, mesures*) accurate, precise ♦ *nm* handbook

précisément [pʀesizemɑ̃] *adv* precisely; **ma vie n'est pas précisément distrayante** my life is not exactly entertaining

préciser [pʀesize] *vt* (*expliquer*) to be more specific about, clarify; (*spécifier*) to state, specify; **se préciser** *vi* to become clear(er)

précision [pʀesizjɔ̃] *nf* precision; accuracy; (*détail*) point *ou* detail (*made clear or to be clarified*); **précisions** *nfpl* further details

précoce [pʀekɔs] *adj* early; (*enfant*) precocious; (*calvitie*) premature

préconçu, e [pʀekɔ̃sy] *adj* preconceived

préconiser [pʀekɔnize] *vt* to advocate

prédécesseur [pʀedesesœʀ] *nm* predecessor

prédilection [pʀedileksjɔ̃] *nf*: **avoir une prédilection pour** to be partial to; **de prédilection** favourite (*BRIT*), favorite (*US*)

prédire [pʀediʀ] *vt* to predict

prédominer [pʀedɔmine] *vi* to predominate; (*avis*) to prevail

préface [pʀefas] *nf* preface

préfecture [pʀefektyʀ] *nf* prefecture; **préfecture de police** police headquarters *pl*; *see boxed note*

PRÉFECTURE

The **préfecture** is the administrative headquarters of the 'département'. The 'préfet', a senior civil servant appointed by the government, is responsible for putting government policy into practice. France's 22 regions, each comprising a number of 'départements', also have a 'préfet de région'.

---

préférable [pʀefeʀabl(ə)] *adj* preferable

préféré, e [pʀefeʀe] *adj, nm/f* favourite (*BRIT*),

favorite (*US*)

préférence [pʀefeʀɑ̃s] *nf* preference; **de préférence** preferably; **de** *ou* **par préférence à** in preference to, rather than; **donner la préférence à qn** to give preference to sb; **par ordre de préférence** in order of preference; **obtenir la préférence sur** to have preference over

préférer [pʀefeʀe] *vt*: **préférer qn/qch (à)** to prefer sb/sth (to), like sb/sth better (than); **préférer faire** to prefer to do; **je préférerais du thé** I would rather have tea, I'd prefer tea

préfet [pʀefɛ] *nm* prefect; **préfet de police** ≃ Chief Constable (*BRIT*), ≃ Police Commissioner (*US*)

préhistorique [pʀeistɔʀik] *adj* prehistoric

préjudice [pʀeʒydis] *nm* (*matériel*) loss; (*moral*) harm *no pl*; **porter préjudice à** to harm, be detrimental to; **au préjudice de** at the expense of

préjugé [pʀeʒyʒe] *nm* prejudice; **avoir un préjugé contre** to be prejudiced against; **bénéficier d'un préjugé favorable** to be viewed favourably

préjuger [pʀeʒyʒe]: **préjuger de** *vt* to prejudge

prélasser [pʀelɑse]: **se prélasser** *vi* to lounge

prélèvement [pʀelɛvmɑ̃] *nm* deduction; withdrawal; **faire un prélèvement de sang** to take a blood sample

prélever [pʀelve] *vt* (*échantillon*) to take; (*argent*): **prélever (sur)** to deduct (from); (: *sur son compte*): **prélever (sur)** to withdraw (from)

prématuré, e [pʀematyʀe] *adj* premature; (*retraite*) early ♦ *nm* premature baby

premier, ière [pʀəmje, -jɛʀ] *adj* first; (*branche, marche, grade*) bottom; (*fig: fondamental*) basic; prime; (*en importance*) first, foremost ♦ *nm* (*premier étage*) first (*BRIT*) *ou* second (*US*) floor ♦ *nf* (*AUTO*) first (gear); (*RAIL, AVIAT etc*) first class; (*SCOL: classe*) penultimate school year (*age 16-17*); (*THÉÂT*) first night; (*CINE*) première; (*exploit*) first; **au premier abord** at first sight; **au** *ou* **du premier coup** at the first attempt *ou* go; **de premier ordre** first-class, first-rate; **de première qualité, de premier choix** best *ou* top quality; **de première importance** of the highest importance; **de première nécessité** absolutely essential; **le premier venu** the first person to come along; **jeune premier** leading man; **le premier de l'an** New Year's Day; **enfant du premier lit** child of a first marriage; **en premier lieu** in the first place; **premier âge** (*d'un enfant*) the first 3 months (of life); **Premier Ministre** Prime Minister

premièrement [pʀəmjɛʀmɑ̃] *adv* firstly

prémonition [pʀemɔnisjɔ̃] *nf* premonition

prémunir [pʀemyniʀ]: **se prémunir contre** to protect o.s. from, guard against

prenant, e [pʀənɑ̃, -ɑ̃t] *vb voir* **prendre** ♦ *adj* absorbing, engrossing

prénatal, e [pʀenatal] *adj* (*MÉD*) antenatal; (*allocation*) maternity *cpd*

prendre [pʀɑ̃dʀ(ə)] *vt* to take; (*ôter*): **prendre qch**

à to take sth from; (*aller chercher*) to get, fetch; (*se procurer*) to get; (*réserver: place*) to book; (*acquérir: du poids, de la valeur*) to put on, gain; (*malfaiteur, poisson*) to catch; (*passager*) to pick up; (*personnel, aussi: couleur, goût*) to take on; (*locataire*) to take in; (*traiter: enfant, problème*) to handle; (*voix, ton*) to put on; (*prélever: pourcentage, argent*) to take off; (*coincer*): **se prendre les doigts dans** to get one's fingers caught in ◆ *vi* (*liquide, ciment*) to set; (*greffe, vaccin*) to take; (*mensonge*) to be successful; (*feu: foyer*) to go; (: *incendie*) to start; (*allumette*) to light; (*se diriger*): **prendre à gauche** to turn (to the) left; **prendre son origine** *ou* **sa source** (*mot, rivière*) to have its source; **prendre qn pour** to take sb for; **prendre pour** to think one is; **prendre sur soi de faire qch** to take it upon o.s. to do sth; **prendre qn en sympathie/horreur** to like/loathe sb; **à tout prendre** all things considered; **s'en prendre à** (*agresser*) to set about; (*passer sa colère sur*) to take it out on; (*critiquer*) to attack; (*remettre en question*) to challenge; **se prendre d'amitié/d'affection pour** to befriend/become fond of; **s'y prendre** (*procéder*) to set about it; **s'y prendre à l'avance** to see to it in advance; **s'y prendre à deux fois** to try twice, make two attempts

preneur [prənœr] *nm*: **être preneur** to be willing to buy; **trouver preneur** to find a buyer

preniez [prənje] *vb voir* **prendre**

prenne *etc* [prɛn] *vb voir* **prendre**

prénom [prenɔ̃] *nm* first name

préoccupation [preɔkypasjɔ̃] *nf* (*souci*) concern; (*idée fixe*) preoccupation

préoccuper [preɔkype] *vt* (*tourmenter, tracasser*) to concern; (*absorber, obséder*) to preoccupy; **se préoccuper de qch** to be concerned about sth; to show concern about sth

préparatifs [preparatif] *nmpl* preparations

préparation [preparasjɔ̃] *nf* preparation; (*SCOL*) piece of homework

préparer [prepare] *vt* to prepare; (*café, repas*) to make; (*examen*) to prepare for; (*voyage, entreprise*) to plan; **se préparer** *vi* (*orage, tragédie*) to brew, be in the air; **se préparer (à qch/à faire)** to prepare (o.s.) *ou* get ready (for sth/to do); **préparer qch à qn** (*surprise etc*) to have sth in store for sb; **préparer qn à qch** (*nouvelle etc*) to prepare sb for sth

prépondérant, e [prepɔ̃derɑ̃, -ɑ̃t] *adj* major, dominating; **voix prépondérante** casting vote

préposé, e [prepoze] *adj*: **préposé à** in charge of ◆ *nm/f* (*gén: employé*) employee; (*ADMIN: facteur*) postman/woman (*BRIT*), mailman/woman (*US*); (*de la douane etc*) official; (*de vestiaire*) attendant

préposition [prepozisjɔ̃] *nf* preposition

près [prɛ] *adv* near, close; **près de** *prép* near (to), close to; (*environ*) nearly, almost; **près d'ici** near here; **de près** *adv* closely; **à 5 kg près** to within about 5 kg; **à cela près que** apart from the fact that; **je ne suis pas près de lui pardonner** I'm nowhere near ready to forgive him; **on n'est pas à**

un jour près one day (either way) won't make any difference, we're not going to quibble over the odd day

présage [prezaʒ] *nm* omen

présager [prezaʒe] *vt* (*prévoir*) to foresee; (*annoncer*) to portend

presbyte [prɛsbit] *adj* long-sighted (*BRIT*), far-sighted (*US*)

presbytère [prɛsbiter] *nm* presbytery

prescription [prɛskripsjɔ̃] *nf* (*instruction*) order, instruction; (*MÉD, JUR*) prescription

prescrire [prɛskrir] *vt* to prescribe; **se prescrire** *vi* (*JUR*) to lapse

présence [prezɑ̃s] *nf* presence; (*au bureau etc*) attendance; **en présence** face to face; **en présence de** in (the) presence of; (*fig*) in the face of; **faire acte de présence** to put in a token appearance; **présence d'esprit** presence of mind

présent, e [prezɑ̃, -ɑ̃t] *adj, nm* present; (*ADMIN, COMM*): **la présente lettre/loi** this letter/law ◆ *nm/f*: **les présents** (*personnes*) those present ◆ *nf* (*COMM: lettre*): **la présente** this letter; **à présent** now, at present; **dès à présent** here and now; **jusqu'à présent** up till now, until now; **à présent que** now that

présentation [prezɑ̃tasjɔ̃] *nf* presentation; introduction; (*allure*) appearance

présenter [prezɑ̃te] *vt* to present; (*invité, candidat*) to introduce; (*félicitations, condoléances*) to offer; (*montrer: billet, pièce d'identité*) to show, produce; (*faire inscrire: candidat*) to put forward; (*soumettre*) to submit ◆ *vi*: **présenter mal/bien** to have an unattractive/a pleasing appearance; **se présenter** *vi* (*sur convocation*) to report, come; (*se faire connaître*) to come forward; (*à une élection*) to stand; (*occasion*) to arise; **se présenter à un examen** to sit an exam; **se présenter bien/mal** to look good/not too good

préservatif [prezɛrvatif] *nm* condom, sheath

préserver [prezɛrve] *vt*: **préserver de** (*protéger*) to protect from; (*sauver*) to save from

président [prezidɑ̃] *nm* (*POL*) president; (*d'une assemblée, COMM*) chairman; **président directeur général (PDG)** chairman and managing director (*BRIT*), chairman and president (*US*); **président du jury** (*JUR*) foreman of the jury; (*d'examen*) chief examiner

présidentiel, le [prezidɑ̃sjɛl] *adj* presidential; **présidentielles** *nfpl* presidential election(s)

présider [prezide] *vt* to preside over; (*dîner*) to be the guest of honour (*BRIT*) *ou* honor (*US*) at; **présider à** *vt* to direct; to govern

présomptueux, euse [prezɔ̃ptɥø, -øz] *adj* presumptuous

presque [prɛsk(ə)] *adv* almost, nearly; **presque rien** hardly anything; **presque pas** hardly (at all); **presque pas de** hardly any; **personne, ou presque** next to nobody, hardly anyone; **la**

presque totalité (de) almost *ou* nearly all

presqu'île [pʀɛskil] *nf* peninsula

pressant, e [pʀɛsɑ̃, -ɑ̃t] *adj* urgent; (*personne*) insistent; **se faire pressant** to become insistent

presse [pʀɛs] *nf* press; (*affluence*): **heures de presse** busy times; **sous presse** gone to press; **mettre sous presse** to send to press; **avoir une bonne/mauvaise presse** to have a good/bad press; **presse féminine** women's magazines *pl*; **presse d'information** quality newspapers *pl*

pressé, e [pʀɛse] *adj* in a hurry; hurried; (*besogne*) urgent ◆ *nm*: **aller au plus pressé** to see to first things first; **être pressé de faire qch** to be in a hurry to do sth; **orange pressée** freshly squeezed orange juice

pressentiment [pʀɛsɑ̃timɑ̃] *nm* foreboding, premonition

pressentir [pʀɛsɑ̃tiʀ] *vt* to sense; (*prendre contact avec*) to approach

presse-papiers [pʀɛspapje] *nm inv* paperweight

presser [pʀɛse] *vt* (*fruit, éponge*) to squeeze; (*interrupteur, bouton*) to press, push; (*allure, affaire*) to speed up; (*débiteur etc*) to press; (*inciter*): **presser qn de faire** to urge *ou* press sb to do ◆ *vi* to be urgent; **se presser** (*se hâter*) to hurry (up); (*se grouper*) to crowd; **rien ne presse** there's no hurry; **se presser contre qn** to squeeze up against sb; **presser le pas** to quicken one's step; **presser qn entre ses bras** to squeeze sb tight

pressing [pʀɛsiŋ] *nm* (*repassage*) steampressing; (*magasin*) dry-cleaner's

pression [pʀɛsjɔ̃] *nf* pressure; (*bouton*) press stud (*BRIT*), snap fastener; **faire pression sur** to put pressure on; **sous pression** pressurized, under pressure; (*fig*) keyed up; **pression artérielle** blood pressure

prestance [pʀɛstɑ̃s] *nf* presence, imposing bearing

prestataire [pʀɛstatɛʀ] *nm/f* person receiving benefits; (*COMM*): **prestataire de services** provider of services

prestation [pʀɛstasjɔ̃] *nf* (*allocation*) benefit; (*d'une assurance*) cover *no pl*; (*d'une entreprise*) service provided; (*d'un joueur, artiste*) performance; **prestation de serment** taking the oath; **prestation de service** provision of a service; **prestations familiales** ≈ child benefit

prestidigitateur, trice [pʀɛstidiʒitatœʀ, -tʀis] *nm/f* conjurer

prestige [pʀɛstiʒ] *nm* prestige

prestigieux, euse [pʀɛstiʒjø, -øz] *adj* prestigious

présumer [pʀezyme] *vt*: **présumer que** to presume *ou* assume that; **présumer de** to overrate; **présumer qn coupable** to presume sb guilty

prêt, e [pʀɛ, pʀɛt] *adj* ready ◆ *nm* lending *no pl*; (*somme prêtée*) loan; **prêt à faire** ready to do; **prêt**

à tout ready for anything; **prêt sur gages** pawnbroking *no pl*

prêt-à-porter, *pl* **prêts-à-porter** [pʀɛtapɔʀte] *nm* ready-to-wear *ou* off-the-peg (*BRIT*) clothes *pl*

prétendre [pʀetɑ̃dʀ(ə)] *vt* (*affirmer*): **prétendre que** to claim that; (*avoir l'intention de*): **prétendre faire qch** to mean *ou* intend to do sth; **prétendre à** *vt* (*droit, titre*) to lay claim to

prétendu, e [pʀetɑ̃dy] *adj* (*supposé*) so-called

prétentieux, euse [pʀetɑ̃sjø, -øz] *adj* pretentious

prétention [pʀetɑ̃sjɔ̃] *nf* pretentiousness; (*exigence, ambition*) claim; **sans prétention** unpretentious

prêter [pʀete] *vt* (*livres, argent*): **prêter qch (à)** to lend sth (to); (*supposer*): **prêter à qn** (*caractère, propos*) to attribute to sb ◆ *vi* (*aussi* **se prêter**: *tissu, cuir*) to give; **prêter à** (*commentaires etc*) to be open to, give rise to; **se prêter à** to lend o.s. (*ou* itself) to; (*manigances etc*) to go along with; **prêter assistance à** to give help to; **prêter attention** to pay attention; **prêter serment** to take the oath; **prêter l'oreille** to listen

prétexte [pʀetɛkst(ə)] *nm* pretext, excuse; **sous aucun prétexte** on no account; **sous (le) prétexte que/de** on the pretext that/of

prétexter [pʀetɛkste] *vt* to give as a pretext *ou* an excuse

prêtre [pʀɛtʀ(ə)] *nm* priest

preuve [pʀœv] *nf* proof; (*indice*) proof, evidence *no pl*; **jusqu'à preuve du contraire** until proved otherwise; **faire preuve de** to show; **faire ses preuves** to prove o.s. (*ou* itself); **preuve matérielle** material evidence

prévaloir [pʀevalwaʀ] *vi* to prevail; **se prévaloir de** *vt* to take advantage of; (*tirer vanité de*) to pride o.s. on

prévenant, e [pʀevnɑ̃, -ɑ̃t] *adj* thoughtful, kind

prévenir [pʀevniʀ] *vt* (*avertir*): **prévenir qn (de)** to warn sb (about); (*informer*): **prévenir qn (de)** to tell *ou* inform sb (about); (*éviter*) to avoid, prevent; (*anticiper*) to anticipate; (*influencer*): **prévenir qn contre** to prejudice sb against

préventif, ive [pʀevɑ̃tif, -iv] *adj* preventive

prévention [pʀevɑ̃sjɔ̃] *nf* prevention; (*préjugé*) prejudice; (*JUR*) custody, detention; **prévention routière** road safety

prévenu, e [pʀevny] *nm/f* (*JUR*) defendant, accused

prévision [pʀevizjɔ̃] *nf*: **prévisions** predictions; (*météorologiques, économiques*) forecast *sg*; **en prévision de** in anticipation of; **prévisions météorologiques** *ou* **du temps** weather forecast *sg*

prévoir [pʀevwaʀ] *vt* (*deviner*) to foresee; (*s'attendre à*) to expect, reckon on; (*prévenir*) to anticipate; (*organiser*) to plan; (*préparer, réserver*) to allow; **prévu pour 4 personnes** designed for 4 people;

prévu pour 10 h scheduled for 10 o'clock

prévoyant, e [prevwajɑ̃, -ɑ̃t] *vb voir* **prévoir** ♦ *adj* gifted with (*ou* showing) foresight, far-sighted

prévu, e [prevy] *pp de* **prévoir**

prier [prije] *vi* to pray ♦ *vt* (*Dieu*) to pray to; (*implorer*) to beg; (*demander*): **prier qn de faire** to ask sb to do; (*inviter*): **prier qn à dîner** to invite sb to dinner; **se faire prier** to need coaxing *ou* persuading; **je vous en prie** (*allez-y*) please do; (*de rien*) don't mention it; **je vous prie de faire** please (would you) do

prière [prijɛʀ] *nf* prayer; (*demande instante*) plea, entreaty; **"prière de faire …"** "please do …"

primaire [primɛʀ] *adj* primary; (*péj: personne*) simple-minded; (: *idées*) simplistic ♦ *nm* (SCOL) primary education

prime [prim] *nf* (*bonification*) bonus; (*subside*) allowance; (COMM: *cadeau*) free gift; (ASSURANCES, BOURSE) premium ♦ *adj*: **de prime abord** at first glance; **prime de risque** danger money *no pl*; **prime de transport** travel allowance

primer [prime] *vt* (*l'emporter sur*) to prevail over; (*récompenser*) to award a prize ♦ *vi* to dominate, prevail

primeur [primœʀ] *nf*: **avoir la primeur de** to be the first to hear (*ou* see etc); **primeurs** *nfpl* (*fruits, légumes*) early fruits and vegetables; **marchand de primeur** greengrocer (BRIT), produce dealer (US)

primevère [primvɛʀ] *nf* primrose

primitif, ive [primitif, -iv] *adj* primitive; (*originel*) original ♦ *nm/f* primitive

primordial, e, aux [primɔʀdjal, -o] *adj* essential, primordial

prince [prɛ̃s] *nm* prince; **prince charmant** Prince Charming; **prince de Galles** *nm inv* (*tissu*) check cloth; **prince héritier** crown prince

princesse [prɛ̃sɛs] *nf* princess

principal, e, aux [prɛ̃sipal, -o] *adj* principal, main ♦ *nm* (SCOL) head (teacher) (BRIT), principal (US); (*essentiel*) main thing ♦ *nf* (LING): **(proposition) principale** main clause

principe [prɛ̃sip] *nm* principle; **partir du principe que** to work on the principle *ou* assumption that; **pour le principe** on principle, for the sake of it; **de principe** *adj* (*hostilité*) automatic; (*accord*) in principle; **par principe** on principle; **en principe** (*habituellement*) as a rule; (*théoriquement*) in principle

printemps [prɛ̃tɑ̃] *nm* spring; **au printemps** in spring

priorité [prijɔrite] *nf* (AUTO): **avoir la priorité (sur)** to have right of way (over); **priorité à droite** right of way to vehicles coming from the right; **en priorité** as a (matter of) priority

pris, e [pri, priz] *pp de* **prendre** ♦ *adj* (*place*) taken; (*billets*) sold; (*journée, mains*) full; (*personne*) busy; (*crème, ciment*) set; (MÉD: *enflammé*): **avoir le nez/la gorge pris(e)** to have a stuffy nose/a bad

throat; (*saisi*): **être pris de peur/de fatigue** to be stricken with fear/overcome with fatigue

prise [priz] *nf* (*d'une ville*) capture; (*PÊCHE, CHASSE*) catch; (*de judo ou catch, point d'appui ou pour empoigner*) hold; (ÉLEC: *fiche*) plug; (: *femelle*) socket; (: *au mur*) point; **en prise** (AUTO) in gear; **être aux prises avec** to be grappling with; to be battling with; **lâcher prise** to let go; **donner prise à** (*fig*) to give rise to; **avoir prise sur qn** to have a hold over sb; **prise en charge** (*taxe*) pick-up charge; (*par la sécurité sociale*) undertaking to reimburse costs; **prise de contact** initial meeting, first contact; **prise de courant** power point; **prise d'eau** water (supply) point; tap; **prise multiple** adaptor; **prise d'otages** hostage-taking; **prise à partie** (JUR) action against a judge; **prise de sang** blood test; **prise de son** sound recording; **prise de terre** earth; **prise de vue** (*photo*) shot; (*action*): **prise de vue(s)** filming, shooting

priser [prize] *vt* (*tabac, héroïne*) to take; (*estimer*) to prize, value ♦ *vi* to take snuff

prison [prizɔ̃] *nf* prison; **aller/être en prison** to go to/be in prison *ou* jail; **faire de la prison** to serve time; **être condamné à 5 ans de prison** to be sentenced to 5 years' imprisonment *ou* 5 years in prison

prisonnier, ière [prizɔnje, -jɛʀ] *nm/f* prisoner ♦ *adj* captive; **faire qn prisonnier** to take sb prisoner

prit [pri] *vb voir* **prendre**

privé, e [prive] *adj* private; (*dépourvu*): **privé de** without, lacking; **en privé, dans le privé** in private

priver [prive] *vt*: **priver qn de** to deprive sb of; **se priver de** to go *ou* do without; **ne pas se priver de faire** to not refrain from doing

privilège [privilɛʒ] *nm* privilege

prix [pri] *nm* (*valeur*) price; (*récompense, SCOL*) prize; **mettre à prix** to set a reserve (BRIT) *ou* an upset (US) price on; **au prix fort** at a very high price; **acheter qch à prix d'or** to pay a (small) fortune for sth; **hors de prix** exorbitantly priced; **à aucun prix** not at any price; **à tout prix** at all costs; **grand prix** (SPORT) Grand Prix; **prix d'achat/de vente/de revient** purchasing/selling/cost price; **prix conseillé** manufacturer's recommended price (MRP)

probable [prɔbabl(ə)] *adj* likely, probable

probablement [prɔbabləmɑ̃] *adv* probably

probant, e [prɔbɑ̃, -ɑ̃t] *adj* convincing

problème [prɔblɛm] *nm* problem

procédé [prɔsede] *nm* (*méthode*) process; (*comportement*) behaviour *no pl* (BRIT), behavior *no pl* (US)

procéder [prɔsede] *vi* to proceed; to behave; **procéder à** *vt* to carry out

procès [prɔsɛ] *nm* (JUR) trial; (: *poursuites*) proceedings *pl*; **être en procès avec** to be involved in a lawsuit with; **faire le procès de qn/qch** (*fig*) to put sb/sth on trial; **sans autre forme de procès**

without further ado

processus [prɔsesys] *nm* process

procès-verbal, aux [prɔsɛvɛrbal, -o] *nm (constat)* statement; *(aussi:* **PV**): **avoir un procès-verbal** to get a parking ticket; to be booked; *(de réunion)* minutes *pl*

prochain, e [prɔʃɛ̃, -ɛn] *adj* next; *(proche)* impending; near ♦ *nm* fellow man; **la prochaine fois/semaine prochaine** next time/week; **à la prochaine!** *(fam)* **à la prochaine fois** see you!, till the next time!; **un prochain jour** (some day) soon

prochainement [prɔʃɛnmɑ̃] *adv* soon, shortly

proche [prɔʃ] *adj* nearby; *(dans le temps)* imminent; close at hand; *(parent, ami)* close; **proches** *nmpl (parents)* close relatives, next of kin; *(amis)*: **l'un de ses proches** one of those close to him *(ou* her); **être proche (de)** to be near be close (to); **de proche en proche** gradually

proclamer [prɔklame] *vt* to proclaim; *(résultat d'un examen)* to announce

procuration [prɔkyrasjɔ̃] *nf* proxy; power of attorney; **voter par procuration** to vote by proxy

procurer [prɔkyre] *vt (fournir)*: **procurer qch à qn** to get *ou* obtain sth for sb; *(causer: plaisir etc)*: **procurer qch à qn** to bring *ou* give sb sth; **se procurer** *vt* to get

procureur [prɔkyrœr] *nm* public prosecutor; **procureur général** public prosecutor *(in appeal court)*

prodige [prɔdiʒ] *nm (miracle, merveille)* marvel, wonder; *(personne)* prodigy

prodiguer [prɔdige] *vt (argent, biens)* to be lavish with; *(soins, attentions)*: **prodiguer qch à qn** to lavish sth on sb

producteur, trice [prɔdyktœr, -tris] *adj*: **producteur de blé** wheat-producing; *(CINE)*: **société productrice** film *ou* movie company ♦ *nm/f* producer

productif, ive [prɔdyktif, -iv] *adj* productive

production [prɔdyksjɔ̃] *nf (gén)* production; *(rendement)* output; *(produits)* products *pl*, goods *pl*; *(œuvres)*: **la production dramatique du XVIIe siècle** the plays of the 17th century

productivité [prɔdyktivite] *nf* productivity

produire [prɔdɥir] *vt, vi* to produce; **se produire** *vi (acteur)* to perform, appear; *(événement)* to happen, occur

produit, e [prɔdɥi, -it] *pp de* **produire** ♦ *nm (gén)* product; **produit d'entretien** cleaning product; **produit national brut (PNB)** gross national product (GNP); **produit net** net profit; **produit pour la vaisselle** washing-up *(BRIT) ou* dishwashing *(US)* liquid; **produit des ventes** income from sales; **produits agricoles** farm produce *sg*; **produits alimentaires** foodstuffs; **produits de beauté** beauty products, cosmetics

prof [prɔf] *nm (fam:* = *professeur)* teacher; professor; lecturer

profane [prɔfan] *adj (REL)* secular; *(ignorant, non initié)* uninitiated ♦ *nm/f* layman

proférer [prɔfere] *vt* to utter

professeur [prɔfesœr] *nm* teacher; *(titulaire d'une chaire)* professor; **professeur (de faculté)** (university) lecturer

profession [prɔfesjɔ̃] *nf (libérale)* profession; *(gén)* occupation; **faire profession de** *(opinion, religion)* to profess; **de profession** by profession; **"sans profession"** "unemployed"; *(femme mariée)* "housewife"

professionnel, le [prɔfesjɔnɛl] *adj* professional ♦ *nm/f* professional; *(ouvrier qualifié)* skilled worker

profil [prɔfil] *nm* profile; *(d'une voiture)* line, contour; **de profil** in profile

profit [prɔfi] *nm (avantage)* benefit, advantage; *(COMM, FINANCE)* profit; **au profit de** in aid of; **tirer *ou* retirer profit de** to profit from; **mettre à profit** to take advantage of; to turn to good account; **profits et pertes** *(COMM)* profit and loss(es)

profitable [prɔfitabl(ə)] *adj* beneficial; profitable

profiter [prɔfite] *vi*: **profiter de** to take advantage of; to make the most of; **profiter de ce que ...** to take advantage of the fact that ...; **profiter à** to be of benefit to, benefit; to be profitable to

profond, e [prɔfɔ̃, -5d] *adj* deep; *(méditation, mépris)* profound; **peu profond** *(eau, vallée, puits)* shallow; *(coupure)* superficial; **au plus profond de** in the depths of, at the (very) bottom of; **la France profonde** the heartlands of France

profondément [prɔfɔ̃demɑ̃] *adv* deeply; profoundly

profondeur [prɔfɔ̃dœr] *nf* depth

progéniture [prɔʒenityr] *nf* offspring *inv*

programme [prɔgram] *nm* programme *(BRIT)*, program *(US)*; *(TV, RADIO)* program(me)s *pl*; *(SCOL)* syllabus, curriculum; *(INFORM)* program; **au programme de ce soir** *(TV)* among tonight's program(me)s

programmer [prɔgrame] *vt (TV, RADIO)* to put on, show; *(organiser, prévoir)* to schedule; *(INFORM)* to program

programmeur, euse [prɔgramœr, -øz] *nm/f* (computer) programmer

progrès [prɔgrɛ] *nm* progress *no pl*; **faire des/être en progrès** to make/be making progress

progresser [prɔgrese] *vi* to progress; *(troupes etc)* to make headway *ou* progress

progressif, ive [prɔgresif, -iv] *adj* progressive

prohiber [prɔibe] *vt* to prohibit, ban

proie [prwa] *nf* prey *no pl*; **être la proie de** to fall prey to; **être en proie à** *(doutes, sentiment)* to be prey to; *(douleur, mal)* to be suffering

projecteur [prɔʒɛktœr] *nm* projector; *(de théâtre, cirque)* spotlight

projectile [prɔʒɛktil] *nm* missile; *(d'arme)* projectile, bullet *(ou* shell *etc)*

projection [prɔʒɛksjɔ̃] nf projection; showing; **conférence avec projections** lecture with slides (ou a film)

projet [prɔʒɛ] nm plan; (ébauche) draft; **faire des projets** to make plans; **projet de loi** bill

projeter [prɔʒte] vt (envisager) to plan; (film, photos) to project; (passer) to show; (ombre, lueur) to throw, cast, project; (jeter) to throw up (ou off ou out); **projeter de faire qch** to plan to do sth

prolétaire [prɔletɛr] adj, nm/f proletarian

prolongement [prɔlɔ̃ʒmɑ̃] nm extension; **prolongements** nmpl (fig) repercussions, effects; **dans le prolongement de** running on from

prolonger [prɔlɔ̃ʒe] vt (débat, séjour) to prolong; (délai, billet, rue) to extend; (suj: chose) to be a continuation ou an extension of; **se prolonger** vi to go on

promenade [prɔmnad] nf walk (ou drive ou ride); **faire une promenade** to go for a walk; **une promenade (à pied)/en voiture/à vélo** a walk/drive/(bicycle) ride

promener [prɔmne] vt (personne, chien) to take out for a walk; (fig) to carry around; to trail round; (doigts, regard): **promener qch sur** to run sth over; **se promener** vi (à pied) to go for (ou be out for) a walk; (en voiture) to go for (ou be out for) a drive; (fig): **se promener sur** to wander over

promesse [prɔmɛs] nf promise; **promesse d'achat** commitment to buy

promettre [prɔmɛtr(ə)] vt to promise ◆ vi (récolte, arbre) to look promising; (enfant, musicien) to be promising; **se promettre de faire** to resolve ou mean to do; **promettre à qn de faire** to promise sb that one will do

promiscuité [prɔmiskɥite] nf crowding; lack of privacy

promontoire [prɔmɔ̃twar] nm headland

promoteur, trice [prɔmɔtœr, -tris] nm/f (instigateur) instigator, promoter; **promoteur (immobilier)** property developer (BRIT), real estate promoter (US)

promotion [prɔmɔsjɔ̃] nf (avancement) promotion; (SCOL) year (BRIT), class; **en promotion** (COMM) on promotion, on (special) offer

promouvoir [prɔmuvwar] vt to promote

prompt, e [prɔ̃, prɔ̃t] adj swift, rapid; (intervention, changement) sudden; **prompt à faire qch** quick to do sth

prôner [prone] vt (louer) to laud, extol; (préconiser) to advocate, commend

pronom [prɔnɔ̃] nm pronoun

prononcer [prɔnɔ̃se] vt (son, mot, jugement) to pronounce; (dire) to utter; (allocution) to deliver ◆ vi (JUR) to deliver ou give a verdict; **prononcer bien/mal** to have good/poor pronunciation; **se prononcer** vi to reach a decision, give a verdict; **se prononcer sur** to give an opinion on; **se prononcer contre** to come down against; **ça se prononce comment?** how do you pronounce this?

prononciation [prɔnɔ̃sjasjɔ̃] nf pronunciation

pronostic [prɔnɔstik] nm (MÉD) prognosis (pl -oses); (fig: aussi: **pronostics**) forecast

propagande [prɔpagɑ̃d] nf propaganda; **faire de la propagande pour qch** to plug ou push sth

propager [prɔpaʒe] vt to spread; **se propager** vi to spread; (PHYSIQUE) to be propagated

prophète [prɔfɛt], **prophétesse** [prɔfetɛs] nm/f prophet/ess

prophétie [prɔfesi] nf prophecy

propice [prɔpis] adj favourable (BRIT), favorable (US)

proportion [prɔpɔrsjɔ̃] nf proportion; **il n'y a aucune proportion entre le prix demandé et le prix réel** the asking price bears no relation to the real price; **à proportion de** proportionally to, in proportion to; **en proportion (de)** in proportion (to); **hors de proportion** out of proportion; **toute(s) proportion(s) gardée(s)** making due allowance(s)

propos [prɔpo] nm (paroles) talk no pl, remark; (intention, but) intention, aim; (sujet): **à quel propos?** what about?; **à propos de** about, regarding; **à tout propos** for no reason at all; **à ce propos** on that subject, in this connection; **à propos** adv by the way; (opportunément) (just) at the right moment; **hors de propos, mal à propos** adv at the wrong moment

proposer [prɔpoze] vt (suggérer): **proposer qch (à qn)/de faire** to suggest sth (to sb)/doing, propose sth (to sb)/to do; (offrir): **proposer qch à qn/de faire** to offer sb sth/to do; (candidat) to nominate, put forward; (loi, motion) to propose; **se proposer (pour faire)** to offer one's services (to do); **se proposer de faire** to intend ou propose to do

proposition [prɔpozisjɔ̃] nf suggestion; proposal; offer; (LING) clause; **sur la proposition de** at the suggestion of; **proposition de loi** private bill

propre [prɔpr(ə)] adj clean; (net) neat, tidy; (qui ne salit pas: chien, chat) house-trained; (: enfant) toilet-trained; (fig: honnête) honest; (possessif) own; (sens) literal; (particulier): **propre à** peculiar to, characteristic of; (approprié): **propre à** suitable ou appropriate for; (de nature à): **propre à faire** likely to do, that will do ◆ nm: **recopier au propre** to make a fair copy of; (particularité): **le propre de** the peculiarity of, the distinctive feature of; **au propre** (LING) literally; **appartenir à qn en propre** to belong to sb (exclusively); **propre à rien** nm/f (péj) good-for-nothing

proprement [prɔprəmɑ̃] adv cleanly; neatly, tidily; **à proprement parler** strictly speaking; **le village proprement dit** the actual village, the village itself

propreté [prɔprəte] nf cleanliness, cleanness; neatness, tidiness

propriétaire [prɔprijetɛr] nm/f owner; (d'hôtel etc) proprietor/tress, owner; (pour le locataire) landlord/lady; **propriétaire (immobilier)** house-owner; householder; **propriétaire récoltant** grower; **propriétaire (terrien)** landowner

propriété [prɔprijete] nf (droit) ownership; (objet, immeuble etc) property gén no pl; (villa) residence, property; (terres) property gén no pl, land gén no pl; (qualité, CHIMIE, MATH) property; (correction) appropriateness, suitability; **propriété artistique et littéraire** artistic and literary copyright; **propriété industrielle** patent rights pl

propulser [prɔpylse] vt (missile) to propel; (projeter) to hurl, fling

proroger [prɔrɔʒe] vt to put back, defer; (prolonger) to extend; (assemblée) to adjourn, prorogue

proscrire [prɔskrir] vt (bannir) to banish; (interdire) to ban, prohibit

prose [proz] nf prose (style)

prospecter [prɔspekte] vt to prospect; (COMM) to canvass

prospectus [prɔspektys] nm (feuille) leaflet; (dépliant) brochure, leaflet

prospère [prɔsper] adj prosperous; (santé, entreprise) thriving, flourishing

prospérer [prɔspere] vi to thrive

prosterner [prɔsterne]: **se prosterner** vi to bow low, prostrate o.s.

prostituée [prɔstitɥe] nf prostitute

prostitution [prɔstitysjɔ̃] nf prostitution

protecteur, trice [prɔtektœr, -tris] adj protective; (air, ton: péj) patronizing ♦ nm/f (défenseur) protector; (des arts) patron

protection [prɔteksjɔ̃] nf protection; (d'un personnage influent: aide) patronage; **écran de protection** protective screen; **protection civile** state-financed civilian rescue service; **protection maternelle et infantile (PMI)** social service concerned with child welfare

protéger [prɔteʒe] vt to protect; (aider, patronner: personne, arts) to be a patron of; (: carrière) to further; **se protéger de/contre** to protect o.s. from

protéine [prɔtein] nf protein

protestant, e [prɔtestɑ̃, -ɑ̃t] adj, nm/f Protestant

protestation [prɔtestasjɔ̃] nf (plainte) protest; (déclaration) protestation, profession

protester [prɔteste] vi: **protester (contre)** to protest (against ou about); **protester de** (son innocence, sa loyauté) to protest

prothèse [prɔtez] nf artificial limb, prosthesis (pl -ses); **prothèse dentaire** (appareil) denture; (science) dental engineering

protocole [prɔtɔkɔl] nm protocol; (fig) etiquette; **protocole d'accord** draft treaty; **protocole opératoire** (MÉD) operating procedure

proue [pru] nf bow (pl s), prow

prouesse [prues] nf feat

prouver [pruve] vt to prove

provenance [prɔvnɑ̃s] nf origin; (de mot, coutume) source; **avion en provenance de** plane (arriving) from

provenir [prɔvnir]: **provenir de** vt to come from; (résulter de) to be due to, be the result of

proverbe [prɔverb(ə)] nm proverb

province [prɔvɛ̃s] nf province

proviseur [prɔvizœr] nm = head (teacher) (BRIT), = principal (US)

provision [prɔvizjɔ̃] nf (réserve) stock, supply; (avance: à un avocat, avoué) retainer, retaining fee; (COMM) funds pl (in account); reserve; **provisions** nfpl (vivres) provisions, food no pl; **faire provision de** to stock up with; **placard ou armoire à provisions** food cupboard

provisoire [prɔvizwar] adj temporary; (JUR) provisional; **mise en liberté provisoire** release on bail

provisoirement [prɔvizwarmɑ̃] adv temporarily, for the time being

provocant, e [prɔvɔkɑ̃, -ɑ̃t] adj provocative

provoquer [prɔvɔke] vt (défier) to provoke; (causer) to cause, bring about; (: curiosité) to arouse, give rise to; (: aveux) to prompt, elicit; (inciter): **provoquer qn à** to incite sb to

proxénète [prɔksenet] nm procurer

proximité [prɔksimite] nf nearness, closeness, proximity; (dans le temps) imminence, closeness; **à proximité** near ou close by; **à proximité de** near (to), close to

prudemment [prydamɑ̃] adv (voir prudent) carefully; cautiously; prudently; wisely, sensibly

prudence [prydɑ̃s] nf carefulness; caution; prudence; **avec prudence** carefully; cautiously; wisely; **par (mesure de) prudence** as a precaution

prudent, e [prydɑ̃, -ɑ̃t] adj (pas téméraire) careful, cautious, prudent; (: en général) safety-conscious; (sage, conseillé) wise, sensible; (réservé) cautious; **ce n'est pas prudent** it's risky; it's not sensible; **soyez prudent** take care, be careful

prune [pryn] nf plum

pruneau, x [pryno] nm prune

prunelle [prynel] nf pupil; (œil) eye; (BOT) sloe; (eau de vie) sloe gin

prunier [prynje] nm plum tree

PS sigle m = parti socialiste; (= post-scriptum) PS

psaume [psom] nm psalm

pseudonyme [psødɔnim] nm (gén) fictitious name; (d'écrivain) pseudonym, pen name; (de comédien) stage name

psychanalyse [psikanaliz] nf psychoanalysis

psychiatre [psikjatr(ə)] nm/f psychiatrist

psychiatrique [psikjatrik] adj psychiatric; (hôpital) mental, psychiatric

psychique [psiʃik] adj psychological

psychologie [psikɔlɔʒi] nf psychology

psychologique [psikɔlɔʒik] adj psychological

psychologue [psikɔlɔg] nm/f psychologist; **être psychologue** (fig) to be a good psychologist

pu [py] *pp de* **pouvoir**

puanteur [pyɑ̃tœʀ] *nf* stink, stench

pub [pyb] *nf (fam = publicité)*: **la pub** advertising

public, ique [pyblik] *adj* public; *(école, instruction)* state *cpd*; *(scrutin)* open ♦ *nm* public; *(assistance)* audience; **en public** in public; **le grand public** the general public

publicitaire [pyblisitɛʀ] *adj* advertising *cpd*; *(film, voiture)* publicity *cpd*; *(vente)* promotional ♦ *nm* adman; **rédacteur publicitaire** copywriter

publicité [pyblisite] *nf (méthode, profession)* advertising; *(annonce)* advertisement; *(révélations)* publicity

publier [pyblije] *vt* to publish; *(nouvelle)* to publicize, make public

publique [pyblik] *adj f voir* **public**

puce [pys] *nf* flea; *(INFORM)* chip; **(marché aux) puces** flea market *sg*; **mettre la puce à l'oreille de qn** to give sb something to think about

pudeur [pydœʀ] *nf* modesty

pudique [pydik] *adj (chaste)* modest; *(discret)* discreet

puer [pɥe] *(péj) vi* to stink ♦ *vt* to stink of, reek of

puéricultrice [pɥeʀikyltʀis] *nf* = nursery nurse

puéril, e [pɥeʀil] *adj* childish

puis [pɥi] *vb voir* **pouvoir** ♦ *adv (ensuite)* then; *(dans une énumération)* next; *(en outre)*: **et puis** and (then); **et puis (après ou quoi)?** so (what)?

puiser [pɥize] *vt*: **puiser (dans)** to draw (from); **puiser dans qch** to dip into sth

puisque [pɥisk(ə)] *conj* since; *(valeur intensive)*: **puisque je te le dis!** I'm telling you!

puissance [pɥisɑ̃s] *nf* power; **en puissance** *adj* potential; **2 (à la) puissance 5** 2 to the power (of) 5

puissant, e [pɥisɑ̃, -ɑ̃t] *adj* powerful

puisse [pɥis] *etc vb voir* **pouvoir**

puits [pɥi] *nm* well; **puits artésien** artesian well; **puits de mine** mine shaft; **puits de science** fount of knowledge

pull(-over) [pyl(ɔvœʀ)] *nm* sweater, jumper *(BRIT)*

pulluler [pylyle] *vi* to swarm; *(fig: erreurs)* to abound, proliferate

pulpe [pylp(ə)] *nf* pulp

pulvérisateur [pylveʀizatœʀ] *nm* spray

pulvériser [pylveʀize] *vt (solide)* to pulverize; *(liquide)* to spray; *(fig: anéantir: adversaire)* to pulverize; *(: record)* to smash, shatter; *(: argument)* to demolish

punaise [pynɛz] *nf (ZOOL)* bug; *(clou)* drawing pin *(BRIT)*, thumb tack *(US)*

punch [pɔ̃ʃ] *nm (boisson)* punch; [pœnʃ] *(BOXE)* punching ability; *(fig)* punch

punir [pyniʀ] *vt* to punish; **punir qn de qch** to punish sb for sth

punition [pynisjɔ̃] *nf* punishment

pupille [pypij] *nf (ANAT)* pupil ♦ *nm/f (enfant)* ward; **pupille de l'État** child in care; **pupille de la Nation** war orphan

pupitre [pypitʀ(ə)] *nm (SCOL)* desk; *(REL)* lectern; *(de chef d'orchestre)* rostrum; *(INFORM)* console; **pupitre de commande** control panel

pur, e [pyʀ] *adj* pure; *(vin)* undiluted; *(whisky)* neat; *(intentions)* honourable *(BRIT)*, honorable *(US)* ♦ *nm (personne)* hard-liner; **en pure perte** fruitlessly, to no avail

purée [pyʀe] *nf*: **purée (de pommes de terre)** = mashed potatoes *pl*; **purée de marrons** chestnut purée; **purée de pois** *(fig)* peasoup(er)

purement [pyʀmɑ̃] *adv* purely

purgatoire [pyʀgatwaʀ] *nm* purgatory

purger [pyʀʒe] *vt (radiateur)* to flush (out), drain; *(circuit hydraulique)* to bleed; *(MÉD, POL)* to purge; *(JUR: peine)* to serve

purin [pyʀɛ̃] *nm* liquid manure

pur-sang [pyʀsɑ̃] *nm inv* thoroughbred, purebred

pus [py] *vb voir* **pouvoir** ♦ *nm* pus

putain [pytɛ̃] *nf (fam!)* whore (!); **ce/cette putain de ...** this bloody *(BRIT)* ou goddamn *(US)* ... (!)

puzzle [pœzl(ə)] *nm* jigsaw (puzzle)

PV *sigle m* = **procès-verbal**

pyjama [piʒama] *nm* pyjamas *pl*, pair of pyjamas

pyramide [piʀamid] *nf* pyramid

Pyrénées [piʀene] *nfpl*: **les Pyrénées** the Pyrenees

— Q q —

QI *sigle m (= quotient intellectuel)* IQ

quadragénaire [kadʀaʒenɛʀ] *nm/f (de quarante ans)* forty-year-old; *(de quarante à cinquante ans)* man/woman in his/her forties

quadriller [kadʀije] *vt (papier)* to mark out in squares; *(POLICE: ville, région etc)* to keep under tight control, be positioned throughout

quadruple [k(w)adʀypl(ə)] *nm*: **le quadruple de** four times as much as

quadruplés, ées [k(w)adʀyple] *nm/fpl* quadruplets, quads

quai [ke] *nm (de port)* quay; *(de gare)* platform; *(de cours d'eau, canal)* embankment; **être à quai** *(navire)* to be alongside; *(train)* to be in the station; **le Quai d'Orsay** offices of the French Ministry for Foreign Affairs; **le Quai des Orfèvres** central police headquarters

qualification [kalifikɑsjɔ̃] *nf* qualification

qualifié, e [kalifje] *adj* qualified; *(main d'œuvre)* skilled

qualifier [kalifje] *vt* to qualify; *(appeler)*: **qualifier qch/qn de** to describe sth/sb as; **se qualifier** *vi (SPORT)* to qualify; **être qualifié pour** to be qualified for

qualité [kalite] *nf* quality; (*titre, fonction*) position; **en qualité de** in one's capacity as; **ès qualités** in an official capacity; **avoir qualité pour** to have authority to; **de qualité** *adj* quality *cpd*; **rapport qualité-prix** value (for money)

quand [kã] *conj, adv* when; **quand je serai riche** when I'm rich; **quand même** (*cependant, pourtant*) nevertheless; (*tout de même*) all the same; really; **quand bien même** even though

quant [kã]: **quant à** *prép* (*pour ce qui est de*) as for, as to; (*au sujet de*) regarding

quant-à-soi [kãtaswa] *nm*: **rester sur son quant-à-soi** to remain aloof

quantité [kãtite] *nf* (*isolement*) quarantine; (*SCIENCE*) quantity; (*grand nombre*): **une ou des quantité(s) de** a great deal of; a lot of; **en grande quantité** in large quantities; **en quantités industrielles** in vast amounts; **du travail en quantité** a great deal of work; **quantité de** many

quarantaine [kaʀãten] *nf* (*isolement*) quarantine; (*âge*): **avoir la quarantaine** to be around forty; (*nombre*): **une quarantaine (de)** forty or so, about forty; **mettre en quarantaine** to put into quarantine; (*fig*) to send to Coventry (*BRIT*), ostracize

quarante [kaʀãt] *num* forty

quart [kaʀ] *nm* (*fraction*) quarter; (*surveillance*) watch; (*partie*): **un quart de poulet/fromage** a chicken quarter/a quarter of a cheese; **un quart de beurre** a quarter kilo of butter, ≈ a half pound of butter; **un quart de vin** a quarter litre of wine; **une livre un quart** *ou* **et quart** one and a quarter pounds; **le quart de** a quarter of; **quart d'heure** quarter of an hour; **2h et** *ou* **un quart** (a) quarter past 2, (a) quarter after 2 (*US*); **il est le quart** it's (a) quarter past *ou* after (*US*); **une heure moins le quart** (a) quarter to one, (a) quarter of one (*US*); **il est moins le quart** it's (a) quarter to; **être de/prendre le quart** to keep/take the watch; **quart de tour** quarter turn; **au quart de tour** (*fig*) straight off; **quarts de finale** (*SPORT*) quarter finals

quartier [kaʀtje] *nm* (*de ville*) district, area; (*de bœuf, de la lune*) quarter; (*de fruit, fromage*) piece; **quartiers** *nmpl* (*MIL, BLASON*) quarters; **cinéma/salle de quartier** local cinema/hall; **avoir quartier libre** to be free; (*MIL*) to have leave from barracks; **ne pas faire de quartier** to spare no one, give no quarter; **quartier commerçant/résidentiel** shopping/residential area; **quartier général (QG)** headquarters (HQ)

quartz [kwaʀts] *nm* quartz

quasi [kazi] *adv* almost, nearly ♦ *préfixe*: **quasi-certitude** near certainty

quasiment [kazimã] *adv* almost, very nearly

quatorze [katɔʀz(ə)] *num* fourteen

quatre [katʀ(ə)] *num* four; **à quatre pattes** on all fours; **tiré à quatre épingles** dressed up to the nines; **faire les quatre cent coups** to be a bit wild; **se mettre en quatre pour qn** to go out of one's

way for sb; **quatre à quatre** (*monter, descendre*) four at a time; **à quatre mains** (*jouer*) four-handed

quatre-vingt-dix [katʀəvɛ̃dis] *num* ninety

quatre-vingts [katʀəvɛ̃] *num* eighty

quatre-vingt-un *num* eighty-one

quatrième [katʀijɛm] *num* fourth

quatuor [kwatyɔʀ] *nm* quartet(te)

┌─────────────┐
│ *MOT CLÉ* │
└─────────────┘

que [kə] *conj* **1** (*introduisant complétive*) that; **il sait que tu es là** he knows (that) you're here; **je veux que tu acceptes** I want you to accept; **il a dit que oui** he said he would (*ou* it was *etc*)

2 (*reprise d'autres conjonctions*): **quand il rentrera et qu'il aura mangé** when he gets back and (when) he has eaten; **si vous y allez ou que vous ...** if you go there or if you ...

3 (*en tête de phrase*: hypothèse, souhait *etc*): **qu'il le veuille ou non** whether he likes it or not; **qu'il fasse ce qu'il voudra!** let him do as he pleases!

4 (*but*): **tenez-le qu'il ne tombe pas** hold it so (that) it doesn't fall

5 (*après comparatif*) than; as; *voir aussi* **plus; aussi; autant** *etc*

6 (*seulement*): **ne ... que** only; **il ne boit que de l'eau** he only drinks water

7 (*temps*): **elle venait à peine de sortir qu'il se mit à pleuvoir** she had just gone out when it started to rain, no sooner had she gone out than it started to rain; **il y a 4 ans qu'il est parti** it is 4 years since he left, he left 4 years ago

♦ *adv* (*exclamation*): **qu'il ou qu'est-ce qu'il est bête/court vite!** he's so silly!/he runs so fast!; **que de livres!** what a lot of books!

♦ *pron* **1** (*relatif*: personne) whom; (: *chose*) that, which; **l'homme que je vois** the man (whom) I see; **le livre que tu vois** the book (that *ou* which) you see; **un jour que j'étais ...** a day when I was ...

2 (*interrogatif*) what; **que fais-tu?, qu'est-ce que tu fais?** what are you doing?; **qu'est-ce que c'est?** what is it?, what's that?; **que faire?** what can one do?; **que préfères-tu, celui-ci ou celui-là?** which (one) do you prefer, this one or that one?

Québec [kebek] *n* (*ville*) Quebec ♦ *nm*: **le Québec** Quebec (Province)

québécois, e [kebekwa, -waz] *adj* Quebec *cpd* ♦ *nm* (*LING*) Quebec French ♦ *nm/f*: **Québécois, e** Quebecois, Quebec(k)er

┌─────────────┐
│ *MOT CLÉ* │
└─────────────┘

quel, quelle [kɛl] *adj* **1** (*interrogatif*: personne) who; (: *chose*) what; **quel est cet homme?** who is this man?; **quel est ce livre?** what is this book?; **quel livre/homme?** what book/man?; (*parmi un certain choix*) which book/man?; **quels acteurs préférez-vous?** which actors do you prefer?; **dans quels pays êtes-vous allé?** which

ou what countries did you go to?
2 (*exclamatif*): **quelle surprise/coïncidence!** what a surprise/coincidence!
3: **quel(le) que soit le coupable** whoever is guilty; **quel que soit votre avis** whatever your opinion (may be)

quelconque [kɛlkɔ̃k] *adj* (*médiocre*) indifferent, poor; (*sans attrait*) ordinary, plain; (*indéfini*): **un ami/prétexte quelconque** some friend/pretext or other; **un livre quelconque suffira** any book will do; **pour une raison quelconque** for some reason (or other)

MOT CLÉ
---

quelque [kɛlkə] *adj* **1** some; a few; (*tournure interrogative*) any; **quelque espoir** some hope; **il a quelques amis** he has a few some friends; **a-t-il quelques amis?** has he any friends?; **les quelques livres qui** the few books which; **20 kg et quelque(s)** a bit over 20 kg; **il habite à quelque distance d'ici** he lives some distance *ou* way (away) from here
2: **quelque ... que** whatever, whichever; **quelque livre qu'il choisisse** whatever (*ou* whichever) book he chooses; **par quelque temps qu'il fasse** whatever the weather
3: **quelque chose** something; (*tournure interrogative*) anything; **quelque chose d'autre** something else; anything else; **y être pour quelque chose** to have something to do with it; **faire quelque chose à qn** to have an effect on sb, do something to sb; **quelque part** somewhere; anywhere; **en quelque sorte** as it were
◆ *adv* **1** (*environ*): **quelque 100 mètres** some 100 metres
2: **quelque peu** rather, somewhat

---

quelquefois [kɛlkəfwa] *adv* sometimes
quelques-uns, -unes [kɛlkəzœ̃, -yn] *pron* some, a few; **quelques-uns des lecteurs** some of the readers
quelqu'un [kɛlkœ̃] *pron* someone, somebody, *tournure interrogative ou négative* + anyone *ou* anybody; **quelqu'un d'autre** someone *ou* somebody else; anybody else
quémander [kemɑ̃de] *vt* to beg for
qu'en dira-t-on [kɑ̃diʀatɔ̃] *nm inv*: **le qu'en dira-t-on** gossip, what people say
querelle [kəʀɛl] *nf* quarrel; **chercher querelle à qn** to pick a quarrel with sb
quereller [kəʀele]: **se quereller** *vi* to quarrel
qu'est-ce que [kɛskə] *voir* **que**
qu'est-ce qui [kɛski] *voir* **qui**
question [kɛstjɔ̃] *nf* (*gén*) question; (*fig*) matter; issue; **il a été question de** we (*ou* they) spoke about; **il est question de les emprisonner** there's talk of them being jailed; **c'est une question de temps** it's a matter *ou* question of time; **de quoi**

est-il question? what is it about?; **il n'en est pas question** there's no question of it; **en question** in question; **hors de question** out of the question; **je ne me suis jamais posé la question** I've never thought about it; **(re)mettre en question** (*autorité, science*) to question; **poser la question de confiance** (*POL*) to ask for a vote of confidence; **question piège** (*d'apparence facile*) trick question; (*pour nuire*) loaded question; **question subsidiaire** tiebreaker
questionnaire [kɛstjɔnɛʀ] *nm* questionnaire
questionner [kɛstjɔne] *vt* to question
quête [kɛt] *nf* (*collecte*) collection; (*recherche*) quest, search; **faire la quête** (*à l'église*) to take the collection; (*artiste*) to pass the hat round; **se mettre en quête de qch** to go in search of sth
quetsche [kwɛtʃə] *nf* damson
queue [kø] *nf* tail; (*fig: du classement*) bottom; (: *de poêle*) handle; (: *de fruit, feuille*) stalk; (: *de train, colonne, file*) rear; (*file: de personnes*) queue (*BRIT*), line (*US*); **en queue (de train)** at the rear (of the train); **faire la queue** to queue (up) (*BRIT*), line up (*US*); **se mettre à la queue** to join the queue *ou* line; **histoire sans queue ni tête** cock and bull story; **à la queue leu leu** in single file; (*fig*) one after the other; **queue de cheval** ponytail; **queue de poisson: faire une queue de poisson à qn** (*AUTO*) to cut in front of sb; **finir en queue de poisson** (*film*) to come to an abrupt end
qui [ki] *pron* (*personne*) who ◆ *prép* + whom; (*chose, animal*) which, that; (*interrogatif indirect: sujet*): **je me demande qui est là?** I wonder who is there?; (: *objet*): **elle ne sait à qui se plaindre** she doesn't know who to complain to *ou* to whom to complain; **qu'est-ce qui est sur la table?** what is on the table?; **à qui est ce sac?** whose bag is this?; **à qui parlais-tu?** who were you talking to?, to whom were you talking?; **chez qui allez-vous?** whose house are you going to?; **amenez qui vous voulez** bring who(ever) you like; **qui est-ce qui ...?** who?; **qui est-ce que ...?** who?; whom?; **qui que ce soit** whoever it may be
quiche [kiʃ] *nf* quiche; **quiche lorraine** quiche Lorraine
quiconque [kikɔ̃k] *pron* (*celui qui*) whoever, anyone who; (*n'importe qui, personne*) anyone, anybody
quiétude [kjetyd] *nf* (*d'un lieu*) quiet, tranquillity; (*d'une personne*) peace (of mind), serenity; **en toute quiétude** in complete peace; (*mentale*) with complete peace of mind
quille [kij] *nf* ninepin, skittle (*BRIT*); (*NAVIG: d'un bateau*) keel; (*jeu de*) **quilles** ninepins *sg*, skittles *sg* (*BRIT*)
quincaillerie [kɛ̃kajʀi] *nf* (*ustensiles, métier*) hardware, ironmongery (*BRIT*); (*magasin*) hardware shop *ou* store (*US*), ironmonger's (*BRIT*)
quincaillier, ière [kɛ̃kaje, -jɛʀ] *nm/f* hardware dealer, ironmonger (*BRIT*)
quinquagénaire [kɛ̃kaʒenɛʀ] *nm/f* (*de*

cinquante ans) fifty-year old; (*de cinquante à soixante ans*) man/woman in his/her fifties

quintal, aux [kɛ̃tal, -o] *nm* quintal (*100 kg*)

quinte [kɛ̃t] *nf*: **quinte (de toux)** coughing fit

quintuple [kɛ̃typl(ə)] *nm*: **le quintuple de** five times as much as

quintuplés, ées [kɛ̃typle] *nm/fpl* quintuplets, quins

quinzaine [kɛ̃zɛn] *nf*: **une quinzaine (de)** about fifteen, fifteen or so; **une quinzaine (de jours)** (*deux semaines*) a fortnight (*BRIT*), two weeks; **quinzaine publicitaire** *ou* **commerciale** (two-week) sale

quinze [kɛ̃z] *num* fifteen; **demain en quinze** a fortnight (*BRIT*) *ou* two weeks tomorrow; **dans quinze jours** in a fortnight('s time) (*BRIT*), in two weeks(' time)

quiproquo [kiprɔko] *nm* (*méprise sur une personne*) mistake; (*malentendu sur un sujet*) misunderstanding; (*THÉAT*) (case of) mistaken identity

quittance [kitɑ̃s] *nf* (*reçu*) receipt; (*facture*) bill

quitte [kit] *adj*: **être quitte envers qn** to be no longer in sb's debt; (*fig*) to be quits with sb; **être quitte de** (*obligation*) to be clear of; **en être quitte à bon compte** to have got off lightly; **quitte à faire** even if it means doing; **quitte ou double** (*jeu*) double or quits; (*fig*): **c'est du quitte ou double** it's a big risk

quitter [kite] *vt* to leave; (*espoir, illusion*) to give up; (*vêtement*) to take off; **se quitter** (*couples, interlocuteurs*) to part; **ne quittez pas** (*au téléphone*) hold the line; **ne pas quitter qn d'une semelle** to stick to sb like glue

qui-vive [kiviv] *nm inv*: **être sur le qui-vive** to be on the alert

quoi [kwa] *pron* (*interrogatif*) what; **quoi de neuf** *ou* **de nouveau?** what's new *ou* the news?; **as-tu de quoi écrire?** have you anything to write with?; **il n'a pas de quoi se l'acheter** he can't afford it, he hasn't got the money to buy it; **il y a de quoi être fier** that's something to be proud of; **"il n'y a pas de quoi"** "(please) don't mention it", "not at all"; **quoi qu'il arrive** whatever happens; **quoi qu'il en soit** be that as it may; **quoi que ce soit** anything at all; **en quoi puis-je vous aider?** how can I help you?; **à quoi bon?** what's the use *ou* point?; **et puis quoi encore!** what(ever) next!; **quoi faire?** what's to be done?; **sans quoi** (*ou sinon*) otherwise

quoique [kwak(ə)] *conj* (al)though

quote-part [kɔtpaʀ] *nf* share

quotidien, ne [kɔtidjɛ̃, -ɛn] *adj* (*journalier*) daily; (*banal*) ordinary, everyday ♦ *nm* (*journal*) daily (paper); (*vie quotidienne*) daily life, day-to-day existence; **les grands quotidiens** the big (national) dailies

quotidiennement [kɔtidjɛnmɑ̃] *adv* daily, every day

rab [ʀab] (*fam*), **rabiot** [ʀabjo] *nm* extra, more

rabâcher [ʀabɑʃe] *vi* to harp on ♦ *vt* keep on repeating

rabais [ʀabɛ] *nm* reduction, discount; **au rabais** at a reduction *ou* discount

rabaisser [ʀabese] *vt* (*rabattre*) to reduce; (*dénigrer*) to belittle

rabat-joie [ʀabaʒwa] *nm/f inv* killjoy (*BRIT*), spoilsport

rabattre [ʀabatʀ(ə)] *vt* (*couvercle, siège*) to pull down; (*col*) to turn down; (*couture*) to stitch down; (*gibier*) to drive; (*somme d'un prix*) to deduct, take off; (*orgueil, prétentions*) to humble; (*TRICOT*) to decrease; **se rabattre** *vi* (*bords, couvercle*) to fall shut; (*véhicule, coureur*) to cut in; **se rabattre sur** (*accepter*) to fall back on

rabbin [ʀabɛ̃] *nm* rabbi

râblé, e [ʀɑble] *adj* broad-backed, stocky

rabot [ʀabo] *nm* plane

rabougri, e [ʀabugʀi] *adj* stunted

rabrouer [ʀabʀue] *vt* to snub, rebuff

racaille [ʀakaj] *nf* (*péj*) rabble, riffraff

raccommoder [ʀakɔmɔde] *vt* to mend, repair; (*chaussette etc*) to darn; (*fam: réconcilier: amis, ménage*) to bring together again; **se raccommoder (avec)** (*fam*) to patch it up (with)

raccompagner [ʀakɔ̃paɲe] *vt* to take *ou* see back

raccord [ʀakɔʀ] *nm* link; **raccord de maçonnerie** pointing *no pl*; **raccord de peinture** join; touch-up

raccorder [ʀakɔʀde] *vt* to join (up), link up; (*suj: pont etc*) to connect, link; **se raccorder à** to join up with; (*fig: se rattacher à*) to tie in with; **raccorder au réseau du téléphone** to connect to the telephone service

raccourci [ʀakuʀsi] *nm* short cut; **en raccourci** in brief

raccourcir [ʀakuʀsiʀ] *vt* to shorten ♦ *vi* (*vêtement*) to shrink

raccrocher [ʀakʀɔʃe] *vt* (*tableau, vêtement*) to hang back up; (*récepteur*) to put down; (*fig: affaire*) to save ♦ *vi* (*TÉL*) to hang up, ring off; **se raccrocher à** *vt* to cling to, hang on to; **ne raccrochez pas** (*TÉL*) hold on, don't hang up

race [ʀas] *nf* race; (*d'animaux, fig: espèce*) breed; (*ascendance, origine*) stock, race; **de race** *adj* purebred, pedigree

rachat [ʀaʃa] *nm* buying; buying back; redemption; atonement

racheter [ʀaʃte] *vt* (*article perdu*) to buy another; (*davantage*): **racheter du lait/3 œufs** to buy more milk/another 3 eggs *ou* 3 more eggs; (*après avoir vendu*) to buy back; (*d'occasion*) to buy; (*COMM: part, firme*) to buy up; (: *pension, rente*) to redeem; (*REL:*

pécheur) to redeem; (: *péché*) to atone for, expiate; (*mauvaise conduite, oubli, défaut*) to make up for; **se racheter** (*REL*) to redeem o.s.; (*gén*) to make amends, make up for it

racial, e, aux [Rasjal, -o] *adj* racial

racine [Rasin] *nf* root; (*fig: attache*) roots *pl*; **racine carrée/cubique** square/cube root; **prendre racine** (*fig*) to take root; to put down roots

raciste [Rasist(ə)] *adj, nm/f* racist, racialist

racket [Raket] *nm* racketeering *no pl*

raclée [Rakle] *nf* (*fam*) hiding, thrashing

racler [Rakle] *vt* (*os, plat*) to scrape; (*tache, boue*) to scrape off; (*fig: instrument*) to scrape on; (*suj: chose: frotter contre*) to scrape (against)

racoler [Rakɔle] *vt* (*attirer: suj: prostituée*) to solicit; (: *parti, marchand*) to tout for; (*attraper*) to pick up

racontars [Rakɔ̃taR] *nmpl* stories, gossip *sg*

raconter [Rakɔ̃te] *vt*: **raconter (à qn)** (*décrire*) to relate (to sb), tell (sb) about; (*dire*) to tell (sb)

racorni, e [Rakɔʀni] *adj* hard(ened)

radar [RadaR] *nm* radar; **système radar** radar system; **écran radar** radar screen

rade [Rad] *nf* (natural) harbour; **en rade de Toulon** in Toulon harbour; **rester en rade** (*fig*) to be left stranded

radeau, x [Rado] *nm* raft; **radeau de sauvetage** life raft

radiateur [RadjatœR] *nm* radiator, heater; (*AUTO*) radiator; **radiateur électrique/à gaz** electric/gas heater *ou* fire

radiation [Radjasjɔ̃] *nf* (*d'un nom etc*) striking off *no pl*; (*PHYSIQUE*) radiation

radical, e, aux [Radikal, -o] *adj* radical ◆ *nm* (*LING*) stem; (*MATH*) root sign; (*POL*) radical

radier [Radje] *vt* to strike off

radieux, euse [Radjø, -øz] *adj* (*visage, personne*) radiant; (*journée, soleil*) brilliant, glorious

radin, e [Radɛ̃, -in] *adj* (*fam*) stingy

radio [Radjo] *nf* radio; (*MÉD*) X-ray ◆ *nm* (*personne*) radio operator; **à la radio** on the radio; **avoir la radio** to have a radio; **passer à la radio** to be on the radio; **se faire faire une radio/une radio des poumons** to have an X-ray/a chest X-ray

radioactif, ive [Radjɔaktif, -iv] *adj* radioactive

radiocassette [Radjɔkaset] *nf* cassette radio

radiodiffuser [Radjɔdifyze] *vt* to broadcast

radiographie [Radjɔgrafi] *nf* radiography; (*photo*) X-ray photograph, radiograph

radiophonique [Radjɔfɔnik] *adj*: **programme/émission/jeu radiophonique** radio programme/broadcast/game

radio(-)réveil [RadjɔRevej] *nm* clock radio

radis [Radi] *nm* radish; **radis noir** horseradish *no pl*

radoter [Radɔte] *vi* to ramble on

radoucir [RadusiR]: **se radoucir** *vi* (*se réchauffer*) to become milder; (*se calmer*) to calm down; to soften

rafale [Rafal] *nf* (*vent*) gust (of wind); (*de balles, d'applaudissements*) burst; **rafale de mitrailleuse** burst of machine-gun fire

raffermir [RafɛRmiR] *vt*: **se raffermir** *vi* (*tissus, muscle*) to firm up; (*fig*) to strengthen

raffiner [Rafine] *vt* to refine

raffinerie [Rafinri] *nf* refinery

raffoler [Rafɔle]: **raffoler de** *vt* to be very keen on

rafistoler [Rafistɔle] *vt* (*fam*) to patch up

rafle [Rafl(ə)] *nf* (*de police*) roundup, raid

rafler [Rafle] *vt* (*fam*) to swipe, nick

rafraîchir [RafRefiR] *vt* (*atmosphère, température*) to cool (down); (*aussi*: **mettre à rafraîchir**) to chill; (*suj: air, eau*) to freshen up; (*boisson*) to refresh; (*fig: rénover*) to brighten up ◆ *vi*: **mettre du vin/une boisson à rafraîchir** to chill wine/a drink; **se rafraîchir** to grow cooler; to freshen up; (*personne: en buvant etc*) to refresh o.s.; **rafraîchir la mémoire** *ou* **les idées à qn** to refresh sb's memory

rafraîchissant, e [RafRefisɑ̃, -ɑ̃t] *adj* refreshing

rafraîchissement [RafRefismɑ̃] *nm* cooling; (*boisson*) cool drink; **rafraîchissements** *nmpl* (*boissons, fruits etc*) refreshments

rage [Raʒ] *nf* (*MÉD*): **la rage** rabies; (*fureur*) rage, fury; **faire rage** to rage; **rage de dents** (raging) toothache

ragot [Rago] *nm* (*fam*) malicious gossip *no pl*

ragoût [Ragu] *nm* (*plat*) stew

raide [Rɛd] *adj* (*tendu*) taut, tight; (*escarpé*) steep; (*droit: cheveux*) straight; (*ankylosé, dur, guindé*) stiff; (*fam: cher*) steep, stiff; (: *sans argent*) flat broke; (*osé, licencieux*) daring ◆ *adv* (*en pente*) steeply; **raide mort** stone dead

raideur [RɛdœR] *nf* steepness; stiffness

raidir [RediR] *vt* (*muscles*) to stiffen; (*câble*) to pull taut, tighten; **se raidir** *vi* to stiffen; to become taut; (*personne: se crisper*) to tense up; (: *devenir intransigeant*) to harden

raie [Rɛ] *nf* (*ZOOL*) skate, ray; (*rayure*) stripe; (*des cheveux*) parting

raifort [RefɔR] *nm* horseradish

rail [Raj] *nm* (*barre d'acier*) rail; (*chemins de fer*) railways *pl* (*BRIT*), railroads *pl* (*US*); **les rails** (*la voie ferrée*) the rails, the track *sg*; **par rail** by rail; **rail conducteur** live *ou* conductor rail

railler [Raje] *vt* to scoff at, jeer at

rainure [RenyR] *nf* groove; slot

raisin [Rezɛ̃] *nm* (*aussi*: **raisins**) grapes *pl*; (*variété*): **raisin blanc/noir** white (*ou* green)/black grape; **raisin muscat** muscat grape; **raisins secs** raisins

raison [Rezɔ̃] *nf* reason; **avoir raison** to be right; **donner raison à qn** (*personne*) to agree with sb; (*fait*) to prove sb right; **avoir raison de qn/qch** to get the better of sb/sth; **se faire une raison** to learn to live with it; **perdre la raison** to become insane; (*fig*) to take leave of one's senses; **recouvrer**

la raison to come to one's senses; ramener qn à la raison to make sb see sense; demander raison à qn de (affront etc) to demand satisfaction from sb for; entendre raison to listen to reason, see reason; plus que de raison too much, more than is reasonable; raison de plus all the more reason; à plus forte raison all the more so; en raison de (à cause de) because of; (à proportion de) in proportion to; à raison de at the rate of; raison d'État reason of state; raison d'être raison d'être; raison sociale corporate name

raisonnable [rɛzɔnabl(ə)] adj reasonable, sensible

raisonnement [rɛzɔnmɑ̃] nm reasoning; arguing; argument

raisonner [rɛzɔne] vi (penser) to reason; (argumenter, discuter) to argue ◆ vt (personne) to reason with; (attitude: justifier) to reason out; **se raisonner** to reason with oneself

rajeunir [raʒœnir] vt (suj: coiffure, robe): **rajeunir qn** to make sb look younger; (suj: cure etc) to rejuvenate; (fig: rafraîchir) to brighten up; (: moderniser) to give a new look to; (: en recrutant) to inject new blood into ◆ vi (personne) to become (ou look) younger; (entreprise, quartier) to be modernized

rajouter [raʒute] vt (commentaire) to add; **rajouter du sel/un œuf** to add some more salt/another egg; **rajouter que** to add that; **en rajouter** to lay it on thick

rajuster [raʒyste] vt (vêtement) to straighten, tidy; (salaires) to adjust; (machine) to readjust; **se rajuster** to tidy ou straighten o.s. up

ralenti [ralɑ̃ti] nm: **au ralenti** (CINÉ) in slow motion; (fig) at a slower pace; **tourner au ralenti** (AUTO) to tick over, idle

ralentir [ralɑ̃tir] vt, vi: **se ralentir** vi to slow down

râler [rɑle] vi to groan; (fam) to grouse, moan (and groan)

rallier [ralje] vt (rassembler) to rally; (rejoindre) to rejoin; (gagner à sa cause) to win over; **se rallier à** (avis) to come over ou round to

rallonge [ralɔ̃ʒ] nf (de table) (extra) leaf (pl leaves); (argent etc) extra (no pl); (ÉLEC) extension (cable ou flex); (fig: de crédit etc) extension

rallonger [ralɔ̃ʒe] vt to lengthen

rallye [rali] nm rally; (POL) march

ramassage [ramɑsaʒ] nm: **ramassage scolaire** school bus service

ramassé, e [ramɑse] adj (trapu) squat, stocky; (concis: expression etc) compact

ramasser [ramɑse] vt (objet tombé ou par terre, fam) to pick up; (recueillir) to collect; (récolter) to gather; (: pommes de terre) to lift; **se ramasser** vi (sur soi-même) to huddle up; to crouch

ramassis [ramɑsi] nm (péj: de gens) bunch; (: de choses) jumble

rambarde [rɑ̃bard(ə)] nf guardrail

rame [ram] nf (aviron) oar; (de métro) train; (de papier) ream; **rame de haricots** bean support; **faire force de rames** to row hard

rameau, x [ramo] nm (small) branch; (fig) branch; **les Rameaux** (REL) Palm Sunday sg

ramener [ramne] vt to bring back; (reconduire) to take back; (rabattre: couverture, visière): **ramener qch sur** to pull sth back over; **ramener qch à** (réduire à, aussi MATH) to reduce sth to; **ramener qn à la vie/raison** to bring sb back to life/bring sb to his (ou her) senses; **se ramener** vi (fam) to roll up ou turn up; **se ramener à** (se réduire à) to come ou boil down to

ramer [rame] vi to row

ramollir [ramɔlir] vt to soften; **se ramollir** vi (os, tissus) to get (ou go) soft; (beurre, asphalte) to soften

ramoner [ramɔne] vt (cheminée) to sweep; (pipe) to clean

rampe [rɑ̃p] nf (d'escalier) banister(s pl); (dans un garage, d'un terrain) ramp; (THÉÂT): **la rampe** the footlights pl; (lampes: lumineuse, de balisage) floodlights pl; **passer la rampe** (toucher le public) to get across the audience; **rampe de lancement** launching pad

ramper [rɑ̃pe] vi (reptile, animal) to crawl; (plante) to creep

rancard [rɑ̃kar] nm (fam) date; tip

rancart [rɑ̃kar] nm: **mettre au rancart** (article, projet) to scrap; (personne) to put on the scrapheap

rance [rɑ̃s] adj rancid

rancœur [rɑ̃kœr] nf rancour (BRIT), rancor (US), resentment

rançon [rɑ̃sɔ̃] nf ransom; (fig): **la rançon du succès** etc the price of success etc

rancune [rɑ̃kyn] nf grudge, rancour (BRIT), rancor (US); **garder rancune à qn (de qch)** to bear sb a grudge (for sth); **sans rancune!** no hard feelings!

rancunier, ière [rɑ̃kynje, -jɛr] adj vindictive, spiteful

randonnée [rɑ̃dɔne] nf ride; (à pied) walk, ramble; hike, hiking no pl

rang [rɑ̃] nm (rangée) row; (de perles) row, string, rope; (grade, condition sociale, classement) rank; **rangs** nmpl (MIL) ranks; **se mettre en rangs/sur un rang** to get into ou form rows/a line; **sur 3 rangs** (lined up) 3 deep; **se mettre en rangs par 4** to form fours ou rows of 4; **se mettre sur les rangs** (fig) to get into the running; **au premier rang** in the first row; (fig) ranking first; **rentrer dans le rang** to get into line; **au rang de** (au nombre de) among (the ranks of); **avoir rang de** to hold the rank of

rangé, e [rɑ̃ʒe] adj (sérieux) orderly, steady

rangée [rɑ̃ʒe] nf row

ranger [rɑ̃ʒe] vt (classer, grouper) to order, arrange; (mettre à sa place) to put away; (voiture dans la rue) to park; (mettre de l'ordre dans) to tidy up; (*arranger, disposer: en cercle etc*) to arrange; (*fig: classer*): **ranger qn/qch parmi** to rank sb/sth among; **se ranger** *vi* (*se placer, se disposer: autour d'une table etc*) to take one's place, sit round; (*véhicule, conducteur: s'écarter*) to pull over; (: *s'arrêter*) to pull in; (*piéton*) to step aside; (*s'assagir*) to settle down; **se ranger à** (*avis*) to come round to, fall in with

ranimer [ʀanime] *vt* (*personne évanouie*) to bring round; (*revigorer: forces, courage*) to restore; (*réconforter: troupes etc*) to kindle new life in; (*douleur, souvenir*) to revive; (*feu*) to rekindle

rap [ʀap] *nm* rap (music)

rapace [ʀapas] *nm* bird of prey ♦ *adj* (*péj*) rapacious, grasping; **rapace diurne/nocturne** diurnal/nocturnal bird of prey

râpe [ʀɑp] *nf* (*CULIN*) grater; (*à bois*) rasp

râper [ʀɑpe] *vt* (*CULIN*) to grate; (*gratter, râcler*) to rasp

rapetisser [ʀaptise] *vt*: **rapetisser qch** to shorten sth; to make sth look smaller ♦ *vi*: **se rapetisser** *vi* to shrink

rapide [ʀapid] *adj* fast; (*prompt*) quick; (*intelligence*) quick ♦ *nm* express (train); (*de cours d'eau*) rapid

rapidement [ʀapidmɑ̃] *adv* fast; quickly

rapiécer [ʀapjese] *vt* to patch

rappel [ʀapɛl] *nm* (*d'un ambassadeur, MIL*) recall; (*THÉÂT*) curtain call; (*MÉD: vaccination*) booster; (*ADMIN: de salaire*) back pay *no pl*; (*d'une aventure, d'un nom*) reminder; (*de limitation de vitesse: sur écriteau*) speed limit sign (*reminder*); (*TECH*) return; (*NAVIG*) sitting out; (*ALPINISME: aussi*: **rappel de corde**) abseiling *no pl*, roping down *no pl*; abseil; **rappel à l'ordre** call to order

rappeler [ʀaple] *vt* (*pour faire revenir, retéléphoner*) to call back; (*ambassadeur, MIL, INFORM*) to recall; (*acteur*) to call back (onto the stage); (*faire se souvenir*): **rappeler qch à qn** to remind sb of sth; **se rappeler** *vt* (*se souvenir de*) to remember, recall; **rappeler qn à la vie** to bring sb back to life; **rappeler qn à la décence** to recall sb to a sense of decency; **ça rappelle la Provence** it's reminiscent of Provence, it reminds you of Provence; **se rappeler que...** to remember that...

rapport [ʀapɔʀ] *nm* (*compte rendu*) report; (*profit*) yield, return; revenue; (*lien, analogie*) relationship; (*corrélation*) connection; (*proportion: MATH, TECH*) ratio (*pl* -s); **rapports** *nmpl* (*entre personnes, pays*) relations; **avoir rapport à** to have something to do with, concern; **être en rapport avec** (*idée de corrélation*) to be related to; **être/se mettre en rapport avec qn** to be/get in touch with sb; **par rapport à** (*comparé à*) in relation to; (*à propos de*) with regard to; **sous le rapport de** from the point of view of; **sous tous (les) rapports** in all respects; **rapports (sexuels)** (sexual) intercourse *sg*; **rapport qualité-prix** value (for money)

rapporter [ʀapɔʀte] *vt* (*rendre, ramener*) to bring back; (*apporter davantage*) to bring more; (*COUTURE*) to sew on; (*suj: investissement*) to yield; (: *activité*) to bring in; (*relater*) to report; (*JUR: annuler*) to revoke ♦ *vi* (*investissement*) to give a good return *ou* yield; (*activité*) to be very profitable; (*péj: moucharder*) to tell; **rapporter qch à** (*fig: rattacher*) to relate sth to; **se rapporter à** (*correspondre à*) to relate to; **s'en rapporter à** to rely on

rapporteur, euse [ʀapɔʀtœʀ, -øz] *nm/f* (*de procès, commission*) reporter; (*péj*) telltale ♦ *nm* (*GÉOM*) protractor

rapprochement [ʀapʀɔʃmɑ̃] *nm* (*réconciliation: de nations, familles*) reconciliation; (*analogie, rapport*) parallel

rapprocher [ʀapʀɔʃe] *vt* (*chaise d'une table*): **rapprocher qch (de)** to bring sth closer (to); (*deux objets*) to bring closer together; (*réunir*) to bring together; (*comparer*) to establish a parallel between; **se rapprocher** *vi* to draw closer *ou* nearer; (*fig: familles, pays*) to come together; to come closer together; **se rapprocher de** to come closer to; (*présenter une analogie avec*) to be close to

rapt [ʀapt] *nm* abduction

raquette [ʀakɛt] *nf* (*de tennis*) racket; (*de ping-pong*) bat; (*à neige*) snowshoe

rare [ʀaʀ] *adj* rare; (*main-d'œuvre, denrées*) scarce; (*cheveux, herbe*) sparse; **il est rare que** it's rare that, it's unusual that; **se faire rare** to become scarce; (*fig: personne*) to make oneself scarce

rarement [ʀaʀmɑ̃] *adv* rarely, seldom

ras, e [ʀɑ, ʀɑz] *adj* (*tête, cheveux*) close-cropped; (*poil, herbe*) short; (*mesure, cuillère*) level ♦ *adv* short; **faire table rase** to make a clean sweep; **en rase campagne** in open country; **à ras bords** to the brim; **au ras de** level with; **en avoir ras le bol** (*fam*) to be fed up; **ras du cou** *adj* (*pull, robe*) crewneck

rasade [ʀɑzad] *nf* glassful

raser [ʀɑze] *vt* (*barbe, cheveux*) to shave off; (*menton, personne*) to shave; (*fam: ennuyer*) to bore; (*démolir*) to raze (to the ground); (*frôler*) to graze, skim; **se raser** to shave; (*fam*) to be bored (to tears)

rasoir [ʀɑzwaʀ] *nm* razor; **rasoir électrique** electric shaver *ou* razor; **rasoir mécanique** *ou* **de sûreté** safety razor

rassasier [ʀasazje] *vt* to satisfy; **être rassasié** (*dégoûté*) to be sated; to have had more than enough

rassemblement [ʀasɑ̃bləmɑ̃] *nm* (*groupe*) gathering; (*POL*) union; association; (*MIL*): **le rassemblement** parade

rassembler [ʀasɑ̃ble] *vt* (*réunir*) to assemble, gather; (*regrouper, amasser*) to gather together, collect; **se rassembler** *vi* to gather; **rassembler ses idées/ses esprits/son courage** to collect one's thoughts/gather one's wits/screw up one's courage

rassis, e [ʀasi, -iz] *adj* (*pain*) stale

rassurer [ʀasyʀe] *vt* to reassure; **se rassurer** to be reassured; **rassure-toi** don't worry

rat [Ra] *nm* rat; **rat d'hôtel** hotel thief (*pl* thieves); **rat musqué** muskrat

rate [Rat] *nf* female rat; (ANAT) spleen

raté, e [Rate] *adj* (*tentative*) unsuccessful, failed ♦ *nm/f* failure ♦ *nm* misfiring *no pl*

râteau, x [Rato] *nm* rake

rater [Rate] *vi* (*ne pas partir: coup de feu*) to fail to go off; (*affaire, projet etc*) to go wrong, fail ♦ *vt* (*cible, train, occasion*) to miss; (*démonstration, plat*) to spoil; (*examen*) to fail; **rater son coup** to fail, not to bring it off

ration [Rasjɔ̃] *nf* ration; (*fig*) share; **ration alimentaire** food intake

ratisser [Ratise] *vt* (*allée*) to rake; (*feuilles*) to rake up; (*suj: armée, police*) to comb; **ratisser large** to cast one's net wide

RATP *sigle f* (= *Régie autonome des transports parisiens*) Paris transport authority

rattacher [Rataʃe] *vt* (*animal, cheveux*) to tie up again; (*incorporer: ADMIN etc*): **rattacher qch à** to join sth to, unite sth with; (*fig: relier*): **rattacher qch à** to link sth with, relate sth to; (*: lier*): **rattacher qn à** to bind ou tie sb to; **se rattacher à** (*fig: avoir un lien avec*) to be linked (*ou* connected) with

rattrapage [Ratrapaʒ] *nm* (SCOL) remedial classes *pl*; (ÉCON) catching up

rattraper [Ratrape] *vt* (*fugitif*) to recapture; (*retenir, empêcher de tomber*) to catch (hold of); (*atteindre, rejoindre*) to catch up with; (*réparer: imprudence, erreur*) to make up for; **se rattraper** *vi* (*regagner: du temps*) to make up for lost time; (*: de l'argent etc*) to make good one's losses; (*réparer une gaffe etc*) to make up for it; **se rattraper (à)** (*se raccrocher*) to stop o.s. falling (by catching hold of); **rattraper son retard/le temps perdu** to make up (for) lost time

rature [Ratyr] *nf* deletion, erasure

rauque [Rok] *adj* raucous; hoarse

ravages [Ravaʒ] *nmpl* ravages; **faire des ravages** to wreak havoc; (*fig: séducteur*) to break hearts

ravaler [Ravale] *vt* (*mur, façade*) to restore; (*déprécier*) to lower; (*avaler de nouveau*) to swallow again; **ravaler sa colère/son dégoût** to stifle one's anger/swallow one's distaste

ravi, e [Ravi] *adj* delighted; **être ravi de/que** to be delighted with/that

ravigoter [Ravigɔte] *vt* (*fam*) to buck up

ravin [Ravɛ̃] *nm* gully, ravine

ravir [Ravir] *vt* (*enchanter*) to delight; (*enlever*): **ravir qch à qn** to rob sb of sth; **à ravir** *adv* delightfully, beautifully; **être beau à ravir** to be ravishingly beautiful

raviser [Ravize]: **se raviser** *vi* to change one's mind

ravissant, e [Ravisɑ̃, -ɑ̃t] *adj* delightful

ravisseur, euse [Raviscœr, -øz] *nm/f* abductor, kidnapper

ravitaillement [Ravitajmɑ̃] *nm* resupplying; refuelling; (*provisions*) supplies *pl*; **aller au ravitaillement** to go for fresh supplies; **ravitaillement en vol** (AVIAT) in-flight refuelling

ravitailler [Ravitaje] *vt* to resupply; (*véhicule*) to refuel; **se ravitailler** *vi* to get fresh supplies

raviver [Ravive] *vt* (*feu*) to rekindle, revive; (*douleur*) to revive; (*couleurs*) to brighten up

rayé, e [Reje] *adj* (*à rayures*) striped; (*éraflé*) scratched

rayer [Reje] *vt* (*érafler*) to scratch; (*barrer*) to cross *ou* score out; (*d'une liste: radier*) to cross *ou* strike off

rayon [Rejɔ̃] *nm* (*de soleil etc*) ray; (GÉOM) radius; (*de roue*) spoke; (*étagère*) shelf (*pl* shelves); (*de grand magasin*) department; (*fig: domaine*) responsibility, concern; (*de ruche*) (honey)comb; **dans un rayon de** within a radius of; **rayons** *nmpl* (*radiothérapie*) radiation; **rayon d'action** range; **rayon de braquage** (AUTO) turning circle; **rayon laser** laser beam; **rayon de soleil** sunbeam, ray of sunlight *ou* sunshine; **rayons X** X-rays

rayonnement [Rejɔnmɑ̃] *nm* radiation; (*fig: éclat*) radiance; (*: influence*) influence

rayonner [Rejɔne] *vi* (*chaleur, énergie*) to radiate; (*fig: émotion*) to shine forth; (*: visage*) to be radiant; (*avenues, axes*) to radiate; (*touriste*) to go touring (*from one base*)

rayure [Rejyr] *nf* (*motif*) stripe; (*éraflure*) scratch; (*rainure, d'un fusil*) groove; **à rayures** striped

raz-de-marée [Radmare] *nm inv* tidal wave

ré [Re] *nm* (MUS) D; (*en chantant la gamme*) re

réacteur [Reaktœr] *nm* jet engine; **réacteur nucléaire** nuclear reactor

réaction [Reaksjɔ̃] *nf* reaction; **par réaction** jet-propelled; **avion/moteur à réaction** jet (plane)/jet engine; **réaction en chaîne** chain reaction

réadapter [Readapte] *vt* to readjust; (MÉD) to rehabilitate; **se réadapter (à)** to readjust (to)

réagir [Reaʒir] *vi* to react

réalisateur, trice [Realizatœr, -tris] *nm/f* (TV, CINÉ) director

réalisation [Realizasjɔ̃] *nf* carrying out; realization; fulfilment; achievement; production; (*œuvre*) production, work; (*création*) creation

réaliser [Realize] *vt* (*projet, opération*) to carry out, realize; (*rêve, souhait*) to realize, fulfil; (*exploit*) to achieve; (*achat, vente*) to make; (*film*) to produce; (*se rendre compte de, COMM: bien, capital*) to realize; **se réaliser** *vi* to be realized

réaliste [Realist(ə)] *adj* realistic; (*peintre, roman*) realist ♦ *nm/f* realist

réalité [Realite] *nf* reality; **en réalité** in (actual) fact; **dans la réalité** in reality; **réalité virtuelle** virtual reality

réanimation [Reanimasjɔ̃] *nf* resuscitation; **service de réanimation** intensive care unit

rébarbatif, ive [Rebarbatif, -iv] *adj* forbidding; (*style*) off-putting (BRIT), crabbed

rebattu, e [Rəbaty] *pp de* **rebattre** ◆ *adj* hackneyed

rebelle [Rəbɛl] *nm/f* rebel ◆ *adj* (*troupes*) rebel; (*enfant*) rebellious; (*mèche etc*) unruly; **rebelle à qch** unamenable to sth; **rebelle à faire** unwilling to do

rebeller [Rəbele]: **se rebeller** *vi* to rebel

rebondi, e [Rəbɔ̃di] *adj* (*ventre*) rounded; (*joues*) chubby, well-rounded

rebondir [Rəbɔ̃diR] *vi* (*ballon: au sol*) to bounce; (: *contre un mur*) to rebound; (*fig: procès, action, conversation*) to get moving again, be suddenly revived

rebondissement [Rəbɔ̃dismɑ̃] *nm* new development

rebord [RəbɔR] *nm* edge

rebours [RəbuR]: **à rebours** *adv* the wrong way

rebrousser [RəbRuse] *vt* (*cheveux, poils*) to brush back, brush up; **rebrousser chemin** to turn back

rebut [Rəby] *nm*: **mettre au rebut** to scrap, discard

rebutant, e [Rəbytɑ̃, -ɑ̃t] *adj* (*travail, démarche*) off-putting, disagreeable

rebuter [Rəbyte] *vt* to put off

récalcitrant, e [Rekalsitrɑ̃, -ɑ̃t] *adj* refractory, recalcitrant

recaler [Rəkale] *vt* (*SCOL*) to fail

récapituler [Rekapityle] *vt* to recapitulate; (*résumer*) to sum up

receler [Rəsəle] *vt* (*produit d'un vol*) to receive; (*malfaiteur*) to harbour; (*fig*) to conceal

receleur, euse [RəsəlœR, -øz] *nm/f* receiver

récemment [Resamɑ̃] *adv* recently

recensement [Rəsɑ̃smɑ̃] *nm* census; inventory

recenser [Rəsɑ̃se] *vt* (*population*) to take a census of; (*inventorier*) to make an inventory of; (*dénombrer*) to list

récent, e [Resɑ̃, -ɑ̃t] *adj* recent

récépissé [Resepise] *nm* receipt

récepteur, trice [ReseptœR, -tRis] *adj* receiving ◆ *nm* receiver; **récepteur (de papier)** (*INFORM*) stacker; **récepteur (de radio)** radio set *ou* receiver

réception [Resɛpsjɔ̃] *nf* receiving *no pl*; (*d'une marchandise, commande*) receipt; (*accueil*) reception, welcome; (*bureau*) reception (desk); (*réunion mondaine*) reception, party; (*pièces*) reception rooms *pl*; (*SPORT: après un saut*) landing; (*du ballon*) catching *no pl*; **jour/heures de réception** day/hours for receiving visitors (*ou* students *etc*)

réceptionniste [Resɛpsjɔnist(ə)] *nm/f* receptionist

recette [Rəsɛt] *nf* (*CULIN*) recipe; (*fig*) formula, recipe; (*COMM*) takings *pl*; (*ADMIN: bureau*) tax *ou* revenue office; **recettes** *nfpl* (*COMM: rentrées*) receipts; **faire recette** (*spectacle, exposition*) to be a winner

receveur, euse [RəsvœR, -øz] *nm/f* (*des contributions*) tax collector; (*des postes*) postmaster/mistress; (*d'autobus*) conductor/conductress; (*MÉD: de sang, organe*) recipient

recevoir [RəsvwaR] *vt* to receive; (*lettre, prime*) to receive, get; (*client, patient, représentant*) to see; (*jour, soleil: pièce*) to get; (*SCOL: candidat*) to pass ◆ *vi* to receive visitors; to give parties; to see patients *etc*; **se recevoir** *vi* (*athlète*) to land; **recevoir qn à dîner** to invite sb to dinner; **il reçoit de 8 à 10** he's at home from 8 to 10, he will see visitors from 8 to 10; (*docteur, dentiste etc*) he sees patients from 8 to 10; **être reçu** (*à un examen*) to pass; **être bien/mal reçu** to be well/badly received

rechange [Rəʃɑ̃ʒ]: **de rechange** *adj* (*pièces, roue*) spare; (*fig: solution*) alternative; **des vêtements de rechange** a change of clothes

réchapper [Reʃape]: **réchapper de** *ou* **à** *vt* (*accident, maladie*) to come through; **va-t-il en réchapper?** is he going to get over it?, is he going to come through (it)?

recharge [RəʃaRʒ(ə)] *nf* refill

rechargeable [RəʃaRʒabl(ə)] *adj* refillable; rechargeable

recharger [RəʃaRʒe] *vt* (*camion, fusil, appareil-photo*) to reload; (*briquet, stylo*) to refill; (*batterie*) to recharge

réchaud [Reʃo] *nm* (portable) stove; plate-warmer

réchauffer [Reʃofe] *vt* (*plat*) to reheat; (*mains, personne*) to warm; **se réchauffer** *vi* to get warmer; **se réchauffer les doigts** to warm (up) one's fingers

rêche [Rɛʃ] *adj* rough

recherche [RəʃɛRʃ(ə)] *nf* (*action*): **la recherche de** the search for; (*raffinement*) affectedness, studied elegance; (*scientifique etc*): **la recherche** research; **recherches** *nfpl* (*de la police*) investigations; (*scientifiques*) research *sg*; **être/se mettre à la recherche de** to be/go in search of

recherché, e [RəʃɛRʃe] *adj* (*rare, demandé*) much sought-after; (*entouré: acteur, femme*) in demand; (*raffiné*) studied, affected

rechercher [RəʃɛRʃe] *vt* (*objet égaré, personne*) to look for, search for; (*témoins, coupable, main-d'œuvre*) to look for; (*causes d'un phénomène, nouveau procédé*) to try to find; (*bonheur etc, l'amitié de qn*) to seek; **"rechercher et remplacer"** (*INFORM*) "search and replace"

rechigner [Rəʃiɲe] *vi*: **rechigner (à)** to balk (at)

rechute [Rəʃyt] *nf* (*MÉD*) relapse; (*dans le péché, le vice*) lapse; **faire une rechute** to have a relapse

récidiver [Residive] *vi* to commit a second (*ou* subsequent) offence; (*fig*) to do it again

récif [Resif] *nm* reef

récipient [Resipjɑ̃] *nm* container

réciproque [ResipRɔk] *adj* reciprocal ◆ *nf*: **la réciproque** (*l'inverse*) the converse

récit [Resi] *nm* (*action de narrer*) telling; (*conte, histoire*) story

récital [Resital] *nm* recital

réciter [Resite] *vt* to recite

réclamation [Reklamɔsjɔ̃] *nf* complaint; **réclamations** *nfpl* (*bureau*) complaints department *sg*

réclame [Reklam] *nf*: **la réclame** advertising; **une réclame** an ad(vertisement), an advert (*BRIT*); **faire de la réclame (pour qch/qn)** to advertise (sth/sb); **article en réclame** special offer

réclamer [Reklame] *vt* (*aide, nourriture etc*) to ask for; (*revendiquer: dû, part, indemnité*) to claim, demand; (*nécessiter*) to demand, require ♦ *vi* to complain; **se réclamer de** to give as one's authority; to claim filiation with

réclusion [Reklyzjɔ̃] *nf* imprisonment; **réclusion à perpétuité** life imprisonment

recoin [Rǝkwɛ̃] *nm* nook, corner; (*fig*) hidden recess

reçois [Rǝswa] *etc vb voir* recevoir

récolte [Rekɔlt(ǝ)] *nf* harvesting, gathering; (*produits*) harvest, crop; (*fig*) crop, collection; (: *d'observations*) findings

récolter [Rekɔlte] *vt* to harvest, gather (in); (*fig*) to get

recommandé [Rǝkɔmɑ̃de] *nm* (*méthode etc*) recommended; (*POSTES*): **en recommandé** by registered mail

recommander [Rǝkɔmɑ̃de] *vt* to recommend; (*suj: qualités etc*) to commend; (*POSTES*) to register; **recommander qch à qn** to recommend sth to sb; **recommander à qn de faire** to recommend sb to do; **recommander qn auprès de qn** *ou* **à qn** to recommend sb to sb; **il est recommandé de faire ...** it is recommended that one does ...; **se recommander à qn** to commend o.s. to sb; **se recommander de qn** to give sb's name as a reference

recommencer [Rǝkɔmɑ̃se] *vt* (*reprendre: lutte, séance*) to resume, start again; (*refaire: travail, explications*) to start afresh, start (over) again; (*récidiver: erreur*) to make again ♦ *vi* to start again; (*récidiver*) to do it again; **recommencer à faire** to start doing again; **ne recommence pas!** don't do that again!

récompense [Rekɔ̃pɑ̃s] *nf* reward; (*prix*) award; **recevoir qch en récompense** to get sth as a reward, be rewarded with sth

récompenser [Rekɔ̃pɑ̃se] *vt*: **récompenser qn (de ou pour)** to reward sb (for)

réconcilier [Rekɔ̃silje] *vt* to reconcile; **réconcilier qn avec qn** to reconcile sb with sb; **réconcilier qn avec qch** to reconcile sb to sth; **se réconcilier (avec)** to be reconciled (with)

reconduire [Rǝkɔ̃dɥiR] *vt* (*raccompagner*) to take *ou* see back; (: *à la porte*) to show out; (: *à son domicile*) to see home, take home; (*JUR, POL: renouveler*) to renew

réconfort [Rekɔ̃fɔR] *nm* comfort

réconforter [Rekɔ̃fɔRte] *vt* (*consoler*) to comfort; (*revigorer*) to fortify

reconnaissance [Rǝkɔnesɑ̃s] *nf* recognition;

acknowledgement; (*gratitude*) gratitude, gratefulness; (*MIL*) reconnaissance, recce; **en reconnaissance** (*MIL*) on reconnaissance; **reconnaissance de dette** acknowledgement of a debt, IOU

reconnaissant, e [Rǝkɔnesɑ̃, -ɑ̃t] *vb voir* **reconnaître** ♦ *adj* grateful; **je vous serais reconnaissant de bien vouloir** I should be most grateful if you would (kindly)

reconnaître [RǝkɔnetR(ǝ)] *vt* to recognize; (*MIL: lieu*) to reconnoitre; (*JUR: enfant, dette, droit*) to acknowledge; **reconnaître que** to admit *ou* acknowledge that; **reconnaître qn/qch à** (*l'identifier grâce à*) to recognize sb/sth by; **reconnaître à qn: je lui reconnais certaines qualités** I recognize certain qualities in him; **se reconnaître quelque part** (*s'y retrouver*) to find one's way around (a place)

reconnu, e [R(ǝ)kɔny] *pp de* reconnaître ♦ *adj* (*indiscuté, connu*) recognized

reconstituant, e [Rǝkɔ̃stitɥɑ̃, -ɑ̃t] *adj* (*régime*) strength-building ♦ *nm* tonic, pick-me-up

reconstituer [Rǝkɔ̃stitɥe] *vt* (*monument ancien*) to recreate, build a replica of; (*fresque, vase brisé*) to piece together, reconstitute; (*événement, accident*) to reconstruct; (*fortune, patrimoine*) to rebuild; (*BIO: tissus etc*) to regenerate

reconstruction [Rǝkɔ̃stRyksjɔ̃] *nf* rebuilding, reconstruction

reconstruire [Rǝkɔ̃stRɥiR] *vt* to rebuild, reconstruct

reconvertir [Rǝkɔ̃vertiR] *vt* (*usine*) to reconvert; (*personnel, troupes etc*) to redeploy; **se reconvertir dans** (*un métier, une branche*) to move into, be redeployed into

record [RǝkɔR] *nm, adj* record; **record du monde** world record

recoupement [Rǝkupmɑ̃] *nm*: **faire un recoupement** *ou* **des recoupements** to crosscheck; **par recoupement** by cross-checking

recouper [Rǝkupe] *vt* (*tranche*) to cut again; (*vêtement*) to recut ♦ *vi* (*CARTES*) to cut again; **se recouper** *vi* (*témoignages*) to tie *ou* match up

recourber [RǝkuRbe] *vt* (*branche, tige de métal*) to bend

recourir [RǝkuRiR] *vi* (*courir de nouveau*) to run again; (*refaire une course*) to race again; **recourir à** *vt* (*ami, agence*) to turn *ou* appeal to; (*force, ruse, emprunt*) to resort to, have recourse to

recours [RǝkuR] *vb voir* recourir ♦ *nm* (*JUR*) appeal; **avoir recours à = recourir à**; **en dernier recours** as a last resort; **sans recours** final; with no way out; **recours en grâce** plea for clemency (*ou* pardon)

recouvrer [RǝkuvRe] *vt* (*vue, santé etc*) to recover, regain; (*impôts*) to collect; (*créance*) to recover

recouvrir [RǝkuvRiR] *vt* (*couvrir à nouveau*) to recover; (*couvrir entièrement: aussi fig*) to cover; (*cacher, masquer*) to conceal, hide; **se recouvrir (se**

superposer) to overlap

récréation [ʀekʀeasjɔ̃] *nf* recreation, entertainment; (*SCOL*) break

récrier [ʀekʀije]: **se récrier** *vi* to exclaim

récriminations [ʀekʀiminasjɔ̃] *nfpl* remonstrations, complaints

recroqueviller [ʀəkʀɔkvije]: **se recroqueviller** *vi* (*feuilles*) to curl *ou* shrivel up; (*personne*) to huddle up

recru, e [ʀəkʀy] *adj*: **recru de fatigue** exhausted ♦ *nf* recruit

recrudescence [ʀəkʀydesɑ̃s] *nf* fresh outbreak

recruter [ʀəkʀyte] *vt* to recruit

rectangle [ʀɛktɑ̃gl(ə)] *nm* rectangle; **rectangle blanc** (*TV*) "adults only" symbol

rectangulaire [ʀɛktɑ̃gylɛʀ] *adj* rectangular

rectificatif, ive [ʀɛktifikatif, -iv] *adj* corrected ♦ *nm* correction

rectifier [ʀɛktifje] *vt* (*tracé, virage*) to straighten; (*calcul, adresse*) to correct; (*erreur, faute*) to rectify, put right

rectiligne [ʀɛktiliɲ] *adj* straight; (*GÉOM*) rectilinear

recto [ʀɛkto] *nm* front (*of a sheet of paper*)

reçu, e [ʀəsy] *pp de* **recevoir** ♦ *adj* (*admis, consacré*) accepted ♦ *nm* (*COMM*) receipt

recueil [ʀəkœj] *nm* collection

recueillir [ʀəkœjiʀ] *vt* to collect; (*voix, suffrages*) to win; (*accueillir: réfugiés, chat*) to take in; **se recueillir** *vi* to gather one's thoughts; to meditate

recul [ʀəkyl] *nm* retreat; recession; decline; (*d'arme à feu*) recoil, kick; **avoir un mouvement de recul** to recoil, start back; **prendre du recul** to stand back; **avec le recul** with the passing of time, in retrospect

reculé, e [ʀəkyle] *adj* remote

reculer [ʀəkyle] *vi* to move back, back away; (*AUTO*) to reverse, back (up); (*fig: civilisation, épidémie*) to (be on the) decline; (*: se dérober*) to shrink back ♦ *vt* to move back; to reverse, back (up); (*fig: possibilités, limites*) to extend; (*: date, décision*) to postpone; **reculer devant** (*danger, difficulté*) to shrink from; **reculer pour mieux sauter** (*fig*) to postpone the evil day

reculons [ʀəkylɔ̃]: **à reculons** *adv* backwards

récupérer [ʀekypeʀe] *vt* (*rentrer en possession de*) to recover, get back; (*: forces*) to recover; (*déchets etc*) to salvage (for reprocessing); (*remplacer: journée, heures de travail*) to make up; (*délinquant etc*) to rehabilitate; (*POL*) to bring into line ♦ *vi* to recover

récurer [ʀekyʀe] *vt* to scour; **poudre à récurer** scouring powder

récuser [ʀekyze] *vt* to challenge; **se récuser** to decline to give an opinion

recycler [ʀəsikle] *vt* (*SCOL*) to reorientate; (*employés*) to retrain; (*matériau*) to recycle; **se recycler** to retrain; to go on a retraining course

rédacteur, trice [ʀedaktœʀ, -tʀis] *nm/f* (*journaliste*) writer; subeditor; (*d'ouvrage de référence*) editor, compiler; **rédacteur en chef** chief editor; **rédacteur publicitaire** copywriter

rédaction [ʀedaksjɔ̃] *nf* writing; (*rédacteurs*) editorial staff; (*bureau*) editorial office(s); (*SCOL: devoir*) essay, composition

redemander [ʀədmɑ̃de] *vt* (*renseignement*) to ask again for; (*nourriture*): **redemander de** to ask for more (*ou* another); (*objet prêté*): **redemander qch** to ask for sth back

redescendre [ʀədesɑ̃dʀ(ə)] *vi* (*à nouveau*) to go back down; (*après la montée*) to go down (again) ♦ *vt* (*pente etc*) to go down

redevance [ʀədvɑ̃s] *nf* (*TÉL*) rental charge; (*TV*) licence (*BRIT*) *ou* license (*US*) fee

rédiger [ʀediʒe] *vt* to write; (*contrat*) to draw up

redire [ʀədiʀ] *vt* to repeat; **trouver à redire à** to find fault with

redonner [ʀədɔne] *vt* (*restituer*) to give back, return; (*du courage, des forces*) to restore

redoubler [ʀəduble] *vi* (*tempête, violence*) to intensify, get even stronger *ou* fiercer etc; (*SCOL*) to repeat a year ♦ *vt* (*SCOL: classe*) to repeat; (*LING: lettre*) to double; **redoubler de** *vt* to be twice as + *adjectif*; **le vent redouble de violence** the wind is blowing twice as hard

redoutable [ʀədutabl(ə)] *adj* formidable, fearsome

redouter [ʀədute] *vt* to fear; (*appréhender*) to dread; **redouter de faire** to dread doing

redressement [ʀədʀɛsmɑ̃] *nm* (*de l'économie etc*) putting right; **maison de redressement** reformatory; **redressement fiscal** repayment of back taxes

redresser [ʀədʀese] *vt* (*arbre, mât*) to set upright, right; (*pièce tordue*) to straighten out; (*AVIAT, AUTO*) to straighten up; (*situation, économie*) to put right; **se redresser** *vi* (*objet penché*) to right itself; to straighten up; (*personne*) to sit (*ou* stand) up; to sit (*ou* stand) up straight; (*fig: pays, situation*) to recover; **redresser (les roues)** (*AUTO*) to straighten up

réduction [ʀedyksjɔ̃] *nf* reduction; **en réduction** *adv* in miniature, scaled-down

réduire [ʀedɥiʀ] *vt* (*gén, aussi CULIN, MATH*) to reduce; (*prix, dépenses*) to cut, reduce; (*carte*) to scale down, reduce; (*MÉD: fracture*) to set; **réduire qn/qch à** to reduce sb/sth to; **se réduire à** (*revenir à*) to boil down to; **se réduire en** (*se transformer en*) to be reduced to; **en être réduit à** to be reduced to

réduit, e [ʀedɥi, -it] *pp de* **réduire** ♦ *adj* (*prix, tarif, échelle*) reduced; (*mécanisme*) scaled-down; (*vitesse*) reduced ♦ *nm* tiny room; recess

rééducation [ʀeedykasjɔ̃] *nf* (*d'un membre*) re-education; (*de délinquants, d'un blessé*) rehabilitation; **rééducation de la parole** speech therapy; **centre de rééducation** physiotherapy *ou* physical therapy (*US*) centre

réel, le [ʀeel] *adj* real ♦ *nm*: **le réel** reality
réellement [ʀeelmɑ̃] *adv* really
réexpédier [ʀeekspedje] *vt* (*à l'envoyeur*) to return, send back; (*au destinataire*) to send on, forward
refaire [ʀəfɛʀ] *vt* (*faire de nouveau, recommencer*) to do again; (*réparer, restaurer*) to do up; **se refaire** *vi* (*en argent*) to make up one's losses; **se refaire une santé** to recuperate; **se refaire à qch** (*se réhabituer à*) to get used to sth again
réfection [ʀefɛksjɔ̃] *nf* repair; **en réfection** under repair
réfectoire [ʀefɛktwaʀ] *nm* refectory
référence [ʀefeʀɑ̃s] *nf* reference; **références** *nfpl* (*recommandations*) reference *sg*; **faire référence à** to refer to; **ouvrage de référence** reference work; **ce n'est pas une référence** (*fig*) that's no recommendation
référer [ʀefeʀe]: **se référer à** *vt* to refer to; **en référer à qn** to refer the matter to sb
refermer [ʀəfɛʀme] *vt* to close again, shut again
refiler [ʀəfile] *vt* (*fam*): **refiler qch à qn** to palm (*BRIT*) *ou* fob sth off on sb; to pass sth on to sb
réfléchi, e [ʀefleʃi] *adj* (*caractère*) thoughtful; (*action*) well-thought-out; (*LING*) reflexive
réfléchir [ʀefleʃiʀ] *vt* to reflect ♦ *vi* to think; **réfléchir à** *ou* **sur** to think about; **c'est tout réfléchi** my mind's made up
reflet [ʀəflɛ] *nm* reflection; (*sur l'eau etc*) sheen *no pl*, glint; **reflets** *nmpl* gleam *sg*
refléter [ʀəflete] *vt* to reflect; **se refléter** *vi* to be reflected
réflexe [ʀeflɛks(ə)] *adj, nm* reflex; **réflexe conditionné** conditioned reflex
réflexion [ʀeflɛksjɔ̃] *nf* (*de la lumière etc, pensée*) reflection; (*fait de penser*) thought; (*remarque*) remark; **réflexions** *nfpl* (*méditations*) thought *sg*, reflection *sg*; **sans réflexion** without thinking; **réflexion faite, à la réflexion, après réflexion** on reflection; **délai de réflexion** cooling-off period; **groupe de réflexion** think tank
refluer [ʀəflye] *vi* to flow back; (*foule*) to surge back
reflux [ʀəfly] *nm* (*de la mer*) ebb; (*fig*) backward surge
réforme [ʀefɔʀm(ə)] *nf* reform; (*MIL*) declaration of unfitness for service; discharge (*on health grounds*) (*REL*): **la Réforme** the Reformation
réformer [ʀefɔʀme] *vt* to reform; (*MIL: recrue*) to declare unfit for service; (*: soldat*) to discharge, invalid out; (*matériel*) to scrap
refouler [ʀəfule] *vt* (*envahisseurs*) to drive back, repulse; (*liquide*) to force back; (*fig*) to suppress; (*PSYCH*) to repress
refrain [ʀəfʀɛ̃] *nm* (*MUS*) refrain, chorus; (*air, fig*) tune
refréner, réfréner [ʀəfʀene, ʀefʀene] *vt* to curb, check

réfrigérateur [ʀefʀiʒeʀatœʀ] *nm* refrigerator; **réfrigérateur-congélateur** fridge-freezer
refroidir [ʀəfʀwadiʀ] *vt* to cool; (*fig*) to have a cooling effect on ♦ *vi* to cool (down); **se refroidir** *vi* (*prendre froid*) to catch a chill; (*temps*) to get cooler *ou* colder; (*fig*) to cool (off)
refroidissement [ʀəfʀwadismɑ̃] *nm* cooling; (*grippe etc*) chill
refuge [ʀəfyʒ] *nm* refuge; (*pour piétons*) (traffic) island; **demander refuge à qn** to ask sb for refuge
réfugié, e [ʀefyʒje] *adj, nm/f* refugee
réfugier [ʀefyʒje]: **se réfugier** *vi* to take refuge
refus [ʀəfy] *nm* refusal; **ce n'est pas de refus** I won't say no, it's very welcome
refuser [ʀəfyze] *vt* to refuse; (*SCOL: candidat*) to fail ♦ *vi* to refuse; **refuser qch à qn/de faire** to refuse sb sth/to do; **refuser du monde** to have to turn people away; **se refuser à qch** *ou* **à faire qch** to refuse to do sth; **il ne se refuse rien** he doesn't stint himself; **se refuser à qn** to refuse sb
réfuter [ʀefyte] *vt* to refute
regagner [ʀəgaɲe] *vt* (*argent, faveur*) to win back; (*lieu*) to get back to; **regagner le temps perdu** to make up (for) lost time; **regagner du terrain** to regain ground
regain [ʀəgɛ̃] *nm* (*herbe*) second crop of hay; (*renouveau*): **un regain de** renewed + *nom*
régal [ʀegal] *nm* treat; **un régal pour les yeux** a pleasure *ou* delight to look at
régaler [ʀegale] *vt*: **régaler qn** to treat sb to a delicious meal; **régaler qn de** to treat sb to; **se régaler** *vi* to have a delicious meal; (*fig*) to enjoy o.s.
regard [ʀəgaʀ] *nm* (*coup d'œil*) look, glance; (*expression*) look (in one's eye); **parcourir/menacer du regard** to cast an eye over/look threateningly at; **au regard de** (*loi, morale*) from the point of view of; **en regard** (*vis à vis*) opposite; **en regard de** in comparison with
regardant, e [ʀəgaʀdɑ̃, -ɑ̃t] *adj*: **très/peu regardant (sur)** quite fussy/very free (about); (*économe*) very tight-fisted/quite generous (with)
regarder [ʀəgaʀde] *vt* (*examiner, observer, lire*) to look at; (*film, télévision, match*) to watch; (*envisager: situation, avenir*) to view; (*considérer: son intérêt etc*) to be concerned with; (*être orienté vers*): **regarder (vers)** to face; (*concerner*) to concern ♦ *vi* to look; **regarder à** *vt* (*dépense, qualité, détails*) to be fussy with *ou* over; **regarder à faire** to hesitate to do; **dépenser sans regarder** to spend freely; **regarder qn/qch comme** to regard sb/sth as; **regarder (qch) dans le dictionnaire/l'annuaire** to look (sth up) in the dictionary/directory; **regarder par la fenêtre** to look out of the window; **cela me regarde** it concerns me, it's my business
régie [ʀeʒi] *nf* (*COMM, INDUSTRIE*) state-owned company; (*THÉÂT, CINÉ*) production; (*RADIO, TV*) control

room; **la régie de l'État** state control

regimber [ʀəʒɛ̃be] vi to balk, jib

régime [ʀeʒim] nm (POL, GÉO) régime; (ADMIN: carcéral, fiscal etc) system; (MÉD) diet; (TECH) (engine) speed; (fig) rate, pace; (de bananes, dattes) bunch; **se mettre au/suivre un régime** to go on/be on a diet; **régime sans sel** salt-free diet; **à bas/haut régime** (AUTO) at low/high revs; **à plein régime** flat out, at full speed; **régime matrimonial** marriage settlement

régiment [ʀeʒimɑ̃] nm (MIL: unité) regiment; (fig: fam): **un régiment de** an army of; **un copain de régiment** a pal from military service ou (one's) army days

région [ʀeʒjɔ̃] nf region; **la région parisienne** the Paris area

régional, e, aux [ʀeʒjɔnal, -o] adj regional

régir [ʀeʒiʀ] vt to govern

régisseur [ʀeʒisœʀ] nm (d'un domaine) steward; (CINÉ, TV) assistant director; (THÉÂT) stage manager

registre [ʀaʒistʀ(ə)] nm (livre) register; logbook; ledger; (MUS, LING) register; (d'orgue) stop; **registre de comptabilité** ledger; **registre de l'état civil** register of births, marriages and deaths

réglage [ʀeglaʒ] nm (d'une machine) adjustment; (d'un moteur) tuning

règle [ʀɛgl(ə)] nf (instrument) ruler; (loi, prescription) rule; **règles** nfpl (PHYSIOL) period sg; **avoir pour règle de** to make it a rule that ou to; **en règle** (papiers d'identité) in order; **être/se mettre en règle** to be/put o.s. straight with the authorities; **en règle générale** as a (general) rule; **être la règle** to be the rule; **être de règle** to be usual; **règle à calcul** slide rule; **règle de trois** (MATH) rule of three

réglé, e [ʀegle] adj well-ordered; stable, steady; (papier) ruled; (arrangé) settled; (femme): **bien réglée** whose periods are regular

règlement [ʀɛglamɑ̃] nm settling; (paiement) settlement; (arrêté) regulation; (règles, statuts) regulations pl, rules pl; **règlement à la commande** cash with order; **règlement de compte(s)** settling of scores; **règlement en espèces/par chèque** payment in cash/by cheque; **règlement intérieur** (SCOL) school rules pl; (ADMIN) by-laws pl; **règlement judiciaire** compulsory liquidation

réglementaire [ʀɛglamɑ̃tɛʀ] adj conforming to the regulations; (tenue, uniforme) regulation cpd

réglementation [ʀɛglamɑ̃tasjɔ̃] nf regulation, control; (règlements) regulations pl

réglementer [ʀɛglamɑ̃te] vt to regulate, control

régler [ʀegle] vt (mécanisme, machine) to regulate, adjust; (moteur) to tune; (thermostat etc) to set, adjust; (emploi du temps etc) to organize, plan; (question, conflit, facture, dette) to settle; (fournisseur) to settle up with, pay; (papier) to rule; **régler qch sur** to model sth on; **régler son compte à qn** to sort sb out, settle sb; **régler un compte avec qn** to settle a score with sb

réglisse [ʀeglis] nf ou m liquorice; **bâton de réglisse** liquorice stick

règne [ʀɛɲ] nm (d'un roi etc, fig) reign; (BIO): **le règne végétal/animal** the vegetable/animal kingdom

régner [ʀeɲe] vi (roi) to rule, reign; (fig) to reign

regorger [ʀəɡɔʀʒe] vi to overflow; **regorger de** to overflow with, be bursting with

regret [ʀəgʀɛ] nm regret; **à regret** with regret; **avec regret** regretfully; **être au regret de devoir/ne pas pouvoir faire** to regret to have to/that one is unable to do; **j'ai le regret de vous informer que …** I regret to inform you that …

regrettable [ʀəgʀɛtabl(ə)] adj regrettable

regretter [ʀəgʀɛte] vt to regret; (personne) to miss; **regretter d'avoir fait** to regret doing; **regretter que** to regret that, be sorry that; **non, je regrette** no, I'm sorry

regrouper [ʀəgʀupe] vt (grouper) to group together; (contenir) to include, comprise; **se regrouper** vi to gather (together)

régulier, ière [ʀegylje, -jɛʀ] adj (gén) regular; (vitesse, qualité) steady; (répartition, pression, paysage) even; (TRANSPORTS: ligne, service) scheduled, regular; (légal, réglementaire) lawful, in order; (fam: correct) straight, on the level

régulièrement [ʀegyljɛʀmɑ̃] adv regularly; steadily; evenly; normally

rehausser [ʀəose] vt to heighten, raise; (fig) to set off, enhance

rein [ʀɛ̃] nm kidney; **reins** nmpl (dos) back sg; **avoir mal aux reins** to have backache; **rein artificiel** kidney machine

reine [ʀɛn] nf queen

reine-claude [ʀɛnklod] nf greengage

réinsertion [ʀeɛ̃sɛʀsjɔ̃] nf rehabilitation

réintégrer [ʀeɛ̃tegʀe] vt (lieu) to return to; (fonctionnaire) to reinstate

rejaillir [ʀəʒajiʀ] vi to splash up; **rejaillir sur** to splash up onto; (fig) to rebound on; to fall upon

rejet [ʀəʒɛ] nm (action, aussi MÉD) rejection; (POÉSIE) enjambement, reject; (BOT) shoot

rejeter [ʀəʒte] vt (relancer) to throw back; (vomir) to bring ou throw up; (écarter) to reject; (déverser) to throw out, discharge; (reporter): **rejeter un mot à la fin d'une phrase** to transpose a word to the end of a sentence; **se rejeter sur qch** (accepter faute de mieux) to fall back on sth; **rejeter la tête/les épaules en arrière** to throw one's head/pull one's shoulders back; **rejeter la responsabilité de qch sur qn** to lay the responsibility for sth at sb's door

rejoindre [ʀəʒwɛ̃dʀ(ə)] vt (famille, régiment) to rejoin, return to; (lieu) to get (back) to; (suj: route etc) to meet, join; (rattraper) to catch up (with); **se rejoindre** vi to meet; **je te rejoins au café** I'll see ou meet you at the café

réjouir [ʀeʒwiʀ] vt to delight; **se réjouir** vi to be delighted; **se réjouir de qch/de faire** to be delighted about sth/to do; **se réjouir que** to be delighted that

réjouissances [reʒwisɑ̃s] *nfpl* (joie) rejoicing *sg*; (fête) festivities, merry-making *sg*

relâche [rəlɑʃ]: **faire relâche** *vi* (navire) to put into port; (CINÉ) to be closed; **c'est le jour de relâche** it's closed today; **sans relâche** *adv* without respite *ou* a break

relâché, e [rəlɑʃe] *adj* loose, lax

relâcher [rəlɑʃe] *vt* (ressort, prisonnier) to release; (étreinte, cordes) to loosen; (discipline) to relax ♦ *vi* (NAVIG) to put into port; **se relâcher** *vi* to loosen; (discipline) to become slack *ou* lax; (élève etc) to slacken off

relais [rəlɛ] *nm* (SPORT): **(course de) relais** relay (race); (RADIO, TV) relay; (intermédiaire) go-between; **équipe de relais** shift team; (SPORT) relay team; **prendre le relais (de)** to take over (from); **relais de poste** post house, coaching inn; **relais routier** = transport café (BRIT), = truck stop (US)

relancer [rəlɑ̃se] *vt* (balle) to throw back (again); (moteur) to restart; (fig) to boost, revive; (personne): **relancer qn** to pester sb; to get on to sb again

relatif, ive [rəlatif, -iv] *adj* relative

relation [rəlɑsjɔ̃] *nf* (récit) account, report; (rapport) relation(ship); **relations** *nfpl* (rapports) relations; relationship; (connaissances) connections; **être/entrer en relation(s) avec** to be in contact *ou* be dealing/get in contact with; **mettre qn en relation(s) avec** to put sb in touch with; **relations internationales** international relations; **relations publiques (RP)** public relations (PR); **relations (sexuelles)** sexual relations, (sexual) intercourse *sg*

relaxer [rəlakse] *vt* to relax; (JUR) to discharge; **se relaxer** *vi* to relax

relayer [rəleje] *vt* (collaborateur, coureur etc) to relieve, take over from; (RADIO, TV) to relay; **se relayer** (dans une activité) to take it in turns

reléguer [rəlege] *vt* to relegate; **reléguer au second plan** to push into the background

relent(s) [rəlɑ̃] *nm(pl)* stench *sg*

relevé, e [rəlve] *adj* (bord de chapeau) turned-up; (manches) rolled-up; (fig: style) elevated; (: sauce) highly-seasoned ♦ *nm* (lecture) reading; (de cotes) plotting; (liste) statement; list; (facture) account; **relevé de compte** bank statement; **relevé d'identité bancaire (RIB)** (bank) account number

relève [rəlɛv] *nf* relief; (équipe) relief team (ou troops *pl*); **prendre la relève** to take over

relever [rəlve] *vt* (statue, meuble) to stand up again; (personne tombée) to help up; (vitre, plafond, niveau de vie) to raise; (pays, économie, entreprise) to put back on its feet; (col) to turn up; (style, conversation) to elevate; (plat, sauce) to season; (sentinelle, équipe) to relieve; (souligner: fautes, points) to pick out; (constater: traces etc) to find, pick up; (répliquer à: remarque) to react to, reply to; (: défi) to accept, take up; (noter: adresse etc) to take down, note;

(: plan) to sketch; (: cotes etc) to plot; (compteur) to read; (ramasser: cahiers, copies) to collect, take in ♦ *vi* (jupe, bord) to ride up; **relever de** *vt* (maladie) to be recovering from; (être du ressort de) to be a matter for; (ADMIN: dépendre de) to come under; (fig) to pertain to; **se relever** *vi* (se remettre debout) to get up; (fig): **se relever (de)** to recover (from); **relever qn de** (vœux) to release sb from; (fonctions) to relieve sb of; **relever la tête** to look up; to hold up one's head

relief [rəljɛf] *nm* relief; (de pneu) tread pattern; **reliefs** *nmpl* (restes) remains; **en relief** in relief; (photographie) three-dimensional; **mettre en relief** (fig) to bring out, highlight

relier [rəlje] *vt* to link up; (livre) to bind; **relier qch à** to link sth to; **livre relié cuir** leather-bound book

religieux, euse [rəliʒjø, -øz] *adj* religious ♦ *nm* monk ♦ *nf* nun; (gâteau) cream bun

religion [rəliʒjɔ̃] *nf* religion; (piété, dévotion) faith; **entrer en religion** to take one's vows

relire [rəlir] *vt* (à nouveau) to reread, read again; (vérifier) to read over; **se relire** to read through what one has written

reliure [rəljyr] *nf* binding; (art, métier): **la reliure** book-binding

reluire [rəlɥir] *vi* to gleam

remanier [rəmanje] *vt* to reshape, recast; (POL) to reshuffle

remarquable [rəmarkabl(ə)] *adj* remarkable

remarque [rəmark(ə)] *nf* remark; (écrite) note

remarquer [rəmarke] *vt* (voir) to notice; (dire): **remarquer que** to remark that; **se remarquer** to be noticeable; **se faire remarquer** to draw attention to o.s.; **faire remarquer (à qn) que** to point out (to sb) that; **faire remarquer qch (à qn)** to point sth out (to sb); **remarquez, ...** mark you, ..., mind you, ...

rembourrer [rɑ̃bure] *vt* to stuff; (dossier, vêtement, souliers) to pad

remboursement [rɑ̃bursəmɑ̃] *nm* repayment; **envoi contre remboursement** cash on delivery

rembourser [rɑ̃burse] *vt* to pay back, repay

remède [rəmɛd] *nm* (médicament) medicine; (traitement, fig) remedy, cure; **trouver un remède à** (MÉD, fig) to find a cure for

remémorer [rəmemɔre]: **se remémorer** *vt* to recall, recollect

remerciements [rəmɛrsimɑ̃] *nmpl* thanks; **(avec) tous mes remerciements** (with) grateful *ou* many thanks

remercier [rəmɛrsje] *vt* to thank; (congédier) to dismiss; **remercier qn de/d'avoir fait** to thank sb for/for having done; **non, je vous remercie** no thank you

remettre [rəmɛtr(ə)] *vt* (vêtement): **remettre qch** to put sth back on, put sth on again; (replacer): **remettre qch quelque part** to put sth back somewhere; (ajouter): **remettre du sel/un sucre** to add more salt/another lump of sugar; (*rétablir: personne*): **remettre qn** to set sb back on his (*ou* her) feet; (*rendre, restituer*): **remettre qch à qn** to give sth back to sb, return sth to sb; (*donner, confier: paquet, argent*): **remettre qch à qn** to hand sth over to sb, deliver sth to sb; (*prix, décoration*): **remettre qch à qn** to present sb with sth; (*ajourner*): **remettre qch (à)** to postpone sth *ou* put sth off (until); **se remettre** *vi* to get better, recover; **se remettre de** to recover from, get over; **s'en remettre à** to leave it (up) to; **se remettre à faire/qch** to start doing/sth again; **remettre une pendule à l'heure** to put a clock right; **remettre un moteur/une machine en marche** to get an engine/a machine going again; **remettre en état/en ordre** to repair/sort out; **remettre en cause/question** to challenge/question again; **remettre sa démission** to hand in one's notice; **remettre qch à neuf** to make sth as good as new; **remettre qn à sa place** (*fig*) to put sb in his (*ou* her) place

remis, e [Rəmi, -iz] *pp de* **remettre** ♦ *nf* delivery; presentation; (*rabais*) discount; (*local*) shed; **remis en marche/en ordre** starting up again/sorting out; **remis en cause/question** calling into question/challenging; **remis de fonds** remittance; **remis en jeu** (*FOOTBALL*) throw-in; **remis à neuf** restoration; **remis de peine** remission of sentence

remontant [Rəmɔ̃tɑ̃] *nm* tonic, pick-me-up

remonte-pente [Rəmɔ̃tpɑ̃t] *nm* ski lift, (ski) tow

remonter [Rəmɔ̃te] *vi* (*à nouveau*) to go back up; (*sur un cheval*) to remount; (*après une descente*) to go up (again); (*dans une voiture*) to get back in; (*jupe*) to ride up ♦ *vt* (*pente*) to go up; (*fleuve*) to sail (*ou* swim *etc*) up; (*manches, pantalon*) to roll up; (*col*) to turn up; (*niveau, limite*) to raise; (*fig: personne*) to buck up; (*moteur, meuble*) to put back together, reassemble; (*garde-robe etc*) to renew, replenish; (*montre, mécanisme*) to wind up; **remonter le moral à qn** to raise sb's spirits; **remonter à** (*dater de*) to date *ou* go back to; **remonter en voiture** to get back into the car

remontrance [Rəmɔ̃tRɑ̃s] *nf* reproof, reprimand

remontrer [Rəmɔ̃tRe] *vt* (*montrer de nouveau*): **remontrer qch (à qn)** to show sth again (to sb); (*fig*): **en remontrer à** to prove one's superiority over

remords [Rəmɔʀ] *nm* remorse *no pl*; **avoir des remords** to feel remorse, be conscience-stricken

remorque [Rəmɔʀk(ə)] *nf* trailer; **prendre/être en remorque** to tow/be on tow; **être à la remorque** (*fig*) to tag along (behind)

remorquer [Rəmɔʀke] *vt* to tow

remorqueur [Rəmɔʀkœʀ] *nm* tug(boat)

remous [Rəmu] *nm* (*d'un navire*) (back)wash *no pl*; (*de rivière*) swirl, eddy ♦ *nmpl* (*fig*) stir *sg*

remparts [Rɑ̃paʀ] *nmpl* walls, ramparts

remplaçant, e [Rɑ̃plasɑ̃, -ɑ̃t] *nm/f* replacement, substitute, stand-in; (*THÉÂT*) understudy; (*SCOL*) supply (*BRIT*) *ou* substitute (*US*) teacher

remplacement [Rɑ̃plasmɑ̃] *nm* replacement; (*job*) replacement work *no pl*; (*suppléance: SCOL*) supply (*BRIT*) *ou* substitute (*US*) teacher; **assurer le remplacement de qn** (*suj: remplaçant*) to stand in *ou* substitute for sb; **faire des remplacements** (*professeur*) to do supply *ou* substitute teaching; (*médecin*) to do locum work

remplacer [Rɑ̃plase] *vt* to replace; (*prendre temporairement la place de*) to stand in for; (*tenir lieu de*) to take the place of, act as a substitute for; **remplacer qch/qn par** to replace sth/sb with

rempli, e [Rɑ̃pli] *adj* (*emploi du temps*) full, busy; **rempli de** full of, filled with

remplir [Rɑ̃pliʀ] *vt* to fill (up); (*questionnaire*) to fill out *ou* up; (*obligations, fonction, condition*) to fulfil; **se remplir** *vi* to fill up; **remplir qch de** to fill sth with

remporter [Rɑ̃pɔʀte] *vt* (*marchandise*) to take away; (*fig*) to win, achieve

remuant, e [Rəmɥɑ̃, -ɑ̃t] *adj* restless

remue-ménage [Rəmymenaʒ] *nm inv* commotion

remuer [Rəmɥe] *vt* to move; (*café, sauce*) to stir ♦ *vi* to move; (*fig: opposants*) to show signs of unrest; **se remuer** *vi* to move; (*se démener*) to stir o.s.; (*fam*) to get a move on

rémunérer [Remyneʀe] *vt* to remunerate, pay

renard [Rənaʀ] *nm* fox

renchérir [Rɑ̃ʃeʀiʀ] *vi* to become more expensive; (*fig*): **renchérir (sur)** to add something (to)

rencontre [Rɑ̃kɔ̃tʀ(ə)] *nf* (*de cours d'eau*) confluence; (*de véhicules*) collision; (*entrevue, congrès, match etc*) meeting; (*imprévue*) encounter; **faire la rencontre de qn** to meet sb; **aller à la rencontre de qn** to go and meet sb; **amours de rencontre** casual love affairs

rencontrer [Rɑ̃kɔ̃tʀe] *vt* to meet; (*mot, expression*) to come across; (*difficultés*) to meet with; **se rencontrer** to meet; (*véhicules*) to collide

rendement [Rɑ̃dmɑ̃] *nm* (*d'un travailleur, d'une machine*) output; (*d'une culture*) yield; (*d'un investissement*) return; **à plein rendement** at full capacity

rendez-vous [Rɑ̃devu] *nm* (*rencontre*) appointment; (: *d'amoureux*) date; (*lieu*) meeting place; **donner rendez-vous à qn** to arrange to meet sb; **recevoir sur rendez-vous** to have an appointment system; **fixer un rendez-vous à qn** to give sb an appointment; **avoir/prendre rendez-vous (avec)** to have/make an appointment (with); **prendre rendez-vous chez le médecin** to make an appointment with the doctor; **rendez-vous spatial** *ou* **orbital** docking (in space)

rendre [Rɑ̃dR(ə)] *vt* (*livre, argent etc*) to give back, return; (*otages, visite, politesse, JUR: verdict*) to return; (*honneurs*) to pay; (*sang, aliments*) to bring up; (*sons: suj: instrument*) to produce, make; (*exprimer, traduire*) to render; (*jugement*) to pronounce, render; (*faire devenir*): **rendre qn célèbre/qch possible** to make sb famous/sth possible; **se rendre** *vi* (*capituler*) to surrender, give o.s. up; (*aller*): **se rendre quelque part** to go somewhere; **se rendre à** (*arguments etc*) to bow to; (*ordres etc*) to comply with; **se rendre compte de qch** to realize sth; **rendre la vue/la santé à qn** to restore sb's sight/health; **rendre la liberté à qn** to set sb free; **rendre la monnaie** to give change; **se rendre insupportable/malade** to become unbearable/make o.s. ill

rênes [ʀɛn] *nfpl* reins

renfermé, e [ʀɑ̃fɛʀme] *adj* (*fig*) withdrawn ♦ *nm*: **sentir le renfermé** to smell stuffy

renfermer [ʀɑ̃fɛʀme] *vt* to contain; **se renfermer (sur soi-même)** to withdraw into o.s.

renflouer [ʀɑ̃flue] *vt* to refloat; (*fig*) to set back on its (*ou* his/her *etc*) feet (again)

renfoncement [ʀɑ̃fɔ̃smɑ̃] *nm* recess

renforcer [ʀɑ̃fɔʀse] *vt* to reinforce; **renforcer qn dans ses opinions** to confirm sb's opinion

renfort [ʀɑ̃fɔʀ]: **renforts** *nmpl* reinforcements; **en renfort** as a back-up; **à grand renfort de** with a great deal of

renfrogné, e [ʀɑ̃fʀɔɲe] *adj* sullen, scowling

rengaine [ʀɑ̃gɛn] *nf* (*péj*) old tune

renier [ʀənje] *vt* (*parents*) to disown, repudiate; (*engagements*) to go back on; (*foi*) to renounce

renifler [ʀənifle] *vi* to sniff ♦ *vt* (*tabac*) to sniff up; (*odeur*) to sniff

renne [ʀɛn] *nm* reindeer *inv*

renom [ʀənɔ̃] *nm* reputation; (*célébrité*) renown; **vin de grand renom** celebrated *ou* highly renowned wine

renommé, e [ʀənɔme] *adj* celebrated, renowned ♦ *nf* fame

renoncer [ʀənɔ̃se] *vi*: **renoncer à** *vt* to give up; **renoncer à faire** to give up the idea of doing; **j'y renonce!** I give up!

renouer [ʀənwe] *vt* (*cravate etc*) to retie; (*fig: conversation, liaison*) to renew, resume; **renouer avec** (*tradition*) to revive; (*habitude*) to take up again; **renouer avec qn** to take up with sb again

renouvelable [ʀ(ə)nuvlabl(ə)] *adj* (*contrat, bail*) renewable; (*expérience*) which can be renewed

renouveler [ʀənuvle] *vt* to renew; (*exploit, méfait*) to repeat; **se renouveler** *vi* (*incident*) to recur, happen again, be repeated; (*cellules etc*) to be renewed *ou* replaced; (*artiste, écrivain*) to try something new

renouvellement [ʀ(ə)nuvɛlmɑ̃] *nm* renewal; recurrence

rénover [ʀenɔve] *vt* (*immeuble*) to renovate, do up; (*meuble*) to restore; (*enseignement*) to reform; (*quartier*) to redevelop

renseignement [ʀɑ̃sɛɲmɑ̃] *nm* information *no pl*, piece of information; (*MIL*) intelligence *no pl*; **prendre des renseignements sur** to make inquiries about, ask for information about;

(guichet des) renseignements information desk; **(service des) renseignements** (*TÉL*) directory inquiries (*BRIT*), information (*US*); **service de renseignements** (*MIL*) intelligence service; **les renseignements généraux** = the secret police

renseigner [ʀɑ̃seɲe] *vt*: **renseigner qn (sur)** to give information to sb (about); **se renseigner** *vi* to ask for information, make inquiries

rentabilité [ʀɑ̃tabilite] *nf* profitability; cost-effectiveness; (*d'un investissement*) return; **seuil de rentabilité** break-even point

rentable [ʀɑ̃tabl(ə)] *adj* profitable; cost-effective

rente [ʀɑ̃t] *nf* income; (*pension*) pension; (*titre*) government stock *ou* bond; **rente viagère** life annuity

rentrée [ʀɑ̃tʀe] *nf*: **rentrée (d'argent)** cash *no pl* coming in; **la rentrée (des classes)** the start of the new school year; **la rentrée (parlementaire)** the reopening *ou* reassembly of parliament; **faire sa rentrée** (*artiste, acteur*) to make a comeback; *see boxed note*

RENTRÉE

La **rentrée (des classes)** in September each year is more than going back to school for children and teachers. It is also the time when political and social life begin again after the long summer break, and it thus marks an important point in the French year.

---

rentrer [ʀɑ̃tʀe] *vi* (*entrer de nouveau*) to go (*ou* come) back in; (*entrer*) to go (*ou* come) in; (*revenir chez soi*) to go (*ou* come) (back) home; (*air, clou: pénétrer*) to go in; (*revenu, argent*) to come in ♦ *vt* (*foins*) to bring in; (*véhicule*) to put away; (*chemise dans pantalon etc*) to tuck in; (*griffes*) to draw in; (*train d'atterrissage*) to raise; (*fig: larmes, colère etc*) to hold back; **rentrer le ventre** to pull in one's stomach; **rentrer dans** to go (*ou* come) back into; to go (*ou* come) into; (*famille, patrie*) to go back *ou* return to; (*heurter*) to crash into; (*appartenir à*) to be included in; (: *catégorie etc*) to fall into; **rentrer dans l'ordre** to get back to normal; **rentrer dans ses frais** to recover one's expenses (*ou* initial outlay)

renverse [ʀɑ̃vɛʀs(ə)]: **à la renverse** *adv* backwards

renverser [ʀɑ̃vɛʀse] *vt* (*faire tomber: chaise, verre*) to knock over, overturn; (*piéton*) to knock down; (*liquide, contenu*) to spill, upset; (*retourner: verre, image*) to turn upside down, invert; (: *ordre des mots etc*) to reverse; (*fig: gouvernement etc*) to overthrow; (*stupéfier*) to bowl over, stagger; **se renverser** *vi* to fall over; to overturn; to spill; **se renverser (en arrière)** to lean back; **renverser la tête/le corps (en arrière)** to tip one's head back/throw oneself back; **renverser la vapeur** (*fig*) to change course

renvoi [ʀɑ̃vwa] *nm* dismissal; return; reflection;

postponement; (*référence*) cross-reference; (*éructation*) belch

renvoyer [ʀɑ̃vwaje] *vt* to send back; (*congédier*) to dismiss; (*TENNIS*) to return; (*lumière*) to reflect; (*son*) to echo; (*ajourner*): **renvoyer qch (à)** to postpone sth (until); **renvoyer qch à qn** (*rendre*) to return sth to sb; **renvoyer qn à** (*fig*) to refer sb to

repaire [ʀəpɛʀ] *nm* den

répandre [ʀepɑ̃dʀ(ə)] *vt* (*renverser*) to spill; (*étaler, diffuser*) to spread; (*lumière*) to shed; (*chaleur, odeur*) to give off; **se répandre** *vi* to spill; to spread; **se répandre en** (*injures etc*) to pour out

répandu, e [ʀepɑ̃dy] *pp de* **répandre** ♦ *adj* (*opinion, usage*) widespread

réparateur, trice [ʀepaʀatœʀ, -tʀis] *nm/f* repairer

réparation [ʀepaʀasjɔ̃] *nf* repairing *no pl*, repair; **en réparation** (*machine etc*) under repair; **demander à qn réparation de** (*offense etc*) to ask sb to make amends for

réparer [ʀepaʀe] *vt* to repair; (*fig: offense*) to make up for, atone for; (*: oubli, erreur*) to put right

repartie [ʀəpaʀti] *nf* retort; **avoir de la repartie** to be quick at repartee

repartir [ʀəpaʀtiʀ] *vi* to set off again; to leave again; (*fig*) to get going again, pick up again; **repartir à zéro** to start from scratch (again)

répartir [ʀepaʀtiʀ] *vt* (*pour attribuer*) to share out; (*pour disperser, disposer*) to divide up; (*poids, chaleur*) to distribute; (*étaler: dans le temps*): **répartir sur** to spread over; (*classer, diviser*): **répartir en** to divide into, split up into; **se répartir** *vt* (*travail, rôles*) to share out between themselves

répartition [ʀepaʀtisjɔ̃] *nf* sharing out; dividing up; distribution

repas [ʀəpa] *nm* meal; **à l'heure des repas** at mealtimes

repassage [ʀəpɑsaʒ] *nm* ironing

repasser [ʀəpɑse] *vi* to come (*ou* go) back ♦ *vt* (*vêtement, tissu*) to iron; (*examen*) to retake, resit; (*film*) to show again; (*lame*) to sharpen; (*leçon, rôle: revoir*) to go over (again); (*plat, pain*): **repasser qch à qn** to pass sth back to sb

repêcher [ʀəpeʃe] *vt* (*noyé*) to recover the body of, fish out; (*fam: candidat*) to pass (*by inflating marks*); to give a second chance to

repentir [ʀəpɑ̃tiʀ] *nm* repentance; **se repentir** *vi*: **se repentir (de)** to repent (of)

répercussions [ʀepɛʀkysjɔ̃] *nfpl* repercussions

répercuter [ʀepɛʀkyte] *vt* (*réfléchir, renvoyer: son, voix*) to reflect; (*faire transmettre: consignes, charges etc*) to pass on; **se répercuter** *vi* (*bruit*) to reverberate; (*fig*): **se répercuter sur** to have repercussions on

repère [ʀəpɛʀ] *nm* mark; (*monument etc*) landmark; **(point de) repère** point of reference

repérer [ʀəpeʀe] *vt* (*erreur, connaissance*) to spot; (*abri, ennemi*) to locate; **se repérer** *vi* to get one's

bearings; **se faire repérer** to be spotted

répertoire [ʀepɛʀtwaʀ] *nm* (*liste*) (alphabetical) list; (*carnet*) index notebook; (*INFORM*) directory; (*de carnet*) thumb index; (*indicateur*) directory, index; (*d'un théâtre, artiste*) repertoire

répéter [ʀepete] *vt* to repeat; (*préparer: leçon: aussi vi*) to learn, go over; (*THÉÂT*) to rehearse; **se répéter** (*redire*) to repeat o.s.; (*se reproduire*) to be repeated, recur

répétition [ʀepetisjɔ̃] *nf* repetition; (*THÉÂT*) rehearsal; **répétitions** *nfpl* (*leçons*) private coaching *sg*; **armes à répétition** repeater weapons; **répétition générale** final dress rehearsal

répit [ʀepi] *nm* respite; **sans répit** without letting up

replier [ʀəplije] *vt* (*rabattre*) to fold down *ou* over; **se replier** *vi* (*troupes, armée*) to withdraw, fall back; **se replier sur soi-même** to withdraw into oneself

réplique [ʀeplik] *nf* (*repartie, fig*) reply; (*objection*) retort; (*THÉÂT*) line; (*copie*) replica; **donner la réplique à** to play opposite; **sans réplique** *adj* nononsense; irrefutable

répliquer [ʀeplike] *vi* to reply; (*avec impertinence*) to answer back; (*riposter*) to retaliate

répondeur [ʀepɔ̃dœʀ] *nm* answering machine

répondre [ʀepɔ̃dʀ(ə)] *vi* to reply, answer; (*freins, mécanisme*) to respond; **répondre à** *vt* to reply to, answer; (*avec impertinence*): **répondre à qn** to answer sb back; (*invitation, convocation*) to reply to; (*affection, salut*) to return; (*provocation: suj: mécanisme etc*) to respond to; (*correspondre à: besoin*) to answer; (*: conditions*) to meet; (*: description*) to match; **répondre que** to answer *ou* reply that; **répondre de** to answer for

réponse [ʀepɔ̃s] *nf* answer, reply; **avec réponse payée** (*POSTES*) reply-paid, post-paid (*US*); **avoir réponse à tout** to have an answer for everything; **en réponse à** in reply to; **carte-/bulletin-réponse** reply card/slip

reportage [ʀəpɔʀtaʒ] *nm* (*bref*) report; (*écrit: documentaire*) story; article; (*en direct*) commentary; (*genre, activité*): **le reportage** reporting

reporter *nm* [ʀəpɔʀtɛʀ] reporter ♦ *vt* [ʀəpɔʀte] (*total*): **reporter qch sur** to carry sth forward *ou* over to; (*ajourner*): **reporter qch (à)** to postpone sth (until); (*transférer*): **reporter qch sur** to transfer sth to; **se reporter à** (*époque*) to think back to; (*document*) to refer to

repos [ʀəpo] *nm* rest; (*fig*) peace (and quiet); (*mental*) peace of mind; (*MIL*): **repos!** (stand) at ease!; **en repos** at rest; **au repos** at rest; (*soldat*) at ease; **de tout repos** safe

reposant, e [ʀ(ə)pozɑ̃, -ɑ̃t] *adj* restful; (*sommeil*) refreshing

reposer [ʀəpoze] *vt* (*verre, livre*) to put down; (*rideaux, carreaux*) to put back; (*délasser*) to rest; (*problème*) to reformulate ♦ *vi* (*liquide, pâte*) to settle, rest; (*personne*): **ici repose ...** here lies ...

reposer sur to be built on; (*fig*) to rest on; **se reposer** *vi* to rest; **se reposer sur qn** to rely on sb

repoussant, e [ʀəpusɑ̃, -ɑ̃t] *adj* repulsive

repousser [ʀəpuse] *vi* to grow again ♦ *vt* to repel, repulse; (*offre*) to turn down, reject; (*tiroir, personne*) to push back; (*différer*) to put back

reprendre [ʀəpʀɑ̃dʀ(ə)] *vt* (*prisonnier, ville*) to recapture; (*objet prêté, donné*) to take back; (*chercher*): **je viendrai te reprendre à 4 h** I'll come and fetch you *ou* I'll come back for you at 4; (*se resservir de*): **reprendre du pain/un œuf** to take (*ou* eat) more bread/another egg; (*COMM: article usagé*) to take back; to take in part exchange; (*firme, entreprise*) to take over; (*travail, promenade*) to resume; (*emprunter: argument, idée*) to take up, use; (*refaire: article etc*) to go over again; (*jupe etc*) to alter; (*émission, pièce*) to put on again; (*réprimander*) to tell off; (*corriger*) to correct ♦ *vi* (*classes, pluie*) to start (up) again; (*activités, travaux, combats*) to resume, start (up) again; (*affaires, industrie*) to pick up; (*dire*): **reprit-il** he went on; **se reprendre** (*se ressaisir*) to recover, pull o.s. together; **s'y reprendre** to make another attempt; **reprendre des forces** to recover one's strength; **reprendre courage** to take new heart; **reprendre ses habitudes/sa liberté** to get back into one's old habits/regain one's freedom; **reprendre la route** to resume one's journey, set off again; **reprendre connaissance** to come to, regain consciousness; **reprendre haleine** *ou* **son souffle** to get one's breath back; **reprendre la parole** to speak again

représailles [ʀəpʀezɑj] *nfpl* reprisals, retaliation *sg*

représentant, e [ʀəpʀezɑ̃tɑ̃, -ɑ̃t] *nm/f* representative

représentation [ʀəpʀezɑ̃tasjɔ̃] *nf* representation; performing; (*symbole, image*) representation; (*spectacle*) performance; (*COMM*): **la représentation** commercial travelling; sales representation; **frais de représentation** (*d'un diplomate*) entertainment allowance

représenter [ʀəpʀezɑ̃te] *vt* to represent; (*donner: pièce, opéra*) to perform; **se représenter** *vt* (*se figurer*) to imagine; to visualize ♦ *vi*: **se représenter à** (*POL*) to stand *ou* run again at; (*SCOL*) to resit

répression [ʀepʀesjɔ̃] *nf* (*voir réprimer*) suppression; repression; (*POL*): **la répression** repression; **mesures de répression** repressive measures

réprimer [ʀepʀime] *vt* (*émotions*) to suppress; (*peuple etc*) repress

repris, e [ʀəpʀi, -iz] *pp* de **reprendre** ♦ *nm*: **repris de justice** ex-prisoner, ex-convict

reprise [ʀəpʀiz] *nf* (*recommencement*) resumption; (*économique*) recovery; (*TV*) repeat; (*CINE*) rerun; (*BOXE etc*) round; (*AUTO*) acceleration *no pl*; (*COMM*) trade-in, part exchange; (*de location*) sum asked for any extras or improvements made to the property; (*raccommodage*) darn; mend; **la reprise des hostilités** the resumption of hostilities; **à plusieurs**

reprises on several occasions, several times

repriser [ʀəpʀize] *vt* to darn; to mend; **aiguille/coton à repriser** darning needle/thread

reproche [ʀəpʀɔʃ] *nm* (*remontrance*) reproach; **ton/air de reproche** reproachful tone/look; **faire des reproches à qn** to reproach sb; **faire reproche à qn de qch** to reproach sb for sth; **sans reproche(s)** beyond *ou* above reproach

reprocher [ʀəpʀɔʃe] *vt*: **reprocher qch à qn** to reproach *ou* blame sb for sth; **reprocher qch à** (*machine, théorie*) to have sth against; **se reprocher qch/d'avoir fait qch** to blame o.s. for sth/for doing sth

reproduction [ʀəpʀɔdyksjɔ̃] *nf* reproduction; **reproduction interdite** all rights (of reproduction) reserved

reproduire [ʀəpʀɔdɥiʀ] *vt* to reproduce; **se reproduire** *vi* (*BIO*) to reproduce; (*recommencer*) to recur, re-occur

réprouver [ʀepʀuve] *vt* to reprove

reptile [ʀɛptil] *nm* reptile

repu, e [ʀəpy] *pp'de* **repaître** ♦ *adj* satisfied, sated

république [ʀepyblik] *nf* republic; **République arabe du Yémen** Yemen Arab Republic; **République Centrafricaine** Central African Republic; **République de Corée** South Korea; **République démocratique allemande (RDA)** German Democratic Republic (GDR); **République dominicaine** Dominican Republic; **République fédérale d'Allemagne (RFA)** Federal Republic of Germany (FRG); **République d'Irlande** Irish Republic, Eire; **République populaire de Chine** People's Republic of China; **République populaire démocratique de Corée** Democratic People's Republic of Korea; **République populaire du Yémen** People's Democratic Republic of Yemen

répugnant, e [ʀepyɲɑ̃, -ɑ̃t] *adj* repulsive, loathsome

répugner [ʀepyɲe]: **répugner à** *vt*: **répugner à qn** to repel *ou* disgust sb; **répugner à faire** to be loath *ou* reluctant to do

réputation [ʀepytasjɔ̃] *nf* reputation; **avoir la réputation d'être ...** to have a reputation for being ...; **connaître qn/qch de réputation** to know sb/sth by repute; **de réputation mondiale** world-renowned

réputé, e [ʀepyte] *adj* renowned; **être réputé pour** to have a reputation for, be renowned for

requérir [ʀəkeʀiʀ] *vt* (*nécessiter*) to require, call for; (*au nom de la loi*) to call upon; (*JUR: peine*) to call for, demand

requête [ʀəkɛt] *nf* request, petition; (*JUR*) petition

requin [ʀəkɛ̃] *nm* shark

requis, e [ʀəki, -iz] *pp* de **requérir** ♦ *adj* required

RER *sigle m* (= *Réseau express régional*) Greater Paris high speed train service

rescapé, e [ʀɛskape] *nm/f* survivor

rescousse [ʀɛskus] *nf*: **aller à la rescousse de qn**

to go to sb's aid *ou* rescue; **appeler qn à la rescousse** to call on sb for help

réseau, x [ʀezo] *nm* network

réservation [ʀezεʀvasjɔ̃] *nf* reservation; booking

réserve [ʀezεʀv(ə)] *nf* (*retenue*) reserve; (*entrepôt*) storeroom; (*restriction, aussi: d'Indiens*) reservation; (*de pêche, chasse*) preserve; (*restrictions*): **faire des réserves** to have reservations; **officier de réserve** reserve officer; **sous toutes réserves** with all reserve; (*dire*) with reservations; **sous réserve de** subject to; **sans réserve** *adv* unreservedly; **en réserve** in reserve; **de réserve** (*provisions etc*) in reserve

réservé, e [ʀezεʀve] *adj* (*discret*) reserved; (*chasse, pêche*) private; **réservé à** *ou* **pour** reserved for

réserver [ʀezεʀve] *vt* (*gén*) to reserve; (*chambre, billet etc*) to book, reserve; (*mettre de côté, garder*): **réserver qch pour** *ou* **à** to keep *ou* save sth for; **réserver qch à qn** to reserve (*ou* book) sth for sb; (*fig: destiner*) to have sth in store for sb; **se réserver le droit de faire** to reserve the right to do

réservoir [ʀezεʀvwaʀ] *nm* tank

résidence [ʀezidɑ̃s] *nf* residence; **résidence principale/secondaire** main/second home; **résidence universitaire** hall of residence; **(en) résidence surveillée** (under) house arrest

résidentiel, le [ʀezidɑ̃sjεl] *adj* residential

résider [ʀezide] *vi*: **résider à** *ou* **dans** *ou* **en** to reside in; **résider dans** (*fig*) to lie in

résidu [ʀezidy] *nm* residue *no pl*

résigner [ʀeziɲe] *vt* to relinquish, resign; **se résigner** *vi*: **se résigner (à qch/à faire)** to resign o.s. (to sth/to doing)

résilier [ʀezilje] *vt* to terminate

résistance [ʀezistɑ̃s] *nf* resistance; (*de réchaud, bouilloire: fil*) element

résistant, e [ʀezistɑ̃, -ɑ̃t] *adj* (*personne*) robust, tough; (*matériau*) strong, hard-wearing ♦ *nm/f* (*patriote*) Resistance worker *ou* fighter

résister [ʀeziste] *vi* to resist; **résister à** *vt* (*assaut, tentation*) to resist; (*effort, souffrance*) to withstand; (*suj: matériau, plante*) to stand up to, withstand; (*personne: désobéir à*) to stand up to, oppose

résolu, e [ʀezɔly] *pp* de **résoudre** ♦ *adj* (*ferme*) resolute; **être résolu à qch/faire** to be set upon sth/doing

résolution [ʀezɔlysjɔ̃] *nf* solving; (*fermeté, décision, INFORM*) resolution; **prendre la résolution de** to make a resolution to

résonner [ʀezɔne] *vi* (*cloche, pas*) to reverberate, resound; (*salle*) to be resonant; **résonner de** to resound with

résorber [ʀezɔʀbe]: **se résorber** *vi* (MÉD) to be resorbed; (*fig*) to be absorbed

résoudre [ʀezudʀ(ə)] *vt* to solve; **résoudre qn à faire qch** to get sb to make up his (*ou* her) mind to do sth; **résoudre de faire** to resolve to do; **se résoudre à faire** to bring o.s. to do

respect [ʀεspε] *nm* respect; **tenir en respect** to keep at bay

respecter [ʀεspεkte] *vt* to respect; **faire respecter** to enforce; **le lexicographe qui se respecte** (*fig*) any self-respecting lexicographer

respectueux, euse [ʀεspεktɥø, -øz] *adj* respectful; **respectueux de** respectful of

respiration [ʀεspiʀasjɔ̃] *nf* breathing *no pl*; **faire une respiration complète** to breathe in and out; **retenir sa respiration** to hold one's breath; **respiration artificielle** artificial respiration

respirer [ʀεspiʀe] *vi* to breathe; (*fig: se reposer*) to get one's breath, have a break; (: *être soulagé*) to breathe again ♦ *vt* to breathe (in), inhale; (*manifester: santé, calme etc*) to exude

resplendir [ʀεsplɑ̃diʀ] *vi* to shine; (*fig*): **resplendir (de)** to be radiant (with)

responsabilité [ʀεspɔ̃sabilite] *nf* responsibility; (*légale*) liability; **refuser la responsabilité de** to deny responsibility (*ou* liability) for; **prendre ses responsabilités** to assume responsibility for one's actions; **responsabilité civile** civil liability; **responsabilité pénale/morale/collective** criminal/moral/collective responsibility

responsable [ʀεspɔ̃sabl(ə)] *adj* responsible ♦ *nm/f* (*du ravitaillement etc*) person in charge; (*de parti, syndicat*) official; **responsable de** responsible for; (*légalement: de dégâts etc*) liable for; (*chargé de*) in charge of, responsible for

resquiller [ʀεskije] *vi* (*au cinéma, au stade*) to get in on the sly; (*dans le train*) to fiddle a free ride

ressaisir [ʀəseziʀ]: **se ressaisir** *vi* to regain one's self-control; (*équipe sportive*) to rally

ressasser [ʀəsase] *vt* (*remâcher*) to keep turning over; (*redire*) to keep trotting out

ressemblance [ʀəsɑ̃blɑ̃s] *nf* (*visuelle*) resemblance, similarity, likeness; (: ART) likeness; (*analogie, trait commun*) similarity

ressemblant, e [ʀəsɑ̃blɑ̃, -ɑ̃t] *adj* (*portrait*) lifelike, true to life

ressembler [ʀəsɑ̃ble]: **ressembler à** *vt* to be like, resemble; (*visuellement*) to look like; **se ressembler** to be (*ou* look) alike

ressemeler [ʀəsəmle] *vt* to (re)sole

ressentiment [ʀəsɑ̃timɑ̃] *nm* resentment

ressentir [ʀəsɑ̃tiʀ] *vt* to feel; **se ressentir de** to feel (*ou* show) the effects of

resserrer [ʀəseʀe] *vt* (*pores*) to close; (*nœud, boulon*) to tighten (up); (*fig: liens*) to strengthen; **se resserrer** *vi* (*route, vallée*) to narrow; (*liens*) to strengthen; **se resserrer (autour de)** to draw closer (around); to close in (on)

resservir [ʀəseʀviʀ] *vi* to do *ou* serve again ♦ *vt*: **resservir qch (à qn)** to serve sth up again (to sb); **resservir de qch (à qn)** to give (sb) a second helping of sth; **resservir qn (d'un plat)** to give sb a second helping (of a dish); **se resservir de** (*plat*) to take a second helping of; (*outil etc*) to use again

ressort [ʀəsɔʀ] *vb voir* **ressortir** ♦ *nm* (*pièce*) spring; (*force morale*) spirit; (*recours*): **en dernier ressort** as a last resort; (*compétence*): **être du ressort de** to fall within the competence of

ressortir [ʀəsɔʀtiʀ] *vi* to go (*ou* come) out (again); (*contraster*) to stand out; **ressortir de** (*résulter de*): **il ressort de ceci que** it emerges from this that; **ressortir à** (*JUR*) to come under the jurisdiction of; (*ADMIN*) to be the concern of; **faire ressortir** (*fig: souligner*) to bring out

ressortissant, e [ʀəsɔʀtisɑ̃, -ɑ̃t] *nm/f* national

ressource [ʀəsuʀs(ə)] *nf*: **avoir la ressource de** to have the possibility of; **ressources** *nfpl* resources; (*fig*) possibilities; **leur seule ressource était de** the only course open to them was to: **ressources d'énergie** energy resources

ressusciter [ʀesysite] *vt* to resuscitate, restore to life; (*fig*) to revive, bring back ♦ *vi* to rise (from the dead); (*fig: pays*) to come back to life

restant, e [ʀɛstɑ̃, -ɑ̃t] *adj* remaining ♦ *nm*: **le restant (de)** the remainder of (of); **un restant de** (*de trop*) some leftover; (*fig: vestige*) a remnant *ou* last trace of

restaurant [ʀɛstɔʀɑ̃] *nm* restaurant; **manger au restaurant** to eat out; **restaurant d'entreprise** staff canteen *ou* cafeteria (*US*); **restaurant universitaire (RU)** university refectory *ou* cafeteria (*US*)

restauration [ʀɛstɔʀasjɔ̃] *nf* restoration; (*hôtellerie*) catering; **restauration rapide** fast food

restaurer [ʀɛstɔʀe] *vt* to restore; **se restaurer** *vi* to have something to eat

reste [ʀɛst(ə)] *nm* (*restant*): **le reste (de)** the rest (of); (*de trop*): **un reste (de)** some leftover; (*vestige*): **un reste de** a remnant *ou* last trace of; (*MATH*) remainder; **restes** *nmpl* leftovers; (*d'une cité etc, dépouille mortelle*) remains; **avoir du temps de reste** to have time to spare; **ne voulant pas être en reste** not wishing to be outdone; **partir sans attendre *ou* demander son reste** (*fig*) to leave without waiting to hear more; **du reste, au reste** *adv* besides, moreover; **pour le reste, quant au reste** *adv* as for the rest

rester [ʀɛste] *vi* (*dans un lieu, un état, une position*) to stay, remain; (*subsister*) to remain, be left; (*durer*) to last, live on ♦ *vb impers*: **il reste du pain/2 œufs** there's some bread/there are 2 eggs left (over); **il reste du temps/10 minutes** there's some time/ there are 10 minutes left; **il me reste assez de temps** I have enough time left; **voilà tout ce qui (me) reste** that's all I've got left; **ce qui reste à faire** what remains to be done; **ce qui reste à faire** what remains for me to do; **(il) reste à savoir/établir si ...** it remains to be seen/established if *ou* whether ...; **il n'en reste pas moins que ...** the fact remains that ..., it's nevertheless a fact that ...; **en rester à** (*stade, menaces*) to go no further than, only go as far as; **restons-en là** let's leave it at that; **rester sur une impression** to retain an impression; **y rester: il a failli y rester** he

nearly met his end

restituer [ʀɛstitɥe] *vt* (*objet, somme*): **restituer qch (à qn)** to return *ou* restore sth (to sb); (*énergie*) to release; (*son*) to reproduce

restreindre [ʀɛstʀɛ̃dʀ(ə)] *vt* to restrict, limit; **se restreindre** (*dans ses dépenses etc*) to cut down; (*champ de recherches*) to narrow

restriction [ʀɛstʀiksjɔ̃] *nf* restriction; (*condition*) qualification; **restrictions** *nfpl* (*mentales*) reservations; **sans restriction** *adv* unreservedly

résultat [ʀezylta] *nm* result; (*conséquence*) outcome *no pl*, result; (*d'élection etc*) results *pl*; **résultats** *nmpl* (*d'une enquête*) findings; **résultats sportifs** sports results

résulter [ʀezylte]: **résulter de** *vt* to result from, be the result of; **il résulte de ceci que ...** the result of this is that ...

résumé [ʀezyme] *nm* summary, résumé; **faire le résumé de** to summarize; **en résumé** *adv* in brief; (*pour conclure*) to sum up

résumer [ʀezyme] *vt* (*texte*) to summarize; (*récapituler*) to sum up; (*fig*) to epitomize, typify; **se résumer** *vi* (*personne*) to sum up (one's ideas); **se résumer à** to come down to

résurrection [ʀezyʀɛksjɔ̃] *nf* resurrection; (*fig*) revival

rétablir [ʀetabliʀ] *vt* to restore, re-establish; (*personne: suj: traitement*): **rétablir qn** to restore sb to health, help sb recover; (*ADMIN*): **rétablir qn dans son emploi/ses droits** to reinstate sb in his post/ restore sb's rights; **se rétablir** *vi* (*guérir*) to recover; (*silence, calme*) to return, be restored; (*GYM etc*): **se rétablir (sur)** to pull o.s. up (onto)

rétablissement [ʀetablismɑ̃] *nm* restoring; recovery; pull-up

retaper [ʀətape] *vt* (*maison, voiture etc*) to do up; (*fam: revigorer*) to buck up; (*redactylographier*) to retype

retard [ʀətaʀ] *nm* (*d'une personne attendue*) lateness *no pl*; (*sur l'horaire, un programme, une échéance*) delay; (*fig: scolaire, mental etc*) backwardness; **être en retard** (*pays*) to be backward; (*dans paiement, travail*) to be behind; **en retard (de 2 heures)** (2 hours) late; **avoir un retard de 2 km** (*SPORT*) to be 2 km behind; **rattraper son retard** to catch up; **avoir du retard** to be late; (*sur un programme*) to be behind (schedule); **prendre du retard** (*train, avion*) to be delayed; (*montre*) to lose (time); **sans retard** *adv* without delay; **retard à l'allumage** (*AUTO*) retarded spark; **retard scolaire** backwardness at school

retardataire [ʀətaʀdatɛʀ] *adj* late; (*enfant, idées*) backward ♦ *nm/f* latecomer; backward child

retardement [ʀətaʀdəmɑ̃]: **à retardement** *adj* delayed action *cpd*; **bombe à retardement** time bomb

retarder [ʀətaʀde] *vt* (*sur un horaire*): **retarder qn (d'une heure)** to delay sb (an hour); (*sur un pro-*

gramme): **retarder qn (de 3 mois)** to set sb back ou delay sb (3 months); (départ, date): **retarder qch (de 2 jours)** to put sth back (2 days), delay sth (for ou by 2 days); (horloge) to put back ♦ vi (montre) to be slow; (: habituellement) to lose (time); **je retarde (d'une heure)** I'm (an hour) slow

retenir [ʀətniʀ] vt (garder, retarder) to keep, detain; (maintenir: objet qui glisse, fig: colère, larmes, rire) to hold back; (: objet suspendu) to hold; (: chaleur, odeur) to retain; (fig: empêcher d'agir): **retenir qn (de faire)** to hold sb back (from doing); (se rappeler) to retain; (réserver) to reserve; (accepter) to accept; (prélever): **retenir qch (sur)** to deduct sth (from); **se retenir** (euphémisme) to hold on; (se raccrocher): **se retenir à** to hold onto; (se contenir): **se retenir de faire** to restrain o.s. from doing; **retenir son souffle** ou **haleine** to hold one's breath; **retenir qn à dîner** to ask sb to stay for dinner; **je pose 3 et je retiens 2** put down 3 and carry 2

retentir [ʀətɑ̃tiʀ] vi to ring out; (salle): **retentir de** to ring ou resound with; **retentir sur** vt (fig) to have an effect upon

retentissant, e [ʀətɑ̃tisɑ̃, -ɑ̃t] adj resounding; (fig) impact-making

retentissement [ʀətɑ̃tismɑ̃] nm (retombées) repercussions pl; effect, impact

retenu, e [ʀətny] pp de **retenir** ♦ adj (place) reserved; (personne: empêché) held up; (propos: contenu, discret) restrained ♦ nf (prélèvement) deduction; (MATH) number to carry over; (SCOL) detention; (modération) (self-)restraint; (réserve) reserve, reticence; (AUTO) tailback

réticence [ʀetisɑ̃s] nf reticence no pl, reluctance no pl; **sans réticence** without hesitation

réticent, e [ʀetisɑ̃, -ɑ̃t] adj reticent, reluctant

rétine [ʀetin] nf retina

retiré, e [ʀətiʀe] adj (solitaire) secluded; (éloigné) remote

retirer [ʀətiʀe] vt to withdraw; (vêtement, lunettes) to take off, remove; (enlever): **retirer qch à qn** to take sth from sb; (extraire): **retirer qn/qch de** to take sb away from/sth out of, remove sb/sth from; (reprendre: bagages, billets) to collect, pick up; **retirer des avantages de** to derive advantages from; **se retirer** vi (partir, reculer) to withdraw; (prendre sa retraite) to retire; **se retirer de** to withdraw from; to retire from

retombées [ʀətɔ̃be] nfpl (radioactives) fallout sg; (fig) fallout; spin-offs

retomber [ʀətɔ̃be] vi (à nouveau) to fall again; (rechuter): **retomber malade/dans l'erreur** to fall ill again/fall back into error; (atterrir: après un saut etc) to land; (tomber, redescendre) to fall back; (pendre) to fall, hang (down); (échoir): **retomber sur qn** to fall on sb

rétorquer [ʀetɔʀke] vt: **rétorquer (à qn) que** to retort (to sb) that

retouche [ʀətuʃ] nf touching up no pl; alteration; **faire une retouche** ou **des retouches à** to touch up

retoucher [ʀətuʃe] vt (photographie, tableau) to touch up; (texte, vêtement) to alter

retour [ʀətuʀ] nm return; **au retour** (en arrivant) when we (ou they etc) get (ou got) back; (en route) on the way back; **pendant le retour** on the way ou journey back; **à mon/ton retour** on my/your return; **au retour de** on the return of; **être de retour (de)** to be back (from); **de retour à …/chez moi** back at …/back home; **en retour** adv in return; **par retour du courrier** by return of post; **par un juste retour des choses** by a favourable twist of fate; **match retour** return match; **retour en arrière** (CINE) flashback; (mesure) backward step; **retour de bâton** kickback; **retour de chariot** carriage return; **retour à l'envoyeur** (POSTES) return to sender; **retour de flamme** backfire; **retour (automatique) à la ligne** (INFORM) wordwrap; **retour de manivelle** (fig) backfire; **retour offensif** renewed attack; **retour aux sources** (fig) return to basics

retourner [ʀətuʀne] vt (dans l'autre sens: matelas, crêpe) to turn (over); (: caisse) to turn upside down; (: sac, vêtement) to turn inside out; (fig: argument) to turn back; (en remuant: terre, sol, foin) to turn over; (émouvoir: personne) to shake; (renvoyer, restituer): **retourner qch à qn** to return sth to sb ♦ vi (aller, revenir): **retourner quelque part/à** to go back ou return somewhere/to; **retourner à** (état, activité) to return to, go back to; (tourner la tête) to turn round; **s'en retourner** to go back; **se retourner contre** (fig) to turn against; **savoir de quoi il retourne** to know what it is all about; **retourner sa veste** (fig) to turn one's coat; **retourner en arrière** ou **sur ses pas** to turn back, retrace one's steps; **retourner aux sources** to go back to basics

retrait [ʀətʀɛ] nm voir **retirer** withdrawal; collection voir **se retirer** withdrawal; (rétrécissement) shrinkage; **en retrait** adj set back; **écrire en retrait** to indent; **retrait du permis (de conduire)** disqualification from driving (BRIT), revocation of driver's license (US)

retraite [ʀətʀɛt] nf (d'une armée, REL, refuge) retreat; (d'un employé) retirement; (revenu) (retirement) pension; **être/mettre à la retraite** to be retired/pension off ou retire; **prendre sa retraite** to retire; **retraite anticipée** early retirement; **retraite aux flambeaux** torchlight tattoo

retraité, e [ʀətʀete] adj retired ♦ nm/f (old age) pensioner

retrancher [ʀətʀɑ̃ʃe] vt (passage, détails) to take out, remove; (nombre, somme): **retrancher qch de** to take ou deduct sth from; (couper) to cut off; **se retrancher derrière/dans** to entrench o.s. behind/in; (fig) to take refuge behind/in

retransmettre [ʀətʀɑ̃smɛtʀ(ə)] vt (RADIO) to

broadcast, relay; (TV) to show

rétrécir [ʀetʀesiʀ] vt (vêtement) to take in ♦ vi to shrink; **se rétrécir** vi to narrow

rétribution [ʀetʀibysjɔ̃] nf payment

rétro [ʀetʀo] adj inv old-style ♦ nm (= rétroviseur) (rear-view) mirror; **la mode rétro** the nostalgia vogue

rétrograde [ʀetʀɔgʀad] adj reactionary, backward-looking

rétroprojecteur [ʀetʀopʀɔʒɛktœʀ] nm overhead projector

rétrospectif, ive [ʀetʀɔspɛktif, -iv] adj, nf retrospective

rétrospectivement [ʀetʀɔspɛktivmɑ̃] adv in retrospect

retrousser [ʀətʀuse] vt to roll up; (fig: nez) to wrinkle; (: lèvres) to curl

retrouvailles [ʀətʀuvaj] nfpl reunion sg

retrouver [ʀətʀuve] vt (fugitif, objet perdu) to find; (occasion) to find again; (calme, santé) to regain; (reconnaître: expression, style) to recognize; (revoir) to see again; (rejoindre) to meet (again), join; **se retrouver** vi to find one's way; (s'orienter) to find one's way; **se retrouver quelque part** to find o.s. somewhere; to end up somewhere; **se retrouver seul/sans argent** to find o.s. alone/with no money; **se retrouver dans** (calculs, dossiers, désordre) to make sense of; **s'y retrouver** (rentrer dans ses frais) to break even

rétroviseur [ʀetʀovizœʀ] nm (rear-view) mirror

réunion [ʀeynjɔ̃] nf bringing together; joining; (séance) meeting

réunir [ʀeyniʀ] vt (convoquer) to call together; (rassembler) to gather together; (cumuler) to combine; (rapprocher) to bring together (again), reunite; (rattacher) to join (together); **se réunir** vi (se rencontrer) to meet; (s'allier) to unite

réussi, e [ʀeysi] adj successful

réussir [ʀeysiʀ] vi to succeed, be successful; (à un examen) to pass; (plante, culture) to thrive, do well ♦ vt to make a success of; to bring off; **réussir à faire** to succeed in doing; **réussir à qn** to go right for sb; (aliment) to agree with sb; **le travail/le mariage lui réussit** work/married life agrees with him

réussite [ʀeysit] nf success; (CARTES) patience

revaloir [ʀəvalwaʀ] vt: **je vous revaudrai cela** I'll repay you some day; (en mal) I'll pay you back for this

revanche [ʀəvɑ̃ʃ] nf revenge; **prendre sa revanche (sur)** to take one's revenge (on); **en revanche** (par contre) on the other hand; (en compensation) in return

rêve [ʀɛv] nm dream; (activité psychique): **le rêve** dreaming; **paysage/silence de rêve** dreamlike landscape/silence; **rêve éveillé** daydreaming no pl, daydream

revêche [ʀəvɛʃ] adj surly, sour-tempered

réveil [ʀevɛj] nm (d'un dormeur) waking up no pl; (fig) awakening; (pendule) alarm (clock); **au réveil** when I (ou you etc) wake (ou woke) up, on waking (up); **sonner le réveil** (MIL) to sound the reveille

réveille-matin [ʀevɛjmatɛ̃] nm inv alarm clock

réveiller [ʀeveje] vt (personne) to wake up; (fig) to awaken, revive; **se réveiller** vi to wake up; (fig) to be revived, reawaken

réveillon [ʀevɛjɔ̃] nm Christmas Eve; (de la Saint-Sylvestre) New Year's Eve; Christmas Eve (ou New Year's Eve) party ou dinner

réveillonner [ʀevɛjɔne] vi to celebrate Christmas Eve (ou New Year's Eve)

révélateur, trice [ʀevelatœʀ, -tʀis] adj: **révélateur (de qch)** revealing (sth) ♦ nm (PHOTO) developer

révéler [ʀevele] vt (gén) to reveal; (divulguer) to disclose, reveal; (dénoter) to reveal, show; (faire connaître au public): **révéler qn/qch** to make sb/sth widely known, bring sb/sth to the public's notice; **se révéler** vi to be revealed, reveal itself ♦ vb avec attribut: **se révéler facile/faux** to prove (to be) easy/false; **se révéler cruel/un allié sûr** to show o.s. to be cruel/a trustworthy ally

revenant, e [ʀəvnɑ̃, -ɑ̃t] nm/f ghost

revendeur, euse [ʀəvɑ̃dœʀ, -øz] nm/f (détaillant) retailer; (d'occasions) secondhand dealer

revendication [ʀəvɑ̃dikasjɔ̃] nf claim, demand; **journée de revendication** day of action (in support of one's claims)

revendiquer [ʀəvɑ̃dike] vt to claim, demand; (responsabilité) to claim ♦ vi to agitate in favour of one's claims

revendre [ʀəvɑ̃dʀ(ə)] vt (d'occasion) to resell; (détailler) to sell; (vendre davantage de): **revendre du sucre/un foulard/deux bagues** to sell more sugar/another scarf/another two rings; **à revendre** adv (en abondance) to spare

revenir [ʀəvniʀ] vi to come back; (CULIN): **faire revenir** to brown; (coûter): **revenir cher/à 15 €** (à **qn)** to cost (sb) a lot/15 €; **revenir à** (études, projet) to return to, go back to; (équivaloir à) to amount to; **revenir à qn** (rumeur, nouvelle) to get back to sb, reach sb's ears; (part, honneur) to go to sb, be sb's; (souvenir, nom) to come back to sb; **revenir de** (fig: maladie, étonnement) to recover from; **revenir sur** (question, sujet) to go back over; (engagement) to go back on; **revenir à la charge** to return to the attack; **revenir à soi** to come round; **n'en pas revenir** : **je n'en reviens pas** I can't get over it; **revenir sur ses pas** to retrace one's steps; **cela revient à dire que/au même** it amounts to saying that/to the same thing; **revenir de loin** (fig) to have been at death's door

revenu, e [ʀəvny] pp de **revenir** ♦ nm income; (de l'État) revenue; (d'un capital) yield; **revenus** nmpl income sg; **revenu national brut** gross national income

rêver [Reve] *vi, vt* to dream; (*rêvasser*) to (day)dream; **rêver de** (*voir en rêve*) to dream of *ou* about; **rêver de qch/de faire** to dream of sth/of doing; **rêver à** to dream of

réverbère [ReveRbER] *nm* street lamp *ou* light

réverbérer [ReveRbere] *vt* to reflect

révérence [ReveRɑ̃s] *nf* (*vénération*) reverence; (*salut: d'homme*) bow; (: *de femme*) curtsey

rêverie [REvRi] *nf* daydreaming *no pl*, daydream

revers [RəveR] *nm* (*de feuille, main*) back; (*d'étoffe*) wrong side; (*de pièce, médaille*) back, reverse; (TENNIS, PING-PONG) backhand; (*de veston*) lapel; (*de pantalon*) turn-up; (*fig: échec*) setback; **revers de fortune** reverse of fortune; **d'un revers de main** with the back of one's hand; **le revers de la médaille** (*fig*) the other side of the coin; **prendre à revers** (MIL) to take from the rear

revêtement [RəvɛtmÃ] *nm* (*de paroi*) facing; (*des sols*) flooring; (*de chaussée*) surface; (*de tuyau etc: enduit*) coating

revêtir [Rəvetir] *vt* (*habit*) to don, put on; (*fig*) to take on; **revêtir qn de** to dress sb in; (*fig*) to endow *ou* invest sb with; **revêtir qch de** to cover sth with; (*fig*) to cloak sth in; **revêtir d'un visa** to append a visa to

rêveur, euse [REvœR, -øz] *adj* dreamy ♦ *nm/f* dreamer

revient [Rəvjɛ̃] *vb voir* **revenir** ♦ *nm*: **prix de revient** cost price

revigorer [RəvigɔRe] *vt* to invigorate, revive, buck up

revirement [RəviRmÃ] *nm* change of mind; (*d'une situation*) reversal

réviser [Revize] *vt* (*texte, SCOL: matière*) to revise; (*comptes*) to audit; (*machine, installation, moteur*) to overhaul, service; (JUR: *procès*) to review

révision [Revizjɔ̃] *nf* revision; auditing *no pl*; overhaul, servicing *no pl*; review; **conseil de révision** (MIL) recruiting board; **faire ses révisions** (SCOL) to do one's revision (BRIT), revise (BRIT), review (US); **la révision des 10 000 km** the 10,000 km service

revivre [RəvivR(ə)] *vi* (*reprendre des forces*) to come alive again; (*traditions*) to be revived ♦ *vt* (*épreuve, moment*) to relive; **faire revivre** (*mode, institution, usage*) to bring back to life

revoir [RəvwaR] *vt* to see again; (*réviser*) to revise (BRIT), review (US) ♦ *nm*: **au revoir** goodbye; **dire au revoir à qn** to say goodbye to sb; **se revoir** (*amis*) to meet (again), see each other again

révoltant, e [Revɔltɑ̃, -ɑ̃t] *adj* revolting

révolte [Revɔlt(ə)] *nf* rebellion, revolt

révolter [Revɔlte] *vt* to revolt, outrage; **se révolter** *vi*: **se révolter (contre)** to rebel (against); **se révolter (à)** to be outraged (by)

révolu, e [Revɔly] *adj* past; (ADMIN): **âgé de 18 ans révolus** over 18 years of age; **après 3 ans révolus** when 3 full years have passed

révolution [Revɔlysjɔ̃] *nf* revolution; **être en**

révolution (*pays etc*) to be in revolt; **la révolution industrielle** the industrial revolution

révolutionnaire [RevɔlysjɔnER] *adj, nm/f* revolutionary

revolver [RevɔlvER] *nm* gun; (*à barillet*) revolver

révoquer [Revɔke] *vt* (*fonctionnaire*) to dismiss, remove from office; (*arrêt, contrat*) to revoke

revu, e [Rəvy] *pp de* **revoir** ♦ *nf* (*inventaire, examen*) review; (MIL: *défilé*) review, march past; (: *inspection*) inspection, review; (*périodique*) review, magazine; (*pièce satirique*) revue; (*de music-hall*) variety show; **passer en revu** to review, inspect; (*fig*) to review; **revu de (la) presse** press review

rez-de-chaussée [Redʃose] *nm inv* ground floor

RF *sigle f* = **République française**

Rhin [Rɛ̃] *nm*: **le Rhin** the Rhine

rhinocéros [RinɔseRɔs] *nm* rhinoceros

Rhône [Ron] *nm*: **le Rhône** the Rhone

rhubarbe [Rybarb(ə)] *nf* rhubarb

rhum [Rɔm] *nm* rum

rhumatisme [Rymatism(ə)] *nm* rheumatism *no pl*

rhume [Rym] *nm* cold; **rhume de cerveau** head cold; **le rhume des foins** hay fever

ri [Ri] *pp de* **rire**

riant, e [Rjɑ̃, -ɑ̃t] *vb voir* **rire** ♦ *adj* smiling, cheerful; (*campagne, paysage*) pleasant

ricaner [Rikane] *vi* (*avec méchanceté*) to snigger; (*bêtement, avec gêne*) to giggle

riche [Riʃ] *adj* (*gén*) rich; (*personne, pays*) rich, wealthy; **riche en** rich in; **riche de** full of; rich in

richesse [Riʃes] *nf* wealth; (*fig*) richness; **richesses** *nfpl* wealth *sg*; treasures; **richesse en vitamines** high vitamin content

ricochet [Rikɔʃe] *nm* rebound; bounce; **faire ricochet** to rebound, bounce; (*fig*) to rebound; **faire des ricochets** to skip stones; **par ricochet** *adv* on the rebound; (*fig*) as an indirect result

rictus [Riktys] *nm* grin; (snarling) grimace

ride [Rid] *nf* wrinkle; (*fig*) ripple

rideau, x [Rido] *nm* curtain; **tirer/ouvrir les rideaux** to draw/open the curtains; **rideau de fer** metal shutter; (POL): **le rideau de fer** the Iron Curtain

rider [Ride] *vt* to wrinkle; (*fig*) to ripple, ruffle the surface of; **se rider** *vi* to become wrinkled

ridicule [Ridikyl] *adj* ridiculous ♦ *nm* ridiculousness *no pl*; **le ridicule** ridicule; (*travers: gén pl*) absurdities *pl*; **tourner en ridicule** to ridicule

ridiculiser [Ridikylize] *vt* to ridicule; **se ridiculiser** to make a fool of o.s.

| MOT CLÉ |

rien [Rjɛ̃] *pron* **1: (ne) ... rien** nothing; *tournure negative* + anything; **qu'est-ce que vous avez? – rien** what have you got? – nothing; **il n'a rien**

dit/fait he said/did nothing, he hasn't said/done anything; **il n'a rien** (*n'est pas blessé*) he's all right; **ça ne fait rien** it doesn't matter; **il n'y est pour rien** he's got nothing to do with it

2 (*quelque chose*): **a-t-il jamais rien fait pour nous?** has he ever done anything for us?

3: rien de: rien d'intéressant nothing interesting; **rien d'autre** nothing else; **rien du tout** nothing at all; **il n'a rien d'un champion** he's no champion, there's nothing of the champion about him

4: rien que just, only; nothing but; **rien que pour lui faire plaisir** only *ou* just to please him; **rien que la vérité** nothing but the truth; **rien que cela** that alone

♦ *excl*: **de rien!** not at all!, don't mention it!; **il n'en est rien!** nothing of the sort!; **rien à faire!** it's no good!, it's no use!

♦ *nm*: **un petit rien** (*cadeau*) a little something; **des riens** trivia *pl*; **un rien** a hint of; **en un rien de temps** in no time at all; **avoir peur d'un rien** to be frightened of the slightest thing

rieur, euse [ʀjœʀ, -øz] *adj* cheerful

rigide [ʀiʒid] *adj* stiff; (*fig*) rigid; (*moralement*) strict

rigole [ʀigɔl] *nf* (*conduit*) channel; (*filet d'eau*) rivulet

rigoler [ʀigɔle] *vi* (*rire*) to laugh; (*s'amuser*) to have (some) fun; (*plaisanter*) to be joking *ou* kidding

rigolo, ote [ʀigɔlo, -ɔt] *adj* (*fam*) funny ♦ *nm/f* comic; (*péj*) fraud, phoney

rigoureusement [ʀiguʀøzmɑ̃] *adv* rigorously; **rigoureusement vrai/interdit** strictly true/forbidden

rigoureux, euse [ʀiguʀø, -øz] *adj* (*morale*) rigorous, strict; (*personne*) stern, strict; (*climat, châtiment*) rigorous, harsh, severe; (*interdiction, neutralité*) strict; (*preuves, analyse, méthode*) rigorous

rigueur [ʀigœʀ] *nf* rigour (*BRIT*), rigor (*US*); strictness; harshness; **"tenue de soirée de rigueur"** "evening dress (to be worn)"; **être de rigueur** to be the usual thing, be the rule; **à la rigueur** at a pinch; possibly; **tenir rigueur à qn de qch** to hold sth against sb

rillettes [ʀijɛt] *nfpl* ≈ potted meat *sg*

rime [ʀim] *nf* rhyme; **n'avoir ni rime ni raison** to have neither rhyme nor reason

rinçage [ʀɛ̃saʒ] *nm* rinsing (out); (*opération*) rinse

rincer [ʀɛ̃se] *vt* to rinse; (*récipient*) to rinse out; **se rincer la bouche** to rinse one's mouth out

ring [ʀiŋ] *nm* (boxing) ring; **monter sur le ring** (*aussi fig*) to enter the ring; (: *faire carrière de boxeur*) to take up boxing

ringard, e [ʀɛ̃gaʀ, -aʀd(ə)] *adj* (*péj*) old-fashioned

rions [ʀjɔ̃] *vb voir* **rire**

riposter [ʀipɔste] *vi* to retaliate ♦ *vt*: **riposter que** to retort that; **riposter à** *vt* to counter; to reply to

rire [ʀiʀ] *vi* to laugh; (*se divertir*) to have fun; (*plaisanter*) to joke ♦ *nm* laugh; **le rire** laughter; **rire de** *vt* to laugh at; **se rire de** to make light of; **tu veux rire!** you must be joking!; **rire aux éclats/aux larmes** to roar with laughter/laugh until one cries; **rire jaune** to force oneself to laugh; **rire sous cape** to laugh up one's sleeve; **rire au nez de qn** to laugh in sb's face; **pour rire** (*pas sérieusement*) for a joke *ou* a laugh

risée [ʀize] *nf*: **être la risée de** to be the laughing stock of

risible [ʀizibl(ə)] *adj* laughable, ridiculous

risque [ʀisk(ə)] *nm* risk; **l'attrait du risque** the lure of danger; **prendre des risques** to take risks; **à ses risques et périls** at his own risk; **au risque de** at the risk of; **risque d'incendie** fire risk; **risque calculé** calculated risk

risqué, e [ʀiske] *adj* risky; (*plaisanterie*) risqué, daring

risquer [ʀiske] *vt* to risk; (*allusion, question*) to venture, hazard; **tu risques qu'on te renvoie** you risk being dismissed; **ça ne risque rien** it's quite safe; **risquer de: il risque de se tuer** he could get *ou* risk getting himself killed; **il a risqué de se tuer** he almost got himself killed; **ce qui risque de se produire** what might *ou* could well happen; **il ne risque pas de recommencer** there's no chance of him doing that again; **se risquer dans** (*s'aventurer*) to venture into; **se risquer à faire** (*tenter*) to dare to do; **risquer le tout pour le tout** to risk the lot

rissoler [ʀisɔle] *vi*, *vt*: **(faire) rissoler** to brown

ristourne [ʀistuʀn(ə)] *nf* rebate; discount

rite [ʀit] *nm* rite; (*fig*) ritual

rivage [ʀivaʒ] *nm* shore

rival, e, aux [ʀival, -o] *adj*, *nm/f* rival; **sans rival** *adj* unrivalled

rivaliser [ʀivalize] *vi*: **rivaliser avec** to rival, vie with; (*être comparable*) to hold its own against, compare with; **rivaliser avec qn de** (*élégance etc*) to vie with *ou* rival sb in

rivalité [ʀivalite] *nf* rivalry

rive [ʀiv] *nf* shore; (*de fleuve*) bank

riverain, e [ʀivʀɛ̃, -ɛn] *adj* riverside *cpd*; lakeside *cpd*; roadside *cpd* ♦ *nm/f* riverside (*ou* lakeside) resident; local *ou* roadside resident

rivet [ʀivɛ] *nm* rivet

rivière [ʀivjɛʀ] *nf* river; **rivière de diamants** diamond rivière

rixe [ʀiks(ə)] *nf* brawl, scuffle

riz [ʀi] *nm* rice; **riz au lait** ≈ rice pudding

rizière [ʀizjɛʀ] *nf* paddy field

RMI *sigle m* (= *revenu minimum d'insertion*) ≈ income support (*BRIT*), ≈ welfare (*US*)

RN *sigle f* = **route nationale**

robe [ʀɔb] *nf* dress; (*de juge, d'ecclésiastique*) robe; (*de professeur*) gown; (*pelage*) coat; **robe de soirée/de mariée** evening/wedding dress; **robe de baptême** christening robe; **robe de chambre** dressing gown; **robe de grossesse** maternity dress

robinet [ʀɔbinɛ] *nm* tap, faucet (*US*); **robinet du gaz** gas tap; **robinet mélangeur** mixer tap

robot [ʀɔbo] *nm* robot; **robot de cuisine** food processor

robuste [ʀɔbyst(ə)] *adj* robust, sturdy

robustesse [ʀɔbystɛs] *nf* robustness, sturdiness

roc [ʀɔk] *nm* rock

rocade [ʀɔkad] *nf* (*AUTO*) bypass

rocaille [ʀɔkaj] *nf* (*pierres*) loose stones *pl*; (*terrain*) rocky *ou* stony ground; (*jardin*) rockery, rock garden ♦ *adj* (*style*) rocaille

roche [ʀɔʃ] *nf* rock

rocher [ʀɔʃe] *nm* rock; (*ANAT*) petrosal bone

rocheux, euse [ʀɔʃø, -øz] *adj* rocky; **les (montagnes) Rocheuses** the Rockies, the Rocky Mountains

rock (and roll) [ʀɔk(ɛnʀɔl)] *nm* (*musique*) rock(-'n'-roll); (*danse*) rock

rodage [ʀɔdaʒ] *nm* running in (*BRIT*), breaking in (*US*); **en rodage** (*AUTO*) running *ou* breaking in

roder [ʀɔde] *vt* (*moteur, voiture*) to run in (*BRIT*), break in (*US*); **roder un spectacle** to iron out the initial problems of a show

rôder [ʀode] *vi* to roam *ou* wander about; (*de façon suspecte*) to lurk (about *ou* around)

rôdeur, euse [ʀodœʀ, -øz] *nm/f* prowler

rogne [ʀɔɲ] *nf*: **être en rogne** to be mad *ou* in a temper; **se mettre en rogne** to get mad *ou* in a temper

rogner [ʀɔɲe] *vt* to trim; (*fig*) to whittle down; **rogner sur** (*fig*) to cut down *ou* back on

rognons [ʀɔɲɔ̃] *nmpl* kidneys

roi [ʀwa] *nm* king; **les Rois mages** the Three Wise Men, the Magi; **le jour** *ou* **la fête des Rois, les Rois** Twelfth Night; *see boxed note*

FÊTE DES ROIS

La **fête des Rois** is celebrated on January 6. Figurines representing the magi are traditionally added to the Christmas crib and people eat la galette des Rois, a plain, flat cake in which a porcelain charm (la fève) is hidden. Whoever finds the charm is king or queen for the day and chooses a partner.

---

rôle [ʀol] *nm* role; (*contribution*) part

romain, e [ʀɔmɛ̃, -ɛn] *adj* Roman ♦ *nm/f*: **Romain, e** Roman ♦ *nf* (*CULIN*) cos (lettuce)

roman, e [ʀɔmɑ̃, -an] *adj* (*ARCHIT*) Romanesque; (*LING*) Romance *cpd*, Romanic ♦ *nm* novel; **roman d'amour** love story; **roman d'espionnage** spy novel *ou* story; **roman noir** thriller; **roman policier** detective novel

romance [ʀɔmɑ̃s] *nf* ballad

romancer [ʀɔmɑ̃se] *vt* to romanticize

romancier, ière [ʀɔmɑ̃sje, -jɛʀ] *nm/f* novelist

romanesque [ʀɔmanɛsk(ə)] *adj* (*fantastique*) fantastic; storybook *cpd*; (*sentimental*) romantic; (*LITTÉRATURE*) novelistic

roman-feuilleton, *pl* **romans-feuilletons** [ʀɔmɑ̃fœjtɔ̃] *nm* serialized novel

romanichel, le [ʀɔmaniʃɛl] *nm/f* gipsy

romantique [ʀɔmɑ̃tik] *adj* romantic

romarin [ʀɔmaʀɛ̃] *nm* rosemary

rompre [ʀɔ̃pʀ(ə)] *vt* to break; (*entretien, fiançailles*) to break off ♦ *vi* (*fiancés*) to break it off; **se rompre** *vi* to break; (*MÉD*) to burst, rupture; **se rompre les os** *ou* **le cou** to break one's neck; **rompre avec** to break with; **à tout rompre** *adv* wildly; **applaudir à tout rompre** to bring down the house, applaud wildly; **rompre la glace** (*fig*) to break the ice; **rompez (les rangs)!** (*MIL*) dismiss!, fall out!

rompu, e [ʀɔ̃py] *pp de* **rompre** ♦ *adj* (*fourbu*) exhausted, worn out; **rompu à** with wide experience of; inured to

ronce [ʀɔ̃s] *nf* (*BOT*) bramble branch; (*MENUISERIE*): **ronce de noyer** burr walnut; **ronces** *nfpl* brambles, thorns

ronchonner [ʀɔ̃ʃɔne] *vi* (*fam*) to grouse, grouch

rond, e [ʀɔ̃, ʀɔ̃d] *adj* round; (*joues, mollets*) well-rounded; (*fam: ivre*) tight; (*sincère, décidé*): **être rond en affaires** to be on the level in business, do an honest deal ♦ *nm* (*cercle*) ring; (*fam: sou*): **je n'ai plus un rond** I haven't a penny left ♦ *nf* (*gén: de surveillance*) rounds *pl*, patrol; (*danse*) round (dance); (*MUS*) semibreve (*BRIT*), whole note (*US*) ♦ *adv*: **tourner rond** (*moteur*) to run smoothly; **ça ne tourne pas rond** (*fig*) there's something not quite right about it; **pour faire un compte rond** to make (it) a round figure, to round (it) off; **avoir le dos rond** to be round-shouldered; **en rond** (*s'asseoir, danser*) in a ring; **à la ronde** (*alentour*): **à 10 km à la ronde** for 10 km round; (*à chacun son tour*): **passer qch à la ronde** to pass sth (a)round; **faire des ronds de jambe** to bow and scrape; **rond de serviette** napkin ring

rondelet, te [ʀɔ̃dlɛ, -ɛt] *adj* plump; (*fig: somme*) tidy; (: *bourse*) well-lined, fat

rondelle [ʀɔ̃dɛl] *nf* (*TECH*) washer; (*tranche*) slice, round

rondement [ʀɔ̃dmɑ̃] *adv* (*avec décision*) briskly; (*loyalement*) frankly

rondin [ʀɔ̃dɛ̃] *nm* log

rond-point, *pl* **ronds-points** [ʀɔ̃pwɛ̃] *nm* roundabout (*BRIT*), traffic circle (*US*)

ronflant, e [ʀɔ̃flɑ̃, -ɑ̃t] *adj* (*péj*) high-flown, grand

ronflement [ʀɔ̃fləmɑ̃] *nm* snore, snoring *no pl*

ronfler [ʀɔ̃fle] *vi* to snore; (*moteur, poêle*) to hum; (: *plus fort*) to roar

ronger [ʀɔ̃ʒe] *vt* to gnaw (at); (*suj: vers, rouille*) to eat into; **ronger son frein** to champ (at) the bit; (*fig*) **se ronger de souci, se ronger les sangs** to worry o.s. sick, fret; **se ronger les ongles** to bite one's nails

rongeur, euse [ʀɔ̃ʒœʀ, -øz] *nm/f* rodent

ronronner [ʀɔ̃ʀɔne] *vi* to purr

rosace [ʀozas] *nf* (*vitrail*) rose window, rosace; (*motif: de plafond etc*) rose

rosbif [ʀɔsbif] *nm*: **du rosbif** roasting beef; (*cuit*) roast beef; **un rosbif** a joint of (roasting) beef

rose [ʀoz] *nf* rose; (*vitrail*) rose window ♦ *adj* pink; **rose bonbon** *adj inv* candy pink; **rose des vents** compass card

rosé, e [ʀoze] *adj* pinkish; (**vin**) **rosé** rosé (wine)

roseau, x [ʀozo] *nm* reed

rosée [ʀoze] *adj f voir* **rosé** ♦ *nf*: **goutte de rosée** dewdrop

rosette [ʀozɛt] *nf* rosette (*gen of the Légion d'honneur*)

rosier [ʀozje] *nm* rosebush, rose tree

rosse [ʀɔs] *nf* (*péj: cheval*) nag ♦ *adj* nasty, vicious

rossignol [ʀɔsiɲɔl] *nm* (*ZOOL*) nightingale; (*crochet*) picklock

rot [ʀo] *nm* belch; (*de bébé*) burp

rotatif, ive [ʀɔtatif, -iv] *adj* rotary ♦ *nf* rotary press

rotation [ʀɔtasjɔ̃] *nf* rotation; (*fig*) rotation, swaparound; (*renouvellement*) turnover; **par rotation** on a rota (*BRIT*) *ou* rotation (*US*) basis; **rotation des cultures** crop rotation; **rotation des stocks** stock turnover

roter [ʀɔte] *vi* (*fam*) to burp, belch

rôti [ʀoti] *nm*: **du rôti** roasting meat; (*cuit*) roast meat; **un rôti de bœuf/porc** a joint of (roasting) beef/pork

rotin [ʀɔtɛ̃] *nm* rattan (cane); **fauteuil en rotin** cane (arm)chair

rôtir [ʀotiʀ] *vt* (*aussi*: **faire rôtir**) to roast ♦ *vi* to roast; **se rôtir au soleil** to bask in the sun

rôtisserie [ʀotisʀi] *nf* (*restaurant*) steakhouse; (*comptoir, magasin*) roast meat counter (*ou* shop)

rôtissoire [ʀotiswaʀ] *nf* (roasting) spit

rotule [ʀɔtyl] *nf* kneecap, patella

roturier, ière [ʀɔtyʀje, -jɛʀ] *nm/f* commoner

rouage [ʀwaʒ] *nm* cog(wheel), gearwheel; (*de montre*) part; (*fig*) cog; **rouages** *nmpl* (*fig*) internal structure *sg*

roucouler [ʀukule] *vi* to coo; (*fig: péj*) to warble; (: *amoureux*) to bill and coo

roue [ʀu] *nf* wheel; **faire la roue** (*paon*) to spread *ou* fan its tail; (*GYM*) to do a cartwheel; **descendre en roue libre** to freewheel *ou* coast down; **pousser à la roue** to put one's shoulder to the wheel; **grande roue** (*à la foire*) big wheel; **roue à aubes** paddle wheel; **roue dentée** cogwheel; **roue de**

secours spare wheel

roué, e [ʀwe] *adj* wily

rouer [ʀwe] *vt*: **rouer qn de coups** to give sb a thrashing

rouge [ʀuʒ] *adj, nm/f* red ♦ *nm* red; (*fard*) rouge; (**vin**) **rouge** red wine; **passer au rouge** (*signal*) to go red; (*automobiliste*) to go through a red light; **porter au rouge** (*métal*) to bring to red heat; **sur la liste rouge** (*TÉL*) ex-directory (*BRIT*), unlisted (*US*); **rouge de honte/colère** red with shame/anger; **se fâcher tout/voir rouge** to blow one's top/see red; **rouge (à lèvres)** lipstick

rouge-gorge [ʀuʒgɔʀʒ(ə)] *nm* robin (redbreast)

rougeole [ʀuʒɔl] *nf* measles *sg*

rougeoyer [ʀuʒwaje] *vi* to glow red

rouget [ʀuʒɛ] *nm* mullet

rougeur [ʀuʒœʀ] *nf* redness; (*du visage*) red face; **rougeurs** *nfpl* (*MÉD*) red blotches

rougir [ʀuʒiʀ] *vi* (*de honte, timidité*) to blush, flush; (*de plaisir, colère*) to flush; (*fraise, tomate*) to go *ou* turn red; (*ciel*) to redden

rouille [ʀuj] *adj inv* rust-coloured, rusty ♦ *nf* rust; (*CULIN*) spicy (*Provençal*) sauce served with fish dishes

rouillé, e [ʀuje] *adj* rusty

rouiller [ʀuje] *vt* to rust ♦ *vi* to rust, go rusty; **se rouiller** *vi* to rust; (*fig: mentalement*) to become rusty; (: *physiquement*) to grow stiff

roulant, e [ʀulɑ̃, -ɑ̃t] *adj* (*meuble*) on wheels; (*surface, trottoir*) moving; **matériel roulant** (*RAIL*) rolling stock; **personnel roulant** (*RAIL*) train crews *pl*

rouleau, x [ʀulo] *nm* (*de papier, tissu, pièces de monnaie, SPORT*) roll; (*de machine à écrire*) roller, platen; (*à mise en plis, à peinture, vague*) roller; **être au bout du rouleau** (*fig*) to be at the end of the line; **rouleau compresseur** steamroller; **rouleau à pâtisserie** rolling pin; **rouleau de pellicule** roll of film

roulement [ʀulmɑ̃] *nm* (*bruit*) rumbling *no pl*, rumble; (*rotation*) rotation; turnover; (: *de capitaux*) circulation; **par roulement** on a rota (*BRIT*) *ou* rotation (*US*) basis; **roulement (à billes)** ball bearings *pl*; **roulement de tambour** drum roll; **roulement d'yeux** roll(ing) of the eyes

rouler [ʀule] *vt* to roll; (*papier, tapis*) to roll up; (*CULIN: pâte*) to roll out; (*fam*) to do, con ♦ *vi* (*bille, boule*) to roll; (*voiture, train*) to go, run; (*automobiliste*) to drive; (*cycliste*) to ride; (*bateau*) to roll; (*tonnerre*) to rumble, roll; (*dégringoler*): **rouler en bas de** to roll down; **rouler sur** (*suj: conversation*) to turn on; **se rouler dans** (*boue*) to roll in; (*couverture*) to roll o.s. (up) in; **rouler dans la farine** (*fam*) to con; **rouler les épaules/hanches** to sway one's shoulders/wiggle one's hips; **rouler les "r"** to roll one's r's; **rouler sur l'or** to be rolling in money, be rolling in it; **rouler (sa bosse)** to go places

roulette [ʀulɛt] *nf* (*de table, fauteuil*) castor; (*de pâtissier*) pastry wheel; (*jeu*): **la roulette** roulette; **à**

roulettes on castors; **la roulette russe** Russian roulette

roulis [ʀuli] *nm* roll(ing)

roulotte [ʀulɔt] *nf* caravan

roumain, e [ʀumɛ̃, -ɛn] *adj* Rumanian, Romanian ◆ *nm* (*LING*) Rumanian, Romanian ◆ *nm/f*: **Roumain, e** Rumanian, Romanian

Roumanie [ʀumani] *nf*: **la Roumanie** Rumania, Romania

rouquin, e [ʀukɛ̃, -in] *nm/f* (*péj*) redhead

rouspéter [ʀuspete] *vi* (*fam*) to moan, grouse

rousse [ʀus] *adj f voir* **roux**

roussir [ʀusiʀ] *vt* to scorch ◆ *vi* (*feuilles*) to go *ou* turn brown; (*CULIN*): **faire roussir** to brown

route [ʀut] *nf* road; (*fig*: *chemin*) way; (*itinéraire, parcours*) route; (*fig*: *voie*) road, path; **par (la) route** by road; **il y a 3 heures de route** it's a 3-hour ride *ou* journey; **en route** *adv* on the way; **en route!** let's go!; **en cours de route** en route; **mettre en route** to start up; **se mettre en route** to set off; **faire route vers** to head towards; **faire fausse route** (*fig*) to be on the wrong track; **route nationale (RN)** ≈ A-road (*BRIT*), ≈ state highway (*US*)

routier, ière [ʀutje, -jɛʀ] *adj* road *cpd* ◆ *nm* (*camionneur*) (long-distance) lorry (*BRIT*) *ou* truck driver; (*restaurant*) ≈ transport café (*BRIT*), ≈ truck stop (*US*); (*scout*) ≈ rover; (*cycliste*) road racer ◆ *nf* (*voiture*) touring car; **vieux routier** old stager; **carte routière** road map

routine [ʀutin] *nf* routine; **visite/contrôle de routine** routine visit/check

routinier, ière [ʀutinje, -jɛʀ] *adj* (*péj*: *travail*) humdrum, routine; (: *personne*) addicted to routine

rouvrir [ʀuvʀiʀ] *vt, vi* to reopen, open again; **se rouvrir** *vi* (*blessure*) to open up again

roux, rousse [ʀu, ʀus] *adj* red; (*personne*) red-haired ◆ *nm/f* redhead ◆ *nm* (*CULIN*) roux

royal, e, aux [ʀwajal, -o] *adj* royal; (*fig*) fit for a king, princely; blissful; thorough

royaume [ʀwajom] *nm* kingdom; (*fig*) realm; **le royaume des cieux** the kingdom of heaven

Royaume-Uni [ʀwajomyni] *nm*: **le Royaume-Uni** the United Kingdom

royauté [ʀwajote] *nf* (*dignité*) kingship; (*régime*) monarchy

RPR *sigle m* (= *Rassemblement pour la République*) political party

ruban [ʀybɑ̃] *nm* (*gén*) ribbon; (*pour ourlet, couture*) binding; (*de téléscripteur etc*) tape; (*d'acier*) strip; **ruban adhésif** adhesive tape; **ruban carbone** carbon ribbon

rubéole [ʀybeɔl] *nf* German measles *sg*, rubella

rubis [ʀybi] *nm* ruby; (*HORLOGERIE*) jewel; **payer rubis sur l'ongle** to pay cash on the nail

rubrique [ʀybʀik] *nf* (*titre, catégorie*) heading, rubric; (*PRESSE*: *article*) column

ruche [ʀyʃ] *nf* hive

rude [ʀyd] *adj* (*barbe, toile*) rough; (*métier, tâche*) hard, tough; (*climat*) severe, harsh; (*bourru*) harsh, rough; (*fruste*) rugged, tough; (*fam*) jolly good; **être mis à rude épreuve** to be put through the mill

rudement [ʀydmɑ̃] *adv* (*tomber, frapper*) hard; (*traiter, reprocher*) harshly; (*fam*: *très*) terribly; (: *beaucoup*) terribly hard

rudimentaire [ʀydimɑ̃tɛʀ] *adj* rudimentary, basic

rudiments [ʀydimɑ̃] *nmpl* rudiments; basic knowledge *sg*; basic principles

rudoyer [ʀydwaje] *vt* to treat harshly

rue [ʀy] *nf* street; **être/jeter qn à la rue** to be on the streets/throw sb out onto the street

ruée [ʀɥe] *nf* rush; **la ruée vers l'or** the gold rush

ruelle [ʀɥɛl] *nf* alley(way)

ruer [ʀɥe] *vi* (*cheval*) to kick out; **se ruer** *vi*: **se ruer sur** to pounce on; **se ruer vers/dans/hors de** to rush *ou* dash towards/into/out of; **ruer dans les brancards** to become rebellious

rugby [ʀygbi] *nm* rugby (football); **rugby à treize/quinze** rugby league/union

rugir [ʀyʒiʀ] *vi* to roar

rugueux, euse [ʀygø, -øz] *adj* rough

ruine [ʀɥin] *nf* ruin; **ruines** *nfpl* ruins; **tomber en ruine** to fall into ruin(s)

ruiner [ʀɥine] *vt* to ruin

ruineux, euse [ʀɥinø, -øz] *adj* terribly expensive to buy (*ou* run), ruinous; extravagant

ruisseau, x [ʀɥiso] *nm* stream, brook; (*caniveau*) gutter; (*fig*): **ruisseaux de larmes/sang** floods of tears/streams of blood

ruisseler [ʀɥisle] *vi* to stream; **ruisseler (d'eau)** to be streaming (with water); **ruisseler de lumière** to stream with light

rumeur [ʀymœʀ] *nf* (*bruit confus*) rumbling; hub-bub *no pl*; (*protestation*) murmur(ing); (*nouvelle*) rumour (*BRIT*), rumor (*US*)

ruminer [ʀymine] *vt* (*herbe*) to ruminate; (*fig*) to ruminate on *ou* over, chew over ◆ *vi* (*vache*) to chew the cud, ruminate

rupture [ʀyptyʀ] *nf* (*de câble, digue*) breaking; (*de tendon*) rupture, tearing; (*de négociations etc*) breakdown; (*de contrat*) breach; (*séparation, désunion*) break-up, split; **en rupture de ban** at odds with authority; **en rupture de stock** (*COMM*) out of stock

rural, e, aux [ʀyʀal, -o] *adj* rural, country *cpd* ◆ *nmpl*: **les ruraux** country people

ruse [ʀyz] *nf*: **la ruse** cunning, craftiness; trickery; **une ruse** a trick, a ruse; **par ruse** by trickery

rusé, e [ʀyze] *adj* cunning, crafty

russe [ʀys] *adj* Russian ◆ *nm* (*LING*) Russian ◆ *nm/f*: **Russe** Russian

Russie [ʀysi] *nf*: **la Russie** Russia; **la Russie blanche** White Russia; **la Russie soviétique** Soviet

Russia

rustine [ʀystin] *nf* repair patch (*for bicycle inner tube*)

rustique [ʀystik] *adj* rustic; (*plante*) hardy

rustre [ʀystʀ(ə)] *nm* boor

rutilant, e [ʀytilɑ̃, -ɑ̃t] *adj* gleaming

rythme [ʀitm(ə)] *nm* rhythm; (*vitesse*) rate; (: *de la vie*) pace, tempo; **au rythme de 10 par jour** at the rate of 10 a day

rythmé, e [ʀitme] *adj* rhythmic(al)

— S s —

s' [s] *pron voir* **se**

SA *sigle f* = **société anonyme**; (= Son Altesse) HH

sa [sa] *adj possessif voir* **son**

sable [sabl(ə)] *nm* sand; **sables mouvants** quicksand(s)

sablé [sable] *adj* (*allée*) sandy ♦ *nm* shortbread biscuit; **pâte sablée** (*CULIN*) shortbread dough

sabler [sable] *vt* to sand; (*contre le verglas*) to grit; **sabler le champagne** to drink champagne

sablier [sablije] *nm* hourglass; (*de cuisine*) egg timer

sablonneux, euse [sablɔnø, -øz] *adj* sandy

saborder [sabɔʀde] *vt* (*navire*) to scuttle; (*fig*) to wind up, shut down

sabot [sabo] *nm* clog; (*de cheval, bœuf*) hoof; **sabot (de Denver)** (wheel) clamp; **sabot de frein** brake shoe

saboter [sabɔte] *vt* (*travail, morceau de musique*) to botch, make a mess of; (*machine, installation, négociation etc*) to sabotage

sac [sak] *nm* bag; (*à charbon etc*) sack; (*pillage*) sack(ing); **mettre à sac** to sack; **sac à provisions/de voyage** shopping/travelling bag; **sac de couchage** sleeping bag; **sac à dos** rucksack; **sac à main** handbag; **sac de plage** beach bag

saccadé, e [sakade] *adj* jerky

saccager [sakaʒe] *vt* (*piller*) to sack, lay waste; (*dévaster*) to create havoc in, wreck

saccharine [sakaʀin] *nf* saccharin(e)

sacerdoce [sasɛʀdɔs] *nm* priesthood; (*fig*) calling, vocation

sache *etc* [saʃ] *vb voir* **savoir**

sachet [saʃɛ] *nm* (small) bag; (*de lavande, poudre, shampooing*) sachet; **thé en sachets** tea bags; **sachet de thé** tea bag

sacoche [sakɔʃ] *nf* (*gén*) bag; (*de bicyclette*) saddlebag; (*du facteur*) (post)bag; (*d'outils*) toolbag

sacquer [sake] *vt* (*fam: candidat, employé*) to sack; (: *réprimander, mal noter*) to plough

sacre [sakʀ(ə)] *nm* coronation; consecration

sacré, e [sakʀe] *adj* sacred; (*fam: satané*) blasted; (: *fameux*): **un sacré ...** a heck of a ...; (*ANAT*) sacral

sacrement [sakʀəmɑ̃] *nm* sacrament; **les derniers sacrements** the last rites

sacrifice [sakʀifis] *nm* sacrifice; **faire le sacrifice de** to sacrifice

sacrifier [sakʀifje] *vt* to sacrifice; **sacrifier à** *vt* to conform to; **se sacrifier** to sacrifice o.s.; **articles sacrifiés** (*COMM*) items sold at rock-bottom *ou* give-away prices

sacristie [sakʀisti] *nf* sacristy; (*culte protestant*) vestry

sadique [sadik] *adj* sadistic ♦ *nm/f* sadist

safran [safʀɑ̃] *nm* saffron

sage [saʒ] *adj* wise; (*enfant*) good ♦ *nm* wise man; sage

sage-femme [saʒfam] *nf* midwife (*pl* -wives)

sagesse [saʒɛs] *nf* wisdom

Sagittaire [saʒitɛʀ] *nm*: **le Sagittaire** Sagittarius, the Archer; **être du Sagittaire** to be Sagittarius

Sahara [saaʀa] *nm*: **le Sahara** the Sahara (Desert); **le Sahara occidental** (*pays*) Western Sahara

saignant, e [sɛɲɑ̃, -ɑ̃t] *adj* (*viande*) rare; (*blessure, plaie*) bleeding

saignée [seɲe] *nf* (*MÉD*) bleeding no *pl*, blood-letting no *pl*; (*ANAT*): **la saignée du bras** the bend of the arm; (*fig: MIL*) heavy losses *pl*; (: *prélèvement*) savage cut

saigner [seɲe] *vi* to bleed ♦ *vt* to bleed; (*animal*) to bleed to death; **saigner qn à blanc** (*fig*) to bleed sb white; **saigner du nez** to have a nosebleed

saillie [saji] *nf* (*sur un mur etc*) projection; (*trait d'esprit*) witticism; (*accouplement*) covering, serving; **faire saillie** to project, stick out; **en saillie, formant saillie** projecting, overhanging

saillir [sajiʀ] *vi* to project, stick out; (*veine, muscle*) to bulge ♦ *vt* (*ÉLEVAGE*) to cover, serve

sain, e [sɛ̃, sɛn] *adj* healthy; (*dents, constitution*) healthy, sound; (*lectures*) wholesome; **sain et sauf** safe and sound, unharmed; **sain d'esprit** sound in mind, sane

saindoux [sɛ̃du] *nm* lard

saint, e [sɛ̃, sɛ̃t] *adj* holy; (*fig*) saintly ♦ *nm/f* saint; **la Sainte Vierge** the Blessed Virgin

sainteté [sɛ̃te] *nf* holiness; saintliness

Saint-Sylvestre [sɛ̃silvɛstʀ(ə)] *nf*: **la Saint-Sylvestre** New Year's Eve

sais [sɛ] *etc vb voir* **savoir**

saisie [sezi] *nf* seizure; **à la saisie** (*texte*) being keyed; **saisie (de données)** (data) capture

saisir [seziʀ] *vt* to take hold of, grab; (*fig: occasion*) to seize; (*comprendre*) to grasp; (*entendre*) to get, catch; (*suj: émotions*) to take hold of, come over; (*INFORM*) to capture, keyboard; (*CULIN*) to fry quickly; (*JUR: biens, publication*) to seize; (: *juridiction*) to refer; **saisir un tribunal d'une affaire** to submit *ou* refer a case to a court; **se saisir de** *vt* to seize; **être saisi** (*frappé de*) to be overcome

saisissant, e [sezisɑ̃, -ɑ̃t] *adj* startling, striking;

(froid) biting

saison [sezɔ̃] nf season; **la belle/mauvaise saison** the summer/winter months; **être de saison** to be in season; **en/hors saison** in/out of season; **haute/basse/morte saison** high/low/slack season; **la saison des pluies/des amours** the rainy/mating season

saisonnier, ière [sezɔnje, -jɛʀ] adj seasonal ◆ nm (travailleur) seasonal worker; (vacancier) seasonal holidaymaker

sait [se] vb voir **savoir**

salade [salad] nf (BOT) lettuce etc (generic term); (CULIN) (green) salad; (fam) tangle, muddle; **salades** nfpl (fam): **raconter des salades** to tell tales (fam); **haricots en salade** bean salad; **salade de concombres** cucumber salad; **salade de fruits** fruit salad; **salade niçoise** salade niçoise; **salade russe** Russian salad; **salade de tomates** tomato salad; **salade verte** green salad

saladier [saladje] nm (salad) bowl

salaire [salɛʀ] nm (annuel, mensuel) salary; (hebdomadaire, journalier) pay, wages pl; (fig) reward; **salaire de base** basic salary (ou wage); **salaire de misère** starvation wage; **salaire minimum interprofessionnel de croissance (SMIC)** index-linked guaranteed minimum wage

salami [salami] nm salami no pl, salami sausage

salarié, e [salaʀje] adj salaried; wage-earning ◆ nm/f salaried employee; wage-earner

salaud [salo] nm (fam!) sod (!), bastard (!)

sale [sal] adj dirty; (fig: avant le nom) nasty

salé, e [sale] adj (liquide, saveur) salty; (CULIN) salted, salt cpd; (fig) spicy, juicy; (: note, facture) steep, stiff ◆ nm (porc salé) salt pork; **petit salé** = boiling bacon

saler [sale] vt to salt

saleté [salte] nf (état) dirtiness; (crasse) dirt, filth; (tache etc) dirt no pl something dirty, dirty mark; (fig: tour) filthy trick; (: chose sans valeur) rubbish no pl; (: obscénité) filth no pl; (: microbe etc) bug; **vivre dans la saleté** to live in squalor

salière [saljɛʀ] nf saltcellar

salin, e [salɛ̃, -in] adj saline ◆ nf saltworks sg

salir [saliʀ] vt to (make) dirty; (fig) to soil the reputation of; **se salir** to get dirty

salissant, e [salisɑ̃, -ɑ̃t] adj (tissu) which shows the dirt; (métier) dirty, messy

salle [sal] nf room; (d'hôpital) ward; (de restaurant) dining room; (d'un cinéma) auditorium; (: public) audience; **faire salle comble** to have a full house; **salle d'armes** (pour l'escrime) arms room; **salle d'attente** waiting room; **salle de bain(s)** bathroom; **salle de bal** ballroom; **salle de cinéma** cinema; **salle de classe** classroom; **salle commune** (d'hôpital) ward; **salle de concert** concert hall; **salle de consultation** consulting room (BRIT), office (US); **salle de danse** dance hall; **salle de douches** shower-room; **salle d'eau** shower-room; **salle**

d'embarquement (à l'aéroport) departure lounge; **salle d'exposition** showroom; **salle de jeux** games room; playroom; **salle des machines** engine room; **salle à manger** dining room; (mobilier) dining room suite; **salle obscure** cinema (BRIT), movie theater (US); **salle d'opération** (d'hôpital) operating theatre; **salle des professeurs** staffroom; **salle de projection** film theatre; **salle de séjour** living room; **salle de spectacle** theatre; cinema; **salle des ventes** saleroom

salon [salɔ̃] nm lounge, sitting room; (mobilier) lounge suite; (exposition) exhibition, show; (mondain, littéraire) salon; **salon de coiffure** hairdressing salon; **salon de thé** tearoom

salope [salɔp] nf (fam!) bitch (!)

saloperie [salɔpʀi] nf (fam!) filth no pl; dirty trick; rubbish no pl

salopette [salɔpɛt] nf dungarees pl; (d'ouvrier) overall(s)

salsifis [salsifi] nm salsify, oyster plant

salubre [salybʀ(ə)] adj healthy, salubrious

saluer [salɥe] vt (pour dire bonjour, fig) to greet; (pour dire au revoir) to take one's leave; (MIL) to salute

salut [saly] nm (sauvegarde) safety; (REL) salvation; (geste) wave; (parole) greeting; (MIL) salute ◆ excl (fam: pour dire bonjour) hi (there); (: pour dire au revoir) see you!, bye!; (style relevé) (all) hail

salutations [salytasjɔ̃] nfpl greetings; **recevez mes salutations distinguées** ou **respectueuses** yours faithfully

samedi [samdi] nm Saturday; voir aussi **lundi**

SAMU [samy] sigle m (= service d'assistance médicale d'urgence) = ambulance (service) (BRIT), = paramedics (US)

sanction [sɑ̃ksjɔ̃] nf sanction; (fig) penalty; **prendre des sanctions contre** to impose sanctions on

sanctionner [sɑ̃ksjɔne] vt (loi, usage) to sanction; (punir) to punish

sandale [sɑ̃dal] nf sandal; **sandales à lanières** strappy sandals

sandwich [sɑ̃dwitʃ] nm sandwich; **pris en sandwich** sandwiched

sang [sɑ̃] nm blood; **en sang** covered in blood; **jusqu'au sang** (mordre, pincer) till the blood comes; **se faire du mauvais sang** to fret, get in a state

sang-froid [sɑ̃fʀwa] nm calm, sangfroid; **garder/perdre/reprendre son sang-froid** to keep/lose/regain one's cool; **de sang-froid** in cold blood

sanglant, e [sɑ̃glɑ̃, -ɑ̃t] adj bloody, covered in blood; (combat) bloody; (fig: reproche, affront) cruel

sangle [sɑ̃gl(ə)] nf strap; **sangles** nfpl (pour lit etc) webbing sg

sanglier [sɑ̃glije] nm (wild) boar

sanglot [sɑ̃glo] nm sob

sangloter [sɑ̃glɔte] vi to sob

sangsue [sɑ̃sy] nf leech

sanguin, e [sɑ̃gɛ̃, -in] *adj* blood *cpd*; (*fig*) fiery ♦ *nf* blood orange; (*ART*) red pencil drawing
sanguinaire [sɑ̃ginɛR] *adj* (*animal, personne*) bloodthirsty; (*lutte*) bloody
sanitaire [sanitɛR] *adj* health *cpd*; **sanitaires** *nmpl* (*salle de bain et w.-c.*) bathroom *sg*; **installation/appareil sanitaire** bathroom plumbing/appliance
sans [sɑ̃] *prép* without; **sans qu'il s'en aperçoive** without him *ou* his noticing; **sans scrupules** unscrupulous; **sans manches** sleeveless
sans-abri [sɑ̃zabRi] *nmpl* homeless
sans-emploi [sɑ̃zɑ̃plwa] *nmpl* jobless
sans-gêne [sɑ̃ʒɛn] *adj inv* inconsiderate ♦ *nm inv* (*attitude*) lack of consideration
santé [sɑ̃te] *nf* health; **avoir une santé de fer** to be bursting with health; **être en bonne santé** to be in good health, be healthy; **boire à la santé de qn** to drink (to) sb's health; **"à la santé de"** "here's to"; **à ta** *ou* **votre santé!** cheers!; **service de santé** (*dans un port etc*) quarantine service; **la santé publique** public health
saoudien, ne [saudjɛ̃, -ɛn] *adj* Saudi (Arabian) ♦ *nm/f:* **Saoudien, ne** Saudi (Arabian)
saoul, e [su, sul] *adj* = **soûl, e**
saper [sape] *vt* to undermine, sap; **se saper** *vi* (*fam*) to dress
sapeur-pompier [sapœRpɔ̃pje] *nm* fireman
saphir [safiR] *nm* sapphire; (*d'électrophone*) needle, sapphire
sapin [sapɛ̃] *nm* fir (tree); (*bois*) fir; **sapin de Noël** Christmas tree
sarcastique [saRkastik] *adj* sarcastic
sarcler [saRkle] *vt* to weed
Sardaigne [saRdɛɲ] *nf:* **la Sardaigne** Sardinia
sardine [saRdin] *nf* sardine; **sardines à l'huile** sardines in oil
SARL [saRl] *sigle f* = **société à responsabilité limitée**
sarrasin [saRazɛ̃] *nm* buckwheat
sas [sas] *nm* (*de sous-marin, d'engin spatial*) airlock; (*d'écluse*) lock
satané, e [satane] *adj* (*fam*) confounded
satellite [satelit] *nm* satellite; **pays satellite** satellite country
satin [satɛ̃] *nm* satin
satire [satiR] *nf* satire; **faire la satire** to satirize
satirique [satiRik] *adj* satirical
satisfaction [satisfaksjɔ̃] *nf* satisfaction; **à ma grande satisfaction** to my great satisfaction; **obtenir satisfaction** to obtain *ou* get satisfaction; **donner satisfaction (à)** to give satisfaction (to)
satisfaire [satisfɛR] *vt* to satisfy; **se satisfaire de** to be satisfied *ou* content with; **satisfaire à** *vt* (*engagement*) to fulfil; (*revendications, conditions*) to satisfy, meet
satisfaisant, e [satisfəzɑ̃, -ɑ̃t] *vb voir* **satisfaire**

♦ *adj* satisfactory; (*qui fait plaisir*) satisfying
satisfait, e [satisfɛ, -ɛt] *pp de* **satisfaire** ♦ *adj* satisfied; **satisfait de** happy *ou* satisfied with
saturer [satyRe] *vt* to saturate; **saturer qn/qch de** to saturate sb/sth with
sauce [sos] *nf* sauce; (*avec un rôti*) gravy; **en sauce** in a sauce; **sauce blanche** white sauce; **sauce chasseur** sauce chasseur; **sauce tomate** tomato sauce
saucière [sosjɛR] *nf* sauceboat; gravy boat
saucisse [sosis] *nf* sausage
saucisson [sosisɔ̃] *nm* (*slicing*) sausage; **saucisson à l'ail** garlic sausage
sauf [sof] *prép* except; **sauf si** (*à moins que*) unless; **sauf avis contraire** unless you hear to the contrary; **sauf empêchement** barring (any) problems; **sauf erreur** if I'm not mistaken; **sauf imprévu** unless anything unforeseen arises, barring accidents
sauf, sauve [sof, sov] *adj* unharmed, unhurt; (*fig: honneur*) intact, saved; **laisser la vie sauve à qn** to spare sb's life
sauge [soʒ] *nf* sage
saugrenu, e [sogRəny] *adj* preposterous, ludicrous
saule [sol] *nm* willow (tree); **saule pleureur** weeping willow
saumon [somɔ̃] *nm* salmon *inv* ♦ *adj inv* salmon (pink)
saumure [somyR] *nf* brine
saupoudrer [supudRe] *vt:* **saupoudrer qch de** to sprinkle sth with
saur [sɔR] *adj m:* **hareng saur** smoked *ou* red herring, kipper
saurai *etc* [sɔRe] *vb voir* **savoir**
saut [so] *nm* jump; (*discipline sportive*) jumping; **faire un saut** to (make a) jump *ou* leap; **faire un saut chez qn** to pop over to sb's (place); **au saut du lit** on getting out of bed; **saut en hauteur/longueur** high/long jump; **saut à la corde** skipping; **saut de page** (*INFORM*) page break; **saut en parachute** parachuting *no pl*; **saut à la perche** pole vaulting; **saut à l'élastique** bungee jumping; **saut périlleux** somersault
saute [sot] *nf:* **saute de vent/température** sudden change of wind direction/in the temperature; **avoir des sautes d'humeur** to have sudden changes of mood
sauter [sote] *vi* to jump, leap; (*exploser*) to blow up, explode; (: *fusibles*) to blow; (*se rompre*) to snap, burst; (*se détacher*) to pop out (*ou* off) ♦ *vt* to jump (over), leap (over); (*fig: omettre*) to skip, miss (out); **faire sauter** to blow up; to burst open; (*CULIN*) to sauté; **sauter à pieds joints/à cloche-pied** to make a standing jump/to hop; **sauter en parachute** to make a parachute jump; **sauter à la corde** to skip; **sauter de joie** to jump for joy; **sauter de colère** to be hopping with rage *ou* hop-

ping mad; **sauter au cou de qn** to fly into sb's arms; **sauter aux yeux** to be quite obvious; **sauter au plafond** (fig) to hit the roof

sauterelle [sotʀɛl] nf grasshopper

sautiller [sotije] vi to hop; to skip

sauvage [sovaʒ] adj (gén) wild; (peuplade) savage; (farouche) unsociable; (barbare) wild, savage; (non officiel) unauthorized, unofficial ♦ nm/f savage; (timide) unsociable type, recluse

sauve [sov] adj f voir **sauf**

sauvegarde [sovgaʀd(ə)] nf safeguard; **sous la sauvegarde de** under the protection of; **disquette/fichier de sauvegarde** (INFORM) backup disk/file

sauvegarder [sovgaʀde] vt to safeguard; (INFORM: enregistrer) to save; (: copier) to back up

sauve-qui-peut [sovkipø] nm inv stampede, mad rush ♦ excl run for your life!

sauver [sove] vt to save; (porter secours à) to rescue; (récupérer) to salvage, rescue; **se sauver** vi (s'enfuir) to run away; (fam: partir) to be off; **sauver qn de** to save sb from; **sauver la vie à qn** to save sb's life; **sauver les apparences** to keep up appearances

sauvetage [sovtaʒ] nm rescue; **sauvetage en montagne** mountain rescue; **ceinture de sauvetage** lifebelt (BRIT), life preserver (US); **brassière** ou **gilet de sauvetage** lifejacket (BRIT), life preserver (US)

sauveteur [sovtœʀ] nm rescuer

sauvette [sovɛt]: **à la sauvette** adv (vendre) without authorization; (se marier etc) hastily, hurriedly; **vente à la sauvette** (unauthorized) street trading, (street) peddling

sauveur [sovœʀ] nm saviour (BRIT), savior (US)

savais etc [save] vb voir **savoir**

savamment [savamɑ̃] adv (avec érudition) learnedly; (habilement) skilfully, cleverly

savant, e [savɑ̃, -ɑ̃t] adj scholarly, learned; (calé) clever ♦ nm scientist; **animal savant** performing animal

saveur [savœʀ] nf flavour (BRIT), flavor (US); (fig) savour (BRIT), savor (US)

savoir [savwaʀ] vt to know; (être capable de): **il sait nager** he knows how to swim, he can swim ♦ nm knowledge; **se savoir** (être connu) to be known; **se savoir malade/incurable** to know that one is ill/incurably ill; **il est petit: tu ne peux pas savoir!** you won't believe how small he is!; **vous n'êtes pas sans savoir que** you are not ou will not be unaware of the fact that; **je crois savoir que ...** I believe that …, I think I know that …; **je n'en sais rien** I (really) don't know; **à savoir (que)** that is, namely; **faire savoir qch à qn** to inform sb about sth, let sb know sth; **pas que je sache** not as far as I know; **sans le savoir** adv unknowingly, unwittingly; **en savoir long** to know a lot

savon [savɔ̃] nm (produit) soap; (morceau) bar ou

tablet of soap; (fam): **passer un savon à qn** to give sb a good dressing-down

savonner [savɔne] vt to soap

savonnette [savɔnɛt] nf bar ou tablet of soap

savons [savɔ̃] vb voir **savoir**

savourer [savuʀe] vt to savour (BRIT), savor (US)

savoureux, euse [savuʀø, -øz] adj tasty; (fig) spicy, juicy

saxo(phone) [saksɔ(fɔn)] nm sax(ophone)

scabreux, euse [skabʀø, -øz] adj risky; (indécent) improper, shocking

scandale [skɑ̃dal] nm scandal; (tapage): **faire du scandale** to make a scene, create a disturbance; **faire scandale** to scandalize people; **au grand scandale de ...** to the great indignation of …

scandaleux, euse [skɑ̃dalø, -øz] adj scandalous, outrageous

scandinave [skɑ̃dinav] adj Scandinavian ♦ nm/f: **Scandinave** Scandinavian

Scandinavie [skɑ̃dinavi] nf: **la Scandinavie** Scandinavia

scaphandre [skafɑ̃dʀ(ə)] nm (de plongeur) diving suit; (de cosmonaute) spacesuit; **scaphandre autonome** aqualung

scarabée [skaʀabe] nm beetle

scarlatine [skaʀlatin] nf scarlet fever

scarole [skaʀɔl] nf endive

sceau, x [so] nm seal; (fig) stamp, mark; **sous le sceau du secret** under the seal of secrecy

scélérat, e [seleʀa, -at] nm/f villain, blackguard ♦ adj villainous, blackguardly

sceller [sele] vt to seal

scénario [senaʀjo] nm (CINÉ) screenplay, script; (: idée, plan) scenario; (fig) pattern; scenario

scène [sɛn] nf (gén) scene; (estrade, fig: théâtre) stage; (entrer en scène to come on stage; **mettre en scène** (THÉÂT) to stage; (CINÉ) to direct; (fig) to present, introduce; **sur le devant de la scène** (en pleine actualité) in the forefront; **porter à la scène** to adapt for the stage; **faire une scène (à qn)** to make a scene (with sb); **scène de ménage** domestic fight ou scene

sceptique [sɛptik] adj sceptical ♦ nm/f sceptic

schéma [ʃema] nm (diagramme) diagram, sketch; (fig) outline

schématique [ʃematik] adj diagrammatic(al), schematic; (fig) oversimplified

sciatique [sjatik] adj: **nerf sciatique** sciatic nerve ♦ nf sciatica

scie [si] nf saw; (fam: rengaine) catch-tune; (: personne) bore; **scie à bois** wood saw; **scie circulaire** circular saw; **scie à découper** fretsaw; **scie à métaux** hacksaw; **scie sauteuse** jigsaw

sciemment [sjamɑ̃] adv knowingly, wittingly

science [sjɑ̃s] nf science; (savoir) knowledge; (savoir-faire) art, skill; **sciences économiques** economics; **sciences humaines/sociales** social sciences; **sciences naturelles** natural science *sg*, biology *sg*; **sciences po** political studies

science-fiction [sjɑ̃sfiksjɔ̃] *nf* science fiction

scientifique [sjɑ̃tifik] *adj* scientific ♦ *nm/f* (*savant*) scientist; (*étudiant*) science student

scier [sje] *vt* to saw; (*retrancher*) to saw off

scierie [siʀi] *nf* sawmill

scinder [sɛ̃de] *vt*: **se scinder** *vi* to split (up)

scintiller [sɛ̃tije] *vi* to sparkle

scission [sisjɔ̃] *nf* split

sciure [sjyʀ] *nf*: **sciure (de bois)** sawdust

sclérose [skleʀoz] *nf* sclerosis; (*fig*) ossification; **sclérose en plaques (SEP)** multiple sclerosis (MS)

scolaire [skɔlɛʀ] *adj* school *cpd*; (*péj*) schoolish; **l'année scolaire** the school year; (*à l'université*) the academic year; **en âge scolaire** of school age

scolariser [skɔlaʀize] *vt* to provide with schooling (*ou* schools)

scolarité [skɔlaʀite] *nf* schooling; **frais de scolarité** school fees (*BRIT*), tuition (*US*)

scooter [skutœʀ] *nm* (motor) scooter

score [skɔʀ] *nm* score; (*électoral etc*) result

scorpion [skɔʀpjɔ̃] *nm* (*signe*): **le Scorpion** Scorpio, the Scorpion; **être du Scorpion** to be Scorpio

scotch [skɔtʃ] *nm* (*whisky*) scotch, whisky; (*adhésif*) Sellotape® (*BRIT*), Scotch tape® (*US*)

scout, e [skut] *adj, nm* scout

script [skʀipt(ə)] *nm* printing; (*CINÉ*) (shooting) script

scrupule [skʀypyl] *nm* scruple; **être sans scrupules** to be unscrupulous; **se faire un scrupule de qch** to have scruples *ou* qualms about doing sth

scruter [skʀyte] *vt* to search, scrutinize; (*l'obscurité*) to peer into; (*motifs, comportement*) to examine, scrutinize

scrutin [skʀytɛ̃] *nm* (*vote*) ballot; (*ensemble des opérations*) poll; **scrutin proportionnel/majoritaire** election on a proportional/majority basis; **scrutin à deux tours** poll with two ballots *ou* rounds; **scrutin de liste** list system

sculpter [skylte] *vt* to sculpt; (*suj: érosion*) to carve

sculpteur [skyltœʀ] *nm* sculptor

sculpture [skyltyʀ] *nf* sculpture; **sculpture sur bois** wood carving

SDF *sigle m* (= *sans domicile fixe*) homeless person; **les SDF** the homeless

MOT CLÉ

se, s' [s(ə)] *pron* **1** (*emploi réfléchi*) oneself; (: *masc*) himself; (: *fém*) herself; (: *sujet non humain*) itself; (: *pl*) themselves; **se voir comme l'on est** to see o.s. as one is

2 (*réciproque*) one another, each other; **ils s'aiment** they love one another *ou* each other

3 (*passif*): **cela se répare facilement** it is easily repaired

4 (*possessif*): **se casser la jambe/laver les mains** to break one's leg/wash one's hands

séance [seɑ̃s] *nf* (*d'assemblée, récréative*) meeting, session; (*de tribunal*) sitting, session; (*musicale, CINÉ, THÉÂT*) performance; **ouvrir/lever la séance** to open/close the meeting; **séance tenante** forthwith

seau, x [so] *nm* bucket, pail; **seau à glace** ice bucket

sec, sèche [sɛk, sɛʃ] *adj* dry; (*raisins, figues*) dried; (*cœur, personne: insensible*) hard, cold; (*maigre, décharné*) spare, lean; (*réponse, ton*) sharp, curt; (*démarrage*) sharp, sudden ♦ *nm*: **tenir au sec** to keep in a dry place ♦ *adv* hard; (*démarrer*) sharply; **boire sec** to be a heavy drinker; **je le bois sec** I drink it straight *ou* neat; **à pied sec** without getting one's feet wet; **à sec** *adj* dried up; (*à court d'argent*) broke

sécateur [sekatœʀ] *nm* secateurs *pl* (*BRIT*), shears *pl*, pair of secateurs *ou* shears

sèche [sɛʃ] *adj f voir* **sec** ♦ *nf* (*fam*) cigarette, fag (*BRIT*)

sèche-cheveux [sɛʃʃəvø] *nm inv* hair-drier

sèche-linge [sɛʃlɛ̃ʒ] *nm inv* drying cabinet

sèchement [sɛʃmɑ̃] *adv* (*frapper etc*) sharply; (*répliquer etc*) drily, sharply

sécher [seʃe] *vt* to dry; (*dessécher: peau, blé*) to dry (out); (: *étang*) to dry up; (*bois*) to season; (*fam: classe, cours*) to skip, miss ♦ *vi* to dry; to dry out; to dry up; (*fam: candidat*) to be stumped; **se sécher** (*après le bain*) to dry o.s.

sécheresse [seʃʀɛs] *nf* dryness; (*absence de pluie*) drought

séchoir [seʃwaʀ] *nm* drier

second, e [s(ə)gɔ̃, -ɔ̃d] *adj* second ♦ *nm* (*assistant*) second in command; (*étage*) second floor (*BRIT*), third floor (*US*); (*NAVIG*) first mate ♦ *nf* second; (*SCOL*) = fifth form (*BRIT*), = tenth grade (*US*); **en second** (*en second rang*) in second place; **voyager en seconde** to travel second-class; **doué de seconde vue** having the (gift of) second sight; **trouver son second souffle** (*SPORT, fig*) to get one's second wind; **être dans un état second** to be in a daze (*ou* trance); **de seconde main** second-hand

secondaire [s(ə)gɔ̃dɛʀ] *adj* secondary

seconder [s(ə)gɔ̃de] *vt* to assist; (*favoriser*) to back

secouer [s(ə)kwe] *vt* to shake; (*passagers*) to rock; (*traumatiser*) to shake (up); **se secouer** (*chien*) to shake itself; (*fam: se démener*) to shake o.s. up; **secouer la poussière d'un tapis** to shake the dust off a carpet; **secouer la tête** to shake one's head

secourir [s(ə)kuʀiʀ] *vt* (*aller sauver*) to (go and) rescue; (*prodiguer des soins à*) to help, assist; (*venir en aide à*) to assist, aid

secourisme [s(ə)kuʀism(ə)] *nm* (*premiers soins*) first aid; (*sauvetage*) life saving

secouriste [sǝkuʀist(ǝ)] *nm/f* first-aid worker

secours [sǝkuʀ] *vb voir* **secourir** ♦ *nm* help, aid, assistance ♦ *nmpl voir sg*; **cela lui a été d'un grand secours** this was a great help to him; **au secours!** help!; **appeler au secours** to shout *ou* call for help; **appeler qn à son secours** to call sb to one's assistance; **porter secours à qn** to give sb assistance, help sb; **les premiers secours** first aid *sg*; **le secours en montagne** mountain rescue

secousse [sǝkus] *nf* jolt, bump; (*électrique*) shock; (*fig: psychologique*) jolt, shock; **secousse sismique** *ou* **tellurique** earth tremor

secret, ète [sǝkʀɛ, -ɛt] *adj* secret; (*fig: renfermé*) reticent, reserved ♦ *nm* secret; (*discrétion absolue*): **le secret** secrecy; **en secret** in secret, secretly; **au secret** in solitary confinement; **secret de fabrication** trade secret; **secret professionnel** professional secrecy

secrétaire [sǝkʀetɛʀ] *nm/f* secretary ♦ *nm* (*meuble*) writing desk, secretaire; **secrétaire d'ambassade** embassy secretary; **secrétaire de direction** private *ou* personal secretary; **secrétaire d'État** ≃ junior minister; **secrétaire général (SG)** Secretary-General; (*COMM*) company secretary; **secrétaire de mairie** town clerk; **secrétaire médicale** medical secretary; **secrétaire de rédaction** sub-editor

secrétariat [s(ǝ)kʀetaʀja] *nm* (*profession*) secretarial work; (*bureau: d'entreprise, d'école*) (secretary's) office; (: *d'organisation internationale*) secretariat; (*POL etc: fonction*) secretaryship, office of Secretary

secteur [sɛktœʀ] *nm* sector; (*ADMIN*) district; (*ÉLEC*): **branché sur le secteur** plugged into the mains (supply); **fonctionne sur pile et secteur** battery or mains operated; **le secteur privé/public** (*ÉCON*) the private/public sector; **le secteur primaire/tertiaire** the primary/tertiary sector

section [sɛksjɔ̃] *nf* section; (*de parcours d'autobus*) fare stage; (*MIL: unité*) platoon; **section rythmique** rhythm section

sectionner [sɛksjɔne] *vt* to sever; **se sectionner** *vi* to be severed

sécu [seky] *nf* (*fam: = sécurité sociale*) ≃ dole (*BRIT*), ≃ Welfare (*US*)

séculaire [sekylɛʀ] *adj* secular; (*très vieux*) age-old

sécuriser [sekyʀize] *vt* to give a sense of security to

sécurité [sekyʀite] *nf* security; (*absence de danger*) safety; **impression de sécurité** sense of security; **la sécurité internationale** international security; **système de sécurité** security (*ou* safety) system; **être en sécurité** to be safe; **la sécurité de l'emploi** job security; **la sécurité routière** road safety; **la sécurité sociale** ≃ (the) Social Security (*BRIT*), ≃ (the) Welfare (*US*)

sédentaire [sedɑ̃tɛʀ] *adj* sedentary

séduction [sedyksjɔ̃] *nf* seduction; (*charme, attrait*) appeal, charm

séduire [sedɥiʀ] *vt* to charm; (*femme: abuser de*) to seduce; (*suj: chose*) to appeal to

séduisant, e [sedɥizɑ̃, -ɑ̃t] *vb voir* **séduire** ♦ *adj* (*femme*) seductive; (*homme, offre*) very attractive

ségrégation [segʀegasjɔ̃] *nf* segregation

seigle [sɛgl(ǝ)] *nm* rye

seigneur [sɛɲœʀ] *nm* lord; **le Seigneur** the Lord

sein [sɛ̃] *nm* breast; (*entrailles*) womb; **au sein de** *prép* (*équipe, institution*) within; (*flots, bonheur*) in the midst of; **donner le sein à** (*bébé*) to feed (at the breast); to breast-feed; **nourrir au sein** to breast-feed

séisme [seism(ǝ)] *nm* earthquake

seize [sɛz] *num* sixteen

seizième [sɛzjɛm] *num* sixteenth

séjour [seʒuʀ] *nm* stay; (*pièce*) living room

séjourner [seʒuʀne] *vi* to stay

sel [sɛl] *nm* salt; (*fig*) wit; spice; **sel de cuisine/de table** cooking/table salt; **sel gemme** rock salt; **sels de bain** bathsalts

sélection [selɛksjɔ̃] *nf* selection; **faire/opérer une sélection parmi** to make a selection from among; **épreuve de sélection** (*SPORT*) trial (for selection); **sélection naturelle** natural selection; **sélection professionnelle** professional recruitment

sélectionner [selɛksjɔne] *vt* to select

self [sɛlf] *nm* (*fam*) self-service

self-service [sɛlfsɛʀvis] *adj* self-service ♦ *nm* self-service (*restaurant*); (*magasin*) self-service shop

selle [sɛl] *nf* saddle; **selles** *nfpl* (*MÉD*) stools; **aller à la selle** (*MÉD*) to have a bowel movement; **se mettre en selle** to mount, get into the saddle

seller [sele] *vt* to saddle

sellette [sɛlɛt] *nf*: **être sur la sellette** to be on the carpet (*fig*)

selon [s(ǝ)lɔ̃] *prép* according to; (*en se conformant à*) in accordance with; **selon moi** as I see it; **selon que** according to, depending on whether

semaine [s(ǝ)mɛn] *nf* week; (*salaire*) week's wages *ou* pay, weekly wages *ou* pay; **en semaine** during the week, on weekdays; **à la petite semaine** from day to day; **la semaine sainte** Holy Week

semblable [sɑ̃blabl(ǝ)] *adj* similar; (*de ce genre*): **de semblables mésaventures** such mishaps ♦ *nm* fellow creature *ou* man; **semblable à** similar to, like

semblant [sɑ̃blɑ̃] *nm*: **un semblant de vérité** a semblance of truth; **faire semblant (de faire)** to pretend (to do)

sembler [sɑ̃ble] *vb avec attribut* to seem ♦ *vb impers*: **il semble (bien) que/inutile de** it (really) seems *ou* appears that/useless to; **il me semble (bien) que** it (really) seems to me that, I (really) think that; **il me semble le connaître** I think *ou* I've a feeling I know him; **sembler être** to seem to be; **comme bon lui semble** as he sees fit; **me semble-**

t-il, à ce qu'il me semble it seems to me, to my mind

semelle [səmɛl] *nf* sole; *(intérieur)* insole, inner sole; **battre la semelle** to stamp one's feet (to keep them warm); *(fig)* to hang around (waiting); **semelles compensées** platform soles

semence [səmɑ̃s] *nf (graine)* seed; *(clou)* tack

semer [səme] *vt* to sow; *(fig: éparpiller)* to scatter; *(confusion)* to spread; *(: poursuivants)* to lose, shake off; **semer la discorde parmi** to sow discord among; **semé de** *(difficultés)* riddled with

semestre [səmɛstʀ(ə)] *nm* half-year; *(SCOL)* semester

séminaire [seminɛʀ] *nm* seminar; *(REL)* seminary

semi-remorque [səmiʀəmɔʀk(ə)] *nf* trailer ♦ *nm* articulated lorry *(BRIT)*, semi(trailer) *(US)*

semoule [səmul] *nf* semolina; **semoule de riz** ground rice

sempiternel, le [sɛ̃pitɛʀnɛl] *adj* eternal, never-ending

sénat [sena] *nm* senate; *see boxed note*

sénateur [senatœʀ] *nm* senator

sens [sɑ̃] *vb voir* **sentir** ♦ *nm* [sɑ̃s] *(signification)* meaning, sense; *(direction)* direction, way ♦ *nmpl (sensualité)* senses; **reprendre ses sens** to regain consciousness; **avoir le sens des affaires/de la mesure** to have business sense/a sense of moderation; **ça n'a pas de sens** that doesn't make (any) sense; **en dépit du bon sens** contrary to all good sense; **tomber sous le sens** to stand to reason, be perfectly obvious; **en un sens, dans un sens** in a way; **en ce sens que** in the sense that; **à mon sens** to my mind; **dans le sens des aiguilles d'une montre** clockwise; **dans le sens de la longueur/largeur** lengthways/width-ways; **dans le mauvais sens** the wrong way; in the wrong direction; **bon sens** good sense; **sens commun** common sense; **sens dessus dessous** upside down; **sens interdit, sens unique** one-way street

sensass [sɑ̃sas] *adj (fam)* fantastic

sensation [sɑ̃sasjɔ̃] *nf* sensation; **faire sensation** to cause a sensation, create a stir; **à sensation** *(péj)* sensational

sensationnel, le [sɑ̃sasjɔnɛl] *adj* sensational

sensé, e [sɑ̃se] *adj* sensible

sensibiliser [sɑ̃sibilize] *vt* to sensitize; **sensibiliser qn (à)** to make sb sensitive (to)

sensibilité [sɑ̃sibilite] *nf* sensitivity; *(affectivité, émotivité)* sensitivity, sensibility

sensible [sɑ̃sibl(ə)] *adj* sensitive; *(aux sens)* perceptible; *(appréciable: différence, progrès)* appreciable, noticeable; **sensible à** sensitive to

sensiblement [sɑ̃siblamɑ̃] *adv (notablement)* appreciably, noticeably; *(à peu près)*: **ils ont sensiblement le même poids** they weigh approximately the same

sensiblerie [sɑ̃siblərie] *nf* sentimentality; squeamishness

sensuel, le [sɑ̃sɥɛl] *adj* sensual; sensuous

sentence [sɑ̃tɑ̃s] *nf (jugement)* sentence; *(adage)* maxim

sentier [sɑ̃tje] *nm* path

sentiment [sɑ̃timɑ̃] *nm* feeling; *(conscience, impression)*: **avoir le sentiment de/que** to be aware of/have the feeling that; **recevez mes sentiments respectueux** yours faithfully; **faire du sentiment** *(péj)* to be sentimental; **si vous me prenez par les sentiments** if you appeal to my feelings

sentimental, e, aux [sɑ̃timɑ̃tal, -o] *adj* sentimental; *(vie, aventure)* love *cpd*

sentinelle [sɑ̃tinɛl] *nf* sentry; **en sentinelle** standing guard; *(soldat: en faction)* on sentry duty

sentir [sɑ̃tiʀ] *vt (par l'odorat)* to smell; *(par le goût)* to taste; *(au toucher, fig)* to feel; *(répandre une odeur de)* to smell of; *(: ressemblance)* to smell like; *(avoir la saveur de)* to taste of; to taste like; *(fig: dénoter, annoncer)* to be indicative of; to smack of; to foreshadow ♦ *vi* to smell; **sentir mauvais** to smell bad; **se sentir bien** to feel good; **se sentir mal** *(être indisposé)* to feel unwell *ou* ill; **se sentir le courage/la force de faire** to feel brave/strong enough to do; **ne plus se sentir de joie** to be beside o.s. with joy; **il ne peut pas le sentir** *(fam)* he can't stand him

séparation [separasjɔ̃] *nf* separation; *(cloison)* division, partition; **séparation de biens** division of property *(in marriage settlement)* **séparation de corps** legal separation

séparé, e [separe] *adj (appartements, pouvoirs)* separate; *(époux)* separated; **séparé de** separate from; separated from

séparément [separemɑ̃] *adv* separately

séparer [separe] *vt (gén)* to separate; *(suj: divergences etc)* to divide; to drive apart; *(: différences, obstacles)* to stand between; *(détacher)*: **séparer qch de** to pull sth (off) from; *(dissocier)* to distinguish between; *(diviser)*: **séparer qch par** to divide sth (up) with; **séparer une pièce en deux** to divide a room into two; **se séparer** *(époux)* to separate, part; *(prendre congé: amis etc)* to part, leave each other; *(adversaires)* to separate; *(se diviser: route, tige etc)* to divide; *(se détacher)*: **se séparer (de)** to split off (from); to come off; **se séparer de** (*époux*) to separate *ou* part from; (*employé, objet personnel*) to part with

sept [sɛt] *num* seven

septante [sɛptãt] *num* (*Belgique, Suisse*) seventy

septembre [sɛptãbʀ(ə)] *nm* September; *voir aussi* **juillet**

septennat [sɛptena] *nm* seven-year term (of office); seven-year reign

septentrional, e, aux [sɛptãtʀijɔnal, -o] *adj* northern

septicémie [sɛptisemi] *nf* blood poisoning, septicaemia

septième [sɛtjɛm] *num* seventh; **être au septième ciel** to be on cloud nine

septique [sɛptik] *adj:* **fosse septique** septic tank

sépulture [sepyltyʀ] *nf* burial; (*tombeau*) burial place, grave

séquelles [sekɛl] *nfpl* after-effects; (*fig*) aftermath *sg*; consequences

séquestrer [sekɛstʀe] *vt* (*personne*) to confine illegally; (*biens*) to impound

serai *etc* [səʀe] *vb voir* **être**

serein, e [səʀɛ̃, -ɛn] *adj* serene; (*jugement*) dispassionate

serez [səʀe] *vb voir* **être**

sergent [sɛʀʒã] *nm* sergeant

série [seʀi] *nf* (*de questions, d'accidents, TV*) series *inv*; (*de clés, casseroles, outils*) set; (*catégorie: SPORT*) rank; class; **en série** in quick succession; (*COMM*) mass *cpd*; **de série** *adj* standard; **hors série** (*COMM*) custom-built; (*fig*) outstanding; **imprimante série** (*INFORM*) serial printer; **soldes de fin de séries** end of line special offers; **série noire** *nf* (*crime*) thriller ◆ *nf* (*suite de malheurs*) run of bad luck

sérieusement [seʀjøzmã] *adv* seriously; reliably; responsibly; **il parle sérieusement** he's serious, he means it; **sérieusement?** are you serious?, do you mean it?

sérieux, euse [seʀjø, -øz] *adj* serious; (*élève, employé*) reliable, responsible; (*client, maison*) reliable, dependable; (*offre, proposition*) genuine, serious; (*grave, sévère*) serious, solemn; (*maladie, situation*) serious, grave; (*important*) considerable ◆ *nm* seriousness; reliability; **ce n'est pas sérieux** (*raisonnable*) that's not on; **garder son sérieux** to keep a straight face; **manquer de sérieux** not to be very responsible (*ou* reliable); **prendre qch/qn au sérieux** to take sth/sb seriously

serin [səʀɛ̃] *nm* canary

seringue [səʀɛ̃g] *nf* syringe

serions *etc* [səʀjɔ̃] *vb voir* **être**

serment [sɛʀmã] *nm* (*juré*) oath; (*promesse*) pledge, vow; **prêter serment** to take the *ou* an oath; **faire le serment de** to take a vow to, swear to; **sous serment** on *ou* under oath

sermon [sɛʀmɔ̃] *nm* sermon; (*péj*) sermon, lecture

séronégatif, ive [seʀonegatif, -iv] *adj* HIV nega-

tive

séropositif, ive [seʀopozitif, -iv] *adj* HIV positive

serpent [sɛʀpã] *nm* snake; **serpent à sonnettes** rattlesnake; **serpent monétaire (européen)** (European) monetary snake

serpenter [sɛʀpãte] *vi* to wind

serpillière [sɛʀpijɛʀ] *nf* floorcloth

serre [sɛʀ] *nf* (*AGR*) greenhouse; **serre chaude** hothouse; **serre froide** unheated greenhouse

serré, e [seʀe] *adj* (*tissu*) closely woven; (*réseau*) dense; (*écriture*) close; (*habits*) tight; (*fig: lutte, match*) tight, close-fought; (*passagers etc*) (tightly) packed; (*café*) strong ◆ *adv:* **jouer serré** to play it close, play a close game; **écrire serré** to write a cramped hand; **avoir la gorge serrée** to have a lump in one's throat

serrer [seʀe] *vt* (*tenir*) to grip *ou* hold tight; (*comprimer, coincer*) to squeeze; (*poings, mâchoires*) to clench; (*suj: vêtement*) to be too tight for; to fit tightly; (*rapprocher*) to close up, move closer together; (*ceinture, nœud, frein, vis*) to tighten ◆ *vi:* **serrer à droite** to keep to the right; to move into the right-hand lane; **se serrer** (*se rapprocher*) to squeeze up; **se serrer contre qn** to huddle up to sb; **se serrer les coudes** to stick together, back one another up; **se serrer la ceinture** to tighten one's belt; **serrer la main à qn** to shake sb's hand; **serrer qn dans ses bras** to hug sb, clasp sb in one's arms; **serrer la gorge à qn** (*suj: chagrin*) to bring a lump to sb's throat; **serrer les dents** to clench *ou* grit one's teeth; **serrer qn de près** to follow close behind sb; **serrer le trottoir** to hug the kerb; **serrer sa droite** to keep well to the right; **serrer la vis à qn** to crack down harder on sb; **serrer les rangs** to close ranks

serrure [seʀyʀ] *nf* lock

serrurier [seʀyʀje] *nm* locksmith

sers, sert [sɛʀ] *vb voir* **servir**

servante [sɛʀvãt] *nf* (*maid*) servant

serveur, euse [sɛʀvœʀ, -øz] *nm/f* waiter/waitress ◆ *adj:* **centre serveur** (*INFORM*) service centre

serviable [sɛʀvjabl(ə)] *adj* obliging, willing to help

service [sɛʀvis] *nm* (*gén*) service; (*série de repas*): **premier service** first sitting; (*pourboire*) service (charge); (*assortiment de vaisselle*) set, service; (*linge de table*) set; (*bureau: de la vente etc*) department, section; (*travail*): **pendant le service** on duty; **services** *nmpl* (*travail, ÉCON*) services, inclusive-/exclusive of service; **faire le service** to serve; **être en service chez qn** (*domestique*) to be in sb's service; **être au service de** (*patron, patrie*) to be in the service of; **être au service de qn** (*collaborateur, voiture*) to be at sb's service; **porte de service** tradesman's entrance; **rendre service à** to help; **il aime rendre service** he likes to help; **rendre un service à qn** to do sb a favour; **heures de service** hours of duty; **être de service** to be on duty; **reprendre du service** to get back into action; **avoir 25 ans de service** to have completed 25 years' service; **être/mettre en service** to be in/put into service ou operation; **hors service** not in use; out of order; **service à thé/café** tea/coffee set ou service; **service après-vente (SAV)** after-sales service; **en service commandé** on an official assignment; **service funèbre** funeral service; **service militaire** military service; see boxed note; **service d'ordre** police (ou stewards) in charge of maintaining order; **services publics** public services, (public) utilities; **services secrets** secret service sg; **services sociaux** social services

SERVICE MILITAIRE

French men over 18 years of age are required to do ten months' **service militaire** if they pass their physical examination. Call-up can be delayed, however, if the conscript is a full-time student in higher education. Conscientious objectors are required to do two years' community service. Since 1970, women have been able to do military service, though few do.

serviette [sɛʀvjɛt] nf (de table) (table) napkin, serviette; (de toilette) towel; (porte-documents) briefcase; **serviette éponge** terry towel; **serviette hygiénique** sanitary towel

servir [sɛʀviʀ] vt (gén) to serve; (dîneur: au restaurant) to wait on; (client: au magasin) to serve, attend to; (fig: aider): **servir qn** to aid sb; to serve sb's interests; to stand sb in good stead; (COMM: rente) to pay ◆ vi (TENNIS) to serve; (CARTES) to deal; (être militaire) to serve; **servir qch à qn** to serve sb with sth, help sb to sth; **qu'est-ce que je vous sers?** what can I get you?; se servir (prendre d'un plat) to help o.s.; (s'approvisionner): **se servir chez** to shop at; **se servir de** (plat) to help o.s. to; (voiture, outil, relations) to use; **servir à qn** (diplôme, livre) to be of use to sb; **ça m'a servi pour faire** it was useful to me when I did; I used it to do; **servir à qch/à faire** (outil etc) to be used for sth/for doing; **ça peut servir** it may come in handy; **à quoi cela sert-il (de faire)?** what's the use of (doing)?; **cela ne sert à rien** it's no use; **servir (à qn) de ...** to serve as ... (for sb); **servir à dîner (à qn)** to serve dinner (to sb)

serviteur [sɛʀvitœʀ] nm servant

ses [se] adj possessif voir **son**

set [sɛt] nm set; (napperon) placemat; **set de table** set of placemats

seuil [sœj] nm doorstep; (fig) threshold; **sur le seuil de la maison** in the doorway of his house, on his doorstep; **au seuil de** (fig) on the threshold ou brink ou edge of; **seuil de rentabilité** (COMM) breakeven point

seul, e [sœl] adj (sans compagnie) alone; (avec nuance affective: isolé) lonely; (unique): **un seul livre** only one book, a single book; **le seul livre** the only book; **seul ce livre, ce livre seul** this book alone, only this book; **d'un seul coup** (soudainement) all at once; (à la fois) at one blow ◆ adv (vivre) alone, on one's own; **parler tout seul** to talk to oneself; **faire qch (tout) seul** to do sth (all) on one's own ou (all) by oneself ◆ nm, nf: **il en reste un(e) seul(e)** there's only one left; **pas un(e) seul(e)** not a single; **à lui (tout) seul** single-handed, on his own; **seul à seul** in private

seulement [sœlmɑ̃] adv (pas davantage): **seulement 5, 5 seulement** only 5; (exclusivement): **seulement eux** only them, them alone; (pas avant): **seulement hier/à 10h** only yesterday/at 10 o'clock; (mais, toutefois): **il consent, seulement il demande des garanties** he agrees, only he wants guarantees; **non seulement ... mais aussi** ou **encore** not only ... but also

sève [sɛv] nf sap

sévère [sevɛʀ] adj severe

sévices [sevis] nmpl (physical) cruelty sg, ill treatment sg

sévir [seviʀ] vi (punir) to use harsh measures, crack down; (suj: fléau) to rage, be rampant; **sévir contre** (abus) to deal ruthlessly with, crack down on

sevrer [səvʀe] vt to wean; (fig): **sevrer qn de** to deprive sb of

sexe [sɛks(ə)] nm sex; (organe mâle) member

sexuel, le [sɛksɥɛl] adj sexual; **acte sexuel** sex act

seyant, e [sejɑ̃, -ɑ̃t] vb voir **seoir** ◆ adj becoming

shampooing [ʃɑ̃pwɛ̃] nm shampoo; **se faire un shampooing** to shampoo one's hair; **shampooing colorant** (colour) rinse; **shampooing traitant** medicated shampoo

short [ʃɔʀt] nm (pair of) shorts pl

MOT CLÉ

si [si] nm (MUS) B; (en chantant la gamme) ti
◆ adv 1 (oui) yes; **"Paul n'est pas venu" – "si!"** "Paul hasn't come" – "Yes he has!"; **je vous assure que si** I assure you he did/she is etc

2 (tellement) so; **si gentil/rapidement** so kind/fast; **(tant et) si bien que** so much so that; **si rapide qu'il soit** however fast he may be
◆ conj if; **si tu veux** if you want; **je me demande si** I wonder if ou whether; **si j'étais toi** if I were you; **si seulement** if only; **si ce n'est que** apart from; **une des plus belles, si ce n'est la plus belle** one of the most beautiful, if not THE most beautiful; **s'il est aimable, eux par contre ...** while ou whereas he's nice, they (on the other hand) ...

Sicile [sisil] nf: **la Sicile** Sicily

SIDA, sida [sida] nm (= syndrome immuno-déficitaire acquis) AIDS sg

sidéré, e [sideʀe] adj staggered

sidérurgie [sideʀyʀʒi] nf steel industry

siècle [sjɛkl(ə)] nm century; (époque): **le siècle des lumières/de l'atome** the age of enlightenment/atomic age; (REL): **le siècle** the world

siège [sjɛʒ] *nm* seat; (*d'entreprise*) head office; (*d'organisation*) headquarters *pl*; (*MIL*) siege; **lever le siège** to raise the siege; **mettre le siège devant** to besiege; **présentation par le siège** (*MÉD*) breech presentation; **siège avant/arrière** (*AUTO*) front/back seat; **siège baquet** bucket seat; **siège social** registered office

siéger [sjeʒe] *vi* (*assemblée, tribunal*) to sit; (*résider, se trouver*) to lie, be located

sien, ne [sjɛ̃, sjɛn] *pron*: **le(la) sien(ne), les siens (siennes)** *m* his; *f* hers; *non humain* its; **y mettre du sien** to pull one's weight; **faire des siennes** (*fam*) to be up to one's (usual) tricks; **les siens** (*sa famille*) one's family

sieste [sjɛst(ə)] *nf* (afternoon) snooze *ou* nap, siesta; **faire la sieste** to have a snooze *ou* nap

sifflement [sifləmɑ̃] *nm* whistle, whistling *no pl*; wheezing *no pl*; hissing *no pl*

siffler [sifle] *vi* (*gén*) to whistle; (*avec un sifflet*) to blow (on) one's whistle; (*en respirant*) to wheeze; (*serpent, vapeur*) to hiss ♦ *vt* (*chanson*) to whistle; (*chien etc*) to whistle for; (*fille*) to whistle at; (*pièce, orateur*) to hiss, boo; (*faute*) to blow one's whistle at; (*fin du match, départ*) to blow one's whistle for; (*fam: verre, bouteille*) to guzzle, knock back (*BRIT*)

sifflet [siflɛ] *nm* whistle; **sifflets** *nmpl* (*de mécontentement*) whistles, boos; **coup de sifflet** whistle

siffloter [sifləte] *vi*, *vt* to whistle

sigle [sigl(ə)] *nm* acronym, (set of) initials *pl*

signal, aux [siɲal, -o] *nm* (*signe convenu, appareil*) signal; (*indice, écriteau*) sign; **donner le signal de** to give the signal for; **signal d'alarme** alarm signal; **signal d'alerte/de détresse** warning/distress signal; **signal horaire** time signal; **signal optique/sonore** warning light/sound; visual/acoustic signal; **signaux (lumineux)** (*AUTO*) traffic signals; **signaux routiers** road signs; (*lumineux*) traffic lights

signalement [siɲalmɑ̃] *nm* description, particulars *pl*

signaler [siɲale] *vt* to indicate; to announce; to report; (*être l'indice de*) to indicate; (*faire remarquer*): **signaler qch à qn/à qn que** to point out sth to sb/to sb that; (*appeler l'attention sur*): **signaler qn à la police** to bring sb to the notice of the police; **se signaler par** to distinguish o.s. by; **se signaler à l'attention de qn** to attract sb's attention

signature [siɲatyR] *nf* signature; (*action*) signing

signe [siɲ] *nm* sign; (*TYPO*) mark; **ne pas donner signe de vie** to give no sign of life; **c'est bon signe** it's a good sign; **c'est signe que** it's a sign that; **faire un signe de la main/tête** to give a sign with one's hand/shake one's head; **faire signe à qn** (*fig*) to get in touch with sb; **faire signe à qn d'entrer** to motion (to) sb to come in; **en signe de** as a sign *ou* mark of; **le signe de la croix** the sign of the Cross; **signe de ponctuation** punctuation mark; **signe du zodiaque** sign of the zodiac; **signes particuliers** distinguishing marks

signer [siɲe] *vt* to sign; **se signer** *vi* to cross o.s.

significatif, ive [siɲifikatif, -iv] *adj* significant

signification [siɲifikɑsjɔ̃] *nf* meaning

signifier [siɲifje] *vt* (*vouloir dire*) to mean, signify; (*faire connaître*): **signifier qch (à qn)** to make sth known (to sb); (*JUR*): **signifier qch à qn** to serve notice of sth on sb

silence [silɑ̃s] *nm* silence; (*MUS*) rest; **garder le silence (sur qch)** to keep silent (about sth), say nothing (about sth); **passer sous silence** to pass over (in silence); **réduire au silence** to silence

silencieux, euse [silɑ̃sjø, -øz] *adj* quiet, silent ♦ *nm* silencer (*BRIT*), muffler (*US*)

silex [silɛks] *nm* flint

silhouette [silwɛt] *nf* outline, silhouette; (*lignes, contour*) outline; (*figure*) figure

silicium [silisjɔm] *nm* silicon; **plaquette de silicium** silicon chip

sillage [sijaʒ] *nm* wake; (*fig*) trail; **dans le sillage de** (*fig*) in the wake of

sillon [sijɔ̃] *nm* (*d'un champ*) furrow; (*de disque*) groove

sillonner [sijɔne] *vt* (*creuser*) to furrow; (*traverser*) to cross, criss-cross

simagrées [simagre] *nfpl* fuss *sg*; airs and graces

similaire [similɛR] *adj* similar

similicuir [similikɥiR] *nm* imitation leather

similitude [similityd] *nf* similarity

simple [sɛ̃pl(ə)] *adj* (*gén*) simple; (*non multiple*) single; **simples** *nmpl* (*MÉD*) medicinal plants; **simple messieurs** *nm* (*TENNIS*) men's singles *sg*; **un simple particulier** an ordinary citizen; **une simple formalité** a mere formality; **cela varie du simple au double** it can double, it can double the price *etc*; **dans le plus simple appareil** in one's birthday suit; **simple course** *adj* single; **simple d'esprit** *nm/f* simpleton; **simple soldat** private

simplicité [sɛ̃plisite] *nf* simplicity; **en toute simplicité** quite simply

simplifier [sɛ̃plifje] *vt* to simplify

simulacre [simylakR(ə)] *nm* enactment; (*péj*): **un simulacre de** a pretence of, a sham

simuler [simyle] *vt* to sham, simulate

simultané, e [simyltane] *adj* simultaneous

sincère [sɛ̃sɛR] *adj* sincere; genuine; heartfelt; **mes sincères condoléances** my deepest sympathy

sincèrement [sɛ̃sɛRmɑ̃] *adv* sincerely; genuinely

sincérité [sɛ̃seRite] *nf* sincerity; **en toute sincérité** in all sincerity

sine qua non [sinekwanɔn] *adj*: **condition sine qua non** indispensable condition

singe [sɛ̃ʒ] *nm* monkey; (*de grande taille*) ape

singer [sɛ̃ʒe] *vt* to ape, mimic

singeries [sɛ̃ʒRi] *nfpl* antics; (*simagrées*) airs and graces

singulariser [sɛ̃gylaʀize] *vt* to mark out; **se singulariser** to call attention to o.s.

singularité [sɛ̃gylaʀite] *nf* peculiarity

singulier, ière [sɛ̃gylje, -jɛʀ] *adj* remarkable, singular; (*LING*) singular ♦ *nm* singular

sinistre [sinistʀ] *adj* sinister; (*intensif*): **un sinistre imbécile** an incredible idiot ♦ *nm* (*incendie*) blaze; (*catastrophe*) disaster; (*ASSURANCES*) damage (*giving rise to a claim*)

sinistré, e [sinistʀe] *adj* disaster-stricken ♦ *nm/f* disaster victim

sinon [sinɔ̃] *conj* (*autrement, sans quoi*) otherwise, or else; (*sauf*) except, other than; (*si ce n'est*) if not

sinueux, euse [sinɥø, -øz] *adj* winding; (*fig*) tortuous

sinus [sinys] *nm* (*ANAT*) sinus; (*GÉOM*) sine

sinusite [sinyzit] *nf* sinusitis, sinus infection

siphon [sifɔ̃] *nm* (*tube, d'eau gazeuse*) siphon; (*d'évier etc*) U-bend

sirène [siʀɛn] *nf* siren; **sirène d'alarme** fire alarm; (*pendant la guerre*) air-raid siren

sirop [siʀo] *nm* (*à diluer: de fruit etc*) syrup, cordial (*BRIT*); (*boisson*) fruit drink; (*pharmaceutique*) syrup, mixture; **sirop de menthe** mint syrup *ou* cordial; **sirop contre la toux** cough syrup *ou* mixture

siroter [siʀote] *vt* to sip

sismique [sismik] *adj* seismic

site [sit] *nm* (*paysage, environnement*) setting; (*d'une ville etc: emplacement*) site; **site (pittoresque)** beauty spot; **sites touristiques** places of interest; **sites naturels/historiques** natural/historic sites

site web [sitwɛb] *nm* website

sitôt [sito] *adv*: **sitôt parti** as soon as he *etc* had left; **sitôt après** straight after; **pas de sitôt** not for a long time; **sitôt (après) que** as soon as

situation [sitɥasjɔ̃] *nf* (*gén*) situation; (*d'un édifice, d'une ville*) situation, position; (*emplacement*) location; **être en situation de faire qch** to be in a position to do sth; **situation de famille** marital status

situé, e [sitɥe] *adj*: **bien situé** well situated, in a good location; **situé à/près de** situated at/near

situer [sitɥe] *vt* to site, situate; (*en pensée*) to set, place; **se situer** *vi*: **se situer à/près de** to be situated at/near

six [sis] *num* six

sixième [sizjɛm] *num* sixth; **en sixième** (*SCOL: classe*) first form (*BRIT*), sixth grade (*US*)

skaï ®[skaj] *nm* ≈ Leatherette®

ski [ski] *nm* (*objet*) ski; (*sport*) skiing; **faire du ski** to ski; **ski alpin** Alpine skiing; **ski court** short ski; **ski évolutif** short ski method; **ski de fond** cross-country skiing; **ski nautique** water-skiing; **ski de piste** downhill skiing; **ski de randonnée** cross-country skiing

skier [skje] *vi* to ski

skieur, euse [skjœʀ, -øz] *nm/f* skier

slip [slip] *nm* (*sous-vêtement*) underpants *pl*, pants *pl* (*BRIT*), briefs *pl*; (*de bain: d'homme*) (bathing *ou* swimming) trunks *pl*; (: *du bikini*) (bikini) briefs *pl* *ou* bottoms *pl*

slogan [slɔgɑ̃] *nm* slogan

SMIC [smik] *sigle m* = **salaire minimum interprofessionnel de croissance**; *see boxed note*

smicard, e [smikaʀ, -aʀd(ə)] *nm/f* minimum wage earner

smoking [smɔkiŋ] *nm* dinner *ou* evening suit

SMS *sigle m* (*short message service*) SMS

SNC *abr* = service non compris

SNCF *sigle f* (= *Société nationale des chemins de fer français*) French railways

snob [snɔb] *adj* snobbish ♦ *nm/f* snob

snobisme [snɔbism(ə)] *nm* snobbery

sobre [sɔbʀ(ə)] *adj* temperate, abstemious; (*élégance, style*) restrained, sober

sobriquet [sɔbʀikɛ] *nm* nickname

social, e, aux [sɔsjal, -o] *adj* social

socialisme [sɔsjalism(ə)] *nm* socialism

socialiste [sɔsjalist(ə)] *adj, nm/f* socialist

société [sɔsjete] *nf* society; (*d'abeilles, de fourmis*) colony; (*sportive*) club; (*COMM*) company; **la bonne société** polite society; **se plaire dans la société de** to enjoy the society of; **l'archipel de la Société** the Society Islands; **la société d'abondance/de consommation** the affluent/consumer society; **société par actions** joint stock company; **société anonyme (SA)** ≈ limited company (Ltd) (*BRIT*), ≈ incorporated company (Inc.) (*US*); **société d'investissement à capital variable (SICAV)** ≈ investment trust (*BRIT*), ≈ mutual fund (*US*); **société à responsabilité limitée (SARL)** *type of limited liability company (with non-negotiable shares)*; **société savante** learned society; **société de services** service company

sociologie [sɔsjɔlɔʒi] *nf* sociology

socle [sɔkl(ə)] *nm* (*de colonne, statue*) plinth, pedestal; (*de lampe*) base

socquette [sɔkɛt] *nf* ankle sock

sœur [sœʀ] *nf* sister; (*religieuse*) nun, sister; **sœur Élisabeth** (*REL*) Sister Elizabeth; **sœur de lait** foster sister

soi [swa] *pron* oneself; **cela va de soi** that *ou* it goes without saying, it stands to reason

soi-disant [swadizɑ̃] *adj inv* so-called ♦ *adv* supposedly

soie [swa] *nf* silk; (*de porc, sanglier : poil*) bristle

soierie [swaʀi] *nf* (*industrie*) silk trade; (*tissu*) silk

soif [swaf] *nf* thirst; (*fig*): **soif de** thirst *ou* craving for; **avoir soif** to be thirsty; **donner soif à qn** to make sb thirsty

soigné, e [swaɲe] *adj* (*tenue*) well-groomed, neat; (*travail*) careful, meticulous; (*fam*) whopping; stiff

soigner [swaɲe] *vt* (*malade, maladie : suj : docteur*) to treat; (: *suj : infirmière, mère*) to nurse, look after; (*blessé*) to tend; (*travail, détails*) to take care over; (*jardin, chevelure, invités*) to look after

soigneux, euse [swaɲø, -øz] *adj* (*propre*) tidy, neat; (*méticuleux*) painstaking, careful; **soigneux de** careful with

soi-même [swamɛm] *pron* oneself

soin [swɛ̃] *nm* (*application*) care; (*propreté, ordre*) tidiness, neatness; (*responsabilité*): **le soin de qch** the care of sth; **soins** *nmpl* (*à un malade, blessé*) treatment *sg*, medical attention *sg*; (*attentions, prévenance*) care and attention *sg*; (*hygiène*) care *sg*; **soins de la chevelure/de beauté** hair/beauty care; **soins du corps/ménage** care of one's body/ the home; **avoir** *ou* **prendre soin de** to take care of, look after; **avoir** *ou* **prendre soin de faire** to take care to do; **faire qch avec (grand) soin** to do sth (very) carefully; **sans soin** *adj* careless; untidy; **les premiers soins** first aid *sg*; **aux bons soins de** c/o, care of; **être aux petits soins pour qn** to wait on sb hand and foot, see to sb's every need; **confier qn aux soins de qn** to hand sb over to sb's care

soir [swaʀ] *nm, adv* evening; **le soir** in the evening(s); **ce soir** this evening, tonight; **à ce soir!** see you this evening (*ou* tonight)!; **la veille au soir** the previous evening; **sept/dix heures du soir** seven in the evening/ten at night; **le repas/journal du soir** the evening meal/newspaper; **dimanche soir** Sunday evening; **hier soir** yesterday evening; **demain soir** tomorrow evening, tomorrow night

soirée [swaʀe] *nf* evening; (*réception*) party; **donner en soirée** (*film, pièce*) to give an evening performance of

soit [swa] *vb voir* **être** ♦ *conj* (*à savoir*) namely, to wit; (*ou*): **soit ... soit** either ... or ♦ *adv* so be it, very well; **soit un triangle ABC** let ABC be a triangle; **soit que ... soit que** *ou* **ou que** whether ... or whether

soixantaine [swasɑ̃tɛn] *nf*: **une soixantaine (de)** sixty or so, about sixty; **avoir la soixantaine** to be around sixty

soixante [swasɑ̃t] *num* sixty

soixante-dix [swasɑ̃tdis] *num* seventy

soja [sɔʒa] *nm* soya; (*graines*) soya beans *pl*; **germes de soja** beansprouts

sol [sɔl] *nm* ground; (*de logement*) floor; (*revêtement*) flooring *no pl*; (*territoire, AGR, GÉO*) soil; (*MUS*) G; (: *en chantant la gamme*) so(h)

solaire [sɔlɛʀ] *adj* solar, sun *cpd*

soldat [sɔlda] *nm* soldier; **Soldat inconnu** Unknown Warrior *ou* Soldier; **soldat de plomb** tin *ou* toy soldier

solde [sɔld(ə)] *nf* pay ♦ *nm* (*COMM*) balance; **soldes** *nmpl ou nfpl* (*COMM*) sales; (*articles*) sale goods; **à la solde de qn** (*péj*) in sb's pay; **solde créditeur/ débiteur** credit/debit balance; **solde à payer** balance outstanding; **en solde** at sale price; **aux soldes** at the sales

solder [sɔlde] *vt* (*compte*) to settle; (*marchandise*) to sell at sale price, sell off; **se solder par** (*fig*) to end in; **article soldé (à) 10 €** item reduced to 10 €

sole [sɔl] *nf* sole *inv* (*fish*)

soleil [sɔlɛj] *nm* sun; (*lumière*) sun(light); (*temps ensoleillé*) sun(shine); (*feu d'artifice*) Catherine wheel; (*ACROBATIE*) grand circle; (*BOT*) sunflower; **il y a** *ou* **il fait du soleil** it's sunny; **au soleil** in the sun; **en plein soleil** in full sun; **le soleil levant/ couchant** the rising/setting sun; **le soleil de minuit** the midnight sun

solennel, le [sɔlanɛl] *adj* solemn; ceremonial

solfège [sɔlfɛʒ] *nm* rudiments *pl* of music; (*exercices*) ear training *no pl*

solidaire [sɔlidɛʀ] *adj* (*personnes*) who stand together, who show solidarity; (*pièces mécaniques*) interdependent; (*JUR : engagement*) binding on all parties; (: *débiteurs*) jointly liable; **être solidaire de** (*collègues*) to stand by; (*mécanisme*) to be bound up with, be dependent on

solidarité [sɔlidaʀite] *nf* (*entre personnes*) solidarity; (*de mécanisme, phénomènes*) interdependence; **par solidarité (avec)** (*cesser le travail etc*) in sympathy (with)

solide [sɔlid] *adj* solid; (*mur, maison, meuble*) solid, sturdy; (*connaissances, argument*) sound; (*personne*) robust, sturdy; (*estomac*) strong ♦ *nm* solid; **avoir les reins solides** (*fig*) to be in a good financial position; to have sound financial backing

soliste [sɔlist(ə)] *nm/f* soloist

solitaire [sɔlitɛʀ] *adj* (*sans compagnie*) solitary, lonely; (*isolé*) isolated, lone; (*lieu*) lonely ♦ *nm/f* recluse; loner ♦ *nm* (*diamant, jeu*) solitaire

solitude [sɔlityd] *nf* loneliness; (*paix*) solitude

solive [sɔliv] *nf* joist

solliciter [sɔlisite] *vt* (*personne*) to appeal to; (*emploi, faveur*) to seek; (*moteur*) to prompt; (*suj : occupations, attractions etc*): **solliciter qn** to appeal to sb's curiosity *etc*; to entice sb; to make demands on sb's time; **solliciter qn de faire** to appeal to sb *ou* request sb to do

sollicitude [sɔlisityd] *nf* concern

soluble [sɔlybl(ə)] *adj* (*sucre, cachet*) soluble; (*problème etc*) soluble, solvable

solution [sɔlysjɔ̃] *nf* solution; **solution de continuité** gap, break; **solution de facilité** easy way out

solvable [sɔlvabl(ə)] *adj* solvent

sombre [sɔ̃bʀ(ə)] *adj* dark; (*fig*) sombre, gloomy; (*sinistre*) awful, dreadful

sombrer [sɔ̃bʀe] *vi* (*bateau*) to sink, go down;

sombrer corps et biens to go down with all hands; **sombrer dans** (*misère, désespoir*) to sink into

sommaire [sɔmɛʀ] *adj* (*simple*) basic; (*expéditif*) summary ♦ *nm* summary; **faire le sommaire de** to make a summary of, summarize; **exécution sommaire** summary execution

sommation [sɔmasjɔ̃] *nf* (*JUR*) summons *sg*; (*avant de faire feu*) warning

somme [sɔm] *nf* (*MATH*) sum; (*fig*) amount; (*argent*) sum, amount ♦ *nm*: **faire un somme** to have a (short) nap; **faire la somme de** to add up; **en somme, somme toute** *adv* all in all

sommeil [sɔmɛj] *nm* sleep; **avoir sommeil** to be sleepy; **avoir le sommeil léger** to be a light sleeper; **en sommeil** (*fig*) dormant

sommeiller [sɔmeje] *vi* to doze, (*fig*) to lie dormant

sommer [sɔme] *vt*: **sommer qn de faire** to command *ou* order sb to do; (*JUR*) to summon sb to do

sommes [sɔm] *vb voir* **être**; *voir aussi* **somme**

sommet [sɔmɛ] *nm* top; (*d'une montagne*) summit, top; (*fig: de la perfection, gloire*) height; (*GÉOM: d'angle*) vertex (*pl* vertices); (*conférence*) summit (conference)

sommier [sɔmje] *nm* bed base, bedspring (*us*); (*ADMIN: registre*) register; **sommier à ressorts** (interior sprung) divan base (*BRIT*), box spring (*US*); **sommier à lattes** slatted bed base

somnambule [sɔmnãbyl] *nm/f* sleepwalker

somnifère [sɔmnifɛʀ] *nm* sleeping drug; (*comprimé*) sleeping pill *ou* tablet

somnoler [sɔmnɔle] *vi* to doze

somptueux, euse [sɔ̃ptɥø, -øz] *adj* sumptuous; (*cadeau*) lavish

son [sɔ̃], **sa** [sa], *pl* **ses** [se] *adj possessif* (*antécédent humain mâle*) his; (: *femelle*) her; (: *valeur indéfinie*) one's, his(her); (: *non humain*) its; *voir note* **sous il**

son [sɔ̃] *nm* sound; (*de blé etc*) bran; **son et lumière** *adj inv* son et lumière

sondage [sɔ̃daʒ] *nm* (*de terrain*) boring, drilling; (*de mer, atmosphère*) sounding; probe; (*enquête*) survey, sounding out of opinion; **sondage (d'opinion)** (opinion) poll

sonde [sɔ̃d] *nf* (*NAVIG*) lead *ou* sounding line; (*MÉTÉOROLOGIE*) sonde; (*MÉD*) probe; catheter; (*d'alimentation*) feeding tube; (*TECH*) borer, driller; (*de forage, sondage*) drill; (*pour fouiller etc*) probe; **sonde à avalanche** pole (*for probing snow and locating victims*) **sonde spatiale** probe

sonder [sɔ̃de] *vt* (*NAVIG*) to sound; (*atmosphère, plaie, bagages etc*) to sound; (*TECH*) to bore, drill; (*fig: personne*) to sound out; (: *opinion*) to probe; **sonder le terrain** (*fig*) to see how the land lies

songe [sɔ̃ʒ] *nm* dream

songer [sɔ̃ʒe] *vi* to dream; **songer à** (*rêver à*) to muse over, think over; (*penser à*) to think of; (*envisager*) to contemplate, think of, consider; **songer que** to consider that; to think that

songeur, euse [sɔ̃ʒœʀ, -øz] *adj* pensive; **ça me laisse songeur** that makes me wonder

sonnant, e [sɔnã, -ãt] *adj*: **en espèces sonnantes et trébuchantes** in coin of the realm; **à 8 heures sonnantes** on the stroke of 8

sonné, e [sɔne] *adj* (*fam*) cracked; (*passé*): **il est midi sonné** it's gone twelve; **il a quarante ans bien sonnés** he's well into his forties

sonner [sɔne] *vi* (*retentir*) to ring; (*donner une impression*) to sound ♦ *vt* (*cloche*) to ring; (*glas, tocsin*) to sound; (*portier, infirmière*) to ring for; (*messe*) to ring the bell for; (*fam: suj: choc, coup*) to knock out; **sonner du clairon** to sound the bugle; **sonner bien/mal/creux** to sound good/bad/hollow; **sonner faux** (*instrument*) to sound out of tune; (*rire*) to ring false; **sonner les heures** to strike the hours; **minuit vient de sonner** midnight has just struck; **sonner chez qn** to ring sb's doorbell, ring at sb's door

sonnerie [sɔnʀi] *nf* (*son*) ringing; (*sonnette*) bell; (*mécanisme d'horloge*) striking mechanism; **sonnerie d'alarme** alarm bell; **sonnerie de clairon** bugle call

sonnette [sɔnɛt] *nf* bell; **sonnette d'alarme** alarm bell; **sonnette de nuit** night-bell

sono [sɔno] *nf* (= *sonorisation*) PA (system); (*d'une discothèque*) sound system

sonore [sɔnɔʀ] *adj* (*voix*) sonorous, ringing; (*salle, métal*) resonant; (*ondes, film, signal*) sound *cpd*; (*LING*) voiced; **effets sonores** sound effects

sonorisation [sɔnɔʀizasjɔ̃] *nf* (*installations*) public address system; (*d'une discothèque*) sound system

sonorité [sɔnɔʀite] *nf* (*de piano, violon*) tone; (*de voix, mot*) sonority; (*d'une salle*) resonance; acoustics *pl*

sont [sɔ̃] *vb voir* **être**

sophistiqué, e [sɔfistike] *adj* sophisticated

sorbet [sɔʀbɛ] *nm* water ice, sorbet

sorcellerie [sɔʀsɛlʀi] *nf* witchcraft *no pl*, sorcery *no pl*

sorcier, ière [sɔʀsje, -jɛʀ] *nm/f* sorcerer/witch *ou* sorceress ♦ *adj*: **ce n'est pas sorcier** (*fam*) it's as easy as pie

sordide [sɔʀdid] *adj* sordid; squalid

sornettes [sɔʀnɛt] *nfpl* twaddle *sg*

sort [sɔʀ] *vb voir* **sortir** ♦ *nm* (*fortune, destinée*) fate; (*condition, situation*) lot; (*magique*): **jeter un sort** to cast a spell; **un coup du sort** a blow dealt by fate; **le sort en est jeté** the die is cast; **tirer au sort** to draw lots; **tirer qch au sort** to draw lots for sth

sorte [sɔʀt(ə)] *vb voir* **sortir** ♦ *nf* sort, kind; **une sorte de** a sort of; **de la sorte** *adv* in that way; **en quelque sorte** in a way; **de sorte à** so as to, in order to; **de (telle) sorte que, en sorte que** (*de* *manière que*) so that; (*si bien que*) so much so that; **faire en sorte que** to see to it that

sortie [sɔʀti] *nf* (*issue*) way out, exit; (*MIL*) sortie; (*fig: verbale*) outburst, sally; (: *parole incongrue*) odd remark; (*d'un gaz, de l'eau*) outlet; (*promenade*) outing; (*le soir: au restaurant etc*) night out; (*de produits*) export; (*de capitaux*) outflow; (*COMM: somme*): **sorties** items of expenditure; outgoings *sans sg*; (*INFORM*) output; (*d'imprimante*) printout; **à sa sortie** as he went out *ou* left; **à la sortie de l'école/l'usine** (*moment*) after school/work; when school/the factory comes out; (*lieu*) at the school/factory gates; **à la sortie de ce nouveau modèle** when this new model comes (*ou* came) out, when they bring (*ou* brought) out this new model; **sortie de bain** (*vêtement*) bathrobe; **"sortie de camions"** "vehicle exit"; **sortie papier** hard copy; **sortie de secours** emergency exit

sortilège [sɔʀtilɛʒ] *nm* (*magic*) spell

sortir [sɔʀtiʀ] *vi* (*gén*) to come out; (*partir, se promener, aller au spectacle etc*) to go out; (*bourgeon, plante, numéro gagnant*) to come up ♦ *vt* (*gén*) to take out; (*produit, ouvrage, modèle*) to bring out; (*boniments, incongruités*) to come out with; (*INFORM*) to output; (: *sur papier*) to print out; (*fam: expulser*) to throw out ♦ *nm*: **au sortir de l'hiver/l'enfance** as winter/childhood nears its end; **sortir qch de** to take sth out of; **sortir qn d'embarras** to get sb out of trouble; **sortir de** (*gén*) to leave; (*endroit*) to go (*ou* come) out of, leave; (*rainure etc*) to come out of; (*maladie*) to get over; (*époque*) to get through; (*cadre, compétence*) to be outside; (*provenir de: famille etc*) to come from; **sortir de table** to leave the table; **sortir du système** (*INFORM*) to log out; **sortir de ses gonds** (*fig*) to fly off the handle; **se sortir de** (*affaire, situation*) to get out of; **s'en sortir** (*malade*) to pull through; (*d'une difficulté etc*) to come through all right; to get through, be able to manage

sosie [sɔzi] *nm* double

sot, sotte [so, sɔt] *adj* silly, foolish ♦ *nm/f* fool

sottise [sɔtiz] *nf* silliness *no pl*, foolishness *no pl*; (*propos, acte*) silly *ou* foolish thing (to do *ou* say)

sou [su] *nm*: **près de ses sous** tight-fisted; **sans le sou** penniless; **sou à sou** penny by penny; **pas un sou de bon sens** not a scrap *ou* an ounce of good sense; **de quatre sous** worthless

soubresaut [subʀəso] *nm* (*de peur etc*) start; (*cahot: d'un véhicule*) jolt

souche [suʃ] *nf* (*d'arbre*) stump; (*de carnet*) counterfoil (*BRIT*), stub; **dormir comme une souche** to sleep like a log; **de vieille souche** of old stock

souci [susi] *nm* (*inquiétude*) worry; (*préoccupation*) concern; (*BOT*) marigold; **se faire du souci** to worry; **avoir (le) souci de** to have concern for; **par souci de** for the sake of, out of concern for

soucier [susje]: **se soucier de** *vt* to care about

soucieux, euse [susjø, -øz] *adj* concerned, worried; **soucieux de** concerned about; **peu soucieux**

de/que caring little about/whether

soucoupe [sukup] *nf* saucer; **soucoupe volante** flying saucer

soudain, e [sudɛ̃, -ɛn] *adj* (*douleur, mort*) sudden ♦ *adv* suddenly, all of a sudden

soude [sud] *nf* soda

souder [sude] *vt* (*avec fil à souder*) to solder; (*par soudure autogène*) to weld; (*fig*) to bind *ou* knit together; to fuse (together); **se souder** *vi* (*os*) to knit (together)

soudoyer [sudwaje] *vt* (*péj*) to bribe, buy over

soudure [sudyʀ] *nf* soldering; welding; (*joint*) soldered joint; weld; **faire la soudure** (*COMM*) to fill a gap; (*fig: assurer une transition*) to bridge the gap

souffert, e [sufɛʀ, -ɛʀt(ə)] *pp de* **souffrir**

souffle [sufl(ə)] *nm* (*en expirant*) breath; (*en soufflant*) puff, blow; (*respiration*) breathing; (*d'explosion, de ventilateur*) blast; (*du vent*) blowing; (*fig*) inspiration; **retenir son souffle** to hold one's breath; **avoir du/manquer de souffle** to have a lot of puff/be short of breath; **être à bout de souffle** to be out of breath; **avoir le souffle court** to be short-winded; **un souffle d'air** *ou* **de vent** a breath of air, a puff of wind; **souffle au cœur** (*MÉD*) heart murmur

soufflé, e [sufle] *adj* (*CULIN*) soufflé; (*fam: ahuri, stupéfié*) staggered ♦ *nm* (*CULIN*) soufflé

souffler [sufle] *vi* (*gén*) to blow; (*haleter*) to puff (and blow) ♦ *vt* (*feu, bougie*) to blow out; (*chasser: poussière etc*) to blow away; (*TECH: verre*) to blow; (*suj: explosion*) to destroy (with its blast); (*dire*): **souffler qch à qn** to whisper sth to sb; (*fam: voler*): **souffler qch à qn** to pinch sth from sb; **souffler son rôle à qn** to prompt sb; **ne pas souffler mot** not to breathe a word; **laisser souffler qn** (*fig*) to give sb a breather

soufflet [sufle] *nm* (*instrument*) bellows *pl*; (*entre wagons*) vestibule; (*COUTURE*) gusset; (*gifle*) slap (in the face)

souffleur, euse [suflœʀ, -øz] *nm/f* (*THÉÂT*) prompter; (*TECH*) glass-blower

souffrance [sufʀɑ̃s] *nf* suffering; **en souffrance** (*marchandise*) awaiting delivery; (*affaire*) pending

souffrant, e [sufʀɑ̃, -ɑ̃t] *adj* unwell

souffre-douleur [sufʀədulœʀ] *nm inv* whipping boy (*BRIT*), butt, underdog

souffrir [sufʀiʀ] *vi* to suffer; (*éprouver des douleurs*) to be in pain ♦ *vt* to suffer, endure; (*supporter*) to bear, stand; (*admettre: exception etc*) to allow *ou* admit of; **souffrir de** (*maladie, froid*) to suffer from; **souffrir des dents** to have trouble with one's teeth; **ne pas pouvoir souffrir qch/que ...** not to be able to endure *ou* bear sth/that ...; **faire souffrir qn** (*suj: personne*) to make sb suffer; (: *dents, blessure etc*) to hurt sb

soufre [sufʀ(ə)] *nm* sulphur (*BRIT*), sulfur (*US*)

souhait [swɛ] *nm* wish; **tous nos souhaits de** good wishes *ou* our best wishes for; **riche etc à**

souhait as rich *etc* as one could wish; **à vos souhaits!** bless you!

souhaitable [swetabl(ə)] *adj* desirable

souhaiter [swete] *vt* to wish for; **souhaiter le bonjour à qn** to bid sb good day; **souhaiter la bonne année à qn** to wish sb a happy New Year; **il est à souhaiter que** it is to be hoped that

souiller [suje] *vt* to dirty, soil; *(fig)* to sully, tarnish

soûl, e [su, sul] *adj* drunk; *(fig):* **soûl de musique/ plaisirs** drunk with music/pleasure ♦ *nm:* **tout son soûl** to one's heart's content

soulagement [sulaʒmã] *nm* relief

soulager [sulaʒe] *vt* to relieve; **soulager qn de** to relieve sb of

soûler [sule] *vt:* **soûler qn** to get sb drunk; *(suj: boisson)* to make sb drunk; *(fig)* to make sb's head spin ou reel; **se soûler** to get drunk; **se soûler de** *(fig)* to intoxicate o.s. with

soulever [sulve] *vt* to lift; *(vagues, poussière)* to send up; *(peuple)* to stir up (to revolt); *(enthousiasme)* to arouse; *(question, débat, protestations, difficultés)* to raise; **se soulever** *vi* *(peuple)* to rise up; *(personne couchée)* to lift o.s. up; *(couvercle etc)* to lift; **cela me soulève le cœur** it makes me feel sick

soulier [sulje] *nm* shoe; **souliers bas** low-heeled shoes; **souliers plats/à talons** flat/heeled shoes

souligner [suliɲe] *vt* to underline; *(fig)* to emphasize, stress

soumettre [sumɛtʀ(ə)] *vt* (*pays*) to subject, subjugate; *(rebelles)* to put down, subdue; **soumettre qn/qch à** to subject sb/sth to; **soumettre qch à qn** *(projet etc)* to submit sth to sb; **se soumettre (à)** *(se rendre, obéir)* to submit (to); **se soumettre à** *(formalités etc)* to submit to; *(régime etc)* to submit o.s. to

soumis, e [sumi, -iz] *pp de* **soumettre** ♦ *adj* submissive; **revenus soumis à l'impôt** taxable income

soumission [sumisjɔ̃] *nf* (*voir se soumettre*) submission; *(docilité)* submissiveness; *(COMM)* tender

soupape [supap] *nf* valve; **soupape de sûreté** safety valve

soupçon [supsɔ̃] *nm* suspicion; *(petite quantité):* **un soupçon de** a hint ou touch of; **avoir soupçon de** to suspect; **au dessus de tout soupçon** above (all) suspicion

soupçonner [supsɔne] *vt* to suspect; **soupçonner qn de qch/d'être** to suspect sb of sth/of being

soupçonneux, euse [supsɔnø, -øz] *adj* suspicious

soupe [sup] *nf* soup; **soupe au lait** *adj inv* quick-tempered; **soupe à l'oignon/de poisson** onion/fish soup; **soupe populaire** soup kitchen

souper [supe] *vi* to have supper ♦ *nm* supper; **avoir soupé de** *(fam)* to be sick and tired of

soupeser [supəze] *vt* to weigh in one's hand(s), feel the weight of; *(fig)* to weigh up

soupière [supjɛʀ] *nf* (soup) tureen

soupir [supiʀ] *nm* sigh; *(MUS)* crotchet rest *(BRIT)*, quarter note rest *(US)*; **rendre le dernier soupir** to breathe one's last

soupirail, aux [supiʀaj, -o] *nm* (small) basement window

soupirer [supiʀe] *vi* to sigh; **soupirer après qch** to yearn for sth

souple [supl(ə)] *adj* supple; *(col)* soft; *(fig: règlement, caractère)* flexible; *(: démarche, taille)* lithe, supple; **disque(tte) souple** *(INFORM)* floppy disk, diskette

souplesse [suples] *nf* suppleness; flexibility

source [suʀs(ə)] *nf* *(point d'eau)* spring; *(d'un cours d'eau, fig)* source; **prendre sa source à/dans** *(suj: cours d'eau)* to have its source at/in; **tenir de bonne source/de source sûre** to have sth on good authority/from a reliable source; **source thermale/d'eau minérale** hot ou thermal/mineral spring

sourcil [suʀsij] *nm* (eye)brow

sourciller [suʀsije] *vi:* **sans sourciller** without turning a hair ou batting an eyelid

sourd, e [suʀ, suʀd(ə)] *adj* deaf; *(bruit, voix)* muffled; *(couleur)* muted; *(douleur)* dull; *(lutte)* silent, hidden; *(LING)* voiceless ♦ *nm/f* deaf person; **être sourd à** to be deaf to

sourdine [suʀdin] *nf* *(MUS)* mute; **en sourdine** *adv* softly, quietly; **mettre une sourdine à** *(fig)* to tone down

sourd-muet, sourde-muette [suʀmyɛ, suʀdmyɛt] *adj* deaf-and-dumb ♦ *nm/f* deaf-mute

souriant, e [suʀjã, -ãt] *vb voir* **sourire** ♦ *adj* cheerful

souricière [suʀisjɛʀ] *nf* mousetrap; *(fig)* trap

sourire [suʀiʀ] *nm* smile ♦ *vi* to smile; **sourire à qn** to smile at sb; *(fig)* to appeal to sb; *(: chance)* to smile on sb; **faire un sourire à qn** to give sb a smile; **garder le sourire** to keep smiling

souris [suʀi] *nf* mouse (*pl* mice); *(INFORM)* mouse

sournois, e [suʀnwa, -waz] *adj* deceitful, underhand

sous [su] *prép* (*gén*) under; **sous la pluie/le soleil** in the rain/sunshine; **sous mes yeux** before my eyes; **sous terre** *adj, adv* underground; **sous vide** *adj, adv* vacuum-packed; **sous l'influence/l'action de** under the influence of/by the action of; **sous antibiotiques/perfusion** on antibiotics/a drip; **sous cet angle/ce rapport** from this angle/in this respect; **sous peu** *adv* shortly, before long

sous-bois [subwa] *nm inv* undergrowth

souscrire [suskʀiʀ]: **souscrire à** *vt* to subscribe to

sous-directeur, trice [sudiʀɛktœʀ, -tʀis] *nm/f* assistant manager/manageress, submanager/manageress

sous-entendre [suzãtãdʀ(ə)] *vt* to imply, infer

sous-entendu, e [suzãtãdy] *adj* implied; *(LING)* understood ♦ *nm* innuendo, insinuation

sous-estimer [suzɛstime] *vt* to underestimate

sous-jacent, e [suʒasɑ̃, -ɑ̃t] *adj* underlying
sous-louer [sulwe] *vt* to sublet
sous-marin, e [sumaʀɛ̃, -in] *adj* (*flore, volcan*) submarine; (*navigation, pêche, explosif*) underwater ♦ *nm* submarine
sous-officier [suzɔfisje] *nm* ≃ non-commissioned officer (NCO)
sous-produit [supʀɔdɥi] *nm* by-product; (*fig: péj*) pale imitation
sous-pull [supul] *nm* thin poloneck sweater
soussigné, e [susiɲe] *adj*: **je soussigné** I the undersigned
sous-sol [susɔl] *nm* basement; (*GÉO*) subsoil
sous-titre [sutitʀ(ə)] *nm* subtitle
soustraction [sustʀaksjɔ̃] *nf* subtraction
soustraire [sustʀɛʀ] *vt* to subtract, take away; (*dérober*): **soustraire qch à qn** to remove sth from sb; **soustraire qn à** (*danger*) to shield sb from; **se soustraire à** (*autorité, obligation, devoir*) to elude, escape from
sous-traitant [sutʀɛtɑ̃] *nm* subcontractor
sous-traiter [sutʀete] *vt, vi* to subcontract
sous-vêtement [suvɛtmɑ̃] *nm* undergarment, item of underwear; **sous-vêtements** *nmpl* underwear *sg*
soutane [sutan] *nf* cassock, soutane
soute [sut] *nf* hold; **soute à bagages** baggage hold
soutenir [sutniʀ] *vt* to support; (*assaut, choc, regard*) to stand up to, withstand; (*intérêt, effort*) to keep up; (*assurer*): **soutenir que** to maintain that; **se soutenir** (*dans l'eau etc*) to hold o.s. up; (*être soutenable: point de vue*) to be tenable; (*s'aider mutuellement*) to stand by each other; **soutenir la comparaison avec** to bear *ou* stand comparison with; **soutenir le regard de qn** to be able to look sb in the face
soutenu, e [sutny] *pp de* **soutenir** ♦ *adj* (*efforts*) sustained, unflagging; (*style*) elevated; (*couleur*) strong
souterrain, e [sutɛʀɛ̃, -ɛn] *adj* underground; (*fig*) subterranean ♦ *nm* underground passage
soutien [sutjɛ̃] *nm* support; **apporter son soutien à** to lend one's support to; **soutien de famille** breadwinner
soutien-gorge, *pl* **soutiens-gorge** [sutjɛ̃gɔʀʒ(ə)] *nm* bra; (*de maillot de bain*) top
soutirer [sutiʀe] *vt*: **soutirer qch à qn** to squeeze *ou* get sth out of sb
souvenir [suvniʀ] *nm* (*réminiscence*) memory; (*cadeau*) souvenir, keepsake; (*de voyage*) souvenir ♦ *vb*: **se souvenir de** *vt* to remember; **se souvenir que** to remember that; **garder le souvenir de** to retain the memory of; **en souvenir de** in memory *ou* remembrance of; **avec mes affectueux/ meilleurs souvenirs, ...** with love from, .../ regards, ...

souvent [suvɑ̃] *adv* often; **peu souvent** seldom, infrequently; **le plus souvent** more often than not, most often
souverain, e [suvʀɛ̃, -ɛn] *adj* sovereign; (*fig: mépris*) supreme ♦ *nm/f* sovereign, monarch
soyeux, euse [swajø, -øz] *adj* silky
soyons *etc* [swajɔ̃] *vb voir* **être**
spacieux, euse [spasjø, -øz] *adj* spacious; roomy
spaghettis [spageti] *nmpl* spaghetti *sg*
sparadrap [spaʀadʀa] *nm* adhesive *ou* sticking (*BRIT*) plaster, bandaid® (*US*)
spatial, e, aux [spasjal, -o] *adj* (*AVIAT*) space *cpd*; (*PSYCH*) spatial
speaker, ine [spikœʀ, -kʀin] *nm/f* announcer
spécial, e, aux [spesjal, -o] *adj* special; (*bizarre*) peculiar
spécialement [spesjalmɑ̃] *adv* especially, particularly; (*tout exprès*) specially; **pas spécialement** not particularly
spécialiser [spesjalize]: **se spécialiser** *vi* to specialize
spécialiste [spesjalist(ə)] *nm/f* specialist
spécialité [spesjalite] *nf* speciality; (*SCOL*) special field; **spécialité pharmaceutique** patent medicine
spécifier [spesifje] *vt* to specify, state
spécimen [spesimɛn] *nm* specimen; (*revue etc*) specimen *ou* sample copy
spectacle [spɛktakl(ə)] *nm* (*tableau, scène*) sight; (*représentation*) show; (*industrie*) show business, entertainment; **se donner en spectacle** (*péj*) to make a spectacle *ou* an exhibition of o.s.; **pièce/ revue à grand spectacle** spectacular (play/revue); **au spectacle de ...** at the sight of ...
spectaculaire [spɛktakylɛʀ] *adj* spectacular
spectateur, trice [spɛktatœʀ, -tʀis] *nm/f* (*CINÉ etc*) member of the audience; (*SPORT*) spectator; (*d'un événement*) onlooker, witness
spéculer [spekyle] *vi* to speculate; **spéculer sur** (*COMM*) to speculate on; (*réfléchir*) to speculate on; (*tabler sur*) to bank *ou* rely on
spéléologie [speleɔlɔʒi] *nf* (*étude*) speleology; (*activité*) potholing
sperme [spɛʀm(ə)] *nm* semen, sperm
sphère [sfɛʀ] *nf* sphere
spirale [spiʀal] *nf* spiral; **en spirale** in a spiral
spirituel, le [spiʀitɥɛl] *adj* spiritual; (*fin, piquant*) witty; **musique spirituelle** sacred music; **concert spirituel** concert of sacred music
splendide [splɑ̃did] *adj* splendid, magnificent
sponsoriser [spɔ̃sɔʀize] *vt* to sponsor
spontané, e [spɔ̃tane] *adj* spontaneous
spontanéité [spɔ̃taneite] *nf* spontaneity
sport [spɔʀ] *nm* sport ♦ *adj inv* (*vêtement*) casual; (*fair-play*) sporting; **faire du sport** to do sport; **sport individuel/d'équipe** individual/team sport; **sport de combat** combative sport; **sports d'hiver**

winter sports

sportif, ive [spɔrtif, -iv] *adj (journal, association, épreuve)* sports *cpd; (allure, démarche)* athletic; *(attitude, esprit)* sporting; **les résultats sportifs** the sports results

spot [spɔt] *nm (lampe)* spot(light); *(annonce)*: **spot (publicitaire)** commercial (break)

square [skwar] *nm* public garden(s)

squelette [skəlɛt] *nm* skeleton

squelettique [skəletik] *adj* scrawny; *(fig)* skimpy

stabiliser [stabilize] *vt* to stabilize; *(terrain)* to consolidate

stable [stabl(ə)] *adj* stable, steady

stade [stad] *nm (SPORT)* stadium; *(phase, niveau)* stage

stage [staʒ] *nm* training period; training course; *(d'avocat stagiaire)* articles *pl;* **stage en entreprise** work experience placement

stagiaire [staʒjɛr] *nm/f, adj* trainee *(cpd)*

stagner [stagne] *vi* to stagnate

stalle [stal] *nf* stall, box

stand [stɑ̃d] *nm (d'exposition)* stand; *(de foire)* stall; **stand de tir** *(à la foire, SPORT)* shooting range; **stand de ravitaillement** pit

standard [stɑ̃dar] *adj inv* standard ♦ *nm (type, norme)* standard; *(téléphonique)* switchboard

standardiste [stɑ̃dardist(ə)] *nm/f* switchboard operator

standing [stɑ̃diŋ] *nm* standing; **immeuble de grand standing** block of luxury flats *(BRIT)*, condo (minium) *(US)*

starter [starter] *nm (AUTO)* choke; *(SPORT: personne)* starter; **mettre le starter** to pull out the choke

station [stɑsjɔ̃] *nf* station; *(de bus)* stop; *(de villégiature)* resort; *(posture)*: **la station debout** standing, an upright posture; **station balnéaire** seaside resort; **station de graissage** lubrication bay; **station de lavage** carwash; **station de ski** ski resort; **station de sports d'hiver** winter sports resort; **station de taxis** taxi rank *(BRIT)* ou stand *(US)*; **station thermale** thermal spa; **station de travail** workstation

stationnement [stasjɔnmɑ̃] *nm* parking; **zone de stationnement interdit** no parking area; **stationnement alterné** parking on alternate sides

stationner [stasjɔne] *vi* to park

station-service [stasjɔ̃sɛrvis] *nf* service station

statistique [statistik] *nf (science)* statistics *sg;* *(rapport, étude)* statistic ♦ *adj* statistical; **statistiques** *nfpl (données)* statistics *pl*

statue [staty] *nf* statue

statu quo [statykwo] *nm* status quo

statut [staty] *nm* status; **statuts** *nmpl (JUR, ADMIN)* statutes

statutaire [statyter] *adj* statutory

Sté *abr (= société)* soc

steak [stɛk] *nm* steak

sténo(graphie) [stenɔ(grafi)] *nf* shorthand; **prendre en sténo(graphie)** to take down in shorthand

stéréo(phonie) [stereɔ(fɔni)] *nf* stereo(phony); **émission en stéréo(phonie)** stereo broadcast

stéréo(phonique) [stereɔ(fɔnik)] *adj* stereo (phonic)

stérile [steril] *adj* sterile; *(terre)* barren; *(fig)* fruitless, futile

stérilet [sterilɛ] *nm* coil, loop

stériliser [sterilize] *vt* to sterilize

stigmates [stigmat] *nmpl* scars, marks; *(REL)* stigmata *pl*

stimulant, e [stimylɑ̃, -ɑ̃t] *adj* stimulating ♦ *nm (MÉD)* stimulant; *(fig)* stimulus *(pl* stimuli *)*; incentive

stimuler [stimyle] *vt* to stimulate

stipuler [stipyle] *vt* to stipulate, specify

stock [stɔk] *nm* stock; **en stock** in stock

stocker [stɔke] *vt* to stock; *(déchets)* to store

stop [stɔp] *nm (AUTO: écriteau)* stop sign; *(: signal)* brake-light; *(dans un télégramme)* stop ♦ *excl* stop!

stopper [stɔpe] *vt* to stop, halt; *(COUTURE)* to mend ♦ *vi* to stop, halt

store [stɔr] *nm* blind; *(de magasin)* shade, awning

strabisme [strabism(ə)] *nm* squint(ing)

strapontin [strapɔ̃tɛ̃] *nm* jump ou foldaway seat

Strasbourg [strazbur] *n* Strasbourg

stratégie [strateʒi] *nf* strategy

stratégique [strateʒik] *adj* strategic

stress [strɛs] *nm inv* stress

stressant, e [stresɑ̃, -ɑ̃t] *adj* stressful

stresser [strese] *vt* to stress, cause stress in

strict, e [strikt(ə)] *adj* strict; *(tenue, décor)* severe, plain; **son droit le plus strict** his most basic right; **dans la plus stricte intimité** strictly in private; **le strict nécessaire/minimum** the bare essentials/minimum

strident, e [stridɑ̃, -ɑ̃t] *adj* shrill, strident

strophe [strɔf] *nf* verse, stanza

structure [stryktyr] *nf* structure; **structures d'accueil/touristiques** reception/tourist facilities

studieux, euse [stydjø, -øz] *adj (élève)* studious; *(vacances)* study *cpd*

studio [stydjo] *nm (logement)* studio flat *(BRIT)* ou apartment *(US)*; *(d'artiste, TV etc)* studio *(pl* studios *)*

stupéfait, e [stypefɛ, -ɛt] *adj* astonished

stupéfiant, e [stypefjɑ̃, -ɑ̃t] *adj* stunning, astonishing ♦ *nm (MÉD)* drug, narcotic

stupéfier [stypefje] *vt* to stupefy; *(étonner)* to stun, astonish

stupeur [stypœr] *nf (inertie, insensibilité)* stupor; *(étonnement)* astonishment, amazement

stupide [stypid] *adj* stupid; *(hébété)* stunned

stupidité [stypidite] *nf* stupidity *no pl; (propos, action)* stupid thing (to say ou do)

style [stil] *nm* style; **meuble/robe de style** piece

of period furniture/period dress; **style de vie** lifestyle

stylé, e [stile] *adj* well-trained

styliste [stilist(ə)] *nm/f* designer; stylist

stylo [stilo] *nm*: **stylo (à encre)** (fountain) pen; **stylo (à) bille** ballpoint pen

su, e [sy] *pp de* savoir ♦ *nm*: **au su de** with the knowledge of

suave [sɥav] *adj* (*odeur*) sweet; (*voix*) suave, smooth; (*coloris*) soft, mellow

subalterne [sybaltɛʀn(ə)] *adj* (*employé, officier*) junior; (*rôle*) subordinate, subsidiary ♦ *nm/f* subordinate, inferior

subconscient [sypkɔsjɑ̃] *nm* subconscious

subir [sybiʀ] *vt* (*affront, dégâts, mauvais traitements*) to suffer; (*influence, charme*) to be under, be subjected to; (*traitement, opération, châtiment*) to undergo; (*personne*) to suffer, be subjected to

subit, e [sybi, -it] *adj* sudden

subitement [sybitmɑ̃] *adv* suddenly, all of a sudden

subjectif, ive [sybʒɛktif, -iv] *adj* subjective

subjonctif [sybʒɔ̃ktif] *nm* subjunctive

subjuguer [sybʒyge] *vt* to subjugate

submerger [sybmɛʀʒe] *vt* to submerge; (*suj: foule*) to engulf; (*fig*) to overwhelm

subordonné, e [sybɔʀdɔne] *adj, nm/f* subordinate; **subordonné à** (*personne*) subordinate to; (*résultats etc*) subject to, depending on

subrepticement [sybʀɛptismɑ̃] *adv* surreptitiously

subside [sypsid] *nm* grant

subsidiaire [sypsidjɛʀ] *adj* subsidiary; **question subsidiaire** deciding question

subsister [sybziste] *vi* (*rester*) to remain, subsist; (*vivre*) to live; (*survivre*) to live on

substance [sypstɑ̃s] *nf* substance; **en substance** in substance

substituer [sypstitɥe] *vt*: **substituer qn/qch à** to substitute sb/sth for; **se substituer à qn** (*représenter*) to substitute for sb; (*évincer*) to substitute o.s. for sb

substitut [sypstity] *nm* (*JUR*) deputy public prosecutor; (*succédané*) substitute

subterfuge [syptɛʀfyʒ] *nm* subterfuge

subtil, e [syptil] *adj* subtle

subtiliser [syptilize] *vt*: **subtiliser qch (à qn)** to spirit sth away (from sb)

subvenir [sybvəniʀ]: **subvenir à** *vt* to meet

subvention [sybvɑ̃sjɔ̃] *nf* subsidy, grant

subventionner [sybvɑ̃sjɔne] *vt* to subsidize

suc [syk] *nm* (*BOT*) sap; (*de viande, fruit*) juice; **sucs gastriques** gastric juices

succédané [syksedane] *nm* substitute

succéder [syksede]: **succéder à** *vt* (*directeur, roi etc*) to succeed; (*venir après: dans une série*) to follow, succeed; **se succéder** *vi* (*accidents, années*) to

follow one another

succès [syksɛ] *nm* success; **avec succès** successfully; **sans succès** unsuccessfully; **avoir du succès** to be a success, be successful; **à succès** successful; **livre à succès** bestseller; **succès de librairie** bestseller; **succès (féminins)** conquests

successeur [syksesœʀ] *nm* successor

successif, ive [syksesif, -iv] *adj* successive

succession [syksesjɔ̃] *nf* (*série, POL*) succession; (*JUR: patrimoine*) estate, inheritance; **prendre la succession de** (*directeur*) to succeed, take over from; (*entreprise*) to take over

succomber [sykɔ̃be] *vi* to die, succumb; (*fig*): **succomber à** to give way to, succumb to

succulent, e [sykylɑ̃, -ɑ̃t] *adj* succulent

succursale [sykyʀsal] *nf* branch; **magasin à succursales multiples** chain *ou* multiple store

sucer [syse] *vt* to suck

sucette [sysɛt] *nf* (*bonbon*) lollipop; (*de bébé*) dummy (*BRIT*), comforter, pacifier (*US*)

sucre [sykʀ(ə)] *nm* (*substance*) sugar; (*morceau*) lump of sugar, sugar lump *ou* cube; **sucre de canne/betterave** cane/beet sugar; **sucre en morceaux/cristallisé/en poudre** lump *ou* cube/granulated/caster sugar; **sucre glace** icing sugar; **sucre d'orge** barley sugar

sucré, e [sykʀe] *adj* (*produit alimentaire*) sweetened; (*au goût*) sweet; (*péj*) sugary, honeyed

sucrer [sykʀe] *vt* (*thé, café*) to sweeten, put sugar in; **sucrer qn** to put sugar in sb's tea (*ou* coffee *etc*); **se sucrer** to help o.s. to sugar, have some sugar; (*fam*) to line one's pocket(s)

sucrerie [sykʀəʀi] *nf* (*usine*) sugar refinery; **sucreries** *nfpl* (*bonbons*) sweets, sweet things

sucrier, ière [sykʀije, -jɛʀ] *adj* (*industrie*) sugar *cpd*; (*région*) sugar-producing ♦ *nm* (*fabricant*) sugar producer; (*récipient*) sugar bowl *ou* basin

sud [syd] *nm*: **le sud** the south ♦ *adj inv* south; (*côte*) south, southern; **au sud** (*situation*) in the south; (*direction*) to the south; **au sud de** (to the) south of

sud-africain, e [sydafʀikɛ̃, -ɛn] *adj* South African ♦ *nm/f*: **Sud-Africain, e** South African

sud-américain, e [sydameʀikɛ̃, -ɛn] *adj* South American ♦ *nm/f*: **Sud-Américain, e** South American

sud-est [sydɛst] *nm, adj inv* south-east

sud-ouest [sydwɛst] *nm, adj inv* south-west

Suède [sɥɛd] *nf*: **la Suède** Sweden

suédois, e [sɥedwa, -waz] *adj* Swedish ♦ *nm* (*LING*) Swedish ♦ *nm/f*: **Suédois, e** Swede

suer [sɥe] *vi* to sweat; (*suinter*) to ooze ♦ *vt* (*fig*) to exude; **suer à grosses gouttes** to sweat profusely

sueur [sɥœʀ] *nf* sweat; **en sueur** sweating, in a sweat; **avoir des sueurs froides** to be in a cold sweat

suffire [syfiʀ] *vi* (*être assez*): **suffire (à qn/pour qch/pour faire)** to be enough *ou* sufficient (for sb/

for sth/to do); (*satisfaire*): **cela lui suffit** he's content with this, this is enough for him; **se suffire** *vi* to be self-sufficient; **cela suffit pour les irriter/qu'ils se fâchent** it's enough to annoy them/for them to get angry; **il suffit d'une négligence/qu'on oublie pour que ...** it only takes one act of carelessness/one only needs to forget for ...; **ça suffit!** that's enough!, that'll do!

suffisamment [syfizamɑ̃] *adv* sufficiently, enough; **suffisamment de** sufficient, enough

suffisant, e [syfizɑ̃, -ɑ̃t] *adj* (*temps, ressources*) sufficient; (*résultats*) satisfactory; (*vaniteux*) self-important, bumptious

suffixe [syfiks(ə)] *nm* suffix

suffoquer [syfɔke] *vt* to choke, suffocate; (*stupéfier*) to stagger, astound ♦ *vi* to choke, suffocate; **suffoquer de colère/d'indignation** to choke with anger/indignation

suffrage [syfraʒ] *nm* (*POL: voix*) vote; (*: méthode*): **suffrage universel/direct/indirect** universal/direct/indirect suffrage; (*du public etc*) approval *no pl*; **suffrages exprimés** valid votes

suggérer [sygʒere] *vt* to suggest; **suggérer que/de faire** to suggest that/doing

suggestion [sygʒɛstjɔ̃] *nf* suggestion

suicide [sɥisid] *nm* suicide ♦ *adj*: **opération suicide** suicide mission

suicider [sɥiside]: **se suicider** *vi* to commit suicide

suie [sɥi] *nf* soot

suinter [sɥɛ̃te] *vi* to ooze

suis [sɥi] *vb voir* **être, suivre**

suisse [sɥis] *adj* Swiss ♦ *nm* (*bedeau*) ≈ verger; ♦ *nm/f*: **Suisse** Swiss *pl inv* ♦ *nf*: **la Suisse** Switzerland; **la Suisse romande/allemande** French-speaking/German-speaking Switzerland; **suisse romand** Swiss French

Suissesse [sɥises] *nf* Swiss (woman *ou* girl)

suite [sɥit] *nf* (*continuation: d'énumération etc*) rest, remainder; (*: de feuilleton*) continuation; (*: second film etc sur le même thème*) sequel; (*série: de maisons, succès*): **une suite de** a series *ou* succession of; (*MATH*) series *sg*; (*conséquence*) result; (*ordre, liaison logique*) coherence; (*appartement, MUS*) suite; (*escorte*) retinue, suite; **suites** *nfpl* (*d'une maladie etc*) effects; **prendre la suite de** (*directeur etc*) to succeed, take over from; **donner suite à** (*requête, projet*) to follow up; **faire suite à** to follow; **(faisant) suite à votre lettre du** further to your letter of the; **sans suite** *adj* incoherent, disjointed ♦ *adv* incoherently, disjointedly; **de suite** *adv* (*d'affilée*) in succession; (*immédiatement*) at once; **par la suite** afterwards, subsequently; **à la suite** *adv* one after the other; **à la suite de** (*derrière*) behind; (*en conséquence de*) following; **par suite de** owing to, as a result of; **avoir de la suite dans les idées** to show great singleness of purpose; **attendre la suite des événements** to (wait and see) what happens

suivant, e [sɥivɑ̃, -ɑ̃t] *vb voir* **suivre** ♦ *adj* next, following; (*ci-après*): **l'exercice suivant** the following exercise ♦ *prép* (*selon*) according to; **suivant que** according to whether; **au suivant!** next!

suivi, e [sɥivi] *pp de* **suivre** ♦ *adj* (*régulier*) regular; (*COMM: article*) in general production; (*cohérent*) consistent; coherent ♦ *nm* follow-up; **très/peu suivi** (*cours*) well-/poorly-attended; (*mode*) widely/not widely adopted; (*feuilleton etc*) widely/not widely followed

suivre [sɥivʀ(ə)] *vt* (*gén*) to follow; (*SCOL: cours*) to attend; (*: leçon*) to follow, attend to; (*: programme*) to keep up with; (*COMM: article*) to continue to stock ♦ *vi* to follow; (*élève: écouter*) to attend, pay attention; (*: assimiler le programme*) to keep up, follow; **se suivre** (*accidents, personnes, voitures etc*) to follow one after the other; (*raisonnement*) to be coherent; **suivre des yeux** to follow with one's eyes; **faire suivre** (*lettre*) to forward; **suivre son cours** (*suj: enquête etc*) to run *ou* take its course; **"à suivre"** "to be continued"

sujet, te [syʒɛ, -ɛt] *adj*: **être sujet à** (*accidents*) to be prone to; (*vertige etc*) to be liable *ou* subject to ♦ *nm/f* (*d'un souverain*) subject ♦ *nm* subject; **un sujet de dispute/discorde/mécontentement** a cause for argument/dissension/dissatisfaction; **c'est à quel sujet?** what is it about?; **avoir sujet de se plaindre** to have cause for complaint; **au sujet de** *prép* about; **sujet à caution** *adj* questionable; **sujet de conversation** topic *ou* subject of conversation; **sujet d'examen** (*SCOL*) examination question; examination paper; **sujet d'expérience** (*BIO etc*) experimental subject

summum [sɔmɔm] *nm*: **le summum de** the height of

super [sypɛʀ] *adj inv* great, fantastic ♦ *nm* (= *supercarburant*) ≈ 4-star (*BRIT*), ≈ premium (*US*)

superbe [sypɛʀb(ə)] *adj* magnificent, superb ♦ *nf* arrogance

supercherie [sypɛʀʃəʀi] *nf* trick, trickery *no pl*; (*fraude*) fraud

supérette [sypeʀet] *nf* minimarket

superficie [sypɛʀfisi] *nf* (*surface*) area; (*fig*) surface

superficiel, le [sypɛʀfisjɛl] *adj* superficial

superflu, e [sypɛʀfly] *adj* superfluous ♦ *nm*: **le superflu** the superfluous

supérieur, e [sypeʀjœʀ] *adj* (*lèvre, étages, classes*) upper; (*plus élevé: température, niveau*): **supérieur (à)** higher (than); (*meilleur: qualité, produit*): **supérieur (à)** superior (to); (*excellent, hautain*) superior ♦ *nm/f* superior; **Mère supérieure** Mother Superior; **à l'étage supérieur** on the next floor up; **supérieur en nombre** superior in number

supériorité [sypeʀjɔʀite] *nf* superiority

superlatif [sypɛʀlatif] *nm* superlative

supermarché [sypɛʀmaʀʃe] *nm* supermarket

superposer [sypɛʀpoze] *vt* to superpose; *(meubles, caisses)* to stack; *(faire chevaucher)* to superimpose; **se superposer** *(images, souvenirs)* to be superimposed; **lits superposés** bunk beds

superproduction [sypɛʀpʀɔdyksjɔ̃] *nf (film)* spectacular

superpuissance [sypɛʀpɥisɑ̃s] *nf* superpower

superstitieux, euse [sypɛʀstisjø, -øz] *adj* superstitious

superviser [sypɛʀvize] *vt* to supervise

supplanter [syplɑ̃te] *vt* to supplant

suppléance [sypleɑ̃s] *nf (poste)* supply post (BRIT), substitute teacher's post (US)

suppléant, e [sypleɑ̃, -ɑ̃t] *adj (juge, fonctionnaire)* deputy *cpd; (professeur)* supply *cpd* (BRIT), substitute *cpd* (US) ♦ *nm/f* deputy; supply *ou* substitute teacher; **médecin suppléant** locum

suppléer [syplee] *vt (ajouter: mot manquant etc)* to supply, provide; *(compenser: lacune)* to fill in; (: *défaut)* to make up for; *(remplacer: professeur)* to stand in for; (: *juge)* to deputize for; **suppléer à** *vt* to make up for; to substitute for

supplément [syplemɑ̃] *nm* supplement; **un supplément de travail** extra *ou* additional work; **un supplément de frites** *etc* an extra portion of chips *etc*; **un supplément de 100 €** a supplement of 100 €, an extra *ou* additional 100 €; **ceci est en supplément** *(au menu etc)* this is extra, there is an extra charge for this; **supplément d'information** additional information

supplémentaire [syplemɑ̃tɛʀ] *adj* additional, further; *(train, bus)* relief *cpd*, extra

supplication [syplikasjɔ̃] *nf (REL)* supplication; **supplications** *nfpl (adjurations)* pleas, entreaties

supplice [syplis] *nm (peine corporelle)* torture *no pl;* form of torture; *(douleur physique, morale)* torture, agony; **être au supplice** to be in agony

supplier [syplije] *vt* to implore, beseech

support [sypɔʀ] *nm* support; *(pour livre, outils)* stand; **support audio-visuel** audio-visual aid; **support publicitaire** advertising medium

supportable [sypɔʀtabl(ə)] *adj (douleur, température)* bearable; *(procédé, conduite)* tolerable

supporter *nm* [sypɔʀtɛʀ] supporter, fan ♦ *vt* [sypɔʀte] *(poids, poussée, SPORT: concurrent, équipe)* to support; *(conséquences, épreuve)* to bear, endure; *(défauts, personne)* to tolerate, put up with; *(suj: chose: chaleur etc)* to withstand; *(suj: personne: chaleur, vin)* to take

supposer [sypoze] *vt* to suppose; *(impliquer)* to presuppose; **en supposant** *ou* **à supposer que** supposing (that)

suppositoire [sypozitwaʀ] *nm* suppository

suppression [sypʀesjɔ̃] *nf (voir supprimer)* removal; deletion; cancellation; suppression

supprimer [sypʀime] *vt (cloison, cause, anxiété)* to remove; *(clause, mot)* to delete; *(congés, service d'autobus etc)* to cancel; *(publication, article)* to suppress; *(emplois, privilèges, témoin gênant)* to do away with; **supprimer qch à qn** to deprive sb of sth

suprême [sypʀɛm] *adj* supreme

MOT-CLÉ

sur [syʀ] *prép* **1** *(position)* on; *(pardessus)* over; *(au-dessus)* above; **pose-le sur la table** put it on the table; **je n'ai pas d'argent sur moi** I haven't any money on me

2 *(direction)* towards; **en allant sur Paris** going towards Paris; **sur votre droite** on *ou* to your right

3 *(à propos de)* on, about; **un livre/une conférence sur Balzac** a book/lecture on *ou* about Balzac

4 *(proportion, mesures)* out of; by; **un sur 10** one in 10; *(SCOL)* one out of 10; **sur 20, 2 sont venus** out of 20, 2 came; **4 m sur 2** 4 m by 2; **avoir accident sur accident** to have one accident after another

5 *(cause)*: **sur sa recommandation** on *ou* at his recommendation; **sur son invitation** at his invitation

sur ce *adv* whereupon; **sur ce, il faut que je vous quitte** and now I must leave you

---

sur, e [syʀ] *adj* sour

sûr, e [syʀ] *adj* sure, certain; *(digne de confiance)* reliable; *(sans danger)* safe; **peu sûr** unreliable; **sûr de qch** sure *ou* certain of sth; **être sûr de qn** to be sure of sb; **sûr et certain** absolutely certain; **sûr de soi** self-assured, self-confident; **le plus sûr est de** the safest thing is to

surcharge [syʀʃaʀʒ(ə)] *nf (de passagers, marchandises)* excess load; *(de détails, d'ornements)* overabundance, excess; *(correction)* alteration; *(POSTES)* surcharge; **prendre des passagers en surcharge** to take on excess *ou* extra passengers; **surcharge de bagages** excess luggage; **surcharge de travail** extra work

surcharger [syʀʃaʀʒe] *vt* to overload; *(timbre-poste)* to surcharge; *(décoration)* to overdo

surchoix [syʀʃwa] *adj inv* top-quality

surclasser [syʀklase] *vt* to outclass

surcroît [syʀkʀwa] *nm*: **un surcroît de** additional + *nom;* **par** *ou* **de surcroît** moreover; **en surcroît** in addition

surdité [syʀdite] *nf* deafness; **atteint de surdité totale** profoundly deaf

surélever [syʀelve] *vt* to raise, heighten

sûrement [syʀmɑ̃] *adv* reliably; safely, securely; *(certainement)* certainly; **sûrement pas** certainly not

surenchère [syʀɑ̃ʃɛʀ] *nf (aux enchères)* higher bid; *(sur prix fixe)* overbid; *(fig)* overstatement; outbidding tactics *pl;* **surenchère de violence** build-up of violence; **surenchère électorale** political (*ou* electoral) one-upmanship

surenchérir [syʀɑ̃ʃeʀiʀ] *vi* to bid higher; to raise one's bid; (*fig*) to try and outbid each other

surent [syʀ] *vb voir* **savoir**

surestimer [syʀɛstime] *vt* (*tableau*) to overvalue; (*possibilité, personne*) to overestimate

sûreté [syʀte] *nf* (*voir sûr*) reliability; safety; (*JUR*) guaranty; surety; **mettre en sûreté** to put in a safe place; **pour plus de sûreté** as an extra precaution; to be on the safe side; **la sûreté de l'État** State security; **la Sûreté (nationale)** *division of the Ministère de l'Intérieur heading all police forces except the gendarmerie and the Paris préfecture de police*

surf [sœrf] *nm* surfing; **faire du surf** to go surfing

surface [syʀfas] *nf* surface; (*superficie*) surface area; **faire surface** to surface; **en surface** *adv* near the surface; (*fig*) superficially; **la pièce fait 100 m² de surface** the room has a surface area of 100m²; **surface de réparation** (*SPORT*) penalty area; **surface porteuse** *ou* **de sustentation** (*AVIAT*) aerofoil

surfait, e [syʀfɛ, -ɛt] *adj* overrated

surfer [sœrfe] *vi*: **surfer sur Internet** to surf the Internet

surgelé, e [syʀʒəle] *adj* (deep-)frozen

surgir [syʀʒiʀ] *vi* (*personne, véhicule*) to appear suddenly; (*jaillir*) to shoot up; (*montagne etc*) to rise up, loom up; (*fig: problème, conflit*) to arise

surhumain, e [syʀymɛ̃, -ɛn] *adj* superhuman

sur-le-champ [syʀləʃɑ̃] *adv* immediately

surlendemain [syʀlɑ̃dmɛ̃] *nm*: **le surlendemain (soir)** two days later (in the evening); **le surlendemain de** two days after

surmenage [syʀmənaʒ] *nm* overwork; **le surmenage intellectuel** mental fatigue

surmener [syʀməne] *vt*, **se surmener** *vi* to overwork

surmonter [syʀmɔ̃te] *vt* (*suj: coupole etc*) to surmount, top; (*vaincre*) to overcome, surmount

surnaturel, le [syʀnatyʀɛl] *adj*, *nm* supernatural

surnom [syʀnɔ̃] *nm* nickname

surnombre [syʀnɔ̃bʀ(ə)] *nm*: **être en surnombre** to be too many (*ou* one too many)

surpeuplé, e [syʀpœple] *adj* overpopulated

surplace [syʀplas] *nm*: **faire du surplace** to mark time

surplomber [syʀplɔ̃be] *vi* to be overhanging ♦ *vt* to overhang; (*dominer*) to tower above

surplus [syʀply] *nm* (*COMM*) surplus; (*reste*): **surplus de bois** wood left over; **au surplus** moreover; **surplus américains** American army surplus *sg*

surprenant, e [syʀpʀənɑ̃, -ɑ̃t] *vb voir* **surprendre** ♦ *adj* amazing

surprendre [syʀpʀɑ̃dʀ(ə)] *vt* (*étonner, prendre à l'improviste*) to amaze, surprise; (*secret*) to discover; (*tomber sur: intrus etc*) to catch; (*fig*) to detect; to chance *ou* happen upon; (*clin d'œil*) to intercept; (*conversation*) to overhear; (*suj: orage, nuit etc*) to catch out, take by surprise; **surprendre la vigi-**

lance/bonne foi de qn to catch sb out/betray sb's good faith; **se surprendre à faire** to catch *ou* find o.s. doing

surpris, e [syʀpʀi, -iz] *pp de* **surprendre** ♦ *adj*: **surpris (de/que)** amazed *ou* surprised (at/that)

surprise [syʀpʀiz] *nf* surprise; **faire une surprise à qn** to give sb a surprise; **voyage sans surprise** uneventful journey; **par surprise** *adv* by surprise

surprise-partie [syʀpʀizpaʀti] *nf* party

sursaut [syʀso] *nm* start, jump; **sursaut de** (*énergie, indignation*) sudden fit *ou* burst of ; **en sursaut** *adv* with a start

sursauter [syʀsote] *vi* to (give a) start, jump

sursis [syʀsi] *nm* (*JUR: gén*) suspended sentence; (*à l'execution capitale, aussi fig*) reprieve; (*MIL*): **sursis (d'appel** *ou* **d'incorporation)** deferment; **condamné à 5 mois (de prison) avec sursis** given a 5-month suspended (prison) sentence

surtaxe [syʀtaks(ə)] *nf* surcharge

surtout [syʀtu] *adv* (*avant tout, d'abord*) above all; (*spécialement, particulièrement*) especially; **il aime le sport, surtout le football** he likes sport, especially football; **cet été, il a surtout fait de la pêche** this summer he went fishing more than anything (else); **surtout pas d'histoires!** no fuss now!; **surtout, ne dites rien!** whatever you do – don't say anything!; **surtout pas!** certainly not *ou* definitely not!; **surtout que …** especially as …

surveillance [syʀvejɑ̃s] *nf* watch; (*POLICE, MIL*) surveillance; **sous surveillance médicale** under medical supervision; **la surveillance du territoire** internal security; *voir aussi* **DST**

surveillant, e [syʀvejɑ̃, -ɑ̃t] *nm/f* (*de prison*) warder; (*SCOL*) monitor; (*de travaux*) supervisor, overseer

surveiller [syʀveje] *vt* (*enfant, élèves, bagages*) to watch, keep an eye on; (*malade*) to watch over; (*prisonnier, suspect*) to keep (a) watch on; (*territoire, bâtiment*) to (keep) watch over; (*travaux, cuisson*) to supervise; (*SCOL: examen*) to invigilate; **se surveiller** to keep a check *ou* watch on o.s.; **surveiller son langage/sa ligne** to watch one's language/figure

survenir [syʀvəniʀ] *vi* (*incident, retards*) to occur, arise; (*événement*) to take place; (*personne*) to appear, arrive

survêt(ement) [syʀvɛt(mɑ̃)] *nm* tracksuit (*BRIT*), sweat suit (*US*)

survie [syʀvi] *nf* survival; (*REL*) afterlife; **équipement de survie** survival equipment; **une survie de quelques mois** a few more months of life

survivant, e [syʀvivɑ̃, -ɑ̃t] *vb voir* **survivre** ♦ *nm/f* survivor

survivre [syʀvivʀ(ə)] *vi* to survive; **survivre à** *vt* (*accident etc*) to survive; (*personne*) to outlive; **la victime a peu de chance de survivre** the victim has little hope of survival

survoler [syʀvɔle] *vt* to fly over; (*fig: livre*) to skim through; (*: question, problèmes*) to skim over

survolté, e [syʀvɔlte] *adj* (*ÉLEC*) stepped up,

boosted; (*fig*) worked up

sus [sy(s)]: **en sus de** *prép* in addition to, over and above; **en sus** *adv* in addition; **sus à** *excl*: **sus au tyran!** at the tyrant! ◆ *vb* [sy] *voir* **savoir**

susceptible [syseptibl(ə)] *adj* touchy, sensitive; **susceptible d'amélioration** *ou* **d'être amélioré** that can be improved, open to improvement; **susceptible de faire** (*capacité*) able to do; (*probabilité*) liable to do

susciter [sysite] *vt* (*admiration*) to arouse; (*obstacles, ennuis*) **susciter (à qn)** to create (for sb)

suspect, e [syspε(kt), -εkt(ə)] *adj* suspicious; (*témoignage, opinions, vin etc*) suspect ◆ *nm/f* suspect; **peu suspect de** most unlikely to be suspected of

suspecter [syspεkte] *vt* to suspect; (*honnêteté de qn*) to question, have one's suspicions about; **suspecter qn d'être/d'avoir fait qch** to suspect sb of being/having done sth

suspendre [syspɑ̃dʀ(ə)] *vt* (*accrocher: vêtement*): **suspendre qch (à)** to hang sth up (on); (*fixer: lustre etc*): **suspendre qch à** to hang sth from; (*interrompre, démettre*) to suspend; (*remettre*) to defer; **se suspendre à** to hang from

suspendu, e [syspɑ̃dy] *pp de* **suspendre** ◆ *adj* (*accroché*): **suspendu à** hanging on (*ou* from); (*perché*): **suspendu au-dessus de** suspended over; (*AUTO*): **bien/mal suspendu** with good/poor suspension; **être suspendu aux lèvres de qn** to hang upon sb's every word

suspens [syspɑ̃]: **en suspens** *adv* (*affaire*) in abeyance; **tenir en suspens** to keep in suspense

suspense [syspɑ̃s] *nm* suspense

suspension [syspɑ̃sjɔ̃] *nf* suspension; deferment; (*AUTO*) suspension; (*lustre*) pendant light fitting; **en suspension** in suspension, suspended; **suspension d'audience** adjournment

sut [sy] *vb voir* **savoir**

suture [sytyʀ] *nf*: **point de suture** stitch

svelte [svεlt(ə)] *adj* slender, svelte

SVP *sigle* (= *s'il vous plaît*) please

sweat-shirt, *pl* **sweat-shirts** [switʃœrt] *nm* sweatshirt

syllabe [silab] *nf* syllable

symbole [sɛ̃bɔl] *nm* symbol; **symbole graphique** (*INFORM*) icon

symbolique [sɛ̃bɔlik] *adj* symbolic; (*geste, offrande*) token *cpd*; (*salaire, dommages-intérêts*) nominal

symboliser [sɛ̃bɔlize] *vt* to symbolize

symétrique [simetʀik] *adj* symmetrical

sympa [sɛ̃pa] *adj inv* (= *sympathique*) nice; friendly; good

sympathie [sɛ̃pati] *nf* (*inclination*) liking; (*affinité*) fellow feeling; (*condoléances*) sympathy; **accueillir avec sympathie** (*projet*) to receive favourably; **avoir de la sympathie pour qn** to like sb, have a liking for sb; **témoignages de sympathie** expressions of sympathy; **croyez à toute ma**

sympathie you have my deepest sympathy

sympathique [sɛ̃patik] *adj* (*personne, figure*) nice, friendly, likeable; (*geste*) friendly; (*livre*) good; (*déjeuner*) nice; (*réunion, endroit*) pleasant, nice

sympathisant, e [sɛ̃patizɑ̃, -ɑ̃t] *nm/f* sympathizer

sympathiser [sɛ̃patize] *vi* (*voisins etc: s'entendre*) to get on (*BRIT*) *ou* along (*us*) (well); (: *se fréquenter*) to socialize, see each other; **sympathiser avec** to get on *ou* along (well) with, to see, socialize with

symphonie [sɛ̃fɔni] *nf* symphony

symptôme [sɛ̃ptom] *nm* symptom

synagogue [sinagɔg] *nf* synagogue

syncope [sɛ̃kɔp] *nf* (*MÉD*) blackout; (*MUS*) syncopation; **tomber en syncope** to faint, pass out

syndic [sɛ̃dik] *nm* managing agent

syndical, e, aux [sɛ̃dikal, -o] *adj* (trade-)union *cpd*; **centrale syndicale** group of affiliated trade unions

syndicaliste [sɛ̃dikalist(ə)] *nm/f* trade unionist

syndicat [sɛ̃dika] *nm* (*d'ouvriers, employés*) (trade(s)) union; (*autre association d'intérêts*) union, association; **syndicat d'initiative (SI)** tourist office *ou* bureau; **syndicat patronal** employers' syndicate, federation of employers; **syndicat de propriétaires** association of property owners

syndiqué, e [sɛ̃dike] *adj* belonging to a (trade) union; **non syndiqué** non-union

syndiquer [sɛ̃dike]: **se syndiquer** *vi* to form a trade union; (*adhérer*) to join a trade union

synonyme [sinɔnim] *adj* synonymous ◆ *nm* synonym; **synonyme de** synonymous with

syntaxe [sɛ̃taks(ə)] *nf* syntax

synthèse [sɛ̃tεz] *nf* synthesis (*pl* syntheses); **faire la synthèse de** to synthesize

synthétique [sɛ̃tetik] *adj* synthetic

Syrie [siʀi] *nf*: **la Syrie** Syria

systématique [sistematik] *adj* systematic

système [sistεm] *nm* system; **le système D** resourcefulness; **système décimal** decimal system; **système expert** expert system; **système d'exploitation à disques** (*INFORM*) disk operating system; **système immunitaire** immune system; **système métrique** metric system; **système solaire** solar system

— T t —

t' [t(ə)] *pron voir* **te**

ta [ta] *adj possessif voir* **ton**

tabac [taba] *nm* tobacco; (*aussi*: **débit** *ou* **bureau de tabac**) tobacconist's (shop) ◆ *adj inv*: (**couleur**) **tabac** buff, tobacco *cpd*; **passer qn à tabac** to beat sb up; **faire un tabac** (*fam*) to be a big hit; **tabac blond/brun** light/dark tobacco; **tabac gris** shag; **tabac à priser** snuff

tabagisme [tabaʒism(ə)] *nm* nicotine addiction;

tabagisme passif passive smoking

tabasser [tabase] *vt* to beat up

table [tabl(ə)] *nf* table; **avoir une bonne table** to keep a good table; **à table!** dinner *etc* is ready!; **se mettre à table** to sit down to eat; (*fig: fam*) to come clean; **mettre** *ou* **dresser/desservir la table** to lay *ou* set/clear the table; **faire table rase de** to make a clean sweep of; **table basse** coffee table; **table de cuisson** (*à l'électricité*) hotplate; (*au gas*) gas ring; **table d'écoute** wire-tapping set; **table d'harmonie** sounding board; **table d'hôte** set menu; **table de lecture** turntable; **table des matières** (table of) contents *pl*; **table de multiplication** multiplication table; **table des négociations** negotiating table; **table de nuit** *ou* **de chevet** bedside table; **table ronde** (*débat*) round table; **table roulante** (tea) trolley; **table de toilette** washstand; **table traçante** (*INFORM*) plotter

tableau, x [tablo] *nm* (*ART*) painting; (*reproduction, fig*) picture; (*panneau*) board; (*schéma*) table, chart; **tableau d'affichage** notice board; **tableau de bord** dashboard; (*AVIAT*) instrument panel; **tableau de chasse** tally; **tableau de contrôle** console, control panel; **tableau de maître** masterpiece; **tableau noir** blackboard

tabler [table] *vi*: **tabler sur** to count *ou* bank on

tablette [tablɛt] *nf* (*planche*) shelf (*pl* shelves); **tablette de chocolat** bar of chocolate

tableur [tablœʀ] *nm* (*INFORM*) spreadsheet

tablier [tablije] *nm* apron; (*de pont*) roadway; (*de cheminée*) (flue-)shutter

tabou, e [tabu] *adj, nm* taboo

tabouret [tabuʀɛ] *nm* stool

tac [tak] *nm*: **du tac au tac** tit for tat

tache [taʃ] *nf* (*saleté*) stain, mark; (*ART: de couleur, lumière*) spot; splash, patch; **faire tache d'huile** to spread, gain ground; **tache de rousseur** *ou* **de son** freckle; **tache de vin** (*sur la peau*) strawberry mark

tâche [taʃ] *nf* task; **travailler à la tâche** to do piecework

tacher [taʃe] *vt* to stain, mark; (*fig*) to sully, stain; **se tacher** *vi* (*fruits*) to become marked

tâcher [taʃe] *vi*: **tâcher de faire** to try to do, endeavour (*BRIT*) *ou* endeavor (*US*) to do

tacheté, e [taʃte] *adj*: **tacheté de** speckled *ou* spotted with

tacot [tako] *nm* (*péj: voiture*) banger (*BRIT*), clunker (*US*)

tact [takt] *nm* tact; **avoir du tact** to be tactful, have tact

tactique [taktik] *adj* tactical ♦ *nf* (*technique*) tactics *sg*; (*plan*) tactic

taie [tɛ] *nf*: **taie (d'oreiller)** pillowslip, pillowcase

taille [taj] *nf* cutting; pruning; (*milieu du corps*) waist; (*hauteur*) height; (*grandeur*) size; **de taille à faire** capable of doing; **de taille** *adj* sizeable; **quelle taille faites-vous?** what size are you?

taille-crayon(s) [tajkʀɛjɔ̃] *nm inv* pencil sharp-ener

tailler [taje] *vt* (*pierre, diamant*) to cut; (*arbre, plante*) to prune; (*vêtement*) to cut out; (*crayon*) to sharpen; **se tailler** *vt* (*ongles, barbe*) to trim, cut; (*fig: réputation*) to gain, win ♦ *vi* (*fam: s'enfuir*) to beat it; **tailler dans** (*chair, bois*) to cut into; **tailler grand/petit** to be on the large/small side

tailleur [tajœʀ] *nm* (*couturier*) tailor; (*vêtement*) suit, costume; **en tailleur** (*assis*) cross-legged; **tailleur de diamants** diamond-cutter

taillis [taji] *nm* copse

taire [tɛʀ] *vt* to keep to o.s., conceal ♦ *vi*: **faire taire qn** to make sb be quiet; (*fig*) to silence sb; **se taire** *vi* (*s'arrêter de parler*) to fall silent, stop talking; (*ne pas parler*) to be silent *ou* quiet; (*s'abstenir de s'exprimer*) to keep quiet; (*bruit, voix*) to disappear; **tais-toi!, taisez-vous!** be quiet!

talc [talk] *nm* talc, talcum powder

talent [talɑ̃] *nm* talent; **avoir du talent** to be talented, have talent

talkie-walkie [tɔkiwɔki] *nm* walkie-talkie

taloche [talɔʃ] *nf* (*fam: claque*) slap; (*TECH*) plaster float

talon [talɔ̃] *nm* heel; (*de chèque, billet*) stub, counterfoil (*BRIT*); **talons plats/aiguilles** flat/stiletto heels; **être sur les talons de qn** to be on sb's heels; **tourner les talons** to turn on one's heel; **montrer les talons** (*fig*) to show a clean pair of heels

talonner [talɔne] *vt* to follow hard behind; (*fig*) to hound; (*RUGBY*) to heel

talus [taly] *nm* embankment; **talus de remblai/déblai** embankment/excavation slope

tambour [tɑ̃buʀ] *nm* (*MUS, aussi TECH*) drum; (*musicien*) drummer; (*porte*) revolving door (*pl* -s); **sans tambour ni trompette** unobtrusively

tambourin [tɑ̃buʀɛ̃] *nm* tambourine

tambouriner [tɑ̃buʀine] *vi*: **tambouriner contre** *ou* **on** to drum against *ou* on

tamis [tami] *nm* sieve

Tamise [tamiz] *nf*: **la Tamise** the Thames

tamisé, e [tamize] *adj* (*fig*) subdued, soft

tampon [tɑ̃pɔ̃] *nm* (*de coton, d'ouate*) pad; (*aussi*: **tampon hygiénique** *ou* **périodique**) tampon; (*amortisseur, INFORM: aussi*: **mémoire tampon**) buffer; (*bouchon*) plug, stopper; (*cachet, timbre*) stamp; (*CHIMIE*) buffer; **tampon buvard** blotter; **tampon encreur** inking pad; **tampon (à récurer)** scouring pad

tamponner [tɑ̃pɔne] *vt* (*timbres*) to stamp; (*heurter*) to crash *ou* ram into; (*essuyer*) to mop up; **se tamponner** (*voitures*) to crash (into each other)

tamponneuse [tɑ̃pɔnøz] *adj f*: **autos tamponneuses** dodgems, bumper cars

tandem [tɑ̃dɛm] *nm* tandem; (*fig*) duo, pair

tandis [tɑ̃di]: **tandis que** *conj* while

tanguer [tɑ̃ge] *vi* to pitch (and toss)

tanière [tanjɛʀ] *nf* lair, den

tanné, e [tane] *adj* weather-beaten

tanner [tane] *vt* to tan

tant [tɑ̃] *adv* so much; **tant de** (*sable, eau*) so much; (*gens, livres*) so many; **tant que** *conj* as long as; **tant que** (*comparatif*) as much as; **tant mieux** that's great; so much the better; **tant mieux pour lui** good for him; **tant pis** too bad; **un tant soit peu** (*un peu*) a little bit; (*même un peu*) (even) remotely; **tant bien que mal** as well as can be expected; **tant s'en faut** far from it, not by a long way

tante [tɑ̃t] *nf* aunt

tantôt [tɑ̃to] *adv* (*parfois*): **tantôt ... tantôt** now ... now; (*cet après-midi*) this afternoon

taon [tɑ̃] *nm* horsefly, gadfly

tapage [tapaʒ] *nm* uproar, din; (*fig*) fuss, row; **tapage nocturne** (*JUR*) disturbance of the peace (*at night*)

tapageur, euse [tapaʒœʀ, -øz] *adj* (*bruyant: enfants etc*) noisy; (*toilette*) loud, flashy; (*publicité*) obtrusive

tape [tap] *nf* slap

tape-à-l'œil [tapalœj] *adj inv* flashy, showy

taper [tape] *vt* (*personne*) to clout; (*porte*) to bang, slam; (*dactylographier*) to type (out); (*INFORM*) to key (board); (*fam: emprunter*): **taper qn de 10 €** to touch sb for 10 €, cadge 10 € off sb ♦ *vi* (*soleil*) to beat down; **se taper** *vt* (*fam: travail*) to get landed with; (: *boire, manger*) to down; **taper sur qn** to thump sb; (*fig*) to run sb down; **taper sur qch** (*clou etc*) to hit sth; (*table etc*) to bang on sth; **taper à** (*porte etc*) to knock on; **taper dans** (*se servir*) to dig into; **taper des mains/pieds** to clap one's hands/ stamp one's feet; **taper (à la machine)** to type

tapi, e [tapi] *adj*: **tapi dans/derrière** (*blotti*) crouching *ou* cowering in/behind; (*caché*) hidden away in/behind

tapis [tapi] *nm* carpet; (*de table*) cloth; **mettre sur le tapis** (*fig*) to bring up for discussion; **aller au tapis** (*BOXE*) to go down; **envoyer au tapis** (*BOXE*) to floor; **tapis roulant** conveyor belt; **tapis de sol** (*de tente*) groundsheet; **tapis de souris** (*INFORM*) mouse mat

tapisser [tapise] *vt* (*avec du papier peint*) to paper; (*recouvrir*): **tapisser qch (de)** to cover sth (with)

tapisserie [tapisʀi] *nf* (*tenture, broderie*) tapestry; (: *travail*) tapestry-making; (: *ouvrage*) tapestry work; (*papier peint*) wallpaper; (*fig*): **faire tapisserie** to sit out, be a wallflower

tapissier, ière [tapisje, -jɛʀ] *nm/f*: **tapissier-décorateur** upholsterer and decorator

tapoter [tapɔte] *vt* to pat, tap

taquin, e [takɛ̃, -in] *adj* teasing

taquiner [takine] *vt* to tease

tarabiscoté, e [taʀabiskɔte] *adj* over-ornate, fussy

tard [taʀ] *adv* late; **au plus tard** at the latest; **plus tard** later (on) ♦ *nm*: **sur le tard** (*à une heure avancée*) late in the day; (*vers la fin de la vie*) late in life

tarder [taʀde] *vi* (*chose*) to be a long time coming; (*personne*): **tarder à faire** to delay doing; **il me tarde d'être** I am longing to be; **sans (plus) tarder** without (further) delay

tardif, ive [taʀdif, -iv] *adj* (*heure, repas, fruit*) late; (*talent, goût*) late in developing

taré, e [taʀe] *nm/f* cretin

tarif [taʀif] *nm* (*liste*) price list, tariff (*BRIT*); (*barème*) rate, rates *pl*, tariff (*BRIT*); (: *de taxis etc*) fares *pl*; **voyager à plein tarif/à tarif réduit** to travel at full/ reduced fare

tarir [taʀiʀ] *vi* to dry up, run dry ♦ *vt* to dry up

tarte [taʀt(ə)] *nf* tart; **tarte aux pommes/à la crème** apple/custard tart

tartine [taʀtin] *nf* slice of bread (and butter (*ou* jam)); **tartine de miel** slice of bread and honey; **tartine beurrée** slice of bread and butter

tartiner [taʀtine] *vt* to spread; **fromage à tartiner** cheese spread

tartre [taʀtʀ(ə)] *nm* (*des dents*) tartar; (*de chaudière*) fur, scale

tas [tɑ] *nm* heap, pile; (*fig*): **un tas de** heaps of, lots of; **en tas** in a heap *ou* pile; **dans le tas** (*fig*) in the crowd; among them; **formé sur le tas** trained on the job

tasse [tɑs] *nf* cup; **boire la tasse** (*en se baignant*) to swallow a mouthful; **tasse à café/thé** coffee/ teacup

tassé, e [tɑse] *adj*: **bien tassé** (*café etc*) strong

tasser [tɑse] *vt* (*terre, neige*) to pack down; (*entasser*): **tasser qch dans** to cram sth into; (*INFORM*) to pack; **se tasser** *vi* (*terrain*) to settle; (*personne: avec l'âge*) to shrink; (*fig*) to sort itself out, settle down

tâter [tɑte] *vt* to feel; (*fig*) to sound out; **tâter de** (*prison etc*) to have a taste of; **se tâter** (*hésiter*) to be in two minds; **tâter le terrain** (*fig*) to test the ground

tatillon, ne [tatijɔ̃, -ɔn] *adj* pernickety

tâtonnement [tɑtɔnmɑ̃] *nm*: **par tâtonnements** (*fig*) by trial and error

tâtonner [tɑtɔne] *vi* to grope one's way along; (*fig*) to grope around (in the dark)

tâtons [tɑtɔ̃]: **à tâtons** *adv*: **chercher/avancer à tâtons** to grope around for/grope one's way forward

tatouage [tatwaʒ] *nm* tattooing; (*dessin*) tattoo

tatouer [tatwe] *vt* to tattoo

taudis [todi] *nm* hovel, slum

taule [tol] *nf* (*fam*) nick (*BRIT*), jail

taupe [top] *nf* mole; (*peau*) moleskin

taureau, x [tɔʀo] *nm* bull; (*signe*): **le Taureau** Taurus, the Bull; **être du Taureau** to be Taurus

tauromachie [tɔʀɔmaʃi] *nf* bullfighting

taux [to] *nm* rate; (*d'alcool*) level; **taux d'escompte** discount rate; **taux d'intérêt** interest rate; **taux de mortalité** mortality rate

taxe [taks(ə)] *nf* taxi (*douanière*) duty; **toutes taxes comprises (TTC)** inclusive of tax; **taxe de base** (*TÉL*) unit charge; **taxe de séjour** tourist tax; **taxe à** *ou* **sur la valeur ajoutée (TVA)** value added tax (VAT)

taxer [takse] *vt* (*personne*) to tax; (*produit*) to put a tax on, tax; (*fig*): **taxer qn de** (*qualifier de*) to call sb + *attribut*; (*accuser de*) to accuse sb of, tax sb with

taxi [taksi] *nm* taxi

Tchécoslovaquie [tʃekɔslɔvaki] *nf*: **la Tchécoslovaquie** Czechoslovakia

tchèque [tʃɛk] *adj* Czech ♦ *nm* (*LING*) Czech ♦ *nm/f*: **Tchèque** Czech

te, t' [t(ə)] *pron* you; (*réfléchi*) yourself

technicien, ne [tɛknisjɛ̃, -ɛn] *nm/f* technician

technico-commercial, e, aux [tɛknikɔkɔmɛʀsjal, -o] *adj*: **agent technico-commercial** sales technician

technique [tɛknik] *adj* technical ♦ *nf* technique

techniquement [tɛknikmɑ̃] *adv* technically

technologie [tɛknɔlɔʒi] *nf* technology

technologique [tɛknɔlɔʒik] *adj* technological

teck [tɛk] *nm* teak

tee-shirt [tiʃœʀt] *nm* T-shirt, tee-shirt

teindre [tɛ̃dʀ(ə)] *vt* to dye; **se teindre (les cheveux)** to dye one's hair

teint, e [tɛ̃, tɛ̃t] *pp de* **teindre** ♦ *adj* dyed ♦ *nm* (*du visage: permanent*) complexion, colouring (*BRIT*), coloring (*US*); (*momentané*) colour (*BRIT*), color (*US*) ♦ *nf* shade, colour, color; (*fig: petite dose*): **une teinte de** a hint of; **grand teint** *adj inv* colourfast; **bon teint** *adj inv* (*couleur*) fast; (*tissu*) colourfast; (*personne*) staunch, firm

teinté, e [tɛ̃te] *adj* (*verres*) tinted; (*bois*) stained; **teinté acajou** mahogany-stained; **teinté de** (*fig*) tinged with

teinter [tɛ̃te] *vt* to tint; (*bois*) to stain

teinture [tɛ̃tyʀ] *nf* dyeing; (*substance*) dye; (*MÉD*): **teinture d'iode** tincture of iodine

teinturerie [tɛ̃tyʀʀi] *nf* dry cleaner's

teinturier, ière [tɛ̃tyʀje, -jɛʀ] *nm/f* dry cleaner

tel, telle [tɛl] *adj* (*pareil*) such; (*comme*): **tel un/des ...** like a/like ...; (*indéfini*) such-and-such a, a given; (*intensif*): **un tel/de tels ...** such (a)/such ...; **rien de tel** nothing like it, no such thing; **tel que** *conj* like, such as; **tel quel** as it is *ou* stands (*ou* was *etc*)

télé [tele] *nf* (= *télévision*) TV, telly (*BRIT*); **à la télé** on TV *ou* telly

télécabine [telekabin] *nm, nf* telecabine, gondola

télécarte [telekaʀt(ə)] *nf* phonecard

télécharger [teleʃaʀʒe] *vt* to download

télécommande [telekɔmɑ̃d] *nf* remote control

télécopie [telekɔpi] *nf* fax, telefax

télécopieur [telekɔpjœʀ] *nm* fax (machine)

télédistribution [teledistribysjɔ̃] *nf* cable TV

téléférique [telefeʀik] *nm* = **téléphérique**

télégramme [telegʀam] *nm* telegram

télégraphier [telegʀafje] *vt* to telegraph, cable

téléguider [telegide] *vt* to operate by remote control, radio-control

téléjournal, aux [teleʒuʀnal, -o] *nm* television news magazine programme

téléobjectif [teleɔbʒɛktif] *nm* telephoto lens *sg*

télépathie [telepati] *nf* telepathy

téléphérique [teleferik] *nm* cable-car

téléphone [telefɔn] *nm* telephone; **avoir le téléphone** to be on the (tele)phone; **au téléphone** on the phone; **les Téléphones** the (tele)phone service *sg*; **téléphone arabe** bush telegraph; **téléphone à carte (magnétique)** cardphone; **téléphone cellulaire** cellphone, cellular phone; **téléphone manuel** manually-operated telephone system; **téléphone rouge** hotline

téléphoner [telefɔne] *vt* to telephone ♦ *vi* to telephone; to make a phone call; **téléphoner à** to phone up, ring up, call up

téléphonique [telefɔnik] *adj* telephone *cpd*, phone *cpd*; **cabine téléphonique** call box (*BRIT*), (tele)phone box (*BRIT*) *ou* booth; **conversation/ appel téléphonique** (tele)phone conversation/call

téléréalité [telerealite] *nf* reality TV

télescope [telɛskɔp] *nm* telescope

télescoper [telɛskɔpe] *vt* to smash up; **se télescoper** (*véhicules*) to collide, crash into each other

téléscripteur [teleskriptœʀ] *nm* teleprinter

télésiège [telesjɛʒ] *nm* chairlift

téléski [teleski] *nm* ski-tow; **téléski à archets** T-bar tow; **téléski à perche** button lift

téléspectateur, trice [telespɛktatœʀ, -tris] *nm/f* (television) viewer

télévente [televɑ̃t] *nf* telesales

téléviseur [televizœʀ] *nm* television set

télévision [televizjɔ̃] *nf* television; (**poste de**) **télévision** television (set); **avoir la télévision** to have a television; **à la télévision** on television; **télévision par câble/satellite** cable/satellite television

télex [telɛks] *nm* telex

telle [tɛl] *adj f voir* **tel**

tellement [tɛlmɑ̃] *adv* (*tant*) so much; (*si*) so; **tellement plus grand (que)** so much bigger (than); **tellement de** (*sable, eau*) so much; (*gens, livres*) so many; **il s'est endormi tellement il était fatigué** he was so tired (that) he fell asleep; **pas tellement** not really; **pas tellement fort/lentement** not (all) that strong/slowly; **il ne mange pas tellement** he doesn't eat (all that) much

téméraire [temeʀɛʀ] *adj* reckless, rash

témérité [temeʀite] *nf* recklessness, rashness

témoignage [temwaɲaʒ] *nm* (*JUR*: *déclaration*) testimony *no pl*, evidence *no pl*; (: *faits*) evidence *no pl*; (*gén*: *rapport, récit*) account; (*fig*: *d'affection etc*) token, mark; expression

témoigner [temwaɲe] *vt* (*manifester: intérêt, gratitude*) to show ◆ *vi* (*JUR*) to testify, give evidence; **témoigner que** to testify that; (*fig*: *démontrer*) to reveal that, testify to the fact that; **témoigner de** *vt* (*confirmer*) to bear witness to, testify to

témoin [temwɛ̃] *nm* witness; (*fig*) testimony; (*SPORT*) baton; (*CONSTR*) telltale ◆ *adj* control *cpd*, test *cpd*; **témoin le fait que …** (as) witness the fact that …; **appartement-témoin** show flat (*BRIT*), model apartment (*US*); **être témoin de** (*voir*) to witness; **prendre à témoin** to call to witness; **témoin à charge** witness for the prosecution; **Témoin de Jehovah** Jehovah's Witness; **témoin de moralité** character reference; **témoin oculaire** eyewitness

tempe [tɑ̃p] *nf* (*ANAT*) temple

tempérament [tɑ̃peʀamɑ̃] *nm* temperament, disposition; (*santé*) constitution; **à tempérament** (*vente*) on deferred (payment) terms; (*achat*) by instalments, hire purchase *cpd*; **avoir du tempérament** to be hot-blooded

température [tɑ̃peʀatyʀ] *nf* temperature; **prendre la température de** to take the temperature of; (*fig*) to gauge the feeling of; **avoir** *ou* **faire de la température** to be running *ou* have a temperature

tempéré, e [tɑ̃peʀe] *adj* temperate

tempête [tɑ̃pɛt] *nf* storm; **tempête de sable/neige** sand/snowstorm; **vent de tempête** gale

temple [tɑ̃pl(ə)] *nm* temple; (*protestant*) church

temporaire [tɑ̃pɔʀɛʀ] *adj* temporary

temps [tɑ̃] *nm* (*atmosphérique*) weather; (*durée*) time; (*époque*) time, times *pl*; (*LING*) tense; (*MUS*) beat; (*TECH*) stroke; **les temps changent/sont durs** times are changing/hard; **il fait beau/mauvais temps** the weather is fine/bad; **avoir le temps/tout le temps/juste le temps** to have time/plenty of time/just enough time; **avoir fait son temps** (*fig*) to have had its (*ou* his *etc*) day; **en temps de paix/guerre** in peacetime/wartime; **en temps utile** *ou* **voulu** in due time *ou* course; **de temps en temps, de temps à autre** from time to time, now and again; **en même temps** at the same time; **à temps** (*partir, arriver*) in time; **à plein/mi-temps** *adv, adj* full-/part-time; **à temps partiel** *adv, adj* part-time; **dans le temps** at one time; **de tout temps** always; **du temps que** at the time when, in the days when; **dans le** *ou* **du** *ou* **au temps où** at the time when; **pendant ce temps** in the meantime; **temps d'accès** (*INFORM*) access time; **temps d'arrêt** pause, halt; **temps mort** (*SPORT*) stoppage (time); (*COMM*) slack period; **temps partagé** (*INFORM*) time-sharing; **temps réel** (*INFORM*) real time

tenable [tənabl(ə)] *adj* bearable

tenace [tənas] *adj* tenacious, persistent

tenailler [tənɑje] *vt* (*fig*) to torment, torture

tenailles [tənɑj] *nfpl* pincers

tenais [t(ə)nɛ] *etc vb voir* **tenir**

tenancier, ière [tənɑsje, -jɛʀ] *nm/f* (*d'hôtel, de bistro*) manager/manageress

tenant, e [tənɑ̃, -ɑ̃t] *adj f voir* **séance** ◆ *nm/f* (*SPORT*): **tenant du titre** title-holder ◆ *nm*: **d'un seul tenant** in one piece; **les tenants et les aboutissants** (*fig*) the ins and outs

tendance [tɑ̃dɑ̃s] *nf* (*opinions*) leanings *pl*, sympathies *pl*; (*inclination*) tendency; (*évolution*) trend; **tendance à la hausse/baisse** upward/downward trend; **avoir tendance à** to have a tendency to, tend to

tendeur [tɑ̃dœʀ] *nm* (*de vélo*) chain-adjuster; (*de câble*) wire-strainer; (*de tente*) runner; (*attache*) elastic strap

tendre [tɑ̃dʀ(ə)] *adj* (*viande, légumes*) tender; (*bois, roche, couleur*) soft; (*affectueux*) tender, loving ◆ *vt* (*élastique, peau*) to stretch, draw tight; (*muscle*) to tense; (*donner*): **tendre qch à qn** to hold sth out to sb; to offer sb sth; (*fig: piège*) to set, lay; (*tapisserie*): **tendu de soie** hung with silk, with silk hangings; **se tendre** *vi* (*corde*) to tighten; (*relations*) to become strained; **tendre à qch/à faire** to tend towards sth/to do; **tendre l'oreille** to prick up one's ears; **tendre la main/le bras** to hold out one's hand/stretch out one's arm; **tendre la perche à qn** (*fig*) to throw sb a line

tendrement [tɑ̃dʀəmɑ̃] *adv* tenderly, lovingly

tendresse [tɑ̃dʀɛs] *nf* tenderness; **tendresses** *nfpl* (*caresses etc*) tenderness *no pl*, caresses

tendu, e [tɑ̃dy] *pp de* **tendre** ◆ *adj* tight; tensed; strained

ténèbres [tenɛbʀ(ə)] *nfpl* darkness *sg*

teneur [tənœʀ] *nf* content, substance; (*d'une lettre*) terms *pl*, content; **teneur en cuivre** copper content

tenir [təniʀ] *vt* to hold; (*magasin, hôtel*) to run; (*promesse*) to keep ◆ *vi* to hold; (*neige, gel*) to last; (*survivre*) to survive; **se tenir** *vi* (*avoir lieu*) to be held, take place; (*être: personne*) to stand; **se tenir droit** to stand up (*ou* sit up) straight; **bien se tenir** to behave well; **se tenir à qch** to hold on to sth; **s'en tenir à qch** to confine o.s. to sth; to stick to sth; **tenir à** *vt* to be attached to, care about (*ou* for); (*avoir pour cause*) to be due to, stem from; **tenir à faire** to want to do, be keen to do; **tenir à ce que qn fasse qch** to be anxious that sb should do sth; **tenir de** *vt* to partake of; (*ressembler à*) to take after; **ça ne tient qu'à lui** it is entirely up to him; **tenir qn pour** to take sb for; **tenir qch de qn** (*histoire*) to have heard *ou* learnt sth from sb; (*qualité, défaut*) to have inherited *ou* got sth from sb; **tenir les comptes** to keep the books; **tenir un rôle** to play a part; **tenir de la place** to take up space *ou* room; **tenir l'alcool** to be able to hold a drink; **tenir le coup** to hold out; **tenir bon** to stand *ou* hold fast; **tenir 3 jours/2 mois** (*résister*) to hold out *ou* last 3 days/2 months; **tenir au chaud/à l'abri** to keep hot/under shelter *ou* cover; **tenir prêt** to have ready; **tenir sa langue** *(fig)* to hold one's tongue; **tiens** *(ou* **tenez), voilà le stylo** there's the pen!; **tiens, Alain!** look, here's Alain!; **tiens?** *(surprise)* really?; **tiens-toi bien!** *(pour informer)* brace yourself!, take a deep breath!

tennis [tenis] *nm* tennis; *(aussi:* **court de tennis**) tennis court ♦ *nmpl ou fpl (aussi:* **chaussures de tennis**) tennis *ou* gym shoes; **tennis de table** table tennis

tennisman [tenisman] *nm* tennis player

tension [tɑ̃sjɔ̃] *nf* tension; *(fig: des relations, de la situation)* tension; (: *concentration, effort)* strain; *(MÉD)* blood pressure; **faire** *ou* **avoir de la tension** to have high blood pressure; **tension nerveuse/raciale** nervous/racial tension

tentation [tɑ̃tasjɔ̃] *nf* temptation

tentative [tɑ̃tativ] *nf* attempt, bid; **tentative d'évasion** escape bid; **tentative de suicide** suicide attempt

tente [tɑ̃t] *nf* tent; **tente à oxygène** oxygen tent

tenter [tɑ̃te] *vt (éprouver, attirer)* to tempt; *(essayer)*: **tenter qch** *ou* **de faire** to attempt *ou* try sth/to do; **être tenté de** to be tempted to; **tenter sa chance** to try one's luck

tenture [tɑ̃tyʀ] *nf* hanging

tenu, e [təny] *pp de* **tenir** ♦ *adj (maison, comptes)*: **bien tenu** well-kept; *(obligé)*: **tenu de faire** under an obligation to do ♦ *nf (action de tenir)* running; keeping; holding; *(vêtements)* clothes *pl*, gear; *(allure)* dress *no pl*, appearance; *(comportement)* manners *pl*, behaviour *(BRIT)*, behavior *(US)*; **être en tenue** to be dressed (up); **se mettre en tenue** to dress (up); **en grande tenue** in full dress; **en petite tenue** scantily dressed *ou* clad; **avoir de la tenue** to have good manners; *(journal)* to have a high standard; **tenue de combat** combat gear *ou* dress; **tenue de pompier** fireman's uniform; **tenue de route** *(AUTO)* road-holding; **tenue de soirée** evening dress; **tenue de sport/voyage** sports/travelling clothes *pl ou* gear *no pl*

ter [tɛʀ] *adj*: **16 ter** 16b *ou* B

térébenthine [teʀebɑ̃tin] *nf*: **(essence de) térébenthine** (oil of) turpentine

tergal® [tɛʀɡal] *nm* Terylene®

terme [tɛʀm(ə)] *nm* term; *(fin)* end; **être en bons/mauvais termes avec qn** to be on good/bad terms with sb; **vente/achat à terme** *(COMM)* forward sale/purchase; **au terme de** at the end of; **en d'autres termes** in other words; **moyen terme** *(solution intermédiaire)* middle course; **à court/long terme** *adj* short-/long-term *ou* -range ♦ *adv* in the short/long term; **à terme** *adj (MÉD)* full-term ♦ *adv* sooner or later, eventually; *(MÉD)* at term; **avant terme** *(MÉD)* ♦ *adj* premature ♦ *adv* prematurely; **mettre un terme à** to put an end *ou* a stop to; **toucher à son terme** to be nearing its end

terminaison [tɛʀminɛzɔ̃] *nf (LING)* ending

terminal, e, aux [tɛʀminal, -o] *adj (partie, phase)* final; *(MÉD)* terminal ♦ *nm* terminal ♦ *nf (SCOL)* ≃ sixth form *ou* year *(BRIT)* ≃ twelfth grade *(US)*

terminer [tɛʀmine] *vt* to end; *(travail, repas)* to finish; **se terminer** *vi* to end; **se terminer par** to end with

terne [tɛʀn(ə)] *adj* dull

ternir [tɛʀniʀ] *vt* to dull; *(fig)* to sully, tarnish; **se ternir** *vi* to become dull

terrain [teʀɛ̃] *nm (sol, fig)* ground; *(COMM)* land *no pl*, plot (of land) ; (: *à bâtir)* site; **sur le terrain** *(fig)* on the field; **terrain de football/rugby** football/rugby pitch *(BRIT) ou* field *(US)*; **terrain d'atterrissage** landing strip; **terrain d'aviation** airfield; **terrain de camping** campsite; **un terrain d'entente** an area of agreement; **terrain de golf** golf course; **terrain de jeu** playground; *(SPORT)* games field; **terrain de sport** sports ground; **terrain vague** waste ground *no pl*

terrasse [teʀas] *nf* terrace; *(de café)* pavement area, terrasse; **à la terrasse** *(café)* outside

terrasser [teʀase] *vt (adversaire)* to floor, bring down; *(suj: maladie etc)* to lay low

terre [tɛʀ] *nf (gén, aussi ÉLEC)* earth; *(substance)* soil, earth; *(opposé à mer)* land *no pl*; *(contrée)* land; **terres** *nfpl (terrains)* lands, land *sg*; **travail de la terre** work on the land; **en terre** *(pipe, poterie)* clay *cpd*; **mettre en terre** *(plante etc)* to plant; *(personne: enterrer)* to bury; **à** *ou* **par terre** *(mettre, être)* on the ground *(ou* floor); *(jeter, tomber)* to the ground, down; **terre à terre** *adj inv* down-to-earth, matter-of-fact; **la Terre Adélie** Adélie Coast *ou* Land; **terre de bruyère** (heath-)peat; **terre cuite** earthenware; terracotta; **la terre ferme** dry land, terra firma; **la Terre de Feu** Tierra del Fuego; **terre glaise** clay; **la Terre promise** the Promised Land; **la Terre Sainte** the Holy Land

terreau [teʀo] *nm* compost

terre-plein [tɛʀplɛ̃] *nm* platform

terrer [teʀe] : **se terrer** *vi* to hide away; to go to ground

terrestre [teʀɛstʀ(ə)] *adj (surface)* earth's, of the earth; *(BOT, ZOOL, MIL)* land *cpd*; *(REL)* earthly, worldly

terreur [teʀœʀ] *nf* terror *no pl*, fear

terrible [teʀibl(ə)] *adj* terrible, dreadful; *(fam: fantastique)* terrific

terrien, ne [teʀjɛ̃, -ɛn] *adj*: **propriétaire terrien** landowner ♦ *nm/f* countryman/woman, man/woman of the soil; *(non martien etc)* earthling; *(non marin)* landsman

terrier [teʀje] *nm* burrow, hole; *(chien)* terrier

terrifier [teʀifje] *vt* to terrify

terrine [teʀin] *nf (récipient)* terrine; *(CULIN)* pâté

territoire [teʀitwaʀ] *nm* territory; **Territoire des Afars et des Issas** French Territory of Afars and Issas

terroir [teʀwaʀ] *nm (AGR)* soil; *(région)* region; **accent du terroir** country *ou* rural accent

terroriser [teʀɔʀize] vt to terrorize

terrorisme [teʀɔʀism(ə)] nm terrorism

terroriste [teʀɔʀist(ə)] nm/f terrorist

tertiaire [teʀsjeʀ] adj tertiary ♦ nm (ÉCON) tertiary sector, service industries pl

tertre [teʀtʀ(ə)] nm hillock, mound

tes [te] adj possessif voir **ton**

tesson [tesɔ̃] nm: **tesson de bouteille** piece of broken bottle

test [test] nm test; **test de grossesse** pregnancy test

testament [testamã] nm (JUR) will; (fig) legacy; (REL): **Testament** Testament; **faire son testament** to make one's will

tester [teste] vt to test

testicule [testikyl] nm testicle

tétanos [tetanos] nm tetanus

têtard [tetaʀ] nm tadpole

tête [tɛt] nf head; (cheveux) hair no pl; (visage) face; (longueur): **gagner d'une (courte) tête** to win by a (short) head; (FOOTBALL) header; **de tête** adj (wagon etc) front cpd; (concurrent) leading ♦ adv (calculer) in one's head, mentally; **par tête** (par personne) per head; **se mettre en tête que** to get it into one's head that; **se mettre en tête de faire** to take it into one's head to do; **prendre la tête de qch** to take the lead in sth; **perdre la tête** (fig: s'affoler) to lose one's head; (: devenir fou) to go off one's head; **ça ne va pas, la tête?** (fam) are you crazy?; **tenir tête à qn** to stand up to ou defy sb; **la tête en bas** with one's head down; **la tête la première** (tomber) head-first; **la tête basse** hanging one's head; **faire une tête** (FOOTBALL) to head the ball; **faire la tête** (fig) to sulk; **en tête** (SPORT) in the lead; at the front ou head; **de la tête aux pieds** from head to toe; **tête d'affiche** (THÉÂT etc) top of the bill; **tête de bétail** head inv of cattle; **tête brûlée** desperado; **tête chercheuse** homing device; **tête d'enregistrement** recording head; **tête d'impression** printhead; **tête de lecture** (playback) head; **tête de ligne** (TRANSPORTS) start of the line; **tête de liste** (POL) chief candidate; **tête de mort** skull and crossbones; **tête de pont** (MIL) bridge- ou beachhead; **tête de série** (TENNIS) seeded player, seed; **tête de Turc** (fig) whipping boy (BRIT), butt; **tête de veau** (CULIN) calf's head

tête-à-queue [tɛtakø] nm inv: **faire un tête-à-queue** to spin round

téter [tete] vt: **téter (sa mère)** to suck at one's mother's breast, feed

tétine [tetin] nf teat; (sucette) dummy (BRIT), pacifier (US)

têtu, e [tety] adj stubborn, pigheaded

texte [tɛkst(ə)] nm text; (SCOL: d'un devoir) subject, topic; **apprendre son texte** (THÉÂT) to learn one's lines; **un texte de loi** the wording of a law

textile [tɛkstil] adj textile cpd ♦ nm textile; (industrie) textile industry

Texto® [tɛksto] nm text (message)

texto [tɛksto] (fam) adj word for word

texture [tɛkstyʀ] nf texture

TGV sigle m = **train à grande vitesse**

thaïlandais, e [tailɑ̃dɛ, -ɛz] adj Thai

Thaïlande [tailɑ̃d] nf: **la Thaïlande** Thailand

thé [te] nm tea; (réunion) tea party; **prendre le thé** to have tea; **thé au lait/citron** tea with milk/lemon

théâtral, e, aux [teatʀal, -o] adj theatrical

théâtre [teatʀ(ə)] nm theatre; (techniques, genre) drama, theatre; (activité) stage, theatre; (œuvres) plays pl, dramatic works pl; (fig: lieu): **le théâtre de** the scene of; (péj) histrionics pl, playacting; **faire du théâtre** (en professionnel) to be on the stage; (en amateur) to do some acting; **théâtre filmé** filmed stage productions pl

théière [tejeʀ] nf teapot

thème [tɛm] nm theme; (SCOL: traduction) prose (composition); **thème astral** birth chart

théologie [teɔlɔʒi] nf theology

théorie [teɔʀi] nf theory; **en théorie** in theory

théorique [teɔʀik] adj theoretical

thérapie [teʀapi] nf therapy; **thérapie de groupe** group therapy

thermal, e, aux [teʀmal, -o] adj thermal; **station thermale** spa; **cure thermale** water cure

thermes [teʀm(ə)] nmpl thermal baths; (romains) thermae pl

thermomètre [teʀmɔmɛtʀ(ə)] nm thermometer

thermos® [teʀmos] nm ou nf: **(bouteille) thermos** vacuum ou Thermos® flask (BRIT) ou bottle (US)

thermostat [teʀmɔsta] nm thermostat

thèse [tɛz] nf thesis (pl theses)

thon [tɔ̃] nm tuna (fish)

thym [tɛ̃] nm thyme

tibia [tibja] nm shin; (os) shinbone, tibia

TIC sigle fpl (= technologies de l'information et de la communication) ICT (sg)

tic [tik] nm tic, (nervous) twitch; (de langage etc) mannerism

ticket [tike] nm ticket; **ticket de caisse** till receipt; **ticket modérateur** patient's contribution towards medical costs; **ticket de quai** platform ticket; **ticket repas** luncheon voucher

tic-tac [tiktak] nm inv tick-tock

tiède [tjed] adj (bière etc) lukewarm; (thé, café etc) tepid; (bain, accueil, sentiment) lukewarm; (air) mild, warm ♦ adv: **boire tiède** to drink things lukewarm

tiédir [tjediʀ] vi (se réchauffer) to grow warmer; (refroidir) to cool

tien, tienne [tjɛ̃, tjɛn] pron: **le tien (la tienne), les tiens (tiennes)** yours; **à la tienne!** cheers!

tiens [tjɛ̃] vb, excl voir **tenir**

tierce [tjɛʀs(ə)] adj f, nf voir **tiers**

tiercé [tjɛʀse] nm system of forecast betting giving first three horses

tiers, tierce [tjɛʀ, tjɛʀs(ə)] adj third ♦ nm (JUR)

third party; (*fraction*) third ◆ *nf* (*MUS*) third; (*CARTES*) tierce; **une tierce personne** a third party; **assurance au tiers** third-party insurance; **le tiers monde** the third world; **tiers payant** direct payment by insurers of medical expenses; **tiers provisionnel** interim payment of tax

tifs [tif] (*fam*) *nmpl* hair

tige [tiʒ] *nf* stem; (*baguette*) rod

tignasse [tiɲas] *nf* (*péj*) shock *ou* mop of hair

tigre [tigʀ(ə)] *nm* tiger

tigré, e [tigʀe] *adj* (*rayé*) striped; (*tacheté*) spotted

tigresse [tigʀɛs] *nf* tigress

tilleul [tijœl] *nm* lime (tree), linden (tree); (*boisson*) lime(-blossom) tea

timbale [tɛ̃bal] *nf* (*metal*) tumbler; **timbales** *nfpl* (*MUS*) timpani, kettledrums

timbre [tɛ̃bʀ(ə)] *nm* (*tampon*) stamp; (*aussi*: **timbre-poste**) (*postage*) stamp; (*cachet de la poste*) postmark; (*sonnette*) bell; (*MUS: de voix, instrument*) timbre, tone; **timbre anti-tabac** nicotine patch; **timbre dateur** date stamp

timbré, e [tɛ̃bʀe] *adj* (*enveloppe*) stamped; (*voix*) resonant; (*fam: fou*) cracked, nuts

timide [timid] *adj* (*emprunté*) shy, timid; (*timoré*) timid, timorous

timidement [timidmɑ̃] *adv* shyly; timidly

timidité [timidite] *nf* shyness; timidity

tintamarre [tɛ̃tamaʀ] *nm* din, uproar

tinter [tɛ̃te] *vi* to ring, chime; (*argent, clés*) to jingle

tique [tik] *nf* tick (*insect*)

tir [tiʀ] *nm* (*sport*) shooting; (*fait ou manière de tirer*) firing *no pl*; (*FOOTBALL*) shot; (*stand*) shooting gallery; **tir d'obus/de mitraillette** shell/machine gun fire; **tir à l'arc** archery; **tir de barrage** barrage fire; **tir au fusil** (*rifle*) shooting; **tir au pigeon** (*d'argile*) clay pigeon shooting

tirage [tiʀaʒ] *nm* (*action*) printing; (*PHOTO*) print; (*INFORM*) printout; (*de journal*) circulation; (*de livre*) (print-)run; edition; (*de cheminée*) draught (*BRIT*), draft (*US*); (*de loterie*) draw; (*fig: désaccord*) friction; **tirage au sort** drawing lots

tirailler [tiʀaje] *vt* to pull at, tug at; (*fig*) to gnaw at ◆ *vi* to fire at random

tire [tiʀ] *nf*: **vol à la tire** pickpocketing

tiré [tiʀe] *adj* (*visage, traits*) drawn ◆ *nm* (*COMM*) drawee; **tiré par les cheveux** far-fetched; **tiré à part** off-print

tire-au-flanc [tiʀoflɑ̃] *nm inv* (*péj*) skiver

tire-bouchon [tiʀbuʃɔ̃] *nm* corkscrew

tirelire [tiʀliʀ] *nf* moneybox

tirer [tiʀe] *vt* (*gén*) to pull; (*extraire*): **tirer qch de** to take *ou* pull sth out of; to get sth out of; to extract sth from; (*tracer: ligne, trait*) to draw, trace; (*fermer: volet, porte, trappe*) to pull to, close; (: *rideau*) to draw; (*choisir: carte, conclusion, aussi COMM: chèque*) to draw; (*en faisant feu: balle, coup*) to fire; (: *animal*)

to shoot; (*journal, livre, photo*) to print; (*FOOTBALL: corner etc*) to take ◆ *vi* (*faire feu*) to fire; (*faire du tir, FOOTBALL*) to shoot; (*cheminée*) to draw; **se tirer** *vi* (*fam*) to push off; **s'en tirer** to pull through; **tirer sur** (*corde, poignée*) to pull on *ou* at; (*faire feu sur*) to shoot *ou* fire at; (*pipe*) to draw on; (*fig: avoisiner*) to verge *ou* border on; **tirer 6 mètres** (*NAVIG*) to draw 6 metres of water; **tirer son nom de** to take *ou* get its name from; **tirer la langue** to stick out one's tongue; **tirer qn de** (*embarras etc*) to help *ou* get sb out of; **tirer à l'arc/la carabine** to shoot with a bow and arrow/with a rifle; **tirer en longueur** to drag on; **tirer à sa fin** to be drawing to an end; **tirer les cartes** to read *ou* tell the cards

tiret [tiʀɛ] *nm* dash; (*en fin de ligne*) hyphen

tireur [tiʀœʀ] *nm* gunman; (*COMM*) drawer; **bon tireur** good shot; **tireur d'élite** marksman; **tireur de cartes** fortuneteller

tiroir [tiʀwaʀ] *nm* drawer

tiroir-caisse [tiʀwaʀkɛs] *nm* till

tisane [tizan] *nf* herb tea

tisonnier [tizɔnje] *nm* poker

tisser [tise] *vt* to weave

tisserand, e [tisʀɑ̃, -ɑ̃d] *nm/f* weaver

tissu [tisy] *nm* fabric, material, cloth *no pl*; (*fig*) fabric; (*ANAT, BIO*) tissue; **tissu de mensonges** web of lies

tissu, e [tisy] *adj*: **tissu de** woven through with

tissu-éponge [tisyepɔ̃ʒ] *nm* (*terry*) towelling *no pl*

titre [titʀ(ə)] *nm* (*gén*) title; (*de journal*) headline; (*diplôme*) qualification; (*COMM*) security; (*CHIMIE*) titre; **en titre** (*champion, responsable*) official, recognized; **à juste titre** with just cause, rightly; **à quel titre?** on what grounds?; **à aucun titre** on no account; **au même titre (que)** in the same way (as); **au titre de la coopération** *etc* in the name of cooperation *etc*; **à titre d'exemple** as an *ou* by way of an example; **à titre exceptionnel** exceptionally; **à titre d'information** for (your) information; **à titre gracieux** free of charge; **à titre d'essai** on a trial basis; **à titre privé** in a private capacity; **titre courant** running head; **titre de propriété** title deed; **titre de transport** ticket

tituber [titybe] *vi* to stagger *ou* reel (along)

titulaire [titylɛʀ] *adj* (*ADMIN*) appointed, with tenure ◆ *nm* (*ADMIN*) incumbent; **être titulaire de** to hold

toast [tost] *nm* slice *ou* piece of toast; (*de bienvenue*) (welcoming) toast; **porter un toast à qn** to propose *ou* drink a toast to sb

toboggan [tɔbɔgɑ̃] *nm* toboggan; (*jeu*) slide; (*AUTO*) flyover (*BRIT*), overpass (*US*); **toboggan de secours** (*AVIAT*) escape chute

toc [tɔk] *nm*: **en toc** imitation *cpd*

tocsin [tɔksɛ̃] *nm* alarm (bell)

toge [tɔʒ] *nf* toga; (*de juge*) gown

tohu-bohu [tɔybɔy] *nm* (*désordre*) confusion;

(tumulte) commotion

toi [twa] *pron* you; **toi, tu l'as fait?** did YOU do it?

toile [twal] *nf (matériau)* cloth *no pl; (bâche)* piece of canvas; *(tableau)* canvas; **grosse toile** canvas; **tisser sa toile** *(araignée)* to spin its web; **toile d'araignée** spider's web; *(au plafond etc: à enlever)* cobweb; **toile cirée** oilcloth; **toile émeri** emery cloth; **toile de fond** *(fig)* backdrop; **toile de jute** hessian; **toile de lin** linen; **toile de tente** canvas

toilette [twalɛt] *nf* wash; *(s'habiller et se préparer)* getting ready, washing and dressing; *(habits)* outfit; dress *no pl;* **toilettes** *nfpl* toilet *sg;* **les toilettes des dames/messieurs** the ladies'/gents' (toilets) *(BRIT),* the ladies'/men's (rest)room *(US);* **faire sa toilette** to have a wash, get washed; **faire la toilette de** *(animal)* to groom; *(voiture etc)* to clean, wash; *(texte)* to tidy up; **articles de toilette** toiletries; **toilette intime** personal hygiene

toi-même [twamɛm] *pron* yourself

toiser [twaze] *vt* to eye up and down

toison [twazɔ̃] *nf (de mouton)* fleece; *(cheveux)* mane

toit [twa] *nm* roof; **toit ouvrant** sun roof

toiture [twatyʀ] *nf* roof

tôle [tol] *nf* sheet metal *no pl; (plaque)* steel *(ou* iron) sheet; **tôles** *nfpl (carrosserie)* bodywork *sg (BRIT),* body *sg;* panels; **tôle d'acier** sheet steel *no pl;* **tôle ondulée** corrugated iron

tolérable [tɔleʀabl(ə)] *adj* tolerable, bearable

tolérant, e [tɔleʀɑ̃, -ɑ̃t] *adj* tolerant

tolérer [tɔleʀe] *vt* to tolerate; *(ADMIN: hors taxe etc)* to allow

tollé [tɔle] *nm:* **un tollé (de protestations)** a general outcry

tomate [tɔmat] *nf* tomato

tombe [tɔ̃b] *nf (sépulture)* grave; *(avec monument)* tomb

tombeau, x [tɔ̃bo] *nm* tomb; **à tombeau ouvert** at breakneck speed

tombée [tɔ̃be] *nf:* **à la tombée du jour** *ou* **de la nuit** at the close of day, at nightfall

tomber [tɔ̃be] *vi* to fall ♦ *vt:* **tomber la veste** to slip off one's jacket; **laisser tomber** to drop; **tomber sur** *vt (rencontrer)* to come across; *(attaquer)* to set about; **tomber de fatigue/sommeil** to drop from exhaustion/be falling asleep on one's feet; **tomber à l'eau** *(fig: projet etc)* to fall through; **tomber en panne** to break down; **tomber juste** *(opération, calcul)* to come out right; **tomber en ruine** to fall into ruins; **ça tombe bien/mal** *(fig)* that's come at the right/wrong time; **il est bien/mal tombé** *(fig)* he's been lucky/unlucky

tombola [tɔ̃bɔla] *nf* tombola

tome [tɔm] *nm* volume

ton, ta, *pl* **tes** [tɔ̃, ta, te] *adj possessif* your

ton [tɔ̃] *nm (gén)* tone; *(MUS)* key; *(couleur)* shade, tone; *(de la voix: hauteur)* pitch; **donner le ton** to set the tone; **élever** *ou* **hausser le ton** to raise one's voice; **de bon ton** in good taste; **si vous le prenez sur ce ton** if you're going to take it like that; **ton sur ton** in matching shades

tonalité [tɔnalite] *nf (au téléphone)* dialling tone; *(MUS)* tonality; *(: ton)* key; *(fig)* tone

tondeuse [tɔ̃døz] *nf (à gazon)* (lawn)mower; *(du coiffeur)* clippers *pl; (pour la tonte)* shears *pl*

tondre [tɔ̃dʀ(ə)] *vt (pelouse, herbe)* to mow; *(haie)* to cut, clip; *(mouton, toison)* to shear; *(cheveux)* to crop

tongs [tɔ̃g] *nfpl* flip-flops

tonifier [tɔnifje] *vt (air, eau)* to invigorate; *(peau, organisme)* to tone up

tonique [tɔnik] *adj* fortifying; *(personne)* dynamic ♦ *nm, nf* tonic

tonne [tɔn] *nf* metric ton, tonne

tonneau, x [tɔno] *nm (à vin, cidre)* barrel; *(NAVIG)* ton; **faire des tonneaux** *(voiture, avion)* to roll over

tonnelle [tɔnɛl] *nf* bower, arbour *(BRIT),* arbor *(US)*

tonner [tɔne] *vi* to thunder; *(parler avec véhémence):* **tonner contre qn/qch** to inveigh against sb/sth; **il tonne** it is thundering, there's some thunder

tonnerre [tɔnɛʀ] *nm* thunder; **coup de tonnerre** *(fig)* thunderbolt, bolt from the blue; **un tonnerre d'applaudissements** thunderous applause; **du tonnerre** *adj (fam)* terrific

tonte [tɔ̃t] *nf* shearing

tonton [tɔ̃tɔ̃] *nm* uncle

tonus [tɔnys] *nm (des muscles)* tone; *(d'une personne)* dynamism

top [tɔp] *nm:* **au 3ème top** at the 3rd stroke ♦ *adj:* **top secret** top secret ♦ *excl* go!

topinambour [tɔpinɑ̃buʀ] *nm* Jerusalem artichoke

topo [tɔpo] *nm (discours, exposé)* talk; *(fam)* spiel

toque [tɔk] *nf (de fourrure)* fur hat; **toque de jockey/juge** jockey's/judge's cap; **toque de cuisinier** chef's hat

toqué, e [tɔke] *adj (fam)* touched, cracked

torche [tɔʀʃ(ə)] *nf* torch; **se mettre en torche** *(parachute)* to candle

torchon [tɔʀʃɔ̃] *nm* cloth, duster; *(à vaisselle)* tea towel *ou* cloth

tordre [tɔʀdʀ(ə)] *vt (chiffon)* to wring; *(barre, fig: visage)* to twist; **se tordre** *vi (barre)* to bend; *(roue)* to twist, buckle; *(ver, serpent)* to writhe; **se tordre le pied/bras** to twist one's foot/arm; **se tordre de douleur/rire** to writhe in pain/be doubled up with laughter

tordu, e [tɔʀdy] *pp de* **tordre** ♦ *adj (fig)* warped, twisted

tornade [tɔʀnad] *nf* tornado

torpille [tɔʀpij] *nf* torpedo

torréfier [tɔʀefje] *vt* to roast

torrent [tɔʀɑ̃] *nm* torrent, mountain stream; (*fig*): **un torrent de** a torrent *ou* flood of; **il pleut à torrents** the rain is lashing down

torsade [tɔʀsad] *nf* twist; (*ARCHIT*) cable moulding (*BRIT*) *ou* molding (*US*)

torse [tɔʀs(ə)] *nm* torso; (*poitrine*) chest

tort [tɔʀ] *nm* (*défaut*) fault; (*préjudice*) wrong *no pl*; **torts** *nmpl* (*JUR*) fault *sg*; **avoir tort** to be wrong; **être dans son tort** to be in the wrong; **donner tort à qn** to lay the blame on sb; (*fig*) to prove sb wrong; **causer du tort à** to harm; to be harmful *ou* detrimental to; **en tort** in the wrong, at fault; **à tort** wrongly; **à tort ou à raison** rightly or wrongly; **à tort et à travers** wildly

torticolis [tɔʀtikɔli] *nm* stiff neck

tortiller [tɔʀtije] *vt* (*corde, mouchoir*) to twist; (*doigts*) to twiddle; **se tortiller** *vi* to wriggle, squirm

tortionnaire [tɔʀsjɔnɛʀ] *nm* torturer

tortue [tɔʀty] *nf* tortoise; (*fig*) slowcoach (*BRIT*), slowpoke (*US*)

tortueux, euse [tɔʀtɥø, -øz] *adj* (*rue*) twisting; (*fig*) tortuous

torture [tɔʀtyʀ] *nf* torture

torturer [tɔʀtyʀe] *vt* to torture; (*fig*) to torment

tôt [to] *adv* early; **tôt ou tard** sooner or later; **si tôt** so early; (*déjà*) so soon; **au plus tôt** at the earliest, as soon as possible; **plus tôt** earlier; **il eut tôt fait de faire ...** he soon did ...

total, e, aux [tɔtal, -o] *adj, nm* total; **au total** in total *ou* all; (*fig*) all in all; **faire le total** to work out the total

totalement [tɔtalmɑ̃] *adv* totally, completely

totaliser [tɔtalize] *vt* to total (up)

totalitaire [tɔtalitɛʀ] *adj* totalitarian

totalité [tɔtalite] *nf*: **la totalité de: la totalité des élèves** all (of) the pupils; **la totalité de la population/classe** the whole population/class; **en totalité** entirely

toubib [tubib] *nm* (*fam*) doctor

touchant, e [tuʃɑ̃, -ɑ̃t] *adj* touching

touche [tuʃ] *nf* (*de piano, de machine à écrire*) key; (*de violon*) fingerboard; (*de télécommande etc*) key, button; (*PEINTURE etc*) stroke, touch; (*fig: de couleur, nostalgie*) touch, hint; (*RUGBY*) line-out; (*FOOTBALL: aussi*: **remise en touche**) throw-in; (*aussi*: **ligne de touche**) touch-line; (*ESCRIME*) hit; **en touche** in (*ou* into) touch; **avoir une drôle de touche** to look a sight; **touche de commande/de fonction/de retour** (*INFORM*) control/function/return key; **touche à effleurement** *ou* **sensitive** touch-sensitive control *ou* key

toucher [tuʃe] *nm* touch ♦ *vt* to touch; (*palper*) to feel; (*atteindre: d'un coup de feu etc*) to hit; (*affecter*) to touch, affect; (*concerner*) to concern, affect; (*contacter*) to reach, contact; (*recevoir: récompense*) to receive, get; (: *salaire*) to draw, get; (*chèque*) to cash; (*aborder: problème, sujet*) to touch on; **au toucher** to the touch; by the feel; **se toucher** (*être en con-*

tact) to touch; **toucher à** to touch; (*modifier*) to touch, tamper *ou* meddle with; (*traiter de, concerner*) to have to do with, concern; **je vais lui en toucher un mot** I'll have a word with him about it; **toucher au but** (*fig*) to near one's goal; **toucher à sa fin** to be drawing to a close

touffe [tuf] *nf* tuft

touffu, e [tufy] *adj* thick, dense; (*fig*) complex, involved

toujours [tuʒuʀ] *adv* always; (*encore*) still; (*constamment*) forever; **depuis toujours** always; **essaie toujours** (you can) try anyway; **pour toujours** forever; **toujours est-il que** the fact remains that; **toujours plus** more and more

toupet [tupɛ] *nm* quiff (*BRIT*), tuft; (*fam*) nerve, cheek (*BRIT*)

toupie [tupi] *nf* (spinning) top

tour [tuʀ] *nf* tower; (*immeuble*) high-rise block (*BRIT*) *ou* building (*US*), tower block (*BRIT*); (*ÉCHECS*) castle, rook ♦ *nm* (*excursion: à pied*) stroll, walk; (: *en voiture etc*) run, ride; (: *plus long*) trip; (*SPORT: aussi*: **tour de piste**) lap; (*d'être servi ou de jouer etc, tournure, de vis ou clef*) turn; (*de roue etc*) revolution; (*circonférence*): **de 3 m de tour** 3 m round, with a circumference *ou* girth of 3 m; (*POL: aussi*: **tour de scrutin**) ballot; (*ruse, de prestidigitation, de cartes*) trick; (*de potier*) wheel; (*à bois, métaux*) lathe; **faire le tour de** to go (a)round; (*à pied*) to walk (a)round; (*fig*) to review; **faire le tour de l'Europe** to tour Europe; **faire un tour** to go for a walk; (*en voiture etc*) to go for a ride; **faire 2 tours** to go (a)round twice; (*hélice etc*) to turn *ou* revolve twice; **fermer à double tour** *vi* to double-lock the door; **c'est au tour de Renée** it's Renée's turn; **à tour de rôle, tour à tour** in turn; **à tour de bras** with all one's strength; (*fig*) non-stop, relentlessly; **tour de taille/tête** waist/head measurement; **tour de chant** song recital; **tour de contrôle** *nf* control tower; **tour de garde** spell of duty; **tour d'horizon** (*fig*) general survey; **tour de Valence** valance; **tour de main** dexterity, knack; **en un tour de main** (as) quick as a flash; **tour de passe-passe** trick, sleight of hand; **tour de reins** sprained back; *see boxed note*

TOUR DE FRANCE

The **Tour de France** is an annual road race for professional cyclists. It takes about three weeks to complete and is divided into daily stages, or 'étapes' of approximately 175km (110 miles) over terrain of varying levels of difficulty. The leading cyclist wears a yellow jersey, the 'maillot jaune'. The route varies; it is not usually confined to France but always ends in Paris. In addition, there are a number of time trials.

---

tourbe [tuʀb(ə)] *nf* peat

tourbillon [tuʀbijɔ̃] *nm* whirlwind; (*d'eau*)

whirlpool; (fig) whirl, swirl

tourbillonner [turbijɔne] vi to whirl, swirl; (objet, personne) to whirl ou twirl round

tourelle [turɛl] nf turret

tourisme [turism(ə)] nm tourism; **agence de tourisme** tourist agency; **avion/voiture de tourisme** private plane/car; **faire du tourisme** to do some sightseeing, go touring

touriste [turist(ə)] nm/f tourist

touristique [turistik] adj tourist cpd; (région) touristic (péj), with tourist appeal

tourment [turmã] nm torment

tourmenter [turmãte] vt to torment; **se tourmenter** vi to fret, worry o.s.

tournage [turnaʒ] nm (d'un film) shooting

tournant, e [turnã, -ãt] adj (feu, scène) revolving; (chemin) winding; (escalier) spiral cpd; (mouvement) circling ♦ nm (de route) bend (BRIT), curve (US); (fig) turning point voir **plaque**, **grève**

tournebroche [turnəbrɔʃ] nm roasting spit

tourne-disque [turnədisk(ə)] nm record player

tournée [turne] nf (du facteur etc) round; (d'artiste, politicien) tour; (au café) round (of drinks); **faire la tournée de** to go (a)round

tournemain [turnəmɛ̃]: **en un tournemain** adv in a flash

tourner [turne] vt to turn; (sauce, mélange) to stir; (contourner) to get (a)round; (CINE) to shoot; to make ♦ vi to turn; (moteur) to run; (compteur) to tick away; (lait etc) to turn (sour); (fig: chance, vie) to turn out; **se tourner** vi to turn (a)round; **se tourner vers** to turn to; to turn towards; **bien tourner** to turn out well; **tourner autour de** to go (a)round; (planète) to revolve (a)round; (péj) to hang (a)round; **tourner autour du pot** (fig) to go (a)round in circles; **tourner à/en** to turn into; **tourner à la pluie/au rouge** to turn rainy/red; **tourner en ridicule** to ridicule; **tourner le dos à** (mouvement) to turn one's back on; (position) to have one's back to; **tourner court** to come to a sudden end; **se tourner les pouces** to twiddle one's thumbs; **tourner la tête** to look away; **tourner la tête à qn** (fig) to go to sb's head; **tourner de l'œil** to pass out; **tourner la page** (fig) to turn the page

tournesol [turnəsɔl] nm sunflower

tournevis [turnəvis] nm screwdriver

tourniquet [turnike] nm (pour arroser) sprinkler; (portillon) turnstile; (présentoir) revolving stand, spinner; (CHIRURGIE) tourniquet

tournoi [turnwa] nm tournament

tournoyer [turnwaje] vi (oiseau) to wheel (a)round; (fumée) to swirl (a)round

tournure [turnyr] nf (LING: syntaxe) turn of phrase; form; (: d'une phrase) phrasing; (évolution): **la tournure de qch** the way sth is developing; (aspect): **la tournure de** the look of; **la tournure des événements** the turn of events; **prendre**

tournure to take shape

tourte [turt(ə)] nf pie

tourterelle [turtərɛl] nf turtledove

tous dét [tu] ♦ pron [tus] voir **tout**

Toussaint [tusɛ̃] nf: **la Toussaint** All Saints' Day; see boxed note

---

TOUSSAINT

La Toussaint, 1 November, or All Saints' Day, is a public holiday in France. People traditionally visit the graves of friends and relatives to lay chrysanthemums on them.

---

tousser [tuse] vi to cough

MOT CLÉ

tout, e [tu, tut] (mpl **tous**, fpl **toutes**) adj 1 (avec article singulier) all; **tout le lait** all the milk; **toute la nuit** all night, the whole night; **tout le livre** the whole book; **tout un pain** a whole loaf; **tout le temps** all the time, the whole time; **c'est tout le contraire** it's quite the opposite; **c'est toute une affaire** ou **histoire** it's quite a business, it's a whole rigmarole

2 (avec article pluriel) every; all; **tous les livres** all the books; **toutes les nuits** every night; **toutes les fois** every time; **toutes les trois/deux semaines** every third/other ou second week, every three/two weeks; **tous les deux** both ou each of us (ou them ou you); **toutes les trois** all three of us (ou them ou you)

3 (sans article): **à tout âge** at any age; **pour toute nourriture, il avait ...** his only food was ...; **de tous côtés, de toutes parts** from everywhere, from every side

♦ pron everything, all; **il a tout fait** he's done everything; **je les vois tous** I can see them all ou all of them; **nous y sommes tous allés** all of us went, we all went; **c'est tout** that's all; **en tout** in all; **en tout et pour tout** all in all; **tout ce qu'il sait** all he knows; **c'était tout ce qu'il y a de chic** it was the last word in chic; **du tout au tout** utterly

♦ nm whole; **le tout** all of it (ou them); **le tout est de ...** the main thing is to ...; **pas du tout** not at all; **elle a tout d'une mère/d'une intrigante** she's a real ou true mother/schemer; **du tout au tout** utterly

♦ adv 1 (très, complètement) very; **tout près** ou **à côté** very near; **le tout premier** the very first; **tout seul** all alone; **il était tout rouge** he was really ou all red; **parler tout bas** to speak very quietly; **le livre tout entier** the whole book; **tout en haut** right at the top; **tout droit** straight ahead

2: **tout en** while; **tout en travaillant** while working, as he etc works

3: **tout d'abord** first of all; **tout à coup** suddenly; **tout à fait** absolutely; **tout à fait!** exactly;

tout à l'heure a short while ago; (*futur*) in a short while, shortly; **à tout à l'heure!** see you later!; **il répondit tout court que non** he just answered no (and that was all); **tout de même** all the same; **tout le monde** everybody; **tout ou rien** all or nothing; **tout simplement** quite simply; **tout de suite** immediately, straight away

toutefois [tutfwa] *adv* however

toux [tu] *nf* cough

toxicomane [tɔksikɔman] *nm/f* drug addict

toxique [tɔksik] *adj* toxic, poisonous

trac [trak] *nm* nerves *pl*; (*THÉAT*) stage fright; **avoir le trac** to get an attack of nerves; to have stage fright; **tout à trac** all of a sudden

tracasser [trakase] *vt* to worry, bother; (*harceler*) to harass; **se tracasser** *vi* to worry o.s., fret

trace [tras] *nf* (*empreintes*) tracks *pl*; (*marques, aussi fig*) mark; (*restes, vestige*) trace; (*indice*) sign; **suivre à la trace** to track; **traces de pas** footprints

tracé [trase] *nm* (*contour*) line; (*plan*) layout

tracer [trase] *vt* to draw; (*mot*) to trace; (*piste*) to open up; (*fig: chemin*) to show

tract [trakt] *nm* tract, pamphlet; (*publicitaire*) handout

tractations [traktasjɔ̃] *nfpl* dealings, bargaining *sg*

tracteur [traktœr] *nm* tractor

traction [traksjɔ̃] *nf* traction; (*GYM*) pull-up; **traction avant/arrière** front-wheel/rear-wheel drive; **traction électrique** electric(al) traction *ou* haulage

tradition [tradisjɔ̃] *nf* tradition

traditionnel, le [tradisjɔnɛl] *adj* traditional

traducteur, trice [tradyktœr, -tris] *nm/f* translator

traduction [tradyksjɔ̃] *nf* translation

traduire [traduir] *vt* to translate; (*exprimer*) to render, convey; **se traduire par** to find expression in; **traduire en français** to translate into French; **traduire en justice** to bring before the courts

trafic [trafik] *nm* traffic; **trafic d'armes** arms dealing; **trafic de drogue** drug peddling

trafiquant, e [trafikɑ̃, -ɑ̃t] *nm/f* trafficker; dealer

trafiquer [trafike] *vt* (*péj*) to doctor, tamper with ◆ *vi* to traffic, be engaged in trafficking

tragédie [traʒedi] *nf* tragedy

tragique [traʒik] *adj* tragic ◆ *nm*: **prendre qch au tragique** to make a tragedy out of sth

trahir [trair] *vt* to betray; (*fig*) to give away, reveal; **se trahir** to betray o.s., give o.s. away

trahison [traizɔ̃] *nf* betrayal; (*JUR*) treason

train [trɛ̃] *nm* (*RAIL*) train; (*allure*) pace; (*fig: ensemble*) set; **être en train de faire qch** to be doing sth; **mettre qch en train** to get sth under way; **mettre qn en train** to put sb in good spirits; **se mettre en train** (*commencer*) to get started; (*faire de la gym-*

nastique) to warm up; **se sentir en train** to feel in good form; **aller bon train** to make good progress; **train avant/arrière** front-wheel/rear-wheel axle unit; **train à grande vitesse (TGV)** high-speed train; **train d'atterrissage** undercarriage; **train autos-couchettes** car-sleeper train; **train électrique** (*jouet*) (electric) train set; **train de pneus** set of tyres *ou* tires; **train de vie** style of living

traîne [trɛn] *nf* (*de robe*) train; **être à la traîne** to be in tow; (*en arrière*) to lag behind; (*en désordre*) to be lying around

traîneau, x [trɛno] *nm* sleigh, sledge

traînée [trene] *nf* streak, trail; (*péj*) slut

traîner [trene] *vt* (*remorque*) to pull; (*enfant, chien*) to drag *ou* trail along; (*maladie*): **il traîne un rhume depuis l'hiver** he has a cold which has been dragging on since winter ◆ *vi* (*être en désordre*) to lie around; (*marcher lentement*) to dawdle (along); (*vagabonder*) to hang about; (*agir lentement*) to idle about; (*durer*) to drag on; **se traîner** *vi* (*ramper*) to crawl along; (*marcher avec difficulté*) to drag o.s. along; (*durer*) to drag on; **se traîner par terre** to crawl (on the ground); **traîner qn au cinéma** to drag sb to the cinema; **traîner les pieds** to drag one's feet; **traîner par terre** to trail on the ground; **traîner en longueur** to drag out

train-train [trɛ̃trɛ̃] *nm* humdrum routine

traire [trɛr] *vt* to milk

trait, e [trɛ, -ɛt] *pp de* **traire** ◆ *nm* (*ligne*) line; (*de dessin*) stroke; (*caractéristique*) feature, trait; (*flèche*) dart, arrow; shaft; **traits** *nmpl* (*du visage*) features; **d'un trait** (*boire*) in one gulp; **de trait** *adj* (*animal*) draught (*BRIT*), draft (*US*); **avoir trait à** to concern; **trait pour trait** line for line; **trait de caractère** characteristic, trait; **trait d'esprit** flash of wit; **trait de génie** brainwave; **trait d'union** hyphen; (*fig*) link

traitant, e [trɛtɑ̃, -ɑ̃t] *adj*: **votre médecin traitant** your usual *ou* family doctor; **shampooing traitant** medicated shampoo; **crème traitante** conditioning cream, conditioner

traite [trɛt] *nf* (*COMM*) draft; (*AGR*) milking; (*trajet*) stretch; **d'une (seule) traite** without stopping (once); **la traite des noirs** the slave trade; **la traite des blanches** the white slave trade

traité [trete] *nm* treaty

traitement [trɛtmɑ̃] *nm* treatment; processing; (*salaire*) salary; **suivre un traitement** to undergo treatment; **mauvais traitement** ill-treatment; **traitement de données** *ou* **de l'information** (*INFORM*) data processing; **traitement hormono-supplétif** hormone replacement therapy; **traitement par lots** (*INFORM*) batch processing; **traitement de texte** (*INFORM*) word processing

traiter [trete] *vt* (*gén*) to treat; (*TECH: matériaux*) to process, treat; (*INFORM*) to process; (*affaire*) to deal with, handle; (*qualifier*): **traiter qn d'idiot** to call sb a fool ◆ *vi* to deal; **traiter de** *vt* to deal with; **bien/mal traiter** to treat well/ill-treat

traiteur [tʀɛtœʀ] *nm* caterer

traître, esse [tʀɛtʀ(ə), -tʀɛs] *adj (dangereux)* treacherous ♦ *nm* traitor; **prendre qn en traître** to make an insidious attack on sb

trajectoire [tʀaʒɛktwaʀ] *nf* trajectory, path

trajet [tʀaʒɛ] *nm* journey; *(itinéraire)* route; *(fig)* path, course

trame [tʀam] *nf (de tissu)* weft; *(fig)* framework; texture; *(TYPO)* screen

tramer [tʀame] *vt* to plot, hatch

trampoline [tʀɑ̃pɔlin], **trampolino** [tʀɑ̃pɔlino] *nm* trampoline; *(SPORT)* trampolining

tramway [tʀamwɛ] *nm* tram(way); *(voiture)* tram (car) *(BRIT)*, streetcar *(US)*

tranchant, e [tʀɑ̃ʃɑ̃, -ɑ̃t] *adj* sharp; *(fig: personne)* peremptory; *(: couleurs)* striking ♦ *nm (d'un couteau)* cutting edge; *(de la main)* edge; **à double tranchant** *(argument, procédé)* double-edged

tranche [tʀɑ̃ʃ] *nf (morceau)* slice; *(arête)* edge; *(partie)* section; *(série)* block; *(d'impôts, revenus etc)* bracket; *(loterie)* issue; **tranche d'âge** age bracket; **tranche (de silicium)** wafer

tranché, e [tʀɑ̃ʃe] *adj (couleurs)* distinct, sharply contrasted; *(opinions)* clear-cut, definite ♦ *nf* trench

trancher [tʀɑ̃ʃe] *vt* to cut, sever; *(fig: résoudre)* to settle ♦ *vi* to be decisive; *(entre deux choses)* to settle the argument; **trancher avec** to contrast sharply with

tranquille [tʀɑ̃kil] *adj* calm, quiet; *(enfant, élève)* quiet; *(rassuré)* easy in one's mind, with one's mind at rest; **se tenir tranquille** *(enfant)* to be quiet; **avoir la conscience tranquille** to have an easy conscience; **laisse-moi/laisse-ça tranquille** leave me/it alone

tranquillisant, e [tʀɑ̃kiliza, -ɑ̃t] *adj (nouvelle)* reassuring ♦ *nm* tranquillizer

tranquillité [tʀɑ̃kilite] *nf* quietness; peace (and quiet); **en toute tranquillité** with complete peace of mind; **tranquillité d'esprit** peace of mind

transat [tʀɑ̃zat] *nm* deckchair ♦ *nf = course transatlantique*

transborder [tʀɑ̃sbɔʀde] *vt* to tran(s)ship

transcription [tʀɑ̃skʀipsjɔ̃] *nf* transcription

transférer [tʀɑ̃sfeʀe] *vt* to transfer

transfert [tʀɑ̃sfɛʀ] *nm* transfer

transformation [tʀɑ̃sfɔʀmasjɔ̃] *nf* transformation; *(RUGBY)* conversion; **industries de transformation** processing industries

transformer [tʀɑ̃sfɔʀme] *vt* to transform, alter *("alter" implique un changement moins radical)*; *(matière première, appartement, RUGBY)* to convert; **transformer en** to transform into; to turn into; to convert into; **se transformer** *vi* to be transformed; to alter

transfusion [tʀɑ̃sfyzjɔ̃] *nf*: **transfusion sanguine** blood transfusion

transgresser [tʀɑ̃sgʀese] *vt* to contravene, disobey

transi, e [tʀɑ̃zi] *adj* numb (with cold), chilled to the bone

transiger [tʀɑ̃ziʒe] *vi* to compromise, come to an agreement; **transiger sur** *ou* **avec qch** to compromise on sth

transistor [tʀɑ̃zistɔʀ] *nm* transistor

transit [tʀɑ̃zit] *nm* transit; **de transit** transit *cpd*; **en transit** in transit

transiter [tʀɑ̃zite] *vi* to pass in transit

transitif, ive [tʀɑ̃zitif, -iv] *adj* transitive

transition [tʀɑ̃zisjɔ̃] *nf* transition; **de transition** transitional

transitoire [tʀɑ̃zitwaʀ] *adj (mesure, gouvernement)* transitional, provisional; *(fugitif)* transient

translucide [tʀɑ̃slysid] *adj* translucent

transmettre [tʀɑ̃smɛtʀ(ə)] *vt (passer)*: **transmettre qch à qn** to pass sth on to sb; *(TECH, TÉL, MÉD)* to transmit; *(TV, RADIO: retransmettre)* to broadcast

transmission [tʀɑ̃smisjɔ̃] *nf* transmission, passing on; *(AUTO)* transmission; **transmissions** *nfpl (MIL)* ≈ signals corps *sg*; **transmission de données** *(INFORM)* data transmission; **transmission de pensée** thought transmission

transparent, e [tʀɑ̃spaʀɑ̃, -ɑ̃t] *adj* transparent

transpercer [tʀɑ̃spɛʀse] *vt* to go through, pierce

transpiration [tʀɑ̃spiʀasjɔ̃] *nf* perspiration

transpirer [tʀɑ̃spiʀe] *vi* to perspire; *(information, nouvelle)* to come to light

transplantation [tʀɑ̃splɑ̃tasjɔ̃] *nf* transplant

transplanter [tʀɑ̃splɑ̃te] *vt (MÉD, BOT)* to transplant; *(personne)* to uproot, move

transport [tʀɑ̃spɔʀ] *nm* transport; *(émotions)*: **transport de colère** fit of rage; **transport de joie** transport of delight; **transport de voyageurs/ marchandises** passenger/goods transportation; **transports en commun** public transport *sg*; **transports routiers** *(BRIT)*, trucking *(US)*

transporter [tʀɑ̃spɔʀte] *vt* to carry, move; *(COMM)* to transport, convey; *(fig)*: **transporter qn (de joie)** to send sb into raptures; **se transporter quelque part** *(fig)* to let one's imagination carry one away (somewhere)

transporteur [tʀɑ̃spɔʀtœʀ] *nm* haulage contractor *(BRIT)*, trucker *(US)*

transvaser [tʀɑ̃svaze] *vt* to decant

transversal, e, aux [tʀɑ̃svɛʀsal, -o] *adj* transverse, cross(-); *(route etc)* cross-country; *(mur, chemin, rue)* running at right angles; *(AUTO)*: **axe transversal** main cross-country road *(BRIT)* ou highway *(US)*

trapèze [tʀapɛz] *nm (GÉOM)* trapezium; *(au cirque)* trapeze

trappe [tʀap] *nf (de cave, grenier)* trap door; *(piège)* trap

trapu, e [tʀapy] *adj* squat, stocky

traquenard [tʀaknaʀ] *nm* trap

traquer [tʀake] *vt* to track down; (*harceler*) to hound

traumatiser [tʀomatize] *vt* to traumatize

travail, aux [tʀavaj, -o] *nm* (*gén*) work; (*tâche, métier*) work *no pl*, job; (*ÉCON, MÉD*) labour (*BRIT*), labor (*US*); (*INFORM*) job ♦ *nmpl* (*de réparation, agricoles etc*) work *sg*; (*sur route*) roadworks; (*de construction*) building (work) *sg*; **être/entrer en travail** (*MÉD*) to be in/go into labour; **être sans travail** (*employé*) to be out of work, be unemployed; **travail d'intérêt général (TIG)** ≈ community service; **travail (au) noir** moonlighting; **travail posté** shiftwork; **travaux des champs** farmwork *sg*; **travaux dirigés (TD)** (*SCOL*) supervised practical work *sg*; **travaux forcés** hard labour *sg*; **travaux manuels** (*SCOL*) handicrafts; **travaux ménagers** housework *sg*; **travaux pratiques (TP)** (*gén*) practical work; (*en laboratoire*) lab work (*BRIT*), lab (*US*); **travaux publics (TP)** ≈ public works *sg*

travailler [tʀavaje] *vi* to work; (*bois*) to warp ♦ *vt* (*bois, métal*) to work; (*pâte*) to knead; (*objet d'art, discipline, fig: influencer*) to work on; **cela le travaille** it is on his mind; **travailler la terre** to work the land; **travailler son piano** to do one's piano practice; **travailler à** to work on; (*fig: contribuer à*) to work towards; **travailler à faire** to endeavour (*BRIT*) ou endeavor (*US*) to do

travailleur, euse [tʀavajœʀ, -øz] *adj* hard-working ♦ *nm/f* worker; **travailleur de force** labourer (*BRIT*), laborer (*US*); **travailleur intellectuel** non-manual worker; **travailleur social** social worker; **travailleuse familiale** home help

travailliste [tʀavajist(ə)] *adj* ≈ Labour *cpd* ♦ *nm/f* member of the Labour party

travers [tʀavɛʀ] *nm* fault, failing; **en travers (de)** across; **au travers (de)** through; **de travers** *adj* askew ♦ *adv* sideways; (*fig*) the wrong way; **à travers** through; **regarder de travers** (*fig*) to look askance at

traverse [tʀavɛʀs(ə)] *nf* (*de voie ferrée*) sleeper; **chemin de traverse** shortcut

traversée [tʀavɛʀse] *nf* crossing

traverser [tʀavɛʀse] *vt* (*gén*) to cross; (*ville, tunnel, aussi: percer, fig*) to go through; (*suj: ligne, trait*) to run across

traversin [tʀavɛʀsɛ̃] *nm* bolster

travesti [tʀavɛsti] *nm* (*costume*) fancy dress; (*artiste de cabaret*) female impersonator, drag artist; (*pervers*) transvestite

trébucher [tʀebyʃe] *vi*: **trébucher (sur)** to stumble (over), trip (over)

trèfle [tʀɛfl(ə)] *nm* (*BOT*) clover; (*CARTES: couleur*) clubs *pl*; (*: carte*) club; **trèfle à quatre feuilles** four-leaf clover

treille [tʀɛj] *nf* (*tonnelle*) vine arbour (*BRIT*) ou arbor (*US*); (*vigne*) climbing vine

treillis [tʀeji] *nm* (*métallique*) wire-mesh; (*toile*) canvas; (*MIL: tenue*) combat uniform; (*pantalon*) combat trousers *pl*

treize [tʀɛz] *num* thirteen

treizième [tʀɛzjɛm] *num* thirteenth; *see boxed note*

TREIZIÈME MOIS

The **treizième mois** is an end-of-year bonus roughly corresponding to one month's salary. For many employees it is a standard part of their salary package.

---

tréma [tʀema] *nm* diaeresis

tremblement [tʀɑ̃bləmɑ̃] *nm* trembling *no pl*, shaking *no pl*, shivering *no pl*; **tremblement de terre** earthquake

trembler [tʀɑ̃ble] *vi* to tremble, shake; **trembler de** (*froid, fièvre*) to shiver ou tremble with; (*peur*) to shake ou tremble with; **trembler pour qn** to fear for sb

trémousser [tʀemuse]: **se trémousser** *vi* to jig about, wriggle about

trempe [tʀɑ̃p] *nf* (*fig*): **de cette/sa trempe** of this/his calibre (*BRIT*) ou caliber (*US*)

trempé, e [tʀɑ̃pe] *adj* soaking (wet), drenched; (*TECH*): **acier trempé** tempered steel

tremper [tʀɑ̃pe] *vt* to soak, drench; (*aussi*: **faire tremper**, **mettre à tremper**) to soak; (*plonger*): **tremper qch dans** to dip sth in(to) ♦ *vi* to soak; (*fig*): **tremper dans** to be involved ou have a hand in; **se tremper** *vi* to have a quick dip; **se faire tremper** to get soaked ou drenched

trempette [tʀɑ̃pɛt] *nf*: **faire trempette** to go paddling

tremplin [tʀɑ̃plɛ̃] *nm* springboard; (*SKI*) ski jump

trentaine [tʀɑ̃tɛn] *nf* (*âge*): **avoir la trentaine** to be around thirty; **une trentaine (de)** thirty or so, about thirty

trente [tʀɑ̃t] *num* thirty; **voir trente-six chandelles** (*fig*) to see stars; **être/se mettre sur son trente et un** to be/get dressed to kill; **trente-trois tours** *nm* long-playing record, LP

trentième [tʀɑ̃tjɛm] *num* thirtieth

trépidant, e [tʀepidɑ̃, -ɑ̃t] *adj* (*fig: rythme*) pulsating; (*: vie*) hectic

trépied [tʀepje] *nm* (*d'appareil*) tripod; (*meuble*) trivet

trépigner [tʀepiɲe] *vi* to stamp (one's feet)

très [tʀɛ] *adv* very; much + *pp*, highly + *pp*; **très beau/bien** very beautiful/well; **très critiqué** much criticized; **très industrialisé** highly industrialized; **j'ai très faim** I'm very hungry

trésor [tʀezɔʀ] *nm* treasure; (*ADMIN*) finances *pl*; (*d'une organisation*) funds *pl*; **trésor (public) (TP)** public revenue; (*service*) public revenue office

trésorerie [tʀezɔʀʀi] *nf* (*fonds*) funds *pl*; (*gestion*) accounts pl; (bureaux) accounts department; (poste) treasurership; **difficultés de trésorerie** cash problems, shortage of cash ou funds; **trésorerie générale (TG)** local government finance office

trésorier, ière [tʀezɔʀje, -jɛʀ] nm/f treasurer

tressaillir [tʀesajiʀ] vi (de peur etc) to shiver, shudder; (de joie) to quiver

tressauter [tʀesote] vi to start, jump

tresse [tʀɛs] nf (de cheveux) braid, plait; (cordon, galon) braid

tresser [tʀese] vt (cheveux) to braid, plait; (fil, jonc) to plait; (corbeille) to weave; (corde) to twist

tréteau, x [tʀeto] nm trestle; **les tréteaux** (fig: THÉÂT) the boards

treuil [tʀœj] nm winch

trêve [tʀɛv] nf (MIL, POL) truce; (fig) respite; **sans trêve** unremittingly; **trêve de ...** enough of this ...; **les États de la Trêve** the Trucial States

tri [tʀi] nm (voir trier) sorting (out) no pl; selection; screening; (INFORM) sort; (POSTES: action) sorting; (: bureau) sorting office

triangle [tʀijɑ̃gl(ə)] nm triangle; **triangle isocèle/équilatéral** isoceles/equilateral triangle; **triangle rectangle** right-angled triangle

triangulaire [tʀijɑ̃gylɛʀ] adj triangular

tribord [tʀibɔʀ] nm: **à tribord** to starboard, on the starboard side

tribu [tʀiby] nf tribe

tribunal, aux [tʀibynal, -o] nm (JUR) court; (MIL) tribunal; **tribunal de police/pour enfants** police/juvenile court; **tribunal d'instance (TI)** ≈ magistrates' court (BRIT), ≈ district court (US); **tribunal de grande instance (TGI)**, ≈ High Court (BRIT), ≈ Supreme Court (US)

tribune [tʀibyn] nf (estrade) platform, rostrum; (débat) forum; (d'église, de tribunal) gallery; (de stade) stand; **tribune libre** (PRESSE) opinion column

tribut [tʀiby] nm tribute

tributaire [tʀibytɛʀ] adj: **être tributaire de** to be dependent on; (GÉO) to be a tributary of

tricher [tʀiʃe] vi to cheat

tricheur, euse [tʀiʃœʀ, -øz] nm/f cheat

tricolore [tʀikɔlɔʀ] adj three-coloured (BRIT), three-colored (US); (français: drapeau) red, white and blue; (: équipe etc) French

tricot [tʀiko] nm (technique, ouvrage) knitting no pl; (tissu) knitted fabric; (vêtement) jersey, sweater; **tricot de corps** vest (BRIT), undershirt (US)

tricoter [tʀikɔte] vt to knit; **machine/aiguille à tricoter** knitting machine/needle (BRIT) ou pin (US)

trictrac [tʀiktʀak] nm backgammon

tricycle [tʀisikl(ə)] nm tricycle

triennal, e, aux [tʀienal, -o] adj (prix, foire, élection) three-yearly; (charge, mandat, plan) three-year

trier [tʀije] vt (classer) to sort (out); (choisir) to select; (visiteurs) to screen; (POSTES, INFORM) to sort

trimestre [tʀimɛstʀ(ə)] nm (SCOL) term; (COMM) quarter

trimestriel, le [tʀimɛstʀijɛl] adj quarterly; (SCOL) end-of-term

tringle [tʀɛ̃gl(ə)] nf rod

trinquer [tʀɛ̃ke] vi to clink glasses; (fam) to cop it; **trinquer à qch/la santé de qn** to drink to sth/sb

triomphe [tʀijɔ̃f] nm triumph; **être reçu/porté en triomphe** to be given a triumphant welcome/be carried shoulder-high in triumph

triompher [tʀijɔ̃fe] vi to triumph; **triompher de** to triumph over, overcome

tripes [tʀip] nfpl (CULIN) tripe sg; (fam) guts

triple [tʀipl(ə)] adj (à trois élements) triple; (trois fois plus grand) treble ♦ nm: **le triple (de)** (comparaison) three times as much (as); **en triple exemplaire** in triplicate; **triple saut** (SPORT) triple jump

tripler [tʀiple] vi, vt to triple, treble, increase threefold

triplés, ées [tʀiple] nm/fpl triplets

tripoter [tʀipɔte] vt to fiddle with, finger ♦ vi (fam) to rummage about

triste [tʀist(ə)] adj sad; (péj): **triste personnage/affaire** sorry individual/affair; **c'est pas triste!** (fam) it's something else!

tristesse [tʀistɛs] nf sadness

trivial, e, aux [tʀivjal, -o] adj coarse, crude; (commun) mundane

troc [tʀɔk] nm (ÉCON) barter; (transaction) exchange, swap

troène [tʀɔɛn] nm privet

trognon [tʀɔɲɔ̃] nm (de fruit) core; (de légume) stalk

trois [tʀwa] num three

troisième [tʀwazjɛm] num third; **le troisième âge** the years of retirement

trois quarts [tʀwakaʀ] nmpl: **les trois quarts de** three-quarters of

trombe [tʀɔ̃b] nf waterspout; **des trombes d'eau** a downpour; **en trombe** (arriver, passer) like a whirlwind

trombone [tʀɔ̃bɔn] nm (MUS) trombone; (de bureau) paper clip; **trombone à coulisse** slide trombone

trompe [tʀɔ̃p] nf (d'éléphant) trunk; (MUS) trumpet, horn; **trompe d'Eustache** Eustachian tube; **trompes utérines** Fallopian tubes

tromper [tʀɔ̃pe] vt to deceive; (fig: espoir, attente) to disappoint; (vigilance, poursuivants) to elude; **se tromper** vi to make a mistake, be mistaken; **se tromper de voiture/jour** to take the wrong car/get the day wrong; **se tromper de 3 cm/20 €** to be out by 3 cm/20 €

tromperie [tʀɔ̃pʀi] nf deception, trickery no pl

trompette [tʀɔ̃pɛt] nf trumpet; **en trompette** (nez) turned-up

trompeur, euse [tʀɔ̃pœʀ, -øz] adj deceptive,

misleading

tronc [tʁɔ̃] *nm* (BOT, ANAT) trunk; (*d'église*) collection box; **tronc d'arbre** tree trunk; **tronc commun** (SCOL) common-core syllabus; **tronc de cône** truncated cone

tronçon [tʁɔ̃sɔ̃] *nm* section

tronçonner [tʁɔ̃sɔne] *vt* (*arbre*) to saw up; (*pierre*) to cut up

trône [tʁon] *nm* throne; **monter sur le trône** to ascend the throne

trop [tʁo] *adv vb* + too much; too + *adjectif*, *adverbe*; **trop (nombreux)** too many; **trop peu (nombreux)** too few; **trop (souvent)** too often; **trop (longtemps)** (for) too long; **trop de** (*nombre*) too many; (*quantité*) too much; **de trop, en trop**: **des livres en trop** a few books too many, a few extra books; **du lait en trop** too much milk; **3 livres/5 € de trop** 3 books too many/5 € too much

tropical, e, aux [tʁɔpikal, -o] *adj* tropical

tropique [tʁɔpik] *nm* tropic; **tropiques** *nmpl* tropics; **tropique du Cancer/Capricorne** Tropic of Cancer/Capricorn

trop-plein [tʁɔplɛ̃] *nm* (*tuyau*) overflow *ou* outlet (pipe); (*liquide*) overflow

troquer [tʁɔke] *vt*: **troquer qch contre** to barter *ou* trade sth for; (*fig*) to swap sth for

trot [tʁo] *nm* trot; **aller au trot** to trot along; **partir au trot** to set off at a trot

trotter [tʁɔte] *vi* to trot; (*fig*) to scamper along (*ou* about)

trotteuse [tʁɔtøz] *nf* (*de montre*) second hand

trottinette [tʁɔtinɛt] *nf* (child's) scooter

trottoir [tʁɔtwaʁ] *nm* pavement (BRIT), sidewalk (US); **faire le trottoir** (*péj*) to walk the streets; **trottoir roulant** moving pavement (BRIT) *ou* walkway

trou [tʁu] *nm* hole; (*fig*) gap; (COMM) deficit; **trou d'aération** (air) vent; **trou d'air** air pocket; **trou de mémoire** blank, lapse of memory; **trou noir** black hole; **trou de la serrure** keyhole

troublant, e [tʁublɑ̃, -ɑ̃t] *adj* disturbing

trouble [tʁubl(ə)] *adj* (*liquide*) cloudy; (*image, mémoire*) indistinct, hazy; (*affaire*) shady, murky ♦ *adv* indistinctly ♦ *nm* (*désarroi*) distress, agitation; (*émoi sensuel*) turmoil, agitation; (*embarras*) confusion; (*zizanie*) unrest, discord; **troubles** *nmpl* (POL) disturbances, troubles, unrest *sg*; (MÉD) disorders; **troubles de la personnalité** personality problems; **troubles de la vision** eye trouble

trouble-fête [tʁublfɛt] *nm/f inv* spoilsport

troubler [tʁuble] *vt* (*embarrasser*) to confuse, disconcert; (*émouvoir*) to agitate; to disturb; to perturb; (*perturber: ordre etc*) to disrupt, disturb; (*liquide*) to make cloudy; **se troubler** *vi* (*personne*) to become flustered *ou* confused; **troubler l'ordre public** to cause a breach of the peace

trouer [tʁue] *vt* to make a hole (*ou* holes) in; (*fig*) to pierce

trouille [tʁuj] *nf* (*fam*): **avoir la trouille** to be

scared stiff, be scared out of one's wits

troupe [tʁup] *nf* (MIL) troop; (*groupe*) troop, group; **la troupe** (MIL: *l'armée*) the army; (: *les simples soldats*) the troops *pl*; **troupe (de théâtre)** (theatrical) company; **troupes de choc** shock troops

troupeau, x [tʁupo] *nm* (*de moutons*) flock; (*de vaches*) herd

trousse [tʁus] *nf* case, kit; (*d'écolier*) pencil case; (*de docteur*) instrument case; **aux trousses de** (*fig*) on the heels *ou* tail of; **trousse à outils** toolkit; **trousse de toilette** toilet *ou* sponge (BRIT) bag

trousseau, x [tʁuso] *nm* (*de mariée*) trousseau; **trousseau de clefs** bunch of keys

trouvaille [tʁuvaj] *nf* find; (*fig: idée, expression etc*) brainwave

trouver [tʁuve] *vt* to find; (*rendre visite*): **aller/venir trouver qn** to go/come and see sb; **je trouve que** I find *ou* think that; **trouver à boire/critiquer** to find something to drink/criticize; **trouver asile/refuge** to find refuge/shelter; **se trouver** *vi* (*être*) to be; (*être soudain*) to find o.s.; **se trouver être/avoir** to happen to be/have; **il se trouve que** it happens that, it turns out that; **se trouver bien** to feel well; **se trouver mal** to pass out

truand [tʁyɑ̃] *nm* villain, crook

truander [tʁyɑ̃de] *vi* (*fam*) to cheat, do

truc [tʁyk] *nm* (*astuce*) way, device; (*de cinéma, prestidigitateur*) trick effect; (*chose*) thing; (*machin*) thingumajig, whatsit (BRIT); **avoir le truc** to have the knack; **c'est pas son** (*ou* **mon** *etc*) **truc** (*fam*) it's not really his (*ou* my *etc*) thing

truelle [tʁyɛl] *nf* trowel

truffe [tʁyf] *nf* truffle; (*nez*) nose

truffé, e [tʁyfe] *adj*: **truffé de** (*fig*) peppered with; (*fautes*) riddled with; (*pièges*) bristling with

truie [tʁyi] *nf* sow

truite [tʁyit] *nf* trout *inv*

truquage [tʁykaʒ] *nm* fixing; (CINÉ) special effects *pl*

truquer [tʁyke] *vt* (*élections, serrure, dés*) to fix; (CINÉ) to use special effects in

TSVP *abr* (= *tournez s'il vous plaît*) PTO

TTC *abr* = **toutes taxes comprises**

tu [ty] *pron* you ♦ *nm*: **employer le tu** to use the "tu" form

tu, e [ty] *pp de* **taire**

tuba [tyba] *nm* (MUS) tuba; (SPORT) snorkel

tube [tyb] *nm* tube; (*de canalisation, métallique etc*) pipe; (*chanson, disque*) hit song *ou* record; **tube digestif** alimentary canal, digestive tract; **tube à essai** test tube

tuberculose [tybɛʁkyloz] *nf* tuberculosis, TB

tuer [tɥe] *vt* to kill; **se tuer** (*se suicider*) to kill o.s.; (*dans un accident*) to be killed; **se tuer au travail** (*fig*) to work o.s. to death

tuerie [tyʁi] *nf* slaughter *no pl*, massacre

tue-tête [tytɛt]: **à tue-tête** *adv* at the top of one's voice

tueur [tɥœʀ] *nm* killer; **tueur à gages** hired killer

tuile [tɥil] *nf* tile; (*fam*) spot of bad luck, blow

tulipe [tylip] *nf* tulip

tuméfié, e [tymefje] *adj* puffy, swollen

tumeur [tymœʀ] *nf* growth, tumour (*BRIT*), tumor (*US*)

tumulte [tymylt(ə)] *nm* commotion, hubbub

tumultueux, euse [tymyltɥø, -øz] *adj* stormy, turbulent

tunique [tynik] *nf* tunic; (*de femme*) smock, tunic

Tunisie [tynizi] *nf*: **la Tunisie** Tunisia

tunisien, ne [tynizjɛ̃, -ɛn] *adj* Tunisian ♦ *nm/f*: **Tunisien, ne** Tunisian

tunnel [tynɛl] *nm* tunnel; **le tunnel sous la Manche** the Channel Tunnel, the Chunnel

turbulences [tyʀbylɑ̃s] *nfpl* (*AVIAT*) turbulence *sg*

turbulent, e [tyʀbylɑ̃, -ɑ̃t] *adj* boisterous, unruly

turc, turque [tyʀk(ə)] *adj* Turkish; (*w.-c.*) seatless ♦ *nm* (*LING*) Turkish ♦ *nm/f*: **Turc, Turque** Turk/ Turkish woman; **à la turque** *adv* (*assis*) cross-legged

turf [tyʀf] *nm* racing

turfiste [tyʀfist(ə)] *nm/f* racegoer

Turquie [tyʀki] *nf*: **la Turquie** Turkey

turquoise [tyʀkwaz] *nf, adj inv* turquoise

tus *etc* [ty] *vb voir* **taire**

tutelle [tytɛl] *nf* (*JUR*) guardianship; (*POL*) trustee-ship; **sous la tutelle de** (*fig*) under the supervision of

tuteur, trice [tytœʀ, -tʀis] *nm/f* (*JUR*) guardian; (*de plante*) stake, support

tutoyer [tytwaje] *vt*: **tutoyer qn** to address sb as "tu"

tuyau, x [tɥijo] *nm* pipe; (*flexible*) tube; (*fam: conseil*) tip; (: *mise au courant*) gen *no pl*; **tuyau d'arrosage** hosepipe; **tuyau d'échappement** exhaust pipe; **tuyau d'incendie** fire hose

tuyauterie [tɥijotʀi] *nf* piping *no pl*

TVA *sigle f* = **taxe à ou sur la valeur ajoutée**

tympan [tɛ̃pɑ̃] *nm* (*ANAT*) eardrum

type [tip] *nm* type; (*personne, chose: représentant*) classic example, epitome; (*fam*) chap, guy ♦ *adj* typical, standard; **avoir le type nordique** to be Nordic-looking

typé, e [tipe] *adj* ethnic (*euph*)

typique [tipik] *adj* typical

tyran [tiʀɑ̃] *nm* tyrant

tyrannique [tiʀanik] *adj* tyrannical

tzigane [dzigan] *adj* gipsy, tzigane ♦ *nm/f* (*Hungarian*) gipsy, Tzigane

— *U u* —

UEM *sigle f* (= *Union économique et monétaire*) EMU

ulcère [ylsɛʀ] *nm* ulcer; **ulcère à l'estomac** stomach ulcer

ulcérer [ylseʀe] *vt* (*MÉD*) to ulcerate; (*fig*) to sicken, appal

ultérieur, e [ylteʀjœʀ] *adj* later, subsequent; **remis à une date ultérieure** postponed to a later date

ultérieurement [ylteʀjœʀmɑ̃] *adv* later

ultime [yltim] *adj* final

┌─────────────────┐
│ MOT CLÉ │
└─────────────────┘

un, une [œ̃, yn] *art indéf* a; (*devant voyelle*) an; **un garçon/vieillard** a boy/an old man; **une fille** a girl

♦ *pron* one; **l'un des meilleurs** one of the best; **l'un ..., l'autre** (the) one ..., the other; **les uns ..., les autres** some ..., others; **l'un et l'autre** both (of them); **l'un ou l'autre** either (of them); **l'un l'autre, les uns les autres** each other, one another; **pas un seul** not a single one; **un par un** one by one

♦ *num* one; **une pomme seulement** one apple only

♦ *nf*: **la une** (*PRESSE*) the front page

unanime [ynanim] *adj* unanimous; **ils sont unanimes (à penser que)** they are unanimous (in thinking that)

unanimité [ynanimite] *nf* unanimity; **à l'unanimité** unanimously; **faire l'unanimité** to be approved unanimously

uni, e [yni] *adj* (*ton, tissu*) plain; (*surface*) smooth, even; (*famille*) close-knit); (*pays*) united

unifier [ynifje] *vt* to unite, unify; (*systèmes*) to standardize, unify; **s'unifier** to become united

uniforme [ynifɔʀm(ə)] *adj* (*mouvement*) regular, uniform; (*surface, ton*) even; (*objets, maisons*) uniform; (*fig: vie, conduite*) unchanging ♦ *nm* uniform; **être sous l'uniforme** (*MIL*) to be serving

uniformiser [ynifɔʀmize] *vt* to make uniform; (*systèmes*) to standardize

union [ynjɔ̃] *nf* union; **union conjugale** union of marriage; **union de consommateurs** consumers' association; **union libre** free love; **l'Union des Républiques socialistes soviétiques (URSS)** the Union of Soviet Socialist Republics (USSR); **l'Union soviétique** the Soviet Union

unique [ynik] *adj* (*seul*) only; (*le même*) **un prix/ système unique** a single price/system; (*exceptionnel*) unique; **ménage à salaire unique** one-salary family; **route à voie unique** single-lane road; **fils/ fille unique** only son/daughter, only child; **unique en France** the only one of its kind in France

uniquement [ynikmɑ̃] *adv* only, solely; *(juste)* only, merely

unir [yniʀ] *vt (nations)* to unite; *(éléments, couleurs)* to combine; *(en mariage)* to unite, join together; **unir qch à** to unite sth with; to combine sth with; **s'unir** to unite; *(en mariage)* to be joined together; **s'unir à** *ou* **avec** to unite with

unitaire [yniteʀ] *adj* unitary; *(POL)* unitarian; **prix unitaire** unit price

unité [ynite] *nf (harmonie, cohésion)* unity; *(COMM, MIL, de mesure, MATH)* unit; **unité centrale (de traitement)** central processing unit (CPU); **unité de valeur (UV)** (university) course, credit

univers [yniveʀ] *nm* universe

universel, le [yniveʀsɛl] *adj* universal; *(esprit)* all-embracing

universitaire [yniveʀsiteʀ] *adj* university *cpd*; *(diplôme, études)* academic, university *cpd* ♦ *nm/f* academic

université [yniveʀsite] *nf* university

urbain, e [yʀbɛ̃, -ɛn] *adj* urban, city *cpd*, town *cpd*; *(poli)* urbane

urbanisme [yʀbanism(ə)] *nm* town planning

urgence [yʀʒɑ̃s] *nf* urgency; *(MÉD etc)* emergency; **d'urgence** *adj* emergency *cpd* ♦ *adv* as a matter of urgency; **en cas d'urgence** in case of emergency; **service des urgences** emergency service

urgent, e [yʀʒɑ̃, -ɑ̃t] *adj* urgent

urine [yʀin] *nf* urine

urinoir [yʀinwaʀ] *nm* (public) urinal

urne [yʀn(ə)] *nf (électorale)* ballot box; *(vase)* urn; **aller aux urnes** *(voter)* to go to the polls

urticaire [yʀtikɛʀ] *nf* nettle rash, urticaria

us [ys] *nmpl*: **us et coutumes** (habits and) customs

USA *sigle mpl* (= *United States of America*) USA

usage [yzaʒ] *nm (emploi, utilisation)* use; *(coutume)* custom; *(éducation)* (good) manners *pl*, (good) breeding; *(LING)*: **l'usage** usage; **faire usage de** *(pouvoir, droit)* to exercise; **avoir l'usage de** to have the use of; **à l'usage** *adv* with use; **à l'usage de** *(pour)* (for use of); **en usage** in use; **hors d'usage** out of service; **à usage interne** to be taken; **à usage externe** for external use only

usagé, e [yzaʒe] *adj (usé)* worn; *(d'occasion)* used

usager, ère [yzaʒe, -ɛʀ] *nm/f* user

usé, e [yze] *adj* worn (down *ou* out *ou* away); ruined; *(banal)* hackneyed

user [yze] *vt (outil)* to wear down; *(vêtement)* to wear out; *(matière)* to wear away; *(consommer: charbon etc)* to use; *(fig: santé)* to ruin; (: *personne)* to wear out; **s'user** *vi* to wear; to wear out; *(fig)* to decline; **s'user à la tâche** to wear o.s. out with work; **user de** *vt (moyen, procédé)* to use, employ; *(droit)* to exercise

usine [yzin] *nf* factory; **usine atomique** nuclear power plant; **usine à gaz** gasworks *sg*; **usine maré-motrice** tidal power station

usité, e [yzite] *adj* in common use, common; **peu usité** rarely used

ustensile [ystɑ̃sil] *nm* implement; **ustensile de cuisine** kitchen utensil

usuel, le [yzɥɛl] *adj* everyday, common

usure [yzyʀ] *nf* wear; worn state; *(de l'usurier)* usury; **avoir qn à l'usure** to wear sb down; **usure normale** fair wear and tear

utérus [yteʀys] *nm* uterus, womb

utile [ytil] *adj* useful; **utile à qn/qch** of use to sb/sth

utilisation [ytilizasjɔ̃] *nf* use

utiliser [ytilize] *vt* to use

utilitaire [ytiliteʀ] *adj* utilitarian; *(objets)* practical ♦ *nm (INFORM)* utility

utilité [ytilite] *nf* usefulness *no pl*; use; **jouer les utilités** *(THÉÂT)* to play bit parts; **reconnu d'utilité publique** state-approved; **c'est d'une grande utilité** it's extremely useful; **il n'y a aucune utilité à ...** there's no use in ...

utopie [ytɔpi] *nf (idée, conception)* utopian idea *ou* view; *(société etc idéale)* utopia

— *V v* —

va [va] *vb voir* **aller**

vacance [vakɑ̃s] *nf (ADMIN)* vacancy; **vacances** *nfpl* holiday(s *pl*) *(BRIT)*, vacation *sg (US)*; **les grandes vacances** the summer holidays *ou* vacation; **prendre des/ses vacances** to take a holiday *ou* vacation/one's holiday(s) *ou* vacation; **aller en vacances** to go on holiday *ou* vacation

vacancier, ière [vakɑ̃sje, -jɛʀ] *nm/f* holiday-maker *(BRIT)*, vacationer *(US)*

vacant, e [vakɑ̃, -ɑ̃t] *adj* vacant

vacarme [vakaʀm(ə)] *nm* row, din

vaccin [vaksɛ̃] *nm* vaccine; *(opération)* vaccination

vaccination [vaksinasjɔ̃] *nf* vaccination

vacciner [vaksine] *vt* to vaccinate; *(fig)* to make immune; **être vacciné** *(fig)* to be immune

vache [vaʃ] *nf (ZOOL)* cow; *(cuir)* cowhide ♦ *adj (fam)* rotten, mean; **vache à eau** (canvas) water bag; **(manger de la) vache enragée** (to go through) hard times; **vache à lait** *(péj)* mug, sucker; **vache laitière** dairy cow; **période des vaches maigres** lean times *pl*, lean period

vachement [vaʃmɑ̃] *adv (fam)* damned, fantastically

vacherie [vaʃʀi] *nf (fam)* meanness *no pl*; *(action)* dirty trick; *(propos)* nasty remark

vaciller [vasije] *vi* to sway, wobble; *(bougie, lumière)* to flicker; *(fig)* to be failing, falter; **vaciller dans ses réponses** to falter in one's replies; **vaciller dans ses résolutions** to waver in one's resolutions

va-et-vient [vaevjɛ̃] *nm inv* (*de pièce mobile*) to and fro (*ou* up and down) movement; (*de personnes, véhicules*) comings and goings *pl*, to-ings and fro-ings *pl*; (ÉLEC) two-way switch

vagabond, e [vagabɔ̃, -ɔ̃d] *adj* wandering; (*imagination*) roaming, roving ♦ *nm* (*rôdeur*) tramp, vagrant; (*voyageur*) wanderer

vagabonder [vagabɔ̃de] *vi* to roam, wander

vagin [vaʒɛ̃] *nm* vagina

vague [vag] *nf* wave ♦ *adj* vague; (*regard*) faraway; (*manteau, robe*) loose(-fitting); (*quelconque*): **un vague bureau/cousin** some office/cousin or other ♦ *nm*: **être dans le vague** to be rather in the dark; **rester dans le vague** to keep things rather vague; **regarder dans le vague** to gaze into space; **vague à l'âme** *nm* vague melancholy; **vague d'assaut** *nf* (MIL) wave of assault; **vague de chaleur** *nf* heatwave; **vague de fond** *nf* ground swell; **vague de froid** *nf* cold spell

vaillant, e [vajɑ̃, -ɑ̃t] *adj* (*courageux*) brave, gallant; (*robuste*) vigorous, hale and hearty; **n'avoir plus un sou vaillant** to be penniless

vaille [vaj] *vb voir* **valoir**

vain, e [vɛ̃, vɛn] *adj* vain; **en vain** *adv* in vain

vaincre [vɛ̃kʀ(ə)] *vt* to defeat; (*fig*) to conquer, overcome

vaincu, e [vɛ̃ky] *pp de* **vaincre** ♦ *nm/f* defeated party

vainqueur [vɛ̃kœʀ] *nm* victor; (SPORT) winner ♦ *adj m* victorious

vais [vɛ] *vb voir* **aller**

vaisseau, x [vɛso] *nm* (ANAT) vessel; (NAVIG) ship, vessel; **vaisseau spatial** spaceship

vaisselier [vɛsəlje] *nm* dresser

vaisselle [vɛsɛl] *nf* (*service*) crockery; (*plats etc à laver*) (dirty) dishes *pl*; **faire la vaisselle** to do the washing-up (BRIT) *ou* the dishes

val, *pl* **vaux** *ou* **vals** [val, vo] *nm* valley

valable [valabl(ə)] *adj* valid; (*acceptable*) decent, worthwhile

valent *etc* [val] *vb voir* **valoir**

valet [valɛ] *nm* valet; (*péj*) lackey; (CARTES) jack, knave (BRIT); **valet de chambre** manservant, valet; **valet de ferme** farmhand; **valet de pied** footman

valeur [valœʀ] *nf* (*gén*) value; (*mérite*) worth, merit; (COMM: *titre*) security; **mettre en valeur** (*bien*) to exploit; (*terrain, région*) to develop; (*fig*) to highlight; to show off to advantage; **avoir de la valeur** to be valuable; **prendre de la valeur** to go up *ou* gain in value; **sans valeur** worthless; **valeur absolue** absolute value; **valeur d'échange** exchange value; **valeur nominale** face value; **valeurs mobilières** transferable securities

valide [valid] *adj* (*en bonne santé*) fit, well; (*indemne*) able-bodied, fit; (*valable*) valid

valider [valide] *vt* to validate

valions [valjɔ̃] *etc vb voir* **valoir**

valise [valiz] *nf* (suit)case; **faire sa valise** to pack one's (suit)case; **la valise (diplomatique)** the diplomatic bag

vallée [vale] *nf* valley

vallon [valɔ̃] *nm* small valley

vallonné, e [valɔne] *adj* undulating

valoir [valwaʀ] *vi* (*être valable*) to hold, apply ♦ *vt* (*prix, valeur, effort*) to be worth; (*causer*): **valoir qch à qn** to earn sb sth; **se valoir** to be of equal merit; (*péj*) to be two of a kind; **faire valoir** (*droits, prérogatives*) to assert; (*domaine, capitaux*) to exploit; **faire valoir que** to point out that; **se faire valoir** to make the most of o.s.; **à valoir** on account; **à valoir sur** to be deducted from; **vaille que vaille** somehow or other; **cela ne me dit rien qui vaille** I don't like the look of it at all; **ce climat ne me vaut rien** this climate doesn't suit me; **valoir la peine** to be worth the trouble, be worth it; **valoir mieux: il vaut mieux se taire** it's better to say nothing; **il vaut mieux que je fasse/comme ceci** it's better if I do/like this; **ça ne vaut rien** it's worthless; **que vaut ce candidat?** how good is this applicant?

valse [vals(ə)] *nf* waltz; **c'est la valse des étiquettes** the prices don't stay the same from one moment to the next

valu, e [valy] *pp de* **valoir**

vandalisme [vɑ̃dalism(ə)] *nm* vandalism

vanille [vanij] *nf* vanilla; **glace à la vanille** vanilla ice cream

vanité [vanite] *nf* vanity

vaniteux, euse [vanitø, -øz] *adj* vain, conceited

vanne [van] *nf* gate; (*fam: remarque*) dig, (nasty) crack; **lancer une vanne à qn** to have a go at sb (BRIT), knock sb

vannerie [vanʀi] *nf* basketwork

vantard, e [vɑ̃taʀ, -aʀd(ə)] *adj* boastful

vanter [vɑ̃te] *vt* to speak highly of, vaunt; **se vanter** *vi* to boast, brag; **se vanter de** to pride o.s. on; (*péj*) to boast of

vapeur [vapœʀ] *nf* steam; (*émanation*) vapour (BRIT), vapor (US), fumes *pl*; (*brouillard, buée*) haze; **vapeurs** *nfpl* (*bouffées*) vapours, vapors; **à vapeur** steam-powered, steam *cpd*; **à toute vapeur** full steam ahead; (*fig*) at full tilt; **renverser la vapeur** to reverse engines; (*fig*) to backtrack, backpedal; **cuit à la vapeur** steamed

vaporeux, euse [vapɔʀø, -øz] *adj* (*flou*) hazy, misty; (*léger*) filmy, gossamer *cpd*

vaporisateur [vapɔʀizatœʀ] *nm* spray

vaporiser [vapɔʀize] *vt* (CHIMIE) to vaporize; (*parfum etc*) to spray

varappe [vaʀap] *nf* rock climbing

vareuse [vaʀøz] *nf* (*blouson*) pea jacket; (*d'uniforme*) tunic

variable [vaʀjabl(ə)] *adj* variable; (*temps, humeur*) changeable; (TECH: *à plusieurs positions etc*) adaptable; (LING) inflectional; (*divers: résultats*) varied, various ♦ *nf* (INFORM, MATH) variable

varice [vaʀis] *nf* varicose vein

varicelle [vaʀisɛl] *nf* chickenpox

varié, e [vaʀje] *adj* varied; *(divers)* various; **hors-d'œuvre variés** selection of hors d'œuvres

varier [vaʀje] *vi* to vary; *(temps, humeur)* to change ◆ *vt* to vary

variété [vaʀjete] *nf* variety; **spectacle de variétés** variety show

variole [vaʀjɔl] *nf* smallpox

vas [va] *vb voir* **aller vas-y!** [vazi] go on!

vase [vɑz] *nm* vase ◆ *nf* silt, mud; **en vase clos** in isolation; **vase de nuit** chamberpot; **vases communicants** communicating vessels

vaseux, euse [vɑzø, -øz] *adj* silty, muddy; *(fig: confus)* woolly, hazy; *(: fatigué)* peaky; *(: étourdi)* woozy

vasistas [vazistas] *nm* fanlight

vaste [vast(ə)] *adj* vast, immense

vaudrai *etc* [vodʀe] *vb voir* **valoir**

vaurien, ne [voʀjɛ̃, -ɛn] *nm/f* good-for-nothing, guttersnipe

vaut [vo] *vb voir* **valoir**

vautour [votuʀ] *nm* vulture

vautrer [votʀe]: **se vautrer** *vi*: **se vautrer dans** to wallow in; **se vautrer sur** to sprawl on

vaux [vo] *pl de* **val** ◆ *vb voir* **valoir**

va-vite [vavit]: **à la va-vite** *adv* in a rush

VDQS *abr* (= vin délimité de qualité supérieure) label guaranteeing quality of wine; see boxed note

---

VDQS

VDQS on a bottle of French wine indicates that it contains high-quality produce from an approved regional vineyard. It is the second-highest French wine classification after 'AOC' and is a step up from 'vin de pays'. In contrast, 'vin de table' or 'vin ordinaire' is table wine of unspecified origin, often blended.

---

veau, x [vo] *nm* *(ZOOL)* calf *(pl* calves*)*; *(CULIN)* veal; *(peau)* calfskin; **tuer le veau gras** to kill the fatted calf

vécu, e [veky] *pp de* **vivre** ◆ *adj* *(aventure)* real(-life)

vedette [vədɛt] *nf* *(artiste etc)* star; *(canot)* patrol boat; launch; **avoir la vedette** to top the bill, get star billing; **mettre qn en vedette** *(CINÉ etc)* to give sb the starring role; *(fig)* to push sb into the limelight; **voler la vedette à qn** to steal the show from sb

végétal, e, aux [veʒetal, -o] *adj* vegetable ◆ *nm* vegetable, plant

végétalien, ne [veʒetaljɛ̃, -ɛn] *adj, nm/f* vegan

végétarien, ne [veʒetaʀjɛ̃, -ɛn] *adj, nm/f* vegetarian

végétation [veʒetasjɔ̃] *nf* vegetation; **végéta-**

tions *nfpl* *(MÉD)* adenoids

véhicule [veikyl] *nm* vehicle; **véhicule utilitaire** commercial vehicle

veille [vɛj] *nf* *(garde)* watch; *(PSYCH)* wakefulness; *(jour):* **la veille** the day before, the previous day; **la veille au soir** the previous evening; **la veille de** the day before; **à la veille de** on the eve of; **l'état de veille** the waking state

veillée [veje] *nf* *(soirée)* evening; *(réunion)* evening gathering; **veillée d'armes** night before combat; *(fig)* vigil; **veillée (mortuaire)** watch

veiller [veje] *vi* *(rester debout)* to stay ou sit up; *(ne pas dormir)* to be awake; *(être de garde)* to be on watch; *(être vigilant)* to be watchful ◆ *vt* *(malade, mort)* to watch over, sit up with; **veiller à** *vt* to attend to, see to; **veiller à ce que** to make sure that, see to it that; **veiller sur** *vt* to keep a watch ou an eye on

veilleur [vejœʀ] *nm*: **veilleur de nuit** night watchman

veilleuse [vejøz] *nf* *(lampe)* night light; *(AUTO)* sidelight; *(flamme)* pilot light; **en veilleuse** *adj* *(lampe)* dimmed; *(fig: affaire)* shelved, set aside

veinard, e [venaʀ, -aʀd] *nm/f* *(fam)* lucky devil

veine [vɛn] *nf* *(ANAT, du bois etc)* vein; *(filon)* vein, seam; *(fam: chance):* **avoir de la veine** to be lucky; *(inspiration)* inspiration

véliplanchiste [veliplɑ̃ʃist(ə)] *nm/f* windsurfer

vélo [velo] *nm* bike, cycle; **faire du vélo** to go cycling

vélomoteur [velomotœʀ] *nm* moped

velours [vəluʀ] *nm* velvet; **velours côtelé** corduroy

velouté, e [vəlute] *adj* *(au toucher)* velvety; *(à la vue)* soft, mellow; *(au goût)* smooth, mellow ◆ *nm*: **velouté d'asperges/de tomates** cream of asparagus/tomato soup

velu, e [vəly] *adj* hairy

venais [vəne] *etc voir* **venir**

venaison [vənɛzɔ̃] *nf* venison

vendange [vɑ̃dɑ̃ʒ] *nf* *(opération, période; aussi:* **vendanges**) grape harvest; *(raisins)* grape crop, grapes *pl*

vendanger [vɑ̃dɑ̃ʒe] *vi* to harvest the grapes

vendeur, euse [vɑ̃dœʀ, -øz] *nm/f* *(de magasin)* shop ou sales assistant *(BRIT)*, sales clerk *(US)*; *(COMM)* salesman/woman ◆ *nm* *(JUR)* vendor, seller; **vendeur de journaux** newspaper seller

vendre [vɑ̃dʀ(ə)] *vt* to sell; **vendre qch à qn** to sell sb sth; **cela se vend à la douzaine** these are sold by the dozen; **"à vendre"** "for sale"

vendredi [vɑ̃dʀədi] *nm* Friday; **Vendredi saint** Good Friday; *voir aussi* **lundi**

vénéneux, euse [venenø, -øz] *adj* poisonous

vénérien, ne [veneʀjɛ̃, -ɛn] *adj* venereal

vengeance [vɑ̃ʒɑ̃s] *nf* vengeance *no pl*, revenge *no pl*; *(acte)* act of vengeance ou revenge

venger [vɑ̃ʒe] *vt* to avenge; **se venger** *vi* to avenge o.s.; (*par rancune*) to take revenge; **se venger de qch** to avenge o.s. for sth; to take one's revenge for sth; **se venger de qn** to take revenge on sb; **se venger sur** to wreak vengeance upon; to take revenge on *ou* through; to take it out on

venimeux, euse [vənimø, -øz] *adj* poisonous, venomous; (*fig: haineux*) venomous, vicious

venin [vənɛ̃] *nm* venom, poison; (*fig*) venom

venir [vəniʀ] *vi* to come; **venir de** to come from; **venir de faire: je viens d'y aller/de le voir** I've just been there/seen him; **s'il vient à pleuvoir** if it should rain, if it happens to rain; **en venir à faire: j'en viens à croire que** I am coming to believe that; **où veux-tu en venir?** what are you getting at?; **il en est venu à mendier** he has been reduced to begging; **en venir aux mains** to come to blows; **les années/générations à venir** the years/generations to come; **il me vient une idée** an idea has just occurred to me; **il me vient des soupçons** I'm beginning to be suspicious; **je te vois venir** I know what you're after; **faire venir** (*docteur, plombier*) to call (out); **d'où vient que ...?** how is it that ...?; **venir au monde** to come into the world

vent [vɑ̃] *nm* wind; **il y a du vent** it's windy; **c'est du vent** it's all hot air; **au vent** to windward; **sous le vent** to leeward; **avoir le vent debout/arrière** to head into the wind/have the wind astern; **dans le vent** (*fam*) trendy; **prendre le vent** (*fig*) to see which way the wind blows; **avoir vent de** to get wind of; **contre vents et marées** come hell or high water

vente [vɑ̃t] *nf* sale; **la vente** (*activité*) selling; (*secteur*) sales *pl*; **mettre en vente** to put on sale; (*objets personnels*) to put up for sale; **vente de charité** jumble (*BRIT*) *ou* rummage (*US*) sale; **vente par correspondance (VPC)** mail-order selling; **vente aux enchères** auction sale

venteux, euse [vɑ̃tø, -øz] *adj* windswept, windy

ventilateur [vɑ̃tilatœʀ] *nm* fan

ventiler [vɑ̃tile] *vt* to ventilate; (*total, statistiques*) to break down

ventouse [vɑ̃tuz] *nf* (*ampoule*) cupping glass; (*de caoutchouc*) suction pad; (*ZOOL*) sucker

ventre [vɑ̃tʀ(ə)] *nm* (*ANAT*) stomach; (*fig*) belly; **prendre du ventre** to be getting a paunch; **avoir mal au ventre** to have (a) stomach ache

ventriloque [vɑ̃tʀilɔk] *nm/f* ventriloquist

venu, e [vəny] *pp de* **venir ♦** *adj*: **être mal venu à** *ou* **de faire** to have no grounds for doing, be in no position to do; **mal venu** ill-timed, unwelcome; **bien venu** timely, welcome **♦** *nf*: coming

ver [vɛʀ] *nm voir aussi* **vers**; worm; (*des fruits etc*) maggot; (*du bois*) woodworm *no pl*; **ver blanc** May beetle grub; **ver luisant** glow-worm; **ver à soie** silkworm; **ver solitaire** tapeworm; **ver de terre** earthworm

verbaliser [vɛʀbalize] *vi* (*POLICE*) to book *ou* report

an offender; (*PSYCH*) to verbalize

verbe [vɛʀb(ə)] *nm* (*LING*) verb; (*voix*): **avoir le verbe sonore** to have a sonorous tone (of voice); (*expression*): **la magie du verbe** the magic of language *ou* the word; (*REL*): **le Verbe** the Word

verdâtre [vɛʀdatʀ(ə)] *adj* greenish

verdict [vɛʀdik(t)] *nm* verdict

verdir [vɛʀdiʀ] *vi, vt* to turn green

verdure [vɛʀdyʀ] *nf* (*arbres, feuillages*) greenery; (*légumes verts*) green vegetables *pl*, greens *pl*

véreux, euse [veʀø, -øz] *adj* worm-eaten; (*malhonnête*) shady, corrupt

verge [vɛʀʒ(ə)] *nf* (*ANAT*) penis; (*baguette*) stick, cane

verger [vɛʀʒe] *nm* orchard

verglacé, e [vɛʀglase] *adj* icy, iced-over

verglas [vɛʀgla] *nm* (black) ice

vergogne [vɛʀgɔɲ]: **sans vergogne** *adv* shamelessly

véridique [veʀidik] *adj* truthful

vérification [veʀifikasjɔ̃] *nf* checking *no pl*, check; **vérification d'identité** identity check

vérifier [veʀifje] *vt* to check; (*corroborer*) to confirm, bear out; (*INFORM*) to verify; **se vérifier** *vi* to be confirmed *ou* verified

véritable [veʀitabl(ə)] *adj* real; (*ami, amour*) true; **un véritable désastre** an absolute disaster

vérité [veʀite] *nf* truth; (*d'un portrait*) lifelikeness; (*sincérité*) truthfulness, sincerity; **en vérité, à la vérité** to tell the truth

vermeil, le [vɛʀmɛj] *adj* bright red, ruby red **♦** *nm* (*substance*) vermeil

vermine [vɛʀmin] *nf* vermin *pl*

vermoulu, e [vɛʀmuly] *adj* worm-eaten, with woodworm

verni, e [vɛʀni] *adj* varnished; glazed; (*fam*) lucky; **cuir verni** patent leather; **souliers vernis** patent (leather) shoes

vernir [vɛʀniʀ] *vt* (*bois, tableau, ongles*) to varnish; (*poterie*) to glaze

vernis [vɛʀni] *nm* (*enduit*) varnish; glaze; (*fig*) veneer; **vernis à ongles** nail varnish (*BRIT*) *ou* polish

vernissage [vɛʀnisaʒ] *nm* varnishing; glazing; (*d'une exposition*) preview

vérole [veʀɔl] *nf* (*variole*) smallpox; (*fam: syphilis*) pox

verrai *etc* [veʀe] *vb voir* **voir**

verre [vɛʀ] *nm* glass; (*de lunettes*) lens *sg*; **verres** *nmpl* (*lunettes*) glasses; **boire** *ou* **prendre un verre** to have a drink; **verre à vin/à liqueur** wine/liqueur glass; **verre à dents** tooth mug; **verre dépoli** frosted glass; **verre de lampe** lamp glass *ou* chimney; **verre de montre** watch glass; **verre à pied** stemmed glass; **verres de contact** contact lenses; **verres fumés** tinted lenses

verrerie [vɛʀʀi] *nf* (*fabrique*) glassworks *sg*; (*activité*) glass-making, glass-working; (*objets*) glassware

verrière [vɛʀjɛʀ] *nf (grand vitrage)* window; *(toit vitré)* glass roof

verrons [vɛʀɔ̃] *etc vb voir* **voir**

verrou [vɛʀu] *nm (targette)* bolt; *(fig)* constriction; **mettre le verrou** to bolt the door; **mettre qn sous les verrous** to put sb behind bars

verrouillage [vɛʀujaʒ] *nm (dispositif)* locking mechanism; *(AUTO)*: **verrouillage central** *ou* **centralisé** central locking

verrouiller [vɛʀuje] *vt* to bolt; to lock; *(MIL: brèche)* to close

verrue [vɛʀy] *nf* wart; *(plantaire)* verruca; *(fig)* eyesore

vers [vɛʀ] *nm* line ♦ *nmpl (poésie)* verse *sg* ♦ *prép (en direction de)* toward(s); *(près de)* around (about); *(temporel)* around, around

versant [vɛʀsɑ̃] *nm* slopes *pl*, side

versatile [vɛʀsatil] *adj* fickle, changeable

verse [vɛʀs(ə)]: **à verse** *adv*: **il pleut à verse** it's pouring (with rain)

Verseau [vɛʀso] *nm*: **le Verseau** Aquarius, the water-carrier; **être du Verseau** to be Aquarius

versement [vɛʀsəmɑ̃] *nm* payment; *(sur un compte)* deposit, remittance; **en 3 versements** in 3 instalments

verser [vɛʀse] *vt (liquide, grains)* to pour; *(larmes, sang)* to shed; *(argent)* to pay; *(soldat: affecter)*: **verser qn dans** to assign sb to ♦ *vi (véhicule)* to overturn; *(fig)*: **verser dans** to lapse into; **verser à un compte** to pay into an account

verset [vɛʀse] *nm* verse; versicle

version [vɛʀsjɔ̃] *nf* version; *(SCOL)* translation *(into the mother tongue)* **film en version originale** film in the original language

verso [vɛʀso] *nm* back; **voir au verso** see over (leaf)

vert, e [vɛʀ, vɛʀt(ə)] *adj* green; *(vin)* young; *(vigoureux)* sprightly; *(cru)* forthright ♦ *nm* green; **dire des vertes (et des pas mûres)** to say some pretty spicy things; **il en a vu des vertes** he's seen a thing or two; **vert bouteille** *adj inv* bottle-green; **vert d'eau** *adj inv* sea-green; **vert pomme** *adj inv* apple-green

vertèbre [vɛʀtɛbʀ(ə)] *nf* vertebra (*pl* -ae)

vertement [vɛʀtəmɑ̃] *adv (réprimander)* sharply

vertical, e, aux [vɛʀtikal, -o] *adj, nf* vertical; **à la verticale** *adv* vertically

verticalement [vɛʀtikalmɑ̃] *adv* vertically

vertige [vɛʀtiʒ] *nm (peur du vide)* vertigo; *(étourdissement)* dizzy spell; *(fig)* fever; **ça me donne le vertige** it makes me dizzy; *(fig)* it makes my head spin *ou* reel

vertigineux, euse [vɛʀtiʒinø, -øz] *adj (hausse, vitesse)* breathtaking; *(altitude, gorge)* breathtakingly high *(ou* deep)

vertu [vɛʀty] *nf* virtue; **une vertu** a saint, a paragon of virtue; **avoir la vertu de faire** to have

the virtue of doing; **en vertu de** *prép* in accordance with

vertueux, euse [vɛʀtɥø, -øz] *adj* virtuous

verve [vɛʀv(ə)] *nf* witty eloquence; **être en verve** to be in brilliant form

verveine [vɛʀvɛn] *nf (BOT)* verbena, vervain; *(infusion)* verbena tea

vésicule [vezikyl] *nf* vesicle; **vésicule biliaire** gall-bladder

vessie [vesi] *nf* bladder

veste [vɛst(ə)] *nf* jacket; **veste droite/croisée** single-/double-breasted jacket; **retourner sa veste** *(fig)* to change one's colours

vestiaire [vɛstjɛʀ] *nm (au théâtre etc)* cloakroom; *(de stade etc)* changing-room *(BRIT)*, locker-room *(US)*; *(métallique)*: **(armoire) vestiaire** locker

vestibule [vɛstibyl] *nm* hall

vestige [vɛstiʒ] *nm (objet)* relic; *(fragment)* trace; *(fig)* remnant, vestige; **vestiges** *nmpl (d'une ville)* remains; *(d'une civilisation, du passé)* remnants, relics

vestimentaire [vɛstimɑ̃tɛʀ] *adj (dépenses)* clothing; *(détail)* of dress; *(élégance)* sartorial

veston [vɛstɔ̃] *nm* jacket

vêtement [vɛtmɑ̃] *nm* garment, item of clothing; *(COMM)*: **le vêtement** the clothing industry; **vêtements** *nmpl* clothes; **vêtements de sport** sportswear *sg*, sports clothes

vétérinaire [veteʀinɛʀ] *adj* veterinary ♦ *nm/f* vet, veterinary surgeon *(BRIT)*, veterinarian *(US)*

vêtir [vetiʀ] *vt* to clothe, dress; **se vêtir** to dress (o.s.)

veto [veto] *nm* veto; **droit de veto** right of veto; **mettre** *ou* **opposer un veto à** to veto

vêtu, e [vety] *pp de* **vêtir** ♦ *adj*: **vêtu de** dressed in, wearing; **chaudement vêtu** warmly dressed

vétuste [vetyst(ə)] *adj* ancient, timeworn

veuf, veuve [vœf, vœv] *adj* widowed ♦ *nm* widower ♦ *nf* widow

veuille [vœj], **veuillez** [vœje] *etc vb voir* **vouloir**

veule [vøl] *adj* spineless

veuve [vœv] *adj f, nf voir* **veuf**

veux [vø] *vb voir* **vouloir**

vexant, e [vɛksɑ̃, -ɑ̃t] *adj (contrariant)* annoying; *(blessant)* upsetting

vexations [vɛksasjɔ̃] *nfpl* humiliations

vexer [vɛkse] *vt* to hurt, upset; **se vexer** *vi* to be hurt, get upset

viable [vjabl(ə)] *adj* viable

viaduc [vjadyk] *nm* viaduct

viager, ère [vjaʒe, -ɛʀ] *adj*: **rente viagère** life annuity ♦ *nm*: **mettre en viager** to sell in return for a life annuity

viande [vjɑ̃d] *nf* meat

vibrer [vibʀe] *vi* to vibrate; *(son, voix)* to be vibrant; *(fig)* to be stirred; **faire vibrer** to (cause to) vibrate; to stir, thrill

vice [vis] *nm* vice; (*défaut*) fault; **vice caché** (*COMM*) latent *ou* inherent defect; **vice de forme** legal flaw *ou* irregularity

vichy [viʃi] *nm* (*toile*) gingham; (*eau*) Vichy water; **carottes Vichy** boiled carrots

vicié, e [visje] *adj* (*air*) polluted, tainted; (*JUR*) invalidated

vicieux, euse [visjø, -øz] *adj* (*pervers*) dirty(-minded); (*méchant*) nasty; (*fautif*) incorrect, wrong

vicinal, e, aux [visinal, -o] *adj*: **chemin vicinal** byroad, byway

victime [viktim] *nf* victim; (*d'accident*) casualty; **être (la) victime de** to be the victim of; **être victime d'une attaque/d'un accident** to suffer a stroke/be involved in an accident

victoire [viktwaʀ] *nf* victory

victuailles [viktɥaj] *nfpl* provisions

vidange [vidɑ̃ʒ] *nf* (*d'un fossé, réservoir*) emptying; (*AUTO*) oil change; (*de lavabo: bonde*) waste outlet; **vidanges** *nfpl* (*matières*) sewage *sg*; **faire la vidange** (*AUTO*) to change the oil, do an oil change; **tuyau de vidange** drainage pipe

vidanger [vidɑ̃ʒe] *vt* to empty; **faire vidanger la voiture** to have the oil changed in one's car

vide [vid] *adj* empty ♦ *nm* (*PHYSIQUE*) vacuum; (*espace*) (empty) space, gap; (*sous soi: dans une falaise etc*) drop; (*futilité, néant*) void; **vide de** empty of; (*de sens etc*) devoid of; **sous vide** *adv* in a vacuum; **emballé sous vide** vacuum-packed; **regarder dans le vide** to stare into space; **avoir peur du vide** to be afraid of heights; **parler dans le vide** to waste one's breath; **faire le vide** (*dans son esprit*) to make one's mind go blank; **faire le vide autour de qn** to isolate sb; **à vide** *adv* (*sans occupants*) empty; (*sans charge*) unladen; (*TECH*) without gripping *ou* being in gear

vidéo [video] *nf, adj inv* video; **vidéo inverse** reverse video

vidéoclip [videoklip] *nm* music video

vidéoclub [videoklœb] *nm* video club

vide-ordures [vidɔʀdyʀ] *nm inv* (rubbish) chute

vidéothèque [videotek] *nf* video library

vide-poches [vidpɔʃ] *nm inv* tidy; (*AUTO*) glove compartment

vider [vide] *vt* to empty; (*CULIN: volaille, poisson*) to gut, clean out; (*régler: querelle*) to settle; (*fatiguer*) to wear out; (*fam: expulser*) to throw out, chuck out; **se vider** *vi* to empty; **vider les lieux** to quit *ou* vacate the premises

videur [vidœʀ] *nm* (*de boîte de nuit*) bouncer

vie [vi] *nf* life (*pl* lives); **être en vie** to be alive; **sans vie** lifeless; **à vie** for life; **membre à vie** life member; **dans la vie courante** in everyday life; **avoir la vie dure** to have nine lives; to die hard; **mener la vie dure à qn** to make life a misery for sb

vieil [vjɛj] *adj m voir* **vieux**

vieillard [vjɛjaʀ] *nm* old man; **les vieillards** old people, the elderly

vieille [vjɛj] *adj f, nf voir* **vieux**

vieilleries [vjɛjʀi] *nfpl* old things *ou* stuff *sg*

vieillesse [vjɛjes] *nf* old age; (*vieillards*): **la vieillesse** the old *pl*, the elderly *pl*

vieillir [vjɛjiʀ] *vi* (*prendre de l'âge*) to grow old; (*population, vin*) to age; (*doctrine, auteur*) to become dated ♦ *vt* to age; **il a beaucoup vieilli** he has aged a lot; **se vieillir** to make o.s. older

vieillissement [vjɛjismɑ̃] *nm* growing old; ageing

Vienne [vjɛn] *n* (*en Autriche*) Vienna

vienne [vjɛn], **viens** [vjɛ̃] *etc vb voir* **venir**

viens [vjɛ̃] *vb voir* **venir**

vierge [vjɛʀʒ(ə)] *adj* virgin; (*film*) blank; (*page*) clean, blank; (*jeune fille*): **être vierge** to be a virgin ♦ *nf* virgin; (*signe*): **la Vierge** Virgo, the Virgin; **être de la Vierge** to be Virgo; **vierge de** (*sans*) free from, unsullied by

Viêtnam, Vietnam [vjɛtnam] *nm*: **le Viêtnam** Vietnam; **le Viêtnam du Nord/du Sud** North/South Vietnam

vietnamien, ne [vjɛtnamjɛ̃, -ɛn] *adj* Vietnamese ♦ *nm* (*LING*) Vietnamese ♦ *nm/f*: **Vietnamien, ne** Vietnamese; **Vietnamien, ne du Nord/Sud** North/South Vietnamese

vieux (vieil), vieille [vjø, vjɛj] *adj* old ♦ *nm/f* old man/woman ♦ *nmpl*: **les vieux** the old, old people; (*fam: parents*) the old folk *ou* ones; **un petit vieux** a little old man; **mon vieux/ma vieille** (*fam*) old man/girl; **pauvre vieux** poor old soul; **prendre un coup de vieux** to put years on; **se faire vieux** to make o.s. look older; **un vieux de la vieille** one of the old brigade; **vieux garçon** *nm* bachelor; **vieux jeu** *adj inv* old-fashioned; **vieux rose** *adj inv* old rose; **vieil or** *adj inv* old gold; **vieille fille** *nf* spinster

vif, vive [vif, viv] *adj* (*animé*) lively; (*alerte*) sharp, quick; (*brusque*) sharp, brusque; (*aigu*) sharp; (*lumière, couleur*) brilliant; (*air*) crisp; (*vent, émotion*) keen; (*froid*) bitter; (*fort: regret, déception*) great, deep; (*vivant*): **brûlé vif** burnt alive; **eau vive** running water; **de vive voix** personally; **piquer qn au vif** to cut sb to the quick; **tailler dans le vif** to cut into the living flesh; **à vif** (*plaie*) open; **avoir les nerfs à vif** to be on edge; **sur le vif** (*ART*) from life; **entrer dans le vif du sujet** to get to the very heart of the matter

vigne [viɲ] *nf* (*plante*) vine; (*plantation*) vineyard; **vigne vierge** Virginia creeper

vigneron [viɲʀɔ̃] *nm* wine grower

vignette [viɲet] *nf* (*motif*) vignette; (*de marque*) manufacturer's label *ou* seal; (*petite illustration*) (small) illustration; (*ADMIN*) ≈ (road) tax disc (*BRIT*), ≈ license plate sticker (*US*); (: *sur médicament*) price label (*on medicines for reimbursement by Social Security*)

vignoble [viɲɔbl(ə)] *nm* (*plantation*) vineyard; (*vignes d'une région*) vineyards *pl*

vigoureux, euse [vigurø, -øz] *adj* vigorous, robust

vigueur [vigœʀ] *nf* vigour (*BRIT*), vigor (*US*); **être/entrer en vigueur** to be in/come into force; **en vigueur** current

vil, e [vil] *adj* vile, base; **à vil prix** at a very low price

vilain, e [vilɛ̃, -ɛn] *adj* (*laid*) ugly; (*affaire, blessure*) nasty; (*pas sage: enfant*) naughty ♦ *nm* (*paysan*) villein, villain; **ça va tourner au vilain** things are going to turn nasty; **vilain mot** bad word

villa [vila] *nf* (detached) house

village [vilaʒ] *nm* village; **village de toile** tent village; **village de vacances** holiday village

villageois, e [vilaʒwa, -waz] *adj* village *cpd* ♦ *nm/f* villager

ville [vil] *nf* town; (*importante*) city; (*administration*): **la ville** ≈ the Corporation; ≈ the (town) council; **aller en ville** to go to town; **habiter en ville** to live in town; **ville jumelée** twin town; **ville nouvelle** new town

villégiature [vileʒjatyʀ] *nf* (*séjour*) holiday; (*lieu*) (holiday) resort

vin [vɛ̃] *nm* wine; **avoir le vin gai/triste** to get happy/miserable after a few drinks; **vin blanc/rosé/rouge** white/rosé/red wine; **vin d'honneur** reception (*with wine and snacks*); **vin de messe** altar wine; **vin ordinaire** *ou* **de table** table wine; **vin de pays** local wine; *voir aussi* **AOC, VDQS**

vinaigre [vinɛgʀ(ə)] *nm* vinegar; **tourner au vinaigre** (*fig*) to turn sour; **vinaigre de vin/d'alcool** wine/spirit vinegar

vinaigrette [vinɛgʀɛt] *nf* vinaigrette, French dressing

vindicatif, ive [vɛ̃dikatif, -iv] *adj* vindictive

vineux, euse [vinø, -øz] *adj* win(e)y

vingt [vɛ̃, vɛ̃t] + *vowel and in 22, 23 etc, num* twenty; **vingt-quatre heures sur vingt-quatre** twenty-four hours a day, round the clock

vingtaine [vɛ̃tɛn] *nf*: **une vingtaine (de)** around twenty, twenty or so

vingtième [vɛ̃tjɛm] *num* twentieth

vinicole [vinikɔl] *adj* (*production*) wine *cpd*; (*région*) wine-growing

vins *etc* [vɛ̃] *vb voir* **venir**

vinyle [vinil] *nm* vinyl

viol [vjɔl] *nm* (*d'une femme*) rape; (*d'un lieu sacré*) violation

violacé, e [vjɔlase] *adj* purplish, mauvish

violemment [vjɔlamɑ̃] *adv* violently

violence [vjɔlɑ̃s] *nf* violence; **violences** *nfpl* acts of violence; **faire violence à qn** to do violence to sb; **se faire violence** to force o.s.

violent, e [vjɔlɑ̃, -ɑ̃t] *adj* violent; (*remède*) drastic; (*besoin, désir*) intense, urgent

violer [vjɔle] *vt* (*femme*) to rape; (*sépulture*) to desecrate, violate; (*loi, traité*) to violate

violet, te [vjɔlɛ, -ɛt] *adj, nm* purple, mauve ♦ *nf* (*fleur*) violet

violon [vjɔlɔ̃] *nm* violin; (*dans la musique folklorique etc*) fiddle; (*fam: prison*) lock-up; **premier violon** first violin; **violon d'Ingres** (artistic) hobby

violoncelle [vjɔlɔ̃sɛl] *nm* cello

violoniste [vjɔlɔnist(ə)] *nm/f* violinist, violin-player; (*folklorique etc*) fiddler

vipère [vipɛʀ] *nf* viper, adder

virage [viʀaʒ] *nm* (*d'un véhicule*) turn; (*d'une route, piste*) bend; (*CHIMIE*) change in colour (*BRIT*) *ou* color (*US*); (*de cuti-réaction*) positive reaction; (*PHOTO*) toning; (*fig: POL*) about-turn; **prendre un virage** to go into a bend, take a bend; **virage sans visibilité** blind bend

virée [viʀe] *nf* (*courte*) run; (: *à pied*) walk; (*longue*) trip; hike, walking tour

virement [viʀmɑ̃] *nm* (*COMM*) transfer; **virement bancaire** (bank) credit transfer, ≈ (bank) giro transfer (*BRIT*); **virement postal** Post Office credit transfer, ≈ Girobank® transfer (*BRIT*)

virent [viʀ] *vb voir* **voir**

virer [viʀe] *vt* (*COMM*): **virer qch (sur)** to transfer sth (into); (*PHOTO*) to tone; (*fam: renvoyer*) to sack, boot out ♦ *vi* to turn; (*CHIMIE*) to change colour (*BRIT*) *ou* color (*US*); (*cuti-réaction*) to come up positive; (*PHOTO*) to tone; **virer au bleu** to turn blue; **virer de bord** to tack; (*fig*) to change tack; **virer sur l'aile** to bank

virevolter [viʀvɔlte] *vi* to twirl around

virgule [viʀgyl] *nf* comma; (*MATH*) point; **4 virgule 2** 4 point 2; **virgule flottante** floating decimal

viril, e [viʀil] *adj* (*propre à l'homme*) masculine; (*énergique, courageux*) manly, virile

virtuel, le [viʀtɥɛl] *adj* potential; (*théorique*) virtual

virtuose [viʀtɥoz] *nm/f* (*MUS*) virtuoso; (*gén*) master

virus [viʀys] *nm* virus

vis *vb* [vi] *voir* **voir, vivre** ♦ *nf* [vis] screw; **vis à tête plate/ronde** flat-headed/round-headed screw; **vis platinées** (*AUTO*) (contact) points; **vis sans fin** worm, endless screw

visa [viza] *nm* (*sceau*) stamp; (*validation de passeport*) visa; **visa de censure** (censor's) certificate

visage [vizaʒ] *nm* face; **à visage découvert** (*franchement*) openly

vis-à-vis [vizavi] *adv* face to face ♦ *nm* person opposite; house *etc* opposite; **vis-à-vis de** *prép* opposite; (*fig*) towards, vis-à-vis; **en vis-à-vis** facing *ou* opposite each other; **sans vis-à-vis** (*immeuble*) with an open outlook

viscéral, e, aux [viseʀal, -o] *adj* (*fig*) deep-seated, deep-rooted

visée [vize] *nf* (*avec une arme*) aiming; (*ARPENTAGE*) sighting; **visées** *nfpl* (*intentions*) designs; **avoir des visées sur qn/qch** to have designs on sb/sth

viser [vize] *vi* to aim ♦ *vt* to aim at; (*concerner*) to be aimed *ou* directed at; (*apposer un visa sur*) to stamp, visa; **viser à qch/faire** to aim at sth/at doing *ou* to do

viseur [vizœʀ] *nm* (*d'arme*) sights *pl*; (*PHOTO*) viewfinder

visibilité [vizibilite] *nf* visibility; **sans visibilité** (*pilotage, virage*) blind *cpd*

visible [vizibl(ə)] *adj* visible; (*disponible*): **est-il visible?** can he see me?, will he see visitors?

visière [vizjɛʀ] *nf* (*de casquette*) peak; (*qui s'attache*) eyeshade

vision [vizjɔ̃] *nf* vision; (*sens*) (eye)sight, vision; (*fait de voir*): **la vision de** the sight of; **première vision** (*CINÉ*) first showing

visionneuse [vizjɔnøz] *nf* viewer

visite [vizit] *nf* visit; (*visiteur*) visitor; (*touristique: d'un musée etc*) tour; (*COMM: de représentant*) call; (*expertise, d'inspection*) inspection; (*médicale, à domicile*) visit, call; **la visite** (*MÉD*) medical examination; (*MIL: d'entrée*) medicals *pl*, (: *quotidienne*) sick parade; **faire une visite à qn** to call on sb, pay sb a visit; **rendre visite à qn** to visit sb, pay sb a visit; **être en visite (chez qn)** to be visiting (sb); **heures de visite** (*hôpital, prison*) visiting hours; **le droit de visite** (*JUR: aux enfants*) right of access, access; **visite de douane** customs inspection *ou* examination; **visite guidée** guided tour

visiter [vizite] *vt* to visit; (*musée, ville*) to visit, go round

visiteur, euse [vizitœʀ, -øz] *nm/f* visitor; **visiteur des douanes** customs inspector; **visiteur médical** medical rep(resentative); **visiteur de prison** prison visitor

vison [vizɔ̃] *nm* mink

visser [vise] *vt*: **visser qch** (*fixer, serrer*) to screw sth on

visuel, le [vizɥɛl] *adj* visual ♦ *nm* (visual) display; (*INFORM*) visual display unit (VDU)

vit [vi] *vb voir* **vivre, voir**

vital, e, aux [vital, -o] *adj* vital

vitamine [vitamin] *nf* vitamin

vite [vit] *adv* (*rapidement*) quickly, fast; (*sans délai*) quickly; soon; **faire vite** (*agir rapidement*) to act fast; (*se dépêcher*) to be quick; **ce sera vite fini** this will soon be finished; **viens vite** come quick(ly)

vitesse [vites] *nf* speed; (*AUTO: dispositif*) gear; **faire de la vitesse** to drive fast *ou* at speed; **prendre qn de vitesse** to outstrip sb, get ahead of sb; **prendre la vitesse** to pick up *ou* gather speed; **à toute vitesse** at full *ou* top speed; **en perte de vitesse** (*avion*) losing lift; (*fig*) losing momentum; **changer de vitesse** (*AUTO*) to change gear; **vitesse acquise** momentum; **vitesse de croisière** cruising speed; **vitesse de pointe** top speed; **vitesse du son** speed of sound

viticole [vitikɔl] *adj* (*industrie*) wine *cpd*; (*région*) wine-growing

viticulteur [vitikyltœʀ] *nm* wine grower

vitrage [vitʀaʒ] *nm* (*cloison*) glass partition; (*toit*) glass roof; (*rideau*) net curtain

vitrail, aux [vitʀaj, -o] *nm* stained-glass window

vitre [vitʀ(ə)] *nf* (window) pane; (*de portière, voiture*) window

vitré, e [vitʀe] *adj* glass *cpd*

vitrer [vitʀe] *vt* to glaze

vitreux, euse [vitʀø, -øz] *adj* vitreous; (*terne*) glassy

vitrine [vitʀin] *nf* (*devanture*) (shop) window; (*étalage*) display; (*petite armoire*) display cabinet; **en vitrine** in the window, on display; **vitrine publicitaire** display case, showcase

vivable [vivabl(ə)] *adj* (*personne*) livable-with; (*endroit*) fit to live in

vivace *adj* [vivas] (*arbre, plante*) hardy; (*fig*) enduring ♦ *adv* [vivatʃe] (*MUS*) vivace

vivacité [vivasite] *nf* (*voir vif*) liveliness, vivacity; sharpness; brilliance

vivant, e [vivɑ̃, -ɑ̃t] *vb voir* **vivre** ♦ *adj* (*qui vit*) living, alive; (*animé*) lively; (*preuve, exemple*) living; (*langue*) modern ♦ *nm*: **du vivant de qn** in sb's lifetime; **les vivants et les morts** the living and the dead

vive [viv] *adj f voir* **vif** ♦ *vb voir* **vivre** ♦ *excl*: **vive le roi!** long live the king!; **vive les vacances!** hurrah for the holidays!

vivement [vivmɑ̃] *adv* vivaciously; sharply ♦ *excl*: **vivement les vacances!** I can't wait for the holidays!, roll on the holidays!

vivier [vivje] *nm* (*au restaurant etc*) fish tank; (*étang*) fishpond

vivifiant, e [vivifjɑ̃, -ɑ̃t] *adj* invigorating

vivions [vivjɔ̃] *vb voir* **vivre**

vivoter [vivɔte] *vi* (*personne*) to scrape a living, get by; (*fig: affaire etc*) to struggle along

vivre [vivʀ(ə)] *vi, vt* to live ♦ *nm*: **le vivre et le logement** board and lodging; **vivres** *nmpl* provisions, food supplies; **il vit encore** he is still alive; **se laisser vivre** to take life as it comes; **ne plus vivre** (*être anxieux*) to live on one's nerves; **il a vécu** (*eu une vie aventureuse*) he has seen life; **ce régime a vécu** this regime has had its day; **être facile à vivre** to be easy to get on with; **faire vivre qn** (*pourvoir à sa subsistance*) to provide (a living) for sb; **vivre mal** (*chichement*) to have a meagre existence; **vivre de** (*salaire etc*) to live on

vlan [vlɑ̃] *excl* wham!, bang!

VO *sigle f* (*CINÉ*: = *version originale*): **voir un film en VO** to see a film in its original language

vocable [vɔkabl(ə)] *nm* term

vocabulaire [vɔkabylɛʀ] *nm* vocabulary

vocation [vɔkasjɔ̃] *nf* vocation, calling; **avoir la vocation** to have a vocation

vociférer [vɔsifeʀe] *vi, vt* to scream

vœu, x [vø] *nm* wish; (*à Dieu*) vow; **faire vœu de** to take a vow of; **avec tous nos vœux** with every good wish *ou* our best wishes; **meilleurs vœux** best wishes; (*sur une carte*) "Season's Greetings"; **vœux de bonheur** best wishes for your future happiness; **vœux de bonne année** best wishes for the New Year

vogue [vɔg] *nf* fashion, vogue; **en vogue** in fashion, in vogue

voguer [vɔge] *vi* to sail

voici [vwasi] *prép* (*pour introduire, désigner*) here is + *sg*, here are + *pl*; **et voici que ...** and now it (*ou* he) ...; **il est parti voici 3 ans** he left 3 years ago; **voici une semaine que je l'ai vue** it's a week since I've seen her; **me voici** here I am; *voir aussi* **voilà**

voie [vwa] *vb voir* **voir** ◆ *nf* way; (*RAIL*) track, line; (*AUTO*) lane; **par voie buccale** *ou* **orale** orally; **par voie rectale** rectally; **suivre la voie hiérarchique** to go through official channels; **ouvrir/montrer la voie** to open up/show the way; **être en bonne voie** to be shaping *ou* going well; **mettre qn sur la voie** to put sb on the right track; **être en voie d'achèvement/de rénovation** to be nearing completion/in the process of renovation; **à voie étroite** narrow-gauge; **à voie unique** single-track; **route à 2/3 voies** 2-/3-lane road; **par la voie aérienne/maritime** by air/sea; **voie d'eau** (*NAVIG*) leak; **voie express** expressway; **voie de fait** (*JUR*) assault (and battery); **voie ferrée** track; railway line (*BRIT*), railroad (*US*); **par voie ferrée** by rail, by railroad; **voie de garage** (*RAIL*) siding; **la voie lactée** the Milky Way; **voie navigable** waterway; **voie prioritaire** (*AUTO*) road with right of way; **voie privée** private road; **la voie publique** the public highway

voilà [vwala] *prép* (*en désignant*) there is + *sg*, there are + *pl*; **les voilà** *ou* **voici** here *ou* there they are; **en voilà** *ou* **voici un** here's one, there's one; **voilà** *ou* **voici deux ans** two years ago; **voilà** *ou* **voici deux ans que** it's two years since; **et voilà!** there we are!; **voilà tout** that's all; **"voilà** *ou* **voici"** (*en offrant etc*) "there *ou* here you are"

voile [vwal] *nm* veil; (*tissu léger*) net ◆ *nf* sail; (*sport*) sailing; **prendre le voile** to take the veil; **mettre à la voile** to make way under sail; **voile du palais** soft palate, velum; **voile au poumon** *nm* shadow on the lung

voiler [vwale] *vt* to veil; (*PHOTO*) to fog; (*fausser: roue*) to buckle; (*: bois*) to warp; **se voiler** *vi* (*lune, regard*) to mist over; (*ciel*) to grow hazy; (*voix*) to become husky; (*roue, disque*) to buckle; (*planche*) to warp; **se voiler la face** to hide one's face

voilier [vwalje] *nm* sailing ship; (*de plaisance*) sailing boat

voilure [vwalyR] *nf* (*de voilier*) sails *pl*; (*d'avion*) aerofoils *pl* (*BRIT*), airfoils *pl* (*US*); (*de parachute*) canopy

voir [vwaR] *vi, vt* to see; **se voir: se voir critiquer/transformer** to be criticized/transformed; **cela se voit** (*cela arrive*) it happens; (*c'est visible*) that's obvious, it shows; **voir à faire qch** to see to it that sth is done; **voir loin** (*fig*) to be far-sighted; **voir**

venir (*fig*) to wait and see; **faire voir qch à qn** to show sb sth; **en faire voir à qn** (*fig*) to give sb a hard time; **ne pas pouvoir voir qn** (*fig*) not to be able to stand sb; **regardez voir** just look; **montrez voir** show (me); **dites voir** tell me; **voyons!** let's see now; (*indignation etc*) come (along) now!; **c'est à voir!** we'll see!; **c'est ce qu'on va voir!** we'll see about that!; **avoir quelque chose à voir avec** to have something to do with; **ça n'a rien à voir avec lui** that has nothing to do with him

voire [vwaR] *adv* indeed; nay; or even

voisin, e [vwazɛ̃, -in] *adj* (*proche*) neighbouring (*BRIT*), neighboring (*US*); (*contigu*) next; (*ressemblant*) connected ◆ *nm/f* neighbo(u)r; (*de table, de dortoir etc*) person next to me (*ou* him *etc*); **voisin de palier** neighbo(u)r across the landing (*BRIT*) *ou* hall (*US*)

voisinage [vwazina3] *nm* (*proximité*) proximity; (*environs*) vicinity; (*quartier, voisins*) neighbourhood (*BRIT*), neighborhood (*US*); **relations de bon voisinage** neighbo(u)rly terms

voiture [vwatyR] *nf* car; (*wagon*) coach, carriage; **en voiture!** all aboard!; **voiture à bras** handcart; **voiture d'enfant** pram (*BRIT*), baby carriage (*US*); **voiture d'infirme** invalid carriage; **voiture de sport** sports car

voix [vwa] *nf* voice; (*POL*) vote; **la voix de la conscience/raison** the voice of conscience/reason; **à haute voix** aloud; **à voix basse** in a low voice; **faire la grosse voix** to speak gruffly; **avoir de la voix** to have a good voice; **rester sans voix** to be speechless; **voix de basse/ténor** *etc* bass/tenor *etc* voice; **à 2/4 voix** (*MUS*) in 2/4 parts; **avoir voix au chapitre** to have a say in the matter; **mettre aux voix** to put to the vote; **voix off** voice-over

vol [vɔl] *nm* (*mode de locomotion*) flying; (*trajet, voyage, groupe d'oiseaux*) flight; (*mode d'appropriation*) theft, stealing; (*larcin*) theft; **vol d'oiseau** as the crow flies; **au vol: attraper qch au vol** to catch sth as it flies past; **saisir une remarque au vol** to pick up a passing remark; **prendre son vol** to take flight; **de haut vol** (*fig*) of the highest order; **en vol** in flight; **vol avec effraction** breaking and entering *no pl*, break-in; **vol à l'étalage** shoplifting *no pl*; **vol libre** hang-gliding; **vol à main armée** armed robbery; **vol de nuit** night flight; **vol plané** (*AVIAT*) glide, gliding *no pl*; **vol à la tire** pickpocketing *no pl*; **vol à voile** gliding

volage [vɔla3] *adj* fickle

volaille [vɔlaj] *nf* (*oiseaux*) poultry *pl*; (*viande*) poultry *no pl*; (*oiseau*) fowl

volant, e [vɔlɑ̃, -ɑ̃t] *adj voir* **feuille** *etc* ◆ *nm* (*d'automobile*) (steering) wheel; (*de commande*) wheel; (*objet lancé*) shuttlecock; (*jeu*) battledore and shuttlecock; (*bande de tissu*) flounce; (*feuillet détachable*) tear-off portion; **le personnel volant, les volants** (*AVIAT*) the flight staff; **volant de sécurité** (*fig*) reserve, margin, safeguard

volcan [vɔlkɑ̃] *nm* volcano; (*fig: personne*) hothead

volée [vɔle] nf (groupe d'oiseaux) flight, flock; (TENNIS) volley; **volée de coups/de flèches** volley of blows/arrows; **à la volée: rattraper à la volée** to catch in midair; **lancer à la volée** to fling about; **semer à la volée** to (sow) broadcast; **à toute volée** (sonner les cloches) vigorously; (lancer un projectile) with full force; **de haute volée** (fig) of the highest order

voler [vɔle] vi (avion, oiseau, fig) to fly; (voleur) to steal ♦ vt (objet) to steal; (personne) to rob; **voler en éclats** to smash to smithereens; **voler de ses propres ailes** (fig) to stand on one's own two feet; **voler au vent** to fly in the wind; **voler qch à qn** to steal sth from sb

volet [vɔle] nm (de fenêtre) shutter; (AVIAT) flap; (de feuillet, document) section; (fig: d'un plan) facet; **trié sur le volet** hand-picked

voleur, euse [vɔlœR, -øz] nm/f thief (pl thieves) ♦ adj thieving; **"au voleur!"** "stop thief!"

volière [vɔljɛR] nf aviary

volley(-ball) [vɔle(bɔl)] nm volleyball

volontaire [vɔlɔ̃tɛR] adj (acte, activité) voluntary; (délibéré) deliberate; (caractère, personne: décidé) self-willed ♦ nm/f volunteer

volonté [vɔlɔ̃te] nf (faculté de vouloir) will; (énergie, fermeté) will(power); (souhait, désir) wish; **se servir/boire à volonté** to take/drink as much as one likes; **bonne volonté** goodwill, willingness; **mauvaise volonté** lack of goodwill, unwillingness

volontiers [vɔlɔ̃tje] adv (de bonne grâce) willingly; (avec plaisir) willingly, gladly; (habituellement, souvent) readily, willingly; **"volontiers"** "with pleasure","I'd be glad to"

volt [vɔlt] nm volt

volte-face [vɔltəfas] nf inv about-turn; (fig) about-turn, U-turn; **faire volte-face** to do an about-turn; to do a U-turn

voltige [vɔltiʒ] nf (ÉQUITATION) trick riding; (au cirque) acrobatics sg; (AVIAT) (aerial) acrobatics sg; **numéro de haute voltige** acrobatic act

voltiger [vɔltiʒe] vi to flutter (about)

volubile [vɔlybil] adj voluble

volume [vɔlym] nm volume; (GÉOM: solide) solid

volumineux, euse [vɔlyminø, -øz] adj voluminous, bulky

volupté [vɔlypte] nf sensual delight ou pleasure

vomi [vɔmi] nm vomit

vomir [vɔmiR] vi to vomit, be sick ♦ vt to vomit, bring up; (fig) to belch out, spew out; (exécrer) to loathe, abhor

vomissements [vɔmismã] nmpl (action) vomiting no pl; **des vomissements** vomit sg

vont [vɔ̃] vb voir **aller**

vorace [vɔRas] adj voracious

vos [vo] adj possessif voir **votre**

vote [vɔt] nm vote; **vote par correspondance/procuration** postal/proxy vote; **vote à main levée** vote by show of hands; **vote secret, vote à bul-**letins secrets secret ballot

voter [vɔte] vi to vote ♦ vt (loi, décision) to vote for

votre [vɔtR(ə)], pl **vos** [vo] adj possessif your

vôtre [votR(ə)] pron: **le vôtre, la vôtre, les vôtres** yours; **les vôtres** (fig) your family ou folks; **à la vôtre** (toast) your (good) health!

voudrai etc [vudRe] vb voir **vouloir**

voué, e [vwe] adj: **voué à** doomed to, destined for

vouer [vwe] vt: **vouer qch à** (Dieu/un saint) to dedicate sth to; **vouer sa vie/son temps à** (étude, cause etc) to devote one's life/time to; **vouer une haine/amitié éternelle à qn** to vow undying hatred/friendship to sb

---
MOT CLÉ
---

vouloir [vulwaR] nm: **le bon vouloir de qn** sb's goodwill; sb's pleasure
♦ vt 1 (exiger, désirer) to want; **vouloir faire/que qn fasse** to want to do/sb to do; **voulez-vous du thé?** would you like ou do you want some tea?; **vouloir qch à qn** to wish sth for sb; **que me veut-il?** what does he want with me?; **que veux-tu que je te dise?** what do you want me to say?; **sans le vouloir** (involontairement) without meaning to, unintentionally; **je voudrais ceci/faire** I would ou I'd like this/to do; **le hasard a voulu que ...** as fate would have it, ...; **la tradition veut que ...** tradition demands that ...; **... qui se veut moderne** ... which purports to be modern

2 (consentir): **je veux bien** (bonne volonté) I'll be happy to; (concession) fair enough, that's fine; **oui, si on veut** (en quelque sorte) yes, if you like; **comme tu veux** as you wish; (en quelque sorte) if you like; **veuillez attendre** please wait; **veuillez agréer ...** (formule épistolaire) yours faithfully

3: **en vouloir** (être ambitieux) to be out to win; **en vouloir à qn** to bear sb a grudge; **je lui en veux d'avoir fait ça** I resent his having done that; **s'en vouloir (de)** to be annoyed with o.s. (for); **il en veut à mon argent** he's after my money

4: **vouloir de** to want; **la compagnie ne veut plus de lui** the firm doesn't want him any more; **elle ne veut pas de son aide** she doesn't want his help

5: **vouloir dire** to mean

---

voulu, e [vuly] pp de **vouloir** ♦ adj (requis) required, requisite; (délibéré) deliberate, intentional

vous [vu] pron you; (objet indirect) (to) you; (réfléchi) yourself (pl yourselves); (réciproque) each other ♦ nm: **employer le vous** (vouvoyer) to use the "vous" form; **vous-même** yourself; **vous-mêmes** yourselves

voûte [vut] nf vault; **la voûte céleste** the vault of heaven; **voûte du palais** (ANAT) roof of the mouth; **voûte plantaire** arch (of the foot)

voûter [vute] vt (ARCHIT) to arch, vault; **se voûter** vi (dos, personne) to become stooped

vouvoyer [vuvwaje] *vt*: **vouvoyer qn** to address sb as "vous"

voyage [vwajaʒ] *nm* journey, trip; (*fait de voyager*): **le voyage** travel(ling); **partir/être en voyage** to go off/be away on a journey *ou* trip; **faire un voyage** to go on *ou* make a trip *ou* journey; **faire bon voyage** to have a good journey; **les gens du voyage** travelling people; **voyage d'agrément/d'affaires** pleasure/business trip; **voyage de noces** honeymoon; **voyage organisé** package tour

voyager [vwajaʒe] *vi* to travel

voyageur, euse [vwajaʒœʀ, -øz] *nm/f* traveller; (*passager*) passenger ◆ *adj* (*tempérament*) nomadic, wayfaring; **voyageur (de commerce)** commercial traveller

voyant, e [vwajā, -āt] *adj* (*couleur*) loud, gaudy ◆ *nm/f* (*personne qui voit*) sighted person ◆ *nm* (*signal*) (warning) light ◆ *nf* clairvoyant

voyelle [vwajɛl] *nf* vowel

voyons [vwajɔ̃] *etc vb voir* **voir**

voyou [vwaju] *nm* lout, hoodlum; (*enfant*) guttersnipe

vrac [vʀak]: **en vrac** *adv* higgledy-piggledy; (*COMM*) in bulk

vrai, e [vʀɛ] *adj* (*véridique: récit, faits*) true; (*non factice, authentique*) real ◆ *nm*: **le vrai** the truth; **à vrai dire** to tell the truth; **il est vrai que** it is true that; **être dans le vrai** to be right

vraiment [vʀɛmā] *adv* really

vraisemblable [vʀɛsāblabl(ə)] *adj* (*plausible*) likely, plausible; (*probable*) likely, probable

vraisemblablement [vʀɛsāblabləmā] *adv* in all likelihood, very likely

vraisemblance [vʀɛsāblās] *nf* likelihood, plausibility; (*romanesque*) verisimilitude; **selon toute vraisemblance** in all likelihood

vrille [vʀij] *nf* (*de plante*) tendril; (*outil*) gimlet; (*spirale*) spiral; (*AVIAT*) spin

vrombir [vʀɔ̃biʀ] *vi* to hum

VRP *sigle m* (= *voyageur, représentant, placier*) (sales) rep

VTT *sigle m* (= *vélo tout-terrain*) mountain bike

vu [vy] *prép* (*en raison de*) in view of; **vu que** in view of the fact that

vu, e [vy] *pp de* **voir** ◆ *adj*: **bien/mal vu** (*personne*) well/poorly thought of; (*conduite*) good/bad form ◆ *nm*: **au vu et au su de tous** openly and publicly; **ni vu ni connu** what the eye doesn't see …!, no one will be any the wiser; **c'est tout vu** it's a foregone conclusion

vue [vy] *nf* (*fait de voir*): **la vue de** the sight of; (*sens, faculté*) (eye)sight; (*panorama, image, photo*) view; (*spectacle*) sight; **vues** *nfpl* (*idées*) views; (*dessein*) designs; **perdre la vue** to lose one's (eye)sight; **perdre de vue** to lose sight of; **à la vue de tous** in full view of everybody; **hors de vue** out of sight; **à première vue** at first sight; **connaître de vue** to know by sight; **à vue** (*COMM*) at sight;

tirer à vue to shoot on sight; **à vue d'œil** *adv* visibly; (*à première vue*) at a quick glance; **avoir vue sur** to have a view of; **en vue** (*visible*) in sight; (*COMM*) in the public eye; **avoir qch en vue** (*intentions*) to have one's sights on sth; **en vue de faire** with the intention of doing, with a view to doing; **vue d'ensemble** overall view; **vue de l'esprit** theoretical view

vulgaire [vylgɛʀ] *adj* (*grossier*) vulgar, coarse; (*trivial*) commonplace, mundane; (*péj: quelconque*): **de vulgaires touristes/chaises de cuisine** common tourists/kitchen chairs; (*BOT, ZOOL: non latin*) common

vulgariser [vylgaʀize] *vt* to popularize

vulnérable [vylneʀabl(ə)] *adj* vulnerable

— W w —

wagon [vagɔ̃] *nm* (*de voyageurs*) carriage; (*de marchandises*) truck, wagon

wagon-lit, *pl* **wagons-lits** [vagɔ̃li] *nm* sleeper, sleeping car

wagon-restaurant, *pl* **wagons-restaurants** [vagɔ̃ʀɛstoʀā] *nm* restaurant *ou* dining car

wallon, ne [walɔ̃, -ɔn] *adj* Walloon ◆ *nm* (*LING*) Walloon ◆ *nm/f*: **Wallon, ne** Walloon

waters [watɛʀ] *nmpl* toilet *sg*, loo *sg* (*BRIT*)

watt [wat] *nm* watt

WC [vese] *nmpl* toilet *sg*, lavatory *sg*

Web [wɛb] *nm inv*: **le Web** the (World Wide) Web

week-end [wikɛnd] *nm* weekend

western [wɛstɛʀn] *nm* western

whisky, *pl* **whiskies** [wiski] *nm* whisky

— X x —

xénophobe [gzenɔfɔb] *adj* xenophobic ◆ *nm/f* xenophobe

xérès [gzeʀɛs] *nm* sherry

xylophone [ksilɔfɔn] *nm* xylophone

— Y y —

y [i] *adv* (*à cet endroit*) there; (*dessus*) on it (*ou* them); (*dedans*) in it (*ou* them) ◆ *pron* (about *ou* on *ou* of) it: *vérifier la syntaxe du verbe employé*; **j'y pense** I'm thinking about it; *voir aussi* **aller**, **avoir**

yacht [jɔt] *nm* yacht

yaourt [jauʀt] *nm* yoghurt

yeux [jø] *pl de* **œil**

yoga [jɔga] *nm* yoga

yoghourt [jɔguʀt] *nm* = **yaourt**

yougoslave [jugɔslav] *adj* Yugoslav(ian) ◆ *nm/f*: **Yougoslave** Yugoslav(ian)

Yougoslavie [jugɔslavi] *nf*: **la Yougoslavie** Yugoslavia

— Z z —

zapper [zape] *vi* to zap

zapping [zapiŋ] *nm*: **faire du zapping** to flick through the channels

zèbre [zɛbʀ(ə)] *nm* (ZOOL) zebra

zébré, e [zebʀe] *adj* striped, streaked

zèle [zɛl] *nm* diligence, assiduousness; **faire du zèle** (*péj*) to be over-zealous

zélé, e [zele] *adj* zealous

zéro [zeʀo] *nm* zero, nought (BRIT); **au-dessous de zéro** below zero (Centigrade), below freezing; **partir de zéro** to start from scratch; **réduire à zéro** to reduce to nothing; **trois (buts) à zéro** 3 (goals to) nil

zeste [zɛst(ə)] *nm* peel, zest; **un zeste de citron** a piece of lemon peel

zézayer [zezeje] *vi* to have a lisp

zigzag [zigzag] *nm* zigzag

zigzaguer [zigzage] *vi* to zigzag (along)

zinc [zɛg] *nm* (CHIMIE) zinc; (*comptoir*) bar, counter

zizanie [zizani] *nf*: **semer la zizanie** to stir up ill-feeling

zizi [zizi] *nm* (fam) willy (BRIT), peter (US)

zodiaque [zɔdjak] *nm* zodiac

zona [zona] *nm* shingles *sg*

zone [zon] *nf* zone, area; (INFORM) field; (*quartiers*): **la zone** the slum belt; **de seconde zone** (*fig*) second-rate; **zone d'action** (MIL) sphere of activity; **zone bleue** = restricted parking area; **zone d'extension** *ou* **d'urbanisation** urban development area; **zone franche** free zone; **zone industrielle (ZI)** industrial estate; **zone piétonne** pedestrian precinct; **zone résidentielle** residential area; **zone tampon** buffer zone

zoo [zoo] *nm* zoo

zoologie [zɔɔlɔʒi] *nf* zoology

zoologique [zɔɔlɔʒik] *adj* zoological

zut [zyt] *excl* dash (it)! (BRIT), nuts! (US)

ENGLISH-FRENCH
ANGLAIS-FRANÇAIS

— A a —

A, a [eɪ] *n* (*letter*) A, a *m*; (*SCOL: mark*) A; (*MUS*): **A** la *m*; **A for Andrew**, (*US*) **A for Able** A comme Anatole; **A road** *n* (*BRIT AUT*) route nationale; **A shares** *npl* (*BRIT STOCK EXCHANGE*) actions *fpl* prioritaires

a [eɪ, ə] (*before vowel or silent h* **an**) *indef art*
1 un(e); **a book** un livre; **an apple** une pomme; **she's a doctor** elle est médecin
2 (*instead of the number "one"*) un(e); **a year ago** il y a un an; **a hundred/thousand** *etc* **pounds** cent/mille *etc* livres
3 (*in expressing ratios, prices etc*): **3 a day/week** 3 par jour/semaine; **10 km an hour** 10 km à l'heure; **30p a kilo** 30p le kilo

AA *n abbr* (*BRIT*: = *Automobile Association*) ≃ ACF *m*; (*US*: = *Associate in/of Arts*) diplôme universitaire; (= *Alcoholics Anonymous*) AA; (= *anti-aircraft*) AA
AAA *n abbr* (= *American Automobile Association*) ≃ ACF *m*; (*BRIT*) = *Amateur Athletics Association*
aback [əˈbæk] *adv*: **to be taken aback** être décontenancé(e)
abandon [əˈbændən] *vt* abandonner ♦ *n* abandon *m*; **to abandon ship** évacuer le navire
abate [əˈbeɪt] *vi* s'apaiser, se calmer
abbey [ˈæbɪ] *n* abbaye *f*
abbot [ˈæbət] *n* père supérieur
abbreviation [əbriːˈveɪʃən] *n* abréviation *f*
abdicate [ˈæbdɪkeɪt] *vt*, *vi* abdiquer
abdomen [ˈæbdəmən] *n* abdomen *m*
abduct [æbˈdʌkt] *vt* enlever
aberration [æbəˈreɪʃən] *n* anomalie *f*; **in a moment of mental aberration** dans un moment d'égarement
abide [əˈbaɪd] *vt* souffrir, supporter
▶ **abide by** *vt fus* observer, respecter
ability [əˈbɪlɪtɪ] *n* compétence *f*; capacité *f*; (*skill*) talent *m*; **to the best of my ability** de mon mieux
abject [ˈæbdʒekt] *adj* (*poverty*) sordide; (*coward*) méprisable; **an abject apology** les excuses les plus plates
ablaze [əˈbleɪz] *adj* en feu, en flammes; **ablaze**

with light resplendissant de lumière
able [ˈeɪbl] *adj* compétent(e); **to be able to do sth** pouvoir faire qch, être capable de faire qch
able-bodied [ˈeɪblˈbɒdɪd] *adj* robuste; **able-bodied seaman** (*BRIT*) matelot breveté
ably [ˈeɪblɪ] *adv* avec compétence *or* talent, habilement
abnormal [æbˈnɔːməl] *adj* anormal(e)
aboard [əˈbɔːd] *adv* à bord ♦ *prep* à bord de; (*train*) dans
abode [əˈbəʊd] *n* (*old*) demeure *f*; (*LAW*): **of no fixed abode** sans domicile fixe
abolish [əˈbɒlɪʃ] *vt* abolir
aborigine [æbəˈrɪdʒɪnɪ] *n* aborigène *m/f*
abort [əˈbɔːt] *vt* (*MED*, *fig*) faire avorter; (*COMPUT*) abandonner
abortion [əˈbɔːʃən] *n* avortement *m*; **to have an abortion** se faire avorter
abortive [əˈbɔːtɪv] *adj* manqué(e)

about [əˈbaʊt] *adv* **1** (*approximately*) environ, à peu près; **about a hundred/thousand** *etc* environ cent/mille *etc*, une centaine (de)/un millier (de) *etc*; **it takes about 10 hours** ça prend environ *or* à peu près 10 heures; **at about 2 o'clock** vers 2 heures; **I've just about finished** j'ai presque fini
2 (*referring to place*) çà et là, deci delà; **to run about** courir çà et là; **to walk about** se promener, aller et venir; **is Paul about?** (*BRIT*) est-ce que Paul est là?; **it's about here** c'est par ici, c'est dans les parages; **they left all their things lying about** ils ont laissé traîner toutes leurs affaires
3: **to be about to do sth** être sur le point de faire qch; **I'm not about to do all that for nothing** (*col*) je ne vais quand même pas faire tout ça pour rien
4 (*opposite*): **it's the other way about** (*BRIT*) c'est l'inverse
♦ *prep* **1** (*relating to*) au sujet de, à propos de; **a book about London** un livre sur Londres; **what is it about?** de quoi s'agit-il?; **we talked about it** nous en avons parlé; **do something about it!** faites quelque chose!; **what** *or* **how about doing**

this? et si nous faisions ceci?
2 (*referring to place*) dans; **to walk about the town** se promener dans la ville

about face, about turn *n* (*MIL*) demi-tour *m*; (*fig*) volte-face *f*

above [ə'bʌv] *adv* au-dessus ♦ *prep* au-dessus de; **mentioned above** mentionné ci-dessus; **costing above £10** coûtant plus de 10 livres; **above all** par-dessus tout, surtout

aboveboard [ə'bʌv'bɔːd] *adj* franc(franche), loyal(e); honnête

abrasive [ə'breɪzɪv] *adj* abrasif(ive); (*fig*) caustique, agressif(ive)

abreast [ə'brest] *adv* de front; **to keep abreast of** se tenir au courant de

abroad [ə'brɔːd] *adv* à l'étranger; **there is a rumour abroad that ...** (*fig*) le bruit court que ...

abrupt [ə'brʌpt] *adj* (*steep, blunt*) abrupt(e); (*sudden, gruff*) brusque

abruptly [ə'brʌptlɪ] *adv* (*speak, end*) brusquement

abscess [ˈæbsɪs] *n* abcès *m*

absence [ˈæbsəns] *n* absence *f*; **in the absence of** (*person*) en l'absence de; (*thing*) faute de

absent [ˈæbsənt] *adj* absent(e); **absent without leave (AWOL)** (*MIL*) en absence irrégulière

absentee [æbsən'tiː] *n* absent/e

absent-minded [ˈæbsənt'maɪndɪd] *adj* distrait(e)

absolute [ˈæbsəluːt] *adj* absolu(e)

absolutely [æbsəˈluːtlɪ] *adv* absolument

absolve [əb'zɔlv] *vt*: **to absolve sb (from)** (*sin etc*) absoudre qn (de); **to absolve sb from** (*oath*) délier qn de

absorb [əb'zɔːb] *vt* absorber; **to be absorbed in a book** être plongé(e) dans un livre

absorbent cotton [əb'zɔːbənt-] *n* (*US*) coton *m* hydrophile

abstain [əb'steɪn] *vi*: **to abstain (from)** s'abstenir (de)

abstract *adj n* [ˈæbstrækt] ♦ *adj* abstrait(e) ♦ *n* (*summary*) résumé *m* ♦ *vt* [əb'strækt] extraire

absurd [əb'sɜːd] *adj* absurde

abundant [ə'bʌndənt] *adj* abondant(e)

abuse *n* [ə'bjuːs] insultes *fpl*, injures *fpl*; (*of power etc*) abus *m* ♦ *vt* [ə'bjuːz] abuser de; **to be open to abuse** se prêter à des abus

abusive [ə'bjuːsɪv] *adj* grossier(ière), injurieux(euse)

abysmal [ə'bɪzməl] *adj* exécrable; (*ignorance etc*) sans bornes

abyss [ə'bɪs] *n* abîme *m*, gouffre *m*

AC *n abbr* (*US*) = *athletic club*

academic [ækə'demɪk] *adj* universitaire; (*pej: issue*) oiseux(euse), purement théorique ♦ *n* universitaire *m/f*; **academic freedom** liberté *f* académique

academic year *n* année *f* universitaire

academy [ə'kædəmɪ] *n* (*learned body*) académie *f*; (*school*) collège *m*; **military/naval academy** école militaire/navale; **academy of music** conservatoire *m*

accelerate [æk'seləreɪt] *vt, vi* accélérer

accelerator [æk'seləreɪtə*] *n* accélérateur *m*

accent [ˈæksent] *n* accent *m*

accept [ək'sept] *vt* accepter

acceptable [ək'septəbl] *adj* acceptable

acceptance [ək'septəns] *n* acceptation *f*; **to meet with general acceptance** être favorablement accueilli par tous

access [ˈækses] *n* accès *m* ♦ *vt* (*COMPUT*) accéder à; **to have access to** (*information, library etc*) avoir accès à, pouvoir utiliser ou consulter; (*person*) avoir accès auprès de; **the burglars gained access through a window** les cambrioleurs sont entrés par une fenêtre

accessible [æk'sesəbl] *adj* accessible

accessory [æk'sesərɪ] *n* accessoire *m*; **toilet accessories** (*BRIT*) articles *mpl* de toilette

accident [ˈæksɪdənt] *n* accident *m*; (*chance*) hasard *m*; **to meet with** *or* **to have an accident** avoir un accident; **accidents at work** accidents du travail; **by accident** par hasard; (*not deliberately*) accidentellement

accidental [æksɪ'dentl] *adj* accidentel(le)

accidentally [æksɪ'dentəlɪ] *adv* accidentellement

accident insurance *n* assurance *f* accident

accident-prone [ˈæksɪdənt'prəun] *adj* sujet(te) aux accidents

acclaim [ə'kleɪm] *vt* acclamer ♦ *n* acclamation *f*

accommodate [ə'kɔmədeɪt] *vt* loger, recevoir; (*oblige, help*) obliger; (*adapt*): **to accommodate one's plans to** adapter ses projets à; **this car accommodates 4 people comfortably** on tient aisément à 4 dans cette voiture

accommodating [ə'kɔmədeɪtɪŋ] *adj* obligeant(e), arrangeant(e)

accommodation, (*US*) **accommodations** [əkɔmə'deɪʃən(z)] *n(pl)* logement *m*; **he's found accommodation** il a trouvé à se loger; **"accommodation to let"** (*BRIT*) "appartement *ou* studio *etc* à louer"; **they have accommodation for 500** ils peuvent recevoir 500 personnes, il y a de la place pour 500 personnes; **the hall has seating accommodation for 600** (*BRIT*) la salle contient 600 places assises

accompany [ə'kʌmpənɪ] *vt* accompagner

accomplice [ə'kʌmplɪs] *n* complice *m/f*

accomplish [ə'kʌmplɪʃ] *vt* accomplir

accomplishment [ə'kʌmplɪʃmənt] *n* accomplissement *m*; (*achievement*) réussite *f*; **accomplishments** *npl* (*skills*) talents *mpl*

accord [ə'kɔːd] *n* accord *m* ♦ *vt* accorder; **of his own accord** de son plein gré; **with one accord**

d'un commun accord
accordance [ə'kɔːdəns] *n*: **in accordance with** conformément à
according [ə'kɔːdɪŋ]: **according to** *prep* selon; **according to plan** comme prévu
accordingly [ə'kɔːdɪŋlɪ] *adv* en conséquence
accordion [ə'kɔːdɪən] *n* accordéon *m*
account [ə'kaunt] *n* (COMM) compte *m*; (*report*) compte rendu, récit *m*; **accounts** *npl* (BOOK-KEEPING) comptabilité *f*, comptes; "**account payee only**" (BRIT) "chèque non endossable"; **to keep an account of** noter; **to bring sb to account for sth/ for having done sth** amener qn à rendre compte de qch/d'avoir fait qch; **by all accounts** au dire de tous; **of little account** de peu d'importance; **to pay £5 on account** verser un acompte de 5 livres; **to buy sth on account** acheter qch à crédit; **on no account** en aucun cas; **on account of** à cause de; **to take into account, take account of** tenir compte de
▶ **account for** *vt fus* expliquer, rendre compte de; **all the children were accounted for** aucun enfant ne manquait; **4 people are still not accounted for** on n'a toujours pas retrouvé 4 personnes
accountable [ə'kauntəbl] *adj*: **accountable (for)** responsable (de)
accountancy [ə'kauntənsɪ] *n* comptabilité *f*
accountant [ə'kauntənt] *n* comptable *m/f*
account number *n* numéro *m* de compte
accrue [ə'kruː] *vi* s'accroître; (*mount up*) s'accumuler; **to accrue to** s'ajouter à; **accrued interest** intérêt couru
accumulate [ə'kjuːmjuleɪt] *vt* accumuler, amasser ◆ *vi* s'accumuler, s'amasser
accuracy ['ækjurəsɪ] *n* exactitude *f*, précision *f*
accurate ['ækjurɪt] *adj* exact(e), précis(e)
accurately ['ækjurɪtlɪ] *adv* avec précision
accusation [ækju'zeɪʃən] *n* accusation *f*
accuse [ə'kjuːz] *vt* accuser
accustom [ə'kʌstəm] *vt* accoutumer, habituer; **to accustom o.s. to sth** s'habituer à qch
accustomed [ə'kʌstəmd] *adj* (*usual*) habituel(le); **accustomed to** habitué(e) *or* accoutumé(e) à
ace [eɪs] *n* as *m*; **within an ace of** (BRIT) à deux doigts *or* un cheveu de
ache [eɪk] *n* mal *m*, douleur *f* ◆ *vi* (*be sore*) faire mal, être douloureux(euse); (*yearn*): **to ache to do sth** mourir d'envie de faire qch; **I've got stomach ache** *or* (US) **a stomach ache** j'ai mal à l'estomac; **my head aches** j'ai mal à la tête; **I'm aching all over** j'ai mal partout
achieve [ə'tʃiːv] *vt* (*aim*) atteindre; (*victory, success*) remporter, obtenir; (*task*) accomplir
achievement [ə'tʃiːvmənt] *n* exploit *m*, réussite *f*; (*of aims*) réalisation *f*
acid ['æsɪd] *adj*, *n* acide (*m*)

acid rain *n* pluies *fpl* acides
acknowledge [ək'nɔlɪdʒ] *vt* (*also*: **acknowledge receipt of**) accuser réception de; (*fact*) reconnaître
acknowledgement [ək'nɔlɪdʒmənt] *n* accusé *m* de réception; **acknowledgements** (*in book*) remerciements *mpl*
acne ['æknɪ] *n* acné *m*
acorn ['eɪkɔːn] *n* gland *m*
acoustic [ə'kuːstɪk] *adj* acoustique
acoustics [ə'kuːstɪks] *n*, *npl* acoustique *f*
acquaint [ə'kweɪnt] *vt*: **to acquaint sb with sth** mettre qn au courant de qch; **to be acquainted with** (*person*) connaître; (*fact*) savoir
acquaintance [ə'kweɪntəns] *n* connaissance *f*; **to make sb's acquaintance** faire la connaissance de qn
acquire [ə'kwaɪə*] *vt* acquérir
acquit [ə'kwɪt] *vt* acquitter; **to acquit o.s. well** s'en tirer très honorablement
acre ['eɪkə*] *n* acre *f* (= 4047 *m*²)
acrid ['ækrɪd] *adj* (*smell*) âcre; (*fig*) mordant(e)
acrobat ['ækrəbæt] *n* acrobate *m/f*
across [ə'krɔs] *prep* (*on the other side*) de l'autre côté de; (*crosswise*) en travers de ◆ *adv* de l'autre côté; en travers; **to walk across (the road)** traverser (la route); **to take sb across the road** faire traverser la route à qn; **a road across the wood** une route qui traverse le bois; **the lake is 12 km across** le lac fait 12 km de large; **across from** en face de; **to get sth across (to sb)** faire comprendre qch (à qn)
acrylic [ə'krɪlɪk] *adj*, *n* acrylique (*m*)
act [ækt] *n* acte *m*, action *f*; (THEAT: *part of play*) acte; (: *of performer*) numéro *m*; (LAW) loi *f* ◆ *vi* agir; (THEAT) jouer; (*pretend*) jouer la comédie ◆ *vt* (*role*) jouer, tenir; **act of God** (LAW) catastrophe naturelle; **to catch sb in the act** prendre qn sur le fait *or* en flagrant délit; **it's only an act** c'est du cinéma; **to act Hamlet** (BRIT) tenir *or* jouer le rôle d'Hamlet; **to act the fool** (BRIT) faire l'idiot; **to act as** servir de; **it acts as a deterrent** cela a un effet dissuasif; **acting in my capacity as chairman, I ...** en ma qualité de président, je ...
▶ **act on** *vt*: **to act on sth** agir sur la base de qch
▶ **act out** *vt* (*event*) raconter en mimant; (*fantasies*) réaliser
acting ['æktɪŋ] *adj* suppléant(e), par intérim ◆ *n* (*of actor*) jeu *m*; (*activity*): **to do some acting** faire du théâtre (*or* du cinéma); **he is the acting manager** il remplace (provisoirement) le directeur
action ['ækʃən] *n* action *f*; (MIL) combat(s) *m(pl)*; (LAW) procès *m*, action en justice; **to bring an action against sb** (LAW) poursuivre qn en justice, intenter un procès contre qn; **killed in action** (MIL) tué au champ d'honneur; **out of action** hors de combat; (*machine etc*) hors d'usage; **to take action** agir, prendre des mesures; **to put a plan into action** mettre un projet à exécution

action replay n (BRIT TV) retour m sur une séquence

activate ['æktɪveɪt] vt (mechanism) actionner, faire fonctionner; (CHEM, PHYSICS) activer

active ['æktɪv] adj actif(ive); (volcano) en activité; **to play an active part in** jouer un rôle actif dans

actively ['æktɪvlɪ] adv activement

activity [æk'tɪvɪtɪ] n activité f

activity holiday n vacances actives

actor ['æktə*] n acteur m

actress ['æktrɪs] n actrice f

actual ['æktjuəl] adj réel(le), véritable

actually ['æktjuəlɪ] adv réellement, véritablement; (in fact) en fait

acute [ə'kju:t] adj aigu(ë); (mind, observer) pénétrant(e)

AD adv abbr (= Anno Domini) ap. J.-C. ◆ n abbr (US MIL) = active duty

ad [æd] n abbr = **advertisement**

adamant ['ædəmənt] adj inflexible

adapt [ə'dæpt] vt adapter ◆ vi: **to adapt (to)** s'adapter (à)

adaptable [ə'dæptəbl] adj (device) adaptable; (person) qui s'adapte facilement

adapter, adaptor [ə'dæptə*] n (ELEC) adaptateur m

add [æd] vt ajouter; (figures) additionner ◆ vi: **to add to** (increase) ajouter à, accroître

▶ **add on** vt ajouter

▶ **add up** vt (figures) additionner ◆ vi (fig): **it doesn't add up** cela ne rime à rien; **it doesn't add up to much** ça n'est pas grand'chose

adder ['ædə*] n vipère f

addict ['ædɪkt] n toxicomane m/f; (fig) fanatique m/f; **heroin addict** héroïnomane m/f; **drug addict** drogué(e) m/f

addicted [ə'dɪktɪd] adj: **to be addicted to** (drink etc) être adonné(e) à; (fig: football etc) être un(e) fanatique de

addiction [ə'dɪkʃən] n (MED) dépendance f

addictive [ə'dɪktɪv] adj qui crée une dépendance

addition [ə'dɪʃən] n addition f; **in addition** de plus, de surcroît; **in addition to** en plus de

additional [ə'dɪʃənl] adj supplémentaire

additive ['ædɪtɪv] n additif m

address [ə'drɛs] n adresse f; (talk) discours m, allocution f ◆ vt adresser; (speak to) s'adresser à; **form of address** titre m; **what form of address do you use for ...?** comment s'adresse-t-on à ...?; **to address (o.s. to) sth** (problem, issue) aborder qch; **absolute/relative address** (COMPUT) adresse absolue/relative

adept ['ædept] adj: **adept at** expert(e) à or en

adequate ['ædɪkwɪt] adj (enough) suffisant(e); **to feel adequate to the task** se sentir à la hauteur de la tâche

adhere [əd'hɪə*] vi: **to adhere to** adhérer à; (fig: rule, decision) se tenir à

adhesive [əd'hi:zɪv] adj adhésif(ive) ◆ n adhésif m; **adhesive tape** (BRIT) ruban adhésif; (US) sparadrap m

ad hoc [æd'hɔk] adj (decision) de circonstance; (committee) ad hoc

adjacent [ə'dʒeɪsənt] adj adjacent(e), contigu(ë); **adjacent to** adjacent à

adjective ['ædʒɛktɪv] n adjectif m

adjoining [ə'dʒɔɪnɪŋ] adj voisin(e), adjacent(e), attenant(e) ◆ prep voisin de, adjacent à

adjourn [ə'dʒə:n] vt ajourner ◆ vi suspendre la séance; lever la séance; clore la session; (go) se retirer; **to adjourn a meeting till the following week** reporter une réunion à la semaine suivante; **they adjourned to the pub** (BRIT col) ils ont filé au pub

adjust [ə'dʒʌst] vt ajuster, régler; rajuster ◆ vi: **to adjust (to)** s'adapter (à)

adjustable [ə'dʒʌstəbl] adj réglable

adjustment [ə'dʒʌstmənt] n ajustage m, réglage m; (of prices, wages) rajustement m; (of person) adaptation f

ad-lib [æd'lɪb] vt, vi improviser ◆ n improvisation f ◆ adv: **ad lib** à volonté, à discrétion

administer [əd'mɪnɪstə*] vt administrer; (justice) rendre

administration [ədmɪnɪs'treɪʃən] n administration f; **the Administration** (US) le gouvernement

administrative [əd'mɪnɪstrətɪv] adj administratif(ive)

admiral ['ædmərəl] n amiral m

Admiralty ['ædmərəltɪ] n (BRIT: also: **Admiralty Board**) ministère m de la Marine

admire [əd'maɪə*] vt admirer

admission [əd'mɪʃən] n admission f; (to exhibition, night club etc) entrée f; (confession) aveu m; **"admission free", "free admission"** "entrée libre"; **by his own admission** de son propre aveu

admission charge n droits d'admission

admit [əd'mɪt] vt laisser entrer; admettre; (agree) reconnaître, admettre; **"children not admitted"** "entrée interdite aux enfants"; **this ticket admits two** ce billet est valable pour deux personnes; **I must admit that ...** je dois admettre or reconnaître que ...

▶ **admit of** vt fus admettre, permettre

▶ **admit to** vt fus reconnaître, avouer

admittance [əd'mɪtəns] n admission f, (droit m d')entrée f; **"no admittance"** "défense d'entrer"

admittedly [əd'mɪtɪdlɪ] adv il faut en convenir

ado [ə'du:] n: **without (any) more ado** sans plus de cérémonies

adolescence [ædəu'lɛsns] n adolescence f

adolescent [ædəu'lɛsnt] adj, n adolescent/e

adopt [ə'dɔpt] vt adopter

adopted [ə'dɔptɪd] adj adoptif(ive), adopté(e)

adoption [ə'dɔpʃən] n adoption f

adore [ə'dɔ:ʳ] vt adorer

adorn [ə'dɔ:n] vt orner

Adriatic (Sea) [eɪdrɪ'ætɪk-] n Adriatique f

adrift [ə'drɪft] adv à la dérive; **to come adrift** (boat) aller à la dérive; (wire, rope, fastening etc) se défaire

adult ['ædʌlt] n adulte m/f

adultery [ə'dʌltərɪ] n adultère m

advance [ad'vɑ:ns] n avance f ♦ vt avancer ♦ vi s'avancer; **in advance** en avance, d'avance; **to make advances to sb** (gen) faire des propositions à qn; (amorously) faire des avances à qn

advanced [ad'vɑ:nst] adj avancé(e); (SCOL: studies) supérieur(e); **advanced in years** d'un âge avancé

advantage [ad'vɑ:ntɪdʒ] n (also TENNIS) avantage m; **to take advantage of** profiter de; **it's to our advantage** c'est notre intérêt; **it's to our advantage to ...** nous avons intérêt à ...

advent ['ædvənt] n avènement m, venue f; **Advent** (REL) avent m

adventure [ad'ventʃəʳ] n aventure f

adverb ['ædvɜ:b] n adverbe m

adverse ['ædvɜ:s] adj contraire, adverse; **adverse to** hostile à; **in adverse circumstances** dans l'adversité

advert ['ædvɜ:t] n abbr (BRIT) = **advertisement**

advertise ['ædvətaɪz] vi, vt faire de la publicité or de la réclame (pour); (in classified ads etc) mettre une annonce (pour vendre); **to advertise for** (staff) recruter par (voie d')annonce

advertisement [ad'vɜ:tɪsmənt] n (COMM) réclame f, publicité f; (in classified ads etc) annonce f

advertising ['ædvətaɪzɪŋ] n publicité f

advice [ad'vaɪs] n conseils mpl; (notification) avis m; **piece of advice** conseil; **to ask (sb) for advice** demander conseil (à qn); **to take legal advice** consulter un avocat

advisable [ad'vaɪzəbl] adj recommandable, indiqué(e)

advise [ad'vaɪz] vt conseiller; **to advise sb of sth** aviser or informer qn de qch; **to advise sb against sth** déconseiller qch à qn; **to advise sb against doing sth** conseiller à qn de ne pas faire qch; **you would be well/ill advised to go** vous feriez mieux d'y aller/de ne pas y aller, vous auriez intérêt à y aller/à ne pas y aller

adviser, advisor [ad'vaɪzəʳ] n conseiller/ère

advisory [ad'vaɪzərɪ] adj consultatif(ive); **in an advisory capacity** à titre consultatif

advocate n ['ædvəkɪt] (upholder) défenseur m, avocat/e ♦ vt ['ædvəkeɪt] recommander, prôner; **to be an advocate of** être partisan(e) de

Aegean (Sea) [i:'dʒi:ən-] n mer f Égée

aerial ['ɛərɪəl] n antenne f ♦ adj aérien(ne)

aerobics [ɛə'rəʊbɪks] n aérobic m

aeroplane ['ɛərəpleɪn] n (BRIT) avion m

aerosol ['ɛərəsɔl] n aérosol m

aesthetic [ɪs'θetɪk] adj esthétique

afar [ə'fɑ:ʳ] adv: **from afar** de loin

affair [ə'fɛəʳ] n affaire f; (also: **love affair**) liaison f; aventure f; **affairs** (business) affaires

affect [ə'fekt] vt affecter

affected [ə'fektɪd] adj affecté(e)

affection [ə'fekʃən] n affection f

affectionate [ə'fekʃənɪt] adj affectueux(euse)

affinity [ə'fɪnɪtɪ] n affinité f

afflict [ə'flɪkt] vt affliger

affluence ['æfluəns] n aisance f, opulence f

affluent ['æfluənt] adj opulent(e); (person) dans l'aisance, riche; **the affluent society** la société d'abondance

afford [ə'fɔ:d] vt (goods etc) avoir les moyens d'acheter or d'entretenir; (behaviour) se permettre; (provide) fournir, procurer; **can we afford a car?** avons-nous de quoi acheter or les moyens d'acheter une voiture?; **I can't afford the time** je n'ai vraiment pas le temps

afloat [ə'fləut] adj à flot ♦ adv: **to stay afloat** surnager; **to keep/get a business afloat** maintenir à flot/lancer une affaire

afoot [ə'fut] adv: **there is something afoot** il se prépare quelque chose

afraid [ə'freɪd] adj effrayé(e); **to be afraid of** or **to** avoir peur de; **I am afraid that** je crains que + sub; **I'm afraid so/not** oui/non, malheureusement

Africa ['æfrɪkə] n Afrique f

African ['æfrɪkən] adj africain(e) ♦ n Africain/e

after ['ɑ:ftəʳ] prep, adv après ♦ conj après que, après avoir or être + pp; **after dinner** après (le) dîner; **the day after tomorrow** après demain; **quarter after two** (US) deux heures et quart; **what/who are you after?** que/qui cherchez-vous?; **the police are after him** la police est à ses trousses; **after you!** après vous!; **after all** après tout

after-effects ['ɑ:ftərɪfekts] npl (of disaster, radiation, drink etc) répercussions fpl; (of illness) séquelles fpl, suites fpl

aftermath ['ɑ:ftəmɑ:θ] n conséquences fpl; **in the aftermath of** dans les mois or années etc qui suivirent, au lendemain de

afternoon ['ɑ:ftə'nu:n] n après-midi m or f; **good afternoon!** bonjour!; (goodbye) au revoir!

afters ['ɑ:ftəz] n (BRIT col: dessert) dessert m

after-sales service [ɑ:ftə'seɪlz-] n service m après-vente, SAV m

after-shave (lotion) ['ɑ:ftəʃeɪv-] n lotion f après-rasage

aftersun ['ɑ:ftəsʌn] n après-soleil m inv

afterthought ['ɑ:ftəθɔ:t] n: **I had an afterthought** il m'est venu une idée après coup

afterwards ['ɑ:ftəwədz] adv après

again [ə'gen] adv de nouveau, encore une fois; **to begin/see again** recommencer/revoir; **not ... again** ne ... plus; **again and again** à plusieurs reprises; **he's opened it again** il l'a rouvert, il l'a de nouveau or l'a encore ouvert; **now and again** de temps à autre

against [ə'gɛnst] *prep* contre; **against a blue background** sur un fond bleu; **(as) against** (*BRIT*) contre

age [eɪdʒ] *n* âge *m* ♦ *vt*, *vi* vieillir; **what age is he?** quel âge a-t-il?; **he is 20 years of age** il a 20 ans; **under age** mineur(e); **to come of age** atteindre sa majorité; **it's been ages since** ça fait une éternité que ... ne

aged ['eɪdʒd] *adj* âgé(e); **aged 10** âgé de 10 ans; **the aged** ['eɪdʒɪd] *npl* les personnes âgées

age group *n* tranche *f* d'âge; **the 40 to 50 age group** la tranche d'âge des 40 à 50 ans

age limit *n* limite *f* d'âge

agency ['eɪdʒənsɪ] *n* agence *f*; **through** or **by the agency of** par l'entremise or l'action de

agenda [ə'dʒɛndə] *n* ordre *m* du jour; **on the agenda** à l'ordre du jour

agent ['eɪdʒənt] *n* agent *m*

aggravate ['ægrəveɪt] *vt* aggraver; (*annoy*) exaspérer, agacer

aggressive [ə'grɛsɪv] *adj* agressif(ive)

agitate ['ædʒɪteɪt] *vt* rendre inquiet(ète) or agité(e) ♦ *vi* faire de l'agitation (politique); **to agitate for** faire campagne pour

AGM *n abbr* = **annual general meeting**

ago [ə'gəʊ] *adv*: **2 days ago** il y a 2 jours; **not long ago** il n'y a pas longtemps; **as long ago as 1960** déjà en 1960; **how long ago?** il y a combien de temps (de cela)?

agony ['ægənɪ] *n* grande souffrance or angoisse; **to be in agony** souffrir le martyre

agree [ə'griː] *vt* (*price*) convenir de ♦ *vi*: **to agree (with)** (*person*) être d'accord (avec); (*statements etc*) concorder (avec); (*LING*) s'accorder (avec); **to agree to do** accepter de or consentir à faire; **to agree to sth** consentir à qch; **to agree that** (*admit*) convenir or reconnaître que; **it was agreed that ...** il a été convenu que ...; **they agree on this** ils sont d'accord sur ce point; **they agreed on going/a price** ils se mirent d'accord pour y aller/sur un prix; **garlic doesn't agree with me** je ne supporte pas l'ail

agreeable [ə'griːəbl] *adj* (*pleasant*) agréable; (*willing*) consentant(e), d'accord; **are you agreeable to this?** est-ce que vous êtes d'accord?

agreed [ə'griːd] *adj* (*time, place*) convenu(e); **to be agreed** être d'accord

agreement [ə'griːmənt] *n* accord *m*; **in agreement** d'accord; **by mutual agreement** d'un commun accord

agricultural [ægrɪ'kʌltʃərəl] *adj* agricole

agriculture ['ægrɪkʌltʃə*] *n* agriculture *f*

aground [ə'graʊnd] *adv*: **to run aground** s'échouer

ahead [ə'hɛd] *adv* en avant; devant; **go right** or

straight ahead allez tout droit; **go ahead!** (*fig*) allez-y!; **ahead of** devant; (*fig: schedule etc*) en avance sur; **ahead of time** en avance; **they were (right) ahead of us** ils nous précédaient (de peu), ils étaient (juste) devant nous

aid [eɪd] *n* aide *f* ♦ *vt* aider; **with the aid of** avec l'aide de; **in aid of** en faveur de; **to aid and abet** (*LAW*) se faire le complice de

aide [eɪd] *n* (*person*) assistant/e

AIDS [eɪdz] *n abbr* (= acquired immune (or immuno-)deficiency syndrome) SIDA *m*

aim [eɪm] *n* but *m* ♦ *vt*: **to aim sth at** (*gun, camera*) braquer or pointer qch sur, diriger qch contre; (*missile*) pointer qch vers or sur; (*remark, blow*) destiner or adresser qch à ♦ *vi* (*also*: **to take aim**) viser; **to aim at** viser; (*fig*) viser (à); avoir pour but or ambition; **to aim to do** avoir l'intention de faire

aimless ['eɪmlɪs] *adj* sans but

ain't [eɪnt] (*col*) = **am not, aren't, isn't**

air [ɛə*] *n* air *m* ♦ *vt* aérer; (*idea, grievance, views*) mettre sur le tapis; (*knowledge*) faire étalage de ♦ *cpd* (*currents, attack etc*) aérien(ne); **by air** par avion; **to be on the air** (*RADIO, TV: programme*) être diffusé(e); (: *station*) émettre

airbed ['ɛəbɛd] *n* (*BRIT*) matelas *m* pneumatique

air-conditioned ['ɛəkən'dɪʃənd] *adj* climatisé(e), à air conditionné

air conditioning [-kən'dɪʃnɪŋ] *n* climatisation *f*

aircraft ['ɛəkrɑːft] *n* (*pl inv*) avion *m*

aircraft carrier *n* porte-avions *m inv*

airfield ['ɛəfiːld] *n* terrain *m* d'aviation

Air Force *n* Armée *f* de l'air

air freshener [-'frɛʃnə*] *m* désodorisant *m*

airgun ['ɛəgʌn] *n* fusil *m* à air comprimé

air hostess (*BRIT*) hôtesse *f* de l'air

air letter *n* (*BRIT*) aérogramme *m*

airlift ['ɛəlɪft] *n* pont aérien

airline ['ɛəlaɪn] *n* ligne aérienne, compagnie aérienne

airliner ['ɛəlaɪnə*] *n* avion *m* de ligne

airmail ['ɛəmeɪl] *n*: **by airmail** par avion

air mile *n* air mile *m*

airplane ['ɛəpleɪn] *n* (*US*) avion *m*

airport ['ɛəpɔːt] *n* aéroport *m*

air raid *n* attaque aérienne

airsick ['ɛəsɪk] *adj*: **to be airsick** avoir le mal de l'air

airtight ['ɛətaɪt] *adj* hermétique

air-traffic controller ['ɛətræfɪk-] *n* aiguilleur *m* du ciel

airy ['ɛərɪ] *adj* bien aéré(e); (*manners*) dégagé(e)

aisle [aɪl] *n* (*of church*) allée centrale; nef latérale; (*in theatre*) allée *f*; (*on plane*) couloir *m*

aisle seat *n* place *f* côté couloir

ajar [ə'dʒɑː*] *adj* entrouvert(e)

akin [ə'kɪn] *adj*: **akin to** semblable à, du même ordre que

alarm [əˈlɑːm] *n* alarme *f* ◆ *vt* alarmer

alarm call *n* coup *m* de fil pour réveiller

alarm clock *n* réveille-matin *m inv*, réveil *m*

alas [əˈlæs] *excl* hélas

album [ˈælbəm] *n* album *m*

alcohol [ˈælkəhɔl] *n* alcool *m*

alcohol-free [ˈælkəhɔlfriː] *adj* sans alcool

alcoholic [ælkəˈhɔlɪk] *adj, n* alcoolique (*m/f*)

ale [eɪl] *n* bière *f*

alert [əˈləːt] *adj* alerte, vif(vive); (*watchful*) vigilant(e) ◆ *n* alerte *f* ◆ *vt*: **to alert sb (to sth)** attirer l'attention de qn (sur qch); **to alert sb to the dangers of sth** avertir qn des dangers de qch; **on the alert** sur le qui-vive; (*MIL*) en état d'alerte

algebra [ˈældʒɪbrə] *n* algèbre *m*

Algeria [ælˈdʒɪərɪə] *n* Algérie *f*

alias [ˈeɪlɪəs] *adv* alias ◆ *n* faux nom, nom d'emprunt

alibi [ˈælɪbaɪ] *n* alibi *m*

alien [ˈeɪlɪən] *n* étranger/ère ◆ *adj*: **alien (to)** étranger(ère) (à)

alight [əˈlaɪt] *adj, adv* en feu ◆ *vi* mettre pied à terre; (*passenger*) descendre; (*bird*) se poser

alike [əˈlaɪk] *adj* semblable, pareil(le) ◆ *adv* de même; **to look alike** se ressembler

alimony [ˈælɪmənɪ] *n* (*payment*) pension *f* alimentaire

alive [əˈlaɪv] *adj* vivant(e); (*active*) plein(e) de vie; **alive with** grouillant(e) de; **alive to** sensible à

KEYWORD

all [ɔːl] *adj* (*singular*) tout(e); (*plural*) tous (toutes); **all day** toute la journée; **all night** toute la nuit; **all men** tous les hommes; **all five** tous les cinq; **all the food** toute la nourriture; **all the books** tous les livres; **all the time** tout le temps; **all his life** toute sa vie

◆ *pron* **1** tout; **I ate it all, I ate all of it** j'ai tout mangé; **all of us went** nous y sommes tous allés; **all of the boys went** tous les garçons y sont allés; **is that all?** c'est tout?; (*in shop*) ce sera tout? **2** (*in phrases*): **above all** surtout, par-dessus tout; **after all** après tout; **at all: not at all** (*in answer to question*) pas du tout; (*in answer to thanks*) je vous en prie!; **I'm not at all tired** je ne suis pas du tout fatigué(e); **anything at all will do** n'importe quoi fera l'affaire; **all in all** tout bien considéré, en fin de compte

◆ *adv*: **all alone** tout(e) seul(e); **it's not as hard as all that** ce n'est pas si difficile que ça; **all the more/the better** d'autant plus/mieux; **all but** presque, pratiquement; **to be all in** (*BRIT col*) être complètement à plat; **all out** *adv* à fond; **the score is 2 all** le score est de 2 partout

---

allege [əˈledʒ] *vt* alléguer, prétendre; **he is alleged to have said** il aurait dit

allegedly [əˈledʒɪdlɪ] *adv* à ce que l'on prétend,

paraît-il

allegiance [əˈliːdʒəns] *n* fidélité *f*, obéissance *f*

allergic [əˈləːdʒɪk] *adj*: **allergic to** allergique à

allergy [ˈælədʒɪ] *n* allergie *f*

alleviate [əˈliːvɪeɪt] *vt* soulager, adoucir

alley [ˈælɪ] *n* ruelle *f*; (*in garden*) allée *f*

alliance [əˈlaɪəns] *n* alliance *f*

allied [ˈælaɪd] *adj* allié(e)

all-in [ˈɔːlɪn] *adj, adv* (*BRIT: charge*) tout compris

all-night [ˈɔːlˈnaɪt] *adj* ouvert(e) *or* qui dure toute la nuit

allocate [ˈæləkeɪt] *vt* (*share out*) répartir, distribuer; (*duties*): **to allocate sth to** assigner *or* attribuer qch à; (*sum, time*): **to allocate sth to** allouer qch à; **to allocate sth for** affecter qch à

allot [əˈlɔt] *vt* (*share out*) répartir, distribuer; (*time*): **to allot sth to** allouer qch à; (*duties*): **to allot sth to** assigner qch à; **in the allotted time** dans le temps imparti

allotment [əˈlɔtmənt] *n* (*share*) part *f*; (*garden*) lopin *m* de terre (*loué à la municipalité*)

all-out [ˈɔːlaut] *adj* (*effort etc*) total(e)

allow [əˈlau] *vt* (*practice, behaviour*) permettre, autoriser; (*sum to spend etc*) accorder, allouer; (*sum, time estimated*) compter, prévoir; (*concede*): **to allow that** convenir que; **to allow sb to do** permettre à qn de faire, autoriser qn à faire; **he is allowed to ...** on lui permet de ...; **smoking is not allowed** il est interdit de fumer; **we must allow 3 days for the journey** il faut compter 3 jours pour le voyage

▶ **allow for** *vt fus* tenir compte de

allowance [əˈlauəns] *n* (*money received*) allocation *f*; (: *from parent etc*) subside *m*; (: *for expenses*) indemnité *f*; (*TAX*) somme *f* déductible du revenu imposable, abattement *m*; **to make allowances for** tenir compte de

alloy [ˈælɔɪ] *n* alliage *m*

all right *adv* (*feel, work*) bien; (*as answer*) d'accord

all-rounder [ɔːlˈraundə*] *n* (*BRIT*): **to be a good all-rounder** être doué(e) en tout

all-time [ˈɔːlˈtaɪm] *adj* (*record*) sans précédent, absolu(e)

ally *n* [ˈælaɪ] allié *m* ◆ *vt* [əˈlaɪ]: **to ally o.s. with** s'allier avec

almighty [ɔːlˈmaɪtɪ] *adj* tout-puissant

almond [ˈɑːmənd] *n* amande *f*

almost [ˈɔːlməust] *adv* presque; **he almost fell** il a failli tomber

alone [əˈləun] *adj, adv* seul(e); **to leave sb alone** laisser qn tranquille; **to leave sth alone** ne pas toucher à qch; **let alone ...** sans parler de ...; encore moins ...

along [əˈlɔŋ] *prep* le long de ◆ *adv*: **is he coming along?** vient-il avec nous?; **he was hopping/limping along** il venait *or* avançait en sautillant/

boitant; **along with** avec, en plus de; (*person*) en compagnie de

alongside [ə'lɒŋ'saɪd] *prep* le long de; au côté de ◆ *adv* bord à bord; côte à côte; **we brought our boat alongside** (*of a pier, shore etc*) nous avons accosté

aloof [ə'luːf] *adj, adv* à distance, à l'écart; **to stand aloof** se tenir à l'écart *or* à distance

aloud [ə'laud] *adv* à haute voix

alphabet ['ælfəbɛt] *n* alphabet *m*

alphabetical [ælfə'bɛtɪkl] *adj* alphabétique; **in alphabetical order** par ordre alphabétique

alpine ['ælpaɪn] *adj* alpin(e), alpestre; **alpine hut** cabane *f or* refuge *m* de montagne; **alpine pasture** pâturage *m* (de montagne); **alpine skiing** ski alpin

Alps [ælps] *npl*: **the Alps** les Alpes *fpl*

already [ɔːl'rɛdɪ] *adv* déjà

alright ['ɔːl'raɪt] *adv* (*BRIT*) = **all right**

Alsatian [æl'seɪʃən] *adj* alsacien(ne), d'Alsace ◆ *n* Alsacien/ne; (*BRIT: dog*) berger allemand

also ['ɔːlsəu] *adv* aussi

altar ['ɔːltə*] *n* autel *m*

alter ['ɔːltə*] *vt, vi* changer, modifier

alternate *adj* [ɔl'tɜːnɪt] alterné(e), alternant(e), alternatif(ive) ◆ *vi* ['ɔltɜːneɪt] alterner; **on alternate days** un jour sur deux, tous les deux jours

alternative [ɔl'tɜːnətɪv] *adj* (*solutions*) interchangeable, possible; (*solution*) autre, de remplacement; (*energy*) doux(douce); (*society*) parallèle ◆ *n* (*choice*) alternative *f*; (*other possibility*) autre possibilité *f*

alternatively [ɔl'tɜːnətɪvlɪ] *adv*: **alternatively one could** une autre *or* l'autre solution serait de

alternator ['ɔltɜːneɪtə*] *n* (*AUT*) alternateur *m*

although [ɔːl'ðəu] *conj* bien que + *sub*

altitude ['æltɪtjuːd] *n* altitude *f*

alto ['æltəu] *n* (*female*) contralto *m*; (*male*) haute-contre *f*

altogether [ɔːltə'gɛðə*] *adv* entièrement, tout à fait; (*on the whole*) tout compte fait; (*in all*) en tout; **how much is that altogether?** ça fait combien en tout?

aluminium [ælju'mɪnɪəm], (*US*) **aluminum** [ə'luːmɪnəm] *n* aluminium *m*

always ['ɔːlweɪz] *adv* toujours

Alzheimer's disease ['æltshaɪməz-] *n* maladie *f* d'Alzheimer

AM *abbr* = amplitude modulation ◆ *n abbr* (= Assembly Member) député *m* au Parlement gallois

am [æm] *vb see* **be**

a.m. *adv abbr* (= ante meridiem) du matin

amalgamate [ə'mælgəmeɪt] *vt, vi* fusionner

amateur ['æmətə*] *n* amateur *m* ◆ *adj* (*SPORT*) amateur *inv*; **amateur dramatics** le théâtre amateur

amateurish ['æmətərɪʃ] *adj* (*pej*) d'amateur, un peu amateur

amaze [ə'meɪz] *vt* surprendre, étonner; **to be amazed (at)** être surpris *or* étonné (de)

amazement [ə'meɪzmənt] *n* surprise *f*, étonnement *m*

amazing [ə'meɪzɪŋ] *adj* étonnant(e), incroyable; (*bargain, offer*) exceptionnel(le)

ambassador [æm'bæsədə*] *n* ambassadeur *m*

amber ['æmbə*] *n* ambre *m*; **at amber** (*BRIT AUT*) à l'orange

ambiguous [æm'bɪgjuəs] *adj* ambigu(ë)

ambition [æm'bɪʃən] *n* ambition *f*

ambitious [æm'bɪʃəs] *adj* ambitieux(euse)

ambulance ['æmbjuləns] *n* ambulance *f*

ambush ['æmbuʃ] *n* embuscade *f* ◆ *vt* tendre une embuscade à

amenable [ə'miːnəbl] *adj*: **amenable to** (*advice etc*) disposé(e) à écouter *or* suivre; **amenable to the law** responsable devant la loi

amend [ə'mɛnd] *vt* (*law*) amender; (*text*) corriger; (*habits*) réformer ◆ *vi* s'amender, se corriger; **to make amends** réparer ses torts, faire amende honorable

amenities [ə'miːnɪtɪz] *npl* aménagements *mpl*, équipements *mpl*

America [ə'mɛrɪkə] *n* Amérique *f*

American [ə'mɛrɪkən] *adj* américain(e) ◆ *n* Américain/e

amiable ['eɪmɪəbl] *adj* aimable, affable

amicable ['æmɪkəbl] *adj* amical(e)

amid(st) [ə'mɪd(st)] *prep* parmi, au milieu de

amiss [ə'mɪs] *adj, adv*: **there's something amiss** il y a quelque chose qui ne va pas *or* qui cloche; **to take sth amiss** prendre qch mal *or* à travers

ammonia [ə'məunɪə] *n* (*gas*) ammoniac *m*; (*liquid*) ammoniaque *f*

ammunition [æmju'nɪʃən] *n* munitions *fpl*; (*fig*) arguments *mpl*

amok [ə'mɔk] *adv*: **to run amok** être pris(e) d'un accès de folie furieuse

among(st) [ə'mʌŋ(st)] *prep* parmi, entre

amorous ['æmərəs] *adj* amoureux(euse)

amount [ə'maunt] *n* (*sum of money*) somme *f*; (*total*) montant *m*; (*quantity*) quantité *f*; nombre *m* ◆ *vi*: **to amount to** (*total*) s'élever à; (*be same as*) équivaloir à, revenir à; **this amounts to a refusal** cela équivaut à un refus; **the total amount** (*of money*) le montant total

amp(ere) ['æmp(ɛə*)] *n* ampère *m*; **a 13 amp plug** une fiche de 13 A

ample ['æmpl] *adj* ample, spacieux(euse); (*enough*): **this is ample** c'est largement suffisant; **to have ample time/room** avoir bien assez de temps/place, avoir largement le temps/la place

amplifier ['æmplɪfaɪə*] *n* amplificateur *m*

amuse [ə'mjuːz] *vt* amuser; **to amuse o.s. with**

sth/by doing sth se divertir avec qch/à faire qch; **to be amused** at être amusé par; **he was not amused** il n'a pas apprécié

amusement [əˈmjuːzmənt] n amusement m

amusement arcade n salle f de jeu

amusement park n parc m d'attractions

an [æn, ən, n] indef art see **a**

anaemic [əˈniːmɪk] adj anémique

anaesthetic [ænɪsˈθetɪk] adj, n anesthésique (m); **under the anaesthetic** sous anesthésie; **local/general anaesthetic** anesthésie locale/générale

analog(ue) [ˈænəlɔɡ] adj (watch, computer) analogique

analyse [ˈænəlaɪz] vt (BRIT) analyser

analysis, pl **analyses** [əˈnæləsɪs, -siːz] n analyse f; **in the final analysis** en dernière analyse

analyst [ˈænəlɪst] n (political analyst etc) analyste m/f; (US) psychanalyste m/f

analyze [ˈænəlaɪz] vt (US) = **analyse**

anarchist [ˈænəkɪst] adj, n anarchiste (m/f)

anarchy [ˈænəkɪ] n anarchie f

anatomy [əˈnætəmɪ] n anatomie f

ancestor [ˈænsɪstə*] n ancêtre m, aïeul m

anchor [ˈæŋkə*] n ancre f ♦ vi (also: **to drop anchor**) jeter l'ancre, mouiller ♦ vt mettre à l'ancre

anchovy [ˈæntʃəvɪ] n anchois m

ancient [ˈeɪnʃənt] adj ancien(ne), antique; (fig) d'un âge vénérable, antique; **ancient monument** m historique

ancillary [ænˈsɪlərɪ] adj auxiliaire

and [ænd] conj et; **and so on** et ainsi de suite; **try and come** tâchez de venir; **come and sit here** venez vous asseoir ici; **better and better** de mieux en mieux; **more and more** de plus en plus

anew [əˈnjuː] adv à nouveau

angel [ˈeɪndʒəl] n ange m

anger [ˈæŋɡə*] n colère f ♦ vt mettre en colère, irriter

angina [ænˈdʒaɪnə] n angine f de poitrine

angle [ˈæŋɡl] n angle m ♦ vi: **to angle for** (trout) pêcher; (compliments) chercher, quêter; **from their angle** de leur point de vue

angler [ˈæŋɡlə*] n pêcheur/euse à la ligne

Anglican [ˈæŋɡlɪkən] adj, n anglican-e

angling [ˈæŋɡlɪŋ] n pêche f à la ligne

Anglo- [ˈæŋɡləu] prefix anglo(-)

angrily [ˈæŋɡrɪlɪ] adv avec colère

angry [ˈæŋɡrɪ] adj en colère, furieux(euse); **to be angry with sb/at sth** être furieux contre qn/de qch; **to get angry** se fâcher, se mettre en colère; **to make sb angry** mettre qn en colère

anguish [ˈæŋɡwɪʃ] n angoisse f

animal [ˈænɪməl] n animal m ♦ adj animal(e)

animate vt [ˈænɪmeɪt] animer ♦ adj [ˈænɪmɪt] animé(e), vivant(e)

animated [ˈænɪmeɪtɪd] adj animé(e)

aniseed [ˈænɪsiːd] n anis m

ankle [ˈæŋkl] n cheville f

ankle socks npl socquettes fpl

annex n [ˈæneks] (BRIT: also: **annexe**) annexe f ♦ vt [əˈneks] annexer

anniversary [ænɪˈvɜːsərɪ] n anniversaire m

announce [əˈnauns] vt annoncer; (birth, death) faire part de; **he announced that he wasn't going** il a déclaré qu'il n'irait pas

announcement [əˈnaunsmənt] n annonce f; (for births etc: in newspaper) avis m de faire-part; (: letter, card) faire-part m; **I'd like to make an announcement** j'ai une communication à faire

announcer [əˈnaunsə*] n (RADIO, TV: between programmes) speaker/ine; (: in a programme) présentateur/trice

annoy [əˈnɔɪ] vt agacer, ennuyer, contrarier; **to be annoyed (at sth/with sb)** être en colère or irrité (contre qch/qn); **don't get annoyed!** ne vous fâchez pas!

annoyance [əˈnɔɪəns] n mécontentement m, contrariété f

annoying [əˈnɔɪɪŋ] adj ennuyeux(euse), agaçant(e), contrariant(e)

annual [ˈænjuəl] adj annuel(le) ♦ n (BOT) plante annuelle; (book) album m

annul [əˈnʌl] vt annuler; (law) abroger

anonymous [əˈnɔnɪməs] adj anonyme; **to remain anonymous** garder l'anonymat

anorak [ˈænəræk] n anorak m

anorexia [ænəˈreksɪə] n (also: **anorexia nervosa**) anorexie f

another [əˈnʌðə*] adj: **another book** (one more) un autre livre, encore un livre, un livre de plus; (a different one) un autre livre; **another drink?** encore un verre?; **in another 5 years** dans 5 ans ♦ pron un(e) autre, encore un(e), un(e) de plus; see also **one**

answer [ˈɑːnsə*] n réponse f; (to problem) solution f ♦ vi répondre ♦ vt (reply to) répondre à; (problem) résoudre; (prayer) exaucer; **to answer the phone** répondre (au téléphone); **in answer to your letter** suite à or en réponse à votre lettre; **to answer the bell** or **the door** aller or venir ouvrir (la porte)

▶ **answer back** vi répondre, répliquer

▶ **answer for** vt fus répondre de, se porter garant de; (crime, one's actions) répondre de

▶ **answer to** vt fus (description) répondre or correspondre à

answerable [ˈɑːnsərəbl] adj: **answerable (to sb/for sth)** responsable (devant qn/de qch); **I am answerable to no-one** je n'ai de comptes à rendre à personne

answering machine [ˈɑːnsərɪŋ-] n répondeur m

ant [ænt] n fourmi f

antagonism [ænˈtæɡənɪzəm] n antagonisme m

antagonize [æn'tægənaɪz] *vt* éveiller l'hostilité de, contrarier

Antarctic [ænt'ɑːktɪk] *adj* antarctique, austral(e) ◆ *n*: **the Antarctic** l'Antarctique *m*

antenatal ['æntɪ'neɪtl] *adj* prénatal(e)

antenatal clinic *n* service *m* de consultation prénatale

anthem ['ænθəm] *n* motet *m*; **national anthem** hymne national

anti- ['æntɪ] *prefix* anti-

anti-aircraft ['æntɪ'ɛəkrɑːft] *adj* antiaérien(ne)

antibiotic ['æntɪbaɪ'ɒtɪk] *adj*, *n* antibiotique (*m*)

antibody ['æntɪbɒdɪ] *n* anticorps *m*

anticipate [æn'tɪsɪpeɪt] *vt* s'attendre à, prévoir; (*wishes, request*) aller au devant de, devancer; **this is worse than I anticipated** c'est pire que je ne pensais; **as anticipated** comme prévu

anticipation [æntɪsɪ'peɪʃən] *n* attente *f*; **thanking you in anticipation** en vous remerciant d'avance, avec mes remerciements anticipés

anticlimax ['æntɪ'klaɪmæks] *n* réalisation décevante d'un événement que l'on escomptait important, intéressant etc

anticlockwise ['æntɪ'klɒkwaɪz] *adj* dans le sens inverse des aiguilles d'une montre

antics ['æntɪks] *npl* singeries *fpl*

antidepressant ['æntɪdɪ'presnt] *n* antidépresseur *m*

antifreeze ['æntɪfriːz] *n* antigel *m*

antihistamine [æntɪ'hɪstəmɪn] *n* antihistaminique *m*

antiquated ['æntɪkweɪtɪd] *adj* vieilli(e), suranné(e), vieillot(te)

antique [æn'tiːk] *n* objet *m* d'art ancien, meuble ancien *or* d'époque, antiquité *f* ◆ *adj* ancien(ne); (*pre-mediaeval*) antique

antique dealer *n* antiquaire *m/f*

antique shop *n* magasin *m* d'antiquités

anti-Semitism ['æntɪ'semɪtɪzəm] *n* antisémitisme *m*

antiseptic [æntɪ'septɪk] *adj*, *n* antiseptique (*m*)

antisocial ['æntɪ'səʊʃəl] *adj* peu liant(e), insociable; (*against society*) antisocial(e)

antlers ['æntləz] *npl* bois *mpl*, ramure *f*

anvil ['ænvɪl] *n* enclume *f*

anxiety [æŋ'zaɪətɪ] *n* anxiété *f*; (*keenness*): **anxiety to do** grand désir *or* impatience *f* de faire

anxious ['æŋkʃəs] *adj* anxieux(euse), (très) inquiet(ète); (*keen*): **anxious to do/that** qui tient beaucoup à faire/à ce que; impatient(e) de faire/que; **I'm very anxious about you** je me fais beaucoup de souci pour toi

┌─────────────────
│ KEYWORD
└─────────────────

any ['enɪ] *adj* **1** (*in questions etc: singular*) du, de l', de la; (*in questions etc: plural*) des; **have you any butter/children/ink?** avez-vous du beurre/des enfants/de l'encre?

2 (*with negative*) de, d'; **I haven't any money/**

books je n'ai pas d'argent/de livres; **without any difficulty** sans la moindre difficulté

3 (*no matter which*) n'importe quel(le), quelconque; (*each and every*) tout(e), chaque; **choose any book you like** vous pouvez choisir n'importe quel livre

4 (*in phrases*): **in any case** de toute façon; **any day now** d'un jour à l'autre; **at any moment** à tout moment, d'un instant à l'autre; **at any rate** en tout cas

◆ *pron* **1** (*in questions etc*) en; **have you got any?** est-ce que vous en avez?; **can any of you sing?** est-ce que parmi vous il y en a qui savent chanter?

2 (*with negative*) en; **I haven't any (of them)** je n'en ai pas, je n'en ai aucun

3 (*no matter which one(s)*) n'importe lequel (*or* laquelle); (*anybody*) n'importe qui; **take any of those books (you like)** vous pouvez prendre n'importe lequel de ces livres

◆ *adv* **1** (*in questions etc*): **do you want any more soup/sandwiches?** voulez-vous encore de la soupe/des sandwichs?; **are you feeling any better?** est-ce que vous vous sentez mieux?

2 (*with negative*): **I can't hear him any more** je ne l'entends plus; **don't wait any longer** n'attendez pas plus longtemps

└─────────────────────────

anybody ['enɪbɒdɪ] *pron* n'importe qui; (*in interrogative sentences*) quelqu'un; (*in negative sentences*): **I don't see anybody** je ne vois personne

anyhow ['enɪhaʊ] *adv* quoi qu'il en soit; (*haphazardly*) n'importe comment; **I shall go anyhow** j'irai de toute façon

anyone ['enɪwʌn] *pron* = **anybody**

anything ['enɪθɪŋ] *pron* n'importe quoi; (*in interrogative sentences*) quelque chose; (*in negative sentences*): **I don't want anything** je ne veux rien; **anything else?** (*in shop*) et avec ça?; **it can cost anything between £15 and £20** (*BRIT*) ça peut coûter dans les 15 à 20 livres

anyway ['enɪweɪ] *adv* de toute façon

anywhere ['enɪwɛə*] *adv* n'importe où; (*in interrogative sentences*) quelque part; (*in negative sentences*): **I don't see him anywhere** je ne le vois nulle part; **anywhere in the world** n'importe où dans le monde

apart [ə'pɑːt] *adv* (*to one side*) à part; de côté; à l'écart; (*separately*) séparément; **10 miles/a long way apart** à 10 milles/très éloignés l'un de l'autre; **they are living apart** ils sont séparés; **apart from** *prep* à part, excepté

apartheid [ə'pɑːteɪt] *n* apartheid *m*

apartment [ə'pɑːtmənt] *n* (*US*) appartement *m*, logement *m*

apartment building *n* (*US*) immeuble *m*; maison divisée en appartements

ape [eɪp] *n* (grand) singe ◆ *vt* singer

apéritif [ə'perɪtiːf] *n* apéritif *m*

aperture ['æpətʃjuə*] *n* orifice *m*, ouverture *f*; (*PHOT*) ouverture (du diaphragme)

APEX ['eɪpeks] *n abbr* (*AVIAT*: = advance purchase excursion) APEX *m*

apologetic [əpɒlə'dʒetɪk] *adj* (*tone, letter*) d'excuse; **to be very apologetic about** s'excuser vivement de

apologize [ə'pɒlədʒaɪz] *vi*: **to apologize (for sth to sb)** s'excuser (de qch auprès de qn), présenter des excuses (à qn pour qch)

apology [ə'pɒlədʒɪ] *n* excuses *fpl*; **to send one's apologies** envoyer une lettre *or* un mot d'excuse, s'excuser (de ne pas pouvoir venir); **please accept my apologies** vous voudrez bien m'excuser

apostle [ə'pɒsl] *n* apôtre *m*

apostrophe [ə'pɒstrəfɪ] *n* apostrophe *f*

appalling [ə'pɔ:lɪŋ] *adj* épouvantable; (*stupidity*) consternant(e); **she's an appalling cook** c'est une très mauvaise cuisinière

apparatus [æpə'reɪtəs] *n* appareil *m*, dispositif *m*; (*in gymnasium*) agrès *mpl*

apparel [ə'pærl] *n* (*US*) habillement *m*, confection *f*

apparent [ə'pærənt] *adj* apparent(e); **it is apparent that** il est évident que

apparently [ə'pærəntlɪ] *adv* apparemment

appeal [ə'pi:l] *vi* (*LAW*) faire *or* interjeter appel ♦ *n* (*LAW*) appel *m*; (*request*) appel *m*, prière *f*; (*charm*) attrait *m*, charme *m*; **to appeal for** demander (instamment); implorer; **to appeal to** (*person*) faire appel à; (*thing*) plaire à; **to appeal to sb for mercy** implorer la pitié de qn, prier *or* adjurer qn d'avoir pitié; **it doesn't appeal to me** cela ne m'attire pas; **right of appeal** droit *m* de recours

appealing [ə'pi:lɪŋ] *adj* (*nice*) attrayant(e); (*touching*) attendrissant(e)

appear [ə'pɪə*] *vi* apparaître, se montrer; (*LAW*) comparaître; (*publication*) paraître, sortir, être publié(e); (*seem*) paraître, sembler; **it would appear that** il semble que; **to appear in Hamlet** jouer dans Hamlet; **to appear on TV** passer à la télé

appearance [ə'pɪərəns] *n* apparition *f*; parution *f*; (*look, aspect*) apparence *f*, aspect *m*; **to put in** *or* **make an appearance** faire acte de présence; (*THEAT*) **by order of appearance** par ordre d'entrée en scène; **to keep up appearances** sauver les apparences; **to all appearances** selon toute apparence

appease [ə'pi:z] *vt* apaiser, calmer

appendicitis [əpendɪ'saɪtɪs] *n* appendicite *f*

appendix, *pl* **appendices** [ə'pendɪks, -si:z] *n* appendice *m*; **to have one's appendix out** se faire opérer de l'appendicite

appetite ['æpɪtaɪt] *n* appétit *m*; **that walk has given me an appetite** cette promenade m'a ouvert l'appétit

appetizer ['æpɪtaɪzə*] *n* (*food*) amuse-gueule *m*;

(*drink*) apéritif *m*

applaud [ə'plɔ:d] *vt*, *vi* applaudir

applause [ə'plɔ:z] *n* applaudissements *mpl*

apple ['æpl] *n* pomme *f*; (*also*: **apple tree**) pommier *m*; **it's the apple of my eye** j'y tiens comme à la prunelle de mes yeux

appliance [ə'plaɪəns] *n* appareil *m*; **electrical appliances** l'électroménager *m*

applicable [ə'plɪkəbl] *adj* applicable; **the law is applicable from January** la loi entre en vigueur au mois de janvier; **to be applicable to** valoir pour

applicant ['æplɪkənt] *n*: **applicant (for)**; (*ADMIN: for benefit etc*) demandeur/euse (de); (*for post*) candidat/e (à)

application [æplɪ'keɪʃən] *n* application *f*; (*for a job, a grant etc*) demande *f*; candidature *f*; **on application** sur demande

application form *n* formulaire *m* de demande

applied [ə'plaɪd] *adj* appliqué(e); **applied arts** *npl* arts décoratifs

apply [ə'plaɪ] *vt*: **to apply (to)** (*paint, ointment*) appliquer (sur); (*theory, technique*) appliquer (à) ♦ *vi*: **to apply to** (*ask*) s'adresser à; (*be suitable for, relevant to*) s'appliquer à, être valable pour; **to apply (for)** (*permit, grant*) faire une demande (en vue d'obtenir); (*job*) poser sa candidature (pour), faire une demande d'emploi (concernant); **to apply the brakes** actionner les freins, freiner; **to apply o.s. to** s'appliquer à

appoint [ə'pɔɪnt] *vt* nommer, engager; (*date, place*) fixer, désigner

appointed [ə'pɔɪntɪd] *adj*: **at the appointed time** à l'heure dite

appointment [ə'pɔɪntmənt] *n* (*to post*) nomination *f*; (*arrangement to meet*) rendez-vous *m*; **to make an appointment (with)** prendre rendez-vous (avec); **"appointments (vacant)"** (*PRESS*) "offres d'emploi"; **by appointment** sur rendez-vous

appraisal [ə'preɪzl] *n* évaluation *f*

appreciate [ə'pri:ʃɪeɪt] *vt* (*like*) apprécier, faire cas de; (*be grateful for*) être reconnaissant(e) de; (*assess*) évaluer; (*be aware of*) comprendre, se rendre compte de ♦ *vi* (*FINANCE*) prendre de la valeur; **I appreciate your help** je vous remercie pour votre aide

appreciation [əpri:ʃɪ'eɪʃən] *n* appréciation *f*; (*gratitude*) reconnaissance *f*; (*FINANCE*) hausse *f*, valorisation *f*

appreciative [ə'pri:ʃɪətɪv] *adj* (*person*) sensible; (*comment*) élogieux(euse)

apprehensive [æprɪ'hensɪv] *adj* inquiet(ète), appréhensif(ive)

apprentice [ə'prentɪs] *n* apprenti *m* ♦ *vt*: **to be apprenticed to** être en apprentissage chez

apprenticeship [ə'prentɪsʃɪp] *n* apprentissage *m*; **to serve one's apprenticeship** faire son apprentissage

approach [ə'prəʊtʃ] *vi* approcher ♦ *vt* (*come near*) approcher de; (*ask, apply to*) s'adresser à; (*subject, passer-by*) aborder ♦ *n* approche *f*; accès *m*, abord *m*; démarche *f* (*auprès de qn*); démarche (*intellectuelle*) **to approach sb about sth** aller *or* venir voir qn pour qch

approachable [ə'prəʊtʃəbl] *adj* accessible

appropriate *vt* [ə'prəʊprieit] (*take*) s'approprier; (*allot*): **to appropriate sth for** affecter qch à ♦ *adj* [ə'prəʊpriɪt] qui convient, approprié(e); (*timely*) opportun(e); **appropriate for** *or* **to** approprié à; **it would not be appropriate for me to comment** il ne me serait pas approprié de commenter

approval [ə'pruːvəl] *n* approbation *f*; **to meet with sb's approval** (*proposal etc*) recueillir l'assentiment de qn; **on approval** (*COMM*) à l'examen

approve [ə'pruːv] *vt* approuver

▶ **approve of** *vt fus* approuver

approximate *adj* [ə'prɒksɪmɪt] approximatif(ive) ♦ *vt* [ə'prɒksɪmeit] se rapprocher de; être proche de

approximately [ə'prɒksɪmətlɪ] *adv* approximativement

apricot ['eɪprɪkɒt] *n* abricot *m*

April ['eɪprəl] *n* avril *m*; **April fool!** poisson d'avril!; *for phrases see also* **July**

April Fools' Day *n* le premier avril; *voir encadré*

apron ['eɪprən] *n* tablier *m*; (*AVIAT*) aire *f* de stationnement

apt [æpt] *adj* (*suitable*) approprié(e); (*able*): **apt (at)** doué(e) (pour); apte (à); (*likely*): **apt to do** susceptible de faire; ayant tendance à faire

Aquarius [ə'kweərɪəs] *n* le Verseau; **to be Aquarius** être du Verseau

Arab ['ærəb] *n* Arabe *m/f* ♦ *adj* arabe

Arabian [ə'reɪbɪən] *adj* arabe

Arabic ['ærəbɪk] *adj, n* arabe (*m*)

arbitrary ['ɑːbɪtrərɪ] *adj* arbitraire

arbitration [ɑːbɪ'treɪʃən] *n* arbitrage *m*; **the dispute went to arbitration** le litige a été soumis à arbitrage

arcade [ɑː'keɪd] *n* arcade *f*; (*passage with shops*) passage *m*, galerie *f*

arch [ɑːtʃ] *n* arche *f*; (*of foot*) cambrure *f*, voûte *f* plantaire ♦ *vt* arquer, cambrer ♦ *adj* mali-

cieux(euse) ♦ *prefix*: **arch(-)** achevé(e); par excellence; **pointed arch** ogive *f*

archaeologist [ɑːkɪ'ɒlədʒɪst] *n* archéologue *m/f*

archaeology [ɑːkɪ'ɒlədʒɪ] *n* archéologie *f*

archbishop [ɑːtʃ'bɪʃəp] *n* archevêque *m*

archeology *etc* [ɑːkɪ'ɒlədʒɪ] (*US*) = **archaeology** *etc*

archery ['ɑːtʃərɪ] *n* tir *m* à l'arc

architect ['ɑːkɪtekt] *n* architecte *m*

architecture ['ɑːkɪtektʃə*] *n* architecture *f*

archives ['ɑːkaɪvz] *npl* archives *fpl*

Arctic ['ɑːktɪk] *adj* arctique ♦ *n*: **the Arctic** l'Arctique *m*

ardent ['ɑːdənt] *adj* fervent(e)

are [ɑː*] *vb see* **be**

area ['eərɪə] *n* (*GEOM*) superficie *f*; (*zone*) région *f*; (: *smaller*) secteur *m*; **dining area** coin *m* salle à manger; **the London area** la région Londonienne

area code *n* (*TEL*) indicatif *m* de zone

aren't [ɑːnt] = **are not**

Argentina [ɑːdʒən'tiːnə] *n* Argentine *f*

Argentinian [ɑːdʒən'tɪnɪən] *adj* argentin(e) ♦ *n* Argentin/e

arguably ['ɑːgjuəblɪ] *adv*: **it is arguably ...** on peut soutenir que c'est ...

argue ['ɑːgjuː] *vi* (*quarrel*) se disputer; (*reason*) argumenter ♦ *vt* (*debate: case, matter*) débattre; **to argue about sth** se disputer (avec qn) au sujet de qch; **to argue that** objecter *or* alléguer que, donner comme argument que

argument ['ɑːgjʊmənt] *n* (*reasons*) argument *m*; (*quarrel*) dispute *f*, discussion *f*; (*debate*) discussion, controverse *f*; **argument for/against** argument pour/contre

argumentative [ɑːgju'mentətɪv] *adj* ergoteur(euse), raisonneur(euse)

Aries ['eərɪz] *n* le Bélier; **to be Aries** être du Bélier

arise, *pt* **arose**, *pp* **arisen** [ə'raɪz, ə'rəʊz, ə'rɪzn] *vi* survenir, se présenter; **to arise from** résulter de; **should the need arise** en cas de besoin

aristocrat ['ærɪstəkræt] *n* aristocrate *m/f*

arithmetic [ə'rɪθmətɪk] *n* arithmétique *f*

ark [ɑːk] *n*: **Noah's Ark** l'Arche *f* de Noé

arm [ɑːm] *n* bras *m* ♦ *vt* armer; **arm in arm** bras dessus bras dessous

armaments ['ɑːməmənts] *npl* (*weapons*) armement *m*

armchair ['ɑːmtʃeə*] *n* fauteuil *m*

armed [ɑːmd] *adj* armé(e); **the armed forces** les forces armées

armed robbery *n* vol *m* à main armée

armour, (*US*) **armor** ['ɑːmə*] *n* armure *f*; (*also*: **armour-plating**) blindage *m*; (*MIL: tanks*) blindés *mpl*

armo(u)red car ['ɑːməd-] *n* véhicule blindé

armpit ['ɑːmpɪt] *n* aisselle *f*

armrest ['ɑːmrest] *n* accoudoir *m*

army ['ɑːmɪ] n armée f
aroma [əˈrəumə] n arôme m
aromatherapy [ərəuməˈθerəpɪ] n aromathérapie f
arose [əˈrəuz] pt of **arise**
around [əˈraund] adv (tout) autour; (nearby) dans les parages ♦ prep autour de; (fig: about) environ; vers; **is he around?** est-il dans les parages or là?
arouse [əˈrauz] vt (sleeper) éveiller; (curiosity, passions) éveiller, susciter; exciter
arrange [əˈreɪndʒ] vt arranger; (programme) arrêter, convenir de ♦ vi: **we have arranged for a car to pick you up** nous avons prévu qu'une voiture vienne vous prendre; **it was arranged that ...** il a été convenu que ..., il a été décidé que ...; **to arrange to do sth** prévoir de faire qch
arrangement [əˈreɪndʒmənt] n arrangement m; (plans etc): **arrangements** dispositions fpl; **to come to an arrangement (with sb)** se mettre d'accord (avec qn); **home deliveries by arrangement** livraison à domicile sur demande; **I'll make arrangements for you to be met** je vous enverrai chercher
array [əˈreɪ] n (of objects) déploiement m, étalage m; (MATH, COMPUT) tableau m
arrears [əˈrɪəz] npl arriéré m; **to be in arrears with one's rent** devoir un arriéré de loyer, être en retard pour le paiement de son loyer
arrest [əˈrest] vt arrêter; (sb's attention) retenir, attirer ♦ n arrestation f; **under arrest** en état d'arrestation
arrival [əˈraɪvl] n arrivée f; (COMM) arrivage m; (person) arrivant/e; **new arrival** nouveau venu/nouvelle venue
arrive [əˈraɪv] vi arriver
► **arrive at** vt fus (fig) parvenir à
arrogant [ˈærəgənt] adj arrogant(e)
arrow [ˈærəu] n flèche f
arse [ɑːs] n (BRIT col!) cul m (!)
arson [ˈɑːsn] n incendie criminel
art [ɑːt] n art m; (craft) métier m; **work of art** œuvre f d'art
artery [ˈɑːtərɪ] n artère f
art gallery n musée m d'art; (small and private) galerie f de peinture
arthritis [ɑːˈθraɪtɪs] n arthrite f
artichoke [ˈɑːtɪtʃəuk] n artichaut m; **Jerusalem artichoke** topinambour m
article [ˈɑːtɪkl] n article m; (BRIT LAW: training): **articles** npl ≈ stage m; **articles of clothing** vêtements mpl
articulate adj [ɑːˈtɪkjulɪt] (person) qui s'exprime clairement et aisément; (speech) bien articulé(e), prononcé(e) clairement ♦ vi [ɑːˈtɪkjuleɪt] articuler, parler distinctement
articulated lorry [ɑːˈtɪkjuleɪtɪd-] n (BRIT) (camion m) semi-remorque m

artificial [ɑːtɪˈfɪʃəl] adj artificiel(le)
artificial respiration n respiration artificielle
artist [ˈɑːtɪst] n artiste m/f
artistic [ɑːˈtɪstɪk] adj artistique
artistry [ˈɑːtɪstrɪ] n art m, talent m
art school n ≈ école f des beaux-arts

KEYWORD

as [æz] conj **1** (time: moment) comme, alors que; à mesure que; (: duration) tandis que; **he came in as I was leaving** il est arrivé comme je partais; **as the years went by** à mesure que les années passaient; **as from tomorrow** à partir de demain
2 (in comparisons): **as big as** aussi grand que; **twice as big as** deux fois plus grand que; **big as it is** si grand que ce soit; **much as I like them, I ...** je les aime bien, mais je ...; **as much or many as** autant que; **as much money/many books as** autant d'argent/de livres que; **as soon as** dès que
3 (since, because) comme, puisque; **as he had to be home by 10 ...** comme il or puisqu'il devait être de retour avant 10h ...
4 (referring to manner, way) comme; **do as you wish** faites comme vous voudrez
5 (concerning): **as for or to that** quant à cela, pour ce qui est de cela
6: as if or though comme si; **he looked as if he was ill** il avait l'air d'être malade; see also **long**; **such**; **well**
♦ prep (in the capacity of) en tant que, en qualité de; **he works as a driver** il travaille comme chauffeur; **as chairman of the company, he ...** en tant que président de la compagnie, il ...; **dressed up as a cowboy** déguisé en cowboy; **he gave me it as a present** il me l'a offert, il m'en a fait cadeau

a.s.a.p. abbr = **as soon as possible**
asbestos [æzˈbestəs] n asbeste m, amiante m
ascend [əˈsend] vt gravir
ascertain [æsəˈteɪn] vt s'assurer de, vérifier; établir
ash [æʃ] n (dust) cendre f; (also: **ash tree**) frêne m
ashamed [əˈfeɪmd] adj honteux(euse), confus(e); **to be ashamed of** avoir honte de; **to be ashamed (of o.s.) for having done** avoir honte d'avoir fait
ashore [əˈfɔː*] adv à terre; **to go ashore** aller à terre, débarquer
ashtray [ˈæftreɪ] n cendrier m
Ash Wednesday n mercredi m des Cendres
Asia [ˈeɪʃə] n Asie f
Asian [ˈeɪʃən] n Asiatique m/f ♦ adj asiatique
aside [əˈsaɪd] adv de côté; à l'écart ♦ n aparté m; **aside from** prep à part, excepté
ask [ɑːsk] vt demander; (invite) inviter; **to ask sb sth/to do sth** demander à qn qch/de faire qch; **to ask sb the time** demander l'heure à qn; **to ask sb**

about sth questionner qn au sujet de qch; se renseigner auprès de qn au sujet de qch; **to ask about the price** s'informer du prix, se renseigner sur le prix du prix; **to ask (sb) a question** poser une question (à qn); **to ask sb out to dinner** inviter qn au restaurant

▶ **ask after** *vt fus* demander des nouvelles de

▶ **ask for** *vt fus* demander; **it's just asking for trouble** *or* **for it** ce serait chercher des ennuis

asking price ['ɑ:skɪŋ-] *n* prix demandé

asleep [ə'sli:p] *adj* endormi(e); **to be asleep** dormir, être endormi; **to fall asleep** s'endormir

asparagus [əs'pærəgəs] *n* asperges *fpl*

aspect ['æspekt] *n* aspect *m*; (*direction in which a building etc faces*) orientation *f*, exposition *f*

aspire [əs'paɪə*] *vi*: **to aspire to** aspirer à

aspirin ['æsprɪn] *n* aspirine *f*

ass [æs] *n* âne *m*; (*col*) imbécile *m/f*; (*us col!*) cul *m* (*!*)

assailant [ə'seɪlənt] *n* agresseur *m*; assaillant *m*

assassinate [ə'sæsɪneɪt] *vt* assassiner

assassination [əsæsɪ'neɪʃən] *n* assassinat *m*

assault [ə'sɔ:lt] *n* (*MIL*) assaut *m*; (*gen: attack*) agression *f*; (*LAW*): **assault (and battery)** voies *fpl* de fait, coups *mpl* et blessures *fpl* ♦ *vt* attaquer; (*sexually*) violenter

assemble [ə'sembl] *vt* assembler ♦ *vi* s'assembler, se rassembler

assembly [ə'semblɪ] *n* (*meeting*) rassemblement *m*; (*construction*) assemblage *m*

assembly line *n* chaîne *f* de montage

assent [ə'sent] *n* assentiment *m*, consentement *m* ♦ *vi*: **to assent (to sth)** donner son assentiment (à qch), consentir (à qch)

assert [ə'sɜ:t] *vt* affirmer, déclarer; établir; **to assert o.s.** s'imposer

assess [ə'ses] *vt* évaluer, estimer; (*tax, damages*) établir *or* fixer le montant de; (*property etc: for tax*) calculer la valeur imposable de

assessment [ə'sesmənt] *n* évaluation *f*, estimation *f*; (*judgment*): **assessment (of)** jugement *m or* opinion *f* (sur)

assessor [ə'sesə*] *n* expert *m* (*en matière d'impôt et d'assurance*)

asset ['æset] *n* avantage *m*, atout *m*; (*person*) atout; **assets** *npl* (*COMM*) capital *m*; avoir(s) *m(pl)*; actif *m*

assign [ə'saɪn] *vt* (*date*) fixer, arrêter; (*task*): **to assign sth to** assigner qch à; (*resources*): **to assign sth to** affecter qch à; (*cause, meaning*): **to assign sth to** attribuer qch à

assignment [ə'saɪnmənt] *n* tâche *f*, mission *f*

assist [ə'sɪst] *vt* aider, assister; (*injured person etc*) secourir

assistance [ə'sɪstəns] *n* aide *f*, assistance *f*; secours *mpl*

assistant [ə'sɪstənt] *n* assistant/e, adjoint/e; (*BRIT:* *also*: **shop assistant**) vendeur/euse

associate *adj, n* [ə'səuʃɪɪt] associé/e ♦ *vb* [ə'səuʃɪeɪt] *vt* associer ♦ *vi*: **to associate with sb** fréquenter qn; **associate director** directeur adjoint; **associated company** société affiliée

association [əsəusɪ'eɪʃən] *n* association *f*; **in association with** en collaboration avec

assorted [ə'sɔ:tɪd] *adj* assorti(e); **in assorted sizes** en plusieurs tailles

assortment [ə'sɔ:tmənt] *n* assortiment *m*

assume [ə'sju:m] *vt* supposer; (*responsibilities etc*) assumer; (*attitude, name*) prendre, adopter

assumption [ə'sʌmpʃən] *n* supposition *f*, hypothèse *f*; **on the assumption that** dans l'hypothèse où; (*on condition that*) à condition que

assurance [ə'ʃuərəns] *n* assurance *f*; **I can give you no assurances** je ne peux rien vous garantir

assure [ə'ʃuə*] *vt* assurer

asthma ['æsmə] *n* asthme *m*

astonish [ə'stɒnɪʃ] *vt* étonner, stupéfier

astonishment [ə'stɒnɪʃmənt] *n* (grand) étonnement, stupéfaction *f*

astound [ə'staund] *vt* stupéfier, sidérer

astray [ə'streɪ] *adv*: **to go astray** s'égarer; (*fig*) quitter le droit chemin; **to go astray in one's calculations** faire fausse route dans ses calculs

astride [ə'straɪd] *adv* à cheval ♦ *prep* à cheval sur

astrology [əs'trɒlədʒɪ] *n* astrologie *f*

astronaut ['æstrənɔ:t] *n* astronaute *m/f*

astronomy [əs'trɒnəmɪ] *n* astronomie *f*

asylum [ə'saɪləm] *n* asile *m*; **to seek political asylum** demander l'asile politique

---

KEYWORD

at [æt] *prep* **1** (*referring to position, direction*) à; **at the top** au sommet; **at home/school** à la maison *or* chez soi/à l'école; **at the baker's** à la boulangerie, chez le boulanger; **to look at sth** regarder qch

2 (*referring to time*): **at 4 o'clock** à 4 heures; **at Christmas** à Noël; **at night** la nuit; **at times** par moments, parfois

3 (*referring to rates, speed etc*) à; **at £1 a kilo** une livre le kilo; **two at a time** deux à la fois; **at 50 km/h** à 50 km/h; **at full speed** à toute vitesse

4 (*referring to manner*): **at a stroke** d'un seul coup; **at peace** en paix

5 (*referring to activity*): **to be at work** être au travail, travailler; **to play at cowboys** jouer aux cowboys; **to be good at sth** être bon en qch

6 (*referring to cause*): **shocked/surprised/annoyed at sth** choqué par/étonné de/agacé par qch; **I went at his suggestion** j'y suis allé sur son conseil

---

ate [eɪt] *pt of* **eat**

atheist ['eɪθɪɪst] *n* athée *m/f*

Athens ['æθɪnz] *n* Athènes *f*

athlete ['æθli:t] *n* athlète *m/f*

athletic [æθ'letik] *adj* athlétique

athletics [æθ'letiks] *n* athlétisme *m*

Atlantic [ət'læntik] *adj* atlantique ◆ *n*: **the Atlantic (Ocean)** l'Atlantique *m*, l'océan *m* Atlantique

atlas ['ætləs] *n* atlas *m*

ATM *abbr* (= *Automated Telling Machine*) guichet *m* automatique

atmosphere ['ætməsfiə*] *n* atmosphère *f*; (*air*) air *m*

atom ['ætəm] *n* atome *m*

atomic [ə'təmik] *adj* atomique

atom(ic) bomb *n* bombe *f* atomique

atomizer ['ætəmaizə*] *n* atomiseur *m*

atone [ə'təun] *vi*: **to atone for** expier, racheter

atrocious [ə'trəuʃəs] *adj* (*very bad*) atroce, exécrable

attach [ə'tætʃ] *vt* (*gen*) attacher; (*document, letter*) joindre; (*employee, troops*) affecter; **to be attached to sb/sth** (*to like*) être attaché à qn/qch; **the attached letter** la lettre ci-jointe

attaché case [ə'tæʃei] *n* mallette *f*, attaché-case *m*

attachment [ə'tætʃmənt] *n* (*tool*) accessoire *m*; (*love*): **attachment (to)** affection *f* (pour), attachement *m* (à)

attack [ə'tæk] *vt* attaquer; (*task etc*) s'attaquer à ◆ *n* attaque *f*; (*also*: **heart attack**) crise *f* cardiaque

attain [ə'tein] *vt* (*also*: **to attain to**) parvenir à, atteindre; acquérir

attempt [ə'tempt] *n* tentative *f* ◆ *vt* essayer, tenter; **attempted theft** *etc* (*LAW*) tentative de vol *etc*; **to make an attempt on sb's life** attenter à la vie de qn; **he made no attempt to help** il n'a rien fait pour m'aider or l'aider *etc*

attempted [ə'temptid] *adj*: **attempted murder/suicide** tentative *f* de meurtre/suicide

attend [ə'tend] *vt* (*course*) suivre; (*meeting, talk*) assister à; (*school, church*) aller à, fréquenter; (*patient*) soigner, s'occuper de; **to attend (up)on** servir; être au service de

▶ **attend to** *vt fus* (*needs, affairs etc*) s'occuper de; (*customer*) s'occuper de, servir

attendance [ə'tendəns] *n* (*being present*) présence *f*; (*people present*) assistance *f*

attendant [ə'tendənt] *n* employé/e; gardien/ne ◆ *adj* concomitant(e), qui accompagne or s'ensuit

attention [ə'tenʃən] *n* attention *f*; **attentions** attentions *fpl*, prévenances *fpl*; **attention!** (*MIL*) garde-à-vous!; **at attention** (*MIL*) au garde-à-vous; **for the attention of** (*ADMIN*) à l'attention de; **it has come to my attention that ...** je constate que ...

attentive [ə'tentiv] *adj* attentif(ive); (*kind*) prévenant(e)

attest [ə'test] *vi*: **to attest to** témoigner de, attester (de)

attic ['ætik] *n* grenier *m*, combles *mpl*

attitude ['ætitju:d] *n* (*behaviour*) attitude *f*, manière *f*; (*posture*) pose *f*, attitude; (*view*): **attitude (to)** attitude (envers)

attorney [ə'tə:ni] *n* (*US: lawyer*) avocat *m*; (*having proxy*) mandataire *m*; **power of attorney** procuration *f*

Attorney General *n* (*BRIT*) = procureur général; (*US*) = garde *m* des Sceaux, ministre *m* de la Justice

attract [ə'trækt] *vt* attirer

attraction [ə'trækʃən] *n* (*gen pl: pleasant things*) attraction *f*, attrait *m*; (*PHYSICS*) attraction; (*fig: towards sth*) attirance *f*

attractive [ə'træktiv] *adj* séduisant(e), attrayant(e)

attribute *n* ['ætribju:t] attribut *m* ◆ *vt* [ə'tribju:t]: **to attribute sth to** attribuer qch à

attrition [ə'triʃən] *n*: **war of attrition** guerre *f* d'usure

aubergine ['əubəʒi:n] *n* aubergine *f*

auction ['ɔ:kʃən] *n* (*also*: **sale by auction**) vente *f* aux enchères ◆ *vt* (*also*: **to sell by auction**) vendre aux enchères; (*also*: **to put up for auction**) mettre aux enchères

auctioneer [ɔ:kʃə'niə*] *n* commissaire-priseur *m*

audience ['ɔ:diəns] *n* (*people*) assistance *f*, auditoire *m*; auditeurs *mpl*; spectateurs *mpl*; (*interview*) audience *f*

audiovisual [ɔ:diəu'vizjuəl] *adj* audio-visuel(le); **audiovisual aids** supports or moyens audiovisuels

audit ['ɔ:dit] *n* vérification *f* des comptes, apurement *m* ◆ *vt* vérifier, apurer

audition [ɔ:'diʃən] *n* audition *f* ◆ *vi* auditionner

auditor ['ɔ:ditə*] *n* vérificateur *m* des comptes

augur ['ɔ:gə*] *vt* (*be a sign of*) présager, annoncer ◆ *vi*: **it augurs well** c'est bon signe or de bon augure, cela s'annonce bien

August ['ɔ:gəst] *n* août *m*; *for phrases see also* **July**

aunt [ɑ:nt] *n* tante *f*

auntie, aunty ['ɑ:nti] *n diminutive of* **aunt**

au pair ['əu'pɛə*] *n* (*also*: **au pair girl**) jeune fille *f* au pair

auspicious [ɔ:s'piʃəs] *adj* de bon augure, propice

Australia [ɔs'treiliə] *n* Australie *f*

Australian [ɔs'treiliən] *adj* australien(ne) ◆ *n* Australien/ne

Austria ['ɔstriə] *n* Autriche *f*

Austrian ['ɔstriən] *adj* autrichien(ne) ◆ *n* Autrichien/ne

authentic [ɔ:'θentik] *adj* authentique

author ['ɔ:θə*] *n* auteur *m*

authoritarian [ɔ:θɔri'tɛəriən] *adj* autoritaire

authoritative [ɔ:'θɔritətiv] *adj* (*account*) digne de foi; (*study, treatise*) qui fait autorité; (*manner*) autoritaire

authority [ɔːˈθɒrɪtɪ] n autorité f; (permission) autorisation (formelle); **the authorities** les autorités, l'administration f; **to have authority to do sth** être habilité à faire qch

authorize [ˈɔːθəraɪz] vt autoriser

auto [ˈɔːtəu] n (US) auto f, voiture f

autobiography [ɔːtəbaɪˈɒgrəfɪ] n autobiographie f

autograph [ˈɔːtəgrɑːf] n autographe m ◆ vt signer, dédicacer

automated [ˈɔːtəmeɪtɪd] adj automatisé(e)

automatic [ɔːtəˈmætɪk] adj automatique ◆ n (gun) automatique m; (washing machine) lave-linge m automatique; (BRIT AUT) voiture f à transmission automatique

automatically [ɔːtəˈmætɪklɪ] adv automatiquement

automation [ɔːtəˈmeɪʃən] n automatisation f

automobile [ˈɔːtəməbiːl] n (US) automobile f

autonomy [ɔːˈtɒnəmɪ] n autonomie f

autumn [ˈɔːtəm] n automne m

auxiliary [ɔːgˈzɪlɪərɪ] adj, n auxiliaire (m/f)

avail [əˈveɪl] vt: **to avail o.s. of** user de; profiter de ◆ n: **to no avail** sans résultat, en vain, en pure perte

availability [əveɪləˈbɪlɪtɪ] n disponibilité f

available [əˈveɪləbl] adj disponible; **every available means** tous les moyens possibles or à sa (or notre etc) disposition; **is the manager available?** est-ce que le directeur peut (me) recevoir?; (on phone) pourrais-je parler au directeur?; **to make sth available to sb** mettre qch à la disposition de qn

avalanche [ˈævəlɑːnʃ] n avalanche f

Ave. abbr (= avenue) Av.

avenge [əˈvɛndʒ] vt venger

avenue [ˈævənjuː] n avenue f

average [ˈævərɪdʒ] n moyenne f ◆ adj moyen(ne) ◆ vt (a certain figure) atteindre or faire etc en moyenne; **on average** en moyenne; **above/below (the) average** au-dessus/en-dessous de la moyenne

▶ **average out** vi: **to average out at** représenter en moyenne, donner une moyenne de

averse [əˈvɜːs] adj: **to be averse to sth/doing** éprouver une forte répugnance envers qch/à faire; **I wouldn't be averse to a drink** un petit verre ne serait pas de refus, je ne dirais pas non à un petit verre

avert [əˈvɜːt] vt prévenir, écarter; (one's eyes) détourner

aviary [ˈeɪvɪərɪ] n volière f

avocado [ævəˈkɑːdəu] n (BRIT: also: **avocado pear**) avocat m

avoid [əˈvɔɪd] vt éviter

await [əˈweɪt] vt attendre; **awaiting attention/ delivery** (COMM) en souffrance; **long awaited** tant attendu(e)

awake [əˈweɪk] adj éveillé(e); (fig) en éveil ◆ vb, pt **awoke** [əˈwəuk], pp **awoken** [əˈwəukən], **awaked** vt éveiller ◆ vi s'éveiller; **awake to** conscient de; **he was still awake** il ne dormait pas encore

awakening [əˈweɪknɪŋ] n réveil m

award [əˈwɔːd] n récompense f, prix m ◆ vt (prize) décerner; (LAW: damages) accorder

aware [əˈwɛəʳ] adj: **aware of** (conscious) conscient(e) de; (informed) au courant de; **to become aware of** avoir conscience de, prendre conscience de; se rendre compte de; **politically/socially aware** sensibilisé(e) aux or ayant pris conscience des problèmes politiques/sociaux; **I am fully aware that** je me rends parfaitement compte que

awareness [əˈwɛənɪs] n conscience f, connaissance f; **to develop people's awareness (of)** sensibiliser le public (à)

away [əˈweɪ] adj, adv (au) loin; absent(e); **two kilometres away** à (une distance de) deux kilomètres, à deux kilomètres de distance; **two hours away by car** à deux heures de voiture or de route; **the holiday was two weeks away** il restait deux semaines jusqu'aux vacances; **away from** loin de; **he's away for a week** il est parti (pour) une semaine; **he's away in Milan** il est (parti) à Milan; **to take away** vt emporter; **to pedal/work/laugh** etc **away** la particule indique la constance et l'énergie de l'action il pédalait etc tant qu'il pouvait; **to fade/ wither** etc **away** la particule renforce l'idée de la disparition, l'éloignement

away game n (SPORT) match m à l'extérieur

awe [ɔː] n respect mêlé de crainte, effroi mêlé d'admiration

awe-inspiring [ˈɔːɪnspaɪərɪŋ], **awesome** [ˈɔːsəm] adj impressionnant(e)

awful [ˈɔːfəl] adj affreux(euse); **an awful lot of** énormément de

awfully [ˈɔːfəlɪ] adv (very) terriblement, vraiment

awkward [ˈɔːkwəd] adj (clumsy) gauche, maladroit(e); (inconvenient) malaisé(e), d'emploi malaisé, peu pratique; (embarrassing) gênant

awning [ˈɔːnɪŋ] n (of tent) auvent m; (of shop) store m; (of hotel etc) marquise f (de toile)

awoke [əˈwəuk] pt of **awake**

awoken [əˈwəukən] pp of **awake**

axe, (US) **ax** [æks] n hache f ◆ vt (employee) renvoyer; (project etc) abandonner; (jobs) supprimer; **to have an axe to grind** (fig) prêcher pour son saint

axes [ˈæksiːz] npl of **axis**

axis, pl **axes** [ˈæksɪs, -siːz] n axe m

axle [ˈæksl] n (also: **axle-tree**) essieu m

ay(e) [aɪ] excl (yes) oui ◆ n: **the ay(e)s** les oui

— B b —

B, b [biː] n (letter) B, b m; (SCOL: mark) B; (MUS): **B** si m;
B for Benjamin, (US) **B for Baker** B comme Berthe;
B road n (BRIT AUT) route départementale
BA n abbr = British Academy; (SCOL) = Bachelor of
Arts
babble ['bæbl] vi babiller ◆ n babillage m
baby ['beɪbɪ] n bébé m
baby carriage n (US) voiture f d'enfant
baby food n aliments mpl pour bébé(s)
baby-sit ['beɪbɪsɪt] vi garder les enfants
baby-sitter ['beɪbɪsɪtə*] n baby-sitter m/f
baby wipe n lingette f (pour bébé)
bachelor ['bætʃələ*] n célibataire m
back [bæk] n (of person, horse) dos m; (of hand)
dos, revers m; (of house) derrière m; (of car, train)
arrière m; (of chair) dossier m; (of page) verso m;
(FOOTBALL) arrière m; **to have one's back to the wall**
(fig) être au pied du mur; **to break the back of a
job** (BRIT) faire le gros d'un travail; **back to front** à
l'envers ◆ vt (financially) soutenir (financièrement);
(candidate: also: **back up**) soutenir, appuyer; (horse:
at races) parier or miser sur; (car) (faire) reculer ◆ vi
reculer; (car etc) faire marche arrière ◆ adj (in compounds) de derrière, à l'arrière; **back seats/wheels**
(AUT) sièges mpl/roues fpl arrière; **back payments/
rent** arriéré m de paiements/loyer; **back garden/
room** jardin/pièce sur l'arrière; **to take a back seat**
(fig) se contenter d'un second rôle, être relégué(e)
au second plan ◆ adv (not forward) en arrière;
(returned): **he's back** il est rentré, il est de retour;
when will you be back? quand seras-tu de
retour?; **he ran back** il est revenu en courant; (restitution): **throw the ball back** renvoie la balle; **can I
have it back?** puis-je le ravoir?, peux-tu me le
rendre?; (again): **he called back** il a rappelé
▶ **back down** vi rabattre de ses prétentions
▶ **back on to** vt fus: **the house backs on to the
golf course** la maison donne derrière sur le terrain
de golf
▶ **back out** vi (of promise) se dédire
▶ **back up** vt (COMPUT) faire une copie de sauvegarde de
backache ['bækeɪk] n maux mpl de reins
backbencher ['bæk'bentʃə*] (BRIT) n membre du
parlement sans portefeuille
backbone ['bækbəʊn] n colonne vertébrale,
épine dorsale; **he's the backbone of the organization** c'est sur lui que repose l'organisation
backdate [bæk'deɪt] vt (letter) antidater; **back-
dated pay rise** augmentation f avec effet rétroactif
backfire [bæk'faɪə*] vi (AUT) pétarader; (plans) mal
tourner
background ['bækgraʊnd] n arrière-plan m; (of

events) situation f, conjoncture f; (basic knowledge)
éléments mpl de base; (experience) formation f
◆ cpd (noise, music) de fond; **background reading**
lecture(s) générale(s) (sur un sujet); **family background** milieu familial
backhand ['bækhænd] n (TENNIS: also: **backhand
stroke**) revers m
backhander ['bæk'hændə*] n (BRIT: bribe) pot-de-
vin m
backing ['bækɪŋ] n (fig) soutien m, appui m;
(COMM) soutien (financier); (MUS) accompagnement
m
backlash ['bæklæʃ] n contre-coup m, répercus-
sion f
backlog ['bæklɔg] n: **backlog of work** travail m
en retard
back number n (of magazine etc) vieux numéro
backpack ['bækpæk] n sac m à dos
backpacker ['bækpækə*] n randonneur/euse
back pain n mal m de dos
back pay n rappel m de salaire
backside ['bæksaɪd] n (col) derrière m, postérieur
m
backstage [bæk'steɪdʒ] adv dans les coulisses
backstroke ['bækstrəʊk] n dos crawlé
backup ['bækʌp] adj (train, plane) supplémentaire, de réserve; (COMPUT) de sauvegarde ◆ n (support)
appui m, soutien m; (COMPUT: also: **backup file**) sauvegarde f
backward ['bækwəd] adj (movement) en arrière;
(measure) rétrograde; (person, country) arriéré(e),
attardé(e); (shy) hésitant(e); **backward and forward movement** mouvement de va-et-vient
backwards ['bækwədz] adv (move, go) en arrière;
(read a list) à l'envers, à rebours; (fall) à la renverse;
(walk) à reculons; (in time) en arrière, vers le passé;
to know sth backwards or (US) **backwards and
forwards**: col) connaître qch sur le bout des doigts
backwater ['bækwɔːtə*] n (fig) coin reculé; bled
perdu
backyard [bæk'jɑːd] n arrière-cour f
bacon ['beɪkən] n bacon m, lard m
bacteria [bæk'tɪərɪə] npl bactéries fpl
bad [bæd] adj mauvais(e); (child) vilain(e); (meat,
food) gâté(e), avarié(e); **his bad leg** sa jambe malade; **to go bad** (meat, food) se gâter; (milk) tourner;
to have a bad time of it traverser une mauvaise
passe; **I feel bad about it** (guilty) j'ai un peu mauvaise conscience; **bad debt** créance douteuse; **in
bad faith** de mauvaise foi
badge [bædʒ] n insigne m; (of policeman) plaque
f; (stick-on, sew-on) badge m
badger ['bædʒə*] n blaireau m ◆ vt harceler
badly ['bædlɪ] adv (work, dress etc) mal; **badly
wounded** grièvement blessé; **he needs it badly** il
en a absolument besoin; **things are going badly**
les choses vont mal; **badly off** adj, adv dans la

gêne

badminton ['bædmɪntən] *n* badminton *m*

bad-tempered ['bæd'tempəd] *adj* (*by nature*) ayant mauvais caractère; (*on one occasion*) de mauvaise humeur

baffle ['bæfl] *vt* (*puzzle*) déconcerter

bag [bæg] *n* sac *m*; (*of hunter*) gibecière *f*, chasse *f* ♦ *vt* (*col: take*) empocher; s'approprier; (*TECH*) mettre en sacs; **bags of** (*col: lots of*) des masses de; **to pack one's bags** faire ses valises *or* bagages; **bags under the eyes** poches *fpl* sous les yeux

baggage ['bægɪdʒ] *n* bagages *mpl*

baggage allowance *n* franchise *f* de bagages

baggage reclaim *n* (*at airport*) livraison *f* des bagages

baggy ['bægɪ] *adj* avachi(e), qui fait des poches

bagpipes ['bægpaɪps] *npl* cornemuse *f*

bail [beɪl] *n* caution *f* ♦ *vt* (*prisoner: also:* **grant bail to**) mettre en liberté sous caution; (*boat: also:* **bail out**) écoper; **to be released on bail** être libéré(e) sous caution *see* **bale**

▶ **bail out** *vt* (*prisoner*) payer la caution de

bailiff ['beɪlɪf] *n* huissier *m*

bait [beɪt] *n* appât *m* ♦ *vt* appâter; (*fig*) tourmenter

bake [beɪk] *vt* (*faire*) cuire au four ♦ *vi* (*bread etc*) cuire (au four); (*make cakes etc*) faire de la pâtisserie

baked beans [beɪkt-] *npl* haricots blancs à la sauce tomate

baked potato *n* pomme *f* de terre en robe des champs

baker ['beɪkə*] *n* boulanger *m*

bakery ['beɪkərɪ] *n* boulangerie *f*; boulangerie industrielle

baking ['beɪkɪŋ] *n* cuisson *f*

baking powder *n* levure *f* (chimique)

balance ['bæləns] *n* équilibre *m*; (*COMM: sum*) solde *m*; (*scales*) balance *f* ♦ *vt* mettre *or* faire tenir en équilibre; (*pros and cons*) peser; (*budget*) équilibrer; (*account*) balancer; (*compensate*) compenser, contrebalancer; **balance of trade/payments** balance commerciale/des comptes *or* paiements; **balance carried forward** solde *m* à reporter; **balance brought forward** solde reporté; **to balance the books** arrêter les comptes, dresser le bilan

balanced ['bælənst] *adj* (*personality, diet*) équilibré(e)

balance sheet *n* bilan *m*

balcony ['bælkənɪ] *n* balcon *m*

bald [bɔːld] *adj* chauve; (*tyre*) lisse

bale [beɪl] *n* balle *f*, ballot *m*

▶ **bale out** *vi* (*of a plane*) sauter en parachute ♦ *vt* (*NAUT: water, boat*) écoper

ball [bɔːl] *n* boule *f*; (*football*) ballon *m*; (*for tennis, golf*) balle *f*; (*dance*) bal *m*; **to play ball (with sb)** jouer au ballon (*or* à la balle) (avec qn); (*fig*) coopé-

rer (avec qn); **to be on the ball** (*fig: competent*) être à la hauteur; (: *alert*) être éveillé(e), être vif(vive); **to start the ball rolling** (*fig*) commencer; **the ball is in their court** (*fig*) la balle est dans leur camp

ballast ['bæləst] *n* lest *m*

ball bearings *n* roulement *m* à billes

ballerina [bælə'riːnə] *n* ballerine *f*

ballet ['bæleɪ] *n* ballet *m*; (*art*) danse *f* (classique)

ballet dancer *n* danseur/euse de ballet

ballet shoe *n* chausson *m* de danse

balloon [bə'luːn] *n* ballon *m*; (*in comic strip*) bulle *f* ♦ *vi* gonfler

ballot ['bælət] *n* scrutin *m*

ballot paper *n* bulletin *m* de vote

ballpoint pen ['bɔːlpɔɪnt-] *n* stylo *m* à bille

ballroom ['bɔːlrʊm] *n* salle *f* de bal

ban [bæn] *n* interdiction *f* ♦ *vt* interdire; **he was banned from driving** (*BRIT*) on lui a retiré le permis (de conduire)

banana [bə'nɑːnə] *n* banane *f*

band [bænd] *n* bande *f*; (*at a dance*) orchestre *m*; (*MIL*) musique *f*, fanfare *f*

▶ **band together** *vi* se liguer

B & B *n abbr* = **bed and breakfast**; *voir encadré*

BED AND BREAKFAST

Un **bed and breakfast** est une petite pension dans une maison particulière ou une ferme où l'on peut louer une chambre avec petit déjeuner compris pour un prix modique par rapport à ce que l'on paierait dans un hôtel. Ces établissements sont communément appelés "B & B", et sont signalés par une pancarte dans le jardin ou au-dessus de la porte.

---

bandage ['bændɪdʒ] *n* bandage *m*, pansement *m* ♦ *vt* (*wound, leg*) mettre un pansement *or* un bandage sur; (*person*) mettre un pansement *or* un bandage à

Band-Aid® ['bændeɪd] *n* (*US*) pansement adhésif

bandit ['bændɪt] *n* bandit *m*

bandy-legged ['bændɪ'legɪd] *adj* aux jambes arquées

bang [bæŋ] *n* détonation *f*; (*of door*) claquement *m*; (*blow*) coup (violent) ♦ *vt* frapper (violemment); (*door*) claquer ♦ *vi* détoner; claquer ♦ *adv*: **to be bang on time** (*BRIT col*) être à l'heure pile; **to bang at the door** cogner à la porte; **to bang into sth** se cogner contre qch

bangs [bæŋz] *npl* (*US: fringe*) frange *f*

banish ['bænɪʃ] *vt* bannir

banister(s) ['bænɪstə(z)] *n(pl)* rampe *f* (d'escalier)

bank [bæŋk] *n* banque *f*; (*of river, lake*) bord *m*, rive *f*; (*of earth*) talus *m*, remblai *m* ♦ *vi* (*AVIAT*) virer sur l'aile; (*COMM*): **they bank with Pitt's** leur banque *or* banquier est Pitt's

▶ **bank on** vt fus miser or tabler sur

bank account n compte m en banque

bank card n = **banker's card**

banker ['bæŋkə*] n banquier m; **banker's card** (BRIT) carte f d'identité bancaire; **banker's order** (BRIT) ordre m de virement

bank holiday n (BRIT) jour férié (où les banques sont fermées); voir encadré

BANK HOLIDAY

Un **bank holiday** en Grande-Bretagne est un lundi férié et donc l'occasion d'un week-end prolongé. La circulation sur les routes et le trafic dans les gares et les aéroports augmentent considérablement à ces périodes. Les principaux **bank holidays**, à part Pâques et Noël, se situent au mois de mai et fin août.

---

banking ['bæŋkɪŋ] n opérations fpl bancaires; profession f de banquier

banknote ['bæŋknəut] n billet m de banque

bank rate n taux m de l'escompte

bankrupt ['bæŋkrʌpt] n failli.e ◆ adj en faillite; **to go bankrupt** faire faillite

bankruptcy ['bæŋkrʌptsɪ] n faillite f

bank statement n relevé m de compte

banner ['bænə*] n bannière f

bannister(s) ['bænɪstə(z)] n(pl) = **banister(s)**

baptism ['bæptɪzəm] n baptême m

bar [ba:*] n barre f; (of window etc) barreau m; (of chocolate) tablette f, plaque f; (fig) obstacle m; mesure f d'exclusion; (pub) bar m; (counter: in pub) comptoir m, bar m; (MUS) mesure f ◆ vt (road) barrer; (window) munir de barreaux; (person) exclure; (activity) interdire; **bar of soap** savonnette f; **behind bars** (prisoner) derrière les barreaux; **the Bar** (LAW) le barreau; **bar none** sans exception

barbaric [ba:'bærɪk] adj barbare

barbecue ['ba:bɪkju:] n barbecue m

barbed wire ['ba:bd-] n fil m de fer barbelé

barber ['ba:bə*] n coiffeur m (pour hommes)

bar code n code m à barres

bare [bɛə*] adj nu.e ◆ vt mettre à nu, dénuder; (teeth) montrer; **the bare essentials** le strict nécessaire

bareback ['bɛəbæk] adv à cru, sans selle

barefaced ['bɛəfeɪst] adj impudent(e), effronté(e)

barefoot ['bɛəfut] adj, adv nu-pieds, (les) pieds nus

barely ['bɛəlɪ] adv à peine

bargain ['ba:gɪn] n (transaction) marché m; (good buy) affaire f, occasion f ◆ vi (haggle) marchander; (trade) négocier, traiter; **into the bargain** par-dessus le marché

▶ **bargain for** vi (col): **he got more than he bar-**

gained for! il en a eu pour son argent!

barge [ba:dʒ] n péniche f

▶ **barge in** vi (walk in) faire irruption; (interrupt talk) intervenir mal à propos

▶ **barge into** vt fus rentrer dans

bark [ba:k] n (of tree) écorce f; (of dog) aboiement m ◆ vi aboyer

barley ['ba:lɪ] n orge f

barley sugar n sucre m d'orge

barmaid ['ba:meɪd] n serveuse f (de bar), barmaid f

barman ['ba:mən] n serveur m (de bar), barman m

bar meal n repas m de bistrot; **to go for a bar meal** aller manger au bistrot

barn [ba:n] n grange f

barometer [bə'rɔmɪtə*] n baromètre m

baron ['bærən] n baron m; **the press/oil barons** les magnats mpl or barons mpl de la presse/du pétrole

baroness ['bærənɪs] n baronne f

barracks ['bærəks] npl caserne f

barrage ['bæra:ʒ] n (MIL) tir m de barrage; (dam) barrage m; **a barrage of questions** un feu roulant de questions

barrel ['bærəl] n tonneau m; (of gun) canon m

barren ['bærən] adj stérile; (hills) aride

barricade [bærɪ'keɪd] n barricade f ◆ vt barricader

barrier ['bærɪə*] n barrière f; (BRIT: also: **crash barrier**) rail m de sécurité

barring ['ba:rɪŋ] prep sauf

barrister ['bærɪstə*] n (BRIT) avocat (plaidant); voir encadré

BARRISTER

En Angleterre, un **barrister**, que l'on appelle également "barrister-at-law", est un avocat qui représente ses clients devant la cour et plaide pour eux. Le client doit d'abord passer par l'intermédiaire d'un "solicitor". On obtient le diplôme de **barrister** après avoir fait des études dans l'une des "Inns of Court", les quatre écoles de droit londoniennes.

---

barrow ['bærəu] n (cart) charrette f à bras

bartender ['ba:tɛndə*] n (US) serveur m (de bar) barman m

barter ['ba:tə*] n échange m, troc m ◆ vt: **to barter sth for** échanger qch contre

base [beɪs] n base f ◆ vt (troops): **to be based at** être basé(e) à; (opinion, belief): **to base sth on** baser or fonder qch sur ◆ adj vil(e), bas(se); **coffee-based** à base de café; **a Paris-based firm** une maison opérant de Paris or dont le siège est à Paris; **I'm based in London** je suis basé(e) à Londres

baseball ['beɪsbɔːl] *n* base-ball *m*

basement ['beɪsmənt] *n* sous-sol *m*

bases ['beɪsiːz] *npl of* **basis** ['beɪsɪz] *npl of* **base**

bash [bæʃ] *vt* (col) frapper, cogner ♦ *n*: **I'll have a bash (at it)** (BRIT col) je vais essayer un coup; **bashed in** *adj* enfoncé(e), défoncé(e)

▶ **bash up** *vt* (col: car) bousiller; (: BRIT: person) tabasser

bashful ['bæʃful] *adj* timide; modeste

basic ['beɪsɪk] *adj* (precautions, rules) élémentaire; (principles, research) fondamental(e); (vocabulary, salary) de base; réduit(e) au minimum, rudimentaire

basically ['beɪsɪklɪ] *adv* (really) en fait; (essentially) fondamentalement

basics ['beɪsɪks] *npl*: **the basics** l'essentiel *m*

basil ['bæzl] *n* basilic *m*

basin ['beɪsn] *n* (vessel, also GEO) cuvette *f*, bassin *m*; (BRIT: for food) bol *m*; (: bigger) saladier *m*; (also: **washbasin**) lavabo *m*

basis, *pl* **bases** ['beɪsɪs, -siːz] *n* base *f*; **on the basis of what you've said** d'après *or* compte tenu de ce que vous dites

bask [bɑːsk] *vi*: **to bask in the sun** se chauffer au soleil

basket ['bɑːskɪt] *n* corbeille *f*; (with handle) panier *m*

basketball ['bɑːskɪtbɔːl] *n* basket-ball *m*

bass [beɪs] *n* (MUS) basse *f*

bass drum *n* grosse caisse *f*

bassoon [bə'suːn] *n* basson *m*

bastard ['bɑːstəd] *n* enfant naturel(le), bâtard/e; (col!) salaud *m* (!)

bat [bæt] *n* chauve-souris *f*; (for baseball etc) batte *f*; (BRIT: for table tennis) raquette *f* ♦ *vt*: **he didn't bat an eyelid** il n'a pas sourcillé *or* bronché; **off one's own bat** de sa propre initiative

batch [bætʃ] *n* (of bread) fournée *f*; (of papers) liasse *f*; (of applicants, letters) paquet *m*; (of work) monceau *m*; (of goods) lot *m*

bated ['beɪtɪd] *adj*: **with bated breath** en retenant son souffle

bath [bɑːθ] *pl*, *n* bain *m*; (bathtub) baignoire *f* ♦ *vt* baigner, donner un bain à; **to have a bath** prendre un bain; *see also* **baths**

bathe [beɪð] *vi* se baigner ♦ *vt* baigner; (wound etc) laver

bathing ['beɪðɪŋ] *n* baignade *f*

bathing costume, (US) **bathing suit** *n* maillot *m* (de bain)

bathrobe ['bɑːθrəub] *n* peignoir *m* de bain

bathroom ['bɑːθrum] *n* salle *f* de bains

baths [bɑːðz] *npl* établissement *m* de bains(-douches)

bath towel *n* serviette *f* de bain

baton ['bætən] *n* bâton *m*; (MUS) baguette *f*; (club) matraque *f*

batter ['bætə*] *vt* battre ♦ *n* pâte *f* à frire

battered ['bætəd] *adj* (hat, pan) cabossé(e); **battered wife/child** épouse/enfant maltraité(e) *or* martyr(e)

battery ['bætərɪ] *n* batterie *f*; (of torch) pile *f*

battery farming *n* élevage *m* en batterie

battle ['bætl] *n* bataille *f*, combat *m* ♦ *vi* se battre, lutter; **that's half the battle** (fig) c'est déjà bien; **it's a** *or* **we're fighting a losing battle** (fig) c'est perdu d'avance, c'est peine perdue

battlefield ['bætlfiːld] *n* champ *m* de bataille

battleship ['bætlʃɪp] *n* cuirassé *m*

Bavaria [bə'vɛərɪə] *n* Bavière *f*

bawl [bɔːl] *vi* hurler, brailler

bay [beɪ] *n* (of sea) baie *f*; (BRIT: for parking) place *f* de stationnement; (: for loading) aire *f* de chargement; (horse) bai/e *m/f*; **to hold sb at bay** tenir qn à distance *or* en échec

bay leaf *n* laurier *m*

bay window *n* baie vitrée

bazaar [bə'zɑː*] *n* bazar *m*; vente *f* de charité

BBC *n* abbr (= British Broadcasting Corporation) office de la radiodiffusion et télévision britannique

---

BBC

La **BBC** est un organisme centralisé dont les membres, nommés par l'État, gèrent les chaînes de télévision publiques (BBC1, qui présente des émissions d'intérêt général, et BBC2, qui est plutôt orientée vers les émissions plus culturelles) et les stations de radio publiques. Bien que non contrôlée par l'État, la **BBC** est responsable devant le parliament quant au contenu des émissions qu'elle diffuse. Par ailleurs, la **BBC** offre un service mondial de diffusion d'émissions, en anglais et dans 43 autres langues, appelé "BBC World Service". La **BBC** est financée par la redevance télévision et par l'exportation d'émissions.

B.C. *adv abbr* (= before Christ) av. J.-C. ♦ *abbr* (Canada) = British Columbia

KEYWORD

be [biː], *pt* **was**, **were**, *pp* **been** *aux vb* **1** (with present participle: forming continuous tenses): **what are you doing?** que faites-vous?; **they're coming tomorrow** ils viennent demain; **I've been waiting for you for 2 hours** je t'attends depuis 2 heures

2 (with pp: forming passives) être; **to be killed** être tué(e); **he was nowhere to be seen** on ne le voyait nulle part

3 (in tag questions): **it was fun, wasn't it?** c'était drôle, n'est-ce pas?; **she's back, is she?** elle est rentrée, n'est-ce pas *or* alors?

4 (+to +infinitive): **the house is to be sold** la maison doit être vendue; **he's not to open it** il ne doit pas l'ouvrir; **am I to understand that ...?** dois-je comprendre que ...?; **he was to have come yesterday** il devait venir hier

5 (*possibility, supposition*): **if I were you, I ...** à votre place, je ...; si j'étais vous, je ...

♦ *vb + complement* 1 (*gen*) être; **I'm English** je suis anglais(e); **I'm tired** je suis fatigué(e); **I'm hot/cold** j'ai chaud/froid; **he's a doctor** il est médecin; **2 and 2 are 4** 2 et 2 font 4

2 (*of health*) aller; **how are you?** comment allez-vous?; **he's fine now** il va bien maintenant; **he's very ill** il est très malade

3 (*of age*) avoir; **how old are you?** quel âge avez-vous?; **I'm sixteen (years old)** j'ai seize ans

4 (*cost*) coûter; **how much was the meal?** combien a coûté le repas?; **that'll be £5, please** ça fera 5 livres, s'il vous plaît

♦ *vi* 1 (*exist, occur etc*) être, exister; **the prettiest girl that ever was** la fille la plus jolie qui ait jamais existé; **be that as it may** quoi qu'il en soit; **so be it** soit

2 (*referring to place*) être, se trouver; **I won't be here tomorrow** je ne serai pas là demain; **Edinburgh is in Scotland** Édimbourg est *or* se trouve en Écosse

3 (*referring to movement*) aller; **where have you been?** où êtes-vous allé(s)?

♦ *impers vb* 1 (*referring to time, distance*) être; **it's 5 o'clock** il est 5 heures; **it's the 28th of April** c'est le 28 avril; **it's 10 km to the village** le village est à 10 km

2 (*referring to the weather*) faire; **it's too hot/cold** il fait trop chaud/froid; **it's windy** il y a du vent

3 (*emphatic*): **it's me/the postman** c'est moi/le facteur

beach [biːtʃ] *n* plage *f* ♦ *vt* échouer

beacon ['biːkən] *n* (*lighthouse*) fanal *m*; (*marker*) balise *f*; (*also*: **radio beacon**) radiophare *m*

bead [biːd] *n* perle *f*; (*of dew, sweat*) goutte *f*; **beads** *npl* (*necklace*) collier *m*

beak [biːk] *n* bec *m*

beaker ['biːkə*] *n* gobelet *m*

beam [biːm] *n* poutre *f*; (*of light*) rayon *m*; (*RADIO*) faisceau *m* radio ♦ *vi* rayonner; **to drive on full** *or* **main** *or* (*US*) **high beam** rouler en pleins phares

bean [biːn] *n* haricot *m*; (*of coffee*) grain *m*

bean sprouts *npl* pousses *fpl* (de soja)

bear [bɛə*] *n* ours *m*; (*STOCK EXCHANGE*) baissier *m* ♦ *vb*, *pt* **bore**, *pp* **borne** [bɔːʳ, bɔːn] *vt* porter; (*endure*) supporter; (*traces, signs*) porter; (*COMM: interest*) rapporter ♦ *vi*: **to bear right/left** obliquer à droite/gauche, se diriger vers la droite/gauche; **to bear the responsibility of** assumer la responsabilité de; **to bear comparison with** soutenir la comparaison avec; **I can't bear him** je ne peux pas le supporter *or* souffrir; **to bring pressure to bear on sb** faire pression sur qn

▶ **bear out** *vt* (*theory, suspicion*) confirmer

▶ **bear up** *vi* supporter, tenir le coup; **he bore up well** il a tenu le coup

▶ **bear with** *vt fus* (*sb's moods, temper*) supporter; **bear with me a minute** un moment, s'il vous plaît

beard [bɪəd] *n* barbe *f*

bearded ['bɪədɪd] *adj* barbu(e)

bearer ['bɛərə*] *n* porteur *m*; (*of passport etc*) titulaire *m/f*

bearing ['bɛərɪŋ] *n* maintien *m*, allure *f*; (*connection*) rapport *m*; (*TECH*): (**ball**) **bearings** *npl* roulement *m* (à billes); **to take a bearing** faire le point; **to find one's bearings** s'orienter

beast [biːst] *n* bête *f*; (*col*): **he's a beast** c'est une brute

beastly ['biːstlɪ] *adj* infect(e)

beat [biːt] *n* battement *m*; (*MUS*) temps *m*, mesure *f*; (*of policeman*) ronde *f* ♦ *vt*, *pt* **beat**, *pp* **beaten** battre; **off the beaten track** hors des chemins *or* sentiers battus; **to beat about the bush** tourner autour du pot; **that beats everything!** c'est le comble!

▶ **beat down** *vt* (*door*) enfoncer; (*price*) faire baisser; (*seller*) faire descendre ♦ *vi* (*rain*) tambouriner; (*sun*) taper

▶ **beat off** *vt* repousser

▶ **beat up** *vt* (*eggs*) battre; (*col: person*) tabasser

beating ['biːtɪŋ] *n* raclée *f*

beautiful ['bjuːtɪful] *adj* beau(belle)

beautifully ['bjuːtɪflɪ] *adv* admirablement

beauty ['bjuːtɪ] *n* beauté *f*; **the beauty of it is that ...** le plus beau, c'est que ...

beauty salon *n* institut *m* de beauté

beauty spot *n* grain *m* de beauté; (*BRIT TOURISM*) site naturel (d'une grande beauté)

beaver ['biːvə*] *n* castor *m*

because [bɪˈkɔz] *conj* parce que; **because of** *prep* à cause de

beck [bɛk] *n*: **to be at sb's beck and call** être à l'entière disposition de qn

beckon ['bɛkən] *vt* (*also*: **beckon to**) faire signe (de venir) à

become [bɪˈkʌm] *vt* (*irreg: like* **come**) devenir; **to become fat/thin** grossir/maigrir; **to become angry** se mettre en colère; **it became known that** on apprit que; **what has become of him?** qu'est-il devenu?

becoming [bɪˈkʌmɪŋ] *adj* (*behaviour*) convenable, bienséant(e); (*clothes*) seyant(e)

bed [bɛd] *n* lit *m*; (*of flowers*) parterre *m*; (*of coal, clay*) couche *f*; (*of sea, lake*) fond *m*; **to go to bed** aller se coucher

▶ **bed down** *vi* se coucher

bedclothes ['bɛdkləuðz] *npl* couvertures *fpl* et draps *mpl*

bedding ['bɛdɪŋ] *n* literie *f*

bed linen *n* draps *mpl* de lit (et taies *fpl*

d'oreillers), literie f

bedraggled [bɪ'drægld] *adj* dépenaillé(e), les vêtements en désordre

bedridden ['bedrɪdn] *adj* cloué(e) au lit

bedroom ['bedrum] *n* chambre *f* (à coucher)

bedside ['bedsaɪd] *n*: **at sb's bedside** au chevet de qn ♦ *cpd* (*book, lamp*) de chevet

bedsit(ter) ['bedsɪt(ə*)] *n* (*BRIT*) chambre meublée, studio *m*

bedspread ['bedspred] *n* couvre-lit, dessus-de-lit *m*

bedtime ['bedtaɪm] *n*: **it's bedtime** c'est l'heure de se coucher

bee [biː] *n* abeille *f*; **to have a bee in one's bonnet** (**about sth**) être obnubilé/e (par qch)

beech [biːtʃ] *n* hêtre *m*

beef [biːf] *n* bœuf *m*

► **beef up** *vt* (*col: support*) renforcer; (: *essay*) étoffer

beefburger ['biːfbə:gə*] *n* hamburger *m*

beefeater ['biːfiːtə*] *n* hallebardier *m* (de la tour de Londres)

beehive ['biːhaɪv] *n* ruche *f*

beeline ['biːlaɪn] *n*: **to make a beeline for** se diriger tout droit vers

been [biːn] *pp of* **be**

beer [bɪə*] *n* bière *f*

beet [biːt] *n* (*vegetable*) betterave *f*; (*us: also*: **red beet**) betterave (potagère)

beetle ['biːtl] *n* scarabée *m*, coléoptère *m*

beetroot ['biːtruːt] *n* (*BRIT*) betterave *f*

before [bɪ'fɔː*] *prep* (*of time*) avant; (*of space*) devant ♦ *conj* avant que + *sub*; avant de ♦ *adv* avant; **before going** avant de partir; **before she goes** avant qu'elle (ne) parte; **the week before** la semaine précédente *or* d'avant; **I've seen it before** je l'ai déjà vu; **I've never seen it before** c'est la première fois que je le vois

beforehand [bɪ'fɔːhænd] *adv* au préalable, à l'avance

beg [beg] *vi* mendier ♦ *vt* mendier; (*favour*) quémander, solliciter; (*entreat*) supplier; **I beg your pardon** (*apologising*) excusez-moi; (: *not hearing*) pardon?; **that begs the question of ...** cela soulève la question de ..., cela suppose réglée la question de ...

began [bɪ'gæn] *pt of* **begin**

beggar ['begə*] *n* (*also*: **beggarman, beggarwoman**) mendiant/e

begin, pt began, pp begun [bɪ'gɪn, -'gæn, -'gʌn] *vt, vi* commencer; **to begin doing** *or* **to do sth** commencer à faire qch; **beginning (from) Monday** à partir de lundi; **I can't begin to thank you** je ne saurais vous remercier; **to begin with** d'abord, pour commencer

beginner [bɪ'gɪnə*] *n* débutant/e

beginning [bɪ'gɪnɪŋ] *n* commencement *m*, début

m; **right from the beginning** dès le début

behalf [bɪ'hɑːf] *n*: **on behalf of**, (*us*) **in behalf of** de la part de; au nom de; pour le compte de

behave [bɪ'heɪv] *vi* se conduire, se comporter; (*well: also*: **behave o.s.**) se conduire bien *or* comme il faut

behaviour, (*us*) **behavior** [bɪ'heɪvjə*] *n* comportement *m*, conduite *f*

behead [bɪ'hed] *vt* décapiter

behind [bɪ'haɪnd] *prep* derrière; (*time*) en retard sur ♦ *adv* derrière; en retard ♦ *n* derrière *m*; **behind the scenes** dans les coulisses; **to leave sth behind** (*forget*) oublier de prendre qch; **to be behind (schedule) with sth** être en retard dans qch

behold [bɪ'həuld] *vt* (*irreg: like* **hold**) apercevoir, voir

beige [beɪʒ] *adj* beige

Beijing ['beɪ'dʒɪŋ] *n* Bei-jing, Pékin

being ['biːɪŋ] *n* être *m*; **to come into being** prendre naissance

Beirut [beɪ'ruːt] *n* Beyrouth

Belarus [belə'rus] *n* Bélarus *f*

belated [bɪ'leɪtɪd] *adj* tardif(ive)

belch [beltʃ] *vi* avoir un renvoi, roter ♦ *vt* (*also*: **belch out**: *smoke etc*) vomir, cracher

Belgian ['beldʒən] *adj* belge, de Belgique ♦ *n* Belge *m/f*

Belgium ['beldʒəm] *n* Belgique *f*

belie [bɪ'laɪ] *vt* démentir; (*give false impression of*) occulter

belief [bɪ'liːf] *n* (*opinion*) conviction *f*; (*trust, faith*) foi *f*; (*acceptance as true*) croyance *f*; **it's beyond belief** c'est incroyable; **in the belief that** dans l'idée que

believe [bɪ'liːv] *vt, vi* croire, estimer; **to believe in** (*God*) croire en; (*ghosts, method*) croire à; **I don't believe in corporal punishment** je ne suis pas partisan des châtiments corporels; **he is believed to be abroad** il serait à l'étranger

believer [bɪ'liːvə*] *n* (*in idea, activity*): **believer in** partisan/e de (*REL*) croyant/e

belittle [bɪ'lɪtl] *vt* déprécier, rabaisser

bell [bel] *n* cloche *f*; (*small*) clochette *f*, grelot *m*; (*on door*) sonnette *f*; (*electric*) sonnerie *f*; **that rings a bell** (*fig*) cela me rappelle qch

belligerent [bɪ'lɪdʒərənt] *adj* (*at war*) belligérant(e); (*fig*) agressif(ive)

bellow ['beləu] *vi* mugir; beugler ♦ *vt* (*orders*) hurler

belly ['belɪ] *n* ventre *m*

belong [bɪ'lɒŋ] *vi*: **to belong to** appartenir à; (*club etc*) faire partie de; **this book belongs here** ce livre va ici, la place de ce livre est ici

belongings [bɪ'lɒŋɪŋz] *npl* affaires *fpl*, possessions *fpl*; **personal belongings** effets personnels

beloved [bɪˈlʌvɪd] *adj* (bien-)aimé(e), chéri(e) ♦ *n* bien-aimé/e

below [bɪˈləu] *prep* sous, au-dessous de ♦ *adv* en dessous; en contre-bas; **see below** voir plus bas *or* plus loin *or* ci-dessous; **temperatures below normal** températures inférieures à la normale

belt [belt] *n* ceinture *f*; (*TECH*) courroie *f* ♦ *vt* (*thrash*) donner une raclée à ♦ *vi* (*BRIT col*) filer (à toutes jambes); **industrial belt** zone industrielle

▶ **belt out** *vt* (*song*) chanter à tue-tête *or* à pleins poumons

▶ **belt up** *vi* (*BRIT col*) la boucler

beltway [ˈbeltweɪ] *n* (*US AUT*) route *f* de ceinture; (: *motorway*) périphérique *m*

bemused [bɪˈmjuːzd] *adj* médusé(e)

bench [bentʃ] *n* banc *m*; (*in workshop*) établi *m*; **the Bench** (*LAW*) la magistrature, la Cour

bend [bend] *vb, pt, pp* **bent** [bent] *vt* courber; (*leg, arm*) plier ♦ *vi* se courber ♦ *n* (*BRIT: in road*) virage *m*, tournant *m*; (*in pipe, river*) coude *m*

▶ **bend down** *vi* se baisser

▶ **bend over** *vi* se pencher

beneath [bɪˈniːθ] *prep* sous, au-dessous de; (*unworthy of*) indigne de ♦ *adv* dessous, au-dessous, en bas

benefactor [ˈbenɪfæktə*] *n* bienfaiteur *m*

beneficial [benɪˈfɪʃəl] *adj*: **beneficial (to)** salutaire (pour), bénéfique (à)

benefit [ˈbenɪfɪt] *n* avantage *m*, profit *m*; (*allowance of money*) allocation *f* ♦ *vt* faire du bien à, profiter à ♦ *vi*: **he'll benefit from it** cela lui fera du bien, il y gagnera *or* s'en trouvera bien

Benelux [ˈbenɪlʌks] *n* Bénélux *m*

benevolent [bɪˈnevələnt] *adj* bienveillant(e)

benign [bɪˈnaɪn] *adj* (*person, smile*) bienveillant(e), affable; (*MED*) bénin(igne)

bent [bent] *pt, pp of* **bend** ♦ *n* inclination *f*, penchant *m* ♦ *adj* (*wire, pipe*) coudé(e); (*col: dishonest*) véreux(euse); **to be bent on** être résolu(e) à

bequest [bɪˈkwest] *n* legs *m*

bereaved [bɪˈriːvd] *n*: **the bereaved** la famille du disparu ♦ *adj* endeuillé(e)

beret [ˈbereɪ] *n* béret *m*

Berlin [bəːˈlɪn] *n* Berlin; **East/West Berlin** Berlin Est/Ouest

berm [bəːm] *n* (*US AUT*) accotement *m*

Bermuda [bəːˈmjuːdə] *n* Bermudes *fpl*

berry [ˈberɪ] *n* baie *f*

berserk [bəˈsəːk] *adj*: **to go berserk** être pris(e) d'une rage incontrôlable; se déchaîner

berth [bəːθ] *n* (*bed*) couchette *f*; (*for ship*) poste *m* d'amarrage, mouillage *m* ♦ *vi* (*in harbour*) venir à quai; (*at anchor*) mouiller; **to give sb a wide berth** (*fig*) éviter qn

beseech, *pt, pp* **besought** [bɪˈsiːtʃ, -ˈsɔːt] *vt* implorer, supplier

beset, *pt, pp* **beset** [bɪˈset] *vt* assaillir ♦ *adj*: **beset with** semé(e) de

beside [bɪˈsaɪd] *prep* à côté de; (*compared with*) par rapport à; **that's beside the point** ça n'a rien à voir; **to be beside o.s. (with anger)** être hors de soi

besides [bɪˈsaɪdz] *adv* en outre, de plus ♦ *prep* en plus de; (*except*) excepté

besiege [bɪˈsiːdʒ] *vt* (*town*) assiéger; (*fig*) assaillir

best [best] *adj* meilleur(e) ♦ *adv* le mieux; **the best part of** (*quantity*) le plus clair de, la plus grande partie de; **at best** au mieux; **to make the best of sth** s'accommoder de qch (du mieux que l'on peut); **to do one's best** faire de son mieux; **to the best of my knowledge** pour autant que je sache; **to the best of my ability** du mieux que je pourrai; **he's not exactly patient at the best of times** il n'est jamais spécialement patient; **the best thing to do is ...** le mieux, c'est de ...

best before date *n* date *f* de limite d'utilisation *or* de consommation

best man *n* garçon *m* d'honneur

bestow [bɪˈstəu] *vt* accorder; (*title*) conférer

bet [bet] *n* pari *m* ♦ *vt, vi, pt, pp* **bet** *or* **betted** parier; **it's a safe bet** (*fig*) il y a de fortes chances

betray [bɪˈtreɪ] *vt* trahir

better [ˈbetə*] *adj* meilleur(e) ♦ *adv* mieux ♦ *vt* améliorer ♦ *n*: **to get the better of** triompher de, l'emporter sur; **a change for the better** une amélioration; **I had better go** il faut que je m'en aille; **you had better do it** vous feriez mieux de le faire; **he thought better of it** il s'est ravisé; **to get better** aller mieux; s'améliorer; **that's better!** c'est mieux!; **better off** *adj* plus à l'aise financièrement; (*fig*): **you'd be better off this way** vous vous en trouveriez mieux ainsi, ce serait mieux *or* plus pratique ainsi

betting [ˈbetɪŋ] *n* paris *mpl*

betting shop *n* (*BRIT*) bureau *m* de paris

between [bɪˈtwiːn] *prep* entre ♦ *adv* au milieu, dans l'intervalle; **the road between here and London** la route d'ici à Londres; **we only had 5 between us** nous n'en avions que 5 en tout

beverage [ˈbevərɪdʒ] *n* boisson *f* (*gén sans alcool*)

beware [bɪˈwɛə*] *vt, vi*: **to beware (of)** prendre garde (à)

bewildered [bɪˈwɪldəd] *adj* dérouté(e), ahuri(e)

beyond [bɪˈjɔnd] *prep* (*in space*) au-delà de; (*exceeding*) au-dessus de ♦ *adv* au-delà; **beyond doubt** hors de doute; **beyond repair** irréparable

bias [ˈbaɪəs] *n* (*prejudice*) préjugé *m*, parti pris; (*preference*) prévention *f*

bias(s)ed [ˈbaɪəst] *adj* partial(e), montrant un parti pris; **to be bias(s)ed against** avoir un préjugé contre

bib [bɪb] *n* bavoir *m*, bavette *f*

Bible [ˈbaɪbl] *n* Bible *f*

bicarbonate of soda [baɪˈkɑːbənɪt-] *n* bicarbonate *m* de soude

bicker ['bɪkə*] *vi* se chamailler

bicycle ['baɪsɪkl] *n* bicyclette *f*

bid [bɪd] *n* offre *f*; (*at auction*) enchère *f*; (*attempt*) tentative *f* ◆ *vb*, *pt* **bid** *or* **bade** [bæd], *pp* **bid** *or* **bidden** ['bɪdn] *vi* faire une enchère *or* offre ◆ *vt* faire une enchère *or* offre de; **to bid sb good day** souhaiter le bonjour à qn

bidder ['bɪdə*] *n*: **the highest bidder** le plus offrant

bidding ['bɪdɪŋ] *n* enchères *fpl*

bide [baɪd] *vt*: **to bide one's time** attendre son heure

bifocals [baɪ'fəʊklz] *npl* lunettes *fpl* à double foyer

big [bɪg] *adj* (*in height*: *person, building, tree*) grand(e); (*in bulk, amount*: *person, parcel, book*) gros (se); **to do things in a big way** faire les choses en grand

bigheaded ['bɪg'hɛdɪd] *adj* prétentieux(euse)

bigot ['bɪgət] *n* fanatique *m/f*, sectaire *m/f*

bigoted ['bɪgətɪd] *adj* fanatique, sectaire

bigotry ['bɪgətrɪ] *n* fanatisme *m*, sectarisme *m*

big top *n* grand chapiteau

bike [baɪk] *n* vélo *m*, bécane *f*

bikini [bɪ'ki:nɪ] *n* bikini *m*

bilingual [baɪ'lɪŋgwəl] *adj* bilingue

bill [bɪl] *n* note *f*, facture *f*; (*POL*) projet *m* de loi; (*US*: *banknote*) billet *m* (de banque); (*in restaurant*) addition *f*, note *f*; (*notice*) affiche *f*; (*THEAT*) **on the bill** à l'affiche; (*of bird*) bec *m* ◆ *vt* (*item*) facturer; (*customer*) remettre la facture à; **may I have the bill please?** est-ce que je peux avoir l'addition, s'il vous plaît?; **"stick** *or* **post no bills"** "défense d'afficher"; **to fit** *or* **fill the bill** (*fig*) faire l'affaire; **bill of exchange** lettre *f* de change; **bill of lading** connaissement *m*; **bill of sale** contrat *m* de vente

billboard ['bɪlbɔ:d] *n* panneau *m* d'affichage

billet ['bɪlɪt] *n* cantonnement *m* (chez l'habitant) ◆ *vt* (*troops*) cantonner

billfold ['bɪlfəʊld] *n* (*US*) portefeuille *m*

billiards ['bɪljədz] *n* (jeu *m* de) billard *m*

billion ['bɪljən] *n* (*BRIT*) billion *m* (*million of millions*); (*US*) milliard *m*

bimbo ['bɪmbəʊ] *n* (*col*) ravissante idiote *f*

bin [bɪn] *n* boîte *f*; (*BRIT*: *also*: **dustbin**, **litterbin**) poubelle *f*; (*for coal*) coffre *m*

bind, *pt*, *pp* **bound** [baɪnd, baʊnd] *vt* attacher; (*book*) relier; (*oblige*) obliger, contraindre

▶ **bind over** *vt* (*LAW*) mettre en liberté conditionnelle

▶ **bind up** *vt* (*wound*) panser; **to be bound up in** (*work, research etc*) être complètement absorbé par, être accroché par; **to be bound up with** (*person*) être accroché à

binding ['baɪndɪŋ] *n* (*of book*) reliure *f* ◆ *adj* (*contract*) qui constitue une obligation

binge [bɪndʒ] *n* (*col*): **to go on a binge** faire la bringue

bingo ['bɪŋgəʊ] *n* sorte de jeu de loto pratiqué dans des établissements publics

binoculars [bɪ'nɒkjʊləz] *npl* jumelles *fpl*

biochemistry [baɪə'kemɪstrɪ] *n* biochimie *f*

biodegradable ['baɪəʊdɪ'greɪdəbl] *adj* biodégradable

biography [baɪ'ɒgrəfɪ] *n* biographie *f*

biological [baɪə'lɒdʒɪkl] *adj* biologique

biology [baɪ'ɒlədʒɪ] *n* biologie *f*

birch [bə:tʃ] *n* bouleau *m*

bird [bə:d] *n* oiseau *m*; (*BRIT col*: *girl*) nana *f*

bird flu *n* grippe *f* aviaire

bird's-eye view ['bə:dzaɪ-] *n* vue *f* à vol d'oiseau; (*fig*) vue d'ensemble *or* générale

bird watcher [-wɒtʃə*] *n* ornithologue *m/f* amateur

Biro® ['baɪərəʊ] *n* stylo *m* à bille

birth [bə:θ] *n* naissance *f*; **to give birth to** donner naissance à, mettre au monde; (*animal*) mettre bas

birth certificate *n* acte *m* de naissance

birth control *n* limitation *f* des naissances, méthode(s) contraceptive(s)

birthday ['bə:θdeɪ] *n* anniversaire *m*

birthplace ['bə:θpleɪs] *n* lieu *m* de naissance

birth rate *n* (taux *m* de) natalité *f*

biscuit ['bɪskɪt] *n* (*BRIT*) biscuit *m*; (*US*) petit pain au lait

bisect [baɪ'sɛkt] *vt* couper *or* diviser en deux

bishop ['bɪʃəp] *n* évêque *m*; (*CHESS*) fou *m*

bit [bɪt] *pt of* **bite** ◆ *n* morceau *m*; (*of tool*) mèche *f*; (*of horse*) mors *m*; (*COMPUT*) bit *m*, élément *m* binaire; **a bit of** un peu de; **a bit mad/dangerous** un peu fou/risqué; **bit by bit** petit à petit; **to come to bits** (*break*) tomber en morceaux, se déglinguer; **bring all your bits and pieces** apporte toutes tes affaires; **to do one's bit** y mettre du sien

bitch [bɪtʃ] *n* (*dog*) chienne *f*; (*col!*) salope *f* (!), garce *f*

bite [baɪt] *vt*, *vi*, *pt* **bit** [bɪt], *pp* **bitten** ['bɪtn] mordre ◆ *n* morsure *f*; (*insect bite*) piqûre *f*; (*mouthful*) bouchée *f*; **let's have a bite (to eat)** mangeons un morceau; **to bite one's nails** se ronger les ongles

bitter ['bɪtə*] *adj* amer(ère); (*criticism*) cinglant(e); (*icy*: *weather, wind*) glacial(e) ◆ *n* (*BRIT*: *beer*) bière *f* (à forte teneur en houblon) **to the bitter end** jusqu'au bout

bitterness ['bɪtənɪs] *n* amertume *f*; goût amer

black [blæk] *adj* noir(e) ◆ *n* (*colour*) noir *m*; (*person*): **Black** noir/e ◆ *vt* (*shoes*) cirer; (*BRIT INDUSTRY*) boycotter; **to give sb a black eye** pocher l'œil à qn, faire un œil au beurre noir à qn; **black coffee** café noir; **there it is in black and white** (*fig*) c'est écrit noir sur blanc; **to be in the black** (*in credit*) avoir un compte créditeur; **black and blue** *adj* couvert(e) de bleus

▶ **black out** vi (faint) s'évanouir

blackberry ['blækbərɪ] n mûre f

blackbird ['blækbɜːd] n merle m

blackboard ['blækbɔːd] n tableau noir

blackcurrant ['blæk'kʌrənt] n cassis m

blacken ['blækn] vt noircir

black ice n verglas m

blackleg ['blækleg] n (BRIT) briseur m de grève, jaune m

blacklist ['blæklɪst] n liste noire ♦ vt mettre sur la liste noire

blackmail ['blækmeɪl] n chantage m ♦ vt faire chanter, soumettre au chantage

black market n marché noir

blackout ['blækaʊt] n panne f d'électricité; (in wartime) black-out m; (TV) interruption f d'émission; (fainting) syncope f

black pudding n boudin (noir)

Black Sea n: **the Black Sea** la mer Noire

black sheep n brebis galeuse

blacksmith ['blæksmɪθ] n forgeron m

black spot n (AUT) point noir

bladder ['blædə*] n vessie f

blade [bleɪd] n lame f; (of oar) plat m; **blade of grass** brin m d'herbe

blame [bleɪm] n faute f, blâme m ♦ vt: **to blame sb/sth for sth** attribuer à qn/qch la responsabilité de qch; reprocher qch à qn/qch; **who's to blame?** qui est le fautif or coupable or responsable?; **I'm not to blame** ce n'est pas ma faute

bland [blænd] adj affable; (taste) doux(douce), fade

blank [blæŋk] adj blanc(blanche); (look) sans expression, dénué(e) d'expression ♦ n espace m vide, blanc m; (cartridge) cartouche f à blanc; **we drew a blank** (fig) nous n'avons abouti à rien

blanket ['blæŋkɪt] n couverture f ♦ adj (statement, agreement) global(e), de portée générale; **to give blanket cover** (subj: insurance policy) couvrir tous les risques

blare [blɛə*] vi (brass band, horns, radio) beugler

blast [blɑːst] n explosion f; (shock wave) souffle m; (of air, steam) bouffée f ♦ vt faire sauter or exploser ♦ excl (BRIT col) zut!; **(at) full blast** (play music etc) à plein volume

▶ **blast off** vi (SPACE) décoller

blast-off ['blɑːstɔf] n (SPACE) lancement m

blatant ['bleɪtənt] adj flagrant(e), criant(e)

blaze [bleɪz] n (fire) incendie m; (flames: of fire, sun etc) embrasement m; (: in hearth) flamme f, flambée f; (fig) flamboiement m ♦ vi (fire) flamber; (fig) flamboyer, resplendir ♦ vt: **to blaze a trail** (fig) montrer la voie; **in a blaze of publicity** à grand renfort de publicité

blazer ['bleɪzə*] n blazer m

bleach [bliːtʃ] n (also: **household bleach**) eau f de Javel ♦ vt (linen) blanchir

bleached [bliːtʃt] adj (hair) oxygéné(e), décoloré(e)

bleak [bliːk] adj morne, désolé(e); (weather) triste, maussade; (smile) lugubre; (prospect, future) morose

bleat [bliːt] n bêlement m ♦ vi bêler

bleed, pt, pp **bled** [bliːd, bled] vt saigner; (brakes, radiator) purger ♦ vi saigner; **my nose is bleeding** je saigne du nez

bleeper ['bliːpə*] n (of doctor etc) bip m

blemish ['blemɪʃ] n défaut m; (on reputation) tache f

blend [blend] n mélange m ♦ vt mélanger ♦ vi (colours etc) se mélanger, se fondre, s'allier

blender ['blendə*] n (CULIN) mixeur m

bless, pt, pp **blessed** or **blest** [bles, blest] vt bénir; **to be blessed with** avoir le bonheur de jouir de or d'avoir

blessing ['blesɪŋ] n bénédiction f; bienfait m; **to count one's blessings** s'estimer heureux; **it was a blessing in disguise** c'est un bien pour un mal

blew [bluː] pt of **blow**

blight [blaɪt] n (of plants) rouille f ♦ vt (hopes etc) anéantir, briser

blimey ['blaɪmɪ] excl (BRIT col) mince alors!

blind [blaɪnd] adj aveugle ♦ n (for window) store m ♦ vt aveugler; **to turn a blind eye (on or to)** fermer les yeux (sur)

blind alley n impasse f

blind corner n (BRIT) virage m sans visibilité

blindfold ['blaɪndfəʊld] n bandeau m ♦ adj, adv les yeux bandés ♦ vt bander les yeux à

blindly ['blaɪndlɪ] adv aveuglément

blindness ['blaɪndnɪs] n cécité f; (fig) aveuglement m

blind spot n (AUT etc) angle m aveugle; (fig) angle mort

blink [blɪŋk] vi cligner des yeux; (light) clignoter ♦ n: **the TV's on the blink** (col) la télé ne va pas tarder à nous lâcher

blinkers ['blɪŋkəz] npl œillères fpl

bliss [blɪs] n félicité f, bonheur m sans mélange

blister ['blɪstə*] n (on skin) ampoule f, cloque f; (on paintwork) boursouflure f ♦ vi (paint) se boursoufler, se cloquer

blizzard ['blɪzəd] n blizzard m, tempête f de neige

bloated ['bləʊtɪd] adj (face) bouffi(e); (stomach) gonflé(e)

blob [blɒb] n (drop) goutte f; (stain, spot) tache f

block [blɒk] n bloc m; (in pipes) obstruction f; (toy) cube m; (of buildings) pâté m (de maisons) ♦ vt bloquer; (COMPUT) grouper; **block of flats** (BRIT) immeuble (locatif); **3 blocks from here** à trois rues d'ici; **mental block** blocage m; **block and tackle** (TECH) palan m

▶ **block up** vt boucher

blockade [blɒ'keɪd] n blocus m ♦ vt faire le blocus de

blockage ['blɔkɪdʒ] *n* obstruction *f*

blockbuster ['blɔkbʌstə*] *n* (*film, book*) grand succès

block letters *npl* majuscules *fpl*

blog [blɔg] *n* (*fam*) blog *m*, blogue *f*

blogger [blɔgə*] *n* blogueur/euse

bloke [bləuk] *n* (*BRIT col*) type *m*

blond(e) [blɔnd] *adj, n* blond/e

blood [blʌd] *n* sang *m*

blood donor *n* donneur/euse de sang

blood group *n* groupe sanguin

bloodhound ['blʌdhaund] *n* limier *m*

blood poisoning *n* empoisonnement *m* du sang

blood pressure *n* tension (artérielle); **to have high/low blood pressure** faire de l'hypertension/ l'hypotension

bloodshed ['blʌdʃed] *n* effusion *f* de sang, carnage *m*

bloodshot ['blʌdʃɔt] *adj*: **bloodshot eyes** yeux injectés de sang

blood sports *npl* sports *mpl* sanguinaires

bloodstream ['blʌdstri:m] *n* sang *m*, système sanguin

blood test *n* analyse *f* de sang

bloodthirsty ['blʌdθə:stɪ] *adj* sanguinaire

blood vessel *n* vaisseau sanguin

bloody ['blʌdɪ] *adj* sanglant(e); (*BRIT col!*): **this bloody ...** ce foutu ..., ce putain de ... (!) **bloody good** (*col!*) vachement *or* sacrément bon

bloody-minded ['blʌdɪ'maɪndɪd] *adj* (*BRIT col*) contrariant(e), obstiné(e)

bloom [blu:m] *n* fleur *f*; (*fig*) épanouissement *m* ♦ *vi* être en fleur; (*fig*) s'épanouir; être florissant(e)

blossom ['blɔsəm] *n* fleur(s) *f(pl)* ♦ *vi* être en fleurs; (*fig*) s'épanouir; **to blossom into** (*fig*) devenir

blot [blɔt] *n* tache *f* ♦ *vt* tacher; (*ink*) sécher; **to be a blot on the landscape** gâcher le paysage; **to blot one's copy book** (*fig*) faire un impair

▶ **blot out** *vt* (*memories*) effacer; (*view*) cacher, masquer; (*nation, city*) annihiler

blotchy ['blɔtʃɪ] *adj* (*complexion*) couvert(e) de marbrures

blotting paper ['blɔtɪŋ-] *n* buvard *m*

blouse [blauz] *n* (*garment*) chemisier *m*, corsage *m*

blow [bləu] *n* coup *m* ♦ *vb, pt* **blew**, *pp* **blown** [blu:, bləun] *vi* souffler ♦ *vt* (*glass*) souffler; (*fuse*) faire sauter; **to blow one's nose** se moucher; **to blow a whistle** siffler; **to come to blows** en venir aux coups

▶ **blow away** *vi* s'envoler ♦ *vt* chasser, faire s'envoler

▶ **blow down** *vt* faire tomber, renverser

▶ **blow off** *vi* s'envoler ♦ *vt* (*hat*) emporter; (*ship*): **to blow off course** faire dévier

▶ **blow out** *vi* (*tyre*) éclater; (*fuse*) sauter

▶ **blow over** *vi* s'apaiser

▶ **blow up** *vi* exploser, sauter ♦ *vt* faire sauter; (*tyre*) gonfler; (*PHOT*) agrandir

blow-dry ['bləudraɪ] *n* (*hairstyle*) brushing *m* ♦ *vt* faire un brushing à

blowlamp ['bləulæmp] *n* (*BRIT*) chalumeau *m*

blow-out ['bləuaut] *n* (*of tyre*) éclatement *m*; (*BRIT col: big meal*) gueuleton *m*

blowtorch ['bləutɔ:tʃ] *n* chalumeau *m*

blue [blu:] *adj* bleu(e); **blue film/joke** film *m*/histoire *f* pornographique; **(only) once in a blue moon** tous les trente-six du mois; **out of the blue** (*fig*) à l'improviste, sans qu'on si attende

bluebell ['blu:bel] *n* jacinthe *f* des bois

bluebottle ['blu:bɔtl] *n* mouche *f* à viande

blueprint ['blu:prɪnt] *n* bleu *m*; (*fig*) projet *m*, plan directeur

bluff [blʌf] *vi* bluffer ♦ *n* bluff *m*; (*cliff*) promontoire *m*, falaise *f* ♦ *adj* (*person*) bourru(e), brusque; **to call sb's bluff** mettre qn au défi d'exécuter ses menaces

blunder ['blʌndə*] *n* gaffe *f*, bévue *f* ♦ *vi* faire une gaffe *or* une bévue; **to blunder into sb/sth** buter contre qn/qch

blunt [blʌnt] *adj* émoussé(e), peu tranchant(e); (*pencil*) mal taillé(e); (*person*) brusque, ne mâchant pas ses mots ♦ *vt* émousser; **blunt instrument** (*LAW*) instrument contondant

blur [blə:*] *n* tache *or* masse floue *or* confuse ♦ *vt* brouiller, rendre flou(e)

blush [blʌʃ] *vi* rougir ♦ *n* rougeur *f*

blustery ['blʌstərɪ] *adj* (*weather*) à bourrasques

boar [bɔ:*] *n* sanglier *m*

board [bɔ:d] *n* planche *f*; (*on wall*) panneau *m*; (*for chess etc*) plateau *m*; (*committee*) conseil *m*, comité *m*; (*in firm*) conseil d'administration; (*NAUT, AVIAT*): **on board** à bord ♦ *vt* (*ship*) monter à bord de; (*train*) monter dans; **full board** (*BRIT*) pension complète; **half board** (*BRIT*) demi-pension *f*; **board and lodging** *n* chambre *f* avec pension; **with board and lodging** logé nourri; **above board** (*fig*) régulier(ère); **across the board** (*fig: adv*) systématiquement; (: *adj*) de portée générale; **to go by the board** être abandonné(e); (*be unimportant*) compter pour rien, n'avoir aucune importance

▶ **board up** *vt* (*door*) condamner (*au moyen de planches, de tôle*)

boarder ['bɔ:də*] *n* pensionnaire *m/f*; (*SCOL*) interne *m/f*, pensionnaire

board game *n* jeu *m* de société

boarding card ['bɔ:dɪŋ-] *n* (*AVIAT, NAUT*) carte *f* d'embarquement

boarding house ['bɔ:dɪŋ-] *n* pension *f*

boarding pass ['bɔ:dɪŋ-] *n* (*BRIT*) = **boarding card**

boarding school ['bɔ:dɪŋ-] *n* internat *m*, pensionnat *m*

board room *n* salle *f* du conseil d'administration

boast [bəʊst] *vi*: **to boast (about** or **of)** se vanter (de) ♦ *vt* s'enorgueillir de ♦ *n* vantardise *f*; sujet *m* d'orgueil or de fierté

boat [bəʊt] *n* bateau *m*; (*small*) canot *m*; barque *f*; **to go by boat** aller en bateau; **to be in the same boat** (*fig*) être logé à la même enseigne

bob [bɔb] *vi* (*boat, cork on water*: *also*: **bob up and down**) danser, se balancer ♦ *n* (BRIT *col*) = *shilling*
▶ **bob up** *vi* surgir or apparaître brusquement

bobby [ˈbɔbɪ] *n* (BRIT *col*) ≃ agent *m* (de police)

bobsleigh [ˈbɔbsleɪ] *n* bob *m*

bode [bəʊd] *vi*: **to bode well/ill (for)** être de bon/ mauvais augure (pour)

bodily [ˈbɔdɪlɪ] *adj* corporel(le); (*pain, comfort*) physique; (*needs*) matériel(le) ♦ *adv* (*carry, lift*) dans ses bras

body [ˈbɔdɪ] *n* corps *m*; (*of car*) carrosserie *f*; (*of plane*) fuselage *m*; (*also*: **body stocking**) body *m*, justaucorps *m*; (*fig*: *society*) organe *m*, organisme *m*; (: *quantity*) masse *f*, ensemble *m*, masse *f*; (*of wine*) corps *m*; **ruling body** organe directeur; **in a body** en masse, ensemble; (*speak*) comme un seul et même homme

body-building [ˈbɔdɪbɪldɪŋ] *n* body-building *m*, culturisme *m*

bodyguard [ˈbɔdɪgɑːd] *n* garde *m* du corps

bodywork [ˈbɔdɪwɜːk] *n* carrosserie *f*

bog [bɔg] *n* tourbière *f* ♦ *vt*: **to get bogged down (in)** (*fig*) s'enliser (dans)

bog-standard [ˈbɔgˈstændəd] (*inf*) *adj* tout à fait ordinaire

bogus [ˈbəʊgəs] *adj* bidon *inv*; fantôme

boil [bɔɪl] *vt* (*faire*) bouillir ♦ *vi* bouillir ♦ *n* (MED) furoncle *m*; **to come to the** or (US) **a boil** bouillir; **to bring to the** or (US) **a boil** porter à ébullition; **boiled egg** œuf *m* à la coque; **boiled potatoes** pommes *fpl* à l'anglaise or à l'eau
▶ **boil down** *vi* (*fig*): **to boil down to** se réduire or ramener à
▶ **boil over** *vi* déborder

boiler [ˈbɔɪlə*] *n* chaudière *f*

boiling point *n* point *m* d'ébullition

boisterous [ˈbɔɪstərəs] *adj* bruyant(e), tapageur(euse)

bold [bəʊld] *adj* hardi(e), audacieux(euse); (*pej*) effronté(e); (*outline, colour*) franc(franche) tranché(e), marqué(e)

bollard [ˈbɔləd] *n* (NAUT) bitte *f* d'amarrage; (BRIT AUT) borne lumineuse or de signalisation

bolt [bəʊlt] *n* verrou *m*; (*with nut*) boulon *m* ♦ *adv*: **bolt upright** droit(e) comme un piquet ♦ *vt* verrouiller; (*food*) engloutir ♦ *vi* se sauver, filer (comme une flèche); **a bolt from the blue** (*fig*) un coup de tonnerre dans un ciel bleu

bomb [bɔm] *n* bombe *f* ♦ *vt* bombarder

bomb disposal *n*: **bomb disposal unit** section *f* de déminage; **bomb disposal expert** artificier *m*

bomber [ˈbɔmə*] *n* caporal *m* d'artillerie; (AVIAT) bombardier *m*; (*terrorist*) poseur *m* de bombes

bombing [ˈbɔmɪŋ] *n* bombardement *m*

bombshell [ˈbɔmʃɛl] *n* obus *m*; (*fig*) bombe *f*

bond [bɔnd] *n* lien *m*; (*binding promise*) engagement *m*, obligation *f*; (FINANCE) obligation; **in bond** (*of goods*) en entrepôt

bondage [ˈbɔndɪdʒ] *n* esclavage *m*

bone [bəʊn] *n* os *m*; (*of fish*) arête *f* ♦ *vt* désosser; ôter les arêtes de

bone-dry [ˈbəʊnˈdraɪ] *adj* absolument sec(sèche)

bone idle *adj* fainéant(e)

bone marrow *n* moelle osseuse

bonfire [ˈbɔnfaɪə*] *n* feu *m* (de joie); (*for rubbish*) feu

bonnet [ˈbɔnɪt] *n* bonnet *m*; (BRIT: *of car*) capot *m*

bonus [ˈbəʊnəs] *n* prime *f*, gratification *f*; (*on wages*) prime

bony [ˈbəʊnɪ] *adj* (*arm, face*: MED: *tissue*) osseux(euse); (*thin*: *person*) squelettique; (*meat*) plein(e) d'os; (*fish*) plein d'arêtes

boo [buː] *excl* hou!, peuh! ♦ *vt* huer ♦ *n* huée *f*

booby trap [ˈbuːbɪ-] *n* guet-apens *m*

book [buk] *n* livre *m*; (*of stamps etc*) carnet *m*; (COMM): **books** *npl* comptes *mpl*, comptabilité *f* ♦ *vt* (*ticket*) prendre; (*seat, room*) réserver; (*driver*) dresser un procès-verbal à; (*football player*) prendre le nom de, donner un carton à; **to keep the books** tenir la comptabilité; **by the book** à la lettre, selon les règles; **to throw the book at sb** passer un savon à qn
▶ **book in** *vi* (BRIT: *at hotel*) prendre sa chambre
▶ **book up** *vt* réserver; **all seats are booked up** tout est pris, c'est complet; **the hotel is booked up** l'hôtel est complet

bookcase [ˈbukkeɪs] *n* bibliothèque *f* (*meuble*)

booking office *n* (BRIT) bureau *m* de location

book-keeping [ˈbukˈkiːpɪŋ] *n* comptabilité *f*

booklet [ˈbuklɪt] *n* brochure *f*

bookmaker [ˈbukmeɪkə*] *n* bookmaker *m*

bookseller [ˈbuksɛlə*] *n* libraire *m/f*

bookshelf [ˈbukʃɛlf] *n* (*single*) étagère *f* (à livres); **bookshelves** rayons *mpl* (de bibliothèque)

bookshop [ˈbukʃɔp] *n* librairie *f*

bookstore [ˈbukstɔː*] *n* = **bookshop**

boom [buːm] *n* (*noise*) grondement *m*; (*busy period*) boom *m*, vague *f* de prospérité ♦ *vi* gronder; prospérer

boon [buːn] *n* bénédiction *f*, grand avantage

boost [buːst] *n* stimulant *m*, remontant *m* ♦ *vt* stimuler; **to give a boost to sb's spirits** or **to sb** remonter le moral à qn

booster [ˈbuːstə*] *n* (TV) amplificateur *m* (de signal); (ELEC) survolteur *m*; (*also*: **booster rocket**) booster *m*; (MED: *vaccine*) rappel *m*

boot [buːt] *n* botte *f*; (*for hiking*) chaussure *f* (de marche); (*for football etc*) soulier *m*; (*ankle boot*) bottine *f*; (BRIT: *of car*) coffre *m* ♦ *vt* (COMPUT) lancer, mettre en route; **to boot** (*in addition*) par-dessus le marché, en plus; **to give sb the boot** (*col*) flanquer qn dehors, virer qn

booth [buːð] *n* (*at fair*) baraque (foraine); (*of cinema, telephone etc*) cabine *f*; (*also*: **voting booth**) isoloir *m*

booze [buːz] (*col*) *n* boissons *fpl* alcooliques, alcool *m* ♦ *vi* boire, picoler

border ['bɔːdə⁎] *n* bordure *f*; bord *m*; (*of a country*) frontière *f*; **the Border** la frontière entre l'Écosse et l'Angleterre; **the Borders** la région frontière entre l'Écosse et l'Angleterre

▶ **border on** *vt fus* être voisin(e) de, toucher à

borderline ['bɔːdəlaɪn] *n* (*fig*) ligne *f* de démarcation ♦ *adj*: **borderline case** cas *m* limite

bore [bɔː⁎] *pt of* **bear** ♦ *vt* (*hole*) percer; (*person*) ennuyer, raser ♦ *n* (*person*) raseur/euse; (*of gun*) calibre *m*; **he's bored to tears** *or* **bored to death** *or* **bored stiff** il s'ennuie à mourir

boredom ['bɔːdəm] *n* ennui *m*

boring ['bɔːrɪŋ] *adj* ennuyeux(euse)

born [bɔːn] *adj*: **to be born** naître; **I was born in 1960** je suis né en 1960; **born blind** aveugle de naissance; **a born comedian** un comédien-né

borne [bɔːn] *pp of* **bear**

borough ['bʌrə] *n* municipalité *f*

borrow ['bɔrəu] *vt*: **to borrow sth (from sb)** emprunter qch (à qn); **may I borrow your car?** est-ce que je peux vous emprunter votre voiture?

Bosnia-Herzegovina ['bɔːsnɪəhɜːzə'gəuviːnə] *n* (*also*: **Bosnia-Hercegovina**) Bosnie-Herzégovine *f*

Bosnian ['bɔznɪən] *adj* bosniaque, bosnien(ne) ♦ *n* Bosniaque *m/f*, Bosnien/ne

bosom ['buzəm] *n* poitrine *f*; (*fig*) sein *m*

boss [bɔs] *n* patron/ne ♦ *vt* (*also*: **boss about**, **boss around**) mener à la baguette

bossy ['bɔsɪ] *adj* autoritaire

bosun ['bəusn] *n* maître *m* d'équipage

botany ['bɔtənɪ] *n* botanique *f*

botch [bɔtʃ] *vt* (*also*: **botch up**) saboter, bâcler

both [bəuθ] *adj* les deux, l'un(e) et l'autre ♦ *pron*: **both (of them)** les deux, tous(toutes) (les) deux l'un(e) et l'autre; **both of us went, we both went** nous y sommes allés tous les deux ♦ *adv*: **they sell both the fabric and the finished curtains** ils vendent (et) le tissu et les rideaux finis), ils vendent à la fois le tissu et les rideaux (finis)

bother ['bɔðə⁎] *vt* (*worry*) tracasser; (*needle, bait*) importuner, ennuyer; (*disturb*) déranger ♦ *vi* (*also*: **bother o.s.**) se tracasser, se faire du souci ♦ *n*: **it is a bother to have to do** c'est vraiment ennuyeux d'avoir à faire ♦ *excl* zut!; **to bother doing** prendre la peine de faire; **I'm sorry to bother you** excusez-

moi de vous déranger; **please don't bother** ne vous dérangez pas; **don't bother** ce n'est pas la peine; **it's no bother** aucun problème

bottle ['bɔtl] *n* bouteille *f*; (*baby's*) biberon *m*; (*of perfume, medicine*) flacon *m* ♦ *vt* mettre en bouteille(s); **bottle of wine/milk** bouteille de vin/lait; **wine/milk bottle** bouteille à vin/lait

▶ **bottle up** *vt* refouler, contenir

bottle bank *n* conteneur *m* (de bouteilles)

bottleneck ['bɔtlnɛk] *n* (*in traffic*) bouchon *m*; (*in production*) goulet *m* d'étranglement

bottle-opener ['bɔtləupnə⁎] *n* ouvre-bouteille *m*

bottom ['bɔtəm] *n* (*of container, sea etc*) fond *m*; (*buttocks*) derrière *m*; (*of page, list*) bas *m*; (*of chair*) siège *m*; (*of mountain, tree, hill*) pied *m* ♦ *adj* du fond; du bas; **to get to the bottom of sth** (*fig*) découvrir le fin fond de qch

bough [bau] *n* branche *f*, rameau *m*

bought [bɔːt] *pt*, *pp of* **buy**

boulder ['bəuldə⁎] *n* gros rocher (*gén lisse, arrondi*)

bounce [bauns] *vi* (*ball*) rebondir; (*cheque*) être refusé (*étant sans provision*) (*also*: **to bounce forward/out etc**) bondir, s'élancer ♦ *vt* faire rebondir ♦ *n* (*rebound*) rebond *m*; **he's got plenty of bounce** (*fig*) il est plein d'entrain *or* d'allant

bouncer ['baunsə⁎] *n* (*col*) videur *m*

bound [baund] *pt*, *pp of* **bind** ♦ *n* (*gen pl*) limite *f*; (*leap*) bond *m* ♦ *vt* (*leap*) bondir; (*limit*) borner ♦ *adj*: **to be bound to do sth** (*obliged*) être obligé(e) *or* avoir obligation de faire qch; **he's bound to fail** (*likely*) il est sûr d'échouer, son échec est inévitable *or* assuré; **bound for** à destination de; **out of bounds** dont l'accès est interdit

boundary ['baundrɪ] *n* frontière *f*

bout [baut] *n* période *f*; (*of malaria etc*) accès *m*, crise *f*, attaque *f*; (BOXING) combat *m*, match *m*

bow¹ [bəu] *n* nœud *m*; (*weapon*) arc *m*; (MUS) archet *m*

bow² [bau] *n* (*with body*) révérence *f*, inclination *f* (du buste *or* corps); (NAUT: *also*: **bows**) proue *f* ♦ *vi* faire une révérence, s'incliner; (*yield*): **to bow to** *or* **before** s'incliner devant, se soumettre à; **to bow to the inevitable** accepter l'inévitable *or* l'inéluctable

bowels [bauəlz] *npl* intestins *mpl*; (*fig*) entrailles *fpl*

bowl [bəul] *n* (*for eating*) bol *m*; (*for washing*) cuvette *f*; (*ball*) boule *f*; (*of pipe*) fourneau *m* ♦ *vi* (CRICKET) lancer (la balle)

▶ **bowl over** *vt* (*fig*) renverser

bow-legged ['bəu'lɛgɪd] *adj* aux jambes arquées

bowler ['bəulə⁎] *n* joueur *m* de boules; (CRICKET) lanceur *m* (de la balle); (BRIT: *also*: **bowler hat**) (chapeau *m*) melon *m*

bowling ['bəulɪŋ] *n* (*game*) jeu *m* de boules, jeu de quilles

bowling alley *n* bowling *m*

bowling green n terrain m de boules (gazonné et carré)

bowls [bəʊlz] n (jeu m de) boules fpl

bow tie [bəʊ-] n nœud m papillon

box [bɒks] n boîte f; (also: **cardboard box**) carton m; (crate) caisse f; (THEAT) loge f; (BRIT AUT) intersection f (matérialisée par des marques au sol) ♦ vt mettre en boîte; (SPORT) boxer avec ♦ vi boxer, faire de la boxe

boxer ['bɒksə*] n (person) boxeur m; (dog) boxer m

boxer shorts npl caleçon m

boxing ['bɒksɪŋ] n (sport) boxe f

Boxing Day n (BRIT) le lendemain de Noël; voir encadré

BOXING DAY

Boxing Day est le lendemain de Noël, férié en Grande-Bretagne. Si Noël tombe un samedi, le jour férié est reculé jusqu'au lundi suivant. Ce nom vient d'une coutume du XIXe siècle qui consistait à donner des cadeaux de Noël (dans des boîtes) à ses employés etc le 26 décembre.

---

boxing gloves npl gants mpl de boxe

boxing ring n ring m

box office n bureau m de location

box room n débarras m; chambrette f

boy [bɔɪ] n garçon m

boycott ['bɔɪkɒt] n boycottage m ♦ vt boycotter

boyfriend ['bɔɪfrɛnd] n (petit) ami

boyish ['bɔɪɪʃ] adj d'enfant, de garçon; **to look boyish** (man: appear youthful) faire jeune

BR abbr = **British Rail**

bra [brɑː] n soutien-gorge m

brace [breɪs] n attache f, agrafe f; (on teeth) appareil m (dentaire); (tool) vilbrequin m; (TYP: also: **brace bracket**) accolade f ♦ vt consolider, soutenir; **to brace o.s.** (fig) se préparer mentalement

bracelet ['breɪslɪt] n bracelet m

bracing ['breɪsɪŋ] adj tonifiant(e), tonique

bracket ['brækɪt] n (TECH) tasseau m, support m; (group) classe f, tranche f; (also: **brace bracket**) accolade f; (also: **round bracket**) parenthèse f; (also: **square bracket**) crochet m ♦ vt mettre entre parenthèses; (fig: also: **bracket together**) regrouper; **income bracket** tranche f des revenus; **in brackets** entre parenthèses or crochets)

brag [bræg] vi se vanter

braid [breɪd] n (trimming) galon m; (of hair) tresse f, natte f

brain [breɪn] n cerveau m; **brains** npl cervelle f; **he's got brains** il est intelligent

brainwash ['breɪnwɒʃ] vt faire subir un lavage de cerveau à

brainwave ['breɪnweɪv] n idée f de génie

brainy ['breɪnɪ] adj intelligent(e), doué(e)

braise [breɪz] vt braiser

brake [breɪk] n frein m ♦ vt, vi freiner

brake light n feu m de stop

bran [bræn] n son m

branch [brɑːntʃ] n branche f; (COMM) succursale f; (: bank) agence f; (of association) section locale ♦ vi bifurquer

▶ **branch out** vi diversifier ses activités; **to branch out into** étendre ses activités à

brand [brænd] n marque (commerciale) ♦ vt (cattle) marquer (au fer rouge); (fig: pej): **to brand sb a communist** etc traiter or qualifier qn de communiste etc

brand-new ['brænd'njuː] adj tout(e) neuf(neuve), flambant neuf(neuve)

brandy ['brændɪ] n cognac m, fine f

brash [bræʃ] adj effronté(e)

brass [brɑːs] n cuivre m (jaune), laiton m; **the brass** (MUS) les cuivres

brass band n fanfare f

brat [bræt] n (pej) mioche m/f, môme m/f

brave [breɪv] adj courageux(euse), brave ♦ n guerrier indien ♦ vt braver, affronter

bravery ['breɪvərɪ] n bravoure f, courage m

brawl [brɔːl] n rixe f, bagarre f ♦ vi se bagarrer

brazen ['breɪzn] adj impudent(e), effronté(e) ♦ vt: **to brazen it out** payer d'effronterie, crâner

brazier ['breɪzɪə*] n brasero m

Brazil [brə'zɪl] n Brésil m

breach [briːtʃ] vt ouvrir une brèche dans ♦ n (gap) brèche f; (estrangement) brouille f; (breaking): **breach of contract** rupture f de contrat; **breach of the peace** attentat m à l'ordre public; **breach of trust** abus m de confiance

bread [brɛd] n pain m; (col: money) fric m; **bread and butter** n tartines (beurrées); (fig) subsistance f; **to earn one's daily bread** gagner son pain; **to know which side one's bread is buttered (on)** savoir où est son avantage or intérêt

breadbin ['brɛdbɪn] n (BRIT) boîte f or huche f à pain

breadcrumbs ['brɛdkrʌmz] npl miettes fpl de pain; (CULIN) chapelure f, panure f

breadline ['brɛdlaɪn] n: **to be on the breadline** être sans le sou or dans l'indigence

breadth [brɛtθ] n largeur f

breadwinner ['brɛdwɪnə*] n soutien m de famille

break [breɪk], vb: pt **broke** [brəʊk], pp **broken** ['brəʊkən] vt casser, briser; (promise) rompre; (law) violer ♦ vi, se briser; (weather) tourner ♦ n (gap) brèche f; (fracture) cassure f; (rest) interruption f, arrêt m; (: short) pause f; (: at school) récréation f; (chance) chance f, occasion f favorable; **to break one's leg** etc se casser la jambe etc; **to break a record** battre un record; **to break the news to sb** annoncer la nouvelle à qn; **to break with sb**

rompre avec qn; **to break even** vi rentrer dans ses frais; **to break free** or **loose** vi se dégager, s'échapper; **to take a break** (few minutes) faire une pause, s'arrêter cinq minutes; (holiday) prendre un peu de repos; **without a break** sans interruption, sans arrêt

▶ **break down** vt (door etc) enfoncer; (resistance) venir à bout de; (figures, data) décomposer, analyser ♦ vi s'effondrer; (MED) faire une dépression (nerveuse); (AUT) tomber en panne

▶ **break in** vt (horse etc) dresser ♦ vi (burglar) entrer par effraction

▶ **break into** vt fus (house) s'introduire or pénétrer par effraction dans

▶ **break off** vi (speaker) s'interrompre; (branch) se rompre ♦ vt (talks, engagement) rompre

▶ **break open** vt (door etc) forcer, fracturer

▶ **break out** vi éclater, se déclarer; **to break out in spots** se couvrir de boutons

▶ **break through** vi: **the sun broke through** le soleil a fait son apparition ♦ vt fus (defences, barrier) franchir; (crowd) se frayer un passage à travers

▶ **break up** vi (partnership) cesser, prendre fin; (marriage) se briser; (friends) se séparer; (line) couper; **the line's** or **you're breaking up** ça coupe ♦ vt fracasser, casser; (fight etc) interrompre, faire cesser; (marriage) désunir

breakage ['breɪkɪdʒ] n casse f; **to pay for breakages** payer la casse

breakdown ['breɪkdaun] n (AUT) panne f; (in communications) rupture f; (MED: also: **nervous breakdown**) dépression (nerveuse); (of figures) ventilation f, répartition f

breakdown van n (BRIT) dépanneuse f

breaker ['breɪkə*] n brisant m

breakfast ['brekfəst] n petit déjeuner m

break-in ['breɪkɪn] n cambriolage m

breaking and entering ['breɪkɪŋənd'entərɪŋ] n (LAW) effraction f

breakthrough ['breɪkθruː] n percée f

breakwater ['breɪkwɔːtə*] n brise-lames m inv, digue f

breast [brest] n (of woman) sein m; (chest) poitrine f

breast-feed ['brestfiːd] vt, vi (irreg: like **feed**) allaiter

breaststroke ['breststrəuk] n brasse f

breath [breθ] n haleine f, souffle m; **to go out for a breath of air** sortir prendre l'air; **out of breath** à bout de souffle, essoufflé(e)

Breathalyser® ['breθəlaɪzə*] n alcootest m

breathe [briːð] vt, vi respirer; **I won't breathe a word about it** je n'en soufflerai pas mot, je n'en dirai rien à personne

▶ **breathe in** vi inspirer ♦ vt aspirer

▶ **breathe out** vt, vi expirer

breather ['briːðə*] n moment m de repos

breathing ['briːðɪŋ] n respiration f

breathless ['breθlɪs] adj essoufflé(e), haletant(e), oppressé(e); **breathless with excitement** le souffle coupé par l'émotion

breath-taking ['breθteɪkɪŋ] adj stupéfiant(e), à vous couper le souffle

breed [briːd], pt, pp **bred** [bred] vt élever, faire l'élevage de; (fig: hate, suspicion) engendrer ♦ vi se reproduire ♦ n race f, variété f

breeding ['briːdɪŋ] n reproduction f; élevage m; (upbringing) éducation f

breeze [briːz] n brise f

breezy ['briːzi] adj frais(fraîche); aéré(e); désinvolte; jovial(e)

brevity ['brevɪti] n brièveté f

brew [bruː] vt (tea) faire infuser; (beer) brasser; (plot) tramer, préparer ♦ vi (tea) infuser; (beer) fermenter; (fig) se préparer, couver

brewery ['bruːəri] n brasserie f (fabrique)

bribe [braɪb] n pot-de-vin m ♦ vt acheter; soudoyer; **to bribe sb to do sth** soudoyer qn pour qu'il fasse qch

bribery ['braɪbəri] n corruption f

brick [brɪk] n brique f

bricklayer ['brɪkleɪə*] n maçon m

bridal ['braɪdl] adj nuptial(e); **bridal party** noce f

bride [braɪd] n mariée f, épouse f

bridegroom ['braɪdgruːm] n marié m, époux m

bridesmaid ['braɪdzmeɪd] n demoiselle f d'honneur

bridge [brɪdʒ] n pont m; (NAUT) passerelle f (de commandement); (of nose) arête f; (CARDS, DENTISTRY) bridge m ♦ vt (river) construire un pont sur; (gap) combler

bridle ['braɪdl] n bride f ♦ vt refréner, mettre la bride à; (horse) brider

bridle path n piste or allée cavalière

brief [briːf] adj bref(brève) ♦ n (LAW) dossier m, cause f ♦ vt (MIL etc) donner des instructions à; **in brief** ... (en) bref ...; **to brief sb (about sth)** mettre qn au courant (de qch)

briefcase ['briːfkeɪs] n serviette f; porte-documents m inv

briefly ['briːfli] adv brièvement; (visit) en coup de vent; **to glimpse briefly** entrevoir

bright [braɪt] adj brillant(e); (room, weather) clair(e); (person) intelligent(e), doué(e); (colour) vif(vive); **to look on the bright side** regarder le bon côté des choses

brighten ['braɪtn] (also: **brighten up**) vt (room) éclaircir; égayer ♦ vi s'éclaircir; (person) retrouver un peu de sa gaieté

brilliance ['brɪljəns] n éclat m; (fig: of person) brio m

brilliant ['brɪljənt] adj brillant(e)

brim [brɪm] n bord m

brine [braɪn] n eau salée; (CULIN) saumure f

bring, *pt, pp* **brought** [brɪŋ, brɔːt] *vt* (*thing*) apporter; (*person*) amener; **to bring sth to an end** mettre fin à qch; **I can't bring myself to fire him** je ne peux me résoudre à le mettre à la porte

▶ **bring about** *vt* provoquer, entraîner

▶ **bring back** *vt* rapporter; (*person*) ramener

▶ **bring down** *vt* (*lower*) abaisser; (*shoot down*) abattre; (*government*) faire s'effondrer

▶ **bring forward** *vt* avancer; (*BOOK-KEEPING*) reporter

▶ **bring in** *vt* (*person*) faire entrer; (*object*) rentrer; (*POL: legislation*) introduire; (*LAW: verdict*) rendre; (*produce: income*) rapporter

▶ **bring off** *vt* (*task, plan*) réussir, mener à bien; (*deal*) mener à bien

▶ **bring out** *vt* (*meaning*) faire ressortir, mettre en relief; (*new product, book*) sortir

▶ **bring round, bring to** *vt* (*unconscious person*) ranimer

▶ **bring up** *vt* élever; (*question*) soulever; (*food: vomit*) vomir, rendre

brink [brɪŋk] *n* bord *m*; **on the brink of doing** sur le point de faire, à deux doigts de faire; **she was on the brink of tears** elle était au bord des larmes

brisk [brɪsk] *adj* vif(vive); (*abrupt*) brusque; (*trade etc*) actif(ive); **to go for a brisk walk** se promener d'un bon pas; **business is brisk** les affaires marchent (bien)

bristle ['brɪsl] *n* poil *m* ◆ *vi* se hérisser; **bristling with** hérissé(e) de

Britain ['brɪtən] *n* (*also:* **Great Britain**) la Grande-Bretagne; **in Britain** en Grande-Bretagne

British ['brɪtɪʃ] *adj* britannique; **the British** *npl* les Britanniques *mpl*; **the British Isles** les îles *fpl* Britanniques

British Rail (BR) *n* compagnie ferroviaire britannique ≃ SNCF *f*

Briton ['brɪtən] *n* Britannique *m/f*

Brittany ['brɪtənɪ] *n* Bretagne *f*

brittle ['brɪtl] *adj* cassant(e), fragile

broach [brəutʃ] *vt* (*subject*) aborder

broad [brɔːd] *adj* large; (*distinction*) général(e); (*accent*) prononcé(e) ◆ *n* (*US col*) nana *f*; **broad hint** allusion transparente; **in broad daylight** en plein jour; **the broad outlines** les grandes lignes

broadcast ['brɔːdkɑːst] *n* émission *f* ◆ *vb, pt, pp* **broadcast** [brɔːdkɑːst] *vt* radiodiffuser; téléviser ◆ *vi* émettre

broaden ['brɔːdn] *vt* élargir ◆ *vi* s'élargir

broadly ['brɔːdlɪ] *adv* en gros, généralement

broad-minded ['brɔːd'maɪndɪd] *adj* large d'esprit

broccoli ['brɔkəlɪ] *n* brocoli *m*

brochure ['brəuʃjuə*] *n* prospectus *m*, dépliant *m*

broil [brɔɪl] *vt* rôtir

broke [brəuk] *pt of* **break** ◆ *adj* (*col*) fauché(e); **to go broke** (*business*) faire faillite

broken ['brəukn] *pp of* **break** ◆ *adj* (*stick, leg etc*) cassé(e); (*promise, vow*) rompu(e); **a broken marriage** un couple dissocié; **a broken home** un foyer désuni; **in broken French/English** dans un français/anglais approximatif *or* hésitant

broken-hearted ['brəukn'hɑːtɪd] *adj* (ayant) le cœur brisé

broker ['brəukə*] *n* courtier *m*

brolly ['brɔlɪ] *n* (*BRIT col*) pépin *m*, parapluie *m*

bronchitis [brɔŋ'kaɪtɪs] *n* bronchite *f*

bronze [brɔnz] *n* bronze *m*

brooch [brəutʃ] *n* broche *f*

brood [bruːd] *n* couvée *f* ◆ *vi* (*hen, storm*) couver; (*person*) méditer (sombrement), ruminer

broom [brum] *n* balai *m*

broomstick ['brumstɪk] *n* manche *m* à balai

Bros. *abbr* (*COMM*: = *brothers*) Frères

broth [brɔθ] *n* bouillon *m* de viande et de légumes

brothel ['brɔθl] *n* maison close, bordel *m*

brother ['brʌðə*] *n* frère *m*

brother-in-law ['brʌðərɪn'lɔː*] *n* beau-frère *m*

brought [brɔːt] *pt, pp of* **bring**

brow [brau] *n* front *m*; (*rare: gen:* **eyebrow**) sourcil *m*; (*of hill*) sommet *m*

brown [braun] *adj* brun(e), marron *inv*; (*hair*) châtain *inv*; (*rice, bread, flour*) complet(ète) ◆ *n* (*colour*) brun *m*, marron *m* ◆ *vt* brunir; (*CULIN*) faire dorer, faire roussir; **to go brown** (*person*) bronzer; (*leaves*) jaunir

brown bread *n* pain *m* bis

Brownie ['braunɪ] *n* jeannette *f*, éclaireuse (cadette)

brown paper *n* papier *m* d'emballage, papier kraft

brown sugar *n* cassonade *f*

browse [brauz] *vi* (*among books*) bouquiner, feuilleter les livres; (*animal*) paître; **to browse through a book** feuilleter un livre

browser ['brauzə*] *n* (*COMPUT*) navigateur *m*

bruise [bruːz] *n* bleu *m*, ecchymose *f*, contusion *f* ◆ *vt* contusionner, meurtrir ◆ *vi* (*fruit*) se taler, meurtrir; **to bruise one's arm** se faire un bleu au bras

brunette [bruː'net] *n* (femme) brune

brunt [brʌnt] *n*: **the brunt of** (*attack, criticism etc*) le plus gros de

brush [brʌʃ] *n* brosse *f*; (*quarrel*) accrochage *m*, prise *f* de bec ◆ *vt* brosser; (*also:* **brush past**, **brush against**) effleurer, frôler; **to have a brush with sb** s'accrocher avec qn; **to have a brush with the police** avoir maille à partir avec la police

▶ **brush aside** *vt* écarter, balayer

▶ **brush up** *vt* (*knowledge*) rafraîchir, réviser

brushwood ['brʌʃwud] *n* broussailles *fpl*, taillis *m*

Brussels ['brʌslz] *n* Bruxelles

Brussels sprout *n* chou *m* de Bruxelles

brutal ['bru:tl] *adj* brutal(e)

brute [bru:t] *n* brute *f* ♦ *adj*: **by brute force** par la force

BSc *n abbr* = Bachelor of Science

BSE *n abbr* (= bovine spongiform encephalopathy) ESB *f*, BSE *f*

bubble ['bʌbl] *n* bulle *f* ♦ *vi* bouillonner, faire des bulles; (*sparkle, fig*) pétiller

bubble bath *n* bain moussant

bubble gum *n* bubblegum *m*

buck [bʌk] *n* mâle *m* (*d'un lapin, lièvre, daim etc*); (*us col*) dollar *m* ♦ *vi* ruer, lancer une ruade; **to pass the buck (to sb)** se décharger de la responsabilité (sur qn)

▶ **buck up** *vi* (*cheer up*) reprendre du poil de la bête, se remonter ♦ *vt*: **to buck one's ideas up** se reprendre

bucket ['bʌkɪt] *n* seau *m* ♦ *vi* (*BRIT col*): **the rain is bucketing (down)** il pleut à verse

Buckingham Palace ['bʌkɪŋhəm-] *n* le palais de Buckingham; *voir encadré*

BUCKINGHAM PALACE

Buckingham Palace est la résidence officielle londonienne du souverain britannique depuis 1762. Construit en 1703, il fut à l'origine le palais du duc de Buckingham. Il a été partiellement reconstruit au début du siècle.

buckle ['bʌkl] *n* boucle *f* ♦ *vt* boucler, attacher; (*warp*) tordre, gauchir; (*: wheel*) voiler

▶ **buckle down** *vi* s'y mettre

bud [bʌd] *n* bourgeon *m*; (*of flower*) bouton *m* ♦ *vi* bourgeonner; (*flower*) éclore

Buddhism ['budɪzəm] *n* bouddhisme *m*

Buddhist ['budɪst] *adj* bouddhiste ♦ *n* Bouddhiste *m/f*

budding ['bʌdɪŋ] *adj* (*flower*) en bouton; (*poet etc*) en herbe; (*passion etc*) naissant(e)

buddy ['bʌdɪ] *n* (*us*) copain *m*

budge [bʌdʒ] *vt* faire bouger ♦ *vi* bouger

budgerigar ['bʌdʒərɪgɑ:*] *n* perruche *f*

budget ['bʌdʒɪt] *n* budget *m* ♦ *vi*: **to budget for sth** inscrire qch au budget; **I'm on a tight budget** je dois faire attention à mon budget

budgie ['bʌdʒɪ] *n* = **budgerigar**

buff [bʌf] *adj* (*couleur f*) chamois ♦ *n* (*enthusiast*) mordu/e

buffalo, *pl* **buffalo** or **buffaloes** ['bʌfələu] *n* buffle *m*; (*us*) bison *m*

buffer ['bʌfə*] *n* tampon *m*; (*COMPUT*) mémoire *f* tampon

buffet *n* ['bufeɪ] (*food, BRIT: bar*) buffet *m* ♦ *vt* ['bʌfɪt] gifler, frapper; secouer, ébranler

buffet car *n* (*BRIT RAIL*) voiture-bar *f*

bug [bʌg] *n* (*insect*) punaise *f*; (*: gen*) insecte *m*, bestiole *f*; (*fig: germ*) virus *m*, microbe *m*; (*spy device*) dispositif *m* d'écoute (électronique), micro clandestin; (*COMPUT: of program*) erreur *f*; (*: of equipment*) défaut *m* ♦ *vt* (*room*) poser des micros dans; (*col: annoy*) embêter; **I've got the travel bug** (*fig*) j'ai le virus du voyage

bugle ['bju:gl] *n* clairon *m*

build [bɪld] *n* (*of person*) carrure *f*, charpente *f* ♦ *vt, pt, pp* **built** [bɪlt] construire, bâtir

▶ **build on** *vt fus* (*fig*) tirer parti de, partir de

▶ **build up** *vt* accumuler, amasser; (*business*) développer; (*reputation*) bâtir

builder ['bɪldə*] *n* entrepreneur *m*

building ['bɪldɪŋ] *n* construction *f*; (*structure*) bâtiment *m*, construction; (*: residential, offices*) immeuble *m*

building society *n* (*BRIT*) société *f* de crédit immobilier; *voir encadré*

BUILDING SOCIETY

Une **building society** est une mutuelle dont les épargnants et emprunteurs sont les propriétaires. Ces mutuelles offrent deux services principaux: on peut y avoir un compte d'épargne duquel on peut retirer son argent sur demande ou moyennant un court préavis et on peut également y faire des emprunts à long terme, par exemple pour acheter une maison. Les building societies ont eu jusqu'en 1985 le quasi-monopole des comptes d'épargne et des prêts immobiliers, mais les banques ont maintenant une part importante de ce marché.

built [bɪlt] *pt, pp of* **build**

built-in ['bɪlt'ɪn] *adj* (*cupboard*) encastré(e); (*device*) incorporé(e); intégré(e)

built-up area ['bɪltʌp-] *n* agglomération (urbaine); zone urbanisée

bulb [bʌlb] *n* (*BOT*) bulbe *m*, oignon *m*; (*ELEC*) ampoule *f*

Bulgaria [bʌl'gɛərɪə] *n* Bulgarie *f*

bulge [bʌldʒ] *n* renflement *m*, gonflement *m*; (*in birth rate, sales*) brusque augmentation *f* ♦ *vi* faire saillie; présenter un renflement; **to be bulging with** être plein(e) à craquer de

bulk [bʌlk] *n* masse *f*, volume *m*; **in bulk** (*COMM*) en gros, en vrac; **the bulk of** la plus grande or grosse partie de

bulky ['bʌlkɪ] *adj* volumineux(euse), encombrant(e)

bull [bul] *n* taureau *m*; (*STOCK EXCHANGE*) haussier *m*; (*REL*) bulle *f*

bulldog ['buldɔg] *n* bouledogue *m*

bulldozer ['buldəuzə*] *n* bulldozer *m*

bullet ['bulɪt] *n* balle *f* (*de fusil etc*)

bulletin ['bulɪtɪn] *n* bulletin *m*, communiqué *m*

bulletin board n (COMPUT) messagerie f (électronique)

bulletproof ['bʊlɪtpruːf] adj à l'épreuve des balles; **bulletproof vest** gilet m pare-balles

bullfight ['bʊlfaɪt] n corrida f, course f de taureaux

bullfighter ['bʊlfaɪtə*] n torero m

bullfighting ['bʊlfaɪtɪŋ] n tauromachie f

bullion ['bʊljən] n or m or argent m en lingots

bullock ['bʊlək] n bœuf m

bullring ['bʊlrɪŋ] n arène f

bull's-eye ['bʊlzaɪ] n centre m (de la cible)

bully ['bʊlɪ] n brute f, tyran m ♦ vt tyranniser, rudoyer; (frighten) intimider

bum [bʌm] n (col: backside) derrière m; (: tramp) vagabond/e, traîne-savates m/f inv; (: idler) glandeur m

▶ **bum around** vi (col) vagabonder

bumblebee ['bʌmblbiː] n bourdon m

bump [bʌmp] n (blow) coup m, choc m; (jolt) cahot m; (on road etc, on head) bosse f ♦ vt heurter, cogner; (car) emboutir

▶ **bump along** vi avancer en cahotant

▶ **bump into** vt fus rentrer dans, tamponner; (col: meet) tomber sur

bumper ['bʌmpə*] n pare-chocs m inv ♦ adj: **bumper crop/harvest** récolte/moisson exceptionnelle

bumper cars npl (US) autos tamponneuses

bumpy ['bʌmpɪ] adj cahoteux(euse); **it was a bumpy flight/ride** on a été secoués dans l'avion/la voiture

bun [bʌn] n petit pain au lait; (of hair) chignon m

bunch [bʌntʃ] n (of flowers) bouquet m; (of keys) trousseau m; (of bananas) régime m; (of people) groupe m; **bunch of grapes** grappe f de raisin

bundle ['bʌndl] n paquet m ♦ vt (also: **bundle up**) faire un paquet de; (put): **to bundle sth/sb into** fourrer or enfourner qch/qn dans

▶ **bundle off** vt (person) faire sortir (en toute hâte); expédier

▶ **bundle out** vt éjecter, sortir (sans ménagements)

bungalow ['bʌŋɡələʊ] n bungalow m

bungle ['bʌŋɡl] vt bâcler, gâcher

bunion ['bʌnjən] n oignon m (au pied)

bunk [bʌŋk] n couchette f; (BRIT col): **to do a bunk** mettre les bouts or les voiles

▶ **bunk off** vi (BRIT col: SCOL) sécher (les cours); **I'll bunk off at 3 o'clock this afternoon** je vais mettre les bouts or les voiles à 3 heures cet aprèsmidi

bunk beds npl lits superposés

bunker ['bʌŋkə*] n (coal store) soute f à charbon; (MIL, GOLF) bunker m

bunting ['bʌntɪŋ] n pavoisement m, drapeaux mpl

buoy [bɔɪ] n bouée f

▶ **buoy up** vt faire flotter; (fig) soutenir, épauler

buoyant ['bɔɪənt] adj (ship) flottable; (carefree) gai(e), plein(e) d'entrain; (COMM: market) actif(ive); (: prices, currency) soutenu(e)

burden ['bəːdn] n fardeau m, charge f ♦ vt charger; (oppress) accabler, surcharger; **to be a burden to sb** être un fardeau pour qn

bureau, pl bureaux ['bjʊərəʊ, -z] n (BRIT: writing desk) bureau m, secrétaire m; (US: chest of drawers) commode f; (office) bureau, office m

bureaucracy [bjʊəˈrɔkrəsɪ] n bureaucratie f

burglar ['bəːɡlə*] n cambrioleur m

burglar alarm n sonnerie f d'alarme

burglary ['bəːɡlərɪ] n cambriolage m

Burgundy ['bəːɡəndɪ] n Bourgogne f

burial ['bɛrɪəl] n enterrement m

burly ['bəːlɪ] adj de forte carrure, costaud(e)

Burma ['bəːmə] n Birmanie f; see also **Myanmar**

burn [bəːn] vt, vi, pt, pp **burned** or **burnt** [bəːnt] brûler ♦ n brûlure f; **the cigarette burnt a hole in her dress** la cigarette a fait un trou dans sa robe; **I've burnt myself!** je me suis brûlé(e)!

▶ **burn down** vt incendier, détruire par le feu

▶ **burn out** vt (writer etc): **to burn o.s. out** s'user (à force de travailler)

burner ['bəːnə*] n brûleur m

burning ['bəːnɪŋ] adj (building, forest) en flammes; (issue, question) brûlant(e)

Burns' Night [bəːnz-] voir encadré

BURNS' NIGHT

Burns' Night est une fête qui a lieu le 25 janvier, à la mémoire du poète écossais Robert Burns (1759–1796), à l'occasion de laquelle les Écossais partout dans le monde organisent un souper, en général arrosé de whisky. Le plat principal est toujours le haggis, servi avec de la purée de pommes de terre et de la purée de rutabagas. On apporte le haggis au son des cornemuses et au cours du repas on lit des poèmes de Burns et on chante ses chansons.

---

burrow ['bʌrəʊ] n terrier m ♦ vt creuser

bursary ['bəːsərɪ] n (BRIT) bourse f (d'études)

burst [bəːst] vb (pt, pp **burst**) vt faire éclater ♦ vi éclater ♦ n explosion f; (also: **burst pipe**) fuite f (due à une rupture) **burst of energy** activité soudaine; **burst of laughter** éclat m de rire; **a burst of applause** une salve d'applaudissements; **a burst of speed** une pointe de vitesse; **burst blood vessel** rupture f de vaisseau sanguin; **the river has burst its banks** le cours d'eau est sorti de son lit; **to burst into flames** s'enflammer soudainement; **to burst out laughing** éclater de rire; **to burst into tears** fondre en larmes; **to burst open** vi s'ouvrir violemment or soudainement; **to be bursting with** être plein(e) (à craquer) de; regorger de

▶ **burst into** vt fus (room etc) faire irruption dans

▶ **burst out of** vt fus sortir précipitamment de

bury ['berɪ] vt enterrer; **to bury one's face in one's hands** se couvrir le visage de ses mains; **to bury one's head in the sand** (fig) pratiquer la politique de l'autruche; **to bury the hatchet** (fig) enterrer la hache de guerre

bus, pl **buses** [bʌs, 'bʌsɪz] n autobus m

bush [buʃ] n buisson m; (scrubland) brousse f

bushy ['buʃɪ] adj broussailleux(euse), touffu(e)

busily ['bɪzɪlɪ] adv: **to be busily doing sth** s'affairer à faire qch

business ['bɪznɪs] n (matter, firm) affaire f; (trading) affaires fpl; (job, duty) travail m; **to be away on business** être en déplacement d'affaires; **I'm here on business** je suis là pour affaires; **he's in the insurance business** il est dans les assurances; **to do business with sb** traiter avec qn; **it's none of my business** cela ne me regarde pas, ce ne sont pas mes affaires; **he means business** il ne plaisante pas, il est sérieux

businesslike ['bɪznɪslaɪk] adj sérieux(euse); efficace

businessman ['bɪznɪsmən] n homme m d'affaires

business trip n voyage m d'affaires

businesswoman ['bɪznɪswumən] n femme f d'affaires

busker ['bʌskə*] n (BRIT) artiste ambulant(e)

bus shelter n abribus m

bus station n gare routière

bus stop n arrêt m d'autobus

bust [bʌst] n buste m ◆ adj (col: broken) fichu(e), fini(e) ◆ vt (col: POLICE: arrest) pincer; **to go bust** faire faillite

bustle ['bʌsl] n remue-ménage m, affairement m ◆ vi s'affairer, se démener

bustling ['bʌslɪŋ] adj (person) affairé(e); (town) très animé(e)

busy ['bɪzɪ] adj occupé(e); (shop, street) très fréquenté(e); (US: telephone, line) occupé ◆ vt: **to busy o.s.** s'occuper; **he's a busy man** (normally) c'est un homme très pris; (temporarily) il est très pris

busybody ['bɪzɪbɔdɪ] n mouche f du coche, âme f charitable

busy signal n (US) tonalité f occupé

KEYWORD

but [bʌt] conj mais; **I'd love to come, but I'm busy** j'aimerais venir mais je suis occupé
◆ prep (apart from, except) sauf, excepté; **nothing but trouble** rien d'autre que; **we've had nothing but trouble** nous n'avons eu que des ennuis; **no-one but him can do it** lui seul peut le faire; **but for you/your help** sans toi/ton aide; **anything but that** tout sauf or excepté ça, tout mais pas ça; **the last but one** (BRIT) l'avant-dernier(ère)

◆ adv (just, only) ne … que; **she's but a child** elle n'est qu'une enfant; **had I but known** si seulement j'avais su; **all but finished** pratiquement terminé; **anything but finished** tout sauf fini, très loin d'être fini

butcher ['butʃə*] n boucher m ◆ vt massacrer; (cattle etc for meat) tuer; **butcher's (shop)** boucherie f

butler ['bʌtlə*] n maître m d'hôtel

butt [bʌt] n (cask) gros tonneau; (thick end) (gros) bout; (of gun) crosse f; (of cigarette) mégot m; (BRIT fig: target) cible f ◆ vt donner un coup de tête à

▶ **butt in** vi (interrupt) interrompre

butter ['bʌtə*] n beurre m ◆ vt beurrer

buttercup ['bʌtəkʌp] n bouton m d'or

butterfly ['bʌtəflaɪ] n papillon m; (SWIMMING: also: **butterfly stroke**) brasse f papillon

buttocks ['bʌtəks] npl fesses fpl

button ['bʌtn] n bouton m ◆ vt (also: **button up**) boutonner ◆ vi se boutonner

buttress ['bʌtrɪs] n contrefort m

buy [baɪ] vb (pt, pp **bought** [bɔ:t]) vt acheter; (COMM: company) (r)acheter ◆ n: **that was a good/ bad buy** c'était un bon/mauvais achat; **to buy sth/sth from sb** acheter qch à qn; **to buy sb a drink** offrir un verre or à boire à qn

▶ **buy back** vt racheter

▶ **buy in** vi (BRIT: goods) acheter, faire venir

▶ **buy into** vt fus (BRIT COMM) acheter des actions de

▶ **buy off** vt (bribe) acheter

▶ **buy out** vt (partner) désintéresser; (business) racheter

▶ **buy up** vt acheter en bloc, rafler

buyer ['baɪə*] n acheteur/euse; **buyer's market** marché m favorable aux acheteurs

buzz [bʌz] n bourdonnement m; (col: phone call) coup m de fil ◆ vi bourdonner ◆ vt (call on intercom) appeler; (with buzzer) sonner; (AVIAT: plane, building) raser; **my head is buzzing** j'ai la tête qui bourdonne

▶ **buzz off** vi (col) s'en aller, ficher le camp

buzzer ['bʌzə*] n timbre m électrique

buzz word n (col) mot m à la mode or dans le vent

KEYWORD

by [baɪ] prep 1 (referring to cause, agent) par, de; **killed by lightning** tué par la foudre; **surrounded by a fence** entouré d'une barrière; **a painting by Picasso** un tableau de Picasso

2 (referring to method, manner, means): **by bus/ car** en autobus/voiture; **by train** par le or en train; **to pay by cheque** payer par chèque; **by saving hard, he …** à force d'économiser, il …

3 (via, through) par; **we came by Dover** nous sommes venus par Douvres

4 (close to, past) à côté de; **the house by the school** la maison à côté de l'école; **a holiday by**

the sea des vacances au bord de la mer; **she sat by his bed** elle était assise à son chevet; **she went by me** elle est passée à côté de moi; **I go by the post office every day** je passe devant la poste tous les jours

5 (*with time: not later than*) avant; (: *during*): **by daylight** à la lumière du jour; **by night** la nuit, de nuit; **by 4 o'clock** avant 4 heures; **by this time tomorrow** d'ici demain à la même heure; **by the time I got here it was too late** lorsque je suis arrivé il était déjà trop tard

6 (*amount*) à; **by the kilo/metre** au kilo/au mètre; **paid by the hour** payé à l'heure; **to increase** *etc* **by the hour** augmenter *etc* d'heure en heure

7 (*MATH: measure*): **to divide/multiply by 3** diviser/multiplier par 3; **a room 3 metres by 4** une pièce de 3 mètres sur 4; **it's broader by a metre** c'est plus large d'un mètre; **the bullet missed him by inches** la balle est passée à quelques centimètres de lui; **one by one** un à un; **little by little** petit à petit, peu à peu

8 (*according to*) d'après, selon; **it's 3 o'clock by my watch** il est 3 heures à ma montre; **it's all right by me** je n'ai rien contre

9: (all) **by oneself** *etc* tout(e) seul(e)

10: **by the way** au fait, à propos

♦ *adv* **1** *see* **go; pass** *etc*

2: **by and by** un peu plus tard, bientôt; **by and large** dans l'ensemble

bye(-bye) [ˈbaɪˈbaɪ] *excl* au revoir!, salut!

by(e)-law [ˈbaɪlɔː] *n* arrêté municipal

by-election [ˈbaɪlekʃən] *n* (*BRIT*) élection (législative) partielle

bygone [ˈbaɪɡɒn] *adj* passé(e) ♦ *n*: **let bygones be bygones** passons l'éponge, oublions le passé

bypass [ˈbaɪpɑːs] *n* (route *f* de) contournement *m*; (*MED*) pontage *m* ♦ *vt* éviter

by-product [ˈbaɪprɒdʌkt] *n* sous-produit *m*, dérivé *m*; (*fig*) conséquence *f* secondaire, retombée *f*

bystander [ˈbaɪstændə*] *n* spectateur/trice, badaud/e

byte [baɪt] *n* (*COMPUT*) octet *m*

byword [ˈbaɪwəːd] *n*: **to be a byword for** être synonyme de (*fig*)

— **C c** —

C, c [siː] *n* (*letter*) C, c *m*; (*SCOL: mark*) C; (*MUS*): **C** do *m*; **C for Charlie** C comme Célestin

C *abbr* (= *Celsius, centigrade*) C

c *abbr* (= *century*) s.; (= *circa*) v.; (*US etc*) = **cent(s)**

CA *n abbr* = **Central America**; (*BRIT*) = **chartered accountant** ♦ *abbr* (*US*) = **California**

cab [kæb] *n* taxi *m*; (*of train, truck*) cabine *f*; (*horse-drawn*) fiacre *m*

cabaret [ˈkæbəreɪ] *n* attractions *fpl*, spectacle *m* de cabaret

cabbage [ˈkæbɪdʒ] *n* chou *m*

cabin [ˈkæbɪn] *n* cabane *f*, hutte *f*; (*on ship*) cabine *f*

cabin crew *n* (*AVIAT*) équipage *m*

cabin cruiser *n* yacht *m* (à moteur)

cabinet [ˈkæbɪnɪt] *n* (*POL*) cabinet *m*; (*furniture*) petit meuble à tiroirs et rayons; (*also*: **display cabinet**) vitrine *f*, petite armoire vitrée

cable [ˈkeɪbl] *n* câble *m* ♦ *vt* câbler, télégraphier

cable-car [ˈkeɪblkɑː*] *n* téléphérique *m*

cable television *n* télévision *f* par câble

cache [kæʃ] *n* cachette *f*; **a cache of food** *etc* un dépôt secret de provisions *etc*, une cachette contenant des provisions *etc*

cackle [ˈkækl] *vi* caqueter

cactus, *pl* **cacti** [ˈkæktəs, -taɪ] *n* cactus *m*

cadet [kəˈdet] *n* (*MIL*) élève *m* officier; **police cadet** élève agent de police

cadge [kædʒ] *vt* (*col*) se faire donner; **to cadge a meal (off sb)** se faire inviter à manger (par qn)

Caesarean, (*US*) **Cesarean** [siːˈzeərɪən] *adj*: **Caesarean (section)** césarienne *f*

café [ˈkæfeɪ] *n* = café(-restaurant) *m* (*sans alcool*)

cage [keɪdʒ] *n* cage *f* ♦ *vt* mettre en cage

cagey [ˈkeɪdʒɪ] *adj* (*col*) réticent(e); méfiant(e)

cagoule [kəˈɡuːl] *n* K-way® *m*

Cairo [ˈkaɪərəu] *n* le Caire

cajole [kəˈdʒəul] *vt* couvrir de flatteries *or* de gentillesses

cake [keɪk] *n* gâteau *m*; **cake of soap** savonnette *f*; **it's a piece of cake** (*col*) c'est un jeu d'enfant; **he wants to have his cake and eat it (too)** (*fig*) il veut tout avoir

caked [keɪkt] *adj*: **caked with** raidi(e) par, couvert(e) d'une croûte de

calculate [ˈkælkjuleɪt] *vt* calculer; (*estimate: chances, effect*) évaluer

▶ **calculate on** *vt fus*: **to calculate on sth/on doing sth** compter sur qch/faire qch

calculation [kælkjuˈleɪʃən] *n* calcul *m*

calculator [ˈkælkjuleɪtə*] *n* machine *f* à calculer, calculatrice *f*

calendar [ˈkæləndə*] *n* calendrier *m*

calendar year *n* année civile

calf, *pl* **calves** [kɑːf, kɑːvz] *n* (*of cow*) veau *m*; (*of other animals*) petit *m*; (*also*: **calfskin**) veau *m*, vachette *f*; (*ANAT*) mollet *m*

calibre, (*US*) **caliber** [ˈkælɪbə*] *n* calibre *m*

call [kɔːl] *vt* (*gen, also TEL*) appeler; (*announce: flight*) annoncer; (*meeting*) convoquer; (*strike*) lancer ♦ *vi* appeler; (*visit: also*: **call in**, **call round**): **to call (for)** passer (prendre) ♦ *n* (*shout*) appel *m*, cri *m*; (*summons: for flight etc, fig: lure*) appel; (*visit*) visite f; (also: **telephone call**) coup m de téléphone; communication f; **to be on call** être de permanence; **she's called Suzanne** elle s'appelle Suzanne; **who is calling?** (TEL) qui est à l'appareil?; **London calling** (RADIO) ici Londres; **please give me a call at 7** appelez-moi à 7 heures; **to make a call** téléphoner, passer un coup de fil; **to pay a call on sb** rendre visite à qn, passer voir qn; **there's not much call for these items** ces articles ne sont pas très demandés

▶ **call at** vt fus (subj: ship) faire escale à; (train) s'arrêter à

▶ **call back** vi (return) repasser; (TEL) rappeler ◆ vt (TEL) rappeler

▶ **call for** vt fus demander

▶ **call in** vt (doctor, expert, police) appeler, faire venir

▶ **call off** vt annuler; **the strike was called off** l'ordre de grève a été rapporté

▶ **call on** vt fus (visit) rendre visite à, passer voir; (request): **to call on sb to do** inviter qn à faire

▶ **call out** vi pousser un cri or des cris ◆ vt (doctor, police, troops) appeler

▶ **call up** vt (MIL) appeler, mobiliser

callbox ['kɔːlbɔks] n (BRIT) cabine f téléphonique

call centre n centre m d'appels

caller ['kɔːlə*] n personne f qui appelle; visiteur m; **hold the line, caller!** (TEL) ne quittez pas, Monsieur (or Madame)!

call girl n call-girl f

call-in ['kɔːlɪn] n (US RADIO, TV) programme m à ligne ouverte

calling ['kɔːlɪŋ] n vocation f; (occupation) état m

calling card n (US) carte f de visite

callous ['kæləs] adj dur(e), insensible

calm [kɑːm] adj calme ◆ n calme m ◆ vt calmer, apaiser

▶ **calm down** vi se calmer, s'apaiser ◆ vt calmer, apaiser

Calor gas® ['kælə*-] n (BRIT) butane m, butagaz® m

calorie ['kælərɪ] n calorie f; **low calorie product** produit m pauvre en calories

calves [kɑːvz] npl of **calf**

camber ['kæmbə*] n (of road) bombement m

Cambodia [kæm'bəudjə] n Cambodge m

camcorder ['kæmkɔːdə*] n caméscope m

came [keɪm] pt of **come**

camel ['kæməl] n chameau m

camera ['kæmərə] n appareil-photo m; (CINE, TV) caméra f; **35mm camera** appareil 24 x 36 or petit format; **in camera** à huis clos, en privé

cameraman ['kæmərəmæn] n caméraman m

camera phone n téléphone m avec appareil photo numérique intégré

camouflage ['kæməflɑːʒ] n camouflage m ◆ vt camoufler

camp [kæmp] n camp m ◆ vi camper; **to go cam-** ping faire du camping

campaign [kæm'peɪn] n (MIL, POL etc) campagne f ◆ vi (also fig) faire campagne; **to campaign for/against** militer pour/contre

campbed ['kæmp'bed] n (BRIT) lit m de camp

camper ['kæmpə*] n campeur/euse

camping ['kæmpɪŋ] n camping m

camping gas® n butane m

camp(ing) site n (terrain m de) camping m

campus ['kæmpəs] n campus m

can¹ [kæn] aux vb see keyword ◆ n (of milk, oil, water) bidon m; (tin) boîte f (de conserve) ◆ vt mettre en conserve; **a can of beer** une canette de bière; **he had to carry the can** (BRIT col) on lui a fait porter le chapeau

KEYWORD

can² [kæn] (negative **cannot, can't**; conditional and pt **could**) aux vb 1 (be able to) pouvoir; **you can do it if you try** vous pouvez le faire si vous essayez; **I can't hear you** je ne t'entends pas

2 (know how to) savoir; **I can swim/play tennis/ drive** je sais nager/jouer au tennis/conduire; **can you speak French?** parlez-vous français?

3 (may) pouvoir; **can I use your phone?** puis-je me servir de votre téléphone?

4 (expressing disbelief, puzzlement etc): **it can't be true!** ce n'est pas possible!; **what CAN he want?** qu'est-ce qu'il peut bien vouloir?

5 (expressing possibility, suggestion etc): **he could be in the library** il est peut-être dans la bibliothèque; **she could have been delayed** il se peut qu'elle ait été retardée; **they could have forgotten** ils ont pu oublier

Canada ['kænədə] n Canada m

Canadian [kə'neɪdɪən] adj canadien(ne) ◆ n Canadien/ne

canal [kə'næl] n canal m

canary [kə'nɛərɪ] n canari m, serin m

cancel ['kænsəl] vt annuler; (train) supprimer; (party, appointment) décommander; (cross out) barrer, rayer; (stamp) oblitérer; (cheque) faire opposition à

▶ **cancel out** vt annuler; **they cancel each other out** ils s'annulent

cancellation [kænsə'leɪʃən] n annulation f; suppression f; oblitération f; (TOURISM) réservation annulée, client etc qui s'est décommandé

cancer ['kænsə*] n cancer m; **Cancer** (sign) le Cancer; **to be Cancer** être du Cancer

candid ['kændɪd] adj (très) franc(franche) sincère

candidate ['kændɪdeɪt] n candidat/e

candle ['kændl] n bougie f; (of tallow) chandelle f; (in church) cierge m

candlelight ['kændllaɪt] n: **by candlelight** à la lumière d'une bougie; (dinner) aux chandelles

candlestick ['kændlstɪk] n (also: **candle holder**)

bougeoir m; (bigger, ornate) chandelier m

candour, (US) **candor** ['kændə*] n (grande) franchise or sincérité

candy ['kændɪ] n sucre candi; (US) bonbon m

candy-floss ['kændɪflɒs] n (BRIT) barbe f à papa

cane [keɪn] n canne f; (for baskets, chairs etc) rotin m ◆ vt (BRIT SCOL) administrer des coups de bâton à

canister ['kænɪstə*] n boîte f (gén en métal)

cannabis ['kænəbɪs] n (drug) cannabis m; (also: **cannabis plant**) chanvre indien

canned ['kænd] adj (food) en boîte, en conserve; (col: music) enregistré(e); (BRIT col: drunk) bourré(e); (US col: worker) mis(e) à la porte

cannon, pl **cannon** or **cannons** ['kænən] n (gun) canon m

cannot ['kænɒt] = **can not**

canoe [kə'nu:] n pirogue f; (SPORT) canoë m

canoeing [kə'nu:ɪŋ] n (sport) canoë m

canon ['kænən] n (clergyman) chanoine m; (standard) canon m

can opener [-'əupnə*] n ouvre-boîte m

canopy ['kænəpɪ] n baldaquin m; dais m

can't [kænt] = **can not**

canteen [kæn'ti:n] n cantine f; (BRIT: of cutlery) ménagère f

canter ['kæntə*] n petit galop ◆ vi aller au petit galop

canvas ['kænvəs] n (gen) toile f; **under canvas** (camping) sous la tente; (NAUT) toutes voiles dehors

canvass ['kænvəs] vt (POL: district) faire la tournée électorale dans; (: person) solliciter le suffrage de; (COMM: district) prospecter; (citizens, opinions) sonder

canyon ['kænjən] n cañon m, gorge f (profonde)

cap [kæp] n casquette f; (for swimming) bonnet m de bain; (of pen) capuchon m; (of bottle) capsule f; (BRIT: contraceptive: also: **Dutch cap**) diaphragme m; (:FOOTBALL) sélection f pour l'équipe nationale ◆ vt capsuler; (outdo) surpasser; **capped with** coiffé(e) de; **and to cap it all, he ...** (BRIT) pour couronner le tout, il ...

capability [keɪpə'bɪlɪtɪ] n aptitude f, capacité f

capable ['keɪpəbl] adj capable; **capable of** (interpretation etc) susceptible de

capacity [kə'pæsɪtɪ] n (of container) capacité f, contenance f; (ability) aptitude f; **filled to capacity** plein(e); **in his capacity as** en sa qualité de; **in an advisory capacity** à titre consultatif; **to work at full capacity** travailler à plein rendement

cape [keɪp] n (garment) cape f; (GEO) cap m

caper ['keɪpə*] n (CULIN: also: **capers**) câpre f

capital ['kæpɪtl] n (also: **capital city**) capitale f; (money) capital m; (also: **capital letter**) majuscule f

capital gains tax n impôt m sur les plus-values

capitalism ['kæpɪtəlɪzəm] n capitalisme m

capitalist ['kæpɪtəlɪst] adj, n capitaliste (m/f)

capitalize ['kæpɪtəlaɪz] vt (provide with capital) financer

▶ **capitalize on** vt fus (fig) profiter de

capital punishment n peine capitale

Capitol ['kæpɪtl] n: **the Capitol** le Capitole; voir encadré

CAPITOL

Le **Capitol** est le siège du "Congress", à Washington. Il est situé sur Capitol Hill.

Capricorn ['kæprɪkɔ:n] n le Capricorne; **to be Capricorn** être du Capricorne

capsize [kæp'saɪz] vt faire chavirer ◆ vi chavirer

capsule ['kæpsju:l] n capsule f

captain ['kæptɪn] n capitaine m ◆ vt commander, être le capitaine de

caption ['kæpʃən] n légende f

captive ['kæptɪv] adj, n captif(ive)

capture ['kæptʃə*] vt capturer, prendre; (attention) capter ◆ n capture f

car [kɑ:*] n voiture f, auto f; (US RAIL) wagon m, voiture; **by car** en voiture

caramel ['kærəməl] n caramel m

caravan ['kærəvæn] n caravane f

caravanning ['kærəvænɪŋ] n: **to go caravanning** faire du caravaning

caravan site n (BRIT) camping m pour caravanes

carbohydrates [kɑ:bəu'haɪdreɪts] npl (foods) aliments mpl riches en hydrate de carbone

carbon ['kɑ:bən] n carbone m

carbon dioxide [-daɪ'ɒksaɪd] n gas m carbonique, dioxyde m de carbone

carbon monoxide [-mɒ'nɒksaɪd] n oxyde m de carbone

carbon paper n papier m carbone

car boot sale n marché aux puces où des particuliers vendent des objets entreposés dans le coffre de leur voiture.

carburettor, (US) **carburetor** [kɑ:bju'retə*] n carburateur m

card [kɑ:d] n carte f; (membership card) carte d'adhérent; **to play cards** jouer aux cartes

cardboard ['kɑ:dbɔ:d] n carton m

card game n jeu m de cartes

cardiac ['kɑ:dɪæk] adj cardiaque

cardigan ['kɑ:dɪgən] n cardigan m

cardinal ['kɑ:dɪnl] adj cardinal(e) ◆ n cardinal m

card index n fichier m (alphabétique)

cardphone ['kɑ:dfəun] n téléphone m à carte (magnétique)

care [kɛə*] n soin m, attention f; (worry) souci m ◆ vi: **to care about** se soucier de, s'intéresser à; **in sb's care** à la garde de qn, confié à qn; **care of (c/o)** (on letter) aux bons soins de; **"with care"** "fragile"; **to take care (to do)** faire attention (à faire); **to take care of** vt s'occuper de, prendre soin de; (details, *arrangements*) s'occuper de; **the child has been taken into care** l'enfant a été placé en institution; **would you care to/for …?** voulez-vous …?; **I wouldn't care to do it** je n'aimerais pas le faire; **I don't care** ça m'est bien égal, peu m'importe; **I couldn't care less** cela m'est complètement égal, je m'en fiche complètement

▶ **care for** *vt fus* s'occuper de; (*like*) aimer

career [kə'rɪə*] *n* carrière *f* ◆ *vi* (*also:* **career along**) aller à toute allure

career woman (*irreg*) *n* femme ambitieuse

carefree ['kɛəfriː] *adj* sans souci, insouciant(e)

careful ['kɛəful] *adj* soigneux(euse); (*cautious*) prudent(e); **(be) careful!** (fais) attention!; **to be careful with one's money** regarder à la dépense

carefully ['kɛəfəlɪ] *adv* avec soin, soigneusement; prudemment

careless ['kɛəlɪs] *adj* négligent(e); (*heedless*) insouciant(e)

carer ['kɛərə*] *n* personne qui s'occupe d'un proche qui est malade

caress [kə'rɛs] *n* caresse *f* ◆ *vt* caresser

caretaker ['kɛəteɪkə*] *n* gardien/ne, concierge *m/f*

car-ferry ['kɑːferɪ] *n* (*on sea*) ferry(-boat) *m*; (*on river*) bac *m*

cargo, *pl* **cargoes** ['kɑːgəu] *n* cargaison *f*, chargement *m*

car hire *n* (*BRIT*) location *f* de voitures

Caribbean [kærɪ'biːən] *adj* des Caraïbes; **the Caribbean (Sea)** la mer des Antilles *or* des Caraïbes

caring ['kɛərɪŋ] *adj* (*person*) bienveillant(e); (*society, organization*) humanitaire

carnation [kɑː'neɪʃən] *n* œillet *m*

carnival ['kɑːnɪvl] *n* (*public celebration*) carnaval *m*; (*US: funfair*) fête foraine

carol ['kærəl] *n*: **(Christmas) carol** chant *m* de Noël

carp [kɑːp] *n* (*fish*) carpe *f*

▶ **carp at** *vt fus* critiquer

car park *n* parking *m*, parc *m* de stationnement

carpenter ['kɑːpɪntə*] *n* charpentier *m*

carpentry ['kɑːpɪntrɪ] *n* charpenterie *f*, métier *m* de charpentier; (*woodwork: at school etc*) menuiserie *f*

carpet ['kɑːpɪt] *n* tapis *m* ◆ *vt* recouvrir (d'un tapis); **fitted carpet** (*BRIT*) moquette *f*

carpet sweeper [-'swiːpə*] *n* balai *m* mécanique

car phone *n* téléphone *m* de voiture

car rental *n* (*US*) location *f* de voitures

carriage ['kærɪdʒ] *n* voiture *f*; (*of goods*) transport *m*; (*: cost*) port *m*; (*of typewriter*) chariot *m*; (*bearing*) maintien *m*, port *m*; **carriage forward** port dû; **carriage free** franco de port; **carriage paid** (en) port payé

carriageway ['kærɪdʒweɪ] *n* (*BRIT: part of road*) chaussée *f*

carrier ['kærɪə*] *n* transporteur *m*, camionneur *m*; (*MED*) porteur/euse; (*NAUT*) porte-avions *m inv*

carrier bag *n* (*BRIT*) sac *m* en papier *or* en plastique

carrot ['kærət] *n* carotte *f*

carry ['kærɪ] *vt* (*subj: person*) porter; (*vehicle*) transporter; (*a motion, bill*) voter, adopter; (*MATH: figure*) retenir; (*COMM: interest*) rapporter; (*involve: responsibilities etc*) comporter, impliquer ◆ *vi* (*sound*) porter; **to be carried away** (*fig*) s'emballer, s'enthousiasmer; **this loan carries 10% interest** ce prêt est à 10% (d'intérêt)

▶ **carry forward** *vt* (*gen, BOOK-KEEPING*) reporter

▶ **carry on** *vi* (*continue*): **to carry on with sth/doing** continuer qch/à faire; (*col: make a fuss*) faire des histoires ◆ *vt* entretenir, poursuivre

▶ **carry out** *vt* (*orders*) exécuter; (*investigation*) effectuer; (*idea, threat*) mettre à exécution

carrycot ['kærɪkɔt] *n* (*BRIT*) porte-bébé *m*

carry-on ['kærɪ'ɔn] *n* (*col: fuss*) histoires *fpl*; (*: annoying behaviour*) cirque *m*, cinéma *m*

cart [kɑːt] *n* charrette *f* ◆ *vt* transporter

carton ['kɑːtən] *n* (*box*) carton *m*; (*of yogurt*) pot *m* (en carton); (*of cigarettes*) cartouche *f*

cartoon [kɑː'tuːn] *n* (*PRESS*) dessin *m* (humoristique); (*satirical*) caricature *f*; (*comic strip*) bande dessinée; (*CINE*) dessin animé

cartridge ['kɑːtrɪdʒ] *n* (*for gun, pen*) cartouche *f*; (*for camera*) chargeur *m*; (*music tape*) cassette *f*; (*of record player*) cellule *f*

carve [kɑːv] *vt* (*meat: also:* **carve up**) découper; (*wood, stone*) tailler, sculpter

carving ['kɑːvɪŋ] *n* (*in wood etc*) sculpture *f*

carving knife *n* couteau *m* à découper

car wash *n* station *f* de lavage (de voitures)

case [keɪs] *n* cas *m*; (*LAW*) affaire *f*, procès *m*; (*box*) caisse *f*, boîte *f*, étui *m*; (*BRIT: also:* **suitcase**) valise *f*; (*TYP*) **lower/upper case** minuscule *f*/majuscule *f*; **to have a good case** avoir de bons arguments; **there's a strong case for reform** il y aurait lieu d'engager une réforme; **in case of** en cas de; **in case he** au cas où il; **just in case** à tout hasard

cash [kæʃ] *n* argent *m*; (*COMM*) argent liquide, numéraire *m*; liquidités *fpl*; (*: in payment*) argent comptant, espèces *fpl* ◆ *vt* encaisser; **to pay (in) cash** payer (en argent) comptant *or* en espèces; **cash with order/on delivery** (*COMM*) payable *or* paiement à la commande/livraison; **to be short of cash** être à court d'argent

▶ **cash in** *vt* (*insurance policy etc*) toucher

▶ **cash in on** *vt fus* profiter de

cashbook ['kæʃbuk] *n* livre *m* de caisse

cash card *n* carte de retrait *or* accréditive

cash desk *n* (*BRIT*) caisse *f*

cash dispenser *n* distributeur *m* automatique

de billets

cashew [kæˈʃuː] n (also: **cashew nut**) noix f de cajou

cashier [kæˈʃɪə*] n caissier/ère ◆ vt (MIL) destituer, casser

cashmere [ˈkæʃmɪə*] n cachemire m

cash register n caisse enregistreuse

casing [ˈkeɪsɪŋ] n revêtement (protecteur), enveloppe (protectrice)

casino [kəˈsiːnəu] n casino m

casket [ˈkɑːskɪt] n coffret m; (US: coffin) cercueil m

casserole [ˈkæsərəul] n cocotte f; (food) ragoût m (en cocotte)

cassette [kæˈset] n cassette f, musicassette f

cassette player n lecteur m de cassettes

cassette recorder n magnétophone m à cassettes

cast [kɑːst] vb (pt, pp **cast**) vt (throw) jeter; (shed) perdre; se dépouiller de; (metal) couler, fondre; (THEAT): **to cast sb as Hamlet** attribuer à qn le rôle d'Hamlet ◆ n (THEAT) distribution f; (mould) moule m; (also: **plaster cast**) plâtre m; **to cast one's vote** voter, exprimer son suffrage

▶ **cast aside** vt (reject) rejeter

▶ **cast off** vi (NAUT) larguer les amarres; (KNITTING) arrêter les mailles ◆ vt (KNITTING) arrêter

▶ **cast on** (KNITTING) vt monter ◆ vi monter les mailles

castaway [ˈkɑːstəweɪ] n naufragé/e

caster sugar [ˈkɑːstə-] n (BRIT) sucre m semoule

casting vote [ˈkɑːstɪŋ-] n (BRIT) voix prépondérante (pour départager)

cast iron n fonte f ◆ adj: **cast-iron** (fig: will) de fer; (: alibi) en béton

castle [ˈkɑːsl] n château-fort m; (manor) château m

castor [ˈkɑːstə*] n (wheel) roulette f

castor oil n huile f de ricin

castrate [kæsˈtreɪt] vt châtrer

casual [ˈkæʒjul] adj (by chance) de hasard, fait(e) au hasard, fortuit(e); (irregular: work etc) temporaire; (unconcerned) désinvolte; **casual wear** vêtements mpl sport inv

casually [ˈkæʒjulɪ] adv avec désinvolture, négligemment; (by chance) fortuitement

casualty [ˈkæʒjultɪ] n accidenté/e, blessé/e; (dead) victime f, mort/e; **heavy casualties** lourdes pertes

cat [kæt] n chat m

catalogue, (US) **catalog** [ˈkætəlɒg] n catalogue m ◆ vt cataloguer

catalyst [ˈkætəlɪst] n catalyseur m

catalytic converter [kætəˈlɪtɪkkənˈvɜːtə*] n pot m catalytique

catapult [ˈkætəpʌlt] n lance-pierres m inv, fronde m; (HISTORY) catapulte f

catarrh [kəˈtɑː*] n rhume m chronique, catarrhe f

catastrophe [kəˈtæstrəfɪ] n catastrophe f

catch [kætʃ] vb (pt, pp **caught** [kɔːt]) vt (ball, train, thief, cold) attraper; (person: by surprise) prendre, surprendre; (understand) saisir; (get entangled) accrocher ◆ vi (fire) prendre; (get entangled) s'accrocher ◆ n (fish etc) prise f; (thief etc) capture f; (trick) attrape f; (TECH) loquet m; cliquet m; **to catch sb's attention** or **eye** attirer l'attention de qn; **to catch fire** prendre feu; **to catch sight of** apercevoir

▶ **catch on** vi (become popular) prendre; (understand): **to catch on (to sth)** saisir (qch)

▶ **catch out** vt (BRIT fig: with trick question) prendre en défaut

▶ **catch up** vi se rattraper, combler son retard ◆ vt (also: **catch up with**) rattraper

catching [ˈkætʃɪŋ] adj (MED) contagieux(euse)

catchment area [ˈkætʃmənt-] n (BRIT SCOL) aire f de recrutement; (GEO) bassin m hydrographique

catch phrase n slogan m; expression toute faite

catchy [ˈkætʃɪ] adj (tune) facile à retenir

category [ˈkætɪgərɪ] n catégorie f

cater [ˈkeɪtə*] vi (provide food): **to cater (for)** préparer des repas (pour)

▶ **cater for** vt fus (BRIT: needs) satisfaire, pourvoir à; (: readers, consumers) s'adresser à, pourvoir aux besoins de

caterer [ˈkeɪtərə*] n traiteur m; fournisseur m

catering [ˈkeɪtərɪŋ] n restauration f; approvisionnement m, ravitaillement m

caterpillar [ˈkætəpɪlə*] n chenille f ◆ cpd (vehicle) à chenille; **caterpillar track** n chenille f

cathedral [kəˈθiːdrəl] n cathédrale f

catholic [ˈkæθəlɪk] adj éclectique; universel(le); libéral(e); **Catholic** adj, n (REL) catholique (m/f)

cat's-eye [ˈkætsˈaɪ] n (BRIT AUT) (clou m à) cataudioptre m

cattle [ˈkætl] npl bétail m, bestiaux mpl

catty [ˈkætɪ] adj méchant(e)

caucus [ˈkɔːkəs] n (US POL) comité électoral (pour désigner des candidats); (BRIT POL: group) comité local (d'un parti politique); voir encadré

CAUCUS

Un **caucus** aux États-Unis est une réunion restreinte des principaux dirigeants d'un parti politique, précédant souvent une assemblée générale, dans le but de choisir des candidats ou de définir une ligne d'action. Par extension, ce terme désigne également l'état-major d'un parti politique.

---

caught [kɔːt] pt, pp of **catch**

cauliflower [ˈkɒlɪflauə*] n chou-fleur m

cause [kɔːz] n cause f ◆ vt causer; **there is no cause for concern** il n'y a pas lieu de s'inquiéter; **to cause sth to be done** faire faire qch; **to cause sb to do sth** faire faire qch à qn

caution [ˈkɔːʃən] n prudence f; (warning) avertissement m ◆ vt avertir, donner un avertissement à

cautious [ˈkɔːʃəs] adj prudent(e)

cavalry [ˈkævəlrɪ] n cavalerie f

cave [keɪv] n caverne f, grotte f ◆ vi: **to go caving** faire de la spéléo(logie)

▶ **cave in** vi (roof etc) s'effondrer

caveman [ˈkeɪvmæn] n homme m des cavernes

caviar(e) [ˈkævɪɑːʳ] n caviar m

CB n abbr (= Citizens' Band (Radio)) CB f; (BRIT: = Companion of (the Order of) the Bath) titre honorifique

CBI n abbr (= Confederation of British Industry) ≈ CNPF m, Conseil national du patronat français

cc abbr (= cubic centimetre) cm³; (on letter etc) = **carbon copy**

CD n abbr (= compact disc) CD m; (MIL) = Civil Defence (Corps) (BRIT), Civil Defense (US) ◆ abbr (BRIT: = Corps Diplomatique) CD

CD writer, CD burner n graveur m de CD

cease [siːs] vt, vi cesser

ceasefire [ˈsiːsfaɪəʳ] n cessez-le-feu m

ceaseless [ˈsiːslɪs] adj incessant(e), continuel(le)

cedar [ˈsiːdəʳ] n cèdre m

ceiling [ˈsiːlɪŋ] n (also fig) plafond m

celebrate [ˈselɪbreɪt] vt, vi célébrer

celebrated [ˈselɪbreɪtɪd] adj célèbre

celebration [selɪˈbreɪʃən] n célébration f

celebrity [sɪˈlebrɪtɪ] n célébrité f

celery [ˈselərɪ] n céleri m (en branches)

cell [sel] n (gen) cellule f; (ELEC) élément m (de pile)

cellar [ˈseləʳ] n cave f

cello [ˈtʃeləu] n violoncelle m

cellphone [ˈselfəun] n téléphone m cellulaire

Celt [kelt, selt] n Celte m/f

Celtic [ˈkeltɪk, ˈseltɪk] adj celte, celtique ◆ n (LING) celtique m

cement [səˈment] n ciment m ◆ vt cimenter

cement mixer n bétonnière f

cemetery [ˈsemɪtrɪ] n cimetière m

censor [ˈsensəʳ] n censeur m ◆ vt censurer

censorship [ˈsensəʃɪp] n censure f

censure [ˈsenʃəʳ] vt blâmer, critiquer

census [ˈsensəs] n recensement m

cent [sent] n (US, euro: coin) cent m (= 1:100 du dollar, de l'euro); see also **per**

centenary [senˈtiːnərɪ], **centennial** [senˈtenɪəl] n centenaire m

center [ˈsentəʳ] n, vt (US) = **centre**

centigrade [ˈsentɪgreɪd] adj centigrade

centimetre, (US) **centimeter** [ˈsentɪmiːtəʳ] n centimètre m

centipede [ˈsentɪpiːd] n mille-pattes m inv

central [ˈsentrəl] adj central(e)

Central America n Amérique centrale

central heating n chauffage central

central reservation n (BRIT AUT) terre-plein central

centre, (US) **center** [ˈsentəʳ] n centre m ◆ vt centrer; (PHOT) cadrer; (concentrate): **to centre (on)** centrer (sur)

centre-forward [ˈsentəˈfɔːwəd] n (SPORT) avant-centre m

centre-half [ˈsentəˈhɑːf] n (SPORT) demi-centre m

century [ˈsentjurɪ] n siècle m; **in the twentieth century** au vingtième siècle

ceramic [sɪˈræmɪk] adj céramique

cereal [ˈsiːrɪəl] n céréale f

ceremony [ˈserɪmənɪ] n cérémonie f; **to stand on ceremony** faire des façons

certain [ˈsɜːtən] adj certain(e); **to make certain of** s'assurer de; **for certain** certainement, sûrement

certainly [ˈsɜːtənlɪ] adv certainement

certainty [ˈsɜːtəntɪ] n certitude f

certificate [səˈtɪfɪkɪt] n certificat m

certify [ˈsɜːtɪfaɪ] vt certifier ◆ vi: **to certify to** attester

cervical [ˈsɜːvɪkl] adj: **cervical cancer** cancer m du col de l'utérus; **cervical smear** frottis vaginal

cervix [ˈsɜːvɪks] n col m de l'utérus

cf. abbr (= compare) cf., voir

CFC n abbr (= chlorofluorocarbon) CFC m

ch. abbr (= chapter) chap

chafe [tʃeɪf] vt irriter, frotter contre ◆ vi (fig): **to chafe against** se rebiffer contre, regimber contre

chain [tʃeɪn] n (gen) chaîne f ◆ vt (also: **chain up**) enchaîner, attacher (avec une chaîne)

chain reaction n réaction f en chaîne

chain-smoke [ˈtʃeɪnsməuk] vi fumer cigarette sur cigarette

chain store n magasin m à succursales multiples

chair [tʃeəʳ] n chaise f; (armchair) fauteuil m; (of university) chaire f ◆ vt (meeting) présider; **the chair** (US: electric chair) la chaise électrique

chairlift [ˈtʃeəlɪft] n télésiège m

chairman [ˈtʃeəmən] n président m

chalk [tʃɔːk] n craie f

▶ **chalk up** vt écrire à la craie; (fig: success etc) remporter

challenge [ˈtʃælɪndʒ] n défi m ◆ vt défier; (statement, right) mettre en question, contester; **to challenge sb to a fight/game** inviter qn à se battre/à jouer (sous forme d'un défi) **to challenge sb to do** mettre qn au défi de faire

challenging [ˈtʃælɪndʒɪŋ] adj de défi, provocateur(trice)

chamber [ˈtʃeɪmbəʳ] n chambre f; **chamber of commerce** chambre de commerce

chambermaid [ˈtʃeɪmbəmeɪd] n femme f de chambre

chamber music n musique f de chambre

champagne [ʃæmˈpeɪn] n champagne m

champion ['tʃæmpɪən] n (also of cause) champion/ne ♦ vt défendre

championship ['tʃæmpɪənʃɪp] n championnat m

chance [tʃɑːns] n hasard m; (opportunity) occasion f, possibilité f; (hope, likelihood) chance f ♦ vt (risk): **to chance it** risquer (le coup), essayer; (happen): **to chance to do** faire par hasard ♦ adj fortuit(e), de hasard; **there is little chance of his coming** il est peu probable or il y a peu de chances qu'il vienne; **to take a chance** prendre un risque; **it's the chance of a lifetime** c'est une occasion unique; **by chance** par hasard

▶ **chance (up)on** vt fus (person) tomber sur, rencontrer par hasard; (thing) trouver par hasard

chancellor ['tʃɑːnsələ*] n chancelier m; **Chancellor of the Exchequer** (BRIT) chancelier de l'Échiquier

chandelier [ʃændə'lɪə*] n lustre m

change [tʃeɪndʒ] vt (alter, replace, COMM: money) changer; (switch, substitute: gear, hands, trains, clothes, one's name etc) changer de; (transform): **to change sb into** changer or transformer qn en ♦ vi (gen) changer; (change clothes) se changer; (be transformed): **to change into** se changer or transformer en ♦ n changement m; (money) monnaie f; **to change one's mind** changer d'avis; **she changed into an old skirt** elle (s'est changée et) a enfilé une vieille jupe; **a change of clothes** des vêtements de rechange; **for a change** pour changer; **small change** petite monnaie; **to give sb change for** or **of £10** faire à qn la monnaie de 10 livres

changeable ['tʃeɪndʒəbl] adj (weather) variable; (person) d'humeur changeante

change machine n distributeur m de monnaie

changeover ['tʃeɪndʒəʊvə*] n (to new system) changement m, passage m

changing ['tʃeɪndʒɪŋ] adj changeant(e)

changing room n (BRIT: in shop) salon m d'essayage; (: SPORT) vestiaire m

channel ['tʃænl] n (TV) chaîne f; (waveband, groove, fig: medium) canal m; (of river, sea) chenal m ♦ vt canaliser; (fig: interest, energies) **to channel into** diriger vers; **through the usual channels** en suivant la filière habituelle; **green/red channel** (CUSTOMS) couloir m vert or sortie f "rien à déclarer"/"marchandises à déclarer"; **the (English) Channel** la Manche

channel-hopping ['tsʃænl'hɔpɪŋ] n (TV) zapping m

chant [tʃɑːnt] n chant m; mélopée f; psalmodie f ♦ vt chanter, scander; psalmodier

chaos ['keɪɔs] n chaos m

chap [tʃæp] n (BRIT col: man) type m; (term of address): **old chap** mon vieux ♦ vt (skin) gercer, crevasser

chapel ['tʃæpl] n chapelle f

chaplain ['tʃæplɪn] n aumônier m

chapped [tʃæpt] adj (skin, lips) gercé(e)

chapter ['tʃæptə*] n chapitre m

char [tʃɑː*] vt (burn) carboniser ♦ vi (BRIT: cleaner) faire des ménages ♦ n (BRIT) = **charlady**

character ['kærɪktə*] n caractère m; (in novel, film) personnage m; (eccentric) numéro m, phénomène m; **a person of good character** une personne bien

characteristic ['kærɪktə'rɪstɪk] adj, n caractéristique (f)

charcoal ['tʃɑːkəʊl] n charbon m de bois

charge [tʃɑːdʒ] n accusation f; (LAW) inculpation f; (cost) prix (demandé); (of gun, battery, MIL: attack) charge f ♦ vt (LAW): **to charge sb (with)** inculper qn (de); (gun, battery, MIL: enemy) charger; (customer, sum) faire payer ♦ vi (gen with: up, along etc) foncer; **charges** npl: **bank/labour charges** frais mpl de banque/main-d'œuvre; **to charge in/out** entrer/sortir en trombe; **to charge down/up** dévaler/grimper à toute allure; **is there a charge?** doit-on payer?; **there's no charge** c'est gratuit, on ne fait pas payer; **extra charge** supplément m; **to take charge of** se charger de; **to be in charge of** être responsable de, s'occuper de; **to have charge of sb** avoir la charge de qn; **they charged us £10 for the meal** ils nous ont fait payer le repas 10 livres, ils nous ont compté 10 livres pour le repas; **how much do you charge for this repair?** combien demandez-vous pour cette réparation?; **to charge an expense (up) to sb** mettre une dépense sur le compte de qn; **charge it to my account** facturez-le sur mon compte

charge card n carte f de client (émise par un grand magasin)

charity ['tʃærɪtɪ] n charité f; (organization) institution f charitable or de bienfaisance, œuvre f (de charité)

charm [tʃɑːm] n charme m ♦ vt charmer, enchanter

charming ['tʃɑːmɪŋ] adj charmant(e)

chart [tʃɑːt] n tableau m, diagramme m; graphique m; (map) carte marine; (weather chart) carte f du temps ♦ vt dresser or établir la carte de; (sales, progress) établir la courbe de; **to be in the charts** (record, pop group) figurer au hit-parade

charter [tʃɑːtə*] vt (plane) affréter ♦ n (document) charte f; **on charter** (plane) affrété(e)

chartered accountant (CA) ['tʃɑːtəd-] n (BRIT) expert-comptable m

charter flight n charter m

chase [tʃeɪs] vt poursuivre, pourchasser ♦ n poursuite f, chasse f

▶ **chase down** vt (US) = **chase up**

▶ **chase up** vt (BRIT: person) relancer; (: information) rechercher

chasm ['kæzəm] n gouffre m, abîme m

chat [tʃæt] vi (also: **have a chat**) bavarder, causer; (on Internet) chatter ♦ n conversation f

▶ **chat up** vt (BRIT col: girl) baratiner

chat show n (BRIT) entretien télévisé

chatter ['tʃætə*] vi (person) bavarder, papoter ♦ n bavardage m, papotage m; **my teeth are chattering** je claque des dents

chatterbox ['tʃætəbɒks] n moulin m à paroles, babillard/e

chatty ['tʃætɪ] adj (style) familier(ière); (person) enclin(e) à bavarder or au papotage

chauffeur ['ʃəufə*] n chauffeur m (de maître)

chauvinist ['ʃəuvɪnɪst] n (also: **male chauvinist**) phallocrate m, macho m; (nationalist) chauvin/e

cheap [tʃiːp] adj bon marché inv, pas cher(chère); (reduced: ticket) à prix réduit; (: fare) réduit(e); (joke) facile, d'un goût douteux; (poor quality) à bon marché, de qualité médiocre ♦ adv à bon marché, pour pas cher; **cheaper** adj moins cher(chère)

cheaply ['tʃiːplɪ] adv à bon marché, à bon compte

cheat [tʃiːt] vi tricher; (in exam) copier ♦ vt tromper, duper; (rob) escroquer ♦ n tricheur/euse; escroc m; (trick) duperie f, tromperie f; **to cheat on sb** (col: husband, wife etc) tromper qn

check [tʃɛk] vt vérifier; (passport, ticket) contrôler; (halt) enrayer; (restrain) maîtriser ♦ vi (official etc) se renseigner ♦ n vérification f; contrôle m; (curb) frein m; (bill) addition f; (pattern: gen pl) carreaux mpl; (US) = **cheque** ♦ adj **checked**: pattern, cloth) à carreaux = **to check with sb** demander à qn = **to keep a check on sb/sth** surveiller qn/qch

▶ **check in** vi (in hotel) remplir sa fiche (d'hôtel); (at airport) se présenter à l'enregistrement ♦ vt (luggage) (faire) enregistrer

▶ **check off** vt cocher

▶ **check out** vi (in hotel) régler sa note ♦ vt (luggage) retirer; (investigate: story) vérifier; (person) prendre des renseignements sur

▶ **check up** vi: **to check up (on sth)** vérifier (qch); **to check up on sb** se renseigner sur le compte de qn

checkered ['tʃɛkəd] adj (US) = **chequered**

checkers ['tʃɛkəz] n (US) jeu m de dames

check-in ['tʃɛkɪn] n (also: **check-in desk**: at airport) enregistrement m

checking account ['tʃɛkɪŋ-] n (US) compte courant

checkmate ['tʃɛkmeɪt] n échec et mat m

checkout ['tʃɛkaut] n (in supermarket) caisse f

checkpoint ['tʃɛkpɔɪnt] n contrôle m

checkup ['tʃɛkʌp] n (MED) examen médical, check-up m

cheek [tʃiːk] n joue f; (impudence) toupet m, culot m

cheekbone ['tʃiːkbəun] n pommette f

cheeky ['tʃiːkɪ] adj effronté(e), culotté(e)

cheep [tʃiːp] n (of bird) piaulement m ♦ vi piauler

cheer [tʃɪə*] vt acclamer, applaudir; (gladden) réjouir, réconforter ♦ vi applaudir ♦ n (gen pl) acclamations fpl, applaudissements mpl; bravos mpl, hourras mpl; **cheers!** (à votre) santé!

▶ **cheer on** vt encourager (par des cris etc)

▶ **cheer up** vi se dérider, reprendre courage ♦ vt remonter le moral à or de, dérider, égayer

cheerful ['tʃɪəful] adj gai(e), joyeux(euse)

cheerio [tʃɪərɪ'əu] excl (BRIT) salut!, au revoir!

cheese [tʃiːz] n fromage m

cheeseboard ['tʃiːzbɔːd] n plateau m à fromages; (with cheese on it) plateau m de fromages

cheetah ['tʃiːtə] n guépard m

chef [ʃɛf] n chef (cuisinier)

chemical ['kɛmɪkl] adj chimique ♦ n produit m chimique

chemist ['kɛmɪst] n (BRIT: pharmacist) pharmacien/ne; (scientist) chimiste m/f; **chemist's (shop)** n (BRIT) pharmacie f

chemistry ['kɛmɪstrɪ] n chimie f

cheque, (US) **check** [tʃɛk] n chèque m; **to pay by cheque** payer par chèque

chequebook, (US) **checkbook** ['tʃɛkbuk] n chéquier m, carnet m de chèques

cheque card n (BRIT) carte f (d'identité) bancaire

chequered, (US) **checkered** ['tʃɛkəd] adj (fig) varié(e)

cherish ['tʃɛrɪʃ] vt chérir; (hope etc) entretenir

cherry ['tʃɛrɪ] n cerise f

chess [tʃɛs] n échecs mpl

chessboard ['tʃɛsbɔːd] n échiquier m

chest [tʃɛst] n poitrine f; (box) coffre m, caisse f; **to get sth off one's chest** (col) vider son sac; **chest of drawers** n commode f

chestnut ['tʃɛsnʌt] n châtaigne f; (also: **chestnut tree**) châtaignier m; (colour) châtain m ♦ adj (hair) châtain inv; (horse) alezan

chew [tʃuː] vt mâcher

chewing gum ['tʃuːɪŋ-] n chewing-gum m

chic [ʃiːk] adj chic inv, élégant(e)

chick [tʃɪk] n poussin m; (US col) pépée f

chicken ['tʃɪkɪn] n poulet m; (col: coward) poule mouillée

▶ **chicken out** vi (col) se dégonfler

chickenpox ['tʃɪkɪnpɔks] n varicelle f

chicory ['tʃɪkərɪ] n chicorée f; (salad) endive f

chief [tʃiːf] n chef m ♦ adj principal(e); **Chief of Staff** (MIL) chef d'État-major

chief executive, (US) **chief executive officer** n directeur général

chiefly ['tʃiːflɪ] adv principalement, surtout

chiffon ['ʃɪfɔn] n mousseline f de soie

chilblain ['tʃɪlbleɪn] n engelure f

child, pl **children** [tʃaɪld, 'tʃɪldrən] n enfant m/f

childbirth ['tʃaɪldbɜːθ] n accouchement m

childhood ['tʃaɪldhud] n enfance f

childish ['tʃaɪldɪʃ] adj puéril(e), enfantin(e)

childlike ['tʃaɪldlaɪk] *adj* innocent(e), pur(e)
child minder *n* (BRIT) garde *f* d'enfants
children ['tʃɪldrən] *npl of* **child**
Chile ['tʃɪlɪ] *n* Chili *m*
chill [tʃɪl] *n* froid *m*; (MED) refroidissement *m*, coup *m* de froid ♦ *adj* froid(e), glacial(e) ♦ *vt* faire frissonner; refroidir; (CULIN) mettre au frais, rafraîchir; **"serve chilled"** "à servir frais"
▶ **chill out** *vi* (col: esp US) se relaxer
chil(l)i ['tʃɪlɪ] *n* piment *m* (rouge)
chilly ['tʃɪlɪ] *adj* froid(e), glacé(e); (sensitive to cold) frileux(euse); **to feel chilly** avoir froid
chime [tʃaɪm] *n* carillon *m* ♦ *vi* carillonner, sonner
chimney ['tʃɪmnɪ] *n* cheminée *f*
chimney sweep *n* ramoneur *m*
chimpanzee [tʃɪmpæn'zi:] *n* chimpanzé *m*
chin [tʃɪn] *n* menton *m*
China ['tʃaɪnə] *n* Chine *f*
china ['tʃaɪnə] *n* porcelaine *f*; (vaisselle *f* en) porcelaine
Chinese [tʃaɪ'ni:z] *adj* chinois(e) ♦ *n* (pl inv) Chinois/e; (LING) chinois *m*
chink [tʃɪŋk] *n* (opening) fente *f*, fissure *f*; (noise) tintement *m*
chip [tʃɪp] *n* (gen pl: CULIN) frite *f*; (: US: also: **potato chip**) chip *m*; (of wood) copeau *m*; (of glass, stone) éclat *m*; (also: **microchip**) puce *f*; (in gambling) fiche *f* ♦ *vt* (cup, plate) ébrécher; **when the chips are down** (fig) au moment critique
▶ **chip in** *vi* (col) mettre son grain de sel
chip shop *n* (BRIT) friterie *f*; voir encadré

CHIP SHOP

Un **chip shop**, que l'on appelle également un "fish-and-chip shop", est un magasin où l'on vend des plats à emporter. Les **chip shops** sont d'ailleurs à l'origine des "takeaways". On y achète en particulier du poisson frit et des frites, mais on y trouve également des plats traditionnels britanniques ("steak pies", saucisses, etc). Tous les plats étaient à l'origine emballés dans du papier journal. Dans certains de ces magasins, on peut s'asseoir pour consommer sur place.

---

chiropodist [kɪ'rɔpədɪst] *n* (BRIT) pédicure *m/f*
chirp [tʃə:p] *n* pépiement *m*, gazouillis *m*; (of crickets) stridulation *f* ♦ *vi* pépier, gazouiller; chanter, striduler
chisel ['tʃɪzl] *n* ciseau *m*
chit [tʃɪt] *n* mot *m*, note *f*
chitchat ['tʃɪttʃæt] *n* bavardage *m*, papotage *m*
chivalry ['ʃɪvəlrɪ] *n* chevalerie *f*; esprit *m* chevaleresque
chives [tʃaɪvz] *npl* ciboulette *f*, civette *f*
chock-a-block ['tʃɔkə'blɔk], **chock-full** [tʃɔk

'ful] *adj* plein(e) à craquer
chocolate ['tʃɔklɪt] *n* chocolat *m*
choice [tʃɔɪs] *n* choix *m* ♦ *adj* de choix; **by** or **from choice** par choix; **a wide choice** un grand choix
choir ['kwaɪə*] *n* chœur *m*, chorale *f*
choirboy ['kwaɪəbɔɪ] *n* jeune choriste *m*, petit chanteur
choke [tʃəuk] *vi* étouffer ♦ *vt* étrangler; étouffer; (block) boucher, obstruer ♦ *n* (AUT) starter *m*
cholesterol [kə'lestərɔl] *n* cholestérol *m*
choose, *pt* **chose**, *pp* **chosen** [tʃu:z, tʃəuz, 'tʃəuzn] *vt* choisir ♦ *vi*: **to choose between** choisir entre; **to choose from** choisir parmi; **to choose to do** décider de faire, juger bon de faire
choosy ['tʃu:zɪ] *adj*: **(to be) choosy** (faire le) difficile
chop [tʃɔp] *vt* (wood) couper (à la hache); (CULIN: also: **chop up**) couper (fin), émincer, hacher (en morceaux) ♦ *n* coup *m* (de hache, du tranchant de la main); (CULIN) côtelette *f*; **to get the chop** (BRIT col: project) tomber à l'eau; (: person: be sacked) se faire renvoyer
▶ **chop down** *vt* (tree) abattre
chopper ['tʃɔpə*] *n* (helicopter) hélicoptère *m*, hélico *m*
choppy ['tʃɔpɪ] *adj* (sea) un peu agité(e)
chopsticks ['tʃɔpstɪks] *npl* baguettes *fpl*
chord [kɔ:d] *n* (MUS) accord *m*
chore [tʃɔ:*] *n* travail *m* de routine; **household chores** travaux *mpl* du ménage
chortle ['tʃɔ:tl] *vi* glousser
chorus ['kɔ:rəs] *n* chœur *m*; (repeated part of song, also fig) refrain *m*
chose [tʃəuz] *pt of* **choose**
chosen ['tʃəuzn] *pp of* **choose**
chowder ['tʃaudə*] *n* soupe *f* de poisson
Christ [kraɪst] *n* Christ *m*
christen ['krɪsn] *vt* baptiser
christening ['krɪsnɪŋ] *n* baptême *m*
Christian ['krɪstɪən] *adj*, *n* chrétien(ne)
Christianity [krɪstɪ'ænɪtɪ] *n* christianisme *m*
Christian name *n* prénom *m*
Christmas ['krɪsməs] *n* Noël *m* or *f*; **happy** or **merry Christmas!** joyeux Noël!
Christmas card *n* carte *f* de Noël
Christmas Day *n* le jour de Noël
Christmas Eve *n* la veille de Noël; la nuit de Noël
Christmas tree *n* arbre *m* de Noël
chrome [krəum] *n* = **chromium**
chromium ['krəumɪəm] *n* chrome *m*; (also: **chromium plating**) chromage *m*
chronic ['krɔnɪk] *adj* chronique; (fig: liar, smoker) invétéré(e)
chronicle ['krɔnɪkl] *n* chronique *f*

chronological [krɔnə'lɔdʒɪkl] *adj* chronologique
chrysanthemum [krɪ'sænθəməm] *n* chrysanthème *m*
chubby ['tʃʌbɪ] *adj* potelé(e), rondelet(te)
chuck [tʃʌk] *vt* lancer, jeter; **to chuck (up** *or* **in)** *vt* (*BRIT: job*) lâcher; (*: person*) plaquer
▶ **chuck out** *vt* flanquer dehors *or* à la porte
chuckle ['tʃʌkl] *vi* glousser
chug [tʃʌg] *vi* faire teuf-teuf; souffler
chum [tʃʌm] *n* copain/copine
chunk [tʃʌŋk] *n* gros morceau; (*of bread*) quignon *m*
church [tʃəːtʃ] *n* église *f*; **the Church of England** l'Église anglicane
churchyard ['tʃəːtʃjɑːd] *n* cimetière *m*
churn [tʃəːn] *n* (*for butter*) baratte *f*; (*for transport: also*: **milk churn**) (grand) bidon à lait
▶ **churn out** *vt* débiter
chute [ʃuːt] *n* glissoire *f*; (*also*: **rubbish chute**) vide-ordures *m inv*; (*BRIT: children's slide*) toboggan *m*
chutney ['tʃʌtnɪ] *n* chutney *m*
CIA *n abbr* (*US*: = *Central Intelligence Agency*) CIA *f*
CID *n abbr* (*BRIT*: = *Criminal Investigation Department*) ≈ P.J. *f* (= *police judiciaire*)
cider ['saɪdə*] *n* cidre *m*
cigar [sɪ'gɑː*] *n* cigare *m*
cigarette [sɪgə'rɛt] *n* cigarette *f*
cigarette case *n* étui *m* à cigarettes
cigarette end *n* mégot *m*
Cinderella [sɪndə'rɛlə] *n* Cendrillon
cinders ['sɪndəz] *npl* cendres *fpl*
cine-camera ['sɪnɪ'kæmərə] *n* (*BRIT*) caméra *f*
cinema ['sɪnəmə] *n* cinéma *m*
cinnamon ['sɪnəmən] *n* cannelle *f*
circle ['səːkl] *n* cercle *m*; (*in cinema*) balcon *m* ◆ *vi* faire *or* décrire des cercles ◆ *vt* (*surround*) entourer, encercler; (*move round*) faire le tour de, tourner autour de
circuit ['səːkɪt] *n* circuit *m*
circuitous [səː'kjuɪtəs] *adj* indirect(e), qui fait un détour
circular ['səːkjulə*] *adj* circulaire ◆ *n* circulaire *f*; (*as advertisement*) prospectus *m*
circulate ['səːkjuleɪt] *vi* circuler ◆ *vt* faire circuler
circulation [səːkju'leɪʃən] *n* circulation *f*; (*of newspaper*) tirage *m*
circumflex ['səːkəmflɛks] *n* (*also*: **circumflex accent**) accent *m* circonflexe
circumstances ['səːkəmstənsɪz] *npl* circonstances *fpl*; (*financial condition*) moyens *mpl*, situation financière; **in the circumstances** dans ces conditions; **under no circumstances** en aucun cas, sous aucun prétexte
circus ['səːkəs] *n* cirque *m*; (*also*: **Circus**: *in place names*) place *f*

CIS *n abbr* (= *Commonwealth of Independent States*) CEI *f*
cistern ['sɪstən] *n* réservoir *m* (d'eau); (*in toilet*) réservoir de la chasse d'eau
citizen ['sɪtɪzn] *n* (*POL*) citoyen/ne; (*resident*): **the citizens of this town** les habitants de cette ville
citizenship ['sɪtɪznʃɪp] *n* citoyenneté *f*
citrus fruit ['sɪtrəs-] *n* agrume *m*
city ['sɪtɪ] *n* ville *f*, cité *f*; **the City** la Cité de Londres (*centre des affaires*)
City Technology College *n* (*BRIT*) établissement *m* d'enseignement technologique (*situé dans un quartier défavorisé*)
civic ['sɪvɪk] *adj* civique
civic centre *n* (*BRIT*) centre administratif (municipal)
civil ['sɪvɪl] *adj* civil(e); (*polite*) poli(e), civil(e)
civil engineer *n* ingénieur civil
civilian [sɪ'vɪlɪən] *adj*, *n* civil(e)
civilization [sɪvɪlaɪ'zeɪʃən] *n* civilisation *f*
civilized ['sɪvɪlaɪzd] *adj* civilisé(e); (*fig*) où règnent les bonnes manières, empreint(e) d'une courtoisie de bon ton
civil law *n* code civil; (*study*) droit civil
civil servant *n* fonctionnaire *m/f*
Civil Service *n* fonction publique, administration *f*
civil war *n* guerre civile
clad [klæd] *adj*: **clad (in)** habillé(e) de, vêtu(e) de
claim [kleɪm] *vt* (*rights etc*) revendiquer; (*compensation*) réclamer; **to claim that/to be** prétendre que/être ◆ *vi* (*for insurance*) faire une déclaration de sinistre ◆ *n* revendication *f*; prétention *f*; (*right*) droit *m*; (*for expenses*) note *f* de frais; **(insurance) claim** demande *f* d'indemnisation, déclaration *f* de sinistre; **to put in a claim for** (*pay rise etc*) demander
claimant ['kleɪmənt] *n* (*ADMIN, LAW*) requérant/e
clairvoyant [klɛə'vɔɪənt] *n* voyant/e, extra-lucide *m/f*
clam [klæm] *n* palourde *f*
▶ **clam up** *vi* (*col*) la boucler
clamber ['klæmbə*] *vi* grimper, se hisser
clammy ['klæmɪ] *adj* humide et froid(e) (au toucher), moite
clamour, (*US*) **clamor** ['klæmə*] *n* (*noise*) clameurs *fpl*; (*protest*) protestations bruyantes ◆ *vi*: **to clamour for sth** réclamer qch à grands cris
clamp [klæmp] *n* étau *m* à main; agrafe *f*, crampon *m* ◆ *vt* serrer; cramponner
▶ **clamp down on** *vt fus* sévir contre, prendre des mesures draconiennes à l'égard de
clan [klæn] *n* clan *m*
clang [klæŋ] *n* bruit *m or* fracas *m* métallique ◆ *vi* émettre un bruit *or* fracas métallique
clap [klæp] *vi* applaudir ◆ *vt*: **to clap (one's hands)** battre des mains ◆ *n* claquement *m*; tape

f; **a clap of thunder** un coup de tonnerre

clapping [ˈklæpɪŋ] n applaudissements mpl

claret [ˈklærət] n (vin m de) bordeaux m (rouge)

clarinet [klærɪˈnet] n clarinette f

clarity [ˈklærɪtɪ] n clarté f

clash [klæʃ] n (sound) choc m, fracas m; (with police) affrontement m; (fig) conflit m ◆ vi se heurter; être or entrer en conflit; (dates, events) tomber en même temps

clasp [klɑːsp] n fermoir m ◆ vt serrer, étreindre

class [klɑːs] n (gen) classe f; (group, category) catégorie f ◆ vt classer, classifier

classic [ˈklæsɪk] adj classique ◆ n (author) classique m; (race etc) classique f

classical [ˈklæsɪkl] adj classique

classified [ˈklæsɪfaɪd] adj (information) secret (ète); **classified ads** petites annonces

classmate [ˈklɑːsmeɪt] n camarade m/f de classe

classroom [ˈklɑːsrum] n (salle f de) classe f

clatter [ˈklætəʳ] n cliquetis m ◆ vi cliqueter

clause [klɔːz] n clause f; (LING) proposition f

claw [klɔː] n griffe f; (of bird of prey) serre f; (of lobster) pince f ◆ vt griffer; déchirer

clay [kleɪ] n argile f

clean [kliːn] adj propre; (clear, smooth) net(te) ◆ vt nettoyer ◆ adv: **he clean forgot** il a complètement oublié; **to come clean** (admit guilt) se mettre à table; **to clean one's teeth** (BRIT) se laver les dents; **clean driving licence** or (US) **record** permis où n'est portée aucune indication de contravention

▶ **clean off** vt enlever

▶ **clean out** vt nettoyer (à fond)

▶ **clean up** vt nettoyer; (fig) remettre de l'ordre dans ◆ vi (fig: make profit): **to clean up on** faire son beurre avec

clean-cut [kliːnˈkʌt] adj (man) soigné; (situation etc) bien délimité(e), net(te), clair(e)

cleaner [ˈkliːnəʳ] n (person) nettoyeur/euse, femme f de ménage; (also: **dry cleaner**) teinturier/ière; (product) détachant m

cleaning [ˈkliːnɪŋ] n nettoyage m

cleanliness [ˈklɛnlɪnɪs] n propreté f

cleanse [klɛnz] vt nettoyer; purifier

cleanser [ˈklɛnzəʳ] n détergent m; (for face) démaquillant m

clean-shaven [kliːnˈʃeɪvn] adj rasé(e) de près

cleansing department [ˈklɛnzɪŋ-] n (BRIT) service m de voirie

clear [klɪəʳ] adj clair(e); (road, way) libre, dégagé(e); (profit, majority) net(te) ◆ vt dégager, déblayer, débarrasser; (room etc: of people) faire évacuer; (woodland) défricher; (cheque) compenser; (COMM: goods) liquider; (LAW: suspect) innocenter; (obstacle) franchir or sauter sans heurter ◆ vi (subj: weather) s'éclaircir; (subj: fog) se dissiper ◆ adv: **clear of** à distance de, à l'écart de ◆ n: **to be in the clear** (out of debt) être dégagé/e de toute dette; (out of suspicion) être lavé/e de tout soupçon; (out of danger) être hors de danger; **to clear the table** débarrasser la table, desservir; **to clear one's throat** s'éclaircir la gorge; **to clear a profit** faire un bénéfice net; **to make o.s. clear** se faire bien comprendre; **to make it clear to sb that ...** bien faire comprendre à qn que ...; **I have a clear day tomorrow** (BRIT) je n'ai rien de prévu demain; **to keep clear of sb/sth** éviter qn/qch

▶ **clear off** vi (col: leave) dégager

▶ **clear up** vi s'éclaircir, se dissiper ◆ vt ranger, mettre en ordre; (mystery) éclaircir, résoudre

clearance [ˈklɪərəns] n (removal) déblayage m; (free space) dégagement m; (permission) autorisation f

clear-cut [ˈklɪəˈkʌt] adj précis(e), nettement défini(e)

clearing [ˈklɪərɪŋ] n (in forest) clairière f; (BRIT BANKING) compensation f, clearing m

clearing bank n (BRIT) banque f qui appartient à une chambre de compensation

clearly [ˈklɪəlɪ] adv clairement; (obviously) de toute évidence

clearway [ˈklɪəweɪ] n (BRIT) route f à stationnement interdit

clef [klef] n (MUS) clé f

cleft [kleft] n (in rock) crevasse f, fissure f

clementine [ˈklɛməntaɪn] n clémentine f

clench [klentʃ] vt serrer

clergy [ˈkləːdʒɪ] n clergé m

clergyman [ˈkləːdʒɪmən] n ecclésiastique m

clerical [ˈklerɪkl] adj de bureau, d'employé de bureau; (REL) clérical(e), du clergé

clerk [klɑːk, (US) kləːrk] n employé/e de bureau; (US: salesman/woman) vendeur/euse; **Clerk of Court** (LAW) greffier m (du tribunal)

clever [ˈklevəʳ] adj (mentally) intelligent(e); (deft, crafty) habile, adroit(e); (device, arrangement) ingénieux(euse), astucieux(euse)

click [klɪk] vi faire un bruit sec or un déclic ◆ vt: **to click one's tongue** faire claquer sa langue; **to click one's heels** claquer des talons

client [ˈklaɪənt] n client/e

cliff [klɪf] n falaise f

climate [ˈklaɪmɪt] n climat m

climate change n changement m climatique

climax [ˈklaɪmæks] n apogée m, point culminant; (sexual) orgasme m

climb [klaɪm] vi grimper, monter; (plane) prendre de l'altitude ◆ vt gravir, escalader, monter sur ◆ n montée f, escalade f; **to climb over a wall** passer par dessus un mur

▶ **climb down** vi (re)descendre; (BRIT fig) rabattre de ses prétentions

climbdown [ˈklaɪmdaun] n (BRIT) reculade f

climber [ˈklaɪməʳ] n (also: **rock climber**) grimpeur/euse, varappeur/euse

climbing ['klaɪmɪŋ] n (also: **rock climbing**) escalade f, varappe f

clinch [klɪntʃ] vt (deal) conclure, sceller

cling, pt, pp **clung** [klɪŋ, klʌŋ], vi: **to cling (to)** se cramponner (à), s'accrocher (à); (of clothes) coller (à)

clinic ['klɪnɪk] n clinique f; centre médical; (session: MED) consultation(s) f(pl), séance(s) f(pl); (:SPORT) séance(s) de perfectionnement

clinical ['klɪnɪkl] adj clinique; (fig) froid(e)

clink [klɪŋk] vi tinter, cliqueter

clip [klɪp] n (for hair) barrette f; (also: **paper clip**) trombone m; (BRIT: also: **bulldog clip**) pince f de bureau; (holding hose etc) collier m or bague f (métallique) de serrage ◆ vt (also: **clip together**: papers) attacher; (hair, nails) couper; (hedge) tailler

clippers ['klɪpəz] npl tondeuse f; (also: **nail clippers**) coupe-ongles m inv

clipping ['klɪpɪŋ] n (from newspaper) coupure f de journal

cloak [kləuk] n grande cape

cloakroom ['kləukrum] n (for coats etc) vestiaire m; (BRIT: W.C.) toilettes fpl

clock [klɔk] n (large) horloge f; (small) pendule f; **round the clock** (work etc) vingt-quatre heures sur vingt-quatre; **to sleep round the clock** or **the clock round** faire le tour du cadran; **30,000 on the clock** (BRIT AUT) 30 000 milles au compteur; **to work against the clock** faire la course contre la montre
▶ **clock in, clock on** vi (BRIT) pointer (en arrivant)
▶ **clock off, clock out** vi (BRIT) pointer (en partant)
▶ **clock up** vt (miles, hours etc) faire

clockwise ['klɔkwaɪz] adv dans le sens des aiguilles d'une montre

clockwork ['klɔkwə:k] n mouvement m (d'horlogerie); rouages mpl, mécanisme m ◆ adj (toy, train) mécanique

clog [klɔg] n sabot m ◆ vt boucher, encrasser ◆ vi se boucher, s'encrasser

cloister ['klɔɪstə*] n cloître m

close adj, adv and derivatives [kləus] ◆ adj (near): **close (to)** près (de), proche (de); (writing, texture) serré(e); (watch) étroit(e), strict(e); (examination) attentif(ive), minutieux(euse); (weather) lourd(e), étouffant(e); (room) mal aéré(e) ◆ adv près, à proximité; **close to** prep près de; **by close at hand** adj, adv tout(e) près; **how close is Edinburgh to Glasgow?** combien de kilomètres y-a-t-il entre Édimbourg et Glasgow?; **a close friend** un ami intime; **to have a close shave** (fig) l'échapper belle; **at close quarters** tout près, à côté ◆ **vb and derivatives** [kləuz] ◆ vt fermer; (bargain, deal) conclure ◆ vi (shop etc) fermer; (lid, door etc) se fermer; (end) se terminer, se conclure ◆ n (end) conclusion f; **to bring sth to a close** mettre fin à qch
▶ **close down** vt, vi fermer (définitivement)
▶ **close in** vi (hunters) approcher; (night, fog) tom-

ber; **the days are closing in** les jours raccourcissent; **to close in on sb** cerner qn
▶ **close off** vt (area) boucler

closed [kləuzd] adj (shop etc) fermé(e); (road) fermé à la circulation

closed shop n organisation f qui n'admet que des travailleurs syndiqués

close-knit ['kləus'nɪt] adj (family, community) très uni(e)

closely ['kləuslɪ] adv (examine, watch) de près; **we are closely related** nous sommes proches parents; **a closely guarded secret** un secret bien gardé

closet ['klɔzɪt] n (cupboard) placard m, réduit m

close-up ['kləusʌp] n gros plan

closure ['kləuʒə*] n fermeture f

clot [klɔt] n (gen) **blood clot** caillot m; (col: person) ballot m ◆ vi (blood) former des caillots; (: external bleeding) se coaguler

cloth [klɔθ] n (material) tissu m, étoffe f; (BRIT: also: **teacloth**) torchon m; lavette f; (also: **tablecloth**) nappe f

clothe [kləuð] vt habiller, vêtir

clothes [kləuðz] npl vêtements mpl, habits mpl; **to put one's clothes on** s'habiller; **to take one's clothes off** enlever ses vêtements

clothes brush n brosse f à habits

clothes line n corde f (à linge)

clothes peg, (US) **clothes pin** n pince f à linge

clothing ['kləuðɪŋ] n = **clothes**

cloud [klaud] n nuage m ◆ vt (liquid) troubler; **to cloud the issue** brouiller les cartes; **every cloud has a silver lining** (proverb) à quelque chose malheur est bon (proverbe)
▶ **cloud over** vi se couvrir; (fig) s'assombrir

cloudburst ['klaudbə:st] n violente averse

cloudy ['klaudɪ] adj nuageux(euse), couvert(e); (liquid) trouble

clout [klaut] n (blow) taloche f; (fig) pouvoir m ◆ vt flanquer une taloche à

clove [kləuv] n clou m de girofle; **clove of garlic** gousse f d'ail

clover ['kləuvə*] n trèfle m

clown [klaun] n clown m ◆ vi (also: **clown about**, **clown around**) faire le clown

cloying ['klɔɪɪŋ] adj (taste, smell) écœurant(e)

club [klʌb] n (society) club m; (weapon) massue f, matraque f; (also: **golf club**) club ◆ vt matraquer ◆ vi: **to club together** s'associer; **clubs** npl (CARDS) trèfle m

club class n (AVIAT) classe f club

clubhouse ['klʌbhaus] n pavillon m

cluck [klʌk] vi glousser

clue [klu:] n indice m; (in crosswords) définition f; **I haven't a clue** je n'en ai pas la moindre idée

clump [klʌmp] n: **clump of trees** bouquet m d'arbres

clumsy ['klʌmzɪ] *adj* (*person*) gauche, maladroit(e); (*object*) malcommode, peu maniable

clung [klʌŋ] *pt, pp of* **cling**

cluster ['klʌstə*] *n* (petit) groupe ♦ *vi* se rassembler

clutch [klʌtʃ] *n* (*grip, grasp*) étreinte *f*, prise *f*; (*AUT*) embrayage *m* ♦ *vt* agripper, serrer fort; **to clutch at** se cramponner à

clutter ['klʌtə*] *vt* (*also*: **clutter up**) encombrer ♦ *n* désordre *m*, fouillis *m*

CND *n abbr* = **Campaign for Nuclear Disarmament**

Co. *abbr* = **company, county**

c/o *abbr* (= *care of*) c/o, aux bons soins de

coach [kəʊtʃ] *n* (*bus*) autocar *m*; (*horse-drawn*) diligence *f*; (*of train*) voiture *f*, wagon *m*; (*SPORT: trainer*) entraîneur/euse; (*school: tutor*) répétiteur/trice ♦ *vt* entraîner; donner des leçons particulières à

coach trip *n* excursion *f* en car

coal [kəʊl] *n* charbon *m*

coal face *n* front *m* de taille

coalfield ['kəʊlfiːld] *n* bassin houiller

coalition [kəʊə'lɪʃən] *n* coalition *f*

coalman ['kəʊlmən] *n* charbonnier *m*, marchand *m* de charbon

coal mine *n* mine *f* de charbon

coarse [kɔːs] *adj* grossier(ère), rude; (*vulgar*) vulgaire

coast [kəʊst] *n* côte *f* ♦ *vi* (*with cycle etc*) descendre en roue libre

coastal ['kəʊstl] *adj* côtier(ère)

coastguard ['kəʊstgɑːd] *n* garde-côte *m*

coastline ['kəʊstlaɪn] *n* côte *f*, littoral *m*

coat [kəʊt] *n* manteau *m*; (*of animal*) pelage *m*, poil *m*; (*of paint*) couche *f* ♦ *vt* couvrir, enduire; **coat of arms** *n* blason *m*, armoiries *fpl*

coat hanger *n* cintre *m*

coating ['kəʊtɪŋ] *n* couche *f*, enduit *m*

coax [kəʊks] *vt* persuader par des cajoleries

cobbler ['kɔblə*] *n* cordonnier *m*

cobbles, cobblestones ['kɔblz, 'kɔblstəʊnz] *npl* pavés (ronds)

cobweb ['kɔbweb] *n* toile *f* d'araignée

cocaine [kə'keɪn] *n* cocaïne *f*

cock [kɔk] *n* (*rooster*) coq *m*; (*male bird*) mâle *m* ♦ *vt* (*gun*) armer; **to cock one's ears** (*fig*) dresser l'oreille

cockerel ['kɔkərl] *n* jeune coq *m*

cockle ['kɔkl] *n* coque *f*

cockney ['kɔknɪ] *n* cockney *m/f* (*habitant des quartiers populaires de l'East End de Londres*) = faubourien/ne

cockpit ['kɔkpɪt] *n* (*in aircraft*) poste *m* de pilotage, cockpit *m*

cockroach ['kɔkrəʊtʃ] *n* cafard *m*, cancrelat *m*

cocktail ['kɔkteɪl] *n* cocktail *m*; **prawn cocktail**, (*US*) **shrimp cocktail** cocktail de crevettes

cocktail cabinet *n* (meuble-)bar *m*

cocktail party *n* cocktail *m*

cocoa ['kəʊkəʊ] *n* cacao *m*

coconut ['kəʊkənʌt] *n* noix *f* de coco

COD *abbr* = **cash on delivery, collect on delivery** (*US*)

cod [kɔd] *n* morue fraîche, cabillaud *m*

code [kəʊd] *n* code *m*; **code of behaviour** règles *fpl* de conduite; **code of practice** déontologie *f*

cod-liver oil ['kɔdlɪvər-] *n* huile *f* de foie de morue

coercion [kəʊ'əːʃən] *n* contrainte *f*

coffee ['kɔfɪ] *n* café *m*; **white coffee**, (*US*) **coffee with cream** (café-)crème *m*

coffee bar *n* (*BRIT*) café *m*

coffee bean *n* grain *m* de café

coffee break *n* pause-café *f*

coffeepot ['kɔfɪpɔt] *n* cafetière *f*

coffee table *n* (petite) table basse

coffin ['kɔfɪn] *n* cercueil *m*

cog [kɔg] *n* dent *f* (d'engrenage)

cogent ['kəʊdʒənt] *adj* puissant(e), convaincant(e)

coil [kɔɪl] *n* rouleau *m*, bobine *f*; (*one loop*) anneau *m*, spire *f*; (*of smoke*) volute *f*; (*contraceptive*) stérilet *m* ♦ *vt* enrouler

coin [kɔɪn] *n* pièce *f* de monnaie ♦ *vt* (*word*) inventer

coinage ['kɔɪnɪdʒ] *n* monnaie *f*, système *m* monétaire

coinbox ['kɔɪnbɔks] *n* (*BRIT*) cabine *f* téléphonique

coincide [kəʊɪn'saɪd] *vi* coïncider

coincidence [kəʊ'ɪnsɪdəns] *n* coïncidence *f*

Coke® [kəʊk] *n* coca *m*

coke [kəʊk] *n* coke *m*

colander ['kɔləndə*] *n* passoire *f* (à légumes)

cold [kəʊld] *adj* froid(e) ♦ *n* froid *m*; (*MED*) rhume *m*; **it's cold** il fait froid; **to be cold** avoir froid; **to catch cold** prendre *or* attraper froid; **to catch a cold** s'enrhumer, attraper un rhume; **in cold blood** de sang-froid; **to have cold feet** avoir froid aux pieds; (*fig*) avoir la frousse *or* la trouille; **to give sb the cold shoulder** battre froid à qn

cold sore *n* bouton *m* de fièvre

coleslaw ['kəʊlslɔː] *n* sorte de salade de chou cru

colic ['kɔlɪk] *n* colique(s) *f(pl)*

collapse [kə'læps] *vi* s'effondrer, s'écrouler ♦ *n* effondrement *m*, écroulement *m*; (*of government*) chute *f*

collapsible [kə'læpsəbl] *adj* pliant(e), télescopique

collar ['kɔlə*] *n* (*of coat, shirt*) col *m*; (*for dog*) collier *m*; (*TECH*) collier, bague *f* ♦ *vt* (*col: person*) pincer

collarbone ['kɔləbəʊn] *n* clavicule *f*

collateral [kə'lætərl] *n* nantissement *m*

colleague ['kɔliːg] *n* collègue *m/f*

collect [kə'lɛkt] *vt* rassembler; (*pick up*) ramasser; (*as a hobby*) collectionner; (*BRIT: call for*) (passer) prendre; (*mail*) faire la levée de, ramasser; (*money owed*) encaisser; (*donations, subscriptions*) recueillir ◆ *vi* (*people*) se rassembler; (*dust, dirt*) s'amasser; **to collect one's thoughts** réfléchir, réunir ses idées; **collect on delivery (COD)** (*US COMM*) payable *or* paiement à la livraison; **to call collect** (*US TEL*) téléphoner en PCV

collection [kə'lɛkʃən] *n* collection *f*; (*of mail*) levée *f*; (*for money*) collecte *f*, quête *f*

collector [kə'lɛktə*] *n* collectionneur *m*; (*of taxes*) percepteur *m*; (*of rent, cash*) encaisseur *m*; **collector's item** *or* **piece** *f* de collection

college ['kɔlɪdʒ] *n* collège *m*; (*of technology, agriculture etc*) institut *m*; **to go to college** faire des études supérieures; **college of education** ≃ école normale

collide [kə'laɪd] *vi*: **to collide (with)** entrer en collision (avec)

colliery ['kɔlɪərɪ] *n* (*BRIT*) mine *f* de charbon, houillère *f*

collision [kə'lɪʒən] *n* collision *f*, heurt *m*; **to be on a collision course** aller droit à la collision; (*fig*) aller vers l'affrontement

colloquial [kə'ləʊkwɪəl] *adj* familier(ère)

colon ['kəʊlən] *n* (*sign*) deux-points *mpl*; (*MED*) côlon *m*

colonel ['kɜːnl] *n* colonel *m*

colony ['kɔlənɪ] *n* colonie *f*

colour, (*US*) **color** ['kʌlə*] *n* couleur *f* ◆ *vt* colorer; peindre; (*with crayons*) colorier; (*news*) fausser, exagérer ◆ *vi* rougir ◆ *cpd* (*film, photograph, television*) en couleur; **colours** *npl* (*of party, club*) couleurs *fpl*

▶ **colour in** *vt* colorier

colo(u)r bar *n* discrimination raciale (*dans un établissement etc*)

colo(u)r-blind ['kʌləblaɪnd] *adj* daltonien(ne)

colo(u)red ['kʌləd] *adj* coloré(e); (*photo*) en couleur

colo(u)rful ['kʌləful] *adj* coloré(e), vif(vive); (*personality*) pittoresque, haut(e) en couleurs

colo(u)ring ['kʌlərɪŋ] *n* colorant *m*; (*complexion*) teint *m*

colo(u)r scheme *n* combinaison *f* de(s) couleur(s)

colt [kəʊlt] *n* poulain *m*

column ['kɔləm] *n* colonne *f*; (*fashion column, sports column etc*) rubrique *f*; **the editorial column** l'éditorial *m*

columnist ['kɔləmnɪst] *n* rédacteur/trice d'une rubrique

coma ['kəʊmə] *n* coma *m*

comb [kəʊm] *n* peigne *m* ◆ *vt* (*hair*) peigner; (*area*) ratisser, passer au peigne fin

combat ['kɔmbæt] *n* combat *m* ◆ *vt* combattre, lutter contre

combination [kɔmbɪ'neɪʃən] *n* (*gen*) combinaison *f*

combine *vb* [kəm'baɪn] ◆ *vt* combiner; (*one quality with another*): **to combine sth with sth** joindre qch à qch, allier qch à qch ◆ *vi* s'associer; (*CHEM*) se combiner ◆ *n* ['kɔmbaɪn] association *f*; (*ECON*) trust *m*; **a combined effort** un effort conjugué

combine (harvester) *n* moissonneuse-batteuse(-lieuse) *f*

come, *pt* **came**, *pp* **come** [kʌm, keɪm] *vi* venir; (*col: sexually*) jouir; **come with me** suivez-moi; **we've just come from Paris** nous arrivons de Paris; ... **what might come of it** ... ce qui pourrait en résulter, ... ce qui pourrait advenir *or* se produire; **to come into sight** *or* **view** apparaître; **to come to** (*decision etc*) parvenir *or* arriver à; **to come undone/loose** se défaire/desserrer; **coming!** j'arrive! **if it comes to it** s'il le faut, dans le pire des cas

▶ **come about** *vi* se produire, arriver

▶ **come across** *vt fus* rencontrer par hasard, tomber sur ◆ *vi*: **to come across well/badly** faire une bonne/mauvaise impression

▶ **come along** *vi* (*pupil, work*) faire des progrès, avancer; **come along!** viens!; allons!, allez!

▶ **come apart** *vi* s'en aller en morceaux; se détacher

▶ **come away** *vi* partir, s'en aller; (*become detached*) se détacher

▶ **come back** *vi* revenir; (*reply*): **can I come back to you on that one?** est-ce qu'on peut revenir là-dessus plus tard?

▶ **come by** *vt fus* (*acquire*) obtenir, se procurer

▶ **come down** *vi* descendre; (*prices*) baisser; (*buildings*) s'écrouler; (: *be demolished*) être démoli(e)

▶ **come forward** *vi* s'avancer; (*make o.s. known*) se présenter, s'annoncer

▶ **come from** *vt fus* venir de; (*place*) venir de, être originaire de

▶ **come in** *vi* entrer

▶ **come in for** *vt fus* (*criticism etc*) être l'objet de

▶ **come into** *vt fus* (*money*) hériter de

▶ **come off** *vi* (*button*) se détacher; (*stain*) s'enlever; (*attempt*) réussir

▶ **come on** *vi* (*lights, electricity*) s'allumer; (*central heating*) se mettre en marche; (*pupil, work, project*) faire des progrès, avancer; **come on!** viens!; allons!, allez!

▶ **come out** *vi* sortir; (*book*) paraître; (*strike*) cesser le travail, se mettre en grève

▶ **come over** *vt fus*: **I don't know what's come over him!** je ne sais pas ce qui lui a pris!

▶ **come round** *vi* (*after faint, operation*) revenir à soi, reprendre connaissance

▶ **come through** *vi* (*survive*) s'en sortir; (*telephone call*): **the call came through** l'appel est bien parvenu

▶ **come to** *vi* revenir à soi ♦ *vt* (*add up to: amount*): **how much does it come to?** ça fait combien?

▶ **come under** *vt fus* (*heading*) se trouver sous; (*influence*) subir

▶ **come up** *vi* monter

▶ **come up against** *vt fus* (*resistance, difficulties*) rencontrer

▶ **come up to** *vt fus* arriver à; **the film didn't come up to our expectations** le film nous a déçu

▶ **come up with** *vt fus*: **he came up with an idea** il a eu une idée, il a proposé quelque chose

▶ **come upon** *vt fus* tomber sur

comeback [ˈkʌmbæk] *n* (*reaction*) réaction *f*; (*response*) réponse *f*; (*THEAT etc*) rentrée *f*

comedian [kəˈmiːdiən] *n* (*in music hall etc*) comique *m*; (*THEAT*) comédien *m*

comedy [ˈkɒmɪdɪ] *n* comédie *f*

comeuppance [kʌmˈʌpəns] *n*: **to get one's comeuppance** recevoir ce qu'on mérite

comfort [ˈkʌmfət] *n* confort *m*, bien-être *m*; (*solace*) consolation *f*, réconfort *m* ♦ *vt* consoler, réconforter

comfortable [ˈkʌmfətəbl] *adj* confortable; **I don't feel very comfortable about it** cela m'inquiète un peu

comfortably [ˈkʌmfətəblɪ] *adv* (*sit*) confortablement; (*live*) à l'aise

comfort station *n* (*US*) toilettes *fpl*

comic [ˈkɒmɪk] *adj* comique ♦ *n* comique *m*; (*magazine*) illustré *m*

comic strip *n* bande dessinée

coming [ˈkʌmɪŋ] *n* arrivée *f* ♦ *adj* (*next*) prochain(e); (*future*) à venir; **in the coming weeks** dans les prochaines semaines

coming(s) and going(s) *n(pl)* va-et-vient *m inv*

comma [ˈkɒmə] *n* virgule *f*

command [kəˈmɑːnd] *n* ordre *m*, commandement *m*; (*MIL: authority*) commandement; (*mastery*) maîtrise *f*; (*COMPUT*) commande *f* ♦ *vt* (*troops*) commander; (*be able to get*) (pouvoir) disposer de, avoir à sa disposition; (*deserve*) avoir droit à; **to command sb to do** donner l'ordre *or* commander à qn de faire; **to have/take command of** avoir/prendre le commandement de; **to have at one's command** (*money, resources etc*) disposer de

commandeer [kɒmənˈdɪə*] *vt* réquisitionner (par la force)

commander [kəˈmɑːndə*] *n* chef *m*; (*MIL*) commandant *m*

commando [kəˈmɑːndəʊ] *n* commando *m*; membre *m* d'un commando

commemorate [kəˈmɛməreɪt] *vt* commémorer

commence [kəˈmɛns] *vt, vi* commencer

commend [kəˈmɛnd] *vt* louer; recommander

commensurate [kəˈmɛnsərɪt] *adj*: **commensurate with/to** en rapport avec/selon

comment [ˈkɒmɛnt] *n* commentaire *m* ♦ *vi* faire des remarques *or* commentaires; **to comment on** faire des remarques sur; **to comment that** faire remarquer que; **"no comment"** "je n'ai rien à déclarer"

commentary [ˈkɒməntərɪ] *n* commentaire *m*; (*SPORT*) reportage *m* (en direct)

commentator [ˈkɒmənteɪtə*] *n* commentateur *m*; (*SPORT*) reporter *m*

commerce [ˈkɒmɜːs] *n* commerce *m*

commercial [kəˈmɜːʃəl] *adj* commercial(e) ♦ *n* (*RADIO, TV*) annonce *f* publicitaire, spot *m* (publicitaire)

commiserate [kəˈmɪzəreɪt] *vi*: **to commiserate with sb** témoigner de la sympathie pour qn

commission [kəˈmɪʃən] *n* (*committee; fee: also for salesman*) commission *f*; (*order for work of art etc*) commande *f* ♦ *vt* (*MIL*) nommer (à un commandement); (*work of art*) commander, charger un artiste de l'exécution de; **out of commission** (*NAUT*) hors de service; (*machine*) hors service; **I get 10% commission** je reçois une commission de 10%; **commission of inquiry** (*BRIT*) commission d'enquête

commissionaire [kəmɪʃəˈnɛə*] *n* (*BRIT: at shop, cinema etc*) portier *m* (en uniforme)

commissioner [kəˈmɪʃənə*] *n* membre *m* d'une commission; (*POLICE*) préfet *m* (de police)

commit [kəˈmɪt] *vt* (*act*) commettre; (*to sb's care*) confier (à); **to commit o.s. (to do)** s'engager (à faire); **to commit suicide** se suicider; **to commit to writing** coucher par écrit; **to commit sb for trial** traduire qn en justice

commitment [kəˈmɪtmənt] *n* engagement *m*; (*obligation*) responsabilité(s) *f (pl)*

committee [kəˈmɪtɪ] *n* comité *m*; commission *f*; **to be on a committee** siéger dans un comité *or* une commission)

commodity [kəˈmɒdɪtɪ] *n* produit *m*, marchandise *f*, article *m*; (*food*) denrée *f*

common [ˈkɒmən] *adj* (*gen, also pej*) commun(e); (*usual*) courant(e) ♦ *n* terrain communal; **in common** en commun; **in common use** d'un usage courant; **it's common knowledge that** il est bien connu *or* notoire que; **to the common good** pour le bien de tous, dans l'intérêt général

commoner [ˈkɒmənə*] *n* roturier/ière

common law *n* droit coutumier

commonly [ˈkɒmənlɪ] *adv* communément, généralement; couramment

Common Market *n* Marché commun

commonplace [ˈkɒmənpleɪs] *adj* banal(e), ordinaire

commonroom [ˈkɒmənrʊm] *n* salle commune; (*SCOL*) salle des professeurs

common sense *n* bon sens

Commonwealth [ˈkɒmənwɛlθ] *n*: **the**

Commonwealth le Commonwealth; *voir encadré*

COMMONWEALTH

Le **Commonwealth** regroupe 50 États indépendants et plusieurs territoires qui reconnaissent tous le souverain britannique comme chef de cette association.

commotion [kə'məuʃən] *n* désordre *m*, tumulte *m*

communal ['kɔmju:nl] *adj* (*life*) communautaire; (*for common use*) commun(e)

commune *n* ['kɔmju:n] (*group*) communauté *f* ♦ *vi* [kə'mju:n]: **to commune with** converser intimement avec; communier avec

communicate [kə'mju:nɪkeɪt] *vt* communiquer, transmettre ♦ *vi*: **to communicate (with)** communiquer (avec)

communication [kəmju:nɪ'keɪʃən] *n* communication *f*

communication cord *n* (*BRIT*) sonnette *f* d'alarme

communion [kə'mju:nɪən] *n* (*also:* **Holy Communion**) communion *f*

communism ['kɔmjunɪzəm] *n* communisme *m*

communist ['kɔmjunɪst] *adj, n* communiste (*m/f*)

community [kə'mju:nɪtɪ] *n* communauté *f*

community centre *n* foyer socio-éducatif, centre *m* de loisirs

community chest *n* (*us*) fonds commun

commutation ticket [kɔmju'teɪʃən-] *n* (*us*) carte *f* d'abonnement

commute [kə'mju:t] *vi* faire le trajet journalier (de son domicile à un lieu de travail assez éloigné) ♦ *vt* (*LAW*) commuer; (*MATH: terms etc*) opérer la commutation de

commuter [kə'mju:tə*] *n* banlieusard/e (qui ... *see vi*)

compact *adj* [kəm'pækt] compact(e) ♦ *n* ['kɔmpækt] contrat *m*, entente *f*; (*also:* **powder compact**) poudrier *m*

compact disc *n* disque compact

compact disc player *n* lecteur *m* de disques compacts

companion [kəm'pænjən] *n* compagnon/compagne

companionship [kəm'pænjənʃɪp] *n* camaraderie *f*

company ['kʌmpənɪ] *n* (*also COMM, MIL, THEAT*) compagnie *f*; **he's good company** il est d'une compagnie agréable; **we have company** nous avons de la visite; **to keep sb company** tenir compagnie à qn; **to part company with** se séparer de; **Smith and Company** Smith et Compagnie

company secretary *n* (*BRIT COMM*) secrétaire général (*d'une société*)

comparative [kəm'pærətɪv] *adj* comparatif(ive); (*relative*) relatif(ive)

comparatively [kəm'pærətɪvlɪ] *adv* (*relatively*) relativement

compare [kəm'pɛə*] *vt*: **to compare sth/sb with/to** comparer qch/qn avec *or* et/à ♦ *vi*: **to compare (with)** se comparer (à); être comparable (à); **how do the prices compare?** comment sont les prix?, est-ce que les prix sont comparables?; **compared with** *or* **to** par rapport à

comparison [kəm'pærɪsn] *n* comparaison *f*; **in comparison (with)** en comparaison (de)

compartment [kəm'pɑ:tmənt] *n* (*also RAIL*) compartiment *m*

compass ['kʌmpəs] *n* boussole *f*; **within the compass of** dans les limites de

compassion [kəm'pæʃən] *n* compassion *f*, humanité *f*

compassionate [kəm'pæʃənɪt] *adj* accessible à la compassion, au cœur charitable et bienveillant; **on compassionate grounds** pour raisons personnelles *or* de famille

compatible [kəm'pætɪbl] *adj* compatible

compel [kəm'pel] *vt* contraindre, obliger

compensate ['kɔmpənseɪt] *vt* indemniser, dédommager ♦ *vi*: **to compensate for** compenser

compensation [kɔmpən'seɪʃən] *n* compensation *f*; (*money*) dédommagement *m*, indemnité *f*

compere ['kɔmpɛə*] *n* présentateur/trice, animateur/trice

compete [kəm'pi:t] *vi* (*take part*) concourir; (*vie*): **to compete (with)** rivaliser (avec), faire concurrence (à)

competent ['kɔmpɪtənt] *adj* compétent(e), capable

competition [kɔmpɪ'tɪʃən] *n* compétition *f*, concours *m*; (*ECON*) concurrence *f*; **in competition with** en concurrence avec

competitive [kəm'petɪtɪv] *adj* (*ECON*) concurrentiel(le); (*sports*) de compétition

competitor [kəm'petɪtə*] *n* concurrent/e

complacency [kəm'pleɪsnsɪ] *n* contentement *m* de soi, autosatisfaction *f*

complain [kəm'pleɪn] *vi*: **to complain (about)** se plaindre (de); (*in shop etc*) réclamer (au sujet de)
▶ **complain of** *vt fus* (*MED*) se plaindre de

complaint [kəm'pleɪnt] *n* plainte *f*; (*in shop etc*) réclamation *f*; (*MED*) affection *f*

complement ['kɔmplɪmənt] *n* complément *m*; (*esp of ship's crew etc*) effectif complet ♦ *vt* compléter

complementary [kɔmplɪ'mentərɪ] *adj* complémentaire

complete [kəm'pli:t] *adj* complet(ète) ♦ *vt* achever, parachever; (*a form*) remplir

completely [kəm'pli:tlɪ] *adv* complètement

completion [kəm'pli:ʃən] *n* achèvement *m*; **to**

be nearing completion être presque terminé; **on completion of contract** dès signature du contrat

complex ['kɒmpleks] *adj* complexe ◆ *n* (*PSYCH, buildings etc*) complexe *m*

complexion [kəm'plekʃən] *n* (*of face*) teint *m*; (*of event etc*) aspect *m*, caractère *m*

compliance [kəm'plaɪəns] *n* (*submission*) docilité *f*; (*agreement*): **compliance with** le fait de se conformer à; **in compliance with** en conformité avec, conformément à

complicate ['kɒmplɪkeɪt] *vt* compliquer

complicated ['kɒmplɪkeɪtɪd] *adj* compliqué(e)

complication [kɒmplɪ'keɪʃən] *n* complication *f*

compliment *n* ['kɒmplɪmənt] compliment *m* ◆ *vt* ['kɒmplɪment] complimenter; **compliments** *npl* compliments *mpl*, hommages *mpl*; vœux *mpl*; **to pay sb a compliment** faire *or* adresser un compliment à qn; **to compliment sb (on sth/on doing sth)** féliciter qn (pour qch/de faire qch)

complimentary [kɒmplɪ'mentərɪ] *adj* flatteur (euse); (*free*) à titre gracieux

complimentary ticket *n* billet *m* de faveur

comply [kəm'plaɪ] *vi*: **to comply with** se soumettre à, se conformer à

component [kəm'pəʊnənt] *adj* composant(e), constituant(e) ◆ *n* composant *m*, élément *m*

compose [kəm'pəʊz] *vt* composer; **to compose o.s.** se calmer, se maîtriser; prendre une contenance

composed [kəm'pəʊzd] *adj* calme, posé(e)

composer [kəm'pəʊzə*] *n* (*MUS*) compositeur *m*

composition [kɒmpə'zɪʃən] *n* composition *f*

composure [kəm'pəʊʒə*] *n* calme *m*, maîtrise *f* de soi

compound ['kɒmpaʊnd] *n* (*CHEM, LING*) composé *m*; (*enclosure*) enclos *m*, enceinte *f* ◆ *adj* composé(e) ◆ *vt* [kəm'paʊnd] (*fig: problem etc*) aggraver

compound fracture *n* fracture compliquée

compound interest *n* intérêt composé

comprehend [kɒmprɪ'hend] *vt* comprendre

comprehension [kɒmprɪ'henʃən] *n* compréhension *f*

comprehensive [kɒmprɪ'hensɪv] *adj* (très) complet(ète)

comprehensive insurance policy *n* assurance *f* tous risques

comprehensive (school) *n* (*BRIT*) école secondaire non sélective avec libre circulation d'une section à l'autre, ≈ CES *m*

compress *vt* [kəm'pres] comprimer ◆ *n* ['kɒmpres] (*MED*) compresse *f*

comprise [kəm'praɪz] *vt* (*also*: **be comprised of**) comprendre

compromise ['kɒmprəmaɪz] *n* compromis *m* ◆ *vt* compromettre ◆ *vi* transiger, accepter un compromis ◆ *cpd* (*decision, solution*) de compromis

compulsion [kəm'pʌlʃən] *n* contrainte *f*, force *f*;

under compulsion sous la contrainte

compulsive [kəm'pʌlsɪv] *adj* (*PSYCH*) compulsif (ive); **he's a compulsive smoker** c'est un fumeur invétéré

compulsory [kəm'pʌlsərɪ] *adj* obligatoire

computer [kəm'pju:tə*] *n* ordinateur *m*; (*mechanical*) calculatrice *f*

computer game *n* jeu *m* vidéo

computer-generated [kəm'pju:tə*'dʒenəreɪtɪd] *adj* de synthèse

computerize [kəm'pju:təraɪz] *vt* traiter *or* automatiser par ordinateur

computer programmer *n* programmeur/euse

computer programming *n* programmation *f*

computer science *n* informatique *f*

computing [kəm'pju:tɪŋ] *n* informatique *f*

comrade ['kɒmrɪd] *n* camarade *m/f*

con [kɒn] *vt* duper; escroquer ◆ *n* escroquerie *f*; **to con sb into doing sth** tromper qn pour lui faire faire qch

conceal [kən'si:l] *vt* cacher, dissimuler

conceit [kən'si:t] *n* vanité *f*, suffisance *f*, prétention *f*

conceited [kən'si:tɪd] *adj* vaniteux(euse), suffisant(e)

conceive [kən'si:v] *vt* concevoir ◆ *vi*: **to conceive of sth/of doing sth** imaginer qch/de faire qch

concentrate ['kɒnsəntreɪt] *vi* se concentrer ◆ *vt* concentrer

concentration [kɒnsən'treɪʃən] *n* concentration *f*

concentration camp *n* camp *m* de concentration

concept ['kɒnsept] *n* concept *m*

concern [kən'sɜ:n] *n* affaire *f*; (*COMM*) entreprise *f*, firme *f*; (*anxiety*) inquiétude *f*, souci *m* ◆ *vt* concerner; **to be concerned (about)** s'inquiéter (de), être inquiet(ète) (au sujet de); **"to whom it may concern"** "à qui de droit"; **as far as I am concerned** en ce qui me concerne; **to be concerned with** (*person: involved with*) s'occuper de; **the department concerned** (*under discussion*) le service en question; (*involved*) le service concerné

concerning [kən'sɜ:nɪŋ] *prep* en ce qui concerne, à propos de

concert ['kɒnsət] *n* concert *m*; **in concert** à l'unisson, en chœur; ensemble

concerted [kən'sɜ:tɪd] *adj* concerté(e)

concert hall *n* salle *f* de concert

concerto [kən'tʃɜ:təʊ] *n* concerto *m*

concession [kən'seʃən] *n* concession *f*

conclude [kən'klu:d] *vt* conclure ◆ *vi* (*speaker*) conclure; (*events*): **to conclude (with)** se terminer (par)

conclusion [kən'klu:ʒən] *n* conclusion *f*; **to come to the conclusion that** (en) conclure que

conclusive [kən'klu:sɪv] *adj* concluant(e), définitif(ive)

concoct [kən'kɔkt] *vt* confectionner, composer

concoction [kən'kɔkʃən] *n* (*food, drink*) mélange *m*

concourse ['kɔŋkɔ:s] *n* (*hall*) hall *m*, salle *f* des pas perdus; (*crowd*) affluence *f*; multitude *f*

concrete ['kɔŋkri:t] *n* béton *m* ♦ *adj* concret(ète); (*CONSTR*) en béton

concur [kən'kə:*] *vi* être d'accord

concurrently [kən'kʌrntlɪ] *adv* simultanément

concussion [kən'kʌʃən] *n* (*MED*) commotion (cérébrale)

condemn [kən'dɛm] *vt* condamner

condensation [kɔndɛn'seɪʃən] *n* condensation *f*

condense [kən'dɛns] *vi* se condenser ♦ *vt* condenser

condensed milk [kən'dɛnst-] *n* lait concentré (sucré)

condition [kən'dɪʃən] *n* condition *f*; (*disease*) maladie *f* ♦ *vt* déterminer, conditionner; **in good/ poor condition** en bon/mauvais état; **a heart condition** une maladie cardiaque; **weather conditions** conditions *fpl* météorologiques; **on condition that** à condition que + *sub*, à condition de

conditional [kən'dɪʃənl] *adj* conditionnel(le); **to be conditional upon** dépendre de

conditioner [kən'dɪʃənə*] *n* (*for hair*) baume démêlant

condolences [kən'dəulənsɪz] *npl* condoléances *fpl*

condom ['kɔndəm] *n* préservatif *m*

condominium [kɔndə'mɪnɪəm] *n* (*US: building*) immeuble *m* (en copropriété); (: *rooms*) appartement *m* (dans un immeuble en copropriété)

condone [kən'dəun] *vt* fermer les yeux sur, approuver (tacitement)

conducive [kən'dju:sɪv] *adj*: **conducive to** favorable à, qui contribue à

conduct *n* ['kɔndʌkt] conduite *f* ♦ *vt* [kən'dʌkt] conduire; (*manage*) mener, diriger; (*MUS*) diriger; **to conduct o.s.** se conduire, se comporter

conducted tour [kən'dʌktɪd-] *n* voyage organisé; (*of building*) visite guidée

conductor [kən'dʌktə*] *n* (*of orchestra*) chef *m* d'orchestre; (*on bus*) receveur *m*; (*US: on train*) chef *m* de train; (*ELEC*) conducteur *m*

conductress [kən'dʌktrɪs] *n* (*on bus*) receveuse *f*

cone [kəun] *n* cône *m*; (*for ice-cream*) cornet *m*; (*BOT*) pomme *f* de pin, cône

confectioner [kən'fɛkʃənə*] *n* (*of cakes*) pâtissier/ière; (*of sweets*) confiseur/euse; **confectioner's (shop)** confiserie(-pâtisserie) *f*

confectionery [kən'fɛkʃənrɪ] *n* (*cakes*) pâtisserie *f*; (*sweets*) confiserie *f*

confer [kən'fə:*] *vt*: **to confer sth on** conférer qch à ♦ *vi* conférer, s'entretenir; **to confer (with sb**

about sth) s'entretenir (de qch avec qn)

conference ['kɔnfərəns] *n* conférence *f*; **to be in conference** être en réunion or en conférence

confess [kən'fɛs] *vt* confesser, avouer ♦ *vi* se confesser

confession [kən'fɛʃən] *n* confession *f*

confetti [kən'fɛtɪ] *n* confettis *mpl*

confide [kən'faɪd] *vi*: **to confide in** s'ouvrir à, se confier à

confidence ['kɔnfɪdns] *n* confiance *f*; (*also*: **self-confidence**) assurance *f*, confiance en soi; (*secret*) confidence *f*; **to have (every) confidence that** être certain que; **motion of no confidence** motion *f* de censure; **to tell sb sth in strict confidence** dire qch à qn en toute confidence

confidence trick *n* escroquerie *f*

confident ['kɔnfɪdənt] *adj* sûr(e), assuré(e)

confidential [kɔnfɪ'dɛnʃəl] *adj* confidentiel(le); (*secretary*) particulier(ère)

confine [kən'faɪn] *vt* limiter, borner; (*shut up*) confiner, enfermer; **to confine o.s. to doing sth/to sth** se contenter de faire qch/se limiter à qch

confined [kən'faɪnd] *adj* (*space*) restreint(e), réduit(e)

confinement [kən'faɪnmənt] *n* emprisonnement *m*, détention *f*; (*MIL*) consigne *f* (au quartier); (*MED*) accouchement *m*

confines ['kɔnfaɪnz] *npl* confins *mpl*, bornes *fpl*

confirm [kən'fə:m] *vt* (*report, REL*) confirmer; (*appointment*) ratifier

confirmation [kɔnfə'meɪʃən] *n* confirmation *f*; ratification *f*

confirmed [kən'fə:md] *adj* invétéré(e), incorrigible

confiscate ['kɔnfɪskeɪt] *vt* confisquer

conflict *n* ['kɔnflɪkt] conflit *m*, lutte *f* ♦ *vi* [kən'flɪkt] être or entrer en conflit; (*opinions*) s'opposer, se heurter

conflicting [kən'flɪktɪŋ] *adj* contradictoire

conform [kən'fɔ:m] *vi*: **to conform (to)** se conformer (à)

confound [kən'faund] *vt* confondre; (*amaze*) rendre perplexe

confront [kən'frʌnt] *vt* confronter, mettre en présence; (*enemy, danger*) affronter, faire face à

confrontation [kɔnfrən'teɪʃən] *n* confrontation *f*

confuse [kən'fju:z] *vt* embrouiller; (*one thing with another*) confondre

confused [kən'fju:zd] *adj* (*person*) dérouté(e), désorienté(e); (*situation*) confus(e), embrouillé(e)

confusing [kən'fju:zɪŋ] *adj* peu clair(e), déroutant(e)

confusion [kən'fju:ʒən] *n* confusion *f*

congeal [kən'dʒi:l] *vi* (*oil*) se figer; (*blood*) se coaguler

congenial [kən'dʒi:nɪəl] *adj* sympathique, agréable

congested [kən'dʒestɪd] *adj* (MED) congestion-né(e); (*fig*) surpeuplé(e); congestionné; bloqué(e); (*telephone lines*) encombré(e)

congestion [kən'dʒestʃən] *n* congestion *f*; (*fig*) encombrement *m*

congratulate [kən'grætjuleɪt] *vt*: **to congratulate sb (on)** féliciter qn (de)

congratulations [kəngrætju'leɪʃənz] *npl*: **congratulations (on)** félicitations *fpl* (pour) ♦ *excl*: **congratulations!** (toutes mes) félicitations!

congregate ['kɔŋgrɪgeɪt] *vi* se rassembler, se réunir

congregation [kɔŋgrɪ'geɪʃən] *n* assemblée *f* (des fidèles)

congress ['kɔŋgres] *n* congrès *m*; (US POL): **Congress** Congrès *m*; *voir encadré*

CONGRESS

Le **Congress** est le parlement des États-Unis. Il comprend la "House of Representatives" et le "Senate". Représentants et sénateurs sont élus au suffrage universel direct. Le Congrès se réunit au "Capitol", à Washington.

congressman ['kɔŋgresmən], **congresswoman** ['kɔŋgreswumən] *n* (US) membre *m* du Congrès

conjunction [kən'dʒʌŋkʃən] *n* conjonction *f*; **in conjunction with** (conjointement) avec

conjunctivitis [kəndʒʌŋktɪ'vaɪtɪs] *n* conjonctivite *f*

conjure ['kʌndʒə*] *vt* faire apparaître (par la prestidigitation) [kən'dʒuə*] conjurer, supplier ♦ *vi* faire des tours de passe-passe

▶ **conjure up** *vt* (*ghost, spirit*) faire apparaître; (*memories*) évoquer

conjurer ['kʌndʒərə*] *n* prestidigitateur *m*, illusionniste *m/f*

conman ['kɔnmæn] *n* escroc *m*

connect [kə'nekt] *vt* joindre, relier; (ELEC) connecter; (*fig*) établir un rapport entre, faire un rapprochement entre ♦ *vi* (*train*): **to connect with** assurer la correspondance avec; **to be connected with** avoir un rapport avec; (*have dealings with*) avoir des rapports avec, être en relation avec; **I am trying to connect you** (TEL) j'essaie d'obtenir votre communication

connection [kə'nekʃən] *n* relation *f*, lien *m*; (ELEC) connexion *f*; (TEL) communication *f*; (*train etc*) correspondance *f*; **in connection with** à propos de; **what is the connection between them?** quel est le lien entre eux?; **business connections** relations d'affaires; **to miss/get one's connection** (*train etc*) rater/avoir sa correspondance

connive [kə'naɪv] *vi*: **to connive at** se faire le complice de

conquer ['kɔŋkə*] *vt* conquérir; (*feelings*) vaincre, surmonter

conquest ['kɔŋkwest] *n* conquête *f*

cons [kɔnz] *npl see* **pro**, **convenience**

conscience ['kɔnʃəns] *n* conscience *f*; **in all conscience** en conscience

conscientious [kɔnʃɪ'enʃəs] *adj* conscien-cieux(euse); (*scruple, objection*) de conscience

conscious ['kɔnʃəs] *adj* conscient(e); (*deliberate: insult, error*) délibéré(e); **to become conscious of sth/that** prendre conscience de qch/que

consciousness ['kɔnʃəsnɪs] *n* conscience *f*; (MED) connaissance *f*; **to lose/regain consciousness** perdre/reprendre connaissance

conscript ['kɔnskrɪpt] *n* conscrit *m*

consent [kən'sent] *n* consentement *m* ♦ *vi*: **to consent (to)** consentir (à); **age of consent** âge nubile (légal); **by common consent** d'un commun accord

consequence ['kɔnsɪkwəns] *n* suites *fpl*, consé-quence *f*; importance *f*; **in consequence** en consé-quence, par conséquent

consequently ['kɔnsɪkwəntlɪ] *adv* par consé-quent, donc

conservation [kɔnsə'veɪʃən] *n* préservation *f*, protection *f*; (*also*: **nature conservation**) défense *f* de l'environnement; **energy conservation** écono-mies *fpl* d'énergie

conservative [kən'sə:vətɪv] *adj* conserva-teur(trice); (*cautious*) prudent(e); **Conservative** *adj, n* (BRIT POL) conservateur/trice; **the Con-servative Party** le parti conservateur

conservatory [kən'sə:vətrɪ] *n* (*greenhouse*) serre *f*

conserve [kən'sə:v] *vt* conserver, préserver; (*sup-plies, energy*) économiser ♦ *n* confiture *f*, conserve *f* (de fruits)

consider [kən'sɪdə*] *vt* considérer, réfléchir à; (*take into account*) penser à, prendre en considéra-tion; (*regard, judge*) considérer, estimer; **to consider doing sth** envisager de faire qch; **consider your-self lucky** estimez-vous heureux; **all things con-sidered** (toute) réflexion faite

considerable [kən'sɪdərəbl] *adj* considérable

considerably [kən'sɪdərəblɪ] *adv* nettement

considerate [kən'sɪdərɪt] *adj* prévenant(e), plein(e) d'égards

consideration [kənsɪdə'reɪʃən] *n* considération *f*; (*reward*) rétribution *f*, rémunération *f*; **out of consideration for** par égard pour; **under consid-eration** à l'étude; **my first consideration is my family** ma famille passe avant tout le reste

considering [kən'sɪdərɪŋ] *prep*: **considering (that)** étant donné (que)

consign [kən'saɪn] *vt* expédier, livrer

consignment [kən'saɪnmənt] *n* arrivage *m*, envoi *m*

consist [kən'sɪst] *vi*: **to consist of** consister en, se composer de

consistency [kən'sɪstənsɪ] *n* consistance *f*; (*fig*) cohérence *f*

consistent [kən'sɪstənt] *adj* logique, cohérent(e); **consistent with** compatible avec, en accord avec

consolation [kɔnsə'leɪʃən] *n* consolation *f*

console *vt* [kən'səul] consoler ♦ *n* ['kɔnsəul] console *f*

consonant ['kɔnsənənt] *n* consonne *f*

conspicuous [kən'spɪkjuəs] *adj* voyant(e), qui attire la vue *or* l'attention; **to make o.s. conspicuous** se faire remarquer

conspiracy [kən'spɪrəsɪ] *n* conspiration *f*, complot *m*

constable ['kʌnstəbl] *n* (*BRIT*) ≃ agent *m* de police, gendarme *m*

constabulary [kən'stæbjulərɪ] *n* ≃ police *f*, gendarmerie *f*

constant ['kɔnstənt] *adj* constant(e); incessant(e)

constantly ['kɔnstəntlɪ] *adv* constamment, sans cesse

constipated ['kɔnstɪpeɪtɪd] *adj* constipé(e)

constipation [kɔnstɪ'peɪʃən] *n* constipation *f*

constituency [kən'stɪtjuənsɪ] *n* circonscription électorale; (*people*) électorat *m*; *voir encadré*

CONSTITUENCY

Une **constituency** est à la fois une région qui élit un député au parlement et l'ensemble des électeurs dans cette région. En Grande-Bretagne, les députés font régulièrement des "permanences" dans leur circonscription électorale lors desquelles les électeurs peuvent venir les voir pour parler de leurs problèmes de logement etc.

---

constituent [kən'stɪtjuənt] *n* électeur/trice; (*part*) élément constitutif, composant *m*

constitution [kɔnstɪ'tjuːʃən] *n* constitution *f*

constitutional [kɔnstɪ'tjuːʃənl] *adj* constitutionnel(le)

constraint [kən'streɪnt] *n* contrainte *f*; (*embarrassment*) gêne *f*

construct [kən'strʌkt] *vt* construire

construction [kən'strʌkʃən] *n* construction *f*; (*fig: interpretation*) interprétation *f*; **under construction** (*building etc*) en construction

constructive [kən'strʌktɪv] *adj* constructif(ive)

consul ['kɔnsl] *n* consul *m*

consulate ['kɔnsjulɪt] *n* consulat *m*

consult [kən'sʌlt] *vt* consulter; **to consult sb (about sth)** consulter qn (à propos de qch)

consultant [kən'sʌltənt] *n* (*MED*) médecin consultant; (*other specialist*) consultant *m*, (expert-)conseil *m* ♦ *cpd*: **consultant engineer** *n* ingénieur-conseil *m*; **consultant paediatrician** *n* pédiatre *m*; **legal/ management consultant** conseiller *m* juridique/

en gestion

consulting room [kən'sʌltɪŋ-] *n* (*BRIT*) cabinet *m* de consultation

consume [kən'sjuːm] *vt* consommer

consumer [kən'sjuːmə*] *n* consommateur/trice; (*of electricity, gas etc*) usager *m*

consumer goods *npl* biens *mpl* de consommation

consumer society *n* société *f* de consommation

consummate ['kɔnsʌmeɪt] *vt* consommer

consumption [kən'sʌmpʃən] *n* consommation *f*; **not fit for human consumption** non comestible

cont. *abbr* = **continued**

contact ['kɔntækt] *n* contact *m*; (*person*) connaissance *f*, relation *f* ♦ *vt* se mettre en contact *or* en rapport avec; **to be in contact with sb/sth** être en contact avec qn/qch; **business contacts** relations *fpl* d'affaires, contacts *mpl*

contact lenses *npl* verres *mpl* de contact

contagious [kən'teɪdʒəs] *adj* contagieux(euse)

contain [kən'teɪn] *vt* contenir; **to contain o.s.** se contenir, se maîtriser

container [kən'teɪnə*] *n* récipient *m*; (*for shipping etc*) conteneur *m*

contaminate [kən'tæmɪneɪt] *vt* contaminer

cont'd *abbr* = **continued**

contemplate ['kɔntəmpleɪt] *vt* contempler; (*consider*) envisager

contemporary [kən'tɛmpərərɪ] *adj* contemporain(e); (*design, wallpaper*) moderne ♦ *n* contemporain/e

contempt [kən'tɛmpt] *n* mépris *m*, dédain *m*; **contempt of court** (*LAW*) outrage *m* à l'autorité de la justice

contemptuous [kən'tɛmptjuəs] *adj* dédaigneux(euse), méprisant(e)

contend [kən'tɛnd] *vt*: **to contend that** soutenir *or* prétendre que ♦ *vi*: **to contend with** (*compete*) lutter avec; **to have to contend with** (*be faced with*) avoir affaire à, être aux prises avec

contender [kən'tɛndə*] *n* prétendant/e; candidat/e

content [kən'tɛnt] *adj* content(e), satisfait(e) ♦ *vt* contenter, satisfaire ♦ *n* ['kɔntɛnt] contenu *m*; teneur *f*; **contents** *npl* contenu *m*; **(table of) contents** table *f* des matières; **to be content with** se contenter de; **to content o.s. with sth/with doing sth** se contenter de qch/de faire qch

contented [kən'tɛntɪd] *adj* content(e), satisfait(e)

contention [kən'tɛnʃən] *n* dispute *f*, contestation *f*; (*argument*) assertion *f*, affirmation *f*; **bone of contention** sujet *m* de discorde

contest *n* ['kɔntɛst] combat *m*, lutte *f*; (*competition*) concours *m* ♦ *vt* [kən'tɛst] contester, discuter; (*compete for*) disputer; (*LAW*) attaquer

contestant [kən'tɛstənt] *n* concurrent/e; (*in fight*)

adversaire *m/f*

context ['kɔntekst] *n* contexte *m*; **in/out of context** dans le/hors contexte

continent ['kɔntɪnənt] *n* continent *m*; **the Continent** (*BRIT*) l'Europe continentale; **on the Continent** en Europe (continentale)

continental [kɔntɪ'nɛntl] *adj* continental(e) ♦ *n* (*BRIT*) Européen/ne (continental)

continental breakfast *n* café (*or* thé) complet

continental quilt *n* (*BRIT*) couette *f*

contingency [kən'tɪndʒənsɪ] *n* éventualité *f*, événement imprévu

continual [kən'tɪnjuəl] *adj* continuel(le)

continuation [kəntɪnju'eɪʃən] *n* continuation *f*; (*after interruption*) reprise *f*; (*of story*) suite *f*

continue [kən'tɪnju:] *vi* continuer ♦ *vt* continuer; (*start again*) reprendre; **to be continued** (*story*) à suivre; **continued on page 10** suite page 10

continuity [kɔntɪ'nju:ɪtɪ] *n* continuité *f*; (*CINE*) script *m*

continuous [kən'tɪnjuəs] *adj* continu(e), permanent(e); **continuous performance** (*CINE*) séance permanente; **continuous stationery** (*COMPUT*) papier *m* en continu

contort [kən'tɔ:t] *vt* tordre, crisper

contour ['kɔntuə*] *n* contour *m*, profil *m*; (*also*: **contour line**) courbe *f* de niveau

contraband ['kɔntrəbænd] *n* contrebande *f* ♦ *adj* de contrebande

contraceptive [kɔntrə'sɛptɪv] *adj* contraceptif(ive), anticonceptionnel(le) ♦ *n* contraceptif *m*

contract *n* ['kɔntrækt] contrat *m* ♦ *cpd* ['kɔntrækt] (*price, date*) contractuel(le); (*work*) à forfait ♦ *vb* [kən'trækt] ♦ *vi* (*become smaller*) se contracter, se resserrer; (*COMM*): **to contract to do sth** s'engager (par contrat) à faire qch ♦ *vt* contracter; **contract of employment/service** contrat de travail/de service

▶ **contract in** *vi* s'engager (par contrat); (*BRIT ADMIN*) s'affilier au régime de retraite complémentaire

▶ **contract out** *vi* se dégager; (*BRIT ADMIN*) opter pour la non-affiliation au régime de retraite complémentaire

contraction [kən'trækʃən] *n* contraction *f*; (*LING*) forme contractée

contractor [kən'træktə*] *n* entrepreneur *m*

contradict [kɔntrə'dɪkt] *vt* contredire; (*be contrary to*) démentir, être en contradiction avec

contraflow ['kɔntrəfləu] *n* (*AUT*): **contraflow lane** voie *f* à contresens; **there's a contraflow system in operation on ...** une voie a été mise en sens inverse sur ...

contraption [kən'træpʃən] *n* (*pej*) machin *m*, truc *m*

contrary¹ ['kɔntrərɪ] *adj* contraire, opposé(e) ♦ *n* contraire *m*; **on the contrary** au contraire; **unless you hear to the contrary** sauf avis contraire; **contrary to what we thought** contrairement à ce que nous pensions

contrary² [kən'trɛərɪ] *adj* (*perverse*) contrariant(e), entêté(e)

contrast *n* ['kɔntrɑ:st] contraste *m* ♦ *vt* [kən'trɑ:st] mettre en contraste, contraster; **in contrast to** *or* **with** contrairement à, par opposition à

contravene [kɔntrə'vi:n] *vt* enfreindre, violer, contrevenir à

contribute [kən'trɪbju:t] *vi* contribuer ♦ *vt*: **to contribute £10/an article to** donner 10 livres/un article à; **to contribute to** (*gen*) contribuer à; (*newspaper*) collaborer à; (*discussion*) prendre part à

contribution [kɔntrɪ'bju:ʃən] *n* contribution *f*

contributor [kən'trɪbjutə*] *n* (*to newspaper*) collaborateur/trice

contrive [kən'traɪv] *vt* combiner, inventer ♦ *vi*: **to contrive to do** s'arranger pour faire, trouver le moyen de faire

control [kən'trəul] *vt* maîtriser; (*check*) contrôler ♦ *n* maîtrise *f*; **controls** *npl* commandes *fpl*; **to take control of** se rendre maître de; (*COMM*) acquérir une participation majoritaire dans; **to be in control of** être maître de, maîtriser; (*in charge of*) être responsable de; **to control o.s.** se contrôler; **everything is under control** j'ai (*or* il a *etc*) la situation en main; **the car went out of control** j'ai (*or* il a *etc*) perdu le contrôle du véhicule; **beyond our control** indépendant(e) de notre volonté

control panel *n* (*on aircraft, ship, TV etc*) tableau *m* de commandes

control room *n* (*NAUT, MIL*) salle *f* des commandes; (*RADIO, TV*) régie *f*

control tower *n* (*AVIAT*) tour *f* de contrôle

controversial [kɔntrə'və:ʃl] *adj* discutable, controversé(e)

controversy ['kɔntrəvə:sɪ] *n* controverse *f*, polémique *f*

convalesce [kɔnvə'lɛs] *vi* relever de maladie, se remettre (d'une maladie)

convector [kən'vɛktə*] *n* radiateur *m* à convection, appareil *m* de chauffage par convection

convene [kən'vi:n] *vt* convoquer, assembler ♦ *vi* se réunir, s'assembler

convenience [kən'vi:nɪəns] *n* commodité *f*; **at your convenience** quand *or* comme cela vous convient; **at your earliest convenience** (*COMM*) dans les meilleurs délais, le plus tôt possible; **all modern conveniences**, (*BRIT*) **all mod cons** avec tout le confort moderne, tout confort

convenient [kən'vi:nɪənt] *adj* commode; **if it is convenient to you** si cela vous convient, si cela ne vous dérange pas

convent ['kɔnvənt] *n* couvent *m*

convention [kən'vɛnʃən] *n* convention *f*

conventional [kən'vɛnʃənl] *adj* conventionnel(le)

convent school n couvent m

conversant [kən'vɜːsnt] adj: **to be conversant with** s'y connaître en; être au courant de

conversation [kɔnvə'seɪʃən] n conversation f

converse n ['kɔnvɜːs] contraire m, inverse m ◆ vi [kən'vɜːs]: **to converse (with sb about sth)** s'entretenir (avec qn de qch)

conversely [kɔn'vɜːslɪ] adv inversement, réciproquement

convert vt [kən'vɜːt] (REL, COMM) convertir; (alter) transformer, aménager; (RUGBY) transformer ◆ n ['kɔnvɜːt] converti/e

convertible [kən'vɜːtəbl] adj convertible ◆ n (voiture f) décapotable f

convey [kən'veɪ] vt transporter; (thanks) transmettre; (idea) communiquer

conveyor belt [kən'veɪə*-] n convoyeur m, tapis roulant

convict vt [kən'vɪkt] déclarer (or reconnaître) coupable ◆ n ['kɔnvɪkt] forçat m, convict m

conviction [kən'vɪkʃən] n condamnation f; (belief) conviction f

convince [kən'vɪns] vt convaincre, persuader; **to convince sb (of sth/that)** persuader qn (de qch/que)

convincing [kən'vɪnsɪŋ] adj persuasif(ive), convaincant(e)

convoluted ['kɔnvəluːtɪd] adj (shape) tarabiscoté(e); (argument) compliqué(e)

convulse [kən'vʌls] vt ébranler; **to be convulsed with laughter** se tordre de rire

cook [kuk] vt (faire) cuire ◆ vi cuire; (person) faire la cuisine ◆ n cuisinier/ière

▶ **cook up** vt (col: excuse, story) inventer

cookbook ['kukbuk] n livre m de cuisine

cooker ['kukə*] n cuisinière f

cookery ['kukərɪ] n cuisine f

cookery book n (BRIT) = **cookbook**

cookie ['kukɪ] n (US) biscuit m, petit gâteau sec

cooking ['kukɪŋ] n cuisine f ◆ cpd (apples, chocolate) à cuire; (utensils, salt) de cuisine

cool [kuːl] adj frais(fraîche); (not afraid) calme; (unfriendly) froid(e); (impertinent) effronté(e) ◆ vt, vi rafraîchir, refroidir; **it's cool** (weather) il fait frais; **to keep sth cool** or **in a cool place** garder or conserver qch au frais

▶ **cool down** vi refroidir; (fig: person, situation) se calmer

coop [kuːp] n poulailler m ◆ vt: **to coop up** (fig) cloîtrer, enfermer

cooperate [kəu'ɔpəreɪt] vi coopérer, collaborer

cooperation [kəuɔpə'reɪʃən] n coopération f, collaboration f

cooperative [kəu'ɔpərətɪv] adj coopératif(ive) ◆ n coopérative f

coordinate vt [kəu'ɔːdɪneɪt] coordonner ◆ n [kəu'ɔːdɪnət] (MATH) coordonnée f; **coordinates** npl (clothes) ensemble m, coordonnés mpl

co-ownership ['kəu'əunəʃɪp] n copropriété f

cop [kɔp] n (col) flic m

cope [kəup] vi s'en sortir, tenir le coup; **to cope with** faire face à; (take care of) s'occuper de

copper ['kɔpə*] n cuivre m; (col: policeman) flic m; **coppers** npl petite monnaie

copy ['kɔpɪ] n copie f; (book etc) exemplaire m; (material: for printing) copie ◆ vt copier; (imitate) imiter; **rough copy** (gen) premier jet; (SCOL) brouillon m; **fair copy** version définitive; propre m; **to make good copy** (PRESS) faire un bon sujet d'article

▶ **copy out** vt copier

copyright ['kɔpɪraɪt] n droit m d'auteur, copyright m; **copyright reserved** tous droits (de reproduction) réservés

coral ['kɔrəl] n corail m

cord [kɔːd] n corde f; (fabric) velours côtelé; whipcord m; corde f; (ELEC) cordon m (d'alimentation), fil m (électrique); **cords** npl (trousers) pantalon m de velours côtelé

cordial ['kɔːdɪəl] adj cordial(e), chaleureux(euse) ◆ n sirop m; cordial m

cordon ['kɔːdn] n cordon m

▶ **cordon off** vt (area) interdire l'accès à; (crowd) tenir à l'écart

corduroy ['kɔːdərɔɪ] n velours côtelé

core [kɔː*] n (of fruit) trognon m, cœur m; (TECH: also of earth) noyau m; (of nuclear reactor, fig: of problem etc) cœur ◆ vt enlever le trognon or le cœur de; **rotten to the core** complètement pourri

cork [kɔːk] n liège m; (of bottle) bouchon m

corkscrew ['kɔːkskruː] n tire-bouchon m

corn [kɔːn] n (BRIT: wheat) blé m; (US: maize) maïs m; (on foot) cor m; **corn on the cob** (CULIN) épi m de maïs au naturel

corned beef ['kɔːnd-] n corned-beef m

corner ['kɔːnə*] n coin m; (AUT) tournant m, virage m; (FOOTBALL: also: **corner kick**) corner m ◆ vt acculer, mettre au pied du mur; coincer; (COMM: market) accaparer ◆ vi prendre un virage; **to cut corners** (fig) prendre des raccourcis

cornerstone ['kɔːnəstəun] n pierre f angulaire

cornet ['kɔːnɪt] n (MUS) cornet m à pistons; (BRIT: of ice-cream) cornet (de glace)

cornflakes ['kɔːnfleɪks] npl cornflakes mpl

cornflour ['kɔːnflauə*] n (BRIT) farine f de maïs, maïzena® f

Cornwall ['kɔːnwəl] n Cornouailles f

corny ['kɔːnɪ] adj (col) rebattu(e), galvaudé(e)

coronary ['kɔrənərɪ] n: **coronary (thrombosis)** infarctus m (du myocarde), thrombose f coronaire

coronation [kɔrə'neɪʃən] n couronnement m

coroner ['kɔrənə*] n coroner m

corporal ['kɔːpərl] n caporal m, brigadier m ◆ adj: **corporal punishment** châtiment corporel

corporate [ˈkɔːpərɪt] *adj* en commun; (COMM) constitué(e) (en corporation)

corporation [kɔːpəˈreɪʃən] *n* (of town) municipalité *f*, conseil municipal; (COMM) société *f*

corps [kɔː*], *pl* **corps** [kɔːz] ♦ *n* corps *m*; **the press corps** la presse

corpse [kɔːps] *n* cadavre *m*

correct [kəˈrɛkt] *adj* (accurate) correct(e), exact(e); (proper) correct, convenable ♦ *vt* corriger; **you are correct** vous avez raison

correction [kəˈrɛkʃən] *n* correction *f*

correspond [kɔrɪsˈpɔnd] *vi* correspondre

correspondence [kɔrɪsˈpɔndəns] *n* correspondance *f*

correspondence course *n* cours *m* par correspondance

correspondent [kɔrɪsˈpɔndənt] *n* correspondant/e

corridor [ˈkɔrɪdɔː*] *n* couloir *m*, corridor *m*

corrode [kəˈrəud] *vt* corroder, ronger ♦ *vi* se corroder

corrugated [ˈkɔrəgeɪtɪd] *adj* plissé(e); ondulé(e)

corrugated iron *n* tôle ondulée

corrupt [kəˈrʌpt] *adj* corrompu(e) ♦ *vt* corrompre; (data) altérer; **corrupt practices** (dishonesty, bribery) malversation *f*

corruption [kəˈrʌpʃən] *n* corruption *f*; altération *f* (de données)

Corsica [ˈkɔːsɪkə] *n* Corse *f*

cosmetic [kɔzˈmɛtɪk] *n* produit *m* de beauté, cosmétique *m* ♦ *adj* (preparation) cosmétique; (surgery) esthétique; (fig: reforms) symbolique, superficiel(le)

cost [kɔst] *n* coût *m* ♦ *vb* (pt, pp **cost**) ♦ *vi* coûter ♦ *vt* établir or calculer le prix de revient de; **costs** *npl* (LAW) dépens *mpl*; **how much does it cost?** combien ça coûte?; **it costs £5/too much** cela coûte 5 livres/trop cher; **what will it cost to have it repaired?** combien cela coûtera de le faire réparer?; **it cost him his life/job** ça lui a coûté la vie/son emploi; **the cost of living** le coût de la vie; **at all costs** coûte que coûte, à tout prix

co-star [ˈkəustɑː*] *n* partenaire *m/f*

cost-effective [ˈkɔstɪˈfɛktɪv] *adj* rentable

costly [ˈkɔstlɪ] *adj* coûteux(euse)

cost-of-living [ˈkɔstəvˈlɪvɪŋ] *adj*: **cost-of-living allowance** indemnité *f* de vie chère; **cost-of-living index** indice *m* du coût de la vie

cost price *n* (BRIT) prix coûtant or de revient

costume [ˈkɔstjuːm] *n* costume *m*; (lady's suit) tailleur *m*; (BRIT: also: **swimming costume**) maillot *m* (de bain)

costume jewellery *n* bijoux *mpl* de fantaisie

cosy, (US) **cozy** [ˈkəuzɪ] *adj* (bed) douillet(te); (scarf, gloves) bien chaud(e); (atmosphere) chaleureux(euse); (room) mignon(ne)

cot [kɔt] *n* (BRIT: child's) lit *m* d'enfant, petit lit; (US:

campbed) lit de camp

cottage [ˈkɔtɪdʒ] *n* petite maison (à la campagne), cottage *m*

cottage cheese *n* fromage blanc (maigre)

cotton [ˈkɔtn] *n* coton *m*; **cotton dress** etc robe etc en or de coton

▶ **cotton on** *vi* (col): **to cotton on (to sth)** piger (qch)

cotton candy (US) *n* barbe *f* à papa

cotton wool *n* (BRIT) ouate *f*, coton *m* hydrophile

couch [kautʃ] *n* canapé *m*; divan *m*; (doctor's) table *f* d'examen; (psychiatrist's) divan ♦ *vt* formuler, exprimer

couchette [kuːˈʃɛt] *n* couchette *f*

cough [kɔf] *vi* tousser ♦ *n* toux *f*

cough sweet *n* pastille *f* pour or contre la toux

could [kud] *pt of* **can**

couldn't [ˈkudnt] = **could not**

council [ˈkaunsl] *n* conseil *m*; **city** or **town council** conseil municipal; **Council of Europe** Conseil de l'Europe

council estate *n* (BRIT) (quartier *m* or zone *f* de) logements loués à/par la municipalité

council house *n* (BRIT) maison *f* (à loyer modéré) louée par la municipalité

councillor [ˈkaunslə*] *n* conseiller/ère

counsel [ˈkaunsl] *n* consultation *f*, délibération *f*; (person) avocat/e ♦ *vt*: **to counsel sth/sb to do sth** conseiller qch/à qn de faire qch; **counsel for the defence/the prosecution** (avocat de la) défense/ avocat du ministère public

counsellor, (US) **counselor** [ˈkaunslə*] *n* conseiller/ère; (US LAW) avocat *m*

count [kaunt] *vt, vi* compter ♦ *n* compte *m*; (nobleman) comte *m*; **to count (up) to 10** compter jusqu'à 10; **to keep count of sth** tenir le compte de qch; **not counting the children** sans compter les enfants; **10 counting him** 10 avec lui, 10 en le comptant; **to count the cost of** établir le coût de; **it counts for very little** cela n'a pas beaucoup d'importance; **count yourself lucky** estimez-vous heureux

▶ **count on** *vt fus* compter sur; **to count on doing sth** compter faire qch

▶ **count up** *vt* compter, additionner

countdown [ˈkauntdaun] *n* compte *m* à rebours

countenance [ˈkauntɪnəns] *n* expression *f* ♦ *vt* approuver

counter [ˈkauntə*] *n* comptoir *m*; (in post office, bank) guichet *m*; (in game) jeton *m* ♦ *vt* aller à l'encontre de, opposer; (blow) parer ♦ *adv*: **counter to** à l'encontre de; contrairement à; **to buy under the counter** (fig) acheter sous le manteau or en sous-main; **to counter sth with sth/by doing sth** contrer or riposter à qch par qch/en faisant qch

counteract [ˈkauntərˈækt] *vt* neutraliser, contrebalancer

counterfeit ['kauntǝfɪt] n faux m, contrefaçon f ♦ vt contrefaire ♦ adj faux(fausse)

counterfoil ['kauntǝfɔɪl] n talon m, souche f

counterpart ['kauntǝpɑːt] n (of document etc) double m; (of person) homologue m/f

countess ['kauntɪs] n comtesse f

countless ['kauntlɪs] adj innombrable

country ['kʌntrɪ] n pays m; (native land) patrie f; (as opposed to town) campagne f; (region) région f, pays; **in the country** à la campagne; **mountainous country** pays de montagne, région montagneuse

country dancing n (BRIT) danse f folklorique

country house n manoir m, (petit) château

countryman ['kʌntrɪmǝn] n (national) compatriote m; (rural) habitant m de la campagne, campagnard m

countryside ['kʌntrɪsaɪd] n campagne f

county ['kauntɪ] n comté m

coup, coups [kuː, -z] n beau coup; (also: **coup d'état**) coup d'État

couple ['kʌpl] n couple m ♦ vt (carriages) atteler; (TECH) coupler; (ideas, names) associer; **a couple of** deux m; (a few) deux ou trois

coupon ['kuːpɒn] n (voucher) bon-prime m, bon-réclame m; (detachable form) coupon m détachable, coupon-réponse m; (FINANCE) coupon

courage ['kʌrɪdʒ] n courage m

courier ['kurɪǝ*] n messager m, courrier m; (for tourists) accompagnateur/trice

course [kɔːs] n cours m; (of ship) route f; (for golf) terrain m; (part of meal) plat m; **first course** entrée f; **of course** adv bien sûr; **(no) of course not!** bien sûr que non!, évidemment que non!; **in the course of the next few days** au cours des prochains jours; **in due course** en temps utile or voulu; **course (of action)** parti m, ligne f de conduite; **the best course would be to ...** le mieux serait de ...; **we have no other course but to ...** nous n'avons pas d'autre solution que de ...; **course of lectures** série f de conférences; **course of treatment** (MED) traitement m

court [kɔːt] n cour f; (LAW) cour, tribunal m; (TENNIS) court m ♦ vt (woman) courtiser, faire la cour à; (fig: favour, popularity) rechercher; (: death, disaster) courir après, flirter avec; **out of court** (LAW: settle) à l'amiable; **to take court** actionner or poursuivre en justice; **court of appeal** cour d'appel

courteous ['kɜːtɪǝs] adj courtois(e), poli(e)

courtesy ['kɜːtǝsɪ] n courtoisie f, politesse f; **by courtesy of** avec l'aimable autorisation de

courtesy bus or **coach** n navette gratuite

court-house ['kɔːthaus] n (US) palais m de justice

courtier ['kɔːtɪǝ*] n courtisan m, dame f de cour

court martial, pl **courts martial** n cour martiale, conseil m de guerre

courtroom ['kɔːtrum] n salle f de tribunal

courtyard ['kɔːtjɑːd] n cour f

cousin ['kʌzn] n cousin/e

cove [kǝuv] n petite baie, anse f

covenant ['kʌvǝnǝnt] n contrat m, engagement m ♦ vt: **to covenant £200 per year to a charity** s'engager à verser 200 livres par an à une œuvre de bienfaisance

cover ['kʌvǝ*] vt couvrir; (PRESS: report on) faire un reportage sur ♦ n (for bed, of book, COMM) couverture f; (of pan) couvercle m; (over furniture) housse f; (shelter) abri m; **to take cover** se mettre à l'abri; **under cover** à l'abri; **under cover of darkness** à la faveur de la nuit; **under separate cover** (COMM) sous pli séparé; **£10 will cover everything** 10 livres suffiront (pour tout payer)

► **cover up** vt (person, object): **to cover up (with)** couvrir (de); (fig: truth, facts) occulter; **to cover up for sb** (fig) couvrir qn

coverage ['kʌvǝrɪdʒ] n (in media) reportage m; (INSURANCE) couverture f

cover charge n couvert m (supplément à payer)

covering ['kʌvǝrɪŋ] n couverture f, enveloppe f

covering letter, (US) **cover letter** n lettre explicative

cover note n (INSURANCE) police f provisoire

covert ['kʌvǝt] adj (threat) voilé(e), caché(e); (attack) indirect(e); (glance) furtif(ive)

cover-up ['kʌvǝrʌp] n tentative f pour étouffer une affaire

covet ['kʌvɪt] vt convoiter

cow [kau] n vache f ♦ cpd femelle ♦ vt effrayer, intimider

coward ['kauǝd] n lâche m/f

cowardice ['kauǝdɪs] n lâcheté f

cowardly ['kauǝdlɪ] adj lâche

cowboy ['kaubɔɪ] n cow-boy m

cower ['kauǝ*] vi se recroqueviller; trembler

coy [kɔɪ] adj faussement effarouché(e) or timide

cozy ['kǝuzɪ] adj (US) = **cosy**

CPA n abbr (US) = certified public accountant

crab [kræb] n crabe m

crab apple n pomme f sauvage

crack [kræk] n fente, fissure f; (in bone, dish, glass) fêlure f; (in wall) lézarde f; (noise) craquement m, coup (sec); (joke) plaisanterie f; (col: attempt): **to have a crack (at sth)** essayer (qch); (DRUGS) crack m ♦ vt fendre, fissurer; fêler; lézarder; (whip) faire claquer; (nut) casser; (solve) résoudre, trouver la clef de; déchiffrer; (col: joke) raconter; **to crack jokes** (col) raconter des blagues; **to get cracking** (col) s'y mettre, se magner

► **crack down on** vt fus (crime) sévir contre, réprimer; (spending) mettre un frein à

► **crack up** vi être au bout de son rouleau, flancher

cracked [krækt] adj (col) toqué(e), timbré(e)

cracker ['krækǝ*] n pétard m; (biscuit) biscuit (salé), craquelin m; **a cracker of a ...** (BRIT col) un(e)

… formidable; **he's crackers** (*BRIT col*) il est cinglé

crackle ['krækl] *vi* crépiter, grésiller

cradle ['kreɪdl] *n* berceau *m* ◆ *vt* (*child*) bercer; (*object*) tenir dans ses bras

craft [krɑːft] *n* métier (artisanal); (*cunning*) ruse *f*, astuce *f*; (*boat*) embarcation *f*, barque *f*

craftsman ['krɑːftsmən] *n* artisan *m*, ouvrier (qualifié)

craftsmanship ['krɑːftsmənʃɪp] *n* métier *m*, habileté *f*

crafty ['krɑːftɪ] *adj* rusé(e), malin(igne), astucieux(euse)

crag [kræg] *n* rocher escarpé

cram [kræm] *vt* (*fill*): **to cram sth with** bourrer qch de; (*put*): **to cram sth into** fourrer qch dans

cramp [kræmp] *n* crampe *f* ◆ *vt* gêner, entraver

cramped [kræmpt] *adj* à l'étroit, très serré(e)

cranberry ['krænbərɪ] *n* canneberge *f*

crane [kreɪn] *n* grue *f* ◆ *vt, vi*: **to crane forward, to crane one's neck** allonger le cou

crank [kræŋk] *n* manivelle *f*; (*person*) excentrique *m/f*

cranny ['krænɪ] *n see* **nook**

crash [kræʃ] *n* fracas *m*; (*of car, plane*) collision *f*; (*of business*) faillite *f*; (*STOCK EXCHANGE*) krach *m* ◆ *vt* (*plane*) écraser ◆ *vi* (*plane*) s'écraser; (*two cars*) se percuter, s'emboutir; (*fig*) s'effondrer; **to crash into** se jeter *or* se fracasser contre; **he crashed the car into a wall** il s'est écrasé contre un mur avec sa voiture

crash course *n* cours intensif

crash helmet *n* casque (protecteur)

crash landing *n* atterrissage forcé *or* en catastrophe

crate [kreɪt] *n* cageot *m*

cravat [krə'væt] *n* foulard (*noué autour du cou*)

crave [kreɪv] *vt, vi*: **to crave for** désirer violemment, avoir un besoin physiologique de, avoir une envie irrésistible de

crawl [krɔːl] *vi* ramper; (*vehicle*) avancer au pas ◆ *n* (*SWIMMING*) crawl *m*; **to crawl on one's hands and knees** aller à quatre pattes; **to crawl to sb** (*col*) faire de la lèche à qn

crayfish ['kreɪfɪʃ] *n* (*pl inv: freshwater*) écrevisse *f*; (*saltwater*) langoustine *f*

crayon ['kreɪən] *n* crayon *m* (de couleur)

craze [kreɪz] *n* engouement *m*

crazy ['kreɪzɪ] *adj* fou(folle); **to go crazy** devenir fou; **to be crazy about sb** (*col*) aimer qn à la folie; **he's crazy about skiing** (*col*) c'est un fana(tique) de ski

creak [kriːk] *vi* (*hinge*) grincer; (*floor, shoes*) craquer

cream [kriːm] *n* crème *f* ◆ *adj* (*colour*) crème *inv*; **whipped cream** crème fouettée

▶ **cream off** *vt* (*fig*) prélever

cream cake *n* (petit) gâteau à la crème

cream cheese *n* fromage *m* à la crème, fromage blanc

creamy ['kriːmɪ] *adj* crémeux(euse)

crease [kriːs] *n* pli *m* ◆ *vt* froisser, chiffonner ◆ *vi* se froisser, se chiffonner

create [kriː'eɪt] *vt* créer; (*impression, fuss*) faire

creation [kriː'eɪʃən] *n* création *f*

creative [kriː'eɪtɪv] *adj* créateur(trice)

creature ['kriːtʃə*] *n* créature *f*

crèche [krɛʃ] *n* garderie *f*, crèche *f*

credence ['kriːdns] *n* croyance *f*, foi *f*

credentials [krɪ'denʃlz] *npl* (*papers*) références *fpl*; (*letters of reference*) pièces justificatives

credit ['krɛdɪt] *n* crédit *m*; (*SCOL*) unité *f* de valeur ◆ *vt* (*COMM*) créditer; (*believe: also*: **give credit to**) ajouter foi à, croire; **to credit sb with** (*fig*) prêter *or* attribuer à qn; **to credit £5 to sb** créditer (le compte de) qn de 5 livres; **to be in credit** (*person, bank account*) être créditeur(trice); **on credit** à crédit; **to one's credit** à son honneur; à son actif; **to take the credit for** s'attribuer le mérite de; **it does him credit** cela lui fait honneur

credit card *n* carte *f* de crédit

creditor ['krɛdɪtə*] *n* créancier/ière

creed [kriːd] *n* croyance *f*, credo *m*, principes *mpl*

creek [kriːk] *n* crique *f*, anse *f*; (*US*) ruisseau *m*, petit cours d'eau

creep, *pt, pp* **crept** [kriːp, krɛpt], *vi* ramper; (*fig*) se faufiler, se glisser; (*plant*) grimper ◆ *n* (*col*) saligaud *m*; **he's a creep** c'est un type puant; **it gives me the creeps** cela me fait froid dans le dos; **to creep up on sb** s'approcher furtivement de qn

creeper ['kriːpə*] *n* plante grimpante

creepy ['kriːpɪ] *adj* (*frightening*) qui fait frissonner, qui donne la chair de poule

cremate [krɪ'meɪt] *vt* incinérer

crematorium, *pl* **crematoria** [krɛmə'tɔːrɪəm, -'tɔːrɪə] *n* four *m* crématoire

crepe [kreɪp] *n* crêpe *m*

crepe bandage *n* (*BRIT*) bande *f* Velpeau®

crept [krɛpt] *pt, pp of* **creep**

crescent ['krɛsnt] *n* croissant *m*; (*street*) rue *f* (en arc de cercle)

cress [krɛs] *n* cresson *m*

crest [krɛst] *n* crête *f*; (*of helmet*) cimier *m*; (*of coat of arms*) timbre *m*

crestfallen ['krɛstfɔːlən] *adj* déconfit(e), découragé(e)

Crete ['kriːt] *n* Crète *f*

crevice ['krɛvɪs] *n* fissure *f*, lézarde *f*, fente *f*

crew [kruː] *n* équipage *m*; (*CINE*) équipe *f* (de tournage); (*gang*) bande *f*

crew-cut ['kruːkʌt] *n*: **to have a crew-cut** avoir les cheveux en brosse

crew-neck ['kruːnɛk] *n* col ras

crib [krɪb] *n* lit *m* d'enfant ◆ *vt* (*col*) copier

crick [krɪk] *n* crampe *f*; **crick in the neck** torticolis *m*

cricket [ˈkrɪkɪt] *n* (*insect*) grillon *m*, cri-cri *m inv*; (*game*) cricket *m*

crime [kraɪm] *n* crime *m*; **minor crime** délit *m* or infraction *f* mineur(e)

criminal [ˈkrɪmɪnl] *adj, n* criminel(le)

crimson [ˈkrɪmzn] *adj* cramoisi(e)

cringe [krɪndʒ] *vi* avoir un mouvement de recul; (*fig*) s'humilier, ramper

crinkle [ˈkrɪŋkl] *vt* froisser, chiffonner

cripple [ˈkrɪpl] *n* boiteux/euse, infirme *m/f* ♦ *vt* estropier, paralyser; (*ship, plane*) immobiliser; (*production, exports*) paralyser; **crippled with rheumatism** perclus(e) de rhumatismes

crisis, *pl* **crises** [ˈkraɪsɪs, -siːz] *n* crise *f*

crisp [krɪsp] *adj* croquant(e); (*fig*) vif(vive) brusque

crisps [krɪsps] *npl* (*BRIT*) (pommes) chips *fpl*

crisscross [ˈkrɪskrɔs] *adj* entrecroisé(e), en croisillons ♦ *vt* sillonner; **crisscross pattern** croisillons *mpl*

criterion, *pl* **criteria** [kraɪˈtɪərɪən, -ˈtɪərɪə] *n* critère *m*

critic [ˈkrɪtɪk] *n* critique *m/f*

critical [ˈkrɪtɪkl] *adj* critique; **to be critical of sb/ sth** critiquer qn/qch

critically [ˈkrɪtɪklɪ] *adv* (*examine*) d'un œil critique; (*speak*) sévèrement; **critically ill** gravement malade

criticism [ˈkrɪtɪsɪzəm] *n* critique *f*

criticize [ˈkrɪtɪsaɪz] *vt* critiquer

croak [krəuk] *vi* (*frog*) coasser; (*raven*) croasser

Croatia [krəuˈeɪʃə] *n* Croatie *f*

crochet [ˈkrəuʃeɪ] *n* travail *m* au crochet

crockery [ˈkrɔkərɪ] *n* vaisselle *f*

crocodile [ˈkrɔkədaɪl] *n* crocodile *m*

crocus [ˈkrəukəs] *n* crocus *m*

croft [krɔft] *n* (*BRIT*) petite ferme

crony [ˈkrəunɪ] *n* copain/copine

crook [kruk] *n* escroc *m*; (*of shepherd*) houlette *f*

crooked [ˈkrukɪd] *adj* courbé(e), tordu(e); (*action*) malhonnête

crop [krɔp] *n* (*produce*) culture *f*; (*amount produced*) récolte *f*; (*riding crop*) cravache *f*; (*of bird*) jabot *m* ♦ *vt* (*hair*) tondre; (*subj: animals: grass*) brouter

▶ **crop up** *vi* surgir, se présenter, survenir

cross [krɔs] *n* croix *f*; (*BIOL*) croisement *m* ♦ *vt* (*street etc*) traverser; (*arms, legs, BIOL*) croiser; (*cheque*) barrer; (*thwart: person, plan*) contrarier ♦ *vi*: **the boat crosses from ... to ...** le bateau fait la traversée de ... à ... ♦ *adj* en colère, fâché(e); **to cross o.s.** se signer, faire le signe de (la) croix; **we have a crossed line** (*BRIT: on telephone*) il y a des interférences; **they've got their lines crossed** (*fig*) il y a un malentendu entre eux; **to be/get cross with sb (about sth)** être en colère/se fâcher contre qn (à propos de qch)

▶ **cross out** *vt* barrer, biffer

▶ **cross over** *vi* traverser

crossbar [ˈkrɔsbɑː*] *n* barre transversale

cross-country (race) [ˈkrɔsˈkʌntrɪ-] *n* cross (-country) *m*

cross-examine [ˈkrɔsɪgˈzæmɪn] *vt* (*LAW*) faire subir un examen contradictoire à

cross-eyed [ˈkrɔsaɪd] *adj* qui louche

crossfire [ˈkrɔsfaɪə*] *n* feux croisés

crossing [ˈkrɔsɪŋ] *n* croisement *m*, carrefour *m*; (*sea passage*) traversée *f*; (*also:* **pedestrian crossing**) passage clouté

cross-purposes [ˈkrɔsˈpəːpəsɪz] *npl*: **to be at cross-purposes with sb** comprendre qn de travers; **we're (talking) at cross-purposes** on ne parle pas de la même chose

cross-reference [ˈkrɔsˈrefrəns] *n* renvoi *m*, référence *f*

crossroads [ˈkrɔsrəudz] *n* carrefour *m*

cross section *n* (*BIOL*) coupe transversale; (*in population*) échantillon *m*

crosswalk [ˈkrɔswɔːk] *n* (*US*) passage clouté

crosswind [ˈkrɔswɪnd] *n* vent *m* de travers

crossword [ˈkrɔswəːd] *n* mots *mpl* croisés

crotch [krɔtʃ] *n* (*of garment*) entre-jambes *m inv*

crouch [krautʃ] *vi* s'accroupir; se tapir; se ramasser

crow [krəu] *n* (*bird*) corneille *f*; (*of cock*) chant *m* du coq, cocorico *m* ♦ *vi* (*cock*) chanter; (*fig*) pavoiser, chanter victoire

crowbar [ˈkrəubɑː*] *n* levier *m*

crowd [kraud] *n* foule *f* ♦ *vt* bourrer, remplir ♦ *vi* affluer, s'attrouper, s'entasser; **crowds of people** une foule de gens

crowded [ˈkraudɪd] *adj* bondé(e), plein(e); **crowded with** plein de

crown [kraun] *n* couronne *f*; (*of head*) sommet *m* de la tête, calotte crânienne; (*of hat*) fond *m*; (*of hill*) sommet *m* ♦ *vt* (*also tooth*) couronner

crown jewels *npl* joyaux *mpl* de la Couronne

crow's-feet [ˈkrəuzfiːt] *npl* pattes *fpl* d'oie (*fig*)

crucial [ˈkruːʃl] *adj* crucial(e), décisif(ive) (*also:* **crucial to**) essentiel(le) à

crucifix [ˈkruːsɪfɪks] *n* crucifix *m*

crucifixion [kruːsɪˈfɪkʃən] *n* crucifiement *m*, crucifixion *f*

crude [kruːd] *adj* (*materials*) brut(e); non raffiné(e); (*basic*) rudimentaire, sommaire; (*vulgar*) cru(e), grossier(ière)

crude (oil) *n* (*pétrole*) brut *m*

cruel [ˈkruəl] *adj* cruel(le)

cruelty [ˈkruəltɪ] *n* cruauté *f*

cruise [kruːz] *n* croisière *f* ♦ *vi* (*ship*) croiser; (*car*) rouler; (*aircraft*) voler; (*taxi*) être en maraude

cruiser [ˈkruːzə*] *n* croiseur *m*

crumb [krʌm] *n* miette *f*

crumble [ˈkrʌmbl] *vt* émietter ♦ *vi* s'émietter; (*plaster etc*) s'effriter; (*land, earth*) s'ébouler; (*build-*

ing) s'écrouler, crouler; (fig) s'effondrer

crumbly ['krʌmblɪ] adj friable

crumpet ['krʌmpɪt] n petite crêpe (épaisse)

crumple ['krʌmpl] vt froisser, friper

crunch [krʌntʃ] vt croquer; (underfoot) faire craquer, écraser; faire crisser ♦ n (fig) instant m or moment m critique, moment de vérité

crunchy ['krʌntʃɪ] adj croquant(e), croustillant(e)

crusade [kru:'seɪd] n croisade f ♦ vi (fig): **to crusade for/against** partir en croisade pour/contre

crush [krʌʃ] n foule f, cohue f; (love): **to have a crush on sb** avoir le béguin pour qn; (drink): **lemon crush** citron pressé ♦ vt écraser; (crumple) froisser; (grind, break up: garlic, ice) piler; (: grapes) presser

crust [krʌst] n croûte f

crutch [krʌtʃ] n béquille f; (TECH) support m; (also: **crotch**) entrejambe m

crux [krʌks] n point crucial

cry [kraɪ] vi pleurer; (shout: also: **cry out**) crier ♦ n cri m; **what are you crying about?** pourquoi pleures-tu?; **to cry for help** appeler à l'aide; **she had a good cry** elle a pleuré un bon coup; **it's a far cry from ...** (fig) on est loin de ...

▶ **cry off** vi se dédire; se décommander

cryptic ['krɪptɪk] adj énigmatique

crystal ['krɪstl] n cristal m

crystal-clear ['krɪstl'klɪə*] adj clair(e) comme de l'eau de roche

CSA n abbr = Confederate States of America; (BRIT: = Child Support Agency) organisme pour la protection des enfants de parents séparés, qui contrôle le versement des pensions alimentaires.

CTC n abbr (BRIT) = **city technology college**

cub [kʌb] n petit m (d'un animal) (also: **cub scout**) louveteau m

Cuba ['kju:bə] n Cuba m

cube [kju:b] n cube m ♦ vt (MATH) élever au cube

cubic ['kju:bɪk] adj cubique; **cubic metre** etc mètre m etc cube; **cubic capacity** (AUT) cylindrée f

cubicle ['kju:bɪkl] n box m, cabine f

cuckoo ['kuku:] n coucou m

cuckoo clock n (pendule f à) coucou m

cucumber ['kju:kʌmbə*] n concombre m

cuddle ['kʌdl] vt câliner, caresser ♦ vi se blottir l'un contre l'autre

cue [kju:] n queue f de billard; (THEAT etc) signal m

cuff [kʌf] n (of shirt, coat etc) poignet m, manchette f; (US: on trousers) revers m; (blow) gifle f ♦ vt gifler; **off the cuff** adv de chic, à l'improviste

cufflinks ['kʌflɪŋks] n boutons m de manchette

cul-de-sac ['kʌldəsæk] n cul-de-sac m, impasse f

cull [kʌl] vt sélectionner; (kill selectively) pratiquer l'abattage sélectif de

culminate ['kʌlmɪneɪt] vi: **to culminate in** finir or se terminer par; (lead to) mener à

culmination [kʌlmɪ'neɪʃən] n point culminant

culottes [kju:'lɒts] npl jupe-culotte f

culprit ['kʌlprɪt] n coupable m/f

cult [kʌlt] n culte m

cultivate ['kʌltɪveɪt] vt (also fig) cultiver

cultivation [kʌltɪ'veɪʃən] n culture f

cultural ['kʌltʃərəl] adj culturel(le)

culture ['kʌltʃə*] n (also fig) culture f

cultured ['kʌltʃəd] adj cultivé(e) (fig)

cumbersome ['kʌmbəsəm] adj encombrant(e), embarrassant(e)

cunning ['kʌnɪŋ] n ruse f, astuce f ♦ adj rusé(e), malin(igne); (clever: device, idea) astucieux(euse)

cup [kʌp] n tasse f; (prize, event) coupe f; (of bra) bonnet m; **a cup of tea** une tasse de thé

cupboard ['kʌbəd] n placard m

cup tie ['kʌptaɪ] n (BRIT FOOTBALL) match m de coupe

curate ['kjuərɪt] n vicaire m

curator [kjuə'reɪtə*] n conservateur m (d'un musée etc)

curb [kə:b] vt refréner, mettre un frein à; (expenditure) limiter, juguler ♦ n frein m (fig); (US) = **kerb**

curdle ['kə:dl] vi (se) cailler

cure [kjuə*] vt guérir; (CULIN) saler; fumer; sécher ♦ n remède m; **to be cured of sth** être guéri de qch

curfew ['kə:fju:] n couvre-feu m

curiosity [kjuərɪ'ɒsɪtɪ] n curiosité f

curious ['kjuərɪəs] adj curieux(euse); **I'm curious about him** il m'intrigue

curl [kə:l] n boucle f (de cheveux); (of smoke etc) volute f ♦ vt, vi boucler; (tightly) friser

▶ **curl up** vi s'enrouler; se pelotonner

curler ['kə:lə*] n bigoudi m, rouleau m; (SPORT) joueur/euse de curling

curly ['kə:lɪ] adj bouclé(e); (tightly curled) frisé(e)

currant ['kʌrnt] n raisin m de Corinthe, raisin sec

currency ['kʌrnsɪ] n monnaie f; **foreign currency** devises étrangères, monnaie étrangère; **to gain currency** (fig) s'accréditer

current ['kʌrnt] n courant m ♦ adj courant(e); (tendency, price, event) actuel(le); **direct/alternating current** (ELEC) courant continu/alternatif; **the current issue of a magazine** le dernier numéro d'un magazine; **in current use** d'usage courant

current account n (BRIT) compte courant

current affairs npl (questions fpl d')actualité f

currently ['kʌrntlɪ] adv actuellement

curriculum, pl **curriculums** or **curricula** [kə'rɪkjuləm, -lə] n programme m d'études

curriculum vitae (CV) [-'vi:taɪ] n curriculum vitae (CV) m

curry ['kʌrɪ] n curry m ♦ vt: **to curry favour with** chercher à gagner la faveur or à s'attirer les bonnes grâces de; **chicken curry** curry de poulet, poulet m au curry

curse [kə:s] vi jurer, blasphémer ♦ vt maudire ♦ n malédiction f; fléau m; (swearword) juron m

cursor ['kə:sə*] n (COMPUT) curseur m

cursory ['kə:sərɪ] adj superficiel(le), hâtif(ive)

curt [kə:t] adj brusque, sec(sèche)

curtail [kə:'teɪl] vt (visit etc) écourter; (expenses etc) réduire

curtain ['kə:tn] n rideau m; **to draw the curtains** (together) fermer ou tirer les rideaux; (apart) ouvrir les rideaux

curts(e)y ['kə:tsɪ] n révérence f ♦ vi faire une révérence

curve [kə:v] n courbe f; (in the road) tournant m, virage m ♦ vt courber ♦ vi se courber; (road) faire une courbe

cushion ['kuʃən] n coussin m ♦ vt (seat) rembourrer; (shock) amortir

custard ['kʌstəd] n (for pouring) crème anglaise

custody ['kʌstədɪ] n (of child) garde f; (for offenders) détention préventive; **to take sb into custody** placer qn en détention préventive; **in the custody of** sous la garde de

custom ['kʌstəm] n coutume f, usage m; (LAW) droit coutumier, coutume; (COMM) clientèle f

customary ['kʌstəmərɪ] adj habituel(le); **it is customary to do it** l'usage veut qu'on le fasse

customer ['kʌstəmə*] n client/e; **he's an awkward customer** (col) ce n'est pas quelqu'un de facile

customized ['kʌstəmaɪzd] adj personnalisé(e)

custom-made ['kʌstəm'meɪd] adj (clothes) fait(e) sur mesure; (other goods: also: **custom-built**) hors série, fait(e) sur commande

customs ['kʌstəmz] npl douane f; **to go through (the) customs** passer la douane

customs officer n douanier m

cut [kʌt] vb (pt, pp **cut**) vt couper; (meat) découper; (shape, make) tailler; couper; creuser; graver; (reduce) réduire; (col: lecture, appointment) manquer ♦ vi couper; (intersect) se couper ♦ n (gen) coupure f; (of clothes) coupe f; (of jewel) taille f; (in salary etc) réduction f; (of meat) morceau m; **cold cuts** npl (US) viandes froides; **to cut teeth** (baby) faire ses dents; **to cut a tooth** percer une dent; **to cut one's finger** se couper le doigt; **to get one's hair cut** se faire couper les cheveux; **to cut sth short** couper court à qch; **to cut sb dead** ignorer (complètement) qn

▶ **cut back** vt (plants) tailler; (production, expenditure) réduire

▶ **cut down** vt (tree) abattre; (reduce) réduire; **to cut sb down to size** (fig) remettre qn à sa place

▶ **cut down on** vt fus réduire

▶ **cut in** vi (interrupt: conversation): **to cut in (on)** couper la parole (à); (AUT) faire une queue de poisson

▶ **cut off** vt couper; (fig) isoler; **we've been cut off** (TEL) nous avons été coupés

▶ **cut out** vt (picture etc) découper; (remove) ôter; supprimer

▶ **cut up** vt découper

cutback ['kʌtbæk] n réduction f

cute [kju:t] adj mignon(ne), adorable; (clever) rusé(e), astucieux(euse)

cutlery ['kʌtlərɪ] n couverts mpl; (trade) coutellerie f

cutlet ['kʌtlɪt] n côtelette f

cutout ['kʌtaut] n coupe-circuit m inv; (paper figure) découpage m

cut-price ['kʌt'praɪs], (US) **cut-rate** ['kʌt'reɪt] adj au rabais, à prix réduit

cut-throat ['kʌtθrəut] n assassin m ♦ adj: **cut-throat competition** concurrence f sauvage

cutting ['kʌtɪŋ] adj tranchant(e), coupant(e); (fig) cinglant(e), mordant(e) ♦ n (BRIT: from newspaper) coupure f (de journal); (: RAIL) tranchée f; (CINE) montage m

CV n abbr = **curriculum vitae**

cwt abbr = **hundredweight**

cyanide ['saɪənaɪd] n cyanure m

cybercafé ['saɪbəkæfeɪ] n cybercafé m

cyberspace ['saɪbəspeɪs] n cyberspace m

cycle ['saɪkl] n cycle m ♦ vi faire de la bicyclette

cycle hire n location f de vélos

cycle lane or **path** n piste f cyclable

cycling ['saɪklɪŋ] n cyclisme m; **to go on a cycling holiday** (BRIT) faire du cyclotourisme

cyclist ['saɪklɪst] n cycliste m/f

cygnet ['sɪgnɪt] n jeune cygne m

cylinder ['sɪlɪndə*] n cylindre m

cylinder-head gasket ['sɪlɪndəhed-] n joint m de culasse

cymbals ['sɪmblz] npl cymbales fpl

cynic ['sɪnɪk] n cynique m/f

cynical ['sɪnɪkl] adj cynique

cynicism ['sɪnɪsɪzəm] n cynisme m

Cypriot ['sɪprɪət] adj cypriote, chypriote ♦ n Cypriote m/f, Chypriote m/f

Cyprus ['saɪprəs] n Chypre f

cyst [sɪst] n kyste m

cystitis [sɪs'taɪtɪs] n cystite f

czar [zɑː*] n tsar m

Czech [tʃek] adj tchèque ♦ n Tchèque m/f; (LING) tchèque m; **the Czech Republic** la République tchèque

Czechoslovak [tʃekə'sləuvæk] adj, n = **Czechoslovakian**

Czechoslovakia [tʃekəslə'vækɪə] n Tchécoslovaquie f

Czechoslovakian [tʃekəslə'vækɪən] adj tchécoslovaque ♦ n Tchécoslovaque m/f

— D d —

D, d [di:] n (letter) D, d m; (MUS): **D** ré m; **D for David**, (US) **D for Dog** D comme Désirée

D abbr (US POL) = **democrat(ic)**

d abbr (BRIT: old) = **penny**

dab [dæb] vt (eyes, wound) tamponner; (paint, cream) appliquer (par petites touches or rapidement); **a dab of paint** un petit coup de peinture

dabble ['dæbl] vi: **to dabble in** faire or se mêler or s'occuper un peu de

dad, daddy [dæd, 'dædi] n papa m

daffodil ['dæfədil] n jonquille f

daft [dɑ:ft] adj (col) idiot(e), stupide; **to be daft about** être toqué(e) or mordu(e) de

dagger ['dægə*] n poignard m; **to be at daggers drawn with sb** être à couteaux tirés avec qn; **to look daggers at sb** foudroyer qn du regard

daily ['deili] adj quotidien(ne), journalier(ière) ♦ n quotidien m; (BRIT: servant) femme f de ménage (à la journée) ♦ adv tous les jours; **twice daily** deux fois par jour

dainty ['deinti] adj délicat(e), mignon(ne)

dairy ['dɛəri] n (shop) crémerie f, laiterie f; (on farm) laiterie ♦ adj laitier(ière)

dairy products npl produits laitier

daisy ['deizi] n pâquerette f

dale [deil] n vallon m

dam [dæm] n barrage m; (reservoir) réservoir m, lac m de retenue ♦ vt endiguer

damage ['dæmidʒ] n dégâts mpl, dommages mpl; (fig) tort m ♦ vt endommager, abîmer; (fig) faire du tort à; **damage to property** dégâts matériels

damn [dæm] vt condamner; (curse) maudire ♦ n (col): **I don't give a damn** je m'en fous ♦ adj (col): **this damn ...** ce sacré or foutu ...; **damn (it)!** zut!

damning ['dæmiŋ] adj (evidence) accablant(e)

damp [dæmp] adj humide ♦ n humidité f ♦ vt (also: **dampen**: cloth, rag) humecter; (: enthusiasm etc) refroidir

damson ['dæmzən] n prune f de Damas

dance [dɑ:ns] n danse f; (ball) bal m ♦ vi danser; **to dance about** sautiller, gambader

dance hall n salle f de bal, dancing m

dancer ['dɑ:nsə*] n danseur/euse

dancing ['dɑ:nsiŋ] n danse f

dandelion ['dændilaiən] n pissenlit m

dandruff ['dændrəf] n pellicules fpl

Dane [dein] n Danois/e

danger ['deindʒə*] n danger m; **there is a danger of fire** il y a (un) risque d'incendie; **in danger** en danger; **he was in danger of falling** il risquait de tomber; **out of danger** hors de danger

dangerous ['deindʒrəs] adj dangereux(euse)

dangle ['dæŋgl] vt balancer; (fig) faire miroiter ♦ vi pendre, se balancer

Danish ['deiniʃ] adj danois(e) ♦ n (LING) danois m

dare [dɛə*] vt: **to dare sb to do** défier qn or mettre qn au défi de faire ♦ vi: **to dare (to) do sth** oser faire qch; **I daren't tell him** (BRIT) je n'ose pas le lui dire; **I dare say he'll turn up** il est probable qu'il viendra

daring ['dɛəriŋ] adj hardi(e), audacieux(euse) ♦ n audace f, hardiesse f

dark [dɑ:k] adj (night, room) obscur(e), sombre; (colour, complexion) foncé(e), sombre; (fig) sombre ♦ n: **in the dark** dans le noir; **in the dark about** (fig) ignorant tout de; **after dark** après la tombée de la nuit; **it is/is getting dark** il fait nuit/commence à faire nuit

darken [dɑ:kn] vt obscurcir, assombrir ♦ vi s'obscurcir, s'assombrir

dark glasses npl lunettes noires

darkness ['dɑ:knis] n obscurité f

darkroom ['dɑ:krum] n chambre noire

darling ['dɑ:liŋ] adj, n chéri(e)

darn [dɑ:n] vt repriser

dart [dɑ:t] n fléchette f ♦ vi: **to dart towards** (also: **make a dart towards**) se précipiter or s'élancer vers; **to dart away/along** partir/passer comme une flèche

dartboard ['dɑ:tbɔ:d] n cible f (de jeu de fléchettes)

darts [dɑ:ts] n jeu m de fléchettes

dash [dæʃ] n (sign) tiret m; (small quantity) goutte f, larme f ♦ vt (missile) jeter or lancer violemment; (hopes) anéantir ♦ vi: **to dash towards** (also: **make a dash towards**) se précipiter or se ruer vers; **a dash of soda** un peu d'eau gazeuse

▶ **dash away** vi partir à toute allure

▶ **dash off** vi = **dash away**

dashboard ['dæʃbɔ:d] n (AUT) tableau m de bord

dashing ['dæʃiŋ] adj fringant(e)

data ['deitə] npl données fpl

database ['deitəbeis] n base f de données

data processing n traitement m (électronique) de l'information

date [deit] n (appointment) rendez-vous m; (fruit) datte f ♦ vt (col: girl etc) sortir avec; **what's the date today?** quelle date sommes-nous aujourd'hui?; **date of birth** date de naissance; **closing date** date de clôture; **to date** adv à ce jour; **out of date** périmé(e); **up to date** à la page, mis(e) à jour, moderne; **to bring up to date** (correspondence, information) mettre à jour; (method) moderniser; (person) mettre au courant; **letter dated 5th July** or (US) **July 5th** lettre (datée) du 5 juillet

dated ['deitid] adj démodé(e)

date rape n viol m (à l'issue d'un rendez-vous galant)

daub [dɔ:b] *vt* barbouiller

daughter ['dɔ:tə*] *n* fille *f*

daughter-in-law ['dɔ:tərɪnlɔ:] *n* belle-fille *f*, bru *f*

daunting ['dɔ:ntɪŋ] *adj* décourageant(e), intimidant(e)

dawdle ['dɔ:dl] *vi* traîner, lambiner; **to dawdle over one's work** traînasser *or* lambiner sur son travail

dawn [dɔ:n] *n* aube *f*, aurore *f* ♦ *vi* (*day*) se lever, poindre; (*fig*) naître, se faire jour; **at dawn** à l'aube; **from dawn to dusk** du matin au soir; **it dawned on him that …** il lui vint à l'esprit que …

day [deɪ] *n* jour *m*; (*as duration*) journée *f*; (*period of time, age*) époque *f*, temps *m*; **the day before** la veille, le jour précédent; **the day after, the following day** le lendemain, le jour suivant; **the day before yesterday** avant-hier; **the day after tomorrow** après-demain; (**on**) **the day that …** le jour où …; **day by day** jour après jour; **by day** de jour; **paid by the day** payé/e à la journée; **these days, in the present day** de nos jours, à l'heure actuelle

daybreak ['deɪbreɪk] *n* point *m* du jour

daydream ['deɪdri:m] *n* rêverie *f* ♦ *vi* rêver (tout éveillé)

daylight ['deɪlaɪt] *n* (lumière *f* du) jour *m*

day return (ticket) *n* (*BRIT*) billet *m* d'aller-retour (valable pour la journée)

daytime ['deɪtaɪm] *n* jour *m*, journée *f*

day-to-day ['deɪtə'deɪ] *adj* (*routine, expenses*) journalier(ière); **on a day-to-day basis** au jour le jour

daze [deɪz] *vt* (*drug*) hébéter; (*blow*) étourdir ♦ *n*: **in a daze** hébété/e, étourdi/e

dazzle ['dæzl] *vt* éblouir, aveugler

DC *abbr* (*ELEC*) = direct current; (*US*) = District of Columbia

D-day ['di:deɪ] *n* le jour J

dead [ded] *adj* mort(e); (*numb*) engourdi(e), insensible ♦ *adv* absolument, complètement; **the dead** *npl* les morts; **he was shot dead** il a été tué d'un coup de revolver; **dead on time** à l'heure pile; **dead tired** éreinté(e), complètement fourbu(e); **to stop dead** s'arrêter pile *or* net; **the line has gone dead** (*TEL*) on n'entend plus rien

deaden [dedn] *vt* (*blow, sound*) amortir; (*make numb*) endormir, rendre insensible

dead end *n* impasse *f*

dead heat *n* (*SPORT*): **to finish in a dead heat** terminer ex aequo

deadline ['dedlaɪn] *n* date *f* or heure *f* limite; **to work to a deadline** avoir des délais stricts à respecter

deadlock ['dedlɔk] *n* impasse *f*; (*fig*)

dead loss *n* (*col*): **to be a dead loss** (*person*) n'être bon/bonne à rien; (*subj: thing*) ne rien valoir

deadly ['dedlɪ] *adj* mortel(le); (*weapon*) meurtrier(ière); **deadly dull** ennuyeux(euse) à mourir, mortellement ennuyeux

deadpan ['dedpæn] *adj* impassible; (*humour*) pince-sans-rire *inv*

Dead Sea *n*: **the Dead Sea** la mer Morte

deaf [def] *adj* sourd(e); **to turn a deaf ear to sth** faire la sourde oreille à qch

deafen ['defn] *vt* rendre sourd(e); (*fig*) assourdir

deafening ['defnɪŋ] *adj* assourdissant(e)

deaf-mute ['defmju:t] *n* sourd/e-muet/te

deafness ['defnɪs] *n* surdité *f*

deal [di:l] *n* affaire *f*, marché *m* ♦ *vt, pt, pp* **dealt** [delt] (*blow*) porter; (*cards*) donner, distribuer; **to strike a deal with sb** faire *or* conclure un marché avec qn; **it's a deal!** (*col*) marché conclu!, tope-là!, topez-là!; **he got a bad deal from them** ils ont mal agi envers lui; **he got a fair deal from them** ils ont agi loyalement envers lui; **a good deal** (*a lot*) beaucoup; **a good deal of, a great deal of** beaucoup de, énormément de

▶ **deal in** *vt fus* (*COMM*) faire le commerce de, être dans le commerce de

▶ **deal with** *vt fus* (*COMM*) traiter avec; (*handle*) s'occuper *or* se charger de; (*be about: book etc*) traiter de

dealer ['di:lə*] *n* marchand *m*

dealings ['di:lɪŋz] *npl* (*in goods, shares*) opérations *fpl*, transactions *fpl*; (*relations*) relations *fpl*, rapports *mpl*

dean [di:n] *n* (*REL, BRIT SCOL*) doyen *m*; (*US SCOL*) conseiller/e (principal(e)) d'éducation

dear [dɪə*] *adj* cher(chère); (*expensive*) cher, coûteux(euse) ♦ *n*: **my dear** mon cher/ma chère; **dear me!** mon Dieu!; **Dear Sir/Madam** (*in letter*) Monsieur/Madame; **Dear Mr/Mrs X** Cher Monsieur/Chère Madame X

dearly ['dɪəlɪ] *adv* (*love*) tendrement; (*pay*) cher

death [deθ] *n* (*ADMIN*) décès *m*

death certificate *n* acte *m* de décès

deathly ['deθlɪ] *adj* de mort ♦ *adv* comme la mort

death penalty *n* peine *f* de mort

death rate *n* taux *m* de mortalité

death toll *n* nombre *m* de morts

debase [dɪ'beɪs] *vt* (*currency*) déprécier, dévaloriser; (*person*) abaisser, avilir

debatable [dɪ'beɪtəbl] *adj* discutable, contestable; **it is debatable whether …** il est douteux que …

debate [dɪ'beɪt] *n* discussion *f*, débat *m* ♦ *vt* discuter, débattre ♦ *vi* (*consider*): **to debate whether** se demander si

debit ['debɪt] *n* débit *m* ♦ *vt*: **to debit a sum to sb** *or* **to sb's account** porter une somme au débit de qn, débiter qn d'une somme

debt [det] *n* dette *f*; **to be in debt** avoir des

dettes, être endetté(e); **bad debt** créance *f* irrécouvrable

debtor ['dɛtə*] *n* débiteur/trice

decade ['dɛkeɪd] *n* décennie *f*, décade *f*

decadence ['dɛkədəns] *n* décadence *f*

decaff ['di:kæf] *n* (*col*) déca *m*

decaffeinated [di'kæfɪneɪtɪd] *adj* décaféiné(e)

decanter [dɪ'kæntə*] *n* carafe *f*

decay [dɪ'keɪ] *n* décomposition *f*, pourrissement *m*; (*fig*) déclin *m*, délabrement *m*; (*also:* **tooth decay**) carie *f* (dentaire) ♦ *vi* (*rot*) se décomposer, pourrir; (*fig*) se délabrer; décliner; se détériorer

deceased [dɪ'si:st] *n*: **the deceased** le/la défunt/e

deceit [dɪ'si:t] *n* tromperie *f*, supercherie *f*

deceitful [dɪ'si:tful] *adj* trompeur(euse)

deceive [dɪ'si:v] *vt* tromper; **to deceive o.s.** s'abuser

December [dɪ'sɛmbə*] *n* décembre *m*; *for phrases see also* **July**

decent ['di:sənt] *adj* décent(e), convenable; **they were very decent about it** ils se sont montrés très chics

deception [dɪ'sɛpʃən] *n* tromperie *f*

deceptive [dɪ'sɛptɪv] *adj* trompeur(euse)

decide [dɪ'saɪd] *vt* (*person*) décider; (*question, argument*) trancher, régler ♦ *vi* se décider, décider; **to decide to do/that** décider de faire/que; **to decide on** décider, se décider pour; **to decide on doing** décider de faire; **to decide against doing** décider de ne pas faire

decided [dɪ'saɪdɪd] *adj* (*resolute*) résolu(e), décidé(e); (*clear, definite*) net(te), marqué(e)

decidedly [dɪ'saɪdɪdlɪ] *adv* résolument; incontestablement, nettement

deciduous [dɪ'sɪdjuəs] *adj* à feuilles caduques

decimal ['dɛsɪməl] *adj* décimal(e) ♦ *n* décimale *f*; **to three decimal places** (jusqu')à la troisième décimale

decimal point *n* = virgule *f*

decipher [dɪ'saɪfə*] *vt* déchiffrer

decision [dɪ'sɪʒən] *n* décision *f*; **to make a decision** prendre une décision

decisive [dɪ'saɪsɪv] *adj* décisif(ive); (*influence*) décisif, déterminant(e); (*manner, person*) décidé(e), catégorique; (*reply*) ferme, catégorique

deck [dɛk] *n* (*NAUT*) pont *m*; (*of bus*): **top deck** impériale *f*; (*of cards*) jeu *m*; **to go up on deck** monter sur le pont; **below deck** dans l'entrepont; **record/cassette deck** platine-disques/-cassettes *f*

deckchair ['dɛktʃɛə*] *n* chaise longue

declare [dɪ'klɛə*] *vt* déclarer

decline [dɪ'klaɪn] *n* (*decay*) déclin *m*; (*lessening*) baisse *f* ♦ *vt* refuser, décliner ♦ *vi* décliner; être en baisse, baisser; **decline in living standards** baisse du niveau de vie; **to decline to do sth** refuser

(poliment) de faire qch

decoder [di:'kəudə*] *n* (*COMPUT, TV*) décodeur *m*

decorate ['dɛkəreɪt] *vt* (*adorn, give a medal to*) décorer; (*paint and paper*) peindre et tapisser

decoration [dɛkə'reɪʃən] *n* (*medal etc, adornment*) décoration *f*

decorator ['dɛkəreɪtə*] *n* peintre *m* en bâtiment

decoy ['di:kɔɪ] *n* piège *m*; **they used him as a decoy for the enemy** ils se sont servis de lui pour attirer l'ennemi

decrease *n* ['di:kri:s] diminution *f* ♦ *vt, vi* [di:'kri:s] diminuer; **to be on the decrease** diminuer, être en diminution

decree [dɪ'kri:] *n* (*POL, REL*) décret *m*; (*LAW*) arrêt *m*, jugement *m* ♦ *vt*: **to decree (that)** décréter (que), ordonner (que); **decree absolute** jugement définitif (de divorce); **decree nisi** jugement provisoire de divorce

dedicate ['dɛdɪkeɪt] *vt* consacrer; (*book etc*) dédier

dedicated ['dɛdɪkeɪtɪd] *adj* (*person*) dévoué(e); (*COMPUT*) spécialisé(e), dédié(e); **dedicated word processor** station *f* de traitement de texte

dedication [dɛdɪ'keɪʃən] *n* (*devotion*) dévouement *m*; (*in book*) dédicace *f*

deduce [dɪ'dju:s] *vt* déduire, conclure

deduct [dɪ'dʌkt] *vt*: **to deduct sth (from)** déduire qch (de), retrancher qch (de); (*from wage etc*) prélever qch (sur), retenir qch (sur)

deduction [dɪ'dʌkʃən] *n* (*deducting*) déduction *f*; (*from wage etc*) prélèvement *m*, retenue *f*; (*deducing*) déduction, conclusion *f*

deed [di:d] *n* action *f*, acte *m*; (*LAW*) acte notarié, contrat *m*; **deed of covenant** (acte *m* de) donation *f*

deep [di:p] *adj* (*water, sigh, sorrow, thoughts*) profond(e); (*voice*) grave ♦ *adv*: **deep in snow** recouvert(e) d'une épaisse couche de neige; **spectators stood 20 deep** il y avait 20 rangs de spectateurs; **knee-deep in water** dans l'eau jusqu'aux genoux; **4 metres deep** de 4 mètres de profondeur; **he took a deep breath** il inspira profondément, il prit son souffle

deepen ['di:pn] *vt* (*hole*) approfondir ♦ *vi* s'approfondir; (*darkness*) s'épaissir

deepfreeze ['di:p'fri:z] *n* congélateur *m* ♦ *vt* surgeler

deep-fry ['di:p'fraɪ] *vt* faire frire (dans une friteuse)

deeply ['di:plɪ] *adv* profondément; jeu (*dig*) en profondeur; (*regret, interest*) vivement

deep-sea ['di:p'si:] *adj*: **deep-sea diver** plongeur sous-marin; **deep-sea diving** plongée sous-marine; **deep-sea fishing** pêche hauturière

deep-seated ['di:p'si:tɪd] *adj* (*belief*) profondément enraciné(e)

deer [dɪə*] *n* (*pl inv*): **the deer** les cervidés *mpl*; (*ZOOL*) **(red) deer** cerf *m*; **(fallow) deer** daim *m*; **(roe) deer** chevreuil *m*

deerskin ['dɪəskɪn] n peau f de daim

deface [dɪ'feɪs] vt dégrader; barbouiller rendre illisible

default [dɪ'fɔːlt] vi (LAW) faire défaut; (gen) manquer à ses engagements ♦ n (COMPUT: also: **default value**) valeur f par défaut; **by default** (LAW) par défaut, par contumace; (SPORT) par forfait; **to default on a debt** ne pas s'acquitter d'une dette

defeat [dɪ'fiːt] n défaite f ♦ vt (team, opponents) battre; (fig: plans, efforts) faire échouer

defect n ['diːfɛkt] défaut m ♦ vi [dɪ'fɛkt]: **to defect to the enemy/the West** passer à l'ennemi/l'Ouest; **physical defect** malformation f, vice m de conformation; **mental defect** anomalie or déficience mentale

defective [dɪ'fɛktɪv] adj défectueux(euse)

defence, (US) **defense** [dɪ'fɛns] n défense f; **in defence of** pour défendre; **witness for the defence** témoin m à décharge; **the Ministry of Defence**, (US) **the Department, of Defense** le ministère de la Défense nationale

defenceless [dɪ'fɛnslɪs] adj sans défense

defend [dɪ'fɛnd] vt défendre; (decision, action, opinion) justifier, défendre

defendant [dɪ'fɛndənt] n défendeur/deresse; (in criminal case) accusé/e, prévenu/e

defender [dɪ'fɛndə*] n défenseur m

defer [dɪ'fɜː*] vt (postpone) différer, ajourner ♦ vi (submit): **to defer to sb/sth** déférer à qn/qch, s'en remettre à qn/qch

defiance [dɪ'faɪəns] n défi m; **in defiance of** au mépris de

defiant [dɪ'faɪənt] adj provocant(e), de défi

deficiency [dɪ'fɪʃənsɪ] n insuffisance f, déficience f; carence f; (COMM) déficit m, découvert m

deficient [dɪ'fɪʃənt] adj insuffisant(e), défectueux(euse), déficient(e); **to be deficient in** manquer de

deficit ['dɛfɪsɪt] n déficit m

define [dɪ'faɪn] vt définir

definite ['dɛfɪnɪt] adj (fixed) défini(e), (bien) déterminé(e); (clear, obvious) net(te), manifeste; (LING) défini(e); **he was definite about it** il a été catégorique; il était sûr de son fait

definitely ['dɛfɪnɪtlɪ] adv sans aucun doute

definition [dɛfɪ'nɪʃən] n définition f

deflate [diː'fleɪt] vt dégonfler; (pompous person) rabattre le caquet à; (ECON) provoquer la déflation de; (: prices) faire tomber or baisser

deflect [dɪ'flɛkt] vt détourner, faire dévier

deformed [dɪ'fɔːmd] adj difforme

defraud [dɪ'frɔːd] vt frauder; **to defraud sb of sth** soutirer qch malhonnêtement à qn; escroquer qch à qn; frustrer qn de qch

defrost [diː'frɔst] vt (fridge) dégivrer; (frozen food) décongeler

deft [dɛft] adj adroit(e), preste

defunct [dɪ'fʌŋkt] adj défunt(e)

defuse [diː'fjuːz] vt désamorcer

defy [dɪ'faɪ] vt défier; (efforts etc) résister à

degenerate vi [dɪ'dʒɛnəreɪt] dégénérer ♦ adj [dɪ'dʒɛnərɪt] dégénéré(e)

degree [dɪ'griː] n degré m; (SCOL) diplôme m (universitaire); **10 degrees below (zero)** 10 degrés au-dessous de zéro; **a (first) degree in maths** (BRIT) une licence en maths; **a considerable degree of risk** un considérable facteur or élément de risque; **by degrees** (gradually) par degrés; **to some degree, to a certain degree** jusqu'à un certain point, dans une certaine mesure

dehydrated [diːhaɪ'dreɪtɪd] adj déshydraté(e); (milk, eggs) en poudre

de-ice ['diː'aɪs] vt (windscreen) dégivrer

deign [deɪn] vi: **to deign to do** daigner faire

dejected [dɪ'dʒɛktɪd] adj abattu(e), déprimé(e)

delay [dɪ'leɪ] vt (journey, operation) retarder, différer; (traveller, train) retarder; (payment) différer ♦ vi s'attarder ♦ n délai m, retard m; **without delay** sans délai, sans tarder

delectable [dɪ'lɛktəbl] adj délicieux(euse)

delegate n ['dɛlɪgɪt] délégué/e ♦ vt ['dɛlɪgeɪt] déléguer; **to delegate sth to sb/sb to do sth** déléguer qch à qn/qn pour faire qch

delete [dɪ'liːt] vt rayer, supprimer; (COMPUT) effacer

deliberate adj [dɪ'lɪbərɪt] (intentional) délibéré(e); (slow) mesuré(e) ♦ vi [dɪ'lɪbəreɪt] délibérer, réfléchir

deliberately [dɪ'lɪbərɪtlɪ] adv (on purpose) exprès, délibérément

delicacy ['dɛlɪkəsɪ] n délicatesse f; (choice food) mets fin or délicat, friandise f

delicate ['dɛlɪkɪt] adj délicat(e)

delicatessen [dɛlɪkə'tɛsn] n épicerie fine

delicious [dɪ'lɪʃəs] adj délicieux(euse), exquis(e)

delight [dɪ'laɪt] n (grande) joie, grand plaisir ♦ vt enchanter; **a delight to the eyes** un régal or plaisir pour les yeux; **to take delight in** prendre grand plaisir à; **to be the delight of** faire les délices or la joie de

delighted [dɪ'laɪtɪd] adj: **delighted (at or with sth)** ravi(e) (de qch); **to be delighted to do sth/that** être enchanté(e) or ravi(e) de faire qch/que; **I'd be delighted** j'en serais enchanté or ravi

delightful [dɪ'laɪtful] adj (person, child) absolument charmant(e), adorable; (evening, view) merveilleux(euse); (meal) délicieux(euse)

delinquent [dɪ'lɪŋkwənt] adj, n délinquant/e

delirious [dɪ'lɪrɪəs] adj (MED, fig) délirant(e); **to be delirious** délirer

deliver [dɪ'lɪvə*] vt (mail) distribuer; (goods) livrer; (message) remettre; (speech) prononcer; (warning, ultimatum) lancer; (free) délivrer; (MED) accoucher; **to deliver the goods** (fig) tenir ses promesses

delivery [dɪ'lɪvərɪ] n (of mail) distribution f; (of

goods) livraison f; (of speaker) élocution f; (MED) accouchement m; **to take delivery of** prendre livraison p

delude [dɪ'lu:d] vt tromper, leurrer; **to delude o.s.** se leurrer, se faire des illusions

delusion [dɪ'lu:ʒən] n illusion f; **to have delusions of grandeur** être un peu mégalomane

demand [dɪ'mɑ:nd] vt réclamer, exiger; (need) exiger, requérir ♦ n exigence f; (claim) revendication f; (ECON) demande f; **to demand sth (from** or **of sb)** exiger qch (de qn), réclamer qch (à qn); **in demand** demandé/e, recherché/e; **on demand** sur demande

demanding [dɪ'mɑ:ndɪŋ] adj (person) exigeant(e); (work) astreignant(e)

demean [dɪ'mi:n] vt: **to demean o.s.** s'abaisser

demeanour, (US) **demeanor** [dɪ'mi:nə*] n comportement m; maintien m

demented [dɪ'mɛntɪd] adj dément(e), fou(folle)

demise [dɪ'maɪz] n décès m

demister [di:'mɪstə*] n (BRIT AUT) dispositif m antibuée inv

demo ['dɛməʊ] n abbr (col: = demonstration) manif f

democracy [dɪ'mɔkrəsɪ] n démocratie f

democrat ['dɛməkræt] n démocrate m/f

democratic [dɛmə'krætɪk] adj démocratique; **the Democratic Party** (US) le parti démocrate

demolish [dɪ'mɔlɪʃ] vt démolir

demonstrate ['dɛmənstreɪt] vt démontrer, prouver ♦ vi: **to demonstrate (for/against)** manifester (en faveur de/contre)

demonstration [dɛmən'streɪʃən] n démonstration f; (POL etc) manifestation f; **to hold a demonstration** (POL etc) organiser une manifestation, manifester

demonstrator ['dɛmənstreɪtə*] n (POL etc) manifestant/e; (COMM: sales person) vendeur/euse; (: car, computer etc) modèle m de démonstration

demote [dɪ'məʊt] vt rétrograder

demure [dɪ'mjuə*] adj sage, réservé(e), d'une modestie affectée

den [dɛn] n tanière f, antre m

denial [dɪ'naɪəl] n (of accusation) démenti m; (of rights, guilt, truth) dénégation f

denim ['dɛnɪm] n coton émerisé

Denmark ['dɛnmɑ:k] n Danemark m

denomination [dɪnɔmɪ'neɪʃən] n (money) valeur f; (REL) confession f; culte m

denounce [dɪ'naʊns] vt dénoncer

dense [dɛns] adj dense; (col: stupid) obtus(e), dur(e) or lent(e) à la comprenette

densely ['dɛnslɪ] adv: **densely wooded** couvert(e) d'épaisses forêts; **densely populated** à forte densité (de population), très peuplé(e)

density ['dɛnsɪtɪ] n densité f; **single/double density disk** (COMPUT) disquette f (à) simple/double densité

dent [dɛnt] n bosse f ♦ vt (also: **make a dent in**) cabosser; **to make a dent in** (fig) entamer

dental ['dɛntl] adj dentaire

dental surgeon n (chirurgien/ne) dentiste

dentist ['dɛntɪst] n dentiste m/f; **dentist's surgery** (BRIT) cabinet m de dentiste

denture(s) ['dɛntʃə(z)] n(pl) dentier m

deny [dɪ'naɪ] vt nier; (refuse) refuser; (disown) renier; **he denies having said it** il nie l'avoir dit

deodorant [di:'əʊdərənt] n désodorisant m, déodorant m

depart [dɪ'pɑ:t] vi partir; **to depart from** (leave) quitter, partir de; (fig: differ from) s'écarter de

department [dɪ'pɑ:tmənt] n (COMM) rayon m; (SCOL) section f; (POL) ministère m, département m; **that's not my department** (fig) ce n'est pas mon domaine or ma compétence, ce n'est pas mon rayon; **Department of State** (US) Département d'État

department store n grand magasin m

departure [dɪ'pɑ:tʃə*] n départ m; (fig): **departure from** écart m par rapport à; **a new departure** une nouvelle voie

departure lounge n salle f de départ

depend [dɪ'pɛnd] vi: **to depend (up)on** dépendre de; (rely on) compter sur; (financially) dépendre (financièrement) de, être à la charge de; **it depends** cela dépend; **depending on the result ...** selon le résultat ...

dependable [dɪ'pɛndəbl] adj sûr(e), digne de confiance

dependant [dɪ'pɛndənt] n personne f à charge

dependent [dɪ'pɛndənt] adj: **to be dependent (on)** dépendre (de) ♦ n = **dependant**

depict [dɪ'pɪkt] vt (in picture) représenter; (in words) (dé)peindre, décrire

depleted [dɪ'pli:tɪd] adj (considérablement) réduit(e) or diminué(e)

deport [dɪ'pɔ:t] vt déporter, expulser

deposit [dɪ'pɔzɪt] n (CHEM, COMM, GEO) dépôt m; (of ore, oil) gisement m; (part payment) arrhes fpl, acompte m; (on bottle etc) consigne f; (for hired goods etc) cautionnement m, garantie f ♦ vt déposer; (valuables) mettre or laisser en dépôt; **to put down a deposit of £50** verser 50 livres d'arrhes or d'acompte; laisser 50 livres en garantie

deposit account n compte m de dépôt

depot ['dɛpəʊ] n dépôt m

depress [dɪ'prɛs] vt déprimer; (press down) appuyer sur, abaisser

depressed [dɪ'prɛst] adj (person) déprimé(e), abattu(e); (area) en déclin, touché(e) par le sous-emploi; (COMM: market, trade) maussade; **to get depressed** se démoraliser, se laisser abattre

depressing [dɪ'prɛsɪŋ] adj déprimant(e)

depression [dɪ'prɛʃən] n (ECON) dépression f

deprivation [dɛprɪ'veɪʃən] *n* privation *f*; (*loss*) perte *f*

deprive [dɪ'praɪv] *vt* (*also*: **to deprive sb of**) priver qn de; enlever à qn

deprived [dɪ'praɪvd] *adj* déshérité(e)

depth [dɛpθ] *n* profondeur *f*; **in the depths of** au fond de; au cœur de; au plus profond de; **at a depth of 3 metres** à 3 mètres de profondeur; **to be out of one's depth** (*BRIT: swimmer*) ne plus avoir pied; (*fig*) être dépassé/e, nager; **to study sth in depth** étudier qch en profondeur

deputize ['depjutaɪz] *vi*: **to deputize for** assurer l'intérim de

deputy ['depjutɪ] *n* (*replacement*) suppléant/e, intérimaire *m/f*; (*second in command*) adjoint/e ◆ *adj*: **deputy chairman** vice-président *m*; **deputy head** (*SCOL*) directeur/trice adjoint(e); sous-directeur/trice; **deputy leader** (*BRIT POL*) vice-président/e, secrétaire adjoint(e)

derail [dɪ'reɪl] *vt* faire dérailler; **to be derailed** dérailler

deranged [dɪ'reɪndʒd] *adj*: **to be (mentally) deranged** avoir le cerveau dérangé

derby ['dɑ:rbɪ] *n* (*US*) (chapeau *m*) melon *m*

derelict ['dɛrɪlɪkt] *adj* abandonné(e), à l'abandon

derisory [dɪ'raɪsərɪ] *adj* (*sum*) dérisoire; (*smile, person*) moqueur(euse), railleur(euse)

derive [dɪ'raɪv] *vt*: **to derive sth from** tirer qch de; trouver qch dans ◆ *vi*: **to derive from** provenir de, dériver de

derogatory [dɪ'rɔgətərɪ] *adj* désobligeant(e), péjoratif(ive)

descend [dɪ'sɛnd] *vt, vi* descendre; **to descend from** descendre de, être issu/e de; **in descending order of importance** par ordre d'importance décroissante

▶ **descend on** *vt fus* (*enemy, angry person*) tomber *or* sauter sur; (*misfortune*) s'abattre sur; (*gloom, silence*) envahir; **visitors descended (up)on us** des gens sont arrivés chez nous à l'improviste

descent [dɪ'sɛnt] *n* descente *f*; (*origin*) origine *f*

describe [dɪs'kraɪb] *vt* décrire

description [dɪs'krɪpʃən] *n* description *f*; (*sort*) sorte *f*, espèce *f*; **of every description** de toutes sortes

desecrate ['dɛsɪkreɪt] *vt* profaner

desert [*n* 'dɛzət] désert *m* ◆ *vb* [dɪ'zə:t] ◆ *vt* déserter, abandonner ◆ *vi* (*MIL*) déserter

deserter [dɪ'zə:tə*] *n* déserteur *m*

desertion [dɪ'zə:ʃən] *n* désertion *f*

desert island *n* île déserte

deserve [dɪ'zə:v] *vt* mériter

deserving [dɪ'zə:vɪŋ] *adj* (*person*) méritant(e); (*action, cause*) méritoire

design [dɪ'zaɪn] *n* (*sketch*) plan *m*, dessin *m*; (*layout, shape*) conception *f*, ligne *f*; (*pattern*) dessin, motif(s) *m(pl)*; (*of dress, car*) modèle *m*; (*art*)

design *m*, stylisme *m*; (*intention*) dessein *m* ◆ *vt* dessiner; (*plan*) concevoir; **to have designs on** avoir des visées sur; **well-designed** *adj* bien conçu(e); **industrial design** esthétique industrielle

designer [dɪ'zaɪnə*] *n* (*ARCHIT, ART*) dessinateur/trice; (*INDUSTRY*) concepteur *m*, designer *m*; (*FASHION*) modéliste *m/f*

desire [dɪ'zaɪə*] *n* désir *m* ◆ *vt* désirer, vouloir; **to desire to do sth/that** désirer faire qch/que

desk [dɛsk] *n* (*in office*) bureau *m*; (*for pupil*) pupitre *m*; (*BRIT: in shop, restaurant*) caisse *f*; (*in hotel, at airport*) réception *f*

desktop publishing ['dɛsktɒp-] *n* publication assistée par ordinateur, PAO *f*

desolate ['dɛsəlɪt] *adj* désolé(e)

despair [dɪs'pɛə*] *n* désespoir *m* ◆ *vi*: **to despair of** désespérer de; **to be in despair** être au désespoir

despatch [dɪs'pætʃ] *n, vt* = **dispatch**

desperate ['dɛspərɪt] *adj* désespéré(e); (*fugitive*) prêt(e) à tout; (*measures*) désespéré, extrême; **we are getting desperate** nous commençons à désespérer

desperately ['dɛspərɪtlɪ] *adv* désespérément; (*very*) terriblement, extrêmement; **desperately ill** très gravement malade

desperation [dɛspə'reɪʃən] *n* désespoir *m*; **in desperation** en désespoir de cause

despicable [dɪs'pɪkəbl] *adj* méprisable

despise [dɪs'paɪz] *vt* mépriser, dédaigner

despite [dɪs'paɪt] *prep* malgré, en dépit de

despondent [dɪs'pɒndənt] *adj* découragé(e), abattu(e)

dessert [dɪ'zə:t] *n* dessert *m*

dessertspoon [dɪ'zə:tspu:n] *n* cuiller *f* à dessert

destination [dɛstɪ'neɪʃən] *n* destination *f*

destined ['dɛstɪnd] *adj*: **to be destined to do sth** être destiné(e) à faire qch; **destined for London** à destination de Londres

destiny ['dɛstɪnɪ] *n* destinée *f*, destin *m*

destitute ['dɛstɪtju:t] *adj* indigent(e), dans le dénuement; **destitute of** dépourvu(e) *or* dénué(e) de

destroy [dɪs'trɔɪ] *vt* détruire

destroyer [dɪs'trɔɪə*] *n* (*NAUT*) contre-torpilleur *m*

destruction [dɪs'trʌkʃən] *n* destruction *f*

detach [dɪ'tætʃ] *vt* détacher

detached [dɪ'tætʃt] *adj* (*attitude*) détaché(e)

detached house *n* pavillon *m*, maison(nette) (individuelle)

detachment [dɪ'tætʃmənt] *n* (*MIL*) détachement *m*; (*fig*) détachement, indifférence *f*

detail ['di:teɪl] *n* détail *m*; (*MIL*) détachement *m* ◆ *vt* raconter en détail, énumérer; (*MIL*): **to detail sb (for)** affecter qn (à), détacher qn (pour); **in detail** en détail; **to go into detail(s)** entrer dans les détails

detailed [ˈdiːteɪld] *adj* détaillé(e)

detain [dɪˈteɪn] *vt* retenir; (*in captivity*) détenir; (*in hospital*) hospitaliser

detect [dɪˈtekt] *vt* déceler, percevoir; (*MED, POLICE*) dépister; (*MIL, RADAR, TECH*) détecter

detection [dɪˈtekʃən] *n* découverte *f*; (*MED, POLICE*) dépistage *m*; (*MIL, RADAR, TECH*) détection *f*; **to escape detection** échapper aux recherches, éviter d'être découvert(e); (*mistake*) passer inaperçu(e); **crime detection** le dépistage des criminels

detective [dɪˈtektɪv] *n* agent *m* de la sûreté, policier *m*; **private detective** détective privé

detective story *n* roman policier

detention [dɪˈtenʃən] *n* détention *f*; (*SCOL*) retenue *f*, consigne *f*

deter [dɪˈtɜː*] *vt* dissuader

detergent [dɪˈtɜːdʒənt] *n* détersif *m*, détergent *m*

deteriorate [dɪˈtɪərɪəreɪt] *vi* se détériorer, se dégrader

determine [dɪˈtɜːmɪn] *vt* déterminer; **to determine to do** résoudre de faire, se déterminer à faire

determined [dɪˈtɜːmɪnd] *adj* (*person*) déterminé(e), décidé(e); (*quantity*) déterminé, établi(e); (*effort*) très gros(se)

deterrent [dɪˈterənt] *n* effet *m* de dissuasion; force *f* de dissuasion; **to act as a deterrent** avoir un effet dissuasif

detest [dɪˈtest] *vt* détester, avoir horreur de

detonate [ˈdetəneɪt] *vi* exploser ◆ *vt* faire exploser *or* détoner

detour [ˈdiːtuə*] *n* détour *m*; (*US AUT: diversion*) déviation *f*

detract [dɪˈtrækt] *vt*: **to detract from** (*quality, pleasure*) diminuer; (*reputation*) porter atteinte à

detriment [ˈdetrɪmənt] *n*: **to the detriment of** au détriment de, au préjudice de; **without detriment to** sans porter atteinte *or* préjudice à, sans conséquences fâcheuses pour

detrimental [detrɪˈmentl] *adj*: **detrimental to** préjudiciable *or* nuisible à

devaluation [dɪvæljuˈeɪʃən] *n* dévaluation *f*

devastate [ˈdevəsteɪt] *vt* dévaster

devastated [ˈdevəsteɪtɪd] *adj* (*fig*) anéanti(e); **he was devastated by the news** cette nouvelle lui a porté un coup terrible

devastating [ˈdevəsteɪtɪŋ] *adj* dévastateur(trice)

develop [dɪˈveləp] *vt* (*gen*) développer; (*habit*) contracter; (*resources*) mettre en valeur, exploiter; (*land*) aménager ◆ *vi* se développer; (*situation, disease: evolve*) évoluer; (*facts, symptoms: appear*) se manifester, se produire; **to develop a taste for sth** prendre goût à qch; **to develop into** devenir

developer [dɪˈveləpə*] *n* (*PHOT*) révélateur *m*; (*of land*) promoteur *m*; (*also: property developer*) promoteur immobilier

development [dɪˈveləpmənt] *n* développement

m; (*of affair, case*) rebondissement *m*, fait(s) nouveau(x)

device [dɪˈvaɪs] *n* (*scheme*) moyen *m*, expédient *m*; (*apparatus*) engin *m*, dispositif *m*; **explosive device** engin explosif

devil [ˈdevl] *n* diable *m*; démon *m*

devious [ˈdiːvɪəs] *adj* (*means*) détourné(e); (*person*) sournois(e), dissimulé(e)

devise [dɪˈvaɪz] *vt* imaginer, concevoir

devoid [dɪˈvɔɪd] *adj*: **devoid of** dépourvu(e) de, dénué(e) de

devolution [diːvəˈluːʃən] *n* (*POL*) décentralisation *f*

devote [dɪˈvəut] *vt*: **to devote sth to** consacrer qch à

devoted [dɪˈvəutɪd] *adj* dévoué(e); **to be devoted to** être dévoué(e) *or* très attaché(e) à; (*book etc*) être consacré(e) à

devotee [dɪvəuˈtiː] *n* (*REL*) adepte *m/f*; (*MUS, SPORT*) fervent/e

devotion [dɪˈvəuʃən] *n* dévouement *m*, attachement *m*; (*REL*) dévotion *f*, piété *f*

devour [dɪˈvauə*] *vt* dévorer

devout [dɪˈvaut] *adj* pieux(euse), dévot(e)

dew [djuː] *n* rosée *f*

diabetes [daɪəˈbiːtiːz] *n* diabète *m*

diabetic [daɪəˈbetɪk] *n* diabétique *m/f* ◆ *adj* (*person*) diabétique; (*chocolate, jam*) pour diabétiques

diabolical [daɪəˈbɒlɪkl] *adj* diabolique; (*col: dreadful*) infernal(e), atroce

diagnosis, *pl* **diagnoses** [daɪəgˈnəusɪs, -siːz] *n* diagnostic *m*

diagonal [daɪˈægənl] *adj* diagonal(e) ◆ *n* diagonale *f*

diagram [ˈdaɪəgræm] *n* diagramme *m*, schéma *m*

dial [ˈdaɪəl] *n* cadran *m* ◆ *vt* (*number*) faire, composer; **to dial a wrong number** faire un faux numéro; **can I dial London direct?** puis-je *or* est-ce-que je peux avoir Londres par l'automatique?

dialect [ˈdaɪəlekt] *n* dialecte *m*

dialling code [ˈdaɪəlɪŋ-], (*US*) **dial code** *n* indicatif *m* (téléphonique)

dialling tone [ˈdaɪəlɪŋ-], (*US*) **dial tone** *n* tonalité *f*

dialogue [ˈdaɪəlɒg] *n* dialogue *m*

diameter [daɪˈæmɪtə*] *n* diamètre *m*

diamond [ˈdaɪəmənd] *n* diamant *m*; (*shape*) losange *m*; **diamonds** *npl* (*CARDS*) carreau *m*

diaper [ˈdaɪəpə*] *n* (*US*) couche *f*

diaphragm [ˈdaɪəfræm] *n* diaphragme *m*

diarrhoea, (*US*) **diarrhea** [daɪəˈriːə] *n* diarrhée *f*

diary [ˈdaɪərɪ] *n* (*daily account*) journal *m*; (*book*) agenda *m*; **to keep a diary** tenir un journal

dice [daɪs] *n* (*pl inv*) dé *m* ◆ *vt* (*CULIN*) couper en dés *or* en cubes

dictate *vt* [dɪkˈteɪt] dicter ◆ *vi*: **to dictate to** (*person*) imposer sa volonté à, régenter; **I won't be dic-**

tated to je n'ai d'ordres à recevoir de personne ♦ *n* ['dɪkteɪt] injonction *f*

dictation [dɪk'teɪʃən] *n* dictée *f*; **at dictation speed** à une vitesse de dictée

dictator [dɪk'teɪtə*] *n* dictateur *m*

dictatorship [dɪk'teɪtəʃɪp] *n* dictature *f*

dictionary ['dɪkʃənrɪ] *n* dictionnaire *m*

did [dɪd] *pt of* **do**

didn't [dɪdnt] = **did not**

die [daɪ] *n* (*pl: dice*) dé *m*; (*pl: dies*) coin *m*; matrice *f*; étampe *f* ♦ *vi*: **to die (of *or* from)** mourir (de); **to be dying** être mourant(e); **to be dying for sth** avoir une envie folle de qch; **to be dying to do sth** mourir d'envie de faire qch

▶ **die away** *vi* s'éteindre

▶ **die down** *vi* se calmer, s'apaiser

▶ **die out** *vi* disparaître, s'éteindre

diesel ['diːzl] *n* diesel *m*

diesel engine *n* moteur *m* diesel

diet ['daɪət] *n* alimentation *f*; (*restricted food*) régime *m* ♦ *vi*: **be on a diet** suivre un régime; **to live on a diet of** se nourrir de

differ ['dɪfə*] *vi*: **to differ from sth** être différent(e) de qch, différer de qch; **to differ from sb over sth** ne pas être d'accord avec qn au sujet de qch

difference ['dɪfrəns] *n* différence *f*; (*quarrel*) différend *m*, désaccord *m*; **it makes no difference to me** cela m'est égal, cela m'est indifférent; **to settle one's differences** résoudre la situation

different ['dɪfrənt] *adj* différent(e)

differentiate [dɪfə'renʃɪeɪt] *vt* différencier ♦ *vi* se différencier; **to differentiate between** faire une différence entre

difficult ['dɪfɪkəlt] *adj* difficile; **difficult to understand** difficile à comprendre

difficulty ['dɪfɪkəltɪ] *n* difficulté *f*; **to have difficulties with** avoir des ennuis *or* problèmes avec; **to be in difficulty** avoir des difficultés, avoir des problèmes

diffident ['dɪfɪdənt] *adj* qui manque de confiance *or* d'assurance, peu sûr(e) de soi

dig [dɪg] *vt, pt, pp* **dug** [dʌg] (*hole*) creuser; (*garden*) bêcher ♦ *n* (*prod*) coup *m* de coude; (*fig*) coup de griffe *or* de patte; (*ARCHAEOLOGY*) fouille *f*; **to dig into** (*snow, soil*) creuser; **to dig into one's pockets for sth** fouiller dans ses poches pour chercher *or* prendre qch; **to dig one's nails into** enfoncer ses ongles dans

▶ **dig in** *vi* (*also:* **dig o.s. in**: *MIL*) se retrancher; (:*fig*) tenir bon, se braquer; (*col: eat*) attaquer (un repas *or* un plat *etc*) ♦ *vt* (*compost*) bien mélanger à la bêche; (*knife, claw*) enfoncer; **to dig in one's heels** (*fig*) se braquer, se buter

▶ **dig out** *vt* (*survivors, car from snow*) sortir *or* dégager (à coups de pelles *or* pioches)

▶ **dig up** *vt* déterrer

digest *vt* [daɪ'dʒest] digérer ♦ *n* ['daɪdʒest] sommaire *m*, résumé *m*

digestion [dɪ'dʒestʃən] *n* digestion *f*

digit ['dɪdʒɪt] *n* chiffre *m* (*de 0 à 9*); (*finger*) doigt *m*

digital ['dɪdʒɪtl] *adj* digital(e); (*watch*) à affichage numérique *or* digital

dignified ['dɪgnɪfaɪd] *adj* digne

dignity ['dɪgnɪtɪ] *n* dignité *f*

digress [daɪ'gres] *vi*: **to digress from** s'écarter de, s'éloigner de

digs [dɪgz] *npl* (*BRIT col*) piaule *f*, chambre meublée

dilapidated [dɪ'læpɪdeɪtɪd] *adj* délabré(e)

dilemma [daɪ'lemə] *n* dilemme *m*; **to be in a dilemma** être pris dans un dilemme

diligent ['dɪlɪdʒənt] *adj* appliqué(e), assidu(e)

dilute [daɪ'luːt] *vt* diluer ♦ *adj* dilué(e)

dim [dɪm] *adj* (*light, eyesight*) faible; (*memory, outline*) vague, indécis(e); (*stupid*) borné(e), obtus(e) ♦ *vt* (*light*) réduire, baisser; (*US AUT*) mettre en code, baisser; **to take a dim view of sth** voir qch d'un mauvais œil

dime [daɪm] *n* (*US*) = 10 cents

dimension [daɪ'menʃən] *n* dimension *f*

diminish [dɪ'mɪnɪʃ] *vt, vi* diminuer

diminutive [dɪ'mɪnjutɪv] *adj* minuscule, tout(e) petit(e) ♦ *n* (*LING*) diminutif *m*

dimmer ['dɪmə*] *n* (*also:* **dimmer switch**) variateur *m*; **dimmers** *npl* (*US AUT:* dipped headlights) phares *mpl* code *inv*; (*parking lights*) feux *mpl* de position

dimple ['dɪmpl] *n* fossette *f*

din [dɪn] *n* vacarme *m* ♦ *vt*: **to din sth into sb** (*col*) enfoncer qch dans la tête *or* la caboche de qn

dine [daɪn] *vi* dîner

diner ['daɪnə*] *n* (*person*) dîneur/euse; (*RAIL*) = **dining car**; (*US: eating place*) petit restaurant

dinghy ['dɪŋgɪ] *n* youyou *m*; (*inflatable*) canot *m* pneumatique; (*also:* **sailing dinghy**) voilier *m*, dériveur *m*

dingy ['dɪndʒɪ] *adj* miteux(euse), minable

dining car ['daɪnɪŋ-] *n* voiture-restaurant *f*, wagon-restaurant *m*

dining room ['daɪnɪŋ-] *n* salle *f* à manger

dinner ['dɪnə*] *n* dîner *m*; (*public*) banquet *m*; **dinner's ready!** à table!

dinner jacket *n* smoking *m*

dinner party *n* dîner *m*

dinner time *n* heure *f* du dîner

dinosaur ['daɪnəsɔː*] *n* dinosaure *m*

dip [dɪp] *n* déclivité *f*; (*in sea*) baignade *f*, bain *m* ♦ *vt* tremper, plonger; (*BRIT AUT:* lights) mettre en code, baisser ♦ *vi* plonger

diploma [dɪ'pləumə] *n* diplôme *m*

diplomacy [dɪ'pləuməsɪ] *n* diplomatie *f*

diplomat ['dɪpləmæt] *n* diplomate *m*

diplomatic [dɪplə'mætɪk] *adj* diplomatique; **to**

break off diplomatic relations (with) rompre les relations diplomatiques (avec)

dipstick ['dɪpstɪk] n (AUT) jauge f de niveau d'huile

dipswitch ['dɪpswɪtʃ] n (BRIT AUT) commutateur m de code

dire [daɪə*] adj extrême, affreux(euse)

direct [daɪ'rɛkt] adj direct(e); (manner, person) direct, franc(franche) ♦ vt diriger, orienter; **can you direct me to ...?** pouvez-vous m'indiquer le chemin de ...?; **to direct sb to do sth** ordonner à qn de faire qch

direct debit n (BANKING) prélèvement m automatique

direction [dɪ'rɛkʃən] n direction f; (THEAT) mise f en scène; (CINE, TV) réalisation f; **directions** npl (instructions: to a place) indications fpl; **directions for use** mode m d'emploi; **to ask for directions** demander sa route or son chemin; **sense of direction** sens m de l'orientation; **in the direction of** dans la direction de, vers

directly [dɪ'rɛktlɪ] adv (in straight line) directement, tout droit; (at once) tout de suite, immédiatement

director [dɪ'rɛktə*] n directeur m; (board member) administrateur m; (THEAT) metteur en scène; (CINE, TV) réalisateur/trice; **Director of Public Prosecutions** (BRIT) ≈ procureur général

directory [dɪ'rɛktərɪ] n annuaire m; (also: **street directory**) indicateur m de rues; (also: **trade directory**) annuaire du commerce; (COMPUT) répertoire m

directory enquiries, (US) **directory assistance** n (TEL: service) renseignements mpl

dirt [də:t] n saleté f; (mud) boue f; **to treat sb like dirt** traiter qn comme un chien

dirt-cheap ['də:t'tʃiːp] adj (ne) coûtant presque rien

dirty ['də:tɪ] adj sale ♦ vt salir; **dirty story** histoire cochonne; **dirty trick** coup tordu

disability [dɪsə'bɪlɪtɪ] n invalidité f, infirmité f

disabled [dɪs'eɪbld] adj infirme, invalide; (maimed) mutilé(e); (through illness, old age) impotent(e)

disadvantage [dɪsəd'vɑːntɪdʒ] n désavantage m, inconvénient m

disagree [dɪsə'griː] vi (differ) ne pas concorder; (be against, think otherwise): **to disagree (with)** ne pas être d'accord (avec); **garlic disagrees with me** l'ail ne me convient pas, je ne supporte pas l'ail

disagreeable [dɪsə'griːəbl] adj désagréable

disagreement [dɪsə'griːmənt] n désaccord m, différend m

disallow ['dɪsə'lau] vt rejeter, désavouer; (BRIT FOOTBALL: goal) refuser

disappear [dɪsə'pɪə*] vi disparaître

disappearance [dɪsə'pɪərəns] n disparition f

disappoint [dɪsə'pɔɪnt] vt décevoir

disappointed [dɪsə'pɔɪntɪd] adj déçu(e)

disappointing [dɪsə'pɔɪntɪŋ] adj décevant(e)

disappointment [dɪsə'pɔɪntmənt] n déception f

disapproval [dɪsə'pruːvəl] n désapprobation f

disapprove [dɪsə'pruːv] vi: **to disapprove of** désapprouver

disarmament [dɪs'ɑːməmənt] n désarmement m

disarray [dɪsə'reɪ] n désordre m, confusion f; **in disarray** (troops) en déroute; (thoughts) embrouillé(e) (clothes) en désordre; **to throw into disarray** semer la confusion or le désordre dans (or parmi)

disaster [dɪ'zɑːstə*] n catastrophe f, désastre m

disastrous [dɪ'zɑːstrəs] adj désastreux(euse)

disband [dɪs'bænd] vt démobiliser; disperser ♦ vi se séparer; se disperser

disbelief ['dɪsbə'liːf] n incrédulité f; **in disbelief** avec incrédulité

disc [dɪsk] n disque m

discard [dɪs'kɑːd] vt (old things) se défaire de, mettre au rencart ou au rebut; (fig) écarter, renoncer à

discern [dɪ'sə:n] vt discerner, distinguer

discerning [dɪ'sə:nɪŋ] adj judicieux(euse), perspicace

discharge vt [dɪs'tʃɑːdʒ] (duties) s'acquitter de; (settle: debt) s'acquitter de, régler; (waste etc) déverser; décharger; (ELEC, MED) émettre; (patient) renvoyer (chez lui); (employee, soldier) congédier, licencier; (defendant) relaxer, élargir ♦ n [ˈdɪstʃɑːdʒ] (ELEC, MED etc) émission f; (also: **vaginal discharge**) pertes blanches; (dismissal) renvoi m; licenciement m; élargissement m; **to discharge one's gun** faire feu; **discharged bankrupt** failli/e, réhabilité/e

discipline ['dɪsɪplɪn] n discipline f ♦ vt discipliner; (punish) punir; **to discipline o.s. to do sth** s'imposer or s'astreindre à une discipline pour faire qch

disc jockey (DJ) n disque-jockey m (DJ)

disclaim [dɪs'kleɪm] vt désavouer, dénier

disclose [dɪs'kləuz] vt révéler, divulguer

disclosure [dɪs'kləuʒə*] n révélation f, divulgation f

disco ['dɪskəu] n abbr = **discotheque**

discomfort [dɪs'kʌmfət] n malaise m, gêne f; (lack of comfort) manque m de confort

disconcert [dɪskən'sə:t] vt déconcerter, décontenancer

disconnect [dɪskə'nɛkt] vt détacher; (ELEC, RADIO) débrancher; (gas, water) couper

discontent [dɪskən'tɛnt] n mécontentement m

discontented [dɪskən'tɛntɪd] adj mécontent(e)

discontinue [dɪskən'tɪnjuː] vt cesser, interrompre; **"discontinued"** (COMM) "fin de série"

discord ['dɪskɔːd] n discorde f, dissension f; (MUS) dissonance f

discotheque ['dɪskəutek] n discothèque f

discount n ['dɪskaunt] remise f, rabais m ♦ vt [dɪs

'kaunt] (*report etc*) ne pas tenir compte de; **to give sb a discount on sth** faire une remise *or* un rabais à qn sur qch; **discount for cash** escompte *f* au comptant; **at a discount** avec une remise *or* réduction, au rabais

discourage [dɪsˈkʌrɪdʒ] *vt* décourager; (*dissuade, deter*) dissuader, décourager

discover [dɪsˈkʌvə*] *vt* découvrir

discovery [dɪsˈkʌvərɪ] *n* découverte *f*

discredit [dɪsˈkrɛdɪt] *vt* mettre en doute; discréditer ♦ *n* discrédit *m*

discreet [dɪˈskriːt] *adj* discret(ète)

discrepancy [dɪˈskrɛpənsɪ] *n* divergence *f*, contradiction *f*

discretion [dɪˈskrɛʃən] *n* discrétion *f*; **use your own discretion** à vous de juger

discriminate [dɪˈskrɪmɪneɪt] *vi*: **to discriminate between** établir une distinction entre, faire la différence entre; **to discriminate against** pratiquer une discrimination contre

discriminating [dɪˈskrɪmɪneɪtɪŋ] *adj* qui a du discernement

discrimination [dɪskrɪmɪˈneɪʃən] *n* discrimination *f*; (*judgment*) discernement *m*; **racial/sexual discrimination** discrimination raciale/sexuelle

discuss [dɪˈskʌs] *vt* discuter de; (*debate*) discuter

discussion [dɪˈskʌʃən] *n* discussion *f*; **under discussion** en discussion

disdain [dɪsˈdeɪn] *n* dédain *m*

disease [dɪˈziːz] *n* maladie *f*

disembark [dɪsɪmˈbɑːk] *vt, vi* débarquer

disentangle [dɪsɪnˈtæŋgl] *vt* démêler

disfigure [dɪsˈfɪgə*] *vt* défigurer

disgrace [dɪsˈgreɪs] *n* honte *f*; (*disfavour*) disgrâce *f* ♦ *vt* déshonorer, couvrir de honte

disgraceful [dɪsˈgreɪsful] *adj* scandaleux(euse), honteux(euse)

disgruntled [dɪsˈgrʌntld] *adj* mécontent(e)

disguise [dɪsˈgaɪz] *n* déguisement *m* ♦ *vt* déguiser; (*voice*) déguiser, contrefaire; (*feelings etc*) masquer, dissimuler; **in disguise** déguisé(e); **to disguise o.s. as** se déguiser en; **there's no disguising the fact that ...** on ne peut pas se dissimuler que ...

disgust [dɪsˈgʌst] *n* dégoût *m*, aversion *f* ♦ *vt* dégoûter, écœurer

disgusting [dɪsˈgʌstɪŋ] *adj* dégoûtant(e), révoltant(e)

dish [dɪʃ] *n* plat *m*; **to do** *or* **wash the dishes** faire la vaisselle

▶ **dish out** *vt* distribuer

▶ **dish up** *vt* servir; (*facts, statistics*) sortir, débiter

dishcloth [ˈdɪʃklɔθ] *n* (*for drying*) torchon *m*; (*for washing*) lavette *f*

dishearten [dɪsˈhɑːtn] *vt* décourager

dishevelled, (*US*) **disheveled** [dɪˈʃɛvəld] *adj* ébouriffé(e), décoiffé(e), débraillé(e)

dishonest [dɪsˈɒnɪst] *adj* malhonnête

dishonour, (*US*) **dishonor** [dɪsˈɒnə*] *n* déshonneur *m*

dishono(u)rable [dɪsˈɒnərəbl] *adj* déshonorant(e)

dishtowel [ˈdɪʃtauəl] *n* torchon *m* (à vaisselle)

dishwasher [ˈdɪʃwɒʃə*] *n* lave-vaisselle *m*; (*person*) plongeur/euse

disillusion [dɪsɪˈluːʒən] *vt* désabuser, désenchanter ♦ *n* désenchantement *m*; **to become disillusioned (with)** perdre ses illusions (en ce qui concerne)

disinfect [dɪsɪnˈfɛkt] *vt* désinfecter

disinfectant [dɪsɪnˈfɛktənt] *n* désinfectant *m*

disintegrate [dɪsˈɪntɪgreɪt] *vi* se désintégrer

disinterested [dɪsˈɪntrəstɪd] *adj* désintéressé(e)

disjointed [dɪsˈdʒɔɪntɪd] *adj* décousu(e), incohérent(e)

disk [dɪsk] *n* (*COMPUT*) disquette *f*; **single-/double-sided disk** disquette une face/double face

disk drive *n* lecteur *m* de disquette

diskette [dɪsˈkɛt] *n* (*COMPUT*) disquette *f*

dislike [dɪsˈlaɪk] *n* aversion *f*, antipathie *f* ♦ *vt* ne pas aimer; **to take a dislike to sb/sth** prendre qn/qch en grippe; **I dislike the idea** l'idée me déplaît

dislocate [ˈdɪsləkeɪt] *vt* disloquer, déboîter; (*services etc*) désorganiser; **he has dislocated his shoulder** il s'est disloqué l'épaule

dislodge [dɪsˈlɒdʒ] *vt* déplacer, faire bouger; (*enemy*) déloger

disloyal [dɪsˈlɔɪəl] *adj* déloyal(e)

dismal [ˈdɪzml] *adj* lugubre, maussade

dismantle [dɪsˈmæntl] *vt* démonter; (*fort, warship*) démanteler

dismay [dɪsˈmeɪ] *n* consternation *f* ♦ *vt* consterner; **much to my dismay** à ma grande consternation, à ma grande inquiétude

dismiss [dɪsˈmɪs] *vt* congédier, renvoyer; (*idea*) écarter; (*LAW*) rejeter ♦ *vi* (*MIL*) rompre les rangs

dismissal [dɪsˈmɪsl] *n* renvoi *m*

dismount [dɪsˈmaunt] *vi* mettre pied à terre

disobedient [dɪsəˈbiːdɪənt] *adj* désobéissant(e), indiscipliné(e)

disobey [dɪsəˈbeɪ] *vt* désobéir à; (*rule*) transgresser, enfreindre

disorder [dɪsˈɔːdə*] *n* désordre *m*; (*rioting*) désordres *mpl*; (*MED*) troubles *mpl*

disorderly [dɪsˈɔːdəlɪ] *adj* (*room*) en désordre; (*behaviour, retreat, crowd*) désordonné(e)

disorientated [dɪsˈɔːrɪənteɪtɪd] *adj* désorienté(e)

disown [dɪsˈəun] *vt* renier

disparaging [dɪsˈpærɪdʒɪŋ] *adj* désobligeant(e); **to be disparaging about sb/sth** faire des remarques désobligeantes sur qn/qch

dispassionate [dɪsˈpæʃənət] *adj* calme, froid(e), impartial(e), objectif(ive)

dispatch [dɪsˈpætʃ] *vt* expédier, envoyer; (*deal*

with: *business*) régler, en finir avec ♦ *n* envoi *m*, expédition *f*; (*MIL*, *PRESS*) dépêche *f*

dispel [dɪs'pel] *vt* dissiper, chasser

dispense [dɪs'pens] *vt* distribuer, administrer; (*medicine*) préparer (et vendre); **to dispense sb from** dispenser qn de

▶ **dispense with** *vt fus* se passer de; (*make unnecessary*) rendre superflu(e)

dispenser [dɪs'pensə*] *n* (*device*) distributeur *m*

dispensing chemist [dɪs'pensɪŋ-] *n* (*BRIT*) pharmacie *f*

disperse [dɪs'pə:s] *vt* disperser; (*knowledge*) disséminer ♦ *vi* se disperser

dispirited [dɪs'pɪrɪtɪd] *adj* découragé(e), déprimé(e)

displace [dɪs'pleɪs] *vt* déplacer

display [dɪs'pleɪ] *n* (*of goods*) étalage *m*; affichage *m*; (*computer display*: *information*) visualisation *f*; (: *device*) visuel *m*; (*of feeling*) manifestation *f*; (*pej*) ostentation *f*; (*show, spectacle*) spectacle *m*; (*military display*) parade *f* militaire ♦ *vt* montrer; (*goods*) mettre à l'étalage, exposer; (*results, departure times*) afficher; (*pej*) faire étalage de; **on display** (*exhibits*) exposé(e), exhibé(e); (*goods*) à l'étalage

displease [dɪs'pli:z] *vt* mécontenter, contrarier; **displeased with** mécontent(e) de

displeasure [dɪs'pleʒə*] *n* mécontentement *m*

disposable [dɪs'pəuzəbl] *adj* (*pack etc*) jetable; (*income*) disponible; **disposable nappy** (*BRIT*) couche *f* à jeter, couche-culotte *f*

disposal [dɪs'pəuzl] *n* (*availability, arrangement*) disposition *f*; (*of property etc*: *by selling*) vente *f*; (: *by giving away*) cession *f*; (*of rubbish*) évacuation *f*, destruction *f*; **at one's disposal** à sa disposition; **to put sth at sb's disposal** mettre qch à la disposition de qn

dispose [dɪs'pəuz] *vt* disposer

▶ **dispose of** *vt fus* (*time, money*) disposer de; (*unwanted goods*) se débarrasser de, se défaire de; (*COMM*: *stock*) écouler, vendre; (*problem*) expédier

disposed [dɪs'pəuzd] *adj*: **disposed to do** disposé(e) à faire

disposition [dɪspə'zɪʃən] *n* disposition *f*; (*temperament*) naturel *m*

disprove [dɪs'pru:v] *vt* réfuter

dispute [dɪs'pju:t] *n* discussion *f*; (*also*: **industrial dispute**) conflit *m* ♦ *vt* contester; (*matter*) discuter; (*victory*) disputer; **to be in** *or* **under dispute** (*matter*) être en discussion; (*territory*) être contesté(e)

disqualify [dɪs'kwɔlɪfaɪ] *vt* (*SPORT*) disqualifier; **to disqualify sb for sth/from doing** (*status, situation*) rendre qn inapte à qch/à faire; (*authority*) signifier à qn l'interdiction de faire; **to disqualify sb (from driving)** (*BRIT*) retirer à qn son permis (de conduire)

disquiet [dɪs'kwaɪət] *n* inquiétude *f*, trouble *m*

disregard [dɪsrɪ'gɑ:d] *vt* ne pas tenir compte de

♦ *n* (*indifference*): **disregard (for)** (*feelings*) indifférence *f* (pour), insensibilité *f* (à); (*danger, money*) mépris *m* (pour)

disrepair ['dɪsrɪ'pɛə*] *n* mauvais état; **to fall into disrepair** (*building*) tomber en ruine; (*street*) se dégrader

disreputable [dɪs'rɛpjutəbl] *adj* (*person*) de mauvaise réputation, peu recommandable; (*behaviour*) déshonorant(e); (*area*) mal famé(e), louche

disrespectful [dɪsrɪ'spɛktful] *adj* irrespectueux(euse)

disrupt [dɪs'rʌpt] *vt* (*plans, meeting, lesson*) perturber, déranger

dissatisfied [dɪs'sætɪsfaɪd] *adj*: **dissatisfied (with)** mécontent(e) *or* insatisfait(e) (de)

dissect [dɪ'sɛkt] *vt* disséquer; (*fig*) disséquer, éplucher

dissent [dɪ'sɛnt] *n* dissentiment *m*, différence *f* d'opinion

dissertation [dɪsə'teɪʃən] *n* (*SCOL*) mémoire *m*

disservice [dɪs'sə:vɪs] *n*: **to do sb a disservice** rendre un mauvais service à qn; desservir qn

dissimilar [dɪ'sɪmɪlə*] *adj*: **dissimilar (to)** dissemblable (à), différent(e) de)

dissipate ['dɪsɪpeɪt] *vt* dissiper; (*energy, efforts*) disperser

dissolute ['dɪsəlu:t] *adj* débauché(e), dissolu(e)

dissolve [dɪ'zɔlv] *vt* dissoudre ♦ *vi* se dissoudre, fondre; (*fig*) disparaître

distance ['dɪstns] *n* distance *f*; **what's the distance to London?** à quelle distance se trouve Londres?; **it's within walking distance** on peut y aller à pied; **in the distance** au loin

distant ['dɪstnt] *adj* lointain(e), éloigné(e); (*manner*) distant(e), froid(e)

distaste [dɪs'teɪst] *n* dégoût *m*

distasteful [dɪs'teɪstful] *adj* déplaisant(e), désagréable

distended [dɪs'tɛndɪd] *adj* (*stomach*) dilaté(e)

distil, (*US*) **distill** [dɪs'tɪl] *vt* distiller

distillery [dɪs'tɪlərɪ] *n* distillerie *f*

distinct [dɪs'tɪŋkt] *adj* distinct(e); (*preference, progress*) marqué(e); **as distinct from** par opposition à, en contraste avec

distinction [dɪs'tɪŋkʃən] *n* distinction *f*; (*in exam*) mention *f* très bien; **to draw a distinction between** faire une distinction entre; **a writer of distinction** un écrivain réputé

distinctive [dɪs'tɪŋktɪv] *adj* distinctif(ive)

distinguish [dɪs'tɪŋgwɪʃ] *vt* distinguer ♦ *vi*: **to distinguish between** (*concepts*) distinguer entre, faire une distinction entre; **to distinguish o.s.** se distinguer

distinguished [dɪs'tɪŋgwɪʃt] *adj* (*eminent, refined*) distingué(e); (*career*) remarquable, brillant(e)

distinguishing [dɪs'tɪŋgwɪʃɪŋ] *adj* (*feature*) distinctif(ive), caractéristique

distort [dɪs'tɔːt] vt déformer

distract [dɪs'trækt] vt distraire, déranger

distracted [dɪs'træktɪd] adj (look etc) éperdu(e), égaré(e)

distraction [dɪs'trækʃən] n distraction f, dérangement m; **to drive sb to distraction** rendre qn fou/folle

distraught [dɪs'trɔːt] adj éperdu(e)

distress [dɪs'tres] n détresse f; (pain) douleur f ♦ vt affliger; **in distress** (ship) en perdition; (plane) en détresse; **distressed area** (BRIT) zone sinistrée

distressing [dɪs'tresɪŋ] adj douloureux(euse), pénible, affligeant(e)

distribute [dɪs'trɪbjuːt] vt distribuer

distribution [dɪstrɪ'bjuːʃən] n distribution f

distributor [dɪs'trɪbjutə*] n (gen, TECH) distributeur m; (COMM) concessionnaire m/f

district [dɪstrɪkt] n (of country) région f; (of town) quartier m; (ADMIN) district m

district attorney n (US) ≃ procureur m de la République

district nurse n (BRIT) infirmière visiteuse

distrust [dɪs'trʌst] n méfiance f, doute m ♦ vt se méfier de

disturb [dɪs'tɜːb] vt troubler; (inconvenience) déranger; **sorry to disturb you** excusez-moi de vous déranger

disturbance [dɪs'tɜːbəns] n dérangement m; (political etc) troubles mpl; (by drunks etc) tapage m; **to cause a disturbance** troubler l'ordre public; **disturbance of the peace** (LAW) tapage injurieux or nocturne

disturbed [dɪs'tɜːbd] adj agité(e), troublé(e); **to be mentally/emotionally disturbed** avoir des problèmes psychologiques/affectifs

disturbing [dɪs'tɜːbɪŋ] adj troublant(e), inquiétant(e)

disuse [dɪs'juːs] n: **to fall into disuse** tomber en désuétude

disused [dɪs'juːzd] adj désaffecté(e)

ditch [dɪtʃ] n fossé m ♦ vt (col) abandonner

dither [dɪðə*] vi hésiter

ditto [dɪtəu] adv idem

dive [daɪv] n plongeon m; (of submarine) plongée f; (AVIAT) piqué m; (pej: café, bar etc) bouge m ♦ vi plonger

diver [daɪvə*] n plongeur m

diversion [daɪ'vɜːʃən] n (BRIT AUT) déviation f; (distraction, MIL) diversion f

divert [daɪ'vɜːt] vt (BRIT: traffic) dévier; (plane) dérouter; (train, river) détourner; (amuse) divertir

divide [dɪ'vaɪd] vt diviser; (separate) séparer ♦ vi se diviser; **to divide (between** or **among)** répartir or diviser (entre); **40 divided by 5** 40 divisé par 5

▶ **divide out** vt: **to divide out (between** or **among)** distribuer or répartir (entre)

dividend [dɪvɪdɛnd] n dividende m

divine [dɪ'vaɪn] adj divin(e) ♦ vt (future) prédire; (truth) deviner, entrevoir; (water, metal) détecter la présence de (par l'intermédiaire de la radiesthésie)

diving [daɪvɪŋ] n plongée (sous-marine)

diving board n plongeoir m

divinity [dɪ'vɪnɪtɪ] n divinité f; (as study) théologie f

division [dɪ'vɪʒən] n (BRIT FOOTBALL) division f; (separation) séparation f; (BRIT POL) vote m; **division of labour** division du travail

divorce [dɪ'vɔːs] n divorce m ♦ vt divorcer d'avec

divorced [dɪ'vɔːst] adj divorcé(e)

divorcee [dɪvɔː'siː] n divorcé/e

DIY adj, n abbr = **do-it-yourself**

dizzy [dɪzɪ] adj (height) vertigineux(euse); **to make sb dizzy** donner le vertige à qn; **I feel dizzy** la tête me tourne, j'ai la tête qui tourne

DJ n abbr = **disc jockey**

DNA fingerprinting [-'fɪŋɡəprɪntɪŋ] n technique f des empreintes génétiques

---
KEYWORD
---

do [duː] pt **did**, pp **done**, n (col: party etc) soirée f, fête f; (: formal gathering) réception f
♦ vb 1 (in negative constructions: non traduit) **I don't understand** je ne comprends pas

2 (to form questions: non traduit) **didn't you know?** vous ne le saviez pas?; **why didn't you come?** pourquoi n'êtes-vous pas venu?

3 (for emphasis, in polite expressions): **she does seem rather late** je trouve qu'elle est bien en retard; **do sit down/help yourself** asseyez-vous/servez-vous je vous en prie; **I DO wish I could go** j'aimerais tant y aller; **but I DO like it!** mais si, je l'aime!

4 (used to avoid repeating vb): **she swims better than I do** elle nage mieux que moi; **do you agree?** vous êtes d'accord?; **she lives in Glasgow – so do I** elle habite Glasgow – moi aussi; **who broke it? – I did** qui l'a cassé? – c'est moi

5 (in question tags): **he laughed, didn't he?** il a ri, n'est-ce pas?; **I don't know him, do I?** je ne crois pas le connaître

♦ vt (gen: carry out, perform etc) faire; (visit: city, museum) faire, visiter; **what are you doing tonight?** qu'est-ce que vous faites ce soir?; **what did he do with the cat?** qu'a-t-il fait du chat?; **to do the cooking/washing-up** faire la cuisine/la vaisselle; **to do one's teeth/hair/nails** se brosser les dents/se coiffer/se faire les ongles; **the car was doing 100** la voiture faisait du 100 (à l'heure)

♦ vi 1 (act, behave) faire; **do as I do** faites comme moi

2 (get on, fare) marcher; **the firm is doing well** l'entreprise marche bien; **how do you do?** com-

ment allez-vous?; (on being introduced) enchanté(e)!

3 (suit) aller; **will it do?** est-ce que ça ira?

4 (be sufficient) suffire, aller; **will £10 do?** est-ce que 10 livres suffiront?; **that'll do** ça suffit, ça ira; **that'll do!** (in annoyance) ça va or suffit comme ça!; **to make do (with)** se contenter (de)

▶ **do away with** vt fus abolir; (kill) supprimer

▶ **do for** vt fus (BRIT col: clean for) faire le ménage chez

▶ **do up** vt (laces, dress) attacher; (buttons) boutonner; (zip) fermer; (renovate: room) refaire; (: house) remettre à neuf; **to do o.s. up** se faire beau(belle)

▶ **do with** vt fus (need): **I could do with a drink/some help** quelque chose à boire/un peu d'aide ne serait pas de refus; **it could do with a wash** ça ne lui ferait pas de mal d'être lavé; (be connected with): **that has nothing to do with you** cela ne vous concerne pas; **I won't have anything to do with it** je ne veux pas m'en mêler; **what has that got to do with it?** quel est le rapport?, qu'est-ce que cela vient faire là-dedans?

▶ **do without** vi s'en passer ♦ vt fus se passer de

dock [dɔk] n dock m; (wharf) quai m; (LAW) banc m des accusés ♦ vi se mettre à quai ♦ vt: **they docked a third of his wages** ils lui ont retenu or décompté un tiers de son salaire

docker ['dɔkə*] n docker m

dockyard ['dɔkjɑːd] n chantier m de construction navale

doctor ['dɔktə*] n médecin m, docteur m; (PhD etc) docteur ♦ vt (cat) couper; (interfere with: food) altérer; (: drink) frelater; (: text, document) arranger; **doctor's office** (US) cabinet m de consultation; **Doctor of Philosophy (PhD)** doctorat m; titulaire m/f d'un doctorat

document n ['dɔkjumənt] document m ♦ vt ['dɔkjumənt] documenter

documentary [dɔkju'mɛntəri] adj, n documentaire (m)

dodge [dɔdʒ] n truc m; combine f ♦ vt esquiver, éviter ♦ vi faire un saut de côté; (SPORT) faire une esquive; **to dodge out of the way** s'esquiver; **to dodge through the traffic** se faufiler or faire de savantes manœuvres entre les voitures

dodgems ['dɔdʒəmz] npl (BRIT) autos tamponneuses

doe [dəu] n (deer) biche f; (rabbit) lapine f

does [dʌz] see **do**

doesn't ['dʌznt] = **does not**

dog [dɔg] n chien/ne ♦ vt (follow closely) suivre de près, ne pas lâcher d'une semelle; (fig: memory etc) poursuivre, harceler; **to go to the dogs** (nation etc) aller à vau-l'eau

dog collar n collier m de chien; (fig) faux-col m

d'ecclésiastique

dog-eared ['dɔgiəd] adj corné(e)

dogged ['dɔgid] adj obstiné(e), opiniâtre

dogsbody ['dɔgzbɔdi] n (BRIT) bonne f à tout faire, tâcheron m

doings ['duːiŋz] npl activités fpl

do-it-yourself ['duːitjɔː'self] n bricolage m

doldrums ['dɔldrəmz] npl: **to be in the doldrums** avoir le cafard; être dans le marasme

dole [dəul] n (BRIT: payment) allocation f de chômage; **on the dole** au chômage

▶ **dole out** vt donner au compte-goutte

doll [dɔl] n poupée f

▶ **doll up** vt: **to doll o.s. up** se faire beau(belle)

dollar ['dɔlə*] n dollar m

dolphin ['dɔlfin] n dauphin m

dome [dəum] n dôme m

domestic [də'mɛstik] adj (duty, happiness) familial(e); (policy, affairs, flight) intérieur(e); (news) national(e); (animal) domestique

domesticated [də'mɛstikeitid] adj domestiqué(e); (pej) d'intérieur; **he's very domesticated** il participe volontiers aux tâches ménagères; question ménage, il est très organisé

dominate ['dɔmineit] vt dominer

domineering [dɔmi'niəriŋ] adj dominateur(trice), autoritaire

dominion [də'miniən] n domination f; territoire m; dominion m

domino, pl **dominoes** ['dɔminəu] n domino m; **dominoes** npl (game) dominos mpl

don [dɔn] n (BRIT) professeur m d'université ♦ vt revêtir

donate [də'neit] vt faire don de, donner

done [dʌn] pp of **do**

donkey ['dɔŋki] n âne m

donor ['dəunə*] n (of blood etc) donneur/euse; (to charity) donateur/trice

donor card n carte f de don d'organes

don't [dəunt] = **do not**

donut ['dəunʌt] (US) n = **doughnut**

doodle ['duːdl] n griffonnage m, gribouillage m ♦ vi griffonner, gribouiller

doom [duːm] n (fate) destin m; (ruin) ruine f ♦ vt: **to be doomed to failure** être voué(e) à l'échec

door [dɔː*] n porte f; (of vehicle) portière f, porte; **to go from door to door** aller de porte en porte

doorbell ['dɔːbɛl] n sonnette f

door handle n poignée f de porte

doorman ['dɔːmən] n (in hotel) portier m; (in block of flats) concierge m

doormat ['dɔːmæt] n paillasson m

doorstep ['dɔːstɛp] n pas m de (la) porte, seuil m

doorway ['dɔːwei] n embrasure f de porte f

dope [dəup] n (col) drogue f; (: information) tuyaux mpl, rancards mpl ♦ vt (horse etc) doper

dormant ['dɔːmənt] *adj* assoupi(e), en veilleuse; (*rule, law*) inappliqué(e)

dormitory ['dɔːmɪtrɪ] *n* dortoir *m*; (*US: hall of residence*) foyer *m* d'étudiants

dormouse, *pl* **dormice** ['dɔːmaus, -maɪs] *n* loir *m*

DOS [dɒs] *n abbr* = disk operating system

dose [dəus] *n* dose *f*; (*BRIT: bout*) attaque *f* ♦ *vt*: **to dose o.s.** se bourrer de médicaments; **a dose of flu** une belle *or* bonne grippe

dosh [dɒʃ] (*inf*) *n* fric *m*

doss house ['dɒs-] *n* (*BRIT*) asile *m* de nuit

dot [dɒt] *n* point *m* ♦ *vt*: **dotted with** parsemé(e) de; **on the dot** à l'heure tapante

dotted line ['dɒtɪd-] *n* ligne pointillée; (*AUT*) ligne discontinue; **to sign on the dotted line** signer à l'endroit indiqué *or* sur la ligne pointillée; (*fig*) donner son consentement

double ['dʌbl] *adj* double ♦ *adv* (*fold*) en deux; (*twice*): **to cost double (sth)** coûter le double (de qch) *or* deux fois plus (que qch) ♦ *n* double *m*; (*CINE*) doublure *f* ♦ *vt* doubler; (*fold*) plier en deux ♦ *vi* doubler; (*have two uses*): **to double as** servir aussi de; **double five two six (5526)** (*BRIT TEL*) cinquante-cinq – vingt-six; **it's spelt with a double "l"** ça s'écrit avec deux "l"; **on the double**, (*BRIT*) **at the double** au pas de course

▶ **double back** *vi* (*person*) revenir sur ses pas

▶ **double up** *vi* (*bend over*) se courber, se plier; (*share room*) partager la chambre

double bass *n* contrebasse *f*

double bed *n* grand lit

double-breasted ['dʌbl'brestɪd] *adj* croisé(e)

double-click ['dʌbl'klɪk] *vi* (*COMPUT*) double-cliquer

double-cross ['dʌbl'krɒs] *vt* doubler, trahir

double-decker ['dʌbl'dekə*] *n* autobus *m* à impériale

double glazing *n* (*BRIT*) double vitrage *m*

double room *n* chambre *f* pour deux

doubly ['dʌblɪ] *adv* doublement, deux fois plus

doubt [daut] *n* doute *m* ♦ *vt* douter de; **without (a) doubt** sans aucun doute; **beyond doubt** *adv* indubitablement ♦ *adj* indubitable; **to doubt that** douter que; **I doubt it very much** j'en doute fort

doubtful ['dautful] *adj* douteux(euse); (*person*) incertain(e); **to be doubtful about sth** avoir des doutes sur qch, ne pas être convaincu de qch; **I'm a bit doubtful** je n'en suis pas certain *or* sûr

doubtless ['dautlɪs] *adv* sans doute, sûrement

dough [dəu] *n* pâte *f*; (*col: money*) fric *m*, pognon *m*

doughnut ['dəunʌt] *n* beignet *m*

dove [dʌv] *n* colombe *f*

Dover ['dəuvə*] *n* Douvres

dovetail ['dʌvteɪl] *n*: **dovetail joint** assemblage *m* à queue d'aronde ♦ *vi* (*fig*) concorder

dowdy ['daudɪ] *adj* démodé(e), mal fagoté(e)

down [daun] *n* (*fluff*) duvet *m*; (*hill*) colline (dénudée) ♦ *adv* en bas ♦ *prep* en bas de ♦ *vt* (*enemy*) abattre; (*col: drink*) siffler; **down there** là-bas (en bas), là au fond; **down here** ici en bas; **the price of meat is down** le prix de la viande a baissé; **I've got it down in my diary** c'est inscrit dans mon agenda; **to pay £2 down** verser 2 livres d'arrhes *or* en acompte; **England is two goals down** l'Angleterre a deux buts de retard; **to down tools** (*BRIT*) cesser le travail; **down with X!** à bas X!

down-and-out ['daunəndaut] *n* (*tramp*) clochard/e

down-at-heel ['daunət'hiːl] *adj* (*fig*) miteux(euse)

downcast ['daunkɑːst] *adj* démoralisé(e)

downfall ['daunfɔːl] *n* chute *f*; ruine *f*

downhearted ['daun'hɑːtɪd] *adj* découragé(e)

downhill ['daun'hɪl] *adv* (*face, look*) en aval, vers l'aval; (*roll, go*) vers le bas, en bas ♦ *n* (*SKI: also*: **downhill race**) descente *f*; **to go downhill** descendre; (*business*) péricliter, aller à vau-l'eau

Downing Street ['daunɪŋ-] *n* (*BRIT*): **10 Downing Street** résidence du Premier ministre; voir encadré

DOWNING STREET

Downing Street est une rue de Westminster (à Londres) où se trouvent la résidence officielle du Premier ministre et celle du ministre des Finances. Le nom **Downing Street** est souvent utilisé pour désigner le gouvernement britannique.

---

downloadable ['daunləudəbl] *adj* téléchargeable

down payment *n* acompte *m*

downpour ['daunpɔː*] *n* pluie torrentielle, déluge *m*

downright ['daunraɪt] *adj* franc(franche); (*refusal*) catégorique

downsize [daun'saɪz] *vt* réduire l'effectif de

Down's syndrome [daunz-] *n* mongolisme *m*, trisomie *f*; **a Down's syndrome baby** un bébé mongolien *or* trisomique

downstairs ['daun'steəz] *adv* (*on or to ground floor*) au rez-de-chaussée; (*on or to floor below*) à l'étage inférieur; **to come downstairs to go downstairs** descendre (l'escalier)

downstream ['daunstriːm] *adv* en aval

down-to-earth ['dauntu'əːθ] *adj* terre à terre *inv*

downtown ['daun'taun] *adv* en ville ♦ *adj* (*US*): **downtown Chicago** le centre commerçant de Chicago

down under *adv* en Australie (*or* Nouvelle Zélande)

downward ['daunwəd] *adj* vers le bas; **a downward trend** une tendance à la baisse, une diminution progressive

downward(s) ['daunwəd(z)] *adv* vers le bas

dowry ['dauri] n dot f

doz. abbr (= dozen) douz

doze [dəuz] vi sommeiller

▶ **doze off** vi s'assoupir

dozen ['dʌzn] n douzaine f; **a dozen books** une douzaine de livres; **80p a dozen** 80p la douzaine; **dozens of times** des centaines de fois

Dr. abbr (= doctor) Dr; (in street names) = **drive**

drab [dræb] adj terne, morne

draft [drɑːft] n brouillon m; (of contract, document) version f préliminaire; (COMM) traite f; (US MIL) contingent m; (: call-up) conscription f ◆ vt faire le brouillon de; (document, report) rédiger une version préliminaire de; see also **draught**

drag [dræg] vt traîner; (river) draguer ◆ vi traîner ◆ n (AVIAT, NAUT) résistance f; (col: person) raseur/euse; (: task etc) corvée f; (women's clothing): **in drag** (en) travesti

▶ **drag away** vt: **to drag away (from)** arracher or emmener de force (de)

▶ **drag on** vi s'éterniser

dragon ['drægn] n dragon m

dragonfly ['drægənflaɪ] n libellule f

drain [dreɪn] n égout m; (on resources) saignée f ◆ vt (land, marshes) drainer, assécher; (vegetables) égoutter; (reservoir etc) vider ◆ vi (water) s'écouler; **to feel drained (of energy or emotion)** être miné(e)

drainage ['dreɪnɪdʒ] n système m d'égouts

draining board ['dreɪnɪŋ-], (US) **drainboard** ['dreɪnbɔːd] n égouttoir m

drainpipe ['dreɪnpaɪp] n tuyau m d'écoulement

drama ['drɑːmə] n (art) théâtre m, art m dramatique; (play) pièce f; (event) drame m

dramatic [drə'mætɪk] adj (THEAT) dramatique; (impressive) spectaculaire

dramatist ['dræmətɪst] n auteur m dramatique

dramatize ['dræmətaɪz] vt (events etc) dramatiser; (adapt) adapter pour la télévision (or pour l'écran)

drank [dræŋk] pt of **drink**

drape [dreɪp] vt draper

drapes [dreɪps] npl (US) rideaux mpl

drastic ['dræstɪk] adj (measures) d'urgence, énergique; (change) radical(le)

draught, (US) **draft** [drɑːft] n courant m d'air; (of chimney) tirage m; (NAUT) tirant m d'eau; **on draught** (beer) à la pression

draughtboard ['drɑːftbɔːd] n (BRIT) damier m

draughts [drɑːfts] n (BRIT) (jeu m de) dames fpl

draughtsman, (US) **draftsman** ['drɑːftsmən] n dessinateur/trice (industriel(le))

draw [drɔː] vb: pt **drew**, pp **drawn** [druː, drɔːn] vt tirer; (attract) attirer; (picture) dessiner; (line, circle) tracer; (money) retirer; (comparison, distinction): **to draw (between)** faire (entre) ◆ vi (SPORT) faire match nul ◆ n match nul; (lottery) loterie f; (: picking of ticket) tirage m au sort; **to draw to a close** toucher à or tirer à sa fin; **to draw near** vi s'approcher; approcher

▶ **draw back** vi (move back): **to draw back (from)** reculer (de)

▶ **draw in** vi (BRIT: car) s'arrêter le long du trottoir; (: train) entrer en gare or dans la station

▶ **draw on** vt (resources) faire appel à; (imagination, person) avoir recours à, faire appel à

▶ **draw out** vi (lengthen) s'allonger ◆ vt (money) retirer

▶ **draw up** vi (stop) s'arrêter ◆ vt (document) établir, dresser; (plan) formuler, dessiner

drawback ['drɔːbæk] n inconvénient m, désavantage m

drawbridge ['drɔːbrɪdʒ] n pont-levis m

drawer [drɔː*] n tiroir m; ['drɔːə*] (of cheque) tireur m

drawing ['drɔːɪŋ] n dessin m

drawing board n planche f à dessin

drawing pin n (BRIT) punaise f

drawing room n salon m

drawl [drɔːl] n accent traînant

drawn [drɔːn] pp of **draw** ◆ adj (haggard) tiré(e), crispé(e)

dread [drɛd] n épouvante f, effroi m ◆ vt redouter, appréhender

dreadful ['drɛdful] adj épouvantable affreux(euse)

dream [driːm] n rêve m ◆ vt, vi, pt, pp **dreamed** or **dreamt** [drɛmt] rêver; **to have a dream about sb/sth** rêver à qn/qch; **sweet dreams!** faites de beaux rêves!

▶ **dream up** vt inventer

dreamy ['driːmɪ] adj (absent-minded) rêveur(euse)

dreary ['drɪərɪ] adj triste; monotone

dredge [drɛdʒ] vt draguer

▶ **dredge up** vt draguer; (fig: unpleasant facts) (faire) ressortir

dregs [drɛgz] npl lie f

drench [drɛntʃ] vt tremper; **drenched to the skin** trempé(e) jusqu'aux os

dress [drɛs] n robe f; (clothing) habillement m, tenue f ◆ vt habiller; (wound) panser; (food) préparer ◆ vi: **she dresses very well** elle s'habille très bien; **to dress o.s., to get dressed** s'habiller; **to dress a shop window** faire l'étalage or la vitrine

▶ **dress up** vi s'habiller; (in fancy dress) se déguiser

dress circle n premier balcon

dresser ['drɛsə*] n (THEAT) habilleur/euse (also: **window dresser**) étalagiste m/f; (furniture) vaisselier m

dressing ['drɛsɪŋ] n (MED) pansement m; (CULIN) sauce f, assaisonnement m

dressing gown n (BRIT) robe f de chambre

dressing room n (THEAT) loge f; (SPORT) vestiaire m

dressing table n coiffeuse f

dressmaker ['drɛsmeɪkə*] n couturière f

dress rehearsal n (répétition f) générale f

drew [dru:] pt of **draw**

dribble ['drɪbl] vi tomber goutte à goutte; (baby) baver ♦ vt (ball) dribbler

dried [draɪd] adj (fruit, beans) sec(sèche); (eggs, milk) en poudre

drier ['draɪə*] n = **dryer**

drift [drɪft] n (of current etc) force f; direction f; (of sand etc) amoncellement m; (of snow) rafale f; coulée f; (: on ground) congère f; (general meaning) sens général ♦ vi (boat) aller à la dérive, dériver; (sand, snow) s'amonceler, s'entasser; **to let things drift** laisser les choses aller à la dérive; **to drift apart** (friends, lovers) s'éloigner l'un de l'autre; **I get** or **catch your drift** je vois en gros ce que vous voulez dire

driftwood ['drɪftwud] n bois flotté

drill [drɪl] n perceuse f; (bit) foret m; (of dentist) roulette f, fraise f; (MIL) exercice m ♦ vt percer; (soldiers) faire faire l'exercice à; (pupils: in grammar) faire faire des exercices à ♦ vi (for oil) faire un or des forage(s)

drink [drɪŋk] n boisson f ♦ vt, vi, pt **drank**, pp **drunk** [dræŋk, drʌŋk] boire; **to have a drink** boire quelque chose, boire un verre; **a drink of water** un verre d'eau; **would you like something to drink?** aimeriez-vous boire quelque chose?; **we had drinks before lunch** on a pris l'apéritif

▶ **drink in** vt (fresh air) inspirer profondément; (story) avaler, ne pas perdre une miette de; (sight) se remplir la vue de

drinker ['drɪŋkə*] n buveur/euse

drinking water n eau f potable

drip [drɪp] n goutte f; (sound: of water etc) bruit m de l'eau qui tombe goutte à goutte; (MED) goutte-à-goutte m inv, perfusion f; (col: person) lavette f, nouille f ♦ vi tomber goutte à goutte; (washing) s'égoutter; (wall) suinter

drip-dry ['drɪp'draɪ] adj (shirt) sans repassage

dripping ['drɪpɪŋ] n graisse f de rôti ♦ adj: **dripping wet** trempé(e)

drive [draɪv] n promenade f or trajet m en voiture; (also: **driveway**) allée f; (energy) dynamisme m, énergie f; (PSYCH) besoin m; pulsion f; (push) effort (concerté); campagne f; (SPORT) drive m; (TECH) entraînement m; traction f; transmission f; (COMPUT: also: **disk drive**) lecteur m de disquette ♦ vb, pt **drove**, pp **driven** [drəuv, 'drɪvn] vt conduire; (nail) enfoncer; (push) chasser, pousser; (TECH: motor) actionner; entraîner ♦ vi (be at the wheel) conduire; (travel by car) aller en voiture; **to go for a drive** aller faire une promenade en voiture; **it's 3 hours' drive from London** Londres est à 3 heures de

route; **left-/right-hand drive** (AUT) conduite f à gauche/droite; **front-/rear-wheel drive** (AUT) traction f avant/arrière; **to drive sb to (do) sth** pousser or conduire qn à (faire) qch; **to drive sb mad** rendre qn fou(folle)

▶ **drive at** vt fus (fig: intend, mean) vouloir dire, en venir à

▶ **drive on** vi poursuivre sa route, continuer; (after stopping) reprendre sa route, repartir ♦ vt (incite, encourage) inciter

drive-by ['draɪvbaɪ] n (also: **drive-by shooting**) tentative d'assassinat par coups de feu tirés d'une voiture

drivel ['drɪvl] n (col) idioties fpl, imbécillités fpl

driver ['draɪvə*] n conducteur/trice; (of taxi, bus) chauffeur m

driver's license n (US) permis m de conduire

driveway ['draɪvweɪ] n allée f

driving ['draɪvɪŋ] adj: **driving rain** n pluie battante ♦ n conduite f

driving instructor n moniteur m d'auto-école

driving lesson n leçon f de conduite

driving licence n (BRIT) permis m de conduire

driving school n auto-école f

driving test n examen m du permis de conduire

drizzle ['drɪzl] n bruine f, crachin m ♦ vi bruiner

drool [dru:l] vi baver; **to drool over sb/sth** (fig) baver d'admiration or être en extase devant qn/qch

droop [dru:p] vi s'affaisser; tomber

drop [drɔp] n goutte f; baisse f; (: in salary) réduction f; (also: **parachute drop**) saut m; (of cliff) dénivellation f; à-pic m ♦ vt laisser tomber; (voice, eyes, price) baisser; (set down from car) déposer ♦ vi (wind, temperature, price, voice) tomber; (numbers, attendance) diminuer; **drops** npl (MED) gouttes fpl; **cough drops** pastilles fpl pour la toux; **a drop of 10%** une baisse or réduction de 10%; **to drop anchor** jeter l'ancre; **to drop sb a line** mettre un mot à qn

▶ **drop in** vi (col: visit): **to drop in (on)** faire un saut (chez), passer (chez)

▶ **drop off** vi (sleep) s'assoupir ♦ vt: **to drop sb off** déposer qn

▶ **drop out** vi (withdraw) se retirer; (student etc) abandonner, décrocher

dropout ['drɔpaut] n (from society) marginal/e; (from university) drop-out m/f, dropé/e

dropper ['drɔpə*] n (MED etc) compte-gouttes m inv

droppings ['drɔpɪŋz] npl crottes fpl

drought [draut] n sécheresse f

drove [drəuv] pt of **drive** ♦ n: **droves of people** une foule de gens

drown [draun] vt noyer; (also: **drown out**: sound) couvrir, étouffer ♦ vi se noyer

drowsy ['drauzı] *adj* somnolent(e)

drug [drʌg] *n* médicament *m*; (*narcotic*) drogue *f* ♦ *vt* droguer; **he's on drugs** il se drogue; (*MED*) il est sous médication

drug addict *n* toxicomane *m/f*

druggist ['drʌgɪst] *n* (*US*) pharmacien/ne-droguiste

drugstore ['drʌgstɔ:ʳ] *n* (*US*) pharmacie-droguerie *f*, drugstore *m*

drum [drʌm] *n* tambour *m*; (*for oil, petrol*) bidon *m* ♦ *vt*: **to drum one's fingers on the table** pianoter or tambouriner sur la table; **drums** *npl* (*MUS*) batterie *f*

▶ **drum up** *vt* (*enthusiasm, support*) susciter, rallier

drummer ['drʌməʳ] *n* (joueur *m* de) tambour *m*

drunk [drʌŋk] *pp of* **drink** ♦ *adj* ivre, soûl(e) ♦ *n* soûlard/e, homme/femme soûl(e); **to get drunk** s'enivrer, se soûler

drunken ['drʌŋkən] *adj* ivre, soûl(e); (*habitual*) ivrogne, d'ivrogne; **drunken driving** conduite *f* en état d'ivresse

dry [draı] *adj* sec(sèche); (*day*) sans pluie; (*humour*) pince-sans-rire; (*uninteresting*) aride, rébarbatif(ive) ♦ *vt* sécher; (*clothes*) faire sécher ♦ *vi* sécher; **on dry land** sur la terre ferme; **to dry one's hands/hair/eyes** se sécher les mains/les cheveux/les yeux

▶ **dry up** *vi* (*also fig: source of supply, imagination*) se tarir; (*speaker*) sécher, rester sec

dry-cleaner's ['draı'kli:nəz] *n* teinturerie *f*

dryer ['draıəʳ] *n* séchoir *m*; (*spin-dryer*) essoreuse *f*

dryness ['draınıs] *n* sécheresse *f*

dry rot *n* pourriture sèche (*du bois*)

DSS *n abbr* (*BRIT*) = **Department of Social Security**

DTP *n abbr* = **desktop publishing**

dual ['djuəl] *adj* double

dual carriageway *n* (*BRIT*) route *f* à quatre voies

dual-purpose ['djuəl'pə:pəs] *adj* à double emploi

dubbed [dʌbd] *adj* (*CINE*) doublé(e); (*nicknamed*) surnommé(e)

dubious ['dju:bıəs] *adj* hésitant(e), incertain(e); (*reputation, company*) douteux(euse); **I'm very dubious about it** j'ai des doutes sur la question, je n'en suis pas sûr du tout

duchess ['dʌtʃıs] *n* duchesse *f*

duck [dʌk] *n* canard *m* ♦ *vi* se baisser vivement, baisser subitement la tête ♦ *vt* plonger dans l'eau

duckling ['dʌklıŋ] *n* caneton *m*

duct [dʌkt] *n* conduite *f*, canalisation *f*; (*ANAT*) conduit *m*

dud [dʌd] *n* (*shell*) obus non éclaté; (*object, tool*): **it's a dud** c'est de la camelote, ça ne marche pas ♦ *adj* (*BRIT: cheque*) sans provision; (: *note, coin*) faux(fausse)

due [dju:] *adj* dû(due); (*expected*) attendu(e); (*fitting*) qui convient ♦ *n* dû *m* ♦ *adv*: **due north** droit vers le nord; **dues** *npl* (*for club, union*) cotisation *f*; (*in harbour*) droits *mpl* (de port); **in due course** en temps utile *or* voulu; (*in the end*) finalement; **due to** dû à; causé par; **the rent is due on the 30th** il faut payer le loyer le 30; **the train is due at 8** le train est attendu à 8 h; **she is due back tomorrow** elle doit rentrer demain; **I am due 6 days' leave** j'ai droit à 6 jours de congé

duet [dju:'et] *n* duo *m*

duffel bag ['dʌfl-] *n* sac marin

duffel coat ['dʌfl-] *n* duffel-coat *m*

dug [dʌg] *pt, pp of* **dig**

duke [dju:k] *n* duc *m*

dull [dʌl] *adj* (*boring*) ennuyeux(euse); (*slow*) borné(e); (*lacklustre*) morne, terne; (*sound, pain*) sourd(e); (*weather, day*) gris(e), maussade; (*blade*) émoussé(e) ♦ *vt* (*pain, grief*) atténuer; (*mind, senses*) engourdir

duly ['dju:lı] *adv* (*on time*) en temps voulu; (*as expected*) comme il se doit

dumb [dʌm] *adj* muet(te); (*stupid*) bête; **to be struck dumb** (*fig*) rester abasourdi(e), être sidéré(e)

dumbfounded [dʌm'faundıd] *adj* sidéré(e)

dummy ['dʌmı] *n* (*tailor's model*) mannequin *m*; (*SPORT*) feinte *f*; (*BRIT: for baby*) tétine *f* ♦ *adj* faux (fausse) factice

dump [dʌmp] *n* tas *m* d'ordures; (*place*) décharge (publique); (*MIL*) dépôt *m*; (*COMPUT*) listage *m* (de la mémoire) ♦ *vt* (*put down*) déposer; déverser; (*get rid of*) se débarrasser de; (*COMPUT*) lister; (*COMM: goods*) vendre à perte (*sur le marché extérieur*) **to be (down) in the dumps** (*col*) avoir le cafard, broyer du noir

dumpling ['dʌmplıŋ] *n* boulette *f* (de pâte)

dumpy ['dʌmpı] *adj* courtaud(e), boulot(te)

dunce [dʌns] *n* âne *m*, cancre *m*

dune [dju:n] *n* dune *f*

dung [dʌŋ] *n* fumier *m*

dungarees [dʌŋgə'ri:z] *npl* bleu(s) *m(pl)*; (*for child, woman*) salopette *f*

dungeon ['dʌndʒən] *n* cachot *m*

duplex ['dju:pleks] *n* (*US: also:* **duplex apartment**) duplex *m*

duplicate *n* ['dju:plıkət] double *m*, copie exacte; (*copy of letter etc*) duplicata *m* ♦ *adj* (*copy*) en double ♦ *vt* ['dju:plıkeıt] faire un double de; (*on machine*) polycopier; **in duplicate** en deux exemplaires, en double; **duplicate key** double *m* de la (*or* d'une) clé

durable ['djuərəbl] *adj* durable; (*clothes, metal*) résistant(e), solide

duration [djuə'reıʃən] *n* durée *f*

during ['djuərıŋ] *prep* pendant, au cours de

dusk [dʌsk] *n* crépuscule *m*

dust [dʌst] n poussière f ♦ vt (furniture) essuyer, épousseter; (cake etc): **to dust with** saupoudrer de
▶ **dust off** vt (also fig) dépoussiérer

dustbin ['dʌstbɪn] n (BRIT) poubelle f

duster ['dʌstə*] n chiffon m

dustman ['dʌstmən] n (BRIT) boueux m, éboueur m

dusty ['dʌstɪ] adj poussiéreux(euse)

Dutch [dʌtʃ] adj hollandais(e), néerlandais(e) ♦ n (LING) hollandais m, néerlandais m ♦ adv: **to go Dutch** or **dutch** partager les frais; **the Dutch** npl les Hollandais, les Néerlandais

Dutchman ['dʌtʃmən], **Dutchwoman** ['dʌtʃwumən] n Hollandais/e

duty ['dju:tɪ] n devoir m; (tax) droit m, taxe f; **duties** npl fonctions fpl; **to make it one's duty to do sth** se faire un devoir de faire qch; **to pay duty on sth** payer un droit or une taxe sur qch; **on duty** de service; (at night etc) de garde; **off duty** libre, pas de service or de garde

duty-free ['dju:tɪ'fri:] adj exempté(e) de douane, hors-taxe; **duty-free shop** boutique f hors-taxe

duvet ['du:veɪ] n (BRIT) couette f

DVD n abbr (= digital versatile disc) DVD m

DVD writer, DVD burner n graveur m de DVD

dwarf [dwɔːf] n nain/e ♦ vt écraser

dwell, pt, pp **dwelt** [dwel, dwelt] vi demeurer
▶ **dwell on** vt fus s'étendre sur

dwindle ['dwɪndl] vi diminuer, décroître

dye [daɪ] n teinture f ♦ vt teindre; **hair dye** teinture pour les cheveux

dying ['daɪɪŋ] adj mourant(e), agonisant(e)

dyke [daɪk] n (embankment) digue f

dynamic [daɪ'næmɪk] adj dynamique

dynamite ['daɪnəmaɪt] n dynamite f ♦ vt dynamiter, faire sauter à la dynamite

dyslexia [dɪs'leksɪə] n dyslexie f

— *E e* —

E, e [iː] n (letter) E, e m; (MUS): **E** mi m; **E for Edward**, (US) **E for Easy** E comme Eugène

E abbr (= east) E ♦ n abbr (DRUGS): **ecstasy**

each [iːtʃ] adj chaque ♦ pron chacun(e); **each one** chacun(e); **each other** se (or nous etc); **they hate each other** ils se détestent (mutuellement); **you are jealous of each other** vous êtes jaloux l'un de l'autre; **each day** chaque jour, tous les jours; **they have 2 books each** ils ont 2 livres chacun; **they cost £5 each** ils coûtent 5 livres (la) pièce; **each of us** chacun de nous

eager ['iːgə*] adj impatient(e), avide; ardent(e), passionné(e); (keen: pupil) plein(e) d'enthousiasme, qui se passionne pour les études; **to be eager to**

do sth être impatient de faire qch, brûler de faire qch; désirer vivement faire qch; **to be eager for** désirer vivement, être avide de

eagle ['iːgl] n aigle m

ear [ɪə*] n oreille f; (of corn) épi m; **up to one's ears in debt** endetté/e jusqu'au cou

earache ['ɪəreɪk] n douleurs fpl aux oreilles

eardrum ['ɪədrʌm] n tympan m

earl [əːl] n comte m

earlier ['əːlɪə*] adj (date etc) plus rapproché(e); (edition etc) plus ancien(ne), antérieur(e) ♦ adv plus tôt

early ['əːlɪ] adv tôt, de bonne heure; (ahead of time) en avance ♦ adj précoce, qui se manifeste (or se fait) tôt or de bonne heure; (Christians, settlers) premier(ière); **have an early night/start** couchez-vous/partez tôt or de bonne heure; **take the early train** prenez le premier train; **in the early** or **early in the spring/19th century** au début or commencement du printemps/19ème siècle; **you're early!** tu es en avance!; **early in the morning** tôt le matin; **she's in her early forties** elle a un peu plus de quarante ans or de la quarantaine; **at your earliest convenience** (COMM) dans les meilleurs délais

early retirement n retraite anticipée

earmark ['ɪəmɑːk] vt: **to earmark sth for** réserver or destiner qch à

earn [əːn] vt gagner; (COMM: yield) rapporter; **to earn one's living** gagner sa vie; **this earned him much praise, he earned much praise for this** ceci lui a valu de nombreux éloges; **he's earned his rest/reward** il mérite or a bien mérité or a bien gagné son repos/sa récompense

earnest ['əːnɪst] adj sérieux(euse) ♦ n (also: **earnest money**) acompte m, arrhes fpl; **in earnest** adv sérieusement, pour de bon

earnings ['əːnɪŋz] npl salaire m; gains mpl; (of company etc) profits mpl, bénéfices mpl

earphones ['ɪəfəunz] npl écouteurs mpl

earring ['ɪərɪŋ] n boucle f d'oreille

earshot ['ɪəʃɔt] n: **out of/within earshot** hors de portée/à portée de voix

earth [əːθ] n (gen, BRIT ELEC) terre f; (of fox etc) terrier m ♦ vt (BRIT ELEC) relier à la terre

earthenware ['əːθnwεə*] n poterie f; faïence f ♦ adj de or en faïence

earthquake ['əːθkweɪk] n tremblement m de terre, séisme m

earthy ['əːθɪ] adj (fig) terre à terre inv (truculent(e))

ease [iːz] n facilité f, aisance f ♦ vt (soothe) calmer; (loosen) relâcher, détendre; (help pass): **to ease sth in/out** faire pénétrer/sortir qch délicatement or avec douceur, faciliter la pénétration/la sortie de qch ♦ vi (situation) se détendre; **with ease** sans difficulté, aisément; **life of ease** vie oisive; **at ease** à l'aise; (MIL) au repos
▶ **ease off, ease up** vi diminuer; (slow down)

ralentir; (*relax*) se détendre

easel ['i:zl] *n* chevalet *m*

easily ['i:zɪlɪ] *adv* facilement

east [i:st] *n* est *m* ♦ *adj* d'est ♦ *adv* à l'est, vers l'est; **the East** l'Orient *m*; (*POL*) les pays *mpl* de l'Est

Easter ['i:stə*] *n* Pâques *fpl* ♦ *adj* (*holidays*) de Pâques, pascal(e)

Easter egg *n* œuf *m* de Pâques

easterly ['i:stəlɪ] *adj* d'est

eastern ['i:stən] *adj* de l'est, oriental(e); **Eastern Europe** l'Europe de l'Est; **the Eastern bloc** (*POL*) les pays *mpl* de l'Est

eastward(s) ['i:stwəd(z)] *adv* vers l'est, à l'est

easy ['i:zɪ] *adj* facile; (*manner*) aisé(e) ♦ *adv*: **to take it** *or* **things easy** ne pas se fatiguer; (*not worry*) ne pas (trop) s'en faire; **payment on easy terms** (*COMM*) facilités *fpl* de paiement; **that's easier said than done** c'est plus facile à dire qu'à faire, c'est vite dit; **I'm easy** (*col*) ça m'est égal

easy chair *n* fauteuil *m*

easy-going ['i:zɪ'gəuɪŋ] *adj* accommodant(e), facile à vivre

eat *pt* **ate**, *pp* **eaten** [i:t, eɪt, 'i:tn] *vt*, *vi* manger

▶ **eat away** *vt* (*subj: sea*) saper, éroder; (*acid*) ronger, corroder

▶ **eat away at, eat into** *vt fus* ronger, attaquer

▶ **eat out** *vi* manger au restaurant

▶ **eat up** *vt* (*food*) finir (de manger); **it eats up electricity** ça bouffe du courant, ça consomme beaucoup d'électricité

eaves [i:vz] *npl* avant-toit *m*

eavesdrop ['i:vzdrɔp] *vi*: **to eavesdrop (on)** écouter de façon indiscrète

ebb [eb] *n* reflux *m* ♦ *vi* refluer; (*fig: also*: **ebb away**) décliner; **the ebb and flow** le flux et le reflux; **to be at a low ebb** (*fig*) être bien bas(se), ne pas aller bien fort

ebony ['ebənɪ] *n* ébène *f*

EC *n abbr* (= *European Community*) CE *f* (= *Communauté européenne*)

ECB *n abbr* (= *European Central Bank*) BCE *f*, Banque centrale européenne

eccentric [ɪk'sentrɪk] *adj*, *n* excentrique *m/f*

echo, *pl* **echoes** ['ekəu] *n* écho *m* ♦ *vt* répéter; faire chorus avec ♦ *vi* résonner; faire écho

eclipse [ɪ'klɪps] *n* éclipse *f* ♦ *vt* éclipser

ecology [ɪ'kɔlədʒɪ] *n* écologie *f*

e-commerce [i:kɔmə:s] *n* commerce *m* électronique

economic [i:kə'nɔmɪk] *adj* économique; (*profitable*) rentable

economical [i:kə'nɔmɪkl] *adj* économique; (*person*) économe

economics [i:kə'nɔmɪks] *n* économie *f* politique ♦ *npl* côté *m* *or* aspect *m* économique

economize [ɪ'kɔnəmaɪz] *vi* économiser, faire des économies

economy [ɪ'kɔnəmɪ] *n* économie *f*; **economies of scale** économies d'échelle

economy class *n* (*AVIAT etc*) classe *f* touriste

economy size *n* taille *f* économique

ecstasy ['ekstəsɪ] *n* extase *f*; (*DRUGS*) ecstasy *m*; **to go into ecstasies over** s'extasier sur

ecstatic [eks'tætɪk] *adj* extatique, en extase

ECU, ecu ['eɪkju:] *n abbr* (= *European Currency Unit*) ECU *m*, écu *m*

eczema ['eksɪmə] *n* eczéma *m*

edge [edʒ] *n* bord *m*; (*of knife etc*) tranchant *m*, fil *m* ♦ *vt* border ♦ *vi*: **to edge forward** avancer petit à petit; **to edge away from** s'éloigner furtivement de; **on edge** (*fig*) = **edgy; to have the edge on** (*fig*) l'emporter (de justesse) sur, être légèrement meilleur que

edgeways ['edʒweɪz] *adv* latéralement; **he couldn't get a word in edgeways** il ne pouvait pas placer un mot

edgy ['edʒɪ] *adj* crispé(e), tendu(e)

edible ['edɪbl] *adj* comestible; (*meal*) mangeable

Edinburgh ['edɪnbərə] *n* Édimbourg

edit ['edɪt] *vt* éditer; (*magazine*) diriger; (*newspaper*) être le rédacteur *or* la rédactrice en chef de

edition [ɪ'dɪʃən] *n* édition *f*

editor ['edɪtə*] *n* (*in newspaper*) rédacteur/trice, rédacteur/trice en chef; (*of sb's work*) éditeur/trice; (*also*: **film editor**) monteur/euse

editorial [edɪ'tɔ:rɪəl] *adj* de la rédaction, éditorial(e) ♦ *n* éditorial *m*; **the editorial staff** la rédaction

educate ['edjukeɪt] *vt* instruire; éduquer; **educated at …** qui a fait ses études à …

educated ['edjukeɪtɪd] *adj* (*person*) cultivé(e)

education [edju'keɪʃən] *n* éducation *f*; (*schooling*) enseignement *m*, instruction *f*; (*at university: subject etc*) pédagogie *f*; **primary** *or* (*us*) **elementary/secondary education** instruction *f* primaire/secondaire

educational [edju'keɪʃənl] *adj* pédagogique; scolaire; (*useful*) instructif(ive); (*game, toy*) éducatif(ive); **educational technology** technologie *f* de l'enseignement

eel [i:l] *n* anguille *f*

eerie ['ɪərɪ] *adj* inquiétant(e), spectral(e), surnaturel(le)

effect [ɪ'fekt] *n* effet *m* ♦ *vt* effectuer; **to take effect** (*LAW*) entrer en vigueur, prendre effet; (*drug*) agir, faire son effet; **to put into effect** (*plan*) mettre en application *or* à exécution; **to have an effect on sb/sth** avoir *or* produire un effet sur qn/qch; **in effect** en fait; **his letter is to the effect that …** sa lettre nous apprend que …

effective [ɪ'fektɪv] *adj* efficace; (*striking: display, outfit*) frappant(e), qui produit *or* fait de l'effet; **to become effective** (*LAW*) entrer en vigueur, prendre effet; **effective date** date *f* d'effet *or* d'entrée en vigueur

effectively [ɪ'fektɪvlɪ] *adv* efficacement; (*strikingly*) d'une manière frappante, avec beaucoup d'effet; (*in reality*) effectivement, en fait

effectiveness [ɪ'fektɪvnɪs] *n* efficacité *f*

effeminate [ɪ'femɪnɪt] *adj* efféminé(e)

effervescent [efə'vesnt] *adj* effervescent(e)

efficiency [ɪ'fɪʃənsɪ] *n* efficacité *f*; rendement *m*

efficient [ɪ'fɪʃənt] *adj* efficace; (*machine, car*) d'un bon rendement

effort ['efət] *n* effort *m*; **to make an effort to do sth** faire *or* fournir un effort pour faire qch

effortless ['efətlɪs] *adj* sans effort, aisé(e)

effusive [ɪ'fju:sɪv] *adj* (*person*) expansif(ive); (*welcome*) chaleureux(euse)

e.g. *adv abbr* (= *exempli gratia*) par exemple, p. ex.

egg [eg] *n* œuf *m*
▶ **egg on** *vt* pousser

eggcup ['egkʌp] *n* coquetier *m*

eggplant ['egplɑ:nt] *n* aubergine *f*

eggshell ['egʃel] *n* coquille *f* d'œuf ◆ *adj* (*colour*) blanc cassé *inv*

ego ['i:gəu] *n* moi *m*

egotism ['egəutɪzəm] *n* égotisme *m*

egotist ['egəutɪst] *n* égocentrique *m/f*

Egypt ['i:dʒɪpt] *n* Égypte *f*

Egyptian [ɪ'dʒɪpʃən] *adj* égyptien(ne) ◆ *n* Égyptien/ne

eiderdown ['aɪdədaun] *n* édredon *m*

Eiffel Tower ['aɪfəl-] *n* tour *f* Eiffel

eight [eɪt] *num* huit

eighteen [eɪ'ti:n] *num* dix-huit

eighth [eɪtθ] *num* huitième

eighty ['eɪtɪ] *num* quatre-vingt(s)

Eire ['eərə] *n* République *f* d'Irlande

either ['aɪðə*] *adj* l'un ou l'autre; (*both, each*) chaque; **on either side** de chaque côté ◆ *pron*: **either (of them)** l'un ou l'autre; **I don't like either** je n'aime ni l'un ni l'autre ◆ *adv* non plus; **no, I don't either** moi non plus ◆ *conj*: **either good or bad** ou bon ou mauvais, soit bon soit mauvais; **I haven't seen either one or the other** je n'ai vu ni l'un ni l'autre

eject [ɪ'dʒekt] *vt* expulser; éjecter ◆ *vi* (*pilot*) s'éjecter

elaborate *adj* [ɪ'læbərɪt] compliqué(e), recherché(e), minutieux(euse) ◆ *vb* [ɪ'læbəreɪt] ◆ *vt* élaborer ◆ *vi* entrer dans les détails

elastic [ɪ'læstɪk] *adj*, *n* élastique (*m*)

elastic band *n* (*BRIT*) élastique *m*

elated [ɪ'leɪtɪd] *adj* transporté(e) de joie

elation [ɪ'leɪʃən] *n* (grande) joie, allégresse *f*

elbow ['elbəu] *n* coude *m* ◆ *vt*: **to elbow one's way through the crowd** se frayer un passage à travers la foule (en jouant des coudes)

elder ['eldə*] *adj* aîné(e) ◆ *n* (*tree*) sureau *m*; **one's elders** ses aînés

elderly ['eldəlɪ] *adj* âgé(e) ◆ *npl*: **the elderly** les personnes âgées

eldest ['eldɪst] *adj*, *n*: **the eldest (child)** l'aîné(e) (des enfants)

elect [ɪ'lekt] *vt* élire; (*choose*): **to elect to do** choisir de faire ◆ *adj*: **the president elect** le président désigné

election [ɪ'lekʃən] *n* élection *f*; **to hold an election** procéder à une élection

electioneering [ɪlekʃə'nɪərɪŋ] *n* propagande électorale, manœuvres électorales

elector [ɪ'lektə*] *n* électeur/trice

electorate [ɪ'lektərɪt] *n* électorat *m*

electric [ɪ'lektrɪk] *adj* électrique

electrical [ɪ'lektrɪkl] *adj* électrique

electric blanket *n* couverture chauffante

electric fire *n* (*BRIT*) radiateur *m* électrique

electrician [ɪlek'trɪʃən] *n* électricien *m*

electricity [ɪlek'trɪsɪtɪ] *n* électricité *f*; **to switch on/off the electricity** rétablir/couper le courant

electrify [ɪ'lektrɪfaɪ] *vt* (*RAIL*) électrifier; (*audience*) électriser

electronic [ɪlek'trɒnɪk] *adj* électronique

electronic mail *n* courrier *m* électronique

electronics [ɪlek'trɒnɪks] *n* électronique *f*

elegant ['elɪgənt] *adj* élégant(e)

element ['elɪmənt] *n* (*gen*) élément *m*; (*of heater, kettle etc*) résistance *f*

elementary [elɪ'mentərɪ] *adj* élémentaire; (*school, education*) primaire

elephant ['elɪfənt] *n* éléphant *m*

elevation [elɪ'veɪʃən] *n* élévation *f*; (*height*) altitude *f*

elevator ['elɪveɪtə*] *n* élévateur *m*, monte-charge *m inv*; (*US: lift*) ascenseur *m*

eleven [ɪ'levn] *num* onze

elevenses [ɪ'levnzɪz] *npl* (*BRIT*) ≃ pause-café *f*

eleventh [ɪ'levnθ] *adj* onzième; **at the eleventh hour** (*fig*) à la dernière minute

elicit [ɪ'lɪsɪt] *vt*: **to elicit (from)** obtenir (de); tirer (de)

eligible ['elɪdʒəbl] *adj* éligible; (*for membership*) admissible; **eligible for a pension** ayant droit à la retraite

elm [elm] *n* orme *m*

elongated ['i:lɒŋgeɪtɪd] *adj* étiré(e), allongé(e)

elope [ɪ'ləup] *vi* (*lovers*) s'enfuir (ensemble)

eloquent ['eləkwənt] *adj* éloquent(e)

else [els] *adv* d'autre; **something else** quelque chose d'autre, autre chose; **somewhere else** ailleurs, autre part; **everywhere else** partout ailleurs; **everyone else** tous les autres; **nothing else** rien d'autre; **is there anything else I can do?** est-ce que je peux faire quelque chose d'autre?; **where else?** à quel autre endroit?; **little else** pas grand-chose d'autre

elsewhere [els'wɛə*] *adv* ailleurs, autre part

elude [ɪ'luːd] *vt* échapper à; (*question*) éluder

elusive [ɪ'luːsɪv] *adj* insaisissable; (*answer*) évasif(ive)

emaciated [ɪ'meɪsɪeɪtɪd] *adj* émacié(e), décharné(e)

email [ˈiːmeɪl] *n abbr* (= electronic mail) courrier *m* électronique ◆ *vt*: **to email sb** envoyer un message électronique à qn

emancipate [ɪ'mænsɪpeɪt] *vt* émanciper

embankment [ɪm'bæŋkmənt] *n* (of road, railway) remblai *m*, talus *m*; (riverside) berge *f*, quai *m*; (dyke) digue *f*

embark [ɪm'bɑːk] *vi*: **to embark (on)** (s')embarquer (à bord de *or* sur) ◆ *vt* embarquer; **to embark on** (journey etc) commencer, entreprendre; (fig) se lancer *or* s'embarquer dans

embarkation [embɑː'keɪʃən] *n* embarquement *m*

embarrass [ɪm'bærəs] *vt* embarrasser, gêner; **to be embarrassed** être gêné(e)

embarrassing [ɪm'bærəsɪŋ] *adj* gênant(e), embarrassant(e)

embarrassment [ɪm'bærəsmənt] *n* embarras *m*, gêne *f*

embassy [ˈembəsɪ] *n* ambassade *f*; **the French Embassy** l'ambassade de France

embedded [ɪm'bedɪd] *adj* enfoncé(e)

embellish [ɪm'belɪʃ] *vt* embellir; enjoliver

embers [ˈembəz] *npl* braise *f*

embezzle [ɪm'bezl] *vt* détourner

embezzlement [ɪm'bezlmənt] *n* détournement *m* (de fonds)

embitter [ɪm'bɪtə*] *vt* aigrir; envenimer

embody [ɪm'bɔdɪ] *vt* (features) réunir, comprendre; (ideas) formuler, exprimer

embossed [ɪm'bɔst] *adj* repoussé(e), gaufré(e); **embossed with** où figure(nt) en relief

embrace [ɪm'breɪs] *vt* embrasser, étreindre; (include) embrasser, couvrir, comprendre ◆ *vi* s'embrasser, s'étreindre ◆ *n* étreinte *f*

embroider [ɪm'brɔɪdə*] *vt* broder; (fig: story) enjoliver

embroidery [ɪm'brɔɪdərɪ] *n* broderie *f*

emerald [ˈemərəld] *n* émeraude *f*

emerge [ɪ'mɜːdʒ] *vi* apparaître, surgir; **it emerges that** (BRIT) il ressort que

emergency [ɪ'mɜːdʒənsɪ] *n* urgence *f*; **in an emergency** en cas d'urgence; **state of emergency** état *m* d'urgence

emergency exit *n* sortie *f* de secours

emergency landing *n* atterrissage forcé

emergency services *npl*: **the emergency services** (fire, police, ambulance) les services *mpl* d'urgence

emery board [ˈemərɪ-] *n* lime *f* à ongles (en carton émerisé)

emigrate [ˈemɪgreɪt] *vi* émigrer

eminent [ˈemɪnənt] *adj* éminent(e)

emissions [ɪ'mɪʃənz] *npl* émissions *fpl*

emit [ɪ'mɪt] *vt* émettre

emotion [ɪ'məuʃən] *n* sentiment *m*; (as opposed to reason) émotion *f*, sentiments

emotional [ɪ'məuʃənl] *adj* (person) émotif(ive), très sensible; (scene) émouvant(e); (tone, speech) qui fait appel aux sentiments

emotive [ɪ'məutɪv] *adj* émotif(ive); **emotive power** capacité *f* d'émouvoir *or* de toucher

emperor [ˈempərə*] *n* empereur *m*

emphasis (pl: **-ases**) [ˈemfəsɪs, -siːz] *n* accent *m*; force *f*, insistance *f*; **to lay** *or* **place emphasis on sth** (fig) mettre l'accent sur, insister sur; **the emphasis is on reading** la lecture tient une place primordiale, on accorde une importance particulière à la lecture

emphasize [ˈemfəsaɪz] *vt* (syllable, word, point) appuyer *or* insister sur; (feature) souligner, accentuer

emphatic [em'fætɪk] *adj* (strong) énergique, vigoureux(euse); (unambiguous, clear) catégorique

empire [ˈempaɪə*] *n* empire *m*

employ [ɪm'plɔɪ] *vt* employer; **he's employed in a bank** il est employé de banque, il travaille dans une banque

employee [ɪmplɔɪ'iː] *n* employé/e

employer [ɪm'plɔɪə*] *n* employeur/euse

employment [ɪm'plɔɪmənt] *n* emploi *m*; **to find employment** trouver un emploi *or* du travail; **without employment** au chômage, sans emploi; **place of employment** lieu *m* de travail

employment agency *n* agence *f or* bureau *m* de placement

empower [ɪm'pauə*] *vt*: **to empower sb to do** autoriser *or* habiliter qn à faire

empress [ˈemprɪs] *n* impératrice *f*

emptiness [ˈemptɪnɪs] *n* vide *m*

empty [ˈemptɪ] *adj* vide; (street, area) désert(e); (threat, promise) en l'air, vain(e) ◆ *n* (bottle) bouteille *f* vide ◆ *vt* vider ◆ *vi* se vider; (liquid) s'écouler; **on an empty stomach** à jeun; **to empty into** (river) se jeter dans, se déverser dans

empty-handed [ˈemptɪ'hændɪd] *adj* les mains vides

EMU *n abbr* (= European Monetary Union) UME *f*

emulate [ˈemjuleɪt] *vt* rivaliser avec, imiter

emulsion [ɪ'mʌlʃən] *n* émulsion *f*; (also: **emulsion paint**) peinture mate

enable [ɪ'neɪbl] *vt*: **to enable sb to do** permettre à qn de faire, donner à qn la possibilité de faire

enamel [ɪ'næməl] *n* émail *m*

enchant [ɪn'tʃɑːnt] *vt* enchanter

enchanting [ɪn'tʃɑːntɪŋ] *adj* ravissant(e), enchanteur(eresse)

enc(l). *abbr* (on letters etc); (= enclosed, enclosure)

PJ

enclose [ɪn'kləʊz] *vt* (*land*) clôturer; (*letter etc*): **to enclose (with)** joindre (à); **please find enclosed** veuillez trouver ci-joint

enclosure [ɪn'kləʊʒə*] *n* enceinte *f*; (*in letter etc*) annexe *f*

encompass [ɪn'kʌmpəs] *vt* encercler, entourer; (*include*) contenir, inclure

encore [ɔŋ'kɔ:*] *excl*, *n* bis *m*

encounter [ɪn'kaʊntə*] *n* rencontre *f* ♦ *vt* rencontrer

encourage [ɪn'kʌrɪdʒ] *vt* encourager; (*industry, growth*) favoriser; **to encourage sb to do sth** encourager qn à faire qch

encouragement [ɪn'kʌrɪdʒmənt] *n* encouragement *m*

encroach [ɪn'krəʊtʃ] *vi*: **to encroach (up)on** empiéter sur

encyclop(a)edia [ɛnsaɪkləʊ'pi:dɪə] *n* encyclopédie *f*

end [ɛnd] *n* fin *f*; (*of table, street, line, rope etc*) bout *m*, extrémité *f*; (*of pointed object*) pointe *f*; (*of town*) bout ♦ *vt* terminer; (*also*: **bring to an end, put an end to**) mettre fin à ♦ *vi* se terminer, finir; **from end to end** d'un bout à l'autre; **to come to an end** prendre fin; **to be at an end** être fini(e), être terminé(e); **in the end** finalement; **on end** (*object*) debout, dressé(e); **to stand on end** (*hair*) se dresser sur la tête; **for 5 hours on end** durant 5 heures d'affilée *or* de suite; **for hours on end** pendant des heures (et des heures); **at the end of the day** (*BRIT fig*) en fin de compte; **to this end with this end in view** à cette fin, dans ce but

▶ **end up** *vi*: **to end up in** finir *or* se terminer par; (*place*) finir *or* aboutir à

endanger [ɪn'deɪndʒə*] *vt* mettre en danger; **an endangered species** une espèce en voie de disparition

endearing [ɪn'dɪərɪŋ] *adj* attachant(e)

endeavour, (*US*) **endeavor** [ɪn'devə*] *n* tentative *f*, effort *m* ♦ *vi*: **to endeavour to do** tenter *or* s'efforcer de faire

ending ['ɛndɪŋ] *n* dénouement *m*, conclusion *f*; (*LING*) terminaison *f*

endive ['ɛndaɪv] *n* (*curly*) chicorée *f*; (*smooth, flat*) endive *f*

endless ['ɛndlɪs] *adj* sans fin, interminable; (*patience, resources*) inépuisable, sans limites; (*possibilities*) illimité(e)

endorse [ɪn'dɔ:s] *vt* (*cheque*) endosser; (*approve*) appuyer, approuver, sanctionner

endorsement [ɪn'dɔ:smənt] *n* (*approval*) caution *f*, aval *m*; (*signature*) endossement *m*; (*BRIT: on driving licence*) contravention *f* (*portée au permis de conduire*)

endure [ɪn'djʊə*] *vt* supporter, endurer ♦ *vi* durer

enemy ['ɛnəmɪ] *adj*, *n* ennemi/e; **to make an enemy of sb** se faire un/e ennemi/e de qn, se

mettre qn à dos

energetic [ɛnə'dʒɛtɪk] *adj* énergique; (*activity*) très actif(ive), qui fait se dépenser (physiquement)

energy ['ɛnədʒɪ] *n* énergie *f*; **Department of Energy** ministère *m* de l'Énergie

enforce [ɪn'fɔ:s] *vt* (*LAW*) appliquer, faire respecter

engage [ɪn'geɪdʒ] *vt* engager; (*MIL*) engager le combat avec; (*lawyer*) prendre ♦ *vi* (*TECH*) s'enclencher, s'engrener; **to engage in** se lancer dans; **to engage sb in conversation** engager la conversation avec qn

engaged [ɪn'geɪdʒd] *adj* (*BRIT: busy, in use*) occupé(e); (*betrothed*) fiancé(e); **to get engaged** se fiancer; **he is engaged in research/a survey** il fait de la recherche/une enquête

engaged tone *n* (*BRIT TEL*) tonalité *f*, occupé *inv*

engagement [ɪn'geɪdʒmənt] *n* obligation *f*, engagement *m*; (*appointment*) rendez-vous *m inv*; (*to marry*) fiançailles *fpl*; (*MIL*) combat *m*; **I have a previous engagement** j'ai déjà un rendez-vous, je suis déjà pris/e

engagement ring *n* bague *f* de fiançailles

engaging [ɪn'geɪdʒɪŋ] *adj* engageant(e), attirant(e)

engine ['ɛndʒɪn] *n* (*AUT*) moteur *m*; (*RAIL*) locomotive *f*

engine driver *n* (*BRIT: of train*) mécanicien *m*

engineer [ɛndʒɪ'nɪə*] *n* ingénieur *m*; (*BRIT: for domestic appliances*) réparateur *m*; (*US RAIL*) mécanicien *m*; **civil/mechanical engineer** ingénieur des Travaux Publics *or* des Ponts et Chaussées/mécanicien

engineering [ɛndʒɪ'nɪərɪŋ] *n* engineering *m*, ingénierie *f*; (*of bridges, ships*) génie *m*; (*of machine*) mécanique *f* ♦ *cpd*: **engineering works** *or* **factory** atelier *m* de construction mécanique

England ['ɪŋglənd] *n* Angleterre *f*

English ['ɪŋglɪʃ] *adj* anglais(e) ♦ *n* (*LING*) anglais *m*; **the English** *npl* les Anglais; **an English speaker** un anglophone

Englishman ['ɪŋglɪʃmən], **Englishwoman** ['ɪŋglɪʃwʊmən] *n* Anglais/e

engraving [ɪn'greɪvɪŋ] *n* gravure *f*

engrossed [ɪn'grəʊst] *adj*: **engrossed in** absorbé(e) par, plongé(e) dans

engulf [ɪn'gʌlf] *vt* engloutir

enhance [ɪn'hɑ:ns] *vt* rehausser, mettre en valeur; (*position*) améliorer; (*reputation*) accroître

enjoy [ɪn'dʒɔɪ] *vt* aimer, prendre plaisir à; (*have benefit of: health, fortune*) jouir de; (: *success*) connaître; **to enjoy o.s.** s'amuser

enjoyable [ɪn'dʒɔɪəbl] *adj* agréable

enjoyment [ɪn'dʒɔɪmənt] *n* plaisir *m*

enlarge [ɪn'lɑ:dʒ] *vt* accroître; (*PHOT*) agrandir ♦ *vi*: **to enlarge on** (*subject*) s'étendre sur

enlargement [ɪn'lɑ:dʒmənt] *n* (*PHOT*) agrandissement *m*

enlighten [ɪnˈlaɪtn] vt éclairer

enlightened [ɪnˈlaɪtnd] adj éclairé(e)

enlightenment [ɪnˈlaɪtnmənt] n édification f; éclaircissements mpl; (HISTORY): **the Enlightenment** ≃ le Siècle des lumières

enlist [ɪnˈlɪst] vt recruter; (support) s'assurer ♦ vi s'engager; **enlisted man** (US MIL) simple soldat m

enmity [ˈenmɪtɪ] n inimitié f

enormous [ɪˈnɔːməs] adj énorme

enough [ɪˈnʌf] adj, n: **enough time/books** assez or suffisamment de temps/livres ♦ adv: **big enough** assez or suffisamment grand; **have you got enough?** (en) avez-vous assez?; **will 5 be enough?** est-ce que 5 suffiront?, est-ce qu'il y en aura assez avec 5?; **that's enough!** ça suffit!, assez!; **that's enough, thanks** cela suffit or c'est assez, merci; **I've had enough!** je n'en peux plus!; **he has not worked enough** il n'a pas assez or suffisamment travaillé, il n'a pas travaillé assez or suffisamment; **enough!** assez!, ça suffit!; **it's hot enough (as it is)!** il fait assez chaud comme ça!; **he was kind enough to lend me the money** il a eu la gentillesse de me prêter l'argent; **... which, funnily enough ...** qui, chose curieuse

enquire [ɪnˈkwaɪə*] vt, vi = **inquire**

enrage [ɪnˈreɪdʒ] vt mettre en fureur or en rage rendre furieux(euse)

enrol, (US) **enroll** [ɪnˈrəul] vt inscrire ♦ vi s'inscrire

enrol(l)ment [ɪnˈrəulmənt] n inscription f

en suite [ˈɒnswiːt] adj: **with en suite bathroom** avec salle de bains en attenante

ensure [ɪnˈʃuə*] vt assurer, garantir; **to ensure that** s'assurer que

entail [ɪnˈteɪl] vt entraîner, nécessiter

entangle [ɪnˈtæŋgl] vt emmêler, embrouiller; **to become entangled in sth** (fig) se laisser entraîner or empêtrer dans qch

enter [ˈentə*] vt (room) entrer dans, pénétrer dans; (club, army) entrer dans; (profession) embrasser; (competition) s'inscrire à or pour; (sb for a competition) (faire) inscrire; (write down) inscrire, noter; (COMPUT) entrer, introduire ♦ vi entrer

▶ **enter for** vt fus s'inscrire à, se présenter pour or à

▶ **enter into** vt fus (explanation) se lancer dans; (negotiations) entamer; (debate) prendre part à; (agreement) conclure

▶ **enter up** vt inscrire

▶ **enter (up)on** vt fus commencer

enterprise [ˈentəpraɪz] n (company, undertaking) entreprise f; (initiative) (esprit m d')initiative f

enterprising [ˈentəpraɪzɪŋ] adj entreprenant(e), dynamique

entertain [entəˈteɪn] vt amuser, distraire; (invite) recevoir (à dîner); (idea, plan) envisager

entertainer [entəˈteɪnə*] n artiste m/f de variétés

entertaining [entəˈteɪnɪŋ] adj amusant(e), distrayant(e) ♦ n: **to do a lot of entertaining** beaucoup recevoir

entertainment [entəˈteɪnmənt] n (amusement) distraction f, divertissement m, amusement m; (show) spectacle m

enthralled [ɪnˈθrɔːld] adj captivé(e)

enthusiasm [ɪnˈθuːzɪæzəm] n enthousiasme m

enthusiast [ɪnˈθuːzɪæst] n enthousiaste m/f; **a jazz etc enthusiast** un fervent or passionné du jazz etc

enthusiastic [ɪnθuːzɪˈæstɪk] adj enthousiaste; **to be enthusiastic about** être enthousiasmé(e) par

entire [ɪnˈtaɪə*] adj (tout) entier(ère)

entirely [ɪnˈtaɪəlɪ] adv entièrement, complètement

entirety [ɪnˈtaɪərətɪ] n: **in its entirety** dans sa totalité

entitle [ɪnˈtaɪtl] vt (allow): **to entitle sb to do** donner (le) droit à qn de faire; **to entitle sb to sth** donner droit à qch à qn

entitled [ɪnˈtaɪtld] adj (book) intitulé(e); **to be entitled to sth/to do sth** avoir droit à qch/le droit de faire qch

entrance n [ˈentrns] entrée f ♦ vt [ɪnˈtrɑːns] enchanter, ravir; **to gain entrance to** (university etc) être admis à

entrance examination n examen m d'entrée or d'admission

entrance fee n droit m d'inscription; (to museum etc) prix m d'entrée

entrance ramp n (US AUT) bretelle f d'accès

entrant [ˈentrnt] n (in race etc) participant/e, concurrent/e; (BRIT: in exam) candidat/e

entrenched [enˈtrentʃt] adj retranché(e)

entrepreneur [ˈɒntrəprəˈnɜː*] n entrepreneur m

entrust [ɪnˈtrʌst] vt: **to entrust sth to** confier qch à

entry [ˈentrɪ] n entrée f; (in register, diary) inscription f; (in ledger) écriture f; **"no entry"** "défense d'entrer", "entrée interdite"; (AUT) "sens interdit"; **single/double entry book-keeping** comptabilité f en partie simple/double

entry form n feuille f d'inscription

entry phone n (BRIT) interphone m (à l'entrée d'un immeuble)

envelop [ɪnˈveləp] vt envelopper

envelope [ˈenvələup] n enveloppe f

envious [ˈenvɪəs] adj envieux(euse)

environment [ɪnˈvaɪərnmənt] n milieu m; environnement m; **Department of the Environment** (BRIT) ministère de l'équipement et de l'aménagement du territoire

environmental [ɪnvaɪərnˈmentl] adj écologique, relatif(ive) à l'environnement; **environmental studies** (in school etc) écologie f

environment-friendly adj écologique

envisage [ɪnˈvɪzɪdʒ] vt envisager; prévoir

envoy [ˈɛnvɔɪ] n envoyé/e

envy [ˈɛnvɪ] n envie f ◆ vt envier; **to envy sb sth** envier qch à qn

epic [ˈɛpɪk] n épopée f ◆ adj épique

epidemic [ɛpɪˈdɛmɪk] n épidémie f

epilepsy [ˈɛpɪlɛpsɪ] n épilepsie f

epileptic [ɛpɪˈlɛptɪk] adj, n épileptique m/f

episode [ˈɛpɪsəʊd] n épisode m

epitome [ɪˈpɪtəmɪ] n (fig) quintessence f, type m

epitomize [ɪˈpɪtəmaɪz] vt (fig) illustrer, incarner

equal [ˈiːkwl] adj égal(e) ◆ n égal/e ◆ vt égaler; **equal to** (task) à la hauteur de; **equal to doing** de taille à or capable de faire

equality [iːˈkwɔlɪtɪ] n égalité f

equalize [ˈiːkwəlaɪz] vt, vi égaliser

equally [ˈiːkwəlɪ] adv également; (just as) tout aussi; **they are equally clever** ils sont tout aussi intelligents

equanimity [ɛkwəˈnɪmɪtɪ] n égalité f d'humeur

equate [ɪˈkweɪt] vt: **to equate sth with** comparer qch à; assimiler qch à; **to equate sth to** mettre qch en équation avec; égaler qch à

equation [ɪˈkweɪʃən] n (MATH) équation f

equator [ɪˈkweɪtə*] n équateur m

equilibrium [iːkwɪˈlɪbrɪəm] n équilibre m

equip [ɪˈkwɪp] vt équiper; **to equip sb/sth with** équiper or munir qn/qch de; **he is well equipped for the job** il a les compétences or les qualités requises pour ce travail

equipment [ɪˈkwɪpmənt] n équipement m; (electrical etc) appareillage m, installation f

equities [ˈɛkwɪtɪz] npl (BRIT COMM) actions cotées en Bourse

equivalent [ɪˈkwɪvələnt] adj équivalent(e) ◆ n équivalent m; **to be equivalent to** équivaloir à, être équivalent(e) à

era [ˈɪərə] n ère f, époque f

eradicate [ɪˈrædɪkeɪt] vt éliminer

erase [ɪˈreɪz] vt effacer

eraser [ɪˈreɪzə*] n gomme f

erect [ɪˈrɛkt] adj droit(e) ◆ vt construire; (monument) ériger, élever; (tent etc) dresser

erection [ɪˈrɛkʃən] n (PHYSIOL) érection f; (of building) construction f; (of machinery etc) installation f

ERM n abbr (= Exchange Rate Mechanism) mécanisme m des taux de change

erode [ɪˈrəʊd] vt éroder; (metal) ronger

erotic [ɪˈrɔtɪk] adj érotique

errand [ˈɛrnd] n course f, commission f; **to run errands** faire des courses; **errand of mercy** mission f de charité, acte m charitable

erratic [ɪˈrætɪk] adj irrégulier(ière), inconstant(e)

error [ˈɛrə*] n erreur f; **typing/spelling error** faute f de frappe/d'orthographe; **in error** par erreur, par méprise; **errors and omissions excepted** sauf erreur ou omission

erupt [ɪˈrʌpt] vi entrer en éruption; (fig) éclater, exploser

eruption [ɪˈrʌpʃən] n éruption f; (of anger, violence) explosion f

escalate [ˈɛskəleɪt] vi s'intensifier; (costs) monter en flèche

escalator [ˈɛskəleɪtə*] n escalier roulant

escapade [ɛskəˈpeɪd] n fredaine f; équipée f

escape [ɪˈskeɪp] n évasion f, fuite f; (of gas etc) fuite; (TECH) échappement m ◆ vi s'échapper, fuir; (from jail) s'évader; (fig) s'en tirer, en réchapper; (leak) fuir; s'échapper ◆ vt échapper à; **to escape from** (person) échapper à; (place) s'échapper de; (fig) fuir; **to escape to** (another place) fuir à, s'enfuir à; **to escape to safety** se réfugier dans or gagner un endroit sûr; **to escape notice** passer inaperçu(e)

escapism [ɪˈskeɪpɪzəm] n évasion f (fig)

escort vt [ɪˈskɔːt] escorter ◆ n [ˈɛskɔːt] escorte f; (to dance etc) cavalier m; **her escort** son compagnon or cavalier; **his escort** sa compagne

Eskimo [ˈɛskɪməʊ] adj esquimau(de), eskimo ◆ n Esquimau/de (LING) esquimau m

especially [ɪˈspɛʃlɪ] adv (specifically) spécialement, exprès; (more than usually) particulièrement; (above all) particulièrement, surtout

espionage [ˈɛspɪɑːnɑːʒ] n espionnage m

Esquire [ɪˈskwaɪə*] n (BRIT: abbr **Esq.**): **J. Brown, Esquire** Monsieur J. Brown

essay [ˈɛseɪ] n (SCOL) dissertation f; (LITERATURE) essai m; (attempt) tentative f

essence [ˈɛsns] n essence f; **in essence** en substance; **speed is of the essence** l'essentiel, c'est la rapidité

essential [ɪˈsɛnʃl] adj essentiel(le); (basic) fondamental(e) ◆ n élément essentiel; **it is essential that** il est essentiel or primordial que

essentially [ɪˈsɛnʃlɪ] adv essentiellement

establish [ɪˈstæblɪʃ] vt établir; (business) fonder, créer; (one's power etc) asseoir, affermir

established [ɪˈstæblɪʃt] adj bien établi(e)

establishment [ɪˈstæblɪʃmənt] n établissement m; création f; (institution) établissement; **the Establishment** les pouvoirs établis; l'ordre établi

estate [ɪˈsteɪt] n (land) domaine m, propriété f; (LAW) biens mpl, succession f; (BRIT: also: **housing estate**) lotissement m

estate agent n (BRIT) agent immobilier

estate car n (BRIT) break m

esteem [ɪˈstiːm] n estime f ◆ vt estimer; apprécier; **to hold sb in high esteem** tenir qn en haute estime

esthetic [ɪsˈθɛtɪk] adj (US) = **aesthetic**

estimate n [ˈɛstɪmət] estimation f; (COMM) devis m ◆ vb [ˈɛstɪmeɪt] ◆ vt estimer ◆ vi (BRIT COMM): **to esti-**

mate for estimer, faire une estimation de; (bid for) faire un devis pour; **to give sb an estimate of** faire or donner un devis à qn pour; **at a rough estimate** approximativement

estimation [ɛstɪ'meɪʃən] n opinion f; estime f; **in my estimation** à mon avis, selon moi

estranged [ɪs'treɪndʒd] adj (couple) séparé(e); (husband, wife) dont on s'est séparé(e)

etc. abbr (= et cetera) etc.

eternal [ɪ'tɜːnl] adj éternel(le)

eternity [ɪ'tɜːnɪtɪ] n éternité f

ethical ['ɛθɪkl] adj moral(e)

ethics ['ɛθɪks] n éthique f ◆ npl moralité f

Ethiopia [iːθɪ'əʊpɪə] n Éthiopie f

ethnic ['ɛθnɪk] adj ethnique; (clothes, food) folklorique, exotique; propre aux minorités ethniques non-occidentales

ethos ['iːθɒs] n (système m de) valeurs fpl

e-ticket ['iːtɪkɪt] n billet m électronique

etiquette ['ɛtɪkɛt] n convenances fpl, étiquette f

EU n abbr (= European Union) UE f

euro ['jʊərəʊ] n (currency) euro m

Euroland ['jʊərəʊlænd] n Euroland m

Europe ['jʊərəp] n Europe f

European [jʊərə'piːən] adj européen(ne) ◆ n Européen/ne

evacuate [ɪ'vækjʊeɪt] vt évacuer

evade [ɪ'veɪd] vt échapper à; (question etc) éluder; (duties) se dérober à

evaporate [ɪ'væpəreɪt] vi s'évaporer ◆ vt faire évaporer

evaporated milk [ɪ'væpəreɪtɪd-] n lait condensé (non sucré)

evasion [ɪ'veɪʒən] n dérobade f; (excuse) faux-fuyant m

eve [iːv] n: **on the eve of** à la veille de

even ['iːvn] adj régulier(ière), égal(e); (number) pair(e) ◆ adv même; **even if** même si + indicative; **even though** quand (bien) même + conditional, alors même que + conditional; **even more** encore plus; **even faster** encore plus vite; **even so** quand même; **not even** pas même; **to break even** s'y retrouver, équilibrer ses comptes; **to get even with sb** prendre sa revanche sur qn
▶ **even out** vi s'égaliser

evening ['iːvnɪŋ] n soir m; (as duration, event) soirée f; **in the evening** le soir; **this evening** ce soir; **tomorrow/yesterday evening** demain/hier soir

evening class n cours m du soir

evening dress n (man's) habit m de soirée, smoking m; (woman's) robe f de soirée

event [ɪ'vɛnt] n événement m; (SPORT) épreuve f; **in the course of events** par la suite; **in the event of** en cas de; **in the event** en réalité, en fait; **at all events** (BRIT), **in any event** en tout cas, de toute manière

eventful [ɪ'vɛntfʊl] adj mouvementé(e)

eventual [ɪ'vɛntʃʊəl] adj final(e)

eventuality [ɪvɛntʃʊ'ælɪtɪ] n possibilité f, éventualité f

eventually [ɪ'vɛntʃʊəlɪ] adv finalement

ever ['ɛvə*] adv jamais; (at all times) toujours; **the best ever** le meilleur qu'on ait jamais vu; **did you ever meet him?** est-ce qu'il vous est arrivé de le rencontrer?; **have you ever been there?** y êtes-vous déjà allé?; **for ever** pour toujours; **hardly ever** ne ... presque jamais; **ever since** adv depuis ◆ conj depuis que; **ever so pretty** si joli; **thank you ever so much** merci mille fois

evergreen ['ɛvəɡriːn] n arbre m à feuilles persistantes

everlasting [ɛvə'lɑːstɪŋ] adj éternel(le)

every ['ɛvrɪ] adj chaque; **every day** tous les jours, chaque jour; **every other/third day** tous les deux/trois jours; **every other car** une voiture sur deux; **every now and then** de temps en temps; **I have every confidence in him** j'ai entièrement or pleinement confiance en lui

everybody ['ɛvrɪbɒdɪ] pron tout le monde, tous pl; **everybody knows about it** tout le monde le sait; **everybody else** tous les autres

everyday ['ɛvrɪdeɪ] adj (expression) courant(e), d'usage courant; (use) courant; (occurrence, experience) de tous les jours, ordinaire

everyone ['ɛvrɪwʌn] = everybody

everything ['ɛvrɪθɪŋ] pron tout; **everything is ready** tout est prêt; **he did everything possible** il a fait tout son possible

everywhere ['ɛvrɪwɛə*] adv partout; **everywhere you go you meet ...** où qu'on aille, on rencontre ...

evict [ɪ'vɪkt] vt expulser

eviction [ɪ'vɪkʃən] n expulsion f

evidence ['ɛvɪdns] n (proof) preuve(s) f(pl); (of witness) témoignage m; (sign): **to show evidence of** donner des signes de; **to give evidence** témoigner, déposer; **in evidence** (obvious) en évidence; en vue

evident ['ɛvɪdnt] adj évident(e)

evidently ['ɛvɪdntlɪ] adv de toute évidence

evil ['iːvl] adj mauvais(e) ◆ n mal m

evoke [ɪ'vəʊk] vt évoquer; (admiration) susciter

evolution [iːvə'luːʃən] n évolution f

evolve [ɪ'vɒlv] vt élaborer ◆ vi évoluer, se transformer

ewe [juː] n brebis f

ex- [ɛks] prefix (former: husband, president etc) ex-; (out of): **the price ex-works** le prix départ usine

exact [ɪɡ'zækt] adj exact(e) ◆ vt: **to exact sth (from)** extorquer qch (à); exiger qch (de)

exacting [ɪɡ'zæktɪŋ] adj exigeant(e); (work) fatigant(e)

exactly [ɪɡ'zæktlɪ] adv exactement; **exactly!** parfaitement!, précisément!

exaggerate [ɪɡ'zædʒəreɪt] *vt, vi* exagérer
exaggeration [ɪɡzædʒə'reɪʃən] *n* exagération *f*
exalted [ɪɡ'zɔːltɪd] *adj* (*rank*) élevé(e); (*person*) haut placé(e); (*elated*) exalté(e)
exam [ɪɡ'zæm] *n abbr* (*SCOL*) = **examination**
examination [ɪɡzæmɪ'neɪʃən] *n* (*SCOL, MED*) examen *m*; **to take** or (*BRIT*) **sit an examination** passer un examen; **the matter is under examination** la question est à l'examen
examine [ɪɡ'zæmɪn] *vt* (*gen*) examiner; (*SCOL, LAW: person*) interroger; (*inspect: machine, premises*) inspecter; (*passport*) contrôler; (*luggage*) fouiller
examiner [ɪɡ'zæmɪnə*] *n* examinateur/trice
example [ɪɡ'zɑːmpl] *n* exemple *m*; **for example** par exemple; **to set a good/bad example** donner le bon/mauvais exemple
exasperate [ɪɡ'zɑːspəreɪt] *vt* exaspérer, agacer
exasperation [ɪɡzɑːspə'reɪʃən] *n* exaspération *f*, irritation *f*
excavate ['ɛkskəveɪt] *vt* excaver; (*object*) mettre au jour
excavation [ekskə'veɪʃən] *n* excavation *f*
exceed [ɪk'siːd] *vt* dépasser; (*one's powers*) outrepasser
exceedingly [ɪk'siːdɪŋlɪ] *adv* excessivement
excellent ['eksələnt] *adj* excellent(e)
except [ɪk'sept] *prep* (*also:* **except for, excepting**) sauf, excepté, à l'exception de ♦ *vt* excepter; **except if/when** sauf si/quand; **except that** excepté que, si ce n'est que
exception [ɪk'sepʃən] *n* exception *f*; **to take exception to** s'offusquer de; **with the exception of** à l'exception de
exceptional [ɪk'sepʃənl] *adj* exceptionnel(le)
excerpt ['eksəːpt] *n* extrait *m*
excess [ɪk'ses] *n* excès *m*; **in excess of** plus de
excess baggage *n* excédent *m* de bagages
excess fare *n* supplément *m*
excessive [ɪk'sesɪv] *adj* excessif(ive)
exchange [ɪks'tʃeɪndʒ] *n* échange *m*; (*also:* **telephone exchange**) central *m* ♦ *vt:* **to exchange (for)** échanger (contre); **in exchange for** en échange de; **foreign exchange** (*COMM*) change *m*
exchange rate *n* taux *m* de change
exchequer [ɪks'tʃekə*] *n* (*BRIT*) Échiquier *m*, ≈ ministère *m* des Finances
excise *n* ['eksaɪz] taxe *f* ♦ *vt* [ek'saɪz] exciser
excite [ɪk'saɪt] *vt* exciter; **to get excited** s'exciter
excitement [ɪk'saɪtmənt] *n* excitation *f*
exciting [ɪk'saɪtɪŋ] *adj* passionnant(e)
exclaim [ɪk'skleɪm] *vi* s'exclamer
exclamation [eksklə'meɪʃən] *n* exclamation *f*
exclamation mark *n* point *m* d'exclamation
exclude [ɪk'skluːd] *vt* exclure
exclusion zone *n* zone interdite
exclusive [ɪk'skluːsɪv] *adj* exclusif(ive); (*club, dis-*

trict) sélect(e); (*item of news*) en exclusivité ♦ *adv* (*COMM*) exclusivement, non inclus; **exclusive of VAT** TVA non comprise; **exclusive of postage** (les) frais de poste non compris; **from 1st to 15th March exclusive** du 1er au 15 mars exclusivement or exclu; **exclusive rights** (*COMM*) exclusivité *f*
excruciating [ɪk'skruːʃɪeɪtɪŋ] *adj* atroce, déchirant(e)
excursion [ɪk'skəːʃən] *n* excursion *f*
excuse *n* [ɪk'skjuːs] excuse *f* ♦ *vt* [ɪk'skjuːz] excuser; (*justify*) excuser, justifier; **to excuse sb from** (*activity*) dispenser qn de; **excuse me!** excusez-moi!, pardon!; **now if you will excuse me, ...** maintenant, si vous (le) permettez ...; **to make excuses for sb** trouver des excuses à qn; **to excuse o.s. for sth/for doing sth** s'excuser de/d'avoir fait qch
ex-directory ['eksdɪ'rektərɪ] *adj* (*BRIT*): **ex-directory (phone) number** numéro *m* (de téléphone) sur la liste rouge
execute ['eksɪkjuːt] *vt* exécuter
execution [eksɪ'kjuːʃən] *n* exécution *f*
executive [ɪɡ'zekjutɪv] *n* (*COMM*) cadre *m*; (*POL*) exécutif *m* ♦ *adj* exécutif(ive); (*position, job*) de cadre; (*secretary*) de direction; (*offices*) de la direction; (*car, plane*) de fonction
exemplify [ɪɡ'zemplɪfaɪ] *vt* illustrer
exempt [ɪɡ'zempt] *adj:* **exempt from** exempté(e) or dispensé(e) de ♦ *vt:* **to exempt sb from** exempter or dispenser qn de
exercise ['eksəsaɪz] *n* exercice *m* ♦ *vt* exercer; (*patience etc*) faire preuve de; (*dog*) promener ♦ *vi* (*also:* **to take exercise**) prendre de l'exercice
exercise book *n* cahier *m*
exert [ɪɡ'zəːt] *vt* exercer, employer; (*strength, force*) employer; **to exert o.s.** se dépenser
exertion [ɪɡ'zəːʃən] *n* effort *m*
exhale [eks'heɪl] *vt* expirer; exhaler ♦ *vi* expirer
exhaust [ɪɡ'zɔːst] *n* (*also:* **exhaust fumes**) gaz *mpl* d'échappement; (*also:* **exhaust pipe**) tuyau *m* d'échappement ♦ *vt* épuiser; **to exhaust o.s.** s'épuiser
exhausted [ɪɡ'zɔːstɪd] *adj* épuisé(e)
exhaustion [ɪɡ'zɔːstʃən] *n* épuisement *m*; **nervous exhaustion** fatigue nerveuse
exhaustive [ɪɡ'zɔːstɪv] *adj* très complet(ète)
exhibit [ɪɡ'zɪbɪt] *n* (*ART*) pièce *f* or objet *m* exposé(e) (*LAW*) pièce à conviction ♦ *vt* exposer; (*courage, skill*) faire preuve de
exhibition [eksɪ'bɪʃən] *n* exposition *f*; **exhibition of temper** manifestation *f* de colère
exhilarating [ɪɡ'zɪləreɪtɪŋ] *adj* grisant(e), stimulant(e)
ex-husband ['eks'hʌzbənd] *n* ex-mari *m*
exile ['eksaɪl] *n* exil *m*; (*person*) exilé/e ♦ *vt* exiler; **in exile** en exil
exist [ɪɡ'zɪst] *vi* exister
existence [ɪɡ'zɪstəns] *n* existence *f*; **to be in ex-**

istence exister

existing [ɪgˈzɪstɪŋ] *adj* (*laws*) existant(e); (*system, regime*) actuel(le)

exit [ˈɛksɪt] *n* sortie *f* ♦ *vi* (COMPUT, THEAT) sortir

exit poll *n* sondage *m* (*fait à la sortie de l'isoloir*)

exit ramp *n* (US AUT) bretelle *f* d'accès

exodus [ˈɛksədəs] *n* exode *m*

exonerate [ɪgˈzɒnəreɪt] *vt*: **to exonerate from** disculper de

exotic [ɪgˈzɒtɪk] *adj* exotique

expand [ɪkˈspænd] *vt* (*area*) agrandir; (*quantity*) accroître; (*influence etc*) étendre ♦ *vi* (*population, production*) s'accroître; (*trade, influence etc*) se développer, s'étendre; (*gas, metal*) se dilater, dilater; **to expand on** (*notes, story etc*) développer

expanse [ɪkˈspæns] *n* étendue *f*

expansion [ɪkˈspænʃən] *n see* **expand** développement *m*; accroissement *m*; extension *f*; dilatation *f*

expect [ɪkˈspɛkt] *vt* (*anticipate*) s'attendre à, s'attendre à ce que + *sub*; (*count on*) compter sur, escompter; (*hope for*) espérer; (*require*) demander, exiger; (*suppose*) supposer; (*await: also baby*) attendre ♦ *vi*: **to be expecting** être enceinte; **to expect sb to do** (*anticipate*) s'attendre à ce que qn fasse; (*demand*) attendre de qn qu'il fasse; **to expect to do sth** penser or compter faire qch, s'attendre à faire qch; **as expected** comme prévu; **I expect so** je crois que oui, je crois bien

expectancy [ɪksˈpɛktənsɪ] *n* attente *f*; **life expectancy** espérance *f* de vie

expectant [ɪkˈspɛktənt] *adj* qui attend (quelque chose); **expectant mother** future maman

expectation [ɛkspɛkˈteɪʃən] *n* attente *f*, prévisions *fpl*; espérance(s) *f(pl)*; **in expectation of** dans l'attente de, en prévision de; **against** or **contrary to all expectation(s)** contre toute attente, contrairement à ce qu'on attendait; **to come** or **live up to sb's expectations** répondre à l'attente or aux espérances de qn

expedient [ɪkˈspiːdɪənt] *adj* indiqué(e), opportun(e), commode ♦ *n* expédient *m*

expedition [ɛkspəˈdɪʃən] *n* expédition *f*

expel [ɪkˈspɛl] *vt* chasser, expulser; (SCOL) renvoyer, exclure

expend [ɪkˈspɛnd] *vt* consacrer; (*use up*) dépenser

expenditure [ɪkˈspɛndɪtʃə*] *n* dépense *f*; dépenses *fpl*

expense [ɪkˈspɛns] *n* (*cost*) coût *m*; (*spending*) dépense *f*, frais *mpl*; **expenses** *npl* frais *mpl*; dépenses; **to go to the expense of** faire la dépense de; **at great/little expense** à grands/peu de frais; **at the expense of** aux frais de; (*fig*) aux dépens de

expense account *n* (note *f* de) frais *mpl*

expensive [ɪkˈspɛnsɪv] *adj* cher(chère) coûteux(euse); **to be expensive** coûter cher; **expensive tastes** goûts *mpl* de luxe

experience [ɪkˈspɪərɪəns] *n* expérience *f* ♦ *vt* connaître; éprouver; **to know by experience** savoir par expérience

experienced [ɪkˈspɪərɪənst] *adj* expérimenté(e)

experiment [ɪkˈspɛrɪmənt] *n* expérience *f* ♦ *vi* faire une expérience; **to experiment with** expérimenter; **to perform** or **carry out an experiment** faire une expérience; **as an experiment** à titre d'expérience

expert [ˈɛkspəːt] *adj* expert(e) ♦ *n* expert *m*; **expert in** or **at doing sth** spécialiste de qch; **an expert on sth** un spécialiste de qch; **expert witness** (LAW) expert *m*

expertise [ɛkspəːˈtiːz] *n* (grande) compétence

expire [ɪkˈspaɪə*] *vi* expirer

expiry [ɪkˈspaɪərɪ] *n* expiration *f*

explain [ɪkˈspleɪn] *vt* expliquer

▶ **explain away** *vt* justifier, excuser

explanation [ɛkspləˈneɪʃən] *n* explication *f*; **to find an explanation for sth** trouver une explication à qch

explanatory [ɪkˈsplænətrɪ] *adj* explicatif(ive)

explicit [ɪkˈsplɪsɪt] *adj* explicite; (*definite*) formel(le)

explode [ɪkˈspləud] *vi* exploser ♦ *vt* faire exploser; (*fig: theory*) démolir; **to explode a myth** détruire un mythe

exploit *n* [ˈɛksplɔɪt] exploit *m* ♦ *vt* [ɪkˈsplɔɪt] exploiter

exploitation [ɛksplɔɪˈteɪʃən] *n* exploitation *f*

exploratory [ɪkˈsplɔrətrɪ] *adj* (*fig: talks*) préliminaire; **exploratory operation** (MED) intervention *f* (à visée) exploratrice

explore [ɪkˈsplɔː*] *vt* explorer; (*possibilities*) étudier, examiner

explorer [ɪkˈsplɔːrə*] *n* explorateur/trice

explosion [ɪkˈspləuʒən] *n* explosion *f*

explosive [ɪkˈspləusɪv] *adj* explosif(ive) ♦ *n* explosif *m*

exponent [ɪkˈspəunənt] *n* (*of school of thought etc*) interprète *m*, représentant *m*; (MATH) exposant *m*

export *vt* [ɛkˈspɔːt] exporter ♦ *n* [ˈɛkspɔːt] exportation *f* ♦ *cpd* d'exportation

exporter [ɛkˈspɔːtə*] *n* exportateur *m*

expose [ɪkˈspəuz] *vt* exposer; (*unmask*) démasquer, dévoiler; **to expose o.s.** (LAW) commettre un outrage à la pudeur

exposed [ɪkˈspəuzd] *adj* (*land, house*) exposé(e); (ELEC: *wire*) à nu; (*pipe, beam*) apparent(e)

exposure [ɪkˈspəuʒə*] *n* exposition *f*; (PHOT) (temps *m* de pose *f*; (: *shot*) pose; **suffering from exposure** (MED) souffrant des effets du froid et de l'épuisement; **to die of exposure** (MED) mourir de froid

exposure meter *n* posemètre *m*

express [ɪkˈsprɛs] *adj* (*definite*) formel(le), exprès(esse); (BRIT: letter etc) exprès inv ◆ n (train) rapide m ◆ adv (send) exprès ◆ vt exprimer; **to express o.s.** s'exprimer

expression [ɪk'sprɛʃən] n expression f

expressly [ɪk'sprɛslɪ] adv expressément, formellement

expressway [ɪk'sprɛsweɪ] n (US) voie f express (à plusieurs files)

exquisite [ɛk'skwɪzɪt] adj exquis(e)

extend [ɪk'stɛnd] vt (visit, street) prolonger; (deadline) reporter, remettre; (building) agrandir; (offer) présenter, offrir; (COMM: credit) accorder ◆ vi (land) s'étendre

extension [ɪk'stɛnʃən] n (see extend) prolongation f; agrandissement m; (building) annexe f; (to wire, table) rallonge f; (telephone: in offices) poste m; (: in private house) téléphone m supplémentaire; **extension 3718** (TEL) poste 3718

extensive [ɪk'stɛnsɪv] adj étendu(e), vaste; (damage, alterations) considérable; (inquiries) approfondi(e); (use) largement répandu(e)

extensively [ɪk'stɛnsɪvlɪ] adv (altered, damaged etc) considérablement; **he's travelled extensively** il a beaucoup voyagé

extent [ɪk'stɛnt] n étendue f; (degree: of damage, loss) importance f; **to some extent** dans une certaine mesure; **to a certain extent** dans une certaine mesure, jusqu'à un certain point; **to a large extent** en grande partie; **to what extent?** dans quelle mesure?, jusqu'à quel point?; **to such an extent that …** à tel point que …

extenuating [ɪk'stɛnjueɪtɪŋ] adj: **extenuating circumstances** circonstances atténuantes

exterior [ɛk'stɪərɪə*] adj extérieur(e), du dehors ◆ n extérieur m; dehors m

external [ɛk'stə:nl] adj externe ◆ n: **the externals** les apparences fpl; **for external use only** (MED) à usage externe

extinct [ɪk'stɪŋkt] adj éteint(e)

extinguish [ɪk'stɪŋgwɪʃ] vt éteindre

extort [ɪk'stɔ:t] vt: **to extort sth (from)** extorquer qch (à)

extortionate [ɪk'stɔ:ʃnɪt] adj exorbitant(e)

extra ['ɛkstrə] adj supplémentaire, de plus ◆ adv (in addition) en plus ◆ n supplément m; (THEAT) figurant/e; **wine will cost extra** le vin sera en supplément; **extra large sizes** très grandes tailles

extract vt [ɪk'strækt] extraire; (tooth) arracher; (money, promise) soutirer ◆ n ['ɛkstrækt] extrait m

extracurricular ['ɛkstrəkə'rɪkjulə*] adj (SCOL) parascolaire

extradite ['ɛkstrədaɪt] vt extrader

extramarital ['ɛkstrə'mærɪtl] adj extraconjugal(e)

extramural ['ɛkstrə'mjuərl] adj hors-faculté inv

extraordinary [ɪk'strɔ:dnrɪ] adj extraordinaire; **the extraordinary thing is that …** le plus étrange or étonnant c'est que …

extravagance [ɪk'strævəgəns] n (excessive spending) prodigalités fpl; (thing bought) folie f, dépense excessive or exagérée

extravagant [ɪk'strævəgənt] adj extravagant(e); (in spending: person) prodigue, dépensier(ière); (: tastes) dispendieux(euse)

extreme [ɪk'stri:m] adj, n extrême (m); **the extreme left/right** (POL) l'extrême gauche f/droite f; **extremes of temperature** différences fpl extrêmes de température

extremely [ɪk'stri:mlɪ] adv extrêmement

extremist [ɪk'stri:mɪst] adj, n extrémiste m/f

extricate ['ɛkstrɪkeɪt] vt: **to extricate sth (from)** dégager qch (de)

extrovert ['ɛkstrəvə:t] n extraverti/e

ex-wife ['ɛkswaɪf] n ex-femme f

eye [aɪ] n œil m (pl yeux); (of needle) trou m, chas m ◆ vt examiner; **as far as the eye can see** à perte de vue; **to keep an eye on** surveiller; **to have an eye for sth** avoir l'œil pour qch; **in the public eye** en vue; **with an eye to doing sth** (BRIT) en vue de faire qch; **there's more to this than meets the eye** ce n'est pas aussi simple que cela paraît

eyebrow ['aɪbrau] n sourcil m

eyedrops ['aɪdrɔps] npl gouttes fpl pour les yeux

eyelash ['aɪlæʃ] n cil m

eyelid ['aɪlɪd] n paupière f

eyeliner ['aɪlaɪnə*] n eye-liner m

eye-opener ['aɪəupnə*] n révélation f

eyeshadow ['aɪʃædəu] n ombre f à paupières

eyesight ['aɪsaɪt] n vue f

eyesore ['aɪsɔ:*] n horreur f, chose f qui dépare or enlaidit

eye witness n témoin m oculaire

— F f —

F, f [ɛf] n (letter) F, f m; (MUS): **F** fa m; **F for Frederick**, (US) **F for Fox** F comme François

F abbr (= Fahrenheit) F

fable ['feɪbl] n fable f

fabric ['fæbrɪk] n tissu m ◆ cpd: **fabric ribbon** n (for typewriter) ruban m (en) tissu

fabulous ['fæbjuləs] adj fabuleux(euse); (col: super) formidable, sensationnel(le)

face [feɪs] n visage m, figure f; expression f; grimace f; (of clock) cadran m; (of building) façade f; (side, surface) face f ◆ vt faire face à; (facts etc) accepter; **face down** (person) à plat ventre; (card) face en dessous; **to lose/save face** perdre/sauver la face; **to pull a face** faire une grimace; **in the face of** (difficulties etc) face à, devant; **on the face of it** à première vue

▶ **face up to** vt fus faire face à, affronter

face cloth n (BRIT) gant m de toilette

face cream n crème f pour le visage

face lift n lifting m; (of façade etc) ravalement m, retapage m

face powder n poudre f (pour le visage)

face value ['feɪs'væljuː] n (of coin) valeur nominale; **to take sth at face value** (fig) prendre qch pour argent comptant

facility [fə'sɪlɪtɪ] n facilité f; **facilities** npl installations fpl, équipement m; **credit facilities** facilités de paiement

facing ['feɪsɪŋ] prep face à, en face de ♦ n (of wall etc) revêtement m; (SEWING) revers m

facsimile [fæk'sɪmɪlɪ] n (exact replica) facsimilé m; (also: **facsimile machine**) télécopieur m; (transmitted document) télécopie f

fact [fækt] n fait m; **in fact** en fait; **to know for a fact that ...** savoir pertinemment que ...

factor ['fæktə*] n facteur m; (COMM) factor m, société f d'affacturage; (: agent) dépositaire m/f ♦ vi faire du factoring; **safety factor** facteur de sécurité

factory ['fæktərɪ] n usine f, fabrique f

factual ['fæktjuəl] adj basé(e) sur les faits

faculty ['fækəltɪ] n faculté f; (US: teaching staff) corps enseignant

fad [fæd] n (col) manie f; engouement m

fade [feɪd] vi se décolorer, passer; (light, sound, hope) s'affaiblir, disparaître; (flower) se faner

▶ **fade in** vt (picture) ouvrir en fondu; (sound) monter progressivement

▶ **fade out** vt (picture) fermer en fondu; (sound) baisser progressivement

fag [fæg] n (BRIT col: cigarette) sèche f; (: chore): **what a fag!** quelle corvée!; (US col: homosexual) pédé m

fail [feɪl] vt (exam) échouer à; (candidate) recaler; (subj: courage, memory) faire défaut à ♦ vi échouer; (supplies) manquer; (eyesight, health, light: also: **be failing**) baisser, s'affaiblir; (brakes) lâcher; **to fail to do sth** (neglect) négliger de or ne pas faire qch; (be unable) ne pas arriver or parvenir à faire qch; **without fail** à coup sûr; sans faute

failing ['feɪlɪŋ] n défaut m ♦ prep faute de; **failing that** à défaut, sinon

failure ['feɪljə*] n échec m; (person) raté/e; (mechanical etc) défaillance f; **his failure to turn up** le fait de n'être pas venu or qu'il ne soit pas venu

faint [feɪnt] adj faible; (recollection) vague; (mark) à peine visible; (smell, breeze, trace) léger(ère) ♦ n évanouissement m ♦ vi s'évanouir; **to feel faint** défaillir

fair [fɛə*] adj équitable, juste; (reasonable) correct(e), honnête; (hair) blond(e); (skin, complexion) pâle, blanc(blanche); (weather) beau(belle); (good enough) assez bon(ne) ♦ adv: **to play fair** jouer franc jeu ♦ n foire f; (BRIT: funfair) fête (foraine); (also: **trade fair**) foire(-exposition) commerciale;

it's not fair! ce n'est pas juste!; **a fair amount of** une quantité considérable de

fairly ['fɛəlɪ] adv équitablement; (quite) assez; **I'm fairly sure** j'en suis quasiment or presque sûr

fairness ['fɛənɪs] n (of trial etc) justice f, équité f; (of person) sens m de la justice; **in all fairness** en toute justice

fairy ['fɛərɪ] n fée f

fairy tale n conte m de fées

faith [feɪθ] n foi f; (trust) confiance f; (sect) culte m, religion f; **to have faith in sb/sth** avoir confiance en qn/qch

faithful ['feɪθful] adj fidèle

faithfully ['feɪθfəlɪ] adv fidèlement; **yours faithfully** (BRIT: in letters) veuillez agréer l'expression de mes salutations les plus distinguées

fake [feɪk] n (painting etc) faux m; (photo) trucage m; (person) imposteur m ♦ adj faux(fausse) ♦ vt (emotions) simuler; (photo) truquer; (story) fabriquer; **his illness is a fake** sa maladie est une comédie or de la simulation

falcon ['fɔːlkən] n faucon m

fall [fɔːl] n chute f; (decrease) baisse f; (US: autumn) automne m ♦ vi, pt **fell**, pp **fallen** [fɛl, 'fɔːlən] tomber; **falls** npl (waterfall) chute f d'eau, cascade f; **to fall flat** vi (on one's face) tomber de tout son long, s'étaler; (joke) tomber à plat; (plan) échouer; **to fall short of** (sb's expectations) ne pas répondre à; **a fall of snow** (BRIT) une chute de neige

▶ **fall apart** vi tomber en morceaux; (col: emotionally) craquer

▶ **fall back** vi reculer, se retirer

▶ **fall back on** vt fus se rabattre sur; **to have something to fall back on** (money etc) avoir quelque chose en réserve; (job etc) avoir une solution de rechange

▶ **fall behind** vi prendre du retard

▶ **fall down** vi (person) tomber; (building) s'effondrer, s'écrouler

▶ **fall for** vt fus (trick) se laisser prendre à; (person) tomber amoureux(euse) de

▶ **fall in** vi s'effondrer; (MIL) se mettre en rangs

▶ **fall in with** vt fus (sb's plans etc) accepter

▶ **fall off** vi tomber; (diminish) baisser, diminuer

▶ **fall out** vi (friends etc) se brouiller

▶ **fall over** vi tomber (par terre)

▶ **fall through** vi (plan, project) tomber à l'eau

fallacy ['fæləsɪ] n erreur f, illusion f

fallout ['fɔːlaut] n retombées (radioactives)

fallow ['fæləu] adj en jachère; en friche

false [fɔːls] adj faux(fausse); **under false pretences** sous un faux prétexte

false alarm n fausse alerte

false teeth npl (BRIT) fausses dents

falter ['fɔːltə*] vi chanceler, vaciller

fame [feɪm] n renommée f, renom m

familiar [fə'mɪlɪə*] adj familier(ière); **to be fa-**

miliar with sth connaître qch; **to make o.s. familiar with sth** se familiariser avec qch; **to be on familiar terms with sb** bien connaître qn

family ['fæmɪlɪ] n famille f

famine ['fæmɪn] n famine f

famished ['fæmɪʃt] adj affamé(e); **I'm famished!** (col) je meurs de faim!

famous ['feɪməs] adj célèbre

famously ['feɪməslɪ] adv (get on) fameusement, à merveille

fan [fæn] n (folding) éventail m; (ELEC) ventilateur m; (person) fan m, admirateur/trice; (SPORT) supporter m/f ♦ vt éventer; (fire, quarrel) attiser

▶ **fan out** vi se déployer (en éventail)

fanatic [fə'nætɪk] n fanatique m/f

fan belt n courroie f de ventilateur

fancy ['fænsɪ] n fantaisie f, envie f; imagination f ♦ cpd (de) fantaisie inv ♦ vt (feel like, want) avoir envie de; (imagine) imaginer; **to take a fancy to** se prendre d'affection pour; s'enticher de; **it took or caught my fancy** ça m'a plu; **when the fancy takes him** quand ça lui prend; **to fancy that ...** se figurer or s'imaginer que …; **he fancies her** elle lui plaît

fancy dress n déguisement m, travesti m

fancy-dress ball [fænsɪ'drɛs-] n bal masqué or costumé

fang [fæŋ] n croc m; (of snake) crochet m

fantastic [fæn'tæstɪk] adj fantastique

fantasy ['fæntəsɪ] n imagination f, fantaisie f; fantasme m

far [fɑː*] adj: **the far side/end** l'autre côté/bout; **the far left/right** (POL) l'extrême gauche f/droite f ♦ adv loin; **is it far to London?** est-ce qu'on est loin de Londres?; **it's not far (from here)** ce n'est pas loin (d'ici); **far away, far off** au loin, dans le lointain; **far better** beaucoup mieux; **far from** loin de; **by far** de loin, de beaucoup; **as far back as the 13th century** dès le 13e siècle; **go as far as the farm** allez jusqu'à la ferme; **as far as I know** pour autant que je sache; **as far as possible** dans la mesure du possible; **how far have you got with your work?** où en êtes-vous dans votre travail?

faraway ['fɑːrəweɪ] adj lointain(e); (look) absent(e)

farce [fɑːs] n farce f

fare [fɛə*] n (on trains, buses) prix m du billet; (in taxi) prix de la course; (passenger in taxi) client m; (food) table f, chère f ♦ vi se débrouiller

Far East n: **the Far East** l'Extrême-Orient m

farewell [fɛə'wɛl] excl, n adieu m ♦ cpd (party etc) d'adieux

farm [fɑːm] n ferme f ♦ vt cultiver

▶ **farm out** vt (work etc) distribuer

farmer ['fɑːmə*] n fermier/ière, cultivateur/trice

farmhand ['fɑːmhænd] n ouvrier/ière agricole

farmhouse ['fɑːmhaus] n (maison f de) ferme f

farming ['fɑːmɪŋ] n agriculture f; **intensive**

farming culture intensive; **sheep farming** élevage m du mouton

farmland ['fɑːmlænd] n terres cultivées or arables

farm worker n = **farmhand**

farmyard ['fɑːmjɑːd] n cour f de ferme

far-reaching ['fɑː'riːtʃɪŋ] adj d'une grande portée

fart [fɑːt] (col!) n pet m ♦ vi péter

farther ['fɑːðə*] adv plus loin ♦ adj plus eloigné(e), plus lointain(e)

farthest ['fɑːðɪst] superlative of **far**

fascinate ['fæsɪneɪt] vt fasciner, captiver

fascinating ['fæsɪneɪtɪŋ] adj fascinant(e)

fascism ['fæʃɪzəm] n fascisme m

fashion ['fæʃən] n mode f; (manner) façon f, manière f ♦ vt façonner; **in fashion** à la mode; **out of fashion** démodé(e); **in the Greek fashion** à la grecque; **after a fashion** (finish, manage etc) tant bien que mal

fashionable ['fæʃnəbl] adj à la mode

fashion show n défilé m de mannequins or de mode

fast [fɑːst] adj rapide; (clock): **to be fast** avancer; (dye, colour) grand or bon teint inv ♦ adv vite, rapidement; (stuck, held) solidement ♦ n jeûne m ♦ vi jeûner; **my watch is 5 minutes fast** ma montre avance de 5 minutes; **fast asleep** profondément endormi; **as fast as I can** aussi vite que je peux; **to make a boat fast** (BRIT) amarrer un bateau

fasten ['fɑːsn] vt attacher, fixer; (coat) attacher, fermer ♦ vi se fermer, s'attacher

▶ **fasten (up)on** vt fus (idea) se cramponner à

fastener ['fɑːsnə*], **fastening** ['fɑːsnɪŋ] n fermeture f, attache f; (BRIT: zip fastener) fermeture éclair® inv or à glissière

fast food n fast food m, restauration f rapide

fastidious [fæs'tɪdɪəs] adj exigeant(e), difficile

fat [fæt] adj gros(se) ♦ n graisse f; (on meat) gras m; **to live off the fat of the land** vivre grassement

fatal ['feɪtl] adj fatal(e); (leading to death) mortel(le)

fatality [fə'tælɪtɪ] n (road death etc) victime f, décès m

fate [feɪt] n destin m; (of person) sort m; **to meet one's fate** trouver la mort

fateful ['feɪtful] adj fatidique

father ['fɑːðə*] n père m

father-in-law ['fɑːðərənlɔː] n beau-père m

fatherly ['fɑːðəlɪ] adj paternel(le)

fathom ['fæðəm] n brasse f (= 1828 mm) ♦ vt (mystery) sonder, pénétrer

fatigue [fə'tiːg] n fatigue f; (MIL) corvée f; **metal fatigue** fatigue du métal

fatten ['fætn] vt, vi engraisser; **chocolate is fattening** le chocolat fait grossir

fatty ['fætɪ] adj (food) gras(se) ♦ n (col) gros/grosse

fatuous ['fætjʊəs] *adj* stupide

faucet ['fɔ:sɪt] *n* (*US*) robinet *m*

fault [fɔ:lt] *n* (*defect*) défaut *m*; (*GEO*) faille *f* ◆ *vt* trouver des défauts à, prendre en défaut; **it's my fault** c'est de ma faute; **to find fault with** trouver à redire *or* à critiquer à; **at fault** fautif(ive), coupable; **to a fault** à l'excès

faulty ['fɔ:ltɪ] *adj* défectueux(euse)

fauna ['fɔ:nə] *n* faune *f*

favour, (*US*) **favor** ['feɪvə*] *n* faveur *f*; (*help*) service *m* ◆ *vt* (*proposition*) être en faveur de; (*pupil etc*) favoriser; (*team, horse*) donner gagnant; **to do sb a favour** rendre un service à qn; **in favour of** en faveur de; **to be in favour of sth/of doing sth** être partisan de qch/de faire qch; **to find favour with sb** trouver grâce aux yeux de qn

favo(u)rable ['feɪvrəbl] *adj* favorable; (*price*) avantageux(euse)

favo(u)rite ['feɪvrɪt] *adj, n* favori/te

fawn [fɔ:n] *n* faon *m* ◆ *adj* (*also:* **fawn-coloured**) fauve ◆ *vi:* **to fawn (up)on** flatter servilement

fax [fæks] *n* (*document*) télécopie *f*; (*machine*) télécopieur *m* ◆ *vt* envoyer par télécopie

FBI *n abbr* (*US:* = *Federal Bureau of Investigation*) FBI *m*

fear [fɪə*] *n* crainte *f*, peur *f* ◆ *vt* craindre ◆ *vi:* **to fear for** craindre pour; **to fear that** craindre que; **fear of heights** vertige *m*; **for fear of** de peur que + *sub or* de + *infinitive*

fearful ['fɪəful] *adj* craintif(ive); (*sight, noise*) affreux(euse), épouvantable; **to be fearful of** avoir peur de, craindre

fearless ['fɪəlɪs] *adj* intrépide, sans peur

feasible ['fi:zəbl] *adj* faisable, réalisable

feast [fi:st] *n* festin *m*, banquet *m*; (*REL: also:* **feast day**) fête *f* ◆ *vi* festoyer; **to feast on** se régaler de

feat [fi:t] *n* exploit *m*, prouesse *f*

feather ['feðə*] *n* plume *f* ◆ *vt:* **to feather one's nest** (*fig*) faire sa pelote ◆ *cpd* (*bed etc*) de plumes

feature ['fi:tʃə*] *n* caractéristique *f*; (*article*) chronique *f*, rubrique *f* ◆ *vt* (*subj: film*) avoir pour vedette(s) ◆ *vi* figurer (en bonne place); **features** *npl* (*of face*) traits *mpl*; **a (special) feature on sth/sb** un reportage sur qch/qn; **it featured prominently in ...** cela a figuré en bonne place sur *or* dans ...

feature film *n* long métrage

February ['februərɪ] *n* février *m*; *for phrases see also* **July**

fed [fed] *pt, pp of* **feed**: **to be fed up** en avoir marre *or* plein le dos

federal ['fedərəl] *adj* fédéral(e)

fee [fi:] *n* rémunération *f*; (*of doctor, lawyer*) honoraires *mpl*; (*of school, college etc*) frais *mpl* de scolarité; (*for examination*) droits *mpl*; **entrance/membership fee** droit d'entrée/d'inscription; **for a small fee** pour une somme modique

feeble ['fi:bl] *adj* faible

feed [fi:d] *n* (*of baby*) tétée *f*; (*of animal*) fourrage *m*; pâture *f*; (*on printer*) mécanisme *m* d'alimentation ◆ *vt, pt, pp* **fed** [fed] nourrir; (*horse etc*) donner à manger à; (*machine*) alimenter; (*data etc*): **to feed sth into** fournir qch à, introduire qch dans

▶ **feed back** *vt* (*results*) donner en retour

▶ **feed on** *vt fus* se nourrir de

feedback ['fi:dbæk] *n* feed-back *m*; (*from person*) réactions *fpl*

feel [fi:l] *n* sensation *f* ◆ *vt, pt, pp* **felt** [felt] (*touch*) toucher; tâter, palper; (*cold, pain*) sentir; (*grief, anger*) ressentir, éprouver; (*think, believe*): **to feel (that)** trouver que; **I feel that you ought to do it** il me semble que vous devriez le faire; **to feel hungry/cold** avoir faim/froid; **to feel lonely/better** se sentir seul/mieux; **I don't feel well** je ne me sens pas bien; **to feel sorry for** avoir pitié de; **it feels soft** c'est doux au toucher; **it feels colder here** je trouve qu'il fait plus froid ici; **it feels like velvet** on dirait du velours, ça ressemble au velours; **to feel like** (*want*) avoir envie de; **to feel about** *or* **around** fouiller, tâtonner; **to get the feel of sth** (*fig*) s'habituer à qch

feeler ['fi:lə*] *n* (*of insect*) antenne *f*; (*fig*): **to put out a feeler** *or* **feelers** tâter le terrain

feeling ['fi:lɪŋ] *n* sensation *f*, sentiment *m*; (*impression*) sentiment; **to hurt sb's feelings** froisser qn; **feelings ran high about it** cela a déchaîné les passions; **what are your feelings about the matter?** quel est votre sentiment sur cette question?; **my feeling is that ...** j'estime que ...; **I have a feeling that ...** j'ai l'impression que ...

feet [fi:t] *npl of* **foot**

feign [feɪn] *vt* feindre, simuler

fell [fel] *pt of* **fall** ◆ *vt* (*tree*) abattre ◆ *n* (*BRIT: mountain*) montagne *f*; (*: moorland*): **the fells** la lande ◆ *adj:* **with one fell blow** d'un seul coup

fellow ['feləu] *n* type *m*; (*comrade*) compagnon *m*; (*of learned society*) membre *m*; (*of university*) universitaire *m/f* (*membre du conseil*) ◆ *cpd:* **their fellow prisoners/students** leurs camarades prisonniers/étudiants; **his fellow workers** ses collègues *mpl* (de travail)

fellow citizen *n* concitoyen/ne

fellow countryman *n* compatriote *m*

fellow men *npl* semblables *mpl*

fellowship ['feləuʃɪp] *n* (*society*) association *f*; (*comradeship*) amitié *f*, camaraderie *f*; (*SCOL*) sorte de bourse universitaire

felony ['felənɪ] *n* (*LAW*) crime *m*, forfait *m*

felt [felt] *pt, pp of* **feel** ◆ *n* feutre *m*

felt-tip pen ['felttɪp-] *n* stylo-feutre *m*

female ['fi:meɪl] *n* (*ZOOL*) femelle *f*; (*pej: woman*) bonne femme ◆ *adj* (*BIOL, ELEC*) femelle; (*sex, character*) féminin(e); (*vote etc*) des femmes; (*child etc*) du sexe féminin; **male and female students** étudiants et étudiantes

feminine ['femɪnɪn] *adj* féminin(e) ◆ *n* féminin *m*

feminist ['femɪnɪst] n féministe m/f

fence [fɛns] n barrière f; (SPORT) obstacle m; (col: person) receleur/euse ♦ vt (also: **fence in**) clôturer ♦ vi faire de l'escrime; **to sit on the fence** (fig) ne pas se mouiller

fencing ['fɛnsɪŋ] n (sport) escrime m

fend [fɛnd] vi: **to fend for o.s.** se débrouiller (tout seul)

▶ **fend off** vt (attack etc) parer

fender ['fɛndə*] n (of fireplace) garde-feu m inv; (on boat) défense f; (US: of car) aile f

ferment vi [fə'mɛnt] fermenter ♦ n ['fə:mɛnt] agitation f, effervescence f

fern [fə:n] n fougère f

ferocious [fə'rəufəs] adj féroce

ferret ['fɛrɪt] n furet m

▶ **ferret about, ferret around** vi fureter

▶ **ferret out** vt dénicher

ferry ['fɛrɪ] n (small) bac m; (large: also: **ferryboat**) ferry(-boat m) m ♦ vt transporter; **to ferry sth/sb across** or **over** faire traverser qch/qn

fertile ['fə:taɪl] adj fertile; (BIOL) fécond(e); **fertile period** période f de fécondité

fertilizer ['fə:tɪlaɪzə*] n engrais m

fester ['fɛstə*] vi suppurer

festival ['fɛstɪvəl] n (REL) fête f; (ART, MUS) festival m

festive ['fɛstɪv] adj de fête; **the festive season** (BRIT: Christmas) la période des fêtes

festivities [fɛs'tɪvɪtɪz] npl réjouissances fpl

festoon [fɛs'tu:n] vt: **to festoon with** orner de

fetch [fɛtʃ] vt aller chercher; (BRIT: sell for) se vendre; **how much did it fetch?** ça a atteint quel prix?

▶ **fetch up** vi (BRIT) se retrouver

fête [feɪt] n fête f, kermesse f

feud [fju:d] n dispute f, dissension f ♦ vi se disputer, se quereller; **a family feud** une querelle de famille

fever ['fi:və*] n fièvre f; **he has a fever** il a de la fièvre

feverish ['fi:vərɪʃ] adj fiévreux(euse), fébrile

few [fju:] adj peu de ♦ pron: **few succeed** il y en a peu qui réussissent, (bien) peu réussissent; **they were few** ils étaient peu (nombreux), il y en avait peu; **a few** quelques ...; **I know a few** j'en connais quelques-uns; **quite a few ...** un certain nombre de ..., pas mal de ...; **in the next few days** dans les jours qui viennent; **in the past few days** ces derniers jours; **every few days/months** tous les deux ou trois jours/mois; **a few more ...** encore quelques ..., quelques ... de plus

fewer ['fju:ə*] adj moins de ♦ pron moins; **they are fewer now** il y en a moins maintenant, ils sont moins (nombreux) maintenant

fewest ['fju:ɪst] adj le moins nombreux

fiancé [fɪ'ã:ŋseɪ] n fiancé m

fiancée [fɪ'ã:ŋseɪ] n fiancée f

fib [fɪb] n bobard m

fibre, (US) **fiber** ['faɪbə*] n fibre f

fibreglass, (US) **fiberglass** ['faɪbəglɑ:s] n fibre f de verre

fickle ['fɪkl] adj inconstant(e) volage, capricieux(euse)

fiction ['fɪkʃən] n romans mpl, littérature f romanesque; (invention) fiction f

fictional ['fɪkʃənl] adj fictif(ive)

fictitious [fɪk'tɪʃəs] adj fictif(ive), imaginaire

fiddle ['fɪdl] n (MUS) violon m; (cheating) combine f; escroquerie f ♦ vt (BRIT: accounts) falsifier, maquiller; **tax fiddle** fraude fiscale, combine f pour échapper au fisc; **to work a fiddle** traficoter

▶ **fiddle with** vt fus tripoter

fidget ['fɪdʒɪt] vi se trémousser, remuer

field [fi:ld] n champ m; (fig) domaine m, champ; (SPORT: ground) terrain m; (COMPUT) champ, zone f; **to lead the field** (SPORT, COMM) dominer; **the children had a field day** (fig) c'était un grand jour pour les enfants

fieldwork ['fi:ldwə:k] n travaux mpl pratiques (or recherches fpl) sur le terrain

fiend [fi:nd] n démon m

fierce [fɪəs] adj (look) féroce, sauvage; (wind, attack) (très) violent(e); (fighting, enemy) acharné(e)

fiery ['faɪərɪ] adj ardent(e), brûlant(e), fougueux(euse)

fifteen [fɪf'ti:n] num quinze

fifth [fɪfθ] num cinquième

fifty ['fɪftɪ] num cinquante

fifty-fifty ['fɪftɪ'fɪftɪ] adv: **to share fifty-fifty with sb** partager moitié-moitié avec qn ♦ adj: **to have a fifty-fifty chance (of success)** avoir une chance sur deux (de réussir)

fig [fɪg] n figue f

fight [faɪt] n bagarre f; (MIL) combat m; (against cancer etc) lutte f ♦ vb, pt, pp **fought** [fɔ:t] vt se battre contre; (cancer, alcoholism) combattre, lutter contre; (LAW: case) défendre ♦ vi se battre; (fig): **to fight (for/against)** lutter (pour/contre)

fighter ['faɪtə*] n lutteur m; (fig: plane) chasseur m

fighting ['faɪtɪŋ] n combats mpl; (brawls) bagarres fpl

figment ['fɪgmənt] n: **a figment of the imagination** une invention

figurative ['fɪgjurətɪv] adj figuré(e)

figure ['fɪgə*] n (DRAWING, GEOM) figure f; (number, cipher) chiffre m; (body, outline) silhouette f, ligne f, formes fpl; (person) personnage m ♦ vt (US) supposer ♦ vi (appear) figurer; (US: make sense) s'expliquer; **public figure** personnalité f; **figure of speech** figure f de rhétorique

▶ **figure on** vt fus (US): **to figure on doing** compter faire

▶ **figure out** vt arriver à comprendre; calculer

figurehead ['fɪgəhed] n (NAUT) figure f de proue

(pej) prête-nom *m*

file [faɪl] *n (tool)* lime *f; (dossier)* dossier *m; (folder)* dossier, chemise *f; (: binder)* classeur *m; (comput)* fichier *m; (row)* file *f* ◆ *vt (nails, wood)* limer; *(papers)* classer; *(law: claim)* faire enregistrer; déposer ◆ *vi:* **to file in/out** entrer/sortir l'un derrière l'autre; **to file past** défiler devant; **to file a suit against sb** *(law)* intenter un procès à qn

filing cabinet *n* classeur *m (meuble)*

fill [fɪl] *vt* remplir; *(vacancy)* pourvoir à ◆ *n:* **to eat one's fill** manger à sa faim

▶ **fill in** *vt (hole)* boucher; *(form)* remplir; *(details, report)* compléter

▶ **fill out** *vt (form, receipt)* remplir

▶ **fill up** *vt* remplir ◆ *vi (aut)* faire le plein; **fill it up, please** *(aut)* le plein, s'il vous plaît

fillet ['fɪlɪt] *n* filet *m* ◆ *vt* préparer en filets

fillet steak *n* filet *m* de bœuf, tournedos *m*

filling ['fɪlɪŋ] *n (culin)* garniture *f*, farce *f; (for tooth)* plombage *m*

filling station *n* station *f* d'essence

film [fɪlm] *n* film *m; (phot)* pellicule *f*, film ◆ *vt (scene)* filmer

film star *n* vedette *f* de cinéma

filter ['fɪltə*] *n* filtre *m* ◆ *vt* filtrer

filter lane *n (brit aut: at traffic lights)* voie *f* de dégagement; *(: on motorway)* voie *f* de sortie

filter tip *n* bout *m* filtre

filth [fɪlθ] *n* saleté *f*

filthy ['fɪlθɪ] *adj* sale, dégoûtant(e); *(language)* ordurier(ière), grossier(ière)

fin [fɪn] *n (of fish)* nageoire *f*

final ['faɪnl] *adj* final, dernier(ière); *(decision, answer)* définitif(ive) ◆ *n (sport)* finale *f;* **finals** *npl (scol)* examens *mpl* de dernière année; **final demand** *(on invoice etc)* dernier rappel

finale [fɪˈnɑːlɪ] *n* finale *m*

finalist ['faɪnəlɪst] *n (sport)* finaliste *m/f*

finalize ['faɪnəlaɪz] *vt* mettre au point

finally ['faɪnəlɪ] *adv (lastly)* en dernier lieu; *(eventually)* enfin, finalement; *(irrevocably)* définitivement

finance [faɪˈnæns] *n* finance *f* ◆ *vt* financer; **finances** *npl* finances *fpl*

financial [faɪˈnænʃəl] *adj* financier(ière); **financial statement** bilan *m*, exercice financier

find [faɪnd] *vt, pt, pp* **found** [faʊnd] trouver; *(lost object)* retrouver ◆ *n* trouvaille *f*, découverte *f;* **to find sb guilty** *(law)* déclarer qn coupable; **to find (some) difficulty in doing sth** avoir du mal à faire qch

▶ **find out** *vt* se renseigner sur; *(truth, secret)* découvrir; *(person)* démasquer ◆ *vi:* **to find out about** se renseigner sur; *(by chance)* apprendre

findings ['faɪndɪŋz] *npl (law)* conclusions *fpl*, verdict *m; (of report)* constatations *fpl*

fine [faɪn] *adj* beau(belle); excellent(e); *(subtle, not coarse)* fin(e) ◆ *adv (well)* très bien; *(small)* fin, finement ◆ *n (law)* amende *f;* contravention *f* ◆ *vt (law)* condamner à une amende; donner une contravention à; **he's fine** il va bien; **the weather is fine** il fait beau; **you're doing fine** c'est bien, vous vous débrouillez bien; **to cut it fine** calculer un peu juste

fine arts *npl* beaux-arts *mpl*

finery ['faɪnərɪ] *n* parure *f*

finger ['fɪŋgə*] *n* doigt *m* ◆ *vt* palper, toucher

fingernail ['fɪŋgəneɪl] *n* ongle *m* (de la main)

fingerprint ['fɪŋgəprɪnt] *n* empreinte digitale ◆ *vt (person)* prendre les empreintes digitales de

fingertip ['fɪŋgətɪp] *n* bout *m* du doigt; *(fig):* **to have sth at one's fingertips** avoir qch à sa disposition; *(knowledge)* savoir qch sur le bout du doigt

finish ['fɪnɪʃ] *n* fin *f; (sport)* arrivée *f; (polish etc)* finition *f* ◆ *vt* finir, terminer ◆ *vi* finir, se terminer; *(session)* s'achever; **to finish doing sth** finir de faire qch; **to finish third** arriver *or* terminer troisième

▶ **finish off** *vt* finir, terminer; *(kill)* achever

▶ **finish up** *vi, vt* finir

finishing line ['fɪnɪʃɪŋ-] *n* ligne *f* d'arrivée

finite ['faɪnaɪt] *adj* fini(e); *(verb)* conjugué(e)

Finland ['fɪnlənd] *n* Finlande *f*

Finn [fɪn] *n* Finnois/e, Finlandais/e

Finnish ['fɪnɪʃ] *adj* finnois(e), finlandais(e) ◆ *n (ling)* finnois *m*

fir [fəː*] *n* sapin *m*

fire ['faɪə*] *n* feu *m;* incendie *m* ◆ *vt (discharge):* **to fire a gun** tirer un coup de feu; *(fig)* enflammer, animer; *(dismiss)* mettre à la porte, renvoyer ◆ *vi* tirer, faire feu ◆ *cpd:* **fire hazard, fire risk: that's a fire hazard** *or* **risk** cela présente un risque d'incendie; **on fire** en feu; **to set fire to sth, set sth on fire** mettre le feu à qch; **insured against fire** assuré contre l'incendie

fire alarm *n* avertisseur *m* d'incendie

firearm ['faɪərɑːm] *n* arme *f* à feu

fire brigade *n (brit)* (régiment *m* de sapeurs-)pompiers *mpl*

fire department *n (us)* = **fire brigade**

fire engine *n* pompe *f* à incendie

fire escape *n* escalier *m* de secours

fire extinguisher *n* extincteur *m*

fireman ['faɪəmən] *n* pompier *m*

fireplace ['faɪəpleɪs] *n* cheminée *f*

fireside ['faɪəsaɪd] *n* foyer *m*, coin *m* du feu

fire station *n* caserne *f* de pompiers

firewood ['faɪəwʊd] *n* bois *m* de chauffage

firework ['faɪəwəːk] *n* feu *m* d'artifice; **fireworks** *npl (display)* feu(x) d'artifice

firing squad *n* peloton *m* d'exécution

firm [fəːm] *adj* ferme ◆ *n* compagnie *f*, firme *f*

first [fəːst] *adj* premier(ière) ◆ *adv (before others)* le premier, la première; *(before other things)* en premier, d'abord; *(when listing reasons etc)* en premier

lieu, premièrement ♦ n (person: in race) premier/
ière; (BRIT SCOL) mention f très bien; (AUT) première f;
the first of January le premier janvier; **at first** au
commencement, au début; **first of all** tout d'abord,
pour commencer; **in the first instance** en premier
lieu; **I'll do it first thing tomorrow** je le ferai tout
de suite demain matin

first aid n premiers secours or soins

first-aid kit ['fɑːst'eɪd-] n trousse f pharmacie

first-class ['fɑːst'klɑːs] adj de première classe

first-hand ['fɑːst'hænd] adj de première main

first lady n (US) femme f du président

firstly ['fɑːstlɪ] adv premièrement, en premier lieu

first name n prénom m

first-rate ['fɑːst'reɪt] adj excellent(e)

fish [fɪʃ] n (pl inv) poisson m; poissons mpl ♦ vt, vi
pêcher; **to fish a river** pêcher dans une rivière; **to
go fishing** aller à la pêche

fisherman ['fɪʃəmən] n pêcheur m

fish farm n établissement m piscicole

fish fingers npl (BRIT) bâtonnets de poisson
(congelés)

fishing boat ['fɪʃɪŋ-] n barque f de pêche

fishing line ['fɪʃɪŋ-] n ligne f (de pêche)

fishing rod ['fɪʃɪŋ-] n canne f à pêche

fishing tackle ['fɪʃɪŋ-] n attirail m de pêche

fishmonger ['fɪʃmʌŋɡə*] n marchand m de poisson; **fishmonger's (shop)** poissonnerie f

fish slice n (BRIT) pelle f à poisson

fish sticks npl (US) = **fish fingers**

fishy ['fɪʃɪ] adj (fig) suspect(e), louche

fist [fɪst] n poing m

fit [fɪt] adj (MED, SPORT) en (bonne) forme; (proper)
convenable; approprié(e) ♦ vt (subj: clothes) aller à;
(adjust) ajuster; (put in, attach) installer, poser;
adapter; (equip) équiper, garnir, munir ♦ vi (clothes)
aller; (parts) s'adapter; (in space, gap) entrer, s'adapter ♦ n (MED) accès m, crise f; (of coughing) quinte f;
fit to en état de; **fit for** digne de; apte à; **to keep fit**
se maintenir en forme; **this dress is a tight/good
fit** cette robe est un peu juste/(me) va très bien; **a
fit of anger** un accès de colère; **to have a fit** (MED)
faire or avoir une crise; (col) piquer une crise; **by fits
and starts** par à-coups

▶ **fit in** vi s'accorder; (person) s'adapter

▶ **fit out** vt (BRIT: also: **fit up**) équiper

fitful ['fɪtful] adj intermittent(e)

fitment ['fɪtmənt] n meuble encastré, élément m

fitness ['fɪtnɪs] n (MED) forme f physique; (of
remark) à-propos m, justesse f

fitted carpet ['fɪtɪd-] n moquette f

fitted kitchen ['fɪtɪd-] n (BRIT) cuisine équipée

fitter ['fɪtə*] n monteur m; (DRESSMAKING) essa-
yeur/euse

fitting ['fɪtɪŋ] adj approprié(e) ♦ n (of dress)
essayage m; (of piece of equipment) pose f, installation f

fitting room n (in shop) cabine f d'essayage

five [faɪv] num cinq

fiver ['faɪvə*] n (col: BRIT) billet m de cinq livres; (: US)
billet de cinq dollars

fix [fɪks] vt fixer; (sort out) arranger; (mend) réparer;
(make ready: meal, drink) préparer; (col: game etc)
truquer ♦ n: **to be in a fix** être dans le pétrin

▶ **fix up** vt (meeting) arranger; **to fix sb up with
sth** faire avoir qch à qn

fixation [fɪkˈseɪʃən] n (PSYCH) fixation f; (fig) obsession f

fixed [fɪkst] adj (prices etc) fixe; **there's a fixed
charge** il y a un prix forfaitaire; **how are you fixed
for money?** (col) question fric, ça va?

fixture ['fɪkstʃə*] n installation f (fixe); (SPORT) rencontre f (au programme)

fizzy ['fɪzɪ] adj pétillant(e), gazeux(euse)

flabbergasted ['flæbəgɑːstɪd] adj sidéré(e), ahu-
ri(e)

flabby ['flæbɪ] adj mou(molle)

flag [flæɡ] n drapeau m; (also: **flagstone**) dalle
♦ vi faiblir; fléchir; **flag of convenience** pavillon n
de complaisance

▶ **flag down** vt héler, faire signe (de s'arrêter) à

flagpole ['flæɡpəul] n mât m

flagship ['flæɡʃɪp] n vaisseau m amiral; (fig) produit m vedette

flair [flɛə*] n flair m

flak [flæk] n (MIL) tir antiaérien; (col: criticism) critiques fpl

flake [fleɪk] n (of rust, paint) écaille f; (of snow, soap
powder) flocon m ♦ vi (also: **flake off**) s'écailler

flamboyant [flæmˈbɔɪənt] adj flamboyant(e),
éclatant(e); (person) haut(e) en couleur

flame [fleɪm] n flamme f

flamingo [fləˈmɪŋɡəu] n flamant m (rose)

flammable ['flæməbl] adj inflammable

flan [flæn] n (BRIT) tarte f

flank [flæŋk] n flanc m ♦ vt flanquer

flannel ['flænl] n (BRIT: also: **face flannel**) gant m
de toilette; (fabric) flanelle f; (BRIT col) baratin m
flannels npl pantalon m de flanelle

flap [flæp] n (of pocket, envelope) rabat m ♦ vt
(wings) battre (de) ♦ vi (sail, flag) claquer; (col: also:
be in a flap) paniquer

flare [flɛə*] n fusée éclairante; (in skirt etc) évase-
ment m

▶ **flare up** vi s'embraser; (fig: person) se mettre en
colère, s'emporter; (: revolt) éclater

flash [flæʃ] n éclair m; (also: **news flash**) flash m
(d'information); (PHOT) flash ♦ vt (switch on) allume
(brièvement); (direct): **to flash sth at** braquer qc
sur; (flaunt) étaler, exhiber; (send: message) câble
♦ vi briller; jeter des éclairs; (light on ambulance etc
clignoter; **in a flash** en un clin d'œil; **to flash one'**
headlights faire un appel de phares; **he flashe**
by or **past** il passa (devant nous) comme un éclai

flashbulb ['flæʃbʌlb] n ampoule f de flash

flashcube ['flæʃkjuːb] n cube-flash m

flashlight ['flæʃlaɪt] n lampe f de poche

flashy ['flæʃi] adj (pej) tape-à-l'œil inv, tapageur(euse)

flask [flɑːsk] n flacon m, bouteille f; (CHEM) ballon m; (also: **vacuum flask**) bouteille f thermos®

flat [flæt] adj plat(e); (tyre) dégonflé(e), à plat; (denial) catégorique; (MUS) bémolisé(e); (: voice) faux (fausse) ◆ n (BRIT: rooms) appartement m; (AUT) crevaison f, pneu crevé; (MUS) bémol m; **flat out** (work) sans relâche; (race) à fond; **flat rate of pay** (COMM) salaire m fixe

flatly ['flætlɪ] adv catégoriquement

flatten ['flætn] vt (also: **flatten out**) aplatir; (house, city) raser

flatter ['flætə*] vt flatter

flattering ['flætərɪŋ] adj flatteur(euse); (clothes etc) seyant(e)

flattery ['flætərɪ] n flatterie f

flaunt [flɔːnt] vt faire étalage de

flavour, (US) **flavor** ['fleɪvə*] n goût m, saveur f; (of ice cream etc) parfum m ◆ vt parfumer, aromatiser; **vanilla-flavoured** à l'arôme de vanille, vanillé(e); **to give** or **add flavour to** donner du goût à, relever

flavo(u)ring ['fleɪvərɪŋ] n arôme m (synthétique)

flaw [flɔː] n défaut m

flawless ['flɔːlɪs] adj sans défaut

flax [flæks] n lin m

flea [fliː] n puce f

fleck [flek] n (of dust) particule f; (of mud, paint, colour) tacheture f, moucheture f ◆ vt tacher, éclabousser; **brown flecked with white** brun moucheté de blanc

flee, pt, pp **fled** [fliː, fled] vt fuir, s'enfuir de ◆ vi fuir, s'enfuir

fleece [fliːs] n toison f ◆ vt (col) voler, filouter

fleet [fliːt] n flotte f; (of lorries, cars etc) parc m; convoi m

fleeting ['fliːtɪŋ] adj fugace, fugitif(ive); (visit) très bref(brève)

Flemish ['flemɪʃ] adj flamand(e) ◆ n (LING) flamand m; **the Flemish** npl les Flamands

flesh [fleʃ] n chair f

flesh wound [-wuːnd] n blessure superficielle

flew [fluː] pt of **fly**

flex [fleks] n fil m or câble m électrique (souple) ◆ vt fléchir; (muscles) tendre

flexible ['fleksəbl] adj flexible; (person, schedule) souple

flick [flɪk] n petite tape; chiquenaude f; sursaut m

▶ **flick through** vt fus feuilleter

flicker ['flɪkə*] vi vaciller ◆ n vacillement m; **a flicker of light** une brève lueur

flier ['flaɪə*] n aviateur m

flight [flaɪt] n vol m; (escape) fuite f; (also: **flight of steps**) escalier m; **to take flight** prendre la fuite; **to put to flight** mettre en fuite

flight attendant n (US) steward m, hôtesse f de l'air

flight deck n (AVIAT) poste m de pilotage; (NAUT) pont m d'envol

flimsy ['flɪmzɪ] adj (partition, fabric) peu solide, mince; (excuse) pauvre, mince

flinch [flɪntʃ] vi tressaillir; **to flinch from** se dérober à, reculer devant

fling [flɪŋ] vt, pt, pp **flung** [flʌŋ] jeter, lancer ◆ n (love affair) brève liaison, passade f

flint [flɪnt] n silex m; (in lighter) pierre f (à briquet)

flip [flɪp] n chiquenaude f ◆ vt donner une chiquenaude à; (US: pancake) faire sauter ◆ vi: **to flip for sth** (US) jouer qch à pile ou face

▶ **flip through** vt fus feuilleter

flippant ['flɪpənt] adj désinvolte, irrévérencieux(euse)

flipper ['flɪpə*] n (of animal) nageoire f; (for swimmer) palme f

flirt [fləːt] vi flirter ◆ n flirteuse f

float [fləut] n flotteur m; (in procession) char m; (sum of money) réserve f ◆ vi flotter; (bather) flotter, faire la planche ◆ vt faire flotter; (loan, business, idea) lancer

flock [flɔk] n troupeau m; (of birds) vol m; (of people) foule f

flog [flɔg] vt fouetter

flood [flʌd] n inondation f; (of words, tears etc) flot m, torrent m ◆ vt inonder; (AUT: carburettor) noyer; **to flood the market** (COMM) inonder le marché; **in flood** en crue

flooding ['flʌdɪŋ] n inondation f

floodlight ['flʌdlaɪt] n projecteur m ◆ vt éclairer aux projecteurs, illuminer

floor [flɔː*] n sol m; (storey) étage m; (of sea, valley) fond m; (fig: at meeting): **the floor** l'assemblée f, les membres mpl de l'assemblée ◆ vt terrasser; (baffle) désorienter; **on the floor** par terre; **ground floor,** (US) **first floor** rez-de-chaussée m; **first floor,** (US) **second floor** premier étage; **top floor** dernier étage; **to have the floor** (speaker) avoir la parole

floorboard ['flɔːbɔːd] n planche f (du plancher)

floor show n spectacle m de variétés

flop [flɔp] n fiasco m ◆ vi (fail) faire fiasco

floppy ['flɔpɪ] adj lâche, flottant(e); **floppy disk** disquette m; **floppy hat** chapeau m à bords flottants

flora ['flɔːrə] n flore f

floral ['flɔːrl] adj floral(e)

florid ['flɔrɪd] adj (complexion) fleuri(e); (style) plein(e) de fioritures

florist ['flɔrɪst] n fleuriste m/f; **florist's (shop)** magasin m or boutique f de fleuriste

flounder ['flaundə*] n (ZOOL) flet m ◆ vi patauger

flour ['flauə*] n farine f

flourish ['flʌrɪʃ] vi prospérer ◆ vt brandir ◆ n floriture f; (of trumpets) fanfare f

flout [flaut] vt se moquer de, faire fi de

flow [fləu] n (of water, traffic etc) écoulement m; (tide, influx) flux m; (of orders, letters etc) flot m; (of blood, ELEC) circulation f; (of river) courant m ◆ vi couler; (traffic) s'écouler; (robes, hair) flotter

flow chart, flow diagram n organigramme m

flower ['flauə*] n fleur f ◆ vi fleurir; **in flower** en fleur

flower bed n plate-bande f

flowerpot ['flauəpɔt] n pot m (à fleurs)

flowery ['flauərɪ] adj fleuri(e)

flown [fləun] pp of **fly**

flu [flu:] n grippe f

fluctuate ['flʌktjueɪt] vi varier, fluctuer

fluent ['flu:ənt] adj (speech, style) coulant(e), aisé(e); **he's a fluent speaker/reader** il s'exprime/lit avec aisance or facilité; **he speaks fluent French, he's fluent in French** il parle le français couramment

fluff [flʌf] n duvet m; peluche f

fluffy ['flʌfɪ] adj duveteux(euse), pelucheux(euse); **fluffy toy** jouet m en peluche

fluid ['flu:ɪd] n fluide m; (in diet) liquide m ◆ adj fluide

fluke [flu:k] n (col) coup m de veine

flung [flʌŋ] pt, pp of **fling**

fluoride ['fluəraɪd] n fluor m

flurry ['flʌrɪ] n (of snow) rafale f, bourrasque f; **flurry of activity/excitement** affairement m/excitation f soudain(e)

flush [flʌʃ] n rougeur f; (fig) éclat m; afflux m ◆ vt nettoyer à grande eau; (also: **flush out**) débusquer ◆ vi rougir ◆ adj (col) en fonds; (level): **flush with** au ras de, de niveau avec; **to flush the toilet** tirer la chasse (d'eau); **hot flushes** (MED) bouffées fpl de chaleur

flushed ['flʌʃt] adj (tout(e)) rouge

flustered ['flʌstəd] adj énervé(e)

flute [flu:t] n flûte f

flutter ['flʌtə*] n agitation f; (of wings) battement m ◆ vi battre des ailes, voleter; (person) aller et venir dans une grande agitation

flux [flʌks] n: **in a state of flux** fluctuant sans cesse

fly [flaɪ] n (insect) mouche f; (on trousers: also: **flies**) braguette f ◆ vb, pt **flew**, pp **flown** [flu:, fləun] vt (plane) piloter; (passengers, cargo) transporter (par avion); (distance) parcourir ◆ vi voler; (passengers) aller en avion; (escape) s'enfuir, fuir; (flag) se déployer; **to fly open** s'ouvrir brusquement; **to fly off the handle** s'énerver, s'emporter

▶ **fly away** vi s'envoler

▶ **fly in** vi (plane) atterrir; (person): **he flew in yesterday** il est arrivé hier (par avion)

▶ **fly off** vi s'envoler

▶ **fly out** vi see **fly in** s'envoler, partir (par avion)

fly-drive ['flaɪdraɪv] n formule f avion plus voiture

flying ['flaɪɪŋ] n (activity) aviation f ◆ adj: **flying visit** visite f éclair inv; **with flying colours** haut la main; **he doesn't like flying** il n'aime pas voyager en avion

flying saucer n soucoupe volante

flying start n: **to get off to a flying start** faire un excellent départ

flyover ['flaɪəuvə*] n (BRIT: overpass) saut-de-mouton m, pont autoroutier

flysheet ['flaɪʃi:t] n (for tent) double toit m

foal [fəul] n poulain m

foam [fəum] n écume f; (on beer) mousse f; (also: **plastic foam**) mousse cellulaire or de plastique ◆ vi écumer; (soapy water) mousser

fob [fɔb] n (also: **watch fob**) chaîne f, ruban m ◆ vt: **to fob sb off with** refiler à qn; se débarrasser de qn avec

focal point n foyer m; (fig) centre m de l'attention, point focal

focus, pl **focuses** ['fəukəs] n foyer m; (of interest) centre m ◆ vt (field glasses etc) mettre au point (light rays) faire converger ◆ vi: **to focus (on)** (with camera) régler la mise au point (sur); (person) fixer son regard (sur); **in focus** au point; **out of focus** pas au point

fodder ['fɔdə*] n fourrage m

foe [fəu] n ennemi m

fog [fɔg] n brouillard m

foggy ['fɔgɪ] adj: **it's foggy** il y a du brouillard

fog lamp, (US) **fog light** n (AUT) phare m anti-brouillard

foil [fɔɪl] vt déjouer, contrecarrer ◆ n feuille f de métal; (kitchen foil) papier m d'alu(minium); (FENCING) fleuret m; **to act as a foil to** (fig) servir de repoussoir or de faire-valoir à

fold [fəuld] n (bend, crease) pli m; (AGR) parc m à moutons; (fig) bercail m ◆ vt plier; **to fold one's arms** croiser les bras

▶ **fold up** vi (map etc) se plier, se replier; (business) fermer boutique ◆ vt (map etc) plier, replier

folder ['fəuldə*] n (for papers) chemise f; (: binder) classeur m; (brochure) dépliant m; (COMPUT) répertoire m

folding ['fəuldɪŋ] adj (chair, bed) pliant(e)

foliage ['fəulɪɪdʒ] n feuillage m

folk [fəuk] npl gens mpl ◆ cpd folklorique; **folk** npl famille f, parents mpl

folklore ['fəuklɔ:*] n folklore m

folksong ['fəuksɔŋ] n chanson f folklorique (contemporary) chanson folk inv

follow ['fɔləu] vt suivre ◆ vi suivre; (result) s'ensuivre; **to follow sb's advice** suivre les conseils de qn; **I don't quite follow you** je ne vous suis plus; **to follow in sb's footsteps** emboîter le pas à qn; (fig) suivre les traces de qn; **it follows that ...** de ce fait, il s'ensuit que ...; **he followed suit** il fit de même

▶ **follow out** vt (idea, plan) poursuivre, mener à terme

▶ **follow through** vt = **follow out**

▶ **follow up** vt (victory) tirer parti de; (letter, offer) donner suite à; (case) suivre

follower ['fɒləʊə*] n disciple m/f, partisan/e

following ['fɒləʊɪŋ] adj suivant(e) ♦ n partisans mpl, disciples mpl

folly ['fɒlɪ] n inconscience f; sottise f; (building) folie f

fond [fɒnd] adj (memory, look) tendre, affectueux(euse); **to be fond of** aimer beaucoup

fondle ['fɒndl] vt caresser

font [fɒnt] n (REL) fonts baptismaux; (TYP) police f de caractères

food [fuːd] n nourriture f

food mixer n mixeur m

food poisoning n intoxication f alimentaire

food processor n robot m de cuisine

foodstuffs ['fuːdstʌfs] npl denrées fpl alimentaires

fool [fuːl] n idiot/e; (HIST: of king) bouffon m, fou m; (CULIN) purée f de fruits à la crème ♦ vt berner, duper ♦ vi (also: **fool around**) faire l'idiot or l'imbécile; **to make a fool of sb** (ridicule) ridiculiser qn; (trick) avoir or duper qn; **to make a fool of o.s.** se couvrir de ridicule; **you can't fool me** vous (ne) me la ferez pas, on (ne) me la fait pas

▶ **fool about, fool around** vi (pej: waste time) traînailler, glandouiller; (: behave foolishly) faire l'imbécile

foolhardy ['fuːlhɑːdɪ] adj téméraire, imprudent(e)

foolish ['fuːlɪʃ] adj idiot(e), stupide; (rash) imprudent(e)

foolproof ['fuːlpruːf] adj (plan etc) infaillible

foot [fut], pl **feet** [fut, fiːt] n (gen) pied m; (measure) pied (= 30.48 cm; 12 inches); (of animal) patte f ♦ vt (bill) casquer, payer; **on foot** à pied; **to find one's feet** (fig) s'acclimater; **to put one's foot down** (AUT) appuyer sur le champignon; (say no) s'imposer

footage ['futɪdʒ] n (CINE: length) ≈ métrage m; (: material) séquences fpl

football ['futbɔːl] n ballon m (de football); (sport) (BRIT) football m; (US) football américain

football player n footballeur m, joueur m de football

football pools npl (US) ≈ loto m sportif, ≈ pronostics mpl (sur les matchs de football); voir encadré

FOOTBALL POOLS

Les **football pools** – ou plus familièrement les **pools** – sont une sorte de loto sportif britannique où l'on parie sur les matches de football qui se jouent tous les samedis. L'expression consacrée en anglais est "to do the pools". Les parieurs envoient à l'avance les fiches qu'ils ont complétées à l'organisme qui gère les paris et ils attendent les résultats, qui sont annoncés à 17h le samedi. Les sommes gagnées se comptent parfois en milliers (ou même en millions) de livres sterling.

footbrake ['futbreɪk] n frein m à pédale

footbridge ['futbrɪdʒ] n passerelle f

foothills ['futhɪlz] npl contreforts mpl

foothold ['futhəʊld] n prise f (de pied)

footing ['futɪŋ] n (fig) position f; **to lose one's footing** perdre pied; **on an equal footing** sur pied d'égalité

footlights ['futlaɪts] npl rampe f

footnote ['futnəʊt] n note f (en bas de page)

footpath ['futpɑːθ] n sentier m; (in street) trottoir m

footprint ['futprɪnt] n trace f (de pied)

footstep ['futstep] n pas m

footwear ['futwɛə*] n chaussure(s) f(pl)

KEYWORD

for [fɔː*] prep 1 (indicating destination, intention, purpose) pour; **the train for London** le train pour (or à destination de) Londres; **he went for the paper** il est allé chercher le journal; **it's time for lunch** c'est l'heure du déjeuner; **what's it for?** ça sert à quoi?; **what for?** (why) pourquoi?; (to what end) pour quoi faire?, à quoi bon?; **for sale** à vendre

2 (on behalf of, representing) pour; **the MP for Hove** le député de Hove; **to work for sb/sth** travailler pour qn/qch; **G for George** G comme Georges

3 (because of) pour; **for this reason** pour cette raison; **for fear of being criticized** de peur d'être critiqué

4 (with regard to) pour; **it's cold for July** il fait froid pour juillet; **a gift for languages** un don pour les langues

5 (in exchange for): **I sold it for £5** je l'ai vendu 5 livres; **to pay 50 pence for a ticket** payer un billet 50 pence

6 (in favour of) pour; **are you for or against us?** êtes-vous pour ou contre nous?

7 (referring to distance) pendant, sur; **there are roadworks for 5 km** il y a des travaux sur or pendant 5 km; **we walked for miles** nous avons marché pendant des kilomètres

8 (referring to time) pendant; depuis; pour; **he**

was away for 2 years il a été absent pendant 2 ans; **she will be away for a month** elle sera absente (pendant) un mois; **I have known her for years** je la connais depuis des années; **can you do it for tomorrow?** est-ce que tu peux le faire pour demain?

9 (with infinitive clauses): **it is not for me to decide** ce n'est pas à moi de décider; **it would be best for you to leave** le mieux serait que vous partiez; **there is still time for you to do it** vous avez encore le temps de le faire; **for this to be possible ...** pour que cela soit possible ...

10 (in spite of): **for all that** malgré cela, néanmoins; **for all his work/efforts** malgré tout son travail/tous ses efforts; **for all his complaints, he's very fond of her** il a beau se plaindre, il l'aime beaucoup

♦ conj (since, as: rather formal) car

forage ['fɒrɪdʒ] n fourrage m ♦ vi fourrager, fouiller

foray ['fɒreɪ] n incursion f

forbid, pt **forbad(e)**, pp **forbidden** [fə'bɪd, -'bæd, -'bɪdn] vt défendre, interdire; **to forbid sb to do** défendre or interdire à qn de faire

forbidding [fə'bɪdɪŋ] adj d'aspect or d'allure sévère or sombre

force [fɔːs] n force f ♦ vt forcer; **the Forces** npl (BRIT) l'armée f; **to force sb to do sth** forcer qn à faire qch; **in force** en force; **to come into force** entrer en vigueur; **a force 5 wind** un vent de force 5; **the sales force** (COMM) la force de vente; **to join forces** unir ses forces

▶ **force back** vt (crowd, enemy) repousser; (tears) refouler

▶ **force down** vt (food) se forcer à manger

force-feed ['fɔːsfiːd] vt nourrir de force

forceful ['fɔːsful] adj énergique, volontaire

forcibly ['fɔːsəblɪ] adv par la force, de force; (vigorously) énergiquement

ford [fɔːd] n gué m ♦ vt passer à gué

fore [fɔː*] n: **to the fore** en évidence

forearm ['fɔːrɑːm] n avant-bras m inv

foreboding [fɔː'bəudɪŋ] n pressentiment m (néfaste)

forecast ['fɔːkɑːst] n prévision f; (also: **weather forecast**) prévisions météorologiques météo f ♦ vt (irreg: like **cast**) prévoir

forecourt ['fɔːkɔːt] n (of garage) devant m

forefinger ['fɔːfɪŋgə*] n index m

forefront ['fɔːfrʌnt] n: **in the forefront of** au premier rang or plan de

foregone ['fɔːgɔn] adj: **it's a foregone conclusion** c'est à prévoir, c'est couru d'avance

foreground ['fɔːgraund] n premier plan ♦ cpd (COMPUT) prioritaire

forehead ['fɒrɪd] n front m

foreign ['fɒrɪn] adj étranger(ère); (trade) extérieur(e)

foreigner ['fɒrɪnə*] n étranger/ère

foreign exchange n (system) change m; (money) devises fpl

Foreign Office n (BRIT) ministère m des Affaires étrangères

foreign secretary n (BRIT) ministre m des Affaires étrangères

foreleg ['fɔːleg] n patte f de devant, jambe antérieure

foreman ['fɔːmən] n contremaître m; (LAW: of jury) président m (du jury)

foremost ['fɔːməust] adj le(la) plus en vue premier(ière) ♦ adv: **first and foremost** avant tout, d'abord

forensic [fə'rensɪk] adj: **forensic medicine** médecine légale; **forensic expert** expert m de la police, expert légiste

forerunner ['fɔːrʌnə*] n précurseur m

foresee, pt **foresaw**, pp **foreseen** [fɔː'siː, -'sɔː, -'siːn] vt prévoir

foreseeable [fɔː'siːəbl] adj prévisible

foreshadow [fɔː'ʃædəu] vt présager, annoncer, laisser prévoir

foresight ['fɔːsaɪt] n prévoyance f

forest ['fɒrɪst] n forêt f

forestry ['fɒrɪstrɪ] n sylviculture f

foretaste ['fɔːteɪst] n avant-goût m

foretell, pt, pp **foretold** [fɔː'tel, -'təuld] vt prédire

forever [fə'revə*] adv pour toujours; (fig) continuellement

foreword ['fɔːwəd] n avant-propos m inv

forfeit ['fɔːfɪt] n prix m, rançon f ♦ vt perdre; (one's life, health) payer de

forgave [fə'geɪv] pt of **forgive**

forge [fɔːdʒ] n forge f ♦ vt (signature) contrefaire; (wrought iron) forger; **to forge documents/a will** fabriquer de faux papiers/un faux testament; **to forge money** (BRIT) fabriquer de la fausse monnaie

▶ **forge ahead** vi pousser de l'avant, prendre de l'avance

forged [fɔːdʒd] adj faux(fausse)

forger [fɔːdʒə*] n faussaire m

forgery ['fɔːdʒərɪ] n faux m, contrefaçon f

forget, pt **forgot**, pp **forgotten** [fə'get, -'gɔt, -'gɔtn] vt, vi oublier

forgetful [fə'getful] adj distrait(e), étourdi(e); **forgetful of** oublieux(euse) de

forget-me-not [fə'getmɪnɔt] n myosotis m

forgive, pt **forgave**, pp **forgiven** [fə'gɪv, -'geɪv, -'gɪvn] vt pardonner; **to forgive sb for sth/for doing sth** pardonner qch à qn/à qn de faire qch

forgiveness [fə'gɪvnɪs] n pardon m

forgo, pt **forwent**, pp **forgone** [fɔː'gəu, -'went, -'gɔn] vt = **forego**

fork [fɔːk] n (for eating) fourchette f; (for gardening) fourche f; (of roads) bifurcation f; (of railways) embranchement *m* ♦ *vi* (*road*) bifurquer

▶ **fork out** (*col: pay*) *vt* allonger, se fendre de ♦ *vi* casquer

fork-lift truck ['fɔːklɪft-] *n* chariot élévateur

forlorn [fə'lɔːn] *adj* abandonné(e), délaissé(e); (*hope, attempt*) désespéré(e)

form [fɔːm] *n* forme *f*; (*SCOL*) classe *f*; (*questionnaire*) formulaire *m* ♦ *vt* former; **in the form of** sous forme de; **to form part of sth** faire partie de qch; **to be in good form** (*SPORT, fig*) être en forme; **in top form** en pleine forme

formal ['fɔːməl] *adj* (*offer, receipt*) en bonne et due forme; (*person*) cérémonieux(euse), à cheval sur les convenances; (*occasion, dinner*) officiel(le) (*ART, PHILOSOPHY*) formel(le); **formal dress** tenue *f* de cérémonie; (*evening dress*) tenue de soirée

formally ['fɔːməlɪ] *adv* officiellement; formellement; cérémonieusement

format ['fɔːmæt] *n* format *m* ♦ *vt* (*COMPUT*) formater

formation [fɔː'meɪʃən] *n* formation *f*

formative ['fɔːmətɪv] *adj*: **formative years** années *fpl* d'apprentissage (*fig*) or de formation (*d'un enfant, d'un adolescent*)

former ['fɔːmə*] *adj* ancien(ne) (*before n*), précédent(e); **the former ... the latter** le premier ... le second, celui-là ... celui-ci; **the former president** l'ex-président; **the former Yugoslavia/Soviet Union** l'ex Yougoslavie/Union Soviétique

formerly ['fɔːməlɪ] *adv* autrefois

formidable ['fɔːmɪdəbl] *adj* redoutable

formula ['fɔːmjulə] *n* formule *f*; **Formula One** (*AUT*) Formule un

forsake, *pt* **forsook**, *pp* **forsaken** [fə'seɪk, -'suk, -'seɪkən] *vt* abandonner

fort [fɔːt] *n* fort *m*; **to hold the fort** (*fig*) assurer la permanence

forte ['fɔːtɪ] *n* (*point*) fort *m*

forth [fɔːθ] *adv* en avant; **to go back and forth** aller et venir; **and so forth** et ainsi de suite

forthcoming [fɔːθ'kʌmɪŋ] *adj* qui va paraître or avoir lieu prochainement; (*character*) ouvert(e), communicatif(ive)

forthright ['fɔːθraɪt] *adj* franc(franche), direct(e)

forthwith ['fɔːθ'wɪθ] *adv* sur le champ

fortify ['fɔːtɪfaɪ] *vt* fortifier

fortitude ['fɔːtɪtjuːd] *n* courage *m*, force *f* d'âme

fortnight ['fɔːtnaɪt] *n* (*BRIT*) quinzaine *f*, quinze jours *mpl*; **it's a fortnight since ...** il y a quinze jours que ...

fortnightly ['fɔːtnaɪtlɪ] *adj* bimensuel(le) ♦ *adv* tous les quinze jours

fortunate ['fɔːtʃənɪt] *adj*: **to be fortunate** avoir de la chance; **it is fortunate that** c'est une chance que, il est heureux que

fortunately ['fɔːtʃənɪtlɪ] *adv* heureusement, par

bonheur

fortune ['fɔːtʃən] *n* chance *f*; (*wealth*) fortune *f*; **to make a fortune** faire fortune

fortune-teller ['fɔːtʃəntɛlə*] *n* diseuse *f* de bonne aventure

forty ['fɔːtɪ] *num* quarante

forward ['fɔːwəd] *adj* (*movement, position*) en avant, vers l'avant; (*not shy*) effronté(e); (*COMM: delivery, sales, exchange*) à terme ♦ *adv* en avant ♦ *n* (*SPORT*) avant *m* ♦ *vt* (*letter*) faire suivre; (*parcel, goods*) expédier; (*fig*) promouvoir, contribuer au développement or à l'avancement de; **to move forward** avancer; **"please forward"** "prière de faire suivre"; **forward planning** planification *f* à long terme

fossil ['fɔsl] *adj, n* fossile *m*; **fossil fuel** combustible *m* fossile

foster ['fɔstə*] *vt* encourager, favoriser

foster child *n* enfant adopté

fought [fɔːt] *pt, pp of* **fight**

foul [faul] *adj* (*weather, smell, food*) infect(e); (*language*) ordurier(ière); (*deed*) infâme ♦ *n* (*FOOTBALL*) faute *f* ♦ *vt* salir, encrasser; (*football player*) commettre une faute sur; (*entangle: anchor, propeller*) emmêler

foul play *n* (*SPORT*) jeu déloyal; **foul play is not suspected** la mort (*or* l'incendie *etc*) n'a pas de causes suspectes, on écarte l'hypothèse d'un meurtre (*or* d'un acte criminel)

found [faund] *pt, pp of* **find** ♦ *vt* (*establish*) fonder

foundation [faun'deɪʃən] *n* (*act*) fondation *f*; (*base*) fondement *m*; (*also:* **foundation cream**) fond *m* de teint; **foundations** *npl* (*of building*) fondations *fpl*; **to lay the foundations** (*fig*) poser les fondements

founder ['faundə*] *n* fondateur *m* ♦ *vi* couler, sombrer

foundry ['faundrɪ] *n* fonderie *f*

fountain ['fauntɪn] *n* fontaine *f*

fountain pen *n* stylo *m* (à encre)

four [fɔː*] *num* quatre; **on all fours** à quatre pattes

four-poster ['fɔː'pəustə*] *n* (*also:* **four-poster bed**) lit *m* à baldaquin

fourteen ['fɔː'tiːn] *num* quatorze

fourth ['fɔːθ] *num* quatrième ♦ *n* (*AUT: also:* **fourth gear**) quatrième *f*

fowl [faul] *n* volaille *f*

fox [fɔks] *n* renard *m* ♦ *vt* mystifier

foyer ['fɔɪeɪ] *n* vestibule *m*; (*THEAT*) foyer *m*

fraction ['frækʃən] *n* fraction *f*

fracture ['fræktʃə*] *n* fracture *f* ♦ *vt* fracturer

fragile ['frædʒaɪl] *adj* fragile

fragment ['frægmənt] *n* fragment *m*

fragrant ['freɪgrənt] *adj* parfumé(e), odorant(e)

frail [freɪl] *adj* fragile, délicat(e)

frame [freɪm] *n* (*of building*) charpente *f*; (*of*

human, animal) charpente, ossature *f*; (*of picture*) cadre *m*; (*of door, window*) encadrement *m*, chambranle *m*; (*of spectacles: also:* **frames**) monture *f* ♦ *vt* encadrer; (*theory, plan*) construire, élaborer; **to frame sb** (*col*) monter un coup contre qn; **frame of mind** disposition *f* d'esprit

framework ['freɪmwəːk] *n* structure *f*

France [frɑːns] *n* la France; **in France** en France

franchise ['fræntʃaɪz] *n* (*POL*) droit *m* de vote; (*COMM*) franchise *f*

frank [fræŋk] *adj* franc(franche) ♦ *vt* (*letter*) affranchir

frankly ['fræŋklɪ] *adv* franchement

frantic ['fræntɪk] *adj* frénétique; (*desperate: need, desire*) effréné(e); (*person*) hors de soi

fraternity [frə'təːnɪtɪ] *n* (*club*) communauté *f*, confrérie *f*; (*spirit*) fraternité *f*

fraud [frɔːd] *n* supercherie *f*, fraude *f*, tromperie *f*; (*person*) imposteur *m*

fraught [frɔːt] *adj* (*tense: person*) très tendu(e); (*: situation*) pénible; **fraught with** (*difficulties etc*) chargé(e) de, plein(e) de

fray [freɪ] *n* bagarre *f*; (*MIL*) combat *m* ♦ *vt* effilocher ♦ *vi* s'effilocher; **tempers were frayed** les gens commençaient à s'énerver; **her nerves were frayed** elle était à bout de nerfs

freak [friːk] *n* phénomène *m* créature ou événement exceptionnel par sa rareté, son caractère d'anomalie; (*pej: fanatic*): **health freak** fana *m/f* ou obsédé/e de l'alimentation saine (or de la forme physique)

▶ **freak out** *vi* (*col: drop out*) se marginaliser; (*: on drugs*) se défoncer

freckle ['frekl] *n* tache *f* de rousseur

free [friː] *adj* libre; (*gratis*) gratuit(e); (*liberal*) généreux(euse), large ♦ *vt* (*prisoner etc*) libérer; (*jammed object or person*) dégager; **to give sb a free hand** donner carte blanche à qn; **free and easy** sans façon, décontracté(e); **admission free** entrée libre; **free (of charge)** gratuitement

freedom ['friːdəm] *n* liberté *f*

Freefone® ['friːfəun] *n* numéro vert

free-for-all ['friːfərɔːl] *n* mêlée générale

free gift *n* prime *f*

freehold ['friːhəuld] *n* propriété foncière libre

free kick *n* (*SPORT*) coup franc

freelance ['friːlɑːns] *adj* (*journalist etc*) indépendant(e); (*work*) à la pige, à la tâche

freely ['friːlɪ] *adv* librement; (*liberally*) libéralement

freemason ['friːmeɪsn] *n* franc-maçon *m*

freepost ['friːpəust] *n* franchise postale

free-range ['friːreɪndʒ] *adj* (*egg*) de ferme

free trade *n* libre-échange *m*

freeway ['friːweɪ] *n* (*US*) autoroute *f*

free will *n* libre arbitre *m*; **of one's own free will** de son plein gré

freeze [friːz] *vb, pt* **froze** [frəuz], *pp* **frozen** ['frəuzn] ♦ *vi* geler ♦ *vt* geler; (*food*) congeler; (*prices, salaries*) bloquer, geler ♦ *n* gel *m*; blocage *m*

▶ **freeze over** *vi* (*river*) geler; (*windscreen*) se couvrir de givre ou de glace

▶ **freeze up** *vi* geler

freeze-dried ['friːzdraɪd] *adj* lyophilisé(e)

freezer ['friːzə*] *n* congélateur *m*

freezing ['friːzɪŋ] *adj*: **freezing (cold)** (*room etc*) glacial(e); (*person, hands*) gelé(e), glacé(e) ♦ *n*: **3 degrees below freezing** 3 degrés au-dessous de zéro

freezing point *n* point *m* de congélation

freight [freɪt] *n* (*goods*) fret *m*, cargaison *f*; (*money charged*) fret, prix *m* du transport; **freight forward** port dû; **freight inward** port payé par le destinataire

freight train *n* (*US*) train *m* de marchandises

French [frentʃ] *adj* français(e) ♦ *n* (*LING*) français *m*; **the French** *npl* les Français

French bean *n* (*BRIT*) haricot vert

French fried potatoes, (*US*) **French fries** *npl* (pommes de terre *fpl*) frites *fpl*

French horn *n* (*MUS*) cor *m* (d'harmonie)

French kiss *n* baiser profond

French loaf *n* ≈ pain *m*, ≈ parisien *m*

Frenchman ['frentʃmən] *n* Français *m*

French window *n* porte-fenêtre *f*

Frenchwoman ['frentʃwumən] *n* Française *f*

frenzy ['frenzɪ] *n* frénésie *f*

frequency ['friːkwənsɪ] *n* fréquence *f*

frequent *adj* ['friːkwənt] fréquent(e) ♦ *vt* [frɪ'kwent] fréquenter

frequently ['friːkwəntlɪ] *adv* fréquemment

fresh [freʃ] *adj* frais(fraîche); (*new*) nouveau(nouvelle); (*cheeky*) familier(ière), culotté(e); **to make a fresh start** prendre un nouveau départ

freshen ['freʃən] *vi* (*wind, air*) fraîchir

▶ **freshen up** *vi* faire un brin de toilette

fresher ['freʃə*] *n* (*BRIT SCOL: col*) = **freshman**

freshly ['freʃlɪ] *adv* nouvellement, récemment

freshman ['freʃmən] *n* (*SCOL*) bizuth *m*, étudiant/e de première année

freshness ['freʃnɪs] *n* fraîcheur *f*

freshwater ['freʃwɔːtə*] *adj* (*fish*) d'eau douce

fret [fret] *vi* s'agiter, se tracasser

friar ['fraɪə*] *n* moine *m*, frère *m*

friction ['frɪkʃən] *n* friction *f*, frottement *m*

Friday ['fraɪdɪ] *n* vendredi *m*; *for phrases see also* **Tuesday**

fridge [frɪdʒ] *n* (*BRIT*) frigo *m*, frigidaire® *m*

fried [fraɪd] *pt, pp of* **fry** ♦ *adj* frit(e); **fried egg** œuf *m* sur le plat

friend [frend] *n* ami/e; **to make friends with** se lier (d'amitié) avec

friendly ['frendlɪ] *adj* amical(e); (*kind*) sympa-

thique, gentil(le); (POL: country, government) ami(e)
◆ n (also: **friendly match**) match amical; **to be
friendly with** être ami/e avec; **to be friendly to**
être bien à l'égard de

friendship ['frendʃɪp] n amitié f

frieze [friːz] n frise f, bordure f

fright [fraɪt] n peur f, effroi m; **to take fright**
prendre peur, s'effrayer; **she looks a fright** elle a
l'air d'un épouvantail

frighten ['fraɪtn] vt effrayer, faire peur à
▶ **frighten away, frighten off** vt (birds, children
etc) faire fuir, effaroucher

frightened ['fraɪtnd] adj: **to be frightened (of)**
avoir peur (de)

frightening ['fraɪtnɪŋ] adj effrayant(e)

frightful ['fraɪtful] adj affreux(euse)

frigid ['frɪdʒɪd] adj frigide

frill [frɪl] n (of dress) volant m; (of shirt) jabot m;
without frills (fig) sans manières

fringe [frɪndʒ] n frange f; (edge: of forest etc) bordure f; (fig): **on the fringe** en marge

fringe benefits npl avantages sociaux or en
nature

Frisbee® ['frɪzbɪ] n Frisbee® m

frisk [frɪsk] vt fouiller

fritter ['frɪtə*] n beignet m
▶ **fritter away** vt gaspiller

frivolous ['frɪvələs] adj frivole

frizzy ['frɪzɪ] adj crépu(e)

fro [frəu] see **to**

frock [frɔk] n robe f

frog [frɔg] n grenouille f; **to have a frog in one's
throat** avoir un chat dans la gorge

frogman ['frɔgmən] n homme-grenouille m

frolic ['frɔlɪk] n ébats mpl ◆ vi folâtrer, batifoler

from [frɔm] prep 1 (indicating starting place, origin etc) de; **where do you come from?, where
are you from?** d'où venez-vous?; **where has he
come from?** d'où arrive-t-il?; **from London to
Paris** de Londres à Paris; **a letter/telephone call
from my sister** une lettre/un appel de ma sœur;
to drink from the bottle boire à (même) la bouteille
2 (indicating time) (à partir) de; **from one o'clock
to or until or till two** d'une heure à deux heures;
from January (on) à partir de janvier
3 (indicating distance) de; **the hotel is one kilometre from the beach** l'hôtel est à un kilomètre
de la plage
4 (indicating price, number etc) de; **the interest
rate was increased from 9% to 10%** le taux
d'intérêt est passé de 9% à 10%
5 (indicating difference) de; **he can't tell red
from green** il ne peut pas distinguer le rouge du
vert

6 (because of, on the basis of): **from what he says**
d'après ce qu'il dit; **weak from hunger** affaibli
par la faim

front [frʌnt] n (of house, dress) devant m; (of coach,
train) avant m; (of book) couverture f; (promenade:
also: **sea front**) bord m de mer; (fig: appearances)
front m; (fig: appearances) contenance f, façade f
◆ adj de devant, premier(ière) ◆ vi: **to front onto
sth** donner sur qch; **in front (of)** devant

frontage ['frʌntɪdʒ] n façade f; (of shop) devanture f

front door n porte f d'entrée; (of car) portière f
avant

frontier ['frʌntɪə*] n frontière f

front page n première page

front room n (BRIT) pièce f de devant, salon m

front-wheel drive ['frʌntwiːl-] n traction f
avant

frost [frɔst] n gel m, gelée f; (also: **hoarfrost**) givre
m

frostbite ['frɔstbaɪt] n gelures fpl

frosted ['frɔstɪd] adj (glass) dépoli(e); (esp US: cake)
glacé(e)

frosty ['frɔstɪ] adj (window) couvert(e) de givre;
(welcome) glacial(e)

froth [frɔθ] n mousse f; écume f

frown [fraun] n froncement m de sourcils ◆ vi
froncer les sourcils
▶ **frown on** vt (fig) désapprouver

froze [frəuz] pt of **freeze**

frozen ['frəuzn] pp of **freeze** ◆ adj (food) conge-
lé(e); (COMM: assets) gelé(e)

fruit [fruːt] n (pl inv) fruit m

fruiterer ['fruːtərə*] n fruitier m, marchand/e de
fruits; **fruiterer's (shop)** fruiterie f

fruitful ['fruːtful] adj fructueux(euse); (plant, soil)
fécond(e)

fruition [fruːˈɪʃən] n: **to come to fruition** se réaliser

fruit juice n jus m de fruit

fruit machine n (BRIT) machine f à sous

fruit salad n salade f de fruits

frustrate [frʌsˈtreɪt] vt frustrer; (plot, plans) faire
échouer

fry, pt, pp **fried** [fraɪ, -d] vt (faire) frire; **the small
fry** le menu fretin

frying pan ['fraɪɪŋ-] n poêle f (à frire)

ft. abbr = **foot, feet**

fudge [fʌdʒ] n (CULIN) sorte de confiserie à base de
sucre, de beurre et de lait ◆ vt (issue, problem) esquiver

fuel [fjuəl] n (for heating) combustible m; (for pro-
pelling) carburant m

fuel oil n mazout m

fuel tank n cuve f à mazout, citerne f; (in vehicle)
réservoir m de or à carburant

fugitive ['fjuːdʒɪtɪv] *n* fugitif/ive

fulfil, (US) **fulfill** [ful'fɪl] *vt* (*function*) remplir; (*order*) exécuter; (*wish, desire*) satisfaire, réaliser

fulfil(l)ment [ful'fɪlmənt] *n* (*of wishes*) réalisation *f*

full [ful] *adj* plein(e); (*details, information*) complet(ète); (*price*) fort(e), normal(e); (*skirt*) ample, large ♦ *adv*: **to know full well that** savoir fort bien que; **full (up)** (*hotel etc*) complet(ète); **I'm full (up)** j'ai bien mangé; **full employment/fare** plein emploi/tarif; **a full two hours** deux bonnes heures; **at full speed** à toute vitesse; **in full** (*reproduce, quote, pay*) intégralement; (*write name etc*) en toutes lettres

full-length [ful'leŋθ] *adj* (*portrait*) en pied; **full-length film** long métrage

full moon *n* pleine lune

full-scale ['fulskeɪl] *adj* (*model*) grandeur nature *inv*; (*search, retreat*) complet(ète), total(e)

full stop *n* point *m*

full-time ['ful'taɪm] *adj* (*work*) à plein temps ♦ *n* (SPORT) fin *f* du match

fully [ful] *adv* entièrement, complètement; (*at least*): **fully as big** au moins aussi grand

fully-fledged ['fulɪ'fledʒd] *adj* (*teacher, barrister*) diplômé(e); (*citizen, member*) à part entière

fumble ['fʌmbl] *vi* fouiller, tâtonner ♦ *vt* (*ball*) mal réceptionner, cafouiller

▶ **fumble with** *vt fus* tripoter

fume [fjuːm] *vi* rager; **fumes** *npl* vapeurs *fpl*, émanations *fpl*, gaz *mpl*

fun [fʌn] *n* amusement *m*, divertissement *m*; **to have fun** s'amuser; **for fun** pour rire; **it's not much fun** ce n'est pas très drôle *or* amusant; **to make fun of** se moquer de

function ['fʌŋkʃən] *n* fonction *f*; (*reception, dinner*) cérémonie *f*, soirée officielle ♦ *vi* fonctionner; **to function as** faire office de

functional ['fʌŋkʃənl] *adj* fonctionnel(le)

fund [fʌnd] *n* caisse *f*, fonds *m*; (*source, store*) source *f*, mine *f*; **funds** *npl* fonds *mpl*

fundamental [fʌndə'mentl] *adj* fondamental(e); **fundamentals** *mpl* principes *mpl* de base

funeral ['fjuːnərəl] *n* enterrement *m*, obsèques *fpl* (*more formal occasion*)

funeral parlour *n* dépôt *m* mortuaire

funeral service *n* service *m* funèbre

funfair ['fʌnfeə*] *n* (BRIT) fête (foraine)

fungus, *pl* **fungi** ['fʌŋgəs, -gaɪ] *n* champignon *m*; (*mould*) moisissure *f*

funnel ['fʌnl] *n* entonnoir *m*; (*of ship*) cheminée *f*

funny ['fʌnɪ] *adj* amusant(e), drôle; (*strange*) curieux(euse), bizarre

fur [fəː*] *n* fourrure *f*; (BRIT: *in kettle etc*) dépôt *m* de) tartre *m*

furious ['fjuərɪəs] *adj* furieux(euse); (*effort*) acharné(e); **to be furious with sb** être dans une fureur

noire contre qn

furlong ['fəːlɔŋ] *n* = 201.17 m (*terme d'hippisme*)

furnace ['fəːnɪs] *n* fourneau *m*

furnish ['fəːnɪʃ] *vt* meubler; (*supply*) fournir; **furnished flat** *or* (US) **apartment** meublé *m*

furnishings ['fəːnɪʃɪŋz] *npl* mobilier *m*, articles *mpl* d'ameublement

furniture ['fəːnɪtʃə*] *n* meubles *mpl*, mobilier *m*; **piece of furniture** meuble *m*

furrow ['fʌrəu] *n* sillon *m*

furry ['fəːrɪ] *adj* (*animal*) à fourrure; (*toy*) en peluche

further ['fəːðə*] *adj* supplémentaire, autre, nouveau(nouvelle) ♦ *adv* plus loin; (*more*) davantage; (*moreover*) de plus ♦ *vt* faire avancer *or* progresser, promouvoir; **how much further is it?** quelle distance *or* combien reste-t-il à parcourir?; **until further notice** jusqu'à nouvel ordre *or* avis; **further to your letter of ...** (COMM) suite à votre lettre du ...

further education *n* enseignement *m* postscolaire (*recyclage, formation professionnelle*)

furthermore [fəːðə'mɔː*] *adv* de plus, en outre

furthest ['fəːðɪst] *superlative of* **far**

fury ['fjuərɪ] *n* fureur *f*

fuse, (US) **fuze** [fjuːz] *n* fusible *m*; (*for bomb etc*) amorce *f*, détonateur *m* ♦ *vt*, *vi* (*metal*) fondre; (*fig*) fusionner; (ELEC): **to fuse the lights** faire sauter les fusibles *or* les plombs; **a fuse has blown** un fusible a sauté

fuse box *n* boîte *f* à fusibles

fuss [fʌs] *n* (*anxiety, excitement*) chichis *mpl*, façons *fpl*; (*commotion*) tapage *m*; (*complaining, trouble*) histoire(s) *f(pl)* ♦ *vi* faire des histoires ♦ *vt* (*person*) embêter; **to make a fuss** faire des façons (*or* des histoires); **to make a fuss of sb** dorloter qn

▶ **fuss over** *vt fus* (*person*) dorloter

fussy ['fʌsɪ] *adj* (*person*) tatillon(ne) difficile, chichiteux(euse); (*dress, style*) tarabis(e); **I'm not fussy** (*col*) ça m'est égal

future ['fjuːtʃə*] *adj* futur(e) ♦ *n* avenir *m*; (LING) futur *m*; **in (the) future** à l'avenir; **in the near/immediate future** dans un avenir proche/immédiat

fuze [fjuːz] *n*, *vt*, *vi* (US) = **fuse**

fuzzy ['fʌzɪ] *adj* (PHOT) flou(e); (*hair*) crépu(e)

— G g —

G, g [dʒiː] *n* (*letter*) G, g *m*; (MUS): **G** sol *m*; **G for George** G comme Gaston

G *n abbr* (BRIT SCOL: = *good*) b = bien; (US CINE: = *general (audience)*) = tous publics

g *abbr* (= *gram, gravity*) g

G8 *n abbr* (= *Group of 8*) G8

gabble ['gæbl] *vi* bredouiller; jacasser

gable ['geɪbl] *n* pignon *m*

gadget ['gædʒɪt] *n* gadget *m*

Gaelic ['geɪlɪk] *adj*, *n* gaélique (*m*)

gag [gæg] *n* bâillon *m*; (*joke*) gag *m* ◆ *vt* (*prisoner etc*) bâillonner ◆ *vi* (*choke*) étouffer

gaiety ['geɪɪtɪ] *n* gaieté *f*

gain [geɪn] *n* gain *m*, profit *m* ◆ *vt* gagner ◆ *vi* (*watch*) avancer; **to gain in/by** gagner en/à; **to gain 3lbs (in weight)** prendre 3 livres; **to gain ground** gagner du terrain

▶ **gain (up)on** *vt fus* rattraper

gal. *abbr* = **gallon**

gale [geɪl] *n* coup *m* de vent; **gale force 10** vent *m* de force 10

gallant ['gælənt] *adj* vaillant(e), brave; (*towards ladies*) empressé(e), galant(e)

gall bladder ['gɔːl-] *n* vésicule *f* biliaire

gallery ['gælərɪ] *n* galerie *f*; (*for spectators*) tribune *f*; (: *in theatre*) dernier balcon; (*also*: **art gallery**) musée *m*; (: *private*) galerie

gallon ['gæln] *n* gallon *m* = 8 *pints*; (*BRIT* = 4.543 *l*; *US* = 3.785 *l*)

gallop ['gæləp] *n* galop *m* ◆ *vi* galoper; **galloping inflation** inflation galopante

gallows ['gæləuz] *n* potence *f*

gallstone ['gɔːlstəun] *n* calcul *m* (biliaire)

galore [gə'lɔː*] *adv* en abondance, à gogo

Gambia ['gæmbɪə] *n* Gambie *f*

gambit ['gæmbɪt] *n* (*fig*): (**opening**) **gambit** manœuvre *f* stratégique

gamble ['gæmbl] *n* pari *m*, risque calculé ◆ *vt*, *vi* jouer; **to gamble on the Stock Exchange** jouer en *or* à la Bourse; **to gamble on** (*fig*) miser sur

gambler ['gæmblə*] *n* joueur *m*

gambling ['gæmblɪŋ] *n* jeu *m*

game [geɪm] *n* jeu *m*; (*event*) match *m*; (*HUNTING*) gibier *m* ◆ *adj* brave; (*ready*): **to be game (for sth/ to do)** être prêt(e) (à qch/à faire), se sentir de taille (à faire); **a game of football/tennis** une partie de football/tennis; **games** (*SCOL*) sport *m*; **big game** gros gibier

gamekeeper ['geɪmkiːpə*] *n* garde-chasse *m*

gammon ['gæmən] *n* (*bacon*) quartier *m* de lard fumé; (*ham*) jambon fumé

gamut ['gæmət] *n* gamme *f*

gang [gæŋ] *n* bande *f*, groupe *m*

▶ **gang up** *vi*: **to gang up on sb** se liguer contre qn

gangster ['gæŋstə*] *n* gangster *m*, bandit *m*

gangway ['gæŋweɪ] *n* passerelle *f*; (*BRIT*: *of bus*) couloir central

gaol [dʒeɪl] *n*, *vt* (*BRIT*) = **jail**

gap [gæp] *n* trou *m*; (*in time*) intervalle *m*; (*fig*) lacune *f*; vide *m*

gape [geɪp] *vi* être *or* rester bouche bée

gaping ['geɪpɪŋ] *adj* (*hole*) béant(e)

garage ['gærɑːʒ] *n* garage *m*

garbage ['gɑːbɪdʒ] *n* ordures *fpl*, détritus *mpl*; (*fig*: *col*) conneries *fpl*

garbage can *n* (*US*) poubelle *f*, boîte *f* à ordures

garbled ['gɑːbld] *adj* déformé(e), faussé(e)

garden ['gɑːdn] *n* jardin *m* ◆ *vi* jardiner; **gardens** *npl* (*public*) jardin public; (*private*) parc *m*

gardener ['gɑːdnə*] *n* jardinier *m*

gardening ['gɑːdnɪŋ] *n* jardinage *m*

gargle ['gɑːgl] *vi* se gargariser ◆ *n* gargarisme *m*

garish ['gɛərɪʃ] *adj* criard(e), voyant(e)

garland ['gɑːlənd] *n* guirlande *f*; couronne *f*

garlic ['gɑːlɪk] *n* ail *m*

garment ['gɑːmənt] *n* vêtement *m*

garrison ['gærɪsn] *n* garnison *f* ◆ *vt* mettre en garnison, stationner

garter ['gɑːtə*] *n* jarretière *f*; (*US*: *suspender*) jarretelle *f*

gas [gæs] *n* gaz *m*; (*used as anaesthetic*): **to be given gas** se faire endormir; (*US*: *gasoline*) essence *f* ◆ *vt* asphyxier; (*MIL*) gazer

gas cooker *n* (*BRIT*) cuisinière *f* à gaz

gas cylinder *n* bouteille *f* de gaz

gas fire *n* (*BRIT*) radiateur *m* à gaz

gash [gæʃ] *n* entaille *f*; (*on face*) balafre *f* ◆ *vt* tailler; balafrer

gasket ['gæskɪt] *n* (*AUT*) joint *m* de culasse

gas mask *n* masque *m* à gaz

gas meter *n* compteur *m* à gaz

gasoline ['gæsəliːn] *n* (*US*) essence *f*

gasp [gɑːsp] *vi* haleter; (*fig*) avoir le souffle coupé

▶ **gasp out** *vt* (*say*) dire dans un souffle *or* d'une voix entrecoupée

gas ring *n* brûleur *m*

gas station *n* (*US*) station-service *f*

gas tap *n* bouton *m* (de cuisinière à gaz); (*on pipe*) robinet *m* à gaz

gastric ['gæstrɪk] *adj* gastrique

gate [geɪt] *n* (*of garden*) portail *m*; (*of farm, at level crossing*) barrière *f*; (*of building, town, at airport*) porte *f*; (*of lock*) vanne *f*

gateau, *pl* **gateaux** ['gætəu, -z] *n* gros gâteau à la crème

gatecrash ['geɪtkræʃ] *vt* s'introduire sans invitation dans

gateway ['geɪtweɪ] *n* porte *f*

gather ['gæðə*] *vt* (*flowers, fruit*) cueillir; (*pick up*) ramasser; (*assemble*) rassembler, réunir; recueillir; (*understand*) comprendre ◆ *vi* (*assemble*) se rassembler; (*dust*) s'amasser; (*clouds*) s'amonceler; **to gather (from/that)** conclure *or* déduire (de/que); **as far as I can gather** d'après ce que je comprends; **to gather speed** prendre de la vitesse

gathering ['gæðərɪŋ] *n* rassemblement *m*

gaudy ['gɔːdɪ] *adj* voyant(e)

gauge [geɪdʒ] *n* (*standard measure*) calibre *m*;

(*RAIL*) écartement *m*; (*instrument*) jauge *f* ◆ *vt* jauger; (*fig: sb's capabilities, character*) juger de; **to gauge the right moment** calculer le moment propice; **petrol gauge**, (*US*) **gas gauge** jauge d'essence

gaunt [gɔːnt] *adj* décharné(e); (*grim, desolate*) désolé(e)

gauntlet ['gɔːntlɪt] *n* (*fig*): **to throw down the gauntlet** jeter le gant; **to run the gauntlet through an angry crowd** se frayer un passage à travers une foule hostile *or* entre deux haies de manifestants *etc* hostiles

gauze [gɔːz] *n* gaze *f*

gave [geɪv] *pt of* **give**

gay [geɪ] *adj* (*homosexual*) homosexuel(le); (*slightly old-fashioned: cheerful*) gai(e), réjoui(e); (*colour*) gai, vif(vive)

gaze [geɪz] *n* regard *m* fixe ◆ *vi*: **to gaze at** *vt* fixer du regard

gazump [gə'zʌmp] *vi* (*BRIT*) revenir sur une promesse de vente pour accepter un prix plus élevé

GB *abbr* = **Great Britain**

GCE *n abbr* (*BRIT*) = *General Certificate of Education*

GCSE *n abbr* (*BRIT*: = *General Certificate of Secondary Education*) examen passé à l'âge de 16 ans sanctionnant les connaissances de l'élève; (= **she's got eight GCSEs**) elle a réussi dans huit matières aux épreuves du GCSE

gear [gɪə*] *n* matériel *m*, équipement *m*; (*TECH*) engrenage *m*; (*AUT*) vitesse *f* ◆ *vt* (*fig: adapt*) adapter; **top** *or* (*US*) **high/low/bottom gear** quatrième (*or* cinquième)/deuxième/première vitesse; **in gear** en prise; **out of gear** au point mort; **our service is geared to meet the needs of the disabled** notre service répond de façon spécifique aux besoins des handicapés

▶ **gear up** *vi*: **to gear up (to do)** se préparer (à faire)

gear box *n* boîte *f* de vitesse

gear lever, (*US*) **gear shift** *n* levier *m* de vitesse

geese [giːs] *npl of* **goose**

gel [dʒel] *n* gelée *f*; (*CHEMISTRY*) colloïde *m*

gem [dʒem] *n* pierre précieuse

Gemini ['dʒemɪnaɪ] *n* les Gémeaux *mpl*; **to be Gemini** être des Gémeaux

gender ['dʒendə*] *n* genre *m*

gene [dʒiːn] *n* (*BIOL*) gène *m*

general ['dʒenərl] *n* général *m* ◆ *adj* général(e); **in general** en général; **the general public** le grand public; **general audit** (*COMM*) vérification annuelle

general delivery *n* poste restante

general election *n* élection(s) législative(s)

general knowledge *n* connaissances générales

generally ['dʒenrəlɪ] *adv* généralement

general practitioner (GP) *n* généraliste *m/f*; **who's your GP?** qui est votre médecin traitant?

generate ['dʒenəreɪt] *vt* engendrer; (*electricity*) produire

generation [dʒenə'reɪʃən] *n* génération *f*; (*of electricity etc*) production *f*

generator ['dʒenəreɪtə*] *n* générateur *m*

generosity [dʒenə'rɒsɪtɪ] *n* générosité *f*

generous ['dʒenərəs] *adj* généreux(euse); (*copious*) copieux(euse)

genetic [dʒɪ'netɪk] *adj* génétique

genetics [dʒɪ'netɪks] *n* génétique *f*

Geneva [dʒɪ'niːvə] *n* Genève; **Lake Geneva** le lac Léman

genial ['dʒiːnɪəl] *adj* cordial(e), chaleureux(euse); (*climate*) clément(e)

genitals ['dʒenɪtlz] *npl* organes génitaux

genius ['dʒiːnɪəs] *n* génie *m*

genteel [dʒen'tiːl] *adj* de bon ton, distingué(e)

gentle ['dʒentl] *adj* doux(douce)

gentleman ['dʒentlmən] *n* monsieur *m*; (*well-bred man*) gentleman *m*; **gentleman's agreement** gentleman's agreement *m*

gently ['dʒentlɪ] *adv* doucement

gentry ['dʒentrɪ] *n* petite noblesse

gents [dʒents] *n* W.-C. *mpl* (pour hommes)

genuine ['dʒenjuɪn] *adj* véritable, authentique; (*person, emotion*) sincère

geographic(al) [dʒɪə'græfɪk(l)] *adj* géographique

geography [dʒɪ'ɒgrəfɪ] *n* géographie *f*

geology [dʒɪ'ɒlədʒɪ] *n* géologie *f*

geometric(al) [dʒɪə'metrɪk(l)] *adj* géométrique

geometry [dʒɪ'ɒmətrɪ] *n* géométrie *f*

geranium [dʒɪ'reɪnɪəm] *n* géranium *m*

geriatric [dʒerɪ'ætrɪk] *adj* gériatrique

germ [dʒɜːm] *n* (*MED*) microbe *m*; (*BIO, fig*) germe *m*

German ['dʒɜːmən] *adj* allemand(e) ◆ *n* Allemand/e; (*LING*) allemand *m*

German measles *n* rubéole *f*

Germany ['dʒɜːmənɪ] *n* Allemagne *f*

gesture ['dʒestjə*] *n* geste *m*; **as a gesture of friendship** en témoignage d'amitié

KEYWORD

get [get], *pt, pp* **got**, *pp* **gotten** (*US*) *vi* **1** (*become, be*) devenir; **to get old/tired** devenir vieux/fatigué, vieillir/se fatiguer; **to get drunk** s'enivrer; **to get ready/washed/shaved** *etc* se préparer/laver/raser *etc*; **to get killed** se faire tuer; **when do I get paid?** quand est-ce que je serai payé?; **it's getting late** il se fait tard

2 (*go*): **to get to/from** aller à/de; **to get home** rentrer chez soi; **how did you get here?** comment es-tu arrivé ici?; **he got across the bridge/under the fence** il a traversé le pont/est passé au-dessous de la barrière

3 (*begin*) commencer or se mettre à; **I'm getting to like him** je commence à l'apprécier; **let's get going** or **started** allons-y

4 (*modal aux vb*): **you've got to do it** il faut que vous le fassiez; **I've got to tell the police** je dois le dire à la police

◆ *vt* **1**: **to get sth done** (*do*) faire faire qch; (*have done*) faire faire qch; **to get sth/sb ready** préparer qch/qn; **to get one's hair cut** se faire couper les cheveux; **to get sb to do sth** faire faire qch à qn; **to get sb drunk** enivrer qn

2 (*obtain*: *money, permission, results*) obtenir, avoir; (*find: job, flat*) trouver; (*fetch: person, doctor, object*) aller chercher; **to get sth for sb** procurer qch à qn; **get me Mr Jones, please** (*on phone*) passez-moi Mr Jones, s'il vous plaît; **can I get you a drink?** est-ce que je peux vous servir à boire?

3 (*receive: present, letter*) recevoir, avoir; (*acquire: reputation*) avoir; (*prize*) obtenir; **what did you get for your birthday?** qu'est-ce que tu as eu pour ton anniversaire?

4 (*catch*) prendre, saisir, attraper; (*hit: target etc*) atteindre; **to get sb by the arm/throat** prendre or saisir or attraper qn par le bras/à la gorge; **get him!** arrête-le!; **he really gets me!** il me porte sur les nerfs!

5 (*take, move*) faire parvenir; **do you think we'll get it through the door?** on arrivera à le faire passer par la porte?; **I'll get you there somehow** je me débrouillerai pour t'y emmener

6 (*catch, take: plane, bus etc*) prendre

7 (*understand*) comprendre, saisir; (*hear*) entendre; **I've got it!** j'ai compris!; **I didn't get your name** je n'ai pas entendu votre nom

8 (*have, possess*): **to have got** avoir; **how many have you got?** vous en avez combien?

▶ **get about** *vi* se déplacer; (*news*) se répandre

▶ **get across** *vt*: **to get across (to)** (*message, meaning*) faire passer (à) ◆ *vi*: **to get across (to)** (*speaker*) se faire comprendre (par)

▶ **get along** *vi* (*agree*) s'entendre; (*depart*) s'en aller; (*manage*) = **get by**

▶ **get at** *vt fus* (*attack*) s'en prendre à; (*reach*) attraper, atteindre; **what are you getting at?** à quoi voulez-vous en venir?

▶ **get away** *vi* partir, s'en aller; (*escape*) s'échapper

▶ **get away with** *vt fus* en être quitte pour; se faire passer or pardonner

▶ **get back** *vi* (*return*) rentrer ◆ *vt* récupérer, recouvrer; **to get back to** (*start again*) retourner or revenir à; (*contact again*) recontacter

▶ **get back at** *vt fus* (*col*): **to get back at sb** rendre la monnaie de sa pièce à qn

▶ **get by** *vi* (*pass*) passer; (*manage*) se débrouiller; **I can get by in Dutch** je me débrouille en hollandais

▶ **get down** *vi*, *vt fus* descendre ◆ *vt* descendre; (*depress*) déprimer

▶ **get down to** *vt fus* (*work*) se mettre à (faire); **to get down to business** passer aux choses sérieuses

▶ **get in** *vi* entrer; (*arrive home*) rentrer; (*train*) arriver ◆ *vt* (*bring in: harvest*) rentrer; (: *coal*) faire rentrer; (: *supplies*) faire des provisions de

▶ **get into** *vt fus* entrer dans; (*car, train etc*) monter dans; (*clothes*) mettre, enfiler, endosser; **to get into bed/a rage** se mettre au lit/en colère

▶ **get off** *vi* (*from train etc*) descendre; (*depart: person, car*) s'en aller; (*escape*) s'en tirer ◆ *vt* (*remove: clothes, stain*) enlever; (*send off*) expédier; (*have as leave: day, time*): **we got 2 days off** nous avons eu 2 jours de congé ◆ *vt fus* (*train, bus*) descendre de; **to get off to a good start** (*fig*) prendre un bon départ

▶ **get on** *vi* (*at exam etc*) se débrouiller; (*agree*): **to get on (with)** s'entendre (avec); **how are you getting on?** comment ça va? ◆ *vt fus* monter dans; (*horse*) monter sur

▶ **get on to** *vt fus* (*BRIT: deal with: problem*) s'occuper de; (*contact: person*) contacter

▶ **get out** *vi* sortir; (*of vehicle*) descendre; (*news etc*) s'ébruiter ◆ *vt* sortir

▶ **get out of** *vt fus* sortir de; (*duty etc*) échapper à, se soustraire à

▶ **get over** *vt fus* (*illness*) se remettre de

◆ *vt* (*communicate: idea etc*) communiquer; (*finish*): **let's get it over (with)** finissons-en

▶ **get round** *vi*: **to get round to doing sth** se mettre (finalement) à faire qch ◆ *vt fus* contourner; (*fig: person*) entortiller

▶ **get through** *vi* (*TEL*) avoir la communication; **to get through to sb** atteindre qn ◆ *vt fus* (*finish: work, book*) finir, terminer

▶ **get together** *vi* se réunir ◆ *vt* rassembler

▶ **get up** *vi* (*rise*) se lever ◆ *vt fus* monter

▶ **get up to** *vt fus* (*reach*) arriver à; (*prank etc*) faire

getaway ['getəweɪ] *n* fuite *f*

geyser ['giːzə*] *n* chauffe-eau *m inv*; (*GEO*) geyser *m*

Ghana ['gɑːnə] *n* Ghana *m*

ghastly ['gɑːstlɪ] *adj* atroce, horrible; (*pale*) livide, blême

gherkin ['gəːkɪn] *n* cornichon *m*

ghetto blaster ['getəublɑːstə*] *n* (*col*) gros radio-cassette

ghost [gəust] *n* fantôme *m*, revenant *m* ◆ *vt* (*sb else's book*) écrire

giant ['dʒaɪənt] *n* géant/e ◆ *adj* géant(e), énorme; **giant (size) packet** paquet géant

gibberish ['dʒɪbərɪʃ] *n* charabia *m*

giblets ['dʒɪblɪts] *npl* abats *mpl*

Gibraltar [dʒɪ'brɔːltə*] *n* Gibraltar *m*

giddy ['gɪdɪ] *adj* (*dizzy*): **to be** (or **feel**) **giddy** avoir le vertige; (*height*) vertigineux(euse);

(*thoughtless*) sot(te), étourdi(e)

gift [gɪft] *n* cadeau *m*, présent *m*; (*donation*) don *m*; (*COMM: also*: **free gift**) cadeau(-réclame) *m*; (*talent*): **to have a gift for sth** avoir des dons pour *or* le don de qch

gifted ['gɪftɪd] *adj* doué(e)

gift shop *n* boutique *f* de cadeaux

gift token, gift voucher *n* bon *m* d'achat

gigantic [dʒaɪ'gæntɪk] *adj* gigantesque

giggle ['gɪgl] *vi* pouffer, ricaner sottement ♦ *n* petit rire sot, ricanement *m*

gill [dʒɪl] *n* (*measure*) = 0.25 pints (*BRIT* = 0.148 *l*; *US* = 0.118 *l*)

gills [gɪlz] *npl* (*of fish*) ouïes *fpl*, branchies *fpl*

gilt [gɪlt] *n* dorure *f* ♦ *adj* doré(e)

gilt-edged ['gɪltedʒd] *adj* (*stocks, securities*) de premier ordre

gimmick ['gɪmɪk] *n* truc *m*; **sales gimmick** offre promotionnelle

gin [dʒɪn] *n* gin *m*

ginger ['dʒɪndʒə*] *n* gingembre *m*

▶ **ginger up** *vt* secouer; animer

ginger ale, ginger beer *n* boisson gazeuse au gingembre

gingerbread ['dʒɪndʒəbred] *n* pain *m* d'épices

gingerly ['dʒɪndʒəlɪ] *adv* avec précaution

gipsy ['dʒɪpsɪ] *n* gitan/e, bohémien/ne ♦ *cpd*: **gipsy caravan** *n* roulotte *f*

giraffe [dʒɪ'rɑ:f] *n* girafe *f*

girder ['gə:də*] *n* poutrelle *f*

girl [gə:l] *n* fille *f*, fillette *f*; (*young unmarried woman*) jeune fille; (*daughter*) fille; **an English girl** une jeune Anglaise; **a little English girl** une petite Anglaise

girlfriend ['gə:lfrend] *n* (*of girl*) amie *f*; (*of boy*) petite amie

girlish ['gə:lɪʃ] *adj* de jeune fille

giro ['dʒaɪrəu] *n* (*bank giro*) virement *m* bancaire; (*post office giro*) mandat *m*

gist [dʒɪst] *n* essentiel *m*

give [gɪv] *n* (*of fabric*) élasticité *f* ♦ *vb*, *pt* **gave**, *pp* **given** [geɪv, 'gɪvn] *vt* donner ♦ *vi* (*break*) céder; (*stretch: fabric*) se prêter; **to give sb sth, give sth to sb** donner qch à qn; **to give sb a cry/sigh** pousser un cri/un soupir; **how much did you give for it?** combien (l')avez-vous payé?; **12 o'clock, give or take a few minutes** midi, à quelques minutes près; **to give way** *vi* céder; (*BRIT AUT*) donner la priorité

▶ **give away** *vt* donner; (*give free*) faire cadeau de; (*betray*) donner, trahir; (*disclose*) révéler; (*bride*) conduire à l'autel

▶ **give back** *vt* rendre

▶ **give in** *vi* céder ♦ *vt* donner

▶ **give off** *vt* dégager

▶ **give out** *vt* (*food etc*) distribuer; (*news*) annoncer ♦ *vi* (*be exhausted: supplies*) s'épuiser; (*fail*) lâcher

▶ **give up** *vi* renoncer ♦ *vt* renoncer à; **to give up smoking** arrêter de fumer; **to give o.s. up** se rendre

glacier ['glæsɪə*] *n* glacier *m*

glad [glæd] *adj* content(e); **to be glad about sth/ that** être heureux(euse) de or bien content de qch/ que; **I was glad of his help** j'étais bien content de (pouvoir compter sur) son aide or qu'il m'aide

gladly ['glædlɪ] *adv* volontiers

glamorous ['glæmərəs] *adj* séduisant(e)

glamour ['glæmə*] *n* éclat *m*, prestige *m*

glance [glɑ:ns] *n* coup *m* d'œil ♦ *vi*: **to glance at** jeter un coup d'œil à

▶ **glance off** *vt fus* (*bullet*) ricocher sur

glancing ['glɑ:nsɪŋ] *adj* (*blow*) oblique

gland [glænd] *n* glande *f*

glare [glɛə*] *n* lumière éblouissante ♦ *vi* briller d'un éclat aveuglant; **to glare at** lancer un *or* des regard(s) furieux à

glaring ['glɛərɪŋ] *adj* (*mistake*) criant(e), qui saute aux yeux

glass [glɑ:s] *n* verre *m*; (*also*: **looking glass**) miroir *m*

glasshouse ['glɑ:shaus] *n* serre *f*

glassware ['glɑ:swɛə*] *n* verrerie *f*

glaze [gleɪz] *vt* (*door*) vitrer; (*pottery*) vernir; (*CULIN*) glacer ♦ *n* vernis *m*; (*CULIN*) glaçage *m*

glazed [gleɪzd] *adj* (*eye*) vitreux(euse); (*pottery*) verni(e); (*tiles*) vitrifié(e)

glazier ['gleɪzɪə*] *n* vitrier *m*

gleam [gli:m] *n* lueur *f* ♦ *vi* luire, briller; **a gleam of hope** une lueur d'espoir

glean [gli:n] *vt* (*information*) recueillir

glee [gli:] *n* joie *f*

glib [glɪb] *adj* qui a du bagou; facile

glide [glaɪd] *vi* glisser; (*AVIAT, bird*) planer ♦ *n* glissement *m*; vol plané

glider ['glaɪdə*] *n* (*AVIAT*) planeur *m*

gliding ['glaɪdɪŋ] *n* (*AVIAT*) vol *m* à voile

glimmer ['glɪmə*] *vi* luire ♦ *n* lueur *f*

glimpse [glɪmps] *n* vision passagère, aperçu *m* ♦ *vt* entrevoir, apercevoir; **to catch a glimpse of** entrevoir

glint [glɪnt] *n* éclair *m* ♦ *vi* étinceler

glisten ['glɪsn] *vi* briller, luire

glitter ['glɪtə*] *vi* scintiller, briller ♦ *n* scintillement *m*

gloat [gləut] *vi*: **to gloat (over)** jubiler (à propos de)

global ['gləubl] *adj* (*world-wide*) mondial(e); (*overall*) global(e)

globe [gləub] *n* globe *m*

gloom [glu:m] *n* obscurité *f*; (*sadness*) tristesse *f*, mélancolie *f*

gloomy ['glu:mɪ] *adj* sombre, triste, mélancolique; **to feel gloomy** avoir *or* se faire des idées noires

glorious ['glɔːrɪəs] *adj* glorieux(euse); (*beautiful*) splendide

glory ['glɔːrɪ] *n* gloire *f*; splendeur *f* ♦ *vi*: **to glory in** se glorifier de

gloss [glɔs] *n* (*shine*) brillant *m*, vernis *m*; (*also*: **gloss paint**) peinture brillante *or* laquée

▶ **gloss over** *vt fus* glisser sur

glossary ['glɔsərɪ] *n* glossaire *m*, lexique *m*

glossy ['glɔsɪ] *adj* brillant(e), luisant(e) ♦ *n* (*also*: **glossy magazine**) revue *f* de luxe

glove [glʌv] *n* gant *m*

glove compartment *n* (AUT) boîte *f* à gants, vide-poches *m inv*

glow [gləu] *vi* rougeoyer; (*face*) rayonner ♦ *n* rougeoiement *m*

glower ['glauə*] *vi* lancer des regards mauvais

glucose ['gluːkəus] *n* glucose *m*

glue [gluː] *n* colle *f* ♦ *vt* coller

glum [glʌm] *adj* maussade, morose

glut [glʌt] *n* surabondance *f* ♦ *vt* rassasier; (*market*) encombrer

glutton ['glʌtn] *n* glouton/ne; **a glutton for work** un bourreau de travail

GM *abbr* (= *genetically modified*) génétiquement modifié(e)

gm *abbr* (= *gram*) g

gnat [næt] *n* moucheron *m*

gnaw [nɔː] *vt* ronger

go [gəu] *vb, pt* **went**, *pp* **gone** [wɛnt, gɔn] *vi* aller; (*depart*) partir, s'en aller; (*work*) marcher; (*be sold*): **to go for £10** se vendre 10 livres; (*fit, suit*): **to go with** aller avec; (*become*): **to go pale/mouldy** pâlir/moisir; (*break etc*) céder ♦ *n* (*pl*: **goes**): **to have a go (at)** essayer (de faire); **to be on the go** être en mouvement; **whose go is it?** à qui est-ce de jouer?; **to go by car/on foot** aller en voiture/à pied; **he's going to do** il va faire, il est sur le point de faire; **to go for a walk** aller se promener; **to go dancing/shopping** aller danser/faire les courses; **to go looking for sb/sth** aller *or* partir à la recherche de qn/qch; **to go to sleep** s'endormir; **to go and see sb, go to see sb** aller voir qn; **how is it going?** comment ça marche?; **how did it go?** comment est-ce que ça s'est passé?; **to go round the back/by the shop** passer par derrière/devant le magasin; **my voice has gone** j'ai une extinction de voix; **the cake is all gone** il n'y a plus de gâteau; **I'll take whatever is going** (BRIT) je prendrai ce qu'il y a (*or* ce que vous avez); **... to go** (US: *food*) ... à emporter

▶ **go about** *vi* (*also*: **go around**) aller çà et là; (*rumour*) se répandre ♦ *vt fus*: **how do I go about this?** comment dois-je m'y prendre (pour faire ceci)?; **to go about one's business** s'occuper de ses affaires

▶ **go after** *vt fus* (*pursue*) poursuivre, courir après; (*job, record etc*) essayer d'obtenir

▶ **go against** *vt fus* (*be unfavourable to*) être

défavorable à; (*be contrary to*) être contraire à

▶ **go ahead** *vi* (*make progress*) avancer; (*get going*) y aller

▶ **go along** *vi* aller, avancer ♦ *vt fus* longer, parcourir; **as you go along (with your work)** au fur et à mesure (de votre travail); **to go along with** (*accompany*) accompagner; (*agree with*: *idea*) être d'accord sur; (: *person*) suivre

▶ **go away** *vi* partir, s'en aller

▶ **go back** *vi* rentrer; revenir; (*go again*) retourner

▶ **go back on** *vt fus* (*promise*) revenir sur

▶ **go by** *vi* (*years, time*) passer, s'écouler ♦ *vt fus* s'en tenir à; (*believe*) en croire

▶ **go down** *vi* descendre; (*ship*) couler; (*sun*) se coucher ♦ *vt fus* descendre; **that should go down well with him** (*fig*) ça devrait lui plaire

▶ **go for** *vt fus* (*fetch*) aller chercher; (*like*) aimer; (*attack*) s'en prendre à; attaquer

▶ **go in** *vi* entrer

▶ **go in for** *vt fus* (*competition*) se présenter à; (*like*) aimer

▶ **go into** *vt fus* entrer dans; (*investigate*) étudier, examiner; (*embark on*) se lancer dans

▶ **go off** *vi* partir, s'en aller; (*food*) se gâter; (*bomb*) sauter; (*lights etc*) s'éteindre; (*event*) se dérouler ♦ *vt fus* ne plus aimer, ne plus avoir envie de; **the gun went off** le coup est parti; **to go off to sleep** s'endormir; **the party went off well** la fête s'est bien passée *or* était très réussie

▶ **go on** *vi* continuer; (*happen*) se passer; (*lights*) s'allumer ♦ *vt fus* (*be guided by*: *evidence etc*) se fonder sur; **to go on doing** continuer à faire; **what's going on here?** qu'est-ce qui se passe ici?

▶ **go on at** *vt fus* (*nag*) tomber sur le dos de

▶ **go on with** *vt fus* poursuivre, continuer

▶ **go out** *vi* sortir; (*fire, light*) s'éteindre; (*tide*) descendre; **to go out with sb** sortir avec qn

▶ **go over** *vi* (*ship*) chavirer ♦ *vt fus* (*check*) revoir, vérifier; **to go over sth in one's mind** repasser qch dans son esprit

▶ **go past** *vt fus*: **to go past sth** passer devant qch

▶ **go round** *vi* (*circulate*: *news, rumour*) circuler; (*revolve*) tourner; (*visit*): **to go round to sb's** passer chez qn; aller chez qn; (*make a detour*): **to go round (by)** faire un détour (par); (*suffice*) suffire (pour tout le monde)

▶ **go through** *vt fus* (*town etc*) traverser; (*search through*) fouiller; (*examine*: *list, book*) lire *or* regarder en détail, éplucher; (*perform*: *lesson*) réciter; (: *formalities*) remplir; (: *programme*) exécuter

▶ **go through with** *vt fus* (*plan, crime*) aller jusqu'au bout de

▶ **go under** *vi* (*sink*: *also fig*) couler; (: *person*) succomber

▶ **go up** *vi* monter; (*price*) augmenter ♦ *vt fus* gravir; (*also*: **to go up in flames**) flamber, s'enflammer brusquement

▶ **go with** vt fus (suit) aller avec

▶ **go without** vt fus se passer de

goad [gəud] vt aiguillonner

go-ahead ['gəuəhed] adj dynamique, entreprenant(e) ◆ n feu vert

goal [gəul] n but m

goalkeeper ['gəulki:pə*] n gardien m de but

goalpost [gəulpəust] n poteau m de but

goat [gəut] n chèvre f

gobble ['gɔbl] vt (also: **gobble down, gobble up**) engloutir

go-between ['gəubitwi:n] n médiateur m

god [gɔd] n dieu m; **God** Dieu

godchild ['gɔdtʃaild] n filleul/e

goddaughter ['gɔdɔ:tə*] n filleule f

goddess ['gɔdis] n déesse f

godfather ['gɔdfɑ:ðə*] n parrain m

god-forsaken ['gɔdfəseikən] adj maudit(e)

godmother ['gɔdmʌðə*] n marraine f

godsend ['gɔdsend] n aubaine f

godson ['gɔdsʌn] n filleul m

goggles ['gɔglz] npl lunettes (protectrices) (de motocycliste etc)

going ['gəuiŋ] n (conditions) état m du terrain ◆ adj: **the going rate** le tarif (en vigueur); **a going concern** une affaire prospère; **it was slow going** les progrès étaient lents, ça n'avançait pas vite

gold [gəuld] n or m ◆ adj en or; (reserves) d'or

golden ['gəuldən] adj (made of gold) en or; (gold in colour) doré(e)

goldfish ['gəuldfiʃ] n poisson m rouge

gold-plated ['gəuld'pleitid] adj plaqué(e) or inv

goldsmith ['gəuldsmiθ] n orfèvre m

golf [gɔlf] n golf m

golf ball n balle f de golf; (on typewriter) boule f

golf club n club m de golf; (stick) club m, crosse f de golf

golf course n terrain m de golf

golfer ['gɔlfə*] n joueur/euse de golf

gone [gɔn] pp of **go** ◆ adj parti(e)

gong [gɔŋ] n gong m

good [gud] adj bon(ne); (kind) gentil(le); (child) sage ◆ n bien m; **good!** bon!, très bien!; **to be good at** être bon en; **it's good for you** c'est bon pour vous; **it's a good thing you were there** heureusement que vous étiez là; **she is good with children/her hands** elle sait bien s'occuper des enfants/sait se servir de ses mains; **to feel good** se sentir bien; **it's good to see you** ça me fait plaisir de vous voir, je suis content de vous voir; **he's up to no good** il prépare quelque mauvais coup; **it's no good complaining** cela ne sert à rien de se plaindre; **for the common good** dans l'intérêt commun; **for good** (for ever) pour de bon, une fois pour toutes; **would you be good enough to ...?** auriez-vous la bonté or l'amabilité de ...?; **that's very good of you** c'est très gentil de votre part; **is this any good?** (will it

do?) est-ce que ceci fera l'affaire?, est-ce que cela peut vous rendre service?; (what's it like?) qu'est-ce que ça vaut?; **a good deal (of)** beaucoup (de); **a good many** beaucoup (de); **good morning/afternoon!** bonjour!; **good evening!** bonsoir!; **good night!** bonsoir!; (on going to bed) bonne nuit!

goodbye [gud'bai] excl au revoir!; **to say goodbye to** dire au revoir à

Good Friday n Vendredi saint

good-looking ['gud'lukiŋ] adj bien inv

good-natured ['gud'neitʃəd] adj (person) qui a un bon naturel; (discussion) enjoué(e)

goodness ['gudnis] n (of person) bonté f; **for goodness sake!** je vous en prie!; **goodness gracious!** mon Dieu!

goods train n (BRIT) train m de marchandises.

goodwill [gud'wil] n bonne volonté; (COMM) réputation f (auprès de la clientèle)

goose (pl: **geese**) [gu:s, gi:s] n oie f

gooseberry ['guzbəri] n groseille f à maquereau; **to play gooseberry** (BRIT) tenir la chandelle

gooseflesh ['gu:sfleʃ], **goosepimples** ['gu:spimplz] npl chair f de poule

gore [gɔ:*] vt encorner ◆ n sang m

gorge [gɔ:dʒ] n gorge f ◆ vt: **to gorge o.s. (on)** se gorger (de)

gorgeous ['gɔ:dʒəs] adj splendide, superbe

gorilla [gə'rilə] n gorille m

gorse [gɔ:s] n ajoncs mpl

gory ['gɔ:ri] adj sanglant(e)

go-slow ['gəu'sləu] n (BRIT) grève perlée

gospel ['gɔspl] n évangile m

gossip ['gɔsip] n bavardages mpl; (malicious) commérage m, cancans mpl; (person) commère f ◆ vi bavarder; cancaner, faire des commérages; **a piece of gossip** un ragot, un racontar

got [gɔt] pt, pp of **get**

gotten ['gɔtn]; (US) pp of **get**

gout [gaut] n goutte f

govern ['gʌvən] vt (gen, LING) gouverner

governess ['gʌvənis] n gouvernante f

government ['gʌvnmənt] n gouvernement m; (BRIT: ministers) ministère m ◆ cpd de l'État; **local government** administration locale

governor ['gʌvənə*] n (of colony, state, bank) gouverneur m; (of school, hospital etc) administrateur/trice; (BRIT: of prison) directeur/trice

gown [gaun] n robe f; (of teacher; BRIT: of judge) toge f

GP n abbr (MED) = **general practitioner**

grab [græb] vt saisir, empoigner; (property, power) se saisir de ◆ vi: **to grab at** essayer de saisir

grace [greis] n grâce f ◆ vt honorer; **5 days' grace** répit m de 5 jours; **to say grace** dire le bénédicité; (after meal) dire les grâces; **with a good/bad grace** de bonne/mauvaise grâce; **his sense of**

humour is his saving grace il se rachète par son sens de l'humour

graceful ['greisful] *adj* gracieux(euse), élégant(e)

gracious ['greiʃəs] *adj* (*kind*) charmant(e), bienveillant(e); (*elegant*) plein(e) d'élégance, d'une grande élégance; (*formal: pardon etc*) miséricordieux(euse) ◆ *excl*: (**good) gracious!** mon Dieu!

grade [greid] *n* (*COMM*) qualité *f*; calibre *m*; catégorie *f*; (*in hierarchy*) grade *m*, échelon *m*; (*US: SCOL*) note *f*; classe *f*; (: *gradient*) pente *f* ◆ *vt* classer; calibrer; graduer; **to make the grade** (*fig*) réussir

grade crossing *n* (*US*) passage *m* à niveau

grade school *n* (*US*) école *f* primaire

gradient ['greidiənt] *n* inclinaison *f*, pente *f*; (*GEOM*) gradient *m*

gradual ['grædjuəl] *adj* graduel(le), progressif(ive)

gradually ['grædjuəlɪ] *adv* peu à peu, graduellement

graduate *n* ['grædjuɪt] diplômé/e d'université; (*US*) diplômé/e de fin d'études ◆ *vi* ['grædjueɪt] obtenir un diplôme d'université (*or* de fin d'études)

graduation [grædju'eɪʃən] *n* cérémonie *f* de remise des diplômes

graffiti [grə'fi:tɪ] *npl* graffiti *mpl*

graft [grɑ:ft] *n* (*AGR, MED*) greffe *f*; (*bribery*) corruption *f* ◆ *vt* greffer; **hard graft** (*col*) boulot acharné

grain [greɪn] *n* grain *m*; (*no pl: cereals*) céréales *fpl*; (*US: corn*) blé *m*; **it goes against the grain** cela va à l'encontre de sa (*or* ma *etc*) nature

gram [græm] *n* gramme *m*

grammar ['græmə*] *n* grammaire *f*

grammar school *n* (*BRIT*) ≃ lycée *m*

grammatical [grə'mætɪkl] *adj* grammatical(e)

gramme [græm] *n* = **gram**

grand [grænd] *adj* splendide, imposant(e); (*terrific*) magnifique, formidable; noble ◆ *n* (*col: thousand*) mille livres *fpl* (*or* dollars *mpl*)

grandchildren ['græntʃɪldrən] *npl* petits-enfants *mpl*

granddad ['grændæd] *n* grand-papa *m*

granddaughter ['grændɔːtə*] *n* petite-fille *f*

grandfather ['grændfɑːðə*] *n* grand-père *m*

grandma ['grænmɑː] *n* grand-maman *f*

grandmother ['grænmʌðə*] *n* grand-mère *f*

grandpa ['grænpɑː] *n* = **granddad**

grandparent ['grændpɛərənt] *n* grand-père/grand-mère

grand piano *n* piano *m* à queue

grandson ['grænsʌn] *n* petit-fils *m*

grandstand ['grændstænd] *n* (*SPORT*) tribune *f*

granite ['grænɪt] *n* granit *m*

granny ['grænɪ] *n* grand-maman *f*

grant [grɑ:nt] *vt* accorder; (*a request*) accéder à; (*admit*) concéder ◆ *n* (*SCOL*) bourse *f*; (*ADMIN*) subside *m*, subvention *f*; (*also:* **to take sth for granted**) considérer qch comme acquis; **to grant that** admettre que

granulated ['grænjuleɪtɪd] *adj*: **granulated sugar** sucre *m* en poudre

grape [greɪp] *n* raisin *m*; **a bunch of grapes** une grappe de raisin

grapefruit ['greɪpfruːt] *n* pamplemousse *m*

graph [grɑːf] *n* graphique *m*, courbe *f*

graphic ['græfɪk] *adj* graphique; (*vivid*) vivant(e)

graphics ['græfɪks] *n* (*art*) arts *mpl* graphiques; (*process*) graphisme *m*; (*pl: drawings*) illustrations *fpl*

grapple ['græpl] *vi*: **to grapple with** être aux prises avec

grasp [grɑːsp] *vt* saisir, empoigner; (*understand*) saisir, comprendre ◆ *n* (*grip*) prise *f*; (*fig*) compréhension *f*, connaissance *f*; **to have sth within one's grasp** avoir qch à sa portée; **to have a good grasp of sth** (*fig*) bien comprendre qch

▶ **grasp at** *vt fus* (*rope etc*) essayer de saisir; (*fig: opportunity*) sauter sur

grasping ['grɑːspɪŋ] *adj* avide

grass [grɑːs] *n* herbe *f*; (*BRIT col: informer*) mouchard/e; (: *ex-terrorist*) balanceur/euse

grasshopper ['grɑːshɒpə*] *n* sauterelle *f*

grass roots *npl* (*fig*) base *f*

grate [greit] *n* grille *f* de cheminée ◆ *vi* grincer ◆ *vt* (*CULIN*) râper

grateful ['greitful] *adj* reconnaissant(e)

grater ['greitə*] *n* râpe *f*

gratifying ['grætifaɪɪŋ] *adj* agréable, satisfaisant(e)

grating ['greitɪŋ] *n* (*iron bars*) grille *f* ◆ *adj* (*noise*) grinçant(e)

gratitude ['grætitjuːd] *n* gratitude *f*

gratuity [grə'tjuːɪtɪ] *n* pourboire *m*

grave [greɪv] *n* tombe *f* ◆ *adj* grave, sérieux(euse)

gravel ['grævl] *n* gravier *m*

gravestone ['greɪvstəun] *n* pierre tombale

graveyard ['greɪvjɑːd] *n* cimetière *m*

gravity ['grævɪtɪ] *n* (*PHYSICS*) gravité *f*; pesanteur *f*; (*seriousness*) gravité, sérieux *m*

gravy ['greɪvɪ] *n* jus *m* (de viande), sauce *f* (au jus de viande)

gray [greɪ] *adj* (*US*) = **grey**

graze [greɪz] *vi* paître, brouter ◆ *vt* (*touch lightly*) frôler, effleurer; (*scrape*) écorcher ◆ *n* écorchure *f*

grease [griːs] *n* (*fat*) graisse *f*; (*lubricant*) lubrifiant *m* ◆ *vt* graisser; lubrifier; **to grease the skids** (*US: fig*) huiler les rouages

greaseproof paper ['griːspruːf-] *n* (*BRIT*) papier sulfurisé

greasy ['griːsɪ] *adj* gras(se), graisseux(euse); (*hands, clothes*) graisseux; (*BRIT: road, surface*) glissant(e)

great [greit] *adj* grand(e); (*heat, pain etc*) très fort(e), intense; (*col*) formidable; **they're great friends** ils sont très amis, ce sont de grands amis; **we had a great time** nous nous sommes bien amusés; **it was great!** c'était fantastique or super!; **the great thing is that ...** ce qu'il y a de vraiment bien c'est que ...

Great Britain n Grande-Bretagne f

great-grandfather [greɪt'grænfɑːðə*] n arrière-grand-père m

great-grandmother [greɪt'grænmʌðə*] n arrière-grand-mère f

greatly ['greɪtlɪ] adv très, grandement; (with verbs) beaucoup

greatness ['greɪtnɪs] n grandeur f

Greece [griːs] n Grèce f

greed [griːd] n (also: **greediness**) avidité f; (for food) gourmandise f

greedy ['griːdɪ] adj avide, gourmand(e)

Greek [griːk] adj grec(grecque) ♦ n Grec/Grecque; (LING) grec m; **ancient/modern Greek** grec classique/moderne

green [griːn] adj vert(e); (inexperienced) (bien) jeune, naïf(ïve); (ecological: product etc) écologique ♦ n (colour, of golf course) vert m; (stretch of grass) pelouse f; (also: **village green**) ≃ place f du village; **greens** npl légumes verts; **to have green fingers** or (US) **a green thumb** (fig) avoir le pouce vert; **Green** (POL) écologiste m/f; **the Green Party** le parti écologiste

green belt n (round town) ceinture verte

green card n (AUT) carte verte

greenery ['griːnərɪ] n verdure f

greengrocer ['griːngrəʊsə*] n (BRIT) marchand m de fruits et légumes

greenhouse ['griːnhaʊs] n serre f

greenhouse effect n: **the greenhouse effect** l'effet m de serre

greenhouse gas n gaz m contribuant à l'effet de serre

greenish ['griːnɪʃ] adj verdâtre

Greenland ['griːnlənd] n Groenland m

greet [griːt] vt accueillir

greeting ['griːtɪŋ] n salutation f; **Christmas/birthday greetings** souhaits mpl de Noël/de bon anniversaire

greeting(s) card n carte f de vœux

gregarious [grə'gɛərɪəs] adj grégaire; sociable

grenade [grə'neɪd] n (also: **hand grenade**) grenade f

grew [gruː] pt of **grow**

grey [greɪ] adj gris(e); (dismal) sombre; **to go grey** (commencer à) grisonner

grey-haired [greɪ'hɛəd] adj aux cheveux gris

greyhound ['greɪhaʊnd] n lévrier m

grid [grɪd] n grille f; (ELEC) réseau m; (US AUT) intersection f (matérialisée par des marques au sol)

gridlock ['grɪdlɔk] n (traffic jam) embouteillage m

gridlocked adj: **to be gridlocked** (roads) être

bloqué par un embouteillage; (talks etc) être suspendu

grief [griːf] n chagrin m, douleur f; **to come to grief** (plan) échouer; (person) avoir un malheur

grievance ['griːvəns] n doléance f, grief m; (cause for complaint) grief

grieve [griːv] vi avoir du chagrin; se désoler ♦ vt faire de la peine à, affliger; **to grieve at** se désoler de; pleurer

grievous ['griːvəs] adj grave, cruel(le); **grievous bodily harm** (LAW) coups mpl et blessures fpl

grill [grɪl] n (on cooker) gril m ♦ vt (BRIT) griller; (question) interroger longuement, cuisiner

grille [grɪl] n grillage m; (AUT) calandre f

grill(room) ['grɪl(rum)] n rôtisserie f

grim [grɪm] adj sinistre, lugubre

grimace [grɪ'meɪs] n grimace f ♦ vi grimacer, faire une grimace

grime [graɪm] n crasse f

grin [grɪn] n large sourire m ♦ vi sourire; **to grin (at)** faire un grand sourire (à)

grind [graɪnd] vb, pt, pp **ground** [graʊnd] vt écraser; (coffee, pepper etc) moudre; (US: meat) hacher; (make sharp) aiguiser; (polish: gem, lens) polir ♦ vi (car gears) grincer ♦ n (work) corvée f; **to grind one's teeth** grincer des dents; **to grind to a halt** (vehicle) s'arrêter dans un grincement de freins; (fig) s'arrêter, s'immobiliser; **the daily grind** (col) le train-train quotidien

grip [grɪp] n (control, grasp) étreinte f; (hold) prise f; (handle) poignée f; (holdall) sac m de voyage ♦ vt saisir, empoigner étreindre; **to come to grips with** se colleter avec, en venir aux prises avec; **to grip the road** (AUT) adhérer à la route; **to lose one's grip** lâcher prise; (fig) perdre les pédales, être dépassé(e)

gripping ['grɪpɪŋ] adj prenant(e), palpitant(e)

grisly ['grɪzlɪ] adj sinistre, macabre

gristle ['grɪsl] n cartilage m (de poulet etc)

grit [grɪt] n gravillon m; (courage) cran m ♦ vt (road) sabler; **to grit one's teeth** serrer les dents; **to have a piece of grit in one's eye** avoir une poussière or saleté dans l'œil

groan [grəʊn] n gémissement m; grognement m ♦ vi gémir; grogner

grocer ['grəʊsə*] n épicier m; **at the grocer's** à l'épicerie, chez l'épicier

groceries ['grəʊsərɪz] npl provisions fpl

groin [grɔɪn] n aine f

groom [gruːm] n palefrenier m; (also: **bridegroom**) marié m ♦ vt (horse) panser; (fig): **to groom sb for** former qn pour

groove [gruːv] n sillon m, rainure f

grope [grəʊp] vi tâtonner; **to grope for** vt fus chercher à tâtons

gross [grəʊs] adj grossier(ière); (COMM) brut(e) ♦ n (pl inv) (twelve dozen) grosse f ♦ vt (COMM): **to gross**

£500,000 gagner 500 000 livres avant impôt

grossly ['grəʊslɪ] *adv* (*greatly*) très, grandement

grotto ['grɒtəʊ] *n* grotte *f*

grotty ['grɒtɪ] *adj* (*BRIT col*) minable

ground [graʊnd] *pt, pp of* **grind** ♦ *n* sol *m*, terre *f*; (*land*) terrain *m*, terres *fpl*; (*SPORT*) terrain; (*reason: gen pl*) raison *f*; (*US: also:* **ground wire**) terre *f* ♦ *vt* (*plane*) empêcher de décoller, retenir au sol; (*US ELEC*) équiper d'une prise de terre, mettre à la terre ♦ *vi* (*ship*) s'échouer ♦ *adj* (*coffee etc*) moulu(e); (*US: meat*) haché(e); **grounds** *npl* (*gardens etc*) parc *m*, domaine *m*; (*of coffee*) marc *m*; **on the ground, to the ground** par terre; **below ground** sous terre; **to gain/lose ground** gagner/perdre du terrain; **common ground** terrain d'entente; **he covered a lot of ground in his lecture** sa conférence a traité un grand nombre de questions *or* la question en profondeur

ground cloth *n* (*US*) = **groundsheet**

grounding ['graʊndɪŋ] *n* (*in education*) connaissances *fpl* de base

groundless ['graʊndlɪs] *adj* sans fondement

groundsheet ['graʊndʃiːt] *n* (*BRIT*) tapis *m* de sol

ground staff *n* équipage *m* au sol

groundwork ['graʊndwɜːk] *n* préparation *f*

group [gruːp] *n* groupe *m* ♦ *vt* (*also:* **group together**) grouper ♦ *vi* (*also:* **group together**) se grouper

grouse [graʊs] *n* (*pl inv*) (*bird*) grouse *f* (*sorte de coq de bruyère*) ♦ *vi* (*complain*) rouspéter, râler

grove [grəʊv] *n* bosquet *m*

grovel ['grɒvl] *vi* (*fig*): **to grovel (before)** ramper (devant)

grow, *pt* **grew,** *pp* **grown** [grəʊ, gruː, grəʊn] *vi* (*plant*) pousser, croître; (*person*) grandir; (*increase*) augmenter, se développer; (*become*): **to grow rich/weak** s'enrichir/s'affaiblir ♦ *vt* cultiver, faire pousser

▶ **grow apart** *vi* (*fig*) se détacher (l'un de l'autre)

▶ **grow away from** *vt fus* (*fig*) s'éloigner de

▶ **grow on** *vt fus:* **that painting is growing on me** je finirai par aimer ce tableau

▶ **grow out of** *vt fus* (*clothes*) devenir trop grand pour; (*habit*) perdre (avec le temps); **he'll grow out of it** ça lui passera

▶ **grow up** *vi* grandir

grower ['grəʊə*] *n* producteur *m*; (*AGR*) cultivateur/trice

growing ['grəʊɪŋ] *adj* (*fear, amount*) croissant(e), grandissant(e); **growing pains** (*MED*) fièvre *f* de croissance; (*fig*) difficultés *fpl* de croissance

growl [graʊl] *vi* grogner

grown [grəʊn] *pp of* **grow** ♦ *adj* adulte

grown-up [grəʊn'ʌp] *n* adulte *m/f*, grande personne

growth [grəʊθ] *n* croissance *f*, développement *m*; (*what has grown*) pousse *f*; poussée *f*; (*MED*) grosseur *f*, tumeur *f*

grub [grʌb] *n* larve *f*; (*col: food*) bouffe *f*

grubby ['grʌbɪ] *adj* crasseux(euse)

grudge [grʌdʒ] *n* rancune *f* ♦ *vt:* **to grudge sb sth** donner qch à qn à contre-cœur; reprocher qch à qn; **to bear sb a grudge (for)** garder rancune *or* en vouloir à qn (de); **he grudges spending** il rechigne à dépenser

gruelling ['grʊəlɪŋ] *adj* exténuant(e)

gruesome ['gruːsəm] *adj* horrible

gruff [grʌf] *adj* bourru(e)

grumble ['grʌmbl] *vi* rouspéter, ronchonner

grumpy ['grʌmpɪ] *adj* grincheux(euse)

grunt [grʌnt] *vi* grogner ♦ *n* grognement *m*

G-string ['dʒiːstrɪŋ] *n* (*garment*) cache-sexe *m inv*

guarantee [gærən'tiː] *n* garantie *f* ♦ *vt* garantir; **he can't guarantee (that) he'll come** il n'est pas absolument certain de pouvoir venir

guard [gɑːd] *n* garde *f*, surveillance *f*; (*squad, BOXING, FENCING*) garde *f*; (*one man*) garde *m*; (*BRIT RAIL*) chef *m* de train; (*safety device: on machine*) dispositif *m* de sûreté; (*also:* **fireguard**) garde-feu *m inv* ♦ *vt* garder, surveiller; (*protect*): **to guard (against** *or* **from)** protéger (contre); **to be on one's guard** (*fig*) être sur ses gardes

▶ **guard against** *vi:* **to guard against doing sth** se garder de faire qch

guarded ['gɑːdɪd] *adj* (*fig*) prudent(e)

guardian ['gɑːdɪən] *n* gardien/ne; (*of minor*) tuteur/trice

guard's van *n* (*BRIT RAIL*) fourgon *m*

guerrilla [gə'rɪlə] *n* guérillero *m*

guess [gɛs] *vi* deviner ♦ *vt* deviner; (*US*) croire, penser ♦ *n* supposition *f*, hypothèse *f*; **to take** *or* **have a guess** essayer de deviner; **to keep sb guessing** laisser qn dans le doute *or* l'incertitude, tenir qn en haleine

guesswork ['gɛswɜːk] *n* hypothèse *f*; **I got the answer by guesswork** j'ai deviné la réponse

guest [gɛst] *n* invité/e; (*in hotel*) client/e; **be my guest** faites comme chez vous

guest-house ['gɛsthaʊs] *n* pension *f*

guest room *n* chambre *f* d'amis

guffaw [gʌ'fɔː] *n* gros rire ♦ *vi* pouffer de rire

guidance ['gaɪdəns] *n* conseils *mpl*; **under the guidance of** conseillé(e) *or* encadré(e) par, sous la conduite de; **vocational guidance** orientation professionnelle; **marriage guidance** conseils conjugaux

guide [gaɪd] *n* (*person, book etc*) guide *m*; (*also:* **girl guide**) guide *f* ♦ *vt* guider; **to be guided by sb/sth** se laisser guider par qn/qch

guidebook ['gaɪdbʊk] *n* guide *m*

guide dog *n* chien *m* d'aveugle

guidelines ['gaɪdlaɪnz] *npl* (*fig*) instructions générales, conseils *mpl*

guild [gɪld] n corporation f; cercle m, association f

guillotine ['gɪləti:n] n guillotine f; (for paper) massicot m

guilt [gɪlt] n culpabilité f

guilty ['gɪltɪ] adj coupable; **to plead guilty/not guilty** plaider coupable/non coupable; **to feel guilty about doing sth** avoir mauvaise conscience à faire qch

guinea pig n cobaye m

guise [gaɪz] n aspect m, apparence f

guitar [gɪ'tɑː*] n guitare f

gulf [gʌlf] n golfe m; (abyss) gouffre m; **the (Persian) Gulf** le golfe Persique

gull [gʌl] n mouette f

gullible ['gʌlɪbl] adj crédule

gully ['gʌlɪ] n ravin m; ravine f; couloir m

gulp [gʌlp] vi avaler sa salive; (from emotion) avoir la gorge serrée, s'étrangler ♦ vt (also: **gulp down**) avaler ♦ n (of drink) gorgée f; **at one gulp** d'un seul coup

gum [gʌm] n (ANAT) gencive f; (glue) colle f; (sweet) boule f de gomme; (also: **chewing-gum**) chewing-gum m ♦ vt coller

▶ **gum up** vt: **to gum up the works** (col) bousiller tout

gumboots ['gʌmbuːts] npl (BRIT) bottes fpl en caoutchouc

gun [gʌn] n (small) revolver m, pistolet m; (rifle) fusil m, carabine f; (cannon) canon m ♦ vt (also: **gun down**) abattre; **to stick to one's guns** (fig) ne pas en démordre

gunboat ['gʌnbəut] n canonnière f

gunfire ['gʌnfaɪə*] n fusillade f

gunman ['gʌnmən] n bandit armé

gunpoint ['gʌnpɔɪnt] n: **at gunpoint** sous la menace du pistolet (or fusil)

gunpowder ['gʌnpaudə*] n poudre f à canon

gunshot ['gʌnʃɔt] n coup m de feu; **within gunshot** à portée de fusil

gurgle ['gəːgl] n gargouillis m ♦ vi gargouiller

gush [gʌʃ] n jaillissement m, jet m ♦ vi jaillir; (fig) se répandre en effusions

gust [gʌst] n (of wind) rafale f; (of smoke) bouffée f

gusto ['gʌstəu] n enthousiasme m

gut [gʌt] n intestin m, boyau m; (MUS etc) boyau ♦ vt (poultry, fish) vider; (building) ne laisser que les murs de; **guts** npl boyaux mpl; (col: courage) cran m; **to hate sb's guts** ne pas pouvoir voir qn en peinture or sentir qn

gutter ['gʌtə*] n (of roof) gouttière f; (in street) caniveau m; (fig) ruisseau m

guy [gaɪ] n (also: **guyrope**) corde f; (col: man) type m; (figure) effigie de Guy Fawkes

Guy Fawkes' Night [gaɪ'fɔːks-] n voir encadré

guzzle ['gʌzl] vi s'empiffrer ♦ vt avaler gloutonnement

gym [dʒɪm] n (also: **gymnasium**) gymnase m; (also: **gymnastics**) gym f

gymnast ['dʒɪmnæst] n gymnaste m/f

gymnastics [dʒɪm'næstɪks] n, npl gymnastique f

gym shoes npl chaussures fpl de gym(nastique)

gymslip ['dʒɪmslɪp] n (BRIT) tunique f (d'écolière)

gynaecologist, (US) **gynecologist** [gaɪnɪ'kɔlədʒɪst] n gynécologue m/f

gypsy ['dʒɪpsɪ] n = **gipsy**

— H h —

haberdashery [hæbə'dæʃərɪ] n (BRIT) mercerie f

habit ['hæbɪt] n habitude f; (costume) habit m, tenue f; **to get out of/into the habit of doing sth** perdre/prendre l'habitude de faire qch

habitual [hə'bɪtjuəl] adj habituel(le); (drinker, liar) invétéré(e)

hack [hæk] vt hacher, tailler ♦ n (cut) entaille f; (blow) coup m; (pej: writer) nègre m; (old horse) canasson m

hacker ['hækə*] n (COMPUT) pirate m (informatique); (: enthusiast) passionné/e m/f des ordinateurs

hackneyed ['hæknɪd] adj usé(e), rebattu(e)

had [hæd] pt, pp of **have**

haddock, pl **haddock** or **haddocks** ['hædək] n églefin m; **smoked haddock** haddock m

hadn't ['hædnt] = **had not**

haemorrhage, (US) **hemorrhage** ['hemərɪdʒ] n hémorragie f

haemorrhoids, (US) **hemorrhoids** ['hemərɔɪdz] npl hémorroïdes fpl

haggle ['hægl] vi marchander; **to haggle over** chicaner sur

Hague [heɪg] *n*: **The Hague** La Haye
hail [heɪl] *n* grêle *f* ♦ *vt* (*call*) héler; (*greet*) acclamer ♦ *vi* grêler; (*originate*): **he hails from Scotland** il est originaire d'Écosse
hailstone ['heɪlstəun] *n* grêlon *m*
hair [hɛə*] *n* cheveux *mpl*; (*on body*) poils *mpl*, pilosité *f*; (*single hair: on head*) cheveu *m*; (: *on body*) poil *m*; **to do one's hair** se coiffer
hairbrush ['hɛəbrʌʃ] *n* brosse *f* à cheveux
haircut ['hɛəkʌt] *n* coupe *f* (de cheveux)
hairdo ['hɛəduː] *n* coiffure *f*
hairdresser ['hɛədrɛsə*] *n* coiffeur/euse
hairdryer ['hɛədraɪə*] *n* sèche-cheveux *m*
hair gel *n* gel *m* pour cheveux
hairgrip ['hɛəgrɪp] *n* pince *f* à cheveux
hairnet ['hɛənɛt] *n* résille *f*
hairpiece ['hɛəpiːs] *n* postiche *m*
hairpin ['hɛəpɪn] *n* épingle *f* à cheveux
hairpin bend, (*US*) **hairpin curve** *n* virage *m* en épingle à cheveux
hair-raising ['hɛəreɪzɪŋ] *adj* à (vous) faire dresser les cheveux sur la tête
hair removing cream *n* crème *f* dépilatoire
hair spray *n* laque *f* (pour les cheveux)
hairstyle ['hɛəstaɪl] *n* coiffure *f*
hairy ['hɛərɪ] *adj* poilu(e), chevelu(e); (*fig*) effrayant(e)
hake [heɪk] *n* colin *m*, merlu *m*
half [hɑːf] *n* (*pl*: **halves**) [hɑːvz] moitié *f*; (*SPORT: of match*) mi-temps *f*; (: *of ground*) moitié (du terrain) ♦ *adj* demi(e) ♦ *adv* (à) moitié, à demi; **half-an-hour** une demi-heure; **half a dozen** une demi-douzaine; **half a pound** une demi-livre ≈ 250 g; **two and a half** deux et demi; **a week and a half** une semaine et demie; **half (of it)** la moitié; **half (of)** la moitié de; **half the amount of** la moitié de; **to cut sth in half** couper qch en deux; **half past three** trois heures et demie; **half empty/closed** à moitié vide/fermé; **to go halves (with sb)** se mettre de moitié avec qn
half-caste ['hɑːfkɑːst] *n* métis/se
half-hearted ['hɑːf'hɑːtɪd] *adj* tiède, sans enthousiasme
half-hour [hɑːf'auə*] *n* demi-heure *f*
half-mast ['hɑːf'mɑːst] *n*: **at half-mast** (*flag*) en berne, à mi-mât
halfpenny ['heɪpnɪ] *n* demi-penny *m*
half-price ['hɑːf'praɪs] *adj* à moitié prix ♦ *adv* (*also*: **at half-price**) à moitié prix
half term *n* (*BRIT SCOL*) congé *m* de demi-trimestre
half-time [hɑːf'taɪm] *n* mi-temps *f*
halfway ['hɑːf'weɪ] *adv* à mi-chemin; **to meet sb halfway** (*fig*) parvenir à un compromis avec qn
hall [hɔːl] *n* salle *f*; (*entrance way*) hall *m*, entrée *f*; (*corridor*) couloir *m*; (*mansion*) château *m*, manoir *m*; **hall of residence** *n* (*BRIT*) pavillon *m* or résidence *f* universitaire
hallmark ['hɔːlmɑːk] *n* poinçon *m*; (*fig*) marque *f*
hallo [hə'ləu] *excl* = **hello**
Hallowe'en ['hæləu'iːn] *n* veille *f* de la Toussaint; *voir encadré*

<table>
<tr><td style="text-align:center">

HALLOWE'EN

Selon la tradition, **Hallowe'en** est la nuit des fantômes et des sorcières. En Écosse et aux États-Unis surtout (beaucoup moins en Angleterre) les enfants, pour fêter **Hallowe'en**, se déguisent ce soir-là et ils vont ainsi de porte en porte en demandant de petits cadeaux (du chocolat, une pomme etc).

</td></tr>
</table>

hallucination [həluːsɪ'neɪʃən] *n* hallucination *f*
hallway ['hɔːlweɪ] *n* vestibule *m*; couloir *m*
halo ['heɪləu] *n* (*of saint etc*) auréole *f*; (*of sun*) halo *m*
halt [hɔːlt] *n* halte *f*, arrêt *m* ♦ *vt* faire arrêter ♦ *vi* faire halte, s'arrêter; **to call a halt to sth** (*fig*) mettre fin à qch
halve [hɑːv] *vt* (*apple etc*) partager *or* diviser en deux; (*reduce by half*) réduire de moitié
halves [hɑːvz] *npl of* **half**
ham [hæm] *n* jambon *m*; (*col: also*: **radio ham**) radio-amateur *m*; (*also*: **ham actor**) cabotin/e
hamburger ['hæmbəːgə*] *n* hamburger *m*
hamlet ['hæmlɪt] *n* hameau *m*
hammer ['hæmə*] *n* marteau *m* ♦ *vt* (*fig*) éreinter, démolir ♦ *vi* (*at door*) frapper à coups redoublés; **to hammer a point home to sb** faire rentrer qch dans la tête de qn
▶ **hammer out** *vt* (*metal*) étendre au marteau; (*fig: solution*) élaborer
hammock ['hæmək] *n* hamac *m*
hamper ['hæmpə*] *vt* gêner ♦ *n* panier *m* (d'osier)
hamster ['hæmstə*] *n* hamster *m*
hand [hænd] *n* main *f*; (*of clock*) aiguille *f*; (*handwriting*) écriture *f*; (*at cards*) jeu *m*; (*measurement: of horse*) paume *f*; (*worker*) ouvrier/ière ♦ *vt* passer, donner; **to give sb a hand** donner un coup de main à qn; **at hand** à portée de la main; **in hand** en main; (*work*) en cours; **we have the situation in hand** nous avons la situation bien en main; **to be on hand** (*person*) être disponible; (*emergency services*) se tenir prêt(e) (à intervenir); **to hand** (*information etc*) sous la main, à portée de la main; **to force sb's hand** forcer la main à qn; **to have a free hand** avoir carte blanche; **to have sth in one's hand** tenir qch à la main; **on the one hand ..., on the other hand** d'une part ..., d'autre part
▶ **hand down** *vt* passer; (*tradition, heirloom*) transmettre; (*US: sentence, verdict*) prononcer
▶ **hand in** *vt* remettre
▶ **hand out** *vt* distribuer

▶ **hand over** vt remettre; (*powers etc*) transmettre

▶ **hand round** vt (*BRIT: information*) faire circuler; (*: chocolates etc*) faire passer

handbag ['hændbæg] n sac m à main

handbook ['hændbuk] n manuel m

handbrake ['hændbreɪk] n frein m à main

handcuffs ['hændkʌfs] npl menottes fpl

handful ['hændful] n poignée f

handicap ['hændɪkæp] n handicap m ◆ vt handicaper; **mentally/physically handicapped** handicapé(e) mentalement/physiquement

handicraft ['hændɪkrɑːft] n travail m d'artisanat, technique artisanale

handiwork ['hændɪwɜːk] n ouvrage m; **this looks like his handiwork** (*pej*) ça a tout l'air d'être son œuvre

handkerchief ['hæŋkətʃɪf] n mouchoir m

handle ['hændl] n (*of door etc*) poignée f; (*of cup etc*) anse f; (*of knife etc*) manche m; (*of saucepan*) queue f; (*for winding*) manivelle f ◆ vt toucher, manier; (*deal with*) s'occuper de; (*treat: people*) prendre; **"handle with care"** "fragile"

handlebar(s) ['hændlbɑː(z)] n(pl) guidon m

hand-luggage ['hændlʌgɪdʒ] n bagages mpl à main

handmade ['hænd'meɪd] adj fait(e) à la main

handout ['hændaut] n documentation f, prospectus m; (*press handout*) communiqué m de presse

handrail ['hændreɪl] n rampe f, main courante

handset ['hændset] n (*TEL*) combiné m

hands-free ['hændzfriː] adj (*phone*) mains libres inv

handshake ['hændʃeɪk] n poignée f de main; (*COMPUT*) établissement m de la liaison

handsome ['hænsəm] adj beau(belle); (*gift*) généreux(euse); (*profit*) considérable

handwriting ['hændraɪtɪŋ] n écriture f

handy ['hændɪ] adj (*person*) adroit(e); (*close at hand*) sous la main; (*convenient*) pratique; **to come in handy** être or s'avérer utile

hang, *pt*, *pp* **hung** [hæŋ, hʌŋ] vt accrocher; (*criminal*) *pt*, *pp* **hanged** pendre ◆ vi pendre; (*hair, drapery*) tomber ◆ n: **to get the hang of (doing) sth** (*col*) attraper le coup pour faire qch

▶ **hang about** vi flâner, traîner

▶ **hang around** vi = **hang about**

▶ **hang back** vi (*hesitate*): **to hang back (from doing)** être réticent(e) (pour faire)

▶ **hang on** vi (*wait*) attendre ◆ vt fus (*depend on*) dépendre de; **to hang on to** (*keep hold of*) ne pas lâcher; (*keep*) garder

▶ **hang out** vt (*washing*) étendre (dehors) ◆ vi pendre; (*col: live*) habiter, percher

▶ **hang together** vi (*argument etc*) se tenir, être cohérent(e)

▶ **hang up** vi (*TEL*) raccrocher ◆ vt accrocher, suspendre; **to hang up on sb** (*TEL*) raccrocher au nez

de qn

hangar ['hæŋə*] n hangar m

hanger ['hæŋə*] n cintre m, portemanteau m

hanger-on [hæŋər'ɔn] n parasite m

hang-gliding ['hæŋglaɪdɪŋ] n vol m libre or sur aile delta

hangover ['hæŋəuvə*] n (*after drinking*) gueule f de bois

hang-up ['hæŋʌp] n complexe m

hanker ['hæŋkə*] vi: **to hanker after** avoir envie de

hankie, hanky ['hæŋkɪ] n abbr = **handkerchief**

haphazard [hæp'hæzəd] adj fait(e) au hasard, fait(e) au petit bonheur

happen ['hæpən] vi arriver, se passer, se produire; **what's happening?** que se passe-t-il?; **she happened to be free** il s'est trouvé (or se trouvait) qu'elle était libre; **if anything happened to him** s'il lui arrivait quoi que ce soit; **as it happens** justement

▶ **happen (up)on** vt fus tomber sur

happening ['hæpnɪŋ] n événement m

happily ['hæpɪlɪ] adv heureusement

happiness ['hæpɪnɪs] n bonheur m

happy ['hæpɪ] adj heureux(euse); **happy with** (*arrangements etc*) satisfait(e) de; **yes, I'd be happy to** oui, avec plaisir or (bien) volontiers; **happy birthday!** bon anniversaire!; **happy Christmas/ New Year!** joyeux Noël/bonne année!

happy-go-lucky ['hæpɪgəu'lʌkɪ] adj insouciant(e)

happy hour n l'heure f de l'apéritif, *heure pendant laquelle les consommations sont à prix réduit*

harass ['hærəs] vt accabler, tourmenter

harassment ['hærəsmənt] n tracasseries fpl

harbour, (*US*) **harbor** ['hɑːbə*] n port m ◆ vt héberger, abriter; (*hopes, suspicions*) entretenir; **to harbour a grudge against sb** en vouloir à qn

hard [hɑːd] adj dur(e) ◆ adv (*work*) dur; (*think, try*) sérieusement; **to look hard at** regarder fixement; regarder de près; **to drink hard** boire sec; **hard luck!** pas de veine!; **no hard feelings!** sans rancune!; **to be hard of hearing** être dur(e) d'oreille; **to be hard done by** être traité(e) injustement; **to be hard on sb** être dur(e) avec qn; **I find it hard to believe that ...** je n'arrive pas à croire que ...

hardback ['hɑːbæk] n livre relié

hard cash n espèces fpl

hard disk n (*COMPUT*) disque dur

harden ['hɑːdn] vt durcir; (*steel*) tremper; (*fig*) endurcir ◆ vi (*substance*) durcir

hard-headed ['hɑːd'hedɪd] adj réaliste; décidé(e)

hard labour n travaux forcés

hardly ['hɑːdlɪ] adv (*scarcely*) à peine; (*harshly*) durement; **it's hardly the case** ce n'est guère le cas; **hardly anywhere/ever** presque nulle part/jamais; **I can hardly believe it** j'ai du mal à le croire

hardship ['hɑːdʃɪp] n épreuves fpl; privations fpl

hard shoulder n (BRIT AUT) accotement stabilisé

hard-up [hɑːd'ʌp] adj (col) fauché(e)

hardware ['hɑːdwɛə*] n quincaillerie f; (COMPUT) matériel m

hardware shop n quincaillerie f

hard-wearing [hɑːd'wɛərɪŋ] adj solide

hard-working [hɑːd'wɜːkɪŋ] adj travailleur(euse), consciencieux(euse)

hardy ['hɑːdɪ] adj robuste; (plant) résistant(e) au gel

hare [hɛə*] n lièvre m

hare-brained ['hɛəbreɪnd] adj farfelu(e), écervelé(e)

harm [hɑːm] n mal m; (wrong) tort m ♦ vt (person) faire du mal or du tort à; (thing) endommager; **to mean no harm** ne pas avoir de mauvaises intentions; **there's no harm in trying** on peut toujours essayer; **out of harm's way** à l'abri du danger, en lieu sûr

harmful ['hɑːmful] adj nuisible

harmless [hɑːmlɪs] adj inoffensif(ive), sans méchanceté

harmony ['hɑːmənɪ] n harmonie f

harness ['hɑːnɪs] n harnais m ♦ vt (horse) harnacher; (resources) exploiter

harp [hɑːp] n harpe f ♦ vi: **to harp on about** parler tout le temps de

harrowing ['hærəuɪŋ] adj déchirant(e)

harsh [hɑːʃ] adj (hard) dur(e), sévère; (rough: surface) rugueux(euse); (: sound) discordant(e); (: taste) âpre

harvest ['hɑːvɪst] n (of corn) moisson f; (of fruit) récolte f; (of grapes) vendange f ♦ vi, vt moissonner; récolter; vendanger

has [hæz] vb see **have**

hash [hæʃ] n (CULIN) hachis m; (fig: mess) gâchis m ♦ n abbr (col) = **hashish**

hasn't ['hæznt] = **has not**

hassle ['hæsl] n (col: fuss) histoire(s) f(pl)

haste [heɪst] n hâte f, précipitation f; **in haste** à la hâte, précipitamment

hasten ['heɪsn] vt hâter, accélérer ♦ vi se hâter, s'empresser; **I hasten to add that ...** je m'empresse d'ajouter que ...

hastily ['heɪstɪlɪ] adv à la hâte, précipitamment

hasty ['heɪstɪ] adj hâtif(ive), précipité(e)

hat [hæt] n chapeau m

hatch [hætʃ] n (NAUT: also: **hatchway**) écoutille f; (BRIT: also: **service hatch**) passe-plats m inv ♦ vi éclore ♦ vt faire éclore; (fig: scheme) tramer, ourdir

hatchback ['hætʃbæk] n (AUT) modèle m avec hayon arrière

hatchet ['hætʃɪt] n hachette f

hate [heɪt] vt haïr, détester ♦ n haine f; **to hate to do** or **doing** détester faire; **I hate to trouble you,**

but ... désolé de vous déranger, mais ...

hateful ['heɪtful] adj odieux(euse), détestable

hatred ['heɪtrɪd] n haine f

haughty ['hɔːtɪ] adj hautain(e), arrogant(e)

haul [hɔːl] vt traîner, tirer; (by lorry) camionner; (NAUT) haler ♦ n (of fish) prise f; (of stolen goods etc) butin m

haulage ['hɔːlɪdʒ] n transport routier

haulier ['hɔːlɪə*], (US) **hauler** ['hɔːlə*] n transporteur (routier), camionneur m

haunch [hɔːntʃ] n hanche f; **haunch of venison** cuissot m de chevreuil

haunt [hɔːnt] vt (subj: ghost, fear) hanter; (person) fréquenter ♦ n repaire m

┌─────────────┐
│ KEYWORD │
└─────────────┘

have [hæv], pt, pp **had** aux vb **1** (gen) avoir; être; **to have arrived/gone** être arrivé(e)/allé(e); **to have eaten/slept** avoir mangé/dormi; **he has been promoted** il a eu une promotion

2 (in tag questions): **you've done it, haven't you?** vous l'avez fait, n'est-ce pas?

3 (in short answers and questions): **no I haven't!/ yes we have!** mais non!/mais si!; **so I have!** ah oui!, oui c'est vrai!; **I've been there before, have you?** j'y suis déjà allé, et vous?

♦ modal aux vb (be obliged): **to have (got) to do sth** devoir faire qch, être obligé(e) de faire qch; **she has (got) to do it** elle doit le faire, il faut qu'elle le fasse; **you haven't to tell her** vous n'êtes pas obligé de le lui dire; (must not) ne le lui dites surtout pas

♦ vt **1** (possess, obtain) avoir; **he has (got) blue eyes/dark hair** il a les yeux bleus/les cheveux bruns; **may I have your address?** puis-je avoir votre adresse?

2 (+noun: take, hold etc): **to have breakfast/a bath/a shower** prendre le petit déjeuner/un bain/une douche; **to have dinner/lunch** dîner/déjeuner; **to have a swim** nager; **to have a meeting** se réunir; **to have a party** organiser une fête; **let me have a try** laissez-moi essayer

3: **to have sth done** faire faire qch; **to have one's hair cut** se faire couper les cheveux; **to have sb do sth** faire faire qch à qn

4 (experience, suffer) avoir; **to have a cold/flu** avoir un rhume/la grippe; **to have an operation** se faire opérer; **I won't have it** cela ne se passera pas ainsi

5 (col: dupe) avoir; **he's been had** il s'est fait avoir or rouler

▶ **have out** vt: **to have it out with sb** (settle a problem etc) s'expliquer (franchement) avec qn

haven ['heɪvn] n port m; (fig) havre m

haven't ['hævnt] = **have not**

havoc ['hævək] n ravages mpl, dégâts mpl; **to play havoc with** (fig) désorganiser complètement; détraquer

hawk [hɔːk] n faucon m ♦ vt (goods for sale) colporter

hay [heɪ] n foin m

hay fever n rhume m des foins

haystack ['heɪstæk] n meule f de foin

haywire ['heɪwaɪə*] adj (col): **to go haywire** perdre la tête; mal tourner

hazard ['hæzəd] n (chance) hasard m, chance f; (risk) danger m, risque m ♦ vt risquer, hasarder; **to be a health/fire hazard** présenter un risque pour la santé/d'incendie; **to hazard a guess** émettre or hasarder une hypothèse

hazard (warning) lights npl (AUT) feux mpl de détresse

haze [heɪz] n brume f

hazelnut ['heɪzlʌt] n noisette f

hazy ['heɪzɪ] adj brumeux(euse); (idea) vague; (photograph) flou(e)

he [hiː] pron il; **it is he who ...** c'est lui qui ...; **here he is** le voici; **he-bear** etc ours etc mâle

head [hɛd] n tête f; (leader) chef m ♦ vt (list) être en tête de; (group) être à la tête de; **heads** pl (on coin) (le côté) face; **heads or tails** pile ou face; **head over heels in love** follement or éperdument amoureux(euse); **to head the ball** faire une tête; **10 francs** a or **per head** 10F par personne; **to sit at the head of the table** présider la tablée; **to have a head for business** avoir des dispositions pour les affaires; **to have no head for heights** être sujet(te) au vertige; **to come to a head** (fig: situation etc) devenir critique

▶ **head for** vt fus se diriger vers

▶ **head off** vt (threat, danger) détourner

headache ['hɛdeɪk] n mal m de tête; **to have a headache** avoir mal à la tête

headdress ['hɛddrɛs] n coiffure f

heading ['hɛdɪŋ] n titre m; (subject title) rubrique f

headlamp ['hɛdlæmp] n = **headlight**

headland ['hɛdlənd] n promontoire m cap m

headlight ['hɛdlaɪt] n phare m

headline ['hɛdlaɪn] n titre m

headlong ['hɛdlɔŋ] adv (fall) la tête la première; (rush) tête baissée

headmaster [hɛd'mɑːstə*] n directeur m, proviseur m

headmistress [hɛd'mɪstrɪs] n directrice f

head office n siège m, direction f (générale)

head-on [hɛd'ɔn] adj (collision) de plein fouet

headphones ['hɛdfəunz] npl casque m (à écouteurs)

headquarters (HQ) ['hɛdkwɔːtəz] npl (of business) siège m, direction f (générale); (MIL) quartier général

headrest ['hɛdrɛst] n appui-tête m

headroom ['hɛdrum] n (in car) hauteur f de plafond; (under bridge) hauteur limite; dégagement m

headscarf ['hɛdskɑːf] n foulard m

headstrong ['hɛdstrɔŋ] adj têtu(e), entêté(e)

head teacher n directeur/trice; (of secondary school) proviseur m

head waiter n maître m d'hôtel

headway ['hɛdweɪ] n: **to make headway** avancer, faire des progrès

headwind ['hɛdwɪnd] n vent m contraire

heady ['hɛdɪ] adj capiteux(euse), enivrant(e)

heal [hiːl] vt, vi guérir

health [hɛlθ] n santé f; **Department of Health** (US) ≈ ministère m de la Santé; **Department of Health (DH)** (BRIT) ≈ ministère m de la Santé

health food(s) n(pl) aliment(s) naturel(s)

health food shop n magasin m diététique

Health Service n: **the Health Service** (BRIT) ≈ la Sécurité Sociale

healthy ['hɛlθɪ] adj (person) en bonne santé; (climate, food, attitude etc) sain(e)

heap [hiːp] n tas m, monceau m ♦ vt entasser, amonceler; **heaps (of)** (col: lots) des tas (de); **to heap favours/praise/gifts** etc **on sb** combler qn de faveurs/d'éloges/de cadeaux etc

hear [hɪə*] , pt, pp **heard** [hɜːd] vt entendre; (news) apprendre; (lecture) assister à, écouter ♦ vi entendre; **to hear about** entendre parler de; (have news of) avoir des nouvelles de; **did you hear about the move?** tu es au courant du déménagement?; **to hear from sb** recevoir des nouvelles de qn; **I've never heard of that book** je n'ai jamais entendu parler de ce livre

▶ **hear out** vt écouter jusqu'au bout

hearing ['hɪərɪŋ] n (sense) ouïe f; (of witnesses) audition f; (of a case) audience f; (of committee) séance f; **to give sb a hearing** (BRIT) écouter ce que qn a à dire

hearing aid n appareil m acoustique

hearsay ['hɪəseɪ] n on-dit mpl, rumeurs fpl; **by hearsay** adv par ouï-dire

hearse [hɜːs] n corbillard m

heart [hɑːt] n cœur m; **hearts** npl (CARDS) cœur m; **at heart** au fond; **by heart** (learn, know) par cœur; **to have a weak heart** avoir le cœur malade; avoir des problèmes de cœur; **to lose heart** perdre courage, se décourager; **to take heart** prendre courage; **to set one's heart on sth/on doing sth** vouloir absolument qch/faire qch; **the heart of the matter** le fond du problème

heart attack n crise f cardiaque

heartbeat ['hɑːtbiːt] n battement m de cœur

heartbreaking ['hɑːtbreɪkɪŋ] adj navrant(e), déchirant(e)

heartbroken ['hɑːtbrəukən] adj: **to be heartbroken** avoir beaucoup de chagrin

heartburn ['hɑːtbɜːn] n brûlures fpl d'estomac

heart failure n (MED) arrêt m du cœur

heartfelt ['hɑːtfɛlt] adj sincère

hearth [hɑːθ] *n* foyer *m*, cheminée *f*

heartily [ˈhɑːtɪlɪ] *adv* chaleureusement; (*laugh*) de bon cœur; (*eat*) de bon appétit; **to agree heartily** être entièrement d'accord; **to be heartily sick of** (*BRIT*) en avoir ras le bol de

hearty [ˈhɑːtɪ] *adj* chaleureux(euse), robuste; vigoureux(euse)

heat [hiːt] *n* chaleur *f*; (*fig*) ardeur *f*; feu *m*; (*SPORT: also:* **qualifying heat**) éliminatoire *f*; (*ZOOL*): **in or on heat** (*BRIT*) en chaleur ◆ *vt* chauffer

▶ **heat up** *vi* (*liquids*) chauffer; (*room*) se réchauffer ◆ *vt* réchauffer

heated [ˈhiːtɪd] *adj* chauffé(e); (*fig*) passionné(e), échauffé(e), excité(e)

heater [ˈhiːtə*] *n* appareil *m* de chauffage; radiateur *m*

heath [hiːθ] *n* (*BRIT*) lande *f*

heather [ˈhɛðə*] *n* bruyère *f*

heating [ˈhiːtɪŋ] *n* chauffage *m*

heatstroke [ˈhiːtstrəuk] *n* coup *m* de chaleur

heatwave [ˈhiːtweɪv] *n* vague *f* de chaleur

heave [hiːv] *vt* soulever (avec effort) ◆ *vi* se soulever; (*retch*) avoir des haut-le-cœur ◆ *n* (*push*) poussée *f*; **to heave a sigh** pousser un gros soupir

heaven [ˈhɛvn] *n* ciel *m*, paradis *m*; **heaven forbid!** surtout pas!; **thank heaven!** Dieu merci; **for heaven's sake!** (*pleading*) je vous en prie!; (*protesting*) mince alors!

heavenly [ˈhɛvnlɪ] *adj* céleste, divin(e)

heavily [ˈhɛvɪlɪ] *adv* lourdement; (*drink, smoke*) beaucoup; (*sleep, sigh*) profondément

heavy [ˈhɛvɪ] *adj* lourd(e); (*work, rain, user, eater*) gros(se); (*drinker, smoker*) grand(e); **it's heavy going** ça ne va pas tout seul, c'est pénible

heavy goods vehicle (HGV) *n* (*BRIT*) poids lourd *m* (P.L.)

heavyweight [ˈhɛvɪweɪt] *n* (*SPORT*) poids lourd

Hebrew [ˈhiːbruː] *adj* hébraïque ◆ *n* (*LING*) hébreu *m*

Hebrides [ˈhɛbrɪdiːz] *n*: **the Hebrides** les Hébrides *fpl*

heckle [ˈhɛkl] *vt* interpeller (*un orateur*)

hectic [ˈhɛktɪk] *adj* agité(e), trépidant(e); (*busy*) trépidant

he'd [hiːd] = **he would, he had**

hedge [hɛdʒ] *n* haie *f* ◆ *vi* se défiler ◆ *vt*: **to hedge one's bets** (*fig*) se couvrir; **as a hedge against inflation** pour se prémunir contre l'inflation

▶ **hedge in** *vt* entourer d'une haie

hedgehog [ˈhɛdʒhɔg] *n* hérisson *m*

heed [hiːd] *vt* (*also:* **take heed of**) tenir compte de, prendre garde à

heedless [ˈhiːdlɪs] *adj* insouciant(e)

heel [hiːl] *n* talon *m* ◆ *vt* (*shoe*) retalonner; **to bring to heel** (*dog*) faire venir à ses pieds; (*fig: person*) rappeler à l'ordre; **to take to one's heels**

prendre ses jambes à son cou

hefty [ˈhɛftɪ] *adj* (*person*) costaud(e); (*parcel*) lourd(e); (*piece, price*) gros(se)

heifer [ˈhɛfə*] *n* génisse *f*

height [haɪt] *n* (*of person*) taille *f*, grandeur *f*; (*of object*) hauteur *f*; (*of plane, mountain*) altitude *f*; (*high ground*) hauteur, éminence *f*; (*fig: of glory*) sommet *m*; (*: of stupidity*) comble *m*; **what height are you?** combien mesurez-vous?, quelle est votre taille?; **of average height** de taille moyenne; **to be afraid of heights** être sujet/te au vertige; **it's the height of fashion** c'est le dernier cri

heighten [ˈhaɪtn] *vt* hausser, surélever; (*fig*) augmenter

heir [ɛə*] *n* héritier *m*

heiress [ˈɛəres] *n* héritière *f*

heirloom [ˈɛəluːm] *n* meuble *m* (*or* bijou *m* *or* tableau *m*) de famille

held [hɛld] *pt, pp of* **hold**

helicopter [ˈhɛlɪkɔptə*] *n* hélicoptère *m*

hell [hɛl] *n* enfer *m*; **a hell of a ...** (*col*) un(e) sacré(e) ...; **oh hell!** (*col*) merde!

he'll [hiːl] = **he will, he shall**

hellish [ˈhɛlɪʃ] *adj* infernal(e)

hello [həˈləu] *excl* bonjour!; salut! (*to sb one addresses as "tu"*); (*surprise*) tiens!

helm [hɛlm] *n* (*NAUT*) barre *f*

helmet [ˈhɛlmɪt] *n* casque *m*

help [hɛlp] *n* aide *f*; (*charwoman*) femme *f* de ménage; (*assistant etc*) employé/e ◆ *vt* aider; **help!** au secours!; **help yourself (to bread)** servez-vous (de pain); **can I help you?** (*in shop*) vous désirez?; **with the help of** (*person*) avec l'aide de; (*tool etc*) à l'aide de; **to be of help to sb** être utile à qn; **to help sb (to) do sth** aider qn à faire qch; **I can't help saying** je ne peux pas m'empêcher de dire; **he can't help it** il n'y peut rien

helper [ˈhɛlpə*] *n* aide *m/f*, assistant/e

helpful [ˈhɛlpful] *adj* serviable, obligeant(e); (*useful*) utile

helping [ˈhɛlpɪŋ] *n* portion *f*

helpless [ˈhɛlplɪs] *adj* impuissant(e); (*baby*) sans défense

hem [hɛm] *n* ourlet *m* ◆ *vt* ourler

▶ **hem in** *vt* cerner; **to feel hemmed in** (*fig*) avoir l'impression d'étouffer, se sentir oppressé(e) *or* écrasé(e)

hemorrhage [ˈhɛmərɪdʒ] *n* (*US*) = **haemorrhage**

hemorrhoids [ˈhɛmərɔɪdz] *npl* (*US*) = **haemorrhoids**

hen [hɛn] *n* poule *f*; (*female bird*) femelle *f*

hence [hɛns] *adv* (*therefore*) d'où, de là; **2 years hence** d'ici 2 ans

henceforth [hɛnsˈfɔːθ] *adv* dorénavant

her [hɑː*] *pron* (*direct*) la, l' + *vowel or h mute*; (*indirect*) lui; (*stressed, after prep*) elle; *see note at* **she** ◆ *adj* son(sa), ses *pl*; **I see her** je la vois; **give her a**

book donne-lui un livre; **after her** après elle

herald ['herəld] n héraut m ◆ vt annoncer

heraldry ['herəldrɪ] n héraldique f; (coat of arms) blason m

herb [hə:b] n herbe f; **herbs** npl (CULIN) fines herbes

herd [hə:d] n troupeau m; (of wild animals, swine) troupeau, troupe f ◆ vt (drive: animals, people) mener, conduire; (gather) rassembler; **herded together** parqués (comme du bétail)

here [hɪə•] adv ici ◆ excl tiens!, tenez!; **here!** présent!; **here is, here are** voici; **here's my sister** voici ma sœur; **here he/she is** le(la) voici; **here she comes la** voici qui vient; **come here!** viens ici!; **here and there** ici et là

hereafter [hɪər'ɑ:ftə•] adv après, plus tard; ci-après ◆ n: **the hereafter** l'au-delà m

hereby [hɪə'baɪ] adv (in letter) par la présente

hereditary [hɪ'redɪtrɪ] adj héréditaire

heresy ['herəsɪ] n hérésie f

heritage ['herɪtɪdʒ] n héritage m, patrimoine m; **our national heritage** notre patrimoine national

hermit ['hə:mɪt] n ermite m

hernia ['hə:nɪə] n hernie f

hero (pl: **heroes**) ['hɪərəu] n héros m

heroin ['herəuɪn] n héroïne f

heroine ['herəuɪn] n héroïne f (femme)

heron ['herən] n héron m

herring ['herɪŋ] n hareng m

hers [hə:z] pron le(la) sien(ne), les siens(siennes); **a friend of hers** un(e) ami(e) à elle, un(e) de ses ami(e)s

herself [hə:'self] pron (reflexive) se; (emphatic) elle-même; (after prep) elle

he's [hi:z] = **he is, he has**

hesitant ['hezɪtənt] adj hésitant(e), indécis(e); **to be hesitant about doing sth** hésiter à faire qch

hesitate ['hezɪteɪt] vi: **to hesitate (about/to do)** hésiter (sur/à faire)

hesitation [hezɪ'teɪʃən] n hésitation f; **I have no hesitation in saying (that) ...** je n'hésiterai pas à dire (que) ...

heterosexual ['hetərəu'seksjuəl] adj, n hétéro-sexuel/le

heyday ['heɪdeɪ] n: **the heyday of** l'âge m d'or de, les beaux jours de

HGV n abbr = **heavy goods vehicle**

hi [haɪ] excl salut!

hiatus [haɪ'eɪtəs] n trou m, lacune f; (LING) hiatus m

hibernate ['haɪbəneɪt] vi hiberner

hiccough, hiccup ['hɪkʌp] vi hoqueter ◆ n hoquet m; **to have (the) hiccoughs** avoir le hoquet

hide [haɪd] n (skin) peau f ◆ vb, pt **hid**, pp **hidden** [hɪd, 'hɪdn] vt: **to hide sth (from sb)** cacher qch (à qn); (feelings, truth) dissimuler qch (à qn) ◆ vi: **to**

hide (from sb) se cacher (de qn)

hide-and-seek ['haɪdən'si:k] n cache-cache m

hideous ['hɪdɪəs] adj hideux(euse), atroce

hiding ['haɪdɪŋ] n (beating) correction f, volée f de coups; **to be in hiding** (concealed) se tenir caché(e)

hierarchy ['haɪərɑ:kɪ] n hiérarchie f

hi-fi ['haɪfaɪ] adj, n abbr (= high fidelity) hi-fi f inv

high [haɪ] adj haut(e); (speed, respect, number) grand(e); (price) élevé(e); (wind) fort(e), violent(e); (voice) aigu(ë); (col: person: on drugs) défoncé(e), fait(e); (: on drink) soûl(e), bourré(e); (BRIT CULIN: meat, game) faisandé(e); (: spoilt) avarié(e) ◆ adv haut, en haut ◆ n: **exports have reached a new high** les exportations ont atteint un nouveau record; **20 m high** haut/e de 20 m; **to pay a high price for sth** payer cher pour qch

highbrow ['haɪbrau] adj, n intellectuel/le

highchair ['haɪtʃeə•] n chaise haute (pour enfant)

higher education n études supérieures

high-handed [haɪ'hændɪd] adj très autoritaire; très cavalier(ière)

high-heeled [haɪ'hi:ld] adj à hauts talons

high jump n (SPORT) saut m en hauteur

highlands ['haɪləndz] npl région montagneuse; **the Highlands** (in Scotland) les Highlands mpl

highlight ['haɪlaɪt] n (fig: of event) point culminant ◆ vt faire ressortir, souligner; **highlights** npl (hairstyle) reflets mpl

highly ['haɪlɪ] adv très, fort, hautement; **highly paid** très bien payé(e); **to speak highly of** dire beaucoup de bien de

highly strung adj nerveux(euse), toujours tendu(e)

highness ['haɪnɪs] n hauteur f; **Her Highness** son Altesse f

high-pitched [haɪ'pɪtʃt] adj aigu(ë)

high-rise (block) ['haɪraɪz-] n tour f (d'habitation)

high school n lycée m; (US) établissement m d'enseignement supérieur; voir encadré

HIGH SCHOOL

Une **high school** est un établissement d'enseignement secondaire. Aux États-Unis, il y a la "Junior High School", qui correspond au collège, et la "Senior High School", qui correspond au lycée. En Grande-Bretagne, c'est un nom que l'on donne parfois aux écoles secondaires; voir "elementary school".

high season n (BRIT) haute saison

high street n (BRIT) grand-rue f

highway ['haɪweɪ] n grand'route f, route nationale; **the information highway** l'autoroute f de l'information

Highway Code n (BRIT) code m de la route

hijack ['haɪdʒæk] vt détourner (par la force) ♦ n (also: **hijacking**) détournement m (d'avion)

hijacker ['haɪdʒækə*] n auteur m d'un détournement d'avion, pirate m de l'air

hike [haɪk] vi aller à pied ♦ n excursion f à pied, randonnée f; (col: in prices etc) augmentation f ♦ vt (col) augmenter

hiker ['haɪkə*] n promeneur/euse, excursionniste m/f

hiking ['haɪkɪŋ] n excursions fpl à pied, randonnée f

hilarious [hɪ'lɛərɪəs] adj désopilant(e)

hill [hɪl] n colline f; (fairly high) montagne f; (on road) côte f

hillside ['hɪlsaɪd] n (flanc m de) coteau m

hill-walking ['hɪl'wɔːkɪŋ] n randonnée f de basse montagne

hilly ['hɪlɪ] adj vallonné(e), montagneux(euse); (road) à fortes côtes

hilt [hɪlt] n (of sword) garde f; **to the hilt** (fig: support) à fond

him [hɪm] pron (direct) le, l' + vowel or h mute; (stressed, indirect, after prep) lui; **I see him** je le vois; **give him a book** donne-lui un livre; **after him** après lui

himself [hɪm'sɛlf] pron (reflexive) se; (emphatic) lui-même; (after prep) lui

hinder ['hɪndə*] vt gêner; (delay) retarder; (prevent): **to hinder sb from doing** empêcher qn de faire

hindrance ['hɪndrəns] n gêne f, obstacle m

hindsight ['haɪndsaɪt] n bon sens après coup; **with the benefit of hindsight** avec du recul, rétrospectivement

Hindu ['hɪnduː] n Hindou/e

hinge [hɪndʒ] n charnière f ♦ vi (fig): **to hinge on** dépendre de

hint [hɪnt] n allusion f; (advice) conseil m ♦ vt: **to hint that** insinuer que ♦ vi: **to hint at** faire une allusion à; **to drop a hint** faire une allusion or insinuation; **give me a hint** (clue) mettez-moi sur la voie, donnez-moi une indication

hip [hɪp] n hanche f; (BOT) fruit m de l'églantier or du rosier

hippie, hippy ['hɪpɪ] n hippie m/f

hippo ['hɪpəu], pl **hippos, hippopotamus**, pl **hippopotamuses** or **hippopotami** [hɪpə'pɔtəmaɪ, -'pɔtəmaɪ] n hippopotame m

hire ['haɪə*] vt (BRIT: car, equipment) louer; (worker) embaucher, engager ♦ n location f; **for hire** à louer; (taxi) libre; **on hire** en location

▶ **hire out** vt louer

hire(d) car ['haɪə(d)-] n (BRIT) voiture louée

hire purchase (H.P.) n (BRIT) achat m (or vente f) à tempérament or crédit; **to buy sth on hire purchase** acheter qch en location-vente

his [hɪz] pron le(la) sien(ne), les siens(siennes) ♦ adj son(sa) ses pl; **this is his** c'est à lui, c'est le sien

hiss [hɪs] vi siffler ♦ n sifflement m

historic(al) [hɪ'stɔrɪk(l)] adj historique

history ['hɪstərɪ] n histoire f; **medical history** (of patient) passé médical

hit [hɪt] vt (pt, pp **hit**) frapper; (knock against) cogner; (reach: target) atteindre, toucher; (collide with: car) entrer en collision avec, heurter; (fig: affect) toucher; (find) tomber sur ♦ n coup m; (success) coup réussi; succès m; (song) chanson f à succès, tube m; (to website) visite f; **to hit it off with sb** bien s'entendre avec qn; **to hit the headlines** être à la une des journaux; **to hit the road** (col) se mettre en route

▶ **hit back** vi: **to hit back at sb** prendre sa revanche sur qn

▶ **hit out at** vt fus envoyer un coup à; (fig) attaquer

▶ **hit (up)on** vt fus (answer) trouver (par hasard); (solution) tomber sur (par hasard)

hit-and-run driver ['hɪtænd'rʌn-] n chauffard m

hitch [hɪtʃ] vt (fasten) accrocher, attacher; (also: **hitch up**) remonter d'une saccade ♦ n (knot) nœud m; (difficulty) anicroche f, contretemps m; **to hitch a lift** faire du stop; **technical hitch** incident m technique

▶ **hitch up** vt (horse, cart) atteler; for phrases see also **hitch**

hitchhike ['hɪtʃhaɪk] vi faire de l'auto-stop

hitchhiker ['hɪtʃhaɪkə*] n auto-stoppeur/euse

hi-tech ['haɪ'tɛk] adj de pointe ♦ n high-tech m

hitherto [hɪðə'tuː] adv jusqu'ici, jusqu'à présent

hitman ['hɪtmæn] n (col) tueur m à gages

HIV n abbr (= human immunodeficiency virus) HIV m, VIH m; **HIV-negative/-positive** séronégatif(ive)/séropositif(ive)

hive [haɪv] n ruche f; **the shop was a hive of activity** (fig) le magasin était une véritable ruche

▶ **hive off** vt (col) mettre à part, séparer

HMS abbr (BRIT) = His (or Her) Majesty's Ship

hoard [hɔːd] n (of food) provisions fpl, réserves fpl; (of money) trésor m ♦ vt amasser

hoarding ['hɔːdɪŋ] n (BRIT) panneau m d'affichage or publicitaire

hoarse [hɔːs] adj enroué(e)

hoax [həuks] n canular m

hob [hɔb] n plaque chauffante

hobble ['hɔbl] vi boitiller

hobby ['hɔbɪ] n passe-temps favori

hobo ['həubəu] n (US) vagabond m

hockey ['hɔkɪ] n hockey m

hog [hɔg] n porc (châtré) m ♦ vt (fig) accaparer; **to go the whole hog** aller jusqu'au bout

hoist [hɔɪst] n palan m ♦ vt hisser

hold [həʊld], *vb: pt, pp* **held** [hɛld] *vt* tenir; (*contain*) contenir; (*keep back*) retenir; (*believe*) maintenir; considérer; (*possess*) avoir; détenir ♦ *vi* (*withstand pressure*) tenir (bon); (*be valid*) valoir ♦ *n* prise *f*; (*fig*) influence *f*; (*NAUT*) cale *f*; **to catch** *or* **get (a) hold of** saisir; **to get hold of** (*fig*) trouver; **to get hold of o.s.** se contrôler; **hold the line!** (*TEL*) ne quittez pas!; **to hold one's own** (*fig*) (bien) se défendre; **to hold office** (*POL*) avoir un portefeuille; **to hold firm** *or* **fast** tenir bon; **he holds the view that ...** il pense *or* estime que …, d'après lui …; **to hold sb responsible for sth** tenir qn pour responsable de qch

▶ **hold back** *vt* retenir; (*secret*) cacher; **to hold sb back from doing sth** empêcher qn de faire qch

▶ **hold down** *vt* (*person*) maintenir à terre; (*job*) occuper

▶ **hold forth** *vi* pérorer

▶ **hold off** *vt* tenir à distance ♦ *vi* (*rain*): **if the rain holds off** s'il ne pleut pas, s'il ne se met pas à pleuvoir

▶ **hold on** *vi* tenir bon; (*wait*) attendre; **hold on!** (*TEL*) ne quittez pas!

▶ **hold on to** *vt fus* se cramponner à; (*keep*) conserver, garder

▶ **hold out** *vt* offrir ♦ *vi* (*resist*): **to hold out (against)** résister (devant), tenir bon (devant)

▶ **hold over** *vt* (*meeting etc*) ajourner, reporter

▶ **hold up** *vt* (*raise*) lever; (*support*) soutenir; (*delay*) retarder; (: *traffic*) ralentir; (*rob*) braquer

holdall ['həʊldɔːl] *n* (*BRIT*) fourre-tout *m inv*

holder ['həʊldə*] *n* (*of ticket, record*) détenteur/trice; (*of office, title, passport etc*) titulaire *m/f*

holding ['həʊldɪŋ] *n* (*share*) intérêts *mpl*; (*farm*) ferme *f*

hold-up ['həʊldʌp] *n* (*robbery*) hold-up *m*; (*delay*) retard *m*; (*BRIT*: *in traffic*) embouteillage *m*

hole [həʊl] *n* trou *m* ♦ *vt* trouer, faire un trou dans; **hole in the heart** (*MED*) communication *f* interventriculaire; **to pick holes (in)** (*fig*) chercher des poux (dans)

▶ **hole up** *vi* se terrer

hole-in-the-wall [həʊlɪnðə'wɔːl] *n* (*cash dispenser*) distributeur *m* de billets

holiday ['hɔlədeɪ] *n* (*BRIT*: *vacation*) vacances *fpl*; (*day off*) jour *m* de congé; (*public*) jour férié; **to be on holiday** être en congé; **tomorrow is a holiday** demain c'est fête, on a congé demain

holiday camp *n* (*BRIT*: *for children*) colonie *f* de vacances; (*also*: **holiday centre**) camp *m* de vacances

holiday-maker ['hɔlədeɪmeɪkə*] *n* (*BRIT*) vacancier/ière

holiday resort *n* centre *m* de villégiature *or* de vacances

Holland ['hɔlənd] *n* Hollande *f*

hollow ['hɔləʊ] *adj* creux(euse); (*fig*) faux(fausse) ♦ *n* creux *m*; (*in land*) dépression *f* (de terrain),

cuvette *f* ♦ *vt*: **to hollow out** creuser, évider

holly ['hɔlɪ] *n* houx *m*

holocaust ['hɔləkɔːst] *n* holocauste *m*

holster ['həʊlstə*] *n* étui *m* de revolver

holy ['həʊlɪ] *adj* saint(e); (*bread, water*) bénit(e); (*ground*) sacré(e)

Holy Ghost, Holy Spirit *n* Saint-Esprit *m*

homage ['hɔmɪdʒ] *n* hommage *m*; **to pay homage to** rendre hommage à

home [həʊm] *n* foyer *m*, maison *f*; (*country*) pays natal, patrie *f*; (*institution*) maison ♦ *adj* de famille; (*ECON, POL*) national(e), intérieur(e); (*SPORT*: *team*) qui reçoit; (: *match, win*) sur leur (*or* notre) terrain ♦ *adv* chez soi, à la maison; au pays natal; (*right in: nail etc*) à fond; **at home** chez soi, à la maison; **to go** (*or* **come**) **home** rentrer (chez soi), rentrer à la maison (*or* au pays); **make yourself at home** faites comme chez vous; **near my home** près de chez moi

▶ **home in on** *vt fus* (*missile*) se diriger automatiquement vers *or* sur

home address *n* domicile permanent

homeland ['həʊmlænd] *n* patrie *f*

homeless ['həʊmlɪs] *adj* sans foyer, sans abri; **the homeless** *npl* les sans-abri *mpl*

homely ['həʊmlɪ] *adj* simple, sans prétention; accueillant(e)

home-made [həʊm'meɪd] *adj* fait(e) à la maison

home match *n* match *m* à domicile

Home Office *n* (*BRIT*) ministère *m* de l'Intérieur

home page *n* (*COMPUT*) page *f* d'accueil

home rule *n* autonomie *f*

Home Secretary *n* (*BRIT*) ministre *m* de l'Intérieur

homesick ['həʊmsɪk] *adj*: **to be homesick** avoir le mal du pays; (*missing one's family*) s'ennuyer de sa famille

home town *n* ville natale

homeward ['həʊmwəd] *adj* (*journey*) du retour ♦ *adv* = **homewards**

homework ['həʊmwəːk] *n* devoirs *mpl*

homoeopathic [həʊmɪəʊ'pæθɪk], (*US* **homeopathic**) *adj* (*medicine, methods*) homéopathique; (*doctor*) homéopathe

homogeneous [həʊməʊ'dʒiːnɪəs] *adj* homogène

homosexual [hɔməʊ'sɛksjʊəl] *adj*, *n* homosexuel/le

honest ['ɔnɪst] *adj* honnête; (*sincere*) franc(franche); **to be quite honest with you ...** à dire vrai …

honestly ['ɔnɪstlɪ] *adv* honnêtement; franchement

honesty ['ɔnɪstɪ] *n* honnêteté *f*

honey ['hʌnɪ] *n* miel *m*; (*col: darling*) chéri/e

honeycomb ['hʌnɪkəʊm] *n* rayon *m* de miel; (*pattern*) nid *m* d'abeilles, motif alvéolé ♦ *vt* (*fig*): **to honeycomb with** cribler de

honeymoon ['hʌnɪmuːn] *n* lune *f* de miel, voyage *m* de noces

honeysuckle ['hʌnɪsʌkl] *n* chèvrefeuille *m*

honk [hɔŋk] *n* (AUT) coup *m* de klaxon ♦ *vi* klaxonner

honorary ['ɔnərərɪ] *adj* honoraire; (*duty, title*) honorifique

honour, (US) **honor** ['ɔnə*] *vt* honorer ♦ *n* honneur *m*; **in honour of** en l'honneur de

hono(u)rable ['ɔnərəbl] *adj* honorable

hono(u)rs degree *n* (SCOL) licence avec mention

hood [hud] *n* capuchon *m*; (BRIT AUT) capote *f*; (US AUT) capot *m*; (col) truand *m*

hoodie ['hudɪ] *n* (top) sweat *m* à capuche

hoof (*pl*: **hoofs** *or* **hooves**) [hu:f, hu:vz] *n* sabot *m*

hook [huk] *n* crochet *m*; (*on dress*) agrafe *f*; (*for fishing*) hameçon *m* ♦ *vt* accrocher; (*dress*) agrafer; **hook and eye** agrafe; **by hook or by crook** de gré ou de force, coûte que coûte; **to be hooked (on)** (col) être accroché(e) (par); (*person*) être dingue (de)

▶ **hook up** *vt* (RADIO, TV ETC) faire un duplex entre

hooligan ['hu:lɪgən] *n* voyou *m*

hoop [hu:p] *n* cerceau *m*; (*of barrel*) cercle *m*

hooray [hu:'reɪ] *excl* hourra

hoot [hu:t] *vi* (AUT) klaxonner; (*siren*) mugir; (*owl*) hululer ♦ *vt* (*jeer at*) huer ♦ *n* huée *f*; coup *m* de klaxon; mugissement *m*; hululement *m*; **to hoot with laughter** rire aux éclats

hooter ['hu:tə*] *n* (BRIT AUT) klaxon *m*; (NAUT, factory) sirène *f*

hoover® ['hu:və*] *n* (BRIT) aspirateur *m* ♦ *vt* (*room*) passer l'aspirateur dans; (*carpet*) passer l'aspirateur sur

hooves [hu:vz] *npl of* **hoof**

hop [hɔp] *vi* sauter; (*on one foot*) sauter à cloche-pied ♦ *n* saut *m*

hope [həup] *vt, vi* espérer ♦ *n* espoir *m*; **I hope so** je l'espère; **I hope not** j'espère que non

hopeful ['həupful] *adj* (*person*) plein(e) d'espoir; (*situation*) prometteur(euse), encourageant(e); **I'm hopeful that she'll manage to come** j'ai bon espoir qu'elle pourra venir

hopefully ['həupfulɪ] *adv* avec espoir, avec optimisme; **hopefully, they'll come back** espérons bien qu'ils reviendront

hopeless ['həuplɪs] *adj* désespéré(e), sans espoir; (*useless*) nul(le)

hops [hɔps] *npl* houblon *m*

horizon [hə'raɪzn] *n* horizon *m*

horizontal [hɔrɪ'zɔntl] *adj* horizontal(e)

horn [hɔ:n] *n* corne *f*; (MUS) cor *m*; (AUT) klaxon *m*

hornet ['hɔ:nɪt] *n* frelon *m*

horoscope ['hɔrəskəup] *n* horoscope *m*

horrendous [hə'rendəs] *adj* horrible, affreux(euse)

horrible ['hɔrɪbl] *adj* horrible, affreux(euse)

horrid ['hɔrɪd] *adj* méchant(e), désagréable

horrify ['hɔrɪfaɪ] *vt* horrifier

horror ['hɔrə*] *n* horreur *f*

horror film *n* film *m* d'épouvante

hors d'œuvre [ɔ:'də:vrə] *n* hors d'œuvre *m*

horse [hɔ:s] *n* cheval *m*

horseback ['hɔ:sbæk] *n*: **on horseback** *adj, adv* à cheval

horse chestnut *n* marron *m* (d'Inde)

horseman ['hɔ:smən] *n* cavalier *m*

horsepower (h.p.) ['hɔ:spauə*] *n* puissance *f* (en chevaux); cheval-vapeur *m* (CV)

horse-racing ['hɔ:sreɪsɪŋ] *n* courses *fpl* de chevaux

horseradish ['hɔ:srædɪʃ] *n* raifort *m*

horseshoe ['hɔ:sʃu:] *n* fer *m* à cheval

hose [həuz] *n* tuyau *m*; (*also*: **garden hose**) tuyau d'arrosage

▶ **hose down** *vt* laver au jet

hospitable ['hɔspɪtəbl] *adj* hospitalier(ière)

hospital ['hɔspɪtl] *n* hôpital *m*; **in hospital**, (US) **in the hospital** à l'hôpital

hospitality [hɔspɪ'tælɪtɪ] *n* hospitalité *f*

host [həust] *n* hôte *m*; (*in hotel etc*) patron *m*; (TV, RADIO) présentateur/trice, animateur/trice; (*large number*): **a host of** une foule de; (REL) hostie *f* ♦ *vt* (TV programme) présenter, animer

hostage ['hɔstɪdʒ] *n* otage *m*

hostel ['hɔstl] *n* foyer *m*; (*also*: **youth hostel**) auberge *f* de jeunesse

hostess ['həustɪs] *n* hôtesse *f*; (AVIAT) hôtesse de l'air; (*in nightclub*) entraîneuse *f*

hostile ['hɔstaɪl] *adj* hostile

hostility [hɔ'stɪlɪtɪ] *n* hostilité *f*

hot [hɔt] *adj* chaud(e); (*more than just warm*) très chaud; (*spicy*) fort(e); (*fig*) acharné(e); brûlant(e); violent(e), passionné(e); **to be hot** (*person*) avoir chaud; (*thing*) être (très) chaud; (*weather*) faire chaud

▶ **hot up** (BRIT col) *vi* (*situation*) devenir tendu(e); (*party*) s'animer ♦ *vt* (*pace*) accélérer, forcer; (*engine*) gonfler

hotbed ['hɔtbed] *n* (*fig*) foyer *m*, pépinière *f*

hot dog *n* hot-dog *m*

hotel [həu'tel] *n* hôtel *m*

hothouse ['hɔthaus] *n* serre chaude

hotline ['hɔtlaɪn] *n* (POL) téléphone *m* rouge, ligne directe

hotly ['hɔtlɪ] *adv* passionnément, violemment

hotplate ['hɔtpleɪt] *n* (*on cooker*) plaque chauffante

hotpot ['hɔtpɔt] *n* (BRIT CULIN) ragoût *m*

hot-water bottle [hɔt'wɔ:tə*] *n* bouillotte *f*

hound [haund] *vt* poursuivre avec acharnement ♦ *n* chien courant; **the hounds** la meute

hour ['auə*] *n* heure *f*; **at 30 miles an hour** ≃ à 50 km à l'heure; **lunch hour** heure du déjeuner; **to pay sb by the hour** payer qn à l'heure

hourly ['auəlɪ] *adj* toutes les heures; (*rate*) horaire; **hourly paid** *adj* payé(e) à l'heure

house *n* [haus] (*pl*: **houses** ['hauzɪz]) maison *f*; (*POL*) chambre *f*; (*THEAT*) salle *f*; auditoire *m* ♦ *vt* [hauz], (*person*) loger, héberger; **at** (*or* **to**) **my house** chez moi; **the House of Commons/of Lords** (*BRIT*) la Chambre des communes/des lords; **the House (of Representatives)** (*US*) la Chambre des représentants; **on the house** (*fig*) aux frais de la maison

house arrest *n* assignation *f* à domicile

houseboat ['hausbəut] *n* bateau (aménagé en habitation)

housebound ['hausbaund] *adj* confiné(e) chez soi

housebreaking ['hausbreɪkɪŋ] *n* cambriolage *m* (avec effraction)

household ['haushəuld] *n* ménage *m*; (*people*) famille *f*, maisonnée *f*; **household name** nom connu de tout le monde

housekeeper ['hauskiːpə*] *n* gouvernante *f*

housekeeping ['hauskiːpɪŋ] *n* (*work*) ménage *m*; (*also*: **housekeeping money**) argent *m* du ménage; (*COMPUT*) gestion *f* (des disques)

house-warming ['hauswɔːmɪŋ] *n* (*also*: **house-warming party**) pendaison *f* de crémaillère

housewife ['hauswaɪf] *n* ménagère *f*; femme *f* du foyer

housework ['hauswɜːk] *n* (travaux *mpl* du) ménage *m*

housing ['hauzɪŋ] *n* logement *m* ♦ *cpd* (*problem, shortage*) de or du logement

housing development, (*BRIT*) **housing estate** *n* cité *f*; lotissement *m*

hovel ['hɔvl] *n* taudis *m*

hover ['hɔvə*] *vi* planer; **to hover round sb** rôder or tourner autour de qn

hovercraft ['hɔvəkrɑːft] *n* aéroglisseur *m*

how [hau] *adv* comment; **how are you?** comment allez-vous?; **how do you do?** bonjour; (*on being introduced*) enchanté(e); **how far is it to ...?** combien y a-t-il jusqu'à ...?; **how long have you been here?** depuis combien de temps êtes-vous là?; **how lovely!** que or comme c'est joli!; **how many/ much?** combien?; **how old are you?** quel âge avez-vous?; **how's life?** (*col*) comment ça va?; **how about a drink?** si on buvait quelque chose?; **how is it that ...?** comment se fait-il que ... + *sub*?

however [hau'ɛvə*] *conj* pourtant, cependant ♦ *adv* de quelque façon or manière que + *sub*; (+ *adjective*) quelque or si ... que + *sub*; (*in questions*) comment

howl [haul] *n* hurlement *m* ♦ *vi* hurler

H.P. *n abbr* (*BRIT*) = **hire purchase**

h.p. *abbr* (*AUT*) = **horsepower**

HQ *n abbr* (= **headquarters**) QG *m*

hub [hʌb] *n* (*of wheel*) moyeu *m*; (*fig*) centre *m*, foyer *m*

hubcap [hʌbkæp] *n* (*AUT*) enjoliveur *m*

huddle ['hʌdl] *vi*: **to huddle together** se blottir les uns contre les autres

hue [hjuː] *n* teinte *f*, nuance *f*; **hue and cry** *n* tollé (général), clameur *f*

huff [hʌf] *n*: **in a huff** fâché(e); **to take the huff** prendre la mouche

hug [hʌg] *vt* serrer dans ses bras; (*shore, kerb*) serrer ♦ *n* étreinte *f*; **to give sb a hug** serrer qn dans ses bras

huge [hjuːdʒ] *adj* énorme, immense

hulk [hʌlk] *n* (*ship*) vieux rafiot; (*car, building*) carcasse *f*; (*person*) mastodonte *m*, malabar *m*

hull [hʌl] *n* (*of ship, nuts*) coque *f*; (*of peas*) cosse *f*

hullo [hə'ləu] *excl* = **hello**

hum [hʌm] *vt* (*tune*) fredonner ♦ *vi* fredonner; (*insect*) bourdonner; (*plane, tool*) vrombir ♦ *n* fredonnement *m*; bourdonnement *m*; vrombissement *m*

human ['hjuːmən] *adj* humain(e) ♦ *n* (*also*: **human being**) être humain

humane [hjuː'meɪn] *adj* humain(e), humanitaire

humanitarian [hjuːmænɪ'tɛərɪən] *adj* humanitaire

humanity [hjuː'mænɪtɪ] *n* humanité *f*

humble ['hʌmbl] *adj* humble, modeste ♦ *vt* humilier

humdrum ['hʌmdrʌm] *adj* monotone, routinier(ière)

humid ['hjuːmɪd] *adj* humide

humiliate [hjuː'mɪlɪeɪt] *vt* humilier

humiliation [hjuːmɪlɪ'eɪʃən] *n* humiliation *f*

humorous ['hjuːmərəs] *adj* humoristique; (*person*) plein(e) d'humour

humour, (*US*) **humor** ['hjuːmə*] *n* humour *m*; (*mood*) humeur *f* ♦ *vt* (*person*) faire plaisir à; se prêter aux caprices de; **sense of humour** sens *m* de l'humour; **to be in a good/bad humour** être de bonne/mauvaise humeur

hump [hʌmp] *n* bosse *f*

hunch [hʌntʃ] *n* bosse *f*; (*premonition*) intuition *f*; **I have a hunch that** j'ai (comme une vague) idée que

hunchback ['hʌntʃbæk] *n* bossu/e

hunched [hʌntʃt] *adj* arrondie(e), voûté(e)

hundred ['hʌndrəd] *num* cent; **about a hundred people** une centaine de personnes; **hundreds of people** des centaines de gens; **I'm a hundred per cent sure** j'en suis absolument certain

hundredweight ['hʌndrɪdweɪt] *n* (*BRIT*) =50.8 kg; 112 lb; (*US*) = 45.3 kg; 100 lb

hung [hʌŋ] *pt, pp of* **hang**

Hungary ['hʌŋgərɪ] *n* Hongrie *f*

hunger ['hʌŋgə*] *n* faim *f* ♦ *vi*: **to hunger for** avoir faim de, désirer ardemment

hungry ['hʌŋgrɪ] *adj* affamé(e); **to be hungry** avoir faim; **hungry for** (*fig*) avide de

hunk [hʌŋk] n gros morceau; (col: man) beau mec
hunt [hʌnt] vt (seek) chercher; (SPORT) chasser ♦ vi
chasser ♦ n chasse f
▶ **hunt down** vt pourchasser
hunter ['hʌntə*] n chasseur m; (BRIT: horse) cheval
m de chasse
hunting ['hʌntɪŋ] n chasse f
hurdle ['həːdl] n (SPORT) haie f; (fig) obstacle m
hurl [həːl] vt lancer (avec violence)
hurrah, hurray [hu'rɑː, hu'reɪ] n hourra m
hurricane ['hʌrɪkən] n ouragan m
hurried ['hʌrɪd] adj pressé(e), précipité(e); (work)
fait(e) à la hâte
hurriedly ['hʌrɪdlɪ] adv précipitamment, à la hâte
hurry ['hʌrɪ] n hâte f, précipitation f ♦ vi se presser, se dépêcher ♦ vt (person) faire presser, faire se
dépêcher; (work) presser; **to be in a hurry** être
pressé(e); **to do sth in a hurry** faire qch en vitesse;
to hurry in/out entrer/sortir précipitamment; **to
hurry home** se dépêcher de rentrer
▶ **hurry along** vi marcher d'un pas pressé
▶ **hurry away, hurry off** vi partir précipitamment
▶ **hurry up** vi se dépêcher
hurt [həːt], vb: pt, pp **hurt** vt (cause pain to) faire
mal à; (injure, fig) blesser; (damage: business, interests etc) nuire à; faire du tort à ♦ vi faire mal ♦ adj
blessé(e); **I hurt my arm** je me suis fait mal au bras;
where does it hurt? où avez-vous mal?, où est-ce
que ça vous fait mal?
hurtful ['həːtful] adj (remark) blessant(e)
hurtle ['həːtl] vt lancer (de toutes ses forces) ♦ vi:
to hurtle past passer en trombe; **to hurtle down**
dégringoler
husband ['hʌzbənd] n mari m
hush [hʌʃ] n calme m, silence m ♦ vt faire taire;
hush! chut!
▶ **hush up** vt (fact) étouffer
husk [hʌsk] n (of wheat) balle f; (of rice, maize)
enveloppe f; (of peas) cosse f
husky ['hʌskɪ] adj rauque; (burly) costaud(e) ♦ n
chien m esquimau or de traîneau
hustle ['hʌsl] vt pousser, bousculer ♦ n bousculade f; **hustle and bustle** n tourbillon m (d'activité)
hut [hʌt] n hutte f; (shed) cabane f
hutch [hʌtʃ] n clapier m
hyacinth ['haɪəsɪnθ] n jacinthe f
hydrant ['haɪdrənt] n prise f d'eau; (also: **fire
hydrant**) bouche f d'incendie
hydraulic [haɪ'drɔːlɪk] adj hydraulique
hydroelectric ['haɪdrəʊɪ'lektrɪk] adj hydro-
électrique
hydrofoil ['haɪdrəfɔɪl] n hydrofoil m
hydrogen ['haɪdrədʒən] n hydrogène m
hyena [haɪ'iːnə] n hyène f
hygiene ['haɪdʒiːn] n hygiène f
hygienic [haɪ'dʒiːnɪk] adj hygiénique

hymn [hɪm] n hymne m; cantique m
hype [haɪp] n (col) matraquage m publicitaire or
médiatique
hypermarket ['haɪpəmɑːkɪt] n (BRIT) hypermarché m
hypertext ['haɪpətekst] n (COMPUT) hypertexte m
hyphen ['haɪfn] n trait m d'union
hypnotize ['hɪpnətaɪz] vt hypnotiser
hypocrisy [hɪ'pɔkrɪsɪ] n hypocrisie f
hypocrite ['hɪpəkrɪt] n hypocrite m/f
hypocritical [hɪpə'krɪtɪkl] adj hypocrite
hypothesis (pl: **hypotheses**) [haɪ'pɔθɪsɪs, -siːz] n
hypothèse f
hysterical [hɪ'sterɪkl] adj hystérique; **to become
hysterical** avoir une crise de nerfs
hysterics [hɪ'sterɪks] npl (violente) crise de nerfs;
(laughter) crise de rire; **to have hysterics** avoir une
crise de nerfs; attraper un fou rire

— I i —

I, i [aɪ] n (letter) I, i m; **I for Isaac**, (US) **I for Item** I
comme Irma
I [aɪ] pron je; (before vowel) j'; (stressed) moi ♦ abbr
(= island, isle) I
ice [aɪs] n glace f; (on road) verglas m ♦ vt (cake)
glacer; (drink) faire rafraîchir ♦ vi (also: **ice over**)
geler; (also: **ice up**) se givrer; **to put sth on ice** (fig)
mettre qch en attente
iceberg ['aɪsbəːg] n iceberg m; **the tip of the iceberg** (also fig) la partie émergée de l'iceberg
icebox ['aɪsbɔks] n (US) réfrigérateur m; (BRIT) compartiment m à glace; (insulated box) glacière f
ice cream n glace f
ice cube n glaçon m
iced [aɪst] adj (drink) frappé(e); (coffee, tea, also
cake) glacé(e)
ice hockey n hockey m sur glace
Iceland ['aɪslənd] n Islande f
ice lolly [-'lɔlɪ] n (BRIT) esquimau m
ice rink n patinoire f
ice-skating ['aɪsskeɪtɪŋ] n patinage m (sur glace)
icicle ['aɪsɪkl] n glaçon m (naturel)
icing ['aɪsɪŋ] n givrage m; (CULIN) glaçage m
icing sugar n (BRIT) sucre m glace
ICT n abbr (BRIT SCOL: = Information and
Communication Technology) TIC fpl
icy ['aɪsɪ] adj glacé(e); (road) verglacé(e); (weather,
temperature) glacial(e)
I'd [aɪd] = I would, I had
idea [aɪ'dɪə] n idée f; **good idea!** bonne idée!; **to
have an idea that ...** avoir idée que ...; **I haven't
the least idea** je n'ai pas la moindre idée

ideal [aɪˈdɪəl] n idéal m ♦ adj idéal(e)

identical [aɪˈdɛntɪkl] adj identique

identification [aɪdɛntɪfɪˈkeɪʃən] n identification f; **means of identification** pièce f d'identité

identify [aɪˈdɛntɪfaɪ] vt identifier ♦ vi: **to identify with** s'identifier à

Identikit® [aɪˈdɛntɪkɪt] n: **Identikit (picture)** portrait-robot m

identity [aɪˈdɛntɪtɪ] n identité f

identity card n carte f d'identité

ideology [aɪdɪˈɔlədʒɪ] n idéologie f

idiom [ˈɪdɪəm] n langue f, idiome m; (phrase) expression f idiomatique

idiosyncrasy [ɪdɪəʊˈsɪŋkrəsɪ] n particularité f, caractéristique f

idiot [ˈɪdɪət] n idiot/e, imbécile m/f

idiotic [ɪdɪˈɔtɪk] adj idiot(e), bête, stupide

idle [ˈaɪdl] adj sans occupation, désœuvré(e); (lazy) oisif(ive), paresseux(euse); (unemployed) au chômage; (machinery) au repos; (question, pleasures) vain(e), futile ♦ vi (engine) tourner au ralenti; **to lie idle** être arrêté, ne pas fonctionner

▶ **idle away** vt: **to idle away one's time** passer son temps à ne rien faire

idol [ˈaɪdl] n idole f

idolize [ˈaɪdəlaɪz] vt idolâtrer, adorer

i.e. abbr (= id est: that is) c. à d., c'est-à-dire

if [ɪf] conj si ♦ n: **there are a lot of ifs and buts in** il y a beaucoup de si mpl et de mais mpl; **I'd be pleased if you could do it** je serais très heureux si vous pouviez le faire; **if necessary** si nécessaire, le cas échéant; **if only he were here** si seulement il était là; **if only to show him my gratitude** ne serait-ce que pour lui témoigner ma gratitude

ignite [ɪgˈnaɪt] vt mettre le feu à, enflammer ♦ vi s'enflammer

ignition [ɪgˈnɪʃən] n (AUT) allumage m; **to switch on/off the ignition** mettre/couper le contact

ignition key n (AUT) clé f de contact

ignorant [ˈɪgnərənt] adj ignorant(e); **to be ignorant of** (subject) ne rien connaître en; (events) ne pas être au courant de

ignore [ɪgˈnɔːʳ] vt ne tenir aucun compte de, ne pas relever; (person) faire semblant de ne pas reconnaître, ignorer; (fact) méconnaître

ill [ɪl] adj (sick) malade; (bad) mauvais(e) ♦ n mal m ♦ adv: **to speak/think ill of sb** dire/penser du mal de qn; **to take** or **be taken ill** tomber malade

I'll [aɪl] = **I will, I shall**

ill-advised [ɪləʳdˈvaɪzd] adj (decision) peu judicieux(euse); (person) malavisé(e)

ill-at-ease [ɪlətˈiːz] adj mal à l'aise

illegal [ɪˈliːgl] adj illégal(e)

illegible [ɪˈlɛdʒɪbl] adj illisible

illegitimate [ɪlɪˈdʒɪtɪmət] adj illégitime

ill-fated [ɪlˈfeɪtɪd] adj malheureux(euse); (day) néfaste

ill feeling n ressentiment m, rancune f

illiterate [ɪˈlɪtərət] adj illettré(e); (letter) plein(e) de fautes

ill-mannered [ɪlˈmænəd] adj impoli(e), grossier(ière)

illness [ˈɪlnɪs] n maladie f

ill-treat [ɪlˈtriːt] vt maltraiter

illuminate [ɪˈluːmɪneɪt] vt (room, street) éclairer; (building) illuminer; **illuminated sign** enseigne lumineuse

illumination [ɪluːmɪˈneɪʃən] n éclairage m; illumination f

illusion [ɪˈluːʒən] n illusion f; **to be under the illusion that** avoir l'illusion que

illustrate [ˈɪləstreɪt] vt illustrer

illustration [ɪləˈstreɪʃən] n illustration f

ill will n malveillance f

I'm [aɪm] = **I am**

image [ˈɪmɪdʒ] n image f; (public face) image de marque

imagery [ˈɪmɪdʒərɪ] n images fpl

imaginary [ɪˈmædʒɪnərɪ] adj imaginaire

imagination [ɪmædʒɪˈneɪʃən] n imagination f

imaginative [ɪˈmædʒɪnətɪv] adj imaginatif(ive), plein(e) d'imagination

imagine [ɪˈmædʒɪn] vt s'imaginer; (suppose) imaginer, supposer

imbalance [ɪmˈbæləns] n déséquilibre m

imitate [ˈɪmɪteɪt] vt imiter

imitation [ɪmɪˈteɪʃən] n imitation f

immaculate [ɪˈmækjulət] adj impeccable; (REL) immaculé(e)

immaterial [ɪməˈtɪərɪəl] adj sans importance, insignifiant(e)

immature [ɪməˈtjuəʳ] adj (fruit) qui n'est pas mûr(e); (person) qui manque de maturité

immediate [ɪˈmiːdɪət] adj immédiat(e)

immediately [ɪˈmiːdɪətlɪ] adv (at once) immédiatement; **immediately next to** juste à côté de

immense [ɪˈmɛns] adj immense; énorme

immerse [ɪˈmɜːs] vt immerger, plonger; **to immerse sth in** plonger qch dans

immersion heater [ɪˈmɜːʃən-] n (BRIT) chauffe-eau m électrique

immigrant [ˈɪmɪgrənt] n immigrant/e; (already established) immigré/e

immigration [ɪmɪˈgreɪʃən] n immigration f

imminent [ˈɪmɪnənt] adj imminent(e)

immoral [ɪˈmɔrl] adj immoral(e)

immortal [ɪˈmɔːtl] adj, n immortel/le

immune [ɪˈmjuːn] adj: **immune (to)** immunisé(e) (contre)

immunity [ɪˈmjuːnɪtɪ] n immunité f; **diplomatic immunity** immunité diplomatique

impact [ˈɪmpækt] n choc m, impact m; (fig) impact m

impair [ɪmˈpɛəʳ] vt détériorer, diminuer

impart [ɪmˈpɑːt] vt (make known) communiquer, transmettre; (bestow) confier, donner

impartial [ɪmˈpɑːʃl] adj impartial(e)

impassable [ɪmˈpɑːsəbl] adj infranchissable; (road) impraticable

impassive [ɪmˈpæsɪv] adj impassible

impatience [ɪmˈpeɪʃəns] n impatience f

impatient [ɪmˈpeɪʃənt] adj impatient(e); **to get** or **grow impatient** s'impatienter

impatiently [ɪmˈpeɪʃəntlɪ] adv avec impatience

impeccable [ɪmˈpekəbl] adj impeccable, parfait(e)

impede [ɪmˈpiːd] vt gêner

impediment [ɪmˈpedɪmənt] n obstacle m; (also: **speech impediment**) défaut m d'élocution

impending [ɪmˈpendɪŋ] adj imminent(e)

imperative [ɪmˈperətɪv] adj nécessaire; urgent(e), pressant(e); (tone) impérieux(euse) ◆ n (LING) impératif m

imperfect [ɪmˈpɜːfɪkt] adj imparfait(e); (goods etc) défectueux(euse) ◆ n (LING: also: **imperfect tense**) imparfait m

imperial [ɪmˈpɪərɪəl] adj impérial(e); (BRIT: measure) légal(e)

impersonal [ɪmˈpɜːsənl] adj impersonnel(le)

impersonate [ɪmˈpɜːsəneɪt] vt se faire passer pour; (THEAT) imiter

impertinent [ɪmˈpɜːtɪnənt] adj impertinent(e), insolent(e)

impervious [ɪmˈpɜːvɪəs] adj imperméable; (fig): **impervious to** insensible à; inaccessible à

impetuous [ɪmˈpetjʊəs] adj impétueux(euse), fougueux(euse)

impetus [ˈɪmpətəs] n impulsion f; (of runner) élan m

impinge [ɪmˈpɪndʒ]: **to impinge on** vt fus (person) affecter, toucher; (rights) empiéter sur

implement n [ˈɪmplɪmənt] outil m, instrument m; (for cooking) ustensile m ◆ vt [ˈɪmplɪment] exécuter, mettre à effet

implicit [ɪmˈplɪsɪt] adj implicite; (complete) absolu(e), sans réserve

imply [ɪmˈplaɪ] vt (hint) suggérer, laisser entendre; (mean) indiquer, supposer

impolite [ɪmpəˈlaɪt] adj impoli(e)

import vt [ɪmˈpɔːt] importer ◆ n [ˈɪmpɔːt] (COMM) importation f; (meaning) portée f, signification f ◆ cpd (duty, licence etc) d'importation

importance [ɪmˈpɔːtns] n importance f; **to be of great/little importance** avoir beaucoup/peu d'importance

important [ɪmˈpɔːtnt] adj important(e); **it is important that** il importe que, il est important que; **it's not important** c'est sans importance, ce n'est pas important

importer [ɪmˈpɔːtə*] n importateur/trice

impose [ɪmˈpəʊz] vt imposer ◆ vi: **to impose on**

sb abuser de la gentillesse de qn

imposing [ɪmˈpəʊzɪŋ] adj imposant(e), impressionnant(e)

imposition [ɪmpəˈzɪʃən] n (of tax etc) imposition f; **to be an imposition on** (person) abuser de la gentillesse or la bonté de

impossible [ɪmˈpɒsɪbl] adj impossible; **it is impossible for me to leave** il m'est impossible de partir

impotent [ˈɪmpətnt] adj impuissant(e)

impound [ɪmˈpaʊnd] vt confisquer, saisir

impoverished [ɪmˈpɒvərɪʃt] adj pauvre, appauvri(e)

impractical [ɪmˈpræktɪkl] adj pas pratique; (person) qui manque d'esprit pratique

impregnable [ɪmˈpregnəbl] adj (fortress) imprenable; (fig) inattaquable, irréfutable

impress [ɪmˈpres] vt impressionner, faire impression sur; (mark) imprimer, marquer; **to impress sth on sb** faire bien comprendre qch à qn

impressed [ɪmˈprest] adj impressionné(e)

impression [ɪmˈpreʃən] n impression f; (of stamp, seal) empreinte f; **to make a good/bad impression on sb** faire bonne/mauvaise impression sur qn; **to be under the impression that** avoir l'impression que

impressionist [ɪmˈpreʃənɪst] n impressionniste m/f

impressive [ɪmˈpresɪv] adj impressionnant(e)

imprint [ˈɪmprɪnt] n empreinte f; (PUBLISHING) notice f; (: label) nom m (de collection or d'éditeur)

imprison [ɪmˈprɪzn] vt emprisonner, mettre en prison

improbable [ɪmˈprɒbəbl] adj improbable; (excuse) peu plausible

improper [ɪmˈprɒpə*] adj (wrong) incorrect(e); (unsuitable) déplacé(e), de mauvais goût; indécent(e)

improve [ɪmˈpruːv] vt améliorer ◆ vi s'améliorer; (pupil etc) faire des progrès

▶ **improve (up)on** vt fus (offer) enchérir sur

improvement [ɪmˈpruːvmənt] n amélioration f; (of pupil etc) progrès m; **to make improvements to** apporter des améliorations à

improvise [ˈɪmprəvaɪz] vt, vi improviser

impudent [ˈɪmpjudnt] adj impudent(e)

impulse [ˈɪmpʌls] n impulsion f; **on impulse** impulsivement, sur un coup de tête

impulsive [ɪmˈpʌlsɪv] adj impulsif(ive)

KEYWORD

in [ɪn] prep 1 (indicating place, position) dans; **in the house/the fridge** dans la maison/le frigo; **in the garden** dans le or au jardin; **in town** en ville; **in the country** à la campagne; **in school** à l'école; **in here/there** ici/là

2 (with place names: of town, region, country): **in**

London à Londres; **in England** en Angleterre; **in Japan** au Japon; **in the United States** aux États-Unis

3 (*indicating time: during*): **in spring** au printemps; **in summer** en été; **in May/1992** en mai/1992; **in the afternoon** (dans) l'après-midi; **at 4 o'clock in the afternoon** à 4 heures de l'après-midi

4 (*indicating time: in the space of*) en; (: *future*) dans; **I did it in 3 hours/days** je l'ai fait en 3 heures/jours; **I'll see you in 2 weeks** *or* **in 2 weeks' time** je te verrai dans 2 semaines; **once in a hundred years** une fois tous les cent ans

5 (*indicating manner etc*) à; **in a loud/soft voice** à voix haute/basse; **in pencil** au crayon; **in writing** par écrit; **in French** en français; **to pay in dollars** payer en dollars; **the boy in the blue shirt** le garçon à *or* avec la chemise bleue

6 (*indicating circumstances*): **in the sun** au soleil; **in the shade** à l'ombre; **in the rain** sous la pluie

7 (*indicating mood, state*): **in tears** en larmes; **in anger** sous le coup de la colère; **in despair** au désespoir; **in good condition** en bon état; **to live in luxury** vivre dans le luxe

8 (*with ratios, numbers*): **1 in 10 (households), 1 (household) in 10** 1 (ménage) sur 10; **20 pence in the pound** 20 pence par livre sterling; **they lined up in twos** ils se mirent en rangs (deux) par deux; **in hundreds** par centaines

9 (*referring to people, works*) chez; **the disease is common in children** c'est une maladie courante chez les enfants; **in (the works of) Dickens** chez Dickens, dans (l'œuvre de) Dickens

10 (*indicating profession etc*) dans; **to be in teaching** être dans l'enseignement

11 (*after superlative*) de; **the best pupil in the class** le meilleur élève de la classe

12 (*with present participle*): **in saying this** en disant ceci

♦ *adv:* **to be in** (*person: at home, work*) être là; (*train, ship, plane*) être arrivé(e); (*in fashion*) être à la mode; **to ask sb in** inviter qn à entrer; **to run/limp** *etc* **in** entrer en courant/boitant *etc*; **their party is in** leur parti est au pouvoir

♦ *n:* **the ins and outs (of)** (*of proposal, situation etc*) les tenants et aboutissants (de)

in. *abbr* = **inch(es)**

inability [ɪnə'bɪlɪtɪ] *n* incapacité *f*; **inability to pay** incapacité de payer

inaccurate [ɪn'ækjʊrət] *adj* inexact(e); (*person*) qui manque de précision

inadequate [ɪn'ædɪkwət] *adj* insuffisant(e), inadéquat(e)

inadvertently [ɪnəd'vɜːtntlɪ] *adv* par mégarde

inadvisable [ɪnəd'vaɪzəbl] *adj* à déconseiller; **it is inadvisable to** il est déconseillé de

inane [ɪ'neɪn] *adj* inepte, stupide

inanimate [ɪn'ænɪmət] *adj* inanimé(e)

inappropriate [ɪnə'prəʊprɪət] *adj* inopportun(e), mal à propos; (*word, expression*) impropre

inarticulate [ɪnɑː'tɪkjʊlət] *adj* (*person*) qui s'exprime mal; (*speech*) indistinct(e)

inasmuch as [ɪnəz'mʌtʃ-] *adv* vu que, en ce sens que

inauguration [ɪnɔːgjʊ'reɪʃən] *n* inauguration *f*; investiture *f*

inborn [ɪn'bɔːn] *adj* (*feeling*) inné(e); (*defect*) congénital(e)

inbred [ɪn'brɛd] *adj* inné(e), naturel(le); (*family*) consanguin(e)

Inc. *abbr* = **incorporated**

incapable [ɪn'keɪpəbl] *adj:* **incapable (of)** incapable (de)

incapacitate [ɪnkə'pæsɪteɪt] *vt:* **to incapacitate sb from doing** rendre qn incapable de faire

incense *n* ['ɪnsɛns] encens *m* ♦ *vt* [ɪn'sɛns] (*anger*) mettre en colère

incentive [ɪn'sɛntɪv] *n* encouragement *m*, raison *f* de se donner de la peine

incessant [ɪn'sɛsnt] *adj* incessant(e)

incessantly [ɪn'sɛsntlɪ] *adv* sans cesse, constamment

inch [ɪntʃ] *n* pouce *m* (=25 mm; 12 in a foot); **within an inch of** à deux doigts de; **he wouldn't give an inch** (*fig*) il n'a pas voulu céder d'un pouce *or* faire la plus petite concession

▶ **inch forward** *vi* avancer petit à petit

incident ['ɪnsɪdnt] *n* incident *m*; (*in book*) péripétie *f*

incidental [ɪnsɪ'dɛntl] *adj* accessoire; (*unplanned*) accidentel(le); **incidental to** qui accompagne; **incidental expenses** faux frais *mpl*

incidentally [ɪnsɪ'dɛntəlɪ] *adv* (*by the way*) à propos

inclination [ɪnklɪ'neɪʃən] *n* inclination *f*

incline *n* ['ɪnklaɪn] pente *f*, plan incliné ♦ *vb* [ɪn'klaɪn] ♦ *vt* incliner ♦ *vi:* **to incline to** avoir tendance à; **to be inclined to do** être enclin(e) à faire; (*have a tendency to do*) avoir tendance à faire; **to be well inclined towards sb** être bien disposé(e) à l'égard de qn

include [ɪn'kluːd] *vt* inclure, comprendre; **the tip is/is not included** le service est compris/n'est pas compris

including [ɪn'kluːdɪŋ] *prep* y compris; **including tip** service compris

inclusive [ɪn'kluːsɪv] *adj* inclus(e), compris(e); **£50 inclusive of all surcharges** 50 livres tous frais compris

income ['ɪnkʌm] *n* revenu *m*; **gross/net income** revenu brut/net; **income and expenditure account** compte *m* de recettes et de dépenses

income tax *n* impôt *m* sur le revenu

incoming ['ɪnkʌmɪŋ] *adj* (*passengers, mail*) à l'arrivée; (*government, tenant*) nouveau(nouvelle);

incoming tide marée montante

incompetent [ɪn'kɔmpɪtnt] *adj* incompétent(e), incapable

incomplete [ɪnkəm'pli:t] *adj* incomplet(ète)

incongruous [ɪn'kɔŋgruəs] *adj* peu approprié(e); (*remark, act*) incongru(e), déplacé(e)

inconsiderate [ɪnkən'sɪdərət] *adj* (*action*) inconsidéré(e); (*person*) qui manque d'égards

inconsistency [ɪnkən'sɪstənsɪ] *n* (*of actions etc*) inconséquence *f*; (*of work*) irrégularité *f*; (*of statement etc*) incohérence *f*

inconsistent [ɪnkən'sɪstnt] *adj* inconséquent(e), irregulier(ière), peu cohérent(e); **inconsistent with** en contradiction avec

inconspicuous [ɪnkən'spɪkjuəs] *adj* qui passe inaperçu(e); (*colour, dress*) discret(ète); **to make o.s. inconspicuous** ne pas se faire remarquer

inconvenience [ɪnkən'vi:njəns] *n* inconvénient *m*; (*trouble*) dérangement *m* ♦ *vt* déranger; **don't inconvenience yourself** ne vous dérangez pas

inconvenient [ɪnkən'vi:njənt] *adj* malcommode; (*time, place*) mal choisi(e), qui ne convient pas; **that time is very inconvenient for me** c'est un moment qui ne me convient pas du tout

incorporate [ɪn'kɔ:pəreɪt] *vt* incorporer; (*contain*) contenir ♦ *vi* fusionner; (*two firms*) se constituer en société

incorporated [ɪn'kɔ:pəreɪtɪd] *adj*: **incorporated company** (*us: abbr* **Inc.**) ≈ société *f* anonyme (S.A.)

incorrect [ɪnkə'rekt] *adj* incorrect(e); (*opinion, statement*) inexact(e)

increase *n* [ɪn'kri:s] augmentation *f* ♦ *vi, vt* [ɪn'kri:s] augmenter; **an increase of 5%** une augmentation de 5%; **to be on the increase** être en augmentation

increasing [ɪn'kri:sɪŋ] *adj* croissant(e)

increasingly [ɪn'kri:sɪŋlɪ] *adv* de plus en plus

incredible [ɪn'kredɪbl] *adj* incroyable

incubator [ɪnkjubeɪtə*] *n* incubateur *m*; (*for babies*) couveuse *f*

incumbent [ɪn'kʌmbənt] *adj*: **it is incumbent on him to ...** il lui appartient de ... ♦ *n* titulaire *m/f*

incur [ɪn'kə:*] *vt* (*expenses*) encourir; (*anger, risk*) s'exposer à; (*debt*) contracter; (*loss*) subir

indebted [ɪn'detɪd] *adj*: **to be indebted to sb (for)** être redevable à qn (de)

indecent [ɪn'di:snt] *adj* indécent(e), inconvenant(e)

indecent assault *n* (*BRIT*) attentat *m* à la pudeur

indecent exposure *n* outrage *m* public à la pudeur

indecisive [ɪndɪ'saɪsɪv] *adj* indécis(e); (*discussion*) peu concluant(e)

indeed [ɪn'di:d] *adv* en effet, effectivement; (*furthermore*) d'ailleurs; **yes indeed!** certainement!

indefinitely [ɪn'defɪnɪtlɪ] *adv* (*wait*) indéfiniment; (*speak*) vaguement, avec imprécision

indemnity [ɪn'demnɪtɪ] *n* (*insurance*) assurance *f*, garantie *f*; (*compensation*) indemnité *f*

independence [ɪndɪ'pendns] *n* indépendance *f*

Independence Day *n* (*us*) fête *or* anniversaire de l'Indépendance américaine; *voir encadré*

independent [ɪndɪ'pendnt] *adj* indépendant(e); **to become independent** s'affranchir

index ['ɪndeks] *n* (*pl*: **indexes**) (*in book*) index *m*; (: *in library etc*) catalogue *m*; (*pl*: **indices** ['ɪndɪsi:z]) (*ratio, sign*) indice *m*

index card *n* fiche *f*

index finger *n* index *m*

index-linked ['ɪndeks'lɪŋkt], (*us*) **indexed** ['ɪndekst] *adj* indexé(e) (sur le coût de la vie *etc*)

India ['ɪndɪə] *n* Inde *f*

Indian ['ɪndɪən] *adj* indien(ne) ♦ *n* Indien/ne

Indian Ocean *n*: **the Indian Ocean** l'océan Indien

indicate ['ɪndɪkeɪt] *vt* indiquer ♦ *vi* (*BRIT AUT*): **to indicate left/right** mettre son clignotant à gauche/à droite

indication [ɪndɪ'keɪʃən] *n* indication *f*, signe *m*

indicative [ɪn'dɪkətɪv] *adj* indicatif(ive) ♦ *n* (*LING*) indicatif *m*; **to be indicative of sth** être symptomatique de qch

indicator ['ɪndɪkeɪtə*] *n* (*sign*) indicateur *m*; (*AUT*) clignotant *m*

indices ['ɪndɪsi:z] *npl of* **index**

indictment [ɪn'daɪtmənt] *n* accusation *f*

indifferent [ɪn'dɪfrənt] *adj* indifférent(e); (*poor*) médiocre, quelconque

indigenous [ɪn'dɪdʒɪnəs] *adj* indigène

indigestion [ɪndɪ'dʒestʃən] *n* indigestion *f*, mauvaise digestion

indignant [ɪn'dɪgnənt] *adj*: **indignant (at sth/ with sb)** indigné(e) (de qch/contre qn)

indignity [ɪn'dɪgnɪtɪ] *n* indignité *f*, affront *m*

indirect [ɪndɪ'rekt] *adj* indirect(e)

indiscreet [ɪndɪ'skri:t] *adj* indiscret(ète); (*rash*) imprudent(e)

indiscriminate [ɪndɪ'skrɪmɪnət] *adj* (*person*) qui manque de discernement; (*admiration*) aveugle; (*killings*) commis(e) au hasard

indisputable [ɪndɪ'spju:təbl] *adj* incontestable, indiscutable

individual [ˌɪndɪˈvɪdjʊəl] *n* individu *m* ♦ *adj* individuel(le); (*characteristic*) particulier(ière), original(e)

indoctrination [ɪndɒktrɪˈneɪʃən] *n* endoctrinement *m*

Indonesia [ɪndəˈniːzɪə] *n* Indonésie *f*

indoor [ˈɪndɔːʳ] *adj* d'intérieur; (*plant*) d'appartement; (*swimming pool*) couvert(e); (*sport, games*) pratiqué(e) en salle

indoors [ɪnˈdɔːz] *adv* à l'intérieur; (*at home*) à la maison

induce [ɪnˈdjuːs] *vt* persuader; (*bring about*) provoquer; **to induce sb to do sth** inciter *or* pousser qn à faire qch

inducement [ɪnˈdjuːsmənt] *n* incitation *f*; (*incentive*) but *m*; (*pej: bribe*) pot-de-vin *m*

indulge [ɪnˈdʌldʒ] *vt* (*whim*) céder à, satisfaire; (*child*) gâter ♦ *vi*: **to indulge in sth** s'offrir qch, se permettre qch; se livrer à qch

indulgence [ɪnˈdʌldʒəns] *n* fantaisie *f* (que l'on s'offre); (*leniency*) indulgence *f*

indulgent [ɪnˈdʌldʒənt] *adj* indulgent(e)

industrial [ɪnˈdʌstrɪəl] *adj* industriel(le); (*injury*) du travail; (*dispute*) ouvrier(ière)

industrial action *n* action revendicative

industrial estate *n* (*BRIT*) zone industrielle

industrialist [ɪnˈdʌstrɪəlɪst] *n* industriel *m*

industrial park *n* (*US*) zone industrielle

industrious [ɪnˈdʌstrɪəs] *adj* travailleur(euse)

industry [ˈɪndəstrɪ] *n* industrie *f*; (*diligence*) zèle *m*, application *f*

inebriated [ɪˈniːbrɪeɪtɪd] *adj* ivre

inedible [ɪnˈɛdɪbl] *adj* immangeable; (*plant etc*) non comestible

ineffective [ɪnɪˈfɛktɪv], **ineffectual** [ɪnɪˈfɛktʃuəl] *adj* inefficace; incompétent(e)

inefficient [ɪnɪˈfɪʃənt] *adj* inefficace

inequality [ɪnɪˈkwɒlɪtɪ] *n* inégalité *f*

inescapable [ɪnɪˈskeɪpəbl] *adj* inéluctable, inévitable

inevitable [ɪnˈɛvɪtəbl] *adj* inévitable

inevitably [ɪnˈɛvɪtəblɪ] *adv* inévitablement, fatalement

inexpensive [ɪnɪkˈspɛnsɪv] *adj* bon marché *inv*

inexperienced [ɪnɪkˈspɪərɪənst] *adj* inexpérimenté(e); **to be inexperienced in sth** manquer d'expérience dans qch

infallible [ɪnˈfælɪbl] *adj* infaillible

infamous [ˈɪnfəməs] *adj* infâme, abominable

infancy [ˈɪnfənsɪ] *n* petite enfance, bas âge; (*fig*) enfance, débuts *mpl*

infant [ˈɪnfənt] *n* (*baby*) nourrisson *m*; (*young child*) petit/e enfant

infant school *n* (*BRIT*) classes *fpl* préparatoires (*entre 5 et 7 ans*)

infatuated [ɪnˈfætjʊeɪtɪd] *adj*: **infatuated with** entiché(e) de; **to become infatuated (with sb)** s'enticher (de qn)

infatuation [ɪnfætjʊˈeɪʃən] *n* toquade *f*; engouement *m*

infect [ɪnˈfɛkt] *vt* infecter, contaminer; (*fig pej*) corrompre; **infected with** (*illness*) atteint(e) de; **to become infected** (*wound*) s'infecter

infection [ɪnˈfɛkʃən] *n* infection *f*; contagion *f*

infectious [ɪnˈfɛkʃəs] *adj* infectieux(euse); (*also fig*) contagieux(euse)

infer [ɪnˈfəːʳ] *vt*: **to infer (from)** conclure (de), déduire (de)

inferior [ɪnˈfɪərɪəʳ] *adj* inférieur(e); (*goods*) de qualité inférieure ♦ *n* inférieur/e; (*in rank*) subalterne *m/f*; **to feel inferior** avoir un sentiment d'infériorité

inferiority [ɪnfɪərɪˈɔrɪtɪ] *n* infériorité *f*

infertile [ɪnˈfəːtaɪl] *adj* stérile

in-fighting [ˈɪnfaɪtɪŋ] *n* querelles *fpl* internes

infinite [ˈɪnfɪnɪt] *adj* infini(e); (*time, money*) illimité(e)

infinitive [ɪnˈfɪnɪtɪv] *n* infinitif *m*

infinity [ɪnˈfɪnɪtɪ] *n* infinité *f*; (*also MATH*) infini *m*

infirmary [ɪnˈfəːmərɪ] *n* hôpital *m*; (*in school, factory*) infirmerie *f*

inflamed [ɪnˈfleɪmd] *adj* enflammé(e)

inflammable [ɪnˈflæməbl] *adj* (*BRIT*) inflammable

inflammation [ɪnfləˈmeɪʃən] *n* inflammation *f*

inflatable [ɪnˈfleɪtəbl] *adj* gonflable

inflate [ɪnˈfleɪt] *vt* (*tyre, balloon*) gonfler; (*fig*) grossir; gonfler; faire monter

inflation [ɪnˈfleɪʃən] *n* (*ECON*) inflation *f*

inflationary [ɪnˈfleɪʃənərɪ] *adj* inflationniste

inflict [ɪnˈflɪkt] *vt*: **to inflict on** infliger à

influence [ˈɪnfluəns] *n* influence *f* ♦ *vt* influencer; **under the influence of** sous l'effet de; **under the influence of drink** en état d'ébriété

influential [ɪnfluˈɛnʃl] *adj* influent(e)

influenza [ɪnfluˈɛnzə] *n* grippe *f*

influx [ˈɪnflʌks] *n* afflux *m*

infomercial [ˈɪnfəʊməːʃl] (*US*) *n* (*for product*) publi-information *f*; (*POL*) émission où un candidat présente son programme électoral

inform [ɪnˈfɔːm] *vt*: **to inform sb (of)** informer *or* avertir qn (de) ♦ *vi*: **to inform on sb** dénoncer qn, informer contre qn; **to inform sb about** renseigner qn sur, mettre qn au courant de

informal [ɪnˈfɔːml] *adj* (*person, manner*) simple, sans cérémonie; (*announcement, visit*) non officiel(le); **"dress informal"** "tenue de ville"

informality [ɪnfɔːˈmælɪtɪ] *n* simplicité *f*, absence *f* de cérémonie; caractère non officiel

informant [ɪnˈfɔːmənt] *n* informateur/trice

information [ɪnfəˈmeɪʃən] *n* information(s) *f(pl)*; renseignements *mpl*; (*knowledge*) connaissances *fpl*; **to get information on** se renseigner sur; **a piece of information** un renseignement; **for your information** à titre d'information

information desk n accueil m

information office n bureau m de renseignements

informative [ɪnˈfɔːmətɪv] adj instructif(ive)

informer [ɪnˈfɔːməʳ] n dénonciateur/trice (also: **police informer**) indicateur/trice

infringe [ɪnˈfrɪndʒ] vt enfreindre ♦ vi: **to infringe on** empiéter sur

infringement [ɪnˈfrɪndʒmənt] n: **infringement (of)** infraction f (à)

infuriating [ɪnˈfjuərɪeɪtɪŋ] adj exaspérant(e)

ingenious [ɪnˈdʒiːnjəs] adj ingénieux(euse)

ingenuity [ɪndʒɪˈnjuːɪtɪ] n ingéniosité f

ingenuous [ɪnˈdʒɛnjuəs] adj franc(franche), ouvert(e)

ingot [ˈɪŋgət] n lingot m

ingrained [ɪnˈgreɪnd] adj enraciné(e)

ingratiate [ɪnˈgreɪʃɪeɪt] vt: **to ingratiate o.s. with** s'insinuer dans les bonnes grâces de, se faire bien voir de

ingredient [ɪnˈgriːdɪənt] n ingrédient m; élément m

inhabit [ɪnˈhæbɪt] vt habiter

inhabitant [ɪnˈhæbɪtnt] n habitant/e

inhale [ɪnˈheɪl] vt inhaler; (perfume) respirer ♦ vi (in smoking) avaler la fumée

inherent [ɪnˈhɪərənt] adj: **inherent (in or to)** inhérent(e) (à)

inherit [ɪnˈherɪt] vt hériter (de)

inheritance [ɪnˈherɪtəns] n héritage m; **law of inheritance** droit m de la succession

inhibit [ɪnˈhɪbɪt] vt (PSYCH) inhiber; **to inhibit sb from doing** empêcher or retenir qn de faire

inhibition [ɪnhɪˈbɪʃən] n inhibition f

inhuman [ɪnˈhjuːmən] adj inhumain(e)

initial [ɪˈnɪʃl] adj initiale f ♦ vt parafer; **initials** npl initiales fpl; (as signature) parafe m

initially [ɪˈnɪʃəlɪ] adv initialement, au début

initiate [ɪˈnɪʃɪeɪt] vt (start) entreprendre; amorcer; lancer; (person) initier; **to initiate sb into a secret** initier qn à un secret; **to initiate proceedings against sb** (LAW) intenter une action à qn, engager des poursuites contre qn

initiative [ɪˈnɪʃətɪv] n initiative f; **to take the initiative** prendre l'initiative

inject [ɪnˈdʒɛkt] vt (liquid, fig: money) injecter; (person) faire une piqûre à

injection [ɪnˈdʒɛkʃən] n injection f, piqûre f; **to have an injection** se faire faire une piqûre

injure [ˈɪndʒəʳ] vt blesser; (wrong) faire du tort à; (damage: reputation etc) compromettre; (feelings) heurter; **to injure o.s.** se blesser

injured [ˈɪndʒəd] adj (person, leg etc) blessé(e); (tone, feelings) offensé(e); **injured party** (LAW) partie lésée

injury [ˈɪndʒərɪ] n blessure f; (wrong) tort m; **to escape without injury** s'en sortir sain et sauf

injury time n (SPORT) arrêts mpl de jeu

injustice [ɪnˈdʒʌstɪs] n injustice f; **you do me an injustice** vous êtes injuste envers moi

ink [ɪŋk] n encre f

inkling [ˈɪŋklɪŋ] n soupçon m, vague idée f

inlaid [ˈɪnleɪd] adj incrusté(e); (table etc) marqueté(e)

inland adj [ˈɪnlənd] intérieur(e) ♦ adv [ɪnˈlænd] à l'intérieur, dans les terres; **inland waterways** canaux mpl et rivières fpl

Inland Revenue n (BRIT) fisc m

in-laws [ˈɪnlɔːz] npl beaux-parents mpl; belle famille

inlet [ˈɪnlet] n (GEO) crique f

inmate [ˈɪnmeɪt] n (in prison) détenu/e; (in asylum) interné/e

inn [ɪn] n auberge f

innate [ɪˈneɪt] adj inné(e)

inner [ˈɪnəʳ] adj intérieur(e)

inner city n (vieux quartiers du) centre urbain (souffrant souvent de délabrement, d'embouteillages etc)

inner tube n (of tyre) chambre f à air

innings [ˈɪnɪŋz] n (CRICKET) tour m de batte; (BRIT fig): **he has had a good innings** il (en) a bien profité

innocent [ˈɪnəsnt] adj innocent(e)

innocuous [ɪˈnɔkjuəs] adj inoffensif(ive)

innuendo, pl innuendoes [ɪnjuˈɛndəu] n insinuation f, allusion (malveillante)

innumerable [ɪˈnjuːmrəbl] adj innombrable

in-patient [ˈɪnpeɪʃənt] n malade hospitalisé(e)

input [ˈɪnput] n (ELEC) énergie f, puissance f; (of machine) consommation f; (of computer) information fournie ♦ vt (COMPUT) introduire, entrer

inquest [ˈɪnkwest] n enquête (criminelle)

inquire [ɪnˈkwaɪəʳ] vi demander ♦ vt demander, s'informer de; **to inquire about** s'informer de, se renseigner sur; **to inquire when/where/whether** demander quand/où/si

▶ **inquire after** vt fus demander des nouvelles de

▶ **inquire into** vt fus faire une enquête sur

inquiry [ɪnˈkwaɪərɪ] n demande f de renseignements; (LAW) enquête f, investigation f; **to hold an inquiry into sth** enquêter sur qch

inquisitive [ɪnˈkwɪzɪtɪv] adj curieux(euse)

ins abbr = **inches**

insane [ɪnˈseɪn] adj fou(folle); (MED) aliéné(e)

insanity [ɪnˈsænɪtɪ] n folie f; (MED) aliénation (mentale)

inscription [ɪnˈskrɪpʃən] n inscription f; (in book) dédicace f

inscrutable [ɪnˈskruːtəbl] adj impénétrable

insect [ˈɪnsekt] n insecte m

insecticide [ɪnˈsektɪsaɪd] n insecticide m

insect repellent *n* crème *f* anti-insectes

insecure [ɪnsɪ'kjuə*] *adj* peu solide; peu sûr(e); (*person*) anxieux(euse)

insensitive [ɪn'sɛnsɪtɪv] *adj* insensible

insert *vt* [ɪn'səːt] insérer ♦ *n* ['ɪnsəːt] insertion *f*

insertion [ɪn'səːʃən] *n* insertion *f*

in-service [ɪn'səː.vɪs] *adj* (*training*) continu(e); (*course*) d'initiation; de perfectionnement; de recyclage

inshore [ɪn'ʃɔː*] *adj* côtier(ière) ♦ *adv* près de la côte; vers la côte

inside ['ɪn'saɪd] *n* intérieur *m*; (*of road: BRIT*) côté *m* gauche (*de la route*); (: *US, Europe etc*) côté droit (*de la route*) ♦ *adj* intérieur(e) ♦ *adv* à l'intérieur, dedans ♦ *prep* à l'intérieur de; (*of time*): **inside 10 minutes** en moins de 10 minutes; **insides** *npl* (*col*) intestins *mpl*; **inside out** *adv* à l'envers; **to turn sth inside out** retourner qch; **to know sth inside out** connaître qch à fond *or* comme sa poche; **inside information** renseignements *mpl* à la source; **inside story** histoire racontée par un témoin

inside lane *n* (*AUT: in Britain*) voie *f* de gauche; (: *in US, Europe*) voie *f* de droite

insider dealing, insider trading *n* (*STOCK EXCHANGE*) délit *m* d'initiés

insight ['ɪnsaɪt] *n* perspicacité *f*; (*glimpse, idea*) aperçu *m*; **to gain (an) insight into** parvenir à comprendre

insignificant [ɪnsɪg'nɪfɪknt] *adj* insignifiant(e)

insincere [ɪnsɪn'sɪə*] *adj* hypocrite

insinuate [ɪn'sɪnjueɪt] *vt* insinuer

insist [ɪn'sɪst] *vi* insister; **to insist on doing** insister pour faire; **to insist that** insister pour que; (*claim*) maintenir *or* soutenir que

insistent [ɪn'sɪstənt] *adj* insistant(e), pressant(e)

insole ['ɪnsəul] *n* semelle intérieure; (*fixed part of shoe*) première *f*

insolent ['ɪnsələnt] *adj* insolent(e)

insolvent [ɪn'sɔlvənt] *adj* insolvable; (*bankrupt*) en faillite

insomnia [ɪn'sɔmnɪə] *n* insomnie *f*

inspect [ɪn'spɛkt] *vt* inspecter; (*BRIT: ticket*) contrôler

inspection [ɪn'spɛkʃən] *n* inspection *f*; contrôle *m*

inspector [ɪn'spɛktə*] *n* inspecteur/trice; contrôleur/euse

inspire [ɪn'spaɪə*] *vt* inspirer

install [ɪn'stɔːl] *vt* installer

installation [ɪnstə'leɪʃən] *n* installation *f*

instalment, (*US*) **installment** [ɪn'stɔːlmənt] *n* acompte *m*, versement partiel; (*of TV serial etc*) épisode *m*; **in instalments** (*pay*) à tempérament; (*receive*) en plusieurs fois

instance ['ɪnstəns] *n* exemple *m*; **for instance** par exemple; **in many instances** dans bien des cas; **in that instance** dans ce cas; **in the first instance** tout d'abord, en premier lieu

instant ['ɪnstənt] *n* instant *m* ♦ *adj* immédiat(e), urgent(e); (*coffee, food*) instantané(e), en poudre; **the 10th instant** le 10 courant

instantly ['ɪnstəntlɪ] *adv* immédiatement, tout de suite

instead [ɪn'stɛd] *adv* au lieu de cela; **instead of** au lieu de; **instead of sb** à la place de qn

instep ['ɪnstɛp] *n* cou-de-pied *m*; (*of shoe*) cambrure *f*

instigate ['ɪnstɪgeɪt] *vt* (*rebellion, strike, crime*) inciter à; (*new ideas etc*) susciter

instil [ɪn'stɪl] *vt*: **to instil (into)** inculquer (à); (*courage*) insuffler (à)

instinct ['ɪnstɪŋkt] *n* instinct *m*

institute ['ɪnstɪtjuːt] *n* institut *m* ♦ *vt* instituer, établir; (*inquiry*) ouvrir; (*proceedings*) entamer

institution [ɪnstɪ'tjuːʃən] *n* institution *f*; (*school*) établissement *m* (scolaire); (*for care*) établissement (psychiatrique *etc*)

instruct [ɪn'strʌkt] *vt* instruire, former; **to instruct sb in sth** enseigner qch à qn; **to instruct sb to do** charger qn *or* ordonner à qn de faire

instruction [ɪn'strʌkʃən] *n* instruction *f*; **instructions** *npl* directives *fpl*; **instructions for use** mode *m* d'emploi

instructor [ɪn'strʌktə*] *n* professeur *m*; (*for skiing, driving*) moniteur *m*

instrument ['ɪnstrumənt] *n* instrument *m*

instrumental [ɪnstru'mɛntl] *adj* (*MUS*) instrumental(e); **to be instrumental in sth/in doing sth** contribuer à qch/à faire qch

instrument panel *n* tableau *m* de bord

insufficient [ɪnsə'fɪʃənt] *adj* insuffisant(e)

insular ['ɪnsjulə*] *adj* insulaire; (*outlook*) étroit(e); (*person*) aux vues étroites

insulate ['ɪnsjuleɪt] *vt* isoler; (*against sound*) insonoriser

insulation [ɪnsju'leɪʃən] *n* isolation *f*; insonorisation *f*

insulin ['ɪnsjulɪn] *n* insuline *f*

insult *n* ['ɪnsʌlt] insulte *f*, affront *m* ♦ *vt* [ɪn'sʌlt] insulter, faire un affront à

insurance [ɪn'ʃuərəns] *n* assurance *f*; **fire/life insurance** assurance-incendie/-vie; **to take out insurance (against)** s'assurer (contre)

insurance policy *n* police *f* d'assurance

insure [ɪn'ʃuə*] *vt* assurer; **to insure sb/sb's life** assurer qn/la vie de qn; **to be insured for £5000** être assuré(e) pour 5000 livres

intact [ɪn'tækt] *adj* intact(e)

intake ['ɪnteɪk] *n* (*TECH*) admission *f*; adduction *f*; (*of food*) consommation *f*; (*BRIT SCOL*): **an intake of 200 a year** 200 admissions par an

integral ['ɪntɪgrəl] *adj* intégral(e); (*part*) intégrant(e)

integrate ['ɪntɪgreɪt] *vt* intégrer ♦ *vi* s'intégrer

intellect [ˈɪntəlekt] *n* intelligence *f*

intellectual [ɪntəˈlektjuəl] *adj, n* intellectuel/le

intelligence [ɪnˈtelɪdʒəns] *n* intelligence *f*; (*MIL etc*) informations *fpl*, renseignements *mpl*

Intelligence Service *n* services *mpl* de renseignements

intelligent [ɪnˈtelɪdʒənt] *adj* intelligent(e)

intend [ɪnˈtend] *vt* (*gift etc*): **to intend sth for** destiner qch à; **to intend to do** avoir l'intention de faire

intense [ɪnˈtens] *adj* intense; (*person*) véhément(e)

intensely [ɪnˈtenslɪ] *adv* intensément; (*moving*) profondément

intensive [ɪnˈtensɪv] *adj* intensif(ive)

intensive care *n*: **to be in intensive care** être en réanimation; **intensive care unit** *n* service *m* de réanimation

intent [ɪnˈtent] *n* intention *f* ♦ *adj* attentif(ive), absorbé(e); **to all intents and purposes** en fait, pratiquement; **to be intent on doing sth** être (bien) décidé à faire qch

intention [ɪnˈtenʃən] *n* intention *f*

intentional [ɪnˈtenʃənl] *adj* intentionnel(le), délibéré(e)

intently [ɪnˈtentlɪ] *adv* attentivement

interact [ɪntərˈækt] *vi* avoir une action réciproque

interactive [ɪntərˈæktɪv] *adj* (*group*) interactif(ive); (*COMPUT*) interactif, conversationnel(le)

interchange *n* [ˈɪntətʃeɪndʒ] (*exchange*) échange *m*; (*on motorway*) échangeur *m* ♦ *vt* [ɪntəˈtʃeɪndʒ] échanger; mettre à la place l'un(e) de l'autre

interchangeable [ɪntəˈtʃeɪndʒəbl] *adj* interchangeable

intercom [ˈɪntəkɔm] *n* interphone *m*

intercourse [ˈɪntəkɔːs] *n* rapports *mpl*; **sexual intercourse** rapports sexuels

interest [ˈɪntrɪst] *n* intérêt *m*; (*COMM: stake, share*) participation *f*, intérêts *mpl* ♦ *vt* intéresser; **compound/simple interest** intérêt composé/simple; **British interests in the Middle East** les intérêts britanniques au Moyen-Orient; **his main interest is ...** ce qui l'intéresse le plus est ...

interesting [ˈɪntrɪstɪŋ] *adj* intéressant(e)

interest rate *n* taux *m* d'intérêt

interface [ˈɪntəfeɪs] *n* (*COMPUT*) interface *f*

interfere [ɪntəˈfɪə*] *vi*: **to interfere in** (*quarrel, other people's business*) se mêler à; **to interfere with** (*object*) tripoter, toucher à; (*plans*) contrecarrer; (*duty*) être en conflit avec; **don't interfere** mêlez-vous de vos affaires

interference [ɪntəˈfɪərəns] *n* (*gen*) intrusion *f*; (*PHYSICS*) interférence *f*; (*RADIO, TV*) parasites *mpl*

interim [ˈɪntərɪm] *adj* provisoire; (*post*) intérimaire ♦ *n*: **in the interim** dans l'intervalle

interior [ɪnˈtɪərɪə*] *n* intérieur *m* ♦ *adj* intérieur(e)

interior decorator, interior designer *n* décorateur/trice d'intérieur

interjection [ɪntəˈdʒekʃən] *n* interjection *f*

interlock [ɪntəˈlɔk] *vi* s'enclencher ♦ *vt* enclencher

interlude [ˈɪntəluːd] *n* intervalle *m*; (*THEAT*) intermède *m*

intermediate [ɪntəˈmiːdɪət] *adj* intermédiaire; (*SCOL: course, level*) moyen(ne)

intermission [ɪntəˈmɪʃən] *n* pause *f*; (*THEAT, CINE*) entracte *m*

intern *vt* [ɪnˈtəːn] interner ♦ *n* [ˈɪntəːn] (*US*) interne *m/f*

internal [ɪnˈtəːnl] *adj* interne; (*dispute, reform etc*) intérieur(e); **internal injuries** lésions *fpl* internes

internally [ɪnˈtəːnəlɪ] *adv* intérieurement; **"not to be taken internally"** "pour usage externe"

Internal Revenue (Service) (IRS) *n* (*US*) fisc *m*

international [ɪntəˈnæʃənl] *adj* international(e) ♦ *n* (*BRIT SPORT*) international *m*

Internet [ˈɪntənet] *n*: **the Internet** l'Internet *m*

interplay [ˈɪntəpleɪ] *n* effet *m* réciproque, jeu *m*

interpret [ɪnˈtəːprɪt] *vt* interpréter ♦ *vi* servir d'interprète

interpreter [ɪnˈtəːprɪtə*] *n* interprète *m/f*

interrelated [ɪntərɪˈleɪtɪd] *adj* en corrélation, en rapport étroit

interrogate [ɪnˈterəugeɪt] *vt* interroger; (*suspect etc*) soumettre à un interrogatoire

interrogation [ɪnterəuˈgeɪʃən] *n* interrogation *f*; interrogatoire *m*

interrupt [ɪntəˈrʌpt] *vt* interrompre

interruption [ɪntəˈrʌpʃən] *n* interruption *f*

intersect [ɪntəˈsekt] *vt* couper, croiser; (*MATH*) intersecter ♦ *vi* se croiser, se couper; s'intersecter

intersection [ɪntəˈsekʃən] *n* intersection *f*; (*of roads*) croisement *m*

intersperse [ɪntəˈspəːs] *vt*: **to intersperse with** parsemer de

intertwine [ɪntəˈtwaɪn] *vt* entrelacer ♦ *vi* s'entrelacer

interval [ˈɪntəvl] *n* intervalle *m*; (*BRIT: THEAT*) entracte *m*; (*: SPORT*) mi-temps *f*; **bright intervals** (*in weather*) éclaircies *fpl*; **at intervals** par intervalles

intervene [ɪntəˈviːn] *vi* (*time*) s'écouler (entre-temps); (*event*) survenir; (*person*) intervenir

intervention [ɪntəˈvenʃən] *n* intervention *f*

interview [ˈɪntəvjuː] *n* (*RADIO, TV etc*) interview *f*; (*for job*) entrevue *f* ♦ *vt* interviewer; avoir une entrevue avec

interviewer [ˈɪntəvjuə*] *n* interviewer *m*

intestine [ɪnˈtestɪn] *n* intestin *m*; **large intestine** gros intestin; **small intestine** intestin grêle

intimacy [ˈɪntɪməsɪ] *n* intimité *f*

intimate *adj* [ˈɪntɪmət] intime; (*knowledge*) approfondi(e) ♦ *vt* [ˈɪntɪmeɪt] suggérer, laisser entendre; (*announce*) faire savoir

into ['ɪntu] *prep* dans; **into pieces/French** en morceaux/français; **to change pounds into dollars** changer des livres en dollars

intolerant [ɪn'tɔlərənt] *adj*: **intolerant (of)** intolérant(e) (de) (*MED*) intolérant (à)

intoxicated [ɪn'tɔksɪkeɪtɪd] *adj* ivre

intractable [ɪn'træktəbl] *adj* (*child, temper*) indocile, insoumis(e); (*problem*) insoluble; (*illness*) incurable

intranet ['ɪntrənet] *n* intranet *m*

intransitive [ɪn'trænsɪtɪv] *adj* intransitif(ive)

intravenous [ɪntrə'vi:nəs] *adj* intraveineux(euse)

in-tray ['ɪntreɪ] *n* courrier *m* "arrivée"

intricate ['ɪntrɪkət] *adj* complexe, compliqué(e)

intrigue [ɪn'tri:g] *n* intrigue *f* ♦ *vt* intriguer ♦ *vi* intriguer, comploter

intriguing [ɪn'tri:gɪŋ] *adj* fascinant(e)

intrinsic [ɪn'trɪnsɪk] *adj* intrinsèque

introduce [ɪntrə'dju:s] *vt* introduire; **to introduce sb (to sb)** présenter qn (à qn); **to introduce sb to** (*pastime, technique*) initier qn à; **may I introduce …?** je vous présente …

introduction [ɪntrə'dʌkʃən] *n* introduction *f*; (*of person*) présentation *f*; **a letter of introduction** une lettre de recommendation

introductory [ɪntrə'dʌktərɪ] *adj* préliminaire, introductif(ive); **introductory remarks** remarques *fpl* liminaires; **an introductory offer** une offre de lancement

intrude [ɪn'tru:d] *vi* (*person*) être importun(e); **to intrude on** *or* **into** (*conversation etc*) s'immiscer dans; **am I intruding?** est-ce que je vous dérange?

intruder [ɪn'tru:də*] *n* intrus/e

intuition [ɪntju:'ɪʃən] *n* intuition *f*

inundate ['ɪnʌndeɪt] *vt*: **to inundate with** inonder de

invade [ɪn'veɪd] *vt* envahir

invalid *n* ['ɪnvəlɪd] malade *m/f*; (*with disability*) invalide *m/f* ♦ *adj* [ɪn'vælɪd] (*not valid*) invalide, non valide

invaluable [ɪn'væljuəbl] *adj* inestimable, inappréciable

invariably [ɪn'veərɪəblɪ] *adv* invariablement; **she is invariably late** elle est toujours en retard

invent [ɪn'vent] *vt* inventer

invention [ɪn'venʃən] *n* invention *f*

inventive [ɪn'ventɪv] *adj* inventif(ive)

inventor [ɪn'ventə*] *n* inventeur/trice

inventory ['ɪnvəntrɪ] *n* inventaire *m*

invert [ɪn'vɜ:t] *vt* intervertir; (*cup, object*) retourner

inverted commas [ɪn'vɜ:tɪd-] *npl* (*BRIT*) guillemets *mpl*

invest [ɪn'vest] *vt* investir; (*endow*): **to invest sb with sth** conférer qch à qn ♦ *vi* faire un investissement, investir; **to invest in** placer de l'argent *or* investir dans; (*acquire*) s'offrir, faire l'acquisition de

investigate [ɪn'vestɪgeɪt] *vt* étudier, examiner; (*crime*) faire une enquête sur

investigation [ɪnvestɪ'geɪʃən] *n* examen *m*; (*of crime*) enquête *f*, investigation *f*

investment [ɪn'vestmənt] *n* investissement *m*, placement *m*

investor [ɪn'vestə*] *n* épargnant/e; (*shareholder*) actionnaire *m/f*

invigilator [ɪn'vɪdʒɪleɪtə*] *n* (*BRIT*) surveillant *m* (d'examen)

invigorating [ɪn'vɪgəreɪtɪŋ] *adj* vivifiant(e), stimulant(e)

invisible [ɪn'vɪzɪbl] *adj* invisible

invitation [ɪnvɪ'teɪʃən] *n* invitation *f*; **by invitation only** sur invitation; **at sb's invitation** à la demande de qn

invite [ɪn'vaɪt] *vt* inviter; (*opinions etc*) demander; (*trouble*) chercher; **to invite sb (to do)** inviter qn (à faire); **to invite sb to dinner** inviter qn à dîner

▶ **invite out** *vt* inviter (à sortir)

▶ **invite over** *vt* inviter (chez soi)

inviting [ɪn'vaɪtɪŋ] *adj* engageant(e), attrayant(e); (*gesture*) encourageant(e)

invoice ['ɪnvɔɪs] *n* facture *f* ♦ *vt* facturer; **to invoice sb for goods** facturer des marchandises à qn

involuntary [ɪn'vɔləntrɪ] *adj* involontaire

involve [ɪn'vɔlv] *vt* (*entail*) impliquer; (*concern*) concerner; (*require*) nécessiter; **to involve sb in** (*theft etc*) impliquer qn dans; (*activity, meeting*) faire participer qn à

involved [ɪn'vɔlvd] *adj* complexe; **to feel involved** se sentir concerné(e); **to become involved** (*in love etc*) s'engager

involvement [ɪn'vɔlvmənt] *n* (*personal role*) participation *f*; (*of resources, funds*) mise *f* en jeu

inward ['ɪnwəd] *adj* (*movement*) vers l'intérieur; (*thought, feeling*) profond(e), intime ♦ *adv* = **inwards**

I/O *abbr* (*COMPUT*: = *input/output*) E/S

iodine ['aɪəudi:n] *n* iode *m*

iota [aɪ'əutə] *n* (*fig*) brin *m*, grain *m*

IOU *n abbr* (= *I owe you*) reconnaissance *f* de dette

iPod® ['aɪpɔd] *n* iPod® *m*

IQ *n abbr* = *intelligence quotient*

IRA *n abbr* (= *Irish Republican Army*) IRA *f*; (*US*) = *individual retirement account*

Iran [ɪ'rɑ:n] *n* Iran *m*

Iraq [ɪ'rɑ:k] *n* Irak *m*

irate [aɪ'reɪt] *adj* courroucé(e)

Ireland ['aɪələnd] *n* Irlande *f*; **Republic of Ireland** République *f* d'Irlande

iris, *pl* **irises** ['aɪrɪs, -ɪz] *n* iris *m*

Irish ['aɪrɪʃ] *adj* irlandais(e) ♦ *n* (*LING*) irlandais *m*; **the Irish** *npl* les Irlandais

Irishman ['aɪrɪʃmən] *n* Irlandais *m*

Irish Sea *n*: **the Irish Sea** la mer d'Irlande

Irishwoman ['aɪrɪʃwumən] *n* Irlandaise *f*

iron ['aɪən] *n* fer *m*; (*for clothes*) fer *m* à repasser ♦ *adj* de or en fer ♦ *vt* (*clothes*) repasser; **irons** *npl* (*chains*) fers *mpl*, chaînes *fpl*
▶ **iron out** (*crease*) faire disparaître au fer; (*fig*) aplanir; faire disparaître

ironic(al) [aɪ'rɒnɪk(l)] *adj* ironique

ironing ['aɪənɪŋ] *n* repassage *m*

ironing board *n* planche *f* à repasser

ironmonger ['aɪənmʌŋgə*] *n* (*BRIT*) quincailler *m*; **ironmonger's (shop)** quincaillerie *f*

irony ['aɪrənɪ] *n* ironie *f*

irrational [ɪ'ræʃənl] *adj* irrationnel(le); déraisonnable; qui manque de logique

irregular [ɪ'regjulə*] *adj* irrégulier(ière)

irrelevant [ɪ'reləvənt] *adj* sans rapport, hors de propos

irresistible [ɪrɪ'zɪstɪbl] *adj* irrésistible

irrespective [ɪrɪ'spektɪv]: **irrespective of** *prep* sans tenir compte de

irresponsible [ɪrɪ'spɒnsɪbl] *adj* (*act*) irréfléchi(e); (*person*) qui n'a pas le sens des responsabilités

irrigate ['ɪrɪgeɪt] *vt* irriguer

irrigation [ɪrɪ'geɪʃən] *n* irrigation *f*

irritate ['ɪrɪteɪt] *vt* irriter

irritating ['ɪrɪteɪtɪŋ] *adj* irritant(e)

irritation [ɪrɪ'teɪʃən] *n* irritation *f*

IRS *n abbr* (*US*) = **Internal Revenue Service**

is [ɪz] *vb see* **be**

Islam ['ɪzlɑ:m] *n* Islam *m*

Islamic [ɪz'læmɪk] *adj* islamique; **Islamic fundamentalists** intégristes *mpl* musulmans

island ['aɪlənd] *n* île *f*; (*also*: **traffic island**) refuge *m* (pour piétons)

islander ['aɪləndə*] *n* habitant/e d'une île, insulaire *m/f*

isle [aɪl] *n* île *f*

isn't ['ɪznt] = **is not**

isolate ['aɪsəleɪt] *vt* isoler

isolated ['aɪsəleɪtɪd] *adj* isolé(e)

isolation [aɪsə'leɪʃən] *n* isolement *m*

ISP *n abbr* = **Internet service provider**

Israel ['ɪzreɪl] *n* Israël *m*

Israeli [ɪz'reɪlɪ] *adj* israélien(ne) ♦ *n* Israélien/ne

issue ['ɪʃu:] *n* question *f*, problème *m*; (*outcome*) résultat *m*, issue *f*; (*of banknotes etc*) émission *f*; (*of newspaper etc*) numéro *m*; (*offspring*) descendance *f* ♦ *vt* (*rations, equipment*) distribuer; (*orders*) donner; (*book*) faire paraître; publier; (*banknotes, cheques, stamps*) émettre, mettre en circulation ♦ *vi*: **to issue from** provenir de; **at issue** en jeu, en cause; **to avoid the issue** éluder le problème; **to take issue with sb (over sth)** exprimer son désaccord avec qn (sur qch); **to make an issue of sth** faire de qch un problème; **to confuse** *or* **obscure the issue** embrouiller la question

it [ɪt] *pron* **1** (*specific: subject*) il(elle); (: *direct object*) le(la, l'); (: *indirect object*) lui; **it's on the table** c'est *or* il (*or* elle) est sur la table; **about/from/of it** en; **what did you learn from it?** qu'est-ce que vous en avez retiré?; **I'm proud of it** j'en suis fier; **I've come from it** j'en viens; **in/to it** y; **put the book in it** mettez-y le livre; **it's on it** c'est dessus; **he agreed to it** il y a consenti; **did you go to it?** (*party, concert etc*) est-ce que vous y êtes allé(s)?; **above it, over it** (au-)dessus; **below it, under it** (en-)dessous; **in front of/behind it** devant/derrière

2 (*impersonal*) il, ce, cela, ça; **it's raining** il pleut; **it's Friday tomorrow** demain, c'est vendredi *or* nous sommes, vendredi; **it's 6 o'clock** il est 6 heures; **it's 2 hours by train** c'est à 2 heures de train; **who is it? – it's me** qui est-ce? – c'est moi

Italian [ɪ'tæljən] *adj* italien(ne) ♦ *n* Italien/ne (*LING*) italien *m*

italic [ɪ'tælɪk] *adj* italique; **italics** *npl* italique *m*

Italy ['ɪtəlɪ] *n* Italie *f*

itch [ɪtʃ] *n* démangeaison *f* ♦ *vi* (*person*) éprouver des démangeaisons; (*part of body*) démanger; **I'm itching to do** l'envie me démange de faire

itchy ['ɪtʃɪ] *adj* qui démange; **my back is itchy** j'ai le dos qui me démange

it'd ['ɪtd] = **it would, it had**

item ['aɪtəm] *n* (*gen*) article *m*; (*on agenda*) question *f*, point *m*; (*in programme*) numéro *m*; (*also*: **news item**) nouvelle *f*; **items of clothing** articles vestimentaires

itemize ['aɪtəmaɪz] *vt* détailler, spécifier

itinerary [aɪ'tɪnərərɪ] *n* itinéraire *m*

it'll ['ɪtl] = **it will, it shall**

its [ɪts] *adj* son(sa), ses *pl* ♦ *pron* le(la) sien(ne), les siens(siennes)

it's [ɪts] = **it is, it has**

itself [ɪt'self] *pron* (*emphatic*) lui-même(elle-même); (*reflexive*) se

ITV *n abbr* (*BRIT*: = **Independent Television**) chaîne de télévision commerciale; voir encadré

ITV

ITV est une chaîne de télévision britannique financée par la publicité. Les actualités, documentaires, débats etc, constituent environ un tiers des émissions de **ITV**, le reste étant partagé entre les sports, les films, les feuilletons, les jeux, les séries etc. Des compagnies indépendantes fournissent des émissions au niveau régional.

IUD *n abbr = intra-uterine device*

I've [aɪv] = **I have**

ivory ['aɪvərɪ] *n* ivoire *m*

ivy ['aɪvɪ] *n* lierre *m*

— **J j** —

jab [dʒæb] *vt*: **to jab sth into** enfoncer *or* planter qch dans ♦ *n* coup *m*; (MED, col) piqûre *f*

jack [dʒæk] *n* (AUT) cric *m*; (BOWLS) cochonnet *m*; (CARDS) valet *m*

▶ **jack in** *vt* (col) laisser tomber

▶ **jack up** *vt* soulever (au cric)

jackal ['dʒækl] *n* chacal *m*

jacket ['dʒækɪt] *n* veste *f*, veston *m*; (of boiler etc) enveloppe *f*; (of book) couverture *f*, jaquette *f*

jacket potato *n* pomme *f* de terre en robe des champs

jackknife ['dʒæknaɪf] *n* couteau *m* de poche ♦ *vi*: **the lorry jackknifed** la remorque (du camion) s'est mise en travers

jack plug *n* (BRIT) jack *m*

jackpot ['dʒækpɔt] *n* gros lot

jaded ['dʒeɪdɪd] *adj* éreinté(e), fatigué(e)

jagged ['dʒægɪd] *adj* dentelé(e)

jail [dʒeɪl] *n* prison *f* ♦ *vt* emprisonner, mettre en prison

jam [dʒæm] *n* confiture *f*; (of shoppers etc) cohue *f*; (also: **traffic jam**) embouteillage *m* ♦ *vt* (passage etc) encombrer, obstruer; (mechanism, drawer etc) bloquer, coincer; (RADIO) brouiller ♦ *vi* (mechanism, sliding part) se coincer, se bloquer; (gun) s'enrayer; **to get sb out of a jam** (col) sortir qn du pétrin; **to jam sth into** entasser *or* comprimer qch dans; enfoncer qch dans; **the telephone lines are jammed** les lignes (téléphoniques) sont encombrées

Jamaica [dʒə'meɪkə] *n* Jamaïque *f*

jam jar *n* pot *m* à confiture

jammed [dʒæmd] *adj* (window etc) coincé(e)

jam-packed [dʒæm'pækt] *adj*: **jam-packed (with)** bourré(e) (de)

jangle ['dʒæŋgl] *vi* cliqueter

janitor ['dʒænɪtə*] *n* (caretaker) huissier *m*; concierge *m*

January ['dʒænjuərɪ] *n* janvier *m*; *for phrases see also* **July**

Japan [dʒə'pæn] *n* Japon *m*

Japanese [dʒæpə'niːz] *adj* japonais(e) ♦ *n* (pl inv) Japonais/e (LING) japonais *m*

jar [dʒɑː*] *n* (container) pot *m*, bocal *m* ♦ *vi* (sound) produire un son grinçant *or* discordant; (colours etc) détonner, jurer ♦ *vt* (shake) ébranler, secouer

jargon ['dʒɑːgən] *n* jargon *m*

jaundice ['dʒɔːndɪs] *n* jaunisse *f*

javelin ['dʒævlɪn] *n* javelot *m*

jaw [dʒɔː] *n* mâchoire *f*

jay [dʒeɪ] *n* geai *m*

jaywalker ['dʒeɪwɔːkə*] *n* piéton indiscipliné

jazz [dʒæz] *n* jazz *m*

▶ **jazz up** *vt* animer, égayer

jealous ['dʒeləs] *adj* jaloux(ouse)

jealousy ['dʒeləsɪ] *n* jalousie *f*

jeans [dʒiːnz] *npl* (blue-)jean *m*

jeer [dʒɪə*] *vi*: **to jeer (at)** huer; se moquer cruellement (de), railler

Jehovah's Witness [dʒɪ'həuvəz-] *n* témoin *m* de Jéhovah

jelly ['dʒelɪ] *n* gelée *f*

jellyfish ['dʒelɪfɪʃ] *n* méduse *f*

jeopardy ['dʒepədɪ] *n*: **in jeopardy** en danger *or* péril

jerk [dʒəːk] *n* secousse *f*; saccade *f*; sursaut *m*, spasme *m*; (col) pauvre type *m* ♦ *vt* donner une secousse à ♦ *vi* (vehicles) cahoter

jersey ['dʒəːzɪ] *n* tricot *m*; (fabric) jersey *m*

Jesus ['dʒiːzəs] *n* Jésus; **Jesus Christ** Jésus-Christ

jet [dʒet] *n* (of gas, liquid) jet *m*; (AUT) gicleur *m*; (AVIAT) avion *m* à réaction, jet *m*

jet-black ['dʒet'blæk] *adj* (d'un noir) de jais

jet engine *n* moteur *m* à réaction

jet lag *n* décalage *m* horaire

jettison ['dʒetɪsn] *vt* jeter par-dessus bord

jetty ['dʒetɪ] *n* jetée *f*, digue *f*

Jew [dʒuː] *n* Juif *m*

jewel ['dʒuːəl] *n* bijou *m*, joyau *m*

jeweller ['dʒuːələ*] *n* bijoutier/ière, joaillier *m*; **jeweller's (shop)** *n* bijouterie *f*, joaillerie *f*

jewellery ['dʒuːəlrɪ] *n* bijoux *mpl*

Jewess ['dʒuːɪs] *n* Juive *f*

Jewish ['dʒuːɪʃ] *adj* juif(juive)

jibe [dʒaɪb] *n* sarcasme *m*

jiffy ['dʒɪfɪ] *n* (col): **in a jiffy** en un clin d'œil

jigsaw ['dʒɪgsɔː] *n* (also: **jigsaw puzzle**) puzzle *m*; (tool) scie sauteuse

jilt [dʒɪlt] *vt* laisser tomber, plaquer

jingle ['dʒɪŋgl] *n* (advertising jingle) couplet *m* publicitaire ♦ *vi* cliqueter, tinter

jinx [dʒɪŋks] *n* (col) (mauvais) sort

jitters ['dʒɪtəz] *npl* (col): **to get the jitters** avoir la trouille *or* la frousse

job [dʒɔb] *n* travail *m*; (employment) emploi *m*, poste *m*, place *f*; **a part-time/full-time job** un emploi à temps partiel/à plein temps; **he's only doing his job** il fait son boulot; **it's a good job that ...** c'est heureux *or* c'est une chance que ...; **just the job!** (c'est) juste *or* exactement ce qu'il faut!

Jobcentre ['dʒɔbsentə*] *n* agence *f* pour l'emploi

jobless ['dʒɔblɪs] *adj* sans travail, au chômage

◆ *npl*: **the jobless** les sans-emploi *m inv*, les chômeurs *mpl*

jockey ['dʒɒkɪ] *n* jockey *m* ◆ *vi*: **to jockey for position** manœuvrer pour être bien placé

jog [dʒɒg] *vt* secouer ◆ *vi* (SPORT) faire du jogging; **to jog along** cahoter; trotter; **to jog sb's memory** rafraîchir la mémoire de qn

jogging ['dʒɒgɪŋ] *n* jogging *m*

join [dʒɔɪn] *vt* unir, assembler; (become member of) s'inscrire à; (meet) rejoindre, retrouver; se joindre à ◆ *vi* (roads, rivers) se rejoindre, se rencontrer ◆ *n* raccord *m*; **will you join us for dinner?** vous dînerez bien avec nous?; **I'll join you later** je vous rejoindrai plus tard; **to join forces (with)** s'associer (à)

▶ **join in** *vi* se mettre de la partie ◆ *vt* se mêler à

▶ **join up** *vi* s'engager

joiner ['dʒɔɪnə*] *n* menuisier *m*

joint [dʒɔɪnt] *n* (TECH) jointure *f*; joint *m*; (ANAT) articulation *f*, jointure; (BRIT CULIN) rôti *m*; (col: place) boîte *f* ◆ *adj* commun(e); (committee) mixte, paritaire; **joint responsibility** coresponsabilité *f*

joint account *n* compte joint

joke [dʒəʊk] *n* plaisanterie *f*; (also: **practical joke**) farce *f* ◆ *vi* plaisanter; **to play a joke on** jouer un tour à, faire une farce à

joker ['dʒəʊkə*] *n* plaisantin *m*, blagueur/euse; (CARDS) joker *m*

jolly ['dʒɒlɪ] *adj* gai(e), enjoué(e) ◆ *adv* (BRIT col) rudement, drôlement ◆ *vt* (BRIT): **to jolly sb along** amadouer qn, convaincre or entraîner qn à force d'encouragements; **jolly good!** (BRIT) formidable!

jolt [dʒəʊlt] *n* cahot *m*, secousse *f* ◆ *vt* cahoter, secouer

Jordan [dʒɔːdən] *n* (country) Jordanie *f*; (river) Jourdain *m*

jostle ['dʒɒsl] *vt* bousculer, pousser ◆ *vi* jouer des coudes

jot [dʒɒt] *n*: **not one jot** pas un brin

▶ **jot down** *vt* inscrire rapidement, noter

jotter ['dʒɒtə*] *n* (BRIT) cahier *m* (de brouillon); bloc-notes *m*

journal ['dʒɜːnl] *n* journal *m*

journalism ['dʒɜːnəlɪzəm] *n* journalisme *m*

journalist ['dʒɜːnəlɪst] *n* journaliste *m/f*

journey ['dʒɜːnɪ] *n* voyage *m*; (distance covered) trajet *m*; **a 5-hour journey** un voyage de 5 heures *m* ◆ *vi* voyager

joy [dʒɔɪ] *n* joie *f*

joyful ['dʒɔɪful], **joyous** ['dʒɔɪəs] *adj* joyeux(euse)

joyrider ['dʒɔɪraɪdə*] *n* voleur/euse de voiture (qui fait une virée dans le véhicule volé)

joystick ['dʒɔɪstɪk] *n* (AVIAT) manche *m* à balai; (COMPUT) manche à balai, manette *f* (de jeu)

JP *n abbr* = **Justice of the Peace**

Jr *abbr* = **junior**

jubilant ['dʒuːbɪlnt] *adj* triomphant(e), réjoui(e)

judge [dʒʌdʒ] *n* juge *m* ◆ *vt* juger; (estimate: weight, size etc) apprécier; (consider) estimer ◆ *vi*: **judging** or **to judge by his expression** d'après son expression; **as far as I can judge** autant que je puisse en juger

judg(e)ment ['dʒʌdʒmənt] *n* jugement *m*; (punishment) châtiment *m*; **in my judg(e)ment** à mon avis; **to pass judg(e)ment on** (LAW) prononcer un jugement (sur)

judicial [dʒuː'dɪʃl] *adj* judiciaire; (fair) impartial(e)

judiciary [dʒuː'dɪʃɪərɪ] *n* (pouvoir *m*) judiciaire *m*

judo ['dʒuːdəʊ] *n* judo *m*

jug [dʒʌg] *n* pot *m*, cruche *f*

juggernaut ['dʒʌgənɔːt] *n* (BRIT: huge truck) mastodonte *m*

juggle ['dʒʌgl] *vi* jongler

juggler ['dʒʌglə*] *n* jongleur *m*

juice [dʒuːs] *n* jus *m*; (col: petrol): **we've run out of juice** c'est la panne sèche

juicy ['dʒuːsɪ] *adj* juteux(euse)

jukebox ['dʒuːkbɒks] *n* juke-box *m*

July [dʒuː'laɪ] *n* juillet *m*; **the first of July** le premier juillet; **(on) the eleventh of July** le onze juillet; **in the month of July** au mois de juillet; **at the beginning/end of July** au début/à la fin (du mois) de juillet, début/fin juillet; **in the middle of July** au milieu (du mois) de juillet, à la mi-juillet; **during July** pendant le mois de juillet; **in July of next year** en juillet de l'année prochaine; **each** or **every July** tous les ans or chaque année en juillet; **July was wet this year** il a beaucoup plu cette année en juillet

jumble ['dʒʌmbl] *n* fouillis *m* ◆ *vt* (also: **jumble up**, **jumble together**) mélanger, brouiller

jumble sale *n* (BRIT) vente *f* de charité; voir encadré

JUMBLE SALE

Les **jumble sales** ont lieu dans les églises, salles des fêtes ou halls d'écoles, et l'on y vend des articles de toutes sortes, en général bon marché et surtout d'occasion, pour collecter des fonds pour une œuvre de charité, une école (par exemple, pour acheter un ordinateur), ou encore une église (pour réparer un toit etc).

---

jumbo ['dʒʌmbəʊ] *adj*: **jumbo jet** (avion) gros porteur (à réaction); **jumbo size** format maxi or extra-grand

jump [dʒʌmp] *vi* sauter, bondir; (start) sursauter; (increase) monter en flèche ◆ *vt* sauter, franchir ◆ *n* saut *m*, bond *m*; sursaut *m*; (fence) obstacle *m*; **to jump the queue** (BRIT) passer avant son tour

▶ **jump about** *vi* sautiller

▶ **jump at** *vt fus* (fig) sauter sur; **he jumped at the offer** il s'est empressé d'accepter la proposition

▶ **jump down** *vi* sauter (pour descendre)

▶ **jump up** *vi* se lever (d'un bond)

jumper ['dʒʌmpə*] *n* (BRIT: *pullover*) pull-over *m*; (US: *pinafore dress*) robe-chasuble *f*; (SPORT) sauteur/euse

jump leads, (US) **jumper cables** *npl* câbles *mpl* de démarrage

jumpy ['dʒʌmpɪ] *adj* nerveux(euse), agité(e)

Jun. *abbr* = **June, junior**

Junr *abbr* = **junior**

junction ['dʒʌŋkʃən] *n* (BRIT: *of roads*) carrefour *m*; (*of rails*) embranchement *m*

juncture ['dʒʌŋktʃə*] *n*: **at this juncture** à ce moment-là, sur ces entrefaites

June [dʒuːn] *n* juin *m*; *for phrases see also* **July**

jungle ['dʒʌŋgl] *n* jungle *f*

junior ['dʒuːnɪə*] *adj, n*: **he's junior to me (by 2 years)**, **he's my junior (by 2 years)** il est mon cadet (de 2 ans), il est plus jeune que moi (de 2 ans); **he's junior to me** (*seniority*) il est en dessous de moi (dans la hiérarchie), j'ai plus d'ancienneté que lui

junior school *n* (BRIT) école *f* primaire, cours moyen

junk [dʒʌŋk] *n* (*rubbish*) bric-à-brac *m inv*; (*ship*) jonque *f* ♦ *vt* (*col*) abandonner, mettre au rancart

junk food *n* snacks vite prêts (*sans valeur nutritive*)

junk mail *n* prospectus *mpl*

junk shop *n* (boutique *f* de) brocanteur *m*

juror ['dʒuərə*] *n* juré *m*

jury ['dʒuərɪ] *n* jury *m*

just [dʒʌst] *adj* juste ♦ *adv*: **he's just done it/left** il vient de le faire/partir; **just as I expected** exactement *or* précisément comme je m'y attendais; **just right/two o'clock** exactement *or* juste ce qu'il faut/deux heures; **we were just going** nous partions; **I was just about to phone** j'allais téléphoner; **just as he was leaving** au moment *or* à l'instant précis où il partait; **just before/enough/here** juste avant/assez/là; **it's just me/a mistake** ce n'est que moi/(rien) qu'une erreur; **just missed/caught** manqué/attrapé de justesse; **just listen to this!** écoutez un peu ça!; **just ask someone the way** vous n'avez qu'à demander votre chemin à quelqu'un; **it's just as good** c'est (vraiment) aussi bon; **it's just as well that you ...** heureusement que vous ...; **not just now** pas tout de suite; **just a minute!, just one moment!** un instant (s'il vous plaît)!

justice ['dʒʌstɪs] *n* justice *f*; **Lord Chief Justice** (BRIT) premier président de la cour d'appel; **this photo doesn't do you justice** cette photo ne vous avantage pas

Justice of the Peace (JP) *n* juge *m* de paix

justify ['dʒʌstɪfaɪ] *vt* justifier; **to be justified in doing sth** être en droit de faire qch

jut [dʒʌt] *vi* (*also*: **jut out**) dépasser, faire saillie

juvenile ['dʒuːvənaɪl] *adj* juvénile; (*court, books*) pour enfants ♦ *n* adolescent/e

— **K k** —

K, k [keɪ] *n* (*letter*) K, k *m*; **K for King** K comme Kléber

K *abbr* (= *kilobyte*) Ko; (BRIT: = *Knight*) titre honorifique ♦ *n abbr* (= *one thousand*) K

kangaroo [kæŋgə'ruː] *n* kangourou *m*

karate [kə'rɑːtɪ] *n* karaté *m*

kebab [kə'bæb] *n* kébab *m*

keel [kiːl] *n* quille *f*; **on an even keel** (*fig*) à flot

▶ **keel over** *vi* (NAUT) chavirer, dessaler; (*person*) tomber dans les pommes

keen [kiːn] *adj* (*interest, desire, competition*) vif (vive); (*eye, intelligence*) pénétrant(e); (*edge*) effilé(e); (*eager*) plein(e) d'enthousiasme; **to be keen to do** *or* **on doing sth** désirer vivement faire qch, tenir beaucoup à faire qch; **to be keen on sth/sb** aimer beaucoup qch/qn; **I'm not keen on going** je ne suis pas chaud pour aller, je n'ai pas très envie d'y aller

keep [kiːp] *vb, pt, pp* **kept** [kɛpt] *vt* (*retain, preserve*) garder; (*hold back*) retenir; (*a shop, the books, a diary*) tenir; (*feed: one's family etc*) entretenir, assurer la subsistance de; (*a promise*) tenir; (*chickens, bees, pigs etc*) élever ♦ *vi* (*food*) se conserver; (*remain: in a certain state or place*) rester ♦ *n* (*of castle*) donjon *m*; (*food etc*): **enough for his keep** assez pour (assurer) sa subsistance; **to keep doing sth** continuer à faire qch; faire qch continuellement; **to keep sb from doing/sth from happening** empêcher qn de faire *or* que qn (ne) fasse/que qch (n')arrive; **to keep sb happy/a place tidy** faire que qn soit content/qu'un endroit reste propre; **to keep sb waiting** faire attendre qn; **to keep an appointment** ne pas manquer un rendez-vous; **to keep a record of sth** prendre note de qch; **to keep sth to o.s.** garder qch pour soi, tenir qch secret; **to keep sth (back) from sb** cacher qch à qn; **to keep time** (*clock*) être à l'heure, ne pas retarder

▶ **keep away** *vt*: **to keep sth/sb away from sb** tenir qch/qn éloigné de qn ♦ *vi*: **to keep away (from)** ne pas s'approcher (de)

▶ **keep back** *vt* (*crowds, tears, money*) retenir ♦ *vi* rester en arrière

▶ **keep down** *vt* (*control: prices, spending*) empêcher d'augmenter, limiter; (*retain: food*) garder ♦ *vi* (*person*) rester assis(e); rester par terre

▶ **keep in** *vt* (*invalid, child*) garder à la maison; (SCOL) consigner ♦ *vi* (*col*): **to keep in with sb** rester en bons termes avec qn

► **keep off** vi ne pas s'approcher; **"keep off the grass"** "pelouse interdite"

► **keep on** vi continuer; **to keep on doing** continuer à faire

► **keep out** vt empêcher d'entrer ◆ vi rester en dehors; **"keep out"** "défense d'entrer"

► **keep up** vi se maintenir; (*fig: in comprehension*) suivre ◆ vt continuer, maintenir; **to keep up with** se maintenir au niveau de; **to keep up with sb** (*in race etc*) aller aussi vite que qn, être du même niveau que qn

keeper ['ki:pə*] n gardien/ne

keep-fit [ki:p'fɪt] n gymnastique f de maintien

keeping ['ki:pɪŋ] n (*care*) garde f; **in keeping with** à l'avenant de; en accord avec

keepsake ['ki:pseɪk] n souvenir m

kennel ['kɛnl] n niche f; **kennels** npl chenil m

kerb [kə:b] n (*BRIT*) bordure f du trottoir

kernel ['kə:nl] n amande f; (*fig*) noyau m

kettle ['kɛtl] n bouilloire f

kettledrum ['kɛtldrʌm] n timbale f

key [ki:] n (*gen, MUS*) clé f; (*of piano, typewriter*) touche f; (*on map*) légende f ◆ cpd (-)clé

► **key in** vt (*text*) introduire au clavier

keyboard ['ki:bɔ:d] n clavier m ◆ vt (*text*) saisir

keyed up [ki:d'ʌp] adj: **to be (all) keyed up** être surexcité(e)

keyhole ['ki:həʊl] n trou m de la serrure

keyhole surgery n chirurgie très minutieuse où l'incision est minimale

keynote ['ki:nəʊt] n (*MUS*) tonique f; (*fig*) note dominante

key ring n porte-clés m

khaki ['kɑ:ki] adj, n kaki m

kick [kɪk] vt donner un coup de pied à ◆ vi (*horse*) ruer ◆ n coup m de pied; (*of rifle*) recul m; (*col: thrill*): **he does it for kicks** il le fait parce que ça l'excite, il le fait pour le plaisir

► **kick around** vi (*col*) traîner

► **kick off** vi (*SPORT*) donner le coup d'envoi

kid [kɪd] n (*col: child*) gamin/e, gosse m/f; (*animal, leather*) chevreau m ◆ vi (*col*) plaisanter, blaguer

kidnap ['kɪdnæp] vt enlever, kidnapper

kidnapper ['kɪdnæpə*] n ravisseur/euse

kidnapping ['kɪdnæpɪŋ] n enlèvement m

kidney ['kɪdnɪ] n (*ANAT*) rein m; (*CULIN*) rognon m

kill [kɪl] vt tuer; (*fig*) faire échouer; détruire; supprimer ◆ n mise f à mort; **to kill time** tuer le temps

► **kill off** vt exterminer; (*fig*) éliminer

killer ['kɪlə*] n tueur/euse; meurtrier/ière

killing ['kɪlɪŋ] n meurtre m; tuerie f, massacre m; (*col*): **to make a killing** se remplir les poches, réussir un beau coup ◆ adj (*col*) tordant(e)

killjoy ['kɪldʒɔɪ] n rabat-joie m inv

kiln [kɪln] n four m

kilo ['ki:ləʊ] n abbr (= kilogram) kilo m

kilobyte ['ki:ləʊbaɪt] n kilo-octet m

kilogram(me) ['kɪləʊɡræm] n kilogramme m

kilometre, (*US*) **kilometer** ['kɪləmi:tə*] n kilomètre m

kilowatt ['kɪləʊwɔt] n kilowatt m

kilt [kɪlt] n kilt m

kin [kɪn] n see **next-of-kin**, **kith**

kind [kaɪnd] adj gentil(le), aimable ◆ n sorte f, espèce f; (*species*) genre m; **to be two of a kind** se ressembler; **would you be kind enough to …?, would you be so kind as to …?** auriez-vous la gentillesse or l'obligeance de …?; **it's very kind of you (to do)** c'est très aimable à vous (de faire); **in kind** (*COMM*) en nature; (*fig*): **to repay sb in kind** rendre la pareille à qn

kindergarten ['kɪndəɡɑ:tn] n jardin m d'enfants

kind-hearted [kaɪnd'hɑ:tɪd] adj bon(bonne)

kindle ['kɪndl] vt allumer, enflammer

kindly ['kaɪndlɪ] adj bienveillant(e), plein(e) de gentillesse ◆ adv avec bonté; **will you kindly …** auriez-vous la bonté or l'obligeance de …; **he didn't take it kindly** il l'a mal pris

kindness ['kaɪndnɪs] n bonté f, gentillesse f

king [kɪŋ] n roi m

kingdom ['kɪŋdəm] n royaume m

kingfisher ['kɪŋfɪʃə*] n martin-pêcheur m

king-size bed ['kɪŋsaɪz-] n grand lit (*de 1,95 m de large*)

king-size(d) ['kɪŋsaɪz(d)] adj (*cigarette*) (*format*) extra-long(longue)

kiosk ['ki:ɔsk] n kiosque m; (*BRIT: also:* **telephone kiosk**) cabine f (téléphonique); (*also:* **newspaper kiosk**) kiosque à journaux

kipper ['kɪpə*] n hareng fumé et salé

kiss [kɪs] n baiser m ◆ vt embrasser; **to kiss (each other)** s'embrasser; **to kiss sb goodbye** dire au revoir à qn en l'embrassant; **kiss of life** n (*BRIT*) bouche à bouche m

kit [kɪt] n équipement m, matériel m; (*set of tools etc*) trousse f; (*for assembly*) kit m; **tool kit** nécessaire m à outils

► **kit out** vt (*BRIT*) équiper

kitchen ['kɪtʃɪn] n cuisine f

kitchen sink n évier m

kite [kaɪt] n (*toy*) cerf-volant m; (*ZOOL*) milan m

kitten ['kɪtn] n petit chat, chaton m

kitty ['kɪtɪ] n (*money*) cagnotte f

km abbr (= kilometre) km

knack [næk] n: **to have the knack (of doing)** avoir le coup (pour faire); **there's a knack** il y a un coup à prendre or une combine

knapsack ['næpsæk] n musette f

knead [ni:d] vt pétrir

knee [ni:] n genou m

kneecap ['ni:kæp] n rotule f ◆ vt tirer un coup de feu dans la rotule de

kneel, *pt, pp* **knelt** [niːl, nɛlt] *vi* (*also*: **kneel down**) s'agenouiller

knew [njuː] *pt of* **know**

knickers [ˈnɪkəz] *npl* (*BRIT*) culotte *f* (de femme)

knife, *pl* **knives** [naɪf] *n* couteau *m* ◆ *vt* poignarder, frapper d'un coup de couteau; **knife, fork and spoon** couvert *m*

knight [naɪt] *n* chevalier *m*; (*CHESS*) cavalier *m*

knighthood [ˈnaɪthud] *n* chevalerie *f*; (*title*): **to get a knighthood** être fait chevalier

knit [nɪt] *vt* tricoter; (*fig*): **to knit together** unir ◆ *vi* (*broken bones*) se ressouder

knitting [ˈnɪtɪŋ] *n* tricot *m*

knitting needle *n* aiguille *f* à tricoter

knitwear [ˈnɪtwɛə*] *n* tricots *mpl*, lainages *mpl*

knives [naɪvz] *npl of* **knife**

knob [nɔb] *n* bouton *m*; (*BRIT*): **a knob of butter** une noix de beurre

knock [nɔk] *vt* frapper; (*make*: *hole etc*): **to knock a hole in** faire un trou dans, trouer; (*force*: *nail etc*): **to knock a nail into** enfoncer un clou dans; (*fig*: *col*) dénigrer ◆ *vi* (*engine*) cogner; (*at door etc*): **to knock at/on** frapper à/sur ◆ *n* coup *m*; **he knocked at the door** il frappa à la porte

► **knock down** *vt* renverser; (*price*) réduire

► **knock off** *vi* (*col*: *finish*) s'arrêter (de travailler) ◆ *vt* (*vase, object*) faire tomber; (*col*: *steal*) piquer; (*fig*: *from price etc*): **to knock off £10** faire une remise de 10 livres

► **knock out** *vt* assommer; (*BOXING*) mettre k.-o.

► **knock over** *vt* (*object*) faire tomber; (*pedestrian*) renverser

knocker [ˈnɔkə*] *n* (*on door*) heurtoir *m*

knockout [ˈnɔkaut] *n* (*BOXING*) knock-out *m*, K.-O. *m*

knot [nɔt] *n* (*gen*) nœud *m* ◆ *vt* nouer; **to tie a knot** faire un nœud

know [nəu] *vt, pt* **knew**, *pp* **known** [njuː, nəun] savoir; (*person, place*) connaître; **to know that** savoir que; **to know how to do** savoir faire; **to know about/of sth** être au courant de/connaître qch; **to get to know sth** (*fact*) apprendre qch; (*place*) apprendre à connaître qch; **I don't know him** je ne le connais pas; **to know right from wrong** savoir distinguer le bon du mauvais; **as far as I know ...** à ma connaissance ..., autant que je sache ...

know-all [ˈnəuɔːl] *n* (*BRIT pej*) je-sais-tout *m/f*

know-how [ˈnəuhau] *n* savoir-faire *m*, technique *f*, compétence *f*

knowing [ˈnəuɪŋ] *adj* (*look etc*) entendu(e)

knowingly [ˈnəuɪŋlɪ] *adv* sciemment; d'un air entendu

knowledge [ˈnɔlɪdʒ] *n* connaissance *f*; (*learning*) connaissances, savoir *m*; **to have no knowledge of** ignorer; **not to my knowledge** pas à ma connaissance; **without my knowledge** à mon insu; **to**

have a working knowledge of French se débrouiller en français; **it is common knowledge that ...** chacun sait que ...; **it has come to my knowledge that ...** j'ai appris que ...

knowledgeable [ˈnɔlɪdʒəbl] *adj* bien informé(e)

knuckle [ˈnʌkl] *n* articulation *f* (des phalanges), jointure *f*

► **knuckle down** *vi* (*col*) s'y mettre

► **knuckle under** *vi* (*col*) céder

Koran [kɔˈrɑːn] *n* Coran *m*

Korea [kəˈrɪə] *n* Corée *f*; **North/South Korea** Corée du Nord/Sud

kosher [ˈkəuʃə*] *adj* kascher *inv*

Kosovo [ˈkɔsɔvəu] *n* Kosovo *m*

— L l —

L, l [ɛl] *n* (*letter*) L, l *m*; **L for Lucy**, (*US*) **L for Love** L comme Louis

L *abbr* (= *lake, large*) L; (= *left*) g; (*BRIT AUT*: = *learner*) signale un conducteur débutant

l *abbr* (= *litre*) l

lab [læb] *n abbr* (= *laboratory*) labo *m*

label [ˈleɪbl] *n* étiquette *f*; (*brand*: *of record*) marque *f* ◆ *vt* étiqueter; **to label sb a ...** qualifier qn de ...

labor *etc* [ˈleɪbə*] (*US*) = **labour** *etc*

laboratory [ləˈbɔrətərɪ] *n* laboratoire *m*

labour, (*US*) **labor** [ˈleɪbə*] *n* (*task*) travail *m*; (*workmen*) main-d'œuvre *f*; (*MED*) travail, accouchement *m* ◆ *vi*: **to labour (at)** travailler dur (à), peiner (sur); **in labour** (*MED*) en travail

labo(u)red [ˈleɪbəd] *adj* lourd(e), laborieux(euse); (*breathing*) difficile, pénible; (*style*) lourd, embarrassé(e)

labo(u)rer [ˈleɪbərə*] *n* manœuvre *m*; (*on farm*) ouvrier *m* agricole

lace [leɪs] *n* dentelle *f*; (*of shoe etc*) lacet *m* ◆ *vt* (*shoe*) lacer; (*drink*) arroser, corser

lack [læk] *n* manque *m* ◆ *vt* manquer de; **through** or **for lack of** faute de, par manque de; **to be lacking** manquer, faire défaut; **to be lacking in** manquer de

lacquer [ˈlækə*] *n* laque *f*

lad [læd] *n* garçon *m*, gars *m*; (*BRIT*: *in stable etc*) lad *m*

ladder [ˈlædə*] *n* échelle *f*; (*BRIT*: *in tights*) maille filée ◆ *vt, vi* (*BRIT*: *tights*) filer

laden [ˈleɪdn] *adj*: **laden (with)** chargé(e) (de); **fully laden** (*truck, ship*) en pleine charge

ladle [ˈleɪdl] *n* louche *f*

lady [ˈleɪdɪ] *n* dame *f*; **Lady Smith** lady Smith; **the ladies' (room)** les toilettes *fpl* des dames; **a lady doctor** une doctoresse, une femme médecin

ladybird ['leɪdɪbə:d], (US) **ladybug** ['leɪdɪbʌg] n coccinelle f

ladylike ['leɪdɪlaɪk] adj distingué(e)

ladyship ['leɪdɪʃɪp] n: **your Ladyship** Madame la comtesse (or la baronne etc)

lag [læg] n = **time lag** ♦ vi (also: **lag behind**) rester en arrière, traîner ♦ vt (pipes) calorifuger

lager ['lɑ:gə*] n bière blonde

lagoon [lə'gu:n] n lagune f

laid [leɪd] pt, pp of **lay**

laid-back [leɪd'bæk] adj (col) relaxe, décontracté(e)

laid up adj alité(e)

lain [leɪn] pp of **lie**

lake [leɪk] n lac m

lamb [læm] n agneau m

lamb chop n côtelette f d'agneau

lame [leɪm] adj boiteux(euse); **lame duck** (fig) canard boiteux

lament [lə'ment] n lamentation f ♦ vt pleurer, se lamenter sur

laminated ['læmɪneɪtɪd] adj laminé(e); (windscreen) (en verre) feuilleté

lamp [læmp] n lampe f

lamppost ['læmppəʊst] n (BRIT) réverbère m

lampshade ['læmpʃeɪd] n abat-jour m inv

lance [lɑ:ns] n lance f ♦ vt (MED) inciser

land [lænd] n (as opposed to sea) terre f (ferme); (country) pays m; (soil) terre; terrain m; (estate) terre(s), domaine(s) m(pl) ♦ vi (from ship) débarquer; (AVIAT) atterrir; (fig: fall) (re)tomber ♦ vt (passengers, goods) débarquer; (obtain) décrocher; **to go/travel by land** se déplacer par voie de terre; **to own land** être propriétaire foncier; **to land on one's feet** (also fig) retomber sur ses pieds

▶ **land up** vi atterrir, (finir par) se retrouver

landfill site ['lændfɪl-] n centre m d'enfouissement des déchets

landing ['lændɪŋ] n (from ship) débarquement m; (AVIAT) atterrissage m; (of staircase) palier m

landing strip n piste f d'atterrissage

landlady ['lændleɪdɪ] n propriétaire f, logeuse f

landlocked ['lændlɔkt] adj entouré(e) de terre(s), sans accès à la mer

landlord ['lændlɔ:d] n propriétaire m, logeur m; (of pub etc) patron m

landmark ['lændmɑ:k] n (point m de) repère m; **to be a landmark** (fig) faire date or époque

landowner ['lændəʊnə*] n propriétaire foncier or terrien

landscape ['lænskeɪp] n paysage m

landscape architect, landscape gardener n paysagiste m/f

landslide ['lændslaɪd] n (GEO) glissement m (de terrain); (fig: POL) raz-de-marée (électoral)

lane [leɪn] n (in country) chemin m; (in town) ruelle f; (AUT) voie f; file f; (in race) couloir m; **shipping**

lane route f maritime or de navigation

language ['læŋgwɪdʒ] n langue f; (way one speaks) langage m; **bad language** grossièretés fpl, langage grossier

language laboratory n laboratoire m de langues

lank [læŋk] adj (hair) raide et terne

lanky ['læŋkɪ] adj grand(e) et maigre, efflanqué(e)

lantern ['læntn] n lanterne f

lap [læp] n (of track) tour m (de piste); (of body): **in** or **on one's lap** sur les genoux ♦ vt (also: **lap up**) laper ♦ vi (waves) clapoter

▶ **lap up** vt (fig) boire comme du petit-lait, se gargariser de; (: lies etc) gober

lapel [lə'pel] n revers m

Lapland ['læplænd] n Laponie f

lapse [læps] n défaillance f; (in behaviour) écart m (de conduite) ♦ vi (LAW) cesser d'être en vigueur; se périmer; **to lapse into bad habits** prendre de mauvaises habitudes; **lapse of time** laps m de temps, intervalle m; **a lapse of memory** un trou de mémoire

laptop ['læptɔp] n (also: **laptop computer**) ordinateur portatif

larceny ['lɑ:sənɪ] n vol m

larch [lɑ:tʃ] n mélèze m

lard [lɑ:d] n saindoux m

larder ['lɑ:də*] n garde-manger m inv

large [lɑ:dʒ] adj grand(e); (person, animal) gros(grosse); **to make larger** agrandir; **a large number of people** beaucoup de gens; **by and large** en général; **on a large scale** sur une grande échelle; **at large** (free) en liberté; (generally) en général; pour la plupart

largely ['lɑ:dʒlɪ] adv en grande partie

large-scale ['lɑ:dʒ'skeɪl] adj (map, drawing etc) à grande échelle; (fig) important(e)

lark [lɑ:k] n (bird) alouette f; (joke) blague f, farce f

▶ **lark about** vi faire l'idiot, rigoler

laryngitis [lærɪn'dʒaɪtɪs] n laryngite f

laser ['leɪzə*] n laser m

laser printer n imprimante f laser

lash [læʃ] n coup m de fouet; (also: **eyelash**) cil m ♦ vt fouetter; (tie) attacher

▶ **lash down** vt attacher; amarrer; arrimer ♦ vi (rain) tomber avec violence

▶ **lash out** vi: **to lash out (at** or **against sb/sth)** attaquer violemment (qn/qch); **to lash out (on sth)** (col: spend) se fendre (de qch)

lass [læs] n (jeune) fille f

lasso [læ'su:] n lasso m ♦ vt prendre au lasso

last [lɑ:st] adj dernier(ière) ♦ adv en dernier ♦ vi durer; **last week** la semaine dernière; **last night** hier soir; la nuit dernière; **at last** enfin; **last but one** avant-dernier(ière); **the last time** la dernière fois; **it lasts (for) 2 hours** ça dure 2 heures

last-ditch [ˌlɑːstˈdɪtʃ] *adj* ultime, désespéré(e)

lasting [ˈlɑːstɪŋ] *adj* durable

lastly [ˈlɑːstlɪ] *adv* en dernier lieu, pour finir

last-minute [ˈlɑːstmɪnɪt] *adj* de dernière minute

latch [lætʃ] *n* loquet *m*

▶ **latch on to** *vt* (*cling to: person*) s'accrocher à; (: *idea*) trouver bon(ne)

late [leɪt] *adj* (*not on time*) en retard; (*far on in day etc*) dernier(ière); tardif(ive); (*recent*) récent(e), dernier; (*former*) ancien(ne); (*dead*) défunt(e) ◆ *adv* tard; (*behind time, schedule*) en retard; **to be late** avoir du retard; **to be 10 minutes late** avoir 10 minutes de retard; **to work late** travailler tard; **late in life** sur le tard, à un âge avancé; **of late** dernièrement; **in late May** vers la fin (du mois) de mai, fin mai; **the late Mr X** feu M. X

latecomer [ˈleɪtkʌmə*] *n* retardataire *m/f*

lately [ˈleɪtlɪ] *adv* récemment

later [ˈleɪtə*] *adj* (*date etc*) ultérieur(e); (*version etc*) plus récent(e) ◆ *adv* plus tard; **later on today** plus tard dans la journée

latest [ˈleɪtɪst] *adj* tout(e) dernier(ière); **the latest news** les dernières nouvelles; **at the latest** au plus tard

lathe [leɪð] *n* tour *m*

lather [ˈlɑːðə*] *n* mousse *f* (de savon) ◆ *vt* savonner ◆ *vi* mousser

Latin [ˈlætɪn] *n* latin *m* ◆ *adj* latin(e)

Latin America *n* Amérique latine

Latin American *adj* latino-américain(e), d'Amérique latine ◆ *n* Latino-Américain/e

latitude [ˈlætɪtjuːd] *n* (*also fig*) latitude *f*

latter [ˈlætə*] *adj* deuxième, dernier(ière) ◆ *n*: **the latter** ce dernier, celui-ci

latterly [ˈlætəlɪ] *adv* dernièrement, récemment

laudable [ˈlɔːdəbl] *adj* louable

laugh [lɑːf] *n* rire *m* ◆ *vi* rire

▶ **laugh at** *vt fus* se moquer de; (*joke*) rire de

▶ **laugh off** *vt* écarter *or* rejeter par une plaisanterie *or* par une boutade

laughable [ˈlɑːfəbl] *adj* risible, ridicule

laughing stock *n*: **the laughing stock of** la risée de

laughter [ˈlɑːftə*] *n* rire *m*; (*people laughing*) rires *mpl*

launch [lɔːntʃ] *n* lancement *m*; (*boat*) chaloupe *f*; (*also*: **motor launch**) vedette *f* ◆ *vt* (*ship, rocket, plan*) lancer

▶ **launch out** *vi*: **to launch out (into)** se lancer (dans)

Launderette® [lɔːnˈdrɛt], (*US*) **Laundromat**® [ˈlɔːndrəmæt] *n* laverie *f* (automatique)

laundry [ˈlɔːndrɪ] *n* blanchisserie *f*; (*clothes*) linge *m*; **to do the laundry** faire la lessive

laurel [ˈlɔrl] *n* laurier *m*; **to rest on one's laurels** se reposer sur ses lauriers

lava [ˈlɑːvə] *n* lave *f*

lavatory [ˈlævətərɪ] *n* toilettes *fpl*

lavender [ˈlævəndə*] *n* lavande *f*

lavish [ˈlævɪʃ] *adj* copieux(euse), somptueux(euse); (*giving freely*): **lavish with** prodigue de ◆ *vt*: **to lavish sth on sb** prodiguer qch à qn

law [lɔː] *n* loi *f*; (*science*) droit *m*; **against the law** contraire à la loi; **to study law** faire du droit; **to go to law** (*BRIT*) avoir recours à la justice; **law and order** *n* l'ordre public

law-abiding [ˈlɔːəbaɪdɪŋ] *adj* respectueux(euse) des lois

law court *n* tribunal *m*, cour *f* de justice

lawful [ˈlɔːful] *adj* légal(e), permis(e)

lawless [ˈlɔːlɪs] *adj* sans loi

lawn [lɔːn] *n* pelouse *f*

lawnmower [ˈlɔːnməuə*] *n* tondeuse *f* à gazon

lawn tennis *n* tennis *m*

law school *n* faculté *f* de droit

lawsuit [ˈlɔːsuːt] *n* procès *m*; **to bring a lawsuit against** engager des poursuites contre

lawyer [ˈlɔːjə*] *n* (*consultant, with company*) juriste *m*; (*for sales, wills etc*) ≃ notaire *m*; (*partner, in court*) ≃ avocat *m*

lax [læks] *adj* relâché(e)

laxative [ˈlæksətɪv] *n* laxatif *m*

lay [leɪ] *pt* de **lie** ◆ *adj* laïque; profane ◆ *vt, pt, pp* **laid** [leɪd], poser, mettre; (*eggs*) pondre; (*trap*) tendre; (*plans*) élaborer; **to lay the table** mettre la table; **to lay the facts/one's proposals before sb** présenter les faits/ses propositions à qn; **to get laid** (*col!*) baiser (*!*), se faire baiser (*!*)

▶ **lay aside, lay by** *vt* mettre de côté

▶ **lay down** *vt* poser; **to lay down the law** (*fig*) faire la loi

▶ **lay in** *vt* accumuler, s'approvisionner en

▶ **lay into** *vi* (*col: attack*) tomber sur; (: *scold*) passer une engueulade à

▶ **lay off** *vt* (*workers*) licencier

▶ **lay on** *vt* (*water, gas*) mettre, installer; (*provide: meal etc*) fournir; (*paint*) étaler

▶ **lay out** *vt* (*design*) dessiner, concevoir; (*display*) disposer; (*spend*) dépenser

▶ **lay up** *vt* (*store*) amasser; (*car*) remiser; (*ship*) désarmer; (*subj: illness*) forcer à s'aliter

layabout [ˈleɪəbaut] *n* fainéant/e

lay-by [ˈleɪbaɪ] *n* (*BRIT*) aire *f* de stationnement (sur le bas-côté)

layer [ˈleɪə*] *n* couche *f*

layman [ˈleɪmən] *n* laïque *m*; profane *m*

layout [ˈleɪaut] *n* disposition *f*, plan *m*, agencement *m*; (*PRESS*) mise *f* en page

laze [leɪz] *vi* paresser

lazy [ˈleɪzɪ] *adj* paresseux(euse)

lb *abbr* (= *libra: pound*) unité de poids

lead[1] [liːd] *n* (*front position*) tête *f*; (*distance, time ahead*) avance *f*; (*clue*) piste *f*; (*to battery*) raccord *m*; (*ELEC*) fil *m*; (*for dog*) laisse *f*; (*THEAT*) rôle principal

◆ *vb, pt, pp* **led** [lɛd] *vt* mener, conduire; (*induce*) amener; (*be leader of*) être à la tête de; (*sport*) être en tête de; (*orchestra: BRIT*) être le premier violon de; (: *US*) diriger ◆ *vi* mener, être en tête; **to lead to** mener à; (*result in*) conduire à; aboutir à; **to lead sb astray** détourner qn du droit chemin; **to be in the lead** (*sport: in race*) mener, être en tête; (: *in match*) mener (à la marque); **to take the lead** (*sport*) passer en tête, prendre la tête; mener; (*fig*) prendre l'initiative; **to lead sb to believe that ...** amener qn à croire que ...; **to lead sb to do sth** amener qn à faire qch

▶ **lead away** *vt* emmener

▶ **lead back** *vt* ramener

▶ **lead off** *vi* (*in game etc*) commencer

▶ **lead on** *vt* (*tease*) faire marcher; **to lead sb on to** (*induce*) amener qn à

▶ **lead up to** *vt* conduire à

lead² [lɛd] *n* (*chemical*) plomb *m*; (*in pencil*) mine *f*

leaded petrol ['lɛdɪd-] *n* essence *f* au plomb

leaden ['lɛdn] *adj* de or en plomb

leader ['liːdə*] *n* (*of team*) chef *m*; (*of party etc*) dirigeant/e, leader *m*; (*in newspaper*) éditorial *m*; **they are leaders in their field** (*fig*) ils sont à la pointe du progrès dans leur domaine; **the Leader of the House** (*BRIT*) le chef de la majorité ministérielle

leadership ['liːdəʃɪp] *n* direction *f*; **under the leadership of ...** sous la direction de ...; **qualities of leadership** qualités *fpl* de chef or de meneur

lead-free ['lɛdfriː] *adj* sans plomb

leading ['liːdɪŋ] *adj* de premier plan; (*main*) principal(e); **a leading question** une question tendancieuse; **leading role** rôle prépondérant or de premier plan

leading lady *n* (*THEAT*) vedette (féminine)

leading light *n* (*person*) sommité *f*, personnalité *f* de premier plan

leading man *n* (*THEAT*) vedette (masculine)

lead singer [liːd-] *n* (*in pop group*) (chanteur *m*) vedette *f*

leaf, *pl* **leaves** [liːf, liːvz] *n* feuille *f*; (*of table*) rallonge *f*; **to turn over a new leaf** (*fig*) changer de conduite or d'existence; **to take a leaf out of sb's book** (*fig*) prendre exemple sur qn

▶ **leaf through** *vt* (*book*) feuilleter

leaflet ['liːflɪt] *n* prospectus *m*, brochure *f*; (*POL, REL*) tract *m*

league [liːg] *n* ligue *f*; (*FOOTBALL*) championnat *m*; (*measure*) lieue *f*; **to be in league with** avoir partie liée avec, être de mèche avec

leak [liːk] *n* (*out: also fig*) fuite *f*; (*in*) infiltration *f* ◆ *vi* (*pipe, liquid etc*) fuir; (*shoes*) prendre l'eau ◆ *vt* (*liquid*) répandre; (*information*) divulguer

▶ **leak out** *vi* fuir; (*information*) être divulgué(e)

lean [liːn] *adj* maigre ◆ *n* (*of meat*) maigre *m* ◆ *vb, pt, pp* **leaned** or **leant** [lɛnt] *vt*: **to lean sth on** appuyer qch sur ◆ *vi* (*slope*) pencher; (*rest*): **to lean against** s'appuyer contre; être appuyé(e) contre; **to lean on** s'appuyer sur

▶ **lean back** *vi* se pencher en arrière

▶ **lean forward** *vi* se pencher en avant

▶ **lean out** *vi*: **to lean out (of)** se pencher au dehors (de)

▶ **lean over** *vi* se pencher

leaning ['liːnɪŋ] *adj* penché(e) ◆ *n*: **leaning (towards)** penchant *m* (pour); **the Leaning Tower of Pisa** la tour penchée de Pise

leant [lɛnt] *pt, pp of* **lean**

leap [liːp] *n* bond *m*, saut *m* ◆ *vi, pt, pp* **leaped** or **leapt** [lɛpt] bondir, sauter; **to leap at an offer** saisir une offre

▶ **leap up** *vi* (*person*) faire un bond; se lever d'un bond

leapfrog ['liːpfrɔg] *n* jeu *m* de saute-mouton

leapt [lɛpt] *pt, pp of* **leap**

leap year *n* année *f* bissextile

learn, *pt, pp* **learned** or **learnt** [ləːn, -t] *vt, vi* apprendre; **to learn how to do sth** apprendre à faire qch; **we were sorry to learn that ...** nous apprenons avec regret que ...; **to learn about sth** (*SCOL*) étudier qch; (*hear*) apprendre qch

learned ['ləːnɪd] *adj* érudit(e), savant(e)

learner ['ləːnə*] *n* débutant/e; (*BRIT: also:* **learner driver**) (conducteur/trice) débutant/e

learning ['ləːnɪŋ] *n* savoir *m*

lease [liːs] *n* bail *m* ◆ *vt* louer à bail; **on lease** en location

▶ **lease back** *vt* vendre en cession-bail

leash [liːʃ] *n* laisse *f*

least [liːst] *adj*: **the least** (+ *noun*) le(la) plus petit(e), le(la) moindre; (*smallest amount of*) le moins de; **the least** (+ *adjective*) le(la) moins; **the least money** le moins d'argent; **the least expensive** le moins cher; **at least** au moins; **not in the least** pas le moins du monde

leather ['lɛðə*] *n* cuir *m* ◆ *cpd* en or de cuir; **leather goods** maroquinerie *f*

leave [liːv] *vb, pt, pp* **left** [lɛft] *vt* laisser; (*go away from*) quitter ◆ *vi* partir, s'en aller ◆ *n* (*time off*) congé *m*; (*MIL, consent*) permission *f*; **to be left** rester; **there's some milk left over** il reste du lait; **to leave school** quitter l'école, terminer sa scolarité; **leave it to me!** laissez-moi faire!, je m'en occupe!; **on leave** en permission; **to take one's leave of** prendre congé de; **leave of absence** *n* congé exceptionnel; (*MIL*) permission spéciale

▶ **leave behind** *vt* (*also fig*) laisser; (*opponent in race*) distancer; (*forget*) laisser, oublier

▶ **leave off** *vt* (*cover, lid, heating*) ne pas (re)mettre; (*light*) ne pas (r)allumer, laisser éteint(e); (*BRIT col: stop*): **to leave off (doing sth)** s'arrêter (de faire qch)

▶ **leave on** *vt* (*coat etc*) garder, ne pas enlever; (*lid*) laisser dessus; (*light, fire, cooker*) laisser allumé(e)

▶ **leave out** vt oublier, omettre

leaves [liːvz] npl of **leaf**

Lebanon ['lebənən] n Liban m

lecherous ['letʃərəs] adj lubrique

lecture ['lektʃə*] n conférence f; (SCOL) cours (magistral) ♦ vi donner des cours; enseigner ♦ vt (reprove) sermonner, réprimander; **to lecture on** faire un cours (or son cours) sur; **to give a lecture (on)** faire une conférence (sur), faire un cours (sur)

lecturer ['lektʃərə*] n (speaker) conférencier/ière; (BRIT: at university) professeur m (d'université), ≈ maître assistant, ≈ maître de conférences; **assistant lecturer** (BRIT) ≈ assistant/e; **senior lecturer** (BRIT) ≈ chargé/e d'enseignement

led [led] pt, pp of **lead**[1]

ledge [ledʒ] n (of window, on wall) rebord m; (of mountain) saillie f, corniche f

ledger ['ledʒə*] n registre m, grand livre

leech [liːtʃ] n sangsue f

leek [liːk] n poireau m

leer [lɪə*] vi: **to leer at sb** regarder qn d'un air mauvais or concupiscent, lorgner qn

leeway ['liːweɪ] n (fig): **to make up leeway** rattraper son retard; **to have some leeway** avoir une certaine liberté d'action

left [left] pt, pp of **leave** ♦ adj gauche ♦ adv à gauche ♦ n gauche f; **on the left, to the left** à gauche; **the Left** (POL) la gauche

left-handed [left'hændɪd] adj gaucher(ère); (scissors etc) pour gauchers

left-hand side ['lefthænd-] n gauche f, côté m gauche

left-luggage locker [left'lʌgɪdʒ-] n (casier m à) consigne f automatique

left-luggage (office) [left'lʌgɪdʒ(-)] n (BRIT) consigne f

leftovers ['leftəuvəz] npl restes mpl

left wing n (MIL, SPORT) aile f gauche; (POL) gauche f ♦ adj: **left-wing** (POL) de gauche

leg [leg] n jambe f; (of animal) patte f; (of furniture) pied m; (CULIN: of chicken) cuisse f; **1st/2nd leg** (SPORT) match m aller/retour; (of journey) 1ère/2ème étape f; **leg of lamb** (CULIN) gigot m d'agneau; **to stretch one's legs** se dégourdir les jambes

legacy ['legəsɪ] n (also fig) héritage m, legs m

legal ['liːgl] adj légal(e); **to take legal action** or **proceedings against sb** poursuivre qn en justice

legal holiday (US) n jour férié

legal tender n monnaie légale

legend ['ledʒənd] n légende f

leggings ['legɪŋz] npl jambières fpl, guêtres fpl

legible ['ledʒəbl] adj lisible

legislation [ledʒɪs'leɪʃən] n législation f; **a piece of legislation** un texte de loi

legislature ['ledʒɪslətʃə*] n corps législatif

legitimate [lɪ'dʒɪtɪmət] adj légitime

leg-room ['legruːm] n place f pour les jambes

leisure ['leʒə*] n (time) loisir m, temps m; (free time) temps libre, loisirs mpl; **at leisure** (tout) à loisir; à tête reposée

leisure centre n centre m de loisirs

leisurely ['leʒəlɪ] adj tranquille, fait(e) sans se presser

lemon ['lemən] n citron m

lemonade [lemə'neɪd] n limonade f

lemon tea n thé m au citron

lend, pt, pp **lent** [lend, lent] vt: **to lend sth (to sb)** prêter qch (à qn); **to lend a hand** donner un coup de main

length [leŋθ] n longueur f; (section: of road, pipe etc) morceau m, bout m; **length of time** durée f; **what length is it?** quelle longueur fait-il?; **it is 2 metres in length** cela fait 2 mètres de long; **to fall full length** tomber de tout son long; **at length** (at last) enfin, à la fin; (lengthily) longuement; **to go to any length(s) to do sth** faire n'importe quoi pour faire qch, ne reculer devant rien pour faire qch

lengthen ['leŋθən] vt allonger, prolonger ♦ vi s'allonger

lengthways ['leŋθweɪz] adv dans le sens de la longueur, en long

lengthy ['leŋθɪ] adj (très) long(longue)

lenient ['liːnɪənt] adj indulgent(e), clément(e)

lens [lenz] n lentille f; (of spectacles) verre m; (of camera) objectif m

Lent [lent] n carême m

lent [lent] pt, pp of **lend**

lentil ['lentl] n lentille f

Leo ['liːəu] n le Lion; **to be Leo** être du Lion

leotard ['liːətɑːd] n maillot m (de danseur etc)

leprosy ['leprəsɪ] n lèpre f

lesbian ['lezbɪən] n lesbienne f ♦ adj lesbien(ne)

less [les] adj moins de ♦ pron, adv moins; **less than that/you** moins que cela/ vous; **less than half** moins de la moitié; **less than one/a kilo/3 metres** moins de un/d'un kilo/de 3 mètres; **less and less** de moins en moins; **the less he works ...** moins il travaille ...

lessen ['lesn] vi diminuer, s'amoindrir, s'atténuer ♦ vt diminuer, réduire, atténuer

lesser ['lesə*] adj moindre; **to a lesser extent** or **degree** à un degré moindre

lesson ['lesn] n leçon f; **a maths lesson** une leçon or un cours de maths; **to give lessons in** donner des cours de; **it taught him a lesson** (fig) cela lui a servi de leçon

let, pt, pp **let** [let] vt laisser; (BRIT: lease) louer; **to let sb do sth** laisser qn faire qch; **to let sb know sth** faire savoir qch à qn, prévenir qn de qch; **he let me go** il m'a laissé partir; **let the water boil and ...** faites bouillir l'eau et ...; **let's go** allons-y; **let him come** qu'il vienne; **"to let"** (BRIT) "à louer"

▶ **let down** vt (lower) baisser; (dress) rallonger

(*hair*) défaire; (*BRIT*: *tyre*) dégonfler; (*disappoint*) décevoir

▶ **let go** *vi* lâcher prise ♦ *vt* lâcher

▶ **let in** *vt* laisser entrer; (*visitor etc*) faire entrer; **what have you let yourself in for?** à quoi t'es-tu engagé?

▶ **let off** *vt* (*allow to leave*) laisser partir; (*not punish*) ne pas punir; (*subj: taxi driver, bus driver*) déposer; (*firework etc*) faire partir; (*smell etc*) dégager; **to let off steam** (*fig: col*) se défouler, décharger sa rate *or* bile

▶ **let on** *vi* (*col*): **to let on that ...** révéler que ..., dire que ...

▶ **let out** *vt* laisser sortir; (*dress*) élargir; (*scream*) laisser échapper; (*rent out*) louer

▶ **let up** *vi* diminuer, s'arrêter

lethal ['li:θl] *adj* mortel(le), fatal(e)

letter ['letə*] *n* lettre *f*; **letters** *npl* (*LITERATURE*) lettres; **small/capital letter** minuscule *f*/majuscule *f*; **letter of credit** lettre *f* de crédit

letter bomb *n* lettre piégée

letterbox ['letəbɔks] *n* (*BRIT*) boîte *f* aux *or* à lettres

lettering ['letərɪŋ] *n* lettres *fpl*; caractères *mpl*

lettuce ['letɪs] *n* laitue *f*, salade *f*

let-up ['letʌp] *n* répit *m*, détente *f*

leukaemia, (*US*) **leukemia** [lu:'ki:mɪə] *n* leucémie *f*

level ['levl] *adj* plat(e), plan(e), uni(e); horizontal(e) ♦ *n* niveau *m*; (*flat place*) terrain plat; (*also*: **spirit level**) niveau à bulle ♦ *vt* niveler, aplanir; (*gun*) pointer, braquer; (*accusation*): **to level (against)** lancer *or* porter (contre) ♦ *vi* (*col*): **to level with sb** être franc(franche) avec qn; **"A" levels** *npl* (*BRIT*: *formerly*) ≃ baccalauréat *m*; **"O" levels** *npl* (*BRIT*: *formerly*) examens passés à l'âge de 16 ans sanctionnant les connaissances de l'élève, ≃ brevet *m* des collèges; **a level spoonful** (*CULIN*) une cuillerée à raser; **to be level with** être au même niveau que; **to draw level with** (*team*) arriver à égalité de points avec, égaliser avec; arriver au même classement que; (*runner, car*) arriver à la hauteur de, rattraper; **on the level** à l'horizontale; (*fig: honest*) régulier(ière)

▶ **level off, level out** *vi* (*prices etc*) se stabiliser ♦ *vt* (*ground*) aplanir, niveler

level crossing *n* (*BRIT*) passage *m* à niveau

level-headed [levl'hedɪd] *adj* équilibré(e)

lever ['li:və*] *n* levier *m* ♦ *vt*: **to lever up/out** soulever/extraire au moyen d'un levier

leverage ['li:vərɪdʒ] *n*: **leverage (on *or* with)** prise *f* (sur)

levy ['levɪ] *n* taxe *f*, impôt *m* ♦ *vt* prélever, imposer; percevoir

lewd [lu:d] *adj* obscène, lubrique

liability [laɪə'bɪlətɪ] *n* responsabilité *f*; (*handicap*) handicap *m*

liable ['laɪəbl] *adj* (*subject*): **liable to** sujet(te) à, passible de; (*responsible*): **liable (for)** responsable

(de); (*likely*): **liable to do** susceptible de faire; **to be liable to a fine** être passible d'une amende

liaise [li:'eɪz] *vi*: **to liaise with** rester en liaison avec

liaison [li:'eɪzɔn] *n* liaison *f*

liar ['laɪə*] *n* menteur/euse

libel ['laɪbl] *n* écrit *m* diffamatoire, diffamation *f* ♦ *vt* diffamer

liberal ['lɪbərl] *adj* libéral(e); (*generous*): **liberal with** prodigue de, généreux(euse) avec ♦ *n*: **Liberal** (*POL*) libéral/e

liberation [lɪbə'reɪʃən] *n* libération *f*

liberty ['lɪbətɪ] *n* liberté *f*; **at liberty to do** libre de faire; **to take the liberty of** prendre la liberté de, se permettre de

Libra ['li:brə] *n* la Balance; **to be Libra** être de la Balance

librarian [laɪ'brɛərɪən] *n* bibliothécaire *m/f*

library ['laɪbrərɪ] *n* bibliothèque *f*

libretto [lɪ'bretəu] *n* livret *m*

Libya ['lɪbɪə] *n* Libye *f*

lice [laɪs] *npl of* **louse**

licence, (*US*) **license** ['laɪsns] *n* autorisation *f*, permis *m*; (*COMM*) licence *f*; (*RADIO, TV*) redevance *f*; (*also*: **driving licence**, (*US*) **driver's license**) permis *m* (de conduire); (*excessive freedom*) licence; **import licence** licence d'importation; **produced under licence** fabriqué/e sous licence

licence number *n* (*BRIT AUT*) numéro *m* d'immatriculation

licence plate *n* plaque *f* minéralogique

license ['laɪsns] *n* (*US*) = **licence** ♦ *vt* donner une licence à; (*car*) acheter la vignette de; délivrer la vignette de

licensed ['laɪsnst] *adj* (*for alcohol*) patenté(e) pour la vente des spiritueux, qui a une patente de débit de boissons

lick [lɪk] *vt* lécher; (*col: defeat*) écraser, flanquer une piquette *or* raclée à ♦ *n* coup *m* de langue; **a lick of paint** un petit coup de peinture

licorice ['lɪkərɪs] *n* = **liquorice**

lid [lɪd] *n* couvercle *m*; **to take the lid off sth** (*fig*) exposer *or* étaler qch au grand jour

lie [laɪ] *n* mensonge *m* ♦ *vi* mentir; *pt* **lay**, *pp* **lain** [leɪ, leɪn] (*rest*) être étendu(e) *or* allongé(e) *or* couché(e); (*in grave*) être enterré(e), reposer; (*of object*: *be situated*) se trouver, être; **to lie low** (*fig*) se cacher, rester caché(e); **to tell lies** mentir

▶ **lie about, lie around** *vi* (*things*) traîner; (*person*) traînasser, flemmarder

▶ **lie back** *vi* se renverser en arrière

▶ **lie down** *vi* se coucher, s'étendre

▶ **lie up** *vi* (*hide*) se cacher

lie-down ['laɪdaun] *n* (*BRIT*): **to have a lie-down** s'allonger, se reposer

lie-in ['laɪɪn] *n* (*BRIT*): **to have a lie-in** faire la grasse matinée

lieutenant [lef'tenənt, (US) lu:'tenənt] n lieutenant m
life, pl: **lives** [laɪf, laɪvz] n vie f ♦ cpd de vie; de la vie; à vie; **true to life** réaliste, fidèle à la réalité; **to paint from life** peindre d'après nature; **to be sent to prison for life** être condamné(e) (à la réclusion criminelle) à perpétuité; **country/city life** la vie à la campagne/à la ville
life assurance n (BRIT) = **life insurance**
lifebelt ['laɪfbelt] n (BRIT) bouée f de sauvetage
lifeboat ['laɪfbəut] n canot m or chaloupe f de sauvetage
lifebuoy ['laɪfbɔɪ] n bouée f de sauvetage
lifeguard ['laɪfgɑːd] n surveillant m de baignade
life insurance n assurance-vie f
life jacket n gilet m or ceinture f de sauvetage
lifeless ['laɪflɪs] adj sans vie, inanimé(e); (dull) qui manque de vie or de vigueur
lifelike ['laɪflaɪk] adj qui semble vrai(e) or vivant(e), ressemblant(e)
lifelong ['laɪflɔŋ] adj de toute une vie, de toujours
life preserver [-prɪ'zɜːvə*] n (US) gilet m or ceinture f de sauvetage
life-saving ['laɪfseɪvɪŋ] n sauvetage m
life sentence n condamnation f à vie or à perpétuité
life-size(d) ['laɪfsaɪz(d)] adj grandeur nature inv
life span n (durée f de) vie f
lifestyle ['laɪfstaɪl] n style m de vie
life-support system n (MED) respirateur artificiel
lifetime ['laɪftaɪm] n: **in his lifetime** de son vivant; **the chance of a lifetime** la chance de ma (or sa etc) vie, une occasion unique
lift [lɪft] vt soulever, lever; (steal) prendre, voler ♦ vi (fog) se lever ♦ n (BRIT: elevator) ascenseur m; **to give sb a lift** (BRIT) emmener or prendre qn en voiture
▶ **lift off** vi (rocket, helicopter) décoller
▶ **lift out** vt sortir; (troops, evacuees etc) évacuer par avion or hélicoptère
▶ **lift up** vt soulever
lift-off ['lɪftɔf] n décollage m
light [laɪt] n lumière f; (daylight) lumière, jour m; (lamp) lampe f; (AUT: traffic light, rear light) feu m; (: headlamp) phare m; (for cigarette etc) **have you got a light?** avez-vous du feu? ♦ vt, pt, pp **lighted** or **lit** [lɪt] (candle, cigarette, fire) allumer; (room) éclairer ♦ adj (room, colour) clair(e); (not heavy, also fig) léger(ère) ♦ adv (travel) avec peu de bagages; **to turn the light on/off** allumer/éteindre; **to cast** or **shed** or **throw light on** éclaircir; **to come to light** être dévoilé(e) or découvert(e); **in the light of** à la lumière de; étant donné; **to make light of sth** (fig) prendre qch à la légère, faire peu de cas de qch
▶ **light up** vi s'allumer; (face) s'éclairer ♦ vt (illuminate) éclairer, illuminer
light bulb n ampoule f

lighten ['laɪtn] vi s'éclairer ♦ vt (give light to) éclairer; (make lighter) éclaircir; (make less heavy) alléger
lighter ['laɪtə*] n (also: **cigarette lighter**) briquet m; (: in car) allume-cigare m inv; (boat) péniche f
light-headed [laɪt'hedɪd] adj étourdi(e), écervelé(e)
light-hearted [laɪt'hɑːtɪd] adj gai(e), joyeux(euse), enjoué(e)
lighthouse ['laɪthaus] n phare m
lighting ['laɪtɪŋ] n (on road) éclairage m; (in theatre) éclairages
lightly ['laɪtlɪ] adv légèrement; **to get off lightly** s'en tirer à bon compte
lightness ['laɪtnɪs] n clarté f; (in weight) légèreté f
lightning ['laɪtnɪŋ] n éclair m, foudre f
lightning conductor, (US) **lightning rod** n paratonnerre m
light pen n crayon m optique
lightweight ['laɪtweɪt] adj (suit) léger(ère) ♦ n (boxer) poids léger inv
like [laɪk] vt aimer (bien) ♦ prep comme ♦ adj semblable, pareil(le) ♦ n: **the like** un(e) pareil(le) or semblable; le(la) pareil(le); (pej) d'autres du même genre or acabit; **his likes and dislikes** ses goûts mpl or préférences fpl; **I would like, I'd like** je voudrais, j'aimerais; **would you like a coffee?** voulez vous du café?; **to be/look like sb/sth** ressembler à qn/qch; **what's he like?** comment est-il?; **what's the weather like?** quel temps fait-il?; **that's just like him** c'est bien de lui, ça lui ressemble; **something like that** quelque chose comme ça; **I feel like a drink** je boirais bien quelque chose; **if you like** si vous voulez; **there's nothing like ...** il n'y a rien de tel que ...
likeable ['laɪkəbl] adj sympathique, agréable
likelihood ['laɪklɪhud] n probabilité f; **in all likelihood** selon toute vraisemblance
likely ['laɪklɪ] adj (result, outcome) probable; (excuse) plausible; **he's likely to leave** il va sûrement partir, il risque fort de partir; **not likely!** (col) pas de danger!
likeness ['laɪknɪs] n ressemblance f
likewise ['laɪkwaɪz] adv de même, pareillement
liking ['laɪkɪŋ] n affection f, penchant m; goût m; **to take a liking to sb** se prendre d'amitié pour qn; **to be to sb's liking** être au goût de qn, plaire à qn
lilac ['laɪlək] n lilas m ♦ adj lilas inv
lily ['lɪlɪ] n lis m; **lily of the valley** muguet m
limb [lɪm] n membre m; **to be out on a limb** (fig) être isolé/e
limber ['lɪmbə*]: **to limber up** vi se dégourdir, se mettre en train
limbo ['lɪmbəu] n: **to be in limbo** (fig) être tombé(e) dans l'oubli
lime [laɪm] n (tree) tilleul m; (fruit) citron vert, lime f; (GEO) chaux f

limelight [ˈlaɪmlaɪt] *n*: **in the limelight** (*fig*) en vedette, au premier plan

limerick [ˈlɪmərɪk] *n* petit poème humoristique

limestone [ˈlaɪmstəʊn] *n* pierre *f* à chaux; (*GEO*) calcaire *m*

limit [ˈlɪmɪt] *n* limite *f* ♦ *vt* limiter; **weight/speed limit** limite de poids/de vitesse

limited [ˈlɪmɪtɪd] *adj* limité(e), restreint(e); **limited edition** édition *f* à tirage limité

limited (liability) company (Ltd) *n* (*BRIT*) ≃ société *f* anonyme (SA)

limousine [ˈlɪməziːn] *n* limousine *f*

limp [lɪmp] *n*: **to have a limp** boiter ♦ *vi* boiter ♦ *adj* mou(molle)

limpet [ˈlɪmpɪt] *n* patelle *f*; **like a limpet** (*fig*) comme une ventouse

line [laɪn] *n* (*gen*) ligne *f*; (*rope*) corde *f*; (*wire*) fil *m*; (*of poem*) vers *m*; (*row, series*) rangée *f*; file *f*, queue *f*; (*COMM: series of goods*) article(s) *m(pl)*, ligne de produits ♦ *vt* (*clothes*): **to line (with)** doubler (de); (*box*): **to line (with)** garnir *or* tapisser (de); (*trees, crowd*) border; **to cut in line** (*US*) passer avant son tour; **in his line of business** dans sa partie, dans son rayon; **on the right lines** sur la bonne voie; **a new line in cosmetics** une nouvelle ligne de produits de beauté; **hold the line please** (*BRIT TEL*) ne quittez pas; **to be in line for sth** (*fig*) être en lice pour qch; **in line with** en accord avec, en conformité avec; **to bring sth into line with sth** aligner qch sur qch; **to draw the line at (doing) sth** (*fig*) se refuser à (faire) qch; ne pas tolérer *or* admettre (qu'on fasse) qch; **to take the line that …** être d'avis *or* de l'opinion que …

▶ **line up** *vi* s'aligner, se mettre en rang(s) ♦ *vt* aligner; (*set up, have ready*) prévoir; trouver; **to have sb/sth lined up** avoir qn/qch en vue *or* de prévu(e)

lined [laɪnd] *adj* (*paper*) réglé(e); (*face*) marqué(e), ridé(e); (*clothes*) doublé(e)

linen [ˈlɪnɪn] *n* linge *m* (de corps *or* de maison); (*cloth*) lin *m*

liner [ˈlaɪnə*] *n* paquebot *m* de ligne

linesman [ˈlaɪnzmən] *n* (*TENNIS*) juge *m* de ligne; (*FOOTBALL*) juge de touche

line-up [ˈlaɪnʌp] *n* file *f*; (*also*: **police line-up**) parade *f* d'identification; (*SPORT*) composition *f* de l'équipe *f*

linger [ˈlɪŋgə*] *vi* s'attarder; traîner; (*smell, tradition*) persister

linguist [ˈlɪŋgwɪst] *n* linguiste *m/f*; personne douée pour les langues

linguistics [lɪŋˈgwɪstɪks] *n* linguistique *f*

lining [ˈlaɪnɪŋ] *n* doublure *f*; (*TECH*) revêtement *m*; (: of brakes) garniture *f*

link [lɪŋk] *n* (*of a chain*) maillon *m*; (*connection*) lien *m*, rapport *m* ♦ *vt* relier, lier, unir; **rail link** liaison *f* ferroviaire

▶ **link up** *vt* relier ♦ *vi* se rejoindre; s'associer

lino [ˈlaɪnəʊ] *n* = **linoleum**

linoleum [lɪˈnəʊlɪəm] *n* linoléum *m*

lion [ˈlaɪən] *n* lion *m*

lioness [ˈlaɪənɪs] *n* lionne *f*

lip [lɪp] *n* lèvre *f*; (*of cup etc*) rebord *m*; (*insolence*) insolences *fpl*

liposuction [ˈlɪpəʊsʌkʃən] *n* liposuccion *f*

lip-read [ˈlɪpriːd] *vi* lire sur les lèvres

lip salve [-sælv] *n* pommade *f* pour les lèvres, pommade rosat

lip service *n*: **to pay lip service to sth** ne reconnaître le mérite de qch que pour la forme *or* qu'en paroles

lipstick [ˈlɪpstɪk] *n* rouge *m* à lèvres

liqueur [lɪˈkjʊə*] *n* liqueur *f*

liquid [ˈlɪkwɪd] *n* liquide *m* ♦ *adj* liquide

liquidize [ˈlɪkwɪdaɪz] *vt* (*BRIT CULIN*) passer au mixer

liquidizer [ˈlɪkwɪdaɪzə*] *n* (*BRIT CULIN*) mixer *m*

liquor [ˈlɪkə*] *n* spiritueux *m*, alcool *m*

liquorice [ˈlɪkərɪs] *n* (*BRIT*) réglisse *m*

liquor store (*US*) *n* magasin *m* de vins et spiritueux

lisp [lɪsp] *n* zézaiement *m*

list [lɪst] *n* liste *f*; (*of ship*) inclinaison *f* ♦ *vt* (*write down*) inscrire; faire la liste de; (*enumerate*) énumérer; (*COMPUT*) lister ♦ *vi* (*ship*) gîter, donner de la bande; **shopping list** liste des courses

listed building [ˈlɪstɪd-] *n* (*ARCHIT*) monument classé

listen [ˈlɪsn] *vi* écouter; **to listen to** écouter

listener [ˈlɪsnə*] *n* auditeur/trice

listless [ˈlɪstlɪs] *adj* indolent(e), apathique

lit [lɪt] *pt, pp of* **light**

liter [ˈliːtə*] *n* (*US*) = **litre**

literacy [ˈlɪtərəsɪ] *n* degré *m* d'alphabétisation, fait *m* de savoir lire et écrire

literal [ˈlɪtərl] *adj* littéral(e)

literally [ˈlɪtrəlɪ] *adv* littéralement

literary [ˈlɪtərərɪ] *adj* littéraire

literate [ˈlɪtərət] *adj* qui sait lire et écrire, instruit(e)

literature [ˈlɪtrɪtʃə*] *n* littérature *f*; (*brochures etc*) copie *f* publicitaire, prospectus *mpl*

lithe [laɪð] *adj* agile, souple

litigation [lɪtɪˈgeɪʃən] *n* litige *m*; contentieux *m*

litre, (us) liter [ˈliːtə*] *n* litre *m*

litter [ˈlɪtə*] *n* (*rubbish*) détritus *mpl*, ordures *fpl*; (*young animals*) portée *f* ♦ *vt* éparpiller; laisser des détritus dans; **littered with** jonché(e) de, couvert(e) de

litter bin *n* (*BRIT*) boîte *f* à ordures, poubelle *f*

little [ˈlɪtl] *adj* (*small*) petit(e); (*not much*): **it's little** c'est peu ♦ *adv* peu; **little milk** peu de lait; **a little** un peu (de); **a little milk** un peu de lait; **for a little while** pendant un petit moment; **with little difficulty** sans trop de difficulté; **as little as possible** le moins possible; **little by little** petit à petit, peu à peu; **to make little of** faire peu de cas de

live *vi* [lɪv] vivre; (*reside*) vivre, habiter ◆ *adj* [laɪv] (*animal*) vivant(e), en vie; (*wire*) sous tension; (*broadcast*) transmis(e)) en direct; (*issue*) d'actualité, brûlant(e); (*unexploded*) non explosé(e); **to live in London** habiter (à) Londres; **to live together** vivre ensemble, cohabiter; **live ammunition** munitions *fpl* de combat

▶ **live down** *vt* faire oublier (avec le temps)

▶ **live in** *vi* être logé(e) et nourri(e); être interne

▶ **live off** *vt* (*land, fish etc*) vivre de; (*pej: parents etc*) vivre aux crochets de

▶ **live on** *vt fus* (*food*) vivre de ◆ *vi* survivre; **to live on £50 a week** vivre avec 50 livres par semaine

▶ **live out** *vi* (*BRIT: students*) être externe ◆ *vt*: **to live out one's days** *or* **life** passer sa vie

▶ **live up** *vt*: **to live it up** (*col*) faire la fête; mener la grande vie

▶ **live up to** *vt fus* se montrer à la hauteur de

livelihood ['laɪvlɪhud] *n* moyens *mpl* d'existence

lively ['laɪvlɪ] *adj* vif(vive) plein(e) d'entrain

liven up ['laɪvn-] *vt* (*room etc*) égayer; (*discussion, evening*) animer

liver ['lɪvə*] *n* foie *m*

lives [laɪvz] *npl of* **life**

livestock ['laɪvstɔk] *n* cheptel *m*, bétail *m*

livid ['lɪvɪd] *adj* livide, blafard(e); (*furious*) furieux(euse), furibond(e)

living ['lɪvɪŋ] *adj* vivant(e), en vie ◆ *n*: **to earn** *or* **make a living** gagner sa vie; **cost of living** coût *m* de la vie; **within living memory** de mémoire d'homme

living conditions *npl* conditions *fpl* de vie

living room *n* salle *f* de séjour

living standards *npl* niveau *m* de vie

living wage *n* salaire *m* permettant de vivre (décemment)

lizard ['lɪzəd] *n* lézard *m*

load [laud] *n* (*weight*) poids *m*; (*thing carried*) chargement *m*, charge *f*; (*ELEC, TECH*) charge ◆ *vt* (*lorry, ship*): **to load (with)** charger (de); (*gun, camera*): **to load (with)** charger (avec); (*COMPUT*) charger; **a load of, loads of** (*fig*) un or des tas de, des masses de

loaded ['laudɪd] *adj* (*dice*) pipé(e); (*question*) insidieux(euse); (*col: rich*) bourré(e) de fric; (: *drunk*) bourré

loaf, *pl* **loaves** [ləuf, ləuvz] *n* pain *m*, miche *f* ◆ *vi* (*also*: **loaf about**, **loaf around**) fainéanter, traîner

loan [ləun] *n* prêt *m* ◆ *vt* prêter; **on loan** prêté(e), en prêt; **public loan** emprunt public

loath [ləuθ] *adj*: **to be loath to do** répugner à faire

loathe [ləuð] *vt* détester, avoir en horreur

loaves [ləuvz] *npl of* **loaf**

lobby ['lɔbɪ] *n* hall *m*, entrée *f*; (*POL*) groupe *m* de pression, lobby *m* ◆ *vt* faire pression sur

lobster ['lɔbstə*] *n* homard *m*

local ['ləukl] *adj* local(e) ◆ *n* (*BRIT: pub*) pub *m* or café *m* du coin; **the locals** *npl* les gens *mpl* du pays or du coin

local anaesthetic *n* anesthésie locale

local authority *n* collectivité locale, municipalité *f*

local call *n* (*TEL*) communication urbaine

local government *n* administration locale or municipale

locality [ləuˈkælɪtɪ] *n* région *f*, environs *mpl*; (*position*) lieu *m*

locate [ləuˈkeɪt] *vt* (*find*) trouver, repérer; (*situate*) situer

location [ləuˈkeɪʃən] *n* emplacement *m*; **on location** (*CINE*) en extérieur

loch [lɔx] *n* lac *m*, loch *m*

lock [lɔk] *n* (*of door, box*) serrure *f*; (*of canal*) écluse *f*; (*of hair*) mèche *f*, boucle *f* ◆ *vt* (*with key*) fermer à clé; (*immobilize*) bloquer ◆ *vi* (*door etc*) fermer à clé; (*wheels*) se bloquer; **lock stock and barrel** (*fig*) en bloc; **on full lock** (*BRIT AUT*) le volant tourné à fond

▶ **lock away** *vt* (*valuables*) mettre sous clé; (*criminal*) mettre sous les verrous, enfermer

▶ **lock in** *vt* enfermer

▶ **lock out** *vt* enfermer dehors; (*on purpose*) mettre à la porte; (: *workers*) lock-outer

▶ **lock up** *vi* tout fermer (à clé)

locker ['lɔkə*] *n* casier *m*

locket ['lɔkɪt] *n* médaillon *m*

locksmith ['lɔksmɪθ] *n* serrurier *m*

lock-up ['lɔkʌp] *n* (*prison*) prison *f*; (*cell*) cellule *f* provisoire; (*also*: **lock-up garage**) box *m*

locum ['ləukəm] *n* (*MED*) suppléant/e (de médecin)

lodge [lɔdʒ] *n* pavillon *m* (de gardien); (*FREEMASONRY*) loge *f* ◆ *vi* (*person*): **to lodge with** être logé(e) chez, être en pension chez ◆ *vt* (*appeal etc*) présenter; déposer; **to lodge a complaint** porter plainte; **to lodge (itself) in/between** se loger dans/entre

lodger ['lɔdʒə*] *n* locataire *m/f*; (*with room and meals*) pensionnaire *m/f*

lodgings ['lɔdʒɪŋz] *npl* chambre *f*, meublé *m*

loft [lɔft] *n* grenier *m*; (*us*) grenier aménagé (en appartement) (*gén dans ancien entrepôt ou fabrique*)

lofty ['lɔftɪ] *adj* élevé(e); (*haughty*) hautain(e); (*sentiments, aims*) noble

log [lɔg] *n* (*of wood*) bûche *f*; (*book*) = **logbook** ◆ *n abbr* (= *logarithm*) log *m* ◆ *vt* enregistrer

▶ **log in, log on** *vi* (*COMPUT*) ouvrir une session, entrer dans le système

▶ **log off, log out** *vi* (*COMPUT*) clore une session, sortir du système

logbook ['lɔgbuk] *n* (*NAUT*) livre *m* or journal *m* de bord; (*AVIAT*) carnet *m* de vol; (*of lorry driver*) carnet *m* de route; (*of movement of goods etc*) registre *m*; (*of car*) ⁓ carte grise

loggerheads ['lɔgəhedz] *npl*: **at loggerheads**

(with) à couteaux tirés (avec)

logic ['lɒdʒɪk] n logique f

logical ['lɒdʒɪkl] adj logique

loin [lɔɪn] n (CULIN) filet m, longe f; **loins** npl reins mpl

loiter ['lɔɪtə*] vi s'attarder; **to loiter (about)** traîner, musarder; (pej) rôder

loll [lɒl] vi (also: **loll about**) se prélasser, fainéanter

lollipop ['lɒlɪpɒp] n sucette f

lollipop lady/man n (BRIT) voir encadré

LOLLIPOP LADIES/MEN

Les **lollipop ladies/men** sont employés pour aider les enfants à traverser la rue à proximité des écoles à l'heure où ils entrent en classe et à la sortie. On les repère facilement à cause de leur long ciré blanc et ils portent une pancarte ronde pour faire signe aux automobilistes de s'arrêter. On les appelle ainsi car la forme circulaire de cette pancarte rappelle une sucette.

lolly ['lɒlɪ] n (col: ice) esquimau m; (: lollipop) sucette f; (: money) fric m

London ['lʌndən] n Londres

Londoner ['lʌndənə*] n Londonien/ne

lone [ləun] adj solitaire

loneliness ['ləunlɪnɪs] n solitude f, isolement m

lonely ['ləunlɪ] adj seul(e); (childhood etc) solitaire; (place) solitaire, isolé(e)

long [lɒŋ] adj long(longue) ♦ adv longtemps ♦ n: **the long and the short of it is that ...** (fig) le fin mot de l'histoire c'est que ... ♦ vi: **to long for sth/to do** avoir très envie de qch/de faire, attendre qch avec impatience/impatience de faire; **he had long understood that ...** il avait compris depuis longtemps que ...; **how long is this river/course?** quelle est la longueur de ce fleuve/la durée de ce cours?; **6 metres long** (long) de 6 mètres; **6 months long** qui dure 6 mois, de 6 mois; **all night long** toute la nuit; **he no longer comes** il ne vient plus; **long before** longtemps avant; **before long** (+ future) avant peu, dans peu de temps; (+ past) peu de temps après; **long ago** il y a longtemps; **don't be long!** fais vite!, dépêche-toi!; **I shan't be long** je n'en ai pas pour longtemps; **at long last** enfin; **in the long run** à la longue; finalement; **so** or **as long as** pourvu que

long-distance [lɒŋ'dɪstəns] adj (race) de fond; (call) interurbain(e)

longer ['lɒŋgə*] adv see long

longhand ['lɒŋhænd] n écriture normale or courante

longing ['lɒŋɪŋ] n désir m, envie f, nostalgie f ♦ adj plein(e) d'envie or de nostalgie

longitude ['lɒŋɡɪtjuːd] n longitude f

long jump n saut m en longueur

long-life [lɒŋ'laɪf] adj (batteries etc) longue durée inv; (milk) longue conservation

long-lost ['lɒŋlɒst] adj perdu(e) depuis longtemps

long-range ['lɒŋ'reɪndʒ] adj à longue portée; (weather forecast) à long terme

long-sighted ['lɒŋ'saɪtɪd] adj (BRIT) presbyte; (fig) prévoyant(e)

long-standing ['lɒŋ'stændɪŋ] adj de longue date

long-suffering [lɒŋ'sʌfərɪŋ] adj empreint(e) d'une patience résignée; extrêmement patient(e)

long-term ['lɒŋtəːm] adj à long terme

long wave n (RADIO) grandes ondes, ondes longues

long-winded [lɒŋ'wɪndɪd] adj intarissable, interminable

loo [luː] n (BRIT col) w.-c. mpl, petit coin

look [luk] vi regarder; (seem) sembler, paraître, avoir l'air; (building etc): **to look south/on the sea** donner au sud/sur la mer ♦ n regard m; (appearance) air m, allure f, aspect m; **looks** npl physique m, beauté f; **to look like** ressembler à; **it looks like him** on dirait que c'est lui; **it looks about 4 metres long** je dirais que ça fait 4 mètres de long; **it looks all right to me** ça me paraît bien; **to have a look at sth** jeter un coup d'œil à qch; **to have a look for sth** chercher qch; **to look ahead** regarder devant soi; (fig) envisager l'avenir

► **look after** vt fus s'occuper de, prendre soin de; (luggage etc: watch over) garder, surveiller

► **look around** vi regarder autour de soi

► **look at** vt fus regarder

► **look back** vi: **to look back at sth/sb** se retourner pour regarder qch/qn; **to look back on** (event, period) évoquer, repenser à

► **look down on** vt fus (fig) regarder de haut, dédaigner

► **look for** vt fus chercher

► **look forward to** vt fus attendre avec impatience; **I'm not looking forward to it** cette perspective ne me réjouit guère; **looking forward to hearing from you** (in letter) dans l'attente de vous lire

► **look in** vi: **to look in on sb** passer voir qn

► **look into** vt fus (matter, possibility) examiner, étudier

► **look on** vi regarder (en spectateur)

► **look out** vi (beware): **to look out (for)** prendre garde (à), faire attention (à)

► **look out for** vt fus être à la recherche de; guetter

► **look over** vt (essay) jeter un coup d'œil à; (town, building) visiter (rapidement); (person) jeter un coup d'œil à; examiner de la tête aux pieds

► **look round** vi (turn) regarder derrière soi, se retourner; **to look round for sth** chercher qch

▶ **look through** vt fus (papers, book) examiner; (: briefly) parcourir; (telescope) regarder à travers

▶ **look to** vt fus veiller à; (rely on) compter sur

▶ **look up** vi lever les yeux; (improve) s'améliorer ◆ vt (word) chercher; (friend) passer voir

▶ **look up to** vt fus avoir du respect pour

loom [luːm] n métier m à tisser ◆ vi surgir; (fig) menacer, paraître imminent(e)

loony ['luːnɪ] adj, n (col) timbré/e, cinglé/e m/f

loop [luːp] n boucle f; (contraceptive) stérilet m

loophole ['luːphəʊl] n porte f de sortie (fig); échappatoire f

loose [luːs] adj (knot, screw) desserré(e); (stone) branlant(e); (clothes) vague, ample, lâche; (animal) en liberté, échappé(e); (life) dissolu(e); (morals, discipline) relâché(e); (thinking) peu rigoureux(euse), vague; (translation) approximatif(ive) ◆ vt (free: animal) lâcher; (: prisoner) relâcher, libérer; (slacken) détendre, relâcher; desserrer; défaire; donner du mou a; donner du ballant à; (BRIT: arrow) tirer; **loose connection** (ELEC) mauvais contact; **to be at a loose end** or (US) **at loose ends** fig ne pas trop savoir quoi faire; **to tie up loose ends** (fig) mettre au point or régler les derniers détails

loose change n petite monnaie

loose chippings [-ˈtʃɪpɪŋz] npl (on road) gravillons mpl

loosely ['luːslɪ] adv sans serrer; approximativement

loosen ['luːsn] vt desserrer, relâcher, défaire

▶ **loosen up** vi (before game) s'échauffer; (col: relax) se détendre, se laisser aller

loot [luːt] n butin m ◆ vt piller

lopsided ['lɒpˈsaɪdɪd] adj de travers, asymétrique

lord [lɔːd] n seigneur m; **Lord Smith** lord Smith; **the Lord** (REL) le Seigneur; **the (House of) Lords** (BRIT) la Chambre des Lords

lordship ['lɔːdʃɪp] n (BRIT): **your Lordship** Monsieur le comte (or le maire or le Juge)

lore [lɔːʳ] n tradition(s) f(pl)

lorry ['lɒrɪ] n (BRIT) camion m

lorry driver n (BRIT) camionneur m, routier m

lose [luːz], pt, pp **lost** vt perdre; (opportunity) manquer, perdre; (pursuers) distancer, semer ◆ vi perdre; **to lose (time)** (clock) retarder; **to lose no time (in doing sth)** ne pas perdre de temps (à faire qch); **to get lost** vi (person) se perdre; **my watch has got lost** ma montre s'est perdue

loser ['luːzəʳ] n perdant/e; **to be a good/bad loser** être beau/mauvais joueur

loss [lɒs] n perte f; **to cut one's losses** limiter les dégâts; **to make a loss** enregistrer une perte; **to sell sth at a loss** vendre qch à perte; **to be at a loss** être perplexe or embarrassé(e); **to be at a loss to do** se trouver incapable de faire

lost [lɒst] pt, pp of **lose** ◆ adj perdu(e); **lost in thought** perdu dans ses pensées; **lost and found property** n (US) objets trouvés; **lost and found** n (US) (bureau m des) objets trouvés

lost property n (BRIT) objets trouvés; **lost property office** or **department** (bureau m des) objets trouvés

lot [lɒt] n (at auctions) lot m; (destiny) sort m, destinée f; **the lot** le tout; tous mpl, toutes fpl; **a lot** beaucoup; **a lot of** beaucoup de; **lots of** des tas de; **to draw lots (for sth)** tirer (qch) au sort

lotion ['ləʊʃən] n lotion f

lottery ['lɒtərɪ] n loterie f

loud [laʊd] adj bruyant(e), sonore, fort(e); (gaudy) voyant(e), tapageur(euse) ◆ adv (speak etc) fort; **out loud** tout haut

loud-hailer [laʊdˈheɪləʳ] n porte-voix m inv

loudly ['laʊdlɪ] adv fort, bruyamment

loudspeaker [laʊdˈspiːkəʳ] n haut-parleur m

lounge [laʊndʒ] n salon m; (of airport) salle f ◆ vi se prélasser, paresser

lounge suit n (BRIT) complet m; (: on invitation) "tenue de ville"

louse ,pl **lice** [laʊs, laɪs] n pou m

▶ **louse up** vt (col) gâcher

lousy ['laʊzɪ] adj (fig) infect(e), moche

lout [laʊt] n rustre m, butor m

lovable ['lʌvəbl] adj très sympathique; adorable

love [lʌv] n amour m ◆ vt aimer; aimer beaucoup; **to love to do** aimer beaucoup or adorer faire; **I'd love to come** cela me ferait très plaisir (de venir); **"15 love"** (TENNIS) "15 à rien or zéro"; **to be/fall in love with** être/tomber amoureux(euse) de; **to make love** faire l'amour; **love at first sight** le coup de foudre; **to send one's love to sb** adresser ses amitiés à qn; **love from Anne, love, Anne** affectueusement, Anne; **I love you** je t'aime

love affair n liaison (amoureuse)

love life n vie sentimentale

lovely ['lʌvlɪ] adj (pretty) ravissant(e); (friend, wife) charmant(e); (holiday, surprise) très agréable, merveilleux(euse); **we had a lovely time** c'était vraiment très bien, nous avons eu beaucoup de plaisir

lover ['lʌvəʳ] n amant m; (amateur): **a lover of** un(e) ami/e de, un(e) amoureux/euse de

loving ['lʌvɪŋ] adj affectueux(euse) tendre, aimant(e)

low [laʊ] adj bas(basse) ◆ adv bas ◆ n (METEOROLOGY) dépression f ◆ vi (cow) mugir; **to feel low** se sentir déprimé(e); **he's very low** (ill) il est bien bas or très affaibli; **to turn (down) low** vt baisser; **to reach a new** or **an all-time low** tomber au niveau le plus bas

low-alcohol [laʊˈælkəhɔl] adj à faible teneur en alcool, peu alcoolisé(e)

low-calorie ['laʊˈkælərɪ] adj hypocalorique

low-cut ['laʊkʌt] adj (dress) décolleté(e)

lower ['ləʊəʳ] adj, adv, comparative of **low** ◆ vt baisser; (resistance) diminuer ◆ vi ['laʊəʳ] (person):

to lower at sb jeter un regard mauvais or noir à qn; (sky, clouds) être menaçant

lower sixth (BRIT) n (SCOL) première f

low-fat ['ləʊ'fæt] adj maigre

lowland(s) ['ləʊlənd(z)] n(pl) plaine(s) f(pl)

lowly ['ləʊlɪ] adj humble, modeste

loyal ['lɔɪəl] adj loyal(e), fidèle

loyalty ['lɔɪəltɪ] n loyauté f, fidélité f

loyalty card n carte f de fidélité

lozenge ['lɒzɪndʒ] n (MED) pastille f; (GEOM) losange m

LP n abbr = long-playing record

L-plates ['elpleɪts] npl (BRIT) plaques fpl (obligatoires) d'apprenti conducteur; voir encadré

L-PLATES

Les **L-plates** sont des carrés blancs portant un "L" rouge que l'on met à l'avant et à l'arrière de sa voiture pour montrer qu'on n'a pas encore son permis de conduire. Jusqu'à l'obtention du permis, l'apprenti conducteur a un permis provisoire et n'a le droit de conduire que si un conducteur qualifié est assis à côté de lui. Il est interdit aux apprentis conducteurs de circuler sur les autoroutes, même s'ils sont accompagnés.

Ltd abbr (COMM) = **limited**

lubricant ['lu:brɪkənt] n lubrifiant m

lubricate ['lu:brɪkeɪt] vt lubrifier, graisser

luck [lʌk] n chance f; **bad luck** malchance f, malheur m; **to be in luck** avoir de la chance; **to be out of luck** ne pas avoir de chance; **good luck!** bonne chance!

luckily ['lʌkɪlɪ] adv heureusement, par bonheur

lucky ['lʌkɪ] adj (person) qui a de la chance; (coincidence) heureux(euse); (number etc) qui porte bonheur

ludicrous ['lu:dɪkrəs] adj ridicule, absurde

lug [lʌg] vt traîner, tirer

luggage ['lʌgɪdʒ] n bagages mpl

luggage rack n (in train) porte-bagages m inv; (: made of string) filet m à bagages; (on car) galerie f

lukewarm ['lu:kwɔ:m] adj tiède

lull [lʌl] n accalmie f ♦ vt (child) bercer; (person, fear) apaiser, calmer

lullaby ['lʌləbaɪ] n berceuse f

lumbago [lʌm'beɪgəʊ] n lumbago m

lumber ['lʌmbə*] n bric-à-brac m inv ♦ vt (BRIT col): **to lumber sb with sth/sb** coller or refiler qch/qn à qn ♦ vi (also: **lumber about**, **lumber along**) marcher pesamment

lumberjack ['lʌmbədʒæk] n bûcheron m

luminous ['lu:mɪnəs] adj lumineux(euse)

lump [lʌmp] n morceau m; (in sauce) grumeau m; (swelling) grosseur f ♦ vt (also: **lump together**)

réunir, mettre en tas

lump sum n somme globale or forfaitaire

lumpy ['lʌmpɪ] adj (sauce) qui a des grumeaux

lunar ['lu:nə*] adj lunaire

lunatic ['lu:nətɪk] n fou/folle, dément/e ♦ adj fou(folle), dément(e)

lunch [lʌntʃ] n déjeuner m ♦ vi déjeuner; **it is his lunch hour** c'est l'heure où il déjeune; **to invite sb to** or **for lunch** inviter qn à déjeuner

luncheon ['lʌntʃən] n déjeuner m

luncheon meat n sorte de saucisson

luncheon voucher n chèque-repas m, ticket-repas m

lung [lʌŋ] n poumon m

lunge [lʌndʒ] vi (also: **lunge forward**) faire un mouvement brusque en avant; **to lunge at sb** envoyer or assener un coup à qn

lurch [lɜ:tʃ] vi vaciller, tituber ♦ n écart m brusque, embardée f; **to leave sb in the lurch** laisser qn se débrouiller or se dépêtrer tout(e) seul(e)

lure [lʊə*] n appât m, leurre m ♦ vt attirer or persuader par la ruse

lurid ['lʊərɪd] adj affreux(euse), atroce

lurk [lɜ:k] vi se tapir, se cacher

luscious ['lʌʃəs] adj succulent(e), appétissant(e)

lush [lʌʃ] adj luxuriant(e)

lust [lʌst] n luxure f; lubricité f; désir m; (fig): **lust for** soif f de

▶ **lust after** vt fus convoiter, désirer

lusty ['lʌstɪ] adj vigoureux(euse), robuste

Luxembourg ['lʌksəmbə:g] n Luxembourg m

luxurious [lʌg'zjʊərɪəs] adj luxueux(euse)

luxury ['lʌkʃərɪ] n luxe m ♦ cpd de luxe

lying ['laɪɪŋ] n mensonge(s) m(pl) ♦ adj (statement, story) mensonger(ère), faux(fausse); (person) menteur(euse)

lyric ['lɪrɪk] adj lyrique; **lyrics** npl (of song) paroles fpl

lyrical ['lɪrɪkl] adj lyrique

— M m —

m abbr (= metre) m; (= million) M; (= mile) mi

MA n abbr (SCOL) = **Master of Arts** ♦ abbr (US) = military academy; (US) = Massachusetts

mac [mæk] n (BRIT) imper(méable m) m

macaroni [mækə'rəʊnɪ] n macaronis mpl

machine [mə'ʃi:n] n machine f ♦ vt (dress etc) coudre à la machine; (TECH) usiner

machine gun n mitrailleuse f

machine language n (COMPUT) langage m machine

machinery [mə'ʃiːnəri] n machinerie f, machines fpl; (fig) mécanisme(s) m(pl)

mackerel ['mækrl] n (pl inv) maquereau m

mackintosh ['mækɪntɔʃ] n (BRIT) imperméable m

mad [mæd] adj fou(folle); (foolish) insensé(e); (angry) furieux(euse): **to go mad** devenir fou; **to be mad (keen) about** or **on sth** (col) être follement passionné de qch, être fou de qch

madam ['mædəm] n madame f; **yes madam** oui Madame; **Madam Chairman** Madame la Présidente

madden ['mædn] vt exaspérer

made [meɪd] pt, pp of **make**

Madeira [mə'dɪərə] n (GEO) Madère f; (wine) madère m

made-to-measure ['meɪdtə'meʒə*] adj (BRIT) fait(e) sur mesure

madly ['mædlɪ] adv follement

madman ['mædmən] n fou m, aliéné m

madness ['mædnɪs] n folie f

magazine [mægə'ziːn] n (PRESS) magazine m, revue f; (MIL: store) dépôt m, arsenal m; (of firearm) magasin m

maggot ['mægət] n ver m, asticot m

magic ['mædʒɪk] n magie f ◆ adj magique

magical ['mædʒɪkl] adj magique

magician [mə'dʒɪʃən] n magicien/ne

magistrate ['mædʒɪstreɪt] n magistrat m; juge m; **magistrates' court** (BRIT) = tribunal m d'instance

magnet ['mægnɪt] n aimant m

magnetic [mæg'netɪk] adj magnétique

magnificent [mæg'nɪfɪsnt] adj superbe, magnifique

magnify ['mægnɪfaɪ] vt grossir; (sound) amplifier

magnifying glass ['mægnɪfaɪŋ-] n loupe f

magnitude ['mægnɪtjuːd] n ampleur f

magpie ['mægpaɪ] n pie f

mahogany [mə'hɔgənɪ] n acajou m ◆ cpd en (bois d')acajou

maid [meɪd] n bonne f; **old maid** (pej) vieille fille

maiden ['meɪdn] n jeune fille f ◆ adj (aunt etc) non mariée; (speech, voyage) inaugural(e)

maiden name n nom m de jeune fille

mail [meɪl] n poste f; (letters) courrier m ◆ vt envoyer (par la poste); **by mail** par la poste

mailbox ['meɪlbɔks] n (US: for letters etc; COMPUT) boîte f aux lettres

mailing list ['meɪlɪŋ-] n liste f d'adresses

mail-order ['meɪlɔːdə*] n vente f or achat m par correspondance ◆ cpd: **mail-order firm** or **house** maison f de vente par correspondance

maim [meɪm] vt mutiler

main [meɪn] adj principal(e) ◆ n (pipe) conduite principale, canalisation f; **the mains** (ELEC) le secteur; **the main thing** l'essentiel m; **in the main** dans l'ensemble

mainframe ['meɪnfreɪm] n (also: **mainframe computer**) (gros) ordinateur, unité centrale

mainland ['meɪnlənd] n continent m

mainly ['meɪnlɪ] adv principalement, surtout

main road n grand axe, route nationale

mainstay ['meɪnsteɪ] n (fig) pilier m

mainstream ['meɪnstriːm] n (fig) courant principal

maintain [meɪn'teɪn] vt entretenir; (continue) maintenir, préserver; (affirm) soutenir; **to maintain that ...** soutenir que ...

maintenance ['meɪntənəns] n entretien m; (LAW: alimony) pension f alimentaire

maize [meɪz] n maïs m

majestic [mə'dʒestɪk] adj majestueux(euse)

majesty ['mædʒɪstɪ] n majesté f

major ['meɪdʒə*] n (MIL) commandant m ◆ adj important(e), principal(e) (MUS) majeur(e) ◆ vi (US SCOL): **to major (in)** se spécialiser (en); **a major operation** (MED) une grosse opération

Majorca [mə'jɔːkə] n Majorque f

majority [mə'dʒɔrɪtɪ] n majorité f ◆ cpd (verdict, holding) majoritaire

make [meɪk] vt, pt, pp **made** [meɪd] faire; (manufacture) faire, fabriquer; (cause to be): **to make sb sad** etc rendre qn triste etc; (force): **to make sb do sth** obliger qn à faire qch, faire faire qch à qn; (equal): **2 and 2 make 4** 2 et 2 font 4 ◆ n fabrication f; (brand) marque f; **to make it** (in time etc) y arriver; (succeed) réussir; **what time do you make it?** quelle heure avez-vous?; **to make good** vi (succeed) faire son chemin, réussir ◆ vt (deficit) combler; (losses) compenser; **to make do with** se contenter de; se débrouiller avec

▶ **make for** vt fus (place) se diriger vers

▶ **make off** vi filer

▶ **make out** vt (write out) écrire; (understand) comprendre; (see) distinguer; (claim, imply) prétendre, vouloir faire croire; **to make out a case for sth** présenter des arguments solides en faveur de qch

▶ **make over** vt (assign): **to make over (to)** céder (à), transférer (au nom de)

▶ **make up** vt (invent) inventer, imaginer; (parcel) faire ◆ vi se réconcilier; (with cosmetics) se maquiller, se farder; **to be made up of** se composer de

▶ **make up for** vt fus compenser; racheter

make-believe ['meɪkbɪliːv] n: **a world of make-believe** un monde de chimères or d'illusions; **it's just make-believe** c'est de la fantaisie; c'est une illusion

maker ['meɪkə*] n fabricant m

makeshift ['meɪkʃɪft] adj provisoire, improvisé(e)

make-up ['meɪkʌp] n maquillage m

making ['meɪkɪŋ] n (fig): **in the making** en formation or gestation; **he has the makings of an**

actor il a l'étoffe d'un acteur

malaria [mə'lɛərɪə] n malaria f, paludisme m

Malaysia [mə'leɪzɪə] n Malaisie f

male [meɪl] n (BIOL, ELEC) mâle m ♦ adj (sex, attitude) masculin(e); mâle; (child etc) du sexe masculin; **male and female students** étudiants et étudiantes

malevolent [mə'lɛvələnt] adj malveillant(e)

malfunction [mæl'fʌŋkʃən] n fonctionnement défectueux

malice ['mælɪs] n méchanceté f, malveillance f

malicious [mə'lɪʃəs] adj méchant(e), malveillant(e) (LAW) avec intention criminelle

malignant [mə'lɪɡnənt] adj (MED) malin(igne)

mall [mɔ:l] n (also: **shopping mall**) centre commercial

mallet ['mælɪt] n maillet m

malpractice [mæl'præktɪs] n faute professionnelle; négligence f

malt [mɔ:lt] n malt m ♦ cpd (whisky) pur malt

Malta ['mɔ:ltə] n Malte f

mammal ['mæml] n mammifère m

mammoth ['mæməθ] n mammouth m ♦ adj géant(e), monstre

man, pl **men** [mæn, mɛn] n homme m; (CHESS) pièce f; (DRAUGHTS) pion m ♦ vt garnir d'hommes; servir, assurer le fonctionnement de; être de service à; **an old man** un vieillard; **man and wife** mari et femme

manage ['mænɪdʒ] vi se débrouiller; y arriver, réussir ♦ vt (business) gérer; (team, operation) diriger; (device, things to do, carry etc) arriver à se débrouiller avec, s'en tirer avec; **to manage to do** se débrouiller pour faire; (succeed) réussir à faire

manageable ['mænɪdʒəbl] adj maniable; (task etc) faisable

management ['mænɪdʒmənt] n administration f, direction f; (persons: of business, firm) dirigeants mpl, cadres mpl; (: of hotel, shop, theatre) direction; **"under new management"** "changement de gérant", "changement de propriétaire"

manager ['mænɪdʒə*] n (of business) directeur m; (of institution etc) administrateur m; (of department, unit) responsable m/f, chef m; (of hotel etc) gérant m; (of artist) impresario m; **sales manager** responsable or chef des ventes

manageress [mænɪdʒə'rɛs] n directrice f; (of hotel etc) gérante f

managerial [mænɪ'dʒɪərɪəl] adj directorial(e); **managerial staff** cadres mpl

managing director (MD) ['mænɪdʒɪŋ-] n directeur général

mandarin ['mændərɪn] n (also: **mandarin orange**) mandarine f; (person) mandarin m

mandatory ['mændətərɪ] adj obligatoire; (powers etc) mandataire

mane [meɪn] n crinière f

manfully ['mænfəlɪ] adv vaillamment

mangle ['mæŋɡl] vt déchiqueter; mutiler ♦ n essoreuse f; calandre f

mango, pl **mangoes** ['mæŋɡəu] n mangue f

mangy ['meɪndʒɪ] adj galeux(euse)

manhandle ['mænhændl] vt (mistreat) maltraiter, malmener; (move by hand) manutentionner

manhole ['mænhəul] n trou m d'homme

manhood ['mænhud] n âge m d'homme; virilité f

man-hour ['mænauə*] n heure-homme f, heure f de main-d'œuvre

manhunt ['mænhʌnt] n chasse f à l'homme

mania ['meɪnɪə] n manie f

maniac ['meɪnɪæk] n maniaque m/f

manic ['mænɪk] adj maniaque

manicure ['mænɪkjuə*] n manucure f ♦ vt (person) faire les mains à

manifest ['mænɪfɛst] vt manifester ♦ adj manifeste, évident(e) ♦ n (AVIAT, NAUT) manifeste m

manifesto [mænɪ'fɛstəu] n manifeste m (POL)

manipulate [mə'nɪpjuleɪt] vt manipuler

mankind [mæn'kaɪnd] n humanité f, genre humain

manly ['mænlɪ] adj viril(e), courageux(euse)

man-made ['mæn'meɪd] adj artificiel(le)

manner ['mænə*] n manière f, façon f; (good) **manners** (bonnes) manières; **bad manners** mauvaises manières; **all manner of** toutes sortes de

mannerism ['mænərɪzəm] n particularité f de langage (or de comportement), tic m

manoeuvre, (US) **maneuver** [mə'nu:və*] vt, vi manœuvrer ♦ n manœuvre f; **to manoeuvre sb into doing sth** manipuler qn pour lui faire faire qch

manor ['mænə*] n (also: **manor house**) manoir m

manpower ['mænpauə*] n main-d'œuvre f

mansion ['mænʃən] n château m, manoir m

manslaughter ['mænslɔ:tə*] n homicide m involontaire

mantelpiece ['mæntlpi:s] n cheminée f

manual ['mænjuəl] adj manuel(le) ♦ n manuel m

manufacture [mænju'fæktʃə*] vt fabriquer ♦ n fabrication f

manufacturer [mænju'fæktʃərə*] n fabricant m

manure [mə'njuə*] n fumier m; (artificial) engrais m

manuscript ['mænjuskrɪpt] n manuscrit m

many ['mɛnɪ] adj beaucoup de, de nombreux(euses) ♦ pron beaucoup, un grand nombre; **how many?** combien?; **a great many** un grand nombre (de); **too many difficulties** trop de difficultés; **twice as many** deux fois plus; **many a ...** bien des ..., plus d'un(e) ...

map [mæp] n carte f ♦ vt dresser la carte de

▶ **map out** vt tracer; (fig: career, holiday) organiser, préparer (à l'avance); (: essay) faire le plan de

maple ['meɪpl] n érable m

mar [mɑː*] *vt* gâcher, gâter

marathon ['mærəθən] *n* marathon *m* ♦ *adj*: **a marathon session** une séance-marathon

marble ['mɑːbl] *n* marbre *m*; (*toy*) bille *f*; **marbles** *npl* (*game*) billes

March [mɑːtʃ] *n* mars *m*; *for phrases see also* **July**

march [mɑːtʃ] *vi* marcher au pas; (*demonstrators*) défiler ♦ *n* marche *f*; (*demonstration*) rallye *m*; **to march out of/into** *etc* sortir de/entrer dans *etc* (*de manière décidée ou impulsive*)

mare [mɛə*] *n* jument *f*

margarine [mɑːdʒə'riːn] *n* margarine *f*

margin ['mɑːdʒɪn] *n* marge *f*

marginal ['mɑːdʒɪnl] *adj* marginal(e); **marginal seat** (*POL*) siège disputé

marigold ['mærɪɡəʊld] *n* souci *m*

marijuana [mærɪ'wɑːnə] *n* marijuana *f*

marina [mə'riːnə] *n* marina *f*

marine [mə'riːn] *adj* marin(e) ♦ *n* fusilier marin; (*US*) marine *m*

marital ['mærɪtl] *adj* matrimonial(e); **marital status** situation *f* de famille

marjoram ['mɑːdʒərəm] *n* marjolaine *f*

mark [mɑːk] *n* marque *f*; (*of skid etc*) trace *f*; (*BRIT SCOL*) note *f*; (*SPORT*) cible *f*; (*currency*) mark *m*; (*BRIT TECH*): **Mark 2/3** 2ème/3ème série *f* or version *f* ♦ *vt* (*also SPORT: player*); (*stain*) tacher; (*BRIT SCOL*) noter; corriger; (*also*: **punctuation marks**) signes *mpl* de ponctuation; **to mark time** marquer le pas; **to be quick off the mark (in doing)** (*fig*) ne pas perdre de temps (pour faire); **up to the mark** (*in efficiency*) à la hauteur

▶ **mark down** *vt* (*prices, goods*) démarquer, réduire le prix de

▶ **mark off** *vt* (*tick off*) cocher, pointer

▶ **mark out** *vt* désigner

▶ **mark up** *vt* (*price*) majorer

marker ['mɑːkə*] *n* (*sign*) jalon *m*; (*bookmark*) signet *m*

market ['mɑːkɪt] *n* marché *m* ♦ *vt* (*COMM*) commercialiser; **to be on the market** être sur le marché; **on the open market** en vente libre; **to play the market** jouer à la or spéculer en Bourse

market garden *n* (*BRIT*) jardin maraîcher

marketing ['mɑːkɪtɪŋ] *n* marketing *m*

marketplace ['mɑːkɪtpleɪs] *n* place *f* du marché; (*COMM*) marché *m*

market research *n* étude *f* de marché

marksman ['mɑːksmən] *n* tireur *m* d'élite

marmalade ['mɑːməleɪd] *n* confiture *f* d'oranges

maroon [mə'ruːn] *vt* (*fig*): **to be marooned (in** or **at)** être bloqué(e) (à) ♦ *adj* bordeaux *inv*

marquee [mɑː'kiː] *n* chapiteau *m*

marriage ['mærɪdʒ] *n* mariage *m*

marriage certificate *n* extrait *m* d'acte de mariage

married ['mærɪd] *adj* marié(e); (*life, love*) conjugal(e)

marrow ['mærəʊ] *n* moelle *f*; (*vegetable*) courge *f*

marry ['mærɪ] *vt* épouser, se marier avec; (*subj: father, priest etc*) marier ♦ *vi* (*also*: **get married**) se marier

Mars [mɑːz] *n* (*planet*) Mars *f*

marsh [mɑːʃ] *n* marais *m*, marécage *m*

marshal ['mɑːʃl] *n* maréchal *m*; (*US: fire, police*) ≈ capitaine *m*; (*for demonstration, meeting*) membre *m* du service d'ordre ♦ *vt* rassembler

marshy ['mɑːʃɪ] *adj* marécageux(euse)

martyr ['mɑːtə*] *n* martyr/e ♦ *vt* martyriser

martyrdom ['mɑːtədəm] *n* martyre *m*

marvel ['mɑːvl] *n* merveille *f* ♦ *vi*: **to marvel (at)** s'émerveiller (de)

marvellous, (*US*) **marvelous** ['mɑːvləs] *adj* merveilleux(euse)

Marxist ['mɑːksɪst] *adj, n* marxiste (*m/f*)

marzipan ['mɑːzɪpæn] *n* pâte *f* d'amandes

mascara [mæs'kɑːrə] *n* mascara *m*

masculine ['mæskjulɪn] *adj* masculin(e) ♦ *n* masculin *m*

mash [mæʃ] *vt* (*CULIN*) faire une purée de

mashed [mæʃt] *adj*: **mashed potatoes** purée *f* de pommes de terre

mask [mɑːsk] *n* masque *m* ♦ *vt* masquer

mason ['meɪsn] *n* (*also*: **stonemason**) maçon *m*; (*also*: **freemason**) franc-maçon *m*

masonry ['meɪsnrɪ] *n* maçonnerie *f*

masquerade [mæskə'reɪd] *n* bal masqué; (*fig*) mascarade *f* ♦ *vi*: **to masquerade as** se faire passer pour

mass [mæs] *n* multitude *f*, masse *f*; (*PHYSICS*) masse *f*; (*REL*) messe *f* ♦ *vi* se masser; **the masses** les masses; **to go to mass** aller à la messe

massacre ['mæsəkə*] *n* massacre *m* ♦ *vt* massacrer

massage ['mæsɑːʒ] *n* massage *m* ♦ *vt* masser

massive ['mæsɪv] *adj* énorme, massif(ive)

mass media *npl* mass-media *mpl*

mass production *n* fabrication *f* en série

mast [mɑːst] *n* mât *m*; (*RADIO, TV*) pylône *m*

master ['mɑːstə*] *n* maître *m*; (*in secondary school*) professeur *m*; (*title for boys*): **Master X** Monsieur X ♦ *vt* maîtriser; (*learn*) apprendre à fond; (*understand*) posséder parfaitement or à fond; **master of ceremonies (MC)** *n* maître des cérémonies; **Master of Arts/Science (MA/MSc)** *n* ≈ titulaire *m/f* d'une maîtrise (en lettres/science); **Master of Arts/Science degree (MA/MSc)** *n* ≈ maîtrise *f*

masterly ['mɑːstəlɪ] *adj* magistral(e)

mastermind ['mɑːstəmaɪnd] *n* esprit supérieur ♦ *vt* diriger, être le cerveau de

masterpiece ['mɑːstəpiːs] *n* chef-d'œuvre *m*

master plan *n* stratégie *f* d'ensemble

mastery ['mɑːstərɪ] *n* maîtrise *f*; connaissance parfaite

mat [mæt] *n* petit tapis; (*also*: **doormat**) paillasson *m* ♦ *adj* = **matt**

match [mætʃ] *n* allumette *f*; (*game*) match *m*, partie *f*; (*fig*) égal/e; mariage *m*; parti *m* ♦ *vt* assortir; (*go well with*) aller bien avec, s'assortir à; (*equal*) égaler, valoir ♦ *vi* être assorti(e); **to be a good match** être bien assorti(e)

▶ **match up** *vt* assortir

matchbox ['mætʃbɒks] *n* boîte *f* d'allumettes

matching ['mætʃɪŋ] *adj* assorti(e)

mate [meɪt] *n* camarade *m/f* de travail; (*col*) copain/copine; (*animal*) partenaire *m/f*, mâle/femelle; (*in merchant navy*) second *m* ♦ *vi* s'accoupler ♦ *vt* accoupler

material [mə'tɪərɪəl] *n* (*substance*) matière *f*, matériau *m*; (*cloth*) tissu *m*, étoffe *f* ♦ *adj* matériel(le); (*important*) essentiel(le); **materials** *npl* matériaux *mpl*; **reading material** de quoi lire, de la lecture

maternal [mə'tə:nl] *adj* maternel(le)

maternity [mə'tə:nɪtɪ] *n* maternité *f* ♦ *cpd* de maternité, de grossesse

maternity dress *n* robe *f* de grossesse

maternity hospital *n* maternité *f*

mathematical [mæθə'mætɪkl] *adj* mathématique

mathematics [mæθə'mætɪks] *n* mathématiques *fpl*

maths [mæθs] *n abbr* (*BRIT*: = *mathematics*) maths *fpl*

matinée ['mætɪneɪ] *n* matinée *f*

mating call *n* appel *m* du mâle

matrices ['meɪtrɪsi:z] *npl of* **matrix**

matriculation [mətrɪkju'leɪʃən] *n* inscription *f*

matrimonial [mætrɪ'məunɪəl] *adj* matrimonial(e), conjugal(e)

matrimony ['mætrɪmənɪ] *n* mariage *m*

matrix, *pl* **matrices** ['meɪtrɪks, 'meɪtrɪsi:z] *n* matrice *f*

matron ['meɪtrən] *n* (*in hospital*) infirmière-chef *f*; (*in school*) infirmière *f*

matted ['mætɪd] *adj* emmêlé(e)

matter ['mætə*] *n* question *f*; (*PHYSICS*) matière *f*, substance *f*; (*content*) contenu *m*, fond *m*; (*MED: pus*) pus *m* ♦ *vi* importer; **it doesn't matter** cela n'a pas d'importance; (*I don't mind*) cela ne fait rien; **what's the matter?** qu'est-ce qu'il y a?, qu'est-ce qui ne va pas?; **no matter what** quoiqu'il arrive; **that's another matter** c'est une autre affaire; **as a matter of course** tout naturellement; **as a matter of fact** en fait; **it's a matter of habit** c'est une question d'habitude; **printed matter** imprimés *mpl*; **reading matter** (*BRIT*) de quoi lire, de la lecture

matter-of-fact ['mætərəv'fækt] *adj* terre à terre, neutre

mattress ['mætrɪs] *n* matelas *m*

mature [mə'tjuə*] *adj* mûr(e); (*cheese*) fait(e) ♦ *vi* mûrir; se faire

maul [mɔ:l] *vt* lacérer

mauve [məuv] *adj* mauve

maximum ['mæksɪməm] *adj* maximum ♦ *n* (*pl* **maxima** ['mæksɪmə]) maximum *m*

May [meɪ] *n* mai *m*; *for phrases see also* **July**

may [meɪ] *vi* (*conditional*): **might** (*indicating possibility*): **he may come** il se peut qu'il vienne; (*be allowed to*): **may I smoke?** puis-je fumer?; (*wishes*): **may God bless you!** (que) Dieu vous bénisse!; **may I sit here?** vous permettez que je m'assoie ici?; **he might be there** il pourrait bien y être, il se pourrait qu'il y soit; **I might as well go** je ferais aussi bien d'y aller, autant y aller; **you might like to try** vous pourriez (peut-être) essayer

maybe ['meɪbi:] *adv* peut-être; **maybe he'll ...** peut-être qu'il ...; **maybe not** peut-être pas

mayday ['meɪdeɪ] *n* S.O.S. *m*

mayhem ['meɪhem] *n* grabuge *m*

mayonnaise [meɪə'neɪz] *n* mayonnaise *f*

mayor [mɛə*] *n* maire *m*

mayoress ['mɛərɛs] *n* maire *m*; épouse *f* du maire

maze [meɪz] *n* labyrinthe *m*, dédale *m*

MD *n abbr* (= *Doctor of Medicine*) titre universitaire; (*COMM*) = **managing director** ♦ *abbr* (*US*) = *Maryland*

me [mi:] *pron* me, m' + *vowel*; (*stressed, after prep*) moi; **it's me** c'est moi; **it's for me** c'est pour moi

meadow ['mɛdəu] *n* prairie *f*, pré *m*

meagre, (*US*) **meager** ['mi:gə*] *adj* maigre

meal [mi:l] *n* repas *m*; (*flour*) farine *f*; **to go out for a meal** sortir manger

mealtime ['mi:ltaɪm] *n* heure *f* du repas

mean [mi:n] *adj* (*with money*) avare, radin(e); (*unkind*) mesquin(e), méchant(e); (*US col: animal*) méchant, vicieux(euse); (: *person*) vache; (*average*) moyen(ne) ♦ *vt, pt, pp* **meant** [mɛnt] (*signify*) signifier, vouloir dire; (*intend*): **to mean to do** avoir l'intention de faire ♦ *n* moyenne *f*; **to be meant for** être destiné(e) à; **do you mean it?** vous êtes sérieux?; **what do you mean?** que voulez-vous dire?

meander [mɪ'ændə*] *vi* faire des méandres; (*fig*) flâner

meaning ['mi:nɪŋ] *n* signification *f*, sens *m*

meaningful ['mi:nɪŋful] *adj* significatif(ive); (*relationship*) valable

meaningless ['mi:nɪŋlɪs] *adj* dénué(e) de sens

meanness ['mi:nnɪs] *n* avarice *f*; mesquinerie *f*

meant [mɛnt] *pt*, *pp of* **mean**

meantime ['mi:ntaɪm] *adv*, **meanwhile** ['mi:nwaɪl] *adv* (*also*: **in the meantime**) pendant ce temps

measles ['mi:zlz] *n* rougeole *f*

measure ['mɛʒə*] *vt*, *vi* mesurer ♦ *n* mesure *f*; (*ruler*) règle (graduée); **a litre measure** un litre; **some measure of success** un certain succès; **to take measures to do sth** prendre des mesures

pour faire qch
▶ **measure up** *vi*: **to measure up (to)** être à la hauteur (de)
measurement ['mɛʒəmənt] *n*: **chest/hip measurement** tour *m* de poitrine/hanches; **measurements** *npl* mesures *fpl*
meat [miːt] *n* viande *f*; **cold meats** (*BRIT*) viandes froides; **crab meat** crabe *f*
meatball ['miːtbɔːl] *n* boulette *f* de viande
Mecca ['mɛkə] *n* la Mecque; (*fig*): **a Mecca (for)** la Mecque (de)
mechanic [mɪ'kænɪk] *n* mécanicien *m*
mechanical [mɪ'kænɪkl] *adj* mécanique
mechanics [mə'kænɪks] *n* mécanique *f* ◆ *npl* mécanisme *m*
mechanism ['mɛkənɪzəm] *n* mécanisme *m*
medal ['mɛdl] *n* médaille *f*
medallion [mɪ'dælɪən] *n* médaillon *m*
medallist, (*US*) **medalist** ['mɛdlɪst] *n* (*SPORT*) médaillé/e
meddle ['mɛdl] *vi*: **to meddle in** se mêler de, s'occuper de; **to meddle with** toucher à
media ['miːdɪə] *npl* media *mpl*
mediaeval [mɛdɪ'iːvl] *adj* = **medieval**
median ['miːdɪən] *n* (*US: also*: **median strip**) bande médiane
mediate ['miːdɪeɪt] *vi* s'interposer; servir d'intermédiaire
Medicaid ['mɛdɪkeɪd] *n* (*US*) assistance médicale aux indigents
medical ['mɛdɪkl] *adj* médical(e) ◆ *n* (*also*: **medical examination**) visite médicale; examen médical
Medicare ['mɛdɪkɛə*] *n* (*US*) régime d'assurance maladie
medication [mɛdɪ'keɪʃən] *n* (*drugs etc*) médication *f*
medicine ['mɛdsɪn] *n* médecine *f*; (*drug*) médicament *m*
medieval [mɛdɪ'iːvl] *adj* médiéval(e)
mediocre [miːdɪ'əʊkə*] *adj* médiocre
meditate ['mɛdɪteɪt] *vi*: **to meditate (on)** méditer (sur)
Mediterranean [mɛdɪtə'reɪnɪən] *adj* méditerranéen(ne); **the Mediterranean (Sea)** la (mer) Méditerranée
medium ['miːdɪəm] *adj* moyen(ne) ◆ *n* (*pl* **media**) (*means*) moyen *m*; (*pl* **mediums**) (*person*) médium *m*; **the happy medium** le juste milieu
medium-sized ['miːdɪəm'saɪzd] *adj* de taille moyenne
medium wave *n* (*RADIO*) ondes moyennes, petites ondes
medley ['mɛdlɪ] *n* mélange *m*
meek [miːk] *adj* doux(douce), humble
meet, *pt, pp* **met** [miːt, mɛt] *vt* rencontrer; (*by arrangement*) retrouver, rejoindre; (*for the first time*) faire la connaissance de; (*go and fetch*): **I'll meet**

you at the station j'irai te chercher à la gare; (*problem*) faire face à; (*requirements*) satisfaire à, répondre à; (*bill, expenses*) régler, honorer ◆ *vi* se rencontrer; se retrouver; (*in session*) se réunir; (*join: objects*) se joindre à; (*in* (*BRIT HUNTING*) rendez-vous *m* de chasse; (*US SPORT*) rencontre *f*, meeting *m*; **pleased to meet you!** enchanté!
▶ **meet up** *vi*: **to meet up with sb** rencontrer qn
▶ **meet with** *vt fus* rencontrer
meeting ['miːtɪŋ] *n* rencontre *f*; (*session: of club etc*) réunion *f*; (*formal*) assemblée *f*; (*SPORT: rally*) rencontre, meeting *m*; (*interview*) entrevue *f*; **she's at a meeting** (*COMM*) elle est en conférence; **to call a meeting** convoquer une réunion
mega ['mɛgə] (*inf*) *adv*: **he's mega rich** il est hyper-riche
megabyte ['mɛgəbaɪt] *n* (*COMPUT*) méga-octet *m*
megaphone ['mɛgəfəʊn] *n* porte-voix *m inv*
megapixel ['mɛgəpɪksl] *n* mégapixel *m*
melancholy ['mɛlənkəlɪ] *n* mélancolie *f* ◆ *adj* mélancolique
mellow ['mɛləʊ] *adj* velouté(e), doux(douce); (*colour*) riche et profond(e); (*fruit*) mûr(e) ◆ *vi* (*person*) s'adoucir
melody ['mɛlədɪ] *n* mélodie *f*
melon ['mɛlən] *n* melon *m*
melt [mɛlt] *vi* fondre; (*become soft*) s'amollir; (*fig*) s'attendrir ◆ *vt* faire fondre
▶ **melt away** *vi* fondre complètement
▶ **melt down** *vt* fondre
meltdown ['mɛltdaʊn] *n* fusion *f* (du cœur d'un réacteur nucléaire)
melting pot ['mɛltɪŋ-] *n* (*fig*) creuset *m*; **to be in the melting pot** être encore en discussion
member ['mɛmbə*] *n* membre *m*; (*of club, political party*) membre, adhérent/e ◆ *cpd*: **member country/state** *n* pays *m*/état *m* membre; **Member of Parliament (MP)** *n* (*BRIT*) député *m*; **Member of the European Parliament (MEP)** *n* Eurodéputé *m*; **Member of the House of Representatives (MHR)** *n* (*US*) membre de la Chambre des représentants
membership ['mɛmbəʃɪp] *n* (*becoming a member*) adhésion *f*; admission *f*; (*being a member*) qualité *f* de membre, fait *m* d'être membre; (*the members*) membres *mpl*, adhérents *mpl*; (*number of members*) nombre *m* des membres or adhérents
membership card *n* carte *f* de membre
memento [mə'mɛntəʊ] *n* souvenir *m*
memo ['mɛməʊ] *n* note *f* (de service)
memoir ['mɛmwɑː*] *n* mémoire *m*, étude *f*; **memoirs** *npl* mémoires
memorandum, *pl* **memoranda** [mɛmə'rændəm, –də] *n* note *f* (de service); (*DIPLOMACY*) mémorandum *m*
memorial [mɪ'mɔːrɪəl] *n* mémorial *m* ◆ *adj* commémoratif(ive)
memorize ['mɛməraɪz] *vt* apprendre or retenir par cœur

memory ['mɛmərɪ] n mémoire f; (recollection) souvenir m; **to have a good/bad memory** avoir une bonne/mauvaise mémoire; **loss of memory** perte f de mémoire; **in memory of** à la mémoire de

memory card n (for camera) carte f mémoire

men [mɛn] npl of **man**

menace ['mɛnɪs] n menace f; (col: nuisance) peste f, plaie f ◆ vt menacer; **a public menace** un danger public

menacing ['mɛnɪsɪŋ] adj menaçant(e)

mend [mɛnd] vt réparer; (darn) raccommoder, repriser ◆ n reprise f; **on the mend** en voie de guérison

mending ['mɛndɪŋ] n raccommodages mpl

menial ['miːnɪəl] adj de domestique, inférieur(e); subalterne

meningitis [mɛnɪn'dʒaɪtɪs] n méningite f

menopause ['mɛnəupɔːz] n ménopause f

menstruation [mɛnstru'eɪʃən] n menstruation f

mental ['mɛntl] adj mental(e); **mental illness** maladie mentale

mentality [mɛn'tælɪtɪ] n mentalité f

mention ['mɛnʃən] n mention f ◆ vt mentionner, faire mention de; **don't mention it!** je vous en prie, il n'y a pas de quoi!; **I need hardly mention that …** est-il besoin de rappeler que …?; **not to mention …, without mentioning …** sans parler de …, sans compter …

menu ['mɛnjuː] n (in restaurant, COMPUT) menu m; (printed) carte f

MEP n abbr = **Member of the European Parliament**

mercenary ['mɜːsɪnərɪ] adj mercantile ◆ n mercenaire m

merchandise ['mɜːtʃəndaɪz] n marchandises fpl ◆ vt commercialiser

merchant ['mɜːtʃənt] n négociant m, marchand m; **timber/wine merchant** négociant en bois/vins, marchand de bois/vins

merchant bank n (BRIT) banque f d'affaires

merchant navy, (US) **merchant marine** n marine marchande

merciful ['mɜːsɪful] adj miséricordieux(euse), clément(e)

merciless ['mɜːsɪlɪs] adj impitoyable, sans pitié

mercury ['mɜːkjurɪ] n mercure m

mercy ['mɜːsɪ] n pitié f, merci f; (REL) miséricorde f; **to have mercy on sb** avoir pitié de qn; **at the mercy of** à la merci de

mere [mɪə*] adj simple

merely ['mɪəlɪ] adv simplement, purement

merge [mɜːdʒ] vt unir; (COMPUT) fusionner, interclasser ◆ vi se fondre; (COMM) fusionner

merger ['mɜːdʒə*] n (COMM) fusion f

meringue [mə'ræŋ] n meringue f

merit ['mɛrɪt] n mérite m, valeur f ◆ vt mériter

mermaid ['mɜːmeɪd] n sirène f

merry ['mɛrɪ] adj gai(e); **Merry Christmas!** joyeux Noël!

merry-go-round ['mɛrɪɡəuraund] n manège m

mesh [mɛʃ] n maille f; filet m ◆ vi (gears) s'engrener; **wire mesh** grillage m (métallique)

mesmerize ['mɛzməraɪz] vt hypnotiser; fasciner

mess [mɛs] n désordre m, fouillis m, pagaille f; (MIL) mess m, cantine f; **to be (in) a mess** être en désordre; **to be/get o.s. in a mess** (fig) être/se mettre dans le pétrin

▶ **mess about, mess around** vi (col) perdre son temps

▶ **mess about** or **around with** vt fus (col) chambarder, tripoter

▶ **mess up** vt salir; chambarder; gâcher

message ['mɛsɪdʒ] n message m; **to get the message** (fig: col) saisir, piger

messenger ['mɛsɪndʒə*] n messager m

Messrs, Messrs. ['mɛsəz] abbr (on letters: = messieurs) MM

messy ['mɛsɪ] adj sale; en désordre

met [mɛt] pt, pp of **meet** ◆ adj abbr (= meteorological) météo inv

metal ['mɛtl] n métal m ◆ vt empierrer

metallic [mɪ'tælɪk] adj métallique

meteorology [miːtɪə'rɔlədʒɪ] n météorologie f

meter ['miːtə*] n (instrument) compteur m; (also: **parking meter**) parc(o)mètre m; (US) = **metre**

method ['mɛθəd] n méthode f; **method of payment** mode m ou modalité f de paiement

methodical [mɪ'θɔdɪkl] adj méthodique

Methodist ['mɛθədɪst] adj, n méthodiste (m/f)

methylated spirit ['mɛθɪleɪtɪd-] n (BRIT: also: **meths**) alcool m à brûler

metre, (US) **meter** ['miːtə*] n mètre m

metric ['mɛtrɪk] adj métrique; **to go metric** adopter le système métrique

metropolitan [mɛtrə'pɔlɪtən] adj métropolitain(e)

mettle ['mɛtl] n courage m

mew [mjuː] vi (cat) miauler

mews [mjuːz] n (BRIT): **mews cottage** maisonnette aménagée dans une ancienne écurie ou remise

Mexico ['mɛksɪkəu] n Mexique m

miaow [miː'au] vi miauler

mice [maɪs] npl of **mouse**

microchip ['maɪkrəutʃɪp] n (ELEC) puce f

micro(computer) ['maɪkrəu(kəm'pjuːtə*)] n micro(-ordinateur m) m

microphone ['maɪkrəfəun] n microphone m

microscope ['maɪkrəskəup] n microscope m; **under the microscope** au microscope

microwave ['maɪkrəuweɪv] n (also: **microwave oven**) four m à micro-ondes

mid [mɪd] adj: **mid May** la mi-mai; **mid afternoon** le milieu de l'après-midi; **in mid air** en plein ciel; **he's in his mid thirties** il a dans les trente-cinq ans

midday ['mɪd'deɪ] n midi m

middle ['mɪdl] n milieu m; (waist) ceinture f, taille f ◆ adj du milieu; **in the middle of the night** au milieu de la nuit; **I'm in the middle of reading it** je suis (justement) en train de le lire

middle-aged [mɪdl'eɪdʒd] adj (people) d'un certain âge, ni vieux ni jeune; (pej: values, outlook) conventionnel(le), rassis(e)

Middle Ages npl: **the Middle Ages** le moyen âge

middle class n: **the middle class(es)** ≃ les classes moyennes; ◆ adj (also: **middle-class**) ≃ (petit(e)-)bourgeois(e)

Middle East n: **the Middle East** le Proche-Orient, le Moyen-Orient

middleman ['mɪdlmæn] n intermédiaire m

middle name n second prénom

middle-of-the-road ['mɪdləvðə'rəud] adj (policy) modéré(e), du juste milieu; (music etc) plutôt classique, assez traditionnel(le)

middleweight ['mɪdlweɪt] n (BOXING) poids moyen

middling ['mɪdlɪŋ] adj moyen(ne)

midge [mɪdʒ] n moucheron m

midget ['mɪdʒɪt] n nain/e ◆ adj minuscule

Midlands ['mɪdləndz] npl comtés du centre de l'Angleterre

midnight ['mɪdnaɪt] n minuit m; **at midnight** à minuit

midriff ['mɪdrɪf] n estomac m, taille f

midst [mɪdst] n: **in the midst of** au milieu de

midsummer [mɪd'sʌmə*] n milieu m de l'été

midway [mɪd'weɪ] adj, adv: **midway (between)** à mi-chemin (entre)

midweek [mɪd'wi:k] adj du milieu de la semaine ◆ adv au milieu de la semaine, en pleine semaine

midwife, pl **midwives** ['mɪdwaɪf, -vz] n sage-femme f

might [maɪt] vb see **may** ◆ n puissance f, force f

mighty ['maɪtɪ] adj puissant(e) ◆ adv (col) rudement

migraine ['mi:greɪn] n migraine f

migrant ['maɪgrənt] n (bird, animal) migrateur m; (person) migrant/e; nomade m/f ◆ adj migrateur(trice); migrant(e); nomade; (worker) saisonnier(ière)

migrate [maɪ'greɪt] vi émigrer

mike [maɪk] n abbr (= microphone) micro m

mild [maɪld] adj doux(douce); (reproach) léger(ère); (illness) bénin(igne) ◆ n bière légère

mildly ['maɪldlɪ] adv doucement; légèrement; **to put it mildly** (col) c'est le moins qu'on puisse dire

mile [maɪl] n mil(l)e m (= 1609 m); **to do 30 miles per gallon** ≃ faire 9, 4 litres aux cent

mileage ['maɪlɪdʒ] n distance f en milles, ≃ kilométrage m

mileometer [maɪ'lɔmɪtə*] n (BRIT) = **milometer**

milestone ['maɪlstəun] n borne f; (fig) jalon m

militant ['mɪlɪtnt] adj, n militant/e

military ['mɪlɪtərɪ] adj militaire ◆ n: **the military** l'armée f, les militaires mpl

militia [mɪ'lɪʃə] n milice f

milk [mɪlk] n lait m ◆ vt (cow) traire; (fig) dépouiller, plumer

milk chocolate n chocolat m au lait

milkman ['mɪlkmən] n laitier m

milk shake n milk-shake m

milky ['mɪlkɪ] adj lacté(e); (colour) laiteux(euse)

Milky Way n Voie lactée

mill [mɪl] n moulin m; (factory) usine f, fabrique f; (spinning mill) filature f; (flour mill) minoterie f ◆ vt moudre, broyer ◆ vi (also: **mill about**) grouiller

millennium bug [mɪ'lɛnɪəm-] n bogue m or bug m de l'an 2000

miller ['mɪlə*] n meunier m

millimetre, (US) **millimeter** ['mɪlɪmi:tə*] n millimètre m

million ['mɪljən] n million m

millionaire [mɪljə'nɛə*] n millionnaire m

milometer [maɪ'lɔmɪtə*] n (BRIT) ≃ compteur m kilométrique

mime [maɪm] n mime m ◆ vt, vi mimer

mimic ['mɪmɪk] n imitateur/trice ◆ vt, vi imiter, contrefaire

min. abbr (= minute) mn.; (= minimum) min.

mince [mɪns] vt hacher ◆ vi (in walking) marcher à petits pas maniérés ◆ n (BRIT CULIN) viande hachée, hachis m; **he does not mince (his) words** il ne mâche pas ses mots

mincemeat ['mɪnsmi:t] n hachis m de fruits secs utilisés en pâtisserie

mince pie n sorte de tarte aux fruits secs

mincer ['mɪnsə*] n hachoir m

mind [maɪnd] n esprit m ◆ vt (attend to, look after) s'occuper de; (be careful) faire attention à; (object to): **I don't mind the noise** je ne crains pas le bruit, le bruit ne me dérange pas; **do you mind if ...?** est-ce que cela vous gêne si ...?; **I don't mind** cela ne me dérange pas; **mind you, ...** remarquez, ...; **never mind** peu importe, ça ne fait rien; **it is on my mind** cela me préoccupe; **to change one's mind** changer d'avis; **to be in two minds about sth** (BRIT) être indécis(e) or irrésolu(e) en ce qui concerne qch; **to my mind** à mon avis, selon moi; **to be out of one's mind** ne plus avoir toute sa raison; **to keep sth in mind** ne pas oublier qch; **to bear sth in mind** tenir compte de qch; **to have sb/sth in mind** avoir qn/qch en tête; **to have in mind to do** avoir l'intention de faire; **it went right out of my mind** ça m'est complètement sorti de la tête; **to bring** or **call sth to mind** se rappeler qch; **to make up one's mind** se décider; **"mind the step"** "attention à la marche"

minder ['maɪndə*] n (child minder) gardienne f;

(*bodyguard*) ange gardien (*fig*)

mindful ['maɪndful] *adj*: **mindful of** attentif(ive) à, soucieux(euse) de

mindless ['maɪndlɪs] *adj* irréfléchie(e); (*violence, crime*) insensé(e)

mine [maɪn] *pron* le(la) mien(ne), les miens(miennes); **this book is mine** ce livre est à moi ◆ *n* mine *f* ◆ *vt* (*coal*) extraire; (*ship, beach*) miner

minefield ['maɪnfiːld] *n* champ *m* de mines

miner ['maɪnə*] *n* mineur *m*

mineral ['mɪnərəl] *adj* minéral(e) ◆ *n* minéral *m*; **minerals** *npl* (*BRIT: soft drinks*) boissons gazeuses (sucrées)

mineral water *n* eau minérale

mingle ['mɪŋgl] *vt* mêler, mélanger ◆ *vi*: **to mingle with** se mêler à

miniature ['mɪnətʃə*] *adj* (en) miniature ◆ *n* miniature *f*

minibus ['mɪnɪbʌs] *n* minibus *m*

minimal ['mɪnɪml] *adj* minimal(e)

minimize ['mɪnɪmaɪz] *vt* minimiser

minimum ['mɪnɪməm] *n* (*pl* **minima** ['mɪnɪmə]) minimum *m* ◆ *adj* minimum; **to reduce to a minimum** réduire au minimum

mining ['maɪnɪŋ] *n* exploitation minière ◆ *adj* minier(ière); de mineurs

miniskirt ['mɪnɪskəːt] *n* mini-jupe *f*

minister ['mɪnɪstə*] *n* (*BRIT POL*) ministre *m*; (*REL*) pasteur *m* ◆ *vi*: **to minister to sb** donner ses soins à qn; **to minister to sb's needs** pourvoir aux besoins de qn

ministerial [mɪnɪs'tɪərɪəl] *adj* (*BRIT POL*) ministériel(le)

ministry ['mɪnɪstrɪ] *n* (*BRIT POL*) ministère *m*; (*REL*): **to go into the ministry** devenir pasteur

mink [mɪŋk] *n* vison *m*

minor ['maɪnə*] *adj* petit(e), de peu d'importance; (*MUS*) mineur(e) ◆ *n* (*LAW*) mineur/e

minority [maɪ'nɔrɪtɪ] *n* minorité *f*; **to be in a minority** être en minorité

mint [mɪnt] *n* (*plant*) menthe *f*; (*sweet*) bonbon *m* à la menthe ◆ *vt* (*coins*) battre; **the (Royal) Mint**, (*US*) **the (US) Mint** ≈ l'hôtel *m* de la Monnaie; **in mint condition** à l'état de neuf

minus ['maɪnəs] *n* (*also*: **minus sign**) signe *m* moins ◆ *prep* moins

minute *adj* [maɪ'njuːt] minuscule; (*detailed*) minutieux(euse) ◆ *n* ['mɪnɪt] minute *f*; (*official record*) procès-verbal *m*, compte rendu; **minutes** *npl* procès-verbal *m*; **it is 5 minutes past 3** il est 3 heures 5; **wait a minute!** (attendez) un instant!; **at the last minute** à la dernière minute; **up to the minute** (*fashion*) dernier cri; (*news*) de dernière minute; (*machine, technology*) de pointe; **in minute detail** par le menu

miracle ['mɪrəkl] *n* miracle *m*

mirage ['mɪrɑːʒ] *n* mirage *m*

mirror ['mɪrə*] *n* miroir *m*, glace *f* ◆ *vt* refléter

mirth [məːθ] *n* gaieté *f*

misadventure [mɪsəd'ventʃə*] *n* mésaventure *f*; **death by misadventure** (*BRIT*) décès accidentel

misapprehension ['mɪsæprɪ'henʃən] *n* malentendu *m*, méprise *f*

misappropriate [mɪsə'prəʊprɪeɪt] *vt* détourner

misbehave [mɪsbɪ'heɪv] *vi* mal se conduire

miscalculate [mɪs'kælkjuleɪt] *vt* mal calculer

miscarriage ['mɪskærɪdʒ] *n* (*MED*) fausse couche; **miscarriage of justice** erreur *f* judiciaire

miscellaneous [mɪsɪ'leɪnɪəs] *adj* (*items, expenses*) divers(es); (*selection*) varié(e)

mischief ['mɪstʃɪf] *n* (*naughtiness*) sottises *fpl*; (*harm*) mal *m*, dommage *m*; (*maliciousness*) méchanceté *f*

mischievous ['mɪstʃɪvəs] *adj* (*naughty*) coquin(e), espiègle; (*harmful*) méchant(e)

misconception ['mɪskən'sepʃən] *n* idée fausse

misconduct [mɪs'kɔndʌkt] *n* inconduite *f*; **professional misconduct** faute professionnelle

misdemeanour, (*US*) **misdemeanor** [mɪsdɪ'miːnə*] *n* écart *m* de conduite; infraction *f*

miser ['maɪzə*] *n* avare *m/f*

miserable ['mɪzərəbl] *adj* malheureux(euse); (*wretched*) misérable; **to feel miserable** avoir le cafard

miserly ['maɪzəlɪ] *adj* avare

misery ['mɪzərɪ] *n* (*unhappiness*) tristesse *f*; (*pain*) souffrances *fpl*; (*wretchedness*) misère *f*

misfire [mɪs'faɪə*] *vi* rater; (*car engine*) avoir des ratés

misfit ['mɪsfɪt] *n* (*person*) inadapté/e

misfortune [mɪs'fɔːtʃən] *n* malchance *f*, malheur *m*

misgiving(s) [mɪs'gɪvɪŋ(z)] *n(pl)* craintes *fpl*, soupçons *mpl*; **to have misgivings about sth** avoir des doutes quant à qch

misguided [mɪs'gaɪdɪd] *adj* malavisé(e)

mishandle [mɪs'hændl] *vt* (*treat roughly*) malmener; (*mismanage*) mal s'y prendre pour faire *or* résoudre *etc*

mishap ['mɪshæp] *n* mésaventure *f*

misinform [mɪsɪn'fɔːm] *vt* mal renseigner

misinterpret [mɪsɪn'təːprɪt] *vt* mal interpréter

misjudge [mɪs'dʒʌdʒ] *vt* méjuger, se méprendre sur le compte de

mislay [mɪs'leɪ] *vt irreg* égarer

mislead [mɪs'liːd] *vt irreg* induire en erreur

misleading [mɪs'liːdɪŋ] *adj* trompeur(euse)

mismanage [mɪs'mænɪdʒ] *vt* mal gérer; mal s'y prendre pour faire *or* résoudre *etc*

misplace [mɪs'pleɪs] *vt* égarer; **to be misplaced** (*trust etc*) être mal placé(e)

misprint ['mɪsprɪnt] *n* faute *f* d'impression

Miss [mɪs] *n* Mademoiselle; **Dear Miss Smith** Chère Mademoiselle Smith

miss [mɪs] *vt* (*fail to get*) manquer, rater; (*appointment, class*) manquer; (*escape, avoid*) échapper à, éviter; (*notice loss of: money etc*) s'apercevoir de l'absence de; (*regret the absence of*): **I miss him/it** il/cela me manque ◆ *vi* manquer ◆ *n* (*shot*) coup manqué; **the bus just missed the wall** le bus a évité le mur de justesse; **you're missing the point** vous êtes à côté de la question

▶ **miss out** *vt* (*BRIT*) oublier

▶ **miss out on** *vt fus* (*fun, party*) rater, manquer; (*chance, bargain*) laisser passer

misshapen [mɪs'ʃeɪpən] *adj* difforme

missile ['mɪsaɪl] *n* (*AVIAT*) missile *m*; (*object thrown*) projectile *m*

missing ['mɪsɪŋ] *adj* manquant(e); (*after escape, disaster: person*) disparu(e); **to go missing** disparaître; **missing person** personne disparue, disparu/e

mission ['mɪʃən] *n* mission *f*; **on a mission to sb** en mission auprès de qn

missionary ['mɪʃənrɪ] *n* missionnaire *m/f*

mission statement *n* déclaration *f* d'intention

mist [mɪst] *n* brume *f* ◆ *vi* (*also*: **mist over, mist up**) devenir brumeux(euse); (*BRIT: windows*) s'embuer

mistake [mɪs'teɪk] *n* erreur *f*, faute *f* ◆ *vt* (*irreg: like* **take**) (*meaning*) mal comprendre; (*intentions*) se méprendre sur; **to mistake for** prendre pour; **by mistake** par erreur, par inadvertance; **to make a mistake** (*in writing*) faire une faute; (*in calculating etc*) faire une erreur; **to make a mistake about sb/sth** se tromper sur le compte de qn/sur qch

mistaken [mɪs'teɪkən] *pp of* **mistake** ◆ *adj* (*idea etc*) erroné(e); **to be mistaken** faire erreur, se tromper

mister ['mɪstə*] *n* (*col*) Monsieur *m*; *see* **Mr**

mistletoe ['mɪsltəʊ] *n* gui *m*

mistook [mɪs'tʊk] *pt of* **mistake**

mistress ['mɪstrɪs] *n* maîtresse *f*; (*BRIT: in primary school*) institutrice *f*; *see* **Mrs**

mistrust [mɪs'trʌst] *vt* se méfier de ◆ *n*: **mistrust (of)** méfiance *f* (à l'égard de)

misty ['mɪstɪ] *adj* brumeux(euse)

misunderstand [mɪsʌndə'stænd] *vt, vi irreg* mal comprendre

misunderstanding ['mɪsʌndə'stændɪŋ] *n* méprise *f*, malentendu *m*

misuse *n* [mɪs'juːs] mauvais emploi; (*of power*) abus *m* ◆ *vt* [mɪs'juːz] mal employer; abuser de

mitigate ['mɪtɪgeɪt] *vt* atténuer; **mitigating circumstances** circonstances atténuantes

mitt(en) ['mɪt(n)] *n* mitaine *f*; moufle *f*

mix [mɪks] *vt* mélanger ◆ *vi* se mélanger ◆ *n* mélange *m*; dosage *m*; **to mix sth with sth** mélanger qch à qch; **to mix business with pleasure** unir l'utile à l'agréable; **cake mix** préparation *f* pour gâteau

▶ **mix in** *vt* incorporer, mélanger

▶ **mix up** *vt* mélanger; (*confuse*) confondre; **to be mixed up in sth** être mêlé(e) à qch ou impliqué(e) dans qch

mixed [mɪkst] *adj* (*assorted*) assortis(ies); (*school etc*) mixte

mixed grill *n* (*BRIT*) assortiment *m* de grillades

mixed-up [mɪkst'ʌp] *adj* (*person*) désorienté(e) (*fig*)

mixer ['mɪksə*] *n* (*for food*) batteur *m*, mixeur *m*; (*person*): **he is a good mixer** il est très sociable

mixture ['mɪkstʃə*] *n* assortiment *m*, mélange *m*; (*MED*) préparation *f*

mix-up ['mɪksʌp] *n* confusion *f*

mm *abbr* (= *millimetre*) mm

moan [məʊn] *n* gémissement *m* ◆ *vi* gémir; (*col: complain*): **to moan (about)** se plaindre (de)

moat [məʊt] *n* fossé *m*, douves *fpl*

mob [mɒb] *n* foule *f*; (*disorderly*) cohue *f*; (*pej*): **the mob** la populace ◆ *vt* assaillir

mobile ['məʊbaɪl] *adj* mobile ◆ *n* (*ART*) mobile *m*; **applicants must be mobile** (*BRIT*) les candidats devront être prêts à accepter tout déplacement

mobile home *n* caravane *f*

mobile phone *n* téléphone portatif

mock [mɒk] *vt* ridiculiser, se moquer de ◆ *adj* faux(fausse)

mockery ['mɒkərɪ] *n* moquerie *f*, raillerie *f*; **to make a mockery of** ridiculiser, tourner en dérision

mock-up ['mɒkʌp] *n* maquette *f*

mod [mɒd] *adj see* **convenience**

mode [məʊd] *n* mode *m*; (*of transport*) moyen *m*

model ['mɒdl] *n* modèle *m*; (*person: for fashion*) mannequin *m*; (: *for artist*) modèle ◆ *vt* modeler ◆ *vi* travailler comme mannequin ◆ *adj* (*railway: toy*) modèle réduit *inv*; (*child, factory*) modèle; **to model clothes** présenter des vêtements; **to model sb/sth on** modeler qn/qch sur

modem ['məʊdɛm] *n* modem *m*

moderate *adj* [ˈmɒdərət] ◆ *adj* modéré(e) ◆ *n* (*POL*) modéré/e ◆ *vb* ['mɒdəreɪt] ◆ *vi* se modérer, se calmer ◆ *vt* modérer

modern ['mɒdən] *adj* moderne; **modern languages** langues vivantes

modernize ['mɒdənaɪz] *vt* moderniser

modest ['mɒdɪst] *adj* modeste

modesty ['mɒdɪstɪ] *n* modestie *f*

modify ['mɒdɪfaɪ] *vt* modifier

mogul ['məʊgl] *n* (*fig*) nabab *m*; (*SKI*) bosse *f*

mohair ['məʊhɛə*] *n* mohair *m*

moist [mɔɪst] *adj* humide, moite

moisten ['mɔɪsn] *vt* humecter, mouiller légèrement

moisture ['mɔɪstʃə*] *n* humidité *f*; (*on glass*) buée *f*

moisturizer [ˈmɔɪstʃəraɪzə*] n produit hydratant

molar [ˈməʊlə*] n molaire f

molasses [məʊˈlæsɪz] n mélasse f

mold [məʊld] n, vt (US) = **mould**

mole [məʊl] n (animal) taupe f; (spot) grain m de beauté

molest [məʊˈlɛst] vt tracasser; molester

mollycoddle [ˈmɔlɪkɔdl] vt chouchouter, couver

molt [məʊlt] vi (US) = **moult**

molten [ˈməʊltən] adj fondu(e)

mom [mɔm] n (US) = **mum**

moment [ˈməʊmənt] n moment m, instant m; (importance) importance f; **at the moment** en ce moment; **for the moment** pour l'instant; **in a moment** dans un instant; **"one moment please"** (TEL) "ne quittez pas"

momentary [ˈməʊməntərɪ] adj momentané(e), passager(ère)

momentous [məʊˈmɛntəs] adj important(e), capital(e)

momentum [məʊˈmɛntəm] n élan m, vitesse acquise; **to gather momentum** prendre de la vitesse

mommy [ˈmɔmɪ] n (US: mother) maman f

Monaco [ˈmɔnəkəʊ] n Monaco f

monarch [ˈmɔnək] n monarque m

monarchy [ˈmɔnəkɪ] n monarchie f

monastery [ˈmɔnəstərɪ] n monastère m

Monday [ˈmʌndɪ] n lundi m; for phrases see also **Tuesday**

monetary [ˈmʌnɪtərɪ] adj monétaire

money [ˈmʌnɪ] n argent m; **to make money** (person) gagner de l'argent; (business) rapporter; **I've got no money left** je n'ai plus d'argent, je n'ai plus un sou

money belt n ceinture-portefeuille f

money order n mandat m

money-spinner [ˈmʌnɪspɪnə*] n (col) mine f d'or (fig)

mongrel [ˈmʌŋgrəl] n (dog) bâtard m

monitor [ˈmɔnɪtə*] n (BRIT SCOL) chef m de classe; (US SCOL) surveillant m (d'examen); (TV, COMPUT) écran m, moniteur m ◆ vt contrôler; (foreign station) être à l'écoute de

monk [mʌŋk] n moine m

monkey [ˈmʌŋkɪ] n singe m

monkey nut n (BRIT) cacahuète f

monopoly [məˈnɔpəlɪ] n monopole m; **Monopolies and Mergers Commission** (BRIT) commission britannique d'enquête sur les monopoles

monotone [ˈmɔnətəʊn] n ton m (or voix f) monocorde; **to speak in a monotone** parler sur un ton monocorde

monotonous [məˈnɔtənəs] adj monotone

monsoon [mɔnˈsuːn] n mousson f

monster [ˈmɔnstə*] n monstre m

monstrous [ˈmɔnstrəs] adj (huge) gigantesque; (atrocious) monstrueux(euse), atroce

month [mʌnθ] n mois m; **every month** tous les mois; **300 dollars a month** 300 dollars par mois

monthly [ˈmʌnθlɪ] adj mensuel(le) ◆ adv mensuellement ◆ n (magazine) mensuel m, publication mensuelle; **twice monthly** deux fois par mois

monument [ˈmɔnjumənt] n monument m

moo [muː] vi meugler, beugler

mood [muːd] n humeur f, disposition f; **to be in a good/bad mood** être de bonne/mauvaise humeur; **to be in the mood for** être d'humeur à, avoir envie de

moody [ˈmuːdɪ] adj (variable) d'humeur changeante, lunatique; (sullen) morose, maussade

moon [muːn] n lune f

moonlight [ˈmuːnlaɪt] n clair m de lune ◆ vi travailler au noir

moonlighting [ˈmuːnlaɪtɪŋ] n travail m au noir

moonlit [ˈmuːnlɪt] adj éclairé(e) par la lune; **a moonlit night** une nuit de lune

moor [mʊə*] n lande f ◆ vt (ship) amarrer ◆ vi mouiller

moorland [ˈmʊələnd] n lande f

moose [muːs] n (pl inv) élan m

mop [mɔp] n balai m à laver ◆ vt éponger, essuyer; **mop of hair** tignasse f

▶ **mop up** vt éponger

mope [məʊp] vi avoir le cafard, se morfondre

▶ **mope about, mope around** vi broyer du noir, se morfondre

moped [ˈməʊpɛd] n cyclomoteur m

moral [ˈmɔrl] adj moral(e) ◆ n morale f; **morals** npl moralité f

morale [mɔˈrɑːl] n moral m

morality [məˈrælɪtɪ] n moralité f

morass [məˈræs] n marais m, marécage m

KEYWORD

more [mɔː*] adj **1** (greater in number etc) plus (de), davantage; **more people/work (than)** plus de gens/de travail (que)

2 (additional) encore (de); **do you want (some) more tea?** voulez-vous encore du thé?; **I have no** or **I don't have any more money** je n'ai plus d'argent; **it'll take a few more weeks** ça prendra encore quelques semaines

◆ pron plus, davantage; **more than 10** plus de 10; **it cost more than we expected** cela a coûté plus que prévu; **I want more** j'en veux plus or davantage; **is there any more?** est-ce qu'il en reste?; **there's no more** il n'y en a plus; **a little more** un peu plus; **many/much more** beaucoup plus, bien davantage

◆ adv: **more dangerous/easily (than)** plus dangereux/facilement (que); **more and more**

expensive de plus en plus cher; **more or less** plus ou moins; **more than ever** plus que jamais; **once more** encore une fois, une fois de plus; **and what's more ...** et de plus ..., et qui plus est ...

moreover [mɔːˈrəʊvə*] *adv* de plus

morning [ˈmɔːnɪŋ] *n* matin *m*; *(as duration)* matinée *f*; **in the morning** le matin; **7 o'clock in the morning** 7 heures du matin; **this morning** ce matin

morning sickness *n* nausées matinales

Morocco [məˈrɒkəʊ] *n* Maroc *m*

moron [ˈmɔːrɒn] *n* idiot/e, minus *m/f*

Morse [mɔːs] *n (also:* **Morse code**) morse *m*

morsel [ˈmɔːsl] *n* bouchée *f*

mortar [ˈmɔːtə*] *n* mortier *m*

mortgage [ˈmɔːgɪdʒ] *n* hypothèque *f*; *(loan)* prêt *m (or* crédit *m)* hypothécaire ♦ *vt* hypothéquer; **to take out a mortgage** prendre une hypothèque, faire un emprunt

mortgage company *n (US)* société *f* de crédit immobilier

mortuary [ˈmɔːtjuərɪ] *n* morgue *f*

mosaic [məuˈzeɪɪk] *n* mosaïque *f*

Moscow [ˈmɒskəʊ] *n* Moscou

Moslem [ˈmɒzləm] *adj, n =* **Muslim**

mosque [mɒsk] *n* mosquée *f*

mosquito, *pl* **mosquitoes** [mɒsˈkiːtəu] *n* moustique *m*

moss [mɒs] *n* mousse *f*

most [məust] *adj* la plupart de; le plus de ♦ *pron* la plupart ♦ *adv* le plus; *(very)* très, extrêmement; **the most** le plus; **most fish** la plupart des poissons; **most of** la plus grande partie de; **most of them** la plupart d'entre eux; **I saw most** j'en ai vu la plupart; c'est moi qui en ai vu le plus; **at the (very) most** au plus; **to make the most of** profiter au maximum de

mostly [ˈməustlɪ] *adv* surtout, principalement

MOT *n abbr (BRIT = Ministry of Transport):* **the MOT (test)** visite technique (annuelle) obligatoire des véhicules à moteur

motel [məuˈtel] *n* motel *m*

moth [mɒθ] *n* papillon *m* de nuit; mite *f*

mother [ˈmʌðə*] *n* mère *f* ♦ *vt (care for)* dorloter

motherhood [ˈmʌðəhud] *n* maternité *f*

mother-in-law [ˈmʌðərɪnlɔː] *n* belle-mère *f*

motherly [ˈmʌðəlɪ] *adj* maternel(le)

mother-of-pearl [ˈmʌðərəvˈpəːl] *n* nacre *f*

Mother's Day [ˈmʌðəz-] *n* fête *f* des Mères

mother-to-be [ˈmʌðətəˈbiː] *n* future maman

mother tongue *n* langue maternelle

motion [ˈməuʃən] *n* mouvement *m*; *(gesture)* geste *m*; *(at meeting)* motion *f*; *(BRIT: also:* **bowel motion)** selles *fpl* ♦ *vt, vi:* **to motion (to) sb to do** faire signe à qn de faire; **to be in motion** *(vehicle)* être en marche; **to set in motion** mettre en

marche; **to go through the motions of doing sth** *(fig)* faire qch machinalement *or* sans conviction

motionless [ˈməuʃənlɪs] *adj* immobile, sans mouvement

motion picture *n* film *m*

motivated [ˈməutɪveɪtɪd] *adj* motivé(e)

motivation [məutɪˈveɪʃən] *n* motivation *f*

motive [ˈməutɪv] *n* motif *m*, mobile *m* ♦ *adj* moteur(trice); **from the best (of) motives** avec les meilleures intentions (du monde)

motley [ˈmɒtlɪ] *adj* hétéroclite; bigarré(e), bariolé(e)

motor [ˈməutə*] *n* moteur *m*; *(BRIT col: vehicle)* auto *f* ♦ *adj* moteur(trice)

motorbike [ˈməutəbaɪk] *n* moto *f*

motorboat [ˈməutəbəut] *n* bateau *m* à moteur

motorcar [ˈməutəkɑː] *n (BRIT)* automobile *f*

motorcycle [ˈməutəsaɪkl] *n* vélomoteur *m*

motorcycle racing *n* course *f* de motos

motorcyclist [ˈməutəsaɪklɪst] *n* motocycliste *m/f*

motoring [ˈməutərɪŋ] *(BRIT) n* tourisme *m* automobile ♦ *adj (accident)* de voiture, de la route; **motoring holiday** vacances *fpl* en voiture; **motoring offence** infraction *f* au code de la route

motorist [ˈməutərɪst] *n* automobiliste *m/f*

motor mechanic *n* mécanicien *m* garagiste

motor racing *n (BRIT)* course *f* automobile

motor trade *n* secteur *m* de l'automobile

motorway [ˈməutəweɪ] *n (BRIT)* autoroute *f*

mottled [ˈmɒtld] *adj* tacheté(e), marbré(e)

motto, *pl* **mottoes** [ˈmɒtəu] *n* devise *f*

mould, *(US)* **mold** [məuld] *n* moule *m*; *(mildew)* moisissure *f* ♦ *vt* mouler, modeler; *(fig)* façonner

mo(u)ldy [ˈməuldɪ] *adj* moisi(e)

moult, *(US)* **molt** [məult] *vi* muer

mound [maund] *n* monticule *m*, tertre *m*

mount [maunt] *n* mont *m*, montagne *f*; *(horse)* monture *f*; *(for jewel etc)* monture *f* ♦ *vt* monter; *(exhibition)* organiser, monter; *(picture)* monter sur carton; *(stamp)* coller dans un album ♦ *vi (also:* **mount up)** s'élever, monter

mountain [ˈmauntɪn] *n* montagne *f* ♦ *cpd* de (la) montagne; **to make a mountain out of a molehill** *(fig)* se faire une montagne d'un rien

mountain bike *n* VTT *m*, vélo *m* tout terrain

mountaineer [mauntɪˈnɪə*] *n* alpiniste *m/f*

mountaineering [mauntɪˈnɪərɪŋ] *n* alpinisme *m*; **to go mountaineering** faire de l'alpinisme

mountainous [ˈmauntɪnəs] *adj* montagneux(euse)

mountain rescue team *n* colonne *f* de secours

mountainside [ˈmauntɪnsaɪd] *n* flanc *m or* versant *m* de la montagne

mourn [mɔːn] *vt* pleurer ♦ *vi:* **to mourn (for)** se lamenter (sur)

mourner ['mɔːnə*] n parent/e or ami/e du défunt; personne f en deuil or venue rendre hommage au défunt

mourning ['mɔːnɪŋ] n deuil m ♦ cpd (dress) de deuil; **in mourning** en deuil

mouse, pl **mice** [maus, maɪs] n (also COMPUT) souris f

mouse mat n (COMPUT) tapis m de souris

mousetrap ['maustræp] n souricière f

mousse [muːs] n mousse f

moustache [məs'tɑːʃ] n moustache(s) f(pl)

mousy ['mausɪ] adj (person) effacé(e); (hair) d'un châtain terne

mouth, pl **mouths** [mauθ, -ðz] n bouche f; (of dog, cat) gueule f; (of river) embouchure f; (of bottle) goulot m; (opening) orifice m

mouthful ['mauθful] n bouchée f

mouth organ n harmonica m

mouthpiece ['mauθpiːs] n (of musical) bec m, embouchure f; (spokesman) porte-parole m inv

mouthwash ['mauθwɔʃ] n eau f dentifrice

mouth-watering ['mauθwɔːtərɪŋ] adj qui met l'eau à la bouche

movable ['muːvəbl] adj mobile

move [muːv] n (movement) mouvement m; (in game) coup m; (: turn to play) tour m; (change of house) déménagement m ♦ vt déplacer, bouger; (emotionally) émouvoir; (POL: resolution etc) proposer ♦ vi (gen) bouger, remuer; (traffic) circuler; (also: **move house**) déménager; **to move towards** se diriger vers; **to move sb to do sth** pousser or inciter qn à faire qch; **to get a move on** se dépêcher, se remuer

► **move about, move around** vi (fidget) remuer; (travel) voyager, se déplacer

► **move along** vi se pousser

► **move away** vi s'en aller, s'éloigner

► **move back** vi revenir, retourner

► **move forward** vi avancer ♦ vt avancer; (people) faire avancer

► **move in** vi (to a house) emménager

► **move off** vi s'éloigner, s'en aller

► **move on** vi se remettre en route ♦ vt (onlookers) faire circuler

► **move out** vi (of house) déménager

► **move over** vi se pousser, se déplacer

► **move up** vi avancer; (employee) avoir de l'avancement

moveable ['muːvəbl] adj = **movable**

movement ['muːvmənt] n mouvement m; **movement (of the bowels)** (MED) selles fpl

movie ['muːvɪ] n film m; **the movies** le cinéma

moving ['muːvɪŋ] adj en mouvement; (touching) émouvant(e) ♦ n (US) déménagement m

mow, pt **mowed**, pp **mowed** or **mown** [məu, -n] vt faucher; (lawn) tondre

► **mow down** vt faucher

mower ['məuə*] n (also: **lawnmower**) tondeuse f à gazon

MP n abbr (= Military Police) PM; (BRIT) = **Member of Parliament**; (Canada) = Mounted Police

mph abbr = miles per hour (60 mph = 96 km/h)

Mr, Mr. ['mɪstə*] n: **Mr X** Monsieur X, M. X

Mrs, Mrs. ['mɪsɪz] n: **Mrs X** Madame X, Mme X

Ms, Ms. [mɪz] n (Miss or Mrs): **Ms X** Madame X, Mme X

MSc n abbr = **Master of Science**

MSP n abbr (= Member of the Scottish Parliament) député m au Parlement écossais

much [mʌtʃ] adj beaucoup de ♦ adv, n or pron beaucoup; **much milk** beaucoup de lait; **how much is it?** combien est-ce que ça coûte?; **it's not much** ce n'est pas beaucoup; **too much** trop (de); **so much** tant (de); **I like it very/so much** j'aime beaucoup/tellement ça; **thank you very much** merci beaucoup; **much to my amazement ...** à mon grand étonnement …

muck [mʌk] n (mud) boue f; (dirt) ordures fpl

► **muck about** vi (col) faire l'imbécile; (: waste time) traînasser; (: tinker) bricoler; tripoter

► **muck in** vi (BRIT col) donner un coup de main

► **muck out** vt (stable) nettoyer

► **muck up** vt (col: ruin) gâcher, esquinter; (: dirty) salir

mucky ['mʌkɪ] adj (dirty) boueux(euse), sale

mud [mʌd] n boue f

muddle ['mʌdl] n pagaille f; désordre m, fouillis m ♦ vt (also: **muddle up**) brouiller, embrouiller; **to be in a muddle** (person) ne plus savoir où l'on en est; **to get in a muddle** (while explaining etc) s'embrouiller

► **muddle along** vi aller son chemin tant bien que mal

► **muddle through** vi se débrouiller

muddy ['mʌdɪ] adj boueux(euse)

mudguard ['mʌdgɑːd] n garde-boue m inv

muesli ['mjuːzlɪ] n muesli m

muffin ['mʌfɪn] n petit pain rond et plat

muffle ['mʌfl] vt (sound) assourdir, étouffer; (against cold) emmitoufler

muffled ['mʌfld] adj étouffé(e), voilé(e)

muffler ['mʌflə*] n (scarf) cache-nez m inv; (US AUT) silencieux m

mug [mʌg] n (cup) tasse f (sans soucoupe); (: for beer) chope f; (col: face) bouille f; (: fool) poire f ♦ vt (assault) agresser; **it's a mug's game** (BRIT) c'est bon pour les imbéciles

► **mug up** vt (BRIT col: also: **mug up on**) bosser, bûcher

mugger ['mʌgə*] n agresseur m

mugging ['mʌgɪŋ] n agression f

muggy ['mʌgɪ] adj lourd(e), moite

mule [mjuːl] n mule f

multi-level ['mʌltɪlevl] adj (US) = **multistorey**

multiple ['mʌltɪpl] *adj* multiple ♦ *n* multiple *m*; (*BRIT: also:* **multiple store**) magasin *m* à succursales (multiples)

multiple sclerosis *n* sclérose *f* en plaques

multiplex ['mʌltɪpleks] *n* (*also:* **multiplex cinema**) (cinéma *m*) multisalles *m*

multiplication [mʌltɪplɪ'keɪʃən] *n* multiplication *f*

multiply ['mʌltɪplaɪ] *vt* multiplier ♦ *vi* se multiplier

multistorey ['mʌltɪ'stɔːrɪ] *adj* (*BRIT: building*) à étages; (: *car park*) à étages *or* niveaux multiples

mum [mʌm] *n* (*BRIT*) maman *f* ♦ *adj:* **to keep mum** ne pas souffler mot; **mum's the word!** motus et bouche cousue!

mumble ['mʌmbl] *vt, vi* marmotter, marmonner

mummy ['mʌmɪ] *n* (*BRIT: mother*) maman *f*; (*embalmed*) momie *f*

mumps [mʌmps] *n* oreillons *mpl*

munch [mʌntʃ] *vt, vi* mâcher

mundane [mʌn'deɪn] *adj* banal(e), terre à terre *inv*

municipal [mjuː'nɪsɪpl] *adj* municipal(e)

murder ['mɜːdə*] *n* meurtre *m*, assassinat *m* ♦ *vt* assassiner; **to commit murder** commettre un meurtre

murderer ['mɜːdərə*] *n* meurtrier *m*, assassin *m*

murderous ['mɜːdərəs] *adj* meurtrier(ière)

murky ['mɜːkɪ] *adj* sombre, ténébreux(euse)

murmur ['mɜːmə*] *n* murmure *m* ♦ *vt, vi* murmurer; **heart murmur** (*MED*) souffle *m* au cœur

muscle ['mʌsl] *n* muscle *m*

▶ **muscle in** *vi* s'imposer, s'immiscer

muscular ['mʌskjulə*] *adj* musculaire; (*person, arm*) musclé(e)

muse [mjuːz] *vi* méditer, songer ♦ *n* muse *f*

museum [mjuː'zɪəm] *n* musée *m*

mushroom ['mʌʃrum] *n* champignon *m* ♦ *vi* (*fig*) pousser comme un (*or* des) champignon(s)

music ['mjuːzɪk] *n* musique *f*

musical ['mjuːzɪkl] *adj* musical(e); (*person*) musicien(ne) ♦ *n* (*show*) comédie musicale

musical instrument *n* instrument *m* de musique

music centre *n* chaîne compacte

musician [mjuː'zɪʃən] *n* musicien/ne

Muslim ['mʌzlɪm] *adj, n* musulman/e

muslin ['mʌzlɪn] *n* mousseline *f*

mussel ['mʌsl] *n* moule *f*

must [mʌst] *aux vb* (*obligation*): **I must do it** je dois le faire, il faut que je le fasse; (*probability*): **he must be there by now** il doit y être maintenant, il y est probablement maintenant; **I must have made a mistake** j'ai dû me tromper ♦ *n* nécessité *f*, impératif *m*; **it's a must** c'est indispensable

mustache ['mʌstæʃ] *n* (*US*) = **moustache**

mustard ['mʌstəd] *n* moutarde *f*

muster ['mʌstə*] *vt* rassembler; (*also:* **muster up:** *strength, courage*) rassembler

mustn't ['mʌsnt] = **must not**

mute [mjuːt] *adj, n* muet/te

muted ['mjuːtɪd] *adj* (*noise*) sourd(e), assourdi(e); (*criticism*) voilé(e); (*MUS*) en sourdine; (: *trumpet*) bouché(e)

mutiny ['mjuːtɪnɪ] *n* mutinerie *f* ♦ *vi* se mutiner

mutter ['mʌtə*] *vt, vi* marmonner, marmotter

mutton ['mʌtn] *n* mouton *m*

mutual ['mjuːtʃuəl] *adj* mutuel(le), réciproque

mutually ['mjuːtʃuəlɪ] *adv* mutuellement, réciproquement

muzzle ['mʌzl] *n* museau *m*; (*protective device*) muselière *f*; (*of gun*) gueule *f* ♦ *vt* museler

my [maɪ] *adj* mon(ma), mes *pl*

myself [maɪ'self] *pron* (*reflexive*) me; (*emphatic*) moi-même; (*after prep*) moi

mysterious [mɪs'tɪərɪəs] *adj* mystérieux(euse)

mystery ['mɪstərɪ] *n* mystère *m*

mystify ['mɪstɪfaɪ] *vt* mystifier; (*puzzle*) ébahir

myth [mɪθ] *n* mythe *m*

mythology [mɪ'θɔlədʒɪ] *n* mythologie *f*

— *N n* —

n/a *abbr* (= *not applicable*) n.a.; (*COMM etc*) = *no account*

naff [næf] (*BRIT inf*) *adj* nul(le)

nag [næg] *vt* (*person*) être toujours après, reprendre sans arrêt ♦ *n* (*pej: horse*) canasson *m*; (*person*): **she's an awful nag** elle est constamment après lui (*or* eux *etc*), elle est terriblement casse-pieds

nagging ['nægɪŋ] *adj* (*doubt, pain*) persistant(e) ♦ *n* remarques continuelles

nail [neɪl] *n* (*human*) ongle *m*; (*metal*) clou *m* ♦ *vt* clouer; **to nail sb down to a date/price** contraindre qn à accepter *or* donner une date/un prix; **to pay cash on the nail** (*BRIT*) payer rubis sur l'ongle

nailbrush ['neɪlbrʌʃ] *n* brosse *f* à ongles

nailfile ['neɪlfaɪl] *n* lime *f* à ongles

nail polish *n* vernis *m* à ongles

nail polish remover *n* dissolvant *m*

nail scissors *npl* ciseaux *mpl* à ongles

nail varnish *n* (*BRIT*) = **nail polish**

naïve [naɪ'iːv] *adj* naïf(ïve)

naked ['neɪkɪd] *adj* nu(e); **with the naked eye** à l'œil nu

name [neɪm] *n* nom *m*; (*reputation*) réputation *f* ♦ *vt* nommer; citer; (*price, date*) fixer, donner; **by**

name par son nom; de nom; **in the name of** au nom de; **what's your name?** quel est votre nom?; **my name is Peter** je m'appelle Peter; **to take sb's name and address** relever l'identité de qn or les nom et adresse de qn; **to make a name for o.s.** se faire un nom; **to get (o.s.) a bad name** se faire une mauvaise réputation; **to call sb names** traiter qn de tous les noms

nameless ['neimlis] *adj* sans nom; (*witness, contributor*) anonyme

namely ['neimli] *adv* à savoir

namesake ['neimseik] *n* homonyme *m*

nanny ['næni] *n* bonne *f* d'enfants

nap [næp] *n* (*sleep*) (petit) somme ♦ *vi*: **to be caught napping** être pris(e) à l'improviste *or* en défaut

nape [neip] *n*: **nape of the neck** nuque *f*

napkin ['næpkin] *n* serviette *f* (de table)

nappy ['næpi] *n* (*BRIT*) couche *f gen pl*

nappy rash *n*: **to have nappy rash** avoir les fesses rouges

narcissus, *pl* **narcissi** [nɑːˈsɪsəs, -saɪ] *n* narcisse *m*

narcotic [nɑːˈkɔtɪk] *n* (*MED*) narcotique *m*; **narcotics** *npl* (*drugs*) stupéfiants *mpl*

narrative ['nærətɪv] *n* récit *m* ♦ *adj* narratif(ive)

narrow ['nærəu] *adj* étroit(e); (*fig*) restreint(e), limité(e) ♦ *vi* devenir plus étroit, se rétrécir; **to have a narrow escape** l'échapper belle; **to narrow sth down to** réduire qch à

narrowly ['nærəuli] *adv*: **he narrowly missed injury/the tree** il a failli se blesser/rentrer dans l'arbre; **he only narrowly missed the target** il a manqué la cible de peu *or* de justesse

narrow-minded [nærəuˈmaɪndɪd] *adj* à l'esprit étroit, borné(e)

nasty ['nɑːstɪ] *adj* (*person*) méchant(e); très désagréable; (*smell*) dégoûtant(e); (*wound, situation*) mauvais(e), vilain(e); (*weather*) affreux(euse); **to turn nasty** (*situation*) mal tourner; (*weather*) se gâter; (*person*) devenir méchant; **it's a nasty business** c'est une sale affaire

nation ['neɪʃən] *n* nation *f*

national ['næʃənl] *adj* national(e) ♦ *n* (*abroad*) ressortissant/e; (*when home*) national/e

national anthem *n* hymne national

national dress *n* costume national

National Health Service (NHS) *n* (*BRIT*) service national de santé, ≃ Sécurité Sociale

National Insurance *n* (*BRIT*) ≃ Sécurité Sociale

nationalism ['næʃnəlɪzəm] *n* nationalisme *m*

nationalist ['næʃnəlɪst] *adj, n* nationaliste *m/f*

nationality [næʃəˈnælɪtɪ] *n* nationalité *f*

nationalize ['næʃnəlaɪz] *vt* nationaliser

nationally ['næʃnəlɪ] *adv* du point de vue national; dans le pays entier

national park *n* parc national

National Trust *n* (*BRIT*) ≃ Caisse *f* nationale des monuments historiques et des sites; *voir encadré*

NATIONAL TRUST

Le **National Trust** est un organisme indépendant, à but non lucratif, dont la mission est de protéger et de mettre en valeur les monuments et les sites britanniques en raison de leur intérêt historique ou de leur beauté naturelle.

---

nationwide ['neɪʃənwaɪd] *adj* s'étendant à l'ensemble du pays; (*problem*) à l'échelle du pays entier ♦ *adv* à travers *or* dans tout le pays

native ['neɪtɪv] *n* habitant/e du pays, autochtone *m/f*; (*in colonies*) indigène *m/f* ♦ *adj* du pays, indigène; (*country*) natal(e); (*language*) maternel(le); (*ability*) inné(e); **a native of Russia** une personne originaire de Russie; **a native speaker of French** une personne de langue maternelle française

Native American *n* Indien/ne d'Amérique

native language *n* langue maternelle

NATO ['neɪtəu] *n abbr* (= *North Atlantic Treaty Organization*) OTAN *f*

natural ['nætʃrəl] *adj* naturel(le); **to die of natural causes** mourir d'une mort naturelle

natural gas *n* gaz naturel

naturalist ['nætʃrəlɪst] *n* naturaliste *m/f*

naturally ['nætʃrəlɪ] *adv* naturellement

nature ['neɪtʃə*] *n* nature *f*; **by nature** par tempérament, de nature; **documents of a confidential nature** documents à caractère confidentiel

naught [nɔːt] *n* = **nought**

naughty ['nɔːtɪ] *adj* (*child*) vilain(e), pas sage; (*story, film*) grivois(e)

nausea ['nɔːsɪə] *n* nausée *f*

naval ['neɪvl] *adj* naval(e)

naval officer *n* officier *m* de marine

nave [neiv] *n* nef *f*

navel ['neɪvl] *n* nombril *m*

navigate ['nævɪgeɪt] *vt* diriger, piloter ♦ *vi* naviguer; (*AUT*) indiquer la route à suivre

navigation [nævɪˈgeɪʃən] *n* navigation *f*

navvy ['nævɪ] *n* (*BRIT*) terrassier *m*

navy ['neɪvɪ] *n* marine *f*; **Department of the Navy** (*US*) ministère *m* de la Marine

navy(-blue) ['neɪvɪ'bluː] *adj* bleu marine *inv*

Nazi ['nɑːtsɪ] *adj* nazi(e) ♦ *n* Nazi/e

NB *abbr* (= *nota bene*) NB; (*Canada*) = *New Brunswick*

near [nɪə*] *adj* proche ♦ *adv* près ♦ *prep* (*also*: **near to**) près de ♦ *vt* approcher de; **near here/ there** près d'ici/non loin de là; **£25,000 or nearest offer** (*BRIT*) 25 000 livres à débattre; **in the near future** dans un proche avenir; **to come near** *vi* s'approcher

nearby [ˈnɪəˈbaɪ] *adj* proche ♦ *adv* tout près, à proximité

nearly [ˈnɪəlɪ] *adv* presque; **I nearly fell** j'ai failli tomber; **it's not nearly big enough** ce n'est vraiment pas assez grand, c'est loin d'être assez grand

near miss *n* collision évitée de justesse; *(when aiming)* coup manqué de peu *or* de justesse

nearside [ˈnɪəsaɪd] *(AUT)* *n* *(right-hand drive)* côté *m* gauche; *(left-hand drive)* côté droit ♦ *adj* de gauche; de droite

near-sighted [nɪəˈsaɪtɪd] *adj* myope

neat [niːt] *adj* *(person, work)* soigné(e); *(room etc)* bien tenu(e) *or* rangé(e); *(solution)* habile; *(spirits)* pur(e); **I drink it neat** je le bois sec *or* sans eau

neatly [ˈniːtlɪ] *adv* avec soin *or* ordre; habilement

necessarily [ˈnɛsɪsrɪlɪ] *adv* nécessairement; **not necessarily** pas nécessairement *or* forcément

necessary [ˈnɛsɪsrɪ] *adj* nécessaire; **if necessary** si besoin est, le cas échéant

necessity [nɪˈsɛsɪtɪ] *n* nécessité *f*; chose nécessaire *or* essentielle; **in case of necessity** en cas d'urgence

neck [nɛk] *n* cou *m*; *(of horse, garment)* encolure *f*; *(of bottle)* goulot *m* ♦ *vi* *(col)* se peloter; **neck and neck** à égalité; **to stick one's neck out** *(col)* se mouiller

necklace [ˈnɛklɪs] *n* collier *m*

neckline [ˈnɛklaɪn] *n* encolure *f*

necktie [ˈnɛktaɪ] *n* *(esp US)* cravate *f*

need [niːd] *n* besoin *m* ♦ *vt* avoir besoin de; **to need to do** devoir faire; avoir besoin de faire; **you don't need to go** vous n'avez pas besoin *or* vous n'êtes pas obligé de partir; **a signature is needed** il faut une signature; **to be in need of** *or* **have need of** avoir besoin de; **£10 will meet my immediate needs** 10 livres suffiront pour mes besoins immédiats; **in case of need** en cas de besoin, au besoin; **there's no need to do ...** il n'y a pas lieu de faire ..., il n'est pas nécessaire de faire ...; **there's no need for that** ce n'est pas la peine, cela n'est pas nécessaire

needle [ˈniːdl] *n* aiguille *f*; *(on record player)* saphir *m* ♦ *vt* *(col)* asticoter, tourmenter

needless [ˈniːdlɪs] *adj* inutile; **needless to say, ...** inutile de dire que ...

needlework [ˈniːdlwɜːk] *n* *(activity)* travaux *mpl* d'aiguille; *(object)* ouvrage *m*

needn't [ˈniːdnt] = **need not**

needy [ˈniːdɪ] *adj* nécessiteux(euse)

negative [ˈnɛɡətɪv] *n* *(PHOT, ELEC)* négatif *m*; *(LING)* terme *m* de négation ♦ *adj* négatif(ive); **to answer in the negative** répondre par la négative

neglect [nɪˈɡlɛkt] *vt* négliger ♦ *n* *(of person, duty, garden)* le fait de négliger; **(state of) neglect** abandon *m*; **to neglect to do sth** négliger *or* omettre de faire qch

neglected [nɪˈɡlɛktɪd] *adj* négligé(e), à l'abandon

negligee [ˈnɛɡlɪʒeɪ] *n* déshabillé *m*

negotiate [nɪˈɡəʊʃɪeɪt] *vi* négocier ♦ *vt* *(COMM)* négocier; *(obstacle)* franchir, négocier; *(bend in road)* négocier; **to negotiate with sb for sth** négocier avec qn en vue d'obtenir qch

negotiation [nɪɡəʊʃɪˈeɪʃən] *n* négociation *f*, pourparlers *mpl*; **to enter into negotiations with sb** engager des négociations avec qn

neigh [neɪ] *vi* hennir

neighbour, *(US)* **neighbor** [ˈneɪbə*] *n* voisin/e

neighbo(u)rhood [ˈneɪbəhud] *n* quartier *m*; voisinage *m*

neighbo(u)ring [ˈneɪbərɪŋ] *adj* voisin(e), avoisinant(e)

neighbo(u)rly [ˈneɪbəlɪ] *adj* obligeant(e); *(relations)* de bon voisinage

neither [ˈnaɪðə*] *adj, pron* aucun(e) (des deux), ni l'un(e) ni l'autre ♦ *conj*: **I didn't move and neither did Claude** je n'ai pas bougé, (et) Claude non plus ♦ *adv*: **neither good nor bad** ni bon ni mauvais; **..., neither did I refuse** ..., (et *or* mais) je n'ai pas non plus refusé

neon [ˈniːɔn] *n* néon *m*

neon light *n* lampe *f* au néon

nephew [ˈnɛvjuː] *n* neveu *m*

nerve [nɜːv] *n* nerf *m*; *(bravery)* sang-froid *m*, courage *m*; *(cheek)* toupet *m*; **he gets on my nerves** il m'énerve; **to have a fit of nerves** avoir le trac; **to lose one's nerve** *(self-confidence)* perdre son sang-froid

nerve-racking [ˈnɜːvrækɪŋ] *adj* angoissant(e)

nervous [ˈnɜːvəs] *adj* nerveux(euse); *(apprehensive)* inquiet(ète), plein(e) d'appréhension

nervous breakdown *n* dépression nerveuse

nest [nɛst] *n* nid *m* ♦ *vi* (se) nicher, faire son nid; **nest of tables** table *f* gigogne

nest egg *n* *(fig)* bas *m* de laine, magot *m*

nestle [ˈnɛsl] *vi* se blottir

net [nɛt] *n* filet *m* ♦ *adj* net(te) ♦ *vt* *(fish etc)* prendre au filet; *(money: subj: person)* toucher; *(: deal, sale)* rapporter; **net of tax** net d'impôt; **he earns £10,000 net per year** il gagne 10 000 livres net par an

netball [ˈnɛtbɔːl] *n* netball *m*

Netherlands [ˈnɛðələndz] *npl*: **the Netherlands** les Pays-Bas *mpl*

nett [nɛt] *adj* = **net**

netting [ˈnɛtɪŋ] *n* *(for fence etc)* treillis *m*, grillage *m*; *(fabric)* voile *m*

nettle [ˈnɛtl] *n* ortie *f*

network [ˈnɛtwɜːk] *n* réseau *m* ♦ *vt* *(RADIO, TV)* diffuser sur l'ensemble du réseau; *(computers)* interconnecter; **there's no network coverage** il n'y a pas de (couverture) réseau

neurotic [njuəˈrɔtɪk] *adj, n* névrosé/e

neuter [ˈnjuːtə*] *adj, n* neutre *m* ♦ *vt* *(cat etc)* châtrer, couper

neutral ['nju:trəl] *adj* neutre ◆ *n* (*AUT*) point mort

neutralize ['nju:trəlaɪz] *vt* neutraliser

never ['nevə*] *adv* (ne …) jamais; **never again** plus jamais; **never in my life** jamais de ma vie; *see also* **mind**

never-ending [nevər'endɪŋ] *adj* interminable

nevertheless [nevəðə'les] *adv* néanmoins, malgré tout

new [nju:] *adj* nouveau(nouvelle); (*brand new*) neuf(neuve); **as good as new** comme neuf

New Age *n* New Age *m*

newborn ['nju:bɔ:n] *adj* nouveau-né(e)

newcomer ['nju:kʌmə*] *n* nouveau venu/nouvelle venue

new-fangled ['nju:fæŋgld] *adj* (*pej*) ultramoderne (et farfelu(e))

new-found ['nju:faund] *adj* de fraîche date; (*friend*) nouveau(nouvelle)

newly ['nju:lɪ] *adv* nouvellement, récemment

newly-weds ['nju:lɪwedz] *npl* jeunes mariés *mpl*

news [nju:z] *n* nouvelle(s) *f(pl)*; (*RADIO, TV*) informations *fpl*; **a piece of news** une nouvelle; **good/bad news** bonne/mauvaise nouvelle; **financial news** (*PRESS, RADIO, TV*) page financière

news agency *n* agence *f* de presse

newsagent ['nju:zeɪdʒənt] *n* (*BRIT*) marchand *m* de journaux

newscaster ['nju:zkɑ:stə*] *n* (*RADIO, TV*) présentateur/trice

news flash *n* flash *m* d'information

newsletter ['nju:zletə*] *n* bulletin *m*

newspaper ['nju:zpeɪpə*] *n* journal *m*; **daily newspaper** quotidien *m*; **weekly newspaper** hebdomadaire *m*

newsprint ['nju:zprɪnt] *n* papier *m* (de) journal

newsreader ['nju:zri:də*] *n* = **newscaster**

newsreel ['nju:zri:l] *n* actualités (filmées)

news stand *n* kiosque *m* à journaux

newt [nju:t] *n* triton *m*

New Year *n* Nouvel An; **Happy New Year!** Bonne Année!; **to wish sb a happy New Year** souhaiter la Bonne Année à qn

New Year's Day *n* le jour de l'An

New Year's Eve *n* la Saint-Sylvestre

New Zealand [-'zi:lənd] *n* Nouvelle-Zélande *f* ◆ *adj* néo-zélandais(e)

New Zealander [-'zi:ləndə*] *n* Néo-Zélandais/e

next [nekst] *adj* (*seat, room*) voisin(e), d'à côté; (*meeting, bus stop*) suivant(e); prochain(e) ◆ *adv* la fois suivante; la prochaine fois; (*afterwards*) ensuite; **next to** *prep* à côté de; **next to nothing** presque rien; **next time** *adv* la prochaine fois; **the next day** le lendemain, le jour suivant *or* d'après; **next week** la semaine prochaine; **the next week** la semaine suivante; **next year** l'année prochaine; **"turn to the next page"** "voir page suivante"; **who's next?** c'est à qui?; **the week after next** dans deux

semaines; **when do we meet next?** quand nous revoyons-nous?

next door *adv* à côté

next-of-kin ['nekstəv'kɪn] *n* parent *m* le plus proche

NHS *n abbr* (*BRIT*) = **National Health Service**

nib [nɪb] *n* (*of pen*) (bec *m* de) plume *f*

nibble ['nɪbl] *vt* grignoter

nice [naɪs] *adj* (*holiday, trip, taste*) agréable; (*flat, picture*) joli(e); (*person*) gentil(le); (*distinction, point*) subtil(e)

nicely ['naɪslɪ] *adv* agréablement; joliment; gentiment; subtilement; **that will do nicely** ce sera parfait

niceties ['naɪsɪtɪz] *npl* subtilités *fpl*

nick [nɪk] *n* encoche *f*; (*BRIT col*): **in good nick** en bon état ◆ *vt* (*cut*): **to nick o.s.** se couper; (*col: steal*) faucher, piquer; (*: BRIT: arrest*) choper, pincer; **in the nick of time** juste à temps

nickel ['nɪkl] *n* nickel *m*; (*US*) pièce *f* de 5 cents

nickname ['nɪkneɪm] *n* surnom *m* ◆ *vt* surnommer

nicotine patch ['nɪkəti:n-] *n* timbre *m* antitabac, patch *m*

niece [ni:s] *n* nièce *f*

Nigeria [naɪ'dʒɪərɪə] *n* Nigéria *m or f*

niggling ['nɪglɪŋ] *adj* tatillon(ne); (*detail*) insignifiant(e); (*doubt, pain*) persistant(e)

night [naɪt] *n* nuit *f*; (*evening*) soir *m*; **at night** la nuit; **by night** de nuit; **in the night, during the night** pendant la nuit; **the night before last** avant-hier soir

nightcap ['naɪtkæp] *n* boisson prise avant le coucher

night club *n* boîte *f* de nuit

nightdress ['naɪtdres] *n* chemise *f* de nuit

nightfall ['naɪtfɔ:l] *n* tombée *f* de la nuit

nightie ['naɪtɪ] *n* chemise *f* de nuit

nightingale ['naɪtɪŋgeɪl] *n* rossignol *m*

nightlife ['naɪtlaɪf] *n* vie *f* nocturne

nightly ['naɪtlɪ] *adj* de chaque nuit *or* soir; (*by night*) nocturne ◆ *adv* chaque nuit *or* soir; nuitamment

nightmare ['naɪtmeə*] *n* cauchemar *m*

night porter *n* gardien *m* de nuit, concierge *m* de service la nuit

night school *n* cours *mpl* du soir

nightshift ['naɪtʃɪft] *n* équipe *f* de nuit

night-time ['naɪttaɪm] *n* nuit *f*

night watchman *n* veilleur *m* de nuit; poste *m* de nuit

nil [nɪl] *n* rien *m*; (*BRIT SPORT*) zéro *m*

Nile [naɪl] *n*: **the Nile** le Nil

nimble ['nɪmbl] *adj* agile

nine [naɪn] *num* neuf

nineteen [naɪn'ti:n] *num* dix-neuf

ninety ['naɪntɪ] *num* quatre-vingt-dix

ninth [naɪnθ] *num* neuvième

nip [nɪp] *vt* pincer ♦ *vi* (*BRIT col*): **to nip out/down/up** sortir/descendre/monter en vitesse ♦ *n* pincement *m*; (*drink*) petit verre; **to nip into a shop** faire un saut dans un magasin

nipple ['nɪpl] *n* (*ANAT*) mamelon *m*, bout *m* du sein

nitrogen ['naɪtrədʒən] *n* azote *m*

⌐ KEYWORD ¬

no [nəu] (*pl* **noes**) *adv* (*opposite of "yes"*) non; **are you coming? – no (I'm not)** est-ce que vous venez? – non; **would you like some more? – no thank you** vous en voulez encore? – non merci ♦ *adj* (*not any*) pas de, aucun(e) (*used with "ne"*); **I have no money/books** je n'ai pas d'argent/de livres; **no student would have done it** aucun étudiant ne l'aurait fait; **"no smoking"** "défense de fumer"; **"no dogs"** "les chiens ne sont pas admis"

♦ *n* non *m*; **I won't take no for an answer** il n'est pas question de refuser

---

nobility [nəu'bɪlɪtɪ] *n* noblesse *f*

noble ['nəubl] *adj* noble

nobody ['nəubədɪ] *pron* personne (*with negative*)

nod [nɔd] *vi* faire un signe de (la) tête (*affirmatif ou amical*); (*sleep*) somnoler ♦ *vt*: **to nod one's head** faire un signe de (la) tête; (*in agreement*) faire signe que oui ♦ *n* signe *m* de (la) tête; **they nodded their agreement** ils ont acquiescé d'un signe de la tête

▶ **nod off** *vi* s'assoupir

noise [nɔɪz] *n* bruit *m*

noisy ['nɔɪzɪ] *adj* bruyant(e)

nominal ['nɔmɪnl] *adj* (*rent, fee*) symbolique; (*value*) nominal(e)

nominate ['nɔmɪneɪt] *vt* (*propose*) proposer; (*elect*) nommer

nominee [nɔmɪ'niː] *n* candidat agréé; personne nommée

non- [nɔn] *prefix* non-

nonalcoholic [nɔnælkə'hɔlɪk] *adj* non-alcoolisé(e)

noncommittal [nɔnkə'mɪtl] *adj* évasif(ive)

nondescript ['nɔndɪskrɪpt] *adj* quelconque, indéfinissable

none [nʌn] *pron* aucun(e); **none of you** aucun d'entre vous, personne parmi vous; **I have none** je n'en ai pas; **I have none left** je n'en ai plus; **none at all** (*not one*) aucun(e); **how much milk? – none at all** combien de lait? – pas du tout; **he's none the worse for it** il ne s'en porte pas plus mal

nonentity [nɔ'nentɪtɪ] *n* personne insignifiante

nonetheless ['nʌnðə'les] *adv* néanmoins

nonexistent [nɔnɪg'zɪstənt] *adj* inexistant(e)

nonfiction [nɔn'fɪkʃən] *n* littérature *f* non-romanesque

nonplussed [nɔn'plʌst] *adj* perplexe

nonsense ['nɔnsəns] *n* absurdités *fpl*, idioties *fpl*; **nonsense!** ne dites pas d'idioties!; **it is nonsense to say that …** il est absurde de dire que …

nonsmoker ['nɔn'sməukə*] *n* non-fumeur *m*

nonsmoking ['nɔn'sməukɪŋ] *adj* non-fumeurs *inv*

nonstick ['nɔn'stɪk] *adj* qui n'attache pas

nonstop ['nɔn'stɔp] *adj* direct(e), sans arrêt (*or* escale) ♦ *adv* sans arrêt

noodles ['nuːdlz] *npl* nouilles *fpl*

nook [nuk] *n*: **nooks and crannies** recoins *mpl*

noon [nuːn] *n* midi *m*

no one ['nəuwʌn] *pron* = **nobody**

noose [nuːs] *n* nœud coulant; (*hangman's*) corde *f*

nor [nɔː*] *conj* = **neither** ♦ *adv see* **neither**

norm [nɔːm] *n* norme *f*

normal ['nɔːml] *adj* normal(e) ♦ *n*: **to return to normal** redevenir normal(e)

normally ['nɔːməlɪ] *adv* normalement

Normandy ['nɔːmandɪ] *n* Normandie *f*

north [nɔːθ] *n* nord *m* ♦ *adj* du nord, nord *inv* ♦ *adv* au *or* vers le nord

North America *n* Amérique *f* du Nord

north-east [nɔːθ'iːst] *n* nord-est *m*

northerly ['nɔːðəlɪ] *adj* (*wind, direction*) du nord

northern ['nɔːðən] *adj* du nord, septentrional(e)

Northern Ireland *n* Irlande *f* du Nord

North Pole *n*: **the North Pole** le pôle Nord

North Sea *n*: **the North Sea** la mer du Nord

northward(s) ['nɔːθwəd(z)] *adv* vers le nord

north-west [nɔːθ'west] *n* nord-ouest *m*

Norway ['nɔːweɪ] *n* Norvège *f*

Norwegian [nɔː'wiːdʒən] *adj* norvégien(ne) ♦ *n* Norvégien(ne; (*LING*) norvégien *m*

nose [nəuz] *n* nez *m*; (*fig*) flair *m* ♦ *vi* (*also:* **nose one's way**) avancer précautionneusement; **to pay through the nose (for sth)** (*col*) payer un prix excessif (pour qch)

▶ **nose about, nose around** *vi* fouiner *or* fureter (partout)

nosebleed ['nəuzbliːd] *n* saignement *m* de nez

nose-dive ['nəuzdaɪv] *n* (*descente f en*) piqué *m*

nosey ['nəuzɪ] *adj* curieux(euse)

nostalgia [nɔs'tældʒɪə] *n* nostalgie *f*

nostril ['nɔstrɪl] *n* narine *f*; (*of horse*) naseau *m*

nosy ['nəuzɪ] *adj* = **nosey**

not [nɔt] *adv* (ne …) pas; **I hope not** j'espère que non; **not at all** pas du tout; (*after thanks*) de rien; **you must not** *or* **mustn't do this** tu ne dois pas faire ça; **he isn't …** il n'est pas …

notably ['nəutəblɪ] *adv* en particulier

notary ['nəutərɪ] *n* (*also:* **notary public**) notaire *m*

notch [nɔtʃ] *n* encoche *f*

▶ **notch up** *vt* (*score*) marquer; (*victory*) remporter

note [nəut] *n* note *f*; (*letter*) mot *m*; (*banknote*) billet *m* ♦ *vt* (*also:* **note down**) noter; (*notice*)

constater; **just a quick note to let you know ...**
juste un mot pour vous dire ...; **to take notes**
prendre des notes; **to compare notes** (fig) échanger des (or leurs etc) impressions; **to take note of**
prendre note de; **a person of note** une personne
éminente

notebook ['nəutbuk] n carnet m; (for shorthand
etc) bloc-notes m

noted ['nəutɪd] adj réputé(e)

notepad ['nəutpæd] n bloc-notes m

notepaper ['nəutpeɪpə*] n papier m à lettres

nothing ['nʌθɪŋ] n rien m; **he does nothing** il ne
fait rien; **nothing new** rien de nouveau; **for
nothing** (free) pour rien, gratuitement; **nothing at
all** rien du tout

notice ['nəutɪs] n avis m; (of leaving) congé m; (BRIT:
review: of play etc) critique f, compte rendu m ◆ vt
remarquer, s'apercevoir de; **without notice** sans
préavis; **advance notice** préavis m; **to give sb
notice of sth** notifier qn de qch; **at short notice**
dans un délai très court; **until further notice** jusqu'à nouvel ordre; **to give notice, hand in one's
notice** (subj: employee) donner sa démission,
démissionner; **to take notice of** prêter attention à;
to bring sth to sb's notice porter qch à la connaissance de qn; **it has come to my notice that ...** on
m'a signalé que ...; **to escape** or **avoid notice**
(essayer de) passer inaperçu or ne pas se faire
remarquer

noticeable ['nəutɪsəbl] adj visible

notice board n (BRIT) panneau m d'affichage

notify ['nəutɪfaɪ] vt: **to notify sth to sb** notifier
qch à qn; **to notify sb of sth** avertir qn de qch

notion ['nəuʃən] n idée f; (concept) notion f

notorious [nəu'tɔ:rɪəs] adj notoire (souvent en
mal)

nought [nɔ:t] n zéro m

noun [naun] n nom m

nourish ['nʌrɪʃ] vt nourrir

nourishing ['nʌrɪʃɪŋ] adj nourrissant(e)

nourishment ['nʌrɪʃmənt] n nourriture f

novel ['nɔvl] n roman m ◆ adj nouveau(nouvelle),
original(e)

novelist ['nɔvəlɪst] n romancier m

novelty ['nɔvəltɪ] n nouveauté f

November [nəu'vɛmbə*] n novembre m; for
phrases see also **July**

now [nau] adv maintenant ◆ conj: **now (that)**
maintenant (que); **right now** tout de suite; **by now**
à l'heure qu'il est; **just now: that's the fashion just
now** c'est la mode en ce moment or maintenant; **I
saw her just now** je viens de la voir, je l'ai vue à
l'instant; **I'll read it just now** je vais le lire à l'instant
or dès maintenant; **now and then, now and again**
de temps en temps; **from now on** dorénavant; **in 3
days from now** dans or d'ici trois jours; **between
now and Monday** d'ici (à) lundi; **that's all for now**
c'est tout pour l'instant

nowadays ['nauədeɪz] adv de nos jours

nowhere ['nəuwɛə*] adv nulle part; **nowhere
else** nulle part ailleurs

nozzle ['nɔzl] n (of hose) jet m, lance f

nuclear ['nju:klɪə*] adj nucléaire

nucleus, pl **nuclei** ['nju:klɪəs, 'nju:klɪaɪ] n noyau m

nude [nju:d] adj nu(e) ◆ n (ART) nu m; **in the nude**
(tout(e)) nu(e)

nudge [nʌdʒ] vt donner un (petit) coup de coude
à

nudist ['nju:dɪst] n nudiste m/f

nuisance ['nju:sns] n: **it's a nuisance** c'est (très)
ennuyeux or gênant; **he's a nuisance** il est assom-
mant or casse-pieds; **what a nuisance!** quelle
barbe!

null [nʌl] adj: **null and void** nul(le) et non avenu(e)

numb [nʌm] adj engourdi(e) ◆ vt engourdir;
numb with cold engourdi(e) par le froid, transi(e)
(de froid); **numb with fear** transi de peur, paraly-
sé(e) par la peur

number ['nʌmbə*] n nombre m; (numeral) chiffre
m; (of house, car, telephone, newspaper) numéro m
◆ vt numéroter; (include) compter; **a number of** un
certain nombre de; **to be numbered among**
compter parmi; **the staff numbers 20** le nombre
d'employés s'élève à or est de 20; **wrong number**
(TEL) mauvais numéro

number plate n (BRIT AUT) plaque f minéralogique or d'immatriculation

numeral ['nju:mərəl] n chiffre m

numerate ['nju:mərɪt] adj (BRIT): **to be numerate**
avoir des notions d'arithmétique

numerical [nju:'mɛrɪkl] adj numérique

numerous ['nju:mərəs] adj nombreux(euse)

nun [nʌn] n religieuse f, sœur f

nurse [nə:s] n infirmière f; (also: **nursemaid**)
bonne f d'enfants ◆ vt (patient, cold) soigner;
(baby: BRIT) bercer (dans ses bras); (: US) allaiter, nourrir; (hope) nourrir

nursery ['nə:sərɪ] n (room) nursery f; (institution)
pouponnière f; (for plants) pépinière f

nursery rhyme n comptine f, chansonnette f
pour enfants

nursery school n école maternelle

nursery slope n (BRIT SKI) piste f pour débutants

nursing ['nə:sɪŋ] n (profession) profession f d'infirmière ◆ adj (mother) qui allaite

nursing home n clinique f; maison f de convalescence

nut [nʌt] n (of metal) écrou m; (fruit) noix f, noisette f,
cacahuète f (terme générique en anglais) ◆ adj
(chocolate etc) aux noisettes; **he's nuts** (col) il est
dingue

nutcrackers ['nʌtkrækəz] npl casse-noix m inv,
casse-noisette(s) m

nutmeg ['nʌtmɛg] n (noix f) muscade f

nutritious [nju:'trɪʃəs] adj nutritif(ive), nourris-
sant(e)

nutshell ['nʌtʃel] n coquille f de noix; **in a nutshell** en un mot

nutter ['nʌtə*] (BRIT inf) n: **he's a complete nutter** il est complètement cinglé

nylon ['naɪlɒn] n nylon m ♦ adj de or en nylon; **nylons** npl bas mpl nylon

— *O o* —

oak [əʊk] n chêne m ♦ cpd de or en (bois de) chêne

OAP n abbr (BRIT) = **old age pensioner**

oar [ɔ:*] n aviron m, rame f; **to put** or **shove one's oar in** (fig: col) mettre son grain de sel

oasis, pl **oases** [əʊ'eɪsɪs, əʊ'eɪsi:z] n oasis f

oath [əʊθ] n serment m; (swear word) juron m; **to take the oath** prêter serment; **on** (BRIT) or **under oath** sous serment; assermenté(e)

oatmeal ['əʊtmi:l] n flocons mpl d'avoine

oats [əʊts] n avoine f

obedience [ə'bi:dɪəns] n obéissance f; **in obedience to** conformément à

obedient [ə'bi:dɪənt] adj obéissant(e); **to be obedient to sb/sth** obéir à qn/qch

obey [ə'beɪ] vt obéir à; (instructions, regulations) se conformer à ♦ vi obéir

obituary [ə'bɪtjuərɪ] n nécrologie f

object n ['ɒbdʒɪkt] vt (block) boucher, obstruer; objet; (LING) complément m d'objet ♦ vi [əb'dʒɛkt]: **to object to** (attitude) désapprouver; (proposal) protester contre, élever une objection contre; **I object!** je proteste!; **he objected that ...** il a fait valoir or a objecté que ...; **do you object to my smoking?** est-ce que cela vous gêne si je fume?; **what's the object of doing that?** quel est l'intérêt de faire cela?; **money is no object** l'argent n'est pas un problème

objection [əb'dʒɛkʃən] n objection f; (drawback) inconvénient m; **if you have no objection** si vous n'y voyez pas d'inconvénient; **to make** or **raise an objection** élever une objection

objectionable [əb'dʒɛkʃənəbl] adj très désagréable; choquant(e)

objective [əb'dʒɛktɪv] n objectif m ♦ adj objectif(ive)

obligation [ɒblɪ'geɪʃən] n obligation f, devoir m; (debt) dette f (de reconnaissance); **"without obligation"** "sans engagement"

obligatory [ə'blɪgətərɪ] adj obligatoire

oblige [ə'blaɪdʒ] vt (force): **to oblige sb to do** obliger or forcer qn à faire; (do a favour) rendre service à, obliger; **to be obliged to sb for sth** être obligé(e) à qn de qch; **anything to oblige!** (col) (toujours prêt à rendre) service!

obliging [ə'blaɪdʒɪŋ] adj obligeant(e), serviable

oblique [ə'bli:k] adj oblique; (allusion) indirect(e) ♦ n (BRIT TYP): **oblique (stroke)** barre f oblique

obliterate [ə'blɪtəreɪt] vt effacer

oblivion [ə'blɪvɪən] n oubli m

oblivious [ə'blɪvɪəs] adj: **oblivious of** oublieux(euse) de

oblong ['ɒblɒŋ] adj oblong(ue) ♦ n rectangle m

obnoxious [əb'nɒkʃəs] adj odieux(euse); (smell) nauséabond(e)

oboe ['əʊbəʊ] n hautbois m

obscene [əb'si:n] adj obscène

obscure [əb'skjuə*] adj obscur(e) ♦ vt obscurcir; (hide: sun) cacher

observant [əb'zə:vnt] adj observateur(trice)

observation [ɒbzə'veɪʃən] n observation f; (by police etc) surveillance f

observatory [əb'zə:vətrɪ] n observatoire m

observe [əb'zə:v] vt observer; (remark) faire observer or remarquer

observer [əb'zə:və*] n observateur/trice

obsess [əb'sɛs] vt obséder; **to be obsessed by** or **with sb/sth** être obsédé(e) par qn/qch

obsessive [əb'sɛsɪv] adj obsédant(e)

obsolete ['ɒbsəli:t] adj dépassé(e), périmé(e)

obstacle ['ɒbstəkl] n obstacle m

obstacle race n course f d'obstacles

obstinate ['ɒbstɪnɪt] adj obstiné(e); (pain, cold) persistant(e)

obstruct [əb'strʌkt] vt (block) boucher, obstruer; (halt) arrêter; (hinder) entraver

obtain [əb'teɪn] vt obtenir ♦ vi avoir cours

obvious ['ɒbvɪəs] adj évident(e), manifeste

obviously ['ɒbvɪəslɪ] adv manifestement; (of course): **obviously, he ...** or **he obviously ...** il est bien évident qu'il ...; **obviously!** bien sûr!; **obviously not!** évidemment pas!, bien sûr que non!

occasion [ə'keɪʒən] n occasion f; (event) événement m ♦ vt occasionner, causer; **on that occasion** à cette occasion; **to rise to the occasion** se montrer à la hauteur de la situation

occasional [ə'keɪʒənl] adj pris(e) (or fait(e) etc) de temps en temps; occasionnel(le)

occasionally [ə'keɪʒənəlɪ] adv de temps en temps; **very occasionally** (assez) rarement

occupation [ɒkju'peɪʃən] n occupation f; (job) métier m, profession f; **unfit for occupation** (house) impropre à l'habitation

occupational hazard [ɒkjupeɪʃənl-] n risque m du métier

occupier ['ɒkjupaɪə*] n occupant/e

occupy ['ɒkjupaɪ] vt occuper; **to occupy o.s. with** or **by doing** s'occuper à faire; **to be occupied with sth** être occupé avec qch

occur [ə'kə:*] vi se produire; (difficulty, opportunity) se présenter; (phenomenon, error) se rencontrer; **to occur to sb** venir à l'esprit de qn

occurrence [ə'kʌrəns] *n* présence *f*, existence *f*; cas *m*, fait *m*

ocean [ˈəuʃən] *n* océan *m*; **oceans of** (*col*) des masses de

o'clock [ə'klɔk] *adv*: **it is 5 o'clock** il est 5 heures

OCR *n abbr* = **optical character reader, optical character recognition**

October [ɔk'təubə*] *n* octobre *m*; **for phrases see also July**

octopus [ˈɔktəpəs] *n* pieuvre *f*

odd [ɔd] *adj* (*strange*) bizarre, curieux(euse); (*number*) impair(e); (*left over*) qui reste, en plus; (*not of a set*) dépareillé(e); **60-odd** 60 et quelques; **at odd times** de temps en temps; **the odd one out** l'exception *f*

oddity [ˈɔdɪtɪ] *n* bizarrerie *f*; (*person*) excentrique *m/f*

odd-job man [ɔd'dʒɔb-] *n* homme *m* à tout faire

odd jobs *npl* petits travaux divers

oddly [ˈɔdlɪ] *adv* bizarrement, curieusement

oddments [ˈɔdmənts] *npl* (*BRIT COMM*) fins *fpl* de série

odds [ɔdz] *npl* (*in betting*) cote *f*; **the odds are against his coming** il y a peu de chances qu'il vienne; **it makes no odds** cela n'a pas d'importance; **to succeed against all the odds** réussir contre toute attente; **odds and ends** de petites choses; **at odds** en désaccord

odour, (*US*) **odor** [ˈəudə*] *n* odeur *f*

KEYWORD
---

of [ɔv, əv] *prep* **1** (*gen*) de; **a friend of ours** un de nos amis; **a boy of 10** un garçon de 10 ans; **that was kind of you** c'était gentil de votre part

2 (*expressing quantity, amount, dates etc*) de; **a kilo of flour** un kilo de farine; **how much of this do you need?** combien vous en faut-il?; **there were 3 of them** (*people*) ils étaient 3; (*objects*) il y en avait 3; **3 of us went** 3 d'entre nous y sont allé(e)s; **the 5th of July** le 5 juillet; **a quarter of 4** (*US*) 4 heures moins le quart

3 (*from, out of*) en, de; **a statue of marble** une statue de *or* en marbre; **made of wood** (fait) en bois

---

off [ɔf] *adj, adv* (*engine*) coupé(e); (*tap*) fermé(e); (*BRIT: food*) mauvais(e), avancé(e); (: *milk*) tourné(e); (*absent*) absent(e); (*cancelled*) annulé(e); (*removed*): **the lid was off** le couvercle était retiré *or* n'était pas mis ♦ *prep* de; sur; **to be off** (*to leave*) partir, s'en aller; **I must be off** il faut que je file; **to be off sick** être absent pour cause de maladie; **a day off** un jour de congé; **to have an off day** n'être pas en forme; **he had his coat off** il avait enlevé son manteau; **the hook is off** le crochet s'est détaché; le crochet n'est pas mis; **10% off** (*COMM*) 10% de rabais; **5 km off (the road)** à 5 km (de la route); **off**

the coast au large de la côte; **a house off the main road** une maison à l'écart de la grand-route; **it's a long way off** c'est loin (d'ici); **I'm off meat** je ne mange plus de viande; je n'aime plus la viande; **on the off chance** à tout hasard; **to be well/badly off** être bien/mal loti; (*financially*) être aisé/dans la gêne; **off and on, on and off** de temps à autre; **I'm afraid the chicken is off** (*BRIT: not available*) je regrette, il n'y a plus de poulet; **that's a bit off** (*fig: col*) c'est un peu fort

offal [ˈɔfl] *n* (*CULIN*) abats *mpl*

off-colour [ˈɔfˈkʌlə*] *adj* (*BRIT: ill*) malade, mal fichu(e); **to feel off-colour** être mal fichu

offence, (*US*) **offense** [ə'fɛns] *n* (*crime*) délit *m*, infraction *f*; **to give offence to** blesser, offenser; **to take offence at** se vexer de, s'offenser de; **to commit an offence** commettre une infraction

offend [ə'fɛnd] *vt* (*person*) offenser, blesser ♦ *vi*: **to offend against** (*law, rule*) contrevenir à, enfreindre

offender [ə'fɛndə*] *n* délinquant/e; (*against regulations*) contrevenant/e

offense [ə'fɛns] *n* (*US*) = **offence**

offensive [ə'fɛnsɪv] *adj* offensant(e), choquant(e); (*smell etc*) très déplaisant(e); (*weapon*) offensif(ive) ♦ *n* (*MIL*) offensive *f*

offer [ˈɔfə*] *n* offre *f*, proposition *f* ♦ *vt* offrir, proposer; **to make an offer for sth** faire une offre pour qch; **to offer sth to sb, offer sb sth** offrir qch à qn; **to offer to do sth** proposer de faire qch; **"on offer"** (*COMM*) "en promotion"

offering [ˈɔfərɪŋ] *n* offrande *f*

offhand [ɔf'hænd] *adj* désinvolte ♦ *adv* spontanément; **I can't tell you offhand** je ne peux pas vous le dire comme ça

office [ˈɔfɪs] *n* (*place*) bureau *m*; (*position*) charge *f*, fonction *f*; **doctor's office** (*US*) cabinet (médical); **to take office** entrer en fonctions; **through his good offices** (*fig*) grâce à ses bons offices; **Office of Fair Trading** (*BRIT*) organisme de protection contre les pratiques commerciales abusives

office automation *n* bureautique *f*

office block, (*US*) **office building** *n* immeuble *m* de bureaux

office hours *npl* heures *fpl* de bureau; (*US MED*) heures de consultation

officer [ˈɔfɪsə*] *n* (*MIL etc*) officier *m*; (*of organization*) membre *m* du bureau directeur; (*also*: **police officer**) agent *m* (de police)

office worker *n* employé/e de bureau

official [ə'fɪʃl] *adj* (*authorized*) officiel(le) ♦ *n* officiel *m*; (*civil servant*) fonctionnaire *m/f*; employé/e

officiate [ə'fɪʃɪeɪt] *vi* (*REL*) officier; **to officiate as Mayor** exercer les fonctions de maire; **to officiate at a marriage** célébrer un mariage

officious [ə'fɪʃəs] *adj* trop empressé(e)

offing [ˈɔfɪŋ] *n*: **in the offing** (*fig*) en perspective

off-licence [ˈɔflaɪsns] *n* (*BRIT: shop*) débit *m* de

vins et de spiritueux; *voir encadré*

OFF-LICENCE

Un **off-licence** est un magasin où l'on vend de l'alcool (à emporter) aux heures où les pubs sont fermés. On peut également y acheter des boissons non alcoolisées, des cigarettes, des chips, des bonbons, des chocolats etc.

---

off line *adj* (*COMPUT*) (en mode) autonome; (: *switched off*) non connecté(e)

off-peak ['ɔf'pi:k] *adj* aux heures creuses

off-putting ['ɔfputɪŋ] *adj* (*BRIT*) rébarbatif(ive); rebutant(e), peu engageant(e)

off-road vehicle ['ɔfrəud-] *n* véhicule *m* tout-terrain

off-season ['ɔf'si:zn] *adj, adv* hors-saison *inv*

offset ['ɔfset] *vt irreg* (*counteract*) contrebalancer, compenser ♦ *n* (*also*: **offset printing**) offset *m*

offshoot ['ɔfʃu:t] *n* (*fig*) ramification *f*, antenne *f*; (: *of discussion etc*) conséquence *f*

offshore [ɔf'ʃɔ:*] *adj* (*breeze*) de terre; (*island*) proche du littoral; (*fishing*) côtier(ière); **offshore oilfield** gisement *m* pétrolifère en mer

offside ['ɔf'said] *n* (*AUT*: *with right-hand drive*) côté droit; (: *with left-hand drive*) côté gauche ♦ *adj* (*AUT*) de droite; de gauche; (*SPORT*) hors jeu

offspring ['ɔfsprɪŋ] *n* progéniture *f*

offstage [ɔf'steidʒ] *adv* dans les coulisses

off-the-peg ['ɔfðə'peg], (*US*) **off-the-rack** ['ɔfðə'ræk] *adv* en prêt-à-porter

off-white ['ɔfwait] *adj* blanc cassé *inv*

Oftel ['ɔftel] *n* (*BRIT*: = *Office of Telecommunications*) *organisme qui supervise les télécommunications*

often ['ɔfn] *adv* souvent; **how often do you go?** vous y allez tous les combien?; **as often as not** la plupart du temps

Ofwat ['ɔfwɔt] *n* (*BRIT*: = *Office of Water Services*) *organisme qui surveille les activités des compagnies des eaux*

oh [əu] *excl* ô!, oh!, ah!

oil [ɔil] *n* huile *f*; (*petroleum*) pétrole *m*; (*for central heating*) mazout *m* ♦ *vt* (*machine*) graisser

oilcan ['ɔilkæn] *n* burette *f* de graissage; (*for storing*) bidon *m* à huile

oilfield ['ɔilfi:ld] *n* gisement *m* de pétrole

oil filter *n* (*AUT*) filtre *m* à huile

oil painting *n* peinture *f* à l'huile

oil refinery *n* raffinerie *f* de pétrole

oil rig *n* derrick *m*; (*at sea*) plate-forme pétrolière

oil slick *n* nappe *f* de mazout

oil tanker *n* pétrolier *m*

oil well *n* puits *m* de pétrole

oily ['ɔili] *adj* huileux(euse); (*food*) gras(se)

ointment ['ɔintmənt] *n* onguent *m*

O.K., okay ['əu'kei] (*col*) *excl* d'accord! ♦ *vt*

approuver, donner son accord à ♦ *n*: **to give sth one's O.K.** donner son accord à qch ♦ *adj* en règle; en bon état; sain et sauf; acceptable; **is it O.K.?, are you O.K.?** ça va?; **are you O.K. for money?** ça va *or* ira question argent?; **it's O.K. with** *or* **by me** ça me va, c'est d'accord en ce qui me concerne

old [əuld] *adj* vieux(vieille); (*person*) vieux, âgé(e); (*former*) ancien(ne), vieux; **how old are you?** quel âge avez-vous?; **he's 10 years old** il a 10 ans, il est âgé de 10 ans; **older brother/sister** frère/sœur aîné(e); **any old thing will do** n'importe quoi fera l'affaire

old age *n* vieillesse *f*

old age pensioner (OAP) *n* (*BRIT*) retraité/e

old-fashioned ['əuld'fæʃnd] *adj* démodé(e); (*person*) vieux jeu *inv*

olive ['ɔliv] *n* (*fruit*) olive *f*; (*tree*) olivier *m* ♦ *adj* (*also*: **olive-green**) (vert) olive *inv*

olive oil *n* huile *f* d'olive

Olympic [əu'limpik] *adj* olympique; **the Olympic Games, the Olympics** les Jeux *mpl* olympiques

omelet(te) ['ɔmlit] *n* omelette *f*; **ham/cheese omelet(te)** omelette au jambon/fromage

omen ['əumən] *n* présage *m*

ominous ['ɔminəs] *adj* menaçant(e), inquiétant(e); (*event*) de mauvais augure

omit [əu'mit] *vt* omettre; **to omit to do sth** négliger de faire qch

---

KEYWORD

on [ɔn] *prep* **1** (*indicating position*) sur; **on the table** sur la table; **on the wall** sur le *or* au mur; **on the left** à gauche; **I haven't any money on me** je n'ai pas d'argent sur moi

2 (*indicating means, method, condition etc*): **on foot** à pied; **on the train/plane** (*be*) dans le train/l'avion; (*go*) en train/avion; **on the telephone/radio/television** au téléphone/à la radio/à la télévision; **to be on drugs** se droguer; **on holiday**, (*US*) **on vacation** en vacances; **on the continent** sur le continent

3 (*referring to time*): **on Friday** vendredi; **on Fridays** le vendredi; **on June 20th** le 20 juin; **a week on Friday** vendredi en huit; **on arrival** à l'arrivée; **on seeing this** en voyant cela

4 (*about, concerning*) sur, de; **a book on Balzac/physics** un livre sur Balzac/de physique

5 (*at the expense of*): **this round is on me** c'est ma tournée

♦ *adv* **1** (*referring to dress, covering*): **to have one's coat on** avoir (mis) son manteau; **to put one's coat on** mettre son manteau; **what's she got on?** qu'est-ce qu'elle porte?; **screw the lid on tightly** vissez bien le couvercle

2 (*further, continuously*): **to walk** *etc* **on** continuer à marcher *etc*; **on and off** de temps à autre; **from that day on** depuis ce jour

♦ *adj* **1** (*in operation: machine*) en marche; (: *radio, TV, light*) allumé(e); (: *tap, gas*) ouvert(e); (: *brakes*)

mis(e); is the meeting still on? (*not cancelled*) est-ce que la réunion a bien lieu?; (*in progress*) la réunion dure-t-elle encore?; **it was well on in the evening** c'était tard dans la soirée; **when is this film on?** quand passe ce film?

2 (*col*): **that's not on!** (*not acceptable*) cela ne se fait pas!; (*not possible*) pas question!

once [wʌns] *adv* une fois; (*formerly*) autrefois ♦ *conj* une fois que; **once he had left/it was done** une fois qu'il fut parti/ que ce fut terminé; **at once** tout de suite, immédiatement; (*simultaneously*) à la fois; **all at once** *adv* tout d'un coup; **once a week** une fois par semaine; **once more** encore une fois; **I knew him once** je l'ai connu autrefois; **once and for all** une fois pour toutes; **once upon a time there was ...** il y avait une fois ..., il était une fois ...

oncoming [ˈɔnkʌmɪŋ] *adj* (*traffic*) venant en sens inverse

KEYWORD

one [wʌn] *num* un(e); **one hundred and fifty** cent cinquante; **one day** un jour

♦ *adj* **1** (*sole*) seul(e), unique; **the one book which** l'unique *or* le seul livre qui; **the one man who** le seul (homme) qui

2 (*same*) même; **they came in the one car** ils sont venus dans la même voiture

♦ *pron* **1**: **this one** celui-ci(celle-ci); **that one** celui-là(celle-là); **I've already got one/a red one** j'en ai déjà un(e)/un(e) rouge; **one by one** un(e) à *or* par un(e); **which one do you want?** lequel voulez-vous?

2: **one another** l'un(e) l'autre; **to look at one another** se regarder

3 (*impersonal*) on; **one never knows** on ne sait jamais; **to cut one's finger** se couper le doigt

4 (*phrases*): **to be one up on sb** avoir l'avantage sur qn; **to be at one (with sb)** être d'accord (avec qn)

one-day excursion [wʌndeɪ-] *n* (*US*) billet *m* d'aller-retour (valable pour la journée)

one-man [ˈwʌnˈmæn] *adj* (*business*) dirigé(e) *etc* par un seul homme

one-man band *n* homme-orchestre *m*

one-off [wʌnˈɔf] (*BRIT col*) *n* exemplaire *m* unique ♦ *adj* unique

oneself [wʌnˈself] *pron* se; (*after prep, also emphatic*) soi-même; **by oneself** tout seul

one-sided [wʌnˈsaɪdɪd] *adj* (*decision*) unilatéral(e); (*judgment, account*) partial(e); (*contest*) inégal(e)

one-to-one [ˈwʌntəwʌn] *adj* (*relationship*) univoque

one-way [ˈwʌnweɪ] *adj* (*street, traffic*) à sens unique

ongoing [ˈɔngəʊɪŋ] *adj* en cours; suivi(e)

onion [ˈʌnjən] *n* oignon *m*

online, on-line [ˈɔnlaɪn] *adj* (*COMPUT*) en ligne; (: *switched on*) connecté(e)

onlooker [ˈɔnlʊkə*] *n* spectateur/trice

only [ˈəʊnlɪ] *adv* seulement ♦ *adj* seul(e), unique ♦ *conj* seulement, mais; **an only child** un enfant unique; **not only** non seulement; **I only took one** j'en ai seulement pris un, je n'en ai pris qu'un; **I saw her only yesterday** je l'ai vue hier encore; **I'd be only too pleased to help** je ne serais que trop content de vous aider; **I would come, only I'm very busy** je viendrais bien mais j'ai beaucoup à faire

onset [ˈɔnset] *n* début *m*; (*of winter, old age*) approche *f*

onshore [ˈɔnʃɔː*] *adj* (*wind*) du large

onslaught [ˈɔnslɔːt] *n* attaque *f*, assaut *m*

onto [ˈɔntʊ] *prep* = **on to**

onward(s) [ˈɔnwəd(z)] *adv* (*move*) en avant

ooze [uːz] *vi* suinter

opaque [əʊˈpeɪk] *adj* opaque

OPEC [ˈəʊpek] *n abbr* (= *Organization of Petroleum-Exporting Countries*) OPEP *f*

open [ˈəʊpn] *adj* ouvert(e); (*car*) découvert(e); (*road, view*) dégagé(e); (*meeting*) public(ique); (*admiration*) manifeste; (*question*) non résolu(e); (*enemy*) déclaré(e) ♦ *vt* ouvrir ♦ *vi* (*flower, eyes, door, debate*) s'ouvrir; (*shop, bank, museum*) ouvrir; (*book etc: commence*) commencer, débuter; **in the open (air)** en plein air; **the open sea** le large; **open ground** (*among trees*) clairière *f*; (*waste ground*) terrain *m* vague; **to have an open mind (on sth)** avoir l'esprit ouvert (sur qch)

▶ **open on to** *vt fus* (*room, door*) donner sur

▶ **open out** *vt* ouvrir ♦ *vi* s'ouvrir

▶ **open up** *vt* ouvrir; (*blocked road*) dégager ♦ *vi* s'ouvrir

opening [ˈəʊpnɪŋ] *n* ouverture *f*; (*opportunity*) occasion *f*; débouché *m*; (*job*) poste vacant

opening hours *npl* heures *fpl* d'ouverture

openly [ˈəʊpnlɪ] *adv* ouvertement

open-minded [əʊpnˈmaɪndɪd] *adj* à l'esprit ouvert

open-necked [ˈəʊpnnekt] *adj* à col ouvert

open-plan [ˈəʊpnˈplæn] *adj* sans cloisons

Open University *n* (*BRIT*) cours universitaires par correspondance; *voir encadré*

OPEN UNIVERSITY

L'**Open University** a été fondée en 1969. L'enseignement comprend des cours (certaines plages horaires sont réservées à cet effet à la télévision et à la radio), des devoirs qui sont envoyés par l'étudiant à son directeur ou sa directrice d'études, et un séjour obligatoire en université d'été. Il faut préparer un certain nombre d'unités de valeur pendant une période de temps déterminée et obtenir la moyenne à un certain nombre d'entre elles pour recevoir le diplôme visé.

opera ['ɔpərə] n opéra m

opera singer n chanteur/euse d'opéra

operate ['ɔpəreɪt] vt (machine) faire marcher, faire fonctionner; (system) pratiquer ♦ vi fonctionner; (drug) faire effet; **to operate on sb (for)** (MED) opérer qn (de)

operatic [ɔpə'rætɪk] adj d'opéra

operating ['ɔpəreɪtɪŋ] adj (COMM: costs, profit) d'exploitation; (MED): **operating table/theatre** table f/salle f d'opération

operation [ɔpə'reɪʃən] n opération f; (of machine) fonctionnement m; **to have an operation (for)** se faire opérer (de); **to be in operation** (machine) être en service; (system) être en vigueur

operative ['ɔpərətɪv] adj (measure) en vigueur ♦ n (in factory) ouvrier/ière; **the operative word** le mot clef

operator ['ɔpəreɪtə*] n (of machine) opérateur/trice; (TEL) téléphoniste m/f

opinion [ə'pɪnjən] n opinion f, avis m; **in my opinion** à mon avis; **to seek a second opinion** demander un deuxième avis

opinionated [ə'pɪnjəneɪtɪd] adj aux idées bien arrêtées

opinion poll n sondage m d'opinion

opponent [ə'pəunənt] n adversaire m/f

opportunity [ɔpə'tjuːnɪtɪ] n occasion f; **to take the opportunity to do** or **of doing** profiter de l'occasion pour faire

oppose [ə'pəuz] vt s'opposer à; **opposed to** adj opposé(e) à; **as opposed to** par opposition à

opposing [ə'pəuzɪŋ] adj (side) opposé(e)

opposite ['ɔpəzɪt] adj opposé(e); (house etc) d'en face ♦ adv en face ♦ prep en face de ♦ n opposé m, contraire m; (of word) contraire; **"see opposite page"** "voir ci-contre"

opposition [ɔpə'zɪʃən] n opposition f

oppressive [ə'presɪv] adj oppressif(ive)

opt [ɔpt] vi: **to opt for** opter pour; **to opt to do** choisir de faire

▶ **opt out** vi (school, hospital) devenir autonome; (health service) devenir privé(e); **to opt out of** choisir de quitter

optical ['ɔptɪkl] adj optique; (instrument) d'optique

optical character reader/recognition (OCR) n lecteur m/lecture f optique

optician [ɔp'tɪʃn] n opticien/ne

optimist ['ɔptɪmɪst] n optimiste m/f

optimistic [ɔptɪ'mɪstɪk] adj optimiste

option ['ɔpʃən] n choix m, option f; (SCOL) matière f à option; (COMM) option; **to keep one's options open** (fig) ne pas s'engager; **I have no option** je n'ai pas le choix

optional ['ɔpʃənl] adj facultatif(ive); (COMM) en option; **optional extras** accessoires mpl en option, options fpl

or [ɔ:*] conj ou; (with negative): **he hasn't seen or heard anything** il n'a rien vu ni entendu; **or else** sinon; ou bien, ou alors

oral ['ɔ:rəl] adj oral(e) ♦ n oral m

orange ['ɔrɪndʒ] n (fruit) orange f ♦ adj orange inv

orbit ['ɔ:bɪt] n orbite f ♦ vt décrire une or des orbite(s) autour de; **to be in/go into orbit (round)** être/entrer en orbite (autour de)

orchard ['ɔ:tʃəd] n verger m; **apple orchard** verger de pommiers

orchestra ['ɔ:kɪstrə] n orchestre m; (US: seating) (fauteuils mpl d')orchestre

orchid ['ɔ:kɪd] n orchidée f

ordain [ɔ:'deɪn] vt (REL) ordonner; (decide) décréter

ordeal [ɔ:'di:l] n épreuve f

order ['ɔ:də*] n ordre m; (COMM) commande f ♦ vt ordonner; (COMM) commander; **in order** en ordre; (of document) en règle; **out of order** hors service; (telephone) en dérangement; **a machine in working order** une machine en état de marche; **in order of size** par ordre de grandeur; **in order to do/that** pour faire/que + sub; **to order sb to do** ordonner à qn de faire; **to place an order for sth with sb** commander qch auprès de qn, passer commande de qch à qn; **to be on order** être en commande; **made to order** fait sur commande; **to be under orders to do sth** avoir ordre de faire qch; **a point of order** un point de procédure; **to the order of** (BANKING) à l'ordre de

order form n bon m de commande

orderly ['ɔ:dəlɪ] n (MIL) ordonnance f ♦ adj (room) en ordre; (mind) méthodique; (person) qui a de l'ordre

ordinary ['ɔ:dnrɪ] adj ordinaire, normal(e); (pej) ordinaire, quelconque; **out of the ordinary** exceptionnel(le)

Ordnance Survey map n (BRIT) ≃ carte f d'État-major

ore [ɔ:*] n minerai m

organ ['ɔ:gən] n organe m; (MUS) orgue m, orgues fpl

organic [ɔ:'gænɪk] adj organique; (crops etc) biologique, naturel(le)

organization [ɔ:gənaɪ'zeɪʃən] n organisation f

organize ['ɔ:gənaɪz] vt organiser; **to get organized** s'organiser

organizer ['ɔ:gənaɪzə*] n organisateur/trice

orgasm ['ɔ:gæzəm] n orgasme m

Orient ['ɔ:rɪənt] n: **the Orient** l'Orient m

oriental [ɔ:rɪ'entl] adj oriental(e) ♦ n Oriental/e

origin ['ɔrɪdʒɪn] n origine f; **country of origin** pays m d'origine

original [ə'rɪdʒɪnl] adj original(e); (earliest) originel(le) ♦ n original m

originally [ə'rɪdʒɪnəlɪ] adv (at first) à l'origine

originate [ə'rɪdʒɪneɪt] *vi*: **to originate from** être originaire de; (*suggestion*) provenir de; **to originate in** prendre naissance dans; avoir son origine dans

Orkney ['ɔːknɪ] *n*: **the Orkneys** (*also*: **the Orkney Islands**) les Orcades *fpl*

ornament ['ɔːnəmənt] *n* ornement *m*; (*trinket*) bibelot *m*

ornamental [ɔːnə'mɛntl] *adj* décoratif(ive); (*garden*) d'agrément

ornate [ɔː'neɪt] *adj* très orné(e)

orphan ['ɔːfn] *n* orphelin/e ♦ *vt*: **to be orphaned** devenir orphelin

orthopaedic, (*US*) **orthopedic** [ɔːθə'piːdɪk] *adj* orthopédique

ostensibly [ɔs'tɛnsɪblɪ] *adv* en apparence

ostentatious [ɔstɛn'teɪʃəs] *adj* prétentieux(euse); ostentatoire

ostracize ['ɔstrəsaɪz] *vt* frapper d'ostracisme

ostrich ['ɔstrɪtʃ] *n* autruche *f*

other ['ʌðə*] *adj* autre ♦ *pron*: **the other (one)** l'autre; **others** (*other people*) d'autres; **some other people have still to arrive** on attend encore quelques personnes; **the other day** l'autre jour; **other than** autrement que; à part; **some actor or other** un certain acteur, je ne sais quel acteur; **somebody or other** quelqu'un; **the car was none other than John's** la voiture n'était autre que celle de John

otherwise ['ʌðəwaɪz] *adv*, *conj* autrement; **an otherwise good piece of work** par ailleurs, un beau travail

otter ['ɔtə*] *n* loutre *f*

ouch [autʃ] *excl* aïe!

ought, *pt* **ought** [ɔːt] *aux vb*: **I ought to do it** je devrais le faire, il faudrait que je le fasse; **this ought to have been corrected** cela aurait dû être corrigé; **he ought to win** il devrait gagner; **you ought to go and see it** vous devriez aller le voir

ounce [auns] *n* once *f* (*28.35g; 16 in a pound*)

our ['auə*] *adj* notre, nos *pl*

ours [auəz] *pron* le(la) nôtre, les nôtres

ourselves [auə'sɛlvz] *pron pl* (*reflexive, after preposition*) nous; (*emphatic*) nous-mêmes; **we did it (all) by ourselves** nous avons fait ça tout seuls

oust [aust] *vt* évincer

out [aut] *adv* dehors; (*published, not at home etc*) sorti(e); (*light, fire*) éteint(e); (*on strike*) en grève ♦ *vt*: **to out sb** révéler l'homosexualité de qn; **out here** ici; **out there** là-bas; **he's out** (*absent*) il est sorti; (*unconscious*) il est sans connaissance; **to be out in one's calculations** s'être trompé dans ses calculs; **to run/back etc out** sortir en courant/en reculant etc; **to be out and about** *or* (*US*) **around again** être de nouveau sur pied; **before the week was out** avant la fin de la semaine; **the journey out** l'aller *m*; **the boat was 10 km out** le bateau était à 10 km du rivage; **out loud** *adv* à haute voix;

out of *prep* (*outside*) en dehors de; (*because of*: *anger etc*) par; (*from among*): **out of 10** sur 10; (*without*): **out of petrol** sans essence, à court d'essence; **made out of wood** en *or* de bois; **out of order** (*machine*) en panne; (*TEL*: *line*) en dérangement; **out of stock** (*COMM*: *article*) épuisé(e); (: *shop*) en rupture de stock

out-and-out ['autəndaut] *adj* véritable

outback ['autbæk] *n* campagne isolée; (*in Australia*) intérieur *m*

outboard ['autbɔːd] *n*: **outboard (motor)** (moteur *m*) hors-bord *m*

outbreak ['autbreɪk] *n* éruption *f*, explosion *f*; (*start*) déclenchement *m*

outburst ['autbɜːst] *n* explosion *f*, accès *m*

outcast ['autkɑːst] *n* exilé/e; (*socially*) paria *m*

outcome ['autkʌm] *n* issue *f*, résultat *m*

outcrop ['autkrɒp] *n* affleurement *m*

outcry ['autkraɪ] *n* tollé (général)

outdated [aut'deɪtɪd] *adj* démodé(e)

outdo [aut'duː] *vt irreg* surpasser

outdoor [aut'dɔː*] *adj* de *or* en plein air

outdoors [aut'dɔːz] *adv* dehors; au grand air

outer ['autə*] *adj* extérieur(e); **outer suburbs** grande banlieue

outer space *n* espace *m* cosmique

outfit ['autfɪt] *n* équipement *m*; (*clothes*) tenue *f*; (*col*: *COMM*) organisation *f*, boîte *f*

outgoing ['autgəuɪŋ] *adj* (*president, tenant*) sortant(e); (*character*) ouvert(e), extraverti(e)

outgoings ['autgəuɪŋz] *npl* (*BRIT*: *expenses*) dépenses *fpl*

outgrow [aut'grəu] *vt* (*irreg*) (*clothes*) devenir trop grand(e) pour

outhouse ['authaus] *n* appentis *m*, remise *f*

outing ['autɪŋ] *n* sortie *f*; excursion *f*

outlaw ['autlɔː] *n* hors-la-loi *m inv* ♦ *vt* (*person*) mettre hors la loi; (*practice*) proscrire

outlay ['autleɪ] *n* dépenses *fpl*; (*investment*) mise *f* de fonds

outlet ['autlɛt] *n* (*for liquid etc*) issue *f*, sortie *f*; (*for emotion*) exutoire *m*; (*for goods*) débouché *m*; (*also*: **retail outlet**) point *m* de vente; (*US*: *ELEC*) prise *f* de courant

outline ['autlaɪn] *n* (*shape*) contour *m*; (*summary*) esquisse *f*, grandes lignes

outlive [aut'lɪv] *vt* survivre à

outlook ['autluk] *n* perspective *f*

outlying ['autlaɪɪŋ] *adj* écarté(e)

outmoded [aut'məudɪd] *adj* démodé(e); dépassé(e)

outnumber [aut'nʌmbə*] *vt* surpasser en nombre

out-of-date [autəv'deɪt] *adj* (*passport, ticket*) périmé(e); (*theory, idea*) dépassé(e); (*custom*) désuet(ète); (*clothes*) démodé(e)

out-of-the-way ['autəvðə'weɪ] *adj* loin de tout;

(fig) insolite

outpatient [ˈaʊtpeɪʃənt] *n* malade *m/f* en consultation externe

outpost [ˈaʊtpəʊst] *n* avant-poste *m*

output [ˈaʊtpʊt] *n* rendement *m*, production *f* ♦ *vt (COMPUT)* sortir

outrage [ˈaʊtreɪdʒ] *n* atrocité *f*, acte *m* de violence; scandale *m* ♦ *vt* outrager

outrageous [aʊtˈreɪdʒəs] *adj* atroce; scandaleux(euse)

outright *adv* [aʊtˈraɪt] complètement; catégoriquement; carrément; sur le coup ♦ *adj* [ˈaʊtraɪt] complet(ète); catégorique

outset [ˈaʊtset] *n* début *m*

outside [aʊtˈsaɪd] *n* extérieur *m* ♦ *adj* extérieur(e); *(remote, unlikely)*: **an outside chance** une (très) faible chance ♦ *adv* (au) dehors, à l'extérieur ♦ *prep* hors de, à l'extérieur de; **at the outside** *(fig)* au plus or maximum; **outside left/right** *n (FOOTBALL)* ailier gauche/droit

outside lane *n (AUT: in Britain)* voie *f* de droite; *(: in US, Europe)* voie de gauche

outside line *n (TEL)* ligne extérieure

outsider [aʊtˈsaɪdə*] *n (in race etc)* outsider *m*; *(stranger)* étranger/ère

outsize [ˈaʊtsaɪz] *adj* énorme; *(clothes)* grande taille *inv*

outskirts [ˈaʊtskəːts] *npl* faubourgs *mpl*

outspoken [aʊtˈspəʊkən] *adj* très franc(franche)

outstanding [aʊtˈstændɪŋ] *adj* remarquable, exceptionnel(le); *(unfinished)* en suspens; en souffrance; non réglé(e); **your account is still outstanding** vous n'avez pas encore tout remboursé

outstay [aʊtˈsteɪ] *vt*: **to outstay one's welcome** abuser de l'hospitalité de son hôte

outstretched [aʊtˈstretʃt] *adj (hand)* tendu(e); *(body)* étendu(e)

outstrip [aʊtˈstrɪp] *vt (also fig)* dépasser

out-tray [ˈaʊttreɪ] *n* courrier *m* "départ"

outward [ˈaʊtwəd] *adj (sign, appearances)* extérieur(e); *(journey)* (d')aller

outweigh [aʊtˈweɪ] *vt* l'emporter sur

outwit [aʊtˈwɪt] *vt* se montrer plus malin que

oval [ˈaʊvl] *adj, n* ovale *m*

Oval Office *n (US POL) voir encadré*

OVAL OFFICE

L'**Oval Office** est le bureau personnel du président des États-Unis à la Maison-Blanche, ainsi appelé du fait de sa forme ovale. Par extension, ce terme désigne la présidence elle-même.

---

ovary [ˈaʊvərɪ] *n* ovaire *m*

oven [ˈʌvn] *n* four *m*

ovenproof [ˈʌvnpruːf] *adj* allant au four

over [ˈəʊvə*] *adv* (par-)dessus; *(excessively)* trop ♦ *adj (or adv) (finished)* fini(e), terminé(e); *(too much)* en plus ♦ *prep* sur; par-dessus; *(above)* au-dessus de; *(on the other side of)* de l'autre côté de; *(more than)* plus de; *(during)* pendant; *(about, concerning)*: **they fell out over money/her** ils se sont brouillés pour des questions d'argent/à cause d'elle; **over here** ici; **over there** là-bas; **all over** *(everywhere)* partout; *(finished)* fini(e); **over and over (again)** à plusieurs reprises; **over and above** en plus de; **to ask sb over** inviter qn (à passer); **to go over to sb's** passer chez qn; **now over to our Paris correspondent** nous passons l'antenne à notre correspondant à Paris; **the world over** dans le monde entier; **she's not over intelligent** *(BRIT)* elle n'est pas particulièrement intelligente

overall *adj n* [ˈaʊvərɔːl] ♦ *adj (length)* total(e); *(study)* d'ensemble ♦ *n (BRIT)* blouse *f* ♦ *adv* [aʊvər ˈɔːl] dans l'ensemble, en général; **overalls** *npl* bleus *mpl* (de travail)

overawe [aʊvərˈɔː] *vt* impressionner

overbalance [aʊvəˈbæləns] *vi* basculer

overboard [ˈaʊvəbɔːd] *adv (NAUT)* par-dessus bord; **to go overboard for sth** *(fig)* s'emballer (pour qch)

overbook [aʊvəˈbuk] *vi* faire du surbooking

overcast [ˈaʊvəkɑːst] *adj* couvert(e)

overcharge [aʊvəˈtʃɑːdʒ] *vt*: **to overcharge sb for sth** faire payer qch trop cher à qn

overcoat [ˈaʊvəkəʊt] *n* pardessus *m*

overcome [aʊvəˈkʌm] *vt irreg* triompher de; surmonter ♦ *adj (emotionally)* bouleversé(e); **overcome with grief** accablé(e) de douleur

overcrowded [aʊvəˈkraudɪd] *adj* bondé(e)

overdo [aʊvəˈduː] *vt (irreg)* exagérer; *(overcook)* trop cuire; **to overdo it, to overdo things** *(work too hard)* en faire trop, se surmener

overdose [ˈaʊvədəus] *n* dose excessive

overdraft [ˈaʊvədrɑːft] *n* découvert *m*

overdrawn [aʊvəˈdrɔːn] *adj (account)* à découvert

overdue [aʊvəˈdjuː] *adj* en retard; *(bill)* impayé(e); **that change was long overdue** ce changement n'avait que trop tardé

overestimate [aʊvərˈestɪmeɪt] *vt* surestimer

overflow *vi* [aʊvəˈfləu] déborder ♦ *n* [ˈaʊvəfləu] trop-plein *m*; *(also:* **overflow pipe***)* tuyau *m* d'écoulement, trop-plein *m*

overgrown [aʊvəˈgrəun] *adj (garden)* envahi(e) par la végétation; **he's just an overgrown schoolboy** *(fig)* c'est un écolier attardé

overhaul *vt* [aʊvəˈhɔːl] réviser ♦ *n* [ˈaʊvəhɔːl] révision *f*

overhead *adv* [aʊvəˈhed] au-dessus ♦ *adj, n* [ˈaʊvəhed] *adj* aérien(ne); *(lighting)* vertical(e); *n (US)* = **overheads**

overhead projector *n* rétroprojecteur *m*

overhear [aʊvəˈhɪə*] *vt irreg* entendre (par

hasard)

overheat [əuvə'hiːt] *vi* devenir surchauffé(e); *(engine)* chauffer

overjoyed [əuvə'dʒɔɪd] *adj* ravi(e), enchanté(e)

overland ['əuvəlænd] *adj, adv* par voie de terre

overlap *vi* [əuvə'læp] se chevaucher ♦ *n* ['əuvəlæp] chevauchement *m*

overleaf [əuvə'liːf] *adv* au verso

overload [əuvə'ləud] *vt* surcharger

overlook [əuvə'luk] *vt (have view of)* donner sur; *(miss)* oublier, négliger; *(forgive)* fermer les yeux sur

overnight *adv* [əuvə'naɪt] *(happen)* durant la nuit; *(fig)* soudain ♦ *adj* ['əuvənaɪt] d'une (or de) nuit; soudain(e); **he stayed there overnight** il y a passé la nuit; **if you travel overnight ...** si tu fais le voyage de nuit ...; **he'll be away overnight** il ne rentrera pas ce soir

overpass ['əuvəpɑːs] *n* pont autoroutier; *(US)* passerelle *f*, pont *m*

overpower [əuvə'pauə*] *vt* vaincre; *(fig)* accabler

overpowering [əuvə'pauərɪŋ] *adj* irrésistible; *(heat, stench)* suffocant(e)

overrate [əuvə'reɪt] *vt* surestimer

override [əuvə'raɪd] *vt (irreg: like* **ride***) (order, objection)* passer outre à; *(decision)* annuler

overriding [əuvə'raɪdɪŋ] *adj* prépondérant(e)

overrule [əuvə'ruːl] *vt (decision)* annuler; *(claim)* rejeter

overrun [əuvə'rʌn] *vt (irreg) (MIL: country etc)* occuper; *(time limit etc)* dépasser ♦ *vi* dépasser le temps imparti; **the town is overrun with tourists** la ville est envahie de touristes

overseas [əuvə'siːz] *adv* outre-mer; *(abroad)* à l'étranger ♦ *adj (trade)* extérieur(e); *(visitor)* étranger(ère)

overshadow [əuvə'ʃædəu] *vt (fig)* éclipser

oversight ['əuvəsaɪt] *n* omission *f*, oubli *m*; **due to an oversight** par suite d'une inadvertance

oversleep [əuvə'sliːp] *vi (irreg)* se réveiller (trop) tard

overstep [əuvə'step] *vt:* **to overstep the mark** dépasser la mesure

overt [əu'vəːt] *adj* non dissimulé(e)

overtake [əuvə'teɪk] *vt irreg* dépasser; *(AUT)* dépasser, doubler

overthrow [əuvə'θrəu] *vt irreg (government)* renverser

overtime ['əuvətaɪm] *n* heures *fpl* supplémentaires; **to do** or **work overtime** faire des heures supplémentaires

overtone ['əuvətəun] *n (also:* **overtones***)* note *f*, sous-entendus *mpl*

overture ['əuvətʃuə*] *n (MUS, fig)* ouverture *f*

overturn [əuvə'təːn] *vt* renverser ♦ *vi* se retourner

overweight [əuvə'weɪt] *adj (person)* trop gros(se); *(luggage)* trop lourd(e)

overwhelm [əuvə'welm] *vt* accabler; submerger; écraser

overwhelming [əuvə'welmɪŋ] *adj (victory, defeat)* écrasant(e); *(desire)* irrésistible; **one's overwhelming impression is of heat** on a une impression dominante de chaleur

overwrought [əuvə'rɔːt] *adj* excédé(e)

owe [əu] *vt* devoir; **to owe sb sth, to owe sth to sb** devoir qch à qn

owing to ['əuɪŋtuː] *prep* à cause de, en raison de

owl [aul] *n* hibou *m*

own [əun] *vt* posséder ♦ *vi (BRIT):* **to own to sth** reconnaître or avouer qch; **to own to having done sth** avouer avoir fait qch ♦ *adj* propre; **a room of my own** une chambre à moi, ma propre chambre; **can I have it for my (very) own?** puis-je l'avoir pour moi (tout) seul?; **to get one's own back** prendre sa revanche; **on one's own** tout(e) seul(e); **to come into one's own** trouver sa voie; trouver sa justification

▶ **own up** *vi* avouer

owner ['əunə*] *n* propriétaire *m/f*

ownership ['əunəʃɪp] *n* possession *f*; **it's under new ownership** *(shop etc)* il y a eu un changement de propriétaire

ox, *pl* **oxen** [ɔks, 'ɔksn] *n* bœuf *m*

oxtail ['ɔksteɪl] *n:* **oxtail soup** soupe *f* à la queue de bœuf

oxygen ['ɔksɪdʒən] *n* oxygène *m*

oyster ['ɔɪstə*] *n* huître *f*

oz. *abbr* = **ounce**

ozone ['əuzəun] *n* ozone *m*

ozone-friendly ['əuzəunfrendlɪ] *adj* qui n'attaque pas or qui préserve la couche d'ozone

ozone hole *n* trou *m* d'ozone

ozone layer *n* couche *f* d'ozone

— *P p* —

p *abbr (= page)* p; *(BRIT)* = **penny, pence**

PA *n abbr* = **personal assistant, public address system** ♦ *abbr (US)* = Pennsylvania

pa [pɑː] *n (col)* papa *m*

p.a. *abbr* = **per annum**

pace [peɪs] *n* pas *m*; *(speed)* allure *f*; vitesse *f* ♦ *vi:* **to pace up and down** faire les cent pas; **to keep pace with** aller à la même vitesse que; *(events)* se tenir au courant de; **to set the pace** *(running)* donner l'allure; *(fig)* donner le ton; **to put sb through his paces** *(fig)* mettre qn à l'épreuve

pacemaker ['peɪsmeɪkə*] *n (MED)* stimulateur *m* cardiaque

pacific [pə'sɪfɪk] *adj* pacifique ♦ *n:* **the Pacific (Ocean)** le Pacifique, l'océan *m* Pacifique

pack [pæk] *n* paquet *m*; ballot *m*; (*of hounds*) meute *f*; (*of thieves, wolves etc*) bande *f*; (*of cards*) jeu *m* ♦ *vt* (*goods*) empaqueter, emballer; (*in suitcase etc*) emballer; (*box*) remplir; (*cram*) entasser; (*press down*) tasser; damer; (*COMPUT*) grouper, tasser ♦ *vi*: **to pack (one's bags)** faire ses bagages; **to pack into** (*room, stadium*) s'entasser dans; **to send sb packing** (*col*) envoyer promener qn

▶ **pack in** (*BRIT col*) *vi* (*machine*) tomber en panne ♦ *vt* (*boyfriend*) plaquer; **pack it in!** laisse tomber!

▶ **pack off** *vt* (*person*) envoyer (promener), expédier

▶ **pack up** *vi* (*BRIT col: machine*) tomber en panne; (: *person*) se tirer ♦ *vt* (*belongings*) ranger; (*goods, presents*) empaqueter, emballer

package ['pækɪdʒ] *n* paquet *m*; (*of goods*) emballage *m*, conditionnement *m*; (*also*: **package deal**) marché global; forfait *m*; (*COMPUT*) progiciel *m* ♦ *vt* (*goods*) conditionner

package tour *n* voyage organisé

packed [pækt] *adj* (*crowded*) bondé(e); **packed lunch** (*BRIT*) repas froid

packet ['pækɪt] *n* paquet *m*

packing ['pækɪŋ] *n* emballage *m*

packing case *n* caisse *f* (d'emballage)

pact [pækt] *n* pacte *m*, traité *m*

pad [pæd] *n* bloc(-notes) *m*; (*for inking*) tampon *m* encreur; (*col: flat*) piaule *f* ♦ *vt* rembourrer ♦ *vi*: **to pad in/about** *etc* entrer/aller et venir *etc* à pas feutrés

padding ['pædɪŋ] *n* rembourrage *m*; (*fig*) délayage *m*

paddle ['pædl] *n* (*oar*) pagaie *f* ♦ *vi* barboter, faire trempette ♦ *vt*: **to paddle a canoe** *etc* pagayer

paddling pool ['pædlɪŋ-] *n* petit bassin

paddock ['pædək] *n* enclos *m*; paddock *m*

padlock ['pædlɔk] *n* cadenas *m* ♦ *vt* cadenasser

paediatrics, (*US*) **pediatrics** [piː'drætrɪks] *n* pédiatrie *f*

pagan ['peɪgən] *adj*, *n* païen/ne

page [peɪdʒ] *n* (*of book*) page *f*; (*also*: **page boy**) groom *m*, chasseur *m*; (*at wedding*) garçon *m* d'honneur ♦ *vt* (*in hotel etc*) (faire) appeler

pageant ['pædʒənt] *n* spectacle *m* historique; grande cérémonie

pageantry ['pædʒəntrɪ] *n* apparat *m*, pompe *f*

pager ['peɪdʒə*] *n* système *m* de téléappel, bip *m* *f*

paid [peɪd] *pt, pp* of **pay** ♦ *adj* (*work, official*) rémunéré(e); **to put paid to** (*BRIT*) mettre fin à, mettre par terre

pail [peɪl] *n* seau *m*

pain [peɪn] *n* douleur *f*; **to be in pain** souffrir, avoir mal; **to have a pain in** avoir mal à *or* une douleur à *or* dans; **to take pains to do** se donner du mal pour faire; **on pain of death** sous peine de mort

pained [peɪnd] *adj* peiné(e), chagrin(e)

painful ['peɪnful] *adj* douloureux(euse); (*difficult*) difficile, pénible

painfully ['peɪnfəlɪ] *adv* (*fig: very*) terriblement

painkiller ['peɪnkɪlə*] *n* calmant *m*

painless ['peɪnlɪs] *adj* indolore

painstaking ['peɪnzteɪkɪŋ] *adj* (*person*) soigneux(euse); (*work*) soigné(e)

paint [peɪnt] *n* peinture *f* ♦ *vt* peindre; (*fig*) dépeindre; **to paint the door blue** peindre la porte en bleu; **to paint in oils** faire de la peinture à l'huile

paintbrush ['peɪntbrʌʃ] *n* pinceau *m*

painter ['peɪntə*] *n* peintre *m*

painting ['peɪntɪŋ] *n* peinture *f*; (*picture*) tableau *m*

paintwork ['peɪntwɜːk] *n* (*BRIT*) peintures *fpl*; (: *of car*) peinture *f*

pair [pɛə*] *n* (*of shoes, gloves etc*) paire *f*; (*couple*) couple *m*; (*twosome*) duo *m*; **pair of scissors** (paire de) ciseaux *mpl*; **pair of trousers** pantalon *m*

▶ **pair off** *vi* se mettre par deux

pajamas [pə'dʒɑːməz] *npl* (*US*) pyjama(s) *m(pl)*

Pakistan [pɑːkɪ'stɑːn] *n* Pakistan *m*

Pakistani [pɑːkɪ'stɑːnɪ] *adj* pakistanais(e) ♦ *n* Pakistanais/e

pal [pæl] *n* (*col*) copain/copine

palace ['pæləs] *n* palais *m*

palatable ['pælɪtəbl] *adj* bon(bonne), agréable au goût

palate ['pælɪt] *n* palais *m* (*ANAT*)

pale [peɪl] *adj* pâle ♦ *vi* pâlir ♦ *n*: **to be beyond the pale** être au ban de la société; **to grow** *or* **turn pale** (*person*) pâlir; **pale blue** *adj* bleu pâle *inv*; **to pale into insignificance (beside)** perdre beaucoup d'importance (par rapport à)

Palestine ['pælɪstaɪn] *n* Palestine *f*

Palestinian [pælɪs'tɪnɪən] *adj* palestinien(ne) ♦ *n* Palestinien/ne

palette ['pælɪt] *n* palette *f*

pall [pɔːl] *n* (*of smoke*) voile *m* ♦ *vi*: **to pall (on)** devenir lassant (pour)

pallet ['pælɪt] *n* (*for goods*) palette *f*

pallid ['pælɪd] *adj* blême

palm [pɑːm] *n* (*ANAT*) paume *f*; (*also*: **palm tree**) palmier *m*; (*leaf, symbol*) palme *f* ♦ *vt*: **to palm sth off on sb** (*col*) refiler qch à qn

Palm Sunday *n* le dimanche des Rameaux

paltry ['pɔːltrɪ] *adj* dérisoire; piètre

pamper ['pæmpə*] *vt* gâter, dorloter

pamphlet ['pæmflət] *n* brochure *f*; (*political etc*) tract *m*

pan [pæn] *n* (*also*: **saucepan**) casserole *f*; (*also*: **frying pan**) poêle *f*; (*of lavatory*) cuvette *f* ♦ *vi* (*CINE*) faire un panoramique ♦ *vt* (*col: book, film*) éreinter; **to pan for gold** laver du sable aurifère

pancake ['pænkeɪk] *n* crêpe *f*

panda ['pændə] *n* panda *m*

pandemonium [pændɪ'məʊnɪəm] *n* tohu-bohu *m*

pander ['pændə*] *vi*: **to pander to** flatter bassement; obéir servilement à

pane [peɪn] *n* carreau *m* (de fenêtre)

panel ['pænl] *n* (*of wood, cloth etc*) panneau *m*; (*RADIO, TV*) panel *m*, invités *mpl*; (*of experts*) table ronde, comité *m*

panelling, (*US*) **paneling** ['pænəlɪŋ] *n* boiseries *fpl*

pang [pæŋ] *n*: **pangs of remorse** pincements *mpl* de remords; **pangs of hunger/conscience** tiraillements *mpl* d'estomac/de la conscience

panic ['pænɪk] *n* panique *f*, affolement *m* ♦ *vi* s'affoler, paniquer

panicky ['pænɪkɪ] *adj* (*person*) qui panique *or* s'affole facilement

panic-stricken ['pænɪkstrɪkən] *adj* affolé(e)

pansy ['pænzɪ] *n* (*BOT*) pensée *f*; (*col*) tapette *f*, pédé *m*

pant [pænt] *vi* haleter

panther ['pænθə*] *n* panthère *f*

panties ['pæntɪz] *npl* slip *m*, culotte *f*

pantihose ['pæntɪhəʊz] *n* (*US*) collant *m*

pantomime ['pæntəmaɪm] *n* (*BRIT*) spectacle *m* de Noël; *voir encadré*

PANTOMIME

Une **pantomime** (à ne pas confondre avec le mot tel qu'on l'utilise en français), que l'on appelle également de façon familière "panto", est un genre de farce où le personnage principal est souvent un jeune garçon et où il y a toujours une "dame", c'est-à-dire une vieille femme jouée par un homme, et un méchant. La plupart du temps, l'histoire est basée sur un conte de fées comme Cendrillon ou Le Chat Botté, et le public est encouragé à participer en prévenant le héros d'un danger imminent. Ce genre de spectacle, qui s'adresse surtout aux enfants, vise également un public d'adultes au travers des nombreuses plaisanteries faisant allusion à des faits d'actualité.

---

pantry ['pæntrɪ] *n* garde-manger *m inv*; (*room*) office *m*

pants [pænts] *n* (*BRIT: woman's*) culotte *f*, slip *m*; (: *man's*) slip *m*, caleçon *m*; (*US: trousers*) pantalon *m*

paper ['peɪpə*] *n* papier *m*; (*also*: **wallpaper**) papier peint; (*also*: **newspaper**) journal *m*; (*study, article*) article *m*; (*exam*) épreuve écrite ♦ *adj* en or de papier ♦ *vt* tapisser (de papier peint); **a piece of paper** (*odd bit*) un bout de papier; (*sheet*) une feuille de papier; **to put sth down on paper** mettre qch par écrit

paperback ['peɪpəbæk] *n* livre *m* de poche; livre broché *or* non relié ♦ *adj*: **paperback edition** édition brochée

paper bag *n* sac *m* en papier

paper clip *n* trombone *m*

paper handkerchief *n*, **paper hankie** *n* (*col*) mouchoir *m* en papier

paperweight ['peɪpəweɪt] *n* presse-papiers *m inv*

paperwork ['peɪpəwɜːk] *n* paperasserie *f*

par [pɑː*] *n* pair *m*; (*GOLF*) normale *f* du parcours; **on a par with** à égalité avec, au même niveau que; **at par** au pair; **above/below par** au-dessus/audessous du pair; **to feel below** *or* **under** *or* **not up to par** ne pas se sentir en forme

parachute ['pærəʃuːt] *n* parachute *m* ♦ *vi* sauter en parachute

parade [pə'reɪd] *n* défilé *m*; (*inspection*) revue *f*; (*street*) boulevard *m* ♦ *vt* (*fig*) faire étalage de ♦ *vi* défiler; **a fashion parade** (*BRIT*) un défilé de mode

paradise ['pærədaɪs] *n* paradis *m*

paradox ['pærədɒks] *n* paradoxe *m*

paradoxically [pærə'dɒksɪklɪ] *adv* paradoxalement

paraffin ['pærəfɪn] *n* (*BRIT*): **paraffin (oil)** pétrole (lampant); **liquid paraffin** huile *f* de paraffine

paragon ['pærəgən] *n* parangon *m*

paragraph ['pærəɡrɑːf] *n* paragraphe *m*; **to begin a new paragraph** aller à la ligne

parallel ['pærəlel] *adj*: **parallel (with** *or* **to)** parallèle (à); (*fig*) analogue (à) ♦ *n* (*line*) parallèle *f*; (*fig, GEO*) parallèle *m*

paralysis, *pl* **paralyses** [pə'rælɪsɪs, -siːz] *n* paralysie *f*

paralyze ['pærəlaɪz] *vt* paralyser

paramount ['pærəmaunt] *adj*: **of paramount importance** de la plus haute *or* grande importance

paranoid ['pærənɔɪd] *adj* (*PSYCH*) paranoïaque; (*neurotic*) paranoïde

paraphernalia [pærəfə'neɪlɪə] *n* attirail *m*, affaires *fpl*

parasol ['pærəsɒl] *n* ombrelle *f*; (*at café etc*) parasol *m*

paratrooper ['pærətruːpə*] *n* parachutiste *m* (*soldat*)

parcel ['pɑːsl] *n* paquet *m*, colis *m* ♦ *vt* (*also*: **parcel up**) empaqueter

▶ **parcel out** *vt* répartir

parchment ['pɑːtʃmənt] *n* parchemin *m*

pardon ['pɑːdn] *n* pardon *m*; grâce *f* ♦ *vt* pardonner à; (*LAW*) gracier; **pardon!** pardon!; **pardon me!** excusez-moi!; **I beg your pardon!** pardon!, je suis désolé!; **(I beg your) pardon?**, (*US*) **pardon me?** pardon?

parent ['peərənt] *n* père *m or* mère *f*; **parents** *npl* parents *mpl*

Paris ['pærɪs] *n* Paris

parish ['pærɪʃ] *n* paroisse *f*; (*civil*) ≈ commune *f* ♦ *adj* paroissial(e)

Parisian [pəˈrɪzɪən] *adj* parisien(ne) ◆ *n* Parisien/ne

park [pɑːk] *n* parc *m*, jardin public ◆ *vt* garer ◆ *vi* se garer

parking [ˈpɑːkɪŋ] *n* stationnement *m*; **"no parking"** "stationnement interdit"

parking lot ᴎ (*US*) parking *m*, parc *m* de stationnement

parking meter *n* parc(o)mètre *m*

parking ticket *n* P.-V. *m*

parliament [ˈpɑːləmənt] *n* parlement *m*

parliamentary [pɑːləˈmɛntərɪ] *adj* parlementaire

parlour, (*US*) **parlor** [ˈpɑːləʳ] *n* salon *m*

parochial [pəˈrəukɪəl] *adj* paroissial(e); (*pej*) à l'esprit de clocher

parole [pəˈrəul] *n*: **on parole** en liberté conditionnelle

parrot [ˈpærət] *n* perroquet *m*

parry [ˈpærɪ] *vt* esquiver, parer à

parsley [ˈpɑːslɪ] *n* persil *m*

parsnip [ˈpɑːsnɪp] *n* panais *m*

parson [ˈpɑːsn] *n* ecclésiastique *m*; (*Church of England*) pasteur *m*

part [pɑːt] *n* partie *f*; (*of machine*) pièce *f*; (*THEAT etc*) rôle *m*; (*MUS*) voix *f*; partie ◆ *adj* partiel(le) ◆ *adv* = **partly** ◆ *vt* séparer ◆ *vi* (*people*) se séparer; (*roads*) se diviser; **to take part in** participer à, prendre part à; **to take sb's part** prendre le parti de qn, prendre parti pour qn; **on his part** de sa part; **for my part** en ce qui me concerne; **for the most part** en grande partie; dans la plupart des cas; **for the better part of the day** pendant la plus grande partie de la journée; **to be part and parcel of** faire partie de; **to take sth in good/bad part** prendre qch du bon/mauvais côté; **part of speech** (*LING*) partie *f* du discours

▶ **part with** *vt fus* se séparer de; se défaire de

part exchange *n* (*BRIT*): **in part exchange** en reprise

partial [ˈpɑːʃl] *adj* partiel(le); (*unjust*) partial(e); **to be partial to** aimer, avoir un faible pour

participate [pɑːˈtɪsɪpeɪt] *vi*: **to participate (in)** participer (à), prendre part (à)

participation [pɑːtɪsɪˈpeɪʃən] *n* participation *f*

participle [ˈpɑːtɪsɪpl] *n* participe *m*

particle [ˈpɑːtɪkl] *n* particule *f*

particular [pəˈtɪkjuləʳ] *adj* particulier(ière); (*specific*) particulier, spécial(e); (*fussy*) difficile, exigeant(e); **particulars** *npl* détails *mpl*; (*information*) renseignements *mpl*; **in particular** surtout, en particulier

particularly [pəˈtɪkjuləlɪ] *adv* particulièrement; (*in particular*) en particulier

parting [ˈpɑːtɪŋ] *n* séparation *f*; (*BRIT: in hair*) raie *f* ◆ *adj* d'adieu; **his parting shot was ...** il lança en partant ....

partisan [pɑːtɪˈzæn] *n* partisan/e ◆ *adj* partisan(e); de parti

partition [pɑːˈtɪʃən] *n* (*POL*) partition *f*, division *f*; (*wall*) cloison *f*

partly [ˈpɑːtlɪ] *adv* en partie, partiellement

partner [ˈpɑːtnəʳ] *n* (*COMM*) associé/e (*SPORT*) partenaire *m/f*; (*at dance*) cavalier/ière ◆ *vt* être l'associé or le partenaire or le cavalier de

partnership [ˈpɑːtnəʃɪp] *n* association *f*; **to go into partnership (with), form a partnership (with)** s'associer (avec)

partridge [ˈpɑːtrɪdʒ] *n* perdrix *f*

part-time [ˈpɑːtˈtaɪm] *adj*, *adv* à mi-temps, à temps partiel

party [ˈpɑːtɪ] *n* (*POL*) parti *m*; (*team*) équipe *f*; groupe *m*; (*LAW*) partie *f*; (*celebration*) réception *f*; soirée *f*; réunion *f*, fête *f*; **dinner party** dîner *m*; **to give** or **throw a party** donner une réception; **we're having a party next Saturday** nous organisons une soirée or réunion entre amis samedi prochain; **it's for our son's birthday party** c'est pour la fête (or le goûter) d'anniversaire de notre garçon; **to be a party to a crime** être impliqué/e dans un crime

party dress *n* robe habillée

pass [pɑːs] *vt* (*time, object*) passer; (*place*) passer devant; (*car, friend*) croiser; (*exam*) être reçu(e) à, réussir; (*candidate*) admettre; (*overtake, surpass*) dépasser; (*approve*) approuver, accepter; (*law*) promulguer ◆ *vi* passer; (*SCOL*) être reçu(e) or admis(e), réussir ◆ *n* (*permit*) laissez-passer *m inv*; carte *f* d'accès or d'abonnement; (*in mountains*) col *m*; (*SPORT*) passe *f*; (*SCOL: also:* **pass mark**): **to get a pass** être reçu(e) (sans mention); **she could pass for 25** on lui donnerait 25 ans; **to pass sth through a ring** *etc* (faire) passer qch dans un anneau *etc*; **could you pass the vegetables round?** pourriez-vous faire passer les légumes?; **things have come to a pretty pass** (*BRIT*) voilà où on en est!; **to make a pass at sb** (*col*) faire des avances à qn

▶ **pass away** *vi* mourir

▶ **pass by** *vi* passer ◆ *vt* négliger

▶ **pass down** *vt* (*customs, inheritance*) transmettre

▶ **pass on** *vi* (*die*) s'éteindre, décéder ◆ *vt* (*hand on*): **to pass on (to)** transmettre (à); (*: illness*) passer (à); (*: price rises*) répercuter (sur)

▶ **pass out** *vi* s'évanouir; (*BRIT MIL*) sortir (*d'une école militaire*)

▶ **pass over** *vt* (*ignore*) passer sous silence

▶ **pass up** *vt* (*opportunity*) laisser passer

passable [ˈpɑːsəbl] *adj* (*road*) praticable; (*work*) acceptable

passage [ˈpæsɪdʒ] *n* (*also:* **passageway**) couloir *m*; (*gen, in book*) passage *m*; (*by boat*) traversée *f*

passbook [ˈpɑːsbuk] *n* livret *m*

passenger [ˈpæsɪndʒəʳ] *n* passager/ère

passer-by [pɑːsəˈbaɪ] *n* passant/e

passing ['pɑːsɪŋ] *adj* (fig) passager(ère); **in passing** en passant

passing place *n* (AUT) aire *f* de croisement

passion ['pæʃən] *n* passion *f*; **to have a passion for sth** avoir la passion de qch

passionate ['pæʃənɪt] *adj* passionné(e)

passive ['pæsɪv] *adj* (also LING) passif(ive)

passive smoking *n* tabagisme passif

Passover ['pɑːsəʊvə*] *n* Pâque juive

passport ['pɑːspɔːt] *n* passeport *m*

passport control *n* contrôle *m* des passeports

passport office *n* bureau *m* de délivrance des passeports

password ['pɑːswɜːd] *n* mot *m* de passe

past [pɑːst] *prep* (further than) au delà de, plus loin que; après; (later than) après ◆ *adj* passé(e); (president etc) ancien(ne) ◆ *n* passé *m*; **quarter/half past four** quatre heures et quart/demie; **ten/twenty past four** quatre heures dix/vingt; **he's past forty** il a dépassé la quarantaine, il a plus de or passé quarante ans; **it's past midnight** il est plus de minuit, il est passé minuit; **for the past few/3 days** depuis quelques/3 jours; ces derniers/3 derniers jours; **to run past** passer en courant; **he ran past me** il m'a dépassé en courant; il a passé devant moi en courant; **in the past** (gen) dans le temps, autrefois; (LING) au passé; **I'm past caring** je ne m'en fais plus; **to be past it** (BRIT col: person) avoir passé l'âge

pasta ['pæstə] *n* pâtes *fpl*

paste [peɪst] *n* (glue) colle *f* (de pâte); (jewellery) strass *m*; (CULIN) pâté *m* (à tartiner); pâte *f* ◆ *vt* coller; **tomato paste** concentré *m* de tomate, purée *f* de tomate

pasteurized ['pæstəraɪzd] *adj* pasteurisé(e)

pastille ['pæstl] *n* pastille *f*

pastime ['pɑːstaɪm] *n* passe-temps *m inv*, distraction *f*

pastry ['peɪstrɪ] *n* pâte *f*; (cake) pâtisserie *f*

pasture ['pɑːstʃə*] *n* pâturage *m*

pasty *n* ['pæstɪ] petit pâté (en croûte) ◆ *adj* ['peɪstɪ] pâteux(euse); (complexion) terreux(euse)

pat [pæt] *vt* donner une petite tape à ◆ *n*: **a pat of butter** une noisette de beurre; **to give sb/o.s. a pat on the back** (fig) congratuler qn/se congratuler; **he knows it (off) pat**, (us) **he has it down pat** il sait cela sur le bout des doigts

patch [pætʃ] *n* (of material) pièce *f*; (spot) tache *f*; (of land) parcelle *f* ◆ *vt* (clothes) rapiécer; **a bad patch** (BRIT) une période difficile

▶ **patch up** *vt* réparer

patchy ['pætʃɪ] *adj* inégal(e)

pâté ['pæteɪ] *n* pâté *m*, terrine *f*

patent ['peɪtnt] ['pætnt] *n* brevet *m* (d'invention) ◆ *vt* faire breveter ◆ *adj* patent(e), manifeste

patent leather *n* cuir verni

paternal [pə'tɜːnl] *adj* paternel(le)

path [pɑːθ] *n* chemin *m*, sentier *m*; allée *f*; (of planet) course *f*; (of missile) trajectoire *f*

pathetic [pə'θetɪk] *adj* (pitiful) pitoyable; (very bad) lamentable, minable; (moving) pathétique

pathological [pæθə'lɔdʒɪkl] *adj* pathologique

pathway ['pɑːθweɪ] *n* chemin *m*, sentier *m*

patience ['peɪʃns] *n* patience *f*; (BRIT: CARDS) réussite *f*; **to lose (one's) patience** perdre patience

patient ['peɪʃnt] *n* patient/e; (in hospital) malade *m/f* ◆ *adj* patient(e)

patio ['pætɪəʊ] *n* patio *m*

patriotic [pætrɪ'ɔtɪk] *adj* patriotique; (person) patriote

patrol [pə'trəʊl] *n* patrouille *f* ◆ *vt* patrouiller dans; **to be on patrol** être de patrouille

patrol car *n* voiture *f* de police

patrolman [pə'trəʊlmən] *n* (us) agent *m* de police

patron ['peɪtrən] *n* (in shop) client/e; (of charity) patron/ne; **patron of the arts** mécène *m*

patronize ['pætrənaɪz] *vt* être (un) client or un habitué de; (fig) traiter avec condescendance

patter ['pætə*] *n* crépitement *m*, tapotement *m*; (sales talk) boniment *m* ◆ *vi* crépiter, tapoter

pattern ['pætən] *n* modèle *m*; (SEWING) patron *m*; (design) motif *m*; (sample) échantillon *m*; **behaviour pattern** mode *m* de comportement

pauper ['pɔːpə*] *n* indigent/e; **pauper's grave** fosse commune

pause [pɔːz] *n* pause *f*, arrêt *m*; (MUS) silence *m* ◆ *vi* faire une pause, s'arrêter; **to pause for breath** reprendre son souffle; (fig) faire une pause

pave [peɪv] *vt* paver, daller; **to pave the way for** ouvrir la voie à

pavement ['peɪvmənt] *n* (BRIT) trottoir *m*; (us) chaussée *f*

pavilion [pə'vɪlɪən] *n* pavillon *m*; tente *f*; (SPORT) stand *m*

paving ['peɪvɪŋ] *n* pavage *m*, dallage *m*

paving stone *n* pavé *m*

paw [pɔː] *n* patte *f* ◆ *vt* donner un coup de patte à; (subj: person: pej) tripoter

pawn [pɔːn] *n* gage *m*; (CHESS, also fig) pion *m* ◆ *vt* mettre en gage

pawnbroker ['pɔːnbrəʊkə*] *n* prêteur *m* sur gages

pawnshop ['pɔːnʃɔp] *n* mont-de-piété *m*

pay [peɪ] *n* salaire *m*; (of manual worker) paie *f* ◆ *vb*, *pt*, *pp* **paid** [peɪd] *vt* payer; (be profitable to: also fig) rapporter à ◆ *vi* payer; (be profitable) être rentable; **how much did you pay for it?** combien l'avez-vous payé?, vous l'avez payé combien?; **I paid £5 for that record** j'ai payé ce disque 5 livres; **to pay one's way** payer sa part; (subj: company) couvrir ses frais; **to pay dividends** (fig) porter ses fruits, s'avérer rentable; **it won't pay you to do that** vous ne gagnerez rien à faire cela; **to pay**

attention (to) prêter attention (à)
► **pay back** vt rembourser
► **pay for** vt fus payer
► **pay in** vt verser
► **pay off** vt (debts) régler, acquitter; (creditor, mortgage) rembourser; (workers) licencier ♦ vi (plan, patience) se révéler payant(e); **to pay sth off in instalments** payer qch à tempérament
► **pay out** vt (money) payer, sortir de sa poche; (rope) laisser filer
► **pay up** vt (debts) régler; (amount) payer
payable ['peɪəbl] adj payable; **to make a cheque payable to sb** établir un chèque à l'ordre de qn
payee [peɪ'iː] n bénéficiaire m/f
pay envelope n (US) (enveloppe f de) paie f
payment ['peɪmənt] n paiement m; (of bill) règlement m; (of deposit, cheque) versement m; **advance payment** (part sum) acompte m; (total sum) paiement anticipé; **deferred payment, payment by instalments** paiement par versements échelonnés; **monthly payment** mensualité f; **in payment for, in payment of** en règlement de; **on payment of £5** pour 5 livres
pay packet n (BRIT) paie f
payphone ['peɪfəʊn] n cabine f téléphonique, téléphone public
payroll ['peɪrəʊl] n registre m du personnel; **to be on a firm's payroll** être employé par une entreprise
pay slip n (BRIT) bulletin m de paie, feuille f de paie
pay television n chaînes fpl payantes
PC n abbr = **personal computer**; (BRIT) = **police constable** ♦ adj abbr = **politically correct** ♦ abbr (BRIT)= Privy Councillor
pc abbr = **per cent, postcard**
pea [piː] n (petit) pois
peace [piːs] n paix f; (calm) calme m, tranquillité f; **to be at peace with sb/sth** être en paix avec qn/qch; **to keep the peace** (subj: policeman) assurer le maintien de l'ordre; (: citizen) ne pas troubler l'ordre
peaceful ['piːsful] adj paisible, calme
peach [piːtʃ] n pêche f
peacock ['piːkɔk] n paon m
peak [piːk] n (mountain) pic m, cime f; (fig: highest level) maximum m; (: of career, fame) apogée m
peak hours npl heures fpl d'affluence
peal [piːl] n (of bells) carillon m; **peals of laughter** éclats mpl de rire
peanut ['piːnʌt] n arachide f, cacahuète f
peanut butter n beurre m de cacahuète
pear [peə*] n poire f
pearl [pəːl] n perle f
peasant ['pɛznt] n paysan/ne
peat [piːt] n tourbe f
pebble ['pɛbl] n galet m, caillou m
peck [pɛk] vt (also: **peck at**) donner un coup de bec à; (food) picorer ♦ n coup m de bec; (kiss)

bécot m
pecking order ['pɛkɪŋ-] n ordre m hiérarchique
peckish ['pɛkɪʃ] adj (BRIT col): **I feel peckish** je mangerais bien quelque chose, j'ai la dent
peculiar [pɪ'kjuːlɪə*] adj (odd) étrange, bizarre, curieux(euse); (particular) particulier(ière); **peculiar to** particulier à
pedal ['pɛdl] n pédale f ♦ vi pédaler
pedantic [pɪ'dæntɪk] adj pédant(e)
peddler ['pɛdlə*] n colporteur m; camelot m
pedestal ['pɛdəstl] n piédestal m
pedestrian [pɪ'dɛstrɪən] n piéton m ♦ adj piétonnier(ière); (fig) prosaïque, terre à terre inv
pedestrian crossing n (BRIT) passage clouté
pedestrianized [pɪ'dɛstrɪənaɪzd] adj: **a pedestrianized street** une rue piétonne
pediatrics [piːdɪ'ætrɪks] n (US) = **paediatrics**
pedigree ['pɛdɪgriː] n ascendance f; (of animal) pedigree m ♦ cpd (animal) de race
pee [piː] vi (col) faire pipi, pisser
peek [piːk] vi jeter un coup d'œil (furtif)
peel [piːl] n pelure f, épluchure f; (of orange, lemon) écorce f ♦ vt peler, éplucher ♦ vi (paint etc) s'écailler; (wallpaper) se décoller
► **peel back** vt décoller
peep [piːp] n (BRIT: look) coup d'œil furtif; (sound) pépiement m ♦ vi (BRIT) jeter un coup d'œil (furtif)
► **peep out** vi (BRIT) se montrer (furtivement)
peephole ['piːphəʊl] n judas m
peer [pɪə*] vi: **to peer at** regarder attentivement, scruter ♦ n (noble) pair m; (equal) pair, égal/e
peerage ['pɪərɪdʒ] n pairie f
peeved [piːvd] adj irrité(e), ennuyé(e)
peg [pɛg] n cheville f; (for coat etc) patère f; (BRIT: also: **clothes peg**) pince f à linge ♦ vt (clothes) accrocher; (BRIT: groundsheet) fixer (avec des piquets); (prices, wages) contrôler, stabiliser
Pekin(g)ese [piːkɪ'niːz] n pékinois m
pelican ['pɛlɪkən] n pélican m
pelican crossing n (BRIT AUT) feu m à commande manuelle
pellet ['pɛlɪt] n boulette f; (of lead) plomb m
pelt [pɛlt] vt: **to pelt sb (with)** bombarder qn (de) ♦ vi (rain) tomber à seaux ♦ n peau f
pelvis ['pɛlvɪs] n bassin m
pen [pɛn] n (for writing) stylo m; (for sheep) parc m; (US col: prison) taule f; **to put pen to paper** prendre la plume
penal ['piːnl] adj pénal(e)
penalize ['piːnəlaɪz] vt pénaliser; (fig) désavantager
penalty ['pɛnltɪ] n pénalité f; sanction f; (fine) amende f; (SPORT) pénalisation f; (FOOTBALL: also: **penalty kick**) penalty m
penance ['pɛnəns] n pénitence f
pence [pɛns] npl (BRIT) see **penny**
pencil ['pɛnsl] n crayon m ♦ vt: **to pencil sth in**

noter qch provisoirement

pencil case n trousse f (d'écolier)

pencil sharpener n taille-crayon(s) m inv

pendant ['pendnt] n pendentif m

pending ['pendɪŋ] prep en attendant ♦ adj en suspens

pendulum ['pendjuləm] n pendule m; (of clock) balancier m

penetrate ['penɪtreɪt] vt pénétrer dans; pénétrer

penfriend ['penfrend] n (BRIT) correspondant/e

penguin ['peŋgwɪn] n pingouin m

penicillin [penɪ'sɪlɪn] n pénicilline f

peninsula [pə'nɪnsjulə] n péninsule f

penis ['pi:nɪs] n pénis m, verge f

penitentiary [penɪ'tenʃərɪ] n (US) prison f

penknife ['pennaɪf] n canif m

pen name n nom m de plume, pseudonyme m

penniless ['penɪlɪs] adj sans le sou

penny, pl **pennies** or **pence** ['penɪ, 'penɪz, pens] n (BRIT) penny m (pl pennies) (new: 100 in a pound; old:12 in a shilling; on tend à employer "pennies" ou "two-pence piece" etc pour les pièces, "pence" pour la valeur); (US) = **cent**

penpal ['penpæl] n correspondant/e

pension ['penʃən] n retraite f; (MIL) pension f

▶ **pension off** vt mettre à la retraite

pensioner ['penʃənə*] n (BRIT) retraité/e

pension fund n caisse f de retraite

pension plan n plan m de retraite

pentagon ['pentəgən] n pentagone m; **the Pentagon** (US POL) le Pentagone; voir encadré

pentathlon [pen'tæθlən] n pentathlon m

Pentecost ['pentɪkɔst] n Pentecôte f

penthouse ['penthaus] n appartement m (de luxe) en attique

pent-up ['pentʌp] adj (feelings) refoulé(e)

penultimate [pɪ'nʌltɪmət] adj pénultième, avant-dernier(ière)

people ['pi:pl] npl gens mpl; personnes fpl; (citizens) peuple m ♦ n (nation, race) peuple m ♦ vt peupler; **I know people who ...** je connais des gens qui ...; **the room was full of people** la salle était pleine de monde or de gens; **people say that ...** on dit or les gens disent que ...; **old people** les personnes âgées; **young people** les jeunes; **a man of the people** un homme du peuple

pepper ['pepə*] n poivre m; (vegetable) poivron m

♦ vt poivrer

pepper mill n moulin m à poivre

peppermint ['pepəmɪnt] n (plant) menthe poivrée; (sweet) pastille f de menthe

peptalk ['peptɔ:k] n (col) (petit) discours d'encouragement

per [pə:*] prep par; **per hour** (miles etc) à l'heure; (fee) (de) l'heure; **per kilo** etc le kilo etc; **per day/person** par jour/personne; **as per your instructions** conformément à vos instructions

perceive [pə'si:v] vt percevoir; (notice) remarquer, s'apercevoir de

per cent adv pour cent; **a 20 per cent discount** une réduction de 20 pour cent

percentage [pə'sentɪdʒ] n pourcentage m; **on a percentage basis** au pourcentage

perception [pə'sepʃən] n perception f; (insight) sensibilité f

perceptive [pə'septɪv] adj (remark, person) perspicace

perch [pə:tʃ] n (fish) perche f; (for bird) perchoir m

♦ vi (se) percher

percolator ['pə:kəleɪtə*] n percolateur m; cafetière f électrique

percussion [pə'kʌʃən] n percussion f

perennial [pə'renɪəl] adj perpétuel(le) (BOT) vivace ♦ n plante f vivace

perfect adj, n ['pə:fɪkt] ♦ adj parfait(e) ♦ n (also: **perfect tense**) parfait m ♦ vt [pə'fekt] parfaire; mettre au point; **he's a perfect stranger to me** il m'est totalement inconnu

perfectly ['pə:fɪktlɪ] adv parfaitement; **I'm perfectly happy with the situation** cette situation me convient parfaitement; **you know perfectly well** vous le savez très bien

perforate ['pə:fəreɪt] vt perforer, percer

perforation [pə:fə'reɪʃən] n perforation f; (line of holes) pointillé m

perform [pə'fɔ:m] vt (carry out) exécuter, remplir; (concert etc) jouer, donner ♦ vi jouer

performance [pə'fɔ:məns] n représentation f, spectacle m; (of an artist) interprétation f; (of player etc) prestation f; (of car, engine) performance f; **the team put up a good performance** l'équipe a bien joué

performer [pə'fɔ:mə*] n artiste m/f

perfume ['pə:fju:m] n parfum m ♦ vt parfumer

perhaps [pə'hæps] adv peut-être; **perhaps he'll ...** peut-être qu'il ...; **perhaps so/not** peut-être que oui/que non

peril ['perɪl] n péril m

perimeter [pə'rɪmɪtə*] n périmètre m

period ['pɪərɪəd] n période f; (HISTORY) époque f; (SCOL) cours m; (full stop) point m; (MED) règles fpl ♦ adj (costume, furniture) d'époque; **for a period of three weeks** pour (une période de) trois semaines; **the holiday period** (BRIT) la période des vacances

periodical [pɪərɪˈɔdɪkl] adj périodique ♦ n périodique m

peripheral [pəˈrɪfərəl] adj périphérique ♦ n (COMPUT) périphérique m

perish [ˈperɪʃ] vi périr, mourir; (decay) se détériorer

perishable [ˈperɪʃəbl] adj périssable

perjury [ˈpəːdʒərɪ] n (LAW: in court) faux témoignage; (breach of oath) parjure m

perk [pəːk] n (col) avantage m, à-côté m
▶ **perk up** vi (col: cheer up) se ragaillardir

perky [ˈpəːkɪ] adj (cheerful) guilleret(te), gai(e)

perm [pəːm] n (for hair) permanente f ♦ vt: **to have one's hair permed** se faire faire une permanente

permanent [ˈpəːmənənt] adj permanent(e); (job, position) permanent, fixe; (dye, ink) indélébile; **I'm not permanent here** je ne suis pas ici à titre définitif; **permanent address** adresse habituelle

permeate [ˈpəːmɪeɪt] vi s'infiltrer ♦ vt s'infiltrer dans; pénétrer

permissible [pəˈmɪsɪbl] adj permis(e), acceptable

permission [pəˈmɪʃən] n permission f, autorisation f; **to give sb permission to do sth** donner à qn la permission de faire qch

permissive [pəˈmɪsɪv] adj tolérant(e); **the permissive society** la société de tolérance

permit n [ˈpəːmɪt] permis m; (entrance pass) autorisation f, laisser-passer m; (for goods) licence f ♦ vt [pəˈmɪt] permettre; **to permit sb to do** autoriser qn à faire, permettre à qn de faire; **weather permitting** si le temps le permet

perpendicular [pəːpənˈdɪkjulə*] adj, n perpendiculaire f

perplex [pəˈpleks] vt rendre perplexe; (complicate) embrouiller

persecute [ˈpəːsɪkjuːt] vt persécuter

persevere [pəːsɪˈvɪə*] vi persévérer

Persian [ˈpəːʃən] adj persan(e) ♦ n (LING) persan m; **the (Persian) Gulf** le golfe Persique

persist [pəˈsɪst] vi: **to persist (in doing)** persister (à faire), s'obstiner (à faire)

persistent [pəˈsɪstənt] adj persistant(e), tenace; (lateness, rain) persistant; **persistent offender** (LAW) multirécidiviste m/f

person [ˈpəːsn] n personne f; **in person** en personne; **on** or **about one's person** sur soi; **person to person call** (TEL) appel m avec préavis

personal [ˈpəːsnl] adj personnel(le); **personal belongings, personal effects** effets personnels; **personal hygiene** hygiène f intime; **a personal interview** un entretien

personal assistant (PA) n secrétaire personnel(le)

personal column n annonces personnelles

personal computer (PC) n ordinateur individuel, PC m

personal identification number (PIN) n (COMPUT, BANKING) numéro m d'identification personnel

personality [pəːsəˈnælɪtɪ] n personnalité f

personally [ˈpəːsnəlɪ] adv personnellement

personal organizer n agenda (personnel) (style Filofax); (electronic) agenda électronique

personal stereo n Walkman® m, baladeur m

personnel [pəːsəˈnel] n personnel m

perspective [pəˈspektɪv] n perspective f; **to get sth into perspective** ramener qch à sa juste mesure

perspex® [ˈpəːspeks] n (BRIT) Plexiglas® m

perspiration [pəːspɪˈreɪʃən] n transpiration f

persuade [pəˈsweɪd] vt: **to persuade sb to do sth** persuader qn de faire qch, amener or décider qn à faire qch; **to persuade sb of sth/that** persuader qn de qch/que

persuasion [pəˈsweɪʒən] n persuasion f; (creed) conviction f

perverse [pəˈvəːs] adj pervers(e); (stubborn) entêté(e), contrariant(e)

pervert n [ˈpəːvəːt] perverti/e ♦ vt [pəˈvəːt] pervertir

pessimist [ˈpesɪmɪst] n pessimiste m/f

pessimistic [pesɪˈmɪstɪk] adj pessimiste

pest [pest] n animal m (or insecte m) nuisible; (fig) fléau m

pester [ˈpestə*] vt importuner, harceler

pet [pet] n animal familier; (favourite) chouchou m ♦ vt choyer ♦ vi (col) se peloter; **pet lion etc** lion etc apprivoisé

petal [ˈpetl] n pétale m

peter [ˈpiːtə*]: **to peter out** vi s'épuiser; s'affaiblir

petite [pəˈtiːt] adj menu(e)

petition [pəˈtɪʃən] n pétition f ♦ vt adresser une pétition à ♦ vi: **to petition for divorce** demander le divorce

petrified [ˈpetrɪfaɪd] adj (fig) mort(e) de peur

petrol [ˈpetrəl] n (BRIT) essence f

petrol can n (BRIT) bidon m à essence

petroleum [pəˈtrəulɪəm] n pétrole m

petrol pump n (BRIT: in car, at garage) pompe f à essence

petrol station n (BRIT) station-service f

petrol tank n (BRIT) réservoir m d'essence

petticoat [ˈpetɪkəut] n jupon m

petty [ˈpetɪ] adj (mean) mesquin(e); (unimportant) insignifiant(e), sans importance

petty cash n caisse f des dépenses f courantes, petite caisse

petty officer n second-maître m

petulant [ˈpetjulənt] adj irritable

pew [pjuː] n banc m (d'église)

pewter [ˈpjuːtə*] n étain m

phantom [ˈfæntəm] n fantôme m; (vision) fantasme m

pharmacy ['fɑːməsɪ] *n* pharmacie *f*

phase [feɪz] *n* phase *f*, période *f* ◆ *vt*: **to phase sth in/out** introduire/supprimer qch progressivement

PhD *abbr* (= *Doctor of Philosophy*) *title* ≃ Docteur *m* en Droit *or* Lettres *etc* ◆ *n* ≃ doctorat *m*, titulaire *m* d'un doctorat; *see also* **doctorate**

pheasant ['feznt] *n* faisan *m*

phenomenon, *pl* **phenomena** [fə'nɒmɪnən, -nə] *n* phénomène *m*

philosophical [fɪlə'sɒfɪkl] *adj* philosophique

philosophy [fɪ'lɒsəfɪ] *n* philosophie *f*

phobia ['fəʊbjə] *n* phobie *f*

phone [fəʊn] *n* téléphone *m* ◆ *vt* téléphoner à ◆ *vi* téléphoner; **to be on the phone** avoir le téléphone; (*be calling*) être au téléphone

▶ **phone back** *vt*, *vi* rappeler

▶ **phone up** *vt* téléphoner à ◆ *vi* téléphoner

phone bill *n* facture *f* de téléphone

phone book *n* annuaire *m*

phone box, phone booth *n* cabine *f* téléphonique

phone call *n* coup *m* de fil *or* de téléphone

phonecard ['fəʊnkɑːd] *n* télécarte *f*

phone-in ['fəʊnɪn] *n* (*BRIT RADIO, TV*) programme *m* à ligne ouverte

phone number *n* numéro *m* de téléphone

phonetics [fə'netɪks] *n* phonétique *f*

phoney ['fəʊnɪ] *adj* faux(fausse), factice ◆ *n* (*person*) charlatan *m*; fumiste *m/f*

photo ['fəʊtəʊ] *n* photo *f*

photocopier ['fəʊtəʊkɒpɪə*] *n* copieur *m*

photocopy ['fəʊtəʊkɒpɪ] *n* photocopie *f* ◆ *vt* photocopier

photograph ['fəʊtəgræf] *n* photographie *f* ◆ *vt* photographier; **to take a photograph of sb** prendre qn en photo

photographer [fə'tɒgrəfə*] *n* photographe *m/f*

photography [fə'tɒgrəfɪ] *n* photographie *f*

phrase [freɪz] *n* expression *f*; (*LING*) locution *f* ◆ *vt* exprimer; (*letter*) rédiger

phrase book *n* recueil *m* d'expressions (pour touristes)

physical ['fɪzɪkl] *adj* physique; **physical examination** examen médical; **physical education** éducation physique; **physical exercises** gymnastique *f*

physically ['fɪzɪklɪ] *adv* physiquement

physician [fɪ'zɪʃən] *n* médecin *m*

physicist ['fɪzɪsɪst] *n* physicien/ne

physics ['fɪzɪks] *n* physique *f*

physiotherapist [fɪzɪəʊ'θerəpɪst] *n* kinésithérapeute *m/f*

physiotherapy [fɪzɪəʊ'θerəpɪ] *n* kinésithérapie *f*

physique [fɪ'ziːk] *n* (*appearance*) physique *m*; (*health etc*) constitution *f*

pianist ['pɪənɪst] *n* pianiste *m/f*

piano [pɪ'ænəʊ] *n* piano *m*

pick [pɪk] *n* (*tool: also*: **pick-axe**) pic *m*, pioche *f* ◆ *vt* choisir; (*gather*) cueillir; (*scab, spot*) gratter, écorcher; **take your pick** faites votre choix; **the pick of** le(la) meilleur(e) de; **to pick a bone** ronger un os; **to pick one's nose** se mettre le doigt dans le nez; **to pick one's teeth** se curer les dents; **to pick sb's brains** faire appel aux lumières de qn; **to pick pockets** pratiquer le vol à la tire; **to pick a quarrel/fight with sb** chercher querelle à/la bagarre avec qn

▶ **pick at** *vt fus*: **to pick at one's food** manger du bout des dents, chipoter

▶ **pick off** *vt* (*kill*) (viser soigneusement et) abattre

▶ **pick on** *vt fus* (*person*) harceler

▶ **pick out** *vt* choisir; (*distinguish*) distinguer

▶ **pick up** *vi* (*improve*) remonter, s'améliorer ◆ *vt* ramasser; (*telephone*) décrocher; (*collect*) passer prendre; (*AUT: give lift to*) prendre; (*learn*) apprendre; (*RADIO, TV, TEL*) capter; **to pick up speed** prendre de la vitesse; **to pick o.s. up** se relever; **to pick up where one left off** reprendre là où l'on s'est arrêté

picket ['pɪkɪt] *n* (*in strike*) gréviste *m/f* participant à un piquet de grève; piquet *m* de grève ◆ *vt* mettre un piquet de grève devant

pickle ['pɪkl] *n* (*also*: **pickles**: *as condiment*) pickles *mpl*; (*fig*): **in a pickle** dans le pétrin ◆ *vt* conserver dans du vinaigre *or* dans de la saumure

pickpocket ['pɪkpɒkɪt] *n* pickpocket *m*

pickup ['pɪkʌp] *n* (*BRIT: on record player*) bras *m* pick-up; (*small truck: also*: **pickup truck, pickup van**) camionnette *f*

picnic ['pɪknɪk] *n* pique-nique *m* ◆ *vi* pique-niquer

picture ['pɪktʃə*] *n* (*also TV*) image *f*; (*painting*) peinture *f*, tableau *m*; (*photograph*) photo(graphie) *f*; (*drawing*) dessin *m*; (*film*) film *m* ◆ *vt* se représenter; (*describe*) dépeindre, représenter; **the pictures** (*BRIT*) le cinéma; **to take a picture of sb/sth** prendre qn/qch en photo; **the overall picture** le tableau d'ensemble; **to put sb in the picture** mettre qn au courant

picture book *n* livre *m* d'images

picturesque [pɪktʃə'resk] *adj* pittoresque

pie [paɪ] *n* tourte *f*; (*of meat*) pâté *m* en croûte

piece [piːs] *n* morceau *m*; (*of land*) parcelle *f*; (*item*): **a piece of furniture/advice** un meuble/conseil; (*DRAUGHTS etc*) pion *m* ◆ *vt*: **to piece together** rassembler; **in pieces** (*broken*) en morceaux, en miettes; (*not yet assembled*) en pièces détachées; **to take to pieces** démonter; **in one piece** (*object*) intact(e); **to get back all in one piece** (*person*) rentrer sain et sauf; **a 10p piece** (*BRIT*) une pièce de 10p; **piece by piece** morceau par morceau; **a six-piece band** un orchestre de six musiciens; **to say one's piece** réciter son morceau

piecemeal ['pi:smi:l] *adv* par bouts

piecework ['pi:swɜ:k] *n* travail *m* aux pièces *or* à la pièce

pie chart *n* graphique *m* à secteurs, camembert *m*

pier [pɪə*] *n* jetée *f*; (*of bridge etc*) pile *f*

pierce [pɪəs] *vt* percer, transpercer; **to have one's ears pierced** se faire percer les oreilles

pig [pɪg] *n* cochon *m*, porc *m*

pigeon ['pɪdʒən] *n* pigeon *m*

pigeonhole ['pɪdʒənhəul] *n* casier *m*

piggy bank ['pɪgɪ-] *n* tirelire *f*

pigheaded ['pɪg'hedɪd] *adj* entêté(e), têtu(e)

piglet ['pɪglɪt] *n* petit cochon, porcelet *m*

pigskin ['pɪgskɪn] *n* (peau *f* de) porc *m*

pigsty ['pɪgstaɪ] *n* porcherie *f*

pigtail ['pɪgteɪl] *n* natte *f*, tresse *f*

pike [paɪk] *n* (*spear*) pique *f*; (*fish*) brochet *m*

pilchard ['pɪltʃəd] *n* pilchard *m*; (*sorte de sardine*)

pile [paɪl] *n* (*pillar, of cards*) pile *f*; (*heap*) tas *m*; (*of carpet*) épaisseur *f* ♦ *vb* (*also*: **pile up**) *vt* empiler, entasser ♦ *vi* s'entasser; **in a pile** en tas

▶ **pile on** *vt*: **to pile it on** (*col*) exagérer

piles [paɪlz] *npl* hémorroïdes *fpl*

pile-up ['paɪlʌp] *n* (*AUT*) télescopage *m*, collision *f* en série

pilfering ['pɪlfərɪŋ] *n* chapardage *m*

pilgrim ['pɪlgrɪm] *n* pèlerin *m*

pill [pɪl] *n* pilule *f*; **the pill** la pilule; **to be on the pill** prendre la pilule

pillage ['pɪlɪdʒ] *vt* piller

pillar ['pɪlə*] *n* pilier *m*

pillar box *n* (*BRIT*) boîte *f* aux lettres (*publique*)

pillion ['pɪljən] *n* (*of motor cycle*) siège *m* arrière; **to ride pillion** être derrière; (*on horse*) être en croupe

pillow ['pɪləu] *n* oreiller *m*

pillowcase ['pɪləukeɪs], **pillowslip** ['pɪləuslɪp] *n* taie *f* d'oreiller

pilot ['paɪlət] *n* pilote *m* ♦ *cpd* (*scheme etc*) pilote, expérimental(e) ♦ *vt* piloter

pilot light *n* veilleuse *f*

pimp [pɪmp] *n* souteneur *m*, maquereau *m*

pimple ['pɪmpl] *n* bouton *m*

PIN *n abbr* = **personal identification number**

pin [pɪn] *n* épingle *f*; (*TECH*) cheville *f*; (*BRIT: drawing pin*) punaise *f*; (*in grenade*) goupille *f*; (*BRIT ELEC: of plug*) broche *f* ♦ *vt* épingler; **pins and needles** fourmis *fpl*; **to pin sb against/to** clouer qn contre/à; **to pin sth on sb** (*fig*) mettre qch sur le dos de qn

▶ **pin down** *vt* (*fig*): **to pin sb down** obliger qn à répondre; **there's something strange here but I can't quite pin it down** il y a quelque chose d'étrange ici, mais je n'arrive pas exactement à savoir quoi

pinafore ['pɪnəfɔ:*] *n* tablier *m*

pinball ['pɪnbɔ:l] *n* flipper *m*

pincers ['pɪnsəz] *npl* tenailles *fpl*

pinch [pɪntʃ] *n* pincement *m*; (*of salt etc*) pincée *f* ♦ *vt* pincer; (*col: steal*) piquer, chiper ♦ *vi* (*shoe*) serrer; **at a pinch** à la rigueur; **to feel the pinch** (*fig*) se ressentir des restrictions (*or de la récession etc*)

pincushion ['pɪnkuʃən] *n* pelote *f* à épingles

pine [paɪn] *n* (*also*: **pine tree**) pin *m* ♦ *vi*: **to pine for** aspirer à, désirer ardemment

▶ **pine away** *vi* dépérir

pineapple ['paɪnæpl] *n* ananas *m*

ping [pɪŋ] *n* (*noise*) tintement *m*

Ping-Pong® ['pɪŋpɔŋ] *n* ping-pong® *m*

pink [pɪŋk] *adj* rose ♦ *n* (*colour*) rose *m*; (*BOT*) œillet *m*, mignardise *f*

pinpoint ['pɪnpɔɪnt] *vt* indiquer (avec précision)

pint [paɪnt] *n* pinte *f* (*BRIT = 0.57 l; US = 0.47 l*); (*BRIT col*) = demi *m*, = pot *m*

pioneer [paɪə'nɪə*] *n* explorateur/trice; (*early settler*) pionnier *m*; (*fig*) pionnier, précurseur *m* ♦ *vt* être un pionnier de

pious ['paɪəs] *adj* pieux(euse)

pip [pɪp] *n* (*seed*) pépin *m*; (*BRIT: time signal on radio*) top *m*

pipe [paɪp] *n* tuyau *m*, conduite *f*; (*for smoking*) pipe *f*; (*MUS*) pipeau *m* ♦ *vt* amener par tuyau; **pipes** *npl* (*also*: **bagpipes**) cornemuse *f*

▶ **pipe down** *vi* (*col*) se taire

pipe cleaner *n* cure-pipe *m*

pipe dream *n* chimère *f*, utopie *f*

pipeline ['paɪplaɪn] *n* (*for gas*) gazoduc *m*, pipeline *m*; (*for oil*) oléoduc *m*, pipeline; **it is in the pipeline** (*fig*) c'est en route, ça va se faire

piper ['paɪpə*] *n* joueur/euse de pipeau (*or de cornemuse*)

piping ['paɪpɪŋ] *adv*: **piping hot** très chaud(e)

pique [pi:k] *n* dépit *m*

pirate ['paɪərət] *n* pirate *m* ♦ *vt* (*record, video, book*) pirater

pirated ['paɪərətɪd] *adj* pirate

Pisces ['paɪsi:z] *n* les Poissons *mpl*; **to be Pisces** être des Poissons

piss [pɪs] *vi* (*col!*) pisser (*!*); **piss off!** tire-toi! (*!*)

pissed [pɪst] *adj* (*BRIT col: drunk*) bourré(e)

pistol ['pɪstl] *n* pistolet *m*

piston ['pɪstən] *n* piston *m*

pit [pɪt] *n* trou *m*, fosse *f*; (*also*: **coal pit**) puits *m* de mine; (*also*: **orchestra pit**) fosse d'orchestre ♦ *vt*: **to pit sb against sb** opposer qn à qn; **to pit o.s. against** se mesurer à; **pits** *npl* (*in motor racing*) aire *f* de service

pitch [pɪtʃ] *n* (*throw*) lancement *m*; (*MUS*) ton *m*; (*of voice*) hauteur *f*; (*fig: degree*) degré *m*; (*also*: **sales pitch**) baratin *m*, boniment *m*; (*BRIT SPORT*) terrain *m*; (*NAUT*) tangage *m*; (*tar*) poix *f* ♦ *vt* (*throw*) lancer; (*tent*) dresser; (*set: price, message*) adapter, positionner ♦ *vi* (*NAUT*) tanguer; (*fall*): **to pitch into/off**

tomber dans/de; **to be pitched forward** être projeté(e) en avant; **at this pitch** à ce rythme
pitch-black ['pɪtʃ'blæk] *adj* noir(e) comme poix
pitched battle [pɪtʃt-] *n* bataille rangée
pitfall ['pɪtfɔːl] *n* trappe *f*, piège *m*
pith [pɪθ] *n* (*of plant*) moelle *f*; (*of orange*) intérieur *m* de l'écorce; (*fig*) essence *f*, vigueur *f*
pithy ['pɪθɪ] *adj* piquant(e); vigoureux(euse)
pitiful ['pɪtɪful] *adj* (*touching*) pitoyable; (*contemptible*) lamentable
pitiless ['pɪtɪlɪs] *adj* impitoyable
pittance ['pɪtns] *n* salaire *m* de misère
pity ['pɪtɪ] *n* pitié *f* ♦ *vt* plaindre; **what a pity!** quel dommage!; **it is a pity that you can't come** c'est dommage que vous ne puissiez venir; **to have** *or* **take pity on sb** avoir pitié de qn
pizza ['piːtsə] *n* pizza *f*
placard ['plækɑːd] *n* affiche *f*
placate [plə'keɪt] *vt* apaiser, calmer
place [pleɪs] *n* endroit *m*, lieu *m*; (*proper position, rank, seat*) place *f*; (*house*) maison *f*, logement *m*; (*in street names*): **Laurel Place** ≃ rue des Lauriers; (*home*): **at/to his place** chez lui ♦ *vt* (*position*) placer, mettre; (*identify*) situer; reconnaître; **to take place** avoir lieu; (*occur*) se produire; **from place to place** d'un endroit à l'autre; **all over the place** partout; **out of place** (*not suitable*) déplacé(e), inopportun(e); **I feel out of place here** je ne me sens pas à ma place ici; **in the first place** d'abord, en premier; **to put sb in his place** (*fig*) remettre qn à sa place; **he's going places** (*fig: col*) il fait son chemin; **it is not my place to do it** ce n'est pas à moi de le faire; **to place an order with sb (for)** (*COMM*) passer commande à qn (de); **to be placed** (*in race, exam*) se placer; **how are you placed next week?** comment ça se présente pour la semaine prochaine?
plague [pleɪg] *n* fléau *m*; (*MED*) peste *f* ♦ *vt* (*fig*) tourmenter; **to plague sb with questions** harceler qn de questions
plaice [pleɪs] *n* (*pl inv*) carrelet *m*
plaid [plæd] *n* tissu écossais
plain [pleɪn] *adj* (*clear*) clair(e), évident(e); (*simple*) simple, ordinaire; (*frank*) franc(franche); (*not handsome*) quelconque, ordinaire; (*cigarette*) sans filtre; (*without seasoning etc*) nature *inv*; (*in one colour*) uni(e) ♦ *adv* franchement, carrément ♦ *n* plaine *f*; **in plain clothes** (*police*) en civil; **to make sth plain to sb** faire clairement comprendre qch à qn
plain chocolate *n* chocolat *m* à croquer
plainly ['pleɪnlɪ] *adv* clairement; (*frankly*) carrément, sans détours
plaintiff ['pleɪntɪf] *n* plaignant/e
plait [plæt] *n* tresse *f*, natte *f* ♦ *vt* tresser, natter
plan [plæn] *n* plan *m*; (*scheme*) projet *m* ♦ *vt* (*think in advance*) projeter; (*prepare*) organiser ♦ *vi* faire des projets; **to plan to do** projeter de faire; **how long do you plan to stay?** combien de temps

comptez-vous rester?
plane [pleɪn] *n* (*AVIAT*) avion *m*; (*tree*) platane *m*; (*tool*) rabot *m*; (*ART, MATH ETC*) plan *m* ♦ *adj* plan(e); plat(e) ♦ *vt* (*with tool*) raboter
planet ['plænɪt] *n* planète *f*
plank [plæŋk] *n* planche *f*; (*POL*) point *m* d'un programme
planner ['plænə*] *n* planificateur/trice; (*chart*) planning *m*; **town** *or* (*US*) **city planner** urbaniste *m/f*
planning ['plænɪŋ] *n* planification *f*; **family planning** planning familial
planning permission *n* (*BRIT*) permis *m* de construire
plant [plɑːnt] *n* plante *f*; (*machinery*) matériel *m*; (*factory*) usine *f* ♦ *vt* planter; (*bomb*) déposer, poser
plaster ['plɑːstə*] *n* plâtre *m*; (*BRIT: also*: **sticking plaster**) pansement adhésif ♦ *vt* plâtrer; (*cover*): **to plaster with** couvrir de; **in plaster** (*BRIT: leg etc*) dans le plâtre; **plaster of Paris** plâtre à mouler
plastered ['plɑːstəd] *adj* (*col*) soûl(e)
plastic ['plæstɪk] *n* plastique *m* ♦ *adj* (*made of plastic*) en plastique; (*flexible*) plastique, malléable; (*art*) plastique
plastic bag *n* sac *m* en plastique
plasticine® ['plæstɪsiːn] *n* pâte *f* à modeler
plastic surgery *n* chirurgie *f* esthétique
plate [pleɪt] *n* (*dish*) assiette *f*; (*sheet of metal, on door, PHOT*) plaque *f*; (*TYP*) cliché *m*; (*in book*) gravure *f*; (*AUT: number plate*) plaque minéralogique; **gold/ silver plate** (*dishes*) vaisselle *f* d'or/d'argent
plateau, *pl* **plateaus** *or* **plateaux** ['plætəu, -z] *n* plateau *m*
plate glass *n* verre *m* à vitre, vitre *f*
platform ['plætfɔːm] *n* (*at meeting*) tribune *f*; (*BRIT: of bus*) plate-forme *f*; (*stage*) estrade *f*; (*RAIL*) quai *m*; **the train leaves from platform 7** le train part de la voie 7
platinum ['plætɪnəm] *n* platine *m*
platter ['plætə*] *n* plat *m*
plausible ['plɔːzɪbl] *adj* plausible; (*person*) convaincant(e)
play [pleɪ] *n* jeu *m*; (*THEAT*) pièce *f* (de théâtre) ♦ *vt* (*game*) jouer à; (*team, opponent*) jouer contre; (*instrument*) jouer de; (*part, piece of music, note*) jouer ♦ *vi* jouer; **to bring** *or* **call into play** faire entrer en jeu; **play on words** jeu de mots; **to play a trick on sb** jouer un tour à qn; **they're playing at soldiers** ils jouent aux soldats; **to play for time** (*fig*) chercher à gagner du temps; **to play into sb's hands** (*fig*) faire le jeu de qn
► **play about**, **play around** *vi* (*person*) s'amuser
► **play along** *vi* (*fig*): **to play along with** (*person*) entrer dans le jeu de ♦ *vt* (*fig*): **to play sb along** faire marcher qn
► **play back** *vt* repasser, réécouter

▶ **play down** vt minimiser

▶ **play on** vt fus (sb's feelings, credulity) jouer sur; **to play on sb's nerves** porter sur les nerfs de qn

▶ **play up** vi (cause trouble) faire des siennes

playboy ['pleɪbɔɪ] n playboy m

player ['pleɪə*] n joueur/euse; (THEAT) acteur/trice; (MUS) musicien/ne

playful ['pleɪful] adj enjoué(e)

playground ['pleɪgraund] n cour f de récréation

playgroup ['pleɪgruːp] n garderie f

playing card ['pleɪɪŋ-] n carte f à jouer

playing field ['pleɪɪŋ-] n terrain m de sport

playmate ['pleɪmeɪt] n camarade m/f, copain/copine

play-off ['pleɪɔf] n (SPORT) belle f

playpen ['pleɪpen] n parc m (pour bébé)

plaything ['pleɪθɪŋ] n jouet m

playtime ['pleɪtaɪm] n (SCOL) récréation f

playwright ['pleɪraɪt] n dramaturge m

plc abbr (BRIT) (= public limited company) SARL f

plea [pliː] n (request) appel m; (excuse) excuse f; (LAW) défense f

plead [pliːd] vt plaider; (give as excuse) invoquer ♦ vi (LAW) plaider; (beg): **to plead with sb (for sth)** implorer qn (d'accorder qch); **to plead for sth** implorer qch; **to plead guilty/not guilty** plaider coupable/non coupable

pleasant ['pleznt] adj agréable

pleasantry ['plezntri] n (joke) plaisanterie f; **pleasantries** npl (polite remarks) civilités fpl

please [pliːz] vt plaire à ♦ vi (think fit): **do as you please** faites comme il vous plaira; **please!** s'il te (or vous) plaît; **my bill, please** l'addition, s'il vous plaît; **please don't cry!** je t'en prie, ne pleure pas!; **please yourself!** (faites) comme vous voulez!

pleased [pliːzd] adj: **pleased (with)** content(e) (de); **pleased to meet you** enchanté (de faire votre connaissance); **we are pleased to inform you that ...** nous sommes heureux de vous annoncer que ...

pleasing ['pliːzɪŋ] adj plaisant(e), qui fait plaisir

pleasure ['pleʒə*] n plaisir m; **"it's a pleasure"** "je vous en prie"; **with pleasure** avec plaisir; **is this trip for business or pleasure?** est-ce un voyage d'affaires ou d'agrément?

pleat [pliːt] n pli m

pledge [pledʒ] n gage m; (promise) promesse f ♦ vt engager; promettre; **to pledge support for sb** s'engager à soutenir qn; **to pledge sb to secrecy** faire promettre à qn de garder le secret

plentiful ['plentiful] adj abondant(e), copieux(euse)

plenty ['plenti] n abondance f; **plenty of** beaucoup de; (sufficient) (bien) assez de; **we've got plenty of time** nous avons largement le temps

pliable ['plaɪəbl] adj flexible; (person) malléable

pliers ['plaɪəz] npl pinces fpl

plight [plaɪt] n situation f critique

plimsolls ['plɪmsəlz] npl (BRIT) (chaussures fpl) tennis fpl

plinth [plɪnθ] n socle m

PLO n abbr (= Palestine Liberation Organization) OLP f

plod [plɔd] vi avancer péniblement; (fig) peiner

plonk [plɔŋk] (col) n (BRIT: wine) pinard m, piquette f ♦ vt: **to plonk sth down** poser brusquement qch

plot [plɔt] n complot m, conspiration f; (of story, play) intrigue f; (of land) lot m de terrain, lopin m ♦ vt (mark out) pointer; relever; (conspire) comploter ♦ vi comploter; **a vegetable plot** (BRIT) un carré de légumes

plough, (US) **plow** [plau] n charrue f ♦ vt (earth) labourer

▶ **plough back** vt (COMM) réinvestir

▶ **plough through** vt fus (snow etc) avancer péniblement dans

ploughman, (US) **plowman** ['plaumən] n laboureur m; **ploughman's lunch** (BRIT) repas sommaire de pain et de fromage

ploy [plɔɪ] n stratagème m

pluck [plʌk] vt (fruit) cueillir; (musical instrument) pincer; (bird) plumer ♦ n courage m, cran m; **to pluck one's eyebrows** s'épiler les sourcils; **to pluck up courage** prendre son courage à deux mains

plug [plʌg] n bouchon m, bonde f; (ELEC) prise f de courant; (AUT: also: **spark(ing) plug**) bougie f ♦ vt (hole) boucher; (col: advertise) faire du battage pour, matraquer; **to give sb/sth a plug** (col) faire de la pub pour qn/qch

▶ **plug in** (ELEC) vt brancher ♦ vi se brancher

plum [plʌm] n (fruit) prune f ♦ adj: **plum job** (col) travail m en or

plumb [plʌm] adj vertical(e) ♦ n plomb m ♦ adv (exactly) en plein ♦ vt sonder

▶ **plumb in** vt (washing machine) faire le raccordement de

plumber ['plʌmə*] n plombier m

plumbing ['plʌmɪŋ] n (trade) plomberie f; (piping) tuyauterie f

plummet ['plʌmɪt] vi plonger, dégringoler

plump [plʌmp] adj rondelet(te), dodu(e), bien en chair ♦ vt: **to plump sth (down) on** laisser tomber qch lourdement sur

▶ **plump for** vt fus (col: choose) se décider pour

▶ **plump up** vt (cushion) battre (pour lui redonner forme)

plunder ['plʌndə*] n pillage m ♦ vt piller

plunge [plʌndʒ] n plongeon m ♦ vt plonger ♦ vi (fall) tomber, dégringoler; **to take the plunge** se jeter à l'eau

plunging ['plʌndʒɪŋ] adj (neckline) plongeant(e)

pluperfect [pluː'pɜːfɪkt] n plus-que-parfait m

plural [ˈpluərl] *adj* pluriel(le) ◆ *n* pluriel *m*

plus [plʌs] *n* (*also*: **plus sign**) signe *m* plus ◆ *prep* plus; **ten/twenty plus** plus de dix/vingt; **it's a plus** c'est un atout

plush [plʌʃ] *adj* somptueux(euse) ◆ *n* peluche *f*

ply [plaɪ] *n* (*of wool*) fil *m*; (*of wood*) feuille *f*, épaisseur *f* ◆ *vt* (*tool*) manier; (*a trade*) exercer ◆ *vi* (*ship*) faire la navette; **three ply (wool)** *n* laine *f* trois fils; **to ply sb with drink** donner continuellement à boire à qn

plywood [ˈplaɪwud] *n* contreplaqué *m*

PM *n abbr* (*BRIT*) = **prime minister**

p.m. *adv abbr* (= *post meridiem*) de l'après-midi

PMS *n abbr* (= *premenstrual syndrome*) syndrome prémenstruel

pneumonia [njuːˈməunɪə] *n* pneumonie *f*

poach [pəutʃ] *vt* (*cook*) pocher; (*steal*) pêcher (*or* chasser) sans permis ◆ *vi* braconner

poached egg [pəutʃt-] *n* œuf poché

poacher [ˈpəutʃə*] *n* braconnier *m*

PO box *n abbr* = **post office box**

pocket [ˈpɔkɪt] *n* poche *f* ◆ *vt* empocher; **to be (£5) out of pocket** (*BRIT*) en être de sa poche (pour 5 livres)

pocketbook [ˈpɔkɪtbuk] *n* (*wallet*) portefeuille *m*; (*notebook*) carnet *m*; (*US: handbag*) sac *m* à main

pocket calculator *n* calculette *f*

pocket knife *n* canif *m*

pocket money *n* argent *m* de poche

pod [pɔd] *n* cosse *f* ◆ *vt* écosser

podcast [ˈpɔdkɑːst] *n* podcast *m* ◆ *vt* diffuser en podcast, podcaster ◆ *vi* faire du podcasting, podcaster

podgy [ˈpɔdʒɪ] *adj* rondelet(te)

podiatrist [pɔˈdiːətrɪst] *n* (*US*) pédicure *m/f*

poem [ˈpəuɪm] *n* poème *m*

poet [ˈpəuɪt] *n* poète *m*

poetic [pəuˈetɪk] *adj* poétique

poetry [ˈpəuɪtrɪ] *n* poésie *f*

poignant [ˈpɔɪnjənt] *adj* poignant(e); (*sharp*) vif(vive)

point [pɔɪnt] *n* (*tip*) pointe *f*; (*in time*) moment *m*; (*in space*) endroit *m*; (*GEOM, SCOL, SPORT, on scale*) point *m*; (*subject, idea*) point, sujet *m*; (*also*: **decimal point**): **2 point 3 (2.3)** 2 virgule 3 (2,3); (*BRIT ELEC: also*: **power point**) prise *f* (de courant) ◆ *vt* (*show*) indiquer; (*wall, window*) jointoyer; (*gun etc*): **to point sth at** braquer *or* diriger qch sur ◆ *vi* montrer du doigt; **to point to** montrer du doigt; (*fig*) signaler; **points** *npl* (*AUT*) vis platinées; (*RAIL*) aiguillage *m*; **good points** qualités *fpl*; **the train stops at Carlisle and all points south** le train dessert Carlisle et toutes les gares vers le sud; **to make a point** faire une remarque; **to make a point of doing sth** ne pas manquer de faire qch; **to make one's point** se faire comprendre; **to get the point** comprendre, saisir; **to come to the point** en venir

au fait; **when it comes to the point** le moment venu; **there's no point (in doing)** cela ne sert à rien (de faire); **to be on the point of doing sth** être sur le point de faire qch; **that's the whole point!** précisément!; **to be beside the point** être à côté de la question; **you've got a point there!** (c'est) juste!; **in point of fact** en fait, en réalité; **point of departure** (*also fig*) point de départ; **point of order** point de procédure; **point of sale** (*COMM*) point de vente; **point of view** point de vue

▶ **point out** *vt* faire remarquer, souligner

point-blank [ˈpɔɪntˈblæŋk] *adv* (*also*: **at point-blank range**) à bout portant ◆ *adj* (*fig*) catégorique

pointed [ˈpɔɪntɪd] *adj* (*shape*) pointu(e); (*remark*) plein(e) de sous-entendus

pointer [ˈpɔɪntə*] *n* (*stick*) baguette *f*; (*needle*) aiguille *f*; (*dog*) chien *m* d'arrêt; (*clue*) indication *f*; (*advice*) tuyau *m*

pointless [ˈpɔɪntlɪs] *adj* inutile, vain(e)

poise [pɔɪz] *n* (*balance*) équilibre *m*; (*of head, body*) port *m*; (*calmness*) calme *m* ◆ *vt* placer en équilibre; **to be poised for** (*fig*) être prêt à

poison [ˈpɔɪzn] *n* poison *m* ◆ *vt* empoisonner

poisonous [ˈpɔɪznəs] *adj* (*snake*) venimeux(euse); (*substance*) vénéneux(euse); (*fumes*) toxique; (*fig*) pernicieux(euse)

poke [pəuk] *vt* (*fire*) tisonner; (*jab with finger, stick etc*) piquer; pousser du doigt; (*put*): **to poke sth into** fourrer *or* enfoncer qch dans ◆ *n* (*jab*) (petit) coup; (*to fire*) coup *m* de tisonnier; **to poke one's head out of the window** passer la tête par la fenêtre; **to poke fun at sb** se moquer de qn

▶ **poke about** *vi* fureter

poker [ˈpəukə*] *n* tisonnier *m*; (*CARDS*) poker *m*

poky [ˈpəukɪ] *adj* exigu(ë)

Poland [ˈpəulənd] *n* Pologne *f*

polar [ˈpəulə*] *adj* polaire

polar bear *n* ours blanc

Pole [pəul] *n* Polonais/e

pole [pəul] *n* (*of wood*) mât *m*, perche *f*; (*ELEC*) poteau *m*; (*GEO*) pôle *m*

pole bean *n* (*US*) haricot *m* (à rames)

pole vault [ˈpəulvɔːlt] *n* saut *m* à la perche

police [pəˈliːs] *npl* police *f* ◆ *vt* maintenir l'ordre dans; **a large number of police were hurt** de nombreux policiers ont été blessés

police car *n* voiture *f* de police

policeman [pəˈliːsmən] *n* agent *m* de police, policier *m*

police station *n* commissariat *m* de police

policewoman [pəˈliːswumən] *n* femme-agent *f*

policy [ˈpɔlɪsɪ] *n* politique *f*; (*also*: **insurance policy**) police *f* (d'assurance); (*of newspaper, company*) politique générale; **to take out a policy** (*INSURANCE*) souscrire une police d'assurance

Polish [ˈpəulɪʃ] *adj* polonais(e) ◆ *n* (*LING*) polonais *m*

polish ['pɒlɪʃ] *n* (for shoes) cirage *m*; (for floor) cire *f*, encaustique *f*; (for nails) vernis *m*; (shine) éclat *m*, poli *m*; (fig: refinement) raffinement *m* ◆ *vt* (put polish on: shoes, wood) cirer; (make shiny) astiquer, faire briller; (fig: improve) perfectionner

▶ **polish off** *vt* (work) expédier; (food) liquider
polished ['pɒlɪʃt] *adj* (fig) raffiné(e)
polite [pə'laɪt] *adj* poli(e); **it's not polite to do that** ça ne se fait pas
politely [pə'laɪtlɪ] *adv* poliment
politeness [pə'laɪtnɪs] *n* politesse *f*
political [pə'lɪtɪkl] *adj* politique
politically correct (PC) *adj* politiquement correct(e)
politician [pɒlɪ'tɪʃən] *n* homme/femme politique, politicien/ne
politics ['pɒlɪtɪks] *n* politique *f*
poll [pəʊl] *n* scrutin *m*, vote *m*; (also: **opinion poll**) sondage *m* (d'opinion) ◆ *vt* obtenir; **to go to the polls** (voters) aller aux urnes; (government) tenir des élections
pollen ['pɒlən] *n* pollen *m*
polling day *n* (BRIT) jour *m* des élections
polling station *n* (BRIT) bureau *m* de vote
pollute [pə'luːt] *vt* polluer
pollution [pə'luːʃən] *n* pollution *f*
polo ['pəʊləʊ] *n* polo *m*
poloneck ['pəʊlənɛk] *n* col roulé ◆ *adj* **poloneck(ed)** à col roulé
polo shirt *n* polo *m*
polythene ['pɒlɪθiːn] *n* polyéthylène *m*
polythene bag *n* sac *m* en plastique
pomegranate ['pɒmɪgrænɪt] *n* grenade *f*
pomp [pɒmp] *n* pompe *f*, faste *m*, apparat *m*
pompous ['pɒmpəs] *adj* pompeux(euse)
pond [pɒnd] *n* étang *m*; (stagnant) mare *f*
ponder ['pɒndə*] *vi* réfléchir ◆ *vt* considérer, peser
ponderous ['pɒndərəs] *adj* pesant(e), lourd(e)
pong [pɒŋ] (BRIT col) *n* puanteur *f* ◆ *vi* schlinguer
pony ['pəʊnɪ] *n* poney *m*
ponytail ['pəʊnɪteɪl] *n* queue *f* de cheval
pony trekking [-trɛkɪŋ] *n* (BRIT) randonnée *f* équestre *or* à cheval
poodle ['puːdl] *n* caniche *m*
pool [puːl] *n* (of rain) flaque *f*; (pond) mare *f*; (artificial) bassin *m*; (also: **swimming pool**) piscine *f*; (sth shared) fonds commun; (money at cards) cagnotte *f*; (billiards) poule *f*; (COMM: consortium) pool *m*; (US: monopoly trust) trust *m* ◆ *vt* mettre en commun; **typing pool**, (US) **secretary pool** pool *m* dactylographique; **to do the (football) pools** (BRIT) ≈ jouer au loto sportif; *see also* **football pools**
poor [puə*] *adj* pauvre; (mediocre) médiocre, faible, mauvais(e) ◆ *npl*: **the poor** les pauvres *mpl*

poorly ['puəlɪ] *adv* pauvrement; médiocrement ◆ *adj* souffrant(e), malade
pop [pɒp] *n* (noise) bruit sec; (MUS) musique *f* pop; (col: drink) soda *m*; (US col: father) papa *m* ◆ *vt* (put) fourrer, mettre (rapidement) ◆ *vi* éclater; (cork) sauter; **she popped her head out of the window** elle passa la tête par la fenêtre

▶ **pop in** *vi* entrer en passant
▶ **pop out** *vi* sortir
▶ **pop up** *vi* apparaître, surgir
popcorn ['pɒpkɔːn] *n* pop-corn *m*
pope [pəʊp] *n* pape *m*
poplar ['pɒplə*] *n* peuplier *m*
popper ['pɒpə*] *n* (BRIT) bouton-pression *m*
poppy ['pɒpɪ] *n* coquelicot *m*; pavot *m*
Popsicle® ['pɒpsɪkl] *n* (US) esquimau *m* (glace)
popular ['pɒpjulə*] *adj* populaire; (fashionable) à la mode; **to be popular (with)** (person) avoir du succès (auprès de); (decision) être bien accueilli(e) (par)
population [pɒpju'leɪʃən] *n* population *f*
pop-up ['pɒp ʌp] *adj* (COMPUT: menu, window) pop up *inv*; ◆ *n inv* pop up *m inv*, fenêtre *f* pop up
porcelain ['pɔːslɪn] *n* porcelaine *f*
porch [pɔːtʃ] *n* porche *m*
porcupine ['pɔːkjupaɪn] *n* porc-épic *m*
pore [pɔː*] *n* pore *m* ◆ *vi*: **to pore over** s'absorber dans, être plongé(e) dans
pork [pɔːk] *n* porc *m*
porn [pɔːn] *adj*, *n* (col) porno *m*
pornographic [pɔːnə'græfɪk] *adj* pornographique
pornography [pɔː'nɔgrəfɪ] *n* pornographie *f*
porpoise ['pɔːpəs] *n* marsouin *m*
porridge ['pɒrɪdʒ] *n* porridge *m*
port [pɔːt] *n* (harbour) port *m*; (opening in ship) sabord *m*; (NAUT: left side) bâbord *m*; (wine) porto *m*; (COMPUT) port *m*, accès *m* ◆ *cpd* portuaire, du port; **to port** (NAUT) à bâbord; **port of call** (port d')escale *f*
portable ['pɔːtəbl] *adj* portatif(ive)
porter ['pɔːtə*] *n* (for luggage) porteur *m*; (doorkeeper) gardien/ne; portier *m*
portfolio [pɔːt'fəʊlɪəʊ] *n* portefeuille *m*; (of artist) portfolio *m*
porthole ['pɔːthəʊl] *n* hublot *m*
portion ['pɔːʃən] *n* portion *f*, part *f*
portrait ['pɔːtreɪt] *n* portrait *m*
portray [pɔː'treɪ] *vt* faire le portrait de; (in writing) dépeindre, représenter
Portugal ['pɔːtjugl] *n* Portugal *m*
Portuguese [pɔːtju'giːz] *adj* portugais(e) ◆ *n* (p inv) Portugais/e; (LING) portugais *m*
pose [pəʊz] *n* pose *f*; (pej) affectation *f* ◆ *vi* poser (pretend): **to pose as** se poser en ◆ *vt* poser, créer **to strike a pose** poser (pour la galerie)

posh [pɒʃ] *adj* (*col*) chic *inv*; **to talk posh** parler d'une manière affectée

position [pə'zɪʃən] *n* position *f*; (*job*) situation *f* ◆ *vt* mettre en place *or* en position; **to be in a position to do sth** être en mesure de faire qch

positive ['pɒzɪtɪv] *adj* positif(ive); (*certain*) sûr(e), certain(e); (*definite*) formel(le), catégorique; (*clear*) indéniable, réel(le)

possess [pə'zɛs] *vt* posséder; **like one possessed** comme un fou; **whatever can have possessed you?** qu'est-ce qui vous a pris?

possession [pə'zɛʃən] *n* possession *f*; **to take possession of sth** prendre possession de qch

possibility [pɒsɪ'bɪlɪtɪ] *n* possibilité *f*; éventualité *f*; **a possibility for the part** c'est un candidat possible pour le rôle

possible ['pɒsɪbl] *adj* possible; (*solution*) envisageable, éventuel(le); **it is possible to do it** il est possible de le faire; **as far as possible** dans la mesure du possible, autant que possible; **if possible** si possible; **as big as possible** aussi gros que possible

possibly ['pɒsɪblɪ] *adv* (*perhaps*) peut-être; **if you possibly can** si cela vous est possible; **I cannot possibly come** il m'est impossible de venir

post [pəust] *n* (*BRIT: mail*) poste *f*; (*: collection*) levée *f*; (*: letters, delivery*) courrier *m*; (*job, situation*) poste *m*; (*pole*) poteau *m*; (*trading post*) comptoir (commercial) ◆ *vt* (*BRIT: send by post, MIL*) poster; (*BRIT: appoint*): **to post to** affecter à; (*notice*) afficher; **by post** (*BRIT*) par la poste; **by return of post** (*BRIT*) par retour du courrier; **to keep sb posted** tenir qn au courant

postage ['pəustɪdʒ] *n* affranchissement *m*; **postage paid** port payé; **postage prepaid** (*US*) franco (de port)

postal order *n* mandat(-poste *m*) *m*

postbox ['pəustbɒks] *n* (*BRIT*) boîte *f* aux lettres (*publique*)

postcard ['pəustkɑːd] *n* carte postale

postcode ['pəustkəud] *n* (*BRIT*) code postal

poster ['pəustə*] *n* affiche *f*

poste restante [pəust'rɛstɑ̃ːnt] *n* (*BRIT*) poste restante

postgraduate ['pəust'grædjuət] *n* = étudiant/e de troisième cycle

posthumous ['pɒstjuməs] *adj* posthume

postman ['pəustmən] *n* facteur *m*

postmark ['pəustmɑːk] *n* cachet *m* (de la poste)

postmortem [pəust'mɔːtəm] *n* autopsie *f*

post office *n* (*building*) poste *f*; (*organization*) postes *fpl*

post office box (PO box) *n* boîte postale (B.P.)

postpone [pəs'pəun] *vt* remettre (à plus tard), reculer

posture ['pɒstʃə*] *n* posture *f*, attitude *f* ◆ *vi* poser

postwar [pəust'wɔː*] *adj* d'après-guerre

postwoman [pəust'wumən] *n* factrice *f*

posy ['pəuzɪ] *n* petit bouquet

pot [pɒt] *n* (*for cooking*) marmite *f*; casserole *f*; (*for plants, jam*) pot *m*; (*piece of pottery*) poterie *f*; (*col: marijuana*) herbe *f* ◆ *vt* (*plant*) mettre en pot; **to go to pot** aller à vau-l'eau; **pots of** (*BRIT col*) beaucoup de, plein de

potato, *pl* **potatoes** [pə'teɪtəu] *n* pomme *f* de terre

potato peeler *n* épluche-légumes *m*

potent ['pəutnt] *adj* puissant(e); (*drink*) fort(e), très alcoolisé(e)

potential [pə'tenʃl] *adj* potentiel(le) ◆ *n* potentiel *m*; **to have potential** être prometteur(euse); ouvrir des possibilités

pothole ['pɒthəul] *n* (*in road*) nid *m* de poule; (*BRIT: underground*) gouffre *m*, caverne *f*

potholing ['pɒthəulɪŋ] *n* (*BRIT*): **to go potholing** faire de la spéléologie

potluck [pɒt'lʌk] *n*: **to take potluck** tenter sa chance

pot plant *n* plante *f* d'appartement

potted ['pɒtɪd] *adj* (*food*) en conserve; (*plant*) en pot; (*fig: shortened*) abrégé(e)

potter ['pɒtə*] *n* potier *m* ◆ *vi* (*BRIT*): **to potter around, potter about** bricoler; **potter's wheel** tour *m* de potier

pottery ['pɒtərɪ] *n* poterie *f*; **a piece of pottery** une poterie

potty ['pɒtɪ] *adj* (*BRIT col: mad*) dingue ◆ *n* (*child's*) pot *m*

pouch [pautʃ] *n* (*ZOOL*) poche *f*; (*for tobacco*) blague *f*

poultry ['pəultrɪ] *n* volaille *f*

pounce [pauns] *vi*: **to pounce (on)** bondir (sur), fondre (sur) ◆ *n* bond *m*, attaque *f*

pound [paund] *n* livre *f* (*weight = 453g, 16 ounces; money = 100 pence*); (*for dogs, cars*) fourrière *f* ◆ *vt* (*beat*) bourrer de coups, marteler; (*crush*) piler, pulvériser; (*with guns*) pilonner ◆ *vi* (*beat*) battre violemment, taper; **half a pound (of)** une demi-livre (de); **a five-pound note** un billet de cinq livres

pour [pɔː*] *vt* verser ◆ *vi* couler à flots; (*rain*) pleuvoir à verse; **to come pouring in** (*water*) entrer à flots; (*letters*) arriver par milliers; (*cars, people*) affluer

▶ **pour away, pour off** *vt* vider

▶ **pour in** *vi* (*people*) affluer, se précipiter

▶ **pour out** *vi* (*people*) sortir en masse ◆ *vt* vider; (*serve: a drink*) verser

pouring ['pɔːrɪŋ] *adj*: **pouring rain** pluie torrentielle

pout [paut] *n* moue *f* ◆ *vi* faire la moue

poverty ['pɒvətɪ] *n* pauvreté *f*, misère *f*

poverty-stricken ['pɒvətɪstrɪkn] *adj* pauvre, déshérité(e)

powder ['paudə*] n poudre f ◆ vt poudrer; **to powder one's nose** se poudrer; (euphemism) aller à la salle de bain; **powdered milk** lait m en poudre

powder compact n poudrier m

powder room n toilettes fpl (pour dames)

power ['pauə*] n (strength) puissance f, force f; (ability, POL: of party, leader) pouvoir m; (MATH) puissance; (of speech, thought) faculté f; (ELEC) courant m ◆ vt faire marcher, actionner; **to do all in one's power to help sb** faire tout ce qui est en son pouvoir pour aider qn; **the world powers** les grandes puissances; **to be in power** être au pouvoir

power cut n (BRIT) coupure f de courant

powered ['pauəd] adj: **powered by** actionné(e) par, fonctionnant à; **nuclear-powered submarine** sous-marin m (à propulsion) nucléaire

power failure n panne f de courant

powerful ['pauəful] adj puissant(e)

powerless ['pauəlis] adj impuissant(e)

power point n (BRIT) prise f de courant

power station n centrale f électrique

power struggle n lutte f pour le pouvoir

pp abbr (= per procurationem: by proxy) p.p.

PR n abbr = proportional representation, **public relations** ◆ abbr (US) = Puerto Rico

practical ['præktɪkl] adj pratique

practicality [præktɪ'kælɪtɪ] n (of plan) aspect m pratique; (of person) sens m pratique; **practicalities** npl détails mpl pratiques

practical joke n farce f

practically ['præktɪklɪ] adv (almost) pratiquement

practice ['præktɪs] n pratique f; (of profession) exercice m; (at football etc) entraînement m; (business) cabinet m; clientèle f ◆ vt, vi (US) = **practise**; **in practice** (in reality) en pratique; **out of practice** rouillé(e); **2 hours' piano practice** 2 heures de travail or d'exercices au piano; **target practice** exercices de tir; **it's common practice** c'est courant, ça se fait couramment; **to put sth into practice** mettre qch en pratique

practise, (US) **practice** ['præktɪs] vt (work at: piano, one's backhand etc) s'exercer à, travailler; (train for: skiing, running etc) s'entraîner à; (a sport, religion, method) pratiquer; (profession) exercer ◆ vi s'exercer, travailler; (train) s'entraîner; **to practise for a match** s'entraîner pour un match

practising, (US) **practicing** ['præktɪsɪŋ] adj (Christian etc) pratiquant(e); (lawyer) en exercice; (homosexual) déclaré

practitioner [præk'tɪʃənə*] n praticien/ne

prairie ['prɛərɪ] n savane f; (US): **the prairies** la Prairie

praise [preɪz] n éloge(s) m(pl), louange(s) f(pl) ◆ vt louer, faire l'éloge de

praiseworthy ['preɪzwə:ðɪ] adj digne de louanges

pram [præm] n (BRIT) landau m, voiture f d'enfant

prance [prɑ:ns] vi (horse) caracoler

prank [præŋk] n farce f

prawn [prɔ:n] n crevette f (rose)

prawn cocktail n cocktail m de crevettes

pray [preɪ] vi prier

prayer [prɛə*] n prière f

preach [pri:tʃ] vt, vi prêcher; **to preach at sb** faire la morale à qn

precaution [prɪ'kɔ:ʃən] n précaution f

precede [prɪ'si:d] vt, vi précéder

precedent ['presɪdənt] n précédent m; **to establish** or **set a precedent** créer un précédent

preceding [prɪ'si:dɪŋ] adj qui précède (or précédait)

precinct ['pri:sɪŋkt] n (round cathedral) pourtour m, enceinte f; (US: district) circonscription f, arrondissement m; **precincts** npl (neighbourhood) alentours mpl, environs mpl; **pedestrian precinct** zone piétonne; **shopping precinct** (BRIT) centre commercial

precious ['preʃəs] adj précieux(euse) ◆ adv (col): **precious little** or **few** fort peu; **your precious dog** (ironic) ton chien chéri, ton chéri chien

precipitate adj [prɪ'sɪpɪtɪt] (hasty) précipité(e), ◆ vt [prɪ'sɪpɪteɪt] précipiter

precise [prɪ'saɪs] adj précis(e)

precisely [prɪ'saɪslɪ] adv précisément

precocious [prɪ'kəuʃəs] adj précoce

precondition ['pri:kən'dɪʃən] n condition nécessaire

predecessor ['pri:dɪsesə*] n prédécesseur m

predicament [prɪ'dɪkəmənt] n situation f difficile

predict [prɪ'dɪkt] vt prédire

predictable [prɪ'dɪktəbl] adj prévisible

predominantly [prɪ'dɔmɪnəntlɪ] adv en majeure partie; surtout

pre-empt [pri:'emt] vt (BRIT) acquérir par droit de préemption; (fig) anticiper sur; **to pre-empt the issue** conclure avant même d'ouvrir les débats

preen [pri:n] vt: **to preen itself** (bird) se lisser les plumes; **to preen o.s.** s'admirer

prefab ['pri:fæb] n abbr (= prefabricated building) bâtiment préfabriqué

preface ['prefəs] n préface f

prefect ['pri:fekt] n (BRIT: in school) élève chargé de certaines fonctions de discipline (in France) préfet m

prefer [prɪ'fə:*] vt préférer; (LAW): **to prefer charges** procéder à une inculpation; **to prefer coffee to tea** préférer le café au thé

preferably ['prefrəblɪ] adv de préférence

preference ['prefrəns] n préférence f; **in preference to sth** plutôt que qch, de préférence à qch

preferential [prefə'renʃəl] adj préférentiel(le); **preferential treatment** traitement m de faveur

prefix ['pri:fɪks] n préfixe m

pregnancy ['pregnənsı] n grossesse f
pregnant ['pregnənt] adj enceinte adj f; **3 months pregnant** enceinte de 3 mois
prehistoric ['pri:hɪs'tɒrɪk] adj préhistorique
prejudice ['predʒudɪs] n préjugé m; (harm) tort m, préjudice m ♦ vt porter préjudice à; (bias): **to prejudice sb in favour of/against** prévenir qn en faveur de/contre; **racial prejudice** préjugés raciaux
prejudiced ['predʒudɪst] adj (person) plein(e) de préjugés; (view) préconçu(e), partial(e); **to be prejudiced against sb/sth** avoir un parti-pris contre qn/qch; **to be racially prejudiced** avoir des préjugés raciaux
premarital ['pri:'mærɪtl] adj avant le mariage; **premarital contract** contrat m de mariage
premature ['premətʃuə*] adj prématuré(e); **to be premature (in doing sth)** aller un peu (trop) vite (en faisant qch)
premier ['premɪə*] adj premier(ière), principal(e) ♦ n (POL: Prime Minister) premier ministre; (POL: President) chef m de l'État
premiere ['premɪeə*] n première f
Premier League n première division
premise ['premɪs] n prémisse f
premium ['pri:mɪəm] n prime f; **to be at a premium** (fig: housing etc) être très demandé(e), être rarissime; **to sell at a premium** (shares) vendre au-dessus du pair
premium bond n (BRIT) obligation f à prime, bon m à lots
premonition [premə'nɪʃən] n prémonition f
preoccupied [pri:'ɒkjupaɪd] adj préoccupé(e)
prep [prep] adj abbr: **prep school** = **preparatory school** ♦ n abbr (SCOL: = preparation) étude f
prepaid [pri:'peɪd] adj payé(e) d'avance
preparation [prepə'reɪʃən] n préparation f; **preparations** (for trip, war) préparatifs mpl; **in preparation for** en vue de
preparatory [prɪ'pærətərɪ] adj préparatoire; **preparatory to sth/to doing sth** en prévision de qch/avant de faire qch
preparatory school n école primaire privée; (US) lycée privé; voir encadré

PREPARATORY SCHOOL

En Grande-Bretagne, une **preparatory school** – ou, plus familièrement, une **prep school** – est une école payante qui prépare les enfants de 7 à 13 ans aux "public schools".

---

prepare [prɪ'peə*] vt préparer ♦ vi: **to prepare for** se préparer à
preposition [prepə'zɪʃən] n préposition f
preposterous [prɪ'pɒstərəs] adj ridicule, absurde
prep school n = **preparatory school**

prerequisite [pri:'rekwɪzɪt] n condition f préalable
presbyterian [prezbɪ'tɪərɪən] adj, n presbytérien/ne
prescribe [prɪ'skraɪb] vt prescrire; **prescribed books** (BRIT SCOL) œuvres fpl au programme
prescription [prɪ'skrɪpʃən] n prescription f; (MED) ordonnance f; **to make up** or (US) **fill a prescription** faire une ordonnance; **"only available on prescription"** "uniquement sur ordonnance"
presence ['prezns] n présence f; **presence of mind** présence d'esprit
present ['preznt] adj présent(e) ♦ n cadeau m; (also: **present tense**) présent m ♦ vt [prɪ'zent] présenter; (give): **to present sb with sth** offrir qch à qn; **to be present at** assister à; **those present** les présents; **at present** en ce moment; **to give sb a present** offrir un cadeau à qn; **to present sb (to sb)** présenter qn (à qn)
presentation [prezn'teɪʃən] n présentation f; (gift) cadeau m, présent m; (ceremony) remise f du cadeau; **on presentation of** (voucher etc) sur présentation de
present-day ['prezntdeɪ] adj contemporain(e), actuel(le)
presenter [prɪ'zentə*] n (BRIT RADIO, TV) présentateur/trice
presently ['prezntlɪ] adv (soon) tout à l'heure, bientôt; (at present) en ce moment; (US: now) maintenant
preservative [prɪ'zə:vətɪv] n agent m de conservation
preserve [prɪ'zə:v] vt (keep safe) préserver, protéger; (maintain) conserver, garder; (food) mettre en conserve ♦ n (for game, fish) réserve f; (often pl: jam) confiture f; (: fruit) fruits mpl en conserve
president ['prezɪdənt] n président/e; (US: of company) président-directeur général, PDG m
presidential [prezɪ'denʃl] adj présidentiel(le)
press [pres] n (tool, machine, newspapers) presse f; (for wine) pressoir m; (crowd) cohue f, foule f ♦ vt (push) appuyer sur; (squeeze) presser, serrer; (clothes: iron) repasser; (pursue) talonner; (insist): **to press sth on sb** presser qn d'accepter qch; (urge, entreat): **to press sb to do** or **into doing sth** pousser qn à faire qch ♦ vi appuyer, peser; se presser; **we are pressed for time** le temps nous manque; **to press for sth** faire pression pour obtenir qch; **to press sb for an answer** presser qn de répondre; **to press charges against sb** (LAW) engager des poursuites contre qn; **to go to press** (newspaper) aller à l'impression; **to be in the press** (being printed) être sous presse; (in the newspapers) être dans le journal
▶ **press ahead** vi = **press on**
▶ **press on** vi continuer
press conference n conférence f de presse
pressing ['presɪŋ] adj urgent(e), pressant(e) ♦ n repassage m

press stud n (BRIT) bouton-pression m

press-up ['presʌp] n (BRIT) traction f

pressure ['preʃə*] n pression f; (stress) tension f
♦ vt = **to put pressure on: to put pressure on sb
(to do sth)** faire pression sur qn (pour qu'il fasse
qch)

pressure cooker n cocotte-minute f

pressure gauge n manomètre m

pressure group n groupe m de pression

prestige [pres'ti:ʒ] n prestige m

prestigious [pres'tɪdʒəs] adj prestigieux(euse)

presumably [prɪ'zju:məblɪ] adv vraisemblablement; **presumably he did it** c'est sans doute lui
(qui a fait cela)

presume [prɪ'zju:m] vt présumer, supposer; **to
presume to do** (dare) se permettre de faire

pretence, (US) **pretense** [prɪ'tens] n (claim) prétention f; (pretext) prétexte m; **she is devoid of all
pretence** elle n'est pas du tout prétentieuse; **to
make a pretence of doing** faire semblant de faire;
on or **under the pretence of doing sth** sous prétexte de faire qch

pretend [prɪ'tend] vt (feign) feindre, simuler ♦ vi
(feign) faire semblant; (claim): **to pretend to sth**
prétendre à qch; **to pretend to do** faire semblant
de faire

pretext ['pri:tekst] n prétexte m; **on** or **under the
pretext of doing sth** sous prétexte de faire qch

pretty ['prɪtɪ] adj joli(e) ♦ adv assez

prevail [prɪ'veɪl] vi (win) l'emporter, prévaloir; (be
usual) avoir cours; (persuade): **to prevail (up)on sb
to do** persuader qn de faire

prevailing [prɪ'veɪlɪŋ] adj dominant(e)

prevalent ['prevələnt] adj répandu(e), courant(e);
(fashion) en vogue

prevent [prɪ'vent] vt: **to prevent (from doing)**
empêcher (de faire)

preventative [prɪ'ventətɪv] adj préventif(ive)

preview ['pri:vju:] n (of film) avant-première f;
(fig) aperçu m

previous ['pri:vɪəs] adj (last) précédent(e); (earlier) antérieur(e); (question, experience) préalable; **I
have a previous engagement** je suis déjà pris(e);
previous to doing avant de faire

previously ['pri:vɪəslɪ] adv précédemment, auparavant

prewar [pri:'wɔ:*] adj d'avant-guerre

prey [preɪ] n proie f ♦ vi: **to prey on** s'attaquer à; **it
was preying on his mind** ça le rongeait or minait

price [praɪs] n prix m; (BETTING: odds) cote f ♦ vt
(goods) fixer le prix de; tarifer; **what is the price of
...?** combien coûte ...?, quel est le prix de ...?; **to
go up** or **rise in price** augmenter; **to put a price
on sth** chiffrer qch; **to be priced out of the market** (article) être trop cher pour soutenir la concurrence; (producer, nation) ne pas pouvoir soutenir la
concurrence; **what price his promises now?** (BRIT)

que valent maintenant toutes ses promesses?; **he
regained his freedom, but at a price** il a retrouvé
sa liberté, mais cela lui a coûté cher

priceless ['praɪslɪs] adj sans prix, inestimable; (col
amusing) impayable

price list n tarif m

prick [prɪk] n piqûre f; (col!) bitte f (!); connard
m (!) ♦ vt piquer; **to prick up one's ears** dresser o
tendre l'oreille

prickle ['prɪkl] n (of plant) épine f; (sensation)
picotement m

prickly ['prɪklɪ] adj piquant(e), épineux(euse); (fig
person) irritable

prickly heat n fièvre f miliaire

pride [praɪd] n (feeling proud) fierté f; (: pej)
orgueil m; (self-esteem) amour-propre m ♦ vt: **to
pride o.s. on** se flatter de; s'enorgueillir de; **to take
(a) pride in** être (très) fier(ère) de; **to take a pride
in doing** mettre sa fierté à faire; **to have pride o
place** (BRIT) avoir la place d'honneur

priest [pri:st] n prêtre m

priesthood ['pri:sthud] n prêtrise f, sacerdoce m

prim [prɪm] adj collet monté inv, guindé(e)

primarily ['praɪmərɪlɪ] adv principalement, essen
tiellement

primary ['praɪmərɪ] adj primaire; (first in impor
tance) premier(ière), primordial(e) ♦ n (US: election
(élection f) primaire f

primary school n (BRIT) école f primaire; voi
encadré

PRIMARY SCHOOL

Les **primary schools** en Grande-Bretagne
accueillent les enfants de 5 à 11 ans. Elles mar-
quent le début du cycle scolaire obligatoire et
elles comprennent deux sections: la section
des petits ("infant school") et la section des
grands ("junior school"); voir "secondary
school".

prime [praɪm] adj primordial(e), fondamental(e
(excellent) excellent(e) ♦ vt (gun, pump) amorce
(fig) mettre au courant; **in the prime of life** dans l
fleur de l'âge

prime minister n Premier ministre

primeval [praɪ'mi:vl] adj primitif(ive)

primitive ['prɪmɪtɪv] adj primitif(ive)

primrose ['prɪmrəuz] n primevère f

primus (stove)® ['praɪməs-] n (BRIT) réchaud
de camping

prince [prɪns] n prince m

princess [prɪn'ses] n princesse f

principal ['prɪnsɪpl] adj principal(e) ♦ n (head
master) directeur m, principal m; (in play) rôle prin
cipal; (money) principal m

principle ['prɪnsɪpl] n principe m; **in principle e**
principe; **on principle** par principe

print [prɪnt] *n* (*mark*) empreinte *f*; (*letters*) caractères *mpl*; (*fabric*) imprimé *m*; (*ART*) gravure *f*, estampe *f*; (*PHOT*) épreuve *f* ♦ *vt* imprimer; (*publish*) publier; (*write in capitals*) écrire en majuscules; **out of print** épuisé(e)

▶ **print out** *vt* (*COMPUT*) imprimer

printed matter ['prɪntɪd-] *n* imprimés *mpl*

printer ['prɪntə*] *n* imprimeur *m*; (*machine*) imprimante *f*

printing ['prɪntɪŋ] *n* impression *f*

print-out ['prɪntaʊt] *n* listing *m*

prior ['praɪə*] *adj* antérieur(e), précédent(e) ♦ *n* (*REL*) prieur *m*; **prior to doing** avant de faire; **without prior notice** sans préavis; **to have a prior claim to sth** avoir priorité pour qch

priority [praɪ'ɔrɪtɪ] *n* priorité *f*; **to have** *or* **take priority over sth/sb** avoir la priorité sur qch/qn

prise [praɪz] *vt*: **to prise open** forcer

prison ['prɪzn] *n* prison *f*

prisoner ['prɪznə*] *n* prisonnier/ière; **the prisoner at the bar** l'accusé/e; **to take sb prisoner** faire qn prisonnier; **prisoner of war** prisonnier de guerre

pristine ['prɪstiːn] *adj* virginal(e)

privacy ['prɪvəsɪ] *n* intimité *f*, solitude *f*

private ['praɪvɪt] *adj* (*not public*) privé(e); (*personal*) personnel(le); (*house, car, lesson*) particulier(ière) ♦ *n* soldat de deuxième classe; **"private"** (*on envelope*) "personnelle"; **in private** en privé; **in (his) private life** dans sa vie privée; **he is a very private person** il est très secret; **to be in private practice** être médecin (*or* dentiste *etc*) non conventionné; **private hearing** (*LAW*) audience *f* à huis-clos

private detective *n* détective privé

private enterprise *n* entreprise privée

private property *n* propriété privée

privatize ['praɪvɪtaɪz] *vt* privatiser

privet ['prɪvɪt] *n* troène *m*

privilege ['prɪvɪlɪdʒ] *n* privilège *m*

privy ['prɪvɪ] *adj*: **to be privy to** être au courant de

prize [praɪz] *n* prix *m* ♦ *adj* (*example, idiot*) parfait(e); (*bull, novel*) primé(e) ♦ *vt* priser, faire grand cas de

prize-giving ['praɪzgɪvɪŋ] *n* distribution *f* des prix

prizewinner ['praɪzwɪnə*] *n* gagnant/e

pro [prəʊ] *n* (*SPORT*) professionnel/le; **the pros and cons** le pour et le contre

probability [prɔbə'bɪlɪtɪ] *n* probabilité *f*; **in all probability** très probablement

probable ['prɔbəbl] *adj* probable; **it is probable/hardly probable that …** il est probable/peu probable que …

probably ['prɔbəblɪ] *adv* probablement

probation [prə'beɪʃən] *n* (*in employment*) (période *f* d')essai *m*; (*LAW*) liberté surveillée; (*REL*) noviciat

m, probation *f*; **on probation** (*employee*) à l'essai; (*LAW*) en liberté surveillée

probe [prəʊb] *n* (*MED, SPACE*) sonde *f*; (*enquiry*) enquête *f*, investigation *f* ♦ *vt* sonder, explorer

problem ['prɔbləm] *n* problème *m*; **to have problems with the car** avoir des ennuis avec la voiture; **what's the problem?** qu'y a-t-il?, quel est le problème?; **I had no problem in finding her** je n'ai pas eu de mal à la trouver; **no problem!** pas de problème!

procedure [prə'siːdʒə*] *n* (*ADMIN, LAW*) procédure *f*; (*method*) marche *f* à suivre, façon *f* de procéder

proceed [prə'siːd] *vi* (*go forward*) avancer; (*go about it*) procéder; (*continue*): **to proceed (with)** continuer, poursuivre; **to proceed to** aller à; passer à; **to proceed to do** se mettre à faire; **I am not sure how to proceed** je ne sais pas exactement comment m'y prendre; **to proceed against sb** (*LAW*) intenter des poursuites contre qn

proceedings [prə'siːdɪŋz] *npl* mesures *fpl*; (*LAW*) poursuites *fpl*; (*meeting*) réunion *f*, séance *f*; (*records*) compte rendu; actes *mpl*

proceeds ['prəʊsiːdz] *npl* produit *m*, recette *f*

process ['prəʊses] *n* processus *m*; (*method*) procédé *m* ♦ *vt* traiter ♦ *vi* ['prə'ses] (*BRIT formal: go in procession*) défiler; **in process** en cours; **we are in the process of doing** nous sommes en train de faire

processing ['prəʊsesɪŋ] *n* traitement *m*

procession [prə'seʃən] *n* défilé *m*, cortège *m*; **funeral procession** cortège funèbre, convoi *m* mortuaire

proclaim [prə'kleɪm] *vt* déclarer, proclamer

procrastinate [prəʊ'kræstɪneɪt] *vi* faire traîner les choses, vouloir tout remettre au lendemain

procure [prə'kjʊə*] *vt* (*for o.s.*) se procurer; (*for sb*) procurer

prod [prɔd] *vt* pousser ♦ *n* (*push, jab*) petit coup, poussée *f*

prodigal ['prɔdɪgl] *adj* prodigue

prodigy ['prɔdɪdʒɪ] *n* prodige *m*

produce *n* ['prɔdjuːs]; (*AGR*) produits *mpl* ♦ *vt* [prə'djuːs] produire; (*show*) présenter; (*cause*) provoquer, causer; (*THEAT*) monter, mettre en scène

producer [prə'djuːsə*] *n* (*THEAT*) metteur *m* en scène; (*AGR, CINE, CINE*) producteur *m*

product ['prɔdʌkt] *n* produit *m*

production [prə'dʌkʃən] *n* production *f*; (*THEAT*) mise *f* en scène; **to put into production** (*goods*) entreprendre la fabrication de

production line *n* chaîne *f* (de fabrication)

productivity [prɔdʌk'tɪvɪtɪ] *n* productivité *f*

profession [prə'feʃən] *n* profession *f*; **the professions** les professions libérales

professional [prə'feʃənl] *n* (*SPORT*) professionnel/le ♦ *adj* professionnel(le); (*work*) de professionnel; **he's a professional man** il exerce une profession libérale; **to take professional advice** consulter un spécialiste

professionally [prəˈfeʃnəlɪ] *adv* professionnellement; (*SPORT: play*) en professionnel; **I only know him professionally** je n'ai avec lui que des relations de travail

professor [prəˈfesə*] *n* professeur *m* (*titulaire d'une chaire*); (*US: teacher*) professeur *m*

proficiency [prəˈfɪʃənsɪ] *n* compétence *f*, aptitude *f*

profile [ˈprəʊfaɪl] *n* profil *m*; **to keep a high/low profile** (*fig*) rester *or* être très en évidence/discret(ète)

profit [ˈprɔfɪt] *n* (*from trading*) bénéfice *m*; (*advantage*) profit *m* ♦ *vi*: **to profit (by** *or* **from)** profiter (de); **profit and loss account** compte *m* de profits et pertes; **to make a profit** faire un *or* des bénéfice(s); **to sell sth at a profit** vendre qch à profit

profitable [ˈprɔfɪtəbl] *adj* lucratif(ive), rentable; (*fig: beneficial*) avantageux(euse); (: *meeting*) fructueux(euse)

profound [prəˈfaund] *adj* profond(e)

profusely [prəˈfjuːslɪ] *adv* abondamment; (*thank etc*) avec effusion

prognosis, *pl* **prognoses** [prɔgˈnəusɪs, -siːz] *n* pronostic *m*

programme, (*US, also BRIT COMPUT*) **program** [ˈprəugræm] *n* programme *m*; (*RADIO, TV*) émission *f* ♦ *vt* programmer

program(m)er [ˈprəugræmə*] *n* programmeur/euse

program(m)ing [ˈprəugræmɪŋ] *n* programmation *f*

progress *n* [ˈprəugres] progrès *m* ♦ *vi* [prəˈgres] progresser, avancer; **in progress** en cours; **to make progress** progresser, faire des progrès, être en progrès; **as the match progressed** au fur et à mesure que la partie avançait

progressive [prəˈgresɪv] *adj* progressif(ive); (*person*) progressiste

prohibit [prəˈhɪbɪt] *vt* interdire, défendre; **to prohibit sb from doing sth** défendre *or* interdire à qn de faire qch; **"smoking prohibited"** "défense de fumer"

project *n* [ˈprɔdʒekt] (*plan*) projet *m*, plan *m*; (*venture*) opération *f*, entreprise *f*; (*gen SCOL: research*) étude *f*, dossier *m* ♦ *vb* [prəˈdʒekt] ♦ *vt* projeter ♦ *vi* (*stick out*) faire saillie, s'avancer

projection [prəˈdʒekʃən] *n* projection *f*; (*overhang*) saillie *f*

projector [prəˈdʒektə*] *n* (*CINE etc*) projecteur *m*

prolong [prəˈlɔŋ] *vt* prolonger

prom [prɔm] *n abbr* = **promenade, promenade concert**; (*US: ball*) bal *m* d'étudiants

promenade [prɔməˈnɑːd] *n* (*by sea*) esplanade *f*, promenade *f*

promenade concert *n* concert *m* (de musique classique); *voir encadré*

PROMENADE CONCERT

En Grande-Bretagne, un **promenade concert** ou **prom** est un concert de musique classique, ainsi appelé car, à l'origine, le public restait debout et se promenait au lieu de rester assis. De nos jours, une partie du public reste debout, mais il y a également des places assises (plus chères). Les Proms les plus connus sont les Proms londoniens. La dernière séance ("the Last Night of the Proms") est un grand événement médiatique où se jouent des airs traditionnels et patriotiques. Aux États-Unis et au Canada, le **prom** ou **promenade** est un bal organisé par le lycée.

---

prominent [ˈprɔmɪnənt] *adj* (*standing out*) proéminent(e); (*important*) important(e); **he is prominent in the field of ...** il est très connu dans le domaine de ...

promiscuous [prəˈmɪskjuəs] *adj* (*sexually*) de mœurs légères

promise [ˈprɔmɪs] *n* promesse *f* ♦ *vt*, *vi* promettre; **to promise sb sth, to promise sth to sb** promettre qch à qn; **a young man of promise** un jeune homme plein d'avenir; **to promise well** *vi* promettre

promising [ˈprɔmɪsɪŋ] *adj* prometteur(euse)

promote [prəˈməut] *vt* promouvoir; (*venture, event*) organiser, mettre sur pied; (*new product*) lancer; **the team was promoted to the second division** (*BRIT FOOTBALL*) l'équipe est montée en 2e division

promoter [prəˈməutə*] *n* (*of event*) organisateur/trice

promotion [prəˈməuʃən] *n* promotion *f*

prompt [prɔmpt] *adj* rapide ♦ *n* (*COMPUT*) message *m* (de guidage) ♦ *vt* inciter; (*cause*) entraîner, provoquer; (*THEAT*) souffler (son rôle *or* ses répliques) à; **they're very prompt** (*punctual*) ils sont ponctuels; **at 8 o'clock prompt** à 8 heures précises; **he was prompt to accept** il a tout de suite accepté; **to prompt sb to do** inciter *or* pousser qn à faire

promptly [ˈprɔmptlɪ] *adv* rapidement, sans délai; ponctuellement

prone [prəun] *adj* (*lying*) couché(e) (face contre terre); (*liable*): **prone to** enclin(e) à; **to be prone to illness** être facilement malade; **to be prone to an illness** être sujet à une maladie; **she is prone to burst into tears if ...** elle a tendance à tomber en larmes si ...

prong [prɔŋ] *n* pointe *f*; (*of fork*) dent *f*

pronoun [ˈprəunaun] *n* pronom *m*

pronounce [prəˈnauns] *vt* prononcer ♦ *vi*: **to pronounce (up)on** se prononcer sur; **they pronounced him unfit to drive** ils l'ont déclaré inapte à la conduite

pronunciation [prənʌnsɪ'eɪʃən] *n* prononciation *f*

proof [pru:f] *n* preuve *f*; (*test, of book*, PHOT) épreuve *f*; (*of alcohol*) degré *m* ♦ *adj*: **proof against** à l'épreuve de ♦ *vt* (BRIT: *tent, anorak*) imperméabiliser; **to be 70° proof** = titrer 40 degrés

prop [prɒp] *n* support *m*, étai *m* ♦ *vt* (*also*: **prop up**) étayer, soutenir; (*lean*): **to prop sth against** appuyer qch contre *or* à

propaganda [prɒpə'gændə] *n* propagande *f*

propel [prə'pɛl] *vt* propulser, faire avancer

propeller [prə'pɛlə*] *n* hélice *f*

propensity [prə'pɛnsɪtɪ] *n* propension *f*

proper ['prɒpə*] *adj* (*suited, right*) approprié(e), bon(bonne); (*seemly*) correct(e), convenable; (*authentic*) vrai(e), véritable; (*col: real*) fini(e), vrai(e); **to go through the proper channels** (ADMIN) passer par la voie officielle

properly ['prɒpəlɪ] *adv* correctement, convenablement; (*really*) bel et bien

proper noun *n* nom *m* propre

property ['prɒpətɪ] *n* (*possessions*) biens *mpl*; (*house etc*) propriété *f*; (*land*) terres *fpl*, domaine *m*; (CHEM *etc*: *quality*) propriété *f*; **it's their property** cela leur appartient, c'est leur propriété

prophecy ['prɒfɪsɪ] *n* prophétie *f*

prophesy ['prɒfɪsaɪ] *vt* prédire ♦ *vi* prophétiser

prophet ['prɒfɪt] *n* prophète *m*

proportion [prə'pɔ:ʃən] *n* proportion *f*; (*share*) part *f*; partie *f* ♦ *vt* proportionner; **to be in/out of proportion to** *or* **with sth** être à la mesure de/hors de proportion avec qch; **to see sth in proportion** (*fig*) ramener qch à de justes proportions

proportional [prə'pɔ:ʃənl], **proportionate** [prə'pɔ:ʃənɪt] *adj* proportionnel(le)

proposal [prə'pəuzl] *n* proposition *f*, offre *f*; (*plan*) projet *m*; (*of marriage*) demande *f* en mariage

propose [prə'pəuz] *vt* proposer, suggérer; (*have in mind*): **to propose sth/to do** *or* **doing sth** envisager qch/de faire qch ♦ *vi* faire sa demande en mariage; **to propose to do** avoir l'intention de faire

proposition [prɒpə'zɪʃən] *n* proposition *f*; **to make sb a proposition** faire une proposition à qn

proprietor [prə'praɪətə*] *n* propriétaire *m/f*

propriety [prə'praɪətɪ] *n* (*seemliness*) bienséance *f*, convenance *f*

prose [prəuz] *n* prose *f*; (SCOL: *translation*) thème *m*

prosecute ['prɒsɪkju:t] *vt* poursuivre

prosecution [prɒsɪ'kju:ʃən] *n* poursuites *fpl* judiciaires; (*accusing side*) accusation *f*

prosecutor ['prɒsɪkju:tə*] *n* procureur *m*; (*also*: **public prosecutor**) ministère public

prospect *n* ['prɒspekt] perspective *f*; (*hope*) espoir *m*, chances *fpl* ♦ *vt*, *vi* [prə'spekt] prospecter; **we are faced with the prospect of leaving** nous risquons de devoir partir; **there is every prospect of an early victory** tout laisse prévoir une victoire rapide

prospecting [prə'spektɪŋ] *n* prospection *f*

prospective [prə'spektɪv] *adj* (*possible*) éventuel(le); (*future*) futur(e)

prospectus [prə'spektəs] *n* prospectus *m*

prosperity [prə'spɛrɪtɪ] *n* prospérité *f*

prostitute ['prɒstɪtju:t] *n* prostituée *f*; **male prostitute** prostitué *m*

protect [prə'tekt] *vt* protéger

protection [prə'tekʃən] *n* protection *f*; **to be under sb's protection** être sous la protection de qn

protective [prə'tektɪv] *adj* protecteur(trice); **protective custody** (LAW) détention préventive

protein ['prəuti:n] *n* protéine *f*

protest *n* ['prəutest] protestation *f* ♦ *vb* [prə'test] ♦ *vi*: **to protest against/about** protester contre/à propos de ♦ *vt* protester de

Protestant ['prɒtɪstənt] *adj*, *n* protestant/e

protester, protestor [prə'testə*] *n* (*in demonstration*) manifestant/e

protracted [prə'træktɪd] *adj* prolongé(e)

protrude [prə'tru:d] *vi* avancer, dépasser

proud [praud] *adj* fier(ère); (*pej*) orgueilleux(euse); **to be proud to do sth** être fier de faire qch; **to do sb proud** (*col*) faire honneur à qn; **to do o.s. proud** (*col*) ne se priver de rien

prove [pru:v] *vt* prouver, démontrer ♦ *vi*: **to prove correct** *etc* s'avérer juste *etc*; **to prove o.s.** montrer ce dont on est capable; **to prove o.s./itself (to be) useful** *etc* se montrer *or* se révéler utile *etc*; **he was proved right in the end** il s'est avéré qu'il avait raison

proverb ['prɒvə:b] *n* proverbe *m*

provide [prə'vaɪd] *vt* fournir; **to provide sb with sth** fournir qch à qn; **to be provided with** (*person*) disposer de; (*thing*) être équipé(e) *or* muni(e) de

▶ **provide for** *vt fus* (*person*) subvenir aux besoins de; (*emergency*) prévoir

provided [prə'vaɪdɪd] *conj*: **provided (that)** à condition que + *sub*

providing [prə'vaɪdɪŋ] *conj* à condition que + *sub*

province ['prɒvɪns] *n* province *f*

provincial [prə'vɪnʃəl] *adj* provincial(e)

provision [prə'vɪʒən] *n* (*supply*) provision *f*; (*supplying*) fourniture *f*; approvisionnement *m*; (*stipulation*) disposition *f*; **provisions** *npl* (*food*) provisions *fpl*; **to make provision for** (*one's future*) assurer; (*one's family*) assurer l'avenir de; **there's no provision for this in the contract** le contrat ne prévoit pas cela

provisional [prə'vɪʒənl] *adj* provisoire ♦ *n*: **Provisional** (*Irish* POL) Provisional *m* (*membre de la tendance activiste de l'IRA*)

proviso [prə'vaɪzəu] *n* condition *f*; **with the pro-**

viso that à la condition (expresse) que

provocative [prə'vɔkətɪv] *adj* provocateur(trice), provocant(e)

provoke [prə'vəuk] *vt* provoquer; **to provoke sb to sth/to do** *or* **into doing sth** pousser qn à qch/à faire qch

prowess ['prauɪs] *n* prouesse *f*

prowl [praul] *vi* (*also:* **prowl about**, **prowl around**) rôder ♦ *n*: **to be on the prowl** rôder

prowler ['praulə*] *n* rôdeur/euse

proxy ['prɔksɪ] *n* procuration *f*; **by proxy** par procuration

prudent ['pru:dnt] *adj* prudent(e)

prune [pru:n] *n* pruneau *m* ♦ *vt* élaguer

pry [praɪ] *vi*: **to pry into** fourrer son nez dans

PS *n abbr* (= *postscript*) PS *m*

psalm [sɑ:m] *n* psaume *m*

pseudonym ['sju:dənɪm] *n* pseudonyme *m*

psyche ['saɪkɪ] *n* psychisme *m*

psychiatrist [saɪ'kaɪətrɪst] *n* psychiatre *m/f*

psychic ['saɪkɪk] *adj* (*also:* **psychical**) (méta)psychique; (*person*) doué(e) de télépathie *or* d'un sixième sens

psychoanalyst [saɪkəu'ænəlɪst] *n* psychanalyste *m/f*

psychological [saɪkə'lɔdʒɪkl] *adj* psychologique

psychologist [saɪ'kɔlədʒɪst] *n* psychologue *m/f*

psychology [saɪ'kɔlədʒɪ] *n* psychologie *f*

PTO *abbr* (= *please turn over*) TSVP (= *tournez s'il vous plaît*)

pub [pʌb] *n abbr* (= *public house*) pub *m*; *voir encadré*

public ['pʌblɪk] *adj* public(ique) ♦ *n* public *m*; **in public** en public; **the general public** le grand public; **to be public knowledge** être de notoriété publique; **to go public** (*COMM*) être coté(e) en Bourse

public address system (**PA**) *n* (système *m* de) sonorisation *f*, sono *f* (*col*)

publican ['pʌblɪkən] *n* patron *m* or gérant *m* de pub

public company *n* société *f* anonyme

public convenience *n* (*BRIT*) toilettes *fpl*

public holiday *n* (*BRIT*) jour férié

public house *n* (*BRIT*) pub *m*

publicity [pʌb'lɪsɪtɪ] *n* publicité *f*

publicize ['pʌblɪsaɪz] *vt* faire connaître, rendre public

public opinion *n* opinion publique

public relations (**PR**) *n* or *npl* relations publiques (RP)

public school *n* (*BRIT*) école privée; (*US*) école publique; *voir encadré*

public-spirited [pʌblɪk'spɪrɪtɪd] *adj* qui fait preuve de civisme

public transport, (*US*) **public transportation** *n* transports *mpl* en commun

publish ['pʌblɪʃ] *vt* publier

publisher ['pʌblɪʃə*] *n* éditeur *m*

publishing ['pʌblɪʃɪŋ] *n* (*industry*) édition *f*; (*of a book*) publication *f*

pub lunch *n* repas *m* de bistrot

pucker ['pʌkə*] *vt* plisser

pudding ['pudɪŋ] *n* (*BRIT: sweet*) dessert *m*, entremets *m*; (*sausage*) boudin *m*; **rice pudding** = riz *m* au lait; **black pudding**, (*US*) **blood pudding** boudin (noir)

puddle ['pʌdl] *n* flaque *f* d'eau

puff [pʌf] *n* bouffée *f* ♦ *vt*: **to puff one's pipe** tirer sur sa pipe; (*also:* **puff out**: *sails, cheeks*) gonfler ♦ *vi* sortir par bouffées; (*pant*) haleter; **to puff out smoke** envoyer des bouffées de fumée

puff pastry, (*US*) **puff paste** *n* pâte feuilletée

puffy ['pʌfɪ] *adj* bouffi(e), boursouflé(e)

pull [pul] *n* (*of moon, magnet, the sea etc*) attraction *f*; (*fig*) influence *f* ♦ *vt* tirer; (*strain: muscle, tendon*) se claquer ♦ *vi* tirer; **to give sth a pull** (*tug*) tirer sur qch; **to pull a face** faire une grimace; **to pull to pieces** mettre en morceaux; **to pull one's punches** (*also fig*) ménager son adversaire; **to pull one's weight** y mettre du sien; **to pull o.s. together** se ressaisir; **to pull sb's leg** (*fig*) faire marcher qn; **to pull strings (for sb)** intervenir (en faveur de qn)

▶ **pull about** *vt* (*BRIT: handle roughly: object*) maltraiter; (: *person*) malmener

▶ **pull apart** *vt* séparer; (*break*) mettre en pièces, démantibuler

▶ **pull down** *vt* baisser, abaisser; (*house*) démolir; (*tree*) abattre

▶ **pull in** *vi* (*AUT*) se ranger; (*RAIL*) entrer en gare

▶ **pull off** *vt* enlever, ôter; (*deal etc*) conclure

▶ **pull out** *vi* démarrer, partir; (*withdraw*) se retirer; (*AUT: come out of line*) déboîter ♦ *vt* sortir; arracher; (*withdraw*) retirer

▶ **pull over** *vi* (*AUT*) se ranger

▶ **pull round** *vi* (*unconscious person*) revenir à soi; (*sick person*) se rétablir

▶ **pull through** *vi* s'en sortir

▶ **pull up** *vi* (*stop*) s'arrêter ♦ *vt* remonter; (*uproot*) déraciner, arracher; (*stop*) arrêter

pulley ['puli] *n* poulie *f*

pullover ['puləuvə*] *n* pull-over *m*, tricot *m*

pulp [pʌlp] *n* (*of fruit*) pulpe *f*; (*for paper*) pâte *f* à papier; (*pej: also:* **pulp magazines** *etc*) presse *f* à sensation *or* de bas étage; **to reduce sth to (a) pulp** réduire qch en purée

pulpit ['pulpit] *n* chaire *f*

pulsate [pʌl'seit] *vi* battre, palpiter; (*music*) vibrer

pulse [pʌls] *n* (*of blood*) pouls *m*; (*of heart*) battement *m*; (*of music, engine*) vibrations *fpl*; **to feel** *or* **take sb's pulse** prendre le pouls à qn

pump [pʌmp] *n* pompe *f*; (*shoe*) escarpin *m* ♦ *vt* pomper; (*fig: col*) faire parler; **to pump sb for information** essayer de soutirer des renseignements à qn

▶ **pump up** *vt* gonfler

pumpkin ['pʌmpkin] *n* potiron *m*, citrouille *f*

pun [pʌn] *n* jeu *m* de mots, calembour *m*

punch [pʌntʃ] *n* (*blow*) coup *m* de poing; (*fig: force*) vivacité *f*, mordant *m*; (*tool*) poinçon *m*; (*drink*) punch *m* ♦ *vt* (*make a hole in*) poinçonner, perforer; (*hit*): **to punch sb/sth** donner un coup de poing à qn/sur qch; **to punch a hole (in)** faire un trou (dans)

▶ **punch in** *vi* (*US*) pointer (en arrivant)

▶ **punch out** *vi* (*US*) pointer (en partant)

punch line *n* (*of joke*) conclusion *f*

punch-up ['pʌntʃʌp] *n* (*BRIT col*) bagarre *f*

punctual ['pʌŋktjuəl] *adj* ponctuel(le)

punctuation [pʌŋktju'eiʃən] *n* ponctuation *f*

puncture ['pʌŋktʃə*] *n* (*BRIT*) crevaison *f* ♦ *vt* crever; **I have a puncture** (*AUT*) j'ai (un pneu) crevé

pundit ['pʌndit] *n* individu *m* qui pontifie, pontife *m*

pungent ['pʌndʒənt] *adj* piquant(e); (*fig*) mordant(e), caustique

punish ['pʌniʃ] *vt* punir; **to punish sb for sth/for doing sth** punir qn de qch/d'avoir fait qch

punishment ['pʌniʃmənt] *n* punition *f*, châtiment *m*; (*fig: col*): **to take a lot of punishment** (*boxer*) encaisser; (*car, person etc*) être mis(e) à dure épreuve

punk [pʌŋk] *n* (*person: also:* **punk rocker**) punk *m/f*; (*music: also:* **punk rock**) le punk; (*US col: hoodlum*) voyou *m*

punt [pʌnt] *n* (*boat*) bachot *m*; (*IRELAND*) livre irlandaise ♦ *vi* (*BRIT: bet*) parier

punter ['pʌntə*] *n* (*BRIT: gambler*) parieur/euse; (: *col*) Monsieur *m* tout le monde; type *m*

puny ['pju:ni] *adj* chétif(ive)

pup [pʌp] *n* chiot *m*

pupil ['pju:pl] *n* élève *m/f*; (*of eye*) pupille *f*

puppet ['pʌpit] *n* marionnette *f*, pantin *m*

puppy ['pʌpi] *n* chiot *m*, petit chien

purchase ['pə:tʃis] *n* achat *m*; (*grip*) prise *f* ♦ *vt* acheter; **to get a purchase on** trouver appui sur

purchaser ['pə:tʃisə*] *n* acheteur/euse

pure [pjuə*] *adj* pur(e); **a pure wool jumper** un pull en pure laine; **pure and simple** pur(e) et simple

purely ['pjuəli] *adv* purement

purge [pə:dʒ] *n* (*MED*) purge *f*; (*POL*) épuration *f*, purge ♦ *vt* purger; (*fig*) épurer, purger

purple ['pə:pl] *adj* violet(te); cramoisi(e)

purpose ['pə:pəs] *n* intention *f*, but *m*; **on purpose** exprès; **for illustrative purposes** à titre d'illustration; **for teaching purposes** dans un but pédagogique; **for the purposes of this meeting** pour cette réunion; **to no purpose** en pure perte

purposeful ['pə:pəsful] *adj* déterminé(e), résolu(e)

purr [pə:*] *n* ronronnement *m* ♦ *vi* ronronner

purse [pə:s] *n* porte-monnaie *m inv*, bourse *f*; (*US: handbag*) sac *m* (à main) ♦ *vt* serrer, pincer

purser ['pə:sə*] *n* (*NAUT*) commissaire *m* du bord

pursue [pə'sju:] *vt* poursuivre; (*pleasures*) rechercher; (*inquiry, matter*) approfondir

pursuit [pə'sju:t] *n* poursuite *f*; (*occupation*) occupation *f*, activité *f*; **scientific pursuits** recherches *fpl* scientifiques; **in (the) pursuit of sth** à la recherche de qch

push [puʃ] *n* poussée *f*; (*effort*) gros effort; (*drive*) énergie *f* ♦ *vt* pousser; (*button*) appuyer sur; (*thrust*): **to push sth (into)** enfoncer qch (dans); (*fig*) mettre en avant, faire de la publicité pour ♦ *vi* pousser; appuyer; **to push a door open/shut** pousser une porte (pour l'ouvrir/pour la fermer);

"**push**" (on door) "pousser"; (on bell) "appuyer"; **to push for** (better pay, conditions) réclamer; **to be pushed for time/money** être à court de temps/d'argent; **she is pushing fifty** (col) elle frise la cinquantaine; **at a push** (BRIT col) à la limite, à la rigueur

▶ **push aside** vt écarter

▶ **push in** vi s'introduire de force

▶ **push off** vi (col) filer, ficher le camp

▶ **push on** vi (continue) continuer

▶ **push over** vt renverser

▶ **push through** vt (measure) faire voter

▶ **push up** vt (total, prices) faire monter

pushchair ['pʊʃtʃɛə*] n (BRIT) poussette f

pusher ['pʊʃə*] n (also: **drug pusher**) revendeur/euse (de drogue), ravitailleur/euse (en drogue)

pushover ['pʊʃəʊvə*] n (col): **it's a pushover** c'est un jeu d'enfant

push-up ['pʊʃʌp] n (US) traction f

pushy ['pʊʃɪ] adj (pej) arriviste

puss, pussy(-cat) [pʊs, 'pʊsɪ(kæt)] n minet m

put, pt, pp **put** [pʊt] vt mettre; (place) poser, placer; (say) dire, exprimer; (a question) poser; (estimate) estimer; **to put sb in a good/bad mood** mettre qn de bonne/mauvaise humeur; **to put sb to bed** mettre qn au lit, coucher qn; **to put sb to a lot of trouble** déranger qn; **how shall I put it?** comment dirais-je?, comment dire?; **to put a lot of time into sth** passer beaucoup de temps à qch; **to put money on a horse** miser sur un cheval; **I put it to you that ...** (BRIT) je (vous) suggère que ..., je suis d'avis que ...; **to stay put** ne pas bouger

▶ **put about** vi (NAUT) virer de bord ◆ vt (rumour) faire courir

▶ **put across** vt (ideas etc) communiquer; faire comprendre

▶ **put aside** vt mettre de côté

▶ **put away** vt (store) ranger

▶ **put back** vt (replace) remettre, replacer; (postpone) remettre; (delay: also watch, clock) retarder; **this will put us back ten years** cela nous ramènera dix ans en arrière

▶ **put by** vt (money) mettre de côté, économiser

▶ **put down** vt (parcel etc) poser, déposer; (pay) verser; (in writing) mettre par écrit, inscrire; (suppress: revolt etc) réprimer, écraser; (attribute) attribuer

▶ **put forward** vt (ideas) avancer, proposer; (date, watch, clock) avancer

▶ **put in** vt (gas, electricity) installer; (application, complaint) faire

▶ **put in for** vt fus (job) poser sa candidature pour; (promotion) solliciter

▶ **put off** vt (light etc) éteindre; (postpone) remettre à plus tard, ajourner; (discourage) dissuader

▶ **put on** vt (clothes, lipstick etc) mettre; (light etc) allumer; (play etc) monter; (extra bus, train etc) mettre en service; (food, meal) servir; (weight) prendre; (assume: accent, manner) prendre; (: airs) se donner, prendre; (brake) mettre; (col: tease) faire marcher; (inform, indicate): **to put sb on to sb/sth** indiquer qn/qch à qn

▶ **put out** vt mettre dehors; (one's hand) tendre; (news, rumour) faire courir, répandre; (light etc) éteindre; (person: inconvenience) déranger, gêner; (BRIT: dislocate) se démettre ◆ vi (NAUT): **to put out to sea** prendre le large; **to put out from Plymouth** quitter Plymouth

▶ **put through** vt (caller) mettre en communication; (call) passer; **put me through to Miss Blair** passez-moi Miss Blair

▶ **put together** vt mettre ensemble; (assemble: furniture, toy etc) monter, assembler; (meal) préparer

▶ **put up** vt (raise) lever, relever, remonter; (pin up) afficher; (hang) accrocher; (build) construire, ériger; (a tent) monter; (increase) augmenter; (accommodate) loger; (incite): **to put sb up to doing sth** pousser qn à faire qch; **to put sth up for sale** mettre qch en vente

▶ **put upon** vt fus: **to be put upon** (imposed on) se laisser faire

▶ **put up with** vt fus supporter

putt [pʌt] vt, vi putter ◆ n putt m

putting green ['pʌtɪŋ-] n green m

putty ['pʌtɪ] n mastic m

put-up ['pʊtʌp] adj: **put-up job** coup monté

puzzle ['pʌzl] n énigme f, mystère m; (jigsaw) puzzle m; (also: **crossword puzzle**) problème m de mots croisés ◆ vt intriguer, rendre perplexe ◆ vi creuser la tête; **to puzzle over** chercher à comprendre; **to be puzzled about sth** être perplexe au sujet de qch

puzzling ['pʌzlɪŋ] adj déconcertant(e), inexplicable

pyjamas [pɪ'dʒɑːməz] npl (BRIT) pyjama m; **a pair of pyjamas** un pyjama

pylon ['paɪlən] n pylône m

pyramid ['pɪrəmɪd] n pyramide f

Pyrenees [pɪrə'niːz] npl: **the Pyrenees** les Pyrénées fpl

— Q q —

quack [kwæk] n (of duck) coin-coin m inv; (pej: doctor) charlatan m ◆ vi faire coin-coin

quad [kwɒd] n abbr = **quadruplet, quadrangle**

quadrangle ['kwɒdræŋgl] n (MATH) quadrilatère m; (courtyard: abbr: **quad**) cour f

quadruple [kwɔ'druːpl] *adj, n* quadruple *m* ♦ *vt, vi* quadrupler

quadruplet [kwɔ'druːplɪt] *n* quadruplé/e

quail [kweɪl] *n* (ZOOL) caille *f*

quaint [kweɪnt] *adj* bizarre; (*old-fashioned*) désuet(ète); au charme vieillot, pittoresque

quake [kweɪk] *vi* trembler ♦ *n abbr* = **earthquake**

qualification [kwɔlɪfɪ'keɪʃən] *n* (*degree etc*) diplôme *m*; (*ability*) compétence *f*, qualification *f*; (*limitation*) réserve *f*, restriction *f*; **what are your qualifications?** qu'avez-vous comme diplômes?; quelles sont vos qualifications?

qualified ['kwɔlɪfaɪd] *adj* diplômé(e); (*able*) compétent(e), qualifié(e); (*limited*) conditionnel(le); **it was a qualified success** ce fut un succès mitigé; **qualified for/to do** qui a les diplômes requis pour/pour faire; qualifié pour/pour faire

qualify ['kwɔlɪfaɪ] *vt* qualifier; (*limit: statement*) apporter des réserves à ♦ *vi*: **to qualify (as)** obtenir son diplôme (de); **to qualify (for)** remplir les conditions requises (pour); (SPORT) se qualifier (pour)

quality ['kwɔlɪtɪ] *n* qualité *f* ♦ *cpd* de qualité; **of good/poor quality** de bonne/mauvaise qualité

quality (news)papers *n* = **quality press**

quality press *n* (BRIT): **the quality press** la presse d'information; *voir encadré*

quality time *n* moments privilégiés

qualm [kwɑːm] *n* doute *m*; scrupule *m*; **to have qualms about sth** avoir des doutes sur qch; éprouver des scrupules à propos de qch

quandary ['kwɔndrɪ] *n*: **in a quandary** devant un dilemme, dans l'embarras

quantity ['kwɔntɪtɪ] *n* quantité *f*; **in quantity** en grande quantité

quantity surveyor *n* (BRIT) métreur vérificateur

quarantine ['kwɔrəntiːn] *n* quarantaine *f*

quarrel ['kwɔrl] *n* querelle *f*, dispute *f* ♦ *vi* se disputer, se quereller; **to have a quarrel with sb** se quereller avec qn; **I've no quarrel with him** je n'ai rien contre lui; **I can't quarrel with that** je ne vois rien à redire à cela

quarry ['kwɔrɪ] *n* (*for stone*) carrière *f*; (*animal*) proie *f*, gibier *m* ♦ *vt* (*marble etc*) extraire

quart [kwɔːt] *n* ≈ litre *m*

quarter ['kwɔːtə*] *n* quart *m*; (*of year*) trimestre *m*; (*district*) quartier *m*; (US, CANADA: 25 cents) (pièce *f* de) vingt-cinq cents *mpl* ♦ *vt* partager en quartiers *or* en quatre; (MIL) caserner, cantonner; **quarters** *npl* logement *m*; (MIL) cantonnement *m*; **a quarter of an hour** un quart d'heure; **it's a quarter to 3, (US) it's a quarter of 3** il est 3 heures moins le quart; **it's a quarter past 3, (US) it's a quarter after 3** il est 3 heures et quart; **from all quarters** de tous côtés

quarter final *n* quart *m* de finale

quarterly ['kwɔːtəlɪ] *adj* trimestriel(le) ♦ *adv* tous les trois mois ♦ *n* (PRESS) revue trimestrielle

quartet(te) [kwɔː'tet] *n* quatuor *m*; (*jazz players*) quartette *m*

quartz [kwɔːts] *n* quartz *m* ♦ *cpd* de *or* en quartz; (*watch, clock*) à quartz

quash [kwɔʃ] *vt* (*verdict*) annuler, casser

quaver ['kweɪvə*] *n* (BRIT MUS) croche *f* ♦ *vi* trembler

quay [kiː] *n* (*also*: **quayside**) quai *m*

queasy ['kwiːzɪ] *adj* (*stomach*) délicat(e); **to feel queasy** avoir mal au cœur

queen [kwiːn] *n* (*gen*) reine *f*; (CARDS etc) dame *f*

queen mother *n* reine mère *f*

queer [kwɪə*] *adj* étrange, curieux(euse); (*suspicious*) louche; (BRIT: sick): **I feel queer** je ne me sens pas bien ♦ *n* (*col*) homosexuel *m*

quell [kwel] *vt* réprimer, étouffer

quench [kwentʃ] *vt* (*flames*) éteindre; **to quench one's thirst** se désaltérer

query ['kwɪərɪ] *n* question *f*; (*doubt*) doute *m*; (*question mark*) point *m* d'interrogation ♦ *vt* (*disagree with, dispute*) mettre en doute, questionner

quest [kwest] *n* recherche *f*, quête *f*

question ['kwestʃən] *n* question *f* ♦ *vt* (*person*) interroger; (*plan, idea*) mettre en question *or* en doute; **to ask sb a question, to put a question to sb** poser une question à qn; **to bring or call sth into question** remettre qch en question; **the question is …** la question est de savoir …; **it's a question of doing** il s'agit de faire; **there's some question of doing** il est question de faire; **beyond question** sans aucun doute; **out of the question** hors de question

questionable ['kwestʃənəbl] *adj* discutable

question mark *n* point *m* d'interrogation

questionnaire [kwestʃə'neə*] *n* questionnaire *m*

queue [kjuː] (BRIT) *n* queue *f*, file *f* ♦ *vi* faire la queue; **to jump the queue** passer avant son tour

quibble ['kwɪbl] *vi* ergoter, chicaner

quick [kwɪk] *adj* rapide; (*reply*) prompt(e), rapide; (*mind*) vif(vive) ♦ *adv* vite, rapidement ♦ *n*: **cut to the quick** (*fig*) touché(e) au vif; **be quick!** dépêche-toi!; **to be quick to act** agir tout de suite

quicken ['kwɪkən] vt accélérer, presser; (rouse) stimuler ♦ vi s'accélérer, devenir plus rapide

quickly ['kwɪklɪ] adv (fast) vite, rapidement; (immediately) tout de suite

quicksand ['kwɪksænd] n sables mouvants

quick-witted [kwɪk'wɪtɪd] adj à l'esprit vif

quid [kwɪd] n (pl inv) (BRIT col) livre f

quiet ['kwaɪət] adj tranquille, calme; (not noisy: engine) silencieux(euse); (reserved) réservé(e); (not busy: day, business) calme; (ceremony, colour) discret(ète) ♦ n tranquillité f, calme m ♦ vt, vi (US) = **quieten; keep quiet!** tais-toi!; **on the quiet** en secret, discrètement; **I'll have a quiet word with him** je lui en parlerai discrètement

quieten ['kwaɪətn] (also: **quieten down**) vi se calmer, s'apaiser ♦ vt calmer, apaiser

quietly ['kwaɪətlɪ] adv tranquillement, calmement; discrètement

quietness ['kwaɪətnɪs] n tranquillité f, calme m; silence m

quilt [kwɪlt] n édredon m; (continental quilt) couette f

quin [kwɪn] n abbr = **quintuplet**

quintuplet [kwɪn'tjuːplɪt] n quintuplé/e

quip [kwɪp] n remarque piquante or spirituelle, pointe f ♦ vt: **... he quipped** ... lança-t-il

quirk [kwəːk] n bizarrerie f; **by some quirk of fate** par un caprice du hasard

quit [kwɪt], pt, pp **quit** or **quitted** vt quitter ♦ vi (give up) abandonner, renoncer; (resign) démissionner; **to quit doing** arrêter de faire; **quit stalling!** (US col) arrête de te dérober!; **notice to quit** (BRIT) congé m (signifié au locataire)

quite [kwaɪt] adv (rather) assez, plutôt; (entirely) complètement, tout à fait; **quite new** plutôt neuf; tout à fait neuf; **she's quite pretty** elle est plutôt jolie; **I quite understand** je comprends très bien; **quite a few of them** un assez grand nombre d'entre eux; **that's not quite right** ce n'est pas tout à fait juste; **not quite as many as last time** pas tout à fait autant que la dernière fois; **quite (so)!** exactement!

quits [kwɪts] adj: **quits (with)** quitte (envers); **let's call it quits** restons-en là

quiver ['kwɪvə*] vi trembler, frémir ♦ n (for arrows) carquois m

quiz [kwɪz] n (on TV) jeu-concours m (télévisé); (in magazine etc) test m de connaissances ♦ vt interroger

quizzical ['kwɪzɪkl] adj narquois(e)

quota ['kwəʊtə] n quota m

quotation [kwəʊ'teɪʃən] n citation f; (of shares etc) cote f, cours m; (estimate) devis m

quotation marks npl guillemets mpl

quote [kwəʊt] n citation f ♦ vt (sentence, author) citer; (price) donner, soumettre; (shares) coter ♦ vi: **to quote from** citer; **to quote for a job** établir un devis pour des travaux; **quotes** npl (col) = **quotation marks; in quotes** entre guillemets; **quote ... unquote** (in dictation) ouvrez les guillemets ... fermez les guillemets

— R r —

rabbi ['ræbaɪ] n rabbin m

rabbit ['ræbɪt] n lapin m ♦ vi: **to rabbit (on)** (BRIT) parler à n'en plus finir

rabbit hutch n clapier m

rabble ['ræbl] n (pej) populace f

rabies ['reɪbiːz] n rage f

RAC n abbr (BRIT: = Royal Automobile Club) ≃ ACF m

ra(c)coon [rə'kuːn] n raton m laveur

race [reɪs] n race f; (competition, rush) course f ♦ vt (person) faire la course avec; (horse) faire courir; (engine) emballer ♦ vi courir; (engine) s'emballer; **the human race** la race humaine; **to race in/out** etc entrer/sortir etc à toute vitesse

race car n (US) = **racing car**

race car driver n (US) = **racing driver**

racecourse ['reɪskɔːs] n champ m de courses

racehorse ['reɪshɔːs] n cheval m de course

racer ['reɪsə*] n (bike) vélo m de course

racetrack ['reɪstræk] n piste f

racial ['reɪʃl] adj racial(e)

racing ['reɪsɪŋ] n courses fpl

racing car n (BRIT) voiture f de course

racing driver n (BRIT) pilote m de course

racism ['reɪsɪzəm] n racisme m

racist ['reɪsɪst] adj, n (pej) raciste (m/f)

rack [ræk] n (also: **luggage rack**) filet m à bagages; (also: **roof rack**) galerie f ♦ vt tourmenter; **magazine rack** porte-revues m inv; **shoe rack** étagère f à chaussures; **toast rack** porte-toast m; **to rack one's brains** se creuser la cervelle; **to go to rack and ruin** (building) tomber en ruine; (business) péricliter

▶ **rack up** vt accumuler

racket ['rækɪt] n (for tennis) raquette f; (noise) tapage m, vacarme m; (swindle) escroquerie f; (organized crime) racket m

racquet ['rækɪt] n raquette f

racy ['reɪsɪ] adj plein(e) de verve, osé(e)

radar ['reɪdɑː*] n radar m ♦ cpd radar inv

radial ['reɪdɪəl] adj (also: **radial-ply**) à carcasse radiale

radiant ['reɪdɪənt] adj rayonnant(e); (PHYSICS) radiant(e)

radiate ['reɪdɪeɪt] vt (heat) émettre, dégager ♦ vi (lines) rayonner

radiation [reɪdɪ'eɪʃən] n rayonnement m; (radio-

active) radiation f

radiator ['reɪdɪeɪtə*] n radiateur m

radical ['rædɪkl] adj radical(e)

radii ['reɪdɪaɪ] npl of **radius**

radio ['reɪdɪəu] n radio f ♦ vi: **to radio to sb** envoyer un message radio à qn ♦ vt (*information*) transmettre par radio; (*one's position*) signaler par radio; (*person*) appeler par radio; **on the radio** à la radio

radioactive ['reɪdɪəu'æktɪv] adj radioactif(ive)

radio cassette n radiocassette m

radio-controlled ['reɪdɪəukən'trəuld] adj radio-guidé(e)

radio station n station f de radio

radish ['rædɪʃ] n radis m

radius, pl **radii** ['reɪdɪəs, -ɪaɪ] n rayon m; (ANAT) radius m; **within a radius of 50 miles** dans un rayon de 50 milles

RAF n abbr (BRIT) = **Royal Air Force**

raffle ['ræfl] n tombola f ♦ vt mettre comme lot dans une tombola

raft [rɑːft] n (*craft; also:* **life raft**) radeau m; (*logs*) train m de flottage

rafter ['rɑːftə*] n chevron m

rag [ræg] n chiffon m; (*pej: newspaper*) feuille f, torchon m; (*for charity*) attractions organisées par les étudiants au profit d'œuvres de charité ♦ vt (BRIT) chahuter, mettre en boîte; **rags** npl haillons mpl; **in rags** (*person*) en haillons; (*clothes*) en lambeaux

rag doll n poupée f de chiffon

rage [reɪdʒ] n (*fury*) rage f, fureur f ♦ vi (*person*) être fou(folle) de rage; (*storm*) faire rage, être déchaîné(e); **to fly into a rage** se mettre en rage; **it's all the rage** cela fait fureur

ragged ['rægɪd] adj (*edge*) inégal(e), qui accroche; (*cuff*) effiloché(e); (*appearance*) déguenillé(e)

raid [reɪd] n (MIL) raid m; (*criminal*) hold-up m inv; (*by police*) descente f, rafle f ♦ vt faire un raid sur or un hold-up dans or une descente dans

rail [reɪl] n (*on stair*) rampe f; (*on bridge, balcony*) balustrade f; (*of ship*) bastingage m; (*for train*) rail m; **rails** npl rails mpl, voie ferrée; **by rail** par chemin de fer, par le train

railing(s) ['reɪlɪŋ(z)] n(pl) grille f

railway ['reɪlweɪ], (US) **railroad** ['reɪlrəud] n chemin m de fer

railway line n ligne f de chemin de fer; (*track*) voie ferrée

railwayman ['reɪlweɪmən] n cheminot m

railway station n gare f

rain [reɪn] n pluie f ♦ vi pleuvoir; **in the rain** sous la pluie; **it's raining** il pleut; **it's raining cats and dogs** il pleut à torrents

rainbow ['reɪnbəu] n arc-en-ciel m

raincoat ['reɪnkəut] n imperméable m

raindrop ['reɪndrɔp] n goutte f de pluie

rainfall ['reɪnfɔːl] n chute f de pluie; (*measure-ment*) hauteur f des précipitations

rainforest ['reɪnfɔrɪst] n forêt tropicale

rainy ['reɪnɪ] adj pluvieux(euse)

raise [reɪz] n augmentation f ♦ vt (*lift*) lever; hausser; (*end: siege, embargo*) lever; (*build*) ériger; (*increase*) augmenter; (*a protest, doubt*) provoquer, causer; (*a question*) soulever; (*cattle, family*) élever; (*crop*) faire pousser; (*army, funds*) rassembler; (*loan*) obtenir; **to raise one's glass to sb/sth** porter un toast en l'honneur de qn/qch; **to raise one's voice** élever la voix; **to raise sb's hopes** donner de l'espoir à qn; **to raise a laugh/a smile** faire rire/sourire

raisin ['reɪzn] n raisin sec

rake [reɪk] n (*tool*) râteau m; (*person*) débauché m ♦ vt (*garden*) ratisser; (*fire*) tisonner; (*with machine gun*) balayer ♦ vi: **to rake through** (*fig: search*) fouiller (dans)

rally ['rælɪ] n (POL etc) meeting m, rassemblement m; (AUT) rallye m; (TENNIS) échange m ♦ vt rassembler, rallier ♦ vi se rallier; (*sick person*) aller mieux; (*Stock Exchange*) reprendre

▶ **rally round** vi venir en aide ♦ vt fus se rallier à; venir en aide à

RAM [ræm] n abbr (COMPUT) = **random access memory**

ram [ræm] n bélier m ♦ vt enfoncer; (*soil*) tasser; (*crash into*) emboutir; percuter; éperonner

ramble ['ræmbl] n randonnée f ♦ vi (*pej: also:* **ramble on**) discourir, pérorer

rambler ['ræmblə*] n promeneur/euse, randonneur/euse; (BOT) rosier grimpant

rambling ['ræmblɪŋ] adj (*speech*) décousu(e); (*house*) plein(e) de coins et de recoins; (BOT) grimpant(e)

ramp [ræmp] n (*incline*) rampe f; dénivellation f; (*in garage*) pont m

rampage [ræm'peɪdʒ] n: **to be on the rampage** se déchaîner ♦ vi: **they went rampaging through the town** ils ont envahi les rues et ont tout saccagé sur leur passage

rampant ['ræmpənt] adj (*disease etc*) qui sévit

ram raiding [-reɪdɪŋ] n pillage d'un magasin en enfonçant la vitrine avec une voiture volée

ramshackle ['ræmʃækl] adj (*house*) délabré(e); (*car etc*) déglingué(e)

ran [ræn] pt of **run**

ranch [rɑːntʃ] n ranch m

rancher ['rɑːntʃə*] n (*owner*) propriétaire m de ranch; (*ranch hand*) cowboy m

rancid ['rænsɪd] adj rance

rancour, (US) **rancor** ['ræŋkə*] n rancune f, rancœur f

random ['rændəm] adj fait(e) or établi(e) au hasard; (COMPUT, MATH) aléatoire ♦ n: **at random** au hasard

random access memory (RAM) n (COMPUT) mémoire vive, RAM f

randy ['rændɪ] *adj* (*BRIT col*) excité(e); lubrique

rang [ræŋ] *pt of* **ring**

range [reɪndʒ] *n* (*of mountains*) chaîne *f*; (*of missile, voice*) portée *f*; (*of products*) choix *m*, gamme *f*; (*also*: **shooting range**) champ *m* de tir; (: *indoor*) stand *m* de tir; (*also*: **kitchen range**) fourneau *m* (de cuisine) ♦ *vt* (*place*) mettre en rang, placer; (*roam*) parcourir ♦ *vi*: **to range over** couvrir; **to range from ... to** aller de ... à; **price range** éventail *m* des prix; **do you have anything else in this price range?** avez-vous autre chose dans ces prix?; **within (firing) range** à portée (de tir); **ranged left/right** (*text*) justifié à gauche/à droite

ranger ['reɪndʒə*] *n* garde *m* forestier

rank [ræŋk] *n* rang *m*; (*MIL*) grade *m*; (*BRIT*: *also*: **taxi rank**) station *f* de taxis ♦ *vi*: **to rank among** compter *or* se classer parmi ♦ *vt*: **I rank him sixth** je le place sixième ♦ *adj* (*smell*) nauséabond(e); (*hypocrisy, injustice etc*) flagrant(e); **he's a rank outsider** il n'est vraiment pas dans la course; **the ranks** (*MIL*) la troupe; **the rank and file** (*fig*) la masse, la base; **to close ranks** (*MIL, fig*) serrer les rangs

ransack ['rænsæk] *vt* fouiller (à fond); (*plunder*) piller

ransom ['rænsəm] *n* rançon *f*; **to hold sb to ransom** (*fig*) exercer un chantage sur qn

rant [rænt] *vi* fulminer

rap [ræp] *n* petit coup sec; tape *f* ♦ *vt* frapper sur *or* à; taper sur

rape [reɪp] *n* viol *m*; (*BOT*) colza *m* ♦ *vt* violer

rape(seed) oil ['reɪp(siːd)-] *n* huile *f* de colza

rapid ['ræpɪd] *adj* rapide

rapids ['ræpɪdz] *npl* (*GEO*) rapides *mpl*

rapist ['reɪpɪst] *n* auteur *m* d'un viol

rapport [ræ'pɔː*] *n* entente *f*

rapturous ['ræptʃərəs] *adj* extasié(e); frénétique

rare [rεə*] *adj* rare; (*CULIN*: *steak*) saignant(e)

raring ['rεərɪŋ] *adj*: **to be raring to go** (*col*) être très impatient(e) de commencer

rascal ['rɑːskl] *n* vaurien *m*

rash [ræʃ] *adj* imprudent(e), irréfléchi(e) ♦ *n* (*MED*) rougeur *f*, éruption *f*; **to come out in a rash** avoir une éruption

rasher ['ræʃə*] *n* fine tranche (de lard)

raspberry ['rɑːzbərɪ] *n* framboise *f*

raspberry bush *n* framboisier *m*

rasping ['rɑːspɪŋ] *adj*: **rasping noise** grincement *m*

rat [ræt] *n* rat *m*

rate [reɪt] *n* (*ratio*) taux *m*, pourcentage *m*; (*speed*) vitesse *f*, rythme *m*; (*price*) tarif *m* ♦ *vt* classer; évaluer; **to rate sb/sth as** considérer qn/qch comme; **to rate sb/sth among** classer qn/qch parmi; **to rate sb/sth highly** avoir une haute opinion de qn/qch; **at a rate of 60 kph** à une vitesse de 60 km/h; **rate of exchange** taux *or* cours *m* du change; **rate of flow** débit *m*; **rate of return** (taux de) rende-

ment *m*; **pulse rate** fréquence *f* des pulsations

rateable value ['reɪtəbl-] *n* (*BRIT*) valeur locative imposable

ratepayer ['reɪtpeɪə*] *n* (*BRIT*) contribuable *m/f* (*payant les impôts locaux*)

rather ['rɑːðə*] *adv* (*somewhat*) assez, plutôt; (*to some extent*) un peu; **it's rather expensive** c'est assez cher; (*too much*) c'est un peu cher; **there's rather a lot** il y en a beaucoup; **I would** *or* **I'd rather go** j'aimerais mieux *or* je préférerais partir; **I had rather go** il vaudrait mieux que je parte; **I'd rather not leave** j'aimerais mieux ne pas partir; **or rather** (*more accurately*) ou plutôt; **I rather think he won't come** je crois bien qu'il ne viendra pas

rating ['reɪtɪŋ] *n* classement *m*; cote *f*; (*NAUT*: *category*) classe *f*; (: *sailor*: *BRIT*) matelot *m*; **ratings** *npl* (*RADIO, TV*) indice(s) *m(pl)* d'écoute

ratio ['reɪʃɪəu] *n* proportion *f*; **in the ratio of 100 to 1** dans la proportion de 100 contre 1

ration ['ræʃən] *n* (*gen pl*) ration(s) *f(pl)* ♦ *vt* rationner

rational ['ræʃənl] *adj* raisonnable, sensé(e); (*solution, reasoning*) logique; (*MED*) lucide

rationale [ræʃə'nɑːl] *n* raisonnement *m*; justification *f*

rationalize ['ræʃnəlaɪz] *vt* rationaliser; (*conduct*) essayer d'expliquer *or* de motiver

rat race *n* foire *f* d'empoigne

rattle ['rætl] *n* cliquetis *m*; (*louder*) bruit *m* de ferraille; (*object*: *of baby*) hochet *m*; (: *of sports fan*) crécelle *f* ♦ *vi* cliqueter; faire un bruit de ferraille *or* du bruit ♦ *vt* agiter (bruyamment); (*col*: *disconcert*) décontenancer; (: *annoy*) embêter

rattlesnake ['rætlsneɪk] *n* serpent *m* à sonnettes

raucous ['rɔːkəs] *adj* rauque

rave [reɪv] *vi* (*in anger*) s'emporter; (*with enthusiasm*) s'extasier; (*MED*) délirer ♦ *n*: **a rave (party)** une rave, une soirée techno ♦ *adj* (*scene, culture, music*) rave, techno ♦ *cpd*: **rave review** (*col*) critique *f* dithyrambique

raven ['reɪvən] *n* grand corbeau

ravenous ['rævənəs] *adj* affamé(e)

ravine [rə'viːn] *n* ravin *m*

raving ['reɪvɪŋ] *adj*: **raving lunatic** *n* fou furieux/folle furieuse

ravishing ['rævɪʃɪŋ] *adj* enchanteur(eresse)

raw [rɔː] *adj* (*uncooked*) cru(e); (*not processed*) brut(e); (*sore*) à vif, irrité(e); (*inexperienced*) inexpérimenté(e); **raw deal** (*col*: *bad bargain*) sale coup *m*; (: *unfair treatment*): **to get a raw deal** être traité(e) injustement

raw material *n* matière première

ray [reɪ] *n* rayon *m*; **ray of hope** lueur *f* d'espoir

raze [reɪz] *vt* (*also*: **raze to the ground**) raser

razor ['reɪzə*] *n* rasoir *m*

razor blade *n* lame *f* de rasoir

Rd *abbr* = **road**

RE *n abbr* (*BRIT*) = religious education; (*BRIT MIL*) = Royal Engineers

re [ri:] *prep* concernant

reach [ri:tʃ] *n* portée *f*, atteinte *f*; (*of river etc*) étendue *f* ♦ *vt* atteindre, arriver à ♦ *vi* s'étendre; (*stretch out hand*): **to reach up/down/out** *etc* (**for sth**) lever/baisser/allonger *etc* le bras (pour prendre qch); **to reach sb by phone** joindre qn par téléphone; **out of/within reach** (*object*) hors de/à portée; **within easy reach (of)** (*place*) à proximité (de), proche (de)

react [ri:ˈækt] *vi* réagir

reaction [ri:ˈækʃən] *n* réaction *f*

reactor [ri:ˈæktə*] *n* réacteur *m*

read, *pt, pp* **read** [ri:d, red] *vi* lire ♦ *vt* lire; (*understand*) comprendre, interpréter; (*study*) étudier; (*subj: instrument etc*) indiquer, marquer; **to take sth as read** (*fig*) considérer qch comme accepté; **do you read me?** (*TEL*) est-ce que vous me recevez?
▶ **read out** *vt* lire à haute voix
▶ **read over** *vt* relire
▶ **read through** *vt* (*quickly*) parcourir; (*thoroughly*) lire jusqu'au bout
▶ **read up** *vt*, **read up on** *vt fus* étudier

readable [ˈri:dəbl] *adj* facile *or* agréable à lire

reader [ˈri:də*] *n* lecteur/trice; (*book*) livre *m* de lecture; (*BRIT: at university*) maître *m* de conférences

readership [ˈri:dəʃip] *n* (*of paper etc*) (nombre *m* de) lecteurs *mpl*

readily [ˈredili] *adv* volontiers, avec empressement; (*easily*) facilement

readiness [ˈredinis] *n* empressement *m*; **in readiness** (*prepared*) prêt(e)

reading [ˈri:diŋ] *n* lecture *f*; (*understanding*) interprétation *f*; (*on instrument*) indications *fpl*

ready [ˈredi] *adj* prêt(e); (*willing*) prêt, disposé(e); (*quick*) prompt(e); (*available*) disponible ♦ *n*: **at the ready** (*MIL*) prêt à faire feu; (*fig*) tout(e) prêt(e); **ready for use** prêt à l'emploi; **to be ready to do sth** être prêt à faire qch; **to get ready** *vi* se préparer ♦ *vt* préparer

ready-made [ˈrediˈmeid] *adj* tout(e) faite(e)

ready-to-wear [ˈreditəˈweə*] *adj* (en) prêt-à-porter

real [riəl] *adj* réel(le); (*genuine*) véritable; (*proper*) vrai(e) ♦ *adv* (*US col: very*) vraiment; **in real life** dans la réalité

real estate *n* biens fonciers *or* immobiliers

realistic [riəˈlistik] *adj* réaliste

reality [ri:ˈæliti] *n* réalité *f*; **in reality** en réalité, en fait

realization [riəlaiˈzeiʃən] *n* prise *f* de conscience; réalisation *f*

realize [ˈriəlaiz] *vt* (*understand*) se rendre compte de, prendre conscience de; (*a project, COMM: asset*) réaliser

really [ˈriəli] *adv* vraiment

realm [relm] *n* royaume *m*

realtor [ˈriəltɔ:*] (*US*) *n* agent immobilier

reap [ri:p] *vt* moissonner; (*fig*) récolter

reappear [ri:əˈpiə*] *vi* réapparaître, reparaître

rear [riə*] *adj* de derrière, arrière *inv*; (*AUT: wheel etc*) arrière ♦ *n* arrière *m*, derrière *m* ♦ *vt* (*cattle, family*) élever ♦ *vi* (*also*: **rear up**: *animal*) se cabrer

rearguard [ˈriəgɑ:d] *n* arrière-garde *f*

rear-view [ˈriəvju:]: **rear-view mirror** *n* (*AUT*) rétroviseur *m*

reason [ˈri:zn] *n* raison *f* ♦ *vi*: **to reason with sb** raisonner qn, faire entendre raison à qn; **the reason for/why** la raison de/pour laquelle; **to have reason to think** avoir lieu de penser; **it stands to reason that** il va sans dire que; **she claims with good reason that ...** elle affirme à juste titre que ...; **all the more reason why** raison de plus pour + *infinitive or* pour que + *sub*

reasonable [ˈri:znəbl] *adj* raisonnable; (*not bad*) acceptable

reasonably [ˈri:znəbli] *adv* (*to behave*) raisonnablement; (*fairly*) assez; **one can reasonably assume that ...** on est fondé à *or* il est permis de supposer que ...

reasoning [ˈri:zniŋ] *n* raisonnement *m*

reassurance [ri:əˈʃuərəns] *n* assurance *f*, garantie *f*; (*comfort*) réconfort *m*

reassure [ri:əˈʃuə*] *vt* rassurer; **to reassure sb of** donner à qn l'assurance répétée de

rebate [ˈri:beit] *n* (*on product*) rabais *m*; (*on tax etc*) dégrèvement *m*; (*repayment*) remboursement *m*

rebel *n* [ˈrebl] rebelle *m/f* ♦ *vi* [riˈbel] se rebeller, se révolter

rebellious [riˈbeljəs] *adj* rebelle

rebound *vi* [riˈbaund] (*ball*) rebondir ♦ *n* [ˈri:baund] rebond *m*

rebuff [riˈbʌf] *n* rebuffade *f* ♦ *vt* repousser

rebuke [riˈbju:k] *n* réprimande *f*, reproche *m* ♦ *vt* réprimander

rebut [riˈbʌt] *vt* réfuter

recall [riˈkɔ:l] *vt* rappeler; (*remember*) se rappeler, se souvenir de ♦ *n* rappel *m*; **beyond recall** *adj* irrévocable

recant [riˈkænt] *vi* se rétracter; (*REL*) abjurer

recap [ˈri:kæp] *n* récapitulation *f* ♦ *vt, vi* récapituler

recd *abbr* = received

recede [riˈsi:d] *vi* s'éloigner; reculer

receding [riˈsi:diŋ] *adj* (*forehead, chin*) fuyant(e); **receding hairline** front dégarni

receipt [riˈsi:t] *n* (*document*) reçu *m*; (*for parcel etc*) accusé *m* de réception; (*act of receiving*) réception *f*; **receipts** *npl* (*COMM*) recettes *fpl*; **to acknowledge receipt of** accuser réception de; **we are in receipt of ...** nous avons reçu ...

receive [riˈsi:v] *vt* recevoir; (*guest*) accueillir; **"received with thanks"** (*COMM*) "pour acquit"; **Received Pronunciation** voir encadré

RECEIVED PRONUNCIATION

En Grande-Bretagne, la **Received Pronunciation** ou **RP** est une prononciation de la langue anglaise qui, récemment encore, était surtout associée à l'aristocratie et à la bourgeoisie, mais qui maintenant est en général considérée comme la prononciation correcte.

---

receiver [rɪ'siːvə*] n (TEL) récepteur m; (RADIO) récepteur; (of stolen goods) receleur m; (COMM) administrateur m judiciaire

recent ['riːsnt] adj récent(e); **in recent years** au cours de ces dernières années

recently ['riːsntlɪ] adv récemment; **as recently as** pas plus tard que; **until recently** jusqu'à il y a peu de temps encore

receptacle [rɪ'septɪkl] n récipient m

reception [rɪ'sepʃən] n réception f; (welcome) accueil m, réception

reception desk n réception f

receptionist [rɪ'sepʃənɪst] n réceptionniste m/f

recess [rɪ'ses] n (in room) renfoncement m; (for bed) alcôve f; (secret place) recoin m; (POL etc: holiday) vacances fpl; (US: LAW: short break) suspension f d'audience; (SCOL: esp US) récréation f

recession [rɪ'seʃən] n (ECON) récession f

recipe ['resɪpɪ] n recette f

recipient [rɪ'sɪpɪənt] n bénéficiaire m/f; (of letter) destinataire m/f

recital [rɪ'saɪtl] n récital m

recite [rɪ'saɪt] vt (poem) réciter; (complaints etc) énumérer

reckless ['rekləs] adj (driver etc) imprudent(e); (spender etc) insouciant(e)

reckon ['rekən] vt (count) calculer, compter; (consider) considérer, estimer; (think): **I reckon (that) ...** je pense (que) ..., j'estime (que) ... ♦ vi: **he is somebody to be reckoned with** il ne faut pas le sous-estimer; **to reckon without sb/sth** ne pas tenir compte de qn/qch

▶ **reckon on** vt fus compter sur, s'attendre à

reckoning ['rekənɪŋ] n compte m, calcul m; estimation f; **the day of reckoning** le jour du Jugement

reclaim [rɪ'kleɪm] vt (land) amender; (: from sea) assécher; (: from forest) défricher; (demand back) réclamer (le remboursement or la restitution de)

recline [rɪ'klaɪn] vi être allongé(e) or étendu(e)

reclining [rɪ'klaɪnɪŋ] adj (seat) à dossier réglable

recluse [rɪ'kluːs] n reclus/e, ermite m

recognition [rekəg'nɪʃən] n reconnaissance f; **in recognition of** en reconnaissance de; **to gain recognition** être reconnu(e); **transformed beyond recognition** méconnaissable

recognizable ['rekəgnaɪzəbl] adj: **recognizable (by)** reconnaissable (à)

recognize ['rekəgnaɪz] vt: **to recognize (by/as)** reconnaître (à/comme étant)

recoil [rɪ'kɔɪl] vi (person): **to recoil (from)** reculer (devant) ♦ n (of gun) recul m

recollect [rekə'lekt] vt se rappeler, se souvenir de

recollection [rekə'lekʃən] n souvenir m; **to the best of my recollection** autant que je m'en souvienne

recommend [rekə'mend] vt recommander; **she has a lot to recommend her** elle a beaucoup de choses en sa faveur

reconcile ['rekənsaɪl] vt (two people) réconcilier; (two facts) concilier, accorder; **to reconcile o.s. to** se résigner à

recondition [riːkən'dɪʃən] vt remettre à neuf; réviser entièrement

reconnoitre, (US) **reconnoiter** [rekə'nɔɪtə*] (MIL) vt reconnaître ♦ vi faire une reconnaissance

reconsider [riːkən'sɪdə*] vt reconsidérer

reconstruct [riːkən'strʌkt] vt (building) reconstruire; (crime) reconstituer

record n ['rekɔːd] rapport m, récit m; (of meeting etc) procès-verbal m; (register) registre m; (file) dossier m; (COMPUT) article m; (also: **police record**) casier m judiciaire; (MUS: disc) disque m; (SPORT) record m ♦ vt [rɪ'kɔːd] (set down) noter; (relate) rapporter; (MUS: song etc) enregistrer; **in record time** dans un temps record inv; **public records** archives fpl; **to keep a record of** noter; **to keep the record straight** (fig) mettre les choses au point; **he is on record as saying that ...** il a déclaré en public que ...; **Italy's excellent record** les excellents résultats obtenus par l'Italie; **off the record** adj officieux(euse) ♦ adv officieusement

record card n (in file) fiche f

recorded delivery letter [rɪ'kɔːdɪd-] n (BRIT POST) ≈ lettre recommandée

recorder [rɪ'kɔːdə*] n (LAW) avocat nommé à la fonction de juge (MUS) flûte f à bec

record holder n (SPORT) détenteur/trice du record

recording [rɪ'kɔːdɪŋ] n (MUS) enregistrement m

record player n électrophone m

recount [rɪ'kaʊnt] vt raconter

re-count n ['riːkaʊnt] (POL: of votes) nouveau décompte (des suffrages) ♦ vt [riː'kaʊnt] recompter

recoup [rɪ'kuːp] vt: **to recoup one's losses** récupérer ce qu'on a perdu, se refaire

recourse [rɪ'kɔːs] n recours m; expédient m; **to have recourse to** recourir à, avoir recours à

recover [rɪ'kʌvə*] vt récupérer ♦ vi (from illness) se rétablir; (from shock) se remettre; (country) se redresser

recovery [rɪ'kʌvərɪ] n récupération f; rétablissement m; redressement m

recreation [rekrɪ'eɪʃən] n récréation f, détente f

recreational [rɛkrɪ'eɪʃənl] *adj* pour la détente, récréatif(ive)

recruit [rɪ'kruːt] *n* recrue *f* ♦ *vt* recruter

rectangle ['rɛktæŋgl] *n* rectangle *m*

rectangular [rɛk'tæŋgjulə*] *adj* rectangulaire

rectify ['rɛktɪfaɪ] *vt* (*error*) rectifier, corriger; (*omission*) réparer

rector ['rɛktə*] *n* (*REL*) pasteur *m*; (*in Scottish universities*) personnalité élue par les étudiants pour les représenter

recuperate [rɪ'kjuːpəreɪt] *vi* (*from illness*) se rétablir

recur [rɪ'kəː*] *vi* se reproduire; (*idea, opportunity*) se retrouver; (*symptoms*) réapparaître

recurrence [rɪ'kəːrns] *n* répétition *f*; réapparition *f*

recurrent [rɪ'kəːrnt] *adj* périodique, fréquent(e)

recycle [riː'saɪkl] *vt, vi* recycler

recycling [riː'saɪklɪŋ] *n* recyclage *m*

red [rɛd] *n* rouge *m*; (*POL, pej*) rouge *m/f* ♦ *adj* rouge; **in the red** (*account*) à découvert; (*business*) en déficit

red carpet treatment *n* réception *f* en grande pompe

Red Cross *n* Croix-Rouge *f*

redcurrant ['rɛdkʌrənt] *n* groseille *f* (rouge)

redden ['rɛdn] *vt, vi* rougir

redecorate [riː'dɛkəreɪt] *vt* refaire à neuf, repeindre et retapisser

redeem [rɪ'diːm] *vt* (*debt*) rembourser; (*sth in pawn*) dégager; (*fig, also REL*) racheter

redeeming [rɪ'diːmɪŋ] *adj* (*feature*) qui sauve, qui rachète (le reste)

redeploy [riːdɪ'plɔɪ] *vt* (*MIL*) redéployer; (*staff, resources*) reconvertir

red-haired [rɛd'hɛəd] *adj* roux(rousse)

red-handed [rɛd'hændɪd] *adj*: **to be caught red-handed** être pris(e) en flagrant délit *or* la main dans le sac

redhead ['rɛdhɛd] *n* roux/rousse

red herring *n* (*fig*) diversion *f*, fausse piste

red-hot [rɛd'hɔt] *adj* chauffé(e) au rouge, brûlant(e)

redirect [riːdaɪ'rɛkt] *vt* (*mail*) faire suivre

red light *n*: **to go through a red light** (*AUT*) brûler un feu rouge

red-light district ['rɛdlaɪt-] *n* quartier réservé

redo [riː'duː] *vt irreg* refaire

redress [rɪ'drɛs] *n* réparation *f* ♦ *vt* redresser; **to redress the balance** rétablir l'équilibre

Red Sea *n*: **the Red Sea** la mer Rouge

redskin ['rɛdskɪn] *n* Peau-Rouge *m/f*

red tape *n* (*fig*) paperasserie (administrative)

reduce [rɪ'djuːs] *vt* réduire; (*lower*) abaisser; **"reduce speed now"** (*AUT*) "ralentir"; **to reduce sth by/to** réduire qch de/à; **to reduce sb to tears** faire pleurer qn

reduction [rɪ'dʌkʃən] *n* réduction *f*; (*of price*) baisse *f*; (*discount*) rabais *m*; réduction

redundancy [rɪ'dʌndənsɪ] *n* (*BRIT*) licenciement *m*, mise *f* au chômage; **compulsory redundancy** licenciement; **voluntary redundancy** départ *m* volontaire

redundant [rɪ'dʌndnt] *adj* (*BRIT: worker*) licencié(e), mis(e) au chômage; (*detail, object*) superflu(e); **to be made redundant** (*worker*) être licencié, être mis au chômage

reed [riːd] *n* (*BOT*) roseau *m*; (*MUS: of clarinet etc*) anche *f*

reef [riːf] *n* (*at sea*) récif *m*, écueil *m*

reek [riːk] *vi*: **to reek (of)** puer, empester

reel [riːl] *n* bobine *f*; (*TECH*) dévidoir *m*; (*FISHING*) moulinet *m*; (*CINE*) bande *f* ♦ *vt* (*TECH*) bobiner; (*also*: **reel up**) enrouler ♦ *vi* (*sway*) chanceler; **my head is reeling** j'ai la tête qui tourne

▶ **reel in** *vt* (*fish, line*) ramener

▶ **reel off** *vt* (*say*) énumérer, débiter

ref [rɛf] *n abbr* (*col: = referee*) arbitre *m*

refectory [rɪ'fɛktərɪ] *n* réfectoire *m*

refer [rɪ'fəː*] *vt*: **to refer sth to** (*dispute, decision*) soumettre qch à; **to refer sb to** (*inquirer: for information*) adresser *or* envoyer qn à; (*reader: to text*) renvoyer qn à; **he referred me to the manager** il m'a dit de m'adresser au directeur

▶ **refer to** *vt fus* (*allude to*) parler de, faire allusion à; (*apply to*) s'appliquer à; (*consult*) se reporter à; **referring to your letter** (*COMM*) en réponse à votre lettre

referee [rɛfə'riː] *n* arbitre *m*; (*TENNIS*) juge-arbitre *m*; (*BRIT: for job application*) répondant/e ♦ *vt* arbitrer

reference ['rɛfrəns] *n* référence *f*, renvoi *m*; (*mention*) allusion *f*, mention *f*; (*for job application: letter*) références; lettre *f* de recommandation; (: *person*) répondant/e; **with reference to** en ce qui concerne; (*COMM: in letter*) me référant à; **"please quote this reference"** (*COMM*) "prière de rappeler cette référence"

reference book *n* ouvrage *m* de référence

refill *vt* [riː'fɪl] remplir à nouveau; (*pen, lighter etc*) recharger ♦ *n* ['riːfɪl] (*for pen etc*) recharge *f*

refine [rɪ'faɪn] *vt* (*sugar, oil*) raffiner; (*taste*) affiner

refined [rɪ'faɪnd] *adj* (*person, taste*) raffiné(e)

refinery [rɪ'faɪnərɪ] *n* raffinerie *f*

reflect [rɪ'flɛkt] *vt* (*light, image*) réfléchir, refléter; (*fig*) refléter ♦ *vi* (*think*) réfléchir, méditer

▶ **reflect on** *vt fus* (*discredit*) porter atteinte à, faire tort à

reflection [rɪ'flɛkʃən] *n* réflexion *f*; (*image*) reflet *m*; (*criticism*): **reflection on** critique *f* de; atteinte *f* à; **on reflection** réflexion faite

reflex ['riːflɛks] *adj, n* réflexe (*m*)

reflexive [rɪˈflɛksɪv] *adj* (*LING*) réfléchi(e)

reform [rɪˈfɔːm] *n* réforme *f* ♦ *vt* réformer

reformatory [rɪˈfɔːmətərɪ] *n* (*US*) centre *m* d'éducation surveillée

refrain [rɪˈfreɪn] *vi*: **to refrain from doing** s'abstenir de faire ♦ *n* refrain *m*

refresh [rɪˈfrɛʃ] *vt* rafraîchir; (*subj: food, sleep etc*) redonner des forces à

refresher course [rɪˈfrɛʃə-] *n* (*BRIT*) cours *m* de recyclage

refreshing [rɪˈfrɛʃɪŋ] *adj* rafraîchissant(e); (*sleep*) réparateur(trice); (*fact, idea etc*) qui réjouit par son originalité *or* sa rareté

refreshment [rɪˈfrɛʃmənt] *n*: **for some refreshment** (*eating*) pour se restaurer *or* sustenter; **in need of refreshment** (*resting etc*) ayant besoin de refaire ses forces; **refreshment(s)** rafraîchissement(s) *m(pl)*

refrigerator [rɪˈfrɪdʒəreɪtə*] *n* réfrigérateur *m*, frigidaire *m*

refuel [riːˈfjuəl] *vt* ravitailler en carburant ♦ *vi* se ravitailler en carburant

refuge [ˈrɛfjuːdʒ] *n* refuge *m*; **to take refuge in** se réfugier dans

refugee [rɛfjuˈdʒiː] *n* réfugié/e

refund *n* [ˈriːfʌnd] remboursement *m* ♦ *vt* [rɪˈfʌnd] rembourser

refurbish [riːˈfɜːbɪʃ] *vt* remettre à neuf

refusal [rɪˈfjuːzəl] *n* refus *m*; **to have first refusal on sth** avoir droit de préemption sur qch

refuse *n* [ˈrɛfjuːs] ordures *fpl*, détritus *mpl* ♦ *vt, vi* [rɪˈfjuːz] refuser; **to refuse to do sth** refuser de faire qch

refuse collection *n* ramassage *m* d'ordures

regain [rɪˈgeɪn] *vt* regagner; retrouver

regal [ˈriːgl] *adj* royal(e)

regard [rɪˈgɑːd] *n* respect *m*, estime *f*, considération *f* ♦ *vt* considérer; **to give one's regards to** faire ses amitiés à; **"with kindest regards"** "bien amicalement"; **as regards, with regard to** en ce qui concerne

regarding [rɪˈgɑːdɪŋ] *prep* en ce qui concerne

regardless [rɪˈgɑːdlɪs] *adv* quand même; **regardless of** sans se soucier de

régime [reɪˈʒiːm] *n* régime *m*

regiment *n* [ˈrɛdʒɪmənt] régiment *m* ♦ *vt* [ˈrɛdʒɪment] imposer une discipline trop stricte à

regimental [rɛdʒɪˈmɛntl] *adj* d'un régiment

region [ˈriːdʒən] *n* région *f*; **in the region of** (*fig*) aux alentours de

regional [ˈriːdʒənl] *adj* régional(e)

register [ˈrɛdʒɪstə*] *n* registre *m*; (*also*: **electoral register**) liste électorale ♦ *vt* enregistrer, inscrire; (*birth*) déclarer; (*vehicle*) immatriculer; (*luggage*) enregistrer; (*letter*) envoyer en recommandé; (*instrument*) marquer ♦ *vi* s'inscrire; (*at hotel*) signer le registre; (*make impression*) être (bien)

compris(e); **to register for a course** s'inscrire à un cours; **to register a protest** protester

registered [ˈrɛdʒɪstəd] *adj* (*design*) déposé(e); (*BRIT: letter*) recommandé(e); (*student, voter*) inscrit(e)

registered trademark *n* marque déposée

registrar [ˈrɛdʒɪstrɑː*] *n* officier *m* de l'état civil; secrétaire général

registration [rɛdʒɪsˈtreɪʃən] *n* (*act*) enregistrement *m*; inscription *f*; (*BRIT AUT: also*: **registration number**) numéro *m* d'immatriculation

registry [ˈrɛdʒɪstrɪ] *n* bureau *m* de l'enregistrement

registry office *n* (*BRIT*) bureau *m* de l'état civil; **to get married in a registry office** ≈ se marier à la mairie

regret [rɪˈgrɛt] *n* regret *m* ♦ *vt* regretter; **to regret that** regretter que + *sub*; **we regret to inform you that …** nous sommes au regret de vous informer que …

regretfully [rɪˈgrɛtfəlɪ] *adv* à *or* avec regret

regular [ˈrɛgjulə*] *adj* régulier(ière); (*usual*) habituel(le), normal(e); (*listener, reader*) fidèle; (*soldier*) de métier; (*COMM: size*) ordinaire ♦ *n* (*client etc*) habitué/e

regularly [ˈrɛgjuləlɪ] *adv* régulièrement

regulate [ˈrɛgjuleɪt] *vt* régler

regulation [rɛgjuˈleɪʃən] *n* (*rule*) règlement *m*; (*adjustment*) réglage *m* ♦ *cpd* réglementaire

rehabilitation [ˈriːəˈbɪlɪˈteɪʃən] *n* (*of offender*) réhabilitation *f*; (*of disabled*) rééducation *f*, réadaptation *f*

rehearsal [rɪˈhəːsəl] *n* répétition *f*; **dress rehearsal** (répétition) générale *f*

rehearse [rɪˈhəːs] *vt* répéter

reign [reɪn] *n* règne *m* ♦ *vi* régner

reimburse [riːɪmˈbəːs] *vt* rembourser

rein [reɪn] *n* (*for horse*) rêne *f*; **to give sb free rein** (*fig*) donner carte blanche à qn

reindeer [ˈreɪndɪə*] *n* (*pl inv*) renne *m*

reinforce [riːɪnˈfɔːs] *vt* renforcer

reinforced concrete [riːɪnˈfɔːst-] *n* béton armé

reinforcement [riːɪnˈfɔːsmənt] *n* (*action*) renforcement *m*; **reinforcements** *npl* (*MIL*) renfort(s) *m(pl)*

reinstate [riːɪnˈsteɪt] *vt* rétablir, réintégrer

reject *n* [ˈriːdʒɛkt] (*COMM*) article *m* de rebut ♦ *vt* [rɪˈdʒɛkt] refuser; (*COMM: goods*) mettre au rebut; (*idea*) rejeter

rejection [rɪˈdʒɛkʃən] *n* rejet *m*, refus *m*

rejoice [rɪˈdʒɔɪs] *vi*: **to rejoice (at *or* over)** se réjouir (de)

rejuvenate [rɪˈdʒuːvəneɪt] *vt* rajeunir

relapse [rɪˈlæps] *n* (*MED*) rechute *f*

relate [rɪˈleɪt] *vt* (*tell*) raconter; (*connect*) établir un rapport entre ♦ *vi*: **to relate to** (*connect*) se rapporter à; (*interact*) établir un rapport or une entente avec

related [rɪ'leɪtɪd] *adj* apparenté(e)

relating [rɪ'leɪtɪŋ]: **relating to** *prep* concernant

relation [rɪ'leɪʃən] *n* (*person*) parent/e; (*link*) rapport *m*, lien *m*; **diplomatic/international relations** relations diplomatiques/internationales; **in relation to** en ce qui concerne; par rapport à; **to bear no relation to** être sans rapport avec

relationship [rɪ'leɪʃənʃɪp] *n* rapport *m*, lien *m*; (*personal ties*) relations *fpl*, rapports; (*also:* **family relationship**) lien de parenté; (*affair*) liaison *f*; **they have a good relationship** ils s'entendent bien.

relative ['relətɪv] *n* parent/e ♦ *adj* relatif(ive); (*respective*) respectif(ive); **all her relatives** toute sa famille

relatively ['relətɪvlɪ] *adv* relativement

relax [rɪ'læks] *vi* se relâcher; (*person: unwind*) se détendre; (*calm down*) se calmer ♦ *vt* relâcher; (*mind, person*) détendre

relaxation [riːlæk'seɪʃən] *n* relâchement *m*; détente *f*; (*entertainment*) distraction *f*

relaxed [rɪ'lækst] *adj* relâché(e); détendu(e)

relaxing [rɪ'læksɪŋ] *adj* délassant(e)

relay ['riːleɪ] *n* (*SPORT*) course *f* de relais ♦ *vt* (*message*) retransmettre, relayer

release [rɪ'liːs] *n* (*from prison, obligation*) libération *f*; (*of gas etc*) émission *f*; (*of film etc*) sortie *f*; (*record*) disque *m*; (*device*) déclencheur *m* ♦ *vt* (*prisoner*) libérer; (*book, film*) sortir; (*report, news*) rendre public, publier; (*gas etc*) émettre, dégager; (*free: from wreckage etc*) dégager; (*TECH: catch, spring etc*) déclencher; (*let go*) relâcher; lâcher; desserrer; **to release one's grip** or **hold** lâcher prise; **to release the clutch** (*AUT*) débrayer

relegate ['reləgeɪt] *vt* reléguer; (*SPORT*): **to be relegated** descendre dans une division inférieure

relent [rɪ'lent] *vi* se laisser fléchir

relentless [rɪ'lentlɪs] *adj* implacable

relevant ['reləvənt] *adj* approprié(e); (*fact*) significatif(ive); (*information*) utile, pertinent(e); **relevant to** ayant rapport à, approprié à

reliable [rɪ'laɪəbl] *adj* (*person, firm*) sérieux(euse), fiable; (*method, machine*) fiable

reliably [rɪ'laɪəblɪ] *adv*: **to be reliably informed** savoir de source sûre

reliance [rɪ'laɪəns] *n*: **reliance (on)** (*trust*) confiance *f* (en); (*dependence*) besoin *m* (de), dépendance *f* (de)

relic ['relɪk] *n* (*REL*) relique *f*; (*of the past*) vestige *m*

relief [rɪ'liːf] *n* (*from pain, anxiety*) soulagement *m*; (*help, supplies*) secours *m(pl)*; (*of guard*) relève *f*; (*ART, GEO*) relief *m*; **by way of light relief** pour faire diversion

relieve [rɪ'liːv] *vt* (*pain, patient*) soulager; (*bring help*) secourir; (*take over from: gen*) relayer; (*: guard*) relever; **to relieve sb of sth** débarrasser qn de qch; **to relieve sb of his command** (*MIL*) relever qn de ses fonctions; **to relieve o.s.** (*euphemism*) se soulager, faire ses besoins

religion [rɪ'lɪdʒən] *n* religion *f*

religious [rɪ'lɪdʒəs] *adj* religieux(euse); (*book*) de piété

relinquish [rɪ'lɪŋkwɪʃ] *vt* abandonner; (*plan, habit*) renoncer à

relish ['relɪʃ] *n* (*CULIN*) condiment *m*; (*enjoyment*) délectation *f* ♦ *vt* (*food etc*) savourer; **to relish doing** se délecter à faire

relocate [riːləʊ'keɪt] *vt* (*business*) transférer ♦ *vi* se transférer, s'installer or s'établir ailleurs; **to relocate in** (déménager et) s'installer or s'établir à, se transférer à

reluctance [rɪ'lʌktəns] *n* répugnance *f*

reluctant [rɪ'lʌktənt] *adj* peu disposé(e), qui hésite; **to be reluctant to do sth** hésiter à faire qch

reluctantly [rɪ'lʌktəntlɪ] *adv* à contrecœur, sans enthousiasme

remain [rɪ'meɪn] *vi* rester; **to remain silent** garder le silence; **I remain, yours faithfully** (*BRIT: in letters*) je vous prie d'agréer, Monsieur *etc*, l'assurance de mes sentiments distingués

remainder [rɪ'meɪndə*] *n* reste *m*; (*COMM*) fin *f* de série

remaining [rɪ'meɪnɪŋ] *adj* qui reste

remains [rɪ'meɪnz] *npl* restes *mpl*

remake ['riːmeɪk] *n* (*CINEMA*) remake *m*

remand [rɪ'mɑːnd] *n*: **on remand** en détention préventive ♦ *vt*: **to remand in custody** écrouer; renvoyer en détention provisoire

remark [rɪ'mɑːk] *n* remarque *f*, observation *f* ♦ *vt* (*faire*) remarquer, dire; (*notice*) remarquer; **to remark on sth** faire une or des remarque(s) sur qch

remarkable [rɪ'mɑːkəbl] *adj* remarquable

remarkably [rɪ'mɑːkəblɪ] *adv* remarquablement

remarry [riː'mærɪ] *vi* se remarier

remedial [rɪ'miːdɪəl] *adj* (*tuition, classes*) de rattrapage

remedy ['remədɪ] *n*: **remedy (for)** remède *m* (contre or à) ♦ *vt* remédier à

remember [rɪ'membə*] *vt* se rappeler, se souvenir de; **I remember seeing it, I remember having seen it** je me rappelle l'avoir vu or que je l'ai vu; **she remembered to do it** elle a pensé à le faire; **remember me to your wife** rappelez-moi au bon souvenir de votre femme

remembrance [rɪ'membrəns] *n* souvenir *m*; mémoire *f*

Remembrance Day n (BRIT) ≈ (le jour de) l'Armistice m, ≈ le 11 novembre; voir encadré

REMEMBRANCE DAY

Remembrance Day ou **Remembrance Sunday** est le dimanche le plus proche du 11 novembre, jour où la Première Guerre mondiale a officiellement pris fin. Il rend hommage aux victimes des deux guerres mondiales. À cette occasion, on observe deux minutes de silence à 11h, heure de la signature de l'armistice avec l'Allemagne en 1918; certaines membres de la famille royale et du gouvernement déposent des gerbes de coquelicots au cénotaphe de Whitehall, et des couronnes sont placées sur les monuments aux morts dans toute la Grande-Bretagne; par ailleurs, les gens portent des coquelicots artificiels fabriqués et vendus par des membres de la légion britannique blessés au combat, au profit des blessés de guerre et de leur famille.

---

remind [rɪ'maɪnd] vt: **to remind sb of sth** rappeler qch à qn; **to remind sb to do** faire penser à qn à faire, rappeler à qn qu'il doit faire; **that reminds me!** j'y pense!

reminder [rɪ'maɪndə*] n rappel m; (note etc) pense-bête m

reminisce [remɪ'nɪs] vi: **to reminisce (about)** évoquer ses souvenirs (de)

reminiscent [remɪ'nɪsnt] adj: **reminiscent of** qui rappelle, qui fait penser à

remiss [rɪ'mɪs] adj négligent(e); **it was remiss of me** c'était une négligence de ma part

remission [rɪ'mɪʃən] n rémission f; (of debt, sentence) remise f; (of fee) exemption f

remit [rɪ'mɪt] vt (send: money) envoyer

remittance [rɪ'mɪtns] n envoi m, paiement m

remnant ['remnənt] n reste m, restant m; **remnants** npl (COMM) coupons mpl; fins fpl de série

remorse [rɪ'mɔːs] n remords m

remorseful [rɪ'mɔːsful] adj plein(e) de remords

remorseless [rɪ'mɔːslɪs] adj (fig) impitoyable

remote [rɪ'məut] adj éloigné(e), lointain(e); (person) distant(e); **there is a remote possibility that ...** il est tout juste possible que ...

remote control n télécommande f

remotely [rɪ'məutlɪ] adv au loin; (slightly) très vaguement

remould ['riːməuld] n (BRIT: tyre) pneu rechapé

removable [rɪ'muːvəbl] adj (detachable) amovible

removal [rɪ'muːvəl] n (taking away) enlèvement m; suppression f; (BRIT: from house) déménagement m; (from office: dismissal) renvoi m; (MED) ablation f

removal van n (BRIT) camion m de déménagement

remove [rɪ'muːv] vt enlever, retirer; (stain) faire partir; (doubt, abuse) supprimer; **first cousin once removed** cousin(e) au deuxième degré

render ['rendə*] vt rendre; (CULIN: fat) clarifier

rendering ['rendərɪŋ] n (MUS etc) interprétation f

rendezvous ['rɒndɪvuː] n rendez-vous m inv ♦ vi opérer une jonction, se rejoindre; **to rendezvous with sb** rejoindre qn

renew [rɪ'njuː] vt renouveler; (negotiations) reprendre; (acquaintance) renouer

renewable [rɪ'njuːəbl] adj renouvelable; **renewable energy, renewables** énergies renouvelables

renewal [rɪ'njuːəl] n renouvellement m; reprise f

renounce [rɪ'nauns] vt renoncer à; (disown) renier

renovate ['renəveɪt] vt rénover; (work of art) restaurer

renown [rɪ'naun] n renommée f

renowned [rɪ'naund] adj renommé(e)

rent [rent] pt, pp of **rend** ♦ n loyer m ♦ vt louer; (car, TV) louer, prendre en location; (also: **rent out**: car, TV) louer, donner en location

rental ['rentl] n (for television, car) (prix m de) location f

reorganize [riː'ɔːgənaɪz] vt réorganiser

rep [rep] n abbr (COMM) = **representative**; (THEAT) = **repertory**

repair [rɪ'peə*] n réparation f ♦ vt réparer; **in good/bad repair** en bon/mauvais état; **under repair** en réparation

repair kit n trousse f de réparations

repatriate [riː'pætrɪeɪt] vt rapatrier

repay [riː'peɪ] vt irreg (money, creditor) rembourser; (sb's efforts) récompenser

repayment [riː'peɪmənt] n remboursement m; récompense f

repeal [rɪ'piːl] n (of law) abrogation f; (of sentence) annulation f ♦ vt abroger; annuler

repeat [rɪ'piːt] n (RADIO, TV) reprise f ♦ vt répéter; (pattern) reproduire; (promise, attack, also COMM: order) renouveler; (SCOL: a class) redoubler ♦ vi répéter

repeatedly [rɪ'piːtɪdlɪ] adv souvent, à plusieurs reprises

repel [rɪ'pel] vt repousser

repellent [rɪ'pelənt] adj repoussant(e) ♦ n: **insect repellent** insectifuge m; **moth repellent** produit m antimite(s)

repent [rɪ'pent] vi: **to repent (of)** se repentir (de)

repentance [rɪ'pentəns] n repentir m

repertory ['repətərɪ] n (also: **repertory theatre**) théâtre m de répertoire

repetition [repɪ'tɪʃən] n répétition f

repetitive [rɪ'petɪtɪv] adj (movement, work) répétitif(ive); (speech) plein(e) de redites

replace [rɪ'pleɪs] vt (put back) remettre, replacer;

(*take the place of*) remplacer; (*TEL*): **"replace the receiver"** "raccrochez"

replacement [rɪ'pleɪsmənt] *n* replacement *m*; remplacement *m*; (*person*) remplaçant/e

replay ['riːpleɪ] *n* (*of match*) match rejoué; (*of tape, film*) répétition *f*

replenish [rɪ'plenɪʃ] *vt* (*glass*) remplir (de nouveau); (*stock etc*) réapprovisionner

replica ['replɪkə] *n* réplique *f*, copie exacte

reply [rɪ'plaɪ] *n* réponse *f* ◆ *vi* répondre; **in reply (to)** en réponse (à); **there's no reply** (*TEL*) ça ne répond pas

report [rɪ'pɔːt] *n* rapport *m*; (*PRESS etc*) reportage *m*; (*BRIT: also*: **school report**) bulletin *m* (scolaire); (*of gun*) détonation *f* ◆ *vt* rapporter, faire un compte rendu de; (*PRESS etc*) faire un reportage sur; (*bring to notice: occurrence*) signaler; (: *person*) dénoncer ◆ *vi* (*make a report*): **to report (on)** faire un rapport (sur); (*for newspaper*) faire un reportage (sur); (*present o.s.*): **to report (to sb)** se présenter (chez qn); **it is reported that** on dit *or* annonce que; **it is reported from Berlin that** on nous apprend de Berlin que

report card *n* (*us, Scottish*) bulletin *m* (scolaire)

reportedly [rɪ'pɔːtɪdlɪ] *adv*: **she is reportedly living in Spain** elle habiterait en Espagne; **he reportedly ordered them to ...** il leur aurait ordonné de ...

reporter [rɪ'pɔːtə*] *n* reporter *m*

repose [rɪ'pəuz] *n*: **in repose** en *or* au repos

represent [reprɪ'zent] *vt* représenter; (*explain*): **to represent to sb that** expliquer à qn que

representation [reprɪzen'teɪʃən] *n* représentation *f*; **representations** *npl* (*protest*) démarche *f*

representative [reprɪ'zentətɪv] *n* représentant/e; (*COMM*) représentant/e (de commerce); (*us POL*) député *m* ◆ *adj*: **representative (of)** représentatif(ive) (de), caractéristique (de)

repress [rɪ'pres] *vt* réprimer

repression [rɪ'prefən] *n* répression *f*

reprieve [rɪ'priːv] *n* (*LAW*) grâce *f*; (*fig*) sursis *m*, délai *m* ◆ *vt* gracier; accorder un sursis *or* un délai à

reprisal [rɪ'praɪzl] *n* représailles *fpl*; **to take reprisals** user de représailles

reproach [rɪ'prəutʃ] *n* reproche *m* ◆ *vt*: **to reproach sb with sth** reprocher qch à qn; **beyond reproach** irréprochable

reproachful [rɪ'prəutʃful] *adj* de reproche

reproduce [riːprə'djuːs] *vt* reproduire ◆ *vi* se reproduire

reproduction [riːprə'dʌkʃən] *n* reproduction *f*

reproof [rɪ'pruːf] *n* reproche *m*

reptile ['reptaɪl] *n* reptile *m*

republic [rɪ'pʌblɪk] *n* république *f*

republican [rɪ'pʌblɪkən] *adj*, *n* républicain/e

repudiate [rɪ'pjuːdɪeɪt] *vt* (*ally, behaviour*) désa-

vouer; (*accusation*) rejeter; (*wife*) répudier

repulsive [rɪ'pʌlsɪv] *adj* repoussant(e), répulsif(ive)

reputable ['repjutəbl] *adj* de bonne réputation; (*occupation*) honorable

reputation [repju'teɪʃən] *n* réputation *f*; **to have a reputation for** être réputé/e pour; **he has a reputation for being awkward** il a la réputation de ne pas être commode

reputed [rɪ'pjuːtɪd] *adj* réputé(e); **he is reputed to be rich/intelligent** *etc* on dit qu'il est riche/intelligent *etc*

reputedly [rɪ'pjuːtɪdlɪ] *adv* d'après ce qu'on dit

request [rɪ'kwest] *n* demande *f*; (*formal*) requête *f* ◆ *vt*: **to request (of or from sb)** demander (à qn); **at the request of** à la demande de

request stop *n* (*BRIT: for bus*) arrêt facultatif

require [rɪ'kwaɪə*] *vt* (*need: subj: person*) avoir besoin de; (: *thing, situation*) nécessiter, demander; (*demand*) exiger, requérir; (*order*): **to require sb to do sth/sth of sb** exiger que qn fasse qch/qch de qn; **if required** s'il le faut; **what qualifications are required?** quelles sont les qualifications requises?; **required by law** requis par la loi

requirement [rɪ'kwaɪəmənt] *n* exigence *f*; besoin *m*; condition *f* (requise)

requisition [rekwɪ'zɪʃən] *n*: **requisition (for)** demande *f* (de) ◆ *vt* (*MIL*) réquisitionner

rescue ['reskjuː] *n* sauvetage *m*; (*help*) secours *mpl* ◆ *vt* sauver; **to come to sb's rescue** venir au secours de qn

rescue party *n* équipe *f* de sauvetage

rescuer ['reskjuə*] *n* sauveteur *m*

research [rɪ'səːtʃ] *n* recherche(s) *f(pl)* ◆ *vt* faire des recherches sur ◆ *vi*: **to research (into sth)** faire des recherches (sur qch); **a piece of research** un travail de recherche; **research and development (R & D)** recherche-développement (R-D)

resemblance [rɪ'zembləns] *n* ressemblance *f*; **to bear a strong resemblance to** ressembler beaucoup à

resemble [rɪ'zembl] *vt* ressembler à

resent [rɪ'zent] *vt* éprouver du ressentiment de, être contrarié(e) par

resentful [rɪ'zentful] *adj* irrité(e), plein(e) de ressentiment

resentment [rɪ'zentmənt] *n* ressentiment *m*

reservation [rezə'veɪʃən] *n* (*booking*) réservation *f*; (*doubt, protected area*) réserve *f*; (*BRIT AUT: also*: **central reservation**) bande médiane; **to make a reservation (in an hotel/a restaurant/on a plane)** réserver *or* retenir une chambre/une table/une place; **with reservations** (*doubts*) avec certaines réserves

reserve [rɪ'zəːv] *n* réserve *f*; (*SPORT*) remplaçant/e ◆ *vt* (*seats etc*) réserver, retenir; **reserves** *npl* (*MIL*) réservistes *mpl*; **in reserve** en réserve

reserved [rɪ'zəːvd] *adj* réservé(e)

reshuffle [riːˈʃʌfl] n: **Cabinet reshuffle** (POL) remaniement ministériel

residence [ˈrezɪdəns] n résidence f; **to take up residence** s'installer; **in residence** (queen etc) en résidence; (doctor) résidant/e

residence permit n (BRIT) permis m de séjour

resident [ˈrezɪdənt] n résident/e ♦ adj résidant(e)

residential [rezɪˈdenʃəl] adj de résidence; (area) résidentiel(le)

residential school n internat m

residue [ˈrezɪdjuː] n reste m; (CHEM, PHYSICS) résidu m

resign [rɪˈzaɪn] vt (one's post) se démettre de ♦ vi: **to resign (from)** démissionner (de); **to resign o.s. to** (endure) se résigner à

resignation [rezɪɡˈneɪʃən] n démission f; résignation f; **to tender one's resignation** donner sa démission

resigned [rɪˈzaɪnd] adj résigné(e)

resilient [rɪˈzɪlɪənt] adj (person) qui réagit, qui a du ressort

resist [rɪˈzɪst] vt résister à

resistance [rɪˈzɪstəns] n résistance f

resit [riːˈsɪt] vt (exam) repasser ♦ n [ˈriːsɪt] deuxième session f (d'un examen)

resolution [rezəˈluːʃən] n résolution f; **to make a resolution** prendre une résolution

resolve [rɪˈzɒlv] n résolution f ♦ vt (decide): **to resolve to do** résoudre or décider de faire; (problem) résoudre

resort [rɪˈzɔːt] n (town) station f (de vacances); (recourse) recours m ♦ vi: **to resort to** avoir recours à; **seaside/winter sports resort** station balnéaire/de sports d'hiver; **in the last resort** en dernier ressort

resounding [rɪˈzaundɪŋ] adj retentissant(e)

resource [rɪˈsɔːs] n ressource f; **resources** npl ressources; **natural resources** ressources naturelles; **to leave sb to his** (or **her**) **own resources** (fig) livrer qn à lui-même (or elle-même)

resourceful [rɪˈsɔːsful] adj plein(e) de ressource, débrouillard(e)

respect [rɪsˈpekt] n respect m; (point, detail): **in some respects** à certains égards ♦ vt respecter; **respects** npl respects, hommages mpl; **to have** or **show respect for sb/sth** respecter qn/qch; **out of respect for** par respect pour; **with respect to** en ce qui concerne; **in respect of** sous le rapport de, quant à; **in this respect** sous ce rapport, à cet égard; **with due respect I …** malgré le respect que je vous dois, je …

respectable [rɪsˈpektəbl] adj respectable; (quite good: result etc) honorable; (player) assez bon (bonne)

respectful [rɪsˈpektful] adj respectueux(euse)

respectively [rɪsˈpektɪvlɪ] adv respectivement

respite [ˈrespaɪt] n répit m

respond [rɪsˈpɒnd] vi répondre; (to treatment) réagir

response [rɪsˈpɒns] n réponse f; (to treatment) réaction f; **in response to** en réponse à

responsibility [rɪspɒnsɪˈbɪlɪtɪ] n responsabilité f; **to take responsibility for sth/sb** accepter la responsabilité de qch/d'être responsable de qn

responsible [rɪsˈpɒnsɪbl] adj (liable): **responsible (for)** responsable (de); (person) digne de confiance; (job) qui comporte des responsabilités; **to be responsible to sb (for sth)** être responsable devant qn (de qch)

responsive [rɪsˈpɒnsɪv] adj qui n'est pas réservé(e) or indifférent(e)

rest [rest] n repos m; (stop) arrêt m, pause f; (MUS) silence m; (support) support m, appui m; (remainder) reste m, restant m ♦ vi se reposer; (be supported): **to rest on** appuyer or reposer sur; (remain) rester ♦ vt (lean): **to rest sth on/against** appuyer qch sur/contre; **the rest of them** les autres; **to set sb's mind at rest** tranquilliser qn; **it rests with him to** c'est à lui de; **rest assured that …** soyez assuré que …

restaurant [ˈrestərɒŋ] n restaurant m

restaurant car n (BRIT) wagon-restaurant m

restful [ˈrestful] adj reposant(e)

restive [ˈrestɪv] adj agité(e), impatient(e); (horse) rétif(ive)

restless [ˈrestlɪs] adj agité(e); **to get restless** s'impatienter

restoration [restəˈreɪʃən] n restauration f; restitution f

restore [rɪˈstɔː*] vt (building) restaurer; (sth stolen) restituer; (peace, health) rétablir

restrain [rɪsˈtreɪn] vt (feeling) contenir; (person): **to restrain (from doing)** retenir (de faire)

restrained [rɪsˈtreɪnd] adj (style) sobre; (manner) mesuré(e)

restraint [rɪsˈtreɪnt] n (restriction) contrainte f; (moderation) retenue f; (of style) sobriété f; **wage restraint** limitations salariales

restrict [rɪsˈtrɪkt] vt restreindre, limiter

restriction [rɪsˈtrɪkʃən] n restriction f, limitation f

rest room n (US) toilettes fpl

result [rɪˈzʌlt] n résultat m ♦ vi: **to result (from)** résulter (de); **to result in** aboutir à, se terminer par; **as a result it is too expensive** il en résulte que c'est trop cher; **as a result of** à la suite de

resume [rɪˈzjuːm] vt (work, journey) reprendre; (sum up) résumer ♦ vi (work etc) reprendre

résumé [ˈreɪzjuːmeɪ] n (summary) résumé m; (US: curriculum vitae) curriculum vitae m inv

resumption [rɪˈzʌmpʃən] n reprise f

resurgence [rɪˈsɜːdʒəns] n réapparition f

resurrection [rezəˈrekʃən] n résurrection f

resuscitate [rɪˈsʌsɪteɪt] vt (MED) réanimer

retail [ˈriːteɪl] n (vente f au) détail m ♦ cpd de or au détail ♦ vt vendre au détail ♦ vi: **to retail at 10 francs** se vendre au détail à 10 francs

retailer [ˈriːteɪlə*] n détaillant/e

retail price n prix m de détail

retain [rɪˈteɪn] vt (keep) garder, conserver; (employ) engager

retainer [rɪˈteɪnə*] n (servant) serviteur m; (fee) acompte m, provision f

retaliate [rɪˈtælɪeɪt] vi: **to retaliate (against)** se venger (de); **to retaliate (on sb)** rendre la pareille (à qn)

retaliation [rɪtælɪˈeɪʃən] n représailles fpl, vengeance f; **in retaliation for** par représailles pour

retarded [rɪˈtɑːdɪd] adj retardé(e)

retch [retʃ] vi avoir des haut-le-cœur

retentive [rɪˈtentɪv] adj: **retentive memory** excellente mémoire

retina [ˈretɪnə] n rétine f

retire [rɪˈtaɪə*] vi (give up work) prendre sa retraite; (withdraw) se retirer, partir; (go to bed) (aller) se coucher

retired [rɪˈtaɪəd] adj (person) retraité(e)

retirement [rɪˈtaɪəmənt] n retraite f

retiring [rɪˈtaɪərɪŋ] adj (person) réservé(e); (chairman etc) sortant(e)

retort [rɪˈtɔːt] n (reply) riposte f; (container) cornue f ♦ vi riposter

retrace [riːˈtreɪs] vt reconstituer; **to retrace one's steps** revenir sur ses pas

retract [rɪˈtrækt] vt (statement, claws) rétracter; (undercarriage, aerial) rentrer, escamoter ♦ vi se rétracter; rentrer

retrain [riːˈtreɪn] vt recycler ♦ vi se recycler

retread vt [riːˈtred] (AUT: tyre) rechaper ♦ n [ˈriːtred] pneu rechapé

retreat [rɪˈtriːt] n retraite f ♦ vi battre en retraite; (flood) reculer; **to beat a hasty retreat** (fig) partir avec précipitation

retribution [retrɪˈbjuːʃən] n châtiment m

retrieval [rɪˈtriːvəl] n récupération f; réparation f; recherche f et extraction f

retrieve [rɪˈtriːv] vt (sth lost) récupérer; (situation, honour) sauver; (error, loss) réparer; (COMPUT) rechercher

retriever [rɪˈtriːvə*] n chien m d'arrêt

retrospect [ˈretrəspekt] n: **in retrospect** rétrospectivement, après coup

retrospective [retrəˈspektɪv] adj (law) rétroactif(ive) ♦ n (ART) rétrospective f

return [rɪˈtɜːn] n (going or coming back) retour m; (of sth stolen etc) restitution f; (recompense) récompense f; (FINANCE: from land, shares) rapport m; (report) relevé m, rapport m ♦ cpd (journey) de retour; (BRIT: ticket) aller et retour; (match) retour ♦ vi (person etc: come back) revenir; (: go back) retourner ♦ vt rendre; (bring back) rapporter; (send back) renvoyer; (put back) remettre; (POL: candidate) élire;

returns npl (COMM) recettes fpl; bénéfices mpl; (: returned goods) marchandises renvoyées; **many happy returns (of the day)!** bon anniversaire!; **by return (of post)** par retour (du courrier); **in return (for)** en échange (de)

reunion [riːˈjuːnɪən] n réunion f

reunite [riːjuːˈnaɪt] vt réunir

reuse [riːˈjuːz] vt réutiliser

rev [rev] n abbr = revolution (AUT) tour m ♦ vb (also: **rev up**) ♦ vt emballer ♦ vi s'emballer

revamp [riːˈvæmp] vt (house) retaper; (firm) réorganiser

reveal [rɪˈviːl] vt (make known) révéler; (display) laisser voir

revealing [rɪˈviːlɪŋ] adj révélateur(trice); (dress) au décolleté généreux or suggestif

revel [ˈrevl] vi: **to revel in sth/in doing** se délecter de qch/à faire

revenge [rɪˈvendʒ] n vengeance f; (in game etc) revanche f ♦ vt venger; **to take revenge** se venger

revenue [ˈrevənjuː] n revenu m

reverberate [rɪˈvɜːbəreɪt] vi (sound) retentir, se répercuter; (light) se réverbérer

reverence [ˈrevərəns] n vénération f, révérence f

reverend [ˈrevərənd] adj vénérable; **the Reverend John Smith** (Anglican) le révérend John Smith; (Catholic) l'abbé John Smith; (Protestant) le pasteur John Smith

reversal [rɪˈvɜːsl] n (of opinion) revirement m

reverse [rɪˈvɜːs] n contraire m, opposé m; (back) dos m, envers m; (AUT: also: **reverse gear**) marche f arrière ♦ adj (order, direction) opposé(e), inverse ♦ vt (turn) renverser, retourner; (change) renverser, changer complètement; (LAW: judgment) réformer ♦ vi (BRIT AUT) faire marche arrière; **to go into reverse** faire marche arrière; **in reverse order** en ordre inverse

reversed charge call [rɪˈvɜːst-] n (BRIT TEL) communication f en PCV

reversing lights [rɪˈvɜːsɪŋ-] npl (BRIT AUT) feux mpl de marche arrière or de recul

revert [rɪˈvɜːt] vi: **to revert to** revenir à, retourner à

review [rɪˈvjuː] n revue f; (of book, film) critique f ♦ vt passer en revue; faire la critique de; **to come under review** être révisé(e)

reviewer [rɪˈvjuːə*] n critique m

revise [rɪˈvaɪz] vt (manuscript) revoir, corriger; (opinion) réviser, modifier; (study: subject, notes) réviser; **revised edition** édition revue et corrigée

revision [rɪˈvɪʒən] n révision f; (revised version) version corrigée

revival [rɪˈvaɪvəl] n reprise f; rétablissement m; (of faith) renouveau m

revive [rɪˈvaɪv] vt (person) ranimer; (custom) rétablir; (hope, courage) redonner; (play, fashion) reprendre ♦ vi (person) reprendre connaissance; (hope) renaître; (activity) reprendre

revoke [rɪ'vəuk] *vt* révoquer; (*promise, decision*) revenir sur

revolt [rɪ'vəult] *n* révolte *f* ◆ *vi* se révolter, se rebeller

revolting [rɪ'vəultɪŋ] *adj* dégoûtant(e)

revolution [revə'lu:ʃən] *n* révolution *f*; (*of wheel etc*) tour *m*, révolution

revolutionary [revə'lu:ʃənrɪ] *adj*, *n* révolutionnaire (*m/f*)

revolve [rɪ'vɔlv] *vi* tourner

revolver [rɪ'vɔlvə*] *n* revolver *m*

revolving [rɪ'vɔlvɪŋ] *adj* (*chair*) pivotant(e); (*light*) tournant(e)

revolving door *n* (porte *f* à) tambour *m*

revulsion [rɪ'vʌlʃən] *n* dégoût *m*, répugnance *f*

reward [rɪ'wɔ:d] *n* récompense *f* ◆ *vt*: **to reward (for)** récompenser (de)

rewarding [rɪ'wɔ:dɪŋ] *adj* (*fig*) qui (en) vaut la peine, gratifiant(e); **financially rewarding** financièrement intéressant(e)

rewind [ri:'waɪnd] *vt irreg* (*watch*) remonter; (*ribbon etc*) réembobiner

rewire [ri:'waɪə*] *vt* (*house*) refaire l'installation électrique de

rewritable [ri:'raɪtəbl] *adj* (*CD, DVD*) réinscriptible

rheumatism ['ru:mətɪzəm] *n* rhumatisme *m*

Rhine [raɪn] *n*: **the Rhine** le Rhin

rhinoceros [raɪ'nɔsərəs] *n* rhinocéros *m*

Rhône [rəun] *n*: **the Rhône** le Rhône

rhubarb ['ru:bɑ:b] *n* rhubarbe *f*

rhyme [raɪm] *n* rime *f*; (*verse*) vers *mpl* ◆ *vi*: **to rhyme (with)** rimer (avec); **without rhyme or reason** sans rime ni raison

rhythm ['rɪðm] *n* rythme *m*

rib [rɪb] *n* (*ANAT*) côte *f* ◆ *vt* (*mock*) taquiner

ribbon ['rɪbən] *n* ruban *m*; **in ribbons** (*torn*) en lambeaux

rice [raɪs] *n* riz *m*

rice pudding *n* riz *m* au lait

rich [rɪtʃ] *adj* riche; (*gift, clothes*) somptueux(euse); **the rich** *npl* les riches *mpl*; **riches** *npl* richesses *fpl*; **to be rich in sth** être riche en qch

richly ['rɪtʃlɪ] *adv* richement; (*deserved, earned*) largement, grandement

rickets ['rɪkɪts] *n* rachitisme *m*

rid, *pt*, *pp* **rid** [rɪd] *vt*: **to rid sb of** débarrasser qn de; **to get rid of** se débarrasser de

riddle ['rɪdl] *n* (*puzzle*) énigme *f* ◆ *vt*: **to be riddled with** être criblé(e) de

ride [raɪd] *n* promenade *f*, tour *m*; (*distance covered*) trajet *m* ◆ *vb*, *pt* **rode**, *pp* **ridden** [rəud, 'rɪdn] *vi* (*as sport*) monter (à cheval), faire du cheval; (*go somewhere: on horse, bicycle*) aller (à cheval ou bicyclette *etc*); (*journey: on bicycle, motor cycle, bus*) rouler ◆ *vt* (*a certain horse*) monter; (*distance*) parcourir, faire; **we rode all day** nous sommes restés toute la journée en selle; **to ride a horse/bicycle/**

camel monter à cheval/à bicyclette/à dos de chameau; **can you ride a bike?** est-ce que tu sais monter à bicyclette?; **to ride at anchor** (*NAUT*) être à l'ancre; **horse/car ride** promenade *or* tour à cheval/en voiture; **to go for a ride** faire une promenade (en voiture *or* à bicyclette *etc*); **to take sb for a ride** (*fig*) faire marcher qn; rouler qn

▶ **ride out** *vt*: **to ride out the storm** (*fig*) surmonter les difficultés

rider ['raɪdə*] *n* cavalier/ière; (*in race*) jockey *m*; (*on bicycle*) cycliste *m/f*; (*on motorcycle*) motocycliste *m/f*; (*in document*) annexe *f*, clause additionnelle

ridge [rɪdʒ] *n* (*of hill*) faîte *m*; (*of roof, mountain*) arête *f*; (*on object*) strie *f*

ridicule ['rɪdɪkju:l] *n* ridicule *m*; dérision *f* ◆ *vt* ridiculiser, tourner en dérision; **to hold sb/sth up to ridicule** tourner qn/qch en ridicule

ridiculous [rɪ'dɪkjuləs] *adj* ridicule

riding ['raɪdɪŋ] *n* équitation *f*

riding school *n* manège *m*, école *f* d'équitation

rife [raɪf] *adj* répandu(e); **rife with** abondant(e) en

riffraff ['rɪfræf] *n* racaille *f*

rifle ['raɪfl] *n* fusil *m* (à canon rayé) ◆ *vt* vider, dévaliser

▶ **rifle through** *vt fus* fouiller dans

rifle range *n* champ *m* de tir; (*indoor*) stand *m* de tir

rift [rɪft] *n* fente *f*, fissure *f*; (*fig: disagreement*) désaccord *m*

rig [rɪg] *n* (*also:* **oil rig**: *on land*) derrick *m*; (: *at sea*) plate-forme pétrolière ◆ *vt* (*election etc*) truquer

▶ **rig out** *vt* (*BRIT*) habiller; (: *pej*) fringuer, attifer

▶ **rig up** *vt* arranger, faire avec des moyens de fortune

rigging ['rɪgɪŋ] *n* (*NAUT*) gréement *m*

right [raɪt] *adj* (*true*) juste, exact(e); (*correctly chosen: answer, road etc*) bon(bonne); (*suitable*) approprié(e), convenable; (*just*) juste, équitable; (*morally good*) bien *inv*; (*not left*) droit(e) ◆ *n* (*title, claim*) droit *m*; (*not left*) droite *f* ◆ *adv* (*answer*) correctement; (*not on the left*) à droite ◆ *vt* redresser ◆ *excl* bon!; **the right time** (*precise*) l'heure exacte; (*not wrong*) la bonne heure; **to be right** (*person*) avoir raison; (*answer*) être juste *or* correct(e); **to get sth right** ne pas se tromper sur qch; **let's get it right this time!** essayons de ne pas nous tromper cette fois-ci!; **you did the right thing** vous avez bien fait; **to put a mistake right** (*BRIT*) rectifier une erreur; **right now** en ce moment même; tout de suite; **right before/after** juste avant/après; **right against the wall** tout contre le mur; **right ahead** tout droit; droit devant; **right in the middle** en plein milieu; **right away** immédiatement; **to go right to the end of sth** aller jusqu'au bout de qch; **by rights** en toute justice; **on the right** à droite; **right and wrong** le bien et le mal; **to be in the right** avoir raison; **film rights** droits d'adaptation cinématographique; **right of way** droit *m* de passage; (AUT) priorité f

right angle n angle droit

righteous ['raɪtʃəs] adj droit(e), vertueux(euse); (anger) justifié(e)

rightful ['raɪtful] adj (heir) légitime

right-handed [raɪt'hændɪd] adj (person) droitier(ière)

right-hand man ['raɪthænd-] n bras droit (fig)

right-hand side ['raɪthænd-] n côté droit

rightly ['raɪtlɪ] adv bien, correctement; (with reason) à juste titre; **if I remember rightly** (BRIT) si je me souviens bien

right wing n (MIL, SPORT) aile droite; (POL) droite f ♦ adj: **right-wing** (POL) de droite

rigid ['rɪdʒɪd] adj rigide; (principle) strict(e)

rigmarole ['rɪgmərəul] n galimatias m, comédie f

rigorous ['rɪgərəs] adj rigoureux(euse)

rile [raɪl] vt agacer

rim [rɪm] n bord m; (of spectacles) monture f; (of wheel) jante f

rind [raɪnd] n (of bacon) couenne f; (of lemon etc) écorce f

ring [rɪŋ] n anneau m; (on finger) bague f; (also: **wedding ring**) alliance f; (for napkin) rond m; (of people, objects) cercle m; (of spies) réseau m; (of smoke etc) rond m; (arena) piste f, arène f; (for boxing) ring m; (sound of bell) sonnerie f; (telephone call) coup m de téléphone ♦ vb, pt **rang**, pp **rung** [ræŋ, rʌŋ] vi (person, bell) sonner; (also: **ring out**: voice, words) retentir; (TEL) téléphoner ♦ vt (BRIT TEL: also: **ring up**) téléphoner à; **to ring the bell** sonner; **to give sb a ring** (TEL) passer un coup de téléphone or de fil à qn; **that has the ring of truth about it** cela sonne vrai; **the name doesn't ring a bell (with me)** ce nom ne me dit rien

▶ **ring back** vt, vi (BRIT TEL) rappeler

▶ **ring off** vi (BRIT TEL) raccrocher

ring binder n classeur m à anneaux

ringing ['rɪŋɪŋ] n (of bell) tintement m; (louder, also of telephone) sonnerie f; (in ears) bourdonnement m

ringing tone n (BRIT TEL) sonnerie f

ringleader ['rɪŋliːdə*] n (of gang) chef m, meneur m

ringlets ['rɪŋlɪts] npl anglaises fpl

ring road n (BRIT) route f de ceinture

ringtone ['rɪŋtəun] n (on mobile) sonnerie f (de téléphone portable)

rink [rɪŋk] n (also: **ice rink**) patinoire f; (for roller-skating) skating m

rinse [rɪns] n rinçage m ♦ vt rincer

riot ['raɪət] n émeute f, bagarres fpl ♦ vi manifester avec violence; **a riot of colours** une débauche or orgie de couleurs; **to run riot** se déchaîner

riotous ['raɪətəs] adj tapageur(euse); tordant(e)

rip [rɪp] n déchirure f ♦ vt déchirer ♦ vi se déchirer

▶ **rip up** vt déchirer

ripcord ['rɪpkɔːd] n poignée f d'ouverture

ripe [raɪp] adj (fruit) mûr(e); (cheese) fait(e)

ripen ['raɪpn] vt mûrir ♦ vi mûrir; se faire

rip-off ['rɪpɔf] n (col): **it's a rip-off!** c'est du vol manifeste!

ripple ['rɪpl] n ride f, ondulation f; égrènement m, cascade f ♦ vi se rider, onduler ♦ vt rider, faire onduler

rise [raɪz] n (slope) côte f, pente f; (hill) élévation f; (increase: in wages: BRIT) augmentation f; (: in prices, temperature) hausse f, augmentation f; (fig) ascension f ♦ vi, pt **rose**, pp **risen** ['rəuz, rɪzn] s'élever, monter; (prices) augmenter, monter; (waters, river) monter; (sun, wind, person: from chair, bed) se lever; (also: **rise up**: rebel) se révolter; se rebeller; **to give rise to** donner lieu à; **to rise to the occasion** se montrer à la hauteur

riser ['raɪzə*] n: **to be an early riser** être matinal(e)

rising ['raɪzɪŋ] adj (increasing: number, prices) en hausse; (tide) montant(e); (sun, moon) levant(e) ♦ n (uprising) soulèvement m, insurrection f

risk [rɪsk] n risque m, danger m; (deliberate) risque ♦ vt risquer; **to take** or **run the risk of doing** courir le risque de faire; **at risk** en danger; **at one's own risk** à ses risques et périls; **it's a fire/health risk** cela présente un risque d'incendie/pour la santé; **I'll risk it** je vais risquer le coup

risky ['rɪskɪ] adj risqué(e)

rite [raɪt] n rite m; **the last rites** les derniers sacrements

ritual ['rɪtjuəl] adj rituel(le) ♦ n rituel m

rival ['raɪvl] n rival/e; (in business) concurrent/e ♦ adj rival(e); qui fait concurrence ♦ vt être en concurrence avec; **to rival sb/sth in** rivaliser avec qn/qch de

rivalry ['raɪvlrɪ] n rivalité f; concurrence f

river ['rɪvə*] n rivière f, fleuve m ♦ cpd (port, traffic) fluvial(e); **up/down river** en amont/aval

riverbank ['rɪvəbæŋk] n rive f, berge f

riverbed ['rɪvəbed] n lit m (de rivière or de fleuve)

rivet ['rɪvɪt] n rivet m ♦ vt riveter; (fig) river, fixer

Riviera [rɪvɪ'eərə] n: **the (French) Riviera** la Côte d'Azur; **the Italian Riviera** la Riviera (italienne)

road [rəud] n route f; (in town) rue f; (fig) chemin, voie f; **main road** grande route; **major road** route principale or à priorité; **minor road** voie secondaire; **it takes four hours by road** il y a quatre heures de route; **"road up"** (BRIT) "attention travaux"

road accident n accident m de la circulation

roadblock ['rəudblɔk] n barrage routier

roadhog ['rəudhɔg] n chauffard m

road map n carte routière

road rage n comportement très agressif de certains usagers de la route

road safety n sécurité routière

roadside ['rəudsaɪd] n bord m de la route, bas-

côté m ♦ *cpd* (situé(e) *etc*) au bord de la route; **by the roadside** au bord de la route

road sign n panneau m de signalisation

roadway ['rəudweɪ] n chaussée f

roadworks ['rəudwɜːks] npl travaux mpl (de réfection des routes)

roadworthy ['rəudwɜːðɪ] adj en bon état de marche

roam [rəum] vi errer, vagabonder ♦ vt parcourir, errer par

roar [rɔːʳ] n rugissement m; (of crowd) hurlements mpl; (of vehicle, thunder, storm) grondement m ♦ vi rugir; hurler; gronder; **to roar with laughter** rire à gorge déployée

roast [rəust] n rôti m ♦ vt (meat) (faire) rôtir

roast beef n rôti m de bœuf, rosbif m

rob [rɒb] vt (person) voler; (bank) dévaliser; **to rob sb of sth** voler or dérober qch à qn; (fig: deprive) priver qn de qch

robber ['rɒbəʳ] n bandit m, voleur m

robbery ['rɒbərɪ] n vol m

robe [rəub] n (for ceremony etc) robe f; (also: **bathrobe**) peignoir m ♦ vt revêtir (d'une robe)

robin ['rɒbɪn] n rouge-gorge m

robot ['rəubɒt] n robot m

robust [rəu'bʌst] adj robuste; (material, appetite) solide

rock [rɒk] n (substance) roche f, roc m; (boulder) rocher m, roche; (BRIT: sweet) ≈ sucre m d'orge ♦ vt (swing gently: cradle) balancer; (: child) bercer; (shake) ébranler, secouer ♦ vi (se) balancer, être ébranlé(e) or secoué(e); **on the rocks** (drink) avec des glaçons; (ship) sur les écueils; (marriage etc) en train de craquer; **to rock the boat** (fig) jouer les trouble-fête

rock and roll n rock (and roll) m, rock'n'roll m

rock-bottom ['rɒk'bɒtəm] n (fig) niveau le plus bas ♦ adj (fig: prices) sacrifié(e); **to reach** or **touch rock-bottom** (price, person) tomber au plus bas

rockery ['rɒkərɪ] n (jardin m de) rocaille f

rocket ['rɒkɪt] n fusée f; (MIL) fusée, roquette f ♦ vi (prices) monter en flèche

rocking chair ['rɒkɪŋ-] n fauteuil m à bascule

rocking horse ['rɒkɪŋ-] n cheval m à bascule

rocky ['rɒkɪ] adj (hill) rocheux(euse); (path) rocailleux(euse); (unsteady: table) branlant(e)

rod [rɒd] n (metallic) tringle f; (TECH) tige f; (wooden) baguette f; (also: **fishing rod**) canne f à pêche

rode [rəud] pt of **ride**

rodent ['rəudnt] n rongeur m

rodeo ['rəudɪəu] n rodéo m

roe [rəu] n (species: also: **roe deer**) chevreuil m; (of fish: also: **hard roe**) œufs mpl de poisson; **soft roe** laitance f

rogue [rəug] n coquin/e

role [rəul] n rôle m

role play, role playing n jeu m de rôle

roll [rəul] n rouleau m; (of banknotes) liasse f; (also: **bread roll**) petit pain; (register) liste f; (sound: of drums etc) roulement m; (movement: of ship) roulis m ♦ vt rouler; (also: **roll up**: string) enrouler; (also: **roll out**: pastry) étendre au rouleau ♦ vi rouler; (wheel) tourner; **cheese roll** ≈ sandwich m au fromage (dans un petit pain)

▶ **roll about, roll around** vi rouler çà et là; (person) se rouler par terre

▶ **roll by** vi (time) s'écouler, passer

▶ **roll in** vi (mail, cash) affluer

▶ **roll over** vi se retourner

▶ **roll up** vi (col: arrive) arriver, s'amener ♦ vt (carpet, cloth, map) rouler; (sleeves) retrousser; **to roll o.s. up into a ball** se rouler en boule

roll call n appel m

roller ['rəuləʳ] n rouleau m; (wheel) roulette f

roller blade n patin m en ligne

roller coaster n montagnes fpl russes

roller skates npl patins mpl à roulettes

roller skating n patin m à roulettes

rolling ['rəulɪŋ] adj (landscape) onduleux(euse)

rolling pin n rouleau m à pâtisserie

rolling stock n (RAIL) matériel roulant

ROM [rɒm] n abbr (COMPUT: = read-only memory) mémoire morte, ROM f

Roman ['rəumən] adj romain(e) ♦ n Romain/e

Roman Catholic adj, n catholique (m/f)

romance [rə'mæns] n histoire f (or film m or aventure f) romanesque; (charm) poésie f; (love affair) idylle f

Romania [rəu'meɪnɪə] n Roumanie f

Romanian [rəu'meɪnɪən] adj roumain(e) ♦ n Roumain/e; (LING) roumain m

Roman numeral n chiffre romain

romantic [rə'mæntɪk] adj romantique; (play, attachment) sentimental(e)

Rome [rəum] n Rome

romp [rɒmp] n jeux bruyants ♦ vi (also: **romp about**) s'ébattre, jouer bruyamment; **to romp home** (horse) arriver bon premier

rompers ['rɒmpəz] npl barboteuse f

roof [ruːf] n toit m; (of tunnel, cave) plafond m ♦ vt couvrir (d'un toit); **the roof of the mouth** la voûte du palais

roofing ['ruːfɪŋ] n toiture f

roof rack n (AUT) galerie f

rook [ruk] n (bird) freux m; (CHESS) tour f ♦ vt (col: cheat) rouler, escroquer

room [ruːm] n (in house) pièce f; (also: **bedroom**) chambre f (à coucher); (in school etc) salle f; (space) place f; **rooms** npl (lodging) meublé m; **"rooms to let"**, (us) **"rooms for rent"** "chambres à louer"; **is there room for this?** est-ce qu'il y a de la place pour ceci?; **to make room for sb** faire de la place à qn; **there is room for improvement** on peut faire mieux

rooming house ['ru:mɪŋ-] *n* (*US*) maison *f* de rapport

roommate ['ru:mmeɪt] *n* camarade *m/f* de chambre

room service *n* service *m* des chambres (*dans un hôtel*)

roomy ['ru:mɪ] *adj* spacieux(euse); (*garment*) ample

roost [ru:st] *n* juchoir *m* ♦ *vi* se jucher

rooster ['ru:stə*] *n* coq *m*

root [ru:t] *n* (*BOT, MATH*) racine *f*; (*fig: of problem*) origine *f*, fond *m* ♦ *vi* (*plant*) s'enraciner; **to take root** (*plant, idea*) prendre racine

▶ **root about** *vi* (*fig*) fouiller

▶ **root for** *vt fus* (*col*) applaudir

▶ **root out** *vt* extirper

rope [rəup] *n* corde *f*; (*NAUT*) cordage *m* ♦ *vt* (*box*) corder; (*climbers*) encorder; **to rope sb in** (*fig*) embringuer qn; **to know the ropes** (*fig*) être au courant, connaître les ficelles

rosary ['rəuzərɪ] *n* chapelet *m*

rose [rəuz] *pt of* **rise** ♦ *n* rose *f*; (*also:* **rosebush**) rosier *m*; (*on watering can*) pomme *f* ♦ *adj* rose

rosé ['rəuzeɪ] *n* rosé *m*

rosebud ['rəuzbʌd] *n* bouton *m* de rose

rosemary ['rəuzmərɪ] *n* romarin *m*

roster ['rɒstə*] *n*: **duty roster** tableau *m* de service

rostrum ['rɒstrəm] *n* tribune *f* (*pour un orateur etc*)

rosy ['rəuzɪ] *adj* rose; **a rosy future** un bel avenir

rot [rɒt] *n* (*decay*) pourriture *f*; (*fig: pej*) idioties *fpl*, balivernes *fpl* ♦ *vt, vi* pourrir; **to stop the rot** (*BRIT fig*) rétablir la situation; **dry rot** pourriture sèche (*du bois*); **wet rot** pourriture (du bois)

rota ['rəutə] *n* liste *f*, tableau *m* de service; **on a rota basis** par roulement

rotary ['rəutərɪ] *adj* rotatif(ive)

rotate [rəu'teɪt] *vt* (*revolve*) faire tourner; (*change round: crops*) alterner; (*: jobs*) faire à tour de rôle ♦ *vi* (*revolve*) tourner

rotating [rəu'teɪtɪŋ] *adj* (*movement*) tournant(e)

rotten ['rɒtn] *adj* (*decayed*) pourri(e); (*dishonest*) corrompu(e); (*col: bad*) mauvais(e), moche; **to feel rotten** (*ill*) être mal fichu(e)

rotund [rəu'tʌnd] *adj* rondelet(te); arrondi(e)

rough [rʌf] *adj* (*cloth, skin*) rêche, rugueux(euse); (*terrain*) accidenté(e); (*path*) rocailleux(euse); (*voice*) rauque, rude; (*person, manner: coarse*) rude, fruste; (*: violent*) brutal(e); (*district, weather*) mauvais(e); (*plan*) ébauché(e); (*guess*) approximatif(ive) ♦ *n* (*GOLF*) rough *m* ♦ *vt*: **to rough it** vivre à la dure; **the sea is rough today** la mer est agitée aujourd'hui; **to have a rough time (of it)** en voir de dures; **rough estimate** approximation *f*; **to play rough** jouer avec brutalité; **to sleep rough** (*BRIT*)

coucher à la dure; **to feel rough** (*BRIT*) être mal fichu(e)

▶ **rough out** *vt* (*draft*) ébaucher

roughage ['rʌfɪdʒ] *n* fibres *fpl* diététiques

rough-and-ready ['rʌfən'redɪ] *adj* (*accommodation, method*) rudimentaire

rough copy, rough draft *n* brouillon *m*

roughly ['rʌflɪ] *adv* (*handle*) rudement, brutalement; (*make*) grossièrement; (*approximately*) à peu près, en gros; **roughly speaking** en gros

roulette [ru:'let] *n* roulette *f*

Romania *etc* [ru:'meɪnɪə] = **Romania** *etc*

round [raund] *adj* rond(e) ♦ *n* rond *m*, cercle *m*; (*BRIT: of toast*) tranche *f*; (*duty: of policeman, milkman etc*) tournée *f*; (*: of doctor*) visites *fpl*; (*game: of cards, in competition*) partie *f*; (*BOXING*) round *m*; (*of talks*) série *f* ♦ *vt* (*corner*) tourner; (*bend*) prendre; (*cape*) doubler ♦ *prep* autour de ♦ *adv*: **right round, all round** tout autour; **the long way round** (par) le chemin le plus long; **all the year round** toute l'année; **in round figures** en chiffres ronds; **it's just round the corner** c'est juste après le coin; (*fig*) c'est tout près; **I'll be round at 6 o'clock** je serai là à 6 heures; **to go round** faire le tour *or* un détour; **to go round to sb's (house)** aller chez qn; **to go round an obstacle** contourner un obstacle; **go round the back** passez par derrière; **to go round a house** visiter une maison, faire le tour d'une maison; **enough to go round** assez pour tout le monde; **she arrived round (about) noon** (*BRIT*) elle est arrivée vers midi; **round the clock** 24 heures sur 24; **to go the rounds** (*disease, story*) circuler; **the daily round** (*fig*) la routine quotidienne; **round of ammunition** cartouche *f*; **round of applause** applaudissements *mpl*; **round of drinks** tournée *f*; **round of sandwiches** (*BRIT*) sandwich *m*

▶ **round off** *vt* (*speech etc*) terminer

▶ **round up** *vt* rassembler; (*criminals*) effectuer une rafle de; (*prices*) arrondir (au chiffre supérieur)

roundabout ['raundəbaut] *n* (*BRIT AUT*) rond-point *m* (à sens giratoire); (*at fair*) manège *m* (de chevaux de bois) ♦ *adj* (*route, means*) détourné(e)

rounders ['raundəz] *npl* (*game*) = balle *f* au camp

roundly ['raundlɪ] *adv* (*fig*) tout net, carrément

round trip *n* (voyage *m*) aller et retour *m*

roundup ['raundʌp] *n* rassemblement *m*; (*of criminals*) rafle *f*; **a roundup of the latest news** un rappel des derniers événements

rouse [rauz] *vt* (*wake up*) réveiller; (*stir up*) susciter; provoquer; éveiller

rousing ['rauzɪŋ] *adj* (*welcome*) enthousiaste

route [ru:t] *n* itinéraire *m*; (*of bus*) parcours *m*; (*of trade, shipping*) route *f*; **"all routes"** (*AUT*) "toutes directions"; **the best route to London** le meilleur itinéraire pour aller à Londres

routine [ru:'ti:n] *adj* (*work*) de routine; (*proce-*

dure) d'usage ♦ _n_ routine _f_; (THEAT) numéro _m_; **daily routine** occupations journalières

rove [rəuv] _vt_ (_area, streets_) errer dans

row¹ [rəu] _n_ (_line_) rangée _f_; (_of people, seats_, KNITTING) rang _m_; (_behind one another: of cars, people_) file _f_ ♦ _vi_ (_in boat_) ramer; (_as sport_) faire de l'aviron ♦ _vt_ (_boat_) faire aller à la rame _or_ à l'aviron; **in a row** (fig) d'affilée

row² [rau] _n_ (_noise_) vacarme _m_; (_dispute_) dispute _f_, querelle _f_; (_scolding_) réprimande _f_, savon _m_ ♦ _vi_ (_also:_ **to have a row**) se disputer, se quereller

rowboat ['rəubəut] _n_ (US) canot _m_ (à rames)

rowdy ['raudɪ] _adj_ chahuteur(euse); bagarreur(euse) ♦ _n_ voyou _m_

rowing ['rəuɪŋ] _n_ canotage _m_; (_as sport_) aviron _m_

rowing boat _n_ (BRIT) canot _m_ (à rames)

royal ['rɔɪəl] _adj_ royal(e)

Royal Air Force (RAF) _n_ (BRIT) armée de l'air britannique

royalty ['rɔɪəltɪ] _n_ (_royal persons_) (membres _mpl_ de la) famille royale; (_payment: to author_) droits _mpl_ d'auteur; (: _to inventor_) royalties _fpl_

rpm _abbr_ (= revolutions per minute) t/mn (= tours/minute)

RSVP _abbr_ (= répondez s'il vous plaît) RSVP

Rt Hon. _abbr_ (= Right Honourable) titre donné aux députés de la Chambre des communes

rub [rʌb] _n_ (_with cloth_) coup _m_ de chiffon _or_ de torchon; (_on person_) friction _f_ ♦ _vt_ frotter; frictionner; **to rub sb up** _or_ **rub sb the wrong way** (US) prendre qn à rebrousse-poil

► **rub down** _vt_ (_body_) frictionner; (_horse_) bouchonner

► **rub in** _vt_ (_ointment_) faire pénétrer

► **rub off** _vi_ partir; **to rub off on** déteindre sur

► **rub out** _vt_ effacer ♦ _vi_ s'effacer

rubber ['rʌbə*] _n_ caoutchouc _m_; (BRIT: _eraser_) gomme _f_ (à effacer)

rubber band _n_ élastique _m_

rubber plant _n_ caoutchouc _m_ (_plante verte_)

rubbish ['rʌbɪʃ] _n_ (_from household_) ordures _fpl_; (fig: pej) choses _fpl_ sans valeur; camelote _f_; (_nonsense_) bêtises _fpl_, idioties _fpl_ ♦ _vt_ (BRIT col) dénigrer, rabaisser; **what you've just said is rubbish** tu viens de dire une bêtise

rubbish bin _n_ (BRIT) boîte _f_ à ordures, poubelle _f_

rubbish dump _n_ (_in town_) décharge publique, dépotoir _m_

rubble ['rʌbl] _n_ décombres _mpl_; (_smaller_) gravats _mpl_

ruby ['ruːbɪ] _n_ rubis _m_

rucksack ['rʌksæk] _n_ sac _m_ à dos

rudder ['rʌdə*] _n_ gouvernail _m_

ruddy ['rʌdɪ] _adj_ (_face_) coloré(e); (_col: damned_) sacré(e), fichu(e)

rude [ruːd] _adj_ (_impolite: person_) impoli(e); (: _word, manners_) grossier(ière); (_shocking_) indécent(e), inconvenant(e); **to be rude to sb** être grossier envers qn

ruffle ['rʌfl] _vt_ (_hair_) ébouriffer; (_clothes_) chiffonner; (_water_) agiter; (fig: _person_) émouvoir, faire perdre son flegme à

rug [rʌg] _n_ petit tapis; (BRIT: _for knees_) couverture _f_

rugby ['rʌgbɪ] _n_ (_also:_ **rugby football**) rugby _m_

rugged ['rʌgɪd] _adj_ (_landscape_) accidenté(e); (_features, kindness, character_) rude; (_determination_) farouche

ruin ['ruːɪn] _n_ ruine _f_ ♦ _vt_ ruiner; (_spoil: clothes_) abîmer; **ruins** _npl_ ruine(s); **in ruins** en ruine

rule [ruːl] _n_ règle _f_; (_regulation_) règlement _m_; (_government_) autorité _f_, gouvernement _m_; (_dominion etc_): **under British rule** sous l'autorité britannique ♦ _vt_ (_country_) gouverner; (_person_) dominer; (_decide_) décider ♦ _vi_ commander; décider; (LAW): **to rule against/in favour of/on** statuer contre/en faveur de/sur; **to rule that** (_umpire, judge etc_) décider que; **it's against the rules** c'est contraire au règlement; **by rule of thumb** à vue de nez; **as a rule** normalement, en règle générale

► **rule out** _vt_ exclure; **murder cannot be ruled out** l'hypothèse d'un meurtre ne peut être exclue

ruled [ruːld] _adj_ (_paper_) réglée(e)

ruler ['ruːlə*] _n_ (_sovereign_) souverain/e; (_leader_) chef _m_ (d'État); (_for measuring_) règle _f_

ruling ['ruːlɪŋ] _adj_ (_party_) au pouvoir; (_class_) dirigeant(e) ♦ _n_ (LAW) décision _f_

rum [rʌm] _n_ rhum _m_ ♦ _adj_ (BRIT col) bizarre

Rumania etc [ruːˈmeɪnɪə] = **Romania** etc

rumble ['rʌmbl] _n_ grondement _m_; gargouillement _m_ ♦ _vi_ gronder; (_stomach, pipe_) gargouiller

rummage ['rʌmɪdʒ] _vi_ fouiller

rumour, (US) **rumor** ['ruːmə*] _n_ rumeur _f_, bruit _m_ (qui court) ♦ _vt_: **it is rumoured that** le bruit court que

rump [rʌmp] _n_ (_of animal_) croupe _f_; (_also:_ **rump steak**) romsteck _m_

rumpus ['rʌmpəs] _n_ (col) tapage _m_, chahut _m_; (_quarrel_) prise _f_ de bec; **to kick up a rumpus** faire toute une histoire

run [rʌn] _n_ (_race etc_) course _f_; (_outing_) tour _m_ _or_ promenade _f_ (en voiture); (_journey_) parcours _m_, trajet _m_; (_series_) suite _f_, série _f_; (THEAT) série de représentations; (SKI) piste _f_; (_in tights, stockings_) maille filée, échelle _f_ ♦ _vb, pt_ **ran**, _pp_ **run** [ræn, rʌn] _vt_ (_business_) diriger; (_competition, course_) organiser; (_hotel, house_) tenir; (COMPUT: _program_) exécuter; (_force through: rope, pipe_): **to run sth through** faire passer qch à travers; (_to pass: hand, finger_): **to run sth over** promener _or_ passer qch sur; (_water, bath_) faire couler ♦ _vi_ courir; (_pass: road etc_) passer; (_work: machine, factory_) marcher; (_bus, train_) circuler; (*continue: play*) se jouer, être à l'affiche; (*: contract*) être valide *or* en vigueur; (*slide: drawer etc*) glisser; (*flow: river, bath*) couler; (*colours, washing*) déteindre; (*in election*) être candidat, se présenter; **to go for a run** aller courir *or* faire un peu de course à pied; (*in car*) faire un tour *or* une promenade (en voiture); **to break into a run** se mettre à courir; **a run of luck** une série de coups de chance; **to have the run of sb's house** avoir la maison de qn à sa disposition; **there was a run on** (*meat, tickets*) les gens se sont rués sur; **in the long run** à longue échéance; à la longue; en fin de compte; **in the short run** à brève échéance, à court terme; **on the run** en fuite; **to make a run for it** s'enfuir; **I'll run you to the station** je vais vous emmener *or* conduire à la gare; **to run errands** faire des commissions; **the train runs between Gatwick and Victoria** le train assure le service entre Gatwick et Victoria; **the bus runs every 20 minutes** il y a un autobus toutes les 20 minutes; **it's very cheap to run** (*car, machine*) c'est très économique; **to run on petrol** *or* (*US*) **gas/on diesel/off batteries** marcher à l'essence/au diesel/sur piles; **to run for president** être candidat à la présidence; **their losses ran into millions** leurs pertes se sont élevées à plusieurs millions; **to be run off one's feet** (*BRIT*) ne plus savoir où donner de la tête

▶ **run about** *vi* (*children*) courir çà et là
▶ **run across** *vt fus* (*find*) trouver par hasard
▶ **run around** *vi* = **run about**
▶ **run away** *vi* s'enfuir
▶ **run down** *vi* (*clock*) s'arrêter (faute d'avoir été remonté) ◆ *vt* (*AUT*) renverser; (*BRIT: reduce: production*) réduire progressivement; (*: factory/shop*) réduire progressivement la production/l'activité de; (*criticize*) critiquer, dénigrer; **to be run down** être fatigué(e) *or* à plat
▶ **run in** *vt* (*BRIT: car*) roder
▶ **run into** *vt fus* (*meet: person*) rencontrer par hasard; (*: trouble*) se heurter à; (*collide with*) heurter; **to run into debt** contracter des dettes
▶ **run off** *vi* s'enfuir ◆ *vt* (*water*) laisser s'écouler
▶ **run out** *vi* (*person*) sortir en courant; (*liquid*) couler; (*lease*) expirer; (*money*) être épuisé(e)
▶ **run out of** *vt fus* se trouver à court de; **I've run out of petrol** *or* (*US*) **gas** je suis en panne d'essence
▶ **run over** *vt* (*AUT*) écraser ◆ *vt fus* (*revise*) revoir, reprendre
▶ **run through** *vt fus* (*instructions*) reprendre, revoir
▶ **run up** *vt* (*debt*) laisser accumuler; **to run up against** (*difficulties*) se heurter à

runaway ['rʌnəweɪ] *adj* (*horse*) emballé(e); (*truck*) fou(folle); (*inflation*) galopant(e)

rung [rʌŋ] *pp of* **ring** ◆ *n* (*of ladder*) barreau *m*

runner ['rʌnə*] *n* (*in race: person*) coureur/euse;

(*: horse*) partant *m*; (*on sledge*) patin *m*; (*for drawer etc*) coulisseau *m*; (*carpet: in hall etc*) chemin *m*

runner bean *n* (*BRIT*) haricot *m* (à rames)

runner-up [rʌnər'ʌp] *n* second/e

running ['rʌnɪŋ] *n* (*in race etc*) course *f*; (*of business*) direction *f*; (*of event*) organisation *f*; (*of machine etc*) marche *f*, fonctionnement *m* ◆ *adj* (*water*) courant(e); (*commentary*) suivi(e); **6 days running** 6 jours de suite; **to be in/out of the running for sth** être/ne pas être sur les rangs pour qch

running commentary *n* commentaire détaillé

running costs *npl* (*of business*) frais *mpl* de gestion; (*of car*): **the running costs are high** elle revient cher

runny ['rʌnɪ] *adj* qui coule

run-of-the-mill ['rʌnəvðə'mɪl] *adj* ordinaire, banal(e)

runt [rʌnt] *n* avorton *m*

run-up ['rʌnʌp] *n* (*BRIT*): **run-up to sth** période *f* précédant qch

runway ['rʌnweɪ] *n* (*AVIAT*) piste *f* (d'envol *or* d'atterrissage)

rupture ['rʌptʃə*] *n* (*MED*) hernie *f* ◆ *vt*: **to rupture o.s.** se donner une hernie

rural ['ruərl] *adj* rural(e)

rush [rʌʃ] *n* course précipitée; (*of crowd*) ruée *f*, bousculade *f*; (*hurry*) hâte *f*, bousculade; (*current*) flot *m*; (*BOT*) jonc *m*; (*for chair*) paille *f* ◆ *vt* transporter *or* envoyer d'urgence; (*attack: town etc*) prendre d'assaut; (*BRIT col: overcharge*) estamper; faire payer ◆ *vi* se précipiter; **don't rush me!** laissez-moi le temps de souffler!; **to rush sth off** (*do quickly*) faire qch à la hâte; (*send*) envoyer d'urgence; **is there any rush for this?** est-ce urgent?; **we've had a rush of orders** nous avons reçu une avalanche de commandes; **I'm in a rush (to do)** je suis vraiment pressé (de faire); **gold rush** ruée vers l'or

▶ **rush through** *vt fus* (*work*) exécuter à la hâte ◆ *vt* (*COMM: order*) exécuter d'urgence

rush hour *n* heures *fpl* de pointe *or* d'affluence

rusk [rʌsk] *n* biscotte *f*

Russia ['rʌʃə] *n* Russie *f*

Russian ['rʌʃən] *adj* russe ◆ *n* Russe *m/f*; (*LING*) russe *m*

rust [rʌst] *n* rouille *f* ◆ *vi* rouiller

rustic ['rʌstɪk] *adj* rustique ◆ *n* (*pej*) rustaud/e

rustle ['rʌsl] *vi* bruire, produire un bruissement ◆ *vt* (*paper*) froisser; (*US: cattle*) voler

rustproof ['rʌstpru:f] *adj* inoxydable

rusty ['rʌstɪ] *adj* rouillé(e)

rut [rʌt] *n* ornière *f*; (*ZOOL*) rut *m*; **to be in a rut** (*fig*) suivre l'ornière, s'encroûter

ruthless ['ru:θlɪs] *adj* sans pitié, impitoyable

rye [raɪ] *n* seigle *m*

— S s —

Sabbath ['sæbəθ] *n* (*Jewish*) sabbat *m*; (*Christian*) dimanche *m*

sabotage ['sæbətɑ:ʒ] *n* sabotage *m* ◆ *vt* saboter

saccharin(e) ['sækərɪn] *n* saccharine *f*

sachet ['sæʃeɪ] *n* sachet *m*

sack [sæk] *n* (*bag*) sac *m* ◆ *vt* (*dismiss*) renvoyer, mettre à la porte; (*plunder*) piller, mettre à sac; **to give sb the sack** renvoyer qn, mettre qn à la porte; **to get the sack** être renvoyé(e) *or* mis(e) à la porte

sacking ['sækɪŋ] *n* toile *f* à sac; (*dismissal*) renvoi *m*

sacrament ['sækrəmənt] *n* sacrement *m*

sacred ['seɪkrɪd] *adj* sacré(e)

sacrifice ['sækrɪfaɪs] *n* sacrifice *m* ◆ *vt* sacrifier; **to make sacrifices (for sb)** se sacrifier *or* faire des sacrifices (pour qn)

sad [sæd] *adj* (*unhappy*) triste; (*deplorable*) triste, fâcheux(euse)

saddle ['sædl] *n* selle *f* ◆ *vt* (*horse*) seller; **to be saddled with sth** (*col*) avoir qch sur les bras

saddlebag ['sædlbæg] *n* sacoche *f*

sadistic [sə'dɪstɪk] *adj* sadique

sadly ['sædlɪ] *adv* tristement; (*regrettably*) malheureusement

sadness ['sædnɪs] *n* tristesse *f*

s.a.e. *abbr* (BRIT: = *stamped addressed envelope*) enveloppe affranchie pour la réponse

safe [seɪf] *adj* (*out of danger*) hors de danger, en sécurité; (*not dangerous*) sans danger; (*cautious*) prudent(e); (*sure: bet etc*) assuré(e) ◆ *n* coffre-fort *m*; **safe from** à l'abri de; **safe and sound** sain(e) et sauf(sauve); **(just) to be on the safe side** pour plus de sûreté, par précaution; **to play safe** ne prendre aucun risque; **it is safe to say that ...** on peut dire sans crainte que ...; **safe journey!** bon voyage!

safe-conduct [seɪf'kɒndʌkt] *n* sauf-conduit *m*

safe-deposit ['seɪfdɪpɒzɪt] *n* (*vault*) dépôt *m* de coffres-forts; (*box*) coffre-fort *m*

safeguard ['seɪfɡɑːd] *n* sauvegarde *f*, protection *f* ◆ *vt* sauvegarder, protéger

safekeeping ['seɪf'kiːpɪŋ] *n* bonne garde

safely ['seɪflɪ] *adv* sans danger, sans risque; (*without mishap*) sans accident; **I can safely say ...** je peux dire à coup sûr ...

safe sex *n* rapports sexuels protégés

safety ['seɪftɪ] *n* sécurité *f*; **safety first!** la sécurité d'abord!

safety belt *n* ceinture *f* de sécurité

safety pin *n* épingle *f* de sûreté *or* de nourrice

safety valve *n* soupape *f* de sûreté

sag [sæg] *vi* s'affaisser, fléchir; pendre

sage [seɪdʒ] *n* (*herb*) sauge *f*; (*man*) sage *m*

Sagittarius [sædʒɪ'tɛərɪəs] *n* le Sagittaire; **to be**

Sagittarius être du Sagittaire

Sahara [sə'hɑːrə] *n*: **the Sahara (Desert)** le (désert du) Sahara *m*

said [sed] *pt, pp* of **say**

sail [seɪl] *n* (*on boat*) voile *f*; (*trip*): **to go for a sail** faire un tour en bateau ◆ *vt* (*boat*) manœuvrer, piloter ◆ *vi* (*travel: ship*) avancer, naviguer; (: *passenger*) aller *or* se rendre (en bateau); (*set off*) partir, prendre la mer; (SPORT) faire de la voile; **they sailed into Le Havre** ils sont entrés dans le port du Havre

▶ **sail through** *vi, vt fus* (*fig*) réussir haut la main

sailboat ['seɪlbəʊt] *n* (US) bateau *m* à voiles, voilier *m*

sailing ['seɪlɪŋ] *n* (SPORT) voile *f*; **to go sailing** faire de la voile

sailing boat *n* bateau *m* à voiles, voilier *m*

sailing ship *n* grand voilier

sailor ['seɪlə*] *n* marin *m*, matelot *m*

saint [seɪnt] *n* saint/e

sake [seɪk] *n*: **for the sake of** (*out of concern for*) pour, dans l'intérêt de; (*out of consideration for*) par égard pour; (*in order to achieve*) pour plus de, par souci de; **arguing for arguing's sake** discuter pour (le plaisir de) discuter; **for the sake of argument** à titre d'exemple; **for heaven's sake!** pour l'amour du ciel!

salad ['sæləd] *n* salade *f*; **tomato salad** salade de tomates

salad bowl *n* saladier *m*

salad cream *n* (BRIT) (sorte *f* de) mayonnaise *f*

salad dressing *n* vinaigrette *f*

salami [sə'lɑːmɪ] *n* salami *m*

salary ['sælərɪ] *n* salaire *m*, traitement *m*

sale [seɪl] *n* vente *f*; (*at reduced prices*) soldes *mpl*; **"for sale"** "à vendre"; **on sale** en vente; **on sale or return** vendu(e) avec faculté de retour; **closing-down** *or* **liquidation sale** (US) liquidation *f* (avant fermeture); **sale and lease back** *n* cession-bail *f*

saleroom ['seɪlruːm] *n* salle *f* des ventes

sales assistant *n* (BRIT) vendeur/euse

salesman ['seɪlzmən] *n* vendeur *m*; (*representative*) représentant *m* de commerce

sales rep *n* (COMM) représentant/e *m/f*

saleswoman ['seɪlzwʊmən] *n* vendeuse *f*

salmon ['sæmən] *n* (*pl inv*) saumon *m*

salon ['sælɒn] *n* salon *m*

saloon [sə'luːn] *n* (US) bar *m*; (BRIT AUT) berline *f*; (*ship's lounge*) salon *m*

salt [sɔːlt] *n* sel *m* ◆ *vt* saler ◆ *cpd* de sel; (CULIN) salé(e); **an old salt** un vieux loup de mer

▶ **salt away** *vt* mettre de côté

salt cellar *n* salière *f*

saltwater ['sɔːlt'wɔːtə*] *adj* (*fish etc*) (d'eau) de mer

salty ['sɔːltɪ] *adj* salé(e)

salute [sə'luːt] *n* salut *m* ◆ *vt* saluer

salvage ['sælvɪdʒ] *n* (*saving*) sauvetage *m*; (*things saved*) biens sauvés *or* récupérés ♦ *vt* sauver, récupérer

salvation [sæl'veɪʃən] *n* salut *m*

Salvation Army *n* Armée *f* du Salut

same [seɪm] *adj* même ♦ *pron*: **the same** le(la) même les mêmes; **the same book** as le même livre que; **on the same day** le même jour; **at the same time** en même temps; **all** *or* **just the same** tout de même, quand même; **they're one and the same** (*person/thing*) c'est une seule et même personne/chose; **to do the same** faire de même, en faire autant; **to do the same as sb** faire comme qn; **and the same to you!** et à vous de même!; (*after insult*) toi-même!; **same here!** moi aussi!; **the same again!** (*in bar etc*) la même chose!

sample ['sɑːmpl] *n* échantillon *m*; (*MED*) prélèvement *m* ♦ *vt* (*food, wine*) goûter; **to take a sample** prélever un échantillon; **free sample** échantillon gratuit

sanction ['sæŋkʃən] *n* sanction *f* ♦ *vt* cautionner, sanctionner; **to impose economic sanctions on** *or* **against** prendre des sanctions économiques contre

sanctity ['sæŋktɪtɪ] *n* sainteté *f*, caractère sacré

sanctuary ['sæŋktjuərɪ] *n* (*holy place*) sanctuaire *m*; (*refuge*) asile *m*; (*for wild life*) réserve *f*

sand [sænd] *n* sable *m* ♦ *vt* sabler; (*also:* **sand down**: *wood etc*) poncer

sandal ['sændl] *n* sandale *f*

sandbox ['sændbɒks] *n* (*US: for children*) tas *m* de sable

sandcastle ['sændkɑːsl] *n* château *m* de sable

sandpaper ['sændpeɪpə*] *n* papier *m* de verre

sandpit ['sændpɪt] *n* (*BRIT: for children*) tas *m* de sable

sandstone ['sændstəun] *n* grès *m*

sandwich ['sændwɪtʃ] *n* sandwich *m* ♦ *vt* (*also:* **sandwich in**) intercaler; **sandwiched between** pris en sandwich entre; **cheese/ham sandwich** sandwich au fromage/jambon

sandwich course *n* (*BRIT*) cours *m* de formation professionnelle

sandy ['sændɪ] *adj* sablonneux(euse); couvert(e) de sable; (*colour*) sable *inv*, blond roux *inv*

sane [seɪn] *adj* (*person*) sain(e) d'esprit; (*outlook*) sensé(e), sain(e)

sang [sæŋ] *pt of* **sing**

sanitary ['sænɪtərɪ] *adj* (*system, arrangements*) sanitaire; (*clean*) hygiénique

sanitary towel, (*US*) **sanitary napkin** *n* serviette *f* hygiénique

sanitation [sænɪ'teɪʃən] *n* (*in house*) installations *fpl* sanitaires; (*in town*) système *m* sanitaire

sanitation department *n* (*US*) service *m* de voirie

sanity ['sænɪtɪ] *n* santé mentale; (*common sense*) bon sens

sank [sæŋk] *pt of* **sink**

Santa Claus [sæntə'klɔːz] *n* le Père Noël

sap [sæp] *n* (*of plants*) sève *f* ♦ *vt* (*strength*) saper, miner

sapling ['sæplɪŋ] *n* jeune arbre *m*

sapphire ['sæfaɪə*] *n* saphir *m*

sarcasm ['sɑːkæzm] *n* sarcasme *m*, raillerie *f*

sarcastic [sɑː'kæstɪk] *adj* sarcastique

sardine [sɑː'diːn] *n* sardine *f*

Sardinia [sɑː'dɪnɪə] *n* Sardaigne *f*

sash [sæʃ] *n* écharpe *f*

sat [sæt] *pt, pp of* **sit**

satchel ['sætʃl] *n* cartable *m*

satellite ['sætəlaɪt] *adj, n* satellite (*m*)

satellite dish *n* antenne *f* parabolique

satellite television *n* télévision *f* par satellite

satin ['sætɪn] *n* satin *m* ♦ *adj* en *or* de satin, satiné(e); **with a satin finish** satiné(e)

satire ['sætaɪə*] *n* satire *f*

satisfaction [sætɪs'fækʃən] *n* satisfaction *f*

satisfactory [sætɪs'fæktərɪ] *adj* satisfaisant(e)

satisfied ['sætɪsfaɪd] *adj* satisfait(e); **to be satisfied with sth** être satisfait de qch

satisfy ['sætɪsfaɪ] *vt* satisfaire, contenter; (*convince*) convaincre, persuader; **to satisfy the requirements** remplir les conditions; **to satisfy sb (that)** convaincre qn (que); **to satisfy o.s. of sth** vérifier qch, s'assurer de qch

satisfying ['sætɪsfaɪɪŋ] *adj* satisfaisant(e)

Saturday ['sætədɪ] *n* samedi *m*; *for phrases see also* **Tuesday**

sauce [sɔːs] *n* sauce *f*

saucepan ['sɔːspən] *n* casserole *f*

saucer ['sɔːsə*] *n* soucoupe *f*

Saudi (Arabian) ['saudi-] *adj* saoudien(ne) ♦ *n* Saoudien/ne

sauna ['sɔːnə] *n* sauna *m*

saunter ['sɔːntə*] *vi*: **to saunter to** aller en flânant *or* se balader jusqu'à

sausage ['sɔsɪdʒ] *n* saucisse *f*; (*salami etc*) saucisson *m*

sausage roll *n* friand *m*

savage ['sævɪdʒ] *adj* (*cruel, fierce*) brutal(e), féroce; (*primitive*) primitif(ive), sauvage ♦ *n* sauvage *m/f* ♦ *vt* attaquer férocement

save [seɪv] *vt* (*person, belongings*) sauver; (*money*) mettre de côté, économiser; (*time*) (faire) gagner; (*food*) garder; (*COMPUT*) sauvegarder; (*avoid: trouble*) éviter ♦ *vi* (*also:* **save up**) mettre de l'argent de côté ♦ *n* (*SPORT*) arrêt *m* (du ballon) ♦ *prep* sauf, à l'exception de; **it will save me an hour** ça me fera gagner une heure; **to save face** sauver la face; **God save the Queen!** vive la Reine!

saving ['seɪvɪŋ] *n* économie *f* ♦ *adj*: **the saving grace of** ce qui rachète; **savings** *npl* économies *fpl*; **to make savings** faire des économies

savings account n compte m d'épargne
savings bank n caisse f d'épargne
saviour, (US) **savior** ['seɪvjə*] n sauveur m
savour, (US) **savor** ['seɪvə*] n saveur f, goût m ◆ vt savourer
savo(u)ry ['seɪvərɪ] adj savoureux(euse); (dish: not sweet) salé(e)
saw [sɔ:] pt of **see** ◆ n (tool) scie f ◆ vt, pt **sawed**, pp **sawed** or **sawn** [sɔ:n] scier; **to saw sth up** débiter qch à la scie
sawdust ['sɔ:dʌst] n sciure f
sawmill ['sɔ:mɪl] n scierie f
sawn-off ['sɔ:nɔf], (US) **sawed-off** ['sɔ:dɔf] adj: **sawn-off shotgun** carabine f à canon scié
sax [sæks] (inf) n saxo m
saxophone ['sæksəfəun] n saxophone m
say [seɪ] n: **to have one's say** dire ce qu'on a à dire ◆ vt, pt, pp **said** [sɛd] dire; **to have a say** avoir voix au chapitre; **could you say that again?** pourriez-vous répéter ceci?; **to say yes/no** dire oui/non; **she said (that) I was to give you this** elle m'a chargé de vous remettre ceci; **my watch says 3 o'clock** ma montre indique 3 heures, il est 3 heures à ma montre; **shall we say Tuesday?** disons mardi?; **that doesn't say much for him** ce n'est pas vraiment à son honneur; **when all is said and done** en fin de compte, en définitive; **there is something** or **a lot to be said for it** cela a des avantages; **that is to say** c'est-à-dire; **to say nothing of** sans compter; **say that ...** mettons or disons que ...; **that goes without saying** cela va sans dire, cela va de soi
saying ['seɪŋ] n dicton m, proverbe m
scab [skæb] n croûte f; (pej) jaune m
scaffold ['skæfəld] n échafaud m
scaffolding ['skæfəldɪŋ] n échafaudage m
scald [skɔ:ld] n brûlure f ◆ vt ébouillanter
scale [skeɪl] n (of fish) écaille f; (MUS) gamme f; (of ruler, thermometer etc) graduation f, échelle (graduée); (of salaries, fees etc) barème m; (of map, also size, extent) échelle ◆ vt (mountain) escalader; (fish) écailler; **pay scale** échelle des salaires; **scale of charges** tarif m (des consultations or prestations etc); **on a large scale** sur une grande échelle, en grand; **to draw sth to scale** dessiner qch à l'échelle; **small-scale model** modèle réduit
▶ **scale down** vt réduire
scallop ['skɔləp] n coquille f Saint-Jacques
scalp [skælp] n cuir chevelu ◆ vt scalper
scampi ['skæmpɪ] npl langoustines (frites), scampi mpl
scan [skæn] vt scruter, examiner; (glance at quickly) parcourir; (poetry) scander; (TV, RADAR) balayer ◆ n (MED) scanographie f
scandal ['skændl] n scandale m; (gossip) ragots mpl
Scandinavia [skændɪ'neɪvɪə] n Scandinavie f

Scandinavian [skændɪ'neɪvɪən] adj scandinave ◆ n Scandinave m/f
scant [skænt] adj insuffisant(e)
scanty ['skæntɪ] adj peu abondant(e), insuffisant(e), maigre
scapegoat ['skeɪpgəut] n bouc m émissaire
scar [skɑ:] n cicatrice f ◆ vt laisser une cicatrice or une marque à
scarce [skɛəs] adj rare, peu abondant(e)
scarcely ['skɛəslɪ] adv à peine, presque pas; **scarcely anybody** pratiquement personne; **I can scarcely believe it** j'ai du mal à le croire
scarcity ['skɛəsɪtɪ] n rareté f, manque m, pénurie f
scare [skɛə*] n peur f, panique f ◆ vt effrayer, faire peur à; **to scare sb stiff** faire une peur bleue à qn; **bomb scare** alerte f à la bombe
▶ **scare away**, **scare off** vt faire fuir
scarecrow ['skɛəkrəu] n épouvantail m
scared ['skɛəd] adj: **to be scared** avoir peur
scarf, pl **scarves** [skɑ:f, skɑ:vz] n (long) écharpe f; (square) foulard m
scarlet ['skɑ:lɪt] adj écarlate
scarlet fever n scarlatine f
scary ['skɛərɪ] adj (col) qui fiche la frousse
scathing ['skeɪðɪŋ] adj cinglant(e), acerbe; **to be scathing about sth** être très critique vis-à-vis de qch
scatter ['skætə*] vt éparpiller, répandre; (crowd) disperser ◆ vi se disperser
scatterbrained ['skætəbreɪnd] adj écervelé(e), étourdi(e)
scavenger ['skævəndʒə*] n éboueur m
scene [si:n] n (THEAT, film etc) scène f; (of crime, accident) lieu(x) m(pl), endroit m; (sight, view) spectacle m, vue f; **behind the scenes** (also fig) dans les coulisses; **to make a scene** (col: fuss) faire une scène or toute une histoire; **to appear on the scene** (also fig) faire son apparition, arriver; **the political scene** la situation politique
scenery ['si:nərɪ] n (THEAT) décor(s) m(pl); (landscape) paysage m
scenic ['si:nɪk] adj scénique; offrant de beaux paysages or panoramas
scent [sɛnt] n parfum m, odeur f; (fig: track) piste f; (sense of smell) odorat m ◆ vt parfumer; (smell: also fig) flairer; (also: **to put** or **throw sb off the scent**: fig) mettre or lancer qn sur une mauvaise piste
sceptical, (US) **skeptical** ['skɛptɪkl] adj sceptique
schedule ['ʃɛdju:l, (US) 'skɛdju:l] n programme m, plan m; (of trains) horaire m; (of prices etc) barème m, tarif m ◆ vt prévoir; **as scheduled** comme prévu; **on schedule** à l'heure (prévue); à la date prévue; **to be ahead of/behind schedule** avoir de l'avance/du retard; **we are working to a very tight schedule** notre programme de travail est très serré or intense; **everything went according to sche-**

dule tout s'est passé comme prévu

scheduled flight [ˈʃedjuːld-, (US) ˈskedjuːld-] *n* vol régulier

scheme [skiːm] *n* plan *m*, projet *m*; (*method*) procédé *m*; (*dishonest plan, plot*) complot *m*, combine *f*; (*arrangement*) arrangement *m*, classification *f*; (*pension scheme etc*) régime *m* ◆ *vt*, *vi* comploter, manigancer; **colour scheme** combinaison *f* de(s) couleurs

scheming [ˈskiːmɪŋ] *adj* rusé(e), intrigant(e) ◆ *n* manigances *fpl*, intrigues *fpl*

scholar [ˈskɔlə*] *n* érudit/e

scholarship [ˈskɔləʃɪp] *n* érudition *f*; (*grant*) bourse *f* (d'études)

school [skuːl] *n* (*gen*) école *f*; (*in university*) faculté *f*; (*secondary school*) collège *m*, lycée *m*; (*of fish*) banc *m* ◆ *cpd* scolaire ◆ *vt* (*animal*) dresser

schoolbook [ˈskuːlbuk] *n* livre *m* scolaire *or* de classe

schoolboy [ˈskuːlbɔɪ] *n* écolier *m*; collégien *m*, lycéen *m*

schoolchild, *pl* **-children** [ˈskuːltʃaɪld, -ˈtʃɪldrən] *n* écolier/ière, collégien/ne, lycéen/ne

schoolgirl [ˈskuːlgɜːl] *n* écolière *f*; collégienne *f*, lycéenne *f*

schooling [ˈskuːlɪŋ] *n* instruction *f*, études *fpl*

schoolmaster [ˈskuːlmɑːstə*] *n* (*primary*) instituteur *m*; (*secondary*) professeur *m*

schoolmistress [ˈskuːlmɪstrɪs] *n* (*primary*) institutrice *f*; (*secondary*) professeur *m*

schoolteacher [ˈskuːltiːtʃə*] *n* (*primary*) instituteur/trice; (*secondary*) professeur *m*

science [ˈsaɪəns] *n* science *f*; **the sciences** les sciences; (*SCOL*) les matières *fpl* scientifiques

science fiction *n* science-fiction *f*

scientific [saɪənˈtɪfɪk] *adj* scientifique

scientist [ˈsaɪəntɪst] *n* scientifique *m/f*; (*eminent*) savant *m*

scissors [ˈsɪzəz] *npl* ciseaux *mpl*; **a pair of scissors** une paire de ciseaux

scoff [skɔf] *vt* (*BRIT col: eat*) avaler, bouffer ◆ *vi*: **to scoff (at)** (*mock*) se moquer (de)

scold [skəuld] *vt* gronder, attraper, réprimander

scone [skɔn] *n* sorte de petit pain rond au lait

scoop [skuːp] *n* pelle *f* (à main); (*for ice cream*) boule *f* à glace; (*PRESS*) reportage exclusif *or* à sensation

▶ **scoop out** *vt* évider, creuser

▶ **scoop up** *vt* ramasser

scooter [ˈskuːtə*] *n* (*motor cycle*) scooter *m*; (*toy*) trottinette *f*

scope [skəup] *n* (*capacity: of plan, undertaking*) portée *f*, envergure *f*; (: *of person*) compétence *f*, capacités *fpl*; (*opportunity*) possibilités *fpl*; **within the scope of** dans les limites de; **there is plenty of scope for improvement** (*BRIT*) cela pourrait être beaucoup mieux

scorch [skɔːtʃ] *vt* (*clothes*) brûler (légèrement), roussir; (*earth, grass*) dessécher, brûler

score [skɔː*] *n* score *m*, décompte *m* des points; (*MUS*) partition *f*; (*twenty*) vingt ◆ *vt* (*goal, point*) marquer; (*success*) remporter; (*cut: leather, wood, card*) entailler, inciser ◆ *vi* marquer des points; (*FOOTBALL*) marquer un but; (*keep score*) compter les points; **on that score** sur ce chapitre, à cet égard; **to have an old score to settle with sb** (*fig*) avoir un (vieux) compte à régler avec qn; **scores of** (*fig*) des tas de; **to score well/6 out of 10** obtenir un bon résultat/6 sur 10

▶ **score out** *vt* rayer, barrer, biffer

scoreboard [ˈskɔːbɔːd] *n* tableau *m*

scorn [skɔːn] *n* mépris *m*, dédain *m* ◆ *vt* mépriser, dédaigner

Scorpio [ˈskɔːpɪəu] *n* le Scorpion; **to be Scorpio** être du Scorpion

Scot [skɔt] *n* Écossais/e

Scotch [skɔtʃ] *n* whisky *m*, scotch *m*

scotch [skɔtʃ] *vt* faire échouer; enrayer; étouffer

scot-free [ˈskɔtˈfriː] *adj*: **to get off scot-free** s'en tirer sans être puni(e); s'en sortir indemne

Scotland [ˈskɔtlənd] *n* Écosse *f*

Scots [skɔts] *adj* écossais(e)

Scotsman [ˈskɔtsmən] *n* Écossais *m*

Scotswoman [ˈskɔtswumən] *n* Écossaise *f*

Scottish [ˈskɔtɪʃ] *adj* écossais(e); **the Scottish National Party** le parti national écossais

Scottish Parliament *n* Parlement écossais

scoundrel [ˈskaundrəl] *n* vaurien *m*

scour [ˈskauə*] *vt* (*clean*) récurer; frotter; décaper; (*search*) battre, parcourir

scout [skaut] *n* (*MIL*) éclaireur *m*; (*also:* **boy scout**) scout *m*

▶ **scout around** *vi* chercher

scowl [skaul] *vi* se renfrogner, avoir l'air maussade; **to scowl at** regarder de travers

scrabble [ˈskræbl] *vi* (*claw*): **to scrabble (at)** gratter; **to scrabble about** *or* **around for sth** chercher qch à tâtons ◆ *n*: **Scrabble®** Scrabble® *m*

scram [skræm] *vi* (*col*) ficher le camp

scramble [ˈskræmbl] *n* bousculade *f*, ruée *f* ◆ *vi* avancer tant bien que mal (à quatre pattes *or* en grimpant); **to scramble for** se bousculer *or* se disputer pour (avoir); **to go scrambling** (*SPORT*) faire du trial

scrambled eggs [ˈskræmbld-] *npl* œufs brouillés

scrap [skræp] *n* bout *m*, morceau *m*; (*fight*) bagarre *f*; (*also:* **scrap iron**) ferraille *f* ◆ *vt* jeter, mettre au rebut; (*fig*) abandonner, laisser tomber; **scraps** *npl* (*waste*) déchets *mpl*; **to sell sth for scrap** vendre qch à la casse *or* à la ferraille

scrapbook [ˈskræpbuk] *n* album *m*

scrap dealer *n* marchand *m* de ferraille

scrape [skreɪp] *vt*, *vi* gratter, racler ◆ *n*: **to get into a scrape** s'attirer des ennuis

▶ **scrape through** *vi* (*in exam etc*) réussir de justesse

▶ **scrape together** *vt* (*money*) racler ses fonds de tiroir pour réunir

scrap heap *n* tas *m* de ferraille; (*fig*): **on the scrap heap** au rancart *or* rebut

scrap merchant *n* (*BRIT*) marchand *m* de ferraille

scrap paper *n* papier *m* brouillon

scratch [skrætʃ] *n* égratignure *f*, rayure *f*; éraflure *f*; (*from claw*) coup *m* de griffe ◆ *adj*: **scratch team** équipe *f* de fortune *or* improvisée ◆ *vt* (*record*) rayer; (*paint etc*) érafler; (*with claw, nail*) griffer; (*COMPUT*) effacer ◆ *vi*; **to start from scratch** partir de zéro; **to be up to scratch** être à la hauteur

scrawl [skrɔ:l] *n* gribouillage *m* ◆ *vi* gribouiller

scrawny ['skrɔ:nɪ] *adj* décharné(e)

scream [skri:m] *n* cri perçant, hurlement *m* ◆ *vi* crier, hurler; **to be a scream** (*col*) être impayable; **to scream at sb to do sth** crier *or* hurler à qn de faire qch

screech [skri:tʃ] *n* cri strident, hurlement *m*; (*of tyres, brakes*) crissement *m*, grincement *m* ◆ *vi* hurler; crisser, grincer

screen [skri:n] *n* écran *m*, paravent *m*; (*CINE, TV*) écran; (*fig*) écran, rideau *m* ◆ *vt* masquer, cacher; (*from the wind etc*) abriter, protéger; (*film*) projeter; (*candidates etc*) filtrer; (*for illness*): **to screen sb for sth** faire subir un test de dépistage de qch à qn

screening ['skri:nɪŋ] *n* (*of film*) projection *f*; (*MED*) test *m* (*or* tests) de dépistage; (*for security*) filtrage *m*

screenplay ['skri:npleɪ] *n* scénario *m*

screw [skru:] *n* vis *f*; (*propeller*) hélice *f* ◆ *vt* visser; (*coll: woman*) baiser (!); **to screw sth to the wall** visser qch au mur; **to have one's head screwed on** (*fig*) avoir la tête sur les épaules

▶ **screw up** *vt* (*paper, material*) froisser; (*col: ruin*) bousiller; **to screw up one's face** faire la grimace

screwdriver ['skru:draɪvə*] *n* tournevis *m*

scribble ['skrɪbl] *n* gribouillage *m* ◆ *vt* gribouiller, griffonner; **to scribble sth down** griffonner qch

script [skrɪpt] *n* (*CINE etc*) scénario *m*, texte *m*; (*in exam*) copie *f*; (*writing*) écriture *f*; script *m*

Scripture ['skrɪptʃə*] *n* Écriture sainte

scroll [skrəul] *n* rouleau *m* ◆ *vt* (*COMPUT*) faire défiler (sur l'écran)

scrounge [skraundʒ] (*col*) *vt*: **to scrounge sth (off** *or* **from sb**) se faire payer qch (par qn), emprunter qch (à qn) ◆ *vi*: **to scrounge on sb** vivre aux crochets de qn

scrounger ['skraundʒə*] *n* parasite *m*

scrub [skrʌb] *n* (*clean*) nettoyage *m* (à la brosse); (*land*) broussailles *fpl* ◆ *vt* (*floor*) nettoyer à la brosse; (*pan*) récurer; (*washing*) frotter; (*reject*) annuler

scruff [skrʌf] *n*: **by the scruff of the neck** par la peau du cou

scruffy ['skrʌfɪ] *adj* débraillé(e)

scrum(mage) ['skrʌm(ɪdʒ)] *n* mêlée *f*

scruple ['skru:pl] *n* scrupule *m*; **to have no scruples about doing sth** n'avoir aucun scrupule à faire qch

scrutiny ['skru:tɪnɪ] *n* examen minutieux; **under the scrutiny of sb** sous la surveillance de qn

scuff [skʌf] *vt* érafler

scuffle ['skʌfl] *n* échauffourée *f*, rixe *f*

sculptor ['skʌlptə*] *n* sculpteur *m*

sculpture ['skʌlptʃə*] *n* sculpture *f*

scum [skʌm] *n* écume *f*, mousse *f*; (*pej: people*) rebut *m*, lie *f*

scurry ['skʌrɪ] *vi* filer à toute allure; **to scurry off** détaler, se sauver

scuttle ['skʌtl] *n* (*NAUT*) écoutille *f*; (*also:* **coal scuttle**) seau *m* (à charbon) ◆ *vt* (*ship*) saborder ◆ *vi* (*scamper*): **to scuttle away, scuttle off** détaler

scythe [saɪð] *n* faux *f*

SDP *n abbr* (*BRIT POL*) = **Social Democratic Party**

sea [si:] *n* mer *f* ◆ *cpd* marin(e) de (la) mer, maritime; **on the sea** (*boat*) en mer; (*town*) au bord de la mer; **by** *or* **beside the sea** (*holiday*) au bord de la mer; (*village*) près de la mer; **by sea** par mer, en bateau; **out to sea** au large; (**out**) **at sea** en mer; **heavy** *or* **rough sea(s)** grosse mer, mer agitée; **a sea of faces** (*fig*) une multitude de visages; **to be all at sea** (*fig*) nager complètement

seaboard ['si:bɔ:d] *n* côte *f*

seafood ['si:fu:d] *n* fruits *mpl* de mer

seafront ['si:frʌnt] *n* bord *m* de mer

seagoing ['si:gəuɪŋ] *adj* (*ship*) de haute mer

seagull ['si:gʌl] *n* mouette *f*

seal [si:l] *n* (*animal*) phoque *m*; (*stamp*) sceau *m*, cachet *m*; (*impression*) cachet, estampille *f* ◆ *vt* sceller; (*envelope*) coller; (*: with seal*) cacheter; (*decide: sb's fate*) décider (de); (*: bargain*) conclure; **seal of approval** approbation *f*

▶ **seal off** *vt* (*close*) condamner; (*forbid entry to*) interdire l'accès de

sea level *n* niveau *m* de la mer

sea lion *n* lion *m* de mer

seam [si:m] *n* couture *f*; (*of coal*) veine *f*, filon *m*; **the hall was bursting at the seams** la salle était pleine à craquer

seaman ['si:mən] *n* marin *m*

seance ['seɪɒns] *n* séance *f* de spiritisme

seaplane ['si:pleɪn] *n* hydravion *m*

search [sɜ:tʃ] *n* (*for person, thing*) recherche(s) *f(pl)*; (*of drawer, pockets*) fouille *f*; (*LAW: at sb's home*) perquisition *f* ◆ *vt* fouiller; (*examine*) examiner minutieusement; scruter ◆ *vi*: **to search for** chercher; **in search of** à la recherche de; **"search and replace"** (*COMPUT*) "rechercher et remplacer"

▶ **search through** vt fus fouiller

searching ['sɜːtʃɪŋ] adj (look, question) pénétrant(e); (examination) minutieux(euse)

searchlight ['sɜːtʃlaɪt] n projecteur m

search party n expédition f de secours

search warrant n mandat m de perquisition

seashore ['siːʃɔː*] n rivage m, plage f, bord m de (la) mer; **on the seashore** sur le rivage

seasick ['siːsɪk] adj: **to be seasick** avoir le mal de mer

seaside ['siːsaɪd] n bord m de la mer

seaside resort n station f balnéaire

season ['siːzn] n saison f ♦ vt assaisonner, relever; **to be in/out of season** être/ne pas être de saison; **the busy season** (for shops) la période de pointe; (for hotels etc) la pleine saison; **the open season** (HUNTING) la saison de la chasse

seasonal ['siːznl] adj saisonnier(ière)

seasoned ['siːznd] adj (wood) séché(e); (fig: worker, actor, troops) expérimenté(e); **a seasoned campaigner** un vieux militant, un vétéran

season ticket n carte f d'abonnement

seat [siːt] n siège m; (in bus, train: place) place f; (PARLIAMENT) siège; (buttocks) postérieur m; (of trousers) fond m ♦ vt faire asseoir, placer; (have room for) avoir des places assises pour, pouvoir accueillir; **are there any seats left?** est-ce qu'il reste des places?; **to take one's seat** prendre place; **to be seated** être assis; **please be seated** veuillez vous asseoir

seat belt n ceinture f de sécurité

sea water n eau f de mer

seaweed ['siːwiːd] n algues fpl

seaworthy ['siːwɜːðɪ] adj en état de naviguer

sec. abbr (= second) sec

secluded [sɪ'kluːdɪd] adj retiré(e), à l'écart

seclusion [sɪ'kluːʒən] n solitude f

second¹ ['sɛkənd] num deuxième, second(e) ♦ adv (in race etc) en seconde position ♦ n (unit of time) seconde f; (in series, position) deuxième m/f, second/e; (BRIT SCOL) ≈ licence f avec mention bien or assez bien; (AUT: also: **second gear**) seconde f; (COMM: imperfect) article m de second choix ♦ vt (motion) appuyer; **Charles the Second** Charles II; **just a second!** une seconde!, un instant!; (stopping sb) pas si vite!; **second floor** (BRIT) deuxième (étage) m; (US) premier (étage) m; **to ask for a second opinion** (MED) demander l'avis d'un autre médecin; **to have second thoughts (about doing sth)** changer d'avis (à propos de faire qch); **on second thoughts** or **thought** (US) à la réflexion

second² [sɪ'kɔnd] vt (employee) détacher, mettre en détachement

secondary ['sɛkəndərɪ] adj secondaire

secondary school n collège m, lycée m; voir encadré

second-class ['sɛkənd'klɑːs] adj de deuxième classe ♦ adv: **to send sth second-class** envoyer qch à tarif réduit; **to travel second-class** voyager en seconde; **second-class citizen** citoyen(ne) de deuxième classe

second hand n (on clock) trotteuse f

secondhand ['sɛkənd'hænd] adj d'occasion ♦ adv (buy) d'occasion; **to hear sth secondhand** apprendre qch indirectement

secondly ['sɛkəndlɪ] adv deuxièmement; **firstly ... secondly ...** d'abord ... ensuite ... or de plus ...

secondment [sɪ'kɔndmənt] n (BRIT) détachement m

second-rate ['sɛkənd'reɪt] adj de deuxième ordre, de qualité inférieure

secrecy ['siːkrəsɪ] n secret m; **in secrecy** en secret

secret ['siːkrɪt] adj secret(ète) ♦ n secret m; **in secret** adv en secret, secrètement, en cachette; **to keep sth secret from sb** cacher qch à qn, ne pas révéler qch à qn; **keep it secret** n'en parle à personne; **to make no secret of sth** ne pas cacher qch

secretary ['sɛkrətrɪ] n secrétaire m/f; (COMM) secrétaire général; **Secretary of State** (US POL) ≈ ministre m des Affaires étrangères; **Secretary of State (for)** (BRIT POL) ministre m (de)

secretive ['siːkrətɪv] adj réservé(e); (pej) cachottier(ière), dissimulé(e)

secretly ['siːkrɪtlɪ] adv en secret, secrètement, en cachette

sectarian [sɛk'tɛərɪən] adj sectaire

section ['sɛkʃən] n coupe f, section f; (department) section m; (COMM) rayon m; (of document) section, article m, paragraphe m ♦ vt sectionner; **the business etc section** (PRESS) la page des affaires etc

sector ['sɛktə*] n secteur m

secular ['sɛkjulə*] adj profane; laïque; séculier(ière)

secure [sɪ'kjuə*] adj (free from anxiety) sans inquiétude, sécurisé(e); (firmly fixed) solide, bien attaché(e) (or fermé(e) etc); (in safe place) en lieu sûr, en sûreté ♦ vt (fix) fixer, attacher; (get) obtenir, se procurer; (COMM: loan) garantir; **to make sth secure** bien fixer or attacher qch; **to secure sth for sb** obtenir qch pour qn, procurer qch à qn

security [sɪ'kjuərɪtɪ] n sécurité f, mesures fpl de sécurité; (for loan) caution f, garantie f; **securities** npl (STOCK EXCHANGE) valeurs fpl, titres mpl; **to**

increase *or* **tighten security** renforcer les mesures de sécurité; **security of tenure** stabilité *f* d'un emploi, titularisation *f*

security guard *n* garde chargé de la sécurité; (*transporting money*) convoyeur *m* de fonds

sedate [sɪ'deɪt] *adj* calme; posé(e) ♦ *vt* donner des sédatifs à

sedative ['sedɪtɪv] *n* calmant *m*, sédatif *m*

seduce [sɪ'djuːs] *vt* séduire

seduction [sɪ'dʌkʃən] *n* séduction *f*

seductive [sɪ'dʌktɪv] *adj* séduisant(e), séducteur(trice)

see [siː] *vb, pt* **saw**, *pp* **seen** [sɔː, siːn] *vt* (*gen*) voir; (*accompany*): **to see sb to the door** reconduire *or* raccompagner qn jusqu'à la porte ♦ *vi* voir ♦ *n* évêché *m*; **to see that** (*ensure*) veiller à ce que + *sub*, faire en sorte que + *sub*, s'assurer que; **there was nobody to be seen** il n'y avait pas un chat; **let me see** (*show me*) fais(-moi) voir; (*let me think*) voyons (un peu); **to go and see sb** aller voir qn; **see for yourself** voyez vous-même; **I don't know what she sees in him** je ne sais pas ce qu'elle lui trouve; **as far as I can see** pour autant que je puisse en juger; **see you!** au revoir!, à bientôt!; **see you soon/later/tomorrow!** à bientôt/plus tard/demain!

▶ **see about** *vt fus* (*deal with*) s'occuper de

▶ **see off** *vt* accompagner (à la gare *or* à l'aéroport *etc*)

▶ **see through** *vt* mener à bonne fin ♦ *vt fus* voir clair dans

▶ **see to** *vt fus* s'occuper de, se charger de

seed [siːd] *n* graine *f*; (*fig*) germe *m*; (*TENNIS etc*) tête *f* de série; **to go to seed** monter en graine; (*fig*) se laisser aller

seedling ['siːdlɪŋ] *n* jeune plant *m*, semis *m*

seedy ['siːdɪ] *adj* (*shabby*) minable, miteux(euse)

seeing ['siːɪŋ] *conj*: **seeing (that)** vu que, étant donné que

seek, *pt, pp* **sought** [siːk, sɔːt] *vt* chercher, rechercher; **to seek advice/help from sb** demander conseil/de l'aide à qn

▶ **seek out** *vt* (*person*) chercher

seem [siːm] *vi* sembler, paraître; **there seems to be ...** il semble qu'il y a ..., on dirait qu'il y a ...; **it seems (that) ...** il semble que ...; **what seems to be the trouble?** qu'est-ce qui ne va pas?

seemingly ['siːmɪŋlɪ] *adv* apparemment

seen [siːn] *pp of* **see**

seep [siːp] *vi* suinter, filtrer

seesaw ['siːsɔː] *n* (jeu *m* de) bascule *f*

seethe [siːð] *vi* être en effervescence; **to seethe with anger** bouillir de colère

see-through ['siːθruː] *adj* transparent(e)

segment ['segmənt] *n* segment *m*

segregate ['segrɪgeɪt] *vt* séparer, isoler

seize [siːz] *vt* (*grasp*) saisir, attraper; (*take posses-*

sion of) s'emparer de; (*LAW*) saisir

▶ **seize up** *vi* (*TECH*) se gripper

▶ **seize (up)on** *vt fus* saisir, sauter sur

seizure ['siːʒə*] *n* (*MED*) crise *f*, attaque *f*; (*LAW*) saisie *f*

seldom ['seldəm] *adv* rarement

select [sɪ'lekt] *adj* choisi(e), d'élite; (*hotel, restaurant, club*) chic *inv*, sélect *inv* ♦ *vt* sélectionner, choisir; **a select few** quelques privilégiés

selection [sɪ'lekʃən] *n* sélection *f*, choix *m*

self [self] *n* (*pl* **selves** [selvz]): **the self** le moi *inv* ♦ *prefix* auto-

self-assured [selfə'ʃuəd] *adj* sûr(e) de soi, plein(e) d'assurance

self-catering [self'keɪtərɪŋ] *adj* (*BRIT: flat*) avec cuisine, où l'on peut faire sa cuisine; (: *holiday*) en appartement (*or* chalet *etc*) loué

self-centred, (*US*) **self-centered** [self'sentəd] *adj* égocentrique

self-confidence [self'kɒnfɪdns] *n* confiance *f* en soi

self-conscious [self'kɒnʃəs] *adj* timide, qui manque d'assurance

self-contained [selfkən'teɪnd] *adj* (*BRIT: flat*) avec entrée particulière, indépendant(e)

self-control [selfkən'trəul] *n* maîtrise *f* de soi

self-defence, (*US*) **self-defense** [selfdɪ'fens] *n* légitime défense *f*

self-discipline [self'dɪsɪplɪn] *n* discipline personnelle

self-employed [selfɪm'plɔɪd] *adj* qui travaille à son compte

self-evident [self'evɪdnt] *adj* évident(e), qui va de soi

self-governing [self'gʌvənɪŋ] *adj* autonome

self-indulgent [selfɪn'dʌldʒənt] *adj* qui ne se refuse rien

self-interest [self'ɪntrɪst] *n* intérêt personnel

selfish ['selfɪʃ] *adj* égoïste

selfishness ['selfɪʃnɪs] *n* égoïsme *m*

selfless ['selflɪs] *adj* désintéressé(e)

self-pity [self'pɪtɪ] *n* apitoiement *m* sur soi-même

self-possessed [selfpə'zest] *adj* assuré(e)

self-preservation ['selfprezə'veɪʃən] *n* instinct *m* de conservation

self-respect [selfrɪs'pekt] *n* respect *m* de soi

self-righteous [self'raɪtʃəs] *adj* satisfait(e) de soi, pharisaïque

self-sacrifice [self'sækrɪfaɪs] *n* abnégation *f*

self-satisfied [self'sætɪsfaɪd] *adj* content(e) de soi, suffisant(e)

self-service [self'sɜːvɪs] *adj, n* libre-service (*m*), self-service (*m*)

self-sufficient [selfsə'fɪʃənt] *adj* indépendant(e)

self-taught [self'tɔːt] *adj* autodidacte

sell, *pt, pp* **sold** [sɛl, səuld] *vt* vendre ◆ *vi* se vendre; **to sell at** *or* **for 10 €** se vendre 10 €; **to sell sb an idea** (*fig*) faire accepter une idée à qn
▶ **sell off** *vt* liquider
▶ **sell out** *vi*: **to sell out (to)** (*COMM*) vendre son fonds *or* son affaire (à) ◆ *vt* vendre tout son stock de; **the tickets are all sold out** il ne reste plus de billets
▶ **sell up** *vi* vendre son fonds *or* son affaire
sell-by date ['sɛlbaɪ-] *n* date *f* limite de vente
seller ['sɛlə*] *n* vendeur/euse, marchand/e; **seller's market** marché *m* à la hausse
selling price ['sɛlɪŋ-] *n* prix *m* de vente
Sellotape® ['sɛləuteɪp] *n* (*BRIT*) papier collant, scotch® *m*
selves [sɛlvz] *npl of* **self**
semblance ['sɛmblns] *n* semblant *m*
semen ['siːmən] *n* sperme *m*
semester [sɪ'mɛstə*] *n* (*esp US*) semestre *m*
semi... ['sɛmɪ] *prefix* semi-, demi-; à demi, à moitié ◆ *n*: **semi** = **semidetached (house)**
semicircle ['sɛmɪsəːkl] *n* demi-cercle *m*
semicolon [sɛmɪ'kəulən] *n* point-virgule *m*
semidetached (house) [sɛmɪdɪ'tætʃt-] *n* (*BRIT*) maison jumelée *or* jumelle
semifinal [sɛmɪ'faɪnl] *n* demi-finale *f*
seminar ['sɛmɪnɑː*] *n* séminaire *m*
seminary ['sɛmɪnəri] *n* (*REL: for priests*) séminaire *m*
semiskilled [sɛmɪ'skɪld] *adj*: **semiskilled worker** ouvrier/ière spécialisé(e)
semi-skimmed milk ['sɛmɪ'skɪmd-] *n* lait demi-écrémé
senate ['sɛnɪt] *n* sénat *m*; (*US*): **the Senate** le Sénat; *voir encadré*

senator ['sɛnɪtə*] *n* sénateur *m*
send, *pt, pp* **sent** [sɛnd, sɛnt] *vt* envoyer; **to send by post** *or* (*US*) **mail** envoyer *or* expédier par la poste; **to send sb for sth** envoyer qn chercher qch; **to send word that ...** faire dire que ...; **she sends (you) her love** elle vous adresse ses amitiés; **to send sb to Coventry** (*BRIT*) mettre qn en quarantaine; **to send sb to sleep** endormir qn; **to send sb into fits of laughter** faire rire qn aux éclats; **to send sth flying** envoyer valser qch
▶ **send away** *vt* (*letter, goods*) envoyer, expédier
▶ **send away for** *vt fus* commander par correspondance, se faire envoyer

▶ **send back** *vt* renvoyer
▶ **send for** *vt fus* envoyer chercher; faire venir; (*by post*) se faire envoyer, commander par correspondance
▶ **send in** *vt* (*report, application, resignation*) remettre
▶ **send off** *vt* (*goods*) envoyer, expédier; (*BRIT SPORT: player*) expulser *or* renvoyer du terrain
▶ **send on** *vt* (*BRIT: letter*) faire suivre; (*luggage etc: in advance*) (faire) expédier à l'avance
▶ **send out** *vt* (*invitation*) envoyer (par la poste); (*emit: light, heat, signals*) émettre
▶ **send round** *vt* (*letter, document etc*) faire circuler
▶ **send up** *vt* (*person, price*) faire monter; (*BRIT: parody*) mettre en boîte, parodier
sender ['sɛndə*] *n* expéditeur/trice
send-off ['sɛndɔf] *n*: **a good send-off** des adieux chaleureux
senior ['siːnɪə*] *adj* (*older*) aîné(e), plus âgé(e); (*of higher rank*) supérieur(e) ◆ *n* aîné/e; (*in service*) personne *f* qui a plus d'ancienneté; **P. Jones senior** P. Jones père
senior citizen *n* personne âgée
seniority [siːnɪ'ɔrɪtɪ] *n* priorité *f* d'âge, ancienneté *f*; (*in rank*) supériorité *f* (hiérarchique)
sensation [sɛn'seɪʃən] *n* sensation *f*; **to create a sensation** faire sensation
sensational [sɛn'seɪʃənl] *adj* qui fait sensation; (*marvellous*) sensationnel(le)
sense [sɛns] *n* sens *m*; (*feeling*) sentiment *m*; (*meaning*) signification *f*; (*wisdom*) bon sens ◆ *vt* sentir, pressentir; **senses** *npl* raison *f*; **it makes sense** c'est logique; **sense of humour** sens de l'humour; **there is no sense in (doing) that** cela n'a pas de sens; **to come to one's senses** (*regain consciousness*) reprendre conscience; (*become reasonable*) revenir à la raison; **to take leave of one's senses** perdre la tête
senseless ['sɛnslɪs] *adj* insensé(e), stupide; (*unconscious*) sans connaissance
sensible ['sɛnsɪbl] *adj* sensé(e), raisonnable; (*shoes etc*) pratique
sensitive ['sɛnsɪtɪv] *adj*: **sensitive (to)** sensible (à); **he is very sensitive about it** c'est un point très sensible (chez lui)
sensual ['sɛnsjuəl] *adj* sensuel(le)
sensuous ['sɛnsjuəs] *adj* voluptueux(euse), sensuel(le)
sent [sɛnt] *pt, pp of* **send**
sentence ['sɛntns] *n* (*LING*) phrase *f*; (*LAW: judgment*) condamnation *f*, sentence *f*; (: *punishment*) peine *f* ◆ *vt*: **to sentence sb to death/to 5 years** condamner qn à mort/à 5 ans; **to pass sentence on sb** prononcer une peine contre qn
sentiment ['sɛntɪmənt] *n* sentiment *m*; (*opinion*) opinion *f*, avis *m*

sentimental [sɛntɪ'mɛntl] *adj* sentimental(e)

sentry ['sɛntrɪ] *n* sentinelle *f*, factionnaire *m*

separate *adj* ['sɛprɪt] séparé(e), indépendant(e), différent(e) ♦ *vb* ['sɛpəreɪt] *vt* séparer ♦ *vi* se séparer; **separate from** distinct(e) de; **under separate cover** (COMM) sous pli séparé; **to separate into** diviser en

separately ['sɛprɪtlɪ] *adv* séparément

separates ['sɛprɪts] *npl* (*clothes*) coordonnés *mpl*

separation [sɛpə'reɪʃən] *n* séparation *f*

September [sɛp'tɛmbə*] *n* septembre *m*; *for phrases see also July*

septic ['sɛptɪk] *adj* septique; (*wound*) infecté(e); **to go septic** s'infecter

septic tank *n* fosse *f* septique

sequel ['si:kwl] *n* conséquence *f*; séquelles *fpl*; (*of story*) suite *f*

sequence ['si:kwəns] *n* ordre *m*, suite *f*; **in sequence** par ordre, dans l'ordre, les uns après les autres; **sequence of tenses** concordance *f* des temps

sequin ['si:kwɪn] *n* paillette *f*

Serbia ['sə:bɪə] *n* Serbie *f*

serene [sɪ'ri:n] *adj* serein(e), calme, paisible

sergeant ['sɑ:dʒənt] *n* sergent *m*; (*POLICE*) brigadier *m*

serial ['sɪərɪəl] *n* feuilleton *m* ♦ *adj* (*COMPUT: interface, printer*) série *inv*; (: *access*) séquentiel(le)

serial killer *n* meurtrier *m* tuant en série

serial number *n* numéro *m* de série

series ['sɪərɪz] *n* série *f*; (*PUBLISHING*) collection *f*

serious ['sɪərɪəs] *adj* sérieux(euse); (*accident etc*) grave; **are you serious (about it)?** parlez-vous sérieusement?

seriously ['sɪərɪəslɪ] *adv* sérieusement, gravement; **seriously rich/difficult** (*col: extremely*) drôlement riche/difficile; **to take sth/sb seriously** prendre qch/qn au sérieux

sermon ['sə:mən] *n* sermon *m*

serrated [sɪ'reɪtɪd] *adj* en dents de scie

servant ['sə:vənt] *n* domestique *m/f*; (*fig*) serviteur/servante

serve [sə:v] *vt* (*employer etc*) servir, être au service de; (*purpose*) servir à; (*customer, food, meal*) servir; (*apprenticeship*) faire, accomplir; (*prison term*) faire, purger ♦ *vi* (*TENNIS*) servir; (*be useful*): **to serve as/for/to do** servir de/à/à faire ♦ *n* (*TENNIS*) service *m*; **are you being served?** est-ce qu'on s'occupe de vous?; **to serve on a committee/jury** faire partie d'un comité/ jury; **it serves him right** c'est bien fait pour lui; **it serves my purpose** cela fait mon affaire

▶ **serve out, serve up** *vt* (*food*) servir

service ['sə:vɪs] *n* (*gen*) service *m*; (*AUT: maintenance*) révision *f*; (*REL*) office *m* ♦ *vt* (*car, washing machine*) réviser; **the Services** *npl* les forces armées; **to be of service to sb, to do sb a service** rendre service à qn; **to put one's car in for service** donner sa voiture à réviser; **dinner service** service de table

serviceable ['sə:vɪsəbl] *adj* pratique, commode

service area *n* (*on motorway*) aire *f* de services

service charge *n* (*BRIT*) service *m*

serviceman ['sə:vɪsmən] *n* militaire *m*

service station *n* station-service *f*

serviette [sə:vɪ'ɛt] *n* (*BRIT*) serviette *f* (de table)

session ['sɛʃən] *n* (*sitting*) séance *f*; (*SCOL*) année *f* scolaire (*or* universitaire); **to be in session** siéger, être en session *or* en séance

set [sɛt] *n* série *f*, assortiment *m*; (*of tools etc*) jeu *m*; (*RADIO, TV*) poste *m*; (*TENNIS*) set *m*; (*group of people*) cercle *m*, milieu *m*; (*CINE*) plateau *m*; (*THEAT: stage*) scène *f*; (: *scenery*) décor *m*; (*MATH*) ensemble *m*; (*HAIRDRESSING*) mise *f* en plis ♦ *adj* (*fixed*) fixe, déterminé(e); (*ready*) prêt(e) ♦ *vb, pt, pp* **set** *vt* (*place*) mettre, poser, placer; (*fix, establish*) fixer; (: *record*) établir; (*assign: task, homework*) donner; (*adjust*) régler; (*decide: rules etc*) fixer, choisir; (*TYP*) composer ♦ *vi* (*sun*) se coucher; (*jam, jelly, concrete*) prendre; **to be set on doing** être résolu(e) à faire; **to be all set to do** être (fin) prêt(e) pour faire; **to be (dead) set against** être (totalement) opposé à; **he's set in his ways** il n'est pas très souple, il tient à ses habitudes; **to set to music** mettre en musique; **to set on fire** mettre le feu à; **to set free** libérer; **to set sth going** déclencher qch; **to set the alarm clock for seven o'clock** mettre le réveil à sonner à sept heures; **to set sail** partir, prendre la mer; **a set phrase** une expression toute faite, une locution; **a set of false teeth** un dentier; **a set of dining-room furniture** une salle à manger

▶ **set about** *vt fus* (*task*) entreprendre, se mettre à; **to set about doing sth** se mettre à faire qch

▶ **set aside** *vt* mettre de côté

▶ **set back** *vt* (*in time*): **to set back (by)** retarder (de); (*place*): **a house set back from the road** une maison située en retrait de la route

▶ **set in** *vi* (*infection, bad weather*) s'installer; (*complications*) survenir, surgir; **the rain has set in for the day** c'est parti pour qu'il pleuve toute la journée

▶ **set off** *vi* se mettre en route, partir ♦ *vt* (*bomb*) faire exploser; (*cause to start*) déclencher; (*show up well*) mettre en valeur, faire valoir

▶ **set out** *vi*: **to set out to do** entreprendre de faire; avoir pour but *or* intention de faire ♦ *vt* (*arrange*) disposer; (*state*) présenter, exposer; **set out (from)** partir (de)

▶ **set up** *vt* (*organization*) fonder, constituer; (*monument*) ériger; **to set up shop** (*fig*) s'établir, s'installer

setback ['sɛtbæk] *n* (*hitch*) revers *m*, contretemps *m*; (*in health*) rechute *f*

set menu *n* menu *m*

settee [sɛ'ti:] *n* canapé *m*

setting ['setɪŋ] *n* cadre *m*; (*of jewel*) monture *f*

settle ['setl] *vt* (*argument, matter, account*) régler; (*problem*) résoudre; (*MED: calm*) calmer; (*colonize: land*) coloniser ♦ *vi* (*bird, dust etc*) se poser; (*sediment*) se déposer; (*also:* **settle down**) s'installer, se fixer; (: *become calmer*) se calmer; se ranger; **to settle to sth** se mettre sérieusement à qch; **to settle for sth** accepter qch, se contenter de qch; **to settle on sth** opter *or* se décider pour qch; **that's settled then** alors, c'est d'accord!; **to settle one's stomach** calmer des maux d'estomac

▶ **settle in** *vi* s'installer

▶ **settle up** *vi*: **to settle up with sb** régler (ce que l'on doit à) qn

settlement ['setlmənt] *n* (*payment*) règlement *m*; (*agreement*) accord *m*; (*colony*) colonie *f*; (*village etc*) établissement *m*; hameau *m*; **in settlement of our account** en règlement de notre compte

settler ['setlə*] *n* colon *m*

setup ['setʌp] *n* (*arrangement*) manière *f* dont les choses sont organisées; (*situation*) situation *f*, allure *f* des choses

seven ['sevn] *num* sept

seventeen [sevn'ti:n] *num* dix-sept

seventh ['sevnθ] *num* septième

seventy ['sevntɪ] *num* soixante-dix

sever ['sevə*] *vt* couper, trancher; (*relations*) rompre

several ['sevərl] *adj, pron* plusieurs *m/fpl*; **several of us** plusieurs d'entre nous; **several times** plusieurs fois

severance ['sevərəns] *n* (*of relations*) rupture *f*

severance pay *n* indemnité *f* de licenciement

severe [sɪ'vɪə*] *adj* sévère, strict(e); (*serious*) grave, sérieux(euse); (*hard*) rigoureux(euse), dur(e); (*plain*) sévère, austère

severity [sɪ'verɪtɪ] *n* sévérité *f*; gravité *f*; rigueur *f*

sew, *pt* **sewed**, *pp* **sewn** [səu, səud, səun] *vt, vi* coudre

▶ **sew up** *vt* (re)coudre; **it is all sewn up** (*fig*) c'est dans le sac *or* dans la poche

sewage ['su:ɪdʒ] *n* vidange(s) *f(pl)*

sewer ['su:ə*] *n* égout *m*

sewing ['səuɪŋ] *n* couture *f*

sewing machine *n* machine *f* à coudre

sewn [səun] *pp of* **sew**

sex [seks] *n* sexe *m*; **to have sex with** avoir des rapports (sexuels) avec

sexism ['seksɪzəm] *n* sexisme *m*

sexist ['seksɪst] *adj* sexiste

sexual ['seksjuəl] *adj* sexuel(le); **sexual assault** attentat *m* à la pudeur; **sexual harassment** harcèlement sexuel; **sexual intercourse** rapports sexuels

sexuality [seksju'ælɪtɪ] *n* sexualité *f*

sexy ['seksɪ] *adj* sexy *inv*

shabby ['ʃæbɪ] *adj* miteux(euse); (*behaviour*) mes-

quin(e), méprisable

shack [ʃæk] *n* cabane *f*, hutte *f*

shackles ['ʃæklz] *npl* chaînes *fpl*, entraves *fpl*

shade [ʃeɪd] *n* ombre *f*; (*for lamp*) abat-jour *m inv*; (*of colour*) nuance *f*, ton *m*; (*us: window shade*) store *m*; (*small quantity*): **a shade of** un soupçon de ♦ *vt* abriter du soleil, ombrager; **shades** *npl* (*us: sunglasses*) lunettes *fpl* de soleil; **in the shade** à l'ombre; **a shade smaller** un tout petit peu plus petit

shadow ['ʃædəu] *n* ombre *f* ♦ *vt* (*follow*) filer; **without** *or* **beyond a shadow of doubt** sans l'ombre d'un doute

shadow cabinet *n* (*BRIT POL*) cabinet parallèle formé par le parti qui n'est pas au pouvoir

shadowy ['ʃædəuɪ] *adj* ombragé(e); (*dim*) vague, indistinct(e)

shady ['ʃeɪdɪ] *adj* ombragé(e); (*fig: dishonest*) louche, véreux(euse)

shaft [ʃɑ:ft] *n* (*of arrow, spear*) hampe *f*; (*AUT, TECH*) arbre *m*; (*of mine*) puits *m*; (*of lift*) cage *f*; (*of light*) rayon *m*, trait *m*; **ventilator shaft** conduit *m* d'aération *or* de ventilation

shaggy ['ʃægɪ] *adj* hirsute; en broussaille

shake [ʃeɪk] *vb, pt* **shook**, *pp* **shaken** [ʃuk, 'ʃeɪkn] *vt* secouer; (*bottle, cocktail*) agiter; (*house, confidence*) ébranler ♦ *vi* trembler ♦ *n* secousse *f*; **to shake one's head** (*in refusal etc*) dire *or* faire non de la tête; (*in dismay*) secouer la tête; **to shake hands with sb** serrer la main à qn

▶ **shake off** *vt* secouer; (*fig*) se débarrasser de

▶ **shake up** *vt* secouer

shaky ['ʃeɪkɪ] *adj* (*hand, voice*) tremblant(e); (*building*) branlant(e), peu solide; (*memory*) chancelant(e); (*knowledge*) incertain(e)

shall [ʃæl] *aux vb*: **I shall go** j'irai

shallow ['ʃæləu] *adj* peu profond(e); (*fig*) superficiel(le), qui manque de profondeur

sham [ʃæm] *n* frime *f*; (*jewellery, furniture*) imitation *f* ♦ *adj* feint(e), simulé(e) ♦ *vt* feindre, simuler

shambles ['ʃæmblz] *n* confusion *f*, pagaïe *f*, fouillis *m*; **the economy is (in) a complete shambles** l'économie est dans la confusion la plus totale

shame [ʃeɪm] *n* honte *f* ♦ *vt* faire honte à; **it is a shame (that/to do)** c'est dommage (que + *sub*/de faire); **what a shame!** quel dommage!; **to put sb/ sth to shame** (*fig*) faire honte à qn/qch

shameful ['ʃeɪmful] *adj* honteux(euse), scandaleux(euse)

shameless ['ʃeɪmlɪs] *adj* éhonté(e), effronté(e); (*immodest*) impudique

shampoo [ʃæm'pu:] *n* shampooing *m* ♦ *vt* faire un shampooing à; **shampoo and set** shampooing et mise *f* en plis

shamrock ['ʃæmrɔk] *n* trèfle *m* (*emblème national de l'Irlande*)

shandy ['ʃændɪ] *n* bière panachée

shan't [ʃɑːnt] = **shall not**

shantytown ['ʃæntɪtaʊn] n bidonville m

shape [ʃeɪp] n forme f ♦ vt façonner, modeler; (clay, stone) donner forme à; (statement) formuler; (sb's ideas, character) former; (sb's life) déterminer; (course of events) influer sur le cours de ♦ vi (also: **shape up**: events) prendre tournure; (: person) faire des progrès, s'en sortir; **to take shape** prendre forme or tournure; **in the shape of a heart** en forme de cœur; **I can't bear gardening in any shape or form** je déteste le jardinage sous quelque forme que ce soit; **to get o.s. into shape** (re)trouver la forme

-shaped [ʃeɪpt] suffix: **heart-shaped** en forme de cœur

shapeless ['ʃeɪplɪs] adj informe, sans forme

shapely ['ʃeɪplɪ] adj bien proportionné(e), beau(belle)

share [ʃɛə*] n (thing received, contribution) part f; (COMM) action f ♦ vt partager; (have in common) avoir en commun; **to share out (among or between)** partager (entre); **to share in** (joy, sorrow) prendre part à; (profits) participer à, avoir part à; (work) partager

shareholder ['ʃɛəhəʊldə*] n actionnaire m/f

shark [ʃɑːk] n requin m

sharp [ʃɑːp] adj (razor, knife) tranchant(e), bien aiguisé(e); (point) aigu(ë); (nose, chin) pointu(e); (outline) net(te); (curve, bend) brusque; (cold, pain) vif(vive); (MUS) dièse; (voice) coupant(e); (person: quick-witted) vif(vive) éveillé(e); (: unscrupulous) malhonnête ♦ n (MUS) dièse m ♦ adv: **at 2 o'clock sharp** à 2 heures pile or tapantes; **turn sharp left** tournez immédiatement à gauche; **to be sharp with sb** être brusque avec qn; **look sharp!** dépêche-toi!

sharpen ['ʃɑːpn] vt aiguiser; (pencil) tailler; (fig) aviver

sharpener ['ʃɑːpnə*] n (also: **pencil sharpener**) taille-crayon(s) m inv; (also: **knife sharpener**) aiguisoir m

sharp-eyed [ʃɑːpˈaɪd] adj à qui rien n'échappe

sharply ['ʃɑːplɪ] adv (abruptly) brusquement; (clearly) nettement; (harshly) sèchement, vertement

shatter ['ʃætə*] vt fracasser, briser, faire voler en éclats; (fig: upset) bouleverser; (: ruin) briser, ruiner ♦ vi voler en éclats, se briser, se fracasser

shave [ʃeɪv] vt raser ♦ vi se raser ♦ n: **to have a shave** se raser

shaver ['ʃeɪvə*] n (also: **electric shaver**) rasoir m électrique

shaving ['ʃeɪvɪŋ] n (action) rasage m; **shavings** npl (of wood etc) copeaux mpl

shaving brush n blaireau m

shaving cream n crème f à raser

shaving foam n mousse f à raser

shawl [ʃɔːl] n châle m

she [ʃiː] pron elle; **there she is** la voilà; **she-elephant** etc éléphant m etc femelle; NB for ships, countries follow the gender of your translation

sheaf, pl **sheaves** [ʃiːf, ʃiːvz] n gerbe f

shear [ʃɪə*] vt, pt **sheared**, pp **sheared** or **shorn** [ʃɔːn] (sheep) tondre

▶ **shear off** vt (also) tondre; (branch) élaguer

shears ['ʃɪəz] npl (for hedge) cisaille(s) f(pl)

sheath [ʃiːθ] n gaine f, fourreau m, étui m; (contraceptive) préservatif m

shed [ʃed] n remise f, resserre f; (INDUSTRY, RAIL) hangar m ♦ vt, pt, pp **shed** (leaves, fur etc) perdre; (tears) verser, répandre; **to shed light on** (problem, mystery) faire la lumière sur

she'd [ʃiːd] = **she had, she would**

sheen [ʃiːn] n lustre m

sheep [ʃiːp] n (pl inv) mouton m

sheepdog ['ʃiːpdɔg] n chien m de berger

sheepskin ['ʃiːpskɪn] n peau f de mouton

sheer [ʃɪə*] adj (utter) pur(e), pur et simple; (steep) à pic abrupt(e); (almost transparent) extrêmement fin(e) ♦ adv à pic, abruptement; **by sheer chance** par pur hasard

sheet [ʃiːt] n (on bed) drap m; (of paper) feuille f; (of glass, metal) feuille, plaque f

sheik(h) [ʃeɪk] n cheik m

shelf, pl **shelves** [ʃelf, ʃelvz] n étagère f, rayon m; **set of shelves** rayonnage m

shell [ʃel] n (on beach) coquillage m; (of egg, nut etc) coquille f; (explosive) obus m; (of building) carcasse f ♦ vt (crab, prawn etc) décortiquer; (peas) écosser; (MIL) bombarder (d'obus)

▶ **shell out** vi (col): **to shell out (for)** casquer (pour)

she'll [ʃiːl] = **she will, she shall**

shellfish ['ʃelfɪʃ] n (pl inv: crab etc) crustacé m; (scallop etc) coquillage m; (pl: as food) crustacés; coquillages

shell suit n survêtement m

shelter ['ʃeltə*] n abri m, refuge m ♦ vt abriter, protéger; (give lodging to) donner asile à ♦ vi s'abriter, se mettre à l'abri; **to take shelter (from)** s'abriter (de)

sheltered housing ['ʃeltəd-] n foyers mpl (pour personnes âgées ou handicapées)

shelve [ʃelv] vt (fig) mettre en suspens or en sommeil

shelves ['ʃelvz] npl of **shelf**

shepherd ['ʃepəd] n berger m ♦ vt (guide) guider, escorter

shepherd's pie ['ʃepədz-] n ≃ hachis m Parmentier

sheriff ['ʃerɪf] n shérif m

sherry ['ʃerɪ] n xérès m, sherry m

she's [ʃiːz] = **she is, she has**

Shetland ['ʃetlənd] n (also: **the Shetlands, the Shetland Isles** or **Islands**) les îles fpl Shetland

shield [ʃiːld] n bouclier m ♦ vt: **to shield (from)** protéger (de or contre)

shift [ʃɪft] n (change) changement m; (of workers) équipe f, poste m ♦ vt déplacer, changer de place; (remove) enlever ♦ vi changer de place, bouger; **the wind has shifted to the south** le vent a tourné au sud; **a shift in demand** (COMM) un déplacement de la demande

shift work n travail m par roulement; **to do shift work** travailler par roulement

shifty [ˈʃɪftɪ] adj sournois(e); (eyes) fuyant(e)

shimmer [ˈʃɪməˀ] n miroitement m, chatoiement m ♦ vi miroiter, chatoyer

shin [ʃɪn] n tibia m ♦ vi: **to shin up/down a tree** grimper dans un/descendre d'un arbre

shine [ʃaɪn] n éclat m, brillant m ♦ vb, pt, pp **shone** [ʃɒn] vi briller ♦ vt faire briller or reluire; (torch): **to shine on** braquer sur

shingle [ˈʃɪŋgl] n (on beach) galets mpl; (on roof) bardeau m

shingles [ˈʃɪŋglz] n (MED) zona m

shiny [ˈʃaɪnɪ] adj brillant(e)

ship [ʃɪp] n bateau m; (large) navire m ♦ vt transporter (par mer); (send) expédier (par mer); (load) charger, embarquer; **on board ship** à bord

shipbuilding [ˈʃɪpbɪldɪŋ] n construction navale

shipment [ˈʃɪpmənt] n cargaison f

shipping [ˈʃɪpɪŋ] n (ships) navires mpl; (traffic) navigation f

shipwreck [ˈʃɪprek] n épave f; (event) naufrage m ♦ vt: **to be shipwrecked** faire naufrage

shipyard [ˈʃɪpjɑːd] n chantier naval

shire [ˈʃaɪəˀ] n (BRIT) comté m

shirt [ʃəːt] n chemise f; **in shirt sleeves** en bras de chemise

shit [ʃɪt] excl (col!) merde (!)

shiver [ˈʃɪvəˀ] n frisson m ♦ vi frissonner

shoal [ʃəul] n (of fish) banc m

shock [ʃɒk] n (impact) choc m, heurt m; (ELEC) secousse f, décharge f; (emotional) choc; (MED) commotion f, choc ♦ vt (scandalize) choquer, scandaliser; (upset) bouleverser; **suffering from shock** (MED) commotionné(e); **it gave us a shock** ça nous a fait un choc; **it came as a shock to hear that …** nous avons appris avec stupeur que …

shock absorber [-əbzɔ:bəˀ] n amortisseur m

shocking [ˈʃɒkɪŋ] adj choquant(e), scandaleux(euse); (weather, handwriting) épouvantable

shoddy [ˈʃɒdɪ] adj de mauvaise qualité, mal fait(e)

shoe [ʃuː] n chaussure f, soulier m; (also: **horseshoe**) fer m à cheval; (also: **brake shoe**) mâchoire f de frein ♦ vt, pt, pp **shod** [ʃɒd] (horse) ferrer

shoelace [ˈʃuːleɪs] n lacet m (de soulier)

shoe polish n cirage m

shoe shop n magasin m de chaussures

shoestring [ˈʃuːstrɪŋ] n: **on a shoestring** (fig) avec un budget dérisoire; avec des moyens très restreints

shone [ʃɒn] pt, pp of **shine**

shook [ʃuk] pt of **shake**

shoot [ʃuːt] n (on branch, seedling) pousse f; (shooting party) partie f de chasse ♦ vb, pt, pp **shot** [ʃɒt] vt (game: BRIT) chasser; tirer; abattre; (person) blesser (or tuer) d'un coup de fusil (or de revolver); (execute) fusiller; (CINE) tourner ♦ vi (with gun, bow): **to shoot (at)** tirer (sur); (FOOTBALL) shooter, tirer; **to shoot past sb** passer en flèche devant qn; **to shoot in/out** entrer/sortir comme une flèche

▶ **shoot down** vt (plane) abattre

▶ **shoot up** vi (fig) monter en flèche

shooting [ˈʃuːtɪŋ] n (shots) coups mpl de feu; (attack) fusillade f; (: murder) homicide m (à l'aide d'une arme à feu); (HUNTING) chasse f; (CINE) tournage m

shooting star n étoile filante

shop [ʃɒp] n magasin m; (workshop) atelier m ♦ vi (also: **go shopping**) faire ses courses or ses achats; **repair shop** atelier de réparations; **to talk shop** (fig) parler boutique

▶ **shop around** vi faire le tour des magasins (pour comparer les prix); (fig) se renseigner avant de choisir or décider

shop assistant n (BRIT) vendeur/euse

shop floor n (BRIT, fig) ouvriers mpl

shopkeeper [ˈʃɒpkiːpəˀ] n marchand/e, commerçant/e

shoplifting [ˈʃɒplɪftɪŋ] n vol m à l'étalage

shopper [ˈʃɒpəˀ] n personne f qui fait ses courses, acheteur/euse

shopping [ˈʃɒpɪŋ] n (goods) achats mpl, provisions fpl

shopping bag n sac m (à provisions)

shopping centre n centre commercial

shop-soiled [ˈʃɒpsɔɪld] adj défraîchi(e), qui a fait la vitrine

shop steward n (BRIT INDUSTRY) délégué/e syndical(e)

shop window n vitrine f

shore [ʃɔːˀ] n (of sea, lake) rivage m, rive f ♦ vt: **to shore (up)** étayer; **on shore** à terre

shorn [ʃɔːn] pp of **shear** ♦ adj: **shorn of** dépouillé(e) de

short [ʃɔːt] adj (not long) court(e); (soon finished) court, bref(brève); (person, step) petit(e); (curt) brusque, sec(sèche); (insufficient) insuffisant(e) ♦ n (also: **short film**) court métrage; **to be short of sth** être à court de or manquer de qch; **to be in short supply** manquer, être difficile à trouver; **I'm 3 short** il m'en manque 3; **in short** bref; en bref; **short of doing** à moins de faire; **everything short of** tout sauf; **it is short for** c'est l'abréviation or le diminutif de; **a short time ago** il y a peu de temps; **in the short term** à court terme; **to cut short** (speech, visit) abréger, écourter; (person) couper la parole à; **to fall short of** ne pas être à la hauteur de; **to stop short** s'arrêter net; **to stop short of** ne pas aller jusqu'à

shortage ['ʃɔːtɪdʒ] n manque m, pénurie f

shortbread ['ʃɔːtbred] n ≃ sablé m

short-change ['ʃɔːt'tʃeɪndʒ] vt: **to short-change sb** ne pas rendre assez à qn

short-circuit ['ʃɔːt'sɜːkɪt] n court-circuit m ♦ vt court-circuiter ♦ vi se mettre en court-circuit

shortcoming ['ʃɔːtkʌmɪŋ] n défaut m

short(crust) pastry ['ʃɔːt(krʌst)-] n (BRIT) pâte brisée

shortcut ['ʃɔːtkʌt] n raccourci m

shorten ['ʃɔːtn] vt raccourcir; (text, visit) abréger

shortfall ['ʃɔːtfɔːl] n déficit m

shorthand ['ʃɔːthænd] n (BRIT) sténo(graphie) f; **to take sth down in shorthand** prendre qch en sténo

shorthand typist n (BRIT) sténodactylo m/f

short list n (BRIT: for job) liste f des candidats sélectionnés

shortly ['ʃɔːtlɪ] adv bientôt, sous peu

short notice n: **at short notice** au dernier moment

shorts [ʃɔːts] npl (also: **a pair of shorts**) un short

short-sighted [ʃɔːt'saɪtɪd] adj (BRIT) myope; (fig) qui manque de clairvoyance

short-staffed [ʃɔːt'stɑːft] adj à court de personnel

short-stay [ʃɔːt'steɪ] adj (car park) de courte durée

short story n nouvelle f

short-tempered [ʃɔːt'tempəd] adj qui s'emporte facilement

short-term ['ʃɔːttɜːm] adj (effect) à court terme

short wave n (RADIO) ondes courtes

shot [ʃɔt] pt, pp of **shoot** ♦ n coup m (de feu); (shotgun pellets) plombs mpl; (person) tireur m; (try) coup, essai m; (injection) piqûre f; (PHOT) photo f; **to fire a shot at sb/sth** tirer sur qn/qch; **to have a shot at (doing) sth** essayer de faire qch; **like a shot** comme une flèche; (very readily) sans hésiter; **to get shot of sb/sth** (col) se débarrasser de qn/qch; **a big shot** (col) un gros bonnet

shotgun ['ʃɔtgʌn] n fusil m de chasse

should [ʃud] aux vb: **I should go now** je devrais partir maintenant; **he should be there now** il devrait être arrivé maintenant; **I should go if I were you** si j'étais vous j'irais; **I should like to** j'aimerais bien, volontiers; **should he phone ...** si jamais il téléphone ...

shoulder ['ʃəuldə*] n épaule f; (BRIT: of road): **hard shoulder** accotement m ♦ vt (fig) endosser, se charger de; **to look over one's shoulder** regarder derrière soi (en tournant la tête); **to rub shoulders with sb** (fig) côtoyer qn; **to give sb the cold shoulder** (fig) battre froid à qn

shoulder bag n sac m à bandoulière

shoulder blade n omoplate f

shouldn't ['ʃudnt] = **should not**

shout [ʃaut] n cri m ♦ vt crier ♦ vi crier, pousser des cris; **to give sb a shout** appeler qn
▶ **shout down** vt huer

shouting ['ʃautɪŋ] n cris mpl

shove [ʃʌv] vt pousser; (col: put): **to shove sth in** fourrer or ficher qch dans ♦ n poussée f; **he shoved me out of the way** il m'a écarté en me poussant
▶ **shove off** vi (NAUT) pousser au large; (fig: col) ficher le camp

shovel ['ʃʌvl] n pelle f ♦ vt pelleter, enlever (or enfourner) à la pelle

show [ʃəu] n (of emotion) manifestation f, démonstration f; (semblance) semblant m, apparence f; (exhibition) exposition f, salon m; (THEAT) spectacle m, représentation f; (CINE) séance f ♦ vb, pt showed, pp shown vt montrer; (courage etc) faire preuve de, manifester; (exhibit) exposer ♦ vi se voir, être visible; **to ask for a show of hands** demander que l'on vote à main levée; **to be on show** être exposé(e); **it's just for show** c'est juste pour l'effet; **who's running the show here?** (col) qui est-ce qui commande ici?; **to show sb to his seat/to the door** accompagner qn jusqu'à sa place/la porte; **to show a profit/loss** (COMM) indiquer un bénéfice/une perte; **it just goes to show that ...** ça prouve bien que ...
▶ **show in** vt faire entrer
▶ **show off** vi (pej) crâner ♦ vt (display) faire valoir; (pej) faire étalage de
▶ **show out** vt reconduire à la porte
▶ **show up** vi (stand out) ressortir; (col: turn up) se montrer ♦ vt démontrer; (unmask) démasquer, dénoncer

show business n le monde du spectacle

showdown ['ʃəudaun] n épreuve f de force

shower ['ʃauə*] n (also: **shower bath**) douche f; (rain) averse f; (of stones etc) pluie f, grêle f; (US: party) réunion organisée pour la remise de cadeaux ♦ vi prendre une douche, se doucher ♦ vt: **to shower sb with** (gifts etc) combler qn de; (abuse etc) accabler qn de; (missiles) bombarder qn de; **to have or take a shower** prendre une douche, se doucher

showerproof ['ʃauəpruːf] adj imperméable

showing ['ʃəuɪŋ] n (of film) projection f

show jumping [-dʒʌmpɪŋ] n concours m hippique

shown [ʃəun] pp of **show**

show-off ['ʃəuɔf] n (col: person) crâneur/euse, m'as-tu-vu/e

showpiece ['ʃəupiːs] n (of exhibition etc) joyau m, clou m; **that hospital is a showpiece** cet hôpital est un modèle du genre

showroom ['ʃəurum] n magasin m or salle f d'exposition

shrank [ʃræŋk] *pt of* **shrink**

shrapnel [ˈʃræpnl] *n* éclats *mpl* d'obus

shred [ʃred] *n* (*gen pl*) lambeau *m*, petit morceau; (*fig: of truth, evidence*) parcelle *f* ♦ *vt* mettre en lambeaux, déchirer; (*documents*) détruire; (*CULIN*) râper; couper en lanières

shredder [ˈʃredə*] *n* (*for vegetables*) râpeur *m*; (*for documents, papers*) déchiqueteuse *f*

shrewd [ʃru:d] *adj* astucieux(euse), perspicace

shriek [ʃri:k] *n* cri perçant *or* aigu, hurlement *m* ♦ *vt, vi* hurler, crier

shrill [ʃrɪl] *adj* perçant(e), aigu(ë), strident(e)

shrimp [ʃrɪmp] *n* crevette grise

shrine [ʃraɪn] *n* châsse *f*; (*place*) lieu *m* de pèlerinage

shrink, *pt* **shrank**, *pp* **shrunk** [ʃrɪŋk, ʃræŋk, ʃrʌŋk] *vi* rétrécir; (*fig*) se réduire; se contracter ♦ *vt* (*wool*) (faire) rétrécir ♦ *n* (*col: pej*) psychanalyste *m/f*; **to shrink from (doing) sth** reculer devant (la pensée de faire) qch

shrink-wrap [ˈʃrɪŋkræp] *vt* emballer sous film plastique

shrivel [ˈʃrɪvl] (*also*: **shrivel up**) *vt* ratatiner, flétrir ♦ *vi* se ratatiner, se flétrir

shroud [ʃraud] *n* linceul *m* ♦ *vt*: **shrouded in mystery** enveloppé(e) de mystère

Shrove Tuesday [ˈʃrauv-] *n* (le) Mardi gras

shrub [ʃrʌb] *n* arbuste *m*

shrubbery [ˈʃrʌbərɪ] *n* massif *m* d'arbustes

shrug [ʃrʌg] *n* haussement *m* d'épaules ♦ *vt, vi*: **to shrug (one's shoulders)** hausser les épaules

▶ **shrug off** *vt* faire fi de; (*cold, illness*) se débarrasser de

shrunk [ʃrʌŋk] *pp of* **shrink**

shudder [ˈʃʌdə*] *n* frisson *m*, frémissement *m* ♦ *vi* frissonner, frémir

shuffle [ˈʃʌfl] *vt* (*cards*) battre; **to shuffle (one's feet)** traîner les pieds

shun [ʃʌn] *vt* éviter, fuir

shunt [ʃʌnt] *vt* (*RAIL: direct*) aiguiller; (: *divert*) détourner ♦ *vi*: **to shunt (to and fro)** faire la navette

shut, *pt*, *pp* **shut** [ʃʌt] *vt* fermer ♦ *vi* (se) fermer

▶ **shut down** *vt* fermer définitivement; (*machine*) arrêter ♦ *vi* fermer définitivement

▶ **shut off** *vt* couper, arrêter

▶ **shut out** *vt* (*person, cold*) empêcher d'entrer; (*noise*) éviter d'entendre; (*block: view*) boucher; (: *memory of sth*) chasser de son esprit

▶ **shut up** *vi* (*col: keep quiet*) se taire ♦ *vt* (*close*) fermer; (*silence*) faire taire

shutter [ˈʃʌtə*] *n* volet *m*; (*PHOT*) obturateur *m*

shuttle [ˈʃʌtl] *n* navette *f*; (*also*: **shuttle service**) (*service m de*) navette *f* ♦ *vi* (*vehicle, person*) faire la navette ♦ *vt* (*passengers*) transporter par un système de navette

shuttlecock [ˈʃʌtlkɔk] *n* volant *m* (*de badminton*)

shuttle diplomacy *n* navettes *fpl* diplomatiques

shy [ʃaɪ] *adj* timide; **to fight shy of** se dérober devant; **to be shy of doing sth** hésiter à faire qch, ne pas oser faire qch ♦ *vi*: **to shy away from doing sth** (*fig*) craindre de faire qch

Siberia [saɪˈbɪərɪə] *n* Sibérie *f*

Sicily [ˈsɪsɪlɪ] *n* Sicile *f*

sick [sɪk] *adj* (*ill*) malade; (*vomiting*): **to be sick** vomir; (*humour*) noir(e), macabre; **to feel sick** avoir envie de vomir, avoir mal au cœur; **to fall sick** tomber malade; **to be (off) sick** être absent(e) pour cause de maladie; **a sick person** un(e) malade; **to be sick of** (*fig*) en avoir assez de

sick bay *n* infirmerie *f*

sicken [ˈsɪkn] *vt* écœurer ♦ *vi*: **to be sickening for sth** (*cold, flu etc*) couver qch

sickening [ˈsɪknɪŋ] *adj* (*fig*) écœurant(e), révoltant(e), répugnant(e)

sickle [ˈsɪkl] *n* faucille *f*

sick leave *n* congé *m* de maladie

sickly [ˈsɪklɪ] *adj* maladif(ive), souffreteux(euse); (*causing nausea*) écœurant(e)

sickness [ˈsɪknɪs] *n* maladie *f*; (*vomiting*) vomissement(s) *m(pl)*

sick note *n* (*from parents*) mot *m* d'absence; (*from doctor*) certificat médical

sick pay *n* indemnité *f* de maladie (*versée par l'employeur*)

side [saɪd] *n* côté *m*; (*of animal*) flanc *m*; (*of lake, road*) bord *m*; (*of mountain*) versant *m*; (*fig: aspect*) côté, aspect *m*; (*team: SPORT*) équipe *f* ♦ *cpd* (*door, entrance*) latéral(e) ♦ *vi*: **to side with sb** prendre le parti de qn, se ranger du côté de qn; **by the side of** au bord de; **side by side** côte à côte; **the right/wrong side** le bon/mauvais côté, l'endroit/l'envers *m*; **they are on our side** ils sont avec nous; **from all sides** de tous côtés; **to take sides (with)** prendre parti (pour); **a side of beef** ≃ un quartier de bœuf

sideboard [ˈsaɪdbɔ:d] *n* buffet *m*

sideboards [ˈsaɪdbɔ:dz] (*BRIT*), **sideburns** [ˈsaɪdbə:nz] *npl* (*whiskers*) pattes *fpl*

side drum *n* (*MUS*) tambour plat, caisse claire

side effect *n* (*MED*) effet *m* secondaire

sidelight [ˈsaɪdlaɪt] *n* (*AUT*) veilleuse *f*

sideline [ˈsaɪdlaɪn] *n* (*SPORT*) (ligne *f* de) touche *f*; (*fig*) activité *f* secondaire

sidelong [ˈsaɪdlɔŋ] *adj*: **to give sb a sidelong glance** regarder qn du coin de l'œil

sideshow [ˈsaɪdʃəu] *n* attraction *f*

sidestep [ˈsaɪdstep] *vt* (*question*) éluder; (*problem*) éviter ♦ *vi* (*BOXING etc*) esquiver

side street *n* rue transversale

sidetrack [ˈsaɪdtræk] *vt* (*fig*) faire dévier de son sujet

sidewalk [ˈsaɪdwɔ:k] *n* (*US*) trottoir *m*

sideways ['saɪdweɪz] *adv* de côté

siding ['saɪdɪŋ] *n* (*RAIL*) voie *f* de garage

siege [siːdʒ] *n* siège *m*; **to lay siege to** assiéger

sieve [sɪv] *n* tamis *m*, passoire *f* ♦ *vt* tamiser, passer (au tamis)

sift [sɪft] *vt* passer au tamis *or* au crible; (*fig*) passer au crible ♦ *vi* (*fig*): **to sift through** passer en revue

sigh [saɪ] *n* soupir *m* ♦ *vi* soupirer, pousser un soupir

sight [saɪt] *n* (*faculty*) vue *f*; (*spectacle*) spectacle *m*; (*on gun*) mire *f* ♦ *vt* apercevoir; **in sight** visible; (*fig*) **out of sight** hors de vue; **at sight** (*COMM*) à vue; **at first sight** à première vue, au premier abord; **I know her by sight** je la connais de vue; **to catch sight of sb/sth** apercevoir qn/qch; **to lose sight of sb/sth** perdre qn/qch de vue; **to set one's sights on sth** jeter son dévolu sur qch

sightseeing ['saɪtsiːɪŋ] *n* tourisme *m*; **to go sightseeing** faire du tourisme

sign [saɪn] *n* (*gen*) signe *m*; (*with hand etc*) signe, geste *m*; (*notice*) panneau *m*, écriteau *m*; (*also*: **road sign**) panneau de signalisation ♦ *vt* signer; **as a sign of** en signe de; **it's a good/bad sign** c'est bon/mauvais signe; **plus/minus sign** signe plus/moins; **there's no sign of a change of mind** rien ne laisse présager un revirement; **he was showing signs of improvement** il commençait visiblement à faire des progrès; **to sign one's name** signer

▶ **sign away** *vt* (*rights etc*) renoncer officiellement à

▶ **sign in** *vi* signer le registre (en arrivant)

▶ **sign off** *vi* (*RADIO, TV*) terminer l'émission

▶ **sign on** *vi* (*MIL*) s'engager; (*as unemployed*) s'inscrire au chômage; (*enrol*): **to sign on for a course** s'inscrire pour un cours ♦ *vt* (*MIL*) engager; (*employee*) embaucher

▶ **sign out** *vi* signer le registre (en partant)

▶ **sign over** *vt*: **to sign sth over to sb** céder qch par écrit à qn

▶ **sign up** (*MIL*) *vt* engager ♦ *vi* s'engager

signal ['sɪɡnl] *n* signal *m* ♦ *vi* (*AUT*) mettre son clignotant ♦ *vt* (*person*) faire signe à; (*message*) communiquer par signaux; **to signal a left/right turn** (*AUT*) indiquer *or* signaler que l'on tourne à gauche/droite; **to signal to sb (to do sth)** faire signe à qn (de faire qch)

signalman ['sɪɡnlmən] *n* (*RAIL*) aiguilleur *m*

signature ['sɪɡnətʃə*] *n* signature *f*

signature tune *n* indicatif musical

signet ring ['sɪɡnət-] *n* chevalière *f*

significance [sɪɡ'nɪfɪkəns] *n* signification *f*; importance *f*; **that is of no significance** ceci n'a pas d'importance

significant [sɪɡ'nɪfɪkənt] *adj* significatif(ive); (*important*) important(e), considérable

sign language *n* langage *m* par signes

signpost ['saɪnpəust] *n* poteau indicateur

silence ['saɪləns] *n* silence *m* ♦ *vt* faire taire, réduire au silence

silencer ['saɪlənsə*] *n* (*on gun, BRIT AUT*) silencieux *m*

silent ['saɪlnt] *adj* silencieux(euse); (*film*) muet(te); **to keep** *or* **remain silent** garder le silence, ne rien dire

silent partner *n* (*COMM*) bailleur *m* de fonds, commanditaire *m*

silhouette [sɪluː'et] *n* silhouette *f* ♦ *vt*: **silhouetted against** se profilant sur, se découpant contre

silicon chip *n* puce *f* électronique

silk [sɪlk] *n* soie *f* ♦ *cpd* de *or* en soie

silky ['sɪlkɪ] *adj* soyeux(euse)

silly ['sɪlɪ] *adj* stupide, sot(te), bête; **to do something silly** faire une bêtise

silt [sɪlt] *n* vase *f*; limon *m*

silver ['sɪlvə*] *n* argent *m*; (*money*) monnaie *f* (en pièces d'argent); (*also*: **silverware**) argenterie *f* ♦ *cpd* d'argent, en argent

silver paper (*BRIT*), **silver foil** *n* papier *m* d'argent *or* d'étain

silver-plated [sɪlvə'pleɪtɪd] *adj* plaqué(e) argent

silversmith ['sɪlvəsmɪθ] *n* orfèvre *m/f*

silvery ['sɪlvrɪ] *adj* argenté(e)

similar ['sɪmɪlə*] *adj*: **similar (to)** semblable (à)

similarly ['sɪmɪləlɪ] *adv* de la même façon, de même

simmer ['sɪmə*] *vi* cuire à feu doux, mijoter

▶ **simmer down** *vi* (*fig: col*) se calmer

simple ['sɪmpl] *adj* simple; **the simple truth** la vérité pure et simple

simplicity [sɪm'plɪsɪtɪ] *n* simplicité *f*

simply ['sɪmplɪ] *adv* simplement; (*without fuss*) avec simplicité

simultaneous [sɪməl'teɪnɪəs] *adj* simultané(e)

sin [sɪn] *n* péché *m* ♦ *vi* pécher

since [sɪns] *adv, prep* depuis ♦ *conj* (*time*) depuis que; (*because*) puisque, étant donné que, comme; **since then** depuis ce moment-là; **since Monday** depuis lundi; **(ever) since I arrived** depuis mon arrivée, depuis que je suis arrivé

sincere [sɪn'sɪə*] *adj* sincère

sincerely [sɪn'sɪəlɪ] *adv* sincèrement; **Yours sincerely** (*at end of letter*) veuillez agréer, Monsieur (*or* Madame) l'expression de mes sentiments distingués *or* les meilleurs

sincerity [sɪn'serɪtɪ] *n* sincérité *f*

sinew ['sɪnjuː] *n* tendon *m*; **sinews** *npl* muscles *mpl*

sing, *pt* **sang**, *pp* **sung** [sɪŋ, sæŋ, sʌŋ] *vt, vi* chanter

Singapore [sɪŋɡə'pɔː*] *n* Singapour *m*

singe [sɪndʒ] *vt* brûler légèrement; (*clothes*) roussir

singer ['sɪŋə*] *n* chanteur/euse

singing ['sɪŋɪŋ] *n* (*of person, bird*) chant *m*; façon *f* de chanter; (*of kettle, bullet, in ears*) sifflement *m*

single ['sɪŋgl] *adj* seul(e), unique; (*unmarried*) célibataire; (*not double*) simple ◆ *n* (*BRIT: also:* **single ticket**) aller *m* (simple); (*record*) 45 tours *m*; **not a single one was left** il n'en est pas resté un(e) seul(e); **every single day** chaque jour sans exception

▶ **single out** *vt* choisir; distinguer

single bed *n* lit *m* à une place

single-breasted ['sɪŋglbrɛstɪd] *adj* droit(e)

single file *n*: **in single file** en file indienne

single-handed [sɪŋgl'hændɪd] *adv* tout(e) seul(e), sans (aucune) aide

single-minded [sɪŋgl'maɪndɪd] *adj* résolu(e), tenace

single parent *n* parent unique (*or* célibataire)

single room *n* chambre *f* à un lit *or* pour une personne

singles ['sɪŋglz] *npl* (*TENNIS*) simple *m*; (*US: single people*) célibataires ◆ *m/fpl*

single-track road [sɪŋgl'træk-] *n* route *f* à voie unique

singly ['sɪŋglɪ] *adv* séparément

singular ['sɪŋgjulə*] *adj* singulier(ière), (*odd*) singulier, étrange; (*LING*) (au) singulier, du singulier ◆ *n* (*LING*) singulier *m*; **in the feminine singular** au féminin singulier

sinister ['sɪnɪstə*] *adj* sinistre

sink [sɪŋk] *n* évier *m* ◆ *vb*, *pt* **sank**, *pp* **sunk** [sæŋk, sʌŋk] *vt* (*ship*) (faire) couler, faire sombrer; (*foundations*) creuser; (*piles etc*): **to sink sth into** enfoncer qch dans ◆ *vi* couler, sombrer; (*ground etc*) s'affaisser; **he sank into a chair/the mud** il s'est enfoncé dans un fauteuil/la boue; **a sinking feeling** un serrement de cœur

▶ **sink in** *vi* s'enfoncer, pénétrer; (*explanation*): **it took a long time to sink in** il a fallu longtemps pour que ça rentre

sinner ['sɪnə*] *n* pécheur/eresse

sinus ['saɪnəs] *n* (*ANAT*) sinus *m inv*

sip [sɪp] *n* petite gorgée ◆ *vt* boire à petites gorgées

siphon ['saɪfən] *n* siphon *m* ◆ *vt* (*also:* **siphon off**) siphonner; (: *fig: funds*) transférer; (: *illegally*) détourner

sir [sə*] *n* monsieur *m*; **Sir John Smith** sir John Smith; **yes sir** oui Monsieur; **Dear Sir** (*in letter*) Monsieur

siren ['saɪərn] *n* sirène *f*

sirloin ['sə:lɔɪn] *n* aloyau *m*

sissy ['sɪsɪ] *n* (*col: coward*) poule mouillée

sister ['sɪstə*] *n* sœur *f*; (*nun*) religieuse *f*, (bonne) sœur; (*BRIT: nurse*) infirmière *f* en chef ◆ *cpd*: **sister organization** organisation *f* sœur; **sister ship** sister(-)ship *m*

sister-in-law ['sɪstərɪnlɔ:] *n* belle-sœur *f*

sit, *pt*, *pp* **sat** [sɪt, sæt] *vi* s'asseoir; (*assembly*) être en séance, siéger; (*for painter*) poser; (*dress etc*) tomber ◆ *vt* (*exam*) passer, se présenter à; **to sit on a committee** faire partie d'un comité; **to sit tight** ne pas bouger

▶ **sit about, sit around** *vi* être assis(e) *or* rester à ne rien faire

▶ **sit back** *vi* (*in seat*) bien s'installer, se carrer

▶ **sit down** *vi* s'asseoir; **to be sitting down** être assis(e)

▶ **sit in** *vi*: **to sit in on a discussion** assister à une discussion

▶ **sit up** *vi* s'asseoir; (*not go to bed*) rester debout, ne pas se coucher

sitcom ['sɪtkɔm] *n abbr* (*TV:* = *situation comedy*) série *f* comique

site [saɪt] *n* emplacement *m*, site *m*; (*also:* **building site**) chantier *m* ◆ *vt* placer

sit-in ['sɪtɪn] *n* (*demonstration*) sit-in *m inv*, occupation *f* de locaux

sitting ['sɪtɪŋ] *n* (*of assembly etc*) séance *f*; (*in canteen*) service *m*

sitting room *n* salon *m*

situated ['sɪtjueɪtɪd] *adj* situé(e)

situation [sɪtju'eɪʃən] *n* situation *f*; **"situations vacant/wanted"** (*BRIT*) "offres/demandes d'emploi"

six [sɪks] *num* six

sixteen [sɪks'ti:n] *num* seize

sixth ['sɪksθ] *adj* sixième; **the upper/lower sixth** (*BRIT SCOL*) la terminale/la première

sixty ['sɪkstɪ] *num* soixante

size [saɪz] *n* dimensions *fpl*; (*of person*) taille *f*; (*estate, area*) étendue *f*; (*of problem*) ampleur *f*; (*of company*) importance *f*; (*of clothing*) taille; (*of shoes*) pointure *f*; (*glue*) colle *f*; **I take size 14** (*of dress etc*) ≃ je prends du 42 *or* la taille 42; **the small/large size** (*of soap powder etc*) le petit/grand modèle; **it's the size of ...** c'est de la taille (*or* grosseur) de ..., c'est grand (*or* gros) comme ...; **cut to size** découpé(e) aux dimensions voulues

▶ **size up** *vt* juger, jauger

sizeable ['saɪzəbl] *adj* assez grand(e) *or* gros(se); assez important(e)

sizzle ['sɪzl] *vi* grésiller

skate [skeɪt] *n* patin *m*; (*fish: pl inv*) raie *f* ◆ *vi* patiner

▶ **skate over, skate around** *vt* (*problem, issue*) éluder

skateboard ['skeɪtbɔ:d] *n* skateboard *m*, planche *f* à roulettes

skateboarding ['skeɪtbɔ:dɪŋ] *n* skateboard *m*

skater ['skeɪtə*] *n* patineur/euse

skating ['skeɪtɪŋ] *n* patinage *m*

skating rink *n* patinoire *f*

skeleton ['skɛlɪtn] *n* squelette *m*; (*outline*) schéma *m*

skeleton staff *n* effectifs réduits

skeptical ['skɛptɪkl] (*US*) *adj* = **sceptical**

sketch [skɛtʃ] *n* (*drawing*) croquis *m*, esquisse *f*;

(THEAT) sketch m, saynète f ◆ vt esquisser, faire un croquis or une esquisse de

sketch book n carnet m à dessin

sketchy ['skɛtʃɪ] adj incomplet(ète), fragmentaire

skewer ['skjuːə*] n brochette f

ski [skiː] n ski m ◆ vi skier, faire du ski

ski boot n chaussure f de ski

skid [skɪd] n dérapage m ◆ vi déraper; **to go into a skid** déraper

skier ['skiːə*] n skieur/euse

skiing ['skiːɪŋ] n ski m; **to go skiing** (aller) faire du ski

ski jump n (ramp) tremplin m; (event) saut m à skis

skilful, (US) **skillful** ['skɪlful] adj habile, adroit(e)

ski lift n remonte-pente m inv

skill [skɪl] n (ability) habileté f, adresse f, talent m; (art, craft) technique(s) f(pl), compétences fpl

skilled [skɪld] adj habile, adroit(e); (worker) qualifié(e)

skim [skɪm] vt (milk) écrémer; (soup) écumer; (glide over) raser, effleurer ◆ vi: **to skim through** (fig) parcourir

skimmed milk [skɪmd-] n lait écrémé

skimp [skɪmp] vt (work) bâcler, faire à la va-vite; (cloth etc) lésiner sur

skimpy ['skɪmpɪ] adj étriqué(e); maigre

skin [skɪn] n peau f ◆ vt (fruit etc) éplucher; (animal) écorcher; **wet** or **soaked to the skin** trempé(e) jusqu'aux os

skin cancer n cancer m de la peau

skin-deep ['skɪn'diːp] adj superficiel(le)

skin diving n plongée sous-marine

skinhead ['skɪnhed] n skinhead m

skinny ['skɪnɪ] adj maigre, maigrichon(ne)

skintight ['skɪntaɪt] adj (dress etc) collant(e), ajusté(e)

skip [skɪp] n petit bond or saut; (container) benne f ◆ vi gambader, sautiller; (with rope) sauter à la corde ◆ vt (pass over) sauter; **to skip school** (esp US) faire l'école buissonnière

ski pass n forfait-skieur(s) m

ski pole n bâton m de ski

skipper ['skɪpə*] n (NAUT, SPORT) capitaine m ◆ vt (boat) commander; (team) être le chef de

skipping rope ['skɪpɪŋ-] n (BRIT) corde f à sauter

skirmish ['skɜːmɪʃ] n escarmouche f, accrochage m

skirt [skɜːt] n jupe f ◆ vt longer, contourner

skirting board ['skɜːtɪŋ-] n (BRIT) plinthe f

ski slope n piste f de ski

ski suit n combinaison f de ski

ski tow n = **ski lift**

skittle ['skɪtl] n quille f; **skittles** (game) (jeu m de) quilles fpl

skive [skaɪv] vi (BRIT col) tirer au flanc

skull [skʌl] n crâne m

skunk [skʌŋk] n mouffette f; (fur) sconse m

sky [skaɪ] n ciel m; **to praise sb to the skies** porter qn aux nues

skylight ['skaɪlaɪt] n lucarne f

skyscraper ['skaɪskreɪpə*] n gratte-ciel m inv

slab [slæb] n plaque f; dalle f; (of wood) bloc m; (of meat, cheese) tranche épaisse

slack [slæk] adj (loose) lâche, desserré(e); (slow) stagnant(e); (careless) négligent(e), peu sérieux(euse) or consciencieux(euse); (COMM: market) peu actif(ive); (: demand) faible; (period) creux(euse) ◆ n (in rope etc) mou m; **business is slack** les affaires vont mal

slacken ['slækn] (also: **slacken off**) vi ralentir, diminuer ◆ vt relâcher

slag heap n crassier m

slag off (BRIT inf) vt dire du mal de

slam [slæm] vt (door) (faire) claquer; (throw) jeter violemment, flanquer; (criticize) éreinter, démolir ◆ vi claquer

slander ['slɑːndə*] n calomnie f; (LAW) diffamation f ◆ vt calomnier; diffamer

slang [slæŋ] n argot m

slant [slɑːnt] n inclinaison f; (fig) angle m, point m de vue

slanted ['slɑːntɪd] adj tendancieux(euse)

slanting ['slɑːntɪŋ] adj en pente, incliné(e); couché(e)

slap [slæp] n claque f, gifle f; (on the back) tape f ◆ vt donner une claque or une gifle (or une tape) à ◆ adv (directly) tout droit, en plein

slapdash ['slæpdæʃ] adj (work) fait(e) sans soin or à la va-vite; (person) insouciant(e), négligent(e)

slapstick ['slæpstɪk] n (comedy) grosse farce (style tarte à la crème)

slap-up ['slæpʌp] adj (BRIT): **a slap-up meal** un repas extra or fameux

slash [slæʃ] vt entailler, taillader; (fig: prices) casser

slat [slæt] n (of wood) latte f, lame f

slate [sleɪt] n ardoise f ◆ vt (fig: criticize) éreinter, démolir

slaughter ['slɔːtə*] n carnage m, massacre m; (of animals) abattage m ◆ vt (animal) abattre; (people) massacrer

slaughterhouse ['slɔːtəhaus] n abattoir m

slave [sleɪv] n esclave m/f ◆ vi (also: **slave away**) trimer, travailler comme un forçat; **to slave (away) at sth/at doing sth** se tuer à qch/à faire qch

slavery ['sleɪvərɪ] n esclavage m

slay, pt **slew**, pp **slain** [sleɪ, sluː, sleɪn] vt (literary) tuer

sleazy ['sliːzɪ] adj miteux(euse), minable

sledge [sledʒ] n luge f

sledgehammer ['sledʒhæmə*] n marteau m de forgeron

sleek [sliːk] adj (hair, fur) brillant(e), luisant(e); (car, *boat*) aux lignes pures or élégantes

sleep [sli:p] *n* sommeil *m* ♦ *vi, pt, pp* **slept** [slept] dormir; (*spend night*) dormir, coucher ♦ *vt:* **we can sleep 4** on peut coucher or loger 4 personnes; **to go to sleep** s'endormir; **to have a good night's sleep** passer une bonne nuit; **to put to sleep** (*patient*) endormir; (*animal: euphemism: kill*) piquer; **to sleep lightly** avoir le sommeil léger; **to sleep with sb** (*euphemism*) coucher avec qn
▸ **sleep around** *vi* coucher à droite et à gauche
▸ **sleep in** *vi* (*lie late*) faire la grasse matinée; (*oversleep*) se réveiller trop tard

sleeper ['sli:pə*] *n* (*person*) dormeur/euse; (*BRIT RAIL: on track*) traverse *f*; (*: train*) train *m* de voitures-lits; (*: carriage*) wagon-lits *m*, voiture-lits *f*; (*: berth*) couchette *f*

sleeping bag *n* sac *m* de couchage

sleeping car *n* wagon-lits *m*, voiture-lits *f*

sleeping partner *n* (*BRIT COMM*) = **silent partner**

sleeping pill *n* somnifère *m*

sleepless ['sli:plɪs] *adj:* **a sleepless night** une nuit blanche

sleepwalker ['sli:pwɔ:kə*] *n* somnambule *m/f*

sleepy ['sli:pɪ] *adj* qui a envie de dormir; (*fig*) endormi(e); **to be** or **feel sleepy** avoir sommeil, avoir envie de dormir

sleet [sli:t] *n* neige fondue

sleeve [sli:v] *n* manche *f*; (*of record*) pochette *f*

sleigh [sleɪ] *n* traîneau *m*

sleight [slaɪt] *n:* **sleight of hand** tour *m* de passe-passe

slender ['slendə*] *adj* svelte, mince; (*fig*) faible, ténu(e)

slept [slept] *pt, pp of* **sleep**

slew [slu:] *vi* (*also:* **slew round**) virer, pivoter ♦ *pt of* **slay**

slice [slaɪs] *n* tranche *f*; (*round*) rondelle *f* ♦ *vt* couper en tranches (or en rondelles); **sliced bread** pain *m* en tranches

slick [slɪk] *adj* brillant(e) en apparence; mielleux(euse) ♦ *n* (*also:* **oil slick**) nappe *f* de pétrole, marée noire

slide [slaɪd] *n* (*in playground*) toboggan *m*; (*PHOT*) diapositive *f*; (*BRIT: also:* **hair slide**) barrette *f*; (*microscope slide*) (lame *f*) porte-objet *m*; (*in prices*) chute *f*, baisse *f* ♦ *vb, pt, pp* **slid** [slɪd] *vt* (faire) glisser ♦ *vi* glisser; **to let things slide** (*fig*) laisser les choses aller à la dérive

sliding ['slaɪdɪŋ] *adj* (*door*) coulissant(e); **sliding roof** (*AUT*) toit ouvrant

sliding scale *n* échelle *f* mobile

slight [slaɪt] *adj* (*slim*) mince, menu(e); (*frail*) frêle; (*trivial*) faible, insignifiant(e); (*small*) petit(e), léger(ère) (*before n*) ♦ *n* offense *f*, affront *m* ♦ *vt* (*offend*) blesser, offenser; **the slightest** le (or la) moindre; **not in the slightest** pas le moins du monde, pas du tout

slightly ['slaɪtlɪ] *adv* légèrement, un peu; **slightly built** fluet(te)

slim [slɪm] *adj* mince ♦ *vi* maigrir, suivre un régime amaigrissant

slime [slaɪm] *n* vase *f*; substance visqueuse

slimming [slɪmɪŋ] *n* amaigrissement *m* ♦ *adj* (*diet, pills*) amaigrissant(e), pour maigrir

sling [slɪŋ] *n* (*MED*) écharpe *f* ♦ *vt, pt, pp* **slung** [slʌŋ] lancer, jeter; **to have one's arm in a sling** avoir le bras en écharpe

slip [slɪp] *n* faux pas; (*mistake*) erreur *f*, bévue *f*; (*underskirt*) combinaison *f*; (*of paper*) petite feuille, fiche *f* ♦ *vt* (*slide*) glisser ♦ *vi* (*slide*) glisser; (*move smoothly*): **to slip into/out of** se glisser or se faufiler dans/hors de; (*decline*) baisser; **to let a chance slip by** laisser passer une occasion; **to slip sth on/off** enfiler/enlever qch; **it slipped from her hand** cela lui a glissé des mains; **to give sb the slip** fausser compagnie à qn; **a slip of the tongue** un lapsus
▸ **slip away** *vi* s'esquiver
▸ **slip in** *vt* glisser
▸ **slip out** *vi* sortir
▸ **slip up** *vi* faire une erreur, gaffer

slipped disc [slɪpt-] *n* hernie discale

slipper ['slɪpə*] *n* pantoufle *f*

slippery ['slɪpərɪ] *adj* glissant(e); (*fig: person*) insaisissable

slip road *n* (*BRIT: to motorway*) bretelle *f* d'accès

slip-up ['slɪpʌp] *n* bévue *f*

slipway ['slɪpweɪ] *n* cale *f* (de construction or de lancement)

slit [slɪt] *n* fente *f*; (*cut*) incision *f*; (*tear*) déchirure *f* ♦ *vt, pt, pp* **slit** fendre; couper; inciser; déchirer; **to slit sb's throat** trancher la gorge à qn

slither ['slɪðə*] *vi* glisser, déraper

sliver ['slɪvə*] *n* (*of glass, wood*) éclat *m*; (*of cheese, sausage*) petit morceau

slob [slɔb] *n* (*col*) rustaud/e

slog [slɔg] *n* (*BRIT*) gros effort; tâche fastidieuse ♦ *vi* travailler très dur

slogan ['sləugən] *n* slogan *m*

slope [sləup] *n* pente *f*; (*side of mountain*) versant *m*; (*slant*) inclinaison *f* ♦ *vi:* **to slope down** être or descendre en pente; **to slope up** monter

sloping ['sləupɪŋ] *adj* en pente, incliné(e); (*handwriting*) penché(e)

sloppy ['slɔpɪ] *adj* (*work*) peu soigné(e), bâclé(e); (*appearance*) négligé(e), débraillé(e); (*film etc*) sentimental(e)

slot [slɔt] *n* fente *f*; (*fig: in timetable, RADIO, TV*) créneau *m*, plage *f* ♦ *vt:* **to slot into** encastrer or insérer dans ♦ *vi:* **to slot into** s'encastrer or s'insérer dans

sloth [sləuθ] *n* (*vice*) paresse *f*; (*ZOOL*) paresseux *m*

slouch [slautʃ] *vi* avoir le dos rond, être voûté(e)
▸ **slouch about, slouch around** *vi* traîner à ne rien faire

slovenly ['slʌvənlɪ] *adj* sale, débraillé(e), négligé(e)

slow [sləʊ] *adj* lent(e); *(watch)*: **to be slow** retarder ♦ *adv* lentement ♦ *vt, vi (also:* **slow down, slow up)** ralentir; **"slow"** *(road sign)* "ralentir"; **at a slow speed** à petite vitesse; **to be slow to act/decide** être lent à agir/décider; **my watch is 20 minutes slow** ma montre retarde de 20 minutes; **business is slow** les affaires marchent au ralenti; **to go slow** *(driver)* rouler lentement; *(in industrial dispute)* faire la grève perlée

slowly ['sləʊlɪ] *adv* lentement

slow motion *n*: **in slow motion** au ralenti

sludge [slʌdʒ] *n* boue *f*

slug [slʌg] *n* limace *f*; *(bullet)* balle *f*

sluggish ['slʌgɪʃ] *adj* mou(molle), lent(e); *(business, sales)* stagnant(e)

sluice [slu:s] *n* écluse *f*; *(also:* **sluice gate)** vanne *f* ♦ *vt*: **to sluice down** *or* **out** laver à grande eau

slum [slʌm] *n* taudis *m*

slump [slʌmp] *n* baisse soudaine, effondrement *m*; crise *f* ♦ *vi* s'effondrer, s'affaisser

slung [slʌŋ] *pt, pp of* **sling**

slur [slɜ:*] *n* bredouillement *m*; *(smear)*: **slur (on)** atteinte *f* (à); insinuation *f* (contre) ♦ *vt* mal articuler; **to be a slur on** porter atteinte à

slush [slʌʃ] *n* neige fondue

slut [slʌt] *n* souillon *f*

sly [slaɪ] *adj* rusé(e), sournois(e); **on the sly** en cachette

smack [smæk] *n (slap)* tape *f*; *(on face)* gifle *f* ♦ *vt* donner une tape à; gifler; *(child)* donner la fessée à ♦ *vi*: **to smack of** avoir des relents de, sentir ♦ *adv (col)*: **it fell smack in the middle** c'est tombé en plein milieu *or* en plein dedans; **to smack one's lips** se lécher les babines

small [smɔ:l] *adj* petit(e); *(letter)* minuscule ♦ *n*: **the small of the back** le creux des reins; **to get** *or* **grow smaller** diminuer; **to make smaller** *(amount, income)* diminuer; *(object, garment)* rapetisser; **a small shopkeeper** un petit commerçant

small ads *npl (BRIT)* petites annonces

small change *n* petite *or* menue monnaie

smallholder ['smɔ:lhəʊldə*] *n (BRIT)* petit cultivateur

small hours *npl*: **in the small hours** au petit matin

smallpox ['smɔ:lpɒks] *n* variole *f*

small talk *n* menus propos

smart [smɑ:t] *adj* élégant(e), chic *inv*; *(clever)* intelligent(e); *(pej)* futé(e); *(quick)* vif(vive), prompt(e) ♦ *vi* faire mal, brûler; **the smart set** le beau monde; **to look smart** être élégant(e); **my eyes are smarting** j'ai les yeux irrités *or* qui me piquent

smart card *n* carte *f* à puce

smarten up ['smɑ:tn-] *vi* devenir plus élégant(e), se faire beau(belle) ♦ *vt* rendre plus élégant(e)

smash [smæʃ] *n (also:* **smash-up)** collision *f*, accident *m*; *(sound)* fracas *m* ♦ *vt* casser, briser, fracasser; *(opponent)* écraser; *(hopes)* ruiner, détruire; *(SPORT: record)* pulvériser ♦ *vi* se briser, se fracasser; s'écraser

► **smash up** *vt (car)* bousiller; *(room)* tout casser dans

smashing ['smæʃɪŋ] *adj (col)* formidable

smattering ['smætərɪŋ] *n*: **a smattering of** quelques notions de

smear [smɪə*] *n* tache *f*, salissure *f*; trace *f*; *(MED)* frottis *m*; *(insult)* calomnie *f* ♦ *vt* enduire; *(fig)* porter atteinte à; **his hands were smeared with oil/ink** il avait les mains maculées de cambouis/d'encre

smear campaign *n* campagne *f* de dénigrement

smell [smɛl] *n* odeur *f*; *(sense)* odorat *m* ♦ *vb, pt, pp* **smelt** *or* **smelled** [smɛlt, smɛld] *vt* sentir ♦ *vi (food etc)*: **to smell (of)** sentir; *(pej)* sentir mauvais; **it smells good** ça sent bon

smelly ['smɛlɪ] *adj* qui sent mauvais, malodorant(e)

smile [smaɪl] *n* sourire *m* ♦ *vi* sourire

smirk [smɜ:k] *n* petit sourire suffisant *or* affecté

smock [smɒk] *n* blouse *f*, sarrau *m*

smog [smɒg] *n* brouillard mêlé de fumée

smoke [sməʊk] *n* fumée *f* ♦ *vt, vi* fumer; **to have a smoke** fumer une cigarette; **do you smoke?** est-ce que vous fumez?; **to go up in smoke** *(house etc)* brûler; *(fig)* partir en fumée

smoked ['sməʊkt] *adj (bacon, glass)* fumé(e)

smoker ['sməʊkə*] *n (person)* fumeur/euse; *(RAIL)* wagon *m* fumeurs

smoke screen *n* rideau *m or* écran *m* de fumée; *(fig)* paravent *m*

smoking ['sməʊkɪŋ] *n*: **"no smoking"** *(sign)* "défense de fumer"; **he's given up smoking** il a arrêté de fumer

smoking compartment, *(US)* **smoking car** *n* wagon *m* fumeurs

smoky ['sməʊkɪ] *adj* enfumé(e)

smolder ['sməʊldə*] *vi (US)* = **smoulder**

smooth [smu:ð] *adj* lisse; *(sauce)* onctueux(euse), *(flavour, whisky)* moelleux(euse); *(cigarette)* doux(douce); *(movement)* régulier(ière), sans à-coups *or* heurts; *(landing, takeoff)* en douceur, *(flight)* sans secousses; *(person)* doucereux(euse), mielleux(euse) ♦ *vt* lisser, défroisser; *(also:* **smooth out)** *creases, difficulties)* faire disparaître

► **smooth over** *vt*: **to smooth things over** *(fig)* arranger les choses

smother ['smʌðə*] *vt* étouffer

smoulder, *(US)* **smolder** ['sməʊldə*] *vi* couver

smudge [smʌdʒ] *n* tache *f*, bavure *f* ♦ *vt* salir, maculer

smug [smʌg] *adj* suffisant(e), content(e) de soi

smuggle ['smʌgl] *vt* passer en contrebande *or* en fraude; **to smuggle in/out** (*goods etc*) faire entrer/sortir clandestinement *or* en fraude

smuggler ['smʌglə*] *n* contrebandier/ière

smuggling ['smʌglɪŋ] *n* contrebande *f*

smutty ['smʌtɪ] *adj* (*fig*) grossier(ière), obscène

snack [snæk] *n* casse-croûte *m inv*; **to have a snack** prendre un en-cas, manger quelque chose (de léger)

snack bar *n* snack(-bar) *m*

snag [snæg] *n* inconvénient *m*, difficulté *f*

snail [sneɪl] *n* escargot *m*

snake [sneɪk] *n* serpent *m*

snap [snæp] *n* (*sound*) claquement *m*, bruit sec; (*photograph*) photo *f*, instantané *m*; (*game*) sorte de jeu de bataille ◆ *adj* subit(e), fait(e) sans réfléchir ◆ *vt* faire claquer; (*break*) casser net; (*photograph*) prendre un instantané de ◆ *vi* se casser net *or* avec un bruit sec; (*fig: person*) craquer; **to snap at sb** (*person*) parler d'un ton brusque à qn; (*: dog*) essayer de mordre qn; **to snap open/shut** s'ouvrir/se refermer brusquement; **to snap one's fingers at** (*fig*) se moquer de; **a cold snap** (*of weather*) un refroidissement soudain de la température

▶ **snap off** *vt* (*break*) casser net

▶ **snap up** *vt* sauter sur, saisir

snappy ['snæpɪ] *adj* prompt(e); (*slogan*) qui a du punch; **make it snappy!** (*col: hurry up*) grouille-toi, magne-toi!

snapshot ['snæpʃɔt] *n* photo *f*, instantané *m*

snare [snɛə*] *n* piège *m* ◆ *vt* attraper, prendre au piège

snarl [snɑːl] *n* grondement *m or* grognement *m* féroce ◆ *vi* gronder ◆ *vt*: **to get snarled up** (*wool, plans*) s'emmêler; (*traffic*) se bloquer

snatch [snætʃ] *n* (*fig*) vol *m*; (*BRIT: small amount*): **snatches of** des fragments *mpl or* bribes *fpl* de ◆ *vt* saisir (*d'un geste vif*); (*steal*) voler ◆ *vi*: **don't snatch!** doucement!; **to snatch a sandwich** manger *or* avaler un sandwich à la hâte; **to snatch some sleep** arriver à dormir un peu

▶ **snatch up** *vt* saisir, s'emparer de

sneak [sniːk] *vi*: **to sneak in/out** entrer/sortir furtivement *or* à la dérobée ◆ *vt*: **to sneak a look at sth** regarder furtivement qch

sneakers ['sniːkəz] *npl* chaussures *fpl* de tennis *or* basket

sneer [snɪə*] *n* ricanement *m* ◆ *vi* ricaner, sourire d'un air sarcastique; **to sneer at sb/sth** se moquer de qn/qch avec mépris

sneeze [sniːz] *n* éternuement *m* ◆ *vi* éternuer

sniff [snɪf] *n* reniflement *m* ◆ *vi* renifler ◆ *vt* renifler, flairer; (*glue, drug*) sniffer, respirer

▶ **sniff at** *vt fus*: **it's not to be sniffed at** il ne faut pas cracher dessus, ce n'est pas à dédaigner

snigger ['snɪgə*] *n* ricanement *m*; rire moqueur

◆ *vi* ricaner; pouffer de rire

snip [snɪp] *n* petit bout; (*bargain*) (bonne) occasion *or* affaire *f* ◆ *vt* couper

sniper ['snaɪpə*] *n* (*marksman*) tireur embusqué

snippet ['snɪpɪt] *n* bribes *fpl*

snob [snɔb] *n* snob *m/f*

snobbish ['snɔbɪʃ] *adj* snob *inv*

snooker ['snuːkə*] *n* sorte de jeu de billard

snoop [snuːp] *vi*: **to snoop on sb** espionner qn; **to snoop about somewhere** fourrer son nez quelque part

snooze [snuːz] *n* petit somme ◆ *vi* faire un petit somme

snore [snɔː*] *vi* ronfler ◆ *n* ronflement *m*

snorkel ['snɔːkl] *n* (*of swimmer*) tuba *m*

snort [snɔːt] *n* grognement *m* ◆ *vi* grogner; (*horse*) renâcler ◆ *vt* (*col: drugs*) sniffer

snout [snaut] *n* museau *m*

snow [snəu] *n* neige *f* ◆ *vi* neiger ◆ *vt*: **to be snowed under with work** être débordé(e) de travail

snowball ['snəubɔːl] *n* boule *f* de neige

snowbound ['snəubaund] *adj* enneigé(e), bloqué(e) par la neige

snowdrift ['snəudrɪft] *n* congère *f*

snowdrop ['snəudrɔp] *n* perce-neige *m*

snowfall ['snəufɔːl] *n* chute *f* de neige

snowflake ['snəufleɪk] *n* flocon *m* de neige

snowman ['snəumæn] *n* bonhomme *m* de neige

snowplough, (*US*) **snowplow** ['snəuplau] *n* chasse-neige *m inv*

snowshoe ['snəuʃuː] *n* raquette *f* (*pour la neige*)

snowstorm ['snəustɔːm] *n* tempête *f* de neige

snub [snʌb] *vt* repousser, snober ◆ *n* rebuffade *f*

snub-nosed [snʌb'nəuzd] *adj* au nez retroussé

snuff [snʌf] *n* tabac *m* à priser ◆ *vt* (*also*: **snuff out**: *candle*) moucher

snug [snʌg] *adj* douillet(te), confortable; **it's a snug fit** c'est bien ajusté(e)

snuggle ['snʌgl] *vi*: **to snuggle down in bed/up to sb** se pelotonner dans son lit/contre qn

KEYWORD

so [səu] *adv* **1** (*thus, likewise*) ainsi, de cette façon; **if so** si oui; **so do** *or* **have I** moi aussi; **it's 5 o'clock – so it is!** il est 5 heures – en effet! *or* c'est vrai!; **I hope/think so** je l'espère/le crois; **so far** jusqu'ici, jusqu'à maintenant; (*in past*) jusque-là; **quite so!** exactement!, c'est bien ça!; **even so** quand même, tout de même

2 (*in comparisons etc: to such a degree*) si, tellement; **so big (that)** si *or* tellement grand (que); **she's not so clever as her brother** elle n'est pas aussi intelligente que son frère

3: **so much** *adj*, *adv* tant (de); **I've got so much work** j'ai tant de travail; **I love you so much** je vous aime tant; **so many** tant (de)

4 (phrases): **10 or so** à peu près or environ 10; **so long!** (inf: goodbye) au revoir!, à un de ces jours!; **so to speak** pour ainsi dire; **so (what)?** (col) (bon) et alors?, et après?

♦ conj **1** (expressing purpose): **so as to do** pour faire, afin de faire; **so (that)** pour que or afin que +sub

2 (expressing result) donc, par conséquent; **so that** si bien que, de (telle) sorte que; **so that's the reason!** c'est donc (pour) ça!

soak [səʊk] vt faire or laisser tremper ♦ vi tremper; **to be soaked through** être trempé jusqu'aux os
▶ **soak in** vi pénétrer, être absorbé(e)
▶ **soak up** vt absorber

soaking ['səʊkɪŋ] adj (also: **soaking wet**) trempé(e)

soap [səʊp] n savon m

soapflakes ['səʊpfleɪks] npl paillettes fpl de savon

soap opera n feuilleton télévisé (quotidienneté réaliste ou embellie)

soap powder n lessive f, détergent m

soapy ['səʊpɪ] adj savonneux(euse)

soar [sɔ:*] vi monter (en flèche), s'élancer; **soaring prices** prix qui grimpent

sob [sɔb] n sanglot m ♦ vi sangloter

sober ['səʊbə*] adj qui n'est pas (or plus) ivre; (sedate) sérieux(euse), sensé(e); (moderate) mesuré(e); (colour, style) sobre, discrète te
▶ **sober up** vt dégriser ♦ vi se dégriser

so-called ['səʊ'kɔ:ld] adj soi-disant inv

soccer ['sɔkə*] n football m

social ['səʊʃl] adj social(e) ♦ n (petite) fête

social club n amicale f, foyer m

socialism ['səʊʃəlɪzəm] n socialisme m

socialist ['səʊʃəlɪst] adj, n socialiste (m/f)

socialize ['səʊʃəlaɪz] vi voir or rencontrer des gens, se faire des amis; **to socialize with** fréquenter; lier connaissance or parler avec

social security n aide sociale

social work n assistance sociale

social worker n assistant/e social(e)

society [sə'saɪətɪ] n société f; (club) société, association f; (also: **high society**) (haute) société, grand monde ♦ cpd (party) mondain(e)

sociology [səʊsɪ'ɔlədʒɪ] n sociologie f

sock [sɔk] n chaussette f ♦ vt (col: hit) flanquer un coup à; **to pull one's socks up** (fig) se secouer (les puces)

socket ['sɔkɪt] n cavité f; (ELEC: also: **wall socket**) prise f de courant; (: for light bulb) douille f

sod [sɔd] n (of earth) motte f; (BRIT col!) con m (!), salaud m (!)
▶ **sod off** vi: **sod off!** (BRIT col!) fous le camp!, va te faire foutre! (!)

soda ['səʊdə] n (CHEM) soude f; (also: **soda water**)

eau f de Seltz; (US: also: **soda pop**) soda m

sofa ['səʊfə] n sofa m, canapé m

soft [sɔft] adj (not rough) doux(douce); (not hard) doux, mou(molle); (not loud) doux, léger(ère); (kind) doux, gentil(le); (weak) indulgent(e); (stupid) stupide, débile

soft drink n boisson non alcoolisée

soften ['sɔfn] vt (r)amollir; adoucir; atténuer ♦ vi se ramollir; s'adoucir; s'atténuer

softly ['sɔftlɪ] adv doucement; légèrement; gentiment

softness ['sɔftnɪs] n douceur f

software ['sɔftweə*] n logiciel m, software m

soggy ['sɔgɪ] adj trempé(e); détrempé(e)

soil [sɔɪl] n (earth) sol m, terre f ♦ vt salir; (fig) souiller

solar ['səʊlə*] adj solaire

solar panel n panneau m solaire

solar power n énergie f solaire

sold [səʊld] pt, pp of **sell**

solder ['səʊldə*] vt souder (au fil à souder) ♦ n soudure f

soldier ['səʊldʒə*] n soldat m, militaire m ♦ vi: **soldier on** persévérer, s'accrocher; **toy soldier** petit soldat

sole [səʊl] n (of foot) plante f; (of shoe) semelle f; (fish: pl inv) sole f ♦ adj seul(e), unique; **the sole reason** la seule et unique raison

solemn ['sɔləm] adj solennel(le); sérieux(euse), grave

sole trader n (COMM) chef m d'entreprise individuelle

solicit [sə'lɪsɪt] vt (request) solliciter ♦ vi (prostitute) racoler

solicitor [sə'lɪsɪtə*] n (BRIT: for wills etc) = notaire m; (: in court) = avocat m

solid ['sɔlɪd] adj (not hollow) plein(e), compact(e), massif(ive); (strong, sound, reliable, not liquid) solide; (meal) consistant(e), substantiel(le); (vote) unanime ♦ n solide m; **to be on solid ground** être sur la terre ferme; (fig) être en terrain sûr; **we waited 2 solid hours** nous avons attendu deux heures entières

solidarity [sɔlɪ'dærɪtɪ] n solidarité f

solitary ['sɔlɪtərɪ] adj solitaire

solitary confinement n (LAW) isolement m (cellulaire)

solo ['səʊləʊ] n solo m

soloist ['səʊləʊɪst] n soliste m/f

soluble ['sɔljʊbl] adj soluble

solution [sə'lu:ʃən] n solution f

solve [sɔlv] vt résoudre

solvent ['sɔlvənt] adj (COMM) solvable ♦ n (CHEM) (dis)solvant m

┌─────────────┐
│ **KEYWORD** │
└─────────────┘

some [sʌm] adj **1** (a certain amount or number of): **some tea/water/ice cream** du thé/de l'eau/

de la glace; **some children/apples** des enfants/pommes

2 (*certain: in contrasts*): **some people say that ...** il y a des gens qui disent que ...; **some films were excellent, but most ...** certains films étaient excellents, mais la plupart ...

3 (*unspecified*): **some woman was asking for you** il y avait une dame qui vous demandait; **he was asking for some book (or other)** il demandait un livre quelconque; **some day** un de ces jours; **some day next week** un jour de la semaine prochaine; **after some time** après un certain temps; **at some length** assez longuement; **in some form or another** sous une forme ou une autre, sous une forme quelconque

♦ *pron* **1** (*a certain number*) quelques-un(e)s, certain(e)s; **I've got some** (*books etc*) j'en ai (quelques-uns); **some (of them) have been sold** certains ont été vendus

2 (*a certain amount*) un peu; **I've got some** (*money, milk*) j'en ai (un peu); **would you like some?** est-ce que vous en voulez?, en voulez-vous?

♦ *adv*: **some 10 people** quelque 10 personnes, 10 personnes environ

somebody ['sʌmbədɪ] *pron* quelqu'un; **somebody or other** quelqu'un, je ne sais qui

somehow ['sʌmhaʊ] *adv* d'une façon ou d'une autre; (*for some reason*) pour une raison ou une autre

someone ['sʌmwʌn] *pron* = **somebody**

someplace ['sʌmpleɪs] *adv* (*US*) = **somewhere**

somersault ['sʌməsɔːlt] *n* culbute *f*, saut périlleux ♦ *vi* faire la culbute *or* un saut périlleux; (*car*) faire un tonneau

something ['sʌmθɪŋ] *pron* quelque chose *m*; **something interesting** quelque chose d'intéressant; **something to do** quelque chose à faire; **he's something like me** il est un peu comme moi; **it's something of a problem** il y a là un problème

sometime ['sʌmtaɪm] *adv* (*in future*) un de ces jours, un jour ou l'autre; (*in past*): **sometime last month** au cours du mois dernier

sometimes ['sʌmtaɪmz] *adv* quelquefois, parfois

somewhat ['sʌmwɔt] *adv* quelque peu, un peu

somewhere ['sʌmwɛə*] *adv* quelque part; **somewhere else** ailleurs, autre part

son [sʌn] *n* fils *m*

song [sɔŋ] *n* chanson *f*

son-in-law ['sʌnɪnlɔː] *n* gendre *m*, beau-fils *m*

soon [suːn] *adv* bientôt; (*early*) tôt; **soon afterwards** peu après; **quite soon** sous peu; **how soon can you do it?** combien de temps vous faut-il pour le faire, au plus pressé?; **how soon can you come back?** quand *or* dans combien de temps pouvez-vous revenir, au plus tôt?; **see you soon!** à bientôt!; *see also* **as**

sooner ['suːnə*] *adv* (*time*) plus tôt; (*preference*): **I would sooner do** j'aimerais autant *or* je préférerais faire; **sooner or later** tôt ou tard; **no sooner said than done** sitôt dit, sitôt fait; **the sooner the better** le plus tôt sera le mieux; **no sooner had we left than ...** à peine étions-nous partis que ...

soot [sʊt] *n* suie *f*

soothe [suːð] *vt* calmer, apaiser

sophisticated [sə'fɪstɪkeɪtɪd] *adj* raffiné(e), sophistiqué(e); (*system etc*) très perfectionné(e), sophistiqué

sophomore ['sɔfəmɔː*] *n* (*US*) étudiant/e de seconde année

sopping ['sɔpɪŋ] *adj* (*also*: **sopping wet**) tout(e) trempé(e)

soppy ['sɔpɪ] *adj* (*pej*) sentimental(e)

soprano [sə'prɑːnəʊ] *n* (*voice*) soprano *m*; (*singer*) soprano *m/f*

sorcerer ['sɔːsərə*] *n* sorcier *m*

sore [sɔː*] *adj* (*painful*) douloureux(euse), sensible; (*offended*) contrarié(e), vexé(e) ♦ *n* plaie *f*; **to have a sore throat** avoir mal à la gorge; **it's a sore point** (*fig*) c'est un point délicat

sorely ['sɔːlɪ] *adv* (*tempted*) fortement

sorrow ['sɔrəʊ] *n* peine *f*, chagrin *m*

sorry ['sɔrɪ] *adj* désolé(e); (*condition, excuse, tale*) triste, déplorable; (*sight*) désolant(e); **sorry!** pardon!, excusez-moi!; **to feel sorry for sb** plaindre qn; **I'm sorry to hear that ...** je suis désolé(e) *or* navré(e) d'apprendre que ...; **to be sorry about sth** regretter qch

sort [sɔːt] *n* genre *m*, espèce *f*, sorte *f*; (*make: of coffee, car etc*) marque *f* ♦ *vt* (*also*: **sort out**: *papers*) trier; classer; ranger; (: *letters etc*) trier; (: *problems*) résoudre, régler; (*COMPUT*) trier; **what sort do you want?** quelle sorte *or* quel genre voulez-vous?; **what sort of car?** quelle marque de voiture?; **I'll do nothing of the sort!** je ne ferai rien de tel!; **it's sort of awkward** (*col*) c'est plutôt gênant

sorting office ['sɔːtɪŋ-] *n* (*POST*) bureau *m* de tri

SOS *n abbr* (= *save our souls*) SOS *m*

so-so ['səʊsəʊ] *adv* comme ci comme ça

sought [sɔːt] *pt*, *pp of* **seek**

soul [səʊl] *n* âme *f*; **the poor soul had nowhere to sleep** le pauvre n'avait nulle part où dormir; **I didn't see a soul** je n'ai vu (absolument) personne

soulful ['səʊlfʊl] *adj* plein(e) de sentiment

sound [saʊnd] *adj* (*healthy*) en bonne santé, sain(e); (*safe, not damaged*) solide, en bon état; (*reliable, not superficial*) sérieux(euse), solide; (*sensible*) sensé(e) ♦ *adv*: **sound asleep** dormant d'un profond sommeil ♦ *n* (*noise*) son *m*; bruit *m*; (*GEO*) détroit *m*, bras *m* de mer ♦ *vt* (*alarm*) sonner; (*also*: **sound out**: *opinions*) sonder ♦ *vi* sonner, retentir; (*fig: seem*) sembler (être); **to be of sound mind** être sain(e) d'esprit; **I don't like the sound of it** ça ne me dit rien qui vaille; **to sound one's horn** (*AUT*) klaxonner, actionner son avertisseur; **to sound like**

ressembler à; **it sounds as if ...** il semblerait que ..., j'ai l'impression que ...

► **sound off** vi (col): **to sound off (about)** la ramener (sur)

sound barrier n mur m du son

sound bite n phrase toute faite (pour être citée dans les médias)

sound effects npl bruitage m

soundly ['saundlı] adv (sleep) profondément; (beat) complètement, à plate couture

soundproof ['saundpru:f] vt insonoriser ◆ adj insonorisé(e)

soundtrack ['saundtræk] n (of film) bande f sonore

soup [su:p] n soupe f, potage m; **in the soup** (fig) dans le pétrin

soup plate n assiette creuse or à soupe

soupspoon ['su:pspu:n] n cuiller f à soupe

sour ['saua*] adj aigre, acide; (milk) tourné(e), aigre; (fig) acerbe, aigre; revêche; **to go** or **turn sour** (milk, wine) tourner; (fig: relationship, plans) mal tourner; **it's sour grapes** c'est du dépit

source [sɔ:s] n source f; **I have it from a reliable source that** je sais de source sûre que

south [sauθ] n sud m ◆ adj sud inv, du sud ◆ adv au sud, vers le sud; **(to the) south of** au sud de; **to travel south** aller en direction du sud; **the South of France** le Sud de la France, le Midi

South Africa n Afrique f du Sud

South African adj sud-africain(e) ◆ n Sud-Africain/e

South America n Amérique f du Sud

South American adj sud-américain(e) ◆ n Sud-Américain/e

south-east [sauθ'i:st] n sud-est m

southerly ['sʌðəlɪ] adj du sud; au sud

southern ['sʌðən] adj (du) sud; méridional(e); **with a southern aspect** orienté(e) or exposé(e) au sud; **the southern hemisphere** l'hémisphère sud or austral

South Pole n Pôle m Sud

South Wales n sud m du Pays de Galles

southward(s) ['sauθwəd(z)] adv vers le sud

south-west [sauθ'west] n sud-ouest m

souvenir [su:və'nıə*] n souvenir m (objet)

sovereign ['sɔvrɪn] adj, n souverain/e

soviet ['səuvɪət] adj soviétique

sow n [sau] truie f ◆ vt [səu], pt **sowed** pt, pp **sown** [səun] semer

soya ['sɔɪə], (US) **soy** [sɔɪ] n: **soya bean** graine f de soja; **soya sauce** sauce f au soja

spa [spa:] n (town) station thermale; (US: also: **health spa**) établissement m de cure de rajeunissement

space [speɪs] n (gen) espace m; (room) place f; espace; (length of time) laps m de temps ◆ cpd spatial(e) ◆ vt (also: **space out**) espacer; **to clear a**

space for sth faire de la place pour qch; **in a confined space** dans un espace réduit or restreint; **in a short space of time** dans peu de temps; **(with)in the space of an hour** en l'espace d'une heure

spacecraft ['speɪskrɑ:ft] n engin spatial

spaceman ['speɪsmæn] n astronaute m, cosmonaute m

spaceship ['speɪsʃɪp] n engin or vaisseau spatial

spacing ['speɪsɪŋ] n espacement m; **single/double spacing** (TYP etc) interligne m simple/double

spacious ['speɪʃəs] adj spacieux(euse), grand(e)

spade [speɪd] n (tool) bêche f, pelle f; (child's) pelle; **spades** npl (CARDS) pique m

Spain [speɪn] n Espagne f

span [spæn] n (of bird, plane) envergure f; (of arch) portée f; (in time) espace m de temps, durée f ◆ vt enjamber, franchir; (fig) couvrir, embrasser

Spaniard ['spænjəd] n Espagnol/e

spaniel ['spænjəl] n épagneul m

Spanish ['spænɪʃ] adj espagnol(e), d'Espagne ◆ n (LING) espagnol m; **the Spanish** npl les Espagnols

Spanish omelette omelette f à l'espagnole

spank [spæŋk] vt donner une fessée à

spanner ['spænə*] n (BRIT) clé f (de mécanicien)

spare [spɛə*] adj de réserve, de rechange; (surplus) de or en trop, de reste ◆ n (part) pièce f de rechange, pièce détachée ◆ vt (do without) se passer de; (afford to give) donner, accorder, passer; (refrain from hurting) épargner; (refrain from using) ménager; (surplus) en surplus, de trop; **there are 2 going spare** (BRIT) il y en a 2 de disponible; **to spare no expense** ne pas reculer devant la dépense; **can you spare the time?** est-ce que vous avez le temps?; **there is no time to spare** il n'y a pas de temps à perdre; **I've a few minutes to spare** je dispose de quelques minutes

spare part n pièce f de rechange, pièce détachée

spare time n moments mpl de loisir

spare wheel n (AUT) roue f de secours

sparingly ['spɛərɪŋlɪ] adv avec modération

spark [spa:k] n étincelle f; (fig) étincelle, lueur f

spark(ing) plug ['spa:k(ɪŋ)-] n bougie f

sparkle ['spa:kl] n scintillement m, étincellement m, éclat m ◆ vi étinceler, scintiller; (bubble) pétiller

sparkling ['spa:klɪŋ] adj étincelant(e), scintillant(e); (wine) mousseux(euse), pétillant(e)

sparrow ['spærəu] n moineau m

sparse [spa:s] adj clairsemé(e)

spartan ['spa:tən] adj (fig) spartiate

spasm ['spæzəm] n (MED) spasme m; (fig) accès m

spasmodic [spæz'mɔdɪk] adj (fig) intermittent(e)

spastic ['spæstɪk] n handicapé/e moteur

spat [spæt] pt, pp of **spit** ◆ n (US) prise f de bec

spate [speɪt] n (fig): **spate of** avalanche f or torrent m de; **in spate** (river) en crue

spawn [spɔːn] *vt* pondre; (*pej*) engendrer ♦ *vi* frayer ♦ *n* frai *m*

speak, *pt* **spoke**, *pp* **spoken** [spiːk, spəuk, 'spəukn] *vt* (*language*) parler; (*truth*) dire ♦ *vi* parler; (*make a speech*) prendre la parole; **to speak to sb/of** *or* **about sth** parler à qn/de qch; **speaking!** (*on telephone*) c'est moi-même!; **to speak one's mind** dire ce que l'on pense; **it speaks for itself** c'est évident; **speak up!** parle plus fort!; **he has no money to speak of** il n'a pas d'argent

▶ **speak for** *vt fus*: **to speak for sb** parler pour qn; **that picture is already spoken for** (*in shop*) ce tableau est déjà réservé

speaker ['spiːkə*] *n* (*in public*) orateur *m*; (*also*: **loudspeaker**) haut-parleur *m*; (*POL*): **the Speaker** le président de la Chambre des communes (*BRIT*) or des représentants (*US*); **are you a Welsh speaker?** parlez-vous gallois?

spear [spɪə*] *n* lance *f* ♦ *vt* transpercer

spearhead ['spɪəhed] *n* fer *m* de lance; (*MIL*) colonne *f* d'attaque ♦ *vt* (*attack etc*) mener

spec [spek] *n* (*BRIT col*): **on spec** à tout hasard; **to buy on spec** acheter avec l'espoir de faire une bonne affaire

special ['speʃl] *adj* spécial(e) ♦ *n* (*train*) train spécial; **take special care** soyez particulièrement prudents; **nothing special** rien de spécial; **today's special** (*at restaurant*) le plat du jour

specialist ['speʃəlɪst] *n* spécialiste *m/f*; **heart specialist** cardiologue *m/f*

speciality [speʃɪ'ælɪtɪ] *n* spécialité *f*

specialize ['speʃəlaɪz] *vi*: **to specialize (in)** se spécialiser (dans)

specially ['speʃlɪ] *adv* spécialement, particulièrement

specialty ['speʃəltɪ] *n* (*US*) = **speciality**

species ['spiːʃiːz] *n* (*pl inv*) espèce *f*

specific [spə'sɪfɪk] *adj* (*not vague*) précis(e), explicite; (*particular*) particulier(ière); (*BOT, CHEM etc*) spécifique; **to be specific to** être particulier à, être le ou un caractère (*or* les caractères) spécifique(s) de

specifically [spə'sɪfɪklɪ] *adv* explicitement, précisément; (*intend, ask, design*) expressément, spécialement; (*exclusively*) exclusivement, spécifiquement

specification [spesɪfɪ'keɪʃən] *n* spécification *f*; stipulation *f*; **specifications** *npl* (*of car, building etc*) spécification

specimen ['spesɪmən] *n* spécimen *m*, échantillon *m*; (*MED*) prélèvement *m*

speck [spek] *n* petite tache, petit point; (*particle*) grain *m*

speckled ['spekld] *adj* tacheté(e), moucheté(e)

specs [speks] *npl* (*col*) lunettes *fpl*

spectacle ['spektəkl] *n* spectacle *m*

spectacular [spek'tækjulə*] *adj* spectaculaire ♦ *n* (*CINE etc*) superproduction *f*

spectator [spek'teɪtə*] *n* spectateur/trice

spectrum, *pl* **spectra** ['spektrəm, -rə] *n* spectre *m*; (*fig*) gamme *f*

speculation [spekju'leɪʃən] *n* spéculation *f*; conjectures *fpl*

speech [spiːtʃ] *n* (*faculty*) parole *f*; (*talk*) discours *m*, allocution *f*; (*manner of speaking*) façon *f* de parler, langage *m*; (*language*) langage *m*; (*enunciation*) élocution *f*

speechless ['spiːtʃlɪs] *adj* muet(te)

speed [spiːd] *n* vitesse *f*; (*promptness*) rapidité *f* ♦ *vi*, *pt*, *pp* **sped** [sped]: **to speed along/by** *etc* aller/passer *etc* à toute vitesse; (*AUT*: **exceed speed limit**) faire un excès de vitesse; **at speed** (*BRIT*) rapidement; **at full** *or* **top speed** à toute vitesse or allure; **at a speed of 70 km/h** à une vitesse de 70 km/h; **shorthand/typing speeds** nombre *m* de mots à la minute en sténographie/dactylographie; **a five-speed gearbox** une boîte cinq vitesses

▶ **speed up**, *pt*, *pp* **speeded up** *vi* aller plus vite, accélérer ♦ *vt* accélérer

speedboat ['spiːdbəut] *n* vedette *f*, hors-bord *m inv*

speedily ['spiːdɪlɪ] *adv* rapidement, promptement

speeding ['spiːdɪŋ] *n* (*AUT*) excès *m* de vitesse

speed limit *n* limitation *f* de vitesse, vitesse maximale permise

speedometer [spɪ'dɔmɪtə*] *n* compteur *m* (de vitesse)

speedway *n* (*SPORT*) piste *f* de vitesse pour motos; (*also*: **speedway racing**) épreuve(s) *f(pl)* de vitesse de motos

speedy [spiːdɪ] *adj* rapide, prompt(e)

spell [spel] *n* (*also*: **magic spell**) sortilège *m*, charme *m*; (*period of time*) (courte) période *f* ♦ *vt*, *pt*, *pp* **spelt** *or* **spelled** [spelt, speld] (*in writing*) écrire, orthographier; (*aloud*) épeler; (*fig*) signifier; **to cast a spell on sb** jeter un sort à qn; **he can't spell** il fait des fautes d'orthographe; **how do you spell your name?** comment écrivez-vous votre nom?; **can you spell it for me?** pouvez-vous me l'épeler?

spellbound ['spelbaund] *adj* envoûté(e), subjugué(e)

spelling ['spelɪŋ] *n* orthographe *f*

spend, *pt*, *pp* **spent** [spend, spent] *vt* (*money*) dépenser; (*time, life*) passer; (*devote*): **to spend time/money/effort on sth** consacrer du temps/de l'argent/de l'énergie à qch

spendthrift ['spendθrɪft] *n* dépensier/ière

sperm [spəːm] *n* spermatozoïde *m*; (*semen*) sperme *m*

sphere [sfɪə*] *n* sphère *f*; (*fig*) sphère, domaine *m*

spice [spaɪs] *n* épice *f* ♦ *vt* épicer

spicy ['spaɪsɪ] *adj* épicé(e), relevé(e); (*fig*) piquant(e)

spider ['spaɪdə*] *n* araignée *f*; **spider's web** toile *f* d'araignée

spike [spaik] *n* pointe *f*; (*ELEC*) pointe de tension; **spikes** *npl* (*SPORT*) chaussures *fpl* à pointes

spill, *pt, pp* **spilt** *or* **spilled** [spil, -t, -d] *vt* renverser; répandre ◆ *vi* se répandre; **to spill the beans** (*col*) vendre la mèche; (*: confess*) lâcher le morceau
▶ **spill out** *vi* sortir à flots, se répandre
▶ **spill over** *vi* déborder

spin [spin] *n* (*revolution of wheel*) tour *m*; (*AVIAT*) (*chute f en*) vrille *f*; (*trip in car*) petit tour, balade *f* ◆ *vb, pt, pp* **spun** [spʌn] *vt* (*wool etc*) filer; (*wheel*) faire tourner; (*BRIT: clothes*) essorer ◆ *vi* tourner, tournoyer; **to spin a yarn** débiter une longue histoire; **to spin a coin** (*BRIT*) jouer à pile ou face
▶ **spin out** *vt* faire durer

spinach [ˈspinitʃ] *n* épinard *m*; (*as food*) épinards *mpl*

spinal [ˈspainl] *adj* vertébral(e), spinal(e)

spinal cord *n* moelle épinière

spin doctor *n* (*col*) personne employée pour présenter un parti politique sous un jour favorable

spin-dryer [spinˈdraiə*] *n* (*BRIT*) essoreuse *f*

spine [spain] *n* colonne vertébrale; (*thorn*) épine *f*, piquant *m*

spineless [ˈspainlis] *adj* invertébré(e); (*fig*) mou(molle), sans caractère

spinning [ˈspiniŋ] *n* (*of thread*) filage *m*; (*by machine*) filature *f*

spinning top *n* toupie *f*

spin-off [ˈspinɔf] *n* sous-produit *m*; avantage inattendu

spinster [ˈspinstə*] *n* célibataire *f*; vieille fille

spiral [ˈspaiərl] *n* spirale *f* ◆ *adj* en spirale ◆ *vi* (*fig: prices rise*) monter en flèche; **the inflationary spiral** la spirale inflationniste

spiral staircase *n* escalier *m* en colimaçon

spire [spaiə*] *n* flèche *f*, aiguille *f*

spirit [ˈspirit] *n* (*soul*) esprit *m*, âme *f*; (*ghost*) esprit, revenant *m*; (*mood*) esprit, état *m* d'esprit; (*courage*) courage *m*, énergie *f*; **spirits** *npl* (*drink*) spiritueux *mpl*, alcool *m*; **in good spirits** de bonne humeur; **in low spirits** démoralisé(e); **community spirit** solidarité *f*; **public spirit** civisme *m*

spirited [ˈspiritid] *adj* vif(vive) fougueux(euse), plein(e) d'allant

spiritual [ˈspiritjuəl] *adj* spirituel(le); religieux(euse) ◆ *n* (*also*: **Negro spiritual**) spiritual *m*

spit [spit] *n* (*for roasting*) broche *f*; (*spittle*) crachat *m*; (*saliva*) salive *f* ◆ *vi, pt, pp* **spat** [spæt] cracher; (*sound*) crépiter

spite [spait] *n* rancune *f*, dépit *m* ◆ *vt* contrarier, vexer; **in spite of** en dépit de, malgré

spiteful [ˈspaitful] *adj* malveillant(e), rancunier(ière)

spittle [ˈspitl] *n* salive *f*; bave *f*; crachat *m*

splash [splæʃ] *n* éclaboussement *m*; (*of colour*) tache *f* ◆ *excl* (*sound*) plouf! ◆ *vt* éclabousser ◆ *vi* (*also*: **splash about**) barboter, patauger

spleen [spli:n] *n* (*ANAT*) rate *f*

splendid [ˈsplendid] *adj* splendide, superbe, magnifique

splint [splint] *n* attelle *f*, éclisse *f*

splinter [ˈsplintə*] *n* (*wood*) écharde *f*; (*metal*) éclat *m* ◆ *vi* se fragmenter

split [split] *n* fente *f*, déchirure *f*; (*fig: POL*) scission *f* ◆ *vb, pt, pp* **split** *vt* fendre, déchirer; (*party*) diviser; (*work, profits*) partager, répartir ◆ *vi* (*break*) se fendre, se briser; (*divide*) se diviser; **let's split the difference** coupons la poire en deux; **to do the splits** faire le grand écart
▶ **split up** *vi* (*couple*) se séparer, rompre; (*meeting*) se disperser

spoil, *pt, pp* **spoilt** *or* **spoiled** [spoil, -t, -d] *vt* (*damage*) abîmer; (*mar*) gâcher; (*child*) gâter; (*ballot paper*) rendre nul ◆ *vi*: **to be spoiling for a fight** chercher la bagarre

spoils [spoilz] *npl* butin *m*

spoilsport [ˈspoilspo:t] *n* trouble-fête *m/f inv*, rabat-joie *m inv*

spoke [spəuk] *pt of* **speak** ◆ *n* rayon *m*

spoken [ˈspəukn] *pp of* **speak**

spokesman [ˈspəuksmən], **spokeswoman** [-wumən] *n* porte-parole *m inv*

sponge [spʌndʒ] *n* éponge *f*; (*CULIN: also*: **sponge cake**) ≈ biscuit *m* de Savoie ◆ *vt* éponger ◆ *vi*: **to sponge on** *or* (*US*) **off of** vivre aux crochets de

sponge bag *n* (*BRIT*) trousse *f* de toilette

sponsor [ˈsponsə*] *n* sponsor *m*, personne *f* (*or* organisme*) *m* qui assure le parrainage; (*of new member*) parrain *m*; /marraine *f* ◆ *vt* (*programme, competition etc*) parrainer, patronner, sponsoriser; (*POL: bill*) présenter; (*new member*) parrainer; **I sponsored him at 3p a mile** (*in fund-raising race*) je me suis engagé à lui donner 3p par mile

sponsorship [ˈsponsəʃip] *n* patronage *m*, parrainage *m*

spontaneous [sponˈteiniəs] *adj* spontané(e)

spooky [ˈspu:ki] *adj* qui donne la chair de poule

spool [spu:l] *n* bobine *f*

spoon [spu:n] *n* cuiller *f*

spoon-feed [ˈspu:nfi:d] *vt* nourrir à la cuiller; (*fig*) mâcher le travail à

spoonful [ˈspu:nful] *n* cuillerée *f*

sport [spo:t] *n* sport *m*; (*amusement*) divertissement *m*; (*person*) chic type/chic fille ◆ *vt* arborer; **indoor/outdoor sports** sports en salle/de plein air; **to say sth in sport** dire qch pour rire

sporting [ˈspo:tiŋ] *adj* sportif(ive); **to give sb a sporting chance** donner sa chance à qn

sport jacket *n* (*US*) = **sports jacket**

sports car *n* voiture *f* de sport

sports jacket *n* veste *f* de sport

sportsman [ˈspo:tsmən] *n* sportif *m*

sportsmanship [ˈspo:tsmənʃip] *n* esprit sportif, sportivité *f*

sportswear [ˈspo:tsweə*] *n* vêtements *mpl* de

sport

sportswoman ['spɔːtswumən] n sportive f

sporty ['spɔːtɪ] adj sportif(ive)

spot [spɔt] n tache f; (dot: on pattern) pois m; (pimple) bouton m; (place) endroit m, coin m; (also: **spot advertisement**) message m publicitaire; (small amount): **a spot of** un peu de ♦ vt (notice) apercevoir, repérer; **on the spot** sur place, sur les lieux; (immediately) sur le champ; **to put sb on the spot** (fig) mettre qn dans l'embarras; **to come out in spots** se couvrir de boutons, avoir une éruption de boutons

spot check n contrôle intermittent

spotless ['spɔtlɪs] adj immaculé(e)

spotlight ['spɔtlaɪt] n projecteur m; (AUT) phare m auxiliaire

spotted ['spɔtɪd] adj tacheté(e), moucheté(e); à pois; **spotted with** tacheté(e) de

spotty ['spɔtɪ] adj (face) boutonneux(euse)

spouse [spauz] n époux/épouse

spout [spaut] n (of jug) bec m; (of liquid) jet m ♦ vi jaillir

sprain [spreɪn] n entorse f, foulure f ♦ vt: **to sprain one's ankle** se fouler or se tordre la cheville

sprang [spræŋ] pt of **spring**

sprawl [sprɔːl] vi s'étaler ♦ n: **urban sprawl** expansion urbaine; **to send sb sprawling** envoyer qn rouler par terre

spray [spreɪ] n jet m (en fines gouttelettes); (container) vaporisateur m, bombe f; (of flowers) petit bouquet ♦ vt vaporiser, pulvériser; (crops) traiter ♦ cpd (deodorant etc) en bombe or atomiseur

spread [spred] n (distribution) répartition f; (CULIN) pâte f à tartiner; (PRESS, TYP: two pages) double page f ♦ vb, pt, pp **spread** vt (paste, contents) étendre, étaler; (rumour, disease) répandre, propager; (repayments) échelonner, étaler; (wealth) répartir ♦ vi s'étendre; se répandre; se propager; **middle-age spread** embonpoint m (pris avec l'âge)

▶ **spread out** vi (people) se disperser

spread-eagled ['spredɪːgld] adj: **to be** or **lie spread-eagled** être étendu(e) bras et jambes écartés

spreadsheet ['spredʃiːt] n (COMPUT) tableur m

spree [spriː] n: **to go on a spree** faire la fête

sprightly ['spraɪtlɪ] adj alerte

spring [sprɪŋ] n (leap) bond m, saut m; (coiled metal) ressort m; (bounciness) élasticité f; (season) printemps m; (of water) source f ♦ vb, pt **sprang**, pp **sprung** [spræŋ, sprʌŋ] vi bondir, sauter ♦ vt: **to spring a leak** (pipe etc) se mettre à fuir; **he sprang the news on me** il m'a annoncé la nouvelle de but en blanc; **in spring, in the spring** au printemps; **to spring into action** passer à l'action; **to walk with a spring in one's step** marcher d'un pas souple

▶ **spring up** vi (problem) se présenter, surgir

springboard ['sprɪŋbɔːd] n tremplin m

spring-clean [sprɪŋ'kliːn] n (also: **spring-cleaning**) grand nettoyage de printemps

springtime ['sprɪŋtaɪm] n printemps m

sprinkle ['sprɪŋkl] vt (pour) répandre; verser; **to sprinkle water etc on, sprinkle with water etc** asperger d'eau etc; **to sprinkle sugar etc on, sprinkle with sugar etc** saupoudrer de sucre etc; **sprinkled with** (fig) parsemé(e) de

sprinkler ['sprɪŋklə*] n (for lawn etc) arroseur m; (to put out fire) diffuseur m d'extincteur automatique d'incendie

sprint [sprɪnt] n sprint m ♦ vi sprinter

sprinter ['sprɪntə*] n sprinteur/euse

sprout [spraut] vi germer, pousser

sprouts [sprauts] npl (also: **Brussels sprouts**) choux mpl de Bruxelles

spruce [spruːs] n épicéa m ♦ adj net(te), pimpant(e)

▶ **spruce up** vt (smarten up: room etc) apprêter; **to spruce o.s. up** se faire beau(belle)

sprung [sprʌŋ] pp of **spring**

spun [spʌn] pt, pp of **spin**

spur [spə:*] n éperon m; (fig) aiguillon m ♦ vt (also: **spur on**) éperonner; aiguillonner; **on the spur of the moment** sous l'impulsion du moment

spurious ['spjuərɪəs] adj faux(fausse)

spurn [spəːn] vt repousser avec mépris

spurt [spəːt] n jet m; (of energy) sursaut m ♦ vi jaillir, gicler; **to put in** or **on a spurt** (runner) piquer un sprint; (fig: in work etc) donner un coup de collier

spy [spaɪ] n espion/ne ♦ vi: **to spy on** espionner, épier ♦ vt (see) apercevoir ♦ cpd (film, story) d'espionnage

spying ['spaɪɪŋ] n espionnage m

sq. abbr (MATH etc) = **square**

squabble ['skwɔbl] n querelle f, chamaillerie f ♦ vi se chamailler

squad [skwɔd] n (MIL, POLICE) escouade f, groupe m; (FOOTBALL) contingent m; **flying squad** (POLICE) brigade volante

squadron ['skwɔdrn] n (MIL) escadron m; (AVIAT, NAUT) escadrille f

squalid ['skwɔlɪd] adj sordide, ignoble

squall [skwɔːl] n rafale f, bourrasque f

squalor ['skwɔlə*] n conditions fpl sordides

squander ['skwɔndə*] vt gaspiller, dilapider

square [skwɛə*] n carré m; (in town) place f; (US: block of houses) îlot m, pâté m de maisons; (instrument) équerre f ♦ adj carré(e); (honest) honnête, régulier(ière); (col: ideas, tastes) vieux jeu inv, qui retarde ♦ vt (arrange) régler; arranger; (MATH) élever au carré; (reconcile) concilier ♦ vi (agree) cadrer, s'accorder; **all square** quitte; à égalité; **a square meal** un repas convenable; **2 metres square** (de) 2 mètres sur 2; **1 square metre** 1 mètre carré; **we're back to square one** (fig) on se retrouve à la case départ

▶ **square up** *vi* (*BRIT: settle*) régler; **to square up with sb** régler ses comptes avec qn

squarely ['skwεəlɪ] *adv* carrément; (*honestly, fairly*) honnêtement, équitablement

squash [skwɒʃ] *n* (*BRIT: drink*): **lemon/orange squash** citronnade/orangeade *f*; (*SPORT*) squash *m*; (*vegetable*) courge *f* ◆ *vt* écraser

squat [skwɒt] *adj* petit(e) et épais(se), ramassé(e) ◆ *vi* s'accroupir; (*on property*) squatter, squattériser

squatter ['skwɒtə*] *n* squatter *m*

squeak [skwiːk] *n* (*of hinge, wheel etc*) grincement *m*; (*of shoes*) craquement *m*; (*of mouse etc*) petit cri aigu ◆ *vi* grincer, crier

squeal [skwiːl] *vi* pousser un *or* des cri(s) aigu(s) *or* perçant(s)

squeamish ['skwiːmɪʃ] *adj* facilement dégoûté(e); facilement scandalisé(e)

squeeze [skwiːz] *n* pression *f*; (*also*: **credit squeeze**) encadrement *m* du crédit, restrictions *fpl* de crédit ◆ *vt* presser; (*hand, arm*) serrer ◆ *vi*: **to squeeze past/under sth** se glisser avec (beaucoup de) difficulté devant/sous qch; **a squeeze of lemon** quelques gouttes de citron

▶ **squeeze out** *vt* exprimer; (*fig*) soutirer

squelch [skwεltʃ] *vi* faire un bruit de succion; patauger

squid [skwɪd] *n* calmar *m*

squiggle ['skwɪgl] *n* gribouillis *m*

squint [skwɪnt] *vi* loucher ◆ *n*: **he has a squint** il louche, il souffre de strabisme; **to squint at sth** regarder qch du coin de l'œil; (*quickly*) jeter un coup d'œil à qch

squirm [skwəːm] *vi* se tortiller

squirrel ['skwɪrəl] *n* écureuil *m*

squirt [skwəːt] *n* jet *m* ◆ *vi* jaillir, gicler

Sr *abbr* (= **senior, sister**) (*REL*)

St *abbr* (= **saint**) St; (= **street**) R

stab [stæb] *n* (*with knife etc*) coup *m* (de couteau *etc*); (*col: try*): **to have a stab at (doing) sth** s'essayer à (faire) qch ◆ *vt* poignarder; **to stab sb to death** tuer qn à coups de couteau

stable ['steɪbl] *n* écurie *f* ◆ *adj* stable; **riding stables** centre *m* d'équitation

stack [stæk] *n* tas *m*, pile *f* ◆ *vt* empiler, entasser; **there's stacks of time** (*BRIT col*) on a tout le temps

stadium ['steɪdɪəm] *n* stade *m*

staff [stɑːf] *n* (*work force*) personnel *m*; (*BRIT SCOL: also*: **teaching staff**) professeurs *mpl*, enseignants *mpl*, personnel enseignant; (*servants*) domestiques *mpl*; (*MIL*) état-major *m*; (*stick*) perche *f*, bâton *m* ◆ *vt* pourvoir en personnel

stag [stæg] *n* cerf *m*; (*BRIT STOCK EXCHANGE*) loup *m*

stage [steɪdʒ] *n* scène *f*; (*profession*): **the stage** le théâtre; (*point*) étape *f*, stade *m*; (*platform*) estrade *f* ◆ *vt* (*play*) monter, mettre en scène; (*demonstration*) organiser; (*fig: recovery etc*) effectuer; **in stages** par étapes, par degrés; **to go through a**

difficult stage traverser une période difficile; **in the early stages** au début; **in the final stages** à la fin

stagecoach ['steɪdʒkəʊtʃ] *n* diligence *f*

stage manager *n* régisseur *m*

stagger ['stægə*] *vi* chanceler, tituber ◆ *vt* (*person*) stupéfier; bouleverser; (*hours, holidays*) étaler, échelonner

staggering ['stægərɪŋ] *adj* (*amazing*) stupéfiant(e), renversant(e)

stagnate [stæg'neɪt] *vi* stagner, croupir

stag night, stag party *n* enterrement *m* de vie de garçon

staid [steɪd] *adj* posé(e), rassis(e)

stain [steɪn] *n* tache *f*; (*colouring*) colorant *m* ◆ *vt* tacher; (*wood*) teindre

stained glass window [steɪnd-] *n* vitrail *m*

stainless ['steɪnlɪs] *adj* (*steel*) inoxydable

stain remover *n* détachant *m*

stair [stεə*] *n* (*step*) marche *f*; **stairs** *npl* escalier *m*; **on the stairs** dans l'escalier

staircase ['stεəkeɪs], **stairway** ['stεəweɪ] *n* escalier *m*

stake [steɪk] *n* pieu *m*, poteau *m*; (*BETTING*) enjeu *m* ◆ *vt* risquer, jouer; (*also*: **stake out**: *area*) marquer, délimiter; **to be at stake** être en jeu; **to have a stake in sth** avoir des intérêts (en jeu) dans qch; **to stake a claim (to sth)** revendiquer (qch)

stale [steɪl] *adj* (*bread*) rassis(e); (*beer*) éventé(e); (*smell*) de renfermé

stalemate ['steɪlmeɪt] *n* pat *m*; (*fig*) impasse *f*

stalk [stɔːk] *n* tige *f* ◆ *vt* traquer ◆ *vi*: **to stalk in/out** *etc* entrer/sortir *etc* avec raideur

stall [stɔːl] *n* (*BRIT: in street, market etc*) éventaire *m*, étal *m*; (*in stable*) stalle *f* ◆ *vt* (*AUT*) caler ◆ *vi* (*AUT*) caler; (*fig*) essayer de gagner du temps; **stalls** *npl* (*BRIT: in cinema, theatre*) orchestre *m*; **a newspaper/ flower stall** un kiosque à journaux/de fleuriste

stallion ['stælɪən] *n* étalon *m* (*cheval*)

stamina ['stæmɪnə] *n* vigueur *f*, endurance *f*

stammer ['stæmə*] *n* bégaiement *m* ◆ *vi* bégayer

stamp [stæmp] *n* timbre *m*; (*mark, also fig*) empreinte *f*; (*on document*) cachet *m* ◆ *vi* (*also*: **stamp one's foot**) taper du pied ◆ *vt* tamponner, estamper; (*letter*) timbrer; **stamped addressed envelope (s.a.e.)** enveloppe affranchie pour la réponse

▶ **stamp out** *vt* (*fire*) piétiner; (*crime*) éradiquer; (*opposition*) éliminer

stamp album *n* album *m* de timbres(-poste)

stamp collecting [-kəlεktɪŋ] *n* philatélie *f*

stampede [stæm'piːd] *n* ruée *f*; (*of cattle*) débandade *f*

stance [stæns] *n* position *f*

stand [stænd] *n* (*position*) position *f*; (*MIL*) résistance *f*; (*structure*) guéridon *m*; support *m*; (*COMM*) étalage *m*, stand *m*; (*SPORT*) tribune *f*; (*also: music stand*) pupitre *m* ♦ *vb, pt, pp* **stood** [stud] *vi* être or se tenir (debout); (*rise*) se lever, se mettre debout; (*be placed*) se trouver ♦ *vt* (*place*) mettre, poser; (*tolerate, withstand*) supporter; **to make a stand** prendre position; **to take a stand on an issue** prendre position sur un problème; **to stand for parliament** (*BRIT*) se présenter aux élections (*comme candidat à la députation*); **to stand guard** or **watch** (*MIL*) monter la garde; **it stands to reason** c'est logique; cela va de soi; **as things stand** dans l'état actuel des choses; **to stand sb a drink/meal** payer à boire/à manger à qn; **I can't stand him** je ne peux pas le voir

▶ **stand aside** *vi* s'écarter

▶ **stand by** *vi* (*be ready*) se tenir prêt(e) ♦ *vt fus* (*opinion*) s'en tenir à

▶ **stand down** *vi* (*withdraw*) se retirer; (*LAW*) renoncer à ses droits

▶ **stand for** *vt fus* (*signify*) représenter, signifier; (*tolerate*) supporter, tolérer

▶ **stand in for** *vt fus* remplacer

▶ **stand out** *vi* (*be prominent*) ressortir

▶ **stand up** *vi* (*rise*) se lever, se mettre debout

▶ **stand up for** *vt fus* défendre

▶ **stand up to** *vt fus* tenir tête à, résister à

standard ['stændəd] *n* (*reference*) norme *f*; (*level*) niveau *m*; (*flag*) étendard *m* ♦ *adj* (*size etc*) ordinaire, normal(e); (*model, feature*) standard *inv*; (*practice*) courant(e); (*text*) de base; **standards** *npl* (*morals*) morale *f*, principes *mpl*; **to be** or **come up to standard** être du niveau voulu or à la hauteur; **to apply a double standard** avoir or appliquer deux poids deux mesures; **standard of living** niveau de vie

standard lamp *n* (*BRIT*) lampadaire *m*

stand-by ['stændbaɪ] *n* remplaçant/e ♦ *adj* (*provisions*) de réserve; **to be on the stand-by** se tenir prêt(e) (à intervenir); (*doctor*) être de garde

stand-by ticket *n* billet *m* stand-by

stand-in ['stændɪn] *n* remplaçant/e; (*CINE*) doublure *f*

standing ['stændɪŋ] *adj* debout *inv*; (*permanent: rule*) immuable; (*army*) de métier; (*grievance*) constant(e), de longue date ♦ *n* réputation *f*, rang *m*, standing; (*duration*): **of 6 months' standing** qui dure depuis 6 mois; **of many years' standing** qui dure or existe depuis longtemps; **he was given a standing ovation** on s'est levé pour l'acclamer; **it's a standing joke** c'est un vieux sujet de plaisanterie; **a man of some standing** un homme estimé

standing order *n* (*BRIT: at bank*) virement permanent; **standing orders** *npl* (*MIL*) règlement *m*

standing room *n* places *fpl* debout

standpoint ['stændpɔɪnt] *n* point *m* de vue

standstill ['stændstɪl] *n*: **at a standstill** à l'arrêt; (*fig*) au point mort; **to come to a standstill** s'immobiliser, s'arrêter

stank [stæŋk] *pt de* **stink**

staple ['steɪpl] *n* (*for papers*) agrafe *f*; (*chief product*) produit *m* de base ♦ *adj* (*food, crop, industry etc*) de base principal(e) ♦ *vt* agrafer

stapler ['steɪplə*] *n* agrafeuse *f*

star [stɑː*] *n* étoile *f*; (*celebrity*) vedette *f* ♦ *vi*: **to star (in)** être la vedette (de) ♦ *vt* (*CINE*) avoir pour vedette; **4-star hotel** hôtel *m* 4 étoiles; **2-star petrol** (*BRIT*) essence *f* ordinaire; **4-star petrol** (*BRIT*) super *m*

starboard ['stɑːbəd] *n* tribord *m*; **to starboard** à tribord

starch [stɑːtʃ] *n* amidon *m*

stardom ['stɑːdəm] *n* célébrité *f*

stare [stɛə*] *n* regard *m* fixe ♦ *vi*: **to stare at** regarder fixement

starfish ['stɑːfɪʃ] *n* étoile *f* de mer

stark [stɑːk] *adj* (*bleak*) désolé(e), morne; (*simplicity, colour*) austère; (*reality, poverty*) nu(e) ♦ *adv*: **stark naked** complètement nu(e)

starling ['stɑːlɪŋ] *n* étourneau *m*

starry ['stɑːrɪ] *adj* étoilé(e)

starry-eyed [stɑːrɪ'aɪd] *adj* (*innocent*) ingénu(e)

start [stɑːt] *n* commencement *m*, début *m*; (*of race*) départ *m*; (*sudden movement*) sursaut *m*; (*advantage*) avance *f* ♦ *vt* commencer; (*found: business, newspaper*) lancer, créer ♦ *vi* partir, se mettre en route; (*jump*) sursauter; **at the start** au début; **for a start** d'abord, pour commencer; **to make an early start** partir or commencer de bonne heure; **to start doing sth** se mettre à faire qch; **to start (off) with ...** (*firstly*) d'abord ...; (*at the beginning*) au commencement ...

▶ **start off** *vi* commencer; (*leave*) partir

▶ **start over** *vi* (*US*) recommencer

▶ **start up** *vi* commencer; (*car*) démarrer ♦ *vt* déclencher; (*car*) mettre en marche

starter ['stɑːtə*] *n* (*AUT*) démarreur *m*; (*SPORT: official*) starter *m*; (: *runner, horse*) partant *m*; (*BRIT CULIN*) entrée *f*

starting point ['stɑːtɪŋ-] *n* point *m* de départ

startle ['stɑːtl] *vt* faire sursauter; donner un choc à

startling ['stɑːtlɪŋ] *adj* surprenant(e), saisissant(e)

starvation [stɑː'veɪʃən] *n* faim *f*, famine *f*; **to die of starvation** mourir de faim or d'inanition

starve [stɑːv] *vi* mourir de faim; être affamé(e) ♦ *vt* affamer; **I'm starving** je meurs de faim

state [steɪt] *n* état *m*; (*pomp*): **in state** en grande pompe ♦ *vt* (*declare*) déclarer, affirmer; (*specify*) indiquer, spécifier; **to be in a state** être dans tous ses états; **state of emergency** état d'urgence; **state of mind** état d'esprit; **the state of the art** l'état actuel de la technologie (or des connaissances)

stately ['steɪtlɪ] *adj* majestueux(euse), imposant(e)

stately home n château m

statement ['steɪtmənt] n déclaration f; (LAW) déposition f; (ECON) relevé m; **official statement** communiqué officiel; **statement of account, bank statement** relevé de compte

statesman ['steɪtsmən] n homme m d'État

static ['stætɪk] n (RADIO) parasites mpl; (also: **static electricity**) électricité f statique ◆ adj statique

station ['steɪʃən] n gare f; (MIL, POLICE) poste m (militaire or de police etc); (rank) condition f, rang m ◆ vt placer, poster; **action stations** postes de combat; **to be stationed in** (MIL) être en garnison à

stationary ['steɪʃnərɪ] adj à l'arrêt, immobile

stationer ['steɪʃənə*] n papetier/ière; **stationer's (shop)** papeterie f

stationery ['steɪʃnərɪ] n papier m à lettres, petit matériel de bureau

stationmaster ['steɪʃənmɑːstə*] n (RAIL) chef m de gare

station wagon n (US) break m

statistic [stə'tɪstɪk] n statistique f

statistics [stə'tɪstɪks] n (science) statistique f

statue ['stætjuː] n statue f

status ['steɪtəs] n position f, situation f; (prestige) prestige m; (ADMIN, official position) statut m

status symbol n marque f de standing, signe extérieur de richesse

statute ['stætjuːt] n loi f; **statutes** npl (of club etc) statuts mpl

statutory ['stætjutrɪ] adj statutaire, prévu(e) par un article de loi; **statutory meeting** assemblée constitutive or statutaire

staunch [stɔːntʃ] adj sûr(e), loyal(e) ◆ vt étancher

stay [steɪ] n (period of time) séjour m; (LAW): **stay of execution** sursis m à statuer ◆ vi rester; (reside) loger; (spend some time) séjourner; **to stay put** ne pas bouger; **to stay with friends** loger chez des amis; **to stay the night** passer la nuit

▶ **stay behind** vi rester en arrière

▶ **stay in** vi (at home) rester à la maison

▶ **stay on** vi rester

▶ **stay out** vi (of house) ne pas rentrer; (strikers) rester en grève

▶ **stay up** vi (at night) ne pas se coucher

staying power ['steɪŋ-] n endurance f

stead [stɛd] n (BRIT): **in sb's stead** à la place de qn; **to stand sb in good stead** être très utile or servir beaucoup à qn

steadfast ['stɛdfɑːst] adj ferme, résolu(e)

steadily ['stɛdɪlɪ] adv régulièrement; fermement; d'une voix etc ferme

steady ['stɛdɪ] adj stable, solide, ferme; (regular) constant(e), régulier(ière); (person) calme, pondéré(e) ◆ vt assurer, stabiliser; (voice) assurer; **to steady oneself** reprendre son aplomb

steak [steɪk] n (meat) bifteck m, steak m; (fish)

tranche f

steal, pt **stole**, pp **stolen** [stiːl, stəul, 'stəuln] vt, vi voler

▶ **steal away, steal off** vi s'esquiver

stealth [stɛlθ] n: **by stealth** furtivement

steam [stiːm] n vapeur f ◆ vt passer à la vapeur; (CULIN) cuire à la vapeur ◆ vi fumer; (ship): **to steam along** filer; **under one's own steam** (fig) par ses propres moyens; **to run out of steam** (fig: person) caler; être à bout; **to let off steam** (fig: col) se défouler

▶ **steam up** vi (window) se couvrir de buée; **to get steamed up about sth** (fig: col) s'exciter à propos de qch

steam engine n locomotive f à vapeur

steamer ['stiːmə*] n (bateau m à) vapeur m; (CULIN) = couscoussier m

steamship ['stiːmʃɪp] n = **steamer**

steamy ['stiːmɪ] adj embué(e), humide

steel [stiːl] n acier m ◆ cpd d'acier

steelworks ['stiːlwəːks] n aciérie f

steep [stiːp] adj raide, escarpé(e); (price) très élevé(e), excessif(ive) ◆ vt (faire) tremper

steeple ['stiːpl] n clocher m

steer [stɪə*] n bœuf m ◆ vt diriger, gouverner; (lead) guider ◆ vi tenir le gouvernail; **to steer clear of sb/sth** (fig) éviter qn/qch

steering ['stɪərɪŋ] n (AUT) conduite f

steering wheel n volant m

stem [stɛm] n (of plant) tige f; (of leaf, fruit) queue f; (of glass) pied m ◆ vt contenir, endiguer, juguler

▶ **stem from** vt fus provenir de, découler de

stench [stɛntʃ] n puanteur f

stencil ['stɛnsl] n stencil m; pochoir m ◆ vt polycopier

stenographer [stɛ'nɔgrəfə*] n (US) sténographe m/f

step [stɛp] n pas m; (stair) marche f; (action) mesure f, disposition f ◆ vi: **to step forward** faire un pas en avant, avancer; **steps** npl (BRIT) = **stepladder**; **step by step** pas à pas; (fig) petit à petit; **to be in step (with)** (fig) aller dans le sens (de); **to be out of step (with)** (fig) être déphasé(e) (par rapport à)

▶ **step down** vi (fig) se retirer, se désister

▶ **step in** vi (fig) intervenir

▶ **step off** vt fus descendre de

▶ **step over** vt fus enjamber

▶ **step up** vt augmenter; intensifier

stepbrother ['stɛpbrʌðə*] n demi-frère m

stepdaughter ['stɛpdɔːtə*] n belle-fille f

stepfather ['stɛpfɑːðə*] n beau-père m

stepladder ['stɛplædə*] n (BRIT) escabeau m

stepmother ['stɛpmʌðə*] n belle-mère f

stepping stone ['stɛpɪŋ-] n pierre f de gué; (fig) tremplin m

stepsister ['stɛpsɪstə*] n demi-sœur f

stepson ['stepsʌn] n beau-fils m

stereo ['steriəu] n (system) stéréo f; (record player) chaîne f stéréo ♦ adj (also: **stereophonic**) stéréophonique; **in stereo** en stéréo

sterile ['sterail] adj stérile

sterilize ['sterilaiz] vt stériliser

sterling ['stə:lɪŋ] adj sterling inv; (silver) de bon aloi, fin(e); (fig) à toute épreuve, excellent(e) ♦ n (currency) livre f sterling inv; **a pound sterling** une livre sterling

stern [stə:n] adj sévère ♦ n (NAUT) arrière m, poupe f

stew [stju:] n ragoût m ♦ vt, vi cuire à la casserole; **stewed tea** thé trop infusé; **stewed fruit** fruits cuits or en compote

steward ['stju:əd] n (AVIAT, NAUT, RAIL) steward m; (in club etc) intendant m; (also: **shop steward**) délégué syndical

stewardess ['stjuədes] n hôtesse f

stick [stik] n bâton m; (of chalk etc) morceau m ♦ vb, pt, pp **stuck** [stʌk] vt (glue) coller; (thrust): **to stick sth into** piquer or planter or enfoncer qch dans; (col: put) mettre, fourrer; (: tolerate) supporter ♦ vi (adhere) coller; (remain) rester; (get jammed: door, lift) se bloquer; **to get hold of the wrong end of the stick** (BRIT fig) comprendre de travers; **to stick to** (one's word, promise) s'en tenir à; (principles) rester fidèle à

▶ **stick around** vi (col) rester (dans les parages)

▶ **stick out** vi dépasser, sortir ♦ vt: **to stick it out** (col) tenir le coup

▶ **stick up** vi dépasser, sortir

▶ **stick up for** vt fus défendre

sticker ['stikə*] n auto-collant m

sticking plaster ['stikiŋ-] n sparadrap m, pansement adhésif

stick-up ['stikʌp] n (col) braquage m, hold-up m

sticky ['stiki] adj poisseux(euse); (label) adhésif(ive)

stiff [stif] adj (gen) raide, rigide; (door, brush) dur(e); (difficult) difficile, ardu(e); (cold) froid(e), distant(e); (strong, high) fort(e), élevé(e); **to be** or **feel stiff** (person) avoir des courbatures; **to have a stiff back** avoir mal au dos; **stiff upper lip** (BRIT: fig) flegme m (typiquement britannique)

stiffen ['stifn] vt raidir, renforcer ♦ vi se raidir; se durcir

stiff neck n torticolis m

stifle ['staifl] vt étouffer, réprimer

stigma, pl (BOT, MED, REL) **stigmata**, (fig) **stigmas** ['stigmə, stig'mɑ:tə] n stigmate m

stile [stail] n échalier m

stiletto [sti'letəu] n (BRIT: also: **stiletto heel**) talon m aiguille

still [stil] adj (motionless) immobile; (calm) calme, tranquille; (BRIT: orange drink etc) non gazeux(euse) ♦ adv (up to this time) encore, toujours; (even) enco-re; (nonetheless) quand même, tout de même ♦ n (CINE) photo f; **to stand still** rester immobile, ne pas bouger; **keep still!** ne bouge pas!; **he still hasn't arrived** il n'est pas encore arrivé, il n'est toujours pas arrivé

stillborn ['stilbɔ:n] adj mort-né(e)

still life n nature morte

stilt [stilt] n échasse f; (pile) pilotis m

stilted ['stiltid] adj guindé(e), emprunté(e)

stimulate ['stimjuleit] vt stimuler

stimulus, pl **stimuli** ['stimjuləs, 'stimjulai] n stimulant m; (BIOL, PSYCH) stimulus m

sting [stiŋ] n piqûre f; (organ) dard m; (col: confidence trick) arnaque m ♦ vt, pt, pp **stung** [stʌŋ] piquer ♦ vi piquer; **my eyes are stinging** j'ai les yeux qui piquent

stingy ['stindʒi] adj avare, pingre, chiche

stink [stiŋk] n puanteur f ♦ vi, pt **stank**, pp **stunk** [stæŋk, stʌŋk] puer, empester

stinking ['stiŋkiŋ] adj (fig: col) infect(e); **stinking rich** bourré(e) de pognon

stint [stint] n part f de travail ♦ vi: **to stint on** lésiner sur, être chiche de

stir [stə:*] n agitation f, sensation f ♦ vt remuer ♦ vi remuer, bouger; **to give sth a stir** remuer qch; **to cause a stir** faire sensation

▶ **stir up** vt exciter

stirrup ['stirəp] n étrier m

stitch [stitʃ] n (SEWING) point m; (KNITTING) maille f; (MED) point de suture; (pain) point de côté ♦ vt coudre, piquer; suturer

stoat [stəut] n hermine f (avec son pelage d'été)

stock [stɔk] n réserve f, provision f; (COMM) stock m; (AGR) cheptel m, bétail m; (CULIN) bouillon m; (FINANCE) valeurs fpl, titres mpl; (RAIL: also: **rolling stock**) matériel roulant; (descent, origin) souche f ♦ adj (fig: reply etc) courant(e); classique ♦ vt (have in stock) avoir, vendre; **well-stocked** bien approvisionné(e) or fourni(e); **in stock** en stock, en magasin; **out of stock** épuisé(e); **to take stock** (fig) faire le point; **stocks and shares** valeurs (mobilières), titres; **government stock** fonds publics

▶ **stock up** vi: **to stock up (with)** s'approvisionner (en)

stockbroker ['stɔkbrəukə*] n agent m de change

stock cube n (BRIT CULIN) bouillon-cube m

stock exchange n Bourse f (des valeurs)

stocking ['stɔkiŋ] n bas m

stock market n (BRIT) Bourse f, marché financier

stockpile ['stɔkpail] n stock m, réserve f ♦ vt stocker, accumuler

stocktaking ['stɔkteikiŋ] n (BRIT COMM) inventaire m

stocky ['stɔki] adj trapu(e), râblé(e)

stodgy ['stɔdʒi] adj bourratif(ive), lourd(e)

stoke [stəuk] vt garnir, entretenir; chauffer

stole [stəul] pt of **steal** ♦ n étole f

stolen ['stəʊln] *pp* of **steal**

stomach ['stʌmək] *n* estomac *m*; (*abdomen*) ventre *m* ♦ *vt* supporter, digérer

stomach ache *n* mal *m* à l'estomac *or* au ventre

stone [stəʊn] *n* pierre *f*; (*pebble*) caillou *m*, galet *m*; (*in fruit*) noyau *m*; (*MED*) calcul *m*; (*BRIT: weight*) = 6.348 kg; 14 pounds ♦ *cpd* de *or* en pierre ♦ *vt* dénoyauter; **within a stone's throw of the station** à deux pas de la gare

stone-cold ['stəʊn'kəʊld] *adj* complètement froid(e)

stone-deaf ['stəʊn'dɛf] *adj* sourd(e) comme un pot

stonework ['stəʊnwɜːk] *n* maçonnerie *f*

stood [stʊd] *pt*, *pp* of **stand**

stool [stuːl] *n* tabouret *m*

stoop [stuːp] *vi* (*also*: **have a stoop**) être voûté(e); (*bend*) se baisser, se courber; (*fig*): **to stoop to sth/ doing sth** s'abaisser jusqu'à qch/jusqu'à faire qch

stop [stɒp] *n* arrêt *m*; (*short stay*) halte *f*; (*in punctuation*) point *m* ♦ *vt* arrêter; (*break off*) interrompre; (*also*: **put a stop to**) mettre fin à; (*prevent*) empêcher ♦ *vi* s'arrêter; (*rain, noise etc*) cesser, s'arrêter; **to stop doing sth** cesser *or* arrêter de faire qch; **to stop sb (from) doing sth** empêcher qn de faire qch; **to stop dead** *vi* s'arrêter net; **stop it!** arrête!

▶ **stop by** *vi* s'arrêter (au passage)

▶ **stop off** *vi* faire une courte halte

▶ **stop up** *vt* (*hole*) boucher

stopgap ['stɒpɡæp] *n* (*person*) bouche-trou *m*; (*also*: **stopgap measure**) mesure *f* intérimaire

stopover ['stɒpəʊvə*] *n* halte *f*; (*AVIAT*) escale *f*

stoppage ['stɒpɪdʒ] *n* arrêt *m*; (*of pay*) retenue *f*; (*strike*) arrêt de travail

stopper ['stɒpə*] *n* bouchon *m*

stop press *n* nouvelles *fpl* de dernière heure

stopwatch ['stɒpwɒtʃ] *n* chronomètre *m*

storage ['stɔːrɪdʒ] *n* emmagasinage *m*; (*of nuclear waste etc*) stockage *m*; (*in house*) rangement *m*; (*COMPUT*) mise *f* en mémoire *or* réserve

storage heater *n* (*BRIT*) radiateur *m* électrique par accumulation

store [stɔː*] *n* provision *f*, réserve *f*; (*depot*) entrepôt *m*; (*BRIT: large shop*) grand magasin; (*US: shop*) magasin *m* ♦ *vt* emmagasiner; (*nuclear waste etc*) stocker; (*in filing system*) classer, ranger; (*COMPUT*) mettre en mémoire; **stores** *npl* provisions; **who knows what is in store for us?** qui sait ce que l'avenir nous réserve *or* ce qui nous attend?; **to set great/little store by sth** faire grand cas/peu de cas de qch

▶ **store up** *vt* mettre en réserve, emmagasiner

storeroom ['stɔːruːm] *n* réserve *f*, magasin *m*

storey, (*US*) **story** ['stɔːrɪ] *n* étage *m*

stork [stɔːk] *n* cigogne *f*

storm [stɔːm] *n* tempête *f*; (*also*: **electric storm**) orage *m* ♦ *vi* (*fig*) fulminer ♦ *vt* prendre d'assaut

stormy ['stɔːmɪ] *adj* orageux(euse)

story [staʊt] *n* histoire *f*; récit *m*; (*PRESS: article*) article *m*; (: *subject*) affaire *f*; (*US*) = **storey**

storybook ['stɔːrɪbʊk] *n* livre *m* d'histoires *or* de contes

stout [staʊt] *adj* solide; (*brave*) intrépide; (*fat*) gros(se), corpulent(e) ♦ *n* bière brune

stove [stəʊv] *n* (*for cooking*) fourneau *m*; (: *small*) réchaud *m*; (*for heating*) poêle *m*; **gas/electric stove** (*cooker*) cuisinière *f* à gaz/électrique

stow [stəʊ] *vt* ranger; cacher

stowaway ['stəʊəweɪ] *n* passager/ère clandestin(e)

straddle ['strædl] *vt* enjamber, être à cheval sur

straggle ['stræɡl] *vi* être (*or* marcher) en désordre; **straggled along the coast** disséminé(e) tout au long de la côte

straight [streɪt] *adj* droit(e); (*frank*) honnête, franc (franche); (*plain, uncomplicated*) simple; (*THEAT: part, play*) sérieux(euse); (*drink*) sec, sans eau ♦ *n*: **the straight** (*SPORT*) la ligne droite; **to put** *or* **get straight** mettre en ordre, mettre de l'ordre dans; **let's get this straight** mettons les choses au point; **10 straight wins** 10 victoires d'affilée; **to go straight home** rentrer directement à la maison; **straight away, straight off** (*at once*) tout de suite; **straight off, straight out** sans hésiter

straighten ['streɪtn] *vt* (*also*: **straighten out**) redresser; **to straighten things out** arranger les choses

straight-faced [streɪt'feɪst] *adj* impassible ♦ *adv* en gardant son sérieux

straightforward [streɪt'fɔːwəd] *adj* simple; (*frank*) honnête, direct(e)

strain [streɪn] *n* (*TECH*) tension *f*; pression *f*; (*physical*) effort *m*; (*mental*) tension (nerveuse); (*MED*) entorse *f*; (*streak, trace*) tendance *f*; élément *m*; (*breed*) variété *f*; (*of virus*) souche *f*; **strains** *npl* (*of music*) accents *mpl*, accords *mpl* ♦ *vt* tendre fortement; mettre à l'épreuve; (*filter*) passer, filtrer ♦ *vi* peiner, fournir un gros effort; **he's been under a lot of strain** il a traversé des moments très difficiles, il est très éprouvé nerveusement

strained [streɪnd] *adj* (*laugh etc*) forcé(e), contraint(e); (*relations*) tendu(e)

strainer ['streɪnə*] *n* passoire *f*

strait [streɪt] *n* (*GEO*) détroit *m*; **to be in dire straits** (*fig*) être dans une situation désespérée

straitjacket ['streɪtdʒækɪt] *n* camisole *f* de force

strait-laced [streɪt'leɪst] *adj* collet monté *inv*

strand [strænd] *n* (*of thread*) fil *m*, brin *m* ♦ *vt* (*boat*) échouer

stranded ['strændɪd] *adj* en rade, en plan

strange [streɪndʒ] *adj* (*not known*) inconnu(e); (*odd*) étrange, bizarre

strangely ['streɪndʒlɪ] *adv* étrangement, bizarrement

stranger ['streɪndʒə*] n (unknown) inconnu/e; (from somewhere else) étranger/ère; **I'm a stranger here** je ne suis pas d'ici

strangle ['stræŋgl] vt étrangler

stranglehold ['stræŋglhəuld] n (fig) emprise totale, mainmise f

strap [stræp] n lanière f, courroie f, sangle f; (of slip, dress) bretelle f ♦ vt attacher (avec une courroie etc)

strappy ['stræpɪ] adj (dress) à bretelles; (sandals) à lanières

strategic [strə'ti:dʒɪk] adj stratégique

strategy ['strætɪdʒɪ] n stratégie f

straw [strɔ:] n paille f; **that's the last straw!** ça c'est le comble!

strawberry ['strɔ:bərɪ] n fraise f; (plant) fraisier m

stray [streɪ] adj (animal) perdu(e), errant(e) ♦ vi s'égarer; **stray bullet** balle perdue

streak [stri:k] n raie f, bande f, filet m; (fig: of madness etc): **a streak of** une or des tendance(s) à ♦ vt zébrer, strier ♦ vi: **to streak past** passer à toute allure; **to have streaks in one's hair** s'être fait faire des mèches; **a winning/losing streak** une bonne/mauvaise série or période

stream [stri:m] n (brook) ruisseau m; (current) courant m, flot m; (of people) défilé m ininterrompu, flot ♦ vt (SCOL) répartir par niveau ♦ vi ruisseler; **to stream in/out** entrer/sortir à flots; **against the stream** à contre courant; **on stream** (new power plant etc) en service

streamer ['stri:mə*] n serpentin m, banderole f

streamlined ['stri:mlaɪnd] adj (AVIAT) fuselé(e), profilé(e); (AUT) aérodynamique; (fig) rationalisé(e)

street [stri:t] n rue f; **the back streets** les quartiers pauvres; **to be on the streets** (homeless) être à la rue or sans abri

streetcar ['stri:tkɑ:*] n (US) tramway m

street lamp n réverbère m

street map, street plan n plan m des rues

streetwise ['stri:twaɪz] adj (col) futé(e), réaliste

strength [streŋθ] n force f; (of girder, knot etc) solidité f; (of chemical solution) titre m; (of wine) degré m d'alcool; **on the strength of** en vertu de; **at full strength** au grand complet; **below strength** à effectifs réduits

strengthen ['streŋθən] vt renforcer; (muscle) fortifier

strenuous ['strenjuəs] adj vigoureux(euse), énergique; (tiring) ardu(e), pénible

stress [stres] n (force, pressure) pression f; (mental strain) tension (nerveuse); (accent) accent m; (emphasis) insistance f ♦ vt insister sur, souligner; **to lay great stress on sth** insister beaucoup sur qch; **to be under stress** être stressé(e)

stretch [stretʃ] n (of sand etc) étendue f; (of time) période f ♦ vi s'étirer; (extend): **to stretch to** or **as far as** s'étendre jusqu'à; (be enough: money, food): **to stretch to** aller pour ♦ vt tendre, étirer; (spread) étendre; (fig) pousser (au maximum); **at a stretch** sans discontinuer, sans interruption; **to stretch a muscle** se distendre un muscle; **to stretch one's legs** se dégourdir les jambes

▶ **stretch out** vi s'étendre ♦ vt (arm etc) allonger, tendre; (to spread) étendre; **to stretch out for sth** allonger la main pour prendre qch

stretcher ['stretʃə*] n brancard m, civière f

stretchy ['stretʃɪ] adj élastique

strewn [stru:n] adj: **strewn with** jonché(e) de

stricken ['strɪkən] adj très éprouvé(e); dévasté(e); (ship) très endommagé(e); **stricken with** frappé(e) or atteint(e) de

strict [strɪkt] adj strict(e); **in strict confidence** tout à fait confidentiellement

stride [straɪd] n grand pas m, enjambée f ♦ vi, pt **strode**, pp **stridden** [strəud, 'strɪdn] marcher à grands pas; **to take in one's stride** (fig: changes etc) accepter sans sourciller

strife [straɪf] n conflit m, dissensions fpl

strike [straɪk] n grève f; (of oil etc) découverte f; (attack) raid m ♦ vb, pt, pp **struck** [strʌk] vt frapper; (oil etc) trouver, découvrir; (make: agreement, deal) conclure ♦ vi faire grève; (attack) attaquer; (clock) sonner; **to go on** or **come out on strike** se mettre en grève, faire grève; **to strike a match** frotter une allumette; **to strike a balance** (fig) trouver un juste milieu

▶ **strike back** vi (MIL, fig) contre-attaquer

▶ **strike down** vt (fig) terrasser

▶ **strike off** vt (from list) rayer; (: doctor etc) radier

▶ **strike out** vt rayer

▶ **strike up** vt (MUS) se mettre à jouer; **to strike up a friendship with** se lier d'amitié avec

striker ['straɪkə*] n gréviste m/f; (SPORT) buteur m

striking ['straɪkɪŋ] adj frappant(e), saisissant(e)

string [strɪŋ] n ficelle f, fil m; (row: of beads) rang m; (: of onions, excuses) chapelet m; (: of people, cars) file f; (MUS) corde f; (COMPUT) chaîne f ♦ vt, pt, pp **strung** [strʌŋ]: **to string out** échelonner; **to string together** enchaîner; **the strings** (MUS) les instruments mpl à cordes; **to get a job by pulling strings** obtenir un emploi en faisant jouer le piston; **with no strings attached** (fig) sans conditions

string(ed) instrument [strɪŋ(d)-] n (MUS) instrument m à cordes

stringent ['strɪndʒənt] adj rigoureux(euse); (need) impérieux(euse)

strip [strɪp] n bande f; (SPORT): **wearing the Celtic strip** en tenue du Celtic ♦ vt déshabiller; (fig) dégarnir, dépouiller; (also: **strip down**: machine) démonter ♦ vi se déshabiller

strip cartoon n bande dessinée

stripe [straɪp] n raie f, rayure f

striped ['straɪpt] adj rayé(e), à rayures

strip lighting (BRIT) n éclairage m au néon or fluorescent

stripper ['strɪpə*] n strip-teaseuse f

strip-search ['strɪpsəːtʃ] n fouille corporelle (en faisant se déshabiller la personne) ◆ vt: **to strip-search sb** fouiller qn (en le faisant se déshabiller)

stripy ['straɪpɪ] adj rayé(e)

strive [straɪv] pt **strove**, pp **striven** [straɪv, strəuv, 'strɪvn] vi: **to strive to do** s'efforcer de faire

strode [strəud] pt of **stride**

stroke [strəuk] n coup m; (MED) attaque f; (caress) caresse f; (SWIMMING: style) (sorte f de) nage f; (of piston) course f ◆ vt caresser; **at a stroke** d'un (seul) coup; **on the stroke of 5** à 5 heures sonnantes; **a stroke of luck** un coup de chance; **a 2-stroke engine** un moteur à 2 temps

stroll [strəul] n petite promenade ◆ vi flâner, se promener nonchalamment; **to go for a stroll** aller se promener or faire un tour

stroller ['strəulə*] n (US) poussette f

strong [strɔŋ] adj (gen) fort(e); (healthy) vigoureux(euse); (object, material) solide; (distaste, desire) vif(vive); (drugs, chemicals) puissant(e) ◆ adv: **to be going strong** (company) marcher bien; (person) être toujours solide; **they are 50 strong** ils sont au nombre de 50

stronghold ['strɔŋhəuld] n bastion m

strongly ['strɔŋlɪ] adv fortement, avec force; vigoureusement; solidement; **I feel strongly about it** c'est une question qui me tient particulièrement à cœur; (negatively) j'y suis profondément opposé(e)

strongroom ['strɔŋruːm] n chambre forte

strove [strəuv] pt of **strive**

struck [strʌk] pt, pp of **strike**

structural ['strʌktʃrəl] adj structural(e); (CONSTR) de construction; affectant les parties portantes

structure ['strʌktʃə*] n structure f; (building) construction f

struggle ['strʌgl] n lutte f ◆ vi lutter, se battre; **to have a struggle to do sth** avoir beaucoup de mal à faire qch

strum [strʌm] vt (guitar) gratter de

strung [strʌŋ] pt, pp of **string**

strut [strʌt] n étai m, support m ◆ vi se pavaner

stub [stʌb] n bout m; (of ticket etc) talon m ◆ vt: **to stub one's toe (on sth)** se heurter le doigt de pied (contre qch)

▶ **stub out** vt écraser

stubble ['stʌbl] n chaume m; (on chin) barbe f de plusieurs jours

stubborn ['stʌbən] adj têtu(e), obstiné(e), opiniâtre

stuck [stʌk] pt, pp of **stick** ◆ adj (jammed) bloqué(e), coincé(e); **to get stuck** se bloquer or coincer

stuck-up [stʌk'ʌp] adj prétentieux(euse)

stud [stʌd] n clou m (à grosse tête); (collar stud) bouton m de col; (of horses) écurie f, haras m; (also:

stud horse) étalon m ◆ vt (fig): **studded with** parsemé(e) or criblé(e) de

student ['stjuːdənt] n étudiant/e ◆ cpd estudiantin(e); universitaire; d'étudiant; **law/medical student** étudiant en droit/médecine

student driver n (US) conducteur/trice débutant(e)

studio ['stjuːdɪəu] n studio m, atelier m

studious ['stjuːdɪəs] adj studieux(euse), appliqué(e); (studied) étudié(e)

studiously ['stjuːdɪəslɪ] adv (carefully) soigneusement

study ['stʌdɪ] n étude f; (room) bureau m ◆ vt étudier ◆ vi étudier, faire ses études; **to make a study of sth** étudier qch, faire une étude de qch; **to study for an exam** préparer un examen

stuff [stʌf] n (gen) chose(s) f(pl), truc m; (belongings) affaires fpl, trucs; (substance) substance f ◆ vt rembourrer; (CULIN) farcir; (animal: for exhibition) empailler; **my nose is stuffed up** j'ai le nez bouché; **get stuffed!** (col!) va te faire foutre! (!); **stuffed toy** jouet m en peluche

stuffing ['stʌfɪŋ] n bourre f, rembourrage m; (CULIN) farce f

stuffy ['stʌfɪ] adj (room) mal ventilé(e) or aéré(e); (ideas) vieux jeu inv

stumble ['stʌmbl] vi trébucher

▶ **stumble across** vt fus (fig) tomber sur

stumbling block ['stʌmblɪŋ-] n pierre f d'achoppement

stump [stʌmp] n souche f; (of limb) moignon m ◆ vt: **to be stumped** sécher, ne pas savoir que répondre

stun [stʌn] vt (blow) étourdir; (news) abasourdir, stupéfier

stung [stʌŋ] pt, pp of **sting**

stunk [stʌŋk] pp of **stink**

stunned [stʌnd] adj sidéré(e)

stunning ['stʌnɪŋ] adj étourdissant(e); (fabulous) stupéfiant(e), sensationnel(le)

stunt [stʌnt] n tour m de force; truc m publicitaire; (AVIAT) acrobatie f ◆ vt retarder, arrêter

stuntman ['stʌntmæn] n cascadeur m

stupendous [stjuː'pɛndəs] adj prodigieux(euse), fantastique

stupid ['stjuːpɪd] adj stupide, bête

stupidity [stjuː'pɪdɪtɪ] n stupidité f, bêtise f

sturdy ['stəːdɪ] adj robuste, vigoureux(euse); solide

stutter ['stʌtə*] n bégaiement m ◆ vi bégayer

sty [staɪ] n (of pigs) porcherie f

stye [staɪ] n (MED) orgelet m

style [staɪl] n style m; (of dress etc) genre m; (distinction) allure f, cachet m, style; **in the latest style** à la dernière mode; **hair style** coiffure f

stylish ['staɪlɪʃ] adj élégant(e), chic inv

stylus, pl **styli** or **styluses** ['staɪləs, -laɪ] n (of record *player*) pointe *f* de lecture

suave [swɑːv] *adj* doucereux(euse), onctueux(euse)

subconscious [sʌb'kɒnʃəs] *adj* subconscient(e) ♦ *n* subconscient *m*

subcontract *n* ['sʌb'kɒntrækt] contrat *m* de sous-traitance ♦ *vt* [sʌbkən'trækt] sous-traiter

subdue [səb'djuː] *vt* subjuguer, soumettre

subdued [səb'djuːd] *adj* contenu(e), atténué(e); (*light*) tamisé(e); (*person*) qui a perdu de son entrain

subject *n* ['sʌbdʒɪkt] sujet *m*; (*SCOL*) matière *f* ♦ *vt* [səb'dʒɛkt]: **to subject to** soumettre à; exposer à; **to be subject to** (*law*) être soumis(e) à; (*disease*) être sujet(te) à; **subject to confirmation in writing** sous réserve de confirmation écrite; **to change the subject** changer de conversation

subjective [səb'dʒɛktɪv] *adj* subjectif(ive)

subject matter *n* sujet *m*; contenu *m*

sublet [sʌb'lɛt] *vt* sous-louer

submarine [sʌbmə'riːn] *n* sous-marin *m*

submerge [səb'məːdʒ] *vt* submerger; immerger ♦ *vi* plonger

submission [səb'mɪʃən] *n* soumission *f*; (*to committee etc*) présentation *f*

submissive [səb'mɪsɪv] *adj* soumis(e)

submit [səb'mɪt] *vt* soumettre ♦ *vi* se soumettre

subnormal [sʌb'nɔːml] *adj* au-dessous de la normale; (*person*) arriéré(e)

subordinate [sə'bɔːdɪnət] *adj, n* subordonné(e)

subpoena [səb'piːnə] (*LAW*) *n* citation *f*, assignation *f* ♦ *vt* citer or assigner (à comparaître)

subscribe [səb'skraɪb] *vi* cotiser; **to subscribe to** (*opinion, fund*) souscrire à; (*newspaper*) s'abonner à; être abonné(e) à

subscriber [səb'skraɪbə*] *n* (*to periodical, telephone*) abonné/e

subscription [səb'skrɪpʃən] *n* (*to fund*) souscription *f*; (*to magazine etc*) abonnement *m*; (*membership dues*) cotisation *f*; **to take out a subscription to** s'abonner à

subsequent ['sʌbsɪkwənt] *adj* ultérieur(e), suivant(e); **subsequent to** *prep* à la suite de

subsequently ['sʌbsɪkwəntlɪ] *adv* par la suite

subside [səb'saɪd] *vi* s'affaisser; (*flood*) baisser; (*wind*) tomber

subsidence [səb'saɪdns] *n* affaissement *m*

subsidiary [səb'sɪdɪərɪ] *adj* subsidiaire; accessoire; (*BRIT SCOL: subject*) complémentaire ♦ *n* filiale *f*

subsidize ['sʌbsɪdaɪz] *vt* subventionner

subsidy ['sʌbsɪdɪ] *n* subvention *f*

substance ['sʌbstəns] *n* substance *f*; (*fig*) essentiel *m*; **a man of substance** un homme jouissant d'une certaine fortune; **to lack substance** être plutôt mince (*fig*)

substantial [səb'stænʃl] *adj* substantiel(le); (*fig*) important(e)

substantially [səb'stænʃəlɪ] *adv* considérablement; en grande partie

substantiate [səb'stænʃɪeɪt] *vt* étayer, fournir des preuves à l'appui de

substitute ['sʌbstɪtjuːt] *n* (*person*) remplaçant/e; (*thing*) succédané *m* ♦ *vt*: **to substitute sth/sb for** substituer qch/qn à remplacer par qch/qn

subterranean [sʌbtə'reɪnɪən] *adj* souterrain(e)

subtitle ['sʌbtaɪtl] *n* (*CINE*) sous-titre *m*

subtitled ['sʌbtaɪtld] *adj* sous-titré(e)

subtle ['sʌtl] *adj* subtil(e)

subtotal [sʌb'təʊtl] *n* total partiel

subtract [səb'trækt] *vt* soustraire, retrancher

subtraction [səb'trækʃən] *n* soustraction *f*

suburb ['sʌbəːb] *n* faubourg *m*; **the suburbs** la banlieue

suburban [sə'bəːbən] *adj* de banlieue, suburbain(e)

suburbia [sə'bəːbɪə] *n* la banlieue

subway ['sʌbweɪ] *n* (*US*) métro *m*; (*BRIT*) passage souterrain

succeed [sək'siːd] *vi* réussir ♦ *vt* succéder à; **to succeed in doing** réussir à faire

succeeding [sək'siːdɪŋ] *adj* suivant(e), qui suit (*or* suivent *or* suivront *etc*)

success [sək'sɛs] *n* succès *m*; réussite *f*

successful [sək'sɛsful] *adj* qui a du succès; (*candidate*) choisi(e), agréé(e); (*business*) prospère, qui réussit; (*attempt*) couronné(e) de succès; **to be successful (in doing)** réussir (à faire)

successfully [sək'sɛsfəlɪ] *adv* avec succès

succession [sək'sɛʃən] *n* succession *f*; **in succession** successivement; **3 years in succession** 3 ans de suite

successive [sək'sɛsɪv] *adj* successif(ive); **on 3 successive days** 3 jours de suite *or* consécutifs

such [sʌtʃ] *adj* tel(telle); (*of that kind*): **such a book** un livre de ce genre *or* pareil, un tel livre ♦ *adv* si; **such books** des livres de ce genre *or* pareils, de tels livres; (*so much*): **such courage** un tel courage; **such a long trip** un si long voyage; **such good books** de si bons livres; **such a long trip that** un voyage si *or* tellement long que; **such a lot of** tellement or tant de; **making such a noise that** faisant un tel bruit que *or* tellement de bruit que; **such a long time ago** il y a si *or* tellement longtemps; **such as** (*like*) tel(telle) que comme; **a noise such as** to un bruit de nature à; **such books as I have** les quelques livres que j'ai; **as such** *adv* en tant que tel (telle) à proprement parler

such-and-such ['sʌtʃənsʌtʃ] *adj* tel(telle) ou tel(telle)

suck [sʌk] *vt* sucer; (*breast, bottle*) téter; (*subj: pump, machine*) aspirer

sucker ['sʌkə*] *n* (*BOT, ZOOL, TECH*) ventouse *f*; (*col*) naïf/ïve, poire *f*

suction ['sʌkʃən] *n* succion *f*

sudden ['sʌdn] *adj* soudain(e), subit(e); **all of a sudden** soudain, tout à coup

suddenly ['sʌdnlɪ] *adv* brusquement, tout à coup, soudain

suds [sʌdz] *npl* eau savonneuse

sue [su:] *vt* poursuivre en justice, intenter un procès à ◆ *vi*: **to sue (for)** intenter un procès (pour); **to sue for divorce** engager une procédure de divorce; **to sue sb for damages** poursuivre qn en dommages-intérêts

suede [sweɪd] *n* daim *m*, cuir suédé ◆ *cpd* de daim

suet ['suɪt] *n* graisse *f* de rognon *or* de bœuf

suffer ['sʌfə*] *vt* souffrir, subir; (*bear*) tolérer, supporter, subir ◆ *vi* souffrir; **to suffer from** (*illness*) souffrir de, avoir; **to suffer from the effects of alcohol/a fall** se ressentir des effets de l'alcool/des conséquences d'une chute

sufferer ['sʌfərə*] *n* malade *m/f*; victime *m/f*

suffering ['sʌfərɪŋ] *n* souffrance(s) *f(pl)*

sufficient [sə'fɪʃənt] *adj* suffisant(e); **sufficient money** suffisamment d'argent

sufficiently [sə'fɪʃəntlɪ] *adv* suffisamment, assez

suffocate ['sʌfəkeɪt] *vi* suffoquer; étouffer

sugar ['ʃugə*] *n* sucre *m* ◆ *vt* sucrer

sugar beet *n* betterave sucrière

sugar cane *n* canne *f* à sucre

suggest [sə'dʒest] *vt* suggérer, proposer; (*indicate*) laisser supposer, suggérer; **what do you suggest I do?** que vous me suggérez de faire?

suggestion [sə'dʒestʃən] *n* suggestion *f*

suicide ['suɪsaɪd] *n* suicide *m*; **to commit suicide** se suicider

suicide bomber *n* kamikaze *m/f*

suit [su:t] *n* (*man's*) costume *m*, complet *m*; (*woman's*) tailleur *m*, ensemble *m*; (CARDS) couleur *f*; (*lawsuit*) procès *m* ◆ *vt* aller à; convenir à; (*adapt*): **to suit sth to** adapter *or* approprier qch à; **to be suited to sth** (*suitable for*) être adapté(e) *or* approprié(e) à qch; **well suited** (*couple*) faits l'un pour l'autre, très bien assortis; **to bring a suit against sb** intenter un procès contre qn; **to follow suit** (*fig*) faire de même

suitable ['su:təbl] *adj* qui convient; approprié(e), adéquat(e); **would tomorrow be suitable?** est-ce que demain vous conviendrait?; **we found somebody suitable** nous avons trouvé la personne qu'il nous faut

suitably ['su:təblɪ] *adv* comme il se doit (*or* se devait *etc*), convenablement

suitcase ['su:tkeɪs] *n* valise *f*

suite [swi:t] *n* (*of rooms, also* MUS) suite *f*; (*furniture*): **bedroom/dining room suite** (ensemble *m* de) chambre *f* à coucher/salle *f* à manger; **a three-piece suite** un salon (canapé et deux fauteuils)

suitor ['su:tə*] *n* soupirant *m*, prétendant *m*

sulk [sʌlk] *vi* bouder

sulky ['sʌlkɪ] *adj* boudeur(euse), maussade

sullen ['sʌlən] *adj* renfrogné(e), maussade; morne

sulphur, (US) **sulfur** ['sʌlfə*] *n* soufre *m*

sultana [sʌl'tɑ:nə] *n* (*fruit*) raisin (sec) de Smyrne

sultry ['sʌltrɪ] *adj* étouffant(e)

sum [sʌm] *n* somme *f*; (SCOL *etc*) calcul *m*

▶ **sum up** *vt* résumer; (*evaluate rapidly*) récapituler ◆ *vi* résumer

summarize ['sʌməraɪz] *vt* résumer

summary ['sʌmərɪ] *n* résumé *m* ◆ *adj* (*justice*) sommaire

summer ['sʌmə*] *n* été *m* ◆ *cpd* d'été, estival(e); **in (the) summer** en été, pendant l'été

summerhouse ['sʌməhaus] *n* (*in garden*) pavillon *m*

summertime ['sʌmətaɪm] *n* (*season*) été *m*

summer time *n* (*by clock*) heure *f* d'été

summit ['sʌmɪt] *n* sommet *m*; (*also:* **summit conference**) (conférence *f* au) sommet *m*

summon ['sʌmən] *vt* appeler, convoquer; **to summon a witness** citer *or* assigner un témoin

▶ **summon up** *vt* rassembler, faire appel à

summons ['sʌmənz] *n* citation *f*, assignation *f* ◆ *vt* citer, assigner; **to serve a summons on sb** remettre une assignation à qn

sun [sʌn] *n* soleil *m*; **in the sun** au soleil; **to catch the sun** prendre le soleil; **everything under the sun** absolument tout

sunbathe ['sʌnbeɪð] *vi* prendre un bain de soleil

sunblock ['sʌnblɒk] *n* écran *m* total

sunburn ['sʌnbə:n] *n* coup *m* de soleil

sunburned ['sʌnbə:nd], **sunburnt** ['sʌnbə:nt] *adj* bronzé(e), hâlé(e); (*painfully*) brûlé(e) par le soleil

Sunday ['sʌndɪ] *n* dimanche *m*; for phrases see also **Tuesday**

Sunday school *n* ≈ catéchisme *m*

sundial ['sʌndaɪəl] *n* cadran *m* solaire

sundown ['sʌndaun] *n* coucher *m* du soleil

sundries ['sʌndrɪz] *npl* articles divers

sundry ['sʌndrɪ] *adj* divers(e), différent(e); **all and sundry** tout le monde, n'importe qui

sunflower ['sʌnflauə*] *n* tournesol *m*

sung [sʌŋ] *pp of* **sing**

sunglasses ['sʌnglɑ:sɪz] *npl* lunettes *fpl* de soleil

sunk [sʌŋk] *pp of* **sink**

sunlight ['sʌnlaɪt] *n* (lumière *f* du) soleil *m*

sunlit ['sʌnlɪt] *adj* ensoleillé(e)

sunny ['sʌnɪ] *adj* ensoleillé(e); (*fig*) épanoui(e), radieux(euse); **it is sunny** il fait (du) soleil, il y a du soleil

sunrise ['sʌnraɪz] *n* lever *m* du soleil

sun roof *n* (AUT) toit ouvrant

sunscreen ['sʌnskri:n] *n* crème *f* solaire

sunset ['sʌnset] *n* coucher *m* du soleil

sunshade ['sʌnʃeɪd] *n* (*lady's*) ombrelle *f*; (*over table*) parasol *m*

sunshine ['sʌnʃaɪn] *n* (lumière *f* du) soleil *m*

sunstroke ['sʌnstrəuk] *n* insolation *f*, coup *m* de soleil

suntan ['sʌntæn] *n* bronzage *m*

suntan lotion *n* lotion *f* or lait *m* solaire

suntan oil *n* huile *f* solaire

super ['su:pə*] *adj* (col) formidable

superannuation [su:pərænju'eɪʃən] *n* cotisations *fpl* pour la pension

superb [su:'pə:b] *adj* superbe, magnifique

supercilious [su:pə'sɪlɪəs] *adj* hautain(e), dédaigneux(euse)

superficial [su:pə'fɪʃəl] *adj* superficiel(le)

superimpose ['su:pərɪm'pəuz] *vt* superposer

superintendent [su:pərɪn'tendənt] *n* directeur/trice; (POLICE) ≃ commissaire *m*

superior [su'pɪərɪə*] *adj* supérieur(e); (COMM: goods, quality) de qualité supérieure; (smug) condescendant(e), méprisant(e) ♦ *n* supérieur/e; **Mother Superior** (REL) Mère supérieure

superiority [supɪərɪ'ɔrɪtɪ] *n* supériorité *f*

superlative [su'pə:lətɪv] *adj* sans pareil(le), suprême ♦ *n* (LING) superlatif *m*

superman ['su:pəmæn] *n* surhomme *m*

supermarket ['su:pəmɑ:kɪt] *n* supermarché *m*

supernatural [su:pə'nætʃərəl] *adj* surnaturel(le)

superpower ['su:pəpauə*] *n* (POL) superpuissance *f*

supersede [su:pə'si:d] *vt* remplacer, supplanter

superstitious [su:pə'stɪʃəs] *adj* superstitieux(euse).

supervise ['su:pəvaɪz] *vt* (children etc) surveiller; (organization, work) diriger

supervision [su:pə'vɪʒən] *n* surveillance *f*; direction *f*; **under medical supervision** sous contrôle du médecin

supervisor ['su:pəvaɪzə*] *n* surveillant/e; (in shop) chef *m* de rayon; (SCOL) directeur/trice de thèse

supper ['sʌpə*] *n* dîner *m*; (late) souper *m*; **to have supper** dîner; souper

supple ['sʌpl] *adj* souple

supplement *n* ['sʌplɪmənt] supplément *m* ♦ *vt* [sʌplɪ'ment] ajouter à, compléter

supplementary [sʌplɪ'mentərɪ] *adj* supplémentaire

supplementary benefit *n* (BRIT) allocation *f* supplémentaire d'aide sociale

supplier [sə'plaɪə*] *n* fournisseur *m*

supply [sə'plaɪ] *vt* (provide) fournir qch (à qn); (people, organization): **to supply sb (with sth)** approvisionner or ravitailler qn (en qch); fournir qn (en qch), fournir qch à qn; (system, machine): **to supply sth (with sth)** alimenter qch (en qch); (a need) répondre à ♦ *n* provision *f*, réserve *f*; (supplying) approvisionnement *m*; (TECH) alimentation *f*; **supplies** *npl* (food) vivres *mpl*; (MIL) subsistances *fpl*; **office supplies** fournitures *fpl* de bureau; **to be in short supply** être rare, manquer; **the electricity/water/gas supply** l'alimentation en électricité/eau/gaz; **supply and demand** l'offre *f* et la demande; **it comes supplied with an adaptor** il (or elle) est pourvu(e) d'un adaptateur

supply teacher *n* (BRIT) suppléant/e

support [sə'pɔ:t] *n* (moral, financial etc) soutien *m*, appui *m*; (TECH) support *m*, soutien ♦ *vt* soutenir, supporter; (financially) subvenir aux besoins de; (uphold) être pour, être partisan de, appuyer; (SPORT: team) être pour; **to support o.s.** (financially) gagner sa vie

supporter [sə'pɔ:tə*] *n* (POL etc) partisan/e; (SPORT) supporter *m*

suppose [sə'pəuz] *vt, vi* supposer; imaginer; **to be supposed to do/be** être censé(e) faire/être); **I don't suppose she'll come** je suppose qu'elle ne viendra pas, cela m'étonnerait qu'elle vienne

supposedly [sə'pəuzɪdlɪ] *adv* soi-disant

supposing [sə'pəuzɪŋ] *conj* si, à supposer que + *sub*

suppress [sə'pres] *vt* (revolt, feeling) réprimer; (publication) supprimer; (scandal) étouffer

supreme [su'pri:m] *adj* suprême

surcharge ['sə:tʃɑ:dʒ] *n* surcharge *f*; (extra tax) surtaxe *f*

sure [ʃuə*] *adj* (gen) sûr(e); (definite, convinced) sûr, certain(e) ♦ *adv* (col: esp US): **that sure is pretty, that's sure pretty** c'est drôlement joli(e); **sure!** (of course) bien sûr!; **sure enough** effectivement; **I'm not sure how/why/when** je ne sais pas très bien comment/pourquoi/quand; **to be sure of o.s.** être sûr de soi; **to make sure of** s'assurer de; vérifier

surely ['ʃuəlɪ] *adv* sûrement; certainement; **surely you don't mean that!** vous ne parlez pas sérieusement!

surf [sə:f] *n* ressac *m*

surface ['sə:fɪs] *n* surface *f* ♦ *vt* (road) poser le revêtement de ♦ *vi* remonter à la surface; faire surface; **on the surface** (fig) au premier abord

surface mail *n* courrier *m* par voie de terre (or maritime)

surfboard ['sə:fbɔ:d] *n* planche *f* de surf

surfeit ['sə:fɪt] *n*: **a surfeit of** un excès de; une indigestion de

surfer ['sə:fə*] *n* (in sea) surfeur/euse; **web** or **net surfer** internaute *m/f*

surfing ['sə:fɪŋ] *n* surf *m*

surge [sə:dʒ] *n* vague *f*, montée *f*; (ELEC) pointe *f* de courant ♦ *vi* déferler; **to surge forward** se précipiter (en avant)

surgeon ['sə:dʒən] *n* chirurgien *m*

surgery ['sə:dʒərɪ] *n* chirurgie *f*; (BRIT: room) cabinet *m* (de consultation); (session) consultation *f*; (of MP etc) permanence *f* (où le député etc reçoit les électeurs etc); **to undergo surgery** être opéré(e)

surgical ['sə:dʒɪkl] *adj* chirurgical(e)

surgical spirit *n* (BRIT) alcool *m* à 90°

surname ['sə:neɪm] *n* nom *m* de famille

surplus ['sə:pləs] n surplus m, excédent m ♦ adj en surplus, de trop; **it is surplus to our requirements** cela dépasse nos besoins; **surplus stock** surplus m

surprise [sə'praɪz] n (gen) surprise f; (astonishment) étonnement m ♦ vt surprendre; étonner; **to take by surprise** (person) prendre au dépourvu; (MIL: town, fort) prendre par surprise

surprising [sə'praɪzɪŋ] adj surprenant(e), étonnant(e)

surprisingly [sə'praɪzɪŋlɪ] adv (easy, helpful) étonnamment, étrangement; **(somewhat) surprisingly, he agreed** curieusement, il a accepté

surrender [sə'rendə*] n reddition f, capitulation f ♦ vi se rendre, capituler ♦ vt (claim, right) renoncer à

surreptitious [sʌrəp'tɪʃəs] adj subreptice, furtif(ive)

surrogate ['sʌrəgɪt] n (BRIT: substitute) substitut m ♦ adj de substitution, de remplacement; **a food surrogate** un succédané alimentaire; **surrogate coffee** ersatz m ou succédané de café

surrogate mother n mère porteuse ou de substitution

surround [sə'raund] vt entourer; (MIL etc) encercler

surrounding [sə'raundɪŋ] adj environnant(e)

surroundings [sə'raundɪŋz] npl environs mpl, alentours mpl

surveillance [sə:'veɪləns] n surveillance f

survey n ['sə:veɪ] enquête f, étude f; (in house buying etc) inspection f, (rapport m d')expertise f; (of land) levé m; (comprehensive view: of situation etc) vue f d'ensemble ♦ vt [sə:'veɪ] passer en revue; enquêter sur; inspecter; (building) expertiser; (land) faire le levé de

surveyor [sə'veɪə*] n (of building) expert m; (of land) (arpenteur m) géomètre m

survival [sə'vaɪvl] n survie f; (relic) vestige m ♦ cpd (course, kit) de survie

survive [sə'vaɪv] vi survivre; (custom etc) subsister ♦ vt survivre à, réchapper de; (person) survivre à

survivor [sə'vaɪvə*] n survivant/e

susceptible [sə'septəbl] adj: **susceptible (to)** sensible (à); (disease) prédisposé(e) (à)

suspect adj, n ['sʌspekt] suspect/e ♦ vt [sə's'pekt] soupçonner, suspecter

suspend [sə's'pend] vt suspendre

suspended sentence [sə's'pendɪd-] n condamnation f avec sursis

suspender belt [sə's'pendə-] n (BRIT) porte-jarretelles m inv

suspenders [sə's'pendəz] npl (BRIT) jarretelles fpl; (US) bretelles fpl

suspense [sə's'pens] n attente f; (in film etc) suspense m

suspension [sə's'penʃən] n (gen, AUT) suspension f; (of driving licence) retrait m provisoire

suspension bridge n pont suspendu

suspicion [sə's'pɪʃən] n soupçon(s) m(pl); **to be under suspicion** être considéré(e) comme suspect(e), être suspecté(e); **arrested on suspicion of murder** arrêté sur présomption de meurtre

suspicious [sə's'pɪʃəs] adj (suspecting) soupçonneux(euse), méfiant(e); (causing suspicion) suspect(e); **to be suspicious of** or **about sb/sth** avoir des doutes à propos de qn/sur qch, trouver qn/qch suspect(e)

sustain [sə's'teɪn] vt supporter; soutenir; corroborer; (suffer) subir; recevoir

sustainable [sə's'teɪnəbl] adj (rate, growth) qui peut être maintenu(e); (agriculture, development) durable

sustained [sə's'teɪnd] adj (effort) soutenu(e), prolongé(e)

sustenance ['sʌstɪnəns] n nourriture f; moyens mpl de subsistance

SUV n abbr (esp US: = sports utility vehicle) SUV m

swab [swɔb] n (MED) tampon m; prélèvement m ♦ vt (NAUT: also: **swab down**) nettoyer

swagger ['swægə*] vi plastronner, parader

swallow ['swɔləu] n (bird) hirondelle f; (of food etc) gorgée f ♦ vt avaler; (fig) gober

▶ **swallow up** vt engloutir

swam [swæm] pt of **swim**

swamp [swɔmp] n marais m, marécage m ♦ vt submerger

swan [swɔn] n cygne m

swap [swɔp] n échange m, troc m ♦ vt: **to swap (for)** échanger (contre), troquer (contre)

swarm [swɔ:m] n essaim m ♦ vi essaimer; fourmiller, grouiller

swastika ['swɔstɪkə] n croix gammée

swat [swɔt] vt écraser ♦ n (BRIT: also: **fly swat**) tapette f

sway [sweɪ] vi se balancer, osciller; tanguer ♦ vt (influence) influencer ♦ n (rule, power): **sway (over)** emprise f (sur); **to hold sway over sb** avoir de l'emprise sur qn

swear, pt **swore**, pp **sworn** [swɛə*, swɔ:*, swɔ:n] vi jurer; **to swear to sth** jurer de qch; **to swear an oath** prêter serment

▶ **swear in** vt assermenter

swearword ['swɛəwə:d] n gros mot, juron m

sweat [swet] n sueur f, transpiration f ♦ vi suer; **in a sweat** en sueur

sweater ['swetə*] n tricot m, pull m

sweaty ['swetɪ] adj en sueur, moite or mouillé(e) de sueur

Swede [swi:d] n Suédois/e

swede [swi:d] n (BRIT) rutabaga m

Sweden ['swi:dn] n Suède f

Swedish ['swi:dɪʃ] adj suédois(e) ♦ n (LING) suédois m

sweep [swi:p] n coup m de balai; (curve) grande

courbe; (*range*) champ *m*; (*also:* **chimney sweep**) ramoneur *m* ◆ *vb, pt, pp* **swept** [swept] *vt* balayer; (*fashion, craze*) se répandre dans ◆ *vi* avancer majestueusement *or* rapidement; s'élancer; s'étendre

▶ **sweep away** *vt* balayer; entraîner; emporter

▶ **sweep past** *vi* passer majestueusement *or* rapidement

▶ **sweep up** *vt, vi* balayer

sweeping ['swi:pɪŋ] *adj* (*gesture*) large; circulaire; (*changes, reforms*) radical(e); **a sweeping statement** une généralisation hâtive

sweet [swi:t] *n* (*BRIT*) dessert *m*; (*candy*) bonbon *m* ◆ *adj* doux(douce); (*not savoury*) sucré(e); (*fresh*) frais((fraîche), pur(e); (*kind*) gentil(le); (*cute*) mignon(ne) ◆ *adv*: **to smell sweet** sentir bon; **to taste sweet** avoir un goût sucré; **sweet and sour** *adj* aigre-doux(douce)

sweetcorn ['swi:tkɔːn] *n* maïs doux

sweeten ['swi:tn] *vt* sucrer; (*fig*) adoucir

sweetheart ['swi:thɑːt] *n* amoureux/euse

sweetness ['swi:tnɪs] *n* douceur *f*; (*of taste*) goût sucré

sweet pea *n* pois *m* de senteur

swell [swɛl] *n* (*of sea*) houle *f* ◆ *adj* (*col: excellent*) chouette ◆ *vb, pt* **swelled**, *pp* **swollen** *or* **swelled** ['swəulən] *vt* augmenter; grossir ◆ *vi* grossir, augmenter; (*sound*) s'enfler; (*MED*) enfler

swelling ['swɛlɪŋ] *n* (*MED*) enflure *f*; grosseur *f*

sweltering ['swɛltərɪŋ] *adj* étouffant(e), oppressant(e)

swept [swept] *pt, pp* of **sweep**

swerve [swəːv] *vi* faire une embardée *or* un écart; dévier

swift [swɪft] *n* (*bird*) martinet *m* ◆ *adj* rapide, prompt(e)

swig [swɪg] *n* (*col: drink*) lampée *f*

swill [swɪl] *n* pâtée *f* ◆ *vt* (*also:* **swill out**, **swill down**) laver à grande eau

swim [swɪm] *n*: **to go for a swim** aller nager *or* se baigner ◆ *vb, pt* **swam**, *pp* **swum** [swæm, swʌm] *vi* nager; (*SPORT*) faire de la natation; (*fig: head, room*) tourner ◆ *vt* traverser (à la nage); (*distance*) faire (à la nage); **to swim a length** nager une longueur; **to go swimming** aller nager

swimmer ['swɪmə*] *n* nageur/euse

swimming ['swɪmɪŋ] *n* nage *f*, natation *f*

swimming cap *n* bonnet *m* de bain

swimming costume *n* (*BRIT*) maillot *m* (de bain)

swimming pool *n* piscine *f*

swimming trunks *npl* maillot *m* de bain

swimsuit ['swɪmsuːt] *n* maillot *m* (de bain)

swindle ['swɪndl] *n* escroquerie *f* ◆ *vt* escroquer

swine [swaɪn] *n* (*pl inv*) pourceau *m*, porc *m*; (*col!*) salaud *m* (!)

swing [swɪŋ] *n* balançoire *f*; (*movement*) balance-

ment *m*, oscillations *fpl*; (*MUS*) swing *m*; rythme *m* ◆ *vb, pt, pp* **swung** [swʌŋ] *vt* balancer, faire osciller; (*also:* **swing round**) tourner, faire virer ◆ *vi* se balancer, osciller; (*also:* **swing round**) virer, tourner; **a swing to the left** (*POL*) un revirement en faveur de la gauche; **to be in full swing** battre son plein; **to get into the swing of things** se mettre dans le bain; **the road swings south** la route prend la direction sud

swing bridge *n* pont tournant

swing door *n* (*BRIT*) porte battante

swingeing ['swɪndʒɪŋ] *adj* (*BRIT*) écrasant(e); considérable

swipe [swaɪp] *n* grand coup; gifle *f* ◆ *vt* (*hit*) frapper à toute volée; gifler; (*col: steal*) piquer; (*credit card etc*) faire passer (dans la machine)

swirl [swəːl] *n* tourbillon *m* ◆ *vi* tourbillonner, tournoyer

Swiss [swɪs] *adj* suisse ◆ *n* (*pl inv*) Suisse/esse

switch [swɪtʃ] *n* (*for light, radio etc*) bouton *m*; (*change*) changement *m*, revirement *m* ◆ *vt* (*change*) changer; (*exchange*) intervertir; (*invert*): **to switch (round** *or* **over)** changer de place

▶ **switch off** *vt* éteindre; (*engine*) arrêter

▶ **switch on** *vt* allumer; (*engine, machine*) mettre en marche; (*BRIT: water supply*) ouvrir

switchboard ['swɪtʃbɔːd] *n* (*TEL*) standard *m*

Switzerland ['swɪtsələnd] *n* Suisse *f*

swivel ['swɪvl] *vi* (*also:* **swivel round**) pivoter, tourner

swollen ['swəulən] *pp* of **swell** ◆ *adj* (*ankle etc*) enflé(e)

swoon [swuːn] *vi* se pâmer

swoop [swuːp] *n* (*by police etc*) rafle *f*, descente *f*; (*of bird etc*) descente *f* en piqué ◆ *vi* (*also:* **swoop down**) descendre en piqué, piquer

swop [swɔp] *n, vt* = **swap**

sword [sɔːd] *n* épée *f*

swordfish ['sɔːdfɪʃ] *n* espadon *m*

swore [swɔː*] *pt* of **swear**

sworn [swɔːn] *pp* of **swear**

swot [swɔt] *vt, vi* bûcher, potasser

swum [swʌm] *pp* of **swim**

swung [swʌŋ] *pt, pp* of **swing**

syllable ['sɪləbl] *n* syllabe *f*

syllabus ['sɪləbəs] *n* programme *m*; **on the syllabus** au programme

symbol ['sɪmbl] *n* symbole *m*

symmetry ['sɪmɪtrɪ] *n* symétrie *f*

sympathetic [sɪmpə'θεtɪk] *adj* (*showing pity*) compatissant(e); (*understanding*) bienveillant(e), compréhensif(ive); **sympathetic towards** bien disposé(e) envers

sympathize ['sɪmpəθaɪz] *vi*: **to sympathize with sb** (*in grief*) être de tout cœur avec qn, compatir à la douleur de qn; (*in predicament*) partager les sentiments de qn; **to sympathize with** (*sb's feelings*) comprendre

sympathizer ['sɪmpəθaɪzə*] n (POL) sympathisant/e

sympathy ['sɪmpəθɪ] n compassion f; **in sympathy with** en accord avec; (strike) en or par solidarité avec; **with our deepest sympathy** en vous priant d'accepter nos sincères condoléances

symphony ['sɪmfənɪ] n symphonie f

symptom ['sɪmptəm] n symptôme m; indice m

syndicate ['sɪndɪkɪt] n syndicat m, coopérative f; (PRESS) agence f de presse

synopsis, pl **synopses** [sɪ'nɒpsɪs, -siːz] n résumé m, synopsis m or f

synthetic [sɪn'θetɪk] adj synthétique ◆ n matière f synthétique; **synthetics** npl textiles artificiels

syphon ['saɪfən] n, vb = **siphon**

Syria ['sɪrɪə] n Syrie f

syringe [sɪ'rɪndʒ] n seringue f

syrup ['sɪrəp] n sirop m; (BRIT: also: **golden syrup**) mélasse raffinée

system ['sɪstəm] n système m; (order) méthode f; (ANAT) organisme m

systematic [sɪstə'mætɪk] adj systématique; méthodique

system disk n (COMPUT) disque m système

systems analyst n analyste-programmeur m/f

— T t —

ta [tɑː] excl (BRIT col) merci!

tab [tæb] n abbr = **tabulator** ◆ n (loop on coat etc) attache f; (label) étiquette f; **to keep tabs on** (fig) surveiller

tabby ['tæbɪ] n (also: **tabby cat**) chat/te tigré(e)

table ['teɪbl] n table f ◆ vt (BRIT: motion etc) présenter; **to lay** or **set the table** mettre le couvert or la table; **to clear the table** débarrasser la table; **league table** (BRIT FOOTBALL, RUGBY) classement m (du championnat); **table of contents** table des matières

tablecloth ['teɪblklɒθ] n nappe f

table d'hôte [tɑːbl'dəut] adj (meal) à prix fixe

table lamp n lampe décorative

tablemat ['teɪblmæt] n (for plate) napperon m, set m; (for hot dish) dessous-de-plat m inv

tablespoon ['teɪblspuːn] n cuiller f de service; (also: **tablespoonful**: as measurement) cuillerée f à soupe

tablet ['tæblɪt] n (MED) comprimé m; (: for sucking) pastille f; (of stone) plaque f; **tablet of soap** (BRIT) savonnette f

table tennis n ping-pong m, tennis m de table

table wine n vin m de table

tabloid ['tæblɔɪd] n (newspaper) tabloïde m; **the tabloids** les journaux mpl populaires

tabloid press n voir encadré

TABLOID PRESS

Le terme **tabloid press** désigne les journaux populaires de demi-format où l'on trouve beaucoup de photos et qui adoptent un style très concis. Ce type de journaux vise des lecteurs s'intéressant aux faits divers ayant un parfum de scandale; voir "quality press".

---

tack [tæk] n (nail) petit clou; (stitch) point m de bâti; (NAUT) bord m, bordée f ◆ vt clouer; bâtir ◆ vi tirer un or des bord(s); **to change tack** virer de bord; **on the wrong tack** (fig) sur la mauvaise voie; **to tack sth on to (the end of) sth** (of letter, book) rajouter qch à la fin de qch

tackle ['tækl] n matériel m, équipement m; (for lifting) appareil m de levage; (FOOTBALL, RUGBY) plaquage m ◆ vt (difficulty) s'attaquer à; (FOOTBALL, RUGBY) plaquer

tacky ['tækɪ] adj collant(e); pas sec(sèche); (col: shabby) moche

tact [tækt] n tact m

tactful ['tæktful] adj plein(e) de tact

tactical ['tæktɪkl] adj tactique; **tactical error** erreur f de tactique

tactics ['tæktɪks] n, npl tactique f

tactless ['tæktlɪs] adj qui manque de tact

tadpole ['tædpəul] n têtard m

tag [tæg] n étiquette f; **price/name tag** étiquette (portant le prix/le nom)

▶ **tag along** vi suivre

tail [teɪl] n queue f; (of shirt) pan m ◆ vt (follow) suivre, filer; **to turn tail** se sauver à toutes jambes; see also **head**

▶ **tail away**

▶ **tail off** vi (in size, quality etc) baisser peu à peu

tailback ['teɪlbæk] n (BRIT) bouchon m

tail end n bout m, fin f

tailgate ['teɪlgeɪt] n (AUT) hayon m arrière

tailor ['teɪlə*] n tailleur m (artisan) ◆ vt: **to tailor sth (to)** adapter qch exactement (à); **tailor's (shop)** (boutique f de) tailleur m

tailoring ['teɪlərɪŋ] n (cut) coupe f

tailor-made ['teɪlə'meɪd] adj fait(e) sur mesure; (fig) conçu(e) spécialement

tailwind ['teɪlwɪnd] n vent m arrière inv

tainted ['teɪntɪd] adj (food) gâté(e); (water, air) infecté(e); (fig) souillé(e)

take [teɪk] vb, pt **took**, pp **taken** [tuk, 'teɪkn] vt prendre; (gain: prize) remporter; (require: effort, courage) demander; (tolerate) accepter, supporter; (hold: passengers etc) contenir; (accompany) emmener, accompagner; (bring, carry) apporter, emporter;

(*exam*) passer, se présenter à; (*conduct: meeting*) présider ◆ *vi* (*dye, fire etc*) prendre ◆ *n* (*CINE*) prise *f* de vues; **to take sth from** (*drawer etc*) prendre qch dans; (*person*) prendre qch à; **I take it that** je suppose que; **I took him for a doctor** je l'ai pris pour un docteur; **to take sb's hand** prendre qn par la main; **to take for a walk** (*child, dog*) emmener promener; **to be taken ill** tomber malade; **to take it upon o.s. to do sth** prendre sur soi de faire qch; **take the first (street) on the left** prenez la première à gauche; **it won't take long** ça ne prendra pas longtemps; **I was quite taken with her/it** elle/cela m'a beaucoup plu

▶ **take after** *vt fus* ressembler à

▶ **take apart** *vt* démonter

▶ **take away** *vt* emporter; (*remove*) enlever; (*subtract*) soustraire ◆ *vi*: **to take away from** diminuer

▶ **take back** *vt* (*return*) rendre, rapporter; (*one's words*) retirer

▶ **take down** *vt* (*building*) démolir; (*dismantle: scaffolding*) démonter; (*letter etc*) prendre, écrire

▶ **take in** *vt* (*deceive*) tromper, rouler; (*understand*) comprendre, saisir; (*include*) couvrir, inclure; (*lodger*) prendre; (*orphan, stray dog*) recueillir; (*dress, waistband*) reprendre

▶ **take off** *vi* (*AVIAT*) décoller ◆ *vt* (*remove*) enlever; (*imitate*) imiter, pasticher

▶ **take on** *vt* (*work*) accepter, se charger de; (*employee*) prendre, embaucher; (*opponent*) accepter de se battre contre

▶ **take out** *vt* sortir; (*remove*) enlever; (*licence*) prendre, se procurer; **to take sth out of** enlever qch de; **don't take it out on me!** ne t'en prends pas à moi!

▶ **take over** *vt* (*business*) reprendre ◆ *vi*: **to take over from sb** prendre la relève de qn

▶ **take to** *vt fus* (*person*) se prendre d'amitié pour; (*activity*) prendre goût à; **to take to doing sth** prendre l'habitude de faire qch

▶ **take up** *vt* (*one's story, a dress*) reprendre; (*occupy: time, space*) prendre, occuper; (*engage in: hobby etc*) se mettre à; (*accept: offer, challenge*) accepter; (*absorb: liquids*) absorber ◆ *vi*: **to take up with sb** se lier d'amitié avec qn

takeaway ['teɪkəweɪ] (*BRIT*) *adj* (*food*) à emporter ◆ *n* (*shop, restaurant*) ≈ traiteur *m* (*qui vend des plats à emporter*)

takeoff ['teɪkɒf] *n* (*AVIAT*) décollage *m*

takeover ['teɪkəʊvə*] *n* (*COMM*) rachat *m*

takings ['teɪkɪŋz] *npl* (*COMM*) recette *f*

talc [tælk] *n* (*also*: **talcum powder**) talc *m*

tale [teɪl] *n* (*story*) conte *m*, histoire *f*; (*account*) récit *m*; (*pej*) histoire; **to tell tales** (*fig*) rapporter

talent ['tælnt] *n* talent *m*, don *m*

talented ['tæləntɪd] *adj* doué(e), plein(e) de talent

talk [tɔːk] *n* propos *mpl*; (*gossip*) racontars *mpl* (*pej*); (*conversation*) discussion *f*; (*interview*) entretien *m*; (*a speech*) causerie *f*, exposé *m* ◆ *vi* (*chatter*) bavarder; **talks** *npl* (*POL etc*) entretiens *mpl*; conférence *f*; **to give a talk** faire un exposé; **to talk about** parler de; (*converse*) s'entretenir or parler de; **talking of films, have you seen …?** à propos de films, avez-vous vu …?; **to talk sb out of/into doing** persuader qn de ne pas faire/de faire; **to talk shop** parler métier or affaires

▶ **talk over** *vt* discuter (de)

talkative ['tɔːkətɪv] *adj* bavard(e)

talk show *n* (*TV, RADIO*) causerie (télévisée or radiodiffusée)

tall [tɔːl] *adj* (*person*) grand(e); (*building, tree*) haut(e); **to be 6 feet tall** ≈ mesurer 1 mètre 80; **how tall are you?** combien mesurez-vous?

tall story *n* histoire *f* invraisemblable

tally ['tælɪ] *n* compte *m* ◆ *vi*: **to tally (with)** correspondre (à); **to keep a tally of sth** tenir le compte de qch

talon ['tælən] *n* griffe *f*; (*of eagle*) serre *f*

tame [teɪm] *adj* apprivoisé(e); (*fig: story, style*) insipide

tamper ['tæmpə*] *vi*: **to tamper with** toucher à (*en cachette ou sans permission*)

tampon ['tæmpən] *n* tampon *m* hygiénique or périodique

tan [tæn] *n* (*also*: **suntan**) bronzage *m* ◆ *vt, vi* bronzer, brunir ◆ *adj* (*colour*) brun roux *inv*; **to get a tan** bronzer

tang [tæŋ] *n* odeur (*or saveur*) piquante

tangent ['tændʒənt] *n* (*MATH*) tangente *f*; **to go off at a tangent** (*fig*) changer complètement de direction

tangerine [tændʒə'riːn] *n* mandarine *f*

tangle ['tæŋgl] *n* enchevêtrement *m* ◆ *vt* enchevêtrer; **to get in(to) a tangle** s'emmêler

tank [tæŋk] *n* réservoir *m*; (*for processing*) cuve *f*; (*for fish*) aquarium *m*; (*MIL*) char *m* d'assaut, tank *m*

tanker ['tæŋkə*] *n* (*ship*) pétrolier *m*, tanker *m*; (*truck*) camion-citerne *m*; (*RAIL*) wagon-citerne *m*

tantalizing ['tæntəlaɪzɪŋ] *adj* (*smell*) extrêmement appétissant(e); (*offer*) terriblement tentant(e)

tantamount ['tæntəmaunt] *adj*: **tantamount to** qui équivaut à

tantrum ['tæntrəm] *n* accès *m* de colère; **to throw a tantrum** piquer une colère

tap [tæp] *n* (*on sink etc*) robinet *m*; (*gentle blow*) petite tape ◆ *vt* frapper or taper légèrement; (*resources*) exploiter, utiliser; (*telephone*) mettre sur écoute; **on tap** (*beer*) en tonneau; (*fig: resources*) disponible

tap-dancing ['tæpdɑːnsɪŋ] *n* claquettes *fpl*

tape [teɪp] *n* ruban *m*; (*also*: **magnetic tape**) bande *f* (magnétique) ◆ *vt* (*record*) enregistrer (au magnétophone or sur bande); **on tape** (*song etc*) enregistré(e)

tape deck *n* platine *f* d'enregistrement

tape measure *n* mètre *m* à ruban

taper ['teɪpə*] n cierge m ♦ vi s'effiler
tape recorder n magnétophone m
tapestry ['tæpɪstrɪ] n tapisserie f
tar [tɑː] n goudron m; **low-/middle-tar cigarettes** cigarettes fpl à faible/moyenne teneur en goudron
target ['tɑːgɪt] n cible f; (fig: objective) objectif m; **to be on target** (project) progresser comme prévu
tariff ['tærɪf] n (COMM) tarif m; (taxes) tarif douanier
tarmac ['tɑːmæk] n (BRIT: on road) macadam m; (AVIAT) aire f d'envol ♦ vt (BRIT) goudronner
tarnish ['tɑːnɪʃ] vt ternir
tarpaulin [tɑː'pɔːlɪn] n bâche goudronnée
tarragon ['tærəgən] n estragon m
tart [tɑːt] n (CULIN) tarte f; (BRIT col: pej: woman) poule f ♦ adj (flavour) âpre, aigrelet(te)
► **tart up** vt (col:): **to tart o.s. up** se faire beau(belle); (: pej) s'attifer
tartan ['tɑːtn] n tartan m ♦ adj écossais(e)
tartar ['tɑːtə*] n (on teeth) tartre m
tartar sauce n sauce f tartare
task [tɑːsk] n tâche f; **to take to task** prendre à partie
task force n (MIL, POLICE) détachement spécial
tassel ['tæsl] n gland m; pompon m
taste [teɪst] n goût m; (fig: glimpse, idea) idée f, aperçu m ♦ vt goûter ♦ vi: **to taste of** (fish etc) avoir le or un goût de; **it tastes like fish** ça a un or le goût de poisson, on dirait du poisson; **what does it taste like?** quel goût ça a?; **you can taste the garlic (in it)** on sent bien l'ail; **can I have a taste of this wine?** puis-je goûter un peu de ce vin?; **to have a taste of sth** goûter (à) qch; **to have a taste for sth** aimer qch, avoir un penchant pour qch; **to be in good/bad** or **poor taste** être de bon/mauvais goût
tasteful ['teɪstful] adj de bon goût
tasteless ['teɪstlɪs] adj (food) qui n'a aucun goût; (remark) de mauvais goût
tasty ['teɪstɪ] adj savoureux(euse), délicieux(euse)
tatters ['tætəz] npl: **in tatters** (also: **tattered**) en lambeaux
tattoo [tə'tuː] n tatouage m; (spectacle) parade f militaire ♦ vt tatouer
tatty ['tætɪ] adj (BRIT col) défraîchi(e), en piteux état
taught [tɔːt] pt, pp of **teach**
taunt [tɔːnt] n raillerie f ♦ vt railler
Taurus ['tɔːrəs] n le Taureau; **to be Taurus** être du Taureau
taut [tɔːt] adj tendu(e)
tax [tæks] n (on goods etc) taxe f; (on income) impôts mpl, contributions fpl ♦ vt taxer; imposer; (fig: strain: patience etc) mettre à l'épreuve; **before/after tax** avant/après l'impôt; **free of tax** exonéré(e) d'impôt
taxable ['tæksəbl] adj (income) imposable
taxation [tæk'seɪʃən] n taxation f; impôts mpl, contributions fpl; **system of taxation** système fiscal

tax avoidance n évasion fiscale
tax disc n (BRIT AUT) vignette f (automobile)
tax evasion n fraude fiscale
tax-free ['tæksfriː] adj exempt(e) d'impôts
taxi ['tæksɪ] n taxi m ♦ vi (AVIAT) rouler (lentement) au sol
taxi driver n chauffeur m de taxi
taxi rank (BRIT), **taxi stand** n station f de taxis
tax payer [-peɪə*] n contribuable m/f
tax relief n dégrèvement or allègement fiscal, réduction f d'impôt
tax return n déclaration f d'impôts or de revenus
TB n abbr = **tuberculosis**
tea [tiː] n thé m; (BRIT: snack: for children) goûter m; **high tea** collation combinant goûter et dîner
tea bag n sachet m de thé
tea break n (BRIT) pause-thé f
teach, pt, pp **taught** [tiːtʃ, tɔːt] vt: **to teach sb sth**, **teach sth to sb** apprendre qch à qn; (in school etc) enseigner qch à qn ♦ vi enseigner; **it taught him a lesson** (fig) ça lui a servi de leçon
teacher ['tiːtʃə*] n (in secondary school) professeur m; (in primary school) instituteur/trice; **French teacher** professeur de français
teaching ['tiːtʃɪŋ] n enseignement m
tea cloth n torchon m
tea cosy n couvre-théière m
teacup ['tiːkʌp] n tasse f à thé
teak [tiːk] n teck m ♦ adj en or de teck
tea leaves npl feuilles fpl de thé
team [tiːm] n équipe f; (of animals) attelage m
► **team up** vi: **to team up (with)** faire équipe (avec)
teamwork ['tiːmwɜːk] n travail m d'équipe
teapot ['tiːpɔt] n théière f
tear[1] n ['tɛə*] déchirure f ♦ vb, pt **tore**, pp **torn** [tɔː*, tɔːn] vt déchirer ♦ vi se déchirer; **to tear to pieces** or **to bits** or **to shreds** mettre en pièces; (fig) démolir
► **tear along** vi (rush) aller à toute vitesse
► **tear apart** vt (also fig) déchirer
► **tear away** vt: **to tear o.s. away (from sth)** (fig) s'arracher (de qch)
► **tear out** vt (sheet of paper, cheque) arracher
► **tear up** vt (sheet of paper etc) déchirer, mettre en morceaux or pièces
tear[2] n ['tɪə*] larme f; **in tears** en larmes; **to burst into tears** fondre en larmes
tearful ['tɪəful] adj larmoyant(e)
tear gas ['tɪə-] n gaz m lacrymogène
tearoom ['tiːruːm] n salon m de thé
tease [tiːz] n taquin/e ♦ vt taquiner; (unkindly) tourmenter
tea set n service m à thé

teaspoon ['ti:spu:n] *n* petite cuiller; (*also:* **tea-spoonful**: *as measurement*) ≃ cuillerée *f* à café

teat [ti:t] *n* tétine *f*

teatime ['ti:taɪm] *n* l'heure *f* du thé

tea towel *n* (*BRIT*) torchon *m* (à vaisselle)

technical ['tɛknɪkl] *adj* technique

technicality [tɛknɪ'kælɪtɪ] *n* technicité *f*; (*detail*) détail *m* technique; **on a legal technicality** à cause de (*or* grâce à) l'application à la lettre d'une subtilité juridique; pour vice de forme

technically ['tɛknɪklɪ] *adv* techniquement; (*strictly speaking*) en théorie, en principe

technician [tɛk'nɪʃən] *n* technicien/ne

technique [tɛk'ni:k] *n* technique *f*

techno ['tɛknəʊ] *n* (*MUS*) techno *f*

technological [tɛknə'lɔdʒɪkl] *adj* technologique

technology [tɛk'nɔlədʒɪ] *n* technologie *f*

teddy (bear) ['tɛdɪ-] *n* ours *m* (en peluche)

tedious ['ti:dɪəs] *adj* fastidieux(euse)

tee [ti:] *n* (*GOLF*) tee *m*

teem [ti:m] *vi:* **to teem (with)** grouiller (de); **it is teeming (with rain)** il pleut à torrents

teenage ['ti:neɪdʒ] *adj* (*fashions etc*) pour jeunes, pour adolescents

teenager ['ti:neɪdʒə*] *n* jeune *m/f*, adolescent/e

teens [ti:nz] *npl:* **to be in one's teens** être adolescent(e)

tee-shirt ['ti:ʃə:t] *n* = **T-shirt**

teeter ['ti:tə*] *vi* chanceler, vaciller

teeth [ti:θ] *npl of* **tooth**

teethe [ti:ð] *vi* percer ses dents

teething troubles ['ti:ðɪŋ-] *npl* (*fig*) difficultés initiales

teetotal ['ti:'təʊtl] *adj* (*person*) qui ne boit jamais d'alcool

telecommunications ['tɛlɪkəmju:nɪ'keɪʃənz] *n* télécommunications *fpl*

teleconferencing [tɛlɪ'kɔnfərənsɪŋ] *n* téléconférence(s) *f(pl)*

telegram ['tɛlɪgræm] *n* télégramme *m*

telegraph ['tɛlɪgrɑ:f] *n* télégraphe *m*

telegraph pole *n* poteau *m* télégraphique

telephone ['tɛlɪfəʊn] *n* téléphone *m* ♦ *vt* (*person*) téléphoner à; (*message*) téléphoner; **to have a telephone**, (*BRIT*) **to be on the telephone** (*subscriber*) être abonné(e) au téléphone; **to be on the telephone** (*be speaking*) être au téléphone

telephone booth, (*BRIT*) **telephone box** *n* cabine *f* téléphonique

telephone call *n* appel *m* téléphonique, communication *f* téléphonique

telephone directory *n* annuaire *m* (du téléphone)

telephone number *n* numéro *m* de téléphone

telephonist [tə'lɛfənɪst] *n* (*BRIT*) téléphoniste *m/f*

telesales ['tɛlɪseɪlz] *npl* télévente *f*

telescope ['tɛlɪskəʊp] *n* télescope *m* ♦ *vi* se télescoper ♦ *vt* télescoper

television ['tɛlɪvɪʒən] *n* télévision *f*

television set *n* poste *m* de télévision, téléviseur *m*

telex ['tɛlɛks] *n* télex *m* ♦ *vt* (*message*) envoyer par télex; (*person*) envoyer un télex à ♦ *vi* envoyer un télex

tell, *pt*, *pp* **told** [tɛl, təʊld] *vt* dire; (*relate: story*) raconter; (*distinguish*): **to tell sth from** distinguer qch de ♦ *vi* (*talk*): **to tell (of)** parler (de); (*have effect*) se faire sentir, se voir; **to tell sb to do** dire à qn de faire; **to tell sb about sth** (*place, object etc*) parler de qch à qn; (*what happened etc*) raconter qch à qn; **to tell the time** (*know how to*) savoir lire l'heure; **can you tell me the time?** pourriez-vous me dire l'heure?; **(I) tell you what ...** écoute, ...; **I can't tell them apart** je n'arrive pas à les distinguer

▶ **tell off** *vt* réprimander, gronder

▶ **tell on** *vt fus* (*inform against*) dénoncer, rapporter contre

teller ['tɛlə*] *n* (*in bank*) caissier/ière

telling ['tɛlɪŋ] *adj* (*remark, detail*) révélateur(trice)

telltale ['tɛlteɪl] *n* rapporteur/euse ♦ *adj* (*sign*) éloquent(e), révélateur(trice)

telly ['tɛlɪ] *n abbr* (*BRIT col:* = *television*) télé *f*

temp [tɛmp] *abbr* (*BRIT col*) = *temporary* ♦ *n* intérimaire *m/f* ♦ *vi* travailler comme intérimaire

temper ['tɛmpə*] *n* (*nature*) caractère *m*; (*mood*) humeur *f*; (*fit of anger*) colère *f* ♦ *vt* (*moderate*) tempérer, adoucir; **to be in a temper** être en colère; **to lose one's temper** se mettre en colère; **to keep one's temper** rester calme

temperament ['tɛmprəmənt] *n* (*nature*) tempérament *m*

temperamental [tɛmprə'mɛntl] *adj* capricieux(euse)

temperate ['tɛmprət] *adj* modéré(e); (*climate*) tempéré(e)

temperature ['tɛmprətʃə*] *n* température *f*; **to have** *or* **run a temperature** avoir de la fièvre

temple ['tɛmpl] *n* (*building*) temple *m*; (*ANAT*) tempe *f*

temporary ['tɛmpərɪ] *adj* temporaire, provisoire; (*job, worker*) temporaire; **temporary secretary** (secrétaire *f*) intérimaire *f*; **a temporary teacher** un professeur remplaçant *or* suppléant

tempt [tɛmpt] *vt* tenter; **to tempt sb into doing** induire qn à faire; **to be tempted to do sth** être tenté(e) de faire qch

temptation [tɛmp'teɪʃən] *n* tentation *f*

tempting ['tɛmptɪŋ] *adj* tentant(e)

ten [tɛn] *num* dix ♦ *n:* **tens of thousands** des dizaines *fpl* de milliers

tenacity [tə'næsɪtɪ] *n* ténacité *f*

tenancy ['tenənsı] n location f; état m de locataire

tenant ['tenənt] n locataire m/f

tend [tend] vt s'occuper de; (sick etc) soigner ♦ vi: **to tend to do** avoir tendance à faire; (colour): **to tend to** tirer sur

tendency ['tendənsı] n tendance f

tender ['tendə*] adj tendre; (delicate) délicat(e); (sore) sensible; (affectionate) tendre, doux(douce) ♦ n (COMM: offer) soumission f; (money): **legal tender** cours légal ♦ vt offrir; **to tender one's resignation** donner or remettre sa démission; **to put in a tender (for)** faire une soumission (pour); **to put work out to tender** (BRIT) mettre un contrat en adjudication

tenement ['tenəmənt] n immeuble m (de rapport)

tennis ['tenɪs] n tennis m ♦ cpd (club, match, racket, player) de tennis

tennis ball n balle f de tennis

tennis court n (court m de) tennis m

tennis player n joueur/euse de tennis

tennis racket n raquette f de tennis

tennis shoes npl (chaussures fpl de) tennis mpl

tenor ['tenə*] n (MUS) ténor m; (of speech etc) sens général

tenpin bowling ['tenpɪn-] n (BRIT) bowling m (à 10 quilles)

tense [tens] adj tendu(e); (person) tendu, crispé(e) ♦ n (LING) temps m ♦ vt (tighten: muscles) tendre

tension ['tenʃən] n tension f

tent [tent] n tente f

tentative ['tentətɪv] adj timide, hésitant(e); (conclusion) provisoire

tenterhooks ['tentəhuks] npl: **on tenterhooks** sur des charbons ardents

tenth [tenθ] num dixième

tent peg n piquet m de tente

tent pole n montant m de tente

tenuous ['tenjuəs] adj ténu(e)

tenure ['tenjuə*] n (of property) bail m; (of job) période f de jouissance; statut m de titulaire

tepid ['tepɪd] adj tiède

term [tə:m] n (limit) terme m; (word) terme, mot m; (SCOL) trimestre m; (LAW) session f ♦ vt appeler; **terms** npl (conditions) conditions fpl; (COMM) tarif m; **term of imprisonment** peine f de prison; **his term of office** la période où il était en fonction; **in the short/long term** à court/long terme; **"easy terms"** (COMM) "facilités de paiement"; **to come to terms with** (problem) faire face à; **to be on good terms with** bien s'entendre avec, être en bons termes avec

terminal ['tə:mɪnl] adj terminal(e); (disease) dans sa phase terminale ♦ n (ELEC) borne f; (for oil, ore etc, also COMPUT) terminal m; (also: **air terminal**) aérogare f; (BRIT: also: **coach terminal**) gare routière

terminally ['tə:mɪnlı] adv: **to be terminally ill** être condamné(e)

terminate ['tə:mɪneɪt] vt mettre fin à ♦ vi: **to terminate in** finir en or par

termini ['tə:mɪnaɪ] npl of **terminus**

terminus, pl **termini** ['tə:mɪnəs, 'tə:mɪnaɪ] n terminus m inv

terrace ['terəs] n terrasse f; (BRIT: row of houses) rangée f de maisons (attenantes les unes aux autres); **the terraces** (BRIT SPORT) les gradins mpl

terraced ['terəst] adj (garden) en terrasses; (in a row: house, cottage etc) attenant(e) aux maisons voisines

terracotta ['terə'kɔtə] n terre cuite

terrain [te'reɪn] n terrain m (sol)

terrible ['terɪbl] adj terrible, atroce; (weather, work) affreux(euse), épouvantable

terribly ['terɪblɪ] adv terriblement; (very badly) affreusement mal

terrier ['terɪə*] n terrier m (chien)

terrific [tə'rɪfɪk] adj fantastique, incroyable, terrible; (wonderful) formidable, sensationnel(le)

terrify ['terɪfaɪ] vt terrifier

territory ['terɪtərɪ] n territoire m

terror ['terə*] n terreur f

terrorism ['terərɪzəm] n terrorisme m

terrorist ['terərɪst] n terroriste m/f

terrorist attack m attaque f terroriste

test [test] n (trial, check) essai m; (: of goods in factory) contrôle m; (of courage etc) épreuve f; (MED) examens mpl; (CHEM) analyses fpl; (exam: of intelligence etc) test m (d'aptitude); (: in school) interrogation f de contrôle; (also: **driving test**) (examen du) permis m de conduire ♦ vt essayer; contrôler; mettre à l'épreuve; examiner; analyser; tester; faire subir une interrogation (de contrôle) à; **to put sth to the test** mettre qch à l'épreuve

testament ['testəmənt] n testament m; **the Old/New Testament** l'Ancien/le Nouveau Testament

testicle ['testɪkl] n testicule m

testify ['testɪfaɪ] vi (LAW) témoigner, déposer; **to testify to sth** (LAW) attester qch; (gen) témoigner de qch

testimony ['testɪmənɪ] n (LAW) témoignage m, déposition f

test match n (CRICKET, RUGBY) match international

test tube n éprouvette f

tetanus ['tetənəs] n tétanos m

tether ['teðə*] vt attacher ♦ n: **at the end of one's tether** à bout (de patience)

text [tekst] n texte m

textbook ['tekstbuk] n manuel m

textile ['tekstaɪl] n textile m

texture ['tekstʃə*] n texture f; (of skin, paper etc) grain m

Thailand ['taɪlænd] n Thaïlande f

Thames [temz] n: **the Thames** la Tamise

than [ðæn, ðən] conj que; (with numerals): **more**

than 10/once plus de 10/d'une fois; **I have more/
less than you** j'en ai plus/moins que toi; **she has
more apples than pears** elle a plus de pommes
que de poires; **it is better to phone than to write**
il vaut mieux téléphoner (plutôt) qu'écrire; **no
sooner did he leave than the phone rang** il
venait de partir quand le téléphone a sonné

thank [θæŋk] *vt* remercier, dire merci à; **thank
you (very much)** merci (beaucoup); **thank
heavens, thank God** Dieu merci

thankful ['θæŋkful] *adj*: **thankful (for)** reconnais-
sant(e) (de); **thankful for/that** (*relieved*) soulagé(e)
de/que

thankless ['θæŋklɪs] *adj* ingrat(e)

Thanksgiving (Day) ['θæŋksgɪvɪŋ-] *n* jour *m*
d'action de grâce; *voir encadré*

THANKSGIVING (DAY)

Thanksgiving (Day) est un jour de congé aux
États-Unis, le quatrième jeudi du mois de
novembre, commémorant la bonne récolte
que les Pèlerins venus de Grande-Bretagne
ont eue en 1621; traditionnellement, c'était un
jour où l'on remerciait Dieu et où l'on organi-
sait un grand festin. Une fête semblable, mais
qui n'a aucun rapport avec les Pères Pèlerins, a
lieu au Canada le deuxième lundi d'octobre.

KEYWORD

that [ðæt] *adj* (*demonstrative: pl* **those**) ce, cet
+*vowel or* h *mute*, *f* cette; **that man/woman/
book** cet homme/cette femme/ce livre; (*not this*)
cet homme-là/cette femme-là/ce livre-là; **that
one** celui-là(celle-là)

♦ *pron* **1** (*demonstrative: pl* **those**) ce; (*not this
one*) cela, ça; (*the one*) celui(celle); **who's that?**
qui est-ce?; **what's that?** qu'est-ce que c'est?; **is
that you?** c'est toi?; **I prefer this to that** je préfère ceci à cela *or* ça; **that's what he said** c'est *or*
voilà ce qu'il a dit; **all that** tout cela, tout ça; **that
is (to say)** c'est-à-dire, à savoir; **at** *or* **with that,
she ...** là-dessus, elle ...; **do it like that** fais-le
comme ça

2 (*relative: subject*) qui; (: *object*) que; (: *indirect*)
lequel(laquelle), lesquels(lesquelles) *pl*; **the
book that I read** le livre que j'ai lu; **the books
that are in the library** les livres qui sont dans la
bibliothèque; **all that I have** tout ce que j'ai; **the
box that I put it in** la boîte dans laquelle je l'ai
mis; **the people that I spoke to** les gens auxquels *or* à qui j'ai parlé; **not that I know of** pas à
ma connaissance

3 (*relative: of time*) où; **the day that he came** le
jour où il est venu

♦ *conj* que; **he thought that I was ill** il pensait
que j'étais malade

♦ *adv* (*demonstrative*): **I can't work that much** je

ne peux pas travailler autant que cela; **I didn't
know it was that bad** je ne savais pas que c'était
si *or* aussi mauvais; **that high** aussi haut; si haut;
it's about that high c'est à peu près de cette
hauteur

thatched [θætʃt] *adj* (*roof*) de chaume; **thatched
cottage** chaumière *f*

thaw [θɔː] *n* dégel *m* ♦ *vi* (*ice*) fondre; (*food*)
dégeler ♦ *vt* (*food*) (faire) dégeler; **it's thawing**
(*weather*) il dégèle

KEYWORD

the [ðiː, ðə] *def art* **1** (*gen*) le, la *f*, l' +*vowel or* h
mute, les *pl* (NB: *à* +*le(s)* = au(x); *de* + *le* = du; *de*
+*les* = des); **the boy/girl/ink** le garçon/la fille/
l'encre; **the children** les enfants; **the history of
the world** l'histoire du monde; **give it to the
postman** donne-le au facteur; **to play the
piano/flute** jouer du piano/de la flûte; **the rich
and the poor** les riches et les pauvres

2 (*in titles*): **Elizabeth the First** Elisabeth première; **Peter the Great** Pierre le Grand

3 (*in comparisons*): **the more he works, the
more he earns** plus il travaille, plus il gagne de
l'argent; **the sooner the better** le plus tôt sera le
mieux

theatre, (*us*) **theater** ['θɪətə*] *n* théâtre *m*

theatre-goer ['θɪətəgəuə*] *n* habitué/e du
théâtre

theatrical [θɪ'ætrɪkl] *adj* théâtral(e); **theatrical
company** troupe *f* de théâtre

theft [θɛft] *n* vol *m* (*larcin*)

their [ðɛə*] *adj* leur, leurs *pl*

theirs [ðɛəz] *pron* le(la) leur, les leurs; **it is theirs**
c'est à eux; **a friend of theirs** un de leurs amis

them [ðɛm, ðəm] *pron* (*direct*) les; (*indirect*) leur;
(*stressed, after prep*) eux(elles); **I see them** je les
vois; **give them the book** donne-leur le livre; **give
me a few of them** donnez m'en quelques uns (*or*
quelques unes)

theme [θiːm] *n* thème *m*

theme park *n* parc *m* à thème

theme song *n* chanson principale

themselves [ðəm'sɛlvz] *pl pron* (*reflexive*) se;
(*emphatic*) eux-mêmes(elles-mêmes); **between
themselves** entre eux(elles)

then [ðɛn] *adv* (*at that time*) alors, à ce moment-là;
(*next*) puis, ensuite; (*and also*) et puis ♦ *conj* (*therefore*) alors, dans ce cas ♦ *adj*: **the then president** le
président d'alors *or* de l'époque; **by then** (*past*) à
ce moment-là; (*future*) d'ici là; **from then on** dès
lors; **before then** avant; **until then** jusqu'à ce
moment-là, jusque-là; **and then what?** et puis
après?; **what do you want me to do then?** (*afterwards*) que veux-tu que je fasse ensuite?; (*in that*

case) bon alors, qu'est-ce que je fais?

theology [θɪˈɒlədʒɪ] *n* théologie *f*

theoretical [θɪəˈrɛtɪkl] *adj* théorique

theory [ˈθɪərɪ] *n* théorie *f*

therapy [ˈθɛrəpɪ] *n* thérapie *f*

KEYWORD
---

there [ðɛə*] *adv* **1: there is, there are** il y a; **there are 3 of them** (*people, things*) il y en a 3; **there has been an accident** il y a eu un accident **2** (*referring to place*) là, là-bas; (*là-bas*): **in/on/up/down there** là-dedans/là-dessus/là-haut/en bas; **he went there on Friday** il y est allé vendredi; **to go there and back** faire l'aller-retour; **I want that book there** je veux ce livre-là; **there he is!** le voilà!
3: there, there (*esp to child*) allons, allons!

---

thereabouts [ˈðɛərəˈbauts] *adv* (*place*) par là, près de là; (*amount*) environ, à peu près

thereafter [ðɛərˈɑːftə*] *adv* par la suite

thereby [ˈðɛəbaɪ] *adv* ainsi

therefore [ˈðɛəfɔː*] *adv* donc, par conséquent

there's [ˈðɛəz] = **there is, there has**

thermal [ˈθəːml] *adj* thermique; **thermal paper/printer** papier *m*/imprimante *f* thermique

thermometer [θəˈmɔmɪtə*] *n* thermomètre *m*

Thermos® [ˈθəːməs] *n* (*also:* **Thermos flask**) thermos® *m or f inv*

thermostat [ˈθəːməustæt] *n* thermostat *m*

thesaurus [θɪˈsɔːrəs] *n* dictionnaire *m* synonymique

these [ðiːz] *pl pron* ceux-ci(celles-ci) ♦ *pl adj* ces; (*not those*): **these books** ces livres-ci

thesis, *pl* **theses** [ˈθiːsɪs, ˈθiːsiːz] *n* thèse *f*

they [ðeɪ] *pl pron* ils(elles); (*stressed*) eux(elles). **they say that ...** (*it is said that*) on dit que ...

they'd [ðeɪd] = **they had, they would**

they'll [ðeɪl] = **they shall, they will**

they're [ðɛə*] = **they are**

they've [ðeɪv] = **they have**

thick [θɪk] *adj* épais(se); (*crowd*) dense; (*stupid*) bête, borné(e) ♦ *n*: **in the thick of** au beau milieu de, en plein cœur de; **it's 20 cm thick** ça a 20 cm d'épaisseur

thicken [ˈθɪkn] *vi* s'épaissir ♦ *vt* (*sauce etc*) épaissir

thickness [ˈθɪknɪs] *n* épaisseur *f*

thickset [θɪkˈsɛt] *adj* trapu(e), costaud(e)

thief, *pl* **thieves** [θiːf, θiːvz] *n* voleur/euse

thigh [θaɪ] *n* cuisse *f*

thimble [ˈθɪmbl] *n* dé *m* (à coudre)

thin [θɪn] *adj* mince; (*person*) maigre; (*soup*) peu épais(se); (*hair, crowd*) clairsemé(e); (*fog*) léger(ère) ♦ *vt* (*hair*) éclaircir; (*also:* **thin down**: *sauce, paint*) délayer ♦ *vi* (*fog*) s'éclaircir; (*also:* **thin out**: *crowd*)

se disperser; **his hair is thinning** il se dégarnit

thing [θɪŋ] *n* chose *f*; (*object*) objet *m*; (*contraption*) truc *m*; **things** *npl* (*belongings*) affaires *fpl*; **first thing (in the morning)** à la première heure, tout de suite (le matin); **last thing (at night), he ...** juste avant de se coucher, il ...; **the thing is ...** c'est que ...; **for one thing** d'abord; **the best thing would be to** le mieux serait de; **how are things?** comment ça va?; **she's got a thing about ...** elle déteste ...; **poor thing!** le (*or* la) pauvre!

think, *pt, pp* **thought** [θɪŋk, θɔːt] *vi* penser, réfléchir ♦ *vt* penser, croire; (*imagine*) s'imaginer; **to think of** penser à; **what do you think of it?** qu'en pensez-vous?; **what did you think of them?** qu'avez-vous pensé d'eux?; **to think about sth/sb** penser à qch/qn; **I'll think about it** je vais y réfléchir; **to think of doing** avoir l'idée de faire; **I think so/not** je crois *or* pense que oui/non; **to think well of** avoir une haute opinion de; **think again!** attention, réfléchis bien!; **to think aloud** penser tout haut

▶ **think out** *vt* (*plan*) bien réfléchir à; (*solution*) trouver

▶ **think over** *vt* bien réfléchir à; **I'd like to think things over** (*offer, suggestion*) j'aimerais bien y réfléchir un peu

▶ **think through** *vt* étudier dans tous les détails

▶ **think up** *vt* inventer, trouver

think tank *n* groupe *m* de réflexion

thinly [ˈθɪnlɪ] *adv* (*cut*) en tranches fines; (*spread*) en couche mince

third [θəːd] *num* troisième ♦ *n* troisième *m/f*; (*fraction*) tiers *m*; (*BRIT SCOL: degree*) = licence *f* avec mention passable; **a third of** le tiers de

thirdly [ˈθəːdlɪ] *adv* troisièmement

third party insurance *n* (*BRIT*) assurance *f* au tiers

third-rate [ˈθəːdˈreɪt] *adj* de qualité médiocre

Third World *n*: **the Third World** le Tiers-Monde

thirst [θəːst] *n* soif *f*

thirsty [ˈθəːstɪ] *adj* qui a soif, assoiffé(e); **to be thirsty** avoir soif

thirteen [θəːˈtiːn] *num* treize

thirty [ˈθəːtɪ] *num* trente

KEYWORD
---

this [ðɪs] *adj* (*demonstrative: pl* **these**) ce, cet +*vowel or h mute*, cette *f*; **this man/woman/book** cet homme/cette femme/ce livre; (*not that*) cet homme-ci/cette femme-ci/ce livre-ci; **this one** celui-ci(celle-ci); **this time** cette fois-ci; **this time last year** l'année dernière à la même époque; **this way** (*in this direction*) par ici; (*in this fashion*) de cette façon, ainsi

♦ *pron* (*demonstrative: pl* **these**) ce; (*not that one*) celui-ci(celle-ci), ceci; **who's this?** qui est-ce?; **what's this?** qu'est-ce que c'est?; **I prefer this to that** je préfère ceci à cela; **they were talking of**

---

this and that ils parlaient de choses et d'autres; **this is what he said** voici ce qu'il a dit; **this is Mr Brown** (in introductions) je vous présente Mr Brown; (in photo) c'est Mr Brown; (on telephone) ici Mr Brown

♦ adv (demonstrative): **it was about this big** c'était à peu près de cette grandeur or grand comme ça; **I didn't know it was this bad** je ne savais pas que c'était si or aussi mauvais

thistle ['θɪsl] n chardon m

thorn [θɔːn] n épine f

thorough ['θʌrə] adj (search) minutieux(euse); (knowledge, research) approfondi(e); (work) consciencieux(euse); (cleaning) à fond

thoroughbred ['θʌrəbred] n (horse) pur-sang m inv

thoroughfare ['θʌrəfeə*] n rue f; **"no thorough-fare"** (BRIT) "passage interdit"

thoroughly ['θʌrəlɪ] adv minutieusement; en profondeur; à fond; **he thoroughly agreed** il était tout à fait d'accord

those [ðəuz] pl pron ceux-là(celles-là) ♦ pl adj ces; (not these): **those books** ces livres-là

though [ðəu] conj bien que + sub, quoique + sub ♦ adv pourtant; **even though** quand bien même + conditional; **it's not easy, though** pourtant, ce n'est pas facile

thought [θɔːt] pt, pp of **think** ♦ n pensée f; (opinion) avis m; (intention) intention f; **after much thought** après mûre réflexion; **I've just had a thought** je viens de penser à quelque chose; **to give sth some thought** réfléchir à qch

thoughtful ['θɔːtful] adj pensif(ive); (considerate) prévenant(e)

thoughtless ['θɔːtlɪs] adj étourdi(e); qui manque de considération

thousand ['θauzənd] num mille; **one thousand** mille; **thousands of** des milliers de

thousandth ['θauzəntθ] num millième

thrash [θræʃ] vt rouer de coups; donner une correction à; (defeat) battre à plate(s) couture(s)

▶ **thrash about** vi se débattre

▶ **thrash out** vt débattre de

thread [θred] n fil m; (of screw) pas m, filetage m ♦ vt (needle) enfiler; **to thread one's way between** se faufiler entre

threadbare ['θredbeə*] adj râpé(e), élimé(e)

threat [θret] n menace f; **to be under threat of** être menacé(e)/de

threaten ['θretn] vi (storm) menacer ♦ vt: **to threaten sb with sth/to do** menacer qn de qch/de faire

three [θriː] num trois

three-dimensional [θriːdɪ'menʃənl] adj à trois dimensions; (film) en relief

three-piece ['θriːpiːs]: **three-piece suit** n complet m (avec gilet); **three-piece suite** n salon m comprenant un canapé et deux fauteuils assortis

three-ply [θriː'plaɪ] adj (wood) à trois épaisseurs; (wool) trois fils inv

threshold ['θreʃhəuld] n seuil m; **to be on the threshold of** (fig) être au seuil de

threw [θruː] pt of **throw**

thrifty ['θrɪftɪ] adj économe

thrill [θrɪl] n frisson m, émotion f ♦ vi tressaillir, frissonner ♦ vt (audience) électriser; **to be thrilled** (with gift etc) être ravi(e)

thriller ['θrɪlə*] n film m (or roman m or pièce f) à suspense

thrilling ['θrɪlɪŋ] adj (book, play etc) saisissant(e); (news, discovery) excitant(e)

thrive [θraɪv], pt **thrived, throve**, pp **thrived, thriven** [θraɪv, θrauv, 'θrɪvn] vi pousser or se développer bien; (subj: business) prospérer; **he thrives on it** cela lui réussit

thriving ['θraɪvɪŋ] adj vigoureux(euse); (industry etc) prospère

throat [θrəut] n gorge f; **to have a sore throat** avoir mal à la gorge

throb [θrɔb] n (of heart) pulsation f; (of engine) vibration f; (of pain) élancement m ♦ vi (heart) palpiter; (engine) vibrer; (pain) lanciner; (wound) causer des élancements; **my head is throbbing** j'ai des élancements dans la tête

throes [θrəuz] npl: **in the throes of** au beau milieu de; en proie à; **in the throes of death** à l'agonie

throne [θrəun] n trône m

throng ['θrɔŋ] n foule f ♦ vt se presser dans

throttle ['θrɔtl] n (AUT) accélérateur m ♦ vt étrangler

through [θruː] prep à travers; (time) pendant, durant; (by means of) par, par l'intermédiaire de; (owing to) à cause de ♦ adj (ticket, train, passage) direct(e) ♦ adv à travers; **(from) Monday through Friday** (US) de lundi à vendredi; **to let sb through** laisser passer qn; **to put sb through to sb** (TEL) passer qn à qn; **to be through** (TEL) avoir la communication; (have finished) avoir fini; **"no through traffic"** (US) "passage interdit"; **"no through way"** (BRIT) "impasse"

throughout [θruː'aut] prep (place) partout dans; (time) durant tout(e) le(la) ♦ adv partout

throw [θrəu] n jet m; (SPORT) lancer m ♦ vt, pt **threw**, pp **thrown** [θruː, θrəun] lancer, jeter; (SPORT) lancer; (rider) désarçonner; (fig) décontenancer; (pottery) tourner; **to throw a party** donner une réception

▶ **throw about**

▶ **throw around** vt (litter etc) éparpiller

▶ **throw away** vt jeter

▶ **throw off** vt se débarrasser de

▶ **throw out** vt jeter dehors; (reject) rejeter

▶ **throw together** vt (clothes, meal etc) assembler à la hâte; (essay) bâcler

▶ **throw up** *vi* vomir

throwaway [ˈθrəʊəweɪ] *adj* à jeter

throw-in [ˈθrəʊɪn] *n* (*SPORT*) remise *f* en jeu

thru [θruː] *prep, adj, adv* (*US*) = **through**

thrush [θrʌʃ] *n* (*ZOOL*) grive *f*; (*MED: esp in children*) muguet *m*; (*BRIT: in women*) muguet vaginal

thrust [θrʌst] *n* (*TECH*) poussée *f* ◆ *vt, pt, pp* **thrust** pousser brusquement; (*push in*) enfoncer

thud [θʌd] *n* bruit sourd

thug [θʌg] *n* voyou *m*

thumb [θʌm] *n* (*ANAT*) pouce *m* ◆ *vt* (*book*) feuilleter; **to thumb a lift** faire de l'auto-stop, arrêter une voiture; **to give sb/sth the thumbs up/thumbs down** donner/refuser de donner le feu vert à qn/qch

▶ **thumb through** *vt* (*book*) feuilleter

thumbtack [ˈθʌmtæk] *n* (*US*) punaise *f* (*clou*)

thump [θʌmp] *n* grand coup; (*sound*) bruit sourd ◆ *vt* cogner sur ◆ *vi* cogner, frapper

thunder [ˈθʌndə*] *n* tonnerre *m* ◆ *vi* tonner; (*train etc*): **to thunder past** passer dans un grondement *or* un bruit de tonnerre

thunderbolt [ˈθʌndəbəʊlt] *n* foudre *f*

thunderclap [ˈθʌndəklæp] *n* coup *m* de tonnerre

thunderstorm [ˈθʌndəstɔːm] *n* orage *m*

thundery [ˈθʌndərɪ] *adj* orageux(euse)

Thursday [ˈθɜːzdɪ] *n* jeudi *m*; *for phrases see also* **Tuesday**

thus [ðʌs] *adv* ainsi

thwart [θwɔːt] *vt* contrecarrer

thyme [taɪm] *n* thym *m*

tiara [tɪˈɑːrə] *n* (*woman's*) diadème *m*

tick [tɪk] *n* (*sound: of clock*) tic-tac *m*; (*mark*) coche *f*; (*ZOOL*) tique *f*; (*BRIT col*): **in a tick** dans un instant; (*BRIT col: credit*): **to buy sth on tick** acheter qch à crédit ◆ *vt* faire tic-tac ◆ *vt* cocher; **to put a tick against sth** cocher qch

▶ **tick off** *vt* cocher; (*person*) réprimander, attraper

▶ **tick over** *vi* (*BRIT: engine*) tourner au ralenti; (*: fig*) aller *or* marcher doucettement

ticket [ˈtɪkɪt] *n* billet *m*; (*for bus, tube*) ticket *m*; (*in shop: on goods*) étiquette *f*; (*: from cash register*) reçu *m*, ticket; (*for library*) carte *f*; (*US POL*) liste électorale (*soutenue par un parti*); **to get a (parking) ticket** (*AUT*) attraper une contravention (*pour stationnement illégal*)

ticket collector *n* contrôleur/euse

ticket office *n* guichet *m*, bureau *m* de vente des billets

tickle [ˈtɪkl] *n* chatouillement *m* ◆ *vt* chatouiller; (*fig*) plaire à; faire rire

ticklish [ˈtɪklɪʃ] *adj* (*person*) chatouilleux(euse); (*which tickles: blanket*) qui chatouille; (*: cough*) qui irrite.

tidal [ˈtaɪdl] *adj* à marée

tidal wave *n* raz-de-marée *m inv*

tidbit [ˈtɪdbɪt] *n* (*esp US*) = **titbit**

tiddlywinks [ˈtɪdlɪwɪŋks] *n* jeu *m* de puce

tide [taɪd] *n* marée *f*; (*fig: of events*) cours *m* ◆ *vt*: **to tide sb over** dépanner qn; **high/low tide** marée haute/basse

tidy [ˈtaɪdɪ] *adj* (*room*) bien rangé(e); (*dress, work*) net(nette) soigné(e); (*person*) ordonné(e), qui a de l'ordre; (*: in character*) soigneux(euse); (*mind*) méthodique ◆ *vt* (*also:* **tidy up**) ranger; **to tidy o.s. up** s'arranger

tie [taɪ] *n* (*string etc*) cordon *m*; (*BRIT: also:* **necktie**) cravate *f*; (*fig: link*) lien *m*; (*SPORT: draw*) égalité *f* de points; match nul; (*: match*) rencontre *f*; (*US RAIL*) traverse *f* ◆ *vt* (*parcel*) attacher; (*ribbon*) nouer ◆ *vi* (*SPORT*) faire match nul; **to tie sth in a bow** faire un nœud à *or* avec qch; **to tie a knot in sth** faire un nœud à qch; **"black/white tie"** "smoking/habit de rigueur"; **family ties** liens de famille; **to tie sth in a bow** faire un nœud à *or* avec qch; **to tie a knot in sth** faire un nœud à qch

▶ **tie down** *vt* attacher; (*fig*): **to tie sb down to** contraindre qn à accepter

▶ **tie in** *vi*: **to tie in (with)** (*correspond*) correspondre (à)

▶ **tie on** *vt* (*BRIT: label etc*) attacher (avec une ficelle)

▶ **tie up** *vt* (*parcel*) ficeler; (*dog, boat*) attacher; (*arrangements*) conclure; **to be tied up** (*busy*) être pris *or* occupé

tier [tɪə*] *n* gradin *m*; (*of cake*) étage *m*

tiger [ˈtaɪgə*] *n* tigre *m*

tight [taɪt] *adj* (*rope*) tendu(e), raide; (*clothes*) étroit(e), très juste; (*budget, programme, bend*) serré(e); (*control*) strict(e), sévère; (*col: drunk*) ivre, rond(e) ◆ *adv* (*squeeze*) très fort; (*shut*) à bloc, hermétiquement; **to be packed tight** (*suitcase*) être bourré(e); (*people*) être serré(e); **everybody hold tight!** accrochez-vous bien!

tighten [ˈtaɪtn] *vt* (*rope*) tendre; (*screw*) resserrer; (*control*) renforcer ◆ *vi* se tendre; se resserrer

tightfisted [taɪtˈfɪstɪd] *adj* avare

tightly [ˈtaɪtlɪ] *adv* (*grasp*) bien, très fort

tightrope [ˈtaɪtrəʊp] *n* corde *f* raide

tights [taɪts] *npl* (*BRIT*) collant *m*

tile [taɪl] *n* (*on roof*) tuile *f*; (*on wall or floor*) carreau *m* ◆ *vt* (*floor, bathroom etc*) carreler

tiled [taɪld] *adj* en tuiles; carrelé(e)

till [tɪl] *n* caisse (*enregistreuse*) ◆ *vt* (*land*) cultiver ◆ *prep, conj* = **until**

tiller [ˈtɪlə*] *n* (*NAUT*) barre *f* (*du gouvernail*)

tilt [tɪlt] *vt* pencher, incliner ◆ *vi* pencher, être incliné(e) ◆ *n* (*slope*) inclinaison *f*; **to wear one's hat at a tilt** porter son chapeau incliné sur le côté; **(at) full tilt** à toute vitesse

timber [ˈtɪmbə*] *n* (*material*) bois *m* de construction; (*trees*) arbres *mpl*

time [taɪm] *n* temps *m*; (*epoch: often pl*) époque *f*, temps; (*by clock*) heure *f*; (*moment*) moment *m*;

(occasion, also MATH) fois f; (MUS) mesure f ◆ vt (race) chronométrer; (programme) minuter; (remark etc) choisir le moment de; **a long time** un long moment, longtemps; **for the time being** pour le moment; **from time to time** de temps en temps; **time after time, time and again** bien des fois; **in time** (soon enough) à temps; (after some time) avec le temps, à la longue; (MUS) en mesure; **in a week's time** dans une semaine; **in no time** en un rien de temps; **on time** à l'heure; **to be 30 minutes behind/ahead of time** avoir 30 minutes de retard/d'avance; **by the time he arrived** quand il est arrivé, le temps qu'il arrive +sub; **5 times 5** 5 fois 5; **what time is it?** quelle heure est-il?; **what time do you make it?** quelle heure avez-vous?; **to have a good time** bien s'amuser; **we** (or **they** etc) **had a hard time** ça a été difficile or pénible; **time's up!** c'est l'heure!; **I've no time for it** (fig) cela m'agace; **he'll do it in his own (good) time** (without being hurried) il le fera quand il en aura le temps; **he'll do it in** or (US) **on his own time** (out of working hours) il le fera à ses heures perdues; **to be behind the times** retarder (sur son temps)

time bomb n bombe f à retardement

time lag n (BRIT) décalage m; (: in travel) décalage horaire

timeless ['taɪmlɪs] adj éternel(le)

timely ['taɪmlɪ] adj opportun(e)

time off n temps m libre

timer ['taɪmə*] n (in kitchen) compte-minutes m inv; (TECH) minuteur m

timescale ['taɪmskeɪl] n délais mpl

time-share ['taɪmʃɛə*] n maison f/appartement m en multipropriété

time switch n (BRIT) minuteur m; (: for lighting) minuterie f

timetable ['taɪmteɪbl] n (RAIL) indicateur (m) horaire m; (SCOL) emploi m du temps; (programme of events etc) programme m

time zone n fuseau m horaire

timid ['tɪmɪd] adj timide; (easily scared) peureux(euse)

timing ['taɪmɪŋ] n minutage m; chronométrage m; **the timing of his resignation** le moment choisi pour sa démission

timpani ['tɪmpənɪ] npl timbales fpl

tin [tɪn] n étain m; (also: **tin plate**) fer-blanc m; (BRIT: can) boîte f (de conserve); (: for baking) moule m (à gâteau); **a tin of paint** un pot de peinture

tinfoil ['tɪnfɔɪl] n papier m d'étain

tinge [tɪndʒ] n nuance f ◆ vt: **tinged with** teinté(e) de

tingle ['tɪŋgl] n picotement m; frisson m ◆ vi picoter

tinker ['tɪŋkə*] n rétameur ambulant; (gipsy) romanichel m

▶ **tinker with** vt fus bricoler, rafistoler

tinkle ['tɪŋkl] vi tinter ◆ n (col): **to give sb a tin-**

kle passer un coup de fil à qn

tinned [tɪnd] adj (BRIT: food) en boîte, en conserve

tin opener [-'əʊpnə*] n (BRIT) ouvre-boîte(s) m

tinsel ['tɪnsl] n guirlandes fpl de Noël (argentées)

tint [tɪnt] n teinte f; (for hair) shampooing colorant ◆ vt (hair) faire un shampooing colorant à

tinted ['tɪntɪd] adj (hair) teint(e); (spectacles, glass) teinté(e)

tiny ['taɪnɪ] adj minuscule

tip [tɪp] n (end) bout m; (protective: on umbrella etc) embout m; (gratuity) pourboire m; (BRIT: for coal) terril m; (: for rubbish) décharge f; (advice) tuyau m ◆ vt (waiter) donner un pourboire à; (tilt) incliner; (overturn: also: **tip over**) renverser; (empty: also: **tip out**) déverser; (predict: winner etc) pronostiquer; **he tipped out the contents of the box** il a vidé le contenu de la boîte

▶ **tip off** vt prévenir, avertir

tip-off ['tɪpɔf] n (hint) tuyau m

tipped ['tɪpt] adj (BRIT: cigarette) (à bout) filtre inv; **steel-tipped** à bout métallique, à embout de métal

tipsy ['tɪpsɪ] adj un peu ivre, éméché(e)

tiptoe ['tɪptəʊ] n: **on tiptoe** sur la pointe des pieds

tiptop ['tɪptɔp] adj: **in tiptop condition** en excellent état

tire ['taɪə*] n (US) = **tyre** ◆ vt fatiguer ◆ vi se fatiguer

▶ **tire out** vt épuiser

tired ['taɪəd] adj fatigué(e); **to be/feel/look tired** être/se sentir/avoir l'air fatigué; **to be tired of** en avoir assez de, être las(lasse) de

tireless ['taɪəlɪs] adj infatigable, inlassable

tiresome ['taɪəsəm] adj ennuyeux(euse)

tiring ['taɪərɪŋ] adj fatigant(e)

tissue ['tɪʃuː] n tissu m; (paper handkerchief) mouchoir m en papier, kleenex® m

tissue paper n papier m de soie

tit [tɪt] n (bird) mésange f; (col: breast) nichon m; **to give tit for tat** rendre coup pour coup

titbit ['tɪtbɪt] n (food) friandise f; (before meal) amuse-gueule m inv; (news) potin m

title ['taɪtl] n titre m; (LAW: right): **title (to)** droit m (à)

title deed n (LAW) titre (constitutif) de propriété

title role n rôle principal

TM n abbr = **trademark**, = transcendental meditation

to [tuː, tə] prep **1** (direction) à; (towards) vers; envers; **to go to France/Portugal/London/ school** aller en France/au Portugal/à Londres/à l'école; **to go to Claude's/the doctor's** aller chez Claude/le docteur; **the road to Edinburgh** la route d'Édimbourg

2 (as far as) (jusqu')à; **to count to 10** compter jusqu'à 10; **from 40 to 50 people** de 40 à 50 personnes

3 (*with expressions of time*): **a quarter to 5** 5 heures moins le quart; **it's twenty to 3** il est 3 heures moins vingt

4 (*for, of*) de; **the key to the front door** la clé de la porte d'entrée; **a letter to his wife** une lettre (adressée) à sa femme

5 (*expressing indirect object*) à; **to give sth to sb** donner qch à qn; **to talk to sb** parler à qn; **it belongs to him** cela lui appartient, c'est à lui

6 (*in relation to*) à; **3 goals to 2** 3 (buts) à 2; **30 miles to the gallon** ≃ 9,4 litres aux cent (km);

7 (*purpose, result*): **to come to sb's aid** venir au secours de qn, porter secours à qn; **to sentence sb to death** condamner qn à mort; **to my surprise** à ma grande surprise

♦ *with vb* 1 (*simple infinitive*): **to go/eat** aller/manger

2 (*following another vb*): **to want/try/start to do** vouloir/essayer de/commencer à faire

3 (*with vb omitted*): **I don't want to** je ne veux pas

4 (*purpose, result*) pour; **I did it to help you** je l'ai fait pour vous aider

5 (*equivalent to relative clause*): **I have things to do** j'ai des choses à faire; **the main thing is to try** l'important est d'essayer

6 (*after adjective etc*): **ready to go** prêt(e) à partir; **too old/young to ...** trop vieux/jeune pour ...

♦ *adv*: **push/pull the door to** tirez/poussez la porte; **to go to and fro** aller et venir

toad [təʊd] *n* crapaud *m*

toadstool ['təʊdstuːl] *n* champignon (vénéneux)

toast [təʊst] *n* (*CULIN*) pain grillé, toast *m*; (*drink, speech*) toast ♦ *vt* (*CULIN*) faire griller; (*drink to*) porter un toast à; **a piece** *or* **slice of toast** un toast

toaster ['təʊstə*] *n* grille-pain *m inv*

tobacco [tə'bækəʊ] *n* tabac *m*; **pipe tobacco** tabac à pipe

tobacconist [tə'bækənɪst] *n* marchand/e de tabac; **tobacconist's (shop)** (bureau *m* de) tabac *m*

toboggan [tə'bɒgən] *n* toboggan *m*; (*child's*) luge *f*

today [tə'deɪ] *adv, n* (*also fig*) aujourd'hui (*m*); **what day is it today?** quel jour sommes-nous aujourd'hui?; **what date is it today?** quelle est la date aujourd'hui?; **today is the 4th of March** aujourd'hui nous sommes le 4 mars; **a week ago today** il y a huit jours aujourd'hui

toddler ['tɒdlə*] *n* enfant *m/f* qui commence à marcher, bambin *m*

toe [təʊ] *n* doigt *m* de pied, orteil *m*; (*of shoe*) bout *m* ♦ *vt*: **to toe the line** (*fig*) obéir, se conformer; **big toe** gros orteil; **little toe** petit orteil

toenail ['təʊneɪl] *n* ongle *m* de l'orteil

toffee ['tɒfɪ] *n* caramel *m*

toffee apple *n* (*BRIT*) pomme caramélisée

together [tə'gɛðə*] *adv* ensemble; (*at same time*) en même temps; **together with** *prep* avec

toil [tɔɪl] *n* dur travail, labeur *m* ♦ *vi* travailler dur; peiner

toilet ['tɔɪlət] *n* (*BRIT: lavatory*) toilettes *fpl*, cabinets *mpl* ♦ *cpd* (*bag, soap etc*) de toilette; **to go to the toilet** aller aux toilettes

toilet bag *n* (*BRIT*) nécessaire *m* de toilette

toilet paper *n* papier *m* hygiénique

toiletries ['tɔɪlətrɪz] *npl* articles *mpl* de toilette

toilet roll *n* rouleau *m* de papier hygiénique

token ['təʊkən] *n* (*sign*) marque *f*, témoignage *m*; (*voucher*) bon *m*, coupon *m* ♦ *cpd* (*fee, strike*) symbolique; **by the same token** (*fig*) de même; **book/record token** (*BRIT*) chèque-livre/-disque *m*

told [təʊld] *pt, pp of* **tell**

tolerable ['tɒlərəbl] *adj* (*bearable*) tolérable; (*fairly good*) passable

tolerant ['tɒlərnt] *adj*: **tolerant (of)** tolérant(e) (à l'égard de)

tolerate ['tɒləreɪt] *vt* supporter; (*MED, TECH*) tolérer

toll [təʊl] *n* (*tax, charge*) péage *m* ♦ *vi* (*bell*) sonner; **the accident toll on the roads** le nombre des victimes de la route

tomato, *pl* **tomatoes** [tə'mɑːtəʊ] *n* tomate *f*

tomb [tuːm] *n* tombe *f*

tomboy ['tɒmbɔɪ] *n* garçon manqué

tombstone ['tuːmstəʊn] *n* pierre tombale

tomcat ['tɒmkæt] *n* matou *m*

tomorrow [tə'mɒrəʊ] *adv, n* (*also fig*) demain (*m*); **the day after tomorrow** après-demain; **a week tomorrow** demain en huit; **tomorrow morning** demain matin

ton [tʌn] *n* tonne *f* (*BRIT: = 1016 kg; US = 907 kg; metric = 1000 kg*); (*also:* **register ton**) tonneau *m* (*= 2.83 cu.m*); **tons of** (*col*) des tas de

tone [təʊn] *n* ton *m*; (*of radio, BRIT TEL*) tonalité *f* ♦ *vi* s'harmoniser

▶ **tone down** *vt* (*colour, criticism*) adoucir; (*sound*) baisser

▶ **tone up** *vt* (*muscles*) tonifier

tone-deaf [təʊn'dɛf] *adj* qui n'a pas d'oreille

tongs [tɒŋz] *npl* pinces *fpl*; (*for coal*) pincettes *fpl*; (*for hair*) fer à friser

tongue [tʌŋ] *n* langue *f*; **tongue in cheek** *adv* ironiquement

tongue-tied ['tʌŋtaɪd] *adj* (*fig*) muet(te)

tongue twister *n* phrase *f* très difficile à prononcer

tonic ['tɒnɪk] *n* (*MED*) tonique *m*; (*MUS*) tonique *f*; (*also:* **tonic water**) tonic *m*

tonight [tə'naɪt] *adv, n* cette nuit; (*this evening*) ce soir; **(I'll) see you tonight!** à ce soir!

tonsil ['tɒnsl] *n* amygdale *f*; **to have one's tonsils out** se faire opérer des amygdales

tonsillitis [tɒnsɪ'laɪtɪs] *n* amygdalite *f*; **to have**

tonsillitis avoir une angine or une amygdalite

too [tu:] adv (excessively) trop; (also) aussi; **it's too sweet** c'est trop sucré; **I went too** moi aussi, j'y suis allé; **too much** adv trop ♦ adj trop de; **too many** adj trop de; **too bad!** tant pis!

took [tuk] pt of **take**

tool [tu:l] n outil m; (fig) instrument m

tool box n boîte f à outils

toot [tu:t] n coup m de sifflet (or de klaxon) ♦ vi siffler; (with car horn) klaxonner

tooth, pl **teeth** [tu:θ, ti:θ] n (ANAT, TECH) dent f; **to have a tooth out** or (US) **pulled** se faire arracher une dent; **to brush one's teeth** se laver les dents; **by the skin of one's teeth** (fig) de justesse

toothache ['tu:θeɪk] n mal m de dents; **to have toothache** avoir mal aux dents

toothbrush ['tu:θbrʌʃ] n brosse f à dents

toothpaste ['tu:θpeɪst] n (pâte f) dentifrice m

toothpick ['tu:θpɪk] n cure-dent m

top [tɒp] n (of mountain, head) sommet m; (of page, ladder) haut m; (of list, queue) commencement m; (of box, cupboard, table) dessus m; (lid: of box, jar) couvercle m; (: of bottle) bouchon m; (toy) toupie f; (DRESS: blouse etc) haut; (of pyjamas) veste f ♦ adj du haut; (in rank) premier(ière); (best) meilleur(e) ♦ vt (exceed) dépasser; (be first in) être en tête de; **the top of the milk** (BRIT) la crème du lait; **at the top of the stairs/page/street** en haut de l'escalier/de la page/de la rue; **on top of** sur; (in addition to) en plus de; **from top to toe** (BRIT) de la tête aux pieds; **at the top of the list** en tête de liste; **at the top of one's voice** à tue-tête; **at top speed** à toute vitesse; **over the top** (col: behaviour etc) qui dépasse les limites

▶ **top up**, (US) **top off** vt remplir

top floor n dernier étage

top hat n haut-de-forme m

top-heavy [tɒp'hevɪ] adj (object) trop lourd(e) du haut

topic ['tɒpɪk] n sujet m, thème m

topical ['tɒpɪkl] adj d'actualité

topless ['tɒplɪs] adj (bather etc) aux seins nus; **topless swimsuit** monokini m

top-level ['tɒplevl] adj (talks) à l'échelon le plus élevé

topmost ['tɒpməʊst] adj le(la) plus haut(e)

topple ['tɒpl] vt renverser, faire tomber ♦ vi basculer; tomber

top-secret ['tɒp'si:krɪt] adj ultra-secret(ète)

topsy-turvy ['tɒpsɪ'tɜ:vɪ] adj, adv sens dessus-dessous

top-up ['tɒpʌp] n (for mobile phone) recharge f, minutes fpl

top-up card n (for mobile phone) recharge f

torch [tɔ:tʃ] n torche f; (BRIT) lampe f de poche

tore [tɔ:*] pt of **tear**

torment n ['tɔ:ment] tourment m ♦ vt [tɔ:'ment] tourmenter; (fig: annoy) agacer

torn [tɔ:n] pp of **tear** ♦ adj: **torn between** (fig) tiraillé(e) entre

tornado, pl **tornadoes** [tɔ:'neɪdəʊ] n tornade f

torpedo, pl **torpedoes** [tɔ:'pi:dəʊ] n torpille f

torrent ['tɒrnt] n torrent m

torrential [tɒ'renʃl] adj torrentiel(le)

tortoise ['tɔ:təs] n tortue f

tortoiseshell ['tɔ:təʃel] adj en écaille

torture ['tɔ:tʃə*] n torture f ♦ vt torturer

Tory ['tɔ:rɪ] adj (BRIT POL) tory, conservateur(trice) ♦ n tory m/f, conservateur(trice)

toss [tɒs] vt lancer, jeter; (BRIT: pancake) faire sauter; (head) rejeter en arrière ♦ vi: **to toss up for sth** (BRIT) jouer qch à pile ou face ♦ n (movement: of head etc) mouvement soudain; (of coin) tirage m à pile ou face; **to toss a coin** jouer à pile ou face; **to toss and turn** (in bed) se tourner et se retourner; **to win/lose the toss** gagner/perdre à pile ou face; (SPORT) gagner/perdre le tirage au sort

tot [tɒt] n (BRIT: drink) petit verre m; (child) bambin m

▶ **tot up** vt (BRIT: figures) additionner

total ['təʊtl] adj total(e) ♦ n total m ♦ vt (add up) faire le total de, totaliser; (amount to) s'élever à; **in total** au total

totally ['təʊtəlɪ] adv totalement

totter ['tɒtə*] vi chanceler; (object, government) être chancelant(e)

touch [tʌtʃ] n contact m, toucher m; (sense, skill: of pianist etc) toucher; (fig: note, also FOOTBALL) touche f ♦ vt (gen) toucher; (tamper with) toucher à; **the personal touch** la petite note personnelle; **to put the finishing touches to sth** mettre la dernière main à qch; **a touch of** (fig) un petit peu de; une touche de; **in touch with** en contact or rapport avec; **to get in touch with** prendre contact avec; **I'll be in touch** je resterai en contact; **to lose touch** (friends) se perdre de vue; **to be out of touch with events** ne pas être au courant de ce qui se passe

▶ **touch on** vt fus (topic) effleurer, toucher

▶ **touch up** vt (paint) retoucher

touch-and-go ['tʌtʃən'gəʊ] adj incertain(e); **it was touch-and-go whether we did it** nous avons failli ne pas le faire

touchdown ['tʌtʃdaʊn] n atterrissage m; (on sea) amerrissage m; (US FOOTBALL) essai m

touched [tʌtʃt] adj touché(e); (col) cinglé(e)

touching ['tʌtʃɪŋ] adj touchant(e), attendrissant(e)

touchline ['tʌtʃlaɪn] n (SPORT) (ligne f de) touche f

touchy ['tʌtʃɪ] adj (person) susceptible

tough [tʌf] adj dur(e); (resistant) résistant(e), solide; (meat) dur, coriace; (journey) pénible; (task, problem, situation) difficile; (rough) dur ♦ n (gangster etc) dur m; **tough luck!** pas de chance!; tant pis!

toughen ['tʌfn] vt rendre plus dur(e) (or plus résistant(e) or plus solide)

toupee ['tu:peɪ] n postiche m

tour ['tʊə*] *n* voyage *m*; (*also:* **package tour**) voyage organisé; (*of town, museum*) tour *m*, visite *f*; (*by artist*) tournée *f* ♦ *vt* visiter; **to go on a tour of** (*museum, region*) visiter; **to go on tour** partir en tournée

tour guide *n* (*person*) guide *m/f*

tourism ['tʊərɪzm] *n* tourisme *m*

tourist ['tʊərɪst] *n* touriste *m/f* ♦ *adv* (*travel*) en classe touriste ♦ *cpd* touristique; **the tourist trade** le tourisme

tourist office *n* syndicat *m* d'initiative

tournament ['tʊənəmənt] *n* tournoi *m*

tousled ['taʊzld] *adj* (*hair*) ébouriffé(e)

tout [taʊt] *vi*: **to tout for** essayer de raccrocher, racoler; **to tout sth (around)** (*BRIT*) essayer de placer *or* (re)vendre qch ♦ *n* (*BRIT*: *ticket tout*) revendeur *m* de billets

tow [taʊ] *n*: **to give sb a tow** (*AUT*) remorquer qn ♦ *vt* remorquer; **"on tow"**, (*US*) **"in tow"** (*AUT*) "véhicule en remorque"

toward(s) [tə'wɔ:d(z)] *prep* vers; (*of attitude*) envers, à l'égard de; (*of purpose*) pour; **toward(s) noon/the end of the year** vers midi/la fin de l'année; **to feel friendly toward(s) sb** être bien disposé envers qn

towel ['taʊəl] *n* serviette *f* (de toilette); (*also:* **tea towel**) torchon *m*; **to throw in the towel** (*fig*) jeter l'éponge

towelling ['taʊəlɪŋ] *n* (*fabric*) tissu-éponge *m*

towel rail, (*US*) **towel rack** *n* porte-serviettes *m inv*

tower ['taʊə*] *n* tour *f* ♦ *vi* (*building, mountain*) se dresser (majestueusement); **to tower above** *or* **over sb/sth** dominer qn/qch

tower block *n* (*BRIT*) tour *f* (d'habitation)

towering ['taʊərɪŋ] *adj* très haut(e), imposant(e)

town [taʊn] *n* ville *f*; **to go to town** aller en ville; (*fig*) y mettre le paquet; **in the town** dans la ville, en ville; **to be out of town** (*person*) être en déplacement

town centre *n* centre *m* de la ville, centre-ville *m*

town council *n* conseil municipal

town hall *n* = mairie *f*

town plan *n* plan *m* de ville

town planning *n* urbanisme *m*

towrope ['taʊrəʊp] *n* (câble *m* de) remorque *f*

tow truck *n* (*US*) dépanneuse *f*

toy [tɔɪ] *n* jouet *m*

▶ **toy with** *vt fus* jouer avec; (*idea*) caresser

trace [treɪs] *n* trace *f* ♦ *vt* (*draw*) tracer, dessiner; (*follow*) suivre la trace de; (*locate*) retrouver; **without trace** (*disappear*) sans laisser de traces; **there was no trace of it** il n'y en avait pas trace

tracing paper ['treɪsɪŋ-] *n* papier-calque *m*

track [træk] *n* (*mark*) trace *f*; (*path: gen*) chemin *m*, piste *f*; (: *of bullet etc*) trajectoire *f*; (: *of suspect, animal*) piste; (*RAIL*) voie ferrée, rails *mpl*; (*on tape, COMPUT, SPORT*) piste; (*on record*) plage *f* ♦ *vt* suivre la trace *or* la piste de; **to keep track of** suivre; **to be on the right track** (*fig*) être sur la bonne voie

▶ **track down** *vt* (*prey*) trouver et capturer; (*sth lost*) finir par retrouver

tracksuit ['træksu:t] *n* survêtement *m*

tract [trækt] *n* (*GEO*) étendue *f*, zone *f*; (*pamphlet*) tract *m*; **respiratory tract** (*ANAT*) système *m* respiratoire

traction ['trækʃən] *n* traction *f*

tractor ['træktə*] *n* tracteur *m*

trade [treɪd] *n* commerce *m*; (*skill, job*) métier *m* ♦ *vi* faire du commerce; **to trade with/in** faire du commerce avec/le commerce de; **foreign trade** commerce extérieur; **Department of Trade and Industry (DTI)** (*BRIT*) ministère *m* du Commerce et de l'Industrie

▶ **trade in** *vt* (*old car etc*) faire reprendre

trade fair *n* foire(-exposition) commerciale

trade-in price *n* prix *m* à la reprise

trademark ['treɪdmɑ:k] *n* marque *f* de fabrique

trade name *n* marque déposée

trader ['treɪdə*] *n* commerçant/e, négociant/e

tradesman ['treɪdzmən] *n* (*shopkeeper*) commerçant *m*; (*skilled worker*) ouvrier qualifié

trade union *n* syndicat *m*

trade unionist [-'ju:njənɪst] *n* syndicaliste *m/f*

tradition [trə'dɪʃən] *n* tradition *f*; **traditions** *npl* coutumes *fpl*, traditions

traditional [trə'dɪʃənl] *adj* traditionnel(le)

traffic ['træfɪk] *n* trafic *m*; (*cars*) circulation *f* ♦ *vi*: **to traffic in** (*pej: liquor, drugs*) faire le trafic de

traffic calming [-'kɑ:mɪŋ] *n* ralentissement *m* de la circulation

traffic circle *n* (*US*) rond-point *m*

traffic jam *n* embouteillage *m*

traffic lights *npl* feux *mpl* (de signalisation)

traffic warden *n* contractuel/le

tragedy ['trædʒədɪ] *n* tragédie *f*

tragic ['trædʒɪk] *adj* tragique

trail [treɪl] *n* (*tracks*) trace *f*, piste *f*; (*path*) chemin *m*, piste; (*of smoke etc*) traînée *f* ♦ *vt* traîner, tirer; (*follow*) suivre ♦ *vi* traîner; **to be on sb's trail** être sur la piste de qn

▶ **trail away**, **trail off** *vi* (*sound, voice*) s'évanouir; (*interest*) disparaître

▶ **trail behind** *vi* traîner, être à la traîne

trailer ['treɪlə*] *n* (*AUT*) remorque *f*; (*US*) caravane *f*; (*CINE*) bande-annonce *f*

trailer truck *n* (*US*) (camion *m*) semi-remorque *m*

train [treɪn] *n* train *m*; (*in underground*) rame *f*; (*of dress*) traîne *f*; (*BRIT: series*): **train of events** série *f* d'événements ♦ *vt* (*apprentice, doctor etc*) former; (*sportsman*) entraîner; (*dog*) dresser; (*memory*) exercer; (*point: gun etc*): **to train sth on** braquer qch sur

♦ *vi* recevoir sa formation; s'entraîner; **one's train of thought** le fil de sa pensée; **to go by train** voyager par le train *or* en train; **to train sb to do sth** apprendre à qn à faire qch; *(employee)* former qn à faire qch

trained [treɪnd] *adj* qualifié(e), qui a reçu une formation; dressé(e)

trainee [treɪ'niː] *n* stagiaire *m/f*; *(in trade)* apprenti/e

trainer ['treɪnə*] *n* (SPORT) entraîneur/euse; *(of dogs etc)* dresseur/euse; **trainers** *npl* (shoes) chaussures *fpl* de sport

training ['treɪnɪŋ] *n* formation *f*; entraînement *m*; dressage *m*; **in training** (SPORT) à l'entraînement; *(fit)* en forme

training college *n* école professionnelle; *(for teachers)* = école normale

training shoes *npl* chaussures *fpl* de sport

trait [treɪt] *n* trait *m* (de caractère)

traitor ['treɪtə*] *n* traître *m*

tram [træm] *n* (BRIT: also: **tramcar**) tram(way) *m*

tramp [træmp] *n* *(person)* vagabond/e, clochard/e; *(col: pej: woman)*: **to be a tramp** être coureuse ♦ *vi* marcher d'un pas lourd ♦ *vt* *(walk through: town, streets)* parcourir à pied

trample ['træmpl] *vt*: **to trample (underfoot)** piétiner, *(fig)* bafouer

trampoline ['træmpəliːn] *n* trampolino *m*

tranquil ['træŋkwɪl] *adj* tranquille

tranquillizer ['træŋkwɪlaɪzə*] *n* (MED) tranquillisant *m*

transact [træn'zækt] *vt* *(business)* traiter

transaction [træn'zækʃən] *n* transaction *f*; **transactions** *npl* *(minutes)* actes *mpl*; **cash transaction** transaction au comptant

transatlantic ['trænzət'læntɪk] *adj* transatlantique

transfer *n* ['trænsfə*] *(gen, also SPORT)* transfert *m*; *(POL: of power)* passation *f*; *(of money)* virement *m*; *(picture, design)* décalcomanie *f*; *(: stick-on)* autocollant *m* ♦ *vt* [træns'fəː*] transférer; passer; virer; décalquer; **to transfer the charges** (BRIT TEL) téléphoner en P.C.V.; **by bank transfer** par virement bancaire

transfer desk *n* (AVIAT) guichet *m* de transit

transform [træns'fɔːm] *vt* transformer

transfusion [træns'fjuːʒən] *n* transfusion *f*

transient ['trænzɪənt] *adj* transitoire, éphémère

transistor [træn'zɪstə*] *n* (ELEC; also: **transistor radio**) transistor *m*

transit ['trænzɪt] *n*: **in transit** en transit

transitive ['trænzɪtɪv] *adj* (LING) transitif(ive)

transit lounge *n* (AVIAT) salle *f* de transit

translate [trænz'leɪt] *vt*: **to translate (from/into)** traduire (du/en)

translation [trænz'leɪʃən] *n* traduction *f*; *(SCOL: as opposed to prose)* version *f*

translator [trænz'leɪtə*] *n* traducteur/trice

transmission [trænz'mɪʃən] *n* transmission *f*

transmit [trænz'mɪt] *vt* transmettre; *(RADIO, TV)* émettre

transparency [træns'pɛərnsɪ] *n* (BRIT PHOT) diapositive *f*

transparent [træns'pærnt] *adj* transparent(e)

transpire [træns'paɪə*] *vi* *(become known)*: **it finally transpired that ...** on a finalement appris que ...; *(happen)* arriver

transplant *vt* [træns'plɑːnt] transplanter; *(seedlings)* repiquer ♦ *n* ['trænsplɑːnt] (MED) transplantation *f*; **to have a heart transplant** subir une greffe du cœur

transport *n* ['trænspɔːt] transport *m* ♦ *vt* [træns'pɔːt] transporter; **public transport** transports en commun; **Department of Transport** (BRIT) ministère *m* des Transports

transportation [trænspɔː'teɪʃən] *n* (moyen *m* de) transport *m*; *(of prisoners)* transportation *f*; **Department of Transportation** (US) ministère *m* des Transports

transport café *n* (BRIT) = routier *m*

trap [træp] *n* *(snare, trick)* piège *m*; *(carriage)* cabriolet *m* ♦ *vt* prendre au piège; *(immobilize)* bloquer; *(jam)* coincer; **to set** *or* **lay a trap (for sb)** tendre un piège (à qn); **to shut one's trap** (col) la fermer

trap door *n* trappe *f*

trapeze [trə'piːz] *n* trapèze *m*

trappings ['træpɪŋz] *npl* ornements *mpl*; attributs *mpl*

trash [træʃ] *n* (pej: goods) camelote *f*; *(: nonsense)* sottises *fpl*; *(US: rubbish)* ordures *fpl*

trash can *n* (US) boîte *f* à ordures

trashy ['træʃɪ] *adj* (col) de camelote, qui ne vaut rien

trauma ['trɔːmə] *n* traumatisme *m*

traumatic [trɔː'mætɪk] *adj* traumatisant(e)

travel ['trævl] *n* voyage(s) *m(pl)* ♦ *vi* voyager; *(move)* aller, se déplacer ♦ *vt* *(distance)* parcourir; **this wine doesn't travel well** ce vin voyage mal

travel agency *n* agence *f* de voyages

travel agent *n* agent *m* de voyages

traveller, *(US)* **traveler** ['trævlə*] *n* voyageur/euse; *(COMM)* représentant *m* de commerce

traveller's cheque, *(US)* **traveler's check** *n* chèque *m* de voyage

travelling, *(US)* **traveling** ['trævlɪŋ] *n* voyage(s) *m(pl)* ♦ *adj* *(circus, exhibition)* ambulant(e) ♦ *cpd* *(bag, clock)* de voyage; *(expenses)* de déplacement

travel sickness *n* mal *m* de la route (*or* de mer *or* de l'air)

trawler ['trɔːlə*] *n* chalutier *m*

tray [treɪ] *n* *(for carrying)* plateau *m*; *(on desk)* corbeille *f*

treacherous ['tretʃərəs] *adj* traître(sse); **road**

conditions are treacherous l'état des routes est dangereux

treacle [ˈtriːkl] n mélasse f

tread [trɛd] n pas m; (sound) bruit m de pas; (of tyre) chape f, bande f de roulement ♦ vi, pt **trod**, pp **trodden** [trɔd, ˈtrɔdn] marcher

▶ **tread on** vt fus marcher sur

treason [ˈtriːzn] n trahison f

treasure [ˈtrɛʒə*] n trésor m ♦ vt (value) tenir beaucoup à; (store) conserver précieusement

treasurer [ˈtrɛʒərə*] n trésorier/ière

treasury [ˈtrɛʒəri] n trésorerie f; **the Treasury**, (US) **the Treasury Department** ≃ le ministère des Finances

treat [triːt] n petit cadeau, petite surprise ♦ vt traiter; **it was a treat** ça m'a (or nous a etc) vraiment fait plaisir; **to treat sb to sth** offrir qch à qn; **to treat sth as a joke** prendre qch à la plaisanterie

treatment [ˈtriːtmənt] n traitement m; **to have treatment for sth** (MED) suivre un traitement pour qch

treaty [ˈtriːti] n traité m

treble [ˈtrɛbl] adj triple ♦ n (MUS) soprano m ♦ vt, vi tripler

treble clef n clé f de sol

tree [triː] n arbre m

trek [trɛk] n voyage m; randonnée f; (tiring walk) tirée f ♦ vi (as holiday) faire de la randonnée

tremble [ˈtrɛmbl] vi trembler

tremendous [trɪˈmɛndəs] adj énorme, formidable; (excellent) fantastique, formidable

tremor [ˈtrɛmə*] n tremblement m; (also: **earth tremor**) secousse f sismique

trench [trɛntʃ] n tranchée f

trend [trɛnd] n (tendency) tendance f; (of events) cours m; (fashion) mode f; **trend towards/away from doing** tendance à faire/à ne pas faire; **to set the trend** donner le ton; **to set a trend** lancer une mode

trendy [ˈtrɛndi] adj (idea) dans le vent; (clothes) dernier cri inv

trespass [ˈtrɛspəs] vi: **to trespass on** s'introduire sans permission dans; (fig) empiéter sur; **"no trespassing"** "propriété privée", "défense d'entrer"

trestle [ˈtrɛsl] n tréteau m

trial [ˈtraɪəl] n (LAW) procès m, jugement m; (test: of machine etc) essai m; (hardship) épreuve f; (worry) souci m; **trials** npl (SPORT) épreuves éliminatoires; **horse trials** concours m hippique; **trial by jury** jugement par jury; **to be sent for trial** être traduit(e) en justice; **to be on trial** passer en jugement; **by trial and error** par tâtonnements

trial period n période f d'essai

triangle [ˈtraɪæŋgl] n (MATH, MUS) triangle m

triangular [traɪˈæŋgjulə*] adj triangulaire

tribe [traɪb] n tribu f

tribesman [ˈtraɪbzmən] n membre m de la tribu

tribunal [traɪˈbjuːnl] n tribunal m

tributary [ˈtrɪbjutəri] n (river) affluent m

tribute [ˈtrɪbjuːt] n tribut m, hommage m; **to pay tribute to** rendre hommage à

trick [trɪk] n ruse f; (clever act) astuce f; (joke) tour m; (CARDS) levée f ♦ vt attraper, rouler; **to play a trick on sb** jouer un tour à qn; **to trick sb into doing sth** persuader qn par la ruse de faire qch; **to trick sb out of sth** obtenir qch de qn par la ruse; **it's a trick of the light** c'est une illusion d'optique causée par la lumière; **that should do the trick** (col) ça devrait faire l'affaire

trickery [ˈtrɪkəri] n ruse f

trickle [ˈtrɪkl] n (of water etc) filet m ♦ vi couler en un filet or goutte à goutte; **to trickle in/out** (people) entrer/sortir par petits groupes

tricky [ˈtrɪki] adj difficile, délicat(e)

tricycle [ˈtraɪsɪkl] n tricycle m

trifle [ˈtraɪfl] n bagatelle f; (CULIN) ≃ diplomate m ♦ adv: **a trifle long** un peu long ♦ vi: **to trifle with** traiter à la légère

trifling [ˈtraɪflɪŋ] adj insignifiant(e)

trigger [ˈtrɪgə*] n (of gun) gâchette f

▶ **trigger off** vt déclencher

trim [trɪm] adj net(te); (house, garden) bien tenu(e); (figure) svelte ♦ n (haircut etc) légère coupe; (embellishment) finitions fpl; (on car) garnitures fpl ♦ vt couper légèrement; (decorate): **to trim (with)** décorer (de); (NAUT: a sail) gréer; **to keep in (good) trim** maintenir en (bon) état

trimmings [ˈtrɪmɪŋz] npl décorations fpl; (extras: gen CULIN) garniture f

trinket [ˈtrɪŋkɪt] n bibelot m; (piece of jewellery) colifichet m

trip [trɪp] n voyage m; (excursion) excursion f; (stumble) faux pas ♦ vi faire un faux pas, trébucher; (go lightly) marcher d'un pas léger; **on a trip** en voyage

▶ **trip up** vi trébucher ♦ vt faire un croc-en-jambe à

tripe [traɪp] n (CULIN) tripes fpl; (pej: rubbish) idioties fpl

triple [ˈtrɪpl] adj triple ♦ adv: **triple the distance/ the speed** trois fois la distance/la vitesse

triplets [ˈtrɪplɪts] npl triplés(ées)

triplicate [ˈtrɪplɪkət] n: **in triplicate** en trois exemplaires

tripod [ˈtraɪpɔd] n trépied m

trite [traɪt] adj banal(e)

triumph [ˈtraɪʌmf] n triomphe m ♦ vi: **to triumph (over)** triompher (de)

trivia [ˈtrɪvɪə] npl futilités fpl

trivial [ˈtrɪvɪəl] adj insignifiant(e); (commonplace) banal(e)

trod [trɔd] pt of **tread**

trodden [ˈtrɔdn] pp of **tread**

trolley [ˈtrɔli] n chariot m

trombone [trɔm'bəun] n trombone m

troop [tru:p] n bande f, groupe m ◆ vi: **to troop in/out** entrer/sortir en groupe; **trooping the colour** (BRIT: ceremony) le salut au drapeau

trophy ['trəufɪ] n trophée m

tropic ['trɔpɪk] n tropique m; **in the tropics** sous les tropiques; **Tropic of Cancer/Capricorn** tropique du Cancer/Capricorne

tropical ['trɔpɪkl] adj tropical(e)

trot [trɔt] n trot m ◆ vi trotter; **on the trot** (BRIT fig) d'affilée

▶ **trot out** vt (excuse, reason) débiter; (names, facts) réciter les uns après les autres

trouble ['trʌbl] n difficulté(s) f(pl), problème(s) m(pl); (worry) ennuis mpl, soucis mpl; (bother, effort) peine f; (POL) conflit(s) m(pl); **troubles** mpl; (MED): **stomach** etc **trouble** troubles gastriques etc ◆ vt déranger, gêner; (worry) inquiéter ◆ vi: **to trouble to do** prendre la peine de faire; **troubles** npl (POL etc) troubles; **to be in trouble** avoir des ennuis; (ship, climber etc) être en difficulté; **to have trouble doing sth** avoir du mal à faire qch; **to go to the trouble of doing** se donner le mal de faire; **it's no trouble!** je vous en prie!; **please don't trouble yourself** je vous en prie, ne vous dérangez pas!; **the trouble is ...** le problème, c'est que ...; **what's the trouble?** qu'est-ce qui ne va pas?

troubled ['trʌbld] adj (person) inquiet(ète); (epoch, life) agité(e)

troublemaker ['trʌblmeɪkə*] n élément perturbateur, fauteur m de troubles

troubleshooter ['trʌblʃu:tə*] n (in conflict) conciliateur m

troublesome ['trʌblsəm] adj ennuyeux(euse), gênant(e)

trough [trɔf] n (also: **drinking trough**) abreuvoir m; (also: **feeding trough**) auge f; (channel) chenal m; **trough of low pressure** (METEOROLOGY) dépression f

trousers ['trauzəz] npl pantalon m; **short trousers** (BRIT) culottes courtes

trout [traut] n (pl inv) truite f

trowel ['trauəl] n truelle f

truant ['truənt] n: **to play truant** (BRIT) faire l'école buissonnière

truce [tru:s] n trêve f

truck [trʌk] n camion m; (RAIL) wagon m à plate-forme; (for luggage) chariot m (à bagages)

truck driver n camionneur m

truck farm n (US) jardin maraîcher

true [tru:] adj vrai(e); (accurate) exact(e); (genuine) vrai, véritable; (faithful) fidèle; (wall) d'aplomb; (beam) droit(e); (wheel) dans l'axe; **to come true** se réaliser; **true to life** réaliste

truffle ['trʌfl] n truffe f

truly ['tru:lɪ] adv vraiment, réellement; (truthfully) sans mentir; (faithfully) fidèlement; **yours truly** (in letter) je vous prie d'agréer, Monsieur (or Madame

etc), l'expression de mes sentiments respectueux

trump [trʌmp] n atout m; **to turn up trumps** (fig) faire des miracles

trumpet ['trʌmpɪt] n trompette f

truncheon ['trʌntʃən] n bâton m (d'agent de police); matraque f

trundle ['trʌndl] vt, vi: **to trundle along** rouler bruyamment

trunk [trʌŋk] n (of tree, person) tronc m; (of elephant) trompe f; (case) malle f; (US AUT) coffre m

truss [trʌs] n (MED) bandage m herniaire ◆ vt: **to truss (up)** (CULIN) brider

trust [trʌst] n confiance f; (LAW) fidéicommis m; (COMM) trust m ◆ vt (rely on) avoir confiance en; (entrust): **to trust sth to sb** confier qch à qn; (hope): **to trust (that)** espérer (que); **to take sth on trust** accepter qch sans garanties (or sans preuves); **in trust** (LAW) par fidéicommis

trusted ['trʌstɪd] adj en qui l'on a confiance

trustee [trʌs'ti:] n (LAW) fidéicommissaire m/f; (of school etc) administrateur/trice

trustful ['trʌstful] adj confiant(e)

trustworthy ['trʌstwə:ðɪ] adj digne de confiance

truth, pl **truths** [tru:θ, tru:ðz] n vérité f

truthful ['tru:θful] adj (person) qui dit la vérité; (description) exact(e), vrai(e)

try [traɪ] n essai m, tentative f; (RUGBY) essai ◆ vt (LAW) juger; (test: sth new) essayer, tester; (strain) éprouver ◆ vi essayer; **to try to do** essayer de faire; (seek) chercher à faire; **to try one's (very) best** or **one's (very) hardest** faire de son mieux; **to give sth a try** essayer qch

▶ **try on** vt (clothes) essayer; **to try it on** (fig) tenter le coup, bluffer

▶ **try out** vt essayer, mettre à l'essai

trying ['traɪɪŋ] adj pénible

T-shirt ['ti:ʃə:t] n tee-shirt m

T-square ['ti:skwɛə*] n équerre f en T

tub [tʌb] n cuve f; baquet m; (bath) baignoire f

tubby ['tʌbɪ] adj rondelet(te)

tube [tju:b] n tube m; (BRIT: underground) métro m; (for tyre) chambre f à air; (col: television): **the tube** la télé

tuberculosis [tjubə:kju'ləusɪs] n tuberculose f

TUC n abbr (BRIT: = Trades Union Congress) confédération f des syndicats britanniques

tuck [tʌk] n (SEWING) pli m, rempli m ◆ vt (put) mettre

▶ **tuck away** vt cacher, ranger

▶ **tuck in** vt rentrer; (child) border ◆ vi (eat) manger de bon appétit; attaquer le repas

▶ **tuck up** vt (child) border

tuck shop n (BRIT SCOL) boutique f à provisions

Tuesday ['tju:zdɪ] n mardi m; **(the date) today is Tuesday 23rd March** nous sommes aujourd'hui le mardi 23 mars; **on Tuesday** mardi; **on Tuesdays** le mardi; **every Tuesday** tous les mardis, chaque

mardi; **every other Tuesday** un mardi sur deux;
last/next Tuesday mardi dernier/prochain;
Tuesday next mardi qui vient; **the following
Tuesday** le mardi suivant; **a week/fortnight on
Tuesday, Tuesday week/fortnight** mardi en huit/
quinze; **the Tuesday before last** l'autre mardi; **the
Tuesday after next** mardi en huit; **Tuesday
morning/lunchtime/afternoon/evening** mardi
matin/midi/après-midi/soir; **Tuesday night** mardi
soir; (*overnight*) la nuit de mardi (à mercredi);
Tuesday's newspaper le journal de mardi

tuft [tʌft] *n* touffe *f*

tug [tʌg] *n* (*ship*) remorqueur *m* ♦ *vt* tirer (sur)

tug-of-war [tʌgəvˈwɔː] *n* lutte *f* à la corde

tuition [tjuːˈɪʃən] *n* (BRIT: *lessons*) leçons *fpl*; (US:
fees) frais *mpl* de scolarité

tulip [ˈtjuːlɪp] *n* tulipe *f*

tumble [ˈtʌmbl] *n* (*fall*) chute *f*, culbute *f* ♦ *vi*
tomber, dégringoler; (*somersault*) faire une or des
culbute(s) ♦ *vt* renverser, faire tomber; **to tumble
to sth** (*col*) réaliser qch

tumbledown [ˈtʌmbldaun] *adj* délabré(e)

tumble dryer *n* (BRIT) séchoir *m* (à linge) à air
chaud

tumbler [ˈtʌmblə*] *n* verre (droit), gobelet *m*

tummy [ˈtʌmɪ] *n* (*col*) ventre *m*

tummy upset *n* maux *mpl* de ventre

tumour, (US) **tumor** [ˈtjuːmə*] *n* tumeur *f*

tuna [ˈtjuːnə] *n* (*pl inv*) (*also*: **tuna fish**) thon *m*

tune [tjuːn] *n* (*melody*) air *m* ♦ *vt* (MUS) accorder;
(RADIO, TV, AUT) régler, mettre au point; **to be in/out
of tune** (*instrument*) être accordé/désaccordé; (*singer*) chanter juste/faux; **to be in/out of tune
with** (*fig*) être en accord/désaccord avec; **she was
robbed to the tune of £10,000** (*fig*) on lui a volé
la jolie somme de 10 000 livres

▶ **tune in** *vi* (RADIO, TV): **to tune in (to)** se mettre à
l'écoute (de)

▶ **tune up** *vi* (*musician*) accorder son instrument

tuneful [ˈtjuːnful] *adj* mélodieux(euse)

tuner [ˈtjuːnə*] *n* (*radio set*) radio-préamplificateur
m; **piano tuner** accordeur *m* de pianos

tunic [ˈtjuːnɪk] *n* tunique *f*

Tunisia [tjuːˈnɪzɪə] *n* Tunisie *f*

tunnel [ˈtʌnl] *n* tunnel *m*; (*in mine*) galerie *f* ♦ *vi*
creuser un tunnel (*or* une galerie)

turbulence [ˈtəːbjuləns] *n* (AVIAT) turbulence *f*

tureen [təˈriːn] *n* soupière *f*

turf [təːf] *n* gazon *m*; (*clod*) motte *f* (de gazon)
♦ *vt* gazonner; **the Turf** le turf, les courses *fpl*

▶ **turf out** *vt* (*col*) jeter; jeter dehors

Turk [təːk] *n* Turc/Turque

Turkey [ˈtəːkɪ] *n* Turquie *f*

turkey [ˈtəːkɪ] *n* dindon *m*, dinde *f*

Turkish [ˈtəːkɪʃ] *adj* turc(turque) ♦ *n* (LING) turc *m*

turmoil [ˈtəːmɔɪl] *n* trouble *m*, bouleversement *m*

turn [təːn] *n* tour *m*; (*in road*) tournant *m*; (*tenden-*

cy: of mind, events) tournure *f*; (*performance*) numéro *m*; (MED) crise *f*, attaque *f* ♦ *vt* tourner; (*collar, steak*) retourner; (*milk*) faire tourner; (*change*): **to
turn sth into** changer qch en; (*shape: wood, metal*)
tourner ♦ *vi* tourner; (*person: look back*) se (re)tourner; (*reverse direction*) faire demi-tour; (*change*)
changer; (*become*) devenir; **to turn into** se changer
en, se transformer en; **a good turn** un service; **a
bad turn** un mauvais tour; **it gave me quite a turn**
ça m'a fait un coup; **"no left turn"** (AUT) "défense de
tourner à gauche"; **it's your turn** c'est (à) votre
tour; **in turn** à son tour; à tour de rôle; **to take
turns** se relayer; **to take turns at** faire à tour de
rôle; **at the turn of the year/century** à la fin de
l'année/du siècle; **to take a turn for the worse**
(*situation, events*) empirer; **his health** *or* **he has
taken a turn for the worse** son état s'est aggravé

▶ **turn about** *vi* faire demi-tour; faire un demi-
tour

▶ **turn away** *vi* se détourner, tourner la tête ♦ *vt*
(*reject: person*) renvoyer; (: *business*) refuser

▶ **turn back** *vi* revenir, faire demi-tour

▶ **turn down** *vt* (*refuse*) rejeter, refuser; (*reduce*)
baisser; (*fold*) rabattre

▶ **turn in** *vi* (*col: go to bed*) aller se coucher ♦ *vt*
(*fold*) rentrer

▶ **turn off** *vi* (*from road*) tourner ♦ *vt* (*light, radio
etc*) éteindre; (*engine*) arrêter

▶ **turn on** *vt* (*light, radio etc*) allumer; (*engine*)
mettre en marche

▶ **turn out** *vt* (*light, gas*) éteindre; (*produce: goods,
novel, good pupils*) produire ♦ *vi* (*appear, attend:
troops, doctor etc*) être présent(e); **to turn out to be
...** s'avérer ..., se révéler ...

▶ **turn over** *vi* (*person*) se retourner ♦ *vt* (*object*)
retourner; (*page*) tourner

▶ **turn round** *vi* faire demi-tour; (*rotate*) tourner

▶ **turn up** *vi* (*person*) arriver, se pointer; (*lost
object*) être retrouvé(e) ♦ *vt* (*collar*) remonter;
(*increase: sound, volume etc*) mettre plus fort

turning [ˈtəːnɪŋ] *n* (*in road*) tournant *m*; **the first
turning on the right** la première (rue *or* route) à
droite

turning point *n* (*fig*) tournant *m*, moment décisif

turnip [ˈtəːnɪp] *n* navet *m*

turnout [ˈtəːnaut] *n* (nombre *m* de personnes
dans l')assistance *f*

turnover [ˈtəːnəuvə*] *n* (COMM: *amount of money*)
chiffre *m* d'affaires; (: *of goods*) roulement *m*; (CULIN)
sorte de chausson; **there is a rapid turnover in
staff** le personnel change souvent

turnpike [ˈtəːnpaɪk] *n* (US) autoroute *f* à péage

turnstile [ˈtəːnstaɪl] *n* tourniquet *m* (d'entrée)

turntable [ˈtəːnteɪbl] *n* (*on record player*) platine *f*

turn-up [ˈtəːnʌp] *n* (BRIT: *on trousers*) revers *m*

turpentine [ˈtəːpəntaɪn] *n* (*also*: **turps**) (essence *f*
de) térébenthine *f*

turquoise [ˈtəːkwɔɪz] n (stone) turquoise f ♦ adj turquoise inv

turret [ˈtʌrɪt] n tourelle f

turtle [ˈtəːtl] n tortue marine

turtleneck (sweater) [ˈtəːtlnek-] n pullover m à col montant

tusk [tʌsk] n défense f (d'éléphant)

tutor [ˈtjuːtə*] n (BRIT SCOL) directeur/trice d'études; (private teacher) précepteur/trice

tutorial [tjuːˈtɔːrɪəl] n (SCOL) (séance f de) travaux mpl pratiques

tuxedo [tʌkˈsiːdəu] n (US) smoking m

TV [tiːˈviː] n abbr (= television) télé f, TV f

twang [twæŋ] n (of instrument) son vibrant; (of voice) ton nasillard ♦ vi vibrer ♦ vt (guitar) pincer les cordes de

tweed [twiːd] n tweed m

tweezers [ˈtwiːzəz] npl pince f à épiler

twelfth [twelfθ] num douzième

twelve [twelv] num douze; **at twelve (o'clock)** à midi; (midnight) à minuit

twentieth [ˈtwentɪɪθ] num vingtième

twenty [ˈtwentɪ] num vingt

twice [twaɪs] adv deux fois; **twice as much** deux fois plus; **twice a week** deux fois par semaine; **she is twice your age** elle a deux fois ton âge

twiddle [ˈtwɪdl] vt, vi: **to twiddle (with) sth** tripoter qch; **to twiddle one's thumbs** (fig) se tourner les pouces

twig [twɪg] n brindille f ♦ vt, vi (col) piger

twilight [ˈtwaɪlaɪt] n crépuscule m; (morning) aube f; **in the twilight** dans la pénombre

twin [twɪn] adj, n jumeau/elle ♦ vt jumeler

twin(-bedded) room [ˈtwɪn(ˈbedɪd)-] n chambre f à deux lits

twin beds npl lits mpl jumeaux

twine [twaɪn] n ficelle f ♦ vi (plant) s'enrouler

twinge [twɪndʒ] n (of pain) élancement m; (of conscience) remords m

twinkle [ˈtwɪŋkl] n scintillement m; pétillement m ♦ vi scintiller; (eyes) pétiller

twirl [twəːl] n tournoiement m ♦ vt faire tournoyer ♦ vi tournoyer

twist [twɪst] n torsion f, tour m; (in wire, flex) tortillon m; (bend: in road) tournant m; (in story) coup m de théâtre ♦ vt tordre; (weave) entortiller; (roll around) enrouler; (fig) déformer ♦ vi s'entortiller; s'enrouler; (road) serpenter; **to twist one's ankle/wrist** (MED) se tordre la cheville/le poignet

twit [twɪt] n (col) crétin/e

twitch [twɪtʃ] n saccade f; (nervous) tic m ♦ vi se convulser; avoir un tic

two [tuː] num deux; **two by two, in twos** par deux; **to put two and two together** (fig) faire le rapport

two-door [tuːˈdɔː*] adj (AUT) à deux portes

two-faced [tuːˈfeɪst] adj (pej: person) faux(fausse)

twofold [ˈtuːfəuld] adv: **to increase twofold** doubler ♦ adj (increase) de cent pour cent; (reply) en deux parties

two-piece [ˈtuːˈpiːs] n (also: **two-piece suit**) (costume m) deux-pièces m inv; (also: **two-piece swimsuit**) (maillot m de bain) deux-pièces

twosome [ˈtuːsəm] n (people) couple m

two-way [ˈtuːweɪ] adj (traffic) dans les deux sens; **two-way radio** émetteur-récepteur m

tycoon [taɪˈkuːn] n: **(business) tycoon** gros homme d'affaires

type [taɪp] n (category) genre m, espèce f; (model) modèle m; (example) type m; (TYP) type, caractère m ♦ vt (letter etc) taper (à la machine); **what type do you want?** quel genre voulez-vous?; **in bold/italic type** en caractères gras/en italiques

typecast [ˈtaɪpkɑːst] adj condamné(e) à toujours jouer le même rôle

typeface [ˈtaɪpfeɪs] n police f (de caractères)

typescript [ˈtaɪpskrɪpt] n texte dactylographié

typewriter [ˈtaɪpraɪtə*] n machine f à écrire

typewritten [ˈtaɪprɪtn] adj dactylographié(e)

typhoid [ˈtaɪfɔɪd] n typhoïde f

typical [ˈtɪpɪkl] adj typique, caractéristique

typing [ˈtaɪpɪŋ] n dactylo(graphie) f

typist [ˈtaɪpɪst] n dactylo m/f

tyrant [ˈtaɪərənt] n tyran m

tyre, (US) **tire** [ˈtaɪə*] n pneu m

tyre pressure n pression f (de gonflage)

— U u —

U-bend [ˈjuːbend] n (BRIT AUT) coude m, virage m en épingle à cheveux; (in pipe) coude

ubiquitous [juːˈbɪkwɪtəs] adj doué(e) d'ubiquité, omniprésent(e)

udder [ˈʌdə*] n pis m, mamelle f

UFO [ˈjuːfəu] n abbr (= unidentified flying object) ovni m (= objet volant non identifié)

Uganda [juːˈgændə] n Ouganda m

ugh [əːh] excl pouah!

ugly [ˈʌglɪ] adj laid(e), vilain(e); (fig) répugnant(e)

UHT adj abbr = ultra-heat treated: **UHT milk** lait m UHT or longue conservation

UK n abbr = **United Kingdom**

ulcer [ˈʌlsə*] n ulcère m; **mouth ulcer** aphte f

Ulster [ˈʌlstə*] n Ulster m

ulterior [ʌlˈtɪərɪə*] adj ultérieur(e); **ulterior motive** arrière-pensée f

ultimate [ˈʌltɪmət] adj ultime, final(e); (authority) suprême ♦ n: **the ultimate in luxury** le summum du luxe

ultimately [ˈʌltɪmətlɪ] adv (in the end) en fin de

compte; (at last) finalement; (eventually) par la suite

ultrasound ['ʌltrəsaund] n (MED) ultrason m

umbilical [ʌmbɪ'laɪkl] adj: **umbilical cord** cordon ombilical

umbrella [ʌm'brelə] n parapluie m; (fig): **under the umbrella of** sous les auspices de; chapeauté(e) par

umpire ['ʌmpaɪə*] n arbitre m; (TENNIS) juge m de chaise ♦ vt arbitrer

umpteen [ʌmp'tiːn] adj je ne sais combien de; **for the umpteenth time** pour la nième fois

UN n abbr = **United Nations**

unable [ʌn'eɪbl] adj: **to be unable to** ne (pas) pouvoir, être dans l'impossibilité de; (not capable) être incapable de

unacceptable [ʌnək'septəbl] adj (behaviour) inadmissible; (price, proposal) inacceptable

unaccompanied [ʌnə'kʌmpənɪd] adj (child, lady) non accompagné(e); (singing, song) sans accompagnement

unaccustomed [ʌnə'kʌstəmd] adj inaccoutumé(e), inhabituel(le); **to be unaccustomed to sth** ne pas avoir l'habitude de qch

unanimous [juː'nænɪməs] adj unanime

unanimously [juː'nænɪməslɪ] adv à l'unanimité

unarmed [ʌn'ɑːmd] adj (person) non armé(e); (combat) sans armes

unattached [ʌnə'tætʃt] adj libre, sans attaches

unattended [ʌnə'tendɪd] adj (car, child, luggage) sans surveillance

unattractive [ʌnə'træktɪv] adj peu attrayant(e)

unauthorized [ʌn'ɔːθəraɪzd] adj non autorisé(e), sans autorisation

unavoidable [ʌnə'vɔɪdəbl] adj inévitable

unaware [ʌnə'weə*] adj: **to be unaware of** ignorer, ne pas savoir, être inconscient(e) de

unawares [ʌnə'weəz] adv à l'improviste, au dépourvu

unbalanced [ʌn'bælənst] adj déséquilibré(e)

unbearable [ʌn'beərəbl] adj insupportable

unbeatable [ʌn'biːtəbl] adj imbattable

unbeknown(st) [ʌnbɪ'nəun(st)] adv: **unbeknown(st) to** à l'insu de

unbelievable [ʌnbɪ'liːvəbl] adj incroyable

unbend [ʌn'bend] vb, vi (irreg) se détendre ♦ vt (wire) redresser, détordre

unbias(s)ed [ʌn'baɪəst] adj impartial(e)

unborn [ʌn'bɔːn] adj à naître

unbreakable [ʌn'breɪkəbl] adj incassable

unbroken [ʌn'brəukn] adj intact(e); (line) continu(e); (record) non battu(e)

unbutton [ʌn'bʌtn] vt déboutonner

uncalled-for [ʌn'kɔːldfɔː*] adj déplacé(e), injustifié(e)

uncanny [ʌn'kænɪ] adj étrange, troublant(e)

unceremonious [ʌnserɪ'məunɪəs] adj (abrupt, rude) brusque

uncertain [ʌn'səːtn] adj incertain(e); **we were uncertain whether ...** nous ne savions pas vraiment si ...; **in no uncertain terms** sans équivoque possible

uncertainty [ʌn'səːtntɪ] n incertitude f, doutes mpl

uncivilized [ʌn'sɪvɪlaɪzd] adj non civilisé(e); (fig) barbare

uncle ['ʌŋkl] n oncle m

uncomfortable [ʌn'kʌmfətəbl] adj inconfortable; (uneasy) mal à l'aise, gêné(e); (situation) désagréable

uncommon [ʌn'kɔmən] adj rare, singulier(ière), peu commun(e)

uncompromising [ʌn'kɔmprəmaɪzɪŋ] adj intransigeant(e), inflexible

unconcerned [ʌnkən'səːnd] adj (unworried): **to be unconcerned (about)** ne pas s'inquiéter (de)

unconditional [ʌnkən'dɪʃənl] adj sans conditions

unconscious [ʌn'kɔnʃəs] adj sans connaissance, évanoui(e); (unaware) inconscient(e) ♦ n: **the unconscious** l'inconscient m; **to knock sb unconscious** assommer qn

unconsciously [ʌn'kɔnʃəslɪ] adv inconsciemment

uncontrollable [ʌnkən'trəuləbl] adj (child, dog) indiscipliné(e); (emotion) irrépressible

unconventional [ʌnkən'venʃənl] adj non conventionnel(le)

uncouth [ʌn'kuːθ] adj grossier(ière), fruste

uncover [ʌn'kʌvə*] vt découvrir

undecided [ʌndɪ'saɪdɪd] adj indécis(e), irrésolu(e)

under ['ʌndə*] prep sous; (less than) (de) moins de; au-dessous de; (according to) selon, en vertu de ♦ adv au-dessous; en dessous; **from under sth** de dessous or de sous qch; **under there** là-dessous; **in under 2 hours** en moins de 2 heures; **under anaesthetic** sous anesthésie; **under discussion** en discussion; **under the circumstances** étant donné les circonstances; **under repair** en (cours de) réparation

underage [ʌndər'eɪdʒ] adj qui n'a pas l'âge réglementaire

undercarriage ['ʌndəkærɪdʒ] n (BRIT AVIAT) train m d'atterrissage

undercharge [ʌndə'tʃɑːdʒ] vt ne pas faire payer assez à

undercoat ['ʌndəkəut] n (paint) couche f de fond

undercover [ʌndə'kʌvə*] adj secret(ète), clandestin(e)

undercurrent ['ʌndəkʌrnt] n courant sous-jacent

undercut [ʌndə'kʌt] vt irreg vendre moins cher que

underdog ['ʌndədɔg] n opprimé m

underdone [ʌndə'dʌn] adj (food) pas assez

cuit(e)

underestimate [ˈʌndərˈestɪmeɪt] *vt* sous-estimer, mésestimer

underfed [ʌndəˈfed] *adj* sous-alimenté(e)

underfoot [ʌndəˈfut] *adv* sous les pieds

undergo [ʌndəˈgəu] *vt irreg* subir; (*treatment*) suivre; **the car is undergoing repairs** la voiture est en réparation

undergraduate [ʌndəˈgrædjuɪt] *n* étudiant/e (qui prépare la licence) ♦ *cpd*: **undergraduate courses** cours *mpl* préparant à la licence

underground [ˈʌndəgraund] *adj* souterrain(e); (*fig*) clandestin(e) ♦ *n* (*BRIT*) métro *m*; (*POL*) clandestinité *f*

undergrowth [ˈʌndəgrəuθ] *n* broussailles *fpl*, sous-bois *m*

underhand(ed) [ʌndəˈhænd(ɪd)] *adj* (*fig*) sournois(e), en dessous

underlie [ʌndəˈlaɪ] *vt irreg* être à la base de; **the underlying cause** la cause sous-jacente

underline [ʌndəˈlaɪn] *vt* souligner

undermine [ʌndəˈmaɪn] *vt* saper, miner

underneath [ʌndəˈniːθ] *adv* (en) dessous ♦ *prep* sous, au-dessous de

underpaid [ʌndəˈpeɪd] *adj* sous-payé(e)

underpants [ˈʌndəpænts] *npl* caleçon *m*, slip *m*

underpass [ˈʌndəpɑːs] *n* (*BRIT*) passage souterrain; (: *on motorway*) passage inférieur

underprivileged [ʌndəˈprɪvɪlɪdʒd] *adj* défavorisé(e), déshérité(e)

underrate [ʌndəˈreɪt] *vt* sous-estimer, mésestimer

undershirt [ˈʌndəʃəːt] *n* (*US*) tricot *m* de corps

undershorts [ˈʌndəʃɔːts] *npl* (*US*) caleçon *m*, slip *m*

underside [ˈʌndəsaɪd] *n* dessous *m*

underskirt [ˈʌndəskəːt] *n* (*BRIT*) jupon *m*

understand [ʌndəˈstænd] *vb* (*irreg: like* **stand**) *vt*, *vi* comprendre; **I understand that …** je me suis laissé dire que …; je crois comprendre que …; **to make o.s. understood** se faire comprendre

understandable [ʌndəˈstændəbl] *adj* compréhensible

understanding [ʌndəˈstændɪŋ] *adj* compréhensif(ive) ♦ *n* compréhension *f*; (*agreement*) accord *m*; **to come to an understanding with sb** s'entendre avec qn; **on the understanding that …** à condition que …

understatement [ˈʌndəsteɪtmənt] *n*: **that's an understatement** c'est (bien) peu dire, le terme est faible

understood [ʌndəˈstud] *pt, pp of* **understand** ♦ *adj* entendu(e); (*implied*) sous-entendu(e)

understudy [ˈʌndəstʌdɪ] *n* doublure *f*

undertake [ʌndəˈteɪk] *vt irreg* (*job, task*) entreprendre; (*duty*) se charger de; **to undertake to do sth** s'engager à faire qch

undertaker [ˈʌndəteɪkə*] *n* entrepreneur *m* des pompes funèbres, croque-mort *m*

undertaking [ˈʌndəteɪkɪŋ] *n* entreprise *f*; (*promise*) promesse *f*

undertone [ˈʌndətəun] *n* (*low voice*): **in an undertone** à mi-voix; (*of criticism etc*) nuance cachée

underwater [ʌndəˈwɔːtə*] *adv* sous l'eau ♦ *adj* sous-marin(e)

underwear [ˈʌndəwɛə*] *n* sous-vêtements *mpl*; (*women's only*) dessous *mpl*

underworld [ˈʌndəwəːld] *n* (*of crime*) milieu *m*, pègre *f*

underwrite [ʌndəˈraɪt] *vt* (*FINANCE*) garantir; (*INSURANCE*) souscrire

undies [ˈʌndɪz] *npl* (*col*) dessous *mpl*, lingerie *f*

undiplomatic [ˈʌndɪpləˈmætɪk] *adj* peu diplomatique, maladroit(e)

undo [ʌnˈduː] *vt* (*irreg*) défaire

undoing [ʌnˈduːɪŋ] *n* ruine *f*, perte *f*

undoubted [ʌnˈdautɪd] *adj* indubitable, certain(e)

undoubtedly [ʌnˈdautɪdlɪ] *adv* sans aucun doute

undress [ʌnˈdres] *vi* se déshabiller ♦ *vt* déshabiller

undue [ʌnˈdjuː] *adj* indu(e), excessif(ive)

undulating [ˈʌndjuleɪtɪŋ] *adj* ondoyant(e), onduleux(euse)

unduly [ʌnˈdjuːlɪ] *adv* trop, excessivement

unearth [ʌnˈəːθ] *vt* déterrer; (*fig*) dénicher

unearthly [ʌnˈəːθlɪ] *adj* surnaturel(le); (*hour*) indu(e), impossible

uneasy [ʌnˈiːzɪ] *adj* mal à l'aise, gêné(e); (*worried*) inquiet(ète); **to feel uneasy about doing sth** se sentir mal à l'aise à l'idée de faire qch

uneconomic(al) [ˈʌniːkəˈnɔmɪk(l)] *adj* peu économique; peu rentable

uneducated [ʌnˈedjukeɪtɪd] *adj* sans éducation

unemployed [ʌnɪmˈplɔɪd] *adj* sans travail, au chômage ♦ *n*: **the unemployed** les chômeurs *mpl*

unemployment [ʌnɪmˈplɔɪmənt] *n* chômage *m*

unending [ʌnˈendɪŋ] *adj* interminable

unerring [ʌnˈəːrɪŋ] *adj* infaillible, sûr(e)

uneven [ʌnˈiːvn] *adj* inégal(e); irrégulier(ière)

unexpected [ʌnɪkˈspektɪd] *adj* inattendu(e), imprévu(e)

unexpectedly [ʌnɪkˈspektɪdlɪ] *adv* contre toute attente; (*arrive*) à l'improviste

unfailing [ʌnˈfeɪlɪŋ] *adj* inépuisable; infaillible

unfair [ʌnˈfɛə*] *adj*: **unfair (to)** injuste (envers); **it's unfair that …** il n'est pas juste que …

unfaithful [ʌnˈfeɪθful] *adj* infidèle

unfamiliar [ʌnfəˈmɪlɪə*] *adj* étrange, inconnu(e); **to be unfamiliar with sth** mal connaître qch

unfashionable [ʌnˈfæʃnəbl] *adj* (*clothes*) démodé(e); (*district*) déshérité(e), pas à la mode

unfasten [ʌnˈfɑːsn] *vt* défaire; détacher

unfavourable, (*US*) **unfavorable** [ʌnˈfeɪvrəbl] *adj* défavorable

unfeeling [ʌnˈfiːlɪŋ] *adj* insensible, dur(e)

unfinished [ʌnˈfɪnɪʃt] *adj* inachevé(e)

unfit [ʌnˈfɪt] *adj* (*physically*) pas en forme; (*incompetent*): **unfit (for)** impropre (à); (*work, service*) inapte (à)

unfold [ʌnˈfəʊld] *vt* déplier; (*fig*) révéler, exposer ◆ *vi* se dérouler

unforeseen [ˈʌnfɔːˈsiːn] *adj* imprévu(e)

unforgettable [ʌnfəˈɡetəbl] *adj* inoubliable

unfortunate [ʌnˈfɔːtʃnət] *adj* malheureux(euse); (*event, remark*) malencontreux(euse)

unfortunately [ʌnˈfɔːtʃnətlɪ] *adv* malheureusement

unfounded [ʌnˈfaʊndɪd] *adj* sans fondement

unfriendly [ʌnˈfrendlɪ] *adj* froid(e), inamical(e)

ungainly [ʌnˈɡeɪnlɪ] *adj* gauche, dégingandé(e)

ungodly [ʌnˈɡɒdlɪ] *adj* impie; **at an ungodly hour** à une heure indue

ungrateful [ʌnˈɡreɪtful] *adj* qui manque de reconnaissance, ingrat(e)

unhappiness [ʌnˈhæpɪnɪs] *n* tristesse *f*, peine *f*

unhappy [ʌnˈhæpɪ] *adj* triste, malheureux(euse); (*unfortunate: remark etc*) malheureux(euse); (*not pleased*): **unhappy with** mécontent(e) de, peu satisfait(e) de

unharmed [ʌnˈhɑːmd] *adj* indemne, sain(e) et sauf(sauve)

UNHCR *n abbr* (= *United Nations High Commission for Refugees*) HCR *m*

unhealthy [ʌnˈhelθɪ] *adj* (*gen*) malsain(e); (*person*) maladif(ive)

unheard-of [ʌnˈhɜːdɒv] *adj* inouï(e), sans précédent

unhurt [ʌnˈhɜːt] *adj* indemne, sain(e) et sauf(sauve)

unidentified [ʌnaɪˈdentɪfaɪd] *adj* non identifié(e)

uniform [ˈjuːnɪfɔːm] *n* uniforme *m* ◆ *adj* uniforme

uninhabited [ʌnɪnˈhæbɪtɪd] *adj* inhabité(e)

unintentional [ʌnɪnˈtenʃənəl] *adj* involontaire

union [ˈjuːnjən] *n* union *f*; (*also*: **trade union**) syndicat *m* ◆ *cpd* du syndicat, syndical(e)

Union Jack *n* drapeau du Royaume-Uni

unique [juːˈniːk] *adj* unique

unison [ˈjuːnɪsn] *n*: **in unison** à l'unisson, en chœur

unit [ˈjuːnɪt] *n* unité *f*; (*section: of furniture etc*) élément *m*, bloc *m*; (*team, squad*) groupe *m*, service *m*; **production unit** atelier *m* de fabrication; **sink unit** bloc-évier *m*

unite [juːˈnaɪt] *vt* unir ◆ *vi* s'unir

united [juːˈnaɪtɪd] *adj* uni(e); unifié(e); (*efforts*) conjugué(e)

United Kingdom (UK) *n* Royaume-Uni *m*

(R.U.)

United Nations (Organization) (UN, UNO) *n* (Organisation *f* des) Nations unies (ONU)

United States (of America) (US, USA) *n* États-Unis *mpl*

unit trust *n* (*BRIT COMM*) fonds commun de placement, FCP *m*

unity [ˈjuːnɪtɪ] *n* unité *f*

universal [juːnɪˈvɜːsl] *adj* universel(le)

universe [ˈjuːnɪvɜːs] *n* univers *m*

university [juːnɪˈvɜːsɪtɪ] *n* université *f* ◆ *cpd* (*student, professor*) d'université; (*education, year, degree*) universitaire

unjust [ʌnˈdʒʌst] *adj* injuste

unkempt [ʌnˈkempt] *adj* mal tenu(e), débraillé(e); mal peigné(e)

unkind [ʌnˈkaɪnd] *adj* peu gentil(le), méchant(e)

unknown [ʌnˈnəʊn] *adj* inconnu(e); **unknown to me** sans que je le sache; **unknown quantity** (*MATH, fig*) inconnue *f*

unlawful [ʌnˈlɔːful] *adj* illégal(e)

unleaded [ʌnˈledɪd] *n* (*also*: **unleaded petrol**) essence *f* sans plomb

unleash [ʌnˈliːʃ] *vt* détacher; (*fig*) déchaîner, déclencher

unless [ʌnˈles] *conj*: **unless he leaves** à moins qu'il (ne) parte; **unless we leave** à moins de partir, à moins que nous (ne) partions; **unless otherwise stated** sauf indication contraire; **unless I am mistaken** si je ne me trompe

unlike [ʌnˈlaɪk] *adj* dissemblable, différent(e) ◆ *prep* à la différence de, contrairement à

unlikely [ʌnˈlaɪklɪ] *adj* (*result, event*) improbable; (*explanation*) invraisemblable

unlimited [ʌnˈlɪmɪtɪd] *adj* illimité(e)

unlisted [ˈʌnˈlɪstɪd] *adj* (*US TEL*) sur la liste rouge; (*STOCK EXCHANGE*) non coté(e) en Bourse

unload [ʌnˈləʊd] *vt* décharger

unlock [ʌnˈlɒk] *vt* ouvrir

unlucky [ʌnˈlʌkɪ] *adj* malchanceux(euse); (*object, number*) qui porte malheur; **to be unlucky** (*person*) ne pas avoir de chance

unmarried [ʌnˈmærɪd] *adj* célibataire

unmistakable [ʌnmɪsˈteɪkəbl] *adj* indubitable; qu'on ne peut pas ne pas reconnaître

unmitigated [ʌnˈmɪtɪɡeɪtɪd] *adj* non mitigé(e), absolu(e), pur(e)

unnatural [ʌnˈnætʃrəl] *adj* non naturel(le), contre nature

unnecessary [ʌnˈnesəsərɪ] *adj* inutile, superflu(e)

unnoticed [ʌnˈnəʊtɪst] *adj* inaperçu(e); **to go unnoticed** passer inaperçu

UNO [ˈjuːnəʊ] *n abbr* = **United Nations Organization**

unobtainable [ʌnəbˈteɪnəbl] *adj* (*TEL*) impossible à obtenir

unobtrusive [ʌnəbˈtruːsɪv] *adj* discret(ète)

unofficial [ʌnəˈfɪʃl] *adj* non officiel(le); (*strike*) ≈ non sanctionné(e) par la centrale

unorthodox [ʌnˈɔːθədɔks] *adj* peu orthodoxe

unpack [ʌnˈpæk] *vi* défaire sa valise, déballer ses affaires

unpalatable [ʌnˈpælətəbl] *adj* (*truth*) désagréable (à entendre)

unparalleled [ʌnˈpærəleld] *adj* incomparable, sans égal

unpleasant [ʌnˈpleznt] *adj* déplaisant(e), désagréable

unplug [ʌnˈplʌg] *vt* débrancher

unpopular [ʌnˈpɔpjulə*] *adj* impopulaire; **to make o.s. unpopular (with)** se rendre impopulaire (auprès de)

unprecedented [ʌnˈpresidentid] *adj* sans précédent

unpredictable [ʌnprɪˈdɪktəbl] *adj* imprévisible

unprofessional [ʌnprəˈfeʃənl] *adj* (*conduct*) contraire à la déontologie

UNPROFOR [ʌnˈprɔufɔː*] *n abbr* (= United Nations Protection Force) FORPRONU *f*

unqualified [ʌnˈkwɔlɪfaɪd] *adj* (*teacher*) non diplômé(e), sans titres; (*success*) sans réserve, total(e)

unquestionably [ʌnˈkwestʃənəblɪ] *adv* incontestablement

unravel [ʌnˈrævl] *vt* démêler

unreal [ʌnˈrɪəl] *adj* irréel(le)

unrealistic [ʌnrɪəˈlɪstɪk] *adj* (*idea*) irréaliste; (*estimate*) peu réaliste

unreasonable [ʌnˈriːznəbl] *adj* qui n'est pas raisonnable; **to make unreasonable demands on sb** exiger trop de qn

unrelated [ʌnrɪˈleɪtɪd] *adj* sans rapport; sans lien de parenté

unreliable [ʌnrɪˈlaɪəbl] *adj* sur qui (*or* quoi) on ne peut pas compter, peu fiable

unremitting [ʌnrɪˈmɪtɪŋ] *adj* inlassable, infatigable, acharné(e)

unreservedly [ʌnrɪˈzəːvɪdlɪ] *adv* sans réserve

unrest [ʌnˈrest] *n* agitation *f*, troubles *mpl*

unroll [ʌnˈrəul] *vt* dérouler

unruly [ʌnˈruːlɪ] *adj* indiscipliné(e)

unsafe [ʌnˈseɪf] *adj* (*machine, wiring*) dangereux(euse); (*method*) hasardeux(euse); **unsafe to drink/eat** non potable/comestible

unsaid [ʌnˈsed] *adj*: **to leave sth unsaid** passer qch sous silence

unsatisfactory [ʌnsætɪsˈfæktərɪ] *adj* qui laisse à désirer

unsavoury, (*us*) **unsavory** [ʌnˈseɪvərɪ] *adj* (*fig*) peu recommandable, répugnant(e)

unscathed [ʌnˈskeɪðd] *adj* indemne

unscrew [ʌnˈskruː] *vt* dévisser

unscrupulous [ʌnˈskruːpjuləs] *adj* sans scrupules

unsettled [ʌnˈsetld] *adj* (*restless*) perturbé(e); (*unpredictable*) instable; incertain(e); (*not finalized*) non résolu(e)

unshaven [ʌnˈʃeɪvn] *adj* non *or* mal rasé(e)

unsightly [ʌnˈsaɪtlɪ] *adj* disgracieux(euse), laid(e)

unskilled [ʌnˈskɪld] *adj*: **unskilled worker** manœuvre *m*

unspeakable [ʌnˈspiːkəbl] *adj* indicible; (*awful*) innommable

unstable [ʌnˈsteɪbl] *adj* instable

unsteady [ʌnˈstedɪ] *adj* mal assuré(e), chancelant(e), instable

unstuck [ʌnˈstʌk] *adj*: **to come unstuck** se décoller; (*fig*) faire fiasco

unsuccessful [ʌnsəkˈsesful] *adj* (*attempt*) infructueux(euse); (*writer, proposal*) qui n'a pas de succès; (*marriage*) malheureux(euse), qui ne réussit pas; **to be unsuccessful** (*in attempting sth*) ne pas réussir; ne pas avoir de succès; (*application*) ne pas être retenu(e)

unsuitable [ʌnˈsuːtəbl] *adj* qui ne convient pas, peu approprié(e); inopportun(e)

unsure [ʌnˈʃuə*] *adj* pas sûr(e); **to be unsure of o.s.** ne pas être sûr de soi, manquer de confiance en soi

unsuspecting [ʌnsəˈspektɪŋ] *adj* qui ne se méfie pas

unsympathetic [ˈʌnsɪmpəˈθetɪk] *adj* hostile; (*unpleasant*) antipathique; **unsympathetic to** indifférent(e) à

untapped [ʌnˈtæpt] *adj* (*resources*) inexploité(e)

unthinkable [ʌnˈθɪŋkəbl] *adj* impensable, inconcevable

untidy [ʌnˈtaɪdɪ] *adj* (*room*) en désordre; (*appearance*) désordonné(e), débraillé(e); (*person*) sans ordre, désordonné; débraillé; (*work*) peu soigné(e)

untie [ʌnˈtaɪ] *vt* (*knot, parcel*) défaire; (*prisoner, dog*) détacher

until [ʌnˈtɪl] *prep* jusqu'à; (*after negative*) avant ♦ *conj* jusqu'à ce que + *sub*, en attendant que + *sub*; (*in past, after negative*) avant que + *sub*; **until now** jusqu'à présent, jusqu'ici; **until then** jusque-là; **from morning until night** du matin au soir *or* jusqu'au soir

untimely [ʌnˈtaɪmlɪ] *adj* inopportun(e); (*death*) prématuré(e)

untold [ʌnˈtəuld] *adj* incalculable; indescriptible

untoward [ʌntəˈwɔːd] *adj* fâcheux(euse), malencontreux(euse)

unused *adj* [ʌnˈjuːzd] (*new*) neuf(neuve); [ʌnˈjuːst]: **to be unused to sth/to doing sth** ne pas avoir l'habitude de qch/de faire qch

unusual [ʌnˈjuːʒuəl] *adj* insolite, exceptionnel(le), rare

unveil [ʌnˈveɪl] *vt* dévoiler

unwanted [ʌnˈwɔntɪd] *adj* non désiré(e)

unwelcome [ʌnˈwelkəm] *adj* importun(e); **to**

feel unwelcome se sentir de trop

unwell [ʌn'wel] *adj* indisposé(e), souffrant(e); **to feel unwell** ne pas se sentir bien

unwieldy [ʌn'wiːldɪ] *adj* difficile à manier

unwilling [ʌn'wɪlɪŋ] *adj*: **to be unwilling to do** ne pas vouloir faire

unwillingly [ʌn'wɪlɪŋlɪ] *adv* à contrecœur, contre son gré

unwind [ʌn'waɪnd] *vb* (*irreg*) ♦ *vt* dérouler ♦ *vi* (*relax*) se détendre

unwise [ʌn'waɪz] *adj* imprudent(e), peu judicieux(euse)

unwitting [ʌn'wɪtɪŋ] *adj* involontaire

unworkable [ʌn'wɜːkəbl] *adj* (*plan etc*) inexploitable

unworthy [ʌn'wɜːðɪ] *adj* indigne

unwrap [ʌn'ræp] *vt* défaire; ouvrir

unwritten [ʌn'rɪtn] *adj* (*agreement*) tacite

```
KEYWORD
```

up [ʌp] *prep*: **he went up the stairs/the hill** il a monté l'escalier/la colline; **the cat was up a tree** le chat était dans un arbre; **they live further up the street** ils habitent plus haut dans la rue

♦ *vi* (*col*): **she upped and left** elle a fichu le camp sans plus attendre

♦ *adv* **1** en haut; en l'air; (*upwards, higher*): **up in the sky/the mountains** (là-haut) dans le ciel/les montagnes; **put it a bit higher up** mettez-le un peu plus haut; **up there** là-haut; **up above** au-dessus; **"this side up"** "haut"

2: **to be up** (*out of bed*) être levé(e); (*prices*) avoir augmenté or monté; (*finished*): **when the year was up** à la fin de l'année; **time's up** c'est l'heure

3: **up to** (*as far as*) jusqu'à; **up to now** jusqu'à présent

4: **to be up to** (*depending on*): **it's up to you** c'est à vous de décider; (*equal to*): **he's not up to it** (*job, task etc*) il n'en est pas capable; (*inf: be doing*): **what is he up to?** qu'est-ce qu'il peut bien faire?

5 (*phrases*): **he's well up in** or **on ...** (*BRIT: knowledgeable*) il s'y connaît en ...; **up with Leeds United!** vive Leeds United!; **what's up?** (*col*) qu'est-ce qui ne va pas?; **what's up with him?** (*col*) qu'est-ce qui lui arrive?

♦ *n*: **ups and downs** hauts et bas *mpl*

up-and-coming [ʌpənd'kʌmɪŋ] *adj* plein(e) d'avenir or de promesses

upbringing ['ʌpbrɪŋɪŋ] *n* éducation *f*

update [ʌp'deɪt] *vt* mettre à jour

upgrade [ʌp'greɪd] *vt* (*person*) promouvoir; (*job*) revaloriser; (*property, equipment*) moderniser

upheaval [ʌp'hiːvl] *n* bouleversement *m*; branle-bas *m*; crise *f*

uphill [ʌp'hɪl] *adj* qui monte; (*fig: task*) difficile, pénible ♦ *adv* (*face, look*) en amont, vers l'amont; (*go, move*) vers le haut, en haut; **to go uphill** monter

uphold [ʌp'həuld] *vt irreg* maintenir; soutenir

upholstery [ʌp'həulstərɪ] *n* rembourrage *m*; (*of car*) garniture *f*

upkeep ['ʌpkiːp] *n* entretien *m*

upon [ə'pɔn] *prep* sur

upper ['ʌpə*] *adj* supérieur(e); du dessus ♦ *n* (*of shoe*) empeigne *f*

upper class *n*: **the upper class** ≃ la haute bourgeoisie; ♦ *adj*: **upper-class** (*district*) élégant(e), huppé(e); (*accent, attitude*) caractéristique des classes supérieures

upper hand *n*: **to have the upper hand** avoir le dessus

uppermost ['ʌpəməust] *adj* le(la) plus haut(e), en dessus; **it was uppermost in my mind** j'y pensais avant tout autre chose

upper sixth *n* terminale *f*

upright ['ʌpraɪt] *adj* droit(e); vertical(e); (*fig*) droit, honnête ♦ *n* montant *m*

uprising ['ʌpraɪzɪŋ] *n* soulèvement *m*, insurrection *f*

uproar ['ʌprɔː*] *n* tumulte *m*, vacarme *m*

uproot [ʌp'ruːt] *vt* déraciner

upset *n* ['ʌpset] dérangement *m* ♦ *vt* [ʌp'set] (*irreg: like* set) (*glass etc*) renverser; (*plan*) déranger; (*person: offend*) contrarier; (*: grieve*) faire de la peine à; bouleverser ♦ *adj* [ʌp'set] contrarié(e); peiné(e); (*stomach*) détraqué(e), dérangé(e); **to get upset** (*sad*) devenir triste; (*offended*) se vexer; **to have a stomach upset** (*BRIT*) avoir une indigestion

upshot ['ʌpʃɔt] *n* résultat *m*; **the upshot of it all was that ...** il a résulté de tout cela que ...

upside down ['ʌpsaɪd-] *adv* à l'envers

upstairs [ʌp'stɛəz] *adv* en haut ♦ *adj* (*room*) du dessus, d'en haut ♦ *n*: **there's no upstairs** il n'y a pas d'étage

upstart ['ʌpstɑːt] *n* parvenu/e

upstream [ʌp'striːm] *adv* en amont

uptake ['ʌpteɪk] *n*: **he is quick/slow on the uptake** il comprend vite/est lent à comprendre

uptight [ʌp'taɪt] *adj* (*col*) très tendu(e), crispé(e)

up-to-date ['ʌptə'deɪt] *adj* moderne; très récent(e)

upturn ['ʌptəːn] *n* (*in economy*) reprise *f*

upward ['ʌpwəd] *adj* ascendant(e); vers le haut ♦ *adv see* **upwards**

upwards ['ʌpwədz] *adv* vers le haut; **and upwards** et plus, et au-dessus

urban ['əːbən] *adj* urbain(e)

urban clearway *n* rue *f* à stationnement interdit

urbane [əː'beɪn] *adj* urbain(e), courtois(e)

urchin ['əːtʃɪn] *n* gosse *m*, garnement *m*

urge [əːdʒ] *n* besoin (impératif), envie (pressante) ♦ *vt* (*caution etc*) recommander avec insistance; (*person*): **to urge sb to do** presser qn de faire,

recommander avec insistance à qn de faire
▶ **urge on** vt pousser, presser
urgency ['ə:dʒənsɪ] n urgence f; (of tone) insistance f
urgent ['ə:dʒənt] adj urgent(e); (plea, tone) pressant(e)
urinal ['juərɪnl] n (BRIT) urinoir m
urine ['juərɪn] n urine f
urn [ə:n] n urne f; (also: **tea urn**) fontaine f à thé
US n abbr = **United States**
us [ʌs] pron nous
USA n abbr = **United States of America**; (MIL) = **United States Army**
use n [ju:s] emploi m, utilisation f; usage m ◆ vt [ju:z] se servir de, utiliser, employer; **in use** en usage; **out of use** hors d'usage; **to be of use** servir, être utile; **to make use of sth** utiliser qch; **ready for use** prêt à l'emploi; **it's no use** ça ne sert à rien; **to have the use of** avoir l'usage de; **what's this used for?** à quoi est-ce que ça sert?; **she used to do it** elle le faisait (autrefois), elle avait coutume de le faire; **to be used to** avoir l'habitude de, être habitué(e) à; **to get used to** s'habituer à
▶ **use up** vt finir, épuiser; (food) consommer
used [ju:zd] adj (car) d'occasion
useful ['ju:sful] adj utile; **to come in useful** être utile
usefulness ['ju:sfəlnɪs] n utilité f
useless ['ju:slɪs] adj inutile
user ['ju:zə*] n utilisateur/trice, usager m
user-friendly ['ju:zə'frendlɪ] adj convivial(e), facile d'emploi
usher ['ʌʃə*] n placeur m ◆ vt: **to usher sb in** faire entrer qn
usherette [ʌʃə'rɛt] n (in cinema) ouvreuse f
usual ['ju:ʒuəl] adj habituel(le); **as usual** comme d'habitude
usually ['ju:ʒuəlɪ] adv d'habitude, d'ordinaire
utensil [ju:'tensl] n ustensile m; **kitchen utensils** batterie f de cuisine
uterus ['ju:tərəs] n utérus m
utility [ju:'tɪlɪtɪ] n utilité f; (also: **public utility**) service public
utility room n buanderie f
utmost ['ʌtməust] adj extrême, le(la) plus grand(e) ◆ n: **to do one's utmost** faire tout son possible; **of the utmost importance** d'une importance capitale, de la plus haute importance
utter ['ʌtə*] adj total(e), complet(ète) ◆ vt prononcer, proférer; émettre
utterance ['ʌtrns] n paroles fpl
utterly ['ʌtəlɪ] adv complètement, totalement
U-turn ['ju:'tə:n] n demi-tour m; (fig) volte-face f inv

— V v —

V abbr = **verse**, (= vide: see) v.; (= versus) c.; (= volt) V.
vacancy ['veɪkənsɪ] n (BRIT: job) poste vacant; (room) chambre f disponible; **"no vacancies"** "complet"
vacant ['veɪkənt] adj (post) vacant(e); (seat etc) libre, disponible; (expression) distrait(e)
vacate [və'keɪt] vt quitter
vacation [və'keɪʃən] n (esp US) vacances fpl; **to take a vacation** prendre des vacances; **on vacation** en vacances
vaccinate ['væksɪneɪt] vt vacciner
vacuum ['vækjum] n vide m
vacuum cleaner n aspirateur m
vacuum-packed ['vækjumpækt] adj emballé(e) sous vide
vagina [və'dʒaɪnə] n vagin m
vagrant ['veɪgrənt] n vagabond/e, mendiant/e
vague [veɪg] adj vague, imprécis(e); (blurred: photo, memory) flou(e); **I haven't the vaguest idea** je n'en ai pas la moindre idée
vaguely ['veɪglɪ] adv vaguement
vain [veɪn] adj (useless) vain(e); (conceited) vaniteux(euse); **in vain** en vain
valentine ['væləntaɪn] n (also: **valentine card**) carte f de la Saint-Valentin
Valentine's day ['væləntaɪnz-] n Saint-Valentin f
valiant ['væliənt] adj vaillant(e), courageux(euse)
valid ['vælɪd] adj valide, valable; (excuse) valable
valley ['vælɪ] n vallée f
valour, (US) **valor** ['vælə*] n courage m
valuable ['væljuəbl] adj (jewel) de grande valeur; (time) précieux(euse); **valuables** npl objets mpl de valeur
valuation [vælju'eɪʃən] n évaluation f, expertise f
value ['vælju:] n valeur f ◆ vt (fix price) évaluer, expertiser; (cherish) tenir à; **you get good value (for money) in that shop** vous en avez pour votre argent dans ce magasin; **to lose (in) value** (currency) baisser; (property) se déprécier; **to gain (in) value** (currency) monter; (property) prendre de la valeur; **to be of great value to sb** (fig) être très utile à qn
value added tax (VAT) [-'ædɪd-] n (BRIT) taxe f à la valeur ajoutée (TVA)
valued ['vælju:d] adj (appreciated) estimé(e)
valve [vælv] n (in machine) soupape f; (on tyre) valve f; (in radio) lampe f
van [væn] n (AUT) camionnette f; (BRIT RAIL) fourgon m
vandal ['vændl] n vandale m/f
vandalism ['vændəlɪzəm] n vandalisme m
vandalize ['vændəlaɪz] vt saccager

vanguard ['vængɑːd] *n* avant-garde *m*

vanilla [vəˈnɪlə] *n* vanille *f* ♦ *cpd* (*ice cream*) à la vanille

vanish ['vænɪʃ] *vi* disparaître

vanity ['vænɪtɪ] *n* vanité *f*

vantage ['vɑːntɪdʒ] *n*: **vantage point** bonne position

vapour, (*US*) **vapor** ['veɪpə*] *n* vapeur *f*; (*on window*) buée *f*

variable ['vɛərɪəbl] *adj* variable; (*mood*) changeant(e) ♦ *n* variable *f*

variance ['vɛərɪəns] *n*: **to be at variance (with)** être en désaccord (avec); (*facts*) être en contradiction (avec)

varicose ['værɪkəus] *adj*: **varicose veins** varices *fpl*

varied ['vɛərɪd] *adj* varié(e), divers(e)

variety [vəˈraɪətɪ] *n* variété *f*; (*quantity*): **a wide variety of ...** une quantité *or* un grand nombre de ... (différent(e)s *or* divers(es)); **for a variety of reasons** pour diverses raisons

variety show *n* (spectacle *m* de) variétés *fpl*

various ['vɛərɪəs] *adj* divers(e), différent(e); (*several*) divers, plusieurs; (*at various times* (*different*) en diverses occasions; (*several*) à plusieurs reprises

varnish ['vɑːnɪʃ] *n* vernis *m*; (*for nails*) vernis (à ongles) ♦ *vt* vernir; **to varnish one's nails** se vernir les ongles

vary ['vɛərɪ] *vt, vi* varier, changer; **to vary with** *or* **according to** varier selon

vase [vɑːz] *n* vase *m*

Vaseline® ['væsɪliːn] *n* vaseline *f*

vast [vɑːst] *adj* vaste, immense; (*amount, success*) énorme

VAT [væt] *n abbr* (*BRIT*) = **value added tax**

vat [væt] *n* cuve *f*

vault [vɔːlt] *n* (*of roof*) voûte *f*; (*tomb*) caveau *m*; (*in bank*) salle *f* des coffres; chambre forte; (*jump*) saut *m* ♦ *vt* (*also*: **vault over**) sauter (d'un bond)

vaunted ['vɔːntɪd] *adj*: **much-vaunted** tant célébré(e)

VCR *n abbr* = **video cassette recorder**

VD *n abbr* = **venereal disease**

VDU *n abbr* = **visual display unit**

veal [viːl] *n* veau *m*

veer [vɪə*] *vi* tourner; virer

vegan ['viːgən] *n* végétalien/ne

vegeburger ['vedʒɪbɑːgə*] *n* burger végétarien

vegetable ['vedʒtəbl] *n* légume *m* ♦ *adj* végétal(e)

vegetarian [vedʒɪˈtɛərɪən] *adj, n* végétarien/ne

vehement ['viːmənt] *adj* violent(e), impétueux(euse); (*impassioned*) ardent(e)

vehicle ['viːɪkl] *n* véhicule *m*

veil [veɪl] *n* voile *m* ♦ *vt* voiler; **under a veil of secrecy** (*fig*) dans le plus grand secret

vein [veɪn] *n* veine *f*; (*on leaf*) nervure *f*; (*fig: mood*) esprit *m*

velocity [vɪˈlɔsɪtɪ] *n* vitesse *f*, vélocité *f*

velvet ['velvɪt] *n* velours *m*

vending machine ['vendɪŋ-] *n* distributeur *m* automatique

veneer [vəˈnɪə*] *n* placage *m* de bois; (*fig*) vernis *m*

venereal [vɪˈnɪərɪəl] *adj*: **venereal disease (VD)** maladie vénérienne

Venetian [vɪˈniːʃən] *adj*: **Venetian blind** store vénitien

vengeance ['vendʒəns] *n* vengeance *f*; **with a vengeance** (*fig*) vraiment, pour de bon

venison ['venɪsn] *n* venaison *f*

venom ['venəm] *n* venin *m*

vent [vent] *n* conduit *m* d'aération; (*in dress, jacket*) fente *f* ♦ *vt* (*fig: one's feelings*) donner libre cours à

ventilator ['ventɪleɪtə*] *n* ventilateur *m*

ventriloquist [venˈtrɪləkwɪst] *n* ventriloque *m/f*

venture ['ventʃə*] *n* entreprise *f* ♦ *vt* risquer, hasarder ♦ *vi* s'aventurer, se risquer; **a business venture** une entreprise commerciale; **to venture to do sth** se risquer à faire qch

venue ['venjuː] *n* (*of conference etc*) lieu *m* de la réunion (*or* manifestation *etc*); (*of match*) lieu de la rencontre

verb [vɜːb] *n* verbe *m*

verbal ['vɜːbl] *adj* verbal(e); (*translation*) littéral(e)

verbatim [vɜːˈbeɪtɪm] *adj, adv* mot pour mot

verdict ['vɜːdɪkt] *n* verdict *m*; **verdict of guilty/ not guilty** verdict de culpabilité/de non-culpabilité

verge [vɜːdʒ] *n* bord *m*; **"soft verges"** (*BRIT*) "accotements non stabilisés"; **on the verge of doing** sur le point de faire

▶ **verge on** *vt fus* approcher de

verify ['verɪfaɪ] *vt* vérifier

vermin ['vɜːmɪn] *npl* animaux *mpl* nuisibles; (*insects*) vermine *f*

vermouth ['vɜːməθ] *n* vermouth *m*

versatile ['vɜːsətaɪl] *adj* polyvalent(e)

verse [vɜːs] *n* vers *mpl*; (*stanza*) strophe *f*; (*in bible*) verset *m*; **in verse** en vers

version ['vɜːʃən] *n* version *f*

versus ['vɜːsəs] *prep* contre

vertical ['vɜːtɪkl] *adj* vertical(e) ♦ *n* verticale *f*

vertigo ['vɜːtɪgəu] *n* vertige *m*; **to suffer from vertigo** avoir des vertiges

verve [vɜːv] *n* brio *m*; enthousiasme *m*

very ['verɪ] *adv* très ♦ *adj*: **the very book which** le livre même que; **the very thought (of it) ...** rien que d'y penser ...; **at the very end** tout à la fin; **the very last** le tout dernier; **at the very least** au moins; **very well** très bien; **very little** très peu; **very much** beaucoup

vessel ['vesl] *n* (*ANAT, NAUT*) vaisseau *m*; (*container*) récipient m

vest [vest] n (BRIT) tricot m de corps; (US) gilet m ◆ vt: **to vest sb with sth, to vest sth in sb** investir qn de qch

vested interest n: **to have a vested interest in doing** avoir tout intérêt à faire; **vested interests** npl (COMM) droits acquis

vet [vet] n abbr (= veterinary surgeon) vétérinaire m/f ◆ vt examiner minutieusement; (text) revoir; (candidate) se renseigner soigneusement sur, soumettre à une enquête approfondie

veteran ['vetərn] n vétéran m; (also: **war veteran**) ancien combattant ◆ adj: **she's a veteran campaigner for ...** cela fait très longtemps qu'elle lutte pour ...

veterinary surgeon n (BRIT) vétérinaire m/f

veto ['viːtəu] n (pl vetoes) veto m ◆ vt opposer son veto à; **to put a veto on** mettre (or opposer) son veto à

vex [veks] vt fâcher, contrarier

vexed [vekst] adj (question) controversé(e)

via ['vaɪə] prep par, via

viable ['vaɪəbl] adj viable

vibrate [vaɪ'breɪt] vi: **to vibrate (with)** vibrer (de); (resound) retentir (de)

vicar ['vɪkə*] n pasteur m (de l'église anglicane)

vicarage ['vɪkərɪdʒ] n presbytère m

vicarious [vɪ'keərɪəs] adj (pleasure, experience) indirect(e)

vice [vaɪs] n (evil) vice m; (TECH) étau m

vice- [vaɪs] prefix vice-

vice squad n ≃ brigade mondaine

vice versa ['vaɪsɪ'vɜːsə] adv vice versa

vicinity [vɪ'sɪnɪtɪ] n environs mpl, alentours mpl

vicious ['vɪʃəs] adj (remark) cruel(le), méchant(e); (blow) brutal(e); **a vicious circle** un cercle vicieux

victim ['vɪktɪm] n victime f; **to be the victim of** être victime de

victor ['vɪktə*] n vainqueur m

Victorian [vɪk'tɔːrɪən] adj victorien(ne)

victory ['vɪktərɪ] n victoire f; **to win a victory over sb** remporter une victoire sur qn

video ['vɪdɪəu] n (video film) vidéo f; (also: **video cassette**) vidéocassette f; (also: **video cassette recorder**) magnétoscope m ◆ vt (with recorder) enregistrer; (with camera) filmer ◆ cpd vidéo inv

video tape n bande f vidéo inv; (cassette) vidéocassette f

video wall n mur m d'images vidéo

vie [vaɪ] vi: **to vie with** lutter avec, rivaliser avec

Vienna [vɪ'enə] n Vienne

Vietnam, Viet Nam ['vjet'næm] n Viêt-nam or Vietnam m

Vietnamese [vjetnə'miːz] adj vietnamien(ne) ◆ n (pl inv) Vietnamien/ne; (LING) vietnamien m

view [vjuː] n vue f; (opinion) avis m, vue ◆ vt (situation) considérer; (house) visiter; **on view** (in museum etc) exposé(e); **in full view of sb** sous les yeux de qn; **to be within view (of sth)** être à portée de vue (de qch); **an overall view of the situation** une vue d'ensemble de la situation; **in my view** à mon avis; **in view of the fact that** étant donné que; **with a view to doing sth** dans l'intention de faire qch

viewer ['vjuːə*] n (viewfinder) viseur m; (small projector) visionneuse f; (TV) téléspectateur/trice

viewfinder ['vjuːfaɪndə*] n viseur m

viewpoint ['vjuːpɔɪnt] n point m de vue

vigorous ['vɪgərəs] adj vigoureux(euse)

vile [vaɪl] adj (action) vil(e); (smell) abominable; (temper) massacrant(e)

villa ['vɪlə] n villa f

village ['vɪlɪdʒ] n village m

villager ['vɪlɪdʒə*] n villageois/e

villain ['vɪlən] n (scoundrel) scélérat m; (criminal) bandit m; (in novel etc) traître m

vindicate ['vɪndɪkeɪt] vt défendre avec succès; justifier

vindictive [vɪn'dɪktɪv] adj vindicatif(ive), rancunier(ière)

vine [vaɪn] n vigne f; (climbing plant) plante grimpante

vinegar ['vɪnɪgə*] n vinaigre m

vineyard ['vɪnjɑːd] n vignoble m

vintage ['vɪntɪdʒ] n (year) année f, millésime m; **the 1970 vintage** le millésime 1970

vintage car n voiture ancienne

vintage wine n vin m de grand cru

viola [vɪ'əulə] n alto m

violate ['vaɪəleɪt] vt violer

violence ['vaɪələns] n violence f; (POL etc) incidents violents

violent ['vaɪələnt] adj violent(e); **a violent dislike of sb/sth** une aversion profonde pour qn/qch

violet ['vaɪələt] adj (colour) violet(te) ◆ n (plant) violette f

violin [vaɪə'lɪn] n violon m

violinist [vaɪə'lɪnɪst] n violoniste m/f

VIP n abbr (= very important person) VIP m

virgin ['vɜːdʒɪn] n vierge f ◆ adj vierge; **she is a virgin** elle est vierge; **the Blessed Virgin** la Sainte Vierge

Virgo ['vɜːgəu] n la Vierge; **to be Virgo** être de la Vierge

virile ['vɪraɪl] adj viril(e)

virtually ['vɜːtjuəlɪ] adv (almost) pratiquement; **it is virtually impossible** c'est quasiment impossible

virtual reality n réalité virtuelle

virtue ['vɜːtjuː] n vertu f; (advantage) mérite m, avantage m; **by virtue of** par le fait de

virtuous ['vɜːtjuəs] adj vertueux(euse)

virus ['vaɪərəs] n virus m

visa ['viːzə] n visa m

visibility [ˌvɪzɪ'bɪlɪtɪ] n visibilité f

visible ['vɪzəbl] adj visible; **visible exports/imports** exportations/importations fpl visibles

vision ['vɪʒən] n (sight) vue f, vision f; (foresight, in dream) vision

visit ['vɪzɪt] n visite f; (stay) séjour m ♦ vt (person) rendre visite à; (place) visiter; **on a private/official visit** en visite privée/officielle

visiting hours npl heures fpl de visite

visitor ['vɪzɪtə*] n visiteur/euse; (in hotel) client/e

visitor centre n hall m or centre m d'accueil

visor ['vaɪzə*] n visière f

vista ['vɪstə] n vue f, perspective f

visual ['vɪzjʊəl] adj visuel(le)

visual aid n support visuel (pour l'enseignement)

visual display unit (VDU) n console f de visualisation, visuel m

visualize ['vɪzjʊəlaɪz] vt se représenter; (foresee) prévoir

visually-impaired ['vɪzjʊəlɪm'pɛəd] adj malvoyant(e)

vital ['vaɪtl] adj vital(e); **of vital importance (to sb/sth)** d'une importance capitale (pour qn/qch)

vitally ['vaɪtəlɪ] adv extrêmement

vital statistics npl (of population) statistiques fpl démographiques; (col: woman's) mensurations fpl

vitamin ['vɪtəmɪn] n vitamine f

vivacious [vɪ'veɪʃəs] adj animé(e), qui a de la vivacité

vivid ['vɪvɪd] adj (account) frappant(e); (light, imagination) vif(vive)

vividly ['vɪvɪdlɪ] adv (describe) d'une manière vivante; (remember) de façon précise

V-neck ['viː'nɛk] n décolleté m en V

vocabulary [vəʊ'kæbjʊlərɪ] n vocabulaire m

vocal ['vəʊkl] adj vocal(e); (articulate) qui n'hésite pas à s'exprimer, qui sait faire entendre ses opinions; **vocals** npl voix fpl

vocal cords npl cordes vocales

vocation [vəʊ'keɪʃən] n vocation f

vocational [vəʊ'keɪʃənl] adj professionnel(le); **vocational guidance/training** orientation/formation professionnelle

vociferous [və'sɪfərəs] adj bruyant(e)

vodka ['vɒdkə] n vodka f

vogue [vəʊg] n mode f; (popularity) vogue f; **to be in vogue** être en vogue or à la mode

voice [vɔɪs] n voix f; (opinion) avis m ♦ vt (opinion) exprimer, formuler; **in a loud/soft** à voix haute/basse; **to give voice to** exprimer

voice mail n (system) messagerie f vocale; (device) boîte f vocale

void [vɔɪd] n vide m ♦ adj (invalid) nul(le); (empty): **void of** vide de, dépourvu(e) de

volatile ['vɒlətaɪl] adj volatil(e); (fig) versatile

volcano, pl **volcanoes** [vɒl'keɪnəʊ] n volcan m

volition [və'lɪʃən] n: **of one's own volition** de son propre gré

volley ['vɒlɪ] n (of gunfire) salve f; (of stones etc) pluie f, volée f; (TENNIS etc) volée

volleyball ['vɒlɪbɔːl] n volley(-ball) m

volt [vəʊlt] n volt m

voltage ['vəʊltɪdʒ] n tension f, voltage m; **high/low voltage** haute/basse tension

volume ['vɒljuːm] n volume m; (of tank) capacité f; (of book) tome m; **volume one/two** (of book) tome un/deux; **his expression spoke volumes** son expression en disait long

voluntarily ['vɒləntrɪlɪ] adv volontairement; bénévolement

voluntary ['vɒləntərɪ] adj volontaire; (unpaid) bénévole

volunteer [vɒlən'tɪə*] n volontaire m/f ♦ vi (MIL) s'engager comme volontaire; **to volunteer to do** se proposer pour faire

vomit ['vɒmɪt] n vomissure f ♦ vt, vi vomir

vote [vəʊt] n vote m, suffrage m; (cast) voix f, vote; (franchise) droit m de vote ♦ vt (bill) voter; (chairman) élire ♦ vi voter; **to put sth to the vote, to take a vote on sth** mettre qch aux voix, procéder à un vote sur qch; **vote for or in favour of/against** vote pour/contre; **to vote to do sth** voter en faveur de faire qch; **vote of censure** motion f de censure; **vote of thanks** discours m de remerciement

voter ['vəʊtə*] n électeur/trice

voting ['vəʊtɪŋ] n scrutin m

vouch [vaʊtʃ]: **to vouch for** vt fus se porter garant de

voucher ['vaʊtʃə*] n (for meal, petrol) bon m; (receipt) reçu m; **travel voucher** bon m de transport

vow [vaʊ] n vœu m, serment m ♦ vi jurer; **to take or make a vow to do sth** faire le vœu de faire qch

vowel ['vaʊəl] n voyelle f

voyage ['vɔɪɪdʒ] n voyage m par mer, traversée f

vulgar ['vʌlgə*] adj vulgaire

vulnerable ['vʌlnərəbl] adj vulnérable

vulture ['vʌltʃə*] n vautour m

— W w —

wad [wɒd] n (of cotton wool, paper) tampon m; (of banknotes etc) liasse f

waddle ['wɒdl] vi se dandiner

wade [weɪd] vi: **to wade through** marcher dans, patauger dans ♦ vt passer à gué

wafer ['weɪfə*] n (CULIN) gaufrette f; (REL) pain m d'hostie; (COMPUT) tranche f (de silicium)

waffle ['wɒfl] n (CULIN) gaufre f; (col) rabâchage m;

remplissage *m* ♦ *vi* parler pour ne rien dire; faire du remplissage

waft [wɔft] *vt* porter ♦ *vi* flotter

wag [wæg] *vt* agiter, remuer ♦ *vi* remuer; **the dog wagged its tail** le chien a remué la queue

wage [weɪdʒ] *n* (*also:* **wages**) salaire *m*, paye *f* ♦ *vt*: **to wage war** faire la guerre; **a day's wages** un jour de salaire

wage earner [-ɑːnə*] *n* salarié/e; (*breadwinner*) soutien *m* de famille

wage packet *n* (*BRIT*) (enveloppe *f* de) paye *f*

wager ['weɪdʒə*] *n* pari *m* ♦ *vt* parier

wag(g)on ['wægən] *n* (*horse-drawn*) chariot *m*; (*BRIT RAIL*) wagon *m* (de marchandises)

wail [weɪl] *n* gémissement *m*; (*of siren*) hurlement *m* ♦ *vi* gémir; hurler

waist [weɪst] *n* taille *f*, ceinture *f*

waistcoat ['weɪskəut] *n* (*BRIT*) gilet *m*

waistline ['weɪstlaɪn] *n* (tour *m* de) taille *f*

wait [weɪt] *n* attente *f* ♦ *vi* attendre; **to wait for sb/sth** attendre qn/qch; **to keep sb waiting** faire attendre qn; **wait a minute!** un instant!; "**repairs while you wait**" "réparations minute"; **I can't wait to ...** (*fig*) je meurs d'envie de ...; **to lie in wait for** guetter

▶ **wait behind** *vi* rester (à attendre)

▶ **wait on** *vt fus* servir

▶ **wait up** *vi* attendre, ne pas se coucher; **don't wait up for me** ne m'attendez pas pour aller vous coucher

waiter ['weɪtə*] *n* garçon *m* (de café), serveur *m*

waiting ['weɪtɪŋ] *n*: "**no waiting**" (*BRIT AUT*) "stationnement interdit"

waiting list *n* liste *f* d'attente

waiting room *n* salle *f* d'attente

waitress ['weɪtrɪs] *n* serveuse *f*

waive [weɪv] *vt* renoncer à, abandonner

wake [weɪk] *vb*, *pt* **woke**, **waked**, *pp* **woken**, **waked** [wəuk, 'wəukn] *vt* (*also:* **wake up**) réveiller ♦ *vi* (*also:* **wake up**) se réveiller ♦ *n* (*for dead person*) veillée *f* mortuaire; (*NAUT*) sillage *m*; **to wake up to sth** (*fig*) se rendre compte de qch; **in the wake of** (*fig*) à la suite de; **to follow in sb's wake** (*fig*) marcher sur les traces de qn

Wales [weɪlz] *n* pays *m* de Galles

walk [wɔːk] *n* promenade *f*; (*short*) petit tour; (*gait*) démarche *f*; (*pace*): **at a quick walk** d'un pas rapide; (*path*) chemin *m*; (*in park etc*) allée *f* ♦ *vi* marcher; (*for pleasure, exercise*) se promener ♦ *vt* (*distance*) faire à pied; (*dog*) promener; **10 minutes' walk from** à 10 minutes de marche de; **to go for a walk** se promener; faire un tour; **I'll walk you home** je vais vous raccompagner chez vous; **from all walks of life** de toutes conditions sociales

▶ **walk out** *vi* (*go out*) sortir; (*as protest*) partir (en signe de protestation); (*strike*) se mettre en grève; **to walk out on sb** quitter qn

walker ['wɔːkə*] *n* (*person*) marcheur/euse

walkie-talkie ['wɔːkɪ'tɔːkɪ] *n* talkie-walkie *m*

walking ['wɔːkɪŋ] *n* marche *f* à pied; **it's within walking distance** on peut y aller à pied

walking shoes *npl* chaussures *fpl* de marche

walking stick *n* canne *f*

Walkman® ['wɔːkmən] *n* Walkman® *m*

walkout ['wɔːkaut] *n* (*of workers*) grève-surprise *f*

walkover ['wɔːkəuvə*] *n* (*col*) victoire *f* or examen *m etc* facile

walkway ['wɔːkweɪ] *n* promenade *f*, cheminement piéton

wall [wɔːl] *n* mur *m*; (*of tunnel, cave*) paroi *f*; **to go to the wall** (*fig: firm etc*) faire faillite

▶ **wall in** *vt* (*garden etc*) entourer d'un mur

walled [wɔːld] *adj* (*city*) fortifié(e)

wallet ['wɔlɪt] *n* portefeuille *m*

wallflower ['wɔːlflauə*] *n* giroflée *f*; **to be a wallflower** (*fig*) faire tapisserie

wallow ['wɔləu] *vi* se vautrer; **to wallow in one's grief** se complaire à sa douleur

wallpaper ['wɔːlpeɪpə*] *n* papier peint

walnut ['wɔːlnʌt] *n* noix *f*; (*tree*) noyer *m*

walrus, *pl* **walrus** or **walruses** ['wɔːlrəs] *n* morse *m*

waltz [wɔːlts] *n* valse *f* ♦ *vi* valser

wand [wɔnd] *n* (*also:* **magic wand**) baguette *f* (magique)

wander ['wɔndə*] *vi* (*person*) errer, aller sans but; (*thoughts*) vagabonder; (*river*) serpenter ♦ *vt* errer dans

wane [weɪn] *vi* (*moon*) décroître; (*reputation*) décliner

wangle ['wæŋgl] (*BRIT col*) *vt* se débrouiller pour avoir; carotter ♦ *n* combine *f*, magouille *f*

want [wɔnt] *vt* vouloir; (*need*) avoir besoin de; (*lack*) manquer de ♦ *n* (*poverty*) pauvreté *f*, besoin *m*; **wants** *npl* (*needs*) besoins *mpl*; **for want of** par manque de, faute de; **to want to do** vouloir faire; **to want sb to do** vouloir que qn fasse; **you're wanted on the phone** on vous demande au téléphone

wanted ['wɔntɪd] *adj* (*criminal*) recherché(e) par la police; "**cook wanted**" "on recherche un cuisinier"

wanting ['wɔntɪŋ] *adj*: **to be wanting (in)** manquer (de); **to be found wanting** ne pas être à la hauteur

war [wɔː*] *n* guerre *f*; **to go to war** se mettre en guerre

ward [wɔːd] *n* (*in hospital*) salle *f*; (*POL*) section électorale; (*LAW: child*) pupille *m/f*

▶ **ward off** *vt* parer, éviter

warden ['wɔːdn] *n* (*BRIT: of institution*) directeur/trice; (*of park, game reserve*) gardien/ne; (*BRIT: also*: **traffic warden**) contractuel/le

warder ['wɔːdə*] *n* (*BRIT*) gardien *m* de prison

wardrobe ['wɔːdrəub] n (cupboard) armoire f; (clothes) garde-robe f; (THEAT) costumes mpl

warehouse ['wɛəhaus] n entrepôt m

wares [wɛəz] npl marchandises fpl

warfare ['wɔːfɛə*] n guerre f

warhead ['wɔːhɛd] n (MIL) ogive f

warily ['wɛərɪlɪ] adv avec prudence, avec précaution

warm [wɔːm] adj chaud(e); (person, greeting, welcome, applause) chaleureux(euse); (supporter) ardent(e), enthousiaste; **it's warm** il fait chaud; **I'm warm** j'ai chaud; **to keep sth warm** tenir qch au chaud; **with my warmest thanks/congratulations** avec mes remerciements/mes félicitations les plus sincères

▶ **warm up** vi (person, room) se réchauffer; (water) chauffer; (athlete, discussion) s'échauffer ♦ vt réchauffer; chauffer; (engine) faire chauffer

warm-hearted [wɔːm'hɑːtɪd] adj affectueux(euse)

warmly ['wɔːmlɪ] adv chaudement; chaleureusement

warmth [wɔːmθ] n chaleur f

warn [wɔːn] vt avertir, prévenir; **to warn sb not to do sth** or **against doing sth** prévenir qn de ne pas faire qch

warning ['wɔːnɪŋ] n avertissement m; (notice) avis m; **without (any) warning** (suddenly) inopinément; (without notifying) sans prévenir; **gale warning** (METEOROLOGY) avis de grand vent

warning light n avertisseur lumineux

warning triangle n (AUT) triangle m de présignalisation

warp [wɔːp] n (TEXTILES) chaîne f ♦ vi (wood) travailler, se voiler or gauchir ♦ vt voiler; (fig) pervertir

warrant ['wɔrnt] n (guarantee) garantie f; (LAW: to arrest) mandat m d'arrêt; (: to search) mandat de perquisition ♦ vt (justify, merit) justifier

warranty ['wɔrəntɪ] n garantie f; **under warranty** (COMM) sous garantie

warren ['wɔrən] n (of rabbits) terriers mpl, garenne f

warrior ['wɔrɪə*] n guerrier/ière

Warsaw ['wɔːsɔː] n Varsovie

warship ['wɔːʃɪp] n navire m de guerre

wart [wɔːt] n verrue f

wartime ['wɔːtaɪm] n: **in wartime** en temps de guerre

wary ['wɛərɪ] adj prudent(e); **to be wary about** or **of doing sth** hésiter beaucoup à faire qch

was [wɔz] pt of **be**

wash [wɔʃ] vt laver; (sweep, carry: sea etc) emporter, entraîner; (: ashore) rejeter ♦ vi se laver ♦ n (paint) badigeon m; (washing programme) lavage m; (of ship) sillage m; **to give sth a wash** laver qch; **to have a wash** se laver, faire sa toilette; **he was washed overboard** il a été emporté par une vague

▶ **wash away** vt (stain) enlever au lavage; (river etc) emporter

▶ **wash down** vt laver; laver à grande eau

▶ **wash off** vi partir au lavage

▶ **wash up** vi faire la vaisselle; (US: have a wash) se débarbouiller

washable ['wɔʃəbl] adj lavable

washbasin ['wɔʃbeɪsn] n lavabo m

washcloth ['wɔʃklɔθ] n (US) gant m de toilette

washer ['wɔʃə*] n (TECH) rondelle f, joint m

washing ['wɔʃɪŋ] n (BRIT: linen etc) lessive f

washing machine n machine f à laver

washing powder n (BRIT) lessive f (en poudre)

washing-up [wɔʃɪŋ'ʌp] n (BRIT) vaisselle f

washing-up liquid n (BRIT) produit m pour la vaisselle

wash-out ['wɔʃaut] n (col) désastre m

washroom ['wɔʃrum] n toilettes fpl

wasn't ['wɔznt] = **was not**

wasp [wɔsp] n guêpe f

wastage ['weɪstɪdʒ] n gaspillage m; (in manufacturing, transport etc) déchet m

waste [weɪst] n gaspillage m; (of time) perte f; (rubbish) déchets mpl; (also: **household waste**) ordures fpl ♦ adj (material) de rebut; (energy, heat) perdu(e); (food) inutilisé(e); (land, ground: in city) à l'abandon; (: in country) inculte, en friche ♦ vt gaspiller; (time, opportunity) perdre; **wastes** npl étendue f désertique; **it's a waste of money** c'est de l'argent jeté en l'air; **to go to waste** être gaspillé(e), **to lay waste** (destroy) dévaster

▶ **waste away** vi dépérir

waste disposal (unit) n (BRIT) broyeur m d'ordures

wasteful ['weɪstful] adj gaspilleur(euse); (process) peu économique

waste ground n (BRIT) terrain m vague

wastepaper basket ['weɪstpeɪpə-] n corbeille à papier

watch [wɔtʃ] n montre f; (act of watching) surveillance f; guet m; (guard: MIL) sentinelle f; (: NAUT homme m de quart; (NAUT: spell of duty) quart m ♦ vt (look at) observer; (: match, programme) regarder; (spy on, guard) surveiller; (be careful of) faire attention à ♦ vi regarder; (keep guard) monter la garde; **to keep a close watch on sb/sth** surveiller qn/qch de près; **watch what you're doing** fais attention à ce que tu fais

▶ **watch out** vi faire attention

watchdog ['wɔtʃdɔg] n chien m de garde; (fig) gardien/ne

watchful ['wɔtʃful] adj attentif(ive), vigilant(e)

watchmaker ['wɔtʃmeɪkə*] n horloger/ère

watchman ['wɔtʃmən] n gardien m; (also: **night watchman**) veilleur m de nuit

watchstrap ['wɔtʃstræp] n bracelet m de montre

water ['wɔːtə*] n eau f ♦ vt (plant) arroser ♦ vi

(*eyes*) larmoyer; **a drink of water** un verre d'eau; **in British waters** dans les eaux territoriales Britanniques; **to pass water** uriner; **to make sb's mouth water** mettre l'eau à la bouche de qn

▶ **water down** *vt* (*milk*) couper d'eau; (*fig: story*) édulcorer

watercolour, (*US*) **watercolor** ['wɔːtəkʌlə*] *n* aquarelle *f*; **watercolours** *npl* couleurs *fpl* pour aquarelle

watercress ['wɔːtəkres] *n* cresson *m* (de fontaine)

waterfall ['wɔːtəfɔːl] *n* chute *f* d'eau

water heater *n* chauffe-eau *m*

watering can ['wɔːtərɪŋ-] *n* arrosoir *m*

water lily *n* nénuphar *m*

waterline ['wɔːtəlaɪn] *n* (*NAUT*) ligne *f* de flottaison

waterlogged ['wɔːtəlɔgd] *adj* détrempé(e); imbibé(e) d'eau

water main *n* canalisation *f* d'eau

watermelon ['wɔːtəmelən] *n* pastèque *f*

waterproof ['wɔːtəpruːf] *adj* imperméable

watershed ['wɔːtəʃed] *n* (*GEO*) ligne *f* de partage des eaux; (*fig*) moment *m* critique, point décisif

water-skiing ['wɔːtəskiːɪŋ] *n* ski *m* nautique

watertight ['wɔːtətaɪt] *adj* étanche

waterway ['wɔːtəweɪ] *n* cours *m* d'eau navigable

waterworks ['wɔːtəwəːks] *npl* station *f* hydraulique

watery ['wɔːtəri] *adj* (*colour*) délavé(e); (*coffee*) trop faible

watt [wɔt] *n* watt *m*

wave [weɪv] *n* vague *f*; (*of hand*) geste *m*, signe *m*; (*RADIO*) onde *f*; (*in hair*) ondulation *f*; (*fig: of enthusiasm, strikes etc*) vague ♦ *vi* faire signe de la main; (*flag*) flotter au vent ♦ *vt* (*handkerchief*) agiter; (*stick*) brandir; (*hair*) onduler; **to wave goodbye to sb** dire au revoir de la main à qn; **short/medium wave** (*RADIO*) ondes courtes/moyennes; **long wave** (*RADIO*) grandes ondes; **the new wave** (*CINE, MUS*) la nouvelle vague

▶ **wave aside, wave away** *vt* (*person*): **to wave sb aside** faire signe à qn de s'écarter; (*fig: suggestion, objection*) rejeter, repousser; (*: doubts*) chasser

wavelength ['weɪvleŋθ] *n* longueur *f* d'ondes

waver ['weɪvə*] *vi* vaciller; (*voice*) trembler; (*person*) hésiter

wavy ['weɪvi] *adj* ondulé(e), onduleux(euse)

wax [wæks] *n* cire *f*; (*for skis*) fart *m* ♦ *vt* cirer; (*car*) lustrer ♦ *vi* (*moon*) croître

waxworks ['wækswəːks] *npl* personnages *mpl* de cire; musée *m* de cire

way [weɪ] *n* chemin *m*, voie *f*; (*path, access*) passage *m*; (*distance*) distance *f*; (*direction*) chemin, direction *f*; (*manner*) façon *f*, manière *f*; (*habit*) habitude *f*, façon *f*; (*condition*) état *m*; **which way? – this way** par où *or* de quel côté? – par ici; **to crawl one's way to ...** ramper jusqu'à ...; **to lie one's way out of it** s'en sortir par un mensonge; **to lose**

one's way perdre son chemin; **on the way (to)** en route (pour); **to be on one's way** être en route; **to be in the way** bloquer le passage; (*fig*) gêner; **to keep out of sb's way** éviter qn; **it's a long way away** c'est loin d'ici; **the village is rather out of the way** le village est plutôt à l'écart *or* isolé; **to go out of one's way to do** (*fig*) se donner beaucoup de mal pour faire; **to be under way** (*work, project*) être en cours; **to make way (for sb/sth)** faire place (à qn/qch); s'écarter pour laisser passer (qn/qch); **to get one's own way** arriver à ses fins; **put it the right way up** (*BRIT*) mettez-le dans le bon sens; **to be the wrong way round** être à l'envers, ne pas être dans le bon sens; **he's in a bad way** il va mal; **in a way** d'un côté; **in some ways** à certains égards; d'un côté; **in the way of** en fait de, comme; **by way of** en passant par, via; (*as a sort of*) en guise de; **"way in"** (*BRIT*) "entrée"; **"way out"** (*BRIT*) "sortie"; **the way back** le chemin du retour; **this way and that** par-ci par-là; **"give way"** (*BRIT AUT*) "cédez la priorité"; **no way!** (*col*) pas question!

waylay [weɪ'leɪ] *vt irreg* attaquer; (*fig*): **I got waylaid** quelqu'un m'a accroché

wayward ['weɪwəd] *adj* capricieux(euse), entêté(e)

WC *n abbr* (*BRIT*: = *water closet*) w.-c. *mpl*, waters *mpl*

we [wiː] *pl pron* nous

weak [wiːk] *adj* faible; (*health*) fragile; (*beam etc*) peu solide; (*tea, coffee*) léger(ère); **to grow weak(er)** s'affaiblir, faiblir

weaken ['wiːkn] *vi* faiblir ♦ *vt* affaiblir

weakling ['wiːklɪŋ] *n* gringalet *m*; faible *m/f*

weakness ['wiːknɪs] *n* faiblesse *f*; (*fault*) point *m* faible

wealth [welθ] *n* (*money, resources*) richesse(s) *f(pl)*; (*of details*) profusion *f*

wealthy ['welθi] *adj* riche

wean [wiːn] *vt* sevrer

weapon ['wepən] *n* arme *f*

wear [weə*] *n* (*use*) usage *m*; (*deterioration through use*) usure *f*; (*clothing*): **sports/babywear** vêtements *mpl* de sport/pour bébés; **town/evening wear** tenue *f* de ville/de soirée ♦ *vb*, *pt* **wore**, *pp* **worn** [wɔː*, wɔːn] *vt* (*clothes*) porter; (*beard etc*) avoir; (*damage: through use*) user ♦ *vi* (*last*) faire de l'usage; (*rub etc through*) s'user; **wear and tear** usure *f*; **to wear a hole in sth** faire (à la longue) un trou dans qch

▶ **wear away** *vt* user, ronger ♦ *vi* s'user, être rongé(e)

▶ **wear down** *vt* user; (*strength*) épuiser

▶ **wear off** *vi* disparaître

▶ **wear on** *vi* se poursuivre; passer

▶ **wear out** *vt* user; (*person, strength*) épuiser

weary ['wɪəri] *adj* (*tired*) épuisé(e); (*dispirited*) las(lasse); abattu(e) ♦ *vt* lasser ♦ *vi*: **to weary of** se lasser de

weasel ['wi:zl] *n* (*ZOOL*) belette *f*

weather ['weðə*] *n* temps *m* ♦ *vt* (*wood*) faire mûrir; (*tempest, crisis*) essuyer, être pris(e) dans; survivre à, tenir le coup durant; **what's the weather like?** quel temps fait-il?; **under the weather** (*fig: ill*) mal fichu(e)

weather-beaten ['weðəbi:tn] *adj* (*person*) hâlé(e); (*building*) dégradé(e) par les intempéries

weathercock ['weðəkɔk] *n* girouette *f*

weather forecast *n* prévisions *fpl* météorologiques, météo *f*

weatherman ['weðəmæn] *n* météorologue *m*

weather vane [-veɪn] *n* = **weather cock**

weave, *pt* **wove**, *pp* **woven** [wi:v, wəuv, 'wəuvn] *vt* (*cloth*) tisser; (*basket*) tresser ♦ *vi* (*fig: pt, pp* **weaved**: *move in and out*) se faufiler

weaver ['wi:və*] *n* tisserand/e

web [web] *n* (*of spider*) toile *f*; (*on foot*) palmure *f*; (*fabric, also fig*) tissu *m*

website ['websaɪt] *n* (*COMPUT*) site *m* web

wed [wed] *vt, pt, pp* **wedded** épouser ♦ *n*: **the newly-weds** les jeunes mariés

we'd [wi:d] = **we had, we would**

wedding ['wedɪŋ] *n* mariage *m*

wedding day *n* jour *m* du mariage

wedding dress *n* robe *f* de mariée

wedding ring *n* alliance *f*

wedge [wedʒ] *n* (*of wood etc*) coin *m*; (*under door etc*) cale *f*; (*of cake*) part *f* ♦ *vt* (*fix*) caler; (*push*) enfoncer, coincer

Wednesday ['wednzdɪ] *n* mercredi *m*; *for phrases see also* **Tuesday**

wee [wi:] *adj* (*Scottish*) petit(e); tout(e) petit(e)

weed [wi:d] *n* mauvaise herbe ♦ *vt* désherber

► **weed out** *vt* éliminer

weedkiller ['wi:dkɪlə*] *n* désherbant *m*

weedy ['wi:dɪ] *adj* (*man*) gringalet

week [wi:k] *n* semaine *f*; **once/twice a week** une fois/deux fois par semaine; **in two weeks' time** dans quinze jours; **Tuesday week, a week on Tuesday** mardi en huit

weekday ['wi:kdeɪ] *n* jour *m* de semaine; (*COMM*) jour ouvrable; **on weekdays** en semaine

weekend [wi:k'end] *n* week-end *m*

weekly ['wi:klɪ] *adv* une fois par semaine, chaque semaine ♦ *adj, n* hebdomadaire (*m*)

weep, *pt, pp* **wept** [wi:p, wept] *vi* (*person*) pleurer; (*MED: wound etc*) suinter

weeping willow ['wi:pɪŋ-] *n* saule pleureur

weigh [weɪ] *vt, vi* peser; **to weigh anchor** lever l'ancre; **to weigh the pros and cons** peser le pour et le contre

► **weigh down** *vt* (*branch*) faire plier; (*fig: with worry*) accabler

► **weigh out** *vt* (*goods*) peser

► **weigh up** *vt* examiner

weight [weɪt] *n* poids *m* ♦ *vt* alourdir; (*fig: factor*) pondérer; **sold by weight** vendu au poids; **to put on/lose weight** grossir/maigrir; **weights and measures** poids et mesures

weighting ['weɪtɪŋ] *n*: **weighting allowance** indemnité *f* de résidence

weightlifter ['weɪtlɪftə*] *n* haltérophile *m*

weightlifting ['weɪtlɪftɪŋ] *n* haltérophilie *f*

weighty ['weɪtɪ] *adj* lourd(e)

weir [wɪə*] *n* barrage *m*

weird [wɪəd] *adj* bizarre; (*eerie*) surnaturel(le)

welcome ['welkəm] *adj* bienvenu(e) ♦ *n* accueil *m* ♦ *vt* accueillir; (*also*: **bid welcome**) souhaiter la bienvenue à; (*be glad of*) se réjouir de; **to be welcome** être le(la) bienvenu(e); **to make sb welcome** faire bon accueil à qn; **you're welcome to try** vous pouvez essayer si vous voulez; **you're welcome!** (*after thanks*) de rien, il n'y a pas de quoi

weld [weld] *n* soudure *f* ♦ *vt* souder

welder ['weldə*] *n* (*person*) soudeur *m*

welfare ['welfeə*] *n* bien-être *m*

welfare state *n* État-providence *m*

well [wel] *n* puits *m* ♦ *adv* bien ♦ *adj*: **to be well** aller bien ♦ *excl* eh bien!; bon!; enfin!; **well done!** bravo!; **I don't feel well** je ne me sens pas bien; **get well soon!** remets-toi vite!; **to do well in sth** bien réussir en *or* dans qch; **to think well of sb** penser du bien de qn; **as well** (*in addition*) aussi, également; **you might as well tell me** tu ferais aussi bien de me le dire; **as well as** aussi bien que *or* de; en plus de; **well, as I was saying ...** donc, comme je disais ...

► **well up** *vi* (*tears, emotions*) monter

we'll [wi:l] = **we will, we shall**

well-behaved ['welbɪ'heɪvd] *adj* sage, obéissant(e)

well-being ['wel'bi:ɪŋ] *n* bien-être *m*

well-built ['wel'bɪlt] *adj* (*house*) bien construit(e); (*person*) bien bâti(e)

well-deserved ['weldɪ'zə:vd] *adj* (bien) mérité(e)

well-dressed ['wel'drest] *adj* bien habillé(e), bien vêtu(e)

well-heeled ['wel'hi:ld] *adj* (*col: wealthy*) fortuné(e), riche

wellingtons ['welɪŋtənz] *npl* (*also*: **wellington boots**) bottes *fpl* de caoutchouc

well-known ['wel'nəun] *adj* (*person*) bien connu(e)

well-mannered ['wel'mænəd] *adj* bien élevé(e)

well-meaning ['wel'mi:nɪŋ] *adj* bien intentionné(e)

well-off ['wel'ɔf] *adj* aisé(e), assez riche

well-read ['wel'red] *adj* cultivé(e)

well-to-do ['weltə'du:] *adj* aisé(e), assez riche

well-wisher ['welwɪʃə*] *n* ami/e, admirateur/trice; **scores of well-wishers had gathered** de nombreux amis et admirateurs s'étaient rassemblés letters from well-wishers des lettres d'encouragement

Welsh [welʃ] *adj* gallois(e) ◆ *n* (*LING*) gallois *m*; **the Welsh** *npl* les Gallois

Welsh Assembly *n* Parlement gallois

Welshman, Welshwoman ['welʃmən, -wumən] *n* Gallois/e

went [went] *pt of* **go**

wept [wept] *pt, pp of* **weep**

were [wəː*] *pt of* **be**

we're [wɪə*] = **we are**

weren't [wəːnt] = **were not**

west [west] *n* ouest *m* ◆ *adj* ouest *inv*, de or à l'ouest ◆ *adv* à or vers l'ouest; **the West** l'Occident *m*, l'Ouest

westerly ['westəlɪ] *adj* (*situation*) à l'ouest; (*wind*) d'ouest

western ['westən] *adj* occidental(e), de or à l'ouest ◆ *n* (*CINE*) western *m*

West Indian *adj* antillais(e) ◆ *n* Antillais/e

West Indies [-'ɪndɪz] *npl*: **the West Indies** les Antilles *fpl*

westward(s) ['westwəd(z)] *adv* vers l'ouest

wet [wet] *adj* mouillé(e); (*damp*) humide; (*soaked*) trempé(e); (*rainy*) pluvieux(euse) ◆ *vt*: **to wet one's pants** or **o.s.** mouiller sa culotte, faire pipi dans sa culotte; **to get wet** se mouiller; **"wet paint"** "attention peinture fraîche"

wet suit *n* combinaison *f* de plongée

we've [wiːv] = **we have**

whack [wæk] *vt* donner un grand coup à

whale [weɪl] *n* (*ZOOL*) baleine *f*

wharf, *pl* **wharves** [wɔːf, wɔːvz] *n* quai *m*

what [wɔt] *adj* quel(le); **what size is he?** quelle taille fait-il?; **what colour is it?** de quelle couleur est-ce?; **what books do you need?** quels livres vous faut-il?; **what a mess!** quel désordre!
◆ *pron* **1** (*interrogative*) que, *prep* + quoi; **what are you doing?** que faites-vous?, qu'est-ce que vous faites?; **what is happening?** qu'est-ce qui se passe?, que se passe-t-il?; **what are you talking about?** de quoi parlez-vous?; **what is it called?** comment est-ce que ça s'appelle?; **what about me?** et moi?; **what about doing ...?** et si on faisait ...?
2 (*relative: subject*) ce qui; (*: direct object*) ce que; (*: indirect object*) ce + *prep* +quoi; **I saw what you did/was on the table** j'ai vu ce que vous avez fait/ce qui était sur la table; **tell me what you remember** dites-moi ce dont vous vous souvenez; **what I want is a cup of tea** ce que je veux, c'est une tasse de thé
◆ *excl* (*disbelieving*) quoi!, comment!

whatever [wɔt'evə*] *adj*: **whatever book** quel que soit le livre que (*or* qui) + *sub*; n'importe quel

livre ◆ *pron*: **do whatever is necessary** faites (tout) ce qui est nécessaire; **whatever happens** quoi qu'il arrive; **no reason whatever** or **whatsoever** pas la moindre raison; **nothing whatever** or **whatsoever** rien du tout

whatsoever [wɔtsəu'evə*] *adj see* **whatever**

wheat [wiːt] *n* blé *m*, froment *m*

wheedle ['wiːdl] *vt*: **to wheedle sb into doing sth** cajoler or enjôler qn pour qu'il fasse qch; **to wheedle sth out of sb** obtenir qch de qn par des cajoleries

wheel [wiːl] *n* roue *f*; (*AUT: also*: **steering wheel**) volant *m*; (*NAUT*) gouvernail *m* ◆ *vt* pousser, rouler ◆ *vi* (*also*: **wheel round**) tourner

wheelbarrow ['wiːlbærəu] *n* brouette *f*

wheelchair ['wiːltʃeə*] *n* fauteuil roulant

wheel clamp *n* (*AUT*) sabot *m* (de Denver)

wheeze [wiːz] *n* respiration bruyante (*d'asthmatique*) ◆ *vi* respirer bruyamment

when [wen] *adv* quand; **when did he go?** quand est-ce qu'il est parti?
◆ *conj* **1** (*at, during, after the time that*) quand, lorsque; **she was reading when I came in** elle lisait quand or lorsque je suis entré
2 (*on, at which*): **on the day when I met him** le jour où je l'ai rencontré
3 (*whereas*) alors que; **I thought I was wrong when in fact I was right** j'ai cru que j'avais tort alors qu'en fait j'avais raison

whenever [wen'evə*] *adv* quand donc ◆ *conj* quand; (*every time that*) chaque fois que; **I go whenever I can** j'y vais quand or chaque fois que je le peux

where [weə*] *adv, conj* où; **this is where** c'est là que; **where are you from?** d'où venez vous?

whereabouts ['weərəbauts] *adv* où donc ◆ *n*: **sb's whereabouts** l'endroit où se trouve qn

whereas [weər'æz] *conj* alors que

whereby [weə'baɪ] *adv* (*formal*) par lequel (*or* laquelle *etc*)

wherever [weər'evə*] *adv* où donc ◆ *conj* où que +*sub*; **sit wherever you like** asseyez-vous (là) où vous voulez

wherewithal ['weəwɪðɔːl] *n*: **the wherewithal (to do sth)** les moyens *mpl* (de faire qch)

whether ['weðə*] *conj* si; **I don't know whether to accept or not** je ne sais pas si je dois accepter ou non; **it's doubtful whether** il est peu probable que; **whether you go or not** que vous y alliez ou non

which [wɪtʃ] *adj* **1** (*interrogative: direct, indirect*) quel(le); **which picture do you want?** quel tableau voulez-vous?; **which one?** lequel(laquelle)?

2: in which case auquel cas

♦ *pron* **1** (*interrogative*) lequel(laquelle), lesquels(lesquelles) *pl*; **I don't mind which** peu importe lequel; **which (of these) are yours?** lesquels sont à vous?; **tell me which you want** dites-moi lesquels *or* ceux que vous voulez

2 (*relative*: *subject*) qui; (: *object*) que, *prep* + lequel(laquelle); (NB: *à* + *lequel* = auquel; *de* + *lequel* = duquel); **the apple which you ate/ which is on the table** la pomme que vous avez mangée/qui est sur la table; **the chair on which you are sitting** la chaise sur laquelle vous êtes assis; **the book of which you spoke** le livre dont vous avez parlé; **he knew, which is true/I feared** il le savait, ce qui est vrai/ce que je craignais; **after which** après quoi

whichever [wɪtʃ'evə*] *adj*: **take whichever book you prefer** prenez le livre que vous préférez, peu importe lequel; **whichever book you take** quel que soit le livre que vous preniez; **whichever way you** de quelque façon que vous + *sub*

while [waɪl] *n* moment *m* ♦ *conj* pendant que; (*as long as*) tant que; (*as, whereas*) alors que; (*though*) quoique + *sub*; **for a while** pendant quelque temps; **in a while** dans un moment; **all the while** pendant tout ce temps-là; **we'll make it worth your while** nous vous récompenserons de votre peine

▶ **while away** *vt* (*time*) (faire) passer

whim [wɪm] *n* caprice *m*

whimper ['wɪmpə*] *n* geignement *m* ♦ *vi* geindre

whimsical ['wɪmzɪkl] *adj* (*person*) capricieux(euse); (*look*) étrange

whine [waɪn] *n* gémissement *m* ♦ *vi* gémir, geindre; pleurnicher

whip [wɪp] *n* fouet *m*; (*for riding*) cravache *f*; (*POL*: *person*) chef *m* de file (*assurant la discipline dans son groupe parlementaire*) ♦ *vt* fouetter; (*snatch*) enlever (*or* sortir) brusquement; *voir encadré*

▶ **whip up** *vt* (*cream*) fouetter; (*col*: *meal*) préparer en vitesse; (*stir up*: *support*) stimuler; (: *feeling*) attiser, aviver

---

WHIP

Un **whip** est un député dont le rôle est, entre autres, de s'assurer que les membres de son parti sont régulièrement présents à la "House of Commons", surtout lorsque les votes ont lieu. Les convocations que les **whips** envoient se distinguent, selon leur degré d'importance, par le fait qu'elles sont soulignées 1, 2 ou 3 fois (les "1-, 2-, ou 3-line whips").

---

whipped cream [wɪpt-] *n* crème fouettée

whip-round ['wɪpraʊnd] *n* (*BRIT*) collecte *f*

whirl [wə:l] *n* tourbillon *m* ♦ *vt* faire tourbillonner; faire tournoyer ♦ *vi* tourbillonner

whirlpool ['wə:lpu:l] *n* tourbillon *m*

whirlwind ['wə:lwɪnd] *n* tornade *f*

whirr [wə:*] *vi* bruire; ronronner; vrombir

whisk [wɪsk] *n* (*CULIN*) fouet *m* ♦ *vt* fouetter, battre; **to whisk sb away** *or* **off** emmener qn rapidement

whiskers ['wɪskəz] *npl* (*of animal*) moustaches *fpl*; (*of man*) favoris *mpl*

whisky, (*Irish, US*) **whiskey** ['wɪskɪ] *n* whisky *m*

whisper ['wɪspə*] *n* chuchotement *m*; (*fig*: *of leaves*) bruissement *m*; (*rumour*) rumeur *f* ♦ *vt*, *v* chuchoter

whistle ['wɪsl] *n* (*sound*) sifflement *m*; (*object*) sifflet *m* ♦ *vi* siffler ♦ *vt* siffler, siffloter

white [waɪt] *adj* blanc(blanche); (*with fear*) blême ♦ *n* blanc *m*; (*person*) blanc/blanche; **to turn** *or* **go white** (*person*) pâlir, blêmir; (*hair*) blanchir; **the whites** (*washing*) le linge blanc; **tennis whites** tenue *f* de tennis

white coffee *n* (*BRIT*) café *m* au lait, (café) crème *m*

white-collar worker ['waɪtkɔlə-] *n* employé/e de bureau

white elephant *n* (*fig*) objet dispendieux et superflu

white lie *n* pieux mensonge

white paper *n* (*POL*) livre blanc

whitewash ['waɪtwɔʃ] *n* (*paint*) lait *m* de chaux ♦ *vt* blanchir à la chaux; (*fig*) blanchir

whiting ['waɪtɪŋ] *n* (*pl inv*: *fish*) merlan *m*

Whitsun ['wɪtsn] *n* la Pentecôte

whizz [wɪz] *vi* aller (*or* passer) à toute vitesse

whizz kid *n* (*col*) petit prodige

who [hu:] *pron* qui

whodunit [hu:'dʌnɪt] *n* (*col*) roman policier

whoever [hu:'evə*] *pron*: **whoever finds it** celui(celle) qui le trouve (, qui que ce soit) quiconque le trouve; **ask whoever you like** demandez à qui vous voulez; **whoever he marries** qui que ce soit *or* quelle que soit la personne qu'il épouse; **whoever told you that?** qui a bien pu vous dire ça?, qui donc vous a dit ça?

whole [həʊl] *adj* (*complete*) entier(ière), tout(e); (*not broken*) intact(e), complet(ète) ♦ *n* (*total*) totalité *f*; (*sth not broken*) tout *m*; **the whole lot (of it)** tout; **the whole lot (of them)** tous (sans exception); **the whole of the time** tout le temps; **the whole of the town** la ville tout entière; **on the whole, as a whole** dans l'ensemble

wholefood(s) ['həʊlfu:d(z)] *n(pl)* aliments complets

wholehearted [həʊl'hɑ:tɪd] *adj* sans réserve(s), sincère

wholemeal ['həʊlmi:l] *adj* (*BRIT*: *flour, bread*) complet(ète)

wholesale ['həulseɪl] n (vente f en) gros m ♦ adj de gros; (destruction) systématique

wholesaler ['həulseɪlə*] n grossiste m/f

wholesome ['həulsəm] adj sain(e); (advice) salutaire

wholewheat ['həulwi:t] adj = **wholemeal**

wholly ['həulɪ] adv entièrement, tout à fait

KEYWORD

whom [hu:m] pron 1 (interrogative) qui; **whom did you see?** qui avez-vous vu?; **to whom did you give it?** à qui l'avez-vous donné?

2 (relative) que, prep + qui; **the man whom I saw/to whom I spoke** l'homme que j'ai vu/à qui j'ai parlé

whooping cough ['hu:pɪŋ-] n coqueluche f

whore [hɔ:*] n (col: pej) putain f

KEYWORD

whose [hu:z] adj 1 (possessive: interrogative): **whose book is this?** à qui est ce livre?; **whose pencil have you taken?** à qui est le crayon que vous avez pris?, c'est le crayon de qui que vous avez pris?; **whose daughter are you?** de qui êtes-vous la fille?

2 (possessive: relative): **the man whose son you rescued** l'homme dont or de qui vous avez sauvé le fils; **the girl whose sister you were speaking to** la fille à la sœur de qui or de laquelle vous parliez; **the woman whose car was stolen** la femme dont la voiture a été volée

♦ pron à qui; **whose is this?** à qui est ceci?; **I know whose it is** je sais à qui c'est

why [waɪ] adv pourquoi ♦ excl eh bien!, tiens!; **the reason why** la raison pour laquelle; **why is he late?** pourquoi est-il en retard?

wicked ['wɪkɪd] adj foncièrement mauvais(e), inique; (mischievous: grin, look) espiègle, malicieux(euse); (terrible: prices, weather) épouvantable

wicket ['wɪkɪt] n (CRICKET) guichet m; espace compris entre les deux guichets

wide [waɪd] adj large; (region, knowledge) vaste, très étendu(e); (choice) grand(e) ♦ adv: **to open wide** ouvrir tout grand; **to shoot wide** tirer à côté; **it is 3 metres wide** cela fait 3 mètres de large

wide-awake [waɪdə'weɪk] adj bien éveillé(e)

widely ['waɪdlɪ] adv (different) radicalement; (spaced) sur une grande étendue; (believed) généralement; **to be widely read** (author) être beaucoup lu(e); (reader) avoir beaucoup lu, être cultivé(e)

widen ['waɪdn] vt élargir

wide open adj grand(e) ouvert(e)

widespread ['waɪdspred] adj (belief etc) très répandu(e)

widow ['wɪdəu] n veuve f

widowed ['wɪdəud] adj (qui est devenu(e)) veuf(veuve)

widower ['wɪdəuə*] n veuf m

width [wɪdθ] n largeur f; **it's 7 metres in width** cela fait 7 mètres de large

wield [wi:ld] vt (sword) manier; (power) exercer

wife, pl **wives** [waɪf, waɪvz] n femme (mariée), épouse f

wig [wɪg] n perruque f

wiggle ['wɪgl] vt agiter, remuer ♦ vi (loose screw etc) branler; (worm) se tortiller

wild [waɪld] adj sauvage; (sea) déchaîné(e); (idea, life) fou(folle); extravagant(e); (col: angry) hors de soi, furieux(euse); (: enthusiastic): **to be wild about** être fou(folle) or dingue de ♦ n: **the wild** la nature; **wilds** npl régions fpl sauvages

wild card n (COMPUT) caractère m de remplacement

wilderness ['wɪldənɪs] n désert m, région f sauvage

wildlife ['waɪldlaɪf] n faune f (et flore f) sauvage(s)

wildly ['waɪldlɪ] adv (applaud) frénétiquement; (hit, guess) au hasard; (happy) follement

wilful, (us) **willful** ['wɪlful] adj (person) obstiné(e); (action) délibéré(e); (crime) prémédité(e)

KEYWORD

will [wɪl] (vt: pt, pp **willed**) aux vb 1 (forming future tense): **I will finish it tomorrow** je le finirai demain; **I will have finished it by tomorrow** je l'aurai fini d'ici demain; **will you do it? – yes I will/no I won't** le ferez-vous? – oui/non; **you won't lose it, will you?** vous ne le perdrez pas, n'est-ce pas?

2 (in conjectures, predictions): **he will** or **he'll be there by now** il doit être arrivé à l'heure qu'il est; **that will be the postman** ça doit être le facteur

3 (in commands, requests, offers): **will you be quiet!** voulez-vous bien vous taire!; **will you help me?** est-ce que vous pouvez m'aider?; **will you have a cup of tea?** voulez-vous une tasse de thé?; **I won't put up with it!** je ne le tolérerai pas!

♦ vt: **to will sb to do** souhaiter ardemment que qn fasse; **he willed himself to go on** par un suprême effort de volonté, il continua

♦ n volonté f; testament m; **to do sth of one's own free will** faire qch de son propre gré; **against one's will** à contre-cœur

willing ['wɪlɪŋ] adj de bonne volonté, serviable ♦ n: **to show willing** faire preuve de bonne volonté; **he's willing to do it** il est disposé à le faire, il veut bien le faire

willingly ['wɪlɪŋlɪ] adv volontiers

willingness ['wɪlɪŋnɪs] n bonne volonté

willow ['wɪləu] n saule m

willpower ['wɪl'pauə*] n volonté f

willy-nilly ['wɪlɪ'nɪlɪ] adv bon gré mal gré

wilt [wɪlt] *vi* dépérir

win [wɪn] *n* (*in sports etc*) victoire *f* ♦ *vb, pt, pp* **won** [wʌn] *vt* (*battle, money*) gagner; (*prize, contract*) remporter; (*popularity*) acquérir ♦ *vi* gagner

▶ **win over** (*BRIT*), **win round** *vt* gagner, se concilier

wince [wɪns] *n* tressaillement *m* ♦ *vi* tressaillir

winch [wɪntʃ] *n* treuil *m*

wind[1] [wɪnd] *n* (*also MED*) vent *m* ♦ *vt* (*take breath away*) couper le souffle à; **the wind(s)** (*MUS*) les instruments *mpl* à vent; **into** *or* **against the wind** contre le vent; **to get wind of sth** (*fig*) avoir vent de qch; **to break wind** avoir des gaz

wind[2], *pt, pp* **wound** [waɪnd, waʊnd] *vt* enrouler; (*wrap*) envelopper; (*clock, toy*) remonter ♦ *vi* (*road, river*) serpenter

▶ **wind down** *vt* (*car window*) baisser; (*fig: production, business*) réduire progressivement

▶ **wind up** *vt* (*clock*) remonter; (*debate*) terminer, clôturer

windfall [ˈwɪndfɔːl] *n* coup *m* de chance

winding [ˈwaɪndɪŋ] *adj* (*road*) sinueux(euse); (*staircase*) tournant(e)

wind instrument *n* (*MUS*) instrument *m* à vent

windmill [ˈwɪndmɪl] *n* moulin *m* à vent

window [ˈwɪndəʊ] *n* fenêtre *f*; (*in car, train: also:* **windowpane**) vitre *f*; (*in shop etc*) vitrine *f*

window box *n* jardinière *f*

window cleaner *n* (*person*) laveur/euse de vitres

window ledge *n* rebord *m* de la fenêtre

window pane *n* vitre *f*, carreau *m*

window-shopping [ˈwɪndəʊʃɔpɪŋ] *n*: **to go window-shopping** faire du lèche-vitrines

windowsill [ˈwɪndəʊsɪl] *n* (*inside*) appui *m* de la fenêtre; (*outside*) rebord *m* de la fenêtre

windpipe [ˈwɪndpaɪp] *n* gosier *m*

wind power *n* énergie éolienne

windscreen [ˈwɪndskriːn], (*US*) **windshield** [ˈwɪndʃiːld] *n* pare-brise *m* *inv*

windscreen washer *n* lave-glace *m* *inv*

windscreen wiper [-waɪpə*] *n* essuie-glace *m* *inv*

windshield [ˈwɪndʃiːld] (*US*) *n* = **windscreen**

windswept [ˈwɪndswept] *adj* balayé(e) par le vent

windy [ˈwɪndɪ] *adj* venté(e), venteux(euse); **it's windy** il y a du vent

wine [waɪn] *n* vin *m* ♦ *vt*: **to wine and dine sb** offrir un dîner bien arrosé à qn

wine bar *n* bar *m* à vin

wine cellar *n* cave *f* à vins

wine glass *n* verre *m* à vin

wine list *n* carte *f* des vins

wine waiter *n* sommelier *m*

wing [wɪŋ] *n* aile *f*; (*in air force*) groupe *m* d'esca-

drilles; **wings** *npl* (*THEAT*) coulisses *fpl*

winger [ˈwɪŋə*] *n* (*SPORT*) ailier *m*

wink [wɪŋk] *n* clin *m* d'œil ♦ *vi* faire un clin d'œil; (*blink*) cligner des yeux

winner [ˈwɪnə*] *n* gagnant/e

winning [ˈwɪnɪŋ] *adj* (*team*) gagnant(e); (*goal*) décisif(ive); (*charming*) charmeur(euse)

winnings [ˈwɪnɪŋz] *npl* gains *mpl*

winter [ˈwɪntə*] *n* hiver *m* ♦ *vi* hiverner

winter sports *npl* sports *mpl* d'hiver

wintry [ˈwɪntrɪ] *adj* hivernal(e)

wipe [waɪp] *n* coup *m* de torchon (*or* de chiffon *or* d'éponge) ♦ *vt* essuyer; **to give sth a wipe** donner un coup de torchon à qch; **to wipe one's nose** se moucher

▶ **wipe off** *vt* essuyer

▶ **wipe out** *vt* (*debt*) régler; (*memory*) oublier; (*destroy*) anéantir

▶ **wipe up** *vt* essuyer

wire [ˈwaɪə*] *n* fil *m* (de fer); (*ELEC*) fil électrique; (*TEL*) télégramme *m* ♦ *vt* (*fence*) grillager; (*house*) faire l'installation électrique de; (*also:* **wire up**) brancher

wireless [ˈwaɪəlɪs] *n* (*BRIT*) télégraphie *f* sans fil; (*set*) T.S.F. *f*

wiring [ˈwaɪərɪŋ] *n* (*ELEC*) installation *f* électrique

wiry [ˈwaɪərɪ] *adj* noueux(euse), nerveux(euse)

wisdom [ˈwɪzdəm] *n* sagesse *f*; (*of action*) prudence *f*

wisdom tooth *n* dent *f* de sagesse

wise [waɪz] *adj* sage, prudent(e), judicieux(euse); **I'm none the wiser** je ne suis pas plus avancé(e) pour autant

▶ **wise up** *vi* (*col*): **to wise up to** commencer à se rendre compte de

wish [wɪʃ] *n* (*desire*) désir *m*; (*specific desire*) souhait *m*, vœu *m* ♦ *vt* souhaiter, désirer, vouloir; **best wishes** (*on birthday etc*) meilleurs vœux; **with best wishes** (*in letter*) bien amicalement; **give her my best wishes** faites-lui mes amitiés; **to wish sb goodbye** dire au revoir à qn; **he wished me well** il me souhaitait de réussir; **to wish to do/sb to do** désirer *or* vouloir faire/que qn fasse; **to wish for** souhaiter; **to wish sth on sb** souhaiter qch à qn

wishful [ˈwɪʃful] *adj*: **it's wishful thinking** c'est prendre ses désirs pour des réalités

wistful [ˈwɪstful] *adj* mélancolique

wit [wɪt] *n* (*gen pl: intelligence*) intelligence *f*, esprit *m*; (*presence of mind*) présence *f* d'esprit; (*wittiness*) esprit; (*person*) homme/femme d'esprit; **to be at one's wits' end** (*fig*) ne plus savoir que faire; **to have one's wits about one** avoir toute sa présence d'esprit, ne pas perdre la tête; **to wit** *adv* à savoir

witch [wɪtʃ] *n* sorcière *f*

witchcraft [ˈwɪtʃkrɑːft] *n* sorcellerie *f*

KEYWORD
---

with [wɪð, wɪθ] *prep* **1** (*in the company of*) avec; (*at the home of*) chez; **we stayed with friends**

nous avons logé chez des amis; **I'll be with you in a minute** je suis à vous dans un instant
2 (descriptive): **a room with a view** une chambre avec vue; **the man with the grey hat/blue eyes** l'homme au chapeau gris/aux yeux bleus
3 (indicating manner, means, cause): **with tears in her eyes** les larmes aux yeux; **to walk with a stick** marcher avec une canne; **red with anger** rouge de colère; **to shake with fear** trembler de peur; **to fill sth with water** remplir qch d'eau
4: I'm with you (I understand) je vous suis; **to be with it** (col: up-to-date) être dans le vent

withdraw [wɪθˈdrɔː] irreg vt retirer ♦ vi se retirer; (go back on promise) se rétracter; **to withdraw into o.s.** se replier sur soi-même
withdrawal [wɪθˈdrɔːəl] n retrait m; (MED) état m de manque
withdrawal symptoms npl: **to have withdrawal symptoms** être en état de manque, présenter les symptômes mpl de sevrage
withdrawn [wɪθˈdrɔːn] pp of **withdraw** ♦ adj (person) renfermé(e)
wither [ˈwɪðəʳ] vi se faner
withhold [wɪθˈhəʊld] vt irreg (money) retenir; (decision) remettre; (permission): **to withhold (from)** refuser (à); (information): **to withhold (from)** cacher (à)
within [wɪðˈɪn] prep à l'intérieur de ♦ adv à l'intérieur; **within sight of** en vue de; **within a mile of** à moins d'un mille de; **within the week** avant la fin de la semaine; **within an hour from now** d'ici une heure; **to be within the law** être légal(e) or dans les limites de la légalité
without [wɪðˈaʊt] prep sans; **without anybody knowing** sans que personne ne le sache; **to go or do without sth** se passer de qch
withstand [wɪθˈstænd] vt irreg résister à
witness [ˈwɪtnɪs] n (person) témoin m; (evidence) témoignage m ♦ vt (event) être témoin de; (document) attester l'authenticité de; **to bear witness to sth** témoigner de qch; **witness for the prosecution/defence** témoin à charge/à décharge; **to witness to sth/having seen sth** témoigner de qch/d'avoir vu qch
witness box, (US) **witness stand** n barre f des témoins
witty [ˈwɪtɪ] adj spirituel(le), plein(e) d'esprit
wives [waɪvz] npl of **wife**
wizard [ˈwɪzəd] n magicien m
wk abbr = **week**
wobble [ˈwɔbl] vi trembler; (chair) branler
woe [wəʊ] n malheur m
woke [wəʊk] pt of **wake**
woken [ˈwəʊkn] pp of **wake**
wolf, pl **wolves** [wʊlf, wʊlvz] n loup m
woman, pl **women** [ˈwʊmən, ˈwɪmɪn] n femme f ♦ cpd: **woman doctor** femme f médecin; **woman**

friend amie f; **woman teacher** professeur m femme; **young woman** jeune femme; **women's page** (PRESS) page f des lectrices
womanly [ˈwʊmənlɪ] adj féminin(e)
womb [wuːm] n (ANAT) utérus m
women [ˈwɪmɪn] npl of **woman**
Women's (Liberation) Movement n (also: **women's lib**) mouvement m de libération de la femme, MLF m
won [wʌn] pt, pp of **win**
wonder [ˈwʌndəʳ] n merveille f, miracle m; (feeling) émerveillement m ♦ vi: **to wonder whether** se demander si; **to wonder at** s'étonner de; s'émerveiller de; **to wonder about** songer à; **it's no wonder that** il n'est pas étonnant que + sub
wonderful [ˈwʌndəful] adj merveilleux(euse)
won't [wəʊnt] = **will not**
wood [wʊd] n (timber, forest) bois m ♦ cpd de bois, en bois
wood carving n sculpture f en or sur bois
wooded [ˈwʊdɪd] adj boisé(e)
wooden [ˈwʊdn] adj en bois; (fig) raide; inexpressif(ive)
woodpecker [ˈwʊdpekəʳ] n pic m (oiseau)
woodwind [ˈwʊdwɪnd] n (MUS) bois m; **the woodwind** (MUS) les bois
woodwork [ˈwʊdwəːk] n menuiserie f
woodworm [ˈwʊdwəːm] n ver m du bois; **the table has got woodworm** la table est piquée des vers
wool [wʊl] n laine f; **to pull the wool over sb's eyes** (fig) en faire accroire à qn
woollen, (US) **woolen** [ˈwʊlən] adj de laine; (industry) lainier(ière) ♦ n: **woollens** lainages mpl
woolly, (US) **wooly** [ˈwʊlɪ] adj laineux(euse); (fig: ideas) confus(e)
word [wəːd] n mot m; (spoken) mot, parole f; (promise) parole; (news) nouvelles fpl ♦ vt rédiger, formuler; **word for word** (repeat) mot pour mot; (translate) mot à mot; **what's the word for "pen" in French?** comment dit-on "pen" en français?; **to put sth into words** exprimer qch; **in other words** en d'autres termes; **to have a word with sb** toucher un mot à qn; **to have words with sb** (quarrel with) avoir des mots avec qn; **to break/keep one's word** manquer à/tenir sa parole; **I'll take your word for it** je vous crois sur parole; **to send word of** prévenir de; **to leave word (with sb/for sb) that ...** laisser un mot (à qn/pour qn) disant que ...
wording [ˈwəːdɪŋ] n termes mpl, langage m; libellé m
word processing n traitement m de texte
word processor [-prəʊsesəʳ] n machine f de traitement de texte
wore [wɔːʳ] pt of **wear**
work [wəːk] n travail m; (ART, LITERATURE) œuvre f ♦ vi travailler; (mechanism) marcher, fonctionner; (plan

etc) marcher; (*medicine*) agir ◆ *vt* (*clay, wood etc*) travailler; (*mine etc*) exploiter; (*machine*) faire marcher *or* fonctionner; **to go to work** aller travailler; **to set to work, to start work** se mettre à l'œuvre; **to be at work (on sth)** travailler (sur qch); **to be out of work** être au chômage; **to work hard** travailler dur; **to work loose** se défaire, se desserrer

▶ **work on** *vt fus* travailler à; (*principle*) se baser sur

▶ **work out** *vi* (*subj: plans etc*) marcher; (*SPORT*) s'entraîner ◆ *vt* (*problem*) résoudre; (*plan*) élaborer; **it works out at £100** ça fait 100 livres

▶ **work up** *vt*: **to get worked up** se mettre dans tous ses états

workable ['wə:kəbl] *adj* (*solution*) réalisable

workaholic [wə:kə'hɔlɪk] *n* bourreau *m* de travail

worker ['wə:kə*] *n* travailleur/euse, ouvrier/ière; **office worker** employé/e de bureau

work experience *n* stage *m*

workforce ['wə:kfɔ:s] *n* main-d'œuvre *f*

working ['wə:kɪŋ] *adj* (*day, tools etc, conditions*) de travail; (*wife*) qui travaille; (*partner, population*) actif(ive); **in working order** en état de marche; **a working knowledge of English** une connaissance toute pratique de l'anglais

working class *n* classe ouvrière ◆ *adj*: **working-class** ouvrier(ière), de la classe ouvrière

workman ['wə:kmən] *n* ouvrier *m*

workmanship ['wə:kmənʃɪp] *n* métier *m*, habileté *f*; facture *f*

works [wə:ks] *n* (*BRIT: factory*) usine *f* ◆ *npl* (*of clock, machine*) mécanisme *m*; **road works** travaux *mpl* (d'entretien des routes)

worksheet *n* (*SCOL*) feuille *f* d'exercices

workshop ['wə:kʃɔp] *n* atelier *m*

work station *n* poste *m* de travail

work-to-rule ['wə:ktə'ru:l] *n* (*BRIT*) grève *f* du zèle

world [wə:ld] *n* monde *m* ◆ *cpd* (*champion*) du monde; (*power, war*) mondial(e); **all over the world** dans le monde entier, partout dans le monde; **to think the world of sb** (*fig*) ne jurer que par qn; **what in the world is he doing?** qu'est-ce qu'il peut bien être en train de faire?; **to do sb a world of good** faire le plus grand bien à qn; **World War One/Two, the First/Second World War** la Première/Deuxième Guerre mondiale; **out of this world** *adj* extraordinaire

worldly ['wə:ldlɪ] *adj* de ce monde

worldwide ['wə:ld'waɪd] *adj* universel(le) ◆ *adv* dans le monde entier

World Wide Web *n* Web *m*

worm [wə:m] *n* ver *m*

worn [wɔ:n] *pp* of **wear** ◆ *adj* usé(e)

worn-out ['wɔ:naut] *adj* (*object*) complètement usé(e); (*person*) épuisé(e)

worried ['wʌrɪd] *adj* inquiet(ète); **to be worried**

about sth être inquiet au sujet de qch

worry ['wʌrɪ] *n* souci *m* ◆ *vt* inquiéter ◆ *vi* s'inquiéter, se faire du souci; **to worry about** *or* **over sth/sb** se faire du souci pour *or* à propos de qch/qn

worse [wə:s] *adj* pire, plus mauvais(e) ◆ *adv* plus mal ◆ *n* pire *m*; **to get worse** (*condition, situation*) empirer, se dégrader; **a change for the worse** une détérioration; **he is none the worse for it** il ne s'en porte pas plus mal; **so much the worse for you!** tant pis pour vous!

worsen ['wə:sn] *vt, vi* empirer

worse off *adj* moins à l'aise financièrement; (*fig*): **you'll be worse off this way** ça ira moins bien de cette façon; **he is now worse off than before** il se retrouve dans une situation pire qu'auparavant

worship ['wə:ʃɪp] *n* culte *m* ◆ *vt* (*God*) rendre un culte à; (*person*) adorer; **Your Worship** (*BRIT: to mayor*) Monsieur le Maire; (: *to judge*) Monsieur le Juge

worst [wə:st] *adj* le(la) pire, le(la) plus mauvais(e) ◆ *adv* le plus mal ◆ *n* pire *m*; **at worst** au pis aller; **if the worst comes to the worst** si le pire doit arriver

worth [wə:θ] *n* valeur *f* ◆ *adj*: **to be worth** valoir; **how much is it worth?** ça vaut combien?; **it's worth it** cela en vaut la peine; **50 pence worth of apples** (pour) 50 pence de pommes

worthless ['wə:θlɪs] *adj* qui ne vaut rien

worthwhile ['wə:θ'waɪl] *adj* (*activity*) qui en vaut la peine; (*cause*) louable; **a worthwhile book** un livre qui vaut la peine d'être lu

worthy ['wə:ðɪ] *adj* (*person*) digne; (*motive*) louable; **worthy of** digne de

---

KEYWORD

would [wud] *aux vb* **1** (*conditional tense*): **if you asked him he would do it** si vous le lui demandiez, il le ferait; **if you had asked him he would have done it** si vous le lui aviez demandé, il l'aurait fait

2 (*in offers, invitations, requests*): **would you like a biscuit?** voulez-vous un biscuit?; **would you close the door please?** voulez-vous fermer la porte, s'il vous plaît?

3 (*in indirect speech*): **I said I would do it** j'ai dit que je le ferais

4 (*emphatic*): **it WOULD have to snow today!** naturellement il neige aujourd'hui! *or* il fallait qu'il neige aujourd'hui!

5 (*insistence*): **she wouldn't do it** elle n'a pas voulu *or* elle a refusé de le faire

6 (*conjecture*): **it would have been midnight** il devait être minuit

7 (*indicating habit*): **he would go there on Mondays** il y allait le lundi

---

would-be ['wudbi:] *adj* (*pej*) soi-disant

wouldn't ['wudnt] = **would not**

wound vb [waund] ♦ pt, pp of **wind** ♦ n, vt [wu:nd] ♦ n blessure f ♦ vt blesser; **wounded in the leg** blessé à la jambe

wove [wəuv] pt of **weave**

woven ['wəuvn] pp of **weave**

wrap [ræp] n (stole) écharpe f; (cape) pèlerine f ♦ vt (also: **wrap up**) envelopper; **under wraps** (fig: plan, scheme) secret(ète)

wrapper ['ræpə*] n (BRIT: of book) couverture f; (on chocolate etc) papier m

wrapping paper ['ræpɪŋ-] n papier m d'emballage; (for gift) papier cadeau

wreak [ri:k] vt (destruction) entraîner; **to wreak havoc** faire des ravages; **to wreak vengeance on** se venger de, exercer sa vengeance sur

wreath, pl **wreaths** [ri:θ, ri:ðz]n couronne f

wreck [rek] n (sea disaster) naufrage m; (ship) épave f; (pej: person) loque (humaine) ♦ vt démolir; (ship) provoquer le naufrage de; (fig) briser, ruiner

wreckage ['rekɪdʒ] n débris mpl; (of building) décombres mpl; (of ship) naufrage m

wren [ren] n (ZOOL) troglodyte m

wrench [rentʃ] n (TECH) clé f (à écrous); (tug) violent mouvement de torsion; (fig) arrachement m ♦ vt tirer violemment sur, tordre; **to wrench sth from** arracher qch (violemment) à or de

wrestle ['resl] vi: **to wrestle (with sb)** lutter (avec qn); **to wrestle with** (fig) se débattre avec, lutter contre

wrestler ['reslə*] n lutteur/euse

wrestling ['reslɪŋ] n lutte f; (also: **all-in wrestling**: BRIT) catch m

wretched ['retʃɪd] adj misérable; (col) maudit(e)

wriggle ['rɪgl] n tortillement m ♦ vi se tortiller

wring, pt, pp **wrung** [rɪŋ, rʌŋ] vt tordre; (wet clothes) essorer; (fig): **to wring sth out of** arracher qch à

wrinkle ['rɪŋkl] n (on skin) ride f; (on paper etc) pli m ♦ vt rider, plisser ♦ vi se plisser

wrinkled ['rɪŋkld] adj, **wrinkly** ['rɪŋklɪ] adj (fabric, paper) froissé(e), plissé(e); (surface) plissé; (skin) ridé(e), plissé

wrist [rɪst] n poignet m

wristwatch ['rɪstwɔtʃ] n montre-bracelet f

writ [rɪt] n acte m judiciaire; **to issue a writ against sb, serve a writ on sb** assigner qn en justice

write, pt **wrote**, pp **written** [raɪt, rəut, 'rɪtn] vt, vi écrire; **to write sb a letter** écrire une lettre à qn

▶ **write away** vi: **to write away for** (information) (écrire pour) demander; (goods) (écrire pour) commander

▶ **write down** vt noter; (put in writing) mettre par écrit

▶ **write off** vt (debt) passer aux profits et pertes; (depreciate) amortir; (smash up: car etc) démolir complètement

▶ **write out** vt écrire; (copy) recopier

▶ **write up** vt rédiger

write-off ['raɪtɔf] n perte totale; **the car is a write-off** la voiture est bonne pour la casse

writer ['raɪtə*] n auteur m, écrivain m

writhe [raɪð] vi se tordre

writing ['raɪtɪŋ] n écriture f; (of author) œuvres fpl; **in writing** par écrit; **in my own writing** écrit(e) de ma main

writing paper n papier m à lettres

wrong [rɔŋ] adj faux(fausse); (incorrectly chosen: number, road etc) mauvais(e); (not suitable) qui ne convient pas; (wicked) mal; (unfair) injuste ♦ adv faux ♦ n tort m ♦ vt faire du tort à, léser; **to be wrong** (answer) être faux(fausse); (in doing/saying) avoir tort (de dire/faire); **you are wrong to do it** tu as tort de le faire; **it's wrong to steal, stealing is wrong** c'est mal de voler; **you are wrong about that, you've got it wrong** tu te trompes; **to be in the wrong** avoir tort; **what's wrong?** qu'est-ce qui ne va pas?; **there's nothing wrong** tout va bien; **what's wrong with the car?** qu'est-ce qu'elle a, la voiture?; **to go wrong** (person) se tromper; (plan) mal tourner; (machine) se détraquer

wrongful ['rɔŋful] adj injustifié(e); **wrongful dismissal** (INDUSTRY) licenciement abusif

wrongly ['rɔŋlɪ] adv à tort; (answer, do, count) mal, incorrectement; (treat) injustement

wrong side n (of cloth) envers m

wrote [rəut] pt of **write**

wrought [rɔ:t] adj: **wrought iron** fer forgé

wrung [rʌŋ] pt, pp of **wring**

wt. abbr (= weight) pds.

WWW n abbr = **World Wide Web**: **the WWW** le Web

— **X x** —

Xmas ['eksməs] n abbr = **Christmas**

X-ray ['eksreɪ] n rayon m X; (photograph) radio(graphie) f ♦ vt radiographier

xylophone ['zaɪləfəun] n xylophone m

— **Y y** —

Y2K n abbr (= year 2000) l'an m 2000

yacht [jɔt] n voilier m; (motor, luxury yacht) yacht m

yachting ['jɔtɪŋ] n yachting m, navigation f de plaisance

yachtsman ['jɔtsmən] n yacht(s)man m

Yank [jæŋk], **Yankee** [ˈjæŋkɪ] n (pej) Amerloque m/f, Ricain/e

yank [jæŋk] vt tirer d'un coup sec

yap [jæp] vi (dog) japper

yard [jɑːd] n (of house etc) cour f; (US: garden) jardin m; (measure) yard m (= 914 mm; 3 feet) **builder's yard** chantier m

yardstick [ˈjɑːdstɪk] n (fig) mesure f, critère m

yarn [jɑːn] n fil m; (tale) longue histoire

yawn [jɔːn] n bâillement m ♦ vi bâiller

yawning [ˈjɔːnɪŋ] adj (gap) béant(e)

yd abbr = **yard**

yeah [jɛə] adv (col) ouais

year [jɪə*] n an m, année f; (SCOL etc) année; **every year** tous les ans, chaque année; **this year** cette année; **a or per year** par an; **year in, year out** année après année; **to be 8 years old** avoir 8 ans; **an eight-year-old child** un enfant de huit ans

yearly [ˈjɪəlɪ] adj annuel(le) ♦ adv annuellement; **twice yearly** deux fois par an

yearn [jɜːn] vi: **to yearn for sth/to do** aspirer à qch/à faire, languir après qch

yeast [jiːst] n levure f

yell [jɛl] n hurlement m, cri m ♦ vi hurler

yellow [ˈjɛləʊ] adj, n jaune (m)

yelp [jɛlp] n jappement m; glapissement m ♦ vi japper; glapir

yes [jɛs] adv oui; (answering negative question) si ♦ n oui m; **to say yes (to)** dire oui (à)

yesterday [ˈjɛstədɪ] adv, n hier (m); **yesterday morning/evening** hier matin/soir; **the day before yesterday** avant-hier; **all day yesterday** toute la journée d'hier

yet [jɛt] adv encore; déjà ♦ conj pourtant, néanmoins; **it is not finished yet** ce n'est pas encore fini or toujours pas fini; **must you go just yet?** dois-tu déjà partir?; **the best yet** le meilleur jusqu'ici or jusque-là; **as yet** jusqu'ici, encore; **a few days yet** encore quelques jours; **yet again** une fois de plus

yew [juː] n if m

yield [jiːld] n production f, rendement m; (FINANCE) rapport m ♦ vt produire, rendre, rapporter; (surrender) céder ♦ vi céder; (US AUT) céder la priorité; **a yield of 5%** un rendement de 5%

YMCA n abbr (= Young Men's Christian Association) ≃ union chrétienne de jeunes gens (UCJG)

yob(bo) [ˈjɔb(əʊ)] n (BRIT col) loubar(d) m

yog(h)ourt, yog(h)urt [ˈjaugət] n yaourt m

yoke [jəʊk] n joug m ♦ vt (also: **yoke together**: oxen) accoupler

yolk [jəʊk] n jaune m (d'œuf)

KEYWORD

you [juː] pron **1** (subject) tu; (polite form) vous; (plural) vous; **you French enjoy your food** vous autres Français, vous aimez bien manger; **you**

and I will go toi et moi or vous et moi, nous irons
2 (object: direct, indirect) te, t' +vowel; vous; **I know you** je te or vous connais; **I gave it to you** je vous l'ai donné, je te l'ai donné
3 (stressed) toi; vous; **I told YOU to do it** c'est à toi or vous que j'ai dit de le faire
4 (after prep, in comparisons) toi; vous; **it's for you** c'est pour toi or vous; **she's younger than you** elle est plus jeune que toi or vous
5 (impersonal: one) on; **fresh air does you good** l'air frais fait du bien; **you never know** on ne sait jamais

---

you'd [juːd] = **you had**, **you would**

you'll [juːl] = **you will**, **you shall**

young [jʌŋ] adj jeune ♦ npl (of animal) petits mpl; (people): **the young** les jeunes, la jeunesse; **a young man** un jeune homme; **a young lady** (unmarried) une jeune fille, une demoiselle; (married) une jeune femme or dame; **my younger brother** mon frère cadet; **the younger generation** la jeune génération

younger [ˈjʌŋgə*] adj (brother etc) cadet(te)

youngster [ˈjʌŋstə*] n jeune m/f; (child) enfant m/f

your [jɔː*] adj ton(ta), tes pl; (polite form, pl) votre, vos pl

you're [juə*] = **you are**

yours [jɔːz] pron le(la) tien(ne), les tiens(tiennes); (polite form, pl) le(la) vôtre, les vôtres; **is it yours?** c'est à toi (or à vous)?; **a friend of yours** un(e) de tes (or de vos) amis

yourself [jɔːˈsɛlf] pron (reflexive) te; (: polite form) vous; (after prep) toi; vous; (emphatic) toi-même; vous-même; **you yourself told me** c'est vous qui me l'avez dit, vous me l'avez dit vous-même

yourselves [jɔːˈsɛlvz] pl pron vous; (emphatic) vous-mêmes

youth [juːθ] n jeunesse f; (young man: pl **youths**) [juːðz] jeune homme m; **in my youth** dans ma jeunesse, quand j'étais jeune

youth club n centre m de jeunes

youthful [ˈjuːθful] adj jeune; (enthusiasm etc) juvénile; (misdemeanour) de jeunesse

youth hostel n auberge f de jeunesse

you've [juːv] = **you have**

YTS n abbr (BRIT: = Youth Training Scheme) ≃ TUC m

Yugoslav [ˈjuːgəʊslɑːv] adj yougoslave ♦ n Yougoslave m/f

Yugoslavia [juːgəʊˈslɑːvɪə] n Yougoslavie f

yuppie [ˈjʌpɪ] n yuppie m/f

YWCA n abbr (= Young Women's Christian Association) union chrétienne féminine

— Z z —

zany ['zeɪnɪ] *adj* farfelu(e), loufoque

zap [zæp] *vt* (*COMPUT*) effacer

zeal [zi:l] *n* (*revolutionary etc*) ferveur *f*; (*keenness*) ardeur *f*, zèle *m*

zebra ['zi:brə] *n* zèbre *m*

zebra crossing *n* (*BRIT*) passage *m* pour piétons

zero ['zɪərəu] *n* zéro *m* ◆ *vi*: **to zero in on** (*target*) se diriger droit sur; **5° below zero** 5 degrés au-dessous de zéro

zest [zɛst] *n* entrain *m*, élan *m*; (*of lemon etc*) zeste *m*

zigzag ['zɪgzæg] *n* zigzag *m* ◆ *vi* zigzaguer, faire des zigzags

Zimbabwe [zɪm'bɑ:bwɪ] *n* Zimbabwe *m*

Zimmer® ['zɪmə*] *n* (*also*: **Zimmer frame**) déam-bulateur *m*

zinc [zɪŋk] *n* zinc *m*

zip [zɪp] *n* (*also*: **zip fastener**, (*US*) **zipper**) ferme-ture *f* éclair® *or* à glissière; (*energy*) entrain *m* ◆ *vt* (*also*: **zip up**) fermer (avec une fermeture éclair®)

zip code *n* (*US*) code postal

zip file *n* (*COMPUT*) fichier *m* zip *inv*

zit [zɪt] (*inf*) *n* bouton *m*

zodiac ['zəudɪæk] *n* zodiaque *m*

zone [zəun] *n* zone *f*

zoo [zu:] *n* zoo *m*

zoom [zu:m] *vi*: **to zoom past** passer en trombe; **to zoom in (on sb/sth)** (*PHOT, CINE*) zoomer (sur qn/qch)

zoom lens *n* zoom *m*, objectif *m* à focale variable

zucchini [zu:'ki:nɪ] *n*(*pl*) (*US*) courgette(s) *f*(*pl*)

Grammar
Grammaire

USING THE GRAMMAR

The Grammar section deals systematically and comprehensively with all the information you will need in order to communicate accurately in French. The boxed numbers, → ☐ etc, direct you to the relevant example in every case.

ABBREVIATIONS

ctd.	continued	**p(p)**	page(s)	**qn**	quelqu'un
fem.	feminine	**perf.**	perfect	**sb**	somebody
infin.	infinitive	**plur.**	plural	**sing.**	singular
masc.	masculine	**qch**	quelque chose	**sth**	something

❐ Simple Tenses: Formation of Regular Verbs

Simple tenses are one-word tenses which are formed by adding endings to a verb stem. The endings show the number and person of the subject of the verb. The stem and endings of regular verbs are totally predictable.

There are three regular patterns (called conjugations), each identifiable by the ending of the infinitive. For irregular verbs see pp 50 ff.

❐ Simple Tenses: First Conjugation

◆ First conjugation verbs end in **-er**, e.g. **donner** to give. The stem is formed as follows:

TENSE	FORMATION	EXAMPLE
Present Imperfect Past Historic Present Subjunctive	infinitive minus **-er**	**donn-**
Future Conditional	infinitive	**donner-**

◆ To the appropriate stem add the following endings

		PRESENT → ①	IMPERFECT → ②	PAST HISTORIC → ③
	1st person	**-e**	**-ais**	**-ai**
sing.	2nd person	**-es**	**-ais**	**-as**
	3rd person	**-e**	**-ait**	**-a**
	1st person	**-ons**	**-ions**	**-âmes**
plur.	2nd person	**-ez**	**-iez**	**-âtes**
	3rd person	**-ent**	**-aient**	**-èrent**

		PRESENT SUBJUNCTIVE → ④	FUTURE → ⑤	CONDITIONAL → ⑥
	1st person	**-e**	**-ai**	**-ais**
sing.	2nd person	**-es**	**-as**	**-ais**
	3rd person	**-e**	**-a**	**-ait**
	1st person	**-ions**	**-ons**	**-ions**
plur.	2nd person	**-iez**	**-ez**	**-iez**
	3rd person	**-ent**	**-ont**	**-aient**

1	PRESENT		2	IMPERFECT
je	donn**e**		je	donn**ais**
tu	donn**es**		tu	donn**ais**
il	donn**e**		il	donn**ait**
elle	donn**e**		elle	donn**ait**
nous	donn**ons**		nous	donn**ions**
vous	donn**ez**		vous	donn**iez**
ils	donn**ent**		ils	donn**aient**
elles	donn**ent**		elles	donn**aient**

I give, I am giving, I do give *etc*   I gave, I was giving, I used to give *etc*

3	PAST HISTORIC		4	PRESENT SUBJUNCTIVE
je	donn**ai**		je	donn**e**
tu	donn**as**		tu	donn**es**
il	donn**a**		il	donn**e**
elle	donn**a**		elle	donn**e**
nous	donn**âmes**		nous	donn**ions**
vous	donn**âtes**		vous	donn**iez**
ils	donn**èrent**		ils	donn**ent**
elles	donn**èrent**		elles	donn**ent**

I gave *etc*   I give/gave *etc*

5	FUTURE		6	CONDITIONAL
je	donner**ai**		je	donner**ais**
tu	donner**as**		tu	donner**ais**
il	donner**a**		il	donner**ait**
elle	donner**a**		elle	donner**ait**
nous	donner**ons**		nous	donner**ions**
vous	donner**ez**		vous	donner**iez**
ils	donner**ont**		ils	donner**aient**
elles	donner**ont**		elles	donner**aient**

I shall give, I shall be giving *etc*   I should/would give,
I should/would be giving *etc*

☐ Simple Tenses: Second Conjugation

◆ Second conjugation verbs end in **-ir**, e.g. **finir** to finish. The stem is formed as follows:

TENSE	FORMATION	EXAMPLE
Present Imperfect Past Historic Present Subjunctive	infinitive minus **-ir**	**fin-**
Future Conditional	infinitive	**finir-**

◆ To the appropriate stem add the following endings:

		PRESENT → ①	IMPERFECT → ②
	1st person	**-is**	**-issais**
sing.	2nd person	**-is**	**-issais**
	3rd person	**-it**	**-issait**
	1st person	**-issons**	**-issions**
plur.	2nd person	**-issez**	**-issiez**
	3rd person	**-issent**	**-issaient**

		PAST HISTORIC → ③	PRESENT SUBJUNCTIVE → ④
	1st person	**-is**	**-isse**
sing.	2nd person	**-is**	**-isses**
	3rd person	**-it**	**-isse**
	1st person	**-îmes**	**-issions**
plur.	2nd person	**-îtes**	**-issiez**
	3rd person	**-irent**	**-issent**

		FUTURE → ⑤	CONDITIONAL → ⑥
	1st person	**-ai**	**-ais**
sing.	2nd person	**-as**	**-ais**
	3rd person	**-a**	**-ait**
	1st person	**-ons**	**-ions**
plur.	2nd person	**-ez**	**-iez**
	3rd person	**-ont**	**-aient**

Grammar

1	PRESENT		2	IMPERFECT
je	fin**is**		je	fin**issais**
tu	fin**is**		tu	fin**issais**
il	fin**it**		il	fin**issait**
elle	fin**it**		elle	fin**issait**
nous	fin**issons**		nous	fin**issions**
vous	fin**issez**		vous	fin**issiez**
ils	fin**issent**		ils	fin**issaient**
elles	fin**issent**		elles	fin**issaient**

I finish, I am finishing, I do finish *etc*

I finished, I was finishing, I used to finish *etc*

3	PAST HISTORIC		4	PRESENT SUBJUNCTIVE
je	fin**is**		je	fin**isse**
tu	fin**is**		tu	fin**isses**
il	fin**it**		il	fin**isse**
elle	fin**it**		elle	fin**isse**
nous	fin**îmes**		nous	fin**issions**
vous	fin**îtes**		vous	fin**issiez**
ils	fin**irent**		ils	fin**issent**
elles	fin**irent**		elles	fin**issent**

I finished *etc*

I finish/finished *etc*

5	FUTURE		6	CONDITIONAL
je	fin**irai**		je	fin**irais**
tu	fin**iras**		tu	fin**irais**
il	fin**ira**		il	fin**irait**
elle	fin**ira**		elle	fin**irait**
nous	fin**irons**		nous	fin**irions**
vous	fin**irez**		vous	fin**iriez**
ils	fin**iront**		ils	fin**iraient**
elles	fin**iront**		elles	fin**iraient**

I shall finish, I shall be finishing *etc*

I should/would finish, I should/would be finishing *etc*

❐ Simple Tenses: Third Conjugation

◆ Third conjugation verbs end in **-re**, e.g. **vendre** to sell. The stem is formed as follows:

TENSE	FORMATION	EXAMPLE
Present Imperfect Past Historic Present Subjunctive	infinitive minus **-re**	**vend-**
Future Conditional	infinitive minus **-e**	**vendr-**

◆ To the appropriate stem add the following endings:

		PRESENT → ①	IMPERFECT → ②
sing.	1st person	**-s**	**-ais**
	2nd person	**-s**	**-ais**
	3rd person	—	**-ait**
plur.	1st person	**-ons**	**-ions**
	2nd person	**-ez**	**-iez**
	3rd person	**-ent**	**-aient**

		PAST HISTORIC → ③	PRESENT SUBJUNCTIVE → ④
sing.	1st person	**-is**	**-e**
	2nd person	**-is**	**-es**
	3rd person	**-it**	**-e**
plur.	1st person	**-îmes**	**-ions**
	2nd person	**-îtes**	**-iez**
	3rd person	**-irent**	**-ent**

		FUTURE → ⑤	CONDITIONAL → ⑥
sing.	1st person	**-ai**	**-ais**
	2nd person	**-as**	**-ais**
	3rd person	**-a**	**-ait**
plur.	1st person	**-ons**	**-ions**
	2nd person	**-ez**	**-iez**
	3rd person	**-ont**	**-aient**

1	PRESENT		2	IMPERFECT
je	vend**s**		je	vend**ais**
tu	vend**s**		tu	vend**ais**
il	vend		il	vend**ait**
elle	vend		elle	vend**ait**
nous	vend**ons**		nous	vend**ions**
vous	vend**ez**		vous	vend**iez**
ils	vend**ent**		ils	vend**aient**
elles	vend**ent**		elles	vend**aient**

I sell, I am selling, I do sell *etc*   I sold, I was selling, I used to sell *etc*

3	PAST HISTORIC		4	PRESENT SUBJUNCTIVE
je	vend**is**		je	vend**e**
tu	vend**is**		tu	vend**es**
il	vend**it**		il	vend**e**
elle	vend**it**		elle	vend**e**
nous	vend**îmes**		nous	vend**ions**
vous	vend**îtes**		vous	vend**iez**
ils	vend**irent**		ils	vend**ent**
elles	vend**irent**		elles	vend**ent**

I sold *etc*   I sell/sold *etc*

5	FUTURE		6	CONDITIONAL
je	vend**rai**		je	vend**rais**
tu	vend**ras**		tu	vend**rais**
il	vend**ra**		il	vend**rait**
elle	vend**ra**		elle	vend**rait**
nous	vend**rons**		nous	vend**rions**
vous	vend**rez**		vous	vend**riez**
ils	vend**ront**		ils	vend**raient**
elles	vend**ront**		elles	vend**raient**

I shall sell, I shall be selling *etc*

I should/would sell,
I should/would be selling *etc*

❏ First Conjugation Spelling Irregularities

Before certain endings, the stems of some '**-er**' verbs may change slightly.

Verbs ending:	**-cer**
Change:	**c** becomes **ç** before **a** or **o** to retain its soft [s] pronunciation
Tenses affected:	Present, Imperfect, Past Historic; Present Participle
Model:	**lancer** *to throw* → 1

Verbs ending:	**-ger**
Change:	**g** becomes **ge** before **a** or **o** to retain its soft [ʒ] pronunciation
Tenses affected:	Present, Imperfect, Past Historic; Present Participle
Model:	**manger** *to eat* → 2

Verbs ending	**-eler**
Change:	**-l** doubles before **-e**, **-es**, **-ent** and throughout the Future and Conditional tenses
Tenses affected:	Present, Present Subjunctive, Future, Conditional
Model:	**appeler** *to call* → 3

◆   EXCEPTIONS: **geler** *to freeze*
            peler *to peel* } like **mener** (p 14)

①	INFINITIVE		PRESENT PARTICIPLE		
	lancer		**lançant**		

PRESENT		IMPERFECT		PAST HISTORIC	
je	lance	**je**	**lançais**	**je**	**lançai**
tu	lances	**tu**	**lançais**	**tu**	**lanças**
il/elle	lance	**il/elle**	**lançait**	**il/elle**	**lança**
nous	**lançons**	nous	lancions	**nous**	**lançâmes**
vous	lancez	vous	lanciez	**vous**	**lançâtes**
ils/elles	lancent	**ils/elles**	**lançaient**	ils/elles	lancèrent

②	INFINITIVE		PRESENT PARTICIPLE		
	manger		**mangeant**		

PRESENT		IMPERFECT		PAST HISTORIC	
je	mange	**je**	**mangeais**	**je**	**mangeai**
tu	manges	**tu**	**mangeais**	**tu**	**mangeas**
il/elle	mange	**il/elle**	**mangeait**	**il/elle**	**mangea**
nous	**mangeons**	nous	mangions	**nous**	**mangeâmes**
vous	mangez	vous	mangiez	**vous**	**mangeâtes**
ils/elles	mangent	**ils/elles**	**mangeaient**	ils/elles	mangèrent

③	PRESENT (+ SUBJUNCTIVE)	FUTURE	
	j'appelle		**j'appellerai**
tu	**appelles**	**tu**	**appelleras**
il/elle	**appelle**	**il**	**appellera** *etc*
nous	appelons		
	(appelions)	CONDITIONAL	
vous	appelez		**j'appellerais**
	(appeliez)	**tu**	**appellerais**
ils/elles	**appellent**	**il**	**appellerait** *etc*

Verbs ending	**-eter**
Change:	**-t** doubles before **-e, -es, -ent** and throughout the Future and Conditional tenses
Tenses affected:	Present, Present Subjunctive, Future, Conditional
Model:	**jeter** *to throw* → ☐1

◆   EXCEPTIONS: **acheter** *to buy*
         haleter *to pant* } like **mener** (*see below*)

Verbs ending	**-yer**
Change:	**y** changes to **i** before **-e, -es, -ent** and throughout the Future and Conditional tenses
Tenses affected:	Present, Present Subjunctive, Future, Conditional
Model:	**essuyer** *to wipe* → ☐2

◆   The change described is optional for verbs ending in **-ayer** e.g. **payer** *to pay*, **essayer** *to try*.

Verbs like:	**mener, peser, lever** etc
Change:	**e** changes to **è** before **-e, -es, -ent** and throughout the Future and Conditional tenses
Tenses affected:	Present, Present Subjunctive, Future, Conditional
Model:	**mener** *to lead* → ☐3

Verbs like:	**céder, régler, espérer** etc
Change:	**é** changes to **è** before **-e, -es, -ent**
Tenses affected:	Present, Present Subjunctive
Model:	**céder** *to yield* → ☐4

	PRESENT (+ SUBJUNCTIVE)	FUTURE	
1			
je	**jette**	**je**	**jetterai**
tu	**jettes**	**tu**	**jetteras**
il/elle	**jette**	**il**	**jettera** *etc*
nous	jetons		
	(jetions)	**CONDITIONAL**	
vous	jetez	**je**	**jetterais**
	(jetiez)	**tu**	**jetterais**
ils/elles	**jettent**	**il**	**jetterait** *etc*

	PRESENT (+ SUBJUNCTIVE)	FUTURE	
2			
	j'essuie		**j'essuierai**
tu	**essuies**	**tu**	**essuieras**
il/elle	**essuie**	**il**	**essuiera** *etc*
nous	essuyons		
	(essuyions)	**CONDITIONAL**	
vous	essuyez		**j'essuierais**
	(essuyiez)	**tu**	**essuierais**
ils/elles	**essuient**	**il**	**essuierait** *etc*

	PRESENT (+ SUBJUNCTIVE)	FUTURE	
3			
je	**mène**	**je**	**mènerai**
tu	**mènes**	**tu**	**mèneras**
il/elle	**mène**	**il**	**mènera** *etc*
nous	menons		
	(menions)	**CONDITIONAL**	
vous	menez	**je**	**mènerais**
	(meniez)	**tu**	**mènerais**
ils/elles	**mènent**	**il**	**mènerait** *etc*

	PRESENT (+ SUBJUNCTIVE)
4	
je	**cède**
tu	**cèdes**
il/elle	**cède**
nous	cédons
	(cédions)
vous	cédez
	(cédiez)
ils/elles	**cèdent**

☐ The Imperative

The imperative is the form of the verb used to give commands or orders. It can be used politely, as in English 'Shut the door, please'.

The imperative is the same as the present tense **tu, nous** and **vous** forms without the subject pronouns:

donne*	**finis**	**vends**
give	*finish*	*sell*

*The final 's' of the present tense of first conjugation verbs is dropped, except before **y** and **en** → [1]

donnons	**finissons**	**vendons**
let's give	*let's finish*	*let's sell*

donnez	**finissez**	**vendez**
give	*finish*	*sell*

◆ The imperative of irregular verbs is given in the verb tables, pp 50 ff.

◆ Position of object pronouns with the imperative:
in POSITIVE commands: they follow the verb and are attached to it by hyphens → [2]
in NEGATIVE commands: they precede the verb and are not attached to it → [3]

◆ For the order of object pronouns, see p 102.

◆ For reflexive verbs – e.g. **se lever** *to get up* – the object pronoun is the reflexive pronoun → [4]

1 Compare: **Tu donnes de l'argent à Paul**
              You give (some) money to Paul
   and: **Donne de l'argent à Paul**
              Give (some) money to Paul

2 **Excusez-moi**   **Envoyons-les-leur**
   Excuse me   Let's send them to them
   Crois-nous   **Expliquez-le-moi**
   Believe us   Explain it to me
   Attendons-la   **Rends-la-lui**
   Let's wait for her/it   Give it back to him/her

3 **Ne me dérange pas**   **Ne leur en parlons pas**
   Don't disturb me   Let's not speak to them about it
   Ne les négligeons pas   **N'y pense plus**
   Let's not neglect them   Don't think about it any more
   Ne leur répondez pas   **Ne la lui rends pas**
   Don't answer them   Don't give it back to him/her

4 **Lève-toi**   **Ne te lève pas**
   Get up   Don't get up
   Dépêchons-nous   **Ne nous affolons pas**
   Let's hurry   Let's not panic
   Levez-vous   **Ne vous levez pas**
   Get up   Don't get up

❏ Compound Tenses: Formation of Regular Verbs

Compound tenses consist of the past participle of the verb together with an auxiliary verb. Most verbs take the auxiliary **avoir,** but some take **être** (see p 22).

Compound tenses are formed in exactly the same way for both regular and irregular verbs, the only difference being that irregular verbs may have an irregular past participle. The past participle of irregular verbs is given for each verb in the verb tables, pp 50 ff.

The past participle

For all compound tenses you need to know how to form the past participle of the verb. For regular verbs this is as follows:

◆ 1st conjugation: replace the **-er** of the infinitive by **-é**:

> **donner** → **donné**
> to give → given

◆ 2nd conjugation: replace the **-ir** of the infinitive by **-i**:

> **finir** → **fini**
> to finish → finished

◆ 3rd conjugation: replace the **-re** of the infinitive by **-u**:

> **vendre** → **vendu**
> to sell → sold

◆ See p 40 for agreement of past participles.

❏ **Compound Tenses** (Continued)

Perfect tense: the present tense of **avoir** or **être** plus the past participle → ① (see pp 20–21)

Pluperfect tense: the imperfect tense of **avoir** or **être** plus the past participle → ② (see pp 20–21)

Future Perfect: the future tense of **avoir** or **être** plus the past participle → ③ (see pp 20–21)

Conditional Perfect: the conditional of **avoir** or **être** plus the past participle → ④ (see pp 20–21)

Perfect Subjunctive: the present subjunctive of **avoir** or **être** plus the past participle → ⑤ (see pp 20–21)

- ◆ Examples of a verb that takes **avoir** and one that takes **être** are conjugated on pp 20 and 21.

- ◆ For a list of verbs and verb types that take the auxiliary **être,** see p 22.

1 PERFECT

j'ai donné	**nous avons donné**
tu as donné	**vous avez donné**
il/elle a donné	**ils/elles ont donné**

I gave, have given *etc*

2 PLUPERFECT

j'avais donné	**nous avions donné**
tu avais donné	**vous aviez donné**
il/elle avait donné	**ils/elles avaient donné**

I had given *etc*

3 FUTURE PERFECT

j'aurai donné	**nous aurons donné**
tu auras donné	**vous aurez donné**
il/elle aura donné	**ils/elles auront donné**

I shall have given *etc*

4 CONDITIONAL PERFECT

j'aurais donné	**nous aurions donné**
tu aurais donné	**vous auriez donné**
il/elle aurait donné	**ils/elles auraient donné**

I should/would have given *etc*

5 PERFECT SUBJUNCTIVE

j'aie donné	**nous ayons donné**
tu aies donné	**vous ayez donné**
il/elle ait donné	**ils/elles aient donné**

I gave/have given *etc*

EXAMPLES

---

1 PERFECT

je suis tombé(e)	**nous sommes tombé(e)s**
tu es tombé(e)	**vous êtes tombé(e)(s)**
il est tombé	**ils sont tombés**
elle est tombée	**elles sont tombées**

I fell, have fallen *etc*

2 PLUPERFECT

j'étais tombé(e)	**nous étions tombé(e)s**
tu étais tombé(e)	**vous étiez tombé(e)(s)**
il était tombé	**ils étaient tombés**
elle était tombée	**elles étaient tombées**

I had fallen *etc*

3 FUTURE PERFECT

je serai tombé(e)	**nous serons tombé(e)s**
tu seras tombé(e)	**vous serez tombé(e)(s)**
il sera tombé	**ils seront tombés**
elle sera tombée	**elles seront tombées**

I shall have fallen *etc*

4 CONDITIONAL PERFECT

je serais tombé(e)	**nous serions tombé(e)s**
tu serais tombé(e)	**vous seriez tombé(e)(s)**
il serait tombé	**ils seraient tombés**
elle serait tombée	**elles seraient tombées**

I should/would have fallen *etc*

5 PERFECT SUBJUNCTIVE

je sois tombé(e)	**nous soyons tombé(e)s**
tu sois tombé(e)	**vous soyez tombé(e)(s)**
il soit tombé	**ils soient tombés**
elle soit tombée	**elles soient tombées**

I fell/have fallen *etc*

❏ Compound Tenses (Continued)

Verbs which take the auxiliary être

◆ Reflexive verbs (see p 24) → ☐1

◆ The following intransitive verbs (i.e. verbs which cannot take a direct object), largely expressing motion or a change of state:

aller	*to go* → ②2	**passer**	*to pass*
arriver	*to arrive; to happen*	**rentrer**	*to go back/in*
descendre	*to go/come down*	**rester**	*to stay* → ⑤5
devenir	*to become*	**retourner**	*to go back*
entrer	*to go/come in*	**revenir**	*to come back*
monter	*to go/come up*	**sortir**	*to go/come out*
mourir	*to die* → ③3	**tomber**	*to fall*
naître	*to be born*	**venir**	*to come* → ⑥6
partir	*to leave* → ④4		

◆ Of these, the following are conjugated with **avoir** when used transitively (i.e. with a direct object):

descendre	*to bring/take down*
entrer	*to bring/take in*
monter	*to bring/take up* → ⑦7
passer	*to pass; to spend* → ⑧8
rentrer	*to bring/take in*
retourner	*to turn over*
sortir	*to bring/take out* → ⑨9

⚠ NOTE that the past participle must show an agreement in number and gender whenever the auxiliary is **être** EXCEPT FOR REFLEXIVE VERBS WHERE THE REFLEXIVE PRONOUN IS THE INDIRECT OBJECT (see p 40).

1. **je me suis arrêté(e)**
I stopped
tu t'es levé(e)
you got up

   elle s'est trompée
she made a mistake
ils s'étaient battus
they had fought (one another)

2. **elle est allée**
she went

3. **ils sont morts**
they died

4. **vous êtes partie**
you left *(addressing a female person)*
vous êtes parties
you left *(addressing more than one female person)*

5. **nous sommes resté(e)s**
we stayed

6. **elles étaient venues**
they *(female)* had come

7. **Il a monté les valises**
He's taken up the cases

8. **Nous avons passé trois semaines chez elle**
We spent three weeks at her place

9. **Avez-vous sorti la voiture?**
Have you taken the car out?

❒ Reflexive Verbs

A reflexive verb is one accompanied by a reflexive pronoun, e.g. **se lever** *to get up;* **se laver** *to wash (oneself).* The pronouns are:

PERSON	SINGULAR	PLURAL
1st	**me (m')**	**nous**
2nd	**te (t')**	**vous**
3rd	**se (s')**	**se (s')**

The forms shown in brackets are used before a vowel, an **h** 'mute', or the pronoun **y** → ①

- In positive commands, **te** changes to **toi** → ②

- The reflexive pronoun 'reflects back' to the subject, but it is not always translated in English → ③

  The plural pronouns are sometimes translated as *one another, each other* (the 'reciprocal' meaning). The reciprocal meaning may be emphasized by **l'un(e) l'autre (les un(e)s les autres)** → ④

- In constructions other than the imperative affirmative the pronoun comes before the verb → ⑤

- In the imperative affirmative, the pronoun follows the verb and is attached to it by a hyphen → ⑥

Past participle agreement

- In most reflexive verbs the reflexive pronoun is a DIRECT object pronoun → ⑦

- When a direct object accompanies the reflexive verb the pronoun is then the INDIRECT object → ⑧

- The past participle of a reflexive verb agrees in number and gender with a direct object which *precedes* the verb (usually, but not always, the reflexive pronoun) → ⑨

  The past participle does not change if the direct object follows the verb → ⑩

1	**Je m'ennuie**	**Ils s'y intéressent**
	I'm bored	They are interested in it
2	**Assieds-toi**	**Tais-toi**
	Sit down	Be quiet
3	**Je me prépare**	**Elle se lève**
	I'm getting (myself) ready	She gets up
4	**Nous nous parlons**	**Ils se ressemblent**
	We speak to each other	They resemble one another

4   **Ils se regardent l'un l'autre**
They are looking at each other

5	**Je me couche tôt**	**Comment vous appelez-vous?**
	I go to bed early	What is your name?
	Il ne s'est pas rasé	**Ne te dérange pas pour nous**
	He hasn't shaved	Don't put yourself out on our account
6	**Renseignons-nous**	**Asseyez-vous**
	Let's find out	Sit down
7	**Je m'appelle**	**Ils se lavent**
	I'm called *(literally: I call myself)*	They wash (themselves)

8   **Elle se lave les mains** *(literally: She's washing to herself the hands)*
She's washing her hands
Nous nous envoyons des cadeaux à Noël
We send presents to each other at Christmas

9   **'Je me suis endormi' s'est-il excusé**
'I fell asleep', he apologized
Pauline s'est dirigée vers la sortie
Pauline made her way towards the exit
Ils se sont levés vers dix heures
They got up around ten o'clock
Elles se sont excusées de leur erreur
They apologized for their mistake

10   **Elle s'est lavé les cheveux**
She (has) washed her hair
Nous nous sommes serré la main
We shook hands

❑ Reflexive Verbs (Continued)

Conjugation of: **se laver** *to wash (oneself)*

I SIMPLE TENSES

Simple tenses of reflexive verbs are conjugated in exactly the same way as those of non-reflexive verbs except that the reflexive pronoun is always used.

PRESENT
je me lave	**nous nous lavons**
tu te laves	**vous vous lavez**
il/elle se lave	**ils/elles se lavent**

IMPERFECT
je me lavais	**nous nous lavions**
tu te lavais	**vous vous laviez**
il/elle se lavait	**ils/elles se lavaient**

FUTURE
je me laverai	**nous nous laverons**
tu te laveras	**vous vous laverez**
il/elle se lavera	**ils/elles se laveront**

CONDITIONAL
je me laverais	**nous nous laverions**
tu te laverais	**vous vous laveriez**
il/elle se laverait	**ils/elles se laveraient**

PAST HISTORIC
je me lavai	**nous nous lavâmes**
tu te lavas	**vous vous lavâtes**
il/elle se lava	**ils/elles se lavèrent**

PRESENT SUBJUNCTIVE
je me lave	**nous nous lavions**
tu te laves	**vous vous laviez**
il/elle se lave	**ils/elles se lavent**

❑ Reflexive Verbs (Continued)

Conjugation of: **se laver** *to wash (oneself)*

II COMPOUND TENSES

Compound tenses of reflexive verbs are formed with the auxiliary **être**.

PERFECT

je me suis lavé(e)	nous nous sommes lavé(e)s
tu t'es lavé(e)	vous vous êtes lavé(e)(s)
il/elle s'est lavé(e)	ils/elles se sont lavé(e)s

PLUPERFECT

je m'étais lavé(e)	nous nous étions lavé(e)s
tu t'étais lavé(e)	vous vous étiez lavé(e)(s)
il/elle s'était lavé(e)	ils/elles s'étaient lavé(e)s

FUTURE PERFECT

je me serai lavé(e)	nous nous serons lavé(e)s
tu te seras lavé(e)	vous vous serez lavé(e)(s)
il/elle se sera lavé(e)	ils/elles se seront lavé(e)s

CONDITIONAL PERFECT

je me serais lavé(e)	nous nous serions lavé(e)s
tu te serais lavé(e)	vous vous seriez lavé(e)(s)
il/elle se serait lavé(e)	ils/elles se seraient lavé(e)s

PERFECT SUBJUNCTIVE

je me sois lavé(e)	nous nous soyons lavé(e)s
tu te sois lavé(e)	vous vous soyez lavé(e)(s)
il/elle se soit lavé(e)	ils/elles se soient lavé(e)s

❏ The Passive

In the passive, the subject *receives* the action (e.g. *I was hit*) as opposed to *performing* it (e.g. *I hit him*). In English the verb 'to be' is used with the past participle. In French the passive is formed in exactly the same way, i.e.:

a tense of **être** + past participle.

The past participle agrees in number and gender with the subject → [1]

A sample verb is conjugated in the passive voice on pp 30 and 31.

◆   The indirect object in French cannot become the subject in the passive:

in **quelqu'un m'a donné un livre** the indirect object **m'** cannot become the subject of a passive verb (unlike English: *someone gave me a book* → *I was given a book*).

◆   The passive meaning is often expressed in French by:

– **on** plus a verb in the active voice → [2]
– a reflexive verb (see p 24) → [3]

1. **Philippe a été récompensé**
Philip has been rewarded

   Cette peinture est très admirée
This painting is greatly admired

   Ils le feront pourvu qu'ils soient payés
They'll do it provided they're paid

   Les enfants seront félicités
The children will be congratulated

   Cette mesure aurait été critiquée si …
This measure would have been criticized if …

   Les portes avaient été fermées
The doors had been closed

2. **On leur a envoyé une lettre**
They were sent a letter

   On nous a montré le jardin
We were shown the garden

   On m'a dit que …
I was told that …

3. **Ils se vendent 30 francs (la) pièce**
They are sold for 30 francs each

   Ce mot ne s'emploie plus
This word is no longer used

❏ The Passive (Continued)

Conjugation of: **être aimé** to *be liked*

PRESENT
je suis aimé(e)
tu es aimé(e)
il/elle est aimé(e)

nous sommes aimé(e)s
vous êtes aimé(e)(s)
ils/elles sont aimé(e)s

IMPERFECT
j'étais aimé(e)
tu étais aimé(e)
il/elle était aimé(e)

nous étions aimé(e)s
vous étiez aimé(e)(s)
ils/elles étaient aimé(e)s

FUTURE
je serai aimé(e)
tu seras aimé(e)
il/elle sera aimé(e)

nous serons aimé(e)s
vous serez aimé(e)(s)
ils/elles seront aimé(e)s

CONDITIONAL
je serais aimé(e)
tu serais aimé(e)
il/elle serait aimé(e)

nous serions aimé(e)s
vous seriez aimé(e)(s)
ils/elles seraient aimé(e)s

PAST HISTORIC
je fus aimé(e)
tu fus aimé(e)
il/elle fut aimé(e)

nous fûmes aimé(e)s
vous fûtes aimé(e)(s)
ils/elles furent aimé(e)s

PRESENT SUBJUNCTIVE
je sois aimé(e)
tu sois aimé(e)
il/elle soit aimé(e)

nous soyons aimé(e)s
vous soyez aimé(e)(s)
ils/elles soient aimé(e)s

❏ The Passive (Continued)

Conjugation of: **être aimé** to *be liked*

PERFECT
j'ai été aimé(e)   **nous avons été aimé(e)s**
tu as été aimé(e)   **vous avez été aimé(e)(s)**
il/elle a été aimé(e)   **ils/elles ont été aimé(e)s**

PLUPERFECT
j'avais été aimé(e)   **nous avions été aimé(e)s**
tu avais été aimé(e)   **vous aviez été aimé(e)(s)**
il/elle avait été aimé(e)   **ils/elles avaient été aimé(e)s**

FUTURE PERFECT
j'aurai été aimé(e)   **nous aurons été aimé(e)s**
tu auras été aimé(e)   **vous aurez été aimé(e)(s)**
il/elle aura été aimé(e)   **ils/elles auront été aimé(e)s**

CONDITIONAL PERFECT
j'aurais été aimé(e)   **nous aurions été aimé(e)s**
tu aurais été aimé(e)   **vous auriez été aimé(e)(s)**
il/elle aurait été aimé(e)   **ils/elles auraient été aimé(e)s**

PERFECT SUBJUNCTIVE
j'aie été aimé(e)   **nous ayons été aimé(e)s**
tu aies été aimé(e)   **vous ayez été aimé(e)(s)**
il/elle ait été aimé(e)   **ils/elles aient été aimé(e)s**

❐ Impersonal Verbs

Impersonal verbs are used only in the infinitive and in the third person singular with the subject pronoun **il**, generally translated *it*.

>e.g. **il pleut**
>*it's raining*
>**il est facile de dire que ...**
>*it's easy to say that ...*

The most common impersonal verbs are:

INFINITIVE	CONSTRUCTIONS
s'agir	**il s'agit de** + noun → ①
	il s'agit de + infinitive → ②
falloir	**il faut** + noun object (+ indirect object) → ③
	il faut + infinitive (+ indirect object) → ④
	il faut que + subjunctive → ⑤
neiger, pleuvoir	**il neige/il pleut** → ⑥
valoir mieux	**il vaut mieux** + infinitive → ⑦
	il vaut mieux que + subjunctive → ⑧

The following are also commonly used in impersonal constructions:

INFINITIVE	CONSTRUCTIONS
avoir	**il y a** + noun → ⑨
être	**il est** + noun → ⑩
	il est + adjective + **de** + infinitive → ⑪
faire	**il fait** + adjective or noun of weather → ⑫
manquer	**il manque** + noun (+ indirect object) → ⑬
paraître	**il paraît que** + subjunctive → ⑭
	il paraît + indirect object + **que** + indicative → ⑮
rester	**il reste** + noun (+ indirect object) → ⑯
sembler	**il semble que** + subjunctive → ⑰
	il semble + indirect object + **que** + indicative → ⑱
suffire	**il suffit de** + infinitive → ⑲
	il suffit de + noun → ⑳

1. **Il ne s'agit pas d'argent**
   It isn't a question/matter of money
2. **Il s'agit de faire vite**
   We must act quickly
3. **Il me faut une chaise de plus**
   I need an extra chair
4. **Il me fallait prendre une décision**
   I had to make a decision
5. **Il faut que vous partiez**
   You have to leave/You must leave
6. **Il neige/Il pleuvait à verse**
   It's snowing/It was raining heavily/It was pouring
7. **Il vaut mieux refuser**
   It's better to refuse; You/He/I had better refuse *(depending on context)*
8. **Il vaudrait mieux que nous ne venions pas**
   It would be better if we didn't come; We'd better not come
9. **Il y a du pain (qui reste)**   **Il n'y avait pas de lettres ce matin**
   There is some bread (left)   There were no letters this morning
10. **Il est dix heures**
    It's ten o'clock
11. **Il était inutile de protester**   **Il est facile de critiquer**
    It was useless to protest   Criticizing is easy
12. **Il fait beau/mauvais**   **Il faisait nuit/du soleil**
    It's lovely/horrible weather   It was dark/sunny
13. **Il manque deux tasses**
    There are two cups missing; Two cups are missing
14. **Il paraît qu'ils partent demain**
    It appears they are leaving tomorrow
15. **Il nous paraît certain qu'il aura du succès**
    It seems certain to us that he'll be successful
16. **Il lui restait cinquante francs**
    He/She had fifty francs left
17. **Il semble que vous ayez raison**
    It seems/appears that you are right
18. **Il me semblait qu'il conduisait trop vite**
    It seemed to me (that) he was driving too fast
19. **Il suffit de téléphoner pour réserver une place**
    You need only phone to reserve a seat
20. **Il suffit d'une seule erreur pour tout gâcher**
    One single error is enough to ruin everything

❏ The Infinitive

The infinitive is the form of the verb found in dictionary entries meaning 'to … ', e.g. **donner** *to give,* **vivre** *to live.*

There are three main types of verbal construction involving the infinitive:

- with the linking preposition **de**
- with the linking preposition **à**
- with no linking preposition

Examples of verbs governing de

s'apercevoir de qch	*to notice sth* → ⬚1
changer de qch	*to change sth* → ⬚2
décider de + infin.	*to decide to* → ⬚3
essayer de + infin.	*to try to do* → ⬚4
finir de + infin.	*to finish doing* → ⬚5
s'occuper de qch/qn	*to look after sth/sb* → ⬚6
oublier de + infin.	*to forget to do* → ⬚7
regretter de + perf. infin.*	*to regret doing, having done* → ⬚8
se souvenir de qn/qch/de + perf. infin.*	*to remember sb/sth/doing, having done* → ⬚9
venir de + infin.	*to have just done* → ⬚10

Examples of verbs governing à

conseiller à qn de + infin.	*to advise sb to do* → ⬚11
défendre à qn de + infin.	*to forbid sb to do* → ⬚12
dire à qn de + infin.	*to tell sb to do* → ⬚13
s'intéresser à qn/qch/à + infin.	*to be interested in sb/sth/in doing* → ⬚14
manquer à qn	*to be missed by sb* → ⬚15
penser à qn/qch	*to think about sb/sth* → ⬚16
réussir à + infin.	*to manage to do* → ⬚17

* The perfect infinitive is formed using the auxiliary verb **avoir** or **être** as appropriate with the past participle of the main verb. It is found after certain verbal constructions and after the preposition **après** *after* → ⬚18

1. **Il ne s'est pas aperçu de son erreur**
He didn't notice his mistake

2. **J'ai changé d'avis**
I changed my mind

3. **Qu'est-ce que vous avez décidé de faire?**
What have you decided to do?

4. **Essayez d'arriver à l'heure**
Try to arrive on time

5. **Avez-vous fini de lire ce journal?**
Have you finished reading this newspaper?

6. **Je m'occupe de ma nièce**
I'm looking after my niece

7. **J'ai oublié d'appeler ma mère**
I forgot to ring my mother

8. **Je regrette de ne pas vous avoir écrit plus tôt**
I'm sorry for not writing to you sooner

9. **Vous vous souvenez de Lucienne?**
Do you remember Lucienne?

10. **Nous venions d'arriver**
We had just arrived

11. **Il leur a conseillé d'attendre**
He advised them to wait

12. **Je leur ai défendu de sortir**
I've forbidden them to go out

13. **Dites-leur de se taire**
Tell them to be quiet

14. **Elle s'intéresse beaucoup au sport**
She's very interested in sport

15. **Tu manques à tes parents**
Your parents miss you

16. **Je pense souvent à toi**
I often think about you

17. **Vous avez réussi à me convaincre**
You've managed to convince me

18. **avoir fini**   **être allé**   **s'être levé**
to have finished   to have gone   to have got up
Après être sorties, elles se sont dirigées vers le parking
After leaving/having left, they headed for the car park

☐ The Infinitive (Continued)

Verbs followed by an infinitive with no linking preposition

- the modal auxiliary verbs:

devoir	*to have to, must* → ①
	to be due to → ②
	in the conditional/conditional perfect:
	should/should have, ought/ought to have → ③
pouvoir	*to be able to, can* → ④
	to be allowed to, can, may → ⑤
	indicating possibility: *may/might/could* → ⑥
savoir	*to know how to, can* → ⑦
vouloir	*to want/wish to* → ⑧
	to be willing to, will → ⑨
	in polite phrases → ⑩
falloir	*to be necessary:* see p 32.

- verbs of seeing or hearing e.g. **voir** *to see*, **entendre** *to hear* → ⑪
- intransitive verbs of motion e.g. **aller** *to go*, **descendre** *to come/go down* → ⑫
- The following common verbs:

adorer	*to love*
aimer	*to like, love*
aimer mieux	*to prefer* → ⑬
compter	*to expect*
désirer	*to wish, want*
détester	*to hate*
envoyer	*to send*
espérer	*to hope*
faillir	→ ⑭
faire	→ ⑮
laisser	*to let, allow* → ⑯
oser	*to dare*
préférer	*to prefer*
sembler	*to seem* → ⑰
souhaiter	*to wish*
valoir mieux	see p 32.

1. **Je dois leur rendre visite**   **Elle a dû partir**
   I must visit them   She (has) had to leave
   Il a dû regretter d'avoir parlé
   He must have been sorry he spoke

2. **Je devais attraper le train de neuf heures mais …**
   I was (supposed) to catch the nine o'clock train but …

3. **Je devrais le faire**   **J'aurais dû m'excuser**
   I ought to do it   I ought to have apologized

4. **Il ne peut pas lever le bras**
   He can't raise his arm

5. **Puis-je les accompagner?**
   May I go with them?

6. **Il peut encore changer d'avis**   **Cela pourrait être vrai**
   He may change his mind yet   It could/might be true

7. **Savez-vous conduire?**
   Can you drive?

8. **Elle veut rester encore un jour**
   She wants to stay another day

9. **Ils ne voulaient pas le faire**
   They wouldn't do it/They weren't willing to do it
   Ma voiture ne veut pas démarrer
   My car won't start

10. **Voulez-vous boire quelque chose?**
    Would you like something to drink?

11. **Il nous a vus arriver**   **On les entend chanter**
    He saw us arriving   You can hear them singing

12. **Allez voir Nicolas**   **Descends leur demander**
    Go and see Nicholas   Go down and ask them

13. **J'aimerais mieux le choisir moi-même**
    I'd rather choose it myself

14. **J'ai failli tomber**
    I almost fell

15. **Ne me faites pas rire!**   **J'ai fait réparer ma valise**
    Don't make me laugh!   I've had my case repaired

16. **Laissez-moi passer**
    Let me pass

17. **Vous semblez être inquiet**
    You seem to be worried

❏ The Present Participle

Formation

- 1st conjugation
  Replace the **-er** of the infinitive by **-ant** → 1

  – Verbs ending in **-cer**: **c** changes to **ç** → 2
  – Verbs ending in **-ger**: **g** changes to **ge** → 3

- 2nd conjugation
  Replace the **-ir** of the infinitive by **-issant** → 4

- 3rd conjugation
  Replace the **-re** of the infinitive by **-ant** → 5

- For irregular present participles, see irregular verbs, pp 50 ff.

Uses

The present participle has a more restricted use in French than in English

- Used as a verbal form, the present participle is invariable. It is found

  – on its own, where it corresponds to the English present participle
  → 6
  – following the preposition **en** → 7

  ⚠ NOTE, in particular, the construction:

  verb + **en** + present participle

  which is often translated by an English phrasal verb, i.e. one
  followed by a preposition like *to run down, to bring up* → 8

- Used as an adjective, the present participle agrees in number and
  gender with the noun or pronoun → 9

  ⚠ NOTE, in particular, the use of **ayant** and **étant** – the present
  participles of the auxiliary verbs **avoir** and **être** – with a past
  participle → 10

1   **donner**   →   **donnant**
      to give   giving

2   **lancer**   →   **lançant**
      to throw   throwing

3   **manger**   →   **mangeant**
      to eat   eating

4   **finir**   →   **finissant**
      to finish   finishing

5   **vendre**   →   **vendant**
      to sell   selling

6   **David, habitant près de Paris, a la possibilité de ...**
      David, living near Paris, has the opportunity of…
      Elle, pensant que je serais fâché, a dit '...'
      She, thinking that I would be angry, said '…'
      Ils m'ont suivi, criant à tue-tête
      They followed me, shouting at the top of their voices

7   **En attendant sa sœur, Richard s'est endormi**
      While waiting for his sister, Richard fell asleep
      Téléphone-nous an arrivant chez toi
      Telephone us when you get home
      En appuyant sur ce bouton, on peut ...
      By pressing this button, you can …
      Il s'est blessé en essayant de sauver un chat
      He hurt himself trying to rescue a cat

8   **sortir en courant**
      to run out *(literally: to go out running)*
      avancer en boîtant
      to limp along *(literally: to go forward limping)*

9   **le soleil couchant**   **une lumière éblouissante**
      the setting sun   a dazzling light
      ils sont déroutants   **elles étaient étonnantes**
      they are disconcerting   they were surprising

10   **Ayant mangé plus tôt, il a pu ...**
      Having eaten earlier, he was able to …
      Étant arrivée en retard, elle a dû ...
      Having arrived late, she had to …

❑ Past Participle Agreement

Like adjectives, a past participle must sometimes agree in number and gender with a noun or pronoun. For the rules of agreement, see below. Example: **donné**

	MASCULINE	FEMININE
SING.	donné	donnée
PLUR.	donnés	données

◆ When the masculine singular form already ends in **-s**, no further **s** is added in the masculine plural, e.g. **pris** *taken*.

Rules of agreement in compound tenses

◆ When the auxiliary verb is **avoir**

The past participle remains in the masculine singular form, unless a direct object precedes the verb. The past participle then agrees in number and gender with the preceding direct object → 1

◆ When the auxiliary verb is **être**

The past participle of a non-reflexive verb agrees in number and gender with the subject → 2

The past participle of a reflexive verb agrees in number and gender with the reflexive pronoun, if the pronoun is a direct object → 3

No agreement is made if the reflexive pronoun is an indirect object → 4

The past participle as an adjective

The past participle agrees in number and gender with the noun or pronoun → 5

[1] **Voici le livre que vous avez demandé**
Here's the book you asked for
Laquelle avaient-elles choisie?
Which one had they chosen?
Ces amis? Je les ai rencontrés à Édimbourg
Those friends? I met them in Edinburgh
Il a gardé toutes les lettres qu'elle a écrites
He has kept all the letters she wrote

[2] **Est-ce que ton frère est allé à l'étranger?**
Did your brother go abroad?
Elle était restée chez elle
She had stayed at home
Ils sont partis dans la matinée
They left in the morning
Mes cousines sont revenues hier
My cousins came back yesterday

[3] **Tu t'es rappelé d'acheter du pain, Georges?**
Did you remember to buy bread, George?
Martine s'est demandée pourquoi il l'appelait
Martine wondered why he was calling her
'Lui et moi nous nous sommes cachés' a-t-elle dit
'He and I hid,' she said
Les vendeuses se sont mises en grève
Shop assistants have gone on strike
Vous vous êtes brouillés?
Have you fallen out with each other?
Les ouvrières s'étaient entraidées
The workers had helped one another

[4] **Elle s'est lavé les mains**
She washed her hands
Ils se sont parlé pendant des heures
They talked to each other for hours

[5] **à un moment donné**   **la porte ouverte**
at a certain point   the open door
ils sont bien connus   **elles semblent fatiguées**
they are well-known   they seem tired

❐ Use of Tenses

The present

◆ Unlike English, French does not distinguish between the simple present (e.g. *I smoke, he reads, we live*) and the continuous present (e.g. *I am smoking, he is reading, we are living*) → ①

◆ To emphasize continuity, the following constructions may be used:

être en train de faire } *to be doing* → ②
être à faire

◆ French uses the present tense where English uses the perfect in the following cases:

   – with certain prepositions of time – notably **depuis** *for/since* – when an action begun in the past is continued in the present → ③
   Note, however, that the perfect is used as in English when the verb is negative or the action has been completed → ④

   – in the construction **venir de faire** *to have just done* → ⑤

The future

The future is generally used as in English, but note the following:

◆ Immediate future time is often expressed by means of the present tense of **aller** plus an infinitive → ⑥

◆ In time clauses expressing future action, French uses the future where English uses the present → ⑦

The future perfect

◆ Used as in English to mean *shall/will have done* → ⑧

◆ In time clauses expressing future action, where English uses the perfect tense → ⑨

1. **Je fume**
   I smoke OR I am smoking
   Il lit
   He reads OR He is reading
   Nous habitons
   We live OR We are living
2. **Il est en train de travailler**
   He's (busy) working
3. **Paul apprend à nager depuis six mois**
   Paul's been learning to swim for six months *(and still is)*
   Je suis debout depuis sept heures
   I've been up since seven
   Il y a longtemps que vous attendez?
   Have you been waiting long?
   Voilà deux semaines que nous sommes ici
   That's two weeks we've been here (now)
4. **Ils ne se sont pas vus depuis des mois**
   They haven't seen each other for months
   Elle est revenue il y a un an
   She came back a year ago
5. **Élisabeth vient de partir**
   Elizabeth has just left
6. **Tu vas tomber si tu ne fais pas attention**
   You'll fall if you're not careful
   Il va manquer le train
   He's going to miss the train
   Ça va prendre une demi-heure
   It'll take half an hour
7. **Quand il viendra vous serez en vacances**
   When he comes you'll be on holiday
   Faites-nous savoir aussitôt qu'elle arrivera
   Let us know as soon as she arrives
8. **J'aurai fini dans une heure**
   I shall have finished in an hour
9. **Quand tu auras lu ce roman, rends-le-moi**
   When you've read the novel, give it back to me
   Je partirai dès que j'aurai fini
   I'll leave as soon as I've finished

☐ Use of Tenses (Continued)

The imperfect

◆ The imperfect describes:
 – an action (or state) in the past without definite limits in time → ①
 – habitual action(s) in the past (often translated by means of *would* or *used to*) → ②

◆ French uses the imperfect tense where English uses the pluperfect in the following cases:
 – with certain prepositions of time – notably **depuis** *for/since* – when an action begun in the remoter past was continued in the more recent past → ③
 Note, however, that the pluperfect is used as in English, when the verb is negative or the action has been completed → ④
 – in the construction **venir de faire** *to have just done* → ⑤

The perfect

◆ The perfect is used to recount a completed action or event in the past. Note that this corresponds to a perfect tense or a simple past tense in English → ⑥

The past historic

◆ Only ever used in *written, literary* French, the past historic recounts a completed action in the past, corresponding to a simple past tense in English → ⑦

The subjunctive

◆ In spoken French, the present subjunctive generally replaces the imperfect subjunctive. See also pp 46 ff.

1. **Elle regardait par la fenêtre**
   She was looking out of the window
   Il pleuvait quand je suis sorti de chez moi
   It was raining when I left the house
   Nos chambres donnaient sur la plage
   Our rooms overlooked the beach

2. **Dans sa jeunesse, il se levait à l'aube**
   In his youth he got up at dawn
   Nous causions des heures entières
   We would talk for hours on end
   Elle te taquinait, n'est-ce pas?
   She used to tease you, didn't she?

3. **Nous habitions à Londres depuis deux ans**
   We had been living in London for two years *(and still were)*
   Il était malade depuis 1985
   He had been ill since 1985
   Il y avait assez longtemps qu'il le faisait
   He had been doing it for quite a long time

4. **Voilà un an que je ne l'avais pas vu**
   I hadn't seen him for a year
   Il y avait une heure qu'elle était arrivée
   She had arrived one hour before

5. **Je venais de les rencontrer**
   I had just met them

6. **Nous sommes allés au bord de la mer**
   We went/have been to the seaside
   Il a refusé de nous aider
   He (has) refused to help us
   La voiture ne s'est pas arrêtée
   The car didn't stop/hasn't stopped

7. **Le roi mourut en 1592**
   The king died in 1592

❐ The subjunctive: when to use it

(For how to form the subjunctive see pp 6 ff.)

◆ After certain conjunctions

quoique **bien que**	*although* → ①
pour que **afin que**	*so that* → ②
pourvu que	*provided that* → ③
jusqu'à ce que	*until* → ④
avant que (... ne)	*before* → ⑤
à moins que (... ne)	*unless* → ⑥
de peur que (... ne) **de crainte que (... ne)**	*for fear that, lest* → ⑦
de sorte que **de façon que** **de manière que**	*so that* (indicating a *purpose*; when they introduce a *result* the indicative is used) → ⑧

⚠ NOTE that **ne** in examples ⑤ to ⑦ has no translation value. It is often omitted in spoken informal French.

◆ After impersonal constructions which express necessity, possibility etc

il faut que **il est nécessaire que**	*it is necessary that* → ⑨
il est possible que	*it is possible that* → ⑩
il semble que	*it seems that* → ⑪
il vaut mieux que	*it is better that* → ⑫
il est dommage que	*it's a pity that* → ⑬

◆ After a superlative → ⑭

◆ After certain adjectives expressing some sort of 'uniqueness'

dernier ... qui/que	*last ... who/that*
premier ... qui/que	*first ... who/that*
meilleur ... qui/que	*best ... who/that* → ⑮
seul **unique** **... qui/que**	*only ... who/that*

◆ In set expressions → ⑯

1. **Bien qu'il fasse beaucoup d'efforts, il est peu récompensé**
   Although he makes a lot of effort, he isn't rewarded for it
2. **Demandez un reçu afin que vous puissiez être remboursé**
   Ask for a receipt so that you can get a refund
3. **Nous partirons ensemble pourvu que Sylvie soit d'accord**
   We'll leave together provided Sylvie agrees
4. **Reste ici jusqu'à ce que nous revenions**
   Stay here until we come back
5. **Je le ferai avant que tu ne partes**
   I'll do it before you leave
6. **Ce doit être Paul, à moins que je ne me trompe**
   That must be Paul, unless I'm mistaken
7. **Parlez bas de peur qu'on ne vous entende**
   Speak softly lest anyone hears you
8. **Retournez-vous de sorte que je vous voie**
   Turn round so that I can see you
9. **Il faut que je vous parle immédiatement**
   I must speak to you right away/It is necessary that I speak …
10. **Il est possible qu'ils aient raison**
    They may be right/It's possible that they are right
11. **Il semble qu'elle ne soit pas venue**
    It appears that she hasn't come
12. **Il vaut mieux que vous restiez chez vous**
    It's better that you stay at home
13. **Il est dommage qu'elle ait perdu cette adresse**
    It's a shame/a pity that she's lost the address
14. **la personne la plus sympathique que je connaisse**
    the nicest person I know
    l'article le moins cher que j'aie jamais acheté
    the cheapest item I have ever bought
15. **Voici la dernière lettre qu'elle m'ait écrite**
    This is the last letter she wrote to me
    David est la seule personne qui puisse me conseiller
    David is the only person who can advise me
16. **Vive le roi!**   **Que Dieu vous bénisse!**
    Long live the king!   God bless you!

☐ The subjunctive: when to use it (Continued)

◆ After verbs of:
  – 'wishing'
    vouloir que
    désirer que   *to wish that, want →* ⬚1
    souhaiter que

  – 'fearing'
    craindre que   *to be afraid that →* ⬚2
    avoir peur que

  ⚠ NOTE that **ne** in example ⬚2 has no translation value. It is often omitted in spoken informal French.

  – 'ordering', 'forbidding', 'allowing'
    ordonner que   *to order that*
    défendre que   *to forbid that*
    permettre que   *to allow that →* ⬚3

  – opinion, expressing uncertainty
    croire que
    penser que   *to think that →* ⬚4
    douter que   *to doubt that*

  – emotion (e.g. regret, shame, pleasure)
    regretter que *to be sorry that →* ⬚5
    être content/surpris etc **que** *to be pleased/surprised etc that →* ⬚6

◆ After   **si (...) que**   *however*   → ⬚7
                 qui que   *whoever*   → ⬚8
                 quoi que   *whatever*   → ⬚9

◆ After **que** in the following:
  – to form the 3rd person imperative or to express a wish → ⬚10
  – when **que** has the meaning *if*, replacing **si** in a clause → ⬚11
  – when **que** has the meaning *whether* → ⬚12

◆ In relative clauses following certain types of indefinite and negative construction → ⬚13

1. **Nous voulons qu'elle soit contente**
   We want her to be happy *(literally: We want that she is happy)*

2. **Il craint qu'il ne soit trop tard**
   He's afraid it may be too late

3. **Permettez que nous vous aidions**
   Allow us to help you

4. **Je ne pense pas qu'ils soient venus**
   I don't think they came

5. **Je regrette que vous ne puissiez pas venir**
   I'm sorry that you cannot come

6. **Je suis content que vous les aimiez**
   I'm pleased that you like them

7. **si courageux qu'il soit**   **si peu que ce soit**
   however brave he may be   however little it is

8. **Qui que vous soyez, allez-vous-en!**
   Whoever you are, go away!

9. **Quoi que nous fassions, …**
   Whatever we do, …

10. **Qu'il entre!**   **Que cela vous serve de leçon!**
    Let him come in!   Let that be a lesson to you!

11. **S'il fait beau et que tu te sentes mieux, nous irons …**
    If it's nice and you're feeling better, we'll go …

12. **Que tu viennes ou non, je …**
    Whether you come or not, I …

13. **Il cherche une maison qui ait deux caves**
    He's looking for a house which has two cellars
    (subjunctive used since such a house may or may not exist)
    J'ai besoin d'un livre qui décrive l'art du mime
    I need a book which describes the art of mime
    (subjunctive used since such a book may or may not exist)

    Je n'ai rencontré personne qui la connaisse
    I haven't met anyone who knows her

❏ Irregular Verb Tables

The verbs on the following pages provide the main patterns for irregular verbs. They are given in their most common simple tenses, together with the imperative and the present participle. The auxiliary (*avoir* or *être*) is also shown, together with the past participle, to enable you to form the compound tenses (see pp 18ff). *Falloir* and *pleuvoir*, which are only used in the 'il' form, are given below. The rest follow in alphabetical order.

falloir *to be necessary* // **pleuvoir** *to rain*		Auxiliary: **avoir**
PAST PARTICIPLE	PRESENT PARTICIPLE	IMPERATIVE
fallu // **plu**	*not used* // **pleuvant**	*not used*
PRESENT	FUTURE	IMPERFECT
il **faut** // il **pleut**	il **faudra** // il **pleuvra**	il **fallait** // il **pleuvait**
PRESENT SUBJUNCTIVE	CONDITIONAL	PAST HISTORIC
il **faille** // il **pleuve**	il **faudrait** // il **pleuvrait**	il **fallut** // il **plut**

acquérir *to acquire*		Auxiliary: **avoir**
PAST PARTICIPLE	PRESENT PARTICIPLE	IMPERATIVE
acquis	**acquérant**	**acquiers** **acquérons** **acquérez**

PRESENT	FUTURE	IMPERFECT
j'**acquiers**	j'**acquerrai**	j'**acquérais**
tu **acquiers**	tu **acquerras**	tu **acquérais**
il **acquiert**	il **acquerra**	il **acquérait**
nous **acquérons**	nous **acquerrons**	nous **acquérions**
vous **acquérez**	vous **acquerrez**	vous **acquériez**
ils **acquièrent**	ils **acquerront**	ils **acquéraient**
PRESENT SUBJUNCTIVE	CONDITIONAL	PAST HISTORIC
j'**acquière**	j'**acquerrais**	j'**acquis**
tu **acquières**	tu **acquerrais**	tu **acquis**
il **acquière**	il **acquerrait**	il **acquit**
nous **acquérions**	nous **acquerrions**	nous **acquîmes**
vous **acquériez**	vous **acquerriez**	vous **acquîtes**
ils **acquièrent**	ils **acquerraient**	ils **acquirent**

aller *to go* Auxiliary: être

PAST PARTICIPLE	PRESENT PARTICIPLE	IMPERATIVE
allé	allant	**va** allons allez

PRESENT	FUTURE	IMPERFECT
je vais **tu vas** **il va** nous allons vous allez **ils vont**	**j'irai** **tu iras** **il ira** **nous irons** **vous irez** **ils iront**	j'allais tu allais il allait nous allions vous alliez ils allaient

PRESENT SUBJUNCTIVE	CONDITIONAL	PAST HISTORIC
j'aille **tu ailles** **il aille** nous allions vous alliez **ils aillent**	**j'irais** **tu irais** **il irait** **nous irions** **vous iriez** **ils iraient**	j'allai tu allas il alla nous allâmes vous allâtes ils allèrent

s'asseoir *to sit down* Auxiliary: être

PAST PARTICIPLE	PRESENT PARTICIPLE	IMPERATIVE
assis	**s'asseyant**	**assieds-toi** **asseyons-nous** **asseyez-vous**

PRESENT	FUTURE	IMPERFECT
je m'assieds *or* **assois** **tu t'assieds** *or* **assois** **il s'assied** *or* **assoit** **nous nous asseyons** *or* **assoyons** **vous vous asseyez** *or* **assoyez** **ils s'asseyent** *or* **assoient**	**je m'assiérai** **tu t'assiéras** **il s'assiéra** **nous nous assiérons** **vous vous assiérez** **ils s'assiéront**	**je m'asseyais** **tu t'asseyais** **il s'asseyait** **nous nous asseyions** **vous vous asseyiez** **ils s'asseyaient**

PRESENT SUBJUNCTIVE	CONDITIONAL	PAST HISTORIC
je m'asseye **tu t'asseyes** **il s'asseye** **nous nous asseyions** **vous vous asseyiez** **ils s'asseyent**	**je m'assiérais** **tu t'assiérais** **il s'assiérait** **nous nous assiérions** **vous vous assiériez** **ils s'assiéraient**	**je m'assis** **tu t'assis** **il s'assit** **nous nous assîmes** **vous vous assîtes** **ils s'assirent**

avoir *to have* — Auxiliary: *avoir*

PAST PARTICIPLE	PRESENT PARTICIPLE	IMPERATIVE
eu	ayant	aie
		ayons
		ayez

PRESENT	FUTURE	IMPERFECT
j'ai	j'aurai	j'avais
tu as	tu auras	tu avais
il a	il aura	il avait
nous avons	nous aurons	nous avions
vous avez	vous aurez	vous aviez
ils ont	ils auront	ils avaient

PRESENT SUBJUNCTIVE	CONDITIONAL	PAST HISTORIC
j'aie	j'aurais	j'eus
tu aies	tu aurais	tu eus
il ait	il aurait	il eut
nous ayons	nous aurions	nous eûmes
vous ayez	vous auriez	vous eûtes
ils aient	ils auraient	ils eurent

battre *to beat* — Auxiliary: *avoir*

PAST PARTICIPLE	PRESENT PARTICIPLE	IMPERATIVE
battu	battant	bats
		battons
		battez

PRESENT	FUTURE	IMPERFECT
je bats	je battrai	je battais
tu bats	tu battras	tu battais
il bat	il battra	il battait
nous battons	nous battrons	nous battions
vous battez	vous battrez	vous battiez
ils battent	ils battront	ils battaient

PRESENT SUBJUNCTIVE	CONDITIONAL	PAST HISTORIC
je batte	je battrais	je battis
tu battes	tu battrais	tu battis
il batte	il battrait	il battit
nous battions	nous battrions	nous battîmes
vous battiez	vous battriez	vous battîtes
ils battent	ils battraient	ils battirent

boire *to drink* — Auxiliary: avoir

PAST PARTICIPLE	PRESENT PARTICIPLE	IMPERATIVE
bu	**buvant**	bois
		buvons
		buvez

PRESENT	FUTURE	IMPERFECT
je bois	je boirai	**je buvais**
tu bois	tu boiras	**tu buvais**
il boit	il boira	**il buvait**
nous buvons	nous boirons	**nous buvions**
vous buvez	vous boirez	**vous buviez**
ils boivent	ils boiront	**ils buvaient**

PRESENT SUBJUNCTIVE	CONDITIONAL	PAST HISTORIC
je boive	je boirais	**je bus**
tu boives	tu boirais	**tu bus**
il boive	il boirait	**il but**
nous buvions	nous boirions	**nous bûmes**
vous buviez	vous boiriez	**vous bûtes**
ils boivent	ils boiraient	**ils burent**

connaître *to know* — Auxiliary: avoir

PAST PARTICIPLE	PRESENT PARTICIPLE	IMPERATIVE
connu	**connaissant**	**connais**
		connaissons
		connaissez

PRESENT	FUTURE	IMPERFECT
je connais	je connaîtrai	**je connaissais**
tu connais	tu connaîtras	**tu connaissais**
il connaît	il connaîtra	**il connaissait**
nous connaissons	nous connaîtrons	**nous connaissions**
vous connaissez	vous connaîtrez	**vous connaissiez**
ils connaissent	ils connaîtront	**ils connaissaient**

PRESENT SUBJUNCTIVE	CONDITIONAL	PAST HISTORIC
je connaisse	je connaîtrais	**je connus**
tu connaisses	tu connaîtrais	**tu connus**
il connaisse	il connaîtrait	**il connut**
nous connaissions	nous connaîtrions	**nous connûmes**
vous connaissiez	vous connaîtriez	**vous connûtes**
ils connaissent	ils connaîtraient	**ils connurent**

coudre to sew — Auxiliary: avoir

PAST PARTICIPLE	PRESENT PARTICIPLE	IMPERATIVE
cousu	cousant	couds
		cousons
		cousez

PRESENT	FUTURE	IMPERFECT
je couds	je coudrai	je cousais
tu couds	tu coudras	tu cousais
il coud	il coudra	il cousait
nous cousons	nous coudrons	nous cousions
vous cousez	vous coudrez	vous cousiez
ils cousent	ils coudront	ils cousaient

PRESENT SUBJUNCTIVE	CONDITIONAL	PAST HISTORIC
je couse	je coudrais	je cousis
tu couses	tu coudrais	tu cousis
il couse	il coudrait	il cousit
nous cousions	nous coudrions	nous cousîmes
vous cousiez	vous coudriez	vous cousîtes
ils cousent	ils coudraient	ils cousirent

courir to run — Auxiliary: avoir

PAST PARTICIPLE	PRESENT PARTICIPLE	IMPERATIVE
couru	courant	cours
		courons
		courez

PRESENT	FUTURE	IMPERFECT
je cours	je courrai	je courais
tu cours	tu courras	tu courais
il court	il courra	il courait
nous courons	nous courrons	nous courions
vous courez	vous courrez	vous couriez
ils courent	ils courront	ils couraient

PRESENT SUBJUNCTIVE	CONDITIONAL	PAST HISTORIC
je coure	je courrais	je courus
tu coures	tu courrais	tu courus
il coure	il courrait	il courut
nous courions	nous courrions	nous courûmes
vous couriez	vous courriez	vous courûtes
ils courent	ils courraient	ils coururent

craindre to fear   Auxiliary: avoir

PAST PARTICIPLE	PRESENT PARTICIPLE	IMPERATIVE
craint	craignant	crains
		craignons
		craignez

PRESENT	FUTURE	IMPERFECT
je crains	je craindrai	je craignais
tu crains	tu craindras	tu craignais
il craint	il craindra	il craignait
nous craignons	nous craindrons	nous craignions
vous craignez	vous craindrez	vous craigniez
ils craignent	ils craindront	ils craignaient

PRESENT SUBJUNCTIVE	CONDITIONAL	PAST HISTORIC
je craigne	je craindrais	je craignis
tu craignes	tu craindrais	tu craignis
il craigne	il craindrait	il craignit
nous craignions	nous craindrions	nous craignîmes
vous craigniez	vous craindriez	vous craignîtes
ils craignent	ils craindraient	ils craignirent

Verbs ending in **-eindre** and **-oindre** are conjugated similarly

....

croire to believe   Auxiliary: avoir

PAST PARTICIPLE	PRESENT PARTICIPLE	IMPERATIVE
cru	croyant	crois
		croyons
		croyez

PRESENT	FUTURE	IMPERFECT
je crois	je croirai	je croyais
tu crois	tu croiras	tu croyais
il croit	il croira	il croyait
nous croyons	nous croirons	nous croyions
vous croyez	vous croirez	vous croyiez
ils croient	ils croiront	ils croyaient

PRESENT SUBJUNCTIVE	CONDITIONAL	PAST HISTORIC
je croie	je croirais	je crus
tu croies	tu croirais	tu crus
il croie	il croirait	il crut
nous croyions	nous croirions	nous crûmes
vous croyiez	vous croiriez	vous crûtes
ils croient	ils croiraient	ils crurent

croître to grow — Auxiliary: avoir

PAST PARTICIPLE	PRESENT PARTICIPLE	IMPERATIVE
crû	**croissant**	**crois**
		croissons
		croissez

PRESENT	FUTURE	IMPERFECT
je croîs	je croîtrai	**je croissais**
tu croîs	tu croîtras	**tu croissais**
il croît	il croîtra	**il croissait**
nous croissons	nous croîtrons	**nous croissions**
vous croissez	vous croîtrez	**vous croissiez**
ils croissent	ils croîtront	**ils croissaient**

PRESENT SUBJUNCTIVE	CONDITIONAL	PAST HISTORIC
je croisse	je croîtrais	**je crûs**
tu croisses	tu croîtrais	**tu crûs**
il croisse	il croîtrait	**il crût**
nous croissions	nous croîtrions	**nous crûmes**
vous croissiez	vous croîtriez	**vous crûtes**
ils croissent	ils croîtraient	**ils crûrent**

cueillir to pick — Auxiliary: avoir

PAST PARTICIPLE	PRESENT PARTICIPLE	IMPERATIVE
cueilli	**cueillant**	**cueille**
		cueillons
		cueillez

PRESENT	FUTURE	IMPERFECT
je cueille	**je cueillerai**	**je cueillais**
tu cueilles	**tu cueilleras**	**tu cueillais**
il cueille	**il cueillera**	**il cueillait**
nous cueillons	**nous cueillerons**	**nous cueillions**
vous cueillez	**vous cueillerez**	**vous cueilliez**
ils cueillent	**ils cueilleront**	**ils cueillaient**

PRESENT SUBJUNCTIVE	CONDITIONAL	PAST HISTORIC
je cueille	**je cueillerais**	je cueillis
tu cueilles	**tu cueillerais**	tu cueillis
il cueille	**il cueillerait**	il cueillit
nous cueillions	**nous cueillerions**	nous cueillîmes
vous cueilliez	**vous cueilleriez**	vous cueillîtes
ils cueillent	**ils cueilleraient**	ils cueillirent

cuire to cook		Auxiliary: avoir
PAST PARTICIPLE	PRESENT PARTICIPLE	IMPERATIVE
cuit	cuisant	cuis
		cuisons
		cuisez

PRESENT	FUTURE	IMPERFECT
je cuis	je cuirai	je cuisais
tu cuis	tu cuiras	tu cuisais
il cuit	il cuira	il cuisait
nous cuisons	nous cuirons	nous cuisions
vous cuisez	vous cuirez	vous cuisiez
ils cuisent	ils cuiront	ils cuisaient
PRESENT SUBJUNCTIVE	CONDITIONAL	PAST HISTORIC
je cuise	je cuirais	je cuisis
tu cuises	tu cuirais	tu cuisis
il cuise	il cuirait	il cuisit
nous cuisions	nous cuirions	nous cuisîmes
vous cuisiez	vous cuiriez	vous cuisîtes
ils cuisent	ils cuiraient	ils cuisirent

nuire *to harm*, conjugated similarly, but past participle **nui**

devoir to have to; to owe		Auxiliary: avoir
PAST PARTICIPLE	PRESENT PARTICIPLE	IMPERATIVE
dû, due	devant	dois
		devons
		devez

PRESENT	FUTURE	IMPERFECT
je dois	je devrai	je devais
tu dois	tu devras	tu devais
il doit	il devra	il devait
nous devons	nous devrons	nous devions
vous devez	vous devrez	vous deviez
ils doivent	ils devront	ils devaient
PRESENT SUBJUNCTIVE	CONDITIONAL	PAST HISTORIC
je doive	je devrais	je dus
tu doives	tu devrais	tu dus
il doive	il devrait	il dut
nous devions	nous devrions	nous dûmes
vous deviez	vous devriez	vous dûtes
ils doivent	ils devraient	ils durent

dire *to say, tell* — Auxiliary: avoir

PAST PARTICIPLE	PRESENT PARTICIPLE	IMPERATIVE
dit	**disant**	dis
		disons
		dites

PRESENT	FUTURE	IMPERFECT
je dis	je dirai	**je disais**
tu dis	tu diras	**tu disais**
il dit	il dira	**il disait**
nous disons	nous dirons	**nous disions**
vous dites	vous direz	**vous disiez**
ils disent	ils diront	**ils disaient**

PRESENT SUBJUNCTIVE	CONDITIONAL	PAST HISTORIC
je dise	je dirais	**je dis**
tu dises	tu dirais	**tu dis**
il dise	il dirait	**il dit**
nous disions	nous dirions	**nous dîmes**
vous disiez	vous diriez	**vous dîtes**
ils disent	ils diraient	**ils dirent**

interdire *to forbid,* conjugated similarly, but 2nd person plural of the present tense is **vous interdisez**

dormir *to sleep* — Auxiliary: avoir

PAST PARTICIPLE	PRESENT PARTICIPLE	IMPERATIVE
dormi	**dormant**	**dors**
		dormons
		dormez

PRESENT	FUTURE	IMPERFECT
je dors	je dormirai	**je dormais**
tu dors	tu dormiras	**tu dormais**
il dort	il dormira	**il dormait**
nous dormons	nous dormirons	**nous dormions**
vous dormez	vous dormirez	**vous dormiez**
ils dorment	ils dormiront	**ils dormaient**

PRESENT SUBJUNCTIVE	CONDITIONAL	PAST HISTORIC
je dorme	je dormirais	je dormis
tu dormes	tu dormirais	tu dormis
il dorme	il dormirait	il dormit
nous dormions	nous dormirions	nous dormîmes
vous dormiez	vous dormiriez	vous dormîtes
ils dorment	ils dormiraient	ils dormirent

écrire to write   Auxiliary: avoir

PAST PARTICIPLE	PRESENT PARTICIPLE	IMPERATIVE
écrit	**écrivant**	écris
		écrivons
		écrivez

PRESENT	FUTURE	IMPERFECT
j'écris	j'écrirai	**j'écrivais**
tu écris	tu écriras	**tu écrivais**
il écrit	il écrira	**il écrivait**
nous écrivons	nous écrirons	**nous écrivions**
vous écrivez	vous écrirez	**vous écriviez**
ils écrivent	ils écriront	**ils écrivaient**

PRESENT SUBJUNCTIVE	CONDITIONAL	PAST HISTORIC
j'écrive	j'écrirais	**j'écrivis**
tu écrives	tu écrirais	**tu écrivis**
il écrive	il écrirait	**il écrivit**
nous écrivions	nous écririons	**nous écrivîmes**
vous écriviez	vous écririez	**vous écrivîtes**
ils écrivent	ils écriraient	**ils écrivirent**

envoyer to send   Auxiliary: avoir

PAST PARTICIPLE	PRESENT PARTICIPLE	IMPERATIVE
envoyé	envoyant	envoie
		envoyons
		envoyez

PRESENT	FUTURE	IMPERFECT
j'envoie	**j'enverrai**	j'envoyais
tu envoies	**tu enverras**	tu envoyais
il envoie	**il enverra**	il envoyait
nous envoyons	**nous enverrons**	nous envoyions
vous envoyez	**vous enverrez**	vous envoyiez
ils envoient	**ils enverront**	ils envoyaient

PRESENT SUBJUNCTIVE	CONDITIONAL	PAST HISTORIC
j'envoie	**j'enverrais**	j'envoyai
tu envoies	**tu enverrais**	tu envoyas
il envoie	**il enverrait**	il envoya
nous envoyions	**nous enverrions**	nous envoyâmes
vous envoyiez	**vous enverriez**	vous envoyâtes
ils envoient	**ils enverraient**	ils envoyèrent

être *to be* Auxiliary: avoir

PAST PARTICIPLE	PRESENT PARTICIPLE	IMPERATIVE
été	étant	sois
		soyons
		soyez

PRESENT	FUTURE	IMPERFECT
je suis	je serai	j'étais
tu es	tu seras	tu étais
il est	il sera	il était
nous sommes	nous serons	nous étions
vous êtes	vous serez	vous étiez
ils sont	ils seront	ils étaient

PRESENT SUBJUNCTIVE	CONDITIONAL	PAST HISTORIC
je sois	je serais	je fus
tu sois	tu serais	tu fus
il soit	il serait	il fut
nous soyons	nous serions	nous fûmes
vous soyez	vous seriez	vous fûtes
ils soient	ils seraient	ils furent

faire *to do; to make* Auxiliary: avoir

PAST PARTICIPLE	PRESENT PARTICIPLE	IMPERATIVE
fait	faisant	fais
		faisons
		faites

PRESENT	FUTURE	IMPERFECT
je fais	je ferai	je faisais
tu fais	tu feras	tu faisais
il fait	il fera	il faisait
nous faisons	nous ferons	nous faisions
vous faites	vous ferez	vous faisiez
ils font	ils feront	ils faisaient

PRESENT SUBJUNCTIVE	CONDITIONAL	PAST HISTORIC
je fasse	je ferais	je fis
tu fasses	tu ferais	tu fis
il fasse	il ferait	il fit
nous fassions	nous ferions	nous fîmes
vous fassiez	vous feriez	vous fîtes
ils fassent	ils feraient	ils firent

fuir *to flee* — Auxiliary: *avoir*

PAST PARTICIPLE	PRESENT PARTICIPLE	IMPERATIVE
fui	**fuyant**	fuis
		fuyons
		fuyez

PRESENT	FUTURE	IMPERFECT
je fuis	je fuirai	**je fuyais**
tu fuis	tu fuiras	**tu fuyais**
il fuit	il fuira	**il fuyait**
nous fuyons	nous fuirons	**nous fuyions**
vous fuyez	vous fuirez	**vous fuyiez**
ils fuient	ils fuiront	**ils fuyaient**

PRESENT SUBJUNCTIVE	CONDITIONAL	PAST HISTORIC
je fuie	je fuirais	je fuis
tu fuies	tu fuirais	tu fuis
il fuie	il fuirait	il fuit
nous fuyions	nous fuirions	nous fuîmes
vous fuyiez	vous fuiriez	vous fuîtes
ils fuient	ils fuiraient	ils fuirent

---

haïr *to hate* — Auxiliary: *avoir*

PAST PARTICIPLE	PRESENT PARTICIPLE	IMPERATIVE
haï	**haïssant**	hais
		haïssons
		haïssez

PRESENT	FUTURE	IMPERFECT
je hais	je haïrai	**je haïssais**
tu hais	tu haïras	**tu haïssais**
il hait	il haïra	**il haïssait**
nous haïssons	nous haïrons	**nous haïssions**
vous haïssez	vous haïrez	**vous haïssiez**
ils haïssent	ils haïront	**ils haïssaient**

PRESENT SUBJUNCTIVE	CONDITIONAL	PAST HISTORIC
je haïsse	je haïrais	**je haïs**
tu haïsses	tu haïrais	**tu haïs**
il haïsse	il haïrait	**il haït**
nous haïssions	nous haïrions	**nous haïmes**
vous haïssiez	vous haïriez	**vous haïtes**
ils haïssent	ils haïraient	**ils haïrent**

lire *to read* — Auxiliary: avoir

PAST PARTICIPLE	PRESENT PARTICIPLE	IMPERATIVE
lu	**lisant**	lis
		lisons
		lisez

PRESENT	FUTURE	IMPERFECT
je lis	je lirai	**je lisais**
tu lis	tu liras	**tu lisais**
il lit	il lira	**il lisait**
nous lisons	nous lirons	**nous lisions**
vous lisez	vous lirez	**vous lisiez**
ils lisent	ils liront	**ils lisaient**

PRESENT SUBJUNCTIVE	CONDITIONAL	PAST HISTORIC
je lise	je lirais	**je lus**
tu lises	tu lirais	**tu lus**
il lise	il lirait	**il lut**
nous lisions	nous lirions	**nous lûmes**
vous lisiez	vous liriez	**vous lûtes**
ils lisent	ils liraient	**ils lurent**

mettre *to put* — Auxiliary: avoir

PAST PARTICIPLE	PRESENT PARTICIPLE	IMPERATIVE
mis	mettant	**mets**
		mettons
		mettez

PRESENT	FUTURE	IMPERFECT
je mets	je mettrai	je mettais
tu mets	tu mettras	tu mettais
il met	il mettra	il mettait
nous mettons	nous mettrons	nous mettions
vous mettez	vous mettrez	vous mettiez
ils mettent	ils mettront	ils mettaient

PRESENT SUBJUNCTIVE	CONDITIONAL	PAST HISTORIC
je mette	je mettrais	**je mis**
tu mettes	tu mettrais	**tu mis**
il mette	il mettrait	**il mit**
nous mettions	nous mettrions	**nous mîmes**
vous mettiez	vous mettriez	**vous mîtes**
ils mettent	ils mettraient	**ils mirent**

mourir *to die* — Auxiliary: être

PAST PARTICIPLE	PRESENT PARTICIPLE	IMPERATIVE
mort	**mourant**	**meurs** **mourons** **mourez**

PRESENT	FUTURE	IMPERFECT
je **meurs**	je **mourrai**	je **mourais**
tu **meurs**	tu **mourras**	tu **mourais**
il **meurt**	il **mourra**	il **mourait**
nous **mourons**	nous **mourrons**	nous **mourions**
vous **mourez**	vous **mourrez**	vous **mouriez**
ils **meurent**	ils **mourront**	ils **mouraient**

PRESENT SUBJUNCTIVE	CONDITIONAL	PAST HISTORIC
je **meure**	je **mourrais**	je **mourus**
tu **meures**	tu **mourrais**	tu **mourus**
il **meure**	il **mourrait**	il **mourut**
nous **mourions**	nous **mourrions**	nous **mourûmes**
vous **mouriez**	vous **mourriez**	vous **mourûtes**
ils **meurent**	ils **mourraient**	ils **moururent**

naître *to be born* — Auxiliary: être

PAST PARTICIPLE	PRESENT PARTICIPLE	IMPERATIVE
né	**naissant**	**nais** **naissons** **naissez**

PRESENT	FUTURE	IMPERFECT
je **nais**	je naîtrai	je **naissais**
tu **nais**	tu naîtras	tu **naissais**
il naît	il naîtra	il **naissait**
nous **naissons**	nous naîtrons	nous **naissions**
vous **naissez**	vous naîtrez	vous **naissiez**
ils **naissent**	ils naîtront	ils **naissaient**

PRESENT SUBJUNCTIVE	CONDITIONAL	PAST HISTORIC
je **naisse**	je naîtrais	je naquis
tu **naisses**	tu naîtrais	tu naquis
il **naisse**	il naîtrait	il naquit
nous **naissions**	nous naîtrions	nous naquîmes
vous **naissiez**	vous naîtriez	vous naquîtes
ils **naissent**	ils naîtraient	ils naquirent

ouvrir *to open* — Auxiliary: avoir

PAST PARTICIPLE	PRESENT PARTICIPLE	IMPERATIVE
ouvert	**ouvrant**	**ouvre**
		ouvrons
		ouvrez

PRESENT	FUTURE	IMPERFECT
j'ouvre	j'ouvrirai	**j'ouvrais**
tu **ouvres**	tu ouvriras	tu **ouvrais**
il **ouvre**	il ouvrira	il **ouvrait**
nous **ouvrons**	nous ouvrirons	nous **ouvrions**
vous **ouvrez**	vous ouvrirez	vous **ouvriez**
ils **ouvrent**	ils ouvriront	ils **ouvraient**

PRESENT SUBJUNCTIVE	CONDITIONAL	PAST HISTORIC
j'ouvre	j'ouvrirais	j'ouvris
tu **ouvres**	tu ouvrirais	tu ouvris
il **ouvre**	il ouvrirait	il ouvrit
nous **ouvrions**	nous ouvririons	nous ouvrîmes
vous **ouvriez**	vous ouvririez	vous ouvrîtes
ils **ouvrent**	ils ouvriraient	ils ouvrirent

offrir *to offer*, **souffrir** *to suffer* are conjugated similarly

paraître *to appear* — Auxiliary: avoir

PAST PARTICIPLE	PRESENT PARTICIPLE	IMPERATIVE
paru	**paraissant**	**parais**
		paraissons
		paraissez

PRESENT	FUTURE	IMPERFECT
je **parais**	je paraîtrai	je **paraissais**
tu **parais**	tu paraîtras	tu **paraissais**
il paraît	il paraîtra	il **paraissait**
nous **paraissons**	nous paraîtrons	nous **paraissions**
vous **paraissez**	vous paraîtrez	vous **paraissiez**
ils **paraissent**	ils paraîtront	ils **paraissaient**

PRESENT SUBJUNCTIVE	CONDITIONAL	PAST HISTORIC
je **paraisse**	je paraîtrais	je **parus**
tu **paraisses**	tu paraîtrais	tu **parus**
il **paraisse**	il paraîtrait	il **parut**
nous **paraissions**	nous paraîtrions	nous **parûmes**
vous **paraissiez**	vous paraîtriez	vous **parûtes**
ils **paraissent**	ils paraîtraient	ils **parurent**

partir *to leave* — Auxiliary: être

PAST PARTICIPLE	PRESENT PARTICIPLE	IMPERATIVE
parti	**partant**	**pars**
		partons
		partez

PRESENT	FUTURE	IMPERFECT
je pars	je partirai	**je partais**
tu pars	tu partiras	**tu partais**
il part	il partira	**il partait**
nous partons	nous partirons	**nous partions**
vous partez	vous partirez	**vous partiez**
ils partent	ils partiront	**ils partaient**

PRESENT SUBJUNCTIVE	CONDITIONAL	PAST HISTORIC
je parte	je partirais	je partis
tu partes	tu partirais	tu partis
il parte	il partirait	il partit
nous partions	nous partirions	nous partîmes
vous partiez	vous partiriez	vous partîtes
ils partent	ils partiraient	ils partirent

---

plaire *to please* — Auxiliary: avoir

PAST PARTICIPLE	PRESENT PARTICIPLE	IMPERATIVE
plu	**plaisant**	plais
		plaisons
		plaisez

PRESENT	FUTURE	IMPERFECT
je plais	je plairai	**je plaisais**
tu plais	tu plairas	**tu plaisais**
il plaît	il plaira	**il plaisait**
nous plaisons	nous plairons	**nous plaisions**
vous plaisez	vous plairez	**vous plaisiez**
ils plaisent	ils plairont	**ils plaisaient**

PRESENT SUBJUNCTIVE	CONDITIONAL	PAST HISTORIC
je plaise	je plairais	**je plus**
tu plaises	tu plairais	**tu plus**
il plaise	il plairait	**il plut**
nous plaisions	nous plairions	**nous plûmes**
vous plaisiez	vous plairiez	**vous plûtes**
ils plaisent	ils plairaient	**ils plurent**

pouvoir *to be able to*   Auxiliary: **avoir**

PAST PARTICIPLE	PRESENT PARTICIPLE	IMPERATIVE
pu	**pouvant**	*not used*

PRESENT	FUTURE	IMPERFECT
je **peux***	je **pourrai**	je **pouvais**
tu **peux**	tu **pourras**	tu **pouvais**
il **peut**	il **pourra**	il **pouvait**
nous **pouvons**	nous **pourrons**	nous **pouvions**
vous **pouvez**	vous **pourrez**	vous **pouviez**
ils **peuvent**	ils **pourront**	ils **pouvaient**

PRESENT SUBJUNCTIVE	CONDITIONAL	PAST HISTORIC
je **puisse**	je **pourrais**	je **pus**
tu **puisses**	tu **pourrais**	tu **pus**
il **puisse**	il **pourrait**	il **put**
nous **puissions**	nous **pourrions**	nous **pûmes**
vous **puissiez**	vous **pourriez**	vous **pûtes**
ils **puissent**	ils **pourraient**	ils **purent**

*In questions: **puis-je?**

prendre *to take*   Auxiliary: **avoir**

PAST PARTICIPLE	PRESENT PARTICIPLE	IMPERATIVE
pris	**prenant**	prends
		prenons
		prenez

PRESENT	FUTURE	IMPERFECT
je prends	je prendrai	je **prenais**
tu prends	tu prendras	tu **prenais**
il prend	il prendra	il **prenait**
nous **prenons**	nous prendrons	nous **prenions**
vous **prenez**	vous prendrez	vous **preniez**
ils **prennent**	ils prendront	ils **prenaient**

PRESENT SUBJUNCTIVE	CONDITIONAL	PAST HISTORIC
je **prenne**	je prendrais	je **pris**
tu **prennes**	tu prendrais	tu **pris**
il **prenne**	il prendrait	il **prit**
nous **prenions**	nous prendrions	nous **prîmes**
vous **preniez**	vous prendriez	vous **prîtes**
ils **prennent**	ils prendraient	ils **prirent**

recevoir *to receive* — Auxiliary: *avoir*

PAST PARTICIPLE	PRESENT PARTICIPLE	IMPERATIVE
reçu	recevant	reçois
		recevons
		recevez

PRESENT	FUTURE	IMPERFECT
je reçois	je recevrai	je recevais
tu reçois	tu recevras	tu recevais
il reçoit	il recevra	il recevait
nous recevons	nous recevrons	nous recevions
vous recevez	vous recevrez	vous receviez
ils reçoivent	ils recevront	ils recevaient

PRESENT SUBJUNCTIVE	CONDITIONAL	PAST HISTORIC
je reçoive	je recevrais	je reçus
tu reçoives	tu recevrais	tu reçus
il reçoive	il recevrait	il reçut
nous recevions	nous recevrions	nous reçûmes
vous receviez	vous recevriez	vous reçûtes
ils reçoivent	ils recevraient	ils reçurent

résoudre *to solve* — Auxiliary: *avoir*

PAST PARTICIPLE	PRESENT PARTICIPLE	IMPERATIVE
résolu	résolvant	résous
		résolvons
		résolvez

PRESENT	FUTURE	IMPERFECT
je résous	je résoudrai	je résolvais
tu résous	tu résoudras	tu résolvais
il résout	il résoudra	il résolvait
nous résolvons	nous résoudrons	nous résolvions
vous résolvez	vous résoudrez	vous résolviez
ils résolvent	ils résoudront	ils résolvaient

PRESENT SUBJUNCTIVE	CONDITIONAL	PAST HISTORIC
je résolve	je résoudrais	je résolus
tu résolves	tu résoudrais	tu résolus
il résolve	il résoudrait	il résolut
nous résolvions	nous résoudrions	nous résolûmes
vous résolviez	vous résoudriez	vous résolûtes
ils résolvent	ils résoudraient	ils résolurent

rire to laugh — Auxiliary: avoir

PAST PARTICIPLE	PRESENT PARTICIPLE	IMPERATIVE
ri	riant	ris
		rions
		riez

PRESENT	FUTURE	IMPERFECT
je ris	je rirai	je riais
tu ris	tu riras	tu riais
il **rit**	il rira	il riait
nous rions	nous rirons	nous riions
vous riez	vous rirez	vous riiez
ils rient	ils riront	ils riaient

PRESENT SUBJUNCTIVE	CONDITIONAL	PAST HISTORIC
je rie	je rirais	**je ris**
tu ries	tu rirais	**tu ris**
il rie	il rirait	**il rit**
nous riions	nous ririons	**nous rîmes**
vous riiez	vous ririez	**vous rîtes**
ils rient	ils riraient	**ils rirent**

rompre to break — Auxiliary: avoir

PAST PARTICIPLE	PRESENT PARTICIPLE	IMPERATIVE
rompu	rompant	romps
		rompons
		rompez

PRESENT	FUTURE	IMPERFECT
je romps	je romprai	je rompais
tu romps	tu rompras	tu rompais
il **rompt**	il rompra	il rompait
nous rompons	nous romprons	nous rompions
vous rompez	vous romprez	vous rompiez
ils rompent	ils rompront	ils rompaient

PRESENT SUBJUNCTIVE	CONDITIONAL	PAST HISTORIC
je rompe	je romprais	je rompis
tu rompes	tu romprais	tu rompis
il rompe	il romprait	il rompit
nous rompions	nous romprions	nous rompîmes
vous rompiez	vous rompriez	vous rompîtes
ils rompent	ils rompraient	ils rompirent

savoir to know   Auxiliary: avoir

PAST PARTICIPLE	PRESENT PARTICIPLE	IMPERATIVE
su	sachant	sache
		sachons
		sachez

PRESENT	FUTURE	IMPERFECT
je sais	je saurai	je savais
tu sais	tu sauras	tu savais
il sait	il saura	il savait
nous savons	nous saurons	nous savions
vous savez	vous saurez	vous saviez
ils savent	ils sauront	ils savaient

PRESENT SUBJUNCTIVE	CONDITIONAL	PAST HISTORIC
je sache	je saurais	je sus
tu saches	tu saurais	tu sus
il sache	il saurait	il sut
nous sachions	nous saurions	nous sûmes
vous sachiez	vous sauriez	vous sûtes
ils sachent	ils sauraient	ils surent

sentir to feel; to smell   Auxiliary: avoir

PAST PARTICIPLE	PRESENT PARTICIPLE	IMPERATIVE
senti	sentant	sens
		sentons
		sentez

PRESENT	FUTURE	IMPERFECT
je sens	je sentirai	je sentais
tu sens	tu sentiras	tu sentais
il sent	il sentira	il sentait
nous sentons	nous sentirons	nous sentions
vous sentez	vous sentirez	vous sentiez
ils sentent	ils sentiront	ils sentaient

PRESENT SUBJUNCTIVE	CONDITIONAL	PAST HISTORIC
je sente	je sentirais	je sentis
tu sentes	tu sentirais	tu sentis
il sente	il sentirait	il sentit
nous sentions	nous sentirions	nous sentîmes
vous sentiez	vous sentiriez	vous sentîtes
ils sentent	ils sentiraient	ils sentirent

servir *to serve* — Auxiliary: avoir

PAST PARTICIPLE	PRESENT PARTICIPLE	IMPERATIVE
servi	**servant**	**sers**
		servons
		servez

PRESENT	FUTURE	IMPERFECT
je sers	je servirai	**je servais**
tu sers	tu serviras	**tu servais**
il sert	il servira	**il servait**
nous servons	nous servirons	**nous servions**
vous servez	vous servirez	**vous serviez**
ils servent	ils serviront	**ils servaient**

PRESENT SUBJUNCTIVE	CONDITIONAL	PAST HISTORIC
je serve	je servirais	je servis
tu serves	tu servirais	tu servis
il serve	il servirait	il servit
nous servions	nous servirions	nous servîmes
vous serviez	vous serviriez	vous servîtes
ils servent	ils serviraient	ils servirent

sortir *to go/come out* — Auxiliary: être

PAST PARTICIPLE	PRESENT PARTICIPLE	IMPERATIVE
sorti	**sortant**	**sors**
		sortons
		sortez

PRESENT	FUTURE	IMPERFECT
je sors	je sortirai	**je sortais**
tu sors	tu sortiras	**tu sortais**
il sort	il sortira	**il sortait**
nous sortons	nous sortirons	**nous sortions**
vous sortez	vous sortirez	**vous sortiez**
ils sortent	ils sortiront	**ils sortaient**

PRESENT SUBJUNCTIVE	CONDITIONAL	PAST HISTORIC
je sorte	je sortirais	je sortis
tu sortes	tu sortirais	tu sortis
il sorte	il sortirait	il sortit
nous sortions	nous sortirions	nous sortîmes
vous sortiez	vous sortiriez	vous sortîtes
ils sortent	ils sortiraient	ils sortirent

suffire to be enough   Auxiliary: avoir

PAST PARTICIPLE	PRESENT PARTICIPLE	IMPERATIVE
suffi	**suffisant**	suffis
		suffisons
		suffisez

PRESENT	FUTURE	IMPERFECT
je suffis	je suffirai	**je suffisais**
tu suffis	tu suffiras	**tu suffisais**
il suffit	il suffira	**il suffisait**
nous suffisons	nous suffirons	**nous suffisions**
vous suffisez	vous suffirez	**vous suffisiez**
ils suffisent	ils suffiront	**ils suffisaient**

PRESENT SUBJUNCTIVE	CONDITIONAL	PAST HISTORIC
je suffise	je suffirais	**je suffis**
tu suffises	tu suffirais	**tu suffis**
il suffise	il suffirait	**il suffit**
nous suffisions	nous suffirions	**nous suffîmes**
vous suffisiez	vous suffiriez	**vous suffîtes**
ils suffisent	ils suffiraient	**ils suffirent**

suivre to follow   Auxiliary: avoir

PAST PARTICIPLE	PRESENT PARTICIPLE	IMPERATIVE
suivi	suivant	**suis**
		suivons
		suivez

PRESENT	FUTURE	IMPERFECT
je suis	je suivrai	je suivais
tu suis	tu suivras	tu suivais
il suit	il suivra	il suivait
nous suivons	nous suivrons	nous suivions
vous suivez	vous suivrez	vous suiviez
ils suivent	ils suivront	ils suivaient

PRESENT SUBJUNCTIVE	CONDITIONAL	PAST HISTORIC
je suive	je suivrais	je suivis
tu suives	tu suivrais	tu suivis
il suive	il suivrait	il suivit
nous suivions	nous suivrions	nous suivîmes
vous suiviez	vous suivriez	vous suivîtes
ils suivent	ils suivraient	ils suivirent

se taire to stop talking — Auxiliary: être

PAST PARTICIPLE	PRESENT PARTICIPLE	IMPERATIVE
tu	se taisant	tais-toi
		taisons-nous
		taisez-vous

PRESENT	FUTURE	IMPERFECT
je me tais	je me tairai	je me taisais
tu te tais	tu te tairas	tu te taisais
il se tait	il se taira	il se taisait
nous nous taisons	nous nous tairons	nous nous taisions
vous vous taisez	vous vous tairez	vous vous taisiez
ils se taisent	ils se tairont	ils se taisaient

PRESENT SUBJUNCTIVE	CONDITIONAL	PAST HISTORIC
je me taise	je me tairais	je me tus
tu te taises	tu te tairais	tu te tus
il se taise	il se tairait	il se tut
nous nous taisions	nous nous tairions	nous nous tûmes
vous vous taisiez	vous vous tairiez	vous vous tûtes
ils se taisent	ils se tairaient	ils se turent

tenir to hold — Auxiliary: avoir

PAST PARTICIPLE	PRESENT PARTICIPLE	IMPERATIVE
tenu	tenant	tiens
		tenons
		tenez

PRESENT	FUTURE	IMPERFECT
je tiens	je tiendrai	je tenais
tu tiens	tu tiendras	tu tenais
il tient	il tiendra	il tenait
nous tenons	nous tiendrons	nous tenions
vous tenez	vous tiendrez	vous teniez
ils tiennent	ils tiendront	ils tenaient

PRESENT SUBJUNCTIVE	CONDITIONAL	PAST HISTORIC
je tienne	je tiendrais	je tins
tu tiennes	tu tiendrais	tu tins
il tienne	il tiendrait	il tint
nous tenions	nous tiendrions	nous tînmes
vous teniez	vous tiendriez	vous tîntes
ils tiennent	ils tiendraient	ils tinrent

---

vaincre *to defeat*   Auxiliary: avoir

PAST PARTICIPLE	PRESENT PARTICIPLE	IMPERATIVE
vaincu	**vainquant**	vaincs
		vainquons
		vainquez

PRESENT	FUTURE	IMPERFECT
je vaincs	je vaincrai	**je vainquais**
tu vaincs	tu vaincras	**tu vainquais**
il vainc	il vaincra	**il vainquait**
nous vainquons	nous vaincrons	**nous vainquions**
vous vainquez	vous vaincrez	**vous vainquiez**
ils vainquent	ils vaincront	**ils vainquaient**

PRESENT SUBJUNCTIVE	CONDITIONAL	PAST HISTORIC
je vainque	je vaincrais	**je vainquis**
tu vainques	tu vaincrais	**tu vainquis**
il vainque	il vaincrait	**il vainquit**
nous vainquions	nous vaincrions	**nous vainquîmes**
vous vainquiez	vous vaincriez	**vous vainquîtes**
ils vainquent	ils vaincraient	**ils vainquirent**

---

valoir *to be worth*   Auxiliary: avoir

PAST PARTICIPLE	PRESENT PARTICIPLE	IMPERATIVE
valu	**valant**	**vaux**
		valons
		valez

PRESENT	FUTURE	IMPERFECT
je vaux	**je vaudrai**	je valais
tu vaux	**tu vaudras**	tu valais
il vaut	**il vaudra**	il valait
nous valons	**nous vaudrons**	nous valions
vous valez	**vous vaudrez**	vous valiez
ils valent	**ils vaudront**	ils valaient

PRESENT SUBJUNCTIVE	CONDITIONAL	PAST HISTORIC
je vaille	**je vaudrais**	**je valus**
tu vailles	**tu vaudrais**	**tu valus**
il vaille	**il vaudrait**	**il valut**
nous valions	**nous vaudrions**	**nous valûmes**
vous valiez	**vous vaudriez**	**vous valûtes**
ils vaillent	**ils vaudraient**	**ils valurent**

venir *to come* — Auxiliary: être

PAST PARTICIPLE	PRESENT PARTICIPLE	IMPERATIVE
venu	venant	viens
		venons
		venez

PRESENT	FUTURE	IMPERFECT
je viens	je viendrai	je venais
tu viens	tu viendras	tu venais
il vient	il viendra	il venait
nous venons	nous viendrons	nous venions
vous venez	vous viendrez	vous veniez
ils viennent	ils viendront	ils venaient

PRESENT SUBJUNCTIVE	CONDITIONAL	PAST HISTORIC
je vienne	je viendrais	je vins
tu viennes	tu viendrais	tu vins
il vienne	il viendrait	il vint
nous venions	nous viendrions	nous vînmes
vous veniez	vous viendriez	vous vîntes
ils viennent	ils viendraient	ils vinrent

vivre *to live* — Auxiliary: avoir

PAST PARTICIPLE	PRESENT PARTICIPLE	IMPERATIVE
vécu	vivant	vis
		vivons
		vivez

PRESENT	FUTURE	IMPERFECT
je vis	je vivrai	je vivais
tu vis	tu vivras	tu vivais
il vit	il vivra	il vivait
nous vivons	nous vivrons	nous vivions
vous vivez	vous vivrez	vous viviez
ils vivent	ils vivront	ils vivaient

PRESENT SUBJUNCTIVE	CONDITIONAL	PAST HISTORIC
je vive	je vivrais	je vécus
tu vives	tu vivrais	tu vécus
il vive	il vivrait	il vécut
nous vivions	nous vivrions	nous vécûmes
vous viviez	vous vivriez	vous vécûtes
ils vivent	ils vivraient	ils vécurent

voir to see — Auxiliary: avoir

PAST PARTICIPLE	PRESENT PARTICIPLE	IMPERATIVE
vu	voyant	vois
		voyons
		voyez

PRESENT	FUTURE	IMPERFECT
je vois	je verrai	je voyais
tu vois	tu verras	tu voyais
il voit	il verra	il voyait
nous voyons	nous verrons	nous voyions
vous voyez	vous verrez	vous voyiez
ils voient	ils verront	ils voyaient

PRESENT SUBJUNCTIVE	CONDITIONAL	PAST HISTORIC
je voie	je verrais	je vis
tu voies	tu verrais	tu vis
il voie	il verrait	il vit
nous voyions	nous verrions	nous vîmes
vous voyiez	vous verriez	vous vîtes
ils voient	ils verraient	ils virent

vouloir to wish, want — Auxiliary: avoir

PAST PARTICIPLE	PRESENT PARTICIPLE	IMPERATIVE
voulu	voulant	veuille
		veuillons
		veuillez

PRESENT	FUTURE	IMPERFECT
je veux	je voudrai	je voulais
tu veux	tu voudras	tu voulais
il veut	il voudra	il voulait
nous voulons	nous voudrons	nous voulions
vous voulez	vous voudrez	vous vouliez
ils veulent	ils voudront	ils voulaient

PRESENT SUBJUNCTIVE	CONDITIONAL	PAST HISTORIC
je veuille	je voudrais	je voulus
tu veuilles	tu voudrais	tu voulus
il veuille	il voudrait	il voulut
nous voulions	nous voudrions	nous voulûmes
vous vouliez	vous voudriez	vous voulûtes
ils veuillent	ils voudraient	ils voulurent

❒ The Gender of Nouns

In French, all nouns are either masculine or feminine, whether denoting people, animals or things. Unlike English, there is no neuter gender for inanimate objects and abstract nouns.

Gender is largely unpredictable and has to be learnt for each noun. However, the following guidelines will help you determine the gender for certain types of nouns.

◆ Nouns denoting male people and animals are usually – but not always – masculine, e.g.

un homme	**un taureau**
a man	*a bull*
un infirmier	**un cheval**
a (male) nurse	*a horse*

◆ Nouns denoting female people and animals are usually – but not always – feminine, e.g.

une fille	**une vache**
a girl	*a cow*
une infirmière	**une brebis**
a nurse	*a ewe*

◆ Some nouns are masculine OR feminine depending on the sex of the person to whom they refer, e.g.

un camarade	**une camarade**
a (male) friend	*a (female) friend*
un Belge	**une Belge**
a Belgian (man)	*a Belgian (woman)*

◆ Other nouns referring to either men or women have only one gender which applies to both, e.g.

un professeur	**une personne**	**une sentinelle**
a teacher	*a person*	*a sentry*
un témoin	**une victime**	**une recrue**
a witness	*a victim*	*a recruit*

NOUNS

◆ Sometimes the ending of the noun indicates its gender. Shown below are some of the most important to guide you:

Masculine endings

-age	**le courage** *courage*, **le rinçage** *rinsing*
	EXCEPTIONS: **une cage** *a cage*, **une image** *a picture*, **la nage** *swimming*, **une page** *a page*, **une plage** *a beach*, **une rage** *a rage*
-ment	**le commencement** *the beginning*
	EXCEPTION: **une jument** *a mare*
-oir	**un couloir** *a corridor*, **un miroir** *a mirror*
-sme	**le pessimisme** *pessimism*, **l'enthousiasme** *enthusiasm*

Feminine endings

-ance, anse	**la confiance** *confidence*, **la danse** *dancing*
-ence, -ense	**la prudence** *caution*, **la défense** *defence*
	EXCEPTION: **le silence** *silence*
-ion	**une région** *a region*, **une addition** *a bill*
	EXCEPTIONS: **un pion** *a pawn*, **un espion** *a spy*
-oire	**une baignoire** *a bath(tub)*
-té, -tié	**la beauté** *beauty*, **la moitié** *half*

◆ Suffixes which differentiate between male and female are shown on p 78.

◆ The following words have different meanings depending on gender:

le crêpe	*crêpe*	**la crêpe**	*pancake*
le livre	*book*	**la livre**	*pound*
le manche	*handle*	**la manche**	*sleeve*
le mode	*method*	**la mode**	*fashion*
le moule	*mould*	**la moule**	*mussel*
le page	*page(boy)*	**la page**	*page* (in book)
le physique	*physique*	**la physique**	*physics*
le poêle	*stove*	**la poêle**	*frying pan*
le somme	*nap*	**la somme**	*sum*
le tour	*turn*	**la tour**	*tower*
le voile	*veil*	**la voile**	*sail*

☐ Gender: the Formation of Feminines

As in English, male and female are sometimes differentiated by the use of two quite separate words, e.g. **mon oncle/ma tante** *my uncle/my aunt*. There are, however, some words in French which show this distinction by the form of their ending.

- ◆ Some nouns add an **e** to the masculine singular form to form the feminine → ①

- ◆ If the masculine singular form already ends in **-e**, no further **e** is added in the feminine → ②

- ◆ Some nouns undergo a further change when **e** is added.

MASC. SING.	FEM. SING.	
-f	-ve	→ ③
-x	-se	→ ④
-eur	-euse	→ ⑤
-teur	⌠-teuse	→ ⑥
	⌡-trice	→ ⑦

Some nouns double the final consonant before adding **e**:

MASC. SING.	FEM. SING.	
-an	-anne	→ ⑧
-en	-enne	→ ⑨
-on	-onne	→ ⑩
-et	-ette	→ ⑪
-el	-elle	→ ⑫

Some nouns add an accent to the final syllable before adding **e**:

MASC. SING.	FEM. SING.	
-er	-ère	→ ⑬

- ◆ Some nouns have unusual feminine forms → ⑭

1	**un ami** a (male) friend	**une amie** a (female) friend
2	**un élève** a (male) pupil	**une élève** a (female) pupil
3	**un veuf** a widower	**une veuve** a widow
4	**un époux** a husband	**une épouse** a wife
5	**un danseur** a dancer	**une danseuse** a dancer
6	**un menteur** a liar	**une menteuse** a liar
7	**un conducteur** a driver	**une conductrice** a driver
8	**un paysan** a countryman	**une paysanne** a countrywoman
9	**un Parisien** a Parisian	**une Parisienne** a Parisian (woman)
10	**un baron** a baron	**une baronne** a baroness
11	**le cadet** the youngest (child)	**la cadette** the youngest (child)
12	**un intellectuel** an intellectual	**une intellectuelle** an intellectual
13	**un étranger** a foreigner	**une étrangère** a foreigner
14	**le comte/la comtesse** count/countess	**le duc/la duchesse** duke/duchess
	le maître/la maîtresse master/mistress	**le prince/la princesse** prince/princess
	le fou/la folle madman/madwoman	**le Turc/la Turque** Turk
	un hôte/une hôtesse host/hostess	**le vieux/la vieille** old man/old woman

NOUNS

☐ The Formation of Plurals

- Most nouns add **s** to the singular form → ①

- When the singular form already ends in **-s**, **-x** or **-z**, no further **s** is added → ②

- For nouns ending in **-au**, **-eau** or **-eu**, the plural ends in **-aux**, **-eaux** or **-eux** → ③

  EXCEPTIONS: **pneu**   *tyre*   (plur: **pneus**)
                  bleu   *bruise*   (plur: **bleus**)

- For nouns ending in **-al** or **-ail**, the plural ends in **-aux** → ④

  EXCEPTIONS: **bal**   *ball*   (plur: **bals**)
                  festival   *festival*   (plur: **festivals**)
                  chandail   *sweater*   (plur: **chandails**)
                  détail   *detail*   (plur: **détails**)

- Forming the plural of compound nouns is complicated and you are advised to check each one individually in a dictionary.

- A word which is singular in English may be plural in French, or vice versa → ⑤

Irregular plural forms

- Some masculine nouns ending in **-ou** add **x** in the plural. These are:

bijou	*jewel*	**genou**	*knee*	**joujou**	*toy*
caillou	*pebble*	**hibou**	*owl*	**pou**	*louse*
chou	*cabbage*				

- Some other nouns are totally unpredictable. Chief among these are:

SINGULAR		PLURAL
œil	*eye*	**yeux**
ciel	*sky*	**cieux**
Monsieur	*Mr*	**Messieurs**
Madame	*Mrs*	**Mesdames**
Mademoiselle	*Miss*	**Mesdemoiselles**

1	**le jardin** the garden	**les jardins** the gardens
	une voiture a car	**des voitures** (some) cars
	l'hôtel the hotel	**les hôtels** the hotels
2	**un tas** a heap	**des tas** (some) heaps
	une voix a voice	**des voix** (some) voices
	le gaz the gas	**les gaz** the gases
3	**un tuyau** a pipe	**des tuyaux** (some) pipes
	le chapeau the hat	**les chapeaux** the hats
	le feu the fire	**les feux** the fires
4	**le journal** the newspaper	**les journaux** the newspapers
	un travail a job	**des travaux** (some) jobs
5	**les bagages** the luggage	**ses cheveux** his/her hair
	le bétail the cattle	**mon pantalon** my trousers

❏ The Definite Article

	WITH MASC. NOUN	WITH FEM. NOUN	
SING.	**le (l')**	**la (l')**	*the*
PLUR.	**les**	**les**	*the*

- The gender and number of the noun determines the form of the article → ①

- **le** and **la** change to **l'** before a vowel or an **h** 'mute' → ②

- While the French definite article is used in much the same way as in English, it is also found:

   - with abstract nouns, except after certain prepositions → ③
   - in generalizations, especially with plural or uncountable nouns (those which cannot be used in the plural or with an indefinite article, e.g. **le lait** *milk*) → ④
   - with names of countries, except after **en** *to/in* → ⑤
   - with parts of the body; 'ownership' is often indicated by an indirect object pronoun or a reflexive pronoun → ⑥
   - in expressions of quantity/rate/price → ⑦
   - with titles/ranks/professions followed by a proper name → ⑧
   - The definite article is NOT used with nouns in apposition → ⑨

- **à + le/la (l'), à + les; de + le/la (l'), de + les**

	à WITH MASC. NOUN	**à** WITH FEM. NOUN		**de** WITH MASC. NOUN	**de** WITH FEM. NOUN	
SING.	**au (à l')**	**à la (à l')**	→ ⑩	**du (de l')**	**de la (de l')**	→ ⑪
PLUR.	**aux**	**aux**		**des**	**des**	

- The definite article combines with the prepositions **à** and **de**, as shown above. You should pay particular attention to the masculine singular forms **au** and **du**, and plural forms **aux** and **des**, since these are not visually the sum of their parts.

Grammar

---

1. **le garçon** — the boy | **la fille** — the girl
   les hôtels — the hotels | **les écoles** — the schools

2. **l'acteur** — the actor | **l'actrice** — the actress
   l'hôpital — the hospital | **l'heure** — the time

3. **Les prix montent** — Prices are rising | **L'amour rayonne dans ses yeux** — Love shines in his eyes
   BUT **avec plaisir** — with pleasure | **sans espoir** — without hope

4. **Je n'aime pas le café** — I don't like coffee | **Les enfants ont besoin d'être aimés** — Children need to be loved

5. **le Japon** — Japan | **les Pays-Bas** — The Netherlands
   BUT **aller en Écosse** — to go to Scotland

6. **Tournez la tête à gauche** — Turn your head to the left | **J'ai mal à la gorge** — My throat is sore, I have a sore throat
   La tête me tourne — My head is spinning | **Elle s'est brossé les dents** — She brushed her teeth

7. **40 francs le mètre/le kilo/rouler à 80 km à l'heure** — 40 francs a metre/a kilo/to go at 50 mph

8. **le roi Georges III** — King George III | **Monsieur le président** — Mr Chairman/President

9. **Victor Hugo, grand écrivain du dix-neuvième siècle** — Victor Hugo, a great author of the nineteenth century

10. **au cinéma** — at/to the cinema | **à la bibliothèque** — at/to the library | **à l'hôpital** — at/to the hospital
    à l'hôtesse — to the hostess | **aux étudiants** — to the students | **aux maisons** — to the houses

11. **du bureau** — from/of the office | **de la réunion** — from/of the meeting
    de l'auteur — from/of the author | **de l'Italienne** — from/of the Italian woman
    des États-Unis — from/of the United States | **des vendeuses** — from/of the saleswomen

❐ The Partitive Article

The partitive article has the sense of *some* or *any*, although the French is not always translated in English.

	WITH MASC. NOUN	WITH FEM. NOUN	
SING.	**du (de l')**	**de la (de l')**	*some, any*
PLUR.	**des**	**des**	*some, any*

- The gender and number of the noun determines the form of the partitive → 1

- The forms shown in brackets in the above table are used before a vowel or an **h** 'mute' → 2

- **des** becomes **de** (**d'** + vowel) before an adjective → 3, unless the adjective and noun are seen as forming one unit → 4

- In negative sentences **de** (**d'** + vowel) is used → 5
  EXCEPTION: after **ne ... que** *only*, the positive forms above are used → 6

❐ The Indefinite Article

	WITH MASC. NOUN	WITH FEM. NOUN	
SING.	**un**	**une**	*a*
PLUR.	**des**	**des**	*some*

- In negative sentences, **de** (**d'** + vowel) is used → 7

- The indefinite article is used in French largely as it is in English EXCEPT:

  - there is no article when a person's profession is being stated → 8
    The article *is* present, however, following **ce** (**c'** + vowel) → 9

  - the English article is not translated by **un/une** in constructions like *what a surprise, what an idiot* → 10

  - in structures of the type given in example 11 the article **un/une** is used in French and not translated in English → 11

1. **Avez-vous du sucre?** **J'ai acheté de la farine**
   Do you have any sugar? I bought (some) flour
   Il a mangé des gâteaux
   He ate some cakes
   Est-ce qu'il y a des lettres pour moi?
   Are there (any) letters for me?

2. **Il me doit de l'argent** **C'est de l'histoire ancienne**
   He owes me (some) money That's ancient history

3. **Cette région a de belles églises**
   This region has some beautiful churches

4. **des grandes vacances** **des jeunes gens**
   summer holidays young people

5. **Vous n'avez pas de timbres/d'œufs?**
   Have you no stamps/eggs?
   Je ne mange jamais de viande/d'omelettes
   I never eat meat/omelettes

6. **Il ne boit que du thé/de la bière/de l'eau**
   He only drinks tea/beer/water
   Je n'ai que des problèmes avec cette machine
   I have nothing but problems with this machine

7. **Je n'ai pas de livre/d'enfants**
   I don't have a book/(any) children

8. **Il est professeur** **Ma mère est infirmière**
   He's a teacher My mother's a nurse

9. **C'est un médecin** **Ce sont des acteurs**
   He's/She's a doctor They're actors

10. **Quelle surprise!** **Quel dommage!**
    What a surprise! What a shame!

11. **avec une grande sagesse/un courage admirable**
    with great wisdom/admirable courage
    un produit d'une qualité incomparable
    a product of incomparable quality

❐ Adjectives

Most adjectives agree in number and in gender with the noun or pronoun

The formation of feminines

◆   Most adjectives add an **e** to the masculine singular form → ①

◆   If the masculine singular form already ends in **-e,** no further **e** i
    added → ②

◆   Some adjectives undergo a further change when **e** is added. These
    changes occur regularly and are shown on p 88.

◆   Irregular feminine forms are shown on p 90.

The formation of plurals

◆   The plural of both regular and irregular adjectives is formed by
    adding an **s** to the masculine or feminine singular form, as
    appropriate → ③

◆   When the masculine singular form already ends in **-s** or **-x**, no further
    s is added → ④

◆   For masculine singulars ending in **-au** and **-eau**, the masculine plural
    is **-aux** and **-eaux** → ⑤

◆   For masculine singulars ending in **-al**, the masculine plural is **-aux**
    → ⑥

    EXCEPTIONS: **final**   (masculine plural **finals**)
                    fatal   (masculine plural **fatals**)
                    naval   (masculine plural **navals**)

1   **mon frère aîné**   **ma sœur aînée**
my elder brother   my elder sister
le petit garçon   **la petite fille**
the little boy   the little girl
un sac gris   **une chemise grise**
a grey bag   a grey shirt
un bruit fort   **une voix forte**
a loud noise   a loud voice

2   **un jeune homme**   **une jeune femme**
a young man   a young woman
l'autre verre   **l'autre assiette**
the other glass   the other plate

3   **le dernier train**   **les derniers trains**
the last train   the last trains
une vieille maison   **de vieilles maisons**
an old house   old houses
un long voyage   **de longs voyages**
a long journey   long journeys
la rue étroite   **les rues étroites**
the narrow street   the narrow streets

4   **un diplomate français**   **des diplomates français**
a French diplomat   French diplomats
un homme dangereux   **des hommes dangereux**
a dangerous man   dangerous men

5   **le nouveau professeur**   **les nouveaux professeurs**
the new teacher   the new teachers
un chien esquimau   **des chiens esquimaux**
a husky (Fr. = an Eskimo dog)   huskies (Fr. = Eskimo dogs)

6   **un ami loyal**   **des amis loyaux**
a loyal friend   loyal friends
un geste amical   **des gestes amicaux**
a friendly gesture   friendly gestures

❐ Regular Feminine Endings

MASC. SING.	FEM. SING.	EXAMPLES	
-f	-ve	neuf, vif	→ 1
-x	-se	heureux, jaloux	→ 2
-eur	-euse	travailleur, flâneur	→ 3
-teur	⎰ -teuse	flatteur, menteur	→ 4
	⎱ -trice	destructeur, séducteur	→ 5

EXCEPTIONS:

> **bref**: see p 90
>
> **doux, faux, roux, vieux:** see p 90
>
> **extérieur, inférieur, intérieur, meilleur, supérieur**: all add **e** to the masculine
>
> **enchanteur**: fem. = **enchanteresse**

MASC. SING.	FEM. SING.	EXAMPLES	
-an	-anne	paysan	→ 6
-en	-enne	ancien, parisien	→ 7
-on	-onne	bon, breton	→ 8
-as	-asse	bas, las	→ 9
-et*	-ette	muet, violet	→ 10
-el	-elle	annuel, mortel	→ 11
-eil	-eille	pareil, vermeil	→ 12

EXCEPTION:

> **ras**: fem. = **rase**

MASC. SING.	FEM. SING.	EXAMPLES	
-et*	-ète	secret, complet	→ 13
-er	-ère	étranger, fier	→ 14

*Note that there are two feminine endings for masculine adjectives ending in **-et**.

1 **un résultat positif**
a positive result

une attitude positive
a positive attitude

2 **d'un ton sérieux**
in a serious tone (of voice)

une voix sérieuse
a serious voice

3 **un enfant trompeur**
a deceitful child

une déclaration trompeuse
a misleading statement

4 **un tableau flatteur**
a flattering picture

une comparaison flatteuse
a flattering comparison

5 **un geste protecteur**
a protective gesture

une couche protectrice
a protective layer

6 **un problème paysan**
a farming problem

la vie paysanne
country life

7 **un avion égyptien**
an Egyptian plane

une statue égyptienne
an Egyptian statue

8 **un bon repas**
a good meal

de bonne humeur
in a good mood

9 **un plafond bas**
a low ceiling

à voix basse
in a low voice

10 **un travail net**
a clean piece of work

une explication nette
a clear explanation

11 **un homme cruel**
a cruel man

une remarque cruelle
a cruel remark

12 **un livre pareil**
such a book

en pareille occasion
on such an occasion

13 **un regard inquiet**
an anxious look

une attente inquiète
an anxious wait

14 **un goût amer**
a bitter taste

une amère déception
a bitter disappointment

❐ Irregular Feminine Forms

MASC. SING.	FEM. SING.		
aigu	aiguë	*sharp; high-pitched*	→ ①
ambigu	ambiguë	*ambiguous*	
beau (bel*)	belle	*beautiful*	
bénin	bénigne	*benign*	
blanc	blanche	*white*	
bref	brève	*brief, short*	→ ②
doux	douce	*soft; sweet*	
épais	épaisse	*thick*	
faux	fausse	*wrong*	
favori	favorite	*favourite*	→ ③
fou (fol*)	folle	*mad*	
frais	fraîche	*fresh*	→ ④
franc	franche	*frank*	
gentil	gentille	*kind*	
grec	grecque	*Greek*	
gros	grosse	*big*	
jumeau	jumelle	*twin*	→ ⑤
long	longue	*long*	
malin	maligne	*malignant*	
mou (mol*)	molle	*soft*	
nouveau (nouvel*)	nouvelle	*new*	
nul	nulle	*no*	
public	publique	*public*	→ ⑥
roux	rousse	*red-haired*	
sec	sèche	*dry*	
sot	sotte	*foolish*	
turc	turque	*Turkish*	
vieux (vieil*)	vieille	*old*	

*This form is used when the following word begins with a vowel or an **h** 'mute' → ⑦

1. **un son aigu**
   a high-pitched sound

   une douleur aiguë
   a sharp pain

2. **un bref discours**
   a short speech

   une brève rencontre
   a short meeting

3. **mon sport favori**
   my favourite sport

   ma chanson favorite
   my favourite song

4. **du pain frais**
   fresh bread

   de la crème fraîche
   fresh cream

5. **mon frère jumeau**
   my twin brother

   ma sœur jumelle
   my twin sister

6. **un jardin public**
   a (public) park

   l'opinion publique
   public opinion

7. **un bel appartement**
   a beautiful flat
   le nouvel inspecteur
   the new inspector
   un vieil arbre
   an old tree

   un bel habit
   a beautiful outfit
   un nouvel harmonica
   a new harmonica
   un vieil hôtel
   an old hotel

❏ Comparatives and Superlatives

Comparatives

These are formed using the following constructions:

plus ... (que)	*more ... (than)*	→ 1
moins ... (que)	*less ... (than)*	→ 2
aussi ... que	*as ... as*	→ 3
si ... que*	*as ... as*	→ 4

*used mainly after a negative

Superlatives

These are formed using the following constructions:

le/la/les plus ... (que)	*the most ... (that)*	→ 5
le/la/les moins ... (que)	*the least ... (that)*	→ 6

◆ When the possessive adjective is present, two constructions are possible → 7

◆ After a superlative the preposition **de** is often translated as *in* → 8

◆ If a clause follows a superlative, the verb is in the subjunctive → 9

Adjectives with irregular comparatives/superlatives

ADJECTIVE	COMPARATIVE	SUPERLATIVE
bon	**meilleur**	**le meilleur**
good	*better*	*the best*
mauvais	**pire** OR	**le pire** OR
bad	**plus mauvais**	**le plus mauvais**
	worse	*the worst*
petit	**moindre*** OR	**le moindre*** OR
small	**plus petit**	**le plus petit**
	smaller;	*the smallest;*
	lesser	*the least*

*used only with abstract nouns

◆ Comparative and superlative adjectives agree in number and in gender with the noun, just like any other adjective → 10

1. **une raison plus grave**
   a more serious reason
   Elle est plus petite que moi
   She is smaller than me

2. **un film moins connu**
   a less well-known film
   C'est moins cher qu'il ne pense
   It's cheaper than he thinks

3. **Robert était aussi inquiet que moi**
   Robert was as worried as I was
   Cette ville n'est pas aussi grande que Bordeaux
   This town isn't as big as Bordeaux

4. **Ils ne sont pas si contents que ça**
   They aren't as happy as all that

5. **le guide le plus utile**   **la voiture la plus petite**
   the most useful guidebook   the smallest car
   les plus grandes maisons
   the biggest houses

6. **le mois le moins agréable**   **la fille la moins forte**
   the least pleasant month   the weakest girl
   les moins belles peintures
   the least attractive paintings

7. **Mon désir le plus cher** } **est de voyager**
   Mon plus cher désir }
   My dearest wish is to travel

8. **la plus grande gare de Londres**
   the biggest station in London
   l'habitant le plus âgé du village/de la région
   the oldest inhabitant in the village/in the area

9. **la personne la plus gentille que je connaisse**
   the nicest person I know

10. **les moindres difficultés**
    the least difficulties
    la meilleure qualité
    the best quality

❏ Demonstrative Adjectives

	MASCULINE	FEMININE	
SING.	**ce (cet)**	**cette**	*this; that*
PLUR.	**ces**	**ces**	*these; those*

- ◆ Demonstrative adjectives agree in number and gender with the noun → 1

- ◆ **cet** is used when the following word begins with a vowel or an **h** 'mute' → 2

- ◆ For emphasis or in order to distinguish between people or objects, **-ci** or **-là** is added to the noun: **-ci** indicates proximity (usually translated *this)* and **-là** distance *(that)* → 3

❏ Interrogative Adjectives

	MASCULINE	FEMININE	
SING.	**quel?**	**quelle?**	*what?; which?*
PLUR.	**quels?**	**quelles?**	*what?; which?*

- ◆ Interrogative adjectives agree in number and gender with the noun → 4

- ◆ The forms shown above are also used in indirect questions → 5

❏ Exclamatory Adjectives

	MASCULINE	FEMININE	
SING.	**quel!**	**quelle!**	*what (a)!*
PLUR.	**quels!**	**quelles!**	*what!*

- ◆ Exclamatory adjectives agree in number and gender with the noun → 6

- ◆ For other exclamations, see p 128.

1. **Ce stylo ne marche pas**
   This/That pen isn't working
   Comment s'appelle cette entreprise?
   What's this/that company called?
   Ces livres sont les miens
   These/Those books are mine
   Ces couleurs sont plus jolies
   These/Those colours are nicer

2. **cet oiseau**   **cet homme**
   this/that bird   this/that man

3. **Combien coûte ce manteau-ci?**
   How much is this coat?
   Je voudrais cinq de ces pommes-là
   I'd like five of those apples
   Est-ce que tu reconnais cette personne-là?
   Do you recognize that person?
   Mettez ces vêtements-ci dans cette valise-là
   Put these clothes in that case

4. **Quel genre d'homme est-ce?**
   What type of man is he?
   Quelle est leur décision?
   What is their decision?
   Vous jouez de quels instruments?
   What instruments do you play?
   Quelles offres avez-vous reçues?
   What offers have you received?

5. **Je ne sais pas à quelle heure il est arrivé**
   I don't know what time he arrived
   Dites-moi quels sont les livres les plus intéressants
   Tell me which books are the most interesting

6. **Quel dommage!**   **Quelle idée!**
   What a pity!   What an idea!
   Quels beaux livres vous avez!   **Quelles jolies fleurs!**
   What fine books you have!   What nice flowers!

☐ **Position of Adjectives**

◆ French adjectives usually follow the noun → ①

◆ Adjectives of colour or nationality *always* follow the noun → ②

◆ As in English, demonstrative, possessive, numerical and interrogative adjectives precede the noun → ③

◆ The adjectives **autre** *other* and **chaque** *each, every* precede the noun → ④

◆ The following common adjectives can precede the noun:

beau	*beautiful*	**jeune**	*young*
bon	*good*	**joli**	*pretty*
court	*short*	**long**	*long*
dernier	*last*	**mauvais**	*bad*
grand	*great*	**petit**	*small*
gros	*big*	**tel**	*such (a)*
haut	*high*	**vieux**	*old*

◆ The meaning of the following adjectives varies according to their position:

	BEFORE NOUN	AFTER NOUN	
ancien	*former*	*old, ancient*	→ ⑤
brave	*good*	*brave*	→ ⑥
cher	*dear (beloved)*	*expensive*	→ ⑦
grand	*great*	*tall*	→ ⑧
même	*same*	*very*	→ ⑨
pauvre	*poor*	*poor*	
	(wretched)	*(not rich)*	→ ⑩
propre	*own*	*clean*	→ ⑪
seul	*single, sole*	*on one's own*	→ ⑫
simple	*mere, simple*	*simple, easy*	→ ⑬
vrai	*real*	*true*	→ ⑭

◆ Adjectives following the noun are linked by **et** → ⑮

1	**le chapitre suivant** the following chapter	**l'heure exacte** the right time
2	**une cravate rouge** a red tie	**un mot français** a French word
3	**ce dictionnaire** this dictionary	**mon père** my father
	le premier étage the first floor	**deux exemples** two examples
	quel homme? which man?	
4	**une autre fois** another time	**chaque jour** every day
5	**un ancien collègue** a former colleague	**l'histoire ancienne** ancient history
6	**un brave homme** a good man	**un homme brave** a brave man
7	**mes chers amis** my dear friends .	**une robe chère** an expensive dress
8	**un grand peintre** a great painter	**un homme grand** a tall man
9	**la même réponse** the same answer	**vos paroles mêmes** your very words
10	**cette pauvre femme** that poor woman	**une nation pauvre** a poor nation
11	**ma propre vie** my own life	**une chemise propre** a clean shirt
12	**une seule réponse** a single reply	**une femme seule** a woman on her own
13	**un simple regard** a mere look	**un problème simple** a simple problem
14	**la vraie raison** the real reason	**les faits vrais** the true facts
15	**un acte lâche et trompeur** a cowardly, deceitful act	
	un acte lâche, trompeur et ignoble a cowardly, deceitful and ignoble act	

❏ Possessive Adjectives

WITH SING. NOUN		WITH PLUR. NOUN	
MASC.	FEM.	MASC./FEM.	
mon	**ma (mon)**	**mes**	*my*
ton	**ta (ton)**	**tes**	*your*
son	**sa (son)**	**ses**	*his; her; its*
notre	**notre**	**nos**	*our*
votre	**votre**	**vos**	*your*
leur	**leur**	**leurs**	*their*

◆ Possessive adjectives agree in number and gender with the noun, NOT WITH THE OWNER → ①

◆ The forms shown in brackets are used when the following word begins with a vowel or an **h** 'mute' → ②

◆ **son**, **sa**, **ses** have the additional meaning of *one's* → ③

---

① **Catherine a oublié son parapluie**
Catherine has left her umbrella
Paul cherche sa montre
Paul's looking for his watch
Mon frère et ma sœur habitent à Glasgow
My brother and sister live in Glasgow
Est-ce que tes voisins ont vendu leur voiture?
Did your neighbours sell their car?
Rangez vos affaires
Put your things away

② **mon appareil-photo**   **ton histoire**
my camera   your story
son erreur   **mon autre sœur**
his/her mistake   my other sister

③ **perdre son équilibre**   **présenter ses excuses**
to lose one's balance   to offer one's apologies

❏ Personal Pronouns: Subject

PERSON	SINGULAR	PLURAL
1st	**je (j')** *I*	**nous** *we*
2nd	**tu** *you*	**vous** *you*
3rd (masc.)	**il** *he; it*	**ils** *they*
(fem.)	**elle** *she; it*	**elles** *they*

je changes to **j'** before a vowel, an **h** 'mute', or the pronoun **y** → ①

◆ **Vous**, as well as being the second person plural, is also used when addressing one person. As a general rule, use **tu** only when addressing a friend, a child, a relative, someone you know very well, or when invited to do so. In all other cases use **vous**. For singular and plural uses of **vous**, see example ②

◆ The form of the third person pronouns (**il/elle; ils/elles**) reflects the number and gender of the noun(s) they replace, referring to animals and things as well as to people. **Ils** also replaces a combination of masculine and feminine nouns → ③

◆ Sometimes stressed pronouns replace the subject pronouns, see p 103.

---

①	**J'arrive!**	**J'en ai trois**
	I'm just coming!	I've got 3 of them
	J'hésite à le déranger	**J'y pense souvent**
	I hesitate to disturb him	I often think about it
②	Compare:	**Vous êtes certain, Monsieur Leclerc?**
		Are you sure, Mr Leclerc?
	and:	**Vous êtes certains, les enfants?**
		Are you sure, children?
③	**Où logent ton père et ta mère quand ils vont à Rome?**
	Where do your father and mother stay when they go to Rome?
	Donne-moi le journal et les lettres quand ils arriveront
	Give me the newspaper and the letters when they arrive

❒ Personal Pronouns: Object

	DIRECT OBJECT PRONOUNS		INDIRECT OBJECT PRONOUNS	
PERSON	SINGULAR	PLURAL	SINGULAR	PLURAL
1st	**me (m')**	**nous**	**me (m')**	**nous**
	me	*us*	*to me*	*to us*
2nd	**te (t')**	**vous**	**te (t')**	**vous**
	you	*you*	*to you*	*to you*
3rd (masc.)	**le (l')**	**les**	**lui**	**leur**
	him; it	*them*	*to him; to it*	*to them*
(fem.)	**la (l')**	**les**	**lui**	**leur**
	her; it	*them*	*to her; to it*	*to them*

The forms shown in brackets are used before a vowel, an **h** 'mute', or the pronoun **y** → ☐1

◆ In positive commands **me** and **te** change to **moi** and **toi** except before **en** or **y** → ☐2

◆ **le** sometimes functions as a 'neuter' pronoun, referring to an idea or information contained in a previous statement or question. It is often not translated → ☐3

◆ The indirect object pronouns replace the preposition **à** + noun, where the noun is a person or an animal → ☐4

◆ The verbal construction affects the translation of the pronoun → ☐5

Position of object pronouns

◆ In constructions other than the imperative affirmative the pronoun comes before the verb → ☐6
The same applies when the verb is in the infinitive → ☐7
In the imperative affirmative, the pronoun follows the verb and is attached to it by a hyphen → ☐8

◆ For further information, see Order of Object Pronouns, p 102.

Reflexive pronouns

These are dealt with under reflexive verbs, p 24.

1 **Il m'a vu**
He saw me

Ils t'ont caché les faits
They hid the facts from you

2 **Avertis-moi de ta décision** → **Avertis-m'en**
Inform me of your decision   Inform me of it
Donnez-moi du sucre → **Donnez-m'en**
Give me some sugar   Give me some

3 **Il n'est pas là. – Je le sais bien.**
He isn't there. – I know that.
Elle viendra demain. – Je l'espère bien.
She'll come tomorrow. – I hope so.

4 **J'écris à Suzanne** → **Je lui écris**
I'm writing to Suzanne   I'm writing to her

5 **arracher qch à qn: Un voleur m'a arraché mon porte-monnaie**
A thief snatched my purse from me
promettre qch à qn: Il leur a promis un cadeau
He promised them a present
demander à qn de faire: Elle nous avait demandé de revenir
She had asked us to come back

6 **Je t'aime**
I love you

Les voyez-vous?
Can you see them?

Ne me faites pas rire
Don't make me laugh

Elle ne nous connaît pas
She doesn't know us

Elle vous a écrit
She's written to you

Vous a-t-elle écrit?
Has she written to you?

Il ne nous parle pas
He doesn't speak to us

Ne leur répondez pas
Don't answer them

7 **Puis-je vous aider?**
May I help you?
Voulez-vous leur envoyer l'adresse?
Do you want to send them the address?

8 **Aidez-moi**
Help me

Donnez-nous la réponse
Tell us the answer

❐ Personal Pronouns: Order of Object Pronouns

◆ When two object pronouns of different persons come before the verb, the order is: indirect before direct, i.e.

| me
te
nous
vous | before | le
la
les | → ① |

◆ When two third person object pronouns come before the verb, the order is: direct before indirect, i.e.

| le
la
les | before | lui
leur | → ② |

◆ When two object pronouns come after the verb (i.e. in the imperative affirmative), the order is: direct before indirect, i.e.

| le
la
les | before | moi
toi
lui
nous
vous
leur | → ③ |

◆ The pronouns **en** and **y** (see pp 104 and 105) always come last → ④

①	**Dominique vous l'envoie demain** Dominique's sending it to you tomorrow **Est-ce qu'il te les a montrés?** Has he shown them to you?	
②	**Elle le leur a emprunté** She borrowed it from them	**Ne la leur donne pas** Don't give it to them
③	**Rends-les-moi** Give them back to me	**Donnez-le-nous** Give it to us
④	**Donnez-leur-en** Give them some	**Je l'y ai déposé** I dropped him there

☐ Personal Pronouns: Stressed or Disjunctive Forms

PERSON	SINGULAR	PLURAL
1st	**moi** *me*	**nous** *us*
2nd	**toi** *you*	**vous** *you*
3rd (masc.)	**lui** *him; it*	**eux** *them*
(fem.)	**elle** *her; it*	**elles** *them*
('reflexive')	**soi** *oneself*	

◆ These pronouns are used:

– after prepositions → ①

– on their own → ②

– following **c'est, ce sont** *it is* → ③

– for emphasis, especially to show contrast; for particular emphasis **-même** (singular) or **-mêmes** (plural) is added to the pronoun → ④

– when the subject consists of two or more pronouns, or a pronoun and a noun → ⑤

– in comparisons → ⑥

– before relative pronouns → ⑦

---

① **Je pense à toi**   **Partez sans eux**
I think about you   Leave without them

② **Qui a fait cela? – Lui**   **Qui est-ce qui gagne? – Moi**
Who did that? – He did   Who's winning? – Me

③ **C'est toi, Simon? – Non, c'est moi, David**
Is that you, Simon? – No, it's me, David

④ **Toi, tu ressembles à ton père, eux pas**
You look like your father, *they* don't
Je l'ai fait moi-même
I did it myself

⑤ **Lui et moi partons demain**
He and I are leaving tomorrow
Mon père et elle ne s'entendent pas
My father and she don't get on

⑥ **plus jeune que moi**   **Il est moins grand que toi**
younger than me   He's smaller than you (are)

⑦ **Ce sont eux qui font du bruit, pas nous**
They're the ones making the noise, not us

❏ The Pronoun *en*

- **en** replaces the preposition **de** + noun → ①
  The verbal construction can affect the translation → ②

- **en** also replaces the partitive article *(English = some, any)* + noun
  → ③

In expressions of quantity **en** represents the noun → ④

- Position:
  en comes before the verb, except in positive commands when it
  follows and is attached to the verb by a hyphen → ⑤

- **en** follows other object pronouns → ⑥

---

①	**Il est fier de son succès**	→	**Il en est fier**
	He's proud of his success		He's proud of it
	Elle est sortie du cinéma	→	**Elle en est sortie**
	She came out of the cinema		She came out (of it)
	Je suis couvert de peinture	→	**J'en suis couvert**
	I'm covered in paint		I'm covered in it

② **avoir besoin de qch: J'en ai besoin**
    I need it/them
  avoir peur de qch: J'en ai peur
    I'm afraid of it/them

③	**Avez-vous de l'argent?**	→	**En avez-vous?**
	Have you any money?		Do you have any?
	Je veux acheter des timbres	→	**Je veux en acheter**
	I want to buy some stamps		I want to buy some

④ **Combien de sœurs as-tu? – J'en ai trois**
  How many sisters do you have? – I have three

⑤	**Elle en a discuté avec moi**	**En êtes-vous content?**
	She discussed it with me	Are you pleased with it/them?
	N'en parlez plus	**Prenez-en**
	Don't talk about it any more	Take some

⑥	**Donnez-leur-en**	**Il m'en a parlé**
	Give them some	He spoke to me about it

Grammar

❑ **The Pronoun *y***

- **y** replaces the preposition **à** + noun → ①
  The verbal construction can affect the translation → ②

- **y** also replaces the prepositions **dans** and **sur** + noun → ③

- **y** can also mean *there* → ④

- Position:
  y comes before the verb, except in positive commands when it
  follows and is attached to the verb by a hyphen → ⑤

- **y** follows other object pronouns → ⑥

---

① **Ne touchez pas à ce bouton** → **N'y touchez pas**
  Don't touch this switch   Don't touch it
  Il participe aux concerts → **Il y participe**
  He takes part in the concerts   He takes part (in them)

② **penser à qch: J'y pense souvent**
    I often think about it
  consentir à qch: Tu y as consenti?
    Have you agreed to it?

③ **Mettez-les dans la boîte** → **Mettez-les-y**
  Put them in the box   Put them in it
  Il les a mis sur les étagères → **Il les y a mis**
  He put them on the shelves   He put them on them

④ **Elle y passe tout l'été**
  She spends the whole summer there

⑤ **Il y a ajouté du sucre**   **Elle n'y a pas écrit son nom**
  He added sugar to it   She hasn't written her name on it
  Comment fait-on pour y aller?
  How do you get there?
  N'y pense plus!   **Réfléchissez-y**
  Don't give it another thought!   Think it over

⑥ **Elle m'y a conduit**   **Menez-nous-y**
  She drove me there   Take us there

❒ Relative Pronouns

qui	*who; which*
que	*who(m); which*

These are subject and direct object pronouns that introduce a clause and refer to people or things.

	PEOPLE	THINGS
SUBJECT	**qui →** 1	**qui →** 3
	who, that	*which, that*
DIRECT OBJECT	**que (qu') →** 2	**que (qu') →** 4
	who(m), that	*which, that*

- **que** changes to **qu'** before a vowel → 2/4

- You cannot omit the object relative pronoun in French as you can in English → 2/4

After a preposition:
- When referring to people, use **qui** → 5
  EXCEPTIONS: after **parmi** *among* and **entre** *between* use **lesquels/ lesquelles** (see below) → 6
- When referring to things, use forms of **lequel:**

	MASCULINE	FEMININE	
SING.	**lequel**	**laquelle**	*which*
PLUR.	**lesquels**	**lesquelles**	*which*

The pronoun agrees in number and gender with the noun → 7

- After the prepositions **à** and **de, lequel** and **lesquel(le)s** contract as follows:

  à + lequel → auquel
  à + lesquels → auxquels   → 8
  à + lesquelles → auxquelles

  de + lequel → duquel
  de + lesquels → desquels   → 9
  de + lesquelles → desquelles

1. **Mon frère, qui a vingt ans, est à l'université**
   My brother, who's twenty, is at university

2. **Les amis que je vois le plus sont …**
   The friends (that) I see most are …
   Lucienne, qu'il connaît depuis longtemps, est …
   Lucienne, whom he has known for a long time, is …

3. **Il y a un escalier qui mène au toit**
   There's a staircase which leads to the roof

4. **La maison que nous avons achetée a …**
   The house (which) we've bought has …
   Voici le cadeau qu'elle m'a envoyé
   This is the present (that) she sent me

5. **la personne à qui il parle**
   the person he's talking to
   la personne avec qui je voyage
   the person with whom I travel
   les enfants pour qui je l'ai acheté
   the children for whom I bought it

6. **Il y avait des jeunes, parmi lesquels Robert**
   There were some young people, Robert among them
   les filles entre lesquelles j'étais assis
   the girls between whom I was sitting

7. **le torchon avec lequel il l'essuie**
   the cloth he's wiping it with
   la table sur laquelle je l'ai mis
   the table on which I put it
   les moyens par lesquels il l'accomplit
   the means by which he achieves it
   les pièces pour lesquelles elle est connue
   the plays for which she is famous

8. **le magasin auquel il livre ces marchandises**
   the shop to which he delivers these goods

9. **les injustices desquelles il se plaint**
   the injustices he's complaining about

❏ Relative Pronouns (Continued)

quoi *which, what*

◆ When the relative pronoun does not refer to a specific noun, **quoi** is used after a preposition → ①

dont *whose, of whom, of which*

◆ **dont** often (but not always) replaces **de qui**, **duquel**, **de laquelle**, and **desquel(le)s** → ②

◆ It cannot replace **de qui**, **duquel** etc in the construction preposition + noun + **de qui/duquel** → ③

◆ If the person (or object) 'owned' is the *object* of the verb, word order is: **dont** + verb + noun → ④
If the person (or object) 'owned' is the *subject* of the verb, word order is: **dont** + noun + verb → ⑤

ce qui, ce que *that which, what*

These are used when the relative pronoun does not refer to a specific noun, and they are often translated as *what* (literally: *that which*)

> **ce qui**   is used as the subject → ⑥
> **ce que***   is used as the direct object → ⑦
>
> ***que** changes to **qu'** before a vowel → ⑦

◆ Note the construction

> **tout ce qui** }
> **tout ce que** } *everything/all that* → ⑧

◆ **de + ce que → ce dont** → ⑨

◆ preposition + **ce que → ce** + preposition + **quoi** → ⑩

◆ When **ce qui, ce que** etc, refers to a previous CLAUSE the translation is *which* → ⑪

1. **C'est en quoi vous vous trompez**
   That's where you're wrong
   À quoi, j'ai répondu '…'
   To which I replied, '…'

2. **la femme dont (= de qui) la voiture est garée en face**
   the woman whose car is parked opposite
   un prix dont (= de qui) je suis fier
   an award I am proud of

3. **une personne sur l'aide de qui on peut compter**
   a person whose help one can rely on
   les enfants aux parents de qui j'écris
   the children to whose parents I'm writing
   la maison dans le jardin de laquelle il y a …
   the house in whose garden there is …

4. **un homme dont je connais la fille**
   a man whose daughter I know

5. **un homme dont la fille me connaît**
   a man whose daughter knows me

6. **Je n'ai pas vu ce qui s'est passé**
   I didn't see what happened

7. **Ce que j'aime c'est la musique classique**
   What I like is classical music
   Montrez-moi ce qu'il vous a donné
   Show me what he gave you

8. **Tout ce qui reste c'est …**
   All that's left is …
   Donnez-moi tout ce que vous avez
   Give me everything you have

9. **Voilà ce dont il s'agit**
   That's what it's about

10. **Ce n'est pas ce à quoi je m'attendais**
    It's not what I was expecting
    Ce à quoi je m'intéresse particulièrement c'est …
    What I'm particularly interested in is …

11. **Il est d'accord, ce qui m'étonne**
    He agrees, which surprises me
    Il a dit qu'elle ne venait pas, ce que nous savions déjà
    He said she wasn't coming, which we already knew

☐ Interrogative Pronouns

In direct questions

qui?	*who; whom?*
que?	*what?*
quoi?	*what?*

These pronouns are used in direct questions. Their form depends on:
- whether it refers to people or to things
- whether it is the subject or object of the verb, or if it comes after a preposition

Qui and **que** have longer forms, as shown in the tables below.

♦ Referring to people:

SUBJECT	**qui?**	
	qui est-ce qui?	→ ①
	who?	
OBJECT	**qui?**	
	qui est-ce que*?	→ ②
	who(m)?	
AFTER PREPOSITIONS	**qui?**	→ ③
	who(m)?	

♦ Referring to things:

SUBJECT	**qu'est-ce qui?**	→ ④
	what?	
OBJECT	**que*?**	
	qu'est-ce que*?	→ ⑤
	what?	
AFTER PREPOSITIONS	**quoi?**	→ ⑥
	what?	

***que** changes to **qu'** before a vowel → ②, ⑤

1 **Qui vient?**
   Qui est-ce qui vient?
   Who's coming?

2 **Qui vois-tu?**
   Qui est-ce que tu vois?
   Who(m) can you see?
   Qui a-t-elle rencontré?
   Qui est-ce qu'elle a rencontré?
   Who(m) did she meet?

3 **De qui parle-t-il?**
   Who's he talking about?
   Pour qui est ce livre?
   Who's this book for?
   À qui avez-vous écrit?
   To whom did you write?

4 **Qu'est-ce qui se passe?**
   What's happening?
   Qu'est-ce qui a vexé Paul?
   What upset Paul?

5 **Que faites-vous?**
   Qu'est-ce que vous faites?
   What are you doing?
   Qu'a-t-il dit?
   Qu'est-ce qu'il a dit?
   What did he say?

6 **À quoi cela sert-il?**
   What's that used for?
   De quoi a-t-on parlé?
   What was the discussion about?
   Sur quoi vous basez-vous?
   What do you base it on?

☐ Interrogative Pronouns (Continued)

In indirect questions

qui	*who; whom*
ce qui	*what*
ce que	*what*
quoi	*what*

These pronouns are used in indirect questions.
The form of the pronoun depends on:
- whether it refers to people or to things
- whether it is the subject or object of the verb, or if it comes after a preposition

- ◆ Referring to people: use **qui** in all instances → ①
- ◆ Referring to things:

SUBJECT	**ce qui** *what*	→ ②
OBJECT	**ce que*** *what*	→ ③
AFTER PREPOSITIONS	**quoi** *what*	→ ④

***que** changes to **qu'** before a vowel → ③

lequel?, laquelle?; lesquels?, lesquelles?

	MASCULINE	FEMININE	
SING.	**lequel?**	**laquelle?**	*which (one)?*
PLUR.	**lesquels?**	**lesquelles?**	*which (ones)?*

- ◆ The pronoun agrees in number and gender with the noun it refers to → ⑤
- ◆ The same forms are used in indirect questions → ⑥
- ◆ After **à** and **de**, **lequel** and **lesquel(le)s** contract as shown on p 106.

1   **Demande-lui qui est venu**
Ask him who came
Je me demande qui ils ont vu
I wonder who they saw
Dites-moi qui vous préférez
Tell me who you prefer
Elle ne sait pas à qui s'adresser
She doesn't know who to apply to
Demandez-leur pour qui elles travaillent
Ask them who they work for

2   **Il se demande ce qui se passe**
He's wondering what's happening
Je ne sais pas ce qui vous fait croire que …
I don't know what makes you think that …

3   **Raconte-nous ce que tu as fait**
Tell us what you did
Je me demande ce qu'elle pense
I wonder what she's thinking

4   **On ne sait pas de quoi vivent ces animaux**
We don't know what these animals live on
Je vais lui demander à quoi il fait allusion
I'm going to ask him what he's hinting at

5   **J'ai choisi un livre – Lequel?**
I've chosen a book – Which one?
Laquelle de ces valises est la vôtre?
Which of these cases is yours?
Amenez quelques amis – Lesquels?
Bring some friends – Which ones?
Lesquelles de vos sœurs sont mariées?
Which of your sisters are married?

6   **Je me demande laquelle des maisons est la leur**
I wonder which is their house
Dites-moi lesquels d'entre eux étaient là
Tell me which of them were there

☐ Possessive Pronouns

SINGULAR		
MASCULINE	FEMININE	
le mien	**la mienne**	*mine*
le tien	**la tienne**	*yours*
le sien	**la sienne**	*his; hers; its*
le nôtre	**la nôtre**	*ours*
le vôtre	**la vôtre**	*yours*
le leur	**la leur**	*theirs*

PLURAL		
MASCULINE	FEMININE	
les miens	**les miennes**	*mine*
les tiens	**les tiennes**	*yours*
les siens	**les siennes**	*his; hers; its*
les nôtres	**les nôtres**	*ours*
les vôtres	**les vôtres**	*yours*
les leurs	**les leurs**	*theirs*

- The pronoun agrees in number and gender with the noun it replaces, NOT WITH THE OWNER → ①

- Alternative translations are *my own, your own* etc; **le sien, la sienne** etc may also mean *one's own* → ②

- After the prepositions **à** and **de** the articles **le** and **les** are contracted in the normal way (see p 82):

à + le mien → au mien
à + les miens → aux miens   → ③
à + les miennes → aux miennes

de + le mien → du mien
de + les miens → des miens   → ④
de + les miennes → des miennes

1   **Demandez à Carole si ce stylo est le sien**
Ask Carole if this pen is hers
Quelle équipe a gagné – la leur ou la nôtre?
Which team won – theirs or ours?
Mon stylo marche mieux que le tien
My pen writes better than yours
Richard a pris mes affaires pour les siennes
Richard mistook my belongings for his
Si tu n'as pas de disques, emprunte les miens
If you don't have any records, borrow mine
Nos maisons sont moins grandes que les vôtres
Our houses are smaller than yours

2   **Est-ce que leur entreprise est aussi grande que la vôtre?**
Is their company as big as your own?
Leurs prix sont moins élevés que les nôtres
Their prices are lower than our own
Le bonheur des autres importe plus que le sien
Other people's happiness matters more than one's own

3   **Pourquoi préfères-tu ce manteau au mien?**
Why do you prefer this coat to mine?
Quelles maisons ressemblent aux leurs?
Which houses resemble theirs?

4   **Leur car est garé à côté du nôtre**
Their coach is parked beside ours
Vos livres sont au-dessus des miens
Your books are on top of mine

❑ Demonstrative Pronouns

celui, celle; ceux, celles

	MASCULINE	FEMININE	
SING.	**celui**	**celle**	*the one*
PLUR.	**ceux**	**celles**	*the ones*

- ◆ **Celui** agrees in number and gender with the noun it replaces → ①
- ◆ Uses:
  - preceding a relative pronoun, meaning *the one(s) who/which* → ①
  - preceding **de**, meaning *the one(s) belonging to, the one(s) of* → ②
  - with **-ci** and **-là**, for emphasis or to distinguish between two things:

	MASCULINE	FEMININE		
SING.	**celui-ci**	**celle-ci**	*this (one)*	→ ③
PLUR.	**ceux-ci**	**celles-ci**	*these (ones)*	
SING.	**celui-là**	**celle-là**	*that(one)*	→ ③
PLUR.	**ceux-là**	**celles-là**	*those (ones)*	

  - **celui-ci/celui-là** etc can also mean *the former/the latter*.

ce (c')   *it, that*

- ◆ **Ce** is usually found in the expressions **c'est**, **ce sont** etc. Note the spelling **ç** when followed by the letter **a** → ④
- ◆ Uses:
  - to identify a person or object → ⑤
  - for emphasis → ⑥
  - as a neuter pronoun, referring to a statement, idea etc → ⑦

ce qui, ce que, ce dont etc

    See Relative Pronouns (p 108), Interrogative Pronouns (p 112).

cela, ça   *it, that*

- ◆ **cela** and **ça** are used as 'neuter' pronouns, referring to a statement, an idea, an object. In everyday spoken language **ça** is preferred → ⑧

ceci   *this* → ⑨

- ◆ **ceci** is not used as often as 'this' in English; **cela**, **ça** are used instead.

---

1 **Cet article n'est pas celui dont vous m'avez parlé**
This article isn't the one you spoke to me about
Quelle robe désirez-vous? – Celle qui est en vitrine
Which dress do you want? – The one which is in the window
Est-ce que ces livres sont ceux qu'il t'a donnés?
Are these the books that he gave you?
Quelles filles? – Celles que nous avons vues hier
Which girls? – The ones we saw yesterday

2 **Comparez vos réponses à celles de votre voisin**
Compare your answers with your neighbour's (answers)
les montagnes d'Écosse et celles du pays de Galles
the mountains of Scotland and those of Wales

3 **Quel tailleur préférez-vous: celui-ci ou celui-là?**
Which suit do you prefer: this one or that one?
De toutes mes jupes, celle-ci me va le mieux
Of all my skirts, this one fits me best

4 **Ç'a été la cause de …**   **C'était moi**
It has been the cause of…   It was me

5 **Qui est-ce?**
Who is it?; Who's this/that?; Who's he/she?
C'est mon frère   **C'est une infirmière***
It's/That's my brother   She's a nurse
Qu'est-ce que c'est?   **Ce sont des trombones**
What's this/that?   They're paper clips

6 **C'est moi qui ai téléphoné**
It was me who phoned

7 **C'est très intéressant**   **Ce serait dangereux**
That's/It's very interesting   That/It would be dangerous

8 **Ça ne fait rien**   **Cela ne compte pas**
It doesn't matter   That doesn't count

9 **À qui est ceci?**   **Ouvrez-le comme ceci**
Whose is this?   Open it like this

* See p 85 for the use of the article with professions

❏ Adverbs

Formation

* Most adverbs are formed by adding **-ment** to the feminine form of the adjective → ①

* **-ment** is added to the *masculine* form when the masculine form ends in **-é, -i** or **-u** → ②
  EXCEPTION: **gai** → ③
  Occasionally the **u** changes to **û** before **-ment** is added → ④

* If the adjective ends in **-ant** or **-ent**, the adverb ends in **-amment** or **-emment** → ⑤
  EXCEPTIONS: **lent**, **présent** → ⑥

Irregular adverbs

ADJECTIVE		ADVERB		
aveugle	*blind*	**aveuglément**	blindly	
bon	*good*	**bien**	well	→ ⑦
bref	*brief*	**brièvement**	briefly	
énorme	*enormous*	**énormément**	enormously	
exprès	*express*	**expressément**	expressly	→ ⑧
gentil	*kind*	**gentiment**	kindly	
mauvais	*bad*	**mal**	badly	→ ⑨
meilleur	*better*	**mieux**	better	
pire	*worse*	**pis**	worse	
précis	*precise*	**précisément**	precisely	
profond	*deep*	**profondément**	deeply	→ ⑩
traître	*treacherous*	**traîtreusement**	treacherously	

Adjectives used as adverbs

Certain adjectives are used adverbially. These include: **bas, bon, cher, clair, court, doux, droit, dur, faux, ferme, fort, haut, mauvais** and **net** → ⑪

	MASC./FEM. ADJECTIVE	ADVERB
1	**heureux/heureuse** fortunate	**heureusement** fortunately
	franc/franche frank	**franchement** frankly
	extrême/extrême extreme	**extrêmement** extremely
2	MASC. ADJECTIVE	ADVERB
	désespéré desperate	**désespérément** desperately
	vrai true	**vraiment** truly
	résolu resolute	**résolument** resolutely
3	**gai** cheerful	**gaiement** OR **gaîment** cheerfully
4	**continu** continuous	**continûment** continuously
5	**constant** constant	**constamment** constantly
	courant fluent	**couramment** fluently
	évident obvious	**évidemment** obviously
	fréquent frequent	**fréquemment** frequently
6	**lent** slow	**lentement** slowly
	présent present	**présentement** presently

7 **Elle travaille bien**
She works well

8 **Il a expressément défendu qu'on parte**
He has expressly forbidden us to leave

9 **Un emploi mal payé**
A badly paid job

10 **J'ai été profondément ému**
I was deeply moved

11 **parler bas/haut**
to speak softly/loudly
coûter cher
to be expensive
voir clair
to see clearly
travailler dur
to work hard
chanter faux
to sing off key
sentir bon/mauvais
to smell nice/horrible

❐ Position of Adverbs

- ◆ When the adverb accompanies a verb in a simple tense, it generally follows the verb → 1

- ◆ When the adverb accompanies a verb in a compound tense, it generally comes between the auxiliary verb and the past participle → 2
  Some adverbs, however, follow the past participle → 3

- ◆ When the adverb accompanies an adjective or another adverb it generally precedes the adjective/adverb → 4

❐ Comparatives and Superlatives of Adverbs

- ◆ Comparatives are formed using the following constructions:

plus ... (que)	*more ... (than)*	→ 5
moins ... (que)	*less ... (than)*	→ 6
aussi ... que	*as ... as*	→ 7
si ... que*	*as ... as*	→ 8

  *used mainly after a negative

- ◆ Superlatives are formed using the following constructions:

le plus ... (que)	*the most ... (that)*	→ 9
le moins ... (que)	*the least ... (that)*	→ 10

Adverbs with irregular comparatives/superlatives

ADVERB	COMPARATIVE	SUPERLATIVE
beaucoup	**plus**	**le plus**
a lot	*more*	*(the) most*
bien	**mieux**	**le mieux**
well	*better*	*(the) best*
mal	**pis** OR **plus mal**	**le pis** OR **le plus mal**
badly	*worse*	*(the) worst*
peu	**moins**	**le moins**
little	*less*	*(the) least*

1. **Il dort encore**
   He's still asleep

   Je pense souvent à toi
   I often think about you

2. **Ils sont déjà partis**
   They've already gone
   J'ai presque fini
   I've almost finished

   J'ai toujours cru que …
   I've always thought that …
   Il a trop mangé
   He's eaten too much

3. **On les a vus partout**
   We saw them everywhere

   Elle est revenue hier
   She came back yesterday

4. **un très beau chemisier**
   a very nice blouse
   beaucoup plus vite
   much faster

   une femme bien habillée
   a well-dressed woman
   peu souvent
   not very often

5. **plus vite**
   more quickly

   plus régulièrement
   more regularly

   Elle chante plus fort que moi
   She sings louder than I do

6. **moins facilement**
   less easily

   moins souvent
   less often

   Nous nous voyons moins fréquemment qu'auparavant
   We see each other less frequently than before

7. **Faites-le aussi vite que possible**
   Do it as quickly as possible
   Il en sait aussi long que nous
   He knows as much about it as we do

8. **Ce n'est pas si loin que je pensais**
   It's not as far as I thought

9. **Marianne court le plus vite**
   Marianne runs fastest
   Le plus tôt que je puisse venir c'est samedi
   The earliest that I can come is Saturday

10. **C'est l'auteur que je connais le moins bien**
    It's the writer I'm least familiar with

❏ Prepositions

◆ It is often difficult to give an English equivalent for French prepositions, since usage varies so much between the two languages. The French preposition may not always be the one that the English sentence leads you to expect, and vice versa. A good dictionary will help you here → ☐1

◆ English verbal constructions often contain a preposition where none exists in French, and vice versa → ☐2

◆ English phrasal verbs (i.e. verbs followed by a preposition e.g. *to run away*, *to fall down*) are often translated by one word in French → ☐3

☐1 **Il y a beaucoup de restaurants à Londres**
There are lots of restaurants in London
Elle est allée à Londres
She went/has gone to London
donner qch à qn
to give sth to sb, to give sb sth
lancer qch à qn   **prendre qch à qn**
to throw sth at sb   to take sth from sb
à pied   **une tasse à thé**
on foot   a teacup
venir de Paris   **une boîte d'allumettes**
to come from Paris   a box of matches
une robe de soie   **d'une façon irrégulière**
a silk dress   in an irregular way
la plus belle ville du monde   **plus de cent personnes**
The most beautiful city in the world   more than a hundred people
je vais en ville   **en janvier**
I'm going (in)to town   in January
déguisé en cowboy   **je suis venue en voiture**
dressed up as a cowboy   I came by car

☐2 **payer**   **regarder**   **écouter**
to pay for   to look at   to listen to
obéir à   **nuire à**   **manquer de**
to obey   to harm   to lack

☐3 **s'enfuir**   **tomber**   **céder**
to run away   to fall down   to give in

❒ Conjunctions

Some conjunctions introduce a main clause, e.g. **et** *and*, **mais** *but*, and some introduce subordinate clauses e.g. **parce que** *because*, **pendant que** *while*. They are used in much the same way as in English, but:

- Some conjunctions in French require a following subjunctive, see p 46

- Some conjunctions are 'split' in French:

et ... et	*both ... and*	→ ⬚1
ni ... ni ... ne	*neither ... nor*	→ ⬚2
ou (bien) ... ou (bien)	*either ... or (else)*	→ ⬚3
soit ... soit	*either ... or*	→ ⬚4

- **si + il(s)** → **s'il(s)** → ⬚5

- **que**
  - meaning *that* → ⬚6
  - replacing another conjunction → ⬚7
  - replacing **si**, see p 48
  - in comparisons, see pp 92 and 120
  - followed by the subjunctive, see p 48

- **aussi** *so*, *therefore*: the subject and verb are inverted if the subject is a pronoun → ⬚8

⬚1 **Ces fleurs poussent et en été et en hiver**
These flowers grow in both summer and winter

⬚2 **Ni lui ni elle ne sont venus**
Neither he nor she came

⬚3 **Ou bien il m'évite ou bien il ne me reconnaît pas**
Either he's avoiding me or else he doesn't recognize me

⬚4 **Il faut choisir soit l'un soit l'autre**
You have to choose either one or the other

⬚5 **Je ne sais pas s'il vient/s'ils viennent**
I don't know if he's coming/if they're coming

⬚6 **Il dit qu'il t'a vu**
He says (that) he saw you

⬚7 **Comme il pleuvait et que je n'avais pas de parapluie, ...**
As it was raining and I didn't have an umbrella, ...

⬚8 **Ceux-ci sont plus rares, aussi coûtent-ils cher**
These ones are rarer, so they're expensive

❑ Negatives

ne … pas	*not*
ne … point (literary)	*not*
ne … rien	*nothing*
ne … personne	*nobody*
ne … plus	*no longer, no more*
ne … jamais	*never*
ne … que	*only*
ne … aucun(e)	*no*
ne … nul(le)	*no*
ne … nulle part	*nowhere*
ne … ni (… ni)	*neither … nor*

- ◆ **Word order**

  – In simple tenses and the imperative:
  ne precedes the verb (and any object pronouns) and the second element follows the verb → ①

  – In compound tenses:

  i   **ne … pas, ne … point, ne … rien, ne … plus, ne … jamais, ne… guère** follow the pattern:
  ne + auxiliary verb + **pas** + past participle → ②

  ii **ne … personne, ne … que, ne … aucun(e), ne … nul(le), ne … nulle part, ne … ni (… ni)** follow the pattern:
  ne + auxiliary verb + past participle + **personne** → ③

  – With a verb in the infinitive:
  ne … pas, ne … point (etc; see i above) come together → ④

- ◆ **Rien**, **personne** and **aucun** can also be used as pronouns. When they are the subject or object of the verb, **ne** is placed immediately before the verb. **Aucun** also needs the pronoun **en** when used as an object → ⑤

- ◆ **Jamais** and **plus** can be combined with some of the negative particles listed above → ⑥

Grammar

☐1 **Je ne fume pas**   **Ne changez rien**
I don't smoke   Don't change anything
Je ne vois personne
I can't see anybody
Nous ne nous verrons plus
We won't see each other any more
Il n'arrive jamais à l'heure   **Il n'avait qu'une valise**
He never arrives on time   He only had one suitcase
Il ne boit ni ne fume
He neither drinks nor smokes
Ni mon fils ni ma fille ne les connaissaient
Neither my son nor my daughter knew them

☐2 **Elle n'a pas fait ses devoirs**
She hasn't done her homework
Ne vous a-t-il rien dit?
Didn't he say anything to you?
Tu n'as guère changé
You've hardly changed

☐3 **Je n'ai vu personne**
I haven't seen anybody
Il n'avait mangé que la moitié du repas
He had only eaten half the meal
Elle ne les a trouvés nulle part
She couldn't find them anywhere

☐4 **Il essayait de ne pas rire**
He was trying not to laugh

☐5 **Je ne vois personne**   **Rien ne lui plaît**
I can't see anyone   Nothing pleases him/her
Aucune des entreprises ne veut …   **Il n'en a aucun**
None of the companies wants …   He hasn't any (of them)

☐6 **Je ne le ferai plus jamais**
I'll never do it again
Ces marchandises ne valaient plus rien
Those goods were no longer worth anything
Ils ne font jamais rien d'intéressant
They never do anything interesting
Je n'ai jamais parlé qu'à sa femme
I've only ever spoken to his wife

❏ Question Forms

Direct questions

There are four ways of forming direct questions in French:

- by inverting the normal word order so that *pronoun subject + verb* → *verb + pronoun subject*. A hyphen links the verb and pronoun → 1

  - When the subject is a noun, a pronoun is inserted after the verb and linked to it by a hyphen → 2

  - When the verb ends in a vowel in the third person singular, **-t-** is inserted before the pronoun → 3

- by maintaining the word order *subject + verb* and using a rising intonation at the end of the sentence → 4

- by inserting **est-ce que** before the construction *subject + verb* → 5

- by using an interrogative word at the beginning of the sentence, together with inversion *or* the **est-ce que** form above → 6

Indirect questions

An indirect question is one that is 'reported', e.g. he asked me *what the time was*, tell me *which way to go*. Word order in indirect questions is as follows:

- *interrogative word* + subject + verb → 7

- when the subject is a noun, and not a pronoun, the subject and verb are often inverted → 8

n'est-ce pas

This is used wherever English would use *isn't it?, don't they?, weren't we?, is it?* etc tagged on to the end of a sentence → 9

1. **Aimez-vous la France?**
   Do you like France?
   Est-ce possible?
   Is it possible?

   Avez-vous fini?
   Have you finished?
   Est-elle restée?
   Did she stay?

2. **Tes parents sont-ils en vacances?**
   Are your parents on holiday?

3. **A-t-elle de l'argent?**
   Does she have any money?
   La pièce dure-t-elle longtemps?
   Does the play last long?

4. **Robert va venir**
   Robert's coming
   Robert va venir?
   Is Robert coming?

5. **Est-ce que tu la connais?**
   Do you know her?
   Est-ce que tes parents sont revenus d'Italie?
   Have your parents come back from Italy?

6. **Quel train** { **prends-tu?**
   { **est-ce que tu prends?**
   What train are you getting?

   Pourquoi { **ne sont-ils pas venus?**
   { **est-ce qu'ils ne sont pas venus?**
   Why haven't they come?

7. **Je me demande s'il viendra**
   I wonder if he'll come
   Dites-moi quel autobus va à la gare
   Tell me which bus goes to the station

8. **Elle nous a demandé comment allait notre père**
   She asked us how our father was
   Je ne sais pas ce que veulent dire ces mots
   I don't know what these words mean

9. **Il fait chaud, n'est-ce pas?**
   It's warm, isn't it?
   Vous n'oublierez pas, n'est-ce pas?
   You won't forget, will you?

❏ Word Order

Word order in French is largely the same as in English, except:

- Object pronouns nearly always come before the verb (see p 100)
- Certain adjectives come after the noun (see p 96)
- Adverbs accompanying a verb in a simple tense usually follow the verb (see p 120)
- After **aussi** *so, therefore*, **à peine** *hardly*, **peut-être** *perhaps*, the verb and subject are inverted → ①
- After the relative pronoun **dont** *whose* certain rules apply (see p 108)
- In exclamations, **que** and **comme** do not affect the normal word order → ②
- Following direct speech:
  - the *verb + subject* order is inverted to become *subject + verb* → ③
  - with a pronoun subject, the verb and pronoun are linked by a hyphen → ④
  - when the verb ends in a vowel in the third person singular, **-t-** is inserted between the pronoun and the verb → ⑤

For word order in negative sentences, see p 124.
For word order in interrogative sentences, see pp 126 and 128.

---

① **Il vit tout seul, aussi fait-il ce qu'il veut**
He lives alone, so he does what he likes
À peine la pendule avait-elle sonné trois heures que …
Hardly had the clock struck three when …
Peut-être avez-vous raison
Perhaps you're right

② **Qu'il fait chaud!**   **Comme c'est cher**
How warm it is!   How expensive it is!

③ **'Je pense que oui' a dit Luc**   **'Ça ne fait rien' répondit Jean**
'I think so', said Luke   'It doesn't matter', John replied

④ **'Quelle horreur!' me suis-je exclamé**
'How awful!' I exclaimed

⑤ **'Pourquoi pas?' a-t-elle demandé**
'Why not?' she asked